Oxford Dictionary of National Biography

Volume 17

Oxford Dictionary of National Biography

IN ASSOCIATION WITH
The British Academy

From the earliest times to the year 2000

Edited by
H. C. G. Matthew
and
Brian Harrison

Volume 17
Drysdale–Ekins

OXFORD
UNIVERSITY PRESS

OXFORD
UNIVERSITY PRESS

Great Clarendon Street, Oxford OX2 6DP

Oxford University Press is a department of the University of Oxford.
It furthers the University's objective of excellence in research, scholarship,
and education by publishing worldwide in

Oxford New York

Auckland Bangkok Buenos Aires Cape Town
Chennai Dar es Salaam Delhi Hong Kong Istanbul Karachi
Kolkata Kuala Lumpur Madrid Melbourne Mexico City Mumbai Nairobi
São Paulo Shanghai Taipei Tokyo Toronto

Oxford is a registered trade mark of Oxford University Press
in the UK and in certain other countries

Published in the United States
by Oxford University Press Inc., New York

British Library Cataloguing in Publication Data
Data available

Library of Congress Cataloging in Publication Data
Data available: for details see volume 1, p. iv

ISBN 0-19-861367-9 (this volume)
ISBN 0-19-861411-X (set of sixty volumes)

Text captured by Alliance Phototypesetters, Pondicherry
Illustrations reproduced and archived by
Alliance Graphics Ltd, UK
Typeset in OUP Swift by Interactive Sciences Limited, Gloucester
Printed in Great Britain on acid-free paper by
Butler and Tanner Ltd,
Frome, Somerset

LIST OF ABBREVIATIONS

1 General abbreviations

AB	bachelor of arts
ABC	Australian Broadcasting Corporation
ABC TV	ABC Television
act.	active
A$	Australian dollar
AD	*anno domini*
AFC	Air Force Cross
AIDS	acquired immune deficiency syndrome
AK	Alaska
AL	Alabama
A level	advanced level [examination]
ALS	associate of the Linnean Society
AM	master of arts
AMICE	associate member of the Institution of Civil Engineers
ANZAC	Australian and New Zealand Army Corps
appx *pl.* appxs	appendix(es)
AR	Arkansas
ARA	associate of the Royal Academy
ARCA	associate of the Royal College of Art
ARCM	associate of the Royal College of Music
ARCO	associate of the Royal College of Organists
ARIBA	associate of the Royal Institute of British Architects
ARP	air-raid precautions
ARRC	associate of the Royal Red Cross
ARSA	associate of the Royal Scottish Academy
art.	article / item
ASC	Army Service Corps
Asch	Austrian Schilling
ASDIC	Antisubmarine Detection Investigation Committee
ATS	Auxiliary Territorial Service
ATV	Associated Television
Aug	August
AZ	Arizona
b.	born
BA	bachelor of arts
BA (Admin.)	bachelor of arts (administration)
BAFTA	British Academy of Film and Television Arts
BAO	bachelor of arts in obstetrics
bap.	baptized
BBC	British Broadcasting Corporation / Company
BC	before Christ
BCE	before the common (*or* Christian) era
BCE	bachelor of civil engineering
BCG	bacillus of Calmette and Guérin [inoculation against tuberculosis]
BCh	bachelor of surgery
BChir	bachelor of surgery
BCL	bachelor of civil law

BCnL	bachelor of canon law
BCom	bachelor of commerce
BD	bachelor of divinity
BEd	bachelor of education
BEng	bachelor of engineering
bk *pl.* bks	book(s)
BL	bachelor of law / letters / literature
BLitt	bachelor of letters
BM	bachelor of medicine
BMus	bachelor of music
BP	before present
BP	British Petroleum
Bros.	Brothers
BS	(1) bachelor of science; (2) bachelor of surgery; (3) British standard
BSc	bachelor of science
BSc (Econ.)	bachelor of science (economics)
BSc (Eng.)	bachelor of science (engineering)
bt	baronet
BTh	bachelor of theology
bur.	buried
C.	command [identifier for published parliamentary papers]
c.	*circa*
c.	*capitulum pl. capitula*: chapter(s)
CA	California
Cantab.	Cantabrigiensis
cap.	*capitulum pl. capitula*: chapter(s)
CB	companion of the Bath
CBE	commander of the Order of the British Empire
CBS	Columbia Broadcasting System
cc	cubic centimetres
C$	Canadian dollar
CD	compact disc
Cd	command [identifier for published parliamentary papers]
CE	Common (*or* Christian) Era
cent.	century
cf.	compare
CH	Companion of Honour
chap.	chapter
ChB	bachelor of surgery
CI	Imperial Order of the Crown of India
CIA	Central Intelligence Agency
CID	Criminal Investigation Department
CIE	companion of the Order of the Indian Empire
Cie	Compagnie
CLit	companion of literature
CM	master of surgery
cm	centimetre(s)

Cmd	command [identifier for published parliamentary papers]
CMG	companion of the Order of St Michael and St George
Cmnd	command [identifier for published parliamentary papers]
CO	Colorado
Co.	company
co.	county
col. *pl.* cols.	column(s)
Corp.	corporation
CSE	certificate of secondary education
CSI	companion of the Order of the Star of India
CT	Connecticut
CVO	commander of the Royal Victorian Order
cwt	hundredweight
$	(American) dollar
d.	(1) penny (pence); (2) died
DBE	dame commander of the Order of the British Empire
DCH	diploma in child health
DCh	doctor of surgery
DCL	doctor of civil law
DCnL	doctor of canon law
DCVO	dame commander of the Royal Victorian Order
DD	doctor of divinity
DE	Delaware
Dec	December
dem.	demolished
DEng	doctor of engineering
des.	destroyed
DFC	Distinguished Flying Cross
DipEd	diploma in education
DipPsych	diploma in psychiatry
diss.	dissertation
DL	deputy lieutenant
DLitt	doctor of letters
DLittCelt	doctor of Celtic letters
DM	(1) Deutschmark; (2) doctor of medicine; (3) doctor of musical arts
DMus	doctor of music
DNA	dioxyribonucleic acid
doc.	document
DOL	doctor of oriental learning
DPH	diploma in public health
DPhil	doctor of philosophy
DPM	diploma in psychological medicine
DSC	Distinguished Service Cross
DSc	doctor of science
DSc (Econ.)	doctor of science (economics)
DSc (Eng.)	doctor of science (engineering)
DSM	Distinguished Service Medal
DSO	companion of the Distinguished Service Order
DSocSc	doctor of social science
DTech	doctor of technology
DTh	doctor of theology
DTM	diploma in tropical medicine
DTMH	diploma in tropical medicine and hygiene
DU	doctor of the university
DUniv	doctor of the university
dwt	pennyweight
EC	European Community
ed. *pl.* eds.	edited / edited by / editor(s)
Edin.	Edinburgh

edn	edition
EEC	European Economic Community
EFTA	European Free Trade Association
EICS	East India Company Service
EMI	Electrical and Musical Industries (Ltd)
Eng.	English
enl.	enlarged
ENSA	Entertainments National Service Association
ep. *pl.* epp.	*epistola(e)*
ESP	extra-sensory perception
esp.	especially
esq.	esquire
est.	estimate / estimated
EU	European Union
ex	sold by (*lit.* out of)
excl.	excludes / excluding
exh.	exhibited
exh. cat.	exhibition catalogue
f. *pl.* ff.	following [pages]
FA	Football Association
FACP	fellow of the American College of Physicians
facs.	facsimile
FANY	First Aid Nursing Yeomanry
FBA	fellow of the British Academy
FBI	Federation of British Industries
FCS	fellow of the Chemical Society
Feb	February
FEng	fellow of the Fellowship of Engineering
FFCM	fellow of the Faculty of Community Medicine
FGS	fellow of the Geological Society
fig.	figure
FIMechE	fellow of the Institution of Mechanical Engineers
FL	Florida
fl.	*floruit*
FLS	fellow of the Linnean Society
FM	frequency modulation
fol. *pl.* fols.	folio(s)
Fr	French francs
Fr.	French
FRAeS	fellow of the Royal Aeronautical Society
FRAI	fellow of the Royal Anthropological Institute
FRAM	fellow of the Royal Academy of Music
FRAS	(1) fellow of the Royal Asiatic Society; (2) fellow of the Royal Astronomical Society
FRCM	fellow of the Royal College of Music
FRCO	fellow of the Royal College of Organists
FRCOG	fellow of the Royal College of Obstetricians and Gynaecologists
FRCP(C)	fellow of the Royal College of Physicians of Canada
FRCP (Edin.)	fellow of the Royal College of Physicians of Edinburgh
FRCP (Lond.)	fellow of the Royal College of Physicians of London
FRCPath	fellow of the Royal College of Pathologists
FRCPsych	fellow of the Royal College of Psychiatrists
FRCS	fellow of the Royal College of Surgeons
FRGS	fellow of the Royal Geographical Society
FRIBA	fellow of the Royal Institute of British Architects
FRICS	fellow of the Royal Institute of Chartered Surveyors
FRS	fellow of the Royal Society
FRSA	fellow of the Royal Society of Arts

FRSCM	fellow of the Royal School of Church Music		ISO	companion of the Imperial Service Order
FRSE	fellow of the Royal Society of Edinburgh		It.	Italian
FRSL	fellow of the Royal Society of Literature		ITA	Independent Television Authority
FSA	fellow of the Society of Antiquaries		ITV	Independent Television
ft	foot *pl.* feet		Jan	January
FTCL	fellow of Trinity College of Music, London		JP	justice of the peace
ft-lb per min.	foot-pounds per minute [unit of horsepower]		jun.	junior
FZS	fellow of the Zoological Society		KB	knight of the Order of the Bath
GA	Georgia		KBE	knight commander of the Order of the British Empire
GBE	knight or dame grand cross of the Order of the British Empire		KC	king's counsel
GCB	knight grand cross of the Order of the Bath		kcal	kilocalorie
GCE	general certificate of education		KCB	knight commander of the Order of the Bath
GCH	knight grand cross of the Royal Guelphic Order		KCH	knight commander of the Royal Guelphic Order
GCHQ	government communications headquarters		KCIE	knight commander of the Order of the Indian Empire
GCIE	knight grand commander of the Order of the Indian Empire		KCMG	knight commander of the Order of St Michael and St George
GCMG	knight or dame grand cross of the Order of St Michael and St George		KCSI	knight commander of the Order of the Star of India
GCSE	general certificate of secondary education		KCVO	knight commander of the Royal Victorian Order
GCSI	knight grand commander of the Order of the Star of India		keV	kilo-electron-volt
GCStJ	bailiff or dame grand cross of the order of St John of Jerusalem		KG	knight of the Order of the Garter
			KGB	[Soviet committee of state security]
GCVO	knight or dame grand cross of the Royal Victorian Order		KH	knight of the Royal Guelphic Order
GEC	General Electric Company		KLM	Koninklijke Luchtvaart Maatschappij (Royal Dutch Air Lines)
Ger.	German		km	kilometre(s)
GI	government (*or* general) issue		KP	knight of the Order of St Patrick
GMT	Greenwich mean time		KS	Kansas
GP	general practitioner		KT	knight of the Order of the Thistle
GPU	[Soviet special police unit]		kt	knight
GSO	general staff officer		KY	Kentucky
Heb.	Hebrew		£	pound(s) sterling
HEICS	Honourable East India Company Service		£E	Egyptian pound
HI	Hawaii		L	lira *pl.* lire
HIV	human immunodeficiency virus		l. *pl.* ll.	line(s)
HK$	Hong Kong dollar		LA	Lousiana
HM	his / her majesty('s)		LAA	light anti-aircraft
HMAS	his / her majesty's Australian ship		LAH	licentiate of the Apothecaries' Hall, Dublin
HMNZS	his / her majesty's New Zealand ship		Lat.	Latin
HMS	his / her majesty's ship		lb	pound(s), unit of weight
HMSO	His / Her Majesty's Stationery Office		LDS	licence in dental surgery
HMV	His Master's Voice		*lit.*	literally
Hon.	Honourable		LittB	bachelor of letters
hp	horsepower		LittD	doctor of letters
hr	hour(s)		LKQCPI	licentiate of the King and Queen's College of Physicians, Ireland
HRH	his / her royal highness		LLA	lady literate in arts
HTV	Harlech Television		LLB	bachelor of laws
IA	Iowa		LLD	doctor of laws
ibid.	*ibidem*: in the same place		LLM	master of laws
ICI	Imperial Chemical Industries (Ltd)		LM	licentiate in midwifery
ID	Idaho		LP	long-playing record
IL	Illinois		LRAM	licentiate of the Royal Academy of Music
illus.	illustration		LRCP	licentiate of the Royal College of Physicians
illustr.	illustrated		LRCPS (Glasgow)	licentiate of the Royal College of Physicians and Surgeons of Glasgow
IN	Indiana			
in.	inch(es)		LRCS	licentiate of the Royal College of Surgeons
Inc.	Incorporated		LSA	licentiate of the Society of Apothecaries
incl.	includes / including		LSD	lysergic acid diethylamide
IOU	I owe you		LVO	lieutenant of the Royal Victorian Order
IQ	intelligence quotient		M. *pl.* MM.	Monsieur *pl.* Messieurs
Ir£	Irish pound		m	metre(s)
IRA	Irish Republican Army			

m. *pl.* mm.	membrane(s)
MA	(1) Massachusetts; (2) master of arts
MAI	master of engineering
MB	bachelor of medicine
MBA	master of business administration
MBE	member of the Order of the British Empire
MC	Military Cross
MCC	Marylebone Cricket Club
MCh	master of surgery
MChir	master of surgery
MCom	master of commerce
MD	(1) doctor of medicine; (2) Maryland
MDMA	methylenedioxymethamphetamine
ME	Maine
MEd	master of education
MEng	master of engineering
MEP	member of the European parliament
MG	Morris Garages
MGM	Metro-Goldwyn-Mayer
Mgr	Monsignor
MI	(1) Michigan; (2) military intelligence
MI1c	[secret intelligence department]
MI5	[military intelligence department]
MI6	[secret intelligence department]
MI9	[secret escape service]
MICE	member of the Institution of Civil Engineers
MIEE	member of the Institution of Electrical Engineers
min.	minute(s)
Mk	mark
ML	(1) licentiate of medicine; (2) master of laws
MLitt	master of letters
Mlle	Mademoiselle
mm	millimetre(s)
Mme	Madame
MN	Minnesota
MO	Missouri
MOH	medical officer of health
MP	member of parliament
m.p.h.	miles per hour
MPhil	master of philosophy
MRCP	member of the Royal College of Physicians
MRCS	member of the Royal College of Surgeons
MRCVS	member of the Royal College of Veterinary Surgeons
MRIA	member of the Royal Irish Academy
MS	(1) master of science; (2) Mississippi
MS *pl.* MSS	manuscript(s)
MSc	master of science
MSc (Econ.)	master of science (economics)
MT	Montana
MusB	bachelor of music
MusBac	bachelor of music
MusD	doctor of music
MV	motor vessel
MVO	member of the Royal Victorian Order
n. *pl.* nn.	note(s)
NAAFI	Navy, Army, and Air Force Institutes
NASA	National Aeronautics and Space Administration
NATO	North Atlantic Treaty Organization
NBC	National Broadcasting Corporation
NC	North Carolina
NCO	non-commissioned officer
ND	North Dakota
n.d.	no date
NE	Nebraska
nem. con.	*nemine contradicente*: unanimously
new ser.	new series
NH	New Hampshire
NHS	National Health Service
NJ	New Jersey
NKVD	[Soviet people's commissariat for internal affairs]
NM	New Mexico
nm	nanometre(s)
no. *pl.* nos.	number(s)
Nov	November
n.p.	no place [of publication]
NS	new style
NV	Nevada
NY	New York
NZBS	New Zealand Broadcasting Service
OBE	officer of the Order of the British Empire
obit.	obituary
Oct	October
OCTU	officer cadets training unit
OECD	Organization for Economic Co-operation and Development
OEEC	Organization for European Economic Co-operation
OFM	order of Friars Minor [Franciscans]
OFMCap	Ordine Frati Minori Cappucini: member of the Capuchin order
OH	Ohio
OK	Oklahoma
O level	ordinary level [examination]
OM	Order of Merit
OP	order of Preachers [Dominicans]
op. *pl.* opp.	opus *pl.* opera
OPEC	Organization of Petroleum Exporting Countries
OR	Oregon
orig.	original
OS	old style
OSB	Order of St Benedict
OTC	Officers' Training Corps
OWS	Old Watercolour Society
Oxon.	Oxoniensis
p. *pl.* pp.	page(s)
PA	Pennsylvania
p.a.	per annum
para.	paragraph
PAYE	pay as you earn
pbk *pl.* pbks	paperback(s)
per.	[during the] period
PhD	doctor of philosophy
pl.	(1) plate(s); (2) plural
priv. coll.	private collection
pt *pl.* pts	part(s)
pubd	published
PVC	polyvinyl chloride
q. *pl.* qq.	(1) question(s); (2) quire(s)
QC	queen's counsel
R	rand
R.	Rex / Regina
r	recto
r.	reigned / ruled
RA	Royal Academy / Royal Academician

RAC	Royal Automobile Club		Skr	Swedish krona
RAF	Royal Air Force		Span.	Spanish
RAFVR	Royal Air Force Volunteer Reserve		SPCK	Society for Promoting Christian Knowledge
RAM	[member of the] Royal Academy of Music		SS	(1) Santissimi; (2) Schutzstaffel; (3) steam ship
RAMC	Royal Army Medical Corps		STB	bachelor of theology
RCA	Royal College of Art		STD	doctor of theology
RCNC	Royal Corps of Naval Constructors		STM	master of theology
RCOG	Royal College of Obstetricians and Gynaecologists		STP	doctor of theology
RDI	royal designer for industry		*supp.*	supposedly
RE	Royal Engineers		suppl. *pl.* suppls.	supplement(s)
repr. *pl.* reprs.	reprint(s) / reprinted		s.v.	*sub verbo* / *sub voce*: under the word / heading
repro.	reproduced		SY	steam yacht
rev.	revised / revised by / reviser / revision		TA	Territorial Army
Revd	Reverend		TASS	[Soviet news agency]
RHA	Royal Hibernian Academy		TB	tuberculosis (*lit.* tubercle bacillus)
RI	(1) Rhode Island; (2) Royal Institute of Painters in Water-Colours		TD	(1) *teachtaí dála* (member of the Dáil); (2) territorial decoration
RIBA	Royal Institute of British Architects		TN	Tennessee
RIN	Royal Indian Navy		TNT	trinitrotoluene
RM	Reichsmark		trans.	translated / translated by / translation / translator
RMS	Royal Mail steamer		TT	tourist trophy
RN	Royal Navy		TUC	Trades Union Congress
RNA	ribonucleic acid		TX	Texas
RNAS	Royal Naval Air Service		U-boat	*Unterseeboot*: submarine
RNR	Royal Naval Reserve		Ufa	Universum-Film AG
RNVR	Royal Naval Volunteer Reserve		UMIST	University of Manchester Institute of Science and Technology
RO	Record Office		UN	United Nations
r.p.m.	revolutions per minute		UNESCO	United Nations Educational, Scientific, and Cultural Organization
RRS	royal research ship			
Rs	rupees		UNICEF	United Nations International Children's Emergency Fund
RSA	(1) Royal Scottish Academician; (2) Royal Society of Arts		unpubd	unpublished
RSPCA	Royal Society for the Prevention of Cruelty to Animals		USS	United States ship
			UT	Utah
Rt Hon.	Right Honourable		*v*	verso
Rt Revd	Right Reverend		v.	versus
RUC	Royal Ulster Constabulary		VA	Virginia
Russ.	Russian		VAD	Voluntary Aid Detachment
RWS	Royal Watercolour Society		VC	Victoria Cross
S4C	Sianel Pedwar Cymru		VE-day	victory in Europe day
s.	shilling(s)		Ven.	Venerable
s.a.	*sub anno*: under the year		VJ-day	victory over Japan day
SABC	South African Broadcasting Corporation		vol. *pl.* vols.	volume(s)
SAS	Special Air Service		VT	Vermont
SC	South Carolina		WA	Washington [state]
ScD	doctor of science		WAAC	Women's Auxiliary Army Corps
S$	Singapore dollar		WAAF	Women's Auxiliary Air Force
SD	South Dakota		WEA	Workers' Educational Association
sec.	second(s)		WHO	World Health Organization
sel.	selected		WI	Wisconsin
sen.	senior		WRAF	Women's Royal Air Force
Sept	September		WRNS	Women's Royal Naval Service
ser.	series		WV	West Virginia
SHAPE	supreme headquarters allied powers, Europe		WVS	Women's Voluntary Service
SIDRO	Société Internationale d'Énergie Hydro-Électrique		WY	Wyoming
sig. *pl.* sigs.	signature(s)		¥	yen
sing.	singular		YMCA	Young Men's Christian Association
SIS	Secret Intelligence Service		YWCA	Young Women's Christian Association
SJ	Society of Jesus			

2 Institution abbreviations

All Souls Oxf.	All Souls College, Oxford
AM Oxf.	Ashmolean Museum, Oxford
Balliol Oxf.	Balliol College, Oxford
BBC WAC	BBC Written Archives Centre, Reading
Beds. & Luton ARS	Bedfordshire and Luton Archives and Record Service, Bedford
Berks. RO	Berkshire Record Office, Reading
BFI	British Film Institute, London
BFI NFTVA	British Film Institute, London, National Film and Television Archive
BGS	British Geological Survey, Keyworth, Nottingham
Birm. CA	Birmingham Central Library, Birmingham City Archives
Birm. CL	Birmingham Central Library
BL	British Library, London
BL NSA	British Library, London, National Sound Archive
BL OIOC	British Library, London, Oriental and India Office Collections
BLPES	London School of Economics and Political Science, British Library of Political and Economic Science
BM	British Museum, London
Bodl. Oxf.	Bodleian Library, Oxford
Bodl. RH	Bodleian Library of Commonwealth and African Studies at Rhodes House, Oxford
Borth. Inst.	Borthwick Institute of Historical Research, University of York
Boston PL	Boston Public Library, Massachusetts
Bristol RO	Bristol Record Office
Bucks. RLSS	Buckinghamshire Records and Local Studies Service, Aylesbury
CAC Cam.	Churchill College, Cambridge, Churchill Archives Centre
Cambs. AS	Cambridgeshire Archive Service
CCC Cam.	Corpus Christi College, Cambridge
CCC Oxf.	Corpus Christi College, Oxford
Ches. & Chester ALSS	Cheshire and Chester Archives and Local Studies Service
Christ Church Oxf.	Christ Church, Oxford
Christies	Christies, London
City Westm. AC	City of Westminster Archives Centre, London
CKS	Centre for Kentish Studies, Maidstone
CLRO	Corporation of London Records Office
Coll. Arms	College of Arms, London
Col. U.	Columbia University, New York
Cornwall RO	Cornwall Record Office, Truro
Courtauld Inst.	Courtauld Institute of Art, London
CUL	Cambridge University Library
Cumbria AS	Cumbria Archive Service
Derbys. RO	Derbyshire Record Office, Matlock
Devon RO	Devon Record Office, Exeter
Dorset RO	Dorset Record Office, Dorchester
Duke U.	Duke University, Durham, North Carolina
Duke U., Perkins L.	Duke University, Durham, North Carolina, William R. Perkins Library
Durham Cath. CL	Durham Cathedral, chapter library
Durham RO	Durham Record Office
DWL	Dr Williams's Library, London
Essex RO	Essex Record Office
E. Sussex RO	East Sussex Record Office, Lewes
Eton	Eton College, Berkshire
FM Cam.	Fitzwilliam Museum, Cambridge
Folger	Folger Shakespeare Library, Washington, DC
Garr. Club	Garrick Club, London
Girton Cam.	Girton College, Cambridge
GL	Guildhall Library, London
Glos. RO	Gloucestershire Record Office, Gloucester
Gon. & Caius Cam.	Gonville and Caius College, Cambridge
Gov. Art Coll.	Government Art Collection
GS Lond.	Geological Society of London
Hants. RO	Hampshire Record Office, Winchester
Harris Man. Oxf.	Harris Manchester College, Oxford
Harvard TC	Harvard Theatre Collection, Harvard University, Cambridge, Massachusetts, Nathan Marsh Pusey Library
Harvard U.	Harvard University, Cambridge, Massachusetts
Harvard U., Houghton L.	Harvard University, Cambridge, Massachusetts, Houghton Library
Herefs. RO	Herefordshire Record Office, Hereford
Herts. ALS	Hertfordshire Archives and Local Studies, Hertford
Hist. Soc. Penn.	Historical Society of Pennsylvania, Philadelphia
HLRO	House of Lords Record Office, London
Hult. Arch.	Hulton Archive, London and New York
Hunt. L.	Huntington Library, San Marino, California
ICL	Imperial College, London
Inst. CE	Institution of Civil Engineers, London
Inst. EE	Institution of Electrical Engineers, London
IWM	Imperial War Museum, London
IWM FVA	Imperial War Museum, London, Film and Video Archive
IWM SA	Imperial War Museum, London, Sound Archive
JRL	John Rylands University Library of Manchester
King's AC Cam.	King's College Archives Centre, Cambridge
King's Cam.	King's College, Cambridge
King's Lond.	King's College, London
King's Lond., Liddell Hart C.	King's College, London, Liddell Hart Centre for Military Archives
Lancs. RO	Lancashire Record Office, Preston
L. Cong.	Library of Congress, Washington, DC
Leics. RO	Leicestershire, Leicester, and Rutland Record Office, Leicester
Lincs. Arch.	Lincolnshire Archives, Lincoln
Linn. Soc.	Linnean Society of London
LMA	London Metropolitan Archives
LPL	Lambeth Palace, London
Lpool RO	Liverpool Record Office and Local Studies Service
LUL	London University Library
Magd. Cam.	Magdalene College, Cambridge
Magd. Oxf.	Magdalen College, Oxford
Man. City Gall.	Manchester City Galleries
Man. CL	Manchester Central Library
Mass. Hist. Soc.	Massachusetts Historical Society, Boston
Merton Oxf.	Merton College, Oxford
MHS Oxf.	Museum of the History of Science, Oxford
Mitchell L., Glas.	Mitchell Library, Glasgow
Mitchell L., NSW	State Library of New South Wales, Sydney, Mitchell Library
Morgan L.	Pierpont Morgan Library, New York
NA Canada	National Archives of Canada, Ottawa
NA Ire.	National Archives of Ireland, Dublin
NAM	National Army Museum, London
NA Scot.	National Archives of Scotland, Edinburgh
News Int. RO	News International Record Office, London
NG Ire.	National Gallery of Ireland, Dublin

NG Scot.	National Gallery of Scotland, Edinburgh
NHM	Natural History Museum, London
NL Aus.	National Library of Australia, Canberra
NL Ire.	National Library of Ireland, Dublin
NL NZ	National Library of New Zealand, Wellington
NL NZ, Turnbull L.	National Library of New Zealand, Wellington, Alexander Turnbull Library
NL Scot.	National Library of Scotland, Edinburgh
NL Wales	National Library of Wales, Aberystwyth
NMG Wales	National Museum and Gallery of Wales, Cardiff
NMM	National Maritime Museum, London
Norfolk RO	Norfolk Record Office, Norwich
Northants. RO	Northamptonshire Record Office, Northampton
Northumbd RO	Northumberland Record Office
Notts. Arch.	Nottinghamshire Archives, Nottingham
NPG	National Portrait Gallery, London
NRA	National Archives, London, Historical Manuscripts Commission, National Register of Archives
Nuffield Oxf.	Nuffield College, Oxford
N. Yorks. CRO	North Yorkshire County Record Office, Northallerton
NYPL	New York Public Library
Oxf. UA	Oxford University Archives
Oxf. U. Mus. NH	Oxford University Museum of Natural History
Oxon. RO	Oxfordshire Record Office, Oxford
Pembroke Cam.	Pembroke College, Cambridge
PRO	National Archives, London, Public Record Office
PRO NIre.	Public Record Office for Northern Ireland, Belfast
Pusey Oxf.	Pusey House, Oxford
RA	Royal Academy of Arts, London
Ransom HRC	Harry Ransom Humanities Research Center, University of Texas, Austin
RAS	Royal Astronomical Society, London
RBG Kew	Royal Botanic Gardens, Kew, London
RCP Lond.	Royal College of Physicians of London
RCS Eng.	Royal College of Surgeons of England, London
RGS	Royal Geographical Society, London
RIBA	Royal Institute of British Architects, London
RIBA BAL	Royal Institute of British Architects, London, British Architectural Library
Royal Arch.	Royal Archives, Windsor Castle, Berkshire [by gracious permission of her majesty the queen]
Royal Irish Acad.	Royal Irish Academy, Dublin
Royal Scot. Acad.	Royal Scottish Academy, Edinburgh
RS	Royal Society, London
RSA	Royal Society of Arts, London
RS Friends, Lond.	Religious Society of Friends, London
St Ant. Oxf.	St Antony's College, Oxford
St John Cam.	St John's College, Cambridge
S. Antiquaries, Lond.	Society of Antiquaries of London
Sci. Mus.	Science Museum, London
Scot. NPG	Scottish National Portrait Gallery, Edinburgh
Scott Polar RI	University of Cambridge, Scott Polar Research Institute
Sheff. Arch.	Sheffield Archives
Shrops. RRC	Shropshire Records and Research Centre, Shrewsbury
SOAS	School of Oriental and African Studies, London
Som. ARS	Somerset Archive and Record Service, Taunton
Staffs. RO	Staffordshire Record Office, Stafford
Suffolk RO	Suffolk Record Office
Surrey HC	Surrey History Centre, Woking
TCD	Trinity College, Dublin
Trinity Cam.	Trinity College, Cambridge
U. Aberdeen	University of Aberdeen
U. Birm.	University of Birmingham
U. Birm. L.	University of Birmingham Library
U. Cal.	University of California
U. Cam.	University of Cambridge
UCL	University College, London
U. Durham	University of Durham
U. Durham L.	University of Durham Library
U. Edin.	University of Edinburgh
U. Edin., New Coll.	University of Edinburgh, New College
U. Edin., New Coll. L.	University of Edinburgh, New College Library
U. Edin. L.	University of Edinburgh Library
U. Glas.	University of Glasgow
U. Glas. L.	University of Glasgow Library
U. Hull	University of Hull
U. Hull, Brynmor Jones L.	University of Hull, Brynmor Jones Library
U. Leeds	University of Leeds
U. Leeds, Brotherton L.	University of Leeds, Brotherton Library
U. Lond.	University of London
U. Lpool	University of Liverpool
U. Lpool L.	University of Liverpool Library
U. Mich.	University of Michigan, Ann Arbor
U. Mich., Clements L.	University of Michigan, Ann Arbor, William L. Clements Library
U. Newcastle	University of Newcastle upon Tyne
U. Newcastle, Robinson L.	University of Newcastle upon Tyne, Robinson Library
U. Nott.	University of Nottingham
U. Nott. L.	University of Nottingham Library
U. Oxf.	University of Oxford
U. Reading	University of Reading
U. Reading L.	University of Reading Library
U. St Andr.	University of St Andrews
U. St Andr. L.	University of St Andrews Library
U. Southampton	University of Southampton
U. Southampton L.	University of Southampton Library
U. Sussex	University of Sussex, Brighton
U. Texas	University of Texas, Austin
U. Wales	University of Wales
U. Warwick Mod. RC	University of Warwick, Coventry, Modern Records Centre
V&A	Victoria and Albert Museum, London
V&A NAL	Victoria and Albert Museum, London, National Art Library
Warks. CRO	Warwickshire County Record Office, Warwick
Wellcome L.	Wellcome Library for the History and Understanding of Medicine, London
Westm. DA	Westminster Diocesan Archives, London
Wilts. & Swindon RO	Wiltshire and Swindon Record Office, Trowbridge
Worcs. RO	Worcestershire Record Office, Worcester
W. Sussex RO	West Sussex Record Office, Chichester
W. Yorks. AS	West Yorkshire Archive Service
Yale U.	Yale University, New Haven, Connecticut
Yale U., Beinecke L.	Yale University, New Haven, Connecticut, Beinecke Rare Book and Manuscript Library
Yale U. CBA	Yale University, New Haven, Connecticut, Yale Center for British Art

3 Bibliographic abbreviations

Adams, *Drama* — W. D. Adams, *A dictionary of the drama*, 1: *A–G* (1904); 2: *H–Z* (1956) [vol. 2 microfilm only]

AFM — J O'Donovan, ed. and trans., *Annala rioghachta Eireann | Annals of the kingdom of Ireland by the four masters*, 7 vols. (1848–51); 2nd edn (1856); 3rd edn (1990)

Allibone, *Dict.* — S. A. Allibone, *A critical dictionary of English literature and British and American authors*, 3 vols. (1859–71); suppl. by J. F. Kirk, 2 vols. (1891)

ANB — J. A. Garraty and M. C. Carnes, eds., *American national biography*, 24 vols. (1999)

Anderson, *Scot. nat.* — W. Anderson, *The Scottish nation, or, The surnames, families, literature, honours, and biographical history of the people of Scotland*, 3 vols. (1859–63)

Ann. mon. — H. R. Luard, ed., *Annales monastici*, 5 vols., Rolls Series, 36 (1864–9)

Ann. Ulster — S. Mac Airt and G. Mac Niocaill, eds., *Annals of Ulster (to AD 1131)* (1983)

APC — *Acts of the privy council of England*, new ser., 46 vols. (1890–1964)

APS — *The acts of the parliaments of Scotland*, 12 vols. in 13 (1814–75)

Arber, *Regs. Stationers* — F. Arber, ed., *A transcript of the registers of the Company of Stationers of London, 1554–1640 AD*, 5 vols. (1875–94)

ArchR — *Architectural Review*

ASC — D. Whitelock, D. C. Douglas, and S. I. Tucker, ed. and trans., *The Anglo-Saxon Chronicle: a revised translation* (1961)

AS chart. — P. H. Sawyer, *Anglo-Saxon charters: an annotated list and bibliography*, Royal Historical Society Guides and Handbooks (1968)

AusDB — D. Pike and others, eds., *Australian dictionary of biography*, 16 vols. (1966–2002)

Baker, *Serjeants* — J. H. Baker, *The order of serjeants at law*, SeldS, suppl. ser., 5 (1984)

Bale, *Cat.* — J. Bale, *Scriptorum illustrium Maioris Brytannie, quam nunc Angliam et Scotiam vocant: catalogus*, 2 vols. in 1 (Basel, 1557–9); facs. edn (1971)

Bale, *Index* — J. Bale, *Index Britanniae scriptorum*, ed. R. L. Poole and M. Bateson (1902); facs. edn (1990)

BBCS — *Bulletin of the Board of Celtic Studies*

BDMBR — J. O. Baylen and N. J. Gossman, eds., *Biographical dictionary of modern British radicals*, 3 vols. in 4 (1979–88)

Bede, *Hist. eccl.* — *Bede's Ecclesiastical history of the English people*, ed. and trans. B. Colgrave and R. A. B. Mynors, OMT (1969); repr. (1991)

Bénézit, *Dict.* — E. Bénézit, *Dictionnaire critique et documentaire des peintres, sculpteurs, dessinateurs et graveurs*, 3 vols. (Paris, 1911–23); new edn, 8 vols. (1948–66), repr. (1966); 3rd edn, rev. and enl., 10 vols. (1976); 4th edn, 14 vols. (1999)

BIHR — *Bulletin of the Institute of Historical Research*

Birch, *Seals* — W. de Birch, *Catalogue of seals in the department of manuscripts in the British Museum*, 6 vols. (1887–1900)

Bishop Burnet's History — *Bishop Burnet's History of his own time*, ed. M. J. Routh, 2nd edn, 6 vols. (1833)

Blackwood — *Blackwood's [Edinburgh] Magazine*, 328 vols. (1817–1980)

Blain, Clements & Grundy, *Feminist comp.* — V. Blain, P. Clements, and I. Grundy, eds., *The feminist companion to literature in English* (1990)

BL cat. — *The British Library general catalogue of printed books* [in 360 vols. with suppls., also CD-ROM and online]

BMJ — *British Medical Journal*

Boase & Courtney, *Bibl. Corn.* — G. C. Boase and W. P. Courtney, *Bibliotheca Cornubiensis: a catalogue of the writings … of Cornishmen*, 3 vols. (1874–82)

Boase, *Mod. Eng. biog.* — F. Boase, *Modern English biography: containing many thousand concise memoirs of persons who have died since the year 1850*, 6 vols. (privately printed, Truro, 1892–1921); repr. (1965)

Boswell, *Life* — *Boswell's Life of Johnson: together with Journal of a tour to the Hebrides and Johnson's Diary of a journey into north Wales*, ed. G. B. Hill, enl. edn, rev. L. F. Powell, 6 vols. (1934–50); 2nd edn (1964); repr. (1971)

Brown & Stratton, *Brit. mus.* — J. D. Brown and S. S. Stratton, *British musical biography* (1897)

Bryan, *Painters* — M. Bryan, *A biographical and critical dictionary of painters and engravers*, 2 vols. (1816); new edn, ed. G. Stanley (1849); new edn, ed. R. E. Graves and W. Armstrong, 2 vols. (1886–9); [4th edn], ed. G. C. Williamson, 5 vols. (1903–5) [various reprs.]

Burke, *Gen. GB* — J. Burke, *A genealogical and heraldic history of the commoners of Great Britain and Ireland*, 4 vols. (1833–8); new edn as *A genealogical and heraldic dictionary of the landed gentry of Great Britain and Ireland*, 3 vols. [1843–9] [many later edns]

Burke, *Gen. Ire.* — J. B. Burke, *A genealogical and heraldic history of the landed gentry of Ireland* (1899); 2nd edn (1904); 3rd edn (1912); 4th edn (1958); 5th edn as *Burke's Irish family records* (1976)

Burke, *Peerage* — J. Burke, *A general* [later edns *A genealogical*] *and heraldic dictionary of the peerage and baronetage of the United Kingdom* [later edns *the British empire*] (1829–)

Burney, *Hist. mus.* — C. Burney, *A general history of music, from the earliest ages to the present period*, 4 vols. (1776–89)

Burtchaell & Sadleir, *Alum. Dubl.* — G. D. Burtchaell and T. U. Sadleir, *Alumni Dublinenses: a register of the students, graduates, and provosts of Trinity College* (1924); [2nd edn], with suppl., in 2 pts (1935)

Calamy rev. — A. G. Matthews, *Calamy revised* (1934); repr. (1988)

CCI — *Calendar of confirmations and inventories granted and given up in the several commissariots of Scotland* (1876–)

CClR — *Calendar of the close rolls preserved in the Public Record Office*, 47 vols. (1892–1963)

CDS — J. Bain, ed., *Calendar of documents relating to Scotland*, 4 vols., PRO (1881–8); suppl. vol. 5, ed. G. G. Simpson and J. D. Galbraith [1986]

CEPR letters — W. H. Bliss, C. Johnson, and J. Twemlow, eds., *Calendar of entries in the papal registers relating to Great Britain and Ireland: papal letters* (1893–)

CGPLA — *Calendars of the grants of probate and letters of administration* [in 4 ser.: *England & Wales, Northern Ireland, Ireland,* and *Éire*]

Chambers, *Scots.* — R. Chambers, ed., *A biographical dictionary of eminent Scotsmen*, 4 vols. (1832–5)

Chancery records — chancery records pubd by the PRO

Chancery records (RC) — chancery records pubd by the Record Commissions

CIPM	Calendar of inquisitions post mortem, [20 vols.], PRO (1904–); also Henry VII, 3 vols. (1898–1955)
Clarendon, Hist. rebellion	E. Hyde, earl of Clarendon, The history of the rebellion and civil wars in England, 6 vols. (1888); repr. (1958) and (1992)
Cobbett, Parl. hist.	W. Cobbett and J. Wright, eds., Cobbett's Parliamentary history of England, 36 vols. (1806–1820)
Colvin, Archs.	H. Colvin, A biographical dictionary of British architects, 1600–1840, 3rd edn (1995)
Cooper, Ath. Cantab.	C. H. Cooper and T. Cooper, Athenae Cantabrigienses, 3 vols. (1858–1913); repr. (1967)
CPR	Calendar of the patent rolls preserved in the Public Record Office (1891–)
Crockford	Crockford's Clerical Directory
CS	Camden Society
CSP	Calendar of state papers [in 11 ser.: domestic, Scotland, Scottish series, Ireland, colonial, Commonwealth, foreign, Spain [at Simancas], Rome, Milan, and Venice]
CYS	Canterbury and York Society
DAB	Dictionary of American biography, 21 vols. (1928–36), repr. in 11 vols. (1964); 10 suppls. (1944–96)
DBB	D. J. Jeremy, ed., Dictionary of business biography, 5 vols. (1984–6)
DCB	G. W. Brown and others, Dictionary of Canadian biography, [14 vols.] (1966–)
Debrett's Peerage	Debrett's Peerage (1803–) [sometimes Debrett's Illustrated peerage]
Desmond, Botanists	R. Desmond, Dictionary of British and Irish botanists and horticulturists (1977); rev. edn (1994)
Dir. Brit. archs.	A. Felstead, J. Franklin, and L. Pinfield, eds., Directory of British architects, 1834–1900 (1993); 2nd edn, ed. A. Brodie and others, 2 vols. (2001)
DLB	J. M. Bellamy and J. Saville, eds., Dictionary of labour biography, [10 vols.] (1972–)
DLitB	Dictionary of Literary Biography
DNB	Dictionary of national biography, 63 vols. (1885–1900), suppl., 3 vols. (1901); repr. in 22 vols. (1908–9); 10 further suppls. (1912–96); Missing persons (1993)
DNZB	W. H. Oliver and C. Orange, eds., The dictionary of New Zealand biography, 5 vols. (1990–2000)
DSAB	W. J. de Kock and others, eds., Dictionary of South African biography, 5 vols. (1968–87)
DSB	C. C. Gillispie and F. L. Holmes, eds., Dictionary of scientific biography, 16 vols. (1970–80); repr. in 8 vols. (1981); 2 vol. suppl. (1990)
DSBB	A. Slaven and S. Checkland, eds., Dictionary of Scottish business biography, 1860–1960, 2 vols. (1986–90)
DSCHT	N. M. de S. Cameron and others, eds., Dictionary of Scottish church history and theology (1993)
Dugdale, Monasticon	W. Dugdale, Monasticon Anglicanum, 3 vols. (1655–72); 2nd edn, 3 vols. (1661–82); new edn, ed. J. Caley, J. Ellis, and B. Bandinel, 6 vols. in 8 pts (1817–30); repr. (1846) and (1970)
DWB	J. E. Lloyd and others, eds., Dictionary of Welsh biography down to 1940 (1959) [Eng. trans. of Y bywgraffiadur Cymreig hyd 1940, 2nd edn (1954)]
EdinR	Edinburgh Review, or, Critical Journal
EETS	Early English Text Society
Emden, Cam.	A. B. Emden, A biographical register of the University of Cambridge to 1500 (1963)
Emden, Oxf.	A. B. Emden, A biographical register of the University of Oxford to AD 1500, 3 vols. (1957–9); also A biographical register of the University of Oxford, AD 1501 to 1540 (1974)
EngHR	English Historical Review
Engraved Brit. ports.	F. M. O'Donoghue and H. M. Hake, Catalogue of engraved British portraits preserved in the department of prints and drawings in the British Museum, 6 vols. (1908–25)
ER	The English Reports, 178 vols. (1900–32)
ESTC	English short title catalogue, 1475–1800 [CD-ROM and online]
Evelyn, Diary	The diary of John Evelyn, ed. E. S. De Beer, 6 vols. (1955); repr. (2000)
Farington, Diary	The diary of Joseph Farington, ed. K. Garlick and others, 17 vols. (1978–98)
Fasti Angl. (Hardy)	J. Le Neve, Fasti ecclesiae Anglicanae, ed. T. D. Hardy, 3 vols. (1854)
Fasti Angl., 1066–1300	[J. Le Neve], Fasti ecclesiae Anglicanae, 1066–1300, ed. D. E. Greenway and J. S. Barrow, [8 vols.] (1968–)
Fasti Angl., 1300–1541	[J. Le Neve], Fasti ecclesiae Anglicanae, 1300–1541, 12 vols. (1962–7)
Fasti Angl., 1541–1857	[J. Le Neve], Fasti ecclesiae Anglicanae, 1541–1857, ed. J. M. Horn, D. M. Smith, and D. S. Bailey, [9 vols.] (1969–)
Fasti Scot.	H. Scott, Fasti ecclesiae Scoticanae, 3 vols. in 6 (1871); new edn, [11 vols.] (1915–)
FO List	Foreign Office List
Fortescue, Brit. army	J. W. Fortescue, A history of the British army, 13 vols. (1899–1930)
Foss, Judges	E. Foss, The judges of England, 9 vols. (1848–64); repr. (1966)
Foster, Alum. Oxon.	J. Foster, ed., Alumni Oxonienses: the members of the University of Oxford, 1715–1886, 4 vols. (1887–8); later edn (1891); also Alumni Oxonienses … 1500–1714, 4 vols. (1891–2); 8 vol. repr. (1968) and (2000)
Fuller, Worthies	T. Fuller, The history of the worthies of England, 4 pts (1662); new edn, 2 vols., ed. J. Nichols (1811); new edn, 3 vols., ed. P. A. Nuttall (1840); repr. (1965)
GEC, Baronetage	G. E. Cokayne, Complete baronetage, 6 vols. (1900–09); repr. (1983) [microprint]
GEC, Peerage	G. E. C. [G. E. Cokayne], The complete peerage of England, Scotland, Ireland, Great Britain, and the United Kingdom, 8 vols. (1887–98); new edn, ed. V. Gibbs and others, 14 vols. in 15 (1910–98); microprint repr. (1982) and (1987)
Genest, Eng. stage	J. Genest, Some account of the English stage from the Restoration in 1660 to 1830, 10 vols. (1832); repr. [New York, 1965]
Gillow, Lit. biog. hist.	J. Gillow, A literary and biographical history or bibliographical dictionary of the English Catholics, from the breach with Rome, in 1534, to the present time, 5 vols. [1885–1902]; repr. (1961); repr. with preface by C. Gillow (1999)
Gir. Camb. opera	Giraldi Cambrensis opera, ed. J. S. Brewer, J. F. Dimock, and G. F. Warner, 8 vols., Rolls Series, 21 (1861–91)
GJ	Geographical Journal

Gladstone, *Diaries* — *The Gladstone diaries: with cabinet minutes and prime-ministerial correspondence*, ed. M. R. D. Foot and H. C. G. Matthew, 14 vols. (1968–94)

GM — *Gentleman's Magazine*

Graves, *Artists* — A. Graves, ed., *A dictionary of artists who have exhibited works in the principal London exhibitions of oil paintings from 1760 to 1880* (1884); new edn (1895); 3rd edn (1901); facs. edn (1969); repr. [1970], (1973), and (1984)

Graves, *Brit. Inst.* — A. Graves, *The British Institution, 1806–1867: a complete dictionary of contributors and their work from the foundation of the institution* (1875); facs. edn (1908); repr. (1969)

Graves, *RA exhibitors* — A. Graves, *The Royal Academy of Arts: a complete dictionary of contributors and their work from its foundation in 1769 to 1904*, 8 vols. (1905–6); repr. in 4 vols. (1970) and (1972)

Graves, *Soc. Artists* — A. Graves, *The Society of Artists of Great Britain, 1760–1791, the Free Society of Artists, 1761–1783: a complete dictionary* (1907); facs. edn (1969)

Greaves & Zaller, *BDBR* — R. L. Greaves and R. Zaller, eds., *Biographical dictionary of British radicals in the seventeenth century*, 3 vols. (1982–4)

Grove, *Dict. mus.* — G. Grove, ed., *A dictionary of music and musicians*, 5 vols. (1878–90); 2nd edn, ed. J. A. Fuller Maitland (1904–10); 3rd edn, ed. H. C. Colles (1927); 4th edn with suppl. (1940); 5th edn, ed. E. Blom, 9 vols. (1954); suppl. (1961) [see also *New Grove*]

Hall, *Dramatic ports.* — L. A. Hall, *Catalogue of dramatic portraits in the theatre collection of the Harvard College library*, 4 vols. (1930–34)

Hansard — *Hansard's parliamentary debates*, ser. 1–5 (1803–)

Highfill, Burnim & Langhans, *BDA* — P. H. Highfill, K. A. Burnim, and E. A. Langhans, *A biographical dictionary of actors, actresses, musicians, dancers, managers, and other stage personnel in London, 1660–1800*, 16 vols. (1973–93)

Hist. U. Oxf. — T. H. Aston, ed., *The history of the University of Oxford*, 8 vols. (1984–2000) [1: *The early Oxford schools*, ed. J. I. Catto (1984); 2: *Late medieval Oxford*, ed. J. I. Catto and R. Evans (1992); 3: *The collegiate university*, ed. J. McConica (1986); 4: *Seventeenth-century Oxford*, ed. N. Tyacke (1997); 5: *The eighteenth century*, ed. L. S. Sutherland and L. G. Mitchell (1986); 6–7: *Nineteenth-century Oxford*, ed. M. G. Brock and M. C. Curthoys (1997–2000); 8: *The twentieth century*, ed. B. Harrison (2000)]

HJ — *Historical Journal*

HMC — Historical Manuscripts Commission

Holdsworth, *Eng. law* — W. S. Holdsworth, *A history of English law*, ed. A. L. Goodhart and H. L. Hanbury, 17 vols. (1903–72)

HoP, *Commons* — *The history of parliament: the House of Commons* [1386–1421, ed. J. S. Roskell, L. Clark, and C. Rawcliffe, 4 vols. (1992); 1509–1558, ed. S. T. Bindoff, 3 vols. (1982); 1558–1603, ed. P. W. Hasler, 3 vols. (1981); 1660–1690, ed. B. D. Henning, 3 vols. (1983); 1690–1715, ed. D. W. Hayton, E. Cruickshanks, and S. Handley, 5 vols. (2002); 1715–1754, ed. R. Sedgwick, 2 vols. (1970); 1754–1790, ed. L. Namier and J. Brooke, 3 vols. (1964), repr. (1985); 1790–1820, ed. R. G. Thorne, 5 vols. (1986); in draft (used with permission): 1422–1504, 1604–1629, 1640–1660, and 1820–1832]

IGI — *International Genealogical Index*, Church of Jesus Christ of the Latterday Saints

ILN — *Illustrated London News*

IMC — Irish Manuscripts Commission

Irving, *Scots.* — J. Irving, ed., *The book of Scotsmen eminent for achievements in arms and arts, church and state, law, legislation and literature, commerce, science, travel and philanthropy* (1881)

JCS — *Journal of the Chemical Society*

JHC — *Journals of the House of Commons*

JHL — *Journals of the House of Lords*

John of Worcester, *Chron.* — *The chronicle of John of Worcester*, ed. R. R. Darlington and P. McGurk, trans. J. Bray and P. McGurk, 3 vols., OMT (1995–) [vol. 1 forthcoming]

Keeler, *Long Parliament* — M. F. Keeler, *The Long Parliament, 1640–1641: a biographical study of its members* (1954)

Kelly, *Handbk* — *The upper ten thousand: an alphabetical list of all members of noble families*, 3 vols. (1875–7); continued as *Kelly's handbook of the upper ten thousand for 1878* [1879], 2 vols. (1878–9); continued as *Kelly's handbook to the titled, landed and official classes*, 94 vols. (1880–1973)

LondG — *London Gazette*

LP Henry VIII — J. S. Brewer, J. Gairdner, and R. H. Brodie, eds., *Letters and papers, foreign and domestic, of the reign of Henry VIII*, 23 vols. in 38 (1862–1932); repr. (1965)

Mallalieu, *Watercolour artists* — H. L. Mallalieu, *The dictionary of British watercolour artists up to 1820*, 3 vols. (1976–90); vol. 1, 2nd edn (1986)

Memoirs FRS — *Biographical Memoirs of Fellows of the Royal Society*

MGH — Monumenta Germaniae Historica

MT — *Musical Times*

Munk, *Roll* — W. Munk, *The roll of the Royal College of Physicians of London*, 2 vols. (1861); 2nd edn, 3 vols. (1878)

N&Q — *Notes and Queries*

New Grove — S. Sadie, ed., *The new Grove dictionary of music and musicians*, 20 vols. (1980); 2nd edn, 29 vols. (2001) [also online edn; see also Grove, *Dict. mus.*]

Nichols, *Illustrations* — J. Nichols and J. B. Nichols, *Illustrations of the literary history of the eighteenth century*, 8 vols. (1817–58)

Nichols, *Lit. anecdotes* — J. Nichols, *Literary anecdotes of the eighteenth century*, 9 vols. (1812–16); facs. edn (1966)

Obits. FRS — *Obituary Notices of Fellows of the Royal Society*

O'Byrne, *Naval biog. dict.* — W. R. O'Byrne, *A naval biographical dictionary* (1849); repr. (1990); [2nd edn], 2 vols. (1861)

OHS — Oxford Historical Society

Old Westminsters — *The record of Old Westminsters*, 1–2, ed. G. F. Barker and A. H. Stenning (1928); suppl. 1, ed. J. B. Whitmore and G. R. Y. Radcliffe [1938]; 3, ed. J. B. Whitmore, G. R. Y. Radcliffe, and D. C. Simpson (1963); suppl. 2, ed. F. E. Pagan (1978); 4, ed. F. E. Pagan and H. E. Pagan (1992)

OMT — Oxford Medieval Texts

Ordericus Vitalis, *Eccl. hist.* — *The ecclesiastical history of Orderic Vitalis*, ed. and trans. M. Chibnall, 6 vols., OMT (1969–80); repr. (1990)

Paris, *Chron.* — *Matthaei Parisiensis, monachi sancti Albani, chronica majora*, ed. H. R. Luard, Rolls Series, 7 vols. (1872–83)

Parl. papers — *Parliamentary papers* (1801–)

PBA — *Proceedings of the British Academy*

Pepys, *Diary*	*The diary of Samuel Pepys*, ed. R. Latham and W. Matthews, 11 vols. (1970–83); repr. (1995) and (2000)
Pevsner	N. Pevsner and others, Buildings of England series
PICE	*Proceedings of the Institution of Civil Engineers*
Pipe rolls	*The great roll of the pipe for . . .*, PRSoc. (1884–)
PRO	Public Record Office
PRS	*Proceedings of the Royal Society of London*
PRSoc.	Pipe Roll Society
PTRS	*Philosophical Transactions of the Royal Society*
QR	*Quarterly Review*
RC	Record Commissions
Redgrave, *Artists*	S. Redgrave, *A dictionary of artists of the English school* (1874); rev. edn (1878); repr. (1970)
Reg. Oxf.	C. W. Boase and A. Clark, eds., *Register of the University of Oxford*, 5 vols., OHS, 1, 10–12, 14 (1885–9)
Reg. PCS	J. H. Burton and others, eds., *The register of the privy council of Scotland*, 1st ser., 14 vols. (1877–98); 2nd ser., 8 vols. (1899–1908); 3rd ser., [16 vols.] (1908–70)
Reg. RAN	H. W. C. Davis and others, eds., *Regesta regum Anglo-Normannorum, 1066–1154*, 4 vols. (1913–69)
RIBA Journal	*Journal of the Royal Institute of British Architects* [later *RIBA Journal*]
RotP	J. Strachey, ed., *Rotuli parliamentorum ut et petitiones, et placita in parliamento*, 6 vols. (1767–77)
RotS	D. Macpherson, J. Caley, and W. Illingworth, eds., *Rotuli Scotiae in Turri Londinensi et in domo capitulari Westmonasteriensi asservati*, 2 vols., RC, 14 (1814–19)
RS	Record(s) Society
Rymer, *Foedera*	T. Rymer and R. Sanderson, eds., *Foedera, conventiones, literae et cuiuscunque generis acta publica inter reges Angliae et alios quosvis imperatores, reges, pontifices, principes, vel communitates*, 20 vols. (1704–35); 2nd edn, 20 vols. (1726–35); 3rd edn, 10 vols. (1739–45); facs. edn (1967); new edn, ed. A. Clarke, J. Caley, and F. Holbrooke, 4 vols., RC, 50 (1816–30)
Sainty, *Judges*	J. Sainty, ed., *The judges of England, 1272–1990*, SeldS, suppl. ser., 10 (1993)
Sainty, *King's counsel*	J. Sainty, ed., *A list of English law officers and king's counsel*, SeldS, suppl. ser., 7 (1987)
SCH	Studies in Church History
Scots peerage	J. B. Paul, ed. *The Scots peerage, founded on Wood's edition of Sir Robert Douglas's Peerage of Scotland, containing an historical and genealogical account of the nobility of that kingdom*, 9 vols. (1904–14)
SeldS	Selden Society
SHR	*Scottish Historical Review*
State trials	T. B. Howell and T. J. Howell, eds., *Cobbett's Complete collection of state trials*, 34 vols. (1809–28)
STC, 1475–1640	A. W. Pollard, G. R. Redgrave, and others, eds., *A short-title catalogue of … English books … 1475–1640* (1926); 2nd edn, ed. W. A. Jackson, F. S. Ferguson, and K. F. Pantzer, 3 vols. (1976–91) [see also Wing, *STC*]
STS	Scottish Text Society
SurtS	Surtees Society
Symeon of Durham, *Opera*	*Symeonis monachi opera omnia*, ed. T. Arnold, 2 vols., Rolls Series, 75 (1882–5); repr. (1965)
Tanner, *Bibl. Brit.-Hib.*	T. Tanner, *Bibliotheca Britannico-Hibernica*, ed. D. Wilkins (1748); repr. (1963)
Thieme & Becker, *Allgemeines Lexikon*	U. Thieme, F. Becker, and H. Vollmer, eds., *Allgemeines Lexikon der bildenden Künstler von der Antike bis zur Gegenwart*, 37 vols. (Leipzig, 1907–50); repr. (1961–5), (1983), and (1992)
Thurloe, *State papers*	*A collection of the state papers of John Thurloe*, ed. T. Birch, 7 vols. (1742)
TLS	*Times Literary Supplement*
Tout, *Admin. hist.*	T. F. Tout, *Chapters in the administrative history of mediaeval England: the wardrobe, the chamber, and the small seals*, 6 vols. (1920–33); repr. (1967)
TRHS	*Transactions of the Royal Historical Society*
VCH	H. A. Doubleday and others, eds., *The Victoria history of the counties of England*, [88 vols.] (1900–)
Venn, *Alum. Cant.*	J. Venn and J. A. Venn, *Alumni Cantabrigienses: a biographical list of all known students, graduates, and holders of office at the University of Cambridge, from the earliest times to 1900*, 10 vols. (1922–54); repr. in 2 vols. (1974–8)
Vertue, *Note books*	[G. Vertue], *Note books*, ed. K. Esdaile, earl of Ilchester, and H. M. Hake, 6 vols., Walpole Society, 18, 20, 22, 24, 26, 30 (1930–55)
VF	*Vanity Fair*
Walford, *County families*	E. Walford, *The county families of the United Kingdom, or, Royal manual of the titled and untitled aristocracy of Great Britain and Ireland* (1860)
Walker rev.	A. G. Matthews, *Walker revised: being a revision of John Walker's Sufferings of the clergy during the grand rebellion, 1642–60* (1948); repr. (1988)
Walpole, *Corr.*	*The Yale edition of Horace Walpole's correspondence*, ed. W. S. Lewis, 48 vols. (1937–83)
Ward, *Men of the reign*	T. H. Ward, ed., *Men of the reign: a biographical dictionary of eminent persons of British and colonial birth who have died during the reign of Queen Victoria* (1885); repr. (Graz, 1968)
Waterhouse, *18c painters*	E. Waterhouse, *The dictionary of 18th century painters in oils and crayons* (1981); repr. as *British 18th century painters in oils and crayons* (1991), vol. 2 of *Dictionary of British art*
Watt, *Bibl. Brit.*	R. Watt, *Bibliotheca Britannica, or, A general index to British and foreign literature*, 4 vols. (1824) [many reprs.]
Wellesley index	W. E. Houghton, ed., *The Wellesley index to Victorian periodicals, 1824–1900*, 5 vols. (1966–89); new edn (1999) [CD-ROM]
Wing, *STC*	D. Wing, ed., *Short-title catalogue of … English books … 1641–1700*, 3 vols. (1945–51); 2nd edn (1972–88); rev. and enl. edn, ed. J. J. Morrison, C. W. Nelson, and M. Seccombe, 4 vols. (1994–8) [see also *STC, 1475–1640*]
Wisden	*John Wisden's Cricketer's Almanack*
Wood, *Ath. Oxon.*	A. Wood, *Athenae Oxonienses … to which are added the Fasti*, 2 vols. (1691–2); 2nd edn (1721); new edn, 4 vols., ed. P. Bliss (1813–20); repr. (1967) and (1969)
Wood, *Vic. painters*	C. Wood, *Dictionary of Victorian painters* (1971); 2nd edn (1978); 3rd edn as *Victorian painters*, 2 vols. (1995), vol. 4 of *Dictionary of British art*
WW	*Who's who* (1849–)
WWBMP	M. Stenton and S. Lees, eds., *Who's who of British members of parliament*, 4 vols. (1976–81)
WWW	*Who was who* (1929–)

Drysdale, Barbara Estelle Dockar- [*née* Barbara Estelle Gordon] (1912–1999), psychotherapist, was born on 17 October 1912 at 8 Fitzwilliam Square, Dublin, the youngest of five daughters of Thomas Eagleston Gordon (1866–1929), surgeon, and his wife, Ellen Marguerite, *née* Blake. Her father was professor of surgery at Trinity College, Dublin, and at his death president of the Royal College of Surgeons in Ireland. Educated at Alexandra College, Dublin, Barbara Gordon had ambitions of following in the steps of her father by studying medicine. However, such hopes were dashed by her father's death in July 1929, which left the family impoverished. Abandoning college, she sought a training that would enable her to fend for herself financially. A married sister arranged for her to stay with the Wittgenstein family in Vienna in order to learn German with a view to studying librarianship. She never became a librarian, but subsequently put her knowledge of German to good use in studying the works of Freud in the original. In 1935 she joined her mother in England. They acquired a cottage in the Berkshire village of Blewbury where they successfully started a daytime playgroup called Cat's Cradle. This childcare work continued when she moved to Radley shortly before her marriage to (Joseph) Stephen Lloyd Dockar-Drysdale (1901/02–1996) on 14 April 1936. He was manager of the large family estate in the village, and the son of William Dockar-Drysdale, gentleman. They had four children, born between 1937 and 1948.

Throughout the years of child rearing that followed her marriage, Barbara Dockar-Drysdale continued caring for other people's children, running a children's nursery, and then, during the Second World War, taking in evacuee children who had been difficult to place (and occasionally their parents). Though she lacked a formal training, her success in dealing with troubled children came to the notice of government representatives who were busy enlisting the best practitioners from the recent evacuation programme for their new child welfare plans. In this post-war climate of innovation Dockar-Drysdale embarked on what became her major practical contribution to childcare in Britain, founding the Mulberry Bush School in Standlake, Oxfordshire. This residential special school for about forty children of junior school age opened in 1948 under the auspices of the Home Office and the Department of Education. Drawing on therapeutic principles deriving from her wartime experiences, she recognized the importance of the qualitative ingredients of family life that many of these children lacked—security based on acceptance, consistency, love, and individual attention—and sought ways of providing them in a communal setting. Her husband actively supported her in launching this venture and was her closest ally throughout. In addition she relied on a network of like-minded psychologists, educationists, and psychiatrists, who valued her therapeutic skills and admired her determination not to give up on even the most dauntingly problematic children.

Keen to make good the absence of formal qualifications, Dockar-Drysdale trained as a psychotherapist. She also gained a broader knowledge of childcare theory through attending courses at the Maudsley Hospital. Her work became more widely known when she was invited to address the British Association for the Advancement of Science in 1956. Her topic was the treatment of 'frozen children'. These were youngsters who, in her terms, had become emotionally and morally desensitized, having grown up without early maternal care. She emphasized the importance of adaptation to the child's needs and of anticipating breakdowns rather than employing corrective or coercive efforts afterwards. The paper was notable for combining intuition, based on empathy, with unsentimentality, based on a realistic appraisal of the depth of such children's deprivation. These qualities became the hallmark of her clinical writing.

In 1954 Dockar-Drysdale first met the psychoanalyst and paediatrician Donald Winnicott, with whom she developed a close professional collaboration. In addition to running the Mulberry Bush School she accepted a number of his patients into analysis, often treating them in her own home. One fruit of their association was her formulation of the place and purpose of symbolic regression within a significant relationship in meeting the emotional needs of deprived children. This for her was the key to solving the major problem of effective residential therapy based on regression, namely, how to provide therapeutically for several children simultaneously and collectively, when what each child had lacked was individual, consistent, personally directed maternal care.

Despite her natural vigour, by the end of the 1950s the extent and variety of Dockar-Drysdale's therapeutic work, added to her family commitments, began taking its toll. Critics of the Mulberry Bush complained that undue emphasis was placed on the inner life and needs of the children at the expense of their social and educational development. Now well established, the Mulberry Bush School needed a more structured management. In 1962 she and her husband stepped down as co-principals. She then became its external therapeutic adviser, a post she held until 1975. From 1968 until her retirement in 1990, much of her energy was devoted to a new role, working with adolescents and their therapeutic management as consultant psychotherapist to the Cotswold Community at Ashton Keynes, Wiltshire. This former approved school, restructured and revitalized in 1968 by Richard Balbernie, saw fresh applications of her thinking about regression, as well as new perspectives on staff consultation and on the effective sharing of therapeutic care.

Dockar-Drysdale produced a steady flow of papers based on lectures and seminars. Three volumes of these were published: *Therapy in Child Care* (1968), *Consultations in Child Care* (1973), and *The Provision of Primary Experience* (1990). In 1993 the two former volumes were reprinted jointly as *Therapy and Consultation in Child Care*. Her writings reflected her character in their simple directness combined with sudden depths of insight. Winnicott described her as 'someone who knew'. In 1986 she was awarded an honorary MA degree by Bristol University. Having missed the opportunity of a university degree, she was gratified by this academic recognition for a highly distinctive and personal contribution to the theory and practice of childcare in Britain. She died of old age at Hyperion House Nursing Home, London Road, Fairford, Gloucestershire, on 18 March 1999, and was buried in the churchyard of St Mary the Virgin, Fairford, on 30 March. Her husband predeceased her. CHRISTOPHER REEVES

Sources *Daily Telegraph* (14 April 1999) · *The Independent* (8 April 1999) · Royal College of Physicians in Ireland, Kirkpatrick archive · personal knowledge (2004) · private information (2004) [Sally Cooper, daughter] · b. cert. · m. cert. · d. cert.
Archives Planned Environmental Therapy Trust, Toddington, Cheltenham, archive
Wealth at death under £200,000—gross; under £10,000—net: probate, 9 April 1999, *CGPLA Eng. & Wales*

Drysdale, Charles Robert (1828/9–1907). *See under* Drysdale, George (1824–1904).

Drysdale, Charles Vickery (1874–1961), electrical engineer and social philosopher, was born at Barnstaple, Devon, on 8 July 1874, the only son of Charles Robert *Drysdale (1828/9–1907) [*see under* Drysdale, George (1824–1904)] and Alice Drysdale *Vickery (1844–1929), both physicians. Although eventually becoming senior physician to the Metropolitan Hospital, London, his father was also adept at engineering and took part in the building of the *Great Eastern* steamship in 1847 and was also engaged in railway surveying in Switzerland and Spain. Both of C. V. Drysdale's parents were founder members of the Malthusian League.

Following private schooling, Drysdale obtained his technical education at Finsbury Technical College, London, and at the Central Technical College, South Kensington, London, where he was awarded the Siemens medal. After a brief period as confidential scientific assistant with Nalder Bros. & Co., electrical instrument makers, he turned to educational work and was associate head of the applied physics and electrical engineering department of the Northampton Institute, London, from 1896 to 1910. During this period he was awarded the degree of DSc (London, 1901) and developed a great interest in the design of electrical measuring instruments. Over the next six years, in association with Messrs H. Tinsley & Co., he supervised the manufacture of many of his inventions. Some of his instruments—for example, the alternating current potentiometer and the polyphase watt meter—survive as high-precision instruments, although perhaps his greatest achievement was the phase shifting transformer which later became the basis of servo-mechanisms throughout the world.

In 1898 Drysdale married Bessie Ingman Edwards (*d.* 1950), a teacher at Stockwell College, south London. They had one daughter, who died at the age of thirteen in 1914, and an adopted son. In January 1918 Drysdale joined the Admiralty Experimental Station at Parkeston Quay, Harwich, Essex. There he became involved in the development of a leader cable system designed to enable a ship to steer along a cable laid on the sea bed. After the end of the war the Admiralty Experimental Station moved to Shandon, Dunbartonshire, Scotland, and Drysdale became the scientific director in 1920. When, later in 1920, the station became the Admiralty research laboratory (ARL), Drysdale was appointed the first superintendent and moved with the laboratory to Teddington, Middlesex, in 1921. While superintendent he also found time to continue his researches into leader cable problems and then turned his attention to the fire control of naval gunnery in which great precision was required to control the elevation and bearing of large warship guns under severe rolling and pitching conditions. In October 1929 Drysdale left ARL to become director of scientific research at the Admiralty and in 1934 he retired from Admiralty service.

Drysdale had a wide range of interests outside his scientific activities. He was a founder member (1907) of the Men's League for Women's Suffrage and its honorary secretary for two years; he also represented it at a women's international conference in Amsterdam. In support of the same cause, he sat on the Men's Committee for Justice to Women. He was a staunch supporter and member of the Malthusian League. On the death of his father in 1907 he and his wife became co-secretaries of the league and he assumed the editorship of the league's journal, *The Malthusian*. In February 1921 he succeeded his mother as president of the league, a position which he retained until it was wound up in September 1952. In 1921 and 1925 he acted as president of neo-Malthusian international conferences in London and New York.

Drysdale's conservative, individualistic philosophy determined his actions and views throughout his life. He changed the Malthusian League from its earlier emphasis on the relationship between over-population and poverty to one of better eugenic selection. His dogged support for Malthusian and neo-Malthusian principles antagonized many of the leading figures of the day and reduced the league's effectiveness in achieving its objectives. Nevertheless it exerted a significant influence upon the family planning movement and led to Drysdale's being made a founder member of the National Birth Control Association in 1930.

Drysdale published many original scientific papers, as well as many contributions on Malthusianism and neo-Malthusianism. He became a fellow of the Physical Society in 1898, a member of its council in 1936–9, and Duddell medallist in 1936. A founder fellow of the Institute of Physics, he served on the board during 1924–5 and was a vice-president during 1932–6. He was also a member of the Optical Society and became its president in 1904. He was made a fellow of the Royal Society of Edinburgh in 1921 and a member of the board of managers of the Royal Institution from 1934 to 1936. He was also a fellow of the Royal Statistical Society. He was appointed OBE in 1920 and CB in 1932. After the death of his wife Drysdale lived with his nephew in Sussex, at Ashley, Filsham Drive, Pebsham, Bexhill; he died at Bexhill on 7 February 1961. A. B. MITCHELL, *rev.*

Sources R. Ledbetter, *A history of the Malthusian League, 1877–1927* (1977) · *Journal of the Institution of Electrical Engineers*, new ser., 7 (1961) · *Year Book of the Royal Society of Edinburgh* (1960–61) · A. B. Wood, *Nature*, 190 (1961), 214–15 · private information (1981) · *The*

Times (9 Feb 1961), 17c · *The Times* (11 Feb 1961), 8e · *CGPLA Eng. & Wales* (1961) · A. V. John and C. Eustance, eds., *The men's share? Masculinities, male support and women's suffrage in Britain, 1890–1920* (1997)
Archives BLPES, papers
Wealth at death £30,280 4s. 10d.: probate, 27 March 1961, *CGPLA Eng. & Wales*

Drysdale, George (1824–1904), freethinker and advocate of contraception, was born at 8 Royal Circus, Edinburgh, on 27 December 1824, the fourth son of the city treasurer and tory leader on Edinburgh council, Sir William Drysdale (1781–1843), who was concerned with sanitary reform and was a correspondent of Edwin Chadwick. The five children of Sir William's two deceased wives lived at their Royal Circus house with Margaret Mary (1823–1891), George, and Charles Robert, the children of his third wife, Elizabeth Copeland, *née* Pew (1787–1887), a widow with one other son. Lady Drysdale was known for her interest in literary and scientific people, and in Edinburgh George and Charles Drysdale met Charles Dickens, Francis Jeffrey (editor of the *Edinburgh Review*), and the secular educationist and phrenologist George Combe. When Margaret Mary and her husband, Dr Edward Wickstead Lane (1822–1891), moved in 1854 to their well-known hydro at Moor Park, Surrey, Lady Drysdale helped to manage it. The Malthusians Combe, James Stuart Laurie, and Alexander Bain, were, like George and Charles, frequent visitors, as was Charles Darwin.

George and Charles Drysdale were educated at Edinburgh Academy, George from 1835. George was particularly brilliant, dux of the school in 1841. About 1839, increasingly overwhelmed by his adolescent sexuality, George's reading convinced him that masturbation was bringing him to mental and physical breakdown. He entered Glasgow University in 1841–2 yet despite excellent results abandoned classics in 1843 and spent two years at home too depressed even to read. He went on a walking tour in May 1844, and was reported drowned in the Danube at Vienna (*The Scotsman*, 17 Sept 1844). To his family's incredulous joy he returned in March 1846, having walked from Hungary, where for two years he had been slowly recovering. Lady Drysdale escaped Edinburgh gossip by going with George to Dublin, where in 1847–9 he was well enough to study medicine at Trinity College; he then finished his undistinguished MD in Edinburgh (1855) and interrupted his studies for two years to write *Physical, Sexual, and Natural Religion* (1855), known after 1857 as *The Elements of Social Science*. It was accepted by the free thought publisher Edward Truelove.

Drysdale hid his personal motives for writing *Physical, Sexual, and Natural Religion* behind a confessional case history which paralleled his own story: early brilliance, adolescent sexual problems, a walking tour and staged drowning, and a return home to attempt life anew after two years of self-imposed exile. The patient recovered only after he had engaged in sex on the advice of Dr François Lallemand, whose theories about the necessity of intercourse (*Des pertes séminales involontaires*, 3 vols., 1836–

42) Drysdale transmuted in his book into his law of exercise—it was everyone's duty to engage in joyous sexual activity to preserve physical health and mental balance.

Drysdale was fired by Thomas Malthus's analysis of the balance between population and food with war, poverty, starvation, disease, and death as the regulators of overpopulation; he totally rejected Malthus's solution of sexual abstinence, choosing instead contraception. Without it single women withered as involuntary nuns; thoughtful men abstained from premarital sex and married late to avoid births; the irresponsible brought about overpopulation, poverty, prostitution, and venereal disease. Prostitutes deserved compassion, even respect, as martyrs to male sexuality. Drysdale believed that the churches had denatured women by prescribing a crippling model of excessive modesty and sexual shame. They had taken from women their female healers, and turned medicine over to the religious orders, whose successors were male. Women could not confide gynaecological problems to men; contemporary physicians were ill-informed, prudish, often incapable of examining them properly, and failed to give patients sexual or contraceptive information. *The Elements* described in plain language male and female sexual anatomy, physiology, and reproduction, the mental and physical results of abstinence, and all the known methods of contraception. Drysdale advocated women doctors, though his profession refused to countenance them. Despite a rather restricted middle-class outlook, he was a feminist when the women's movement had hardly started. Unusual in equating women's sexual nature with men's, he believed contraception would free both sexes to live naturally. He looked forward to a smaller population, where women, whose minds were as good as men's, would have an education as thorough as theirs, be their equally matched companions, and compete with them in all professions and trades. For years Drysdale lived with Letitia Gallafent, *née* Radley (*bap.* 1825), who was probably his partner.

Drysdale was led by his logic to revolutionary conclusions. Since contraception would permit early marriage, youthful errors would require new divorce legislation. With divorce effectively on demand, marriage would become meaningless. He found himself advocating permissive but publicly avowed relationships, a change of partners when relationships failed, and contracts to protect the children. His sexual permissiveness brought *The Elements* notoriety as 'the Bible of the brothel'. *The Elements* sold 90,000 copies and was translated into eleven languages, including Hungarian. The cost of new stereotype plates made revision impossible. In 1878 and after Drysdale added appendices, including *The State Remedy for Poverty*, where he proposed fines for those who did not limit their families. He elaborated his views in his *Political Economist and Journal of Social Science* (1856–7) and *Population Fallacies* (1860). As 'G.R.' (George Rex, his school nickname) he wrote articles for Charles Bradlaugh's *National Reformer* during the 1860s. Later expanded as pamphlets, they discussed J. S. Mill, Irish home rule, and European federation. Bradlaugh (accused by his enemies of having written *The*

Elements) did not know his contributor's identity; they communicated through Truelove. Known only as Charles's reclusive brother, George was never suspected of writing anything, though he did little else. George Drysdale, who died at 75 Palace Road, Penge, London on 19 November 1904, had begged Charles to fight on for *The State Remedy* and left him nearly £18,000. He was buried in unconsecrated ground, without a memorial, at West Norwood, London.

Charles Robert Drysdale (1828/9–1907), freethinker and birth control activist, attended Edinburgh Academy from 1836 to 1842, but he was eclipsed at school by his elder brother, and began to shine only after George left. He began to read mathematics at Edinburgh University in 1843, but was probably with his brother in Vienna in May 1844. The shock of his idolized brother's supposed death made Charles a mediocre student until George's return. Charles read mathematics at Trinity College, Cambridge (1846–7), then joined the family in Dublin and registered at the school of engineering (16 January 1848). As a pupil of his cousin, George Willoughby Hemans, he surveyed railways in Ireland and on the continent. His paper 'On steep gradients' (8 April 1856) won the Telford medal (1856), yet he registered in medicine at University College, London (1855), obtaining a first-class MD at St Andrews (1859). He had seen poverty in Ireland, studied *The Elements*, and abandoned his career to become George's disciple and mouthpiece. George remained unknown: Charles, as a Malthusian propagandist, accepted scurrilous abuse as the supposed author of *The Elements*. Both poured their considerable fortunes into the cause. Charles claimed in his *Memoir*, appended to the posthumous thirty-fifth edition of 1905, that George retained his anonymity to protect his mother; the sensitivity of the material makes it as likely that he was protecting his privacy. Their choice of a profession meant secrecy if they were to implement George's conclusions. Charles and Dr Alice *Vickery (1844–1929) began their relationship when she was his student at the Ladies' Medical College in the 1870s; they never married and kept secret two children, one of whom was Charles Vickery *Drysdale (1874–1961). Charles put his property in their joint names; when Alice died it was worth about £30,000. Both brothers guarded their domesticity at addresses which never reached the *Medical Directory*. George refused requests (made through Truelove) to debate his ideas. Charles and Alice, needing to work in their profession and maintain a platform presence as Malthusian propagandists, trumpeted George's theories while chafing at a secrecy which humiliatingly compromised their own integrity.

It was Charles who worked among the poor and in a Lock Hospital, specialized in women's diseases and syphilis, lectured on the need for female doctors, and instructed his patients and students on 'preventive intercourse'. When the brothers realized that the Contagious Diseases Acts (1864 and 1866) did not protect but rather penalized prostitutes, George changed a paragraph in *The State Remedy*, but Charles publicly joined those campaigning against the extension of the act. In 1877 'G.R.' wrote medical notes to Charles Knowlton's contraceptive manual, *The Fruits of Philosophy*, but after the trial of Bradlaugh and Annie Besant for publishing it, it was Charles who became president of their newly formed Malthusian League and editor of *The Malthusian*. After 1895 they all lived at 28 Carson Road, West Dulwich. At the Malthusian League's annual general meeting in 1907 Charles refused congratulations for his supposed success in lowering the birth-rate, attributing it all to George. A founder member in 1907 (with his son C. V. Drysdale) of the Men's League for Women's Suffrage, there was no time for him to contribute in any way. He edited his last *Malthusian* in November 1907, and died a fortnight later, on 2 December at Carson Road. Inscribed on his tomb in Brookwood cemetery is George's authorship of *The Elements*.   J. MIRIAM BENN

Sources C. R. Drysdale, *Memoir*, in G. Drysdale, *The elements of social science, or, Physical, sexual, and natural religion*, 35th edn (1905) · *People's Paper* (March–June 1855) [review of 1st edn of *Physical, sexual, and natural religion* (1855)] · *The Reasoner* (May 1857) [review of latest edn of *Physical, sexual, and natural religion*] · *The Investigator* (Aug 1857) [review of latest edn of *Physical, sexual, and natural religion*] · reviews of latest edn of *Physical, sexual, and natural religion*, *National Reformer* (May 1860); (June–Aug 1861); (March 1869); (Aug 1869) · J. M. Benn, *Predicaments of love* (1992) · T. Sato, 'George Drysdale's supposed death and the *Elements of social science*', *Hitotsubashi Ronso*, 78/2 (Aug 1977), 19–38 [in Japanese] · T. Sato, 'E. W. Lane's hydropathic establishment at Moor Park', *Hitotsubashi Journal of Arts and Sciences*, 10/1 (1978), 45–9 · d. cert. [Charles Robert Drysdale] · private information (2004)
Likenesses photographic proof (after portrait), priv. coll.
Wealth at death £19,722 6s. 11d.: probate, 10 Dec 1904, CGPLA Eng. & Wales · £2964 10s. 11d.—Charles Robert Drysdale: probate, 21 Dec 1907, CGPLA Eng. & Wales

Drysdale, Hugh (d. 1726), army officer and colonial governor, was born in Ireland, the son of an archdeacon of Ossory. In 1688 he matriculated at Queen's College, Oxford, where he was a classmate of Edmund Gibson, later bishop of London. Nothing is known of his years at Oxford or until June 1701, when he settled on a career in the army, enlisting as an ensign in Thomas Brudnell's regiment of foot. Drysdale was promoted to captain and brevet major in Charles Churchill's marine regiment in 1709, and in 1715 he became a major in Churchill's dragoons. He was appointed lieutenant-governor of Virginia on 3 April 1722 by Sir Robert Walpole, though the reason for his choosing Drysdale is not clear. It is possible that his name was recommended by Bishop Gibson, a close friend of Walpole. Drysdale's military service, especially under the earl of Orkney, the non-resident governor of Virginia, may have also played a role.

Drysdale arrived in Virginia on 25 September 1722 to replace Alexander Spotswood, whose administration was characterized in its later years by dispute with the colony's leadership. Drysdale met with the council of state on 27 September and was sworn into office. The governor reported a few months later that 'there is a universall sign of contentment on the change made in the government here' (*CSP col.*, 32.304). Councillor Robert Carter confirmed this estimate when he wrote that all found Drysdale 'of a mild Temperate & courteous disposition' and that the 'generality' were 'happy in him' (Carter's letter-book, 2 July 1723). From an early date Drysdale took positions that endeared him to a wide spectrum of the population. He urged the Board of Trade to press for the 'remittance' of quit-rents in the new frontier counties of Spotsylvania and Brunswick, and that there be no limitation on the amount of land one could patent (*CSP col.*, 33.140). He also approved two much desired laws, one which provided for a tax on liquor and slaves, and another limiting the amount of tobacco that could be planted—a response to poor revenues and low tobacco prices. The tax on liquor and slaves was disallowed.

Drysdale's popularity remained high. He was sensitive to Virginia's political world and developed good relations with most of the leadership. Only against Alexander Spotswood did he exhibit hostility, pointing to the former governor's land-grabbing as well as his manufacture of iron products, which, he implied, was against the spirit of British economic regulation. This animosity may well have been fuelled by councillor and commissary James Blair, an inveterate enemy of Spotswood. In general, however, Drysdale's approach was cautious and his governorship contributed to political harmony. By September 1725 it was reported that he had been in poor health for some considerable time. By the following spring he had determined to return to England to recover his health. In early July he appeared to improve and decided against the trip home, but he died at Williamsburg 'of a pleurisie' on 22 July 1726 (Carter's diary). He was survived by his wife, Hester, about whom no further details are known. Councillor John Custis wrote, probably in 1726 or 1727, that the 'irreperable loss … of the colony … of upright Mr. Drisdals is beyond all expression' (Custis's letter-book). Drysdale was buried at Bruton parish church in Williamsburg on 2 August. EMORY G. EVANS

Sources M. C. Kaduboski, 'The administration of Lieutenant-Governor Hugh Drysdale, 1722–1726', MA diss., College of William and Mary, 1967 · *CSP col.*, vols. 32–5 · *Journals of the council of trade and plantations*, vols. 4–5 · *Executive journals of the council of colonial Virginia*, 4, ed. H. R. McIlwaine (1930), vol. 4 · H. R. McIlwaine and J. P. Kennedy, eds., *Journals of the house of burgesses of Virginia, 1619–1776*, 13 vols. (1905–15), vol. 5 · Robert Carter's diary, 1722–7, University of Virginia · Robert Carter's letter-book, 1723–4, University of Virginia · 'Robert Carter to Philip Ludwell, July 23, 1726', *Virginia Magazine of History and Biography*, 3 (1895–6), 355–6 · will, 23 July 1721/23 July 1722, Principal Registry of the Family Division, London, TCC register, 255 Plymouth [photostat, Colonial Williamsburg] · M. Tinling, ed., *The correspondence of the three William Byrds of Westover, Virginia, 1684–1776*, 2 vols. (1977) · J. Custis, letter-book, 1717–42, L. Cong. · W. M. Billings, J. E. Selby, and T. W. Tate, *Colonial Virginia: a history* (1986) · P. Rouse, *James Blair of Virginia* (1971) · J. H. Plumb, *Sir Robert Walpole*, 2 (1960)

Drysdale, John (1718–1788), Church of Scotland minister, was born on 20 April 1718, the third son of John Drysdale (c.1681–1726), minister of Kirkcaldy, on the Fife coast, and Anne Ferguson, daughter of William Ferguson, a provost of Kirkcaldy. He was educated at the Kirkcaldy parish school along with his brother George, who would also serve as provost of Kirkcaldy, and their lifelong friend Adam Smith. In 1732 he entered the University of Edinburgh, where he studied arts and divinity in the company of Hugh Blair, William Robertson, and other future leaders of the moderate party. He enjoyed a particularly close connection with Robertson through the Adam family of architects, and on 11 June 1749 married Mary Adam (d. 1799), Robertson's first cousin on his father's side. Robertson would later refer to Drysdale as 'among the oldest and most intimate of my companions' (W. Robertson to G. Elliot, 12 Aug 1762, NL Scot., MS 11009, fols. 153–4) and his wife as 'an accomplished prudent woman' (*Selections from the Caldwell Papers*, 2, pt 2, 23–4).

After receiving a licence to preach from the presbytery of Kirkcaldy in 1740 Drysdale passed most of the 1740s in Edinburgh as the assistant of Blair's uncle, the Revd James Bannatyne of Trinity Church. On 18 February 1749 he was presented by the crown, through the interest of the earl of Hopetoun, to the parish of Kirkliston in the presbytery of Linlithgow, several miles west of Edinburgh. On 1 December 1762 he was presented by the town council of Edinburgh to Lady Yester's Church, setting off an intense controversy that lasted until he was finally admitted on 14 August 1764, following a ruling by the House of Lords. The dispute concerned the town council's right of patronage, not the credentials of Drysdale himself, who was widely respected as a diligent minister and an excellent preacher, 'not less masterly than original', according to one contemporary (Somerville, 60). Upon coming to Edinburgh he served as Robertson's ecclesiastical manager during the moderates' greatest age of ascendancy in church affairs, earning the respect even of opponents such as Sir Henry Moncreiff Wellwood for his 'indefatigable industry and talents' (Wellwood, 462).

Drysdale was made an honorary DD of Marischal College, Aberdeen, on 15 April 1765. The following year Robertson arranged his appointments as one of his majesty's chaplains in ordinary and a dean of the Chapel Royal, and on 22 October 1767 he was translated to the Tron Church. On 29 May 1778 his colleague at the Tron, George Wishart, was prevailed upon to admit Drysdale as his assistant and successor as principal clerk of the general assembly, an office that Drysdale held alone after Wishart's death in 1785. He served as moderator of the general assembly on 20 May 1773, and eleven years later had the distinction of holding that office a second time, just as he had earlier had the rare honour of preaching twice before the lord high commissioner, in 1754 and 1762. His son-in-law believed that a decisive victory in the moderator election of 1784 demonstrated that Drysdale had become the most influential minister in the Church of Scotland after the retirement of William Robertson in 1780 (Dalzel, 48–9). Unlike Robertson, however, Drysdale was no ecclesiastical orator, perhaps because his 'invincible modesty prevented him from speaking in public' (*Autobiography*, ed. Burton, 452), and he built his power base behind the scenes, by means of an extensive correspondence with parish ministers throughout Scotland, but especially in the highlands. He was also no man of letters, publishing nothing in his lifetime and being rejected on 2 November 1756 for admission to the élite Edinburgh debating club, the Select Society. On 26 January 1784 he was elected a fellow of the Royal Society of Edinburgh, however, and his two volumes of *Sermons*, edited for posthumous publication in 1793 by the Edinburgh University professor of Greek, Andrew Dalzel, who had married the elder of Drysdale's two daughters, Anne (1751–1826), in 1786, reveal a concern for education, improvement, sociability, Christian-Stoic resignation, and social conservatism that was characteristic of the dominant values of the Scottish Enlightenment. Drysdale died on 16 June 1788. A biographical sketch that Dalzel read to the Royal Society of Edinburgh on 17 December 1792 was prefixed to Drysdale's *Sermons* and also appeared in the society's *Transactions* for 1794.   RICHARD B. SHER

Sources W. Adam, *Sequel to the gift of a grandfather* (1836) · *The autobiography of Dr Alexander Carlyle of Inveresk, 1722–1805*, ed. J. H. Burton (1910) · A. Dalzel, 'Account of John Drysdale, DD', *Transactions of the Royal Society of Edinburgh*, 3/1 (1794), 37–53 · J. Dwyer, *Virtuous discourse: sensibility and community in late eighteenth-century Scotland* (1987) · R. L. Emerson, 'The social composition of Enlightened Edinburgh: the Select Society of Edinburgh, 1754–1764', *Studies on Voltaire and the Eighteenth Century*, 114 (1973), 291–329 · N. M. [N. Morren], *Annals of the general assembly of the Church of Scotland*, 2 vols. (1838–40) · *DNB* · I. S. Ross, *The life of Adam Smith* (1995) · *Fasti Scot.*, new edn, vol. 8 · [W. Mure], ed., *Selections from the family papers preserved at Caldwell*, 2 vols. in 3 (1883–5) · R. B. Sher, 'Moderates, managers and popular politics in mid-eighteenth-century Edinburgh: the Drysdale "bustle" of the 1760s', *New perspectives on the politics and culture of early modern Scotland*, ed. J. Dwyer, R. A. Mason, and A. Murdoch (1982), 179–209 · R. B. Sher, *Church and university in the Scottish Enlightenment: the moderate literati of Edinburgh* (1985) · T. Somerville, *My own life and times, 1741–1814*, ed. W. Lee (1861) · H. M. Wellwood, *Account of the life and writings of John Erskine* (1818), appx
Archives NL Scot., Robert Douglas MSS, MS 3116 · NL Scot., Minto MSS (Sir Gilbert Elliot), MS 11009

Drysdale, (George John) Learmont (1866–1909), composer, was born on 3 October 1866 at 37 George Street, Edinburgh, the youngest of the three children of Andrew Drysdale (1831–1918), builder, and his wife, Jane Elspeth Learmont (1827–1909), who was descended from the border poet Thomas the Rhymer. Educated at the Royal High School, Edinburgh, he afterwards studied architecture, pursuing his musical interests through organ playing and the composition of songs and piano pieces. Anxious to further his musical training, Drysdale abandoned architecture in 1887, moving to London as sub-organist of All Saints' Church, Kensington. The following year he entered the Royal Academy of Music, studying composition with Frederick Corder and piano under Wilhelm Kuhe. He had an excellent career there, having several orchestral works performed at the St James Hall, notably *The Spirit of the Glen* (1889) and *Thomas the Rhymer* (1890), winning praise from both teachers and critics. He gained several prizes including the prestigious Charles Lucas medal for composition in 1890 for his *Overture to a Comedy* and the Glasgow Society of Musicians' prize with his colourful overture *Tam o'Shanter* (written in 1890 but not published until 1921), his best-known work. Headstrong and opinionated, Drysdale left the Royal Academy of Music in

1892 without graduating, after a disagreement with the principal, Alexander Mackenzie.

From 1892 to 1904 Drysdale mainly resided in Edinburgh earning his living by composing and conducting. His notable successes included the cantata *The Kelpie* (1891–4), the Borders-inspired overture *Herondean* (1893–4), and striking incidental music for the mystical play *The Plague* (c.1894). His dramatic bent found expression in the romantic comic opera *Red Spider* (1895–8), which received more than 100 performances to much critical acclaim. The tone poem *Border Romance* (1904) was composed at the request of Henry Wood for the Queen's Hall, London. From 1904 to 1905 Drysdale was composition and theory master at the Glasgow Athenaeum; he also composed the dramatic cantata *Tamlane* (c.1905) and incidental music of great beauty for Euripides' *Hippolytus* (1905). His numerous original settings of Scots lyrics and folk-song arrangements show great insight into his native song; a number of the latter are included in *The Dunedin Collection of Scots Songs* (1908), which he edited. He collaborated with the ninth duke of Argyll on *The Scottish Tribute to France* and the unfinished opera *Fionn and Tera* (1908–9), furthering their mutual interest in the burgeoning Celtic renaissance.

Drysdale's music is idiomatically Scottish and demonstrates much originality, versatility, and inspiration. He was respected by many leading musical figures of his time, but poor self-promotion, with a corresponding lack of published work, his untimely death, and a musical style that fell out of fashion led to his music falling into obscurity. In 1937 a monument was erected in his honour near Traquair, Peeblesshire. His archive is in Glasgow University Library. He died, unmarried, of pneumonia at 22 Braid Crescent, Edinburgh, on 18 June 1909 and was buried on 22 June at Peebles churchyard, Peeblesshire.

MOIRA ANN HARRIS

Sources J. Drysdale, 'Learmont Drysdale', 1942, U. Glas., Drysdale collection, Cb10-x.14 · M. Harris, 'The life and work of (George John) Learmont Drysdale', BMus hons diss., U. Glas., 1998 · J. Drysdale, 'Scottish composers: Learmont Drysdale', *Dunedin Magazine*, 3 (1914–15), 15–30 [with work list] · H. G. Farmer, *A history of music in Scotland* (1947) · H. G. Farmer, 'Drysdale, Learmont', *Die Musik in Geschichte und Gegenwart*, 3, 832–4 [with work list] · *DNB* · J. M. Allen, 'Drysdale, Learmont', *New Grove* [incl. work list] · b. cert., district of St Andrew, burgh of Edinburgh, entry 800, 24 Oct 1866 · d. cert., district of Morningside, burgh of Edinburgh, entry 549, 19 June 1909
Archives Edinburgh Central Reference Library, music department · Mitchell L., Glas. · NL Scot., items · U. Glas., manuscript compositions, letters, and ephemera | U. Glas., Farmer collection
Likenesses photographic plate, U. Glas. L.; repro. in Farmer, *History of music*
Wealth at death £14 10s. 4d.: confirmation, 21 April 1911, *CCI*

Drysdale, Sir (George) Russell (1912–1981), painter, was born on 7 February 1912 at Millbrook, 9 Aldwick Road, Bognor Regis, Sussex, the son of George Russell (Leigh) Drysdale, a grazier, and his wife, Isobel, formerly Gates. His family had long-standing Australian connections, and Drysdale's parents settled permanently near Albury, on the Victoria–New South Wales border, in 1923. He was educated at Geelong grammar school, and remembered for his passion for cricket and his talent for caricature; his schooling ended early due to a detached retina. He lost the sight of one eye, later being exempted from military service. After a happy period with the family company, Pioneer Sugar in north Queensland, he eventually found his direction.

While recovering from an illness, Drysdale was introduced by his doctor, who had noticed his talent, to Daryl Lindsay, later director of the National Gallery of Victoria. Lindsay introduced Drysdale to George Bell, whose new art school in Melbourne followed principles of modern European art, and where he was shown reproductions of works by such artists as Cézanne and Modigliani. Drysdale decided that he would become a painter, and after a trip to Europe looking at collections of modern art he joined the Bell School and studied there from 1935 to 1938. He continued his studies in Paris and at the Grosvenor School of Art in London, but his time there was cut short because of the threat of war, and he was back in Melbourne in time to join in the inaugural exhibition (June 1939) of the Contemporary Art Society, formed in 1938 in opposition to the reactionary Australian Academy of Art, established in 1937. Drysdale married Elizabeth (*d.* 1963), daughter of J. Stephen, in 1935; they had a daughter, Lynne, and a son, Timothy.

Drysdale now devoted himself to painting, no longer inspired by the school of Paris, but by essential characteristics of Australian life. His development was quick and masterly. Within a few years he produced some of the most memorable paintings in twentieth-century Australian art. The first series in 1942–3 featured the lonely life of people on the land—tall, lean figures who lived a life of hardship in the aftermath of the great depression.

Drysdale moved to Sydney in 1940, where he spent almost all the rest of his life. In 1944 he was sent on a tour of the drought-devastated outback of New South Wales by the *Sydney Morning Herald*. The resulting drawings were minimal, but the experience provided material for an exceptional series of landscapes.

With reminiscences of Graham Sutherland (Drysdale probably saw Sutherland's first exhibition in 1938), incorporating some surrealist elements, Drysdale created an atmosphere charged full of psychological foreboding, capturing the drama and uncertainty of wartime existence. Richly painted in warm reds and yellows, these paintings present a dark, spiritual landscape, partly objective, partly subjective, the poetry of which has the dignified authority of great art. One of Drysdale's most memorable images, *The Drover's Wife*, was developed from a small sketch made during this tour.

In 1950 Drysdale had the first of several exhibitions at the Leicester Galleries in London, following advice from Kenneth Clark, who had met him in Australia in 1949 and had acquired a landscape of the gold mining town Hill End. Appointed a director of Pioneer Sugar in 1951, Drysdale frequently visited Queensland, extending his experience of Australian Aborigines. In his portrayal of striking, typical attitudes, he extracted the essence of their timid and gentle nature, and their characteristic shapes, with a compassionate and understanding eye, presenting them with a melancholic dignity.

By 1953 Drysdale had begun to use a 'black oil' medium which imparted a greater fluidity and impasto to his work. It became more painterly, more dependent on the brush rather than his detailed drawing in Indian ink, which was not always entirely covered by the finished work. The result was a series of sonorous musical paintings, restrained in colour and intensely felt. His 1953 exhibition, which featured many of his finest Aboriginal subjects, possibly marks the peak of his achievement as a painter and his fame continued to mount. With Sidney Nolan and William Dobell he represented Australia at the 1954 Venice Biennale. He spent 1957–8 in London, his only extended period away from Australia, working on the paintings for his 1958 London exhibition. These works were the result of an extensive tour of central and western Australia made with his son during May–November 1956. The large retrospective by the Art Gallery of New South Wales in 1960 made Drysdale nationally revered. And his next exhibition sold out within a few hours. He was knighted in 1969.

Drysdale's personal life was tragic. His son died in 1962, and his wife in 1963, both by their own hands at the time when he reached the peak of his fame. In 1965 he married Maisie Joyce, the widow of his close friend Peter Purves Smith. He had a house and studio built on Kilcare Heights, an hour's drive from Sydney, and he lived there for the rest of his life. He never quite regained the greatness of the 1950s, but he did make some remarkable drawings and painted a magnificent poster for the 1980 Festival of Perth. Never a prolific painter, his output was only a fraction of that of his contemporaries Sidney Nolan and Arthur Boyd. He died in Westmead Hospital, Westmead, Sydney, on 29 June 1981 from cancer.

Drysdale was a major figure of Australian twentieth-century art. Coming to prominence during the 1940s amid the cultural and social changes precipitated by the Second World War, he initiated a new vision of Australian landscape which would replace the outmoded pastoralism of the Heidelberg school. With Nolan and Boyd, Drysdale presented a penetrating and realistic view more in line with modern ideas and perceptions. He revealed the vastness, emptiness, and dryness of the landscape, and its effect on the people who survived in these sparse, arid conditions. He created a host of characters, totally identified with the lost world of 'the outback', which in his paintings can also be interpreted as a metaphor for the essential loneliness of the human soul.   LOU KLEPAC

Sources J. Burke, *The paintings of Russell Drysdale* (Sydney, 1951) · G. Dutton, *Russell Drysdale* (1964) · L. Klepac, ed., *The drawings of Russell Drysdale* (1980) [exhibition catalogue, Art Gallery of Western Australia, 21 Feb – 15 March, 1980] · L. Klepac, *The life and work of Russell Drysdale* (Sydney, 1983) · diaries, 1942–89, NL Aus., MSS of Donald Friend · R. Drysdale, correspondence, Mitchell L., NSW, Russell Drysdale MSS · b. cert.

Archives State Library of New South Wales, Sydney, corresp. | SOUND ABC archives, speech, broadcast on ABC radio on 18 Nov 1979 · Art Gallery of Western Australia, interview with Lou Klepac, February 1980 · NL Aus., interview with Hazel de Berg, February

1960 • NL Aus., interview with James Gleeson, 19 Oct 1978 • NL Aus., interview with David Muir, 7 May 1980 • priv. coll., interview with Geoffrey Dutton, Sydney, 1963 • State Library of Victoria, Melbourne, La Trobe collection, interview with James Mellen, 12 July 1972 • State Library of Victoria, Melbourne, La Trobe collection, interview with Richard Haese, 21 May 1975

Duane, James (1733–1797), lawyer and revolutionary politician in America, was born in New York city on 6 February 1733, the son of Anthony Duane (1682–1741), merchant of New York city, and Althea, *née* Kettletas. He was of Irish descent through his father and Dutch through his mother. He was associated in his law practice and political life with New York city and, through his land speculations, with western New York. He was a lifelong Anglican/Episcopalian.

James Duane's biographer, Edward Alexander, characterizes him as a 'revolutionary conservative', and though the description may seem oxymoronic, it is accurate. He virtually typifies the sort of colonial American who decided with pain and regret that separation from Britain was a necessity, but who wanted virtually no social change as a result. But he also typifies the kind of American conservative who found himself not only accepting change but participating in it.

Despite being the son of a prosperous Irish-born merchant who had married into an established New York Dutch family, Duane did not receive a formal education. King's College was not founded until he was a young adult, and his parents did not choose to send him to Harvard or Yale. He received private tutoring instead, and proceeded to legal study in the office of James Alexander. After his independent legal practice began in 1754 he rapidly acquired a strong reputation. His argument in *Forsey* v. *Cunningham* (1763) helped to undercut the position that a royal governor and his appointed council formed the final court of colonial appeals. Since the council provided a rough American equivalent of the House of Lords (at least in American eyes), the case helped to establish the American constitutional principle of separation of powers.

Duane was no friend to the growing revolutionary movement in his province, but during the independence crisis (1774–6) he was drawn almost against his will towards the American side. He served in the first continental congress (1774), which established a common ground of resistance to the punishments visited upon Massachusetts after the Boston Tea Party (December 1773). He was a delegate from New York to the second continental congress almost continuously from 1775 until 1783. His shift during the early summer of 1776 from temporizing on the problem of declaring independence to accepting its necessity typifies both the larger problem faced by his group and their eventual solution for that problem. They would break with Britain, but they would remain in control for the sake of their own perspective and interests.

Duane's chance to further that perspective came when he was appointed mayor of New York on 4 February 1784. As mayor he presided over the mayor's court, the city's highest judicial body, where he decided the important case of *Rutgers* v. *Waddington* (1784). Based on common law, his ruling partially undermined the strong anti-loyalist legislation that his state had adopted during the war and was continuing to enforce. He held the mayoralty until 1789, serving also in New York state's convention that ratified the federal constitution in 1788, in the state senate from 1782 until 1790, and from 1789 until 1795 as a federal judge.

On 21 October 1759 Duane married Mary, the daughter of Robert Livingston jun., lord of the manor of Livingston in the Hudson valley. Duane became involved in upstate land developments, founding the community of Duanesburgh, west of Schenectady, and also purchasing a great deal of land in what became the state of Vermont. He abandoned the manorial principle of creating a landed estate whose tenants' rents and other quasi-feudal dues supported their landlord, substituting the capitalist developer's idea of selling off some plots in order to raise the value of others. Ill health caused him to retire to Schenectady in 1795, and he died there on 1 February 1797 from unknown causes. He was buried in the Episcopal church in Duanesburgh. His wife survived him.

EDWARD COUNTRYMAN

Sources E. Alexander, *A revolutionary conservative: James Duane of New York* (1938) • M. Bellesiles, *Revolutionary outlaws* (1993) • C. Matson, 'Duane, James', *ANB*
Archives New York Historical Society

Duane, Matthew (1707–1785), lawyer and art patron, was of obscure family origins. It seems likely that he came from Ireland and that his education took place in a Catholic school on the continent. Prevented by his religion from being called to the bar, he was by his mid-thirties practising with great success as a 'chamber counsel' and conveyancer in Newcastle and London. On 21 October 1742 he married Dorothy Dawson (1722–1799), a Newcastle heiress and the daughter of Thomas Dawson and Barbara Pearath. In 1748 he purchased estates at Wideopen and Donnington and had chambers in Pilgrim Street, Newcastle, in a house which had once belonged to the Pearath family, from which his wife was descended. But his chief centre remained London. A member of Lincoln's Inn since 10 June 1748, he had a house in New Square until 1782, when it was destroyed by fire, after which he moved to Bedford Row. He contributed to Matthew Bacon's *A New Abridgement of Law* (4th edn, 1736–66) and had as his pupil John Scott, later earl of Eldon, who spoke highly of his character and legal skills.

Duane devoted his leisure to the acquisition of an expert knowledge of ancient coins and the patronage of contemporary artists and engravers, notably Giles Hussey. He was elected member of the Society of Arts and fellow of the Society of Antiquaries in 1757, fellow of the Royal Society in 1763, and trustee of the British Museum in 1766. In 1763 he was elected one of the two chairmen of the Society of Arts' committee of polite arts. He held this office for twenty years and was active in it for over ten, which makes his record of service to the society quite outstanding. For his assistance in the complicated negotiations between Robert and James Adam and the society over the

Matthew Duane
(1707–1785), by
James Mitan, pubd
1798 (after Giles
Hussey, 1774)

350, 519; 33.200; 41.119 • D. G. C. Allan, 'Matthew Duane FRS, FSA (1707–85): gold medallist and active member of the society', *RSA Journal*, 144 (Oct 1996), 35–7 • minutes, correspondence, RS Friends, Lond. • minutes, S. Antiquaries, Lond. • BM, minutes of trustees, BM • W. P. Baildon, ed., *The records of the Honorable Society of Lincoln's Inn: admissions*, 1 (1896), 528 • M. Bacon, *A new abridgement of law*, 4th edn (1736–66) • C. Butler, *Historical memoirs of the English, Irish, and Scottish Catholics since the Reformation*, 3rd edn, 4 (1822), 460 • L. Dutens, *Explication de quelques médailles pheniciennes du cabinet de M. Duane* (1774) • A. MacGregor, ed., *Sir Hans Sloane: collector, scientist, antiquary, founding father of the British Museum* (1994), 150, 163 • mural monument, St Nicholas's Church, Newcastle upon Tyne

Archives RSA, MS corresp. | BL, Stowe MS 940 G1, 222–32, Add. MS 35258

Likenesses J. Mitan, line engraving, pubd 1798 (after G. Hussey, 1774), BM, NPG, RS [*see illus.*]

Wealth at death £700 p.a. to widow: will, PRO, PROB 11/1126, fols. 167*v*–181*r*

building of the society's house in the Adelphi he was awarded the society's honorary gold medal in 1775.

Duane was called 'the most skilful medallist in England' and his medallic collection was said to be 'famous over Europe' (Butler, 4.460). He had a special knowledge of the coins of the Macedonian kings and of the successors of Alexander the Great in Syria. Lewis Dutens, the diplomatist, made Duane's collection known through a book published in 1774. In 1776 Duane sold his Syriac medals to William Hunter, who presented them to Glasgow University. Duane listed the duplicate coins in Sir Hans Sloane's collection at the British Museum, and he assisted in the arrangement of the coins given to the museum by Lord Maynard in 1780. He was also a collector of manuscripts and discovered ten volumes of state papers relating to the accession of George I (now in the Stowe manuscripts of the British Library); he was also said to possess Sir Robert Walpole's papers.

In 1779 Duane purchased an ancient property called The Grove in Twickenham, and was soon afterwards chosen by Horace Walpole, who was now his neighbour, to mediate in a family legal dispute, which he settled in 1784 to the satisfaction of the parties involved and without requiring any payment for himself. Walpole was 'charmed with his handsome behaviour. It confirms the character I gave of him' (Walpole, 25.519).

Duane died of an attack of apoplexy on 6 February 1785 at his London home in Bedford Row. He left most of his furniture and collection of paintings, prints, gems, and busts to his nephew Michael Bray, and an income for life and the houses in Bedford Row and at Twickenham to his widow. She arranged for him to be buried in the St George's porch of St Nicholas's Church in Newcastle and erected a monument recording his work as a patron of the arts and paying tribute to the generosity of his nature. A wider historical perspective would note the contribution he and his pupils made to the attainment of religious toleration in England.   D. G. C. ALLAN

Sources R. Welford, *Men of mark 'twixt Tyne and Tweed*, 3 vols. (1895) [annotated edn in Newcastle public library] • Nichols, *Illustrations*, 8.458 • Nichols, *Lit. anecdotes*, 2.280; 3.37, 147, 497–9, 759; 4.705; 6.302; 8.189 • Walpole, *Corr.*, 24.207, 220; 25.216–17, 266, 331,

Dub dá Leithe [Dubhdalethe] (*d.* 1064), abbot of Armagh, was the son of Máel Maire mac Eochada (*d.* 1020). By the eleventh century Armagh was pre-eminent among the churches of Ireland and the abbots had been members of Dub dá Leithe's family, Clann Sínaich (located in what is now co. Armagh), since the tenth century. His family was to acquire a fame of sorts when its control of the monastery was condemned by Bernard of Clairvaux in his life of Malachy (Máel Máedoc Ua Morgair) (*d.* 1148), where he notes that for two hundred years before Malachy's tenure, the succession to the abbacy was hereditary. Dub dá Leithe's father and brother both preceded him as abbot, and he would be succeeded by his nephew Máel Ísu. As abbot, Dub dá Leithe was the *comarba* ('heir') of St Patrick; he seems not to have been in major orders, nor was he a priest. He is important as a historian and credit for much of the precise information about Armagh in the early eleventh century should probably be given to him.

Dub dá Leithe mac Máel Maire first comes to notice in 1046, when he was appointed to the office of *fer léiginn*, the head of the church's school. Three years later he was elected abbot of Armagh on the same day that his brother and predecessor, Amalgaid, died. The tenure of Dub dá Leithe was stormy. In 1050 he made a visitation on the northern Irish kingdom of Cenél nEógain where he brought away a tithe of 300 cows. Five years later, in 1055, he led the army of the church of Armagh to victory in the 'Battle of the Relic-house' fought at Martry (near Navan) against Murchad Ua Maíl Sechlainn, the *comarba* of the churches of Clonard and Kells. The cause of the conflict is nowhere stated, but its location suggests that Dub dá Leithe was the aggressor. These battles were not unknown among the secular clergy and show how slight, at this period, was the difference between a *comarba* and the Irish lay aristocracy. Dub dá Leithe's martial career seems to have provoked opposition to his leadership of Armagh, and in 1060 a rival named Cumuscach Ua hErodáin conducted a 'great war' with respect to the abbacy. The outcome is not clear, but the near-contemporary annals of Inisfallen claim that Dub dá Leithe was expelled; Cumuscach follows Dub dá Leithe in the list of the 'heirs' of St Patrick. Dub dá Leithe apparently retired with honour, since he was styled *comarba* when he died in 1064, 'in good penance'.

A noteworthy aspect of Dub dá Leithe's career was his scholarship, as reflected in Bernard of Clairvaux's admission that the abbots of Armagh were learned men. He laboured during an important time for historical writing in Ireland, but his literary career may, in part, have been an attempt to make good the losses resulting from a fire which devastated Armagh on 30 May 1020, when the great stone church, other buildings, and many antiquities were destroyed; his father's death three days later may have been from injuries sustained in the blaze. The building that contained the manuscripts survived, although the texts in the students' dwellings were burned; the abbot would have had the sources for his compositions and the incentive to copy them. A manuscript composed, or commissioned, by Dub dá Leithe, containing various works, including a chronicle, was used by Irish historians of the later middle ages. It survives only in extracts in later compilations; the annals of Ulster, calling it simply the book of Dub dá Leithe, cites it as a source, for example, s.a. 629, 963, and 1021. The identified extracts suggest that Dub dá Leithe was most interested in the northern Irish dynasty of Cenél nEógain, which had controlled Armagh since the ninth century; they also show his interest in geography and political affairs. His historical interests extended to reworking an earlier tract known as *Baile in Scáil* ('The phantom's vision'), which was copied in the manuscript that bears his name. The text is in the form of an *echtra* ('narrative'), in which a king named Conn of the Hundred Battles has an adventure where he is entertained by a lady, representing the sovereignty of Ireland, and a phantom. When the lady asks who is to receive the ale of sovereignty, the phantom begins to recite the names of those who will have lordship over Ireland after Conn. The remainder of the tale is a list of the prominent Irish kings together with important events of their reigns, extending from Conn to the eleventh century. *Baile in Scáil* was composed probably between 1022 and 1036. Again, there is much important geographical information, including the burial-place of many of the monarchs.

Dub dá Leithe mac Máel Maire died on 1 September 1064 in Armagh, where he is assumed to have been buried. Nothing is known of his marriage(s), but he was survived by a son named Áed who died in 1108.

Benjamin T. Hudson

Sources Ann. Ulster · S. Mac Airt, ed. and trans., *The annals of Inisfallen* (1951) · AFM · H. J. Lawlor and R. I. Best, 'The ancient list of the coarbs of Patrick', *Proceedings of the Royal Irish Academy*, 35C (1918–20), 316–62 · K. Hughes, *The church in early Irish society* (1966) · R. Thurneysen, 'Baile in Scáil', *Zeitschrift für Celtische Philologie*, 20 (1933–6), 213–27 · G. Murphy, 'A poem in praise of Aodh úa Foirréidh, bishop of Armagh, 1032–56', *Measgra i gcuimhne Mhichíl Uí Chléirigh / Miscellany of historical and linguistic studies in honour of Brother Michael Ó Cléirigh*, ed. S. O'Brien (1944), 140–64 · B. T. Hudson, *Prophecy of Berchán* (1996) · T. W. Moody and others, eds., *A new history of Ireland*, 9: *Maps, genealogies, lists* (1984)

Du Bellay, Jean (1498–1560), diplomat and bishop of Paris, was born at Glatigny, the second son of Louis Du Bellay and Marguerite de la Tour-Landry. He studied first at the University of Angers, then in Paris at the Collège de Navarre, and finally at Orléans, where he studied law. In 1526 he was given the abbey of Breteuil, in Picardy, and appointed bishop of Bayonne. Like many of his fellow bishops, he did not reside in his diocese, but merely drew its revenues while living at court. In September 1527 he accompanied the constable, Anne de Montmorency, on an embassy to England, and remained in London as resident ambassador from November 1527 until February 1529. His main task was to ensure that England fulfilled her obligations under the two treaties of Westminster. After a brief sojourn in France, he returned to England in May 1529, remaining there until January 1530, when he was replaced as resident by his elder brother, Guillaume. Both men were keen to prevent Henry VIII's breach with Rome. They supported his divorce and were deemed broadly sympathetic to the evangelical cause.

In August 1530 Jean Du Bellay returned to London, remaining there until September, when he hastily went back to France. The reports which he sent back to the French king or his chief minister are an invaluable source of information on Wolsey and Henry VIII's divorce. Meanwhile, a group of theologians of the University of Paris, who had opposed the divorce, spread a false rumour to the effect that Du Bellay had been charged with heresy by the *parlement* of Paris. Although the rumour was shown to be false, Du Bellay insisted on his name being cleared. The matter was referred to the *grand conseil*, which presumably found in his favour, since he was sent back to England as ambassador-extraordinary in October 1531, remaining there until 25 October. In September 1532 he became bishop of Paris, and as such accompanied François I to his meeting with Henry VIII at Boulogne in the following month. It was even rumoured that Henry would marry Anne Boleyn in François's presence, and that the bishop, whom Anne liked, would be the officiating priest. In 1533 Du Bellay accompanied François to Marseilles for his meeting with Pope Clement VII. The king tried to have Henry VIII's excommunication deferred for six months, but the pope would only concede one. However, Henry's appeal to a general council angered François almost as much as the pope, and in November Du Bellay returned to England for the last time, to complain of Henry's provocative behaviour. In November 1533, as the rise of protestantism in France caused tension in Paris, Du Bellay was accused of neglecting to prosecute heretics, a charge vigorously rejected by his vicar-general. On 10 January 1534 he was back at the French court, and a year later, on 21 January 1535, figured prominently in a public procession in Paris aimed at demonstrating François I's orthodoxy.

On 21 May 1535 Du Bellay was created a cardinal by Pope Paul III, and in June was sent to Italy, primarily to win over the pope to the side of François I, and to dissuade him from calling a general council. He used his visit to strengthen France's ties with her allies in Italy and to recruit mercenary captains. In July 1536, following the outbreak of war between François and the empire, Du Bellay took charge of the defence of Paris as the king's lieutenant-general in the capital and the Île-de-France. In September 1544 he was a plenipotentiary appointed to make peace with England. The notion that Du Bellay lost influence at court following the accession of Henri II in March 1547 is unfounded: as a friend of Montmorency he kept his place in the king's council. After resigning the see of Paris on 16 March 1551, he retired to Rome, acquired four Italian sees, and became dean of the Sacred College. Despite failing health, he defended French interests in Italy with tenacity. He lived luxuriously in a palace near the baths of Diocletian. A noted collector of antiquities, he was also a patron of humanists, including Rabelais. Du Bellay died in Rome on 16 February 1560 and was buried in the church of Trinità dei Monti. R. J. KNECHT

Sources *Catalogue des actes de François 1er*, 10 vols. (Paris, 1887–1908) · V.-L. Bourrilly and P. de Vaissière, eds., *Ambassades en Angleterre de Jean du Bellay* (1905) · *Catalogue des actes de Henri II*, [6 vols.] (1979–) · *Correspondance du Cardinal Jean du Bellay*, ed. R. Scheurer, 2 vols. (1969–73) · V.-L. Bourrilly, *Guillaume du Bellay* (1905) · V.-L. Bourrilly, 'Le cardinal Jean du Bellay en Italie', *Revue des Études Rabelaisiennes*, 5 (1907), 246–53, 262–74 · V.-L. Bourrilly and N. Weiss, 'Jean du Bellay, les protestants et la Sorbonne', *Bulletin* [Société de l'Histoire du Protestantisme Français], 52 (1903), 97–127, 193–231; 53 (1904), 97–143 · L. Romier, *Les origines politiques des guerres de religion*, 2 vols. (1913) · A. Tallon, *La France et le concile de Trente (1518–1563)* (Rome, 1997) · *LP Henry VIII* · H. O. Evennett, 'Pie IV et les bénéfices de Jean du Bellay', *Revue d'Histoire de l'Église de France*, 22 (1936), 425–61 · F. J. Baumgartner, *Change and continuity in the French episcopate: the bishops and the wars of religion, 1547–1610* (1986) · J. Balteau and others, eds., *Dictionnaire de biographie française*, [19 vols.] (Paris, 1933–)

Duberly [*née* Locke], **Frances Isabella** [Fanny] (1829–1902), diarist, was born on 27 September 1829 at Rowdeford House, Devizes, Wiltshire, the youngest of the eight children of Sir Wadham Locke, a banker in Devizes, and his wife, Anna Maria Selina Powell. Her father died when she was six, her mother when she was eight. Her upbringing owed much to her eldest sister, Selina; she received a sound education at a boarding-school in High Wycombe, Buckinghamshire, and became a skilled horsewoman. In 1846 she met a 24-year-old lieutenant, Henry Duberly (1822–1891), at a family wedding; they married at New Alresford, Hampshire, four years later, on 21 February 1850.

In February 1854 Fanny accompanied her husband when his regiment, the 8th hussars, sailed to Constantinople on the eve of the Crimean War. She ignored orders from the commander, Lord Raglan, excluding wives from the war zone and remained with the hussars at Varna and in the Crimea longer than any other woman, in her last months sharing her husband's hut in the light brigade lines. Although she missed the battle of the Alma and saw only the aftermath of the battle of Inkerman, she witnessed the cavalry charges at Balaklava and the assault on Malakhov, experienced the winter privations, and rode into Sevastopol soon after it fell.

Fanny recorded these events daily. She possessed a ready pen, eyes perceptive to detail, youthful self-confidence, and an incisive style softened by candid pathos. Anonymous extracts from her letters home were leaked to the London press, encouraging her to ask her sister Selina's husband, Francis Marx, to edit her journal for publication. He toned down suspected indiscretions and the book reads less vividly than her letters (now held in the British Library), but a convincing realism survived the excisions and the *Journal Kept during the Russian War* sold well at Christmas 1855. Readers who anticipated a more heroic romanticism were, however, left uneasy, while Queen Victoria was offended by Fanny's ingenuous wilfulness. The queen had already declined an optimistically proffered dedication, and in May 1856 she snubbed Mrs Duberly when the hussars were inspected on returning to Portsmouth. Fanny was never appreciated as much in England as she had been in the Crimea, notably by the French chasseurs d'Afrique.

After two years in Ireland the 8th hussars sailed for India, in October 1857, with Fanny again accompanying her husband. She kept a journal covering the next twelve months and chronicling a march across Rajputana, during which she was in the saddle for 1800 miles. By this time, however, she was writing self-consciously and with mounting weariness; the earlier spontaneity had gone. *Campaigning Experiences in Central India and Rajputana during the Suppression of the Mutiny* appeared in July 1859 but was less successful than her earlier book.

At Balaklava, Fanny 'prayed that [she] might *wear* out [her] life and not rust it out' (*Journal Kept during the Russian War*, 102). However, she was denied this hope. The hussars returned from India in 1864; thereafter she remained the dutiful wife of a serving officer in dull garrison towns until Henry retired, as a lieutenant-colonel, in 1881. The Duberlys purchased St Clair, a villa in The Park, Cheltenham, Gloucestershire. Henry died there in 1891; Fanny outlived him by almost twelve years. She died at St Clair on 19 November 1902. ALAN PALMER

Sources E. E. P. Tisdall, *Mrs Duberly's campaigns* (1963) · A. W. Palmer, *The banner of battle: the story of the Crimean War* (1987) · m. cert. · d. cert.
Archives BL, letters to F. Marx and Mrs F. Marx, Add. MS 47218
Likenesses R. Fenton, photograph, 1855, NAM
Wealth at death £8828 9s. 3d.: administration with will, 21 April 1903, *CGPLA Eng. & Wales*

Dubh [Duff; Dub mac Mael Coluim] (*d.* 966), king in Scotland, was the son of *Malcolm I (*d.* 954). His brother (probably younger) was *Kenneth II (*d.* 995). Dubh succeeded *Indulf as king on the latter's death in 962 and it is arguable that, until his reign, the two branches of the royal dynasty had maintained a degree of solidarity ever since the reign of Dubh's grandfather, *Donald II (*r.* 889–900) [*see under* Constantine II]. In 965, however, Dubh (of the branch descended from Constantine I) was challenged by *Culen, of the branch descended from King Aed (*d.* 878). Culen was defeated by Dubh at the battle of Duncrub in Strathearn (modern Perthshire), but in the following year Dubh was killed by the men of Moray at Forres, an event which apparently coincided with an eclipse of the sun on 20 July 966, and was succeeded by Culen. It has been argued cogently that the vivid depiction of a battle and its aftermath on the huge stone monument at Forres (known as 'Sueno's stone') represents Dubh's defeat and death. This defeat no doubt undid the probable success of Dubh's father, Malcolm I, in subduing Moray. According to a late (and debatable) source, Dubh's body was taken to Iona for burial. He had one son, King *Kenneth III (d. 1005).

Dubh is the eponymous ancestor of the Clann Duib (Macduffs), the earls of Fife from the mid-eleventh to the mid-fourteenth century. Their status as descendants of a line of kings, albeit ones who failed to maintain themselves as plausible claimants to the throne, is surely reflected in the privileged position which the earls later enjoyed, and above all in the prominent position which they came to play in the ceremonies which marked the inauguration of Scottish kings at Scone. A further sign of their pre-eminence among the Scottish nobility may be the role which late medieval chroniclers allot to a certain **Macduff** [Macduib] (*fl.* 1057–1058), 'thane' of Fife, who is represented as a key supporter of Malcolm III in his campaign for the throne against Macbeth. The earls of Fife were certainly close supporters of the kings of Scots in the twelfth century [*see* Macduff family, earls of Fife]. If Macduff and his description as earl or thane of Fife are not literary inventions, then he may have been a descendant, perhaps the great-grandson, of King Dubh, through the latter's son, Kenneth III. The first to bear the style Macduib, who established his family as earls of Fife (thereby displacing the Clann Conaill Cirr), he could have been the father or grandfather of Constantine, earl of Fife between 1095 and *c.*1130, and/or of Gille Micheil, earl of Fife from *c.*1130 to 1133.   DAUVIT BROUN

Sources A. O. Anderson, ed. and trans., *Early sources of Scottish history, AD 500 to 1286*, 1 (1922), 471–4 · M. O. Anderson, *Kings and kingship in early Scotland*, rev. edn (1980), 249–53, 265–89 · A. A. M. Duncan, 'The kingdom of the Scots', *The making of Britain: the dark ages*, ed. L. M. Smith (1984) · J. Bannerman, 'Macduff of Fife', *Medieval Scotland: crown, lordship and community: essays presented to G. W. S. Barrow*, ed. A. Grant and K. J. Stringer (1993), 20–38

Dubhdalethe. *See* Dub dá Leithe (d. 1064).

Dublin. For this title name *see* Vere, Robert de, ninth earl of Oxford, marquess of Dublin, and duke of Ireland (1362–1392).

Dublitter (d. 796). *See under* Meath, saints of (*act. c.*400–*c.*900).

Dubnovellaunus (*fl. c.*40 BC). *See under* Roman Britain, British leaders in (*act.* 55 BC–AD 84).

Dubnovellaunus (*fl. c.*30 BC). *See under* Roman Britain, British leaders in (*act.* 55 BC–AD 84).

Dubois, Charles (1656–1740), botanist, was the eldest son of John Dubois (d. 1684), a weaver in London, and his wife, Anne, the daughter of Charles Herle of Winwick, Lancashire. He was bred to the cloth trade but on his half-brother's death in 1702, he succeeded him as cashier-general of the East India Company. He retained this position until 1737. He inherited from his father a home at Mitcham, Surrey, where he had a garden rich in plants newly introduced from India and China. He became acquainted with a group of natural historians around London, including James Petiver, William Sherard, and Hans Sloane, with whom he shared plants and observations on cultivation. He was elected a fellow of the Royal Society in 1700, and admitted more than a decade later, in 1714. Dubois contributed observations to the third edition of Ray's *Synopsis* (1724) and subscribed to Catesby's expedition to Carolina. He collected shells, fossils, and coins but only his herbarium has survived. Dubois bequeathed his books, his herbarium, and all his other curiosities to his brother-in-law Ebenezer Dubois. His dried plants occupy seventy-four folio volumes, the entire number of specimens being about thirteen thousand, and are in excellent preservation; they now form part of the herbarium at the Oxford Botanic Garden. He died on 20 October 1740 and was buried at Mitcham on 28 October.

B. D. JACKSON, *rev.* P. E. KELL

Sources C. Dubois, 'Notes on insects, 1692 and 1695', *Bulletin of the British Museum (Natural History)* [Historical Series], 17 (1989), 1–165 · B. Henrey, *British botanical and horticultural literature before 1800*, 2 (1975), 431 · C. Daubeny, *Oxford Botanic Garden* (1853), 60 · Nichols, *Illustrations*, 1.366 · H. M. Clokie, *An account of the herbaria of the department of botany in the University of Oxford* (1964), 30 · Desmond, *Botanists* · will, PRO, PROB 11/705, sig. 264
Archives Bodl. Oxf. · NHM · Oxford Botanic Garden, plants

Du Bois [*née* Annesley], **Lady Dorothea** (1728–1774), writer and poet, was the eldest of the seven daughters of Richard *Annesley, sixth earl of Anglesey (*bap.* 1693, d. 1761), and Ann Simpson (*c.*1700–1765), daughter of John Simpson, a wealthy citizen of Dublin. She was born in Ireland in 1728, the year after her father became Lord Altham. In 1737 he succeeded to the earldom. During an illness in November 1740 the earl drew up a deed of settlement to provide for his wife and three surviving daughters after his death, assigning £2000 a year to the countess and £10,000, £8000, and £7000 to Dorothea, Caroline, and Elizabeth respectively, to be inherited when they reached eighteen or married, whichever happened first. Soon after this, however, the earl, having begun an affair with Juliana Donovan (a woman described by Dorothea in her *Case of Ann Countess of Anglesey*, 1766, as the daughter of a local alehouse keeper), repudiated his marriage and turned his wife and daughters out of his house. The countess promptly sued in the ecclesiastical courts and gained, Dorothea tells us, 'an Order against him for an interim Alimony of Four Pounds a Week until a full Answer should be pronounced in the said Suit' (Du Bois, *Case*, 15). The earl, however, declined to pay and was excommunicated as a result. From then on the only means of support for the countess and her three daughters was a pension of £200 a year granted by George II.

In 1752 Dorothea married a French musician, M. Du Bois. Little is known about him, but he had lived 'on a familiar foot' in the family of George Berkeley, bishop of Cloyne, for some years and was, in the bishop's opinion, 'much above the common level of those amongst whom fortune had placed him' (letter to Dorothea, 1752, NL Ire., MS 987); he also delighted Dorothea by converting to protestantism. The couple seem to have married privately in the first instance and were strongly advised by the bishop to 'satisfy the Laws by a public legal marriage' (ibid.). They went on to have six children in the next eight years. In the meantime legal wrangles between the earl and the countess continued; shortly after the birth of her sixth child in 1760 Dorothea travelled to the family seat at Camolin Park, co. Wexford, accompanied only by two servants, in an attempt to persuade her father, whom she knew to be seriously ill, to acknowledge his marriage with her mother, and thus the legitimacy of herself and her sisters. The attempt, however, was a disaster and resulted only in Dorothea's being roughly repulsed by her father's new wife and their son, Arthur (the couple had married in September 1752 and subsequently claimed a prior marriage in September 1741). The scene is vividly described in both Dorothea's *Poems on Several Occasions*, published by subscription in 1764, and her later prose tract, *The Case of Ann Countess of Anglesey*. She also published a novel, *Theodora* (1770), closely based on her own history, of which the *Critical Review* wrote,

> When a writer, particularly a female one, is prompted by *necessity* to take up her pen, criticism ought to give way to compassion. Lady Dorothea calls her 'Theodora' a novel; but we cannot possibly look upon her as a mere novelist … We sincerely pity lady Dorothea as a woman of distinction in distress; but, as impartial reviewers, we must own that we cannot think the emolument arising from the publication of her novel will be adequate to her wishes. (*Critical Review*, 29, 1770, 474)

Dorothea also published *The Lady's Polite Secretary, or, New Female Letter Writer* (1772?) and wrote several musical entertainments for Marylebone Gardens, as well as *The Haunted Grove*, a piece performed about 1772 in Fishamble Street, Dublin, but removed 'when a verse in the Finale, which was deemed indelicate, occasioned its sudden condemnation' (*Thespian Dictionary*).

There seems little doubt that Dorothea Du Bois's writing career was motivated mainly by the dual aims of raising much-needed money and of publicizing the case of her mother's abandonment by her father, and thus the poverty-stricken plight of herself and her sisters. Still, her work has more than purely archival interest: it registers strongly a consciousness of her powerlessness as a woman attempting to establish her rights. In her poem 'The Amazonian Gift' she asks:

> Is Courage in a Woman's Breast,
> Less pleasing than in Man?
> And is a smiling Maid allow'd
> No Weapon but a Fan?

The poem concludes,

> Then since the Arms that Women use
> Successless are in me;
> I'll take the Pistol, Sword or Gun,
> And thus equip'd, live free.
>
> The Pattern of the *Spartan* Dame,
> I'll copy as I can;
> To Man, degen'rate Man, I'll give
> That simple Thing, a *Fan*.
> (Du Bois, *Poems*, 85–6)

The defiant spirit to which she gives voice in these lines

sits somewhat bathetically beside her account in *The Case of Ann Countess of Anglesey* of her fruitless visit to her father in 1760, in which she confesses that when his servants made to throw her out of his room she drew from her pocket 'a small silver-mounted Pistol … which I blush to say was, with its Fellow, unloaded; and only meant to keep those Ruffians, I expected to meet, at a Distance' (Du Bois, *Case*, 5). The subsequent struggle concluded with Dorothea's half-brother, Arthur, holding a pistol to her head; there followed a humiliating sequence of events over two days, at the end of which Dorothea was only saved from being sent to gaol by, she tells us, 'the Town of Ferns' which, 'sensible of my cruel usage, rose in my Defence' (ibid., 7). Dorothea died of what is described in the *Gentleman's Magazine* as 'an apoplectic fit', in Grafton Street, Dublin, early in 1774. GILLIAN SKINNER

Sources D. Du Bois, *The case of Ann countess of Anglesey, lately deceased; lawful wife of Richard Annesley, late earl of Anglesey, and of her three surviving daughters, Lady Dorothea, Lady Caroline, and Lady Elizabeth, by the said earl* (1766) • DNB • copies of a letter from Lady Dorothy Annesley to George Berkeley, bishop of Cloyne, on her proposed marriage to M. Dubois, with Berkeley's answer, 1752, NL Ire., MS 987 • *The thespian dictionary, or, Dramatic biography of the present age*, 2nd edn (1805) • D. Du Bois, *Poems on several occasions, by a lady of quality* (1764) • GM, 1st ser., 44 (1774), 94
Archives NL Ire., MS 987
Wealth at death given penurious life, probably insignificant

Du Bois, Edward (1619–1696). *See under* Du Bois, Simon (1632–1708).

Dubois, Edward (1774–1850), writer, was born in Love Lane, London, on 4 January 1774, the son of William Dubois, a merchant originally from the neighbourhood of Neufchâtel, and his wife, Jane. He was baptized on 29 January 1774 at St Mary Woolnoth, London. His education was conducted at home and at Christ's Hospital, and he acquired a considerable knowledge of the classics and a fair acquaintance with French, Italian, and Spanish. He adopted literature as his profession, publishing quite a few works at this time, including: *A Piece of Family Biography* (1799), dedicated to George Colman; *The wreath: selections from Sappho, Theocritus, Bion, and Moschus, with a prose translation and notes* (1799), in which he was assisted by Capel Lofft; and *The fairy of misfortune, or, The loves of Octar and Zuleima, an Italian tale translated from the French* (1799). More characteristic of his later work, however, were *Old Nick: a Satirical Story* (1801), and an edition of Boccaccio's *Decameron*, which appeared in 1804, and which represented a revision of the anonymous translation of 1741. Although Dubois was called to the bar at the Inner Temple on 5 May 1809, he continued to supplement his income by writing. He was a regular contributor to various periodicals, and especially to the *Morning Chronicle* under James Perry. Art notices, dramatic criticisms, and verses on the topics of the day were his principal contributions; and to the last day of his life he retained his position of art critic on the staff of *The Observer*.

Dubois was the editor of the *Monthly Mirror* during the

ownership of Thomas Hill, and at the urging of that periodical's publishers, Thomas Hood (1759?–1811) and his partner Sharpe, he produced a satirical pamphlet entitled *My pocket-book, or, Hints for a 'ryghte merrie and conceitede tour', in quarto, to be called, 'The stranger in Ireland'* (1805). This was an effective satire of the travel literature of Sir John Carr, and quickly passed through two editions. It was answered by *Old Nick's Pocket-Book* (1808), written in ridicule of Dubois by a friend of Carr, who was stung into bringing legal action against Hood and Sharpe, in defence of his literary character. The case came before Lord Ellenborough and a special jury at Guildhall on 1 August 1808, when the judge summed up strongly in favour of the defendants, and the verdict was given for them. A report of the proceedings was appended to the third edition of *My Pocket-Book*.

In August 1815 Dubois married Harriet, the daughter of Richard Cheslyn Cresswell, registrar of the arches court of Canterbury. They had three sons and one daughter. Dubois continued to work for the *Monthly Mirror*, and had Theodore Hook as one of his assistants. It was R. H. Barham who obtained, when writing Hook's life, 'many of the most interesting details' of the wit's early history. On the death in 1840 of Hill, the periodical's owner, Dubois was left a considerable legacy as one of the will's two executors and residuary legatees. He went on to assist Thomas Campbell in editing the first number of Colburn's *New Monthly Magazine*, but before the second number could be issued differences broke out and they separated. For a few years he was the editor of the *Lady's Magazine*, and for the same period he conducted the *European Magazine*.

Dubois is sometimes said to have been 'a connection' of Sir Philip Francis, at other times his private secretary, and they were certainly on intimate terms of friendship from 1807 until Francis's death in 1818. In 1807 Dubois edited and issued in four volumes a new edition of Francis's *Poetical Translations of the Works of Horace*. He compiled Francis's biography in the *Monthly Mirror* for 1810, and wrote the life of Francis which appeared in the *Morning Chronicle* for 28 December 1818. When Lord Campbell was composing his *Memoir* of Lord Loughborough, Dubois obtained for him a long memorandum from Lady Francis on the authorship of the *Letters of Junius* (Campbell, 6.344–7). The first of these lives is said to have prompted the publication of John Taylor's *Junius Identified*, and it has been wrongly suggested that Dubois was the real author of that volume, a suggestion refuted by Taylor's assurance that he 'never received the slightest assistance from Mr. Dubois' (*N&Q*, 1850, 258–9).

For at least twenty years Dubois was assistant to Serjeant Heath, judge of the court of requests, and when county courts were established, a judgeship was offered to Dubois, but he preferred to continue as Heath's deputy. In 1833 he was appointed by Lord Brougham to the office of treasurer and secretary of the Metropolitan Lunacy Commission, and on the abolition of that body in 1845 was employed under the new commission without any special duties. These appointments he retained until his death,

which took place in Sloane Street, Chelsea, on 10 January 1850. One of his last acts had been to raise a subscription for the family of the late R. B. Peake, playwright.

W. P. COURTNEY, *rev.* REBECCA MILLS

Sources IGI · J. Parkes and H. Merivale, *Memoirs of Sir Philip Francis*, 2 vols. (1867), vol.1, pp. xxiii, 327; vol. 2, pp. 383–5 · *Literary Gazette* (19 Jan 1850), 52–3 · [J. Watkins and F. Shoberl], *A biographical dictionary of the living authors of Great Britain and Ireland* (1816) · *GM*, 2nd ser., 33 (1850), 326–7 · H. Smith, 'A greybeard's gossip about his literary acquaintance, no. VII', *New Monthly Magazine*, new ser., 81 (1847), 83–7, esp. 83–4 · *N&Q*, 2 (1850), 258–9 · S. Halkett and J. Laing, *A dictionary of the anonymous and pseudonymous literature of Great Britain*, 3 (1885), 1911, 2207, 2250 · J. Collier, *An old man's diary, forty years ago*, 4 pts in 1 vol. (1871–2), pt 4, p. 23 · C. Redding, *Fifty years' recollections, literary and personal*, 2nd edn, 2 (1858), 161–5 · Allibone, *Dict.* · Watt, *Bibl. Brit.*, 1.319–20 · J. Campbell, *Lives of the lord chancellors*, 8 vols. (1845–69), vol. 6, pp. 344–7 · will, PRO, PROB 11/2106, sig. 22

Likenesses E. Dumée, stipple, 1794 (after A. Van Assen), BM; repro. in *Thespian Magazine* (1794) · Ridley, stipple, pubd 1839 (after Allingham), NPG · stipple, BM

Dubois, John (*bap.* 1622, *d.* 1684), local politician, was baptized on 24 February 1622 in Canterbury, Kent, the son of Jean Dubois (*d.* 1680), physician of Canterbury, and his wife, Catherine de l'Espine. Reared in the French Reformed community of Canterbury, Dubois became active in the French church at Threadneedle Street, London, by the 1650s and eventually became a deacon and an elder. On 11 January 1652 he married Anne (*d.* 1659), daughter of Charles *Herle, presbyterian rector of Winwick, Lancashire, and one-time prolocutor of the Westminster assembly. The following year he became free of the London Weavers' Company, presumably upon the completion of an apprenticeship, and he eventually developed a lucrative overseas trade, chiefly as a silk importer from France.

On 27 July 1662, after the death of his first wife, Dubois married Sarah (*d.* 1715), daughter of Daniel Waldo and Anne Claxton. His second marriage further strengthened his ties to English nonconformity, connecting him to a leading London Independent family. His commercial and political career would keep him associated with civic nonconformists thereafter. In 1670, for instance, he joined London dissenters in a major loan to Charles II intended to undermine implementation of the new Conventicle Act. Upset by French commercial competition and tariffs, Dubois joined Thomas Papillon, Sir Patience Ward, and other prominent dissenting and French Reformed merchants in promoting the proposals for English commerce put forward in *A Scheme of the Trade … between England and France* (1674). He also became a trustee for presbyterian Dr Thomas Gouge's fund to establish schools and to promote literacy in Wales. From 1672 or earlier Dubois resided in St Mary Aldermanbury, London, where he served as churchwarden in 1672–4, and where his children were baptized. Dubois was also a friend of Canterbury dean John Tillotson, who was a trustee for Gouge's fund, and who retained numerous dissenting connections after conforming.

Dubois was elected to the London common council for Cripplegate Within ward in 1674, and served until 1682.

He quickly became a leader of the opposition that emerged in the city as the ministry of Thomas Osborne, earl of Danby, sought to revive the coercive Anglican polity first erected in 1662–5. In March 1675, just before the dramatic parliamentary session of that year, Dubois confronted Danby's civic protégé, Lord Mayor Sir Robert Vyner, in common council, claiming that Vyner and the court of aldermen had 'invaded' the rights of the court of common council in making a minor corporation judicial appointment (Coventry MS 16, fol. 9). At court Dubois was counted among those in the city who 'hate Prerogative' and who were provoking trouble for the benefit of country spokesmen in the Commons (BL, Add. MS 34362, fol. 14). He was nevertheless appointed as a London assessment commissioner for 1677–80. Drawing upon the influence of his business associate and brother-in-law, the Liverpool merchant Charles Herle, he was also returned as Liverpool MP for each of the parliaments of 1679–81.

Dubois was at the centre of parliamentary and London affairs during the crisis of 1679–83. He believed that English protestantism was as vulnerable in those years as it had been in the 1640s, accusing the Jesuits of advancing their cause again by 'divid[ing] Protestants from Protestants' (Grey, 7.414). Parliament must 'determine the Succession' through the exclusion of the Catholic duke of York, he urged his fellow MPs in May 1679, and he served on a Commons' committee for the speedier conviction of recusants (ibid., 7.238). Between parliaments Dubois aided in the election of the dissenters Henry Cornish and Slingsby Bethel as sheriffs of London and Middlesex for 1680–81. In the 1680–81 parliament he was the first speaker on behalf of the Exclusion Bill, warning that, 'If the Catholics have such an influence upon the Government under a Protestant Prince, what will they have under a Popish?' (ibid., 7.396). He was equally supportive of endeavours to promote protestant union, and served on the Commons' committee to prepare a bill to achieve it. When the Commons adopted the Exclusion Bill, Dubois served on a corporation of London committee that addressed Charles II on its behalf. And when Charles instead prorogued parliament, in January 1681, Dubois sat on another civic committee that drafted a petition to the crown for an immediate resumption of the session. Dubois took a similar role in the short-lived third Exclusion Parliament of March 1681, serving on committees for another Exclusion Bill and for conferring with the Lords about the irregular loss of a bill, approved in the previous parliament, for repealing the Elizabethan statute against sectarians. His outspoken views did not prevent him from serving with the archbishop of Canterbury and the bishop of London on a committee that met weekly in 1681 to distribute money for the relief of arriving French protestant refugees.

As Charles II's efforts to resolve the crisis on his terms moved from parliament to the city, Dubois stood firmly against him. He was among those who out-manoeuvred civic loyalists in securing another corporation address on behalf of a new parliament in May 1681. He was impanelled by the city's whig sheriffs for the jury that rejected the crown's treason case against the earl of Shaftesbury.

On that occasion his detractors claimed that he called the king a papist. In January 1682 he was chosen as a member of the corporation committee to defend the London charter against the crown's *quo warranto*. As the 1682 midsummer's election of sheriffs approached, and as the crown embarked upon strategies to secure the election of loyalists, the London whigs settled upon Dubois and Thomas Papillon as their candidates. Just prior to the election, a whig effort to secure a vacant aldermanic place for Dubois miscarried. The shrieval election itself was the most protracted contest in the city's electoral history, requiring several common halls and polls between June and September, by which time Dubois had also been elected master of the Weavers' Company. A majority of civic electors clearly favoured Dubois and Papillon, but the crown was determined to prevent their election.

Dubois and Papillon appeared at the Guildhall on 28 September 1682 for the taking of the shrieval oaths. Loyalist Lord Mayor Sir John Moore instead swore in tory candidates Dudley North and Peter Rich and forced their whig rivals from the hustings. As the court and London loyalists celebrated victory, the whig aldermen took bonds from Dubois and Papillon to serve as sheriffs; and the pair were feasted by Shaftesbury and other whig lords as sheriffs-elect. Indeed, the following day the two whigs wrangled with North and Rich about who should preside, as sheriffs, at the beginning of the mayoral election for 1682–3. After loyalist aldermen adjusted a mayoral poll to advance tory Sir William Pritchard over whig Henry Cornish, the contest for the corporation entered the courts. Recognized by the whigs as the legitimate civic magistrates, Dubois and Papillon sued in king's bench for the shrievalty, and Henry Cornish sued for the mayoralty. The whigs advanced Dubois, without success, for another vacant aldermanic place in December. He was apparently the object of an attempted legal entrapment when a government informer offered him seditious papers; and Cripplegate loyalists secured his replacement on common council for 1683. In the meantime, the government's interference in the London elections turned some whigs to plotting resistance, and John Locke and Algernon Sidney to defending it.

The legal contest for the London shrievalty reached its climax in April 1683. Lord Mayor Pritchard and several loyalist aldermen were then briefly arrested, on writs taken out by attorney Richard Goodenough, for their failure to respond to Dubois's and Papillon's suits for office. Dubois and his colleague hastily distanced themselves from Goodenough's action. Whether they had any awareness of the seditious conspiracy in which Goodenough and several of his accomplices in making the arrests were already involved seems unlikely. Plot ringleader Robert West apparently feared that Dubois and Papillon might hesitate to seize office in an insurrection, in which case they would need to be 'knocked on the head' (*State trials*, 9.420). Dubois's hope of securing the shrievalty by legal means collapsed in May when king's bench convicted several leading London whigs of committing a riot in the course of the election. He was disarmed after the disclosure of whig plotting in June, but the government took no further action against him.

Dubois died in October 1684 and was buried on 30 October at St Mary Aldermanbury; he was survived by his wife. His death occurred just days before the hearing of Sir William Pritchard's suit against him and Papillon for false arrest. Dubois's personal estate was valued at over £35,000. He owned land in Carmarthen, Kent, and Surrey, where he had a house at Mitcham. He also owned stock in the East India Company and served on its directing committee from 1681 until his death. At his request, John Tillotson preached his funeral sermon.

GARY S. DE KREY

Sources I. Cassidy and E. Cruickshanks, 'Dubois, John', HoP, *Commons, 1660–90*, 2.237–8 · *CSP dom.*, *1678*, 490; *1680–81*, 256, 280, 603; *1682*, 244, 264, 295, 304, 315, 381, 401, 404, 412, 430, 433, 478, 513, 544, 556; *Jan–June 1683*, 39, 41, 49, 204–6, 210, 214, 259–60; *July–Sept 1683*, 154, 164; *1683–4*, 391–2; *1684–5*, 177 · N. Luttrell, *A brief historical relation of state affairs from September 1678 to April 1714*, 1 (1857), 87, 158, 191, 194, 197, 203, 206–8, 210, 217–21, 223, 224, 230, 235, 237, 239, 240, 241–2, 243, 247, 256, 260 · J. R. Woodhead, *The rulers of London, 1660–1689* (1965), 62 · *Memoirs of Thomas Papillon, of London, merchant*, ed. A. F. W. Papillon (1887), 214–34 · L. Cong., manuscript division, London newsletters collection, 7.300, 302; 8.70, 121, 123–4, 322 (17 June, 28, 30 Sept, 5 Oct, 14, 16 Dec 1682; 22 April 1683) · Newdigate newsletters, 28 Sept 1682, Folger, L.c.1280; 24 Oct 1682, Folger, L.c.1291; 28 Nov 1682, Folger, L.c.1305; 5 Dec 1682, Folger, L.c.1308; 14 Dec 1682, Folger, L.c.1312; 3–6 Feb 1683, Folger, L.c.1333–4; 24 Feb 1683, Folger, L.c.1342; 26 April 1683, Folger, L.c.1368 · A. Grey, ed., *Debates of the House of Commons, from the year 1667 to the year 1694*, 10 vols. (1763), vol. 7, pp. 238, 396, 414; vol. 8, pp. 90, 117 · K. H. D. Haley, *The first earl of Shaftesbury* (1968), 234, 582, 620, 640, 675, 699–700, 702–3 · M. Knights, *Politics and opinion in crisis, 1678–81* (1994), 24, 51, 123, 125, 138, 278, 280n. · G. de F. Lord and others, eds., *Poems on affairs of state: Augustan satirical verse, 1660–1714*, 7 vols. (1963–75), vol. 3, pp. 44, 215, 217, 222, 234–5, 238, 244, 262, 269, 275, 345–6, 370, 383, 385, 410, 541 · BL, Add. MS 34362, fols. 13–14 · Bath Papers, BL, M/863/11, Coventry MS, 16, fols. 9–11, 16 · PRO, SP 29/425/43 · CLRO, Journal 49, fols. 156–7, 170, 205, 281 · CLRO, Repertory 88, fols. 13, 128 · CLRO, MS 40/30 · ward assessment books for six-months' tax, Cripplegate Within, 1680, CLRO · M. Priestley, 'London merchants and opposition politics in Charles II's reign', *BIHR*, 29 (1956), 205–19 · *State trials*, 9.187–298, 420; 10.320–72 · R. Gwynn, ed., *Minutes of the consistory of the French Church of London, Threadneedle Street, 1679–1692*, Huguenot Society, quarto series, 58 (1994), 6, 61, 68n., 73, 101, 101n. · W. B. Bannerman, ed., *The registers of St Mary the Virgin, Aldermanbury, London*, 1–2, Harleian Society, register section, 61–2 (1931–2), vol. 1, p. 161; vol. 2, pp. 186–9, 194, 201–2, 237, 262, 291 · P. Ward and others, *London, 29 Nov. 1674. A scheme of the trade* [1674] · R. Morrice, 'Ent'ring book', DWL, p. 337 · *Moderate Intelligencer*, 2 (14–17 June 1682) · *JHC*, 9 (1667–87), 584, 597, 645, 653, 686, 708, 711 · W. A. Shaw, ed., *Calendar of treasury books*, 5, PRO (1911), 1375; 6 (1913), 275, 276, 424 · R. Hovenden, ed., *Registers of the Walloon or strangers' church in Canterbury*, Publications of the Huguenot Society of London, 5 (1891), 121, 472, 605 · W. J. C. Moens, ed., *Registers of the French Church Threadneedle Street, London, 1637–1685*, Publications of the Huguenot Society of London, 13 (1899), 33, 44 · *Memoirs of Thomas, earl of Ailesbury*, ed. W. E. Buckley, 1, Roxburghe Club, 122 (1890), 71 · 'Gouge, Thomas (1609–1681)', *DNB* · 'Herle, Charles', *DNB* · 'Tillotson, John', *DNB* · Tai Liu, *Puritan London: a study of religion and society in the City parishes* (1986), 200–01, 225 · R. L. Greaves, *Secrets of the kingdom: British radicals from the Popish Plot to the revolution of 1688–89* (1992), 96, 149, 189 · G. S. De Krey, 'Trade, religion, and politics in London in the reign of William III', PhD diss., Princeton, 3 vols., 1978, 3.548–9 · R. D. Gwynn, 'The ecclesiastical organization of French protestants in London', PhD diss., Massy University, 1976, 433 · PRO, PROB 11/378, fols. 221r–233r · PRO, PROB 11/378, fols. 296v–297v

Wealth at death over £35,000; land in Carmarthen, Kent, Surrey: will, PRO, PROB 11/378, fols. 296v–297v; Woodhead, *Rulers*; Cassidy and Cruickshanks, 'Dubois, John', vol. 2, p. 238

Du Bois, Simon (1632–1708), painter, was born in Antwerp, the son of Hendrik Dubois (*c*.1589–1646), a portrait painter and art dealer, and Helena, the daughter of Eland Gysbrechts Tromper. They were married in Antwerp in 1614, and Simon was baptized there on 26 July 1632. He lived in Rotterdam from 1638 until 1646, when he moved to Haarlem with his older brother, Edward, and studied with Nicolaes (or Claes) Pieterszoon Berchem. He also studied with Philips Wouwermans from April 1652 to October 1653. He and Edward then went to Italy; he was in Venice in 1657 and in Rome in 1667, when he was paid for a portrait of Pope Alexander VII.

Du Bois painted portraits, oil miniatures on copper, animals, landscapes, battle and history scenes, and copied Italian old masters. The latter he sold as originals, saying that if he put his own name to them their merit would never be recognized. There are six of his drawings after earlier compositions by Italian artists in the British Museum, London. According to Vertue he began painting portraits in Italy. It is thought that he lived there for about twenty-five years before joining his brother in London, *c*.1680. They shared an establishment in Covent Garden, and 'by their extraordinary industry … made one of the finest collections, of closet pieces especially, of any in England' (Buckeridge, 359). There were 363 pictures in the collection when it was sold in 1709, and it is likely that he dealt in works of art.

Du Bois was fortunate in securing the patronage and friendship of the lord chancellor, John Somers, who sat for his portrait (*c*.1698; priv. coll.) and paid him liberally; James Elsum wrote an epigram on this portrait. Among the portraits painted by Du Bois in England were those of Archbishop Thomas Tenison (*c*.1700; Lambeth Palace, London); William Bentinck, earl of Portland (engraved by Robert Williams and Jacob Houbraken); Adrian Beverland (engraved by Isaac Beckett); and a man and a woman called Sir William and Lady Jones (1682; Dulwich Picture Gallery, London). His oil miniatures of William III and Mary II (priv. coll.) were originally owned by the miniaturist Bernard Lens and another of his miniatures, of an unknown man (1682), is at the Fitzwilliam Museum, Cambridge.

On 16 September 1706, Du Bois married Sarah Atkins (*b.* *c*.1671), the widowed daughter of the painter Willem Van de Velde II, at St Paul's, Covent Garden. She was thirty-nine years younger than Du Bois. They are said to have become acquainted when he painted her portrait. He died between 16 May 1708, when a second codicil was added to his will of 7 May, and 20 May, when the will was proved. He was buried on 26 May in the church where he had been married. His widow later married a Mr Burgess and dissipated Du Bois's fortune.

In his will, among legacies to his wife and relations, Du

Bois left to Lord Somers 'my father's and mother's pictures drawn by Van Dyke, and my case of books and the books therein', and to his wife 'the copper-plates of my father and mother, and the prints printed from the same'. The painting of his father is now in Frankfurt (Städelsches Kunstinstitut und Städtische Galerie) and that of his mother in the Art Institute of Chicago (both *c*.1626–32). They were engraved by Cornelis Visscher.

Du Bois's elder brother, **Edward** [Eduard] **Du Bois** (1619–1696), was born in Antwerp and baptized on 9 December 1619. He was a painter of histories and Italianate landscapes, though of inferior merit, according to Vertue. He moved to Rotterdam with his father in 1638, and was probably his pupil. He is also said to have been the pupil of the landscape painter Pieter Anthoniszoon van Groenewegen. He was probably the Du Bois who became a member of the guild of painters in Haarlem in 1648. He was in Italy for about eight years studying antiquities. He worked for a time in Paris, and for Archduke Carlo Emmanuele II of Savoy. He went to London about 1662. Seven of his animal studies are in the British Museum, and a painting is in the Haags Gemeentemuseum in The Hague. His name appears as publisher on Visscher's prints of the portraits of his parents. Edward Du Bois gave up painting *c*.1694 and died in 1696. He was buried at St Giles-in-the-Fields, London, on 6 September 1696.

L. H. CUST, rev. ARIANNE BURNETTE

Sources [B. Buckeridge], 'An essay towards an English school of painting', in R. de Piles, *The art of painting, with the lives and characters of above 300 of the most eminent painters*, 3rd edn (1754), 354–439 · E. Croft-Murray and P. H. Hulton, eds., *Catalogue of British drawings*, 1 (1960) · Vertue, *Note books*, vols. 1, 2, 4 · F. W. H. Hollstein, *Dutch and Flemish etchings, engravings and woodcuts, ca. 1450–1700*, 6 (1951) · *Engraved Brit. ports.* · G. Scharf, 'Extracts from the will of Simon Du Bois', 'Portraits in private collections', NPG, Heinz Archive and Library, vol. 4, p. 183 · J. de Maere and M. Wabbes, *Illustrated dictionary of 17th century Flemish painters*, ed. J. A. Martin (1994) · R. Jeffree, 'Du Bois [Dubois], Simon', *The dictionary of art*, ed. J. Turner (1996) · Thieme & Becker, *Allgemeines Lexikon* · will, PRO, PROB 11/501, sig. 113 · E. Larsen, *The paintings of Anthony Van Dyck*, 2 (1988) · E. K. Waterhouse, *The dictionary of British 16th and 17th century painters* (1988) · C. H. C. Baker, *Lely and the Stuart portrait painters: a study of English portraiture before and after van Dyck*, 2 (1912) · H. V. S. Ogden and M. S. Ogden, *English taste in landscape in the seventeenth century* (1955) · H. Walpole, *Anecdotes of painting in England: with some account of the principal artists*, ed. R. N. Wornum, new edn, 2 (1849); repr. (1862)
Archives BL, Harley MS 5947 · BL, Sloane MS 1985, fols. 2, 7
Likenesses A. Bannerman, line engraving, BM, NPG; repro. in H. Walpole, *Anecdotes of painting in England*, 4 vols. (1762)
Wealth at death extensive; bequests of £200 to the poor of Covent Garden; £128 annuity from the exchequer; £110 relating to funeral expenses and mourning; bonds; art collection; silver plate: will, PRO, PROB 11/501, sig. 113; Scharf, 'Extracts'

Du Bosc, Claude (*b*. 1682, *d*. in or after **1746**), engraver and printseller, was born in France. His earliest prints were published in Paris by Gaspard Duchange; those for Duchange's *Recueil de cent estampes représentant différentes nations du Levant* (1714) are dated 1712 or 1713. Du Bosc was invited to England by Nicolas Dorigny in order to assist him with the engraving of the Raphael cartoons at Hampton Court, and in 1713 Vertue listed Du Bosc among the

engravers working in London. He immediately found good employment. In 1714 Thomas Bowles and Henry Overton offered him £80 for each of six large plates of Louis Laguerre's paintings of the duke of Marlborough's victories. Du Bosc sent for Bernard Baron and Nicolas-Dauphin de Beauvais from France to help, and the set was published in April 1717. For Bowles, Du Bosc also engraved allegorical prints of the death of Queen Anne and the coronation of George I (1715), some engravings of the Raphael cartoons (1721), and the trial of Charles I from the series of his life (1728); in addition he worked with Baron on the tapestry cartoons by Rubens of the story of Achilles, 'upon wch undertaking there was much discord & some law between the two brother Gravers' although they were 'at length accomodated' (Vertue, *Note books*, 6.190). For James Thornhill he engraved two of the designs for his cupola of St Paul's Cathedral (1719); for Bowles and Peter Tillemans he helped to engrave three of the earliest sets of sporting subjects.

In 1729 Du Bosc went with Baron to Paris, 'upon Settling affairs relating to trade of print selling haveing now sett up shop to sell prints &c.' (Vertue, *Note books*, 3.73). From then on he was his own publisher and sold modern English, imported, and old master prints from his shop at the Golden Head in Charles Street, Covent Garden; in 1740, for instance, he sold the dealer Arthur Pond a volume of Rembrandt prints for £36 1s. He published copies of contemporary French paintings, including at least eighteen prints after Watteau, and certain innovative English prints, including the first of Lord Burlington's garden at Chiswick. He also published translations of several illustrated books originally issued in Amsterdam. In 1733 he launched a subscription in weekly parts for *The Ceremonies and Religious Customs of the Various Nations of the Known World*, translated and with new illustrations. In 1736 he published an English translation of the *Military History of the Duke of Marlborough*, and in 1737 *Antiquities Explained*, a collection of classical gems. During this period he entered into partnership with William Darres in a shop selling imported books and prints at the Three Flower de Luces at the corner of Haymarket and Piccadilly. By 1743 he was a member of the Rose and Crown Club but he was last mentioned as a publisher, in 1746, for a plan of the battle of Culloden. The business was apparently continued by Darres, who remained a prominent auctioneer and dealer in prints until 1768. The British Museum, London, and the Bibliothèque Nationale de France, Paris, hold examples of Du Bosc's work.

TIMOTHY CLAYTON

Sources Vertue, *Note books*, vols. 3, 6 · T. Clayton, *The English print, 1688–1802* (1997) · M. Roux and others, eds., *Inventaire du fonds français: graveurs du dix-huitième siècle*, 7 (1951), 360–74 · M. Harris, 'Scratching the surface: engravers, printsellers and the London book trade in the mid-eighteenth century', *The book trade and its customers, 1450–1900: historical essays for Robin Myers*, ed. A. Hunt, G. Mandelbrote, and A. Shell (1997) · L. Lippincott, 'Arthur Pond's journal … 1734–1750', *Walpole Society*, 54 (1988), 220–333 · *British Magazine*, 1 (May 1746), 125 · I. Bignamini, 'George Vertue, art historian, and art institutions in London, 1689–1768', *Walpole Society*, 54 (1988), 1–148 · P. Fuhring, 'The print privilege in eighteenth-century France—1', *Print Quarterly*, 2 (1985), 174–93

Likenesses J. B. van Loo, portrait, 1729 • Smibert, portrait

Dubourdieu, Isaac (1597?–1700?), Reformed minister, was the son of Pierre Dubourdieu, governor of the château of Bergerac, from a family originating in Béarn, in the kingdom of Navarre. About 1620 he married into a noble family called Le Valet or La Valade, and had a daughter, Andrée Le Valet (*b. c.*1622), and a son, Jacques (*d.* 1683). Having graduated in 1629 from the protestant academy at Montauban, he became minister of a congregation in Bergerac. In 1641 he married Marie, daughter of Jean de Costebadie, also a minister, and they had four sons, Isaac (*d. c.*1685), Jean *Dubourdieu (*c.*1643–1720?), Armand (1651–1685), and Jean Armand (*b.* 1652). On 10 May 1651 he moved to Montpellier, where he became senior pastor at the protestant temple. Following the death of his second wife, in 1660 he married Jeanne de Poyteuin.

While at Montpellier Dubourdieu became a prominent figure within the French protestant church, and his publications gained him notice outside it. In 1659 he represented the province of Lower Languedoc at the national synod at Londure; on 10 June 1678 he addressed to the whole church a letter on behalf of protestants at St Hippolyte, who had been accused of showing insufficient respect for the sacrament as it passed in public procession, in which he urged the faithful to endure and to unify in testing times. He published at Geneva a catechism designed for young people, and trained in his household prospective ministers, like the son of his long-standing friend Monsieur Claude, minister of the premier French protestant church at Charenton. Dubourdieu's *Deux traitez d'un docteur Romain, pour le retranchement de la coupe au sacrament de l'eucharistie* (1681), a 540-page work dedicated to Claude, is a reasoned, learned, and lucid exposition of the case for communion in both kinds.

About the time the book appeared Dubourdieu was barred from preaching in French pulpits. Following a judgment against him in 1682 by the Toulouse *parlement*, and the demolition of the temple at Montpellier (the latter marked by contemporary epigrams translated into English by Isaac Watts), he left France. On 2 January 1684 Pastor Primerose reported to the consistory of the French Reformed Church of London, Threadneedle Street, that Dubourdieu, wishing 'to exercise his ministry while God granted him the strength, and to do so in a church following the forms of the French churches which he had served for 44 years' (Gwynn, 123), had offered his services, but the consistory was hesitant about accepting them owing to his advanced age and the church's financial weakness. By 29 May, Dubourdieu had been inducted as a minister at the French conformist chapel at the Savoy, which used the Church of England liturgy in translation. Here he was described as holding 'a primary rank', despite his age, and 'what he was in Montpellier, that he is in London—wise, laborious, and entirely devoted to the welfare of the Refugee church' (Agnew, 2.345). In his *A Discourse of Obedience unto Kings and Magistrates*, published that year with a dedication by its translator to Henry Savile, he expressed his profound thanks to 'a Monarch, who is the Sanctuary of

the Oppressed, and the Refuge of the persecuted' (p. 1), for his reception of great numbers of protestants, and called on fellow Huguenots to 'be examples of fidelity and subjection' (p. 15) to a king established by the providence of God and whom they could serve with purity of conscience.

Dubourdieu had been joined in England by his sons Jean and (briefly) Jean Armand, by his great-nephew Matthieu Dubourdieu, and by numerous grandchildren including Jean's son Jean Armand *Dubourdieu (1677–1727), Jacques's son Jean Armand Dubourdieu (1682/3–1723?) and Andrée's son (or grandson) Armand Boybellaud de La Chapelle (1676–1746), all of whom finished their education under Isaac's care. Although they and several other of the patriarch's descendants were ordained in the Church of England, and published in English, Dubourdieu himself never joined the English church, continuing to preach at the Savoy in extreme old age but hoping always to return to France. The inscription on his portrait states that he died in 1699, aged 102, but evidence from chapel records indicates that he died late in 1700; he was certainly buried at the Savoy Chapel. VIVIENNE LARMINIE

Sources W. J. DuBourdieu, *Baby on her back: a history of the Huguenot family DuBourdieu* (1967) • R. Gwynn, ed., *Minutes of the consistory of the French church of London, Threadneedle Street, 1679–1692*, Huguenot Society of Great Britain and Ireland, 58 (1994), 123 • D. C. A. Agnew, *Protestant exiles from France, chiefly in the reign of Louis XIV, or, The Huguenot refugees and their descendants in Great Britain and Ireland*, 3rd edn, 2 (1886), 345 • E. Haag and E. Haag, *La France protestante*, 10 vols. (Paris, 1846–59), vol. 3, pp. 332–3 • C. E. Lart, 'Some letters from France, 1585 and 1685', *Proceedings of the Huguenot Society*, 16 (1937–41), 50–76
Likenesses P. van Somer, mezzotint (after original in French chapel at the Savoy?), BM

Dubourdieu, Jean (*c.*1643–1720?), Church of England clergyman, was born at Bergerac in south-western France, one of the four sons of Isaac *Dubourdieu (1597?–1700?) and his second wife, Marie de Costebadie (*d.* 1652x60). He was educated at the protestant seminary at Puylaurens, east of Toulouse, but when it was closed in 1665 transferred to the academy of Geneva, where he enrolled on 30 May. By licence dated 27 January 1667 he married Marguerite, daughter of Jean Voysine, chief syndic of the Genevan republic, and on 21 June that year was ordained in Lausanne in the Pays de Vaud. He then returned to France, and served as minister from April 1668 at St Pargoire and from 1672 at Uzes, and in 1676 became an assistant to his father at Montpellier, succeeding him as preacher at the Grand Temple there when Dubourdieu the elder was barred from the pulpit in 1680.

Engagement in theological controversy brought Dubourdieu, like his father, to the attention of those at the highest levels of the Roman Catholic church in France. His *Avis de la Sainte Vierge sur ce que tous les siecles doivent dire d'elle* (1682), an attack on mariolatry dedicated to Madame Schomberg (to whose husband he may have been chaplain while at Uzes), led to an exchange of correspondence with the bishop of Meaux, Jacques-Benigne Bossuet. Dubourdieu was briefly imprisoned in the autumn of 1682, but was released on 7 December after the demolition of the Montpellier temple had been completed. Probably late in 1683 he left France, accompanied by a number of his relatives but leaving behind his two daughters, Anne (*b.* 1680) and Elisabeth, who had been taken from their parents and placed in a convent. As John and Margaret Dubourdieu he and his wife received denization in London on 24 August 1684.

As a convinced Gallican, devoted to the ideal of one independent French national church, about the time of his flight Dubourdieu had produced a 'projet de réunion des deux religions', subsequently printed as an appendix to Bossuet's works. It is thus he, rather than his father, who (as Du Bourdieu) heads the list of signatories to *A True Copy of a Project for the Reunion of both Religions in France*, published in London in 1685. With a foreword in which the Reformed ministers emphasize their preparedness to compromise, this remarkable statement adheres to the limits set to the pope's authority by the last assembly of the French clergy, accepts the opinion of Augustine and the exposition of the bishop of Meaux on the merits of good works and the power of grace, and tolerates numerous rites and practices of the Roman church provided they are optional or shorn of abuses. While Dubourdieu retained his belief in national churches, his experience over subsequent decades caused his stance on 'idolatry' to harden.

For thirty-five years from 1685 Dubourdieu exercised a ministry at the French chapel at the Savoy, London. Initially, during James II's reign he felt insecure, writing to someone close to the archbishop of Canterbury in December 1687 that, menaced by plotting Jesuits seeking to evict them from the Savoy, and by rival refugee churches, his congregation risked being 'plus malheureux que nous n'etions en France' ('in a more unhappy state than we were in France'; Bodl. Oxf., MS Tanner 92, fol. 171). Later his tenure was secure enough to cope with frequent absences abroad in the service of the dukes of Schomberg. As chaplain to Frederick Herman, the first duke, he delivered the public address to William III at his coronation and was at Schomberg's side when he was fatally wounded at the battle of the Boyne in 1690. He accompanied Charles, the second duke, when he went as lieutenant-general to Savoy in 1691, wrote the duke's manifesto to the French people issued to accompany his expedition to Dauphiné on 29 August the following year, and personally accepted the abjurations of protestants who took advantage of Schomberg's local success to reject conversions to Catholicism previously made under duress. Dubourdieu was the chief witness to Schomberg's will, made on 14 October 1693 at Turin, and when he died accompanied his body to Lausanne to be buried and then carried his heart back to England.

On 4 March 1695 Dubourdieu preached a sermon on the eve of Queen Mary's funeral, published later that year as *Sermon prononcé la veille des funérailles de la reyne*. Dedicated to the duke of Leeds, it likened the queen to a Tabitha, who had done much for the church. Notwithstanding 'a sense of gratitude to a People that shewed so much good

nature to me a Stranger, and a Protestant minister' (*Historical Dissertation*, 6), Dubourdieu's experiences at Turin of civic celebration of local 'martyrs' prompted him to publish in 1696 *An Historical Dissertation upon the Thebean Legion, Plainly Proving it to be Fabulous*, in which, after displaying a grasp of current European affairs as well as of English and French writers on primitive Christianity and of the Greek fathers, he concluded that the 'fabulous relations of pretended martyrs [are] sufficient to destroy all Reasons brought by the Roman church to justify the worship they pay to Saints' (ibid., 173). It is dedicated to Ralph Montagu, Viscount Monthermer, a patron of French protestant refugees, but the continuing connection to the Schombergs is proclaimed on the title-page, and in 1704 Dubourdieu accompanied the third duke's son to Portugal.

By this time, however, Dubourdieu also had other patrons and concerns. In April 1703 he offered to Lord Nottingham, as a polite but well-known supplicant, his advice on whether the protestants of the Cévennes might be helped by an English maritime expedition; speaking with the knowledge of one who had bathed in twenty places along the coast of Languedoc, he concluded that the plan was impracticable. Another attachment was to the Churchill family: in an undated letter he sought the earl of Sunderland's assistance in keeping Sunderland's father-in-law, the duke of Marlborough, to a promise of securing him a £60 pension. Dubourdieu's *A Sermon Preached on the 7th Day of September* (1704), dedicated to the countess of Sunderland, celebrates the presence of God with her father's army at Blenheim and Europe's escape from enslavement. Adducing the example of Constantine, he asserts the lawfulness of making leagues 'with the princes of idolatrous nations' (p. 17) in order to defeat Louis XIV, 'the Adversary of God, the implacable Enemy of Goodness, and the Barbarous Persecutor of the Saints, who has everywhere declared war against Christ and his Church' (p. 22). In *The Triumphs of Providence* (1707), Dubourdieu's acclamation of Marlborough's victory at Ramilies, Louis is a pharaoh finally brought down by the judgment of God against persecuting emperors, and the duke 'the hook which God has put through the nose of that wild Boar' (p. 19). France, so lately at 'a pitch of grandeur' (p. 9), 'the idolaters of France, the slaves of arbitrary power … the false Protestants', and other enemies should put on sackcloth and cry that judgment had come to Babylon, but the French refugees in England were exhorted to throw off the insinuation that they were disloyal to the queen and, remembering that 'we are men, that we are Protestants … [and] this Day England is our country', exult, giving 'salvation to our God' (p. 21).

Dubourdieu made his will, written in French, on 15 February 1718 in the parish of St Martin-in-the-Fields. By this time three of his sons were Church of England clergymen. Jean Armand *Dubourdieu (1677–1727) was not mentioned by his father, but annuities were given to the eldest, Peter (*d.* 1755?), vicar of Kirby Misperton, Yorkshire, and to Armand (1671/2–1733), vicar of Sawbridgeworth, Hertfordshire. Dubourdieu's books and papers were to go to Armand's son John (d. 1754), also later vicar of Sawbridgeworth and eventually chancellor of the diocese of St Asaph, while the residue of his estate was to be divided between John Dubourdieu, son of Armand Bigué Prevenom (who remains unidentified), and Peter's eldest daughter. Legacies to Dubourdieu's own daughters were to be paid only if they abjured Catholicism and lived in England as protestants. He probably died on 26 July 1720 and he was buried beside his father at the Savoy chapel. His will was proved on 3 August 1720 by his nephew and executor, Armand Boybelland de La Chapelle, by this time minister of the Huguenot church at Wandsworth.

VIVIENNE LARMINIE

Sources W. J. DuBourdieu, *Baby on her back: a history of the Huguenot family DuBourdieu* (1967) · J. Dubourdieu, *An historical dissertation upon the Thebean legion* (1696) · W. Minet and S. Minet, eds., *Registers of the churches of the Savoy, Spring Gardens and les Grecs*, Huguenot Society of London, quatro ser., 26 (1922) · will, PRO, PROB 11/575, fols. 203–4 · Bodl. Oxf., MS Tanner 92, fol. 171 · E. Haag and E. Haag, *La France protestante*, 10 vols. (Paris, 1846–59), vol. 3, pp. 332–3 · D. C. A. Agnew, *Protestant exiles from France, chiefly in the reign of Louis XIV, or, The Huguenot refugees and their descendants in Great Britain and Ireland*, 3rd edn, 2 (1886), 345 · B. Cottret, *The Huguenots in England: immigration and settlement, c.1550–1700* (1985), 176, 203 · BL, Add. MS 32556, fols. 440–45 · BL, Add. MS 61590, fol. 27
Archives BL, letter to Lord Nottingham, Add. MS 32556, fols. 440–45 · BL, letter to Sir H. Sloane, Sloane MS 4058, fol. 269 · BL, letter to earl of Sunderland, Add. MS 61590, fol. 27
Wealth at death see will, PRO, PROB 11/575, fols. 203–4

Dubourdieu, Jean Armand (1677–1727), Church of England clergyman and religious controversialist, was born in Montpellier, where his father, Jean *Dubourdieu (c.1643–1720?), and grandfather Isaac *Dubourdieu were ministers in the Reformed church; his mother was Marguerite Voysine. Following the destruction of the protestant temple, in 1683 most of the family made their hazardous way to England, and both his grandfather and father were soon ministering to fellow Huguenots at the French chapel at the Savoy in London. Tough in adversity and resourceful in exile, the family secured valuable patronage, and Jean Dubourdieu became chaplain to the first duke of Schomberg.

Naturalized on 21 January 1685 Jean Armand Dubourdieu was educated in his grandfather's house before he matriculated from Gloucester Hall, Oxford, in February 1694. He became chaplain to the duke of Devonshire, who presented him to the rectory of Sawtry Moines in 1701. He was also appointed chaplain of the Smyrna factory. He married Esther, daughter of William and Clare Trafford of 304 Queen Anne Street, London; they had four daughters and one son. Following his grandfather's death, probably late in 1700, Jean Armand succeeded as minister at the Savoy Chapel in 1701. As a preacher he earned a formidable reputation for his denunciations of Louis XIV and Catholicism and for his fervent support for the protestant succession in Britain. Typical of his published sermons was one condemning the persecution in France, *The Silence of the Faithful in their Affliction* (1712), and another entitled *A comparison of the penal laws of France against protestants, with those of England against papists* (1717). In May 1713 Dubourdieu was summoned before the bishop of London

to answer charges brought by the French ambassador that he had insulted Louis XIV; he successfully defended himself and no further action was taken against him.

Jean Armand Dubourdieu died at his lodgings in Green Street, near Leicester Fields, London, on 25 March 1727, aged forty-nine. He was buried two days later in the churchyard of St Martin-in-the-Fields. He is easily confused with his uncle, Jean Armand Dubourdieu (b. 1652), who was his father's younger brother, and with his cousin, Jean Armand Dubourdieu (1682/3–1723?), who also ministered at the Savoy Chapel in the 1710s and 1720s and published a number of sermons. The son of Jacques Dubourdieu (d. 1683), this Jean Armand Dubourdieu was smuggled out of France when an infant in 1683 by his mother, who brought him to London after an epic journey from their home near Bergerac. He married Charlotte Massey, countess of Esponage, at St Martin-in-the-Fields on 4 September 1716 and had one son, Saumarez (1717–1812), who became minister at Lisburn in Ireland.

GEOFFREY TREASURE

Sources D. C. A. Agnew, *Protestant exiles from France in the reign of Louis XIV, or, The Huguenot refugees and their descendants in Great Britain and Ireland*, 2nd edn, 3 (1874), 38, 39 · *Proceedings of the Huguenot Society*, 3 (1965), 20 · J. Dubordier, 'Hic sistamus tandem: the story of the Dubordier family', 1958 · C. T. Wilmshurst, *Pedigree of a noble family, Ashby de la Zouch* (1864) · W. J. DuBourdieu, *Baby on her back: a history of the Huguenot family DuBourdieu* (1967) · Foster, *Alum. Oxon.* · *DNB*
Likenesses P. Pelham, mezzotint (after D. Firmin), BM, NPG · engraving, repro. in DuBourdieu, *Baby on her back*, 309 · line engraving, NPG

Dubourg, George (1799?–1882), writer on the violin, was the grandson of Matthew *Dubourg (1703–1767). His most important work is *The Violin, being an Account of that Leading Instrument and its most Eminent Professors*, which was first published c.1832, and was frequently reprinted during the rest of the nineteenth century. He was also the author of the words to many songs, one of the best known at the time being John Parry's 'Wanted a Governess'. During the greater part of his long life Dubourg contributed to various newspapers, especially in Brighton, where he lived for several years. He finally settled in Maidenhead, where he died on 17 April 1882.

W. B. SQUIRE, rev. DAVID J. GOLBY

Sources J. D. Brown, *Biographical dictionary of musicians: with a bibliography of English writings on music* (1886) · private information (1888) · Grove, *Dict. mus.* (1954)

Dubourg, Matthew (1703–1767), violinist and composer, was born probably in London in 1703, a natural son of Isaac or Isaacs (*fl. c.1655–1720), who had been dancing master to Queen Anne before her accession. His mother's identity is unknown. He learned the violin at an early age and probably first appeared in public at Thomas Britton's concerts, perhaps in 1712, when he played a solo by Arcangelo Corelli, standing on a stool. When Francesco Geminiani came to England in 1714 Dubourg became his pupil. He played a sonata at the Queen's Theatre on 4 March 1714, and gave his first benefit concert on 27 May 1714 at Hickford's room. Thereafter he regularly appeared as a soloist and, from 1721, as an orchestral leader. In 1719 he performed a concerto by Handel, possibly op. 3 no. 2, at Hickford's room on 18 February, and his own compositions at the Theatre Royal, Drury Lane, on 4 March. On 17 June 1727, at Stanmore, Middlesex, he married Frances, the daughter of Bernard Gates, master of the children of the Chapel Royal. They had a daughter, who married the oboist Redmond Simpson.

In 1728, four years after his first appearance in Dublin, Dubourg succeeded Kusser as master and composer of the state music in Ireland, the post having been refused by Geminiani. Dubourg's duties in Ireland were not onerous, and he frequently visited England, where he taught Frederick, prince of Wales (into whose service he entered in 1736), his children, and his brother William, duke of Cumberland. At Dublin he composed birthday odes (several to poems by Benjamin Victor) and other ceremonial music. Autograph sources of these odes are at the Royal College of Music, London. None of these larger works has been printed, but some smaller instrumental pieces were published during his lifetime and in early twentieth-century editions. Dubourg directed the first Dublin performances of works by Handel and Arne, and led the orchestra for Handel's visit to Ireland in 1741–2, taking part in the first performance of *Messiah* on 13 April 1742. He also played in Handel's oratorio concerts in London in 1743. On 3 March 1751 Dubourg was elected a member of the Royal Society of Musicians, and in 1752 he succeeded Festing as master of the king's band in England. He was appointed master of her majesty's band of musick in 1761. Although some sources report his having finally left Ireland in 1765 this is unlikely, for birthday odes by him were performed there in 1766 and 1767. Dubourg remained on close terms with his London-based contemporaries. He was the chief mourner at Pietro Castrucci's funeral on 10 March 1752, Handel left him £100 on his death in 1759, and Geminiani was staying at Dubourg's house in Dublin when he died in 1762. Dubourg died in the parish of St Marylebone on 3 July 1767 and was buried on 7 July in Paddington churchyard. The epitaph on his gravestone was printed by Hawkins.

Dubourg's style of playing, which he passed on to his celebrated pupil John Clegg, differed from Geminiani's gentler style. Its fire and energy were praised by, among others, Burney, who, having accompanied him in a Corelli sonata in 1743 or 1744, commented on his 'fullness of tone' and 'spirit of execution'. His elaborate ornamentations of Corelli's sonatas show considerable invention, but he could overreach himself. Burney tells of an occasion when Dubourg, improvising a long cadenza, lost sight of the original key. When finally he arrived safely at the concluding trill Handel, who was conducting, said, 'to the great delight of the audience' and 'loud enough to be heard in the most remote parts of the theatre, "Welcome home, welcome home, Mr. Dubourg!"'.

ANTHONY FORD

Sources M. Tilmouth, 'A calendar of references to music in newspapers published in London and the provinces (1660–1719)', *Royal Musical Association Research Chronicle*, 1 (1961) • Burney, *Hist. mus.*, new edn, vol. 2 • J. Hawkins, *A general history of the science and practice of music*, new edn, 3 vols. (1853); repr. in 2 vols. (1963) • C. Burney, 'Sketch of the life of Handel', in C. Burney, *An account of the musical performances … in commemoration of Handel* (1785), 1–38 • E. L. Avery, ed., *The London stage, 1660–1800*, pt 2: *1700–1729* (1960) • A. H. Scouten, ed., *The London stage, 1660–1800*, pt 3: *1729–1747* (1961) • G. W. Stone, ed., *The London stage, 1660–1800*, pt 4: *1747–1776* (1962) • G. Dubourg, *The violin* (1836) • G. Dubourg, *The violin*, 5th edn, rev. J. Bishop (1887) • O. E. Deutsch, ed., *Handel: a documentary biography* (1955) • D. Lysons, *The environs of London*, 3 (1795) • T. J. Walsh, *Opera in Dublin, 1705–1797: the social scene* (1973) • A. Ford, 'Dubourg, Matthew', *Die Musik in Geschichte und Gegenwart*, ed. F. Blume (Kassel and Basel, 1949–86) • D. D. Boyden, 'Corelli's solo violin sonatas "grac'd" by Dubourg', *Festkrift Jens Peter Larsen*, ed. N. Schiørring, H. Glahn, and C. E. Hatting (1972), 113–25 • H. J. Marx, 'The origins of Handel's op. 3', *Handel tercentenary collection*, ed. S. Sadie and A. Hicks (1987), 254–70 • B. Boydell, 'Dubourg, Matthew', *New Grove* • G. B. L. W. [G. B. L. Wilson], 'Isaac', *Enciclopedia dello spettacolo*, ed. S. D'Amico, 6 (Rome, 1959) • Royal Society of Musicians, London

Archives BL, acquittance for expenses, Egerton MS 2159, fol. 51

Dubricius. See Dyfrig (*supp. fl. c.475–c.525*).

Dubsky, Mario Peter (1939–1985), painter and poet, was conceived in Vienna and born in London on 14 May 1939. He was one of two sons, non-identical twins, whose parents were refugees from Austria. His parents, who later had a daughter, were Christians of Jewish origin who spoke German at home when he was young; they made belts and decorative flowers from leather. He failed the 11-plus examination twice, and was educated at a progressive school, Burgess Hill. Passionately interested in art from childhood, in 1955 he hitch-hiked to Vallauris, where he waited for two weeks in the hope of seeing Picasso. He travelled during the summer of 1956 to Greece, Rome, and Venice, before attending the Slade School of Fine Art, 1956–60. At the Slade he was influenced by Dorothy Mead, a founder member of the Borough Group with David Bomberg, who was at that time a mature student along with Dennis Creffield, another member of the same group. Dubsky made vigorous charcoal drawings and used paint thickly at this period. He was a postgraduate student at the Slade in 1960–61, and in 1963 won an Abbey major scholarship for two years in Rome. He travelled there via Amsterdam and Berlin, where he encountered the homosexual scene, and also visited Prague and Vienna, where he met relations who had survived the Nazi period. In 1964 he travelled through Serbia, Macedonia, and Turkey to Jerusalem and during that time came to terms with his homosexuality, although he had had relationships with women. He was later to be awarded a Harkness fellowship in painting to work in New York, 1969–71.

He had already, as a student, participated in the British Art Exhibition in Moscow (1959) and, when in Rome, in 'Ospiti di Roma' at the Galleria Feltrinelli (1969). His work was also included in the contemporary British art exhibition at the Palazzo Strozzi in Florence in 1968. In 1969 he had his first solo exhibition at the Grosvenor Gallery, showing brightly coloured highly abstracted paintings, and in 1971 exhibited 'Works on Paper' at the Penthouse Gallery of the Museum of Modern Art, New York. Friendship with Keith Vaughan contributed to his use of flatter areas of paint and brighter colours, as in *Allegro negro*

(1967/8). The relatively brief period of brilliant colour in his work, exemplified by *Shades* of 1970 (nearly abstract, with hard edges to flat passages of paint), gave way to a darker palette and to denser textures in the mid-1970s. Dark-toned and jewelled passages appeared to be trapped in fields or curtains of black: *Firebrand* and *City Nights* were large (7 foot) paintings of 1973.

During the 1970s it seemed to critics that he was faltering as he introduced a wide range of imagery into some of his pictures, which became dedicated to social and political causes. Through his friendship with John Button, he had been commissioned in 1971 to create a 40 by 8 foot mural for The Firehouse, the New York SoHo headquarters of the Gay Activists Alliance; here he employed photomontage, stencilled words, and slogans. *The Trial* of 1974 represented three archetypal heads and threatening axes, while *Handshake over Europe* (1975) introduced floating, almost surrealist figures and bone-like forms. The 18 foot triptych on the theme of time and human development (he had been making many drawing studies in the Natural History Museum), when shown in the 'British Painting, 1957–77' exhibition at the Royal Academy in 1977, received a hostile press. He was artist in residence at the British School in Rome in 1982.

A fiery and ebullient man, Dubsky lived at a very intense pitch, and engaged in many conflicts in his personal life; he read widely in philosophy and anthropology, and in 1981 published a book of drawings, *Tom Pilgrim's Progress among the Consequences of Christianity*, reproducing the often tortured poses of a favourite model, Tom Dawson. His last exhibition at the South London Art Gallery in 1984 included *Caberet Valhalla* (oil on canvas, 1983), a characteristically menacing, figurative painting, which is now in the Tate collection. He felt confident of that recent work, saying 'at last I am doing the painting I had dreamed of doing when I was 15' (*Mario Dubsky*, 3). Some of his expressive poems were published in his statement entitled 'X factor', for that exhibition. He was a dark, handsome man of medium-small build who usually had a close-cropped beard, emphasizing the strong bone structure of his face. He lived alone for most of his adult life, in New York or at the Archway in London. He died of an AIDS-related illness in the Middlesex Hospital on 24 August 1985 and was buried in Highgate cemetery. ALAN WINDSOR

Sources autobiographical statement, *Mario Dubsky, paintings and drawings, 1973–84: x factor 1984* (1984) [exhibition catalogue, South London Art Galleries, May–June 1984] · E. Cooper, 'Mario Dubsky', *Gay News*, 169 (1978/9) · d. cert. · private information (2004) [E. Cooper] · private information (2004) [A. Katz] · *The Times* (14 Sept 1985), 10 · papers, Tate collection · *CGPLA Eng. & Wales* (1986)
Archives Tate collection, press cuttings | Boundary Gallery, London, papers
Likenesses E. Cooper, photograph, repro. in Cooper, 'Mario Dubsky'
Wealth at death £135,432: administration, 11 Sept 1986, *CGPLA Eng. & Wales*

Dubthach maccu Lugair (*supp. fl.* 432), poet, was said in the seventh century to have been chief poet of the men of Ireland in the reign of Lóegaire mac Néill, high-king of Ireland, at the time of Patrick's arrival there, traditionally dated to 432. He is a figure of dubious historicity but major ideological importance. In a range of texts from the late seventh century onwards Dubthach represented Irish native learning, especially the legal and poetical learning, as it came to terms with Christianity. The two earliest surviving versions of the story are in Muirchú's life of Patrick and the legal tract *Córus béscnai* ('The proper arrangement of custom'); more elaborate later versions are in the tripartite life of Patrick and the later preface to the law book, the *Senchas már*. As far as can be seen, each of the earlier versions is independent of the other. The common elements of the story are that Dubthach was at Tara when Patrick first confronted Lóegaire mac Néill. Dubthach was the first to 'rise up before Patrick', in other words, to go through the ritual act of respect due from an inferior to a superior. This act of reverence implied Christian faith, since Patrick, as a British alien in Ireland, could have commanded such respect only as the acknowledged apostle of the truth. The full significance of Dubthach's act, however, only emerges if one remembers who did not show such reverence to Patrick. The readiness of Dubthach, a poet and a lawyer, to accept the apostle of the Irish is contrasted with the reluctance of the king of Tara, Lóegaire mac Néill, and the outright opposition of his druids. Secular power might ultimately have yielded to the new faith; but it was the chief poet and lawyer who, at Tara, most willingly gave it a welcome. Thus native learning was aligned with Christian learning in an implicit alliance between men of knowledge. But not all native learning was accorded such a treatment: the *magi*, called druids in vernacular texts, clashed directly with Patrick; and their power, so it is implied, perished with the triumph of Christianity.

Córus béscnai has a more detailed story to tell:

> Dubthach maccu Lugair recited to Patrick the laws of the men of Ireland according to the law of nature and according to the law of prophecy, for prophecy prevailed according to the law of nature in the judicial tradition of the island of Ireland. Prophets among them prophesied that 'the white language of the *beati*' [Psalm 118 in the Vulgate] would come, that is, the written law.   (Binchy, 528)

The 'language of the *beati*' is a reference to the first lines of the psalm: 'Beati immaculati in via, quia ambulant in lege Domini' ('Blessed are the undefiled in the way, who walk in the law of the Lord'; Psalm 119, Authorized Version). The psalm was interpreted as a prophecy of the new law of Christ. As a result of the collaboration between Dubthach and Patrick, anything contrary to Christianity was purged from the laws of the Irish. It even became part of the Patrician legend that the most important Irish law book, the *Senchas már*, had been written during Patrick's mission: according to the annals of Ulster, this event occurred in 438 (at much the same date as the promulgation of the Theodosian code of Roman law).

The nature and grounds of this reconciliation between native law and the Christian faith can be inferred from Dubthach's position as a *fili* ('poet', but originally 'seer') and from the appeal to the laws of nature and prophecy.

The men who prophesied Patrick's arrival, according to the story in Muirchú and *Córus béscnai*, were the druids, those committed to paganism. Yet Dubthach appealed to the law of prophecy as well as to the law of nature. It is quite unclear what kind of distinction was made between druid and *fili* before the Irish were converted to Christianity, but later evidence at least suggests that their functions overlapped in that both claimed a knowledge of the future or of things remote in space superior to any available to ordinary men. This makes it especially interesting that, in the story told by *Córus béscnai*, while druids prophesied to Lóegaire that Patrick 'would steal the living and the dead from him', Dubthach appealed to the law of prophecy. Moreover, this was a prophecy within Ireland: Irish prophets had foretold the coming of Christianity just as Jewish prophets had foretold Christ. Such prophecy required divine grace and thus conferred a Christian legitimacy on a legal tradition which, it was admitted, went back to a time before Patrick had ever set foot in Ireland. For these reasons, it was not surprising that a *fili* should be the authority chosen to represent native law to the new Christian order.

Dubthach maccu Lugair is, however, an odd figure at the court of Lóegaire for another reason: he had close connections with Leinster, although in the genealogies of the saints his family is said to have been from Connacht. He appears in Bridgettine hagiography as well as that of Patrick. In a story in the Book of Armagh, Dubthach was the master of Fíacc, the supposed first bishop of the Leinstermen and founder of the church of Sleaty (Sletty), near Carlow. In Tírechán's *Collectanea* concerning Patrick, written in the late seventh century at much the same time as Muirchú's life of Patrick, Dubthach is not mentioned: his place is taken by Erc, the supposed founder and patron saint of Slane on the Boyne (a church allied with Armagh) and also supposed, in the tripartite life, to have been Patrick's judge. When compared with Erc, Dubthach had a much less close connection with the lands of the southern Uí Néill and no direct connection with Armagh. Erc was part of Patrick's household; Dubthach was not. There may be a connection between Dubthach and the saint Mo Laisse maccu Lugair, whose church is said in the martyrologies of Tallaght and Óengus to have been among the Uí Fhairchelláin (near Mountrath, Laois). In the tract on the mothers of Irish saints, Dediu, Dubthach's granddaughter, was said to have been the mother of thirty male saints and virgins (many of them clearly fictitiously related). Dubthach's connection with Patrick had made him a desirable ancestor.   T. M. CHARLES-EDWARDS

Sources Muirchú, 'Vita S. Patricii', *The Patrician texts in the Book of Armagh*, ed. and trans. L. Bieler, Scriptores Latini Hiberniae, 10 (1979), 62–122, esp. 119 • 'Additamenta, 13', *The Patrician texts in the Book of Armagh*, ed. and trans. L. Bieler, Scriptores Latini Hiberniae, 10 (1979), 166–77 • D. A. Binchy, ed., *Corpus iuris Hibernici* (1976), 527–8 • J. Carey, 'An edition of the pseudo-historical prologue to the *Senchas Már*', *Ériu*, 45 (1994), 1–32 • P. Ó Riain, ed., *Corpus genealogiarum sanctorum Hiberniae* (Dublin, 1985) • 'Vita prima sanctae Brigidae', *Acta sanctorum: Februarius*, 1, 119–35 • S. Connolly, trans., 'Vita prima sanctae Brigidae', *Journal of the Royal Society of Antiquaries of Ireland*, 119 (1989), 14–49 • *Bethu Brigte*, ed. and trans. D. Ó hAodha (1978) • R. I. Best and H. J. Lawlor, eds., *The martyrology of Tallaght*, HBS, 68 (1931) • *Félire Óengusso Céli Dé / The martyrology of Oengus the Culdee*, ed. W. Stokes, HBS, 29 (1905); repr. (1984) • *Ann. Ulster* • D. Bracken, 'Immortality and capital punishment: patristic concepts in Irish law', *Peritia*, 9 (1995), 167–86 • J. Carey, 'The two laws in Dubthach's judgment', *Cambridge Medieval Celtic Studies*, 19 (1990), 1–18 • K. McCone, 'Dubthach maccu Lugair and a matter of life and death in the pseudo-historical prologue to the *Senchas már*', *Peritia*, 5 (1986), 1–35

Du Cane, **Sir Edmund Frederick** (1830–1903), prison administrator and army officer, born at Colchester on 23 March 1830, was the youngest of the four sons and two daughters of Major Richard Du Cane (1788–1832), and Eliza (1791–1870), daughter of Thomas Ware of Woodfort, Mallow, co. Cork, Ireland. Du Cane was educated at Dedham grammar school, Essex, until 1843, and at Major Horton's Wimbledon crammer between 1843 and 1846. He entered the Royal Military Academy at Woolwich in November 1846 and passed out at the head of his class; significantly, he took first place in fortification and mathematical studies. He was commissioned second lieutenant in the Royal Engineers on 19 December 1848. In December 1850 he was posted to the sappers at Woolwich, and was assistant superintendent of the foreign side of the International Exhibition of 1851 and assistant secretary to the juries of awards.

Later in 1851 Du Cane was sent to the Swan River penal labour depot of Western Australia to organize convict labour on public works under the command of Captain Edmund Henderson. On 17 February 1854 Du Cane was promoted first lieutenant, supervising the building of roads, bridges, barracks, and prisons, and was also appointed a magistrate of the colony. On 18 July 1855 he married Mary Dorothea (1834–1881), daughter of Lieutenant-Colonel John Molloy of Western Australia; they had three sons and five daughters.

In 1856 Du Cane was recalled to serve in the Crimean War, but by the time he arrived in England on 21 June 1856 that war was over. From August 1856 until 1863 he was an important designer of land forts and other dockyard and naval defence works, chiefly at Dover and around Plymouth. In 1858 he was promoted second captain. He had developed a close interest in the convict prison service through his experience of convict labour in Australia, but entry to this service was blocked because Du Cane had deeply offended the then chairman of directors of convict prisons, Sir Joshua Jebb, in an 1862 article ridiculing one of Jebb's projects. However, on Jebb's death in 1863 Du Cane's former commander, Henderson, was appointed chairman, and in 1863 Du Cane was appointed one of the directors of convict prisons and an inspector of military prisons. He was therefore deeply involved in the implementation of penal servitude—the system of long-term imprisonment of convicts in convict prisons in Britain, which had entirely replaced the transportation of criminals overseas by 1870.

In 1869 Du Cane replaced Henderson as chairman of the convict prison directors, surveyor-general of prisons, and inspector-general of military prisons. On 5 July 1872 he was promoted major, on 11 December 1873 lieutenant-colonel, and four years later brevet colonel. He was placed on the supernumerary list in August 1877. As chairman of convict prisons until his retirement in 1895, Du Cane served under eight home secretaries and three permanent under-secretaries. In the early years his influence with the Home Office was prodigious, and in 1873 he proposed that local prisons administered by local magistrates should be placed under central control. The 1877 Prisons Act gave control of all 116 local prisons of England and Wales to a new London-based Prison Commission, of which Du Cane was also the chairman.

Du Cane's historical significance as a prison administrator is great. He exercised a profound influence on the direction of penal policy between 1870 and 1895, and he based his projects upon a general thesis about crime and punishment. He was enthusiastic for preventive measures of education and instruction to be made available to children and to young, impulsive first-time offenders, advocating that social enquiry and medical reports be made available to sentencers, and that punishment of the wayward and impulsive first-time offender be suspended. He was a strong supporter of the Church of England Waifs and Strays Society, on the basis that destitute and abandoned children needed both nurturing and moral and technical education if they were to become industrious and law-abiding adults. However, Du Cane was deeply sceptical about all projects for reforming adult criminals, and he consistently advanced a straightforward penological theory to legitimate the system of imprisonment which he created. He emphasized that the offender was a rational, cognitive actor, who must be made to know that the sure consequences of his or her actions would be the pains of severe imprisonment. Therefore, a severe short sentence in a local prison would deter most early offenders. But Du Cane also believed that social environment had a habituating effect in the training of human beings, particularly criminals, and, because he believed that the effect of early habituation was so deep, he was most pessimistic about the possibility of reforming the repetitive offender. Indeed, he believed that the habitual offender belonged to a lower moral and mental order than the honest industrious citizen. Du Cane was well aware of contemporary Darwinian theorizing on this subject, but there is no consensus as to the influence this exercised on him. He certainly rejected the Italian positivist Lombrosian belief in the born criminal with innate physical and psychological stigmata, but he clearly did view habitual criminals as predatory, self-indulgent, cunning, and reckless of consequence to others, and he regarded them as an unreformable, inferior, subnormal social group. It is, surely, no accident that Du Cane was a close associate of the famous theorist on crime, pauperism, and lunacy and their relation to inherited constitution, Sir Francis Galton: indeed it was he who prompted Galton to study the different types of physical feature among prisoners.

Du Cane advocated more effective detective methods, pioneering registers and descriptions of criminals to facilitate this from 1877 onwards, because he believed that the most effective deterrent was sureness of detection. He also believed that the supreme purpose of punishment was prevention through general deterrence, in addition to deterring the individual imprisoned offender. Although Du Cane favoured schemes for the care of former prisoners, he relegated reformatory schemes of spiritual, moral, and educational instruction in prisons to the margins of prison discipline, and was outrightly contemptuous towards the early Victorian evangelical prison chaplains and earlier convict prison directors, such as Jebb, who had pioneered these methods. He required all stages of a penal servitude or local prison sentence to operate uniformly and consistently in their severity. Here came into play Du Cane's abiding belief that sentencers should know the exact content of a sentence, the precise degree of 'pain' which the offender would experience, so that their sentence could be precisely adjusted to the penalty to be endured. Indeed, one of Du Cane's strongest criticisms of the local prison system, which he did so much to centralize, was that regimes varied hugely and that this made it impossible to have standardized and uniform systems of deterrent punishment. But, in addition, Du Cane viewed economy as a guiding penal principle: a centralized prison system should be less wasteful than the former local one and more rational in its expenditure. Here he emphasized his faith in convict public works as a means by which the convict repaid society not only for the injury inflicted by the crime but also for the cost of his penal servitude. Du Cane publicized his views in two books, including *The Punishment and Prevention of Crime* (1885), as well as in a pamphlet and some sixteen lengthy articles in journals such as the *Nineteenth Century*, the *Fortnightly Review*, and the *Cornhill Magazine*.

The Prison Commission and directors of convict prisons therefore defined every element of the regime in minute detail as to diet, labour, confinement in cells, rule of silence, worship, punishment for prison offences, release on parole licence (ticket of leave), permitted reading and writing materials, visits, and so forth. Under penal servitude the convict began with nine months of confinement in the cells and proceeded thereafter to a second stage of associated hard labour on public works. The third and final stage was conditional release under police supervision. Throughout stages one and two the convict had to earn marks to enable progress through the system: Du Cane set high store on the marks system as a means of inducing compliance. In the local prisons where short sentences were served, most prisoners spent all their sentence in solitary confinement, and initially faced extremely severe conditions such as a plank bed, a very coarse diet, no visits, no library books or writing materials, and gruelling hard labour often including oakum picking or the treadmill. The fact that during the late nineteenth century prison populations were falling enabled Du Cane to claim the effectiveness of his deterrent system.

During the 1870s and early 1880s, despite allegations that this severe system involved systematic institutionalized brutality to convicts and prisoners, one instance being Dartmoor in the 1870s, Du Cane's position was unchallenged, and he administered the Prison Commission as a personal satrapy. However, he made many enemies, for he was an autocratic and imperious figure, on occasion uncontrolledly giving vent to rages against any whom he conceived had thwarted him. Indeed, in 1878 he nearly sacrificed his career by his extreme behaviour towards the gate-warder at Strangeways prison. He ferociously harried all who failed to obey his orders and, following one row, the home secretary, Sir William Vernon Harcourt, banished Du Cane from his office. The two permanent under-secretaries of state, Adolphus Liddell (1867–85) and Sir Godfrey Lushington (1885–95), sought to restrain him in such matters as his habitual disdain for the magistracy and contempt towards Home Office officials.

In 1889 a prisoner called William Gatcliffe was savagely done to death in Strangeways prison. Although the staff charged with his killing were acquitted, the Home Office was extremely concerned by Du Cane's cavalier rejection of any criticism, and thereafter was looking to be rid of him. By 1893 there was a growing clamour against him. Among the most determined of his critics were the new Liberal home secretary, Herbert Asquith; the chaplain of Wandsworth prison, William Douglas Morrison; the *News Chronicle*; a cadre of Labour and Liberal members of parliament; the magistrates; and William Tallack, secretary of the Howard Association, all of whom, from differing standpoints, launched major attacks on the 'Du Cane system'. At that time the new Liberalism, with its vision of a morally uplifting society cemented by voluntary effort, knowledge, and a social crusade against crime and the vice-inducing environment, was significantly shifting the popular attitude to such groups as offenders. Du Cane's clumsy attempts to mislead parliament did not help him, and a departmental inquiry into the prison system was set up. During the process of this Gladstone committee inquiry, Du Cane reached retirement age on 23 March 1895, having done all he could to avoid giving evidence to the Gladstone committee, which had to show immense persistence in its attempts to get hold of him. While Gladstone was careful to avoid any personal criticism of Du Cane, his system was described as overly severe, regimented, and unresponsive to modern thinking. A range of important reforms was proposed, and a young, recently appointed prison commissioner, who was also a Home Office civil servant, Evelyn Ruggles-Brise, was appointed in Du Cane's place.

Du Cane was made CB (civil division) in 1873 and KCB (civil division) in 1877. He received the honorary rank of major-general on 31 December 1887. In his retirement he wrote letters to the press and articles deploring the direction of penal policy, and he followed his wide interests in archaeology, architecture, and Napoleonic literature, publishing articles on fortifications and warfare. He was an accomplished painter in water-colours, and his sketches of Peninsular War battlefields were exhibited at the Royal Military Exhibition at Chelsea in 1890. He was also interested in the history of his Huguenot family and published an account of them in 1876. His first wife died in 1881, and on 2 January 1883 Sir Edmund married Florence Victoria (d. 1914), daughter of Colonel Hardress Saunderson and widow of Colonel Marmaduke J. Grimston of Grimston Garth and Kilnwick, Yorkshire. He died at his home, 10 Portman Square, London, on 7 June 1903 and was buried at Great Braxted church, Essex.

Du Cane had an exact mind and a phenomenal mastery of detail. It was, in part, his wide knowledge of prison discipline which made him intolerant of those who, as he saw it, knew not of what they spoke. His legacy of a centralized prison system has endured.   BILL FORSYTHE

Sources *The Times* (8 June 1903) · PRO, HO 45 · PRO, HO 144 · PRO, PCOM · Bodl. Oxf., MSS Du Cane · L. Radzinowicz and R. Hood, *A history of English criminal law and its administration from 1750*, rev. edn, 5: *The emergence of penal policy in Victorian and Edwardian England* (1990) · S. McConville, *English local prisons, 1860–1900: next only to death* (1995) · W. Forsythe, *The reform of prisoners, 1830–1900* (1987) · W. Forsythe, *Penal discipline, reformatory projects and the English prison commission* (1991) · S. Webb and B. Webb, *English local government*, 6: *English prisons under local government* (1922) · W. J. Forsythe, 'Local autonomy and centralisation: the experience of English local prisons, 1820–1877', *Journal of Historical Sociology*, 4/3 (1991), 317–45 · Burke, *Gen. GB*

Archives BL · Bodl. Oxf., family and official papers · PRO, HO 45 · PRO, HO 144 | BL, letters to H. J. Gladstone and others

Likenesses photograph, repro. in *The Graphic* (20 June 1903)

Wealth at death £24,883 17s. 2d.: resworn probate, Oct 1903, CGPLA Eng. & Wales

Ducarel, Andrew Coltée (1713–1785), librarian and antiquary, was born on 9 June 1713 in Paris, the eldest of three sons of Jacques Coltée Ducarel (1680–1718), banker, merchant, and sieur de Muids, and his wife, Jeanne Crommelin (1690–1723), daughter of André Crommelin and his wife, Marie Jeanne le Maître. His parents were both Huguenots from Normandy, and his mother's family were international bankers and merchants. His father died on 1 March 1718, just as a fresh wave of Huguenot persecution was beginning in France, and in 1719 his mother fled with her infant sons to the protection of her relatives in Amsterdam (the Dutch branch was called Crommelinck). In 1721 they crossed to England, where, in 1722, she married her second husband, Jacques Girardot, a wealthy Huguenot timber merchant in Greenwich. She died in 1723 in childbirth, leaving a daughter, Jeanne, by the second marriage. The three boys were tutored at home by a Calvinist refugee, Pierre Issanchon, until in 1728 the elder boys, Andrew and James, were sent to Eton College.

Character and education Francis Grose described Ducarel as a 'great black man' (F. Grose, *The Olio*, 2nd edn, 1793, 142), by which was meant that he had a dark, Gallic appearance; as his portrait (1751) by Antonio Soldi shows, he suffered from a squint, having lost the sight of his right eye in an accident at Eton. He suffered frequent eye infections, often so bad that he could neither read nor write, and at those times his clerk wrote his letters for him. At best he had, according to Grose, 'a focus not exceeding half an inch; so that whatever he wished to see clearly, he was obliged to put close to his nose' (ibid., 142). He was a convivial man, a great drinker of both wine and tea, although he ate no meat nor drank wine until he was fourteen. He had a deep-seated desire to be more English than

Andrew Coltée Ducarel (1713–1785), by Francis Perry, pubd 1757 (after Andrea Soldi, 1746)

the English, although he could mask his lack of confidence with a bullying exterior at times. The Huguenot church in Greenwich was strongly conformist at that time and adopted the Anglican liturgy in French, so Ducarel would have had no difficulty in subscribing to the Thirty-Nine Articles of the Church of England to get to Oxford or hold his legal and library posts in later life.

Ducarel went up to Oxford in 1731, matriculated from Trinity College, then moved to St John's. He and his brother were naturalized while undergraduates (1734). Ducarel graduated BCL from St John's in 1738, then moved to Trinity Hall, Cambridge, to study canon law and was awarded the degree of DCL. He shared chambers in the Inner Temple with his brother James from 1739 to 1742. He was admitted to the College of Advocates (Doctors' Commons) in November 1743, and leased a house in the Commons complex, where he entertained his friends and transacted his legal business for the rest of his life. He served as librarian of Doctors' Commons (1754–7) and as treasurer (1757–61). He was appointed commissary of the royal peculiar of St Katharine by the Tower by Archbishop Herring in 1755, of the city and diocese of Canterbury by Archbishop Secker in 1758, and of the subdeaneries of South Malling, Pagham, and Tarring, Sussex, by Archbishop Cornwallis in 1776.

Ducarel married his housekeeper, Sarah Desborough (1696–1791), a widow seventeen years his senior, in 1749

and the same year bought a house in Peckham which he rarely lived in. There were no children of the marriage. Ducarel was devoted to his wife, and when she fell off a ladder in her garden at the age of sixty-eight he 'was distracted' and 'only recovered [his] spirits' when she was completely out of danger (Ducarel to Philip Morant, 13 Oct 1764, BL, Add. MS 37219).

Fellow of the Society of Antiquaries Ducarel was admitted fellow of the Society of Antiquaries on 22 September 1737, at the age of twenty-four. He took an active part in meetings at The Mitre tavern in Fleet Street, where fellows exhibited antiquarian objects in their possession, and he sat on the publications committee for several years. Among older antiquary friends who influenced the bent of his studies was Samuel Gale, with whom he toured England in the summer law vacation. 'They usually took up quarters at an inn; and penetrated into the country for three or four miles round. After dinner, Mr Gale smoked his pipe, while Dr Ducarel took notes, which he regularly transcribed' (Nichols, *Lit. anecdotes*, 6.402). In July 1752, in company of a friend, Thomas Bever, Ducarel made an architectural tour of Lower Normandy and visited his uncle at the family château of Muids and other relatives in Paris. He was one of the first Englishmen to see and realize the importance of the Bayeux tapestry. On his return he set to work to turn his journal of the tour into an account for his circle of antiquary friends, at first intending to circulate it in manuscript. It was eventually published in a slim quarto, without illustrations, as *A Tour through Normandy in a Letter to a Friend* (1754); the friend was George North, the numismatist, who had encouraged Ducarel to make the tour. Years later he revised and enlarged it, omitting some of the more personal detail and adding material supplied in letters from his brother James. The latter, having returned to live in France, had visited many of the places his brother had seen in 1752, and commissioned drawings and engravings, which were included in *Anglo-Norman architecture considered in a tour through part of Normandy, illustrated with 27 copper-plates* (1767); it included an appendix of drawings of the Bayeux tapestry with an account of it by Smart Letheuiller. The work now ranks as a pioneer comparative study of medieval architecture.

Another of Ducarel's antiquarian interests was coins and medals. The advantage over native English numismatists which his family connections gave him made him well placed to specialize in collecting Anglo-Aquitain coins. While in Paris he visited Monsieur de Boze, the keeper of the king's medals, and he incorporated a unique set of plates which de Boze sent him in his next book, *A series of above two hundred Anglo-Gallic, or Norman and Aquitain coins of the ancient kings of England; exhibited in sixteen copper-plates and illustrated in twelve letters, addressed to the Society of Antiquaries of London … to which is added, a map of the antient dominions of the kings of England in France* (1757). One of the letters was written by Philip Morant. Ducarel was elected a member of the Society of Antiquaries of Cortona in 1760, a fellow of the Royal Society in 1762, of the Society of Antiquaries of Cassel in 1778, and of the Society of Antiquaries of Scotland in 1781.

Ducarel first turned author in 1753 with 'A summary account of Doctors Commons', based on extant documents, which he presented to the dean of arches, Sir George Lee. He gave another copy to a brilliant young friend, later arch-enemy, Edward Rowe Mores. Still a basic reference work on Doctors' Commons, it was not published until 1931. In March 1754 Archbishop Thomas Herring, who resided at Croydon Palace in preference to Lambeth, asked Ducarel to prepare an account of Croydon for him, with, at Ducarel's request, Edward Rowe Mores to assist him. 'Some account of the town, church, and archiepiscopal palace of Croydon' was presented to the archbishop in 1755, but not published until 1783. Mores was furious to find that, although his help was acknowledged as the author of chapter 8, his name was not on the title-page, and after relieving his feelings in two vitriolic letters, he went his separate way. While they had worked together, Mores had searched the records in the Tower of London, and at Lambeth the two had spent

> 60 successive week-days (Sundays being excepted) from 9 in the morning, till between 4 and 5 in the afternoon. During all that time we lived upon an halfpenny roll and a pint of wine which we carried in our pockets … Mr Mores and myself did with our own hands sort and put to rights almost 2000 old records in the Lambeth Library, which were labelled and put into proper order. (Nichols, *Illustrations*, 6.672)

Librarian of Lambeth After his herculean labour at Lambeth, Ducarel, who was tiring of Doctors' Commons and thought of taking holy orders, hoped that the archbishop would offer him a lucrative job with living accommodation at the British Museum, which was in his gift. But it was already spoken for, and it was not until the arrival of Matthew Hutton, Herring's successor, at Lambeth in May 1757 that Ducarel was offered the Lambeth librarianship at a salary of £30 per annum. 'It was intended to be … a sinecure, & I to continue to act at Doctors Commons as usual' (Ducarel to Morant, 21 May 1757, BL, Add. MSS 37217–37219). 'Thus it hath pleased God to have committed to my care', he wrote to Morant with gusto, 'the greatest MSS collection in this kingdom as relates to ecclesiastical affairs', and he was determined to prove himself a worthy successor to the great scholars who had preceded him in the post (Ducarel to Morant, 30 June 1757, BL, Add. MSS 37217–37219). He was Lambeth's first lay librarian and turned out to be the longest-serving, working for five archbishops during twenty-eight years. All his predecessors and several of his successors combined the duties of librarian with that of private chaplain to the archbishop. The job proved to be anything but a sinecure; besides the normal duties of a librarian, he was required to undertake legal negotiation, find documentation for surveys and reports on palace dilapidations and repairs, and to research and write historical accounts. Although the library was, up to a point, open to the public, its costs were entirely met by the archbishop personally; he paid for the services of Ducarel's clerk as amanuensis, but all other assistance was voluntary and so Ducarel called upon scholarly friends when the work overwhelmed him. Thomas Secker was the most exigent and the longest-

lasting of his employers, whose early years as archbishop coincided with a heavy workload at Doctors' Commons and at the Admiralty. Ducarel called on two willing friends, Revd Henry Hall, his predecessor at Lambeth and a schoolfellow, and Philip Morant, the Essex historian. The amount of publicly unacknowledged help Ducarel got from them would today be considered thoroughly reprehensible, but in an age when gentlemen of leisure abounded, and the fruits of research were handed around in manuscript, it was not uncommon to call, as Ducarel did, on friendly assistance from fellow scholars.

Hall was able to guide him on the running of the library and to help him find books and manuscripts. He was invaluable in assisting in the indexing of the registers from February 1756, after Mores had departed, until his untimely death in June 1763. He checked Ducarel's transcriptions against the originals, which were sent down by carrier to Hall's Kent rectory, and gave useful information on palace alterations and repairs for inclusion in the history of the palace which the archbishop was clamouring for. He also collected data for *The Repertory of Endowments of Vicarages* (1763; rev. edn, 1782). Morant was equally happy to be involved in Ducarel's work and in the course of a long working collaboration (1752–70) became an even closer personal friend than Hall. Ducarel introduced into the Morant family circle his young friend and fellow antiquary Thomas Astle, who became Morant's son-in-law.

On the outbreak of the Seven Years' War Ducarel was appointed to the high court of Admiralty to take depositions for prize ships, which meant working throughout the usually slack time of the law vacation, both for the Admiralty and at Lambeth, where he was forging ahead with indexing the archiepiscopal registers. It began to tell on his health and his doctor 'plainly told [him] that if [he] did not use air and exercise [he] was gone and must not expect to see the end of the registers' (Ducarel to Morant, 30 June 1757, BL, Add. MSS 37217–37219). Ducarel took heed and leased a house formerly belonging to the Tradescants, near Lambeth Palace, where he lived to the end of his life.

Later career and achievement Morant, an experienced biographer, wrote with journalistic ease, whereas Ducarel seemed to suffer from writer's block, and on several occasions Morant willingly undertook to write up Ducarel's researches for the archbishop. Twice Ducarel paid him for his work, but he seems to have enjoyed the involvement without counting the cost or caring about attribution. Their correspondence began because they failed to meet when Morant paid a visit to London in 1752, and continued unbroken until Morant moved from Colchester to London in 1768. Ducarel first sought Morant's advice on the writing and printing of *A Tour through Normandy* and the *Anglo-Gallic Coins*. In 1757, when Ducarel was at his most hard-pressed, Morant agreed to relieve Ducarel of the writing of the 'Memoirs of the Hutton family' which the late archbishop's brother John Hutton of Marske had asked for. It was presented to Mr Hutton in a single manuscript copy

(1758). At the same time Secker was pressing for 'The history and antiquities of the archiepiscopal palace of Lambeth from its foundation to the present time' (BL, Add. MS 37219), most of which was written by Morant and presented by Ducarel to the archbishop in 1758. The published version (1785) was dedicated to Archbishop Moore. Pressed by Secker to catalogue Bishop Gibson's voluminous papers in forty volumes, Ducarel again enlisted the help of Morant, who had been the bishop's protégé. Morant also wrote most of 'The history of the royal hospital and collegiate church of St Katharine, near the Tower of London, from the foundation in the year 1273, to the present time', presented to Queen Charlotte (1762) and published by Nichols (1782).

In 1763 Ducarel was appointed, with Sir Joseph Ayloffe and Thomas Astle, 'to methodise … and make catalogues, calendars and indexes' of the state papers in Whitehall, and thereafter of those of the augmentation office. They received a royal warrant to complete their work in 1765, which they continued to the end of their respective lives. This was the precursor of the first commission of the public records, leading to the setting up of a public record office.

Shortly before publication of *A Tour through Normandy*, Ducarel decided that 'it would not be amiss to add … by way of appendix some account of the alien priories, abbies etc which had formerly lands in England' (Ducarel to Morant, July 1754, BL, Add. MSS 37217–37219); but he could not then gain access to the relevant records which were in the augmentation office and had to wait until he was himself appointed to 'methodise' those records in 1763. The resulting book, published anonymously in 1778, was *Some account of the alien priories and of such lands as they are known to have possessed in England and Wales* (2 vols., 1778); the authors were Ducarel and the Somerset herald, Thomas Warburton.

Ducarel's lasting importance is as a historian of Anglo-Norman architecture on the one hand, and as Lambeth's first professional librarian on the other. He laid the foundations of the present-day library at Lambeth. He found considerable chaos and disorder and an imperfect and partial catalogue. He worked hard to enlarge the collection and to put the official records in order. His monument, among the many indexes and catalogues that bear his name, remains the forty-eight volumes of epitomes of the archiepiscopal registers from Peccham (1279) to Potter (1747) which, in the hand of his clerk, with his engraved portrait as frontispiece, have been in daily use since 1761 and still stand on the open shelves of the reading-room.

Ducarel died at his home in South Lambeth on 29 May 1785, after hurrying home from Canterbury on hearing that his wife was on the point of death. She survived him for six years. In his will he left her his Peckham house and £3000 in South Sea stock, and to his youngest nephew, Gustavus Gerard Ducarel, son of his deceased youngest brother, Adrian, he left his books and medals. He was buried in St Katharine by the Tower.   ROBIN MYERS

Sources DNB • Nichols, *Lit. anecdotes*, 6.380 ff. • Nichols, *Illustrations* • correspondence with Philip Morant, BL, Add. MSS 37217–37219 • correspondence with James Ducarel, 1761–6, LPL [microfilm] [orig. correspondence privately held] • correspondence with Henry Hall, 1756–63, LPL, MS 1163 • correspondence with Archbishop Thomas Secker, 1758–68, LPL • correspondence in English and French; family papers, Glos. RO, D2091 • R. Myers, 'Dr Andrew Coltée Ducarel (1713–1785): a pioneer of Anglo-Norman studies', *Antiquaries, book collectors and the circles of learning*, ed. R. Myers and M. Harris (1996), 45–70 • R. Myers, 'Dr Andrew Coltée Ducarel, Lambeth librarian, civilian and keeper of the public records', *The Library*, 6th ser., 21 (1999), 199–222 • M. D. Slatter, 'A. C. Ducarel and the Lambeth MSS', *Archives* (1957), 97–104 • J. Cave-Brown, *Lambeth Palace and its associations* (1882) • H. Carter and C. Ricks, introduction, in E. R. Mores, *A dissertation upon English typographical founders and foundries*, ed. H. Carter and C. Ricks, new edn (1961) • N. Savage and others, eds., *Early printed books, 1478–1840: catalogue of the British Architectural Library early imprints collection*, [5 vols.] (1994–), vol. 1, pp. 83–5 • G. D. Squibb, *Doctors' Commons: a history of the College of Advocates and Doctors of Law* (1977) • Venn, *Alum. Cant.* • Foster, *Alum. Oxon.* • IGI • *A catalogue of the very valuable library of books, manuscripts, and prints, of the late A. C. Ducarel* (1786) [sale catalogue, Leigh and Sotheby, 3 April 1786] • will, 2 Aug 1784, PRO, PROB 11/1131

Archives BL, abstracts of archiepiscopal registers and catalogue of court, rolls, deeds, etc. at Lambeth, Add. MSS 5707, 6062–6109, 6297 • BL, collections and papers relating to church and hospital history, index to charters in the Augmentation Office, Stowe MSS 163, 356, 545, 796, 863–865 • BL, copy of the *British Librarian* with Ducarel's MS notes and additions • BL, corresp. and catalogue of his collections, Add. MSS 15935, 23990, 40103–40106 • BL, miscellanies, Eg MS 834 • Bodl. Oxf., catalogue of collection of coins and medals made by George North with Ducarel's own MS notes and additions; copies with annotations of answers to an ecclesiastical questionnaire sent to Cambridgeshire and Essex incumbents in 1705; corresp. and papers; topographical collections, incl. prints and drawings • CCC Cam., list of obituaries of antiquaries made by William Stukeley with Ducarel's MS annotations • Glos. RO, corresp. and papers, incl. draft and corrected printed copy of *Tour through Normandy* • Lambeth archives, London, memorandum book • LPL, account of St Katharine by the Tower; land papers; papers relating to the history of Croydon, Lambeth and the society of Doctors' Commons; corresp. • S. Antiquaries, Lond., notes relating to the revision of Martin Folkes's table of coins • U. Birm. L., index to Bishop Gibson's papers | BL, corresp. with Philip Morant, Add. MSS 37217–37219 • BL, letters to Thomas Birch, Add. MSS 4224, 4305 *passim* • Bodl. Oxf., corresp. with John Loveday sen. and jun. • CUL, corresp. with James Bentham, Add. MS 2960 • Norfolk RO, letters to Thomas Martin

Likenesses A. Soldi, oils, 1751, priv. coll. • P. Audinet, line engraving, 1818 (after F. Towne), BM, NPG; repro. in Nichols, *Illustrations* • F. Perry, etching (after A. Soldi, 1746), BM, NPG; repro. in A. C. Ducarel, *Norman coins* (1757) [*see illus.*]

Wealth at death library of books, manuscripts, coins and medals to nephew; £3000 in South Sea stock and Peckham house to widow: will, PRO, PROB 11/1131

Ducarel, Gerard Gustavus (1745–1800), East India Company servant, was born on 15 April 1745 in London, the youngest of the four children of Adrian Coltée Ducarel (1718–1745), a merchant and director of the South Sea Company, and his wife, Elizabeth, *née* Hamilton (1719–1792). He was a nephew of the antiquarian Andrew Coltée Ducarel. The Huguenot family emigrated to England from Caen around 1715.

In 1758 Gusty Ducarel was a midshipman in the Royal Navy and present at the siege of Louisburg. He was still in the navy in 1762 but, under Lord Clive's patronage, he obtained a writership in the East India Company, arriving in Calcutta in December 1765. Almost at once he placed himself in an invidious position by improvidently signing a memorial objecting to Clive's plan to transfer Madras officials to Bengal. Full of remorse he hurriedly withdrew his name. After brief spells as deputy paymaster to the 1st brigade, assistant cash keeper to the governor, and Persian translator to the resident at Murshidabad, he was appointed supervisor at Purnea in 1770. Purnea was a poverty-stricken district with tracts of wasteland and depressed smallholdings. Ducarel disapproved of the official policy of short-term revenue farming, but his measures to revive the local economy were vitiated by famine and the obtuseness of the superior revenue authorities. Although he left Purnea in 1772, his service there earned him recognition as an able and imaginative fiscal administrator. Several short appointments followed until he became fourth member of the Calcutta committee of revenue in 1775.

In October 1774 Philip Francis alighted in Calcutta as a member of the newly established Bengal supreme council. Like Ducarel he was attached to the Clive interest, and Ducarel soon became his adviser on the revenue and a personal friend. Ducarel declined an important part in Warren Hastings's survey of the revenue system (the *amini* commission) inaugurated in 1776. His appointment as superintendent of the *khalsa* (treasury) in July 1778 was managed by Francis. Beyond the call of official duty, Ducarel assisted in the escapade at the house of G. F. Grand on 8 December 1778 which culminated in Francis's appearance in court as defendant in an action for criminal conversation during which Ducarel was called as a witness. In December 1779 he was an intermediary in the opening of negotiations to try to arrange an accommodation between Francis and Hastings.

When Francis left India in December 1780 his associates were left without a patron and protector. Although Hastings listed Ducarel among 'the lees of Mr. Francis' (Gleig, 2.384–6), he conceded an obligation to indemnify him for loss of office when a centralized revenue committee formed in Calcutta in 1781 absorbed the functions of the *khalsa*. Thus, in 1782, Ducarel was appointed commissioner at Burdwan, where he remained until he retired and returned to England in 1784.

Ducarel began a relationship with Elizabeth (Bibi) Mirza (*c*.1758–1822) in the early 1770s. They had six children: five were born in India and one in England. She accompanied Ducarel back to his retirement home in Exmouth, Devon. Presumably at some stage she converted from Islam to Christianity, and they probably married, most likely in India between 1780 and 1784 (they had not married by 22 April 1780, when the youngest of three recorded natural children was born). An Indian traveller, Abu Taleb, wrote of visiting Ducarel's house, seemingly in London, about 1799 or 1800. He saw portraits of Indian acquaintances and described Mrs Ducarel as 'very fair and so accomplished in all the English manners and language, that I was sometime in her company before I could be convinced she was a native of India' (Abu Taleb Khan, 1.198–9). Philip Francis facetiously alluded to Ducarel's diminutive stature (he was 5 feet ½ inch tall) in a letter to his wife written from Paris, where Ducarel and he were on a visit in September 1784 (Parkes and Merivale, 2.219). Although a good deal occupied with family affairs in retirement, two letters from Francis in 1795 suggest that Ducarel was anxious about the effects of the continuance of the war with France. Ducarel died at Stilton, Huntingdonshire, on 14 December 1800 while travelling. He was an efficient and principled administrator, respected though regarded warily by Hastings for his closeness to Francis.

T. H. BOWYER

Sources Glos. RO, Palmer (Ducarel) MSS · Mrs J. Whiting, 'G. G. Ducarel and the East India Company, 1765–1784', *Indian Archives*, 16 (1965–6), 62–71 · Bengal civilians, BL OIOC, O/6/23 · R. Guha, *A rule of property for Bengal: an essay on the idea of permanent settlement*, 2nd edn (New Delhi, 1982), 50–55 · Abu Taleb Khan, *Travels of Mirza Abu Taleb Khan in Asia, Africa, and Europe during the years 1799, 1800, 1801, 1802, and 1803: written by himself, in the Persian language*, trans. C. Stewart, 2 vols. (1810) · ecclesiastical returns, BL OIOC · research file, Ducarel family, UCL, Huguenot Library · Nichols, *Lit. anecdotes*, 6.404–5 · J. Parkes and H. Merivale, *Memoirs of Sir Philip Francis*, 2 vols. (1867) · *GM*, 1st ser., 15 (1745), 388 · *GM*, 1st ser., 70 (1800), 1293 · *GM*, 1st ser., 92/1 (1822), 285 · *Memoirs of the life of the Right Hon. Warren Hastings, first governor-general of Bengal*, ed. G. R. Gleig, 3 vols. (1841) · parish register (births), St Thomas Apostle, London
Archives Glos. RO, Palmer (Ducarel) MSS, D2091 | BL OIOC, Francis MSS

Ducart, Davis (*d.* 1780x86), engineer and architect, has been variously described as 'an English Engineer who had been long in the Sardinian service' (Mullins, 26), 'an Italian Engineer and very ingenious architect' (Hutton, 2.127), and a 'French architect' (*Freeman's Journal*, 3–4 Feb 1773). His origins have not been traced; according to his own account, he was born and bred as an engineer in the 'hilly parts adjacent to the Alps … so often visited by the English nobility and Gentry' (McCutcheon, 61), and he signed his will as 'Daviso de Arcrt'. It is not known what took him to Ireland; he is first heard of in Cork in 1761, when Cork corporation ordered a payment of £25 to him 'for his trouble in taking the level of the river Lee, and drawing several plans of waterworks to supply this City with water' (Caulfield, 752). At some point after this he worked as an engineer on the Newry Canal, and by 1767 he was engaged in works on the River Boyne and in the design of a new canal to link the co. Tyrone collieries with the Coalisland Canal. Here he introduced a system of inclined planes known as 'dry hurries', rather than locks, to raise or lower the vessels from one level to another. The innovation was not a success, and the canal soon fell into disuse. Ducart's aqueduct at Newmills, co. Tyrone, built about 1768, survives.

Ducart also practised as an architect. His first dated building in Ireland is the mayoralty house in Cork, begun in 1765: this project proceeded very slowly, and he was accused of not giving due attention to the work. At the same time he designed the custom house in Limerick, which was built under the supervision of the architect Christopher Colles between 1765 and 1770. From 1765 onwards Ducart also designed several country houses, including Lota, co. Cork (1765), Kilshannig, co. Cork (c.1765–1766), Brockley Park, Queen's county (1768), Crosshaven House, co. Cork (1769), and Castletown Cox, co. Kilkenny (c.1770). Ducart's style was eclectic, drawing both on continental baroque and on English Palladian pattern books for its sources, with an element of unorthodox detailing. A critic in the *Freeman's Journal* of 13–16 May 1769 accused him of producing designs 'such as our forefathers (that might have lived in Vitruvius or Palladio's time) never saw' and of being 'utterly ignorant of the given rules and proportions of architecture, although he contrives to make five or six hundred pounds a year by it as his profession'. No further commissions are recorded after 1770. Ducart may have fallen out of favour because of dissatisfaction with his unreliability rather than with his stylistic idiosyncrasies. According to further hostile comment in the *Freeman's Journal* for 3–4 February 1773, he had given up architecture after 'eternally committing mistakes and blunders, and confounding and contradicting his own directions, until he himself saw the folly of such proceedings, and (not without certain admonitions) quitted the profession'.

By November 1767 Ducart had an address in Dublin; he also acquired property in Drumrea, co. Tyrone, where he had an interest in a glassworks in the early 1770s. He died between 30 November 1780, when he wrote his will, and 29 March 1786, when the will was proved. In it he made bequests to friends in France and Italy; he named no relatives, but alluded to his friendship with Frederick Hervey, earl of Bristol and bishop of Derry, for whom he had earlier prepared two proposals for a bridge over the River Foyle at Londonderry.   A. M. ROWAN

Sources abstract of Ducart's will, NL Ire., Genealogical Office MS 424, fols. 237–8 [summary in *Georgian Society Records*, 5 (1913), 72] · *Public Register, or, Freeman's Journal* (13–16 May 1769) · *Public Register, or, Freeman's Journal* (2–4 Feb 1773) · R. Caulfield, ed., *The council book of the corporation of the city of Cork* (1876), 752, 815–16 · W. A. McCutcheon, *The industrial archaeology of Northern Ireland* (1980), 61–5 · D. Fitzgerald, 'The architecture of Davis Duckart [pts 1–2]', *Country Life*, 142 (1967), 735–9, 798–801 · signed and dated drawings of Crosshaven House, priv. coll. · *Finn's Leinster Journal* (27 June–1 July 1767) · *Arthur Young's tour in Ireland (1776–1779)*, ed. A. W. Hutton, 2 vols. (1892), vol. 2, p. 127 · M. B. Mullins, 'An historical sketch of engineering in Ireland', *Transactions of the Institution of Civil Engineers of Ireland*, 6 (1859–61), 26 · P. Rankin, *Irish building ventures of the earl bishop of Derry* (1972), 11 · M. S. Dudley Westropp, *Irish glass*, rev. edn (1978), 99–101

Duchal, James (*d.* 1761), non-subscribing Presbyterian minister, was a very private person who seems to have communicated little of his background even to his few close friends. Andrew Kippis remarked on the anonymous 'Letter to a friend' which was prefixed to the second volume of Duchal's posthumous *Sermons* (1764), and was probably the work of the prominent layman Gabriel Cornwall (*d.* 1786), that 'we never met with a piece of biographical writing more idly declamatory, or less specific in the narration' (Kippis, 410). He noted but discounted an old report that Duchal was born in Scotland. The family name, always rare and now extinct, nevertheless is found in west-central Scotland in the seventeenth and early

eighteenth centuries, and still survives as a topographical name in Renfrewshire.

Duchal entered Glasgow University in the session 1709–10, when he went directly into the *prima classis*—the final-year or natural philosophy class, conducted that year by Gershom Carmichael—and identified himself in the register as *Scoto-Hibernus*, an Ulster Scot. He postponed his graduation until 1726. The author of 'Letter to a friend' believed that Duchal was sixty-four when he died; that would place his birth in the twelve months prior to May 1697 and would mean that he entered the graduating class, already trained in other parts of philosophy and mathematics, at twelve or thirteen. This is unlikely, and Duchal himself portrayed John Abernethy's entry, aged thirteen, into the *tertia classis*—the first of the three years of the philosophy course—as premature forcing. Before going to university Duchal had been educated by an unidentified uncle. He seems to have had a sister, since his one named relative is a nephew surnamed Cuningham, identified in a letter to the English dissenter George Benson in 1754. This was probably James Cuningham, who acquired and annotated some of Duchal's manuscripts after his death and whose name appears on a letter wrapper bound into one set.

Surviving class lists give no evidence that Duchal continued into the divinity class, although the time interval before his ministerial trials would be consistent with his having done so. He was entered on trials in 1717–18 and licensed in 1718–19 by the Antrim presbytery, and was one of the commissioners from the Antrim congregation to the general synod who opposed Abernethy's removal to Dublin in 1718; he is therefore likely to have been domiciled in Antrim or its locality for some years. He came deeply under Abernethy's influence during his ministerial training and remained in awe of 'that astonishing man' (Hincks, 78–9). He was associated with the Belfast Society and his 'Brief memoirs' of some of the non-subscribing divines appeared in an appendix to his memorial sermon for Abernethy in 1741. He appears to have been ordained in England. In 1721 he became minister to the Presbyterian congregation at Green Street, Cambridge, an appointment he later considered the happiest of his life. Manuscript sermons from this period show him theologically orthodox but not Calvinistic. In 1729 he was a candidate for the pulpit of the Scots church at Founders' Hall, London, which went to William Wishart, another preacher with Arminian leanings; this suggests, however, that Duchal may at this time have taken a relaxed view of the controversy in Irish presbyterianism over confessional subscription.

Duchal twice succeeded Abernethy, at Antrim in 1730 and at Wood Street, Dublin, in 1741. In Antrim he tried unsuccessfully, through publication, to heal the rift between subscribers and non-subscribers among the congregation that he had known in his youth; on leaving he was succeeded by Abernethy's son-in-law Alexander Maclaine. In Dublin, Duchal avoided any part in church politics. He was a pastor of exemplary diligence, strongly humanitarian, and like many ministers acquired and applied a certain amount of medical knowledge in the course of his ministrations. The responsibilities of preparing Abernethy's work for publication and providing it with appropriate prefatory material occupied his spare energies for some years; he consulted with Abernethy's lay collaborator William Bruce on the theoretical grounding of his mentor's position. Duchal himself prepared fresh sermons each week, rehearsing them thoroughly and committing them to a minutely written aide-mémoire; where he had not time to complete the preparation he would set down summary notes in a larger hand to be easily legible in the pulpit.

Duchal's life's message was consistently one of moral reformation. Three sermons published in 1728 as *The Practice of Religion Recommended as Excellent and Reasonable* show already a deeply philosophical approach and a concern to understand the psychology of religion: a conviction that it is first and foremost a matter of disciplining and orienting the affections, and that reason and revelation are complementary guides to the same end; a belief in the efficacy of conscience that suggests familiarity with Joseph Butler's work; and a theory of rational taste that probably reflects the fashion for adapting Shaftesbury's ideas to the service of religion. These themes come to maturity in works published after his return to Ireland: *Presumptive Arguments for the Truth and Divine Authority of the Christian Religion* (1753; translated into German, Gustow, 1773), which earned him the DD degree from Glasgow, and the posthumous *Sermons*, of which the first thirteen had been picked by Duchal himself for publication. His 'presumptive arguments' are studies in moral and historical coherence.

Duchal was open to new ideas, both in his personal thinking and in his reading. Writing to Bruce in 1742 he expressed concern at the disruptive potential of the seceders who had lately crossed from Scotland, but he was tolerant of the fanaticism of the Cambuslang revival if the end result was a return to virtue. He corresponded on theology with rational dissenters like Benson, and John Taylor of Norwich. After his death his work was promoted by Kippis and Priestley; the latter would have published further materials if manuscripts had not been lost at sea. A famous letter of 1754 from Duchal to Taylor on the atonement, first published by Priestley in the *Theological Repository* and later republished by W. Graham of Leeds, shows greater theological probing than the sermons in seeking a fully consistent and convincing Arminian stance. Late in life Duchal studied, and rejected, the Hebraistic work of John Hutchinson. Alexander Gerard encouraged reference to Duchal's work in his lectures at Aberdeen. Kippis levels a veiled charge of plagiarism against William Leechman for a discourse published in 1768 that he considers to be a distillation of three sermons by Duchal on the spirit of Christianity. Leechman would have known Duchal's handling of the theme but the charge is unwarranted: the identity of structure is determined by the form of the Pauline text (2 Timothy 1: 7) and the conventions of preaching upon a text; but the text was a commonplace and the substance of their narratives is plainly different.

Although there are philosophical affinities between Duchal and Francis Hutcheson, and it is reasonable to think that Hutcheson attended Duchal's meeting-house on visits to Dublin, there was never the rapport between them that there was between Duchal and Abernethy or between Abernethy and Hutcheson. When Thomas Drennan (1696–1768) of Belfast consulted him about a memorial to Hutcheson consistent with Hutcheson's instructions Duchal found the terms of the instructions distasteful. He died, unmarried, in Dublin on 4 May 1761.

M. A. STEWART

Sources MS sermons, mostly by Duchal, 8 vols., Magee University College, Londonderry, MSS 14–21 · correspondence, PRO NIre., D 1759/3B/6 [typescript copies] · James Duchal, two sermons; letter to T. Drennan, Presbyterian Historical Society of Ireland, Belfast · 'Letter to a friend', J. Duchal, *Sermons*, 3 vols. (1762–4), 2.i–xxxv · A. Kippis, 'Duchal', *Biographia Britannica, or, The lives of the most eminent persons who have flourished in Great Britain and Ireland*, ed. A. Kippis and others, 2nd edn, 5 (1793), 410–14 · *Records of the General Synod of Ulster, from 1691 to 1820*, 1 (1890), 456, 460, 487 · J. Duchal to G. Benson, 28 Sept 1754, JRL, Unitarian College collection · T. D. Hincks, 'Notices of William Bruce, and of his contemporaries and friends, Hutcheson, Abernethy, Duchal, and others', *Christian Teacher*, new ser., 5 (1843), 72–92 · register of diplomas, U. Glas., Archives and Business Records Centre, MS 21320 · C. Innes, ed., *Munimenta alme Universitatis Glasguensis / Records of the University of Glasgow from its foundation till 1727*, 3, Maitland Club, 72 (1854), 194 · W. Wilson, *The history and antiquities of the dissenting churches and meeting houses in London, Westminster and Southwark*, 4 vols. (1808–14), vol. 2, p. 494 · R. B. Barlow, 'The career of James Duchal (1697–1761)', *Non-Subscribing Presbyterian*, 978 (March 1988), 26–9; 979 (April 1988), 38–41 · DNB

Archives PRO NIre., Duchal corresp., D/1759/3B/6 [typescript copies; originals lost in fire] · University of Ulster, Magee Campus, Derry, sermons MS

Ducie. For this title name *see* Moreton, Henry George Francis, second earl of Ducie (1802–1853).

Duck, Arthur (1580–1648), civil lawyer, was the second son of Richard Duck (*d.* 1603), of Heavitree, Devon, and his wife, Joanna; he was the younger brother of Nicholas *Duck. He matriculated from Exeter College, Oxford, in 1595, and graduated BA in 1599. He then migrated to Hart Hall, from where he proceeded MA in 1602. Two years later he was elected a fellow of All Souls College, of which he was a bursar in 1608 and sub-warden in 1610. He took the degree of BCL in 1607 and, after a period in France, Italy, and Germany, DCL in 1612. He was admitted an advocate of Doctors' Commons in 1614, and was later employed on a mission to Scotland. In 1617 he published in Oxford a life of the founder of All Souls: the *Vita Henrici Chichele, archiepiscopi Cantuariensis sub regibus Henrici V et VI* was in effect an ecclesiastical and constitutional history of England in the fifteenth century.

From 1616 Duck was chancellor of the diocese of Bath and Wells. Within a few years he was married by the bishop, Arthur Lake, to Margaret, younger daughter of Henry Southworth, a London merchant who also had strong ties to Wells. They had nine children, of whom only two daughters, Mary and Martha, survived. Lake had close connections to the court and Duck himself began to accumulate offices. In 1615 he became a commissioner for policies and assurances, in 1617 a master in chancery extraordinary, in 1622 a commissioner for the admiralty in Dorset and Middlesex and for piracy in London, and from 1623 king's advocate in the court of chivalry, dealing with crimes committed overseas. In 1624, probably through Lake's influence, he was elected MP for Minehead, Somerset. During the debate on the bill to prohibit arbitrary imprisonment contrary to Magna Carta, he objected on the grounds that it restricted the powers of the lord marshal, the lord admiral, and the high commissioners; owing to his and others' exceptions, the bill did not pass. While still retaining his position at Bath and Wells and property in Somerset, on 11 December that year Duck was appointed vicar-general and chancellor of the London diocese by Bishop George Montaigne. He subsequently moved to London, first to Blackfriars and then to Chiswick, and made only periodic visits to Somerset in the later 1620s and 1630s. In 1625 he became a member of the court of delegates and a master of requests, and the following year gave an opinion upholding the validity of a statute drafted by William Laud (then bishop of Bath and Wells) for Wadham College, Oxford, which imposed fines on absentee fellows. Following Laud's translation to London in 1628 the bishop made Duck his commissary on 12 December 1629. When Laud became archbishop of Canterbury in 1633 Duck was appointed to the high commission, although when called before the privy council on 3 November that year to give his learned opinion in the St Gregory by Paul case, he failed to support Laud's arguments for the positioning of the altar. In 1634 he was made visitor of hospitals, poorhouses, and schools in the diocese of Canterbury.

By 1640, when in the Short Parliament Duck again served as MP for Minehead, he had become closely associated with the campaign for ecclesiastical conformity, and took it to greater lengths than most in his illegal attempt to make London churchwardens take the oath attached to the canons of that year. In 1641 he defended the high commission before parliament and attracted hostile petitioning. Having lost his chancellorships and been sequestered by parliament in 1642, he was permitted to compound for his estate at a tenth, reckoned to be £2000. Despite his continuing support for the king, to whose cause he gave £6000, Duck's career was not over: in 1645 he again became a master in chancery. That his family had friends among the godly is evident from the 'life' of Margaret Duck, included by Samuel Clarke in his *A Collection of the Lives of Ten Eminent Divines* (1662); here the charity and piety of both wife and husband are celebrated and their living at Blackfriars under the ministry of the notable puritan minister William Gouge is noted. Margaret died on 15 August 1646, and was buried on 24 August at Chiswick. In 1648 Duck was involved in negotiating for the king on the Isle of Wight, but a few months later, on 12 or 16 December, he died suddenly in Chelsea church; he was buried in Chiswick the following May. Although the *Dictionary of National Biography* calls him Sir Arthur, there is no evidence that he was ever knighted.

Duck had spent his last years working, together with Gerard Langbaine, provost of Queen's College, Oxford, on his *magnum opus*, *De usu et authoritate juris civilis Romanorum*, which was published posthumously in 1653. Although the work was reprinted in several European countries, and also translated into French and German, the only part translated into English is the chapter on civil law in England, published in 1724. Duck's motive was to refute the view of two French writers that England did not use Roman civil law at all. In tracing the fortunes of Roman law in the various kingdoms of Europe, he produced the first history of law on a European scale, based on the best authorities. The chapter on England ends with a gloomy forecast that civil law would not last long in England (a passage omitted in the English translation).

PETER STEIN

Sources *CSP dom.*, 1611–43 · B. P. Levack, *The civil lawyers in England, 1603–1641* (1973) · G. D. Squibb, *Doctors' Commons: a history of the College of Advocates and Doctors of Law* (1977) · E. Heward, *Masters in ordinary* (1990) · Wood, *Ath. Oxon.*, new edn, 3.257–8 · *DNB* · S. Clarke, *A collection of the lives of ten eminent divines* (1662), 488–500 · J. Davies, *The Caroline captivity of the church: Charles I and the remoulding of Anglicanism, 1625–1641* (1992) · C. Russell, *Parliaments and English politics, 1621–1629* (1979) · GL, MS 25630/7, fols. 19r–20r, 188v

Duck, Sir John, baronet (1631/2–1691), local politician, was of unknown parentage. He was apprenticed to a Durham butcher, John Heslope, although there seems to have been some opposition in 1657 within the guild to his employment in that trade. This may relate to his marriage in St Margaret's, Durham, on 30 July 1655, to Heslope's daughter, Anne (*bap.* 1635, *d.* 1695). According to legend Duck's subsequent fortunes were laid in the following incident in his youth: 'As he was straying in melancholy idleness by the water side, a raven appeared hovering in the air, and from chance or fright dropped from his bill a gold *Jacobus* at the foot of the happy butcher boy'. This adventure was depicted on a panel in the house which he afterwards built for himself in Durham.

Duck was trading as a butcher in 1670, and in 1673–4 was wealthy enough to rent a pew in St Nicholas's Church. He also seems to have invested in land and coal deposits. He served as mayor of Durham in 1680–81 and was elected to the Butchers' Company that same year. By 1680 he had a house in Silver Street and purchased the manor of Haswell on the Hill.

However, despite Duck's wealth and political usefulness to the government, he was generally treated as a parvenu. His appointment to the bench raised opposition on the grounds of 'inferior birth or an upstart in point of fortune' (*CSP dom.*, *Jan–June 1683*, 164), but this cut little ice with Secretary Jenkins in London, or with Bishop Crew of Durham. Indeed, his political loyalty was rewarded on 19 March 1687 with the grant of a baronetcy. During the preparations for the elections to James II's abortive parliament in 1688, Duck promised to vote for candidates recommended by Crew, and he was named a deputy lieutenant of Durham in July 1688. By that year he had also acquired the leases of coalmines at Rainton. As late as October 1688 he was searching for the putative rebel Lord Lumley, although it is unknown what part he played in the events following the Dutch invasion.

Duck died, aged fifty-nine, on 26 August 1691, and was buried at St Margaret's, Durham, on the 31st. His will mentioned a niece, Anne, the daughter of his brother Robert, 'if she be alive', but the chief beneficiary was his widow, who followed him to the grave on 14 December 1695, amid much comment about her fortune (Burke, 173). Another beneficiary was the son of her niece Jane, James Nicholson, the future MP for Durham, who received Haswell and Rainton. His widow's other niece, Elizabeth, received 'an old rotten house at the bottom of Silver Street' (Surtees, 4.54).   C. J. ROBINSON, *rev.* STUART HANDLEY

Sources GEC, *Baronetage* · R. Surtees, *The history and antiquities of the county palatine of Durham*, 4 vols. (1816–40), 4.53–4, 156 · J. Burke and J. B. Burke, *A genealogical and heraldic history of the extinct and dormant baronetcies of England, Ireland, and Scotland* (1838), 173 · G. Duckett, ed., *Penal laws and Test Act*, 1 (1882), 115, 436 · *CSP dom., Jan–June 1683*, 164; *1686–7*, 379; *1687–9*, 233, 331 · J. Barmby, ed., *Churchwardens' accounts of Pittington and other parishes in the diocese of Durham, from AD 1580 to 1700*, SurtS, 84 (1888), 232–3

Duck, Nicholas (1570–1628), lawyer, was born at Heavitree, Devon, the eldest son of Richard Duck (*d.* 1603) of Exeter and his wife, Joanna, and elder brother of Arthur *Duck. He matriculated from Exeter College, Oxford, on 10 July 1584, aged fourteen, but took no degree. He then entered Lincoln's Inn and in 1599 was called to the bar. In 1614 he was elected a bencher of his inn and he thereafter divided his time between the inn and the city of Exeter, of which he became a freeman in 1609. Duck married Grace, daughter of Thomas Walker, alderman of Exeter, and in 1614 he bought Mount Radford, Exeter, from Sir John Doddridge. In 1617 he was made counsel to the corporation of Exeter and in the following year he was Lent reader of Lincoln's Inn and he became recorder of Exeter. In 1622 he was one of the civic figures who planned the city's strategy of blocking Bishop Valentine Cary's moves to extend his jurisdiction in Exeter. Duck was returned to parliament as MP for the city in 1625; he served on several committees, including two concerned with religious issues, and he spoke on questions relating to the imprisonment of debtors. He produced some law reports (BL, Hargrave MS 51), but they were never printed. He died on 28 August 1628 and was buried in Exeter Cathedral.
                                              J. M. RIGG, *rev.* PETER STEIN

Sources W. R. Prest, *The rise of the barristers: a social history of the English bar, 1590–1640* (1986), 357 · W. P. Baildon, ed., *The records of the Honorable Society of Lincoln's Inn: the black books*, 2 (1898) · Foster, *Alum. Oxon.* · W. T. MacCaffrey, *Exeter, 1540–1640: the growth of an English county town*, 2nd edn (Cambridge, MA, 1975), 218, 224 · M. Jansson and W. B. Bidwell, eds., *Proceedings in parliament, 1625* (1987)

Duck, Stephen (1705?–1756), poet, was born at Charlton, near Pewsey, Wiltshire. His parents were said to have been poor; otherwise there is no information about his family. He attended a charity school, leaving at about his fourteenth year to work as an agricultural labourer. He married Ann (*d.* 1730) on 22 June 1724; they had three children: Emey (*b.* 1725), William (*b.* 1727), and Ann (*b.* 1729).

Joseph Spence records that it was about the time of his marriage that Duck began his attempts at self-improvement. He bought a few books, which he studied by night. Spence adds: 'Considering the difficulties … the

inclination for Knowledge must have been very strong in him', and lists Duck's early reading, including Milton, Dryden, *The Spectator*, and Matthew Prior (Spence, 6–11). Duck was fortunate in the support he received for his intellectual and poetical development. He came to the attention of Dr Alured Clarke, prebendary of Winchester Cathedral, who drew Duck to the attention of Mrs Charlotte Clayton, lady of the bedchamber, and thence to the queen herself. Early fragmentary attempts at verse culminated in *The Thresher's Labour*, suggested by another early supporter, the Revd Stanley, rector of Pewsey. Duck then wrote, at the instigation of Mrs Stanley, *The Shunammite*, based on a scriptural theme and on which much of his early reputation was founded.

In early October 1730 Duck travelled to Windsor to be presented to the queen. While he was engaged in these travels his wife, Ann, died; Clarke advised that he should not be informed until after his interview with Caroline. Duck's reputation had spread first locally and then nationally, supported by Clarke and Spence, with whom Duck spent considerable time and remained a lifelong friend. Spence's account of Duck appeared without authority in the *Gentleman's Magazine* for March 1731, and subsequently prefaced later (authorized) editions of the poems. Duck's poems were published in up to ten pirate editions from 1730 to 1733 under the title of *Poems on Several Subjects*. Duck was well received by the queen, who gave him an annuity of £30 or £50 and a house. In 1733 she made him a yeoman of the guard, and in 1735 keeper of the queen's library in Merlin's Cave, a Gothic building in Richmond Gardens, a post he filled with diligence and taste. On 17 July 1733 he married Sarah Big, housekeeper to the queen at Kew. She bore two daughters (born in 1736 and 1738), and died at some date before 1744 when, on 16 September, he married a third wife (name unknown) who died in 1749.

Duck's first authorized publication was an ode to the duke of Cumberland (1732) and the first authorized collection—*Poems on Several Occasions*—appeared in 1736, the subscribers including royalty, the archbishops, and Swift. The frontispiece is probably the only surviving likeness of Duck. His works can be divided into three periods. Many early poems he is said to have destroyed; apart from *The Thresher's Labour* and *The Shunammite* only slight pieces remain. The period of his patronage by the queen is the most productive, characterized by occasional verses and long descriptive or didactic poems, of which *A Description of a Journey* is of some biographical interest. The period after the death of the queen produced eight long and largely uninspired poems.

Duck's poems, though without genius, are not without interest. He was in a unique position to write from his farm labouring experience, but the Georgian establishment refined him into an imitation of many another court poet, so that *The Thresher's Labour* stands alone as a testimony to his early life. It would be easy to underestimate Duck's reputation in the 1730s. It was rumoured that he was considered for the laureateship; he was satirized by many, including Swift. He had a personality which attracted those who met him; his simple uprightness and naïve charm won a measure of personal liking from even such harsh judges as Pope and Swift, neither of whom had a kind word for him as a poet.

The death of Queen Caroline in 1737 left Duck without his benefactor, and, his fame as a literary novelty waning, he applied himself to scholarship, taking holy orders in 1746. He secured positions first in 1747 as chaplain to Lieutenant-General H. Cornwall's (7th) regiment of marines, then, in 1750, as chaplain to Ligonier's dragoons, and in August the following year as preacher to Kew chapel. In January 1752 he was appointed to the rectory of Byfleet, Surrey, probably through the agency of Spence, who lived there. He proved a hard working and popular parish priest, but between 30 March and 2 April 1756 committed suicide by drowning at Reading.

LESLIE STEPHEN, rev. WILLIAM R. JONES

Sources R. M. Davis, *Stephen Duck, the thresher poet* (1927) · J. Spence, *A full and authentick account of Stephen Duck, the Wiltshire poet* (1731) · R. Southey, *The lives and works of the uneducated poets*, ed. J. S. Childers (1925) · C. B. Tinker, *Nature's simple plan* (1922) · A. Kippis and others, eds., *Biographia Britannica, or, The lives of the most eminent persons who have flourished in Great Britain and Ireland*, 2nd edn, 5 (1793) · *DNB* · *IGI*

Likenesses attrib. B. Lens, miniature, *c*.1740, NPG · G. Bickham the elder, line engraving (after J. Thornhill), BM, NPG; repro. in S. Duck, *Poems on several occasions* (privately printed, London, 1736), frontispiece · line engraving, BM, NPG

Duckenfield [Duckenfeild], **Robert** (1619–1689), parliamentarian army officer, was possibly born at Portwood Hall, Stockport, Cheshire, the eldest of the seven children of Robert Duckenfield, esquire (*bap.* 1597, *d.* 1630), and his wife, Frances (*d.* 1663), daughter of George Preston of Holker, Lancashire. The family, first recorded at Dukinfield in the thirteenth century, held the manors of Dukinfield and Brinnington, two of fourteen townships of the parish of Stockport in north-east Cheshire. The Duckenfields' holdings placed them in the second tier of county gentry. Duckenfield's early education is unknown though the stipulations of his father's will in 1630 suggest a strong puritan influence. In 1637 he entered Gray's Inn. Before 1642 Duckenfield, who throughout his life consistently spelt his name Duckenfeild, married Martha Fleetwood (*d.* 1669), daughter of Sir Miles *Fleetwood of Aldwincle, Northamptonshire, receiver of the court of wards, and sister to the future parliamentarian general Charles *Fleetwood. Robert and Martha were to have four boys and two girls. In 1651 Martha's brother married Henry Ireton's widow, Oliver Cromwell's eldest daughter.

North-east Cheshire was overwhelmingly for parliament during the civil wars, and through family and neighbours—and particularly his Cheshire kinsman Sir William Brereton—Duckenfield was all but predestined to the side of rebellion. At Brinnington Moor, Stockport, on Whit Tuesday 1642 he mustered under his captaincy a company of foot—in 1647 payment was disallowed, there 'being no Comysson' (PRO, SP 28/128, pt 10). Duckenfield led this and a similarly raised troop of horse to the siege of Manchester in September 1642 when they were formally

commissioned into the parliamentarian army. He was among the first to join Brereton at Nantwich in February 1643 and under his command fought throughout Cheshire and the adjacent English and Welsh counties. Commissioned colonel in November 1643, he raised a regiment consisting of up to ten companies of foot. His soldierly qualities seem to have lain less in field skills—he was in joint command of the force that retreated before Prince Rupert at Stockport in 1644—than in an ability to raise and largely retain men, and in his loyalty to Brereton. He became acting governor of the Chester suburbs during Brereton's absence in 1645. His regiment's disbandment in 1647 coincided with his appointment as governor of Chester, a post he held until 1653 and one placing him at the centre of the region's military affairs. During the second and third civil wars he again raised soldiers. There is no record of him in action in 1648 but in 1651 he commanded the force that captured the Isle of Man from the countess of Derby. Duckenfield was appointed governor of the island.

Support for parliament and Brereton brought public responsibilities: membership of the Macclesfield Hundred's sequestration committee, and, more crucially, of the radical group in the county committee. Duckenfield was appointed a justice of the peace but was rarely active. In 1649 he served as high sheriff for Cheshire. The Fleetwood family connections may have furthered his career. Having been nominated to, but non-attendant at, the commission to try Charles I, he participated in the trial of the earl of Derby. Shortly before his execution Derby wrote his wife that 'Colonel Duckenfield … being so much a gentleman born, will doubtless for his own honour's sake deal fairly with you' (Raines, 1.201). He was a commissioner for the propagation of the gospel in Wales and for the monthly assessment. With his friend Henry Birkenhead he was one of two Cheshire representatives in Barebone's Parliament. A contemporary listing reckoned him 'for the Godly Learned Ministry and Universities' (Woolrych, 416) but the journals of the House of Commons note only his request for absence. He served on no committees. His loyalty to the regime outlasted the fall of Barebone's—he was appointed an ejector in 1654—but was clearly waning. In March 1655, on the occasion of Penruddock's rising, Major-General Worsley reported to Thurloe that Duckenfield was 'the onely person that refuses … the orders and instructions of his highness and councell' (Thurloe, *State papers*, 4.485). Duckenfield explained his refusal to raise a regiment in a much quoted letter to Cromwell. Awareness of a local reluctance to serve combined with his own disenchantment with Cromwell. Though 'the roote and tree of piety is alive in your lordship … the leaves theirof, through abundance of temptations and flatteries, seeme to mee to be withered much of late …'. More pointedly

> wheirwith I am much delighted, for a season to accept of some hansome military command, if your lordshipp think well theirof; soe as the men that I serve with may not be cast of afterwards unrequited; and that they be selected in the best way from such as be your superficiall and dissembling

friends, whom I know well, and will have little to doe with them, unless forced theirto.   (Thurloe, *State papers*, 3.294)

Duckenfield's absence from the Cheshire elections of 1654 and 1656 emphasizes his withdrawal from national and local affairs. This withdrawal was briefly reversed in 1659 when he supported John Bradshaw in the election and raised a troop of horse to oppose Sir George Booth (Nevell, *The People who Made Tameside*, 24–5). His support for the Good Old Cause may have been more than political. As a regimental commander Duckenfield in 1651 had been the country's sixth largest purchaser of crown estates, in particular the large manor of Denbigh and other estates in Cheshire, Huntingdonshire, and Staffordshire. Potentially he had much to lose from a change of regime.

Duckenfield's adoption of the Independency of his mentor Brereton suggests that the puritanism of kin and neighbours deeply influenced him. In 1643 he appointed Samuel Eaton chaplain to his regiment. Subsequently Eaton became pastor of a congregation established at Dukinfield Hall chapel. Reputedly the country's first Independent church, its success probably reflected the puritanism of the district and the attachment to alternative worship of Duckenfield's soldiers. Opposed to presbyterianism, the chapel was to be a focus for religious radicals. According to Martindale 'such as were stiffest for the congregationall government joyned at Duckenfield' (Martindale, 74). The congregation framed the local petition against the new form of church government in 1646 and permitted George Fox to preach there in 1647. Noted for brethren gifted in lay preaching, the body was to split over anti-Trinitarianism in the early 1650s when 'the opinions that were rampant in the armie infected also the countrey, and some belonging to the Church of Duckenfield (so called) were thought to be deeply tainted' (ibid., 110). However, a church was to continue at Dukinfield until the Restoration. References to Duckenfield's beliefs are few. To Cromwell he expressed his wish 'not to seek a confederacy with those who limit God to their passions' (Thurloe, *State papers*, 3.294). And in a letter to old Sir George Booth in 1652 suggesting the non-enforcement of tithes he urged 'it is better to connive att the endevers of hott spirits sometimes than to reduce things to extremitie' (Morrill, 274). His patronage of the congregation at Dukinfield is probably the best guide to his views.

The Restoration brought Duckenfield victimization: loss of the purchased crown estates, attempted prosecution by the countess dowager of Derby in 1660, suspicion of plotting in 1664, arrest in 1665, and detention at Hull. Subsequently he was held at the Tower and in the Isle of Wight, but released in 1668 after petitioning the king 'for clemency, in spite of the flying calumnies wherewith he has been aspersed' (*CSP dom., 1668–9*, 128). He has frequently been confused with his younger and possibly more radical brother Lieutenant-Colonel John Duckenfield, who played a significant part during Booth's revolt and in the conflict between the army and parliament. He too was imprisoned during the 1660s. Another brother, Lieutenant-Colonel William, also fought for parliament during the 1640s. There is no evidence that Robert

supported local nonconformists in the 1660s. Though the family was to maintain its links with excluded clergy the church at Dukinfield lost its public status. The elevation of his eldest son to a baronetcy in 1665 reflects the mixed attitudes of the authorities towards the family.

Duckenfield's first wife, Martha, died in 1669. On 20 August 1678 he married Judith Bottomley (1653?–1739), daughter of Nathaniel Bottomley of Cawthorne, Yorkshire; they too had four boys and two girls. Both wives seem to have shared his nonconformist faith. In 1681, as tension heightened during the exclusion crisis, the family again gave its support to nonconformist worship at Dukinfield. Cheshire did not forget the old soldier; in June 1689, as forces were being raised to defend the new regime, it was reported that 'old Colonel Duckenfield undertook for a regiment of true old stagers' (*Kenyon MSS*, 223). He died in September 1689 and was buried on 21 September at Denton Chapel, the preferred place of local nonconformists.   J. J. MASON

Sources M. Nevell, *The people who made Tameside* (1994) · M. Nevell, *Tameside, 1066–1700* (1991) · J. S. Morrill, *Cheshire 1630–1660: county government and society during the English revolution* (1974) · R. N. Dore, *The civil wars in Cheshire: a history of Cheshire*, 8 (1966) · *The letter books of Sir William Brereton*, ed. R. N. Dore, 2 vols., Lancashire and Cheshire RS, 123, 128 (1984–90) · C. H. Firth and G. Davies, *The regimental history of Cromwell's army*, 2 vols. (1940) · A. Woolrych, *Commonwealth to protectorate* (1982) · J. P. Earwaker, *East Cheshire: past and present, or, A history of the hundred of Macclesfield*, 2 (1880) · G. F. Nuttall, *Visible saints: the Congregational way, 1640–1660* (1957) · A. M. Dodd, *Studies in Stuart Wales* (1971) · Thurloe, *State papers*, vols. 3–4 · *DNB* · *CSP dom., 1644–69* · James, seventh earl of Derby, *The Stanley papers, pt 3*, ed. F. R. Raines, 3 vols., Chetham Society, 66–7, 70 (1867) · I. Gentles, 'The debentures market and military purchases of crown land, 1649–1660', PhD diss., U. Lond., 1969 · *The life of Adam Martindale*, ed. R. Parkinson, Chetham Society, 4 (1845) · T. Edwards, *Gangraena, pt 3* (1646) · *The manuscripts of Lord Kenyon*, HMC, 35 (1894) · Coll. Arms, C 83.31 · *Visitation of Cheshire, 1663*
Archives PRO, accounts, SP 28/128
Likenesses engraving, repro. in Nevell, *People who made Tameside*, 23
Wealth at death held manors of Dukinfield and Brinnington and miscellaneous family properties in Lancashire and Cheshire · rated at £13 in early to mid-seventeenth century subsidies; twenty-second in the list of county wealth holders; lost almost £20,000 in crown land at the Restoration: M. Wanklyn, 'Landed Society and allegiance in Cheshire and Shropshire in the first civil wars', PhD diss., Manchester University, 1976, p. 375

Duckett, George (1684–1732), author, of Hartham, Wiltshire, and Dewlish, Dorset, was born on 19 February 1684, the second son and heir of Lionel Duckett MP (1651–1693) and Martha, daughter of Samuel Ashe of Langley Burrell, Wiltshire. He matriculated at Trinity College, Oxford, on 29 November 1700, and entered the Middle Temple on 14 January 1703. He was elected member for the family borough of Calne, Wiltshire, on 11 May 1705, and was again returned in 1708 and 1722, and supported the whig administration. He acted as one of the commissioners of excise between 1722 and 1732. He married on 23 March 1711 Grace (d. 1755), the only daughter and heiress of Thomas and Grace Skinner of Dewlish. They had nine children (six sons and three daughters), one of whom died young. All six sons died childless. Duckett was on friendly terms with

Addison and Edmund Smith, both of whom were frequent visitors to Hartham, where Smith died in July 1710.

In 1715, in conjunction with Sir Thomas Burnet (1694–1753), Duckett published *Homerides, or, A letter to Mr. Pope, occasion'd by his intended translation of Homer; by Sir Iliad Doggrel*, and in 1716 the same authors produced *Homerides, or, Homer's First Book Moderniz'd*. In 1715 also Curll published *An Epilogue to a Puppet Show at Bath Concerning the same Iliad*, by Duckett alone. According to Curll, several things published under Burnet's name were in reality by Duckett.

In 1717 there appeared anonymously *A Summary of All the Religious Houses in England and Wales*, which contained titles and valuations at the time of their dissolution, and an approximate estimate of their value, if existing, in 1717. James West, in a letter dated 18 January 1730, says: 'George Duckett, the author of the "Summary Account of the Religious Houses", is now a commissioner of excise' (quoted in Duckett, 245). Burnet was at the time considered co-author of this interesting tract. Burnet and Duckett promoted two weekly papers, *The Grumbler* and *Pasquin* respectively. The first number of the former was dated 14 February 1715 (1714 OS). Nichols and Drake, through a careless reading of the notes to *The Dunciad*, ascribe *The Grumbler* to Duckett alone. Burnet is bracketed with him in book three of *The Dunciad*. *Pope Alexander's Supremacy and Infallibility Examin'd*, in which Duckett co-operated with John Dennis, appeared in 1729. Duckett was the patron of another of Pope's Dunces, John Oldmixon.

About twenty years after the death of Edmund Smith, Duckett informed Oldmixon that Clarendon's *History* was before publication corrupted by Aldrich, Smalridge, and Atterbury, and that Smith before he died confessed to having helped them, and pointed out some spurious passages. A bitter controversy resulted; Duckett's charge entirely broke down, and it is now unknown who was primarily responsible. Duckett, who is sometimes alluded to as Colonel (the title of his brother William), died on 6 October 1732, his wife surviving until 1755.

WILLIAM ROBERTS, rev. FREYA JOHNSTON

Sources G. F. Duckett, *Duchetiana, or, Historical and genealogical memoirs of the family of Duket* (1874) • Nichols, *Lit. anecdotes*, vols. 4, 8 • A. Pope, *The Dunciad*, ed. J. Sutherland (1943), vol. 5 of *The Twickenham edition of the poems of Alexander Pope*, ed. J. Butt (1939–69) • S. Johnson, *Lives of the English poets*, ed. G. B. Hill, [new edn], 3 vols. (1905) • [E. Curll], *The Curliad* (privately printed, Edinburgh, 1729) • J. Oldmixon, *Remarks upon a scandalous book lately publish'd, called the history of the Royal House of Stuart* (1731) • *The critical and miscellaneous prose works of John Dryden*, ed. E. Malone, 3 vols. (1800), vol. 1 • R. Blackmore, *A compleat key to the Dunciad* (1728) • HoP, *Commons, 1715–54* • Foster, *Alum. Oxon.*

Duckett [*formerly* Jackson], **Sir George**, **first baronet** (1725–1822), naval administrator and judge, was born on 24 October 1725, probably in Yorkshire, the third but oldest surviving son of George Jackson (1687/8–1758) of Hill House, Richmond, Yorkshire, and Ellerton Abbey, Yorkshire, and Hannah, daughter of William Ward of Guisborough, Yorkshire. Joshua *Ward (1684/5–1761) was his uncle. George entered the Navy Office as clerk to the clerk of the acts on 24 June 1743. On 24 September 1745 at St Benet Paul's Wharf, London, he married his cousin Mary,

daughter of William Ward of Guisborough, and his wife, Frances, daughter of Sir Francis Vincent, fifth baronet. She died in 1754, leaving three surviving daughters. Jackson became chief clerk to the clerk of the acts on 22 February 1755 and from 11 May 1758 to 11 November 1766 he was assistant clerk of the acts. On the recommendation of the new premier, William Pitt, earl of Chatham, he was then transferred to the admiralty as second secretary to the board and first clerk of the marine department by the first lord, Sir Charles Saunders. On 19 February 1768 he was also made judge advocate of the fleet, a position he held until his death. Jackson was a zealous patron of the career of James Cook whose father had been a dependant of the family and who had worked as stable-boy with Jackson's sister at Ayton, Yorkshire. In gratitude Cook named Point Jackson in New Zealand and Port Jackson, New South Wales, in his honour. On 9 September 1775 at St Margaret's, Westminster, he married his second wife, Grace (d. 1798), daughter and heir of a London merchant, Gwyn Goldstone of Goldstone, Shropshire, and his wife, Grace Duckett, and widow of Robert Neale of Shaw House, Melksham, Wiltshire. They had a son, George (1777–1856), subsequently MP and banker (the failure of whose bank in 1832 destroyed the Duckett fortunes) and the father of Sir George Floyd *Duckett, who claimed that Duckett had been the political writer Junius.

Jackson was a faithful public servant of successive ministries, but subsequently suffered for his friendship with Lord North's first lord of the admiralty, John Montagu, fourth earl of Sandwich, by becoming involved in the aftermath of the controversial court martial of Admiral Augustus Keppel, an opposition supporter, on whose acquittal in 1779 Jackson as judge advocate accepted the poisoned chalice of prosecuting Keppel's accuser, Sir Hugh Palliser, a ministerialist admiral. When Palliser too was acquitted, Keppel and the opposition refused to believe that the prosecution had not been deliberately mishandled, and Jackson had to defend himself vigorously in a two-hour examination by the House of Lords. When Keppel replaced Sandwich at the admiralty on the fall of North's ministry, he took his revenge by dismissing Jackson from his post as second secretary on 12 June 1782—the first political dismissal of a senior admiralty official since 1690—with a pension of £400 p.a. The episode was subject of debate in the Commons on 12 May 1783 when John Buller senior deplored the dismissal of 'probably the most useful man at the board' adding that 'a more able and honest man never served the public' (Debrett, 4).

Instead of returning to the admiralty on Keppel's departure from office—reportedly he twice turned down the offer of secretary to the admiralty—Jackson opted for a political life, being recorded by William Pitt the younger's political manager, John Robinson, as willing to pay £1500 or perhaps more for a seat at the 1784 election. He stood as government candidate at Penrhyn but was defeated, being however returned for Weymouth and Melcombe Regis on 27 March 1786 in place of its pro-government patron. In December 1788 he vacated the seat to contest the expensive borough of Colchester with government support, being returned but unseated on petition, though he regained the seat at the 1790 election and held it until the next election in 1796.

On 28 July 1791 Jackson was created a baronet. In 1797 he inherited the Hartham estate of his second wife's uncle, Thomas Duckett, at Corsham, Wiltshire, taking the name Duckett by royal licence, in accordance with his benefactor's will, on 3 February 1797. He had been described as 'of Hartham House' on being created a baronet, and so presumably had lived on the Duckett estate for several years. He also had a residence at Roydon, near Bishop's Stortford, Hertfordshire, where from 1760 to 1769 he had applied himself to making part of the River Stort navigable from the River Lea to Bishop's Stortford, a step that reportedly produced an income of £4000 a year until the coming of the railway.

Duckett died at his London home in Upper Grosvenor Street on 15 December 1822 at the age of ninety-seven, and was buried at Bishop's Stortford, Hertfordshire. His obituary in the *Gentleman's Magazine* declared that 'Those who knew Sir George Duckett can testify to his strong mind, his gentlemanly manners, and his loyal and religious feelings' (*GM*, 644).   MICHAEL DUFFY

Sources M. M. Drummond, 'Jackson, George', HoP, *Commons, 1754–90* · J. A. Cannon, 'Colchester', 'Weymouth and Melcombe Regis', HoP, *Commons, 1754–90*, 1.276–8, 272–3 · *GM*, 1st ser., 92/2 (1822), 644–5 · *DNB* · R. G. Thorne, 'Jackson, Sir George', HoP, *Commons, 1790–1820* · R. G. Thorne, 'Colchester', HoP, *Commons, 1790–1820*, 2.158–60 · J. C. Sainty, *Office holders in modern Britain*, 4: *Admiralty officials, 1660–1870* (1975) · D. Syrett, *The Royal Navy in European waters during the American Revolutionary War*, Columbia SC (1998) · N. A. M. Rodger, *The insatiable earl: a life of John Montagu, fourth earl of Sandwich* (1993) · J. Debrett, ed., *The Parliamentary Register*, 2nd ser., 10 · Cobbett, *Parl. hist.*, vol. 20 · GEC, *Baronetage*, 5.273

Archives BL, corresp., Add. MSS 9343–9344 · NMM, papers | Birm. CA, letters to Matthew Boulton · NMM, corresp. with Lord Sandwich · PRO, letters to Admiral Rodney, PRO 30/20

Likenesses Copley, miniature; formerly in possession of Duckett family · G. Dance, portrait; formerly in possession of Duckett family

Duckett, Sir George Floyd, third baronet (1811–1902), antiquary and lexicographer, born at 15 Spring Gardens, Westminster, London, on 27 March 1811, was the eldest child of Sir George Duckett, second baronet (1777–1856), MP for Lymington (1807–12), and his first wife, Isabella (1781–1844), the daughter of Stainbank Floyd of Barnard Castle, co. Durham. His grandfather Sir George Jackson, first baronet (1725–1822), assumed in 1797 the surname of Duckett, having married the heiress of the Duckett family [see Duckett, Sir George]. After attending private schools at Putney and Wimbledon Common, Duckett was educated at Harrow School from 1820 to 1823. He was then placed with a private tutor in Bedfordshire, and in 1827 spent a year in Germany, at Gotha and Dresden, where he acquired a thorough knowledge of the language. He matriculated on 13 December 1828 as a gentleman commoner of Christ Church, Oxford, but left Oxford without a degree, having devoted himself chiefly to hunting.

After Oxford, Duckett joined the West Essex yeomanry, and on 4 May 1832 was commissioned a sub-lieutenant in the 2nd regiment of Life Guards. By the time he came of age in 1832, his father, whose means had been large, had been ruined by wild speculations. Faced by beggary, Duckett practised thrift by moving through a succession of decreasingly costly regiments. On 21 June 1845 he married Isabella (*d*. 31 Dec 1901), the daughter of Lieutenant-General Sir Lionel Smith, first baronet; they had no children.

During this period Duckett concentrated on the compilation of a *Technological Military Dictionary* in German, English, and French. To make the work accurate he obtained leave to visit the arsenals of Woolwich, Paris, Brussels, and Berlin, and retired on half pay to complete his task. The work was published in 1848, although its merits were recognized mainly abroad. He received gold medals from the emperor of Austria in 1850, Frederick William IV of Prussia, and Napoleon III. On resuming his commission on full pay he was placed at the bottom of the captains' list of the reserve battalion of the 69th regiment, and thirty-two years later, in 1890, he was awarded £200.

When his father died, on 15 June 1856, Duckett became third baronet. He abandoned his interest in military matters, and thenceforth devoted himself to historical and genealogical studies, to which he brought immense industry but little judgement or scholarship. He published accounts of the Duckett ancestry which, although lengthy, are not of great genealogical value. One reviewer commented: 'It will be found a tough morsel by the most robust genealogical digestion' (Allibone, *Dict.*). In pursuing this research Duckett delved into the history of the first Cluniac monastery in England, at Lewes in 1077, using the Bibliothèque Nationale, Paris, further fruits of which were the privately printed *Record Evidences among the Archives of the Ancient Abbey of Cluni from 1077 to 1534* (1886) and a monumental compilation of charters and records from the same dates, *Monasticon Cluniacense Anglicanum* (2 vols., 1888). There followed *Visitations of English Cluniac Foundations, 1262–1279* (1890) and *Visitations and Chapters-General of the Order of Cluni* (1893). These works have retained their value for the primary source material they make available. For the *Monasticon Cluniacense* Duckett received in 1888 the decoration of an officer of public instruction in France. Besides the works already mentioned, and numerous contributions to local archaeological societies, Duckett published several other works of variable scholarship and interest. He continued his literary pursuits until 1895, when he published his *Anecdotal Reminiscences of an Octo-Nonogenarian*. Blindness then put an end to his literary activities. He was elected FSA on 11 February 1869. He died at Cleeve House, Cleeve, Somerset, on 13 May 1902, whereupon the baronetcy became extinct. He was buried in the cemetery at Wells.

CHARLES WELCH, rev. MICHAEL ERBEN

Sources Burke, *Peerage* (1902) · *The Times* (6 May 1902) · *The Standard* (14 May 1902) · *The Athenaeum* (31 Aug 1895), 285–6 · *BL cat.* · private information (1912) · Allibone, *Dict.* · *Men of the time* (1875) · *Men of the time* (1887) · *Men and women of the time* (1899)

Archives Bodl. Oxf., corresp. with Sir Thomas Phillipps

Wealth at death £1518 10s. 5d.: probate, 3 June 1902, CGPLA Eng. & Wales

Duckett, James (*d*. 1601), bookseller, was a younger son of Duckett of Gilthwaiterigg, in the parish of Skelsmergh, Westmorland, and was brought up as a protestant. He had, however, for godfather James Leybourne of Skelsmergh, who was executed at Lancaster on 22 March 1583 for denial of the queen's supremacy.

Duckett was apprenticed to a bookseller in London: there is no record of his being bound to a member of the Stationers' Company, which means he was bound during the gap in the company records (1571–6), or was apprenticed to a non-stationer, or was not formally bound. During his apprenticeship he converted to Roman Catholicism, and was imprisoned for not attending church. He bought out the remainder of his time, set up as a bookseller, was received into the Roman Catholic church, and about 1589 married a widow. Nine out of the next twelve years of his life were passed in prison. His last arrest was caused by Peter Bullock, a bookbinder (who may have been the Bullock bound to William Norton for 1562–9, but was more probably the namesake bound to Gabriel Cawood for 1591–8), who gave information that Duckett had in stock a number of copies of Southwell's *An Humble Supplication to her Maiestie* (1600). These were not found, but a quantity of other Roman Catholic books were seized on the premises. Duckett was imprisoned in Newgate on 4 March 1601, and brought to trial during the following sessions, with Bullock testifying against him. The jury initially pronounced Duckett not guilty, but the judge urged them to reconsider. Sentence of death was then pronounced against him and three priests, and he was hanged at Tyburn with Bullock on 19 April 1601. His wife survived him.

Duckett's son was prior of the English Carthusians at Nieuwpoort in Flanders. His manuscript account of his father's life was later sent to Challoner, who quoted extensively from it in his account of Duckett.

H. R. TEDDER, *rev.* I. GADD

Sources Gillow, *Lit. biog. hist.*, 2.133–5 • R. Challoner, *Memoirs of missionary priests*, another edn, 2 vols. (1803), vol. 1, pp. 216–19 • H. R. Plomer, 'Bishop Bancroft and a Catholic press', *The Library*, new ser., 8 (1907), 164–76

Duckett, John (*bap.* 1614, *d.* 1644), Roman Catholic priest, was descended from an ancient family settled at Skelsmergh, Westmorland, and was born at Underwinder, in the parish of Sedbergh, Yorkshire. He was baptized on 24 February 1614, the third son of James Duckett, a minor landowner, and his wife, Frances Girlington. His parents were protestant but he converted to Rome and was educated from 1 March 1633 in the English College, Douai, where he was ordained priest in September 1639. He continued his studies for a further three years in the college of Arras at Paris, and at Christmas 1643 was sent on the English mission, working in co. Durham. On 2 July 1644 he was captured by soldiers of the parliamentary army near Lanchester (a roadside cross at the top of Redgate Bank was erected to mark the place) and was taken for examination to Sunderland, where, to save his companions, he admitted his priesthood. In company with Ralph Corbie, a Jesuit captured at Hamsterley, co. Durham, on 18 July, he

was sent to Newgate prison, London. They were tried on 4 September and having confessed to being priests they were condemned to death for treason. Preparatory to execution they were permitted, exceptionally, to have their heads tonsured and to wear clerical dress, Duckett in the cassock of a secular priest and Corbie in his Jesuit habit. On 7 September they were drawn on a hurdle from Newgate to Tyburn, where they suffered death by being hanged, drawn, and quartered.

An account of Duckett's capture and imprisonment entitled 'A relation concerning Mr. Duckett', by John Horsley, Corbie's cousin and a fellow prisoner in Newgate, was printed by Henry Foley in his *Records of the English Province* (1877–1884) from a manuscript preserved at Stonyhurst College. Duckett was beatified as a martyr in 1929.

THOMPSON COOPER, *rev.* ROBIN M. GARD

Sources H. Foley, ed., *Records of the English province of the Society of Jesus*, 3 (1878), 73–90 • R. Challoner, *Memoirs of missionary priests*, ed. J. H. Pollen, rev. edn (1924), 457–61 • T. F. Knox and others, eds., *The first and second diaries of the English College, Douay* (1878), 38, 40, 287, 421 • E. H. Burton and T. L. Williams, eds., *The Douay College diaries, third, fourth and fifth, 1598–1654*, 1, Catholic RS, 10 (1911), 311 • *Westmonasterien. beatificationis seu declarationis martyrii venerabilium servorum Dei Georgii Haydock et sociorum … in Anglia interfectorum Positio super martyrio et causa martyrii* (1928), 1.177, 334–5; 2.187–8, 303–6 • Gillow, *Lit. biog. hist.*, 2.135–7 • G. Anstruther, *The seminary priests*, 2 (1975), 90 • W. J. Nicholson, 'Blessed John Duckett (1613–1644), priest and martyr', *Northern Catholic History*, 17 (1983), 10–12 • D. A. Bellenger, ed., *English and Welsh priests, 1558–1800* (1984) • J. A. Myerscough, *The martyrs of Durham and the north-east* (1956), 142–9 • parish register, Sedbergh, Cumbria AS, Kendal, 24 Feb 1614 [baptism] • Stonyhurst College Archives, ref. Anglia, 5, n. 18

Archives Stonyhurst College, Lancashire, Anglia, vol. 5, n. 18

Likenesses portrait, *c*.1640–1649, church of Sts Peter and Paul, Newport, Shropshire

Duckett, Sir Lionel (*d.* 1587), merchant and local politician, was the son of William Duckett of Flintham, Nottinghamshire, and his wife, Jane Redman, of Harwood Castle, Yorkshire. His first wife was Mary, the daughter of Hugh Leighton, of Leighton, Shropshire, with whom he had one son, George, who died young, and his second was Jane, the daughter of Humphrey Packington and the wealthy widow of Humphrey Baskerfeld (or Baskerville) of London, who had four daughters from her first marriage and with whom he had a son, Thomas.

In 1537, after his apprenticeship to John Colet in London, Duckett gained the freedom of the Mercers' Company. Thereafter he developed extensive commercial and business interests and became one of the most successful merchants in the city of London. He was a prominent member of the Company of Merchant Adventurers, trading extensively in cloth at Antwerp and other markets in northern Europe and importing wine in exchange. In 1557 he secured a patent for the import of felts and hats from Spain and Portugal in partnership with Henry Viner. During his career he was a powerful supporter of new commercial initiatives. He was a founder member of the Russia Company in 1555, and served as an assistant in 1569 and a governor in 1575 and 1577. He was involved in promoting trading ventures to Guinea in 1558 and 1562. He was also a backer of John Hawkins's slaving voyages of

1562 and 1567. He was a member of the Spanish Company in 1577, and a supporter of Martin Frobisher's attempts to find a north-west passage from 1577 to 1579. Although Frobisher's voyages failed, Duckett later joined Adrian Gilbert's abortive fellowship for the discovery of the passage. In 1577 he was a leading promoter of the Russia Company's attempts to establish a whale fishery in the Arctic, with the help of certain Biscayan mariners skilled in whaling.

Duckett acquired other business interests in the city, which brought him into close contact with the court. With a small group of leading merchant adventurers, which included his close business associate Sir Thomas Gresham, he advanced money to the crown, including a loan of £30,000 to Elizabeth in 1560 at 10 per cent interest. He loaned £160 to the crown in 1562 to pay for an English garrison in Normandy, and other royal loans were arranged in 1569 and 1570. In 1560 or 1561 he was involved in a loan of £12,000 to the king of Sweden, though it remained unpaid in 1582. He was associated with Gresham in building the Royal Exchange from 1565 to 1568, and with Gresham he served as a commissioner for clearing the accounts for Frobisher's north-west ventures. In 1567 he became heavily involved in the attempt to mine and smelt copper at Keswick, using the expertise of German miners. He was a shareholder in the Company of Mines Royal, and was appointed governor of the company in May 1568. The venture brought Duckett into close contact with Sir William Cecil, who was an investor in the company. In 1568 he became involved with Geoffrey Duckett, possibly a kinsman, in the manufacture of light cloth at Coventry.

Commercial success enabled Duckett to become a leading figure in the city of London. He was master of the Mercers' Company in 1567, 1572, 1578, and 1584. He served as an auditor for the city from 1559 to 1561 and again from 1585 to 1586. In 1564–5 he served as one of the city's sheriffs. He was elected alderman of Aldersgate ward in 1564, but moved to Bassishaw during 1567, and served there in this capacity until 1587. He was mayor of London in 1572–3 during a difficult period of dearth and discontent. To maintain good order in London he advised that the issue of writs of habeas corpus be restricted for cases brought by the city authorities against disturbers of the peace. As mayor he attempted also to curb excessive feasting and drinking in the city, especially by the meaner sort, though at the risk of encouraging personal criticism and complaint. He was knighted on 2 February 1573. That same year he was elected president of St Thomas's Hospital; and he served as president of Bethlem and Bridewell hospitals from 1569 to 1573 and from 1580 to 1586. In 1576 he was appointed to a commission investigating criminal activity throughout the realm.

Although several of his business ventures were unprofitable, Duckett became one of the wealthiest merchants in London during his lifetime. He also acquired wide-ranging landed interests. He began purchasing former monastic and chantry lands in Surrey, Staffordshire, and Derbyshire in 1553, additional lands in Somerset and Devon were acquired in 1556 and 1557, and by the time of his death he owned other property in Gloucestershire, Wiltshire, Berkshire, and Kent. His wealth was so great that he reputedly gave 8000 marks to each of his four stepdaughters, and would have given them more had it not appeared unbecoming. He died in August 1587 in London. By the terms of his will, drawn up in 1585 but later modified, he left £200 to the Mercers' Company to provide loans for its younger members, £100 to Christ's Hospital, and various smaller bequests to the poor. The bulk of his personal estate was left to his wife and only son, Thomas, though the latter's share was reduced because of his marriage to Margaret Nelson without his father's approval.

JOHN C. APPLEBY

Sources CSP dom., 1547–80; rev. edn, 1547–53; addenda, 1566–79 · CPR, 1554–80 · A. B. Beaven, ed., The aldermen of the City of London, temp. Henry III–[1912], 2 vols. (1908–13) · G. F. Duckett, Duchetiana, or, Historical and genealogical memoirs of the family of Duket (1874) · BL, Lansdowne MS 14, fol. 92 · BL, Lansdowne MS 16, fols. 160–61, 162–3 · BL, Lansdowne MS 18, fols. 107–9 · Analytical index, to the series of records known as Remembrancia, preserved among the archives of the City of London, Corporation of London, ed. [W. H. Overall and H. C. Overall] (1878) · R. Hakluyt, The principall navigations, voiages and discoveries of the English nation (1589) · CSP for., 1553–8 · CSP for., 1564–5 · CSP for., 1572–4 · CSP for., 1583–4 · APC, 1558–75, 1577–8, 1586–7 · T. S. Willan, The Muscovy merchants of 1555 (1953) · M. B. Donald, Elizabethan copper: the history of the Company of Mines Royal, 1568–1605 (1955) · G. D. Ramsay, ed., John Isham, mercer and merchant adventurer: two account books of a London merchant in the reign of Elizabeth I, Northamptonshire RS, 21 (1962) · G. D. Ramsay, The City of London in international politics at the accession of Elizabeth Tudor (1975) · PRO, E134/24 Eliz./Hil. 7 · PRO, E134/31 and 32 Eliz./Mich. 30
Archives BL, Lansdowne MSS · PRO, exchequer, port books · PRO, state papers | CLRO, City records, court of aldermen proceedings · CLRO, Mercers' Company records · Hatfield House, Hertfordshire, Cecil MSS
Likenesses reputed H. Holbein, portrait, Mercers' Company, London
Wealth at death gave 8000 marks to each of his four stepdaughters; £200 to Mercers' Company; £100 to Christ's Hospital; bulk of estate to wife and son: will

Duckett, William (1768–1841), Irish nationalist, born at Killarney, was sent to the Irish College at Paris, and gained a scholarship at Sainte-Barbe, then conducted by the Abbé Badnel. In November 1792 he was a signatory to an address to the National Convention from the English-speaking residents of Paris, congratulating the French on their recent military successes. In 1793 Duckett returned to Ireland to disseminate propaganda in favour of the French Revolution. Subsequently, he divided his time between England and Ireland, becoming involved with radical groups in both countries.

Duckett contributed to the revolutionary Northern Star, under the signature of Junius Redivivus, and also to the Morning Chronicle. These letters, according to his own account, made it prudent for him to quit Ireland, and in 1796 he was in Paris. Wolfe Tone, who was also in Paris, regarded him as a spy, and complained that he interfered with his own plans for interesting the French in Ireland, and that by addressing him in English, he betrayed his incognito. When, moreover, Tone arrived with Hoche at Brest, Duckett was there, intending to accompany them, but was not allowed to embark. In 1798 he was reported to Castlereagh as having been sent to Hamburg with money destined for a mutiny in the British fleet and for burning the dockyards. This, coupled with his outlawry by the Irish parliament, ought to have vouched for his sincerity, but he was suspected of betraying Tandy and Blackwell to the English resident at Hamburg.

Duckett married a Danish lady attached to the Augustenburg family, returned to Paris about 1803, and became a professor at the resuscitated Collège de Sainte-Barbe. He seems to have shunned, or been shunned by, Irish exiles in Paris, yet Durozoir, one of his pupils, testified to his anti-English feeling and to his admiration of the French Revolution. In 1819, no longer apparently connected with Sainte-Barbe, he conducted English literature classes, and also girls' classes on the Lancastrian system. Between 1816 and 1821 he published a number of political odes. In 1828 he issued a *Nouvelle grammaire anglaise*. He died in 1841, before 10 April, in Paris after a long illness, quoting Horace on his deathbed, and receiving the last rites. He left two sons, Alexander, a physician, and William (1803–1873), a French journalist, translator of German works, and editor or compiler of the *Dictionnaire de la conversation*, completed in 1843. This William had a son, William Alexander (1831–1863), who contributed to the new edition of the *Dictionnaire* and published an illustrated work on French monuments; he also had a daughter, Mathilde (1842–1884?), who studied under Rosa Bonheur, exhibited at the Paris salon (1861–8), and taught drawing in Paris.   J. G. ALGER, *rev.* GERARD MCCOY

Sources *Moniteur Universel* (10 April 1841), 935–6 · R. R. Madden, *The United Irishmen: their lives and times*, 3rd ser., 3 vols. (1846) · W. T. W. Tone, *Life of Theobald Wolfe Tone*, 2 vols. (1826) · *Memoirs and correspondence of Viscount Castlereagh, second marquess of Londonderry*, ed. C. Vane, marquess of Londonderry, 12 vols. (1848–53), vols. 1–8 · M. Elliott, *Partners in revolution: the United Irishmen and France* (1982) · R. Hayes, *Biographical dictionary of Irishmen in France* (1949)
Archives Archives Nationales, Paris | Ministère des Affaires etrangères, Paris, corresp. politique: angleterre, Cote 592 · NL Ire., Salvandy MSS

Duckham, Sir Arthur McDougall (1879–1932), gas engineer, was born on 8 July 1879 at Blackheath, London, the second of the three sons of Frederick Elliot Duckham (1841–1918), a noted civil engineer, and his wife, Maud Mary, *née* McDougall. All the sons achieved prominence in their chosen careers: the eldest, William Duckham, ran a harbour works company, and Alexander Duckham, the youngest, established the Duckham oil company. Arthur, known to family and close friends as Bob, was educated at Blackheath proprietary school; he left aged seventeen to become an articled pupil in the South Metropolitan Gas Company under the chief engineer, Frank Livesey, younger brother of the chairman, Sir George Livesey.

During his training Duckham studied carbonization, furnace work, and chemical engineering, supplementing his practical work with evening study in engineering at King's College, London. At the age of twenty he was appointed assistant superintendent of the Old Kent Road works of South Metropolitan. Two years later he left to become assistant engineer of the Bournemouth Gas and Water Company under Harold Woodall, who was to become a lifelong friend. With Woodall's active encouragement, Duckham began experimenting with methods of changing the carbonization process from a cyclical to a continuous one. He concentrated on the development of vertical retorts (in place of the traditional horizontal retorts), where coal fell by gravity and, after gasification, was extracted from the bottom as coke. He and Woodall entered into partnership in 1903 and set up Woodall-Duckham Ltd in 1906 to exploit Duckham's process. At first the company provided only a design service and relied on specialist suppliers and contractors to meet its production specifications, but by the early 1920s it was also undertaking installations on its own account. As an indication of the economic advantages of the process, within twenty years approximately half of all the coal used in British gasworks was carbonized in continuous vertical retorts.

The success of the Woodall–Duckham company owed at least as much to Duckham's character and his ability as a salesman as to his technical expertise. He was a dominating figure, 6 feet tall and weighing 18 stone, but with the knack of making and keeping friends and of inspiring others, even at the gasworks, by both his example and his ideas. In the early years of the company there were problems of cash flow, but a number of important firms which supplied the gas industry with steelwork, refractories, and other construction parts took shares in the company to ensure its survival. As the company prospered, the minority holdings were later bought out.

After war broke out in 1914, it became essential to supply certain by-products of carbonization, notably toluene and phenol, for the manufacture of explosives. It was therefore natural that Duckham should join the munitions invention department, becoming deputy controller of munitions supply late in 1915. He adapted very well to life in Whitehall, and held a number of executive and administrative appointments during the war: he was chairman of the advisory committee to the minister of munitions, a member of the Munitions Council, director-general for aircraft production, and in 1919 a member of the Air Council. His services were recognized in 1917 when he was made a KCB.

After the war, business at Woodall–Duckham again gathered momentum, expanding to produce plant not only for gasworks but also for other chemical processes. Duckham's career now extended into much wider spheres. Having joined the Institution of Civil Engineers in 1918 he came to believe that chemical engineers needed a professional body of their own; he chaired a committee formed in 1922 to create what became the Institution of Chemical Engineers and was elected its founder president. He was also president of the Society of British Gas Industries for two years. In 1919 he was appointed to the coal industry commission chaired by Mr Justice Sankey to examine ways to make the industry more economically efficient. Unwilling to support full nationalization, he produced a minority report commending state ownership of mineral rights, the efficient exploitation of coal reserves, minimum wages for miners, and a role for miners in the direction of the industry. As a leading businessman, Duckham was in great demand as a speaker on the problems of both sides of industry.

At the request of the Australian prime minister, in 1928 Duckham was appointed by the British government to lead a group of prominent businessmen on an economic mission to Australia to advise on trade opportunities. The subsequent report described the vast resources in Australia, strongly advocated a firm trade partnership between the two countries (later to be extended to all the Commonwealth), and recommended higher levels of emigration to Australia. Following this mission Duckham was created a GBE in 1929. Further government work followed and Duckham's status as a leading industrial statesman was endorsed by his election as deputy president and president-elect of the Federation of British Industries (FBI). He was also a member of the Légion d'honneur.

In 1903 Arthur Duckham married Maud, eldest daughter of the painter A. D. Peppercorn; they had three children. Through his wife's interest he became an enthusiast for the arts. He was also something of a gourmet, and he enjoyed golf, dancing, tennis, and squash. Before he could take office as president of the FBI he collapsed at his home, High Warren, Ashtead, Surrey, after his regular game of squash, and died on 14 February 1932, aged fifty-two. He was buried at St Giles, Ashtead, and there was a memorial service for him at St Martin-in-the-Fields, London, on 17 February. His wife survived him.

FRANCIS GOODALL

Sources D. Teasdale, 'Duckham, Sir Arthur McDougall', *DBB* • *The Times* (15 Feb 1932) • *Gas World* (20 Feb 1932) • T. I. Williams, *A history of the British gas industry* (1981)
Wealth at death £78,338 0s. 9d.: probate, 27 May 1932, *CGPLA Eng. & Wales*

Duckworth, Sir Dyce, first baronet (1840–1928), physician, the fourth and youngest son of Robinson Duckworth (1794–1875), a Liverpool merchant, and his wife, Elizabeth Forbes (d. 1868), daughter of William Nicol, a naval surgeon, of Stonehaven, Kincardineshire, was born in Liverpool on 24 November 1840. He was educated at the Royal Institution School, Liverpool, and at the University of Edinburgh, where he graduated MB (1862) and MD (1863) and was president of the Royal Medical Society. He was awarded a gold medal for his thesis on the anatomy of the suprarenal capsules.

After graduation Duckworth held the post of resident physician (house physician) at the Royal Infirmary, Edinburgh, but he left a year later, in 1864, in order to enter the naval medical service, in which his maternal grandfather had served as an assistant surgeon. Duckworth left the service in 1865. The death in December 1864 of Dr Henry Jeaffreson had caused a vacancy for a medical tutor at St Bartholomew's Hospital, London, and Duckworth was appointed to the post. He nevertheless retained a special affection for the navy throughout his life.

Duckworth followed the career of a teacher of medicine and consulting physician in London from 1865 onwards. He held a series of posts at St Bartholomew's Hospital:

assistant physician (1869), head of the skin department (1870–75), and ultimately full physician to the hospital (1883–1905) and joint lecturer on medicine (1890–1901). On his retirement he became consulting physician to, and governor of, the hospital.

The Royal College of Physicians also claimed Duckworth's services. He was elected member in 1865 and fellow in 1870, and served in turn as councillor, examiner, censor, and senior censor. He was treasurer to the college for almost forty years, and on his retirement from that office in 1923 was elected emeritus treasurer. He delivered the Lumleian lectures in 1896, entitled *The Sequels of Diseases*, and the Harveian oration in 1898, when he took as his subject 'The influence of character and right judgement in medicine'.

Always interested in the nursing profession, Duckworth was for some years vice-president of the Royal British Nurses' Association. He was physician to the prince of Wales from 1890 to 1901. He was a knight of justice and almoner of the order of St John of Jerusalem in England, and he was president of the Clinical Society (1891–3). Duckworth acted as examiner in medicine at the universities of Edinburgh, Durham, and Manchester, for the Royal Naval Medical Service, and for the conjoint board.

On his retirement from St Bartholomew's in 1905, Duckworth was appointed physician to the Royal Naval Hospital at Greenwich, and lectured in its school. He was consulting physician to the Italian Hospital, Queen Square, in London, medical referee to the Treasury (1900–11), and a member of the pensions commutation board (1904–10). A volume of his collected papers and addresses appeared in 1915 under the title *Views on some Social Subjects*.

Duckworth received many honours: he was knighted in 1886 and created a baronet in 1909; he was accorded the honorary degrees of LLD of Liverpool and Edinburgh universities and MD of Belfast, of the Royal University of Ireland, and of Cincinnati, USA; he was also honorary FRCP (Ireland) and corresponding member of the Académie de Médecine of Paris.

Duckworth had all the attributes of the courtly physician. He always dressed in frock coat and top hat and had a courteous though somewhat formal manner, with a strong sense of propriety. He liked everything done in order and with due ceremony. He could be impatient with others and had no time for fads, but he had a sense of humour and could laugh at his own expense. Duckworth was 'in politics a Tory, by religious profession an Anglican and good churchman, [and] he did not suffer gladly the trend of modern manners. He disliked the intrusion of women into the medical profession, and maintained stoutly that the proper place for them was at home, or at most as nurses' (*BMJ*, 161). He was a cultured man, widely travelled, and a linguist. He had a good knowledge of French and great sympathy with the ideas of French medicine, especially as regards diathesis, in which his early teacher, Thomas Laycock, had first awakened his interest.

Duckworth was above all an exponent of the art of

medicine, and feared that this art might be lost in what he regarded as the futile effort to make medicine into an exact science. His pupils learned more from example than from precept, and to watch his handling of a case of acute illness, his resource in emergencies, his foresight of possible accidents, and his meticulous care of all details of medical treatment and nursing was a valuable training in the art of medicine. He made many minor contributions to medical literature but his chief work was his *Treatise on Gout* (1889), which was popular at the time and was translated into French and German.

Duckworth was married twice: first, in 1870, to Annie Alicia (*d.* 1889), daughter of Alexander Hopkins, of Limavady, co. Antrim, and widow of John Smith, East India merchant, of Mickleham Hall, Dorking, with whom he had a son and two daughters; and second, in 1890, to Ada Emily, daughter of George Arthur Fuller of Dorking and his wife, Georgiana Craven, with whom he had two sons. The anatomist Wynfrid Laurence Henry Duckworth (1870–1956) was his nephew. Duckworth died in London on 20 January 1928 and was buried on 23 January in Betchworth, Surrey; he was survived by his wife and was succeeded as second baronet by his eldest son, Edward Dyce Duckworth (1875–1945), later a judge of the high court of judicature in Rangoon.

A. E. GARROD, *rev.* PATRICK WALLIS

Sources Munk, *Roll* · *BMJ* (28 Jan 1928), 161–2 · *The Lancet* (28 Jan 1928), 211 · W. S. C. Copeman, *A short history of the gout* (1964) · V. C. Medvei and J. L. Thornton, eds., *The royal hospital of Saint Bartholomew, 1123–1973* (1974) · personal knowledge (1937) · private information (1937) · Burke, *Peerage* · *WWW, 1941–50* [Edward Dyce Duckworth; Dyce Duckworth] · *CGPLA Eng. & Wales* (1928)
Archives RCP Lond., some requirements for modern clinical teaching
Likenesses photograph, repro. in *BMJ*, 161 · wood-engraving (after a photograph by Barraud), NPG; repro. in *ILN* (3 April 1886)
Wealth at death £7711 0s. 6d.: probate, 16 March 1928, *CGPLA Eng. & Wales*

Duckworth, Gerald L'Étang (1870–1937), publisher, was born on 29 October 1870, probably in London, five weeks after the death of his father, Herbert Duckworth (1833–1870). Herbert was a barrister whose family were landed gentry from the county of Somerset. His mother, Julia, *née* Jackson (1846–1895), had aristocratic connections and her aunts included Julia Margaret Cameron, the well-known photographer, and Sarah Prinsep, mother of the painter Valentine Prinsep. Gerald was his mother's favourite, a delicate and petted child who liked to write to her in baby language. His elder brother, George Herbert Duckworth (1868–1934), was at one time private secretary to Austen Chamberlain and was knighted in 1927; he married Lady Margaret Herbert (1870–1958), daughter of the fourth earl of Carnarvon, with whom he had three sons. His sister Stella (1869–1897) died just three months after marrying John Waller Hills (*d.* 1938).

Gerald's mother remarried in 1878. Her new husband, Leslie *Stephen, was to become well known through his editorship of the *Dictionary of National Biography* (1882–91). Together Leslie and Julia had four children, two boys, Thoby (1880–1906) and Adrian (1883–1948), and two girls,

Vanessa *Bell (1879–1961) and Virginia *Woolf (1882–1941). Over the years the family divided their time between 22 Hyde Park Gate in London, and Talland House at St Ives in Cornwall. Gerald did not take kindly to his stepbrothers and stepsisters and was not above telling tales on the Stephen children, mocking them with his sneering, teasing, and treacherous laughter. Virginia Woolf's diaries suggest that both he and his brother sexually molested her over a period of years, starting when she was just six years old (Schulkind).

Duckworth, like his brother and stepfather, was educated at Eton College and then went on to Clare College, Cambridge, but he was not given to hard work, preferring instead the pleasures of the stomach and the delights of London nightlife. Virginia Woolf likened him to 'a pampered overfed pug dog with white hair, hardly a gleam of life, let alone intelligence in his eye' and 'with no opinions, merely a seaweed drift in the prevailing current' (King, 242).

In 1898 Duckworth decided to go into publishing, apparently believing it to be an occupation suitable for a gentleman. Gerald Duckworth & Co. was established at Henrietta Street, Covent Garden, and A. R. Waller, a literary adviser and bookman, left the firm of J. M. Dent to join the company. The first list included Leslie Stephen's Ford lectures, *English Literature and Society in the Eighteenth Century* (1898); a translation of August Strindberg's *Der Fater* (*The Father*, 1899); Henry James's *In the Cage* (1898); and *Jocelyn* (1898) by the unknown John Sinjohn, an early pseudonym of John Galsworthy.

It was at Waller's instigation that Galsworthy's fiction was published by Duckworth, though Gerald, a lifelong friend of the author, did turn down *The Man of Property* (1906)—the first of the novels that were to become *The Forsyte Saga* (1922)—with the words 'Stick to plays, my man, stick to plays'. Duckworth published all of Galsworthy's plays over a period of twenty years from 1909, and in 1929 produced a limited omnibus edition. Much to his horror, Galsworthy was required to sign all 1250 copies. On being told however that he would receive a royalty of 15s. 9d. on each copy, he placed his watch on the table and said: 'It will be interesting to see how long it takes me to earn £984 7s. 6d.' (Beare, 103–7).

Despite Virginia Woolf's antipathy to her stepbrother, it was Duckworth & Co. that published her first two novels. She rewrote *The Voyage Out* several times before submitting it, but Edward Garnett, who had joined the company in 1901 as a reader, was enthusiastic, and the book was published in 1915. Her second book, *Night and Day*, came out in 1919 and Woolf recorded her feelings, saying that

> I thought of my novel destined to be pawed and snored over by him … I don't like the Club man's view of literature … [yet] I can't think of stout smooth Gerald smoking a cigar over my pages without a smile. (King, 243)

On 2 March 1921 Duckworth married Cecil Alice Scott-Chad (*b.* 1891/2), the daughter of Charles Scott-Chad, a barrister. Virginia Woolf commented that he would either marry 'an older woman for money or a younger, sexually inexperienced woman for the same purpose' (King, 290).

The marriage proved childless. Duckworth's publishing venture, however, prospered. Edward Garnett, considered by many to be the greatest reader of his time, stayed for nearly twenty years. He brought a number of authors to the firm including W. H. Hudson, Charles M. Doughty, and D. H. Lawrence. He initiated the Popular Library of Art series (1902) which included volumes on D. G. Rossetti, and the Pre-Raphaelite Brotherhood, and the Studies in Theology series (1907).

Thomas Balston joined the company in 1921 and became a partner in 1923. His interest in avant-garde literature was reflected in the firm's publications of Evelyn Waugh and practically everything produced by Edith, Osbert, and Sacheverell Sitwell. He left Duckworth ten years later having never forgiven the company for the loss of Waugh's *Decline and Fall* which had happened while he was away on holiday. The following year, 1924, the firm became a limited company.

Anthony Powell joined as literary editor in 1926 and in his novel *What's become of Waring?* (1939) the publishing firm of Judkins and Judkins is based on Duckworth's. Powell said that Gerald's interest in books, as far as reading was concerned, 'was as slender as that of any man I have ever encountered'. As for his appearance, he was at this time 'a big, burly man with a slight grey moustache, small baleful eyes behind steel spectacles, a vaguely dissatisfied air and he moved gloomily through the office, a haze of port-fumes and stale cigar-smoke in his wake' (Garnett, 198).

Duckworth died on 28 September 1937 while on holiday in Milan. Apart from his publishing interests he was honorary secretary of the Savile Club and was remembered for his considerable zest and skill at billiards. E. Phillips Oppenheim, a popular fiction writer, described Duckworth as having a 'severe smile and a rather school mastery air which disappeared suddenly when he heard a familiar voice' (Phillips Oppenheim, 195). Of the few people who had a good word for him, Leonard Woolf said that he had found him to be 'a kindly, uncensorious man' (Garnett, 198). His publishing company continued to prosper and in 1969 it moved to a spacious Victorian building in Camden Town which was once owned by the piano makers Collard and Collard. It successfully celebrated its centenary in 1998.   GERALDINE BEARE

Sources G. Beare, 'Gerald Duckworth and Company', *British literary publishing houses, 1881–1965*, ed. J. Rose and P. J. Anderson, DLitB, 112 (1991), 103–7 · H. Lee, *Virginia Woolf* (1996) · J. King, *Virginia Woolf* (1994) · R. Garnett, *Constance Garnett: a heroic life* (1991) · Q. Bell, *Virginia Woolf* (1972), vol. 1, 1882–1912 · *The Times* (30 Sept 1937) · *The diary of Virginia Woolf*, ed. A. O. Bell and A. McNeillie, 1 (1977) · V. Woolf, *Moments of being: unpublished autobiographical writings*, ed. J. Schulkind (1976) · E. Phillips Oppenheim, *The pool of memory* (1941) · m. cert. · *CGPLA Eng. & Wales* (1937)

Archives BL, corresp. with Albert Mansbridge, Add. MS 65259

Wealth at death £7870 2s. 6d.: administration with will, 13 Nov 1937, *CGPLA Eng. & Wales*

Duckworth, Sir John Thomas, first baronet (1748–1817), naval officer, descended from a family long settled in mid-Lancashire and the second son of the Revd Henry Duckworth (1711/12–1794) and Sarah Johnson (1716/17–

Sir John Thomas Duckworth, first baronet (1748–1817), by Sir William Beechey, c.1809–10

1780), was born on 9 February 1748 at Leatherhead in Surrey where his father (afterwards vicar of Stoke Poges and a minor canon of Windsor) was curate.

Early career Duckworth entered Eton College in 1757 but was removed in 1759 when Admiral Edward Boscawen, a neighbour, invited him to replace a protégé who had withdrawn when due to go to sea. He entered his patron's flagship, the *Namur* (74 guns), as a captain's servant on 22 February 1759 and, aged eleven, fought in two major fleet actions, off Lagos and in Quiberon Bay. He went on to the *Prince of Orange* (70 guns), under Captain Samuel Wallis the circumnavigator, whose niece he was to marry, and then to the *Guernsey* (48 guns) under Captain Hugh Palliser; it was from her that he first saw Newfoundland, which he was later to govern.

Duckworth passed for lieutenant in 1766 but his acting commission was not confirmed until 1771 while he was serving in the *Rainbow* (44 guns) where, according to John Jervis, 'he came under the high hand of Captain Fielding' (*Private Papers of George, second Earl Spencer*, 2.487), with whom he served until they shifted to the *Kent* (74 guns); Fielding and Duckworth survived the explosion of her quarter deck in Plymouth Sound before they went in the *Diamond* (32 guns) to North America. There Duckworth, her first lieutenant, had the unusual experience of being tried twice by court martial for the same offence. The *Diamond*, returning from a cruise with her guns loaded, had to fire a salute. Duckworth had the shot removed, counted them and found the total correct. But one had been double shotted, and the remaining round killed five men in a nearby ship. The ensuing court martial acquitted Duckworth of neglect of duty and commended his counting the shot, but this did not satisfy Lord Howe, who reconvened the reluctant court to try Duckworth for murder, of which he was also acquitted. Howe intended the second trial to pre-empt any action in a civil court.

While serving in John Byron's flagship, the *Princess Royal* (90 guns) in the West Indies in June 1779, Duckworth was sent to reconnoitre a French squadron in Fort Royal, Martinique. Bamboozled by transports armed *en flute* and failing to approach near enough to perceive the stratagem, he misled the admiral but redeemed himself in the action off Grenada on 6 July; ten days later he was promoted master and commander into the sloop *Rover* and within a year (and within nine years of promotion to lieutenant) he was made post captain (16 June 1780) in the *Terrible* (74 guns), before returning to the *Princess Royal* as flag captain to Sir Joshua Rowley, with whom he went to Jamaica in 1781. This was a notable start to his career as a senior officer. He had no political interest to favour him but he had impressed his superiors; he was also fortunate to have been made post before the peace which followed the American War of Independence. He brought a convoy home in 1781, made three channel cruises, and on 7 April 1783 disappeared onto half pay.

Middle years Duckworth had married Anne Wallis (1750/51–1797) at Stoke Damerel in July 1776, but then went to sea for five years; in June 1782 they had a son, George Henry, and in September 1784 a daughter, Sarah Anne. The family were dependent on the father's pay of 6s. a day and he was unemployed until January 1790, though he was one of the first twenty-six captains mobilized for the Spanish armament. Having been retained when the Ochakov crisis threatened a Russian war, he remained on active service until 1813, a signal achievement in itself. After nearly two years in the *Bombay Castle* (74 guns), he commanded the *Orion* of the same rate until 1795 when he took her people into the newer *Leviathan*, his last private ship and first flagship. He was awarded his first gold medal for his conduct during the battle of 1 June 1794; he also gained the respect of Howe and Jervis who regarded him as a captain who took particular care in the welfare, education, and training of young gentlemen entrusted to him, of whom the future admiral of the fleet Sir William Parker is the best known. This characteristic brought him the useful patronage of William Baker, MP for Hertford.

From May 1795 until February 1797 Duckworth was in the West Indies, his time dominated by the affairs of the main French colony, San Domingo. He was involved in the ill-conceived and fruitless attack on Fort Léogane in March 1796 and then suddenly found himself commanding the Leeward Islands station when Rear-Admiral William Parker, taken sick, sailed for home, pausing only to leave, with no formal turn-over, his Admiralty instructions and an order for Duckworth to hoist a commodore's pennant. Duckworth's letters to George, Earl Spencer, first lord of the Admiralty, reveal that this golden moment seemed almost too much for him. Similar misgivings appear later

in his career. Spencer's replies show great understanding and forbearance, and he and others among the commodore's superiors did not allow this apparent weakness to diminish their high professional regard for him.

In April 1797 Duckworth came home to find his wife near to death. Within a month he was deprived of his ship by the spread of the naval mutinies from Portsmouth to Plymouth. His command was soon restored and his confidence reassured by a colonelcy of marines. His wife died in August. Duckworth blockaded Brest and Ushant until detached in November, as senior captain under Robert Brice Kingsmill, to watch the western approaches from Berehaven. From there he was sent in a squadron under Roger Curtis to reinforce St Vincent off Cadiz in May 1798. He did not see his daughter again until 1805, and had it not been for his son's undergraduate misadventures (which led Duckworth to obtain for him a commission in the army) father and son would not have been reunited in the West Indies in 1801.

In November 1798 Duckworth again became a commodore, commanding the naval element in General the Hon. Charles Stuart's recapture of Minorca. All went well afloat and ashore until as a reward for the victory Stuart was made KB. With a tactlessness which became characteristic, Duckworth made plain his expectation of the same red ribbon, if not a baronetcy, 'a pretension on which St Vincent, representing the matter to Lord Spencer, threw a sufficiency of cold water' (*DNB*). Nevertheless on 14 February 1799 the commodore was promoted to the flag list as a rear-admiral of the white, the only one of the sixteen new admirals ordered to hoist his flag that day—and this in his own ship, a particular and professional compliment intended by the Admiralty board. After joining the unsuccessful pursuit of Bruix, Duckworth reinforced Nelson at Naples and as his second in command covered Minorca against a Spanish relief before taking over the blockade of Cadiz. Here he had the good luck to intercept a convoy from Peru, from which he took quicksilver worth at least £70,000 and a colonial archbishop.

Later career and reputation To his professional pride and parental regret, he was sent directly to the Leeward Islands station as commander-in-chief in 1801 where his thirst for glory was temporarily assuaged when he was made knight of the Bath after he and General Trigge snapped up the Danish and Swedish islands with great speed, good luck, and no losses in 1802. His son George came out as aide-de-camp to the general. The peace brought the admiral reinforcements rather than respite. On the death of Lord Hugh Seymour in 1803 he assumed the chief command at Jamaica where he was again preoccupied with the affairs of San Domingo. Considerable French reinforcements there threatened the American mainland as well as British possessions. He got on well with Governor Nugent and his wife in Jamaica; the former welcomed George as an aide-de-camp. Duckworth was promoted vice-admiral in April 1804.

On learning that he was soon to be relieved Duckworth placed his protégé Captain Richard Dalling Dunn in command of the newly arrived frigate *Acasta* (40 guns), having removed her captain, James Athol Wood, on grounds of alleged ill health. He brought her to Plymouth with a prodigious cargo of merchandise, including logs of mahogany for his new house outside Exeter. This led to his third court martial. Several eminent counsel thought that he had contravened at least two of the articles of war, but the court accepted his assurance that everything which he had imported was for his own use or as gifts, criticized the prosecution, and acquitted him. Duckworth was once again professionally reassured by selection to relieve Lord Northesk as third in command to Nelson.

Duckworth missed Trafalgar, partly because of Admiralty procrastination about his flagship but partly through his insistence on waiting for his old officers and for his band, a quartet of fiddlers. He joined Vice-Admiral Cuthbert Collingwood off Cadiz on 15 November, relieved him of its blockade, and within two weeks lifted it in order to pursue a French force said to have quit Rochefort. He failed to find it, but while returning to his station on 24 December met a French squadron equal to his own. After thirty hours he called off the chase; only his flagship was in sight of the enemy. This decision was condemned by the naval historian William James, a persistent and often unreasonable critic of the admiral, perhaps because of a clash in the admiralty court at Jamaica where James had been a proctor when Duckworth commanded the station. Like Nelson earlier in the year, Duckworth ran for water to the West Indies. He sent a ship to warn the Cape and East Indies stations that the French were out and on 1 February 1806 he learnt that a French force was off San Domingo. It comprised five ships of the line (one of 120 guns), two frigates, and a corvette; Duckworth had seven ships of the line and two frigates. He brought the French to action on 6 February, making the interesting but seldom quoted signal 'This is glorious' before relying on the now traditional and in this case needless exhortation to 'engage the enemy more closely'. Two Frenchmen ran ashore, three were taken and the frigates escaped, to the derision of James.

It was a neat and well fought little battle, and following Sir Richard Strachan's victory (4 November 1805) completed the Trafalgar campaign. It was also the last action for which the large gold medal was awarded, and the three flag officers—never were there so many in so small a squadron—each received one. Moreover Duckworth's victory pre-empted any danger of a fourth court martial; to abandon a blockade or to forbear 'the chase of an enemy beaten or flying' are serious matters. But Thomas Louis, his second in command, became a baronet (which gave him precedence over his commander-in-chief) and Alexander Cochrane, his third, a KB. Duckworth was infuriated by an annuity of £1000 and mourned for the Irish peerage he had expected. It is astonishing that so publicly disgruntled a senior officer was allowed to continue in a reasonably distinguished career; it suggests that despite the competition of the times, his services were still worth keeping.

Duckworth was allowed home when he rejoined Collingwood, which enabled him to congratulate his son who had survived a bad fall from his horse, attained a majority in the Yorkshire Volunteers and was about to marry Penelope Fanshawe, daughter of the commissioner at Plymouth. He also saw his daughter for the first time since 1797; she was now twenty-two years old and in 1803 had married Captain Richard King. Duckworth was then back off Cadiz for the first anniversary of Trafalgar, his flag in the *Royal George* (100 guns, Captain Dunn). He was notified by Thomas Grenville, the first lord, that affairs in Constantinople required the presence of a naval force and that he was instructing Collingwood to detach Duckworth with five ships. His orders for so ambiguous and difficult a mission could scarcely have been more unrealistic. He was to safeguard the British ambassador, Charles Arbuthnot, and to require Ottoman compliance with British demands, by anchoring close off the city. Collingwood augmented his force but advised him to open fire if he did not receive satisfaction within half an hour. This naïvety suggested a post-Trafalgar euphoria. Duckworth confided his professional doubts to Collingwood—'stuffing a cushion against a fall' (James, 4.300)—but carried out his orders as far as he was able. He forced the Dardanelles on 19 February 1807, no small feat under sail even if not under fire. But wind and tide kept him 8 miles off the city. Arbuthnot fell ill. Duckworth was no diplomatic negotiator, but realized that the Turks were stalling him while strengthening their defences. Without troops or even a full complement of Royal Marines a landing was pointless. Appreciating that the Dardanelles would be harder to re-pass and that prudence was wiser than blind valour, he sailed as soon as the wind was favourable, and fought his way out on 3 March, suffering more casualties than on his way in. In a letter to the duke of Northumberland (30 August 1807), Collingwood defended Duckworth:

> that all was not performed that was expected is only to be attributed to difficulties that could not be surmounted; and if they baffled his skill, I do not know where to look for the officer to whom they would have yielded. (*Private Correspondence*, 220)

Others were less accommodating. The brother of the captain whom Duckworth had replaced in Jamaica suggested unsuccessfully in the Commons that he should be court martialled. William James inevitably thought him wanting in 'ability and firmness' though even he admitted that the board's orders were puzzling (James, 4.311). Duckworth was impenitent; 'as the public varies of this service, I shall not offer an observation farther than that I pride myself more upon my conduct on this occasion than in any other service I have performed' (Ralfe, 4.298–9).

Orders awaited him to command in the Baltic, but they were too late and Saumarez had been sent. He became second in command of the Channel Fleet, with little to do. He married Susannah Catharine Buller (1768–1840), daughter of the bishop of Exeter and sister of the local MP, on 14 May 1808. Their first son, named after his father, was born in the following spring. In 1810 Duckworth accepted the appointment of governor and commander-in-chief of Newfoundland, a three-year post for an ageing but seemingly deserving admiral, to which rank he was promoted that June. He was expected to reside in his colony for only a few weeks each summer; that September he was still there when his wife had their second child, William, who died within days. Duckworth seems to have done well in both his civilian and military roles, though the island was, oddly, little involved in the American war. In 1811 his son George, now a lieutenant-colonel and commanding the 2nd battalion 48th foot, was killed leading the battalion at Albuera; in the same week George's only son died in Devon.

Duckworth was elected to the Admiralty seat of New Romney in 1812 and on his final return home in 1813 was created a baronet. He was an infrequent attender at Westminster; his main claim to fame as an MP seems to have been making Robert Peel laugh at his pigtail, the last (so far) to have been worn in the Commons. In January 1815, after a period of unemployment, he became port admiral at Plymouth and, on the reconstitution of the Order of the Bath, a knight grand cross. He declined to receive the exiled Napoleon, but attended to the mobilization and victualling of Sir Israel Pellew's Algerian expedition in 1816, after which he died in his bed at Admiralty House, signing papers until 'Discharged, dead' on 31 August 1817. There were three military bands in his funeral procession, and 2500 silver gilt nails in his coffin when he was buried at Topsham, near Exeter, on 9 September.

A century ago Laughton said that of all the distinguished British naval officers 'there was none whose character has been more discussed and more confusedly described', and that is still true. Brave and reliable, eager for glory because ambitious for recognition, Duckworth also remained curiously uncertain of himself. With less influence than many of his contemporaries, he was prone to scent criticism and to exaggerate it if it was confirmed. In some ways his own worst enemy, he was nevertheless unfairly criticized.   A. B. SAINSBURY

Sources DNB · NMM, Duckworth MSS · PRO, ADM 1, 12, 35–7, 50 · BL, Add. MS 35138 · BL, Add. MS 34913, fol. 104 · BL, Add. MS 34914, fol. 361 · BL, Add. MS 23207, fol. 285 · Private papers of George, second Earl Spencer, ed. J. S. Corbett and H. W. Richmond, 4 vols., Navy RS, 46, 48, 58–9 (1913–24) · Letters and papers of Charles, Lord Barham, ed. J. K. Laughton, 3 vols., Navy RS, 32, 38–9 (1907–11) · The private correspondence of Admiral Lord Collingwood, ed. E. Hughes, Navy RS, 98 (1957) · J. Ralfe, The naval biography of Great Britain, 4 vols. (1828) · 'Biographical memoir of Sir John Thomas Duckworth', Naval Chronicle, 18 (1807), 1–27 · E. P. Brenton, The naval history of Great Britain, from the year 1783 to 1822, 5 vols. (1823–5) · W. James, The naval history of Great Britain, from the declaration of war by France in 1793, to the accession of George IV, [4th edn], 6 vols. (1847) · P. Mackesy, The war in the Mediterranean, 1803–1810 (1957) · Lady Nugent's journal of her residence in Jamaica from 1801 to 1805, ed. P. Wright, new edn (1966) · J. M. Collinge, 'Duckworth, John', HoP, Commons, 1790–1820

Archives Hispanic Society of America Library, New York, corresp. · Hispanic Society of America Library, New York, letters and papers · NMM, corresp. and papers · NMM, letter-book · NMM, official and private corresp. and papers · Queen's University, Kingston, Ontario, corresp. and papers · University of Florida Libraries, Gainsville, corresp. mainly relating to Jamaica · University of the West Indies, Mona, Jamaica, corresp. relating to the Caribbean · Yale U., Beinecke L., corresp. and papers | Alnwick Castle, corresp. with duke of Northumberland · BL, letters to Lord Collingwood, etc., Add. MS 40098 · BL, letters to Lord Nelson, Add. MSS 34913–34931 · Bodl. RH, corresp. with Sir George Nugent · Herts. ALS, Baker MSS · Hunt. L., letters to Grenville family · NA Canada, corresp. and papers relating to Newfoundland · NA Scot., corresp. with Lord Melville · NL Scot., letters to Sir Alexander Cochrane · NL Scot., letters to Sir Charles Stuart · NMM, corresp. with Lord Barham · NMM, corresp. with Lord Mulgrave · NMM, corresp. with Lord Nelson · NRA, priv. coll., letters to Lord Lansdowne · Provincial Archives of Newfoundland and Labrador, St John's, Newfoundland, corresp. and papers relating to Newfoundland · Rice University, Houston, Texas, Woodson Research Center, corresp. with Sir Charles Stirling · U. Durham, Gray MSS · University of Chicago Library, corresp. and papers relating to Newfoundland

Likenesses H. R. Cook, stipple, 1807 (after R. Bowyer), BM, NPG; repro. in Naval Chronicle (1807) · W. Beechey, oils, c.1809–1810; Christies, New York, 4 Oct 1996, lot 53 [see illus.] · W. Beechey, oils, second version, NMM · G. Mills, medal, NMM

Duckworth, Richard (bap. 1631?, d. 1706), writer on campanology, a native of Lancashire, may have been the person of that name who was baptized at St Peter's, Bolton, on 20 July 1631, the son of John Duckworth. He went to Oxford and on 4 May 1648 was one of the undergraduates of New Inn Hall who submitted to the visitors of the university appointed by the Long Parliament. He matriculated at New Inn Hall in 1649, graduated BA in 1651, and proceeded MA in 1653. He is thought to have acted subsequently as a schoolmaster for a period. After becoming a Lancashire fellow at Brasenose College, in 1661 he became BD. He was junior bursar from 1661 to 1664, and at various times between 1665 and 1679 he held the posts of viceprincipal and senior bursar of Brasenose. Subsequently he seems to have held several livings in plurality, that of Tolland, Somerset, from 1671 to 1680, and St Martin's, Carfax, Oxford, from 1676 to 1682. He was instituted as rector of Steeple Aston, Oxfordshire, on 30 March 1680. While at Steeple Aston he continued to act as a schoolmaster, and was said to have been severe to his scholars, some of whom were of good birth. In later years he became principal of St Alban Hall, Oxford (some accounts say that he was vice-principal).

Duckworth was evidently deeply interested in church bells, and in 1676, during his incumbency of St Martin's, Carfax, the bells were recast and hung in a new frame with new fittings. It is possible that he also had the bells at Steeple Aston augmented to a ring of six while he was there, but the evidence is not clear. His lasting legacy is his authorship of Tintinnalogia, or, The Art of Ringing, published in 1668, the first book published on the art of change ringing. It was published by Fabian Stedman, for many years incorrectly thought to be the author. This well-written book gives a clear exposition of the state of development of the art at the time. It has a final section giving advice on the hanging of bells, incorrectly described by Anthony Wood as a separate publication. There was enough demand for the book for a second edition to be published in 1671; this was a reprint of the first edition without any additional material. The only known copy of the second edition is in the Bodleian Library in Oxford. Duckworth died at Steeple Aston on 19 July 1706 and was buried there the following day. A fine memorial tablet in his memory was erected on the south wall of the chancel of the church there.   JOHN C. EISEL

Sources *Remarks and collections of Thomas Hearne*, ed. C. E. Doble and others, 9, OHS, 65 (1914), 86 • Wood, *Ath. Oxon.*, new edn, 4.734 • J. Buchan, *Brasenose College* (1898) • *Ringing World* (1944) • IGI • *Ringing World* (1973), 213

Duckworth, Wynfrid Laurence Henry (1870–1956), anatomist, was born at Toxteth Park, Liverpool, on 5 June 1870, the eldest child of Henry Duckworth JP FRGS, of Chester, and his wife, Mary J. Bennett. An uncle was Sir Dyce *Duckworth, a consulting physician at St Bartholomew's Hospital. A younger brother, F. R. G. Duckworth (1881–1964), became senior chief inspector at the Ministry of Education. Educated at Birkenhead School and the École Libre des Cordéliers in Dinan, Brittany, Duckworth became an exhibitioner of Jesus College, Cambridge, in 1889, was elected a scholar in 1890, and obtained a double first in the natural sciences tripos (1892–3). As an undergraduate he also rowed in the college boat. He was elected in 1893 into a college fellowship which he retained until his death; he was rarely out of office in the college, serving as its steward for over thirty years and as its bursar for some ten years. In the war years 1940–45 he was master of the college, and after superannuation from that post he continued to live in a fellow's set of rooms until his final illness.

Duckworth proceeded to his MA in 1896, completed his medical studies at St Bartholomew's Hospital, took his MD in 1905 (winning the Raymond Horton Smith prize), and his ScD in 1906. In 1902 he married Eva Alice (*d.* 1955), widow of Charles Cheyne, Indian Staff Corps, and daughter of Frederick Wheeler; there were no children of the marriage. A stepdaughter, Mariot Ysobel Cheyne, married William Edmund Ironside (1880–1959).

Duckworth was senior proctor (1904); university lecturer in physical anthropology (a lectureship established for him in 1898 which he held until 1920); additional demonstrator of human anatomy (1898–1907); senior demonstrator of anatomy (1907–20); and reader in human anatomy (1920–40). He represented his university on the General Medical Council from 1923 to 1926. During the First World War he was commissioned as a captain in the Royal Army Medical Corps; owing to severe injuries sustained in a riding accident, however, he never saw active service. He was president of the Anatomical Society of Great Britain and Ireland in 1941–3.

Duckworth's scientific interests covered a very wide field extending far beyond human anatomy into those of many related disciplines. The breadth of his biological knowledge was reflected in his publications, which included many contributions to physical anthropology, archaeology, primatology, embryology, teratology, and general natural history. He was a field as well as a laboratory anthropologist and in the furtherance of his investigations in archaeology and physical anthropology he travelled widely and studied peoples and prehistoric sites in the Balkans, Greece, Crete, and the Iberian peninsula. Much of Duckworth's earlier work was collected and published in 1904 by Cambridge University Press in *Studies from the Anthropological Laboratory, Anatomy School*. In the same year there appeared his *Morphology and Anthropology*, which covered structural studies in both physical anthropology and human anatomy. It is important in the history of preclinical education as an early attempt to present the medical student with a wider view of anatomy than the purely vocational; its field later came to be called human biology. Another popular volume was his *Prehistoric Man* (1912).

A devoted student of the history of biology, Duckworth possessed a detailed and firsthand acquaintance of most of the major historical works on anatomy and embryology. A good classical scholar, he was widely read in the contributions to biological literature of the sixteenth and seventeenth centuries. Moreover, his excellent knowledge of several modern European languages enabled him to be well orientated in the historical and critical studies relating to these contributions. Duckworth became a most assiduous student of Galen's works and devoted his Linacre lecture (1948) to aspects of Galen's anatomy, and his rendering into English of Simon's German version of the Arabic translation of the later books of *On Anatomical Procedures* was published in 1962, edited by M. C. Lyons and B. Towers.

Duckworth took his teaching duties, both in the anatomy school and in college, very seriously. In his years of maturity his formal teaching was most impressive. A complete command of the facts, a precision in description, consummate, and ambidextrous, skill with chalk on blackboard, and an elegance in manners all combined to give an unforgettable character to his lectures. In more intimate teaching he was less successful, for his eager attempts to impart knowledge tended to swamp the recipients. His attention to his college students, however, was much appreciated; his affection for them was shown by his bequest, after a life interest, of a considerable fortune to forward medical studies in Jesus College.

Duckworth was an insatiable collector. The museum in the Cambridge anatomy school owes much to him and to his worldwide contacts. In later years he placed much of his anthropological collection in the newly created Duckworth Laboratory in the University Museum of Archaeology and Anthropology. Duckworth died at the Evelyn Nursing Home, Cambridge, on 14 February 1956, exactly one year after his wife.   J. D. BOYD, *rev.*

Sources WWW • Venn, *Alum. Cant.* • *The Times* (15 Feb 1956) • *CGPLA Eng. & Wales* (1956) • personal knowledge (1971) • private information (1971)
Likenesses J. Wood, oils, Jesus College, Oxford
Wealth at death £45,919 2s. 11d.: probate, 17 April 1956, *CGPLA Eng. & Wales*

Duclaux [*née* Robinson; *other married name* Darmesteter], **(Agnes) Mary Frances** (1857–1944), writer, was born on 27 February 1857 in Leamington Spa, Warwickshire, daughter of George Thomas Robinson (1828–1897), an architect, and his wife, Frances Sparrow (1831–1916). She had one sister, (Frances) Mabel *Robinson. Having moved to Kensington, London, the Robinsons belonged to a circle of writers and artists; the atmosphere in which the sisters were brought up was extremely cultivated and lively.

They were acquainted with Robert Browning, were familiar with Walter Pater and his sisters, and were great friends with William Rossetti. George Moore entered this circle on his arrival in London and described it later with admiration and humour in *Avowals*. He remained a faithful friend of the sisters until his death in 1933.

Mary was a precocious and serious child, very fond of reading the learned volumes of her father's library and writing verse from early childhood. She was first educated at home, then in a finishing school in Brussels, and finally read classics at University College, London, from 1875 probably until 1878. She was said to be at that time the only woman in the advanced Greek course. Physically, she was small and dainty, with striking large dark eyes, a sweet voice, and a charm which was to last all her life. Her character was always firm; but she was, in her youth, in need of intellectual guidance. She found it especially from two great friends: John Addington Symonds (1840–1893) and Violet Paget (Vernon Lee), whom she often visited in Tuscany.

Mary's first volume of verse was published in 1878 by Kegan Paul and reviewed quite favourably. The forty-five poems of *A Handful of Honeysuckle* are either philosophical or the legendary and historical narratives of the sort then fashionable. The keynote is the intimate blending of fantasy and the past, which remained characteristic of her work. She was hailed as a promising new talent and began to be translated abroad. An ambitious enterprise, the translation of Euripides from the Greek, followed in 1881, together with personal poetry, in *The Crowned Hippolytus*.

In her third volume Mary veered to social themes, on the advice of Dante Gabriel Rossetti. Under the satirical title *A New Arcadia, Idylls of Country Life* (1884) she depicted scenes of rural England, viewed in Epsom, which made her indignant. She had by then lost her Christian faith, which was replaced by an ardent desire to be helpful to her fellows. This inspiration was not well received, for her first successes had made critics expect more tender, imaginative—perhaps feminine—poetry. So when her most famous book, *An Italian Garden* (1886), appeared two years later, after a single attempt at novel writing, *Arden* (1883), *The Athenaeum* congratulated her not only on its perfect form but also for having returned to natural themes. It was followed by *Songs, Ballads and a Garden-Play* (1888), in which *The Spectator* saw a touch of real genius.

Mary's literary production had made her known to lovers of poetry beyond England, and one of them became her husband. In 1888 she married the French orientalist James Darmesteter (1849–1894), a specialist in Indian and Persian religion, and translator of and commentator on the Zend Avesta. They lived six happy years in Paris, during which period James received a professorship at the Collège de France, where he succeeded Renan, the author of *La vie de Jésus*. But he was frail, and died from overwork in 1894.

In 1893 Mary had published *Retrospect*, poems about the past but also about philosophy: leaving behind the anguished questionings of her adolescence, these poems drew on doctrines, beliefs, and legends which she owed to her companionship with James Darmesteter. She chose to stay in France among his cultivated Jewish acquaintances, writing articles on French literature for English reviews, and vice versa. She became a regular contributor to the *Times Literary Supplement*, and an occasional one to the great reviews such as the *Contemporary Review* and the *Nineteenth Century Review*. She naturally supported the cause of Dreyfus in the famous trial. So did, among many others, the biologist Emile Duclaux (1840–1904), successor of Pasteur. He became her second husband in 1901. This marriage introduced her to the world of science as well as to the French province of Auvergne, both providing new centres of interest and poetical themes.

In 1901 Mary Duclaux selected her favourite poetry for her *Collected Poems*, a volume of 304 pages, with sixteen new poems, the fruit of the sombre years she had lately lived. But equanimity and interest in life returned. She showed in the forty-seven poems of *The Return to Nature* (1904) and in her prose work *The Fields of France* (1905) her gift of intelligent sympathy. Her last published poetry was called *Images and Meditations* (1923). It partly reflects the emotion caused by the First World War, but is also concerned with more personal thoughts in grave, but not sad, introspection.

If the poems of the later period had a limited echo, Mary was, on the contrary, well established as a French literary critic. She had become a sort of 'official interpreter' of French and English literature. She had a salon, always open to young authors whom she liked to support, to the Irish acquaintances of her sister Mabel, who lived near her, and to a great number of distinguished French authors. She was a co-founder of the famous literary award the *prix femina*, still in existence at the end of the twentieth century. She died on 7 February 1944 at Aurillac, Cantal, France, where she was buried.

There is no doubt that Mary Duclaux is far better remembered in France than in England. She is the subject of studies in comparative literature in France. Her poems, despite their appeal in the 1880s, have now fallen into almost total obscurity. Yet she was a born poet. Her flexible art explored a wide variety of styles and subjects—love, death, beauty, and the past being her hallmarks, and rhythmic felicity her natural gift. Her attractive and complex personality, her poise, her immense culture may be what will endure, through the many written testimonies left by contemporaries.   SYLVAINE MARANDON

Sources S. Marandon, *L'oeuvre poétique de Mary Robinson* (1967) · D. Halévy, 'Les trois Mary', in D. Halévy, *Mary Duclaux et Maurice Barrès: lettres échangées* (1959) · E. Berl, *Rachel et autres grâces* (1965) · D. Halévy, 'Les trois Mary', *Revue des Deux Mondes* (15 March 1948), 286–97 · J. Pollock, 'Mary Duclaux', *Contemporary Review*, 167 (1945), 201–8 · A. Symons, 'A. Mary F. Robinson-Darmesteter', in A. Symons, *Robert Bridges and contemporary poets* (1892), vol. 8 of *The poets and the poetry of the century* · *The Athenaeum* (11 Aug 1888), 181–2 · *The Spectator* (7 July 1888), 936–8 · E. S. Robertson, *English poetesses* (1883) · H. Lynch, 'A. Mary F. Robinson', *Fortnightly Review*, 77 (1902), 260–76

Archives Bibliothèque Nationale, Paris | U. Leeds, Brotherton L., letters to Edmund Gosse

Du Cros, Sir **Arthur Philip**, first baronet (1871–1955), industrialist, was born in Dublin on 26 January 1871, the third of seven sons of (William) Harvey *Du Cros (1846–1918) and his first wife, Annie Jane (d. 1899), daughter of James Roy, a small landowner and farmer of Durrow, Queen's county, Ireland.

Du Cros was brought up in modest circumstances, but the family was a happy one. His father, at that time a book-keeper, had an income of only £170 a year. Harvey Du Cros, a noted athlete, was also president of the Irish Cyclists' Association and it was this intimate connection with the sport which led him to appreciate the potential of the pneumatic tyre. All his sons were brought up in a spartan manner to be keen athletes, particularly cyclists.

In 1888 John Boyd Dunlop was granted a patent for pneumatic tyres. Later he made over his rights verbally to William Bowden, a Dublin cycle agent, who, with Dunlop's consent, brought in J. M. Gillies, manager of a leading Dublin newspaper, to share his responsibilities. Both men felt Harvey Du Cros was the very man to organize and develop the pneumatic tyre. He agreed, with the stipulation that he should assume complete control. The company, originally called the Pneumatic Tyre and Booth's Cycle Agency Ltd, was thus founded in 1889 under Harvey Du Cros's chairmanship.

Arthur Du Cros attended a national school in Dublin and then, at the age of fifteen, entered the civil service in the lowest grade at 12s. 6d. per week. In 1892 he joined his father and brothers in the infant company, becoming general manager and in 1896, when it was floated as a public company—the Dunlop Pneumatic Tyre Company—he was made joint managing director. In 1895 he married Maude (1876/7–1938), daughter of William Gooding, a watch manufacturer, of Coventry, Warwickshire; they had two sons and two daughters before the marriage was dissolved in 1923. Du Cros laid the foundations of the pneumatic tyre industry in England at Coventry, while his five surviving brothers directed its development abroad: Alfred, Harvey, and George in America and Canada, and William and Frederick in Belgium and France.

In 1901 Du Cros founded the Dunlop Rubber Company, subsequently developing the 400 acres at Fort Dunlop in Birmingham for the complete process of the manufacture of tyres. In 1912 he obtained the consent of the shareholders of the original company to the sale of all the goodwill and trading rights to the Dunlop Rubber Company, thus making the latter entirely independent. During these years the tyre business was revolutionized by the development of the motor car, and Du Cros played a major role in Dunlop's successful response to the growing market opportunities. The firm diversified into making rubber products other than tyres, and also acquired its own sources of supply. Du Cros personally selected estates in Ceylon and Malaya for purchase by the company, which by 1917 owned about 60,000 acres of rubber plantations.

In 1906 Du Cros entered the political field, contesting unsuccessfully as a Conservative the Bow and Bromley constituency, for which his eldest brother, Alfred, was elected in 1910. In 1908, however, Du Cros was elected

Sir Arthur Philip Du Cros, first baronet (1871–1955), by H. Walter Barnett

member for Hastings in succession to his father. In 1909 he formed, and became honorary secretary of, the parliamentary aerial defence committee, to try to ensure the funding of aeronautical development in the army. He and his father were strong advocates of the military uses of aviation and they jointly gave to the army its first airship.

During the First World War Du Cros worked in an honorary capacity for the Ministry of Munitions. He financed, at a cost of £50,000, three motor ambulance convoys, which he maintained at his own expense throughout the war. He also raised an infantry battalion and was for some years honorary colonel of the 8th battalion of the Warwickshire regiment. Du Cros was created a baronet in 1916. He continued to represent Hastings until 1918, but in that year he was elected as a coalition Unionist for the Clapham division of Wandsworth, resigning four years later. He was a founder and the first chairman of the Junior Imperial League.

During the latter stages of Du Cros's career his earlier achievements were overshadowed by errors of judgement. He experienced difficulties in distinguishing between personal interests and those of Dunlop Rubber, using company funds to support Du Cros family business interests, and placing members of the family in senior positions regardless of merit. Du Cros also engaged in financial manipulation of various kinds. He became closely involved with the activities of the financier James White, a specialist in share rigging and other forms of malpractice; the latter's transactions had a major effect on Dunlop, and it came close to collapse in 1921. Du Cros himself had lost influence within the organization by the end of the war. He was made titular president in February 1919 in succession to his father, and was given a consultancy agreement, but this connection was ended in the aftermath of the company's crash. In the 1920s Du Cros continued to be engaged in various financial activities, and became a substantial shareholder in the interests of the fraudulent financier Clarence Hatry. The collapse of the Hatry group in 1929 and the subsequent criminal fraud proceedings left Du Cros's company, Parent Trust and Finance, with £3 million in losses. It was wound up in 1932 with a considerable loss to Du Cros's personal fortunes, which seem never to have recovered.

Before these financial disasters Du Cros was a generous benefactor to many causes, and privately a very generous man. He is said to have lent more than £60,000 to Frances, countess of Warwick, who was in financial difficulties, a debt which he eventually agreed to overlook. When he learned that she was considering the publication of intimate letters written to her by Edward VII he warned court officials of this possibility; the latter promptly took steps which prevented it. In his public benevolence he patronized particularly art and architecture and at Craigweil House, his home near Bognor Regis, he had the rooms in which he displayed his pictures designed to take advantage of the clean, pure air of that part of the Sussex coast. He put the house at the disposal of George V for his convalescence in 1929. Du Cros had a great love of beautiful things and, like his father, who had been known as the best-dressed man in the House of Commons, was always immaculate in his personal appearance. This is reflected in the character portrait of him by 'H. C. O.' which appeared in *Vanity Fair* in 1910.

Du Cros's second marriage, in Paris in 1928, was to Florence May Walton King, daughter of James Walton King, of Walton, Buckinghamshire. She died in 1951 and he married later in that year Mary Louise Joan (d. 1956), daughter of Wilhelm Bühmann, a railway official of Hanover, Germany, who on her naturalization in 1934 assumed the surname of Beaumont. Du Cros died at his home, Nancy Downs House, Oxhey, Watford, Hertfordshire, on 28 October 1955. His elder son, Philip Harvey (1898–1975) succeeded as second baronet.

G. K. S. HAMILTON-EDWARDS, rev. G. JONES

Sources A. du Cros, *Wheels of fortune, a salute to pioneers* (1938) · G. Jones, 'Du Cros, Sir Arthur Philip', *DBB* · G. Jones, 'The growth and performance of British multinational firms before 1939: the case of Dunlop', *Economic History Review*, 2nd ser., 37 (1984) · H. A. Meredith, *The drama of money making* (1931) · m. cert., 1895 · d. cert.

Likenesses H. W. Barnett, photograph, NPG [*see illus.*] · H. C. O., caricature, NPG; repro. in *VF* (6 Jan 1910) · W. Orpen, portrait; formerly in possession of Philip Harvey Du Cros, his elder son

Wealth at death £18,817 3s. 3d.: resworn probate, 1956, *CGPLA Eng. & Wales*

Du Cros, (William) Harvey (1846–1918), pneumatic tyre manufacturer, was born in Dublin on 19 June 1846, son of Edouard Pierce Du Cros and his wife, Maria Molloy. The family was of Huguenot origin, an ancestor, Jean Peter Du Cros, having settled in Dublin at the beginning of the eighteenth century as a refugee from religious persecution. Du Cros was briefly educated at a blue coat school for the children of distressed gentlefolk, King's Hospital, Dublin (1855–60), and when he was fifteen started on a series of minor commercial posts as clerk and later as an unqualified book-keeper. At the same time he left home, according to his son Arthur, because of differences between his parents. In 1866 he married Annie Jane Roy (d. 1899); he had six sons by his mid-twenties. At twenty-three he became part-time assistant secretary of the fledgeling Irish Commercial Travellers' Association.

A small, wiry, but immensely determined man, with a long and carefully waxed moustache, Du Cros was once described as 'of no particular physique' but 'never known to acknowledge defeat'. He was advised to take up sport for the sake of his health at thirty, and followed the prescription so enthusiastically that he became boxing champion of Ireland at two weights, its fencing champion, and founder and captain of the Bective Rangers Football Club, which won the Irish Rugby championship. He was also a leading amateur cyclist and president of the Irish Cyclists' Association. He insisted his sons follow his example, boxing against them in the gym and forming them into a successful team of racing cyclists on the solid-tyred penny-farthing machines then popular.

A turning point came for Du Cros when two of his sons were defeated by an unfancied Ulster cyclist using the rudimentary pneumatic tyres invented by John Boyd Dunlop, a Belfast vet. Du Cros instantly appreciated their possibilities and after successful racing trials of the tyres was invited by William Bowden, a Dublin cycle agent to whom Dunlop had informally made over the rights, to set up a company to exploit them. Du Cros insisted on complete control, wrote the prospectus, and effected the public issue of 15,010 £1 shares in 1889. Shrewdly he linked the company with an established cycle agency as the Pneumatic Tyre and Booth's Cycle Agency Ltd, providing early cash flow, and absorbed the Belfast cycle firm which had made the early tyres.

Du Cros's practical commercial sense and public relations flair carried the company through in spite of the revocation of Dunlop's patent in 1890, barely a year after the flotation, when it was found to have been anticipated. Du Cros rapidly arranged to purchase a separate patent relating to the way the tyre was attached, a key problem for early tyres, and employed the inventor, Charles Kingston Welch. Six years later the owner of a rival patent was bought out. Du Cros inserted his team of sons into the business, sending them to different countries to establish the company. Arthur *Du Cros became general manager and another, Harvey, became a major investor in the Austin motor company.

In 1896 Du Cros secured his fortune when he sold the company, with an issued capital of £260,000, to a group including the motor speculator Ernest T. Hooley for £3 million, subsequently taking part in the reflotation as the Dunlop Pneumatic Tyre Company. He and Arthur became joint managing directors and the company expanded in step with the motor industry, producing its first motor tyre in 1900 (though significantly later than Michelin in France) and later diversifying into golf balls and aerotyres. Manufacture moved to Coventry in 1893 and was expanded into the production of rubber, cotton, and other components for the tyres. The style was so confident that when the crucial Welch patent expired, Du Cros held a wake, inviting 400 people to celebrate. Among other activities, he helped finance the first airship for the British army and organize the first motorized movement of British troops. In 1906 he became a Conservative MP against the run of Liberal success, standing for Hastings on a platform of tariff controls to protect industry.

Du Cros's first wife died in 1899 and he later married Florence Gibbings of Bow in Devon. By the time of his death at Inniscorrig, Dalkey, co. Dublin, on 21 December 1918, Dunlop was Britain's fourteenth biggest manufacturing company. Without Du Cros, his contemporaries believed, it could never have survived.

Martin Adeney

Sources A. du Cros, *Wheels of fortune, a salute to pioneers* (1938) · E. Tompkins, *History of the pneumatic tyre* (1981) · R. Storrs, *Dunlop in war and peace* (1946) · G. Jones, 'The growth and performance of British multinational firms before 1939: the case of Dunlop', *Economic History Review*, 2nd ser., 37 (1984) · G. Jones, 'Du Cros, William Harvey', *DBB* · *The Times* (2 Jan 1919) · *WWW*
Likenesses photograph, National Motor Museum, Beaulieu
Wealth at death £42,143: Jones, 'Du Cros, William Harvey'

Du Cros [*née* Rees], **Rosemary Theresa**, Lady Du Cros (1901–1994), aviator, was born at 2 Walton Street, Brompton, London, on 23 September 1901, the daughter of Sir John David Rees, first baronet (1854–1922), and his wife, Mary Catherine Dormer. She had an older brother, Richard. Having already retired from the Indian Civil Service her father became Conservative MP for East Nottingham, and remained in the House of Commons until his death. Rosemary always maintained that she had no formal education other than that gained from listening to her parents' conversation and from avid reading. However, while living for a short time at Harrow on the Hill she joined the daughters of housemasters at Harrow School for tuition in French, German, and English by visiting governesses. She also attended ballet classes in Chelsea, and later pursued a career as a dancer in revue. For most of the 1920s she travelled the country with concert parties and musical comedies.

In 1932 Rees travelled round the world with her brother, Richard. On their return they renewed acquaintance with Gordon Selfridge junior, a former fellow undergraduate of Richard's at Cambridge. A keen aviator, Selfridge owned an aeroplane and persuaded Rees to have a trial flight. So began her second obsession. Though still dancing she had to decide between the two careers: she chose aviation, and obtained a pilot's licence in 1933. The 1930s were the palmy days of aviation, when the air over Europe was free; aircraft owners could fly to parties given by European aero clubs where they were wined and dined by the local mayors. Having bought a Miles Hawk Major aircraft (to be replaced later by a Miles Whitney Straight) Rees could

spend the summers touring and the winters skiing in Europe. In this way she accrued over 600 hours' flying time.

With war on the horizon this hedonistic existence ended in 1938. The Civil Air Guard was formed to train more pilots through subsidies to aero clubs. The need for more instructors gave experienced women pilots, who had previously had little chance of a career in aviation, the opportunity of obtaining an instructor's licence. Having done this Rees was employed by army co-operation; this entailed flying her aircraft to and fro while anti-aircraft gunners practised aiming their guns. For this she was paid £10 per hour.

On the outbreak of war in 1939 Gerard d'Erlanger, a director of British Overseas Airways Corporation, persuaded the government to make use of experienced civilian pilots not eligible for the armed forces. Forty male pilots were recruited initially to ferry aircraft from the factories to the squadrons in what became the Air Transport Auxiliary (ATA). Meanwhile an equally persuasive woman pilot, Pauline Gower, had lobbied on behalf of women. When she was allowed to choose eight pilots to form a small women's section Rees became one of these first eight so-called ATA girls, caught up in an unwelcome storm of publicity and even antagonism from some quarters.

At first cleared only to fly open-cockpit Tiger Moths (the RAF's elementary trainer) in the freezing winter of 1939–40 Rees was far from happy. Yet her situation improved when she was sent to the RAF Central Flying School at Upavon for training on more advanced twin-engine trainers. In July 1941 women were cleared to fly operational aircraft in consequence of the pressing need for more experienced ferry pilots. Rees was one of four women chosen to convert to flying Hurricanes.

In September 1941 no. 15 Ferry Pool, Hamble, became an all-woman pool under the command of Captain Margot Gore, with Flight Captain Rees as her deputy. Rees remained there for the duration of the war, qualifying to fly all five classes of operational aircraft from light singles through to heavy, four-engine bombers. Towards the end of the war she was lucky enough to ferry a Vampire and a Meteor jet aircraft. She was appointed MBE in 1945 for her wartime services and later joined the volunteer reserve of the RAF, gaining her commission.

On leaving the ATA after six and a half years Rees bought a war-surplus Percival Proctor and obtained a commercial flying licence in order to fly for hire and reward. She operated her air-taxi charter firm, Ski Taxi, for five years until increasing post-war bureaucracy and deteriorating eyesight eventually terminated her flying career.

Rees married, as his second wife, Sir Philip Harvey Du Cros, second baronet (1898–1975), at Westminster register office on 3 November 1950 and went to live with him in Parkham, north Devon, where he was an active member of the Torrington parliamentary constituency. She involved herself in politics and became chairman of the Bideford area Conservative Association. Her husband died in 1975, but she remained mentally and physically active well into old age. She died at Little Bocombe, Parkham, on 8 March 1994, aged ninety-two.

Enid deBois

Sources R. du Cros, 'ATA girl': memoirs of a wartime ferry pilot (1983) · L. Curtis, The forgotten pilots (1971); 2nd edn (1989) · WWW · Burke, Peerage (2000) · b. cert. · m. cert. · d. cert. · personal knowledge (2004)
Archives FILM The forgotten pilots, BBC documentary (1986)
Wealth at death £612,827: probate, 16 Aug 1994, CGPLA Eng. & Wales

Ducrow, Andrew (1793–1842), equestrian performer, was born at the Nag's Head, 102 High Street, Southwark, Surrey, on 10 October 1793, the eldest of at least six children. His father, Peter Ducrow (c.1765–1815), a native of Bruges in west Flanders, and his mother, Margaret (c.1768–1854), were both circus performers. Peter appeared as an equestrian, wire-dancer, juggler, and bird-imitator, but later excelled as a strongman, known as the 'Flemish Hercules'. He arrived in London by June 1793 with Thomas Franklin's circus, in which he served primarily as a leaper. A stern taskmaster, he put his children through rigorous physical training from their earliest years. Andrew regularly worked sixteen hours a day from the age of three to fifteen, learning gymnastics, fencing, and circus skills, and, more surreptitiously, drawing, painting, and music; he was whipped severely for breaking his leg during a performance. His earliest billed performance seems to have been as the 'Infante Hercules' in Lisbon (25 October 1797). In May 1800 he may have taken part in a fête given at Frogmore in the presence of George III, when his father balanced on his chin three coach-wheels and a ladder, to which were affixed two chairs with two children on them, and held on his hands a table bearing eight persons.

When Astley's Amphitheatre reopened in London in 1801, the Ducrows were among its company. About this time Andrew Ducrow learned from the example and tutelage of the choreographer J. H. D'Egville, the rope-dancer Jack Richer, and the equestrian performer Collett, and with his family performed in circuses throughout England and Scotland. His earliest steps in drama came as the Child in Perouse, or, The Desolate Island, a pantomimic drama staged at the Olympic Circus, Glasgow (15 February 1806), and he first won the special attention of the critics in 1814 as Eloi the Dumb Boy in The Dog of Montargis, or, The Forest of Bondy by William Barrymore (Royal Circus, 6 October 1814). He later made a speciality of playing idiots capable of expressing themselves exclusively in mime. He perfected his 'equestrian exercises' or 'poses plastiques', posing as classical statuary, while circling the arena on horseback. His entrance from the audience as a rustic interloper and his quick changes on horseback in 'The Peasant's Frolic, or, The Flying Wardrobe' became part of the standard circus repertory.

From 1818 to 1823 Ducrow toured the Netherlands, Belgium, Switzerland, Italy, Spain, and France, with great success. He was especially prominent at the Cirque Olympique in Paris during the 1818–19 season, where he shared in the nightly profits. With a company made up in part of his family, in part of recruits, the Vestris à Cheval, as Ducrow was termed, evolved a form of equestrian pantomimes to music as the best showcase for his talents; they ranged from comic scenarios to the death of Othello. On 5 November 1823 he and his horses took part in Planché's drama Cortez, or, The Conquest of Mexico, at Covent Garden, but the piece was not a great success. After a few more appearances at the theatre, both in spectacular melodrama and pantomime, and a brief engagement at the

Andrew Ducrow (1793–1842), by William Heath [in the ring at Astley's]

Bristol Theatre Royal, Ducrow's troupe, combined with that of William Davis, moved to Astley's Amphitheatre. This was to be the scene of Ducrow's triumphs until the end of his career. Their opening production (19 April 1824) was J. H. Amherst's *The Battle of Waterloo*, in which Ducrow's 'foreign equestrian evolutions' contributed mightily to the public favour long bestowed on this patriotic recreation. Ducrow and the equestrian showman James West took a seven-year contract on Astley's, and commenced their management with *Bonaparte's Invasion of Russia, or, The Conflagration of Moscow*. Expert at grouping large masses of men and animals, with a faultless eye for stage effect, Ducrow was adept at drawing performances equally from 'supers' (or extras) and horses. The *London Magazine* for August 1824 called him 'the first true horseman that ever gave a meaning to the display of fine riding', for he shed an artistic hue over what had previously been a display of mechanical, quasi-military feats. The most obvious example was *Raphael's Dream, or, The Mummy and Study of Living Pictures* (1830), an exhibition on horseback of *tableaux vivants* drawn from classical painting and sculpture. Ducrow added to horsemanship both a narrative and a theatrical element, insisting on continuous action, and his innovations were rapidly imitated and diffused throughout the circus world. In the ring, Ducrow's brother John (1796–1843) acted Mr Merryman the clown, serving tea to his ponies Darby and Joan. There too, Ducrow introduced his 'most daring creation', 'The Courier of St Petersburg', in which he bestrode four (later five) horses running at top speed; and in 1831 he staged what was to become the most imitated and longest-running equestrian play in history, H. M. Milner's *Mazeppa and the Wild Horse of Tartary*, in which the undraped hero, bound to a fiery steed, courses a treadmill through the wilds of Poland. He also initiated the vogue for lion dramas by featuring Isaac Van Amburgh and his beasts in *The Brute Tamer of Pompeii* (1838). From 1828 Ducrow's shows began to be patronized by the royal family, and in 1832 William IV had the royal carpenter convert a riding school behind the Brighton Pavilion into a circus for Ducrow's appearance there. The next year, under Alfred Bunn's management, Ducrow produced at Drury Lane the spectacle of *St George and the Dragon*, followed by *King Arthur and the Knights of the Round Table*; the critics found that the dullness of the proceedings was recompensed only by Ducrow's dumbshow and fight scenes, but the public thronged to see them. By this time his fame had grown so great that his name was a byword, and allusions to his mastery could be found in Dickens, Thackeray, Disraeli, *The Bon Gaultier Ballads*, and *The Ingoldsby Legends*.

Ducrow was 5 feet 8 inches tall, with a fair complexion, regular features, and a wiry, muscular build. He was famed for his quick temper and peremptory behaviour, which he deliberately unleashed to get results from his performers. Astley's employed more than 150 persons, with a weekly expenditure of £500, so discipline had to be maintained. His language was notoriously foul, especially at rehearsals, and got him into trouble when he directed at Drury Lane. It was also a habit of journalists to insist on his illiteracy, cockney pronunciation, and malapropisms, although these were evidently much exaggerated and even invented. His proverbial admonition to 'cut out the dialect and come to the 'osses' (later corrupted to 'cut the cackle') may date from a direction given when staging his 1838 spectacle *Charlemagne*. His charity was generous and in keeping with professional standards.

Ducrow married, first, in 1818, Margaret Griffith of Liverpool, a well-educated woman with limited talents as a circus rider; she died, probably of influenza, in 1836, and at the rainy funeral Ducrow threw a tantrum about the water in her grave. In June 1838 he wed Louisa Woolford (c.1814–1900), a very gifted and popular equestrian performer, who had joined his company ten years earlier; they had two sons and a daughter, none of whom went into the circus. On 8 June 1841 Astley's Amphitheatre and Ducrow's adjacent residence were totally destroyed by fire, along with all his costumes, *objets d'art*, scenery, and stage machinery. Uninsured, the managers attempted to pay their company and announced a new season at the Surrey Theatre. But this latest in a series of domestic disasters seriously enfeebled Ducrow's mind and body, and he underwent a paralytic stroke. Following a second stroke, he died at 19 York Road, Lambeth, on 27 January 1842. His spectacular funeral, attended by vast crowds of people, took place on 5 February in Kensal Green cemetery, where an Egyptian-style mausoleum, the work of his designer Danson, was erected to his memory. Despite his losses by fire, Ducrow left property valued at approximately £60,000.

LAURENCE SENELICK

Sources A. H. Saxon, *The life and art of Andrew Ducrow and the romantic age of the English circus* (1978) · *Oxberry's Dramatic Biography* · P. Egan, 'Theatrical sketch of Mr A. Ducrow, the unparalleled equestrian', *Anecdotes of the turf, the chase, the ring and the stage* (1827) · A. H. Coxe, *A study of Andrew Ducrow* (privately printed, 1957)

Archives Harvard U. · priv. coll., album · Theatre Museum, London | BL, Astley's Amphitheatre scrapbooks, playbills · University of Kansas, Lawrence, Kenneth Spencer Research Library, M. Willson Disher MSS

Likenesses G. Charton, lithograph, 1820 (after J. Bergman), Harvard TC · Engelmann, print, 1827 (after E. F. Lambert), Harvard TC · Danson, mausoleum, 1837, Kensal Green cemetery, London · J. Howe, bust, 1841 · J. W. Gear, drawing, Harvard TC · W. Heath, drawing, Theatre Museum, London [*see illus.*] · Madeley, lithograph, Harvard TC · J. Rogers, line engraving (after Wagerman), Harvard TC · Villain, lithograph (after Reverchon), Harvard TC · oils, Harvard TC · prints, NPG · prints, Harvard TC

Wealth at death approx. £60,000—£500 for funeral; £200 for widow's immediate expenses; £200 to two sisters, £150 for third surviving sister and £150 for her husband; legacies of £25–£300 were left to eight individuals; residue of nearly £47,560 in securities alone left in trust to wife and children: will

Duddell, Benedict (c.1695–1759x67), surgeon and oculist, about whose life few details are known, was probably educated in France and served his surgical apprenticeship in a town about 4 leagues from Paris. In 1718 he was in practice at Worksop, Nottinghamshire. Upset by his failure to save the sight of a poor labourer under his care, Duddell resolved to make a special study of eye diseases. He went back to Paris and attended the eye clinic at the Hospice des Quinze-Vingts run by John Thomas Woolhouse, who was renowned as a teacher and attracted many bright young students of promise. Duddell thought highly of him, calling him 'that great man', 'a very great Oculist at Paris', and 'my master'.

After his stay in France, Duddell returned to Worksop. He worked as an itinerant surgeon, travelling to places such as Castleton in Derbyshire, and Sheffield. In the early 1720s he moved south and set up in Hammersmith on the outskirts of London, where he continued his itinerant work, seeing patients east and west of the capital.

Duddell's first book, *A Treatise of the Diseases of the Horny-Coat of the Eye, and the Various Kinds of Cataracts*, was published in 1729. It was a response to the views of his contemporary, the flamboyant eye surgeon 'Chevalier' John Taylor. Duddell disliked Taylor's treatment of corneal scars, and he discussed the problem of the recurrence of cataract after couching. In his second book, *An Appendix to the Treatise* (1733), he criticized the new operation devised by Cheselden to form an artificial pupil, and described his own method following the precedent set by Charles St Yves in 1707 of extracting the lens through the cornea, usually employed after a failed couching. Duddell's third book, *A Supplement to the Treatise* (1736), virulently attacked the ideas and practice of Chevalier Taylor, though Duddell denied that it was written out of personal malice.

Duddell dealt with a large variety of eye troubles, and his views were based on his experience and his wide acquaintance with the developments in his field. He did not unreservedly accept the opinions of the eminent, preferring to rely on his own observations. He dissected the cornea and described the laminae; 'Duddell's membrane' is one name for the posterior elastic lamina of the cornea. Unlike his admired teacher, John Woolhouse, Duddell asserted that the cause of cataract was the opacity of the lens. Contrary to St Yves he maintained that the retina and not the choroid was the immediate organ of sight. He disputed the originality of Dominique Anel's treatment in 1713 of the obstruction of the lachrymal duct. Duddell was bitter towards the regular surgeons who treated eye diseases without any special knowledge, and he was equally scathing of quacks who were extravagant with their promises of cure. He was a great believer in the value of scarifying the cornea in various conditions, and although he claimed that his method was original, it had been borrowed without acknowledgement from Woolhouse.

Duddell was largely ignored in Britain but on the continent his writings were taken seriously. In 1799 Professor Bertrandi of Turin praised Duddell's skill with the needle in couching, and drew attention to his method of cataract extraction (Bertrandi, 2.119, 153). Belatedly, in the early twentieth century, an English ophthalmologist, G. Coats, acknowledged that Duddell was 'the best English writer on ophthalmic subjects in the first half of the eighteenth century' (James, 93).

Little is known about Duddell's personal life. In January 1724 his son Albanus was baptized by a Catholic priest in Hammersmith, the mother being Joanna. Between 1734 and 1745 Duddell fathered four other children (two of whom died in infancy). Two relationships are known from this time, first with Amy Smith and then with Mary Green. The offspring were labelled 'bastard' or 'base', but this may be because the parents, being Catholic, were not married in an Anglican church.

In his later years Duddell worked as a parish surgeon. Again his contentious nature asserted itself. In 1740 he began a legal action against some of the overseers and churchwardens of Hammersmith, but the cause and outcome are unknown. In 1759 he was paid by the parish of Fulham for curing scald heads. It is likely that Duddell died between that date and 1767, as he appears to be absent from the Hammersmith section of the Return of Papists for the diocese of London.

Perhaps because of his personal failings, or perhaps because of the civil disabilities attached to his religion, Duddell failed to receive the recognition his ability and originality deserved.   A. L. WYMAN

Sources A. L. Wyman, 'Benedict Duddell: pioneer oculist of the 18th century', *Journal of the Royal Society of Medicine*, 85 (1992), 412–15 · A. Bertrandi, *Opere anatomiche e cerusiche: trattato delle malattie degli occhi* (1799) · R. R. James, ed., *Studies in the history of ophthalmology in England prior to the year 1800* (1933) · J. H. Harting, ed., 'Catholic registers of Hammersmith, Middlesex, 1710–1838', *Miscellanea, XIII*, Catholic RS, 26 (1926), 58–130, esp. 68
Archives Hammersmith and Fulham Archives, London, church register of St Paul's, Hammersmith, vestry minutes, poor rates overseers' accounts

Duddell, William Du Bois (1872–1917), electrical engineer, was born on 1 July 1872 at 23 Westmoreland Place, Kensington, London, the son of Frances Kate Du Bois. The identity of his father is unknown. In 1881 his mother married George Duddell (*d.* 1887), a landowning gentleman of Queen's Park, Brighton. An asthmatic, delicate child, William received his early education privately in England, and at the Collège Stanislas, Cannes, where the family had moved for the benefit of his health. William showed mechanical ability at an early age. When only four, he is said to have fitted a toy mouse with a clockwork motor. From 1890 to 1893 he was apprenticed to the firm of Davey, Paxman & Co. at Colchester. His skills were obviously known to his friends, as his landlady is said to have complained at the number of clocks being brought to her house for repair.

William Duddell studied at the Central Technical College (later the City and Guilds College), South Kensington, under professors Ayrton and Mather, obtaining a Whitworth exhibition in 1896, and a Whitworth scholarship in 1897. There he became interested in the alternating-current electric arc. His work was hindered by the clumsiness of the Joubert 'point to point' method used at that time to delineate alternating-current waveforms. André Blondel, in Paris, had suggested modifying a moving-coil meter by reducing it to a rudimentary form consisting simply of one single loop of wire under tension, thereby reducing its mechanical inertia to the point where the coil could follow the instantaneous variations of the current. Movement of the loop was observed by directing a light beam at a small mirror fixed to it. Projection of the reflected beam on to a screen or photographic plate by a vibrating mirror then revealed the waveform. Using his great skills, Duddell developed this idea into a fully engineered oscillograph. He and his colleague, E. W. Marchant, described both the oscillograph and the results of their observations on the arc in a paper published in the *Journal of the Institution of Electrical Engineers* in 1899 (28, 1–107). The demonstration of the oscillograph caused a sensation, since those present realized that they now had, for the first time, a convenient and speedy method of displaying waveforms. The Cambridge Scientific Instrument Co. manufactured many different models of these oscillographs and they were used until the Second World War when they were gradually superseded by cathode-ray oscillographs (or oscilloscopes as they then became known).

Duddell developed many other instruments, including a vibration galvanometer; a thermo-ammeter based on Boys's radio-micrometer; a twisted-strip galvanometer; and a version of Einthoven's string galvanometer. All bore the stamp of his manual skills and his minute attention to detail. He retained his interest in the electric arc and in 1901 revealed his discovery that an arc connected across a capacitor and an inductor could oscillate—the so-called 'musical arc' or 'singing arc'. He demonstrated the effect at a public lecture by causing an arc to play the tune 'God Save the King'. This phenomenon became the basis of the arc method of radio transmission, developed most notably by Valdemar Poulsen.

William Duddell also played an active part in his profession, and received many honours, being president of the Röntgen Society in 1907, of the Institution of Electrical Engineers from 1912 to 1914, and of the Commission Internationale de Télégraphie sans Fils in 1914. He was also vice-president and honorary treasurer of the Physical Society. He was elected fellow of the Royal Society of London on 2 May 1907 and he received their Hughes medal in 1912. He was awarded gold medals from the Paris Exhibition in 1900 and the St Louis Exhibition in 1904.

Duddell, who was unmarried, lived at 47 Hans Place, Knightsbridge, London, moving about 1904 to 36 Walton Street, Chelsea. He died at Newlands House, 180 Tooting Bec Road, London, on 4 November 1917, of general paralysis, aged only forty-five; he was buried four days later at Brighton. It was thought that the drastic deterioration in his health was caused by the intensive government war work on which he was engaged. He was survived by his mother, by then Mrs Smithers, and by his younger sister, Mrs Blanche Gladys Du Bois Colston. He left effects worth £4735 7s. 11d. Some months before his death he was appointed commander in the Order of the British Empire. However, he was too ill to go the palace, and the insignia were received by his mother two days after he died. By all accounts William Duddell was an extremely well-liked person. Descriptions of him in various obituaries refer to 'an unassuming and kindly man', and 'a man of charming courtesy' with 'lightness of manner, approachable by all

and sundry'. Although his major achievements, the oscillograph and the musical arc, are no longer of any practical importance, they were crucial to the development of electrical engineering and wireless telegraphy.

V. J. PHILLIPS

Sources W. M. Mordey, *Journal of the Institution of Electrical Engineers*, 56 (1918), 54–5 · E. W. Marchant, *Journal of the Institution of Electrical Engineers*, 56 (1918), 538–40 · *Electrical Review*, 81 (9 Nov 1917), 449 · 'William Du Bois Duddell, president of the IEE', *Electrical Review*, 71 (1912), 749–50 · *PRS*, 94A (1917–18), xxxiv–xxxv · *The Electrician* (9 Nov 1917), 199–200 · R. T. Smith, letter, *The Electrician* (16 Nov 1917), 240 · W. D. Duddell and E. W. Marchant, 'Experiments on alternate current arcs by aid of oscillographs', *Journal of the Institution of Electrical Engineers*, 28 (1899), 1–107 · V. J. Phillips, *Waveforms: a history of early oscillography* (1987), chap. 4 · W. D. Duddell, 'On rapid variations in the current through the direct-current arc', *Journal of the Institution of Electrical Engineers*, 30 (1900–01), 232–67 · V. J. Phillips, *Early radio wave detectors* (1980), 155–7, 166–7 · *CGPLA Eng. & Wales* (1918) · b. cert. · d. cert. · will, George Duddell, 7 Oct 1881, administration 10 Feb 1888 · joint will, William Du Bois Duddell and Blanche Gladys Du Bois Duddell, 26 April 1904; William Du Bois Duddell, 1 May 1904, codicil 1 June 1917; proved 22 March 1918

Archives Inst. EE, notebooks, SC MSS 49 · Sci. Mus.

Likenesses Lafayette Ltd, photograph, repro. in *PRS*, 94A (1918), facing p. xxxiv · C. Vandyk Ltd, photograph, repro. in R. Appleyard, *The history of the Institution of Electrical Engineers, 1871–1931* (1939), facing p. 294 · portrait, Inst. EE

Wealth at death £4735 7s. 11d.: probate, 22 March 1918, *CGPLA Eng. & Wales*

Dudgeon, (John) Alastair (1916–1989), microbiologist, was born on 9 November 1916 in Stanhope Place, Bayswater, London, the youngest in the family of two sons and one daughter of Leonard Stanley *Dudgeon (1876–1938), professor of pathology and dean of St Thomas's Hospital, London, and his wife, Norah Edith, daughter of Sir Richard Orpen, solicitor and later president of the Irish Law Society. His childhood was spent in London, and his summer holidays in Aldeburgh, a place which was to mean much to him throughout his life. He was educated at Repton School, Derbyshire, and at Trinity College, Cambridge, where he graduated second class in part one of the natural sciences tripos (1937). He then went to St Thomas's Hospital medical school.

Dudgeon had joined the Territorial Army in 1936 and at the outbreak of the Second World War in 1939 he interrupted his medical studies to serve as a combatant officer. His career in the north Africa campaign as a company commander in the 7th rifle brigade was distinguished. In 1942 he was awarded the MC, to which a bar was added in 1943. Having been wounded twice, he was evacuated back to Britain in 1943. His army service had left a deep imprint on him; he had cared for the soldiers under his command with the sense of responsibility which he was later to feel for patients, colleagues, research workers, and technicians, and his friendships made in the army were lasting.

He completed his medical studies at St Thomas's, qualifying MRCS, LRCP and MB, BCh in 1944. He transferred to the Royal Army Medical Corps in 1944 and served in the Territorial Army until 1962, gaining the rank of colonel and the Territorial decoration and three clasps (1947). In 1945 he married Patricia Joan (d. 1969), daughter of Gilbert

Ashton, schoolmaster; they had two sons. He received an MD from Cambridge University in 1947. After qualification he specialized in microbiology, particularly virology. In 1945–6 he worked at the National Institute for Medical Research, under Christopher Andrewes. In 1948 he was appointed assistant pathologist (virus diseases) at the Hospital for Sick Children, Great Ormond Street, London—another institution to benefit from his lifelong loyalty. In 1953 he became senior lecturer in virology at St George's Hospital, keeping his links with Great Ormond Street as honorary consultant virologist. From 1958 to 1960 he was director of virus research at the Glaxo laboratories. He returned to Great Ormond Street in 1960, as consultant microbiologist and lecturer at the Institute of Child Health. He built up a splendid department and in 1972 became professor of microbiology and in 1974 dean of the institute. In 1963 he had become FRCPath. He was an excellent administrator, serving on many hospital and institute committees, usually as chairman. After the death of his first wife he married in 1974 Joyce Kathleen, widow of Stanley Tibbetts and daughter of James Counsell, farmer and businessman.

Dudgeon's researches related to viral diseases of the foetus and new-born child. His most original contribution concerned the trials of a vaccine against the rubella virus. After a link between an attack of rubella during the early weeks of pregnancy and malformations in the offspring had been demonstrated, a live vaccine against the virus was produced in 1967 in the United States and was awaiting clinical trials. Dudgeon thought that the trials should be undertaken in closed religious communities, in order to avoid accidental transferral of rubella to pregnant women. With the enthusiastic co-operation of those communities he showed that the vaccine was not transmitted from person to person and was safe, and that the resulting immunity lasted for many years. These studies laid the foundation for the vaccine's routine use and resulted in the declining incidence of rubella malformations. For this contribution Dudgeon received the Harding award (1972) and the Bissett Hawkins medal of the Royal College of Physicians (1977), of which he had become a member in 1970 and a fellow in 1974. His expertise in the field of immunization was recognized internationally and he became chairman of several government and World Health Organization committees. He was appointed an officer of the order of St John of Jerusalem (1958), deputy lieutenant of Greater London (1973), and CBE (1977). After his retirement in 1981 he worked for medical charities and the South-East Kent Health Authority. He became senior warden (1984–5) and master (1985–6) of the Society of Apothecaries.

Dudgeon valued tradition. He had a rocklike dependability and a strong sense of right. On first acquaintance he appeared austere, but underneath he had great warmth, a sense of humour, and a humility which prevented him from mentioning his achievements. He enjoyed gardening and collected antique porcelain, glass, silver, and apothecary jars. Always correctly dressed, he was of medium height, with a fine head of black hair, which remained unchanged into old age, and dark brown eyes. Dudgeon died on 9 October 1989 at his home, Cherry Orchard Cottage, Bonnington, near Ashford, Kent.

OTTO WOLFF, *rev.*

Sources *The Times* (16 Oct 1989) · *WWW* · personal knowledge (1996) · private information (1996)
Wealth at death £161,912: probate, 19 Feb 1990, *CGPLA Eng. & Wales*

Dudgeon, Leonard Stanley (1876–1938), pathologist, was born in London on 7 October 1876, the second son and youngest of the eight children of John Hepburn Dudgeon of Haddington, East Lothian, and his wife, Catherine, daughter of Alexander Pond. He was educated at University College School and St Thomas's Hospital, London, and qualified in 1899. His association with Louis Leopold Jenner and Samuel Shattock led him to become one of the earliest workers in the specialisms of pathology and bacteriology.

After a short period as a pathologist at the West London Hospital, Dudgeon returned in 1903 to St Thomas's where he spent the rest of his working life, and became superintendent of the Louis Jenner Clinical Laboratory. He found students eager to be taught and colleagues willing to take advantage of the application of pathology and bacteriology to medicine and surgery. His collaboration was constantly sought over obscure cases in the wards, and under his direction the clinical laboratory became one of the most important departments of the hospital. He was appointed director of the pathological laboratory and bacteriologist (1905), professor of pathology in the University of London (1919), curator of the Shattock Museum (1927), and dean of the medical school (1928). In 1909 Dudgeon married Norah Edith, third daughter of Richard Orpen of Kenmare, co. Kerry; they had one daughter and two sons, the younger of whom was (John) Alastair *Dudgeon.

In the First World War Dudgeon served in the Near East as a temporary colonel in the Army Medical Services, and carried out valuable investigations of infectious diseases prevalent among the troops. An account of his work on dysentery in Macedonia was published by the Medical Research Council in 1919. For his war services he was mentioned in dispatches three times; he was appointed CMG in 1918 and CBE in 1919, and awarded the order of St Sava of Serbia.

During Dudgeon's term as dean, the St Thomas's Hospital medical school was largely rebuilt and modernized. Dudgeon was for many years honorary secretary of the voluntary hospitals' committee, chairman of the deans' committee, and a member of the senate of London University. He was an active member of the Sankey commission on voluntary hospitals which reported in 1937. In these positions he exerted considerable influence on the course of medical education and hospital policy, and in particular he took a leading part in securing co-operation, for teaching purposes, between the voluntary and the London county council hospitals.

Administration, teaching, and a large consulting practice left little time for research. Nevertheless, Dudgeon published work that was both sound and original. He was the author of *The Bacteriology of Peritonitis*, in collaboration with Percy Sargent (1905), and of *Bacterial Vaccines and their Position in Therapeutics* (1927). He wrote many papers on tropical diseases, and on bacteriology and immunity. During the latter years of his life he developed a technique by means of smears for the rapid diagnosis of tumours and for the detection of malignant cells in bodily secretions, which found wide application. At the Royal College of Physicians, of which he was elected a fellow in 1908, he was Horace Dobell lecturer (1908) and Croonian lecturer (1912). He gave the Erasmus Wilson lecture at the Royal College of Surgeons in 1905 and 1908, and was president of the section of tropical diseases of the Royal Society of Medicine (1923–5).

Dudgeon was a kindly and humorous man, who endeavoured to disguise his warm humanity by a somewhat brusque manner. He died at 5 Collingham Gardens, London, on 22 October 1938, and was buried at Holy Trinity Church, Sloane Street, London. His wife survived him.

W. J. BISHOP, *rev.* MARY E. GIBSON

Sources H. Dean, 'In memoriam: Leonard Stanley Dudgeon, 1876–1938', *Journal of Pathology and Bacteriology*, 48 (1939), 231–9 · 'Leonard Stanley Dudgeon', *St Thomas's Hospital Gazette*, 36 (1937–8), 545–7 · *The Times* (24 Oct 1938) · *The Times* (27 Oct 1938), 17 · private information (1949) · *The Lancet* (29 Oct 1938), 1031; (5 Nov 1938), 1088 · *BMJ* (29 Oct 1938), 922 · *CGPLA Eng. & Wales* (1938)
Likenesses H. Wrightson, photograph, repro. in Dean, 'In memoriam', pl. 26
Wealth at death £16,982 6s. 6d.: probate, 7 Dec 1938, *CGPLA Eng. & Wales*

Dudgeon, Robert Ellis (1820–1904), homoeopathic physician, born at Leith on 17 March 1820, was the younger son of a timber merchant and shipowner in that town. After attending a private school he received his medical education at Edinburgh, partly in the university and partly in the extra-academical medical school. At the age of nineteen he received the licence of the Royal College of Surgeons of Edinburgh and also passed all the examinations for the MD degree. He attended lectures in Paris until he was old enough to graduate MD on 1 August 1841. He then spent a semester at Vienna, where his fellow students John Drysdale and Rutherfurd Russell, were studying homoeopathy, which was then at the height of its popularity in the city. Dudgeon was not at the time attracted by Hahnemann's system of homoeopathy. From Vienna he went to Berlin to study diseases of the eye under Juengken, and of the ear under Kramer, and organic chemistry under Simon; finally he travelled to Dublin for instruction by Graves, Stokes, Corrigan, and Marsh.

Dudgeon started practice in Liverpool, in 1843. The *British Journal of Homoeopathy* was first issued in this year, and Dudgeon translated German articles for it. This introduction to the subject enabled Drysdale to induce him to study homoeopathy. After a second sojourn in Vienna to study homoeopathic practice there, Dudgeon began to practise in London in 1845. He was editor of the *British Journal of Homoeopathy* conjointly with Drysdale and Russell from 1846 until 1884, when the journal ceased. He was a prolific writer and was best known for his English translations of Hahnemann's writings, of which the *Organon* appeared in 1849 and the *Materia medica pura* in 1880. In 1850 he helped to found the Hahnemann Hospital in Bloomsbury Square, London. Dudgeon lectured in the school on the theory and practice of homoeopathy and published his lectures in 1854. These lectures made clear his devotion to the *Similimum* principle but his inability to accept Hahnemann's explanatory theories. In 1869 he was for a short time assistant physician to the homoeopathic hospital. He was secretary of the British Homoeopathic Society in 1848, vice-president in 1874–5, and president in 1878 and 1890. Although elected president of the International Homoeopathic Congress which met in Atlantic City in 1904 he did not attend, owing to ill health.

Dudgeon's patients included Lord Lyndhurst, John Bright, Lord Ebury, and Samuel Butler, who became his intimate friend. In 1858 with the aid of Lord Ebury he succeeded in defeating the efforts of Sir James Simpson to preclude homoeopaths from practice. A clause drafted by Dudgeon was inserted into the new Medical Act, which prevented universities and colleges from withholding degrees on the grounds that the candidate was a homoeopath. In 1869, despairing of ever convincing his colleagues in conventional medicine, he formed the Homoeopathic League for which he wrote numerous tracts for distribution to the public and the profession.

Dudgeon was twice married, and had two sons and three daughters. He was a man with many interests outside clinical homoeopathy. For many years he was a member of the London Scottish regiment of the rifle brigade and was a keen golfer. He invented spectacles for use under water and at the age of seventy he published his book *On the Prolongation of Life* (1890). He was best known in orthodox medicine for his modification of Marey's sphygmograph, a device for recording the pulse, so that it was small enough for clinical work. It was in general use in physiological research for a decade and was employed by Sir James Mackenzie in his early research on the heart.

Dudgeon recognized the merits of current scientific advances and wished homoeopathy to have a place within the medical establishment. He was what later came to be known as a 'pathological prescriber', though most of his contemporaries shared his viewpoint. It is perhaps fortunate that his life ended just as new ideas, which were to sweep away everything that he stood for, appeared from America in the first decade of the twentieth century. Dudgeon died at 22 Carlton Hill, St John's Wood, London, on 8 September 1904 and was cremated at Golders Green, his ashes being buried in Willesden cemetery. He was survived by his second wife, Dora Anna Dudgeon.

D'A. POWER, *rev.* BERNARD LEARY

Sources *Homoeopathic World*, 39 (1904), 433, 464 · *Journal* [British Homoeopathic Society], 13 (1905), 55 · C. Lawrence, 'The Dudgeon sphygmograph and its descendants', *Medical History*, 23 (1979), 96–101, esp. 100 · *CGPLA Eng. & Wales* (1904) · *Daily News* (10 Sept 1904)
Likenesses London Stereoscopic Company, photograph, Wellcome L.
Wealth at death £2479 19s. 4d.: probate, 19 Oct 1904, *CGPLA Eng. & Wales*

Dudgeon, William (1705/6–1743), freethinker and philosopher, is of unknown origins. A tenant farmer who resided at Lennel Hill Farm, near Coldstream, Berwickshire, he was one of several philosophers active in the borders area of Scotland during this period. Other figures in this group include Andrew Baxter, Henry Home (Lord Kames), and most importantly David Hume.

Dudgeon's first major study was *The State of the Moral World Considered* (1732). In this work he defended a metaphysical optimism that is similar to that of Lord Shaftesbury, as well as a necessitarian doctrine not unlike that of Anthony Collins. This work drew a hostile reply from Andrew Baxter, who was Scotland's most prominent defender of the philosophy of Samuel Clarke. Baxter accused Dudgeon of both 'atheism' and 'scepticism'. These charges encouraged the local clergy in the presbytery of Chirnside to prosecute Dudgeon on the ground that he was the author of a work that 'contains many gross errors subversive of Christianity'. One of the clerics involved was an uncle of David Hume (who was also living in Chirnside at this time with his family).

Among Dudgeon's other major works is *Philosophical Letters* (1737), written to John Jackson, another prominent defender of Clarke's philosophy. In this work Dudgeon criticized Clarke's Newtonian metaphysics and morals. By way of alternative he defended a form of pantheistic immaterialism that blended Berkeley and Spinoza, along with a moral sense ethics in line with Shaftesbury. This work was favourably reviewed in the journal *History of the Works of the Learned* (1737/8), where Dudgeon's 'Spinozism' was noted.

In another controversy Dudgeon tangled with William Warburton on the subject of Pope's *Essay on Man*. Warburton, a friend of Baxter's (and later a celebrated enemy of Hume's), referred to Dudgeon as belonging to 'the tribe of Free-thinkers' and placed him in the same company as John Toland, Matthew Tindal, and Collins (Warburton, preface). Some years later John Witherspoon, in his satirical work *Ecclesiastical Characteristics* (maxim 4), mentioned Dudgeon along with a number of thinkers, including Shaftesbury, Leibniz, Collins, and Kames, whose ideas had been influential on the 'moderate' party in the Church of Scotland. These controversies and references suggest that Dudgeon's philosophy enjoyed some influence on both sides of the border.

There is no evidence that Dudgeon and Hume had any direct contact. Nevertheless, given their close proximity when Hume was young and philosophically active, and the role of Hume's uncle in Dudgeon's prosecution, it is reasonable to assume that Hume knew of Dudgeon's philosophical work and the associated controversies involving Baxter and Warburton. Suffice it to note that Dudgeon and Hume shared philosophical interests and that on a number of significant issues they took up similar positions.

Dudgeon, a resolute defender of the thesis that all is for the best, died of consumption, aged thirty-seven, on 28 January 1743 at Upsettlington, Berwickshire. His most important works were gathered into a single volume, which was published without a printer's name attached in 1765.   P. RUSSELL

Sources W. Dudgeon, *The philosophical works* (1765); repr. with a new introduction by D. Berman (1994) • W. Warburton, *A critical and philosophical commentary on Pope's 'Essay'* (1742) • J. Witherspoon, *Ecclesiastical characteristics*, 5th edn (1762) • A. Baxter, *Some reflections on a late pamphlet called, 'The state of the moral world considered'* (1732) • J. McCosh, *The Scottish philosophy, biographical, expository, critical, from Hutcheson to Hamilton* (New York, 1875) • P. Russell, 'Dudgeon, William', *The dictionary of eighteenth-century British philosophers*, ed. J. W. Yolton, J. V. Price, and J. Stephens (1999)
Archives NA Scot., CH2/516/3, CH2/265/2, CH1/3

Dudgeon, William (1758–1813), poet, was born on 13 October 1758 at Oldhamstocks, Haddington, the son of John Dudgeon, farmer, and his wife, Jannet Spence. His mother was an aunt of Robert Ainslie, writer to the signet, a friend of Robert Burns. Dudgeon was educated alongside John Rennie the engineer at Dunbar. His father procured for him a thirty-year lease of an extensive farm near Duns in Berwickshire, which Dudgeon called Primrose Hill and which he cultivated successfully for many years. He wrote a number of unpublished pieces as well as the song 'The Maid that Tends the Goats', which became very popular and was included in Allan Cunningham's edition of Burns's *Works* (p. 533). His other hobbies included painting and music. In May 1787 he met Burns, then visiting the father of Robert Ainslie at Berrywell, near Duns. Burns called Dudgeon 'a Poet at times' and thought him to have 'a worthy, remarkable character, a good deal of penetration, a great deal of information, some genius, and extreme Modesty' (Lindsay, 111). Dudgeon died at Duns on 28 October 1813, and was buried in the churchyard of Prestonkirk.   J. M. RIGG, rev. SARAH COUPER

Sources Anderson, *Scot. nat.* • C. Rogers, *The modern Scottish minstrel, or, The songs of Scotland of the past half-century*, 1 (1855), 151 • Irving, *Scots.* • M. Lindsay, *The Burns encyclopedia*, 3rd edn (1980) • bap. reg. Scot.

Dudhope. For this title name *see* Scrymgeour, John, first Viscount Dudhope (*d.* 1643) [*see under* Scrymgeour, Sir James, of Dudhope (*c.*1550–1612)]; Scrymgeour, James, second Viscount Dudhope (*d.* 1644) [*see under* Scrymgeour, Sir James, of Dudhope (*c.*1550–1612)].

Dudley. For this title name *see* individual entries under Dudley; *see also* Sutton, John (VI), first Baron Dudley (1400–1487); Sutton, Edward, fourth Baron Dudley (*c.*1515–1586); Ward, John William, earl of Dudley (1781–1833); Ward, William Humble, second earl of Dudley (1867–1932); Millar, Gertrude [Gertrude Ward, countess of Dudley] (1879–1952).

Dudley and Ward. For this title name *see* Ward, John, second Viscount Dudley and Ward (1725–1788).

Dudley, Alice, Lady Dudley (1579–1669). *See under* Dudley, Sir Robert (1574–1649).

Dudley, Ambrose, earl of Warwick (*c.*1530–1590), magnate, was the fourth son of John *Dudley, duke of Northumberland (1504–1553), royal minister, and his wife, Jane

Ambrose Dudley, earl of Warwick (*c*.1530–1590), by unknown artist [left, with a page]

*Dudley (1508/9–1555) [*see under* Dudley, John, duke of Northumberland], noblewoman, daughter of Sir Edward Guildford of Halden and Hemsted, Kent, and his first wife, Eleanor. His brothers included John *Dudley, earl of Warwick (1527?–1554) [*see under* Dudley, John, duke of Northumberland], Henry *Dudley (1531?–1557) [*see under* Dudley, John, duke of Northumberland], Robert *Dudley, earl of Leicester (1532/3–1588), and Guildford *Dudley (*c*.1535–1554), and his sisters included Mary *Sidney, *née* Dudley (1530x35–1586). As is the case with most of his siblings, his year of birth is conjectural and little is known of the circumstances of his childhood. Thomas Wilson may have had some involvement in his education.

Early career, 1549–1559 Ambrose Dudley is first encountered serving with his father against the Norfolk rebels in 1549. Shortly afterwards he married his first wife, Anne (*d.* 1552), daughter and coheir of William Whorwood, of London, and his first wife, Cassandra. Ambrose's marriage may have been the occasion of his appointment as constable of Kenilworth Castle, Warwickshire, on 20 December 1549. His wife died of the sweating sickness on 26 May 1552, shortly after the birth of a daughter (possibly named Margaret), who died about the same time. By Edward VI's death in July 1553, Dudley had married an older woman,

Elizabeth (1520–1563), daughter and heir of Gilbert *Tailboys, first Baron Tailboys of Kyme (*d.* 1530) [*see under* Tailboys, William], and his wife, Elizabeth, and widow of Thomas Wimbish.

Ambrose Dudley followed his father to disaster in July 1553 and surrendered with him at Cambridge, but it was not until 13 November that he was arraigned, together with his brothers Henry and Guildford, and his sister-in-law, Lady Jane Dudley [*see* Grey, Lady Jane (1537–1554)], found guilty of treason, and subsequently attainted. The appeal to Philip of Spain that Ambrose's wife commissioned Roger Ascham to draft in November 1554 reveals that he alone of the Dudley brothers was still in the Tower of London then. The reason may be that the death of his brother Warwick in September left him the Dudley heir. Elizabeth Dudley's appeal seems to have worked, for in December Ambrose joined Robert in the tournaments arranged by Philip to cement Anglo-Spanish relations. The three surviving brothers now enjoyed considerable royal benevolence. In January 1555 they were pardoned, though they remained attainted. Their mother died at the same time, leaving her fee simple lands to Ambrose, which Mary I permitted him to inherit despite his attainder. Following a further appeal by Elizabeth Dudley in February she and Ambrose were granted her substantial inheritance on 17 July 1556, also despite the attainder. Henry's wife received similar favour on 5 July 1556, but Robert's wife had still to inherit. In November 1555 Ambrose (with Henry's agreement) sold the dowager duchess's estate to Robert for £800.

In spring 1555 Elizabeth Dudley suffered a hysterical pregnancy and their marriage proved subsequently childless. Together with Robert and Henry (who was killed there), Ambrose served in the expedition to St Quentin in 1557, largely out of obligation to Philip. In return, the attainders of the four remaining Dudley children were repealed in 1558, though in the process they also had to surrender any claim of right to their father's lands, titles, or offices. The cost of his service at St Quentin nearly broke Ambrose and his wife and, as their music tutor recorded, they were forced to reduce their household.

Restoration, 1559–1572 What, if any, connection Ambrose Dudley had with Princess Elizabeth is unknown, but like Robert and their sister Mary he was an immediate beneficiary of the new reign. In March 1559 he was granted the manor of Knebworth Beauchamp, Leicestershire, and, more importantly, the office of master of the ordnance, though he was cautious about taking it on because of the debts accrued by his predecessor, Sir Richard Southwell, and his patent did not pass until 12 April 1560. More difficult were the family titles and lands, given the surrender of the claim of right. On 25 December 1561 (after some hesitation) Elizabeth I created him Baron Lisle and then, the following day, earl of Warwick. Several months later (6 April 1562) he was granted the lordship of Warwick Castle and other estates in the county. At the same time he and his brother readopted the bear and ragged staff device.

In the autumn of 1562 Warwick was given command of

the expeditionary force to Newhaven (Le Havre), possibly the major episode of his life. His commission was dated 1 October, but he was delayed by bad weather and did not arrive until the 29th. There seems no doubt that Robert wanted this post, but Elizabeth would not let him go and Warwick went to some extent as his surrogate. The operation was complicated from the start by the fact that the purpose of Warwick's force was unclear, and at the end of the year Elizabeth ordered him not to give active military support to the French protestants. In March 1563 the two French sides made peace and Elizabeth responded by ordering that Newhaven be held until Calais was returned. Warwick had warned throughout that 'I fear [you] are too much abused in the good opinion you have in the strength of this town' (BL, Harley MS 6990, fol. 55r). The landward fortifications were minimal and a major engineering effort would be necessary to make a long-term defence possible. Nevertheless he did the best he could and his surrender in July 1563 was an honourable one forced by an outbreak of plague that decimated the English garrison.

However much a disaster the expedition was in political terms, Warwick gained widespread commendation. The garrison was well-disciplined, its morale high, and it was free from the internal wranglings that crippled so many other Elizabethan military operations. He also maintained good relations with the French civil population. He received his reward in the form of election as a KG in April 1563 (he was installed by proxy on 23 May) and a second large grant of land on 23 June 1564. This was a combination of west midlands manors and the lordship of Ruthin, Denbighshire. On the other hand, his wife died early in 1563 and he returned with a nasty leg wound, from which he never fully recovered. His indifferent health rendered abortive proposals in subsequent years to appoint him either lord president of the north or lord deputy of Ireland.

On 11 November 1565 Warwick married his third and best-known wife, the sixteen-year-old Anne Russell (1548/9–1604) [see Dudley, Anne], noblewoman, eldest of three daughters of Francis *Russell, second earl of Bedford (1526/7–1585), and his first wife, Margaret. It was one of the grandest of the Elizabethan court marriages. Yet whatever dynastic hopes were pinned on it, this marriage too was childless. Warwick's last active military appointment came in November 1569 when he was given command, together with Edward Fiennes de Clinton, ninth Baron Clinton, of the army raised in the south of England against the northern uprising. This appointment lasted only two months for the rising collapsed in November and, because of worries about his health, Warwick was given permission to return early. His brother Robert (now earl of Leicester) went to meet him at Kenilworth in January 1570 and found him well: 'all this hard whether [he] hath every day travelled on horse, your majesty's service hath made him forget his payne', but 'assuredly he ys marvelous weary, though in my Judgement hit hath done his boddy much good' (PRO, SP 15/17, fols. 51r–51v). For this service Warwick received some of the forfeited estates in Yorkshire and Northumberland in 1571 and 1572. On 4 May 1571 he was granted the office of chief butler of England.

The Dudley partnership 1572–1588 During the last two decades of his life Warwick lived mainly at North Hall, the house he built at Northaw, Hertfordshire, when not at court or in London. He was sworn of the privy council on 5 September 1573 and was initially an active member, but after 1578 his attendance declined to half its previous level, which may reflect the steady deterioration of his health during the 1580s.

Owing to the disappearance of most of its records prior to the 1590s, Warwick's administration of the ordnance office is not easy to detail. The office underwent a dramatic expansion during the sixteenth century from its modest origins as a minor court department. It was now a highly centralized commissioning and storing agency for ordnance, munitions, and small arms. The handling of commodities with a potential market value made it, like the navy, an obvious target for charges of peculation. The daily running of the office was the responsibility of the lieutenant of the ordnance, who from 1567 to 1587 was Warwick's Newhaven colleague, Sir William Pelham, but Warwick's estate was charged with a debt of £2005 for 'munitions of war' released into his custody (CSP dom., 1591–4, 526). Precisely what those were is unclear, though Warwick appears to have interpreted liberally the master's perquisite of selling off old and worn-out equipment. A more controversial issue was his possible generosity to William of Orange, a major consumer of English ordnance. This was the subject of a formal complaint by Frederic Perrenot, seigneur de Champigny, Philip II's ambassador, in 1576. On 21 July 1585 Warwick's nephew Sir Philip *Sidney (1554–1586) was appointed joint master with him, possibly in response to the earl's declining health, but Sidney's departure for Flushing several months later made his appointment irrelevant.

With the exception of a few fragments, Warwick's papers were destroyed after his widow's death. Their disappearance has made him difficult to delineate as an individual and has reinforced the impression that he was very much in his younger brother's shadow. The affection between the two was undoubted and they were almost inseparable. Warwick's only recorded visits to the midlands were with his brother (1566, 1571, 1580) or on progress (1572, 1575). They visited the spa at Buxton, Derbyshire, together in 1577 and Bath and Bristol in 1587. Leicester regularly referred to his brother as 'him I love as myself' ('An unpublished letter', 284) and Warwick reciprocated, 'lett me have your best advyce what is best for me to doe for that I meane to take soche partt as you doe' (Bruce, 151). When encountered together, as in the accounts in the Black Book of Warwick or their correspondence with Thomas Wood, they are as one, Warwick informing Wood that 'there is no man knoweth his [Leicester's] doings better than I myself' ('Letters of Thomas Wood', 93).

The brothers employed the same men as estate and legal officers in both the west midlands and Wales and their provincial affinity was essentially a joint one. Warwick supported Leicester in reviving the 'great Berkeley lawsuit', and they shared the regained manors between them. Leicester held Warwick's proxy for the parliaments of 1566, 1571, and 1584. Warwick's wider interests mirrored his brother's. He invested in the Fenton voyage of 1582 and Leicester's Barbary Company of 1585. His literary patronage as reflected in the twenty-five works dedicated to him was not as extensive as his brother's, but included many of the same authors, about half of whom were puritan divines. The one investment in which he was possibly more adventurous was Martin Frobisher's north-west passage voyage of 1576.

Both men were no less closely involved in each other's personal affairs. If Leicester arranged Warwick's third marriage, in 1564–5, Warwick was godfather to Leicester's illegitimate son Robert *Dudley (1574–1649) in 1574 and one of the witnesses to his marriage in 1578 to Lettice *Dudley, dowager countess of Essex (b. after 1540, d. 1634). For Warwick the consequences of their closeness were unfortunate. He held the senior peerage and the one that really mattered to both men; moreover there is some evidence that in the 1560s he was expected to predecease Leicester. Leicester's legitimate son, Robert Dudley, Baron Denbigh (d. 1584), would have been Warwick's heir as well. When Leicester made his first will (1582) he nominated Warwick overseer on the assumption that his young son would inherit both men's estates. By the time he made his final will in 1587, Denbigh was dead and Leicester left Warwick all his lands (except for those in the countess's jointure) for life. Leicester's unexpected death in 1588 probably hastened Warwick's own for with his brother's estate came his massive debts. The last year of his life was dominated by the settlement of Leicester's affairs, which included giving his widow £5000 towards the debts.

Final years, 1588–1590 Warwick made his own will on 28 January 1590, probably just before his leg, which had turned gangrenous, was amputated. He left certain fee simple lands including North Hall in a use to his wife, and the remainder to trustees for the repayment of his debts. The residual heirs to anything left over were his wife, then his sister Katherine Hastings, countess of Huntingdon (c.1538–1620), and ultimately his nephew, Sir Robert *Sidney (1563–1626). It was later claimed that Elizabeth came to see him shortly before his death, but what transpired is unknown. Two days before he died he summoned Sir Edward Stafford to entrust him with the interests of Leicester's illegitimate son. Stafford found him in great pain 'in his bedd the Hickocke [spasms] havinge already taken him which lasted him unto his death' (CKS, MS U1475/L2/4, item 3, m. 79). Warwick died at Bedford House on the Strand on 21 February 1590. His funeral took place on 9 April and, like Leicester, he was buried in the Beauchamp chapel of St Mary's, Warwick. His elegant tomb was presumably erected by his widow, for he had specified only that his body 'be disposed in Christian Burial' at her discretion. The dowager countess died at Northaw on 9 February 1604 and was buried at Chenies, Buckinghamshire.

None of the reputed portraits of Warwick can be relied on as a likeness, but he certainly lacked his brother's polish, which was the subject of a joke by Elizabeth in 1563 that 'she wished to God the Earl of Warwick had the grace and good looks of Lord Robert in which case each [Elizabeth and Mary, queen of Scots] could have one' (Hume, 313). By the mid-seventeenth century Warwick's homeliness had become part of the legend of the good earl. He was 'a little crooked man but a man of exemplary piety, one of the great friends of religion and one of the ornaments of those times. He had great influence upon his brother the Earl of Leicester, which made him so much to patronise religion and the godly ministers' (BL, Harley MS 6071, fol. 61v). Warwick certainly possessed the fervent loyalty of his former Newhaven subordinates—Wood was already referring to him as the 'Good Earll of Warwick' in 1574 ('Letters of Thomas Wood', 6)—but the reality behind the legend is less obvious. Warwick endowed no charities. He was not a spectacularly generous landlord—there were anti-enclosure riots at Northaw in the spring of 1579. Nor was the puritan survey of the ministry of Warwickshire in 1586 uniformly impressed by his appointments. It is possible that he was closer to such quasi-presbyterian ministers as John Field and John Knewstub than his brother was, but, given the closeness between them, Warwick's reputation may owe as much to Leicester's sexual and political notoriety as his own personal rectitude.

SIMON ADAMS

Sources T. Wilson, *A discourse upon usurye by waye of dialogue* (1572); repr., ed. R. H. Tawney (1925) · D. Loades, *John Dudley, duke of Northumberland, 1504–1553* (1996) · PRO, DL [duchy of Lancaster] · *The visitation of Staffordshire by Robert Glover … 1583*, ed. H. S. Grazebrook (1883) · *The whole works of Roger Ascham*, ed. G. A. Giles, 3 vols. (1865) · R. C. McCoy, 'From the Tower to the tiltyard: Robert Dudley's return to glory', *HJ*, 27 (1984), 425–35 · *CPR, 1553–82* · S. Adams, *Leicester and the court: essays on Elizabethan politics* (2002) · *The autobiography of Thomas Wythorne*, ed. J. M. Osborne (1961) · Longleat House, Wiltshire, Marquess of Bath MSS, Dudley MSS · papiers d'état et de l'audience, National State Archives, Brussels · Harley MSS, BL · *CSP for.*, 1558–89 · state papers, domestic, addenda, PRO, SP 15 · R. W. Stewart, *The English ordnance office, 1585–1625: a case-study in bureaucracy* (1996) · *CSP dom.*, 1547–80, with addenda 1547–1625 · 'An unpublished letter of Robert Dudley, earl of Leicester, 1564', *N&Q*, 6th ser., 3 (1881), 283–4 · J. Bruce, ed., *Correspondence of Robert Dudley, earl of Leycester*, CS, 27 (1844) · T. Kemp, ed., *The Black Book of Warwick* [1898] · 'Letters of Thomas Wood, puritan, 1566–1577', ed. P. Collinson, *BIHR*, special suppl., 5 (1960) [whole issue]; repr. in P. Collinson, *Godly people: essays on English protestantism and puritanism* (1983), 45–107 · S. Adams, 'The papers of Robert Dudley, earl of Leicester, 3: the countess of Leicester's collection', *Archives*, 22 (1996), 1–26 · H. Sydney and others, *Letters and memorials of state*, ed. A. Collins, 2 vols. (1746) · CKS, Penshurst papers, MS U1475 · M. A. S. Hume, ed., *Calendar of letters and state papers relating to English affairs, preserved principally in the archives of Simancas*, 4 vols., PRO (1892–9) · *APC* · A. Peel, ed., *The seconde parte of a register*, 2 vols. (1915)

Archives Berkeley Castle, Gloucestershire, estate papers, chiefly related to the Berkeley lawsuit · Warks. CRO, Warwick Castle deposit, estate papers, C1886 | BL, Harley MSS, corresp. · BL, Lansdowne MSS, corresp. · BL, Cotton MSS, corresp. · Hatfield House, Cecil papers, corresp. · PRO, state papers domestic, Elizabeth I, SP12 · PRO, state papers foreign, Elizabeth I, SP70

Likenesses M. Gheeraerts senior, etching (*Procession of Garter knights 1578*), BM · W. & M. van de Passe, line engraving, BM, NPG; repro. in H. Holland, *Herwologia* (1620) · alabaster tomb effigy, St

Mary's Church, Warwickshire, Beauchamp chapel • oils, Longleat House, Wiltshire [*see illus.*] • portrait (of Dudley?), Charlecote House • portrait (of Dudley?), Parham Park • portrait (of Dudley?), Hatfield House, Hertfordshire • portrait (of Dudley?), Woburn Abbey, Bedfordshire

Wealth at death debts of £7000 charged on estate: *CSP dom.*, 1601–3, 278; will, PRO, PROB 11/75, fol. 43 printed in Collins; Warks. CRO CR136/C1482 (1590); inquisition post mortem, Gloucestershire; surveys Warwickshire estates 1590 E 178/2351; LR2/255/83–111

Dudley [*née* Robsart], **Amy, Lady Dudley** (1532–1560), gentlewoman, was born on 7 June 1532, probably at Stanfield Hall, Norfolk, the only child and heir of Sir John Robsart (*d.* 1554), landowner, of Syderstone, Norfolk, and his wife, Elizabeth (*d.* 1557), daughter of John Scott of Camberwell, Surrey. Elizabeth Robsart was the widow of Roger Appleyard (*d.* 1528), of Stanfield, Norfolk, and mother of four children including John Appleyard (*b.* 1529, *d.* in or after 1574). Sir John Robsart held three manors near King's Lynn, as well as one in Suffolk, and was a substantial grazier, leaving over 3000 sheep at his death in 1554 (there were 4900 on the estate in 1563). However, his seat, Syderstone Hall, was uninhabitable and he may have lived outside Norfolk until he married Elizabeth Appleyard between 1528 and 1531, for he is not among the resident gentry in the subsidy lists of the 1520s. Thereafter he resided at the Appleyard house, Stanfield Hall, and from 1532 he was a Norfolk JP.

A printed missal, *Missale adusum insignis ac preclare ecclesie Sarum* (1512), now known as the 'Robsart missal', contains the inscription 'Amea Robsart generosa filia Johno Robsart Armiger nata fuit in vij die Junij in Anno Dom Angelismo cccccxxxii' (Durham University Library, Bamburgh Select 15, p. 4). Robsart's inquisition post mortem of 16 October 1554 gives his daughter's age as twenty-three, making her a year older, but if the missal is correct she was almost exactly the same age as Robert *Dudley, later earl of Leicester (1532/3–1588), courtier and magnate, fifth son of John *Dudley, duke of Northumberland, and his wife, Jane *Dudley, *née* Guildford [*see under* Dudley, John]. The missal also contains anti-papal marginalia, which suggests that its owner was someone of strong reformist views. Further evidence of Sir John Robsart's allegiances are found in the precocious reference in his will of 6 October 1535 to Henry VIII as 'within his realme supreame hede of the church immediately under God' and in the dedication to him by Thomas Becon of *The Fortresse of the Faithful* (1550), in honour of the 'godly affection and christian zeal which both you and … your wife have borne toward the pure religion of God these many years' (Norwich commissary court, Walpoole, fol. 77r; Becon, 592). His wife shared his views. He is said to have been a receiver for Thomas Howard, third duke of Norfolk, but significantly it was only after the fall of the Howards in 1546 that he became prominent in county government. He was made KB at Edward VI's coronation on 20 February 1547 and appointed sheriff of Norfolk and Suffolk for 1547–8.

Nothing else is known of Amy Robsart herself until her marriage to Robert Dudley at Sheen on 4 June 1550. Robsart had named her his sole heir in his will, although he

also had an illegitimate son, Arthur. Under the marriage contract he made with Warwick on 24 May he granted Amy and her husband an annuity of £20 per annum until they inherited the Robsart estate after his and his wife's death. Warwick for his part obtained for them the lands of Coxford Priory, which were adjacent to Robsart's own. The two estates combined would make the couple major figures in the county. How they met is unknown, but it was presumably during the campaign against Ket's rebellion in 1549, when Warwick and his sons stayed near Stanfield. Sir William Cecil's sardonic observation on Dudley's marriage in 1565 that 'nuptii carnales a laetitia incipiunt et in luctu terminantur' ('carnal marriages begin in joy and end in weeping'), suggests that it was a romantic one (Hatfield House, Cecil MS 155, art. 29).

Although Robsart and his son-in-law were active in Norfolk local government between 1550 and 1553, the Dudleys do not appear to have lived in the county. Dudley was knighted in 1551. On the eve of Edward's death the couple were residing at Somerset House, where Dudley was keeper. Amy appears to have remained in London during her husband's imprisonment in 1553–4, for she was given permission to visit him in the Tower of London. Robsart died on 8 June 1554 (without revising his 1535 will), but Lady Elizabeth lived on until June 1557. It was not until then that the Dudleys inherited the Robsart estate. In the years immediately after Dudley's release in October 1554 they were technically landless (he had lost the Coxford lands in his attainder), but the Robsarts appear to have given them financial assistance and he received help from his brothers in 1556.

Amy Dudley's earliest surviving letter is dated simply from Mr Hyde's, 7 August, and was written to John Flowerdew. Hyde has been identified recently as William Hyde of Throcking, Hertfordshire, rather than one of the Berkshire Hydes as previously thought. The letter can also be dated to 1557, when Dudley left for the St Quentin campaign: 'he beyng sore trubeled with wayty affars and I not beyng altogether in quyet for his soden departyng' (BL, Harley MS 4712, fol. 275r). She was still living at Throcking in the spring of 1559, but this may have been a prolonged temporary arrangement, while the couple found a residence. On 22 July 1558 Dudley was negotiating the purchase of the manor of Flitcham, Norfolk, as, given the unsuitability of Syderstone, 'I must if to dwell in that countrey take some house other than my none [own]' (BL, Harley MS 4712, fol. 273r).

Amy Dudley did not follow her husband to court on Elizabeth I's accession, but remained at Throcking until he visited her there immediately after Easter 1559. Six weeks later (mid-May) she went to London, where she shopped and then went on to Camberwell. In the middle of June Dudley left on the royal progress into Kent and she departed from Camberwell. Thereafter her movements are difficult to trace, but in September she may have been staying at Sir Richard Verney's house at Compton Verney, Warwickshire, and by December had moved to Cumnor Place in Berkshire, 3 miles from Oxford. This was a former house of the abbot of Abingdon, recently leased by

Anthony Foster. Foster later became keeper of Dudley's wardrobe, but their association was not of long standing in 1559, and it is just possible that he was a relative of Amy's. At Cumnor she had a household of some ten servants and there were other gentlewomen living in the house as well. Up to the eve of her death she was ordering gowns and other clothes from London. Berkshire was a novel part of the country for her, but her residence there may have been a consequence of Dudley's appointment as lieutenant of Windsor Castle in November 1559.

Amy Dudley was found dead at Cumnor in the evening of 8 September 1560. Dudley was then with the court at Windsor, which was on its return from the progress in Hampshire. All that is known about the immediate circumstances comes from a correspondence of five letters between him and his household officer Thomas Blount of Kidderminster, Worcestershire, between 9 and 15 September. Amy Dudley was alone at the time (although the other women were elsewhere in the house) and no obvious cause of death could be discovered. The verdict of the coroner's jury was death by misadventure. Blount learned that she had rather emotionally and suddenly ordered her servants to go to a fair at Abingdon, which makes it difficult to credit a murder planned in advance. He worried initially about suicide, but this was denied strongly by her servants. In early 1567 John Appleyard tried to reopen the case, claiming that his half-sister had been murdered, though not by Dudley. He received short shrift from the privy council, was shown the verdict of the inquest, and then announced that he was satisfied.

Amy Dudley was buried at St Mary's, Oxford, on 22 September with the full dignities of her rank. Her husband appeared in mourning for the next six months, but his absence from the funeral (although this was within convention) and his failure to erect any memorial to her have been held to his discredit. The main literary source for a murder plot is the famous libel, *Leicester's Commonwealth*, published in 1584. It claimed that Dudley 'when his lordship was in full hope to marry her Majesty … did but set her [his wife] aside to the house of his servant Foster of Cumnor by Oxford'. Having failed to poison her, he had her murder arranged by Verney, disguising it as a broken neck from a fall down a flight of stairs (Peck, 81-2, 90-92). In recent years a near contemporary version of this account including the role played by Verney has come to light, possibly written by John Hales, which suggests that it was in circulation immediately after Amy's death (BL, Add. MS 48023, fols. 353r-353v).

In the nineteenth century the murder theory was sustained by the discovery of the contemporary Spanish ambassadorial correspondence. This repeated rumours that Amy Dudley was ill and that Dudley was trying to poison or divorce her as early as the spring of 1559. The only report to survive from the period immediately following her death, dated 11 September 1560, suggests that Cecil believed that Dudley was intending to murder his wife. In 1956 Ian Aird advanced a challenging alternative. On the basis of a reference in a Spanish report of April 1559 to her suffering from a malady in one of her breasts,

he suggested that the cause of her death was advanced breast cancer. This theory accounts for a number of the known circumstances, but a serious illness in April 1559 is difficult to reconcile with her extensive travelling in the following months.

The Dudleys' domestic life presents as many mysteries as Amy Dudley's death. There is not a hint of pregnancy or even miscarriage during the ten years of their marriage. It is also clear that after the summer of 1559 Dudley never saw his wife again. He was clearly shocked by her death, but possibly more by the political damage it might cause. The key role was possibly played by Elizabeth, as hinted at in the 'Journal of matters of state': 'when the Lord Rob. went to his wife he wentt all in black, and howe he was commanded to saye that he did nothing with her, when he cam to her, as seldom he did' (BL, Add. MS 48023, fol. 353r). Although the tradition that Amy Dudley was incarcerated or secluded at Cumnor has been disproved, Elizabeth's favour to Dudley clearly did not extend to his wife.

SIMON ADAMS

Sources C. E. Moreton, *The Townshends and their world: gentry, law and land in Norfolk, c.1450-1551* (1992) · D. MacCulloch, *Suffolk and the Tudors: politics and religion in an English county, 1500-1600* (1986) · Longleat House, Wiltshire, Dudley MSS · Bamburgh Select 15, U. Durham L. · PRO, E 150/650 · PRO, E 315/37 · register Walpoole, Norfolk RO, Norwich commissary court · T. Becon, *Works*, Parker Society (1844) · *The chronicle and political papers of King Edward VI*, ed. W. K. Jordan (1966) · Hatfield House, Hertfordshire, Cecil MSS · BL, Harley MS 4712 · S. Adams, *Leicester and the court: essays on Elizabethan politics* (2002) · S. Adams, ed., *Household accounts and disbursement books of Robert Dudley, earl of Leicester, 1558-1561, 1584-1586*, CS, 6 (1995) · S. Adams, 'The papers of Robert Dudley, earl of Leicester: III, the countess of Leicester's collection', *Archives*, 22 (1996), 1-26 · letters of state II, Magd. Cam., Pepys Library · D. C. Peck, ed., *Leicester's commonwealth: the copy of a letter written by a master of art of Cambridge (1584) and related documents* (1985) · I. Aird, 'The death of Amy Robsart: accident, suicide, or murder—or disease?', *EngHR*, 71 (1956), 69-79

Archives Longleat House, Wiltshire, Dudley papers IV | Birm. CL, Hagley Hall MSS

Dudley, Sir Andrew (c.1507-1559). *See under* Sutton, Henry (d. 1564?).

Dudley, Anne, countess of Warwick (1538-1587). *See under* Seymour, Lady Jane (1541-1561).

Dudley [née Russell], **Anne, countess of Warwick** (1548/9-1604), courtier, was the eldest of the three daughters of Francis *Russell, second earl of Bedford (1526/7-1585), magnate, and his first wife, Margaret (d. 1562), daughter of Sir John St John of Bletsoe, Bedfordshire, and his wife, Margaret. Thanks to the loss of most of the Russell family papers for the sixteenth century her childhood is effectively a blank. How well educated she was is equally unknown. She was said to have been 'no good secretary' in 1600 (*Letters*, ed. Collins, 2.192), and her sister Margaret was taught no language other than English.

Anne Russell's life was shaped by two events in her adolescence: her appointment as a maid of honour to Elizabeth I in 1559 and then her marriage at the age of sixteen to Ambrose *Dudley, earl of Warwick (c.1530–1590), magnate, fourth son of John Dudley, duke of Northumberland, and his wife, Jane, in the queen's chapel at Whitehall Palace on 11 November 1565. It is possible that she entered Elizabeth's household before the accession. In 1564 Warwick's brother Robert *Dudley, earl of Leicester (1532/3–1588), referred to Bedford having 'as it were bequeathed' ('Unpublished lettter', 284) his daughter to the queen, and Warwick in his will requested Elizabeth 'to continue her good favour towards my said wife, whom I leave to continue her most faithfull and devoted servant' (Letters, ed. Collins, 1.42). Anne Russell's marriage to Warwick was arranged between her father and Leicester in autumn 1564. Leicester carefully sought Elizabeth's permission and she gave the union her enthusiastic backing. The marriage was celebrated with great ceremony and was pregnant with political symbolism, for it not only sealed the alliance of two of the leading protestant dynasties, but was also vital for the Dudley succession. Warwick was nearly twenty years older than Anne and no children had survived from his two previous marriages, while Leicester was unmarried at the time. Yet this marriage proved childless too, and was accepted by Leicester as such early in the 1570s.

According to her admiring niece and goddaughter, Lady Anne *Clifford (1590–1676), the countess was 'a mother in affection' to her youngest brother, William *Russell, first Baron Russell of Thornhaugh (c.1553–1613), and her sisters Elizabeth Bourchier, countess of Bath (1558–1605), and Margaret *Clifford, countess of Cumberland (1560–1616), following the early death of their mother, and later to their children (Williamson, 37). Anne may have had a particular influence on her father, which gave her a leading role in the family crisis that broke out after his death on 28 July 1585. As a result of the deaths of Bedford's three elder sons the earldom was inherited by his grandson Edward Russell. The third earl of Bedford was a minor and, since his mother was dead as well, Leicester and Warwick claimed and initially received his wardship on behalf of the countess of Warwick. However, this settlement was challenged by Elizabeth *Russell (1528–1609), linguist and courtier, the widow of Bedford's uncle, John Russell, Baron Russell. She was a notoriously combative woman, who accused the countess of Warwick of persuading the second earl of Bedford to revoke an earlier settlement for John Russell and his heirs in the will he made on 7 April 1584, thus disinheriting her two daughters. She appealed to her brother-in-law, William Cecil, Baron Burghley, and to the queen, who had second thoughts. This in turn provoked Warwick to complain on 31 August 1585 about the queen's treatment of 'my poor afflicted wyfe' (PRO, SP 12/181/238). The Dudleys were ultimately successful in obtaining the wardship, but Lady Russell was still charging the countess with 'cruelty' as late as 1601 (Salisbury MSS, 9.562).

The countess's marriage appears to have been a model of domestic harmony and partnership. When Sir Edward Stafford came to see the dying Warwick at Bedford House in February 1590 (he died on the 21st), he found her distraught, 'sitting by the fire so full of teares that she could not speak' (CKS, U 1475/L2/4, item 3, m. 80). She was no less close to Warwick's family. In his first will (1582) Leicester effusively left 'my noble & worthy sister the countys of Warwyk at whose hands I have ever found great love & kindnes [a gift worth 100 marks] praying hir to accept yt as from hym that in his lyffe tyme did both honor & esteme hir asmoch as any brother did his syster' (Longleat House, Dudley papers, box 3, article 56, m. 10). However, there was a less fortunate side to the Dudley connection. When he died Warwick left her North Hall, his house at Northaw, Hertfordshire, and his fee simple lands as an estate of inheritance, and she lived there for the rest of her life. But he also left her debts totalling over £7000. After her own death the heir to her Dudley lands, Sir Robert Sidney, inherited a residual debt of £2700. In 1574 Warwick added the lands he had gained from the 'Great Berkeley Law-Suit' to her jointure (Berkeley Castle, charter 5211), and as a result she faced legal battles with Henry Berkeley, seventh Baron Berkeley, in 1593 and 1597. In 1599 she lamented to Sir Robert Cecil that 'suits and troubles at law have emptied my purse' (Salisbury MSS, 9.21).

During the 1570s and 1580s the earl and countess of Warwick lived either at North Hall or at court, and her attendance on the queen was thus uninterrupted. The countess served as an extraordinary gentlewoman of the privy chamber until the end of the reign and, according to Anne Clifford, was 'more beloved and in greater favour with the queen than any other woman in the kingdom' (Gilson, 24–5). Since Anne Clifford was only thirteen when Elizabeth died, there is an element of legend here. Nevertheless in the 1590s the countess, her sister-in-law, Katherine *Hastings, countess of Huntingdon (after she was widowed in 1595), and Charles Howard, first earl of Nottingham, the lord admiral, were widely understood to be the queen's closest intimates, and Anne was among those attending Elizabeth at her death on 24 March 1603. Interestingly, she feared Elizabeth's death might cause a 'commotion' and advised her sister and niece to take refuge in her London house. Although she was graciously received by King James on his arrival, Anne Clifford later remembered that Anne of Denmark 'shewed no favour to the elderly ladies'. In the autumn of 1603 the countess retired to North Hall 'something ill and melancholy' (Diaries of Lady Anne Clifford, 21, 23–4, 27). On 11 October she made her will and in the following month gave all of Leicester's and Warwick's pictures at North Hall to the countess of Huntingdon (PRO, PROB 11/103, fols. 100r–103r). Her fee simple lands she left to her beloved brother William, who was also her executor. The remaining Dudley lands went to her nephew, Sidney. She died at North Hall on 9 February 1604 in the presence of her immediate relatives, having outlived Elizabeth by less than a year. At her own request she was interred with the Russells at Chenies, Buckinghamshire, not with Warwick. An alabaster effigy and altar-tomb of black marble were then erected for her.

Thanks to the countess's intimacy with Elizabeth her

influence was believed to be extensive and much solicited, but owing to the destruction of her papers after her death it can be gauged only from the comments of others. The prevailing impression is of a very effective advocate and medium for submitting petitions and letters, as, for example, John Dee found. Anne Clifford described her as 'a great friend to virtue and helper to many petitioners' (Gilson, 24–5). Both before and after Warwick's death the countess's hand can be found in a wide range of lesser patronage. Best known is her help to various puritan divines, but she was also involved in university and ecclesiastical appointments, wardships, pensions, lawsuits, minor military postings, and land transactions. Whether she gained in any material way from her influence is a moot point. In 1594 Sir Thomas Shirley was quick to dismiss as slander gossip that she had received a share of his purchase of office. Some twenty books were dedicated to her, about half in her widowhood. Quite a few were by men her husband patronized, among them several puritan divines, but in the 1590s the authors were more literary and included Edmund Spenser. Yet there were also limits to her influence. The most extensive series of references to her help comes from the correspondence of Sidney's agent, Rowland Whyte, from 1595 to 1600. If, in Whyte's words, 'she doth labour as if it were for her owne brother for your sake' (*Letters*, ed. Collins, 2.74), Sidney used her primarily to lobby for home leave from his command at Flushing. When he wished to pursue offices, she advised him to employ 'a man of greatness and authority' (ibid., 2.122). When her brother William was lord deputy of Ireland from 1594 to 1596, Elizabeth commanded her 'not to meddle in Irish causes' (*Salisbury MSS*, 5.481). The countess was undoubtedly one of the pivotal women in Elizabeth's court, but her intimacy with the queen may, in the last resort, have depended on her not overstepping the mark.

SIMON ADAMS

Sources H. Sydney and others, *Letters and memorials of state*, ed. A. Collins, 2 vols. (1746) · 'An unpublished letter of Robert Dudley, earl of Leicester, 1564', *N&Q*, 6th ser., 3 (1881), 283–4 · 'A letter from Robert, earl of Leicester, to a lady', ed. C. Read, *Huntington Library Bulletin*, 9 (1936), 14–26 · G. C. Williamson, *Lady Anne Clifford, countess of Dorset, Pembroke and Montgomery (1590–1676)*, 2nd edn (1967) · state papers, domestic, Elizabeth I, PRO · S. Adams, ed., *Household accounts and disbursement books of Robert Dudley, earl of Leicester, 1558–1561, 1584–1586*, CS, 6 (1995) · *CSP dom.*, 1547–1625 · *Calendar of the manuscripts of the most hon. the marquis of Salisbury*, 24 vols., HMC, 9 (1883–1976) · Penshurst papers, CKS, U 1475 · Longleat House, Wiltshire, Marquess of Bath MSS, Dudley MSS · M. P. Hannay, *Philip's phoenix: Mary Sidney, countess of Pembroke* (1990) · Berkeley Castle muniments, Berkeley Castle, Gloucestershire · J. P. Gilson, ed., *Lives of Lady Anne Clifford, countess of Dorset, Pembroke and Montgomery (1590–1676)* · *The diaries of Lady Anne Clifford*, ed. D. J. H. Clifford (1990) · S. Adams, *Leicester and the court: essays on Elizabethan politics* (2002) · *The diaries of John Dee*, ed. E. Fenton (1998) · P. Collinson, *The Elizabethan puritan movement* (1967) · P. E. J. Hammer, *The polarisation of Elizabethan politics: the political career of Robert Devereux, 2nd earl of Essex, 1585–1597* (1999)
Archives Berkeley Castle, Gloucestershire, Berkeley Castle collection, estate papers and legal papers relating to Berkeley lawsuit
Likenesses portrait, *c*.1565, Bedford Estate, Woburn?; repro. in R. Strong, *The Elizabethan image: painting in England, 1540–1620*

(1969), item 44 [exhibition catalogue, Tate Gallery, London, 28 Nov 1969–8 Feb 1970] · portrait (after Appleby triptych)
Wealth at death see will, PRO, PROB 11/103/100–03, printed in Collins, *Sidney papers*, 1.42–4

Dudley, Charles Stokes (1780–1862). *See under* Dudley, Mary (1750–1823).

Dudley, Dud (1600?–1684), ironmaster, was probably born in spring 1600, the fourth illegitimate son of Edward Sutton, fifth Baron Dudley (1567–1643), and his long term 'concubine', Elizabeth Tomlinson (*d*. 1629). He was educated at Balliol College, Oxford, from 1619 to 1622. Lord Dudley was generous to his illegitimate family during Elizabeth's life, but in 1628 married his legitimate granddaughter Frances (1611–1697) to Humble Ward (later Lord Ward), whose father redeemed the heavily mortgaged Dudley estates; also Dud Dudley fell out with his mother in 1627, having in the previous year (on 12 October) married Eleanor (*d*. 3 Dec 1675), daughter of Francis Heaton of Groveley Hall, Worcestershire, and Mary, daughter of Francis Dincley or Dingley of Charlton in the same county.

Dud Dudley is the best-known and most persistent of those, starting with Thomas Proctor in 1589, who attempted to smelt iron ore with a fuel other than charcoal, thus opening the way to producing iron in quantities not limited by the availability (and hence the speed of growth) of wood. He claimed in his book, *Dud Dudley's Metallum martis* (1665), to have succeeded, but this has been the subject of modern doubt: the best view is probably that he made something like iron, but contaminated with sulphur and therefore too brittle at red heat to be forged. His claim to have made pots and other cast-ware is more credible, but this probably provided insufficient work to keep a blast furnace busy.

Initial experiments in pit-coal smelting began before Dudley's father in May 1618 obtained a licence from John Robinson (or Rovenson), an earlier patentee; Lord Dudley obtained a new patent in his own name in February 1622. Dud Dudley, who may have been concerned in these experiments, was fetched from Balliol College, Oxford, probably in March 1622 to manage his father's ironworks at Cradley (then part of Pensnett Chase), one of four or five ironworks that had been built by his father on his Dudley estates, but the works were destroyed by the 'Mayday flood' in the following year, shortly after Dudley had begun to make iron with pit coal. He rebuilt the works, but being 'outed of his works' (Dudley, 11), moved to his father's Himley furnace, where, lacking a forge, he had 'to sell pig iron to charcoal ironmasters who did him much prejudice by not only detaining his stock but also disparaging the iron' (ibid., 12). As a result his father let the furnace to Richard Foley (1580–1657) in 1625. Dudley then used the nearby Hascoe furnace (now Askew Bridge) at Gornal Wood, also belonging to his father. This was leased by William Smallman, Dudley's trustee, in January 1626 and transferred to Francis Heaton in 1631. There, using larger bellows, Dudley cast 7 tons of pig iron per week, then a record for pit-coal iron; but, evidently again unsuccessful, he sublet his furnace and mines in November 1627 to an agent of Richard Foley. Foley was evicted in 1631 by Lord Dudley, who said Dud Dudley had no right but in trust for Lord Dudley. Further litigation from 1634 with the Ward family over title to the manor of Himley ended with Dudley's imprisonment about November 1638 in London for contempt, the dispute being settled in April 1639 by his resigning all claim to the family estates in exchange for confirmation of his lease of Greens Lodge (in Wombourne, Staffordshire).

In 1638 Dudley and others obtained a new patent for smelting with pit coal, but probably did not then develop it. In 1651 he erected a 'bloomery' for smelting lead (perhaps a reverberatory furnace) at Okham Slade in Clifton, near Bristol, but his partners there, Walter Stephens, a linen draper, and John Stone, a merchant, harassed him for debt; he claimed this was unjust and because he was a royalist, but Stephens's widow replied that he had failed to repay a loan guaranteed by her husband. Despite failing to get his patent renewed after the Restoration, he built a unique furnace at Dudley 'for making iron or melting ironstone with charcoal made of wood and pitcoal together to be blown ... by the strength of men and horses without the help of water' (PRO, E112/538/95), but was no longer a partner by 1671. With Edward Chamberlain he did, however, in 1662 obtain a patent to make tin plate, and, although they did not exploit it, it was Chamberlain's questionable renewal of this patent in 1672 that prevented Joshua Newborough and Philip Foley from exploiting the tin-plate researches of Andrew Yarranton and Ambrose Crowley at Wolverley Lower Mill, near Kidderminster. Dudley also tried to use coal in the next stage of the production of iron, in which pig iron was fined and drawn out into bar iron in a forge, and he complained that his process was in use at Greens, Swin, Heath, and Cradley forges, all in south Staffordshire and then belonging to Thomas Foley (1616–1676), 'yet the author hath had no benefit thereby' (Dudley, 35); despite his belief, however, this was not his invention.

In 1637 Dudley visited Scotland in the train of the marquess of Hamilton. He served against the Scots in 1640 and as a royalist officer throughout the civil war, being promoted to colonel after the fall of Lichfield, where he had been responsible for successfully mining the walls. In addition he organized ordnance supplies in Staffordshire and Worcestershire and was general of ordnance to Prince Maurice and then Lord Astley, being taken at the fall of Worcester. In 1648 he mustered 200 men in Boscobel Woods in order to seize Dawley Castle, Shropshire, but they were captured by Andrew Yarranton; he was imprisoned but escaped, and was retaken in London, again escaping the day before he was due to be shot. For the next two years he lived at Bristol under a false name, Dr Hunt. Unable to compound for his delinquency, he lost his property, except a house in Friarsgate, Worcester, until the Restoration, when he petitioned the king for redress and was appointed a serjeant-at-arms.

In 1665, probably to find a financial backer, Dudley wrote *Dud Dudley's Metallum martis, or, Iron Made with Pit-Coale, Sea-Cole, etc.*, the work that has caused him to be remembered. His diagrammatic map of the coalfield around Dudley Castle is an early move towards geological mapping. The secrets of his process (if there were any) were not disclosed in this and they therefore probably died with him. However, it is possible that Sir Clement Clerke, one of his successors at the Dudley furnace, was his pupil. If so, what Dud Dudley discovered may have enabled Clerke and his sons to establish the successful copper and lead smelting works using reverberatory furnaces. These became the basis of two of the new chartered companies of the 1690s and for much of the eighteenth-century metal smelting industry. Dudley remarried as an old man and had a son, but the name of his second wife is not known. He died in October 1684 at his house in Friarsgate, Worcester, and was buried at St Helen's Church, on 25 October, a fact not added to the memorial he set up there to his wife. P. W. KING

Sources D. Dudley, *Dud Dudley's Metallum martis, or, Iron made with pit-coale, sea-cole, &c.* (1665); repr. (1854) · A. Bedord-Smith, 'Dudonius Dudley, a short summary of his life and works', typescript, Birm. CL, local studies class 78.1 DUD · P. W. King, 'Dud Dudley's contribution to metallurgy', *Historical Metallurgy*, 36 (2002), 43–53 · PRO, C 5/420/77 · PRO, SP 29/11/54. i · William Salt Library, Stafford, Salt MS 393(ii) [transcript of Royalist composition papers], 25–43

Dudley, Edmund (c.1462–1510), administrator, was the eldest son of John Dudley of Atherington (d. 1502) and his wife, Elizabeth (d. 1498), daughter and coheir of John Bramshott of Bramshott (d. 1481). His father, a Sussex gentleman and justice of the peace, was the second son of John *Sutton, first Baron Dudley, and brother of William *Dudley, bishop of Durham.

Early career and royal service Dudley apparently began his education at Oxford, where he was studying about 1474, but some four years later, when he would have been about sixteen, he moved on, perhaps via Davy's Inn, to Gray's Inn. There he took a prominent part in the inn's learning exercises. In the later 1480s he gave the first known reading in any inn on *quo warranto*, the procedure by which the king challenged the exercise of private jurisdictions. Thus he demonstrated the interest in the king's rights which was to be a hallmark of his career. Then, in Lent term 1496, he dealt with Westminster II c. 25, in a reading which attracted admiration from his contemporaries. He was elected to parliament in 1491–2, representing Lewes, and again in 1495 as knight of the shire for Sussex. By 1494 he had been named to the commission of the peace for the county and for the next ten years he often attended sessions. In November 1496 he was chosen one of the two under-sheriffs of London, and until he gave up the post in December 1502 he sat in the city's courts to the apparent satisfaction of the citizens. In 1501 he served on a commission to investigate infringements of the king's feudal rights and prerogatives in Sussex.

In October 1503 Dudley was about to take the next step in a successful legal career, the promotion to serjeant-at-law which was the last stage before appointment as a judge, when he suddenly changed direction, seeking exemption from the promotion. This was probably because Henry VII had already decided he would like Dudley to serve as speaker of the Commons in the forthcoming parliament. He duly acted as speaker in the troubled session of January–April 1504. Then, in October, he began to receive a fee of £66 13s. 4d. as a retained councillor of the king. By July 1506 he was president of the king's council, the first layman to hold the position. It was a post of central importance in the council's growing judicial function rather than one of wider political pre-eminence. He does not seem, for example, to have taken much part in dealings with foreign ambassadors. None the less, his rise to power had been real and rapid.

Dudley's role outside the council was as significant as that within. His period in office was that in which Henry VII's exploitation of his subjects' wealth reached its most extreme level. One arm of this was the council's offshoot concerned with the profitable enforcement of the king's rights, the council learned in the law: this was chaired by Dudley's colleague Sir Richard Empson, and Dudley was not himself much involved in its work. He operated rather to fill a vacuum left by the deaths in 1503 of Sir Reynold Bray (who had probably acted as a patron earlier in his own career), and in 1504 of Sir John Mordaunt. His accounts, surviving with various degrees of completeness in at least four early seventeenth-century transcripts, run from 9 September 1504 to May 1508. They suggest his role was to manage the king's use of a miscellaneous range of opportunities for financial exploitation of his greater subjects. He sold offices, wardships, and licences to marry the widows of tenants-in-chief; pardons for treason, sedition, murder, riot, retaining, and other offences. In less than four years he collected some £219,316 6s. 11d. in cash and bonds for future payment. He also enforced the king's rights and capitalized on his resources in a more specialized way as chief justice of the royal forests south of the Trent.

Profit and unpopularity Such activity brought Dudley into confrontation with three groups in particular. Aristocrats found it advisable to keep him sweet with pensions and other *douceurs*: as the great chronicle of London put it, 'the Chyeff lordys of England were gladd to be In his Favour, and were Fayn to swe to hym for many urgent cawsys' (Thomas and Thornley, 348). Londoners found that he took an unwelcome interest in customs fraud and coinage offences, in raising customs rates and forcing the king's candidates for civic office on the citizens, and in extracting £3333 6s. 8d. from the city in return for the king's confirmation of its liberties. Meanwhile his associates in the city, notably John Camby, keeper of the Poultry Compter prison, and John Baptist Grimaldi, a Genoese merchant, acquired a bad reputation for extortionate use of their influence. Thus in effect 'whoo soo evyr hadd the sword born beffore hym, Dudley was mayer, and what his pleasure was, was doon' (ibid.). Finally, churchmen had to negotiate large fines with Dudley for the king's favour in securing their appointments, for the restitution of their temporalities when they took up new sees, for pardons for the

escape of prisoners from episcopal prisons, for licences to acquire lands in mortmain, and for confirmations of the privileges of religious houses. It seemed, as Polydore Vergil put it, as though Empson and Dudley were 'plotting to snatch all lay and ecclesiastical wealth' (*Anglica historia*, 131). Preachers inveighed against them at Paul's Cross and elsewhere.

Dudley profited greatly from his position. By 1509 he had built up a landed estate in sixteen counties, worth some £550 a year gross, plus £5000 or more in goods. The largest concentration of his landholdings, about two-thirds by value, lay in Sussex, Hampshire, and the Isle of Wight, but there were important outliers as far away as Lancashire, Derbyshire, and Cambridgeshire. He gained some direct reward from the king—a dozen stewardships of crown estates and grants of wardships between 1505 and 1508 and occasional sums in cash—but the profits to be gained indirectly from the exercise of his influence were far greater. Those litigating before the king's council and others in need of his favour readily bought it. In converting this money into land Dudley used all the advantages at his disposal. He bought up weak titles and litigated upon them. He paid off fines due to the king in return for the lands of those with whom he dealt, allegedly setting fines sufficiently high to force them to sell. In one instance he secured a pardon for murder for a gentleman and settled with the family of his victim in exchange for a grant of the murderer's lands. Dudley's associates also benefited from his rise. A notable example was his cousin Richard Dudley, a theologian and fellow of Oriel College, Oxford, who received a rash of clerical promotions in 1505–8 from the crown and from noblemen and bishops anxious to secure Edmund's goodwill. The inventory of Edmund's goods taken in 1509, featuring foreign armour, books, glassware, chairs, and hangings, suggests that his style of life was fashionable, though not outrageously pompous.

Fall from power At Henry VII's death Dudley had many enemies and few friends even among his fellow councillors. Henry died late on 21 April 1509, but the fact was not announced until the evening of the 23rd. Early on the 24th Dudley and Empson were arrested and sent to the Tower of London, blamed for the oppressions of the late reign. Dudley was tried in London in July and convicted of treason on the 18th, the charge being that on 22 April he had conspired to 'hold, guide and govern the King and his Council' by summoning a force of men to London under the leadership of various named associates (*Report of the Deputy Keeper*, 226). He may well have summoned the men, a prudent and possibly widespread precaution at a time of political uncertainty, but it is highly unlikely he intended such a *coup d'état*. In the parliament of 1510, when several statutes blamed him for the injustices of the previous regime, a bill to attaint him and Empson passed the Commons but failed in the Lords. Unaware of its failure, Dudley made an unsuccessful attempt to escape from the Tower. Afterwards he made his will, making provision for some of those from whom he had purchased land to repurchase it from his executors, arranging the payment of his debts and seeking to provide for his wife and children: he asked the earl of Shrewsbury to see his eldest son 'maryed in a honest stok' (PRO, SP 1/2, fol. 5r). The will seems never to have been proved, but was referred to in subsequent lawsuits. His fate was finally settled when Henry VIII's progress took him through the midlands in summer 1510. There the king heard a fresh wave of complaints about the injustices of his father's ministers, and resolved on their execution. Dudley was beheaded on Tower Hill on 17 August 1510 and buried at the London Blackfriars.

Dudley made a convenient scapegoat for Henry VII's exactions. Certainly he had exploited his position as the king's executive, but so to a less extreme degree had most of Henry's other councillors. There are many signs that the general shape of policy was the king's. Dudley himself fell foul of Henry's insistence on his rights at least once, having to secure a pardon in 1508 for taking possession of lands inherited from his mother without suing livery from the king. Henry's close involvement with his work is evident from the references in his accounts to books, bonds, and indictments passed backwards and forwards between them. Surviving warrants discharging bonds bear his signature and the king's, and the king regularly signed his accounts. Henry's responsibility for the policy was also reflected in the petition Dudley composed in the Tower. In it he listed those he felt had been too harshly treated by the king and identified scores of bonds taken for debts which Henry to his knowledge intended as a means to guarantee the good behaviour of the debtors rather than as a means to extract full payment of the specified sum: a distinction he felt it important to make lest his colleagues act unjustly (and to the peril of the king's soul) in insisting such debts be settled in full.

The Tree of Commonwealth In prison Dudley also wrote a treatise on government and society, *The Tree of Commonwealth*, which survives in three sixteenth-century manuscripts and one seventeenth-century. It aimed to advise Henry VIII on the restoration of the common wealth of his realm. Its allegory is laborious. The polity is a tree, upheld by roots of godliness, justice, truth, concord, and peace. Each of these virtues must be actively pursued by the king and by each order of society in its own appropriate way. Each social group should also enjoy its own distinctive fruit of worldly reward, which however requires proper peeling to temper its effects and must be consumed with God-fearing sauce for fear of its poisonous core of mortal sin.

For all its conventionality, the book does shed suggestive light on the attitudes of English statesmen of Dudley's generation. It illustrates its arguments not only from English history and the Old Testament, but also on occasion from ancient Rome, medieval France, and the Turks. It denounces most of the abuses of royal power over the church in which Dudley himself had been so intimately involved, yet it takes royal leadership in church affairs for granted, berates clerical shortcomings, and urges a revival on the universities and their theologians. Its

detailed prescriptions for the judicial system and its suspicion of noble self-assertion, mercantile chicanery, and popular idleness and disorder look very like those pursued by Henry VII's regime. Reflections upon the previous reign and forebodings for the new meet in warnings against royal covetousness, fleshliness, warmongering, and indulgence in dangerous sports.

Family and descendants Dudley's first wife was Anne (d. 1500x03), daughter of Thomas Windsor of Stanwell, Middlesex, sister of Andrew Windsor, later first Baron Windsor, who became one of Dudley's close colleagues in the service of Henry VII, and widow of Roger Corbet of Moreton Corbet. Their only child was a daughter, Elizabeth (c.1499–c.1560), who married William, seventh Baron Stourton (1505–1548). His second marriage, contracted between 1500 and 1504, was a measure of his increasing standing: he married Elizabeth (1482x4–1525/6), sister and eventually heir of John Grey, fourth Viscount Lisle (d. 1504). They had three sons, John *Dudley, Jerome, and Andrew. John, granted his grandfather's title of Viscount Lisle in 1542, rose to be duke of Northumberland and father of the Elizabethan earls of Leicester and Warwick; Andrew played a supporting role to John in war and politics; but Jerome, intended by his father to be educated for the priesthood, though he survived until at least 1555, did so in a state of mental or physical incapacity. After Edmund's death his widow married Arthur Plantagenet, illegitimate son of Edward IV, who was created Viscount Lisle in 1523.

Edmund Dudley's rapid rise and his disgrace were used against his illustrious descendants, notably in the vicious tract of 1584, *Leicester's Commonwealth*. By the late sixteenth century rumours were current that he was the son of a carpenter. William Cecil knew better, but still, contemplating the unwelcome possibility of a match between Elizabeth and Leicester, noted dryly 'His grandfather but a solicitor' (Starkey, 157). Yet later Dudleys found much to be proud of not only in Edmund's descent from the barons Dudley, but also in his political reflections. Thus the earliest extant manuscript of *The Tree of Commonwealth* may have been made for Northumberland, and the antiquary John Stow presented another to Lord Robert Dudley, the future earl of Leicester, in 1562. As his descendants might have hoped, Edmund Dudley, long typecast as the evil minister, has been more recently recognized as a forerunner of the educated lay statesmen of later sixteenth-century England.

S. J. GUNN

Sources E. Dudley, *The tree of commonwealth*, ed. D. M. Brodie (1948) · C. J. Harrison, 'The petition of Edmund Dudley', *EngHR*, 87 (1972), 82–99 · Emden, *Oxf.*, 1.597–8 · A. H. Thomas and I. D. Thornley, eds., *The great chronicle of London* (1938) · *The Anglica historia of Polydore Vergil, AD 1485–1537*, ed. and trans. D. Hay, CS, 3rd ser., 74 (1950) · *Report of the Deputy Keeper of the Public Records*, 3 (1842), appx 2, pp. 226–7 · D. R. Starkey, ed., *Rivals in power: lives and letters of the great Tudor dynasties* (1990) · S. J. Gunn, 'Edmund Dudley and the church', *Journal of Ecclesiastical History*, 51 (2000), 609–26 · D. C. Peck, ed., *Leicester's commonwealth: the copy of a letter written by a master of art of Cambridge (1584) and related documents* (1985) · M. St C. Byrne, ed., *The Lisle letters*, 6 vols. (1981) · J. S. Roskell, *The Commons and their speakers in English parliaments, 1376–1523* (1965) · M. R. Horowitz,

'Richard Empson, minister of Henry VII', *BIHR*, 55 (1982), 35–49 • will, PRO, Henry VIII general series, state papers, SP1/2, fols. 4–9 • account of estates, PRO, special collections, ministers' accounts, SC6/Henry VIII/6217 • inventory of goods, PRO, exchequer, king's remembrancer, inventories of goods and chattels, E154/2/17 • S. E. Thorne and J. H. Baker, eds., *Readings and moots at the inns of court in the fifteenth century*, 1, SeldS, 71 (1954); 2, SeldS, 105 (1990) • J. H. Baker, ed., *John Spelman's reading on Quo warranto*, SeldS, 113 (1997) **Archives** BL, accounts, Lansdowne MS 127 [copies] • BL, accounts, Harley MS 1877, fol. 47 [copies] • Bodl. Oxf., accounts, MS Eng. Hist. D. 421, fols. 7–18 [copies] • CUL, law readings, MS Hh.3.10 • Hunt. L., accounts, Ellesmere MS 1518 [copies] • Keele University, marquess of Anglesey papers, petition **Wealth at death** £5000 in goods • £333 6s. 8d.: *Report of the Deputy Keeper*, appx 2, 227

Dudley, Edward. *See* Sutton, Edward, fourth Baron Dudley (c.1515–1586).

Dudley, Elizabeth (1779–1849), Quaker minister, was born on 1 September 1779 at Suirville Mills, Clonmel, co. Tipperary, Ireland, the eldest of the eight children of Robert Dudley (1732?–1807) and his third wife, Mary (1750–1823), daughter of Joseph and Mary Stokes of Bristol. She was educated at Suir Island School, Clonmel. In 1798 her mother reluctantly accepted medical advice stipulating 'a sea voyage and short residence at Bristol Hot-wells' (*Life of Mary Dudley*, 228) and was accompanied by Elizabeth, her three sisters, and her brother Charles: they remained there until early 1800. Her mother's gift in the vocal ministry had been acknowledged by her Quaker meeting shortly before Elizabeth's birth and in 1802 she accompanied her mother on a religious visit to England.

After her husband's death in 1807, Mary Dudley moved to London in 1810 with her three surviving daughters. In the following year Southwark monthly meeting acknowledged Elizabeth's gift in the ministry, which 'though full of gospel love and human sympathies … was less tender and winning' than that of her mother, for she 'was endowed with a more masculine understanding' and 'possessed in a large degree the power of close reasoning, with a clearness of judgment which was seldom at fault' (*Memoirs*, 328).

Elizabeth Dudley's travels in the ministry were, except for one visit to Ireland in 1845, confined to Britain. She held meetings in many places where there were no Quakers and was broad in her religious sympathies; the evangelical Joseph John Gurney (1788–1847) and Josiah Forster (1782–1870) were frequent correspondents. Nevertheless, when faced with more extreme evangelical views, she could write (probably in 1836): 'Mary J. Graham is too strong in her views of election and assurance for my Quakerly expansiveness, and seems to overlook numerous Scripture assertions bearing on universal grace and love' (*Memoirs of Elizabeth Dudley*, 237). Perhaps her firmest friendship, lasting from 1802 until her death, was with Lucy Alexander (1774–1856), the wife of Thomas Maw of Needham Market from 1804.

Elizabeth Dudley was a not infrequent visitor to Newgate and by 1818 had recorded her conviction that the death penalty was inconsistent with Christian principles and must be abolished. She was clerk to the women's yearly meeting of British Quakers in 1817 and from 1826 to 1834. She was an active member of the morning meeting (the body which acted as a publications committee for British Friends) and she herself prepared the *Life* (1825) of her mother. Her sister Charlotte (1786–1825) was also acknowledged a minister in 1825, shortly before she died.

Elizabeth Dudley was deeply affected by her sister Mary's death in 1847. In August 1849, on returning from a visit to Lucy and Thomas Maw, she found cholera raging with great violence in Southwark. On 6 September she became unwell, signs of cholera appeared, and she died shortly after midnight at The Priory, Peckham. Her body was interred in the Quaker burial-ground, Peckham, on 10 September. EDWARD H. MILLIGAN

Sources *Memoirs of Elizabeth Dudley*, ed. C. Tylor (1861) • digest of deaths, 1837–1961, RS Friends, Lond. • *The life of Mary Dudley, with some account of the illness and death of her daughter, Hannah*, ed. E. Dudley (1825) **Archives** RS Friends, Lond. **Likenesses** silhouette, c.1830, RS Friends, Lond.

Dudley, Lord Guildford (c.1535–1554), husband of Lady Jane Grey, was the fourth surviving son of John *Dudley, duke of Northumberland (1504–1553), and his wife, Lady Jane Guildford (d. 1555), the daughter of Sir Edward *Guildford of Halden and Hemsted, Kent. Northumberland originally planned to marry Guildford to Lady Margaret Clifford, daughter of Henry Clifford, first earl of Cumberland, great-niece of Henry VIII. Edward VI spoke in support of this plan to Cumberland, and on 4 July 1552 the privy council wrote to the earl urging his agreement to the marriage. However, in early 1553 Northumberland substituted his younger brother, Andrew, for Guildford in these marriage plans.

Guildford Dudley was instead married to Lady Jane Grey [*see* Dudley, Lady Jane (1537–1554)], the daughter of Henry Grey, duke of Suffolk, and so became involved in the plans to divert the succession of the crown from Mary Tudor. The marriage took place on 21 May 1553 at Durham House, Northumberland's London residence. Edward VI's 'device for the crown' provided that the crown was to go, not to his sisters Mary and Elizabeth, but to the male heirs of Frances, duchess of Suffolk, provided that they were born before the king's death. If the king died first, the crown was to pass directly to Lady Jane, as the duchess's daughter, and to her male heirs.

Following the death of Edward VI on 6 July 1553, Lady Jane was proclaimed queen. On 10 July Dudley joined his wife in specially prepared apartments in the Tower. But by 19 July Mary Tudor had established her authority and Dudley was arrested with Jane. At the Guildhall on 13 November he was arraigned for treason, together with his wife, his brothers Ambrose and Henry, and Thomas Cranmer, archbishop of Canterbury. He was found guilty and sentenced to death, but was not finally executed until after Wyatt's rebellion. To ensure the security of Philip II's marriage to Mary, Dudley was beheaded on Tower Hill on 12 February 1554, immediately before the execution of Lady Jane, and was buried in the church of St Peter ad Vincula within the Tower.

Of Guildford Dudley's character or his feelings for Lady Jane there is only slight evidence. He wrote a short and rather formulaic farewell letter to his father-in-law. Monsignor Commendone, a papal agent in London in 1554, reported that Dudley had wanted to see and embrace Jane again before his execution. She had refused, apparently fearing that such a painful encounter would unsettle both of them too much, but sent him a message that they would soon be together eternally. Contemporaries were sympathetic to him, regarding him more as a victim of his father's intrigues than a willing accomplice. Grafton's *Abridgement of the Chronicles of England* (1563) described him as a 'comely, vertuous and goodly gentleman' who 'most innocently was executed' and who was much lamented at his death (Nichols, *Chronicle of Queen Jane*, 55).

G. J. RICHARDSON

Sources *Literary remains of King Edward the Sixth*, ed. J. G. Nichols, 2, Roxburghe Club, 75 (1857) · GEC, *Peerage*, new edn · J. G. Nichols, ed., *The chronicle of Queen Jane, and of two years of Queen Mary*, CS, old ser., 48 (1850) · J. G. Nichols, ed., *The chronicle of the grey friars of London*, CS, 53 (1852) · *The diary of Henry Machyn, citizen and merchant-taylor of London, from AD 1550 to AD 1563*, ed. J. G. Nichols, CS, 42 (1848) · C. V. Malfatti, ed., *The accession, coronation and marriage of Mary Tudor as related in four manuscripts of the Escorial* (1961) · N. H. Nicholas, ed., *Memoirs and remains of Lady Jane Grey* (1831) · *DNB* · BL, Harleian MS 2342 · BL, Stowe MS 652 [pedigree]

Dudley, Harold Ward (1887–1935), biochemist, was born in Derby on 30 October 1887, the elder son of Joshua Dudley, a Methodist minister, and his wife, Florence. His father's work necessitated several moves around the country, and Dudley was educated principally at Truro College and King Edward VI Grammar School, Morpeth, before entering Leeds University to read chemistry. There he was influenced towards organic chemistry by his teacher, J. B. Cohen, with whom he studied for an MSc (awarded in 1910), before travelling to Berlin to work for his PhD, which he gained in 1912. He then moved to New York, to join Henry Dakin in the private research laboratories established by Christian Herter, where they worked on the biochemistry of carbohydrates and proteins.

Returning to Leeds in 1914, as a lecturer in biochemistry in the Animal Nutrition Research Institute, Dudley obtained a commission on the outbreak of the First World War, and worked for the RAMC, initially under Ernest Starling, on the biochemical and physiological effects of chemical warfare. In 1919 he was created OBE, and also accepted an appointment with Henry Dale at the Medical Research Committee's National Institute for Medical Research in Hampstead, where he remained until his death. In 1921 he married (Louisa) Mary Nettleship (*d.* 1935); they had no children.

Dudley's research work concentrated on the chemical isolation and identification of biologically active substances, and he was elected FRS in 1930 for his notable contributions to this field. Alone or in collaboration he made a number of significant discoveries, three of which, the standardization of insulin, the isolation of histamine and acetylcholine, and the discovery of ergometrine, were of particular importance. After the discovery of insulin by researchers at the University of Toronto in 1922, the MRC

Harold Ward Dudley (1887–1935), by Walter Stoneman, 1931

sent Dale and Dudley to Canada to learn about this new therapy for diabetes. On their return, Dudley took the major part in developing production and standardization techniques, initially on an experimental basis, but later to accelerate commercial production by pharmaceutical companies. In 1923 an international conference asked Dudley, on behalf of the MRC, to prepare the first international standard for insulin, which was used to ensure uniform production throughout the world, and to define the unit of activity with which to measure that standard.

Shortly afterwards Dudley became interested in histamine, a chemical known from the fungus ergot, but not unequivocally identified from animal sources. With Dale he succeeded in isolating it from a variety of biological tissues, thus establishing it as a normal constituent of the animal body. While searching for histamine, Dale and Dudley also identified acetylcholine as an endogenous component of the animal body. This was a vital contribution to work by Dale and others in establishing that acetylcholine acted as a chemical transmitter in the nervous system: work for which Dale shared the Nobel Prize for physiology and medicine in 1936.

Dudley's final researches were further concerned with the chemistry of ergot. For centuries an extract of ergot had been used to assist labour, although by the late nineteenth century its use was restricted to the prevention of post-partum haemorrhage. However, the precise chemical nature of the active principle was not determined until a British obstetrician, John Chassar Moir, began a re-examination of ergot in 1932. Dudley joined him in a clinical–chemical investigation, resulting in the isolation and description of ergometrine. Unfortunately, their announcement in 1935 was closely followed by other claims to the discovery, an episode that coincided with Dudley's declining health and premature death in the Royal Northern Hospital, London, on 3 October 1935. His wife, whom he had nursed through illness for many years, had died just six months earlier. The successful resolution of the disagreements, and acceptance of Moir and Dudley's priority, were carried forward by Dudley's junior partner at the National Institute, Harold King.

E. M. TANSEY

Sources H. H. Dale, *Obits. FRS*, 1 (1932–5), 595–606 · A. S. V. Burgen, 'Dale and Dudley's discovery of acetylcholine in mammals', *Trends in Neuroscience*, 2 (1979), xii · E. M. Tansey, 'Sir Henry Dale and autopharmacology: the role of acetylcholine in neurotransmission', *Essays in the history of the physiological sciences*, ed. C. Debru (1995), 180–93 · E. M. Tansey, 'From ergot to ergometrine—the history of an obstetric drug', *Women and medicine*, ed. L. Conrad and A. Hardy [forthcoming] · *The Times* (4 Oct 1935) · T. W. Goodwin, *History of the Biochemical Society, 1911–1986* (1987) · WWW

Archives Medical Research Council, London · National Institute for Medical Research, London | RS, Dale MSS

Likenesses W. Stoneman, photograph, 1931, NPG [*see illus.*] · photograph, repro. in Dale, *Obits. FRS*

Wealth at death £8224 1s. 0d.: administration, 20 Nov 1935, *CGPLA Eng. & Wales*

Dudley, Henry. *See* Sutton, Henry (d. 1564?).

Dudley, Lord Henry (1531?–1557). *See under* Dudley, John, duke of Northumberland (1504–1553).

Dudley, Sir Henry Bate, baronet (1745–1824), newspaper editor, was born at Fenny Compton, Warwickshire, on 25 August 1745, the second son of the Revd Henry Bate, who held a living for many years at St Nicholas, Worcester, and afterwards became rector of North Fambridge in Essex, and his wife, who was the sister of a Dr White of Warwickshire. Although he was said to have been educated at Queen's College, Oxford, Bate does not appear to have been awarded a degree. However, he still took up orders and succeeded to the rectory of North Fambridge upon his father's death. Little of Bate's time was spent in Essex, since he preferred to be in London. In the summer of 1773 he was celebrated for defending the honour of the actress Mrs Elizabeth Hartley, his future sister-in-law, from the unwarranted attention of a group of macaronis at Vauxhall Gardens. The incident led to a planned duel (not carried out) and a boxing match between Bate and one Captain Miles, supposedly a gentleman defender of the macaronis but in fact the footman of their ringleader, George Robert Fitzgerald. Bate easily defeated Miles, who was sent home 'with his face a perfect jelly' (*Morning Chronicle*, 26 July 1773). Reports of what became known as the Vauxhall affray established Bate's reputation for manly courage in the face of provocation from effeminate men of fashion. Around this time he became the curate to James Townley, vicar of Hendon and author of the farce *High Life*

Sir Henry Bate Dudley, baronet (1745–1824), by Thomas Gainsborough, exh. RA 1780

below Stairs. Bate himself began to write comic operas at this point, and produced at least eight during the next twenty years.

However, it was for his journalistic writing that Bate became famous. In 1775 he was taken on as editor of the *Morning Post* at 4 guineas a week. At some point after this he also became a proprietor of the paper, possibly after 1780, when he was left a large inheritance by his uncle, and in return assumed the additional surname of Dudley. Despite this change in his fortunes, Bate Dudley lost none of his love of risk-taking. James Stephen, parliamentary reporter for the *Post*, described him as an 'able and witty, but profligate man … who, by his prowess as a noted bruiser and duellist, not less than by the power of his pen, was become a very conspicuous and formidable character' (*Memoirs*, 1.289). His constant involvement in fist fights and duels won him fame and the nickname the Fighting Parson. Bate Dudley was also fond of political contests in his newspaper, but this landed him in more serious trouble. On 25 July 1781 he was convicted of a libel on the duke of Richmond in the *Post* in February 1780 and sentenced to twelve months' imprisonment. Bate was responsible for numerous attacks which had labelled Richmond the 'Gallic Duke' and 'patriotic agent vender of his Majesty's dominions!' (*Morning Post*, 7 Dec 1779). Before this point, James Stephen asserted that Bate Dudley's 'domineering spirit had so much subdued the Proprietors of the paper, among whom were Alderman Skinner and some other individuals of pecuniary consequence, that he was allowed to conduct it without controul [sic] as to its political tone or otherwise' (*Memoirs*, 1.288). The confusion caused by the Richmond affair seems to have upset this tight command, and Bate Dudley was forced to leave. Perhaps not surprisingly, considering his reputation as the Fighting Parson, the political struggle which erupted among the partners in 1780 ended in a duel between Bate Dudley and Joseph Richardson, another proprietor. In November 1780 Bate Dudley set up the *Morning Herald* in opposition to the *Post*. It was soon acknowledged to be the capital's best-selling newspaper. In the same year he married Mary White, daughter of James White of Berrow, Somerset, and sister of Elizabeth Hartley; their marriage produced no children.

Bate Dudley was, without doubt, the most prominent, and the most notorious, newspaper editor in London during the 1780s. Some press historians have charged him with producing an entirely new kind of newspaper in this period, in which scandal, gossip, and ribald assaults were increasingly prominent. However, to suggest that Bate Dudley was responsible for this degree of innovation is an overstatement, since all of these elements were present in the London press before he took control at the *Post*. There is no doubt, however, that Bate Dudley published an unprecedented volume of scurrilous material in his paper, and that his many pronouncements on public figures were considered particularly outrageous. This policy won him few friends. According to James Grant, 'his extravagant habits and immoral conduct were assailed alike in Parliament and out of it' (Grant, 1.314). Samuel Johnson reputedly said of Bate Dudley: 'I will not allow this man to have merit; no, Sir, what he has is rather the contrary. I will, indeed, allow him courage, and on this account we so far give him credit' (J. Boswell, *Life of Johnson*, ed. P. Rogers, 1925, 1295). James Taylor was more forgiving, and wrote that

It is my sincere opinion, from a full consideration of the character of Sir Henry Bate Dudley, that the spirit, acuteness, and vigour, which animated his pen as a public censor, would have rendered him conspicuous for heroism, judgement, zeal, and enterprise, in the military or naval service, at once honourable to himself, and glorious to his country. (Taylor, 1.102–6)

As a result of his notoriety Bate Dudley featured in many contemporary satirical prints. In the 1779 print *A Baite for the Devil* he was described as

A Canonical Buck, Vociferous Bully
A Duellist, Boxer, Gambler & Cully …
A Government Runner of Falsehood a Vender
Staunch Friend to the Devil, the Pope & Pretender
A Managers parasite, Opera Writer
News paper Editor, Pamphlet Indictor.

Other prints attributed to him a great deal of political power. In *Ministerial Purgations, or, State Gripings*, for example, a print from 1780, Bate is set alongside both leading figures in the government and the devil, who refers to

him as 'my best child of all'. The implication that Bate could influence the nation's affairs through his newspaper was repeated in other hostile prints from this period.

Bate Dudley was also constantly accused of corruption. The *London Evening-Post* proclaimed that he was patronized by the North ministry and 'a prostituted hireling and betrayer of his country' (24 Feb 1780). Such accusations were not unwarranted. In 1781 Bate Dudley received large sums from the government, perhaps as much as £3000, in return for backing the prime minister at a time when most newspapers were highly critical of his administration. Lord North wrote to the king in 1782 that Bate had kept his newspaper 'open for all writings in favour of Government … to do Mr. Bate justice, he was a very constant, diligent, zealous and able, though perhaps too warm a writer on the part of the government' (North to George III, 18 April 1782, *Correspondence of George III*, 5.471). In 1784 the *Herald* was again receiving money from the Treasury, and during the early 1790s Bate Dudley was given an annual subsidy of £600. Yet he was no servant of the government, and the *Morning Herald* was famous for its virulent attacks on politicians of all political persuasions. Thus even though he was given £100 in 1784 from secret service funds, the *Herald* opposed the government line and remained militantly Foxite while defending the prince of Wales.

Bate Dudley was at least constant in his pursuit of personal advantage. His newspaper business made him a good deal of money, but he also craved the sort of social status which such work could not provide. This he attempted to do by chasing ecclesiastical preferment. Between 1797 and 1801 Bate Dudley battled to gain the living of Bradwell in Essex. He failed in this instance, but in 1804 was presented to the living of Kilscoran in co. Wexford—at which point he appears to have finally given up his newspaper interests—and in 1805 he was appointed chancellor of the diocese of the Ferns. Two years later he became rector of Kilnglass in co. Longford. In 1812 he resigned his Irish benefices and was presented to the rectory of Willingham in Cambridgeshire. Bate Dudley had always maintained that the prince of Wales had promised him both church preferment and a baronetcy some time before 1793 'for the faithful discharge of antecedent duties' and owing to the 'pecuniary losses and personal privations' he had faced in the prince's 'most confidential service' (BL, Add. MS 38292, fol. 152).

In 1806 the prince unsuccessfully recommended Bate Dudley for an Irish deanery, and in 1812 he made him a baronet, while five years later he gave him a stall in Ely Cathedral. At some point Bate Dudley also became a magistrate for seven English counties, including Essex, and on 23 May 1816 helped put down riots near Ely. Despite Bate Dudley's best efforts, he failed subsequently to become dean either of Ely or of Peterborough. In 1823 he wrote to the prime minister, Lord Liverpool, in an aggrieved mood. He was in debt and declared that owing to 'a continuance of embarrassing disappointments' he was no longer able to remain a resident magistrate at Ely.

Bate Dudley threatened Liverpool, none too subtly, that unless he received some form of further preferment he might expose the contents of a 'private letter' about an 'exalted personage': apparently the prince of Wales (BL, Add. MS 38292, fol. 152 and Add. MS 38293, fol. 389). The following December Bate Dudley was given a pension of £300 a year. However, he was unable to make much use of it as he died in Cheltenham on 1 February 1824. According to one source, Bate Dudley's

> person was finely formed, and possessed all of its symmetry beyond the age of sixty. His countenance, which was handsome, preserved its animation till a few days preceding his death; and his naturally cheerful mind never lost its vivacity till within a few months before he took leave of Ely College and its friendly inhabitants, for the last time. (GM, 276)

HANNAH BARKER

Sources H. Barker, *Newspapers, politics and public opinion in late eighteenth-century England* (1998) · A. Aspinall, *Politics and the press, c.1780–1850* (1949) · J. Taylor, *Records of my life*, 2 vols. (1832) · *Memoirs of James Stephen*, ed. M. Bevington, 2 vols. (1949) · *The correspondence of King George the Third from 1760 to December 1783*, ed. J. Fortescue, 6 vols. (1927–8) · J. Grant, *The newspaper press: its origin, progress, and present position*, 3 vols. (1871–2) · H. R. F. Bourne, *English newspapers*, 2 vols. (1887) · BL, Add. MSS 38292, fol. 152; 38293, fol. 389 · *GM*, 1st ser., 94/1 (1824), 276 · *The Vauxhall affray, or, Macaronies defeated* (1773) · H. Angelo, *Reminiscences*, 1 (1828) · W. Hindle, *The Morning Post, 1772–1937: portrait of a newspaper* (1937)
Archives BL, letters to George IV, Add. MSS 38277–38288 · BL, corresp. with Lord Hardwicke and others · BL, letters to third Lord Hardwicke, Add. MSS 35652–35753 · BL, corresp. with second earl of Liverpool, Add. MSS 38288–38293 · BL, corresp. with R. Peel, Add. MSS 40347–40359
Likenesses line engraving, caricature, pubd 1779 (*A baite for the devil*), BM · T. Gainsborough, oils, exh. RA 1780, priv. coll.; on loan to Marlborough House, London [see illus.] · T. Gainsborough, oils, c.1780, Tate collection · line engraving, caricature, pubd 1780 (*Ministerial purgations, or, State gripings*), BM

Dudley, Howard (1820–1864), wood-engraver and illustrator, born in Salisbury Square, Fleet Street, London, was the only son of George Dudley (d. 1827) of Tipperary and his wife, Sarah, daughter of Nathaniel Cove, coal merchant, of Salisbury Square. His parents were Quakers but his nurse surreptitiously arranged for his baptism in St Leonard, Shoreditch. After the death of his father the family moved to Easebourne, near Midhurst, Sussex. Here he devoted his holidays to exploring the history and antiquities of the area, and in 1835 he published *Juvenile researches, or, A description of some of the principal towns in the western part of Sussex and the borders of Hants*. Printed on his own printing press, this small work was illustrated with his crude but effective wood-engravings and contained poetry by his sister. (He had set the types himself and learned wood-engraving on the job.) As it met with some success, he reprinted it in a slightly enlarged form, and in 1836 published another volume, entitled *The History and Antiquities of Horsham*, containing thirty woodcuts and four lithographic views, all his own work. He also planned to print a quarto volume on the history and antiquities of Midhurst, with 150 illustrations, but other commitments as a wood-engraver prevented him from carrying out this project. From 1845 Dudley lived and worked in Edinburgh,

where he married Jane Ellen, the second daughter of Alexander Young; they had no children. He and his wife moved to London in 1852 and he was one of the illustrators of Charles Dolman's 1854–5 edition of John Lingard's *History of England*: these competent but uninspiring illustrations suggest a penchant for melodrama. Howard Dudley died at his home, 12 Holford Square, Pentonville, London, on 4 July 1864. His wife and her brothers, also illustrators, continued his business. In the *Gentleman's Magazine* of 1865 he was described as 'a mild and amiable man, affectionate in his domestic relations, and his gentlemanly manners, bright ideas, pungent remarks and very great choice of words made him a delightful companion' (p. 101).

L. H. CUST, *rev.* CHLOE JOHNSON

Sources GM, 3rd ser., 18 (1865), 101 · Bénézit, *Dict.*, 3rd edn · J. Glover, 'Juvenile researches, or, The diligent Dudleys', *Sussex County Magazine*, 22 (1948), 50–52 · M. A. Lower, *The worthies of Sussex* (1865), 339 · CGPLA Eng. & Wales (1865)
Archives Bodl. Oxf., corresp. with Sir Thomas Phillipps
Wealth at death under £800: probate, 4 July 1865, CGPLA Eng. & Wales

Dudley, Jane, duchess of Northumberland (1508/9–1555). *See under* Dudley, John, duke of Northumberland (1504–1553).

Dudley, Lady Jane. *See* Grey, Lady Jane (1537–1554).

Dudley, John. *See* Sutton, John (VI), first Baron Dudley (1400–1487).

Dudley, John, duke of Northumberland (1504–1553), royal servant, was born in London, the eldest of three sons and heir of Edmund *Dudley (c.1462–1510), administrator, of Atherington in Sussex, and his second wife, Elizabeth (1482×4–1525/6), daughter of Edward Grey, first Baron Lisle, and his wife, Elizabeth, and sister and coheir of John Grey, second Baron Lisle. He was named for his grandfather John Dudley (d. 1502) of Atherington, the second son of John Sutton (or Dudley), first Baron Dudley. His brothers were Sir Andrew *Dudley (c.1507–1559) [see under Sutton, Henry (d. 1564?)] and Jerome (d. in or after 1555).

Childhood, youth and early career, 1504–1532 At the time of John Dudley's birth his father was a highly trusted servant of Henry VII. Nothing is known of his early childhood, but it was probably spent at his father's main house in Candlewick Street, London. The king's death in April 1509 led directly to Edmund Dudley's downfall and execution on 17 August 1510. All his children were under six at that time, and presumably remained with their mother, although it is not known where, all his property being forfeit to the crown.

On 12 November 1511 Elizabeth Dudley remarried, her second husband being Arthur *Plantagenet (b. before 1472, d. 1542), the illegitimate son of Edward IV. Plantagenet was granted such of Edmund Dudley's lands as still remained in the hands of the crown but not, apparently, the custody of any of his children. Either at the time of Elizabeth's marriage, or very soon afterwards, John was placed in the care of Edward *Guildford (c.1479–1534), a well-connected esquire of the body, who was formally granted his wardship in February 1512. At the same time

John Dudley was restored in blood 'being not yet eight years old' and his father's attainder was annulled by statute (*Statutes of the Realm*, 11 vols., 1810–28, 3 Hen. VIII c. 19). Why this arrangement was made, and on whose initiative, is not known, and there are some hints that Plantagenet felt aggrieved about it.

Guildford seems to have received little for his pains beyond the modest profits of those lands which Edmund Dudley had enfeoffed to his son's use before his attainder. His principal seat was at Halden in Kent, and it was there that the young John Dudley was brought up. He probably had only the haziest memory of his father, and the attainder—so obviously a matter of political convenience—seems to have cast no shadow upon his childhood, although in later life he complained that Edmund Dudley had been treated unfairly. John Dudley would have left his mother's care in any case at about seven to be brought up in a friendly household, so he had lost nothing by becoming Guildford's ward. There is no direct evidence of that upbringing, which seems to have been entirely conventional. As an adult Dudley was literate in English, but claimed to have no knowledge of Latin, which probably means that he had forgotten the little he had learned. He had no conventional intellectual skills, and it is unlikely that his interest in cosmography and navigation was acquired as a child. He was almost certainly taught at home by a tutor, which was the normal education provided for the son (or ward) of a substantial gentleman, and probably shared his lessons with Guildford's own children, Richard and Jane [*see below*]. Consequently, instead of following his father in the study of the law he followed his guardian to become a soldier and courtier.

In 1514 Guildford became master of the Tower armouries and *ex officio* master of ceremonies for Henry VIII's jousts, a very responsible and high profile position at court at that time. By twelve or thirteen Dudley would have been old enough to have served as a page under his guardian, but there is no mention of his having done so. He must at some point have been introduced to the court, because in 1521, aged seventeen, he was selected to serve in Cardinal Thomas Wolsey's retinue during his abortive mission to negotiate peace between François I of France and the young emperor, Charles V. This was a purely educational trip—he was given no specific task—but it represented his first small exposure to public life. Guildford had been appointed knight marshal of Calais in 1519, and in 1522 with the outbreak of war with France he gave his young ward a very minor command within the garrison. Dudley seems to have gained his first taste of military service in the minor skirmishes which took place around the pale towards the end of that year. At about the same time he became betrothed to Jane Guildford. Whether this was by his wish or hers—or someone else's—is not known. He appears to have felt that the arrangement was made by his mother and Guildford, but the subsequent marriage was happy and fruitful. Richard Guildford seems to have been a sickly or inadequate youth (at least in his father's eyes), and Dudley was always favoured before him. This could

have caused serious problems later had not Richard Guildford predeceased his father.

Meanwhile, when Charles Brandon, first duke of Suffolk, was appointed to lead an army royal against France in 1523 Guildford was among his senior officers, taking Dudley in his retinue. The campaign was a failure, but on 7 November the nineteen-year-old Dudley was knighted by the duke. Suffolk was somewhat generous with knighthoods at this point, perhaps because he had nothing else to be generous with, and this gesture may have been no more than a favour to his old friend Guildford, but his action attracted no criticism, either at the time or later. Dudley, who subsequently acquired a reputation for physical courage, had distinguished himself at the crossing of the Somme. By 1524 he was back at court as an esquire of the body. Since the rise of the privy chamber during Henry VII's reign this no longer implied a close relationship with the king, but it was a position of honour, made more significant by the fact that Dudley also began to appear prominently among the jousters. Guildford was in a good position to give him his chance in this respect, but the fact that he was able to grasp the opportunity and to gain Henry VIII's favour in consequence tells us that he had both courage and skill. Jousting was a demanding occupation in 1524.

Jane Guildford reached her sixteenth birthday in 1525, and John his twenty-first, and they must have married before the end of the year. By 1528 they had at least two, and probably three children, although the exact dates of birth are not known. Their eight sons included John Dudley, earl of Warwick (1527?–1554) [*see below*], Ambrose *Dudley, earl of Warwick (c.1530–1590), Henry Dudley (1531?–1557) [*see below*], Robert *Dudley, earl of Leicester (1532/3–1588), and Guildford *Dudley (c.1535–1554); their daughters were Mary *Sidney (1530x35–1586) and Katherine *Hastings, later countess of Huntingdon (c.1538–1620).

Because Dudley had not been required to sue livery of his lands there is no exact record of what he inherited. The value was estimated at £200 a year, and he probably received more as Jane Guildford's jointure, which would have given him a reasonable competence for a man in his position. Where the young couple lived is not clear either, but it was probably upon one of the manors in Surrey or Sussex which Dudley is known to have held later. In 1527 he again accompanied Wolsey to France, but he was never in the cardinal's service, and was unaffected by his fall in 1529. His only known patron was Guildford, and Guildford himself was the king's man. Neither followed the contemporary rule that an aspiring hop needed a strong pole. By 1530 Dudley was an active and successful courtier, but he always seems to have been guided by his own reading of Henry's mind rather than by allegiance to any particular court party. This had its risks, but avoided dependence upon intermediaries for favour. At some point between 1525 and 1528 his mother, Lady Elizabeth Plantagenet, died. This should have conferred upon him the barony of Lisle, but Plantagenet had already been created Viscount

Lisle and Dudley's claim (if he put it forward) was not recognized. He may have inherited some property from his mother, but the bulk of her estate was also tied up in a life interest to Lisle, so he seems to have benefited hardly at all from her death. During the critical years 1528 to 1532, when the court was becoming increasingly divided over Henry's great matter, Dudley kept a low profile—so low that no one commented upon his alignment at all. He was not yet important enough to get himself into danger, but he remained at court, not making any attempt to promote a career in the country. He did not even serve upon a commission of the peace for Surrey or Sussex (for which he was well qualified by 1525) until 1531.

By 1532 Dudley was a minor member of what at this point was the Boleyn / Cromwell party, which was clearly in the ascendant by the end of that year. Perhaps as a result, in March he gained his first office, the constableship of Warwick Castle, which he held jointly in survivorship with the established favourite, Sir Francis Bryan. A number of minor offices (which were not shared) were granted with the constableship, carrying fees of about £45 a year, and enough status in the county for him to be added to the commission of the peace during the same year. At the age of about twenty-eight Dudley's career begins to emerge from the shadows. He obtained his first wardship, that of Anthony Norton of Worcestershire, and stood surety for a substantial sum which his friend Sir Edward Seymour borrowed from the king.

Royal service, 1532–1544 Also during 1532 Dudley entered into a complex, and eventually acrimonious, financial relationship with his kinsman, Edward *Sutton (known as Dudley), fourth Baron Dudley (c.1515–1586), the grandson of his grandfather's elder brother. Lord Dudley was deep in debt, partly as a result of his father's extravagance, and partly his own incompetence. Dudley loaned him £1400, for which he bound himself to repay £2000 over five years at an annual interest rate of about eight per cent. At the same time Lord Dudley appears to have borrowed smaller sums from other people, and to have mortgaged most of his estate to Dudley for another £6000. Dudley must himself have borrowed to raise a capital sum of nearly £7500, which he probably did at a favourable rate through contacts in London. From his point of view it was purely a business arrangement, and when Lord Dudley began to get into trouble with his repayments Dudley had no option but to apply pressure. Lord Dudley, however, does not seem to have understood this, and complained loudly that a kinsman could so misuse him. By 1533 he was thoroughly mired, but received little sympathy from Thomas Cromwell, then the near all powerful secretary. Eventually Dudley foreclosed on the mortgage, and in 1537 Lord Dudley sold his entire estate to a London syndicate, who were probably John Dudley's financial backers, and now became his feoffees to uses. By 1540 he had moved his principal seat from Sussex to Dudley Castle in Worcestershire and was known as Sir John Dudley of Dudley.

By 1534 his father-in-law and patron was obviously ailing, and Dudley took over Guildford's parliamentary seat

as knight of the shire for Kent, and his mastership of the Tower armoury (10 July). Now that the king had virtually retired from jousting this latter office had lost some of its importance, but it was still a position of prestige, and Dudley was supervising the making of armour for Henry as late as 1540. Guildford died on 4 June 1534, leaving his nephew, John Guildford (b. in or before 1508, d. 1565), as his principal heir. Dudley however, pursued claims against the estate, both on his own and his wife's behalf. Cromwell arbitrated the quarrel, but it is not known how successful the Dudley claim was. What is clear is that Dudley, although not unscrupulous, was a shrewd and hardheaded man of business. This can also be seen in his land dealings. By 1535 he had already sold his reversionary interest in his mother's estate, and by 1536, in spite of sitting for the county in the House of Commons, he had parted with most of his land in Kent to Cromwell, who was keen to build up an estate close to London. At the same time he was buying land in Staffordshire and the Welsh marches. The fall of the Boleyns in that year did not touch him because he had already attached himself to the victorious Cromwell, the price of whose favour was no doubt the Kentish lands at a favourable rate. Later in 1536 he commanded 200 Sussex men against the Pilgrimage of Grace, but did not see any active service. At about this time Cromwell posited appointing him vice-chamberlain and captain of the guard, but either changed his mind or was overruled by the king, because the appointment was not made. Instead he received in 1537 the honourable but not particularly exciting post of chief trencher, at £50 a year (16 February 1537 to 12 January 1553). In spite of Cromwell's favour, and the increasing prosperity of his landholdings, at the age of thirty-four Dudley was still only a minor office-holder and middle-ranking courtier. However, in February 1537 he was appointed a vice-admiral to keep the narrow seas. There was no war, and his service in that capacity was low key, but the king was pleased with his achievement and Dudley seems to have found the sea congenial. He was mostly occupied in chasing pirates between July and September, and his reports, of which a number survive, give a lively impression of the difficulties of dealing with an elusive quarry, and with the channel weather. He also went on embassy with Sir Thomas Wyatt the younger to Spain in October, but his role in the mission was a subordinate one, not much more distinguished than that in Wolsey's abortive mission ten years earlier.

In spite of his sea service, by 1540 Dudley had still obtained no major preferment. Appointment as master of the horse to Anne of Cleves did not represent the hoped for breakthrough at court, and in June disaster befell his friend and mentor Cromwell. Dudley had been close enough to Cromwell to make it prudent for him to retire from the court for a few months, and his domestic affairs probably benefited from some attention. However, the conservative victory was less decisive than it appeared, and by the end of 1541 he was back at court, giving close support to Thomas Cranmer, archbishop of Canterbury, in unravelling the distasteful and dangerous story of Catherine Howard's infidelities. The arrest and imprisonment of his stepfather, Lisle, on 19 May 1540 on suspicion of Catholic sympathies may have been an embarrassment, but Dudley was by this time a recognized member of the reforming party in religious matters, so he was not touched by the association. He later claimed to have embraced the new ideas before 1540, and his contemporary reputation supports that. On 3 March 1542 Lisle died in prison, and nine days later Dudley was created Viscount Lisle 'by the right of his mother, Lady Elizabeth, sister and heir to Sir John Grey, Viscount Lisle, who was late wife to Arthur Plantagenet, Viscount Lisle, deceased' (*LP Henry VIII*, 17.163). So he owed his title neither to his service nor his wealth, but simply to his kinship. Although by custom Dudley could have inherited the barony of Lisle from his mother, once his stepfather's life interest was ended, the viscountcy was a new creation by letters patent, and reflected the king's favour. No chief minister followed Cromwell, and for the remainder of Henry's reign the court was divided between conservative and reforming groups. The former was a somewhat uneasy alliance between survivors of the old nobility such as Thomas Howard, third duke of Norfolk, and William FitzAlan, eleventh earl of Arundel, and senior prelates like Stephen Gardiner, bishop of Winchester, and Cuthbert Tunstall, bishop of Durham. These men were close to the king in terms of their religious policy, but suspect for their political pretensions. Against them stood a group of service nobles led by Seymour, now earl of Hertford, closely allied to Cranmer, and Henry's last queen, Katherine Parr. The king trusted these people, but suspected them (rightly) of heretical inclinations. To this latter group belonged the new Viscount Lisle. Within the court the conflict swung backwards and forwards, and it was not until the last months of 1546 that Henry's political suspicions overcame his theological ones, and the reformers emerged as clearly victorious. The Howards were disgraced, Gardiner was rusticated, and the list of executors of the king's will was dominated by Hertford, Cranmer, Sir William Paget—and Lisle.

Lisle's political progress between 1542 and 1547 was very marked. He was knight of the shire for Staffordshire in the heart of his new landed base in 1542. On 8 November that year, as Henry prepared to renew his war with France by attacking Scotland, Lisle was appointed warden-general of the Scottish marches. It was twenty years since he had seen any military service, and the appointment was a political one. He played no part in the victory at Solway Moss on 25 November, but had to deal with a Scotland left in chaos by that defeat, and by the death of James V a few days later. He often did not know who he was supposed to deal with, but his reports disclose a sharp and pragmatic mind. He dealt successfully with the Scottish regency council, and made some progress in building up a party among the border lairds who could see an accommodation with England as being to their greatest advantage.

Henry decided to follow up his victory by pressing the Scots for a marriage alliance between their infant queen Mary and his own five-year-old son, Prince Edward, and bound the Scottish lords taken prisoner at Solway Moss to

purchase their freedom by swearing to support this match. Lisle's progress with the border lairds supported this policy effectively, and although the warden-general achieved no spectacular success the king was pleased with his service. However, precisely because it was a political rather than a military position, Lisle was soon agitating for a move, and only two months after his appointment he was promoted to higher things. On 26 January 1543 he became lord high admiral and thus an *ex officio* member of the privy council. Deeply immersed in the affairs of the north it was three months before he could come south to take up his new duties. He was sworn of the privy council on 23 April, and nominated a knight of the Garter on the same day (installed on 5 May). In less than a year he had moved from being a frustrated middle-ranking courtier to a great officer of state.

This success (a little belated from Lisle's point of view) was not owed to any particular talent—certainly not great military ability—but to hard political graft. He was competent, did what he was bidden, and the king trusted him. However, as lord high admiral he was a conspicuous success. Henry had had a standing navy for over twenty years, but its administration had developed in a ramshackle and unplanned fashion. In 1545 and 1546 the structure was overhauled, the number of officers augmented from three to seven, and a professional salary structure established. The officers were then constituted into the king's council for marine causes, and became a department of state with defined responsibilities and a considerable degree of autonomy. This structure, which was the most developed in Europe at the time, gave the English navy the edge over its rivals in mobilization, supply, victualling, and logistics for the remainder of the century. The extent to which Lisle was personally responsible for the ideas embodied in this institution is not known, but as lord high admiral at the time he was formally responsible, and such a pragmatic and businesslike arrangement bears the stamp which all his projects show. As a fleet commander he was successful without ever winning a battle. Full-scale battles at sea were rare at this date, and in 1544 he supported both Hertford's campaign against Edinburgh and Henry's siege of Boulogne. The Scottish regent, James Hamilton, second earl of Arran, having signed a treaty accepting the English marriage proposal at Greenwich in 1543, then defected to the French party, to Henry's enormous indignation, and Hertford's punitive expedition was the result.

The French war, 1544–1546 The king's obsessive siege of Boulogne, which was successful in September 1544, cost him his alliance with the emperor and left him in dangerous isolation against the French and the Scots. This did not dent Henry's satisfaction, and he wasted no time in arranging for the government and defence of his conquest. For this front line responsibility he might have been expected to choose his favourite soldier, Hertford, but instead he entrusted it to the lord high admiral. Lisle was less than delighted by this demonstration of trust, fearing that he might lose the admiralty, by which he clearly set great store. However, he need not have worried. After four months he was recalled from Boulogne, and in January 1545 began to mobilize the fleet for what was likely to be a busy and dangerous summer. François was determined to recover Boulogne, and by June was assembling a fleet of some 300 ships for that purpose. Lisle determined upon a pre-emptive strike, and on 25 June attempted to enter the Seine estuary with 160 ships. The weather frustrated him and no more than a skirmish resulted, but the lord high admiral had shown a better grasp of large-scale tactics than anyone had a right to expect. His French antagonist, Claude d'Annebaut, also had a problem because his large fleet was ready well ahead of the army which it was supposed to accompany, and could not be kept on hold. Consequently, on 19 July he moved against Portsmouth and the Isle of Wight. Although his intentions are uncertain, this was a very dangerous moment for the English. Lisle confronted him in the Solent with about 200 ships. Partly because of the fickle winds, and partly because the English were obviously ready for him, d'Annebaut backed off, mindful that his main objective was supposed to be Boulogne. This confrontation is best known for the controversial loss of the *Mary Rose*, which cost over 500 lives, but the engagement was really a victory for the new admiralty.

D'Annebaut discharged his main function, landing 7000 troops at Boulogne, and then brought a part of his fleet back to the Sussex coast, apparently looking for a fight. Lisle went after him with seventy ships, and the two fleets met on 15 August. However, after an exchange of gunfire the French unexpectedly retreated under cover of darkness. It was subsequently learned that plague had broken out in the fleet, and d'Annebaut was forced to return and demobilize. Lisle thus emerged victorious without having fought a battle, but having shown a conspicuous ability to be ready for one. The battle orders which he issued in August 1545 also show a tactical awareness which was altogether new in English sea commanders, who were usually noted for their extreme conservatism. Lisle was familiar with the latest French and Spanish ideas, and envisaged fighting his fleet in functional squadrons to make better use of their firepower, which was a major advance upon the mêlée of one-to-one encounters envisaged in Thomas Audley's fleet orders of 1530. The lord high admiral's stock was understandably raised. As early as January 1544 Eustache Chapuys, the well informed imperial ambassador, had thought him to be one of Henry's must influential privy councillors, and when Suffolk died in August 1545 some thought that Lisle would inherit his unique place in the king's estimation. That did not happen, and Lisle secured no further preferment during Henry's life, but his services did not go unrewarded. He acted along with Paget as a principal commissioner for the negotiation of peace with France from 17 April to 14 June 1546, and his good personal relations with d'Annebaut were a significant factor in the success of that mission. Henry was able to retain Boulogne, at least for the time being, and was able to keep his options open in Scotland.

The peace treaty was signed, and appropriately it was Lisle who was sent to the French court to receive François's ratification on 1 August. In recognition of this achievement he was granted a number of former ecclesiastical properties, including the substantial priory of St John, Clerkenwell, and the opportunity to purchase from the crown on favourable terms lands in Birmingham and Richard's Castle. When the subsidy assessments were drawn up towards the end of 1545 his lands were valued at £1376 a year. This was almost certainly an underassessment, but it made him the eighth or ninth richest peer, outranking several earls. He was also by this time a gentleman of the privy chamber, and his income from fees and the other perquisites of office amounted to at least £1000 per year. When the king died on 28 January 1547 Lisle was one of the richest as well as one of the most important subjects of the crown.

By contrast little is known of Lisle's domestic life. Although he spent so much of his time at court he seems not to have owned a London house, and his wife is scarcely ever mentioned. He rented a house in Holborn, but she probably remained in Worcestershire, looking after her growing family. Eight children survived to adulthood, six sons and two daughters. Nothing is known about their education, but the second son, John Dudley, earned generous praise from the mathematician Dr John Dee, and the two sons who survived into Elizabeth I's reign, Ambrose and Robert Dudley, were both regarded as polished gentlemen. It was later claimed that Dee had been their tutor, but by the time of his known association with Dudley the latter's sons were all grown men. Mary Dudley, mother of Sir Philip Sidney, had received the benefit of a good education too. Robert Dudley seems to have shared the lessons of the young Prince Edward in the 1540s, but how long that arrangement continued is not apparent. Lisle's eldest son and heir, Sir Henry Dudley (1525/6–1544), served under his father in the Boulogne campaign of 1544, and died of an illness not long after the capture of the town, aged eighteen. None of Lisle's surviving letters from the period allude to his loss, but whether this was stoicism or the random survival of evidence is not clear. Other letters suggest that he was an affectionate parent, who showed a proper concern for his children's welfare, and that Henry Dudley, who was then newly knighted, had been his favourite. Even Lisle's worst enemies (who were numerous) never alleged any sexual scandal against him, and his family life seems to have been a model of propriety.

The protectorate, 1547–1549 Henry's death in January 1547 converted the reformers' ascendancy into power. Edward was a little over nine years old, and a longish minority was in prospect. Within a few days Hertford, Edward's maternal uncle, and his friends set about converting Henry's somewhat indeterminate arrangements into a workable regency. Hertford became lord protector and governor of the king's person on 31 January and was promoted duke of Somerset. Thomas Wriothesley, Baron Wriothesley, remained lord chancellor and became first earl of Southampton; Lisle became earl of Warwick and on 17 February lord great chamberlain; and Sir Thomas Seymour became Baron Seymour of Sudeley and lord high admiral. These arrangements were not effected as smoothly as the official records make them appear. Seymour was deeply disgruntled at getting only a barony, and thought he should have been made the governor. Southampton was strongly opposed to the powers conferred on the new lord protector, and was consequently disgraced by him in March. Warwick was gratified by his title, and by his court office, which satisfied his long felt need for estimation, but was not particularly happy to lose the admiralty. Seymour secured a sort of revenge on his brother by marrying Katherine, the dowager queen, against the lord protector's wishes, and relations between the two brothers steadily deteriorated. It was alleged in Elizabeth's reign that Warwick had encouraged Seymour's disaffection for reasons of his own, but no contemporary evidence from 1547 suggests that. All the indications are that at that time Somerset and Warwick were working closely together and in reasonable harmony. Outside observers thought that the earl was the second or third most important person in England, and well satisfied with his position. He received a legacy of £500 in Henry VIII's will, and in March a grant of the manor, castle, and town of Warwick, together with extensive properties in eleven counties to an annual value of £498, following his elevation to the title. In spite of his concern with estimation he made no attempt to create an old-fashioned power base for himself in the west midlands, and in fact had sold most of this grant within a few months of receiving it, buying elsewhere for reasons which are now impossible to recover. He subsequently repurchased much of this land.

Somerset believed that he had a duty to complete the old king's unfinished business in Scotland, and in autumn 1547 he made another attempt to enforce the defunct treaty of Greenwich. In September he crossed the Tweed at the head of about 18,000 men, with Warwick as his lieutenant and commander of the cavalry. The resulting battle of Pinkie on 10 September was an overwhelming English victory, but it achieved little, except to make French intervention more likely. Warwick distinguished himself by his personal courage, receiving warm compliments from the lord protector and another £100 worth of land as a reward, but he kept a low profile for the remainder of the year, and may have been suffering from one of those bouts of ill health which become increasingly noticeable over the last six years of his life. There was still no suggestion of a rift with Somerset at this time. Odete de Selve, the French ambassador, considered them to be close allies, and many petitioners approached Warwick because of his presumed influence with the lord protector. In March 1548 he was appointed president of the king's council in the marches of Wales, and soon afterwards gave his first hint of dissatisfaction with Somerset's style of government when his proposals for appointments which he thought should have been in his gift were ignored.

By summer 1548 Somerset's administration was running into increasing difficulties. His policy of controlling Scotland through strategic garrisons was proving an expensive failure, and his attempts to defend what some saw as traditional social values by prohibiting enclosure and changes of land use were alienating the aristocratic support upon which he depended. There were enclosure riots, and in June the French sent an expeditionary force of 6000 men to Scotland. The English garrisons were forced out over the next eighteen months, and Mary, queen of Scots, was betrothed to the dauphin, François. In August 1548 she departed for France, and the lord protector's Scottish policy, to which he had devoted so much energy and money, was in ruins. Warwick disapproved of Somerset's agrarian policy, and clashed bitterly with the commonwealth man John Hales, but he assiduously maintained good relations with Somerset's familiars, Sir John Thynne and William Cecil, and at the end of 1548 still seems to have thought good relations with the lord protector to be the best guarantee of his own interests. He warmly supported the moves towards protestantism which produced the first Book of Common Prayer in January 1549, and conservatives noted with disapproval that the mass had been discontinued in his household by the end of 1547.

By the end of 1548 Somerset's relations with Seymour had also reached a crisis. Katherine had died in September, and Seymour began a reckless and irresponsible bid to secure the hand of the fifteen-year-old Princess Elizabeth. He also attempted to use the House of Lords to annul his brother's patent. Having discovered that the under-treasurer of the Bristol mint, Sir William Sharrington, was corrupt, he persuaded or browbeat him into illicitly coining large sums of money which he spent on weapons, claiming that he had a substantial following who would support his cause. In January 1549 the lord protector felt compelled to act. Seymour was arrested and charged with treason. He was not tried by his peers, but condemned by act of attainder and executed on 20 March. This may have been because he refused to answer some of the charges, or perhaps because the evidence was insecure. It was later claimed that Warwick engineered this situation as part of a plot to destroy Somerset, but he said at the time that he had tried to reconcile the brothers. Every effort was made to blacken Seymour's name, but there is no contemporary evidence that Somerset was seriously weakened by the execution of his brother. The privy council solidly supported him, accepting that he had no option, and expressed their sympathy with his painful dilemma.

Nevertheless all was not well between lord protector and privy council. The latter had become increasingly marginalized as Somerset grew more autocratic, and less sensitive to either advice or criticism. With more persistence than good sense he began to mobilize in spring 1549 to recover the initiative in Scotland, but was forced to abandon his plans when rebellion, riots, and other major disorders engulfed about fifteen English counties in June and July. In some places, particularly in Devon and Cornwall, the introduction of the new Book of Common Prayer at Whitsun was the trigger, but most of the troubles were caused by economic grievances. Sometimes it was the alleged loss of homes and employment to enclosing landlords, more often the engrossing of common land by those with the greatest interests. In many cases the protesters were encouraged to act by the belief that the king and the lord protector were sympathetic to their cause, a belief encouraged by the enclosure commissions which Somerset had established to determine the extent of the problem (1 June 1548, 11 April 1549). In spite of strenuous warnings that subjects should not take the law into their own hands yeomen farmers and minor gentlemen like the brothers Robert and William Kett in Norfolk were often convinced that it was the greater gentry, who dominated county government, who stood in the way of a policy wanted by both the crown and the common people. These protests enjoyed very different fortunes. In many counties strong local leadership either suppressed or pacified the troubles, and significantly it was in two places where the dominant county nobility, the Howards and the Courtenays, had recently been removed, Norfolk and Devon, that matters got out of hand. At first Somerset was reluctant to act firmly, partly because he saw the justice of some of the demands, and partly because it took time to recall his forces (many of them foreign mercenaries) from the Scottish border. This proved disastrous.

The coup against Somerset, 1549 Eventually, in mid-August John Russell, first Baron Russell, put down the western rebellion, but in Norfolk the first attempt under William Parr, marquess of Northampton, was defeated in late July, and if the rebels had had any aggressive strategy or political leadership the situation could have become serious. However, because they saw themselves simply as a protest movement they merely repeated their demands and waited for the next government move. In this crisis Somerset called upon his most trusted ally and skilled soldier, Warwick, who moved against the camp on Mousehold Heath outside Norwich on 23 August. Warwick had not fought this kind of campaign before, but he had good and reliable troops and a clear strategic objective. Going about his task carefully and systematically he retook the city of Norwich and defeated the rebels at the so-called battle of Dussindale on 27 August. About 2000 of the insurgents were killed on the field, but Warwick refused to allow the local gentry to exact revenge for the humiliation which they had suffered, and, in sharp contrast to what was taking place in the west country, judicial executions following the rising numbered only a few dozen.

By early September Warwick was back in the capital, but he did not disband his troops, and his attitude towards the lord protector seems to have undergone a radical change. In July his amicable correspondence with Sir John Thynne, Somerset's steward, came to an end, and according to François Van der Delft, the imperial ambassador, it was then that he joined a group of leading peers who were plotting the duke's overthrow. The others, particularly Henry FitzAlan, twelfth earl of Arundel, and Southampton, were religious conservatives who were already attempting unsuccessfully to persuade Princess Mary to accept the regency. Whether Warwick was the leader, or merely the most powerful member of this group is not clear, but the troops which he had retained since the Norfolk campaign proved vital to the outcome of the coup.

Most of the privy council rallied to the conspirators, and gathered in London at the beginning of October. Somerset was with the king at Hampton Court when he discovered what was afoot on 5 October. Apart from the king's guard of about 200 men he had no troops, and he issued a general summons to Edward's loyal subjects to defend him against a traitorous plot. This was a major error, reinforcing the privy councillors' claim that he was favouring the commons against their natural lords. There was a strong response from the commons to Somerset's pleas for assistance and thousands gathered at Hampton Court, but nothing of military significance, and on 6 October the lord protector removed the king to the greater security of Windsor Castle. At that point it also became clear that Russell and Sir William Herbert, leading the forces in the west, would not commit their forces to Somerset's cause. A tense stand-off then followed as letters passed between those with the king, particularly Paget and Cranmer, and the council in London. On 10 October, realizing that no useful help was coming, and having strained his relations with the young king, Somerset surrendered.

This was a negotiated settlement that Sir Philip Hoby brokered in which Somerset agreed to surrender and even give up his protectorship, 'if ye will again for your partes use equitie' (PRO, SP 10/9/26, M. fols. 39v–40r). Probably the key figures behind this were Warwick and Cranmer, who shared a common interest in continuing the lord protector's religious reforms, although for rather different reasons. After the coup Somerset was imprisoned and the protectorate dissolved (13 October), and the privy council assumed a collective responsibility for government, ostensibly under the leadership of Southampton. A religious reaction was generally expected, and Van der Delft was puzzled by Cranmer's continued presence on the privy council. As late as 7 November the ambassador believed that Southampton was still the leader, but in fact his influence was waning, and the appointment of the protestant Henry Grey, third marquess of Dorset, to the privy council at the end of November signalled that Warwick's power was growing. Realizing that they were losing ground, in December a group of conservative privy councillors led by Southampton apparently decided to try and remove Warwick by condemning Somerset as a traitor, and then alleging Warwick's complicity in his crimes. Warned in advance, probably by William Paulet, Baron St John, on 13 December Warwick staged a dramatic scene, declaring that Southampton did 'seek his [Somerset's] bloude and he that seekethe his bloude woulde have myne also' (BL, Add. MS 48126, fol. 16r). The privy council rallied to him and the conservative leaders were removed. Shortly afterwards Somerset was allowed to compound for his offences and was released into house arrest. The conservative plot may have been real, or it may have been fabricated, but the outcome was decisive. Warwick became the unchallenged leader, assuming the title of lord president of the privy council in February 1550, and the policy of religious reform continued. He was again briefly lord high admiral from 28 October 1549 to 14 May

1550. At this time he relinquished his office of chamberlain (1 February 1550), becoming instead great master of the royal household on 20 February.

Lord president of the privy council, 1550–1552 Throughout this period of domestic crisis England had been at war. In August 1549, seeing his opportunity, Henri II had attacked Boulogne. Most of the Boullonais was quickly overrun, but the town itself held out, and repeated attacks were defeated. Faced with a financial crisis at home, with characteristic pragmatism Warwick decided to cut his losses. Capitalizing on Henri's own difficulties, and the failure of his military strategy, in March 1550 he sold Boulogne back to the French for the equivalent of £180,000. He then redeployed the garrison to improve domestic security and used the money to pay off some of the king's debts. Later in the year he also quietly abandoned Somerset's aggressive policy towards Scotland. Military expenditure continued to be high because a protestant England had few friends abroad, so the navy, and the garrisons of Berwick and Calais were maintained at full strength, but this was nothing like as costly as waging war. By 1550 the crown was £300,000 in debt, inflation had risen by about 75 per cent in two years, and the sterling exchange rate had collapsed. Warwick's policy of retrenchment was thus not only urgent but long overdue. Unfortunately, although he knew what had to be done he could not resist the temptation for one last round of debasement before finally listening to the advice of his London friends, including Sir Thomas Gresham, and restoring a sound level of purity to the mint output. Unfortunately he also made the mistake of announcing his intention in advance. The decline was halted, and some confidence restored, but the problem was not solved because the privy council judged that it could not afford to recall the base coin. However, by strict economy, and by appointing Gresham as the king's agent in Antwerp early in 1552, Warwick managed to restore the exchange rate, and made a start on reducing the burden of debt. Some loans were recycled, and some recalled to London where the support of the city reduced the difficulty of servicing them. Warwick's declared intention of removing the king's debts was aimed at least as much at gratifying his supporters in London as easing the administrative burden on the privy council.

The social tensions of 1549 had not gone away, but Warwick avoided his predecessor's critical mistake. No one believed that he had any sympathy with agrarian malcontents, justified or not. He judged that the unity of the ruling class was more important for the preservation of order than strict social justice and, in the circumstances of a minority, he was right. It was for this reason that he restored the privy council to an effective administrative body, licensed his friends and allies to maintain men in their liveries, regularized the appointment of lords lieutenant from 1550, and distributed favours and rewards with a generous hand. For all these things he was severely criticized, both at the time and since, but as long as Edward was alive the policy worked. Not only was there no repetition of 1549, but conservative gentry who detested his continued protestant reforms nevertheless

enforced them rather than give the commons another excuse for rebellion. The severe outbreaks of sweating sickness which afflicted the country in 1551 and 1552 probably helped to keep the lid on discontent, but the critical factor was that the privy council and the county commissions spoke with a single voice. It was this urgent need for unity which made Somerset such a problem. The former lord protector was restored to the privy council in April 1550, and both he and Warwick made public gestures of reconciliation, particularly the marriage between the earl's eldest surviving son, John Dudley, Viscount Lisle, and Anne Seymour, the duke's daughter, which took place on 3 June 1550.

Unfortunately Somerset lacked his supplanter's pragmatic realism. He did not like Warwick's repressive social policy, or his tentative friendship with France, and he was deeply offended by the abandonment of his Scottish policy. Nor was he prepared to retire with a good grace. Rumours gathered around him from mid-1550 on, and some of Warwick's enemies tried to use him by hinting at his restoration to power. Apart from making his dissatisfaction with Warwick obvious, and failing to discourage his over-zealous adherents, Somerset confined his activity to intrigue. However, after making several indirect and unsuccessful attempts to persuade him to desist Warwick decided that the danger of another split in the ruling élite was too grave to be ignored. This attack was presaged by Warwick's promotion to duke of Northumberland on 11 October 1551. Northumberland bought support through granting titles: Dorset was promoted duke of Suffolk, St John to marquess of Winchester (having already been made earl of Wiltshire), and Herbert to earl of Pembroke. On 16 October Somerset was arrested, and was tried on 1 December on charges of treason which were largely fabricated, as was the custom in such cases. When he was acquitted and the crowds outside thought he would go free there were scenes of rejoicing in London which demonstrated how right Northumberland had been to fear him. However, Somerset was convicted of felony under the statute of 3 & 4 Edward VI c. 5 for having assembled an illegal force—an offence of which he was probably guilty—and executed on 22 January 1552. Somerset was destroyed by a combination of ruthlessness and trickery, but he was partly the author of his own downfall. The privy council remained united, as was politically necessary, despite his death.

By this time Edward was fourteen; precocious, opinionated, and very much aware of who he was. Somerset, who never seems to have noticed that the boy was growing up, had made the serious mistake of ignoring him, except for ceremonial purposes. During the crisis of October 1549 had given his sovereign lord a severe fright and a bad cold by hastily removing him from Hampton Court to Windsor, and there was no affection thereafter in their relationship. Edward was easily convinced of his uncle's guilt at the time of his final fall. Northumberland did not make the same error, controlling the privy chamber through his office of great master. He knew (or thought he knew) that the king would achieve his majority in October 1555, and he had no intention of losing his influence at that point. Whatever his own religious views he judged that Edward's adolescent enthusiasm for radical protestantism was not a passing phase, and did everything in his power to humour him. He even risked making an enemy of his erstwhile ally Cranmer by advancing the more radical protestantism of men he favoured such as John Hooper and John Knox. Cranmer resented being outbid in Erastianism, and perhaps suspected that Northumberland's radicalism was largely assumed—or 'carnal' as he put it.

Edward was completely convinced, and the duke's personal ascendancy became unshakeable. According to one contemporary French observer the young king would do nothing without consulting Northumberland, whom he regarded as almost a father. Northumberland also took great pains with the king's political education, recruiting the services of William Thomas, one of the clerks of the privy council, to help by introducing the king to political essays, along Machiavellian lines, and even staging special meetings of the privy council for Edward to practise the skills of kingship. Perhaps even those taking part hardly knew how real these exercises were. Northumberland's main service to the crown during these years was the restoration of effective conciliar government, and the establishment of a relationship between king and privy council which he envisaged as surviving into the time of Edward's personal rule. The fact that his own authority would probably be confirmed and reinforced by this process accounts for the largely negative opinions which his efforts attracted from contemporaries. He was not an idealist, but like Cromwell he had a political strategy: to reduce the king's debts, to consolidate his position as supreme head of the church, and to reinforce the privy council's administrative machinery. He also encouraged the boy to take more vigorous exercise, which Edward greatly enjoyed, particularly archery and running at the quintain. Fortunately he was too young for the dangerous sport of jousting.

The rewards of power For John Dudley political power also brought generous rewards. After his fall he was bitterly denounced for his pride and greed, but in fact what he gained was not out of proportion to his position. He became earl marshal on 20 April 1551 and warden-general of the marches of Scotland on 20 October. The latter position carried the apparently large fee of £1333 6s. 8d. per annum, but out of that he was supposed to maintain the warden's retinue, and even if it had all been profit it would not have compared with the £5333 6s. 8d. a year which Somerset had awarded himself in 1547. The charge that Northumberland intended to add the palatinate jurisdiction of Durham and much diocesan property to his growing estates in the north is not substantiated by the position which he actually achieved, which was that of steward of the crown lands in the north and leader of the king's tenants (2 May 1553). The choice of Northumberland as his ducal title may be significant, but he had handled the Warwick lands fairly cavalierly, and there is no more sign of his having a power base in the north than in

the west midlands. He continued to trade in land, as he had done all his life, and between 1550 and 1553 acquired property with a capital value of about £40,000. Some of this was indeed granted on terms which amounted virtually to gift, but much was purchased or obtained by exchange, and some was sold almost immediately. When he fell his lands were valued at £4300 per annum; great wealth, but not as great as that of Somerset, or indeed of the Talbot earls of Shrewsbury. His promotion to duke of Northumberland gave him the highest dignity possible for a subject. He had at last satisfied his craving for estimation, but he made no attempt to follow it up with the creation of a ducal retinue. He had a household of more than 200, including many gentlemen, and several residences, but his devoted personal following was very small; a few soldiers like Sir John Gates. His estate was large, but constantly changing, and he had no *manred* in the traditional sense. His power base was the central government, and he could not command the loyal following of a Stanley, or a Talbot, or even a FitzAlan. He also used the crown's resources to buy support, although that did not have the damaging effect which has sometimes been alleged. As long as Edward was alive this preserved the unity of the government, but few of those who had benefited from his patronage felt beholden to Dudley personally. He was what Henry VIII had made him, a service peer on a grand scale, not an overmighty subject.

The succession crisis, 1553 The true nature of Northumberland's position was ruthlessly exposed by the events of 1553. At the beginning of the year the king was unwell. He was not sickly by nature, and had cast off previous infections with encouraging resilience, so at first anxiety was muted. However on 1 March he was forced to open the parliament with a special ceremony at Whitehall Palace instead of the usual procession at Westminster, and his physicians began to be concerned. By the end of the month he was better. In April he was able to take the air and a normal recovery was expected. However, that did not happen, and he was still ill in May. By then some pessimists, including Jehan Scheyfve, the imperial ambassador, were declaring that his sickness was mortal, but as late as the end of that month some who were in a position to know pronounced that he was recovering. In early June Edward collapsed, and even the most sanguine recognized that his days were numbered. Months before, perhaps before his illness had commenced, Edward had toyed with ideas about the succession, and jotted them down. They were not very coherent, but they show him to have been obsessed with legitimacy, and with a male succession. Bypassing both his half-sisters as illegitimate he started with an unborn son of his cousin Frances *Grey, duchess of Suffolk (1517–1559), and proceeded through the even more remote sons of her young daughters. This was not serious politics. It was never discussed by the privy council, and was not mentioned in the parliament. It is not even certain that anyone other than Edward knew of the existence of the 'Device'. However, when the king collapsed it came urgently into the public domain. There was no Salic law in England and a female successor would have to be considered. No one wanted the duchess of Suffolk as queen, so the 'Device' was altered to settle the succession on her eldest daughter, Lady Jane *Grey (1537–1554) 'and her heires masles' (Inner Temple Library, Petyt MS 538/47, fol. 317r).

The responsibility for this somewhat bizarre outcome has been fiercely debated ever since. The most commonly held view is that Northumberland bullied or persuaded the dying boy to designate an heir whom he considered to be biddable and amenable to his own designs. Jane had married his son Guildford on 21 May with the king's blessing, and if Northumberland could not have the puppet king he had been preparing, then he would have a puppet queen instead. The marriage between Jane and Guildford had been designed to bring that about. It is impossible to disprove this theory, which now has centuries of credibility, but there is some contemporary evidence against it. In the first place the marriage was part of a wider scheme of dynastic alliances, and Jane had not been the duke's first choice for his son; nor, at the time of the marriage, did anyone suggest that it had significance for the succession. Secondly, the king was almost sixteen, and very conscious of his responsibilities. Much as he may have respected Northumberland this was not a decision for a subject. Nor is it likely that anyone other than the king would have ventured to treat a statute so cavalierly. The 'Device' is in his own hand, and no one would have altered it without his full knowledge and consent. Moreover, when his law officers demurred at the breach of his father's statute it was (and could only have been) Edward who commanded them upon their allegiance to obey him, asserting that he would obtain parliament's assent retrospectively. Northumberland was totally committed to do the king's bidding, but such an attitude was inevitable in the circumstances, and does not prove that he was the originator of the scheme. He certainly had little to hope for from Mary, whom he had bullied unmercifully since 1550 over her religious nonconformity, but he would have had no reason to obstruct Elizabeth's succession, except that the king would have it so.

The real question is not how the scheme to settle the crown on Jane came about, but why it was adhered to when Edward died on 6 July and his driving will was removed. In this connection Northumberland's leadership was certainly critical. Against all sorts of doubts and uncertainties it was he who insisted that Edward's wishes should be respected and the claim which Mary promptly advanced rejected on 10 July. Whether this was calculated self interest, a reckless gamble, or an honest endeavour to honour a commitment, is not known. What is known is that there was no real planning for a coup of the kind which a seasoned politician like Northumberland would surely have made if his scheme had been premeditated. His actions after 6 July bear every sign of hasty improvisation. For about five days he held the privy council together, and most outside observers believed that he would succeed, but as soon as he was compelled to leave London to face the growing force which Mary was building around her in Norfolk conciliar unity collapsed.

Northumberland was personally unpopular, largely because he seems to have been incapable of establishing cordial relations with any of his colleagues, or indeed with anyone else apart from his wife and children. Moreover, what he was trying to do was generally regarded as unlawful. Even the protestants, in whose interests he claimed to be acting, distrusted and disliked him. Most of them declared for the lawful heir, in spite of the threat which she represented, although according to John Foxe the men of Suffolk attempted to make their allegiance conditional. For the majority who were not protestants Mary's high profile conservatism was an asset rather than a liability. Within a few days the duke's political position collapsed, and the fact that he had no old-fashioned affinity to fall back on left him totally exposed. When most of his troops deserted he surrendered at Cambridge on 23 July, along with his sons and a few friends, and was imprisoned in the Tower of London two days later.

Trial, death, and reputation The last weeks of Northumberland's life were a sad anticlimax for a man who had frequently displayed high levels of political skill. Tried for high treason on 18 August he claimed to have done nothing save by the king's command and the privy council's consent. Implicitly that argument was accepted for events before 6 July, but he was inevitably convicted for having acted on Jane's (invalid) authority after Edward's death. It was in this context of imminent death that he took the notorious step of renouncing the protestantism which he had long been promoting. Northumberland's religion has always been a matter of controversy, and this spectacular change of course has probably done more than anything else both to shape his image as the stereotypical wicked duke, a reverse figure of the godly, as well as good, duke of Somerset, and to fuel doubts as to whether he had any true religion at all.

In fact Dudley's conversion to an evangelical religion had taken place at much the same time as Seymour's. He himself assured Sir William Cecil in December 1552 that 'I have for xx yere stand to oon kynd of religion in the same which I doo nowe profes' (PRO, SP 10/15/66, M. fol. 137r), and this is borne out by the dedication to him of Latin poems by Nicholas Bourbon in 1533, one of which urges him and his wife to continue to follow the banners of Christ. Clearly Bourbon saw him as one of the group of evangelicals who gathered round Anne Boleyn. Informed comment from 1546–7 similarly placed him firmly in the reformist camp. The imperial ambassador Eustache Chapuys, for instance, on 29 January 1547 described Dudley as one of the new king's 'stirrers-up of heresy'. Less than a year earlier he had not been so far committed as to be unwilling to put pressure on the radical protestant Anne Askew, but it is significant that she rebuked him and his colleague Baron Parr of Kendal, saying 'it was great shame for them to counsell contrarye to their knowlege' (Bellin, 96). By December 1547 it was reported that mass was no longer said in his house.

During Edward VI's reign there were no doubts of Dudley's religious allegiance. He was a committed supporter of protestantism who also favoured reducing the powers of bishops and the confiscation of their estates. In part his stance was anti-papal. He owned a copy of Bernardino Ochino's *Dialoge of the Unjuste Usurped Primacie of the Bishop of Rome* (1549), and was also the dedicatee of one of John Bale's attacks on papistry. But it is significant that Bale also declared that he had always known Dudley as 'a most mighty, zealous, and ardent supporter, maintainer, and defender of God's lively word' (MacCulloch, *Tudor Church Militant*, 53). Nor was Bale's the only voice raised in praise of Dudley's religious zeal. As late as 28 February 1553 John Hooper, an advanced reformer, praised him as 'a diligent promoter of the glory of God' (Robinson, 1.99).

His collapse later in 1553, following the failure of his attempt to divert the succession from Princess Mary, appalled English protestants, not least his own daughter-in-law, who angrily denounced him: 'wo worthe him! he hathe brought me and my stocke in most myserable callamyty and mysery by his exceeding ambicion' (Nichols, 25). But it is noteworthy that Jane did not impugn Northumberland's religious sincerity; ambition, and simple fear of death, were her charges—'But life was swete, it appeered; so he might have lyved, you wyl saye, he dyd (not) care howe' (ibid., 26). A sudden breakdown of faith, both in himself and in the religion which had long underpinned his actions, at a time of overwhelming crisis, is certainly suggested by Northumberland's very moving letter to the earl of Arundel on the eve of his execution, begging him to move the queen to mercy: 'O that it would please her good grace to give me life, yea, the life of a dog, that I might live and kiss her feet … O my good lord remember how sweet life is, and how bitter ye contrary' (Loades, 269). In his letter the duke referred to his long service to the crown. In a time of agonized fear it may have been easy for him to be persuaded, or to have persuaded himself, that his defeat was a sign of God's wrath at his having deserted both the guiding principle of his secular life—loyalty to the Tudor dynasty—and the religion of his fathers, and to have turned for succour to the Catholicism he had once spurned.

Northumberland's appeal for clemency fell on deaf ears. Having extracted every propaganda advantage which he was willing to give, Mary had him executed at Tower Hill on 22 August. He made a carefully stage-managed speech before his death, in which he departed from the script in references to the recent plot to advance Jane to the throne, but otherwise said what the government wanted to hear. In particular he warned the crowd to remain loyal to the Catholic church, and to 'beware and take hede that yow be not ledde—and deceavyd by thes sedycyowse and lewde preachers that have openid the booke and knowe not how to shutt yt'. Protestantism, he said, caused God to plague the realm 'with warres commocions rebellyon pestelence & famyne besydes manye more greate and grevouse plagues to the greate decaye of our commonwealthe' (BL, Cotton MS Titus B. ii, fols. 144v–145r). The speech was printed by John Cawood, the royal printer, with Latin and German translations, and widely circulated. He was buried at the Tower of London.

Beyond his own family few tears were shed for Northumberland and the 'black legend' of his pride, greed, and tyranny in power developed almost immediately, not least because he became a convenient scapegoat for all those who had accepted Jane, and because Mary had to find excuses for those whom she wished to employ. Until recently he has received very little credit for the major services which he performed in maintaining a viable government from 1549 to 1553. Nor is it always remembered that it was his patronage of the visionary Dee and the ageing Sebastian Cabot, and his close relations with prominent Londoners like Sir John York, which launched England's first officially sponsored voyage of discovery to attempt to find the north-east passage in 1553. Like Cromwell, upon whom he may have modelled himself, he saw himself first and foremost as a servant of the crown, and believed that he had well earned the titles and rewards which he had received. He was not a magnate in the traditional mould, but a businessman and politician. No doubt if he had remained an avowed protestant, like Somerset, or his otherwise feeble friend Suffolk, rather than having abjured, he would have been rehabilitated by Foxe, but as it was no one had a good word to say for him. All his sons were imprisoned, but only Guildford, Jane's husband, shared his fate, being executed with her on 12 February 1554. This resulted from the alleged intention of the rebel Sir Thomas Wyatt the younger to restore Jane to the throne, but the conviction upon which he suffered was for aiding the schemes of his father. Ambrose and Robert Dudley were partly rehabilitated, and survived in modest circumstances to enjoy the favour of Elizabeth, but the large Dudley clientele simply evaporated, as usually happened with the destruction of a major figure. This was made easier by the fact that it was so shallow rooted. When Ambrose and Robert became earls of Warwick and of Leicester many old Dudley servants were employed by them, but both their retinues were essentially new creations.

Northumberland was created by Henry for his own purposes, like many others. Very little is known about the private man, and even his personality is largely a matter of deduction from circumstantial evidence. In some respects he was a conventional royal servant, and although brought up in the context of the court, never a great courtier himself. In spite of his reputation in England, as a soldier he was a mere amateur beside Claude de Lorraine Guise, first duc de Guise, or Charles III, duke of Savoy, his experience of serious campaigning being confined to the years 1544 and 1545, but as a politician he was a hardened professional. Eventually he destroyed himself by a major miscalculation, which left his reputation as discredited as his career, but he was a major figure in English government for a crucial decade in the sixteenth century, and a case study in the politics of the period.

Jane Dudley, duchess of Northumberland (1508/9–1555), noblewoman, was born in Kent in 1508 or 1509, being forty-six at the time of her death in 1555, the daughter of Sir Edward Guildford, administrator, and his first wife, Eleanor, daughter of Thomas *West, eighth Baron

West and ninth Baron de la Warr (1472–1554), soldier and courtier. She was a member of Anne Boleyn's privy chamber and became interested in religious reform during the 1530s, even contacting Anne Askew during her imprisonment in 1545–6. Jane Dudley played an important part in her husband's circle, with men like Sir Richard Morison and Gresham seeking her favour, although she suffered from poor health from 1548, when London surgeons considered amputating one of her legs. Despite her modesty ('I have not loved to be very bold afore women'), she was a leading social figure at court from 1550 to 1553 (PRO, PROB 11/37, sig. 26). Like Northumberland she had a close relationship with her children, adding a postscript to a letter of 1552 or 1553 from her husband to their eldest son, Warwick, from 'your lovynge mothere that wyshes you helthe dayli Jane Northumberland' (*Pepys MSS*, 70, 1911, 1–2). She herself was sent to the Tower on 23 July 1553 but was released shortly afterwards. Initially she kept to herself. However, she petitioned to have her children restored to some favour and did what she could to provide for them financially. In her will she exhorted her executors to aid her brother-in-law, Sir Andrew Dudley, and her sons. She spent her final years at Chelsea and died there on 15 January 1555 and was buried there on 1 February.

John Dudley, earl of Warwick (1527?–1554), nobleman, was probably born in 1527 in Sussex, the third but first surviving son of Northumberland and his wife. He was made a knight of the Bath on 20 February 1547 and was styled Viscount Lisle from 1547 to 1551, then earl of Warwick. Warwick was more of a courtier than a soldier and was criticized for keeping light company and amassing debts, which, his parents felt, was to his discredit. His wardrobe account survives for the years 1545 to 1551, listing, among other things, an impressive collection of books for a young man studying the new learning, including 'thone part of Tullie', 'a tragedie in english of the unjust supremacie of the bushope of Rome', 'a Greek grammar' and 'a Terence' (Bodl. Oxf., Add. MS C 94, fols. 13r–14r). From 20 April 1551 to November 1552 he was master of the buckhounds and on 28 April 1552 was appointed master of the horse for life. With his father he was named lord lieutenant of Warwickshire on 16 May 1552 and again on 24 May 1553. Having signed the letters patent settling the crown on Jane on 16 June 1553 he accompanied Northumberland's expedition against Mary and was arrested and tried with him. He was found guilty of treason and condemned to death but his life was spared though his titles were forfeited. During his time in the Tower, where he was lodged in the Beauchamp Tower, he was permitted to walk on the leads, 'being crased for want of ayer', and carved a rebus on the wall of his cell (*APC, 1554–6*, 72). Underneath it he wrote an unfinished inscription:

> Yow that these beasts do wel behold and se
> May deme with ease wherefore here made they be
> With borders eke wherein [there may be found]
> 4 brothers names who list to serche the ground.
> (Lindsay, 176–7)

John Dudley was released shortly before 20 October 1554, when he was placed in the custody of his brother-in-law,

Sir Henry *Sidney (1529–1586), at Penshurst in Kent, and died there the following day. His widow, Anne, daughter of Somerset and his wife, Anne, suffered from bouts of madness and died late in 1587. Northumberland's third surviving son, **Lord Henry Dudley** (1531?–1557), soldier, was probably born at Dudley in Worcestershire or in Sussex. Little is known about him. In 1553 he married Margaret (1540–1564), daughter and coheir of Thomas Audley, Baron Audley of Walden, and his second wife, Elizabeth. On 27 September 1557 Dudley died from disease or wounds resulting from the siege of St Quentin and his widow later married, as his second wife, Thomas Howard, fourth duke of Norfolk; she died on 10 January 1564.

DAVID LOADES

Sources PRO, SP1, SP10 · PRO, SP2, SP11, SP12, SP15, SP46, SP68 · Cecil MSS, Hatfield House, Hertfordshire · Longleat House, Wiltshire, Seymour MSS · Longleat House, Wiltshire, Thynne MSS · office of the auditors of land revenue, PRO, LR 2 · exchequer, king's remembrancer and treasury of receipt, inventories of goods and chattels, PRO, E 154 · BL, Royal MS 18 C xxiv · *Literary remains of King Edward the Sixth*, ed. J. G. Nichols, 2 vols., Roxburghe Club, 75 (1857) · J. G. Nichols, ed., *The chronicle of Queen Jane, and of two years of Queen Mary*, CS, old ser., 48 (1850) · D. MacCulloch, 'The *Vita Mariae Angliae Reginae* of Robert Wingfield of Brantham', *Camden miscellany, XXVIII*, CS, 4th ser., 29 (1984), 181–301 · M. St C. Byrne, ed., *The Lisle letters*, 6 vols. (1981) · HoP, *Commons, 1509–58*, 2.63–6 · GEC, *Peerage* · B. L. Beer, *Northumberland: the political career of John Dudley, earl of Warwick and duke of Northumberland* (Kent, Ohio, 1973) · D. Loades, *John Dudley, duke of Northumberland, 1504–1553* (1996) · W. K. Jordan, *Edward VI, 1: The young king* (1968) · W. K. Jordan, *Edward VI, 2: The threshold of power* (1970) · J. Hayward, *The life and raigne of King Edward the sixth*, ed. B. L. Beer (Kent, Ohio, 1993) · J. Loach, *Edward VI* (1999) · J. Loach, *Protector Somerset: a reassessment* (1994) · M. L. Bush, *The government policy of Protector Somerset* (1976) · D. E. Hoak, *The king's council in the reign of Edward VI* (1976) · M. Aston, *The king's bedpost: reformation and iconography in a Tudor group portrait* (1993) · S. Alford, *Kingship and politics in the reign of Edward VI* (2002) · *CSP Spain, 1509–53* · *CSP dom., 1547–58* · *CSP for., 1547–58* · *CSP Venice, 1509–54* · D. E. Hoak, 'Rehabilitating the duke of Northumberland: politics and political control, 1549–1553', *The mid-Tudor polity, c.1540–1560*, ed. J. Loach and R. Tittler (1980), 29–51 · D. MacCulloch, *Tudor church militant: Edward VI and the protestant Reformation* (1999) · P. F. Tytler, ed., *England under the reigns of Edward VI and Mary*, 2 vols. (1839) · LP Henry VIII · P. Lindsay, *The queen-maker: a portrait of John Dudley, Viscount Lisle, earl of Warwick, and duke of Northumberland, 1502–1553* (1951) · E. Bellin, ed., *The examinations of Anne Askew* (1996) · *Report on the Pepys manuscripts*, HMC, 70 (1911) · H. Robinson, ed. and trans., *Original letters relative to the English Reformation*, 1 vol. in 2, Parker Society, [26] (1846–7) · BL, Cotton MS Titus B ii · will, PRO, PROB 11/37, sig. 26 [duchess of Northumberland]

Archives BL, letters and papers, Add. MSS 32648–32654, *passim* · Bodl. Oxf., wardrobe lists | BL, Cotton MSS · BL, Harley MSS · Hatfield House, Hertfordshire, Cecil MSS · Longleat House, Wiltshire, Dudley MSS · Longleat House, Wiltshire, Seymour MSS · Longleat House, Wiltshire, Thynne MSS · PRO, state papers

Likenesses oils on panel, c.1570 (*Edward VI and the Pope*; identification of John Dudley uncertain), NPG

Wealth at death approx. total value of lands £86,000; goods £10,000: PRO, LR 2/118; PRO E154/2/39 (1553)

Dudley, John, earl of Warwick (1527?–1554). *See under* Dudley, John, duke of Northumberland (1504–1553).

Dudley, John (1762–1856), Church of England clergyman and writer, eldest son of the Revd John Dudley, was born in Humberstone, Leicestershire, where his father was vicar. He was at Uppingham School, and then at Clare College, Cambridge. He proceeded BA in 1785 (when he was second wrangler and mathematical prizeman), and MA in 1788. In 1787 he was elected fellow of Clare, and in 1788 tutor. In 1794 he succeeded his father in the living of Humberstone. His grandfather had previously held the benefice, which continued in the family for three generations during 142 years. In 1795 he was also presented to the vicarage of Sileby, Leicestershire. According to his own account (in the advertisement to *Naology*), Dudley spent 'a long and happy life' as 'a retired student', occupying himself chiefly with mythological and philosophical studies, including a sermon on translation (1807), *The Metamorphosis of Sona: a Hindu Tale* (in verse, 1810), *A Dissertation Showing the Identity of the Rivers Niger and Nile* (1821), *Naology, or, A treatise on the origin, progress, and symbolical import of the sacred structures of the most eminent nations and ages of the world* (1846). *The Anti-Materialist, Denying the Reality of Matter and Vindicating the Universality of Spirit* (1849) is a treatise written under the influence of the philosophy of Berkeley, to whose memory it is dedicated. Dudley died at Sileby on 7 January 1856; he was probably married (for a Charles Dudley of Humberstone matriculated from Clare in 1818), but his wife's name has not been traced.

FRANCIS WATT, *rev.* H. C. G. MATTHEW

Sources *GM*, 2nd ser., 45 (1856), 197–8 · Venn, *Alum. Cant.* · Boase, *Mod. Eng. biog.*

Joseph Dudley (1647–1720), by unknown artist, *c.*1701

Dudley, Joseph (1647–1720), colonial governor, was born on 23 September 1647 at Roxbury in Massachusetts Bay Colony, the seventh child of Thomas Dudley (1576–1653), the colony's second governor, and his second wife, Catherine Hackburn (*née* Dighton), the widow of Samuel Hackburn of Roxbury. When Joseph was a small boy, his father died and his mother remarried. He was brought up by his stepfather, John Allin, minister of the church at Dedham. He graduated from Harvard College in 1665 intending to be a minister, but for unknown reasons decided to enter politics. He was elected to the lower house of the colony's legislature, the general court, as a representative from Roxbury in 1672, and later became a member of the court of assistants, the legislature's upper house. His political career was enhanced by family connections. In 1668 he married Rebecca Tyng (1651–1722), the daughter of Edward Tyng, a member of the court of assistants; their son Paul *Dudley later achieved prominence as a politician and judge. One of Dudley's sisters was the wife of Major-General Daniel Denison, a leading supporter of royal authority who became his political ally. Another sister married Simon Bradstreet, a leading figure in the colonial government.

Dudley was one of two men chosen to go to England in 1682 to make Massachusetts Bay's case against a *quo warranto* proceeding that, if successful, would lead to the loss of the charter. Despite his commission he did not oppose the threatened revocation energetically, and his political opponents later claimed that his lack of enthusiasm grew from the opportunities he saw for personal advancement if the charter were vacated. Whatever the reasons for his actions, the stay in the mother country transformed his public image. Before crossing the Atlantic he had been a popular figure among the colonial citizenry, but the conciliatory line he adopted throughout the negotiations caused many in the Bay Colony to consider him a traitor. Upon his return he found himself an object of hatred, and his reputation never entirely recovered.

On 23 October 1684 the charter was revoked and a provisional government created. Dudley was appointed president of the temporary council and named interim governor of Massachusetts, Maine, New Hampshire, and a portion of western Rhode Island known as the King's Province. His brief administration lasted until 19 December 1686, when Edmund Andros arrived to install the permanent government. Dudley's career prospered under Governor Andros's administration. He received an appointment to the colony's council and was named to several other influential posts. In addition, he assisted in enforcing obedience to several unpopular laws enacted during the period. Feeling ran so strongly against him for his unswerving support of the government that when Andros was deposed in 1689 he was placed in gaol for his own safety.

Dudley remained in protective custody for almost a year before being released. He was then taken to England, where a group of leading Massachusetts citizens had lodged 119 charges against him, the most serious of which alleged that he administered justice illegally and extracted excessive fines and fees. He was ultimately acquitted on all counts, and through the influence of powerful English friends received an appointment as chief of the council in New York. In this post Dudley became as unpopular for supporting the royal prerogative as he had been in Massachusetts, and his service as chief justice during the trial of the insurgent leader Jacob Leisler only increased his unpopularity. Although the proceeding was entirely legal, many in New York regarded the execution of Leisler and his son-in-law as judicial murder.

In 1692 Dudley resigned from office, returned briefly to Roxbury, and by February 1693 was in England. Again, through the influence of well-placed acquaintances— including William Blathwayt, clerk of the privy council, and John Cutts, a hero of the battle of the Boyne and a friend of the king—he was appointed deputy governor of the Isle of Wight. At about this time, he became a member of parliament, abandoned his dissenting religious beliefs, conformed to the Church of England, and joined the Society for the Propagation of the Gospel in Foreign Parts.

Despite his apostasy and his comfortable position in English society, Dudley nursed the hope that he might some day return to his native province. Blathwayt and Cutts again exerted influence on his behalf, and, along with the support of colonials resident in London, several colonial merchants, and the leading Boston cleric Cotton Mather, he succeeded. In spring 1702 he was named governor of Massachusetts. Contention characterized Dudley's tenure from his first days in office, not only because of substantive disagreements with local legislators but because of his difficult character. He was a cold and ambitious man who relished exercising power and had no qualms about increasing his personal fortune while in public office. Throughout his service as governor he exhibited the commitment to royal prerogative that had characterized his entire political career. On one occasion he was forced to return to England to rebut another series of charges levelled against him, but, even though he was absolved of any wrongdoing, his opponents grew in strength and eventually overwhelmed him and his influential English supporters. In 1715 he was replaced as governor by Samuel Shute.

Historians at first drew largely unsympathetic portraits of Joseph Dudley and his legacy. More recently it has been conceded that he dealt effectively with American Indian tribes, ably handled the colony's military efforts, and possessed a measure of personal charm; otherwise there has been no attempt to burnish his unsavoury reputation. In the four years between his leaving office and his death in Massachusetts on 2 April 1720 he managed to regain at least some measure of his former popularity. Massachusetts gave him one of the most lavish funerals in the colony's history. He was buried in Roxbury, the town of his birth, on 14 April.   B. R. BURG

Sources E. Kimball, *The public life of Joseph Dudley: a study of the colonial policy of the Stuarts in New England, 1660–1715* (1911) · J. T. Adams, 'Dudley, Joseph', *DAB* · J. T. Adams, 'Dudley, Thomas', *DAB* · R. E. Moody and R. C. Simmons, eds., *The glorious revolution in Massachusetts: selected documents, 1689–1692* (1988) · T. H. Breen, *The character of a good ruler: a study of puritan political ideas in New England, 1630–1730* (1970) · *The diary of Samuel Sewall, 1674–1729: newly edited from the manuscript at the Massachusetts Historical Society*, ed. M. H. Thomas, 2 vols. (1973) · M. G. Hall, *The last American puritan: the life of Increase Mather, 1639–1723* (1988) · M. G. Hall, *Edward Randolph and the American colonies, 1676–1703* (1960) · R. I. Melvoin, *New England outpost: war and society in colonial Deerfield* (1989) · *The deplorable state of New-England, by reason of a covetous and treacherous governour, and pusillanimous counsellors ... To which is added an account of the shameful miscarriage of the late expedition against Port-Royal* (1708) · C. Mather, *A memorial of the present deplorable state of New-England* (1707) · *A modest enquiry into the grounds and occasions of a late pamphlet, intitled, A memorial of the present deplorable state of New-England* (1707)

Archives Bodl. Oxf., Rawlinson MSS · PRO, board of trade MSS, colonial entry books, New England; journals of the board of trade; original papers New England; original papers New York · PRO, register of the privy council (MS), Charles II · PRO, register of the privy council (MS), James II, pts i–ii · PRO, register of the privy council (MS), William III · PRO, register of the privy council (MS), Anne · PRO, register of the privy council (MS), George I

Likenesses portrait, *c*.1701, Mass. Hist. Soc. [*see illus.*]

Wealth at death unspecified number of houses, approx. 6000 acres, 'stock', plus unspecified amount of money to be distributed, incl. £50 to the Free School in Roxbury; household goods, plate, 'mansion house and gardens', £200, and £100 annually from his estates to wife; two farms, one of 150 acres, another of 1000 acres, and £300 to build a house to son; 1000 acres each and £100 each to daughters; to his nephew Daniel Allen and niece Ann Hilton £40 to be paid on marriage; plus 500 acres; remaining house or houses, the rest of his lands (approx. 450 acres), his 'stock', and remaining money to eldest son: Kimball, *Public life*

Dudley [*née* Knollys; *other married name* Devereux], **Lettice, countess of Essex and countess of Leicester** (*b.* after 1540, *d.* 1634), noblewoman, was the eldest of the sixteen children of Sir Francis *Knollys (1511/12–1596), politician, and his wife, Katherine (1529/30–1569), daughter of William Carey of Aldenham, Berkshire, and his wife, Mary *Stafford, *née* Boleyn (*d.* 1543). She was born at the Knollys house, Rotherfield Greys, near Henley-on-Thames, Oxfordshire, and named after her paternal grandmother—hence the Anglicized form of Laetitia. Between 1544 and 1546 her father was master of the horse to Edward, prince of Wales, and it was probably in those years that the close family relationship with Princess Elizabeth was formed. The Knollys family took five of their children with them when they went into exile in Frankfurt from 1556 to 1558, but they are not identified, and it is possible that Lettice Knollys was left with Elizabeth at Hatfield in Hertfordshire. On their return in January 1559 Knollys was appointed vice-chamberlain, his wife one of the four ladies of the bedchamber, and Lettice Knollys a salaried gentlewoman of the privy chamber.

Marriage to Essex and affair with Leicester, 1560–1578 In late 1560 Lettice Knollys married Walter *Devereux, second Viscount Hereford (1539–1576), nobleman and adventurer, eldest son of Sir Richard Devereux and his wife, Dorothy. In the following year her privy chamber salary ceased. The probable reason was her withdrawal from the court to Chartley in Staffordshire, the principal Devereux house, where the majority of her five children with Hereford were born. However, she was presumably at court in summer 1565, for in September the Spanish ambassador, Diego de Guzman de Silva, was told that Robert *Dudley, earl of Leicester (1532/3–1588), courtier and magnate, had been paying court to her in a ploy to force Elizabeth I's

Lettice Dudley, countess of Essex and countess of Leicester
(*b.* 1540, *d.* 1634), attrib. George Gower

hand. He described her as one of the best-looking women of the court and a favourite of the queen. She was also heavily pregnant with Leicester's godson, Robert *Devereux, later second earl of Essex (1565–1601), who was born on 10 November, so too much should not be read into this episode.

In May 1572 Hereford was created earl of Essex and he resided at court until summer 1573, when his proposal for a plantation in Ulster was accepted. He departed for Ireland in the autumn, not to return until November 1575. He then appears to have remained at court until summer 1576, when he went back to Ireland via Chartley, only to die of dysentery in Dublin on 22 September. In December 1575 the resident Spanish agent, Antonio de Guaras, reported London gossip that Essex had discovered that his wife had given birth to two children by Leicester in his absence. Almost two years to the day after Essex died, his widow and Leicester married discreetly at Wanstead House in Essex on the morning of 21 September 1578, and their marriage gave retrospective credibility to both the earlier alleged adultery and rumours that Essex had been poisoned. *Leicester's Commonwealth* (1584) claimed that Essex was murdered because he was about to return to England to revenge himself on Leicester for having fathered a daughter by the countess. A later version ('The letter of estate') has Leicester encouraging Essex's Ulster expedition in order to separate him from his wife, like King David and Uriah the Hittite. Leicester was certainly among the initial supporters of the Ulster enterprise, but by 1576 Essex appears to have believed that he was trying

to block his return to Ireland. The difficulties of reconciling adultery with the known political tensions are well illustrated by William Camden's account. Although Camden denied that Essex was poisoned, he saw his return to Ireland in 1576 as engineered 'by the court subteltie of Leicester, who was afraid of him, and by the peculiar mysteries of the Court' (Camden, 2.366).

Essex's references to his wife in his will are perfunctory, and they may well have been estranged in the years immediately prior to his death, but where she was living and her possible contacts with Leicester are not easy to establish. She may have accompanied Essex to court in 1572, but when he went to Ireland she seems to have retired to Chartley. Leicester had deer sent to her from Kenilworth Castle, Warwickshire, in 1573, and she hunted there with her sister Anne West, Lady De La Warr, in 1574. She was at Kenilworth again during the famous progress of 1575, which included a visit to Chartley at the beginning of August. It is not clear whether she joined her husband at court at the end of the year. The much quoted reference to her as Elizabeth's 'nearest kinswoman' in the entry for a letter from Elizabeth to Essex provisionally dated November 1575 in the *Calendar of State Papers Relating to Ireland, 1575–84* (1860) is in fact an editorial interpolation. The letter itself does not mention her.

In 1576 the countess of Essex is found hunting at Kenilworth again and then attending her husband's funeral at Carmarthen on 26 November, but by the beginning of 1577 she had retired to Rotherfield Greys. From there she conducted a forthright correspondence with William Cecil, Baron Burghley, about her jointure. It was both too small to live on and excluded Chartley, thus forcing her to seek accommodation from her friends. To the fury of Essex's officers she threatened 'by some froward advice' to sue out a writ of dower if a compromise was not reached (*Bath MSS*, 5.249). The last letter in the series (30 April 1577) was written from Colshill in Warwickshire, the home of George Digby, who had been a ward of her father and was then a rising figure in Leicester's Warwickshire affinity. *Leicester's Commonwealth* specifically mentions Digby's house in its jibe that Leicester sent her 'up and down the country from house to house by privy ways' (Peck, *Leicester's Commonwealth*, 76, 208, n. 140). She hunted at Kenilworth in summer 1577 together with her daughter Penelope *Rich, *née* Devereux (1563–1607), and her brother William *Knollys (*c.*1545–1632) and his wife, Dorothy. Thereafter, until her marriage at Wanstead, her movements are unknown. She may have gone to court, but it is also possible that she was living at Benington in Hertfordshire, a house assigned to her when her jointure was increased in the winter of 1577–8.

Marriage to Leicester, 1578–1588 The details of the Wanstead marriage are found in the depositions made by the witnesses before a notary on 13 March 1581. They included the officiating clergyman, Leicester's chaplain, Humphrey Tyndall, the countess's father, her brother Richard Knollys, Ambrose *Dudley, earl of Warwick (*c.*1530–1590), Henry Herbert, second earl of Pembroke, and Roger North, second Baron North. In March 1581 the countess was pregnant with Leicester's son Robert Dudley, Baron Denbigh (1581–1584), who was born at Leicester House on 6 June. The depositions were to ensure that his legitimacy would be beyond question. The witnesses confirmed that Leicester had discussed marriage to the countess with them for nearly a year prior to 1578, but what has attracted most attention is Tyndall's passing comment that she was 'attired as he now remembereth in a loose gown' (PRO, SP 12/148, fol. 83r). *Leicester's Commonwealth* claimed that the marriage 'was celebrated twice—the first at Killingworth and secondly at Wanstead (in presence of the Earl of Warwick [etc.])' (Peck, *Leicester's Commonwealth*, 95). Camden repeated this story and explained the second wedding as a demand by her father that the ceremony be repeated before a notary. In recent literature Tyndall's comment has been read as a hint that the countess was pregnant in September 1578. In 1981 Derek Wilson advanced an elaborate theory of a secret marriage at Kenilworth in spring 1578 forced by her pregnancy, Leicester informing Elizabeth about it in April, and a second marriage demanded by his wife and her father. However, the latest occasion Leicester and the countess could have been at Kenilworth together was in summer 1577, and the actual date of Denbigh's birth was unknown until it was discovered in 1992 in a document at Longleat House, Wiltshire. A failed pregnancy in 1578 cannot be ruled out entirely, but no reference to one survives.

The debate over these issues has obscured the fact that the Wanstead wedding fulfilled the two-year mourning for Essex almost to the day—in 1582 there was a portrait of the countess 'in mourning weeds' in Leicester House (Evelyn MS 264, unfoliated). The depositions also reveal that Leicester was worried about Elizabeth's reaction and wished to keep his marriage secret. Yet it was open knowledge practically from the start, Thomas Radcliffe, third earl of Sussex, informing the French ambassador, Castelnau de Mauvissière, about it early in November 1578. How and when Elizabeth found out and what the political consequences were have been no less debated. What can be said with assurance is that Leicester's marriage did not become an issue until December 1579, and that the immediate crisis—so far as he was concerned—was over in spring 1580. It is, however, very likely that what the queen 'discovered' was not simply that Leicester had married the dowager countess of Essex, but that he was supposed to be already married to Douglas Sheffield, dowager Baroness Sheffield. This is certainly the impression given by Sir Edward Stafford in 1604.

Over the next few years the countess of Leicester appears to have behaved very discreetly and continued to style herself only countess of Essex. Mauvissière reported in February 1580 that she was living with her father and was about to give birth. She was still at Rotherfield Greys in October, when she wrote to Burghley to excuse her keeping her brother, the younger Francis Knollys (c.1550–1648), with her. In September 1582 Mauvissière reported that she was 'grosse de son segond enfant', but the outcome of this pregnancy is unknown (PRO 31, 3/28/417). By 1584 she was living openly at Leicester House. She had

obviously moved there for Denbigh's birth in 1581, but the report in summer 1583 that Elizabeth was angry with Leicester 'abowt his maryage, for he opened the same more playnly then ever before' suggests that she had recently taken up permanent residence as his wife (*Bath MSS*, 5.44). Mauvissière recorded being invited by Leicester to dine with them in December 1583 and that she had 'toute puissance sur luy' (Harley MS 1582, fol. 334v).

Leicester's household accounts and inventories supply many details of their domestic life, from the bed the countess gave him as a new year's present in 1585 to the cushions and close stool cover at Leicester House made from her old gowns. He had been close to her family since the beginning of the reign (several of her brothers were in his service), and he was no less benevolent to her children by Essex. Catholic sources paint a more lurid picture. Like Mauvissière, *Leicester's Commonwealth* emphasizes her influence over him, and adds the gratuitous innuendo that Sir Francis Knollys may not have been the father of all his children. The 'addition' to the 1585 French edition claimed that her influence over Leicester was for sale. Both *Leicester's Commonwealth* and 'The letter of estate' make much of her regal pretensions. The latter is the source of the story that Elizabeth banned her from the court for attempting to outdress her, and that she responded by parading round London in state. The Spanish ambassador, Bernardino de Mendoza, reported Elizabeth's explosion ('se incendio en la materia') in June 1583 over reports that Leicester was trying to marry Dorothy Devereux (1564?–1619) to James VI. She would not allow James to marry 'the daughter of such a she-wolf' ('con hija de una loba') and to stop the intrigue she would expose Leicester as a cuckold (Hume, 1580–6, 477; *Coleccion de documentos*, 92.507). A year later, both Mary, queen of Scots, and *Leicester's Commonwealth* claimed that Leicester and the countess were scheming to marry Denbigh to Arabella Stewart. The source for both these stories may have been Lord Henry Howard, on whom Mendoza and Mary relied for their court information in 1583 and 1584.

All speculation about Denbigh's future was brought to an end by his death at Wanstead on 19 July 1584. Leicester left the court for several weeks 'to comfort my sorrowfull wyfe', and received generous letters of condolence from his colleagues and friends (PRO, SP 52/36/7). *Leicester's Commonwealth* is the source for the story that Denbigh was a sickly child. There is a tradition that the small suit of armour with one thigh piece longer than the other, now in the Warwick Castle collection, was made for him, and it has been cited by Elizabeth Jenkins as evidence that he was deformed. However, the armour is probably of seventeenth-century manufacture, it is far too big for a child who died aged three and a half, and not a single bear and ragged staff (Leicester's device) adorns it.

The death of Denbigh, Mauvissière observed in October 1584, meant the end of Leicester's hopes for a legitimate heir, as the countess was 'fort agée'; she would have been no older than forty-four (Chéruel, 341). In summer 1585 they went on holiday to Kenilworth together, triggering Elizabeth's anger again. Gossip (whether malicious or not) that the countess was planning to join him in the Netherlands in February 1586 'with suche a train of ladies … as hir majestie had none' was one reason for the queen's furious reaction to his acceptance of the governor-generalship. The countess was 'greatly troubled with the tempestuous newes she receaved from the court' (Bruce, 112, 144). Ironically, they were innocent of this ambition, for it was precisely at this point (20 February) that Leicester drew up a commission for her to set and let his lands in his absence. When Leicester returned to the Netherlands in June 1587, her son the young second earl of Essex described her as in mourning.

The countess was with Leicester when he died at Cornbury House in Oxfordshire on 4 September 1588, and was given his last will immediately afterwards. She may also have been present at his funeral in Warwick on 10 October. Leicester appointed her executor of both his surviving wills (30 January 1582 and August 1587) and provided for her generously. In 1582 he left her a substantial jointure, which was augmented first on 15 July 1584 and again in 1587 when he added Drayton Basset in Staffordshire. She was nominally a very wealthy widow. Her combined jointures from Essex and Leicester gave her an income of £3000 a year, and she possessed £6000 worth of plate and household furniture. Set against her assets was the responsibility of settling Leicester's estate—a burden so great she was advised to refuse to act as executor. Only a month after his death her possession of Drayton Basset was challenged, and she had to call on her son for help. The inheritance of Kenilworth by Leicester's illegitimate son Robert Dudley in 1590 initiated a much more serious legal battle, for many of the adjacent manors were in her jointure. Even greater was the problem of Leicester's debts, which totalled some £50,000. Warwick, who was his immediate heir, helped the countess initially, but after his death in 1590 she was on her own. Paying off the debts cost her a large part of her jointure, including Leicester House, which she sold to her son, who renamed it Essex House in 1593.

After Leicester, 1588–1634 In July 1589 the countess suddenly married Sir Christopher *Blount (1555/6–1601), soldier and conspirator, second son of Thomas Blount of Kidderminster, Worcestershire, and his wife, Margery, and Leicester's former master of the horse. She defended her marriage—which even her son termed 'this unhappy choyce'—as a necessity for a defenceless widow (Hammer, 34, n. 120). The marriage soon inspired gossip that she had poisoned Leicester. By the Restoration a baroque tale (*Leicester's Ghost*) was in circulation: she had begun an adulterous affair with Blount in 1587, Leicester had found out about it and planned their murder, but she killed him first.

The countess was still an extraordinary gentlewoman of the privy chamber, and both her son and a number of her brothers and sisters remained at the centre of the court, but Leicester's death did not melt Elizabeth's hostility. In 1595 she retired to Drayton Basset, where she lived for the rest of her life. Her correspondence with Essex (whom she addressed as 'Sweet Robin') between 1595 and 1599 reveals

that her retirement was in effect a strike. She would not return to court unless reconciled to Elizabeth: 'to obtain that favour without which I live there as you know with greater disgrace' (Craik, 1.30, 148–52). In late 1597 'my friends there make me believe that her majesty is very well prepared to hearken to terms of pacification', and if Essex thought 'it be to any purpose' she was prepared to make 'a winter journey' (Birch, 2.362). She spent January to March 1598 at Essex House, but, despite Essex's attempts to arrange a meeting, Elizabeth avoided her. Her only concession was to allow the countess to kiss hands before she returned to Drayton Basset. Essex's imprisonment in 1599 caused his mother to come up to London again, this time to intercede for his release. Although she purchased a gown worth £100 as a present, Penelope Rich, Baroness Rich's, notoriously arrogant letter to Elizabeth doomed the appeal. Elizabeth refused to receive the gown or even let the countess kiss hands.

The countess was at Drayton Basset during Essex's revolt in February 1601, but has left no comment on the executions of her son and her husband (25 February and 18 March respectively). Their attainders led to a dispute over her remaining possessions in Essex House, and it was in the course of this that she claimed the penniless Blount had swindled her out of much of her wealth. However, the new reign brought a change of climate. Lady Rich was in favour with Anne of Denmark, and James VI and I restored the Essex lands to Robert *Devereux, third earl of Essex (1591–1646), in July 1603. On 18 August he waived repayment of the remaining £3967 of Leicester's debts. The benevolence of the court also helped her in the culmination of her legal battles with Sir Robert Dudley, 'the great cause' of 1603–5. If Dudley were to be successful in his attempt to prove himself Leicester's legitimate son, her marriage would be judged bigamous and her jointure overturned. She already had one not entirely comfortable ally in Sir Robert Sidney, who claimed to be the only legitimate male heir to Leicester and Warwick. By 1603 she had agreed with Sidney (under threat of litigation, she later claimed) that in exchange for his assistance in the defence of her jointure lands she would assign them to him on her death. Her most effective protector was Sir Robert Cecil, who decided that the existing settlement of Warwick's and Leicester's lands was too complex to be overturned. It was undoubtedly with his backing that she filed a bill of complaint against Dudley in the court of star chamber on 10 February 1604, alleging that he had defamed her by challenging the legitimacy of her marriage in his suit. As well as submitting the 1581 depositions on her marriage she cited fifty-six witnesses to testify that Leicester had never considered Dudley legitimate. In the course of delivering the judgment against Dudley on 10 May 1605, Cecil:

> much commended the Countes of Lester, how well she lyved with him [Leicester] all his time notwithstanding all his humours, how for her marriage with him she was long disgraced with the Queene … & good Lady for her part he thoughte she weyghed not Sir Robert Dudlie's fine the garter upon her legge. (Hawarde, 220)

Of more immediate importance to her than this curious compliment was the decision that the evidence from the case be sequestered so it could not be reopened.

The countess was very close to her daughters Penelope and Dorothy, whose stormy personal lives rivalled her own. Their deaths in 1607 and 1619 left her dependent on her surviving siblings and her grandchildren, especially the third earl of Essex. During the last fifteen years of her life he spent every winter with her either at Chartley or at Drayton Basset. She died at Drayton on Christmas day 1634, having enjoyed a robust good health almost to the eve of her death. When her brother William Knollys, first earl of Banbury, died in 1632, she was reported as still able to walk a mile a day. She was the last survivor of the great Elizabethans, and there was considerable public mourning at court and in London. She had made her will on 15 October 1622. Despite her disclaimer, 'because I have lived all my life to my full proportion it cannot be looked for that I should have much to bestow', she died a wealthy woman (PRO, PROB 11/167, sig. 1). Her probate inventory valued her possessions at £6645 11s. 4d. Essex was her executor and heir to her Devereux jointure lands and Drayton Basset, but her remaining jointure lands from Leicester (the Warwickshire manors of Balsall and Long Itchington) remained in dispute. In 1628 Sir Robert Dudley's abandoned wife, Alice, brought a fresh suit against her in the court of chancery. Her jointure was not at issue, but she was accused of conspiring with the Sidneys against Dudley's daughters. The legal battle over Balsall and Long Itchington continued until 1655, when the Sidneys finally admitted defeat.

In her will the countess requested to be buried without pomp 'at Warwick by my deere lord and husband the Earle of Leicester with whom I desire to be entombed' (PRO, PROB 11/167, sig. 1). After she was buried in St Mary's, Warwick, in February 1635, his effigy had to be shifted in order to fit hers onto his tomb. The verse inscription added for her—written by her grandson Gervase Clifton—makes no reference to her other husbands or even that she had been countess of Essex. The triangle she formed with Leicester and Elizabeth is possibly the central enigma of the queen's reign. If, as all the domestic evidence suggests, she and Leicester enjoyed a close and contented marriage, major questions are begged about his relations with Elizabeth. Elizabeth's animosity towards her after 1579 was bitter and unforgiving. It was also very specific; Leicester escaped most of its effects, and it did not do her son Essex any damage. Sexual jealousy is the obvious explanation, but Elizabeth did not display any towards Sheffield, whom she consistently regarded as a victim. Was it because she considered that the countess had deliberately seduced Leicester away from both of them?   SIMON ADAMS

Sources C. H. Garrett, *The Marian exiles: a study in the origins of Elizabethan puritanism* (1938); repr. (1966) • wardrobe account, coronation of Elizabeth I, PRO, E 101/429/3 • cofferer of the house accounts, Elizabeth I, PRO, E 351/1795, mm 11–13 • M. A. S. Hume, ed., *Calendar of letters and state papers relating to English affairs, preserved principally in the archives of Simancas*, 4 vols., PRO (1892–9) • P. E. J. Hammer, *The polarisation of Elizabethan politics: the political career of Robert Devereux, 2nd earl of Essex, 1585–1597* (1999) • D. C. Peck, ed., *Leicester's commonwealth: the copy of a letter written by a master of art of Cambridge* (1584) *and related documents* (1985) • E. Jenkins, *Elizabeth and Leicester* (1961) • CKS, Penshurst papers, U1475 [incl. Kenilworth game book, 1568–78, U1475/E 93 and Stafford deposition, [1604], U1475/L2/4, it. 3] • *Calendar of the manuscripts of the marquis of Bath preserved at Longleat, Wiltshire*, 5 vols., HMC, 58 (1904–80) • *CSP Ire.*, *1574–85* • BL, Lansdowne MS 24, arts. 12, 13, 85 • S. Adams, *Leicester and the court: essays on Elizabethan politics* (2002) • D. C. Peck, ed., '"The letter of estate": an Elizabethan libel', *N&Q*, 227 (1981), 21–35 • W. Camden, *Annales: the true and royall history of the famous Empresse Elizabeth*, trans. A. Darcie (1625) • state papers domestic, Elizabeth, PRO, SP 12 • S. Adams, 'The papers of Robert Dudley, earl of Leicester: III. The countess of Leicester's collection', *Archives*, 22 (1996), 1–26 • D. Wilson, *Sweet Robin: a biography of Robert Dudley, earl of Leicester, 1533–1588* (1981) • BL, Evelyn MSS • registre de Michel de Castelnau, seigneur de Mauvissière, 1578–81, Bibliothèque Nationale de France, MS français 15793 • PRO, 31, 3/28, French transcripts • misc. Mauvissière correspondence, BL, Harley MS 1582 • S. Adams, ed., *Household accounts and disbursement books of Robert Dudley, earl of Leicester, 1558–1561, 1584–1586*, CS, 6 (1995) • Longleat House, Wiltshire, Dudley MSS • *Coleccion de documentos inéditos para la historia de España*, 29: *Correspondencia de Felipe II con sus embajadores en la córte de Inglaterra 1558 a 1584*, V (1888) • state papers, Scotland, Elizabeth I, PRO, SP 52 • A. Chéruel, *Marie Stuart et Catherine de Médicis* (Paris, 1858) • J. Bruce, ed., *Correspondence of Robert Dudley, earl of Leycester*, CS, 27 (1844) • *The manuscripts of his grace the duke of Rutland*, 4 vols., HMC, 24 (1888–1905) • Folger, La; Gb4; Xd63 [Bagot papers; Sir Michael Stanhope; collections relating to the trial of the earl of Essex] • *CSP dom.*, *1547–1625* • *Leicester's ghost*, ed. F. B. Williams (Chicago, Ill., 1972) • G. L. Craik, *The romance of the nobility, or, Curiosities of family history*, 4 vols. (1848–9) • T. Birch, *Memoirs of the reign of Queen Elizabeth*, 2 vols. (1754) • H. Sydney and others, *Letters and memorials of state*, ed. A. Collins, 2 vols. (1746) • S. Freedman, *Poor Penelope: Lady Penelope Rich, an Elizabethan woman* (1983) • answer of the countess of Leicester to the complaint of Lady Alice Dudley, 5 May 1629, Warks. CRO, Arbury MS 1 [deposit by Viscount Daventry] it. 11 • *Les reportes del cases in camera stellata, 1593 to 1609, from the original ms. of John Hawarde*, ed. W. P. Baildon (privately printed, London, 1894) • V. F. Snow, *Essex the rebel: the life of Robert Devereux, the third earl of Essex, 1591–1646* (Lincoln, Ne., 1970) • probate inventory, BL, Add. MS 18985 • will, PRO, PROB 11/167, sig. 1 • *HoP, Commons, 1558–1603*

Archives Longleat House, Wiltshire, Dudley MSS | BL, corresp. with second earl of Essex, Sloane MS 4214 [transcripts]

Likenesses portrait, 1590–99, repro. in V. J. Watney, *Cornbury and the Forest of Wychwood* (1910), facing p. 84; formerly in possession of Lord St Leven, 1910 • attrib. G. Gower, oils, Longleat, Wiltshire [*see illus.*] • Hubbard, double portrait (with the young Lord Denbigh); at Leicester House in 1583 • portrait; 1582 Leicester House inventory

Wealth at death £6645 11s. 4d.: probate inventory of possessions, BL, 7 Jan 1635, Add. MS 18985, printed in J. O. Halliwell, ed., *Ancient inventories … illustrative of the domestic manners of the English* (1854)

Dudley [*née* Stokes], **Mary** (1750–1823), Quaker minister, was born on 8 June or 8 August 1750 at Bristol, the daughter of Joseph (d. 1773) and Mary Stokes. It has been claimed that there were thirty children and that on one occasion half were in Temple Church, Bristol, to hear a brother preach. Mary had a strict Church of England upbringing, and also enjoyed 'most of the vain amusements of the world' (Dudley, *Life*, 2) but, becoming increasingly serious in her later teens, she attended Methodist meetings. By the time she was twenty-one, however, she started to go to Quaker meetings, causing John Wesley (who had much esteemed her) to write in strong terms of disapprobation—to which she made a spirited reply. By 1773 she was a decided Friend and soon afterwards sometimes spoke in meeting for worship. Her mother's chance presence on one such occasion helped to reconcile the outraged relatives to her Quakerism. She later moved from Bristol to Frenchay and was married there on 9 July 1777 to Robert Dudley (1732?–1807) of Prior Park, Clonmel, co. Tipperary. She was his third wife and had the care of five stepsons; the couple also had four sons, the eldest being Charles Stokes Dudley [see below], and four daughters. By 1806 all her stepsons had died, the longest-lived being forty-two. Clonmel, her home until 1810, had a substantial and cultured Quaker population.

By the time of her marriage Dudley's vocation for the ministry was formally acknowledged, and in 1786 she first travelled in the ministry. In 1788, when her seventh child was but ten weeks old, she was away for six months as a member of a small group of Friends travelling in Holland, Germany, and France, visiting Moravians, Inspirants, and the groups near Nîmes who came to form a Quaker meeting at Congénies. She was away from home for much of the rest of her life, visiting Quaker meetings throughout Britain and Ireland, and appointing special meetings to which townspeople or villagers would flock in large numbers.

Dudley's travels in the ministry in Ireland throughout the 1790s were considerable, as were those of more than half a dozen Irish, English, and American ministering Friends. Apart from the political events of the decade, it is almost as though they recognized the theological tensions which were also brewing and which would decimate Irish Quakerism between 1798 and 1801. The paths of these ministering Friends crossed and recrossed and—as they stayed at Prior Park or were companions with Mary Dudley on journeys, or simply met her in out-of-the-way places—their affection as well as their regard is in no doubt. Her vocal ministry was 'tender and winning' (*Memoirs*, 328), her sympathies broad, and her pastoral gifts sensitive. Her significance in the history of Irish Quakerism during this decade may be greater than has hitherto been recognized.

Dudley suffered a persistent affliction of the lungs, which cannot have been helped by constant travelling in all weathers, by a succession of different houses or inns to sleep in, and by the strain of almost daily meetings. She often had to take to her bed when travelling in the ministry and in 1795, seriously ill, finally journeyed to her native Bristol to take the waters. Within six weeks her health had markedly improved. She returned to Ireland and was once again on the move. However, she was soon affected by ill health and in 1798 her life was in danger. Reluctantly, she accepted medical advice stipulating 'a sea voyage and short residence at Bristol Hotwells' (Dudley, *Life*, 228). Her son Charles, who accompanied her and her four daughters, later claimed that they had left Ireland because of the rising. Robert Dudley may well have been grateful for the medical advice: that it was genuine seems equally certain.

The family returned to Ireland in 1800, and the succession of travels in the ministry resumed. In 1807 Dudley's

husband and a son died, and in March 1810 a daughter. Later that year she and her three surviving daughters moved to London, settling in Southwark. Apart from a visit to Yorkshire, Dudley's ministerial labours were now confined to London and the home counties. In winter 1818–19 (she had just returned from a 400 mile journey) she was confined to the house for a considerable time, 'her body and mind suffering under a combination of afflicting circumstances' (Dudley, *Life*, 301). One affliction was the bankruptcy of the business run by two of her sons, bringing serious loss to their creditors. She continued her Quaker activities until 18 April 1823 when palpitations of the heart and faintness confined her to bed. Despite a slight remission in July, when she was able to be taken for drives, she never regained strength and died on 24 September 1823, at her home in George Street, Peckham, Surrey. She was buried on 2 October at the Bunhill Fields Friends' burial-ground in London.

Dudley's eldest son, **Charles Stokes Dudley** (1780–1862), administrator and writer, was born on 18 September 1780 at Clonmel, co. Tipperary. He was educated at Ballitore School, co. Kildare, under Abraham Shackleton, and in 1798, aged seventeen, he was entrusted with the care of his four sisters and desperately ill mother, on their journey to Bristol. While there he found employment in a large commercial house and also met Samuel Taylor Coleridge, Robert Southey, and others to whom he was attracted by his literary tastes. When the rest of the family returned to Ireland in 1800 he went to London and then, or a little later, set up in business as a provision merchant. In 1802 he married Hester (1777–1803), daughter of Joseph Savory (1745–1821), a London goldsmith, and Anna, *née* Bellamy (1745?–1785). His wife's death in 1803, along with that of their child, prompted Charles Lamb's poem 'When maidens such as Hester die'.

In 1810 Charles Dudley joined his mother and sisters following their move to Southwark. His brother George (*b.* 1789) had already moved to London and entered his provision business. Charles, who now began to use his mother's maiden name as a second forename, became involved in the British and Foreign Bible Society's Southwark auxiliary. His organization was so successful that he was asked to visit other auxiliaries and demonstrate his system. From 1812 he gave a substantial part of his time to this work and from 1815 (partly also on account of ill health) was virtually a sleeping partner in the business.

In December 1818 Dudley was recalled from Bible Society business in Plymouth to find that his brother, who had assured him that the firm was lucrative, had suspended payment to creditors and that business was at a total stop, with debts amounting to £20,000 against assets of £7200. Both brothers were disowned by their respective monthly meetings. Charles Stokes Dudley had probably, in any event, been increasingly drawn to the Church of England, which he joined about 1820.

Hitherto, the work of the Bible Society from its foundation in 1804 had been entirely on a voluntary basis. Dudley now became salaried. Until 1852 he continued travelling the country, organizing and fostering auxiliaries. He published in 1821 a work entitled *An Analysis of the System of the Bible Society*, a 600 page volume of historical background, with guidance on the setting up and regulation of auxiliaries and branches. On 12 May 1824 he married Sarah Haycock, at Farnham, Surrey; the marriage produced thirteen children, eight of whom survived him. In 1852 he retired, having been the guiding hand behind the Bible Society's work for forty years. He died on 4 November 1862.

EDWARD H. MILLIGAN

Sources E. Dudley, ed., *The life of Mary Dudley* (1825) · *Memoirs of Elizabeth Dudley*, ed. C. Tylor (1861) · G. T. Edwards, 'Old friends of the Bible Society', *Bible Society Reporter* (1892), 152–4, 167–9 · Kingston monthly meeting, MS minutes, 1818–19, RS Friends, Lond. **Archives** RS Friends, Lond., MSS

Dudley, Paul (1675–1751), politician and judge in America, was born in Roxbury, Massachusetts, on 3 September 1675, the fourth of thirteen children of Massachusetts governor Joseph *Dudley (1647–1720) and Rebecca Tyng (1651–1722). He graduated from Harvard College in 1690 after his father had been briefly imprisoned and ousted for his role in the dominion of New England headed by Sir Edmund Andros. In 1693 Dudley moved to England. He studied law at the Inner Temple, London, from 1698 until 1702, when his father was called to govern Massachusetts. On his return Paul Dudley's credentials as the only trained lawyer in the province justified the apparent nepotism of his appointment as the province's attorney-general. On 15 September 1703 he married Lucy (1684–1756), the daughter of Colonel John Wainwright of Ipswich. Their six children all died in infancy.

The younger Dudley took to his job with zeal, prosecuting pirates who had hitherto fenced stolen goods in Boston, but over the objections of his father's numerous political enemies, who feared 'betwixt the Governor and his son Paul … there is no Justice to be had without Money' ('A memorial of the present deplorable state of New England', *Collections of Massachusetts Historical Society*, 5th ser., 6.42). Nevertheless, both Dudleys weathered such charges as they conscientiously directed Massachusetts's efforts in the War of the Spanish Succession (1702–13).

As his father aged Dudley became a leader of the political faction that favoured increasing co-operation with Britain. During the war, and immediately after, he enjoyed considerable success. In 1707 the legislature refused to sanction charges that the Dudleys had been trading with the French-Canadian enemy. In 1714 Paul Dudley successfully led those who opposed establishing a private land bank in Massachusetts. He persuaded the legislature to issue public bills of credit instead, on the grounds that allowing directors of a private fund to control the money supply would lead to inflation rather than to the revival of an economy suffering from post-war doldrums. In 1718 Governor Samuel Shute rewarded him with an appointment to the Massachusetts supreme court, on which he served until his death. In 1745 he became chief justice.

Yet by 1720 Dudley's faction went into an eclipse. Governor Shute quarrelled with the anti-prerogative group headed by Boston's Elisha Cooke. Dudley did his cause no good, for he had picked up aristocratic ways in England which played into his enemies' hands. At the contested elections for Boston representatives in 1720 he sarcastically proposed that the town meeting bar from voting anyone who refused to take an oath of allegiance to the crown, implying the people still retained their puritan independence. Perhaps the virulent response to Dudley's intervention persuaded him to move that year to Roxbury, the town immediately south-west of Boston. He thereby became one of the first leading Bostonians to escape the disorder and unhealthiness of the city by retreating to a country house in the manner of the English gentry. Dudley's learned conversation and hospitality endeared him far more to this class of people than to those of Boston, to which he regularly commuted to perform his judicial duties.

Dudley quit politics in his final years and devoted himself more exclusively to his intellectual interests, which had led to his election as fellow of the Royal Society for his contribution to its *Philosophical Transactions* in 1720, 'An account of the method of making of sugar from the juice of the maple tree in New England' (31.27–8). He published eleven more articles in the *Transactions*, on topics including a description of Niagara Falls (32.69–72), accounts of moose (31.165–9), rattlesnakes (32.292–5), the value of American Indian hot-houses in curing disease (33.129–32), whales (33.265–9), and earthquakes (39.67–73). In his secular, scholarly pursuits, rejection of town democracy for country gentility, and support of royal government, Dudley was a principal figure in the Anglicization of a provincial Massachusetts that was transformed from the most intransigent opponent of royal power under the puritans to the most co-operative province during the great Anglo-American wars of the mid-eighteenth century. He died on 25 January 1751 at Roxbury, Massachusetts.

WILLIAM PENCAK

Sources C. K. Shipton, 'Dudley, Paul', *Sibley's Harvard graduates: biographical sketches of those who attended Harvard College*, 4 (1933), 42–54 · J. Murrin, 'Anglicizing an American colony', PhD diss., Yale U., 1966 · W. Pencak, *War, politics and revolution in provincial Massachusetts* (1981) · P. Ranlet, 'Dudley, Paul', *ANB* · H. W. H. Knott, 'Dudley, Paul', *DAB* **Archives** American Antiquarian Society, MSS · Mass. Hist. Soc., MSS **Likenesses** portrait, repro. in Shipton, 'Dudley, Paul' **Wealth at death** substantial property: Shipton, 'Dudley, Paul', 4.42–54

Dudley, Robert, earl of Leicester (1532/3–1588), courtier and magnate, was born on 24 June 1532 or 1533, the fifth son of John *Dudley, duke of Northumberland (1504–1553), royal minister, and his wife, Jane *Dudley (1508/9–1555) [see under Dudley, John, duke of Northumberland (1504–1553)], noblewoman, daughter of Sir Edward *Guildford, of Halden and Hemsted, Kent, and his first wife, Eleanor. None of the numerous Dudley genealogies supplies dates of birth for their thirteen children, but in a letter to William Cecil, Baron Burghley, in 1587 Robert Dudley mentioned that 24 June was his birthday (*CSP for.*, 1587, 129). A portrait miniature by Nicholas Hilliard dated

Robert Dudley, earl of Leicester (1532/3–1588), by unknown artist, *c*.1575

1576 (NPG, 4197) gives his age then as forty-four, so 1532 is the most likely year of his birth. Dudley's brothers included John *Dudley, Viscount Lisle and earl of Warwick (1527?–1554) [*see under* Dudley, John], Ambrose *Dudley, earl of Warwick (*c*.1530–1590), Henry *Dudley (1531?–1557) [*see under* Dudley, John (1504–1553)], and Lord Guildford *Dudley (*c*.1535–1554), and his sisters included Mary *Sidney (1530x35–1586) and Katherine *Hastings, later countess of Huntingdon (*c*.1538–1620).

Early life and education, 1532/3–1558 Few details survive of the Dudley children's education, though the list of books in the wardrobe account in 1550 of John Dudley, Viscount Lisle, gives some idea of their cultural milieu (Bodl. Oxf., MS Addit. C. 94, fol. 13). Both Roger Ascham (who later teased him about giving up Cicero for Euclid) and Thomas Wilson had some involvement in Robert Dudley's education, and there are references to other schoolmasters, including his uncle Sir Francis *Jobson (*b*. in or before 1509, *d*. 1573). His correspondence displays none of the academic humanism of university-educated contemporaries such as Cecil, but he both spoke and wrote Italian fluently, could read Latin and French and possibly speak Latin, and retained an interest in mathematics, engineering, and navigation throughout his life.

Perhaps the most tantalizing aspect of Dudley's early years is his childhood friendship with Princess Elizabeth. All that is known is the allusion he made to it in 1566:

> his true opinion was that she would never marry … he knew her majesty as well as or better than anyone else of her close acquaintance, for they had first become friends before she

was eight years old. Both then and later (when she was old enough to marry) she said she never wished to do so. (Bibliothèque Nationale de France, Paris, MS français 15970, fol. 14)

The best explanation is that he was attached to the household of Edward, prince of Wales, in the early 1540s. Although he is not found in any of the extant lists of the king's henchmen or the 'young lords' educated with Edward, a number of them became his lifelong friends: Henry Sidney (1529–1586), Henry Hastings, third earl of Huntingdon (1536?–1595), Henry Stanley, fourth earl of Derby, and, possibly, George Talbot, sixth earl of Shrewsbury. Among them were two Irishmen, Barnaby Fitzpatrick, second Baron Upper Ossory, who also became a good friend, and Thomas Butler, eleventh earl of Ormond, who became one of his bitterest enemies.

Robert Dudley is not otherwise encountered until 1549, when he and his brother Ambrose Dudley accompanied their father in the campaign against Ket's rebellion. It is generally assumed that it was while he was in Norfolk that he met Amy (1532–1560) [*see* Dudley, Amy], gentlewoman, daughter of Sir John Robsart of Syderstone, Norfolk, and his wife, Elizabeth, whom he married at Sheen, Surrey, on 4 June 1550. Although her father was a prosperous grazier and a committed protestant, the marriage had no overt political motive or significance, and there is no reason to doubt that it was a romantic one. John Dudley, then earl of Warwick, was an indulgent parent and made the best of the marriage by using it to establish his son in the county. The Robsart estate was held by Sir John Robsart and his wife in survivorship and would not be inherited by Robert and Amy Dudley until both died. Under the marriage settlement of 24 May 1550, Warwick provided the couple with the lands of the nearby priory of Coxford, with the obvious intention that they would be combined with the Robsart lands in due course. In February 1553 he added the manor of Hemsby near Great Yarmouth, 'so his son might be able to keep a good house in Norfolk' (Adams, *Leicester and the Court*, 159).

Dudley served an apprenticeship in Norfolk local government with his father-in-law; they shared the lord lieutenancy in 1552, and he was elected a knight of the shire for Norfolk, first in a by-election in autumn 1551 and then in the parliament of March 1553. However, he and his wife usually resided at court or with his parents at Ely Place in London, and it was at court that his real interests lay. On 15 August 1551 he was appointed a gentleman of the privy chamber together with his friend Fitzpatrick. He had been knighted the previous year, probably about the time of his wedding, but he was generally styled Lord Robert Dudley, the courtesy title for a duke's younger son. Dudley did not visit France in 1551 (as once thought), though he did take part in the reception for Mary of Guise on her return to Scotland in October. He was appointed master of the buckhounds on 29 September 1552 and chief carver on 27 February 1553. On 27 December 1552 he was appointed keeper of Somerset Place, where he and his wife lived for the remaining months of Edward's reign. At the same time Princess Elizabeth begrudgingly agreed to exchange

Durham Place for Somerset Place; although she never resided there before Edward's death, the coincidence is intriguing.

Dudley played a larger role than did his brothers in the disaster that overwhelmed his family in July 1553. Immediately after Edward died on 6 July, Northumberland sent Dudley to Hunsdon, Hertfordshire, to bring Princess Mary to court. Forewarned, however, she had already left for Kenninghall. He followed her into Norfolk, but outnumbered by her supporters retired to King's Lynn, which he held until his father surrendered at Cambridge on 20 July. He was brought to the Tower of London on 26 July, the day after his brothers. His trial posed an awkward legal problem because Mary's privy council had determined that the primary act of treason was appearing in arms with Northumberland at Cambridge on 16–17 July. Dudley had to be tried on a separate charge of treason for having proclaimed Lady Jane Grey at King's Lynn on 18 July. Because a Norfolk jury had to be empanelled first, he was not in fact arraigned until 22 January 1554, the eve of the rebellion of Sir Thomas Wyatt the younger. Although he admitted guilt on the following day and was condemned, he was not attainted until the second parliament of 1554, along with the Wyatt rebels—by which time he had actually been released. Moreover Dudley had an unused defence: like many others who had also proclaimed Jane, he had simply carried out the orders of the privy council. In 1571 he sought and obtained a reversal of the attainder in the court of king's bench.

At his trial on 18 August 1553 Northumberland appealed for mercy for his five sons 'consydering that they went by my commandment who am their father, and not of their own free wills', though ironically the duchess was prepared to sacrifice them to save her husband (Nichols, 17). Northumberland was beheaded on Tower Hill on 22 August but there is no evidence that Mary intended to carry out the sentences in full. Only Lord Guildford Dudley suffered execution, but that he owed to his father-in-law's participation in Wyatt's rebellion. Otherwise their imprisonment was not harsh: their wives were allowed to visit them and they were given liberty to walk on the leads. In June 1554 their mother—accurately assessing what mattered to the queen—obtained liberty for them to hear mass. The four surviving brothers (John Dudley, earl of Warwick, Robert, Ambrose, and Henry) carved an elaborate memorial to each other in the wall of the Beauchamp tower, and Robert Dudley wrote a verse translation of Psalm 94:

O Mightie Lord to whom
all vengeance doth belong

This is the only poetry he is known to have composed (Haughey, 1.24–5). Despite Robert Dudley's pronounced loyalty to his family in all other respects, he has left no other comment on the fate of his father or that of Lord Guildford Dudley.

In spring 1554 the numerous prisoners from Wyatt's rebellion joined the Dudley brothers in the Tower, among them Elizabeth. Ever since then there has been recurrent speculation about a romance in the Tower, but Elizabeth

was there for only two months (mid-March to mid-May) and under quite tight restrictions. Contact between them cannot be ruled out, but its significance may be doubted. The continued imprisonment of the Dudleys over the summer of 1554 is best explained by the nervousness of Mary's government about another rising to disrupt the marriage to Philip of Spain. Both the duchess of Northumberland and Sidney were working hard for their release, particularly with Philip and his companions. Robert Dudley also enjoyed the avuncular benevolence of two key privy councillors, William Paget, first Baron Paget, and William Herbert, first earl of Pembroke. By autumn Warwick's health began to deteriorate from the effects of incarceration, and on 18 October he left the Tower, only to die at Sidney's house, Penshurst Place in Kent, on the 21st. Robert and Henry Dudley were probably released with him, for on 14 November, Ambrose Dudley's wife, Elizabeth, appealed to Philip for his freedom on the grounds that he was the only one still in the Tower.

The brothers owed their release to Philip's desire to win loyalty by generosity. They were not the only beneficiaries, but they also enjoyed several further gestures of good will. In December Robert and Ambrose Dudley participated in the Anglo-Spanish tournaments that Philip organized to improve relations. On 22 January 1555 they were pardoned, although they remained attainted. Coincidentally their mother died on either 15 or 22 January, and Mary allowed Ambrose to inherit her estate of inheritance despite his attainder. The attainders had cost all of them their existing estates, but Ambrose and Henry Dudley were married to major heiresses. Robert Dudley, however, faced a more critical financial situation. Sir John Robsart died on 8 June 1554, but his wife lived on until June 1557. Although Robert received some financial assistance from the Robsarts, it was Ambrose and Henry Dudley who came to his aid. In a family agreement on 20 November 1556, Ambrose Dudley gave him the lands he had inherited from the duchess of Northumberland (the estates of the former monastery of Halesowen in Worcestershire) for £800 and responsibility for paying off her debts. Mary also helped; in January 1557 he was permitted to inherit the Robsart estate despite the attainder, and Hemsby was restored to him.

Nevertheless, suspicion remained. In summer 1555 the Dudleys were among the gentlemen ordered to leave London during Mary's confinement. After the breaking of the Dudley plot in March 1556, the French ambassador, Antoine de Noailles, reported them as being in flight. However, Robert Dudley is next heard of on 17 March 1557, bringing news that Philip was about to arrive from Calais on his last visit to England. This has led to speculation that he went to the Low Countries with Philip in August 1555, but in fact he was probably a member of the party that Pembroke took to inspect Calais in December 1556, and which remained there to escort the king to England. Together with many others who had debts of honour to Philip, the three Dudley brothers joined the expeditionary force that Pembroke led to France in August 1557 to assist him at the siege of St Quentin. Robert Dudley was appointed master of the ordnance, an unusual position for someone of his relative youth, but probably the result of Pembroke's appreciation of his talents. Lord Henry Dudley was killed in the storming of St Quentin on 27 September—'before his own eyes', Robert Dudley recalled in 1576 (Archives Générales du Royaume, Brussels, papiers d'état et de l'audience 361, fol. 156v). The expedition had at least one material benefit, for in the first session of the parliament of 1558 Northumberland's four surviving children were restored in blood, though in exchange they surrendered any claim of right to their father's lands or offices. It also widened Robert Dudley's horizons: at St Quentin he met the famous German soldier Lazarus von Schwendi, Antoine Perrenot, the future Cardinal Granvelle, and possibly also William, prince of Orange.

Dudley's departure for St Quentin was the occasion for his wife's well-known letter that concludes, 'not being altogether in quiet for my lord's sudden departing' (BL, Harley MS 4712, fol. 275r). She was then living with William Hyde at Throcking, Hertfordshire, where she was still residing in spring 1559. Although the couple now possessed the Robsart estate, the main house, Syderstone Hall, was uninhabitable. Robert Dudley may have lived with her at Throcking as well, although they also used Christchurch, the large house in London owned by his brother Henry Dudley, and possibly those of some of her maternal relations, the Scotts of Camberwell. His earliest surviving letter, dated 22 July 1558, was written from a Scott house, Hay's Court in Kent. The subject was the significant one of purchasing a house in Norfolk in order to settle there (ibid., fol. 273r).

Amy Dudley's residence in Hertfordshire strengthens the case for a close association between Dudley and Princess Elizabeth in 1557–8. After her accession on 17 November 1558 there was speculation that the favour she showed him then was a reward for having supplied her with money earlier. This cannot be confirmed; Halesowen was certainly heavily mortgaged, but for that his own weak finances provide an adequate explanation. However, he was identified as one of Elizabeth's intimates on the eve of the accession, and he was among the witnesses to the surrender of the Marian great seal at Hatfield, Hertfordshire, in the morning of 18 November. On the same day he was nominated master of the horse, and he served in that office from then on, although his letters patent did not pass the great seal until 11 January 1559. In December 1558 Elizabeth also gave him Kew House in Surrey, where he resided until he sold it about 1564.

The queen's favourite, 1559–1562 Both Ambrose Dudley and Lady Mary Sidney were appointed to the new court at the same time as their brother, and the Dudley presence there does not appear to have occasioned much surprise. It was only in April 1559 that Robert Dudley's peculiar relationship to Elizabeth began to attract comment. This relationship—which defined the rest of his life—was characterized by her almost total emotional dependence on him and her insistence on his constant presence at court. It explains why, for example, a suggestion made on the eve

of the accession that he should be sent as special ambassador to announce it to Philip was not followed up and why he took no part in the Scottish campaign in 1560. It also helps to explain his separation from his wife, who came to London from Throcking in May 1559, but spent only a month or so there. In autumn 1559 she was probably living in Warwickshire, and in spring 1560 moved to Cumnor House near Oxford.

Dudley did not become a member of the privy council until October 1562, and his prominence at court had little immediate political impact. He was elected one of the Norfolk knights of the shire for the parliament of 1559, but has left no trace of any role in the making of the religious settlement—except using the Easter recess to pay a quick visit to his wife at Throcking. At the beginning of 1559 he asked the secretary of the Merchant Adventurers in the Netherlands to supply him with newsletters. While this suggests an interest in wider political affairs, his involvement in the making of foreign policy was limited to the reception of the French embassy that came to ratify the treaty of Cateau Cambrésis in May. The author of the 'Journrall of matters of state' (BL, Add. MS 48023), the much cited contemporary narrative of these years, probably John Hales, saw Dudley as Paget's mouthpiece, but he had an animus against both the Dudleys and Paget, and his claims are difficult to confirm from other sources.

The sudden death of his wife at Cumnor on 8 September 1560 was almost as important as Elizabeth's favour in shaping Dudley's future. The court was then at Windsor Castle, Berkshire, on its return from the progress in Hampshire, and ironically he was closer to his wife geographically than he had been for over a year. A near hysterical servant of theirs brought the news to Windsor on the 9th. On the road from Abingdon he had encountered Dudley's chief household officer, Thomas Blount of Kidderminster, who coincidentally was making his way home from Windsor. Blount decided on his own initiative to investigate, and the subsequent correspondence between him and Dudley is the only reliable source for the circumstances of Amy Dudley's death (Magdalene College, Cambridge, Pepys MSS, letters of state 2). No obvious explanation as to how she came to break her neck could be found, and while Blount worried about suicide, the verdict of the coroner's jury was death by misadventure.

Dudley retired to Kew in a state of shock, provided his wife with a full funeral, and went into mourning for six months. His letters to Blount reveal his concern to have her death fully investigated, but possibly more with an eye to the damage it might do to him than from grief at her loss. In 1584 *Leicester's Commonwealth* made notorious the story of a murder plot involving Sir Richard Verney, and the discovery of the 'Journrall of matters of state' has revealed that it was already in circulation by 1563. However, this is no more than public gossip and speculation. The more serious evidence against Dudley is provided by the single surviving report of the Spanish ambassador, Alvaro de la Quadra, bishop of Aquila, written from Windsor on 11 September 1560. In it Quadra records Cecil's complaints to him about Dudley's influence over the queen:

that he was encouraging her to spend all her time hunting, that he (Cecil) wished to retire, and that Elizabeth and Dudley intended to do away with Dudley's wife. The day after this conversation Elizabeth told him in confidence that Amy Dudley was dead or almost so, and in a postscript he added that the queen had just made public her death from a broken neck. The internal chronology of this letter is not entirely clear, but it would appear that Elizabeth made her confidential admission on the 10th, and that the conversation with Cecil occurred on the 9th, just after the first news reached Windsor (Archivo General de Simancas, secreteria de estado 814, fol. 24).

Certain elements ring true. Cecil's correspondence of late August and September 1560 reveals him as very unhappy and wishing to retire. Precisely why is not clear, though it appears related to Elizabeth's attitude to the negotiations over Scotland—the now missing letter he wrote to Thomas Randolph on 11 September would be very interesting to see. Dudley himself confirmed Cecil's concern about the queen's taking up potentially dangerous sports such as riding and hunting. On the 7th he wrote to Thomas Radcliffe, third earl of Sussex, to order horses from Ireland for Elizabeth, who 'is now become a great huntress and doth follow it daily from morning to night' (BL, Cotton MS Titus B. xiii, fol. 17r). If even Cecil was hinting that Amy Dudley's life was in danger, then Dudley's worries about the effects of her death on his own position were fully justified. On the other hand, Dudley's influence on the Anglo-Scots negotiations is not clear, while any assumption that Cecil believed he had murdered his wife must take into account the fact that a week later he went to Kew to condole with Dudley, for which he received a fulsome if semi-coherent letter of thanks.

The inconclusive verdict on his wife's death haunted Dudley for the rest of his life. As Cecil bluntly put it several years later, he was 'infamed by the deth of his wife' (Hatfield House, Hertfordshire, Cecil MS 155, article 28). Even if innocent of murder, he may well have been guilty of abandoning her. The legend that she was sequestered in the country has been disproved, but nevertheless she played no part in his life at court. This may well have been Elizabeth's doing. The 'Journall of matters of state' comments, 'he was commanded to saye that he did nothing with her [his wife], when he cam to her, as seldom he did' (BL, Add. MS 48023, fol. 353r). Elizabeth was not going to share him with anyone else.

As important as its causes was the fact that Amy Dudley's death freed her husband to marry Elizabeth. There is absolutely no evidence that they were ever lovers—or that Elizabeth lost her virginity to anyone. But from early 1559 it was appreciated that her affection for him was an effective barrier to her marrying anyone else. The answer to the conundrum of their relations after 1560 depends on the credence placed in the sincerity of Elizabeth's protestations of her preference for virginity and in his appreciation that she would never marry. Yet she was also under constant pressure to marry to save the Tudor succession, and whether or not she would bow to it eventually was no less an issue for the immediate future. In Dudley's favour

as a consort were their apparent compatibility and the widespread preference for a domestic marriage—particularly among protestants—in the aftermath of Mary's marriage to Philip. There were no serious domestic rivals. The case for a foreign marriage was weakened by the absence of suitable protestant candidates with the exceptions of Eric XIV of Sweden and James Hamilton, third earl of Arran—and Elizabeth showed no interest in either of them.

Nevertheless, there were strong personal objections to Dudley. These were less birth and his father's treason, whatever polemical capital might be made of them, than that marrying someone who was technically her servant and whose wife had just died in compromising circumstances would tarnish if not destroy Elizabeth's reputation, as Sir Nicholas Throckmorton argued stridently in autumn 1560. Equally significant in some quarters was fear of his revenge for 1553. It is conventionally argued that the winter of 1560–61 was the moment when Elizabeth might have married Dudley, but it can equally well be suggested that the nature of Amy Dudley's death actually provided her with an excuse not to do so.

On 20 January 1561 Francis Russell, second earl of Bedford, was commissioned a special ambassador to France. He had two major assignments: co-ordinating a joint response with France to the papal summoning of what became the last session of the council of Trent and preventing a rumoured marriage between the recently widowed Mary, queen of Scots, and Philip's son, Don Carlos. On the 22nd Quadra was approached by Sidney with the suggestion that Philip give his public support for a marriage between Dudley and Elizabeth, in return for which they would reform religion in England in accordance with the new general council. It was clear that Sidney was speaking initially on Dudley's behalf and ultimately on Elizabeth's. Quadra claimed to be sceptical from the start, but he immediately reported Sidney's proposal, and in the meantime informed various English Catholics that he was negotiating with Elizabeth for the restoration of religion. During February and March he discussed the scheme in general terms with Dudley, Elizabeth, and Cecil.

Philip's response (dated 17 March) did not reach England until early April. He too was sceptical and required a signed statement from Elizabeth as to her intentions; he further suggested that as a gesture of good faith she release the imprisoned Marian bishops and include them in a delegation to the new council. On receipt of this instruction Quadra told Dudley that he would judge their sincerity by the reception given to the nuncio bringing the invitation to the council, and also let it be known that he expected shortly to see the release of one or two of the bishops. Whether by accident or design, it soon became public knowledge that Quadra had informed the imprisoned bishops that they would be freed as Dudley and the queen had offered to restore the church in exchange for support for their marriage. On 25 April, Cecil accused Quadra of conspiring with the imprisoned bishops and stated that the nuncio would probably not be admitted into England. The formal announcement that Elizabeth would neither receive the nuncio nor send a delegation to Trent was made on 1 May. In the meantime Quadra had complained to both Dudley and Elizabeth that he had been misrepresented, and the queen responded by denying that either she or Dudley had ever proposed the restoration of Catholicism.

This episode first came to light when J. A. Froude explored the Spanish diplomatic correspondence in the 1860s, and since then it has been repeatedly cited as evidence of Dudley's opportunistic pursuit of marriage to Elizabeth. Denounced by protestants for the death of his wife, he had swung round to the opposite pole. However, it is doubtful that this was an initiative on his part. It was neither the first nor the last time that Elizabeth employed indirect hints about her marriage for diplomatic ends, and unauthorized private interventions received short shrift. What, though, were her motives? By June, Quadra was convinced that it had been a ploy to divert Philip from a Habsburg marriage for Mary. The coincidence with the Bedford embassy is striking, not least because on 11 February he wrote to Dudley about the good prospects for protestantism in France. The English effort to organize a general council free from papal control made the offer to reform religion in accord with it a distinctly ambiguous one.

All other evidence about Dudley's religious convictions reveals a remarkable consistency. In 1576 he answered the concerns of his puritan follower Thomas Wood with a now famous lengthy defence of his commitment:

> there is no man I knowe in this realme … that hath shewed a better minde to the furthering of true religion then I have done, even from the first day of her Majestie's reigne to this … I take Almighty God to my record, I never altered my mind or thought from my youth touching my religion, and yow know I was ever from my cradle brought up in it.   ('Letters of Thomas Wood', 95)

Although little is known of the religious outlook of the Dudley family in the 1530s and 1540s, strong protestantism was marked among all his siblings, none of whom joined their father in public recantation in 1553. The very lengthy will that the duchess of Northumberland wrote in January 1555 reveals no allegiance to the old church and is suspiciously perfunctory about her faith, although as noted above she encouraged her sons to attend mass to win over Mary I in 1554. There is no reason to doubt that Dudley, like Elizabeth and Cecil, conformed publicly for the rest of Mary's reign, but from Elizabeth's accession his patronage of former Edwardian clergymen and Marian exiles was extensive. His domestic chaplains in 1559 and 1560 had both been exiles. During the next three decades he employed an extraordinary number of chaplains—twenty-seven can be definitely identified—which suggests he may have used some form of annual rotation. Nine of his chaplains became bishops, and at least twelve became heads of Oxford and Cambridge colleges. Since many of these appointments occurred after his death, it is clear that the advancement of his chaplains was not solely the result of his own patronage; rather it reflected his own close association with the intellectual élite of the Elizabethan church. That one or two of his chaplains may have reconciled themselves to Rome—the main example was the mathematician John Bridgewater—should cause no surprise.

There is some evidence that after the general council affair became public Dudley offered to leave the country and serve in the wars against the Turks. However, Elizabeth would not permit it and his position at court was unaltered. He was now known simply as 'the favourite', a job description that he and she wrote between them. Favourites to male monarchs had been either cronies or homosexual partners; a male favourite to a virgin queen was without precedent. Elizabeth repeatedly described their relationship as that between sister and brother, but he was more than that: he was practically a surrogate husband. His widower status meant that there was now no other woman competing for his attention, and she could be assured of what she really wanted—his constant companionship. On those occasions when he left the court for any period of time—effectively not until 1566, or regularly until after 1570—a stream of letters was expected. Francis Walsingham reminded him in April 1576, 'her majesty doth accept in good part your lordship's often sending unto her sithence your departure, therefore your lordship will do well to continue that course until your return' (BL, Cotton MS Titus B. vii, fol. 12r). Of the extensive familiar correspondence between them, only some twenty-odd letters of his (exclusive of those from the Netherlands in 1586–7) have survived. Elizabeth appears to have saved them in a packet tied up with ribbon that was discovered after her death. Hers to him were destroyed, and there is only a copy of one (written on 19 July 1586) to provide an example of her intimate style. By 1570 his letters included the 'eyes' motif that had become her nickname for him. Nicknames were one of the clearest symbols of membership in her circle of intimates, but their origins are unfortunately lost in obscure private jokes.

For Dudley's companionship Elizabeth was prepared to pay well—though not immediately. He was elected to the Order of the Garter on 24 April 1559 and installed on 3 June. In November he was appointed lieutenant of Windsor Castle (constable in February 1562). However, no great estates followed Kew. Instead she granted him a licence to export wool free of customs worth £6000 in 1560, a further licence together with an annuity from the customs of London worth £1000 in 1562, and then a similar licence to export cloth, worth £6666, in 1563. These were early examples of what became her favourite type of reward, but the customs annuity was explicitly a temporary measure pending a grant of lands of similar annual value. Why the landed endowment (and with it a peerage) was so delayed is still unexplained. The surrender of the claim of right to Northumberland's lands and titles in 1558 may have been a consideration, while Ambrose Dudley's seniority would involve endowing two peers rather than one. It is also possible that her hesitation over a peerage was caused by the fear it would make Dudley too independent.

What amounted to a cash subsidy kept him closer to the court.

Ambrose Dudley was finally created Baron Lisle and earl of Warwick at Christmas 1561. Earlier in the year (1 March) Robert Dudley had received a small group of Northumberland's outlying lands, chiefly in the East Riding of Yorkshire—the significance of which appears to lie in the Dudley claim of descent from the Anglo-Saxon lords of Sutton in Holderness. On 9 June 1563 Elizabeth granted him what became the core of his estate, the lordships of Kenilworth (Warwickshire), Denbigh, and Chirk, and he was created earl of Leicester and baron of Denbigh on 29 September 1564. The justification for his promotion to the peerage in 1564 was that it would qualify him as a consort for Mary, queen of Scots, although his simultaneous election to the order of St Michael by Charles IX may also have been an influence. However, Kenilworth had a historic association with the earldom of Leicester, and why the relevant estates were granted a year before the titles remains a mystery.

The new earl of Leicester received two further large grants of estates, one in 1566, most of which he later sold, and the other in 1572, which included the Montgomeryshire lordships of Arwystli and Cyfeiliog. The cumulative effect of Elizabeth's generosity was to make the two Dudley brothers the leading landed interest in the west midlands and north Wales. The affection between them was one of the constants in their lives, and in their estate management, as in so many other areas, they operated in close accord. They employed the same officers and men of business, many of whom had previously worked for Northumberland. Leicester attached a particular sentimental value to his Warwickshire estates and the Dudley claim of descent from the Beauchamp earls of Warwick. As Northumberland had done earlier, both brothers adopted the Beauchamp device of the bear and ragged staff in 1562. Yet Leicester did not even see Kenilworth until the progress of 1566. Following the sale of Kew he moved initially to Durham Place, Westminster. After spending the second half of the 1560s there, he purchased Paget Place near Temple Bar, London, from Thomas Paget, third Baron Paget, in January 1570, and immediately renamed it Leicester House.

Privy councillor and politics, 1561–1570 Leicester's political role and influence—unlike Cecil's or (later) Walsingham's—has been obscured by the dispersal of his papers and correspondence. While theirs has survived in great quantity and forms the core of the Elizabethan state papers, his is scattered in a number of private collections. Theirs is easily accessible through the various volumes of *Calendar of State Papers* (1856–)—from which too much Elizabethan history has been written—but only small sections from his are in print.

Give or take the general council affair, Leicester's first clear involvement in making high policy occurred in autumn 1561, following Mary's return to Scotland and Elizabeth's refusal to recognize her formally as her presumptive. Together with Cecil he was the architect of a policy of maintaining good relations between the queens

to protect the political *status quo* of the newly protestant Scotland. This brought him into close association with the Scottish leaders William Maitland of Lethington and James Stewart, earl of Moray, the first of his international political friendships. Cecil and he were also the architects of policy towards France following the outbreak of the first war of religion in summer 1562. Although there is a historiographical tradition that the ill-fated occupation of Le Havre in winter 1562–3 was a victory for Dudley's irresponsible adventurism over Cecil's caution, all the correspondence relating to Le Havre shows them working closely together. A number of the officers at Le Havre ('Newhaven') were Dudley followers, and there is evidence that he would have liked the command himself. Once again, though, Elizabeth would not let him leave, and it went to Warwick instead. It is revealing of the conflict of loyalties under which he operated that his earliest surviving letter to Elizabeth, dated 7 August 1563, is an apology for leaving the court to greet Warwick on his return from Le Havre (PRO, SP 12/29/122). A final early political intervention was his support for the attempt to reach a settlement with Shane O'Neill over Ulster that took place during the Irish chief's visit to court in winter 1561–2. This has been portrayed as an episode in a wider factional struggle in which Dudley tried to wrest control of the Irish military establishment from Sussex, the lord deputy. However, this argument advances the date of their hostility by several years.

Dudley's appointment to the privy council in October 1562 effectively recognized and formalized his existing political influence. His intimacy with Elizabeth made him automatically one of the privy council's senior members. 'You knowe the quene and her nature best of anny man', wrote Sir Thomas Shirley in March 1586, but it was no less true twenty years earlier when the Spanish ambassador, Diego Guzman de Silva, described him on 16 August 1566 as the person who had most influence over her (*Correspondance*, 176; Hume, 1558–67, 671). However, the twin issues of the queen's marriage and the settlement of the succession quickly overshadowed the French intervention. Elizabeth's marriage posed an inherent conflict between Leicester's own perceived interest as a potential consort and his function as an adviser. Clarification of his role has not been helped by the repeated efforts to write the political history of the 1560s as a factional struggle between his friends and his enemies. This has never been very convincing because the nature and range of the issues involved were such that shifting alliances rather than coherent factions were the reality.

Over the succession, which became a matter of public controversy in the parliament of 1563, there was a serious difference of opinion between Leicester and Cecil. Cecil never trusted Mary and was always anxious to prevent her succeeding Elizabeth, while Leicester, like Elizabeth, seems to have believed that her claim to the succession was unstoppable. Yet unlike the queen, Leicester considered that some form of formal agreement with her had to be reached in advance. This helped to shape his political friendship with Maitland, about whom he later wrote, 'I protest I loved as derely as ever I loved man not born in England and not many in England better' (Cameron, 1.189). Cecil's solution was an heir of Elizabeth's body, a hope to which he clung as late as 1579. To this end he was the architect of the revival of the proposal for her marriage to Archduke Charles of Styria, son of Ferdinand I, during the course of 1563.

However, such a course involved persuading Elizabeth to marry. An earlier Austrian marriage scheme had collapsed in 1559 when Vienna had refused her demand that Charles visit her first without preconditions. It may have been revived initially to prevent the marriage of Charles to Mary, which Charles de Guise, cardinal of Lorraine, had been negotiating at the beginning of 1563. It then obtained the backing of several Lutheran princes who wished to see England tied more closely to the empire, but, having been bitten once, Vienna responded very cautiously to the English approaches in 1563–4. Assurance was required that Elizabeth was now serious and that Dudley was not a rival. In another counter to the cardinal's negotiations, Elizabeth intimated to Mary during 1563 that she must choose a friendly second husband if her rights of succession were to be protected. When pressed to nominate a candidate, Elizabeth proposed Dudley.

The Dudley–Mary marriage plan has been so universally regarded as one of Elizabeth's worst misjudgements that it has never been given serious consideration. From her perspective it was both a gesture of goodwill to Mary and a demonstration of her own commitment to virginity—and it has also been suggested that she saw the marriage as means of making the Stuart succession palatable in England. There were, however, two issues to be surmounted. If as her servant Dudley was not a suitable consort for her, how could he be for Mary, and how serious was Elizabeth in wishing to deprive herself of his company? Her answers were Dudley's promotion to the earldom of Leicester and the proposal that after the marriage he and Mary should live at the English court. The combination of the two marriages thus had a tidy logic: Leicester as husband to Mary would assure Scotland and at the same time leave the field open to Charles in England.

Mary had never been interested in marrying Charles. Her choice was Don Carlos (Philip was unwilling to inform her directly that this marriage was not possible), but she did not reject the Leicester proposal out of hand. Instead she sought to see what concessions Elizabeth would make over recognition as heir presumptive. Not until March 1565 did Elizabeth make it clear there would be no concessions apart from the offer to house her and Leicester in the English court. Leicester himself had the common sense to appreciate that the proposed *ménage à trois* was a recipe for disaster and was almost openly unco-operative. His opposition to marrying Mary has inspired recurrent speculation that he deliberately engineered the visit of Henry Stewart, Lord Darnley, to Scotland in February 1565. However, this theory rests on the assumption that Mary would marry Darnley as soon as it was possible. All reliable evidence suggests that her decision was a sudden and unexpected one taken in April, after Darnley had been in Scotland for two months.

An ambassador arrived from Vienna in May 1565, but in July a basic problem was encountered when Maximilian II made it clear that the English would have to fund Charles's household and that he and his household must enjoy public Catholic worship. Although Elizabeth was ultimately prepared to compromise on the funding question, she refused to take a husband of a different religion, and it was on this rock that the Austrian marriage foundered. It was a major setback to Cecil, who appears to have believed that Charles could be persuaded to convert. In the face of this impasse, interest in Leicester as a consort revived and the French, always eager to inhibit an Anglo-Habsburg alliance, offered him their support. The current Spanish ambassador (de Silva) openly doubted that Elizabeth would marry anyone else. Cecil's difficulties are revealed in the famous memorandum that he drafted comparing Charles and Leicester as potential husbands, greatly to the latter's disadvantage. Although usually dated later, Cecil's confidence that Charles would fund himself and other internal evidence suggest that it must have been drafted before July 1565. Nowhere in the memorandum is religion mentioned.

Leicester had nailed his religious colours to the mast at the beginning of the year, in the course of the vestiarian controversy, the first major rift within the Elizabethan church. On 31 December 1564 he was elected chancellor of Oxford University (at the recommendation of the retiring chancellor, Sir John Mason), and this office gave him an increased role in the church at all levels in subsequent years. The driving force for conformity on vestments was the queen, for neither Matthew Parker, archbishop of Canterbury, nor Cecil was happy with it, and by March 1565 they were seriously worried by the possible extent of nonconformity. Like Cecil, Leicester was the recipient of appeals from the nonconformist clergy, two of whose leaders—Thomas Sampson and Lawrence Humphrey—were also key figures in the Oxford protestant establishment. On this occasion, as in later disciplinarian disputes within the church, he took the common-sense view that, given the shortage of committed protestant clergy, depriving men for what appeared to be minor acts of nonconformity made no sense. The precise effect of his influence is unclear, but the drive for conformity petered out in 1566. More important was the reputation he gained as the privy councillor most sympathetic to, and protective of, protestant nonconformity, a reputation that came increasingly to worry Parker.

The stalemate over the Austrian marriage was followed quickly by the marriage of Mary and Darnley on 29 July 1565. This led to a clash between Mary and Moray, and early in September, Moray and a number of the Scottish peers were in revolt. Leicester was deeply involved in supporting Moray in this revolt—the chaseabout raid—and late in September the privy council held a formal debate on the issue of open military assistance. Leicester was widely understood to be in favour, but Cecil argued that the justification for such a step was not clear enough. The confrontation with Mary was postponed, but the crisis inspired a new Irish policy, based on fears of an alliance between Mary and Shane. Leicester's brother-in-law Sidney was appointed lord deputy in the autumn, and, together with a number of former Le Havre officers, left for Dublin in December.

What has encouraged the wider factional interpretation of the events of 1565 has been a long-established misreading of two episodes. In March, Leicester and Thomas Howard, fourth duke of Norfolk, were said to have come to blows after a tennis match, evidence—it has been claimed—of Norfolk's resentment of his familiarity with Elizabeth. This incident was in fact relayed gossip from the Scottish court and is not confirmed by any English source. Filed among the state papers under June 1565 is an undated letter from Sussex complaining at the threatening behaviour of Leicester's followers; this undoubtedly refers to their quarrel in June 1566 (PRO, SP 12/36/152).

In mid-September 1565 there was a mysterious altercation between Elizabeth and Leicester. There was much speculation as to its cause, and there is no clear answer, though it may have been inspired by mutual recriminations over Scottish policy. Nevertheless it was short-lived and Elizabeth's affection for him remained unabated. In November the wedding of his brother Warwick and Bedford's daughter Anne Russell (1538–1587) [see Dudley, Anne], a marriage he had arranged, was celebrated with Elizabeth's enthusiastic backing in one of the grandest of the court ceremonials. In February 1566 he finally obtained permission to visit Kenilworth and his other estates. He never got there, because the illness or miscarriage of his sister Katherine, the countess of Huntingdon, diverted him. Nevertheless, Elizabeth grew increasingly restless at his absence, and came to meet him when he returned to London in April, 'kissing him thrice' on their encounter (Gairdner, 137).

During Leicester's journey Sidney sent him a long report on the state of Ireland for forwarding to Elizabeth. Sidney openly blamed Sussex for the situation, yet most of the new policies he proposed—especially an all-out campaign against Shane—were in fact Sussex's. Leicester's defence of Sidney in the face of Sussex's not totally unjustified resentment (abetted by Ormond) caused their open clash in June 1566. Cecil—equally committed to Sidney's campaign—and Elizabeth reconciled them, but thereafter their relations were guarded at best. In July the queen left on progress towards Lincolnshire, with Leicester urging her to visit Kenilworth as well. She hesitated for several days before she finally agreed—ostensibly because she feared he would be too extravagant, though possibly also because it might send the wrong signals to Vienna. She was greeted by the first of the grand Kenilworth entertainments.

It was during the progress that Leicester told a French diplomat that he did not believe Elizabeth would ever marry. At the same time she agreed to the recall of the prorogued parliament of 1563 on 30 September 1566, primarily to raise money for Sidney's Ulster campaign, an issue that reunited Leicester and Cecil. This was the first session in which Leicester sat in the House of Lords, and he held seven proxies. The birth of the future James VI on 19 June raised temperatures over the succession, and this issue came to dominate the parliamentary session. To fight off pressure to resolve the succession Elizabeth declared her serious intent to marry—Archduke Charles being her thinly veiled candidate. Yet such was the scepticism about her sincerity that this concession did not end the succession debate. Late in October, Leicester and Pembroke were temporarily banned from the presence chamber, apparently for persuading the Lords to join the House of Commons in a petition to the queen over the succession. The purpose of this manoeuvre is not entirely clear, but Leicester fell ill early in November and did not take an active role in parliament for the rest of the month.

Elizabeth's commitment to the Austrian marriage led to Sussex's embassy to Vienna in June 1567 and his attempt to resolve the religious issue by offering Charles private worship. This alternative (which the Austrians had not in fact accepted) Elizabeth rejected on 10 December, thus bringing the negotiations finally to an end. One of Sussex's followers reported that the privy council had divided on the question, with Leicester leading the opponents and possibly tuning the pulpit as well. This has been read as evidence that Leicester had persuaded Elizabeth to reject the proposal. He actually sent Sussex an angry denial of the story, but both accounts may have been true. The privy council may have been divided on the issue initially, but then united to leave the decision in the queen's hands.

The last phase of the Austrian negotiations was overshadowed first by the murder of Darnley (15 February 1567) and then by Mary's demission (abdication) in July. Elizabeth's unwillingness to accept Mary's abdication led to another reuniting of the protestant wing of the privy council in support of Moray's regency. This unity (whatever the disagreements over the Austrian marriage) was sustained by the outbreak of religious conflict in France and the Low Countries during 1568. Leicester was now widely observed to be the most sympathetic to protestant appeals for assistance, and in the autumn he was active in trying to organize support for the Huguenots. He also assisted Cecil in the famous seizure of the Spanish treasure ships in December.

Mary's flight to England in May 1568 introduced further complexities. Leicester was not directly involved in the 'first trial' in autumn 1568, but the inclusive adjournment of the trial and Mary's continued confinement in England led in the early months of 1569 to what has been considered the most notorious example of his political opportunism. This was the attempted overthrow of Cecil in the so-called Ash Wednesday plot of 23 February 1569. Ash Wednesday was supposedly the date of the incident at court in which Leicester denounced Cecil to Elizabeth, and was supported by Norfolk and William Parr, marquess of Northampton. However, the only source is the papal agent Roberto de Ridolfi, who recounted it in a letter to the Spanish ambassador, Don Guerau de Spes (who was under house arrest over the seizure of the treasure ships), on 22 February. Ridolfi later repeated the story to the

French ambassador, Bertrand de Salignac de La Motte-Fénélon, who dated it to the 23rd.

Ridolfi and Spes were certainly trying to encourage the overthrow of Cecil by cultivating fears in England that the seizure of the ships would provoke a war with Philip. Ridolfi believed that with Cecil gone Elizabeth could be persuaded to restore Catholicism, though he may in fact have intended Cecil's dismissal as the first stage in the queen's deposition in favour of Mary. The anonymous Catholic tract *A Treatise of Treasons*, published in 1572 and erroneously attributed to John Leslie, bishop of Ross, made public the plans to overthrow Cecil—and claimed that Cecil engineered the later fall of Norfolk out of revenge. However, both the Ash Wednesday incident and Leicester's involvement in the plot were undoubtedly the products of Ridolfi's overheated imagination. All reliable evidence suggests that Cecil and Leicester were united over foreign policy both before and after Ash Wednesday. Only one aspect has some grounding in fact. Ridolfi told Fénélon that Leicester was boycotting the privy council on the excuse that he had a cold. On 3 March 1569 Leicester apologized to Shrewsbury for not having written to him for some time owing to a cold.

The context has been further distorted by the conflation of this episode with the simultaneous discussions between Leicester and Norfolk over the duke's possible marriage with Mary. These negotiations are described in detail in Norfolk's self-serving confession in late 1571, which in turn (with some blatant editorializing) forms the basis of William Camden's account of the events of 1569. The marriage was part of a plan for a conditional (compromise) restoration of Mary to Scotland, a solution to the inclusive outcome of her first trial. The plan originated with Maitland, who first suggested it to Norfolk in autumn 1568, but since then it had circulated quite widely. Norfolk's claim of innocence until approached by Throckmorton on Leicester's behalf about Lent 1569 is—at the least—disingenuous.

Leicester's involvement in the scheme is entirely consistent with his belief in the need to reach an agreement with Mary. Pembroke and he drafted a set of terms for Mary's restoration to Scotland that he had Richard Cavendish take to her in May. The text is printed in Camden, and the conditions—the maintenance of protestantism in Scotland and a close alliance with England—are what one would expect. Mary expressed agreement, but the plan hinged on Moray's backing, for it was intended that the Scots—Leicester's choice was Maitland—should propose it to Elizabeth. Moray took until the end of the summer to decide against it. Leicester had demanded secrecy until Scottish agreement was secured, but Norfolk informed his friends and allies, and rumours reached Elizabeth through what Leicester termed 'some bablinge women' (*CSP Scot.*, 1571–4, 36).

On 8 September, after Moray's rejection arrived, Leicester revealed the whole scheme to Elizabeth. Camden's editing makes Leicester's 'confession' a craven exercise in which he sacrificed Norfolk to save his own skin. Yet in order to persuade Norfolk to admit his part as well, Cecil significantly reassured him that he would suffer no more than Leicester and Pembroke had done in 1566. Norfolk, however, vacillated, possibly because he feared that he would be forced to reveal the more dangerous activities of his friends, and was formally arrested. Worries about what Norfolk might confess frightened Henry Percy, eighth earl of Northumberland, and Charles Neville, sixth earl of Westmorland, into taking arms, however much they tried to disguise their rising as a response to the persecution of the old nobility. Leicester did not play a direct role in the defeat of the northern uprising, although men associated with him—Sir George Bowes, Sir John Forster, and Sir Simon Musgrave—provided the core of northern loyalism. The French ambassador reported that he had requested command of the forces against the rebels, but Elizabeth wished to hold him for a reserve army should one be necessary, and Warwick and Edward Fiennes de Clinton, ninth Baron Clinton, were appointed instead.

Captain-general of the puritans, 1570–1577 Ironically, Leicester was very active in promoting the proposed marriage of Elizabeth with Henri, duc d'Anjou (later Henri III), the last serious marriage scheme. It had originated with French friends of his in 1568, and was taken up in the winter of 1570–71 as a way of both settling the French religious wars and building an alliance with England. It collapsed in summer 1571 because Elizabeth would not budge from the terms she had offered Charles and because (more importantly) Anjou was not interested in compromising. As Leicester observed to Robert Beale on 7 July, 'it seems that he [Anjou] means earnestly to stand upon his demands for his religion, which will never be granted unto him, and so will the matter break off I suppose' (BL, Egerton MS 1693, fol. 9r). Catherine de' Medici then offered her younger son, François, duc d'Alençon, claiming that he might be more flexible in religion, but the age difference posed an apparently insuperable barrier. Both Elizabeth and Alençon kept the scheme in play during the 1570s for their respective political advantage, but few others took it seriously.

After 1571 Elizabeth's approaching middle age eliminated an heir of her body as a solution to the succession. As a result Leicester's own position underwent some significant changes. He grew restive over what he later described as being 'tied in more than unequal and unreasonable bonds … almost more than a bond man' (BL, Harley MS 6992, fol. 114v). In either 1570 or 1571 he began his affair with Douglas *Sheffield, *née* Howard, dowager Lady Sheffield (1542/3–1608), the eldest daughter of William *Howard, first Baron Howard of Effingham (*c*.1510–1573), and his second wife, Margaret. This was the first liaison he is known to have conducted since the death of his wife. In August 1574 the couple had a son, Robert *Dudley (1574–1649), and it was later claimed—though denied by Sheffield—that they had also had a daughter who died stillborn in the winter of 1572–3. From this affair there survives perhaps the most personal item of all Leicester's correspondence, a long undated letter that he wrote to Sheffield before 1574 in the course of a series of rows between them over his refusal to marry. He advised her to break off the affair and marry someone else, for he could offer her nothing more than what they had. He described his dilemma in quite moving terms:

> For you must think hit ys some marvelous cause … that forceth me thus to be cause almost of the ruyne of my none [own] howse; for ther ys no lykelyhoode that any of our boddyes of menkind lyke to have ayres; my brother you se long maryed and not lykke to have Children, yet resteth so now in myself, and yet such occasions ys ther … as yf I shuld marry I am seure never to have favor of them that I had rather yet never have wyfe than lose them, yet ys ther nothing in the world next that favor that I wold not gyve to be in hope of leaving some childern behind me, being nowe the last of our howse. ('A letter from Robert, earl of Leicester', 24)

There are a number of mysteries surrounding this affair. One is the nature of its connection to Norfolk, for Sheffield claimed many years later that he had encouraged it and that Elizabeth kept Leicester obedient by retaining a letter from the duke that would ruin him. The second is the question of whether the queen knew about the affair. There was gossip at court about it in 1573, and in May 1574 she gave Sheffield a gown for her daughter Elizabeth, which suggests that she was at court then, despite being six months pregnant. Was she prepared to turn a blind eye to a liaison? Lastly, there is the curious coincidence of the sudden rise of Christopher Hatton, Leicester's first real rival as a favourite, between 1572 and 1574. Was Hatton part of a private game that Elizabeth was playing with him?

No less mysterious are the circumstances under which the affair came to an end, and why Leicester decided to risk Elizabeth's anger by marrying on 21 September 1578 Lettice Devereux, née Knollys, dowager countess of Essex (b. after 1540, d. 1634) [see Dudley, Lettice], eldest child of Sir Francis *Knollys (1511/12–1596) and his wife, Katherine. The dowager countess of Essex had been widowed on 22 September 1576, but there were rumours about a liaison in 1575, which encouraged the story that Leicester had poisoned her husband, Walter Devereux, first earl of Essex. However, it is possible that the affair with Sheffield had died out naturally by then. According to her second husband, Sir Edward Stafford, at the time of their marriage in 1579 she simply wished it forgotten. By then she and Leicester had reached an amicable settlement over the custody of their son—whatever was said later.

Leicester also began to pay greater attention to his own estates in the early 1570s. In January 1570 he went to Kenilworth to meet Warwick on his return from the north. Thereafter every summer or autumn until 1586 he visited Kenilworth for about a fortnight, the only exception being 1583, when he had to cancel at the last minute owing to the discovery of the Throckmorton plot. In 1568 he initiated his building works at Kenilworth, and the subsequent years saw the construction of the large range now known as Leicester's Buildings. Leicester had initiated an ambitious reorganization of the tenurial structure of his Welsh lordships (Denbigh and Chirk in Denbighshire) in the late 1560s, which took to the mid-1570s to complete. He also built up the Kenilworth estate by the purchase of adjacent lands. Overall, his estate policy appears to have been one of consolidation and the creation of an estate of inheritance. In the absence of an heir of his own, his nephew Philip *Sidney (1554–1586), to whom he was more than the usual benevolent uncle, was the potential beneficiary.

Elizabeth's extensive generosity towards Leicester did not diminish. Hatton never actually became a rival; instead by the late 1570s the two settled into a genuine friendship. If the last large estates Leicester received from the queen were the lordships of Arwystli and Cyfeiliog in 1572, in 1574 he obtained several extensive grants of small parcels for immediate resale. His archives contain agreements with the ultimate purchasers in advance of the grants. In December 1576 Elizabeth loaned him £15,000, secured on the lordship of Denbigh, to be repaid by three instalments of £5000 over the next fifteen years. A final major financial asset was the farm of the customs on sweet (Mediterranean) wines. He obtained a ten-year lease of the farm from the crown in 1577, though he appears to have bought out the previous leaseholders in 1573.

The queen's backing also lay behind two subsequently notorious episodes in 1573–4: the revival of 'the great Berkeley lawsuit' and the encroachments in the forest of Snowdon. The Berkeley lawsuit had rumbled on since the early fifteenth century and, apparently, had been settled in favour of Henry Berkeley, seventh Baron Berkeley, under Mary I. Leicester's interest came from his descent from the rival claimants, but it was largely antiquarian—he actually undertook considerable historical research himself. Why he went to this trouble is curious, not least because his relations with Berkeley had previously been friendly. There was a definite political aspect to it, which involved Lady Berkeley—Norfolk's sister, Katherine—more than Berkeley himself. She had apparently blamed Elizabeth for her brother's death and also had rejected a proposal that Leicester made of a marriage between Sidney and one of her daughters.

There had undoubtedly been extensive encroachments into the lands of the forest of Snowdon by local families in north Wales who now claimed them as their freehold. Leicester, who held the office of ranger of Snowdon Forest under the crown, was able to keep the proceeds, but reclaiming the lands was a mammoth process. He offered an initial compromise, but this encountered resistance, and then the business dragged on through the decade, absorbing much of the time and energies of his estate officers. In later years both affairs were cited as evidence of his harrying of the ancient nobility and his tyrannical oppression. Yet it was equally the case that neither could have proceeded without Elizabeth's active consent—though who precisely was the instigator remains unclear.

What Leicester did with the money is an interesting point, for his accounts for the 1570s have not survived. During this decade he flourished as one of the great patrons of Elizabeth's reign, and his influence spread throughout the country. He was high steward of ten boroughs (Bristol, Great Yarmouth, King's Lynn, Abingdon, Windsor, Reading, Wallingford, Tewkesbury, St Albans, and Evesham) and had a less formal but no less powerful influence in Southampton, Chester, Coventry, and Beverley. He was an investor in the Company of Mines Royal, the Mineral and Battery Works, and the Society for the New Art. Maritime ventures were a particular interest, and he backed John Hawkins's second voyage (his profit was £301) and probably his third, the Frobisher voyage of 1576, the Gilbert voyage of 1583, and Drake's circumnavigation and West Indies voyages. The unfortunate Fenton voyage of 1582 was largely of his inspiration, and the Barbary Company of 1585 was his own creation. As part of his investment in the Fenton voyage he purchased a first-rate warship, the *Galleon Leicester*, which later took part in the West Indies voyage and the defeat of the Armada. He owned at least two other ships as well, the *White Bear* and a flyboat named the *White Lion*, which he employed in the 1570s in a lucrative trade supplying barrel staves from his Worcestershire woodlands to Spain.

Leicester was no less active in intellectual and artistic patronage. At least ninety-eight books were dedicated to him, making him one of the greatest literary patrons of the reign. As chancellor of Oxford University he sponsored the revival of the university press in 1584–5. His own library contained several hundred volumes, but unfortunately his numerous surviving household inventories do not list them. However, more than ninety-five books, both manuscript and printed, have been identified (chiefly by their bindings), scattered in libraries throughout the world. His collection of paintings and maps—distributed among his various houses—is inventoried individually, and it comprises one of the largest of the reign for which lists survive. The paintings are almost entirely portraits, and only a few can be located today. He was himself the subject of some twelve separate portraits, and (counting copies as well as originals) more survive of him than of any other Elizabethan except Burghley.

There is, however, a mystery surrounding Leicester's influence as an intellectual patron: the nature of his own involvement. It can be argued that patronage of this range was a consequence of his rank and position and was no indication of any positive commitment. Yet personal tastes and interests cannot be eliminated entirely, and his are difficult to identify, apart from history and mathematics. Many of his surviving books are presentation copies. His company of players, which was already in existence in 1559, was prominent and controversial to many of his puritan followers, yet he does not appear to have shaped the growth of the theatre in any way. He surrounded himself with some impressive intellects. His chief secretary from 1574, Arthur Atye, was the former public orator at Oxford, and he also employed the French jurist Jean Hotman. Leicester House has been seen as the centre of an important circle of poets (Sidney, Edward Dyer, and Edmund Spenser) in the early 1580s. Yet details of his own contribution remain vague, and his household was not identified with a specific intellectual or artistic ambience.

Leicester's personal tastes were not otherwise particularly extravagant, except perhaps with regard to clothes, as was expected by the queen. He was always an active sportsman, though not as much of a jouster as has been claimed. The tone of the lecture that he gave to Elizabeth on fresh air and exercise in February 1573 reveals a lot about their relations:

> So good a medycyne I have alway found exersise with the open good ayre as yt hath ever byn my best remedye ageynst those dellycate deceases gotten about yor deynty cytty of London, which place but for necessyty Lord he knoweth how sorrey I am to se yor Majesty remayne … Yf when season shall serve yor good determynacion may hold to spend some tyme abroade to finde the difference about and furder of from London, hit shalbe wel begonne now, but I wold God hit had byn long before put in profe, God graunt now that yow may finde much good therof, as yet for yor tyme heareafter yow may reape the benefytt of good contynuance of yor desired health. You se swette Lady with howe weighty matters I trowble yow withal.   (PRO, SP 15/17/205)

Leicester suffered a riding accident in April 1565 and another in August 1585, and it may have been the long-term effects of the first that caused him to visit the baths at Buxton, Derbyshire, in 1577 and 1578 for a swelling in his leg. He was relatively abstemious in diet and drink, which may account for the slurs on his gluttony in *Leicester's Commonwealth* and other Catholic libels. He followed the court fashion towards lighter white wines (in the choice of which he took a close interest), and possibly set one for salads. The corporation of Chester understood in advance of his visit in 1584 that 'his honour delighteth not in banquets' (Chester RO, AB/1/192). One of his difficulties in the Netherlands in 1586 may have been that like other Englishmen (and very much unlike Orange) he did not enjoy the Dutch passion for carousing. When his father-in-law Knollys heard of his ultimately fatal illness in September 1588 he was confident of his speedy recovery 'through your lordship's foresight and good order of diet' (Longleat House, Wiltshire, Dudley MS 2, fol. 273r). In 1585 the French ambassador Guillaume de l'Aubespeine, baron de Châteauneuf, described him as a 'beau gentilhomme … devenu fort replet', but they were all getting on a bit then (Teulet, 5.79). Leicester's almost ceaseless travelling in the Netherlands and elsewhere almost to the day of his death suggests that he was still in good shape for a man in his mid-fifties.

The Kenilworth building project was possibly Leicester's major single extravagance, but compared with the building works of colleagues such as Burghley, it was relatively modest. How much it cost is unknown. Despite hostile rumours that Leicester was fortifying Kenilworth, the purpose, like that of so many other Elizabethan courtier houses, was to accommodate the queen on future progresses. The progress of 1566 initiated a series that went much further afield than the earlier ones, and from the early 1570s Leicester encouraged the queen to undertake more. She visited Kenilworth again in 1568, 1572, and then, most famously, in 1575. There is an established tradition that the festivities at Kenilworth in 1575 marked a climax in Leicester's relations with Elizabeth, for she never went there again. However, during the following ten years the progresses in general were greatly reduced, and in the winter of 1577–8 Leicester purchased Wanstead

House in Essex, only a short distance from Greenwich Palace in Kent. His regular entertainment of Elizabeth at Wanstead suggests there was no real change in their relations. The entertainment of 1575 may well have been intended to celebrate the completion of the Kenilworth building works, and any references to marriage were less a last bid to persuade her to marry him than a signal to free him to marry someone else.

The area where Leicester's patronage became increasingly prominent, and in some circles notorious, was his continued protection for protestant nonconformity. The years from 1571 to 1573 saw a second major crisis in the church—the admonition controversy—in which the nonconformists now openly attacked the episcopate and some publicly advocated presbyterianism. Although Leicester's response was to shelter and protect individuals as he had done in the vestiarian controversy, the new context made it difficult to avoid giving the impression of deliberately supporting attacks on the episcopate, particularly when among those he protected were such leading presbyterians as Thomas Cartwright. His own assessment is best expressed in his lament to Beale of July 1571:

> For surely it is too much to see in a church professing the truth, being so well learned, so agreeable in doctrine, as generally they be, to see such squares and differences as there is among them for trifles. And it cannot be excused almost of neither party, for as some of the higher sort hath been over hard in persuasion to some of their inferior brethren, so are they of the inferior sort that use more wilfulness in some causes than reason or charity will allow. (BL, Egerton MS 1693, fol. 9r)

What his influence achieved is neatly illustrated by the case of Christopher Goodman, whom William Downham, bishop of Chester, appointed archdeacon of Richmond at his persuasion early in 1573. Downham effectively held Leicester responsible for Goodman's good behaviour: 'percase he is somewhat singular by fervent zeal of God's truth, which now more temperately he useth and by your lordship's good means and advertisement to him will be more easily reformed' (BL, Add. MS 32091, fol. 268r).

It was in the course of the admonition controversy that nonconformists were first labelled puritans. Shortly afterwards the term acquired a political definition, thanks in part to Mary, queen of Scots, who used it to describe those who were trying to remove her from the English succession in favour of Leicester's brother-in-law Huntingdon. She actually warned Leicester about this in November 1579. In the 1580s Catholic polemic claimed that, like his father, Leicester was seeking to secure the succession for his own family by keeping Elizabeth unmarried and seeking Mary's execution. The puritans were his faction, whose hostility to Mary he was exploiting. A variant also gained currency in the disciplinarian wing of the church: he was encouraging the presbyterians to overthrow the episcopate so that he and his friends could seize the estates of the church. His political motives were further highlighted by his personal behaviour, which was not easy to reconcile with the aims of puritan moralism.

By the end of the decade the combination of widespread quasi-presbyterian activity, symbolized by exercises and prophesyings, and increasing attacks on the bishops led the queen to order prophesyings to be abolished, and when Edmund Grindal, archbishop of Canterbury, stood up for them in 1577 she suspended him from office. Accusations that Leicester had been involved in the suspension of prophesyings and criticisms of his personal life inspired his famous defence to Wood on 19 August 1576: 'I stand on the topp of the hill, where I know the smallest slipp semeth a fall'. He was proud that:

> when tymes of some troble hath bene amonge the preachers and ministers of the Church for matters of ceremonies and such like, knowing many of them to be hardly handled for so small causes, who did move for them, bothe at the bishops' handes and at the Prince's?

However, he was not prepared to destroy the episcopal order—'I am so resolved to the defence of that is already established'—and the present crisis 'I feared long agoe wold prove the fruict of our discention for trifles and since for other matters' ('Letters of Thomas Wood', 94–8).

As important as Leicester's protection of nonconformity in the shaping of his puritan image was the new context of foreign policy in the 1570s. The years 1570 and 1571 saw the final efforts to rehabilitate Norfolk and to negotiate a conditional restoration of Mary to Scotland. Ironically, the terms were very similar to Leicester's proposals of 1569, but the scheme collapsed again, initially in the face of Scottish opposition, but finally after Mary and Norfolk were incriminated by the exposure of the Ridolfi plot in 1571. After his execution, Norfolk was portrayed variously as a martyr for the ancient nobility and as a victim of court treachery, with Leicester or Burghley as the villain of the piece.

The Ridolfi plot also marked the beginning of an open breach with Spain, which quickly focused on the future of the Netherlands. During the winter of 1571–2 an Anglo-French alliance in support of a new revolt led by Orange was discussed, and Leicester wished to lead the embassy to sign the Anglo-French treaty (the treaty of Blois). Once again Elizabeth would not let him go. The French alliance collapsed following the massacre of St Bartholomew's eve (24 August 1572), and Leicester was one of many who drew the conclusion, when writing to James Douglas, fourth earl of Morton, on 7 September, that:

> these my lord be good warnings to all those that be professors of the trew religion to take heed in tyme … we cannot but stand in no small danger except there be a full concurrence together of all such as mean faithfully to continue such as they profess. (Edinburgh University Library, MS De 1.12/4)

Distrust of the French crown was the key to the complexities of Elizabeth's foreign policy in the years 1573 to 1576. If it persuaded her to support Morton in Scotland, she was unsure about backing the Orangeist cause in the Netherlands and antagonizing Spain unnecessarily, when her only ally was the small and poor Palatinate.

Yet an almost emotional drive towards a confessional alliance led to the forming of a number of informal personal alliances. Within England the appointment of Walsingham as secretary of state in December 1573, with the joint backing of both Leicester and Burghley, brought one of the most active of these alliance-makers into a key position. Leicester helped to form another by sponsoring Sidney's grand tour in 1572–4, which forged closer links with the elector palatine Friedrich III and his son Johan Casimir. Between them Leicester and Walsingham seem to have been able to encourage Elizabeth to employ as diplomatic agents men sympathetic to this confessional outlook. Yet with Orange close relations were slow to develop, not least because he regarded Elizabeth with suspicion and showed more interest in the empire and France.

A transformation occurred in 1576 when the collapse of Spanish authority in the Low Countries offered the opportunity for the creation of a native government, while Philip's appointment of Don Juan of Austria—already widely associated with the 'enterprise of England'—as governor-general frightened Elizabeth. From this point Orange was seen as an ally to be backed. At the end of 1576 Elizabeth made it clear that if Don Juan did not reach a compromise with the states general of the United Provinces and the war was resumed, she would assist Orange openly. In January 1577 it was proposed that Leicester should act as commander if an army was sent. In April, Orange responded to the new climate by inviting Leicester and Elizabeth to be godparents for his daughter Elizabeth, an 'honneur que j'estime vraiment d'autant plus grand qu'en cela je vois une demonstration singuliere de la bonne affection que votre excellence me porte' (BL, Cotton MS Galba C. vi, fol. 43v).

The breakdown in relations between Don Juan and the states general in summer 1577 made the sending of the English expeditionary force a strong possibility, and in September, Leicester began actively preparing to go. However, at this point both Orange and Elizabeth drew back, Orange initially because he was worried by the political effects of an openly protestant ally on the Catholic Netherlanders, the queen because she thought it still possible that Philip would be prepared to settle. Only a small English force, commanded by Leicester's protégé John Norris, was sent over in spring 1578, while the large expedition was held in reserve. In the interval Alençon (now duc d'Anjou) approached the states general with grandiose offers of assistance.

The Anjou episode, 1578–1584 Elizabeth responded to Anjou's intervention by hinting indirectly in May 1578 that she was ready to entertain a proposal of marriage, which had being lying dormant since 1576, and that he should come for an interview. Her purpose appears to have been to divert him from his Netherlands enterprise, but he responded enthusiastically, offering to be guided entirely by her. In September 1578 Elizabeth reiterated that the unconditional interview was the necessary first step. Instead Anjou sent a delegation led by his chamberlain Jean de Simier, who on his arrival in January 1579 demanded that the marriage treaty be concluded first. This led to a stalemate not broken until late March, when Anjou agreed to come without a treaty and Elizabeth agreed to an initial discussion of terms. The all-important

issue of the exercise of his religion was reserved for discussion between Elizabeth and Anjou at the interview. Anjou eventually visited between 17 and 28 August, but he and Elizabeth spent the time very secretly at Greenwich, and after he departed it was not clear what had been agreed. Simier now pressed for a draft treaty to carry to France. The privy council discussed the marriage in general terms early in October without much enthusiasm, and it was only after pressure from Simier that a draft was agreed (with the religious clause still reserved), and he returned to France on 29 November.

Leicester's disappointment with the direction of Elizabeth's policy during summer 1578 was pronounced. On 20 July he told Walsingham that:

> I meane not to leave as long as I may have leave &
> opportunyte to put hir Majesty in better remembrance of
> this manner of course which maketh me afrayd & the more I
> love hir the more fearfull am I to see such dangerous ways
> taken, God of his mercy help all.   (PRO, SP 83/7/73)

However, at this stage no one knew how serious Elizabeth was about marrying Anjou. As a result the timing of Leicester's discreet marriage to the dowager countess of Essex at Wanstead on 21 September 1578, while the court was returning from the progress into East Anglia, is all the more curious. The officiating clergyman was his current resident chaplain, Humphrey Tyndall, and the witnesses were Warwick, Henry *Herbert, second earl of Pembroke (b. in or after 1538, d. 1601), his close friend Roger North, second Baron North, the countess's father, Sir Francis Knollys, and brother Richard Knollys, who was then in his service. In March 1581 Tyndall and the witnesses all made notarized depositions confirming the marriage (PRO, SP 12/148/75–85). The purpose of the depositions was to assure the legitimacy of the child the countess of Leicester was then carrying, their son Robert Dudley, Baron Denbigh (1581–1584), who was born at Wanstead on 6 June 1581. The witnesses gave slightly different accounts of the background to the marriage, but it is clear that with North and Warwick at least Leicester had previously discussed his desire to marry the countess and raise a family. He had also mentioned his worries about Elizabeth's reaction, and North on his own admission had encouraged him to persevere. The most obvious significance in the timing is that it fulfilled the customary two years' mourning for Essex almost to the day. If this was the case then it was devoid of any wider political import.

Yet however discreetly performed, the marriage did not remain secret for long, for Sussex told the French ambassador, Castelnau de Mauvissière, about it in early November 1578. The later revelation of the marriage to Elizabeth by Simier proved one of the most dramatic episodes of the Anjou courtship, but it is shrouded in legend. Thanks to the accounts in *Leicester's Commonwealth* and Camden's *Annales* (1615, 1628), it has been generally assumed that Simier told Elizabeth in May or June of 1579, and that Leicester was then briefly imprisoned and in revenge tried to have him murdered. This is a myth. Leicester's troubles began in November 1579 and lasted until March 1580.

There are numerous references to them by both Mauvissière (at some length) and the Spanish ambassador, Bernardino de Mendoza. Elizabeth deliberately caused Leicester major financial difficulties by demanding early repayment of the first £5000 instalment of the 1576 loan. Among the Dudley papers at Longleat House in Wiltshire are a series of draft indentures dated between 4 December 1579 and 6 January 1580 in which Leicester assigned many of his major lands and offices to family, friends, and servants as a means of raising money (Dudley MS, box 3, items 43–52). In the end he sold a number of estates to Elizabeth and on 10 March 1580 mortgaged Wanstead for £5000 to the London clothier Thomas Skinner in order to buy them back.

The sequel is equally revealing. Early in January 1580 Elizabeth informed Anjou that she would be unable to grant him the liberty of worship he had demanded. The negotiations should have petered out at this point, but there was a dramatic change in the diplomatic context. Anjou's Netherlands ambitions had been in abeyance during 1579, but early in 1580 Orange decided to renounce all allegiance to Philip and offer the sovereignty to him. The death of Enriques, king of Portugal, on 31 January 1580 also raised the question of France's challenging Philip over the Portuguese succession. For Anjou, good relations with England and with Leicester in particular—given the respect in which he was held in the Netherlands—were now essential. In April 1580 he sought to mend relations by blaming Simier and his legal adviser, the président de Combelles. Combelles had, as William Herle told Leicester on 18 May, cultivated 'such as had the worst humours and dispositions towards your lordship that might be, with whom he had his secret cabala … to undermyne your estate' (BL, Cotton MS Caligula E. vii, fol. 174v).

The timing of Leicester's troubles suggests that whatever Simier told Elizabeth he told her just before his departure, and this raises the question of the precise causes. Leicester had been appointed one of the commissioners to negotiate with him in January 1579. Unlike many of his colleagues Leicester has not left any memoranda on the subject—unless one considers that Sidney's famous letter to Elizabeth (written before the interview, not afterwards, as has often been thought) reflects his views. Early in February Leicester had a guarded conversation with Mauvissière in which he emphasized the necessity of the interview and Elizabeth's desire for an alliance with Henri III. As a gesture of goodwill he was in favour of discussing the articles of the treaty in advance. Later in the month he informed William Davison that it:

> doth seem to us all that she will marry if she may like the person and if the person adventure without condition or assurance to come. If she then like him, it is like she will have him … As for my own opinion, if I should speak according to former disposition, I should hardly believe it will take place. (BL, Harley MS 285, fols. 77r–78r)

He confessed to Shrewsbury on 10 September that he was in the dark about the outcome of Anjou's visit, despite all the speculation, 'believe me, my lord, I know no more but that he is departed even as he came hitherto' (Bath MSS, 5.24). According to the notes Burghley made of the discussions at the privy council on 6 October, Leicester like Hatton stated that he had changed his mind and now opposed the marriage owing to 'new reasons' (Murdin, 335). Immediately afterwards Leicester went on holiday to Kenilworth. From there he wrote to Burghley on 20 October that 'I doe assure your lordship since Queen Mary's time the papists were never in that jollity they be at present in this country', which suggests what the 'new reasons' were (BL, Harley MS 6992, fol. 112r).

This late reversal of opinion may have been one reason why Simier decided to attack Leicester at this stage. Another may have been John Stubbe's tract *A Gaping Gulf*, which was published in September. As in December 1567, there was widespread speculation that Leicester or Walsingham was behind it, although there is no firm evidence either way. As for the actual date, the best evidence is two undated letters from Leicester to Hatton and Burghley in which he stated his refusal to attend the privy council owing to the 'bitterness in her majesty to me' (Nicolas, 97; BL, Harley MS 6992, fol. 114r). Burghley endorsed the second letter with the date, 12 November 1579, but it is too early. There is conflicting evidence over whether Leicester was a member of the commission that negotiated the draft marriage articles with Simier between 20 and 24 November, but his only sustained absence from the privy council was between 25 and 30 November. The very eve of Simier's departure is therefore the most probable date.

No less important is what Simier told Elizabeth. Traditionally it has been assumed that he revealed the marriage at Wanstead, but since Mauvissière had reported it in November 1578, discovering it took no great detective work on Simier's part. However, it is also possible that he told her that Leicester was already married to Sheffield, who married Stafford on the eve of his own departure to France. In 1604 Stafford deposed that in February 1580 Elizabeth had tried to persuade Sheffield to admit she had been married to Leicester, for which there is some confirmation in Mauvissière's report of 8 February 1580. Sheffield's refusal to do so may have been one of the reasons for the end of the crisis. Simier's source for her marriage to Leicester may have been Combelles's allies, Charles Arundel and Lord Henry Howard. Both very prominently escorted Simier to Dover in November 1579, and he was worried about their fate after his departure.

The role Sussex played may also have been important, for there was a marked hostility between Leicester and him from this point until his death in 1583. They actually came to blows on 12 July 1581 in an incident widely recorded at the time. The cause was a dispute over the liberty of Havering atte Bower in Essex. Influence in Essex, where Sussex had lived for most of the reign and where Leicester had become a leading figure after the purchase of Wanstead, may have been the underlying issue, but the clash probably also reflected the wider tension between them. Equally curious is the long-term effect of Leicester's marriage on his relations with Elizabeth. While she appears to have regarded Sheffield as wronged, the queen never forgave the countess of Leicester, and her hostility to her was a major problem for Leicester for the rest of his life. He was forced to keep his marriage half concealed, so much so that the date of birth of his cherished son remained unknown until discovered in 1992 (Adams, 'Papers, III', 3, n. 11). Yet Elizabeth's emotional attachment to him remained unchanged, and there is no evidence of any permanent decline in his favour.

Relations with Anjou dominated Elizabeth's foreign policy between 1580 and his death on 10 June 1584, not least because he was the key to an alliance with France over the Netherlands and Portugal. The marriage itself was less important, despite the final negotiation of a marriage treaty in spring 1581. On this occasion Leicester left his strongest recorded opposition to the marriage in a letter of 26 May to Huntingdon: 'so great appearance of myslike is there in her majesty's heart toward this marriage as assuredly I can neither account him loving nor loyal that will indirectly seek to press her to it' (Hunt. L., MS HA 2377). He was also concerned over the physical danger she would risk in attempting to conceive, a worry already widely expressed in 1579. As a demonstration of English support, Elizabeth appointed him to escort Anjou to his *joyeuse entrée* in Antwerp in February 1582, the first time he had crossed the channel since 1557. The *joyeuse entrée* did at least enable him to meet Orange. In the meantime he found the cause of the Portuguese pretender Dom Antonio more attractive, and in 1581 he was deeply involved in plans for a maritime expedition to help Dom Antonio hold the Azores. Owing to difficulties in co-operation with France, this expedition was suspended, and the only result was the Fenton voyage of 1582, an attempt to open commercial contact with the East Indies, of which Leicester was the chief promoter.

Elizabeth's wider foreign policy was also inhibited by the rebellion in Ireland of Gerald fitz James Fitzgerald, fourteenth earl of Desmond (1579–83), and the unstable state of Scotland following Morton's fall at the end of 1580. During Sir Henry Sidney's lord deputyships, Leicester had become heavily involved in Irish government, not least because Sidney relied on a number of his followers and friends, such as Sir Nicholas Bagnall, Sir Nicholas Maltby, and Lord Upper Ossory. Sidney's successors, Sir William Drury and Sir William Pelham, were also among Leicester's followers. They kept Leicester fully informed of Irish affairs, and he was even mentioned as a possible lord deputy himself in 1575. On the other hand he showed no interest in confiscated Irish estates when they were suggested to him in 1580.

The Spanish-assisted landing of James fitz Maurice Fitzgerald—which inspired the Desmond rebellion—coincided with Anjou's visit and undoubtedly contributed to the tension surrounding it. The privy council united on a rapid military response, and Leicester's hand can be seen in the appointment of the new lord deputy, Arthur Grey, fourteenth Baron Grey of Wilton, in 1580. The danger posed by the Desmond rebellion probably accounted for his bleak reaction to the massacre at Smerwick on 10 November—'I trust hit wylbe a warning how theyr fellows attempt the lyke'. He was more upset by the death there of Sir John Cheke's son, 'Mr John Cheke, a querry under my rule, a tall valiant gentleman he was' (*Bath MSS*, 5.31). More curious was his possible role in the replacement of Grey by Ormond as lord-general in Munster at the end of 1582, for he was on the receiving end of much of the running criticism of Ormond's more discriminating policy. There was even gossip in Ireland that:

> the erles sending hether was a practice of the erle of Leicester to banish the woulfe from the doore, holding it a great pollicie in your lordship to rid so greate an enemy as hee is to yow from the presence of the Queene. (BL, Cotton MS Titus B. xiii, fols. 357*v*–358*r*)

Morton's fall provoked a major debate over the military intervention to save him in spring 1581, which Leicester appears to have supported. Thereafter Leicester provided a friendly reception for Morton's nephew Archibald Douglas, eighth earl of Angus, when he went into exile in England after Morton's execution in June 1581. The next few years saw a complex struggle for control of the young Scottish king. Leicester had an agent, Roger Aston, in James's privy chamber. It was to counter Leicester's possible influence over her son in 1583 that Mary began spreading stories that he was scheming to marry James to his step-daughter Dorothy Devereux (*b*. 1564?) and his son Denbigh to Arabella Stuart. Scottish policy in summer 1584 was the subject of the one political memorandum Leicester wrote to Elizabeth, in which he noted that he 'never used lyke before'. He urged her not to fear war with James and to embody any agreement with Mary and the Scottish king in an act of parliament. Their claims to the succession were to be forfeit if Elizabeth was harmed in any way, an arrangement that possibly inspired the bond of association several months later. In the winter of 1584–5 Leicester achieved an important success when he won over James's current favourite, Patrick Gray, master of Gray, and laid the groundwork for the treaty of 1586.

The Netherlands, 1584–1587 It was to the death of Anjou and the assassination of Orange in summer 1584 that Leicester owed the climax of his political career, his governor-generalship of the Netherlands. The death of Sussex, followed by the discovery of the Throckmorton plot at the end of 1583, had ushered in an unusual degree of harmony on the privy council. However, there was a cloud on the horizon: the promotion in August 1583 of John Whitgift as archbishop of Canterbury after several senior bishops had for various reasons been excluded. There is evidence that Whitgift gave Leicester an assurance that he intended to follow a moderate policy towards puritan nonconformity before his election. However, he then ordered a new campaign for subscription in the autumn, and Leicester's attempt to engineer a compromise in the Lambeth conference of December 1584 failed. Whitgift and his allies responded by emphasizing the threat to the church lands. After 1584 there was a distinct personal animus between them that lasted until Leicester's death.

With the decline in royal progresses in the 1580s Leicester's own holiday journeys expanded, and 1584 saw the most extensive. It took him to Denbigh and Chester for the first and only time, and according to Mauvissière at least sparked some jealousy in Elizabeth. On his return he was faced both by the crisis in the Netherlands and by a personal tragedy, the death of his three-year-old son, Denbigh, at Wanstead on 19 July. Leicester left the court to mourn with his wife, but neither appears to have attended Denbigh's funeral at Wanstead on 1 August. Nor was Leicester present at his interment in the Beauchamp chapel of St Mary's, Warwick, on 20 October, though he left the court at that point to see his illegitimate son at Witney in Oxfordshire. He presumably commissioned Denbigh's funeral monument, though no records survive. Denbigh's death meant the end of his hopes for a legitimate heir of his body and undoubtedly coloured the remaining years of his life.

In September 1584 the first copies of the tract *Leicester's Commonwealth* were discovered in London. It was compiled in Paris in the previous spring and went to press at Robert Persons's printer at Rouen just before Denbigh's death. There has been much debate over the authorship and purpose of the tract, but the origins lie in Persons's plan to distribute propaganda about Leicester's and Huntingdon's threat to Mary and 'la tirannide delli ministri' in advance of a Catholic invasion in 1582 (Kretzschmar, 144). Coincidentally a copy of this plan fell into Walsingham's hands, and he at least appreciated the context of *Leicester's Commonwealth*. It was a deliberate exercise in character assassination, relating a number of incidents in Leicester's life beginning with the death of Amy Dudley in a way that revealed him as a lecher, a murderer, and a tyrant. The tract also displays a considerable knowledge of the court politics surrounding the Anjou marriage, which has suggested that some of Simier's former allies were the actual authors. The leading candidate was Arundel, who had gone into exile in Paris in December 1583 after the exposure of the Throckmorton plot. The tract also made public Leicester's affair with Sheffield, and since she was then residing in Paris with Stafford, who was ambassador at the French court, a question mark hangs over her role as well.

Whatever malicious pleasure *Leicester's Commonwealth* gave to exile circles at the time, its real impact came later, when it appeared to offer a secret history of Elizabeth's court and by discrediting their champion supplied ammunition to anti-puritan polemic. It has been noted that the majority of the large number of surviving manuscript copies date from the seventeenth century. Although possibly the most spectacular, it was not the first (or last) violent Catholic polemic against Elizabeth's government and if anything helped to draw the regime together in the face of the Netherlands crisis in the winter of 1584–5. It is one of the myths of the reign that the military intervention in the Netherlands was a factional victory by a war party led by Leicester and Walsingham over a peace party led by Burghley. The apparent English hesitation was caused by the Dutch decision to pursue what appeared to be a more generous offer by Henri and Elizabeth's wish to co-operate with France. Once it was known in February 1585 that

Henri would not intervene, the English moved very rapidly. It was a combination of complicated Dutch decision-making and bad weather in the channel that delayed the arrival of the Dutch embassy until the end of June. Leicester's willingness to lead any large-scale English expeditionary force was known in February 1585—if not before—but his involvement was not a primary issue in the negotiation of the two treaties at Nonsuch in August. Immediately afterwards he departed for a holiday at Kenilworth, taking his wife with him (possibly for the first time). There he injured his foot in a riding accident, and while lying in bed at nearby Stoneleigh he was informed that, on learning of the surrender of Antwerp, Elizabeth had decided to send him to the Netherlands.

Between Leicester's return to court in September and his departure for Flushing in December, the preparation of his expedition was plagued by a series of debates over its structure and purpose. Although Elizabeth was angry with him for taking his wife to Warwickshire (not, as often thought, to the Netherlands), she also raised objections to his denuding the country of trained military officers. Even more serious were her personal reservations about letting him depart at all. After spending the night of 27 September with her, he sent Walsingham what is perhaps his most revealing description of their relationship:

> Mr. Secretary, I find hir majesty very desirous to stey me, she makes the cause only the dowtfullnes of hir owen self, by reason of hir often decease taking hir of late & this last night worst of all. She used very pittyfull words to me of hir fear she shall not lyve & wold not have me from hir. You can consider what manner of perswasion this must be to me from hir. (PRO, SP 12/182/41)

To finance his expenses he took out a fresh and crippling mortgage of the lordship of Denbigh for £17,000. His possible political role presented further difficulties. Elizabeth had strong views about what she wanted accomplished, including the dangerous issue of forcing the Dutch to co-operate in the English blockade of Spain. Yet he was provided with no authority other than his military command over the English forces and only an informal instruction to advise the Dutch on political matters. When he left England he was far from confident about his prospects, telling Burghley on 5 December:

> My lord, no man feleth comfort but they have cause of grefe and no men have so much nede of relyfe and comfort as those that goe in these dowbtfull servyces. I pray you my lord help us to be kept in comfort, for we wyll hazard our lyves for yt. (*Correspondance*, 24)

Despite the season Leicester had a rapid and easy passage to Flushing over the night of 9 December, but was then delayed by fog on his way to Holland, while bad weather in the North Sea severely restricted communication with England over the next two months. As a result he felt abandoned, while Elizabeth, always restive when he was away, grew suspicious. It was against this background that he took his fateful decision to accept appointment as governor-general of the Netherlands from the states general, and was sworn in on 15 January 1586 os. It has been claimed that the grand reception he received went to his head, but the disputes over his role before he left England suggest that there was more design to it. The main justification was the belief held widely in both England and the Netherlands that the main weakness of Dutch government was the lack of a central authority. A more interesting role was played by rumours that Elizabeth was entering peace discussions with Alessandro Farnese, duke of Parma, loudly relayed from Antwerp, which Leicester felt necessary to counter with a demonstration of commitment. The delayed notification of Elizabeth provoked the dispatch of Sir Thomas Heneage with her celebrated order to Leicester to resign of 10 February. However, when she cooled down, she grudgingly accepted that Leicester 'had no other meaning and intent then to advaunce our service [and] to think of sum waye how the point concerning the absolut title may be qualified, in such sort as the authoritie may, notwithstanding, remayn' (ibid., 209–10). It may have been Heneage, though, who advised Leicester to lay the blame on William Davison, the commander of Flushing. This was one of the shabbiest actions of Leicester's life, not least because Davison was easily able to disprove the claim that 'you dyd chifely perswade me' (ibid., 169).

Elizabeth's public repudiation of his office dealt a blow to his prestige from which he never recovered, but Leicester was also probably too old and lacking in experience in military high command for the role he undertook. His assumption of both political and military authority was a huge task, particularly when he was caught between Elizabeth and the states general (or more effectively the states of Holland), who had radically different views of the role he was to perform. He appreciated that the Dutch needed an effective field army and took immediate measures to create one. Yet to fund it he was dependent on a supplementary levy from the states general, for Elizabeth restricted her financial assistance to what was agreed at Nonsuch. He also decided to recruit a further large contingent from England—above those Elizabeth had agreed to at Nonsuch—and they were to be paid for by the Dutch supplementary levy. The payment of the original English contingent was already in difficulties before he arrived, and he worsened the situation by issuing a full pay to all the English troops on his arrival. From this point on his finances were always seriously in arrears, and such money as he received from England was frequently used to supply advances supposedly to be reimbursed by the Dutch.

Leicester was also inhibited by Elizabeth's instructions to fight a defensive war, which meant conceding the strategic initiative to Parma. Although delayed by the dispute over the governor-generalship, in spring 1586 he undertook a subtle manoeuvre to cut out the garrison of Nijmegen, only to have it collapse when the governor of the key town of Grave capitulated on 28 May without a fight. The decision to court-martial and execute the governor looked like a petty act of vengeance and stimulated Dutch resentment of an English take-over. This was already brewing over the proclamation (*placcart*) banning trade with Spain that—following Elizabeth's instructions—he had issued

in April. There were also major personality clashes with two key figures: his former protégé Norris, who had commanded the initial English contingent, and Paul Buys, *landsadvocaat* of Utrecht and one of the architects of the Anglo-Dutch alliance. Both men were notoriously difficult to deal with, and the responsibility was probably mutual. Nevertheless, the clash with Norris split the English army, while the arrest of Buys in Utrecht on 9 July (which Leicester at least winked at) revealed Leicester's political commitment to the more open Calvinists. They were his most fervent Dutch supporters, but they were a minority, and many of them émigrés from the southern Netherlands, far from popular with the natives of the northern provinces.

After the surrender of Grave, the deliberate foot-dragging of the states of Holland over the supplementary levy (partly in retaliation for the ban on trade) and delays in the arrival of his new English levies forced Leicester onto the defensive. However, Parma was under orders to clear out the remaining protestant garrisons in the archbishopric of Cologne, and moved south-west, taking Venlo (18 June) and then Neuss (25 July). Leicester's enemies made capital out of his failure to relieve these towns, but they were distant and not of immediate importance. However, Parma then laid siege to Rheinberg, and the danger of his crossing the Rhine released the necessary funds in late July. In mid-August, Leicester advanced into Gelderland to break the siege of Rheinberg. At the end of August he laid siege to the outlying garrison at Doesburg, taking such an interest in the planting of the batteries that he and Pelham got themselves lost in the middle of the night of 30 August 'insomuch as we found ourselves suddenly almost at the verie gate of the town', and Pelham was wounded (*Correspondance*, 401). Doesburg surrendered on 2 September, and he then invested Zutphen, the principal Spanish garrison in the province. The investment forced Parma to march north to resupply Zutphen and led to the skirmish in which Sidney was mortally wounded (22 September). Although the death of his nephew and heir on 17 October blighted his success, Leicester rounded off the campaign by taking several of the key forts outside Zutphen, before dispersing the army into garrison in early October.

The beginning of Leicester's Gelderland campaign coincided with the discovery of the Babington plot, and both Burghley and Walsingham wanted him to return to assist in overcoming Elizabeth's reluctance to proceed to the execution of Mary. He also hoped to use the occasion to lobby for a greater commitment from Elizabeth for the following year. Norris was left in command of the English troops, but in a disastrous conclusion to their earlier disputes, Leicester gave commissions to Norris's enemies that freed them from his authority. As a result Norris was able to do little to prevent Sir William Stanley and Rowland Yorke from negotiating with Parma and defecting with their garrisons on 18–19 January 1587. Stanley's motive may have been fear of implication in the Babington plot, but the episode did grave damage to the political credibility of English military assistance.

Leicester returned to England on 24 November 1586. His main role in the final stages of Mary's life appears to have been to work on the Scottish king. Through the ambassadors James sent to plead for his mother, he emphasized the necessity for the king to concede her execution if he wished to retain his place in the English succession. In the event that the king did, however, Leicester promised his support and the neutralization of any challenge from Huntingdon (Cameron, 1.242–3). This advice James appears to have accepted, for when Leicester died eighteen months later he was very worried that he had lost his chief supporter in England. Leicester was with Burghley when Davison brought the signed warrant for Mary's execution to him on 1 February 1587 and backed the decision to go ahead, but on 6 February he went on holiday to Wanstead and was absent when Elizabeth exploded at the news.

For Leicester the fate of Mary was overshadowed by a major dispute over the financing of the war. In September 1586 the states general had charged that he had committed them to expenditures they could not meet and then wasted their money by incompetence and maladministration, grossly inflating the sums they had actually supplied. Thomas Wilkes forwarded their complaints to Elizabeth without criticism, and when Leicester returned he faced a grilling over his financial administration: 'I thought myself very hardly handled … considering the cause apperteined to the examynacion of commissioners & audytors, and no wey possible for me to gyve her majesty such a partycular reckonyng of the expenses as she looked for' (PRO, SP 12/198/40). The defections of Stanley and Yorke provided an excuse for the states of Holland, now led by Johan van Oldenbarnevelt, who had recently become *landsadvocaat* of Holland, to oppose a resumption of Leicester's governor-generalship and to dismantle the structure he had created in the previous year. Wilkes, who remained as resident agent in the Netherlands, sent highly critical reports to Walsingham, blaming Leicester, thinly disguised under the code name Themistocles, for the whole crisis.

Whether Leicester would return to the Netherlands was now an open question, and in an effort to resolve the differences Elizabeth sent Thomas Sackville, first Baron Buckhurst, as a special envoy to the states general in March 1587, ostensibly to learn their response to Leicester's counter-charges. However, like Wilkes, Buckhurst accepted most of the Dutch case. The situation was further complicated by the queen's demand that the Dutch participate in her negotiations for a peace settlement. At the beginning of April 1587 Leicester and Warwick went to Bath to take the waters. Leicester now wished his 'speedy discharge of any charge in the Low Countries', but on his way back he was informed by Walsingham that Elizabeth wanted him to return as soon as possible, having received reports that Parma was about to attack the Flemish ports of Ostend and Sluys (BL, Harley MS 287, fol. 22r). Since 1584 the two towns had been outposts which the states of Holland (though not Zealand) had little interest in defending, but because they were of possible use in an invasion of England, English garrisons had been placed in them. With his usual opportunism Parma began with Sluys, the less important port of the two, and at the beginning of June 1587 Sir Roger Williams brought a small Anglo-Dutch reinforcement for the garrison.

To relieve Sluys substantial reinforcements from England were necessary, and it was not until the day after his birthday (25 June 1587) that Leicester crossed from Margate, Kent, to Flushing. There he found great difficulty in gaining co-operation from Holland. In mid-July he attempted to raise the siege by sending his army via Ostend, but Parma got there first. On 25 July he tried to destroy the boom across the harbour by a fireship, but it failed to ignite and he did not rush the barrier. On the following day Williams finally surrendered. Yet the loss of Sluys was not a total disaster: it made Williams's reputation ('he is to be cherished', Leicester wrote) and cost Parma such heavy casualties that Ostend was safe for the rest of the summer (*CSP for.*, 1587, 233). On Leicester's arrival in Zealand his English critics, Buckhurst, Norris, and Wilkes, had left for England, Wilkes and Norris without meeting him. They were imprisoned on their return, and a long series of charges and counter-charges were exchanged, which, however informative as to the issues, did not clarify them. Leicester was reconciled to Buckhurst and Norris when he returned to England, but Wilkes remained under arrest until the earl's death.

Elizabeth also wanted Leicester to persuade the Dutch to co-operate with her peace negotiations, but he had little taste for this role as he considered the negotiations fruitless at best. The states of Holland had informed Buckhurst that they would not take part, and the queen gave Leicester the potentially dangerous instruction to use his influence with 'such as have best credit with the common sort of people to like and embrace peace' (Oosterhoff, 175). There was considerable resentment against the states of Holland (particularly in Zealand) for the loss of Sluys, and Leicester sought to capitalize on it in order to create an English party in Holland. Early in October a conspiracy (which possibly had his sympathy) to overturn the town council of Leiden was broken, and this led to charges that he was planning a military coup against the states.

Leicester's health had not been good throughout the summer, and he received permission to return to England in October. He was then delayed by rumours of a Spanish attack on Zealand and did not depart until 4 December. Elizabeth rewarded his services by appointing him to the post of lord steward of the household, an office vacant since 1570. Just before his departure to the Netherlands he had surrendered the mastership of the horse to his stepson Robert *Devereux, second earl of Essex (1565–1601), but he was not promoted then; he is first referred to as lord steward on 2 November 1587. An immediate consequence of this appointment was his introduction of a system of compounding for purveyance at the beginning of 1588, a much needed reform, but one not fully completed by the time he died.

Leicester's final year, 1588 Leicester's return to England coincided with the great debates over the threatened Spanish naval attack in 1588. He was quite convinced it was coming, but his direct influence on the overall strategy to be adopted against the Armada is not immediately clear, not least because he was ill for a fortnight during the crucial period at the end of April. He was, however, very much involved in the military preparations, particularly the construction of a boom across the Thames at Tilbury, Essex, and the establishing of a fortified camp there. The camp was based on the assumption that the Armada would attempt to enter the Thames and land its troops in Essex, though a bridge of boats was also built in case the landing was made in Kent. On 21 July he left the court for Gravesend, where he was sent a commission as lord lieutenant of the southern parts should he need to operate in Kent; this was the origin of Camden's story that Elizabeth appointed him lord lieutenant of England and Ireland. For all the effort he put into organizing the camp, it was not put to the test, and Leicester's most enduring contribution to the defeat of the Armada was in arranging Elizabeth's visit to Tilbury on 8 and 9 August. This revealed a perceptive grasp of public relations. After Elizabeth had acquainted him 'with yor secret determynacion for yor person', he advised against 'imploying yor owne person in this daungerous action … yet wyll I not that in some sort, so princely and so rare a magnanymytye shold not appere to yor people and the world as yt ys'. As a compromise she should 'spend two or three days to se both the camp and the fort' (PRO, SP 12/213/79). Yet even the visit was controversial, for the privy council was seriously worried that Elizabeth might be the target for an assassination attempt if she left the safety of Richmond Palace, Surrey.

After disbanding the Tilbury camp in mid-August Leicester returned briefly to court and then left on the 27th, initially for a holiday at Kenilworth with his wife and the earl and countess of Warwick. At Rycote on the 29th he wrote Elizabeth a brief note, which she later endorsed 'his last letter' (PRO, SP 12/215/114). A day or two later he suddenly fell ill—probably of a malarial infection—at Cornbury House in the forest of Wychwood, Oxfordshire, and he died there on 4 September. The room in which he is believed to have died still bears his name. The suddenness of Leicester's death was a major surprise, but in retrospect it was clear that the two years in the Netherlands had definitely weakened his health, and his exertions in summer 1588 had not helped.

Leicester's first surviving will was drafted on 30 January 1582, the date of his departure to escort Anjou to Antwerp, a channel crossing being the conventional occasion for doing so. He nominated his wife his executrix and left her a generous jointure, but assumed Denbigh would inherit. If Denbigh died without heirs the estate was to go to Sidney, while Robert Dudley, referred to simply as 'an infant', was left only a small property (Longleat House, Wiltshire, Dudley MS, box 3, item 56). Leicester does not appear to have made a will when he went to the Netherlands in 1585, presumably because Sidney was already named his heir. However, soon after he arrived there (6 February 1586) he made a settlement leaving further lands to Dudley. His last will was drafted at Middelburg in the week after the loss of Sluys. The main change was his nomination of Warwick as his heir, and Dudley after him; he left only a minor bequest to his godson and nephew Robert *Sidney, later first earl of Leicester (1563–1626). In both wills he requested to be buried in St Mary's, Warwick, 'where sundry myne ancestors do lie' (Warks. CRO, CR 1600/LH4).

Leicester's will was given to his widow immediately after his death, and as executrix she inherited the nightmare of his debts. Although his assets in both land and moveables were formidable, so were his debts, notably the outstanding loan from Elizabeth and the mortgage of Denbigh for his Netherlands expenses. The Netherlands effectively broke him: his financial state would have been much healthier had he died in 1585. An unintended consequence of the settlement of his estate was the assembly of his various household inventories and accounts, which now form one of the largest collections of personal material left by any Elizabethan. It is famously said that only Elizabeth mourned his passing. However, this is to discount the large numbers—led by his wife, Essex, and Huntingdon—who attended his funeral at Warwick on 10 October 1588, as well as those in the Netherlands, like Henry Killigrew, who wished to do so.

The posthumous destruction of Leicester's reputation has a number of causes. Robert Dudley and Essex had their own battles to fight, and the Dudley family interest disintegrated. There were also two institutions that had a direct interest in discrediting him. One was the episcopate, for whom Whitgift's defence of the church and its lands against Leicester's grasping designs was a victory in its campaign against the puritan clergy and their lay sympathizers. The other was the states of Holland, proud of their defence of their provincial liberties against the 'Leicesterian tyranny'. The image of the arrogant English courtier seen off by the stout-hearted burghers of Holland became enshrined in Dutch republican historiography. Yet these negative images also reflected the failure of the two policies with which he was most closely associated. Calvinist confessionalism was not a solution to the complexities of Dutch politics. His protection of individual puritan nonconformists was increasingly difficult to justify in the face of Whitgift's charges of presbyterian conspiracy.

The decisive blow was struck several decades later by Camden's portrayal of Leicester as the ambitious and malign favourite in the *Annales*. Camden embodies much of *Leicester's Commonwealth*, but the overall portrait is almost openly derived from Tacitus's Sejanus. The precise grounds for Camden's hostility to Leicester remain obscure, but his opposition to puritanism was undoubtedly one. Burghley's initial patronage of the *Annales* has led some to argue that Camden was simply the mouthpiece for his long-standing resentment of Leicester, but whether Camden actually wrote anything in the 1590s is still debated. More significant was the possible influence of Henry Howard, now earl of Northampton, and Sir Robert Cotton on the final version, for Northampton definitely had old scores to pay off. Whoever was ultimately responsible, the *Annales* quickly established Elizabeth's reign as an age of equipoise and balance, and in the process 'the great earl' was reduced to a mere by-product of her feminine weakness.   SIMON ADAMS

Sources wardrobe account: John Dudley, Viscount Lisle and earl of Warwick, 1550, Bodl. Oxf., MS Add. C. 94 · registre de Michel de Castelnau, seigneur de Mauvissière, 1578–81, Bibliothèque Nationale de France, Paris, MS français 15793 · papiers d'état et de l'audience, National State Archives, Brussels · BL, Harley MSS · BL, Cotton MSS · BL, Add. MSS · BL, Egerton MSS · Longleat House, Wiltshire, Dudley MSS · Longleat House, Wiltshire, Talbot MSS · letters of state, Magd. Cam. · secretaria de estado, Archivo General de Simancas · Cecil MSS, Hatfield House, Hertfordshire · CKS, Penshurst papers, U1475 · state papers domestic, Elizabeth I, PRO, SP 12 · state papers domestic, addenda, PRO, SP 15 · state papers Ireland, Elizabeth I, PRO, SP 63 · state papers Holland and Flanders, PRO, SP 83 · close rolls, PRO, C54 · will, PRO, PROB 11/37, sig. 26 [duchess of Northumberland] · assembly minute books, Ches. & Chester ALSS · U. Edin. L., Drummond of Hawthornden MSS, MS De · J. Woolley, letter-book, CUL, department of manuscripts and university archives, letters 8 · Child family estates: Wanstead, Essex RO, DCw · Hunt. L., Hastings papers · Lancs. RO, Lord Lilford of Bankhall papers, Ddli · Leicester's Hospital records, Warks. CRO, CR 1600/LH · *CSP for.*, 1547–88 · *The whole works of Roger Ascham*, ed. G. A. Giles, 3 vols. (1865) · J. G. Nichols, ed., *The chronicle of Queen Jane, and of two years of Queen Mary*, CS, old ser., 48 (1850) · 'A letter of Jane, duchess of Northumberland in 1553', ed. S. J. Gunn, *EngHR*, 114 (1999), 1268–71 · R. J. Haughey, ed., *The Arundel Harrington MS. of Tudor poetry*, 2 vols. (1960) · S. Adams, ed., *Household accounts and disbursement books of Robert Dudley, earl of Leicester, 1558–1561, 1584–1586*, CS, 6 (1995) · I. W. Archer, S. Adams, and G. Bernard, eds., 'A "journall" of matters of state … untill the yere 1562', *Religion, politics and society in sixteenth-century England*, CS [forthcoming] · Baron Kervyn de Lettenhove [J. M. B. C. Kervyn de Lettenhove] and L. Gilliodts-van Severen, eds., *Relations politiques des Pays-Bas et de l'Angleterre sous le règne de Philippe II*, 11 vols. (Brussels, 1882–1900) · M. A. S. Hume, ed., *Calendar of letters and state papers relating to English affairs, preserved principally in the archives of Simancas*, 4 vols., PRO (1892–9) · 'Letters of Thomas Wood, puritan, 1566–1577', ed. P. Collinson, *BIHR*, special suppl., 5 (1960) [whole issue]; repr. in P. Collinson, *Godly people: essays on English protestantism and puritanism* (1983), 45–107 · J. Bruce, ed., *Correspondence of Robert Dudley, earl of Leycester*, CS, 27 (1844) · A. I. Cameron, ed., *The Warrender papers*, Scottish History Society, 3rd ser., 18–19 (1931–2) · J. Gairdner, ed., *Three fifteenth-century chronicles*, CS, new ser., 28 (1880) · *Correspondance diplomatique de Bertrand de Salignac de la Mothe Fénélon*, ed. A. Teulet, 7 vols., Bannatyne Club, 67 (1838–40) · *CSP Scot.*, 1547–88 · W. Camden, *Annales: the true and royall history of the famous Empresse Elizabeth*, trans. A. Darcie (1625) · 'A letter from Robert, earl of Leicester, to a lady', ed. C. Read, *Huntington Library Bulletin*, 9 (1936), 14–26 · J. B. A. T. Teulet, ed., *Relations politiques de la France et de l'Espagne avec l'Écosse au XVIème siècle: papiers d'état, pièces et documents inédits*, new edn, 5 vols. (Paris, 1862) · *Calendar of the manuscripts of the marquis of Bath preserved at Longleat, Wiltshire*, 5 vols., HMC, 58 (1904–80) · N. H. Nicolas, ed., *Memoirs of the life and times of Christopher Hatton KG* (1847) · W. Murdin, ed., *Collection of state papers … left by William Cecil, Lord Burghley … 1571–96* (1759) · *The diaries of John Dee*, ed. E. Fenton (1998) · D. C. Peck, ed., *Leicester's commonwealth: the copy of a letter written by a master of art of Cambridge (1584) and related documents* (1985) · *APC* · S. Adams, *Leicester and the court: essays on Elizabethan politics* (2002) · S. Adams, 'The papers of Robert Dudley, earl of Leicester, I', *Archives*, 20 (1992), 63–85 · S. Adams, 'The papers of Robert Dudley, earl of Leicester, II', *Archives*, 20 (1993), 131–44 · S. Adams, 'The papers of Robert Dudley, earl of Leicester, III', *Archives*, 22 (1996), 1–26 · S. Adams, 'The release of Lord Darnley

and the failure of the amity', *Mary Stewart: queen in three kingdoms*, ed. M. Lynch (1988), 123–53 · J. Kretzschmar, *Die Invasionsprojekte der katholischen Mächte gegen England zur Zeit Elizabeths* (Leipzig, 1892) · F. G. Oosterhoff, *Leicester and the Netherlands, 1586–1587* (1988) · P. E. J. Hammer, *The polarisation of Elizabethan politics: the political career of Robert Devereux, 2nd earl of Essex, 1585–1597* (1999) · E. Rosenberg, *Leicester patron of letters* (1956) · W. E. Moss, *Bindings from the library of Robert Dudley, earl of Leicester, 1533–1588* (1934) · H. R. Woudhuysen, 'Leicester's literary patronage: a study of the English court, 1578–1582', DPhil diss., U. Oxf., 1981 · J. E. L. Clark, 'The building and art collections of Robert Dudley, earl of Leicester (with notes on his portraits)', MA diss., U. Lond., 1981 · J. Voorthuis, 'Portraits of Leicester', *The Dutch in crisis, 1585–1588: people and politics in Leicester's time* (Leiden, 1988), 53–70 · Bibliothèque Nationale de France, Paris, MS français 15970 · *Correspondance inédite de Robert Dudley, comte de Leycester, et de François et Jean Hotman*, ed. P. J. Blok (Haarlem, 1911) · *Correspondentie van Robert Dudley graaf van Leycester en andere documenten betreffende zijn gouvernement-generaal in de Nederlanden, 1585–1588*, ed. H. Brugmans, 3 vols. (Utrecht, 1931) · R. Broesma and G. Busken Huet, eds., *Brieven over het Leycestersche tijdvak uit de papieren van Jean Hotman* (Utrecht, 1913) · F. von Bezold, ed., *Briefe des Pfalzgaven Johann Casimer mit verwandten Schriftstücken*, 3 vols. (Munich, 1882–1903)

Archives Christ Church Oxf., corresp. and papers · Longleat House, Wiltshire, corresp. · V&A NAL, copy of the 1583 wardrobe inventory of his household | Archives du Ministère des Affaires Étrangères, Paris, corresp. 1584–87, correspondance politique, Hollande, vols. 2–4 · Arundel Castle, West Sussex, corresp. with earls of Shrewsbury · Bayerisches Hauptstaatsarchiv, Munich, corresp. 1580–87, Kurpfälzischen Bestände, Kasten Schwartz 16691–16694 · BL, Evelyn papers · BL, Cotton MSS, corresp. and papers · BL, Harley MSS, corresp. relating to Low Countries, etc. · BL, corresp. relating to Low Countries, Add. MS 29302 · BL, journal written in Holland, Add. MS 48014 [transcript] · BL, corresp., Add. MSS 32091–32092, 33207, 33271 · Hatfield House, Hertfordshire, letters and papers · Inner Temple, London, letters and papers · Lincs. Arch., corresp. relating to the Netherlands, Ancaster (Willoughby d'Eresby) · Magd. Cam., corresp. · NL Scot., corresp. relating to Mary, queen of Scots, MS 3657 · Rigsarkivet, Copenhagen, corresp. 1582–88, Tyske Kancellis Udenrigske Afdeling, England, A.II.9, items 100–123 · Staffs. RO, corresp. with Lords Paget · Teylers Museum, Haarlem, corresp. 1581–88, MS 2376

Likenesses attrib. S. van der Meulen, oils, c.1560–1565, Wallace Collection, London · attrib. S. van der Meulen, oils, c.1564, priv. coll.; copy, Yale U. CBA · miniature, c.1565, Belvoir Castle, Leicestershire · R. Hogenberg, woodcut, 1568, BL · oils, c.1570–1572, NPG · F. Zuccaro, pencil drawing, 1575, BM · oils, c.1575, NPG [*see illus.*] · N. Hilliard, miniature, 1575–80, priv. coll. · N. Hilliard, miniature, 1576, NPG · oils, c.1585–1586, Parham, West Sussex · N. Hilliard, miniature, c.1585–1588, Penshurst Place, Kent · W. Segar, oils, c.1587, Hatfield House, Hertfordshire; versions, Warwick Castle, Warwickshire, Penhurst Place, Kent · J. Hollemans, tomb effigy, c.1588, St Mary's Church, Warwick, Beauchamp chapel · M. Gheeraerts senior, group portrait, etching (*Procession of Garter knights, 1576*), BM · R. Hogenberg, woodcut, BL; repro. in *The bishop's Bible* (1568) · W. Passe, line engraving (after W. Segar, c.1585–1586), BM, NPG; repro. in H. Holland, *Heröologia* (1620) · G. Scharf, drawing, NPG · oils, second version, Hatfield House, Hertfordshire

Wealth at death assets incl. debts owing £59,006; £2544 p.a. landed income: probate inventory, BL, Harley MSS, roll D 35 · lands (excl. leasehold) valued at £2600 p.a., 20 Dec 1588: Hunt. L., EL 763

Dudley, Sir Robert (1574–1649), mariner and landowner, was born at Sheen House, Richmond, Surrey, on 7 August 1574, the son of Robert *Dudley, earl of Leicester (1532/3–1588), and Douglas *Sheffield (née Howard), Lady Sheffield (1542/3–1608). The status of his birth, which was to

Sir Robert Dudley (1574–1649), by Nicholas Hilliard, *c.*1591–3

become the leading obsession of his life, is still debated, as are the circumstances of his early life, due in part to his own deliberate exaggerations and falsifications. Despite his mother's later claim that she refused to surrender him to Leicester for fear he would have him killed, he was in fact brought up in the households first of Leicester's cousin and servant John Dudley of Stoke Newington and then of his friend Lord North. In the early 1580s he appears to have moved freely between his parents. He was undoubtedly the 'Roben my lords bastard by my lady of Essex' whom Richard Madox saw in Leicester House in March 1582 (Donno, 92), rather than Leicester's legitimate son, Robert (1581–1584), lord of Denbigh, who was only nine months old at the time. After Denbigh's death the earl transferred his affections to his illegitimate son. By then Dudley was living near Witney (possibly with his godfather Sir Henry Lee at Woodstock), but in spring 1585 he moved to Sir Thomas West's house at Offington, Sussex. He was probably the Robert Dudley who was a mourner at the funeral of the third Lord Dudley (who had married his aunt) in August 1586.

Disputes over inheritance Dudley matriculated as an undergraduate of Christ Church, Oxford, on 7 May 1588. His later claim that his father appointed him a colonel in the army at Tilbury in the summer of 1588 is a typical exaggeration, but he may well have been in Leicester's company. Two wills by Leicester have survived, the earlier dated 30 January 1582. In this he named Denbigh his heir but left the manor of Cleobury Mortimer, Shropshire, to 'an infant', undoubtedly Robert Dudley (Longleat, Dudley box III, art. 56, fol. 8). In a separate indenture of 1 February his 'reputed bastard son' was also left a group of newly purchased fee simple manors (Warks. CRO, Arbury MS I, fol. 142ff.). However, when he assigned a body of manors to his wife's jointure in July 1584 he revoked the 1 February 1582 settlement. In 1582 he had nominated Philip Sidney as Denbigh's heir, should he die heirless, which is probably why he did not make a will when he went to the Netherlands in 1585. But on 6 February 1586, soon after his arrival, he made a new settlement for 'his welbeloved Robert Dudley base son', leaving him a group of Lancashire estates known as Butler's Lands that he had obtained somewhat obscurely. In his last will, dated August 1587, Leicester designated his brother, the earl of Warwick, his heir but with the remainder to his base son.

Dudley came into his inheritance on Warwick's death in February 1590. The lordships of Denbigh, Chirk, and Kenilworth formed the core of his inheritance, but Leicester had assigned his main residences, Leicester House and Wanstead, together with a number of the manors surrounding Kenilworth, to the countess's jointure; she was also his executrix. Since Dudley was still a minor Warwick confirmed his inheritance of the jointure lands with his other uncle (his mother's brother), the lord admiral, Howard of Effingham, on 2 June 1589, although he remained concerned about the future. Only a few months after Warwick's death the overseers of Leicester's will brought suit in chancery against the countess in Robert Dudley's name. The case was primarily over whether the manor of Honiley (included in her jointure) was part of Kenilworth, but she was also charged with removing muniments and other items from the castle. Litigation between them continued throughout the decade. Their relations were further exacerbated by Leicester's debts. To redeem these Warwick had sold Denbigh and Chirk before he died, thus reducing Dudley's immediate inheritance to Kenilworth. Yet Dudley escaped any further liability for the debts, which fell on the countess as executrix. He also faced a challenge from Sir Robert Sidney, who regarded himself as the only legitimate male heir to both Leicester and Warwick. By the end of the 1590s Sidney had reached an understanding with the countess in which he would protect her remaining jointure lands in exchange for her leasing them to him in the meantime.

On the day that Leicester died, 4 September 1588, Dudley's mother returned from France where she had lived since 1583 with her husband Sir Edward Stafford, ambassador to the French court. She then resumed her service as a gentlewoman of the privy chamber, and was active in looking after her son's interests at court. He was at court himself by October 1591 when he was temporarily barred for publicly kissing a maid of honour. She was Margaret (*d.* 1595), daughter of Richard Cavendish, a former friend of his father's, whom Dudley married about this time. The marriage brought with it some interesting connections, for Margaret's sister was married to Richard Hakluyt and her cousin was the navigator Thomas Cavendish.

Naval expeditions Dudley later stated that his fascination with maritime affairs and navigation began when he was seventeen, roughly 1591. There were a number of possible influences apart from his wife's family: his uncle the lord admiral, his father, who had extensive maritime and mathematical interests, and his Oxford tutor, Thomas Chaloner (1564–1615).

Dudley's interest in navigation led him to purchase scientific instruments made by the five leading craftsmen of his day: Humfrey Cole, Augustin Ryther, James Kynvyn, and Charles Whitwell; the astrolabe of Thomas Gemini, dated 1558?, may have been inherited from his father. Whitwell's lunar computer, a brass disc of 72 cm diameter overall, is the most complex instrument made during the sixteenth century. Inscribed 'Sir Robert Dudley was the inventor of this instrument', its purpose was to calculate the place of the moon over a period of thirty years. Nineteen of these instruments are now in the Museo di Storia della Scienza in Florence.

During the 1590s Dudley's main ambition was to circumnavigate the globe. He was a backer of Thomas Cavendish's circumnavigation voyage of 1591–3, which included his father's old ship, the *Galleon Leicester*. In 1594 he prepared a voyage that he intended to command himself. The queen refused him permission to attempt a circumnavigation because she considered it too dangerous, and only allowed him to go to the West Indies. At this stage his voyage may have been co-ordinated with one to Guiana that Sir Walter Ralegh was planning, but in the event Dudley left England with his three ships in November 1594 before Ralegh was ready. He made for the Canaries, crossed the Atlantic to Trinidad (which he claimed for Elizabeth), made a limited exploration of the mouth of the Orinoco, and then returned via Puerto Rico and the Azores, reaching Cornwall in May 1595. He considered that the voyage was 'so common … as it is not worth the recording' (Warner, 67), but Hakluyt was keen to publicize it, and it appears to have excited the jealousy of Ralegh, who was always territorial about Guiana. There is evidence that Dudley wished to set out on a new major voyage at the end of 1595. Instead he was given the command of one of the queen's larger warships, *Nonpareil*, in the expedition to Cadiz in 1596, receiving his knighthood on his return to Plymouth on 8 August. This was the last time he went to sea himself, but at the end of the year he finally financed a circumnavigation voyage. This was a total disaster, all the ships being lost and only one man returning alive in 1601.

Dudley returned from the West Indies to find that Margaret had died of plague in spring 1595. On 11 September 1596 at Ashow, Warwickshire, he married Alice [**Alice Dudley** (1579–1669)], daughter of Sir Thomas Leigh (*d.*

1625) of Stoneleigh. A daughter was baptized on 25 September 1597, the first of seven daughters, five of whom survived to adulthood. Little is known about Dudley between 1597 and 1603, but there seems to be no real evidence to support the suggestion (Lee, 98–9) that he took part in Essex's rebellion in 1601.

The 'great cause' 'The great cause of Sir Robert Dudley', the culmination of his legal battles with the countess of Leicester and Sir Robert Sidney, was heard in the court of Star Chamber in 1604–5. It arose from his attempt to prove himself Leicester's legitimate son and thus heir to both his father and Warwick, something he had not claimed in the litigation of the 1590s. This was held against him in Star Chamber. The judgment included the impounding of the evidence files, which, with one possible exception (the depositions concerning Leicester's marriage to the countess in 1578, now SP 12/148/75–85) have disappeared. As a result for a long time the only account was that of Sir William Dugdale. Dugdale saw the Star Chamber order book before it was destroyed, but he also numbered Dudley's daughter Lady Katherine Leveson among his patrons and was misled by Charles I's letters patent of 1644. However, during the nineteenth century parts of two separate sets of copies of the evidence files, probably made for Sidney's and the countess of Leicester's legal counsel (see Adams, *Papers*, 19–20), were discovered at Penshurst Place and Longleat House.

Thanks to the account in John Hawarde's *Les reportes de cases in camera stellata*, the course of the Star Chamber proceedings is reasonably clear, but the immediate background to the trial is murky. Dudley's first known move was to obtain a licence to examine witnesses from the court of arches on 20 May 1603, only two months after Elizabeth I died. Having presumably collected his evidences of legitimacy during the summer, in September he brought a suit for defamation in the commissary court of the bishop of Coventry and Lichfield against a citizen of Coventry for calling him a bastard. The apparent purpose of this collusive suit was to have his evidence entered in the legal record. The case, which became known as the 'Lichfield suit', was redirected to the court of arches, but before it could begin the countess of Leicester filed a bill of complaint in Star Chamber (10 February 1604) alleging that Dudley was seeking to defame her and threaten her possession of her jointure lands, for if his claim of legitimacy were upheld her marriage would become a bigamous one and her jointure invalid.

The case certainly stretched the bounds of the jurisdiction of Star Chamber (which did not extend to rights over real property) as well as its practice, for all the parties were represented by counsel and the crown by the attorney-general, Sir Edward Coke. The verdict was effectively in the hands of the privy council. If the countess and Sidney were then in favour with James I, Dudley had his own supporters, among them the lord admiral and the earl of Northampton, and Essex and Howard loyalties may have come into play. What seems to have tipped the scales against him was a decision (possibly by Robert Cecil) that the consequences of overturning the existing settlement of Leicester's and Warwick's estates were too great to be contemplated. None the less there was sympathy for Dudley and his mother. He was therefore to be let down lightly by the charge that he had been suborned into bringing the Lichfield case by others, in particular Thomas Drury (a relation by marriage of Sir Edward Stafford), who had conveniently died in August 1603.

On the substantive question of his legitimacy Dudley could produce only four relevant witnesses, his mother, two former servants of hers, Magdalen Salisbury and Henry Frodsham, and a single former servant of Leicester's, Owen Jones. His mother testified in detail to her marriage to Leicester, but she could supply no supporting evidence and her testimony was largely discredited by her husband, who claimed that Dudley had browbeaten her into it. Except for Magdalen Salisbury, who deposed that as a girl she had been present at the wedding in 1573, and Frodsham (whose deposition has disappeared), all those Douglas Sheffield named as witnesses to her marriage had died. Jones, who had been assigned to Robert Dudley when he went to Sussex in 1585, deposed that Leicester had confided to him that Robert was legitimate. However, the countess produced a phalanx of Leicester's surviving friends and servants who testified uniformly to the contrary.

The crown was interested solely in the alleged conspiracy behind the Lichfield suit—not the substantive issue—which made it possible to evade calling Douglas Sheffield's veracity into question. The council was unhappy about open discussion of the sexual misadventures of the peerage, but in general considered that it was only natural for Dudley to 'seek his perfection' (as the earl of Devonshire put it), although he had been ill advised and unorderly (Hawarde, 221). The majority found that Salisbury, Frodsham, and Jones had offered their testimony for gain and that Salisbury had been coached by Drury. This judgment effectively obscured Dudley's own role. Reading the case papers literally (as Lee does in *Son of Leicester*, 100–02), Dudley was progressively persuaded of his legitimacy by Drury and it was merely coincidence that Elizabeth died before he could mount his suit. This does at least explain why the claim was absent in his earlier litigation. On the other hand, without his pressure his mother would not have testified. She (apparently) had not been involved in the Lichfield suit, but only agreed afterwards—'although she hath been often moved by her son for such purpose' (CKS, U 1475/L/2/3, it. 13, fol. 1). His stepfather, Stafford, who was an openly hostile witness, saw him as the driving force from the start and that his mother 'should have cause to curse the tyme that ever shee bore [him]' (Stafford deposition, fol. 69). From this perspective Dudley had been waiting for Elizabeth to die, as he was well aware that she would not have allowed him to raise the issue.

Exile in Florence It is doubtful whether Dudley would have accepted anything other than a judgment in his favour, but two further developments undoubtedly influenced his response. Only days before the judgment was delivered (4 May 1605) Sidney was created Viscount Lisle, a Dudley title, while the sealing of the evidences was a clear signal that the case could not be reopened. Just over a month after the verdict Dudley obtained a licence to travel abroad for three years and left early in July. It was soon discovered that he was accompanied by the nineteen-year-old Elizabeth Southwell (1585/6–1631), his first cousin once removed (she was the lord admiral's granddaughter) and a maid of honour. The two spent the winter of 1605–6 in Lyons, where they announced their conversion to Catholicism and applied to the Vatican for a dispensation to marry on grounds of consanguinity. To escape his existing marriage Dudley claimed (or more likely invented) a contract with the maid of honour Frances Vavasour in 1591 to invalidate both his earlier marriages. He also adopted the style earl of Warwick and Leicester.

In 1606 Dudley approached the grand duke of Tuscany, Ferdinand I, with an offer to build warships for the navy which Ferdinand was assembling for a campaign against the Turks. Ferdinand had no desire to alienate James I and responded cautiously, but in the autumn he was satisfied with Dudley's bona fides. During the winter of 1606–7 he and his wife moved to Florence, where they made their home for the rest of their lives. Their daughter Maria was born in 1609, the first of twelve or thirteen children. Dudley quickly established his credibility with Ferdinand by building an English style galleon, *San Giovanni Battista*, which was launched in March 1608. He also recruited English seamen to serve in the Tuscan navy and organized an expedition to the West Indies under the Tuscan flag.

Ferdinand died in 1608 and was succeeded by his son Cosimo II (r. 1609–21), who in some respects was a more important patron. Dudley also won the sympathy of the two grand duchesses, Ferdinand's widow, Christina of Lorraine, and Cosimo's wife, Maria Maddelena (sister of the Emperor Ferdinand II). Dudley's accomplishments were not diminished in the subsequent relating, but they were real enough and earned him the reputation of one of the first of the English *virtuosi*. Although the new harbour at Livorno (Leghorn) had been started before he arrived he is credited with the design and construction of the mole which was completed in 1621. In 1610 he was given a patent for a machine to improve silk weaving. Several years later (c.1614) he discovered a curative powder that was made public in 1620 under the name of *Pulvis Warwicensis*. However, he is most famous for his nautical and navigational writings. In 1610 he wrote two manuscript volumes in English and in 1619–20 the 'Direttorio marittimo', a volume in Italian for the instruction of officers of the Tuscan navy.

Dudley did not necessarily intend his exile to be a permanent one, but his return to England was to be on his own terms and he did not make things easy for himself. His abandoning of his wife and daughters destroyed the sympathy he had previously enjoyed. Moreover bigamy was now a felony under 1 James I c. 11 (1604), which may have been inspired by his case. The aftermath of the Gunpowder Plot was not the most politic time to convert to

Catholicism. He claimed several years later that his conversion was not a consequence of his exile, 'he was different many years before' (Adlard, 313), but on arriving in Florence he and his wife joined a group of English exiles presided over by the celebrated Jesuit Robert Persons. In April 1607 Elizabeth Dudley supplied Persons with her notorious account of Elizabeth I's death.

On 2 February 1607 Dudley's licence to travel was formally revoked and he was ordered to return. When the revocation was presented to him in April he refused to accept it because it did not style him earl of Warwick. This arrogant response caused James to order the sequestration of Kenilworth and terminated a discreet attempt involving his mother (and possibly Ferdinand I as well) to reach a compromise with Sidney over the earldom of Warwick. There was a serious danger that Kenilworth could escheat to the crown and be regranted to Sidney, but Northampton (who hated Sidney) blocked it on the ground that Dudley's offence was contempt, not treason. In the meantime James awarded Lady Alice and her daughters an annuity of £300 out of the revenues.

Negotiations over English estates Dudley now initiated a complex series of negotiations with Henry, prince of Wales, who was attracted by his maritime skills in much the same way as he was by the imprisoned Ralegh's. Dudley's old tutor Chaloner, who was Henry's chamberlain, was the intermediary, but the various strands are not easy to disentangle. One was the proposal for a marriage between Henry and Cosimo's sister Caterina, which surfaced in 1611. If Dudley was not the instigator he was certainly heavily involved. A second was the sale of Kenilworth to Henry, possibly in the beginning a collusive sale in which Henry would safeguard Dudley's property until his return, as he had just done for Ralegh. The sale was concluded in November 1611. Kenilworth had been valued in 1609 at £38,000 clear, but Dudley apparently accepted £15,000 (£14,500 according to Charles I in 1644), although Henry's agent later stated that he had agreed to only £7000. In mid-1612 James assigned Henry £7000 towards the purchase, but Henry had received only half this sum before he died in November and how much had been remitted to Dudley by then is unknown.

Dudley sold Kenilworth cheaply on the understanding that he was effectively buying his pardon with the difference. However, it was also made clear that he needed to redeem his contempt by an act of service, and to this end on 14 November 1612 NS he sent Henry a scheme to make England master of the seas. This would be achieved by building a fleet of *gallizabras*, a warship of his own invention, a hybrid between a galleon and a galley, smaller than (and he claimed superior to) the earlier Spanish *galleass*. There was in fact nothing particularly novel about this type of ship; several Elizabethan naval theorists had proposed similar vessels, but English shipwrights considered them impractical.

Unfortunately for Dudley, Henry died only two days after he wrote, leaving the pardon and the balance of the sale unresolved. For his pardon Dudley turned to James's favourite Robert Carr, earl of Somerset, with another version of his naval construction scheme, and then more notoriously with his famous 'Proposition to bridle the impertinence of parliaments' in July 1614. This was a response to the Addled Parliament and proposed the imposition by force of an openly absolutist government. Although Somerset apparently showed it to James nothing more was heard of the tract until 1629, when a major scandal broke out after copies made in Sir Robert Cotton's library were discovered to be in circulation.

Henry's heir was his brother Charles, but he did not come of age until 1617. In 1614 Dudley built a house on the via della Vigna Nuova in the parish of San Pancrazio, which was to be his town house in Florence for the rest of his life. Although he received an annual income of 2000 scudi (about £500) from the grand duke, he was dependent on loans secured on his English estates. With the Kenilworth remittances in abeyance he turned to selling the inheritance of the countess of Leicester's jointure lands, which by then amounted to little more than the Warwickshire manors of Long Itchington and Balsall. When Sir Thomas Leigh learned of this he appealed to James on behalf of his daughter and granddaughters and in 1616 James barred the transmission to Dudley of any remittances from the sale of his lands. Sidney also claimed an interest in the manors and received a judgment confirming his existing leases in return for taking over the pension to Lady Alice. A further disaster for Dudley occurred in 1618 when James sold the earldoms of Leicester and Warwick to Sidney and Lord Rich respectively, effectively rejecting any claim he had to them. Finally, unlike his brother, Charles had strong views on domestic propriety and was more sympathetic to Lady Alice's interests in Kenilworth than Dudley's. Her jointure was secured on the woods (valued at £10,000), and in order to buy her out Charles supported the passing of a private act in the parliament of 1621 giving her the right to act as a feme sole. In 1622 she accepted £4000 down and an annual pension for her jointure and Charles then leased Kenilworth to the earl of Monmouth.

Last years in Florence Dudley responded by turning to the Medici. In 1619 Maria Maddelena appointed him her great chamberlain and shortly afterwards Christina followed suit. When the two grand duchesses became joint regents for the young Ferdinand II in 1621 his place at the Medici court was assured. At the same time Cosimo gave him the use of the Villa di Castello, adjacent to the grand-ducal Villa della Retraia, as a country house. Lastly, through Maria Maddelena he appealed to Emperor Ferdinand II to recognize him as duke of Northumberland. Ferdinand was unwilling to grant the title on his own authority, but on 9 March 1620 NS he issued a patent (possibly drafted by Dudley) recognizing his right to the dukedom by inheritance from his grandfather, which he had lost through his adherence to the Roman church. This patent inspired Dudley to make his most extravagant demand. In 1627 he obtained from the church power to collect what he claimed the English crown owed him by confiscating the cargoes of English merchants trading at Livorno. He valued this debt at £8 million for the whole of the dukedom, plus £200,000 interest. Even the young grand duke was unhappy with the involvement of the church in Dudley's private affairs, and he gave his support to a fresh attempt to reach a compromise in the early 1630s. An agreement was reached in the summer of 1632. In December, Dudley transferred his rights to the countess of Leicester's jointure lands to his four surviving daughters by Lady Alice. In the following year he received 8000 scudi from Charles I for the arrears from the Kenilworth sale.

Thanks to this agreement Dudley played no direct role in the last phase of the settlement of his father's will, which was initiated by the death of the countess of Leicester in December 1634. Robert Sidney, second earl of Leicester, advanced the old Sidney claim to the jointure lands, only to be challenged by three of Dudley's daughters: Frances (d. 1663), the wife of Sir Gilbert Kniveton, Anne (d. 1663), the wife of Sir Robert *Holborne, and Katherine (d. 1673), the wife of Sir Richard Leveson. The fourth (Douglas) transferred her rights to her sisters in December 1635. The case was finally settled in their favour in 1655. In the meantime there was a bizarre last twist to the tale, when on 23 May 1644 Charles I created Lady Alice Duchess Dudley for life. He gave several reasons for doing so. He wished to reward Holborne (his solicitor-general) and Leveson who were prominent royalists. He also admitted to a guilty conscience over the failure to pay Dudley the full value of Kenilworth and Lady Alice her pension. But he was also convinced from a perusal of the files of the Star Chamber case that Dudley was indeed Leicester's legitimate son and that the verdict of 1605 was unjust.

The 1632 settlement also meant that Dudley's exile was now permanent. His beloved wife's death from plague on 13 September 1631 NS was a blow from which he never fully recovered, and his last years were embittered by a feud with his heir, Carlo. In the early 1640s he retired to the Villa di Castello and devoted himself to writing on naval matters, drawing on his experience to compose the encyclopaedic *Dell'arcano del mare* (1646–7), dedicated to Grand Duke Ferdinand II. The first of its six books dealt with methods of calculating longitude, including those of his own invention; the second contained charts and sailing directions. The third contained much of the material in the earlier 'Direttorio marittimo', plus proposals for the creation of a navy; the fourth book, concerned with shipbuilding and fortifications, recalled his practical experience at Livorno. Book five built on the work of the Portuguese navigator Pedro Nunez. The final book was an atlas of 127 maps, the first to employ Mercator's projections. In the Florence Museum there are also instruments associated with Dudley but not made in London, although their inscriptions claiming his invention are dated prior to his arrival in Italy.

Dudley died at the Villa di Castello on 6 September 1649 NS. It is assumed that he wished to be buried with his wife, to whom he had erected a large monument in the church of San Pancrazio. Owing to his estrangement from his heir no funeral took place. As late as 1674 his corpse was still deposited in the nearby monastery at Boldrone and its fate is unknown. There is no record that he was ever interred in San Pancrazio and the monument to his wife was destroyed in 1798. He left his navigational instruments and manuscripts to Ferdinand II. It is still debated whether he and his wife were the source for the Holbein portrait of Sir Richard Southwell now in the Uffizi.

Duchess Alice lived on at Dudley House, St Giles-in-the-Fields, Westminster, and had her title confirmed by Charles II in 1660. She was a great benefactor of the church and parish of St Giles and bequeathed large sums to the parochial charities on her death, at Dudley House, on 22 January 1669. She was buried at Stoneleigh.

The supposed stigma of bastardy did little real harm to Dudley. He received a generous bequest from his father and enjoyed considerable public sympathy, which he forfeited by his treatment of his first family. In Florence he successfully exploited his 'martyrdom' for his adherence to the Roman Catholic church, but that was irrelevant to his self-imposed exile. He did English Catholics few favours with the 'Proposition for bridling parliaments', which helped to substantiate the growing popular association of Catholicism with absolutism. Although he is regularly compared to his father, the comparison with Ralegh, whose path crossed his at several interesting points, is more relevant. Both were men of many talents, but among them were those for self-aggrandizement and self-destruction.   SIMON ADAMS

Sources CKS, Penshurst papers, U1475 [esp. Stafford deposition, 1604, U1475/L2/4, it. 3 and deposition of Douglas, Lady Sheffield, 6–7 June 1604, U1475/L2/3, it. 13] · *An Elizabethan in 1582: the diary of Richard Madox, fellow of All Souls*, ed. E. S. Donno, Hakluyt Society, 2nd ser., 147 (1976) · G. L. Craik, *The romance of the nobility, or, Curiosities of family history*, 4 vols. (1848–9) · S. Adams, ed., *Household accounts and disbursement books of Robert Dudley, earl of Leicester, 1558–1561, 1584–1586*, CS, 6 (1995) · W. Dethick, 'Book of funerals of the nobility', 1586–1603, Coll. Arms · Longleat House, Wiltshire, Marquess of Bath MSS, Dudley MSS · Warks. CRO, Newdegate of Arbury papers, Arbury MS 1 [a vol. subsequently deposited by Viscount Daventry] · Lancs. RO, Lord Lilford of Bankhall papers, DDli · W. Beamont, *Annals of the lords of Warrington*, Chetham Society, 87–8 (1872–3) · APC, 1590–91, 1615–19 · depositions in the case of *Robert Dudley v. the countess of Leicester*, 1590, PRO, C 21/ElizI/D/5/2 · G. F. Warner, ed., *The voyage of Robert Dudley … to the West Indies, 1594–1595*, Hakluyt Society, 2nd ser. (1899); repr. (1967), (1991) · M. Feingold, *The mathematicians' apprenticeship: science, universities and society in England, 1560–1640* (1984) · A. G. Lee, *The son of Leicester: the story of Sir Robert Dudley* (1964) · state papers domestic, Elizabeth, PRO, SP 12 · W. Dugdale, *The baronage of England*, 2 vols. (1675–6) · S. Adams, 'The papers of Robert Dudley, earl of Leicester: III: the countess of Leicester's collection', *Archives*, 22 (1996), 1–26 · *Les reportes del cases in camera stellata, 1593 to 1609, from the original ms. of John Hawarde*, ed. W. P. Baildon (privately printed, London, 1894) · J. Temple-Leader, *Life of Sir Robert Dudley* (Florence, 1895); repr. (Amsterdam, 1977) · [V. Thomas], *The Italian biography of Sir Robert Dudley, Knt.* (1859); repr. (Amsterdam, 1977) · G. Adlard, *Amye Robsart and the earl of Leycester … and a history of Kenilworth Castle* (1870) · R. Strong, *Henry prince of Wales and England's lost Renaissance* (1986) · R. Strong, 'England and Italy: the marriage of Henry prince of Wales', *For Veronica Wedgwood these: studies in seventeenth-century history*, ed. R. Ollard and P. Tudor-Craig (1986), 59–87 · G. L'E. Turner, *Elizabethan instrument makers: the origins of the London trade in precision instrument making* (2000), chap. 5 · W. Martigli, 'Sir Robert Dudley e l'arsenale di Livorno', *Quaderni Stefaniani*, 3 (1984) · W. Martigli,

'L'arcano del mare di Robert Dudley e l'idrografia della marina stefaniana', *Quaderni Stefaniani*, 4 (1985), 197–200

Archives BL, account of journey to West Indies, Sloane MS 358 · Museo di Storia della Scienza, Florence, scientific papers | Lancs. RO, Lilford of Bankhall MSS, estate muniments for Butler's Lands, DDL · Warks. CRO, Newdegate of Arbury MSS, estate muniments and legal papers relating to Long Itchington and Balsall

Likenesses N. Hilliard, miniature, *c.*1591–1593, National Museum, Stockholm [*see illus.*] · J. Brown, line engraving (after N. Hilliard), BM, NPG; repro. in T. Moule, *Portraits of illustrious persons in English history* (1869) · portrait?, repro. in V. J. Watney, *Cornbury and the forest of Wychwood* (1910), facing p. 82; at Lilleshall, Shropshire, 1908

Dudley, Thomas (*fl.* 1678–1679), etcher, signs himself on one plate as 'quondam condicipulus W. Hollar' ('a former pupil of Wenceslaus Hollar'), and his plates are etched in a manner resembling, but greatly inferior to, his master's style. His most important work was a series of twenty-six etchings executed in 1678–9, representing the life of Aesop, from drawings by Francis Barlow (now in the British Museum), and added by Barlow to the second edition of his *Fables of Aesop* in 1687. A few portraits by him are known, including one of Titus Oates on a broadside entitled *A Prophesy of England's Future Happiness* (British Museum). In 1679 Dudley went to Lisbon, where he etched portraits of John IV and Peter II of Portugal, of Theodosius Lusitanus (1679), of Bishop Russel of Portalegre (1679), and of an unidentified man in armour, the last being signed 'Tho. Dudley fecit Vlissippone'. He also made a bookplate which he signed 'Tho. Dudley Anglus fecit'. He was presumably a Roman Catholic, and there is no reason to think that he ever returned to England.

L. H. CUST, rev. ANTONY GRIFFITHS

Sources F. G. Stephens and M. D. George, eds., *Catalogue of prints and drawings in the British Museum, division 1: political and personal satires*, 11 vols. in 12 (1870–1954), vol. 1, no. 1078

Dudley, William (*d.* 1483), bishop of Durham, was the son (probably the third) of John (VI) *Sutton, first Baron Dudley (1400–1487), and Elizabeth (*d.* 1478), daughter of Sir John Berkeley of Beverstone, Gloucestershire. His date of birth is unknown. He was educated at Oxford where he graduated BA in 1454, and MA, following a dispensation, in 1456. His first living was that of Malpas in Cheshire, of which he became rector in 1457. He had been ordained deacon in July that year. His father fought for Henry VI, but made his peace with the Yorkists. William Dudley was one of the king's chaplains by 1467, by which date he already held three benefices with cure of souls.

Dudley's career in royal service was transformed when he was one of the first to rally to Edward IV on his return to recover his kingdom in March 1471, joining the king at Doncaster at the head of 160 troops. A grateful Edward promoted him to dean of the Chapel Royal a few months later, in charge of an establishment incorporated a decade later with three canons and twenty-four chaplains. He was Queen Elizabeth's chancellor from 1471 to 1474, and benefices and offices subsequently flowed his way. He was dean of St George's Chapel, Windsor, from November 1473, and archdeacon of Middlesex from November 1475. By 1476 he held prebends in York, Salisbury, Chichester, and Wells.

As dean of St George's he witnessed the beginning of the building of the new chapel. In his capacity as dean of the Chapel Royal he accompanied Edward IV on his expedition to France and was one of his envoys who negotiated the treaty of Picquigny; he was subsequently employed by Edward in further negotiations with the French. He was provided to Durham on 31 July 1476, was consecrated some time between 1 September and 12 October, and received the temporalities on 14 October.

Although Dudley was by no means the first royal confidant to be provided to Durham, his lack of administrative experience made him a somewhat surprising choice. But as the senior cleric in the royal household his promotion was in tune with Edward IV's preference for government through the personnel of his own affinity, and one might suppose that the king anticipated that he would dance to his tune in the palatinate. To some extent he did. A pliant Dudley was content to allow royal commissioners to take over the repairs of Norham Castle, and to find an annuity for the king's knight of the body, Sir John Pilkington. Edward no doubt also expected the new bishop to be more amenable to Richard, duke of Gloucester, than his predecessor, Laurence Booth, had been. He might not have anticipated, however, that Dudley would come so completely under the sway of the king's brother. As early as 1477 the bishop was seeking the duke's advice. In 1479 he granted the Forest of Weardale and Stanhope Park to Richard for life, the equivalent of an annuity of £100. A year later he extended to the palatinate Gloucester's appointment as the king's lieutenant for the war against Scotland, with full power to call out his subjects, and renewed this in 1482. The bishop's council was before long dominated by the duke's servants, while several offices and fees were steered the way of the duke's men. In 1477 Dudley had been advised by Prior Richard Bell to cherish the family and affinity of the earl of Westmorland, since if they stood as one 'ye may rule and guide all other that inhabit the country' (Raine, cclxxiv, 359). But in truth by 1480 he had placed his palatinate at the service of the duke of Gloucester, in a manner and to a degree remarkably similar to Bishop Robert Neville in his dealings with the earl of Salisbury three decades earlier.

Dudley was at court when Edward IV died in 1483, for he sang a requiem mass during the funeral rites on 20 April. But he was quick to support Richard III, officiating at his coronation on 6 July, and taking the place of honour in the absence of the archbishop of Canterbury at the banquet afterwards. He accompanied the royal progress through the midlands in August and took the leading role in place of the archbishop of York in the investiture of the new Prince of Wales in York Minster on 8 September. He was elected chancellor of the University of Oxford on 20 October. He had probably already returned to Westminster with the king, for it was there that he died suddenly on 29 November. He was buried in the chapel of St Nicholas in Westminster Abbey, and the outline of his effigy, from a now lost brass, survives under a canopied table tomb. Not one of the more distinguished bishops of Durham, he had been foolishly promoted beyond his ability by Edward IV to a position for which he possessed neither the necessary experience nor sufficient strength of character.

A. J. POLLARD

Sources PRO, Durham chancery records, Durh 3 · U. Durham L., archives and special collections, Durham Church Commission records, estate accounts · Emden, *Oxf.* · W. Hutchinson, *The history and antiquities of the county palatine of Durham*, [2nd edn], 1 (1823), 443–9 · A. J. Pollard, '"St Cuthbert and the Hog": Richard III and the county palatine of Durham, 1471–85', *Kings and nobles in the later middle ages*, ed. R. A. Griffiths and J. Sherborne (1986), 109–29 · C. Ross, *Edward IV* (1974) · *Historiae Dunelmensis scriptores tres: Gaufridus de Coldingham, Robertus de Graystanes, et Willielmus de Chambre*, ed. J. Raine, SurtS, 9 (1839) · A. J. Pollard, *North-eastern England during the Wars of the Roses: lay society, war and politics, 1450–1500* (1990)
Wealth at death approx. £3000: Pollard, *North-eastern England*, 53–4

Dudley, Sir William Edward (1868–1938), co-operative society administrator, was born on 29 May 1868 at 1 Loch Street, Runcorn, Cheshire, the son of William Dudley, house painter, and his wife, Rebecca Cottrell. Dudley attended Runcorn parish church school until 1883, when he began work with Bridgewater Navigation as an office boy. Dudley transferred to the engineer's office, which he eventually headed. He was prominent in local public life as a leading churchman and, from 1914, as an independent member of Runcorn urban district council. Dudley was council chairman in 1921–3; he also served as an overseer of the poor and a JP, and he was involved with numerous local societies and charities.

Born into a family already involved in co-operative trading, Dudley joined the Runcorn Co-operative Society in 1893, on his marriage to Theresa Sutton (d. 1927). In 1895 he was elected to the society's management committee, and in 1896 he became chairman. Dudley directed the reform of the society, which enjoyed unprecedented growth.

Dudley had larger ambitions to co-operative leadership. He campaigned for better representation for the Cheshire and north Wales district within the north-western section of the Co-operative Union, and he took the new seat created on its board in 1904. By 1911 he was chairman of the union's central board, and he oversaw revision of the Co-operative Union's rules at congress. This success assisted his election to the Co-operative Wholesale Society (CWS) board in the same year. Dudley then resigned from Bridgewater Navigation and as chairman of Runcorn and Widnes Co-operative Society.

Dudley served on the grocery committee of the CWS, acting as chairman from 1916. He was central to co-operative attempts to influence government food controls during the First World War. In 1918 Dudley was one of six co-operative nominees to the consumers' council at the Ministry of Food. He served on fourteen wartime governmental departmental committees and helped to revise post-war import restrictions. He served on the royal commission on food prices of 1924 and the National Food Council established in 1925.

Dudley was appointed CWS president in 1933, overseeing an operation with sales of around £100 million. His presidency saw extension into storekeeping, through the formation of the CWS Retail Society in 1934. From 1919 Dudley represented the CWS as a director of the Manchester Ship Canal and from 1930 he chaired the committee controlling Bridgewater Navigation. He was also a director of Bridgewater and Manchester collieries. Dudley was honoured through election as president of the 1925 Co-operative Congress. He was appointed OBE in 1920 for his work with the Ministry of Food and a knighthood in 1926. Dudley was in addition decorated by the governments of the CWS's trading partners, particularly of Denmark and Quebec.

Dudley's health was already failing at his retirement as CWS president in 1936. He died on 7 May 1938 at his Runcorn home, Cranleigh, Weston Road. Lady Dudley had died in 1927, but he was survived by his son and daughter. His funeral, on 11 May, at Runcorn parish church, was attended by co-operative and civic dignitaries. Dudley's energy as a self-made man was combined with a practical view of co-operation: 'I am for doing one job well, and my business is to improve and extend co-operative trading' (Co-operative Union, *57th Congress*, 348).

MARTIN PURVIS

Sources *Co-operative News* (14 May 1938) · *Runcorn Weekly News* (13 May 1938) · W. Millington, *Runcorn and Widnes Industrial Co-operative Society Ltd: jubilee history of the society* (1912) · P. Redfern, *The new history of the CWS* (1938) · *Runcorn Weekly News* (14 March 1930) · *The Producer* (May 1933) · *Proceedings of the 57th Annual Co-operative Congress* [Co-operative Union] (1925) · *Proceedings of the 43rd Annual Co-operative Congress* [Co-operative Union] (1911) · J. Bellamy and H. F. Bing, 'Dudley, Sir William Edward', *DLB*, vol. 1 · b. cert. · d. cert.
Likenesses photograph, c.1912, repro. in Millington, *Runcorn and Widnes Industrial Co-operative Society Ltd*, frontispiece · photograph, c.1925, repro. in *Co-operative Union, Proceedings of the 57th Annual Co-operative Congress*, 3 · photograph, c.1933, Co-operative College, Manchester, National Co-operative Archive, William Dudley biographical file
Wealth at death £15,283 4s. 7d.: probate, 25 June 1938, resworn

Duesbury, William (*bap.* 1725, *d.* 1786), china manufacturer, was baptized in Cannock, Staffordshire, on 7 September 1725, the son of William Duesbury (*d.* 1768), currier, of Cannock, and his wife, Sarah. He practised as an enameller in London from 1751 to 1753, moving in 1754 to Longton Hall in Staffordshire, where there was a small china works. About 1750 he married Sarah James (1724–1780) of Shrewsbury. With the help of his father, who in September 1755 had assigned all his possessions to his son in return for lifelong maintenance, Duesbury was enabled on 1 January 1756 to become a co-partner with John Heath, 'Gentleman', and Andrew Planché, 'China Maker', both of Derby, in 'the Art of making English China' (Jewitt, 2.67). Porcelain had been first made in Derby about 1750, probably by Andrew Planché (1728–1805), a French Huguenot who had been apprenticed to a London goldsmith, and that early factory had produced some of the most admired porcelain figures ever made in England. Planché seems to have left Derby not long after the agreement, and under Duesbury's management, with Heath's financial backing, new and larger premises were acquired in the Nottingham Road. A London agent was appointed in April 1757 and the business grew in size and importance. In February 1770 Duesbury purchased the failing Chelsea manufactory, whose premises he probably then used primarily as a decorating establishment until 1784 when all operations were centred in Derby. Using the prestige of its famous name Duesbury at first continued the Chelsea practice of holding annual auctions until he opened his own London warehouse in Bedford Street, Covent Garden, in June 1774, and in March 1775 Messrs Duesbury and Heath were appointed 'China Manufacturers in Ordinary to His Majesty' (PRO, LC3/67/73). George, prince of Wales, became a patron and an important customer in 1783 when he was furnishing Carlton House. Duesbury had survived John Heath's bankruptcy in 1779 and in August 1780 had been able to buy the china works property from Heath's assignees, so becoming the sole proprietor of the business which he had built up to be the leading porcelain manufacturer in England producing vases, figures, and a range of table wares for luxury use. He died on 30 October 1786 at the china manufactory in Nottingham Road, Derby, incapacitated by a stroke, 'much respected by all who had the pleasure of his acquaintance' (*Derby Mercury*), and was buried on 2 November in St Alkmund's, Derby. Of his four surviving children, **William Duesbury** (1763–1796), china manufacturer, the elder son, succeeded to the proprietorship. He was born in February 1763, at the china manufactory in Derby, and baptized on 2 March 1763 at St Alkmund's, Derby. He had been brought up in the business, becoming an equal partner with his father in July 1785. On 4 January 1787 he married Elizabeth (1767–1828), daughter of William Edwards, a solicitor of Derby. Teawares soon became the mainstay of the factory's sales and Duesbury recruited additional skilled porcelain painters, and introduced the fashion for decorating services with named landscapes and botanical specimens. He also supplied the clockmaker Benjamin Vulliamy with specially commissioned biscuit figures. Duesbury's health had never been strong and in November 1795 he took into partnership an Irish miniature painter, Michael *Kean. Duesbury died, intestate, after a long illness, on 8 October 1796 at the Nottingham Road manufactory, and was buried on 12 October in St Alkmund's, Derby, His widow was left with five young children, of whom the eldest son, William (1787–1845), inherited but did not take part in the business. Kean took over the sole management of the factory and married the widow Elizabeth Duesbury in 1798, but the marriage did not last. In 1811, having failed to find other buyers, Kean sold the factory to his chief clerk, Robert Bloor. Representative collections of Derby porcelain may be seen in the Derby Museum and Art Gallery, Derby, and the Victoria and Albert Museum, London.

L. H. Cust, *rev.* A. P. Ledger

Sources L. F. W. Jewitt, 'Derby china', *The ceramic art of Great Britain, from pre-historic times*, 1 (1878), 174–87; 2 (1878), 60–114 · BM, department of medieval and modern Europe, Bemrose MSS, documents of the Derby porcelain factory · Derby Local Studies Library, Duesbury MSS, documents relating to the Duesburys and the Derby porcelain manufactory, DL82, files 1–21 · W. Bemrose, *Bow, Chelsea and Derby porcelain* (1898) · E. Adams, *Chelsea porcelain* (1987), 172–97 · *Drewry's Derby Mercury* (1 Nov 1786) · *Public Advertiser* (4 April 1757) · *Daily Advertiser* [London] (1 June 1774) · parish register, St Alkmund's Church, Derby · PRO, PROB 11/1152 [William Duesbury (1725–1786)], fols. 77r and v, 78 · PRO, IR 26/179 [William Duesbury (1763–1796)], fol. 32

Archives BM, account book, ref. M&LA 1962, 10–21; London work book [part of the Bemrose Bequest] · Derby Local Studies Library, MSS, DL82, files 1–21 · V&A, letters and papers relating to Duesbury and the Derby porcelain factory, etc. | BM, Bemrose MSS

Likenesses lithograph, silhouette on cream wove, c.1775, Royal Crown Derby Museum, Derby · M. Kean, miniature, watercolour on ivory, 1795 (William Duesbury the younger), Derby Museum and Art Gallery

Wealth at death most to elder son; annuities to other children: will, PRO, PROB 11/1152, fols. 77r–77v

Duesbury, William (1763–1796). *See under* Duesbury, William (*bap.* 1725, *d.* 1786).

Duff, Adrian Grant- (1869–1914), army officer, was born on 29 September 1869, the third son of the Liberal MP who was to become governor of Madras, Sir Mountstuart Elphinstone Grant *Duff (1829–1906), and his wife, Anna Julia Webster (*d.* 1915). Having been educated at Wellington College and the Royal Military College, Sandhurst, Grant-Duff was commissioned second lieutenant in the Black Watch on 23 March 1889. He received his lieutenancy on 22 October 1890 and was further promoted to captain on 3 August 1898 following active service as commandant of the base depot during the Tirah expedition in 1897. He also served in the Transvaal during the closing stages of the Second South African War in 1902 before serving as adjutant to a rifle volunteer battalion. After passing through the Staff College, Camberley, he was appointed to the War Office in February 1905 as staff captain, becoming successively deputy assistant quartermaster-general and general staff officer, grade 2, there in March 1906. On 22 October 1906 he married the Hon. Ursula Lubbock (*b.* 1885), daughter of first Baron Avebury: they had one son and three daughters.

In October 1910 Grant-Duff, who had been promoted major on 12 December 1907, was appointed assistant military secretary to the committee of imperial defence, working on the 'war book', the catalogue of procedures to be followed by government departments in the event of war. Having received the CB for his services in 1913, Grant-Duff returned to his regiment at Aldershot in October and took command with the rank of lieutenant-colonel on 24 May 1914. Despite his father's political affiliation, Grant-Duff was utterly contemptuous of politicians and especially of the Asquith government, whose muddled handling of the Curragh incident in March 1914 he regarded as an appalling case of dragging the army into politics. Indeed he was deeply conservative and extremely pessimistic as to the future of British society. Nor did he approve of Haldane's army reforms although, unlike many contemporaries, he did not advocate conscription as a solution to the army's perceived manpower difficulties. Regarded as a brilliant and able soldier, Grant-Duff took his battalion to war in August 1914 but was killed in action in the battle of the Aisne in France on 21 September 1914. He was buried in Moulins new communal cemetery, Aisne; his son was also killed in action, with the Black Watch, in the Second World War.　　　IAN F. W. BECKETT

Sources E. Spiers, 'The regular army', *A nation in arms: a social study of the British army in the First World War*, ed. I. F. W. Beckett and K. Simpson (1985), 38–60 · I. F. W. Beckett, ed., *The army and the Curragh incident, 1914* (1986) · *WWW* · *Army List* · D. French, *British economic and strategic planning, 1905–1915* (1982) · N. D'Ombrain, *War machinery and high policy* (1973) · S. Grant, 'The origins of the war book', *Journal of the Royal United Service Institute for Defence Studies*, 117/3 (1972), 65–9 · Burke, *Peerage* (1939) · *CGPLA Eng. & Wales* (1914) · CWGC

Archives CAC Cam., journals and papers · IWM, diaries | FILM BFI NFTVA, news footage

Wealth at death £5539 18*s*. 6*d*.: probate, 1914, *CGPLA Eng. & Wales*

Duff, Alexander (1806–1878), missionary, was born to James Duff and Jean Rattray at Auchnahyle Farm in the parish of Moulin, Perthshire, on 26 April 1806.

Education and early ministry Through his parents and his early schooling Duff was strongly influenced by the evangelical revival then taking root in Scottish parishes. He attended a parish boarding-school from the age of eight and a day school at Kirkmichael, and then spent another year at school in Perth before he was sent up at the age of fifteen to study arts and theology at St Andrews University. He found the place dull and lifeless until the arrival in 1823 of Thomas Chalmers as professor of moral philosophy. Under Chalmers's influence and the inspiration of visits to St Andrews by the pioneering missionaries Joshua Marshman and Robert Morrison, Duff, his friend John Urquhart, and a few other students started a student branch of the St Andrews University Missionary Society. Other missionaries had been sent out by the Scottish Missionary Society, but Duff accepted appointment from the general assembly to be its first missionary to India under the scheme drawn up by John Inglis in 1824. On 9 July 1829 Duff married Anne Scott Drysdale (*d*. 1865) of Edinburgh. He was ordained in August 1829 and the couple then proceeded to India. After being twice shipwrecked on the voyage and losing nearly all of a library of 800 books representing 'every department of knowledge', they reached Calcutta in May 1830.

Duff was immediately impressed with the considerable intellectual ferment then in evidence among young men educated in the first English-medium schools, which has since been labelled 'young India' or the 'Bengali renaissance'. He determined to make Calcutta his base of operations, and to conduct the mission in a different manner from others already established. His plan was to open an English-medium school aimed specifically at the sons of the Bengali élite and to give them a liberal education in Western arts and sciences as well as Christian religious instruction. The use of English and his specific focus on

Alexander Duff (1806–1878), by John Faed, 1851

the élite constituted a major innovation among missionary schools and was widely criticized. But Duff was persuaded that the popularity of English was already established among the leading families of Bengal, that Western education had already begun to undermine the foundations of their Hindu beliefs, and that what was wanted was a positive push in the direction of Christianity. The influence of this newly enlightened élite would 'filter down' the social order and thus be the instrument of the eventual transformation of Indian society and its conversion to Christianity. It was a leading feature of his plan to train teachers and preachers of the gospel from among the converts of the mission.

Teaching in Calcutta Shortly after his arrival in Calcutta, Duff was introduced to Raja Rammohan Roy, the most renowned Bengali intellectual of that era. Roy helped him locate a house where he could open his school and introduced him to his first pupils. Soon Duff was joined by another Scottish missionary, W. S. Mackay. From the beginning the school was highly successful in attracting students, the vast majority of whom eagerly learned the English language and absorbed Western knowledge. Very few, however, embraced Christianity. Yet there were in the first years a number of notable conversions bringing on a storm of protest and withdrawals from the school. The most prominent among these representatives of 'young Bengal' were Krishna Mohan Banerjea, who joined the Church of England and became a renowned pastor, polemicist, and teacher at the Bishop's College, and Lal Bihari De, a Christian pastor who later wrote a vivid remembrance of life in Duff's school. A third convert,

Gopinath Nandi, was killed in the Indian Mutiny in 1857. Despite temporary set-backs, the General Assembly Institution, as it was called, prospered, expanded into a missionary college, and gained the reputation of being among the best schools in India.

As a prolific writer of pamphlets and letters to government Duff entered the lists as an advocate of English-language education in the debate between Anglicists and orientalists which resulted in the minute of the governor-general in council on 7 March 1835, promoting English education. A pamphlet of Duff's, entitled *New Era of the English Language and Literature in India* (1837) showed the immense importance which he attached to this new governmental policy. Duff also petitioned the government on behalf of Western medical education and, with C. E. Trevelyan, proposed the application of the Roman alphabet to all the vernacular languages of India.

Return to Scotland Broken down in health Duff returned to Scotland in 1834. Here his missionary enthusiasm did not at first receive a very flattering response; but when he was called to address the general assembly, and when the young man of twenty-nine was able to hold the whole audience for nearly three hours in an empassioned speech, his triumph was complete. In this speech he called English 'the lever which, as the instrument of conveying the entire range of knowledge, was destined to move all Hindustan'. The speech was published as *The Church of Scotland's India Mission* (1835) and went through two printings totalling 15,000 copies. With these in hand Duff visited nearly every parish in Scotland gathering moral and monetary support for his project. He travelled to England and addressed the annual meeting of the Church Missionary Society and visited Cambridge University. Duff elaborated his plans and answered his critics in a second speech to the general assembly in 1837, published as *A Vindication of the Church of Scotland's India Mission*.

In 1839 Duff articulated a strategy for female education in which the first generation of educated males would demand educated wives and thus provide an opening for missionaries into the seclusion of the zenana and access to the mothers who would become the moral teachers of the next generation. Before leaving Scotland, Duff completed his theoretical exposition of missionary work in a 700 page treatise called *India and Indian Missions* (1840). These documents taken together constituted a full exposition of Duff's vision of missionary purpose and strategy and are among the most comprehensive in missionary literature.

During this time in Scotland and England, Duff's wife, Anne, gave birth to five children, the first of whom died after six months. When Duff determined to return to India in 1840 Anne accompanied him and left the four children in the care of Dr Brunton, professor of Hebrew at Edinburgh University, and his niece.

In India again When he reached Calcutta, Duff found many indications of the growth of Western ideas and values. His own institution was now accommodated on Cornwallis Square and was attended by nearly 700 pupils. It now had an established collegiate department. Duff was also able to open a girls' school with money he had raised in Scotland and England. The General Assembly Institution was a model for other schools established by the Church of Scotland in Madras under John Anderson and in Bombay under John Wilson. In all these schools English was the medium of the higher classes with the vernacular used in elementary classes, though in the Bombay and Madras schools much more emphasis was placed on vernacular.

Following the Disruption of the Church of Scotland in 1843, Duff with all the other foreign missionaries of the church adhered to the Free Church of Scotland, and all the buildings, books, and apparatus of every description that had been collected for his mission had to be surrendered. Once more he found himself destitute, but he soon recovered with support from the Free Church in Britain. Duff and his wife moved from Cornwallis Square to a house in Bow Bazaar. A house in Nimtollah Street in the heart of the town was found for the school. Duff was now a prominent figure in the intellectual life of Calcutta. He continued to hold evening lectures and discussions in his home attended by young men from other mission colleges, the government colleges, and his own school. Duff was an initiator of and frequent contributor to the *Calcutta Christian Observer*, an outlet for missionaries and other Christians of all denominations, and in 1844 he helped to found the *Calcutta Review*, a journal for a more general audience. Duff contributed frequently to early numbers of the magazine and was editor from 1845 to 1849, when ill health drove him away.

On hearing rumours of his failing health, several of Duff's friends made overtures to the general assembly to offer him the theological chair at New College, Edinburgh, vacated through the death of Dr Chalmers. Duff turned down the offer, characteristically in a public letter, saying that he was dedicated to missionary work. Nevertheless he returned to Scotland in 1849 for recuperation. On his way home he traversed India, seeing many of the chief seats of mission work and providing inspirational descriptions for missionary magazines and pamphlet publication. On his second visit home in 1851 he was elected moderator of the general assembly of the Free Church of Scotland. He made another tour of Scottish parishes with the aim of securing increased funding for the missions of the church. Duff was now undoubtedly the most prominent British missionary to India, and in 1853 he appeared before a select committee of the House of Lords. His testimony, and an extensive memorandum that he submitted to the president of the Board of Control, Sir Charles Wood (later Viscount Halifax), were influential in shaping the famous education dispatch of 1854 which established the framework for Indian education. It proceeded on the principle that it was the duty of the British government to provide India with 'improved European knowledge' by means of the English language in the higher branches of education, and by that of the vernacular languages to the great mass of the people.

The plan, both in Duff's draft and in the official dispatch, included the establishment of universities modelled on the University of London, setting examination standards and granting degrees to successful students trained in affiliated English and Anglo-vernacular colleges. It provided grants-in-aid—the system then in force in England—to all schools that met standards determined by government inspectors, the principal beneficiaries of this aid likely in the first instance to be mission schools. Duff was quite naturally delighted with this new policy of government, though he and his missionary colleagues fought a continuing battle against unsympathetic government officials to get its provisions fully and fairly carried into effect.

In 1854 Duff, at the earnest solicitation of George H. Stuart of Philadelphia, paid a visit to the United States and Canada. His travels and orations carried him as far west as St Louis and across Ontario and Quebec. The University of New York conferred on him the degree of LLD. The University of Aberdeen had previously made him DD.

'Mutiny' in India After returning to India in 1856 Duff recorded his reactions to the upheavals of 1857 in a series of twenty-five letters to the convener of the foreign missions committee; these were published serially in the *Witness* newspaper, and afterwards collected in a volume which went through several editions, entitled *The Indian Mutiny: its Causes and Results* (1858). Despite the title Duff warned his readers that this was not a mere mutiny of troops but a true rebellion precipitated by hatred and jealousy of advancing Christian civilization on the part of every religious group in India. Nevertheless, he argued that missionaries *per se* were not responsible for the outbreak, citing the tranquillity of south India, where Christian missions were the most advanced. The uprising, he wrote, was a providential warning that Britain had failed to advance the cause of the Christian church with energy and determination; the only true security for Britain was to eradicate these religious differences through the conversion of the masses to the Christian religion. In his letters he pointed to the steadfast loyalty of Indian Christians in the face of persecution by the rebels.

Establishing the University of Calcutta After the suppression of the rebellion, life in Calcutta resumed its normal course and Duff his accustomed activities. In 1859 he agreed to assume the presidency of the Bethune Society on the condition that the rules be changed to permit reference in its discussions to 'the Being, Providence, or works of God'. Duff was appointed by the governor-general to be one of those who drew up the constitution of the University of Calcutta, the first of the universities to be established under the 1854 dispatch. 'For the first six years of the history of the university', says his biographer, George Smith, 'in all that secured its catholicity, and in such questions as pure text-books and the establishment of the chair of physical science contemplated in the despatch, Dr Duff led the party in the senate' (Smith). In 1863 the office of vice-chancellor was pressed upon him by Sir Charles Trevelyan, to whose recommendation the viceroy

would probably have acceded. However, the state of things in Britain was such that the church recalled him to preside over its missions committee, and Duff himself was so unwell that his doctors sent him on a sea voyage to China. It was thought to be time that Duff should leave India.

Retirement, later years, and death On his leaving India the memorials devised for Duff in his honour were very numerous. In the centre of the educational buildings of Calcutta a marble hall was erected, and four Duff scholarships were instituted in the university. Portraits were placed in the Bethune Society and in Doveton College; a bust was mounted in his own college. A few Scots in India and adjacent countries offered him a gift of £11,000: he was able to live off the interest while the capital was destined for the invalided missionaries of his own church. Conspicuous among those who gave utterance to their esteem for him as he was leaving them was Sir Henry Maine, who had succeeded to the post of vice-chancellor of the university. Maine expressed his admiration for Duff's thorough self-sacrifice, and for his faith in the harmony of truth, remarking that it was very rare to see such a combination of the enthusiasm of religious conviction with fearlessness in encouraging the spread of knowledge.

Anne Duff preceded her husband to a home in Edinburgh given to them by friends and admirers. Duff chose the Cape route home in order to become practically acquainted with other missions of his church. He visited South Africa and traversed the country in a wagon, inspecting the mission stations. He reached Scotland at the end of 1864. His wife died early in the next year and Duff entered the last phase of his career alone with a daughter and a son for support. The two eldest children had died earlier. In 1865 Duff learned that his school in Calcutta had for the first time been visited by a governor-general, Sir John Lawrence, who wrote to him that it was calculated to do much good among the upper classes of Bengal society. Installed as convener of the foreign missions committee, Duff set himself to promote the work in every available way. To endow a missionary chair in New College, Edinburgh, he raised a sum of £10,000. He had never thought of occupying the chair, but circumstances altered his purpose and he became first missionary professor. He superintended all the arrangements for carrying into effect the scheme so dear to David Livingstone, of a Free Church mission on the banks of Lake Nyasa. He travelled to Syria to inspect a mission in Lebanon, and he visited the Netherlands, St Petersburg, and Moscow. He co-operated with Lady Aberdeen and Lord Polwarth in the establishment of a mission in Natal, the Gordon Memorial Mission, designed to commemorate the two sons of Lady Aberdeen. In 1873, when the state of the Free Church was critical, on account of a threatened schism, Duff was a second time called to the chair. This danger, strange to say, arose from a proposal for union between the Free and the United Presbyterian churches, which Duff greatly encouraged. Among his last acts was to take an active part in the formation of the Alliance of Reformed Churches holding the Presbyterian System. Before its first meeting, in 1877, Duff's health broke; he died in Edinburgh on 12 February 1878. His personal property he bequeathed for a lectureship on missions on the model of the Bampton lectures at Oxford. W. G. BLAIKIE, *rev.* DAVID W. SAVAGE

Sources G. Smith, *The life of Alexander Duff*, 2 vols. (1879) • A. A. Millar, *Alexander Duff of India* (1992) • L. B. Day, *Recollections of Alexander Duff* (1879) • W. P. Duff, *Memorials of Alexander Duff* (1890) • *Proceedings of the Bethune Society* (1862) • G. Viswanathan, *Masks of conquest: literary study and British rule in India* (1989) • S. Neill, *A history of Christianity in India, 1707–1858* (1985) • A. Porter, 'Scottish missions and education in nineteenth-century India: the changing face of trusteeship', *Journal of Imperial and Commonwealth History*, 16/3 (1987–8), 35–57 [special issue] • M. A. Laird, *Missionaries and education in Bengal, 1793–1837* (1972) • D. Chambers, 'The Church of Scotland's nineteenth-century foreign missions scheme', *Journal of Religious History*, 9 (1976–7) • R. J. Moore, *Sir Charles Wood's Indian policy, 1853–1866* [1966]

Archives U. St Andr. L. | NL Scot., letters to foreign mission committee • NL Scot., letters to David Maclagan • Rhodes University, Grahamstown, South Africa, Cory Library for Historical Research, letters to Bryce Ross • SOAS, letters to Sir William Mackinnon

Likenesses J. Faed, mezzotint, pubd 1851 (after J. Faed), BM, NPG • J. Faed, oils, 1851, Scot. NPG; on loan from Church of Scotland [*see illus.*] • J. Hutchison, plaster bust, Scot. NPG • C. H. Jeens, stipple, NPG • bust, General Assembly Institution, Calcutta • mezzotint, BM • portrait, Bethune Society, Calcutta • portrait, Doveton College, Calcutta

Duff, Sir Alexander Ludovic (1862–1933), naval officer, was born at Knockleith, Aberdeenshire, on 20 February 1862, the fourth son and seventh of the fourteen children of Colonel James Duff (*b.* 1820), of Knockleith, and his wife, Jane Bracken, daughter of Alan Colquhoun Dunlop, of Edinburgh. He entered the navy in 1875, and served as midshipman in the Mediterranean from 1877 to 1881. He served as sub-lieutenant in the royal yacht *Victoria and Albert*, and was promoted to lieutenant in September 1884, serving on the China station for two years in the *Agamemnon*.

Having qualified as torpedo lieutenant, Duff served for three years in the *Imperieuse*, flagship of the China station, and afterwards (1891) in the *Blake*, flagship of the North America station, and the torpedo depot-ship *Vulcan*. He was promoted commander in 1897. After two years in command of the destroyer *Bat* on training service at Devonport, he joined the cruiser *St George* as executive officer. He was promoted captain in 1902 and became flag captain in the battleship *Albemarle*, flagship of the rear-admiral, first in the Mediterranean and later in the Channel Fleet. On 3 September 1886 he married his cousin Janet Douglas (*d.* 1908), daughter of Garden William Duff, of Hatton Castle, Aberdeenshire. They had two daughters. On 10 January 1924 he married (Alice) Marjorie, who survived him, daughter of Charles Hill-Whitson, of Parkhill, Perthshire. They had no children.

In 1905 Duff became naval assistant to the controller of the navy for three years, then returned to sea service in command of the battleship *Temeraire*. In 1910 he was appointed commodore of the naval barracks at Portsmouth for a year before becoming director of naval mobilization (entitled director of the mobilization division

after the creation of the naval war staff in 1912), and he continued to hold this appointment after his promotion to rear-admiral in March 1913. In October 1914 he returned to sea service as rear-admiral, 4th battle squadron in the Grand Fleet. The commander-in-chief, Admiral Sir John Jellicoe, recognizing Duff's technical abilities, put him in charge, jointly with Rear-Admiral Arthur Cavenagh Leveson, of experiments with devices for defending ships from submarine mines and with other inventions; during the battle of Jutland, Duff flew his flag in the *Superb*.

When in December 1916 Jellicoe left the fleet to become first sea lord in order to cope with the immense problem of the U-boat war, he took Duff with him to the Admiralty as director of the anti-submarine division which was then formed in the naval staff. Duff formulated the detailed proposals which finally led to the adoption of the convoy system, as well as many other important initiatives in this area, which provided much improved protection for British vessels from the submarines. Six months later he joined the Board of Admiralty with the title of assistant chief of the naval staff, with specific responsibility across all divisions for issues concerning anti-submarine warfare. With others, Duff threatened to resign after Jellicoe's dismissal in 1917, but pertinently commented that it was the muddled approach and arguing within the Admiralty that 'put us entirely in the wrong and the politicians were quick to seize it' (Marder, 4.345).

Duff was promoted vice-admiral in 1918 and appointed KCB. On leaving the Admiralty in 1919 he was appointed commander-in-chief of the China station and while there convened a conference with the commanders-in-chief of adjoining stations which recommended the establishment of the naval base at Singapore. He was promoted admiral in 1921 and relinquished the China command the following year. He was appointed CB (civil in 1912 and military in 1916), GCB in 1926, KCVO in 1922, and GBE in 1924. For his services he was awarded, among other foreign orders, the commandership of the Légion d'honneur and the American DSM. He retired in 1925, and settled at Copdock, Ipswich. He died in London on 22 November 1933 and was cremated at Golders Green on 24 November. His ashes were scattered at sea off Harwich.

H. G. THURSFIELD, *rev.* MARC BRODIE

Sources *The Times* (23 Nov 1933) • *The Times* (25 Nov 1933) • Burke, *Gen. GB* • A. J. Marder, *From the Dreadnought to Scapa Flow: the Royal Navy in the Fisher era, 1904–1919*, 5 vols. (1961–70) • J. Terraine, *Business in great waters: the U-boat wars, 1916–1945* (1989) • J. Jellicoe, *The crisis of the naval war* (1920) • WWW • private information (1949) • CGPLA *Eng. & Wales* (1934)

Archives NMM, corresp. and papers

Likenesses W. Stoneman, photograph, 1917, NPG • J. A. M. Hay, oils, 1925, NMM • W. Stoneman, photograph, 1931, NPG • photograph, repro. in Marder, *From the Dreadnought to Scapa Flow*, vol. 4, facing p. 41 • photograph, repro. in *The Times* (23 Nov 1933), 18

Duff, Sir (Arthur) Antony (1920–2000), diplomatist and intelligence officer, was born on 25 February 1920 at Var Trees, Moreton, near Dorchester, Dorset, the son of Admiral Sir Arthur Allan Morison Duff (1874–1952), naval officer, and his wife, Margaret Grace, daughter of Commander Wyatt Rawson, naval officer. He had a brother and two sisters. In 1933 he entered the Royal Naval College, Dartmouth, where he passed out top of his term; he was commissioned a midshipman in 1937.

Duff served in the battleship *Malaya* and in the destroyer *Beagle* but volunteered for submarine service shortly after the outbreak of the Second World War. He was mentioned in dispatches before being given command of the submarine *Stubborn* at the age of twenty-two. In 1943 *Stubborn* conveyed the midget submarine X-7 to Norway, where it placed two charges beneath the German battleship *Tirpitz*, effectively crippling her. The commander of the X-7 was awarded the VC and Duff a DSC for this operation. The following year *Stubborn* sank two enemy ships off Trondheim but shortly afterwards was herself subjected to heavy and accurate attack by depth-charges, which jammed her hydroplanes in the dive position. As *Stubborn* plunged well beyond her safe limit Duff first tried to balance her by shifting the crew around the vessel and then diverted their last remaining compressed air supplies to the ballast tanks. After several hours stuck on the bottom *Stubborn* dislodged herself and shot to the surface at an angle of 70°. Duff managed to get his ship home without a single casualty, attributing her rescue to 'our guardian angel' (*Daily Telegraph*); the Admiralty, however, attributed it to Duff's calm and courage and awarded him an immediate DSO. On 28 March 1944 he married Pauline Marion (Polly), the 24-year-old widow of Flight-Lieutenant J. A. Sword and daughter of Captain Robert Hesketh Bevan RN; she brought one stepson to the marriage and together they had one further son and two daughters.

When the war ended Duff's eyesight was found to have been adversely affected, and his naval career could not be continued. Despite having no university degree he was accepted into the foreign service in January 1946 and deployed in a number of demanding posts. He was in Greece as a third secretary during the civil war there, from 1946 to 1948, then in Cairo as a second secretary (1949–52) before being transferred to the Foreign Office as private secretary to the minister of state, with the rank of first secretary. Appointments to Paris (1954–57) and Bonn (1960–64) followed, and he was promoted counsellor in 1962. His first ambassadorial appointment was to Nepal (1964–5), where he was made a CMG, and after a further spell at home, in the Commonwealth Office (1965–8) and Foreign and Commonwealth Office (1968–9), he was posted as deputy high commissioner to Malaysia (1969–72) and as high commissioner to Kenya (1972–5). He was promoted KCMG in 1973. In all these appointments he established a reputation for running outstandingly happy missions, a task in which he was much assisted by his wife. His final normal appointment in the diplomatic service was as a deputy under-secretary of state at the Foreign and Commonwealth Office in London (1975–80), in the course of which he stood in for the permanent under-secretary when the latter was away. It was during this period in London that he led the official team to the Lancaster House talks on the independence of Rhodesia, and in 1979–80 he went out to Salisbury as deputy to the political-appointee governor, Christopher Soames, during the final months before the handover. The calm and dependable Duff was a perfect foil to the flamboyant Soames, and on the conclusion of his mission Duff (who was promoted GCMG in 1980) was given the unusual honour for a diplomat of being sworn of the privy council.

Duff might have retired with these honours but instead he was asked to act as deputy secretary and intelligence co-ordinator in the Cabinet Office from 1980 until 1985. This period spanned the Falklands War, when the intelligence community was much criticized for not foreseeing the Argentinian invasion, and Duff found himself defending his own and his colleagues' actions to the Franks commission of inquiry. It was also during this period that he was instrumental in persuading Margaret Thatcher, as prime minister, that Gorbachov was the coming man in the Soviet Union and one with whom she could do business.

It was therefore not altogether surprising that, when the Bridge inquiry revealed that the Security Service (MI5) was suffering from low morale and poor performance following a series of scandals, Thatcher asked Duff to take over as director-general and sort matters out. His easy way with people did much to restore a sense of purpose to the service, and his shift of emphasis towards countering terrorism and away from concentrating too exclusively on communist subversion, or (as it had been alleged) domestic issues, did much to instil a contemporary sense of direction. He also took significant steps towards making the service more open and accountable. But problems persisted, including notably the attempts to silence Peter Wright (a former MI5 officer), who intended to publish damaging allegations in his book *Spycatcher* (1987). All in all Duff was relieved to stand down and retire finally from public service in 1987.

Duff's last years were spent serving the community in a very different role: he worked at a day centre for the homeless, performing the most humble tasks—making and serving tea while chatting to the clients, who knew him simply as Tony. He also served on the board of London's Homeless Network, where his Whitehall connections were occasionally deployed to good use. But it was his hands-on work with the down-and-out that gave him greatest satisfaction.

Tall, well-built, and good-looking, Duff possessed an unusual capacity to inspire trust in others; frightened young submariners, lonely junior diplomats in far-flung countries, harassed prime ministers and foreign secretaries, resentful African freedom fighters, confused intelligence officers, and disorientated homeless drifters—all felt that when Duff's reassuring figure was looming over them nothing could go too badly wrong. They were never let down and seldom disappointed. He died on 13 August 2000, of bronchopneumonia, at Yeovil District Hospital and was survived by his wife, Polly, and their four children.   JOHN URE

Sources *The Times* (17 Aug 2000) · *The Guardian* (18 Aug 2000) · *Daily Telegraph* (21 Aug 2000) · WWW · Burke, *Peerage* · private information (2004) · personal knowledge (2004) · b. cert. · m. cert. · d. cert.

Likenesses photograph, 1979, Hult. Arch. • photograph, c.1979–1980, repro. in *The Guardian* • Marc [M. Boxer], caricature, 1985, repro. in *Daily Telegraph* • photograph, repro. in *The Times*

Duff, Sir Beauchamp (1855–1918), army officer, was born in Aberdeenshire on 17 February 1855, the second son of Garden William Duff of Hatton Castle, Turriff, Aberdeenshire, and his wife, Douglas Isabella Maria, daughter of Beauchamp C. Urquhart of Meldrum. He was educated at Trinity College, Glenalmond, and the Royal Military Academy, Woolwich. Duff joined the Royal Artillery in 1874 and served with the regiment during the Second Anglo-Afghan War in 1879–80. In 1877 he married, in India, Grace Maria, daughter of Oswald Wood, Indian Civil Service, of Glenalmond, Perthshire, and had two sons and one daughter (who died in 1897).

In 1881 Duff transferred to the Bengal staff corps and was appointed a lieutenant in the 9th Bengal infantry, with which he served until he reached the rank of captain. Duff attended the Staff College at Camberley, passing out with distinction in 1889. He was appointed a deputy assistant adjutant-general in September 1891, and then held a succession of staff and administrative appointments in India. Duff served on the north-west frontier as a brigade major during the Isazai expedition in 1892, and later in the same role with the escort accompanying the delimitation commission in Waziristan. Following an attack on the commission at Wana in November 1894, he again served as brigade major during the ensuing punitive expedition against the Mahsuds and Wazirs. Duff was mentioned in dispatches, and after being promoted major in 1894 he was made brevet lieutenant-colonel in 1895 in recognition of his services. The same year he was appointed military secretary to the commander-in-chief, Sir George Stuart White, and held this post for more than three years, being made a CIE in 1897 and promoted substantive colonel in 1898. He was then appointed assistant military secretary for Indian affairs at the War Office in January 1899, a post created some years earlier to liaise with the India Office and assist in the conduct of Indian military affairs.

After the Second South African War broke out Duff was sent to Natal in September 1899 as military secretary to Sir George White, serving with him throughout the siege of Ladysmith. Following the relief, he served on Roberts's staff as assistant adjutant-general until October 1899 during the operations in the Orange Free State, the Transvaal, and Cape Colony. He was mentioned in dispatches and made a CB.

Duff served for eighteen months at headquarters on his return to India as deputy assistant adjutant-general (1901–2). He then commanded Allahabad district as a brigadier-general for nine months, during part of which he also served as acting adjutant-general. Duff was then appointed adjutant-general with the rank of major-general in June 1903. For more than six years he acted as the commander-in-chief's right-hand man while Lord Kitchener introduced a range of sweeping changes in the organization and administration of the army in India. Duff's administrative skill and experience made him invaluable at the time these reforms were introduced and

during the clash with the viceroy, Lord Curzon, over the abolition of the post of military member of council. He was appointed to the newly created post of chief of staff in March 1906 and was made a KCVO. Duff returned to England in 1907 to provide the secretary of state, Lord Morley, with detailed explanations of Kitchener's further proposals to reorganize the army commands in India. In 1907 he was appointed military secretary at the India Office, and was appointed KCSI in 1910 and promoted GCB in 1911.

Duff took over command of the army in India from Sir O'Moore Creagh in March 1914. The army in India was still equipped primarily for military operations on the north-west frontier and the maintenance of internal security. His predecessor had battled against rigid financial restrictions imposed by the government of India which had prevented the full completion of Kitchener's scheme and proposals to remedy deficiencies in equipment. A committee headed by Lord Nicholson, including Sir William Meyer of the finance department, had only recently reviewed military organization in India and had further deprecated any reforms involving additional expenditure. Within five months of his appointment, Duff's dual responsibilities as commander-in-chief and member of council under the changes of 1905 were dramatically increased by the outbreak of war in 1914, which also deprived him of the services of Sir William Birdwood, his secretary in the army department. His duties placed an immense strain on Duff, who was severely overworked and lacked a deputy with whom he could share some of the burden. His elder son, Captain Beauchamp Oswald Duff, was killed in action near Ypres on 7 November 1914.

The army in India dispatched two fully organized and equipped mixed divisions and two cavalry divisions, with four extra brigades of artillery, to France and Flanders in response to urgent demands from the home government. Additionally twelve battalions of infantry and auxiliary services were sent to east Africa. These forces were soon followed, for service in France and Egypt, by fifty-two British and Indian battalions and twenty batteries of artillery, which were replaced by Territorial Army units from England; reinforcements for Aden and other British colonies absorbed nearly 6000 additional troops from India. Turkey entered the war on 29 October 1914 before these demands had all been fully met, and the home government ordered an expedition, control of which was vested with the government of India, to be sent to Mesopotamia. A fully equipped Indian division of all arms was landed and had captured Basrah, the base of future operations, by the end of November 1914. However, India was depleted of supplies and reserves after equipping so many expeditions, despite the insistent threat posed by Afghanistan, the border tribes, and the needs of internal security. India was almost entirely dependent on Britain for their replacement, but the demands of the War Office and Admiralty meant little was available. The gradual extension of operations in Mesopotamia made it more and more difficult to keep up the necessary supplies, while

Indian reserves of medical personnel were quickly exhausted.

The campaign in Mesopotamia was strategically defensive initially, with operations halting after Nasiriyyah, Kut al-Amara, and ʿAziziyyah had been occupied. During the summer and autumn of 1915 the possibility of a further advance was discussed, to provide a decisive victory that would offset failure in the Dardanelles. The authorities both in England and in India agreed, however, that to capture Baghdad and then to be forced to retreat would have a worse effect than to remain in current positions. Moreover, in order to hold it and secure a line of communications, an additional one or two divisions would be necessary as reinforcements. Duff warned that such an advance was unwise with existing forces, and in a draft telegram to the secretary of state, submitted to the viceroy, Lord Hardinge of Penshurst, he expressed doubt 'whether in the present state of the river combined with our present insufficient number of light-draught steamers, we could adequately supply our troops there' ('War in Mesopotamia', 22–3). His opinion, however, was not communicated by the viceroy to the secretary of state, and the urgent need for increasing the amount of river transport available to support a further advance, for the conveyance of supplies and reinforcements, and for the evacuation of sick and wounded, was not realized by the government in England. A large supply of tugs and barges was ordered from England in August 1915 by the government of India after Sir John Nixon, commanding in Mesopotamia, requested them. It was clear, however, that they could not arrive in India for many months, as they had to be built. Despite this the secretary of state telegraphed the viceroy stating that Nixon might advance on Baghdad as long as he was satisfied that he had sufficient forces at his disposal; two divisions from France were promised as reinforcements. Duff passed on this telegram to Nixon without comment and, whatever his personal doubts, seems to have believed that it was not for him to interfere with the man on the spot.

When Sir Charles Townshend advanced (against his own judgement and with serious misgivings), under orders from Nixon, he met a reinforced Turkish army occupying a prepared defensive position at Ctesiphon, and after a severe engagement conducted a fighting withdrawal to Kut al-Amara. Townshend was encircled there and after a defence lasting five months surrendered on 29 April 1916. The available river transport quickly proved hopelessly insufficient to convey large numbers of sick and wounded from Kut al-Amara or the casualties suffered by the forces attempting to relieve the beleaguered garrison. It was also impossible to convey up river the large numbers of troops, artillery, and supplies waiting at Basrah as reinforcements.

The failure to capture Baghdad was a striking contrast to the brilliant successes that had marked the earlier operations. This and reports that the sick and wounded were suffering badly caused great consternation in England, and a royal commission was appointed in August 1916 to inquire into the origin and conduct of the operations in Mesopotamia, and into responsibility of the government departments concerned. Duff, who had been appointed GCSI in January 1916, was recalled from India in order to give evidence, and in consequence vacated his appointment as commander-in-chief. In December he underwent four days of examination and cross-examination. The commission's report (17 May 1917) assigned to him a large share of the blame, ranking him next after Sir John Nixon and Lord Hardinge, the viceroy, in responsibility among officials in India for the expedition's shortcomings. The main grounds for criticism were: the shortage of medical personnel and supplies; delay in investigating the unofficial reports of medical breakdown (which were subsequently confirmed); the deficiency of water transport for the greatly increased numbers of troops deployed; and provision for the sick and wounded after the advance on Baghdad had commenced. The commission also blamed Duff for not leaving his post and visiting Mesopotamia or Bombay to ascertain what was happening, though he appears to have felt himself bound to stay with the viceroy, having no deputy to leave in charge of the army department. The commission's censures were, however, qualified in part by the statement that 'the combination of duties of commander-in-chief and military member of council cannot adequately be performed by any one man in time of war' ('War in Mesopotamia', 116). Duff had, in fact, been set a wellnigh impossible task in the circumstances. The Mesopotamian expedition differed from any pre-war schemes contemplated by the Indian general staff, and in conjunction with so many other undertakings it posed immense practical difficulties for the military authorities in India, given that the army had been starved of the necessary funds to prepare adequately for a campaign against European troops.

Duff did not live long enough to complete the defence of his actions during the campaign in Mesopotamia which he proposed to write. The mental strain of the war had gradually eroded his health from the spring of 1915, and he suffered badly from insomnia. When he returned to England the effects were all too apparent to those that knew him. He died on 20 January 1918 at the Caledonian Club, Charles Street, St James's Square, London.

J. H. SEABROOKE, rev. T. R. MOREMAN

Sources *Indian Army List* (July 1916) · 'Commission … to enquire into the operations of war in Mesopotamia', *Parl. papers* (1917), 16.773, Cd 8610 · F. J. Moberly, ed., *The campaign in Mesopotamia, 1914–1918*, 4 vols. (1923–7) · Summary of the administration of Lord Hardinge of Penshurst, 11/1910–3/1916, 1916 · A. J. Barker, *The neglected war: Mesopotamia, 1914–1918* (1967) · C. V. F. Townshend, *My campaign in Mesopotamia* (1920) · 'Correspondence regarding the administration of the army in India', *Parl. papers* (1905), vol. 57, Cd 2572, 2615 · 'Correspondence regarding the administration of the army in India', *Parl. papers* (1906), vol. 81, Cd 2718, 2642 · CGPLA Eng. & Wales (1918) · *Army List*

Archives CUL, corresp. with Lord Hardinge, etc. · PRO, letters to Lord Kitchener on Indian affairs, PRO30/57; Wo159

Wealth at death £4151 12s. 2d.: probate, 8 May 1918, CGPLA Eng. & Wales

Duff, Edward Gordon (1863–1924), bibliographer, was born on 16 February 1863 in Liverpool, the youngest of four sons (there were no daughters) of Robert Duff, merchant, of Prince's Park, Liverpool, and his wife, Jane Gordon. He was educated at Cheltenham College, entered Wadham College, Oxford, in 1883, and took a pass degree in classics in 1887. While at Oxford he began to draw up a catalogue of the fifteenth-century books in the Bodleian Library. Neither the Bodleian nor the British Museum, however, would offer him a place, and in 1889 he began to read for the bar.

Duff had to wait for more congenial work until 1893, when Mrs Rylands appointed him her librarian. He had the task of cataloguing her books (including the Spencer library) advising on new purchases, organizing the collection, and supervising its transfer to the new John Rylands Library in Manchester. The library opened in 1900, but Duff resigned shortly afterwards, having quarrelled with the trustees. He never took another permanent job, but supported himself with freelance work (he catalogued books for the London booksellers Pearson & Co.), with academic appointments (he was Sandars reader in bibliography at Cambridge in 1899, 1904, and 1911), and with the income from his books.

Duff's first work, *Early Printed Books*, was published in 1893, followed by *Early English Printing* in 1896. His works on early printing included two textbooks, *The Printers, Stationers and Bookbinders of Westminster and London from 1476 to 1535* (1906) and *The English Provincial Printers, Stationers and Bookbinders to 1557* (1912), a biographical dictionary, *A Century of the English Book Trade, 1457–1557* (1905), and a bibliography, twenty-eight years in the making, of *Fifteenth Century English Books* (1917). A work on armorial book-stamps remained unpublished.

Duff regarded bibliography as a science: his work set new standards of accuracy. He was scathing in his criticism of colleagues whose work did not match these standards. A Liverpool friend remembered him as 'a tall spare man with alert eyes and a very beautiful voice, but with an ironic and often unkind humour about his contemporaries'.

Duff never married. He lived in Liverpool until 1915, and thereafter in Oxford. He died at his home, 293 Woodstock Road, Oxford, on 28 September 1924.

ARNOLD HUNT, *rev.*

Sources *The Library*, 4th ser., 5 (1924–5), 264–6 · *Library Association Record*, 26 (1924), 226–8 · A. S. Marsh, 'Edward Gordon Duff: a bibliography', diploma diss., U. Lond., 1953 · letters and MSS, CUL, Add. MSS 6463, 8294–7, 8591–8631 · correspondence, Hunt. L. · *CGPLA Eng. & Wales* (1924) · private information (2004)
Archives Bodl. Oxf., list of books · CUL, Add. MSS 6463, 8294–8297, 8591–8631 · Hunt. L., corresp. · JRL, MS catalogue of books printed on vellum; minutes and address book of Bibliographical Society of Lancashire
Wealth at death £16,241 16s. 5d.: probate, 17 Nov 1924, *CGPLA Eng. & Wales*

Duff, James, second Earl Fife (1729–1809), landowner, was born on 28 September 1729 in Banff, the eldest surviving son in the family of five sons and five daughters of William Duff, Lord Braco of Kilbryde (d. 1763), and his second wife, Jean, daughter of Sir James Grant of Grant, bt. His father was MP for Banffshire (1727–34), and was created

Lord Braco in the peerage of Ireland on 28 July 1735, and Earl Fife and Viscount Macduff, also in the peerage of Ireland, by patent dated 26 April 1759, after proving his descent from Macduff, earl of Fife. James Duff was educated at home by William Guthrie, later author of *A Geographical Grammar* (1770); intended for a legal career, he was then sent to the University of Edinburgh. In 1754 he was elected MP for Banff, and he was re-elected in 1761, 1768, 1774, and 1780; from 1784 to 1790 he represented the county of Elgin. As an MP Duff seldom spoke, but his enmity towards Pitt led him to speak in the House of Lords on 2 February 1801, attacking Pitt's conduct of the war.

On 30 September 1763 Duff succeeded his father in the title and estates, mainly in Aberdeen and Moray, and he devoted himself to the improvement of the property, which he greatly increased by the purchase of land in the north of Scotland. He settled at Banff and built Duff House, and he planted trees on 14,000 acres of hills and heath around it. For this he was twice awarded the gold medal of the Society for the Encouragement of Arts, Manufactures, and Commerce. He set an example to the farmers on his estates by setting up a model farm near each of his estates, where agriculture and cattle breeding were carried on under his personal supervision. In 1782 and 1783, when all the crops failed, Duff reduced the rents paid by his tenants by 20 per cent, and sold grain to the poor considerably below the market price, importing several cargoes from England, which he sold at a loss of £3000.

On 5 June 1759, Duff had married Lady Dorothea Sinclair, only child of Alexander Sinclair, ninth earl of Caithness, but they had no children. He did, however, have three illegitimate children with a woman from Keith, Margaret Adam. The eldest of these children was Sir James *Duff (1753–1839). James Duff was created a British peer with the title of Baron Fife in 1793. He also served as lord lieutenant of Banffshire and founded the town of Macduff, changing its name from Doune to Macduff. It cost him £5000 to build the harbour. Duff died at his home, Fife House in Whitehall, London, on 24 January 1809, and was buried in the mausoleum at Duff House, Banffshire. His British peerage became extinct on his death. He was succeeded in his Irish earldom by his next brother, Alexander.

ANNE PIMLOTT BAKER

Sources R. Douglas, *The peerage of Scotland*, 2nd edn, ed. J. P. Wood, 1 (1813), 578 · J. Foster, *Members of parliament, Scotland … 1357–1882*, 2nd edn (privately printed, London, 1882) · Burke, *Peerage*
Archives U. Aberdeen L., corresp.; corresp. and papers | BL, corresp. with George Grenville, Add. MS 57815 · BL, letters to Lord Grenville, Add. MS 58987 · CKS, letters to Lord Amherst · Duke U., Perkins L., letters to Henry Dundas · NA Scot., letters to the Duffs of Fetteresso · NA Scot., letters to Henry Dundas · NA Scot., corresp. with William Rose
Likenesses F. Cotes, portrait, 1765, North Carolina Museum of Art, Raleigh · R. Dunkarton, mezzotint (after A. W. Devis, 1805), NPG

Duff, Sir James (1753–1839), army officer, was born at Keith, Aberdeenshire, the eldest illegitimate son of James *Duff, second Earl Fife (1729–1809), and Margaret Adam, of Keith. His mother was of humble status, and her three children with Fife were taken at an early age and placed under William Rose, Fife's factor. Duff was handsome, and Fife lavished affection on him. He was educated at Keith Academy and at King's College, Aberdeen, where he graduated MA in 1771. Fife paid for his education, his army promotions, and for his small Aberdeenshire estate of Kinstair, and made him his constant companion. Commissioned ensign and lieutenant, 1st foot guards, in April 1769 and lieutenant and captain in April 1775, and appointed battalion adjutant in 1777, Duff served as brigade-major in 1780 during the Gordon riots. He was knighted in April 1779, as proxy for his father's friend Sir James Harris (later first earl of Malmesbury; 1746–1820) at Harris's installation as KB, and promoted captain and lieutenant-colonel in July 1780. On 12 August 1785 he married Basilia (*d.* 1849), daughter and heir of James Dawes of Rockspring, Jamaica; they had one son and three daughters. Marriage brought him financial independence and a sugar plantation. He was MP for Banffshire, where the Duff family electoral influence was dominant, from 1784 to 1788, and opposed his father and the government during the Regency crisis of 1788. The resulting estrangement lasted until February 1793, when, on the eve of Duff's departure for active service in the Netherlands, Fife initiated a reconciliation. Duff fought at Valenciennes and commanded the guards' light infantry battalion in 1794. Promoted colonel in November 1790 and major-general in October 1794, he was appointed colonel of the 50th regiment in August 1798.

As general officer commanding the Limerick district from 1797 Duff helped to crush the Irish rebellion of 1798. His capture in May of Kildare with a flying column earned the commendation of the Irish government. He led his force of dragoons and militia towards the rebel camp at the Curragh of Kildare. Inflamed by rebel outrages, and especially by the murder of the seventeen-year-old son of a militia officer, they were determined to 'make a dreadful example of the rebels' (Pakenham, 163). However, unknown to Duff and his force the Curragh rebels had begun to make terms with Sir Ralph Dundas, who offered generous conditions. On 29 May, at the Curragh, rebels reportedly fired on Duff's advancing men, who attacked, killing about 200; Dundas wrote that 'nothing could stop the Rage of the troops' (ibid.). The episode ended the process of peacemaking, embarrassed the government, and prolonged the rising, but was praised by the Dublin ultras.

Promoted lieutenant-general in January 1801 and general in October 1809, Duff died, the oldest general officer in the army, at his home, Funtington House, near Chichester, Sussex, on 5 December 1839, and was buried in Funtington parish churchyard.

H. M. STEPHENS, *rev.* STEPHEN WOOD

Sources A. Tayler and H. Tayler, *The book of the Duffs*, 2 vols. (1914), vol. 2, pp. 506–16 · HoP, *Commons, 1754–90*, vol. 2, p. 350 · F. W. Hamilton, *The origin and history of the first or grenadier guards*, 2 (1874) · A. Tayler and H. Tayler, *Lord Fife and his factor* (1925) · *GM*, 2nd ser., 14 (1840), 319 · GEC, *Peerage* · T. Pakenham, *The year of liberty: the story of the great Irish rebellion of 1798* (1969)

Likenesses engraving, repro. in Tayler and Tayler, *The book of the Duffs*, 506 · portrait, repro. in Tayler and Tayler, *Lord Fife and his factor*, 35; formerly at Duff House, 1925

Duff, James, **fourth Earl Fife** (1776–1857), army officer in the Spanish service, elder son of the Hon. Alexander Duff (1731–1811), advocate (who succeeded his brother as third Earl Fife in 1809), and his wife, Mary, daughter of George Skene, was born at Aberdeen on 6 October 1776. His mother was considered unfit to care for her children—she later eloped with a criminal cousin—and when Duff was six the second Earl Fife, without legitimate issue and wanting to groom the child as his heir, removed him and his brother from their parents and supervised their education. Duff was educated by Dr Chapman at Inchdrewer, Banffshire, in 1783; at Westminster School, London; and at Christ Church, Oxford, where he matriculated in February 1794. He was admitted to Lincoln's Inn on 9 April 1794, but in 1796 he abandoned his legal studies. He joined the allied army on the continent and was present at the Congress of Radstadt (1798). On 9 September 1799 he married Maria Caroline (*b.* 1775), third daughter of John Manners of Grantham Grange, Lincolnshire. After his marriage he mixed with the Carlton House set and lost money gambling. His wife was bitten on the nose by her rabid pet Newfoundland dog, and she died of rabies at Edinburgh on 20 December 1805.

In 1808 Duff sought distraction from his wife's death by volunteering to join the Spanish in their war against Napoleon. His assistance was gladly received, especially as he came full of enthusiasm and with a full purse, and he became a staff officer in the Spanish service. In January 1809 he became Viscount Macduff on his father's accession to the Irish earldom of Fife, but he still continued to serve in Spain, and was present at the battle of Talavera, and also at the siege of Cadiz, where he was severely wounded in the attack on Fort Matagorda in 1810. On 17 April 1811 he succeeded his father as fourth Earl Fife, and as lord lieutenant of Banffshire, and he returned to England after being awarded the order of San Fernando and promoted to the rank of lieutenant-general. He was grand master of freemasons in 1814–16, Canningite tory MP for Banffshire from 1818 to 1827, and a lord of the bedchamber in 1819–21 and from 1827 to 1835. He was created a peer of the United Kingdom as Lord Fife on 27 April 1827, at Canning's premiership, and in September was made a KT. He soon afterwards retired altogether to Scotland, where he lived at Duff House, Banffshire. A popular, improving landlord, he pursued his interests in farming and cattle raising. In later life he was a whig. He died, childless, at Duff House on 9 March 1857, and the United Kingdom barony of Fife thereby became extinct. He was succeeded as fifth Earl Fife by his nephew, James Duff, the elder son of his only brother, General the Hon. Sir Alexander Duff (*d.* 1851), who commanded the 88th foot (Connaught Rangers) from 1798 to 1810, serving at its head in Sir David Baird's expedition from India to Egypt in 1801, and in the attack on Buenos Aires in 1806.

H. M. STEPHENS, *rev.* CHARLES ESDAILE

Sources GM, 3rd ser., 2 (1857) · *A memoir of the services of Lieutenant-General Sir Samuel Ford Whittingham*, ed. F. Whittingham, new edn (1868) · Foster, *Alum. Oxon.* · D. R. Fisher, 'Duff, James', HoP, *Commons* · GEC, *Peerage*, new edn
Archives U. Aberdeen L., corresp. and papers | U. Aberdeen L., letters to R. W. Duff
Likenesses R. Dighton, coloured etching, pubd 1821, NPG · W. Holl, stipple, 1830 (after F. Rochard), BM, NPG · W. Holl, stipple (after Birnie), BM, NPG

Duff, James Cuninghame Grant (1789–1858), army officer in the East India Company and historian, was born on 8 July 1789 in Banff, the eldest son of John Grant (*d.* 1799) of Kincardine O'Neil and Margaret Miln Duff (*d.* 1824) of Eden, near Aberdeen. He took the additional surname Duff in 1825 after succeeding to the estate of Eden. He took the additional name Cuninghame in 1850 after succeeding to an estate in Fife through his wife's mother. After his father's death, Grant's mother moved to Aberdeen, where he went to school and to the Marischal College. He was to have joined the civil service of the East India Company, but impatient at the prospect of delay in obtaining a post he accepted a cadetship in 1805 and sailed for Bombay. Having studied at the cadet establishment there, he joined the 1st Bombay native infantry (Bombay Grenadiers).

Grant was present in 1808 as ensign in command at the storming of Malia, the fortified stronghold of a gang of freebooters, where he displayed conspicuous gallantry. On 6 February 1811 he became adjutant to his regiment and Persian interpreter, and was even more influential than this position indicated. Promoted lieutenant on 16 November 1811, he attracted the attention of Mountstuart Elphinstone, then resident of Poona, and became, along with Captain Henry Pottinger, his assistant and devoted friend. Elphinstone characterized him in 1858 as 'a man of much ability, and what is more, much good sense'. Contemporaries regarded him as particularly successful in understanding the Indian character, and in discovering the mean between too rapid reform and too great deference to custom and tradition.

During the long operations against Peshwa Baji Rao, terminating in his overthrow, Grant took a considerable part, both in a civil and in a military capacity. On the settlement of the country he was appointed in April 1818 to the office of resident of Satara, based in the heart of a warlike province, the centre of the Maratha confederacy, with but one European companion and a body of native infantry. By proclamation, on 11 April 1818, Elphinstone made over to Grant full powers for the arrangement of the affairs of Satara. He was made brevet captain on 8 January 1819, and captain on 20 December the same year.

After the battle of Ashta in February 1819, the raja of Satara, Pertab Singh, who had been held captive by Baji Rao, was restored to the throne under the tutelage of Grant. By treaty of 25 September 1819 Grant was to administer the country in the raja's name until 1822, and then transfer it to him and his officers when they should prove fit for the task. Grant impressed upon the raja that any

relations with other princes, except such as the treaty provided for, would be punished with annexation of his territory, and trained him so successfully in the habits of business that Pertab Singh was made direct ruler of Satara in 1822. During this time Grant concluded treaties with the various Satara *jagirdars*, and the arrangements which he prescribed both for the etiquette of the durbar and for the management of the revenue remained as he left them for many years. Under Grant's successor, General Briggs, however, relations between Satara and the East India Company once more deteriorated.

After five years the anxiety and toil of his work in Satara had broken down Grant's health, and compelled his return to Scotland. There he occupied himself in writing his *History of the Mahrattas* (1826), the materials for which he had long been collecting from state papers, family and temple archives, and personal conversations with the Maratha chiefs. In 1825 he married Jane Catharine, the only daughter of Sir Whitelaw Ainslie, an eminent physician and author of the *Materia medica Indica*. They had a daughter and two sons, and she survived her husband. Their elder son was Sir Mountstuart Elphinstone Grant-*Duff, Liberal MP and governor of Madras. James Grant Duff died at his home, Eden House, near Aberdeen, on 23 September 1858.   J. A. HAMILTON, *rev.* ALEX MAY

Sources *Indian Army List* · C. A. Kincaid, *A history of the Maratha people* (1925) · J. G. Duff, *A history of the Mahrattas*, 3 vols. (1826) · M. Edwardes, *Glorious sahibs: the romantic as empire-builder* (1968) · Boase, *Mod. Eng. biog.*
Archives BL OIOC, corresp. and papers · Royal United Services Institute, London, coatee, epaulette, and sash
Wealth at death £43,354 10s. 1d.: Scottish confirmation sealed in London, 23 Dec 1858, NA Scot., SC 1/36/43/751–4

Duff, Sir James Fitzjames (1898–1970), educationist and academic administrator, was born in Cambridge on 1 February 1898, the second of three sons and two daughters of James Duff Duff (1860–1940), a distinguished Latinist who was a fellow and classical tutor of Trinity College, Cambridge, and his wife, Laura Eleanor (1871–1956), daughter of Sir William Lenox-Conyngham of Springhill, co. Londonderry. He was descended from the Duffs of Hatton Castle and Knockleith in Aberdeenshire and the Lenox-Conynghams long resident in Ulster. An uncle on his father's side was Admiral Sir Alexander Duff and on his mother's side was Sir Gerald Lenox-Conyngham, geodesist, also a fellow of Trinity College. James showed early promise and took every advantage of his family connections; he became a scholar of Winchester College in 1910, secured a Trinity College entrance scholarship at sixteen, and published a prize poem in 1916. He was commissioned in the Royal Flying Corps and qualified as a pilot, but a crash landing led to his being invalided out in 1917. After teaching temporarily at Winchester he went up to Trinity in January 1919; he took a first in the classical tripos, part one, and a second in economics, part two, but more particularly he established himself as a character full of wit and learning, and gave masterly performances in the debates of a club devoted to the absurd, the Magpie and Stump. In later life he upheld the Trinity tradition of a

June house party known as the Lake Hunt, which was held at Seatoller at the foot of the Honister Pass. A lack of handiness characterized his family, and his flying accident may have made him nervous of any machine more powerful than a bicycle. Certainly he never learned to drive and his incompetence at golf seemed almost cultivated, but he mesmerized his friends and larger audiences of diverse kinds throughout his life by his conversation and his command of language.

Assistant lecturer in classics at Manchester University in 1921, Duff became lecturer in education at Armstrong College, Newcastle upon Tyne, in 1922 under Godfrey Thomson. He was heavily involved in the pioneer work of intelligence testing, especially when he was seconded to Northumberland county council in 1925 as educational superintendent. The work took him to rural schools in the county and he claimed later to have visited all of them at one time or another. This was after Sir Theodore Morison, the principal of Armstrong College, refused to consider him for a chair in education (to the annoyance of Duff's father). He returned to Manchester as senior lecturer in education in 1927 and was made professor of education in 1932. His ability at communication was recognized by his being public orator. He was later described as 'a progressive conservative in education', and 'a warm admirer of the grammar school'; he was said to have been highly successful in training teachers for that type of school (*DNB*).

In 1937, apparently at the suggestion of Sir Walter Moberly, chairman of the University Grants Committee and formerly vice-chancellor of Manchester, Duff was offered the newly created wardenship of the Durham colleges. In the words of Sidney Holgate, who served under him as secretary of the colleges and was later master of Grey College, 'he found the Durham challenge more exacting and intricate than the weekly machinations of Torquemada to which he was predictably addicted' (*Durham University Gazette*, 8). A fearsome internecine quarrel in the Newcastle division, actually confined to the college of medicine but affecting also Armstrong College, had precipitated the appointment of a royal commission on Durham University (see E. M. Bettenson, 'A persistent myth', *Durham University Journal*, 55, July 1994, 161–4).

Until 1937 Durham was governed by a council, the membership of which was largely *ex officio*, with only three members appointed by readers and lecturers of the university and presided over by a layman who had held office since 1911. There was no overall academic head of the eight colleges, only two of which were fully maintained by the university, and the non-maintained colleges, notably the teacher training colleges, provided about 300 of the fewer than 500 undergraduates. A grant from Durham county council had allowed the university to develop a school of pure science, and that department, along with the department of education, enabled the Durham colleges to double in size between 1920 and 1937. But the price paid was that half the members of the joint board, which managed the departments of science and education, were appointed by the local authority, a unique situation among British universities, as was noted by the royal

commission in its 1935 report. The commission recommended the appointment, to full-time posts, of a warden of the Durham colleges and a principal of Armstrong College and the college of medicine at Newcastle—combined as King's College—who would alternate as vice-chancellor on a two-yearly basis.

Duff accepted the wardenship with mixed feelings and misgivings. His correspondence with his close-knit family makes it clear that he was under no illusions—'There is a certain air of spiritual mildew about Durham, with a strong clerical flavour that goes ill with the sort of University that a local University in an industrial area should aim at being' (Duff to his mother, 1 July 1937, Duff MS, III A/151). But he was attracted to the north-east and its people and he had the good fortune to have Lord Eustace Percy as his counterpart in Newcastle. Duff remarked that 'If the holder of the post (of Warden) does his job he'll not be popular' (ibid.), and, inevitably, he proved a great success. Student numbers almost quadrupled in his time to 1600 or so. His classical education gave him a sense of order. He never forgot that he had been a professor of education and constantly sought to promote learning outside as well as within the university. He believed fervently in the value of beautiful surroundings for study and in the effect of a feeling of fellowship among tutors and students. He modernized and he expanded, but he respected the traditions of the university.

Duff took early retirement in 1960. By then he was prodigiously busy in the world at large. He was a member of the Asquith commission on higher education in the colonies (1943–5), of the Elliot commission on higher education in west Africa (1943–4)—which gave him a loyalty to Fourah Bay, the Durham-linked college—of the Indian government's universities commission (1948–9), and of an inquiry into university government in Canada, which he particularly enjoyed (1964). He was chairman of the academic advisory committee for the new University of Sussex (1961) and a governor of the BBC (1959–65), an appointment which caused him to acquire a television set. He was knighted in 1949 and he received honorary degrees from the universities of Aberdeen (1942), Durham (1950), and Sussex (1964); he was a visiting professor at Toronto University in 1967. He was especially touched to be invited to be mayor of Durham City (1959–60) and lord lieutenant of the county (1964–70).

Duff never married, but his homes at Elvet Garth and afterwards at Low Middleton Hall, near Darlington, witnessed much hospitality. His mother shared his home after his father's death in 1940 until her own death in 1956, when his sister Hester joined him. He died suddenly at Dublin airport, Ireland, on 24 April 1970, and was cremated in Belfast.

G. R. BATHO

Sources U. Durham L., archives and special collections, Duff MSS · private information (2004) [Hester Duff, Dr Sidney Holgate] · *University of Durham Gazette* (30 Sept 1970) · *Durham University Journal* (July 1988) · *The Times* (27 April 1970) · *Sunday Times* (17 Sept 1916) · *DNB*
Archives PRO, corresp., BW 90; International Universities Council MSS · U. Durham L., MSS and family corresp. | BL, letters to

Albert Mansbridge, Add. MSS 65257B–8 | FILM BFI NFTVA, news footage
Likenesses W. Stoneman, three photographs, 1917–50, NPG • D. Edis, photograph, c.1937, U. Durham • H. Lamb, portrait, 1958, University College, Durham • W. Bird, photograph, 1960, NPG • L. A. Wilcox, portrait, 1966, Grey College, Durham
Wealth at death £29,192: probate, 13 July 1970, *CGPLA Eng. & Wales*

Duff, Sir Lyman Poore (1865–1955), judge in Canada, was born on 7 January 1865 at Parker Street, Meaford, Grey county, Upper Canada (Ontario), the second son of the Revd Charles Duff (d. 1905) and his wife, Isabella Johnson (d. 1902). His father, the son of a stone carver from Perth who migrated first to England and later to Canada in search of work, became a Congregationalist clergyman in 1862. His mother was the daughter of an emigrant Irish Roman Catholic lawyer and converted to protestantism on her marriage. Lyman himself was to become a nominal Anglican. He spent his childhood at Liverpool, Nova Scotia, where two sisters were born before the family returned to southern Ontario. After graduating from the University of Toronto (BA 1887) Lyman supported himself through teaching while studying law, and was called to the Ontario bar in 1893. When teaching in Barrie, Ontario, Duff met his future wife, Elizabeth Bird (1859/60–1926), also a teacher and the daughter of a local shoe merchant, whom he married on 2 July 1898; they had no children. Of average height and slight build, Duff none the less possessed a definite presence with his keen eyes, red hair, and Vandyke beard.

Attracted by the west's booming economy, Duff settled in Victoria, British Columbia, and was called to the bar on 28 February 1895. His success depended on careful preparation and mastery of the law rather than rhetorical skill. These talents and Liberal Party connections led to his appointment as QC in 1900 and a brief to plead Canada's case in London in the 1903 Alaska Panhandle boundary dispute, where Duff provided the Canadian government 'good value in a lost cause' (Williams, 51). After a short stint on the provincial supreme court (1904–6) Duff became the first British Columbian appointed to the supreme court of Canada, where his thirty-seven years' service remains a record.

The supreme court of Canada in the early twentieth century was somewhat overshadowed by the judicial committee of the privy council. Decisions of the provincial courts of appeal could be appealed directly to London, bypassing the supreme court. Throughout Duff's tenure, the division of powers within Canada's federal system remained a contentious issue. Duff was largely in sympathy with the judicial committee's decentralist view of the Canadian constitution, probably because of his familiarity with all regions of the country. While in Ottawa he became fluent in French and very familiar with Quebec's civil law tradition.

Duff's legal prowess was accompanied by alcoholism and financial incapacity, which only worsened after his wife Lizzie's death on 8 July 1926. A bout with bowel cancer and renewed drinking nearly killed him by 1932, when his unmarried sister Annie moved to Ottawa and took charge of her brother and his household. So successful was she that Prime Minister R. B. Bennett had few qualms in appointing Duff chief justice in 1933 and recommending his knighthood in 1934.

Appointments of the chief justice of Canada to the privy council had begun in the 1890s in an effort to cement imperial ties. Duff, the first puisne judge so honoured, was appointed on 1 January 1919 and sworn in on 1 July. Every July until Lizzie's death he would spend with her in London, hearing judicial committee appeals. Impressed by his colleague, Lord Birkenhead invited Duff to be an honorary bencher of Gray's Inn in 1924, the same year that he sat on the Ulster boundary reference. In the late 1920s Duff resumed his summer sojourn in London, which gradually became more holiday than work. None the less he participated in some eighty appeals in all, mainly Canadian cases, although he never sat on appeals from the supreme court of Canada while a member of it. In 1946 Duff made a final journey to London, aged eighty-one, to hear five Canadian appeals. The last of these confirmed the legality of the deportation of nearly 4000 Japanese-Canadian citizens to Japan after the war.

The decision is a fitting epitaph for Duff's ungenerous approach to civil rights. While on the supreme court, he refused to invalidate racially discriminatory legislation and practices, and held that women could not be appointed senators because they were not 'persons' within the meaning of the relevant article of the Canadian constitution. After the judicial committee overturned this decision, the Hon. Cairine Wilson was named Canada's first female senator in 1930. Ironically, she and Duff were neighbours and remained lifelong friends.

In 1939 parliament extended Duff's term of office by three years from his seventy-fifth birthday, the statutory retirement age. In 1942 Prime Minister Mackenzie King pressed Duff to carry out a public inquiry into the decimation of Canadian troops at the fall of Hong Kong. The Canadian government had sent two ill-prepared battalions in response to Britain's plea for assistance late in 1941. Duff's report was a cover-up, exacerbated when King extended his term for another year to stifle criticism, and the episode was thought to have 'shadowed an otherwise illustrious life' (*Globe and Mail*). Duff retired in 1944 but remained healthy until his ninetieth birthday. He then declined rapidly and died of kidney failure in Ottawa Civic Hospital on 26 April 1955. He was buried on 28 April in Beechwood cemetery, Ottawa.

Duff cherished his opportunities to interact with the English bench and bar. Yet when the Canadian government in 1939 referred to the supreme court draft legislation abolishing privy council appeals, Duff upheld it. This judgment, in Duff's opinion the most important of his career, was adopted by the judicial committee in 1947; abolition followed in 1949. Severance of the ties linking the English and Canadian legal élites was one of the casualties of dismantling the empire. Duff was the last Canadian of whom it could be said: 'Sir Lyman is more than a great Canadian judge: He is an Empire figure' (Victoria *Daily Colonist*, 22 April 1939). PHILIP GIRARD

Sources D. R. Williams, *Duff: a life in the law* (1984) · NA Canada, Sir Lyman Poore Duff collection, MG30-E141 · *The law reports: House of Lords judicial committee of the privy council and peerage cases* (1919–47) · *Report on the Canadian expeditionary force to the crown colony of Hong Kong* (1942) · *Reports of the supreme court of Canada, Toronto, Canada law book, 1906–1920* (1921–2), vols. 37–60 · *Canada law reports: supreme court of Canada* (1923–44) · DNB · *Globe and Mail* [Toronto] (27 April 1955)

Archives NA Canada, Sir Lyman Poore Duff collection, MG30-E141

Likenesses E. Fosberry, oils, 1944, Supreme Court of Canada, Ottawa · O. Wheeler, bronze bust, 1947, Supreme Court of Canada, Ottawa

Wealth at death approx. C$10,000

Duff, Sir Mountstuart Elphinstone Grant- (1829–1906), politician and author, elder son of James Cuninghame Grant *Duff (1789–1858), of the East India Company, and his wife, Jane Catharine, daughter of Sir Whitelaw *Ainslie, was born at Eden, Aberdeenshire, on 21 February 1829. He was named after his father's mentor the Indian administrator Mountstuart Elphinstone. He was educated at Edinburgh Academy, the Grange School, Sunderland, and at Balliol College, Oxford (1847–50). Among his contemporary friends at Oxford were Henry Smith, Henry Oxenham, Charles Pearson, Goldwin Smith, Charles Parker, and John Coleridge Patteson. He graduated BA in 1850 with a second class in *literae humaniores*, and proceeded MA in 1853. On leaving Oxford he settled in London and read for the bar, and in 1854 passed with honours in the LLB examination of London University; he was second to James Fitzjames Stephen, who later became a close friend of Grant-Duff and also of his wife. In the same year (17 November) he was called to the bar by the Inner Temple, and while a pupil in the chambers of William Ventris Field joined the midland circuit, and obtained his first brief because he was the only person present who could speak German. He was one of the earliest contributors to the *Saturday Review*, and lectured at the Working Men's College, of which Frederick Denison Maurice was first principal.

In December 1857 Grant-Duff succeeded George Skene Duff as the Liberal MP for Elgin burghs, holding the seat until 1881, when he was appointed governor of Madras. He never had to fight a contested election, except in 1880, when he was opposed by J. M. Maclean, a Conservative, whom he easily defeated. Grant-Duff enjoyed the sturdy, independent character of the small fishing towns and villages he represented. From 1860 he annually addressed his constituents in a major speech. Many of these speeches were published as pamphlets (reprinted in *Elgin Speeches*, 1871), and many of them were on foreign affairs, Grant-Duff's chief interest. He travelled widely in Europe, the Near East, and India (in 1874). He was in Darmstadt during the Franco-Prussian War of 1870. His cosmopolitanism led him to meet Garibaldi, and to correspond with Ollivier about the origins of the Franco-Prussian War and with the Empress Frederick of Germany. He was a close and long-standing friend of Ernest Renan, whose memorial volume he published in 1893. He also wrote memoirs of Henry Maine (1892) and Lord De Tabley (1899). His travels and reading were reflected in *Studies in European Politics*

Sir Mountstuart Elphinstone Grant-Duff (1829–1906), by John Watkins

(1866). He was active in the British Association and in the National Association for the Promotion of Social Science, some of his addresses being reprinted in his *Miscellanies* (1878). He had extracts from his writings and speeches reprinted by the government printing press, Madras, in 1884 as *Brief Comments*.

On 13 April 1859 Grant-Duff married Anna Julia (d. 1915), only daughter of Edward Webster of North Lodge, Ealing; they had four sons and four daughters. Their third son was Adrian Grant-*Duff (1869–1914). His growing status was marked by his election as lord rector of Aberdeen University in 1866 (with a second term until 1872). As an MP he was not always successful in the house, Sir John Trelawny noting: 'Grant-Duff could not get a hearing. What an odd little intellectual ferret it is! Clever, cultivated & industrious (as I fancy)—why does he not succeed?' (*Parliamentary Diaries*, 281). Even so, in December 1868 Gladstone made him under-secretary for India, with Argyll, the secretary, in the Lords. Grant-Duff had thus to handle most Indian business in the Commons. Here he took his lead from Argyll, his 'quite ideal chief'. Though initially apprehensive of each other, Argyll and Grant-Duff worked well together, with the latter 'rather deliberately obedient to Argyll; and always in agreement with him on policy' (Duthie, 49). Grant-Duff recalled his speeches on central Asian policy of 9 July 1869 and 22 April 1873 as 'almost the only official speeches which it gave me real pleasure to deliver' (Duff, 1.7). Grant-Duff was made a freeman of Elgin when the government was defeated in 1874, after which he visited India (recorded in *Notes on an Indian Journey*, 1876).

In the Eastern question debates in the 1876–80 period Grant-Duff sought a middle way between the rival positions of Gladstone and Disraeli, and proposed his own settlement (see his speeches in his *Miscellanies*, 1878). He resolutely attacked the tories in *The Afghan Policy of the Beaconsfield Government* (n.d. [1880?]) as 'one vast web of crime'. In April 1880 Gladstone made him under-secretary for the colonies (with the colonial secretary, Lord Kimberley, in the Lords), with membership of the privy council. This may have been less than Grant-Duff expected, and he was never fully at ease in Gladstone's second government. When W. P. Adam, formerly Liberal chief whip, died in May 1881, Grant-Duff agreed to succeed him as governor of Madras, for which he left with his wife in October 1881. Faced with stiff controversies in India over the Ilbert Bill and the relations of the European community to the Indians, Grant-Duff was cautious, and had to be encouraged in his support of government policy by Lord Ripon, the viceroy. The Indian government 'met with inordinate delay and an indifference to instructions' from Madras (though this was less than the direct hostility it experienced from Bombay) and, in the view of Professor Gopal, Grant-Duff became 'narrow-minded' in India (Gopal, 219). Grant-Duff recorded his view of his governorship, during which he visited all twenty-two districts of Madras, in two forthright minutes, of September–November 1884 and 20 September 1886. They show him to have taken an especial interest in forests and in fauna and flora generally. The Grant-Duffs left Madras in November 1886, returning to Britain by Syria. In March 1887 he was invested with the GCSI, having been made CIE in 1881. In July 1886 Gladstone considered a peerage for Grant-Duff, but nothing came of this.

This was in effect the end of Grant-Duff's political career, though he was later chairman of the Liberty and Property Defence League and was concerned about what he saw as socialistic tendencies in the Liberal Party of the 1890s. His opinions on India, as stated in articles written after his return, were sharply attacked by D. Naoroji in *Sir M. E. Grant Duff's Views about India* (1887). After his return to Britain he devoted himself chiefly to what was perhaps his natural role, that of a leading clubman and intellectual socialite. From the start of his parliamentary career he was a member of the Athenaeum and the Cosmopolitan clubs; he also joined the Literary Society (1872) and Grillion's Club (1889), and in 1866 founded the Breakfast Club. He was a member of Brooks's and The Club. Through these clubs and other meeting places he maintained an extensive network of cosmopolitan contacts, to which his diaries testify. He became a diarist in 1851, and from 1873 wrote it with the intention of publication. He published extracts, as *Notes from a Diary*, from the years 1851 to 1872 in 1897, with six further releases of two volumes, published between 1898 and 1905, and taking the record down to 23 January 1901, when he kissed hands with Edward VII on the latter's accession. Some of the *Notes* are retrospective, and the diaries await a scholarly edition. He largely excluded politics from his extracts, which are mostly records of the intellectual gossip of the day, with many pleasant stories about eminent individuals. They constitute a voluminous record of the social life of the day. He also published biographical essays, *Out of the Past* (2 vols., 1903) and *Gems from a Victorian Anthology* (1904). His contemporary eminence was marked by his presidency of the Royal Geographical Society (1889–93) and of the Royal Historical Society (1892–9). He was elected FRS in 1901 and was a crown trustee of the British Museum from 1903. He was 'slight, delicately made, and habitually gentle in speech and manner, though he would upon occasion express himself with great animation' (*DNB*). His health was always uncertain and he suffered from astigmatic vision to the extent that it was difficult for him to read or write.

Grant-Duff liked to live and entertain in grand houses, and took tenancies in Hampden House, Berkshire, York House, Twickenham, and Knebworth House, Hertfordshire. He eventually bought Lexden Park, near Colchester. He died at his London house, 11 Chelsea Embankment, on 12 January 1906, and was buried at Elgin Cathedral. His wife died on 13 March 1915. Two of his sons were diplomatists, the elder, Sir Arthur Cuninghame Grant-Duff (1861–1948), having an eminent career especially in Europe and Latin America and in naval intelligence 1916–19. Another son, Adrian Grant-*Duff, became an army officer.

H. C. G. MATTHEW

Sources DNB · *The Times* (13 Jan 1906) · *Banffshire Herald* (16 Jan 1906) · M. E. G. Duff, *Notes from a diary, kept chiefly in southern India, 1881–1886*, 2 vols. (1899) · *The parliamentary diaries of Sir John Trelawny, 1858–1865*, ed. T. A. Jenkins, CS, 4th ser., 40 (1990) · Gladstone, *Diaries* · S. Gopal, *The viceroyalty of Lord Ripon, 1880–1884* (1953) · J. L. Duthie, 'Pressure from within: the "Forward" group in the India office during Gladstone's first ministry', *Journal of Asian History*, 15 (1981), 36–71 · C. Tolley, *Domestic biography: the legacy of evangelicalism in four nineteenth-century families* (1997)
Archives BL OIOC, corresp. and papers, MS Eur. F 234 | BL, corresp. with Sir Charles Dilke, Add. MS 43894 · BL, corresp. with W. E. Gladstone, Add. MSS 44412–44785 · BL OIOC, corresp. with Lord Cross, MS Eur. E 243 · BL OIOC, letters to Arthur Godley, MS Eur. F 102 · BL OIOC, corresp. with Sir Alfred Lyall, MS Eur. F 132 · BL OIOC, corresp. with Lord Northbrook, MS Eur. C 144 · Bodl. Oxf., letters to Lord Kimberley · Bodl. Oxf., letters to C. H. Pearson · CUL, letters to Lord Acton and others · Hove Central Library, Sussex, letters to Lord Wolseley · King's AC Cam., corresp. with Oscar Browning · NL Wales, corresp. with Lord Rendel · PRO, corresp. with Odo Russell, FO 918 · U. Birm. L., corresp. with Joseph Chamberlain · U. St Andr. L., letters to Wilfrid Ward
Likenesses R. Lehman, drawing, 1872, BM · Ape [C. Pellegrini], chromolithograph caricature, NPG; repro. in *VF* (2 Oct 1869) · W. Roffe, stipple (after H. T. Wells), NPG · J. Watkins, carte-de-visite, NPG [*see illus.*] · H. T. Wells, drawing, priv. coll.
Wealth at death £85,998 5s. 2d.: probate, 8 March 1906, CGPLA Eng. & Wales

Duff, Robert (1721–1787), naval officer, was a cousin of William Duff, first Earl Fife, and connected with the earl of Bute. Details of his parents are unknown. He was listed a lieutenant by 9 March 1739, promoted commander on 4 December 1744, and in 1746 had command of the bomb-vessel *Terror* on the coast of Scotland. On 23 October he was promoted captain of the new ship *Anglesea* (44 guns), which he commanded on the coast of Ireland and the home station until the peace of Aix-la-Chapelle (1748). In 1755 he was appointed to the *Rochester* (50 guns), which was employed during the following years on the coast of France either in independent cruising or as part of the Grand Fleet. In 1758 Duff was with Commodore Richard Howe in the squadron covering the expeditions against St

Malo, Cherbourg, and St Cas. In 1759 he was senior officer of the little squadron stationed on the south coast of Brittany to keep watch over the movements of the French in Morbihan, while Edward Hawke with the fleet blockaded Brest. He was lying at anchor in Quiberon Bay, his squadron consisting of four 50-gun ships and four frigates, when, on the morning of 20 November, his outlook frigate informed him of the French fleet to the south of Belle Île. Duff hastily put to sea and stood to the southward, chased by the French. Engagement was prevented by the appearance of the British fleet in pursuit of the French, who were overtaken and attacked before they could reach safety.

Duff was afterwards appointed to the *Foudroyant* (80 guns), a crack ship in which he accompanied Rear-Admiral George Brydges Rodney to the West Indies, and took part in the capture of Martinique during January and February 1762. However, because of his seniority he refused to serve as Rodney's flag-captain, and was sent home. In 1764 he married Helen, the daughter of his cousin the Earl Fife; they had several children.

On 31 March 1775 Duff was promoted rear-admiral, and in April he was sent out as commander-in-chief at Newfoundland. In September 1777 he was appointed to the command of the Mediterranean, with his flag in the *Panther*. When the siege of Gibraltar was begun in 1779, Duff co-operated with the garrison in so far as the very limited force at his disposal permitted. The government, not being able to strengthen his command, recalled him early in the following year. He had been promoted vice-admiral on 29 January 1778, but held no further command after his return to England in 1780. During his later years he was grievously afflicted with gout, his death being attributed to an attack of gout in the stomach. He died at Queensferry on 6 June 1787.

Robert Duff's grandnephew George Duff was killed at Trafalgar in command of the *Mars*, and before the battle had command of the inshore squadron watching the motions of the enemy in Cadiz.

J. K. LAUGHTON, *rev.* NICHOLAS TRACY

Sources J. Charnock, ed., *Biographia navalis*, 6 vols. (1794–8) · PRO, ADM 1/307; 30/20/8 p. 168 · D. Syrett and R. L. DiNardo, *The commissioned sea officers of the Royal Navy, 1660–1815*, rev. edn, Occasional Publications of the Navy RS, 1 (1994) · HMC
Archives NA Scot., corresp. and papers · NMM, log books, letter books, papers | PRO, ADM 1/307, Rodney 1 July 1762; 30/20/8 p. 168

Duff [*formerly* Duff Abercromby], **Sir Robert William** (1835–1895), colonial governor, was born at Fetteresso, Kincardineshire, on 8 May 1835, the only son of the three children of Arthur Duff Abercromby (d. 1859), of Glasnaugh, Banffshire, and his wife, Elizabeth Davidson (d. 1838), the daughter of John Innes of Cowie, Kincardineshire. His father had taken his mother's family name, Abercromby, at the time of inheriting her estates. Robert was educated at Blackheath School, London, before joining the Royal Navy in 1848. He served until 1870, attaining the rank of commander. Upon inheriting the estates of his uncle Robert Duff in 1861 he discontinued the use of the surname Abercromby. On 21 February 1871 he married

Sir Robert William Duff (1835–1895), by Elliott & Fry, pubd 1893

Louisa, the daughter of Sir William Scott, ninth baronet, of Ancrum, Roxburghshire. They had three sons and four daughters.

In May 1861 Duff was elected as a Liberal to the House of Commons for the constituency of Banffshire, which he retained throughout his time in parliament. He was neither a 'frequent speaker' nor 'widely known', but towards the end of his term was 'somewhat conspicuous as the oldest Scottish member' (*Sydney Morning Herald*, 16 March 1895). Duff was a government whip from 1882 to 1885, junior lord of the Treasury in the same period, and a civil lord of the Admiralty in 1886. He was sworn of the privy council in 1892, but refused Gladstone's offer of appointment to a household position. In the following year he was appointed to the post of governor of New South Wales and was knighted.

Duff arrived in Sydney in May 1893 and by the end of the year found himself at the centre of political controversy. In October he had agreed to an Electoral Act which abolished the existing electoral registers and constituency boundaries, as part of a reform by the premier, Sir George Dibbs, of the chaotic and undemocratic New South Wales electoral system. Unfortunately, it was not going to be possible to complete new registers before January 1894. In December two ministers of the Dibbs government resigned over irregularities, and it was expected that Dibbs would follow. Instead he requested that Duff prorogue parliament. Duff noted that, under 'ordinary circumstances, I should have declined to give my assent to a prorogation' (Mackerras, 299), but without registers or constituency boundaries he believed he could not compel the holding of an election.

Duff was severely criticized for agreeing to Dibbs's request. Sir Henry Parkes condemned the governor for doing 'a thing which his Sovereign would never have dreamed of doing' (Mackerras, 300). Duff, who 'privately disapproved of Dibbs's actions' (Rutledge) and was affronted by the criticism from Parkes and others, agreed to a press interview to justify his position. He was later attacked by the Colonial Office for what was seen as his indiscretion. Further controversy arose with his viceregal rejection of ministerial advice from Dibbs, who, after losing the election finally held in July 1894, recommended the appointment of ten supporters of his party to the legislative council.

Duff was a prominent freemason, being appointed grand master of the united grand lodge of New South Wales soon after his arrival in the colony. He was 'handsome, bearded', and able to carry out 'his duties with dignity' (Rutledge), although in his personal dealings, particularly in times of crisis, he was seen to be 'highly strung and nervous' (Mackerras, 309). Duff died in office, at Government House, Sydney, on 15 March 1895, from a liver disorder and septicaemia. He was buried at Waverley cemetery, Sydney, on 17 March, though his remains were later taken to Scotland; he was survived by his wife.

MARC BRODIE

Sources *Sydney Morning Herald* (16 March 1895) · *Sydney Morning Herald* (18 March 1895) · C. B. Mackerras, 'Dibbs versus Duff: the sad story of a colonial governor', *Journal of the Royal Australian Historical Society*, 56 (1970), 296–314 · M. Rutledge, 'Duff, Sir Robert William', *AusDB*, vol. 8 · IGI · *The Times* (16 March 1895), 12 · *Sydney Morning Herald* (11 Dec 1893) · *Sydney Morning Herald* (12 Dec 1893) · *DNB* · m. cert.
Archives NA Scot., corresp. and papers | BL, Ripon MSS
Likenesses photograph, 1893, Mitchell L., NSW · Elliott & Fry, photograph, BM, NPG; repro. in *ILN* (4 March 1893) [*see illus.*] · chromolithograph caricature, NPG; repro. in *VF* (16 June 1883) · photograph, repro. in *Wadivian Review* (1893)

Duff, William (1732–1815), Church of Scotland minister and author, was born, of unknown parentage, at King Edward manse in the parish of King Edward, Aberdeenshire. He studied at Marischal College, Aberdeen, graduating MA in 1750. He was licensed to preach on 25 June 1755, called to the parish of Glenbucket in the presbytery of Alford, Aberdeenshire, on 18 September of that year and ordained on 8 October 1755. On 4 March 1767 he moved to the parish of Peterculter in the presbytery of Aberdeen, where he served as minister for eight years. Three years later, on 4 September 1770, he married Ann Mitchell (*d.* 1797); they had three sons and seven daughters. On the presentation of George III he was transferred to the parish of Foveran in the presbytery of Ellon, also in Aberdeenshire, in 1775. Duff remained minister of Foveran for the rest of his life, contributing an account of the parish to Sir John Sinclair's *Statistical Account of Scotland* (1791–9) and opening a new church there in 1794.

Duff is best remembered for his two works on genius, *An Essay on Original Genius* (1767) and *Critical Observations on the Writings of the most Celebrated Original Geniuses in Poetry* (1770), which are often cited for their contribution to eighteenth-century Scottish primitivism. Characterizing poetic genius in terms of its simplicity, spontaneity, and enthusiasm, Duff argued that poetry reaches its utmost perfection 'in the early and uncultivated periods of social life', when the 'wild exuberance and plastic forces' of the poetic imagination have yet to be constrained by 'the progress of Literature, Criticism and Civilization' (Duff, *Essay on Original Genius*, 295–6).

Duff was a great admirer of Ossian, the so-called Scottish Homer, whose supposedly ancient highland epics *Fingal* and *Temora* were 'translated' by the eighteenth-century poet James Macpherson. In his *Critical Observations*, Duff confidently asserted that in the area of 'fabulous composition' Ossian had no superior and could be rivalled only by Shakespeare, and he seems never to have considered the possibility that the poems might be spurious. Yet alongside his somewhat naïve belief in the complete authenticity of the Ossianic verses, in both his *Essay on Original Genius* and his *Critical Observations* Duff offered sophisticated accounts of the material and cultural forces that led to historical shifts in modes of artistic representation and literary composition. Indeed, if Duff's notion of the singular and solitary 'man of genius' is often seen as a precursor of nineteenth-century English Romantic conceptions of originality and creativity, his historical approach to poetry should be viewed against the backdrop of eighteenth-century Scottish conjectural, or natural, history, which sought to trace the progress of manners, laws, customs, language, arts, and sciences from 'savage' to 'civil' society.

Given his interest in epic poetry, it is not surprising that Duff responded with enthusiasm to James Beattie's poem *The Minstrel*: writing to Beattie in August 1774 he offered high praise for Beattie's 'natural and pleasing, often highly picturesque, and sometimes … perfectly luxuriant and enchanting' poetic descriptions (Duff to Beattie). Duff's penchant for primitive and oriental literature also found expression in his novel *The History of Rhedi, the Hermit of Mount Ararat* (1773), which was translated into French as *Histoire de Rhedy* in 1777, and reprinted at Dublin in 1781, with a title page mistakenly attributing it to Henry Mackenzie.

Like many Scottish ministers of the time, Duff also contributed to the period's proliferation of female conduct books with his *Letters on the Intellectual and Moral Character of Women*, published by subscription in 1807. Subscribers to the work included such luminaries as the judge Francis Jeffrey, and the philosopher Dugald Stewart. Dedicated to the duchess of Gordon and addressed to the 'Ladies of Great Britain', *Letters on Women* denounced the 'encroaching spirit' and 'licentious principles' of Mary Wollstonecraft, but also called for improvements in female education and reforms in male behaviour. The influence of Scottish conjectural history can again be seen in Duff's account of the progress of women from 'savage' to 'civilized' life. In addition to the titles mentioned above Duff also published several volumes of sermons (1785, 1786, 1800) and a final work entitled *Letters to his Daughters* (1814). He died at Foveran on 23 February 1815.

MARY CATHERINE MORAN

Sources *DNB* · W. Duff, letter to James Beattie, 1 Aug 1774, U. Aberdeen, MS 30/2/202 · D. M. Foerster, 'Scottish primitivism and the historical approach', *Philological Quarterly*, 29 (1950), 307–23 · W. B. Johnson, introduction, in W. Duff, *Critical observations on the writings of the most celebrated original geniuses in poetry* (1973) · W. Duff, *Letters on the intellectual and moral character of women* (1807); repr. with introduction by G. Luria (1974) · W. Duff, *An essay on original genius* (1767); repr. with introduction by J. V. Price (1994) · J. V. Price, 'Ossian the

canon in the Scottish Enlightenment', *Ossian revisited*, ed. H. Gaskill (1991), 109–28 • *Scots Magazine and Edinburgh Literary Miscellany*, 77 (1815), 319 • *Fasti Scot.*
Archives U. Aberdeen L., letter to James Beattie, MS 30/2/202

Dufferin and Ava. For this title name *see* Blackwood, Frederick Temple Hamilton-Temple-, first marquess of Dufferin and Ava (1826–1902); Blackwood, Hariot Georgina Hamilton-Temple-, marchioness of Dufferin and Ava (1843–1936).

Dufferin and Claneboye. For this title name *see* Hay, Helen Selina, countess of Gifford [Helen Selina Blackwood, Lady Dufferin and Claneboye] (1807–1867).

Duffett [Duffet], **Thomas** (*fl.* 1673–1676), playwright, remains a shadowy figure; little is known of his life. He may have been Irish. Before he turned to playwriting, he was a milliner at the New Exchange on the Strand, one of Restoration London's most fashionable resorts, patronized by a predominantly upper-class clientele.

Duffett's works appeared during the 1670s. *The Spanish Rogue* was probably performed by the King's Men at Lincoln's Inn Fields in March 1673. It can thus be considered a Lenten play, one in which the company's hirelings, rather than its actor-sharers, comprised a large part of the cast. The text was published, with a dedication to Nell Gwyn, the following year. The anonymous comedy *The Amorous Old-Woman, or, 'Tis Well if it Take* (published 1674), a coarsely entertaining farce 'Written by a Person of Honour' according to the title-page and first produced at Lincoln's Inn Fields no later than March 1674, has been attributed to Duffett. (The text was subsequently reissued as *The Fond Lady* in 1684.) *Beauties Triumph, a Masque* (1676), a versification of the judgment of Paris, was (to cite its title-page) 'Presented by the Scholars of Mr Jeffrey Banister, and Mr James Hart, at their New Boarding-School for Young Ladies and Gentlewomen' in Chelsea.

Duffett also wrote a number of burlesques which are of importance in the history of London's Restoration theatres. In November or December 1673 the King's Company performed *The Empress of Morocco* (published 1674), the first of his travesties, which satirized not only Elkanah Settle's popular tragedy of that title, and, in an epilogue, William Davenant's adaptation of *Macbeth*, but also the spectacularly visual productions both plays had received earlier that summer at the rival house, the Duke's Theatre, Dorset Garden. This sequence of events established a pattern. In November 1674, having moved to Drury Lane, the King's Company performed *The Mock-Tempest, or, The Enchanted Castle* (published 1675, in which text it is also headed 'The New Tempest', p. 1, sig. B1r), Duffett's farcical response to Thomas Shadwell's opera, a musical version of Dryden's and Davenant's reworking of Shakespeare's play. As a commercial attempt to lure some of the audience from the Dorset Garden's popular autumn production, it was a success. And in May 1675, again with a mainly hireling cast, the Drury Lane company put on *Psyche Debauch'd* (published 1678), Duffett's most sophisticated play, a burlesque of Shadwell's operatic tragedy which had been produced three months earlier. Duffett also

wrote non-dramatic and lyric verse. Several of the songs included in his plays were republished in contemporary anthologies and his own collection of *New Poems, Songs, Prologues and Epilogues* (1676). This volume, moreover, offers considerable evidence of private and vacation performances in the early 1670s and provides the only known record of the Duchess of Portsmouth's Company. It is as the witness of theatrical and literary history that Duffett's works are now remembered. The frontispiece to the published text of *The Empress of Morocco* answers—and ridicules—the six engraved 'sculptures' included in the quarto of Settle's *Empress* (1673), for example, and *The Songs and Masque in The New Tempest* (1674), a mock-libretto, deliberately echoes—and apes—*Songs and Masques in The Tempest* (1674), the pamphlet which accompanied Settle's opera and which was sold at the door of the Duke's Theatre.

Duffett disappears from view as silently as he appears. It is possible that the 'Severall Deeds and Writings forged and Counterfeited by one Thomas Duffett' adduced in Sir Robert Cotton's petition of May 1677 refer to his later activities (this Duffett had been 'pricked in Conscience' to reveal his crimes; *CSP dom.*, fol. 112), but the identification is not certain. It is not known when Duffett died.

JONATHAN PRITCHARD

Sources [C. Gildon], *The lives and characters of the English dramatick poets … first begun by Mr Langbain* [1699], 48 • [D. E. Baker], *The companion to the play-house*, 2 (1764), sig. L2v • P. E. Lewis, 'The three dramatic burlesques of Thomas Duffett', *Durham University Journal*, 58 (1965–6), 149–56 • K. M. Cameron, 'Duffett's *New poems* and vacation plays', *Theatre Survey*, 5 (1964), 64–70 • C. Haywood, '"The songs and masque in the new *Tempest*": an incident in the battle of the two theaters, 1674', *Huntington Library Quarterly*, 19 (1955–6), 39–56 • J. H. Wilson, *Mr Goodman: the player* (1964), 54 • *CSP dom.*, 1675–8, fol. 112 • *Three burlesque plays of Thomas Duffett*, ed. R. E. DiLorenzo (1972) • V. C. Clinton-Baddeley, *The burlesque tradition in the English theatre after 1660* (1952), 38–43 • P. H. Gray, 'Lenten casts and the nursery: evidence for the dating of certain Restoration plays', *Publications of the Modern Language Association of America*, 53 (1938), 781–94 • A. Nicoll, *Restoration drama, 1660–1700*, 4th edn (1952), vol. 1 of *A history of English drama, 1660–1900* (1952–9), 37, 249 • W. Van Lennep and others, eds., *The London stage, 1660–1800*, pt 1: *1660–1700* (1965), 204, 212, 214, 224, 235, 238, 307, 322 • L. Stone, 'Inigo Jones and the New Exchange', *Archaeological Journal*, 114 (1957), [106]–21 • W. H. Godfrey, 'The New Exchange in the Strand', in A. W. Clapham and W. H. Godfrey, *Some famous buildings and their story: being the results of recent research in London and elsewhere* [1913], [152]–64 • T. N. Brushfield, *Britain's burse, or, The new exchange* (1903)

Duff Gordon. For this title name *see* Gordon, Lucie Duff, Lady Duff Gordon (1821–1869); Gordon, Lucy Christiana Duff, Lady Duff Gordon (1862–1935).

Duffield, Alexander James (1821/2–1890), translator and mining engineer, was born at Tettenhall, near Wolverhampton, Staffordshire. He was intended for the clerical profession, and studied at Trinity College, Dublin, but did not take orders. Instead, after marriage, he emigrated to South America. He worked for some years in Bolivia and Peru as a mining chemist, and acquired a knowledge of Spanish. During this period he interested himself in numerous enterprises, one of the most important being an attempt, which proved unsuccessful, to introduce alpacas into Australia. He visited Brisbane several times; on one occasion he made a six-month cruise on a vessel employed in the trade to supply native labourers for the sugar plantations, and provided the Queensland government with a report on that subject. Subsequently he travelled in Spain and other countries, and for some time held an appointment under the government of Canada.

In 1877 Duffield produced in London, in collaboration with Walter Herries Pollock, a novel entitled *Masston: a Story of these Modern Days*. In the same year appeared *Peru in the Guano Age: being a Short Account of a Recent Visit to the Guano Deposits*. A second monograph on Peru was published in 1881 under the title *The Prospects of Peru: the End of the Guano Age and a Description Thereof*. In 1880 Duffield issued a work advocating a scheme by which English parishes might purchase land in Canada for the profitable employment of paupers and workhouse children; this was entitled *Needless misery at home and abounding treasure in the west under our own flag: old town and new domains, or, Birmingham and Canada revisited*.

In 1888 Duffield published a translation of *Don Quixote*. Nearly twenty years before, during his travels in Spain, he had conceived the idea of the translation, and the work was begun in conjunction with H. Watts, but differences arose, with the result that the translators finished their labours independently, and two versions appeared. Duffield's version, which he dedicated to W. E. Gladstone, bore the title, *The ingenious knight Don Quixote de la Mancha: a new translation from the originals of 1605 and 1608, with some notes of Bowle, J. A. Pellicer, Clemencin, and others* (3 vols., 1881). The rendering of the text was accurate and careful, and was preceded by an introduction which compared the original text with previous translations of importance, and by a bibliographical account of the books of chivalry connected with the story. The passages in verse were rendered by James Young Gibson. In the same year, 1881, Duffield published *Don Quixote: his critics and commentators, with a brief account of the minor works of Cervantes*, a treatise more remarkable for enthusiasm than for sound critical judgement. Duffield's other works include *The Beauty of the World: a Story of this Generation* (1886), and *Recollections of Travels Abroad*, with a map (1889). Duffield died at the age of sixty-eight, after a brief illness and an operation, on 9 October 1890. C. E. HUGHES, rev. NILANJANA BANERJI

Sources *The Times* (11 Oct 1890) · *The Times* (17 Oct 1890) · *The Athenaeum* (18 Oct 1890), 514 · *Chambers's biographical dictionary*, ed. D. Patrick and F. H. Groome (1897)

Duffield, William (1816–1863), still-life painter, was born at Bath, the second son of Charles Duffield, at one time proprietor of the Royal Union Library. Educated in Bath, at an early age Duffield displayed a decided predilection and talent for drawing. George Doo, the engraver, having been struck by Duffield's highly elaborated pen-and-ink sketches and faithful copies of his engravings, offered to take him as his pupil without a premium. A few years later he placed himself under the still-life painter George Lance, and was noted for his unremitting attention and assiduity as a student of the Royal Academy. After completing the usual course of study in London he returned to

Bath, and later on proceeded to Antwerp, where, under Baron Wappers, he worked for two years.

On 28 February 1850 Duffield married **Mary Elizabeth Rosenberg** (1819–1914), the daughter of Thomas Elliot Rosenberg (1790–1835) of Bath, a painter of landscapes and miniatures with a substantial teaching practice. Mary was born in Bath on 2 April 1819, and was educated in that town. A highly accomplished painter of fruit and flowers, she won a silver medal from the Society of Arts in 1834 and exhibited between 1848 and 1912 at the Royal Academy (1857–74), the British Institution, the Grosvenor Gallery, and the New Society of Painters in Water Colours, of which she was elected a member in 1861. As Mrs William Duffield she published *The Art of Flower Painting* in 1856, which reached eighteen editions by 1882. William and Mary Duffield had one son, probably the landscape and figure painter William L. Duffield (*fl*. 1873–1880). Mary Duffield died on 14 January 1914 at her home, Stowting rectory, Hythe, Kent.

In 1857 William Duffield lived in Bayswater, London; he exhibited with an increasing reputation at the Royal Academy and the Society of British Artists at Suffolk Street. He died at Sunninghill, Egham, Surrey, on 3 September 1863, from an infection thought to have been caught from a dead deer that he was painting in his room.

L. A. FAGAN, rev. MARK POTTLE

Sources Redgrave, *Artists* · *Art Journal*, 25 (1863) · Mallalieu, *Watercolour artists* · Wood, *Vic. painters*, 2nd edn · *WWW*, 1897–1915 · Bryan, *Painters* (1903–5) · m. cert. · d. cert.
Wealth at death under £4000: will, 25 Sept 1863, *CGPLA Eng. & Wales*

Duffy, Sir Charles Gavan (1816–1903), journalist and politician, was born in the town of Monaghan on 12 April 1816, the youngest child of John Duffy (*d*. 1826/7), a shopkeeper, and his wife, Anne (Annie) Gavan (*d. c*.1837), the daughter of Patrick Gavan of Aughabog, co. Monaghan, gentleman farmer, and his wife, Judith McMahon of Oriel.

Early years Duffy was mainly self-educated, since co. Monaghan had insufficient schooling for Catholics. In Monaghan town he spent some time at a poor school run by Neil Quinn, and five years at the Revd John Bleckley's classical academy, where he was the only Catholic. When he was eighteen, Duffy became a contributor to Charles Hamilton Teeling's nationalist paper, the *Northern Herald*. In 1836 he moved to Dublin, where he joined the staff of the Liberal paper the *Dublin Morning Register* as an unpaid trainee, and worked his way up to become its sub-editor. In 1839 he left Dublin to edit (and soon own) *The Vindicator*, organ of Belfast's Catholics. At the end of the year he entered as a law student at the King's Inns, Dublin.

In 1842 Duffy married Emily McLaughlin (1819/20–1845), daughter of Francis McLaughlin of Belfast. Their only surviving son, John Gavan Duffy, succeeded his father as a member of the legislative assembly of Victoria. The same year saw Duffy in the court of the queen's bench, Dublin, accused of false and seditious libel. He was found guilty but was not sentenced, since he retracted his views.

Sir Charles Gavan Duffy (1816–1903), by J. C. McRae

Young Ireland In the autumn of 1841 Duffy met John Blake Dillon and Thomas Davis, both writers on the *Morning Register*. He suggested to his friends a new weekly journal, which should support the policies of Daniel O'Connell's Loyal National Repeal Association and impart to the people the ideas of Irish cultural nationalism. The resultant paper was called *The Nation*, of which Duffy was proprietor and editor. The first number, of 15 October 1842, sold out immediately. By 1843 the paper had an average circulation of 10,730. W. E. H. Lecky wrote later:

> What *The Nation* was when Gavan Duffy edited it, when Davis, [Denis Florence] McCarthy, and their brilliant associates contributed to it, and when its columns maintained with unqualified zeal the cause of liberty and nationality in every land, Irishmen can never forget. Seldom has any journal of the kind exhibited a more splendid combination of eloquence, of poetry and of reasoning.

Duffy wrote under the pseudonyms the Black Northern, Ben Heder, the O'Donnell, and C.G.D. In 1843 the *Nation* writers (later known as Young Ireland) published a collection of nationalist ballads, entitled *The Spirit of the Nation*, which contained two of Duffy's most famous songs, 'Fag an Bealach' and 'The muster of the north, A.D. 1641'. The Young Irelanders also began to publish the Library of Ireland, a series of shilling volumes of historical and literary works, which included Duffy's *Ballad Poetry of Ireland* (1845; fifty editions).

In January 1844 O'Connell, Duffy, and other 'traversers' were indicted for seditious conspiracy. On 30 May 1844 Duffy was sentenced to nine months' imprisonment, was fined £50, and was compelled to provide a security of £1000 for his good behaviour. While in Richmond prison

he was nominated for the Dublin corporation. The packed jury's verdict against all 'traversers' was quashed by the House of Lords on 7 September 1844. Relations between O'Connell and the Young Irelanders became strained when Duffy criticized O'Connell's *rapprochement* with federalists in an open letter to *The Nation* of 7 October 1844. In 1845 more serious differences arose over Peel's proposed scheme of new non-denominational universities, which the Young Irelanders supported and O'Connell opposed.

In Michaelmas term 1845 Duffy was called to the Irish bar, but he never practised. Within less than two weeks in September he lost both his friend Thomas Davis and his wife. When John Blake Dillon and Thomas McNevin also fell ill, the existence of *The Nation* was threatened. However, Duffy managed to continue the paper, and persuaded John Mitchel to become sub-editor. He also attracted new writers such as Thomas D'Arcy McGee, who later described Duffy as follows:

> He struck me as of a dyspeptic constitution … His manner was frank, short and decided, like that of a General after a campaign has begun. He was always in action, planning, suggesting and negotiating. … He was brave, yet gentle, firm though full of feeling, a soldier in resolve, a woman in affection.   (O'Sullivan, 13)

As editor of *The Nation*, Duffy stood trial in June 1846 for seditious libel for John Mitchel's article, 'Irish railways', of 22 November 1845, which had suggested sabotaging the railways as an act of self-defence. Since the jury disagreed, Duffy was discharged.

Together with the other Young Irelanders present, Duffy walked out of the special meeting of the Repeal Association on 27–8 June 1846, which passed an O'Connell-backed resolution against the use of physical force. When the split became permanent, he was one of the founders of the Irish Confederation, which disclaimed alliances with English parties and repelled O'Connell's moral force doctrine. Its first public meeting took place on 13 January 1847. On 8 February 1847 Duffy married his cousin (and sister of fellow Young Irelander Margaret *Callan) Susan Hughes (1826–1878), a teacher and the daughter of Philip Hughes and Susanna Gavan. Their six surviving children included Sir Frank Gavan *Duffy, chief justice of Australia, and Susan Duffy, a well-known writer.

By December 1847 John Mitchel, who had adopted the radical views of James Fintan Lalor, could no longer agree with Duffy on a common policy and left *The Nation* to start the *United Irishman*. Although they parted as friends, the two were soon engaged in a bitter personal battle. Duffy, as an alternative to Mitchel's radical ideas, suggested in a report to the council of the Irish Confederation that an independent Irish party should be sent to the House of Commons, pledged not to accept office from any government until repeal was conceded. The report was adopted by 317 votes to 188.

The revolutions in Europe of 1848 inspired the Confederate leaders to organize an Irish rising, to which Duffy gave support in *The Nation*. However, he was arrested on 8 July, and *The Nation* was closed down on 28 July. Whereas the leaders of the failed insurrection and Confederate editors of radical newspapers were quickly sentenced, it proved difficult to get a verdict against Duffy. Between July 1848 and April 1849 he was arraigned five times, his trial was postponed three times, and on two occasions the juries disagreed. Eventually, in April 1849, he was discharged. This outcome was surprising, for he was one of the most prominent Young Ireland leaders. No evidence of secret deals between Duffy and the government has come to light, and the conclusion may be drawn that he was just unusually lucky. However, Mitchel accused him of cowardice and betraying his principles, nicknaming him 'Give-in-Duffy'.

Tenant right On regaining freedom Duffy revived *The Nation*, but the paper never again expressed the same optimism and vigour. Focusing on the urgent question of tenant right, with Frederick Lucas he formed the Irish Tenant League, which campaigned for legislation granting the 'three Fs': fixity of tenure, fair rents, and free sale. At the general election of 1852 Duffy was elected MP for New Ross and founded the party of independent opposition (which he had proposed in 1847), pledged to oppose any government which would not support the demands of the Tenant League. The party had around fifty adherents. In November 1852 Lord Derby's government introduced a land bill to secure compensation for evicted Irish tenants for any improvements made by them on the property. The bill passed the House of Commons in 1853 and 1854, but failed to pass the House of Lords. The unity of the independent parliamentary party had already begun to crumble when two members took junior government posts in 1852. The party was also weakened by frequent attacks from Dr Cullen, archbishop of Dublin, who regarded Duffy as an 'Irish Mazzini'.

Australia By 1855 Duffy believed that his parliamentary work had failed, and that 'there was no more hope for the Irish cause then for a corpse on the dissecting table' (*The Nation*, 15 Aug 1855). He also had financial worries. On 8 October 1855 he sailed with his family to Australia, where he was welcomed with enthusiasm by his émigré fellow countrymen, and began a new life as a barrister in Melbourne. But after supporters raised £5000 to give him the property qualification necessary for membership of the legislative assembly of Victoria, he entered politics again. In 1856 he became a member of the house of assembly for Villiers and Hytesbury, and acted as 'parliamentary schoolmaster' to secure close adherence to British procedure, which sat somewhat at odds with his reputation as an 'Irish rebel'. However, Duffy wanted to prove that one who had been indicted for treason in Ireland could have a successful political career in a self-governing colony of Britain. He was in charge of the lands department in the O'Shanassy ministry in 1858–9, but resigned office in 1859 after differences with the premier over land policy. After some years in opposition, he again became minister of land and works in 1861. He carried 'Duffy's Land Act', the main object of which was to facilitate land purchase by industrious inhabitants of Victoria and deserving immigrants. However, the act did not meet its aim of preventing speculators from buying most of the land. When the O'Shanassy ministry resigned in 1863, Duffy had been in office long enough to qualify for a life pension of £1000, which enabled him to live as a gentleman. In 1865 he visited his friends in England and Ireland, and spent some months on the continent. The constituency of Dalhousie in north-western Victoria elected him as its legislative representative in 1867. The following year he launched *The Advocate*, a Catholic lay journal which encouraged Catholics to make use of their electoral power.

In June 1871 Duffy became prime minister of Victoria, uniting the free-traders with the increasingly influential protectionists, who were led by Sir Graham Berry. Duffy was not a very popular prime minister: his free-trade principles clashed with the views of Berry's progressive party, and his Catholicism and support for Catholic emancipation marked him out from the majority of liberals. Thus he suffered from anti-Catholic prejudices, but did not benefit from well-organized Catholic support. In 1872 his government was defeated by five votes in a no-confidence motion over political jobbery.

Duffy had also been prominent in the discussions about the federation of the Australian states, chairing several select committees on the issue between 1857 and 1862. In 1870 he chaired the royal commission on federation, when the withdrawal of British troops was proposed. When it recommended that the colonies had the right to remain neutral if Britain was at war, Duffy was accused of wanting to sever the connection with Britain. Hosting the intercolonial conference in Melbourne in September 1871, Duffy, the premier of a protectionist state, did little to reduce the rivalry between Victoria and New South Wales, and did not involve himself in the federation debate again until he wrote 'The road to Australian federation' for the *Contemporary Review* in 1890. Duffy's contribution to Australian federalism has been neglected in historical writing.

In 1873 Duffy was knighted in recognition of his services to Victoria. While visiting England, Ireland, and the continent in 1874–6, he was asked to stand for election to parliament but could not accept Isaac Butt's home rule policy. He was unanimously elected speaker of the legislative assembly of Victoria in 1877, and was made KCMG. During his early days as speaker he was an interested but independent observer of the struggle between the legislature's two branches in 1877–8 over payment of members.

Retirement and historical significance In 1880 Duffy resigned as speaker and left Victoria for good. He spent the remainder of his life mainly in southern Europe, where he was always looking for suitable pieces to send to the Melbourne Public Library and National Gallery, of both of which he was a trustee. A widower since the death of Susan Duffy from tuberculosis on 21 September 1878, he married Louise Hall (*d.* 1889), a young woman in her twenties and eldest daughter of George Hall of Rock Ferry, Cheshire, on 16 November 1881. The couple had four children, including George Gavan *Duffy, president of the Irish high court, and Louise Gavan *Duffy [see under Duffy, George Gavan], an Irish nationalist and Gaelic scholar. When his third wife died, on 17 February 1889, Duffy brought his daughters over from Australia to look after the household.

Having always considered himself a 'poet–statesman', Duffy devoted himself to literary work, and published valuable accounts of his own experiences in *Young Ireland: a Fragment of Irish History, 1840–45* (2 vols., 1880–83; rev. edn, 1896); *Four Years of Irish History, 1845–1849* (1883); *The League of North and South: an Episode in Irish History, 1850–4* (1886); *Thomas Davis: the Memoirs of an Irish Patriot, 1840–1846* (1890); *Conversations with Thomas Carlyle* (1892; new edn, 1896); and *My Life in Two Hemispheres* (1898). These works were highly contentious, insisting that Young Ireland had been not a revolutionary but a constitutional movement. However, they contributed to the revival of interest in Young Ireland and cultural nationalism at the turn of the century. Duffy also projected and edited a New Irish Library, based on the principles of the old, but his choice of books was considered too old-fashioned by the younger generation in the Irish Literary Society, of which he was president in 1892. He died at his home, 12 boulevard Victor Hugo, Nice, on 9 February 1903, and was buried in Glasnevin cemetery, Dublin, on 8 March 1903.

Duffy was one of the most important and long-lived figures of nineteenth-century Irish nationalism, but was not a charismatic leader. A talented writer, good networker, and excellent organizer, he often worked behind the scenes and promoted the prominence of others, for example Thomas Davis. A moderate constitutional Irish nationalist at heart, his willingness to embrace insurrection in 1848 gave the impression that he was a revolutionary, and when he reverted to moderate policies, he was vulnerable to attack for being insincere. His acceptance of a knighthood from a British queen was open to similar criticism. In essence Duffy was a political survivor, ambitious, shrewd, and practical. Emphasizing proper procedures, propriety, and middle-class respectability in all his affairs, he was criticized as being vain, formal, meticulous, and fastidious. In Australian politics his European liberalism was often perceived as outdated. The relative lack of recent historical research on Duffy, especially in Ireland, belies his significance.

R. B. O'Brien, *rev.* Brigitte Anton

Sources C. Pearl, *The three lives of Gavan Duffy* (1979) • *AusDB* • C. G. Duffy, *Young Ireland: a fragment of Irish history, 1840–1845*, rev. edn, 2 vols. (1896) • C. G. Duffy, *Four years of Irish history, 1845–1849: a sequel to 'Young Ireland'* (1883) • C. G. Duffy, *My life in two hemispheres*, 1 (1898); facs. edn (Shannon, 1969) • L. O'Bróin, *Charles Gavan Duffy: patriot and statesman* (1967) • T. F. O'Sullivan, *The Young Irelanders*, 2nd edn (1945) • R. J. Hayes, ed., *Manuscript sources for the history of Irish civilisation*, 1 (1965) • R. J. Hayes, ed., *Manuscript sources for the history of Irish civilisation: first supplement, 1965–1975*, 1 (1979) • S. R. Knowlton, 'The enigma of Sir Charles Gavan Duffy: looking for clues in Australia', *Éire–Ireland*, 31/3–4 (1996), 189–208 • B. Anton, 'Northern voices: Ulsterwomen in the Young Ireland movement', *Coming into the light: the work, politics and religion of women in Ulster*, ed. J. Holmes and D. Urquhart (1994), 60–92 • 'The women of Young Ireland', anonymous MS, *c.*1920x29, NL Ire., MS 10906 • *Irish Press* (12 Sept 1945), suppl. • Newry Catholic Church records, PRO NIre.,

MIC ID 26 • 'Death of Mrs C. G. Duffy', *The Nation* (27 Sept 1845), 832 • *The Nation* (13 Feb 1847), 302 [marriage announcement] • 'State prisoner Charles Gavan Duffy to be nominated for Dublin corporation', *The Nation* [Dublin] (24 Aug 1844), 721 • J. Mitchel, *Jail journal ... with a continuation of the journal in New York and Paris* (1913); repr. (*c.*1940)

Archives Monaghan County Museum, Monaghan, papers • NL Ire., commonplace book, MS 1627 • NL Ire., corresp. • NL Ire., corresp. and papers, MSS 340; 3040–3042; 4193–4198; 4760; 5756–5758; 7404; 8005–8006; 8098; 15744–15745 • NL Ire., scrapbook, MS 3739 • NL Ire., scrapbook, MS 4722 • PRO NIre., letters, T1143 [repr.] • Royal Irish Acad., corresp. and papers • Royal Irish Acad., list of collection, MS 67E4 • Royal Irish Acad., MSS, MS 12 • Royal Irish Acad., scrapbook, MS 23047 • State Library of Victoria, Melbourne, La Trobe manuscript collection, MSS • State Library of Victoria, Melbourne, corresp. | BL, corresp. with Lord Carnarvon, Add. MS 60821 • BL, corresp. with Lord Ripon, Add. MS 43545 • Mitchell L., NSW, Long MSS • Mitchell L., NSW, Parks MSS • NL Ire., Hickey collection, MS 3227 • NL Ire., Michael MacDonagh MSS, MS 11444 • NL Ire., corresp. with James Clarence Mangan, MS 138 • NL Ire., Monsell MSS, MS 8319 • NL Ire., J. F. X. O'Brien MSS, MSS 13418–13477 • NL Ire., corresp. with Smith O'Brien, MSS 434; 441; 445–446; 2642; 8660; 15742 • NL Ire., Léon O'Bróin MSS, MSS 24893–24895 • NL Ire., journals, William J. O'Neill, MSS 3040–3042 • NL Ire., Redmond MSS, MS 15186 • NL Ire., Sigerson MSS, MSS 8100; 10904–10905 • NL Ire., Sullivan MSS, MS 8237 • NL Scot., corresp. with Thomas Carlyle and family • PRO NIre., corresp. with Sharman Crawford, MS 856 • PRO NIre., letters to Lord Goderich • PRO NIre., John Kells Ingram MSS, D2808 • State Library of Victoria, Melbourne, corresp. relating to Australian federation

Likenesses M. H. Gill & Son, photograph, 1846, repro. in Mitchel, *Jail journal*, 336 • drawing, 1880, repro. in Pearl, *Three lives*, 223 • print, 1880, repro. in Duffy, *My life*, vol. 2, frontispiece • M. de Carnawsky, terracotta plaque, 1891, NG Ire. • Beard, photograph, repro. in *ILN* (7 May 1853) • J. P. Haverty, group portrait, lithograph (after his drawing; *The monster meeting of the 20th September 1843, at Clifden in the Irish Highlands*), NG Ire. • J. C. MacRae, line engraving (after daguerreotype), NG Ire. • J. C. McRae, stipple, NPG [see illus.] • H. O'Neill, lithograph (after daguerreotype by L. Gluckman), BM, NG Ire. • oils (after daguerreotype), NG Ire.

Wealth at death £137 10s. 0d.: probate, 6 May 1903, CGPLA Ire. • £3121: resworn probate, Aug 1903, CGPLA Eng. & Wales

Duffy, Edward (1840–1868), Fenian leader, was born at Ballaghaderreen, co. Mayo, one of a large family. In 1861 or earlier, while an assistant in a Dublin retail store, he joined the Irish Republican Brotherhood (IRB). By 1862 he was foreman of a hardware store in Castlerea, co. Roscommon and had become the pioneer of Fenian recruitment in the west. In 1863 he was persuaded to become a full-time organizer with responsibility for Connaught and for Longford, Cavan, and Westmeath. He specialized in recruiting members of 'ribbon' societies.

Duffy was arrested on 11 November 1865, with James Stephens, Charles J. Kickham, and Hugh Brophy, at Fairfield House, Sandymount, but after a brief imprisonment was released on bail in January 1866, in the belief that he was dying of consumption. When Stephens, the Fenian chief, escaped from Ireland in March 1866, he left Duffy as his deputy. When a collective IRB leadership emerged in Ireland in February 1867, Duffy was the member for Connaught. Meeting in London, his group set up the provisional government incorporating Irish-American officers which authorized the attempted rising of 5 March 1867 in Ireland. Duffy was rearrested at Boyle on 11 March 1867, tried on 21 May, and sentenced to fifteen years' penal servitude. He was found dead in his cell at Millbank prison, London, on 17 January 1868. Following a private funeral he was buried in Glasnevin cemetery, Dublin.

GORDON GOODWIN, *rev.* R. V. COMERFORD

Sources S. Ó Luing, 'A contribution to a study of Fenianism in Breifne', *Breifne*, 3/10 (1967), 156–74 • NA Ire., Fenian MSS • R. V. Comerford, *The Fenians in context: Irish politics and society, 1848–82* (1985) • *The Irishman* (25 Jan 1868)

Duffy, Sir Frank Gavan (1852–1936), judge, was born in Dublin on 29 February 1852, the elder son of the Irish nationalist and colonial politician Charles Gavan *Duffy (1816–1903) and his second wife, Susan (1826–1878), daughter of Philip Hughes, of Newry, co. Down. He was educated at Stonyhurst College, Lancashire, from 1865 to 1869, and at the University of Melbourne, where he graduated BA in 1872 and took his MA and LLB in 1882. On 3 April 1880, he married Ellen Mary (*d.* 1943), daughter of John Richard Torr, warehouseman, of Melbourne. They were to have six sons and one daughter, of whom only three sons survived their father.

On 7 July 1874, Duffy had been admitted to practise as a barrister in Victoria. After serving as an officer of the Victorian treasury, he began legal practice, first in the county court, and later in the supreme court. Short of stature, vigorous in manner, quick witted, and of sparkling vitality, he was regarded as a brilliant cross-examiner and advocate and became a leader of the bar. Sir Owen Dixon recorded that Duffy practised advocacy 'with extraordinary success', adding that 'if ever there was a man who could make bricks without straw in open court', it was he (Dixon, 259).

Duffy was appointed king's counsel on 4 February 1901. He found time to lecture in law at the University of Melbourne, to edit the *Australian Law Times* (1879–82) and the *Victorian Law Reports* (1907–13), and to write several legal works on property and insolvency. On 11 February 1913 he was appointed a justice of the high court of Australia. In addition to its appellate work in all types of cases, that court is called upon to determine constitutional issues of far-reaching importance. In general, Duffy was unfavourable to an extended interpretation of commonwealth powers. He was a member of the court which decided the famous *Engineers' case* (1920), overruling earlier decisions holding that state instrumentalities were not subject to the operation of federal law. Duffy was the sole dissentient, and in a short and closely reasoned judgment expounded a view of the federal character of the constitution which denied to commonwealth legislation a general power to bind the states as such.

In an earlier (and almost equally famous) case, *Farey* v. *Burvett* (1916), decided in the course of the First World War, Duffy also dissented. The majority there held that the defence power conferred by the constitution upon the commonwealth supported the fixing of the price of bread. Duffy's view was that while the ambit of defence might be more extensive in time of war than in peace, a power to legislate with respect to the naval and military defence of the commonwealth did not justify a general regulation of the national economy. Similarly, he tended to interpret restrictively the powers conferred by the commonwealth on its (later superseded) arbitration court. However, towards the close of his judicial career, in the *Clothing Factory case* of 1935 (a decision again involving the interpretation of the defence power), Duffy was among the majority in deciding that the peacetime activities of the Commonwealth Clothing Factory were authorized by the constitution.

Duffy was appointed KCMG in 1929. On 22 January 1931, at the age of seventy-eight, he was appointed chief justice of the high court, resigning on 1 October 1935. He had never liked sitting on the bench and as chief justice did not show himself a leader. He was sworn of the privy council in 1932. He died in Melbourne on 29 July 1936 and was buried the next day in the Boroondara general cemetery at Kew, near Melbourne.

PETER BALMFORD

Sources O. Dixon, *Jesting Pilate and other papers and addresses* (1965) • G. Sawer, *Australian federalism in the courts* (1967) • A. Dean, *A multitude of counsellors: a history of the bar of Victoria* (1968) • Z. Cowen, *Sir John Latham and other papers* (1965) • J. Rickard, *H. B. Higgins: the rebel as judge* (1984) • *DNB* • *Commonwealth Law Reports* • *AusDB* • J. M. Bennett, *Keystone of the federal arch: a historical memoir of the high court of Australia to 1980* (1980) • J. L. Forde, *The story of the bar of Victoria* (c.1915) • F. Johns, *An Australian biographical dictionary* (1934) • private information (2004) • *The Argus* [Melbourne] (29 July 1936) • *The Argus* [Melbourne] (30 July 1936)
Archives NL Ire., papers
Likenesses W. B. McInnes, oils, c.1935, High Court Buildings, Melbourne, Australia • Lafayette, photograph, NPG • P. I. White, portrait, Victorian Bar, 205 William Street, Melbourne, Australia, Owen Dixon Chambers (West) • photograph, High Court Building, Canberra, Australia

Duffy, George Gavan [Seoirse Ui Gabháin] (1882–1951), politician and judge, was born at Rose Cottage, Rock Ferry, Cheshire, on 21 October 1882, the eldest of the four children of Sir Charles Gavan *Duffy (1816–1903), the Irish nationalist who became prime minister of Victoria, Australia, and his third wife, Louise Hall (c.1860–1889). He received his early education at the Petit Séminaire in Nice, and at Stonyhurst College. In 1907 he qualified as a solicitor in London. On 23 December 1908 he married, in Paris, Margaret (1876–1967), the daughter of Alexander Martin *Sullivan, journalist and Irish nationalist MP. There were two children of the marriage, Colum and Máire. His papers in the National Library of Ireland show that he was in regular correspondence with leaders of Irish opinion, both Unionist and nationalist, from as early as 1906. He was associated with societies exploring separatist and cultural ideas (his wife was secretary to the Irish Literary Society in London), and his interest and goodwill were actively solicited by a wide spectrum of prominent persons.

Duffy was forced out of legal practice in London by his partners when he acted as solicitor to Roger Casement in his trial for treason in 1916. He moved to Dublin with his family and was called to the Irish bar in 1917. In December 1918 he was elected Sinn Féin MP for South Dublin, taking his seat in the secessionist Dáil Éireann, which opened as a constituent assembly in Dublin on 21 January 1919. He went as Dáil representative to Paris, where the peace congress was being held, but was expelled from France. Fluent in Italian, as well as in French and Irish, he continued his propaganda work for Irish independence in Rome. Appointed a member of the five-man delegation to the London peace talks in October 1921, he signed the Anglo-Irish treaty two months later but made no secret of his disappointment that only dominion status had been achieved. He pleaded, without success, that the constitution of the Irish Free State be drafted to minimize the position of the crown in Irish affairs.

Duffy was foreign minister in the Dáil cabinet from January 1922 but six months later, when the government abruptly closed the separatist Dáil courts to prevent the hearing of habeas corpus applications, he resigned in protest. An unswerving advocate of human rights and the rule of law, he proposed a series of amendments in Dáil Éireann to limit the army's emergency powers, although his efforts aroused the unremitting hostility of his kinsman Kevin O'Higgins, minister for home affairs.

When he lost his seat in the 1923 election Duffy devoted himself to his law practice, taking silk in 1929. He appeared in several leading cases and was appointed to the High Court in 1936, becoming its president in 1946. He was a dark-haired man with a pointed beard, well-dressed and of a decidedly continental appearance; he spoke in a precise, beautifully modulated voice with an English accent. A Roman Catholic of conviction, he possessed a strong religious sense. He had considerable personal charm but, socially shy, he spent the brief time he spared from work and study with his family. He died of lung cancer at St Vincent's Hospital, 96 Lower Leeson Street, Dublin, on 10 June 1951 and was buried in Glasnevin cemetery two days later.

Duffy's influence on the development of Irish jurisprudence, particularly in judicial review, is widely acknowledged. He roundly defended the liberty of the individual and the concept of the rule of law against undue interference by government in cases such as *The State (Burke)* v. *Lennon* (1940) and *Buckley & Ors.* v. *Attorney-General* (1950). The forceful language of these judgments mirrors the conviction of his Dáil speeches in 1922–3 opposing the draconian application of emergency powers, and his principled resignation from the cabinet in July 1922. In actions arising from charitable bequests he regularly and insistently expressed the belief, almost to the point of a crusade, that Irish law should evolve with some independence from common law precedent and look instead to pre-Reformation common law in construing testamentary gifts of a religious nature; he felt this particularly to be so in the light of the 1937 constitution. Modern commentators find his trenchant Catholicism—although explicable by his background and times—uncomfortable, and are undecided how inherent a part it played in his reasoning. No one, however, doubts the impact he has had on Irish judicial development, his remarkable intellectual energy, and his role as a champion of human rights. Professor Osborough, the legal historian, ranks him as 'the first judge to appreciate the significance of the Constitution for the Irish legal system. Scholarly and with an interest in law reform, Duffy demonstrated an approach to pre-1922 English and Irish case law … that was critical and heterodox' (Osborough, 160).

Duffy's only sister, **Louise Gavan Duffy** [Luise Gabhánach Ní Dhufaigh] (1884–1969), was born at Cimiez, Nice, France, on 17 July 1884, and left Nice for Dublin in 1907. After being educated at home she attended University College, Dublin, where she graduated BA in 1911 (MA 1916), and the teachers' training college at Eccles Street, Dublin. She was joint secretary of the nationalist women's organization, Cumann na mBan, and worked in the kitchens of the General Post Office during the Easter rising. In 1917 she founded Scoil Bhríde, an Irish-speaking girls' school which enjoyed a considerable cultural and academic reputation. She died at 1 Kenilworth Square, Rathgar, Dublin, on 12 October 1969, and was buried in Glasnevin cemetery, Dublin.   MARY KOTSONOURIS

Sources private information (2004) · NL Ire., G. Gavan Duffy MSS · two statements given to Bureau of Military History, 1913–21, Military Archives, Cathal Brugha Barracks, Dublin · Dáil debates, 1921–3, NL Ire. · G. M. Golding, *George Gavan Duffy, 1882–1951: a legal biography* (1982) · catalogue, University College, Dublin, G. Gavan Duffy MSS · W. N. O. [W. N. Osborough], 'Duffy, George Gavan', *Biographical dictionary of the common law*, ed. A. W. B. Simpson (1984) **Archives** NL Ire., papers · University College, Dublin | Irish Defence Forces Museum, Dublin, Bureau of Military History MSS | SOUND Bureau of Military History, 'The aftermath of the treaty', 20 Jan 1951 **Likenesses** J. Lavery, group portrait, oils, 1916 (*High treason*), King's Inns, Dublin · S. O'Sullivan, pencil drawing, King's Inns, Dublin **Wealth at death** £2844: probate, 16 Aug 1951, CGPLA Éire · £9108—Louise Gavan Duffy: probate, 26 Feb 1970, CGPLA Éire

Duffy, Louise Gavan (1884–1969). *See under* Duffy, George Gavan (1882–1951).

Duffy, Patrick Vincent (1832–1909), landscape painter, was born in Dublin, the son of James Duffy, a jeweller and art dealer, and his wife, Mary Anne, daughter of Bartholomew Lamb, auctioneer. He was admitted to the schools of the Royal Dublin Society in 1847, and while still a pupil he began to exhibit at the Royal Hibernian Society, showing *Exterior of St Patrick's* in 1851. He was a regular exhibitor there throughout his life, and exhibited one painting, *Flood in the Dargle*, at the Royal Academy in London, in 1876. All his paintings were landscapes, although in his early years he also did a little sculpture, exhibiting a model of the cross at Monasterboice in 1854.

Duffy was elected a member of the Royal Hibernian Academy in 1860, and in 1870 was appointed keeper. He held this post until his death, and was also treasurer for the last few years of his life. He died in the Richmond Hospital, Dublin, on 22 November 1909, after a long illness. He was survived by his wife, Elizabeth, daughter of James Malone, and his daughter. One of his paintings, *A Wicklow Common*, is in the National Gallery of Ireland.

ANNE PIMLOTT BAKER

Sources W. G. Strickland, *A dictionary of Irish artists*, 1 (1913); facs. edn with introduction by T. J. Snoddy (1969), 306–7 · DNB

Likenesses M. Saunders, portrait, repro. in Strickland, *A dictionary of Irish artists*, facing p. 302
Wealth at death £368 17s. 10d.: probate, 18 Feb 1910, *CGPLA Ire.*

Duffy, Terence (1922–1985), trade unionist, was born on 3 May 1922 in Wolverhampton, the second child in a family of five sons and six daughters of John Duffy, an engineering worker at Thomson's Motor Pressings, Wolverhampton, and his wife, Ann Lockrey. He was educated at two local Roman Catholic schools—St Patrick's and St Joseph's—and left school at the age of fourteen to take a job as a sheet-metal worker in the Standard Motor Company factory. As a youth his main hobby was boxing—and he was very good at it, winning several local championships. He might easily have turned professional but for the war. In the army he became a regimental boxing champion.

At the outbreak of war in 1939 Duffy was only seventeen, but enlisted in the 70th battalion (the boys' battalion) of the Hampshire regiment before transferring later to the Leicestershire regiment as an infantryman. He served with distinction for six years, rising to the rank of regimental sergeant-major, and saw front-line service on the north African and Italian fronts, and in Greece, and was in the occupation force in Austria. In 1946 he married Eileen Stokes (d. 1954) from Wolverhampton, with whom he had two sons and a daughter. Following her death he married, in 1957, Joyce, the daughter of Alexander Sturgess, a metal machinist at Guys' Motors in Wolverhampton. They had a son and a daughter.

When he was demobbed in 1945 Duffy returned to the engineering industry and worked in various local plants until joining the Norton motorcycle factory, where in 1951 he was elected as a shop steward. That was the first rung on the ladder which was to take him to the presidency of his union, the Amalgamated Union of Engineering Workers (AUEW). He became increasingly involved in the broader trade union and labour movement, and from 1955 served for twenty years on the executive of the Wolverhampton Trades Council. He was also active in the Wolverhampton constituency Labour Party, of which he was chairman from 1965 to 1970. By the early 1960s Duffy had moved to a job with Lucas Aerospace, where he became senior shop steward. In 1969 he made his first bid for a full-time elected office in the AUEW and was elected as assistant divisional organizer for his area, the union's no. 16 division in the midlands. He was re-elected again for that post in 1973.

Duffy's election in 1969 was fiercely contested against strong left-wing and communist opposition. He had already established a reputation as a scourge of the left in the midlands area, and the communist opposition to him in 1969 and again in 1973 was intense. He had no pretensions as an intellectual but drew his voting strength from his basic, down-to-earth attitudes on the shop floor and his shrewd, often quite open, tactical scheming. The midlands' region of the union became a political battleground and in it he was a fearless fighter. It was this which attracted the attention of the union's national leaders, and in 1975 he was encouraged to stand for the AUEW national executive.

The contest for the executive seat turned into a *cause célèbre* in the AUEW. The sitting member was Bob Wright, a popular left-winger and friend of the union's president, Hugh Scanlon. Duffy appeared to have little chance against him. But before the election Duffy successfully challenged his opponent in a court case over the election procedure. That cleared the path for a narrow victory by Duffy against the favourite, Bob Wright. In six years Duffy had moved from the shop floor to the union's executive boardroom. And in 1978 he repeated his victory over Bob Wright, but this time for the presidency of the union after the retirement of Hugh Scanlon. It was a narrow victory, since Bob Wright, again, was the favourite. But in a subsequent election three years later Duffy repeated his triumph, this time beating Wright by an overwhelming majority. Thereafter he remained president until his death.

Duffy was not a giant in terms of trade union leadership. Nor was he, in the tradition of engineering union presidents, a skilled craftsman. Indeed he was the first in the union's long history not to have served a craft apprenticeship. His strength lay in his ordinariness; in his intuitive understanding of the average workers' feelings, views, and even prejudices. He judged all issues by a measure of what he himself described as 'sensible practicalities'. He also drew upon his Roman Catholic faith, which was part of a deeper culture among groups of workers in the midlands: three of the last five presidents of the engineers' union had been Catholics from the midlands. His religious beliefs shaped his attitude towards the communists and contributed to his intolerance of radical views elsewhere in the trade union movement and the Labour Party. He often declared that his view of socialism was based on his personal Catholicism. Consequently his eight-year period of office as president of the AUEW was dominated so much by internal battles with the union's left wing, who openly disapproved of him but at the same time respected his guile and tenacity.

One of Duffy's outstanding achievements was to win a reduction in the forty-hour working week—by one hour—after a ten-week national strike in the industry in 1979. This shorter week agreement set a pattern for other European metal trade unions, especially since Duffy had been elected president of the International Metalworkers Federation. He was also chairman of the Confederation of Shipbuilding and Engineering Unions, a member of the TUC general council, the National Economic Development Council (Neddy), the British Overseas Trade Board, and the Think British campaign.

One of Duffy's more controversial achievements was to persuade his union to accept the Thatcher government's proposals to fund postal balloting in trade union elections. The policy was strongly opposed by Duffy's TUC colleagues, who were against accepting any money from the Conservative government. Duffy's more pragmatic view brought the threat of expulsion of the AUEW from the TUC, but Duffy fought his corner tenaciously and defied the majority of congress. Eventually the TUC accepted

Duffy's line and amended its own policy. The whole episode had a marked effect on the way in which the TUC handled its subsequent relations with the Thatcher government, even though it did not increase Duffy's popularity with many of his fellow union leaders. He also laid the foundation for his union's merger with the electricians' union to form the Amalgamated Engineering and Electrical Union, though this was not finally established until after his death.

In his younger days Duffy had always prided himself on his fitness, his physical stance, and compact military-style bearing, the legacy of his wartime service. In later years there still remained the sergeant-major's pencil-line moustache, the squared shoulders, and the quick step, even when the ageing process had begun to show. He was always neatly, though not expensively, dressed: never without a tie. He carried a quick and responsive smile which easily softened his sometimes stern features; he was always ready with a helping hand. The straight and simple virtues of the ordinary working man were never a cliché where he was concerned. Nor did they disguise the shrewdness behind his eyes. Duffy died after a long illness from lung cancer and lung infection in Brompton Hospital, London, on 1 October 1985.

GEOFFREY GOODMAN

Sources AUEW records, Amalgamated Engineering and Electrical Union, London · Trades Union Congress Library · *The Times* (2 Oct 1985) · *The Guardian* (2 Oct 1985) · *Daily Telegraph* (2 Oct 1985) · *Daily Mail* (2 Oct 1985) · *Terry Duffy: an appreciation* (1986) [pubd by AUEW and Mirror Group Newspapers] · private information (2004) [Joyce Duffy, Denis Duffy, Sir John Boyd] · personal knowledge (2004) · *DNB*
Archives FILM BFI NFTVA, current affairs footage · BFI NFTVA, news footage
Likenesses M. Haywood, photograph, 5 Feb 1949, Hult. Arch. · photograph, 30 Sept 1980, Hult. Arch.
Wealth at death £77,609: probate, 30 Jan 1986, *CGPLA Eng. & Wales*

Dufief, Nicolas Gouin (1776?–1834), teacher of French, was a native of Nantes. His father, Nicolas-Henri Dufief, a knight of the order of St Louis, served during the French Revolution as a volunteer under the French princes in Germany; his mother, the Comtesse Victoire Aimée Libault Gouin Dufief, was personally engaged in the many battles fought by her relative, General Charette, against the revolutionaries, for which she was afterwards known as the 'heroine of La Vendée'. Dufief, though a stripling of fifteen, joined in 1792 the royal naval corps assembled under the Comte d'Hector at Enghien, and went through the campaign with his regiment in the army of the brothers of Louis XVIII until its disbandment. The same year he sought refuge in England, but soon afterwards sailed for the West Indies, and from there travelled to Philadelphia, which he reached in July 1793.

In America, Dufief became an influential bookseller, supplying Thomas Jefferson over a number of years, and becoming acquainted with Joseph Priestley. His rapid success in teaching himself English caused him to publish an essay on *The Philosophy of Language*, in which he first explained to the world how he was led to make those discoveries 'from which my system of universal and economical instruction derives such peculiar and manifold advantages'. This system, which relied on the learning of sentences and phrases rather than grammatical rules, he applied in the teaching of French both in America and in England, to which he returned about 1818. It was described in his principal work, *Nature displayed in her mode of teaching language to man: being a new and infallible method of acquiring languages with unparalleled rapidity*, first published in Philadelphia (1804) and later reprinted in two volumes (London, 1818). Despite its size and costliness this work reached a twelfth edition in the author's lifetime. Dufief appears to have remained unmarried, bequeathing the rights to his literary works to Elizabeth Clarke, widow of Robert Clarke, who had attended him during his final illness. He died at Pentonville, London, on 12 April 1834.

GORDON GOODWIN, rev. M. C. CURTHOYS

Sources *GM*, 2nd ser., 1 (1834), 561 · M. B. Stern, *Nicholas Gouin Dufief of Philadelphia* (1988) · E. Philips, *Louis Hue Girardin and Nicholas Gouin Dufief and their relations with Thomas Jefferson* (1926) · will, PRO, PROB 11/1830/204
Archives L. Cong., corresp. with T. Jefferson
Likenesses P. J. Meance, miniature, Hist. Soc. Penn.

Dufour [married name Sarratt], (**Elizabeth**) **Camilla** (d. 1846), singer and writer, made her début in a concert at the King's Theatre, Haymarket, on 11 February 1796 and that season sang at the Pantheon and in Johann Peter Salomon's Hanover Square concerts. Her father arranged that Michael Kelly and Anna Maria Crouch should give her lessons in singing and acting in return for a percentage of her salary. She was to have been introduced at Kelly's benefit in May 1797 and then have a summer season at the Haymarket, with a specially written prologue for the début there of 'this little native of Britannia's Isle' (Young, 277). However, her parents broke with Kelly and negotiated a lucrative contract with Richard Brinsley Sheridan at Drury Lane, where she made her first stage appearance in the soprano role of Adela in Stephen Storace's *The Haunted Tower* on 19 October 1797. She sang well but lacked the acting skills to compensate for her short, plump figure, and during that season made only four appearances as Adela and four more as Amphitrite in *The Tempest*.

Miss Dufour was a soloist in the Covent Garden oratorios in Lent 1798 and sang again at Drury Lane only as one of the priestesses in Sheridan's *Pizarro* in May and June 1799. She turned to writing, producing stories for periodicals and, in 1803, *Aurora, or, The Mysterious Beauty*, a translation of J. J. M. Duperche's French novel based on F. J. H. von Soden's play *Aurora, oder, Das Kind der Hölle*. Jacob Henry Sarratt [see below], the future 'professor of chess', was writing for the same publisher and they married at St Leonard, Shoreditch, on 30 December 1804. Mary Julia Young, in her *Memoirs of Mrs. Crouch* (1806), wrote: 'it would be difficult to find a more accomplished, a more amiable, or a happier couple, than Mr. and Mrs. Sarrat' (Young, 312). Mrs Sarratt was for a time the leading singer in John Philip Conway Astley's company, which performed at Astley's Amphitheatre, Wesminster Bridge, in summer and at the

Royalty Theatre, Wellclose Square, in winter. In 1809 she played Polly to Robert Elliston's Macheath in his burletta version of *The Beggar's Opera* at the Royal Circus. Her last stage appearance seems to have been at the Royal Circus on 30 October 1809. Sarratt died, after a long illness, in 1819. By 1843 his widow had been living in Paris for some years, giving chess lessons to numerous pupils, including members of the aristocracy. Over the next three years a subscription was raised for her, to which King Louis-Philippe and many French and English chess amateurs contributed. In December 1846 the chess magazine *Le Palamède*, which had been active in her support, reported that she had died in Paris after a short illness, aged eighty-five, although she was probably about fifteen years younger than that.

Mrs Sarratt's husband, **Jacob Henry Sarratt** (1772/3–1819), was remembered as 'the famous Sarratt, the great chess teacher, whose fee was a guinea a lesson' (Tuckwell, 65). His early life is obscure. He married his first wife, Marie Bruzard (d. 1802x4), at St Saviour, Jersey, on 3 July 1790, and they were settled in London by late 1799. They had at least two children, Mary Ann Louisa, born on 11 December 1799, and Susan Catherine, born on 1 February 1802. He worked as a schoolmaster, and wrote *The History of Man ... Adapted to the Capacities of Youth*, two translations of Gothic novels, *The Three Monks!!!* and *Koenigsmark the Robber, or, The Terror of Bohemia*, and a useful pocket guide, *A View of London*, all published between 1802 and 1804. As 'Lieut. Sarratt, of the Royal York Mary-le-bone Volunteers', he published his *Life of Buonaparte* (1803), a rousing attack on 'the tyrant who swears eternal hatred to Britons' (p. 285). Sarratt had become interested in chess before the death of the French master François-André Danican Philidor in 1795 and learned much from Verdoni, Philidor's successor as professional at the English Chess Club. With Hippolyte de Bourblanc he enjoyed 'an uninterrupted friendship of fifteen years' duration' (J. H. Sarratt, *A New Treatise on the Game of Chess* 1821, 29), until Bourblanc's death in 1813. They frequently played chess together without a board 'while strolling in the pleasant meadows then skirting the north of London' (Walker, 117). After Verdoni's death in 1804 Sarratt became London's leading chess professional. Under his influence the London Chess Club (founded in 1807) adopted the continental rule that a game ending in stalemate was a draw, not a win for the player stalemated, as hitherto in England. *A Treatise on the Game of Chess* by 'J. H. Sarratt *Professor of Chess*' came out in 1808, and he later published *The Works of Damiano, Ruy-Lopez, and Salvio* (1813) and *The Works of Gianutio, and Gustavus Selenus* (1817), translations which made the writings of earlier masters accessible to English players. William Hazlitt came to know 'old S[arratt], tall and gaunt' as a fellow habitué of the Salopian Coffee House. Hazlitt's *On Coffee-House Politicians* includes a portrait of this extraordinary man, who had once been a prize-fighter and was still proud of his strength, a great reader who could recite Ossian by heart but whose memory 'tyrannised over and destroyed all power of selection' (*Complete Works*, 195–6). Sarratt's health was apparently in decline by autumn 1817,

and he died on 6 November 1819, when he was said to be in his forty-seventh year. His last work, *A New Treatise on the Game of Chess*, which included a beginners' section in question-and-answer form, was published in 1821. William Lewis, his most distinguished pupil, oversaw a revised version of Sarratt's 1808 *Treatise* in 1822. In the same year Lewis, in his preface to his own translation of Pietro Carrera, described Sarratt as 'the finest and most finished player' he had ever seen, 'alike excellent in attack and defence'. OLIVE BALDWIN and THELMA WILSON

Sources C. B. Hogan, ed., *The London stage, 1660–1800*, pt 5: *1776–1800* (1968) • *Oracle* (11 Feb 1796) • *Oracle* (13 Feb 1796) • *Oracle* (26 Feb 1796) • *The Times* (17 July 1809) • *The Times* (25 Oct 1809) • *The Times* (30 Oct 1809) • M. J. Young, *Memoirs of Mrs Crouch*, 2 (1806) • *Monthly Mirror*, 3 (Oct 1797) • *Le Palamède*, 3 (1843), 566 • *Le Palamède*, 4 (1844), 233–4, 280 • *Le Palamède*, 5 (1845), 181–2 • *Le Palamède*, 6 (1846), 139, 569 • *Chess Player's Chronicle*, 5 (1845), 156 • P. Garside and R. Schöwerling, *The English novel, 1770–1829: a bibliographical survey of prose fiction published in the British Isles*, 2: *1800–1829* (2000) • M. Summers, *A Gothic bibliography* (1940) • H. J. R. Murray, 'J. H. Sarratt', *British Chess Magazine*, 57 (1937), 353–9, letter from P. W. Sergeant, 474 • *The complete works of William Hazlitt*, ed. P. P. Howe, 8 (1931) • W. Tuckwell, *Reminiscences of Oxford* (1900) • D. P. Carrera, *A treatise on the game of chess*, trans. W. Lewis (1822) • G. Walker, *Chess & chess-players* (1850) • F. M. Edge, *The exploits and triumphs in Europe of Paul Morphy, the chess champion* (1859) • D. Hooper and K. Whyld, *The Oxford companion to chess*, 2nd edn (1992) • H. J. R. Murray, *A history of chess* (1913) • *GM*, 1st ser., 89/2 (1819), 477 • parish register, Jersey, St Saviour, 3 July 1790 [marriage: Jacob Henry Sarratt and Marie Bruzard] • parish register, Shoreditch, St Leonard, 30 Dec 1804 [marriage] • parish register, London, St Pancras, 19 March 1800 and 7 March 1802 [baptism: Susan Catherine and Mary Ann Louisa, daughters of Sarratt's first marriage]

DuGard [Dugard], **Samuel** (1642/3–1697), Church of England clergyman and author, the son of Thomas *Dugard (*bap*. 1608, *d*. 1683), master of Warwick School between 1633 and 1648, and his first wife, Hannah, *née* Hanks or Hancks (*d*. 1655), was probably baptized at nearby Barford in 1643. His father was inducted to the rectory of Barford in 1648. Samuel had a sister, Anne, still alive in 1683, and a brother, Henry, five years his junior, who followed in his brother's educational footsteps. In 1661, aged eighteen, DuGard matriculated at Trinity College, Oxford, as a commoner; he was admitted a scholar on 24 May 1662. He graduated BA on 20 October 1664 and was then ordained a minister of the Church of England. He was elected a fellow of Trinity College in June 1667, proceeding MA the following October. He married his cousin Lydia Dugard (1649/50–1675) of Barford, daughter of William *Dugard, by licence dated 4 April 1672, when he was described as being of Trinity College, implying that it was only upon his marriage that he resigned his fellowship. Their first child, Thomas, was baptized at Barford a year later. In November 1674 DuGard sent to Ralph Bathurst, the president of his old college (and an active member of the Oxford branch of the Royal Society), a 'Relation concerning a strange kind of bleeding in a little child at Lilleshall in Shropshire', which was printed in the *Philosophical Transactions* (9.193)

Samuel DuGard is credited with an anonymous publication, *The marriages of cousin germans vindicated from the censures of unlawfulness and inexpediency: being a letter written to his much honour'd T.D.* in 1673. The dedication may refer to his father Thomas, a former puritan, who may have objected strongly to his son's choice of marital partner on religious grounds. Samuel DuGard was inducted to the rectory of Forton in Staffordshire later that year. His next two children, Richard and Lydia, were baptized at Forton in 1674 and 1675 respectively. Sadly, Lydia's baptism took place on the same day as her mother's burial. Samuel subsequently married another cousin, Elizabeth Kimberley, and they had a further seven children—Elizabeth, William, Hannah, Phebe, Samuel, Susanna, and Charles—baptized between 1679 and 1692. While his family was growing Samuel wrote his best-known literary work, published in 1687, *The True Nature of Divine Law, and of Disobedience Thereunto; in Nine Discourses*. This theological work was dedicated to the patron of the rectory, Edwin Skrymsher of Aqualate Hall, a lawyer and MP for Stafford in 1681, also a graduate of Trinity College.

Criticism of the size of his family may have encouraged DuGard to publish in 1695 *A discourse concerning many children, in which the prejudices against a numerous offspring are removed, and the objections answered, in a letter to a friend*. Despite unspecified poor health mentioned in his will, written in June 1696, DuGard became a canon of Lichfield Cathedral, collated to the prebend of Pipa Minor in January 1697. He died at Forton three months later and was buried there on 13 April. His goods were valued at about £300, and property and land in Warwickshire and Worcestershire was left to support his widow, five sons, and five daughters.　　　　　　　　　　ANNE TARVER

Sources Wood, *Ath. Oxon.*, new edn, 4.679 • Wood, *Ath. Oxon.: Fasti* (1820), 277 • *Fasti Angl.* (Hardy), 1.619 • parish register, Forton, transcript, William Salt Library, Stafford • F. R. Twemlow, 'History of the manor of Mere and Forton', William Salt Library, Stafford • will and inventory of Samuel DuGard, 1697, Lichfield Joint RO • will and inventory, 1683, Worcs. RO [Thomas Dugard] • parish registers, Barford, 1634–46, Warks. CRO, DR 48 • A. F. Leach, *History of Warwick School* (1906) • Foster, *Alum. Oxon.* • IGI • Wadley, Worcestershire, marriage licences • memorial, Forton church, Staffordshire [Lydia DuGard]
Wealth at death £301 10s.—goods only, incl. books valued at £100: will and inventory, Lichfield Joint RO, 1697

Dugard, Thomas (*bap.* 1608, *d.* 1683), Church of England clergyman and diarist, was baptized on 10 April 1608, at Bromsgrove, Worcestershire, the second son of Henry Dugard (*d.* 1635) a clergyman and schoolmaster, and his wife, Elizabeth Kimberley. With his elder brother, William *Dugard (1606–1662), he was educated at Worcester School and the puritan Sidney Sussex College, Cambridge, where his uncle Richard was a noted tutor. Admitted as a sizar in March 1626, he graduated BA in 1630 and proceeded MA in 1633. Soon afterwards Dugard obtained the post of master of Warwick School through the patronage of Robert Greville, second Baron Brooke, to whom he had been introduced by the noted puritan Thomas Gataker, a former fellow of Sidney Sussex. Dugard was ordained as deacon at Gloucester in December 1634 and priest at Worcester in June 1636, but remained at Warwick until 1647. On 24 August 1635 he married Hannah Hanks or Hancks

(*d.* 1655); the couple had several children, of whom Anne and Samuel *DuGard (1642/3–1697) outlived their father.

Dugard's surviving diary (covering exactly ten years, from March 1632 to March 1642) offers important insights into the social, professional, and ideological networks of a young provincial clergyman moving in puritan, oppositional circles in the 1630s. With his clerical friends he swapped pulpits, preaching frequently even before ordination, discussed sermons, edited manuscripts, and debated the troubling issues of ceremonial conformity, emigration to New England, and attitudes to the Scots. He helped co-ordinate local protests against the Laudian canons of 1640, and through Brooke was acquainted with a range of eminent puritan ministers such as Simeon Ashe and Peter Sterry as well as several of the leading lay opponents of Charles I's personal rule such as John Pym, Lord Saye and Sele, and the earl of Lincoln.

In 1647 Dugard acquired the wealthy living of Barford, near Warwick. Here in the 1640s and 1650s he followed a mainstream puritan or presbyterian course. He signed the Warwickshire ministers' testimony of 1648 against the growth of error and division, and in a funeral sermon for Alice, Lady Lucy, *Death and the Grave* (1649), bemoaned the growth of radical sectarianism. He was active in the voluntary association of Warwickshire ministers known as the Kenilworth classis. Hannah Dugard died in December 1655, and on 26 April 1660 Dugard married Mary Hugford (*d.* 1669).

Unlike most of his closest associates Dugard conformed in August 1662, taking the declarations required by the Act of Uniformity five days before the deadline. In 1663 he was briefly questioned for preaching that Charles I's issue of the Book of Sports 'was the cause of all blood that was shed in this nation' (PRO, SP 29/85/101). This perhaps triggered the publication of a collection of orations and poems, *Philobasileus, philoepiscopus, philophilus*, (1664) in which he eulogized Charles I and various bishops and conformist clergy, while conspicuously ignoring the nonconformists among his friends. Dugard's second wife was buried on 4 October 1669. By 1677 he had married Anne, daughter of Hugh Musson or Muston of Kingsbury, Warwickshire, probably born in 1637 or 1638. Dugard died at his rectory within a very short time of her death; Anne Dugard was buried at Barford on 4 October 1683, Dugard eight days later on 12 October.

Thomas Dugard was an inveterate writer of mostly terrible verse which can be found in the Barford parish register and prefacing the works of colleagues such as Ashe, Samuel Clarke, and John Trapp, as well as in his own publications. He was a cautious and pedantic man, whose career was apparently equally conventional and conformist, as well as successful. Shortly before his death he was enrolled by the heralds among the Warwickshire gentry, and he left a substantial estate. His life does, however, reveal the readjustments and tensions inevitable as a moderate puritan negotiated the complex religious changes of the 1630s to the 1660s.　　　ANN HUGHES

Sources A. Hughes, 'Thomas Dugard and his circle in the 1630s—a "parliamentary–puritan" connexion?', *HJ*, 29 (1986), 771–93 • J. L.

Salter, 'Warwickshire clergy, 1660–1714', PhD diss., U. Birm., 1975 • Dugard's diary, BL, Add. MS 23146 • W. H. Rylands, ed., *The visitation of the county of Warwick … 1682 … 1683*, Harleian Society, 62 (1911) • Venn, *Alum. Cant.* • P. Styles, 'The heralds' visitation of Warwickshire, 1682/3', in P. Styles, *Studies in seventeenth century west midlands history* (1978) • S. Clarke, *The lives of thirty two English divines*, in *A general martyrologie*, 3rd edn (1677) • parish register, Barford, Warks. CRO • *The Warwickshire ministers testimony to the trueth of Jesus Christ and to the solemn league and covenant* (1648) • J. Ley, *A discourse of disputations, chiefly concerning matters of religion* (1658) • diocesan records, Worcs. RO, BA 2736 [subscription book, 1661–1681] • diocesan records, Worcs. RO, BA 2951 [liber cleri, 1661] • diocesan records, Worcs. RO, BA 2697 [subscription book, 1662–3] • PRO, SP 29/85/101 • will, Worcs. RO, WP 5 Nov 1683

Archives BL, diary, Add. MS 23146 • Warks. CRO, administrative material in diocesan archives | Warks. CRO, Barford parish register

Wealth at death substantial; two yard-lands and a house; £138 in money; £100 in books; £188 in good debts: will, Worcs. RO, WP 5 Nov 1683

Dugard, William (1606–1662), schoolmaster and printer, was born on 9 January 1606 at The Hodges, in Bromsgrove, Worcestershire, the eldest son of Henry Dugard (d. 1635), clergyman and schoolmaster, and his wife, Elizabeth Kimberley, and elder brother of Thomas *Dugard (bap. 1608, d. 1683). A king's scholar at Worcester School, he was admitted to Sidney Sussex College, Cambridge, on 13 September 1622, graduated BA in 1627, and proceeded MA in 1630.

In 1626 Dugard began what was to be in many respects a distinguished teaching career as usher at Oundle School, and in 1630 became master of Stamford School. Probably soon afterwards he married his first wife, Elizabeth; a son, Richard, was born in 1633 or 1634. At Stamford, Dugard's strength of purpose and taste for controversy first became apparent in a dispute with the corporate authorities, which eventually led to his departure from the school. From 1637 to 1643 he was a highly energetic and successful master of Colchester School, but, notwithstanding the support of powerful interests, was forced to resign when a 'disaffected party in the town' (Morant, 1.177) threatened to set up another school. Meanwhile, his wife having died in July 1641, he married in March 1642 Lydia Tiler, a widow.

Dugard's fine qualities as scholar and schoolmaster were recognized in 1644 by his appointment as chief schoolmaster of the Merchant Taylors' School in London, a post which gave full scope to his organizational powers and innovational teaching methods. The latter were based on sensible and logical progression and the active involvement of the pupils in the process of learning. Existing textbooks were inadequate to his purpose, and, influenced by Comenius, he wrote a series of works for the study of Latin and Greek composition, initially for the use of his own pupils; these subsequently appeared in many editions, and in 1648 spawned a second, and equally significant, career as a printer and publisher, when he was invited to join the Stationers' Company to correct its school books. He acquired a number of presses and printed his own and other school manuals, books on scientific and general subjects, and political tracts, pursuing this work within the confines of Merchant Taylors' School despite the disapproval of the school authorities.

Through the 1640s Dugard was a royalist, and he printed and published books, including *Eikon basilike*, which justified the king's cause and challenged the Commonwealth government. In 1650, when he printed Claude de Saumaise's *Defensio regia*, a denunciation of regicide, the council of state ordered his committal to Newgate. His presses were seized and he was dismissed from Merchant Taylors' School; his wife and six children were turned out of doors. After a month in Newgate he was released upon the intervention of his friends Sir James Harrington and John Milton (also a close friend of his uncle Richard Dugard (d. 1654), rector of Fullerby, Lincolnshire). His incarceration brought about a remarkable, or at least expedient, conversion, and, with his school post and presses later restored, he took the republican side with some vigour. As a 'printer for the state', he printed and published, alone or in partnership with Henry Hills, books in support of the Commonwealth government, most notably, in 1651, Milton's *Pro populo Anglicano defensio*, the official reply to de Saumaise.

Dugard's publication in 1652 of the *Racovian Catechism*, a translation of the anti-Trinitarian work issued at Rakow in 1605, for a while brought further trouble on his head. The *Catechism* had already been condemned by the Church of England, and after examination by a parliamentary committee Dugard was found guilty of publishing this 'blasphemous and scandalous book' (*JHC*, 7.113–14), all copies of which were ordered to be seized and publicly burnt. However, his relations with the government were not ruptured by this incident and he continued to print tracts praising the policies and victories of the Commonwealth and its army. In 1652 he printed Milton's Latin translation of the council of state's declaration of war against the states of Holland and, on the order of the committee for foreign affairs, English and Latin versions of John Selden's *Mare clausum*. Among the non-political works bearing his imprint were books by the physicians William Harvey and Francis Glisson and the agriculturalist Sir Richard Weston.

Dugard's activities as printer and publisher declined after reaching a peak in 1654. Continuing poor relations with his school governors reached a head in 1660 and he was again dismissed, this time finally. Thereafter he prospered as master of his own school in White Alley, Coleman Street, London. Even his action in December 1660 of sheltering Harrington from the pursuing forces of the Restoration government apparently escaped prosecution. By 27 November 1662, when he drew up his will, he was 'sicke and weake in body' (PRO, PROB 11/309, fols. 358v–359v), and he died on 3 December 1662, leaving his daughter Lydia, apparently his only surviving child, as his heir and executor; his second wife had predeceased him.

W. R. MEYER

Sources L. Rostenberg, 'William Dugard, pedagogue and printer to the Commonwealth', *Papers of the Bibliographical Society of America*, 52 (1958), 179–204 • H. B. Wilson, *The history of Merchant-Taylors'*

School, 1 (1812), 268–70, 288–9, 304–28 · PRO, PROB 11/309, fols. 358–9 [Dugard's will] · *CSP dom.*, *1650*, 27, 76, 514–15, 535; *1649–50*, 500, 523, 568; *1651–2*, 99, 132, 303, 483; *1660–61*, 413; *1661–2*, 32 · *JHC*, 7 (1651–9), 113–14 · P. Morant, *The history and antiquities of the county of Essex*, 1 (1768), 177 · F. F. Madan, 'Milton, Salmasius, and Dugard', *Transactions of the Bibliographical Society*, 2nd ser., 4 (1923–4), 119–45 · W. R. Parker, *Milton: a biography*, 2 vols. (1968), vol. 1, pp. 378, 395, 423; vol. 2, p. 973 · Venn, *Alum. Cant.* · *DNB*

Dugdale, Amy Katherine. *See* Browning, Amy Katherine (1881–1978).

Dugdale [*née* Balfour], **Blanche Elizabeth Campbell** (1880–1948), author and Zionist, was born on 23 May 1880 at 32 Addison Road, Holland Park, London. Generally known as Baffy, she was the eldest of the five children of Eustace James Anthony Balfour (1854–1911), an architect and the youngest brother of the prime minister Arthur James *Balfour, and his wife, Lady Frances Campbell (1858–1931), daughter of George *Campbell, eighth duke of Argyll.

In her memoir, *Family Homespun* (1940), Baffy describes her family: on her mother's side the Campbells at Inveraray, ducal, Celtic, and feudal, on her father's the Balfours at Whittingehame, logical and tolerant, revering accuracy as much as the Campbells scorned it. It was at Whittingehame, where Arthur Balfour lived, adored by his numerous relations—including Baffy—that she spent much of her childhood. Her family spent half of the year at 32 Addison Road and half in Scotland. They felt very consciously Scottish: on their way north when exactly half-way across the Tweed they all cheered. On the southbound journey they 'hissed like serpents' (Dugdale, *Family Homespun*, 65).

Baffy had no formal education; but her mother read to her, mainly from the novels of Sir Walter Scott, and she learned to read by puzzling out the words in Macaulay's *Lays of Ancient Rome*, which she knew by heart. As she grew up 'the multiplication tables might remain a sealed book but if you had asked me the difference between a Conservative and a Liberal Unionist I could have told you by the time I was ten' (Dugdale, *Family Homespun*, 143). According to her difficult and passionately political mother, conversation was the one essential accomplishment: it was a high priority both at Whittingehame and at Hatfield, where she often stayed with her Cecil cousins.

Baffy 'came out' and was presented at one of Queen Victoria's last drawing-rooms in March 1898. On 18 November 1902 she married Edgar Trevelyan Stratford Dugdale (1876–1964), an underwriting member of Lloyds, the second son of William Stratford Dugdale of Merevale Hall, Atherstone, Warwickshire. They had two children, Frances and Michael, and lived at 1 Roland Gardens, South Kensington.

Baffy was jolted into public life by the First World War. From 1915 to 1919 she worked in the department of naval intelligence at the Admiralty. After the war, enthusiastic for international co-operation, she joined her cousin Robert Cecil in founding the League of Nations Union and was head of the union's intelligence department from 1920 to 1928. In 1932 she was a member of the British government delegation to the assembly of the League of Nations.

Blanche Elizabeth Campbell Dugdale (1880–1948), by unknown photographer

Meanwhile 1 Roland Gardens became well known for amusing, often political lunch parties; good conversationalists like Bob Boothby, Harold Nicolson, and Robert Cecil were frequent guests. Tall, with wide-apart eyes and a generous mouth, Baffy was excellent company; her enthusiasms were infectious, though she was also 'capable of deflating pretension with deadly effect' (*The Times*, 18 May 1948).

When Arthur Balfour retired from public life Baffy encouraged him to write his memoirs (published as *Chapters of Autobiography*, 1930), organizing his papers and acting as his secretary. When he died she wrote *Arthur James Balfour* (1936), his authorized biography. *The Times* described it as 'penetrating' and 'the most intimate since Boswell'. It is a magisterial work in two volumes and is a standard work for students of Balfour's life. As well as describing his political career it gives a sensitive, entertaining, and of course well-informed picture of his life at Whittingehame, his friends the Souls, and his passion for golf. Baffy also wrote numerous political articles for newspapers and journals, and her perceptive and entertaining memoir *Family Homespun* was published in 1940.

Baffy had been deeply impressed by the Balfour declaration. The idea of the British government helping to establish a national home for the Jewish people fired her imagination, and as a woman of action she started working for the cause. By 1936, the year in which her diary (edited by N. A. Rose as *Baffy*, 1973) begins, she was working at the headquarters of the Jewish Agency and Zionist Federation at 77 Great Russell Street, promoting the Jewish viewpoint and drafting articles and speeches with the historian Lewis Namier, also a dedicated Zionist. She became an effective speaker, especially to Jewish audiences.

Baffy thought of Palestine as her second country and often stayed with Chaim Weizmann, leader of the Zionists, and his wife, Vera, at Rehovoth, their house near Jerusalem. Weizmann, a charismatic figure whom she much admired, made her one of his team: the only gentile on the inner circle of his policy making group. He respected her political judgement, but perhaps for him her greatest asset was that she knew several members of the British government well and had friends in the cabinet, where the decisions about Israel were made. She could act on diplomatic missions trusted by both sides. She was, for instance, able to give Weizmann a synopsis of the contents of the Peel report concerning the partitioning of Palestine a fortnight before it was published in July 1937. Walter Elliot, minister of agriculture (1936–8) and then of health (1938–40), was her greatest friend in the government and the member of the cabinet who was most willing to give her information.

Baffy was a Conservative, but she was also a convinced non-appeaser, and she became so disillusioned by the government's attitude to Hitler that in 1937 she joined the National Labour Party and was adopted as its candidate for Central Southwark. However, when National Labour did not oppose the government on the issue of Czechoslovakia she resigned. The diary as it is edited is mainly a day-by-day account of her work for the Jews, but it includes brilliant snapshots of the great political events of the day as seen by someone on gossiping terms with those involved. The Mrs Simpson drama unfolds, and she and Walter Elliot and Colin Coote, then leader writer for *The Times*, and his wife settle down to a game of poker as the Munich crisis accelerates.

Blanche Dugdale loved the young and was devoted to her four grandchildren, and if one of her nieces was in London on leave during the Second World War she would sweep her off to a pub in William IV Street where Baffy and her friends met, all paying for their own lunches, and where conversation sparkled.

When war broke out Blanche Dugdale continued to work for the Jewish Agency, helping to persuade the British government to allow a Jewish fighting force but frustrated by how little could be done about the atrocities in occupied Europe. In 1942 she wrote of the Jews in Poland: 'It is an extermination policy now, but what can one do?' (*Baffy*, 198, 28 Nov 1942). She supported the National Committee for Rescue from Nazi Terror led by Victor Cazalet and Victor Gollancz. She fought against the indifference of the Foreign Office, and she brought pressure to bear on the Colonial Office to allow Jews, particularly children, in the refugee ships to disembark in Palestine.

Blanche Dugdale hated the in-fighting that occurred between the Jewish leaders, and when Weizmann lost the leadership in 1946 she realized her work was done; her health also was declining. She died on 16 May 1948 (the day after she heard that the state of Israel had been established) at the house of her daughter and son-in-law Sir James Fergusson of Kilkerran House, by Maybole, Ayrshire. She was buried on 22 May. Undoubtedly she would have considered her work for the Jews her most important achievement, and she is still honoured in Israel, but in Britain she is best remembered as an author.

CLAIRE PERCY

Sources *Baffy: the diaries of Blanche Dugdale, 1936–47*, ed. N. A. Rose (1973) [incl. introduction by N. A. Rose] · B. E. C. Dugdale, *Family homespun* (1940) · B. E. C. Dugdale, *Arthur James Balfour*, 2 (1936) · A. James, first earl of Balfour, *Chapters of autobiography*, ed. Mrs E. Dugdale (1930) · Burke, *Peerage* (1999) · *The Times* (18 May 1948) · *The Times* (21 May 1948) · private information (2004) [Adam Fergusson, grandson; Ann Balfour Fraser, cousin]
Archives BL, corresp. and papers mostly relating to Arthur James Balfour · priv. coll., MSS
Likenesses photograph, repro. in *Baffy*, ed. Rose [*see illus.*] · photographs, priv. coll.
Wealth at death £3917 3s.: probate, 11 Sept 1948, *CGPLA Eng. & Wales*

Dugdale, Sir John (1628–1700). *See under* Dugdale, Sir William (1605–1686).

Dugdale, Richard [*called* the Surey Demoniack] (*b. c.*1670), demoniac, was the son of Thomas Dugdale of Surey, near Whalley, Lancashire, who was a gardener and servant to Thomas Lister of Westby, Yorkshire. An otherwise obscure individual, Dugdale owed his contemporary notoriety to a series of pamphlets published in the late 1690s concerning his alleged possession and exorcism. According to these pamphlets, Dugdale and his father approached the dissenting minister Thomas Jolly on 29 April 1689, informing this divine that in July 1688, when about eighteen years of age, Dugdale had attended a rush-bearing at Whalley where, having drunk to excess, he 'offered himself to the Devil, on condition the Devil would make him a good dancer' (Jolly, *Surey Demoniack*, 2). Dugdale subsequently quarrelled and fought with one of the revellers, and having returned home began to experience a 'burning pain' in his side. Jolly was further told that during subsequent nights Dugdale had been alarmed by the door to his room opening and a mist entering, followed by various supernatural appearances, and that he had become subject to violent fits and an uncontrollable urge to dance. Despite the ministrations of a local physician the fits had continued and increased.

Jolly was convinced that Dugdale's illness was attributable to demonic possession, and initiated a series of meetings at which he and a number of other nonconformist ministers prayed and fasted for the exorcism of Dugdale. Dugdale's fame spread throughout the county, and several thousand people attended these prayer meetings, held at a variety of locations in and around Whalley. Such crowds were attracted by reports of the startling physical manifestations of Dugdale's possession, some of which were detailed by the dissenting ministers and, in declarations before local magistrates, those who attended these meetings. In addition to violent fits of rage and anger, it was claimed that Dugdale foretold future events; spoke languages of which he was ignorant, on occasion with two voices at once; was at times wildly blasphemous, and at others preached sermons. Progress towards curing Dugdale proved slow, however, and by September 1689 the demoniac was threatening to seek other remedies and had complained to his father's landlord, Sir Edmund Assheton, third baronet, of Whalley Abbey, of his frustration at the ineffectiveness of the dissenters' ministrations. Though Dugdale's fits and the dissenters' prayer meetings continued, Assheton arranged for Dugdale to be given a 'physic' on 25 March 1690. Dugdale's symptoms ceased from this date, though the nonconformist ministers claimed that this was due to the effects of their final prayer meeting on 24 March rather than the medicine administered the following day.

Despite uncertainties as to the nature of Dugdale's affliction and the reason for its apparent cure, the young man's plight attracted the interest of such leading figures as Richard Baxter and Increase Mather, both of whom, it was claimed, wished to quote the case in their works upon witchcraft. Publication of such details did not, however, occur until the appearance in 1697 of *The Surey Demoniack*, which prompted the Anglican clergyman Zachary Taylor to publish *The Surey Impostor* (1698), a critique of both the claims made for Dugdale's actions and the behaviour of the dissenting ministers, which in turn led to further pamphlets on the topic.

Little more is known of Dugdale's life. *The Surey Demoniack* claimed that shortly after his exorcism Dugdale married and returned to his duties as a gardener, and all the pamphlets generated by this controversy agreed that down to the late 1690s Dugdale had not suffered a significant recurrence of his malady of the late 1680s.

A. C. BICKLEY, *rev.* RICHARD D. HARRISON

Sources [T. Jolly and J. Carrington], *The Surey Demoniack, or, An account of Satan's strange and dreadful actings in and about the body of Richard Dugdale of Surey, near Whalley in Lancashire* (1697) · Z. Taylor, *The Surey impostor: being an answer to a late fanatical pamphlet entituled 'The Surey Demoniack'* (1698) · T. Jolly, *A vindication of the Surey Demoniack as no impostor, or, A reply to a certain pamphlet publish'd by Mr Zach. Taylor, called 'The Surey impostor'* (1698) · M. F. Snape, '"The Surey impostor": demonic possession and religious conflict in seventeenth-century Lancashire', *Transactions of the Lancashire and Cheshire Antiquarian Society*, 90 (1994), 93–114 · J. Westaway and R. D. Harrison, '"The Surey Demoniack": defining protestantism in 1690s Lancashire', *Unity and diversity in the church*, ed. R. N. Swanson, SCH, 32 (1996), 263–82
Likenesses woodcut, BM; repro. in Taylor, *Surey impostor*, frontispiece · woodcut, BM; repro. in Z. Taylor, *Popery, superstition, ignorance, and knavery confess'd and fully proved on the Surey dissenters* (1699); facsimile, 1793, NPG

Dugdale, Stephen (*d.* 1683), informer, may have come from a minor gentry family of Staffordshire, but his parentage is unknown. He later claimed that as a young man he was converted to Roman Catholicism by a priest named Knight, and was in his care until Knight fell ill. He was then passed to Francis Evers, a Jesuit, and became his great intimate. By 1677 he was steward to Walter Aston, third Lord Aston, a Catholic landowner of Tixall, Staffordshire. Dugdale apparently cheated the estate men of their wages and also stole from his employer to pay for his gambling debts and debauchery. Sacked by Lord Aston, he was arrested and imprisoned for debt in Stafford in November 1678. To escape from this he turned informer, claiming to have knowledge of the Catholic plot to assassinate the king which had recently been revealed by Titus Oates, and was brought up to London for questioning.

Dugdale's gentlemanly speech and bearing enabled him to give a good account of himself, and he even managed to half convince Charles II of his sincerity. Burnet claimed that Dugdale was 'a man of sense and temper ... behaved himself decently, and had somewhat in his air and deportment that disposed people to believe him' (*Burnet's History*, 2.190). Beginning in December 1678, when he gave information to the privy council, Dugdale made various accusations, conveniently confirming the evidence of Oates against the Catholic lords in the Tower and the associated Jesuit conspiracy, and creating a minor sub-plot in Staffordshire. He claimed that he had been offered £500 to kill the king by William Howard, Viscount Stafford, and that Stafford had told him of the plot in September 1678. He also said that he had had many conversations with Evers and others in which they declared that 'it would not be long before we might expect some good times' (Dugdale, *Information*, 2), and made much of the duke of York's conversion to the Catholic religion. He had also heard rumours of plotting and of weapons being gathered in Staffordshire, a point which cost many of the Catholic Staffordshire gentry their liberty. By implicating those he knew in the plot rather than resorting to the exaggerations of fellow informer William Bedloe, Dugdale generally seems to have settled for relatively safe accusations.

At the Popish Plot trials of 1679, however, Dugdale was not a great success. His first court appearance was at the trial of the five Jesuits on 13 June 1679. He also gave evidence at the trial of Sir George Wakeman in July, but he had already begun to embroider his tales further, and his apparent respectability soon ebbed away under bouts of venereal disease and drunkenness. In October 1679 John Tasborough and Anne Price, a former lover and fellow servant of Lord Aston, apparently offered Dugdale £1000 to recant his evidence, which he refused. They were tried and convicted in January 1680 for subornation of perjury.

Dugdale led a shifting life in the latter days of the plot crisis. He was an associate of Edmund Warcup, the magistrate who involved himself with many informers, and apparently wrote pamphlets about the plot. His supposed gentlemanly background ensured that he was one of the best-paid of the informers of the day, netting some £475 from the government in 1678–9; in 1681 his expenses bill came to £251 15s. 6d. Other gifts of £100 also came his way. Although his allowance of £5 per week was cut to £3 in July 1680 and £2 in April 1681, it continued until his death. Having been present at the searching of Lord Stafford's house in May 1679, he gave evidence against Stafford at his trial in December 1680. Dugdale fell out with Oates at the trials for sedition of the violently anti-Catholic Stephen College in July and August 1681, testifying for the prosecution while Oates was for the defence. Afterwards it was reported that he had quite 'lost his credit, and [was] absolutely ruin'd' (Luttrell, 1.123). It had long been rumoured that he was suffering from a venereal disease (Dugdale having claimed that he had been poisoned), and in October 1681 he complained to the privy council that his own doctor had libelled him. Upon investigation the council found the doctor to be telling the truth, and Dugdale was dismissed with a warning 'not to trouble them any more' (ibid., 1.136–7). In his last days alcoholism and disease seem to have caught up with him, and he claimed to have seen the ghosts of his victims. Dugdale died in London shortly before 26 March 1683, a minor informer and an example of the opportunists whom the plot scare pushed to the forefront of political life.   ALAN MARSHALL

Sources S. Dugdale, *The information of Stephen Dugdale, gent., delivered at the bar of the House of Commons Monday the first day of November in the year of our Lord 1680* (1680) • S. Dugdale, *The further information of Stephen Dugdale (30 October 1680) November 2nd 1680* (1680) • *The manuscripts of the House of Lords*, 4 vols., HMC, 17 (1887–94), vol. 1 • N. Luttrell, *A brief historical relation of state affairs from September 1678 to April 1714*, 6 vols. (1857) • 'The journals of Edmund Warcup, 1676–84', ed. K. G. Feiling and F. R. D. Needham, *EngHR*, 40 (1925), 235–60 • *Burnet's History of my own time*, ed. O. Airy, new edn, 2 vols. (1897–1900) • J. Kenyon, *The Popish Plot* (1972) • J. Pollock, *The Popish Plot* (1903) • S. Dugdale, *A narrative of unheard-of popish cruelties towards protestants beyond the seas, or, A new account of the bloody Spanish inquisition, published as a caveat to protestants* (1680) • R. North, *Examen, or, An enquiry into the credit and veracity of a pretended complete history* (1740) • A. Clifford, ed., *Tixall letters, or, The correspondence of the Aston family and their friends during the seventeenth century*, 2 vols. (1815) • *The tryal and conviction of John Tasborough and Ann Price for subornation of perjury in endeavouring to persuade Mr Stephen Dugdale to retract and deny his evidence about the horrid Popish Plot* (1680)
Likenesses engraving, 1681, BM • R. White, line engraving, BM, NPG

Dugdale, Thomas Lionel, first Baron Crathorne (1897–1977)

Dugdale, Thomas Lionel, first Baron Crathorne (1897–1977), politician, was born at Bucklands Hotel, Brooke Street, London, on 20 July 1897, the only son (he had one sister) of James Lionel Dugdale (1862–1941), of Crathorne, Yorkshire, an army captain, and his wife, Maud Violet (d. 1940), daughter of George William Plukenett Woodroffe, of the Royal Horse Guards. He was educated at Eton College, and the Royal Military College, Sandhurst. In 1916 he joined the Royal Scots Greys and served in France and Belgium. After the war he was captain (1923), and later adjutant (1927) in the Yorkshire hussars (Alexandra, Princess of Wales's Own) yeomanry (TA).

Dugdale's parliamentary career began when he was elected Conservative MP for the Richmond division of the North Riding of Yorkshire in 1929. He retained this seat until 1959. In 1931 he became parliamentary private secretary (PPS) to Sir Philip Cunliffe-Lister, president of the Board of Trade in the National Government, and he continued as his PPS when Cunliffe-Lister became colonial secretary and secretary of state for air. In 1935 Stanley Baldwin, the prime minister, selected Dugdale to be his own PPS.

Dugdale was therefore deeply involved from the first moment when the prime minister became aware of the relationship between Edward VIII and Mrs Simpson and was totally in the prime minister's confidence, in fact long before the members of the cabinet ascertained what Baldwin was doing. He was in attendance on the prime minister on almost every occasion when he saw either the king or other members of the royal family and later on when the cabinet colleagues were consulted. He was also present at the final dinner at Fort Belvedere before the king abdicated. He gave Baldwin much moral support and helped him to deal with an immensely difficult task so that the matter could be concluded with as little disturbance as possible to the country as a whole, and with the minimum amount of damage to the monarchy.

From 1937 to 1940 Dugdale was a junior lord of the Treasury, and then was on active service in Egypt with the Yorkshire hussars. In February 1941 he returned to England and became deputy chief government whip. He left that office in 1942 to become chairman of the Conservative Party Organization (he had been vice-chairman in 1941–2), but became ill and resigned in October 1944. He received a baronetcy in the new year honours in 1945.

During the Labour government after 1945 Dugdale was opposition spokesman on agriculture, a position for which his landowning interests in Yorkshire well fitted him. He was therefore an obvious choice as minister of agriculture in Winston Churchill's government in 1951. At the same time he was admitted to the privy council, and in September 1953 he was made a member of the cabinet.

Dugdale inherited, like most other ministers, a vast amount of wartime regulations which the Labour government had done little to remove and this was largely the cause of the mishandling of the Crichel Down affair. The Air Ministry had taken over some land in Dorset for use as a bombing range and had later passed it on to the Ministry of Agriculture. The original owners wished to repurchase the land, but the crown land commissioners instead found another tenant without informing the owners. This action aroused the anger of farmers and MPs, who demanded a public inquiry. Dugdale resisted this, without avail, and the inquiry's report severely criticized various civil servants who, it was said, had deliberately deceived the minister. Dugdale was a man of very high principles who firmly believed that if a ministry made a mistake, the minister, as ultimately responsible, should resign. This he did, although many of his colleagues tried to dissuade him as he bore no personal responsibility. The ending of Dugdale's political career in this way forced ministers and senior civil servants to think seriously about the reduction or elimination of the vast powers they had acquired during the war.

One of Dugdale's passions in life was racing and as a young officer in the Royal Scots Greys he occasionally rode on the flat and in point-to-points and over fences. He had often watched his father's horses working on Middleham Moor, where his own horses were subsequently trained. In 1951 he owned a good horse, Socrates, which was beaten, although favourite, in the Cambridgeshire; it subsequently won the Zetland and Manchester cups. His contribution to racing administration was unobtrusive but extremely effective, stemming from his friendly, unassuming nature and his integrity. In 1959–60, when the issue of a levy on horse-racing was an extremely controversial subject, it was he who played a key role in the departmental committee which resolved the matter. Subsequently he served as one of the first Jockey Club representatives on the Horserace Betting Levy Board from 1964 to 1973.

Deeply interested in European affairs, in 1958 Dugdale became a member of the Council of Europe. He also joined the NATO parliamentarians' conference, of which he became president in 1962–3. He did a great deal of work through both organizations to interest British MPs in the vital importance of European countries and the USA working together to guarantee peace. When he retired from the Commons in July 1959 Dugdale was created Baron Crathorne. He was chairman of the north of England advisory committee for civil aviation from 1964 to 1972, and chairman of the political honours scrutiny committee from 1961.

On 22 September 1936 Dugdale married Nancy (d. 1969), formerly wife of Sylvester Govett Gates and daughter of Sir Charles *Tennant, merchant and art patron. They had two sons, of whom the elder, Charles James (born 1939), succeeded his father in the barony when he died at home at Crathorne Hall, Crathorne, near Yarm, Yorkshire, on 26 March 1977.   ST ALDWYN, rev.

Sources Dugdale family MSS · personal knowledge (1986) · private information (1986) · Burke, *Peerage* · *The Times* (28 March 1977)
Archives NRA, priv. coll.
Likenesses F. Man, double portrait, photograph, 1943 (with Kingsley Wood), Hult. Arch.
Wealth at death £57,298: probate, 21 Sept 1977, *CGPLA Eng. & Wales* · £71,300: further grant, 14 Nov 1977, *CGPLA Eng. & Wales*

Dugdale, Una Harriet Ella Stratford. *See* Duval, Una Harriet Ella Stratford (1879–1975).

Dugdale, Sir William (1605–1686), antiquary and herald, was born on 12 September 1605 at Shustoke rectory, north Warwickshire, the son of John Dugdale (1552–1624), the rector, a native of Clitheroe, Lancashire, and his wife, Elizabeth Swynfen, from a Staffordshire gentry family. According to William Lilly, 'the famous Figure-flinger' or astrologer, his birth was marked by a swarm of bees in his father's garden, a sure sign that William 'should in time prove a prodigy of industry'—though it should be remarked that Lilly made this observation with the benefit of hindsight (Wood, *Ath. Oxon.*: *Fasti*, 693). Until the age of ten he was educated by Thomas Sibley, the curate at the nearby village of Nether Whitacre; then he was sent to the free school at Coventry, where his master was James Cranford. After leaving school at fifteen, he was set by his father on a course of reading in history and law. Dugdale never attended university. His father, being elderly, wanted to see his son married, and so at the age of sixteen, on 17 March 1622, William Dugdale was married to Margery Huntbach (d. 1681), the daughter of a Staffordshire gentleman. It was a companionable marriage that produced nineteen children in twenty-four years. When his father died William purchased in 1625 the manor of Blyth

GULIELMUS   DUGDALE
Ætatis. 50.   A. MDCLVI.

Ovid:
Nescio qua natale solum dulcedine cunctos
ducit et immemores non sinit esse sui.

Sir William Dugdale (1605–1686), by Wenceslaus Hollar, pubd 1656

in the parish of Shustoke, and Blyth Hall remained the family home for the rest of his life.

Early career and friendships, c.1630–1640   Dugdale's life can be reconstructed in some detail, because he left a brief autobiography that was later enlarged by Anthony Wood and printed in *Fasti Oxonienses* (1692). From this work we learn that Dugdale's antiquarian interests developed as a result of a series of felicitous encounters that brought him into contact with a network of historically minded gentlemen in his native Warwickshire and further afield. His kinsman Samuel Roper, a barrister of Lincoln's Inn, seems first to have aroused his curiosity about antiquities, and this curiosity was given a distinct direction by his reading William Burton's *Description of Leicester Shire* (1622). William Burton was the brother of Robert Burton, the anatomist of melancholy, and a near neighbour of Dugdale's; they met, and Burton encouraged Dugdale to make collections of material relating to the history of Warwickshire, a project that had already taken shape in Dugdale's mind. Towards this end, Burton about the year 1630 introduced Dugdale to Sir Simon Archer of Umberslade near Tamworth, who had already gathered together a large amount of information about the history of Warwickshire families, intending himself to compile a record of the county gentry. Archer was happy to make his collections available to Dugdale, and also introduced him to most of the gentlemen of note in Warwickshire, who seem to have been remarkably favourable to Dugdale's design, as tending to the honour of their own families and of the county at large; they proved very willing to give him sight of their ancient deeds and papers.

In 1638 Archer took Dugdale to London to introduce him to Sir Henry Spelman, the learned lawyer and antiquary who had been a founder member of the Elizabethan Society of Antiquaries and who was then in his eightieth year. Impressed by Dugdale's skill as a collector and organizer of antiquarian material, Spelman determined to advance his fortunes and used his own great influence and reputation to draw Dugdale away from the county arena and to push him onto the national scene. He recommended him to Thomas Howard, earl of Arundel, the earl marshal, as a person worthy to serve in the office of arms as a herald, and he also brought about the connection that would ensure Dugdale's lasting reputation by suggesting that he engage in research into the monastic foundations of England. Anthony Wood recorded that Spelman:

> told him that one Roger Dodsworth a Gent. of Yorkshire had taken indefatigable pains in searching of Records and other ancient Memorials relating to the Antiquities of that County, but especially touching the foundations of Monasteries there, and in the northern parts of the Realm ... much importuning Mr Dugdale to joyn with Dodsworth in that most commendable work. (Wood, *Ath. Oxon.*: *Fasti*, 694)

Dugdale met Dodsworth shortly thereafter, and they agreed to co-operate, with the understanding that the Warwickshire project should not be neglected.

During this same stay in London in 1638 Dugdale was introduced to Sir Christopher Hatton, whose father had been Elizabeth's lord chancellor, and who was 'a person highly affected to Antiquities'. He arranged for Dugdale to have access to the records in the exchequer and in the Tower of London, two of the major repositories of ancient documents in the country. The plea rolls and ledger books that he found there were indispensable to an understanding of land ownership, tenure, and finance in the middle ages. Another antiquarian sanctuary, the library of Sir Robert Cotton, was opened to him by an introduction to Cotton's son Thomas brought about by his kinsman Samuel Roper. Roper also arranged for him to have special access to the Domesday Book in the exchequer, with its invaluable accounts of land tenure at the conquest. This astonishing transformation in Dugdale's prospects was completed when Sir Christopher Hatton reinforced Spelman's appeal to Arundel to make Dugdale a herald. He was created blanch lyon pursuivant in 1638, and was advanced to rouge croix pursuivant the next year. These appointments gave him a lodging at the office of heralds in London, and a modest income, augmented by funeral fees.

Research and royal service 1641–1654 In 1641, conscious that the political climate was deteriorating and that the anti-episcopal party was becoming dominant, Dugdale undertook a heroic antiquarian mission to the cathedrals and major churches of London, the midlands, and the north in order to record the monuments, inscriptions, and coats of arms in these places. Such memorials were the working stock of antiquarians, with their records of kinship lines and regional history, and Dugdale rightly feared that the cathedrals, as the seats of bishops, would become the particular targets of the iconoclastic fervour that was now becoming apparent. He took a draughtsman with him named William Sedgwick, whose drawings would become a valuable repository of pre-civil war memorials.

In June 1642 Dugdale was summoned by the king to York in his capacity as herald, and then sent into Warwickshire to demand the submission of the garrisons at Banbury, Warwick, and later Coventry. Banbury submitted to the king's authority, but the other two garrisons resisted. Dugdale's listing of the seventy-eight gentlemen and two peers who appeared at royalist musters is an important guide to local allegiances at this date. Dugdale was present at the battle of Edgehill in October 1642, as a herald not as a combatant, and then followed the king to Oxford, where he remained until the surrender of the city in June 1646, residing for the most part at Hart Hall. His estate was sequestrated, and he supplemented his reduced income during his Oxford years by overseeing the conduct of royalist funerals. He was advanced to the position of Chester herald in April 1644 and continued to take an active interest in the course of the conflict: in 1645 he published anonymously *A Full Relation of the Passages Concerning the Late Treaty for a Peace*, describing the negotiations which had taken place at Uxbridge on 30 January that year.

During his time in Oxford, Dugdale was busy in the libraries studying some of the monastic charters and deeds which had been scattered everywhere after the Reformation, and also collecting information about the history of the nobility that he would eventually put to use in his *Baronage of England*. In the summer of 1646 he went to London to compound for his estate, thereafter enjoying the free use of it, and at this time renewed his acquaintance with Roger Dodsworth; the two men discussed the prospects for the book on monastic foundations, so much delayed by the wars. Dugdale made his sole visit abroad in May 1648, when he accompanied Lord Hatton to Paris, where he stayed for about three months, improving the time by gathering information about the outposts of French religious houses in England.

On his return to London, Dugdale joined up with Dodsworth once more, and together they combed through the Tower of London and the Cottonian library for monastic records that had escaped their earlier researches. By August 1651 they had material enough to make two folio volumes, but Dugdale had to spend several months ordering Dodsworth's collections before the books were ready for the press. Then, however, no bookseller could be found who was willing to bear the costs of publication, so the two authors decided to borrow money to finance their project. In order to meet the additional expenses of the illustrations, large engraved plates with views of the great abbeys executed by Wenceslaus Hollar and Daniel King, Dugdale instituted a system of subscription whereby well-wishers contributed the cost of a plate, usually £5, and had their name, arms, and an appropriate phrase included on the plate. Dodsworth inconveniently died in August 1654, leaving Dugdale to see the work through the press.

Monasticon, Antiquities of Warwickshire, and History of St Paul's

The first volume of *Monasticon Anglicanum* appeared in 1655 (with Dodsworth and Dugdale named as joint authors) and was purchased by a small but appreciative audience; Dugdale himself sold the copies on to booksellers. It gave the history of the various orders in England, and an account of all the individual monasteries. The surviving foundation charters, and charters relating to the growth of the monastery, were printed in full, and all known benefactions of land made to the monastery were set down. *Monasticon Anglicanum* established for the first time the importance of charters as a primary source for the writing of medieval history, and as a source for understanding the legal practice of earlier centuries and aspects of the feudal system relating to conditions of tenure. Equally it established for the first time since the Reformation the importance of monasteries and the scale of their territorial possessions. In Elizabethan and Jacobean times monasteries had been a reviled institution, associated only with superstition, idleness, and all the faults of the old religion. William Camden admitted that it was difficult to discuss their role in the life of the middle ages in his *Britannia* of 1586, or in its enlarged edition of 1607, for it was hard to consider the subject objectively. At first *Monasticon* evoked protests that it was a covert plea for the revival of Catholicism, and also that it might provide a basis for the recovery of former church lands that had been sold into private hands at the Reformation. But overall Dugdale established monastic history as a legitimate subject of study.

Dugdale waited for the money to come in from the sales of the first volume of *Monasticon* before he proceeded with the second, and in the meantime devoted himself to completing *The Antiquities of Warwickshire*. This appeared in 1656, the author bearing the entire costs of publication. Over twenty-five years in the making, it stood in the tradition pioneered by William Lambarde's *Perambulation of Kent* (1576). It is also indebted in its method to Camden's *Britannia*, following the rivers of the shire in order to progress from site to site. The history of the towns is briefly given, with speculations on the meanings of the placenames. Regional commodities are noted. But the main business is to record the families associated with each place, to record their notable deeds and to list their intermarryings and burials. The hundreds of coats of arms that fill the pages make it clear that genealogy is the prime concern of the book. *Warwickshire* was extensively illustrated with etchings by Hollar, including an authoritative frontispiece depicting Dugdale surrounded by manuscripts; his continued desire thus to enliven his books with illustrations was a commendable advance in the production of antiquarian works at this period.

Project followed project. Even as *Warwickshire* was being printed, an acquaintance drew Dugdale's attention to a collection of records relating to St Paul's Cathedral. Following this trail he was led to Scriveners' Hall, where he was lent 'ten porters' burthens' of charters and rolls and other manuscripts 'in bags and hampers'—unsorted like many legal and state documents at that time, and in mouldering neglect. With the spectacle close at hand of the great church slowly deteriorating from years of maltreatment and sacrilegious use, Dugdale rapidly compiled *The History of St Paul's Cathedral*, which was published in 1658. Not only did this book print the surviving documentary records of the cathedral, it also preserved the appearance of the building. Its Norman and Gothic details and the alterations made by Inigo Jones in the 1630s were recorded in extensive plates, once again prepared by Hollar, several of them based on drawings made by William Sedgwick in 1641. With the destruction of the cathedral in the great fire of 1666 Dugdale's book became the lasting memorial of old St Paul's.

Restoration scholar and herald, 1660–1686

The Restoration allowed Dugdale to re-enter the mainstream of public life. The new lord chancellor, the earl of Clarendon, was an admirer of his learning, and persuaded Charles II to advance him to Norroy king of arms. He received in 1662 a commission to carry out a visitation of his province, which comprised Derbyshire, Nottinghamshire, Staffordshire, Cheshire, Lancashire, Cumberland, Westmorland, Northumberland, Durham, and Yorkshire. He took his duties seriously, and throughout the 1660s he made series of visitations to confirm the status of gentry families in these counties after a generation in which the authority of the College of Arms had not been exercised. He took a severe view of those who had falsely claimed arms or the title of esquire or gentleman, or intruded on heraldic functions, such as the marshalling of funerals, in his province.

His scholarly activities continued unabated; the second volume of *Monasticon* and a work on the knights of the Bath appeared in 1661, and in the next year he published *The History of Imbanking and Drayning of Diverse Fenns and Marshes*, an account of the great drainage schemes that had been carried out in the fens, mainly during the Commonwealth years, by the initiative of Lord Gorges and John Thurloe, secretary to the council of state. This book was effectively commissioned by Gorges to advertise the success of the project. His next enterprise combined personal piety with antiquarian scholarship, for it involved the completion of two works left unfinished by his old mentor Sir Henry Spelman, who had died in 1641: *Concilia* and the 'Glossary'. *Concilia* was a detailed account of the church councils of Saxon England, where much doctrine and discipline that would be relevant to the post-Reformation church had been decided. Spelman had published the first part in 1639, but now with the renewal of the Church of England a number of important members of the establishment wished to see the completion of this work which clarified the doctrinal inheritance of the church. Clarendon and the new archbishop of Canterbury, Gilbert Sheldon, were the most prominent figures who encouraged Dugdale to continue the work on the basis of Spelman's notes and new research of his own. The 'Glossary' or *Archaeologus* was an alphabetical series of definitions of and disquisitions on the obscure legal words and terms used in Anglo-Saxon and Norman documents. Spelman's enquiry into archaic terms resulted in a detailed reconstruction of the legal framework of Saxon and Norman societies, with an understanding of the workings of the feudal system, the hierarchy of ranks and the ties and obligations between them, and the structure of government in state and church. The work allowed scholars to make sense of the emergent society of the early medieval world. The first half of the 'Glossary' had been published in 1628, and no more had appeared, but Dugdale was able to bring it to completion from Spelman's notes and further research; the new volumes of *Concilia* and the 'Glossary' both appeared in 1664.

Dugdale's scholarly industry from the 1650s to the 1670s was prodigious. He brought out *Origines juridiciales* in 1666, a substantial history of the law, lawyers, and the inns of court. The work had only just reached the booksellers when most of the stock was destroyed in the great fire, a fate shared by the unsold copies of *Concilia* and the 'Glossary'. After thirty years of accumulating material towards a history of the nobility, Dugdale energetically applied himself to its completion in the later 1660s and the early seventies. Long delayed in the press, the first volume of *The Baronage of England* eventually appeared in 1676; the second and third were printed together in 1677. It is a history of the aristocracy and its deeds since Saxon times, an immense work of genealogical scholarship derived from sound sources that retains its value to the present day. In 1671 an enlarged edition of *Origines juridiciales* came out, and in 1673 Dugdale published a third and final volume of *Monasticon Anglicanum*, containing a great deal of new documentation that had come into his hands since the publication of the second volume in 1661, including some contributed by Wood.

Dugdale's career as a herald reached its height in 1677 when he was appointed Garter king of arms after the death of Sir Edward Walker, with a salary of £100 a year and a residence at Windsor. In accordance with the dignity of his office, he was knighted at this time. His last major production was *A Short View of the Late Troubles in England* (1681), another large folio, which traced the course of the dissensions that grew into civil war. It is a highly partisan chronicle of events which has never found much recognition among historians, although it is useful for its copiousness and the precision of its dates. He issued two further small compilations: *The Ancient Usage in Bearing … Arms* (1681), mainly composed of lists of knights of the Garter, of baronets to 1681, and of the shires and boroughs that returned members to parliament in England and Scotland, and *A perfect copy of all summons of the nobility to the great councils and parliaments of this realm* (1685), containing the peerage lists from the reign of Henry III onwards.

Family life and death Little is known of Dugdale's large family. All his sons died young, except for **Sir John Dugdale** (1628–1700), who joined the household of the earl of Clarendon, and later followed a heraldic career,

becoming Norroy herald and being knighted by James II. Dugdale had twelve daughters, of whom nine were living in 1655. Elizabeth (1632–1701) became in 1668 the third wife of Elias *Ashmole, thus providing Dugdale with a congenial son-in-law with whom he shared extensive antiquarian interests, and whose career he forwarded.

A verse letter from Ashmole to Mistress Dugdale thanking her for hospitality at Christmas 1656 offers an extremely rare glimpse of Dugdale's family life at Blyth Hall: it describes the traditional celebrations that were being maintained through the Commonwealth years, with a seasonal feast, yule games, a masque of mummers, a bagpiper, and a tambour player (Josten, 1.115). This picture is compatible with another personal view offered by Anthony Wood when he and Dugdale were working on the records in the Tower in 1676 and used to dine together cheerfully there at a cook's house. These images of Dugdale as a good companion with a large capacity for enjoyment should be set against the serious and urbane tone of his correspondence.

Dugdale died on 10 February 1686 'in his chair' at Blyth Hall, having caught cold 'from tarrying too long in the moist meadows near his house' (*Life*, ed. Hamper, 30). Wood noted in his account of Dugdale that the day of his death was St Scholastica's day, a suitable time for the departure of so learned a man. He was buried on 12 February in the church at Shustoke, on the north side of the chancel, along with his wife, Margery, who had died on 18 December 1681.

Scholarship and legacy Editions of Dugdale's work continued to appear after his death as scholars polished and quarried his researches. His place in the annals of historical scholarship is an honourable one. His speciality was the retrieval of factual information relating to the great institutions of the middle ages: the monasteries, the legal system, and the aristocracy. The scale of his operations was greater than any previous endeavour, and its achievements were astonishing, especially in view of the disorder of the records from which he worked. *Monasticon Anglicanum* opened up a new area of historical research, and provided the foundations for such future investigations as Henry Wharton's *Anglia sacra* (1691) and Thomas Tanner's *Notitia monastica* (1695), while *The Antiquities of Warwickshire* (of which the second edition of 1730 was republished in facsimile in the twentieth century) continues to be regarded as the finest of seventeenth-century county histories on account of its thoroughness of documentation and attractive presentation.

It is true that Dugdale benefited to some extent from other men's labours without giving them sufficient acknowledgement. This was a complaint lodged against him in the eighteenth century, but it is beside the point, and characteristic of an age more jealous of individual achievement in scholarship. In the seventeenth century antiquarian research was a co-operative activity, and scholars were desirous of having their protracted schemes brought to fulfilment by another if age or death curtailed their designs. Dugdale's relations with his fellow antiquaries were almost invariably cordial. Just as he benefited from the advice, encouragement, and the collections of older scholars such as Hatton, Burton, Archer, Spelman, and Dodsworth, so in turn he was able to help other antiquaries like Ashmole and Wood with their designs. As Spelman had been Dugdale's true patron, so the latter had an especial regard for Spelman's protégé William Somner, the Canterbury historian and the most proficient Anglo-Saxon scholar of the century. Somner had helped Dugdale to understand the Anglo-Saxon documents printed in *Monasticon* and instructed him in the rudiments of the language. They had a close working relationship, and Dugdale often turned to Somner for advice. When Somner had completed his great dictionary, which became the indispensable foundation of Anglo-Saxon linguistic studies, it was Dugdale who took the lead in recruiting subscribers who would ensure the publication of the volume. Somner's acknowledgement of this initiative was idiosyncratic, for hidden away in the text of *Dictionarium Saxonico-Anglicum* (1659), under the entry *hlaeye: agger: tumulus*, the reader comes across a sentence in English in praise of 'the great retriever of our English Antiquities, my noble friend Mr William Dugdale; one (to do him right) without whose most active and effectual assistance in the publication of it, this work had never seen the light'.

In his long life Dugdale had exchanged letters with many of the learned antiquaries of his day, including Sir Simonds D'Ewes, Francis Junius, Meric Casaubon, Gerard Langbaine, Sir Roger Twysden, Sir Thomas Browne, and Thomas Peck; his letters were collected and edited by William Hamper as *The Life, Diary and Correspondence of Sir William Dugdale* (1827). His papers were bequeathed to the Ashmolean Museum in Oxford, established by his son-in-law, and transferred to the Bodleian Library in 1858. In the twentieth century the Dugdale Society began publishing sources for and occasional papers on Warwickshire history. GRAHAM PARRY

Sources *The life, diary, and correspondence of Sir William Dugdale*, ed. W. Hamper (1827) · Wood, *Ath. Oxon.: Fasti*, 1st edn, vol. 2 · E. Gibson, 'The life of Sir Henry Spelman', *Reliquiae Spelmanniae* (1698) · *Elias Ashmole (1617–1692): his autobiographical and historical notes*, ed. C. H. Josten, 5 vols. (1966 [i.e. 1967]) · G. Parry, *The trophies of time* (1995) · D. C. Douglas, *English scholars* (1939) · S. A. E. Mendyk, *Speculum Britanniae: regional study, antiquarianism and science in Britain to 1700* (1989) · *The letters of Sir Thomas Browne*, ed. G. Keynes (1931) · H. Ellis, 'The life of Sir William Dugdale', in W. Dugdale, *History of St Paul's Cathedral* (1818) · *DNB* · A. Hughes, *Politics, society and civil war in Warwickshire, 1620–1660* (1987)
Archives BL, annotated copy of plea rolls, Stowe MS 394 · BL, Book of Monuments, Add. MS 71474 · BL, journal of his itinerary through the fens, Lansdowne MS 722 · BL, heraldic corresp., collections, and papers, Add. MSS 29570, 32116, 38017, 38140–38141 · BL, visitations of Staffordshire and Derbyshire, etymological notes, papers relating to fen drainage, Harley MSS 1129, 5011, 6104 · Bodl. Oxf., collections and papers, MSS Wood D 12, 20; F 32–33, 51 · Bodl. Oxf., corresp., collections, and papers · Bodl. Oxf., copy of Speed's catalogue of the religious houses of England and Wales, MS Eng. hist. c 485 · Bodl. Oxf., heraldic papers, MSS Ashmole 818, 836, 840, 853–854, 857–858, 1118, 1131, 1134, 1137 · Bodl. Oxf., notebooks and transcript of 1656 diary · JRL, arms of the gentry of Cheshire · JRL, history of the Mainwaring family, Eng. MS 923 · Northants. RO,

papers incl. indexes to Christopher Hatton's antiquarian collections · Shakespeare Birthplace Trust RO, Stratford upon Avon, autograph pedigree, DR 85 · Staffs. RO, letters, D868/5 · Staffs. RO, letters, D593, 868, 4092, 4401; D(W) 0/5–6 · Warks. CRO, genealogical notes relating to the Newdegate family · Warks. CRO, papers and letters · Warks. CRO, working papers, diaries, pedigrees, and corresp., CR 721 | BL, corresp. with Sir Simon Archer, Add. MS 28564 [copies] · Bodl. Oxf., corresp. with Sir Simon Archer, MS Eng. lett. b 1 · Bodl. Oxf., corresp. with Nathaniel Johnston and copies of MSS in his possession, MSS Top. Yorks. c 17–18, 27, 36; Top. gen. c 57 · Bodl. Oxf., letters to Anthony Wood, MS Wood, fol. 41 · Cumbria AS, Kendal, letters to Sir Daniel Fleming · Folger, Warwickshire collections · NRA, priv. coll., letters to Huntbach family · Warks. CRO, corresp. with Henry Firebrace, CR 2017
Likenesses portrait, c.1675, NPG; version, Bodl. Oxf. · W. Hollar, etching, BM, NPG; repro. in W. Dugdale, *Antiquities of Warwickshire* (1656) [*see illus.*] · H. Robinson, print (after P. Borsselaer), BM; repro. in *Life*, ed. Hamper

Dugdale, William (1799/1800–1868), publisher, was born in Stockport. Little is known of his early life, though a government spy reported that he was the son of a tailor–bookseller in Stockport and attended a Quaker school there, working briefly as a tailor and basket-weaver before moving to London at the age of eighteen with the aim of entering the book trade (McCalman, 156). Influenced in his youth by Painite freethought, he moved in ultra-radical circles and was employed by William Benbow and James Watson in publishing 'infidel' literature. He was said to have been on the fringes of the Cato Street conspiracy of 1820. During the mid-1820s he set up his publishing business in the Covent Garden area of London. He used at least four aliases: Henry Smith, Henry Young, Henry Brown, and Henry Turner. During the 1840s he made his name as the largest publisher of obscene titles in England, a position unchallenged for over twenty years. Four addresses are known: 3 Wych Street and numbers 5, 16, and 37 Holywell Street. By 1830 he was married with children. Thomas Frost, a compositor employed by Dugdale, described him as a 'stout, middle-aged man' with a 'sodden, sensual countenance' and in a continuous state of 'semi-intoxification' (Frost, 52–4).

Dugdale's early publishing lists in the 1840s, under the alias Henry Smith of 37 Holywell Street, Strand, were mildly pornographic. Titles include *The Amorous Quaker: a Boarding School Biography* (c.1848) and *The Tale of a Bedstead* (date unknown). Under the same name he also published the three-volume magazine *The Boudoir* (1860), writing some of the worst passages himself. As Henry Young, at the same address, he published, among others, *The Cherub:- another Boarding School Tale* (c.1860).

As a publisher of the obscene and the satanic, Dugdale's preference was for literature on flogging, with titles such as *The Bedfellows, or, A Manual for Young Ladies* (c.1860), *Exhibition of Female Flagellants* (c.1870), published by John Camden Hotten, and *Nunnery Tales, or, Cruising under False Colours* (mid-1860s). In the last, as Dugdale put it, 'every stretch of voluptuous imagination is here fully depicted, rogering, ramming, one unbounded scene of lust, lechery and licentiousness' (Pearsall, 364).

During the late 1850s Dugdale acquired *The Great Secret*

Revealed. This was a reprint of *Leon to Annabella*, which Lord Byron was supposed to have written, and Dugdale's intention was to use it to blackmail Lady Byron. Dugdale sought advice on its authenticity, and was furious when told it was not by the poet, particularly when he was also advised not to approach Lady Byron in case he was then charged with an attempt to extort money. He nevertheless published the poem.

The fitful efforts of the Society for the Suppression of Vice, aided by Lord Campbell's act (1857), failed to control obscene publishers such as Dugdale. He was repeatedly prosecuted, convicted, and imprisoned, though on one occasion he was released by order of the home secretary, on the advice of the surgeon of the gaol, certifying that his life would be endangered if he was incarcerated for any length of time.

On 13 July 1868 Dugdale was sentenced to eighteen months' hard labour and died in the house of correction, Coldbath Fields, near Gray's Inn Road, London, on 11 November 1868.   GERALDINE BEARE

Sources P. Fraxi, *Index librorum prohibitorum* (1877) · T. Frost, *Reminiscences of a country journalist* (1886) · Boase, *Mod. Eng. biog.*, vol. 5 · R. Pearsall, *The worm in the bud* (1969) · P. Fraxi, *Catena librorum tacendorum* (1885) · I. McCalman, *Radical underworld: prophets, revolutionaries, and pornographers in London, 1795–1840* (1988)
Archives BL, Index librorum prohibitum, P. C. 18. b. 9 · BL, Catena librorum tacendorum, P. C. 18. b. 9

Duggan, Mary Beatrice (1925–1973), cricketer, was born on 7 November 1925 at 106 High Street, Worcester, the youngest of three children of Norman Duggan, physician and surgeon, and his wife, Mary Heath Gattey. She attended Alice Ottley School, Worcester, and Royal School, Bath, from where she went on to Dartford College of Physical Education to train as a physical education teacher. She held several schoolteaching posts, was employed by the London county council as a physical education organizer, and eventually returned to Dartford College as vice-principal.

Duggan, who had first played cricket with her two elder brothers in the family's back garden, joined the Women's Cricket Association in 1946. As a young and unknown player, she was chosen for the representative match that traditionally marks the annual women's cricket week at Colwall, near Malvern. She made her début for the England women's team in 1948, and toured Australia in 1948–9. She went on to captain Yorkshire, the north, Middlesex, and the south as her teaching positions took her around the country. She started as a left-arm fast bowler and matured into a highly successful spinner, as well as being good enough with the bat to score two test centuries. Against the Australian tourists in 1951 Duggan took a record twenty wickets in the three test series, including a match analysis of nine for 104 as England won the final test at the Oval. Her seven wickets for 6 runs against Australia at Melbourne during the 1957–8 tour remains England's best individual bowling performance in women's test cricket. In her seventeen match test career she took seventy-seven wickets (average 13.49). 'Big in build, big in heart, kind, generous, and gentle' (Flint and Rheinberg,

134), she captained England from 1957 to 1963. Her playing career ended in glory in the final test at the Oval against the Australians in 1963, when her 101 not out and match bowling analysis of seven for 82 contributed to England's match and series win.

Duggan's charming manner and careful application made her an effective and sought-after cricket coach. In 1962 she and Ruth Westbrook became the first two women to be awarded the MCC's advanced coaching certificate. In undertaking one of the exercises Duggan's lofted drive back over the bowler hit the target on the far wall on no fewer than thirty-six consecutive occasions in five minutes; over a decade later men and women were still striving to better this feat. In 1971 she became president of the Women's Cricket Association, and her death occurred just four months before the association's achievement of organizing the women's cricket world cup, the first such competition held for either men or women. Signs of the brain tumour that was eventually to bring about her early death had first become apparent when she was captaining England on the 1957–8 tour of Australia, and she showed considerable courage as the disease progressed. She died at her father's home, Tarradale, Ballards Drive, Colwall, Herefordshire, on 10 March 1973.

CAROL SALMON

Sources Women's Cricket Association archives · R. H. Flint and N. Rheinberg, *Fair play: the story of women's cricket* (1976) · J. L. Hawes, *Women's test cricket: the golden triangle, 1934–84* (1987) · *Wisden* (1974) · b. cert. · d. cert. · private information (2004)
Archives FILM BFI NFTVA, news footage
Likenesses photographs, repro. in Flint and Rheinberg, *Fair play* · photographs, repro. in Hawes, *Women's test cricket*
Wealth at death £54,825: probate, 9 April 1973, *CGPLA Eng. & Wales*

Dugrès [Du Grès], **Gabriel** (*fl.* 1631–1643), grammarian, was born at Saumur in France at an unknown date. In his biography of Cardinal Richelieu, Dugrès claimed that his father was born in Angers, while he himself had lived 'at severall times' in Loudon, just to the west of Richelieu (*Jean Arman Du Plessis*, 1643, sig. B2v). Dugrès left France in 1631—possibly for religious reasons—and he settled in Cambridge, where he taught French. In 1636, with the help of his students, he published a French grammar in Latin at the university press, *Breve et accuratum grammaticae Gallicae compendium*, with a dedication to the university (a variant edition of the same year replaced this with a dedication to the students of Oxford); the work followed continental and London practices by distinguishing the three languages through different typefaces. The grammar was reissued in London in 1650.

By 1639 Dugrès was teaching at Oxford when he published there a trilingual dialogue, *Dialogi Gallico–Anglico–Latini*. Dedicated to Charles, prince of Wales, and including observations about English and French society, the dialogues, printed in three columns, 'are animated, and since synonyms are juxtaposed to give an impression of garrulous fluency not without humour' (Francis, 81–2). The university press republished the work in 1652 and 1660. In 1643 Dugrès produced two works about Richelieu:

a short summary of the cardinal's will, as *The Will, and Legacies, of Cardinall Richelieu*, and a biography, *Jean Arman du Plessis, Duke of Richelieu, and Peere of France*. In the latter Dugrès emphasized his own familial links with the French court during Richelieu's rise to power, particularly through the Messieurs les Botrus, who were close to the French queen, though Dugrès 'spare[d] telling what relation he had to them' (sig. B3r). His biography was intended to 'honour that brave mans memory' but he was very conscious of widely divergent contemporary opinions of the cardinal; none the less, he went so far as to hint that the cardinal may have had protestant sympathies (sig. B2v).

GORDON GOODWIN, *rev.* I. GADD

Sources D. McKitterick, *A history of Cambridge University Press*, 1 (1992) · Wood, *Ath. Oxon.*, new edn · E. A. Francis, 'Some comments on French teaching at Oxford: Pierre du Ploich and Gabriel Du Grès', *Proceedings of the Huguenot Society of London*, 18 (1947–52), 73–87

Du Guernier, Louis (1687–1716), engraver, was born in Paris and was probably descended from the miniaturist, Louis du Guernier (1614–1659). After receiving some instruction from Louis de Châtillon, he moved to London in 1708, at a time when many French engravers were being tempted to England to work on the production of prestigious prints. Du Guernier was soon recognized as 'a good designer, etcher and engraver, especially [of] small historical subjects for books or plays, of which he did a great many' (Vertue, *Note books*, 2.131). He worked in particular for Jacob Tonson, notably on editions of the works of Otway (1712) and Horace and Virgil (both 1715), and he also produced plates for one of John Baskett's folio Bibles.

Although Du Guernier's work fell short of the standard achieved by the first-rank French engravers of his time, he was involved in many prestigious undertakings, particularly for noble patrons. His engraving of *Lot and his Daughters*, after Michelangelo di Caravaggio, engraved at the instance of Charles Montagu, earl of Halifax, was one of many significant attempts at the time to produce prints of fine paintings in British collections. Yet more important was his work with Claude du Bosc to produce engravings after Laguerre's frescoes in Marlborough House, depicting the battles of the duke of Marlborough. He engraved very few portraits, but a pair of half-length engravings, measuring 22 x 16 inches, of James Douglas, second duke of Queensberry, with a companion piece of the duchess, both after Kneller, are notable exceptions.

Chosen, with Dorigny, to serve as a director of the academy for artists established in Great Queen Street by Sir Godfrey Kneller, Du Guernier seemed assured of a successful career when he fell a victim to smallpox. He died in London on 19 September 1716. Vertue remembered him as 'rather low than middle size, very obliging, good temper, gentleman-like and well beloved by all his acquaintance' (Vertue, *Note books*, 2.131).

L. H. CUST, *rev.* RICHARD SHARP

Sources Vertue, *Note books*, vol. 2 · T. Clayton, *The English print, 1688–1802* (1997) · L. G. Geddes, 'Du Guernier', *The dictionary of art*, ed. J. Turner (1996) · Thieme & Becker, *Allgemeines Lexikon*, 15.234–5 · *Engraved Brit. ports.* · DNB

Duhigg, Bartholomew (*c.*1751–1813), antiquary and barrister, was the fourth son of Bartholomew Duhigg (*d.* before 1771), gentleman, of Ballyhigh, co. Limerick, Ireland. His father appears to have been brought up a Catholic but to have conformed to the established church in 1725, thereby escaping the effects of the penal laws. In 1769 he entered Trinity College, Dublin, but there is no record of his having graduated. Admitted to the Middle Temple in London on 6 November 1771, Duhigg was called to the bar in 1775. He later wrote that 'my professional exertions were first known or encouraged by the people of Cork' (Duhigg, *History*, 560). In 1777 he married Maryanne Montgomery of Kilkee, co. Cork. The couple made a home in Dublin, and had one son and at least one daughter.

Described by Chief Baron Yelverton as 'a man of general reading and information, not only in his own profession but in every branch of science' (National Archives), Duhigg served part-time as the assistant librarian (1794–1801) and then junior librarian (1801–13) of King's Inns, Dublin, and also acted as its under-treasurer in 1803–4. He published the first catalogue of the library of King's Inns (1801) and was instrumental in securing for that society the benefit of the Copyright Act of 1801 (this being the right to receive on demand and free of charge any new book published in the United Kingdom). The arrangement was, however, terminated in 1836.

Duhigg wrote two books, *King's Inns Remembrances* (1805) and *History of the King's Inns* (1806). The latter is unreliable in some important respects (Kenny, 'Counsellor Duhigg', 318–20; *King's Inns*, 10–13, 22, 75n.). He also penned at least seven extended 'letters' or 'observations' which were published as pamphlets and which addressed political, legal, and administrative topics. Duhigg's surviving manuscripts, which include 'Irish parliaments' and papers relating to his published works, have remained at King's Inns.

A member of the volunteer movement for national reform and an independent whig, Duhigg claimed later to have incurred the abiding enmity of John Fitzgibbon, the future lord chancellor and earl of Clare, by publishing in 1785–6 an attack on the latter's prosecution as attorney-general of the co. Dublin sheriff, Henry Stevens Reily. Unlike many other protestants, Duhigg supported demands for the political emancipation of Catholics and even praised those Catholics who in 1690–91 had resisted at the siege of Limerick the forces of King William. If Duhigg's father was indeed a convert, then some of his own ancestors may have been among those besieged in that city. Duhigg's name was noticeably absent from a declaration in favour of the Union signed by 300 Limerickmen, including the senior librarian of King's Inns, which was published by direction of Fitzgibbon in the *Limerick Chronicle* on 14 September 1799. However, notwithstanding various indications that he had once opposed the political union of Britain and Ireland, near the end of his life he was to declare his support for it.

Duhigg was one of the first lawyers to be appointed an 'assistant barrister' to the justices of the peace, in his case for co. Wexford (1796–1808). Although silent on the local effects of the Irish rising of 1798, which most directly impinged upon that very county where he sat 'at the foot of Vinegar Hill' as its assistant barrister, Duhigg strongly condemned the manifesto of the United Irishmen and poured scorn on certain supporters of the outbreak, whom he described as 'briefless barristers and physicians without practice' (Kenny, 'Counsellor Duhigg', 314–15).

He undertook research on public documents for William Burton Conyngham of the Royal Irish Academy who, before his death in 1796, had intended to publish a volume for Ireland in the style of Rymer's *Foedera*. Thereafter, Duhigg long advocated and was partly responsible for the establishment of a record commission for Ireland, publishing two pamphlets on the subject (1801 and 1810). He was one of four barristers appointed in 1810 as the first sub-commissioners for records. According to Duhigg's widow 'his indefatigable attention to the laborious duties of the Record Commission which he first recommended to this country was the immediate cause of his death' (Maryanne Duhigg to Charles Abbot, BL, Add. MS 40232, fol. 172). Duhigg died some time between 17 October and 9 December 1813.

Although Duhigg's prose style was often inelegant, he is significant not only as the first modern historian of the Irish legal profession but also as a writer of passion and a lawyer of deep conviction of the social value of his profession.   COLUM KENNY

Sources C. Kenny, 'Counsellor Duhigg—antiquarian and activist', *Irish Jurist*, new ser., 21 (1986), 300–25 · B. Duhigg, *Letters of William Russell on the doctrine of constructive contempt, with a true copy of the original affidavit upon which the sheriff of the county of Dublin was attached* (1786) · B. T. Duhigg, *History of the King's Inns* (1806) · C. Kenny, *King's Inns and the kingdom of Ireland* (1992) · state papers, law, 1728–96, NA Ire., OP/9/25/33 · *Limerick Chronicle* (14 Sept 1799) · Maryanne Duhigg to Charles Abbot, BL, Add. MS 40232, fol. 172
Archives BL, Add. MS 40232, fol. 172 · King's Inns, Dublin · NA Ire., state papers, law, 1728–96, OP/9/25/33

Duigenan, Patrick (1734/5–1816), lawyer and politician, was born in co. Londonderry, the son of Hugh Duigenan, of Dublin, 'gentleman', and his wife, who was probably Priscilla Lake (1713/14–1792). It was rumoured that he had been born a Catholic and had in his youth conformed to the Church of Ireland but after his death it was stated authoritatively that although his name was of 'aboriginal Irish import' (*GM*, 1st ser., 87/2, 1817, 605), his grandfather and father had belonged to the established church. J. W. Stubbs, in his *History of the University of Dublin*, stated that Duigenan's father was a schoolmaster. Duigenan entered Trinity College as a sizar in 1753, was elected to scholarship in 1756, graduated in 1757, and was elected to fellowship in 1761. As a jurist—a fellow who was a student of the civil law—he was not obliged to take orders. In 1766 he was appointed regius professor of laws and in 1767 he was called to the Irish bar. Later he became a KC and a bencher of the King's Inns.

The appointment in 1774 of John Hely-Hutchinson, a barrister and MP, to the provostship of Trinity College aroused Duigenan's ire. Hely-Hutchinson, who had benefited greatly from political bargaining, was enlightened, self-interested, and very self-assured, and Duigenan, a

Patrick Duigenan (1734/5–1816), by James Heath, pubd 1810 (after John Comerford)

man of integrity and a crusted, cantankerous academic conservative, opposed him with such vigour that in 1775 the board (the governing body of Trinity College) censured him for using 'improper and disrespectful expressions' to the provost (twenty years later, shortly after Hely-Hutchinson's death, the board, referring to the 1775 censure, expressed its high opinion of Dr Duigenan). In 1776 Duigenan resigned his regius professorship and was appointed professor of feudal and English law at an enhanced salary. This arrangement removed a thorn from the provost's side and placed Duigenan out of the provost's power. In 1777 Duigenan published a bulky pamphlet, *Lachrymae academicae*, a philippic against the provost, whom he accused of arrogance, petulance, ignorance, oppressive misuse of his powers, 'a disposition to mountebanking' (Duigenan, 63), and unscrupulous electioneering. Hely-Hutchinson, Duigenan wrote, displayed 'all the low artifice and wheedling of an Old-Baily solicitor' (ibid., 204), delivered 'frothy harangues' (ibid., 64) at the board, and offended against academic decorum by allowing his children to be wheeled in 'go-carts' (ibid., 55) through college. About 1782 Duigenan married his first wife, Angelina (1741/2–1799), daughter of James and Angelina Cusack of Coolmines, co. Dublin, and of Ballyronan, co. Wicklow. It may well have been the Catholicism of the Cusack family that gave rise to later misapprehensions about Duigenan's religion.

Duigenan practised as a civilian, being appointed in 1790 advocate in the Court of Admiralty. He was also vicar-general of the metropolitan court of Armagh, of the consistorial court of Dublin, and of the diocesan courts of Meath and Elphin, and in 1793 he was appointed judge of the prerogative court. Naturally he was a strong defender of ecclesiastical rights, and during the Munster disturbances of the 1780s he published a work entitled *An Address to the Nobility and Gentry* (1786) in which he asserted that the established church was the main pillar of the constitution and that its subversion would lead to the ruin of the protestant religion and the destruction of the liberties of Europe.

Duigenan was returned to the Irish parliament, representing Old Leighlin from 1790 to 1797 and Armagh from 1797 to 1800, both episcopal boroughs. In parliament he was conspicuous for his opposition to Catholic relief. In 1798, in his *An Answer to the Address of Henry Grattan*, he attacked the patriot leader as an ally of radical republicans and bigoted Roman Catholics and for seeking the separation of Ireland from Great Britain. In the same year, along with John Fitzgibbon, earl of Clare, he conducted a visitation of Trinity College with the aim of detecting disloyalty. However, he scarcely spoke, being completely overshadowed by his colleague. Duigenan supported the Union, and continued to sit for Armagh in the United Kingdom parliament. At Westminster he maintained his unbending opposition to Catholic emancipation. A dogged doctrinaire, he was convinced that the Roman Catholic church, a close-knit body, claimed an exclusive jurisdiction in the spiritual sphere—a sphere which the church expanded to embrace many matters which others felt did not belong to it. Catholics, he argued, could not be loyal subjects and the Irish Catholics, resolved on the destruction of the protestant ascendancy and separation from Great Britain, were ready to seek the aid of revolutionary radicals and France.

In his speeches and writings Duigenan was excessively erudite, prolix, ponderous, and badly lacking in a sense of proportion. Extreme in opinion, often archaic in argument, old-fashioned in dress, and overburdened with learning—he was always referred to as Doctor, sometimes probably ironically—Duigenan's crude vigour and obvious sincerity fortified intellectually those who agreed with him while he aroused ridicule rather than violent hostility among his opponents. In 1808 his admission to the Irish privy council, shortly after he had attacked the parliamentary grant to Maynooth College, was strongly criticized in the House of Commons and unenthusiastically defended by Sir Arthur Wellesley (later first duke of Wellington), the chief secretary, who emphasized that Duigenan would only be consulted on ecclesiastical affairs. A few days later Wellesley wrote to Duigenan suggesting he should not speak in the coming debate on the Catholic petition, 'or that if you should speak you should confine yourself within very narrow limits, and deliver yourself in moderate language', 'having so frequently delivered your opinions upon this subject' (*Supplementary Despatches*, 5.440). In 1812 another chief secretary, Robert Peel, while admiring Duigenan for his 'labours', referred to his 'cumbrous armour' (HoP, *Commons, 1790–1820*) and regretted that his zeal was not tempered with more discretion.

Duigenan seems to have taken part in drafting the act of 1808 for building churches and glebe houses, and was responsible in 1814 for a measure improving the working of the Irish ecclesiastical courts. He was a member of two important commissions, the Union compensation commission and the commission of inquiry into the state of the Irish public records. His published works, in addition to those already mentioned, included two pamphlets on Irish affairs and four speeches. Duigenan's first wife had died on 7 November 1799 and was buried in co. Wicklow. On 2 October 1807 he married Hester, *née* Watson, widow of George Heppenstall, attorney and clerk to the police of the city of Dublin; she survived him. He died at his home in Parliament Street or Bridge Street, Westminster, on 11 April 1816, aged eighty-one.   R. B. McDowell

Sources J. W. Stubbs, *The history of the University of Dublin, from its foundation to the end of the eighteenth century* (1889) · *GM*, 1st ser., 86/1 (1816), 371 · *GM*, 1st ser., 87/2 (1817), 604–5 · H. Grattan, *Memoirs of the life and times of the Rt Hon. Henry Grattan*, 5 vols. (1839–46), vol. 2, pp. 96–7 · P. J. Jupp, 'Duigenan, Patrick', HoP, *Commons, 1790–1820* · *Supplementary despatches (correspondence) and memoranda of Field Marshal Arthur, duke of Wellington*, ed. A. R. Wellesley, second duke of Wellington, 15 vols. (1858–72), vol. 5, pp. 432, 440 · P. Duigenan, *Lachrymae academicae* (1777) · BL, Add. MS 40235 · National University of Ireland, O'Hart pedigrees [MS] · *DNB*

Likenesses J. Heath, stipple (after J. Comerford), BM, NPG; repro. in J. Barrington, *Historic anecdotes and secret memoirs of the legislative union*, 2 vols. (1810) [*see illus.*]

Du Jon, Franciscus. See Junius, Franciscus (1591–1677).

Duke, Edward (1779–1852), antiquary, was baptized at Hungerford, Berkshire, on 24 September 1779, the only surviving son of Edward Duke (*b.* 1731), of Lake House, Wilsford, Salisbury, and his wife, Fanny, daughter of John Field of Islington. He was educated from 1799 at Magdalen Hall, Oxford, where he graduated BA in 1803 and proceeded MA in 1807. He was ordained in 1802, and served at Turkdean, Gloucestershire, and Salisbury. In 1805 he came into the estates and the mansion at Lake, which had been in his family since 1578. On 19 January 1813 he married Harriet, daughter of Henry Hinxman of Ivy Church House, Wiltshire. They had four sons and four daughters.

With Sir Richard Colt Hoare, Duke excavated the barrows on his estates. The resulting finds were described in Hoare's *Ancient Wiltshire* (1811–12), and were preserved in the museum at Lake House until their sale in 1895. Most are now in the British Museum, London. Between 1823 and 1828 Duke contributed to the *Gentleman's Magazine*, chiefly on Wiltshire antiquities. In his *Druidical Temples of the County of Wilts* (1846) he maintained that the early inhabitants of Wiltshire had 'pourtrayed on the Wiltshire downs, planetarium or stationary orrery' (p. 6), the earth being represented by Silbury Hill, and the sun and planets, revolving round it, by seven 'temples', four of stone and three of earth, placed at relevant distances.

Duke was also an active Wiltshire magistrate, and was a fellow of the Society of Antiquaries and of the Linnean Society. He died at Lake House on 28 August 1852, and was buried in the family vault at Wilsford church on 6 September. His eldest son, Edward, also a clergyman, succeeded to the estates, which were eventually sold by Edward's widow in 1897.   W. W. Wroth, *rev.* Penelope Rundle

Sources *GM*, 2nd ser., 38 (1852), 643–4 · Burke, *Gen. GB* · *Wiltshire Archaeological and Natural History Magazine*, 17 (1878), 36 [Stonehenge excursion] · 'The sale of the collection of antiquities belonging to the Rev E. Duke of Lake House', *Wiltshire Archaeological and Natural History Magazine*, 28 (1894–6), 260–62 · Foster, *Alum. Oxon.* · *Wiltshire Notes and Queries*, 8 (1914–16), 247 · parish register, Alderbury, Wiltshire, 19 Jan 1813 [marriage] · parish register, Wilsford, Wiltshire, 6 Sept 1852 [burial]

Archives BM, excavation finds | Bodl. Oxf., letters to Sir Thomas Phillipps · Devizes Museum, Wiltshire Archaeological and Natural History Society, letters to John Britton; letters to William Cunnington · Salisbury and South Wiltshire Museum, Salisbury, letters mainly to J. B. Nichols

Wealth at death exact sum unknown: *Wiltshire Notes and Queries*; *VCH Wiltshire*, vol. 6

Duke, Henry Edward, first Baron Merrivale (1855–1939), judge and politician, was the second son of William Edward Duke (*d.* 1898), then a clerk at the granite works at Walkhampton, south Devon, where Henry was born on 5 November 1855. His mother was Elizabeth Ann Lord. Without any advantage of family or fortune, he was educated locally, did not attend any public school, nor was he a member of any university. He married in 1876 Sarah (*d.* 1914), daughter of John Shorland, of Shrewsbury; they had one son, Edward (1883–1951), and one daughter. At first Duke was a journalist on the *Western Morning News*, but he went to London at the age of twenty-five, and entered the press gallery of the House of Commons. While there he read for the bar and was called by Gray's Inn in 1885. He joined the western circuit and acquired a considerable practice at assizes and in the local courts. His reputation as an advocate soon reached London, where he built up a large junior practice and took silk in 1899. He was recorder of Devonport and Plymouth from 1897 to 1900, retaining the recordership of Devonport (which he held until 1914) when he became Unionist member of parliament for Plymouth in 1900. He lost his seat in 1906 but was returned for Exeter in January 1910. In December 1910 his opponent headed the poll by four votes, but after a scrutiny Duke was awarded the seat by one vote and held it until 1918.

At the height of his career at the bar Duke found himself opposed to such famous advocates of the day as Sir Edward Clarke, Sir Edward Carson, and Sir Rufus Isaacs. Although his industry and experience had given him a wealth of legal knowledge, he was better in cases tried by judge and jury than by a judge alone. No one would dispute his claim to be one of the finest *nisi prius* advocates of his time. He understood well the outlook and reactions of the ordinary juryman. Tall, with a commanding presence, he was a slow and deliberate speaker, and had a slight Devon accent which attracted attention. In court he was always serious and profoundly believed in the cause he was pleading. Above all he was imperturbable and never upset when things appeared to go against him. As a cross-examiner he was formidable, and often turned to the advantage of his client what had seemed to be a damaging answer. Among many famous cases in which Duke was engaged were those of *Adam v. Ward* (1914), a libel action brought against the permanent under-secretary of state for war, and the *Slingsby baby* (1915). In 1915 he was sworn of

Henry Edward Duke, first Baron Merrivale (1855–1939), by Sir William Orpen, 1925

the privy council and was appointed attorney-general to the prince of Wales, a post which he held until 31 July 1916.

Duke did well in the House of Commons, achieving more success than lawyers usually do in that assembly. During the early days of the coalition government of 1915 he presided over the royal commissions on the defence of the realm losses and on the liquor trade control losses. When Augustine Birrell resigned as chief secretary for Ireland in the aftermath of the Easter rising in 1916, Asquith appointed Duke, on 31 July, to the post with a seat in the cabinet; Asquith regarded Duke as 'almost persuaded' to be a home-ruler. Duke played a major part in inducing the Irish parties (except Sinn Féin) to attend the convention which began in July 1917. He respected the idealism of the Sinn Féin leaders and declined the demands of the army and police for systematic coercion in the wake of the death (following forced feeding) of Thomas Ashe, a young republican leader, in September 1917. He had some success in containing political violence. But the failure of the convention in the spring of 1918 showed that a united, self-governing Ireland was, then at least, an impossibility, and failure further helped the rapid rise of Sinn Féin. Until March 1918 he successfully resisted cabinet demands for Irish conscription, arguing that unless conscription was the consequence or at least the accompaniment of a home-rule settlement it would make Ireland ungovernable. Lloyd George's announcement on 9 April 1918 of Irish conscription led to Duke's resignation, formally made on 2 May.

On his resignation Duke was knighted and made a lord justice of appeal, an office which he held for eighteen months until he was appointed in November 1919 president of the Probate, Divorce, and Admiralty Division of the High Court. His natural seriousness admirably fitted him for the discharge of the duties of a divorce judge. He was dignified and efficient. There were no 'scenes' in his court, no bandying of jokes, no laughter during the hearing of a case. During his presidency there was passed the Matrimonial Causes Act (1923), which placed the sexes on an equal footing as regards grounds for divorce. The work increased and necessitated the appointment of an additional judge in 1925. Duke in his summings up and judgments showed great power in clarifying the issues and marshalling the facts. He was an urbane judge, always courteous to counsel. In the Admiralty court he was satisfactory but lacked technical knowledge. It fell to him to wind up the work of the prize court. He retired in 1933.

Duke was raised to the peerage in 1925 as Baron Merrivale of Walkhampton, in the county of Devon. He was a devoted member of Gray's Inn, serving as treasurer in 1908 and 1927. Duke died in London on 20 May 1939 and was succeeded as second baron by his son.

SANKEY, *rev.* H. C. G. MATTHEW

Sources *The Times* (22 May 1939) • E. H. Butcher, 'The late master Lord Merrivale', *Graya* [magazine of Gray's Inn], 23 (Easter 1940), 37–40 • D. G. Boyce and C. Hazlehurst, 'The unknown chief secretary', *Irish Historical Studies*, 20 (1976–7), 286–311 • R. B. McDowell, *The Irish Convention, 1917–18* (1970) • Burke, *Peerage*
Archives Bodl. Oxf., corresp. and papers, Eng. lett. MSS c213, 714–717 | Bodl. Oxf., Asquith MSS, corresp. with Herbert Asquith • HLRO, corresp. with David Lloyd George • Plunkett Foundation, Long Hanborough, Oxfordshire, corresp. with Sir Horace Plunkett
Likenesses W. Stoneman, photographs, 1922–32, NPG • W. Orpen, oils, 1925, Gray's Inn, London [*see illus.*]
Wealth at death £94,510 8s. 9d.: probate, 23 Aug 1939, CGPLA Eng. & Wales

Duke, Richard (1658–1711), poet and Church of England clergyman, was born on 13 June 1658 in London, and baptized on 20 June 1658 at St Michael Cornhill, the second, but first surviving, son of Richard Duke (*fl.* 1644–1668), a citizen of London and scrivener, and his second wife, Anne Peirce (*d.* 1668). From 1670 he was educated at Westminster School, before proceeding to Trinity College, Cambridge, where he was admitted pensioner on 25 June 1675. He was elected a scholar the following year. He matriculated in 1678, taking his BA in 1678–9 and his MA in 1682. In 1681 he was elected to a fellowship of the college, and wrote a verse panegyric which was rehearsed before the queen when the court visited Cambridge in September of that year. He was also said to have been for a time tutor to Charles Lennox, duke of Richmond, the illegitimate son of Charles II and Louise de Kéroualle, duchess of Portsmouth.

The verse Duke wrote in his time at Cambridge essays a variety of genres. John Dryden, who had also attended Westminster and Trinity, was an early friend to Duke; several of Duke's works, including two renderings of Ovid and translations of a number of Horatian odes, initially appeared in the Dryden–Tonson miscellanies *Ovid's Epistles* (1680) and *Miscellany Poems* (1684), and a couple of amorous English songs were later included in *Examen poeticum* (1693). Duke continued to translate Ovid, but turned his hand to Theocritus, Virgil, and, at Dryden's behest, Juvenal as well, and translated the lives of Theseus, the legendary king of Athens, and Marcus Iunius Brutus, conspirator in the murder of Caesar, in Tonson's five-volume edition of *Plutarch's Lives* (1683–6). He also composed a number of Latin poems, among which were his lines addressed 'Ad Thomam Otway'. The friendship of Otway and Dryden intimates the society of courtiers, playwrights, and actors Duke enjoyed; he offered commendatory verses for Dryden's *Troïlus and Cressida* (1679) and *Absalom and Achitophel* (1681), wrote a prologue to Nathaniel Lee's *Lucius Junius Brutus* (1681), extolled Thomas Creech in the second edition of his translation of Lucretius (1682; 1683), and complimented Edmund Waller. Duke's civic verse includes *Floriana. A Pastoral, upon the Death of her Grace the Duchess of Southampton* (1681), a conventional four-page lamentation in dialogue form, and lines 'On the Marriage of George Prince of Denmark, and the Lady Anne' (1683), and 'On the Death of King Charles the Second. And the Inauguration of King James the Second' (1685). And the verses he addressed 'To the people of England; a detestation of civil war' indicate that he further interested himself in political concerns. *A Panegyric upon Oates* (1679), the first of a series of satirical broadsides which lampooned the principal informers in the Popish Plot, has been attributed to Duke on the grounds that he acknowledged as his own its companion piece, *An Epithalamium upon the Marriage of Capt. William Bedloe* (1679). *The Funeral Tears upon the Death of Captain William Bedloe* (1680), published nine months later, has also been ascribed to the poet. Little of his verse appeared in his own name. Duke's work was collected after his death as 'Poems upon Several Occasions', a compilation appended to *Poems by the Earl of Roscomon* (1717) which reveals a facility for the heroic couplet, and ambition in other verse forms, and which prints for the first time 'The Review', a composition which Thomas Sheridan, the sometime Jacobite, persuaded him to undertake, probably in 1682; 'finding Mr. *Sheridan* design'd to make use of his Pen to vent his Spleen against several Persons at Court that were of another Party', however, the poet 'broke off proceeding in it, and left it as it is now printed' ('To the reader', *Poems by the Earl of Roscomon*, sig. A2v).

Duke was ordained before the accession of James II and in 1687 he was presented in the rectorship of Blaby, Leicestershire, an incumbency he held until 1708. In 1688 he was made a prebend of Gloucester Cathedral, and soon afterwards became proctor in convocation for the diocese. He was also appointed a chaplain-in-ordinary to Queen Anne. In 1696 he is thought to have married Mary Ben. The Revd Dr Jonathan Trelawney, bishop of Winchester, made Duke his chaplain in June 1707, and in July 1710 presented him in the wealthy living of Witney, Oxfordshire, a position worth £500 per annum. From that town came Duke's second wife, Martha, daughter of Thomas Jordan, whom he had married on 3 December 1708. His clerical career was quietly uneventful; three sermons were printed during his lifetime at royal or shrieval command. A posthumous collection of *Fifteen Sermons Preach'd on Several Occasions* (1714) was received with critical approval; indeed, Duke was well regarded during his life as a conscientious minister and, as one of the group of translator-poets associated with Dryden's and Tonson's miscellanies, an able versifier.

Duke died late on 10 February 1711 or in the early hours of Sunday 11 February, having returned home from an evening's entertainment. He was buried in St Andrew's, Holborn; his friends Francis Atterbury and Matthew Prior attended the interment. JONATHAN PRITCHARD

Sources *Old Westminsters*, 1.290 • Venn, *Alum. Cant.*, 1/2.73 • [G. Jacob], *The poetical register, or, The lives and characters of the English dramatick poets*, [2] (1720), 2.50–51 • J. Yeowell, 'Richard Duke, the poet', *N&Q*, 3rd ser., 12 (1867), 21–2; corrected in part by 'H.', 'Richard Duke', *N&Q*, 3rd ser., 12 (1867), 69 • A. Sherbo, 'The Dryden-Cambridge translation of Plutarch's *Lives*', *Études Anglaises*, 32 (1979), [177]–84 • S. R. Maitland, 'Duke the poet', *N&Q*, 2nd ser., 2 (1856), 4–5 • S. Johnson, *Lives of the English poets*, ed. G. B. Hill, [new edn], 3 vols. (1905), 2.[24]–5 • J. Swift, *Journal to Stella*, ed. H. Williams, 2 vols. (1948), letter 16, 1.191–2, 193 • N. Luttrell, *A brief historical relation of state affairs from September 1678 to April 1714*, 6 vols. (1857), vol. 1, p. 130; vol. 6, pp. 183, 332, 690 • J. Anderson Winn, *John Dryden and his world* (1987), 338, 372, 595 • *The poems of John Dryden*, ed. P. Hammond and D. Hopkins, 4 vols. (1995–2000), headnote to no. 133, 3.[302]–10, 'Appendix B: the contents of *Ovid's epistles*', 1.[539], 'Appendix C: commendatory poems on *Absalom and Achitophel*', 1.[540]–43, 'Appendix A: the contents of *Miscellany poems* and *Sylvae*', 2.[431]–6, 'Appendix A: the contents of *Examen poeticum* and *The annual miscellany: for the year 1694*', 4.[365]–70

Duke, Sir (Frederick) William (1863–1924), administrator in India, born at Arbroath on 8 December 1863, was the eldest son of William Duke DD, parish minister of St Vigean's, Forfarshire, and his wife, Annie, daughter of Surgeon Peter Alexander Leonard RN, inspector-general of hospitals. Educated as a child at a dame-school at Norwood, he returned to Scotland and spent seven years at the Arbroath high school, from where he went to Messrs Wren and Gurney's to be coached for the Indian Civil Service examination, which he passed, eleventh on the list, in 1882. His two-year probation was passed at University College, London.

Assigned to Bengal, where he remained throughout his Indian career, William Duke served for twenty-four years in the districts, before becoming Bengal chief secretary in 1909. The experience gave him a very thorough knowledge of Bengal and of district administration. His long apprenticeship was very unusual for someone destined to rise to high office. But, modest, kindly, and shrewd, he seems not to have resented the delay in his promotion, and he gained clear views on the agrarian and political issues of his day. From 1897 to 1902, as magistrate and chairman of the municipality at Howrah, adjacent to Calcutta, he was brought into touch with members of the European business community, among whom he made many friends. He restored the disordered finances of the Howrah municipality, and for a short time acted as chairman of the Calcutta corporation.

In 1905 he was promoted to be commissioner in Orissa. In Sir Andrew Fraser he found a sympathetic lieutenant-governor; and his appointment to officiate as Bengal chief secretary in 1908, which came as somewhat of a surprise, was continued by Sir Edward Baker, a brilliant but difficult chief, whom Duke's imperturbable good temper and quiet loyalty gradually impressed. As the leading Indian Civil Service officer in the province it fell to him to draft the rules of business for the Bengal legislative council set up in 1909; he demonstrated unexpected political imagination by framing them so as to encourage non-official Indian participation.

An executive council was also created in Bengal in 1910, and Duke became one of its members. While Baker was on leave in July 1911, and again after he retired in the following September, Duke acted as the last of Bengal's lieutenant-governors. Then the royal durbar at Delhi (12 December 1911) reversed the partition of Bengal of 1905, reuniting the eastern and western wings as a new province (excluding Assam, Bihar, and Orissa). Its first governor, Lord Carmichael, was not well regarded in the government of India; and thus the experienced Duke, as senior member of the council, remained the leading figure in policy-making, with P. C. Lyon. The chief problems were the reorganization of the administration after 1911 and the curbing of Bengali terrorism.

In November 1914 Duke retired from the Indian Civil Service, and was appointed a member of the Council of India. Though the ordinary work of the council in Whitehall was diminished by war conditions, the political problems of India became increasingly insistent. Duke joined a study group of Round Table and India Office members, to discuss moves towards Indian self-government. He produced a memorandum in 1915 which summed up the findings of the group, criticizing the 1909 reforms and calling for 'dyarchy', then meaning a horizontal division of Indian government, providing for Indian self-government in sub-provincial levels. This document was sent to Lord Chelmsford, the incoming viceroy, who also met members of the group before leaving London. Thus began Duke's role as a conduit for ideas which helped to shape the Montagu–Chelmsford reforms of 1919. He chaired an India Office committee on the proposals sent from India in 1916, introducing the idea that legislative power should not be conceded to Indians without also fixing upon them some executive responsibility—to avoid perpetuating the false line of the 1909 reforms, which he called a 'vicious system' of irresponsible critics, and 'no progress in or towards self-government'. This view influenced the wording, interpretation, and impact of the Montagu declaration of 1917 which promised India the 'progressive realization of responsible government'.

To represent the Council of India (with Sir Malcolm Seton of the India Office), Duke then accompanied Edwin Montagu, the secretary of state, on his tour of India in 1917–18 to work out the reforms proposals. The story of these deliberations was long dominated by the account in Montagu's diary (published in 1930) but it is now thought to have exaggerated its author's (still considerable) contributions, and underplayed those of others, including Duke.

Some recognition of this was implied when, in January 1920, on the retirement of Sir Thomas Holderness (the only other Indian civilian to hold the office), Montagu made Duke permanent under-secretary of state at the India Office. In this post, confronted by the difficult task of adjusting the degree of control exercised by the secretary of state in council to the new conditions in India, as well as by the unfamiliar duties of the head of the major office in the home civil service, Duke earned the confidence of Montagu's successors, Lord Peel and Lord Olivier, as well as the regard of the permanent staff.

Duke thoroughly enjoyed Indian life, especially in its outdoor aspects, was a fair shot, and acquired a good field knowledge of the fauna and flora of Bengal. An indefatigable walker, he liked to explore his districts and to get to know the villagers, by whom he was called 'the sahib who does all his *daks* (journeys) on foot'. Genuinely interested in Indian archaeology, he was able to do useful work at Gaya in the conservation of Buddhist remains.

Duke had married on 15 August 1889 Mary Eliza (1864/5–1939x42), daughter of James Addison Scott, of Wooden, Roxburghshire; they had two sons and one daughter. He was created CSI in 1910, KCIE in 1911, KCSI in 1915, and GCIE in 1918. An unofficial distinction which he valued highly was his election to the Athenaeum under rule II in 1922. On 11 June 1924 he died suddenly in London of a heart attack due to arteriosclerosis. His wife survived him.   P. G. ROBB

Sources P. G. Robb, *The government of India and reform, 1916–21* (1976) • P. G. Robb, *The evolution of British policy towards Indian politics, 1880–1920* (1992) • *DNB* • L. Curtis, *Dyarchy* (1920) • E. S. Montagu, *An Indian diary*, ed. V. Montagu (1930) • S. D. Waley, *Edwin Montagu* (1964) • S. R. Mehrotra, *India and the commonwealth, 1885–1929* (1965) • M. Carmichael, ed., *Lord Carmichael of Skirling: a memoir prepared by his wife* [1929] • J. H. Broomfield, *Elite conflict in a plural society: twentieth century Bengal* (1968) • *CGPLA Eng. & Wales* (1924) • m. cert.

Archives BL OIOC, corresp. and papers as permanent under-secretary of state of India | BL OIOC, letters to Sir B. P. Blackett, MS Eur. E 397 • CUL, corresp. with Lord Hardinge • State Library of New South Wales, Dixson Wing, letters to second earl of Lytton

Wealth at death £9157 4s. 3d.: confirmation, 12 Dec 1924, *CCI*

Dukes, Ashley (1885–1959), playwright and theatre critic, was born on 29 May 1885 at Bridgwater, Somerset, the son of the Revd Edwin Joshua Dukes, Congregational minister, and his wife, Edith Mary Pope. Educated at Silcoates School, Yorkshire, he graduated in science at Manchester University in 1905 and went to London to lecture in science, though also (as he put it later) as 'an aspirant to the humanities'. In London he became interested in the modern drama. The naturalistic methods—the staging rather than the acting—of the famous Edwardian productions of Harley Granville Barker at the Court Theatre dissatisfied him, and when in the early autumn of 1907 he had the opportunity of combining a postgraduate course at Munich University with private tutoring, he began eagerly to study the progressive German theatre on its own ground. He was abroad for two years, based first at Munich, and then, in 1908, at Zürich.

On Dukes's return to England in 1909 he became a full-time professional writer, and he acted as drama critic for A. R. Orage on the *New Age* (for this he received only 10s. a week), with freedom—as he said—'to train the batteries of Continental criticism' upon such writers as Barrie, Galsworthy, and Maugham. During 1910 the Stage Society put on the first of his plays, a comedy, *Civil War*; in 1911 he published his *New Age* essays on *Modern Dramatists*. In 1912–14 he was drama critic for *Vanity Fair*; in 1913–14 for *The Star*; and he also wrote short essays, known as 'turnovers', for *The Globe*.

In 1914 Dukes adapted for the Stage Society (Haymarket) Anatole France's *Comedy of a Man who Married a Dumb Wife*. He was thoroughly cosmopolitan, loving the European scene and reading widely in German and French. These early days indicated a future which was interrupted during the First World War by western front service in the machine-gun corps, from which he retired with the rank of major after holding every rank—except that of sergeant—between private and company commander. On 7 March 1918 he married the dancer Cyvia Myriam Ramberg (1888–1982) [*see* Rambert, Marie], daughter of Yakof Ramberg, a Polish publisher. She had studied with Émile Jaques-Dalcroze and later with Diaghilev; after leaving Diaghilev's company she went to London where she met Dukes.

During 1920–24 Dukes wrote drama criticism for the *Illustrated Sporting and Dramatic News* as well as contributing to the *New Statesman* and other journals. He adapted Georg Kaiser's *From Morn to Midnight* (1920) and Ernst Toller's *The Machine Wreckers* (1923) from their original German. But it was his own *The Man with a Load of Mischief* which established his name. This, produced at the New Theatre by the Stage Society in December 1924, ran for 261 performances at the Haymarket from June 1925 and in later years had revivals at three London theatres. It was a Regency fable by a man who had always cared for the spoken word in the theatre and whose poetic sense showed in his prose rhythms. The play excited people whose ears had become accustomed to the period's fashionably curt dialogue, which had reminded the actress Mrs Patrick Campbell of typewriters tapping away into the night. The plot was slight, set in an inn where a valet, a Jacobin, wooed a lady, and a lord was left in helpless anger, but the dialogue and Dukes's judgement and balance create a sense of enchantment.

The success of this comedy gave Dukes his independence. He made many other adaptations and dramatizations, notably two for Matheson Lang—*Such Men are Dangerous* (Duke of York's, 1928) from the German of Alfred Neumann's *Der Patriot*, and *Jew Süss* (Duke of York's, 1929) from Lion Feuchtwanger's novel—and *Elizabeth of England*, from the German of Ferdinand Bruckner, in which Lang also appeared (with Phyllis Neilson-Terry) at the Cambridge Theatre in 1931. Further, Dukes wrote a good deal of original work, including the heroic comedy *The Song of Drums*, or *Ulenspiegel*, performed at the Royal Flemish Theatre, Brussels, but not in London; *The Fountain-Head*, and *Matchmaker's Arms*. His other activities also show his preoccupation with theatre, especially European theatre. He acted as British delegate from the Critics' Circle at the International Congress of Critics in Paris (1926) and Salzburg (1927); he wrote the volume *Drama* (1926) for the Home University Library; and he became one of the editors of the international *Theatre Arts Monthly*.

In 1933 Dukes opened his own theatre, the Mercury, in a converted church hall in Ladbroke Road, close to his home in Campden Hill. He turned it eventually into a workshop for poets' drama and for his wife's Ballet Rambert, the senior English ballet company. The Mercury became his primary interest in this period, and its great day came in November 1935 when he brought T. S. Eliot's *Murder in the Cathedral* from the chapter house at Canterbury for a run of 225 nights. (It was transferred later to the West End.) Various other poets' plays—among them *The Ascent of F6* by W. H. Auden and Christopher Isherwood—followed on Dukes's small stage; and the Mercury, governed by its owner's taste and urbanity, moved safely into the history of the theatre. Simultaneously, Dukes still worked for the West End, as in *The Mask of Virtue* (Ambassadors, 1935), a very free rendering of Carl Sternheim's *Die Marquise von Arcis*, in itself a dramatic version of a play by Denis Diderot; it was this which brought Vivien Leigh to the West End stage.

In 1945–9 Dukes held the kind of post for which no man was better fitted, despite its cumbrous title: theatre and music adviser, main headquarters Allied Control Commission for Germany (British element). Later in London, though he had to pause in his work at the Mercury, he continued his series of adaptations. Sir Donald Wolfit toured during 1958 in Dukes's versions of two German plays, Heinrich von Kleist's *The Broken Jug* and Frank Wedekind's *The Maestro*. Dukes died at the Princess Beatrice Hospital, London, on 4 May 1959; his wife (who was made a DBE in 1962) died in 1982. Two daughters survived them.

Ashley Dukes, a man of great charm and unobtrusive common sense, with the means to back his judgement, had much influence on the intellectual theatre of his time. Smilingly, he rejected any form of insularity; he was a European with a taste in wine as sure as his taste in the theatre and the fastidious cadences of his prose. *The Man with a Load of Mischief* and his one not very factual venture into autobiography, *The Scene is Changed* (1942), are likely to live on when much else in the theatrical record of the period is lost.   J. C. TREWIN, *rev.* SAYONI BASU

Sources *The Times* (5 May 1959) · A. Dukes, *The scene is changed* (1942) · E. H. Mikhail, 'Ashley Dukes', *Modern British dramatists, 1900–1945*, ed. S. Weintraub, DLitB, 10 (1982) · J. Ritchie, 'Ashley Dukes and the German theatre between the wars', *Affinities: essays in German and English literature*, ed. R. W. Last (1971), 97–109 · M. Rambert [C. M. Ramberg], *Quicksilver* (1972) · *CGPLA Eng. & Wales* (1959)
Archives BL, corresp. with League of Dramatists, corresp. with Society of Authors, Add. MSS 63372–63373; Add. MS 56695

Likenesses photographs, 1925–35, Hult. Arch. · H. Coster, photographs, NPG · Kostia [C. Irinski], portrait, priv. coll. · photograph, repro. in Dukes, *The scene is changed*
Wealth at death £45,066 14s. 3d.: probate, 29 July 1959, *CGPLA Eng. & Wales*

Dukes, Charles, Baron Dukeston (1880–1948), trade unionist, was born on 28 October 1880 at Bedcote, Stourbridge, Worcestershire, the first child of George Harry Dukes, a spade plater, and his wife, Ann Hatton. After leaving elementary school at the age of eleven he was employed as an errand boy. When he was thirteen his parents moved to Stockton Heath, Warrington, where he worked with his father in an iron forge and then had a series of labouring jobs, including one as a 'ripper' with navvies on the Manchester Ship Canal. At the age of seventeen he joined the United Builders' Labourers' Union and later the National Union of Gasworkers and General Labourers—the union which in 1924 became the National Union of General and Municipal Workers (NUGMW). In his early working life he took a leading part in local disputes, which made employers reluctant to employ him, and in 1911 he became full-time secretary of the Gasworkers' Warrington branch, living on commission. In three years he increased the membership from thirty to 3000, and he was appointed district officer in 1915, the year of his marriage to Emily Forster (1879–1969). A tall, imposing figure, 'with the voice of a gentle sergeant-major' (*County Express*, 22 May 1948), he was an outstanding organizer and a thoughtful and skilful negotiator. In 1924 he was appointed temporary district secretary for the NUGMW Leeds district and in 1925 he was elected district secretary for Lancashire.

Throughout these years Dukes was active in politics. When he was nineteen he had joined the Independent Labour Party (ILP) and a year later he was secretary of the Warrington branch. He served on Stockton Heath parish council, was secretary of the Warrington Trades Council and Labour Representation Committee, and fought municipal elections. In 1912 he became a member of the national executive of the newly formed British Socialist Party (BSP), to which members of the ILP left were drawn, and he was among the majority within the BSP who opposed war. In 1916, when conscripted into the Cheshire regiment, he refused to obey military orders, was court-martialled, and served a prison sentence. None the less, in the 1923 general election he became Warrington's first Labour MP, but he lost the seat in the following year's general election. He again represented Warrington in the Commons from 1929 to 1931.

Dukes's election as district secretary for Lancashire in 1925 automatically placed him on the union's national executive, where he rapidly established himself as the dominant force. He supported the decision of the general council of the Trades Union Congress (TUC) to call off the general strike, and in 1927 vigorously enforced his own union executive's rule against members of the Communist Party or minority movement holding office in the NUGMW. When, in 1933, Will Thorne, the general secretary of the NUGMW since 1889, announced his impending retirement, Dukes was the obvious successor; following his election he took office in 1934. Between 1936 and 1938 he carried through a much needed reorganization of the union, bringing in compulsory retirement at sixty-five for full-time officers, redrawing the boundaries of the union's districts, abolishing the office of president, and enhancing the authority of national officers. Under his leadership the NUGMW was on the right of labour politics.

The general secretaryship gave Dukes a seat on the general council of the TUC, where, after Ernest Bevin and Walter Citrine, he was recognized as its strongest personality. After Bevin became minister of labour in 1940 it was Dukes who moved many of the council's most important resolutions during the war. He was made a CBE in 1942. In 1945–6 he was president of the TUC. Following his retirement from the general secretaryship of the NUGMW in 1946 he received a peerage in the new year's honours in 1947, and was later appointed a director of the Bank of England. His career epitomizes that of many trade union leaders of his generation who, in their early days, combined militant political views with trade union activism and then, as their trade union responsibilities increased and they experienced the inter-war depression and the failure of the general strike, became political moderates.

Dukes died from a lympho sarcoma in Granard House Royal Cancer Hospital on 14 May 1948, and was buried in St Leonard's churchyard, Chesham Bois, near Amersham, on 19 May. He left no heir and his barony became extinct.

JOE ENGLAND

Sources H. A. Clegg, *General union in a changing society: a short history of the National Union of General and Municipal Workers, 1889–1964* (1964) · H. A. Clegg, *General union: a study of the National Union of General and Municipal Workers* (1954) · H. A. Clegg, A. Fox, and A. F. Thompson, *A history of British trade unions since 1889*, 2 (1985) · *Warrington Guardian year book* (1930) · *County Express for Worcestershire and Staffordshire* (22 May 1948) · *The Times* (15 May 1948) · *Warrington Examiner* (22 May 1948) · *Warrington Guardian* (19 May 1948) · *Fifty years of the National Union of General and Municipal Workers* (1939) · *Sixty years of the National Union of General and Municipal Workers* (1949) · election leaflets, 1914, Warrington Public Library · *The Labour who's who* (1927)
Archives FILM BFI NFTVA, propaganda film footage (TUC)
Likenesses photograph, General, Municipal and Boilermakers Union Head Office, London
Wealth at death £7144 10s. 1d.: probate, 19 July 1948, CGPLA Eng. & Wales

Dukes, Sir Paul (1889–1967), intelligence officer and author, was born on 10 February 1889 at North Field, Bridgwater, the son of Edwin Joshua Dukes, a Congregational minister, and his wife, Edith Mary Pope. Dukes was educated at Caterham School before travelling to St Petersburg to study music, and he was to write in his memoirs that 'I felt at home from the moment of arrival in the city' (Dukes, *The Story of 'ST 25'*, 14). He worked at the Marinsky Theatre with the conductor Albert Coates, and was convinced for a time that he was destined to pursue a musical career. The outbreak of war upset his plans, though, and at the start of 1916 Dukes joined the Anglo-Russian commission established the previous year. For

Sir Paul Dukes (1889–1967), by Karl Pollak, *c.*1948

the next two years he was involved in promoting the somewhat nebulous range of propaganda activities carried out by the commission, serving both in the Russian capital and at the Foreign Office in London.

In the summer of 1918 Dukes was summoned back to Britain where he was recruited into the Secret Intelligence Service. Allied military intervention in post-revolutionary Russia was already under way, and the British authorities were keen to place an agent in the country before it was sealed off from the outside world. At the end of 1918 Dukes (using the codename ST 25) crossed the Finnish border and travelled to Petrograd, equipped with the false papers he needed to carry out his work. Dukes already spoke fluent Russian and boasted a formidable range of contacts in the Russian capital. During his time in Russia he passed himself off as a member of the secret police (the *Cheka*), and later enlisted in the Red Army. He also joined the Bolshevik Party and developed links with at least one individual who had good access to some of its leading figures. Dukes showed himself to be a master of disguises during his time in Russia, frequently changing his appearance and using more than a dozen names to conceal his identity. He recounted some of his extraordinary adventures in his books *Red Dusk and the Morrow* (1922) and *The Story of 'ST 25'* (1938), which remain among the most gripping examples of real-life espionage literature.

Dukes was deliberately vague when describing his activities in Russia, implying in his memoirs that he spent his time collecting information about a wide range of social and political developments. The most valuable material he obtained was in fact concerned with the operational effectiveness and morale of Bolshevik naval forces in the eastern Baltic, a subject of vital concern to British military planners during the time of allied intervention. Many of Dukes's reports were smuggled out of Russia by couriers transported on the boats of a special naval unit headed by Captain Augustus *Agar, who later won the Victoria Cross for his activities. A mission by Agar's unit to extract Dukes himself failed, however, with the result that ST 25 was forced to make his own escape across the Latvian border.

Dukes and Agar met in person only after they had returned to London. George V was deeply impressed by the bravery and daring of the two men, and awarded Dukes a KBE in 1920 since he was not, as a civilian, eligible to receive the Victoria Cross. Despite the success of his activities in Russia the Secret Intelligence Service appeared unwilling to make further use of Dukes between the wars. This may have been a consequence of the cuts in the organization's budget that followed the end of the First World War, though it probably also reflected unease among its senior members about Dukes's somewhat eccentric interest in various forms of eastern mysticism. About 1922 he joined a tantric community at Nyack, 15 miles from New York, led by Dr Pierre Arnold Bernard (known as the 'Omnipotent Oom'). While living there Dukes married Margaret Rutherford, but the couple were divorced in 1929. He married Diana Fitzgerald in 1959.

Dukes engaged in a good deal of journalistic work after returning to Britain from Russia, serving as a special correspondent of *The Times*, as well as lecturing widely in the United States and Canada. He was chairman of British Continental Press from 1930 to 1937. On the eve of the Second World War he was asked by some acquaintances to visit Germany in order to trace the whereabouts of a wealthy Czech businessman who had fled from house arrest following his imprisonment by the Nazis. He described his adventures in *An Epic of the Gestapo* (1940), in which he argued that there were clear parallels between soviet communism and German Nazism, but the book lacked the drama of his earlier works. In the Second World War, Dukes lectured on behalf of the Ministry of Information, and served as a director of companies involved in aircraft production. In later years he developed his interest in yoga, writing a number of books on the subject, including *Yoga for the Western World* (1955), and *The Yoga of Health, Youth and Joy* (1960), as well as making a series of broadcasts for the BBC.

Paul Dukes possessed many of the qualities that helped to forge the reputation of members of the Secret Intelligence Service in the public mind. His arrival in Russia on secret service took place soon after several other British agents, including Sidney Reilly, had been forced to flee the country following their involvement in an abortive plot to destroy the youthful Bolshevik regime. Dukes's role in Russia during 1919 was essentially the more modest one of observer and reporter, but he played his part with a high degree of courage and intelligence.

Sir Paul Dukes died in Cape Town, South Africa, on 27 August 1967.   MICHAEL HUGHES

Sources P. Dukes, *Red dusk and the morrow* (1922) • P. Dukes, *The story of 'ST 25'* (1938) • P. Dukes, *An epic of the Gestapo* (1940) • A. Agar, *Baltic episode* (1963) • C. Andrew, *Secret service: the making of the British intelligence community* (1985) • G. Brook-Shepherd, *Iron maze … the western secret services and the Bolsheviks* (1998) • *The Times* (28 Aug 1967) • *WW* • 'The great fuss and fume over the Omnipotent Oom', www.vanderbilt.edu • b. cert.
Likenesses W. Stoneman, photograph, 1947, NPG • K. Pollak, photograph, c.1948, NPG [*see illus.*] • photographs, repro. in Dukes, *Red dusk* • photographs, repro. in Dukes, *Story of 'ST 25'*
Wealth at death £374: probate, 23 Oct 1970, *CGPLA Eng. & Wales*

Dukeston. For this title name *see* Dukes, Charles, Baron Dukeston (1880–1948).

Dulac, Edmund [Edmond] (1882–1953), artist, was born at 56 rue Montaudron, Toulouse, on 22 October 1882, the only child of Pierre Henri Aristide Dulac (1848–1923?), a commercial traveller in textiles, and his wife, Marie Catherine Pauline Rieu (b. 1858). His father dealt in paintings as a sideline, and his uncle sold Japanese prints and oriental *objets d'art* which Dulac saw regularly. Dulac was educated at the *petit lycée* in Toulouse from 1890 to 1899 and then read law at Toulouse University, and graduated in 1902. He also studied drawing and painting at the city's École des Beaux-Arts (1900–03), where he discovered the illustrations of Aubrey Beardsley, Edward Burne-Jones, Walter Crane, and William Morris. He briefly attended the Académie Julian in Paris in the following year. An Anglophile, he took English lessons, habitually dressed in the English fashion, with tight trousers, spats, white gloves, and a cane, and gained the nickname 'l'Anglais'. On 13 December 1903 he married Alice May de Marini (b. c.1869), an American thirteen years his senior. The course of his life was leading him towards England, and, his marriage having ended within weeks, he moved in 1904 to London, where he Anglicized the spelling of his forename, and settled. He became naturalized in 1912.

Dulac's flair for book illustration brought him an early commission from the publishers J. M. Dent for illustrations to the Brontë novels, for which he supplied sixty watercolours. This was followed by regular work as a caricaturist and illustrator for the *Pall Mall Magazine*, but his status as a popular artist was assured when he was commissioned by Hodder and Stoughton to illustrate a new edition of *The Arabian Nights* (1907) with fifty colour plates. Editions of *The Tempest* (1908) and *The Rubáiyát of Omar Khayyám* (1909) followed (the limited, de luxe editions were bound in vellum and signed by the illustrator), and these confirmed Dulac to be a direct challenger in the illustrated gift book market to the work of Arthur Rackham. Susan Lambert noted that, compared to Rackham, Dulac 'made greater use of the breakthrough in four-colour printing, conceiving and modelling his pictures in colour rather than adding colours to a linear design' (private information).

The exotic stories he illustrated struck a new chord in

'The shadows in it are blue. Blue—the *only* blue, a blue to make you drunk'. The journey had the effect of brightening his palette, and introducing to his work harder, opaque colours with a greater dependence on pattern and outline. This is evident in the illustrations to *Sinbad the Sailor and other Stories* (1914), which are in marked contrast to the earlier *Arabian Nights*.

During the First World War the illustrated gift book market collapsed, and with it a contract Dulac had negotiated in 1914 with Hodder and Stoughton for three new books. He worked instead for the war effort, designing stamps and gift books for charity, and posters and other ephemera, for little or no money. From 1919 he made caricatures for publication in *The Outlook*, taking Kitchener, Winston Churchill, Lloyd George, and others as his subjects, and made a series of society portraits comparable to those by his contemporaries Gerald Brockhurst or James Gunn. Though they share the heightened detail and sharp sense of line of Brockhurst or Gunn, Dulac's little portraits lack the haunting intensity characteristic of the work of these artists, remaining by comparison elegantly charming, decorative, and unengaged.

Out of the friendship between Dulac and Yeats a variety of artistic projects grew, including the design at Yeats's suggestion of a proposed coinage for the Irish Free State, and collaboration on his play *At the Hawk's Well*. For this Dulac designed the scenery and costumes, composed the incidental music, and took part in the first performance in 1916.

After the war, Dulac's work as a theatrical designer broadened. He designed productions such as C. B. Cochran's *Cyrano de Bergerac* (1919), *Phoebus and Pan* (1919) for Thomas Beecham, and the Cochran revue *Phi-Phi* (1922). He collaborated in the 1930s with Rupert Doone on the management of the Group Theatre Company, based at the progressive Mercury Theatre, where he also designed ballet productions for Marie Rambert's Camargo Society.

Book illustration, though still a significant part of Dulac's output, had to make way for these and other new areas of design that now attracted him and brought him his living. He designed stamps, coins, and medals, including the king's poetry medal (1935), and wallpaper, industrial brochures, playing cards, and banknotes. His profile of George VI for coins and stamps has since become a classic image. Dulac's technique was always meticulous, his banknote designs in particular being derived from hundreds of measured studies. Dulac was an obsessive maker—from caricature dolls to stencils, book bindings, and musical instruments. As an illustrator his most sustained output in this second half of his career was his series of covers for the magazine *American Weekly*. This relationship lasted for twenty-five years from 1924, and took his work to a wide audience across the United States.

Dulac separated from his wife in 1923, and lived until his death with the writer Helen Beauclerk (1894?–1969), *née* Bellingham (her name had changed in childhood), whose books he illustrated. They had no children. In 1939 the couple moved to Morecombelake in Dorset, where they lived until 1944. In 1941, General de Gaulle visited Dulac

Dulac. They allowed him to enlarge his skill at caricature, and at the same time to sharpen his miniaturist's technique and to develop his lyrical sense of tone and composition. The sources he turned to were Japanese prints, which he had studied in his youth, with their flat colour and assymetry, and the high detail and colour of Indian and Persian miniatures.

Dulac quickly made friends with other illustrators, such as John Hassall, Arthur Rackham, William Heath Robinson, and Edmund Sullivan, fellow members of the London Sketch Club. However, he was never fully at home in the knockabout atmosphere of the club, instead forming more lasting friendships in the cosmopolitan circles of London, particularly with the philanthropist and collector Edmund Davis. In April 1911 Dulac married, in Marylebone, Elsa Arnalice Bignardi, a violinist, the daughter of a professor of singing, and the following year the couple moved into one of a group of studios that Edmund Davis had built in Ladbroke Road. Dulac flourished in the social and artistic world of this part of north London, where, at Davis's house nearby, he met the artists Charles Ricketts, Charles Shannon, and Glyn Philpot, and others, including the pianist Arthur Rubinstein and W. B. Yeats, with whom he formed a lifelong friendship.

Despite the exotic nature of Dulac's paintings, he had himself travelled only between France and England until, in 1913, he and Elsa went on a Mediterranean cruise with Edmund Davis. The diary Dulac kept (priv. coll., Baltimore) records the impact on him of the light and colour he witnessed—describing the sea off Taormina, he wrote:

and commissioned designs for the Free French stamps and banknotes. Dulac's last years, after his return to London, were taken up by book illustration, in a series of three titles for the Limited Editions Club of America, *The Golden Cockerel* (1950), *The Marriage of Cupid and Psyche* (1951) and *Comus* (1955), a commission which built on the popularity of his *American Weekly* covers.

After his death at St Mary's Hospital, London, on 25 May 1953, which followed a heart attack brought on by a bout of flamenco dancing, a memorial exhibition of Dulac's work was held at the Leicester Galleries, London. His centenary was marked by a touring exhibition of his work shown in Sheffield, Bristol, and London during 1982–3. Original watercolours for Dulac's illustrations are in the collections of the British Museum and the Victoria and Albert Museum, London, and the University of Texas.

JAMES HAMILTON

Sources C. White, *Edmund Dulac* (1975) · J. Hamilton and C. White, *Edmund Dulac, 1882–1953* (1982) [exhibition catalogue] · D. Larkin, ed., *Edmund Dulac* (1975) · *CGPLA Eng. & Wales* (1953) · private information (2004) [Susan Lambert]
Archives BL, corresp. with Society of Authors, Add. MS 56695 · GL, corresp. with publishers · priv. coll., corresp. · priv. coll., diaries · priv. coll., notebooks · priv. coll., sketchbooks · priv. coll., studies
Likenesses A. L. Coburn, photogravure photograph, 1914, NPG · photograph, c.1929, Hult. Arch. · H. Coster, photographs, 1930–39, NPG [*see illus.*] · E. Dulac, self-portrait, pen-and-ink caricature, FM Cam. · H. L. Oakley, silhouette, NPG · R. S. Sherriffs, pencil caricature, NPG
Wealth at death £2308 18s. 6d.: probate, 8 Aug 1953, *CGPLA Eng. & Wales*

Dulanty, John Whelan (1883–1955), diplomat and civil servant, was born in Manchester, the son of John Dulanty; his mother was probably named Ellen, and both parents were of Irish extraction. He was educated at St Mary's, Failsworth, Manchester School of Commerce, and Manchester University, where he read law and became secretary of the faculty of technology. He entered the Middle Temple and in 1910 was appointed educational adviser to Indian students attending the northern universities of England. He also worked on *GK's Weekly* and at *The Clarion* under Robert Blatchford. He knew Yeats, and was a friend of Shaw and Joyce, and later became guardian to Joyce's grandson. He became honorary director of Redmond's United Irish League of Great Britain, and supported Winston Churchill's 1908 campaign to secure the North-West Manchester seat. On 7 April 1909 he married Annie (1885/6–1952), the daughter of George Hutton, an education inspector of Charlton-cum-Hardy, Lancashire. They had two sons and one daughter. In 1913 he joined the civil service as a Board of Education examiner, and became in turn principal assistant secretary to Churchill at the Ministry of Munitions and assistant secretary at the Treasury in 1920. He was awarded a CB and CBE for his services. In 1921 he declined Lloyd George's offer of Irish treasury remembrancer and resigned from the civil service in protest against the government's Irish policy.

In the same year Dulanty became chairman of Peter Jones Ltd, the department store. He was involved in the Anglo-Irish treaty negotiations which resulted in the establishment of the Irish Free State. In 1926 he was appointed Irish trade commissioner for the free state in the United Kingdom, and in 1930 as high commissioner. At this time the status of the dominions was in flux and their advance to separate sovereignty was confirmed in the Statute of Westminster (1931). Dulanty was charged with negotiating direct access to the sovereign and facilitating the acquisition of autonomous treaty-making power, finally conceded in the granting of a great seal in 1931.

Following the victory of Eamon De Valera's Fianna Fáil in 1932, Dulanty, with his Redmondite background, unconcealed British honours, and pro-treatyite connections, was widely expected to be replaced by a republican ideologue. Surprisingly De Valera, impressed by his extensive Westminster and dominion contacts and insider's contacts in the civil service and industry, decided to retain him. Until the appointment of Sir John Maffey as British representative in Éire in 1939 he provided the chief diplomatic conduit between the two governments.

These were difficult years for Anglo-Irish relations, as De Valera sought to abolish the monarchical symbols and financial and military obligations embodied in the treaty, and the British responded with punitive tariffs on Irish goods. Dulanty aimed to blunt British retaliation by arguing that the Irish leader had been moderated by political office, and that British concessions would greatly assist De Valera in containing extreme republican elements. Dulanty often suggested that he did not personally agree with many of De Valera's policies and raised the spectre of Britain's being supplanted by Germany as Ireland's leading trading partner. He attended the Imperial Economic Conference at Ottawa in 1932, helping to prevent a Commonwealth quarantine by carefully cultivating dominion statesmen, including Smuts, Hertzog, Mackenzie King, and Stanley Bruce. In 1933 he used a secret visit to George V at Balmoral to help secure the resignation of the governor-general, James McNeill, thus avoiding a serious constitutional crisis.

Crucially Dulanty was personally friendly with Dominions Office and Treasury officials, especially Sir Warren Fisher, who enabled him to initiate negotiations leading to the coal-cattle pact of 1934. From 1935 his influence began to wane as De Valera began to negotiate directly with the new dominions secretary, Malcolm MacDonald. Dulanty was forbidden by De Valera to attend the abdication council of 1936, but he continued to lay official armistice day wreaths at the Cenotaph. He attended the Imperial Conference of 1937 as an unofficial observer, as well as meetings of Commonwealth high commissioners until the outbreak of war in 1939 (even if, as he once observed, such occasions made him feel 'like a whore at a christening' (Massey, 298). He failed to persuade De Valera into an Anglo-Irish defence relationship, although his diplomatic assistance in the transfer of British naval facilities was recognized in his attendance in 1938 at the British withdrawal from Queenstown (Cobh), regarded by the British commander as 'a particularly graceful act' (Fisk, 4–5). 'Mr

Dulanty is thoroughly friendly to England', Churchill cynically remarked: 'He acts as a general smoother, representing everything Irish in the most favourable light' (Churchill, 582–3).

Dulanty's diplomatic skills were severely tested during the Second World War, when he forcefully conveyed De Valera's opposition to extending conscription to Northern Ireland. Privately he remained sceptical about any immediate prospect of Irish reunification. He facilitated the wartime visits to Dublin of Deneys Reitz, South African deputy prime minister, and the Australian prime minister, Robert Menzies. A member of several London clubs, he did much of his work on the telephone. He promoted Irish commerce abroad and was inveterately what a later generation would call a networker. He survived another Irish change of government in 1948, with the election of John A. Costello's administration. Following the declaration of a republic in the following year he became for a few weeks before his retirement the first Irish ambassador to the court of St James.

After retirement he held directorships of the National Bank and the department store McBirney & Co. of Dublin, remaining a consultant to the Irish embassy in London. His honorary degrees included LLDs from Leeds University (1939) and the National University of Ireland (1940). He died after a short illness at the Westminster Hospital, London, on 11 February 1955. A requiem mass was held at Westminster Cathedral on 17 February.

DONAL LOWRY

Sources *The Times* (12 Feb 1955) • *Irish Times* (12 Feb 1955) • *Irish Press* (Feb 1955) • *Manchester Guardian* (Feb 1955) • *WWW, 1951–60* • H. J. Hood, ed., *The Catholic who's who* (1952) • R. Fisk, *In time of war: Ireland, Ulster and the price of neutrality, 1939–45* (1983) • D. W. Harkness, *The restless dominion: the Irish Free State and the British Commonwealth of Nations* (1969) • D. W. Harkness, 'Mr de Valera's dominion: Irish relations with Britain and the commonwealth, 1932–8', *Journal of Commonwealth Political Studies*, 8 (1970) • D. McMahon, *Republicans and imperialists: Anglo-Irish relations in the 1930s* (1984) • D. Reitz, *No outspan* (1943) • C. Sanger, *Malcolm Macdonald: bringing an end to empire* (1995) • V. Massey, *What's past is prologue* (1965) • I. McCabe, *A diplomatic history of Ireland 1948–1949: the republic, the commonwealth and NATO* (1991) • D. Lowry, 'New Ireland, old empire and the outside world, 1922–1949: the strange evolution of a "dictionary republic"', *Ireland: the politics of independence, 1922–49*, ed. M. Cronin and J. Regan (2000) • D. Lowry, 'Irish-South African relations and the British commonwealth, c.1902–1961', *Ireland and South Africa in modern times*, ed. D. P. McCracken (1996) • earl of Longford and T. P. O'Neill, *Eamon de Valera* (1970) • N. Mansergh, *The unresolved question: the Anglo-Irish settlement and its undoing, 1910–72* (1994) • N. Mansergh, 'Ireland: external relations 1926–39', *The years of the great test*, ed. F. MacManus (1967) • J. O'Brien, 'Ireland's departure from the British commonwealth', *Round Table*, 306 (1988), 170–94 • P. Canning, *British policy towards Ireland, 1921–1941* (1985) • D. W. Dean, 'Final exit? Britain, Eire, the commonwealth and the repeal of the External Relations Act, 1945–1949', *Journal of Imperial and Commonwealth History*, 20 (1992), 391–418 • L. Lloyd and A. James, 'The external relations of the dominions, 1919–1948', *The British Yearbook of International Law, 1996* (1997) • W. S. Churchill, *The Second World War*, 1 (1948) • m. cert. • d. cert.

Archives JRL, letters to the *Manchester Guardian* • NA Ire., department of foreign affairs, secretary's office index • NA Ire., department of the Taoiseach, private office files • National Archives of South Africa, Pretoria, Jan Christian Smuts papers • National Archives of South Africa, Pretoria, Charles te Water papers • PRO, Cabinet: conclusions • PRO, Cabinet: memoranda • PRO, Dominions Office • TCD, corresp. with Thomas Bodkin • U. Durham, Malcolm MacDonald papers • University College, Dublin, Patrick McGilligan papers

Dulany, Daniel (1685–1753), lawyer and politician in America, was born in Queen's county, Ireland, one of three sons of Thomas Dulany. He attended the University of Dublin, but after his father's remarriage the family could no longer afford his tuition. Dulany and his two brothers emigrated to Maryland, arriving in spring 1703. His indenture was purchased by Colonel George Plater (c.1664–1709), a wealthy planter and office-holder, who employed Daniel as a clerk in his law office.

Dulany completed a legal apprenticeship with Plater, was admitted to the Charles county bar in 1709, and soon qualified to practise in several county courts and the provincial court. In the following year he married Charity Smallwood (c.1692–1711), daughter of Colonel John Courts (1656–1702) and widow of Bayne Smallwood. Charity brought two plantations and a slave to the marriage, but Dulany retained only the slave and her child after Charity's death in 1711.

About 1713 Dulany moved his law practice to Nottingham town in Prince George's county and began to buy land there, now styling himself as 'gentleman'. In 1716 he travelled to England and was admitted to Gray's Inn on 20 February 1717, although he returned to Maryland that spring. In the same year he married Rebecca (c.1695–1737), daughter of Colonel Walter Smith (d. 1711) of Calvert county.

In 1720 Dulany, ready for a larger arena for his talents and ambition, established himself in Annapolis. He practised in the courts of central Maryland and represented clients in the provincial courts of appeal and chancery. In September 1721 Annapolis voters selected Dulany as a common councilman and in 1722 sent him to the lower house. Between 1721 and 1725 he served as attorney-general and from 1721 until 1724 as one of the commissaries-general. Despite his proprietary offices, early in his political career Dulany and his fellow lawyer Thomas Bordley led lower house efforts to circumscribe the proprietor's prerogative powers through the protection of English statute and common law. In 1728 Dulany argued his position in *The Rights of the Inhabitants of Maryland to the Benefit of the English Laws*. Maryland's proprietor, Charles Calvert, fifth Baron Baltimore, is known to have possessed a copy of the pamphlet (the only one that survives), but never responded directly to Dulany's arguments.

However, an implicit response may be inferred from Baltimore's actions on his visit to Maryland in the winter of 1732–3. Before returning to England the proprietor disarmed lower house opposition by offering Dulany three of the most lucrative patronage positions at his disposal: agent- and receiver-general, vice-admiralty court judge, and attorney-general. Dulany's acceptance ensured that the services of the ablest lawyer in the province (Bordley, his closest rival, having died) were now employed on behalf of the proprietor.

During these years Dulany did not confine his interests to the law and politics. Already one of the province's largest landowners, Dulany in the 1720s began to survey and patent extensive holdings in the undeveloped Piedmont backcountry. As frontier conditions stabilized, he promoted settlement through sale of family-sized tracts at modest prices or leaseholds that eventually sold as improved farms. To serve the needs of the farmers of this region, the fastest growing in Maryland, Dulany laid out a market town, named Frederick after Lord Baltimore's son, which by 1750 had become the colony's largest settlement.

In 1731 Dulany joined four other investors to found the Baltimore Ironworks Company. His initial capital outlay of £700 increased in value to £10,000 by the time of his death, as the company became the most profitable of the Maryland ironworks. Enhanced personal wealth allowed Dulany to engage in money-lending on a large scale; he dealt in sterling, currency, and tobacco loans to small tradesmen and planters: he also invested in the slave trade, profiting both from slave sales and loans made to their buyers.

Daniel and Rebecca Dulany had three sons and four daughters, including the younger Daniel *Dulany (1722–1797), before Rebecca's death in March 1737. In September 1738 he married for the third time, his new wife being Henrietta Maria Chew (d. 1766), daughter of Philemon Lloyd (c.1674–1733) and widow of Samuel Chew (c.1704–1737). Dulany added six stepchildren (three boys and three girls) to his family by this marriage, and had two more sons with Henrietta Maria.

Dulany continued to serve in the lower house until appointed to the governor's council in 1742, a position he retained until his death. He resigned as agent- and receiver-general in November 1734 to become commissary-general, or judge of the probate court, a position also held at his death. Dulany's principal achievement during his last decade was a successful correspondence in which he persuaded Lord Baltimore to compromise over the issue of officers' fees. Strong public support existed during the 1740s for a tobacco inspection act to improve the quality and therefore the prices paid for Maryland's tobacco, but the lower house refused to accept inspection and the resulting elimination of poor-quality tobacco without a compensatory scaling down of officers' fees and clerical salaries. The proprietor had long rejected any legislation that regulated fees as an infringement of the prerogative. The arguments offered by Dulany, himself a recipient of substantial fees, at last convinced the proprietor and in 1747 resulted in legislation that mandated inspection and reduced fees and tithes accordingly.

Daniel Dulany died at his home in Annapolis, after a 'long and lingering Illness' (Land, *Dulanys*, 211), on 5 December 1753, and was buried in the family vault in St Anne's churchyard, Annapolis, six days later. He left a substantial estate that included personal property worth £10,921 9s. 8d. current money of Maryland (including 187 slaves and 2594 ounces of plate), sizeable sums out on loan, and about 10,000 acres of land in five counties.

EDWARD C. PAPENFUSE

Sources E. C. Papenfuse and others, eds., *A biographical dictionary of the Maryland legislature, 1635–1789*, 1 (1985) [this entry was produced as part of the Maryland State Archives project] • A. C. Land, *The Dulanys of Maryland: a biographical study of Daniel Dulany, the elder (1685–1753) and Daniel Dulany, the younger (1722–1797)* (Baltimore, MD, 1955); repr. (1968) • A. C. Land, *Colonial Maryland—a history* (1981) • R. J. Brugger, *Maryland: a middle temperament* (1988) • M. D. M. [M. D. Mereness], 'Dulany, Daniel (1685–1753)', *DAB* • A. Day, *A social study of lawyers in Maryland* (1989)
Archives Maryland Historical Society, Baltimore, family papers, MSS 1562, 1919
Likenesses J. E. Kuhn, oils, Maryland Historical Society, Baltimore
Wealth at death £10,921 9s. 8 d. current money of Maryland, incl. 187 slaves and 2594 ounces of plate, but excl. substantial sums out on loan; c.10,000 acres in five counties and lots in Annapolis: Papenfuse and others, eds., *Biographical dictionary*, vol. 1, p. 286

Dulany, Daniel (1722–1797), politician in America, was born in Annapolis, Maryland, on 28 June 1722, the eldest son of Daniel *Dulany (1685–1753), lawyer and politician, and his second wife, Rebecca (c.1695–1737), the daughter of Colonel Walter Smith of Calvert county, Maryland. Dulany had two brothers and four sisters, as well as three stepbrothers, three stepsisters, and two half-brothers from his father's later marriage to Henrietta Maria Chew (d. 1766). Dulany's father was one of the colony's most astute lawyers, holder of major proprietary offices, successful land developer, and investor in the Baltimore Ironworks Company. He provided his son with both a superior education and the connections needed to pursue an equally successful career.

After attending Eton College, Dulany matriculated at Clare College, Cambridge, in January 1739, entered the Middle Temple of the inns of court in March 1742, and was called to the English bar in June 1746, one of the few Maryland lawyers to claim that distinction. He returned to America in 1747 and soon qualified to practise in Maryland's provincial and chancery courts as well as in several county courts.

On 16 September 1749 Dulany married Rebecca Tasker (1724–1822), second daughter of Benjamin Tasker (c.1690–1768) and his wife, Anne Bladen (d. 1775). Rebecca's father was president of the governor's council and served as agent- and receiver-general, among numerous other offices. Her uncle was the former governor Thomas Bladen. In 1741 her sister Anne had married governor Samuel Ogle, and a second sister, Frances, later married Robert Carter of Nomini Hall, Virginia. The marriage thus united two politically powerful families as well as bringing Dulany 'a handsome fortune' (Day, 322). The couple had two sons and one daughter during the next decade.

Dulany represented Frederick, the county his father had done so much to develop, in the lower house from 1751 to 1754 and sat as an Annapolis delegate from 1756 to 1757 before being named to the governor's council, where he served from 1757 until 1774. From 1754 to 1756 he shared the office of commissary-general with his father-in-law and occupied it exclusively from 1759 to 1761. In July 1761 Dulany arrived in England in the hope of improving his health, with an extended stay at Bath. During this visit he also sought to solidify his position with the proprietary establishment. When Dulany returned to Maryland in July 1763, he held the lucrative post of deputy secretary, which he retained until the revolution.

In autumn 1763, before ceasing publication in response to the Stamp Act, the *Maryland Gazette* advertised an anonymous pamphlet, *Considerations on the propriety of imposing taxes in the British colonies, for the purpose of raising a revenue*. The author, soon revealed as Dulany, argued that because colonists enjoyed neither direct nor virtual representation in parliament, only the Maryland assembly, its members chosen by the electorate, had the right to impose internal taxes. 'Easily the most influential American protest' against the Stamp Act, Dulany's essay was printed not only in other colonies but also in London, where its arguments were quoted in parliamentary debates (Brugger, 106).

During his stay in London, Dulany had several encounters with a fellow Marylander, the young Charles Carroll of Carrollton (1737–1832), whose father had encouraged him to call upon Dulany, 'the best Lawyer on this Continent', in the elder Carroll's opinion (Hoffman, 173). The exchanges did not go well; Carroll, insulted, described Dulany as 'un homme bizarre' (Brugger, 111). A decade later, and after further hostilities between the families, the two men had their most significant encounter, taking opposite sides on the perennially contentious issue of Maryland politics, the question of officials' fees.

In January 1773 Dulany, hoping to influence elections later that spring, wrote a dialogue for the *Gazette* in which he debated the merits of the governor's fee proclamation from 1770. In Dulany's account, 'Second Citizen' finally convinced 'First Citizen' of the proclamation's legality. In February, however, a new author took up the role of 'First Citizen' and carried on a six-month exchange of letters with Dulany, now writing as 'Antilon'. 'First Citizen', known to all to be the younger Charles Carroll, espoused the popular position against encroachments by the executive, arguing that fees constituted a tax which could only be enacted by the legislature, that as a new law the proclamation could not be enacted unilaterally by the governor, and that the constitution would be unbalanced if legislative control over finance were compromised. Dulany, writing in defence of the established form of government, argued that fees were not taxes and had historically been levied by various branches of government. Dulany saw all branches of government as competing for power; to function effectively there had to be a final authority—that of the executive—over the legislature. Dulany marshalled cogent legal arguments but Carroll claimed victory in the exchange, as Maryland voters returned a lower house favourable to his views.

The election results of early 1773 confirmed a gradual diminution of Dulany's political authority. The death of Benjamin Tasker in 1768 had deprived him of a major source of his political strength; a trip to England in 1771–2 to bolster his position with the proprietary establishment alienated the governor, while his exchange with Carroll dissipated the popular support he had earlier achieved with *Considerations*. The Dulanys, wrote Carroll to his father, 'have great reason to fear an end of their powers, influence, and future promotion' (Brugger, 111).

Without the movement for independence it might have been possible for Dulany to consolidate his position. However, Carroll's prediction came true as events in Maryland and elsewhere moved towards revolution. Neither Dulany's intellectual position nor his strong affiliation with England would permit him to do more than maintain a position of neutrality during the ensuing war, although after the war he wrote a number of unsigned pamphlets supporting the opposition to the ratification of the constitution and continued to give legal advice. During the revolution he retired to his Hunting Ridge estate near Baltimore, where he lived from 1776 until 1781, when the property was confiscated along with other loyalist holdings. In that year Dulany moved to Baltimore town, where he died on 17 March 1797 and was buried in St Paul's churchyard.   EDWARD C. PAPENFUSE

Sources E. C. Papenfuse and others, eds., *A biographical dictionary of the Maryland legislature, 1635–1789*, 1 (1985) [this entry was produced as part of the Maryland State Archives project] · A. C. Land, *The Dulanys of Maryland: a biographical study of Daniel Dulany, the elder (1685–1753) and Daniel Dulany, the younger (1722–1797)* (Baltimore, MD, 1955); repr. (1968) · R. J. Brugger, *Maryland: a middle temperament* (1988) · R. Hoffman, *Princes of Ireland, planters of Maryland: a Carroll saga, 1500–1782* (2000) · P. Onuf, ed., *Maryland and the empire, 1773: The Antilon–First Citizen letters* (1974) · A. C. Land, *Colonial Maryland — a history* (1981) · M. D. M. [M. D. Mereness], 'Dulany, Daniel (1722–1797)', *DAB* · A. Day, *A social study of lawyers in Maryland* (1989)
Archives Maryland Historical Society, Baltimore, family papers, MSS 1562, 1919
Likenesses oils, Maryland Historical Society, Baltimore
Wealth at death approx. 3000 acres in two counties: Papenfuse and others, eds., *Biographical dictionary*, vol. 1. p. 287

Duleep Singh, Princess **Sophia Alexandra** (1876–1948), suffragette, was born on 8 August 1876 probably at Elveden Hall, Norfolk, the fifth of six children of Maharaja Duleep *Singh (1838–1893), exiled by the British at the annexation of the Punjab, and his first wife, Bamba Muller (d. 1887). Her mother was the daughter of Ludwig Muller, a partner in the German firm of merchant bankers Todd, Muller & Co. of Alexandria, and an Ethiopian woman. Her father, a Sikh convert to Christianity (who later re-embraced Sikhism), was a naturalized British citizen, living on a pension of £25,000 per annum; her mother was Christian. She had three brothers and four sisters, two from her father's second marriage. Educated at home, Princess Sophia became an enthusiastic photographer. She lived at Faraday House, Hampton Court, Middlesex, and like her sisters, inherited the sum of £23,200 after the death of her father.

An Indian princess, brought up as a member of the British aristocracy, Princess Sophia none the less retained a sense of Sikh family heritage and pride in Indian culture. This involved her in the patronage of Indians in Britain, and her generous assistance was instrumental in establishing the Lascar Club in London's East End. Her chief

Princess Sophia Alexandra Duleep Singh (1876–1948), by unknown photographer, pubd 1913

activity, however, was campaigning to win votes for women in Britain through the Women's Social and Political Union (WSPU) and the Women's Tax Resistance League (WTRL). Mrs Blathwayt recorded that she had been converted to the views of WSPU at the home of Una Dugdale, and she became an active campaigner between 1909 and 1914, both nationally and locally, in the Richmond and Kew branch as well as the Kingston and District branch of WSPU. Her sister Princess Catherine Duleep Singh was an active member of the Esher and Molesey branch of the WSPU.

Princess Sophia took a prominent part in the first deputation to parliament on 18 November 1910, 'black Friday', heading the deputation with Mrs Pankhurst, Elizabeth Garrett Anderson, Dorinda Neligan, and others. She played an active role in publicity campaigns, in July 1911 driving in the first cart in the parade of 'press carts' delivering copies of Votes for Women to various pitches in London. An energetic fund-raiser for WSPU, in April 1911 she contributed cake and sweets for the opening of the Pankhursts' Streatham tea-shop. Listed as a collector, she was also a regular seller of The Suffragette at her 'pitch' outside Hampton Court. Locally, the branch reports are peppered with 'special thanks' for her fund-raising activities. She regularly spoke at meetings of the Richmond branch, and in March 1913 chaired a meeting of the Kingston and District branch.

It was as a tax resister, however, that Sophia Duleep

Singh, the sole Indian member of the WTRL, made her greatest impression. Taking her stand on the principle that taxation without representation was tyranny, she registered her defiance on several occasions by refusing to pay her taxes. Refusal to pay taxes and fines levied could lead to goods being impounded by the bailiffs under 'distraint' and sold by public auction to recover sums due. In May 1911, at Spelthorne petty sessions, her refusal to pay licences for her five dogs, carriage, and manservant led to a fine of £3. In July 1911, against arrears of 6s. in rates, she had a seven stone diamond ring impounded and auctioned at Ashford for £10. The ring was bought by a member of the WTRL and returned to her. In December 1913 she was summoned again to Feltham police court for employing a male servant and keeping two dogs and a carriage without licence. Her refusal to pay a fine of £12 10s. resulted in a pearl necklace, comprising 131 pearls, and a gold bangle studded with pearls and diamonds, being seized under distraint and auctioned at Twickenham town hall, both items being bought by members of WTRL, the necklace fetching £10 and the bangle £7. Such actions were a means of achieving publicity. Members of the WTRL, by buying articles under distraint, and organizing protest demonstrations and meetings after the auction, generated interest and sympathy in the movement. Sophia Duleep Singh's high-profile stand was thus significant, and an important contribution to women's struggle before the First World War, especially in the Richmond and Twickenham district.

In 1915 Sophia Duleep Singh was part of the 10,000-strong women's war work procession led by Emmeline Pankhurst. After the death of Mrs Pankhurst in 1928 she was appointed president of the committee which provided flowers for her statue. She joined the Suffragette Fellowship, remaining a member until her death. Her passionate commitment to the women's cause continued, as demonstrated by the fact that in the 1934 edition of Women's Who's Who she listed 'Advancement of Women' as her one and only interest.

In 1935 Sophia Duleep Singh lent to the Inverness Museum her brother Prince Frederick Duleep Singh's collection of Stuart relics. She remained unmarried. She died of cardiac failure on 22 August 1948 at her home, Hilden Hall, Tylers Green, Chepping, Wycombe, Buckinghamshire; she was cremated at Golders Green on 26 August.

ROZINA VISRAM

Sources R. Visram, *Asians in Britain: four hundred years of history* (2002) · G. D. Heath and J. Heath, *The women's suffrage movement in and around Richmond and Twickenham* (1968) · financial settlement of Maharajah Dalip Singh, BL OIOC, L/P&S/18/D/105 · *The Times* (25 Aug 1948) · *Daily Telegraph* (24 Aug 1948) · d. cert. · C. Campbell, *The maharajah's box: an imperial story of conspiracy, love and a guru's prophecy* (2000) · E. Crawford, *The women's suffrage movement: a reference guide, 1866–1928* (1999)

Archives BL OIOC, India Office records, L/P&S/18/D collection · Museum of London, Suffragette Fellowship collection · Women's Library, London, Women's Tax Resistance League collection

Likenesses photograph, Museum of London, Women's Library, London; repro. in *The Suffragette* (18 April 1913) [see illus.]

Wealth at death £58,040 0s. 11d.: probate, 8 Nov 1948, CGPLA Eng. & Wales

Dumaresq, Philippe [Philip] (**1637–1690**), topographer, was born on 2 May 1637 at Samarès Manor, St Clement, Jersey, the eldest son of Henry Dumaresq (c.1614–1654), seigneur of Samarès, and his wife, Marguerite (d. 1683), daughter of Abraham Herault. Philippe became seigneur of Samarès after his father's death. His father and maternal grandfather, both staunch parliamentarians, had been dismissed from the office of jurat of the royal court by Sir George Carteret but were reinstated by the council of state in 1653. The son, however, appears to have held different views. According to Baker, he entered the navy at an early age and attained the rank of captain. However, his name does not appear in Samuel Pepys's register of sea officers for the reigns of Charles II and James II and he describes himself in the 'Survey' as 'a Stranger to the Profession of the Sea'. He was sworn jurat of the royal court on 2 February 1681, having apparently lived in London for some time before then. By licence bearing the date 24 June 1672 he married at the Savoy Chapel, London, Deborah (d. 1720), daughter of William Trumbull of Easthampstead, Berkshire.

On the accession of James II in 1685, he presented him with his work 'A survey of the island of Jersey', the main motivation for which was concern for the security and defence of Jersey and its neighbouring islands. The work remained unpublished until 1935 though much of its content had already been widely disseminated as a result of the substantial use made of it by Philip Falle in his history of Jersey. Falle acknowledged that he had 'received some help from those imperfect Notes' imparted to him by Dumaresq 'sometime before his Decease', and includes Dumaresq's map in his work. Though he says that Dumaresq 'had begun a Survey of this Island, and had made good Progress in it, but Death gave him not leave to finish it', the 'Survey' itself bears no sign of incompleteness. Falle describes Dumaresq as 'a very ingenious and inquisitive Person' (Falle, preface).

From his letters Dumaresq seems to have been an amiable, well-informed man, who devoted most of his time to gardening, fruit, and tree culture. He was the friend and correspondent of John Evelyn. A few of his letters to Christopher, Lord Hatton, when governor of Jersey, also survive. Dumaresq died in 1690 in London and was buried there on 3 June. His widow died in 1720 at Hertford and desired to be buried at Easthampstead 'as near my dear father as may be'. Their only child, Deborah, married Philip, son of Benjamin Dumaresq. Having no children, she was the last of her family who held the seigneurie of Samarès, and conveyed it to the Seale family.

GORDON GOODWIN, rev. HELEN M. E. EVANS

Sources register of baptisms, marriages and burials in the parish of St Clement, Jersey, 1623–87, St Clement's rectory • 'Mémoires de la famille La Cloche', *Annual Bulletin* [Société Jersiaise], 2 (1885–9), 461–507 • J. L. Chester and J. Foster, eds., *London marriage licences, 1521–1869* (1887) • C. Langton, 'Seigneurs of Samarès', *Annual Bulletin* [Société Jersiaise], 11 (1928–31), 375–427 • J. A. Messervy, 'Liste des jurés-justiciers de la cour royale de Jersey, 1274–1665', *Annual Bulletin* [Société Jersiaise], 4 (1897–1901), 213–36 • *Diary and correspondence of John Evelyn*, ed. W. Bray, new edn, ed. [J. Forster], 4 vols. (1850–52), vol. 3 • G. R. Balleine, *A biographical dictionary of Jersey*, [1] [1948] • P. Falle, *An account of the isle of Jersey* (1694) • J. R. Tanner, ed., *A descriptive catalogue of the naval manuscripts in the Pepysian Library at Magdalene College, Cambridge*, 1, Navy RS, 26 (1903) • T. Baker, *Caesarea: the island of Jersey* (1840) • [P. Dumaresq], 'A survey of the island of Jersey', *Annual Bulletin* [Société Jersiaise], 12 (1932–5), 415–46
Archives BL, corresp. with John Evelyn, Add. MS 15857, fols. 225–7 • BL, corresp. with Christopher, Lord Hatton, Add. MS 29560, fols. 108, 212, 318 • BL, letters to William Trumbull

Du Maurier [*married name* Browning], **Dame Daphne** (**1907–1989**), novelist, was born on 13 May 1907 at 24 Cumberland Terrace, Regent's Park, London, the second of three daughters (there were no sons) of Sir Gerald Hubert Edward Busson *Du Maurier (1873–1934), actor–manager, and his wife, Muriel (1881–1957), actress, daughter of Harry Beaumont, solicitor. She was educated mainly at home by governesses (of whom one, Maud Waddell, was highly influential) and afterwards spent three terms at a finishing school near Paris. She began writing stories and poetry in her childhood and was encouraged by her father, with whom she had a very close relationship. He longed for her to emulate her grandfather, George *Du Maurier, artist and author of three novels, including the best-selling *Trilby* (1894). But the circumstances of her upbringing, with its constant emphasis on pleasure and distraction, called for self-discipline of a kind she did not manage to exert until she was twenty-two, when she finally completed several short stories. The first published story was 'And now to God the Father', which appeared in *The Bystander* (May 1929), a magazine edited by her uncle. It was a cynical view of society as she saw it. Her ambition then was to write a novel, and she settled down to do so in the winter of 1929–30 at Bodinnick by Fowey in Cornwall, where her parents had bought Ferryside to be their country home. Here she wrote *The Loving Spirit*, the story of four generations of a Cornish family, which was published to considerable acclaim by Heinemann in February 1931. She immediately wrote second and third novels which confounded expectations by differing radically from her first, but it was her fourth book, *Gerald*, a frank biography of her father, written when he died in 1934, which made the greatest impact. It was published by Victor Gollancz, with whom she then began a long and fruitful partnership. Gollancz recognized that her strengths lay in narrative drive and the evocation of atmosphere. He encouraged her to develop these and the result was *Jamaica Inn* (1936), an instant best-seller. At this point in her career she was obliged, as an army wife, to go abroad, to Egypt, with her husband, Major Frederick Arthur Montague (Boy) *Browning (1896–1965), the son of Frederick Henry Browning. Boy Browning ran various businesses and also worked for MI5, and had a distinguished army career as well. They had married in 1932 and in 1933 had a daughter, Tessa, who later married, as her second husband, the son of the first Viscount Montgomery of Alamein.

This was a deeply unhappy period in Daphne Du Maurier's life—she was an untypical army wife, being very anti-social, and she loathed Egypt and was profoundly homesick—but it produced *Rebecca* (1938). This was meant to be a psychological study of jealousy and was based on her own feelings of jealousy towards a former fiancée of her

Dame Daphne Du Maurier (1907–1989), by Bassano, 1930

husband's, Jan Ricardo, but it was hailed as a romantic novel in the tradition of *Jane Eyre*. She was astonished by the success of *Rebecca*—hardback copies in Britain alone passed the million mark in 1992—and mystified by the readers' interpretation of the novel. In 1941 she produced *Frenchman's Creek* and in 1943 *Hungry Hill*.

In 1943, while her husband was away fighting in the war, Daphne Du Maurier went to live in Cornwall with her three children, Tessa, her other daughter, Flavia (*b*. 1937), and her son, Christian (*b*. 1940). She took on the lease of Menabilly, near Par, a house (owned by the Rashleigh family) with which she had become obsessed. The war years affected her marriage deeply and adversely. She felt estranged from her husband, in spite of her love for him, and wrote a play, *The Years Between* (performed in 1944), about how war affected marriages. After the war her husband became comptroller of the household and treasurer to Princess Elizabeth, which meant that he lived in London while she stayed in Cornwall, with only weekends shared. This led to tensions which heavily influenced her work. Outwardly charming, witty, and light-hearted, she was struggling inwardly with feelings of rejection and uncertainty about her personal life. In *The Apple Tree* (1952) and *The Breaking Point* (1959), two collections of short stories of great biographical significance, she expressed the extent of her confusion and frustration. Her career flourished, though not precisely in the way she wished. *My Cousin Rachel* appeared in 1951. Her novels translated well

into films and *Jamaica Inn* (1939), *Rebecca* (1940), *Frenchman's Creek* (1944), and *Hungry Hill* (1946) were notable successes. Her short story *The Birds* became famous in the hands of Alfred Hitchcock in 1963. (Hitchcock had also directed Laurence Olivier and Joan Fontaine in *Rebecca*.) *Rebecca* had made her a popular, worldwide, best-selling author, but she felt her later, more serious, work was not given its due. In *The Scapegoat* (1957) she was writing at a deeper level, but the novel was treated as a romantic thriller. She turned to biography, partly in an attempt to show she could do serious work, though it was also true that she had temporarily lost the creative urge to write fiction. *The Infernal World of Branwell Brontë* (1960) gave her great satisfaction and was well researched, but it did little to alter her image.

In 1965 Daphne Du Maurier's husband died. Her grief, together with the distress caused by her fear that her imagination was deserting her, made her depressed. The news that she could not renew her lease on Menabilly again added to her misery but in 1969, the year in which she was made a DBE, she moved to Kilmarth in Par, Menabilly's dower house, where she wrote *The House on the Strand* (1969), which restored her confidence. Her last novel, *Rule Britannia* (1972), destroyed it again; she was unable to write any more fiction afterwards. In 1977 she wrote a slim volume of autobiography (*Growing Pains*), which she regretted producing. In 1981 she had a nervous breakdown and then a mild coronary. The last eight years of her life were spent mourning her lost talent, without which she felt her days were empty and meaningless.

Daphne Du Maurier was in her youth an extremely beautiful woman, of medium height, fine-boned and slender, with thick blonde hair and arresting eyes of a startlingly bright, clear blue. She was a very complex person, well aware, through constant self-analysis, that she acted out her life to an extraordinary degree. Her novels were her fantasies and seemed more real to her than her actual life. She needed them, to give expression to what she called, through her fascination with Jungian theory, her 'no. 2' self. This was a darker, violent self which she suppressed in a most determined manner. Part of this suppression was sexual: she believed she should have been born a boy and that she had to keep this masculine side of herself hidden, which she did, except while writing, for most of her life. The problem of her life she herself defined as 'a fear of reality'. Only when she was alone, and especially alone at Menabilly, was she able to still this fear. Her work has been consistently underrated, in spite of critical acknowledgement that *Rebecca* and *The Scapegoat*, at least, are of literary worth. Her influence on the growth of 'women's writing' as a separate division, and on writing for the cinema (eight of her novels and stories were made into successful films), was significant in the 1930s and 1940s, but it is as a popular novelist that her position remains secure, especially among the young. She died of heart failure at her home in Par, Cornwall, on 19 April 1989. She was cremated and her ashes were scattered at Kilmarth.　　MARGARET FORSTER, *rev.*

Sources M. Forster, *Daphne du Maurier* (1993) · priv. coll., Du Maurier MSS · personal knowledge (1996) · private information (1996) · P. Beer, 'Something about her eyes', *London Review of Books* (24 June 1993) [review]
Archives Princeton University, New Jersey, Ellen Doubleday collection, corresp. · priv. coll. | CUL, letters to Regis Bovis · JRL, corresp. with Basil Dean · U. Warwick Mod. RC, corresp. with Victor Gollancz · W. Yorks. AS, Bradford, notebooks on life of Branwell Brontë
Likenesses Bassano, photograph, 1930, NPG [*see illus.*] · photographs, Hult. Arch. · portrait, NPG
Wealth at death £467,992: probate, 21 Sept 1989, *CGPLA Eng. & Wales*

Du Maurier, George Louis Palmella Busson (1834–

1896), illustrator, cartoonist, and novelist, was born on 6 March 1834 at 80 Champs Elysées, Paris, and baptized in May 1835 at Rotherfield, Sussex, the eldest of the three children of Louis-Mathurin Busson Du Maurier (1797–1856) and his wife, Ellen Clarke (1797–1870). Louis-Mathurin Du Maurier, an improvident scientist and inventor, gave his son the name Palmella in a bid to attract the patronage of a Portuguese noble family. Louis-Mathurin was a Frenchman, Ellen Clarke an Englishwoman, and George Du Maurier's childhood was spent moving between France, England, and Belgium. This Anglo-French parentage set a pattern for the first part of his life and was to have a considerable effect on his future role as a satirist of Victorian middle- and upper-class society.

Family and education Du Maurier's paternal grandfather claimed that he was an aristocrat, exiled to England during the French Revolution. His name had, however, been Busson, and he came from a family of glass-blowers working in La Sarthe in northern France. George Du Maurier never knew the truth, which was discovered only in 1962 by his granddaughter, the novelist Daphne *Du Maurier. George Du Maurier's maternal grandmother, Mary-Anne Clarke, was a former lover of Frederick, duke of York, a son of George III. She had supplemented her income by selling military commissions, obtained through her lover, the commander-in-chief of the army. The money which she gained in a settlement from the duke eventually paid for George Du Maurier's art education. Du Maurier believed himself to be the grandson of the duke of York, but this, like his French aristocratic origins, was a fantasy. Mary-Anne Clarke did not meet the duke until after her daughter Ellen was born.

From 1835 to 1837 the Du Mauriers were living in Laeken, near Brussels, while Louis-Mathurin looked for work. In 1836, through Palmella influence, he became scientific adviser to the Portuguese embassy to Belgium. When he lost the post in 1837 the family lived in London for a time until, in 1839, the mother and children settled with Mary-Anne Clarke in Boulogne. Only in 1842 did they rejoin Louis-Mathurin in Paris where they lived in the village of Passy, then on the outskirts of the city. Du Maurier described these Passy years in his first novel, *Peter Ibbetson*, where he recalls his delight in the old Bois de Boulogne and in the park of St Cloud. Du Maurier later said that he had attended many schools. In Passy he was at the pension

George Louis Palmella Busson Du Maurier (1834–1896), self-portrait, *c.*1856

Pelieu, and in 1847 he enrolled at the pension Froussard in the avenue Bois de Boulogne. This involved a move away from Passy and into the city, where the Du Mauriers lived in the rue du Bac. The pension Froussard, thinly disguised, is the subject of the opening chapters of Du Maurier's third novel, *The Martian*.

Du Maurier failed the *baccalauréat* in 1851 but, at his father's insistence, he travelled to London in the same year to begin a scientific training at the Birkbeck Chemical Laboratory of University College, London. After two years there, his father set him up in his own laboratory for scientific analysis in Barge Yard, Bucklersbury. Du Maurier received only two commissions, one for the analysis of deposits in a Devonian mine, a post which came to an abrupt end when he declared that there was no gold. Du Maurier described this experience in a short story, 'Recollections of an English Goldmine', published in *Once a Week* in 1861.

On the death of his father in 1856, Du Maurier thankfully abandoned science and England, returning to Paris to become an art student. He had shown a talent for drawing from early childhood and was known for his sketches of people he met. From 1852 he had been drawing from classical sculpture in the British Museum. He now enrolled at the atelier of Charles Gleyre, later known as the master of several impressionist painters. Du Maurier lived at home with his mother and sister, first in the faubourg Poissonnière and then in Passy. He shared a studio with a group of English artists, Thomas Armstrong, Edward Poynter, and Thomas Reynolds Lamont. Among their friends was the American painter James McNeill Whistler. During this period Du Maurier sold a small oil painting of a scene from Walter Scott's *Rob Roy*, made a number of drawings from the life at Gleyre's atelier, and sketched his friends in the studio. This artist life in Paris was to provide the background of his second novel, *Trilby*.

In 1857 Du Maurier left Paris for Antwerp where he enrolled at the Academy of Fine Arts under the tuition of Jacob Van Lerius, the professor of painting. The reasons for Du Maurier's move are not clear but he evidently believed that the Antwerp academy had more to offer a young painter. An oil painting of an old woman with a young boy in her lap, known only from a friend's drawing, suggests that he was now working in a realist style. Du Maurier had been three or four months in Antwerp when, during a session in the life class, he suddenly lost the sight of his left eye, almost certainly as the result of a detached retina. He moved to Malines and received treatment from a Jesuit priest who practised as an oculist in Louvain. Du Maurier had formed a friendship with another Antwerp art student, Felix Moscheles, son of the pianist, composer, and teacher Ignaz Moscheles, and Moscheles's account of life in Malines in his *In Bohemia with George Du Maurier* supplements Du Maurier's own version in *The Martian*.

The loss of sight in his left eye altered the course of Du Maurier's life. He understood that he could not risk the remaining eye by continuing his career as a painter, and he turned instead to work as an artist in black and white. In 1859 he moved to Düsseldorf in order to consult another doctor, Hofrath de Leeuwe. Once there, he became a student at the Düsseldorf Academy, to which Thomas Armstrong had also transferred. After a year Du Maurier returned to London, drawn by rumours of a demand for illustrators for books and magazines. He had also met his sister's friend Emma Wightwick (1840/41–1915), whom he was to marry on 3 January 1863, and the fact that she lived in London was another inducement to return there.

Book illustrations In London, Du Maurier discovered that it was far more difficult than he had expected to find work. The development in black and white illustration which is generally associated with the 1860s was already underway, and a number of other artists, among them John Everett Millais, Frederick Sandys, and Frederick Walker, had established a firm hold on the most prestigious illustrated magazines of the period and on the *Cornhill Magazine* in particular. Du Maurier's first published woodcuts were accepted by Mark Lemon, the editor of *Punch*, and, between 1860 and 1864, he slowly began to establish himself on other magazines, among them *Once a Week*, *London Society*, the *Cornhill*, and the *Leisure Hour*. Having imagined that drawing for the woodblock would be easy, Du Maurier was shocked to have an illustration turned down. He then took advice from Frederick Sandys who told him to draw everything from life and not from the imagination and to create detailed landscapes for out of door scenes. The immediate result was Du Maurier's fine drawings for *The Notting Hill Mystery* and *Santa, or, A Woman's Tragedy* by the author of *Agnes Tremorne*, both published in *Once a Week* in 1862 and 1863.

Du Maurier continued to work as an illustrator for the rest of his life, although the volume of such work declined in the 1880s and 1890s. The best of his drawings were almost all made in the 1860s and, between 1863 and 1867, he worked on an eight-volume collected edition of the novels and stories of Elizabeth Gaskell, a novelist whom he particularly admired. Taken together, they probably represent his finest achievement as an illustrator of books. Among the other authors whose work he illustrated were Shirley Brooks, *Sooner or Later* (1868); Wilkie Collins, for whom he worked on four reissues, including *The Moonstone* and *The Frozen Deep*, in 1875; Thomas Hardy, *The Hand of Ethelberta* (*Cornhill Magazine*, 1875, and book publication, 1877) and *A Laodicean* (*Harper's Magazine*, 1880–81); Douglas Jerrold, *The Story of a Feather* (1867); George Meredith, *The Adventures of Harry Richmond* (*Cornhill Magazine*, 1870–71); Florence Montgomery, *Misunderstood* (1874); Margaret Oliphant, six stories and novels (*Cornhill Magazine*, 1868–76); Adelaide Proctor, *Legends and Lyrics: Second Series* (1866); Charles Reade and Dion Boucicault, *Foul Play* (*Once a Week*, 1867, and book publication, 1868); Anne Thackeray Ritchie, 'Sola' (*Cornhill Magazine*, 1869); and W. M. Thackeray, *Henry Esmond* (1868) and *Ballads* (1879).

Cartoons After publishing a number of cartoons and initial letters in the magazine, Du Maurier became a regular member of the *Punch* staff after the death of John Leech in 1864. He held the post of social cartoonist from then until his death thirty-two years later. In all he contributed over three thousand cartoons at the rate of two a week with around ten more each year for the *Punch Almanack*. Many of Du Maurier's cartoons were aimed at the vagaries of fashion and at the idiocies of social behaviour. His admiration for the satirical writing of Thackeray had a large effect upon his work as a cartoonist, and, as someone who had lived abroad for many years, Du Maurier had, at least initially, the eye of an outsider.

Du Maurier's regular cartoon characters, such as the *nouveau riche* Sir Gorgius Midas, the snobbish Lady Clara Robinson, *née* Vere de Vere, and the hostesses Mrs Ponsonby de Tomkyns and Mrs Lyon Hunter, move in high society, which he presented as self-seeking and pretentious. Like his father, George Du Maurier was a talented amateur singer, and, in the *Music at Home* series, he directed his satire at manipulative hostesses who tried to capture the best performers at no expense to themselves, or at inattentive audiences who talked through the music. The *Music at Home* drawings clearly reflected some personal experiences.

Another large group of cartoons was concerned with middle-class domestic life, giving a humorous view of relations between husbands and wives, parents and children, and employers and servants, or making jokes at the expense of fathers and mothers trying to find husbands for their daughters. Du Maurier's own family and friends supplied him with many situations and phrases and his children and huge St Bernard, Chang, were regular characters in these cartoons.

Du Maurier was not a religious man, and those of his cartoons that deal with the theories of Charles Darwin are light-hearted rather than disturbing. For him evolutionary theory was not a source of anxiety but of stimulation.

In his later years, however, Du Maurier found some changes in behaviour and practice distasteful. He took up the subject of the 'new woman' in a series of patronizing attacks on women who turned to writing or who entered the professions.

Unlike the political cartoonists, whose subjects were decided at the weekly staff dinner, Du Maurier had to think of his jokes himself, and he was often grateful to friends, and Canon Alfred Ainger in particular, for suggesting ideas to him. For his cartoons, both for *Punch* and, in the 1880s and 1890s, for *Harper's Magazine*, Du Maurier relied heavily upon the caption. In some cases, the caption *is* the joke, as in the long series entitled *Things One Would Rather Have Left Unsaid*, where the humour lies in the embarrassing *faux pas*. Not many of Du Maurier's *Punch* drawings are intrinsically funny although, in conjunction with the caption, the comedy of the drawing frequently becomes apparent. The most famous of Du Maurier's cartoons, *True Humility* of 9 November 1895 (better known as *The Curate's Egg*) wittily contrasts an obsequious 1890s curate with a hawkish old-style bishop. The sharply turned caption reads:

> Right Reverend Host. 'I'm afraid you've got a bad egg, Mr. Jones!' The Curate. 'Oh no, my Lord, I assure you! Parts of it are excellent!'

The typical Du Maurier cartoon is a small picture, very detailed and carefully structured. A small man himself, Du Maurier particularly liked tall statuesque men and, more particularly, women. Many of his cartoon characters have a classical dignity which suggests the painter he might have become. Those cartoons that have no captions are usually lyrical or nostalgic, often scenes involving his family on holiday in Whitby, a seaport that he loved. These were fine drawings and not in any real sense *Punch* cartoons.

The development of aestheticism in the later 1870s and 1880s gave Du Maurier a perfect subject for some of his sharpest and most successful cartoons. He greatly disliked the affectations of the aesthetes, often showing them in juxtaposition to true blue British characters. His target was what he regarded as their effeminacy and absurdity. There was a regular aesthetic clientele, Mrs Cimabue Brown, the hostess, and her acolytes, Maudle the painter and Postlethwaite the poet. A few of the aesthetic cartoons are clearly aimed at the musical titles that James Whistler, Du Maurier's former friend, gave to his pictures.

Du Maurier was the father of five children, born between 1864 and 1873. The fifth, Gerald *Du Maurier, was to become famous as an actor–manager. Du Maurier began his married life at 91 Great Russell Street in London, moving to 12 Earls Terrace in Kensington in 1868. From 1869 the family were living in Hampstead, with which Du Maurier is particularly associated. Having rented a number of houses there, the Du Mauriers settled at 27 Church Row in 1870, before moving to New Grove House in 1874. For George Du Maurier, Hampstead was a second Passy, and Hampstead Heath, seen in many of his cartoons, was a new Bois de Boulogne. More remote from London then

than now, Hampstead also set Du Maurier outside the social world with which so many of his cartoons were concerned, reinforcing his role as an outsider.

Du Maurier retained an air of youthfulness well into middle age, partly as a result of his short stature and boyish face. His own features sometimes appear in his *Punch* cartoons, and he painted at least three self-portraits, two when he was in his twenties and one, now in the National Portrait Gallery, London, around 1879–80. There is an oil portrait of 1882 by his friend John Millais in the MacDonald collection of artists' portraits, now in the Aberdeen Art Gallery.

Writings Du Maurier's remaining eye occasionally troubled him, but he was able to continue working, and even, in the 1880s, painted a number of watercolours for exhibition, including the portrait of Canon Ainger of 1881 in the National Portrait Gallery, London. However, by the late 1880s Du Maurier's sight began to show signs of failing. This helped to trigger his decision to seek alternative means of earning a living. He published two articles on illustration from the artist's point of view in the *Magazine of Art* for 1890, and prepared a lecture, 'Social pictorial satire', which he gave on several occasions. It was eventually published as a book in 1898, after his death. A number of his original drawings were sold at three exhibitions held at the Fine Art Society in 1884, 1887, and 1895. The catalogue introduction for the 1884 show was by Henry James.

Most important of all, Du Maurier turned to fiction. He had intermittently published poems and satirical stories in *Punch*, including his Pre-Raphaelite parody *A Legend of Camelot* of 1866 and an aesthetic skit, 'Rise and Fall of the Jack Sprats' of 1878. In March 1889 Du Maurier offered his close friend Henry James the plot of a novel which he had conceived, and which eventually became *Trilby*. In response James suggested that Du Maurier should write the book himself. Du Maurier returned home and completed the opening chapters of a different novel, *Peter Ibbetson*. This, probably the best of his books, sets an account of his own Passy childhood into a supernatural story. A couple meet in dreams after they are separated in life. Like all of Du Maurier's novels it is illustrated by the author himself. The comparative success of *Peter Ibbetson* encouraged Du Maurier to write a second novel, *Trilby*. Parisian student days gave him a background for the first part of the novel, which concludes, like *Peter Ibbetson*, with supernatural events. Here the musician Svengali mesmerizes a tone-deaf Irish model, Trilby O'Ferrall, who becomes a world-famous singer.

The popularity of *Trilby*, which gave two expressions (the trilby hat and Svengali) to the English language, overwhelmed and exhausted Du Maurier, particularly after the book was adapted into a play and produced by Herbert Beerbohm Tree at the Haymarket Theatre, with Gerald Du Maurier playing the minor role of Dodor. The novel nearly plunged George Du Maurier into a libel suit. The initial serialization in *Harper's Magazine* included a character, Joe Sibley, who was clearly drawn from James Whistler. Whistler threatened to sue, and the passages and most of the illustrations in which he appeared were removed before publication in book form. Du Maurier wrote a third novel, *The Martian*, again using the formula of mingled autobiography and science fiction, but the book, which began serialization only in the month of his death, was weaker than its two predecessors.

Du Maurier moved from Hampstead to 17 Oxford Square, Paddington, in 1895. His health was failing and it was hoped that life would be easier in London. The move was not a success, however, and he died at home of heart disease on 8 October 1896. The following day he was cremated at Woking, an unusual choice which aroused comment. On 13 October the ashes were interred in the graveyard of Hampstead parish church.   LEONÉE ORMOND

Sources L. Ormond, *George Du Maurier* (1969) • *The young George Du Maurier: a selection of his letters, 1860–67*, ed. D. Du Maurier (1951) • E. V. Lucas, 'George Du Maurier at thirty-three', *Cornhill Magazine*, [3rd] ser., 150 (1934), 385–410 • F. Moscheles, *In Bohemia with Du Maurier* (1896) • *CGPLA Eng. & Wales* (1896) • T. M. Wood, *George du Maurier: the satirist of the Victorians* (1913) • C. C. H. Millar, *George du Maurier and others* (1937) • D. P. Whiteley, *George du Maurier: his life and work* (1948) • T. Armstrong, 'Reminiscences of George Du Maurier', *Thomas Armstrong C.B.: a memoir*, ed. L. M. Lamont (1912), 111–67 • d. cert. • private information (2004)

Archives Hunt. L., letters • Morgan L., corresp., literary MSS, and papers • V&A NAL, letters | Dorset County Museum, Dorchester, letters to Thomas Hardy • FM Cam., letters to Burne-Jones • JRL, holograph article, possibly with author's corrections and editor's markings, submitted to M. H. Spielmann, *The illustrating of books from the serious artist's point of view* • Man. City Gall., letters relating to the setting up and running of Manchester Art Museum • NL Scot., letters to *Cornhill Magazine* • Sheff. Arch., letters to first earl of Wharncliffe • U. Glas., corresp. with J. A. M. Whistler

Likenesses G. Du Maurier, self-portrait, oils, *c.*1856, priv. coll. [*see illus.*] • G. Du Maurier, self-portrait, watercolour, *c.*1856, priv. coll.; repro. in Ormond, *George du Maurier*, pl. 1 • G. Du Maurier, self-portrait, oils, *c.*1879, NPG • H. Furniss, pen-and-ink drawings, *c.*1880–1910, NPG • J. E. Millais, oils, 1882, Aberdeen Art Gallery • W. & D. Downey, photographs, woodburytype, 1891, NPG; repro. in W. Downey and D. Downey, *The cabinet portrait gallery*, 2 (1891) • E. J. Sullivan, pen-and-ink drawing, 1891, NPG • Elliott & Fry, cabinet photograph, NPG • Spy [L. Ward], caricature, watercolour study, NPG; repro. in *VF* (23 Jan 1896) • woodcut, BM

Wealth at death £47,555 6s. 7d.: probate, 17 Nov 1896, *CGPLA Eng. & Wales*

Du Maurier, Sir Gerald Hubert Edward Busson (1873–1934), actor and theatre manager, was born on 26 March 1873 at 27 Church Row, Hampstead, London, the last and fifth child of George Louis Palmella Busson *Du Maurier (1834–1896), artist and writer, and his wife, Emma Wightwick (1840/41–1915). His father, celebrated *Punch* artist and author of *Trilby*, was of Anglo-French parentage and settled in England during the early 1860s. Gerald was a born actor and when a boy he often dressed up as various characters to pose for his father's drawings. After leaving Harrow School, where he was a popular mimic rather than a keen scholar, he took to amateur acting as relief from a short-lived office job. His father, reluctantly, used influence to get him into John Hare's company at the Garrick, where he made his professional début playing a waiter in Sydney Grundy's *The Old Jew* (6 January 1894). His apprenticeship continued with Johnston Forbes-Robertson and

Sir Gerald Hubert Edward Busson Du Maurier (1873–1934), by Howard Coster, 1930s

Herbert Beerbohm Tree, under whom he spent four years. He then joined a company run by the formidable Mrs Patrick Campbell (1899–1901), who set the seal on both his professional and his sentimental education.

A long and fruitful association with J. M. Barrie began in 1902. As Ernest Woolley in *The Admirable Crichton*, Du Maurier achieved West End renown; he also married a fellow member of the cast, Muriel Beaumont (1881–1957), on 11 April 1903, at St Peter's Church, Cranley Gardens, Kensington. They set up house at 5 Chester Place, Regent's Park, subsequently moving in days of prosperity (from 1916) to the more spacious Cannon Hall, Hampstead. The Barrie connection continued with *Peter Pan* (1904), his professional avidity for plum parts inspiring him to double Hook and Darling, and with *What Every Woman Knows* (1908). Perhaps his best interpretation was that of the failed artist Dearth in Barrie's *Dear Brutus* (1917). Besides other Barrie ventures he delighted audiences as the gentleman thief in *Raffles* (1906); as the gentleman burglar in *Arsène Lupin* (1909); and as the gentleman adventurer in *Bull-Dog Drummond* (1921).

From 1910 to 1925, in partnership with Frank Curzon, Du Maurier managed Wyndhams Theatre, after which he joined Gilbert Miller at the St James's Theatre to direct and star in Frederick Lonsdale's *The Last of Mrs Cheyney* (1925), among others. With him in the cast was Gladys Cooper, one of his earlier discoveries, and he teamed up with her at the Playhouse in H. M. Harwood's *Cynara* (1930). His other leading ladies included Tallulah Bankhead (*The Dancers*, 1924), Gracie Fields (*SOS*, 1928), and Gertrude Lawrence (*Behold we Live*, 1932). Among his greatest triumphs were Edgar Wallace's *The Ringer* (1926) and *The Green Pack* (1932), which both owed as much to his directorial stagecraft as they did to Wallace's gift for suspense. The four disappointing films he made at the end of his career arose from financial necessity and the demands of the Inland Revenue. He was knighted in 1922.

Apart from brief military service in 1918, the theatre was Du Maurier's life and he could never have envisaged any other career than that of actor. He was also a gifted director, as he proved in his collaboration with Edgar Wallace and with his brother Guy in the latter's drama *An Englishman's Home* (1915). Except for an American tour with Beerbohm Tree early on and a few trips into the provinces, Gerald remained very much the Londoner, an ornament of the West End stage and a leading light of the Garrick Club. He was a naturally gifted performer who never attended drama school and who owed his technique to intuition and observation. He lacked conventional good looks and never appeared in the great Shakespearian roles and other classic parts, preferring to transform generally mediocre plays with his personal flair. To those who criticized him for 'always being himself' in performance, James Agate retorted that Du Maurier was 'himself in a way that what he put on stage was an urgent, heightened, theatrical presentation of *Geraldism*' (Agate, 183). Reacting against the flamboyant claptrap of *monstres sacrés* such as Beerbohm Tree, he introduced a revolutionary, naturalistic style more in tune with everyday life. This deceptively easy technique, much imitated by the less talented, grew from long solitary rehearsals in front of a looking-glass perfecting each phrase and polishing such banal details as lighting a cigarette or pouring a drink. Although he seemed to 'throw away' lines, his attack, precision, and audibility remained impeccable. Mercurial, easily bored, something of a Peter Pan himself, he loathed the thought of growing old and no longer being able to charm young women. Daphne *Du Maurier, second of his three daughters, later became a best-selling novelist and playwright; it has been rumoured, though not proved, that he regarded her with rather more than paternal affection. He died of cancer on 11 April 1934 at 20 Devonshire Place, London, and was buried a week later, on 18 April, in the family grave in Hampstead parish church graveyard.

JAMES HARDING

Sources J. Harding, *Gerald Du Maurier* (1989) • D. Du Maurier, *Gerald: a portrait* (1934) • J. Gielgud, J. Miller, and J. Powell, *An actor and his time* (1979) • J. Agate, *Ego 6: once more the autobiography of James Agate* (1944) • G. Fields, *Sing as we go* (1960) • S. Morley, *Gladys Cooper* (1979) • private information (2004)
Archives FILM BFI NFTVA, news footage
Likenesses H. Furniss, pen-and-ink drawing, before 1905, NPG • J. Collier, oils, 1922, Hampstead town hall, London • E. Kapp, drawing, 1928, Barber Institute of Fine Arts, Birmingham • H. Coster, photograph, 1930–34, NPG [*see illus.*] • E. Burra, ink drawing, 1932, NPG • C. A. Buchel, oils, Garr. Club • C. A. Buchel & Hassall, lithograph, NPG • H. Coster, photographs, NPG • Foulsham & Banfield, photograph, NPG • C. Harris, photograph, NPG • A. John, oils, Park-Bernet Gallery, New York • Spy [L. Ward], caricature, Hentschel-colourtype, repro. in *VF* (25 Dec 1907)
Wealth at death £17,996 4*s.* 3*d.*: resworn probate, 5 July 1934, CGPLA Eng. & Wales

Dumbarton. For this title name *see* Douglas, George, earl of Dumbarton (*c.*1636–1692).

Dumbleton, John (*d.* 1349?), natural philosopher, may well have hailed from the ancient Cotswold village of Dumbleton in Gloucestershire. By 1338 he was a fellow of Merton College, Oxford, and, despite having been named as one of the original fellows of Queen's College in 1341, he was still at Merton in 1347; he may have died of the plague in 1349. Before that he had spent some time at the Sorbonne in Paris studying theology, perhaps in 1345–6; this would have been part of the course for the degree of bachelor in sacred theology, with which he is credited in a manuscript of one of his works.

Only two works can be ascribed with any certainty to Dumbleton. One, known as the *Compendium sex conclusionum* (edited in Weisheipl, 'Early fourteenth-century physics', 392–9), was designed to explicate six conclusions on circular motion found in Part IV of Thomas Bradwardine's influential *Tractatus de proportionibus*. It restricts itself to the geometrical as opposed to the kinematic parts of these, and if anything serves to obfuscate rather than elucidate Bradwardine's intent. It may be taken as a sign (supported in other parts of the corpus) of Dumbleton's limited powers of mathematical insight and penetration, especially when compared with such Mertonian natural philosophers as Bradwardine himself and Richard Swineshead. The only known manuscript may be in the hand of the noted Parisian scholar, Themo Judei, and seems to have been written in 1348.

Dumbleton's major work was the huge *Summa logicae et philosophiae naturalis* (Vatican City, Biblioteca Apostolica Vaticana, MS Vat. lat. 6750, and other MSS). Verbatim correspondences between opinions rejected by Dumbleton, but upheld in William Heytesbury's *Regulae solvendi sophismata* of 1335, make it fairly clear that the *Summa* was subsequent to that work, and probably it should be dated to the 1340s. Dumbleton was very consciously composing a *summa*, forming, as he said, a bundle of scattered ears of corn ('quandam summam, veluti spicarum dispersarum manipulum'), and in the textually corrupt prologue (edited in Weisheipl, 'Early fourteenth-century physics', 401–8) he seems to be taking a sideswipe at those colleagues who would multiply sophistical opinions for the sheer delight of it. Dumbleton's aim was instead to give an account of the natural world that was coherent and realistic (in the non-technical sense of that term, for philosophically he veered towards nominalism); and in general he eschewed talking of situations that were merely imaginary and not even approximately realized in practice.

Part 1 of the *Summa* concerns logic, and treats of such customary topics as the signification of terms, what it is to be better known to ourselves and to nature, universals and particulars, and *insolubilia*; but interestingly

Dumbleton also includes a section on the intension and remission of knowledge and doubt with respect to the evidence available. In this he uses language more often to be found in late medieval discussions of the intensities of qualities and motions, and Dumbleton himself applies it in this way later in the treatise. How original he was in extending it to epistemological issues must await further investigation.

The subject matter of parts 2–9 is natural philosophy, and, as Dumbleton himself indicates, parallels (but not completely) five works by Aristotle, *Physics*, *De coelo*, *De generatione et corruptione*, *Meteorologica*, and *De anima*. Special attention is understandably given to issues of the moment, and in the early parts, especially, many disputed questions are discussed. In what may be regarded as his updating of Aristotle, Dumbleton has a particular eye to the quantitative, and in this he usually displays an abstractionist attitude, in which the mathematical properties are firmly rooted in physical objects. An exception occurs in part 9, when he discusses the status of the lines, angles, and geometrical figures employed by writers on geometrical optics: he allows them minimal physical reality, and instead sees them as useful fictions for calculating where an object seen by reflection or refraction would appear.

In his discussions of motion in part 3 of the *Summa*, Dumbleton accepts Thomas Bradwardine's quantitative law of motion relating speeds to forces and resistances, which (understandably in the context of the time) he regards as the position of Aristotle and Averroes (Ibn Rushd). Dumbleton's proof of what has come to be called the 'Merton rule', which equates a uniformly accelerated motion with a uniform motion at the speed which the former has at half-time, deploys procedures akin to those used in the ancient geometrical method of exhaustion, and is at variance with his general lack of mathematical acumen noted above; it may reasonably be concluded that he took this from another source. On the vexed question of the continuance of projectile motion after contact with the original mover has been lost, Dumbleton appeals to an overriding form of natural motion in which bodies might move against their own particular nature in order that they remain in contact with other bodies and thus avoid a vacuum. In this he might be seen as in a tradition developing from Roger Bacon (*d.* 1294), but, curiously, when (in another context) he mentions Bacon by name, it is simply as 'unus qui Bakun cognominatur' ('one who is called Bacon').

Although Dumbleton did not acquire in Italy or elsewhere on the continent the fame that accrued to William Heytesbury or Richard Swineshead, the number of extant manuscripts (at least twenty-one) of his *Summa* testifies to a considerable, if largely local, influence, and at least one work by the later fourteenth-century writer John Chilmark was explicitly based on part of Dumbleton's treatise.   GEORGE MOLLAND

Sources J. A. Weisheipl, 'Ockham and some Mertonians', *Mediaeval Studies*, 30 (1968), 163–213 • E. D. Sylla, 'The Oxford calculators and mathematical physics: John Dumbleton's *Summa logicae et philosophiae naturalis*, Parts II and III', *Physics, cosmology and astronomy, 1300–1700: tension and accommodation*, ed. S. Unguru (1991), 129–61 • J. A. Weisheipl, 'The place of John Dumbleton in the Merton School', *Isis*, 50 (1959), 439–54 • J. A. Weisheipl, 'Early fourteenth-century physics of the Merton "School" with special reference to Dumbleton and Heytesbury', DPhil diss., U. Oxf., 1956 • Emden, *Oxf.*, 1.603 • A. G. Molland, 'John Dumbleton and the status of geometrical optics', *Actes du XIIIe Congrès International d'Histoire des Sciences* [Moscow 1971], 3–4 (Moscow, 1974), 125–30; repr. in A. G. Molland, *Mathematics and the medieval ancestry of physics* (1995) • M. Clagett, *The science of mechanics in the middle ages* (1959) • J. A. Weisheipl, 'Repertorium Mertonense', *Mediaeval Studies*, 31 (1969), 174–224 • W. J. Courtenay, *Schools and scholars in fourteenth-century England* (1987) • A. Maier, *Zwei Grundprobleme der Scholastischen Naturphilosophie*, 2nd edn (1951) • P. Duhem, 'Roger Bacon et l'horreur du vide', *Roger Bacon: essays*, ed. A. G. Little (1914), 241–84 • H. Hugonnard-Roche, *L'oeuvre astronomique de Thémon Juif, maître parisien du XIVe siècle* (1973)

Archives Biblioteca Apostolica Vaticana, Vatican City, MS Vat. lat. 6750; and MSS

Dumbreck, Sir David (1805–1876), army medical officer, the only son of Thomas Dumbreck, collector of Inland Revenue in Kincardine O'Neil, Aberdeenshire, and his wife, Elizabeth, youngest daughter of David Sutherland of the same service, was born in Kincardine O'Neil, on 25 October 1805. He was educated at the University of Edinburgh, where he graduated MD in 1830, having previously, in 1825, passed as a licentiate of the Royal College of Surgeons of Edinburgh.

Dumbreck entered the army as a hospital assistant on 3 November 1825. He became assistant surgeon in 1826, surgeon in 1841, surgeon-major in 1847, and deputy inspector-general on 28 March 1854. Prior to the outbreak of the Crimean War he was sent on a special mission early in 1854 to the expected theatre of war to assess the medical problems it might present. He traversed Serbia, Bulgaria, and part of Romania, crossing the Balkans on his route. In his report he warned of the problems the climate and endemic malaria could present, highlighting many of the difficulties that eventually dogged the British campaign.

Dumbreck was attached to the staff of the commander-in-chief, Lord Raglan, as a deputy inspector-general for much of the war, and was for a short time principal medical officer with the army. He was present at the time of the affair of Bulganac, the Alma, the capture of Balaklava, the battles of Balaklava and Inkerman, and the siege of Sevastopol. The efforts of Dumbreck and the other senior medical officers to alleviate the chronic health problems of the troops were unfortunately not successful in overcoming Raglan's ineptitude and conservatism. Dumbreck's rewards were a medal with four clasps, the fourth class of the Mejidiye, and the Turkish medal. He was gazetted CB on 4 February 1856, became KCB on 20 May 1871, and was named honorary physician to the queen on 21 November 1865.

After the cessation of hostilities Dumbreck served as principal medical officer in Cape Town. On 19 July 1859 he was promoted to be an inspector-general of the medical department, and on 1 May in the following year he was placed on half pay and received a special pension for distinguished services. He had married, on 27 February 1844, Elizabeth Campbell, only daughter of George Gibson of Leith, with whom he had a son. Dumbreck died at via Montebello 34, Florence, Italy, on 24 January 1876. He was survived by his wife.

G. C. BOASE, *rev.* PATRICK WALLIS

Sources *Hart's Army List* (1876), 593 · *ILN* (5 Feb 1876), 143 · *ILN* (15 April 1876), 383 · *BMJ* (5 Feb 1876), 179 · N. Cantlie, *A history of the army medical department*, 2 vols. (1974) · *Dod's Peerage* (1876) · *Nomina eorum, qui gradum medicinae doctoris in academia Jacobi sexti Scotorum regis, quae Edinburgi est, adepti sunt, ab anno 1705 ad annum 1845*, University of Edinburgh (1846) · Walford, *County families* · parish register, Aberdeenshire, Kincardine O'Neil, 25 Oct 1805 [birth]
Archives U. Nott. L., corresp. relating to hospitals (Scutari), etc. | Wellcome L., corresp. with Sir John Hall
Wealth at death £12,000: probate, 21 March 1876, *CGPLA Eng. & Wales*

Dumbuya, Alimami **Dala Muhammadu** [Dala Modu] (*c.*1760–1841), political leader in Sierra Leone, was born in Bambouk in the upper Senegal River region, the eldest son of Fenda Muhammadu Dumbuya and Mama Dalu of Bambouk. He was a member of the Dumbuya, one of the most distinguished merchant (*jula*) and military clans in western Africa. Fenda Muhammadu was a very successful merchant who had trade contacts from the interior to the Guinea coast, and some time during the 1770s Dala Muhammadu, known as Dala Modu, and his five brothers accompanied their father to Sumbuya kingdom in Guinea and settled at Bolobinneh (Conakry). Over a period of two decades they developed several villages and extensive agricultural plantations, and they facilitated long-distance trade in cattle, gold, hides, and other products.

Dala Modu attended local Muslim schools, became proficient in Arabic, and acquired great skill as a merchant. In 1794 he and his father visited Freetown, the British port at the mouth of the Sierra Leone River. They perceived that Freetown would become a major centre of trade, and in 1799 Dala Modu and sixty associates established Dalamodia on the eastern edge of Freetown. Quickly, he became a notable leader among Susu and other Mande immigrants and the main agent for trade with the interior. He assumed the title of *alimami* (ruler) of the Susu community. Although he had rendered mediation services to the British administration and had formed good relations with several British officials, he was suspected of supporting a local African uprising and was accused of being a dealer in slaves. After a formal hearing Dala Modu was expelled from Sierra Leone by Governor Thomas Ludlam, and on 22 November 1806 he acquired a location from the king of Kafu Bullom to build a new town, Madina (Lungi), across the river.

With Madina as his base, Dala Modu built several villages in Kafu Bullom and in the neighbouring kingdom of Loko, and established plantations for the production of rice, palm oil, cotton, tobacco, and other products. He also became an agent for Zachary Macaulay, a timber merchant and colonial official in Sierra Leone. He maintained his contacts with several important kingdoms and small

states in the northern hinterland and developed extensive trade networks. His plantations and import business provided a considerable quantity of foodstuffs, hides, timber, gold, horses, and other goods for the colony. Dala Modu was a notable patron of the Muslim community, and he provided the funds to build many mosques and schools and to support scholars and teachers. He continued to use the title *alimami* and was the most prominent leader among immigrant Africans in the colony of Sierra Leone.

After his resettlement at Madina, Dala Modu became the British administration's most important African representative in the Sierra Leone hinterland. He was a colonial mediator and a 'king-maker' in three nearby African states: Kafu Bullom (where he was the most powerful political leader), Loko (where he was regent from 1829 to 1838), and Port Loko (where he participated in the crowning of two rulers in 1825 and 1841). His most significant contribution in Sierra Leone affairs, however, was as a colonial negotiator with African rulers in the northern hinterland.

As Sierra Leone developed from a small British outpost to a robust colony, its relations with African states became increasingly crucial to its economic vitality. Alimami Dala Modu's ties of kinship, and political and economic connections in several northern states, made him particularly useful to the colony. In 1818, 1825, 1826, and 1827 he negotiated treaties for the British administration which expanded British interests and influence and which formed the basis for formal relations between Great Britain and west African rulers during the nineteenth century. In 1836 he convinced Lieutenant-Governor H. D. Campbell that, rather than use European merchants as intermediaries, African rulers would prefer to send their representative directly to Freetown to consult with colonial administrators; this method of communication had become common by 1850. In return for his many services, Dala Modu received rents on his properties under treaty with Sierra Leone, an annual stipend, and recognition as the principal leader of Mande immigrants from the northern hinterland.

Alimami Dala Modu died at the Dalamodia compound in Madina late in 1841, soon after negotiating an important treaty in Port Loko. His remains were buried in Madina. As the principal African representative for the colonial administration, his death at a crucial juncture in African affairs was a serious loss. In 1846 Thomas George Lawson was retained as the personal interpreter for Governor N. W. Macdonald to fill the gap left by Dala Modu's death. Lawson himself wrote about the important services rendered by Dala Modu and his successors in a report to the colonial administration on 24 July 1875.

DAVID E. SKINNER

Sources D. E. Skinner, *Thomas George Lawson: African historian and administrator in Sierra Leone* (1980) · D. E. Skinner, 'Mande settlement and the development of Islamic institutions in Sierra Leone', *International Journal of African Historical Studies*, 11 (1978), 32–62 · B. E. Harrell-Bond and others, *Community leadership and the transformation of Freetown, 1801–1976* (1978) · D. E. Skinner, interview with the elders of Madina (Lungi) Sierra Leone, 21 March 1976, Fourah Bay College Library, Freetown, Sierra Leone Collection [copy; original in author's possession] • Government interpreter's memoranda, 24 July 1875, Sierra Leone Archives, Freetown

Archives PRO, CO 267, 270, 879/35/411 | Sierra Leone Archives, Freetown, government interpreter T. G. Lawson memoranda

Du Mitand, Louis Huguenin (*b.* 1748, *d.* in or after 1816), educational writer, was born in Paris, the son of Huguenin Du Mitand. His father possessed an ample fortune, which he ultimately lost. Louis was educated for five years at a private academy in the rue de Montmartre, Paris, by 'the Pedantic, very Pedantic, and superlative Pedantic Mr L***', to whom he later waspishly dedicated his *New Treatise on the Method of Teaching Languages*. He was married in the Parisian church in which he had been baptized, but the name of his wife is not known.

About 1777 Du Mitand moved to London, where he made a living teaching Greek, Latin, French, and Italian according to the principles laid down in his *Plan d'une nouvelle méthode pour enseigner les langues*. This, his most successful work, was first published in London in 1778 and translated into English as *A New Treatise on the Method of Teaching Languages*. Du Mitand also printed for his pupils' use a Greek and Latin grammar; grammatical tables of French, English, Italian, Spanish, Portuguese, German, and Dutch; and several spelling books. By 1782 he was advertising 'genteel accommodation' in his house for eight boys who would be taught languages and also 'attended by capital masters in the different arts of Writing, Drawing, Dancing, Fencing, &c. for 100 Guineas a Year and 6 Guineas entrance' (Du Mitand, preface).

Du Mitand contributed a number of Latin verses on various public events to the *Morning Chronicle*, and printed these in 1780. He edited the eighth edition of John Palairet's *Abrégé sur les sciences et sur les arts*, printed in 1788, and published an improved edition of Abel Boyer's French–English dictionary in 1816. Nothing further is known of his life.   GORDON GOODWIN, *rev.* S. J. SKEDD

Sources L. Du Mitand, preface and dedication, *A new treatise on the method of teaching languages*, 4th edn (1782) • [J. Watkins and F. Shoberl], *A biographical dictionary of the living authors of Great Britain and Ireland* (1816)

Dummer, Edmund (*bap.* 1651, *d.* 1713), civil engineer, was baptized on 28 August 1651 at North Stoneham church, Southampton, the eldest of four sons born to Thomas Dummer (1626–1710), gentleman farmer of Chickenhall, in the parish of North Stoneham, and his wife, Joanne Newman. Serving his shipwright apprenticeship under John Tippetts at Portsmouth naval dockyard, he subsequently became a master carpenter at sea, appointed to HMS *Woolwich* in July 1682. During a period of service in the Mediterranean he made drawings of naval arsenals and ships seen. Subsequently, William III requested an account of these observations, especially those on the French use of fireships. (They are preserved as BL, King's MS 40.) On his return from sea Dummer became first assistant master shipwright at Chatham in 1686–9 before appointment to the Navy Board as assistant surveyor in 1689–92 and surveyor in 1692–9. In the last two offices he oversaw establishment of a naval dockyard at Plymouth, together with enlargement programmes to other naval dockyards, these works representing the largest civil engineering project of the century and resulting in his pioneering a number of innovatory ideas. Most important was his insistence on the use of stone and brick for many of the new structures. Previously the Navy Board had relied upon timber as the major building material, which resulted in high maintenance costs and was also a fire risk. The docks Dummer designed were stronger with more secure foundations and stepped sides that made it easier for men to work beneath the hull of a docked vessel. These innovations also allowed rapid erection of staging and greater workforce mobility. He discarded the earlier three-sectioned hinged gate, which was labour intensive in operation, and replaced it with the simpler and more mobile two-sectioned gate. He wished to ensure that naval dockyards were efficient working units that maximized available space, as evidenced by the simplicity of his design layout for Plymouth. He introduced a centralized storage area and a logical positioning of buildings, and his double rope-house combined the previously separate tasks of spinning and laying while allowing the upper floor to be used for the repair of sails. Another achievement was that he oversaw the raising and repairing of the 34-gun *St David* after that ship had, in November 1691, capsized and partially blocked Portsmouth harbour. In 1698 he headed a survey to identify a site for a third naval dockyard on the south coast, but the commission, which included members of Trinity House, concluded that no further yards should be built between Dover and Land's End. When in 1698 he laid charges of 'indirect practices' against Fitch, the main contractor undertaking building works at Portsmouth Dockyard, he faced a countercharge of soliciting bribes and was suspended from office with effect from Christmas eve 1698. Although his name was cleared by a court of inquiry and a civil court awarded him damages of £500, his career at the Navy Office was abruptly terminated. He was allowed the title and salary for 1699 but was not reinstated. He turned his attention to other matters. In December 1701 he became owner-manager of iron works at Sowley, near Lymington, Hampshire, and in 1702 he inaugurated a pioneering scheme that resulted in the first regular mail link between Britain and plantations in the West Indies. Despite government financial support, the project resulted in his falling heavily into debt. For this reason his father, in 1708, entrusted South Stoneham House into his hands with the intention that it should provide security for his debts. Loss of several of his ships from enemy action and natural hazards led to the government reviewing the mail contract in 1711 and his effects were seized by creditors. Although he was left with South Stoneham House, this had to be sold two years later when, upon his death, his wife, Sarah, paid off outstanding debts. In December 1713, a petition from Sarah and his only remaining daughter, Jane, who were close to destitution, was presented to the Navy Board. In the light of Dummer's earlier services as a civil engineer, they were granted a pension of £150 per annum.

PHILIP MacDOUGALL

Sources parish registers, Southampton, North Stoneham, 1640–1837 · parish registers, Southampton, South Stoneham, 1663–1837 · J. G. Coad, *The royal dockyards, 1690–1850* (1989) · J. M. Collinge, *Navy Board officials, 1660–1832* (1978) · A. W. Dickinson, 'The unfortunate Mr Dummer', *Hampshire: the county magazine* (Oct 1979), 66–8 · E. Dummer, 'A voyage into the Mediterranean', 1689, BL, King's MS 40 · A. J. Holland, *Ships of British oak* (1971) · J. H. Kemble, 'England's first Atlantic mail line', *Mariner's Mirror*, 26 (1940), 33–54, 185–98 · J. Vale, 'The lost houses of Southampton', 1980, Southampton Museum · BL, King's MS 40 · PRO, T1/167, no. 6 · PRO, ADM 7/810 · BL, Lansdowne MS 847 · BL, Harleian MS 4318
Archives BL, 'A voyage into the Mediterranean', King's MS 40 | BL, letters to Robert Harley
Wealth at death in debt; South Stoneham House was sold to meet debts

Du Moulin, Lewis (1605?–1680), physician and religious controversialist, was born in Paris, probably on 25 October 1605, the third but second surviving son of Pierre *Du Moulin (1568–1658) and his first wife, Marie Colignon (d. in or before 1622); Peter *Du Moulin (1601–1684) was his elder brother. After education at the Huguenot academy at Saumur, he was admitted to the University of Leiden on 8 July 1627, 'aged twenty-one'. He proceeded MD on 23 January 1630 with a thesis entitled 'De morbo acuto'. By March he was with his brother Peter in London. Over the next decade, during which on 10 October 1634 his MD was incorporated at Cambridge, he probably practised as a physician in London. Although on his own telling he was slow to acquire fluency in English, he took up the burning issues of the day and became an energetic controversialist.

Having published *Anatome missae* (1637), a translation of one of his father's anti-Catholic works, in 1639 Du Moulin 'wrote a piece in Latin against the corrupted party of the English hierarchy' (*Of the Right of Churches*, 1658, preface). Admitted a licenciate of the College of Physicians on 7 February 1640, on 20 November the following year he submitted to parliament a set of proposals, unanimously endorsed (he claimed) by the medical establishment. Showing a knowledge of local population and parish structure, these called for a small group of salaried doctors to serve Londoners in time of plague. His characteristically systematic thinking and grasp of context are also apparent in his other 'motions' to parliament of 1641, published anonymously as *Vox populi*. Its 'thirty-five' (actually thirty-four) clauses 'for reforming the present corrupt state of the Church' included proposals for a convocation of English, Scottish, and foreign divines, to include such men as James Ussher, John Prideaux, his uncle André Rivet, and his father, for synods working with and over bishops; and for a more equal and carefully chosen clerical estate. He admitted authorship in *Ludovici Molinaei … apologia* (1641), but adopted pseudonyms in many subsequent works such as *Sabbato dominica* (1643), in which he argued as Irenaeus Philalethes against a legalistic interpretation of the sabbath, and *Aytomaxia* (1643), in which as Irenaeus Philanax he staged a debate on church government between 'Religion' and 'Reason'. Reason conceded that both episcopacy and presbytery might be considered of divine institution, but rejected the notion that 'God himselfe did expresly prescribe the one or the other': he 'onely left generall rules as according unto which hee would have church government at all times either established or altered in respect of severall circumstances of persons, times and places' (*Aytomaxia*, 70). The primacy of human reasoning in church discipline was to be a fundamental of his polemical writing, and set him on a different tack from his father and his brother, but like them he wrote in the context of pan-European Reformed thought: Latin works like *Declaratio regnorum Angliae et Scotiae* (1645) paralleled Peter's attempts to mediate events in Britain to the continental Reformed community.

In his early search for preferment too, Du Moulin resembled others in his family. His petition to parliament for a college headship or professorship was recommended for acceptance on 4 August 1646. Reiterating his request on 2 April 1647 'for a place perhaps at Harts Hall or Mary Hall, joined with a prebend of Christ Church', he explained that it would 'afford him with more leisure and freedom from domestic employments to bend the force of his studies to the service of Church and State', especially 'to follow his intention of compiling a history of these times in Latin to justify the Parliament's proceedings for the better satisfaction of foreign nations' (*Sixth Report*, HMC, 167b). Finally inaugurated on 4 August 1648 to the Camden professorship in history at Oxford, in April 1649 he was voted a £100 annuity from money granted for the augmentation of ministers' and academics' salaries (a scheme he had himself promoted) and on 14 July his MD was incorporated at the university.

Du Moulin's pledge to public service was redeemed early in 1650 with *The Power of the Christian Magistrate in Sacred Things*, his justification for subscription to the engagement. Dedicated to the lords commissioners of the great seal, whom he thanked for their favours and to whom he apologized for his 'starke naked' English (sig. A2*v*v), it developed his earlier pragmatism and his suspicion of ecclesiastical jurisdiction into a distinctly Hobbesian position. Convinced that 'there cannot be in a well-composed state (and so doth Scripture teach us) more than one sovereign power' (p. 17) and that it was the magistrate's duty 'equally to order religion and civil government' (p. 59), he castigated the reformers who 'usurped power like Richard III' (pp. 84–5) in retaining the power of keys. Primary obedience was due to God, but Christian duty was not dependent on the magistrate; religion was essentially a matter of private conscience and the pastor's only weapons those of persuasion, counselling, and prayer. Thus, while episcopal and presbyterian systems both had some positive features, 'the meetings of the congregations of those called Independents' (p. 74) made the least disturbance to the peace of the state.

Academically Du Moulin was less adept at fulfilling the needs of the moment. Although he clearly knew English and French history, he was distracted by his medical practice in London and found his lectures, when he gave them, ill-attended. In dedicating to his friend the vice-chancellor, John Owen, *Oratio auspicalis*, his inaugural lecture belatedly published in 1652, he complained of the laziness of students and of general suspicion of foreigners. However, his nationality was addressed first by denization on 28 June 1655 and then naturalization, finally approved by Oliver Cromwell on 9 July 1657, and in the meantime he gained scholarly recognition, if not always approbation. Joseph Hall gave him a complimentary copy of his *Annales veteris testamenti* (1654), while the appearance of Du Moulin's *De fidei partibus in justificatione* (1653) inaugurated a short-lived confrontation and a long-standing correspondence with Richard Baxter, whose criticism of his work did not dint Du Moulin's respect and goodwill.

In *Paranesis ad aedificatores imperii in imperio* (1656), an answer to the celebrated Saumur professor Moïse Amyraut, dedicated to Cromwell and with a preface by Owen, and in *The Right of Churches* (1658), Du Moulin returned to the theme of authority. Aligning himself with, among others, Zwingli, Bullinger, and Jeremiah Burroughes, he favoured 'the legalistic theory of the state and the pietistic theory of the church' (Nobbs, *Theocracy*, 233). While the state was a unique coercive power, the church was brought together 'not by constraint … but with a ready mind' (*The Right of Churches*, 7), although he assumed a fundamental doctrinal consensus grounded in Reformed theology. Once again he did not explicitly reject episcopacy or presbyterianism, but since the existence of one national church was neither politically prudent nor spiritually sanctioned, 'private churches' were naturally preferred. In practice both works were read as attacks on presbyterianism, and as such met with a mixed response. Applause from the professor of ecclesiastical history at Leiden and from the elector palatine, who apparently offered Du Moulin a chair at Heidelberg, and grim satisfaction from Anthony Wood, were matched by disparagement from Utrecht professor Gisbertus Voetius. Baxter thought *Paranesis* 'a work unprofitable, tedious' and considered that Du Moulin had misunderstood what was at issue between presbyterians and Independents (Keeble and Nuttall, no. 387, 1.259). Unabashed, Du Moulin presented to parliament *Proposals and Reasons* (1659) for a new political and religious order, which incorporated suggestions for elections and for the composition of the council of state, as well as for enhanced clerical salaries, educational endowment, and foreign missionary work. Because the printer demanded a round number of pages, he included the summary of a plan to 'preserve Democracy and keep it from going back to Monarchy' through the introduction of equal inheritance among children (pp. 39–40).

At the Restoration, Du Moulin was ejected by the university visitors from his place at Oxford. Peter Du Moulin's plea to the king that summer for the transference to Lewis of the living at Llanrhaeadr, Denbighshire, that he had himself regained, was unsurprisingly rejected. With financial help from his brother, Lewis seems to have returned to his London medical practice, but he was not silenced. *Discours d'un bourgeois de Paris* (1665), an anonymous parallel French/English text exposing how the 'Empire of the Pope' had 'captivated the bodies of Monarchs and People' (p. 224), was followed by *Papa ultrajectinus* (1668), dedicated to Louis XIV's Huguenot secretary Henri Justel. A direct attack on Voetius's *Politica ecclesiastica*, it dismissed the Dutchman's claims for the political power of the church as even less plausible than those of the pope. When Du Moulin reiterated his arguments in *Jugulum causae* (1671), Voetius was finally provoked into furious reply. Baxter, a kinder critic, told Du Moulin in acknowledging his complimentary copy that his approach was inaccurate and that he had severely underrated divinely appointed pastoral power.

In 1669 Du Moulin discussed with Baxter a project more likely to find them in accord—a refutation of Jean Durel's *Vindication of the Church of England*, which had asserted the superiority of Anglican episcopacy over other forms of Reformed church discipline. Durel, who had married Du Moulin's kinswoman Marie de l'Angle, was a member of the circle of French conformist clergy in England who included Peter Du Moulin and Marie's brother Jean Maximilien de l'Angle. By this time the maverick Lewis was at odds with all of them, and Peter had withdrawn his financial support. When the answer to Durel appeared as *Patronus bonae fidei in causa puritanorum contra hierarchicos Anglos* (1672), it cost Lewis a spell of imprisonment. *La tyrannie des prejugez* (1678) saw him on the defensive against his sister Marie Du Moulin, his nephew Pierre Jurieu, and a phalanx of leading protestant ministers in France. Dedicated to Monsieur Menjot, Louis XIV's physician, it upheld the right of a medical man, 'd'une profession plus désintéressée & dégagée de tout prejugé' ('a profession more disinterested and unencumbered by prejudice'; sig. a4) to pronounce on ecclesiastical matters such as excommunication. Clearly wounded, with embarrassing directness Du Moulin upbraided his family, including his more prosperous brother, for their failure to grasp the force of his arguments.

In the aftermath of the Popish Plot the urgency of pleading his case only increased, and Du Moulin scraped together money for private publication and for complimentary copies for a wide range of influential people. *Declaratory Considerations upon the Present State of England* (1679) and, more forcefully, *A Short and True Account of the Several Advances the Church of England hath Made towards Rome* (1680) drew on post-Reformation history and many English clerical writers to demonstrate that 'the prevailing and most numerous Party of that Church', disowning communion with Calvin, had 'been these twenty years endeavouring to make their advances towards Rome, and have run themselves into Pelagianism and Socinianism' (p. 31). The puritans or Calvinists had secured the accession of the Stuarts in England and Henri IV in France, and had restored the crown to Charles II, but 'most of these kings have paid them with ingratitude' (p. 13). Good protestants within the church like Joseph Hall, Ralph Brownrigg, Thomas Barlow, and James Ussher had been overwhelmed first by men like John Bramhall, John Pocklington, and Peter Heylyn, and later by Samuel Parker and Simon Patrick, corrupted by rich benefices. Rejecting in *A Short and True Account* and its appendixed *A True Report* his brother's argument that the Anglican church polity was the closest to that of the primitive church, he acknowledged Peter's sincerity but roundly condemned his church's corruption, 'reigning spirit of persecution' (p. 74), 'popish ordination', and compulsory ceremonies. He also both recounted and rejected his kinsman l'Angle's attempts to deflect him from 'that Enmity which I testified with so much heat and bitterness against the Church of England' (p. 71). In a flurry of defiant activity he issued *The Conformity of Discipline and Government of the Independents to that of Ancient Primitive Christians* (1680), *Moral Reflections upon the Number of the Elect* (1680), and *An Appeal of the Nonconformists of England to God and All the Protestants of Europe in Order to Manifest their Sincerity in Point of Obedience to God and the King* (1681).

By the time the last appeared, Du Moulin was dead. Having been taken ill at the end of September 1680, he died on 20 October and was buried two days later at St Paul's, Covent Garden, with Simon Patrick, the dean of Peterborough whose stance he had previously attacked, officiating. According to *The Last Words of Lewis Du Moulin* (1680), on 4 October he had requested a visit from Gilbert Burnet (whom he perhaps respected as a fellow church historian). As a result of several encounters with Burnet and with Patrick, he repented of some of his writings, and signed on 5 and 17 October what the title-page of *The Last Words* announced as a 'Retraction of all the personal reflections he had made on the divines of the Church of England' (*The Last Words of Lewis Du Moulin*, 1680). Conceding that he had 'vented too much of my own Passion and Bitterness' in his books, he expressed hearty regret and begged both 'worthy men of the Church of England' and dissenters to exhibit charity, respect, and mutual forbearance so that they might unite for 'the defence and preservation of the Holy Reformed Religion' (ibid., 11). His wife was with him when he died. Although a family life is hinted at in his early requests for preferment, her identity is unclear and there is no certain evidence of children; no will has come to light. A Mistress Priscilla Du Moulin was buried at St Paul's, Covent Garden on 20 July 1687 and Rebecca, wife of Lewis Du Moulin, on 23 November 1702; the former could be his wife or his daughter, the latter his wife or his daughter-in-law. For all their doubts about his arguments and exasperation with his behaviour, Du Moulin also left at least some good friends. Although Anthony Wood, a natural critic, had thought him ill-tempered, those responsible for *The Last Words* depicted a man of dignity as well as spirit. Baxter 'found him more patient of confutation, contradiction and reproof than most men that I ever disputed with'. He had 'never heard that the doctor gave me any uncivil or uncharitable word', nor taken offence at this criticism. This, he concluded, 'showed a forgiving mind' (Nobbs, 'New light', 491).

VIVIENNE LARMINIE

Sources F. N. L. Poynter, 'A seventeenth-century London plague document in the Wellcome Historical Medicine Library: Dr Du Moulin's proposals for a corps of salaried plague doctors', *Bulletin of the History of Medicine*, 34 (1960), 365–72 [incl. biographical note on Louis Du Moulin by W. le Fanu] • D. Nobbs, 'New light on Louis Du Moulin', *Proceedings of the Huguenot Society of London*, 15 (1936), 489–509 • *Calendar of the correspondence of Richard Baxter*, ed. N. H. Keeble and G. F. Nuttall, 2 vols. (1991) • Venn, *Alum. Cant.* • Foster, *Alum. Oxon.* • W. H. Hunt, ed., *The registers of St Paul's Church, Covent Garden, London*, 4, Harleian Society, register section, 36 (1908), 89, 195 • Munk, *Roll* • R. W. Innes Smith, *English-speaking students of medicine at the University of Leyden* (1932), 74 • E. Haag and E. Haag, *La France protestante*, 2nd edn, 6 vols. (Paris, 1877–88), vol. 5, pp. 824–8 • Wood, *Ath. Oxon.: Fasti* (1820), 125–8 • *Calamy rev.*, 172 • *Hist. U. Oxf.* 4: *17th-cent. Oxf.* • D. Nobbs, *Theocracy and toleration: a study of the disputes in Dutch Calvinism from 1600 to 1650* (1938) • G. F. Nuttall, 'Dr Du Moulin and Papa ultrajectinus', *Nederlands Archief voor Kerkgeschiedenis*, 61 (1981), 205–13 • *Sixth report*, HMC, 5 (1877–8)
Archives Wellcome L., proposal to House of Commons for salaried corps of physicians | DWL, corresp. with Richard Baxter

Du Moulin, Peter [Pierre] (**1601–1684**), Church of England clergyman and religious controversialist, was born in Paris on 24 April 1601, the eldest of six children of Pierre *Du Moulin (1568–1658), minister of the French Reformed church, and his first wife, Marie Colignon (*d.* in or before 1622); his younger brothers included Lewis (Louis) *Du Moulin (1605?–1680) and Cyrus (*b.* 1608, *d.* before 1680). He studied at the protestant academy at Sedan and under his uncle André Rivet at the University of Leiden, presenting dissertations in 1623 and 1625, and proceeding DD from Leiden. In 1625 he also published in London a verse celebration of James I, *Petri Molinaei filii carmen heroicum ad regem*, apparently signalling an intention to exploit his father's manifold connections and join his search for ecclesiastical preferment in Britain.

It has been asserted that Du Moulin first held the living of St John's, Chester, although there is no confirmation of this. Already acquainted with Joseph Hall (from 1627 bishop of Exeter), by 1628 Du Moulin had become chaplain to James Stanley, Lord Strange, perhaps on the recommendation of the family of Strange's wife, Charlotte de la Trémoille. About 1630 he visited Oxford and met Jean Verneuil, sub-librarian and translator of Du Moulin senior's works. Early in March that year Gilbert Primrose, minister of the French church in London, wrote to Rivet that he had encountered the Du Moulin brothers. Peter, Primrose considered, had migrated to the episcopalian ministry because its infrequent preaching and mere reading of the liturgy was less demanding and he was lazy: 'il fuit le labeur' (Poynter, 370). This opinion was held by others, and for a while royal favour eluded Du Moulin. In February 1631 he wrote to secretary of state Dudley Carleton, Viscount Dorchester, justifying his possession of an unnamed living worth £80 a year: he feared the king had a bad opinion of him, for his 'enemies' had reported him as 'consuming an ecclesiastical benefice in idleness' and as being 'a lewd and debauched fellow' (*CSP dom.*, 1629–31, 497), accusations he denied. He was living in the parish of St Martin-in-the-Fields, London, when, on 7 May 1633, he was licensed to marry Anne Claver, aged about twenty-seven, daughter of the late Matthew Claver of Foscott, Buckinghamshire, and his wife, Jane. That year he became rector of Witherley, Leicestershire, and by 23 November 1634, when he was admitted to Lincoln's Inn, he had succeeded his father as rector of Llanarmon-yn-Lâl, Denbighshire; like his father he probably regarded it as a sinecure. As the 'pretended rector of Witherley' (*CSP dom.*, 1635, 200), he was summoned to answer before high commission in 1635, but the outcome is unclear.

Perhaps inspired by Hall, early in 1640 Du Moulin entered the debate over episcopacy with *A Letter of a French Protestant to a Scotishman of the Covenant*, signed from Chester on 1 March. While he acknowledged the auld alliance between France and Scotland, and the ties between their protestant churches since the Reformation, as a 'Frenchman borne' 'happily engrafted into the body of the Church of England' (p. 3), Du Moulin both denied French Reformed support for Scottish presbyterian discipline and affirmed its acceptance of English bishops. The Reformed of all three countries were united (with the Dutch) in doctrine, but their ceremonies in practice differed according to circumstance; in the British context the necessity of obedience to the king required submission to the episcopal system desired by the king and even approved by Calvin. As Du Moulin indicated, his views were derived from his father; they were to underpin his own writings for the next forty years.

The same year Du Moulin's establishment in England was sealed by the incorporation of his DD at Cambridge. In 1641 he became rector of Wheldrake, Yorkshire, and he seems to have taken up residence there. On 29 March 1645, as he explained in a letter to Lord Fairfax dated at York the following day, he was forcibly ejected from his living without having seen the articles against him, an action for which he blamed local ministers rather than soldiers. His subsequent movements are unknown, but his wife, Anne's, dispute over her fifths with his successor at Wheldrake was before the committee for plundered ministers in 1646–7. By 1649, which saw the appearance of his anonymous protest against the 'martyrdom' of Charles I, *Ecclesiae gemitus sub anabaptistica tyrannide*, he was rector of Londesborough on the Yorkshire estates of Richard Boyle, second earl of Cork. That June he compounded for his sequestration under the York articles; a successor was instituted on 19 January 1652. He seems to have been chiefly responsible for a second anonymous tract against the regicide (and John Milton) designed for European circulation, *Regii sanguinis clamor ad coelum adversus paricidas Anglicanos* (1652), and this may have been one motive for accompanying Cork to the relative obscurity of Ireland. Anthony Wood asserted that he lived under Cork's patronage at Lismore, Youghal, and Dublin; Du Moulin indicated in the dedication to the third edition of *A Week of Soliloquies and Prayers* (1677) that the work first published in 1657 had

its origins in meditations presented about 1654 to Elizabeth Clifford, countess of Cork, while he was in her household. 'The favourable retreat in the publick and my private calamity' (fol. A3v) gave him the leisure, and the troubles themselves the motivation, for a second devotional work, *A Treatise of Peace and Contentment of the Mind*, also first published in 1657.

In the meantime, however, Du Moulin had resumed a more active life and gained some measure of political rehabilitation. In 1656, on his petition, he was given leave by the council of state to hold ministerial office. Having been on 10 October incorporated DD at Oxford, where his brother Lewis was reader in history, he accompanied Cork's sons Charles Boyle, Viscount Dungarvon, and Richard Boyle to Christ Church, from where they matriculated on 25 November. During the next two years he preached frequently at St Peter-in-the-East in the city, and evidently gained wide acceptance. Writing from Christ Church on 9 June 1658 the first of several letters to Richard Baxter, he reverenced the latter 'above all the divines of this age', commending him particularly 'for setting your brethren of the Ministers upon the neglected duty of private conference with their people' (*Calendar*, no. 459, 1.312–13). Baxter expressed his admiration for both Du Moulin and his father (who had died that March) and agreed to the son's request that he add a postscript to *The History of the Devil of Mascon*, Peter the younger's translation of his father's work published that year. Following his admittance by the triers to the vicarage of Bradwell, Buckinghamshire, on 20 October 1657, Du Moulin seems to have remained largely in Oxford; he moved to Kent on his institution to the rectory of Adisham on 8 October 1658. Encouraged by Baxter, he continued translating another work by Pierre despite his fears, as he wrote to Baxter on 27 September 1659, 'that present ruine is at hand for the Ministry, the ready way for the extinction of the Gospell, & the setting up of Atheisme'. Thanking Baxter for defending orthodox royalist clergy against those who claimed that 'the Episcopal are halfe Papists', he declared himself 'a French Protestant' who was 'nothing ingaged to the Episcopal party but an hereditary dislike of all violent ways of subjects with their soveraine' (*Calendar*, no. 606, 1.412–13).

This disclaimer is more surprising than his apparently comfortable existence of the previous few years. The latter has several possible explanations: the standing of his brother and Cork's brother Broghill under the protectorate; general respect for his father; an amiable personality which contrasted with his brother's abrasiveness; a recognition from both sides of the integrity of one whom the royalist Anthony Wood dubbed 'an honest, zealous Calvinist' (Wood, *Ath. Oxon.: Fasti*, 2.198). But Du Moulin's attachment to episcopacy, albeit implicitly a primitive kind in the tradition of Hall, was otherwise as constant as it was to monarchy. In *The History of the English and Scotch Presbytery*, first published in 1659 and reissued in 1660, he returned to the themes of *A Letter of a French Protestant*. He prefaced the work with Charles I's declaration to Reformed protestants of May 1644 denying an intention to introduce popery and affirming his attachment to an Anglican church they had accepted, and with a letter apparently of his own to the ministers of the Reformed church in Paris setting out to show 'that it's impossible to alter the foundation of Church and State, without pulling down the house, which is the work of the blind, as Sampson' (sig. a4, 2): the covenanters had wronged their king, their countrymen, and the Reformed churches.

After the Restoration, Du Moulin retained the rectory of Adisham. At an early stage he urged Baxter to retract in print what he had written under 'other powers and another forme of State' and 'to declare how you acknowledge & adore the hand of God in this great revolution of Church & State' lest he be deprived and silenced (*Calendar*, no. 650, 2.5). Probably in August, Du Moulin unsuccessfully petitioned the king that the rectory of Llanrhaeadr, Denbighshire, granted to him by the king, be transferred to his brother Lewis, who had lost his place at Oxford.

Peter supported Lewis financially for several years but, although they shared a vehement anti-Catholicism, in other respects their opinions and fortunes diverged further as the former found favour. He became a royal chaplain and on 29 June 1660 was presented by the king to his father's former prebend at Canterbury, which he held for the rest of his life in congenial company that included his friend Thomas Turner and his younger kinsman Jean Maximilien de l'Angle; his younger brother Cyrus was for a while pastor of the French congregation that met in the cathedral. Du Moulin's warmly expressed letters of 1661 to William Sancroft, chaplain to John Cosin, bishop of Durham, indicate that he was among those French immigrants who enjoyed Cosin's patronage.

Like de l'Angle's brother-in-law Jean Durel, Du Moulin used his privileged position to mediate the restored Church of England to the Reformed world and to counter Catholicism. The translation work of 1659 appeared as *The Novelty of Popery* (1662), while 'in answer to a Jesuitical Libel, entituled Philanax Anglicus' he wrote *A vindication of the sincerity of the protestant religion in the point of obedience to sovereigns* (1664). Dedicated, like *Philanax Anglicus*, to Archbishop Gilbert Sheldon, it directly challenged British Catholics to face up to the implications of their loyalty to the pope. Exposure of effectively treasonable activity by Catholic 'royalists' during the 1640s and 1650s was a risky business in the context of the Restoration court, and Du Moulin chose a particularly dangerous path when he drew on William Prynne as his source. There ensued what Du Moulin termed a 'storme from Somerset House' (BL, Add. MS 8880, fol. 190). Feeling obliged by his oath to the king to explain himself further, he wrote to secretary of state Sir William Morrice on 12 January 1665 naming Sir Kenelm Digby as the head of a Jesuit delegation at Paris and Rome in 1648 to plan the destruction of Charles I because they had concluded he would never turn Catholic. The precise upshot is unclear, but Du Moulin was not cowed. Further editions of *A Vindication* were complemented by *The Great Loyalty of the Papists to K. Charles I … Discovered* (1673), *The Papal Tyranny* (1674; dedicated to Sir Robert Hales and William Longueville), *A Replie to a Person of Honour* (1675), and

The Ruine of Papacy (1678); in the context of the Popish Plot these took on a new relevance. He also defended the re-established church against its lay opponents in *A Letter to a Person of Quality Concerning the Fines Received by the Church* at its restoration (1668).

In the meantime, and more calmly, Du Moulin crossed swords with his fellow prebendary Meric Casaubon over natural experimental philosophy. Non-controversial works included funeral sermons for Mabella, Lady Fordwitch, and for Thomas Turner, and *Directions for the Education of a Young Prince* (1673). Still in touch with his origins and on good terms with powerful patrons, about 1671 he wrote to Lucy Hastings, countess of Huntingdon, explaining a detail of 'the 69th page of my reflections upon la Politique de France': 'it is an allusion to French cookery of mackerels which are always served with fennel. And in France un maquereau signifies both that fish & a pimp' (*Hastings MSS*, 2.157). Even in a period of estrangement between the brothers Lewis could write that 'His natural temper … is meek and humble and full of benignity' (Agnew, 133). By the time his *Ten Sermons Preached upon Several Occasions* appeared in 1684 he was 'barred from the Pulpit by the infirmities of Old Age, yet very loth to give over my sacred and beloved Office of Evangelist' (preface). He died on 10 October that year, and was buried on 13 October in Canterbury Cathedral.   VIVIENNE LARMINIE

Sources E. Haag and E. Haag, *La France protestante*, 2nd edn, 6 vols. (Paris, 1877–88), vol. 5, pp. 824–7 · *Walker rev.*, 392 · Foster, *Alum. Oxon.* · Venn, *Alum. Cant.* · Wood, *Ath. Oxon.: Fasti* (1820), 195 · *Fasti Angl., 1541–1857*, [Canterbury], 23 · *Calendar of the correspondence of Richard Baxter*, ed. N. H. Keeble and G. F. Nuttall, 2 vols. (1991) · *CSP dom.*, 1629–31, 1635–6; 1660 · J. L. Chester and G. J. Armytage, eds., *Allegations for marriage licences issued by the bishop of London*, 2, Harleian Society, 26 (1887), 211 · W. P. Baildon, ed., *The records of the Honorable Society of Lincoln's Inn: admissions*, 1 (1896), 225 · BL, Add. MSS, 8880, fol. 190; 30305, fol. 78 · BL, Harley MS 3784, fols. 21, 33 · *Report on the manuscripts of the late Reginald Rawdon Hastings*, 4 vols., HMC, 78 (1928–47), vol. 2, p. 157 · J. Pannier, 'Un pasteur à Paris: canoine de Canterbury et recteur dans le Pays de Galles. Pierre Du Moulin (1615–1625)', *Proceedings of the Huguenot Society of London*, 13 (1924–9), 173–81 · D. C. A. Agnew, *Protestant exiles from France, chiefly in the reign of Louis XIV, or, The Huguenot refugees and their descendants in Great Britain and Ireland*, 3rd edn, 2 vols. (1886), 130–33 · F. N. L. Poynter, 'A seventeenth-century London plague document in the Wellcome Historical Medicine Library: Dr Du Moulin's proposals for a corps of salaried plague doctors', *Bulletin of the History of Medicine*, 34 (1960), 365–72 [incl. biographical note on Louis Du Moulin by W. le Fanu]

Archives DWL, corresp. with Richard Baxter

Du Moulin, Pierre (1568–1658), Reformed minister and religious controversialist, was born in the Château de Buhy in north-east Normandy, France, the eldest of three sons of Joachim Du Moulin, seigneur de Lorme Grigny (*c.*1538–*c.*1618), pastor in the Reformed church in the Orléans area, and his wife, Françoise Gabet, widow of Jacques Du Plessis. In his autobiography he was proud to relate that he first drew breath in the same room as the great Philippe Du Plessis-Marly Du Mornay (1549–1623), the Huguenot controversialist whose family owned the château, and to recount the subsequent sufferings of his own family in the wars of religion.

Early life in France and England According to the life written by Pierre's son Peter *Du Moulin (1601–1684), Joachim, from an ancient noble house, was disinherited by his mother when about 1558 he chose to enter the protestant ministry; his sixty years in the pastorate thereafter were conducted in conditions of extreme difficulty. Pierre recalled that, as a child of five, during a raid on their home by Roman Catholic forces, he was first concealed in the straw bedding and then under the long skirt of a servant girl, thus escaping with his life. Less reliably (Peter gives a different account) he related that his younger brother Eléazar, taken captive in such a raid, had his fingers and toes chopped off before being buried alive. In family letters there appears to be some evidence that their mother, Françoise, who died during this period, took her own life, possibly as a result of the same hereditary depression which was later to afflict her eldest son. What is clear is that Pierre's childhood experiences, combined with his sense of honour derived from his noble heritage, contributed to his characteristically fiery and combative nature. He developed a fractious and highly independent spirit, with a powerful dislike for the Roman Catholic church and what it represented, and a white-hot animosity towards those Catholics who had sought out and slaughtered many of his friends and relatives.

Fleeing for safety from Normandy, Du Moulin finally settled in the early 1580s at Sedan, a protestant enclave on the Meuse governed by the powerful Guillaume Robert de la Marck, duc de Bouillon. There Pierre entered first the Huguenot college and then the academy, where he was powerfully influenced by the principal, Toussaint Berchet, who taught a love for letters, a passion for teaching, reverence for monarchical authority as a remedy for chaos and conflict in the body politic, and an early form of patriotism, all of which were reflected in his later activities and writings. Following the death of Bouillon in 1588 Sedan became less secure, and Du Moulin senior considered that his son, who had completed his studies with distinction, should establish himself elsewhere. Reluctantly, Pierre went first to Paris, where he served as tutor to the protestant de Cussy family, and then to England.

In London, Du Moulin attached himself to the French church. Its pastor, the highly regarded René Bochart, sieur du Mesnillet, whose son Etienne or Stephen had married Du Moulin's elder sister Esther, became his mentor as he underwent training for the ministry. His period of probationary preaching successfully completed, in 1589 Mesnillet helped find him employment as a servant in the household of the young Roger Manners, eighth earl of Rutland, then a student at Cambridge. Du Moulin himself was thereby able to study for three years in the university, where he was profoundly influenced by the strictly Calvinist William Whitaker and made the acquaintance of the future bishop James Montagu (1568–1618). The former armed him with a theology of combat which was to render him a very difficult opponent in the art of disputation; the latter became his closest friend and confidant in England. Having emerged from Cambridge with a profound biblical knowledge and a deeply engrained and rationalized Reformed theology, Du Moulin preached before the French church consistory and was called to be pastor of the Reformed church of Paris by one of its ministers who happened to be present, but he declined the invitation.

Leiden and early works, 1592–1598 Instead, in 1592, perhaps with the primary object of studying with the celebrated scholar Francis Junius or Du Jon, whom he had befriended in England, Du Moulin went to the University of Leiden. En route he lost his luggage when it was thrown overboard in a violent storm; a poem about the episode, 'Votiva tabella', composed on his safe arrival in the Netherlands, drew high praise from many quarters and made him something of a reputation. Although in his letters to English friends he complained of poverty and humiliation, this seems to have been more the product of the dramatic shifts in mood characteristic of his manic-depressive condition than a reflection of reality. Taking advantage of his prior acquaintance with the French ambassador, de Buzenval, he secured an introduction to Louise de Coligny, princess of Orange, and thus access to the Dutch court and to leaders of the republic. With the support of the princess and of his brother-in-law André Rivet, then professor of logic at Leiden, he established himself as 'corrector' at the Staaten College, where he was by all accounts a dynamic and popular teacher of logic and Greek. Later he became professor of languages, philosophy, and finally logic. He shared both teaching and lodgings with the distinguished Reformed scholar Joseph Justus Scaliger, who arrived in 1593 and whose learning and enormous mastery of the classics was a great inspiration to him. Their students included the young Daniel Heinsius (1580–1655) and Hugo Grotius (1583–1645): both acknowledged their considerable debt to this instruction, although the latter later deprecated Du Moulin's precipitance, hauteur, penchant for debating contested issues, and theological programme of dogmatic hair-splitting.

While at Leiden, Du Moulin began what was to become a formidable career as a publishing scholar spanning seventy years. Poetry which appeared in 1592 was followed by perhaps the most popular logic textbook of the age, his *Elementa logica*: the first of more than forty separate editions was published in 1598. In *Batavia*, a striking panegyric in two parts of more than 400 verses, he manifested an ability of no small measure in poetic expression. By this time he had also become very proficient in languages, especially Greek, skilled in oratory, and highly competent in disputation. Profoundly influenced by the principles of Aristotelian logic which he had taught, he considered the logic-based beliefs of the Dutch Reformed church more useful in debate than the biblically based positions of French protestantism, even if, on certain points, there was much agreement.

Minister in Paris and international controversialist, 1598–1615 In February 1598, having somewhat reluctantly turned his back on an offer of diplomatic employment and on the further pursuit of an academic career, Du Moulin returned to France, where Henri IV's ratification of the edict of Nantes was transforming the Huguenots into an officially recognized minority group. The following year Du Moulin became a minister of the protestant church in Paris, originally meeting in the home of Henri's sister Catherine de Bourbon, but then established at the citadel of Charenton. That year he also married Marie (d. 1622), daughter of Nicolas de Colignon, sieur de Chalette en Parthois, and his wife, Jeanne Prudhomme; among their children were Peter, Lewis *Du Moulin (1605?–1680), and Esther, who later married Daniel Jurieu of Rotterdam and became the mother of the celebrated Pierre Jurieu. Keenly aware of his noble ancestry and comporting himself as a member of the aristocracy, Du Moulin developed many contacts and friendships with high-placed officials of the French and other governments and acquired, almost certainly through purchase, the largely honorary title of counsellor and master of requests to the king. Until her death in 1604 he served as chaplain to Catherine and her household, accompanying her each spring on visits to her Catholic husband, the duc de Bar, in Lorraine, and earning her high regard.

Du Moulin soon became the leading voice of French protestantism, a role he retained through the first half of the seventeenth century. Rising with enthusiasm to the challenge, he defended both himself and the Reformed church against perceived enemies from without and within. He 'duelled' at court with prominent Roman Catholic scholars (who according to his son Peter never defeated him in debate) while pursuing a constant war of polemics in printed broadsides. In the course of a long life, his literary output was truly astonishing, covering ethics, logic, natural science, apologetics, spirituality, monarchy, and human power and privileges. At the very minimum, taking account only of those works published as a separate treatise, there are more than 1200 separate editions or printings in ten or more languages. This figure would rise dramatically if one were to count each individual title, especially his sermons, and it is doubtful if any other Calvinist writer, except perhaps Calvin and Théodore Beza, was more frequently published.

By the end of the first decade of the seventeenth century, Du Moulin's writings, controversies, and personal contacts had combined to make him a well-known figure in the eyes of the British social and clerical élite. When James VI, before his accession to the English throne, had sent his friendly greetings to the Paris consistory, Du Moulin (according to his son) had been deputed to reply. His verbal sparring match with Pierre Cayer was published by the Scot Archibald Adaire in 1602, while a little later his young family had close ties with that of Gilbert Primrose, the Scottish minister of the Reformed church at Bordeaux. In addition to James Montagu, from 1603 dean of the chapel royal, Du Moulin had other well-placed friends in successive ambassadors and agents in Paris—Sir Henry Neville, Sir Ralph Winwood, Sir Thomas Parry, Sir George Carew, and, particularly, Sir Thomas Edmondes, as well as the Dutch envoy Francis Aerssens. Du Moulin's devotional treatise Théophile, ou, L'amour divine (1609) became enormously popular, and was soon translated into English,

Dutch, and German. Influential too was his pessimistic Héraclite, ou, De la vanité et misère de la vie humaine (1609), in which he presented a fallen world as the platform for the providence of God as revealed through his church. In this context, and especially given Du Moulin's engagement in polemic, it is not surprising that when King James issued that year as an accompaniment to the second edition of his An Apologie for the Oath of Allegiance, a Premonition to All most Mightie Monarches, he should send Du Moulin a personal copy. Attacks on the king's books by Cardinal Bellarmine and by the French Dominican Nicolas Coëffeteau prompted Du Moulin to write an officially sanctioned reply to the latter, which appeared in 1610 in a three-part version, Défense de la foy Catholique, which also contained general observations on papal usurpations and on prophecy, and in the shorter Defence of the Catholique Faith Contained in the Booke of … King James the First. Gliding over James's firmly expressed commitment to divine-right episcopacy, and his criticism of his puritan as well as his papist subjects, Du Moulin explained for his international protestant audience that the king did not aim to impose the polity of the English church on others, while James seems to have swallowed a potentially embarrassing divergence of opinion because of Du Moulin's effective defence of royal authority. Subsequently Du Moulin's De monarchia temporali pontificis Romani (1614), which appeared in London and Geneva, attempted to refute Bellarmine in the same vein.

Meanwhile, although not always in agreement with all his trenchant opinions and his combative style, James continued to be convinced of Du Moulin's worth. In December 1611 he wrote to Du Moulin criticizing several of the interpretations of scripture contained in his writing on prophecy. However, when early in 1612 a controversy developed between Du Moulin and Daniel Tilenus, with the former accusing the latter of undermining the doctrine of justification by an over-distinction between the two natures of Christ and a consequent underemphasis on his humanity, James joined those urging Du Moulin towards peace. Acting through Edmondes and the current duc de Bouillon, Henri de la Tour d'Auvergne, the king pressed for an end to damaging divisions among French protestants. Perhaps influenced by Du Plessis Mornay, who had already attempted to nudge James himself into a more active role in promoting unity among European protestants, Du Moulin replied in a letter of 19 February / 1 March 1613 enclosing articles entitled 'Overtures for striving for the union of the churches of Christendom'. The document proposed in the first instance an international conference of Reformed representatives from Britain, France, the Netherlands, Switzerland, and Germany in order to arrive at a doctrinal consensus and issue an agreed confession. Subsequently overtures would be made first to the Lutherans and then, once a concord had been reached, perhaps also to the Roman Catholic church. Even if the last aim proved unattainable Du Moulin felt that the protestant voice in Europe would be greatly strengthened. James gave a cautious welcome to the plan, in which it was envisaged he would play a major role; a version revised by Du Moulin and Du Plessis Mornay was presented by the king's emissary David Home to the twenty-first national synod of the French Reformed churches at Tonneins in 1614 and accepted. In October or November Du Moulin gratefully acknowledged James's part in his reconciliation with Tilenus, brokered chiefly by Du Plessis Mornay and Home, and in return received in February 1615 via Théodore Turquet de Mayerne the king's invitation to visit England.

English preferment, James I, and protestant unity, 1615–1625 Obtaining leave of absence from his consistory, Du Moulin arrived in England in March. Staying close to James for nearly three months, he assisted the king with his defence of monarchical rights against the papal deposing powers championed by the Cardinal Du Perron. Du Moulin subsequently gave conflicting accounts of the extent of his part in James's *Declaration du serenissime Roy Jaques I … pour le droit des rois* (1615) (issued in English as *Remonstrance of the most Gracious King James I*, 1616), but he clearly earned the king's high favour. Accompanying James to Cambridge, he was awarded a DD and on 7 June was collated to a prebend in Canterbury Cathedral. A week later he delivered in French an address later translated by Jean Verneuil as *A Sermon Preached before the Kings Majesty at Greenwich* (1620), in which he spoke of Christian reconciliation and commended James's aspirations towards unity. Although he also took the opportunity to criticize the theatricals he had witnessed at Cambridge, the king again chose not to take offence, and the prince of Wales presented him with a valuable jewel. Having renewed his acquaintance with some old friends, and made a new one in the bishop of Winchester, Lancelot Andrewes, Du Moulin returned to Paris, from where he kept up a wide correspondence with England.

Plunging back into controversy, a challenge from the Jesuit court preacher Arnoux led Du Moulin to publish his most popular work, *Le bouclier de la foi* (1618), translated into English as *The Buckler of Faith*, in which he adduced the intercommunion of the French Reformed and English churches as a defence against accusations that they were divided by fundamental differences. His inflammable personal honour aroused, he defended the Reformed ministry the same year in *De la vocation des pasteurs*. Characteristically, he did so by attacking Roman Catholic orders, but unlike most other Reformed commentators, he did not deny the possibility of apostolic succession and/or the validity of the Anglican position. This delicate balancing act was appreciated neither by Reformed luminaries such as François Hotman and Isaac Casaubon, who disliked Du Moulin and had for some years suspected him of closet episcopalianism, nor by Andrewes. Writing to Du Moulin in 1618–19 Andrewes, advancing significantly beyond the previous Jacobean orthodoxy, made a robust assertion of episcopacy as a separate ministerial order existing by divine right. In reply Du Moulin pointed out that if he concurred he would effectively render the French Reformed church guilty of heretical error; the exchange did not lead him to review his assumption that the English episcopacy and the French pastorate were reconcilable.

When an international synod was convoked at Dordrecht in 1618 Du Moulin and his brother-in-law Rivet were among those chosen to represent the French church. Du Moulin wrote a fiercely anti-Remonstrant account of the issues in dispute in *Anatomia Arminianismi* (published in 1619, and in English translation in 1620). Rendered suspect by their foreign links, the French delegates were prevented by their government from attending in November, but Du Moulin sent on a shortened version of his work as a communiqué to the synod, where it was read out in open session on 27 April 1619. Among the other issues on the agenda, James I was keen to promote discussion of Du Moulin's plan of union, but the British representatives were less enthusiastic, and although they promoted moderation, little progress was made. None the less, the canons that did come out of Dort were endorsed at the next French synod, at Alès in 1620, where Du Moulin presided with quasi-episcopal authority.

Du Moulin's long-standing Anglophilia, association with James I's interests in Europe, and correspondence with the king finally exhausted the patience of the French council of state and, warned by his fellow pastor Charles Drelincourt of impending arrest, early in 1621 he fled to Sedan. He took with him his brother, Captain Jean Du Moulin, who over the years acted as his bodyguard in the face of several serious assassination attempts. At Sedan he combined pastoral work with the professorship of theology at the academy. With 1500 livres a year from these positions, a continued salary (at least at first) from the Charenton pastorate, and the revenue of his Canterbury prebend he was comfortably off, and he continued to attract respect and approbation from many students, scholars, and readers of his published works, but he remained prey both to feelings of financial insecurity and to depression, which once kept him in his study for six months at a time and frequently required his family to invent excuses to preserve his reputation. A particularly acute period followed the death of his wife in 1622 and partly coincided with a visit to London in 1623, during which he was informed that his church at Charenton had been destroyed by an arson attack. This engendered what his nephew Samuel de l'Angle described as a prolonged catatonic stupor, but it also produced a treatise, *Du combat chrestien*, in which he sought to provide heart-felt encouragement and consolation to his old flock. Published also as *A Preparation to Suffer for the Gospel* (1623), it tried to forewarn the English of the possibility of troubles analogous to those already being experienced by their continental co-religionists.

For the time being, however, England had much to offer Du Moulin, despite the fact that, or perhaps because, that year he married again, his new wife being Sarah, daughter of Captain Louis de Gelhay, and began a second family. By October 1623 he was given the free choice of permanent residence; by the following August, when he was again in London, he had been awarded £100 and the sinecure rectory of Llanrhaeadr, Denbighshire. When he contracted what seemed a terminal illness that summer, his most pressing request in a letter to James was that his English livings might devolve upon two of his sons so they should not be left unprovided for. Reassured on this point via Secretary Conway on 2 September, Du Moulin (now temporarily joined by members of his family) recovered, only to make a more audacious request. On 24 October, a few days after the death of Miles Smith, bishop of Gloucester, he wrote to Conway proposing himself as Smith's successor. Gauchely expressed, naive in its assumptions about the current state of the English church, and embarrassing to his English sympathizers, the approach was none the less neither illogical nor entirely out of the blue. The austere episcopal style of the scholarly Smith had been a long way from the divine-right sacerdotalism espoused by Andrewes, and Du Moulin probably expected to continue in his footsteps. That he was favourable to a 'primitive' form of episcopacy had long been evident to some, and that it suited his personality had been revealed by his conduct in recent synods. The English rebuff, delivered via Conway on 3 November, took the form of polite silence and further assurances of good will and imminent alternative rewards, a tribute to the high standing Du Moulin continued to enjoy with the king despite his disconcerting attributes and opinions. On 20 November he received from James a free gift of £200, and although the deanery of Ripon mooted for him on 27 November did not eventually come his way, on 11 January 1625 he was presented to the sinecure rectory of Llanarmon-yn-Lâl, Denbighshire.

Sedan and last years, 1625–1658 This was to be the sum of Du Moulin's preferments in the Church of England. That spring the illness and subsequent death of James sent him, still in poor health, back to Sedan, and he never attained the same level of intimacy and respect with Charles I, despite attempts to keep contact through intermediaries such as the dowager duchess de la Trémoille and secretary of state, Dudley Carleton, Viscount Dorchester. In common with other foreign apologists, he found that further editions of works of controversy in support of King James received no reward from his son, despite dedicating to him his massive *Nouveauté du papisme* (1627). Although his own sons Peter and Lewis settled in England (the former succeeding to Llanarmon by 1634), and although the conversion to Catholicism of the duc de Bouillon rendered life at Sedan precarious from the later 1630s, Du Moulin remained at his post in the university and in his pastorate. The shifting political situation in England threatened his Canterbury prebend from 1641, but that in France permitted a brief return to his old congregation at Charenton about 1644, although the reunion did not last. On 11 November 1648 an order from the committee for plundered ministers that both he and Gerard Vossius should receive the profit of their prebends, being 'aged divines and forrainers' (*Walker rev.*, 2), demonstrated that his reputation was still high in England, even though his letter to Speaker William Lenthall protesting that he had always supported the puritan cause must have rung hollow. Perhaps the definitive cession of Sedan to France on 20 March 1651, with attendant extension to the city of the fragile safeguards for protestants contained in the

now precarious edict of Nantes, was sufficient to convince a very old man not to risk a final move to England.

In spite of insecurity and danger Du Moulin continued to court controversy. In a remarkable volte-face, having once promoted united protestantism, he launched a violent and long-lasting campaign for the condemnation of the views of the Scottish theologian John Cameron (1579/80–1625) and his chief French disciple, Moïse Amyraut (1596–1664) of the Reformed academy of Saumur, who taught that the sacrifice of Christ was sufficient to atone for the sins of all humankind. Du Moulin's tirade against this 'preposterous' position was given added bite by his contempt for Amyraut's humble social origins (shared with Arminius) and added bitterness in its extension to Amyraut's circle of supporters, who included such celebrated pastors at the Charenton church as Drelincourt and Jean Daillé. The sword he customarily wore to signal his noble origins was echoed in his verbal and written duelling.

About the autumn of 1655 Du Moulin sustained an injury in falling from his horse from which he never fully recovered. He died at Sedan on 10 March 1658, just as negotiations were underway in the circle of the minister Richard Baxter for the translation into English of his 'treasure' and 'masterpiece' *Nouveauté du papisme* (*Calendar of the Correspondence of Richard Baxter*, 1.306, 316). He was buried at Sedan; a description of his last hours was published there that year and at Geneva in 1666. He left behind several copies of an autobiography, primarily given over to self-aggrandizement and to his perceived victories in debates with Catholics, but also capturing the trauma, if not the detail, of his early years. His works continued to appear in several languages, and at least four of his children, Peter, Lewis, Cyrus, and Marie, his daughter from his second marriage, perpetuated his tradition of scholarship and controversialism.

BRIAN G. ARMSTRONG and VIVIENNE LARMINIE

Sources L. Rimbault, *Pierre du Moulin, 1568–1658: un pasteur classique à l'age classique* (1966) • 'Autobiographie de Pierre du Moulin, d'après le manuscript autographe, 1564–1658', *Bulletin de la Société de l'Histoire du Protestantisme Français*, 71 (1858), 170–82, 333–44, 456–77 • B. G. Armstrong, 'The changing face of French protestantism: the influence of Pierre du Moulin', *Calviniana*, ed. R. V. Schnucker (1988), 131–49 • B. G. Armstrong, 'Pierre du Moulin and James I: the Anglo-French programme', *De l'humanisme aux lumières: Bayle et le protestantisme en l'honneur d'Elisabeth Labrousse*, ed. M. Magdelaine and others (Paris, 1996), 17–29 • B. G. Armstrong, *Bibliographia Molinaei* (Geneva, 1997) • J. van der Meij, 'Pierre du Moulin in Leiden, 1592–1598', *Lias*, 14/1 (1987), 15–40 • W. B. Patterson, 'Pierre du Moulin's quest for protestant unity, 1613–1618', *Unity and diversity in the church*, ed. R. Swanson, SCH, 32 (1996), 235–50 • W. B. Patterson, *King James VI and I and the reunion of Christendom* (1997) • A. Milton, *Catholic and Reformed: the Roman and protestant churches in English protestant thought, 1600–1640* (1995) • *CSP dom.*, 1611–37 • Venn, *Alum. Cant.* • *Fasti Angl., 1541–1857*, [Canterbury] • E. Labrousse, 'Great Britain as envisaged by the Huguenots of the seventeenth century', *Huguenots in Britain and their French background, 1550–1800*, ed. I. Scouloudi (1987), 143–57 • H. Kretzer, *Calvinismus und französische Monarchie im 17. Jahrhundert* (Berlin, 1975) • J. Pannier, *L'Eglise Réformée de Paris sous Henri IV* (Paris, 1911) • P. Bayley, *French pulpit oratory, 1598–1650: a study in themes and styles* (1980) • Calendar of the

correspondence of Richard Baxter, ed. N. H. Keeble and G. F. Nuttall, 1 (1991), 306, 313, 316, 327, 332
Archives BL, letters, Add. MSS 4285, 19402, 22960 · BL, letters and papers, Stowe MSS 172–176 · LPL, volume of lecture notes and commentaries | BL, letters to Bishop Lancelot Andrewes, Sloane MS 118

Du Moulin, Pierre (d. 1676), political propagandist, was born in Dunois, France, the son of Cyrus Du Moulin (b. 1608), a Reformed church minister, and his wife, Marie de Marbois or Marbais. He came from a family of distinguished Huguenot scholars, which included his grandfather, Pierre *Du Moulin (1568–1658), and uncles Peter *Du Moulin (1601–1684) and Lewis *Du Moulin (1605?–1680). It is not known where Du Moulin was educated, but he had a knowledge of classical languages and of English, Spanish, Dutch, and French. The date of his arrival in England is uncertain, but he was naturalized by act of parliament in May 1664.

Du Moulin found work as a clerk in the office of the secretary of state, Sir Henry Bennet, earl of Arlington from 1665. With Arlington as a patron, Du Moulin then embarked on a career in the diplomatic service. He served as secretary to the envoy Sir Gilbert Talbot in Denmark (1664–6) and to the ambassador Sir Thomas Clifford in Denmark and Sweden (1665–6). Talbot was impressed by Du Moulin's abilities and recommended him as 'a man of very good parts, and perfect honesty' (Haley, 17). The following year Du Moulin joined the entourage of the English ambassadors at the peace negotiations with the Dutch at Breda, whence he supplied Arlington with political and military intelligence. A warrant exists appointing Du Moulin as assistant to the master of ceremonies, Sir Charles Cotterell, but if he held this office it was not for long, as in March 1668 Clement Cotterell was named to the post. From February to August 1668 Du Moulin was secretary to Sir John Trevor, envoy-extraordinary to France, the French ambassador to England noting that Du Moulin was highly intelligent and in Arlington's confidence. In October 1668 Du Moulin was appointed secretary to the council of trade, following a recommendation from Arlington and against a nominee of the duke of York, but at the beginning of 1669 he was named to the entourage of Ralph Montagu, the new ambassador-extraordinary to France: his post was not that of secretary to the ambassador, but Montagu was told it would 'do well for his credit to let it pass so' (ibid., 20). Du Moulin, however, did not find relations with Montagu easy, and, given the new pro-French direction of English foreign policy, his days in favour were numbered. He was recalled after only a few months and left for England on 26 June 1669.

Du Moulin continued to serve the council of trade, but he was increasingly out of sympathy with the new pro-French foreign policy, and especially with the Dutch war which began at the start of 1672. He eventually left England following an order from the privy council on 31 July 1672 for his arrest for visiting the Dutch deputies residing at Hampton Court. He blamed three years' persecution by his former patron, Arlington, for his predicament. Du Moulin now entered the service of William, prince of

Orange, who had been stadholder of the states general since June. In the autumn of 1672 Du Moulin wrote to his English contacts soliciting information upon which to base Dutch policy, and as early as September 1672 Dutch agents were active in England following policies developed by Du Moulin in a series of memoranda to William. Initially the aim was to divide the English ministers, particularly the earls of Lauderdale and Shaftesbury. However, hopes of disrupting the Franco-English alliance came to focus on influencing parliament to refuse to grant supplies for carrying on the war. It was in these circumstances that Du Moulin penned *England's Appeal from the Private Cabal at Whitehall to the Great Council of the Nation*, which may have been in Arlington's possession at the end of January 1673, but which became widely available in England only in March, near the end of the parliamentary session.

In the summer of 1673 Du Moulin was employed by William as a confidential secretary to deal with foreign correspondence, and he continued his efforts to force England out of the war. Meanwhile in England there was a marked growth in anti-French sentiment, for which *England's Appeal* had some responsibility, with its clever play on the consequences of the French alliance for England's politics, religion, and trade. The result was two very uncomfortable parliamentary sessions for Charles II's ministers in October–November 1673 and January–February 1674, which forced England to the negotiating table, a peace with the Dutch being signed on 19 February 1674.

In 1674 Du Moulin was still serving as William's secretary, but English ministers were determined to use the desire of William for good relations with Charles II to force him from favour, and Arlington came to the Netherlands with the intention of forcing his dismissal. Du Moulin, realizing his position could not be sustained, wished to be appointed governor of Surinam, but this required the assent of all the Dutch provinces and for some time Zeeland proved recalcitrant. Du Moulin's last official letter to William was written on 17 November 1674, although he was still available to offer informal advice. In the summer of 1675 Du Moulin was sent as Dutch representative to the imperial general Montecuculi.

Du Moulin's commission as governor of Surinam was dated 24 February 1676, and he was also voted a pension of 1600 gulden. However, he never took up his post. On 13 June 1676 he took a vomit which caused him to burst several blood vessels, and he died at The Hague, 'strangled in his blood' (Haley, 217). He was buried in the Kloosterkerk in The Hague on 16 June, and his papers were seized by the judge of the high court of the Netherlands to prevent them from falling into the wrong hands.

STUART HANDLEY

Sources K. H. D. Haley, *William of Orange and the English opposition, 1672–4* (1953) · J. C. Sainty, ed., *Officials of the board of trade, 1660–1870* (1974), 95 · W. A. Shaw, ed., *Letters of denization and acts of naturalization for aliens in England and Ireland, 1603–1700*, Huguenot Society of London, 18 (1911) · G. M. Bell, *A handlist of British diplomatic representatives, 1509–1688*, Royal Historical Society Guides and Handbooks, 16 (1990), 37, 117, 277 · E. Berwick, ed., *The Rawdon papers* (1819), 237–8 · V. Barbour, *Henry Bennet, earl of Arlington* (1914), 211 · Bishop

Burnet's History, 2.56, 63 • D. T. Witcombe, *Charles II and the cavalier House of Commons, 1663–1674* (1966), 141–6 • *Report on the manuscripts of his grace the duke of Buccleuch and Queensberry … preserved at Montagu House*, 3 vols. in 4, HMC, 45 (1899–1926), vol. 1, pp. 423, 428 • S. B. Baxter, *William III and the defense of European liberty, 1650–1702* (New York, 1966), 109, 139

Archives Nationaal Archief, The Hague, Fagel papers, folder 244

Dun. For this title name *see* Erskine, David, Lord Dun (*bap.* 1673, *d.* 1758).

Dun [Donne], **Sir Daniel** (1544/5–1617), ecclesiastical lawyer, was the eldest of three known sons of Robert Dun of St Botolph, Aldersgate, London (*d.* 1552/3), gentleman (in his will, though in 1576 held to have been a villein regardant to the honour of Eye in Suffolk), and his wife, Anne (*d.* 1611×13), daughter of John Branche and Joan Wilkenson. Their father entrusted the care of Daniel and his brothers, together with their £100 portions, to his brothers-in-law John and Thomas Branche, London drapers, while allowing his widow to have their keeping if she wished. Dun was admitted a fellow of All Souls College, Oxford, in 1567, BCL on 14 July 1572, and DCL on 20 July 1580, the year in which he became principal of New Inn Hall. Commissioned as an advocate in the court of arches on 3 October 1580, he was admitted to Doctors' Commons on 22 January 1582. He was a commissary during the vacancy of the see of Peterborough in 1585, official of the archdeaconry of Essex in 1585–6, and from 1598 chancellor of Rochester diocese (until 1604), the archbishop of Canterbury's *auditor causarum*, official principal of the court of arches, and dean of arches. In 1584 and 1586 he was one of the commissioners empowered to preside in convocation in Archbishop Whitgift's absence. He was one of nine civilians responsible for a treatise of *c.*1590 defending the oaths used in the ecclesiastical courts. A member of the high commission from 1601, he was in 1603 also included in an ecclesiastical commission for the diocese of Winchester. He attended in 1604 the third session of the Hampton Court conference, at which the *ex officio* oath was discussed, and was included in a commission for the suppression of books printed or imported without authority, which was set up pursuant to a decision taken at the conference. He became an honorary member of Gray's Inn in 1599.

From 1598 onwards, while continuing to act as an ecclesiastical judge, Dun was very often instructed or commissioned, along with other expert civil lawyers, to inquire into delicate and complicated maritime matters, including merchants' grievances, disputes between English and foreign merchants, and cases concerning doubtful prizes, embezzlement, or piracy. He was included in two commissions appointed in 1599 to hear and determine cases brought by Danish and French subjects respectively against English pirates, and in 1601 and 1609 in two other commissions, headed by the earl of Nottingham, to inquire into the depredations committed by such pirates against the subjects of the king of France and other friendly states. In August 1602 he was sent on embassy, together with Lord Eure and Sir John Herbert, to treat at Bremen with Danish ambassadors concerning tolls on English ships going through the sound or to Muscovy and attempts to prevent English fishing in waters claimed by the Danish crown. Just before this mission he was sworn extraordinary master of requests (1 August 1602). He was knighted (23 July 1603), and by July 1609 had been appointed lieutenant principal judge and president of the high court of admiralty. In 1611, together with Henry Marten, he complained to the privy council about growing interference with admiralty jurisdiction by means of prohibitions, but with little success.

Dun was elected MP for Taunton, probably as a nominee of the bishop of Winchester, in the parliament of 1601, where he served on a committee concerned with the penal laws and on 16 November opposed a bill against pluralities. He worked to gain representation for the universities, and in 1604 and 1614 he was elected by Oxford University; on the latter occasion the votes of the heads of houses were decisive, despite widespread support for his opponent among the electors. In 1604 he was one of the MPs appointed to consult with Scottish commissioners concerning a closer union of the two kingdoms, and (in connection with the proposed bill for abolishing hostile laws) defended in the Commons on 28 May 1607 the remanding by the king from either England or Scotland of prisoners accused of crimes in the other country.

In 1613, when he was a justice of assize in north Wales, Dun and his colleagues were instructed to investigate a complaint by Shropshire drapers about the export of undressed Welsh cloth to France. In 1615 he was included in the commission to investigate the complicity of the earl and countess of Somerset in the murder of Sir Thomas Overbury. A tract defending the annulment of the countess's first marriage, to the earl of Essex, is probably by Dun, as is also a treatise upholding the supervisory and prerogative jurisdiction of the Canterbury archiepiscopal courts. A collection of statutes concerning the court of arches bears his signature on its flyleaf and was presumably compiled under his aegis, as a set of reports of arches cases (1598–1604), may also have been. All these works survive only in manuscript.

Dun had married by 1587 Joan (*d.* 1640), daughter of William Aubrey, his predecessor as principal of New Inn Hall and the subject of a short account in Dun's hand. According to his epitaph they had sixteen children, seven of whom were alive in 1607. He held a messuage on Aldersgate Street, London, and the manor of Theydon Garnon, Essex, in which county he was a justice of the peace in both 1601 and 1609, and was named a member of the Virginia Company in its charter of 1609. He died on 26 September 1617 probably at Theydon Garnon, where he was buried on 28 September. His epitaph in the church there gives his age at death as seventy-two. Administration of his estate was granted to John, his son and heir, in April 1618. There is a bust of Dun by Sir Henry Cheere, executed many years after Dun's death, in the Codrington Library, All Souls College, Oxford.   RALPH HOULBROOKE

Sources epitaph, Essex, Theydon Garnon church • will, PRO, PROB 11/36, fols. 38v–39r [Robert Dun] • *CPR, 1578–8*, 111, no. 706 • B. P. Levack, *The civil lawyers in England, 1603–1641* (1973), 226–7 •

HoP, *Commons, 1558–1603* · Rymer, *Foedera*, 16.362–4, 412–13, 429–36, 430–33, 464–5, 546–51, 600, 781–3 · J. L. Chester and G. J. Armytage, eds., *Allegations for marriage licences issued by the bishop of London*, 1, Harleian Society, 25 (1887), 295, 312–13 · Foster, *Alum. Oxon.* · J. Strype, *The life and acts of John Whitgift*, new edn, 3 vols. (1822) · M. B. Rex, *University representation in England, 1604–1690* (1954) · G. D. Squibb, *Doctors' Commons: a history of the College of Advocates and Doctors of Law* (1977) · APC, 1590–91; 1597–1601; 1613–17, xx, xxviii–xxxi · *VCH Essex* · M. J. Prichard and D. E. C. Yale, eds., *Hale and Fleetwood on admiralty jurisdiction*, SeldS, 108 (1993) · *The parliamentary diary of Robert Bowyer, 1606–1607*, ed. D. H. Willson (1931) · T. L. Moir, *The Addled Parliament of 1614* (1958) · W. A. Shaw, *The knights of England*, 2 vols. (1906) · parish register, Theydon Garnon, Essex RO, Chelmsford · private information (2004) [R. Helmholz]

Archives NL Scot., memorandum book
Likenesses H. Cheere, bust, All Souls Oxf., Codrington Library

Dun, Finlay (1795–1853), composer and violinist, was born on or before 24 July 1795 in Aberdeen, the son of Barclay Dun (1771–1843/1844?), a dancing-master, and his wife, Helen (*b*. 1777), the daughter of John Duthie and his wife, Bathie. He was a nephew of David Dun (*b*. 1773), the author of 'A Volume of Shreds, & Patches' (NL Scot., MS 2715), which includes verses 'On Mr Finlay Dun's Marrying Miss Juliet White, Edin^r' and other references. From Aberdeen the family seems to have moved to Perth, where Finlay attended the grammar school, and thence to Edinburgh, where as a talented violinist he assisted his father. 'Dun and Son' were teachers of dancing in Edinburgh's New Town from 1812 until Finlay's visit to Italy (1821–5); thereafter Barclay Dun alone was listed in this capacity until 1843. In 1815–16 Finlay was a student at the University of Edinburgh, then went on to Paris, where he became a pupil of the great violinist Pierre Baillot. He is credited with introducing the quadrille to Scotland; the nineteen-year-old Elizabeth Grant of Rothiemurchus remembered practising 'all the most graceful steps from Paris' under his instruction in the winter of 1816. At the Edinburgh music festival of 1819 he played in Sir George Smart's orchestra. In the 1820s, Dun spent 'upwards of four years' in Italy. In Milan he studied with Franciszek Mirecki; in Naples, where he was engaged as principal viola at the royal theatre of San Carlo, he took lessons in counterpoint and composition in 1823–4 from Pietro Raimondi and in singing from the castrato Girolamo Crescentini.

By 1828 Dun was established as a teacher of music and singing in Edinburgh. On 25 August 1828 he married Juliet (1800/01–1876), the youngest daughter of John White, a paper maker, and his wife, Ann; they had at least four sons and two daughters. Mendelssohn dined at their home (6 Howe Street) on 28 July 1829, and the following day accompanied his host to the triennial highland pipers' competition. Dun led the orchestra at Paganini's Edinburgh concerts in October–November 1831, and was principal viola at the first Reid memorial concert conducted by John Thomson on 13 February 1841 and at the Edinburgh music festival conducted by Sir Henry Bishop in October 1843. When Thomson died in May 1841 Dun applied for the Reid chair of music at the university, supported by testimonials from Mendelssohn and others, but was passed over in favour of Bishop. In 1852, however, his advice was sought by the Reid trustees during their legal dispute with Professor John Donaldson. He died suddenly from a heart attack on 28 November 1853 at 41 Heriot Row, Edinburgh, where he had lived since 1835, and was buried in the Dean cemetery.

Dun's compositions include a prize-winning glee, 'The Parted Spirit' (1831); a fine dramatic song to words by Clementina Stirling Graham, 'The Fisherman's Home' (autograph MS in the Reid Music Library, Edinburgh); and a setting of Robert Gilfillan's ode to the memory of Sir Walter Scott (1832). He also wrote two overtures which were performed by the Edinburgh Professional Society of Musicians on 8 April 1825 and 26 January 1827, but these are lost. His doxologies and harmonized psalms were part of a Presbyterian musical revival centred on St George's, Charlotte Square, where he was a member of the congregation. But it is as an arranger of Scots songs that he is chiefly remembered. He collaborated with John Thomson on *The Vocal Melodies of Scotland* (1836–8) and with George Farquhar Graham on *The Songs of Scotland* (1848–53), and was responsible for a book of Lady Nairne's songs, *Lays from Strathearn* (1846), and one of Gaelic songs, *Orain na'h-Albain* (1848). Together with his writings—notable among which is an 'Analysis of the structure of the music of Scotland' (published in 1838 as an appendix to William Dauney's *Ancient Scottish Melodies*)—these reveal an intelligent and accomplished musician. In disposition he was 'exceedingly mild, gentle, and amiable' (*The Scotsman*); Baptie characterized him as 'a man of great ability, refined taste and genius, an excellent linguist and scholar and courteous gentleman'.   CHRISTOPHER D. S. FIELD

Sources *The Scotsman* (30 Nov 1853) · F. Dun, application for the Reid chair of music with supporting testimonials, 1841, U. Edin., Box Da 46.9 · D. Baptie, ed., *Musical Scotland, past and present: being a dictionary of Scottish musicians from about 1400 till the present time* (1894) · J. D. Brown, *Biographical dictionary of musicians: with a bibliography of English writings on music* (1886) · F. Dun, notes for the trustees of General Reid's fund, 1852, U. Edin., Box Da 46.13(2) · *Memoirs of a highland lady: the autobiography of Elizabeth Grant of Rothiemurchus*, ed. J. M. Strachey, 2nd edn (1911) · F. Mendelssohn, *Felix Mendelssohn Bartholdy Briefe*, ed. R. Elvers (1984) · *Leaves from the journals of Sir George Smart*, ed. H. B. Cox and C. L. E. Cox (1907) · W. Dauney, *Ancient Scottish melodies* (1838) · parish register (baptism), Aberdeen, 24 July 1795 [GRO Scotland 168.A/9] · parish register (marriage), Edinburgh, 25 Aug 1828 [GRO Scotland 685.I/63] · parish register, death [GRO Scotland 685/4 no. 378] · postal directories, Edinburgh, 1812–53 · D. Baptie, *Sketches of the English glee composers: historical, biographical and critical (from about 1735–1866)* [1896] · DNB · *Edinburgh Advertiser* (1 April 1825) · *Edinburgh Advertiser* (12 April 1825) · *Edinburgh Advertiser* (30 Jan 1827)

Dun, John (1723/4–1792), Church of Scotland minister and tutor, was born in Eskdale, Dumfriesshire, and was educated for the ministry under Professor Patrick Cuming at the University of Edinburgh. In the late 1740s he was taken to Auchinleck in Ayrshire by Alexander Boswell, Lord Auchinleck, to be his family chaplain and the tutor to his eight-year-old son, James. In an autobiographical sketch he prepared for Rousseau in 1764, James Boswell credited Dun with his initial exposure to *The Spectator*, the Roman poets, and moderate religion, though in an unused draft he criticized his early tutors for their subservience to Lord Auchinleck, their lack of manners, and their mean education, on account of which, Boswell states, he treated them 'with contempt' (Pottle, 18, 28). Yet surviving correspondence and documents among the Boswell papers demonstrate that Boswell remained respectful and supportive of Dun throughout his life, even after the minister grew difficult in old age.

While in Lord Auchinleck's service Dun received his licence to preach from the presbytery of Irvine on 11 September 1750. Boswell lost his tutor at the age of twelve, when Lord Auchinleck secured for Dun a call (dated 11 August 1752, and reproduced in *Sermons*, 1.253–4) to the church at Auchinleck, where he was ordained on 9 November 1752 and remained until his death forty years later. He married, on 21 November 1757, Mary Wilson (1730?–1762); they had two daughters, Elizabeth (*b*. 1758) and Isabella (1760–1833), who married the minister of Kilmaurs, Alexander Gillies (*d*. 1786). On 28 December 1770 Dun married Deborah Blackstock (1732?–1795), who gave birth to a son, Alexander Boswell, on 3 July 1772. Dun published two occasional sermons during his career, one preached on 19 January 1766 on the occasion of Lady Auchinleck's death, which also prompted him to write to James expressing his sympathy and lecturing him on his new responsibilities toward his father (Cole, 12–13), and the other preached at Kirkconnel on 24 June 1780 on the Lord's supper. The sermon Dun preached at the time of Lord Auchinleck's death in 1782, 'The immortality of the righteous', appeared in his *Sermons, in Two Volumes*, an odd mixture of political, religious, and literary writings published by subscription in 1790 with the assistance of James Boswell (Boswell MSS, C 1129, P 49), who subscribed for six copies (and his wife for three more) but expressed concern that 'Poor John Dun will be a sad loser by his *Sermons*' (*Letters of Johnson*, 2.387). If so, his former tutor was at least well prepared for the outcome, having begun the preface to his second volume with this memorable sentence: 'To commence author, is like going forth to stand on the pillory'.

The first edition of Boswell's *Tour to the Hebrides* (1785) records that when Samuel Johnson visited Auchinleck in November 1773 he was 'so highly offended' by Dun's gross characterizations of the Anglican clergy that he said to him, 'Sir, you know no more of our church than a Hottentot', but Dun hotly denied that the word 'Hottentot' had been used, and in spite of supporting documentation Boswell removed his name from the anecdote in the second edition (Boswell, *Life*, 5.382; *Tour*, 375; Boswell MSS, L 925, M 254).

Dun was an aggressive whig in secular and ecclesiastical politics. Although his theology was moderate he sided with the popular party in the Church of Scotland on the burning issue of church patronage, and his speech in the general assembly of 1784 was published as a pamphlet with the title *The Law of Patronage in Scotland an Unjust Law*. He commiserated with Boswell in 1769 on the defeat of General Paoli of Corsica, praised Lord Auchinleck for accepting lower rents from older tenants, corresponded with Richard Price in 1791, and filled his *Sermons* with poems and remarks that celebrated the revolution of 1688

for securing 'the rights of mankind' and that reminded Scottish heritors (landowners) of their responsibility to maintain the parish poor (Boswell MSS, C 1126, C 1129, C 2292). He died on 11 October 1792, naming James Boswell one of his trustees in his will (Boswell MSS, C 1122, L 446).

RICHARD B. SHER

Sources Boswell, *Life* · *Boswell's journal of a tour to the Hebrides with Samuel Johnson*, ed. F. A. Pottle and C. H. Bennett (1963), vol. 9 of *The Yale editions of the private papers of James Boswell*, trade edn (1950–89) · *Boswell, laird of Auchinleck, 1778–1782*, ed. J. W. Reed and F. A. Pottle (1977), vol. 11 of *The Yale editions of the private papers of James Boswell*, trade edn (1950–89) · *Boswell: the English experiment, 1785–1789*, ed. I. S. Lustig and F. A. Pottle (1986), vol. 13 of *The Yale editions of the private papers of James Boswell*, trade edn (1950–89) · F. Brady, *James Boswell: the later years, 1769–1795* (1984) · *The general correspondence of James Boswell, 1766–1769*, ed. R. C. Cole and others, 1 (1993), vol. 5 of *The Yale editions of the private papers of James Boswell*, research edn · F. A. Pottle, *James Boswell: the earlier years, 1740–1769* (1966) · *Fasti Scot.*, new edn, 3.4 · R. B. Sher, 'Scottish divines and legal lairds: Boswell's Scots Presbyterian identity', *New light on Boswell: critical and historical essays on the occasion of the bicentenary of the 'Life of Johnson'*, ed. G. Clingham (1991), 28–55 · *Letters of James Boswell*, ed. C. B. Tinker, 2 vols. (1924) · *Boswell: the applause of the jury, 1782–1785*, ed. I. S. Lustig and F. A. Pottle (1981), vol. 12 of *The Yale editions of the private papers of James Boswell*, trade edn (1950–89) · *The correspondence of James Boswell with James Bruce and Andrew Gibb, overseers of the Auchinleck estate*, ed. N. P. Hankins and J. Strawhorn (1998), vol. 8 of *The Yale editions of the private papers of James Boswell*, research edn (1966–) · Yale U., Beinecke L., Boswell papers
Archives Yale U., Boswell MSS

Dun [Dune, Dunne], **Patrick** (*bap*. 1581, *d*. 1652), college head and benefactor, was baptized on 23 July 1581 at St Nicholas Church, New Aberdeen, the son of Andrew Dun, a burgess of the city. It is likely that he attended Aberdeen grammar school, before progressing to either King's College in Old Aberdeen or Marischal College in New Aberdeen to take his first degree. By 1603 he had followed his townsman Duncan Liddel to the German University of Helmstedt in the duchy of Brunswick. He studied medicine there under Liddel for four years, until Liddel left Helmstedt, and then visited the University of Heidelberg and the Huguenot academy at Nîmes, before graduating in medicine at Basel in 1607.

By 1610 Dun had returned to Aberdeen, and was teaching logic in Marischal College, being described as 'ane verie famous professor of Germanie' in the *Buik of Register* (Lang, 43). He also became involved in Bishop Patrick Forbes's attempts to re-establish Bishop Elphinstone's original foundation at King's College in Old Aberdeen. A member of Forbes's commission of visitation to King's in 1619, Dun was appointed to the newly re-established post of mediciner. In 1621 he was appointed first lay principal of Marischal College, but on admission to the post was granted leave to continue his medical practice to the nobility and gentry of the burgh's hinterland. However, it is not for his academic position or medical career that Dun is now chiefly remembered, but for the benefactions he made to educational causes in Aberdeen. In 1629 he bought the lands of Ferryhill to the south of the burgh, with a view to mortifying them—that is, gifting them in perpetual trust—to the town for the endowment of its grammar school. In his deed of mortification of 1631 he stated his intention that after his death the profit from the lands should be used to support four full-time teachers at the school. Poor scholars should be educated free, and Dun hoped that sufficiently endowed posts would improve the quality and commitment of their teachers. He also contributed 2000 merks (approximately £111), the largest individual contribution, to a fund to restore the buildings of Marischal College after a serious fire in 1639.

Although, probably due to pressure of work, Dun demitted his post at King's in 1632, he continued to take an interest in the affairs of that college, and was in 1634 elected to the newly revived post of dean of medicine there. His position as a layman rather than theologian appears to have helped him avoid the censure directed at the 'Aberdeen doctors' by the covenanting authorities. His son-in-law Alexander Jaffray bitterly, if not necessarily reliably, observed of his principalship of Marischal College that he was 'unfit for training up youths' (*Diary*, 43), but he remained principal until 1649, when he was succeeded by William Moir. Dun showed little interest in publishing on his own account, but he edited and was instrumental in securing the posthumous publication of the *Artis sanitatem conservandi* (1651) of his old mentor Duncan Liddel. Dun died in 1652. He had married, but no details of his wife are known.

A portrait of Dun by George Jamesone hung in the hall of the grammar school until it was destroyed in a fire in 1986, but copies survive in print. Dun's daughter, Jean, predeceased him by eight years, and his heirs were the sons of his brother Charles, one of whom was the father of the physician Sir Patrick *Dun (1642–1713).

SHONA MACLEAN VANCE

Sources council register, Aberdeen City Archive, vols. 49–53/1 · mortification accounts, Aberdeen City Archive, vol. 1 · P. J. Anderson and J. F. K. Johnstone, eds., *Fasti academiae Mariscallanae Aberdonensis: selections from the records of the Marischal College and University, MDXCIII–MDCCCLX*, 3 vols., New Spalding Club, 4, 18–19 (1889–98) · D. Liddel, *Artis conservandi sanitatem libri duo* (1651) · *Mortifications under the charge of the provost, magistrates, and town council of Aberdeen* (1849) · J. F. Kellas Johnstone and A. W. Robertson, *Bibliographia Aberdonensis*, ed. W. D. Simpson, 2 vols., Third Spalding Club (1929–30) · J. K. Cameron, 'Some Aberdeen students on the continent in the late sixteenth and seventeenth centuries', *The universities of Aberdeen and Europe: the first three centuries*, ed. P. Dukes (1995), 57–78 · G. Molland, 'Scottish-continental intellectual relations as mirrored in the career of Duncan Liddel (1561–1613)', *The universities of Aberdeen and Europe: the first three centuries*, ed. P. Dukes (1995), 79–101 · R. French, 'Medical teaching in Aberdeen: from the foundation of the university to the middle of the seventeenth century', *History of Universities*, 3 (1983) · D. Stevenson, *King's College, Aberdeen, 1560–1641: from protestant Reformation to covenanting revolution* (1990) · parochial register, St Nicholas, New Aberdeen, vol. 1, 1563–91, NA Scot., OPR 168 A/1 [baptism], fol. 237, 23 July 1581 · H. F. Morland Simpson, ed., *Bon record: records and reminiscences of Aberdeen grammar school* (1906) · J. M. Lang, 'Hector Boece and the principals', *Studies in the history of the University of Aberdeen*, ed. P. J. Anderson (1906), 21–56 · *Diary of Alexander Jaffray*, ed. J. Barclay, 3rd edn (1856) · W. C. Taylor, 'Scottish students in Heidelberg', *SHR*, 5 (1907–8), 67–75 · J. Durkan, 'The French connection in the sixteenth century and early seventeenth century', *Scotland and Europe*, ed. T. C. Smout (1986)

Likenesses G. Jamesone, oils, 1631, repro. in Morland Simpson, ed., *Bon record*, frontispiece; destroyed by fire, 1986

Wealth at death 1600 merks—left to the town council of Aberdeen: *Mortifications under the charge of the provost*, 84; mortification accounts, vol. 1, Ferryhill a/c, 1652–3, Aberdeen City Archive

Dun, Sir Patrick (1642–1713), physician, was born on 13 January 1642 at Aberdeen, the second son of Charles Dun (*d.* 1667), dyer, and his second wife, Catherine Burnet. His great-uncle Dr Patrick Dun was principal of Marischal College, Aberdeen, and dean of the faculty of medicine; he also endowed Aberdeen grammar school. Patrick Dun graduated in arts at Marischal College in 1658 and also studied at Valence in France. He became a doctor of physic of Trinity College, Dublin, and in 1677 was also incorporated *in absentia* MD at Oxford. His name does not appear on the list of graduates of the school of physic of Dublin University, but it is known that this list is not complete, and in his portrait by Sir Godfrey Kneller Dun is depicted in the robes of a doctor of physic of the university.

Dun's appointment as physician to the state and to James, duke of Ormond, lord lieutenant of Ireland, may have been the reason for his arrival in Dublin. The date of the appointment is not recorded, but it is known from a letter written from Dublin by Sir John Hill on 14 February 1676 that Dun was in the city at that time. He was elected as one of the fourteen fellows of the Irish College of Physicians, probably in 1677, and delivered an address before the college on 4 April 1677. He was elected president of the college on 24 June 1681 and continued in office until 1687. Dun was among the founder members of the Dublin Philosophical Society in 1683, and read a paper on the analysis of mineral waters to the society. Dun also supported the study of anatomy, and an account is given in the records of the society of the anatomical dissection of the body of an executed criminal, obtained for the purpose by Dun, in February 1684.

Dun became one of the leading physicians in Dublin and counted among his friends many of the most eminent men in the city. He supported the Williamite side in 1688 and is listed among the refugees who fled the country in that year. He returned in 1689 and was appointed physician to King William's army. He cared for soldiers in army camps on the campaign and at the Royal Hospital, Kilmainham, Dublin. He was also responsible for distributing medical supplies to the army surgeons in camps around the country. As there was a great shortage of resources, he requested that his pay should be deferred. His generosity however was not appreciated, as many years later his widow was still seeking payment of the money from the English government.

Dun was re-elected president of the College of Physicians in 1690, and the college was granted a new charter two years later, giving it greater powers. Having played a leading part in bringing this about, Dun was elected first president under the new charter in 1692. He was re-elected to this position in the years 1693, 1696, 1698, and 1706. Dun was elected to the Irish House of Commons in 1692, but did not play a very active role in its affairs. He was appointed as physician to the Royal Hospital, Kilmainham, in 1705 at a salary of 10 shillings a day.

On 11 December 1694 Dun, then aged fifty-two, married Mary (d. 1748), daughter of Colonel John Jephson of Mallow, co. Cork, and his wife, Bridget, daughter of Richard Boyle, archbishop of Tuam, and a great-niece of the first earl of Cork. The marriage took place at St Michan's Church in Dublin. They had one son, Boyle, who died at a very early age. Dun was knighted on 29 July 1696.

Dun died on Sunday, 24 May 1713, following a short illness. He was buried three days later at St Michan's Church. He left provision in his will for the endowment of a professorship of physic in the College of Physicians. Disputes between Dun's widow and the college delayed the implementation of his scheme. In 1740 it was finally agreed that the trust would support three professors, to be known as king's professors, in physic, surgery, midwifery, materia medica, and pharmacy. The appointments were to be made by the provost of Trinity College, the regius professor of physic of the university, and the president and two senior censors of the College of Physicians. Additional professorships were founded in 1785. The income from the bequest was also sufficient to support the foundation of a teaching hospital. In 1800 the School of Physic Act of the Irish parliament made provision for the establishment of the hospital, which was to be called Sir Patrick Dun's Hospital: it became an important teaching hospital for Trinity College, Dublin, until its closure in 1987, when the staff and patients were moved to the new St James's Hospital. The funds which accrued from the sale of the hospital buildings were used to develop postgraduate medical education at the Royal College of Physicians of Ireland, to build a new teaching centre for Trinity College, and to support laboratories for clinical research, which are known as the Sir Patrick Dun's Research Laboratories. The teaching centre and the research laboratories are based at St James's Hospital, Dublin.

DAVIS COAKLEY

Sources T. W. Belcher, *Memoir of Sir Patrick Dun* (1866) · T. P. C. Kirkpatrick, 'Sir Patrick Dun's library', *Irish Journal of Medical Science*, 149 (1920), 49–68 · J. Osborne, *Annals of Sir Patrick Dun's Hospital* (1831) · T. G. Moorhead, *A short history of Sir Patrick Dun's Hospital* (1942) · E. O'Brien, A. Crookshank, and G. Wolstenholme, *A portrait of Irish medicine* (1984) · T. P. C. Kirkpatrick, *History of the medical teaching in Trinity College, Dublin, and of the School of Physic in Ireland* (1912) · J. D. H. Widdess, *A history of the Royal College of Physicians of Ireland, 1654–1963* (1963) · M. D. Jephson, *An Anglo-Irish miscellany: some records of the Jephsons of Mallow* (1964) · T. P. C. Kirkpatrick, *Sir Patrick Dun* (1945) · *Fasti academiae Mariscallanae Aberdonensis: selections from the records of the Marischal College and University, MDXCIII–MDCCCLX*, 2, ed. P. J. Anderson, New Spalding Club, 18 (1898), 226 · Wood, *Ath. Oxon.*
Archives Bodl. Oxf., Locke MSS · Marsh's Library, Dublin, King MSS · TCD, Clarke Correspondence Library · TCD, Lyons Collection Library, corresp. with Archbishop William King
Likenesses G. Kneller, oils, Royal College of Physicians of Ireland · G. Kneller, oils, Sir Patrick Dun's Hospital, Dublin · W. Lizars, engraving (after an oil painting by G. Kneller), Wellcome L.; repro. in Belcher, *Memoir of Sir Patrick Dun*

Wealth at death £5936 personal estate; also real estate: personal estate of Sir Patrick Dun in the hand of Lady Dun, Marsh's Library, Dublin; Widdess, *History*, 47–54

Dúnán [Donatus] (d. 1074), bishop of Dublin, was the first bishop of that Hiberno-Scandinavian town. The only certain date connected with him is his death, but his career was long, and witnessed the passing of Dublin from government by an independent Hiberno-Scandinavian prince to rule by powerful Irish princes.

Before the arrival of the vikings in Ireland, there had been ecclesiastical houses in the neighbourhood of a crossing of the River Liffey known as Áth Clíath ('the ford of the hurdles'). By the eleventh century Dublin (Baile Átha Clíath in Irish) had been accepted as part of the Irish political sphere, but its place in ecclesiastical affairs remained ambiguous. There had been a Christian element among Dublin's rulers since the tenth century, and its king Olaf Cuarán (Sihtricson) died in religious retirement at Iona in 981. His son Sihtric Silkiskegg (d. 1042) was also a Christian and in 1028 he made a pilgrimage to Rome. Some time before his abdication in 1036, Sihtric founded a church dedicated to the Holy Trinity, possibly on the site of an earlier church whose arches and vaults were said to have been used as its foundation. Dúnán was consecrated the first bishop and he began the construction of his cathedral on the site of Holy Trinity, completing the nave and two collateral structures. On the north side he had built a chapel dedicated to St Nicholas and at the entrance he had an image of the crucifixion. Dúnán is also credited with building a church dedicated to St Michael Archangel, which was probably the chapel to St Michael that was attached to his own residence. Sihtric was the patron of these enterprises and in addition to supplying the gold and silver to pay for the construction of the buildings, he also contributed to the support of the bishop and his curia. Estates with workers and livestock at St Doulogh's, Lambay, and Portrane were given to the new bishop. These lands are all in the north of Fine Gall, or Fingal, the limits of Dublin's territory. The archbishops' residence in Dublin was built in an orchard belonging to the convent of Holy Trinity.

An unanswered question about the establishment of the see of Dublin concerns whether or not Dúnán was consecrated by the archbishop of Canterbury and, if so, whether this was a formal submission. The question is relevant because after Dúnán's death his successors for the rest of the century would go to Canterbury for consecration and offer their submissions according to ancestral custom. By the twelfth century the claims of Canterbury were being actively contested by Armagh, which was probably responsible for the late eleventh-century legend claiming that St Patrick had brought Christianity to the vikings of Dublin. Although there is evidence for close ties between Sihtric and King Cnut of England, the matter of Dúnán's consecration must remain open. The conquest of the town in 1052 by the Leinster king Diarmait mac Máel na mBó brought it under direct Irish control and Dúnán continued as bishop. At the time of his death the town was under the lordship of the king of Munster, Toirdelbach Ó

Briain. Dúnán died on 15 May 1074, according to the contemporary chronicler Marianus Scottus; he was buried to the left of the great altar in Christ Church, Dublin.

BENJAMIN T. HUDSON

Sources D. G. Waitz, ed., 'Mariani Scotti chronicon', [*Annales et chronica aevi Salici*], ed. G. H. Pertz, MGH Scriptores [folio], 5 (Stuttgart, 1844), 481–568 • H. J. Lawlor, 'A calendar of the *Liber niger* and *Liber albus* of Christ Church, Dublin', *Proceedings of the Royal Irish Academy*, 27C (1908–9), 1–93 • A. Gwynn, 'The origins of the see of Dublin', *Irish Ecclesiastical Record*, 5th ser., 57 (1941), 40–55, 97–112 • A. Gwynn, ed., 'Some unpublished texts from the Black Book of Christ Church, Dublin', *Analecta Hibernica*, 16 (1946), 281–337 • B. T. Hudson, 'Knútr and viking Dublin', *Scandinavian Studies*, 66 (1994), 321–35 • *Ann. Ulster* • *AFM* • Annals of St Mary's, Dublin, s.a. 1074

Dunbar. For this title name *see* individual entries under Dunbar; *see also* Patrick, fourth earl of Dunbar (*d.* 1232); Home, George, earl of Dunbar (*d.* 1611); Constable, Henry, first Viscount Dunbar (1588–1645).

Dunbar family, earls of Moray (*per. c.*1370–1430), was important in the conduct of Anglo-Scottish warfare in the late fourteenth and early fifteenth centuries. **John Dunbar**, first earl of Moray (*d.* 1391/2), and his elder brother George *Dunbar, later ninth earl of Dunbar, were the sons of Sir Patrick Dunbar and his wife, Isabel Randolph. They first came to prominence as royal favourites late in the reign of David II when their sister Agnes became the king's mistress. In 1370 John made a prestigious marriage with Marjory Stewart (*d.* after 1403), the daughter of David's nephew and heir apparent, Robert the Steward (the future Robert II). Later chroniclers suggest that the Steward was less than happy with his daughter's marriage, which may have been arranged by David II, no doubt influenced by his mistress. In autumn 1370 the king granted John the lordship of the earldom of Fife, a territory that the Steward and his family had long coveted. After David II's death on 22 February 1371 and the accession of Robert II, however, Dunbar found his hold on Fife challenged by the new king's son (and Dunbar's brother-in-law) Robert Stewart, earl of Menteith and later duke of Albany. The dispute between Dunbar and Earl Robert was ended about 9 March 1372, when the former gave up his claims to Fife, receiving in compensation a grant of the earldom of Moray, to which he had a claim through his mother. Moray's hold on the northern earldom was made problematic by the conditions of the 1372 grant. Strategic lordships such as Lochaber, Badenoch, and the castle and barony of Urquhart, which had been part of the earldom created for Thomas Randolph in 1312, were specifically excepted from the grant because they had been seized by or gifted to other powerful lords in the years after the death of the third and last Randolph earl in 1346. The truncated earldom proved difficult to defend, and Moray soon found himself embroiled in a series of territorial and jurisdictional clashes with forceful neighbours, including Alexander Stewart, another son of Robert II who was lord of Badenoch and later earl of Buchan, and Alexander Bur, bishop of Moray. Earl John was prepared to invest in his new lordship and he seems to have been responsible for the building of a new hall at Darnaway Castle (now

known, mistakenly, as Randolph's Hall) in the years shortly before his death. Overall, however, the evidence suggests that the Dunbar earls lacked the local network of kin and allies to maintain a firm hold on the upland zones surrounding the Moray coastal plain.

Moreover, despite his acquisition of an important northern earldom, Moray also retained an active role in Anglo-Scottish warfare and diplomacy. He was involved in the escalation of pressure on English-occupied lands in the south of Scotland in the years after the death of Edward III in 1377 and took a leading role in the major Franco-Scottish campaign against targets in the north of England during 1385, when he received a large payment (1000 livres tournois) from the French war-chest for his services and was regarded by the chronicler Froissart as one of the principal Scottish leaders. He also played a prominent part, alongside his brother, George, and James, second earl of Douglas, in the Scottish campaign in the north of England which culminated in the battle of Otterburn on 5 August 1388. Moray's role in the engagement is commemorated in Thomas Barry's contemporary Latin poem and in Walter Bower's *Scotichronicon*, where the earl is said to have fought bareheaded after a surprise English attack on the Scottish force.

Moray's interest in warfare and the display of martial prowess was not blunted by the conclusion of an Anglo-Scottish truce in 1389. In the next two years he received several safe conducts to allow his participation in jousts and tournaments in England and he was a prominent figure at a tournament held at Smithfield in the summer of 1390 by Richard II. The exact date and circumstances surrounding his death are difficult to determine. Later English chronicles contain garbled accounts suggesting that he died at York of injuries sustained in a joust with Thomas Mowbray, earl of Nottingham. There were indeed plans for a duel between the two men in May 1390, but either the combat did not take place then or Moray survived it, for he was still alive on 13 June 1391, when he applied for a further English safe conduct. He died between the latter date and 15 February 1392; his demise may have occurred in England as a result of wounds received in a tournament, but there is no conclusive evidence.

Moray's marriage to Marjory Stewart produced at least four children, Thomas, Alexander, James, and Euphemia. He was succeeded as earl of Moray by their eldest son, **Thomas Dunbar**, second earl of Moray (*d.* in or before 1422), who was using the comital style by 15 February 1392. Thomas also inherited the strategic problems of the Moray earldom. Even before he became earl he had been made aware of the difficulties of protecting lowland Moray from neighbouring lordships, when in 1390 he replaced Alexander Stewart as sheriff of Inverness and entered into an agreement to protect the bishop of Moray's lands and estates from the exactions of Stewart's followers. In response Stewart's men burnt the bishop's houses and property in Elgin and Forres in May and June, with Moray apparently unable to intervene, and in August Robert III supported Bishop Bur when he asserted that the agreement with Moray was no longer binding because he had failed to protect the bishop's property. The weakness of the Dunbar earls and the vulnerability of Moray was further emphasized in Thomas's agreement of September 1394 with Alastair MacDomhnaill, lord of Lochaber, whereby the latter was to receive an annual payment from the earl in return for preventing his men from raiding or living off lands inside the earldom. The problem of disorder in the highland zones around Moray resurfaced in 1396, when Thomas played a leading part in arranging the famous 'Clan Fight' on the north inch of Perth, a formal conflict designed to bring an end to a long-running and violent feud between two highland kindreds. Thereafter references to him are few. He was among the many Scots captured by the English at the battle of Hamildon Hill on 14 September 1402 and remained a prisoner in England until July 1405. He was apparently still alive in June 1415, but had died before August 1422. The identity of his wife is unknown; they had a son and heir, also Thomas, who succeeded to the earldom before 9 August 1422.

Most aspects of the short career of the younger **Thomas Dunbar**, third earl of Moray (*d.* in or after 1425), remain obscure. In June 1415, before he became earl, it was evidently intended that he should marry Euphemia Leslie, countess of Ross, and a papal dispensation for the marriage was obtained. However, the match was never finalized and instead Euphemia resigned her lands and earldom in favour of John Stewart, earl of Buchan. Moray was one of the Scottish lords named as a surety for the payment of James I's ransom when the king was released from English captivity in 1424, and was consequently warded in England from March 1424 until July 1425. He died shortly afterwards, to be succeeded by his cousin **James Dunbar**, fourth earl of Moray (*d.* 1430), the son of Alexander Dunbar and Matilda Fraser and grandson of the first earl. The exact date of James's accession to the earldom is unknown, but he seems to have been acting as earl before he died. Like his cousin, James was one of the hostages for James I's release and between 1425 and November 1427 he was held in England. He died on or about 10 August 1430, leaving two daughters from his marriage to Margaret Seton: Janet, who married James, second Lord Crichton between 1442 and 1446, and Elizabeth, who before 26 April 1442 married Archibald Douglas, the third son of James, seventh earl of Douglas. His widow married Alexander Stewart, twelfth earl of Mar. The Moray title went with Elizabeth, and by 3 July 1445 Archibald Douglas was styling himself earl of Moray. The line of Dunbar earls thus ended, although James had an illegitimate son, also James, who founded the Dunbar of Westfield line which retained a local influence inside Moray.

S. I. BOARDMAN

Sources J. M. Thomson and others, eds., *Registrum magni sigilli regum Scotorum / The register of the great seal of Scotland*, 11 vols. (1882–1914), vols. 1–2 · G. Burnett and others, eds., *The exchequer rolls of Scotland*, 3–4 (1880) · *CDS*, vols. 2–4 · W. Bower, *Scotichronicon*, ed. D. E. R. Watt and others, new edn, 9 vols. (1987–98), vol. 6 · J. Froissart, *Chronicles*, ed. T. Johnes, 2 vols. (1868) · J. Robertson, ed., *Illustrations of the topography and antiquities of the shires of Aberdeen and* Banff, 3–4, Spalding Club, 29, 32 (1857–62) · *RotS*, vol. 2 · S. I. Boardman, *The early Stewart kings: Robert II and Robert III, 1371–1406* (1996) · M. Brown, *James I* (1994) · *Scots peerage*, vol. 6

Dunbar, Agnes, countess of Dunbar or of March (*d.* 1369). *See under* Dunbar, Patrick, eighth earl of Dunbar or of March, and earl of Moray (1285–1369).

Dunbar, Andrea (1961–1990), playwright, was born on 22 May 1961 at 23 Oliver Street, East Bowling, Bradford, the third of the eight children of John Brian Dunbar (1936–1989), a wool warehouseman, and his wife, Alma (*b.* 1935), a worsted twister, daughter of John Chippendale of Bradford and his wife, Millicent. Both Andrea's grandfathers were woolcombers and both her parents were textile workers at the time of their marriage in 1958. However, with the decline of the textile industry her father found alternative employment as a demolition worker until an injury left him partially disabled. His consequent feckless drinking, and foul-mouthed and sometimes violently abusive behaviour towards his wife and children at their council-house home on Bradford's notorious Buttershaw estate, has been identified as the dramatic centre of Andrea's childhood.

Andrea Dunbar was educated at Horton Bank Top junior school from 1966 to 1972 and Buttershaw high school from 1972 to 1977. She showed little interest in school until her repeated failure to bring the required ingredients to her domestic science lessons resulted in an imposition, which turned into a spontaneously hilarious, pertinently intelligent two-page essay questioning the relevance to her family situation of the confection of a raspberry pavlova. Sympathetic teachers recognized, in her talent for observation of the foibles of human behaviour, her potential as a writer: she was encouraged to develop a taped dialogue for submission as coursework for CSE English. She later confessed that at that time she read little other than horror comics, and learned to write dramatic dialogue by copying out the Victorian melodrama *Maria Marten, or, Murder in the Red Barn*, the story of a rich seducer and an innocent country lass. Her education was interrupted when she became pregnant at fourteen and lost the baby she was carrying following a car crash. She subsequently returned to school to develop her burgeoning interest in drama, leaving with three CSEs at sixteen with no particular plans or aspirations for her future, and obtaining employment French combing at Bowling Mills in Bradford.

In 1980 Dunbar entered the script of her first play, *The Arbor*—written when she was a fifteen-year-old schoolgirl in green biro on pages torn from a school exercise book—in a national competition for young writers. Her work impressed Max Stafford-Clark, director of London's Royal Court Theatre, and the play was produced at the Theatre Upstairs before transfer to the main stage, where it followed Richard Eyre's celebrated production of *Hamlet*. 'For most of the Royal Court audience', one sympathetic critic observed, 'the language and substance of the play were as remote as a piece of anthropology' (Ritchie).

Revolving around the pregnancy and subsequent miscarriage of the central character, the semi-autobiographical play was set against a background of domestic violence, boredom, poverty, and overcrowding in Brafferton Arbor, the crescent on the Bradford council estate where Andrea had spent her childhood and adolescence. Its success resulted in the commissioning of a second play, *Rita, Sue and Bob too*, a ribald comedy-drama in which a pair of teenage schoolgirls living on a run-down Bradford council estate are seduced by an older married man for whom they work as babysitters. Opening at the Royal Court in 1982, it was awarded the George Devine award for promising young playwrights and subsequently adapted for the cinema in 1986. A third play, *Shirley*, centring upon the infidelity of the play's eponymous heroine while her longstanding boyfriend serves a short prison sentence, opened at the Theatre Upstairs in 1985 and was acclaimed by the critic Michael Billington as 'a short, sharp, brutally funny slice of Bradford life' ('Andrea Dunbar a tribute', Bradford Libraries and Information Services).

Dunbar's three plays about contemporary working-class urban life were widely praised for their earthy realism and sharp wit. The playwright Shelagh Delaney pronounced her 'the genius from the slums' (*Mail on Sunday*, quoted in *Bradford Telegraph and Argus*, 21 Dec 1990), while the drama critic Benedict Nightingale dubbed Dunbar 'the bard of the West Riding council-estate jungle' and hailed her achievement in 'steeping herself in a distinctive geographical, social and human area', making it 'unmistakably her own' (B. Nightingale, *New Statesman*, undated, 'Andrea Dunbar a tribute', Bradford Libraries and Information Services). The tabloid press sensationally represented her work as 'Thatcher's Britain with its Knickers Down' (*The Guardian*, 30 Aug 2000). However, her writing was as devoid of political and social comment as it was of moralizing and self-pity. She simply recorded her raw experiences of social and cultural deprivation in the depressed environment of the council estate which she knew best in the 1980s, revealing an acute ear for idiom, a firm grasp of a dramatic narrative, an impressive capacity for total recall, and an ability to import humour into the direst of circumstances.

Dunbar's personal life was certainly tumultuous and ultimately tragic. After the trauma of her initial teenage pregnancy and miscarriage she never married, but had three more children by different fathers between 1979 and 1983, seeking refuge from the first of these partners, an Asian taxi driver, in an eighteen-month sojourn in a refuge for battered women at Keighley. Moreover, the release of the film version of *Rita, Sue and Bob too* created a furore in her native Bradford, where 'all hell broke loose ... at news of the contents of the film' (*Bradford Telegraph and Argus*, 21 Dec 1990). Dunbar recognized that the film

> probably upset councillors who would like to show a fairytale side of Bradford and ignore the darker elements of it, the Tourist Office who also shut their eyes to the rundown parts and even some residents on the Buttershaw estate itself. (*Bradford Telegraph and Argus*, 11 Sept 1987)

The film also received some hostile reviews. The *Yorkshire Post* critic pronounced it 'without doubt the crudest film I have ever seen' (9 Sept 1987), while the *Daily Express* complained of ninety minutes of 'unmitigated abusive gloom ... filmed with an inexperienced cast and an appalling script' (quoted in *Sunday Times*, 6 Sept 1987). Her unofficial agent, Rob Ritchie, commented: 'I think the film was the point at which whatever dreams she might have had about being a writer collapsed. It unleashed all those problems for her family and the community that she was living in' (*The Guardian*, 30 Aug 2000). However, Dunbar insisted on riding out the storm of controversy by remaining close to her roots in Bradford with the children she adored, even after arousing further controversy when she was fined by Bradford magistrates for claiming social security without declaring her royalty payments.

Grotesquely caricatured in appearance by some journalists as 'boot-faced' with 'black teeth' and hard-bitten fingernails (*Mail on Sunday*), others commented more sympathetically on Dunbar's watchful eyes, strong chin, and brilliant smile. She was usually photographed informally, sometimes at her local enjoying a pint of ale or in the bleaker surroundings of the desolate Buttershaw estate with its boarded-up windows, graffiti-vandalized walls, and tangled, overgrown gardens. Beneath a belligerent façade she displayed a disarming modesty, shyness, and sensitivity, but also an impermeable stoicism and dour stubbornness. A heavy drinker and smoker, and a victim of both domestic violence and sexual harassment, she suffered a brain haemorrhage and collapsed while drinking alone in her local public house on the afternoon of 20 December 1990 and was rushed to the Bradford Royal Infirmary, where she died at the age of twenty-nine. She professed no religious faith, but a neighbour on the Buttershaw estate, the Revd Arthur Tuffee, a Baptist minister, conducted her funeral service at Scholemoor Crematorium, Bradford, on 28 December 1990, describing her as a 'happy-go-lucky character, who spoke up for the poor and disadvantaged' (*Yorkshire Post*, 29 Dec 1990). New facilities for creative writers were established at Bradford Central Library as a living memorial to her in 1997, and the actor and playwright Robin Soans wrote a new play, *A State Affair*, a sequel to *The Arbor*, after revisiting the Buttershaw estate with Max Stafford-Clark in July 2000, which was premièred in Liverpool in October 2000.

JOHN A. HARGREAVES

Sources 'Andrea Dunbar a tribute', unpublished cuttings book, June 1991, Bradford Libraries and Information Services • R. Ritchie, introduction, in A. Dunbar, *Rita, Sue and Bob too* (1988) • *The Guardian* (30 Aug 2000) • *Sunday Times* (15 Oct 2000) • *Sunday Times* (6 Sept 1987) • *Yorkshire Post* (9 Sept 1987) • *Bradford Telegraph and Argus* (21 Dec 1990) • M. Cantrell, 'Writing a living memorial', *Yorkshire Journal* (Jan 1997) • personal knowledge (2004) [Pamela Dunbar, sister] • personal knowledge (2004) [Max Fowler, former teacher] • Newspaper cuttings file on A. Dunbar, Bradford Libraries • J. Yaakov, *Play Index 1978–1982* (New York, H.W. Wilson Co., 1983) • b. cert. • d. cert. • b. cert. [J. B. Dunbar] • m. cert. [J. B. Dunbar] • d. cert. [J. B. Dunbar] • b. cert. [Alma Dunbar]

Archives FILM *Great North show*, 'In praise of bad girls', Yorkshire Television (31 Jan 1986), profile of Andrea Dunbar

Likenesses photograph, repro. in *The Guardian* • photograph (on Buttershaw estate), repro. in *Sunday Express Magazine* (9 Aug 1987) • photographs, repro. in *Bradford Telegraph and Argus*
Wealth at death died on social security: *Guardian* • prosecuted Jan 1986 for claiming social security while receiving royalties: *Bradford Telegraph and Argus* (15 Dec 1988)

Dunbar, Columba (*c.*1386–1435). *See under* Dunbar, George, ninth earl of Dunbar or of March (*c.*1336–1416x23).

Dunbar, Eliza Louisa Walker (1845–1925), physician, was born Eliza Louisa Walker in 1845 in Bombay, the daughter of Alexander Walker, a medical practitioner originally from Edinburgh. She later assumed the family surname of Dunbar. As a girl she was educated at Cheltenham Ladies' College. By 1867 she had begun studying medicine in London, hoping to follow Elizabeth Garrett (later Garrett Anderson) on to the medical register by passing the licentiate examinations of the Society of Apothecaries. Excluded from all medical schools Walker was receiving private tuition and clinical training at Garrett's St Mary's Dispensary in Marylebone when the Society of Apothecaries revised its regulations in order to exclude from its examinations those who had not attended regular medical schools. Walker then followed two other British women, Frances Morgan Hoggan and Louisa Atkins, who had been following the same path in London, to the University of Zürich, where medical classes had been open to women since 1865. She spent four years in Zürich, passing her final examination with special distinction and submitting her MD thesis on blockage of the arteries of the brain in 1872. While a student Walker became the first female assistant in Zürich cantonal hospital, working in the women's ward. She then went to Vienna for a year's postgraduate study.

In 1873 Walker returned to England and was appointed to the post of house surgeon at the Bristol Royal Hospital for Sick Children, the only female among thirteen candidates. Prior to her appointment the medical staff had informed the lay managing committee of the hospital that they would resign if Walker were appointed. Only two carried out this threat immediately on her appointment. Five weeks later an altercation between Walker and one of the honorary medical staff led to the resignation of the rest of the hospital's doctors and she was left in sole medical charge of the hospital for five days. Although supported by the management committee she then resigned to save the hospital further embarrassment. After this she set up in private practice as an unregistered medical practitioner in Clifton, Bristol, establishing the Read Dispensary for Women and Children in the Hotwells area of the city in 1876 with her friend and active supporter of the women's movement Miss Read. In 1877, when the King and Queen's College of Physicians in Ireland opened its licentiate examinations to women, following Russell Gurney's enabling act of 1876, she was able to place her name on the medical register.

Walker Dunbar continued in medical practice in Bristol, being for many years medical officer to the Red Lodge Reformatory for Girls, the Bristol Training College for Elementary Teachers, and the department of education (women) of Bristol University from its inception. She was always an active campaigner for the women's cause as well as devoted to her friends and patients. In 1895 she established the Bristol Private Hospital for Women and Children in Berkeley Square, Clifton, with provision, initially, for twelve patients. The hospital aimed to provide hospital experience for medical women and to fill a gap in Bristol's hospital service by bringing hospital treatment for women by women within reach, 'not only of the so-called poor, but of women higher in the social scale, yet to whom the advantages of such treatment are equally needful' (*The Englishwoman's Review*, 15 Jan 1896, 43). In 1906 she published an article in the *Bristol Medical Chirurgical Journal* on 'The new theory and prophylactic treatment of puerperal eclampsia'. Walker Dunbar was still on the honorary staff of the Bristol Private Hospital and active in private practice when she died following a fall at her home, 9 Oakfield Road, Clifton, Bristol, on 25 August 1925.

M. A. ELSTON

Sources T. N. Bonner, *To the ends of the earth: women's search for education in medicine* (1992) • J. Manton, *Elizabeth Garrett Anderson* (1965) • M. A. Elston, 'Run by women, (mainly) for women: medical women's hospitals in Britain, 1866–1948', *Women in modern medicine*, ed. A. Hardy and L. Conrad (1998) • *BMJ* (12 Sept 1925), 496–7 • *Medical Women's Federation Newsletter* (Nov 1925) • 'Events of the quarter', *Englishwoman's Review* (15 Jan 1874) • *The Lancet* (16 Aug 1873), 241 • *The Lancet* (27 Sept 1873) • d. cert.
Wealth at death £3535 10s. 10d.: administration, 8 May 1926, *CGPLA Eng. & Wales*

Dunbar [*married name* Folley], **Evelyn Mary** (1906–1960), painter, was born at 179 Oxford Road, Reading, Berkshire, on 18 December 1906, the daughter of William Dunbar of Moray, a master tailor, and Florence Murgatroyd of Yorkshire. She was educated at Rochester Girls' Grammar School, and first studied art at Rochester School of Art. At the age of twenty-three she won a Kent exhibition (a county scholarship) to study at the Royal College of Art, which she did from 1929 to 1933. One of her studies of that period, *Flight* (oil and watercolour on paper, 1930) intended for a mural decoration, is now in the Tate collection. Dunbar first came to public notice as one of the outstanding young graduates of the college working on decorations for Brockley county school, Suffolk, depicting scenes drawn from Aesop's *Fables* and other sources, under the direction of Cyril Mahoney, 1933–6. Her composition *The Country Girl and the Pail of Milk* was especially praised. Following this she embarked on a career as a freelance painter and illustrator. She enjoyed gardening subjects—the Tate collection includes her *Winter Garden* (oil on canvas, *c.*1929–36), a painting in the long horizontal format which she favoured in some other works. A characteristic painting of the late 1930s is *Rochester from Strood* (oil on canvas, 1938), in which the tower of the castle and the spire of the cathedral are seen from a distance, the foreground being a garden dominated by a humble potting-shed. In 1937 she turned to book illustration, working with Cyril Mahoney on *Gardner's Choice* and later with Michael Greenhill on *A Book of Farmcraft* (*c.*1942).

During the Second World War, Dunbar became an official war artist (1940–45); her *Convalescent Nurses Making Camouflage Nets* was reproduced in colour in Eric Newton's *War through Artists' Eyes* (1945). She concentrated mainly, however, on subjects taken from the activities of the Women's Land Army. Typical of her unusual vision is the painting in Manchester City Galleries, *A 1944 Pastoral: Land Girls Pruning at East Malling* (oil on canvas, 1944). The scene, of the girls climbing trees and moving their triangular ladders about, has a painted surround of compartments depicting disembodied hands using saws, knives, and pruning shears, as well as decorative compositions of fruit. In the same collection is *Potato Sorting, Berwick* (oil on canvas), an austere frieze-like composition of seven farm workers in a bleak landscape, gathered near the large wheeled piece of equipment used for their task, while in *Sprout Picking, Monmouthshire* (oil on canvas, also in Manchester City Galleries) the bent figures in it are in a field receding sharply in perspective to a row of greenhouses, above which the trees and hills are surmounted by a glowing cloudy sky. A major work now in the Tate collection is *A Land Girl with the Bail Bull* (oil on canvas, 1945), another long horizontal picture. On 17 August 1942 Dunbar married, at St Nicholas, Strood, Kent, Roger Roland Westwell Folley (*b.* 1912/13), a flying officer in the RAF and later an agricultural economist at Oxford. She was for many years friendly with the painter Percy Horton, and he invited Dunbar to teach at the Ruskin School of Drawing, which she did for a number of years from 1950. She painted lunette murals at Bletchley Park Training College, Bedfordshire (1958–60), as well as *The Seasons* at Wye College. She was a member of the Society of Mural Painters and, from 1945, the New English Art Club. She died on 12 May 1960 near her home, Staple Farm, Hastingleigh, East Ashford, Kent. She was survived by her husband.

ALAN WINDSOR

Sources *The Times* (16 May 1960), 16 · *The Times* (19 May 1960), 19 · *WWW*, 1951–60 · *Concise catalogue of British paintings*, Man. City Gall., 2 (1978) · *Concise catalogue of the Tate Gallery collection*, 9th edn (1991) · *Arts Council collection: concise illustrated catalogue* (1979) · b. cert. · m. cert. · d. cert. · *CGPLA Eng. & Wales* (1960)
Wealth at death £3913 7s. 4d.: administration, 11 July 1960, *CGPLA Eng. & Wales*

Dunbar, Gavin (1454×6–1532), administrator and bishop of Aberdeen, was the son of Sir Alexander Dunbar of Westfield, son of James Dunbar, fourth earl of Moray (*d.* 1430), and Elizabeth (or Isabella), daughter of Alexander Sutherland of Duffus, Moray. He was probably born at the family home of Westfield, near Elgin. As a younger son unlikely to inherit the family estates, he was drawn to an ecclesiastical career early in life; he graduated MA at the University of St Andrews in 1475 and then, possibly through family connections, entered the king's civil service. Rising steadily through the ranks, he had become dean of Moray by 31 January 1487 and was finally appointed clerk register of the kingdom on 21 October 1501. This office controlled and authenticated all the charters and muniments issued

by the chancery, the accounts of the exchequer, and the records of parliament and the king's council. In addition, the clerk register was by now a member of the judicial council and of the king's daily council, placing Dunbar at the very centre of government affairs. Hence we find him closely involved in the terms of the Anglo-Scottish peace treaty of 1502 and a party to the marriage arrangements of James IV and Margaret Tudor in 1503. He remained in office after the death of James IV at Flodden on 9 September 1513, playing a full part in the council's restoration of the country's political stability, including the negotiations for a truce with England, and at the same time supporting the return from France of John Stewart, duke of Albany (*d.* 1536), to become governor of the kingdom during the minority of Albany's cousin James V. This was a difficult balancing act between the two Stewart factions concerned which caused the Dowager Queen Margaret to incarcerate Dunbar in Edinburgh Castle between August and November 1524 for his pro-French stance.

Dunbar's true greatness, however, did not fully emerge until he was provided to the see of Aberdeen on 5 November 1518 (consecrated 20 February 1519). The uncertainty of the times following the disaster of Flodden, combined with the indifferent health of Bishop Alexander Gordon during his years in office from 1515 to 1518, meant that the diocese had been virtually leaderless since the death of William Elphinstone in 1514. It was Dunbar's achievement to provide the needed leadership. Besides completing the south transept of St Machar's, his cathedral, he extended its choir eastwards, added twin spires at its west end, and created a unique heraldic ceiling for its nave. He enlarged the body of his vicars choral and presented them with a beautiful *epistolare*; he also built or extended an existing residence for them near by. All this has to be viewed within the context of his liturgical reforms, which, being based on Bishop Elphinstone's Aberdeen breviary of 1510, were devised to bring added meaning and dignity to the singing of the divine office in his cathedral. As chancellor of the University of Aberdeen, Dunbar immediately set about completing those of its buildings left unfinished by its founder, resuscitating the administration of its funds, and enforcing those of its bulls and charters which had become ineffective by having them reconfirmed by the crown and the papacy. By 1529 he had seen to the completion, opening, and maintenance of the bridge of Dee and in that year, remembering his family roots, he endowed two chaplaincies at Elgin Cathedral in Moray. And finally, in 1532, he endowed and built an almshouse for twelve poor elderly men near the west end of his cathedral in Aberdeen. His emoluments as clerk register of Scotland and bishop of Aberdeen, and also as dean of Moray and archdeacon of St Andrews (1504–19) before he became a bishop, were substantial. In the prologue of his almshouse charter he stated that 'whatever was left from the fruits of his church, after satisfying its necessities, a prelate was bound to devote to the poor and disadvantaged' (Munro, 2.280). Those who knew him all record that as bishop of Aberdeen, and indeed throughout his career, Dunbar saw this responsibility as his own. He died at St Andrews on 10 March 1532, and was buried in the south transept of his cathedral.

LESLIE J. MACFARLANE

Sources *Hectoris Boetii murthlacensium et aberdonensium episcoporum vitae*, ed. and trans. J. Moir, New Spalding Club, 12 (1894), ii–viii, 115–23 · C. Innes, ed., *Registrum episcopatus Aberdonensis*, 2 vols., Spalding Club, 13–14 (1845) · D. E. R. Watt, ed., *Fasti ecclesiae Scoticanae medii aevi ad annum 1638*, [2nd edn], Scottish RS, new ser., 1 (1969), 4, 220, 308 · A. I. Dunlop, ed., *Acta facultatis artium universitatis Sanctiandree, 1413–1588*, 2, Scottish History Society, 3rd ser., 55 (1964), 188, 194, 198, 207 · A. L. Murray, 'The lord clerk register', *SHR*, 53 (1974), 124–56 · A. M. Munro, ed., *Records of old Aberdeen*, 2 vols., New Spalding Club, 20, 36 (1899–1909), vol. 2, pp. 257, 276–91, 294–5, 311 · *The letters of James V*, ed. R. K. Hannay and D. Hay (1954), 107 · D. McRoberts, *The heraldic ceiling of St Machar's Cathedral, Aberdeen*, 2 (1976) · J. Stuart, ed., *Extracts from the council register of the burgh of Aberdeen*, 1: *1398–1570*, Spalding Club, 12 (1844), 116–19, 125–30 · C. Innes, ed., *Fasti Aberdonenses … 1494–1854*, Spalding Club, 26 (1854), 77–108, 296, 300, 533 · E. J. Powell, 'Bishop Gavin Dunbar: second founder of the University of Aberdeen', *Aberdeen University Review*, 56 (1995–6), 151–61 · J. Dowden, *The bishops of Scotland … prior to the Reformation*, ed. J. M. Thomson (1912), 137–9 · C. Innes, ed., *Registrum episcopatus Moraviensis*, Bannatyne Club, 58 (1837), 417–18 · *Scots peerage*
Archives BL, Cotton MSS · NA Scot. · NL Scot. · St Machar's Cathedral, Aberdeen · U. Aberdeen, King's College, special collection
Likenesses effigy, St Machar's Cathedral, Aberdeen · oils (as bishop of Aberdeen), St Machar's Cathedral, Aberdeen; copy, U. Aberdeen

Dunbar, Gavin (*c.*1490–1547), administrator and archbishop of Glasgow, was the third son of Sir John Dunbar of Mochrum, Wigtownshire, and his second wife, Janet Stewart, daughter of Alexander Stewart, third Lord Garlies. His date of birth is unknown, but his progression in the church suggests that he was born about 1490. His early years are shrouded in obscurity. It has been suggested that he was educated at Glasgow University, but there is no record of his presence there, and it seems more likely that he attended St Andrews, where several Gavin Dunbars were enrolled in the early 1500s. He had evidently gained his master's degree by 1517, when he first appears on record as Master Gavin Dunbar.

Early career The first significant advance in Dunbar's career came in early 1517 when he was appointed tutor of the five-year-old James V. There is no evidence for the nature of the connection that brought this political appointment, but Dunbar evidently owed his place to the then governor of Scotland, the fourth duke of Albany, with whom he subsequently maintained a close association. Rapid promotion within the church followed: in September 1517 his uncle Gavin Dunbar resigned the deanery of Moray with reservation and secured the provision for his nephew. After being appointed to the bishopric of Aberdeen on 5 November 1518 Dunbar senior was instructed to resign the deanery, thereby releasing the fruits to the younger Gavin. Early the following month, Albany recommended Dunbar junior to Pope Leo X for provision to the priory of Whithorn. This was a contested office, with Albany's brother Alexander and the cardinal of Cortona also claiming possession. Protracted negotiation conducted by Albany secured the priory for Dunbar by August 1520, and

thereafter the latter held it *in commendam* along with the deanery.

About August 1522 Dunbar travelled to meet Albany in France, Lord Erskine assuming his responsibilities as tutor to the king. His return was linked to the vacancy in the see of Glasgow, from which the translation of Archbishop James Beaton to St Andrews, first proposed in December 1521, had finally been effected in June 1523. On 15 August 1523, described as elect of Glasgow, Dunbar returned to Scotland while Albany, who arrived the following month, confirmed his nomination to the pope. He received his *pallium* on 8 July 1524 and gained possession of the temporalities of his see on 27 September 1524. He remained prior of Whithorn until the publication on 21 December 1524 of the papal bulls confirming his provision to Glasgow, and continued to hold the deanery of Moray until his consecration at Edinburgh on 5 February 1525.

The dispute over primacy As archbishop Dunbar became immediately embroiled in the long-running controversy between Glasgow and St Andrews over the latter's claims to primacy over the former. Although Archbishop Beaton was also an adherent of the governor's party, at Albany's request Pope Clement VII had confirmed Dunbar's exemption from Beaton's jurisdiction. This had not ended the matter, however. In May 1524 Albany had left Scotland for good and his erstwhile protégé shifted his allegiance to the political party gathered around the queen mother, Margaret Tudor, and James Hamilton, first earl of Arran. On 26 July 1524 Dunbar accompanied Margaret and Arran from Stirling to Edinburgh, where they proclaimed James V of age and prepared for the formal ending of Albany's governorship. Beaton remained loyal to Albany and the French alliance and was warded briefly as a consequence, but on his release in October 1524 he was courted by Arran's rival Archibald Douglas, sixth earl of Angus, and his English allies. Beaton next sought English diplomatic aid at the curia to overturn Dunbar's exemption, offering in return his aid in securing peace between Scotland and England, while Dunbar, with Margaret's support, also courted English aid to have his exemption secured, currying English favour through firm action against border reivers, albeit action which also had a spiritual dimension. About this time Dunbar launched his remarkable 'greit cursing' against the reivers, a broadside of some 1500 words condemning them to 'all the vengeance that evir was takin sen the warlde began for oppin synnys, and all the plagis and pestilence that ever fell on man or beist' (Fraser, 335).

From 1528 Dunbar enjoyed the active support of James V in his efforts to resist Beaton's claims, the king in 1530 blocking Beaton's efforts to secure a legatine commission and instead advancing the candidacy of Dunbar, whom he also suggested for elevation to cardinal. In response the pope issued a bull in September 1531 confirming Glasgow's exemption from Beaton's jurisdiction. However, although the issue was thus apparently settled, the summoning of a provincial council of the Scottish church in June 1535—the first held since 1470—exposed continuing tensions over the question of jurisdiction. In November 1535 Beaton defied the bull of September 1531, and having had his processional cross raised he processed through Dumfries in Glasgow diocese in a declaration of his authority over Dunbar. The precedent was followed in May 1539 when the new archbishop of St Andrews, Cardinal David Beaton, repeated the challenge. Like his predecessor Beaton made little headway while Dunbar had the support of the king, but following James's death in December 1542 the cardinal renewed the offensive. In 1544 Beaton secured a commission as legate *a latere* that was stipulated to run throughout the entire kingdom, implicitly including Dunbar's diocese: St Andrews's metropolitan supremacy had been regained. On 4 June 1545 Beaton sought to demonstrate his authority on a visit to Glasgow by having his processional cross borne into the cathedral, an action which ended in a brawl between the clerical attendants of the rival archbishops in which the crosses of both were broken. The bitter rivalry between Dunbar and Beaton continued until the latter's assassination in 1546. It had been a debilitating struggle, the chief effect of which had been to ensure that there was little concerted action against heresy and insignificant movement towards internal reform of the church.

Combating heresy and the Douglases Dunbar's elevation to the archbishopric in 1525 had coincided with the first Scottish legislation to combat Lutheranism, represented by parliamentary acts against heresy in 1525 and 1527. As archbishop Dunbar was prominent in the attempted suppression: he concurred in February 1528 with the sentence of death passed on the leading dissident cleric, Patrick Hamilton; in 1539 he sat on the tribunals that condemned Jerome Russell, Thomas Forret, vicar of Dollar, and five others; and in March 1543 he led clerical opposition to the act permitting reading of the New Testament in Scots. As early as 1539, however, there are indications that he favoured the more lenient policy of suppression of heretical opinion over the execution of dissidents. In 1545 Dunbar attempted to neutralize the effects of George Wishart's preaching at Ayr by himself preaching in the church there, but he was humiliated when his congregation largely deserted him to hear Wishart in the market place. The archbishop had his revenge in February 1546, however, when he joined Beaton at St Andrews for Wishart's trial and watched his public execution from the castle walls, an act presented by Knox as symbolizing the reconciliation of the archbishops after previous public demonstrations of enmity between them.

The manoeuvres by James Beaton and Dunbar over the exemption issue in 1524 formed the prelude to the conflict for control of the young king between Angus and his opponents. In the parliament of February 1525, when Dunbar was appointed to the council, an agreement was drawn up between the rival factions whereby possession of the king's person was to move between them in rotation. Dunbar was supposed to retain custody until November 1525, but Angus gained possession of him and refused to give him up, thereby taking control of government and effectively ending the archbishop's tutorship. Dunbar was

now confirmed in his opposition to the Douglas party, and on 4 February 1526 entered into a bond with Angus's rival, the earl of Lennox, who, however, was killed on 4 September in an attempt to seize James at Linlithgow.

Despite his association with Lennox, Dunbar served in the Douglas-dominated government. In August 1525 he acted as a commissioner in negotiations for peace with England; in the 1526 parliament he served as a lord of the articles; and in March 1527 he was made president of the council and sat as a judge in the session. Nevertheless, when James escaped from Angus in June 1528 Dunbar immediately joined the king and was prominent among the clergy and lords who accompanied him to Edinburgh on 6 July. As early as 26 June James had appointed Dunbar as chancellor in succession to Angus, thereby alienating Beaton, who had been chancellor until August 1526 and who had expected restoration to that office. In July 1528 Dunbar was confirmed as a lord of council, and he became deeply involved in advancing government action against the Douglases. On 6 November he was among the lords who swore an oath to James that they would never take the part of the exiled Angus, a stance that Dunbar maintained thereafter.

Chancellor of Scotland Tradition credits Dunbar, in his office of chancellor, with a key role in the development of the college of justice, which was established by act of parliament on 17 May 1532, but this view is now largely discredited. His main role, rather, appears to have been in the formalizing of the 'session' as a specialized judicial branch of the council. The aims of the session were to speed the process and administration of civil justice, and to improve the quality of the judges. Movement in this direction had begun early in the fifteenth century, but the emergence of the session as an institution dates largely from the reign of James IV (*r.* 1488–1513). The process had stalled somewhat in the disturbed minority of James V, but in early 1526 eight individuals were named to sit in the session. In March 1527 Dunbar held the presidency of the session and initiated a trend towards the professionalizing of the judiciary. It was probably under his guidance that between 1527 and 1531 legislation was laid down concerning procedural rules and the constitution of what became the court of session. Dunbar may have envisaged the development of a professional, salaried judiciary, but the moves towards that goal which emerged in 1531 originated with the king and were motivated by aims other than the improvement of justice.

The college of justice, the structure within which these professional judges were to be incorporated, was ostensibly to be financed by taxation of the church. James V secured papal approval for a tax initially designated as being for the defence of the realm but clearly intended primarily to improve crown finances. Dunbar was named as one of the executors in the collection and allocation of the funds, his involvement possibly secured by James's steady support for him in the struggle with St Andrews. The move met with stiff clerical opposition, not least from Dunbar's rivals, the Beatons, who refused payment of their share of the tax until 1541, when the institution of the college was confirmed. Dunbar's own contribution, however, was considerably in arrears at that date.

As chancellor Dunbar was an active member of the royal administration throughout James V's personal rule, his presence at all meetings of the royal council confirmed by his perfect record as a witness to charters issued under the great seal. Opinion varies on the extent of his influence over James's policy, ranging from his portrayal as a central figure in a clerical clique upon which the king was dependent, to his presentation as a pliant instrument who preferred acquiescence in royal plans for church taxation to the possibility of a Scottish reformation along English lines. That the king set great store by his abilities, however, is indicated by his successful tenure of the chancellorship for the remainder of the reign. As chancellor not only was he automatically nominated as one of the six vice-regents appointed to govern Scotland in August 1536 during James's absence in France for his marriage, but he was also the only one of the six whose attendance at all quorate meetings of the regents was mandatory. Dunbar's consistent support for the king throughout the 1530s, which often placed him out of sympathy with the views of the main body of the senior clergy, received its final recognition in July 1538 when the pope granted James V's request for his provision to the commendatorship of Inchaffray Abbey, an office that Dunbar held until his death.

Dunbar has been credited with significant influence over Scottish diplomacy in the period 1528–42, particularly in respect of England. Here, however, he can be seen to operate in accord with royal policy rather than as its formulator. In 1528–9, following James V's wishes, he pursued a strongly anti-Douglas line in his dealings with Henry VIII. On 14 December 1529 he concluded a five years' peace with England. A more hostile attitude towards England emerged in 1531, and in 1532 it was reported that Dunbar was involved in secret negotiations with the O'Neills in Ireland against the English administration there. Peace nevertheless held, despite Henry's breach with Rome in 1536, and Dunbar wrote as chancellor in February and April 1537 to assure the English king that the Scots would take no action to threaten the peace and that justice would be strictly administered to English rebels against Henry's policies who had sought refuge in Scotland. By 1539 a more strongly anti-English policy had emerged among the Scottish hierarchy, but this was largely due to the growing influence of David Beaton rather than to Dunbar. Indeed, as the two kingdoms slid towards war in 1542, Dunbar was reported to be out of step with his clerical colleagues and the king in that he favoured peace, and there are suggestions that he maintained that position until his final removal from the chancellorship in December 1543.

Last years On 10 January 1543 Dunbar was temporarily removed from office as chancellor and replaced by Beaton. He was restored by 15 February and assumed an active role in the administration set in place by the earl of Arran, governor in the name of the infant Queen Mary. In June 1543 he was appointed one of the commissioners and auditors of exchequer, and by September he had been appointed to the council of state set up to direct the governor. In December 1543, however, Dunbar was again obliged to relinquish the chancellorship to Beaton, and he was soon associated with the political opposition to Arran and the cardinal. It is unclear to what extent Dunbar was complicit in the seizure and fortification of the bishop's castle at Glasgow against the governor by Matthew Stewart, thirteenth earl of Lennox, but by 1544 he had been firmly identified with the faction that on 10 June suspended Arran from office. Dunbar did not regain the chancellorship, however, and cannot be seen to have exercised any active role in the administrations that governed Scotland thereafter in Queen Mary's name.

Dunbar died on 30 April 1547, apparently in the archiepiscopal castle at Glasgow, and in the following month was interred in the elaborate tomb that he had prepared for himself in the choir of the adjacent cathedral. The superstructure of the tomb was destroyed thirteen years later when the cathedral was 'purged' by protestant reformers, but what were believed to be his remains were found beneath floor level during building work in 1855.

RICHARD D. ORAM

Sources D. E. Easson, *Gavin Dunbar, chancellor of Scotland, archbishop of Glasgow* (1947) · R. K. Hannay, *The college of justice* (1933) · I. H. Shearer, ed., *Selected cases from the Acta dominorum concilii et sessionis, 1532–33*, Stair Society, 14 (1951) · R. K. Hannay, ed., *Acts of the lords of council in public affairs, 1501–1554* (1932) · *The letters of James V*, ed. R. K. Hannay and D. Hay (1954) · J. Cameron, *James V: the personal rule, 1528–1542*, ed. N. Macdougall (1998) · J. M. Thomson and others, eds., *Registrum magni sigilli regum Scotorum / The register of the great seal of Scotland*, 11 vols. (1882–1914), vol. 3 · T. Thomson, ed., *A diurnal of remarkable occurrents that have passed within the country of Scotland*, Bannatyne Club, 43 (1833) · F. C. H. Blair, ed., *Charters of the Abbey of Crosraguel*, 2 vols., Ayrshire and Galloway Archaeological Association (1886), vol. 1 · W. A. Lindsay, J. Dowden, and J. M. Thomson, eds., *Charters, bulls and other documents relating to the abbey of Inchaffray*, Scottish History Society, 56 (1908) · M. Lynch, *Scotland: a new history* (1991) · D. E. R. Watt, ed., *Fasti ecclesiae Scoticanae medii aevi ad annum 1638*, [2nd edn], Scottish RS, new ser., 1 (1969) · G. M. Fraser, *The steel bonnets: the story of the Anglo-Scottish border reivers* (1971)
Wealth at death £3815 1s. 4d. Scots: will and inventory, Blair, ed., *Charters*, 1.65

Dunbar, George, ninth earl of Dunbar or of March (*c.*1336–1416×23), magnate and soldier, was the son of Sir Patrick Dunbar (*d.* 1357) and his wife, Isabel Randolph. On 25 July 1368 he became earl of Dunbar or March by grant from David II, to whom George's paternal great-uncle Patrick, the eighth earl, had resigned what was a single earldom, its titles increasingly interchangeable from the late thirteenth century. George's paternal inheritance included extensive lands in the Scottish east march, while from his mother, the coheir of the Randolph earls of Moray, he inherited territories elsewhere, including the lordship of Annandale, which made him a significant figure on the western borders too. Moreover he inherited a claim to the Isle of Man which he took seriously, making a grant of lands there *c.*1372. March's regional influence was initially hampered by English control of large areas of southern Scotland, notably in Berwickshire and Annandale, and it is in his efforts to gain full possession of his inheritance that his military abilities, the hallmark of his career, can first be perceived. He was greatly successful in re-establishing Scottish control in Berwickshire; outside Berwick itself and a small area around it, this had been achieved by the early 1370s. The conquest of Annandale took longer and was completed only with the seizure of the castle of Lochmaben on 4 or 5 February 1384. These military activities of the 1370s and 1380s entailed much more than the reoccupation of disputed border lands. March was engaged in broader, national endeavours as well as personal ones. The Anglo-French war which began again in 1369 went generally badly for the English and was accompanied by sometimes bloody crises in English government and society for over twenty years. These were circumstances ripe for exploitation by the Scots led by March and other belligerent Scottish nobles.

The government of Robert II (1371–90) supported attacks on England, first under the cover of an official Anglo-Scottish truce and then, from 1384, as acts of open war. March was the most effective tool of this new and aggressive Scottish approach. He was responsible for burning English-controlled Roxburgh in 1377 and took part in subsequent heavy raiding which led to his capture of Sir Thomas Musgrave, the keeper of Berwick, in the same year. He also terrorized northern English communities into making blackmail payments to him—in 1379/80 the townsmen of Berwick claimed to be paying tribute to him in money, wine, and victuals. The culmination of Scottish attacks in what was still a time of truce came in 1380, when March defeated and captured Ralph, Baron Greystoke, and most of his force on the eastern border while another Scottish force raided deep into the English west march. March was the main figure in establishing a local Scottish military ascendancy unparalleled since the reign of Robert I. When the Scottish government chose to make open war upon England in 1384, 1385, and 1388–9, March was again heavily involved. An indication of his perceived military value is the 4000 livres tournois he received when a French expeditionary force, complete with treasure chest, arrived in Scotland in 1385. Only the king's eldest son, John, earl of Carrick, and James and Archibald Douglas were given more. In 1388 March was in the Scottish raiding force which encountered Henry Percy (Hotspur) at the battle of Otterburn. James, second earl of Douglas, was killed in the battle, and much credit for the final Scottish victory went to March, who, in English chronicle accounts, also saved the captive Hotspur from death at the hands of enraged retainers of the dead earl of Douglas.

Despite an extremely active career in border warfare and diplomacy, March often kept a low profile on the domestic political scene. In the later years of David II's reign he and his brother John *Dunbar [see under Dunbar family, earls of Moray (per. c.1370–1430)] were high in royal favour, a position they owed at least in part to the fact that no later than 1369 their sister Agnes had become the king's mistress. On the accession of Robert II in 1371

March does not seem to have suffered for his association with the previous regime; indeed, he and John Dunbar were prominent in supporting the new king against the obscure Douglas 'demonstration' which preceded his coronation. Thereafter March's links with the royal court appear to have been distant, but not hostile. In the longer term the earl was on good terms with Robert II's second son, Robert Stewart, who later became duke of Albany and guardian of Scotland. In the 1370s and 1380s he also co-operated happily, especially in the military field, with the other great magnates of the south. In the 1390s, however, he was to assume a more prominent place in national politics. His higher profile came with the relationship, from 1395 at the latest, between his daughter, Elizabeth, and the heir to the throne, David Stewart, earl of Carrick. There was political opposition to this match: Robert III, whose relations with March had probably long been cool, is reported to have besieged Dunbar Castle, the earl's chief seat, probably in autumn 1396, in a bid to oppose his son's connection with Elizabeth Dunbar. The couple may have been forced to separate, but Earl George clearly still expected the union to go ahead. His reaction was furious when David Stewart, now duke of Rothesay, rejected Elizabeth in 1400 in favour of Mary Douglas, a daughter of the aged Archibald the Grim, third earl of Douglas, and sister of Archibald, master of Douglas. The younger Archibald became fourth earl in 1402 and was March's great political and military rival for several years. March responded to his family's dishonour by appealing to the new king of England, Henry IV. Accounts of the earl's subsequent defection to English allegiance stress power politics and the quest for increased authority within Scotland. There was no doubt an element of this, but from March's point of view the issue of outraged honour evident in the contemporary sources needs to be considered as well. A man previously content to take care of his regional interests and play little part in central politics felt driven to take drastic action which was hardly a coldly calculated political move; indeed, its results were disastrous for his family.

The repercussions of March's defection were important; and just as his actions impacted on great events he remained an important player in them. In Scotland his switch of allegiance ushered in an extremely turbulent period which resulted in the (highly probable) murder of Rothesay in 1402 and the long-lasting political dominance of the duke of Albany. In regional terms it helped bring about an unprecedented dominance of southern Scotland by the Douglas family, not least because March was deserted by a number of his leading tenants and retainers, including his nephew Robert Maitland, the keeper of Dunbar Castle. In an international context March had a role in spurring Henry IV to mount an ineffective invasion of Scotland in 1400, which in turn inspired continued Scottish belligerence in the following years. One factor that now worked against Anglo-Scottish rapprochement was the ferocious personal feud between March and the fourth earl of Douglas. In the former's absence Douglas took over his lands in Annandale and the east march. Warfare in the borders increasingly came to be driven by local rivalries and regional concerns. Military success continued to accompany March. He defeated a major Scottish raiding force at Nisbet on 22 June 1402 and was with the English host on 14 September following when a full-scale Scottish army met disaster at the battle of Homildon Hill. Although overall command lay with the earl of Northumberland and Henry Percy, the tactics that brought victory were March's. The earl of Douglas was taken captive, as was Murdoch Stewart, Albany's son; much of the higher nobility of Scotland was captured or killed.

Homildon Hill had important consequences: it decisively ended a thirty-year period in which the Scots felt they could pursue ambitious political objectives through military means. They were never so confident nor consistently belligerent again. In a real sense the battle ended (in stalemate) the century-long Scottish wars of independence. It also acted as a spur (for various reasons) for the Percy family to rise against Henry IV in 1403. March remained true to his royal master and his advice helped bring about the defeat at Shrewsbury of the greatest challenge to Henry IV's rule. For a second time March defeated both Hotspur (who was killed) and Douglas (who was captured again). His military career was outstanding, as his contemporaries noticed. In the words of Walter Bower, 'He was accounted most fortunate in every fighting encounter, for his side always prevailed' (Bower, 8.117). For his efforts on King Henry's behalf he and his family were given lands and annuities, while by a more symbolic reward he was permitted to style his herald Shrewsbury. Yet March was unable to retain a power-base in Scotland and the impecunious Henry could hardly endow him in a manner commensurate with his previous lofty standing. The Dunbar family seem to have been in desperate financial straits in England, as their recurrent appeals for money show. Finally in 1408 a return to Scotland was arranged and a truncated earldom of March was regained in 1409. He was now an old man, aged over seventy, but March's military expertise apparently continued to be appreciated, since in the following year he was one of a small group of nobles consulted by Albany as to how to counter the growing threat from the lord of the Isles. But such services did nothing to win back his lordship of Annandale, and the fortunes of his family never recovered.

That March was able to switch allegiance to the English crown while maintaining at least a measure of support in south-east Scotland says much about aristocratic mentalities and the bonds of loyalty that powerful magnates could inspire. Before 1400 he seems to have been an implacable, militant enemy of England. Yet this perception obscures another strand in the earl's career, his long-standing links of friendship and co-operation across the border. In the 1380s and 1390s he consistently attempted to maintain the traditional attachment of Coldingham Priory in Berwickshire to Durham Cathedral priory in spite of attempts to introduce Scottish monks there. His efforts were recognized when he and his wife, Christiana

(probably *née* Seton), were admitted to the confraternity of Durham in 1418. Affection for Durham perhaps indicates an attachment to the cross-border cult of St Cuthbert, and more certainly a recognizably east march sensibility. March also had amicable contacts with the gentry and aristocracy of Northumberland and trading links with Newcastle and further afield. This aristocratic internationalism reached further than Northumberland. A major exporter of wool, the earl had direct trading links in the Low Countries and fiscal connections in the Baltic. Yet despite foreign ties and membership of the brotherhood of the international aristocracy it was the misfortune of March to defect to England at a time when national sentiments were gaining increasing power, so that his lands in Scotland were swiftly taken over by those who could claim to represent an undiluted animosity to the traditional enemy. The Dunbar family, meanwhile, clearly encountered hostility in northern England, especially after Henry Percy's death at Shrewsbury. And indeed the earl's own followers, despite his apparently smooth transition from Scottish marcher lord to English agent, show that the power of national sentiment was on the increase. Fully seven years after his defection, in 1407, some eighty of his followers occupied the village of Navenby in Lincolnshire. They held it to ransom, terrorized the inhabitants, and defied resistance, shouting at the 'tailed English dogs' who hesitated to confront them.

The ninth earl of March was in a British context the foremost warrior of his time and he had a lofty conception of his own status to match this prominence. A now lost tomb inscription gives vivid testimony of local and familial pride. It speaks of a man who ruled in his own sphere, the eastern borders of Scotland, for some fifty years and whose family prestige and kinship ties with three royal houses put him on a par with monarchy. His historical standing, however, has not been overly prominent, no doubt partly because he was a turncoat to both the Scottish and the English crowns. In view of this relative obscurity it is somehow fitting that there is no certain dating for March's death, contradictory evidence suggesting dates ranging between 1416 and 1423. He was buried in Dunbar collegiate church.

The ninth earl of March had six recorded sons and a daughter from his marriage (*c*.1360) to Christiana (*d*. after 1418) and also an illegitimate son, Nicholas. He was succeeded as earl by his eldest son, another **George Dunbar** (*c*.1370–1455×7), who gave firm support to James I at the beginning of his reign and was made warden of the east march by him, probably in 1424. But his hopes of further recovering his family's position were disappointed. His Douglas rivals were now too firmly entrenched in south-east Scotland, and in 1430 March was replaced as warden of the east march by William Douglas, second earl of Angus. In 1432 a quarrel with Angus led to royal intervention, and James may have decided that March's loyalty could not be trusted, for in 1434 he had the earl arrested and forfeited him a year later. A grant of the earldom of Buchan was little compensation and may not have become effective, not least because Dunbar withdrew to

England in search of support there. He retained the barony of Kilconquhar, Fife, held from the bishop of St Andrews, and eventually retired there, supported by a pension of 400 merks from the revenues of his former earldom, but neither he nor any of his descendants held comital rank again. He may have married twice. His wife, Beatrice (surname unknown), with whom he had three sons and two daughters, had died by 1421, when he had licence to marry Alice Hay of Yester, but the marriage may not have taken place. He died between 1455 and 1457.

Among George's younger brothers was **Columba Dunbar** (c.1386–1435), bishop of Moray, who withdrew to England with the rest of his family in 1400 and was dispensed to hold benefices without cure of souls in that year. Presented to the deanship of the royal free chapel in Bridgnorth in 1403, he studied arts at Oxford. He lost his position at Bridgnorth on returning to Scotland in 1409, but was dean of Dunbar collegiate church by 1412 and was made archdeacon of Lothian in 1419. He had been ordained priest by 3 April 1422, when he was provided to the see of Moray. Little is known of his activities as bishop, but he attended to the restoration of his cathedral, devastated by the earl of Buchan in 1390—Dunbar's arms appear on the west gable of the nave. In 1429 he went to Rome as the king's envoy and in 1434 had an English safe conduct to attend the council of Basel, though it seems unlikely that he went. He died at Spynie, near Elgin, in 1435, some time before his successor was recorded as bishop-elect on 7 November. He may be represented by the effigy of a bishop in Elgin Cathedral, where he was probably buried.   ALASTAIR J. MACDONALD

Sources W. Bower, *Scotichronicon*, ed. D. E. R. Watt and others, new edn, 9 vols. (1987–98) · *Scots peerage* · *Chancery records* · Andrew of Wyntoun, *The orygynale cronykil of Scotland*, ed. D. Laing, 3 (1879) · PRO · J. M. Thomson and others, eds., *Registrum magni sigilli regum Scotorum / The register of the great seal of Scotland*, 11 vols. (1882–1914), vol. 1 · BL, Cotton MS Vespasian F vii · A. J. Macdonald, *Border bloodshed: Scotland, England and France, 1369–1403* (2000) · S. I. Boardman, *The early Stewart kings: Robert II and Robert III, 1371–1406* (1996) · M. Brown, *The Black Douglases: war and lordship in late medieval Scotland, 1300–1455* (1998) · A. L. Brown, 'The priory of Coldingham in the late fourteenth century', *Lunes Review*, 23 (1972), 91–101 · D. E. R. Watt, *A biographical dictionary of Scottish graduates to AD 1410* (1977) · GEC, *Peerage*, new edn, 4.508–9 · M. Brown, *James I* (1994) · J. Dowden, *The bishops of Scotland … prior to the Reformation*, ed. J. M. Thomson (1912) · R. Fawcett, *Scottish architecture from the accession of the Stewarts to the Reformation, 1371–1560* (1994)
Likenesses coat of arms (Armorial de Gelre) · seal, repro. in H. Laing, *Supplemental descriptive catalogue of ancient Scottish seals* (1866), 55, no. 317
Wealth at death extensive landed base at death, but much reduced from period of greatest prominence

Dunbar, George, tenth earl of Dunbar or of March (c.**1370–1455×7**). *See under* Dunbar, George, ninth earl of Dunbar or of March (c.1336–1416×23).

Dunbar, George (1777–1851), classical scholar, the child of humble parents, John Dunbar and his wife, Margaret Home, was born at Coldingham in Berwickshire on 30 March 1777. He was employed in youth as a gardener, but was incapacitated from manual labour by a fall from a tree. Dunbar then had the good fortune to attract the notice of a neighbouring proprietor, who aided him to acquire a classical education. About the beginning of the nineteenth century he went to Edinburgh, and was employed as tutor in the family of William Fettes, lord provost of Edinburgh. Within a few months he was selected as assistant to Andrew Dalzel, the professor of Greek at the university, and on the death of the latter in 1806 was appointed his successor, when he received the degree of MA from the university (February 1807). Dunbar filled the Greek chair until his death, though in his last months his duties were performed by a substitute by the name of Kirkpatrick. He was twice married and died at Rose Park, Trinity, Edinburgh, on 6 December 1851.

As a classical scholar Dunbar did not leave behind him a very enduring reputation, and the bulk of his work had little permanent value. His industry, however, was very great. He completed in 1814 a Greek grammar left unfinished by Dalzel and added a third volume to Dalzel's *Collectanea Graeca majora* (1820). On his own account he published an edition of Herodotus, with derivative Latin notes (7 vols., 1806–7), a very foolish *Inquiry into the structure and affinity of the Greek and Latin languages … with an appendix in which the derivation of the Sanskrit from the Greek is endeavoured to be established* (1827), and various elementary works. Dunbar's best work was the compilation of lexicons. In conjunction with E. H. Barker he wrote a *Greek and English and English and Greek Lexicon* (1831), which was well received. His own *Greek and English and English and Greek Lexicon* (1840) was the result of eight years' labour, with very considerable assistance from Dr Francis Adams. It was a carefully arranged and thorough piece of research, but was soon superseded.

L. C. SANDERS, *rev.* RICHARD SMAIL

Sources *GM*, 2nd ser., 37 (1852), 195–6 · Boase, *Mod. Eng. biog.* · b. cert.
Archives BL, corresp. with Sir Robert Peel, Add. MSS 40379–40593
Likenesses J. Watson-Gordon, oils, U. Edin.

Dunbar, James, fourth earl of Moray (d. **1430**). *See under* Dunbar family, earls of Moray (*per. c.*1370–1430).

Dunbar, James (d. **1798**), university teacher and writer on moral philosophy, of whose upbringing and parentage details are unknown, was educated at King's College, Aberdeen, from where he received the degree of LLD. In 1765 he began a thirty-year career as a lecturer in moral philosophy at King's; in the following year he was elected a regent of the college. Dunbar's lectures comprised three principal elements: the philosophy of mind, in which he was greatly influenced by Thomas Reid; ethics, which saw him draw on Francis Hutcheson's idea of innate human sociability and a universal moral code based on natural benevolence; and political economy, a new subject at King's and one influenced by Adam Smith's *Wealth of Nations* (1776).

Dunbar himself published *De primordiis civitatum oratio in qua agitur de bello civili inter Magnam Britanniam et colonias nunc flagrante* (1779) and *Essays on the History of Mankind in*

Rude and Uncultivated Ages (1780), which provided discussion on the 'primeval form of society', 'language as an universal accomplishment', 'the criterion of a polished tongue', and the 'hereditary genius of nations'. Dunbar was a promoter of the unsuccessful bid to amalgamate King's with Marischal College in 1786–7. He retired from teaching in April 1794, and died in his rooms at King's College on 28 May 1798.   J. M. RIGG, *rev.* PHILIP CARTER

Sources W. Thom, *The history of Aberdeen*, 2 vols. (1811) · *GM*, 1st ser., 68 (1798), 539, 622 · Nichols, *Illustrations*, 4.822 · P. B. Wood, *The Aberdeen Enlightenment: the arts curriculum in the eighteenth century* (1993) · D. Allan, *Virtue, learning and the Scottish Enlightenment: ideas of scholarship in early modern history* (1993)

Archives N. Yorks. CRO, corresp. with Christopher Wyvill

Dunbar, John, first earl of Moray (*d.* 1391/2). *See under* Dunbar family, earls of Moray (*per. c.*1370–1430).

Dunbar, Patrick, fifth earl of Dunbar (*c.*1186–1248). *See under* Dunbar, Patrick, eighth earl of Dunbar or of March, and earl of Moray (1285–1369).

Dunbar, Patrick, sixth earl of Dunbar (*c.*1213–1289). *See under* Dunbar, Patrick, eighth earl of Dunbar or of March, and earl of Moray (1285–1369).

Dunbar, Patrick, seventh earl of Dunbar or of March (1242–1308). *See under* Dunbar, Patrick, eighth earl of Dunbar or of March, and earl of Moray (1285–1369).

Dunbar, Patrick, eighth earl of Dunbar or of March, and earl of Moray (1285–1369), soldier and magnate, was the first member of his family for nearly a century to attain national prominence. His great-great-grandfather Patrick, the fourth earl, died in December 1232 and was succeeded by his son, also Patrick. **Patrick Dunbar**, fifth earl of Dunbar (*c.*1186–1248), continued the family tradition of endowing religious houses, most notably Dryburgh and Melrose abbeys. He took part in Alexander II's campaign against Thomas, illegitimate son of Alan of Galloway, in 1235 and in 1242 became involved in the aftermath of the murder, through arson, of the young earl of Atholl by the Bissets. The Comyns, together with Dunbar, pushed for retribution, and the Bissets were forced to flee the country. In 1247 Earl Patrick decided to go on crusade, supposedly because he had offended the monastic house of Tynemouth, and sold his stud horses in Lauderdale to Melrose Abbey to pay for his expenses. He and a number of other Scots died at the (successful) siege of Damietta in Egypt in 1248. Matthew Paris describes him as 'earl Patrick … who was held to be the most powerful among the magnates of Scotland' (Anderson, 360), though his career suggests that any distinction he achieved was due to his position rather than his abilities. He married, some time before 1213, Euphemia (*fl.* 1193), daughter of Walter Fitzalan, and was succeeded by their son, another Patrick.

Patrick Dunbar, sixth earl of Dunbar (*c.*1213–1289), featured in the power struggle of the minority of Alexander III. Identifying himself with the Durwards against the Comyns, the earl participated in the English-backed seizure of the young king from Edinburgh Castle in 1255. The

Comyns returned to power two years later, but a compromise between the two factions was reached soon after, which left Dunbar out. The earl was present at the battle of Largs against the Norwegians in 1263, apparently in command of the left division; despite injury, he then went with the earls of Atholl and Carrick to subdue the Western Isles. He witnessed the main events of King Alexander's reign, such as the marriage contract between Princess Margaret and Erik II of Norway in 1281; he later swore to uphold their daughter, Margaret, as heir to the Scottish throne. Perhaps the most significant event in his career, though, was the alleged visit to Dunbar Castle of Thomas Erceldoune, when Alexander III's tragic death was prophesied. After this became a reality in 1286 the earl, with his three sons, subscribed to the Turnberry Bond of the same year, effectively backing the Brus claim to the throne. Earl Patrick reputedly married Christian Bruce, daughter of Robert (V) de Brus of Annandale (*d.* 1295), the Competitor, which may explain his otherwise unexpected presence at Turnberry; however, his only recorded spouse was one 'Cecilia filia Johannis', possibly a Fraser. Earl Patrick died in 1289, well into his seventies. Like that of his father, his career indicates that, while he took part in events, he was not the main author of them.

He was succeeded by his son, Patrick 'with the blak beard'. **Patrick Dunbar**, seventh earl of Dunbar or of March (1242–1308), was the first to designate himself earl of March. He attended the parliament at Birgham in 1290 and subsequently put forward a claim to the vacant throne through his great-grandmother Ada, illegitimate daughter of King William the Lion, but soon withdrew. When war broke out in 1296, Earl Patrick quickly joined the English side, proving so useful that he was appointed captain of the Berwick garrison in May 1298 and promoted to chief commander of English forces in southern Scotland the following November. He was with the English army at the siege of Caerlaverock in 1300, yet for some reason failed to take up his appointment as a Scottish commissioner to the English parliament in 1305. On the resumption of hostilities in 1306 the earl does not appear to have played an active part and he died, aged sixty-six, on 10 October 1308. He was married to Marjory Comyn, a daughter of Alexander, earl of Buchan (*d.* 1289), and their son, the inevitable Patrick, became eighth earl. This Patrick, like his father, initially consistently backed the English: he participated in the siege of Caerlaverock, aged fifteen, and received orders, with his father, to keep the peace on Edward II's accession. In 1313 Earl Patrick and Sir Adam Gordon (*d.* 1328), a prominent Lothian landowner, approached Edward II on behalf of the 'people of Scotland' who were suffering from English raids. Dunbar's own lands were also under attack from the English garrisons at Berwick and Roxburgh.

The earl's faith in the ability of the English government to protect his property survived until Bannockburn; although he allowed Edward II to shelter at Dunbar, he submitted to King Robert immediately thereafter. He proved an active supporter, taking part in the siege of Berwick in 1318 and attesting the declaration of Arbroath in

April 1320. The presence of Adam Gordon in the embassy that took this letter to Rome has led to the suggestion that Earl Patrick was also in the party; while travelling back through France he heard rumours of a pro-Balliol plot, which, on his return to Scotland, resulted in the arrest of those associated with the so-called Soulis conspiracy. Following the death of King Robert in 1329 the earl remained loyal to the late king's son; the brigade he commanded after the battle of Dupplin Moor in 1332 besieged Edward Balliol (d. 1363) in Perth until a lack of supplies caused their withdrawal. Indeed, it was claimed in the sixteenth century that the earl was a joint guardian, with the earl of Mar, appointed specifically 'to governe the realme on the south side of Forth' (Boece, 2.414). Later in 1332 he and Sir Archibald Douglas (d. 1333), guardian of Scotland, tried and failed to make peace with the invading army. Earl Patrick was given command of Berwick Castle in 1333, but surrendered it to Edward III after the Scottish defeat at Halidon Hill in that year. Having then decided to rejoin the English, he received a grant of £100 of land and attended Balliol's parliament in 1334, which effectively handed Scotland over to Edward III. The devastation caused by the English army in the south-east in 1334, however, forced Dunbar to change sides again; he deserted Edward Balliol in 1335, took part in the Scottish siege of Perth in 1339, and commanded the left wing of the Scottish army at Nevilles Cross in 1346. His son and heir, possibly called John, was sent to England as a hostage while King David visited Scotland in 1351 and also in 1354, but not in 1357, suggesting that he was dead by that date. John's mother was probably Patrick's first wife, Ermigarda, who was recorded as pregnant in 1304.

About 1320 Earl Patrick married Agnes [**Agnes Dunbar**, countess of Dunbar or of March (d. 1369)], the eldest daughter of Thomas *Randolph, first earl of Moray (d. 1332), and Isabel, daughter of Sir John Stewart of Bunkle. According to the chronicler Pitscottie, the countess was popularly called Black Agnes 'be ressone sho was blak skynnit', presumably meaning that she was swarthy in complexion. Pitscottie goes on to add that she was also 'of greater spirit than it became a woman to be' (CDS, 4.xxi), a remark which the few known facts about her life would seem to corroborate. She was Patrick's cousin, and a papal dispensation was needed before they could marry. She played as prominent a part as her husband in the cause of Scottish independence.

With the resumption of war in the 1330s the strategically important castle of Dunbar became a focal point for both sides. The castle was rebuilt in 1333 at Edward III's expense, yet by 1337 it was held against him. Control of English affairs in the north lay with Richard (II) Fitzalan, earl of Arundel (d. 1376), and William Montagu, earl of Salisbury (d. 1344); the two resolved to launch an English offensive by attacking Dunbar. The siege was begun in January 1338, when a vast array of professional engineers ensured that the castle faced a formidable barrage of missiles. Earl Patrick had absented himself, but his wife was ready. Appearing on the battlements even during bombardment, she mocked Salisbury's efforts and, according

to Sir Walter Scott, set her maids to dusting the walls struck by the missiles. When a particular engine, called a sow owing to its shape, was drawn up, she taunted the English earl by saying, 'Beware, Montagow, for farrow shall they sow', and destroyed it with a specially prepared fragment of rock. As the English ran for cover, she reputedly shouted after them, 'Behold the litter of English pigs' (Scott, 99). Edward III was so impressed by this resistance that he interrupted his continental preparations to visit Salisbury and Arundel. Ultimately they decided to lift the siege, pleading the need to devote all resources overseas. This ineffective expedition cost almost £6000, which prompted one English chronicler to remark that its conclusion was 'wasteful, and neither honourable nor secure, but useful and advantageous to the Scots' (Historia Anglicana, 1.200).

With the death of his wife's brother, John Randolph, at Nevilles Cross, Earl Patrick assumed the title of earl of Moray. David II, on his release in 1357, granted the earldom to the English duke of Lancaster, though Dunbar seems to have held on to both the title and the rents. Agnes and her younger sister, Isabel, jointly inherited their brother's considerable lands in Dumfriesshire, Ayrshire, Aberdeenshire, and Fife. Isabel was married to Earl Patrick's cousin, Sir Patrick Dunbar, with whom she had a son, George. Since Agnes and Patrick remained childless, George became their heir. In November 1355 Earl Patrick participated in the raid which for a short time took the town of Berwick and in 1358 he was briefly captured by Sir James Lindsay for some unknown reason. He joined with Robert Stewart, the heir to the throne, and the earl of Douglas in 1363 in a rebellion ostensibly directed against David II's extravagance, but more truthfully associated with Stewart's royal ambitions in the face of the king's impending marriage to Margaret Logie. Earl Patrick, who continued to witness royal charters until July 1368, remained active up to his death in 1369. Although Countess Agnes was still alive in 1367, this is the last mention of her before her death, also in 1369.   FIONA WATSON

Sources W. Scott, Tales of a grandfather, ed. E. M. Lang, abridged edn (1925), 98–9 · Scots peerage, 3.268 · R. Nicholson, Scotland: the later middle ages (1974), vol. 2 of The Edinburgh history of Scotland, ed. G. Donaldson (1965–75) · CDS, 3, no. 1233; vol. 4, p. xxi · G. Burnett and others, eds., The exchequer rolls of Scotland, 1 (1878) · J. M. Thomson and others, eds., Registrum magni sigilli regum Scotorum / The register of the great seal of Scotland, 2nd edn, 1, ed. T. Thomson (1912), no. 149 · accounts, various, PRO, E 101/20/25 · Scalacronica, by Sir Thomas Gray of Heton, knight: a chronical of England and Scotland from AD MLXVI to AD MCCCLXII, ed. J. Stevenson, Maitland Club, 40 (1836), 168 · CEPR letters, 2.201, 235 · H. Boece, The history and chronicles of Scotland, trans. J. Bellenden, 2 vols. (1821) · A. A. M. Duncan, 'The war of the Scots, 1306–23', TRHS, 6th ser., 2 (1992), 125–51 · A. O. Anderson, ed., Scottish annals from English chroniclers, AD 500 to 1286 (1908) · Thomae Walsingham, quondam monachi S. Albani, historia Anglicana, ed. H. T. Riley, 2 vols., pt 1 of Chronica monasterii S. Albani, Rolls Series, 28 (1863–4), vol. 1 · G. W. S. Barrow and others, eds., Regesta regum Scottorum, 6, ed. B. Webster (1982) · History of Dunbar

Dunbar, Patrick (1598–1646), army officer in the Danish service, was born at Cumnoch, Moray, the son of Patrick Dunbar of Cumnoch, justice of Moray, and his wife, Maria Weyer. Such was the parentage ascribed to him in his funeral sermon, though it has not been possible to confirm these claims from Scottish sources. In all essentials his coat of arms is the same as that belonging to the Dunbars of Mochrum. Dunbar attended Marischal College, Aberdeen, and King's College, Aberdeen, and later stayed with his kinsman Thomas Hamilton, earl of Melrose (later of Haddington), secretary of state in Scotland and president and later lord privy seal in Scotland for Charles I.

Dunbar entered Danish service in 1625 as an ensign in the company under Sir Patrick Mackay of Lairg, in the regiment levied by Sir Donald Mackay. With four companies of 800 men Dunbar defended successfully Boizenburg on the Elbe against Tilly's army of 10,000 men, at the end of July 1627, and in 1628 was sent to Stralsund to relieve the besieged city. Here he was wounded in action, and when the regiment was reformed in the same year his company was disbanded. He must have chosen to remain in Denmark, as he did not transfer with the regiment to Swedish service in the summer of 1629. Dunbar had taken over a company in Scania as a captain in 1628 and on 2 April 1631 he was appointed a major of Scanian conscript peasants, giving him a part in creating a national Danish army (conscription had been introduced only in 1614). By the time he asked for leave to go to Scotland two years later, he held the rank of *overvagtmester* of a regiment of foot, which could indicate that he had been assigned to another unit. If he went to Scotland, Dunbar must have returned to Denmark in the following year, as on 24 September 1634 he was reappointed major with effect from the previous 1 May.

Dunbar married on 3 September 1637 at Sønderskov, Jutland, Maren Munk (*d.* 1652), daughter of Frands Nielsen Munk of Ørs (*d.* by 1625) and his wife, Mette Thomesdatter Orning (who was still alive at the time of the marriage). Dunbar's marriage into a noble family made his naturalization on 4 May 1638 possible, and at the same time his noble birth was recognized, which enabled him to own land in Denmark. He acquired the manor of Spannarp in north-west Scania; no noble title was linked to the manor, despite the assertions of older literature. Dunbar's concern about the arrangement of his parish church of Ausås in May 1641 may indicate that he held the patronage of it as owner of Spannarp.

As major of a Scanian regiment from 1 May 1641, Dunbar was to have commanded a company of conscripts from Halland, but he exchanged the position for another—with conscripts from the *len* (administrative district) of Helsingborg. His own manor, Spannarp, was situated there, which appears to have influenced this arrangement. He was appointed commander *ad interim* of Halmstad Castle on 20 August 1641 and of Christianopel Castle on 16 May 1642. Both castles were of strategic significance in the event of war with Sweden: Halmstad Castle commanded the end of one of the most important roads, which, following the River Nissan, led from the Kattegat coast to Jönköping on Lake Vättern. Christianopel had been built as a fortress town close to the Danish–Swedish frontier and commanded the southern entrance to Kalmar Sound. As support for naval operations in this region, Christianopel was important. During Torstensson's War (named after the Swedish commander-in-chief) between Denmark and Sweden in 1643–5, Dunbar was garrisoned with his company at Halmstad from new year 1644 until the following October. He was then to be found in the camp by Malmö and in Zealand, before he was again garrisoned with two companies at Halmstad until the end of the war. On 12 December 1644 he was appointed lieutenant-colonel of Falk Lykke's Scanian regiment, but he retired from service at the end of the war. Dunbar died on 7 February 1646 at Spannarp and was buried in the church of Ausås, South Åsbo, Scania.

Dunbar has sometimes been confused with his namesake, Patrick Dunbar, who on 11 November 1657 married Elisabeth Grubbe at Elsinore (Elisabeth was buried at St Mary's, Elsinore, on 15 December 1658). Patrick Dunbar also appears to have fought in Torstensson's War, as his company was disbanded in 1645; from 1657 to 1661 he was a major in Nadelwitz's (later Münchhausen's) infantry regiment of mercenaries in Danish service. Captured by the Swedes at Elsinore in 1658, Patrick Dunbar had to remain in captivity for eighteen months, and in 1661 he appears to have left Denmark, having asked for a passport and for settlement of his accounts.   THOMAS RIIS

Sources S. Murdoch and A. Grosjean, 'Scotland, Scandinavia and Northern Europe, 1580–1707', www.abdn.ac.uk/ssne/, June 1999, no. 272 • T. Riis, *Should auld acquaintance be forgot ... Scottish–Danish relations, c.1450–1707*, 2 (1988), 86, 145 • *Danmarks Adels Aarbog*, 22 (1905), 321 • *Danmarks Adels Aarbog*, 24 (1907), 338 • *Danmarks Adels Aarbog*, 37 (1920), 459–60 • *Danmarks Adels Aarbog*, 61 (1944), 111 • A. Mackay, *The book of Mackay* (1906), 133–4
Wealth at death owner of Spannarp manor, Scania

Dunbar, Robert Nugent- (*d.* 1866), poet, lived many years in the Antilles and elsewhere in the West Indies. He recorded his impressions of the scenery and romance of the western archipelago in several volumes of verse, which were suggestive of Byron and Moore to nineteenth-century readers. His published works include *The cruise, or, A prospect of the West Indian archipelago ... with notes, historical and illustrative* (1835), *The Caraguin: a tale of the Antilles* (1837), *Indian hours* (1839), and *Beauties of tropical scenery: lyrical sketches, and love-songs. With notes, historical and illustrative* (1862; 2nd edn, 1864; 3rd edn, 1866). The latter work, and a poem, 'The Nuptials of Barcelona' (first published in *Indian Hours*, then separately in 1851) were his best known. In his introduction to the revised second edition of *Beauties of tropical scenery*, he described his artistic project, maintaining: 'I have not sought to present merely light agreeable pictures; but have endeavoured to combine with poetical sentiment much interesting historical and general information' (p. xii), and indeed, the author's notes to his poetry were highly valued in his day.

Nugent-Dunbar died at the Hotel du Louvre, Paris, on 25 July 1866, survived by his widow Annette Ellen. Before his death, Nugent-Dunbar had settled at 59 Brompton Square, Brompton, London.

GORDON GOODWIN, *rev.* MEGAN A. STEPHAN

Sources GM, 4th ser., 2 (1866), 424 • R. N. Dunbar, *Beauties of tropical scenery*, 2nd edn (1864) • Allibone, *Dict.* • BL cat., [CD-ROM] • CGPLA Eng. & Wales (1866)
Wealth at death under £5000: administration, 4 Oct 1866, CGPLA Eng. & Wales

Dunbar, Rudolph (1899–1988), clarinettist and conductor, was born at either Nabaclis or Clonbrook, near Georgetown, British Guiana, on 5 April 1899; his father was a pharmacist, and his mother, Selena, had supposedly worked as a nursemaid. The birth date quoted is adequately attested by early official sources, but Dunbar himself quoted progressively later dates, ranging from about 1904 in 1931 to about 1916 at the time of his death. His parents moved to Georgetown when he was a child, and he attended the Wesleyan Methodist school, then Christ Church Anglican school. In 1913 he was apprenticed in the British Guiana militia band; after serving for five years he became bugler and boatswain boy on the SS *Caraquet* on a voyage via New Brunswick to Barbados, where he resided for six months in 1918–19 as a member of the Barbados police band. In mid-1919 he moved to New York, where he studied under Percy Goetschius at the Institute of Musical Art of Columbia University, rising to become clarinet soloist in the institute's orchestra and giving several recitals. To help support his studies he started to play jazz. After graduating in May 1924, he played with Will Vodery's Plantation Orchestra accompanying the show *Dixie to Broadway* on a road tour.

Early in 1925 Dunbar applied for a British passport, cancelling his United States 'first papers', and in May he travelled to Paris, where he studied at the conservatory under Louis Costes (1925–30), learning conducting with Philippe Gaubert, composition with Paul Vidal, and the clarinet with Louis Cahuzac. He also studied philosophy and journalism at the University of Paris. He joined a succession of jazz groups, including the Crutcher and Evans Palm Beach Six in Biarritz and Paris (1925–6) and then Benny Peyton's Jazz Kings in Rome (December 1926 to January 1927), distinguishing himself in rescue attempts when a fire broke out during an appearance of the band at the Apollo. After playing in Dan Parrish's band at Le Grand Écart, he rejoined Will Vodery's Plantation Orchestra in summer 1927 for a British tour accompanying *Blackbirds of 1927*. He was a member of Thompson's Negro Band for the 1928 summer season at La Baule, France, and on an international tour the following winter, which visited Hamburg, Amsterdam, Rotterdam, Oslo, Copenhagen, and Madrid. In March 1930 he went to London with the band of the African-American violinist Leon Abbey. He continued to give classical recitals in Paris and continued his studies in 1930–31, first in Leipzig and then in Vienna, where he studied conducting under Felix Weingartner.

By August 1931 Dunbar had settled in London, and in December he founded the Rudolph Dunbar School of Clarinet Playing. Teaching remained his main activity for a decade, during which he regularly contributed technical articles to *Melody Maker* and in 1939 published *A Treatise on the Clarinet (Boehm System)*. He was also an active jazz musician, leading in 1933–5 a band sometimes called Rudolph

Dunbar and His All-British Coloured Band, which held residencies at the Cossack Restaurant, Jermyn Street, and the Prince's Restaurant, Piccadilly. It recorded only once, accompanying the singer Gladys Keep. The band worked frequently in Cambridge, where Dunbar became an honorary member of the Footlights. In 1936 he led bands at the Jacobite Club in Brick Street, London, and at the Florence Mills Social Parlour in Carnaby Street, an enterprise of Marcus Garvey's former wife Amy Ashwood, for which he also acted as host. Two 'symphonic jazz' pieces, *Opus in Rhythm* and *Dance of the 21st Century*, were premièred in 1935 and 1938 respectively.

In 1932 Dunbar had become the London correspondent of the Associated Negro Press, in which capacity he was granted special facilities for the 1936 Abyssinia debates in the Commons. He visited the USA from October 1938 to July 1939, giving lectures and conducting his music. In 1940 he formed a new jazz band, Rudolph Dunbar's Harlem Knights, and began broadcasting regularly with his Negro Choir, the latter work representing his last involvement with vernacular music. In May 1941 the Colonial Office, despite misgivings expressed by the security services, decided to give 'cautious encouragement' to his promotion of a 'black-British' viewpoint in the African-American press, and to his career as a broadcaster and conductor, as likely to boost colonial morale. He made his London conducting début with the London Philharmonic at the Royal Albert Hall on 26 July 1942. Thereafter he toured as a guest conductor, notably conducting the Berlin Philharmonic in 1945 and the Hollywood Bowl Orchestra in 1948. He was again in the Caribbean in 1951–2, guest conducting the British Guiana militia band.

After returning to Britain in the early 1950s Dunbar, though he continued to teach, was unable to sustain a career as a conductor and came to believe that he was the victim of a conspiracy motivated by his racial origins which excluded him in particular from broadcasting with the BBC. He died of cancer at St Mary's Hospital, Westminster, London, on 10 June 1988. He was unmarried.

HOWARD RYE

Sources R. Dunbar, 'Triumph and tragedy: the trials and tribulations of a black symphony conductor', priv. coll. [including H. Rye, 'Rudolph Dunbar: the jazz years, a chronology'] • 'Rudolph Dunbar', *Flamingo* (Dec 1961), 9–12 • 'In retrospect: W. Rudolph Dunbar: pioneering orchestra conductor', *Black Perspective in Music*, 9/2 (autumn 1981), 193–7 • J. Croker, 'British Guiana captured Europe, England, America in the person of Rudolph Dunbar', *Daily Chronicle* [Georgetown, British Guiana] (5 Aug 1951) • E. Southern, *Biographical dictionary of African-American and African musicians* (1982) • 'Rudolph Dunbar still suffers from BBC's falsehood and hypocrisy', *Frontline* (1981) • *The Independent* (5 July 1988) • *The Guardian* (7 July 1988) • d. cert. • *Daily Chronicle* [Georgetown, British Guiana] (27 Dec 1940), 1
Likenesses portrait, repro. in *Daily Chronicle* [Georgetown] (27 Dec 1940), 1 • portrait, repro. in *Daily Chronicle* [Georgetown] (11 Jan 1941), 3 • portrait, repro. in *Trinidad Guardian* (13 July 1951) • portrait, repro. in *The Independent* • portrait, repro. in *The Guardian* • portraits, repro. in *Melody Maker* (1934–9) • portraits, repro. in 'Rudolph Dunbar', *Flamingo* • portraits, repro. in 'Rudolph Dunbar still suffers', *Frontline*
Wealth at death under £70,000: administration, 10 Nov 1988, CGPLA Eng. & Wales

Dunbar, Thomas, second earl of Moray (*d.* in or before 1422). *See under* Dunbar family, earls of Moray (*per. c.*1370–1430).

Dunbar, Thomas, third earl of Moray (*d.* in or after 1425). *See under* Dunbar family, earls of Moray (*per. c.*1370–1430).

Dunbar, William (1460?–1513x30), poet and courtier, is of obscure origins.

Early years and education, 1460?–1480 The birth date of 1460 normally assigned to Dunbar by critics and editors itself derives from a hypothesis. Among the lists of students preserved in the *acta* of St Andrews University for the later 1470s the name William Dunbar does appear: this individual completed formal studies in 1477 and became a licentiate of the university in 1479, which makes 1460 a plausible birth date. Also, in the admittedly vituperative context of *The Flyting of Dunbar and Kennedie*, Gavin Kennedy dates his opponent's life from the year of the great eclipse. While this event was not visible in Scotland, it was widely reported and did occur in 1460. Whether this graduate may certainly be identified with the poet remains in question. Later records in the accounts of the lord high treasurer of Scotland during the reign of James IV do refer to Dunbar as 'maister', the proper title for a licentiate. The attribution is confirmed in the manuscript headings to some of his poems. 'The Tretis of the Twa Mariit Wemen and the Wedo', for example, is recorded as having been 'Compylit be maister William Dunbar', while Kennedy in the *Flyting* maintains that he had managed to graduate while still remaining 'an ignorant elf' (Dunbar and Kennedy, 36). Smeaton claimed to have discovered further records, proving that one 'Gul Donbere' also attended the University of Paris in 1480–81 (Baxter, 23–5). Although the truthfulness of this claim has been questioned, many Scottish graduates did go to Europe to round off their studies. Dunbar's verse does show an awareness of European culture and institutions, while Kennedy describes him as one accustomed to European travelling.

Early biographers also attempted to place Dunbar within the influential family of the earls of Dunbar and March. Kennedy traces his genealogical origins back to Gospatrick, earl of Northumberland, and uses this to question his loyalty to king and country. Concentrating only on treacherous examples, he then links the poet with Patrick, eighth Earl Dunbar, who fought against Wallace, and the Archibald Dunbar who later opposed James Douglas. But flyting is a mode whose conventions demand imaginative denigration. It may well be, therefore, that this genealogical branding of his opponent as a traitor derives only from a shared name. Indeed the poet's threadbare figure and lack of nobility form another leitmotif in Kennedy's attack.

To deduce biographical evidence from imaginative verse of any kind is, of course, a dangerous procedure. Certainly, Dunbar's own rhetorical enthusiasm for English poets ('Chaucere, rose of rhetoris all'; 'The Goldyn Targe', line 253), and his designating London the flower of all cities, are much more likely to stem from his belief that poetry transcends national boundaries than confirm the unpatriotic claims of Kennedy. Yet Dunbar so often writes about himself that it is tempting to boost the scant autobiographical evidence in this way. If Baxter, Smeaton, and others tended to use such material uncritically, their successors have sometimes moved to the opposite pole of excessive scepticism. Even within so overtly vituperative a climate as that of the *Flyting* it would be inept to falsify the most basic facts, as understood by the contemporary audience.

A general picture of Dunbar may be built up from repeated evidence of this sort. He appears to have been a small man—Kennedy regularly refers to him as a dwarf—whose roots are in the Scottish lowlands. He is most often associated with the east coast and especially the Lothians. He usually defines himself, in Aristotelian terms, as a 'makar', or poet. In 'Ane Dance in the Quenis Chalmer' he combines that definition with a satiric picture of his own awkwardness in romantic situations. Hopping around like a wanton colt, he trips and loses one of his dancing shoes rather than attracting the woman he hoped to impress (lines 22–8).

Dunbar uses the complaint form so often and so personally that the image of a touchy, insecure individual also emerges. Lyrically he laments the inadequacy of his pension, the pains caused by toothache, the malicious behaviour of other courtiers towards him, the undeserved favouring of scientist over artist, and (especially) the length of time he has had to wait for an ecclesiastical living. Indeed, a poem which begins by addressing the wretchedness of the world in general uses its refrain to identify the poet's own lack of a benefice as the major symptom of universal injustice:

> Sum men hes sevin and I nocht ane;
> Quhilk to consider is ane pane.
> ('This Waverand Warldis Wretchidnes', lines 47–8)

Middle years, 1480–1500 The next twenty years provide only one piece of clear documentary evidence, and it comes at the very end of the period. In 1500 the privy seal registers for 15 August record that a pension of 10 pounds is to be paid to Dunbar 'for al the dais of his life or quhil he be promovit be our soverane lord to ane benefice' (Baxter, 60). This payment heralds his entry as 'servitour' into the court of James IV and initiates a period during which his name will appear with some frequency in court documents. The fact remains that hypotheses regarding his early life are followed by twenty years of silence.

Dunbar's career after graduation has, therefore, to be deduced retrospectively. This applies to the poetic evidence as well as documents. Dunbar's verse survives in a number of later anthology collections, Bannatyne, Maitland, Reidpeth, and Osborn. Only the verses in the Chepman and Myllar prints, the Aberdeen sasine register, and the Asloan and Arundel manuscripts belong to the poet's lifetime. Within these the earliest certain attribution date for poems by Dunbar is 1503. The marriage of James IV to Margaret Tudor, celebrated in 'The Thrissill and the Rois', took place in that year.

Most critics assume, when assessing his activities between 1479 and 1500, that the poet's own evidence in 'How Dunbar was Desyrd to be Ane Freir' may be taken at face value. In that lyric Dunbar describes himself in Franciscan habit, preaching 'Off all Yngland frome Berwick to Kalice' (line 34), as well as crossing on the ferry from Dover and reaching Picardy. Although the poem recounts a devilish dream, a career as an itinerant preacher is consistent with the absence of his name from domestic records at the time. It also fits in with the body of his verse, which deals with the major events of the Christian story and with the sacraments of the church. The major critical debate in this area centres on whether he was a novice or a full Franciscan brother at this time. Baxter believes the former (Baxter, 13). If so, Dunbar would not have been qualified to do the preaching he describes in the poem. Matthew McDiarmid, therefore, when reviewing the book regarded this as an unnecessary hypothesis.

If uncertainty exists over details, the general assumption that Dunbar followed a religious career which regularly took him beyond Scotland seems reliable. He was definitely a priest by 16 March 1504, as an entry in the treasurer's accounts bears witness. The entry records the award, by James IV, of 7 French crowns, for the poet's first mass. By then he had become a paid 'servitour' of the court. Further progress within the clerical establishment is suggested by an entry in the protocol book of John Foular (1503–13). On 13 March 1508 'Maister William Dunbar' and Sir Edward Bog are recorded as witnesses to various resignations of property in Edinburgh. The poet is described as 'chaplain' (McDiarmid, 51). This probably refers to one of the many chaplaincies associated with St Giles, though a similar position in Queen Margaret's household is another possibility.

The poet at court, 1500–1513 The pension awarded in 1500 marks a continued period of courtly employment. Indeed, its precise terms suggest that Dunbar may have proved himself to the king earlier. A lifelong pension of £10, guaranteed against an ecclesiastical living of £40, was quite a substantial annuity. An untried newcomer would be unlikely to be offered so much for so long. The usual registration fee was also benevolently waived in this case.

The payment was to be made in two equal portions, the first at Whitsun and the second at Martinmas. Although the first was duly received on 23 May 1501, the accounts record that the second was delayed until 'efter he com furth of Ingland' (*Compota*, 2.95). While no definite proof exists, Kennedy does mention martial and ambassadorial roles for the poet, and he may have been employed earlier on courtly as well as church business when travelling beyond Scotland.

From 1501 until 1509 the pension was paid regularly to Dunbar. A number of additional payments are also recorded at this time. When specified, they usually refer to clothing, especially the gowns and livery needed for holiday celebrations. An entry for Yule 1508 itemizes the length of material needed to make him a gown of 'Parise blake' for these festivities. By this time Dunbar had certainly composed a number of official poems celebrating royal functions, and so had consolidated his artistic reputation. James IV wished to make his court a centre of cultural excellence: as a composer of songs and of dramatic entertainments, including a dance of the seven deadly sins and a mock tournament between cobbler and tailor, Dunbar would be at the centre of such occasions and so had to look the part.

The year 1510 marks an astonishing rise in Dunbar's income. The privy seal registers record £80 per year as the new sum, and it is guaranteed against a higher evaluation of the (still unforthcoming) benefice at a hundred pounds (Baxter, 182). Although Dunbar was now an established cleric, poet, and courtier, the degree of the increase remains surprising.

But it is as a 'makar' or word-builder that Dunbar most often refers to himself—'Than cam in Dunbar the Mackar'; 'This day to mak that I na micht'. The teachings of Aristotle dominated the university curriculum and his account of art derives from the basic premises of causality as established in his *Physics* and *Metaphysics*. The artist as 'efficient cause' shaped words like any artificer but, in so doing, he also imitated the creative act of the first Maker or 'original cause'. In these terms Dunbar is at once a careful and an inspired word-builder: a verbal perfectionist, whether he is creating a short, low-style lyric or a lengthy, high-style allegory. The frequency with which he uses an artificial form (formal cause) to underline sense (material cause) would also have been approved by his teachers. For example, the powerful satire he advances against medieval marriage in 'The Tretis of the Twa Mariit Wemen and the Wedo' has a form which exactly underlines the hypocrisy described. A high-style opening and conclusion surround a predominantly low-style centre, just as the high ideals of Christian marriage and courtly love are mocked by the actual evidence.

'The Tretis' at 530 lines is a fairly long narrative poem. Generally, however, Dunbar prefers shorter lyrical forms. He experiments with a wide variety of stanzaic forms, is a master of rhetorical figures, and is adept at assuming different voices for different purposes. As a cleric he can act as the court's conscience, reminding it of the higher values of Christianity. The mystery of Christ's birth is triumphantly celebrated in 'Rorate celi desuper', the joyous catharsis of the crucifixion is re-enacted in 'The Passioun of Christ', while the victories of cross and harrowing are at once celebrated martially and regretted penitentially in 'Done is a battell on the dragon blak'.

Although some of Dunbar's verse is bawdy and scurrilous, there is nothing in it that is inconsistent with a priestly vocation. Indeed, the Christian value system sounds clearly in most of his secular writing. The *contemptus mundi* topos is a favourite motif in his moral lyrics. Behind it lies the conventional Christian view of this world as, analogically, a stormy voyage leading to the port of eternal rest, or a desert in which we must wander before coming to our heavenly home. These ideas are most clearly presented in 'Of the Warldis Vanitie':

Walk furth, pilgrame, quhill thow hes dayis lycht;
Dres fra desert, draw to thy dwelling-place.
(lines 1–2)

Variations on the theme also infiltrate Dunbar's amorous writings. Although he sometimes celebrates physical love in and for itself, more usually a phrase or an aside will remind readers that there co-exists a higher, spiritual perspective:

Now of wemen, this I say for me
Off erthly thingis nane may bettir be.
('In Prays of Wemen', lines 1–2)

In the debate form as well, when charity and love are directly opposed the former gains the victory. In 'The Merle and the Nychtingall' alternating refrains put the case for 'a lusty life' and 'God allone' for the first twelve stanzas. After the nightingale has concluded charity's case and the blackbird confessed her error, the first refrain ceases and the final three, literally, sound out for God alone.

When dealing with physical love Dunbar's power to 'contradict' himself imaginatively in a wide range of modes and stanzaic forms comes into its own. At one moment he can use a male voice lyrically to imitate the humility of a genuine courtly lover ('My Hartis Tresure'); at the next he will employ the voices of married women and widows to satirize dramatically the same conventions. Allegorical analyses of the passion ('Bewty and the Presoneir'; 'The Goldyn Targe') mingle with light-hearted bawdry and misogynistic satire ('In Secreit Place'; 'Now of wemen, this I say for me'). Self-evidently these poetic strengths are ideal for a poet who may wish to eulogize a marriage or an entry into Aberdeen, to amuse the court by commenting on the arrival of a black woman, or to indulge in the vituperative verbal gymnastics of the flyting form.

Final years and reputation The last record of Dunbar's pension being paid is dated 14 May 1513. If that entry in the treasury accounts indicates the earliest possible date for his death, David Lyndsay's inclusion of his name in his 'Testament of our Soverane Lordis Papyngo' makes 1530, its composition date, the latest likely limit. In that poem Dunbar's name precedes that of Gavin Douglas. As it was usual for such lists to be chronological, and in the absence of any contradictory evidence, it seems likely that he was dead before Douglas's death in 1522.

While the sudden disappearance of a leading courtier from the records makes 1513 the single most likely date for Dunbar's death, there remains one poem that refers to an event probably of 1517: 'Ane Orisoun: Quhen the Governour Past in France'. This is not an inspired work, and some critics are inclined to reject the attribution on literary grounds alone. Further, while it is attributed to Dunbar in the version in the Maitland manuscript, Reidpeth has no attribution. As the governor in question is, almost certainly, Albany, those who accept the attribution conclude that Dunbar was still alive in 1517, the year in which the duke left Scotland. Current scholarship makes it impossible to know which of these two views is correct. While the two most popular precise dates offered are 1513

and 1520, the only certainty is that Dunbar died between 1513 and 1530.

Dunbar's poetic contemporaries and immediate successors recognized his talents. Gavin Douglas included him among his court of muses in the *Palice of Honour* (1579), while David Lyndsay praised his 'language at large' in 'The Papyngo' (printed in his *Works*, 1568). As earlier noted, selections of Dunbar's verse were preserved in the manuscript collections of the sixteenth and early seventeenth centuries, as well as appearing in the early printed texts of Chepman and Myllar. Yet, while most of the other major Scottish makars saw further editions of their work appearing at this period, Dunbar did not. In the seventeenth century he appears to have been almost forgotten, and the task of more widely disseminating his poetry was left to Allan Ramsay.

Ramsay's *Evergreen* of 1724 is a curious work. He was a careless editor, who felt free to omit, abridge, and expand texts. Indeed, Dunbar's list of the great poets of Scotland in 'The Lament for the Makaris' is extended to advertise the talents of Ramsay himself! But he did present a wide range of the shorter lyrics, along with 'The Goldyn Targe' and 'The Thrissill and the Rois'. Since then the poet's reputation among scholars and poets has remained high. The first major edition of his work, drawn from the Bannatyne manuscript selection, was published by Lord Hailes in his *Ancient Scottish Poems* of 1778. At the same time Warton in *The History of English Poetry* was praising Dunbar's thematic range and linking his poetic energy with Langland. David Laing's collected edition of 1834 consolidated his reputation in the early nineteenth century and marked the beginning of serious biographical research. Later in the same century the German scholar Jakob Schipper drew the attention of Europe to the poet in his *William Dunbar: sein Leben und Gedichte* of 1884.

Dunbar's virtuosity impressed Hugh MacDiarmid, the poet who led the early twentieth-century literary renaissance. Coming from a communist and anglophobe, MacDiarmid's call for Scottish lyricists to rally to the warcry 'Not Burns—Dunbar' had to be poetic rather than political. Having had to recreate a Scots poetic language synthetically, MacDiarmid at once envied Dunbar's inheritance of Middle Scots in its most subtly developed form and the way in which he pushed every level of style to its fullest limits. 'Ane Ballat of Our Lady', in which each stanza offers twenty-one rhymes on only two sounds, might represent one extreme—the intricate word-cathedral decorously associated with its divine heroine. But there is just as much craft dedicated to creating the alliterative ingenuity and staccato rhythms of the low style in *The Flyting*. MacDiarmid's support played a major part in confirming or establishing Dunbar's reputation among poets and literati in the early years of the twentieth century. Since then critics and teachers, benefiting from a series of scholarly editions and critical monographs, have transmitted an awareness of Dunbar's supreme craftsmanship. Ironically the linguistic and rhetorical virtuosity thus praised also denies him the popular reputation enjoyed in Scotland by Burns. If the latter remained the people's bard, however, in the twentieth century, Dunbar has certainly advanced his claim to be the poets' poet.   R. D. S. JACK

Sources J. W. Baxter, *William Dunbar* (1951) · P. Bawcutt, *Dunbar the makar* (1992) · *The poems of William Dunbar*, ed. P. Bawcutt, 2 vols., Association of Scottish Literary Studies (1998) · W. Scheps and J. A. Looney, eds., *Middle Scots poets: a reference guide* (1986) · W. Geddie, *A bibliography of Middle Scots poets, with an introduction on the history of their reputations*, STS, 61 (1912) · W. Dunbar and G. Kennedy, [*The flyting of Dunbar and Kennedie*] (c.1508) · M. P. McDiarmid, review, *SHR*, 33 (1954), 46–52 · J. Schipper, *William Dunbar: sein Leben und Gedichte* (1884) · J. B. Paul, ed., *Compota thesaurariorum regum Scotorum / Accounts of the lord high treasurer of Scotland*, 2–5 (1900–03) · R. D. S. Jack, *The poetry of William Dunbar* (1997) · D. Fox, 'The chronology of William Dunbar', *Philological Quarterly*, 39 (1960), 413–25 · *DNB* · H. MacDiarmid, *Albyn, or, Scotland and the future* (1927) · L. Ebin, *Illuminator, makar, vates: visions of poetry in the fifteenth century* (1988) · A. I. Dunlop, ed., *Acta facultatis artium universitatis Sanctiandree, 1413–1588*, 2 vols., Scottish History Society, 3rd ser., 54–5 (1964)

Dunbar, Sir William, seventh baronet (1812–1889), railway director and politician, was born on 2 March 1812, the eldest of the eight children of James Dunbar (1778–1840) and his wife, Anna Catherina (d. 1860), daughter of William Ferdinand, Baron de Reede d'Oudtshoorn of the Netherlands. He was educated at Edinburgh University, graduating on 5 January 1828. In 1835 he was admitted advocate at the Scottish bar, but never practised, and in 1841 he succeeded his uncle, Sir William Rowe Dunbar, sixth baronet, of Mochrum. On 7 January 1842 he married Catherine Hay (1807–1890), eldest daughter of James Paterson of Carpow, Perthshire. They had two children, Uthred James Hay (1843–1904) and William Cospatrick (1844–1931).

By 1852 Dunbar was deputy chairman of the Edinburgh, Perth, and Dundee Railway Company, particularly involved with feeder lines for the counties of Fife and Kinross. On 29 July 1862 the company amalgamated with the North British Railway, of which Dunbar then became a director. He was also active in the establishment of the Portpatrick railway, becoming vice-chairman on 10 November 1857, and 'went begging for the railway' in Manchester and Liverpool as well as in Wigtownshire. On 1 October 1864 he negotiated an advantageous working agreement with the Caledonian Railway; when this was due to expire in 1885 he helped to negotiate a take-over by a joint committee of the London and North Western, the Caledonian, the Glasgow and South Western, and the Midland railways.

In 1856 Dunbar became deputy lieutenant of Wigtownshire. In April 1857 he became Liberal MP for the Wigtown burghs, and on 10 June 1858 he delivered a notable speech in the Commons during the debate on the Universities (Scotland) Bill, which 'saved Edinburgh from total extinction in the University business'. In 1859 he became a lord of the Treasury in Palmerston's second administration and keeper of the prince of Wales's privy seal for Scotland during the prince's minority. After the prince attained his majority in 1863, Dunbar became his keeper of the great seal for Scotland and a member of the council of the duchy of Cornwall. On 27 July 1865 he resigned his parliamentary seat and in 1867 he was appointed to the newly

established posts of comptroller-general of the exchequer and auditor-general of public accounts, which he held until his retirement in 1888.

The family estates in the parish of Mochrum, Wigtownshire, had been dispersed; in 1859 Dunbar purchased the Grange and Torhousekie estates in Wigtown parish, and in 1872 added Cullach in Penninghame parish to his possessions. From October 1879 he made his home at the renamed Mochrum Park on the Grange estate. He died there on 19 December 1889, following a stroke. An Episcopalian in religion, he was buried on 24 December at All Saints', Challoch, Newton Stewart. He was succeeded in the baronetcy by his elder son.   JOHN MACQUEEN

Sources P. H. M'Kerlie, *History of the lands and their owners in Galloway*, new edn, 2 vols. (1906), 2.67 · *Galloway Advertiser and Wigtownshire Free Press* (25 July 1844); (3 April 1856); (2 April 1857); (17 June 1858); (21 April 1859); (23 June 1859); (11 Aug 1859); (1 March 1860); (5 Sept 1872); (23 Oct 1879); (1 Nov 1888); (26 Dec 1889); (10 April 1890) · NA Scot., BR/POR/1/1–7 · NA Scot., BR/EDP/1/1–14 · NA Scot., BR/NBR/1/10–11 · *ILN* (11 April 1863), 400 · *ILN* (4 Jan 1890), 28 · D. Laing, ed., *A catalogue of the graduates ... of the University of Edinburgh*, Bannatyne Club, 106 (1858), 222 · m. cert., Scotland · Burke, *Peerage* · *Dod's Peerage* (1890)
Archives NL Scot., journal, corresp., and papers | BL, memoranda and corresp. with W. E. Gladstone, Add. MSS 44406–44499
Likenesses engraving, repro. in *ILN* (11 April 1863), 400
Wealth at death £86,790 12s. 10d.: confirmation, 28 March 1890, *CCI*

Dunboyne. For this title name *see* Butler, John, styled twelfth Baron Dunboyne (1731–1800).

Duncan I [Donnchad ua Maíl Choluim] (d. 1040), king of Scots, was the son of Crinán, abbot of Dunkeld (d. 1045), and Bethóc, daughter of *Malcolm II (d. 1034). The belief that he had a brother, Maldred, who married a daughter of Earl Uhtred of Northumbria (d. 1016), is erroneous. Duncan married an unnamed cousin of Siward, earl of Northumbria, and had three sons: *Malcolm III (Malcolm Canmore) (d. 1093), king of Scots from 1058 to 1093; *Donald III (Donalbane) (b. in or before 1040, d. 1099?), king of Scots in 1093–4 and 1094–7; and Mael Muire, ancestor of the earls of Atholl.

It is often argued that Duncan I was favoured by Malcolm II, as his heir to the Scottish throne. The exiguous evidence can be interpreted differently, but a sign of Malcolm's support for Duncan may have been Duncan's installation as king of Strathclyde ('king of the Cumbrians') some time after King Owain's death, perhaps in 1018. Probably this did not occur until nearer the end of Malcolm's reign, for it is unlikely that Duncan reached adulthood much before c.1030: a (probably) contemporary source describes him as being 'at an immature age' (Anderson, *Early Sources*, 1.581) when he was killed in 1040. It may be noted, moreover, that Duncan does not appear among the northern kings who submitted to Cnut in 1031–2. It is not impossible, indeed, that Duncan actually made himself 'king of Strathclyde' following his successful claim to the Scottish kingship on Malcolm II's death in 1034. The fact that Duncan was ever king of Strathclyde rests chiefly on the description of his son, Malcolm, as 'son of the king of the Cumbrians' (Anderson, *Scottish*

Annals, 85 n. 4) by a northern English source reporting Malcolm's Northumbrian-backed invasion of Scotland in 1054. He is the last known 'king of the Cumbrians' (though his grandson, *David I, was 'prince of the Cumbrians' (Lawrie, no. 50) for a decade or more before 1124).

Malcolm II died on 25 November 1034, the last member of the male lineage descended from Kenneth I to hold the kingship. He was not, however, the last male member of the dynasty: the Clann Duib, descendants of King Dubh (*d.* 966) continued unbroken in the male line until the mid-fourteenth century. Perhaps no adult male descendant of Kenneth I was active in 1034. Perhaps Duncan was simply an out-and-out opportunist. Certainly the succession of someone whose claim had descended primarily through his mother is highly unusual in this period. Be this as it may, within days of Malcolm's death, Duncan I was formally inaugurated as king on 30 November.

Duncan's first recorded venture out of his kingdoms was provoked by the devastation of Strathclyde by Earl Eadulf of Northumbria in 1038—possibly extending his control over Cumberland and other areas. Duncan I's response was to launch an invasion of northern England the following year. He laid siege to Durham, but suffered a comprehensive defeat at the hands of the besieged. As a result Strathclyde may have been left open to Northumbrian penetration, as well as to invasion from the Gall Gaedhil, suffering a mortal blow to its integrity. Duncan, however, was also preoccupied with problems in the north, which saw him campaigning in 1040 against the ruler of Moray, Macbeth (*d.* 1057), who had married the daughter of Boite mac Cinaeda (probably brother of Malcolm II). Duncan's efforts ended in failure and death: he was killed by Macbeth in battle at Both Gobhanán (probably Pitgaveny, near Elgin, in Moray) on 14 August 1040. He was perhaps only in his mid-twenties; certainly not the old man depicted in Shakespeare's *Macbeth*. A late and debatable source claims that he was buried on Iona.

DAUVIT BROUN

Sources A. O. Anderson, ed. and trans., *Early sources of Scottish history, AD 500 to 1286*, 1 (1922), 571–82 · A. O. Anderson, ed., *Scottish annals from English chroniclers, AD 500 to 1286* (1908), 83–5 · A. A. M. Duncan, *Scotland: the making of the kingdom* (1975), vol. 1 of *The Edinburgh history of Scotland*, ed. G. Donaldson (1965–75), 99 · G. W. S. Barrow, 'Some problems in 12th and 13th century Scottish history: a genealogical approach', *Scottish Genealogist*, 25 (1978), 97–112 · M. O. Anderson, *Kings and kingship in early Scotland*, rev. edn (1980), 265–89 · A. C. Lawrie, ed., *Early Scottish charters prior to AD 1153* (1905), no. 50

Duncan II (*b.* before 1072, *d.* 1094), king of Scots, was the son of *Malcolm III (*d.* 1093) and his first wife, Ingibiorg, of the house of Orkney earls. He was described by William of Malmesbury as *nothus*, bastard, a slur intended to explain the succession in the kingship of the sons of Malcolm's second wife, *Margaret (*d.* 1093): when William I of England took Duncan as hostage from Malcolm he is unlikely to have taken an illegitimate son. William Rufus released and knighted Duncan in 1087, along with Ulf, son of Harold II, but Duncan was intermittently at Rufus's court until the death of his father in 1093, when, in return for homage, he obtained the English king's consent to his

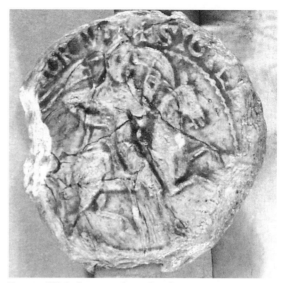

Duncan II (*b.* before 1072, *d.* 1094), seal

seeking the Scottish throne. He seems to have scraped together a force of English and French, but was successful in driving out his uncle *Donald III and became king before the end of 1093.

Probably on his way north, Duncan sought the help of St Cuthbert, to whom he restored the long-lost lands of Tyninghame, in what is the earliest Scottish charter, whether in original or copy. In it Duncan describes himself as 'heritably undoubted king of *Scotia*' (Lawrie, no. 12); he makes the gift for his father, brothers, wife, and infants, but adds as reassurance that he has caused his brothers to make the grant; his mother is not mentioned. The signatories include *Edgar, presumably Duncan's half-brother, and a Malcolm who is usually taken to be a full brother—not an impossibility but lacking any confirmation. Duncan's seal is single-faced and shows him armed as mounted knight with lance and pennon; perhaps it was produced for the occasion by the monks of Durham. He granted land to Dunfermline Priory, the foundation of his stepmother, Margaret, thus confirming that he was on good terms with her sons.

Duncan's reign was brief and stormy; first some Scots attacked and drove out his foreign contingent, and he had to swear that he would never reintroduce them to Scotland. Then in a second rising, under Donald III and Edmund, son of Malcolm III, he was killed, apparently with some treachery, by the local mormaer at Mondynes in the Mearns on 12 November 1094, a date preserved by an obit at Durham, where he was highly regarded, though he was allegedly buried on Iona. Donald III resumed the throne; Duncan, despite his Gaelic name, Donnchad, was too Anglo-French for Scotland. He had married Etheldreda (or Octreda), daughter of *Gospatric, the earl of Northumbria who fled to Scotland in 1072, but only one of their children is known, **William fitz Duncan** (*d.* 1151x4).

William probably came to Scotland with his uncle *David before 1124, and supported the latter loyally and effectively after he became king in 1124. He led the contingent which attacked Wark Castle in January 1138, ravaged in Yorkshire fiercely, won a victory at Clithero, and devastated Craven before joining the king at Cowton Moor in August, where he angrily opposed the attempts of Robert (I) de Brus (d. 1142) to persuade David to go home. He then fought at the battle of the Standard, but does not seem to have accompanied David south in 1141, and, apart from witnessing charters, is not heard of again until David I confirmed him by force in the honour of Skipton and Craven in 1151. William married Alice de Rumilly, who inherited lands in Copeland and Skipton, and himself inherited Allerdale, south of Derwent, through his mother. It is surely likely that he also had Scottish lands, and in an English inquest of the thirteenth century he is called 'earl of Moray', a province forfeited to the crown in 1130; but he is never so called in Scotland. According to charter evidence William fitz Duncan had died by 1154.

William had two sons, a Gospatric who is once mentioned and may have been a child of an earlier marriage, and William, 'the boy of Egremont', who succeeded to his father's English lands and died childless in or soon after 1163, so that the inheritance passed to his three sisters. William fitz Duncan made no known claim to the throne of Scotland, nor did his lawful heirs in 1291, although *Orkneyinga Saga* (about 1200–40) makes the striking comment that the son of Malcolm and Ingibiorg 'was Duncan, king of Scots, father of William who was a great man, and whose son, William the noble, every Scotsman wanted for his king' (*Orkneyinga Saga*, 72). This may, however, be a confusion with William's son, Donald *MacWilliam [see under Macwilliam family] (probably illegitimate), who from 1179 led a rebellion against King William the Lion with support from Moray and Ross.   A. A. M. DUNCAN

Sources A. O. Anderson, ed. and trans., *Early sources of Scottish history, AD 500 to 1286*, 2 (1922), 89–94 · A. O. Anderson, ed., *Scottish annals from English chroniclers, AD 500 to 1286* (1908), 117–18 · W. Farrer and others, eds., *Early Yorkshire charters*, 12 vols. (1914–65), vol. 7, pp. 9–16 · A. A. M. Duncan, 'Yes, the earliest Scottish charters', *SHR*, 78 (1999), 1–38 · A. C. Lawrie, ed., *Early Scottish charters prior to AD 1153* (1905), no. 12 and pp. 271–3 · A. H. Dunbar, *Scottish kings*, 2nd edn (1906) · H. Pálsson and P. Edwards, eds. and trans., *The Orkneyinga saga: the history of the earls of Orkney* (1978)
Archives Durham Cath. CL, charter
Likenesses seal, U. Durham L., Durham Cathedral muniments, Misc. ch. 554 [*see illus.*]

Adam Duncan, Viscount Duncan (1731–1804), by Henry Pierre Danloux, 1792

Duncan, Adam, Viscount Duncan (1731–1804), naval officer, was born on 1 July 1731 at the town house of the Stewarts of Grandtully, Seagait, Dundee, the third of seven children of Alexander Duncan (1703–1765) of Lundie, Forfarshire, provost of Dundee (1744–6), and Helen Haldane (d. 1777), daughter of John Haldane of Gleneagles, Perthshire, and Helen Erskine.

Early career and Keppel's influence Having been educated in Dundee, Duncan entered the navy in 1746 on board the sloop *Trial*, which was under the command of his cousin, Lieutenant Robert Haldane, and was engaged in convoying troop transports from Leith to Inverness, part of the government's reaction to the Jacobite rising. After the battle of Culloden in April 1746 the *Trial* cruised off the Western Isles and Ireland until September 1747, before returning to Plymouth in November. Duncan joined Haldane when the latter was promoted post captain of the frigate *Shoreham* in February 1748, and he remained with him until the peace in October. On 25 January 1749 Duncan became a midshipman in the *Centurion*, then commissioned for the Mediterranean by the Hon. Augustus Keppel. The connection then begun with Keppel dictated Duncan's subsequent career; Keppel became strongly attached to Duncan and formed the highest opinion of him as an officer. When General Edward Braddock was sent to North America in 1755 Keppel commanded the convoy for the army transports. On his warm recommendation, on 10 January 1755 Duncan was appointed lieutenant to the *Norwich* (50 guns); he moved to Keppel's *Centurion* on arrival in North America. In August 1755 he moved with Keppel to the *Swiftsure*, and in January 1756 to the *Torbay*. He was present in the expedition to Basque Roads in 1757, and at the taking of Goree in 1758, and the blockade of Brest in 1759. Promotion to the rank of commander on 21 September 1759 and the command of the *Royal Exchange*, a hired merchant vessel briefly employed on convoy duty, between October 1759 and April 1760, meant that Duncan missed the battle of Quiberon Bay. He saw no further service until promoted captain (21 February 1761) and appointed to the *Valiant* (74 guns), fitting for Keppel's broad pennant as second in command to Sir George Pocock. Thereafter Duncan had an important share in the capture of Belle Île in June 1761, and of Havana in August 1762. He remained with Keppel at Jamaica until the end of the war, but his health had been affected by his service in the West Indies and for the next three years he spent much time at Bath and Cheltenham.

More than a decade of peace after 1763 condemned Duncan, like most naval officers, to unemployment. He returned to Dundee, after his father's death, helping his widowed sister, Mrs Haldane, with the education of her three children and visiting his recently widowed aunt by marriage, Lady Mary Duncan, in Italy in 1774. On 6 June 1777 he married Henrietta Dundas (1748/9–1832), third daughter of the Rt Hon. Robert Dundas of Arniston, Edinburghshire, lord president of the court of session, and his first wife, Henrietta Carmichael. She was the niece of Henry Dundas, the political manager of Scotland, and eighteen years Duncan's junior, but it was a very happy marriage.

War with the American colonies brought Duncan employment. In May 1778 he was appointed to the *Suffolk* (74 guns), joining the Channel Fleet under Admiral Keppel, and in December he moved to the *Monarch* (74 guns). As 'a follower and dependent upon Mr Keppel' (*Correspondence of George III*, 4.226) Duncan was reluctant to be a member of Keppel's court martial in January 1779, and is said to have interfered several times during the course of the trial to prevent irrelevant or leading questions or misinterpreted answers. Lord Sandwich considered Duncan 'a quiet man' (ibid.); he was not a violent political partisan. Nevertheless the Admiralty did not wish Keppel's adherents to sit on Sir Hugh Palliser's court martial in April, and ordered the *Monarch* to St Helens. But the crew refused to weigh anchor until they were paid their advance and as this could not be done in time, Duncan sat on the court martial, though he does not seem to have shown any bias against Palliser.

During the anxious summer of 1779 the *Monarch* was part of the Channel Fleet under Sir Charles Hardy, and in December the ship was one of Sir George Rodney's squadron ordered to the relief of Gibraltar. Duncan played a prominent part in the 'moonlight battle' off Cape St Vincent on 16 January 1780. The uncoppered *Monarch* was slow, but Duncan, declaring 'I wish to be among them' (*Naval Chronicle*, 12.87), hurried into the action against three Spanish ships. Though the *Monarch* took the *San Augustin* (70 guns) she suffered considerable damage and her prize was retaken by the Spaniards. Duncan returned to England with Admiral Robert Digby and the bulk of the fleet, but when the *Monarch* was ordered to the West Indies in 1781 Duncan's health made him decline the command and he thus missed the battle of the Saints (April 1782).

The change of ministry in March 1782 brought Keppel to the Admiralty. Duncan was appointed to the *Blenheim* (90 guns) and commanded her, under Lord Howe, at the relief of Gibraltar and the encounter with the Franco-Spanish fleet off Cape Spartel in October, but he left her in November when she was ordered to the West Indies. He then succeeded Sir John Jervis in command of the *Foudroyant* (84 guns) and after the peace in 1783 commanded the Portsmouth guardship *Edgar* (74 guns) for three years. Though

he was promoted rear-admiral of the blue on 24 September 1787, peace again brought unemployment, which he spent chiefly in Scotland, living in the house in George Square, Edinburgh, which he had recently bought from Henry Dundas.

Duncan was promoted rear-admiral of the white on 21 September 1790, vice-admiral of the blue on 1 February 1793, and just over a year later, on 12 April 1794, vice-admiral of the white. But despite the outbreak of the French Revolutionary War in 1793 he was not employed until February 1795, when he was appointed commander-in-chief in the North Sea. Traditionally Lord Spencer, then first lord of the Admiralty, is reported to have enquired of Henry Dundas why Duncan had not been employed. Dundas replied that he thought Duncan, married to his niece, would like employment and Duncan was forthwith appointed. There is nothing inherently improbable in this story, so typical of eighteenth-century politics. Spencer, a whig who had joined the coalition government under Pitt in December 1794, could be expected to look favourably on the protégés of political friends. Combined with Dundas's patronage and Duncan's professional reputation, this proved decisive.

Blockading the Dutch and the battle of Camperdown, 1797
The command Duncan was given was no sinecure and the political/strategic situation was grave. Since January, Britain had imposed an embargo on all Dutch shipping. In May an alliance between the Netherlands and France increased the threat to British security and trade. Duncan's force was a motley collection of ships of various rates and ages, comprising captured prizes, converted Indiamen and worn out war ships, numerically inadequate for the area he had to cover, from the far north of Scotland to the channel, and always being taken from him for other stations and duties. Duncan, though he complained occasionally of his force, endeavoured to do the best he could with it. At first he was appointed to the *Prince George* (98 guns) but she proved to have too deep a draft for blockading the Dutch coast and on 11 March 1795 he transferred to the *Venerable* (74 guns); he hoisted his flag in her on 31 March and was promoted admiral of the blue on 1 June.

Duncan now began a private correspondence with Spencer, keeping the first lord abreast of his situation. The correspondence engendered mutual respect and it was at this time too that Duncan became acquainted with William Pitt, visiting Walmer Castle, Pitt's residence as warden of the Cinque Ports, when his ships were in the Downs and becoming something of a naval consultant to these politicians. When Admiral William Hotham was recalled from the Mediterranean in the summer of 1795 the station was offered to Duncan, but he declined as he thought the Dutch fleet were about to leave their base at the Texel. Consulted by Pitt, Spencer, and Dundas on a replacement Duncan recommended Sir John Jervis, whose seamanship and officer-like qualities Duncan had recognized when in the Channel Fleet with him in 1779, and when he later succeeded Jervis as captain of the *Foudroyant* in 1782. In October 1795 it was proposed that

Duncan take Sir Charles Middleton's place at the Admiralty but Spencer declared the admiral could not be spared from the North Sea.

A Russian squadron of twelve ships of the line and six frigates, under Vice-Admiral Hanickoff, had joined Duncan in July 1795. Their unpreparedness and inactivity during the summer, and the threat posed by the Dutch fleet to the British Baltic trade and to homeward bound convoys, led Spencer to insist on Duncan's blockading the Texel as closely as possible. For two years, despite appalling weather and an inadequate force, the admiral achieved this. But matters worsened in 1797. Rumours that the Dutch were preparing to put to sea, as part of an invasion force, increased at a time when mutiny paralysed first the Channel Fleet at Spithead in April and May and then that at the Nore in May.

Duncan's squadron was also affected. Though he dealt with mutiny on the *Venerable* and *Adamant* by a direct appeal to the crews and by his commanding presence and physical strength, he was unable to prevent the rest of his force, then blockading the enemy and based at Yarmouth, from joining the mutinous ships at the Nore. Yet the admiral determined to continue the blockade of the Dutch fleet 'and make up as well as I can for the want of my fleet by making a number of signals as if the fleet was in the offing …' (Corbett, 2.147). He continued this gallant pretence off the Texel for some days with only the *Venerable* and *Adamant*. Fortunately the Dutch were unprepared to take advantage of the opportunity and Duncan was reinforced, first by Sir Roger Curtis and six ships from the Channel Fleet, then by the Russian squadron, and finally, after the mutiny had ended, by his own squadron. Any projected Dutch invasion of Ireland was frustrated by prolonged adverse weather and by the death of General Hoche, the commander of the expedition. It is something of a mystery why the Dutch fleet finally left the Texel on 6 October 1797, too late in the year for an invasion attempt. It has generally been attributed to a display of national prestige by the Dutch government. Duncan was revictualling his ships at Yarmouth when the news was brought to him on 9 October. Immediately he weighed anchor and stood over to the Dutch coast. Steering south, he sighted the Dutch fleet on the morning of 11 October, about 5 miles from the shore, nearly half way between the villages of Egmont and Camperdown, forming their line of battle and heading north for their base. The opposing fleets were equal in numbers, sixteen sail of the line, though the Dutch ships were lighter and had a shallower draught. The wind was blowing straight on shore. It was clear that the Dutch would speedily get into shoal water, where the British would be unable to follow, unless Duncan attacked immediately, cutting off the Dutch retreat by getting between them and the land. Without waiting for his ships astern to come up, and without waiting to form a regular line of battle, 'I made the signal to bear up, break the enemy's line, and engage them to leeward, each ship her opponent, by which I got between them and the land, whither they were fast approaching' (13 October, ADM 1/524). His fleet formed into two irregular groups, led by

himself in the *Venerable* and Vice-Admiral Richard Onslow in the *Monarch*. The manoeuvre was a success but the engagement was long and bloody. The British had the advantage of carronades on their ships and their gunnery was superior, but the Dutch fought with great courage and tenacity. For a time the *Venerable*, engaging the Dutch flagship, *Vrijheid*, was surrounded by enemy ships and suffered heavily. Duncan later declared that the pilot and himself were the only two left alive on the quarterdeck, while when the *Vrijheid* finally surrendered only Admiral de Winter remained unhurt. Nine severely damaged Dutch ships were taken, and the rest escaped in the rising gale. But the immediate threat from the Dutch fleet had been removed.

Public hero and later career News of the victory was received in Britain with delight and as confirmation that the mutinies of the summer had not destroyed the power and prestige of the navy. Duncan was granted a pension of £2000 p.a. for himself and his two succeeding heirs, and created Baron Duncan of Lundie and Viscount Duncan of Camperdown on 21 October 1797, a reward thought inadequate by, among others, his aunt, Lady Mary Duncan. Writing to Henry Dundas, on 18 October she remarked, 'my nephew is only made a viscount … the whole nation thinks the least you can do is to give him an English earldom …' (Omond, 251). But if the official reward seemed niggardly, this was compensated for by the public response. Duncan was granted the freedom of the city of London, on 19 October, and a sword worth 200 guineas. Bath, Bristol, Yarmouth, Liverpool, Portsmouth, and many other English towns made him an honorary freeman, while others and several marine societies voted him their thanks or bestowed membership on him. In Scotland, where he was particularly fêted as a local hero, Glasgow, Edinburgh, and Dundee, which also voted him a piece of plate, conferred their freedom on him. His native county of Forfarshire presented him with a piece of plate worth 200 guineas and commissioned a portrait by John Hoppner to hang, as it continued to do over two centuries later, in the town hall of Forfar. A Duncan tartan was advertised in *The Morning Chronicle* (11 January 1798), 'emblematical of the species of tactics pursued by the British Admiral' in response to a demand for the many newly formed Scottish Camperdown clubs (Murray, 51). Civic receptions and celebratory dinners all signalled the delighted relief which marked the news of the victory.

Duncan was created admiral of the white in February 1799, and remained in command of the North Sea Fleet until 1800. The British government had considered landing an army in Europe in 1797 but it was not until August 1800 that such an expedition was launched to The Helder, in northern Holland, under the command of the duke of York and General Sir Ralph Abercromby. Duncan, as senior admiral, commanded a fleet of 250 transports in addition to his own ships. The naval part of the expedition was a success. Thirteen Dutch warships and three Indiamen, lying at The Helder, surrendered and a few days later a further twelve, some of them the ships which had escaped after Camperdown, surrendered at the Texel. The rest of the expedition was a failure and British forces had to be evacuated in November, with the loss of four ships. This marked the end of Duncan's active career. He struck his flag on 28 April 1800 and although he offered his services on the renewal of the war in 1803, these were refused because of his age. He retired to Lundie House, near Dundee, which he had inherited on the death of his brother in 1796. Though his constitution had been strong, he suffered, increasingly, from bouts of ill health from 1799. He died suddenly on 4 August 1804 at The Inn, Cornhill-on-Tweed, while on the way to Edinburgh. He was buried at Dundee, and succeeded by his third, but first surviving, son, Robert Dundas Duncan (b. 1785), who was created earl of Camperdown (12 September 1831) and assumed the name of Haldane after Duncan. Duncan's second surviving son, Henry, died a captain in the navy and KCH in 1835. Four of Duncan's five daughters married members of the Scots peerage or gentry. His wife died in Edinburgh on 8 December 1832, aged eighty-three, and was buried at Dundee.

Reputation Duncan's reputation for coolness, courage, and daring was well deserved. A highly skilled seaman, he kept an indifferent collection of ships cruising in all weathers on a lee shore and maintained a strict blockade of the dangerous Dutch coast for years without serious loss. In his youth he was an exceptionally handsome man who, at over 6 feet in height, had an imposing physical presence, which he retained into old age, and which is apparent in his portraits. His kindly, unaffected, and modest nature, noted by contemporaries, is a feature of his correspondence. Writing to Robert Dundas a week after his victory he declared, 'Honours seem to flow on me. I hope my head will keep right, tho' if I at all know myself neither riches or titles will have no other affect in me than to be able to do more good' (Murray, 38). He earned the respect and friendship of the umbrageous Russian admirals, and the emperor Paul created him a knight of the imperial order of St Alexander Nevsky on 19 July 1797. He quickly gained and retained de Winter's friendship, arranging for the Dutch admiral's repatriation when he learned of his wife's illness.

Duncan was reluctant to find fault with subordinates, but he could be severe with those who failed in their duty. His care for his seamen earned their gratitude and affection, his courage and endurance their respect. One sailor wrote of him after Camperdown 'They can't make too much of him. He is heart of oak; he is a seaman every inch of him, and as to a bit of broadside it only makes the old cock young again' (Lloyd, 158).

Duncan was a deeply religious man, as his speeches to his crews during the mutinies illustrate, and he often displayed an unaffected piety. When the *Venerable* was bearing down on the Dutch fleet before the battle, he called his officers on deck and knelt in prayer; and on the conclusion of the battle, 'he called up the clergyman and made all in his ship that were able return thanks to God Almighty for all his mercies showered upon them and him' (ibid., 138).

Duncan was criticized by some contemporaries for his lack of tactical skill at Camperdown, and for attacking 'without attention to form or order' (Lloyd, 141). He had met John Clerk of Eldin, had a copy of his book *Essay on Naval Tactics* (1782), which stressed that the key to victory in a naval battle lay in breaking the enemy's line, and acknowledged his indebtedness to it. But for Duncan time was the deciding tactical factor as he approached the Dutch fleet and coast. He could not afford to wait to form his line, as he originally intended, to break the enemy line at all points. He was forced to approach the Dutch, in no particular order, in two groups of ships. He first signalled a general chase, then to pass through the enemy's line and engage to leeward; finally the signal for close action was kept flying. He thus left much to the initiative and common sense of his captains, all of whom, except Williamson in the *Agincourt*, responded in the way he had hoped. De Winter's remark to Duncan, after the battle, makes clear both Duncan's tactics and the results: 'Your not waiting to form line ruined me: if I had got nearer the shore and you had attacked, I should probably have drawn both fleets on it, and it would have been a victory for me, being on my own coast' (ibid., 142).

P. K. CRIMMIN

Sources NL Scot., Duncan MSS, M.1995 · correspondence between Lord Spencer and Admiral Duncan, 1796, BL, Althorp MS G.184 · BL, Add. MS 23207, fols. 160b, 161, 162 · *The Naval Chronicle*, 12 (1804), 87 · J. Charnock, ed., *Biographia navalis*, 4 (1796) · J. Ralfe, *Naval biography*, vol. 1 · C. Lloyd, *St Vincent and Camperdown* (1963) · Lord Camperdown, *Admiral Duncan* (1898) · D. Syrett and R. L. DiNardo, *The commissioned sea officers of the Royal Navy, 1660–1815*, rev. edn, Occasional Publications of the Navy RS, 1 (1994), 135 · J. Murray, ed., *Glorious victory: Admiral Duncan and the battle of Camperdown, 1797* (1997) · *Private papers of George, second Earl Spencer*, ed. J. S. Corbett and H. W. Richmond, 4 vols., Navy RS, 46, 48, 58–9 (1913–24), vols. 1–2 · G. W. T. Omond, *The Arniston memoirs* (1888) · J. Aylmer Haldane, *The Haldanes of Gleneagles* (1929) · *Scots peerage* · Chambers, *Scots.* (1855), 3.162–9 · Burke, *Peerage* · J. K. Laughton, ed., 'The pedigree of the naval Duncans', *The naval miscellany*, 2, Navy RS, 40 (1912), 387 · E. H. Turner, 'The Russian squadron with Admiral Duncan's north sea fleet, 1795–1800', *Mariner's Mirror*, 72 (1986), 212–22 · R. D. Franks, 'Admiral Sir Richard Onslow', *Mariner's Mirror*, 67 (1981), 327–37 · P. K. Crimmin, 'George Canning and the battle of Camperdown', *Mariner's Mirror*, 67 (1981), 319–25 · *The correspondence of King George the Third from 1760 to December 1783*, ed. J. Fortescue, 4 (1928), 226 · PRO, ADM 1/524 · Keppel's court martial, Palliser's court martial, both 1779, PRO, Adm MSS, ADM 1/5312–5313

Archives Dundee City Archives, corresp., letter-books, and legal and other papers · priv. coll., corresp. and papers relating to 1797 mutiny · Scottish United Services Museum, Edinburgh, Duncan MSS, official, miscellaneous, and family papers, M.1995 | BL, corresp. with Earl Spencer, Althorp MS G184 · NL Scot., letters, information on mutinies of 1797 [copies]

Likenesses J. Reynolds, portrait, 1760–61, National Galleries of Scotland · H.-P. Danloux, portrait, c.1780, National Galleries of Scotland · H.-P. Danloux, oils, 1792, NPG [see illus.] · J. Hoppner, portrait, 1797, Forfar Town and County Hall · J. S. Copley, portrait, 1798, National Galleries of Scotland · H. Raeburn, portrait, 1798 (Incorporation of the Shipmasters of the of Trinity House, Leith), repro. in Murray, ed., *Glorious victory* · D. Orme, miniature, repro. in D. Foskett, *Dictionary of British miniature painters* (1972), vol. 2, pl. 257 · J. Tassie, paste enamel, repro. in Murray, ed., *Glorious victory* · engraving (after picture by R. M. Payne), National Galleries of Scotland · portrait, National Galleries of Scotland; repro. in Murray, ed., *Glorious victory*, p. 38

Wealth at death c.£17,200–17,500 p.a.; possibly £35,000: Scottish United Services Museum, Edinburgh, Duncan MSS, M.1995.2.23–4, statement of affairs 1786; M.1995.2.80, 1787; M.1995.2.22, memo book, 1783–1804

Duncan, Andrew, the elder (1744–1828), physician, was born at Pinkerton, near St Andrews, on 17 October 1744, the second son of Andrew Duncan, merchant and shipmaster, of Crail, afterwards of St Andrews, and his wife, Catherine, daughter of Professor William Vilant, and related to William Drummond of Hawthornden. Duncan was educated first by Sandy Don of Crail, celebrated in the song of 'Crail Town', and afterwards by Richard Dick of St Andrews. He proceeded next to St Andrews University, where he obtained the MA degree in 1762. As a youth he was known as the 'smiling boy', and he retained his good nature throughout his life. In 1762 he entered Edinburgh University as a medical student, being the pupil of William Cullen, John Gregory, Monro secundus, John Hope, and William Black. He was president of the Royal Medical Society in 1767, and from 1769 to 1774; he later declared that he considered it an essential part of the medical school at Edinburgh.

On the completion of his studies in 1768, Duncan went on a voyage to China as surgeon of the East India Company's ship *Asia*. He refused an offer of 500 guineas to undertake a second voyage, choosing instead to pursue a career as university lecturer. The first step was to obtain the necessary qualifications. Duncan graduated MD at St Andrews in October 1769, and in May 1770 became a licentiate of the Edinburgh College of Physicians. In the same year he was an unsuccessful candidate for the professorship of medicine in St Andrews University, and published the first of his many books, *Elements of Therapeutics*. In August 1770 he married Mary Knox, daughter of John Knox, surgeon; they had twelve children. His eldest son, Andrew *Duncan (1773–1832), also became a professor at Edinburgh. His third son, Alexander (1780–1859), became a general in the army, and distinguished himself in India.

During the absence of Dr Drummond, professor-elect of medicine at Edinburgh, Duncan was appointed to lecture in 1774–6. When Drummond failed to return, James Gregory was elected professor. Disappointed that he had not been elected, Duncan started an extra-academical course on the theory and practice of medicine, with special attention to chronic diseases, which led him to found a public dispensary, an institution for giving free medicines and medical advice to the poor. This afterwards became the Royal Public Dispensary, incorporated by royal charter in 1818. In 1773 Duncan founded the Aesculapian Club, and in 1782 the Harveian Club, in order to promote friendship between members of the College of Physicians and the College of Surgeons. Though primarily supper clubs, they gave Duncan the same kind of professional contacts among practitioners in Edinburgh as his membership in the Royal Medical Society did among students. Both sets of contacts proved valuable in his publication of *Medical and Philosophical Commentaries*, a quarterly journal of medicine, begun in 1773. It was the first medical review journal published regularly in Great Britain; by 1775 it was translated into German, and by the end of the decade it printed news from medical societies throughout Great Britain, France,

Andrew Duncan the elder (1744–1828), by John Brown, c.1780

Denmark, Russia, and America. In 1775 the name of the publication was changed to *Annals of Medicine*; in 1804 this was discontinued in favour of the *Edinburgh Medical and Surgical Journal*, edited by Andrew Duncan the younger.

In 1790, Duncan was elected president of the Royal College of Physicians of Edinburgh. On Cullen's resignation of the professorship of medicine in that year, he was succeeded by James Gregory, whom Duncan followed in the chair of the theory or institutes of medicine. The subject matter of this course was not well defined, and Duncan taught it to his own interests, including therapeutics and medical police (public health), as well as physiology. In 1795 he began teaching a course in medical jurisprudence and medical police, and worked for several years to have a chair in medical jurisprudence established at the University of Edinburgh. This was done in 1807, and Andrew Duncan the younger was the first professor.

Duncan continued to promote new institutions in Edinburgh. In 1792 he proposed the erection of a public lunatic asylum, finally built in 1807 at Morningside. In 1808 the freedom of Edinburgh was conferred on him for his services in the foundation of the dispensary and the asylum. In 1809 he founded the Caledonian Horticultural Society, and in later years he was actively occupied in promoting the establishment of a public experimental garden. In 1819 his son became joint professor of medical theory with him. In 1821, on the death of James Gregory, Duncan became first physician to the king in Scotland, having held the same office to the prince of Wales for more than thirty years. During the same year he was elected president of the Edinburgh Medico-Chirurgical Society at its foundation. In 1824 he was again elected president of the Edinburgh College of Physicians.

Duncan was an industrious and perspicuous lecturer who, in common with other members of the medical faculty, took seriously the task of keeping up with the literature and presenting a comprehensive course in his field. He was both generous and hospitable to his pupils, and was much loved for the geniality and benevolence of his character. For more than half a century he walked to the top of Arthur's Seat on May day morning, accomplishing this for the last time on 1 May 1827. He died on 5 July 1828, and was buried in Buccleuch churchyard, Edinburgh. He bequeathed to the College of Physicians of Edinburgh seventy volumes of manuscript notes from the lectures of the founders of the Edinburgh school of medicine, and a hundred volumes of practical observations on medicine in his own handwriting.

Duncan's reputation has suffered by comparison with his more famous colleagues, but the comparison is unfair, for he was not a scientific but an institutional innovator. He was particularly noteworthy in drawing on continental models when proposing new institutions, and did much to break the insularity of the Edinburgh medical community. He was particularly far-sighted in promoting the unity of physicians and surgeons at a time of great professional rivalry; and Andrew Duncan the younger, unusually for the period, received a thorough education both in medicine and in surgery.

G. T. Bettany, rev. Lisa Rosner

Sources A. Duncan, *Miscellaneous poems* (1818) · R. Huie, *Harveian oration for 1829: being a tribute of respect for the memory of A. Duncan* (1829) · Chambers, *Scots.* (1835) · J. Gray, *History of the Royal Medical Society, 1737–1937*, ed. D. Guthrie (1952) · H. L. W. Wemyss, *A record of the Edinburgh Harveian Society* (1933) · L. Rosner, *Andrew Duncan, MD, FRSE* (1981) · parish register (birth), Crail, Fife, 20 Oct 1744 · parish register (marriage), Lady Yester's Kirk, 19 Aug 1770 · private information (2004)
Archives NL Scot. · Royal College of Physicians of Edinburgh, corresp. and papers · Royal Medical Society, Edinburgh · U. Edin. L., lecture notes · Wellcome L., lecture notes | Royal College of Physicians of Edinburgh, Aesculapian Society MSS
Likenesses J. Brown, pencil drawing, *c*.1780, Scot. NPG [*see illus.*] · T. Trotter, line engraving, 1784 (after W. Weir), Wellcome L. · J. Kay, caricature, etching, 1785, BM, NPG, Wellcome L. · J. Kay, caricature, etching, 1797, BM · E. Mitchell, engraving, 1819 (after H. Raeburn), Wellcome L. · J. Watson-Gordon, oils, 1825, Scot. NPG; loaned by Royal Medical Society, Edinburgh · D. Martin, oils, Scot. NPG · H. Raeburn, oils, Royal College of Physicians of Edinburgh · P. Slater, porcelain bust (after B. Cheverton), Scot. NPG · W. H. Worthington, line engraving, Wellcome L. · oils (after a portrait), Scot. NPG

Duncan, Andrew (1773–1832), physician and expert in forensic science, was born in Edinburgh on 10 August 1773, the eldest of the twelve children born to Andrew *Duncan (1744–1828), professor of the institutes of medicine, and his wife, Mary Knox. He was the only child to follow his father into the medical profession, and shared many interests with him; the elder Duncan greatly fostered his son's career. Having soon shown a strong bias

towards medicine, the younger Duncan was apprenticed between 1787 and 1792 to Alexander and George Wood, surgeons of Edinburgh. He graduated MA at Edinburgh in 1793 and MD 1794, and then studied in London in 1794–5 at the Great Windmill Street school of medicine under Matthew Baillie, William Cruickshank, and James Wilson.

At about this time Duncan twice visited Europe to study medical practice in all the chief cities and medical schools, including Göttingen, Vienna, Pisa, Naples, and many others, and he was befriended by such men as J. F. Blumenbach, J. P. Frank, A. Scarpa, and L. Spallanzani. His European visits were facilitated by the extensive connections of his father, with whom he maintained a regular correspondence on his medical progress and on the consignments of European textbooks he sent back to Edinburgh. During these visits Duncan gained a knowledge of continental languages and practice, and of people of importance, that few others of his time could boast. He returned to Edinburgh in 1796 at his father's request, and became a fellow of the Royal College of Physicians and physician to the Royal Public Dispensary. He afterwards became physician to the Fever Hospital at Queensberry House, Edinburgh.

Duncan also assisted his father in editing the *Annals of Medicine*. In 1803 he brought out the *Edinburgh New Dispensatory*, a much improved version of William Lewis's work. This became very popular, a tenth edition appearing in 1822. It was translated into German and French, and was republished several times in the United States. The preparation of successive editions occupied much of Duncan's time. For many years from 1805, he was in addition the chief editor of the newly founded *Edinburgh Medical and Surgical Journal*, which quickly gained a leading position in medical publishing. Duncan also served between 1809 and 1822 as an efficient secretary of senate and librarian to the University of Edinburgh, and from 1816 until his death he was an active member of the 'college commission' for rebuilding the university; it was largely due to him that the Adam-Playfair buildings were built.

During his earlier stay in Vienna, Duncan had studied clinical medicine under Johann Peter Frank, whose interest in state medicine formed the basis of his encyclopaedic work, translated as *A Complete System of Medical Police* and published in 1778–88. The work envisaged the state regulation and care of any given population from the cradle to the grave. The general thrust of Frank's ideal appealed to both Duncan and his father, and they in turn replaced the state's role with philanthropic endeavour as being more suited to British traditions. From the mid-1790s the elder Duncan introduced lectures on medical jurisprudence and medical police (public health) into his teaching as professor of the institutes of medicine, while his son publicized the subjects in the *Edinburgh Medical and Surgical Journal*.

In 1807 Fox's whig government imposed the regius chair of medical jurisprudence and medical police (forensic medicine and public health) upon an unwilling University of Edinburgh and the younger Andrew Duncan became the first professor of these subjects in Britain. The chair's foundation was achieved through the exertions of his father, along with the whig lord advocate, Henry Erskine, and resulted in the royal signature on the warrant. The deeply suspicious medical faculty not only refused to admit the subjects but also prevented the new professor from teaching any subject contained in the medical curriculum. With no compulsion upon his lectures either for medical or legal students, few took his course and thus his fee salary was minimal; his professorial salary, paid from the civil list, was £100 per annum and presumably he derived the greater part of his income from private practice. Like the third professor of medical jurisprudence at Edinburgh, Robert Christison, Duncan had other commercial opportunities to augment his financial position. In 1815 he became a founder member of, and medical adviser to, the Scottish Widows' Fund and Life Assurance Society. During his service with the society it was noted that much of its success stemmed from 'that entire freedom of litigated claims … attributed to the great professional ability and attention with which Dr Duncan's duties were discharged' (Maxwell, 92).

In 1819 Duncan resigned his professorship of medical jurisprudence on being appointed joint professor with his father of the institutes of medicine. In 1821 he was elected without opposition professor of materia medica, in which chair he achieved great success. He worked indefatigably, always improving his lectures and studying every new publication on medicine, British or foreign. He was often at his desk by three in the morning. To his chief academic work, the *Dispensatory*, Duncan added a supplement, published in 1829. In 1809 he had contributed to the *Transactions* of the Highland Society a 'Treatise on the diseases which are incident to sheep in Scotland'. He also published, in 1818, *Reports of the Practice in the Clinical Wards of the Royal Infirmary of Edinburgh*. Perhaps his most distinctive discovery was the isolation of the principle 'cinchonin' from cinchona, as related in *Nicholson's Journal* (2nd ser., vol. 6, December 1803). Besides writing copiously in his own *Journal*, he also wrote occasionally for the *Edinburgh Review*.

Duncan's visits, his *Dispensatory*, and his *Journal* made him widely known on the continent, and few foreigners came to Edinburgh without introductions to him; his foreign correspondence also was extensive. He was well versed in the fine arts, music, and foreign literature. His manner was unaffected, his feelings sensitive, and his character honourable. However, though Duncan was more cultured than his father, he lacked his strong constitution and balanced temperament. In 1827 he had a severe attack of fever, after which his strength gradually declined. He lectured until nearly the end of the session 1831–2, and died on 13 May 1832, in his fifty-eighth year, only four years after his father. It is not known if his wife survived him.   G. T. BETTANY, *rev.* BRENDA M. WHITE

Sources The Lancet (26 May 1832), 249 • Chambers, *Scots*. (1835) • *Nicholson's Journal*, 2nd ser., 6 (Dec 1803) • G. Thomson, *History of Edinburgh University* • A. Duncan, letters to his father, 1794–6, U. Edin. L., special collections division, DC.1.90 • A. Duncan, *Head of lectures on medical jurisprudence and medical police* (1801) • memorial, presented to patrons of Edinburgh University, Dr Duncan snr and Hon. H. Erskine, lord advocate, 1806, U. Edin. L., special collections division • G. Rosen, *From medical police to social medicine* (1974), 142–58 • B. M. White, 'Medical police, politics and police: the fate of John Roberton', *Medical History*, 27 (1983), 407–22 • M. A. Crowther and B. White, *On soul and conscience: the medical expert and crime* (1988), 7–10 • B. M. White, 'Training medical policemen', *Legal medicine in history*, ed. M. Clark and C. Crawford (1994), 145–63 • H. Maxwell, *Annals of the Scottish Widows' Fund and Life Assurance Society during the hundred years 1815–1914* (1914) • private information (2004)

Archives Royal College of Physicians of Edinburgh, corresp. • U. Edin. L., corresp. and papers | NL Scot., corresp. with Archibald Constable

Duncan, Sir Andrew Rae (1884–1952), industrial administrator and public servant, was born at Bower Lodge, Waterside, Irvine, Ayrshire, on 3 June 1884, one of eight children of George Duncan, a missionary and social worker, and his wife, Jessie Rae. He was educated at Irvine Royal Academy, and at Glasgow University, where he graduated MA two months before his nineteenth birthday. He was a pupil teacher at Ayr Academy, but having decided against teaching as a career, he entered the office of Biggart, Lumsden & Co., solicitors, of Glasgow and studied law part-time at the university, graduating LLB in 1911. Before the age of thirty he was made a partner, specializing on the industrial side, and through his senior, Sir Thomas Biggart, honorary secretary of the Shipbuilding Employers' Federation, he was introduced to many of the problems and personalities of the shipbuilding and engineering industries. In 1916 he married Annie, daughter of Andrew Jordan; they had two sons, the elder of whom was killed in action in 1940.

The Shipbuilding Employers' Federation moved to London during the First World War, and on becoming its full-time secretary Duncan took one of the decisive steps of his career. In 1916 he was appointed secretary of the Merchant Shipbuilding Advisory Committee by the shipping controller, Sir Joseph Paton Maclay, and later joint secretary of the Admiralty shipbuilding council by Sir Eric Geddes, then first lord of the Admiralty. Lloyd George and other Liberal politicians regarded Duncan as a man of uncommon ability. After the war he twice unsuccessfully contested parliamentary elections as a Liberal candidate at Cathcart (1918), and at Dundee (1922), where he was defeated by E. D. Morel, as Labour consolidated a major base in Scottish urban areas. In October 1919 he became coal controller for the finite purpose of restoring the industry to private enterprise by August 1921. As the government's chief negotiator he proposed that a network of consultative pit committees would reconcile the interests of miners and management, but the inevitability of decontrol forestalled their acceptance. On the completion of this sub-ministerial work in 1921, he received a knighthood. During the 1920s he contributed to the development of the research department of the National Confederation of Employers' Organization. He was committed to presenting the interests of large-scale employers to government and to using statistical expertise to enhance their clarity of viewpoint when evidence was sought by

Sir Andrew Rae Duncan (1884–1952), by Howard Coster, 1940s

negotiating position with hostile suppliers during the construction of the grid in 1929–33. In promoting the eventual benefits of cheaper electricity supply he maintained the momentum of pylon construction, especially through initiatives to advertise new electrical goods. Consequently, he was a central figure in campaigns to present the industry as a potent provider of material improvement for all and the dominant industrial expression of modernity. Though the economies of scale were barely apparent by 1934, his survival and achievements at this juncture of politics and business drew attention to the strategic utility of the 'public corporation' in the economy in the 1930s.

Duncan became a friend and confidant of Montagu Norman, governor of the Bank of England, and served as a director of the bank from 1929 to 1940. He acted as one of Norman's key industrial advisers and was especially influential with regard to the Bank of England-sponsored rationalization of the shipbuilding industry. He also served as the go-between linking Norman and Sir James *Lithgow (1883–1952) [see under Lithgow family (per. c.1870–1952)], head of a great Scottish shipbuilding and industrial firm. The ensuing discussions led to the setting up of the National Shipbuilders' Security Limited, a shipbuilding rationalization company in which Lithgow was the central figure. Under its auspices, the major companies collectively agreed to fund the acquisition of redundant shipyards, which were then closed down. It eliminated up to one-third of redundant capacity in the industry from 1930 to 1939 and proved to be a major success for the policies promoted by Norman and Duncan.

Similar restructuring was also urgently required in the steel industry and, with his contacts in Whitehall and with the Bank of England, Duncan was the obvious figure to undertake it. In January 1935, at the behest of the government, he became chairman of the executive committee of the British Iron and Steel Federation. Part of his brief included obtaining voluntary co-operation among producers for amalgamations and plant closures within the context of a protective tariff on steel imports, and also the co-ordination of production quotas. However, the high prices derived from monopolistic trading conditions ensured that the steel industry subsequently became the focus of political disagreement.

Duncan's experience was subsequently further widened by his service as a non-executive director on the boards of a number of major British companies, including Imperial Chemical Industries, the Dunlop Rubber Company, and the North British Locomotive Company. The climax of his career, however, was his contribution to the organization of the nation's industrial life during the Second World War. He had taken an important part in the plans drawn up against the contingency of war, and on its outbreak he became iron and steel controller.

On 5 January 1940 Duncan was appointed president of the Board of Trade, which reassured the Federation of British Industries. That year he also became a nominal Conservative MP for the City of London, and in the turbulent months which followed many Conservative MPs

royal commissions and for use at periodic conferences. For example, in December 1929 he participated in Ramsay MacDonald's conferences on the industrial situation and urged the Labour government to establish an expert staff who would study economic trends and markets and co-ordinate statistical information. As a consequence of fulfilling this role as a representative industrialist, he became a member of the Economic Advisory Council.

In 1927 Stanley Baldwin appealed to the Shipbuilding Employers' Federation to release Duncan for work of national importance. He became full-time chairman of the newly created Central Electricity Board (CEB) and was therefore responsible for the development of an interconnected system of power generation—the national grid. The legislative framework for co-ordination under the Electricity (Supply) Act of 1926 could not be implemented without the co-operation of diverse and often highly localized electricity supply undertakings of variable efficiency. Duncan's appointment at this 'corporatist' intersection of state intervention and business efficiency reflected his growing reputation as an able arbitrator of conflicting capitalist interests whose rationalization was sought by the Conservative government. He worked hard to ensure that the CEB was relatively free of Treasury control. His emphasis on management autonomy and on taking electricity generation and supply out of politics enhanced his expected him to become the economics supremo in the war cabinet. However, Winston Churchill's reshuffle on 3 October 1940 took him to the Ministry of Supply and, apart from a further period at the Board of Trade from 29 June 1941 to 4 February 1942—whose regulatory functions irked him—he remained supervisor of the productive capacity of war industries until May 1945. Lord Woolton described him as an able administrator and he was admired by Oliver Lyttelton for his firm management of the supply of priority materials for the scheduled completion of the artificial (Mulberry) harbours for the Normandy invasion. Although he was not naturally at home in the House of Commons, he was widely respected for his mastery of business issues.

Throughout the war Duncan remained sceptical of 'pump-priming' measures which might diversify productive activity in depressed areas. He opposed the state requisitioning of coalmines during the war on the (arguable) grounds that it had been tried and had failed in the First World War, and he was hesitant to respond to the more 'total' demands of the war effort by rationing coal in May 1942. Increasingly, he disputed the early intimations of Labour's post-war industrial policy. For example, in the autumn months of 1944 plans for the nationalization of the iron and steel industry were hotly contested with Hugh Dalton, president of the Board of Trade. Duncan highlighted the success that the steel industry had had after 1935 and refused to concede the need for an outside inquiry, let alone the prospect of public ownership.

Duncan continued to represent the City of London in the House of Commons until 1950. However, after the general election of 1945 he became once more chairman of the British Iron and Steel Federation. In 1946 he was in frequent contact with Labour ministers who were inclined to postpone steel nationalization or obtain a 'halfway' measure. Early in 1947 he discussed the issue with Clement Attlee, the prime minister, who, thereafter, preferred the solution of an un-nationalized industry under public supervision. Consequently, Duncan's effective advocacy of the status quo was a contributory factor in the government's 'steel crisis', whereby the Parliamentary Labour Party forced Attlee to confirm that the nationalization of the industry would be pursued in 1948–9. Duncan's argument of the irrelevance to efficiency of a change in the ownership of this 'commanding height' industry, of diverse units of output and product specialisms, was stated in the House of Commons on 17 November 1948 in his detailed critique of the government's intentions, which was subsequently published by the British Iron and Steel Federation in 1949 as a pamphlet.

Had Duncan's convictions been other than they were, he might have become a distinguished head of one of the nationalized industries. When Winston Churchill became prime minister again in 1951 he reluctantly felt morally bound to denationalize the steel industry. Churchill's wartime leadership was an inspiration to Duncan, who was described by some Conservatives, right to the end of the war, as an outsider. Like other businessmen-in-government Duncan's adherence to Conservatism

stemmed from its association with the organization of the nation's resources in the First World War, the rapid decline in the links of the manufacturing industry and the Liberal Party after 1918, and its inter-war preference for co-ordination and rationalization in industrial policy which enabled administrators with business experience to represent the government's interest on public corporations. Duncan's career as an 'independent' chairman was successful in the sense that he personified the apparent separateness of politics and business. In August 1947 he believed the formation of a coalition government, led by Ernest Bevin, to be imminent, and he was ready to serve in it, largely because it would curb nationalization beyond the public utilities. He remained to the end unconvinced that the running of industries could be subject to political control and yet be adaptable enough to answer the challenge of events at home or of competition from abroad. Thus he ended his career where he began—in the private sector.

Duncan presided over several royal commissions in Canada. In 1925 (and again in 1932) he chaired inquiries into the coal industry in Nova Scotia. In 1926 he also served as chairman of the royal commission set up to investigate the grievances of the maritime provinces. The Canadian prime minister W. L. Mackenzie King paid a warm tribute to his work and he was given an honorary degree by Dalhousie University in Nova Scotia. In the United Kingdom he was a member in 1924 of the royal commission on national health insurance; in the same year he served on the dock strike inquiry. He was chairman of the Sea-Fish Commission in 1933–5 and a technical assessor of the Permanent Court of International Justice (labour section) at The Hague. He was made GBE (1938), was sworn of the privy council (1940), was high sheriff for the county of London (1939–40), was one of his majesty's lieutenants for the City of London and a bencher of Gray's Inn, and was made an honorary LLD of Glasgow University (1939). From his formative years in Ayrshire he derived companionship and a continuing sense of cultural identity, and in 1948 he was admitted to the burgess roll at Irvine, his birthplace, amid civic pomp. He died at the Dorchester Hotel, London, on 30 March 1952. He was survived by his wife.

Duncan's career was spent as a new type of industrial administrator, whose legal training and specialist knowledge of organizations equipped him for translating industrial initiatives into practice, and for a readiness to acknowledge the limitations of direct governmental expertise in the industrial arena. He espoused the notion of harmony of interests at the workplace with sincerity and had a reserved, unselfish, and unspectacular demeanour in negotiations alongside a forensic grasp of detail and an understanding of statistical techniques. He benefited from the 'managerial revolution' of the inter-war years. His qualities of leadership, his work ethic, and his meritocratic regard for other people's abilities were evident in the roles he undertook. He sustained many friendships, which originated in his work for shipbuilders in

Glasgow, while domiciled, from the end of the First World War, in the London suburb of Beckenham.

Duncan was one of those notable industrialists who organized the mobilization of the nation's resources in the two world wars and provided a continuity of experience in the production sphere. His work in the Second World War demanded sustained effort and caused great strain, which was exacerbated by political strife. He was unconvinced by the comprehensive plans for a 'New Jerusalem', for his life's work had taught him that the state's planning procedures were inadequate economic instruments for managing change in times of peace.

KEITH GRIEVES

Sources 'Andrew Rae Duncan, 3.6.84–30.3.52', British Iron and Steel Federation (privately printed, 1952) • *The Times* (31 March 1952) • *The Times* (4 April 1952) • *The Times* (7 April 1952) • *The Times* (15 July 1952) • *Iron and Steel Bill: report of speech by Sir A. Duncan in the House of Commons, 17th November 1948* (1949) • A. Duncan, 'The electricity industry', memorandum for war cabinet committee on reconstruction problems, 4 Dec 1942, PRO, CAB 117/240 • L. Hannah, *Electricity before nationalisation: a study in the development of the electricity supply industry in Britain to 1948* (1979) • J. E. Vaizey, *The history of British steel* (1974) • K. Burk, *The first privatization* (1988) • B. Supple, *The political economy of decline: 1913–1946* (1987), vol. 4 of *The history of the British coal industry* (1984–93) • *The Second World War diary of Hugh Dalton, 1940–1945*, ed. B. Pimlott (1986) • H. Dalton, *High tide and after: memoirs, 1945–1960* (1962) • T. Jones, *Whitehall diary*, ed. K. Middlemas, 2 (1969) • A. Jones, 'Duncan, Sir Andrew Rae', *DBB* • A. Slaven, 'Lithgow, Sir James', *DSBB* • *WWW, 1951–60* • Burke, *Peerage* (1927) • Kelly, *Handbk* (1924) • *DNB* • personal knowledge (1971) [*DNB*] • private information (1971) • Lord Chandos [O. Lyttleton, first Viscount Chandos], *The memoirs of Lord Chandos: an unexpected view from the summit* (1962) • K. Middlemas, *Politics in industrial society: the experience of the British system since 1911* (1979); pbk edn (1980) • *My dear Max: the letters of Brendan Bracken to Lord Beaverbrook, 1925–1958*, ed. R. Cockett (1990) • d. cert.

Archives PRO, papers, letters, BT 231, T228/75–79, 151–167 | Nuffield Oxf., corresp. with Lord Cherwell • PRO, Avia 2 | FILM BFI, 'Rt Hon. Sir Andrew Rae Duncan. Eminent in the National 'Grid' System of electricity supply' (Institute of Electrical Engineers, 1948)

Likenesses W. Stoneman, photograph, 1938, NPG • H. Coster, photograph, 1940–49, NPG [*see illus.*] • H. Coster, photographs, NPG • F. Eastman, oils (after a photograph, 1954), British Iron and Steel Corporation, London

Wealth at death £48,088 2s. 7d. in England and Scotland: confirmation, 25 June 1952, CCI

Duncan, Charles (1865–1933), trade unionist and politician, was born on 8 June 1865 at 93 Stockton Street, Middlesbrough, the son of Alexander Duncan, a ship's pilot, and his wife, Jane Dobson. The family had a comfortable lifestyle and Charles was able to attend the local church school until he was sixteen. He then served an engineering apprenticeship, joining the Amalgamated Society of Engineers (ASE) in 1888. He served as its district secretary for a time, and retained his membership of this skilled union for the rest of his life. In 1890 he married Lydia Copeland.

Duncan became a socialist in 1887, apparently primarily motivated by a concern to improve the lives of those less fortunate than himself, and this led to his active involvement in local welfare issues and his election to Middlesbrough town council as an Independent Labour Party

member from 1895 to 1900. At the same time Duncan was a supporter of Tom Mann's campaign to reform the ASE and this led to his appointment as a full-time official of the new Workers' Union in 1898. Formed in the aftermath of the defeat of the engineers in the 1897 lock-out, this body was based on Mann's political ideals: it aimed to create a single union for all workers, devoted to industrial militancy and the promotion of Labour candidates in local and national elections. However, in 1901 the union still had fewer than 5000 members, and Mann emigrated to Australia in the course of that year. Duncan, who had been appointed general secretary the year before, became the dominant influence.

In Duncan's first years as leader, the Workers' Union faced a period of rising unemployment and falling membership, and he responded not only with rigid economies in administration but also with two fundamental departures from the organization's original aims. First, influenced by his own experiences in the ASE, he introduced elementary welfare benefits to provide individuals with a financial incentive for steady membership. Second, he gradually shifted recruitment towards semi-skilled workers with some security of employment. These departures helped to stabilize membership and finances, but not to develop internal democracy: patchy recruitment undermined the branch structure, and lack of resources inhibited district and national procedures. However, the union was now well-placed for explosive growth in the 1910–14 boom when its membership rose from 5000 to over 140,000 members.

Despite Tom Mann's return after ten years and his appearance on the union's platforms as a prophet of syndicalism, Duncan retained the real control and maintained his cautious emphasis on financial strength and steady recruitment, especially among semi-skilled workers in light engineering in the midlands. This focus of recruitment became even more marked during the First World War when the expansion of munitions production led to a flood of new labour, including women, into the engineering industry and also into the Workers' Union, which by 1919 claimed to be the largest single union in the country with half a million members.

It was unlikely that this position could be maintained after the end of the exceptional wartime conditions, but the boom of the immediate post-war years encouraged optimism and Duncan introduced a more generous scheme of unemployment benefits late in 1920, in an effort to stabilize the still highly volatile membership. Unfortunately the almost immediate onset of heavy unemployment initiated a sharp downward spiral in which membership collapsed, income from subscriptions fell, and the insecurity of benefit provision led to further losses of members: by the end of 1922 the union had only 150,000 members and a deficit of £30,000. Duncan's best efforts at rigid economy and new recruitment were unfortunately undermined by the general strike of 1926, which involved almost half of the union's members and cost almost £60,000: in order to avoid terminal collapse he had to negotiate a merger with the Transport and General

Workers' Union (TGWU) in 1929. Although its own history had thus come to a rather depressing conclusion, the Workers' Union was to have a major influence within the TGWU, giving it the skeleton organization to make a long-term shift away from dockers and transport workers into what were to be more dynamic fields of recruitment, above all in the motor industry.

In parallel with his career as a trade union leader, Duncan had a long, but not very distinguished, career in parliament. He was first elected as an MP for Barrow in Furness in 1906, sponsored by the ASE, and he held this seat until 1918, serving for a time as a Labour whip. He was an enthusiastic patriot during the First World War and a member of the British Workers' League, until it became clear that it would oppose Labour candidates in the 1918 general election. However, Duncan's resignation from the league was too late to save his seat. Keen to return to parliament he was unsuccessful in two by-elections in 1920, but held the safe Derbyshire mining seat of Clay Cross from 1922 until 1933. After the union amalgamation of 1929 he retained a nominal official position with the TGWU but was restricted mainly to a role as one of its parliamentary representatives.

Charles Duncan was a quiet, well-dressed man with an unusually alert and upright appearance, possibly due to prowess as an athlete in his youth. In addition to his trade union and parliamentary careers he was active in the Willesden co-operative society, and became a JP for Middlesex in 1919. After a long illness Duncan died in Manor House Hospital, North End Road, Hampstead, on 6 July 1933. He was survived by his wife.   ALASTAIR J. REID

Sources D. E. Martin, 'Duncan, Charles', *DLB*, vol. 2 · R. Hyman, *The worker's union* (1971) · *CGPLA Eng. & Wales* (1933) · b. cert. · d. cert.
Archives People's History Museum, Manchester, papers
Wealth at death £3883 10s.: resworn probate, 16 Aug 1933, *CGPLA Eng. & Wales*

Duncan, Daniel (1649–1735), physician, was born in 1649 in Montauban, Languedoc, France, the only son of Peter Duncan (*c*.1615–1649), professor of physic, and his wife, a member of a prominent protestant family. His father's family, originally of landed Scottish stock, boasted a number of distinguished physicians. Both of his parents died while Duncan was an infant and he was left in the care of his maternal uncle, Daniel Paul, a leading counsellor of the parliament of Toulouse. He followed the other male members of his family to the academy of Puylaurens and then to Montpellier, where he also studied medicine. His ability attracted the attention of Charles Barbeyrac, the famous clinician, who invited him to live in his house. He took the degree of MD (Montpellier) in 1673, moving to Paris shortly after graduation.

In 1677 Duncan's patron Colbert appointed him physician-general to the army before St Omer, commanded by the duke of Orléans. His service was recognized by the award of letters of nobility. After the peace of Nijmegen, he returned to Paris, where in 1678, he published his first medical book, *Explication nouvelle et méchanique des actions animals, ou il est traité des fouctions de*

l'âme, in which he attempted to disprove Descartes's theory that the pineal gland is the seat of the soul and was the first person to describe the *cavum septum pellucidi* of the brain, which is still eponymously known as Duncan's ventricle (Dobson). Also in 1678 he commenced the first of many journeys and travelled to London to research the effects of plague. He was recalled to Paris two years later by Colbert, whose health was declining. Soon after his return, he published *La chymie naturelle, ou l'explication chymique et méchanique de la nourriture de l'animal*, his first major work, in which he attempted to reconcile contemporary theories on the corpuscular and chemical workings of the body with anatomical findings. As this 'raised rather than satisfied the curiosity of the learned' (Kippis, 497) he subsequently wrote two further parts, which were eventually published as a single volume in 1687.

Despite the success of his medical works, Duncan's popularity was dampened by his 'zeal for Protestantism, and his avowed abhorrence of Popery' (Kippis, 497) and after the death of Colbert in 1683, he decided to move back to England. He returned to Montauban to sell his property, but was prevailed upon to stay there for several years. In 1687 he also published *Historie de l'animal, ou la connoissance du corps, animé par la méchanique et par la chymie*, which cemented his reputation both as a scholar and as a physician. Despite remaining in France after the revocation of the edict of Nantes, he finally withdrew to Geneva in 1690, planning to return to England. However, 'great numbers of his persuasion, encouraged by his liberality in defraying their expenses on the road to Geneva had followed him thither' (ibid., 497) and he remained there helping other refugees. He was then invited to Bern, where he was made professor of anatomy and chemistry, while continuing his medical practice and providing assistance to other protestants. In 1699 Philip, landgrave of Hesse, whose wife was seriously ill, sent for him to Kassel. Duncan's diagnosis was an abuse of hot liquors, such as tea and coffee, and he recounted both the condition and his successful cure in a treatise, which was circulated in manuscript form before being published several years later.

Duncan's continuing largesse to protestant refugees attracted the attention of Prince Frederick of Prussia and he was summoned to Berlin, where he was appointed professor of physic and physician to the royal household, as well as 'distributor of his [Frederick's] prudent munificence' (Kippis, 498). Court life did not, however, agree with him and he moved to The Hague in 1703. While in The Hague he corresponded with both Boerhaave and Richard Mead and published further medical books. Unfortunately, no trace of this correspondence appears to have survived, but Duncan seems to have insisted on the transmission of smallpox by some infective means rather than by miasmas or bad airs, as was commonly thought at the time. In 1714, he finally resolved to make the long-awaited move to London. However, he was struck by a palsy, from which he recovered sufficiently to move the following year, but was left with a persistent shaking of his head. He continued to practise in London, although there is no record of his joining the Royal College of Physicians. From the age of seventy he refused to accept any fees from his patients, having vowed that if he lived to that age, 'he would consecrate the remainder of it to the gratuitous service of those who sought his advice' (ibid., 499). He remained true to this promise, despite losing a substantial part of his fortune in the South Sea Bubble.

Very little is known about Duncan's personal life. He had a sole surviving son of the same name, an Anglican minister, but there is no record of his presumed marriage. However, there can be no doubt as to his commitment to the Christian faith and his multiple works of charity. His conversation was said to be 'easy, chearful, and interesting, pure from all taint of party-scandal or idle raillery. This made his company a blessing' (Kippis, 500). He died at his London residence on 30 April 1735.

L. K. VAUGHAN

Sources *Bibliothèque Britannique* (1735), 219–23 · A. Kippis and others, eds., *Biographia Britannica, or, The lives of the most eminent persons who have flourished in Great Britain and Ireland*, 2nd edn, 5 (1793), 492–500 · J. Dobson, *Journal of the History of Medicine and Allied Sciences*, 4 (1949), 471–3 · *DNB*

Duncan, Edward (1803–1882), engraver and watercolour painter, was born on 21 October 1803 in Frederick Street, Hampstead Road, London, the son of Edward Duncan, artist and engraver, and his wife, Peggy. His talents were obvious from childhood: his early drawings, according to Joseph Jenkins, 'for delicacy and precision of line foreshadow the character and care of his later works' (Roget, 2.308). At the age of sixteen he was apprenticed to Robert Havell, an aquatint engraver, and his son; for many years afterwards he made his living primarily as an engraver, specializing in sporting and marine aquatints. One of the artists he worked for was the marine painter William John *Huggins, whose daughter Berthia he married. Duncan also studied drawing at the Artists' Academy in Clipstone Street, London, and there he made lifelong friends such as Joseph Jenkins, Frank Topham, and Henry Riviere. Two watercolours of 1825, *Wild Duck Shooting* and *Pheasant Shooting*, are in the Paul Mellon collection. He had five pictures in the first exhibition of the New Watercolour Society in 1832 and was a member of the society until 1847, serving as both vice-president and treasurer.

From 1843 to 1851 Duncan was on the staff of the *Illustrated London News*; his wood-engravings for this thriving paper included pictures of the Great Exhibition (Gov. Art Coll.). In 1848 he was elected an associate of the Society (subsequently Royal Society) of Painters in Water Colours; he became a full member in the following year. In all he exhibited 187 works with the New Society of Painters in Water Colours and 180 with the old. He is best-known for his marine subjects: examples include *Billingsgate; First Day of Oysters; Early Morning* (exh. New Watercolour Society, 1843; Guildhall Art Gallery, London); and *A Wreck on the Mumbles, Near Swansea, South Wales* (exh. Old Watercolour Society, 1865; priv. coll.). According to Roget, a drawing by Duncan exhibited at the New Watercolour Society for 160 guineas sold at Christies in 1875 for £504. He usually signed his work E. Duncan. His obituarist in *The Builder* (22 April 1882) described him as:

a very industrious man. Hardly in England a drawing room owned by any one of taste but had drawings of his ... He was a very liberal man too; kept an open house, a dinner party weekly; and his billiard room was open to all comers.

Photographs show him as a balding and heavily built figure, with a full, clean-shaven face.

Duncan lived all his life in north London, from 1869 until his death residing at 36 Upper Park Road, Haverstock Hill. He died there on 11 April 1882 and was buried at Highgate cemetery in London on 19 April. Sales of his remaining works by Christie, Manson, and Woods Ltd in 1883 and 1885 included 125 albums containing over 5000 sketches and studies. The Victoria and Albert Museum in London has nineteen of his watercolour drawings; the National Maritime Museum, Greenwich, has a far larger collection of his watercolours, engravings, and mixed media drawings of marine and river subjects. He left a large family; three of his sons—Lawrence Duncan (*b.* 1835/6), Allan Duncan (*b.* 1844), and Walter Duncan (1848–1932)—were also painters. Walter Duncan was an associate member of the Royal Society of Painters in Water Colours from 1874 until his expulsion in 1906 for drunk and disorderly behaviour.

SIMON FENWICK

Sources C. Lack, 'Edward Duncan RWS, 1803–1882', *OWCS Club*, 60 (1985), 1–46 · J. L. Roget, *A history of the 'Old Water-Colour' Society*, 2 vols. (1891) · *The Builder*, 42 (1882), 480–81 · Bankside Gallery, London, RWS MSS · E. H. H. Archibald, *Dictionary of sea painters* (1980) · parish registers, St Pancras, LMA · 'Catalogue of prints and drawings', www.nmm.ac.uk, 1 March 1999 · *CGPLA Eng. & Wales* (1882)
Archives Bankside Gallery, London, Royal Watercolour Society MSS
Likenesses Elliott & Fry, photograph, *c.*1860, Bankside Gallery, London · G. Lance, oils, Royal Institution of South Wales, Swansea · J. Watkins and C. Watkins, carte-de-visite, NPG · carte-de-visite, NPG · engraving, repro. in *ILN* (29 April 1882) · group portrait, wood-engraving (*Our artists, past and present*), NPG; repro. in *ILN* (14 May 1892)
Wealth at death £12,001 16*s.* 2*d.*: probate, 6 May 1882, *CGPLA Eng. & Wales*

Duncan, Francis (1836–1888), army officer, was born at Aberdeen on 4 April 1836, the eldest son of John Duncan, advocate, and Helen Drysdale, daughter of Andrew Douglass of Berwick upon Tweed. John Duncan took a leading role in the 1841 Marnoch intrusion case, which contributed to the disruption of the Church of Scotland, and joined the Free Church. He was a successful railway company promoter and director, known as 'the Scottish railway king', and his house was 'by far the largest and best in the granite city' (Blogg, 6).

Francis Duncan was educated at the West-End Academy, the grammar school, and Marischal College, all in Aberdeen. In 1855 he graduated MA, 'honourably distinguished', failed the Indian Civil Service examination, but passed the open competitive examination for a direct commission in the Royal Artillery, and was commissioned lieutenant on 24 September. From 1857 to 1862 he served in British North America, largely at Halifax, Nova Scotia. There he married, on 24 August 1858, Mary Kate, daughter of the Revd William Cogswell, rector of St Paul's, Halifax; she survived her husband. He was promoted captain on 10 August 1864, and was made adjutant of the 7th brigade. In

Francis Duncan (1836–1888), by unknown engraver, pubd 1888

1871 he was appointed superintendent of regimental records at Woolwich, and this led him to write his two-volume *History of the Royal Regiment of Artillery* (1872). He wrote several other books. Under the pseudonym 'a staff officer', in 1872 he published, with 'an Oxford tutor' (F. J. Jayne of Keble), a pamphlet *The Universities and the Scientific Corps*, arguing that engineer and artillery officers should be educated at the universities, and citing in support those graduates directly commissioned from 1855 to 1857 and his own *History*.

Duncan was promoted major on 4 February 1874, and in May 1876 was sent to Jamaica, where he wrote a report on its defence. From January 1877 to 1882 he was a gunnery instructor, training militia and volunteer artillery officers at the Repository, Woolwich. He was one of the army officers who founded the Oxford Military College, Cowley, a private-venture school to prepare boys for entrance to Woolwich and Sandhurst, opened in 1876. In 1877 he became chairman of its executive committee. Despite his efforts, the patronage of the duke of Cambridge, and a distinguished council, the college had a troubled and precarious existence and survived only until 1896. He was a keen member of the order of St John, which he joined in 1875, director of its ambulance department, and an assiduous publicist of the St John Ambulance Association. He was active in other philanthropic movements, including the establishment of 'coffee palaces'—intended as counter-attractions to alcohol and prostitutes—in garrison towns. He taught a Sunday school class and later a young men's class at Woolwich.

Duncan became lieutenant-colonel in the army in July 1881, and in the Royal Artillery in October 1881. From January 1883 to November 1885 he commanded the artillery of the reconstituted British-officered Egyptian army commanded by Sir Evelyn Wood. At Cairo, the khedive said, Duncan 'had done the work of two men' (Blogg, 97), and at Wadi Halfa in 1884 he worked to forward the Gordon relief expedition. He was promoted colonel in the British army in June 1885, and was made CB in August. He also received the order of the Osmanieh (third class). He commanded the artillery of the southern division at Portsmouth until late January 1886, then commanded the garrison artillery at Woolwich.

Duncan was unsuccessful Conservative candidate in February 1874 at Morpeth (defeated by Thomas Burt), in June 1874 at Durham City, and in April 1880 at Finsbury. In November 1885 he was elected MP for the Holborn division of Finsbury, a largely middle-class and non-resident constituency, and was re-elected in July 1886. He spoke frequently in parliament on Egypt—advocating British reforms and eventual withdrawal—and on military and other subjects, notably advocating Moncrieff disappearing mountings for coastal artillery. In February 1888 he seconded the address, gaining Gladstone's praise. He was awarded honorary degrees by Aberdeen and Durham universities and by King's College, Canada.

In 1888 Duncan's health deteriorated from a liver disease, probably contracted in Egypt, followed by dropsy and an operation, and he died at his home, Connaught House, Woolwich Common, on 16 November 1888. Ambitious, energetic, and hard-working, a keen professional soldier who was never in battle, he was described by an acquaintance as, in the Anglo-Indian phrase, 'the sort of man to go tiger-hunting with' (Blogg, 141). The Duncan prize medals of the Royal Artillery Institution were founded in his memory.　　　ROGER T. STEARN

Sources H. B. Blogg, *The life of Francis Duncan* (1892) · *The Times* (17 Nov 1888) · J. Tecklenborough [H. Naidley], *Seven years' cadet-life: containing the records of the Oxford Military College* (1885) · H. S. Loyd-Lindsay, *Lord Wantage, V.C., K.C.B.: a memoir* (1907) · J. Headlam, *The history of the royal artillery*, 2 (1937) · H. Pelling, *Social geography of British elections, 1885–1910* (1967) · *WWBMP*, vol. 2 · F. W. S. Craig, *British parliamentary election results, 1832–1885* (1977) · F. W. S. Craig, *British parliamentary election results, 1885–1918* (1974) · *DNB* · *CGPLA Eng. & Wales* (1889)

Archives Royal Artillery Institution, Woolwich, London, papers

Likenesses Ape [C. Pellegrini], caricature, chromolithograph, NPG; repro. in *VF* (March 1887) · J. Tecklenborough, engraving, repro. in Tecklenborough, *Seven years' cadet-life*, 37 · engraving, NPG; repro. in *The Graphic* (18 Feb 1888), 132 [*see illus.*]

Wealth at death £1125 18s. 4d. effects in England: probate, 12 Feb 1889, *CGPLA Eng. & Wales*

Duncan, George Simpson (1884–1965), New Testament scholar, was born in Forfar on 8 March 1884, the son of Alexander Duncan, tailor's cutter, and his wife, Isabella Brown. From Forfar Academy he went on to Edinburgh University where he obtained first-class honours in classics in 1906 and then went as an exhibitioner and sizar to Trinity College, Cambridge, where he obtained a first class in part one of the classical tripos in 1909. He studied also at St Andrews, Marburg, Jena, and Heidelberg.

In 1915 Duncan was ordained to the ministry of the Church of Scotland and became an army chaplain. On the second Sunday after Sir Douglas Haig took command of the British armies in France, Duncan was appointed to general headquarters. A remarkable bond of affection developed between them, the older man during the dark days of war deeply appreciating the sermons of his chaplain. A photograph in St Mary's College, St Andrews, bears the inscription 'to my Chaplain, 1916 to the end, in all gratitude, D. Haig'. In 1966 Duncan published *Douglas Haig as I Knew Him*. He was twice mentioned in dispatches and was appointed OBE. He married first, in 1923, Amelia Hay Norden (*d.* 1924); in 1929 he married (Eliza) Muriel, daughter of the late James Smith, doctor of medicine, of Edinburgh; they had one son.

In 1919 Duncan succeeded to the chair of biblical criticism in St Andrews. His work in the New Testament field brought him an international reputation. The latest of his three chief works, *Jesus Son of Man* (1948), interprets freshly the message of Jesus in the light of the elusive concept 'son of man', thus anticipating later more detailed interest. In 1934 he contributed *Galatians* to the series of Moffatt commentaries—at the time probably the best exposition in the English language. His earliest major work, *Saint Paul's Ephesian Ministry* (1929), boldly and independently proposed an Ephesian origin for all the 'imprisonment epistles'. Duncan wrote that 'the Ephesian origin of [the epistle to the Philippians] ought to remain no longer a matter of dispute'. New Testament scholars are not so easily silenced, but the view has never been better presented. Reviewers said that 'it read like a detective story'; and this remains true even if it is possible to think that in the end the wrong man is charged. In 1948 Duncan became president of the Society for New Testament Studies, of which he was a founder member.

Appointed principal of St Mary's College, St Andrews, in 1940, Duncan ranked second only to the principal of the university and began to exercise an increasing influence in academic affairs. He was deeply involved in the discussions which in 1954 issued in an act 'making provision for the reorganization of university education in St Andrews and Dundee'. At the same time he upheld with tenacity the ancient privileges and position of the college of which he was principal. Crossing swords with Principal Sir James Irvine demanded courage. But his fairness and reasonableness were recognized when he was appointed vice-chancellor (1952–3).

Already in 1949 Duncan had been moderator of the general assembly of the Church of Scotland, the duke of Gloucester being lord high commissioner. He visited Germany as a guest of the Foreign Office, to 'strengthen the links between the Church of Scotland and the Evangelical Churches, Luther and Reformed'. Thus, after a second world war he met on cordial terms church leaders of the people fought by the army he had served in the first.

Among his friends Duncan numbered Bishop Hans Lilje of Berlin, and Bishop Bergrav of the Church of Sweden. His knowledge of and admiration for the Reformed churches in Czechoslovakia and France grew. This appreciation was reciprocated: he became honorary D.Theol of Paris and honorary professor of the Reformed Church College of Debreçen and of Budapest. Honorary doctorates in divinity came from Edinburgh and Glasgow and in laws from Edinburgh and St Andrews.

Duncan showed an immediate interest in the *New English Bible* venture. He was present at the first meeting of the joint committee in 1947 and was member of the New Testament panel and a translator. His contributions were always scholarly and sensible. He broadcast on television when the New Testament appeared and was acclaimed as a natural in this exacting medium.

Duncan possessed an enviable common touch, always breaking through an external appearance of peppery pomposity. Academic eminence never distanced him from ordinary people, whether soldier or former serviceman, parish minister or parishioner. But his students claimed his principal attention. Their interests he assiduously promoted: in the classroom, from which they went out knowing better the exacting standards that true scholarship demands; in university court among the crosscurrents of academic politics; in his own home, where the perplexed probationer or ordained man was always welcome and never left without help. With less fire he would not have accomplished what he did; with less humanity he would not have engendered such affection. He died in Dundee on 8 April 1965; his second wife, Muriel, survived him.   J. K. S. REID, *rev.*

Sources personal knowledge (1981) · private information, 1981 · *CGPLA Eng. & Wales* (1965) · *The Times* (9 April 1965)
Archives U. St Andr. L., corresp. and papers
Likenesses A. Morocco, portrait, U. St Andr., St Mary's College

Duncan [*née* MacFarlane], **(Victoria) Helen McCrae** (1897–1956), medium, was born on 25 November 1897 at 96 Main Street, Callander, Perthshire, the fourth child of Archibald MacFarlane, slater, and his wife, Isabella Rattray. As a child she earned the nickname Hellish Nell for her tomboyish exploits, but alienated her peers with hysterical outbursts and sinister predictions. Fearing shame for their Presbyterian family, Helen's mother said she would be burnt as a witch. After leaving school in her early teens, Helen worked as a hotel waitress, but in 1914 became pregnant and was banished to Dundee, where she was employed in the jute mills and as a nursing auxiliary. Her daughter Isabella was born in 1915, and on 27 May 1916 Helen married Henry Anderson Horne Duncan (1897–1967), an invalided soldier whom she had first met in her dreams, and son of Henry Horne Duncan, an iron driller, and his wife, Ann, *née* Mearns. They set up home in Edinburgh, where Henry devoted time not spent on his cabinet-maker's business to her development as a psychic.

In 1926 the Duncans returned to Dundee, where Helen held seances, progressing from clairvoyance to materialization, allegedly manifesting spirits of the dead from a mysterious substance known as ectoplasm. Her spirit guide was 'Albert', a Scots émigré to Australia. In October 1930 the London Spiritualist Alliance invited the Duncans to the English capital. There Helen's powers were tested for several months, but with a negative conclusion. In May 1931 she was exposed by the leading psychical researcher Harry Price, who argued that she draped herself in regurgitated cheesecloth. Ironically, her reputation soared among many spiritualists. In January 1933 she was again caught red-handed in Edinburgh (where the family had returned) at a seance impersonating a spirit of a small girl using a stockinet vest. At the instigation of the outraged sitter who exposed her, Duncan was tried at the sheriff court for fraudulently procuring money from members of the public, and was fined £10. Demand for her services increased, the Spiritualists' National Union renewed her diploma, and she was given a column in a Saturday newspaper, the *People's Journal*. Although her health was poor—she suffered from obesity and, from the early 1940s, diabetes, and endured several difficult pregnancies—Helen toured Britain giving seances for which she charged about 10s. a head. Six of her children survived to adulthood.

Fond of coastal resorts, Helen worked hard in Portsmouth, the war having intensified anxiety about men serving overseas. In 1941 Albert foresaw the sinking of HMS *Hood*, and at the Master Temple Psychic Centre—a room above a chemist's shop—Helen was reported to have materialized the spirit of a sailor from HMS *Barham* several weeks before the sinking was announced. These apparent breaches of security were noted by the authorities who, by 1943, were stepping up prosecutions of mediums for exploiting the bereaved. Charges under the 1824 Vagrancy Act now drew upon the language of the 1735 Witchcraft Act which outlawed the pretence to conjure spirits. In January 1944 the Master Temple was raided during a seance and Helen arrested. Amid a storm of publicity, her trial at the Old Bailey opened on 22 March. Supporters subsequently attributed this extreme reaction to fear that she might disclose secrets concerning the preparations for D-day.

Helen and three others were indicted under the Witchcraft Act. She had dishonestly made £112 in six days, alleged the prosecution. The defence, paid for by the Spiritualists' National Union, argued that as a genuine medium she could not have acted fraudulently; but the act of 1735 ensured that by conspiring even to attempt conjuration she would be found guilty. The forty-five defence witnesses, who amazed the packed courtroom with accounts of tearful reunions with deceased relatives, therefore spoke in vain. The eight-day trial was reported by the press as a witchcraft prosecution, and an offer to hold a seance in court—declined by the jury—caused a sensation. At its conclusion the Master Temple's owners were bound over, and Helen and her travelling companion received sentences of nine and four months respectively. An appeal failed—the hearing being held in an air-raid shelter because the court had been blitzed. Helen served six months in Holloway prison, where her health improved, but mentally she was strained by the bombing. Meanwhile, she was depicted as spiritualism's Joan of Arc.

Post-war idealism fuelled demands from the Spiritualists' National Union for a change in the law, and in the Labour government the union found sponsors more sympathetic than in previous administrations. Activists exploited fully the fact that Winston Churchill (to whom many spiritualists had appealed) had asked the home secretary Herbert Morrison why the Duncan trial had been allowed to happen. Disillusioned, but now a legend among spiritualists, Helen drifted back into physical mediumship, and lived to see the replacement of the Witchcraft Act with the Fraudulent Mediums Act of 1951, which at last granted spiritualists freedom of worship.

Lord Dowding, victor of the battle of Britain, and a supporter of spiritualism, supported the bill's passage through the House of Lords.

There was no boom in spiritualism after the Second World War (as following 1918), and Duncan's powers appeared to be waning. In 1956 police stormed a materialization seance at Nottingham, after which she displayed strange burns where traumatized ectoplasm had supposedly rushed back into her body. Probably on legal advice, the police did not press charges. Helen was left to languish in hospital and at her home, 36 Rankeillor Street, Edinburgh, where she died early on 6 December 1956; she was cremated at Warriston crematorium, Edinburgh, on 10 December, and her ashes were scattered at Kilmahog cemetery, Callander. The official causes of death were given as diabetes and cardiac failure; the family blamed the authorities.

Despite a lack of consensus about her genuineness, Helen Duncan is remembered as a figurehead for the spiritualist movement during its finest hour. From the day she died, mediums have claimed that she is in touch, although it seems that her feelings are mixed about a campaign to have her conviction quashed. MALCOLM GASKILL

Sources M. Gaskill, *Hellish Nell: last of Britain's witches* (2001) · G. Brealey and K. Hunter, *The two worlds of Helen Duncan* (1985) · C. E. Bechhofer Roberts, ed., *The trial of Mrs Duncan* (1945) · M. Barbanell, *The case of Helen Duncan* (1945) · LUL, Harry Price Library, Helen Duncan box · CUL, Society for Psychical Research archives, Helen Duncan file · Home Office papers relating to Helen Duncan, PRO, HO 144/22172 · director of public prosecutions' files, 1944, PRO, DPP 2/1204, 1234 · H. Price, *Regurgitation and the Duncan mediumship* (1931) · D. J. West, 'The trial of Mrs Helen Duncan', *Proceedings of the Society for Psychical Research*, 48 (1946–9), 32–64 · A. E. Crossley, *The story of Helen Duncan: materialization medium* (1975) · M. Cassirer, *Medium on trial: the story of Helen Duncan and the Witchcraft Act* (1996) · d. cert. · m. cert. · *Psychic News* (15 Dec 1956) · b. cert. · b. cert. [Henry Duncan] · d. cert. [Henry Duncan]

Archives College of Psychic Studies, London, corresp. · LUL · PRO, Home Office reports, HO 144/22172 · PRO, depositions relating to the trial, CRIM 1/1581 | CUL, Society for Psychical Research archives · Island Archives Service, Guernsey, Loseby collection · PRO, director of public prosecutions' files, DPP 2/1204, 1234 | FILM BFI NFTVA, *Secret history*, Channel 4, 20 July 1998

Likenesses photograph, repro. in Gaskill, *Hellish Nell* (2001) · photograph, repro. in Duncan, ed., *Trial*, frontispiece · photograph, repro. in Cassirer, *Medium on trial*, 142

Duncan, Henry (1774–1846), Church of Scotland minister and savings bank founder, was born at Lochrutton, Kirkcudbrightshire, on 8 October 1774, the third son of the minister George Duncan (1738–1807) and his first wife, Anne M'Murdo (d. 1824). He was educated at Dumfries Academy, before studying at St Andrews University for two sessions from 1788 to 1790. A family friend offered him a junior post with the Liverpool bankers Arthur Heywood, Sons & Co., which he held until 1793, when he went to Edinburgh and Glasgow universities to study for the ministry of the Church of Scotland. While he was still in Liverpool his literary and theological interests had already manifested themselves (to the detriment of his work, according to his employers), and he had published a pamphlet opposing Unitarianism (1793). At the universities Duncan was strongly influenced by the lectures of the

Henry Duncan (1774–1846), by David Octavius Hill and Robert Adamson, c.1843–6

jurist John Miller and the moral philosopher Dugald Stewart. In Edinburgh, he joined the Edinburgh University Speculative Society, where he met Francis Horner (1778–1817) and Henry Brougham (1778–1868).

In 1799 Duncan was ordained minister of Ruthwell in Dumfriesshire, where he spent the rest of his life; from the first he involved himself in a range of social activities not strictly clerical. When a French invasion seemed imminent he raised a troop of volunteers, of which he was captain. During a bad harvest he arranged for the transport of corn from Liverpool, to be sold at cost price, and he encouraged the women of his parish to supplement their income by spinning. One of Duncan's main concerns, however, was raising the standard of popular education and advancing the 'march of the mind'. He started a local newspaper, the *Dumfries and Galloway Courier*, with the financial assistance of his brothers, and a popular journal entitled the *Scotch Cheap Repository*, which was modelled on Hannah More's *Cheap Magazine*. The *Repository* chiefly consisted of moral tales: Duncan himself wrote a story called 'The Cottage Fireside', which was published separately in 1815. He also gave lectures on astronomy and physics to his parishioners, holding, with George Miller of Dunbar and Thomas Dick of Methven, that knowledge of the natural world would instruct the rural lower orders in their place in the divinely ordered scheme of things. Such a natural theology, compounded of Enlightenment ideas and evangelical enthusiasm, contrasted with the more

dynamic and secular emphasis of the popular scientific education of urban mechanics' institutes. It was readily apparent in *The Philosophy of the Seasons* (1835–6), where he described 'True Science' as the 'Handmaid of Religion'.

As an advocate of the self-improvement of the individual, Duncan was opposed to a compulsory poor rate, feeling that it would undermine the independence of the lower classes and encourage idleness. His interest in encouraging self-help and thrift among the poor led him in 1796 to revitalize a local friendly society formed in the previous year; such was its success that he founded another for women. However, Duncan was not convinced that friendly societies were the best vehicle for encouraging the poor to save: influenced by the writings of John Bone, he became interested in the idea of savings banks and, while writing on the subject of poverty in the *Dumfries and Galloway Courier* in the spring of 1810, he outlined the advantages and possible form of parish savings banks. Late that year he founded the first savings bank in Ruthwell: he was the governor and other dignitaries served as the court of directors. The Ruthwell bank aimed to attract long-term deposits: withdrawal was made difficult, and those savers who failed to deposit 4s. a year or more were subject to fines, but a good rate of interest—5 per cent—was offered to depositors of more than three years' standing and there were bonuses for regular savers. The bank was decidedly successful, and by its fourth year held £922 in deposits. Subsequently Duncan gave unstinting support, in the form of speeches, lectures, and pamphlets such as *An Essay on the Nature and Advantages of Savings Banks* (1815), to the spread of such institutions. In 1817 he travelled to London to give his personal support to George Rose's bill for the protection and encouragement of banks for saving, which, when passed, placed the deposits of savings banks in England and Wales on account with the commissioners of the national debt.

In the 1820s Duncan gave his support to several radical causes, including the abolition of slavery and Catholic emancipation. In support of the latter he published *A Letter to the Parishioners of Ruthwell on Catholic Emancipation* (1829). His evangelical opinions, the result of a conversion experience in 1804, led him to become an opponent of patronage and a friend of Thomas Chalmers (1780–1847) and Andrew Thomson (1779–1831). In the crisis preceding the Disruption he corresponded with his old acquaintance Brougham, and also with Lord Melbourne. In 1839 he was appointed moderator of the general assembly, and he headed a deputation to congratulate Queen Victoria on her marriage in 1840. In 1843 Duncan joined the Free Church, leaving a manse which he had considerably improved for more humble lodgings in a nearby cottage. He did not long survive the Disruption, dying on 19 February 1846 from a stroke which he suffered while conducting a service in the cottage of an elder.

Duncan was an accomplished man of many varied interests, who dabbled in the arts of drawing, modelling, sculpture, gardening, and architecture. Keenly interested in history, he was also the author of a historical novel, *William Douglas, or, The Scottish Exiles* (1826), which was intended to redress the unfavourable depiction of the covenanters in Scott's *Old Mortality* (1816), and he restored a runic cross which he discovered in his parish, sending a description of it to the *Transactions of the Scottish Antiquarian Society*. He made a small contribution to geology, too, by the discovery of the footmarks of quadrupeds on the New Red Sandstone of Corncockle Muir, near Lochmaben. His private life was apparently very happy. He married Agnes, daughter of his predecessor, James Craig, on 10 September 1803; they had two sons and one daughter. After her death in January 1832 he married again on 24 October 1836. His second wife was Mary (*d.* 1877), daughter of George Grey of West Ord, widow of Revd Robert Lundie of Kelso, and aunt of Josephine Butler (1828–1906). She published several works, including *Missionary Life in Samoa* (1846), which was based on her son's journal. Duncan was a man of an appealing personality: Thomas Carlyle, who frequently visited Duncan's house while teaching at Annan and benefited from his introductions to literary and learned men, described him as 'the aimabliest and kindliest of men, … the one cultivated man whom I could feel myself permitted to call *friend* as well' (*Fasti*, 2.256).

ROSEMARY MITCHELL

Sources G. J. C. Duncan, *Memoir of the Reverend Henry Duncan, minister of Ruthwell* (1848) · S. Hall, *Dr Duncan of Ruthwell* (1910) · Chambers, *Scots.* (1856), 5.201–11 · *Fasti Scot.* · J. V. Smith, 'Manners, morals, and mentalities: reflections on the popular enlightenment of early nineteenth century Scotland', *Scottish culture and Scottish education, 1800–1980*, ed. W. M. Humes and H. M. Paterson (1983), 25–54 · M. Moss and I. Russell, *An invaluable treasure: a history of the TSB* (1994)
Archives Dumfries and Galloway Libraries, Dumfries, papers · Savings Banks Museum, Ruthwell, letters relating to bill to encourage savings banks | NL Scot., letters to John Lee, MSS 3435–3440 · U. Edin., New Coll. L., letters to Thomas Chalmers
Likenesses D. O. Hill and R. Adamson, photograph, *c.*1843–1846, NPG [*see illus.*] · D. O. Hill and R. Adamson, calotype photograph, priv. coll. · oils (in middle age), Lloyds TSB Group plc, London; repro. in Moss and Russell, *Invaluable treasure*, 22

Duncan [*née* Clark], **Isabelle Wight** (1812–1878), author, was born on 2 July 1812 at Dumfries, Scotland, the third and youngest daughter of Samuel Clark (1768–1814), Dumfriesshire clerk of the peace, and his second wife, Elizabeth Nicolson (*fl.* 1790–1864), of Kendal, Westmorland. Although complaining of a lack of rigour in her education, which appears to have inclined to the secular, Isabelle developed a taste for literature by her early twenties. On 23 June 1833 she married the Revd George John Craig Duncan (1806–1868), minister at Kirkpatrick Durham, and through this union became associated with the illustrious clerical family of her husband's father, the Revd Henry *Duncan DD (1774–1846). George Duncan remained minister at Kirkpatrick Durham until 1843, when the family joined the evangelical Free Church in the Disruption of that year—a decision that brought temporary financial hardship. Thereafter he served as minister of the fledgeling Free Church in Kirkpatrick Durham (1843–4) and the Presbyterian churches of North Shields (1844–51) and Greenwich, London (1851–61), rising to the rank of general secretary of the English Presbyterian church in 1861. Improvements in their financial affairs allowed the family

to move to a comfortable home in Blackheath, and then to relocate in 1861 to Bayswater, in west London. Isabelle bore nine children between 1834 and 1852, five of whom survived to adulthood.

During this period of stability Isabelle emerged from her husband's shadow and published *Pre-Adamite Man, or, The story of our old planet and its inhabitants told by scripture and science* (1860). Her aim was to reconcile the Bible with recent findings in geology—a motivation that reveals her commitment to the Christian philosophy promoted by such evangelicals as her father-in-law and his ally Thomas Chalmers. Duncan's book tackled two problems: the first concerned harmonizing the Bible with science and the second was more exclusively theological in nature. Duncan founded her response to the first challenge on Free Church natural historian Hugh Miller's day-age theory, which interpreted the creation days of Genesis as long geological epochs. This allowed her to accept the then rapidly expanding geological timescale. Duncan also deployed Chalmers's gap theory, except that she shifted the gap between creations from Genesis 1: 1 to 2: 4, contending that the account before 2: 4 described the creation of a pre-adamite race, and the one afterwards the creation of Adam and his descendants only. The end of the pre-adamites' tenancy on earth came with the Ice Age—a geological event only recently explicated by Louis Agassiz and which Duncan skilfully wove into her brilliant sacralization of secular geology, illustrated though a quadripartite lithograph that fitted prehistoric animal life into the pre-adamite epoch and which was bisected by a depiction of the lifeless desolation of the Ice Age.

This pre-adamite theory also served to answer a second problem: namely, that the Bible does not provide a specific record for the origin of angels and demons. Duncan finds their derivation in the pre-adamite population, with the righteous pre-adamites becoming angels and the rebellious denizens demons after a probationary period. Careful to stress that there was no genetic continuity between the pre-adamites and Adamites (thus preserving Calvinist orthodoxy on the atonement), this evangelical writer looked back to Christian tradition using the pre-adamite angels as an analogy for what human beings might become when saved. Here is seen the greatest contrast between Duncan's evangelical system and that of evolutionary theorists like Darwin, who were beginning to base their anthropologies on similarities between humans and apes.

The startling revelations of September 1859 that early human beings had lived among extinct mammoths added immediacy to Duncan's work. The coincidental appearance of *Pre-Adamite Man* a few weeks after the release of Darwin's *Origin of Species* undoubtedly also heightened interest in her book and projected it into the midst of lively current debate over human origins. The book certainly did attract both curiosity and controversy, and was reviewed in many leading journals: the Edinburgh daily the *Caledonian Mercury* claimed in February 1861 that it was 'making no small stir in circles which cleave to the idea that the Mosaic cosmogony squares with the discoveries of modern geological science'. Several reviewers also noted that regardless of what one thought of its main conclusions, the book conveniently summarized recent findings in natural history.

The first edition of *Pre-Adamite Man* sold out within weeks; it went through five editions in six printings by 1866. A large excerpt was also published in 1862 as *Geological Wonders of London and its Vicinity*. Although Duncan argued her case passionately, her works did not bear her name until the final edition of *Pre-Adamite Man*; the decision to reveal her authorship stemmed partly from her irritation that most reviewers assumed she was a male. Ironically, she also revealed at this time that her husband had provided stylistic and theological assistance, even though he had withheld his assent from the book's main thesis. One of many popular evangelical works on science long overlooked by historians of science, Isabelle Duncan's *Pre-Adamite Man* was the first full-length defence by a theological conservative of pre-adamism—a theory with sceptical associations. Although controversial, the work was cited by later pre-adamite theorists and played an important role in propelling pre-adamite anthropology and angelology into the currents of evangelical thought. Isabelle died at her home, 18 Pembridge Gardens, Bayswater, London, on 26 December 1878.

STEPHEN D. SNOBELEN

Sources S. D. Snobelen, 'Of stones, men and angels: the competing myth of Isabelle Duncan's *Pre-adamite man* (1860)', *Studies in the History and Philosophy of Biology and Biomedical Sciences*, 32 (2001), 59–104 · I. Duncan, correspondence, Savings Banks Museum, Ruthwell, Scotland · G. J. C. Duncan, journal, Savings Banks Museum, Ruthwell, Scotland · G. J. C. Duncan, *Memoir of the Rev. Henry Duncan* (1848) · *Fasti Scot.*, new edn · C. Rogers, *The book of Robert Burns: genealogical and historical memoirs of the poet, his associates and those celebrated in his writings*, 3 vols. (1889–91) · A. Sedgwick, *A discourse on the studies of the university* (1833) · b. cert. · m. cert. · d. cert. · *CGPLA Eng. & Wales* (1879)

Archives Savings Banks Museum, Ruthwell, corresp.

Likenesses oils, priv. coll.

Wealth at death under £1500: administration with will, 19 April 1879, *CCI*

Duncan, James Bruce (1848–1917). *See under* Greig, Gavin (1856–1914).

Duncan, James Matthews (1826–1890), obstetric physician, was born and baptized in Aberdeen on 29 April 1826, the fifth child of William Duncan, a merchant and later shipowner, and his wife, Isabella Matthews. After education at the local grammar school and at Marischal College, Aberdeen, where he graduated MA in April 1843, Duncan began to study medicine at the same college. He continued his studies in Edinburgh in 1845, where he rapidly emerged as James Young Simpson's most promising midwifery student. On returning to Aberdeen in 1846 Duncan took his MD degree. He spent the winter of 1846–7 as a student in Paris and in April 1847 he returned to Edinburgh to take up an appointment as Simpson's assistant. He helped Simpson in his experiments with anaesthetics, and on 4 November 1847 took part in the famous experiment which established the anaesthetic property of chloroform.

In 1849, after some months of travel as personal physician to the marquess of Bute, Duncan settled in Edinburgh and soon established his reputation as one of the leading obstetricians of his day. In 1851 he became a fellow of the Royal College of Physicians of Edinburgh and in May 1853 he began a course as an extra-academical lecturer on midwifery. In 1861 he was elected physician to the ward for diseases of women at the Edinburgh Royal Infirmary. He was instrumental in founding the Sick Children's Hospital (1860) and for a while he was one of its physicians. He was a member of the Royal Society of Edinburgh and from 1873 to 1875 was president of the Obstetrical Society of Edinburgh.

On the death of Sir James Young Simpson in 1870, Duncan was widely expected to be his successor in the chair of obstetrics at the university, but he was passed over, and Simpson's nephew Alexander Russell Simpson was elected to the professorship. Duncan bore his disappointment with equanimity and continued to practise in Edinburgh until 1877, when he was offered the posts of lecturer on midwifery and obstetric physician to St Bartholomew's Hospital, London. He accepted and went to live at 71 Brook Street, Grosvenor Square. After becoming MRCP, in 1883 Duncan was elected a fellow of the Royal College of Physicians of London, and on 7 June 1883 he became FRS; in the same year he was nominated a member of the General Medical Council. Duncan received many honours, including LLD degrees from the universities of Cambridge and Edinburgh, an MD from Dublin University, and the honorary fellowship of the King and Queen's College of Physicians, and he was a member of the most important medical societies in the United States, Russia, Austria, Germany, and Norway.

Besides contributions to various medical journals, Duncan published *Researches in Obstetrics* (1868); *Treatise on Parametritis and Perimetritis* (1869); *The Mortality of Childbed and Maternity Hospitals* (1870); *Papers on the Female Perineum* (1879); and *Clinical Lectures on Diseases of Women* (1879, 1883, 1886, 1889). His chief claim to fame, however, was his influential work *Fecundity, Fertility and Sterility* (1866), a subject he further developed in the Goulstonian lectures entitled 'On sterility in woman' delivered at the Royal College of Physicians in 1883. Duncan's approach, based on extensive statistical work, was widely regarded as a breakthrough in the study of fecundity and sterility, establishing the book's reputation well into the twentieth century.

Duncan was a great admirer of William Harvey, of William Hunter, and of William Smellie. He was well known as a fierce critic of surgical gynaecology and vehemently opposed the view propounded by his chief rival in London, Robert Barnes, that ovariotomy should be performed by obstetricians rather than by general surgeons. As one of the leaders of the Obstetrical Society of London, Duncan was prominently involved in the dispute that led Barnes to found the British Gynaecological Society in 1884. Powerfully built, with a massive head and an impassive expression, Duncan was a reserved man with few great friends and no hobby other than reading. Kind but inflexible, he was a dedicated teacher who always aimed at clarity rather elegance in his lectures.

On 21 August 1860 Duncan married Jane Hart Hotchkis (*b*. 1838/9) of Castlemilk, Dumfriesshire; they had thirteen children. In 1890 he began to suffer from angina and did not finish his usual course of lectures. He died at the Hotel Minerva, Baden-Baden, Germany, on 1 September 1890, of a heart attack, and was buried at Islington cemetery, London, on 8 September 1890. Queen Victoria informed his widow that 'the country and Europe at large have lost one of their most distinguished men' (Munk, 287).

ORNELLA MOSCUCCI

Sources *The Lancet* (13 Sept 1890), 594–6 · *BMJ* (13 Sept 1890), 655–6 · *CGPLA Eng. & Wales* (1890) · Munk, *Roll*, 4.286–7 · O. Moscucci, *The science of woman: gynaecology and gender in England, 1800–1929* (1990), 172–3 · *Edinburgh Medical Journal*, 36 (1890–91), 392–7
Archives Royal College of Physicians of Edinburgh · Wellcome L.
Likenesses G. Jerrard, photograph, 1881, Wellcome L. · Barraud, photograph, Wellcome L. · Dawsons, photogravure, Wellcome L. · wood-engraving (after photograph by Bassano), NPG; repro. in *ILN* (13 Sept 1890)
Wealth at death £86,436 11*s*. 8*d*. in UK: probate, 8 Nov 1890, *CGPLA Eng. & Wales*

Duncan, Jane. *See* Cameron, Elizabeth Jane (1910–1976).

Duncan, John (1721–1808), Church of England clergyman and religious writer, was born on 3 November 1721, a younger son of Dr Daniel Duncan and grandson of the physician Daniel *Duncan (1649–1735), whose memoir John Duncan contributed to the *Biographia Britannica*. He entered Merchant Taylors' School at the age of twelve, and in 1739 went to St John's College, Oxford, as probationary fellow. After graduating MA in 1746 he took holy orders and became chaplain to the forces. He served with the King's Own regiment during the Scots' uprising in 1745–6, and afterwards at the siege of St Philip's, Minorca. Made DD by degree of convocation in 1757, in 1763 he gained the college living of South Warnborough, Hampshire, which he retained until his death.

Duncan wrote mostly on theological and moral subjects. Several of his publications, such as *An Essay on Happiness* (1762), went into second editions, and most of his output was collected in his *Miscellaneous Works* (1793). Duncan was twice married, first to Ellen and second to Mary, and had several children. He died at Bath, where he owned property, on 28 December 1808.

C. J. ROBINSON, *rev.* EMMA MAJOR

Sources *GM*, 1st ser., 79 (1809), 89 · *ESTC* · will, PRO, PROB 11/1491, fols. 174–6 · Foster, *Alum. Oxon.* · C. J. Robinson, ed., *A register of the scholars admitted into Merchant Taylors' School, from AD 1562 to 1874*, 2 (1883), 82
Wealth at death over £12,700; excl. property: will, PRO, PROB 11/1491, fols. 174–6

Duncan, John (1794–1881), hand-loom weaver and botanist, was born on 19 December 1794 at Stonehaven, Kincardineshire, the illegitimate son of John Duncan, weaver and soldier, from Drumlithie, and Ann Caird (*c*.1773–*c*.1830), also of Drumlithie, who decided to support herself and her child by weaving stockings and harvesting at nearby Stonehaven. Duncan never attended school but

John Duncan (1794–1881), by unknown engraver, *c*.1865–6

rambled in the countryside collecting rushes to make pith wicks for sale. From the age of ten he worked as a herdboy at various farms, where he was often treated harshly. While tending herds in Dunnottar, Duncan began to observe wild plants but illiteracy prevented his learning more. At fifteen, rather than become a ploughman, he chose to be apprenticed to a weaver in his parents' village of Drumlithie, a weaving community where interest in politics engendered skills in literacy. Duncan's master, Charles Pirie, a pugilist, gin smuggler, and owner of an illicit still, was violent and treated Duncan cruelly. Pirie's wife, however, possessed a library and secretly taught Duncan to read. After her unexpected death, Duncan continued his education with the help of others in the village and by trying to make out his Bible after hearing the text read in church. He did not learn to write until he was thirty-four.

Duncan spent his free time looking for plants, especially after reading Culpeper's *Herbal* from which he learned the herbs needed for medical remedies. By 1814 his apprenticeship had become so intolerable that he ran away and lived with his mother in Stonehaven for two years, earning his keep by weaving. Extreme frugality allowed him to save £1, with which he purchased his own copy of Culpeper, thus stimulating his interest in herbalism, astronomy, and meteorology. In 1816 he moved to Aberdeen to perfect his weaving skills, learning a variety of techniques and mastering every stage of the process.

In 1818 Duncan married Margaret Wise, whom he had met shortly after she had given birth to an illegitimate son. They had two daughters, but separated in 1824 when Duncan discovered his wife's adultery. After this he never mentioned his marriage, even to close friends, and moved from place to place to escape any association with his wife, who pursued him for money. From Aberdeen he went to Auchleven and surrounding places before moving from village to village in the Vale of Alford. He used his weaving skills in a variety of jobs and served in the Aberdeen militia for part of each year until his wife's death some time between 1844 and 1849. From 1852 he settled at Droughsburn.

In 1836 Duncan met Charles Black, gardener to local gentry at Whitehouse, who was to become his most important friend. Black taught Duncan the Linnaean system and together they scoured the surrounding country for plants to make a scientific herbarium. They used George Dickie's list of plants growing within fourteen miles of Aberdeen (included in H. C. Watson, *New Botanist's Guide*, vol. 2, 1837, 489–97, and later published as *Flora Aberdonensis*, 1838), but required W. J. Hooker's *British Flora* (1830), a work too expensive to buy, for identifying their rarities. Drinking, however, gave them access to the book, for they discovered a copy owned by a local innkeeper, to whose deceased son it had been presented when he worked as a gardener.

Duncan took summer harvesting jobs in different parts of Scotland in order to collect more widely. He collected over two-thirds of the British flora and, despite having only a tiny loft area to live in for many years, found space for his specimens. In his later life he cultivated wild plants in his garden at Droughsburn, many of which he used in herbal remedies. Duncan was an active member of the Auchleven Mutual Improvement Class, 1850–52, giving talks on botany, astronomy, weaving, and gardening.

Charles Black's brother James summed up Duncan as 'human protoplasm, man in his least complex form … a survival of those "rural swains" who lived in idyllic simplicity' (Jolly, *Life*, 482). Duncan's old age, however, was far from idyllic; destitution forced him to apply for poor relief in 1874 to supplement the pittance he earned from weaving. His only indulgence had been the purchase of books but even in extreme poverty he never considered selling his library. From 1879, Duncan having been judged a deserving pauper, the parish also paid for his lodging. Deeply humiliated, Duncan kept this secret until the following year. The educationist and phrenologist William Jolly, who had published an account of Duncan in *Good Words* in 1878, was appalled to discover that Duncan was a pauper. He launched a nationwide appeal and raised £326.

After Duncan began to suffer from heart disease in 1878, his botanical friend James Taylor impressed on him the need to add names and localities to his herbarium sheets while his memory was still intact. Although many specimens had decayed, Duncan presented the remainder to Aberdeen University in 1880. His pleasure in knowing his gift might inspire students to study botany was also reflected in the use of the remaining portion of the money raised for him to found prizes to encourage botanical studies by local schoolchildren. The only request Duncan made for himself was for a decent funeral in Alford. Duncan died at Droughsburn on 9 August 1881 and was buried, shrouded by plants symbolizing his life, on 15 August in Alford churchyard. His grave was marked with a volcanic boulder as Duncan had requested, and also with a granite obelisk recording the donations made by his many admirers.

Duncan was often ridiculed for his appearance, his seeming simplicity, and his pursuit of science. A sartorial oddity, Duncan possessed two tall hats and two best blue suits of his own unusual design and weaving, as well as his work clothes which he wore with Tam o' Shanter bonnets with great tassels on the top. By wearing his trousers rolled up, he preserved the same clothes for fifty years. He was nicknamed Johnnie Moon or the Nogman from his pronunciation of the gnomon, an astronomical instrument he used. Duncan's seemingly strange behaviour was compounded by his shortsightedness, which forced him to crawl along the ground when botanizing. He was unsuccessful in his attempts to remarry after his wife's death and his life was lonely. Considered shy and aloof by many, Duncan occasionally encountered sympathy and formed warm friendships, especially with those who shared his botanical interests. Duncan's devotion to these few friends never overwhelmed his strongly held opinions on the political rights of weavers, his stern Calvinism, nor his support of the Free Church. His dearest friend, Charles Black, loved the poetry of Robert Burns but could never sway Duncan, who thought the poet 'a filthy loon' (Jolly, *Life*, 488).

ANNE SECORD

Sources W. Jolly, *The life of John Duncan, Scotch weaver and botanist* (1883) · W. Jolly, 'John Duncan: the Alford weaver and botanist', *Nature*, 23 (1880–81), 269–70 · 'John Duncan, the Alford weaver-botanist', *Nature*, 24 (1881), 6 · *Nature*, 24 (1881), 361 · 'John Duncan, weaver and botanist', *Gardeners' Chronicle*, 3rd ser., 84 (1928), 22 · *Journal of Botany, British and Foreign*, 19 (1881), 287–8
Likenesses engraving, c.1865–1866, NPG [see illus.] · etching, repro. in Jolly, *Life of John Duncan*, frontispiece
Wealth at death under £326: Jolly, *Life*; *Nature*

Duncan, John (1796–1870), biblical scholar and missionary to the Jews, was born at Aberdeen of very humble parentage. Receiving a small bursary he attended Marischal College, Aberdeen, and showed promise as a linguist and philosopher. While a student of divinity, first at the Divinity Hall of the Anti-Burghers and then at that of the established church, he was at one time troubled by religious doubts. After temporary employment as a probationer he was ordained, on 28 April 1836, to the charge of Milton church, Glasgow. On the occurrence of a vacancy in the chair of oriental languages in the University of Glasgow, he offered himself as a candidate, stating in his application that he knew Hebrew, Syriac, Arabic, Persian, Sanskrit, Bengali, Hindustani, and Marathi. His application failed but his college gave him the degree of LLD in 1840.

On 7 October 1840 the committee of the Church of Scotland for the conversion of the Jews appointed him their first missionary to Pest in Hungary. Here his missionary work, with that of like-minded colleagues, had a remarkable effect. The Archduchess Maria Dorothea, wife of the prince palatine and daughter of the king of Württemberg, was most friendly, and helped the mission in many ways. Duncan's learning and character attracted great attention; many pastors of the Reformed church of Hungary were much influenced by him, and even some Roman Catholic priests attended some of his lectures. Among his converts from Judaism were the biblical scholar Alfred *Edersheim and Adolph *Saphir of the English Presbyterian church in London. He also worked among Italian Jews at Leghorn.

In 1843 he joined the Free Church of Scotland and took up the chair of oriental languages in New College, Edinburgh, the city's theological institution. He quickly became a well-known Edinburgh character. He was very poorly qualified for the chair in one sense, but very admirably in another. His habits utterly unfitted him for teaching the elements of Hebrew or other languages, as well as for the general conduct of a class. However:

> his vast learning, his still more remarkable power of exact thought, and, above all, the profound reaches of his spiritual experience, which penetrated and illuminated from within the entire range of his scientific acquirements, admirably qualified him to handle the exegesis of scripture, and especially that of the Old Testament.

It was in discourse with minds trained to abstract thought that his power as a thinker chiefly appeared. The results of his thought were usually given in sententious aphorisms, much in the manner of a rabbi (he was known as Rabbi Duncan), while in concision and precision of language he showed the influence of Aristotle. He had very little faith in the achievements of philosophy, believing that its constructive power was very small and that it could never raise man to the heights to which he aspired. He relied for the discovery of truth on the voice of God, which he claimed to have heard in the scriptures, and he disliked the emerging school of biblical criticism.

Duncan wrote very little. He edited, in 1838, a British edition of Robinson's *Lexicon of the Greek New Testament* and published several lectures and occasional addresses; *Rich Gleanings* was published in 1925. Such contributions, however, give only a partial impression of the man. Much of him may be learned from the *Colloquia peripatetica* (1870) of William Knight of the University of St Andrews, a favourite and most admiring student, who, living with Duncan for two summers in his student days, took notes of his idiosyncratic conversation and later published them.

Duncan died at his home, 10 Dalrymple Crescent, Edinburgh, on 26 February 1870, aged seventy-four, his wife, Janet, *née* Douglas, having died on 28 October 1852.

W. G. BLAIKIE, rev. H. C. G. MATTHEW

Sources D. Brown, *Life of the late John Duncan, LL.D.* (1872) • W. A. Knight, *Colloquia peripatetica*, 5th edn (1879) • *DSCHT* • J. Macleod, *Scottish theology in relation to church history since the Reformation*, [3rd edn] (1974) • D. Chambers, 'The Church of Scotland's mission to the Jews', *Records of the Scottish Church History Society*, 19 (1975–7), 43–58 • NA Scot., SC 70/1/150/284
Wealth at death £1858 6s. 10d.: confirmation, 1 Nov 1870, NA Scot., SC 70/1/150/284

Duncan, John (1805–1849), traveller in Africa, was the son of a small farmer of Culdoach, near Kirkcudbright, Scotland. He had a strong frame and little education. In 1822 he enlisted in the 1st regiment of Life Guards. He taught himself drawing during his service, and in 1839 left the army with a high character. He next obtained an appointment as master-at-arms in the *Albert*, under Captain H. D. Trotter, which with the *Wilberforce* and the *Soudan* sailed on the ill-fated Niger expedition in 1841. The enterprise was sponsored by the British government with the backing of Thomas Fowell Buxton's Society for the Extinction of the Slave Trade and the Civilization of Africa, with the aim of exploration and the establishment of commercial treaties. On the voyage out Duncan was wounded by a poisoned arrow in fighting at the Cape Verde Islands. He held a conspicuous position in all the treaties made with the local chiefs since he was selected to march at the head of the party, in the cumbrous uniform of a life-guardsman in the extreme heat, the personification of British military might, splendour, and foolhardiness. When at Egga, the highest point reached by the *Albert* on the Niger, he tried to explore further upstream, but sickness compelled the abandonment of the project. On reaching Fernando Po, Duncan was attacked by fever, the effects of which were aggravated by his previous wound. He was one of a minority of Europeans in the Niger expedition to survive the unhealthy climate, despite the fact that the expedition had a light-draught steamer for speedy passage through fever areas. He reached England in a most emaciated condition.

As soon as his health improved Duncan proposed to explore the unknown land from the western coast to the Kong Mountains, and between the Lagos and Niger rivers. His plans were approved by the Royal Geographical Society, and the lords of the Admiralty granted him a free passage in the *Prometheus*, which left England on 17 June 1844, and reached Cape Castle on 22 July following. After an attack of fever he commenced his journey from the coast to Ouidah, and explored Dahomey to Adofidiah, areas previously unknown to Europeans. He sent particulars to the Royal Geographical Society, dated 19 April and 4 October 1845. He was refused passage through the Asante country, but was favourably received by the king of Dahomey. Another attack of fever was followed by a breaking out of the old wound, and Duncan made preparations, happily unnecessary, to amputate his own leg, fearing that gangrene had set in. He succeeded, however, in returning to Cape Coast where he arrived destitute. He was forced to borrow money which it would have taken years of labour to work off, had not supporters in the Royal Geographical Society sent him funds. There, early in 1846, he planned a journey to Timbuktu, but poor health forced him to sail for home in February 1846.

In 1847 Duncan published *Travels in Western Africa* (2 vols.), and, in *Bentley's Miscellany*, an 'Account of the late expedition to the Niger'. In 1849 he proposed to continue his explorations, and the government appointed him vice-consul at Ouidah in the kingdom of Dahomey. He arrived in the Bight of Benin, but died on board HMS *Kingfisher* on

John Duncan (1805–1849), by G. Cook, pubd 1847 (after
C. Durham)

3 November 1849. His widow, of whom nothing is known, was left impoverished. Although uneducated Duncan wrote well from his own experience and his book was favourably received by a public eager for adventurous tales from Africa and rightly impressed by his extraordinary courage.

JOHN WESTBY-GIBSON, rev. ELIZABETH BAIGENT

Sources Chambers, *Scots.* (1835) · Anderson, *Scot. nat.* · Irving, *Scots.* · *Journal of the Royal Geographical Society*, 16 (1846), xlii · *Journal of the Royal Geographical Society*, 18 (1848), lviii · *Journal of the Royal Geographical Society*, 19 (1849), lxxviii · *Journal of the Royal Geographical Society*, 20 (1850), xxxviii–xxxix · *GM*, 2nd ser., 33 (1850), 327–8 · R. A. Stafford, *Scientist of empire: Sir Roderick Murchison, scientific exploration and Victorian imperialism* (1989) · R. Robinson, J. Gallagher, and A. Denny, *Africa and the Victorians* (1961)
Archives RGS, African travel accounts
Likenesses G. Cook, line print (after C. Durham), AM Oxf., BM; repro. in *Bentley's Miscellany* (1847) [*see illus.*] · Durham, steel engraving, repro. in J. Duncan, *Travels in western Africa* (1847)

Duncan, Sir **John Norman Valette** [Val] (1913–1975), international mining executive, was born on 18 July 1913, at Pinner, Middlesex, the eldest of four children of Norman Duncan, barrister, and his wife, Gladys Marguerite Dauvergne Valette. From 1927 to 1932 he was educated at Harrow School, of which he became a governor in 1972; he went on to Brasenose College, Oxford (BA, 1936), of which he became an honorary fellow in 1974. Val Duncan, as he was known, was called to the bar at Gray's Inn in 1938 but never practised law. Instead he became a transport trainee with the Southern Railway in 1938–9. Commissioned in the Royal Engineers following the outbreak of war, he was a railway transport officer at general headquarters of the British expeditionary force in France and Belgium in 1939–40, before attending the staff college at Camberley in 1941. He was then deputy adjutant and quartermaster-

general (1942), acting quartermaster-general in north Africa and Italy (1943), and colonel of Q movements (planning and supervising military operations) in France, Belgium, and Germany (1944–5); he was appointed OBE in 1944. As an acting brigadier he was assistant secretary at the Control Office for Germany and Austria (1946–7), before becoming assistant director of marketing at the National Coal Board—co-ordinating transport arrangements and re-establishing British coal exports in Europe (1947–8). In 1950 Duncan married Lorna Frances (c.1922–1963), daughter of Robert Eyre Archer-Houblon and great-granddaughter of Alexander Lindsay, twenty-fifth earl of Crawford. They were childless.

In July 1948 Duncan was recruited by Sir Mark Turner, who had been his superior at the Control Office, as commercial manager of the Rio Tinto company (which had been formed by Hugh Matheson in 1873 to operate pyrites mines in south-west Spain). He succeeded Turner as managing director in 1951. He had an exceptional strategic grasp of industrial affairs. Supported by Turner he pursued a strategy of large-scale, capital-intensive projects concentrated in politically stable regions, especially in Commonwealth countries. By the early 1960s these policies had established Rio Tinto as a world force in mining.

At first it was essential to rescue Rio Tinto from the chauvinistic policies of Franco's dictatorship, and Duncan masterminded the negotiations whereby the company sold its Spanish assets in return for £7,667,000 and a one-third share in the new Spanish operating company, in 1954. He had meanwhile supervised its diversification. Rio Tinto's new interests included Ugandan copper, South African copper and diamonds, Rhodesian emeralds, gold, and nickel, Australian iron, and Portuguese tin and wolfram. After the company was freed from the Spanish imbroglio, it bought uranium mines in Canada and Australia, in 1955; by the end of the decade it produced 15 per cent of the world's uranium oxide.

Following Rio Tinto's merger with the Consolidated Zinc Corporation, Duncan became managing director in 1962 of the newly formed Rio Tinto Zinc Corporation (RTZ); in 1964 he became chairman and chief executive. RTZ was a conspicuous success at a time when other British multinationals were disarrayed and British political prestige was ebbing, and its overseas earnings helped Britain through the economic crises of the Wilson and Heath administrations after 1964. It developed an aluminium business in Australasia, and in 1968 it acquired borax deposits in Death valley, USA. Explorations were undertaken in Papua New Guinea, South-West Africa, and elsewhere, ultimately leading to new mining projects. Some of these activities, together with lead pollution from RTZ's Avonmouth smelter, and the company's proposals to mine in Snowdonia, were reviled by environmentalists. Duncan's experiences under Spanish economic autarky had made him sensitive to nationalistic susceptibilities. Under his guidance RTZ sought to minimize conflict with foreign governments. It encouraged local autonomy in decision making, employed host country nationals at high levels in overseas management, and encouraged foreign government investment.

Duncan was knighted in 1968. George Brown thought him 'most impressive' (Brown, 163). Following the merger of the Foreign and Commonwealth offices Duncan was appointed to chair a committee on overseas diplomatic representation in 1968–9. His report recommended prioritizing diplomatic strategies, dividing the world into either areas of concentration or outer areas; and it also proposed a more commercially orientated diplomatic service. Harold Wilson 'deplored Duncan's division of the world "literally into black and white"' (*Castle Diaries, 1964–70*, 729).

Duncan, who was a director of the Bank of England from 1969 and of British Petroleum from 1974, held strong views about British national strategy and developed a taste for politicking. Cecil King recorded a confidential discussion with him in 1969: 'He apologized profusely for being one minute late—and stayed till three o'clock. He is an almost fanatical European and thinks the E.E.C. provides the answer to our problems.' Duncan had advised Edward Heath, 'whom he likes … that a general strike—or its equivalent—will be encountered and thinks that the [next Conservative] Government should very carefully pick the timing and the issue and stage the whole thing' (King, 271–2). After the European referendum in 1975 Duncan entertained several newspaper editors, including W. F. (Bill) Deedes, Lord Robens (the advocate of a national government), and two ex-staff officers of his former military chief, Field Marshal Bernard Montgomery.

> Duncan had called them in to head off the revolution. He said, 'When anarchy comes, we are going to provide a lot of essential generators to keep electricity going, and we have invited you, the Editors, to tell us if you can maintain communications to people, then the army will play its proper role.' (Benn, 531)

From boyhood Duncan was a Christian Scientist. Keen, energetic, clear-headed, and forceful, he was outstanding among the post-war generation of entrepreneurs for whom improved civil aviation, and jet aircraft particularly, provided an unprecedented global mobility. However, the stress of international travel undoubtedly hastened his death. Superb in negotiations he was a generous and sympathetic friend. He died of heart failure, on 19 December 1975, in Beaumont House, Beaumont Street, Marylebone, London, and was cremated privately.

RICHARD DAVENPORT-HINES

Sources D. Avery, *Not on Queen Victoria's birthday: the story of the Rio Tinto mines* (1974) · C. E. Harvey, *The Rio Tinto Company: an economic history of a leading international mining concern, 1873–1954* (1981) · C. King, *Diary, 1965–70* (1972) · G. Brown, *In my way* (1971) · *The Times* (20 Dec 1975) · *The Times* (30 Dec 1975) · *Financial Times* (20 Dec 1975) · *Daily Telegraph* (22 Dec 1975) · R. West, *River of tears* (1972) · *The Castle diaries, 1964–1970* (1984) · T. Benn, *Against the tide: diaries, 1973–1976* (1989) · *DNB* · A. C. Fox-Davies, ed., *Armorial families: a directory of gentlemen of coat-armour*, 7th edn, 1 (1929) · *CGPLA Eng. & Wales* (1976)

Archives Rio Tinto Zinc Corporation, London | PRO, Foreign Office archives

Likenesses photograph, c.1960, repro. in Avery, *Not on Queen Victoria's birthday*, 395 · photograph, Hult. Arch.

Wealth at death £654,590: probate, 10 Feb 1976, *CGPLA Eng. & Wales*

Duncan, John Shute (1769–1844), museum curator, was born at South Warnborough, Hampshire, the elder son of John Duncan DD, rector of South Warnborough. He was educated at Winchester College and matriculated in 1787 at New College, Oxford, where he took a BA in 1791 and became a fellow in the same year. He proceeded MA in 1794. He was called to the bar from Lincoln's Inn in 1798, but practised for only a short time. His earlier writings include the anonymous *Hints to the Bearers of Walking Sticks and Umbrellas* (1808; 3rd edn, 1809). On 17 November 1823 he was elected keeper of the Ashmolean Museum, Oxford, and he promptly started to repair the museum's premises and audit and rearrange its contents, himself underwriting these improvements without waiting for approval from the hebdomadal board, which eventually provided funds.

Duncan was a man of strong religious principle as well as being knowledgeable about natural history. His rearranged displays of natural objects illustrated William Paley's *Natural Theology* (1802) and the animals followed Cuvier's classification. Antiquities were set in chronological order but the works of art were mostly kept in storage, since Duncan believed pictures to be foreign to the purpose of a museum. The collections, especially in ornithology, were much expanded, and among his own benefactions was the formation of a reference library. Once the reforms were well set up, Duncan delegated much of the routine conduct of the museum to his loyal and able under-keeper William Kirtland.

On 6 July 1829, aged sixty, Duncan married a Miss Welch, twenty years his junior and sister-in-law of Philip Shuttleworth, warden of New College; he resigned his keepership, and was succeeded by his younger brother Philip Bury *Duncan (1772–1863). The university made him a DCL in June 1830. He was the author of *Botano-Theology* (1825; 2nd edn, 1826), and of *Analogies of Organised Beings* (1831), a compendium drawing mainly on the naturalists Smith, Keith, and Thomson. An anonymous tract, *Collections Relative to the Systematic Relief of the Poor* (1815) demonstrates a special interest in active benevolence; in 1814 he founded the Anti-Mendicity Society in Oxford, based on the success of similar activities in Bath. He died at Westfield Lodge, near Bath, on 14 May 1844.

ALAN BELL

Sources *GM*, 2nd ser., 22 (1844), 97–8 · G. V. Cox, *Recollections of Oxford*, 2nd edn (1870) · R. F. Ovenell, *The Ashmolean Museum, 1683–1894* (1986) · H. H. E. Craster, *History of the Bodleian Library, 1845–1945* (1952) · Foster, *Alum. Oxon.* · *GM*, 3rd ser., 16 (1864), 122–7 [obit. of Philip Bury Duncan] · J. Hunter, 'Biographical notices of some of my contemporaries who have gained some celebrity', BL, Add. MS 36527

Likenesses J. S. Deville, plaster bust, exh. RA 1825, Oriel College, Oxford · T. Kirkby, oils, c.1825–1826, AM Oxf. · Kilbert, oils, Winchester College, Hampshire · W. Smith, oils, New College, Oxford

Duncan, Jonathan (*bap.* 1756, *d.* 1811), administrator in India, was the son of James Duncan in Blairno, and his wife, Jean Meeky. He was baptized on 16 May 1756 in the parish of Lethnot and Navar in Forfarshire. Shortly afterwards his parents moved to Wardhouse, where he spent his boyhood. He was only sixteen when, in 1771, he secured, through the influence of his uncle John Michie, who was a director of the East India Company, a writership in the company's service in Bengal. Duncan typically ascribed all his good fortune to his uncle, whose advice he sought assiduously, but there is reliable testimony that it was his own industry and integrity which attracted the favourable judgement, first of Hastings, and later of Cornwallis, who sought men with these qualities to purge the company's service of corruption and mismanagement.

Duncan's knowledge of Dutch, Persian, and Bengali shows the linguistic gifts which assisted him in his early career as a revenue collector. This was the field where he excelled, and where his attention to detail was needed. Unfortunately it was not accompanied by the gift of concise expression. The prolixity of his reports, and the volume of his later official correspondence, irritated even his friends, and they help to explain why William Hickey described him as 'a heavy, dull man, without a particle of genius' (*Memoirs of William Hickey*, 4.129). His letters also exhibit the lack of self-confidence which made him easily influenced by his fellow Europeans and a poor judge of their characters. These failings were apparent in his youth, and they undermined his capacity for leadership in high office.

Duncan's happiest and most fruitful years in India were spent from 1787 to 1795 as resident of Benares. There he lived detached from European society and had the full support of Cornwallis to cleanse the province of the rapacious influence of his predecessors, which had reduced Benares to a deplorable state. Duncan worked tirelessly to restore some semblance of order and justice, to encourage the recovery of trade, and to advance public health and education. He established the Hindu College, and was one of the founder members of the Asiatic Society of Bengal. Sir James Mackintosh was to say of Duncan at the end of his career that 'Four and thirty years' residence, in this country have Braminised his mind and body' (*Memoirs of … Sir James Mackintosh*, 1.207). But Duncan's respect for Indian culture did not allow him to condone slavery or infanticide, which he tried to repress. His main task in Benares was to introduce a permanent revenue settlement of the kind which had been imposed on Bengal, and which inevitably incorporated the defects of that system. None the less, Cornwallis, no partial judge, declared that Duncan had 'saved the province from ruin' (Cornwallis MS 30/11/188). Bishop Heber reported thirty years after Duncan left that he still lived in the hearts of the people.

Duncan's expertise in revenue settlements led Cornwallis to second him in 1792–4 to Malabar, on the west coast of India. The province was ceded to the company after the First Anglo-Mysore War, and Duncan wrote most of the lengthy report which proposed its future administration. Malabar's chief importance lay in producing pepper, which the company needed for its trade with China and Europe. However, the local rajas and private European traders, including the Bombay civil servants in their private capacity, competed with the company for the profits of the spice trade and Duncan unwisely trusted the advice of self-interested men. The province was exploited for private profit, the coinage devalued, and its economy shattered. The company gained no benefit from its acquisition, and in 1797, two years after Duncan had arrived in Bombay as its governor, rebellion broke out in Malabar. To Duncan's mortification Wellesley transferred the province to the Madras presidency in 1800.

Duncan was unable to retire to Scotland, because in 1799 he discovered that his private fortune had been embezzled, and his only hope of financial recovery was to stay in Bombay as governor. He turned for support to David Scott, the former Bombay private trader who had become one of the company's most influential directors. Scott supported Duncan as governor, and preserved the Bombay presidency, which Wellesley wanted to dissolve. But the price was Duncan's acquiescence in the policy of territorial acquisitions which the Bombay civil servants, some of them Scott's trading partners, were pursuing to advance their private commercial interests in the Gujarat cotton trade. Duncan provided the political excuses which persuaded Wellesley and the directors to permit the extension of Bombay's power over Surat, Gujarat, Cutch, and Kathiawar, while the private traders provided the funds which supplied Bombay's troops in the Second Anglo-Maratha War. Only in 1804 did the court of directors force the Bombay civil servants to give up their private commercial interests.

In 1791 Duncan had married Anne Mercer, the sister of a captain in the Bengal army. She may have died soon afterwards, because she did not accompany him to Bombay. He had an illegitimate son, Jonathan *Duncan the younger, through his connection with Mrs Jane Allen. She returned to England in 1801, and Duncan referred to her in his will as an excellent woman who had deserved well of him. Duncan died at Bombay on 11 August 1811 and was buried in St Thomas's Church. The inhabitants of Bombay paid for a memorial to Duncan, which was inscribed, 'He was a good man and a just' (Higginbotham, 114). Unfortunately his good nature contributed to his weakness as governor, which others exploited to expand British territory with the aim of increasing their private trade in western India.

PAMELA NIGHTINGALE

Sources V. A. Narain, *Jonathan Duncan in Varanasi* (1959) • P. Nightingale, *Trade and empire in western India, 1784–1806* (1970) • *The correspondence of David Scott, director and chairman of the East India Company, relating to Indian affairs, 1787–1805*, ed. C. H. Philips, CS, 3rd ser., 75–6 (1951) • H. Furber, *John Company at work* (1948) • *Memoirs of William Hickey*, ed. A. Spencer, 4 vols. (1913–25) • R. Heber, *Narrative of a journey through the upper provinces of India*, 2 vols. (1828) • J. J. Higginbotham, *Men whom India has known: biographies of eminent Indian characters*, 8 pts (1870–71) • *Memoirs of the life of the Right Honourable Sir James Mackintosh*, ed. R. J. Mackintosh, 2 vols. (1835) • parish register (baptisms), Lethnott and Navar, Forfarshire, Scotland, 16 May 1756 • DNB • will, Jonathan Duncan, BL OIOC, L/AG 34/29 • PRO, Cornwallis MSS, 30/11/188

Archives BL OIOC, corresp. and papers relating to India, home misc. series | BL, corresp. with Lord Wellesley, Add. MSS 13693–13712 • Bucks. RLSS, letters to Lord Hobart • GL, corresp. with John Michie • Herefs. RO, corresp. with Sir Harford Jones • Hunt. L., letters to Grenville family • NA Scot., letters to Lord Melville; précis of letters to H. Dundas • National War Museum of Scotland, corresp. with Sir David Baird • NL Scot., corresp. with Lord Melville • NL

Scot., corresp. with first earl of Minto · NL Scot., corresp. with Alexander Walker · NL Wales, corresp. with Lord Clive · PRO, Cornwallis MSS, 30/11/188 · U. Southampton L., corresp. with Arthur Wellesley

Likenesses W. Ward, mezzotint (after J. J. Masquerier, 1792), NPG

Wealth at death see will, BL OIOC, L/AG 34/29

Duncan, Jonathan, the younger (1799–1865), currency reformer, born at Bombay, was the illegitimate son of Jonathan *Duncan (*bap.* 1756, *d.* 1811), governor of the presidency, and Mrs Jane Allen. His mother returned to Britain soon after his birth. He received his preliminary training under a private tutor named Cobbold. On 24 January 1817 he was entered a pensioner of Trinity College, Cambridge, and took the ordinary BA degree in 1821. He considered the law, and was admitted to the Inner Temple in June 1830, but decided on a literary life, having adequate means from his father. He wrote on the legality of religious prosecutions (1825) and *The Religions of Profane Antiquity* (1830?). In 1836–7 he edited the first four volumes of the short-lived *Guernsey and Jersey Magazine*; it seems he lived for a time in Guernsey. In 1840 he published a translation of F. Bodin's *Résumé de l'histoire d'Angleterre*. He wrote *A History of Russia from the Foundation of the Empire by Rourick to the Close of the Hungarian Wars* (2 vols., 1854), part of which is a translation from the French of A. Rabbe.

After 1841 Duncan lived chiefly in London. He published a history of Guernsey (1841), but subsequently became drawn into the anti-bullionist campaign. Duncan became one of the campaign's most strident pamphleteers, with Sir Robert Peel and S. J. Loyd (Lord Overstone) as his chief targets. He believed that Peel's Currency Act of 1821 and Bank Act of 1844 had 'permanently reduced the wages of labour 50 per cent. He has made money dear and industry cheap' (Duncan, 48). Duncan's pamphlet *How to Reconcile the Rights of Property, Capital, and Labour* was the first tract of the Currency Reform Association (1846). Despite this, Duncan was a strong free-trader, and was willing to have gold used to balance international exchange. He also wrote *The National Anti-Gold League: the Principles of the League Explained* (1847), *The Principles of Money Demonstrated* (1849), and *The Bank Charter Act … with Remarks on the Monetary Crisis of November 1857* (1857). In 1850 he began the *Journal of Industry*, but it failed after sixteen numbers. Duncan died at his house, 33 Norland Square, Notting Hill, London, on 20 October 1865.   H. C. G. MATTHEW

Sources *The Times* (24 Oct 1865) · *GM*, 3rd ser., 19 (1865), 662 · Venn, *Alum. Cant.* · Boase, *Mod. Eng. biog.* · J. Duncan, *How to reconcile the rights of property, capital, and labour* (1846) · *DNB* · d. cert.

Duncan, Mark (*d.* 1640), physician and philosopher, was probably born in London to Thomas Duncan of Maxpoffle, Roxburghshire, and Janet, daughter of Patrick Oliphant of Sowdoun in the same county. He appears to have been educated partly in Scotland and partly on the continent. He took the degree of MD, but at what university is not known.

In 1606 Duncan became a professor at the protestant University of Saumur, and taught philosophy and Greek there. He became regent of the university in 1616. While teaching, he also practised medicine, and gained such a good reputation that James I offered him the post of physician-in-ordinary at the English court, and even forwarded to him the necessary patent. However, Duncan declined the royal invitation out of consideration for his second wife, who was French and was reluctant to leave her native land. He ceased working actively as regent in 1624, although he retained the title until his death.

Duncan's *Institutiones logicae* appeared in 1612: it was influential and went into several editions. In 1634 he published, anonymously, *Discours de la possession des religieuses Ursulines de Loudun*, an investigation of the supposed cases of demoniacal possession among the Ursuline nuns of Loudun. The phenomena had been attributed to the sorcery of Urbain Grandier, curé and canon of Loudun, who had been burnt at the stake in consequence. Duncan ascribed them instead to a psychological origin, that of melancholy. This opinion displeased the religious authorities, from whose anger he was reputedly shielded by the influence of the wife of the maréchal de Brézé, then governor of Saumur. The *Discours* attracted criticism in the form of a *Traité de la mélancholie* by H. J. Pilet de la Mesnardière, and that in turn prompted, *c.*1636, an *Apologie pour Mr. Duncan, docteur en médecine, dans laquelle les plus rares effects de la mélancholie et de l'imagination sont expliquez contre les reflexions du Sieur de la* MRE *par le Sieur de la F. M.* (that is, Duncan).

Duncan lived in Saumur until his death in 1640. He left three sons, who took the names respectively of Cérisantis, Saint Helène, and Montfort.

His eldest son, **Mark Duncan de Cérisantis** (*d.* 1648), was for a time tutor to the marquis de Faure, and was employed by Richelieu in negotiations at Constantinople in 1641; but he was forced to leave France after a quarrel with M. de Caudale, and entered the Swedish service. He returned to France as the Swedish ambassador resident in 1645. Shortly afterwards he left the Swedish service, renounced his protestantism, and went to Rome, where in 1647 he met the duc de Guise, who was then planning his attempt to wrest the kingdom of Sicily from Spain. Cérisantis accompanied the duc to Naples as his secretary. He is said also to have been secretly employed by the French king to spy on the duc's plans and movements.

Cérisantis was considered an elegant Latinist, and published a number of poems. He died of gangrene from a musket-ball wound in the ankle, received in a battle with the Spanish in February 1648. The duc de Guise's *Mémoires* (1668) refer to Cérisantis as vainglorious, although brave and skilful in battle. His brother, Saint Helène, took exception to this, to the point of challenging the authenticity of the memoirs.   J. M. RIGG, *rev.* SARAH BAKEWELL

Sources W. Anderson, *The Scottish nation*, 2 (1877), 84–5 · A. J. L. Jourdan, ed., *Biographie médicale*, 7 vols. (1820–25), vol. 3, p. 553 · Y. Destianges, 'Duncan, Marc', *Dictionnaire de biographie française*, ed. J. Balteau and others, 12 (Paris, 1970), 275–6 · R. D. Amat, 'Cerisantes, Marc Duncan de', *Dictionnaire de biographie française*, ed. J. Balteau and others, 8 (Paris, 1959), 60 · Watt, *Bibl. Brit.*, vol. 1 · A.-A. Barbier, *Dictionnaire des ouvrages anonymes* (1872–9), 1.1010

Duncan, Sir Patrick (1870–1943), politician in South Africa and governor-general of the Union of South Africa, was born on his father's remote farm at Fortrie, in King Edward parish, Banffshire, Scotland, on 21 December 1870, the second of the five children of John Duncan and his wife, Janet Taylor of Balmand, Banffshire. He attended the small King Edward parish school where Dr John Milne encouraged him to read Cicero and Xenophon by the time he was twelve. He also educated himself, winning a scholarship to George Watson's College, Edinburgh, and emerging as dux and gold medallist with a scholarship to Edinburgh University where he drew the attention of two remarkable mentors, W. Y. Sellar and S. H. Butcher. In 1888 he won a classical scholarship to Balliol College, Oxford. He was awarded, successively, a Warner exhibition in the college and a Craven scholarship (1890), gaining first classes in classical moderations (1891) and *literae humaniores* (1893).

Early career and friendships Duncan spent some time in London, studying Aristotle and working at the Toynbee Hall settlement, before starting his career in the Inland Revenue in 1894 as secretary to the chairman, Alfred Milner, and his successor, G. H. Murray. Duncan became principal clerk in 1898, leaving three years later when Milner offered him the colonial treasurership of Transvaal, newly annexed in the Second South African War. Duncan thus joined Milner's 'Kindergarten' of administrators in a senior position. He was a safe pair of hands— scholarly, unassuming, habitually cautious, fair-minded, firm, and precise. In 1903 he was appointed Transvaal colonial secretary to institute a new system of civil administration in the colony with Lionel Curtis as his assistant colonial secretary (urban affairs). Close friendships evolved among the Kindergarten; throughout his life Duncan maintained a weekly political correspondence with Lady Maud Selborne, wife of Milner's successor and mentor to the young men of the administration.

Duncan advocated an early return to colonial responsible government as a preliminary to a united South Africa. As chairman of the railway committee of the intercolonial council for Transvaal and Orange River Colony he developed the core of a unified railway system. He presided over the discussions among his colleagues in the Kindergarten and their friends, the results codified in the Selborne memorandum as a focus for the debates on closer union already current in each of the four South African colonies. In his last few months before the Transvaal elections in 1907 Duncan was appointed acting lieutenant-governor. He was made a CMG at the end of his term of office.

The Het Volk party of Louis Botha and J. C. Smuts won the election. Duncan had decided that it would be inappropriate to make a living solely from politics and, while publicly declaring his intention to return to South Africa, joined the chambers of J. A. (later Viscount) Simon in London. He was called to the bar at the Inner Temple in 1908. He practised as an advocate in Johannesburg and joined his friends Richard Feetham and Hugh Wyndham in the Progressive Party supporting British interests

Sir Patrick Duncan (1870–1943), by Walter Stoneman, 1937

against the Het Volk ministers. With Lionel Curtis he produced the technical factual compilation published as *The Government of South Africa*, and toured the country to increase public understanding of the constitutional issues at stake in union. Duncan and R. H. Brand were invited to be legal advisers to the impressive Transvaal delegation to the national convention led by Smuts and Botha. With Brand and N. J. de Wet, Duncan drafted many of the convention's programmes and general principles in terms of legislative enactment. Duncan's was the resolution from the chair ensuring that the conference of the popular Closer Union societies endorsed union.

Association with Smuts Duncan's collaboration over union with Smuts, his exact contemporary, began a lifelong association. As early as 1908 Duncan noted the disjunction between Smuts's lofty sentiments and his political actions; equally, Duncan was detached from his colleagues in the Progressive Party and from the Unionists, their union-wide successors. He spoke Afrikaans, favoured consensus between Boer and Briton, and instinctively sympathized with country rather than town, workers rather than magnates, quoting Bacon, 'wealth is like muck—not good but it is spread' (Duncan to Lady Selborne, 31 Oct 1922, Duncan MS D5.16). After inquiring into poverty with the indigency commission he had become a lifelong proponent of a free labour market, with opportunities for skilled black workers and special inducements to safeguard the employment of unskilled white workers.

In the first union-wide elections of 1910 Duncan won the polyglot working class Rand seat of Fordsburg as the Unionist candidate, holding the seat until 1920. It was said that his dry wit and capacity to dispatch a stiff glass won him popularity; more probably his appeal derived from his opposition to imported indentured labour and his principled foregoing of the pension due to him as colonial secretary. Though leader of the Transvaal Unionists in the new parliament, Duncan considered that Sir L. S. Jameson, his Cape senior colleague, had fatally undermined the British cause by his famous raid on the Transvaal in 1895. In 1913 Duncan led the Young Unionists for a year, criticizing the party's conservatism on questions of social reform and its alliance with magnate wealth. Thereafter he acted increasingly independently, as when he denounced the deportation of the British-born leaders of the 1914 miners' strike. He was interested in social conditions: miners' silicosis, the protection of children, and the wages of women and young persons working in industry, his private member's bill giving rise to an inquiry by select committee and legislation in 1918. His other interest was education, from technical schools and reformatories to the evolution of the South African School of Mines into the autonomous University of the Witwatersrand.

In 1912 Duncan had published *Suggestions for a Native Policy* (reprinted with an introduction in 1927), arguing that the policy of low wages had led to appalling social conditions for black people while giving no security to white workers. Segregation was no formula for a solution: it was both impracticable—'the mere statement of what it would involve condemns it as impossible' (P. Duncan, *Suggestions for a Native Policy*, 1927, 7)—and undesirable. The idea that the native would develop along his own lines was 'plausible but unsound' (ibid., 8). His own proposal was equally implausible: to improve the conditions of life and work for black people, assimilating them into civilized society while avoiding social integration or political equality because the numerical imbalance was so great. He was thus driven to criticize the Cape's colour-blind franchise (although it was assimilationist in tone) and to advocate large-scale white immigration (although he was inclined to oppose the influx of Jewish immigrants from eastern Europe). Many Unionists dismissed his *Suggestions*. Nevertheless, Duncan was widely trusted: he was chosen to chair the sensitive parliamentary select committee enquiring into the 1914 uprising opposing South Africa's participation in the First World War.

In 1916 Duncan married Alice Dora Amanda (1893–1948), daughter of Victor Dold, a trader at Kokstad, East Griqualand. They were a strikingly handsome couple, and she complemented her husband's shy temperament. Three of their four children (John, Andrew, and Deborah) moved home between Cape Town and Pretoria with the parliamentary sessions; the fourth, Patrick, was sent to school in England.

Cabinet minister and QC 1920–1927 Duncan was to become a naturalized South African, and the most prominent English-speaking politician in South Africa between the First and Second World Wars. By 1920 Afrikaner nationalist opposition to the First World War and the government had grown; Botha was dead and Smuts looked to the Unionists to merge with his South African Party. Duncan lost Fordsburg to Maurice Kentridge (Labour) in the 1920 election, but in 1921 won the predominantly Jewish constituency of Yeoville, which he held until 1937. He became minister of the interior, health, and education in Smuts's cabinet and a key figure in managing the various groupings clustered round Smuts as politics developed on a national scale. The government was divided on provincial lines as well as on the great questions of economic doctrine and race policy. Duncan's overriding consideration was to keep the whole political show on the road. He warmed to Smuts's largeness of outlook—'money and place mean simply nothing to him. He reads, and prefers to talk about things that are really interesting' (Duncan to Lady Selborne, 15 Nov 1920, Duncan MS D4.14.26). But Duncan and J. H. Hofmeyr, Smuts's other lieutenant, never resolved their mutual suspicion after 1923 when Duncan intervened in the constitutional row that erupted early in Hofmeyr's principalship of the new University of the Witwatersrand. Where Hofmeyr articulated his principles, Duncan's quiet idealism acknowledged a gap between what needed doing and what could be done (about Asian immigration, or black political rights, or the politics of the provincial councils). He confided to his son that 'my imagination is subject, perhaps enslaved, to a severely practical control' (Driver, 22).

When the Smuts government fell in 1924 to a coalition of Nationalists and Labour led by Hertzog, Duncan took silk. He acted at various times as legal commissioner and legal adviser to the British high commissioner on Bechuanaland, and chaired the special court of the Bechuanaland protectorate (1929–33). In opposing Hertzog's proposed segregationist legislation of 1926–7 he wrote 'Race questions in South Africa' (*Foreign Affairs*, 5, 1927, 293–306). His talent at taking the heat out of an issue was as useful in opposition as in office—he was the sole member of the deadlocked committee determining the national flag who went on to join the small group of four who resolved the issue in 1927. He was generally held to be the most honest politician of his generation.

Policies and alliances, 1927–1937 Duncan's diplomatic skills were decisively deployed when South African politics fragmented in the wake of the 1931 gold standard crisis. He led the opposition's campaign to leave the gold standard and later, with Hofmeyr and Deneys Reitz, persuaded a reluctant Smuts in February 1933 to serve with Hertzog against the right-wing Nationalists rather than ally with the opportunistic lawyer Tielman Roos. As minister of mines and industry in Hertzog's cabinet, Duncan introduced an excess profits tax on gold premiums. He cemented a friendship with Hertzog (whom he liked personally better than Smuts) over the passage of the Status Bill confirming South Africa's autonomy within the Commonwealth, and in opposing Natal's jingoistic bid for secession. In 1934 Smuts chose Duncan to accompany him in negotiating with Hertzog and N. C. Havenga the transition from coalition to full political fusion in a new United Party. Hertzog's segregationist race legislation had been opposed by the South African Party in the 1920s and glossed over in 1933; now Duncan thought demography dictated that South Africa was unlikely to remain a white-dominated country. Hofmeyr and other liberals opposed the bills but did not resign. Duncan, believing that it would be less divisive to abolish the Cape non-racial franchise than to limit it, acquiesced in the removal of the 11,000 black voters in the Cape to a separate voters' roll: 'it is still possible ... to do it peacefully; therefore let it be done now' (private information). His overriding consideration was to keep the new political alignment in existence:

> we should not have got the necessary two-thirds majority [to alter the terms of the bills] and then we should have had the whole native question as a battleground in a general election with Hertzog on one side and Smuts on the other, and the great United Party would have gone up in smoke.
> (Driver, 23)

In 1935 Duncan accompanied Hertzog to London for the silver jubilee of George V. The Imperial Conference of 1930 had established the right of a dominion to advise the crown on the appointment of the governor-general. In 1936 Hertzog broke with all precedent, choosing Duncan—a South African citizen, active in politics and a cabinet minister—to fill the role. The choice was formally debated; Duncan himself needed much persuading to undertake the task. The appointment was announced on 17 November 1936. Duncan returned to London where he was made a GCMG, despite a longstanding resolution that South African citizens should eschew honours bestowed by the crown. He was sworn officially on 5 April 1937 and nominated privy councillor.

Governor-general, 1937–1943 Duncan's years as governor-general were not happy. He was a private man, shy, with no small-talk, never so much at ease as when on trek with an ox-wagon. Living in an official residence next door to parliament in Cape Town, he felt misplaced. On the outbreak of the Second World War in September 1939 he was called upon to make a decision which Smuts hailed as an imperishable service to South Africa and the world. Hertzog had pledged in May 1938 that the issue of whether or not South Africa should be neutral in wartime would be decided in parliament. When war was declared the cabinet was divided on the issue; parliament happened to be sitting in special session. On 4 September two motions were put: Hertzog's, advocating neutrality (but with existing obligations unimpaired), and Smuts's amendment that the union should sever relations with the Reich and refuse to adopt neutrality. Smuts won by thirteen votes; fusion was at an end. Hertzog resigned the premiership, advising the governor-general to dissolve parliament. After consulting works of constitutional law flown from Pretoria overnight, Duncan declined to follow the advice, carefully recording the grounds for his decision: a general election would provoke intense bitterness,

even bloodshed; the government had been divided, but Smuts's motion had been adopted by a substantial majority and the decision of the house must stand. Duncan wrote personally to Hertzog and unhesitatingly called on Smuts to form a ministry. On 6 September South Africa entered the war. Duncan's decision was controversial and it remains debatable whether Hertzog would have won an election on the strength of his support from rural voters, to whom the electoral system gave a weighted preference.

Duncan's appointment was renewed in April 1942, but within six months he was relieved of his duties to undergo an operation for cancer. At the same time Andrew, his second son, a major on active service in north Africa, was reported missing. Duncan took refuge in intellectual pursuits. He had been awarded honorary doctorates of civil law by the universities of Edinburgh and Cape Town, and in 1936 had been made a fellow of Balliol. He had published a translation of Plato's *Phaedo* (1928); now he published 'Socrates and Plato' (*Philosophy*, 15, 1940, 339–62) and 'Immortality of the soul in the Platonic dialogues and Aristotle' (*Philosophy* 17, 1942, 304–23). Smuts persuaded him not to resign his office, but he was able to resume for only a few months in 1943 before he died at Government House, Pretoria, on 17 July 1943. Smuts spoke movingly at the state funeral: 'If he was not the stuff which makes popular leaders, he had in him the stuff which leads the leaders ... We all trusted him' (*DNB*). The *Round Table* recorded that in the course of a distinguished political career in intensely volatile circumstances, Duncan never made an enemy (*Round Table*, 33, 1943, 305). In 1945 his ashes were interred within the stone pillar on which is inscribed the name of the Duncan Dock in Cape Town.

DEBORAH LAVIN

Sources P. Duncan and M. Selborne, correspondence, 1907–43, Bodl. Oxf., MSS Film 1324–7 · *Selections from the Smuts papers*, ed. W. K. Hancock and J. van der Poel, 7 vols. (1966–73) · C. J. Driver, *Patrick Duncan, South African and pan-African* (1980) · L. M. Thompson, *The unification of South Africa, 1902–1910* (1960) · D. Lavin, *From empire to international commonwealth: a biography of Lionel Curtis* (1995) · K. Ingham, *Jan Christian Smuts: the conscience of a South African* (1986) · M. Paton, *Hofmeyr* (1964) · O. Pirow, *James Barry Munnik Hertzog* (1957) · N. Mansergh, *Survey of British commonwealth affairs: problems of wartime co-operation and change, 1939–52* (1958) · W. K. Hancock, *Smuts*, 2 vols. (1962–8) · B. K. Murray, *WITS, the early years: a history of the University of the Witwatersrand, Johannesburg, and its precursors, 1896–1939* (1982) · L. E. Neame, *Some South African politicians* (1929) · P. Duncan, *Suggestions for a native policy* (1912) · private information · *Round Table*, 33 (1943), 305 · *DNB* · *WWW*

Archives Borth. Inst., administrative and political papers and corresp. · University of Cape Town Library, corresp. and papers · University of York | BLPES, corresp. with Violet Markham · Bodl. Oxf., corresp. with L. G. Curtis · Bodl. Oxf., corresp. with Geoffrey Dawson · Bodl. Oxf., Milner MSS · Bodl. Oxf., Selborne MSS · Bodl. RH, corresp. with Sir Herbert Baker · Bodl. RH, corresp. with Lady Selborne [copies] · Borth. Inst., letters to Patrick Duncan · HLRO, letters to Herbert Samuel · NA Scot., corresp. with Lord Lothian · NA Scot., Lothian MSS · U. Cam., J. C. Smuts MSS | FILM BFI NFTVA, documentary footage · BFI NFTVA, news footage

Likenesses W. Stoneman, photographs, 1937, NPG [*see illus.*] · M. Kottler, bust, Houses of Parliament, Cape Town, South Africa, Queen's Hall

Duncan, Peter Martin (1824–1891), geologist, was born at Twickenham, on 20 April 1824, the son of Peter King Duncan, a leather merchant and descendant of an old Scottish family, and Jemima, daughter of Captain R. Martin RN of Ilford, Essex. Duncan was educated at the grammar school, Twickenham, and at Nyon, by Lake Geneva. In 1840 he was apprenticed to a London surgeon. Two years later, he began studying medicine at King's College, London; he graduated MB (London) in 1846.

For a time Duncan was assistant to Dr Martin at Rochester, but from 1848 to 1860 he had his own practice at Colchester. At nearby Lexden, on 12 May 1852, he married Jane Emily (b. 1828/9), daughter of Samuel Green Cooke; they had at least four sons and seven daughters. As a young married professional, Duncan became active in Colchester's municipal affairs, and in 1857 was elected mayor.

Despite professional and civic commitments, Duncan was attracted by the natural history and archaeology of the district, and the arrangement of the town museum was largely his work. His first scientific paper, 'Observations on the pollen tube', published in 1856 in the *Proceedings* of the Edinburgh Botanical Society, was soon followed by others. In 1860 he moved to Blackheath, where he practised until 1870. There he found more time for scientific study, particularly the study of corals.

More freedom for scientific research was obtained when Duncan was elected in 1870 to the professorship of geology at King's College; he became a fellow in the following year. Shortly afterwards he was appointed as lecturer of geology at the Royal Indian Engineering College, Cooper's Hill. In 1877 he settled in London near Regent's Park, residing there until 1883, when he moved to Gunnersbury. In 1881 he was elected to the chair of geology in King's College.

Duncan was elected a fellow of the Geological Society in 1849, and was secretary from 1864 to 1870 and president from 1876 to 1878. In 1879 he was president of the geological section of the British Association meeting, and in 1881 he received the Wollaston medal. He was also a fellow of the Zoological and Linnean societies, holding office in both, and an active member of the Microscopical Society, being president from 1881 to 1883. He was elected FRS on 4 June 1868.

Duncan's industry was unflagging. He undertook a great amount of work, of both a popular and a scientific character. He was editor of Cassell's *Natural History* (1876–82), to which he contributed several important articles. He wrote a *Primer of Physical Geography* (1882); a small volume of biographies of botanists, geologists, and zoologists entitled *Heroes of Science* (1882); another on *The Seashore* (1879); and an *Abstract of the Geology of India* (1875), which reached a third edition in 1881. He also assisted in preparing the third edition of Griffith and Henfrey's *Micrographic Dictionary* (1875), and in revising the fourth edition of Lyell's *Student's Elements of Geology* (1885). Duncan was also author of at least a hundred scientific papers.

Duncan made a special study of corals and echinids, although he also took much interest in ophiurids, sponges, and protozoa. He adopted the viewpoint of a philosophical zoologist for this research, but also investigated the relationship between species distribution and palaeoenvironments. He described fossil coral fauna from different parts of the world, and the echinids of Sind. The results of these researches were summed up in two valuable papers, *Revision of the Madreporaria*, published by the Linnean Society (1885), and *Revision of the Genera and Great Groups of the Echinoidea*. Other papers on the *Physical geology of western Europe during Mesozoic and Cainozoic times, elucidated by the coral fauna*, on *The Formation of Land Masses*, and *On Lakes and their Origin* were at the time, important contributions to science. He was also considered an excellent teacher, a genial companion, and a true friend.

Duncan's health began to fail from about 1889 and a painful illness led to his death at his home, 6 Grosvenor Road, Gunnersbury, on 28 May 1891. He was buried in Chiswick churchyard. Duncan was survived by his second wife, Mary Jane Emily Liddell Whitmarsh, whom he had married in 1869 after his first wife's death, and with whom he had one son. T. G. BONNEY, *rev.* YOLANDA FOOTE

Sources *Proceedings of the Linnean Society of London* (1890–92), 65 · *Geological Magazine*, new ser., 3rd decade, 8 (1891), 332–6 · *Quart. Journ. Geol. Soc.*, 48, 47 · *Nature*, 44 (1891), 387 · private information (1901) [F. Martin Duncan] · Boase, *Mod. Eng. biog.* · L. C. Sanders, *Celebrities of the century: being a dictionary of men and women of the nineteenth century* (1887) · m. cert. · letter, *Colchester Historical Record* (28 Dec 1911) · IGI · d. cert.
Archives U. Edin. L., letters to Sir Charles Lyell
Likenesses photograph, RS
Wealth at death £3312 7s. 0d.: probate, 17 Aug 1891, CGPLA Eng. & Wales

Duncan, Philip Bury (1772–1863), museum curator, was born at South Warnborough, Hampshire, where his father, John Duncan, was rector. John Shute *Duncan (1769–1844) was an elder brother. He was educated at Winchester College (where he was a schoolfellow of Sydney Smith and William Howley, and where he later founded the Duncan prizes for mathematics) and at New College, Oxford, where he matriculated on 17 July 1791, and took his BA in 1794 and MA in 1798. He was called to the bar from Lincoln's Inn in 1800 and practised for some time on the home and western circuits. From 1801 he lived mainly at Bath, where with his brother he promoted local philanthropic schemes, including a savings bank and a society for the suppression of mendicity. In Oxford he gave generously to a scheme for promoting the establishment of wash-houses and baths for the working classes, set up in 1850. His *Essays and Miscellanea* (1840) include several pieces read at the Bath Royal Literary and Scientific Institution, and in 1841 he was president of the Bath United Hospital.

In November 1829 Duncan succeeded his brother John Shute as keeper of the Ashmolean Museum, Oxford. As a boy, he had delighted in Sir Ashton Lever's private museum in London, the Holophusikon. Assisted by an able under-keeper, William Kirtland, Duncan applied himself keenly to his Oxford duties. He added to the cast collection, and arranged for catalogues to be compiled and printed. He supported the museum generously from his own pocket, but missed no opportunity to remind a reluctant university of its duty to give the Ashmolean adequate financial support and to find it urgently needed additional space for teaching and for display.

During Duncan's quarter-century in office many gifts and bequests were received, aggravating the congestion. At the end of his keepership the campaign for a new museum in the Parks found more general support. On his resignation in 1855 he was awarded an honorary DCL for his services to the university. He retired to Bath, where he died, unmarried, at his home, Westfield Lodge, parish of Weston, on 12 November 1863. His schoolfellow Archbishop Howley said of the Duncan brothers, 'I question whether any two men, with the same means, have ever done the same amount of good' (*GM*, 122).

ALAN BELL

Sources *GM*, 3rd ser., 16 (1864), 122–6 · G. V. Cox, *Recollections of Oxford*, 2nd edn (1870) · R. F. Ovenell, *The Ashmolean Museum, 1683–1894* (1986) · H. H. E. Craster, *History of the Bodleian Library, 1845–1945* (1952) · Foster, *Alum. Oxon.* · *DNB* · *CGPLA Eng. & Wales* (1863) · A. MacGregor and A. Headon, 'Re-inventing the Ashmolean: natural history and natural theology at Oxford in the 1820s to 1850s', *Archives of Natural History*, 27 (2000), 369–406
Archives AM Oxf., corresp.
Likenesses T. Kirkby, oils, exh. RA 1825, New College, Oxford · W. Smith junior, oils, New College, Oxford · portrait, Winchester College
Wealth at death under £45,000: probate, 16 Jan 1864, *CGPLA Eng. & Wales*

Duncan [*married name* Cotes], **Sara Jeannette** (1861–1922), novelist and journalist, was born in Brantford, Upper Canada (now Ontario), on 22 December 1861, the oldest surviving of the eleven children of Charles Lees Duncan (1832–1907), a prosperous Scottish Presbyterian dry goods merchant, and Jane, *née* Bell (1837–1931), from New Brunswick and of Irish descent. Educated at Brantford Ladies' College and Brantford Collegiate Institute, Duncan satisfied the expectations of her class and time by training as a teacher (at Brant County model school in 1879 and Toronto normal school in 1882). Between 1880 and 1884 she published poems and essays in Ontario newspapers, vigorously seeking a full-time position as a journalist. In 1884 she suggested to *The Globe* (Toronto) and *The Advertiser* (London, Ontario) that she might report on the New Orleans cotton centennial fair; her articles (under the pen-name Garth) appeared in several Canadian and American newspapers. From 1885 to 1888 she wrote for *The Globe*, the *Washington Post*, and the *Montreal Star*, and contributed to the important Toronto journal *The Week*. In the spring of 1888, though Canadian women were still unenfranchised, she was one of the *Montreal Star*'s parliamentary correspondents in Ottawa.

In September 1888, with the Montreal journalist Lily Lewis, Duncan began the unchaperoned round-the-world trip which produced her first book, *A Social Departure: how Orthodocia and I Went Around the World by Ourselves* (1890), dedicated irreverently 'to Mrs Grundy'. It was a great success, making possible the international career which she had resolved upon as a young woman in Canada. Its journalistic flair and sharp social observation recur in all her later writing, whether in popular magazine genres or the one-volume commercial best-seller addressed to a middle-class audience. She wrote an interesting 'new woman' novel (*A Daughter of Today*, 1894) and experimented with both Henry James's 'international' themes, in the charming *An American Girl in London* (1891) and *Cousin Cinderella* (1908), and his style, in the tedious *The Path of a Star* (1899). But Duncan's edgy satire would eventually isolate her between John Galsworthy, whose bourgeois subjects and audience she shared, and E. M. Forster, whose modernist vision she anticipated in her later critiques of Anglo-Indian life. In 1912 Forster described her as 'clever and odd—nice to talk to alone, but at times the Social Manner descended like a pall' (*Selected Letters*, 1.159).

Presented at court on 17 March 1890, Duncan married Everard Charles Cotes (1862–1944), entomologist at the Indian Museum in Calcutta on 6 December 1890 in St Thomas's Church in that city. A child (undocumented) was reportedly born in 1900 but died within days. She resided in Calcutta, Simla, and Delhi and shuttled between India and London to manage her career. Her Canadian journalism of the 1880s has been studied, but her extensive Indian journalism (assisting her husband in editing the *Indian Daily News* from 1895) remains untraced; a formidable anonymous attack on Lord Curzon in the *Contemporary Review* of August 1900 has recently been identified. Her novels were usually serialized in London and the USA before publication in Britain and America. Duncan was market-wise and tailored much of her writing to popular expectations—the children's book *The Story of Sonny Sahib* (1894) generated royalties until 1940—but her experience of Anglo-India produced a core group of successful novels of increasing depth and post-colonial political insight: *The Simple Adventures of a Memsahib* (1893), *His Honor, and a Lady* (1896), *Set in Authority* (1906), and *The Burnt Offering* (1909). These novels centre on the Anglo-Indian professional class into which she had married; their social wit and ruthless irony sharply distinguish them from the popular Anglo-Indian romances of the period, a genre which she repeatedly satirized.

It is *The Imperialist* (1904), however, that is Duncan's major novel. A richly envisioned chronicle of political inexperience set in Brantford (here called 'Elgin'), its combination of bourgeois subject and ironic viewpoint make it the first recognizably 'modern' Canadian novel. It was, however, initially rejected by Canadian readers. Duncan invested funds in Canada and strove to have her books published there; she retained a strong belief in its tradition of egalitarian civility. Late-twentieth-century appreciation of *The Imperialist* would have consoled her for the post-1920 oblivion of her Anglo-Indian novels—too conventional for modern readers and too sceptical for Edwardians.

Duncan's husband became proprietor of the Eastern News Agency, and when they were separated by the First World War, she turned London playwright, but without success; she never returned to India after 1915. Reunited in 1919, the Coteses established themselves prosperously in England, where family recollections describe Redney (as she was nicknamed) holding court, a formidable personality but of frail physique. Between 1914 and her death she published four late novels of lesser distinction. She died of pneumonia and emphysema on 22 July 1922 at her home, Barnett Wood Lodge, Ashtead, Surrey, leaving her estate to her husband, who remarried in 1924. She was buried in St Giles's Church, Ashtead. GERMAINE WARKENTIN

Sources M. Fowler, *Redney: a life of Sara Jeannette Duncan* (1983) · University of North Carolina, Chapel Hill, Wilson Library, A. P. Watt MSS · R. Goodwin, 'The early journalism of Sara Jeannette Duncan', MA diss., University of Toronto, 1964 · *Brantford Expositor* (7 Oct 1907) · *Brantford Expositor* (22 April 1931) · entry of marriage, ecclesiastical records, BL OIOC, N/1/214, fol. 338 · d. cert. · M. E. R. [Mrs Sandford (Nellie) Ross], 'Sara Jeannette Duncan—personal glimpses', *Canadian Literature*, no. 27 (winter 1962), 15–19 · interview with Dr John Cotes and Mrs Alison Payne, York, 20 June 1997 · *Selected letters of E. M. Forster*, ed. M. Lago and P. N. Furbank, 1 (1983) · S. J. Duncan [Mrs Everard Cotes], *On the other side of the latch* (1901) · *WWW* · S. J. Duncan, *Set in authority*, ed. G. Warkentin, new edn (1996), introduction, chronology, and appxs · University of Western Ontario, London, Ontario, D. B. Weldon Library, Carl Klinck MSS · Archibald MacMechan to Lorne Pierce, 11 Nov 1926, Queen's University Archives, Kingston, Ontario, Lorne Pierce MSS · R. W. Noble, '*A passage to India*: the genesis of E. M. Forster's novel', *Encounter*, 54/2 (1980), 51–61 · G. B. Burgin, 'A chat with Sara Jeannette Duncan', *The Idler*, 8 (Aug 1895), 113–18 · F. Donaldson, 'Mrs Everard Cotes', *The Bookman*, 14 (1898), 65–7 · M. MacMurchy, 'Mrs Everard Cotes', *The Bookman*, 48 (1915), 39–40 · T. E. Tausky, *Sara Jeannette Duncan: novelist of empire* (1980) · M. Dean, *A different point of view: Sara Jeannette Duncan* (1991)

Archives University of North Carolina, Chapel Hill, Wilson Library, A. P. Watt MSS · University of Western Ontario, London, Ontario, D. B. Weldon Library, Carl Klinck MSS

Likenesses photographs, repro. in Fowler, *Redney*

Wealth at death £150 7s. 0d.: probate, 17 Oct 1922, CGPLA Eng. & Wales

Duncan, Thomas (1807–1845), history and portrait painter, was born at Kinclaven, near Perth, on 4 May 1807, the third child of Samson Duncan (1767–1837), musician, and Janet Alexander (d. 1841). Duncan was educated at Perth Academy, where the drawing-master, David Junor, encouraged his interest in art and no doubt that of his schoolmate D. O. Hill, who also went on to become an artist and who remained a lifelong friend. On 22 June 1818, while still at school, Duncan painted the scenery for the first ever stage adaptation of Walter Scott's novel *Rob Roy*, which had been published the previous year. Before he could take up painting as a profession, however, Duncan, to satisfy his father's wish, served a three-year apprenticeship in Perth with the legal firm of John and James Miller, writers to the signet, before successfully applying to study at the Trustees' Academy in Edinburgh, where he enrolled on 22 March 1827. His application was supported by Hill, who had preceded him there three years earlier, and by David Junor. William Allan had recently replaced Andrew Wilson as master of the academy. Duncan had evidently pursued his interest in painting in the intervening years: in 1828, only a year after enrolling as a student, he exhibited at the Scottish Academy and was elected a full member a year later in 1829. Thereafter he exhibited at the Scottish Academy (later Royal Scottish Academy) every year until his death, but he also exhibited at the West of Scotland Exhibition of Fine Art in Glasgow with some

regularity between 1830 and 1842. It was as a result of this exposure, perhaps, that he developed a significant portrait practice in Glasgow as well as in Edinburgh. He exhibited for the first time in London in 1832 at the Society of British Artists.

The majority of Duncan's exhibited work throughout his life consisted of portraiture, for example *Lady Stewart of Allanbank* (exh. Royal Scottish Academy, 1838; NG Scot.) and *Professor James Miller* (exh. Royal Scottish Academy, 1845; Royal College of Surgeons of Edinburgh). He also made several portraits of dogs such as *Bran, a Celebrated Scottish Deerhound* (exh. Royal Scottish Academy, 1842; NG Scot.). Other portraits, such as *Professor John Wilson, 'Christopher North'* (n.d., Scot. NPG) were engraved though apparently not exhibited. From an early date, however, he also exhibited the kind of historical narrative pictures for which he is best remembered. These are principally of subjects taken from the novels of Walter Scott and, in the spirit of Scott, of scenes from Scottish history of the kind that William Allan had begun to paint a few years earlier. Duncan exhibited *Jeanie Deans on her Way to London* (possibly his Royal Scottish Academy diploma work later withdrawn because of its condition; see Rinder, 94) at the Scottish Academy in 1830, for instance, and in 1835 *Mary Queen of Scots Compelled to Sign her Abdication* (priv. coll.), a picture he had begun as early as 1831. The strength of these pictures lies in their subtlety of expression and definition of character, and when in 1836 he exhibited for the first time at the Royal Academy in London, he chose a light-hearted character study from Shakespeare for his début, *Anne Page Inviting Slender to Dinner* (NG Scot.).

In 1828 Duncan's first recorded Edinburgh address was 74 Rose Street. It may have been as a neighbour, therefore, that he met his future wife, Mary (d. 18 Feb 1905), whose father, William Steele, tinplate worker, was also a resident of Rose Street. A portrait of Mary Steele aged seventeen is recorded in the notes for a biography of Duncan prepared in the 1930s by a Perth art teacher, J. Finlayson (NL Scot., MS 9297), but never completed. Her age when this was painted indicates that Mary Steele was still a girl when Duncan first met her. The couple were married on 16 January 1832 and lived first at 1 Darnaway Street, where their first child, Thomas Alexander Duncan, was born on 17 June 1833. Five further children followed, three sons and two daughters. Before his marriage, for a period in 1830 Duncan had been lodging with William Allan at 8 Scotland Street, Edinburgh, and in the following year, 1831, in Allan's absence, he worked as his substitute, teaching at the Trustees' Academy.

On 5 July 1838 Duncan was appointed to a permanent post at the Trustees' Academy as professor of colour, filling the position left vacant by the resignation of William Dyce. The links between the London Scots and Edinburgh were close. William Allan was in regular touch with David Wilkie, for instance, and wrote to him in 1838 about Duncan's work on *Bonnie Prince Charlie Entering Edinburgh*. Allan's advocacy may have helped him achieve recognition in the south. Certainly, his application for this post was supported by testimonials not only from his Edinburgh friends, but also from the two leading Scottish artists in London, Wilkie and David Roberts (*Testimonials in favour of Thomas Duncan, SA: candidate for the office of master of the school of colour*, 1838). Finally in July 1844 he succeeded Allan in the senior position at the Trustees' Academy, the chair of drawing from the antique. For his appointment this position was combined with his previous post of professor of colour. In December 1844 he was additionally appointed to the related position of manager of the Royal Institution galleries. (The galleries were housed in the same building as the Trustees' Academy.) The testimonials he collected on this occasion included not only those of Wilkie and Roberts again, but also that of Andrew Geddes, and attest to the reputation Duncan enjoyed among the Scottish artists in London. Indeed in the previous year, with the same support, he had been elected an associate of the Royal Academy. This certainly also reflected the public success that he enjoyed with his major exhibits at the Royal Academy in London during these years, especially *Bonnie Prince Charlie Entering Edinburgh*, exhibited in 1840 (priv. coll.) and *Prince Charles Edward Stuart Asleep in one of his Hiding Places after Culloden*, exhibited in 1843 (priv. coll.). Both these pictures were purchased for 400 guineas for the purpose of engraving them by D. O. Hill's brother, the publisher Alexander Hill. The success of these engravings contributed greatly to Duncan's popular reputation.

Duncan sympathized with the evangelical party in the Scottish kirk. In 1843 at the Disruption of the kirk he joined the new Free Church and in the same year painted a portrait of Thomas Chalmers, leader of the evangelicals (Scot. NPG). In their opposition to the established church, the members of the Free Church identified themselves with the covenanters. Duncan's best-known picture, the *Martyrdom of John Brown of Priesthill* (exh. RA, 1844; Glasgow Art Gallery) reflects this. In this large picture Brown's murder in front of his family by government troops in 1685 is recounted with sympathy, but without sentimentality.

After a few months of illness which affected his sight, Duncan died of a brain tumour at his home at 3 Gloucester Place, Edinburgh, on 25 April 1845, attended by his family and by his friend D. O. Hill. The 300 mourners at his funeral on 30 April included all the members of the Royal Scottish Academy in procession, testifying to the high regard in which he was held by his fellow artists. His last projects, both left unfinished, were a commission from the marquess of Breadalbane for a large picture recording the visit of Queen Victoria and Prince Albert to Taymouth Castle in September 1842 (sketch, priv. coll.) and a projected major history painting, *George Wishart dispensing the sacrament in the prison of St Andrews Castle on the morning of his execution* (sketch, Perth Museum and Art Gallery). Both in subject and in composition the sketch for the latter reveals a debt to Wilkie's unfinished painting *John Knox Administering the Sacrament at Calder House*, a debt that had shaped Duncan's art generally. The contents of his studio, including a number of paintings and 700 drawings, were sold over three days on 19–21 June 1845. Perth town council bought Duncan's portrait *The Hon. Fox Maule-Ramsay, Member of Parliament for Perth* (exh. Royal Scottish Academy, 1839; Perth Museum and Art Gallery). Shortly before his death his *Self-Portrait* was purchased by his fellow artists and gifted to the Royal Scottish Academy (now NG Scot.). Lady Eastlake admired the picture at the Royal Scottish Academy in 1845 and noted its affinity with Hill's and Adamson's calotype portraits.

DUNCAN MACMILLAN

Sources *Perthshire Advertiser* (1 May 1845) · R. Rodger, *The brightest ornament: Thomas Duncan RSA, ARA* (1995) [exhibition catalogue, Perth Museums and Art Galleries] · W. D. McKay and F. Rinder, *The Royal Scottish Academy, 1826–1916* (1917); repr. (1975) · J. Finlayson, notes on Thomas Duncan, NL Scot., MS 9297 [7 vols.] · *Testimonials in favour of Thomas Duncan, S.A.: candidate for the office of master of the school of colour* (1838) · D. Irwin and F. Irwin, *Scottish painters at home and abroad, 1700–1900* (1975), 213–14 · *Journals and correspondence of Lady Eastlake*, ed. C. E. Smith, 1 (1895), 157–8
Likenesses R. S. Lauder, oils, *c*.1839, Scot. NPG · T. Duncan, self-portrait, 1844, NG Scot. · D. O. Hill & Adamson, calotype portraits, Scot. NPG · D. Macnee, oils, Scot. NPG · P. Port, bust, Royal Scot. Acad. · J. Smyth, line engraving (after T. Duncan), BM; repro. in *Art union* (1847)

Duncan, William (1717–1760), university professor, elder son of William Duncan, an Aberdeen tradesman, and his wife, Euphemia Kirkwood, daughter of a wealthy farmer in Haddingtonshire, was born in Aberdeen in July 1717. He had several sisters and a younger brother, John, who became a merchant and served three times as chief magistrate of Aberdeen. He was sent to the Aberdeen grammar school, and afterwards to Foveran boarding-school under George Forbes. When sixteen he entered Marischal College, Aberdeen, and graduated MA in 1737. Having a dislike for the ministry, for which he was intended, he moved soon after to London. He worked for Robert Dodsley as a translator of French novels, and generously assisted David Watson with his *Works of Horace* (1741). At this time he was close friends with the mathematician George Lewis Scott and the poet John Armstrong.

In 1748 Duncan published *The Elements of Logic*. Its plan, to 'introduce *scientifical* Reasoning into natural Knowledge', was consonant with the Baconian curriculum reforms shortly to be introduced at Aberdeen University by Thomas Blackwell, with whom Duncan had once studied Greek. The work's success led to Duncan's appointment in May 1752 as one of three professors of philosophy at Marischal College. Specializing in experimental and natural philosophy, Duncan lectured alongside Francis Skene and Alexander Gerard. The latter's *Plan of Education in the Marischal College* (1755) proposed that logic was the natural history of human understanding and should therefore be grounded in natural philosophy, an argument which reflects Duncan's earlier ideas.

Alongside his academic commitments, Duncan continued to produce popular translations of the classics. *The Commentaries of Caesar, Translated* (1753) was published in a lavish folio edition, prefixed with 'A discourse concerning the Roman art of war'. *Cicero's Select Orations* (1756) was an annotated parallel-text translation. Both books were still in print during the 1830s.

Duncan, remembered as a man of exemplary morals, became an elder of the church session at Aberdeen. Gerard described him as sociable, though prone to depression. He had in hand both a translation of Plutarch's *Lives* and a continuation of Blackwell's *Court of Augustus* (1753) when he died, unmarried, in Aberdeen on 1 May 1760.

JOHN WESTBY-GIBSON, rev. PATRICK BULLARD

Sources A. Chalmers, ed., *The general biographical dictionary*, new edn, 32 vols. (1812–17) • J. Stark, *Biographia Scotia* (1805) • J. Aikin and others, *General biography, or, Lives, critical and historical of the most eminent persons*, 10 vols. (1799–1815) • P. B. Wood, *The Aberdeen Enlightenment: the arts curriculum in the eighteenth century* (1993) • *Fasti academiae Mariscallanae Aberdonensis: selections from the records of the Marischal College and University, MDXCIII–MDCCCLX*, 2, ed. P. J. Anderson, New Spalding Club, 18 (1898), 45 • A. Gerard, *Plan of education in the Marischal College and University of Aberdeen* (1755) • BL, Egerton MS 738, fol. 9 [pubn agreement between Duncan and Robert Dodsley regarding *Commentaries of Caesar*] • *The correspondence of Robert Dodsley, 1733–1764*, ed. J. E. Tierney (1988), 30–32, 121 • A. Kippis and others, eds., *Biographia Britannica, or, The lives of the most eminent persons who have flourished in Great Britain and Ireland*, 2nd edn, 5 (1793), 500 • *Monthly Review*, 7 (1752), 467–8 • Nichols, *Lit. anecdotes*, 3.268 • J. Sinclair, *Statisical account of Scotland*, 12 (1794), 1191

Duncan, William Augustine (1811–1885), newspaper editor and customs official in Australia, was born on 12 March 1811 at Bluefield, Towie, Aberdeenshire, the son of Peter Duncan and his wife, Mary, *née* Macdougal. He was educated with a view to being ordained in the Church of Scotland. However, he converted to Roman Catholicism during his adolescence. He was accepted as a student at the Scots Benedictine College, Regensburg, and afterwards at the new college at Blairs, Kincardineshire, but having offended the authorities there by too outspoken criticism on a sermon, he withdrew from the college and gave up all thoughts of entering the priesthood. He started a publishing and bookselling business in Aberdeen, out of which he came some five years later rather poorer than when he began. In 1831 he married, in Aberdeen, Mary Yates (or Yeats; *d.* 1880); they had one son, Lewis (1834–1845), and six daughters.

With his business failed, Duncan resorted to teaching and to writing for the press, and was a strong supporter of the Reform Bill of 1832 and of Lord Stanley's Irish education scheme. In 1837 Duncan went out to New South Wales as a Catholic schoolteacher, and soon became involved in religious controversy, defending Catholicism against Anglicanism. In 1839 he was appointed editor of a newly established Roman Catholic journal, the *Australasian Chronicle*, published in Sydney; it strongly opposed the landowning interest. He quarrelled with his fellow Roman Catholics, for he disliked the Irish, and in 1842 was forced from his editorship—Duncan publishing *An Appeal from the Unjust Decision of the … Vicar General* (1843). In 1843 he began his own paper, *Duncan's Weekly Register of Politics, Facts, and General Literature*, in which he encouraged Australian poetry and the integration of Roman Catholics into the community; squatters replaced landowners as his chief political target, and he was associated with the governor, Sir George Gipps, in the land controversy of 1844.

His *Register* was forced to close in 1845 and, despite accusations of jobbery, Duncan was appointed by Gipps sub-collector of customs at Moreton Bay in 1846. For the rest of his time in Australia he held a succession of such posts, initially in Brisbane, eventually becoming collector of customs for New South Wales in January 1859, a post he held until 1881.

Duncan was active in various spheres of Australian public life, including being first president of the School of Arts in Brisbane (1850–54). He became involved in educational disputes—taking a literal Roman Catholic line—and was for thirteen years on the national board of education, and chairman of the free public library in Sydney. In 1856 he published *A Plea for the New South Wales Constitution*, supporting continuation of the nominated legislative council.

Duncan maintained his intellectual interests. He compiled an unpublished history of New South Wales, wrote a memoir of Joseph Monnier (1876), and translated from the Spanish of Pedro Fernandes de Queiros an *Account of a memorial presented to his majesty [Philip III, king of Spain], concerning the population and discovery of the fourth part of the world, Australia the unknown, its great riches and fertility, printed anno 1610* (1874). On retirement in 1881 Duncan was made CMG. He died at his house, The Boulevard, Petersham, New South Wales, on 25 June 1885, and was buried in Devonshire Street cemetery.

GORDON GOODWIN, rev. H. C. G. MATTHEW

Sources *AusDB* • W. A. Duncan, 'Autobiography', Mitchell L., NSW

Duncan, William Henry (1805–1863), physician and medical officer of health, was born in Liverpool on 27 January 1805, the third son and fifth of the seven children of George Duncan, merchant of Liverpool, and his wife, Christian, the youngest daughter of James Currie, minister of Middlebie and of Kirkpatrick Fleming, Dumfriesshire, and a sister of James Currie MD FRS of Liverpool. He was educated under the supervision of his uncle, the Revd Henry *Duncan DD, at Ruthwell manse, his tutors including Robert Mitchell. From 1825 to 1829 he studied at Edinburgh University. He graduated MD in 1829; the dedicatees of his thesis, 'De ventris in reliquum corpus potestate' ('On the influence of the abdomen over the body in general'), included professors William P. Alison and James Home.

By 1830 Duncan was in medical practice in Liverpool, also serving as a physician at the Central and North dispensaries. His published analysis of the cholera cases he attended during the 1832 epidemic drew attention to the correlations between disease and environment (in particular the habitations, principally in cellars and courts, of the poor). In 1804 Currie had also written on the relationship between health and environment in Liverpool. Duncan submitted evidence to the inquiry into the corporation of Liverpool (1833), the commission on the condition of the poor in Ireland (1836 report), and the House of Commons' select committee on the health of towns (1840), detailing the deplorable 'sanitary state of the labouring classes' in Liverpool, whose population was rapidly increasing, principally by migration from Ireland and elsewhere. His paper 'On the physical causes of the high rate of mortality in Liverpool' (1843) was particularly influential; Liverpool he declared to be 'the most unhealthy town in England'. He was a prominent member of the Liverpool branch of the Health of Towns Association, established in 1845.

It was largely due to Duncan's efforts that the corporation of Liverpool promoted the Liverpool Sanitary Act 1846, which established a public health service as an essential activity of local government. Under the act Duncan was appointed medical officer of health for the borough of Liverpool, from 1 January 1847. The first such appointment in England, initially part-time, the post became full-time in 1848 at an annual salary of £750.

A most conscientious man, of generally a quiet and retiring disposition, Duncan, as a pioneer in sanitary reform, faced opposition but robustly defended his actions and publications against criticism. He enjoyed a good relationship with the corporation and particularly with its able engineer, James Newlands. However, he encountered difficulties with the select vestry (responsible for poor-law institutions), particularly during the years when epidemics of typhus (1847) and cholera (1849, 1854) ravaged the town. To his influence and actions may be attributed a significant reduction in the population living in cellars and other 'unhealthy dwellings', and a general improvement in environmental hygiene. He established methods of work, and initiated courses of improvement under which, by 1890, the average general death rate of Liverpool was declared by Sir John Simon to have been reduced by 'probably at least a fourth part' of the rate which prevailed when Duncan had become medical officer of health.

Duncan was a physician at Liverpool's Northern Hospital from 1837 to 1838 and at Liverpool Infirmary from 1843 to 1848. He lectured at the Liverpool Royal Institution school of medicine and surgery (from 1844 the Liverpool Infirmary medical school) from 1835 to 1848, and was the school's secretary in 1844–5. He helped to establish the Liverpool Medical Society (of which he was secretary from 1833 and president from 1836 to 1838) and also the Liverpool Medical Institution (in 1840 he became its first secretary). He was an active member of the Literary and Philosophical Society of Liverpool from 1837 onwards and served as its treasurer.

Duncan was twice married: in 1848 to Philadelphia (d. 1850), eldest daughter of James Rickarby, merchant, of Liverpool; and secondly, in 1853, to Catherine (d. 1909), daughter of William Duncan MacAndrew, merchant, of Liverpool. He and his second wife had a son and a daughter. Duncan, whose health had been failing for several years, died in West Park, Elgin, on 23 May 1863.

ADRIAN R. ALLAN, rev.

Sources W. M. Frazer, *Duncan of Liverpool* (1947) • P. Laxton, 'Fighting for public health: Dr Duncan and his adversaries, 1847–1863', *Body and city: histories of urban public health*, ed. S. Sheard and H. Power (2000), 59–88 • E. Kearns, 'Town hall and Whitehall: sanitary intelligence in Liverpool, 1840–63', *Body and city: histories of urban public health*, ed. S. Sheard and H. Power (2000), 89–108 • E. Midwinter, *Old Liverpool* (1971) • medical officer of health for Liverpool, reports, 1847–63 • medical officer of health for Liverpool, letter books, 1849–63 • private information (1993)

Likenesses I. C. Ferranti, portrait, 1864, repro. in Frazer, *Duncan of Liverpool* (1947); photograph of the portrait held by Museum of Liverpool Life, Pier Head, Liverpool

Wealth at death under £3000: probate, 7 Sept 1863, *CGPLA Eng. & Wales*

Duncannon. For this title name *see* Ponsonby, William, first Viscount Duncannon (1658/9–1724) [*see under* Ponsonby, Henry (d. 1745)].

Duncan-Sandys. For this title name *see* Sandys, (Edwin) Duncan, Baron Duncan-Sandys (1908–1987).

Duncanson, Robert (d. 1705), army officer, was of a branch of the Duncanson family of Fossachie, Stirlingshire, which had settled at Inveraray, Argyllshire. His father, the Revd John Duncanson MA (c.1630–1687), was minister of Kilmartin, Argyllshire, from 1655 until deprived for presbyterianism in 1662. Robert, the younger son, was one of four children of his first marriage, in 1656, to Beatrix, daughter of Dugald Oig Campbell of Stronchormaig (a second produced at least one more daughter). John Duncanson became an indulged minister in the parish of Kilbrandon and Kilchattan, Argyllshire, from 1670 until deprived again in 1684. Robert Duncanson in Degnish (within the parish) joined the ninth earl of Argyll's rising in 1685. Captain Duncanson, after bold exploits, was, as the rising finally collapsed, one of the last four men accompanying Argyll, who sent him back with Sir Duncan Campbell of Auchinbreck to attempt to raise new levies in Argyllshire. He evidently escaped to the Netherlands and returned with William III. On 28 February 1689 he was commissioned lieutenant, and on 24 September captain-lieutenant, in Beveridge's English regiment, which was sent to Scotland after Killiecrankie. During 1690 he transferred to the tenth earl of Argyll's Highland regiment, and by early 1691 was its major and was commanding it on active service.

At the end of 1691 Duncanson marched 400 men from the regiment through Argyllshire to Fort William for an intended winter campaign against the Jacobite clans. *En route* they quartered peaceably overnight in Glencoe. At Fort William the clans were submitting, and the regiment lay, again peaceably, among the Keppoch Macdonalds. In late January Lieutenant-Colonel James Hamilton, of Colonel John *Hill's garrison regiment, planned the massacre at Glencoe with Duncanson. They followed official orders, but added on their own initiative its most outrageous feature, the quartering in the glen for twelve days beforehand of two companies of Argyll's regiment, who then slaughtered their hosts. Duncanson evidently selected their commander, the feckless Captain Robert Campbell of Glenlyon, whom he left in ignorance of the plan. On 12 February Duncanson was at Ballachulish, near Glencoe, with the rest of Argyll's regiment. Hamilton extorted from Hill a command to proceed, and prepared to march with a detachment. He wrote ordering Duncanson to attack Glencoe with his force next morning at 7 a.m. (by which time he hoped to join him), taking no prisoners and killing all males younger than seventy, particularly the chief, Alexander *Macdonald, 'the old fox', and his sons. Duncanson repeated these savage commands in his order, sent that night, to Glenlyon, whom he frightened into obeying by threats of cashiering or worse. He advanced the time significantly:

> This you are to putt in execution att fyve of the clock precisely; and by that time, or verie shortly after it, I'le strive to be att you with a stronger party: if I doe not come to you att fyve, you are not to tary for me, butt to fall on. (Original order, NL Scot. MS Adv. 23.6.24)

As Duncanson did not, like Hamilton, have a long night march through blizzards to delay him, he evidently wished, from whatever motives, to avoid personal involvement. By the time his force reached the glen, almost all the surviving inhabitants had fled, though one captain killed a sick man and his infant son.

From 1693 Argyll's regiment fought in William III's Flanders campaigns; Argyll's son Lord Lorne was colonel from 1694. In 1695 the regiment was in the garrison of Dixmude near Ostend. Two days into a siege the Danish commander called a council of war to endorse immediate surrender as prisoners of war. Duncanson, although the youngest member, protested that this was premature and dishonourable, and refused to sign the capitulation upon which nine regiments surrendered on 18 July. This earned him a lieutenant-colonel's commission, dated 22 August. The regiment's capture enabled William to avoid responding to the Scottish parliament's address of 10 July upon the report on Glencoe, requesting that Duncanson should either be interrogated in Flanders regarding his knowledge and the orders he gave, or sent home for trial along with the actual killers. That December Argyll presented him to William. However, Duncanson was imprisoned for debt at Edinburgh for several years as liable for the regiment's new uniforms lost at the surrender, until the English Treasury paid for them. Meanwhile, Lorne's regiment was disbanded in 1698.

As war approached again, Duncanson became lieutenant-colonel of the earl of Huntingdon's new foot regiment (the 33rd, later the Duke of Wellington's) on 22 February 1702. On 1 March 1703 he received a brevet colonelcy as the actual commander. The regiment served in Portugal. He was promoted colonel on 12 February 1705, but fell at the allied siege of Valencia de Alcántara on the following 8 May.   PAUL HOPKINS

Sources P. A. Hopkins, *Glencoe and the end of the highland war* (1986); rev. edn (1998) · J. Gordon, ed., *Papers illustrative of the political condition of the highlands of Scotland, 1689–1696* (1845) · R. M. Holden, 'The first highland regiment: the Argyllshire highlanders', *SHR*, 3 (1905–6), 27–40 · J. Prebble, *Glencoe: the story of the massacre* (1966) · 'Information of the murder of the Glenco men 1692', Blair Castle, Duke of Atholl's MSS, box 43/VI/15 · *Fasti Scot.*, new edn · R. Wodrow, *The history of the sufferings of the Church of Scotland from the Restoration to the revolution*, ed. R. Burns, 4 vols. (1828–30) · C. Dalton, ed., *English army lists and commission registers, 1661–1714*, 6 vols. (1892–1904) · E. D'Auvergne, *The history of the campagne in Flanders, for the year 1695. With an account of the siege of Namur* (1696) · unsigned notes, *N&Q*, 2nd ser., 8 (1859), 109, 193, 253 · unsigned notes, *N&Q*, 3rd ser., 7 (1865), 96–7 · W. A. Shaw, ed., *Calendar of treasury books*, 15, PRO (1933) · J. Redington, ed., *Calendar of Treasury papers*, 2, PRO (1871) · D. C. MacTavish, ed., *The commons of Argyll: name-lists of 1685 and 1692* (1935)

Dunch, Edmund (1677–1719), politician, was descended from an ancient family long resident at Little Wittenham, Berkshire. He was born on 14 December 1677 in Little Jermyn Street, London, and baptized on the following new year's day at St Martin-in-the-Fields. He was the only son of Hungerford Dunch MP (1639–1680), of Little Wittenham and Down Ampney, and Catherine Oxton (1660/61–1697), daughter of William Oxton, brewer, of Westminster and Hertfordshire. On 2 May 1702 Dunch married Elizabeth Godfrey (1683–1761). She was the younger daughter and coheir of Charles Godfrey MP, successively master of the jewel house (1698–1704) and clerk of the green cloth (1704–15), and Arabella *Churchill, daughter of Sir Winston Churchill MP, sister of John Churchill, first duke of Marlborough, and sometime mistress of James II. Elizabeth Dunch was a great beauty and a Kit-Cat toast, but the marriage was not, apparently, a happy one: according to Philip Lempriere 'Dunch had a lewd, handsome wife who lived many years with other persons', James Craggs the younger in particular (Piper, 117).

The connection established between Dunch and the court circle of the Churchills, combined with Dunch's adherence to the whigs in parliament, eventually led to his political advancement. As early as 1702 there were rumours that he would be created a peer. By 1704 he was being spoken of to succeed his father-in-law as master of the jewel house. It was not, however, until 16 November 1708 that he was appointed master of the household. In addition, he was said to have been granted £1000 per annum on the Post Office revenue during the queen's life, but there is no evidence that this was confirmed.

The politics of the Dunch family had been republican during the civil war: the subject's grandfather, Sir Edmund Dunch MP (*d.* 1678), was a kinsman of and ennobled by Oliver Cromwell. In 1701 Edmund Dunch ran on the interest of his Gloucester estate to secure the representation of Cricklade. He served for Cricklade from February 1701 to July 1702. Defeated in 1702, he was returned for Cricklade again from May 1705 to August 1713, then served for Boroughbridge from November 1713 to January 1715, and for Wallingford from the latter date until his death. As a parliamentarian he was an infrequent committeeman, serving on an average of but one per session under Anne. Politically he was, from the first, labelled a whig. Indeed, he tended to vote consistently along party lines whether in office or out. Specifically, he voted for John Smith as speaker in 1705; for the naturalization of the Poor Palatines in 1709; against Henry Sacheverell in 1710; for No Peace Without Spain in 1711; against the French commercial treaty in 1713; and against the expulsion of Richard Steele in 1714. This voting record cost him his mastership of the household in June 1712, but he was reappointed upon the accession of George I. Thereafter, he voted with the government until his death.

Edmund Dunch was a man about town. He was a member of the Kit-Cat Club, and had a reputation for wit and, prior to his marriage, for being something of a ladies' man. According to Hearne, he was also 'a very great gamester', having been 'drawn into gaming purely to please his Lady' (*Remarks*, 7.17). The effect upon his estate was, apparently, deleterious. That estate consisted of lands in Sussex worth £6000 and in Buckinghamshire worth £4000, as well as those at Little Wittenham and Down Ampney. Thomas Pelham-Holles, the future duke of Newcastle, gave out a figure of £4000 when he recommended Dunch to the electors of Boroughbridge in 1713 as 'a true Whig, and a very honest, civil, well-bred, and good-natured gentleman' (T. Lawson-Tancred, *Records of a Yorkshire Manor*, 1937, 249, 255).

Dunch died on 31 May 1719 at Little Wittenham, and was buried at the church there on 4 June. Though he was said to have left a very good estate at Little Wittenham, Down Ampney had to be sold to pay off a gambling debt of £26,000. Edmund and Elizabeth had four daughters: Elizabeth, Harriet, Catherine, and Arabella. The younger Elizabeth married Sir George Oxendon of Dean, Wingham, Kent, baronet and MP for Sandwich. Harriet married Robert, third duke of Manchester, privy councillor, lord lieutenant, and *custos rotulorum* of Huntingdon. Catherine died young and unmarried. Arabella married Edmund Thompson MP, of Marston, York.   R. O. BUCHOLZ

Henry Dunckley (1823–1896), by Alfred Edward Emslie, 1889

Sources HoP, *Commons, 1715–54* · G. S. Holmes, *British politics in the age of Anne* (1967) · M. Noble, *Memoirs of the protectorate-house of Cromwell*, 2 vols. (1784), vol. 2, pp. 196–203 · HoP, *Commons, 1690–1715* [draft] · *Remarks and collections of Thomas Hearne*, ed. C. E. Doble and others, 7, OHS, 48 (1906), 17 · 'Pedigree of Dunch of Little Wittenham, Berks.', *Miscellanea Genealogica et Heraldica*, 3rd ser., 2 (1896–7), 43–8 · D. Piper, *Catalogue of seventeenth-century portraits in the National Portrait Gallery, 1625–1714* (1963), 116–17

Likenesses G. Kneller, oils, *c.*1700 (Kit-Cat Club), NPG · J. Faber junior, mezzotint, 1733 (after G. Kneller), BM, NPG

Dúnchad mac Cind Fháelad (d. **717**). *See under* Iona, abbots of (*act.* 563–927).

Dunckley, Henry (1823–1896), journalist, was born in Warwick on 24 December 1823, the son of James Dunckley. Intending to become a minister, he went to the Baptist college at Accrington, Lancashire, and then, in 1846, with financial assistance from the Dr Ward Trust, to the University of Glasgow, where he graduated BA in 1847 and MA in 1848. In 1848 he became minister of the Baptist church at Great George Street, Salford, and on 7 October of the same year he married Elizabeth Arthur, the daughter of Thomas Wood of Coventry; they had several children, of whom two sons and three daughters survived him.

Dunckley soon began to help to publicize for the Lancashire Public School Association, and to look into the needs and conditions of the working classes. When the Religious Tract Society invited essays on this subject he submitted one which was awarded a first prize of £100 and published in 1851 as *The glory and the shame of Britain: an essay on the condition and claims of the working classes, together*

with the means of securing elevation. In 1852 the Anti-Corn Law League offered prizes for essays showing the results of the repeal of the corn-law and the free-trade policy, and Dunckley gained the first prize of £250 for his 'Charter of the nations, or, Free trade and its results'. After its publication in 1854 it attracted wide attention. A Dutch translation by P. P. van Bosse was printed at Hoogesand in 1856.

In 1854 Dunckley began to write for the *Manchester Examiner and Times*, a leading Liberal newspaper of the day, and in 1855, under pressure from his congregation to make a choice, relinquished his ministerial position to become editor, succeeding Abraham Walter Paulton. He continued in office until 25 January 1889, when the paper was transferred to new proprietors and its policy changed. His powerful leading articles greatly increased the influence of the paper and his own reputation, and he received several invitations to join the staff of London newspapers, including *The Times*, which, however, he declined. Haslam Mills, in his centenary history of the *Manchester Guardian* (1921), endorsed the general assessment of Dunckley's cogent writing, but commented:

> It is just possible that as an editor he was a little too sedentary even for the quiet days in which his lot was cast. People who remember him in his office speak of his velvet jacket and cigar, and the sanctity of his meditations. ... a housekeeper in a black alpaca used to go about at ten at night administering tea to the stylists and the thinkers.

The same sources said that the *Examiner* missed the Tay Bridge disaster in 1879 because soon after the first news arrived the sub-editors all went home in a cab: 'The editor thought the excuse not an unreasonable one, seeing that it had certainly been snowing hard'.

In 1877 Dunckley began a series of letters on current affairs in the *Manchester Weekly Times*, an offshoot of the *Examiner*, under the pseudonym Verax. Among these letters were five entitled 'The crown and the cabinet', inspired by certain doctrines set forth in Sir Theodore Martin's *Life of the Prince Consort* which seemed to him incompatible with the English constitution. A caustic criticism of the letters appeared in the *Quarterly Review* for April 1878, and Dunckley replied in seven letters entitled 'The crown and the constitution'. His exposition of the rights and functions of government ministers gave great satisfaction to his friends and political associates who, on 15 January 1879, gave him a complimentary banquet at the Manchester Reform Club. At the same time he was presented with 300 volumes of books and 81 pieces of silver. The Verax letters were continued in the *Weekly Times* until 1888, and afterwards in the *Manchester Guardian*. A selection of the earliest letters was reprinted in a volume in 1878. Others, entitled 'Our hereditary legislators', were issued separately in 1882, and those on capital punishment appeared in 1884. In 1890 he wrote a biography of Lord Melbourne for the series The Queen's Prime Ministers and in 1893 edited Bamford's *Passages in the Life of a Radical and Early Days*. He contributed several political articles to the *Contemporary Review* (1889 and 1891) and *Cosmopolis* (1896), and six articles on the English constitution, the South Sea Bubble, stock exchanges, privileged classes, and nationalization of railways in the *Co-Operative Wholesale Society's Annual* (1891–5).

In 1878 Dunckley was elected a member of the London Reform Club in recognition of services rendered to the Liberal Party. In 1883 the University of Glasgow conferred on him the honorary degree of LLD, and in 1886 he became a commissioner of the peace for Manchester. A further mark of esteem was the presentation to his wife of his portrait, painted by Emslie, in February 1889. Dunckley died suddenly on 29 June 1896 while travelling from his home at 9 Egerton Road, Fallowfield, Manchester, in a tram. His body was cremated at the Manchester crematorium, Withington, on 2 July.

C. W. SUTTON, rev. GEOFFREY TAYLOR

Sources *Men and women of the time* (1895) · *Manchester Guardian* (30 June 1896) · *Manchester City News* (4 July 1898) · W. H. Mills, *The Manchester Guardian: a century of history* (1921) · *Biograph and Review*, 2 (1879), 83–9 · 'Verax testimonial: address delivered to Mr Dunckley, and his speech in reply, 14 Jan 1879' (privately printed, Manchester, 1879) · private information (1901)

Likenesses A. E. Emslie, oils, 1889, Manchester City Art Gallery [*see illus.*] · portrait, repro. in *ILN* (1896)

Wealth at death £6793 18s. 3d.: probate, 28 July 1896, *CGPLA Eng. & Wales*

Duncombe, Sir Charles (*bap.* 1648, *d.* 1711), financier, baptized on 16 November 1648 at Drayton, Buckinghamshire, was the second son of (Alexander) Sanders Duncombe, a Buckinghamshire yeoman. He had two brothers and a sister. Possibly because his father was steward to a local landowner, whose daughter married the eldest son of Edward

Sir Charles Duncombe (*bap.* 1648, *d.* 1711), by Charles Beale

*Backwell, Duncombe was apprenticed to this leading figure among the goldsmith–bankers in 1665.

Rise to wealth From an early stage Duncombe proved to be no ordinary apprentice. By 1666 he was acting as Backwell's cashier and principal assistant; by about 1670 he was himself a tax receiver for the three counties of Bedfordshire, Buckinghamshire, and Huntingdonshire, probably thanks to the patronage of a fairly remote relative, Sir John Duncombe, a native of Bedfordshire (Treasury commissioner from 1667 to 1672, and chancellor of the exchequer from 1672 to 1676). Duncombe's apprenticeship ended in the summer of 1672, when he was admitted to the freedom of the Goldsmiths' Company; so far as can be seen, he was never a practising goldsmith or silversmith. Following the notorious 'Stop' of the exchequer in January 1672 and Backwell's financial embarrassment arising therefrom, Duncombe in effect succeeded to his master's banking business. Whether any of Backwell's funds were secretly transferred to Duncombe's name, in order to escape the former's creditors, cannot be demonstrated, but is not impossible. The received explanation for Duncombe's sudden rise to wealth is that he was already banker to Lord Ashley, later earl of Shaftesbury, and that the latter warned him in advance of the forthcoming stop, thus enabling Duncombe to withdraw his funds from the exchequer and to tip off another of his clients, Charles Paulet, Lord St John, later duke of Bolton, who was thereby able to avoid losing £30,000, and whose lasting gratitude was expressed by his casting vote against Duncombe's impeachment for malversation of public funds a quarter of a century later.

Unfortunately the sole source for these details appears to be the annotations made by William Legge, the first earl of Dartmouth, to Gilbert Burnet's *History*, but Legge was born only in 1672. Moreover, there is no other evidence of Duncombe as Shaftesbury's banker, and his own future party allegiance was tory rather than whig. It is at least possible that Bolton or Dartmouth or both confused the two Duncombes in their recollections. Sir John, like Lord Ashley, was unhappy about the Stop and would have known that it was impending. The notes of the then secretary of the Treasury, Sir Robert Howard, include an entry for 19 December 1671: 'Sir John Duncombe commanded me to carry Lord St John's sign manual to Lord Ashley to read tonight for signing tomorrow'; and on 20 December an order was passed to secure, on the hearth tax, the large advance which St John and his partners had made as prospective customs farmers, before their intended lease was aborted at the beginning of October 1671 and the customs transferred to direct management by salaried commissioners (*Calendar of Treasury Books*, 3.1002). The notion that either Charles Duncombe or Lord St John could have made large withdrawals of money shows a misunderstanding both of exchequer procedure and of the stop itself. This seems pardonable in the case of Lord Dartmouth, writing in the early eighteenth century, but less so for all those historians who have subsequently accepted his story.

Credit financier Since none of Duncombe's ledgers or account books and very few of his other banking records are known to have survived, it is hard to assess the scale of his business. He may always have been more important as a credit financier and receiving official for the crown than as a banker for private individuals. By the later 1670s he and his principal partner, Richard Kent, not himself a goldsmith but a dependant of the great Sir Stephen Fox, had become large-scale operators in this capacity; Duncombe had already been acting with William Bartlett, son of a Cromwellian official and also a former apprentice of Edward Backwell, in making advances to the excise commissioners on the security of their forthcoming rent due from the farmers of that revenue, of whom Duncombe was one; this had led to a dispute with the commissioners in 1675–6. After that it was Kent and Duncombe who made the advances jointly. Their position was strengthened by Kent's appointment as receiver- and cashier-general of the customs in 1677, and a similar post was created for Duncombe at the excise in 1680. Loans of £50,000 and £70,000 are recorded in 1677–8; the fact that the Treasury opened a separate 'interest' account for them would seem to indicate that their advances were almost assuming the character of a long-term funded debt on the crown's part. The total of what they were owed peaked at over £236,000 in June 1681, and again at £235,000 at the end of 1684. This was a massive sum, equivalent to almost one-fifth of the crown's annual income; yet it was significantly less than the total advances of Sir Robert Vyner at the time of the Stop, and more or less comparable to what Backwell was then owed. However, by April 1687 the Kent–Duncombe debt was reduced to a mere £105,000—a tribute to prudent Treasury management and buoyant royal revenues. At its height the amount owing on the interest account had been £4,000, and this too was reduced to a few hundred pounds.

In 1680 Duncombe became one of three commissioners in charge of the Royal Mint, following the discovery of malpractices by the then master, Henry Slingsby, who was suspended from office but on full pay. By contrast his tenure as one of the six clerks in chancery was so brief (for nine and a half months in 1682–3) that it can only have been intended as an investment, though his partner Kent, who preceded him in the post, held it for only two and a half weeks. In 1684 Duncombe was appointed treasurer and cashier-general of the hearth tax (often known as the 'chimney money'), which was then being managed by the same body of commissioners as the excise, which had followed the customs out of farm into direct management in 1683. Although there is evidence of periodic tension, which could hardly have been avoided, Duncombe's overall position was surprisingly little affected by successive political changes from the time of the Popish Plot to the eve of the Revolution.

According to a newsletter writer in July 1687 Duncombe and the merchant and financier Sir John Banks both sold their entire holdings in the East India Company, on a scale sufficient to trade down the value of the company's shares; either they both judged the company was becoming overextended, or they may have foreseen the coming crisis at home and wanted to have their assets as liquid as possible (despite the fact that, until the pregnancy of James II's queen was known at the end of that year, there was no reason to expect an immediate denouement). During the critical months of 1688–9 Duncombe made two calculated moves where politics would seem to have overridden or at least dictated finance: he refused an immediate request for cash from James II following the Orangist invasion; but he joined Banks in advancing money to William III shortly after his accession, though not on the scale of his earlier loans.

Land dealings Meanwhile Duncombe's interests and investments had indeed been changing. Although he never married, Duncombe set about establishing landed estates for his nephews much as if they had been his own sons. He had property in the City and at Teddington in Middlesex, and he had acquired what became his main country seat at Barford, near Downton, in Wiltshire. The latter property was settled on the son of his elder brother, Anthony; this nephew, also Anthony, was created Lord Feversham, but in spite of three marriages he left no legitimate male heir. The third and youngest brother, Valentine, was apprenticed to Charles Duncombe and became a partner in the banking business, but died in 1689 leaving no issue. Their sister, Ursula, was married to Thomas Browne of London, gentleman, also a financier, who became the hearth-tax receiver for Buckinghamshire and Oxfordshire from 1669 to 1670, having had an account with Sir Robert Vyner as early as 1666 (as, coincidentally, had Richard Kent). Their children, Thomas and Mary Browne, were to inherit a large part of their uncle's wealth.

In 1695 Duncombe took one of the most dramatic steps in his career. For £86,000 (magnified by gossip and family tradition to £90,000), he bought out the great scrivener-banker Sir Robert Clayton, along with Thomas Sprat, bishop of Rochester, the executors and residuary mortgagees of the second duke of Buckingham's north Yorkshire estates, to become the owner of Helmsley and a large area to the west. Thomas Browne junior's inheritance of this property was made conditional on his taking his mother's and his uncle's surname, Duncombe; and it was he who undertook the building of Duncombe Park, near Helmsley, a house which, though it did not rival Castle Howard or Blenheim Palace in size and grandeur, was nevertheless high in the next bracket. Although Thomas Browne, alias Duncombe, was outlived by his first cousin Anthony, it was his descendants who inherited the Wiltshire as well as the Yorkshire estates and, eventually, the revived Feversham title. His sister Mary was sufficiently well-endowed to be married to John Campbell, Lord Lorne, who became the second duke of Argyll, another illustration of social fluidity, but resulting in a most unhappy match.

Duncombe is said to have ceased to act as a banker after 1688, though his name was still associated with the 'grasshopper' until 1695, and the earliest receipts of Martin's Bank still included some with his signature in the early 1700s. Whatever the case, Duncombe certainly remained active in the field of public finance. Another story, told by the indefatigable and usually reliable newshound Narcissus Luttrell, is that Duncombe sold his entire holding in the newly formed Bank of England, supposedly in order to buy the Villiers estate. Although there is independent evidence of his hostility to the new institution, perhaps on political grounds, modern historians of the bank have found no evidence that he ever held shares in it, unless in the names of other people.

Accusations of corruption It was probably party politics which led to Duncombe's being charged with corrupt practices by the whig-dominated House of Commons in 1698. Duncombe admitted having bought £10,000 worth of Treasury bills at a discount, and then having had them cashed at full face value in the exchequer. This was not improper, still less a serious crime, by the standards of the day; moreover, the sum involved seems trivial for someone of his wealth. However, he was found technically guilty of entering forged endorsements on the bills in question, rather than for the profit he had made. The Commons proceeded against him by a bill of pains and penalties (which would have deprived him of two-thirds of his estate and disqualified him perpetually from holding office), not by an impeachment as that term is properly understood. The Lords finally rejected this by one vote, including that of his old patron, Thomas Osborne, now first duke of Leeds, as well as that of Charles Paulet, now first duke of Bolton, and the Commons simply voted for his re-arrest and committal to the Tower, where he remained for another three months. He was then brought to trial in king's bench, where he was acquitted once on a technicality and summarily at a second trial. Formal expression of royal approval, to clear his name, took another two years; even so he became sheriff of London and was knighted on 20 October 1699, his position seeming to fluctuate with what came to be called 'the rage of party'. Duncombe never regained the prominence as a credit financier of the crown which he had held in the 1680s, though he and a group of prospective partners did offer King William an attractive package as an alternative to royal dependence on the bank.

Parallel with this involvement in high finance, Duncombe continued to pursue an active career in the City and as an MP, latterly with a controlling electoral interest in the borough of Downton. He was not particularly notable as an MP, though he sat in most of the parliaments from 1685 to the end of his life. From 1685 to 1687 he was MP for Hedon, Yorkshire. He represented Yarmouth (Isle of Wight) in the Commons from 1690 to 1695. He was MP for Downton from October 1695 until he was expelled from the House of Commons in 1698, and again from 1702 to the year of his death. He contested the seat of the City of London, without success, in 1700, 1701, and 1702.

Final years and significance Duncombe agreed to pay to have his portrait painted for the Goldsmiths' Company, of which he was prime warden in 1684, but this never seems to have been carried out. There are two portraits (in oils) at Duncombe Park, one of a slightly effeminate-looking young man, the other of a portly and aldermanic gentleman. The summit of Duncombe's ambitions was probably his election as lord mayor of London in 1708. He left no will, presumably by design, his main assets having already been settled. His sister was awarded the administration of his estate, provision also having been made for their mother, who lived to the age of about ninety-six. This longevity was not, however, transmitted to her immediate descendants, Duncombe himself dying at the age of about sixty-two; even the redoubtable Ursula only attained seventy-one years of age.

There are a number of unresolved issues in the story of Charles Duncombe's career. They include the reliability or otherwise of the facts about him and the Stop of the exchequer, and the later significance of this. His reported or alleged sale of shares in the East India Company and later in the bank is also significant, as this may have affected his capital resources in the late 1680s and the 1690s. The other two principal enigmas are the reasons for his trial by the House of Commons and for his acquittal by the Lords; and, more personally, why he never married. Malicious rumour credited him with several young mistresses; gossip put his total fortune at £400,000. Whatever the answers to these questions, the main importance of his career, besides exemplifying upward economic and social mobility, lies in the history of royal-cum-public finance. Duncombe's role in the late 1670s and the 1680s undoubtedly served the fiscal interests of the English state and strengthened the monarchy as it was inherited by James from Charles II. Duncombe died on 9 April 1711 at Teddington, Middlesex. Although his place of burial is unknown, a funeral monument of him was erected at Downton church, Wiltshire.   G. E. AYLMER

Sources LUL, Goldsmiths' Company of London [incl. small Duncombe collection] · N. Yorks. CRO, Duncombe Park papers, ZEW · BL, Blathwayt MSS, Add. MS 38714, fol. 64 · W. A. Shaw, ed., *Calendar of treasury books*, 3–25, PRO (1908–61) · *CSP dom.*, 1670–1700 · *Burnet's History of my own time*, ed. O. Airy, new edn, 1 (1897), 550, n. 3 · *Report on the manuscripts of the marquis of Downshire*, 6 vols. in 7, HMC, 75 (1924–95), vol. 1, pt 1, p. 253 · N. Luttrell, *A brief historical relation of state affairs from September 1678 to April 1714*, 3 (1857), 513 · P. Duncombe, *Great goldsmith: the life of Sir Charles Duncombe* (2002) · J. Clapham, *The Bank of England: a history*, 1 (1944) · D. C. Coleman, *Sir John Banks, baronet and businessman* (1963) · A. Heal, ed., *The London* *goldsmiths, 1200–1800: a record of the names and addresses of the crafts-men, their shop-signs and trade-cards* (1935) · F. G. Hilton Price, *A hand-book of London bankers*, enl. edn (1890–91) · P. Watson, 'Duncombe, Charles', HoP, *Commons* · HoP, *Commons* [draft] · H. Horwitz, *Parliament, policy and politics in the reign of William III* (1977) · J. B. Martin, *"The Grasshopper" in Lombard Street* (1892) · G. O. Nichols, 'Intermediaries and the development of English government borrowing: the case of Sir John James and Major Robert Huntington, 1675–79', *Business History*, 29 (1987), 27–46 · R. D. Richards, *The early history of banking in England* (1929) · J. E. T. Rogers, *The first nine years of the Bank of England* (1887) · *VCH Wiltshire*, vol. 11 · G. Matcham and R. C. Hoare, *The history of modern Wiltshire*, 3/4: *Hundred of Downton* (1834) · GEC, *Peerage*, new edn · J. R. Woodhead, *The rulers of London, 1660–1689* (1965) · C. Saunders, *Downton's richest family* (1992)

Archives N. Yorks. CRO, family papers · N. Yorks. CRO, family deeds and papers; proceedings against subject in House of Commons

Likenesses C. Beale, miniature, priv. coll. [*see illus.*] · two portraits, oils, Duncombe Park, Yorkshire

Wealth at death very wealthy; approx. £400,000 in cash and property

Duncombe, Sir John (*bap.* 1622, *d.* 1687), politician and government official, was baptized on 20 July 1622 in Battlesden, Bedfordshire, the second but eldest surviving son of William Duncombe (*d.* 1655) of Battlesden, landowner, and his wife, Elizabeth, daughter of Sir John Poyntz of South Ockenden, Essex. Educated at Eton College, from about 1634 to 1638, he was briefly enrolled at Christ's College, Cambridge, in 1638, but between 1641 and 1646 was abroad, registering at Leiden University in 1643. On his return he faced a conflict of loyalties. His father actively supported the parliamentarian cause in the English civil war but John Duncombe's sympathies were royalist and his marriage, on 12 July 1646, to Elizabeth, daughter of a former chancellor of the duchy of Lancaster, Sir Humphrey *May, allied him to one of the Stuarts' most loyal families of servants. In 1648 a knighthood was conferred upon Duncombe and in 1655, upon his father's death, he succeeded to his Bedfordshire estates.

Duncombe entered parliament in 1660 as member for Bury St Edmunds, which he represented until 1678. Active in committees and a frequent speaker he was given office as a commissioner of the Ordnance office in May 1664. The appointment, held until 1670, associated him with an energetic department and Duncombe here acquired a modest reputation for administrative skills. However, in May 1667 the political world was surprised by Duncombe's selection as member of a powerful Treasury commission and elevation to the privy council. Eclipsed by more dynamic colleagues, such as Anthony Ashley Cooper (first Baron Ashley and later first earl of Shaftesbury), Sir Thomas Clifford (later first Baron Clifford of Chudleigh), and Sir William Coventry, Duncombe was nevertheless recognized by Samuel Pepys as a painstaking, if pompous, public servant of the kind he could respect. His personal weaknesses and his deference to Sir William Coventry were satirized by George Villiers, second duke of Buckingham, in a play, *The Country Gentleman* (1669), but unlike Coventry he survived the humiliation and continued to serve Charles II as a ministerial spokesman on financial legislation.

In November 1672 Duncombe succeeded Lord Ashley as chancellor of the exchequer. This was still a minor office with little independent authority, and Duncombe continued to play second fiddle to the successive lords treasurer with whom he served. It was a role to which he seemed well suited, for he displayed little originality of mind and almost no strong convictions—except in defence of the Church of England. On the key religious policies of this first age of half tolerated dissent Duncombe took a consistently conservative stance, sharing Anglican prejudices against nonconformists and Roman Catholics alike. He helped to frame much of the persecuting legislation of the reign, such as the Conventicle Acts of 1664 and 1670. However, it was on financial policies that he chose to oppose his senior colleague, the lord treasurer, Thomas Osborne, first earl of Danby, and in May 1676 he was dismissed, losing his pension in 1678 and his place in the council in 1679. He died in Battlesden on 4 March 1687 and was succeeded in his estates by his son William (*c.*1647–1704) whose undistinguished career in parliament and administration was a paler shadow of his own. There were six other children.   H. G. ROSEVEARE, *rev.*

Sources P. Watson, 'Duncombe, Sir John', HoP, *Commons, 1660–90* · J. C. Sainty, ed., *Treasury officials, 1660–1870* (1972) · S. B. Baxter, *The development of the treasury, 1660–1702* (1957) · H. C. Tomlinson, *Guns and governments: the ordnance office under the later Stuarts* (1979)

Duncombe, John [*pseud.* Crito] (1729–1786), Church of England clergyman and writer, only child of the writer William *Duncombe (1690–1769) and Elizabeth Hughes (*d.* 1736), was born in London on 29 September 1729 and baptized on 2 November 1729 at St Andrew's, Holborn. He was first educated at two schools in Essex, then entered on 1 July 1745 Corpus Christi College, Cambridge, where he graduated BA in 1748 and proceeded MA in 1752. He was afterwards chosen fellow of his college. In 1753 he was ordained at Kew Chapel by Dr Thomas, bishop of Peterborough, and appointed, by the recommendation of Archbishop Herring, to the curacy of Sundridge in Kent; after which he became assistant preacher at St Anne's, Soho. In 1757 Archbishop Herring, his constant friend, presented him to the united livings of St Andrew and St Mary Bredman, Canterbury.

Duncombe was made one of the six preachers in the cathedral, and appointed master of St John's Hospital. In 1773 he received the living of Herne, near Canterbury, which he held with his other preferments.

On 20 April 1761 Duncombe married the artist and poet Susanna Highmore [*see* Duncombe, Susanna (1725–1812)], daughter of Joseph and Susanna Highmore, and a childhood friend who shared his taste for literature. They had four children, only one of whom, Anna Maria, survived infancy. Duncombe became known as a conscientious, benevolent pastor, and an accomplished preacher. Three of his sermons were published at the request of his congregations. He also served as acting magistrate in Canterbury and Herne. Duncombe enjoyed a prolific career as a writer. He was a frequent contributor to the *Gentleman's*

Magazine (often under the pen-name Crito), especially during the final two decades of his life, as a book reviewer, literary critic, biographer, and author of articles on a wide variety of topics. He published several translations, most notably of Horace (1766–7), edited the works of Emperor Julian (1784) and several collections of correspondence, and printed a description of Canterbury Cathedral (1772) and other local historical studies.

Duncombe acquired a considerable reputation as a poet, and published many occasional works independently and in the periodical press and the miscellanies. Their subjects ranged from panegyric, epitaph, and social satire to patriotic commemoration of British successes during the Seven Years' War. Through his wide-ranging literary pursuits he became acquainted with many of the era's leading writers, and was a valued friend of Samuel Richardson. In assessing Duncombe's verse, an early nineteenth-century critic declared that 'his distinguishing talent was chastened humour, and he was very happy in his attempts at parody' (Freeman, 2.349). This quality was exemplified in two of his most popular poems, a burlesque of Thomas Gray's *Elegy in a Country Churchyard*, entitled *An Evening's Contemplation in a College* (1753), and a mock-heroic description of a cricket match, *Surry Triumphant, or, The Kentish-Men's Defeat* (1773), modelled upon the ballad *Chevy Chase*.

In 1754 Duncombe published another successful work, for which he is chiefly remembered, the *Feminead*, which celebrated the artistic achievements of British women poets who had been writing since the reign of Charles I. Although his verse was favourably received by his contemporaries, he was not an innovative poet, and interest in his works declined soon after his death. The inclusion of a passage from the *Feminead* in *The Stuffed Owl: an Anthology of Bad Verse* (1948) by Wyndham Lewis and Charles Lee emphasizes the hostility of some later evaluations of Duncombe's poetry. However, literary historians recently have demonstrated a renewed interest in the *Feminead*, as an important reflection of a mid-eighteenth-century movement which encouraged the literary aspirations of women.

Duncombe suffered a paralytic attack in June 1785 and, following a second attack, he died at Canterbury on 19 January 1786. He was buried at St Mary Bredman, Canterbury. He was survived by his wife and their daughter, Anna Maria. At his death a close friend and fellow clergyman, John Greene, wrote, 'An intimacy with Mr. Duncombe for 40 years entitles me to say that, in addition to a strong, natural, and highly cultivated understanding, he possessed a consummate sweetness of temper and a thorough goodness of heart' (*GM*, 190).

M. JOHN CARDWELL

Sources A. Kippis and others, eds., *Biographia Britannica, or, The lives of the most eminent persons who have flourished in Great Britain and Ireland*, 2nd edn, 5 (1793), 509–12 · *GM*, 1st ser., 56 (1786), 187–90 · R. Freeman, *Kentish poets: a series of writers in English poetry, natives or residents in the county of Kent*, 2 vols. (1821), 2.338–86 · Nichols, *Lit. anecdotes*, 8.271–6 · Nichols, *Illustrations*, 8.589 · *N&Q*, 4th ser., 8 (1871), 243 · *European Magazine and London Review*, 9 (1786), 66 · IGI · DNB

Likenesses group portrait, engraving, 1751 (*Mr Richardson, reading the manuscript of Sir Charles Grandison in 1751, to his friends in the grotto of his house at North End*; after drawing by S. Highmore), repro. in A. L. Barbauld, ed., *The correspondence of Samuel Richardson* (1804), vol. 2, frontispiece · J. Highmore, oils, 1766, CCC Cam.

Duncombe [*née* Highmore], **Susanna** (1725–1812), artist and poet, was born on 5 December 1725 at the Two Lions, 24 Holborn Row, Lincoln's Inn Fields, London, the second child of Joseph *Highmore (1692–1780), a painter, and his wife, Susanna Hiller (1689/90–1750) [*see* Highmore, Susanna], a poet. Susanna was 'educated with the greatest care, and under every possible advantage' by her parents, who looked to John Locke's *Some Thoughts Concerning Education* (1693) for guidance (Freeman, 342). Under their instruction Susanna became proficient in Latin, Spanish, French, and Italian, published verse translations of Petrarch, Metastasio, and Guarini, and learned sketching and painting. Allowed rather more freedom than her older brother, Anthony *Highmore [*see under* Highmore, Joseph], she came into close but limited contact with many of the artists who frequented her father's studio in their London home. However, like her father, she became noticeably more attached to the literary set into which her parents' friends William and Elizabeth Duncombe had introduced them. Among these were the editor Dr John Hawkesworth, the retired lawyer Thomas Edwards, Elizabeth Carter (to whom Susanna would later become quite close), and Samuel Richardson.

The friendship between the Highmores and Samuel Richardson flourished in the years after Joseph Highmore's announcement that he would illustrate scenes from Richardson's *Pamela*. Susanna often accompanied her mother and father on their visits to Richardson's home at North End where she 'instantly became a perplexing but persisting member of the troupe of young admirers' (Mild, 254). Included in this group were Thomas and Edward Mulso, their sister Hester, later an active participant in the literary 'bluestocking' set, Mary Prescott, John Chapone, and John Duncombe. Susanna, Hester, and Mary were close friends and rivals, styling themselves Sackey, Hecky, and Pressy, each taking up her perch as one of Richardson's celebrated 'song birds', gathering not only to hear the latest extracts from his manuscripts, but also to exchange gossip and partake in discussions of love 'in an atmosphere charged with the delicacies of actual love affairs' (*Selected Letters of Samuel Richardson*, 19). Susanna herself was something of a 'heart snatcher', and her beauty inspired verses from Thomas Mulso and possibly Christopher Smart published in the *Gentleman's Magazine* and *London Magazine* respectively (Mild, 240). However, these attentions did not distract her from her longer-term designs on John *Duncombe (1729–1786), the son of her father's good friend William Duncombe, and a frequenter of the set despite his residence at Cambridge.

Susanna's talents endeared her to Richardson who 'claimed her for an adoptive daughter' (Mild, 306), and the two began to correspond regularly from 1748. According to Richardson it was not everyone, who, like Miss Highmore, can write a great deal in a little compass … who can figure out in still superior lights, the beauties of contemplation which she enjoys in her Clarissa-closet (as she is pleased to call it) with pen, pencil and books! (*Correspondence of Samuel Richardson*, 2.207–8)

In addition to striking descriptions of natural scenery, her letters included reflections on the characters and situations within Richardson's novels, and often focused on topics of general interest such as nature, education, and social customs. Richardson in turn offered Susanna fatherly advice and a sympathetic understanding of her resistance to the 'parental restrictions' that enforced her separation from John Duncombe (Thomson, 98). Yet such seriousness was tempered by Richardson's gentle sense of humour, as he often teased her about a 'certain young man' of whom he playfully withheld news (ibid., 2.229).

Susanna thrived in this genteel set where she gained recognition for her talented wielding of both the 'pencil and the lyre' (Mild, 236). In addition to a number of poetical imitations, she wrote a number of poems that appeared in the *Poetical Calendar* and Nichols's *Select Collection* (1782). Her literary reputation was firmly established by her allegory of Fidelio and Honoria—a couple who chose to live in the 'House of Content' after failing to find the 'Palace of Happiness'—which was circulated among her friends in manuscript form. Susanna's allegory should not be confused with Hester Mulso's work *Fidelia*, a prose story published in John Hawkesworth's *The Adventurer* (Mild, 317). Like Thomas Edwards, who encouraged Susanna to publish as she wrote, John Duncombe also attempted to arouse public interest in her work through making reference to her within the lines of his poem *The Feminead* (1754). Duncombe celebrates Susanna ('Eugenia') as the 'Muses' pupil' on whose labours the 'sister arts smile' (Freeman, 360). Despite his encouragement, Susanna's allegory remained unpublished and is now lost (Mild, 236). Susanna captured the informal intimacy of the group of 'young learners' at North End not only in her correspondence and poetry, but also in her group portrait of Richardson reading from the manuscript of *Sir Charles Grandison* (Pierpont Morgan Library, New York; reproduced in Barbauld, 2, frontispiece). The little group ultimately dispersed as a result of Richardson's failing health, Hester Mulso's marriage to John Chapone, and the death of Susanna's mother in 1750 which required Susanna to assume the duties of her father's house. There appears to be no further correspondence between Susanna and Richardson after 1757.

After a protracted courtship Susanna and John Duncombe finally married on 20 April 1761 and moved to Duncombe's Canterbury home where they were joined by her father a year later. As one of the six preachers in the cathedral, Duncombe was entitled to a house within the precincts; this he and Susanna occupied with their only surviving daughter, Anna Maria, their other daughter, Elizabeth, having died when ten months old. While at the precincts they had two other children, William and John, who both died in infancy.

Susanna acquired artistic skills at an early age and continued to develop them throughout her life. In its formal aspects her work was influenced largely by her father's use of elongated figures and clear compositional structure. Most of the early drawings included in the family scrapbook (Tate collection) depict fanciful creatures and figures couched in tranquil rural scenes. The years following her marriage and move to Kent were her most productive. All her published illustrations date from this period and include designs for popular publications such as *Orlando Furioso*, *The Castle of Otranto*, and John Hughes's *Siege of Damascus* (1773). However, she undertook illustrations primarily for the works of close friends and family, choosing to remain within the familiar confines of the small and intimate circles that she cherished. Susanna provided topographical and figurative designs for John Duncombe's 'The history and antiquities of Recalver and Herne' in *Bibliotheca Topographica Britannica* (1779), his edition of *Letters from Italy in the Years 1754 and 1755*, his translation of *The Works of Horace in English Verse by Several Hands* (1767), and E. Halsted's *The History and Topographical Survey of the County of Kent* (1778). While many of her illustrations remained unpublished, those that were published suffered severely at the hands of the 'miserable engraving' which according to Freeman was a 'disgrace to the arts' (Freeman, 342). The primary collection of her designs and engravings after her designs is at the Tate Gallery.

After her husband's death in 1786 Susanna and her unmarried 'bookish' daughter lived a reclusive life in the cathedral precincts where they gained a reputation for keeping cats. Susanna died on 28 October 1812 in Canterbury and is buried in the same vault as her husband at St Mary Bredman, Canterbury.   SHANNON R. MCBRIAR

Sources W. Mild, *Joseph Highmore of Holborn Row* (1990) · J. Riding, 'Susanna Duncombe', *Dictionary of women artists*, ed. D. Gaze, 1 (1997) · R. Freeman, *Kentish poets: a series of writers in English poetry, natives or residents in the county of Kent*, 2 vols. (1821) · *The correspondence of Samuel Richardson*, ed. A. L. Barbauld, 6 vols. (1804) · C. L. Thomson, *Samuel Richardson: a biographical and critical study* (1900) · *Selected letters of Samuel Richardson*, ed. J. Carroll (1964) · T. C. D. Eaves and B. D. Kimpel, *Samuel Richardson: a biography* (1971) · F. Doherty, 'An autograph of Samuel Richardson', *N&Q*, 230 (1985), 230 · Nichols, *Illustrations*, vol. 8 · *GM*, 1st ser., 31 (1761), 188

Archives Tate collection, scrapbook with sketches by members of the Highmore family

Likenesses J. Highmore, group portrait, oils, *c.*1727, Art Gallery of South Australia, Adelaide; *see illus. in* Highmore, Susanna (1689/90–1750) · J. Highmore, oils, *c.*1745–1750, National Gallery of Victoria, Melbourne; repro. in biography, pl. 10 · S. Duncombe, group portrait (Samuel Richardson reading Sir Charles Grandison), Morgan L.; repro. in Barbauld, ed., *Correspondence of Samuel Richardson*, vol. 2, frontispiece · S. Highmore, drawing, Tate collection, Highmore scrapbook; repro. in C. R. Beard, 'Highmore's Scrapbook', *Connoisseur*, 93 (1934), 294

Duncombe, Thomas Slingsby (1796–1861), politician, was the eldest son of Thomas Duncombe of Copgrove, near Boroughbridge, West Riding of Yorkshire, and his wife, Emma (*d.* 1840), eldest daughter of John Hinchliffe, bishop of Peterborough and nephew of Charles, first Baron Feversham. He was sent to Harrow School in 1808. Shortly before leaving school in December 1811 he was

Thomas Slingsby Duncombe (1796–1861), by James Warren Childe, 1836

commissioned as an ensign in the Coldstream Guards, and in November 1813 he was sent to the Netherlands. During the latter portion of the Peninsular War he acted as aide-de-camp to General Ronald Craufurd Ferguson, the whig politician and supporter of parliamentary reform. He returned to England before the battle of Waterloo and rose to the rank of lieutenant on 23 November 1815, but retired from the army on 17 November 1819.

Duncombe began his long political career when he unsuccessfully contested Pontefract in 1820 and Hertford in 1823, as a whig candidate. He was returned for Hertford in 1826, when he defeated Henry Lytton Bulwer by a majority of ninety-two, and he retained his seat in 1830 and 1831, but was defeated at the general election in December 1832. The local magnate, the marquess of Salisbury, had used unlawful methods in opposing Duncombe's return and the election was afterwards declared void on the ground of bribery, with both writs being suspended for the remainder of the parliament. Duncombe's five contests for the borough are estimated to have cost him at least £40,000.

Financial insecurity dogged Duncombe's political career. A patron of the turf, a gambler, and a frequenter of whig salons and London clubs, Duncombe's extravagant tastes—he had a reputation as the best-dressed man in the House of Commons—led him into massive debt. When his father died, on 7 December 1847, the Yorkshire estate Duncombe inherited had to be sold for the benefit of his numerous creditors. He was a member of Count D'Orsay's circle, and Lady Blessington based the character of Lord Arlington in her novel *The Two Friends* (1835) upon him (M. Sadleir, *Blessington-D'Orsay*, 1933, 251). He sought the company of actresses, though he was eventually married, reportedly in 1840 to a cousin, Emma Margaret, widow of Charles Slingsby (d. 1832). They had a son, Thomas H. Duncombe, who in 1868 produced an unrevealing biography of his father.

After his defeat at Hertford, Duncombe became more advanced in his political views and joined the radical groups associated with Lord Brougham and his friend Lord Durham. On 1 July 1834 he was returned for the newly created borough of Finsbury; he continued to sit for that constituency until his death, sharing with his fellow Finsbury MP Thomas Wakley solid support from working-class radicals such as James Watson, Henry Hetherington, and Richard Moore. He was an early supporter of corn law repeal and of the Ten Hours Bill, and was an opponent of the new poor law and administrative centralization. On 30 May 1836 Duncombe moved that an address be presented to the king asking for his assistance in persuading Louis-Philippe to free the former Bourbon minister Prince Polignac from imprisonment. In the summer of 1838 he visited Canada, and on his return to Britain allied himself with John Stuart Mill in the defence of the liberal self-government policy of the recent governor-general Lord Durham.

In 1840 Duncombe took up the case of the imprisoned Chartist insurgents, and in March he spoke in favour of an address to the queen for the free pardon of Frost, Jones, and Williams. This action received the support of only seven MPs, though including Benjamin Disraeli, and was rejected by a majority of sixty-three. Duncombe's motion in the following year for the merciful consideration of all political offenders then imprisoned in England and Wales was more successful, and was only lost by the casting vote of the speaker. On 2 May 1842 he presented to the Commons the second 'monster' people's petition for the six points of the Charter. His motion on the following day, that the petitioners should 'be heard by themselves or their counsel at the bar of the House', was defeated by a majority of 236. In 1844 he sent his friend Disraeli material on Chartism for use in his novel *Sybil*.

On 14 June 1844 Duncombe presented a petition from Mazzini, William Linton, William Lovett, and Serafino Calderera (an old associate of Lovett and Linton in the London Working Men's Association), complaining that their letters had, without reason, been opened by the Post Office, thereby 'introducing ... the spy system of foreign states [so] repugnant to every principle of the British Constitution' (Smith, 55). Sir James Graham, the home secretary, handled the matter very badly, and Duncombe succeeded in rousing the other parliamentary radicals against Graham, who acknowledged that he had issued a warrant for the opening of letters of one of the petitioners. Duncombe presented further damaging petitions from Karl Stolzman and Stanislaus Worcell on 24 June and demanded an investigation into the probability that Graham had broken the law by issuing a general warrant for opening all their correspondence. The affair quickly became a national question, but Duncombe was unprepared to work publicly with those he regarded as artisanal demagogues and refused to become a radical martyr. However, in 1847 he joined Linton's fledgeling People's International League as a committee member and worked with Linton, Mazzini, Watson, Thomas Cooper, and others with the object of influencing the formation of Foreign Office policy.

Duncombe, according to his biographer, took part in the plot which led to Prince Louis Napoleon's escape from Ham Castle in May 1846. In the same year he presented the petition of Charles, duke of Brunswick, to the House of Commons. Though unsuccessful in his attempt to induce parliament to interfere, Duncombe continued to interest himself in the affairs of the duke, who in December 1846 made an extraordinary will in his favour. Subsequently Duncombe for some years employed his secretary on secret missions to the duke and the emperor of the French.

Although Duncombe had to a great extent identified himself with the Chartists, he entirely rejected physical force, and opposed the 10 April 1848 demonstration. However, after the events of 1848, the Chartist leadership began to take a much greater interest in the potential of parliamentary reformers and the Chartist National Association of United Trades again looked to Duncombe as its parliamentary representative. By the end of the 1840s he had become disillusioned by the politics of the whig-Liberal alliance, which he had supported in the 1830s and 1840s, and increasingly saw his parliamentary position as that of an independent Liberal, free to speak on matters of personal interest. However, though having the status of a radical reformer, in reality Duncombe rarely recorded a vote against Liberal administrations. Indeed, his belief that Palmerstonian governments had seen the end of the whiggism he too rejected led him to praise Palmerston on a number of occasions. Only on the question of foreign affairs was Duncombe fundamentally to reject Palmerstonian politics.

In the 1850s Duncombe was a parliamentary spokesman for the Liberation Society, which supported the claims of religious dissenters in the House of Commons and helped bring in a motion for the abolition of church rates. In 1858 he supported the admission of Jews to parliament, carrying a motion to place Baron Rothschild on a committee that was to hold a conference with the House of Lords. He also was in favour of the regulation of small workshop trades, the establishment of large urban constituencies, the secret ballot, and the redistribution of seats. From a pro-interventionist stance in 1852–4, Duncombe became isolationist during the later stages of the Crimean War. In 1851, at the request of Mazzini, he became a member of the council of the 'Friends of Italy'. On 9 February 1858 he defended the emperor, Louis Napoleon, from the attack that had been made upon him in the debate on the motion for leave to bring in the Conspiracy to Murder Bill, and, opposing the radicals, took no part in the division. In 1861 he acted on behalf of Kossuth in the question of the Hungarian notes.

Despite ill health, which for many years before his death prevented regular parliamentary attendance, Duncombe did continue to speak on occasion. He died on 13 November 1861 at South House, Lancing, and was buried eight days later at Kensal Green cemetery. A handsome man, popular among constituents and metropolitan society alike, Duncombe was a fluent, though eccentric, speaker.

MATTHEW LEE

Sources *The life and correspondence of Thomas Slingsby Duncombe*, ed. T. H. Duncombe, 2 vols. (1868) • J. F. Waller, ed., *The imperial dictionary of universal biography*, 3 vols. (1857–63) • Boase, *Mod. Eng. biog.* • *A dictionary of contemporary biography* (1861) • P. W. Kingsford, 'Radical dandy: Thomas Slingsby Duncombe, 1796–1861', *History Today*, 14 (1964), 399–407 • J. L. Sturgis, 'Duncombe, Thomas Slingsby', *BDMBR*, vol. 2 • M. Taylor, *The decline of British radicalism, 1847–1860* (1995) • *Benjamin Disraeli letters*, ed. J. A. W. Gunn and others (1982–) • A. M. Pflaum, 'The parliamentary career of Thomas S. Duncombe, 1836–1861', PhD diss., University of Minnesota, 1975 • F. B. Smith, *Radical artisan: William James Linton, 1812–97* (1973), 55–9 **Archives** Bodl. Oxf., Disraeli MSS, corresp. with Benjamin Disraeli • Lambton estate office, Chester-le-Street, letters to first earl of Durham • UCL, letters to Society for the Diffusion of Useful Knowledge **Likenesses** S. W. Reynolds senior, mezzotint, pubd 1831 (after S. W. Reynolds junior), BM • F. Bromley, group portrait, etching, pubd 1835 (after B. Haydon, *The reform banquet, 1832*), NPG • J. W. Childe, pen and wash drawing, 1836, NPG [*see illus.*] • J. C. Bromley, group portrait, mezzotint, pubd 1837, BM • Count D'Orsay, pencil and chalk drawing, 1839, NPG • Wilkins, crayon, exh. Exhibition of National Portraits 1868 • D. J. Pound, stipple and line print (after a photograph by Mayall), NPG

Duncombe, William (1690–1769), writer, was born on 9 January 1690 in Hatton Garden, London, the youngest son of John Duncombe of Stocks, Aldbury, Hertfordshire, and his wife, Hannah. He was educated in 'two private seminaries' at Cheney, Buckinghamshire, and Pinner, Middlesex. In December 1706 Duncombe was entered as a clerk in the Navy Office, where he remained for nineteen years, eventually leaving to pursue a life of 'literary leisure'. His marriage on 1 September 1726 to Elizabeth Hughes (*b. c.*1692), 'a woman of excellent sense and temper', sister of his friends John Hughes and Jabez Hughes, was facilitated by a large lottery win on a joint ticket (Kippis, 505). From 1730 Duncombe lived in the house that he had built for himself in Frith Street, Soho. Elizabeth died in January 1736, but William survived into old age.

Duncombe's earliest literary attempts took the form of translation. His version of Horace's 'Carmen saeculare', a competent performance, appeared in 1721, and was later included in Matthew Concanen's miscellany (*The Flower-Piece: a Collection of Miscellany Poems*, 1731); *Athaliah*, his translation of Racine's *Athalie*, was published in 1722, with a second edition in 1726. Duncombe's most ambitious work was the tragedy *Junius Brutus*, modelled on Voltaire's *Brutus* but, as he hints in the 'Preface', adapted to the English taste for the sentimental, notably in the fifth act. It is an example of the whiggish political tragedy, heroic and idealizing, then in fashion, represented also in the work of James Thomson; liberty is constantly invoked. The quality of the blank verse leaves something to be desired. The tragedy was performed at Drury Lane for six nights, in November 1734, 'when the town was empty, the parliament not sitting, and Farinelli in full song and feather at the Hay-Market'. 'The quivering Italian eunuch', the

William Duncombe (1690–1769), by Joseph Highmore, 1721

author himself noted ironically if regretfully, 'proved too powerful for the rigid Roman consul' (Kippis, 506–7). *Junius Brutus* was published in 1735, surprisingly reaching a second edition in the same year.

Several of Duncombe's fugitive pieces appeared in the *Whitehall Evening Post*, in which he had a financial share, and he also published in the *London Journal*. In March 1728 a letter by Duncombe condemning the *Beggar's Opera* for its likely deleterious effect on public morality was published in the *London Journal*; his praise for a sermon on the same subject by Thomas Herring, preacher at Lincoln's Inn and later archbishop of Canterbury, led to a lifelong friendship. Herring's letters to Duncombe, written between 1728 and 1757, were published posthumously in 1777. In 1744 Duncombe published an *Oration on the Usefulness of Dramatic Interludes in the Education of Youth*, a characteristically moralizing piece translated from the Latin of Samuel Werenfels. 'The Choice of Hercules', a not inconsiderable poem concerned with moral choice, is the opening piece of the third volume of Dodsley's miscellany (*A Collection of Poems. By Several Hands*, 1748). *The Works of Horace in English Verse. By Several Hands*, partly translated by Duncombe himself and partly by his son, appeared in two volumes in 1757–9. Duncombe clearly had a gift for friendship, and his generosity was apparent in the efforts he made in the posthumous publication of his friends' work, including that of Henry Needler, John Hughes, Jabez Hughes, and Samuel Say; he also published Herring's *Seven Sermons on Public Occasions* (1763). In his later years he became a friend of John Boyle, fifth earl of Orrery.

Duncombe died in Margaret Street, Cavendish Square, where he lived, on 26 February 1769; he was buried in the church of St John the Baptist, Aldbury. He had one son, John *Duncombe, who shared his literary interests.

ROBERT INGLESFIELD

Sources A. Kippis and others, eds., *Biographia Britannica, or, The lives of the most eminent persons who have flourished in Great Britain and Ireland*, 2nd edn, 5 vols. (1778–93), vol. 5 · *GM*, 1st ser., 39 (1769), 168 · J. Duncombe, ed., *Letters by several eminent persons deceased*, 3 vols. (1773)
Likenesses J. Highmore, oils, 1721, CCC Cam. [*see illus.*] · T. Cook, line engraving (after J. Highmore), BM, NPG; repro. in J. Nichols, *A select collection of poems* (1780)

Duncon, Edmund (1600/01–1673). *See under* Duncon, Eleazar (1597/8–1660).

Duncon, Eleazar (1597/8–1660), Church of England clergyman, was the eldest of at least three sons of Eleazar Duncon MD of Ipswich and Gipping, Suffolk, a graduate of Pembroke College, Cambridge, author of a treatise on tobacco, *The Copy of a Letter* (1606). Eleazar junior attended St Paul's School, London, and was admitted to Gonville and Caius College, Cambridge, in February 1614 at the age of sixteen. He graduated BA in 1618, was elected a fellow of Pembroke College, and proceeded MA in 1621.

On 13 March 1625 Duncon was ordained deacon by Bishop William Laud of St David's and in September 1626 was ordained priest by Bishop Richard Neile of Durham, who acted as his patron and seems to have been responsible for all his subsequent appointments; John Cosin, former fellow of Caius and then Neile's chaplain, was a lifelong friend. Duncon's enthusiastic support for Laud's high-church policy ensured that, like Cosin, he was appointed to a number of valuable offices [*see* Durham House group]. In 1628 he proceeded BD and was made a prebendary of Durham Cathedral; the following year he obtained a similar post at Winchester. He came into conflict with a number of puritans over the implementation of the Laudian programme in Durham Cathedral. In 1631, by which time he had become Neile's chaplain, he became rector of Wyke Regis, Dorset, and two years later was made rector of Haughton-le-Skern, co. Durham. That year he also proceeded DD. His commencement determination, of the question whether 'good works are efficaciously necessary to salvation', gained an approving reference in the Franciscan Christopher Davenport's *Deus, natura, gratia*, published at Lyons in 1634, while the thesis was appended to the second discourse, 'Preferring holy charitie before faith, hope and knowledge', in Robert Shelford's *Five Pious and Learned Discourses* (1635). This book, dedicated to Charles I, sought to 'reconcile the doctrinal teachings of the English Church with those of Roman Catholicism' (N. Tyacke, *Anti-Calvinists: the Rise of English Arminianism, c.1590-1640*, 1987, 54, 227). In 1635 Duncon also became vicar of Powick in Worcester. On 8 May 1639 he was appointed a royal chaplain-extraordinary at Newcastle, while in April 1640 he resigned his Winchester position in order to become a prebendary of York Minster.

At the outbreak of the civil war Duncon removed the plate from Durham Cathedral and sent it in a trunk to Lady Hammond, who arranged for it to be buried for safe keeping. During the war he was removed from all his preferments, and on 10 September 1644 was sequestrated by the committee for compounding. He apparently went to the continent shortly afterwards in order to avoid arrest. In 1650 he was acting as chaplain to the Levant Company at Leghorn in Italy. In 1651 John Evelyn heard him preach at the royal court in exile in Paris, and in May 1652 he was appointed a temporary replacement for the recently deceased chaplain of the Levant Company at Smyrna. While in exile he acted as tutor to Sir George Savile, future marquess of Halifax (Hardacre, 361–2).

Duncon returned to England some time before September 1654, but the following March travelled to France with £100 for Charles II. He was directed by Edward Hyde to liaise with a number of bishops concerning the appointment of deacons, priests, and bishops to vacant church positions in England. In December 1655 he was at Saumur, about 40 km east of Nantes, but one year later he was in Lyons. He moved to Italy before August 1659, when Cosin remarked that Duncon's sole employment was 'to make sermons before the English merchants at Ligorne and Florence' (Correspondence of John Cosin, 1.290). He died at Leghorn on his way back to England shortly after the Restoration, and was given a 'very honourable' burial by order of the duke of Tuscany (Walker rev., 141). His only published works—De adoratione Dei versus altare (1660) and Of Worshiping God towards the Altar (1661)—appeared posthumously. These were based on his doctoral disputation and argued that 'to worship with the bowing of the body is a Worship most pious and humble, as testifying humane abjection, and asserting the excellency of God' (E. Duncon, Of Worshiping God, 1661, 13).

Eleazar's brother **Edmund Duncon** (1600/01–1673), Church of England clergyman, matriculated in the Michaelmas term of 1624 from Trinity Hall, Cambridge, of which he was a fellow from 1628 to 1631. He graduated LLB in 1630 and was ordained priest at St David's the same year. He was vicar of Wood Dalling from 1629 and rector of Swannington, Norfolk, from 1630. He was a friend of Nicholas Ferrar and George Herbert; it was reported that the latter, on his deathbed, gave Duncon a manuscript of 'The Temple', from the proceeds of which he was able to build a parsonage house at Swannington.

In 1639 Edmund Duncon married Elizabeth Eston. By 25 August 1646 he had been sequestered from Swannington; fifths from Wood Dalling were granted to his wife, Elizabeth, on 21 November that year. Between 1654 and 1656 he was a curate to Richard Ball at Tattingstone, Suffolk. Restored to both his livings in 1660, he lost them again in 1662, but the following year was appointed rector of Friern Barnet, Middlesex. He died in possession of this living on 4 October 1673, aged seventy-two; a monument was erected in the church. His son, John Duncon, succeeded him as rector, but died a few weeks later.

Eleazar's brother **John Duncon** (1602/3–1652), Church of England clergyman, matriculated from Pembroke College, Cambridge, in 1620 aged seventeen. He graduated BA in 1624, was elected a fellow of the college in 1625, and proceeded MA in 1627 and BD in 1634. From 1636 he was

appointed to a number of parishes in Cambridge, Suffolk, and Norfolk. In 1640 the parishioners of Stoke by Ipswich, where he had been made rector in 1637, petitioned the House of Commons that, as chaplain to Bishop Matthew Wren of Norwich, Duncon had been inducted into the living without the patron's consent. He was named in articles against Wren, and by 1641 had been removed from Stoke. That year he became rector of Rattendon, Essex, but within a few years was sequestered. He then became chaplain to Lettice Cary, Viscountess Falkland (d. 1646), in whose house he enjoyed 'full Accommodations and plentifull Conveniencies' (J. Duncon, The Returns of Spirituall Comfort, 2nd edn, sig. A4r). His biography of the viscountess, The Returns of Spirituall Comfort, went through three editions between 1648 and 1653. Sequestration of Duncon's estate was discharged by 1648. He probably died at the house of Sir John Pettus, Cheston Hall, Suffolk, on 6 October 1652.   JASON Mᶜ ELLIGOTT

Sources Venn, Alum. Cant. • Walker rev., 141, 151, 267 • Calendar of the Clarendon state papers preserved in the Bodleian Library, ed. O. Ogle and others, 5 vols. (1869–1970) • Diary of John Evelyn, ed. W. Bray, new edn, ed. H. B. Wheatley, 4 vols. (1906) • M. A. E. Green, ed., Calendar of the proceedings of the committee for compounding … 1643–1660, 5 vols., PRO (1889–92) • CSP dom., 1625–31; 1639–40; 1651–2 • C. Wren, Parentalia (1750), 82, 106 • The correspondence of John Cosin D.D., lord bishop of Durham, ed. [G. Ornsby], 2 vols., SurtS, 52, 55 (1869–72) • P. H. Hardacre, 'The royalists in exile during the puritan revolution, 1642–1660', Huntington Library Quarterly, 16 (1952–3), 353–70
Archives BL, Add. MS 4275, fols. 197, 198

Duncon, John (1602/3–1652). See under Duncon, Eleazar (1597/8–1660).

Duncon, Samuel (fl. 1633–1663), pamphleteer and haberdasher, was the son of Robert Duncon (d. 1670), tanner and three times bailiff of Ipswich, and his wife, Elizabeth Smith. Duncon became a freeman of Ipswich in 1633 and held minor offices there during the 1630s. He was married to Helen, of whom nothing further is known. Duncon opposed the personal rule of Charles I, refusing to pay ship money or to enlist in the bishops' wars of 1639–40, and in 1636 was excommunicated for refusing to take the sacrament at the altar rail. In 1640 he entered the corporation's assembly as one of the twenty-four common councilmen. After the shire election held in Ipswich in October 1640, Duncon wrote two affidavits condemning the riotous disruption of the poll by armed royalist supporters. In 1642 he contributed money, arms, and horse in response to the parliamentary propositions, and drafted the petition of the high constables and freeholders of Suffolk, which was aggressively critical of the king's refusal to negotiate. By the eve of war, his support for parliament was unequivocal, and its onset saw Duncon actively raising forces in Suffolk. In November 1642 he sought advice from Colchester about the fortification of Ipswich, and argued that Norfolk, Suffolk, and Essex should form an association for their common defence.

Acting on a commission of April 1643 to secure and disarm 'malignants', Duncon requisitioned material from which he formed a foot company, and spent £300 himself raising a troop of seventy-five horse which he escorted to join Oliver Cromwell's forces at Huntingdon. Cromwell persuaded him to stay and raise more forces there. Duncon thus contributed directly to the creation of the Ironsides. He continued recruiting 'honest able men' throughout the war, and also had the 'hazardous, dangerous and troublesome' post of high collector of assessments in Suffolk until 1651 (S. Duncon, *Several Proposals … in Reference to a Settlement of Peace and Truth in this Nation*, 1659, 5). In 1650 he was also appointed a provisioner of supplies for the parliamentary armies in Ireland and Scotland.

During the 1640s and 1650s, Duncon's religious and political outlook became more radical. He gave damning evidence against three Laudian 'scandalous ministers'. In 1649 he signed a petition to Cromwell from the Particular Baptists in Ipswich, asking for his support for them to congregate freely. His first tract, published in March 1652, *Severall propositions of publick concernment presented to his excelency the Lord Generall Cromwel* (BL, Thomason tracts, E656 (18)), shows the range of his ideas. Duncon urged the Commonwealth parliament to make good 'that which have been fought for, Payed for, and Prayed for … that the Just Rights and Liberties of the people may be ratified, and Confirmed' (S. Duncon, *Severall Propositions*, 1). His proposals included: full liberty of conscience; the abolition of tithes; the relief of maimed soldiers and widows; punishment for any authority that allowed beggary; and an act to maintain the army by using revenue from confiscated crown, ecclesiastical, royalist, and recusant estates, thus reducing taxation. Most revolutionary were his act for peace keeping, whereby arbitrators would be chosen by all communities to settle disputes before any lawsuit commenced, and his proposal that MPs and civil officers be elected annually by 'the free people' (ibid., 4).

In 1653, during the Barebones Parliament, Duncon shared lodgings in London, provided by the council of state, with one of the members for Suffolk, his fellow townsman Jacob Caley. In the later 1650s he acted as 'a friend in compassion' on behalf of imprisoned Quakers in Ipswich (*Christian Progress*, 79). A second pamphlet, *Several Proposals … in Reference to a Settlement of Peace and Truth in this Nation*, of 1659 (BL, Thomason tracts, E989 (10)), epitomizes the radical demands and millenarian expectations of the Good Old Cause of the English revolution which died with the Restoration in 1660: Duncon declared that 'it is in the wisdom of GOD' that men be appointed to draw up a model constitution, an 'Agreement among the people … that all may set their hands to' (p. 3). The last notice of him is a letter of March 1663, dated in Quaker style, asking to be 'discharged for matters of worship' relating to the anti-puritan Clarendon code, and hinting at a quietist resignation, willing to 'love his enemies and pray for them that persecute' (Suffolk RO, HD, 36/A/270).

FRANK GRACE

Sources Two petitions … the other to the right worshipfull the justices of the peace now assembled at the assizes holden at Bury St. Edmonds for the county of Suffolk [1642] [Thomason tract E 112(9)] • T. Carlyle, 'An election to the Long Parliament', *Fraser's Magazine*, 30 (1844), 382–7 • S. Duncon to the mayor of Colchester, 1642, Essex RO, D/Y 2/7, 291 • S. Duncon to —, 1663, Suffolk RO, HD 36/A/270 • S. Duncon to Captain Baynes (2 letters), BL, Add. MSS 21418, 21419 • A. J. Klaiber, The story of the Suffolk Baptists (1931), appx 2, 204–5 • The Christian progress of that ancient servant and minister of Jesus Christ, George Whitehead, ed. [J. Besse?] (1725), 79 • CSP dom., 1650, 517, 603; 1651, 537 • parish register, Ipswich, St Lawrence [marriage]

Duncumb, John (1765–1839), topographer, was the second son of Thomas Duncumb, rector of Shere, Surrey. He was educated at a school in Guildford, kept by a clergyman named Cole, and at Trinity College, Cambridge. He graduated BA in 1787, and proceeded MA in 1796. In 1788 he settled at Hereford in the dual capacity of editor and printer of Pugh's *Hereford Journal*. Duncumb married in 1792 Mary (d. 1841), daughter of William Webb of Holmer, near Hereford. They had three children: Thomas Edward (d. 1823), William George (d. 1834), and a daughter. Duncumb was secretary to the Herefordshire Agricultural Society from its formation in 1797, and published works on agriculture, including a *General View of the Agriculture of the County of Hereford* (1805) as well as sermons. By 1809 he had become a fellow of the Society of Antiquaries.

In 1780 Duncumb was engaged by Charles, eleventh duke of Norfolk, the owner of extensive estates in the county, to compile and edit a history of Herefordshire. The terms were £2 2s. per week for collecting materials, the resulting work being the property of the duke. The first volume, containing a general history of the county and account of the city, was published in 1804; and the first part of a second volume, containing the hundreds of Broxash and Ewyas-Lacy, with a few pages of Greytree hundred, in 1812. At the death of the duke in December 1815 payments ceased and Duncumb stopped work. The unsold portions of the work, with the pages of Greytree hundred then printed but not published, since they were part of the duke's personal estate, were taken from Hereford to London, where the parcels remained in a warehouse until 1837. The whole stock was then purchased by Thomas Thorpe, the bookseller, who disposed of his copies of the first and second volumes, with the section on Greytree, to which he appended an index. The second volume was completed with an index in 1866 by Judge W. H. Cooke, who issued a third volume, containing the remainder of Greytree, in 1882 and volume 7, covering the parishes in the hundred of Grimsworth, in 1892. Subsequently, volume 4, edited by the Revd Morgan G. Watkins, appeared in 1897, covering Huntington and Radlow hundreds. Volumes 5 and 6 appeared in 1912 and 1913 respectively, compiled by John H. Matthews and covering Wormelow hundred.

Duncumb's connection with the *Hereford Journal* ceased in 1791, when he was ordained. He was instituted to the rectory of Tâlachddû in Brecknockshire in 1793 and to Frilsham, Berkshire, in the same year. In 1809 he became rector of Tortington, Sussex, but he resigned the living soon afterwards on his institution to Abbey Dore, Herefordshire, the duke of Norfolk being the patron of both benefices. In 1815 he obtained the vicarage of Mansel-Lacy, Herefordshire, from Uvedale Price, and he held both these Herefordshire benefices at his death. However, he was never resident at his livings, and remained in Hereford from 1788 until his death on 19 September 1839. He was buried in the church of Abbey Dore, where there is a monument to him. His manuscript collections were sold by his widow to a local bookseller.

GORDON GOODWIN, rev. ROBIN WHITTAKER

Sources Venn, *Alum. Cant.* · private information (1888) · *GM*, 2nd ser., 12 (1839), 660–61 · *GM*, 1st ser., 93/2 (1823), 644 · *GM*, 2nd ser., 1 (1834), 219 · *GM*, 2nd ser., 5 (1836), 209 [death of William George Duncombe] · *GM*, 2nd ser., 16 (1841), 664
Archives Hereford Library, Herefordshire collections

Dundas family of Fingask and Kerse (*per.* 1728/9–1820), landowners and politicians, came to prominence with **Thomas** [i] **Dundas of Fingask** (1681?–1762), woollen-draper, the son of John Dundas (*b.* before 1670, *d.* 1724) and grandson of Sir John Dundas of Fingask (*d.* 1670). In 1650 Sir John's Perthshire estate had been confiscated by the Scottish covenanting regime as punishment for the family's royalism, an action his descendants sought to redress. Having prospered in business, and after receiving a small inheritance, Thomas [i] was able to borrow money and in 1728–9 he purchased Letham and other lands in Airth, Stirlingshire. He obtained a crown charter for this property 'by which the names and designations thereof were to be changed into that of Fingask' (Dundas, 40), and he was henceforth known as Thomas Dundas of Fingask or of Letham. He married Bethia Baillie (*fl.* 1686–1732), sister of Bernard Baillie (1673–1743), abbot of St James's at Ratisbon in Bavaria.

Notwithstanding this Roman Catholic connection the Dundas family conformed to the Church of Scotland and accepted the Hanoverian succession. Thomas [i] and Bethia had two children—Thomas [ii] Dundas of Fingask (*c.*1708–1786) and **Sir Lawrence Dundas of Kerse**, first baronet (1712–1781), army contractor and landowner—both of whom were born at Edinburgh and probably were educated at the city's high school. Lawrence, though the younger son, benefited as the namesake, godson, and favoured nephew of Professor Lawrence Dundas of Edinburgh, who, in 1734, left him £1500 sterling. In 1737 Thomas [ii] married his first wife, Anne, daughter of James Graham, a judge of the Scottish court of admiralty. Following her death he married on 11 November 1744 Lady Janet (1721–1805), daughter of Charles Maitland, sixth earl of Lauderdale, and Elizabeth Ogilvie; the couple had five daughters and two sons, Thomas *Dundas (1750–1794) and Charles *Dundas, later Baron Amesbury (1751–1832). On 9 April 1738 Thomas [ii]'s brother Lawrence married Margaret (1716–1802), daughter of Alexander Bruce of Kennet, Clackmannanshire. The couple had one son, Thomas [iii] Dundas of Kerse.

Sir Lawrence Dundas: Nabob of the North At the time of Thomas [iii]'s birth Lawrence Dundas was established as a wine merchant. Shortly afterwards, however, he became involved as an army contractor, in which business he soon made his fortune. In the wake of the Jacobite rising of 1745 he accompanied the duke of Cumberland as commissary for bread and forage in Scotland (1746–8), and by his favour he was appointed commissary for stores in Flanders (1747–8) and in Scotland (1748–57). With seven battalions stationed in Scotland and a major building project beginning at Fort George, Ardersier, Lawrence grew rich. He used his wealth to buy a residence in Argyle Square, Edinburgh, and in 1747 he obtained the estate of Kerse, near the mouth of the River Carron in Stirlingshire, which, bought in the name of his father, passed to him in 1750. In 1747 Lawrence was elected to parliament as MP for Linlithgow Burghs, having paid what Scotland's political manager, the third duke of Argyll, described as 'the greatest sum to purchase an election that was ever known in the country' (HoP, *Commons, 1715–54*, 1.628). He also helped his friend, George Haldane, to win Stirling Burghs. Both Argyll and the prime minister, Henry Pelham, objected to Dundas's successful campaign, for which he had not sought government approval. Argyll collected evidence of bribery against the new MP and displayed his hostility by ensuring that the post of barrack-master in Scotland was given neither to Dundas nor to his nominee, Lord Lauderdale. Dundas was unseated, on the grounds of electoral corruption, in March 1748. His attempt to return to parliament at the election of 1754 was unsuccessful, and it became clear that his political career would be blocked during Argyll's lifetime.

Thwarted in politics, Lawrence Dundas focused his efforts on social advancement. He joined the Society of Dilettanti in 1750 and sent his son, Thomas [iii], to Eton College. In 1756 he purchased the house and lands of Castlecary, Stirlingshire, formerly owned by members of the Baillie family. Lawrence's career as an army contractor was furthered by the outbreak of the Seven Years' War (1756–63), which generated supply contracts for a combined force of British and allied troops in north-west Germany numbering 100,000 men with 60,000 horses. Dundas was soon involved in creating magazines for forage (1757–8), and on 16 March 1759 he engaged to supply the Hanoverian army with bread for six months. Although this contract was not renewed he secured others for a series of wagon trains, and from these and other activities he had acquired massive profits by the end of the war. James Boswell's claim that Dundas would 'bring home a couple of hundred thousand pounds' (11 Dec 1762, *Boswell's London Journal*, ed. F. A. Pottle, 1950, 75) underestimates the scale of profits, which others have put at between £600,000 and £800,000. Yet whatever the potential for corruption it appears that Dundas's gross profit rate (estimated at 17 per cent in 1762; see Little, 383) was not excessive; rather his success may be attributed to the huge scale of the contracts with which he was involved.

In 1762, through his involvement with Lord Shelburne, whom he had met in Germany, Dundas negotiated a baronetcy and the purchase of a parliamentary seat. Shelburne accepted a large loan and on 19 August 1762 informed Henry Fox that 'Dundas, the Nabob of the North, writes me to desire I'll get him made a baronet; this made me go to Lord Bute yesterday' (HoP, *Commons, 1754–90*, 2.358). He received his title on 20 October, and by the end of the year had become MP for Newcastle under Lyme.

1762 also saw the death of his father, Thomas [i], who was buried in the Old Greyfriars churchyard, Edinburgh, on 2 June.

Throughout this period Sir Lawrence continued his series of considerable land purchases. Between 1759 and 1762 he paid £63,696 for an estate in the counties of Sligo and Roscommon, in Ireland, and a further £31,000 for Ballinbreich, Fife. In 1762 he acquired Marske and Upleatham, in the North Riding of Yorkshire, and Aske Hall, with its Richmond estate and pocket borough, on the west side of the North Riding. In December he paid about £22,000 for most of the Clackmannan estate, once the patrimony of his wife's relatives, while leaving the last Bruce laird in the castle, which was purchased later. Following the peace of 1763 he purchased the palatial Moor Park, Hertfordshire, for £25,000 and a house in Arlington Street, London, for £15,000. In the following year he added Loftus to his Yorkshire properties, and in 1766 acquired the Earldom estate, Orkney, and the lordship of Shetland for £63,000. Two years later he purchased Burray and its associated lands on other Orkney islands for £16,500. All these acquisitions made him one of the great landowners of the United Kingdom. He also became owner of two slave estates in the West Indies; one in Dominica and the other in Grenada. Later acquisitions were few but significant. In 1773 he bought Letham from his elder brother, Thomas [ii]. His culminating achievement came later that year, in Edinburgh, when he used his influence with the town council to obtain the best site in the New Town, originally intended for a church, and there built Dundas House, St Andrew Square (designed by Sir William Chambers and now head office of the Royal Bank of Scotland).

Besides his taste for property Dundas was also active in commerce and finance. He had a preponderant interest in the Forth and Clyde Navigation Company and dug the first spadeful of earth when work began on the canal in June 1768. The line surveyed ran conveniently via Castlecary, Carron Hall and Kerse, enhancing the value of these Dundas properties. He was a governor of the Royal Bank of Scotland (1764–77), and in 1767 secured the parliamentary act that led to the building of Edinburgh's New Town. Other campaigns in the Commons included his (only partly successful) attempt to have Treasury commissioners settle war contractors' accounts in full. He also failed in another aim—elevation to the House of Lords and a leading role in Scotland's political management—for which he needed more influence than even his wealth and connections could achieve. Re-elected for Edinburgh in 1768, 1774, and 1781, he established himself at the head of a small parliamentary group of relatives and friends whose support was useful for the prime minister, Lord North. Denied a peerage by George III, despite assisting the Grafton ministry to influence the election of East India Company directors, Sir Lawrence was given a consolation position on the privy council in October 1771.

However, by the mid-1770s relations with North had grown increasingly strained. Dundas was now subject to attacks from a distant kinsman, Henry Dundas of Melville (1742–1811), later Viscount Melville, who entered the Commons in 1774 and became lord advocate in Scotland in the following year. In alliance with the duke of Buccleuch, Henry Dundas was soon in a position to influence Lord North and to challenge Sir Lawrence's control of Edinburgh town council. Sir Lawrence's success, not to mention his often controversial business practices, had provoked envy and opposition for a number of years. Under Henry Dundas's co-ordination he now became the target of a pamphlet war that exposed his alleged corruption and vanity. Trade guilds were encouraged to break free of his control and in 1777 he was ousted from his governorship of the Royal Bank of Scotland. Increasingly disgruntled with North's refusal to curb the actions of his lord advocate, Sir Lawrence began building bridges to the opposition Rockingham whigs. At the election of 1780 he faced a concerted attack from the Henry Dundas–Buccleuch interest but was still able to bargain successfully to retain control of three Scottish seats: Stirlingshire, held by his son, Thomas [iii]; Orkney and Shetland, held by his nephew Charles Dundas; and his own Edinburgh constituency. James Boswell, who met Dundas for the first time during the contest, commented that to his surprise he was not the 'cunning shrewd man of the world as I had imagined' but a 'comely jovial Scotch gentleman of good address but not bright parts … I liked him much. I even felt for him as a man ungratefully used in his old age' (20 Sept 1780, *J. Boswell: Laird of Auchinleck, 1778–1782*, ed. J. W. Reed and F. A. Pottle, 1977, 251). Sir Lawrence was now sixty-eight. He died on 18 September 1781 at Aske Hall, near Richmond, Yorkshire, and was buried in the Dundas mausoleum attached to Falkirk parish church, in Stirlingshire. According to the *Annual Register* he left £900,000 in personal effects and landed property, together with debts in mortgages, bonds, and annuities amounting to £400,000.

Later politics   It was clear, certainly by the mid-eighteenth century, that Sir Lawrence had emerged as the dominant figure in the Dundas family. This is not to say that his elder brother, **Thomas** [ii] **Dundas of Fingask** (c.1708–1786), was an insignificant figure in Scottish property markets and politics but rather that Sir Lawrence's immense and rapidly made fortune enabled him to become the principal agent for the advancement, or rescue, of other family members, of which his purchase of Letham, in 1773, was the most eloquent statement. Thomas [ii] had previously worked as Lawrence's agent during his period as an army contractor. It was an association that brought him wealth also and, as in the case of his brother, facilitated his establishment as a significant owner of property. Purchase of Drumdryan House, Edinburgh, was followed by that of Quarrell, near Larbert, Stirlingshire, together with its coalworks and collier serfs, in January 1749. Having sold Drumdryan, Thomas then enlarged the old manor house at Quarrell and renamed it Carron Hall. In 1751 he bought lands at Torwood, north of Larbert. Notwithstanding his involvement with his brother's commercial enterprise Thomas clearly lacked Sir Lawrence's business talent, displaying instead a gentlemanly interest in genealogy and heraldry that led to his appointment as deputy lyon king of arms (1744–54). In 1768 he was elected MP for Orkney and Shetland, from which he retired two years later in favour of his son Thomas (1750–1794). Thomas [ii] died at Carron Hall on 17 April 1786 after a long period of ill health. He was survived by his wife, Lady Janet, who retired to Northumberland Street, Edinburgh, where she died on 29 December 1805.

Sir Lawrence's only son, **Thomas** [iii] **Dundas of Kerse**, first Baron Dundas of Aske (1741–1820), politician, was born in Edinburgh on 16 February 1741. The beneficiary of his father's considerable wealth, he followed his education at Eton College with two years at St Andrews University (1756–8). He was introduced by Sir Lawrence to the freemasons of St Giles Lodge, Edinburgh, and in December 1758, aged seventeen, was elected master of St John's Lodge, Falkirk. Between 1759 and 1763 he toured Europe, visiting France, Switzerland, and Italy. He was summoned home in order to enter parliament as MP for Richmond in Yorkshire (for which he sat between 1763 and 1768), and to take his place in metropolitan society. Writing to his wife from Aske Hall, Sir Lawrence Dundas requested that she did not leave London before Thomas (known as Thomie) was:

> properly presented at Court and has seen Lord Bute, Lord Northumberland, [and] if possible the Duke of Bedford … Tell Thomie that I wish my friends to be his and these are the people I desire him to be known to … Order him to have his teeth put in and let him dress like an Englishman. (Ashcroft, 20–21)

On 24 May 1764 Thomas [iii] married Lady Charlotte Fitzwilliam (1746–1833), daughter of the third Earl Fitzwilliam and a niece of the marquess of Rockingham. The couple, who lived principally at the family's Yorkshire estate of Upleatham, had fourteen children, eleven of whom reached adulthood.

During the late 1770s Thomas [iii] Dundas, now MP for Stirlingshire, actively defended his father's national and local political reputation from the attack led by their kinsman Henry Dundas. Thomas followed his father into the Rockingham camp, a position that, in view of his opposition to political corruption and sympathy for moderate reform, was a more natural association than that effectively forced on Sir Lawrence. On his father's death, in September 1781, Thomas became second baronet and, with property yielding £16,000 per annum, securities valued at £300,000, and numerous art treasures, was the principal beneficiary of Sir Lawrence's will.

During the 1780s Sir Thomas emerged as a supporter of Charles James Fox and secured a few favours for associates and relatives; a close friend of the prince of Wales, he was also made one of George's councillors of state. With his father dead, Sir Thomas now negotiated the family's removal from the costly world of Edinburgh politics, effected in return for a government loan of £50,000 to the Forth and Clyde Navigation Company, in which, like Sir Lawrence, Thomas was involved. However, he did maintain his political influence elsewhere in Scotland. In 1784 he held Stirlingshire and once more secured Orkney and Shetland for his cousin Thomas (1750–1794). He also contented himself with choosing MPs for his pocket borough of Richmond, one of whom was his cousin, Charles, who sat from 1784 to 1786. He also maintained what proved a never particularly effective parliamentary opposition to Henry Dundas. Thomas's position was later weakened further with the success of a government-sponsored candidate, John Balfour, at Orkney and Shetland in the election of 1790, which also reduced Thomas's influence in the northern burghs. During the 1780s he had combined opposition with a campaign for political reform. However, his appetite for change was deadened by the increasingly violent course of the French Revolution. Shocked by the excesses of the revolutionaries, he left Fox and sided with the Portland whigs in their support of the Pitt administration. His reward was a peerage, and on 13 August 1794 he became Baron Dundas of Aske. Thereafter he was denied further political advancement and was unable to restore the family's former Scottish influence until 1818, when his sixth son, the naval officer George Heneage Lawrence Dundas, agreed with a fellow officer, Captain William Balfour RN, that their families should share representation of Orkney and Shetland in alternate parliaments.

As a friend of the prince of Wales Lord Dundas enjoyed an active social life, being a member of Brooks's Club, the United Service Club, the Society of Dilettanti, and the Society of Antiquaries. From 1793 to 1813 he was the effective commander of the Yorkshire militia, and was lord lieutenant and vice-admiral of Orkney and Shetland between 1794 and 1820. An enthusiastic agricultural improver, he spent his income from rents on draining and enclosing land, experimenting with new crops and breeds (including merino sheep), using bone and gypsum manures, and building water- or horse-powered threshing mills. The family's alum works at Loftus were enlarged and he ran a successful alkali works at Dalmuir, Dunbartonshire. As governor of the Forth and Clyde Navigation Company (1786–1816), he presided over the canal's completion and the creation of Grangemouth and Port Dundas. He also persuaded the company to test the first practical steam-tug, the *Charlotte Dundas*. Lady Charlotte had herself always advocated retrenchment, and she was occasionally heeded. In 1785 Dundas sold Moor Park, without its contents, for £25,000 and, three years later, Dundas House, Edinburgh, for £10,000. After selling numerous paintings from the family collection in May 1794, he parted with most of the family's Irish estate in 1809 for £177,490. In 1812 he obtained an act of parliament allowing him to sell feu and teind duties in Orkney and Shetland.

Lord Dundas died at Aske Hall, near Richmond, on 14 July 1820, and was buried some days later in the Dundas mausoleum at Falkirk parish church, Stirlingshire. He was survived by his wife, who died on 11 February 1833; the barony passed to their eldest son, Lawrence Dundas (1766–1839), a determined whig politician who was created first earl of Zetland in 1838.

The Dundas family owed its place in late eighteenth- and early nineteenth-century national society to the remarkable career of Sir Lawrence Dundas of Kerse. Starting behind a shop counter in the Luckenbooths, Edinburgh, he amassed the wealth that enabled the family to buy its way into the whig oligarchy, to further the careers of other successful relatives, and to play a prominent role in the politics and land management of Scotland. The best monument to Sir Lawrence's success, as well as his determination, underhand methods, and excellent taste, remains Dundas House, St Andrew's Square, Edinburgh, which is still the New Town's finest building. Yet for all their wealth and local influence the Dundases of Fingask and of Kerse remained subordinate to a kinsman whose still crucial attachment to king and prime minister gave him precedence. Appropriately the statue in the centre of St Andrew's Square is not of Sir Lawrence, his brother, or nephew but of their rival Henry Dundas, later Lord Melville. In death, as in life, Harry IX succeeded and overshadows the Nabob of the North and his kind.

R. P. FEREDAY

Sources M. Dundas, *Dundas of Fingask: some memorials of the family* (1891) · M. Y. Ashcroft, 'The Zetland (Dundas) archive', *North Riding Record Office annual report* (1971), 12–18 · J. Harris, 'The Dundas empire', *Apollo* (Sept 1967), 170–79 · D. Sutton, 'The Dundas pictures', *Apollo*, 86 (1967), 204–13 · E. Haden-Guest, 'Dundas, Lawrence', HoP, *Commons, 1715–54* · E. Haden-Guest, 'Dundas, Lawrence', 'Dundas, Thomas (c.1708–86)', 'Dundas, Thomas (1741–1820)', HoP, *Commons, 1754–90*; D. G. Henry, 'Dundas, Thomas', HoP, *Commons, 1790–1820* · A. Murdoch, 'The importance of being Edinburgh: management and opposition in Edinburgh politics, 1746–1784', *SHR*, 62 (1983), 1–16 · H. M. Little, 'The treasury, the commissariat and the supply of the combined army in Germany during the seven years war, 1756–1763', PhD diss., U. Lond., 1981 · J. Lindsay, *The canals of Scotland* (1968) · M. Fry, *The Dundas despotism* (1992) · I. G. Brown, 'John Kay's satires on Lawrence Dundas', *Book of the Old Edinburgh Club*, new ser., 3 (1994), 123–30 · R. P. Fereday, *The Orkney Balfours, 1747–99* (1990) · 'Dundas, Thomas (1750–1794)', *DNB* · T. Johnston, *The old masonic lodge of Falkirk* (1887) · J. Smith, 'Notes on lands of High Riggs, Drumdryan and Tolcross', *Book of the Old Edinburgh Club*, 18 (1932), 169–71 · Burke, *Gen. GB* · Burke, *Peerage* · *Scots Magazine* (1781), 503 · NA Scot., CC 8/129/1, fol. 165 [death of Lawrence Dundas] · parish register, Edinburgh, North Kirk, 28 Oct 1712 [baptism: Lawrence Dundas] · parish register, Edinburgh, North Kirk, 16 Feb 1741 [baptism: Thomas [iii] Dundas] · IGI

Archives Berks. RO, family corresp. and papers incl. genealogical notes · N. Yorks. CRO, corresp. and papers [Sir Lawrence Dundas] · N. Yorks. CRO, Zetland (Dundas) archive · NA Scot., Dundas of Fingask papers · NA Scot., Dundas of Kerse estate records · NA Scot., Dundas and Wilson papers · NL Scot., letter-book in Germany [Sir Lawrence Dundas] · Orkney Archives, Kirkwall, earldom of Orkney (Dundas) papers | Edinburgh City Archives · NA Scot., Carlops and Abbotskerse muniments · NA Scot., Mar and Kellie muniments · NMM, letters to Lord Sandwich [Sir Lawrence Dundas] · PRO, Treasury records

Likenesses T. Hudson, oils, 1760–69 (Lawrence Dundas (1712–1781)), Aske, Richmond, North Yorkshire · P. Batoni, oils, 1764 (Thomas [iii] Dundas (1741–1820) of Castle Cary), Aske, Richmond, North Yorkshire · J. Zoffany, oils, 1769 (Lawrence Dundas (1712–1781) and his grandson, Lawrence Dundas), Aske, Richmond, North Yorkshire

Wealth at death £16,000 p.a. devolved on son; also £900,000 in personalties and landed property: *Annual register* (1781), 214 · £400,000 debts: Ashcroft, 'The Zetland (Dundas) archive', 27

Dundas, Ada Charlotte (*b.* **1864**, *d.* after **1931**). *See under* Women artists in Ruskin's circle (*act.* 1850s–1900s).

Dundas, Charles, Baron Amesbury (1751–1832), politician, was born on 5 April 1751, second son of Thomas *Dundas (c.1708–1786) [*see under* Dundas family of Fingask and Kerse], landowner, of Fingask, Stirlingshire, and his second wife, Lady Janet Maitland (1721–1805), daughter of Charles Maitland, sixth earl of Lauderdale and Elizabeth Ogilvy. His family's fortunes had been made by his uncle Sir Lawrence Dundas (c.1710–1781) [*see under* Dundas family of Fingask and Kerse] as commissary-general in the Seven Years' War; this wealth bought the clan lands and connections from Shetland to Berkshire, and political influence usually cast on the whig side.

Dundas was educated at Edinburgh high school then, from 1768, Edinburgh University and from 1769 Trinity College, Cambridge (BA 1773, MA 1776). He was admitted to the Middle Temple in 1774 and called to the bar in 1777. On 16 February 1782, having come into his inheritance, he married Anne Whitley (*d.* 1812), daughter of Ralph Whitley of Aston Hall, Flintshire; his marriage brought him the estates of Kentbury–Amesbury in Berkshire, which had descended to his wife from her grandmother, Anne Loder. They had one daughter, Janet.

In 1775 Dundas entered parliament for Richmond, Yorkshire, one of his family's seats. In 1780 he switched to another, Orkney and Shetland, which his father had represented briefly from 1768 to 1770, then back to Richmond in 1784–6. His allegiances were also wayward. Starting in support of Lord North, he drifted into opposition and stayed there during the ministry of Lord Shelburne, then voted successively with William Pitt the younger and Charles James Fox. To Fox, however, he remained attached until his cousin Sir Thomas Dundas, a leader of the Portland whigs, moved over with them in 1794–5 to support the government in the French war. One reward was his return to parliament in August 1794, after eight years' absence, as MP for Berkshire, which he represented until 1832.

Dundas's political waywardness matured into an independence which made his local position unassailable. While 'disposed to vote in general with ministers', he was a 'friend to peace' (HoP, *Commons*, 3.633) and other causes enjoying little ministerial approval: abolition of the slave trade, parliamentary reform, Catholic emancipation. He disliked personal animosities and reserved his energy for measures useful to a county: to regulate the sale of corn by weight, to promote planting of potatoes on common land, to relieve hardship caused by collection of tax, and to encourage inland navigation. In 1802 he declined to become speaker when proposed by Sheridan and Lord George Cavendish. By 1814 he had fallen out of the habit of regular attendance but afterwards always voted with the whigs, while refusing to put his name to anything or attend partisan meetings.

Dundas's second marriage on 25 January 1822 was to his cousin, Margaret Erskine (*d.* 1841), daughter of the Hon. Charles Barclay Maitland and Isabel Barclay, and widow successively of Charles Ogilvy of Inchmartin and of Major Archibald Erskine of Venlaw. Dundas was ennobled on 16

May 1832, but died of cholera at his home in Pimlico, London on 30 June 1832. The title became extinct and his only child, Janet, who had married Sir James Whitley Deans Dundas in 1808, died in April 1846.   MICHAEL FRY

Sources D. R. Fisher, 'Dundas, Charles', HoP, *Commons* • *DNB* • GEC, *Peerage* • *GM*, 1st ser., 102/2 (1832), 177–8 • Venn, *Alum. Cant.* **Archives** N. Yorks. CRO, corresp. • Wilts. & Swindon RO, letters | Berks. RO, Benyon MSS • Berks. RO, Neville MSS • Hants. RO, Tierney MSS
Likenesses W. Say, mezzotint (after W. Beechey), BM, NPG

Dundas, Sir David (1735?–1820), army officer and military writer, was born in Edinburgh, the third of the four sons of Robert Dundas, a prosperous Edinburgh merchant, and his wife, Margaret (*b.* 1707), daughter of Robert Watson of Muirhouse. Through his mother's family he was a half-cousin of Henry Dundas, Viscount Melville. He entered the Royal Military Academy, Woolwich, as a cadet in 1750, and from 1752 until 1756 accompanied his maternal uncle, Lieutenant-Colonel David Watson, on the Ordnance's first major cartographical survey of Scotland. Dundas graduated from Woolwich as a lieutenant fireworker in the Royal Artillery on 1 March 1755 but resigned soon afterwards when, on 21 December 1755, he was appointed a practitioner engineer in the corps of engineers. In that capacity, in 1756, he was made assistant quartermaster on Watson's survey. His early technical training in the ordnance corps will have been crucial to his later development, as to his tactician's eye for distances and ground.

Dundas retained his commission in the engineers until September 1757, even after he obtained a lieutenancy in the new raising 58th foot on 3 January 1756; and it was as an engineer that he accompanied the expeditions which raided St Malo and Cherbourg in 1758, taking part in the brutal rearguard action at St Cast on 11 September. He joined the army in Germany, again as an engineer, in the autumn of 1758, but returned to England early in 1759 to obtain a captaincy, dated 21 March 1759, in the Hon. George Augustus Eliott's new raising 15th light dragoons, the regiment in which he was to serve until 1775. Although promoted sub-engineer on 17 March 1759, Dundas resigned his engineer's commission on 9 September 1759. In July 1760 he embarked with the 15th for service in Germany, where Eliott, commanding a cavalry brigade in the allied army under Ferdinand of Brunswick, made Dundas his aide-de-camp; and Dundas took part in the battles of Warburg and Kloster Kamp on 31 July and 16 October 1760 and the battle of Vellinghausen on 15–16 July 1761. When, after the campaign of 1761, Eliott was made second in command of Albemarle's upcoming Cuban expedition, Dundas went with him, again as his aide-de-camp, and was present at the fall of Havana in August 1762.

After returning to Britain in January 1763, Dundas was in France in 1764, embarking on the professional studies that were to bear fruit later in his career. From the peace until 1774 he served in England as a regimental officer in the 15th, in which corps, on 28 May 1770, he was promoted major, probably by purchase. He returned to the continent in 1774 to observe the French and Austrian training

camps. Made lieutenant-colonel in the army by brevet on 11 September 1775, he eleven days later purchased the lieutenant-colonelcy of the 12th light dragoons, a regiment on the Irish establishment. He passed the American War of Independence on the Dublin staff, having been made Irish quartermaster-general in 1778, a post which he was to retain until 1789. On 19 November 1781 he left the 12th for the lieutenant-colonelcy of another Irish regiment, the 2nd horse; he was promoted colonel in the army, by brevet, on 14 February 1782.

On 31 August 1783 Dundas resigned his commission in the 2nd horse, leaving regimental service in order to devote himself to his staff duties and to the studies that were to result in his major treatise on drill. Already long in draft when he attended the Prussian manoeuvres in 1785, 1786, and 1787, his *Principles of Military Movements, Chiefly Applied to Infantry* was published in London in 1788 (2nd edn, 1795). The work was an immediate success because it not only laid bare the irregularity prevailing in the army's current training and drill, but also served as a critique of the widespread influence in the army of an unsound tactical doctrine deriving from its experience in the Americas. Dundas severely criticized the fad for unrealistic light formations and tactics—the result of operations against irregular forces bereft of cavalry—which were characterized by thin lines, open intervals, and speedy movements, all at the expense of solidity, mobility, and fire control, the decisive factors in linear tactics. The work, and the drill regulations developed from it, were to be criticized for paying too little attention to the training and tactics of light infantry, already an important element in European tactical theory and soon to play an important battlefield role; but it was Dundas's purpose to restore the heavy infantry, and in this he was eminently successful.

Opening with a discussion of the basic mechanics of linear movements and the tactical principles on which they should be based—which provided in turn the foundation for training, for uniformity, and thus for advanced manoeuvres—the *Principles* went on to lay out a sound and sophisticated system of drill and tactics designed for the battalion and the larger line, which could be adopted army-wide. Attached to the book, for the benefit of regimental officers (who were to nickname him 'Old Pivot' for his pains), was an abstract of the whole, in which his system of drill was reduced to eighteen comprehensive manoeuvres.

With the firm support of George III and the Irish lord lieutenant, the marquess of Buckingham, and in conjunction with generals Sir William Pitt and the earl of Ross in Dublin and, in London, the duke of York, Lord Heathfield, and (undoubtedly the crucial catalyst) the adjutant-general Sir William Fawcett, Dundas was able to begin to test and revise his drill for army-wide issue. Over the years 1788–91 the large Dublin garrison, with the expanses of Phoenix Park close at hand, was exercised in Dundas's drill and under his direction. His principles were tested and refined, and with such success that an official abridged version of his book (the interim *Rules and Regulations for the Field Exercise and Movements of the Army in Ireland*) was issued to the whole of the army in Ireland as early as 1 July 1789. In 1789 he was made adjutant-general in Ireland, the staff post most to the purpose; and during this period he was promoted major-general on 28 April 1790, and on 2 April 1791 was rewarded with the colonelcy of the 22nd foot. Further tests and revision resulted in the issue to the army generally, on 1 June 1792, of the *Rules and regulations for the formations, field-exercise, and movements, of his majesty's forces*, the regulations that were to see the British heavy infantry through the French Revolutionary and Napoleonic wars, and indeed well beyond. There were many subsequent imprints, widely published; and that section of his *Principles* in which he had abstracted his system into eighteen comprehensive manoeuvres, and which was included in the 1792 *Rules and Regulations*, was also widely reprinted in various handy versions.

After resigning his adjutant-generalcy in 1791, Dundas left the Irish staff in 1793 when he joined the duke of York's army in Flanders, from where, late in the campaign, he travelled overland to Toulon. Appointed second in command of the British and allied troops holding the town for the royalists, he took the command when General O'Hara was captured. He and Admiral Hood evacuated Toulon on 19 December 1793, taking the troops to Elba and, in early February, on to Corsica to assist Paoli's insurgents against the French. Early in the Corsican operations, however, Dundas, ill and at odds with Hood, went home on sick leave. In 1794 he joined the duke of York's contingent of the allied army in Flanders, where, commanding a cavalry brigade, he took part in the heavy fighting about Tournai late in May; and he remained with the army as it was slowly pushed back into north Brabant, retreating into northern Germany early in 1795 and embarking in January 1796 with the remnants.

After his experience with the mounted regiments in the Netherlands and Germany during the operations of 1794–5, Dundas prepared a cavalry drill based upon the system which he had used in the light dragoons, modified to correspond with the plan and tactical system of his *Principles*. This work, combined with a revision of the standing orders prepared by Lord Pembroke for the 2nd dragoon guards, was issued by authority as the interim *Rules and Regulations for the Cavalry* (1795). Dundas revised this drill extensively, working it up in a cavalry camp, again under Sir William Pitt's command; and on 17 June 1796 the results were issued army-wide as the *Instructions and Regulations for the Formations and Movements of the Cavalry*. Like his drill for the heavy infantry, these cavalry regulations were to appear in revised editions and abridgements over subsequent years.

On 23 December 1795 Dundas was given the colonelcy of the 7th dragoons, and on 8 November 1796 he was appointed quartermaster-general on the London staff, a post that he held until 1803. He was promoted lieutenant-general on 26 January 1797. During his years on the London staff, and notably during the anti-invasion planning of 1796–9, he played an instrumental role in the preparations for Britain's home defence. In September 1799 he accompanied the duke of York, with reinforcements including a large Russian contingent, when the duke took command of the force recently landed by Sir Ralph Abercromby on the Dutch coast near The Helder. Dundas, serving with Abercromby as one of the four lieutenant-generals in the British contingent, commanded columns at the battles of Bergen on 19 September and Egmond aan Zee on 2 October 1799. He was rewarded on 15 February 1800 with the sinecure governorship of Landguard Fort.

With his professional interests, it was natural that Dundas should be a member of the committee of general officers that in 1801 presided over the creation of the Royal Military College. He was made colonel of the 2nd dragoons on 16 May 1801, and made governor of Fort George the same year; on 29 April 1802 he was promoted full general. He resigned as quartermaster-general on 15 March 1803, and in 1804–5 was in command of the crucial southern district of Kent and Sussex, the most likely place for a French landing. In 1804 he was made knight of the Bath and appointed governor of Chelsea Hospital. He resigned the southern district in 1805, owing to illness, and retired to Chelsea, where he made his home for the remainder of his life. It was only now that Dundas married: on 21 July 1807, at Westelleon in Hampshire, he married Charlotte (*d.* 1840), daughter of General Oliver De *Lancey (*c.*1749–1822), army officer. In 1808 he acted as president of the court of inquiry into the convention of Cintra, and, during the duke of York's temporary eclipse following the Mary Anne Clarke affair, he was commander-in-chief of the army from 18 March 1809 until 26 May 1811, when the duke was able to return to the Horse Guards. As commander-in-chief Dundas was sworn of the privy council; he was also made colonel-in-chief of the 95th rifles on 31 August 1809 and given the additional colonelcy of the 1st dragoon guards on 27 January 1813, retaining both corps until his death.

Dundas, who had no children, predeceased his wife, dying of old age at Chelsea Hospital on 18 February 1820; he was buried in the grounds of the hospital. When Charlotte died in April 1840, Dundas's property was left to a nephew, Robert Dundas of Beechwood in Midlothian, principal clerk of the court of session in Scotland.

Although Dundas was described by the unsympathetic Sir Henry Bunbury as 'a tall, spare man, crabbed and austere, dry in his looks and demeanour', his dress and style earning 'some ridicule among young officers' (Bunbury, *Narrative of some Passages in the Great War with France from 1799 to 1810*, 1854, 46), the written work from his middle age and later years shows him to have been among the most intelligent and knowledgeable of his officer contemporaries. He assisted throughout in the duke of York's reforming efforts, which were of untold value to the British army. The duke of Wellington's superb peninsular and Waterloo heavy infantry was his professional legacy.

J. A. HOULDING

Sources J. A. Houlding, *Fit for service: the training of the British army, 1715–1795* (1981) • R. Glover, *Peninsular preparation: the reform of the British army, 1795–1809* (1963) • *Army Lists* (1754–1804) • J. Philippart, ed., *The royal military calendar*, 3rd edn, 1 (1820), 284–301 • R. F. Edwards, ed., *Roll of officers of the corps of royal engineers from 1660 to 1898* (1898) • Succession Books, PRO, WO.25/209, fols. 63, 137; WO.25/211, fol. 12th D; WO.25/212, fol. 2nd H • Fortescue, *Brit. army*, 2nd edn, vol. 4 • P. Mackesy, *Statesmen at war: the strategy of overthrow, 1798–1799* (1974) • N. B. Leslie, *The succession of colonels of the British army from 1660 to the present day* (1974) • P. Mackesy, 'What the British army learned', *Arms and independence: the military character of the American Revolution*, ed. R. Hoffman and P. J. Albert (1984), 191–215 • D. W. Marshall, 'The British military engineers, 1741–1783', PhD diss., U. Mich., 1976 • J. E. Cookson, *The British armed nation, 1793–1815* (1997) • *DNB* • *GM*, 1st ser., 77 (1807), 681 • *GM*, 2nd ser., 13 (1840), 667 • *GM*, 1st ser., 90/1 (1820), 274–5 • S. G. P. Ward, 'Three watercolour portraits', *Journal of the Society for Army Historical Research*, 66 (1988), 63–71 • will, PRO, PROB 11, 11/1626, sig. 135

Archives BL, papers and corresp., Add. MSS 27594–27600; 38245–38246; 38361; 46702–46711; King's MSS 240–242 • NAM, corresp. and papers as quartermaster general | BL, corresp. with Spencer Perceval and Lord Palmerston, Add. MS 27598 • NA Scot., letters to Sir Alexander Hope • NA Scot., corresp. with Lord Melville • NAM, corresp. with J. Drinkwater relating to Toulon prize money • NMM, letters to Lord Hood • NRA Scotland, priv. coll., MSS • PRO NIre., corresp. with Lord Castlereagh • West Highland Museum, Fort William, corresp. with Henry Dundas

Likenesses H. Raeburn, oils, 1809, Arniston House, Lothian • S. W. Reynolds, uncoloured mezzotint, *c.*1809 (after W. Owen), NAM • R. Deighton, caricature, coloured etching, pubd 1810, BM, NPG • F. Chantrey, pencil drawing, NPG • H. R. Cook, stipple (after W. Owen), BM, NPG; repro. in *Royal Military Panorama* • S. Drummond, oils, Scot. NPG

Wealth at death £25,000 in Bank of England stock; shares in the Globe Insurance Co.; also held sinecures at Fort George and the Royal Hospital; also emoluments of his colonelcies and general officer's pay: will, PRO, PROB 11/1626, sig. 135

Dundas, Sir David (1799–1877), politician, the eldest surviving son of James Dundas of Ochtertyre, Perthshire, and his wife, Elizabeth, daughter of William Graham of Airth, Stirlingshire, was born in Edinburgh. He attended Westminster School and then went in 1816 to Christ Church, Oxford, where he graduated BA in 1820, and was elected a student; he proceeded MA in 1822. He was called to the bar at the Inner Temple on 7 February 1823, and went on the northern circuit. He was also a member of the Scottish bar. In February 1840 he was appointed QC, later being elected a bencher of his inn.

From March 1840 until 1852, and again from March 1861 until May 1867 Dundas represented Sutherland as a Liberal. On 10 July 1846 he was appointed solicitor-general under Lord John Russell, receiving the customary knighthood on 4 February 1847. Indifferent health obliged him to resign office on 25 March 1848, when it was thought he would have accepted the permanent and more comfortable post of principal clerk of the House of Lords. He, however, declined it. In May 1849 he again took office, this time as judge-advocate-general, was sworn of the privy council on the following 29 June, and retired with his party in 1852. Thereafter it was understood that he did not care for further professional or political advancement. An accomplished scholar, he lived a somewhat retired life at his chambers, 13 King's Bench Walk, Inner Temple, where he had brought together a fine library. He died unmarried at his chambers, on 30 March 1877. Dundas was an honorary MA of Durham University, and from 1861 to 1867 a trustee of the British Museum. He always gave his steady support to Westminster School, and was a constant attendee at its anniversaries and plays. He was one of those 'Old Westminsters' who (successfully) most strongly opposed the proposal of removing the school into the country.   GORDON GOODWIN, *rev.* H. C. G. MATTHEW

Sources J. Welch, *The list of the queen's scholars of St Peter's College, Westminster*, ed. [C. B. Phillimore], new edn (1852) • Boase, *Mod. Eng. biog.* • *Law Times* (18 July 1846) • *Law Times* (1 April 1848) • *Law Times* (7 April 1877)

Archives NL Scot., corresp. and papers | Castle Howard, Yorkshire, letters to C. W. G. Howard • Dalkeith Palace, Midlothian, Buccleuch MSS • NL Scot., corresp. incl. with Lord Rutherford • NL Scot., letters to the duke of Sutherland • NRA, corresp. with Lord Panmure • NRA, priv. coll., letters to Robert Stewart • PRO, corresp. with Lord John Russell, PRO 30/22 • Staffs. RO, letters to the duke of Sutherland

Wealth at death under £40,000: probate, 27 April 1877, *CGPLA Eng. & Wales*

Dundas, Francis (1759?–1824), army officer, of Sanson, Berwickshire, was the second son of Robert *Dundas, Lord Arniston (1713–1787), who held various important judicial posts in Scotland, and his second wife, Jean, daughter of William Grant, Lord Prestongrange. He was appointed ensign 1st foot guards on 4 April 1775, and became lieutenant and captain in January 1778. In May 1777 he was one of the officers of the guards sent out to relieve a similar force in America. He fought at the battle of the Brandywine and at Germantown, in the attack on the Delaware forts, and in the battle of Monmouth during the march from Philadelphia to New York. He was frequently employed on detached services during the campaigns of 1778–9, and being appointed to the light company of his regiment, commanded it under Lord Cornwallis in Carolina and Virginia, where it formed the advance guard of the army, and was daily engaged with the enemy. He was one of the officers who surrendered with Cornwallis at Yorktown, on 19 October 1781.

Dundas became captain and lieutenant-colonel on 11 April 1783, exchanged as lieutenant-colonel to 45th foot, and then in 1787 to 1st Royals, a battalion of which he commanded in Jamaica from 1787 to 1791. He was adjutant-general with Sir Charles Grey at the capture of Martinique and Guadeloupe in 1794. He was made major-general in 1795. In October 1794 he became colonel-commandant of the Scots brigade, for which he raised an additional battalion. The same year he was ordered to the West Indies with the expedition under Sir Ralph Abercromby, but, being driven back by bad weather to Southampton, was countermanded and appointed to command the troops at the Cape of Good Hope, and went there in August 1796.

The chief events of Dundas's military command in South Africa were the mutiny on board the men-of-war in Table Bay in 1797, and the Cape Frontier War on the Sundays River in 1800. Together with the command of the troops he held the post of acting governor from Lord Macartney's departure in November 1798 until the arrival of the new governor, Sir George Yonge, in December 1799, and again from the recall of the latter in 1801 until the colony was restored to the Dutch in 1803.

In 1800 Dundas married Eliza, daughter of Sir John

Cumming of the East India Company; they had two sons and a daughter. He commanded the Kent division of the army collected on the south coast of England under Sir David Dundas during part of the invasion alarms of 1804–5, commanded a division under Lord Cathcart in the Hanover expedition of 1805–6, and again commanded on the Kentish coast after his return. He became lieutenant-general in 1802, and general in 1812.

In 1809 Dundas had been appointed colonel of the 71st Highland light infantry. He was also transferred from the governorship of Carrickfergus, to which he was appointed in 1817, to that of Dumbarton Castle. He was never on half pay. He died at Dumbarton on 15 January 1824.

H. M. CHICHESTER, *rev.* LYNN MILNE

Sources M. Arkin, 'Dundas, Francis', *DSAB* · Burke, *Peerage* (1939) · *GM*, 1st ser., 94/1 (1824), 378–9 · F. W. Hamilton, *The origin and history of the first or grenadier guards*, 3 vols. (1874) · Chambers, *Scots.* (1835)
Archives Brenthurst Library, Johannesburg, papers relating to Cape Colony · Duke U., Perkins L., estate accounts and papers · NA Scot., observations on the preparation for invasion at Boulogne
Likenesses J. Downman, chalk and watercolour drawing, 1793, Arniston House, Midlothian · D. Gardner, pastel and gouache drawing, Arniston House, Midlothian · J. Kay, etching, BM · H. Raeburn, oils, Arniston House, Midlothian

Dundas, Henry, first Viscount Melville (1742–1811), politician, was born on 28 April 1742 at Arniston House, Edinburghshire, Scotland, fourth son among seven children of Robert *Dundas, Lord Arniston (1685–1753), and his second wife, Ann (1705–1797), daughter of Sir William Gordon of Invergordon (*d.* 1742) and Isabel Hamilton of Halcraig. The Dundases of Arniston were the most distinguished legal family in Scotland, three generations having already served as lords of session and in other offices. The mother's family were northern whigs.

Early life Dundas went to the grammar school of Dalkeith, the Royal High School, Edinburgh, and the University of Edinburgh. He wrote his 'Disputatio juridica' on the status of acts by guardians and was called to the bar in 1763; he would take the degree of doctor of laws only in 1789, in return for raising money to complete the new university then being built to the design of Robert Adam. As a student his attainments had been social rather than academic, in the Speculative Society, Belles Lettres Society, and also as a freemason, circles where much of the social life of enlightened Edinburgh went on. He was so clubbable that a club, the Feast of Tabernacles, formed round him.

On 16 August 1765 Dundas married Elizabeth (1751–1843), coheir of David Rannie (1712–1764), merchant and shipbuilder. She had a fortune of £10,000 but Dundas squandered it on investment in the Ayr Bank, which crashed in 1772. They inherited Rannie's seat of Melville Castle, Edinburghshire; Dundas was to have it rebuilt in 1786–98 by James Playfair. In Edinburgh they lived at 5 George Square. They had four children: Elizabeth (1766–1852), who married her first cousin, Robert Dundas of Arniston (1758–1819); Anne (1768–1852), who married Henry Drummond (1762–1794), and James Strange (1753–

Henry Dundas, first Viscount Melville (1742–1811), by Sir Thomas Lawrence, 1810

1840); Robert *Dundas, second Viscount Melville (1771–1851); and Montague (1772–1837), who married George, second Lord Abercromby (1776–1843). Divorce took place in 1778 on grounds of Elizabeth's adultery with Everard Fawkener whom she subsequently married. Dundas remarried on 2 April 1793; his second wife was Lady Jane Hope (1766–1829), daughter of John, second earl of Hopetoun (1704–1781), and his second wife, Jean Oliphant of Rossie (*d.* 1767). They had no children.

At the start of his career Dundas had to supplement his income with work for the corporation of Edinburgh and the Church of Scotland. But his legal connections soon brought him big cases, including a part as junior counsel in the Douglas cause, the disputed succession to the vast patrimony of the extinct dukedom of Douglas. In 1766 he was appointed solicitor-general for Scotland, an office involving management of official business with the kirk. He at once made his mark in that year's general assembly by repelling the evangelical party's 'schism overture', a move to end lay patronage, much to the relief of the religious and political authorities. He also gained experience of electoral law, notably over a disputed poll at Cromarty in 1768, where he acted for his uncle Sir John Gordon of Invergordon.

Yet Dundas complained that the routine of the courts tired and bored him. With a few professional feathers in his cap he resolved to enter parliament. His family held the effective patronage of Edinburghshire (Midlothian), which since 1761 they had given to Sir Alexander Gilmour. They hinted heavily, to no effect, that he should step aside. Dundas went ahead and opposed Gilmour anyway, and won with ease in his only ever contested poll on 20 October 1774. He lost little time in impressing himself on Westminster. He made his maiden speech on 20 February 1775. In May he became lord advocate in succession to Sir James Montgomery.

Management of Scotland Since abolition of the post of secretary of state for Scotland after the last Jacobite rising in 1746, the lord advocate had become the country's chief officer of government, responsible for what administration and legislation remained necessary. More to the point for his compatriots, he was also a fount of patronage, though his ability to dispense it tended to depend on some unofficial Scottish manager, generally noble, closer to the hub of power. After the fall of the earl of Bute in 1763, however, there was no such person, a lack acutely felt by Scots. Dundas's domestic achievement was to arrogate the manager's functions to the office of lord advocate, so as in effect to subject Scottish affairs to one man, in the first instance himself, and ensure *de facto* that a minister for Scotland continued to exist.

One means to this end was to make Scottish government more active. In general, however, no more than an eye had to be kept on the national institutions guaranteed by the treaty of union. The universities were embarking on their most brilliant era, while the church of Scotland remained subdued under the leadership of principal William Robertson and his moderate party. The sole trouble on the religious front came from Dundas's attempt in 1778–9 to grant relief from the worst of the penal laws to Roman Catholics, following similar measures in Quebec and Ireland, now in preparation for England too. Though approved in the general assembly, his plans aroused furious popular protest, with riots in Edinburgh, Glasgow, and elsewhere. He had to back down. In reaction Robertson confined himself for the future to academic business, while management of the assembly passed to Dundas's nephew and solicitor-general, Robert Dundas, later to Dr George Hill, principal of St Mary's College, St Andrews. The two non-Presbyterian religious minorities, Episcopalians and Roman Catholics, had to wait until 1792–3 for relief.

Scots law was also enjoying a golden age under Henry's elder brother Robert *Dundas (1713–1787), lord president of the court of session, who expeditiously adapted the system to social and economic change. But it was run on a shoestring, with rewards for judges meagre compared to the volume of business. Henry Dundas proposed in 1785 a diminishing bill to reduce the number of gowns through natural wastage from fifteen to ten, the salary left over to be divided among the rest. Once more he met fierce opposition, now from electors in the counties condemning this as an infringement of the treaty of union. Once more he gave way, and no major legal reform was to take place until 1806–7. Such episodes showed that the terms of the union could not yet, even with the best intentions, be easily tampered with.

Where Dundas avoided touching on these sensitivities he achieved more. Half a highlander himself, he took a close interest in the north of Scotland. Problems there

came to his attention in 1775 through heavy emigration to America by men of military age who might be tempted to join the colonists' revolt. He forbade the Scottish board of customs to clear from its ports any more ships carrying them. But he knew this to be only a temporary answer to deep difficulties arising from the collapse of the old social order since 1746. Some of his remedies were symbolic. In 1781 he repealed the Disarming Act to allow highlanders to wear kilt and tartan again. He lobbied for restoration of forfeited Jacobite estates to families which originally owned them, many having since served the house of Hanover. He became a commissioner of the estates in 1783 with a brief to wind the old policy up. The next year he introduced a bill to disannex them from the crown (himself taking the chance to acquire a small estate at Dunira, near Comrie, Perthshire, which became his favourite residence). Still he wanted some agency, if no longer an agency of the state, to pay heed to the region as a whole, and promoted foundation of the Highland Society in 1784, then the British Fisheries Society in 1785. Later he was to encourage Thomas Telford to lay down the modern system of communications in the north. He impotently deplored the onset of the clearances.

Dundas most clearly established his authority in electoral control of Scotland. Manipulation of fictitious votes was becoming common through perversion of the Scots law of the franchise. This Dundas first tried to salvage. He inherited a bill from Montgomery to define voters' qualifications more strictly, but could not carry it. He then gave up reform as a bad job and began to use the system for his own ends. He formed alliances with great noblemen, the dukes of Buccleuch and of Hamilton in the south, dukes of Atholl and of Gordon in the north, and proved adept at bringing landowners into complex schemes for sharing spoils. For himself, he carried on a costly campaign against his kinsman Sir Lawrence Dundas, and his allies the Rockingham whigs, over the city of Edinburgh, which the latter's death in 1781 resolved in Henry's favour. He became its MP in 1790, representation of the capital now being consonant with his dignity. By the general election of 1796, at his apogee, he had Scotland so well organized that in the whole country just four polls took place. He serenely held forty-three seats, failing only by a fluke to win the remaining two.

Uniting the kingdoms Dundas's concern to make his mark in Scotland was linked to wider ambitions. From the outset he meant to be in equal measure a Scottish and British politician. He was well prepared for opportunities that came his way with the political upheaval unleashed by the lost war in America. He supported Lord North until the fall of the government in 1782, but smoothly went over to his successors, first Lord Rockingham (this not in a spirit of amity), then Lord Shelburne, becoming treasurer of the navy under the latter.

Each change involved long, complex negotiations. During one such round Dundas at first took no notice when, in an aside, Shelburne ventured that they might all end up serving under William Pitt the younger, a parliamentary novice wearing the aura of an illustrious father. Somehow the words lodged in Dundas's mind, though, and came back to him in March 1783 amid plots that led to coalition between Charles James Fox and Lord North. This, bringing together Dundas's worst enemy (as residual legatee of the Rockingham whigs) and his best patron to date, menaced his career. He tried to foil it by pushing Pitt as prime minister instead. The effort came to nothing and the coalition was formed anyway. To Dundas's surprise it kept him on as lord advocate, until a terse letter of dismissal arrived from Fox in August. The eclipse proved only temporary as George III set about destroying the coalition. In December he succeeded. Dundas meanwhile firmly allied himself with Pitt, and the pair stood ready to take over. For four months they faced a hostile House of Commons, refusing either to resign or dissolve, while Dundas did more than anyone else to help Pitt to frustrate and wear down the opposition. At a division in March 1784 they lost by a single vote and went straight to the country. The election brought ample victory for Pitt, if only modest gains for Dundas in Scotland.

Partnership with Pitt proved the key to Dundas's career. Forged in this initial adversity, it strengthened as they worked in unison on complex administrative problems for the rest of the decade and in the following one fought a war together. Amid the vagaries of public life it later loosened somewhat, but never broke. At the end of Pitt's days, in 1805 and 1806, it was restored to being as close as it had ever been.

To begin with, most observers regarded Dundas as a politician decidedly of the second rank, doubtless diligent and useful but at the limit of his capacities. Also, being a Scot, Dundas was an outsider at Westminster, by no stretch of the imagination a rival to his chief. What made the difference was Pitt's disdain of his cabinet, which he reduced to a nullity. This opened the way for Dundas to reach a powerful informal position as friend, adviser, and factotum. They would discuss and settle public business while riding or walking at the beginning and end of the day, often round the mansion of Cannizaro (named after an Italian duke formerly resident there) on Wimbledon Common which Dundas bought in 1786. Their intimacy still seemed belied by the difference, indeed stark contrast, between the bluff, practical, knowing Scot and his boyish, reserved, high-minded leader. Many held that Dundas corrupted Pitt with his cynicism and hard drinking. In fact they complemented each other. Pitt provided inspiration, while Dundas saw to the hard labour and the dirty work. Ready to find time for intellectuals and eager for their ideas, he himself was a man of action, a shrewd judge of people and events able to tell as if by instinct who would win and what would work. Loyal and even-tempered, he was content to discharge his duties without seeking more than he knew Pitt was willing to give. Where his chief came across as stiff and cold, Dundas remained always human, interested in those he had to deal with while entertaining no illusions about them. A master of expediency, he also knew the meaning of a fair deal.

Dundas's role was recognized in 1791 when he became home secretary in place of William Grenville. Pitt meant Dundas only to keep the seat warm for Lord Cornwallis, who had to be recalled from India. All the same, Dundas set about his duties with a will. He suppressed popular unrest sparked off by the French Revolution, beginning with Church and King riots in Birmingham in July 1791. In Scotland disturbances erupted with a riot in Edinburgh on the king's birthday, 4 June 1792, when Dundas's residence in George Square was attacked and he himself burned in effigy. He acquitted himself well enough to be confirmed in office after the arrival of Cornwallis, for whom Pitt found something else. Dundas then remained in the cabinet until 1801.

Dundas thus became the first Scot since 1707 to reach the top of British politics and stay there. In Scotland he henceforth exercised only general supervision, leaving detail to his nephew Robert, now lord advocate. Where he impressed his countrymen was by supplying them with official patronage in Britain and the empire which they thought had been wanting so far. Their cupidity evoked jealousy or scorn from Englishmen, but their rewards were the small change of common exertions by which, in the French wars especially, the two nations came to feel they were equal partners. Still, Dundas took care not to overdo things, treated Englishmen with good-natured fellowship, and would have offered the same services to the Irish had he been able.

Dundas saw the answer to Ireland's complaints in replicating what he had done for Scotland. He intended, after union with Great Britain and indulgence to Catholics, to make Henry Grattan Irish secretary in London, as counterpart to himself. For Dundas, as for Pitt, rebellion in 1798 clinched the argument in favour of union, which by their efforts was inaugurated on 1 January 1801. Attempting to proceed straight to Catholic emancipation, they brought on the crisis which ended their years in power. George III refused his assent to anything likely to violate the oath he had taken at his coronation to uphold protestantism. Even Dundas's urgings could not move him. He ended them during a levee at St James's with, 'None of your damned Scotch metaphysics, Mr Dundas!' (*Diaries of Sylvester Douglas*, 1.147). Pitt had no choice but to resign, and Dundas handed in his seals on 17 March. They had unified the British Isles but, contrary to their will, in a form which would not in the long run endure.

Imperial strategy The new British bonds forged by Dundas could not have been so strong unless linked also to the empire, which remained an abiding interest of his. The first imperial problem he met, as he began his career at Westminster, was the outbreak of the American War of Independence. It formed the subject of his maiden speech, when he urged the hardest possible line against the rebels. He thus aligned himself with those hawks who enjoyed a parliamentary ascendancy until the first big British defeat at Saratoga in 1777. This, followed by France's joining in on the American side, brought a change of mind. When North again proposed conciliation Dundas issued him a veiled challenge to say if the war could still be won. He himself toyed with the notion of federal union as preferable to losing the colonies or letting them fall into the hands of France. Later, when the war reached stalemate, and later yet, when fortune attended British arms in the Carolinas, he once more seemed to turn aggressive. But it is clear from his private correspondence that by the end of 1780 he had decided the war could not be won. He bided his time to make this judgement public until the surrender of Yorktown a year later. The subsequent king's speech opening the new parliamentary session ignored what had happened, prompting Dundas's most significant intervention in the Commons to date. He broke the official façade of unity and revealed within the government men like himself who now differed little from the opposition's view that the fighting had somehow to be ended. It was a bold and astute stance to be taken up by a minor politician, with as much to lose as to gain from saying the unsayable, articulating the flaws in an untenable policy. In any event he added his weight to the pressures which brought down North and opened the way to peace.

Afterwards Dundas constantly bore in mind the genesis of the United States. The peopling of colonies would, he believed, create demands for autonomy, then independence, with disruption or loss of British commerce. Under his subsequent Indian regime, therefore, he prohibited permanent residence by British subjects, who were allowed out only under licence and urged to come home once their business was done. Where settlers were already present, as in Canada, he retarded political development. He conceived of this second British empire, after 1783, as a trading rather than colonizing one, built on commercial outposts for the exploitation of resources which remained in the hands of alien peoples, though this last point had to be modified in the light of geostrategic developments.

In India also Dundas took an early interest. It had personal origins. His family never quite made the grade as nabobs, though not for want of trying. Like many a needy Scots clan they sent sons to the east. Three of Dundas's brothers went and two died there. His contributions to Indian debates brought a reward in 1781 with appointment as chairman of the secret committee inquiring into the recent war in the Carnatic with Haidar Ali, sultan of Mysore. His organization of the proceedings so as to give malcontents a say without embarrassing a shaky government was a godsend. A year later he wound up this work in forty-five resolutions calling on parliament to intervene and send out commissioners with authority to remedy the evils. He then proposed another resolution blaming Warren Hastings for having condoned incompetence at Madras—which presaged, for those with eyes to see, his decisive vote three years later in favour of the governor-general's impeachment.

In April 1783 Dundas essayed legislation of his own which embodied a clear new maxim for Indian government. Effective sovereignty was to be vested in central authorities, both in an administration at home under a secretary of state, and in a governor-general's office in India given the power to match its responsibilities. The measure, if widely praised, had no chance of passing amid the current political confusion, and was overtaken by the India Bill of the Fox–North coalition. When the coalition fell and Pitt came to power, Indian reform remained outstanding. Without fixed ideas of his own, the new prime minister was content to take over several of his lieutenant's.

What became the India Act of 1784, and remained the primary legislation for government of the subcontinent until 1857, thus owed a great deal to Dundas. He did not this time try to do so much, but concentrated on relations between the British government and the East India Company. Compared to previous schemes his bill took less power for the first and left greater independence to the second. The government was not to rule India directly but to entrust that to a board of control. The first members were nevertheless senior political figures, including Dundas and Pitt. Dundas took effective charge of it, the main instrument of administration being the correspondence between him and the governor-general. He enjoyed specially good relations with Cornwallis, whom he induced to take the job by an amending act in 1786 which further enhanced executive power. The office as thus established to Dundas's satisfaction was his most durable achievement, lasting in essentials until the end of the raj. His declaratory act of 1788, ending disputes over the army maintained by the company, then put its directors in their place. Finally, his legislation of 1793 renewing its charter won a yet larger share for the crown in the joint administration. The main departure was to formalize Dundas's unofficial role, creating for him a post of president of the Board of Control, at £2000 a year, and a permanent, salaried staff.

The company yet remained in existence and in business. British hegemony rested on it and required a degree of indulgence to it, so that its privileges could only be dismantled if no political risk was entailed. Dundas nominally upheld the monopoly, but in piecemeal fashion regulated it so as to encourage gains from trade through new channels. He found scope to attack weak links in the abuses which monopoly threw up. He thus reconciled vested interests to novel economic principles, which can be broadly described as more free-trading (and owed to Dundas's mentor, Adam Smith). They were still set in the framework of an imperial system and so remained limited compared to what would be taken for granted in the nineteenth century. To Dundas's mind they were above all conceived as answers to practical problems.

Dundas found, for example, that the biggest adverse item in Britain's balance of payments arose from a growing deficit against imports of tea from China. He sought a remedy through construction of a trading triangle, with more British goods going to India and development of commerce from there to China. This required that still closed empire to be opened up, for which purpose he sent out three unsuccessful embassies. A better bait was new products, of which opium would be the most fateful. Dundas did not want to operate any mercantilist system of colonial exclusion, as Britain had earlier done in America and other powers still did in their possessions. If foreigners possessed the capital and kept out of trouble, they should be free to enter the commerce and would then have no grievances to justify subversion. Spain concluded an agreement in 1788. The Compagnie des Indes was granted a limited trade under British protection in the French commercial treaty of 1786. Britain's real competitor was the Netherlands, to which Dundas put a package for division of the oriental spoils, though no agreement on it could be reached. A further aspect of his Indian economic policy was to promote the 'country trade', by which the company's servants deployed their private fortunes outside the monopoly. From 1793 he obliged the company to offer in its ships room for goods owned by individuals worth £300,000 a year. In 1796 he tried to break the British circle through which the company financed and built all its ships, in particular by opening this market to cheaper vessels constructed in the subcontinent, but succeeded only to a limited extent.

More important in the event than commercial regulation was the political context in which the company operated, since its business could hardly flourish without peace. A prime purpose of Dundas's reforms had been to put an end to its expensive, corrupting record of petty wars and random annexations. His legislation provided that the authorities in India might neither take up arms against nor even conclude a treaty with any native prince, except if London consented. They were only to interfere at all should a European power take one side, in which case they were to take the other. Tipu Sahib, successor to Haidar in Mysore, severely tested these good intentions. His aggressions provoked the British to attack him in 1789, but only after three years could Cornwallis oblige him to sue for peace and hand over half his territory. At this point the governor-general returned home, leaving the bitter sultan to plot revenge, soon by cultivating relations with revolutionary France.

As global war developed in the next decade Dundas hoped to send Cornwallis back for a second term, but his services were needed elsewhere. At length, in 1798, the earl of Mornington, granted the British title of Lord Wellesley, became governor-general. He made conquest again the centrepiece of policy. Given Dundas's desire to keep trade open, a military solution was doubtless inevitable for the problems of security created by France's resurgent oriental ambitions, evinced in her attention to Egypt. Wellesley's assault on Mysore in 1798 ended with the death of Tipu at Seringapatam and annexation of much of the rest of the sultanate, a measure soon emulated in the Carnatic and in Oudh. This solved problems dogging even the reformed British administration. It settled the balance of power for good. Neutrality among native princes had not in fact maintained a balance nor mitigated the prevailing anarchy. France was under a standing temptation to exploit this. To such a tangle of problems British supremacy offered the simplest answer.

After twenty years of reform, the crown otherwise won what it wanted in the east: control of the broad lines of policy, without stifling restriction, on the contrary with some liberalization, of commercial interests. Pitt and Dundas thus set up a dual system, one which served well until the complete overhaul required after 1857. The caution and economy of Dundas's methods ought not to obscure the boldness of his conceptions. Change took place not only in personnel and instruments, but also in purposes and attitudes. The whole amounted to a fresh start, a new philosophy in Indian government turning it from mercantilist pillage to imperial administration. Only the question how much of India should be ruled directly remained open.

War with France Dundas became secretary of state for war in July 1794. Pitt shifted him sideways to create scope for strengthening the government by the accession of the duke of Portland's whigs. In return the duke demanded the Home Office for himself. But Pitt thought him incapable of handling the military responsibilities which would thus pass to him, for the defence of Britain and her colonies. He therefore created a new post in order to entrust them to Dundas.

Since the outbreak of war early in 1793 its conduct on the allied side had turned into a shambles, and the first coalition was already crumbling. The failures could not be divorced from the processes of British policy making by a triumvirate of Pitt, Grenville, and Dundas. Dundas was a realist interested in the empire, Grenville a precisian captivated by the concert of Europe, while the mediation of their quarrels fell to Pitt, closer in outlook to the former, in character to the latter, but coming to value Grenville's judgement above Dundas's. The man left in the minority felt vexed and unsettled by this, above all by the fretful niggling with Pitt and Grenville brought out in each other and which found release in bouts of impulsiveness. Dundas, by contrast, was the least opportunistic, the least likely in crises to fall for hasty, ill-judged expedients. His nerve showed itself steadier when things kept going wrong in Europe, and he refused to be deflected from the colonial campaigns he wanted to fight.

Dundas saw the war as essentially economic, the war of a worldwide trading nation. Since the rise of European empires it had become normal in their conflicts for them to seize one another's possessions overseas, which at the peace could be swapped against other advantages or held as compensation for any adverse change in the balance of power. To Dundas this was how Britain should now exploit her maritime strength to damage the enemy in every way possible, attacking his outposts, ruining his trade, sapping his naval resources. Europe therefore had to take second place. Britain, with a population one-third the size of France's, could anyway only ever have a relatively small army, too small to hope for successful continental campaigns. As in previous general wars, the French would instead have to be defeated on land by a European coalition. Britain's most useful contribution would come from her ample resources of money to subsidize allies. So, from the security offered by command of the narrow seas, she should above all 'protect the essential interests of commerce and navigation' (Cobbett, *Parl. hist.*, 33.582). She would then be neutralizing the one threat to her own ability to sustain the struggle. And even if war went badly, as it did for a Britain now standing alone in 1797–8, she could still maintain an effective defensive posture against invasion behind a naval blockade of the enemy.

In practice, with divided counsels at the top, Britain made no clear choice of strategy. Dundas did win agreement early in the war for a major expedition to the West Indies. It set off in November 1793 and quickly captured several islands. This was enough to make the tactic worth trying again when, two years later, the war in Europe seemed lost. Despite extreme pressure on resources, the second expedition was the biggest ever to leave these shores. In the spring of 1796 about 30,000 troops set out, but half were to die of tropical sickness. With such appalling casualties and no chance of adequate reinforcement, Britain could after all do no more than make sure of what she had. The last months of 1796 saw a final assault on Spain's possessions, prompted by her declaration of war on Britain. The capture of Trinidad marked the close of the main conflict in this theatre, with little to show for it other than an extended string of outposts requiring protection at a cost Britain could no longer afford. A maritime strategy evidently had its penalties too.

In other theatres it proved hard to maintain clear strategic priorities. From the start Pitt felt obliged to offer some material help to allies, however unreliable. He could not stop France defeating Austria, Prussia, and the Netherlands, from the last of which Britain recalled in the spring of 1795 a now impotent expeditionary force. With the declaration of the Batavian Republic, Dundas had at once to secure the route to India and send out squadrons to capture the chain of Dutch stations to the east: Cape Town, Colombo, Trincomalee, and Malacca.

Then Napoleon Bonaparte's brilliant conquest of Italy in 1797 increased the naval forces ranged against Britain and turned almost the whole northern seaboard of the Mediterranean into a hostile one. Grenville, believing losses had to be cut somewhere, demanded abandonment of the entire theatre. For this he carried the cabinet against the opposition of Dundas, who felt sure the French, left unchallenged, would try through Egypt to seize the overland route to India and imperil Britain's eastern empire. He was at once alerted when Napoleon started massing troops at Toulon in 1798, whence indeed they sailed to Alexandria. The British rushed every possible ship eastwards but the fleet, commanded by Admiral Horatio Nelson, could only follow a good three weeks behind, too late to stop the French landing. But Nelson, by a smashing victory at Abu Qir Bay, did ensure that Napoleon would stay marooned by the Nile for the time being. Dundas's colleagues were forced to admit he had been right, and that Britain could still deprive France of control in the Mediterranean if she wanted to.

This signal success at long last for British arms spurred other powers to re-enter the war. Austria, Naples, Portugal, Prussia, Russia, and Turkey did so in the second coalition. Dundas remained unimpressed. In a long memorandum on the strategic situation, put to Pitt in December 1798, he cautioned against a premature belief in the defeat of France or a trusting reliance on fair-weather friends, so that Britain should not drop her guard over her interests for the prospect of an early peace (NA Scot., GD 51/1/772/1). His warnings against European entanglements were all the same ignored. After the coalition had made headway by concerted offensives, the British government responded not just with subsidies but also with an expedition to the island of Walcheren, intended to launch an allied reconquest of the Netherlands. But it was defeated, and this marked the end of serious activity by the second coalition.

Then, in October 1799, Napoleon slipped past the British ships patrolling off Egypt and regained his own country, to stage the *coup d'état* of 18 Brumaire and set himself up as dictator. He fulfilled both French and foreign expectations by launching at once into vigorous attacks on his continental foes. Britain's expedients, in the face of this renewed aggression, seemed exhausted. Her own territory and most of her colonies were in practice unassailable; she remained free of the mastery established by the French over western Europe, while she had mastered the Orient as far as she needed. But resources for successful initiatives elsewhere did not exist. The British government remained divided all through 1800: with one or two, like Dundas, still hoping for energetic prosecution of the war. The fact of the matter was that Britain could make neither peace nor war.

The one blemish in the tidy division of global control was the army left by Napoleon in Egypt. Dundas feared that the French aimed to establish a colony on this land bridge between east and west which would pose a permanent, mortal danger to the British empire. It was therefore vital to get them out as a preliminary to treating with France; to throw the same object into negotiation might require the sacrifice in exchange of some other captured points of strategic importance. But a war-weary government could not summon up the will for a fresh trial of strength. Dundas took it upon himself to relieve his colleagues of any collective responsibility by declaring he would answer for the enterprise personally. On that understanding, opposition was withdrawn. Dundas then had to go again over all the same ground, and resort to the same expedient, to persuade an unwilling George III. Sir Ralph Abercromby landed in Egypt in 1801 and in a couple of months won a decisive victory, though also a glorious death, at the battle of Alexandria. The French surrendered and were expelled. With them went for ever their country's hopes of dominion in India. Meanwhile, Nelson had beaten the enemy fleets at Copenhagen. The war seemed to have turned again in Britain's favour. The king rode out in person to Wimbledon to toast the minister who had dared to stand up to him and had been vindicated.

The government shortly fell all the same. Dundas, retired to Scotland, did not stand on bad terms with Pitt's successor, Henry Addington, who raised him to the peerage at the end of 1802 as Viscount Melville and Baron Dunira. But he had been open in criticism of the peace of Amiens, and his relations with the government worsened once war resumed. By the spring of 1804, when Napoleon was camped with the *grande armée* at Boulogne, a stronger ministry had become imperative. All Addington's enemies concerted their strength, and Melville hurried to London to help in restoring Pitt. The latter, however, found himself unable to form the broad-based government he wanted. Indeed he had trouble keeping Melville, the sole figure of the first rank remaining to him, now accused by the king of having been too disloyal to Addington.

The post Melville wanted and at length got was first lord of the Admiralty. The country felt no less alarmed than in 1797, but he was sure invasion could be defeated. Against it he devised a triple shield: blockade of the enemy's ports, control of the narrow seas, and means of resistance along the coasts. It occurred to him that he could demonstrate to the French the vanity of their designs by running fire ships into the harbours and destroying the transports. He himself sailed across to stand off Boulogne and observe an experiment on these lines—the nearest he ever got to going abroad.

On Melville's taking office the navy had eighty-one ships of the line afloat. The number of vessels launched during his term at the Admiralty was higher than in any similar period of its history. By the summer of 1805 Britain boasted 105 ships of the line on active service, and five others almost of the same standard. That autumn she would have 120, including 26 new ones. Of these, 80 were deployed round Europe, most on the dreary and arduous duty of blockading; 24 rode off Brest alone. This meant that the French, Dutch, and Spanish fleets, though together bigger than the Royal Navy, were useless because they could not get out of harbour. Britain then ruled the rest of the world's oceans. Melville maintained that, since there was no chance of challenging Napoleon on land, a bigger and better navy offered the only chance of renewing offensive operations. He was promptly vindicated by Nelson's victory at the battle of Trafalgar. This settled the naval war for the duration. Never again would France dare to challenge Britain at sea. That meant Britain could not be defeated, even while she and her allies were still a long way off defeating France. Nelson had been an untiring importuner at the Admiralty for ever more vessels to deploy in his actions, and Melville had done everything possible to satisfy these demands. He could claim to be the man who made the dead hero's triumph possible.

Impeachment and death By the time of Trafalgar, however, Melville had left the Admiralty, the events which led to his impeachment being under way. They arose from legislation which he himself had passed in 1785 to sort out the chaotic finances of the navy. As its treasurer he failed, however, to follow his own regulations. This inconvenient fact now came to the notice of a commission of inquiry. It found out in particular that Melville had not, as required, kept at the Bank of England official disbursements allocated to him though not yet spent. Since he refused to co-operate in showing where else they had gone, the focus of the investigation switched to his subordinate, Alexander Trotter, paymaster of the navy. Trotter eventually admitted to having drawn money from the bank and laid it out in investments of his own, a practice by no means uncommon among public servants at the time, if in this case expressly prohibited by law.

The commission's report came out in March 1805. While it stopped short of saying that Melville had lined his own pockets, it blamed him for what had been going on. This threatened not only to end his career but also to bring down the government. To win time Pitt offered a parliamentary inquiry, but Samuel Whitbread countered with a motion of censure. It was called on 8 April and, in the division at the end of a tense all-night debate, the ayes and noes stood each at 216. Mr Speaker Abbot sat 'white as a sheet' (R. G. Thorne, 'Abbot, Charles', HoP, *Commons, 1790–1820*, 5) for ten minutes before giving his casting vote against an inquiry, after which Whitbread's motion was carried without further division. Melville had no choice but to resign. Complex manoeuvres during the rest of the summer resulted in the Commons' voting articles of impeachment drawn up by Whitbread. Both Melville and Pitt thought this better than any form of prosecution, since the peers were more likely than the courts to acquit.

The impeachment, the last ever of a British minister, went to the House of Lords as its first ordinary business in the session of 1806, the day before Pitt's death in January. The trial itself opened on 29 April amid huge public excitement, in a Westminster Hall thronged by notables. But in the full light of day the prosecution's case looked thin. Only the first of ten articles charged Melville with corruption. The rest concerned Trotter, so far arraigned of nothing. Whitbread set out his case with a scoff—'Scotland bowed down before this idol'—but that was his last good line (*Memorials … by Henry Cockburn*, 203). It all grew a trifle boring, amid the rehearsal of evidence heard dozens of times before and the erection by Melville's lawyers of a maze of technicalities. On 12 June he was acquitted of nearly all charges by comfortable majorities: only on two dealing with Trotter's embezzlement were they smaller.

But to Melville full vindication meant return to office. Frustrated at his exclusion, he wasted his last years in futile fulminations and vain plots, fuelled by heavy drinking. Despite help from well-wishers, the cost of the trial had been ruinous and he could barely afford to attend parliament. He even vented his wrath on his son, whose political advancement he tried to block in case this hindered his own comeback. It was something of a relief to those around him when he died in his sleep on 27 May 1811 at 55 George Square, Edinburgh, apparently of a condition of the heart. He was buried on 8 June in the family's lair at the old kirk of Lasswade, Edinburghshire.

Melville stood high in the estimation of Scotland, Britain, and the empire at the time of his death, as attested by tributes written and monuments erected to him. But he aroused peculiar rancour among the Scots whigs whom he kept so long in the wilderness. His kinsman Henry Cockburn gave them ammunition in his memoirs with many *aperçus* which were still generous in a personal sense but harped on the plenitude of his power. This was the prelude to a sharp fall in Melville's reputation in the later nineteenth and the twentieth century. It created a conventional view of him as a monster of corruption and oppression who had sold out his country and countrymen to the English. For good measure Sir John Fortescue's military history condemned Melville's conduct of war, which certainly looked the worse if no account was taken of his maritime strategy. But Vincent Harlow's imperial history, stressing his creative rethinking, began a rehabilitation which in the military sphere was completed by Michael Duffy's and David Geggus's effective refutation of Fortescue's strictures. More recent scholarship has pointed to his role in maintaining the cohesion of Scottish government and in averting the subordination that Irish government suffered, while making the union of 1707 a partnership which justified calling the empire a British rather than an English one.　　　　　　　　　　MICHAEL FRY

Sources M. Fry, *The Dundas despotism* (1992) · H. Furber, *Henry Dundas, first Viscount Melville, 1742–1811* (1931) · C. Matheson, *The life of Henry Dundas, first Viscount Melville, 1742–1811* (1933) · *Memorials of his time, by Henry Cockburn* (1856) · *The diaries of Sylvester Douglas (Lord Glenbervie)*, ed. F. Bickley, 2 vols. (1928) · Fortescue, *Brit. army*, vol. 4 · V. T. Harlow, *The founding of the second British empire, 1763–1793*, 2 vols. (1952–64) · G. W. T. Ormond, ed., *The Arniston memoirs, 1571–1838* (1887) · H. W. Meikle, *Scotland and the French Revolution* (1912) · W. L. Mathieson, *The awakening of Scotland: a history from 1747 to 1797* (1910) · J. Dwyer, R. A. Mason, and A. Murdoch, eds., *New perspectives on the politics and culture of early modern Scotland* (1982) · M. Duffy, *Soldiers, sugar, and sea power: the British expeditions to the West Indies and the war against revolutionary France* (1987) · D. Geggus, 'The case of Pitt's Caribbean campaigns', *HJ*, 26 (1983), 699–706 · D. J. Brown, 'The government of Scotland under Henry Dundas and William Pitt', *History*, new ser., 83 (1998), 265–79 · J. Ehrman, *The younger Pitt*, 3 vols. (1969–96) · *DNB* · *Scots peerage* · NL Scot., MS 547, pp. 459–60

Archives Bank of Scotland, Edinburgh, corresp. as governor of Bank of Scotland · BL, corresp. and papers, Add. MSS 27594–27596, 40100–40102, 41079–41085, 41345, 41767–41768, 43770 · BL, military and political corresp., loan 57 · BL OIOC, corresp. and papers · BL OIOC, corresp. and papers relating to India · BLPES, corresp. and papers relating to Scottish transport · Bodl. Oxf., papers relating to East India Company · Bodl. RH, corresp. relating to West Indies · Brenthurst Library, Johannesburg, corresp. relating to Cape Colony · Duke U., corresp. and MSS · Harvard U., business school, commercial corresp. and MSS · Harvard U., corresp. · JRL, corresp. and papers relating to India · L. Cong., corresp. and MSS · NA Scot., corresp. and papers · NA Scot., family corresp. · NL Ire., corresp. and papers relating to Ireland · NL Scot., additional corresp. · NL Scot., corresp. and papers · NL Scot., corresp. · NMM, naval corresp. and papers · PRO NIre., papers relating to Ireland · SOAS, letters relating to India · U. Aberdeen, corresp. and MSS relating to the Isle of Man · U. Mich., Clements L., corresp. and papers · U. St Andr., corresp. and papers relating to St Andrews · Wellcome L., corresp. and papers relating to medical service in India · Wellcome L., corresp. and papers mainly relating to Scotland · West Highland Museum, Fort William, corresp. relating to highland military affairs · Yale U., Beinecke L., corresp. mostly relating to Scottish affairs | BL, corresp. with Lord Auckland, Add. MSS 34412–34460 · BL, corresp. with Lord Grenville, Add. MSS 58914–58918 · BL, corresp. with Warren Hastings, Add. MSS 29168–29192, 29234 · BL, letters to Lord Hardwick, Add. MSS 35662–35754 · BL, corresp. with William Huskisson, Add. MSS 38734–38737 · BL, corresp. with Harford Jones, Add. MS 41767 · BL, corresp. with Lord Liverpool, Add. MSS 38192–38424 · BL, corresp. with Lord Wellesley, Add. MSS 13456–13459, 37274–37276, 37285,

37309–37310 · BL, letters to Earl Spencer · BL, corresp. with William Windham, Add. MSS 37874–37879 · Bucks. RLSS, corresp. with Scrope Bernard · Bucks. RLSS, corresp. with Lord Hobart · CKS, letters to Frederick North · Cumbria AS, Carlisle, letters to Lord Lonsdale · Devon RO, corresp. with Lord Sidmouth · Devon RO, letters to J. G. Simcoe · Falkirk Museums History Research Centre, letters to Forbes family · Harrowby Manuscript Trust, Sandon Hall, Staffordshire, letters to Lord Harrowby · Herefs. RO, corresp. with Harford Jones · JRL, letters to William Pitt · Kimberley Public Library, letters to Lord Macartney · Morgan L., letters to Sir James Murray-Pulteney · NA Ire., corresp. with Lord Westmorland · NA Scot., corresp. with Lord Buccleuch · NA Scot., corresp. with Sir John Gordon, letters to his mother · NA Scot., letters to Sir James Grant · NA Scot., corresp. with Sir Alexander Hope · NA Scot., letters to William Macdowall · New York Historical Society, letters incl. Rufus King · NL Scot., corresp. with Sir Alexander Cochrane · NL Scot., letters to Sir William Forbes · NL Scot., corresp. with Lord Keith · NL Scot., corresp. with Lord Lynedoch · NL Scot., corresp. with Lord Minto · NL Scot., corresp with Donald Robertson · NL Scot., letters to Sir William Young · NL Wales, corresp. with Lord Clive · NMM, corresp. with Lord Barham · NMM, letters to Sir William Cornwallis · NMM, letters to Lord Nelson · NRA, priv. coll., letters to William Adam · NRA, priv. coll., letters to Sir Adam Fergusson · NRA, priv. coll., corresp. with Spencer Perceval · NRA, priv. coll., letters to Lord Shelburne · NRA, priv. coll., letters to Sir John Sinclair · NRA, priv. coll., letters to Stewart family · Orkney Archives, Kirkwall, corresp. with Balfour family · PRO, dispatches to Lord Cornwallis, 30/11 · PRO, corresp. with William Pitt, 30/8 · PRO NIre., corresp. with Lord Castlereagh, D 3030 · PRO NIre., letters to G. V. Hart · Royal Arch., letters to George III · U. Durham L., letters to Lord Grey · U. Edin., letters to Lord Arniston · U. Edin. L., letters to Charles Gordon · U. Nott. L., letters to the duke of Portland · University of Sheffield, corresp. with Edmund Burke · Worcs. RO, letters to Lord Coventry · Yale U., corresp. with James Boswell

Likenesses D. Martin, oils, 1770, Scot. NPG · J. Reynolds, group portrait, oils, 1777–9 (*The Society of Dilettanti*), Brooks's Club, London, Society of Dilettanti · J. Sayers, etching, pubd 6 April 1782 (after his portrait), BM, NPG · Hill and Pugin, group portrait, coloured aquatint, pubd 1806 (*The trial of Henry Lord Viscount Melville in Westminster Hall*; after Nattes), Palace of Westminster, London · T. Lawrence, oils, 1810, priv. coll. [*see illus.*] · H. H. Meyer, stipple, pubd 1810 (after T. Lawrence), BM, NPG · E. McInnes, mezzotint, pubd 1843 (after T. Lawrence), BM, NPG · F. Chantrey, bust, admiralty, London · F. Chantrey, bust, AM Oxf. · F. Chantrey, statue, Parliament House, Edinburgh · K. A. Hickel, group portrait, oils (*The House of Commons, 1793*), NPG · J. Kay, caricatures, etchings, BM, NPG · Maurin, coloured lithograph (after H. Raeburn), BM, NPG · H. Raeburn, oils (in robes), National Bank of Scotland · H. Raeburn, oils (in robes), Buccleuch estates, Selkirk · attrib. J. Reynolds, oils, Arniston House, Lothian · J. Rising, oils, Scot. NPG · G. Romney, oils (in robes), Arniston House, Lothian · A. Scirving, pastel drawing (after D. Martin), Arniston House, Lothian · J. Tassie, paste medallion, Scot. NPG · Wedgwood medallion (after a paste medallion by J. Tassie), Scot. NPG

Wealth at death debts of £65,000: NA Scot., GD 235/10/10/3; 10/18/175; GD 51/11/42; 11/35/14; Fry, *Dundas despotism*, 313

Dundas, Henry, **third Viscount Melville** (1801–1876), army officer, eldest son of Robert Saunders *Dundas, second Viscount Melville (1771–1851), and his wife, Anne (*d.* 10 Sept 1841), daughter of Richard Huck-Saunders MD, was born at Melville Castle, near Lasswade, Midlothian, on 25 February 1801. Sir Richard Saunders *Dundas (1802–1861), naval officer, was his younger brother. Dundas entered the army as an ensign and lieutenant in the 3rd (Scots guards) on 18 November 1819, and was promoted captain into the 83rd regiment in April 1824, major on 11 July 1826, and lieutenant-colonel on 3 December 1829. He was tory MP for Rochester from 1826 to 1830, and for Winchelsea in 1830–31. His regiment was in Canada when the rebellion of 1837 broke out, and Dundas showed such vigour in its suppression, and in repelling American brigands who landed near Prescott in Upper Canada in 1838, that he was made a CB (March 1839); he was promoted colonel and appointed an aide-de-camp to the queen on 28 November 1841.

Dundas exchanged into the 60th rifles in 1844, and accompanied his battalion to India, where he was appointed a brigadier-general on the Bombay staff in 1847. He was chosen to command the column sent from Bombay to co-operate with Lord Gough's army in the Second Anglo-Sikh War, and was present at the siege and capture of Multan as second in command to General Whish, joining the main army just before the battle of Gujrat. In that battle his division played a leading part; he was mentioned in dispatches, received the thanks of parliament and of the directors of the East India Company, and was made a KCB (June 1849). He returned to England in 1850, and succeeded his father as third viscount in 1851.

Melville was promoted major-general on 20 June 1854, and commanded the forces in Scotland from 1856 to 1860, in which year he was made governor of Edinburgh Castle. He was promoted lieutenant-general on 5 May 1860, and was colonel of the 100th foot (1858–62) and of the 32nd foot (1862–3). He became colonel-commandant of the 60th rifles on 1 April 1863, GCB in March 1865, and general on 1 January 1868. He was president of the royal archers (the royal bodyguard for Scotland) from 1860 until his death. He died unmarried at Melville Castle on 1 February 1876.

H. M. STEPHENS, *rev.* JAMES LUNT

Sources The Times (4 Feb 1876) · H. C. B. Cook, *The Sikh wars: the British army in the Punjab, 1845–1849* (1975) · Burke, *Peerage* · *Hart's Army List* · Boase, *Mod. Eng. biog.* · GEC, *Peerage*
Archives NA Scot., corresp.
Wealth at death under £1500—in England: probate, 26 June 1876, CGPLA Eng. & Wales

Dundas, Sir James, Lord Arniston (*b.* in or after **1619**, *d.* **1679**), presbyterian leader and judge, was the son of Sir James Dundas of Arniston (1570–1628), MP for Edinburghshire in 1612 and 1625 and governor of Berwick under James VI, and his second wife, Mary (*d.* 1661), daughter of George Home of Wedderburn; his parents married in 1619. Dundas succeeded to his father's estates at an early age, his guardians being Dundas of Dundas, Home of Blackadder, and Sir Patrick Murray of Elibank. However, the family estates were managed by his mother, a lady of strong presbyterian convictions. In 1635 Dundas was sent to St Andrews University. On 12 December 1639 he signed the national covenant at the presbytery of Dalkeith and by July 1640 he was an elder of the church. On 12 November 1641 he was contracted to marry Marion (*b.* after 1617), daughter of Robert Boyd, seventh Lord Boyd (*d.* 1628), and Christian Hamilton (*d.* 1646), another ardent presbyterian. Marion brought a portion of 17,000 merks. They had one son, Robert *Dundas (*d.* 1726), and three daughters. On 16 November Dundas was knighted by Charles I.

Dundas served on the committee of war in 1643–4 and 1647–8 and was a commissioner for runaways in 1644. He was elected to parliament for Edinburghshire in 1648, and served as a colonel of foot and on the committee of estates and the commission for the plantation of kirks. Apparently an engager Dundas did not take the solemn league and covenant until 1650, having expressed to the presbytery of Dalkeith certain scruples, but thereafter came to see the engagement as unlawful. Little is known of his activities in the 1650s although he served as a commissioner of the cess in 1655. Some time after the death, on 10 May 1657, of Sir John Cockburn of Ormiston, Dundas married as his second wife his widow, Janet (*bap.* 1630, *d.* 1665), daughter of Sir Adam Hepburn of Humbie and Agnes Fowlis. They had three sons.

Following the Restoration Dundas was appointed a commissioner of supply and a commissioner for the plantation of kirks in 1661. Dundas was able to garner significant presbyterian support from such notables as the earls of Crawford and Lauderdale to promote his ambition to become a lord of session. Although not a trained lawyer he was duly nominated an ordinary lord of session on 16 May 1662, and having satisfied the court of his legal acumen he was admitted to the college of justice on 4 June, taking the title Lord Arniston. His tenure of office was brief, however, because he refused to subscribe to the declaration imposed on all office-holders by the act of 1663 whereby they had to abjure the national and solemn league and covenant and declare it unlawful to take up arms against the sovereign. Dundas and his supporters spent much activity trying to gain exemption from the act, but to no avail. Dundas was absent from the court when most of his fellow judges signed the declarations on 18 November 1663, and when he was summoned on 8 January 1664 he sent a letter refusing the declarations. Although his place was declared vacant it remained unfilled until 28 August 1665 while attempts were made to find a compromise. In the end Dundas refused any solution which did not allow him to qualify his declaration abjuring the covenant with the words 'in so far as it led to deeds of actual rebellion' (*DNB*). He also refused the concession of a private audience with Charles II in which he could make his reservations known to the king: 'if my subscription is to be public, I cannot be satisfied that the salvo should be latent' (*DNB*).

Shortly before 4 July 1665 Dundas lost his second wife. In 1666 he married as his third wife Helen (*bap.* 1619), daughter of Sir James Skene of Curriehill, first baronet, president of the court of session and widow successively of Sir Robert Bruce of Broomhall and Sir Charles Erskine of Alva (*d.* 1663). Dundas was named as a commissioner of supply in 1678. He died at Arniston in September or October 1679. He was survived by his wife. STUART HANDLEY

Sources DNB · G. W. T. Omond, *The Arniston memoirs* (1887) · M. D. Young, ed., *The parliaments of Scotland: burgh and shire commissioners*, 2 vols. (1992–3) · G. Brunton and D. Haig, *An historical account of the senators of the college of justice, from its institution in MDXXXII* (1832), 380–82 · Scots peerage, vol. 5 · IGI · J. Nicoll, *A diary of public transactions and other occurrences, chiefly in Scotland, from January 1650 to June 1667*, ed. D. Laing, Bannatyne Club, 52 (1836) · Collins peerage of

England: genealogical, biographical and historical, ed. E. Brydges, 9 vols. (1812), vol. 6 · Anderson, *Scot. nat.*
Likenesses oils, Arniston House, Lothian region

Dundas, James (1842–1879), army officer, was born in Edinburgh on 12 September 1842, the eldest son of George Dundas, a judge of the court of session in Scotland, and his wife, Elizabeth, daughter of Colin Mackenzie of Portmore, Peeblesshire. He was educated at the Edinburgh Academy, at Trinity College, Glenalmond, and at Addiscombe College (1858–60). He received a commission as first-lieutenant in the Royal Engineers on 8 June 1860. After the usual course at Chatham, Dundas proceeded to India in March 1862, and was appointed to the public works department in Bengal.

In 1865 Dundas accompanied the expedition to Bhutan under General Sir Henry Tombs, and was awarded the Victoria Cross (gazetted on 31 December 1867) for his distinguished bravery in storming a blockhouse at Dewangiri on 30 April 1865, which was the key of the enemy's position, and held after the retreat of the main body. Major W. S. Trevor and Dundas, who had volunteered to lead a body of Sikh soldiers, had to climb a wall 14 feet high, enter a house occupied by some two hundred desperate men, and force their way through a narrow opening.

After the Bhutan expedition Dundas rejoined the public works department, in which his ability and varied and accurate engineering knowledge won him a high position. On 3 August 1872 he was promoted captain. In 1877 he succeeded to the estate of his uncle, the Rt Hon. Sir David Dundas, at Ochtertyre, Stirlingshire. The following year he gained fame for rescuing an Indian tradesman from a burning house in the bazaar at Simla, where he was serving with the military works department.

In 1879, on the fresh outbreak of the Afghan War, Dundas found his way to the front, and was killed with his subaltern, Lieutenant Nugent RE, on 23 December 1879, in attempting to blow up a fort at Sherpur, near Kabul, in Afghanistan. A general order referring to Dundas's services in this campaign was issued by Sir Frederick Roberts. There is a monument to him in St Giles's Cathedral, Edinburgh, and a window in Rochester Cathedral.

R. H. VEITCH, *rev.* ALEX MAY

Sources *Indian Army List* · P. A. Wilkins, *The history of the Victoria Cross* (1904) · O'M. Creagh and E. M. Humphris, *The V.C. and D.S.O.*, 1 [1920] · H. M. Vibart, *Addiscombe: its heroes and men of note* (1894) · B. Robson, *The road to Kabul: the Second Afghan War, 1878–1881* (1986)
Archives NL Scot., corresp. relating to India
Likenesses photograph, repro. in Wilkins, *History of the Victoria cross*, 202
Wealth at death £8145 8s. 3d.: probate, 12 April 1880, *CCI*

Dundas, Sir James Whitley Deans (1785–1862), naval officer and politician, son of Dr James Deans of Calcutta, was born on 4 December 1785. He entered the navy on 19 March 1799, and, after serving in the Mediterranean, on the west coast of France, and in the North Sea, was promoted lieutenant by Lord Keith on 25 May 1805. The following year, after being for a few weeks flag lieutenant to Admiral the Hon. George Berkeley, he was made commander (8 October 1806). On 13 October 1807 he was posted

Sir James Whitley Deans Dundas (1785–1862), by W. J. Edwards

captain, and continued employed in the Baltic or the North Sea until the peace of 1815. On 2 April 1808 he married his first cousin, Janet (d. 1846), only daughter and heir of Charles *Dundas, Baron Amesbury, and took the surname of Dundas. Through her he had a life interest in large estates in Flintshire and Berkshire. From 1815 to 1819 he commanded the frigate *Tagus* in the Mediterranean; from 1830 to 1832 he was flag captain to Sir William Parker on board the *Prince Regent* (120 guns) on the coast of Portugal, where Parker observed his mania for neatness and his limited abilities as a seaman; and from 1836 to 1838 he commanded the *Britannia* at Portsmouth as flag captain to Sir Philip Durham. On 25 October 1839 he was nominated CB, and he became a rear-admiral on 23 November 1841. He was Liberal MP for Greenwich from 1832 to 1834, for Devizes from 1836 to 1838, and for Greenwich again between 1841 and 1852, proving an astute and effective party politician. For some months in 1841, and again from 1846 to 1852, he sat on the Board of Admiralty; between 1848 and 1852 he was the senior naval lord. Dundas's first wife died in April 1846, and on 3 August 1847 he married Lady Emily Moreton (d. 27 April 1900), daughter of the first earl of Ducie, and his wife, Frances, and younger sister of Lady Charlotte Moreton, who had married Admiral Berkeley in 1834.

In January 1852 Dundas was appointed commander-in-chief in the Mediterranean, and on 17 December of the same year was advanced to the rank of vice-admiral. In this post, his first seagoing command, Dundas quarrelled with the first lord (the duke of Northumberland) in 1852, with Lord Stratford de Redcliffe in early 1854, and, after the outbreak of the Crimean War, with Lord Raglan. However, Dundas's handling of the 1854 campaign, in which he accepted without demur the role of supporting the allied armies, to the extent of carrying out the unnecessary and dangerous bombardment of Sevastopol on 17 October 1854, was exemplary. Despite pressure from the first lord, Sir James Graham, ill health, and the incessant attacks of *The Times*, which reflected the ambitions of his second in command, Sir Edmund Lyons, he conveyed the armies to the Crimea, supported them there with transport, men, and guns, gave up the chance of any purely naval operations, and endured the unjustified attacks of ill-informed junior officers. Dundas was a solid second-rank officer who ran a professional campaign in trying circumstances, only to be sacrificed as a scapegoat by the first lord. His GCB, conferred in July 1855, after his return to England at the end of his term of command in January, was by way of a payment for his silence at a time of great difficulty for the government. Promoted admiral on 8 December 1857, he had no further service. He died at Weymouth on 3 October 1862.

Dundas's reputation suffered at the hands of the ignorant, whose attacks he never condescended to rebut. He was a competent officer rather than an outstanding one, and his service at the Admiralty was dominated by the needs of party, but he served his country well and deserved better treatment than he received.

J. K. LAUGHTON, *rev.* ANDREW LAMBERT

Sources J. W. D. Dundas and C. Napier, *Russian war, 1854, Baltic and Black Sea: official correspondence*, ed. D. Bonner-Smith and A. C. Dewar, Navy RS, 83 (1943) • A. D. Lambert, *The Crimean War: British grand strategy, 1853–56* (1990) • C. J. Bartlett, *Great Britain and sea power, 1815–1853* (1963) • A. D. Lambert, *The last sailing battlefleet: maintaining naval mastery, 1815–1850* (1991) • A. Phillimore, *Sir William Parker* (1879) • NMM, Dundas MSS • O'Byrne, *Naval biog. dict.* • *CGPLA Eng. & Wales* (1863) • *Annual Register* (1862) • J. Marshall, *Royal naval biography*, 4/2 (1835) • *GM*, 3rd ser., 13 (1862), 782 • Burke, *Peerage*
Archives Berks. RO, corresp. and papers • Glos. RO, corresp. and orders during Crimean War • NMM, corresp. and papers; letterbook | Alnwick Castle, corresp. with duke of Northumberland • BL, corresp. with Sir T. B. Martin, Add. MS 41370 • BL, corresp. with Sir Charles Napier, Add. MSS 40022–40023, 40040–40041 • Cumbria AS, Carlisle, corresp. with Sir James Graham • NAM, corresp. with Lord Raglan • PRO, corresp. with Stratford Canning • W. Sussex RO, Lyons MSS
Likenesses W. H. Gibbs, stipple, pubd 1855 (after F. Piercy), NPG • W. J. Edwards, engraving, NPG [*see illus.*] • R. Fenton, photograph • G. Hayter, group portrait, oils (*The House of Commons, 1833*), NPG • D. J. Pound, stipple and line engraving, NPG
Wealth at death under £16,000: administration with will, 30 March 1863, *CGPLA Eng. & Wales*

Dundas, John (*fl.* 1698–1731), lawyer, was the second son of James Dundas (third son of George Dundas of Dundas) and Elizabeth, daughter of John Haliburton of Garvock. It is possible, but far from certain, that he was the John Dundas who matriculated as a law student at Utrecht in 1695, aged twenty-three. He was admitted advocate on 29 June 1698.

Details of Dundas's career are obscure, but he was procurator of the Church of Scotland from 1706 to 1731, and principal clerk to the general assembly. His experience in the legal affairs of the church shaped his career as a commentator. He was the author of *Method of Procedure by Presbyteries in Settling of Schools in any Parish* (1709) and An

Abridgement of the Acts of the General Assemblies of the Church of Scotland, 1638–1720 (1721), together with some shorter compilations on contemporary church matters. At its institution in 1709, he became a charter member of the Society in Scotland for the Propagation of Christian Knowledge. He may perhaps be the John Dundas who wrote *A summary view of the feudal law, with the differences of the Scots law from it: together with a dictionary of the select terms of the Scots and English law by way of appendix* (1710). An alternative author might be John Dundas (c.1682–1769), writer to the signet, fifth son of John Dundas of Duddingston.

On 17 December 1703, at Abercorn, Linlithgowshire, Dundas married Euphame (*d.* 1727), daughter and heir of David Dundas of Philpstoun, Linlithgowshire, and Katharine, daughter of George Swinton of Chesters. With his wife he had three daughters and a son, James Dundas of Philpstoun, who was admitted advocate on 9 February 1734.

W. D. H. SELLAR

Sources F. J. Grant, ed., *The Faculty of Advocates in Scotland, 1532–1943*, Scottish RS, 145 (1944) • D. Whyte, 'The Dundas family: old cadet branches of West Lothian (IV): 3. Dundas of Philpstoun', *Scottish Genealogist*, 5/4 (Oct 1958), 65–8 • R. Douglas, 'Dundas of Dundas', *Baronage of Scotland* (1798) • R. Douglas, 'Dundas of Newliston', *Baronage of Scotland* (1798) • D. M. Walker, *The Scottish jurists* (1985) • J. M. Pinkerton, ed., *The minute book of the Faculty of Advocates*, 1: *1661–1712*, Stair Society, 29 (1976) • J. M. Pinkerton, ed., *The minute book of the Faculty of Advocates*, 2: *1713–1750*, Stair Society, 32 (1980) • IGI

Dundas, Sir Lawrence, of Kerse, first baronet (1712–1781). *See under* Dundas family of Fingask and Kerse (*per.* 1728/9–1820).

Dundas, Lawrence John Lumley, second marquess of Zetland (1876–1961), administrator in India, politician, and author, was born in London on 11 June 1876, the elder surviving son of Lawrence Dundas, third earl, later first marquess, of Zetland (1844–1929), viceroy of Ireland (1889–92), and his wife, Lady Lilian Selina Elizabeth Lumley (*d.* 1943), third daughter of the ninth earl of Scarbrough. Educated at Harrow School and at Trinity College, Cambridge, he joined the staff of Lord Curzon, then viceroy of India, as an aide-de-camp in 1900.

Early career In certain respects the career of the earl of Ronaldshay, as he was from 1892 until he succeeded his father in 1929, seemed to parallel that of Lord Curzon, whose official biographer he was later to become. The young Ronaldshay travelled extensively in Asia over a period of ten years, and published a number of travel studies, culminating in *An Eastern Miscellany* (1911). He used his expertise in foreign affairs to good effect when he became a Conservative member of parliament for the Hornsey division of Middlesex in 1907. Like Curzon he could bring firsthand knowledge from his travels to bear on his speeches in parliament. However, although he was to become a widely acclaimed governor of Bengal (1917–22) and later secretary of state for India (1935–40), he never attained the viceroyalty of India, a post which many knowledgeable observers thought would be the inevitable pinnacle of his career. While an imperialist, he was a much more liberal imperialist than Curzon, and he

Lawrence John Lumley Dundas, second marquess of Zetland (1876–1961), by Lafayette, 1927

devoted his life to finding a means of blending Indian culture and aspirations with the continuance of what he saw as the benefits of British rule.

Governor of Bengal, 1917–1922 Having visited India on several occasions during the first decade of the century, he was appointed to the public service commission, which visited India twice during 1913–14. In March 1917 he was appointed governor of Bengal, one of the most important posts within the empire. Bengal was politically the most advanced province in British India, and one where there was a tradition of political terrorism and turbulence. Its capital, Calcutta, contained the largest European community in Asia. The appointment was for five years, and it involved a good deal of disruption to family life. Ronaldshay had married Cicely Alice Archdale (1885/6–1973) on 3 December 1907, and they had three young children (one son and two daughters) at the time of his appointment; a fifth child, a son, was born during his governorship. Ronaldshay's appointment was met with an outcry from Bengali nationalist politicians, who were dismayed by his Curzonian reputation, and who were fond of his predecessor, the easy-going and liberal Lord Carmichael. It is some mark of the success of Ronaldshay's regime that when he retired from office in 1922 he was publicly lauded by the veteran nationalist politician Sir Surendranath Banerjea, who had been vocal in the initial protests.

Ronaldshay arrived in Bengal at a critical time for British rule, when an unprecedented degree of nationalist unity had been forged between the Muslim League and the Indian National Congress in December 1916. Political terrorism in Bengal had been contained by the use of wartime powers of detention without trial, but this in itself had stirred political controversy, and the war had created political demands which needed to be addressed. Moderate Indian nationalists, especially those in Bengal, were finding themselves under pressure from younger and more radical nationalists, inspired by the home rule movements of B. G. Tilak and Annie Besant. Muslim loyalty, which was shaken by the overturning of the partition of Bengal in 1911, was being tested even further by the war against the *khalifah* or leader of the Islamic world, the sultan of Turkey. Ronaldshay's approach was to rule firmly, but to show a willingness to empathize with Bengali aspirations, and to talk to Bengali leaders directly when necessary.

True to the Curzonian style, Ronaldshay's first emphasis was on good government rather than self-rule: expansion of irrigation, agricultural improvement schemes, and an anti-malarial campaign were all undertaken. Realizing that members of the public services in Bengal, who would implement these reforms, were demoralized by his predecessor's liberal policies, he made it a priority to support them. His second concern was to deal with the Bengali intelligentsia and their political aspirations. Ronaldshay believed that he had an insight into the mind of the educated élite. He admired India's ancient culture and believed that modern Bengalis were suffering from a natural resentment at the undermining of their culture. For decades they had been taught that Western civilization was superior to their own. Naturally, they rejected this view and tended to over-compensate by demanding a return to an idealized pre-British India, and a rejection of Western civilization, artefacts and, most of all, rule. Bengali terrorism, in Ronaldshay's view, had psychological or spiritual rather than material roots, and, therefore, it was impossible to assuage it by concession or by reasoning: it must be dealt with by firm measures. He suggested as early as May 1917 that a semi-judicial commission be appointed to examine revolutionary crime and to use this evidence as the basis for persuading public opinion of the need to retain special measures to counter terrorism after the war was over. This suggestion led to the appointment of the Rowlatt committee and thence to the legislation which sparked off nationwide agitation in India and brought Gandhi into prominence as a national leader.

However, the other side of Ronaldshay's tough policy against Indian revolutionaries was his belief that it ought to be possible to find a way of integrating reasonable Indian aspirations with the best aspects of British rule in India. This was the argument that underlay his later study, *The heart of Aryavarta: a study of the psychology of Indian unrest* (1925). In practice, Ronaldshay was surprisingly open to some of the political demands of Indian nationalists. He had always believed, contrary to official statements at the time, that the Morley–Minto reforms (1909) implied the development of a parliamentary system in India. He had doubts about the straightforward transferability of Western political institutions to India, in particular feeling that it was wrong at the local level to ignore India's indigenous tradition of village democracy. However, he was convinced that educated Indians were committed to the demand for parliamentary democracy. The promised goal of responsible government within the empire, which was made by E. S. Montagu, secretary of state for India, in August 1917, was seen by Ronaldshay as the basis of all future political developments in India. He was one of the few provincial governors to recognize at the outset that diarchy—division of the provincial governments into two halves, one made up of Indian ministers responsible to the elected legislature and the other directly under the provincial governor—was the only workable means of starting the process of the devolution of political power. Therefore Montagu, one of the most radical secretaries of state for India, was to find Ronaldshay a surprisingly sympathetic political partner, operating the new system of diarchy very much as its authors intended.

Ronaldshay was forced by the Congress boycott of the elections to the new provincial legislatures in 1920 to choose his Indian ministers from among moderate Indian nationalists. He encouraged the two halves of his government to meet to discuss all issues, but made it clear where the responsibility for particular decisions ultimately lay. The most difficult problems under the new constitution were provincial finance and the Gandhian non-co-operation movement. Bengal had suffered particularly badly under the allocation of finance between the centre and the provinces. Ronaldshay dealt with the situation skilfully by negotiating a three-year moratorium on Bengal's payments to the centre, while at the same time tactfully persuading the legislative council to restore a cut in the police budget which it had made. The biggest crisis he faced, however, arose from the dissatisfaction with the tough measures he used to deal with opposition to the prince of Wales's visit to Bengal in November 1921. Once again a mixture of calm, firmness, tact, and a readiness to avoid unnecessarily wounding the pride of Indians carried him through. It helped that in his view there was no contradiction between firm handling of non-co-operation and a belief in the devolution of power to elected Indians. It was typical that in the discussion on further Indian reforms in the 1930s he favoured the handing of the law and order portfolio to elected Indian representatives, arguing that only when Indians had power and responsibility would they deal with these issues sensibly.

Landowner and author On returning to Britain in 1922, at the end of his term of office, Ronaldshay made no attempt to re-enter the House of Commons. He declined the high commissionership in Egypt and was disappointed of the viceroyalty of India in succession to Lord Reading. He settled into a life of scholarly activities. In his autobiography, *Essayez* (1956), he modestly describes the next decade of his life as 'A ten year interlude with Pen, Rifle, and Race-Glasses'. This description encompasses his love of shooting on his family estate at Letterewe in the Scottish highlands and of horse-racing, where he continued the family

tradition as an owner and breeder, and became steward of the Jockey Club in 1928. In the latter post he introduced several reforms to ensure the integrity of the sport and to place it on a more stable economic basis, including the introduction of the totalizator, of which he had had experience in Calcutta. However, it was as an author that he made most mark. He was active in the Royal Central Asian, the India, and the Royal Asiatic societies. He was made president of the Royal Geographical Society in 1922 and in the following year wrote a travel book, *Lands of the Thunderbolt: Sikhim, Chumbi and Bhutan* (1923), the first of a trilogy on south Asia. Probably the best received was *The Heart of Aryavarta* (1925), which was translated into Sanskrit, and earned him election to the British Academy in 1929. This book displayed Ronaldshay's profound interest in Indian religion and philosophy, which were central, he believed, to an understanding of Indian nationalism and revolutionary crime. Some critics argued that Ronaldshay too readily assumed that the prevailing beliefs of Bengali Hindus could stand for all India, but modern scholars would also criticize the author's fundamentally 'orientalist' assumptions that sharply divided the traditional 'Hindu race civilization' from that of modern Western civilization. It was typical of Ronaldshay that, while he could understand and even admire many of Gandhi's ideas, he believed that the Mahatma was making a profound mistake in turning his back on Western civilization and British rule. His heroes were Indians such as Rabindranath Tagore, the philosopher–poet and Brajendra Nath Seal, prime minister of Mysore, who, he believed, could integrate the best of Indian and Western civilizations.

Ronaldshay was a sound choice for the role of official biographer of Lord Curzon. His three-volume biography appeared in 1928 and was met with general critical acclaim. The author showed assiduous research into Curzon's voluminous manuscripts, and drew a sober and tactful but also psychologically perceptive portrait of a multi-faceted statesman. In 1932 he wrote the authorized biography of Lord Cromer, another great imperial statesman. In a different vein, he edited the letters of Disraeli to Lady Bradford and Lady Chesterfield (2 vols., 1929) and was recognized for his literary achievements by the award of honorary doctorates from the universities of Cambridge, Glasgow, and Leeds.

Ronaldshay took pride in his role as a large landowner in Yorkshire and Scotland, becoming second marquess of Zetland on his father's death in 1929. It was probably because of his standing among landed families that he was invited to join the executive committee of the National Trust in 1932. As chairman until 1945, Zetland presided over a period of expansion of the trust's activities in taking on country houses and their estates from owners threatened with the breakup of their property because of increased taxation. By means of parliamentary legislation (1937) owners were able to avoid death duties by donating their properties to the trust. They were required to endow them with enough income for their future maintenance and open them to the public, while their families could continue living in part of the property. This very British arrangement formed an important basis for the future development of the National Trust. Those who worked with Zetland at this time have provided some of the best pen-portraits of the man. Lord Chorley, who admired Zetland's skills as a chairman, remembered him as

> a slightly dandified figure who looked as if he wore a corset; his voice was rather unattractive and his delivery somewhat pompous. Indeed as a speaker he had little ability either to make his subject attractive or to hold the attention of his audience, all of which disadvantages were underlined by an irritating gesture he made by a jerking movement of the head repeated continuously.   (Jenkins and James, 77)

Indian constitutional reform India was never far from Zetland's concerns, and during the 1930s he played an important role in the development and implementation of the 1935 constitutional reforms. He served on the Indian round-table conferences and the joint select committee of the two houses of parliament, before being invited in 1935 to join Baldwin's cabinet as secretary of state for India. In this capacity he steered the enormously long Government of India Bill through its final stages in the House of Lords. He managed to hold out against Conservative die-hard opposition to steps towards future dominion status for India through the granting of complete provincial responsibility. In later years, historians have tended to emphasize the fundamental conservatism of the reforms, particularly in the safeguards which were built into the concessions at central and provincial level. Zetland supported the reforms as representing the fulfilment of the pledges of the Montagu declaration of 1917 within a framework of a federal constitution that would bring in the princely states and the Muslims to counterbalance the more radical Indian National Congress. Typically he described the reforms as 'a synthesis of all that was best in both East and West', and 'an outstanding landmark in the new conception of cooperative imperialism'.

It was one thing to enact the new legislation, but another to persuade the Indian National Congress to work the reforms fully and the Indian princes to sign up to the federal part of the scheme, without which responsibility at the centre could not be inaugurated. Zetland's role in both processes has proved somewhat controversial. He is criticized, along with the viceroy, Lord Linlithgow (viceroy from 1937 to 1943), for not doing enough to achieve these outcomes, yet the obstacles that were in his way should not be underestimated. Congress, which had done much better in the 1937 provincial elections than Zetland or other British politicians had expected, used its negotiating stance with the British as a means of covering over divisions within its own leadership. Zetland believed, correctly as it turned out, that Congress would succumb to the temptation of provincial office without any significant concessions from the British. As for the federal scheme, which required half of the princely states to agree to join before it came into operation, Zetland was probably over-cautious and unwilling to allow Linlithgow the freedom that he desired to make concessions to bring

in the princes. However, the odds were stacked against success, in that many of the princes had turned against federation as early as 1931, and their scepticism was strengthened by a combination of fear of the financial and constitutional implications of federation, and Congress campaigns to democratize the princely states. Furthermore, Zetland had the additional consideration of the need to consider die-hard opposition to the new constitution within his own Conservative Party. Before federation could be finally instituted it required the approval of both houses of parliament, and Zetland was always aware of the power that this gave to Winston Churchill and others to revive the bitter debates of the early 1930s. Despite differences with Linlithgow over the issue of possible concessions to the princes, viceroy and secretary of state generally worked in harmony. Unlike the viceroy, however, Zetland had not only his Indian responsibilities but also a role in the whole range of affairs that tested the Baldwin and Chamberlain governments. For instance, Zetland was closely affected by Edward VIII's abdication, and played a part in the dealings with Hitler's Germany, where he managed to take a rather more outspokenly critical view of the Führer than many other cabinet colleagues.

In September 1939, when the Second World War broke out in Europe, a crisis was precipitated by the viceroy's failure to consult representative Indian opinion before declaring India to be at war. Linlithgow's decision, though constitutionally correct, lacked imagination and betrayed an underlying arrogance in the assumption that Congress, however much it might protest, would ultimately have to agree to participate in the war against fascism. By November 1939 the Congress provincial ministries had resigned and a political stalemate was created which led inexorably to Congress non-co-operation and declared hostility to the war effort. Zetland, perhaps looking back to his experience in India during the First World War, was much more aware than Linlithgow that the war might, by its very nature, upset the British plans for a steady devolution of power along the lines of the 1935 act. However, it was the viceroy, fortified by the awareness of the ever-present die-hard critics in parliament, who was able to set the limits to any bold act of political concession to Congress at this time.

Resignation and retirement In March 1940 Zetland had a miraculous escape from death when a Punjabi patriot, Udham Singh, shot at close range at a number of dignitaries attending a meeting at Caxton Hall, killing Sir Michael O'Dwyer, governor of the Punjab at the time of the Amritsar massacre in 1919. Zetland was only slightly grazed by a bullet and was soon able to return to his desk at the India Office. Shortly afterwards, when Churchill replaced Chamberlain as prime minister, Zetland resigned from office, aware that his approach to the Indian issue was so fundamentally different from the premier's that he could not remain in the government.

In 1942 Zetland was made a knight of the Order of the Garter. He now concentrated on his many non-official interests, especially in Yorkshire and Scotland. He served as lord lieutenant of the North Riding, and found more time for his long-standing role as provincial grand master of the freemasons of the North and East Ridings of Yorkshire. He was also a long-serving governor of the Bank of Scotland. He died in his family home of Aske on 6 February 1961. His wife survived him. PHILIP WOODS

Sources marquess of Zetland [L. J. L. Dundas], *Essayez* (1956) • *DNB* • G. Rizvi, *Linlithgow and India: a study of British policy and political impasse in India, 1936–43* (1978) • C. Bridge, *Holding India to the empire: the British conservative party and the 1935 constitution* (1986) • J. Jenkins and P. James, *From acorn to oak tree: the growth of the National Trust, 1895–1994* (1994) • J. H. Broomfield, *Elite conflict in a plural society: twentieth century Bengal* (1968) • P. G. Robb, *The government of India and reform: policies towards politics and the constitution, 1916–1921* (1976) • m. cert. • Burke, *Peerage*
Archives BL OIOC, Indian corresp. and papers, MS Eur. D 609 • N. Yorks. CRO, corresp. and papers | BL OIOC, corresp. with Sir John Anderson, MS Eur. F 207 • BL OIOC, corresp. with Lord Brabourne, MS Eur. F 97 • BL OIOC, corresp. with Lord Erskine, MS Eur. D 596 • BL OIOC, Montagu MSS • BL OIOC, letters to Lord Reading, MSS Eur. E 238, F 118 • CAC Cam., corresp. with Sir Henry Page Croft • NA Scot., corresp. with Lord Lothian • PRO NIre., corresp. with Lord Dufferin • St Ant. Oxf., Middle East Centre, letters to Harry Boyle | FILM BFI NFTVA, news footage
Likenesses Lafayette, photograph, 1927, NPG [*see illus.*] • W. Stoneman, photographs, 1927–43, NPG • O. Birley, portrait, RGS • T. C. Dugdale, portrait, Freemasons' Hall, Duncombe Place, York • R. Healey, portrait, Aske, Yorkshire
Wealth at death £92,805 11s. 11d.—save and except settled land: probate, 5 April 1961, *CGPLA Eng. & Wales* • under £800,000: probate limited to settled land, 5 May 1961, *CGPLA Eng. & Wales*

Dundas, Sir Richard Saunders (1802–1861), naval officer, born on 11 April 1802, was the second son of Robert Saunders *Dundas, second Viscount Melville (1771–1851), and his wife, Anne (died 10 Sept 1841), daughter of Richard Huck-Saunders and his wife, Jane, *née* Kinsey; Anne was also the grand-niece and coheir of Admiral Sir Charles Saunders. Henry *Dundas, army officer, was his brother. After attending Harrow School, he entered the Royal Naval College at Portsmouth in 1815, and on 15 June 1817 became a volunteer on the frigate *Ganymede*, under the Hon. Robert Cavendish Spencer, in the Mediterranean. As the son of the first lord of the Admiralty his promotions were as rapid as the rules of the service permitted: on 18 June 1821 lieutenant, on 23 June 1823 commander, and on 17 July 1824 captain, during which time he was employed on the Mediterranean and North American stations. In September 1825 he was appointed to the frigate *Volage*, in which he went to the East Indies and New South Wales, where he transferred to the *Warspite* (74 guns); he returned to England in October 1827. For the next three years he was private secretary to his father.

In November 1830 Dundas commissioned the frigate *Belvidera* for three years in the Mediterranean, and in September 1837 was appointed to the *Melville* (72 guns). In her he participated in the First Opium War, being especially mentioned for his conduct at the capture of Fort Taecockow on 7 January 1841 and of the Bogue (Humen) forts on 26 February. For these services he was nominated a CB on 29 June. At the end of 1841 he returned to England. In 1845 he was private secretary to the earl of Haddington, first lord of the Admiralty, and in 1853 was appointed a

junior lord of the Admiralty under Sir James Graham. Promoted rear-admiral on 4 July 1853, in February 1855 he was appointed commander-in-chief of the fleet in the Baltic, where he led the fleet with discretion and caution. Dundas carried out a strict blockade, bombarded Sveaborg on 9–11 August, conducted minor coastal operations—including the first ever sustained mine clearance—and in 1856 prepared for operations against Kronstadt.

Despite a reputation for caution (the first lord believing him not to be an enterprising officer), Dundas was reappointed after attending the allied council of war in Paris in January 1856 and was made a KCB on 4 February. After a brief period as second in command of the Mediterranean Fleet he joined the Admiralty as second, and later first sea lord. He stepped down to second lord during the Derby ministry, before resuming the senior post in Palmerston's government of 1859. A liberal conservative with no strong political views, Dundas refused to sit in the House of Commons, helping to take party politics out of the naval service. He was an experienced and capable administrator who contributed significantly to defence and technical debates and was particularly concerned to improve lower-deck conditions of service. Liked by those who served with him, Dundas was the antithesis of the popular image of a naval officer: quiet, reserved, undemonstrative, and cautious. These qualities made him an effective fleet commander and a major participant in defence debates. At the Admiralty he had many of his father's qualities, leavened by professional experience. He was promoted vice-admiral on 24 February 1858 and died, unmarried, of a heart attack at 13 New Street, Spring Gardens, London, on 3 June 1861.

J. K. LAUGHTON, rev. ANDREW LAMBERT

Sources A. D. Lambert, *The Crimean War: British grand strategy, 1853–56* (1990) • A. C. Dewar, ed., *Russian war, 1855, Black Sea: official correspondence*, Navy RS, 85 (1945) • J. Wells, *The immortal warrior* (1987) • J. H. Briggs, *Naval administrations, 1827 to 1892: the experience of 65 years*, ed. Lady Briggs (1897) • Dundas MSS, NA Scot. • BL, Wood MSS. Add. MSS 49533–49534 • York University, Wood MSS • Bucks. RLSS, Somerset MSS • C. I. Hamilton, *Anglo-French naval rivalry, 1840–1870* (1993) • *CGPLA Eng. & Wales* (1861) • O'Byrne, *Naval biog. dict.* • *GM*, 3rd ser., 11 (1861), 87 • J. Marshall, *Royal naval biography*, 3/1 (1831), 183–4 • GEC, *Peerage*
Archives NA Scot., Melville Castle muniments • NA Scot., private and official papers • priv. coll., service corresp. | BL, corresp. with Sir Charles Wood, Add. MSS 49533–49534 • Bucks. RLSS, Somerset MSS • U. Nott. L., letters to Sir Andrew Buchanan • U. Nott. L., letters to duke of Newcastle • University of York, letters to Sir Charles Wood
Likenesses M. Alophe, group portrait, lithograph, pubd 1854 (*Les défenseurs du droit et de la liberté de l'Europe*), BM • portrait, repro. in Wells, *Immortal warrior*, 19
Wealth at death £16,000: probate, 16 July 1861, *CGPLA Eng. & Wales*

Dundas, Robert, Lord Arniston (d. 1726), judge, was the eldest son of Sir James *Dundas, Lord Arniston (d. 1679), covenanter, and his first wife, Marion, daughter of Robert, Lord Boyd. Many of his forebears had held high judicial office, and were related by marriage with the highest families throughout Scotland. Dundas was educated abroad, but returned to Scotland as a supporter of William of

Robert Dundas, Lord Arniston (d. 1726), by unknown artist

Orange. His marriage on 4 January 1683 to Margaret, daughter of Sir Robert *Sinclair of Stevenston, brought six sons, of whom the eldest, James, predeceased him; the second, known as Robert *Dundas the elder (1685–1753), became lord president of the court of session. There were also four daughters.

Dundas was appointed judge of the court of session on 1 November 1689, taking the title Lord Arniston, and he sat on the bench for thirty years. He was commissioner for Edinburghshire in the parliaments of 1700–01 and 1703–7, during which time he voted in favour of an act to declare Caledonia a lawful colony and spoke against the Wine Act of 1703. He was a commissioner for the Union in 1706. Arniston took pleasure in retirement and study, reading chiefly books in Italian. He died on 25 November 1726.

J. M. RIGG, rev. ANITA MCCONNELL

Sources M. D. Young, ed., *The parliaments of Scotland: burgh and shire commissioners*, 1 (1992), 215 • G. W. T. Omond, *The Arniston memoirs* (1887), 40–57 • G. Brunton and D. Haig, *An historical account of the senators of the college of justice, from its institution in MDXXXII* (1832) • R. Douglas, *The peerage of Scotland*, 2nd edn, ed. J. P. Wood, 1 (1813) • J. Foster, *Members of parliament, Scotland … 1357–1882*, 2nd edn (privately printed, London, 1882)
Likenesses W. Hole, drawing, repro. in Omond, *Arniston memoirs*, facing p. 42 • oils, priv. coll. [*see illus.*]

Dundas, Robert, Lord Arniston (1685–1753), politician and advocate, was born on 9 December 1685, the second son of Robert *Dundas, whose judicial title was also Lord Arniston (d. 1726), and his wife, Margaret, daughter of Sir Robert Sinclair of Stevenson. Following a period spent at the University of Utrecht, and possibly also at Edinburgh University, Dundas was admitted to the Faculty of Advocates in July 1709. Scottish politics at this time was marked by bitter rivalry between the squadrone and the Argathelians, followers of John Campbell, second duke of Argyll, and his brother Archibald, earl of Ilay. In June 1717, already a rising figure in the squadrone hierarchy, Dundas was appointed solicitor-general by the squadrone secretary of state, John Ker, first duke of Roxburghe. In 1720 he was promoted to lord advocate and the following year became dean of the Faculty of Advocates. At the 1722 general election he stood on the squadrone interest for Edinburghshire, where he was returned with the support of Jacobite electors on the understanding that he would protect their estates from confiscation. He continued to represent the constituency until his elevation to the bench in 1737.

Dundas married first, in 1712, Elizabeth, eldest daughter of Robert Watson of Muirhouse, who, with three of their children, died in January 1734 of smallpox; their son Robert *Dundas (1713–1787) later became lord president. On 3 June 1734 he married Ann (d. 1797), daughter of Sir William Gordon of Invergordon, with whom he had six sons and a daughter. One of these sons was Henry *Dundas, first Viscount Melville.

During the early 1720s, with the squadrone in the ascendancy, Dundas acted as one of Roxburghe's principal agents in Scotland on political, patronage, and electoral matters, as well as undertaking the more routine tasks of his office. He played a leading but ultimately unsuccessful role in the bitter squadrone–Argathelian struggle to secure the nomination of Patrick Haldane, a squadrone supporter, to the bench. In 1725 he vigorously opposed Walpole's proposal to extend the malt tax to Scotland. As a result he was dismissed as lord advocate in May, returning to the bar. He then openly fomented opposition to the tax, acting on behalf of the Glasgow magistrates who had been arrested for failing to quell disturbances in the city and encouraging the Edinburgh brewers to stop brewing. With Walpole and the Argathelians firmly in control, Dundas continued in opposition after the 1727 general election, leading the small group of squadrone members attacking the ministry in the Commons. In particular, he helped organize resistance, in the end unsuccessful, to the return of the king's list of representative peers for Scotland at the 1734 election.

At a time when the quality of the court of session was at one of its lowest ebbs, Dundas took a keen interest in law reform. In 1725, after several years of pressure from him as lord advocate, public funds were established to pay the cost of crown prosecutions and to maintain public prisoners. In 1728, in the trial of Carnegie of Finavon for the murder of Charles Lyon, earl of Strathmore, Dundas persuaded the jury to reverse the previous practice of the jury determining whether the facts were 'proven' or 'not proven', leaving it to the judge to determine whether the facts, if proven, inferred guilt, and instead to return a general verdict of not guilty. This practice was adopted in all subsequent cases. Early in 1737 the lord president of the court of session, Sir David Dalrymple, died. Dundas applied for the post but it was given to Duncan Forbes. Nevertheless, Ilay and Walpole were keen to remove

Dundas from Westminster and he was therefore promoted to the bench on 24 March as Lord Arniston to fill the vacancy created by the death of Lord Newhall.

In 1742, with the fall of Walpole, John Hay, fourth marquess of Tweeddale, a leading squadrone peer and political ally of Carteret, was appointed secretary of state for Scotland. Tweeddale sought to manage Scotland with the help of a small group of advisers in Edinburgh, including Arniston, his son Robert, who was appointed solicitor general, and Lord Advocate Robert Craigie. Arniston and Craigie, his erstwhile protégé, frequently quarrelled. Moreover, Arniston suffered constantly from gout throughout the period and consequently played only an intermittent part in public affairs. He grew increasingly frustrated and disillusioned at Tweeddale's inability to purge the administration of Argathelian supporters and at the marquess's lack of interest in his plans to reform the law courts in Scotland. Since being dismissed as lord advocate he had struggled to make ends meet and Tweeddale's failure to obtain a prestigious post for him increased the tension between them. Thus, while Arniston's abilities made him a useful ally, he was difficult to work with and he became an increasingly disruptive force. The outbreak of the Jacobite rising of 1745 finally ended Tweeddale's secretaryship.

Lord President Forbes died in December 1747. The choice of his successor lay between the Argathelian Charles Erskine, Lord Tinwald, and Arniston, who threatened to resign if he was passed over. Initially Pelham favoured Tinwald while Chesterfield and particularly Hardwicke, who was anxious to improve the quality of the Scottish bench, were for Arniston. Finally, in May 1748 Pelham effected a compromise: Arniston was appointed lord president on 15 June while Tinwald replaced Milton as lord justice clerk.

Arniston had a keen legal mind and as an advocate was both eloquent and ingenious. He was, however, extremely hot-tempered, his appearance was unprepossessing, and his voice harsh, speaking in a broad Scots dialect. Even for his day he was a heavy drinker. He embarked on the rebuilding of Arniston House, near Gorebridge, Edinburghshire, and effected many improvements to the estate. In his later years he suffered ill health and grew increasingly cantankerous. He continued in office, increasingly sapped by age and illness, until his death at Abbey Hill, Edinburgh, on 26 August 1753. By the end he was said to be 'very doited'. He was buried on 31 August in the family tomb at Borthwick.   RICHARD SCOTT

Sources M. Fry, *The Dundas despotism* (1992) · letter books kept at Arniston House, Midlothian, NA Scot., Arniston MSS, RH/4/15/2-4, vols. 2-5 [microfilm] · G. W. T. Omond, ed., *The Arniston memoirs: three centuries of a Scottish house, 1571–1838* (1887) · R. Scott, 'The politics and administration of Scotland, 1725–48', PhD diss., U. Edin., 1982 · G. W. T. Omond, *The lord advocates of Scotland from the close of the fifteenth century to the passing of the Reform Bill*, 2 vols. (1883) · J. Hay, fourth marquess of Tweeddale, correspondence, NL Scot., Yester MSS YP 7044-7119; SYP Acc. 7174 · U. Nott. L., Newcastle Clumber MSS, NEC 2016-2017 · *DNB* · R. R. Sedgwick, 'Dundas, Robert', HoP, *Commons, 1715-54* · matriculation records, U. Edin. L., special collections division, university archives

Archives NA Scot., papers | BL, corresp. with first earl of Hardwicke, Add. MSS 35446–35447 · NA Scot., letters to John Clerk · NL Scot., corresp. with fourth marquess of Tweeddale
Likenesses attrib. J. B. Medina, oils, Arniston House, Lothian

Dundas, Robert, of Arniston (1713–1787), judge and politician, was born in Edinburgh on 18 July 1713, the eldest son of Robert *Dundas (1685–1753), lord president of the court of session, and his first wife, Elizabeth (d. 1734), eldest daughter of Robert Watson of Muirhouse (d. before 1712). He was educated partly at home, and nothing is known about his other schooling. He proceeded to the University of Edinburgh, then in 1733 to Utrecht, celebrated for the teaching of Roman law, and he also visited the universities of Frankfurt and Paris. He returned to Scotland in 1737 and was admitted an advocate in 1738. He was quick, ingenious, and eloquent, and had a retentive memory. Like his father, he was convivial and shirked drudgery. He is said, though a good scholar, never to have read through a book after leaving college, and being solely ambitious of attaining to the bench, he refused many cases, especially those which involved writing papers, and took only such work as seemed to lead to advancement. For his first five years his fees only averaged £280 per annum. On 17 October 1741 he married Henrietta (d. 13 May 1755), daughter of Sir James Carmichael, of Lamington and Bountytoun, and his wife, Margaret Baillie. They had four daughters, of whom Elizabeth married Sir John Lockhart *Ross, sixth baronet, naval officer, Henrietta married Adam *Duncan, Viscount Duncan, and Margaret married General John Scott MP.

Through the favour of the Wilmington administration Dundas was appointed solicitor-general on 11 August 1742, serving under John Hay, fourth marquess of Tweeddale as secretary of state for Scotland. This fractious and incompetent administration had to face the Jacobite rising of 1745. It was found wanting and most of its members, including Dundas, had to flee into England during Prince Charles's occupation of Edinburgh. Early in 1746 they were all sacked, but Dundas was soon afterwards elected dean of the Faculty of Advocates. He kept his distance from politics and declined requests to stand for Edinburghshire (Midlothian) in 1747 and Lanarkshire in 1750. There followed a period when the Scottish political factions tried to pull together to avert English anger at their failure to counter the Jacobite threat. Dundas was at length able to benefit from this trend. At the general election of 1754 he was returned as MP for Edinburghshire, and in August that year became lord advocate, now (since abolition of the secretary's post in 1746) the chief officer of government in Scotland. While in parliament Dundas opposed the establishment of a militia in Scotland, and, as lord advocate, was largely occupied in settling the new conditions of the highlands, and in disposing of his patronage so as to enhance the family influence. He was appointed a commissioner of fisheries on 17 June 1755. He was critical of the great Scots whig families and in June 1755 attempted to supplant Archibald Campbell, third duke of Argyll, as government manager in Scotland, but he received no encouragement and allied himself with

Argyll in order to obtain financial support for his family after he lost control of the Carmichael estates following his wife's death. In December 1755 he spoke in parliament in favour of press-gangs.

Dundas remained faithful to Argyll and the duke of Newcastle during the political crises of the late 1750s. He cemented new alliances by his marriage on 7 September 1756 to Jean, daughter of the outgoing lord advocate William *Grant, Lord Prestongrange (1700/01–1764), and his wife, Grizel Miller (d. 1792). They had four sons, Robert [see below], Francis *Dundas (1759?–1824), William *Dundas (1762–1845), and Philip (1763–1807), and two daughters, Grizel (b. 1761) and Janet (b. 1763). Dundas was the only Scots MP to speak against the Militia Bill in April 1760, fearing it would arm a hostile populace. He had already been assured of his reward, and on 14 June 1760 was appointed lord president of the court of session, in succession to Robert Craigie. He found upwards of two years' arrears of cases undecided, and the effort required to resolve them led him never to allow his cause-list to fall into arrear again. He was short but weighty in his judgments, thorough in his grasp of the cases, indignant at chicane, a punctilious guardian of the dignity of the court, a chief who called forth all the faculties of his colleagues. Having, on 7 July 1767, given the casting vote against the claimant, Archibald Stewart, in the Douglas cause, he became very unpopular, and during the tumultuous rejoicings at Edinburgh, after the House of Lords had reversed that decision on 2 March 1769, the mob insulted him and attacked his house. He continued to exercise political influence in the interest of his half-brother Henry *Dundas. In his latter years his eyesight failed, and after a short illness he died at his house in Adam's Square on 13 December 1787, and was buried with great pomp at Borthwick parish church on 18 December.

His eldest son, **Robert Dundas of Arniston** (1758–1819), born on 6 June 1758, was educated at the high school and the University of Edinburgh and admitted advocate in 1779. By the patronage of his uncle Henry Dundas he succeeded Alan Wight as solicitor-general for Scotland in 1784. In 1787, on inheriting Arniston, he married his first cousin, Elizabeth (1766–1852), daughter of Henry Dundas; they had three sons and two daughters. He became lord advocate in 1789, and from 1790 to 1801 was MP for Edinburghshire. He appeared for the crown in the great prosecutions for sedition at Edinburgh in 1793. He was joint clerk and keeper of the general registers for seisins and other writs in Scotland from 1799 until on 1 June 1801 he was appointed chief baron of the exchequer in Scotland, and from then on took only an advisory role in politics. He refused offers of the lord presidency in 1801 and 1811. He died at Arniston, Midlothian, on 17 June 1819. His zeal as a prosecutor was belied by Henry Cockburn's portrait of him as a 'little, alert, handsome, gentleman-like man, with a countenance and air beaming with sprightliness and gaiety, and dignified by considerable fire: altogether inexpressibly pleasing' (*Memorials*, 151).

J. A. HAMILTON, rev. MICHAEL FRY

Sources M. Fry, *The Dundas despotism* (1992) • *Memorials of his time, by Henry Cockburn*, another edn, ed. H. A. Cockburn (1910) • E. Haden-Guest, 'Dundas, Robert', HoP, *Commons, 1754–90* • R. G. Thorne, 'Dundas, Robert', HoP, *Commons, 1790–1820* • G. W. T. Omond, ed., *The Arniston memoirs: three centuries of a Scottish house, 1571–1838* (1887) • G. W. T. Omond, *The lord advocates of Scotland from the close of the fifteenth century to the passing of the Reform Bill*, 2 vols. (1883) • G. Brunton and D. Haig, *An historical account of the senators of the college of justice of Scotland, from its institution in 1532* (1849) • Chambers, *Scots.* (1856), 183–7 • *Transactions of the Royal Society of Edinburgh*, 2 (1784), 37 • H. Drummond, *Histories of noble British families* (1846) • *Scots peerage* • *Scots Magazine*, 49 (1787) • J. Foster, *Members of parliament, Scotland … 1357–1882*, 2nd edn (privately printed, London, 1882) • Anderson, *Scot. nat.* • J. Paterson, *Kay's Edinburgh portraits: a series of anecdotal biographies chiefly of Scotchmen*, ed. J. Maidment, 2 vols. (1885) • Burke, *Peerage* (1967)
Archives NA Scot., corresp. and papers [Robert Dundas, son] • NA Scot., corresp., mainly letters to his wife • NL Scot., corresp. [Robert Dundas, son] • priv. coll., corresp. and papers, incl. diaries and journals [Robert Dundas, son] • U. Edin., corresp. [Robert Dundas, son] | BL, letters to first earl of Hardwicke, Add. MSS 35448–35449 • BL, Newcastle papers • BL, corresp. with duke of Newcastle, Add. MSS 32732–32970, *passim* • CKS, letters to William Pitt [Robert Dundas, son] • Harrowby Manuscript Trust, Sandon Hall, Staffordshire, corresp. with R. Ryder, etc. [Robert Dundas, son] • NA Scot., letters to Robert Craigie • NA Scot., Melville papers • NA Scot., letters to Lord Melville [Robert Dundas, son] • NA Scot., letters to Sir Andrew Mitchell • NL Scot., corresp. with Sir Alexander Cochrane [Robert Dundas, son] • NL Scot., Melville papers • NL Scot., corresp. with Lord Melville [Robert Dundas, son] • NL Scot., letters to Lord Robertson [Robert Dundas, son] • NL Scot., corresp. mainly with fourth marquess of Tweeddale • priv. coll., corresp. with Spencer Perceval [Robert Dundas, son] • U. Aberdeen, corresp. with G. Ogilvie [Robert Dundas, son]
Likenesses A. Soldi, oils, 1757, Faculty of Advocates, Parliament House, Edinburgh • J. Kay, caricature, etching, 1790 (Robert Dundas, son, with Lord Melville), BM, NPG • J. Kay, caricature, etching, 1799 (Robert Dundas, son), BM, NPG • F. Chantrey, marble bust, exh. RA 1817? (Robert Dundas, son), Arniston House • F. Chantrey, marble statue, 1824 (Robert Dundas, son), Faculty of Advocates, Parliament Hall, Edinburgh • J. Edgar, group portrait, wash drawing, c.1854 (*Robert Burns at an evening party of Lord Monboddo's, 1786*), Scot. NPG • F. Chantrey, pencil drawing (Robert Dundas, son), NPG • K. A. Hickel, group portrait, oils (*The House of Commons, 1793*; Robert Dundas, son), NPG • J. Kay, etching (Robert Dundas, son), repro. in Paterson, *Kay's Edinburgh portraits* • J. J. Masquerier, oils (Robert Dundas, son), Arniston House • attrib. W. Mosman, oils (as a boy), Arniston House • H. Raeburn, oils, Arniston House; copy, Parliament Hall, Edinburgh • H. Raeburn, oils (Robert Dundas, son), Arniston House • plaster medallion (Robert Dundas, son; after J. Henning), Scot. NPG

Dundas, Robert, of Arniston (1758–1819). *See under* Dundas, Robert, of Arniston (1713–1787).

Dundas, Robert Hamilton (1884–1960), classical scholar, was born on 30 August 1884 at 14 Athole Crescent, Edinburgh, the only son of George Smythe Dundas of Duns (1842–1909) and his wife, Georgina Lockhart Ross (d. 1927). His father, a lawyer, was later sheriff substitute of Roxburgh, Berwick, and Selkirk. Robert was a descendant of the younger Pitt's cabinet colleague Lord Melville, but seldom if ever mentioned him. From Summer Fields, Oxford, Dundas went to Eton College as king's scholar (ninth on the list) in 1897, and thence to New College, Oxford, as a scholar in classics in 1903; he was taught by Alfred Zimmern, and after firsts in classical moderations and *literae* *humaniores* (1905, 1907) was appointed to a lectureship in classics at Liverpool University in 1908, his superior (and another strong influence) being Professor Sir John Myres. In the following year he was elected to a studentship and tutorship at Christ Church, Oxford, where he taught Greek history for most of the next forty-six years.

Dundas quickly made an impression on his Christ Church colleagues, and was elected (junior) censor and put on two key committees on 2 December 1914, in the knowledge that he would soon accept a commission in the Black Watch. He served briefly in France in 1915 and then in Mesopotamia; wounded during the Kut campaign, he was posted to India, where he was a military censor in Delhi, Simla, and Rangoon. He was twice mentioned in dispatches, and ended the war as a captain. Back at Christ Church by May 1919, he was at once reinstated as censor (to 1924); from 1925 his tutorial rooms, once occupied by C. L. Dodgson, and borrowed by A. Einstein during Dundas's world tour in 1930–31, were known to a long succession of Christ Church undergraduates, whatever their subject, as the place where Dundas had interrogated them on their arrival as to their knowledge of life and particularly of its financial and sexual aspects; some public schoolboys, forewarned by others, may have pulled his leg.

Dundas regarded his tutorial and counselling activities as more demanding calls on his time than printed contributions to classical scholarship. He had long been intending to publish a work on Thucydides, but the material which he had collected was stolen or lost on a wartime train journey to Scotland and, given the advance of scholarship, it was then too late for him to start all over again. His publications were therefore limited to a rather overwritten reminiscence entitled 'The last place in India' (1920), and the privately published Christ Church reports. Nevertheless, he taught many distinguished classicists, including E. S. G. Robinson. Sir John Masterman, Dundas's fellow censor, later commended him as 'the best-known and most honoured of all Christ Church tutors … the type of tutor who devoted his life to his pupils without any other competing activity'.

In the senior common room, though never elected curator, Dundas often presided at formal sessions by seniority; here his inquisition had little place, the new arrivals being older (and, latterly, former service personnel); but he sang the praises of Christ Church—without, it seemed, much detailed knowledge of its earlier history. He believed that he had lived in and had contributed to a golden age which his hearer, if Dundas's hopes were realized, could help to continue, especially if he held what to Dundas was the House's most important office: the censorship itself. When he reached retirement age (1955) Dundas was allowed to retain his rooms, and remained an active senior member. It is from this period that most reminiscences survive. In a stern reassessment, 'Mercurius Oxoniensis' (H. R. Trevor-Roper) held that 'as a scholler he was no great shakes', but for fifty years Christ Church was the centre of his life and efforts: to that institution

and its members, and to his relatives and house in Scotland, he gave the time and affection which others would have lavished on immediate family and home.

His *Times* obituarist (K. G. Feiling, a colleague from 1909 to 1946 in Oxford and briefly in India) attributed Dundas's attitudes and values to his experience of Lothian and to the influence of his mother's 'long and admirable' life; the same writer thought that to Dundas college life was a 'training ground for action', and called him 'a pillar, in some ways the central pillar, of Christ Church'. There Dundas much enjoyed a duty which he performed from 1938 to 1959: compiling the Christ Church annual report circulated to all members of the House. Each year he accumulated and brought together all that he could discover of the activities of members, with lapidary comments on the deeds and attitudes of many; his first six reports described the impact of war (he was himself again censor in 1944–5), and the remainder the adjustment to peace and its novelties—all this in economical and deeply considered prose (not without its Scotticisms), some of it rehearsed in advance to his often hard-pressed colleagues. The task allowed him to welcome, in somewhat guarded terms, the spouses of colleagues to the House's first Ladies Nights.

Dundas was an example of the lay bachelor don after 1882: a kind if idiosyncratic host to many pupils, former pupils, and friends (there were 1648 names in his visitors' book). He was a generous and unproclaimed benefactor of the needy young, and by his will left £2000 to assist their travel (music, swimming, and travel were his own chief pleasures). He died at his home at Laurel Hill, Stirling, on 1 October 1960; his last words ('You women always want to have the last word'—to his nurse), cited by Venables, are among the few such recorded of members of Christ Church.

J. F. A. MASON

Sources E. W. Gray, *Christ Church annual report for 1960*, 4–8 · *Christ Church annual reports* (1938×9–1960) · R. Venables, *'D': portrait of a don* (1967) · G. E. Williams, *George: an early autobiography* (1961), 281–2 · J. C. Masterman, *On the chariot wheel* (1975) · *The Times* (3 Oct 1960) · private information (2004) [M. G. Beecroft; E. G. W. Bill; A. L. Binney; Henry Chadwick; N. G. Painting; P. J. Parsons; Lord Blake; Lord Armstrong of Ilminster] · personal knowledge (2004) · R. Boothby, *My Oxford*, ed. A. Thwaite (1977), 19–34 · [H. R. Trevor-Roper], *The letters of Mercurius* (1970), 103–6 · b. cert. · R. H. Dundas, 'The last place in India', *Blackwood*, 208 (1920), 519–27
Archives Bodl. Oxf., corresp. with Sir J. L. Myres · King's AC Cam., letters to John Maynard Keynes
Likenesses photograph, repro. in Venables, *'D'* · photograph, repro. in Masterman, *On the chariot wheel* · photographs, Christ Church Oxf.; repro. in *SCR Album*
Wealth at death £49,791 16s. 7d.: confirmation, 17 Nov 1960, *CCI*

Dundas, Robert Saunders, second Viscount Melville

(1771–1851), politician, was born in Edinburgh on 14 March 1771, the only son of Henry *Dundas, first Viscount Melville (1742–1811), and Elizabeth (1751–1843), daughter of David Rannie. Educated at Edinburgh high school, he went in 1786 on a continental tour and enrolled at Göttingen University. He studied afterwards at Edinburgh University and at Emmanuel College, Cambridge, and matriculated at Lincoln's Inn in 1788. Although he came of the foremost legal family in Scotland, Dundas showed no interest in the law. His father found him unpromising and

Robert Saunders Dundas, second Viscount Melville (1771–1851), by Charles Turner, pubd 1827 (after Sir Thomas Lawrence, 1826)

resorted to employing him as a private secretary from 1794, though thinking it also useful for him to be in parliament: he was brought in as MP for Hastings in 1794, then Rye in 1796. The same year, on 29 August, he married an heiress, Anne Saunders (d. 10 Sept 1841), and took her name beside his own. They had four sons and two daughters; their eldest son, Henry *Dundas, later third Viscount Melville, became an army officer while their second son, Richard Saunders *Dundas, became a vice-admiral in the navy.

Not until his father retired in 1801 could Dundas win some independence and emerge as heir apparent to his family's large electoral interest. His personality blossomed: he was hard-working but sociable, a keen sportsman, a loyal friend. He remained close all his life to a schoolmate, Sir Walter Scott, who described him thus: 'Though not a literary man, he is judicious, clairvoyant and uncommonly sound-headed, like his father' (Grierson, 1.123). His cousin, but political opponent, Henry Cockburn wrote that 'he had fully as much good sense, excellent business habits and as much candour as, I suppose, a party leader can practise' (Memorials, 216). Lord Liverpool called him 'an excellent man of business' (Aspinall, 5.405). Dundas was appointed keeper of the signet and elected MP for Midlothian (Edinburghshire) in 1801. He remained silent in parliament until his speeches of 1805 and 1806 in defence of his father, who was then being impeached. His first real test came in negotiating to be left

in charge of Scotland by a hostile 'ministry of all the talents'. He got nowhere, but won the respect of his own side, and the problem vanished with the ministry's collapse. He was rewarded with the presidency of the Board of Control for India by the duke of Portland in 1807.

Dundas's main task here was to frustrate any possibility that Napoleon might exploit his alliance with Russia to make some attempt on British India. He sent a mission to the shah of Persia, at whose court French agents were intriguing. He formed alliances with the princes of Lahore and Kabul. He ordered occupation of the Portuguese factories in India and China, of the Dutch colony of Java, and of the French stations on Mauritius and Réunion. He had also to deal with a sharp deterioration, through loss of trade during the war, in the finances of the East India Company. A series of reports on its development since the India Act of 1784, written by a select committee which he chaired, concluded that it should give up its inefficient trading privileges, at least in the subcontinent. Dundas drafted the legislation which ended them at the renewal of the company's charter in 1813. He was otherwise concerned that British government should not offend the Indians' immemorial customs: so, for example, he banned evangelical missions among them, a policy reversed after 1813.

Dundas's Indian administration was interrupted for six months in 1809 when he served as chief secretary for Ireland. Spencer Perceval, succeeding Portland, then wanted to promote him to the cabinet as secretary for war. His father, vainly hoping for a political comeback after the impeachment, tried to prevent this. It nearly came to an open breach between the two, averted only by the prospective consequences for their influence in Scotland. Dundas returned to the Board of Control, still without a place in cabinet. He succeeded as Viscount Melville on 27 May 1811. The next year, under Liverpool, he was promoted first lord of the Admiralty.

At the Admiralty Melville gave of his best. A diligent administrator ably balancing the pressures on him, he was regarded by the navy as a thoroughly reliable representative of its interests, and by his political colleagues as a man who could be ruthless when necessary. While the wars went on, his job was to maintain the British maritime supremacy established at the battle of Trafalgar. In a state paper of February 1813 he pointed out that France, with the shipbuilding resources of Holland and Italy at her disposal, would be able to construct a fleet to match Britain's if the struggle continued much longer. The point was underlined by complaints from Wellington in Spain of inadequate protection for the convoys supplying him, especially after the outbreak of hostilities with the United States in 1812 unleashed hordes of American privateers on the Atlantic. With resources everywhere stretched, Melville yet coped.

Drastic cuts followed the peace, but Britain, now the only colonial power of any importance, found her maritime commitments increased. Melville did not think the fleet could be reduced much below 100 ships of the line. The cabinet set a limit of forty-four. The following years saw a constant struggle by Melville to find every possible economy while he avoided meeting a target he regarded as unreal. He quietly got his way, not least by improving the design and durability of ships, research on which benefited from his close personal interest. Yet he resisted the introduction of steamers, since an infant technology seemed bound to prove expensive and unreliable; moreover, if navies were to be rebuilt all round as steam driven, Britain would place herself on the same level as her rivals. After some years, his colleagues stopped interfering and usually let his estimates through on the nod. By the late 1820s he was able to construct new and larger classes of ship, matching those in France and the United States. Even out of tight budgets he never failed to squeeze something for another scientific interest, in exploration. He sent expeditions to the Arctic and northern Australia, where he is commemorated respectively by the Melville Sound and Melville Island.

A second part of his duties was the political management of Scotland. He stepped into, but did not fill, his father's shoes. Appointed a governor of the Bank of Scotland, he was elected chancellor of the University of St Andrews in 1814, and made a knight of the Thistle in 1821. He was the efficient dispenser of a stock of patronage diminished by the drive for public economy. He solved the perennial problem of getting Scottish legislation through by not introducing much of it. He continued to control thirty or more of the forty-five Scottish seats, but never showed his father's zest for the hustings and allowed some regrettable lapses. The crisis of the system came in 1827 on the resignation of Liverpool and the succession of George Canning, who was set on Catholic emancipation. Melville said that, while he personally supported it, he could not approve of a policy which would split the outgoing cabinet. Thus muddling his stance, he refused office.

His exit shocked Scotland, used to a representative at the centre of power. The whigs in Canning's coalition now persuaded him that a Scottish manager was unnecessary; the home secretary could do all the work with a native adviser or two. The old governing interest in Scotland began to break up, a process which did not halt when Melville returned under Wellington and Sir Robert Peel as president of the Board of Control in 1828, then again at the Admiralty. The Reform Act would anyway end the arrangements under which the Dundases had ruled Scotland. Melville resigned in 1830, never to hold office again. But he made himself useful in good works, notably chairmanship of the royal commission which in 1845 proposed reform of the Scots poor law. He died on 10 June 1851 at Melville Castle, and was buried at the Old Kirk, Lasswade, Edinburghshire, on 17 June. MICHAEL FRY

Sources M. R. G. Fry, *The Dundas despotism* (1993) · *The letters of Sir Walter Scott*, ed. H. J. C. Grierson and others, centenary edn, 12 vols. (1932–79) · *Memorials of his time, by Henry Cockburn* (1856) · *The later correspondence of George III*, ed. A. Aspinall, 5 vols. (1962–70) · HoP, *Commons, 1790–1820* · J. W. McCleary, 'Anglo-French naval rivalry', PhD diss., Johns Hopkins University, 1947 · Venn, *Alum. Cant.*
Archives BL, corresp., loan 57 · BL, corresp. and papers, Add. MSS 40100–40102; 41079–41085, 41345, 41767–41768, 43370 · BLPES,

corresp. and papers relating to Highland roads and bridges · Duke U., Perkins L., corresp. relating to naval matters · Hunt. L., corresp. and papers · NA Canada, papers · NA Scot., corresp. and papers · NA Scot., family and personal corresp. · NL Scot., corresp. · NL Scot., corresp. and papers · NMM, naval corresp. and papers · SOAS, corresp. relating to India · U. Mich., Clements L., corresp. and papers · U. St Andr. L., corresp. and papers relating to Scotland | Bank of Scotland, Edinburgh, corresp. as governor of Bank of Scotland · BL, corresp. with Lord Bathurst, loan 57 · BL, letters to J. W. Croker, RP 706 [microfilm] · BL, corresp. with Sir Harford Jones, Add. MS 41768 · BL, corresp. with Lord Liverpool, Add. MSS 38245–38328, 38411, 38571–38576 · BL, corresp. with Sir Robert Peel, Add. MSS 40221–40601 · BL, letters to Lord Spencer · BL, Wellesley papers · BL, corresp. with C. P. Yorke, Add. MSS 45044–45046 · Bodl. Oxf., corresp. with Charles Grant and Edward Parry · Bodl. RH, corresp. relating to West Indies · Edinburgh Central Reference Library, letters to Robert Christie · Harrowby Manuscript Trust, Sandon Hall, Staffordshire, corresp. with Lord Harrowby · L. Cong., corresp. and papers relating to Admiralty administration · N. Yorks. CRO, corresp. with Lord Bolton · NA Scot., letters to Thomas, Lord Cochrane · NA Scot., letters to Lord Dalhousie · NA Scot., letters to Sir Alexander Hope · NA Scot., corresp. with J. A. Stewart-Mackenzie · NA Scot., corresp. with duke of Wellington · NL Ire., corresp. and papers relating to Ireland · NL Scot., corresp. with John Borthwick of Crookston, Lord Rutherford, and Thomas Graham Stirling · NL Scot., corresp. with Sir Alexander Cochrane · NL Scot., corresp., mainly on Indian affairs · NL Scot., corresp. with Lord Keith · NL Scot., corresp. with John Lee · NL Scot., corresp. with Sir David Milne and earl of Seafield · NL Scot., corresp. with Lord Minto · NL Scot., corresp. with Sir Walter Scott · NMM, letters to Sir Thomas Foley · NMM, corresp. with Sir John Warren · Northumbd RO, Newcastle upon Tyne, letters to Lord Wallace · NRA, priv. coll., letters to J. J. Hope Johnstone · NRA, priv. coll., corresp. with Spencer Perceval · Orkney Archives, Kirkwall, corresp. with Balfour family · PRO NIre., corresp. with Lord Castlereagh · PRO NIre., corresp. with John Foster · Surrey HC, letters to Henry Goulburn · U. Durham L., corresp. with second Earl Grey · U. Leeds, Brotherton L., corresp. with Lord Minto and Lady Minto · U. Mich., Clements L., corresp. with George Canning · U. Southampton L., letters to duke of Wellington · W. Yorks. AS, Leeds, Canning papers · Wellcome L., corresp., mainly relating to Edinburgh
Likenesses C. Turner, mezzotint, pubd 1827 (after T. Lawrence, 1826), BM, NPG [*see illus.*] · C. Smith, oils, *c.*1831, Scot. NPG · D. Wilkie, oils, 1831, U. St Andr. · J. Steell, statue, 1857, Melville Crescent, Edinburgh · G. Hayter, group portrait, oils (*The trial of Queen Caroline, 1820*), NPG

Dundas, Thomas, of Fingask (1681?–1762). *See under* Dundas family of Fingask and Kerse (*per.* 1728/9–1820).

Dundas, Thomas, of Fingask (*c.*1708–1786). *See under* Dundas family of Fingask and Kerse (*per.* 1728/9–1820).

Dundas, Thomas, of Kerse, first Baron Dundas of Aske (1741–1820). *See under* Dundas family of Fingask and Kerse (*per.* 1728/9–1820).

Dundas, Thomas (1750–1794), army officer and politician, of Fingask and Carron Hall, Stirlingshire, was born on 30 June 1750 into an old but minor Scottish gentry family. He was one of two sons and five daughters born to Thomas *Dundas of Fingask (*c.*1708–1786), businessman and MP for Orkney and Shetland (1768–70) [*see under* Dundas family of Fingask and Kerse], and his second wife, Lady Janet Maitland (1721–1805), daughter of Charles, sixth earl of Lauderdale. Dundas was the brother of Charles *Dundas, later Baron Amesbury, and nephew of Sir Lawrence

*Dundas, army contractor and MP [*see under* Dundas family of Fingask and Kerse]. Having been educated at Edinburgh high school, Dundas obtained through Sir Lawrence's influence a purchase cornetcy, dated 25 April 1766, in the 1st dragoon guards, at that time stationed in Scotland. He purchased next a captaincy, dated 20 May 1769, in the 63rd foot, a corps in Ireland, where he served until he sailed with the 63rd from Cork, in April 1775, in the first embarkation of reinforcements for the beleaguered army in Boston.

By this time Dundas was in parliament, having replaced his father, in his uncle's interest, as MP for Orkney and Shetland on 31 January 1771. Although he is not known to have spoken in the house he voted with Sir Lawrence in support of Lord North's ministry and retained his seat until, absent on service, he was replaced at the 1780 election by his brother, Charles, on the instruction of Sir Lawrence.

On 20 January 1776 Dundas purchased the majority of the 65th foot, then in Halifax, Nova Scotia, a regiment that was drafted shortly thereafter, the cadre being sent home in May to recruit. When early in 1778 the corporation of Edinburgh, at Sir Lawrence's prompting, raised a regiment (the 80th foot, Royal Edinburgh volunteers) Dundas was appointed its lieutenant-colonel, his commission dated 27 December 1777. He embarked with the 80th in May 1779 and joined the army at New York in August; he and his regiment were with Clinton at the capture of Charlestown, South Carolina, in May 1780; and he himself was with Cornwallis's army in the southern campaigns of 1780–81. He was one of the commissioners who arranged the surrender at Yorktown in October 1781. The 80th was disbanded at Edinburgh on 5 April 1784, its officers having been put on the half-pay list, and there Dundas chose to remain until the outbreak of war with revolutionary France.

On 9 May 1784 Dundas married Lady Eleonora Elizabeth (1759–1837), daughter of Alexander, ninth earl of Home; they had a son, Thomas (d. 1860), who entered the army, and six daughters. The little time that he had at home Dundas spent at Carron Hall, a Stirlingshire estate purchased by his father in 1749. He was returned MP for his former constituency in the election of 1784 but, having in June 1783 been made a member of the board appointed to examine the claims of dispossessed American loyalists, he embarked for Nova Scotia in September 1785, and remained in the Canadian maritimes until 1788. His return to England in 1788 coincided with the regency crisis, and in December 1788 and February 1789 he voted with the opposition on the regency question. He declined the appointment, offered him early in 1789, of confidential secretary to the duke of York, a decision that his cousin Sir Thomas Dundas ascribed to his 'diffidence' (Dundas, 93), but in 1793 he briefly held office as governor of Guernsey. At the 1790 general election he was defeated for Orkney and Shetland and, primarily concerned with his military career, he did not attempt to re-enter parliament.

Dundas returned to active service in summer 1793,

when he was given command of a brigade (with local rank of 'brigadier in America', dated 26 September 1793) in Sir Charles Grey's expedition that was forming for the West Indies. He was promoted major-general on 12 October and sailed with the expedition in November. While the troops were prepared in Barbados in January, Dundas, with his experience of light infantry tactics gained in the southern campaigns, drilled the assembled flank companies, formed into six élite, composite battalions; they went on to perform well during Grey's campaign of 1794 in the French Windward Islands. Dundas played a leading role in these operations, commanding brigades at the capture of Martinique in February and March, and of St Lucia, Martinique, and Guadeloupe in April. Tropical disease, however, halted the operations by early May. Dundas, recently appointed governor of Guadeloupe, died of yellow fever at Basse Terre, Guadeloupe, on 3 June 1794 and was buried the following day 'in the principal Bastion of Fort Matilda' (*GM*, 155). He thus did not enjoy the colonelcy of the 68th foot awarded him on 30 April, a mark of recognition which, his letters to his wife showed, he felt he had been unjustly denied. Reinforcements not having arrived, all these gains, except Martinique, were lost in 1795, by which time the struggle, already bitter, had become savage. After the British evacuated Fort Matilda, their last toehold in Basse Terre, in December 1794, Dundas's remains were disinterred by the French and, in the words of Victor Hugues, the notorious republican commissioner, 'given as prey to the birds of the air' (*GM*, 255). Hugues ordered the erection of a monument inscribed 'This ground, restored to liberty by the bravery of the Republicans, was polluted by the body of Thomas Dundas, Major-General and Governor of Guadaloupe, for the bloody George III' (ibid.). In 1795 a monument to Dundas was voted by parliament and placed in St Paul's Cathedral. A mother's advice to her son, a young ensign in the 80th foot, had already summed up Dundas: 'everybody speaks well of him, and whatever character he gives of the officers of his regiment will be believed before anybody' (Dundas, 63).

J. A. HOULDING

Sources M. I. Dundas, *Dundas of Fingask* (1891) · HoP, *Commons, 1754–90*, 1.356–61, 364–7 · M. Duffy, *Soldiers, sugar, and sea power: the British expeditions to the West Indies and the war against revolutionary France* (1987) · GM, 2nd ser., 20 (1843), 155–60, 249–56 · succession books, PRO, WO.25/210, p. 39; WO.25/211, 65th and 80th foot · *Army List* (1770) · *Army List* (1794) · DNB · P. R. N. Katcher, *King George's army, 1775–1783* (1973) · M. Fry, *The Dundas despotism* (1992) · Burke, *Gen. GB* (1871) · Burke, *Peerage* (1963) · N. B. Leslie, *The succession of colonels of the British army from 1660 to the present day* (1974)

Archives PRO, corresp., CO 318/12–13 | U. Durham, Earl Grey papers

Likenesses W. Nutter, stipple (after G. Romney), NAM

Wealth at death left estate of Carron Hall, Stirlingshire to son

Dundas, William (1762–1845), politician, was the third son of Robert *Dundas, Lord Arniston (1713–1787), lord president of the court of session in 1760, and his wife, Jean, daughter of William Grant, Lord Prestongrange, and his wife, Grizel. William's brother Robert *Dundas [*see under* Dundas, Robert, of Arniston] suspected his legitimacy (see the entry in *History of Parliament*). He was born in

1762 and was educated at Westminster School from 1770 (the first of his family to be sent south) and at University College, Oxford, in 1780, where he took no degree. He entered Lincoln's Inn in 1780 and was called to the bar on 31 January 1788.

Dundas's uncle, Henry *Dundas, first Viscount Melville, arranged for his entry to the Commons as MP for Anstruther burghs in 1794 and he transferred to Tain burghs in 1796, which he held until 1802. He then transferred, under Lady Sutherland's patronage, to the Sutherland constituency, for which he sat from 1802 to 1808. Like other members of his family, he was a Pittite. He was on the Board of Control, 1796–1803, was sworn of the privy council in 1800, and from 1804 to 1806 was secretary at war. George III found him to have 'the appearance of a man of sense'. On Pitt's death in 1806 Dundas was the first of his followers to join Lord Grenville. When he took an independent line in considering the offer of the lieutenant-governorship of Upper Canada in 1806, his uncle, now Lord Melville, was furious. In 1808, estranged from his family and his patrons, Dundas resigned his seat. However, he returned in 1810 as MP for Elgin burghs under Sir James Grant's patronage. His relations with his uncle restored, he was elected for Edinburgh on taking office in March 1812 as a lord of the Admiralty. He held the seat until 1831. In August 1814 he resigned the Admiralty lordship to succeed his brother Robert as keeper of the signet; to this he added the sinecures of keeper of the sasines in 1819 and lord clerk register in June 1821.

In 1814 Dundas married Mary, daughter of J. A. Stuart Wortley Mackenzie; she brought him £40,000 p.a. With an income from his offices of over £4000 p.a. he died at St Leonards on 14 November 1845. Though not the most notorious of the Dundas family of placemen, he certainly was a worthy representative of its ethos.

H. C. G. MATTHEW

Sources HoP, Commons • Annual Register (1845) • G. W. T. Omond, ed., The Arniston memoirs: three centuries of a Scottish house, 1571–1838 (1887) • GM, 2nd ser., 25 (1846), 312 • M. Fry, The Dundas despotism (1992)
Archives NA Scot., corresp. with Henry Dundas and Robert Dundas
Likenesses J. Downman, watercolour drawing, Arniston House, Lothian • J. Hoppner, oils, Arniston House, Lothian; version, Scot. NPG

Dundee. For this title name see Scrymgeour, John, first earl of Dundee (d. 1668) [see under Scrymgeour, Sir James, of Dudhope (c.1550–1612)]; Graham, John, first viscount of Dundee (1648?–1689).

Dunderdale, Wilfred Albert (1899–1990), intelligence officer, was born in Russia on 24 December 1899, the son of Richard Albert Dunderdale, a British shipowner, whose vessels traded between Constantinople and the Russian ports on the Black Sea, and his wife, Sophie. He was educated in Russia, at the Gymnasium in Nikolayev, Ukraine, and was studying naval engineering at Petrograd University when the Russian Revolution broke out in 1917. Much of the Russian navy remained in White Russian hands. Dunderdale was contacted by the Royal Navy, who found his great knowledge of the Russian language and the Russian navy invaluable.

At this time Constantinople, where Dunderdale had numerous friends, had been occupied by the allies. On one occasion in 1919 a submarine was being handed over by the allies to the White Russian navy. Dunderdale discovered that the crew were Bolsheviks who intended to murder the tsarist officers together with the liaison officer (himself) as soon as the vessel sailed. The crew was arrested and Dunderdale was appointed MBE in 1920. In the same year he became a sub-lieutenant in the Royal Naval Volunteer Reserve. During this period he was also sent as the British observer and interpreter to accompany the imperial procurator on his investigation into the murder of the Russian imperial family at Yekaterinburg, which had been recaptured by the White Russian army. As a result he remained convinced of the falseness of the pretender Anastasia, who he said was merely the Polish girlfriend of one of the Bolshevik gaolers who had occasionally done some sewing for the tsarina.

The world of Constantinople, from the end of the First World War until Kemal Atatürk deposed Sultan Muhammad in 1922, was one of classical Byzantine intrigue on a grand scale. The only stabilizing factor was the heavy guns of the Royal Navy, which were trained on the centre of the city. Dunderdale was in his element and in 1921 he was recruited by MI6, with whom he remained until 1959. He had found his spiritual home. He always maintained that his first job for MI6 was to pay off, with gold sovereigns, all the foreign members of the sultan's harem and to repatriate them through the good offices of the Royal Navy.

In 1926 Dunderdale was posted to Paris to represent MI6's interests and to liaise with the French Deuxième Bureau. He stayed in Paris until 1940. The central weapon in his armoury was his personality. He spoke several languages well, and was debonair and a wonderful host. There was about him an element of the pirate; he was a romantic with enormous vitality and a gift for friendship. If the truth of past dramatic events was occasionally expanded in telling the story, his friends readily forgave him. His flat in Paris became a meeting-place for international visitors and a venue for political gossip. His relations with the Deuxième Bureau became close and he played a major role in one great intelligence coup. He had become a close personal friend of Colonel Gustave Bertrand, the Deuxième Bureau chief signals officer, and they were both friendly with the Polish intelligence service in Paris. Shortly after the outbreak of the Second World War in 1939, they managed to smuggle out of Poland to Paris a model of the top secret German encoding machine known as Enigma. Dunderdale took it over to London himself, in romantic circumstances. It was the biggest single contribution to the vital intelligence results achieved by the British decoding centre at Bletchley Park, and was perhaps the greatest allied intelligence coup of the war. He was appointed CMG in 1942.

In the summer of 1940 Dunderdale had to return to London. He ran a small group of agents into French seaports, but his contribution gradually diminished. Part of the reason for this was that, as Charles De Gaulle became increasingly powerful in London and set up his own intelligence organization, Dunderdale's contacts with the old Deuxième Bureau became an object of suspicion: a number of its officers were indeed working with the Vichy government. After the war Dunderdale refused to have an office in MI6's headquarters because the aura of Whitehall was intolerable to him; he was allowed to set up a small office nearby. There, with lovely oriental carpets, portraits of the queen and the tsar, a whiff of incense, and a fine model of a Russian destroyer of 1912, he provided a home from home for many foreign visitors from pre-war days. He also made two further contributions. When De Gaulle resigned early in 1946 an intelligence amalgamation took place in Paris between the pre-war professionals and those who worked for the French general. Dunderdale played a useful role in bridging the gap between the new generation of MI6 officers and his pre-war French colleagues. Second, in his final period with MI6 his company and his worldly knowledge were a constant pleasure and profit to his younger colleagues. He was an officer of the French Légion d'honneur, a holder of the French Croix de Guerre (with palm), and an officer of the American Legion of Merit.

Always known as Biffy, Dunderdale was neat, dark, immaculately dressed, and stubby in build, and he always had a Balkan cigarette, in a long, black, ivory holder, in his hand. In 1928 he married June Woodbridge Ament-Morse of Washington, USA. The marriage was dissolved in 1947 and in 1952 he married Dorothy Mabel Brayshaw Hyde, daughter of James Murray Crofts DSc. They had a happy marriage and lived in London until her death in 1978. After his wife died there was little left to keep Dunderdale in England and he went to live in New York, where he had some old friends. In 1980 he married Deborah, widow of Harry McJ. McLeod and daughter of Eugene B. Jackson, of Boston, Massachusetts. There were no children of any of the marriages. Dunderdale died on 13 November 1990 in New York. JOHN BRUCE LOCKHART, rev.

Sources personal knowledge (1996) · private information (1996) · *The Times* (16 Nov 1990) · *CGPLA Eng. & Wales* (1991)
Wealth at death £199,876—effects in England: probate, 23 April 1991, *CGPLA Eng. & Wales*

Dundonald. For this title name *see* Cochrane, William, first earl of Dundonald (1605–1685); Cochrane, Archibald, ninth earl of Dundonald (1748–1831); Cochrane, Thomas, tenth earl of Dundonald (1775–1860); Cochrane, Douglas Mackinnon Baillie Hamilton, twelfth earl of Dundonald (1852–1935).

Dundrennan. For this title name *see* Maitland, Thomas, Lord Dundrennan (1792–1851).

Dunedin. For this title name *see* Murray, Andrew Graham, first Viscount Dunedin (1849–1942); Murray, Jane Elmslie Henderson, Viscountess Dunedin (1885–1944).

Dunfermline. For this title name *see* Seton, Alexander, first earl of Dunfermline (1556–1622); Seton, Charles, second earl of Dunfermline (1615–1672); Abercromby, James, first Baron Dunfermline (1776–1858).

Dúngal (*d. c.*736). *See under* Dál Riata, kings of (*act. c.*500–*c.*850).

Dúngal (*fl. c.*800–827), astronomer and theologian, went to Francia *c.*800, taught at Pavia, and died as a monk, probably at Bobbio. His presence in Francia and his Irish origins are attested in a letter of Alcuin written probably in the early 790s to the monks of Ireland, which mentions a Bishop Dúngal as 'a venerable brother, a doctor of your learning … a most devout person leading a regular life' (Dümmler, ed., *Epistolae Karolini Aevi*, 4, no. 280); this must imply that he was a monk. Various persons named Dúngal are mentioned in ninth-century continental contexts. Although Traube, writing in 1892, believed that there were at least three separate Dúngals, one active at St Denis, one at Bobbio, and one who was the friend of Sedulius Scottus, more recent scholarship has suggested that the first two are identical. But the canon of Dúngal's writings is still in need of a careful study.

In 801 Dúngal was consulted by Charlemagne on the topic of the substance of nothing, which had been discussed by Fridugis of Tours (*d.* 833). In 811 he was a monk at the abbey of St Denis and responded to a question from Charlemagne to his abbot, Waldo (*d.* 813), asking for an explanation of the supposed occurrence of solar eclipses in both June and November 810 and for an explanation of how such an event could be predicted. His reply treats the sequence and motion of the planets, drawing extensively on Macrobius's early fifth-century commentary on the *Dream of Scipio* (a text known to the Irish) for an account of the ordered structure of the heavens and the position of the sun and the moon. Dúngal's letter shows a readiness to revise Macrobius in the light of Pliny the Elder (*d.* AD 79), though he explains that he does not have a copy of Pliny to hand. Following Pliny, Dúngal prefers the Ciceronian placement of the planets, with the sun in the fourth position, in contrast to the Platonic view defended by Macrobius, which put the sun in the sixth position. He concludes by explaining how the eclipses of 810 occurred at times of luni-solar conjunction, six lunar cycles apart. The letter is noteworthy for its praise of Charlemagne as a patron of science and learning (Dümmler, ed., *Epistolae Karolini Aevi*, 4.570–77).

Dúngal has been identified as the insular scribe who corrected the text of the oldest surviving manuscript of Lucretius's *De rerum natura*, probably copied at Charlemagne's court (Leiden, MS Vossianus Lat. F.30). His corrections can be found on almost every page, and they range from deciphering passages which the main scribe could not read to orthographic and textual emendation.

Further letters, in which Dúngal describes himself as a recluse, a pilgrim, and an orator, contain appeals for alms from an unidentified abbot to relieve his unaccustomed poverty, a request for a horse from Abbot Adam of Jumièges, and accompany a gift of silver. In 814 he congratulated Charlemagne's daughter Theodrada on her entry into a nunnery after her father's death. Verses convincingly attributed to Dúngal include a poem to Gundrada, the cousin of Charlemagne (Dümmler, ed., *Poetae Latini aevi Carolini*, 1.395–6), verse tituli for St Denis (ibid., 401–2), and epitaphs for Fulrad and Fardulf, abbots of St Denis, and for the graves of Dagobert I (*d.* 639) and Pippin III (*d.* 768) at St Denis (ibid., 404–5). Dúngal also wrote brief verses addressed to Baldo of Salzburg, Hildoard, bishop of Cambrai (*d.* 816), and Hilduin, abbot of St Denis (*d.* 855×61) (Dümmler, ed., *Poetae Latini aevi Carolini*, 1.393–5, 411–13; 2.664–5).

In 825 a capitulary of the emperor Lothar recommends Dúngal's school in the Carolingian capital at Pavia as the chief centre for those seeking instruction in Milan, Lombardy, and Piedmont. He is the only teacher named in this document. In 827 Dúngal wrote his chief work, a treatise responding to the iconoclastic teachings of Bishop Claudius of Turin, a protégé of the emperor Louis the Pious (*Patrologia Latina*, 105.465–530). Claudius had attacked the widespread cult of images as worship of idols, and objected to the practice of pilgrimage. Both Dúngal and Bishop Jonas of Orléans were asked to reply. Dúngal, who dedicated his reply to Louis the Pious and Lothar, had access only to excerpts from a letter of Claudius to Abbot Theutmir of Psalmody, Provence. His treatise of 'answers plucked and extracted from the authority and doctrine of the holy fathers' defended the worship of images and of the cross and its representations, and charged that Claudius was contemptuous of Christ's passion. He traced the history of images in the church and defended their function in educating and as an aid to memory. He also affirmed that the saints can intercede for the living and their relics can act as mediators between earth and heaven. The work assembled quotations from Ambrose, Jerome, Augustine, and Gregory the Great, and from the poets Paulinus of Nola, Prudentius, and Venantius Fortunatus, which supplement authorities quoted by the Council of Paris of 825. Dúngal may also have composed an account of the translation of the relics of St Syrus, the first bishop of Pavia, to the new cathedral there.

The Bobbio library catalogue lists some twenty-eight manuscripts which Dúngal, called *praecipuus Scottorum* ('most distinguished of the Irish'), donated to Bobbio, of which six survive. Apart from a sixth-century Italian copy of the poems of Prudentius, they were all copied at the abbey of St Denis in the early ninth century. Some contain Dúngal's corrections and one has a brief presentation poem.

The year of Dúngal's death is unknown. He was buried at Bobbio and his epitaph, which he may have composed himself, was printed from a Brussels manuscript of Prudentius by H. Silvestre. DAVID GANZ

Sources M. Esposito, 'The poems of Colmanus "Nepos Cracavist" and Dungalus "Praecipuus Scottorum"', *Journal of Theological Studies*, 33 (1931–2), 113–31 • M. Ferrara, 'In Papia conveniant ad Dungalum', *Italia Medioevale e Umanistica*, 15 (1972), 1–52 • C. Leonardi, 'Gli Irlandesi in Italia: Dungal e la controversia iconoclastica', *Die Iren und Europa im früheren Mittelalter*, ed. H. Löwe, 2 (Stuttgart, 1982), 746–57 • J. Vezin, 'Observations sur l'origine des manuscrits légués à Bobbio par Dungal', *Paläographie 1981: Colloquium des Comité International de Paléographie* [Munich 1981], ed. G. Silagi (Munich, 1982), 125–44 • B. Eastwood, 'The astronomy of Macrobius in Carolingian Europe: Dungal's letter of 811 to Charles the Great', *Early Medieval Europe*, 3 (1994), 112–34 • J. F. Kenney, *The sources for the early history of Ireland* (1929), 538–42 • M. Lapidge and R. Sharpe, *A bibliography of Celtic-Latin literature, 400–1200* (1985), 173 • W. Wattenbach, W. Levison, and H. Löwe, *Deutschlands Geschichtsquellen im Mittelalter: Vorzeit und Karolinger*, 4 (Weimar, 1963), 422–3 • H. Silvestre, 'La véritable épitaphe de Dungal, reclus de St Denis et auteur des "*Responsa contra Claudium*"?', *Revue Bénédictine*, 61 (1952), 256–9 • Dungal, *Patrologia Latina*, 105 (1831) • E. Dümmler, ed., *Epistolae Karolini aevi*, MGH Epistolae [quarto], 4 (Berlin, 1895) • E. Dümmler, ed., *Poetae Latini aevi Carolini*, MGH Poetae Latini Medii Aevi, 1–2 (Berlin, 1881–4) • A. Boretius, ed., *Capitularia regum Francorum*, MGH Capitularia Regum Francorum, 1 (Hanover, 1883) • C. Prelini, ed., *San Siro primo vescovo e patrono della citta e diocesi di Pavia*, 1 (1880)

Archives Biblioteca Apostolica Vaticana, Vatican City, MS Regin. lat. 200 • Bibliothèque Nationale, Paris, MS nouv. acq. lat. 1096 • BL, MS Harley 208

Dungannon. For this title name *see* Trevor, Marcus, first Viscount Dungannon (1618–1670); Trevor, Arthur Hill-, first Viscount Dungannon (*d.* 1771) [*see under* Trevor, Arthur Hill-, third Viscount Dungannon (1798–1862)]; Trevor, Arthur Hill-, third Viscount Dungannon (1798–1862).

Dunglison, Robley (1798–1869), physician and medical writer, was born on 4 January 1798, at Keswick in Cumberland, the son of William Dunglison, who was possibly engaged in woollen manufacture, and his wife, Elizabeth Jackson (*d.* 1854). He attended Green Row Academy at Abbey Holme on the Solway, but a plan that he should receive a merchant's education and join his great-uncle Joseph Robley, a wealthy planter in the West Indies, was frustrated by the latter's death. Dunglison resolved to study medicine and was apprenticed at seventeen to a Keswick surgeon, John Edmundson. Next he attended hospital lectures and joined a practice in London as a pupil of the obstetrician Charles T. Haden, and he then spent the session of 1815–16 at Edinburgh University and Edinburgh Royal Infirmary, followed by another session in Paris.

Dunglison passed the examinations of the Royal College of Surgeons and the Society of Apothecaries in 1818 and commenced practice in 1819. He was appointed physician accoucheur to the Eastern Dispensary in London and in 1823 he received the degree of MD by examination from the University of Erlangen, having submitted a thesis on neuralgia. He had also written articles on medical and literary subjects, and in 1824 he published his first major medical work, *Commentaries on Diseases of the Stomach and Bowels of Children*. In the same year he announced a course of lectures in practical midwifery.

Dunglison was never to teach the course, for in the summer of 1824, after being recommended by Dr George Birkbeck to a representative of the newly established University of Virginia, he accepted an appointment to its faculty. The salary was $1500, to which certain student fees and the occupancy of a house were added. With an income assured, Dunglison married on the eve of his departure for America Harriette Leadam (*d.* 1853), daughter of John

Leadam, a medical practitioner of Southwark, London. They were to have six children, of whom two sons became physicians.

Dunglison's professorship included the full sweep of medical knowledge—anatomy, surgery, physiology, materia medica, pharmacy, and history of medicine. These lectures were meant to be historical and cultural rather than professional and practical; but in 1827 the curriculum was revised and in 1827 four degrees in medicine were conferred. In Charlottesville Dunglison became physician and friend of Thomas Jefferson, former president of the United States and the university's founder, who, despite his low regard for medicine and doctors, proved to be 'one of the most attentive and respectful of patients' (*Autobiographical ana*, 26).

The duties of his professorship left Dunglison ample time to write. He founded, edited, and contributed to the *Virginia Museum and Journal of Belles Lettres, Arts, Sciences* (1829–30) and published a syllabus of his lectures on medical jurisprudence in 1827. He wrote a textbook, *Human Physiology* (2 vols., 1832), which presented the subject systematically for the first time in the United States, and *A New Dictionary of Medical Science and Literature* (2 vols., 1833). *Human Physiology*, which appeared in eight editions, had 'a decided influence in modifying the heroic practice, which generally prevailed at that time' (*Autobiographical ana*, 74); and his dictionary, which contained definitions of French medical terms and sold more than 55,000 copies in nineteen editions during his lifetime, introduced contemporary French medicine to English-speaking physicians.

Dunglison left Virginia in 1833 for the University of Maryland, where anatomical and clinical facilities were greater; and after three years in Baltimore he moved, as professor of the institutes of medicine and of medical jurisprudence, to Jefferson Medical College in Philadelphia, then the principal medical centre of the country. Amid the often bitter clashes of personalities in the Jefferson faculty and the rivalries of partisans of Jefferson and the University of Pennsylvania, Dunglison acted frequently as a peacemaker. As dean of the medical faculty from 1854 to 1868, he was conservative in curricular matters and methods of teaching; he wisely discouraged faculty meetings, which he reckoned were likely sources of difference and dispute.

In Baltimore and Philadelphia Dunglison continued his industrious schedule of writing, translating, and editing. He published *Elements of Hygiene* (1835), *General Therapeutics* (1836), a manual for medical students (1837), *New Remedies* (1839), and *Practice of Medicine* (2 vols., 1842). He edited the *American Medical Library and Intelligencer* (1837–42), which reprinted standard works, and revised and contributed new articles to John Forbes's *Cyclopedia of Medicine* (4 vols., 1845).

Dunglison was not an original thinker; he had neither the taste nor the aptitude for research or experiment, and his name is associated with no discovery, practice, or principle in medicine. He did not dispute this criticism but believed that his principal opportunity and obligation were to communicate accepted medical knowledge to his students and to the profession at large. 'He was too much of a closet man, too much shut up in his library, and too much given to authorship, to be a great practitioner', was the judgement of his colleague Samuel D. Gross. 'He was a medical philosopher, a savant, rather than a physician' (Gross, 303). Most of his writing during the last twenty years of his life was spent on new editions of his books. It was calculated in 1875 that 134,875 copies of his works had been sold; they made him a wealthy man.

Dunglison was one of the physicians of the Philadelphia Hospital from 1839 to 1845. He was also a sponsor of the Pennsylvania State Lunatic Asylum. Interested in the education of blind people, he co-authored a three-volume dictionary in raised letters, in 1860, and he served for thirty years as vice-president of the Pennsylvania Institution for the Blind. Passionately fond of music, he was for many years president of the Musical Fund Society. He was elected a member or honorary member of scores of American and European medical, scientific, and literary societies, and he served for eighteen years as secretary or vice-president of the American Philosophical Society. Dunglison's library contained 4000 volumes; Thackeray was a favourite author, and *Clarissa Harlowe*, *Pickwick Papers*, and Humboldt's *Cosmos* were on his reading table when he died. He was an ardent fisherman and, until prevented by ill health, enjoyed long walks in the country.

Because of his ailing constitution Dunglison retired from his chair in 1868; suffering from gout and angina, he died at his home, 1116 Girard Avenue, Philadelphia, on 1 April 1869. His body was buried later in the month, in Laurel Hill cemetery in west Philadelphia.

WHITFIELD J. BELL, JR

Sources *The autobiographical ana of Robley Dunglison*, ed. S. X. Radbill (1963) • S. D. Gross, 'Memoir of Robley Dunglison, M.D., LL.D.', *Transactions of the College of Physicians of Philadelphia*, new ser., 4 (1874), 294–313 • F. B. Wagner, *Thomas Jefferson University: tradition and heritage*, 3 vols. (1989–96) • J. M. Dorsey, ed., *The Jefferson–Dunglison letters* (1960)
Archives College of Physicians of Philadelphia • Thomas Jefferson University, Philadelphia
Likenesses oils, *c*.1830, University of Virginia, Charlottesville • T. Sully, oils, 1868, College of Physicians of Philadelphia

Dunham, Samuel Astley (1795/6–1858), historian, was the author of several scholarly and well-researched works published by Dionysius Lardner in his *Cabinet Cyclopaedia*. Little is known of him personally. According to his acquaintance Robert Southey, writing in 1832 (*New Letters*, 2.377), he had been a laborious student from the age of seven and had made four European tours, sparing neither time, trouble, nor expense in historical research. His *History of Poland* (1831) was followed by a *History of Spain and Portugal* (5 vols., 1832–3), long regarded as the best work on the subject, which was translated into Spanish by Antonio Alcalá Galiano in 1844. It earned the author honorary membership of the Royal Spanish Academy. Equal praise was given to his four-volume *History of Europe during the Middle Ages* (1833–4).

By 1836 Dunham was reduced to extreme poverty. A dispute with the publisher Benjamin Fellowes led to the abandonment of a projected biographical dictionary. He himself spent time in a debtors' prison; his wife, Mary Elizabeth, *née* Charnley, and the five eldest of their ten children were dependent on parish relief while the five youngest were put in a workhouse. A printed appeal launched on Dunham's behalf by a number of Durham clergymen headed by George Townsend quoted glowing tributes to the writer from H. J. Rose, John Lingard, and others, and attracted contributions from eminent benefactors, but in June 1842 Dunham petitioned W. E. Gladstone to obtain a royal bounty of £50 to assist himself and his family to emigrate to Canada. However, he remained in London and continued to work for Lardner, publishing a *History of Denmark, Sweden and Norway* (3 vols., 1839–40) and a *History of the Germanic Empire* (3 vols., 1844–5). The entries on dramatists and early writers which he contributed to Lardner's *Lives of the most Eminent Literary and Scientific Men of Great Britain* (1836–7) were later published as separate volumes. His continuing interest in Spain is evident in reviews written for the *Monthly Chronicle* and *Dublin Review* (1838–9).

Dunham's connection with the city of Durham is proved by his offer in 1836 to Macvey Napier, the editor of the *Edinburgh Review*, of an article on the 'deficiencies' of the newly established University of Durham (BL, Add. MS 34616, fol. 81). Three of his sons are recorded as having been baptized in Roman Catholic chapels in, or near, Durham between 1834 and 1835; John Lingard was godfather to one of these. Robert Southey Dunham (*b*. 1835) was a Benedictine monk of Ramsgate Abbey who later served as a secular priest in England, Australia, and New Zealand, where he died in 1902. Francis Augustus (*b*. 1836), became a priest in the archdiocese of Liverpool and went on the Australian mission in 1871.

Dunham died suddenly on 17 July 1858 at his home, 22 Murray Street, Camden Town, London. His work, distinguished by original research and sound judgement, won recognition only among *cognoscenti*. In its obituary notice of 24 July 1858 *The Athenaeum* commented: 'We fear the general public will only learn that he was lately alive amongst us on now hearing of his death'.

C. W. SUTTON, rev. G. MARTIN MURPHY

Sources 'Extraordinary statement addressed to the patrons of literature on behalf of a well-known historian', *c*.1841, BL, Add. MS 34574 [n.p.], fols. 435–7 • *New letters of Robert Southey*, ed. K. Curry, 2 (1965), 377 • Boase, *Mod. Eng. biog.* • *The Athenaeum* (24 July 1858), 111 • C. Fitzgerald-Lombard, *English and Welsh priests, 1801–1914* (1993) • BL, Gladstone and Napier MSS • *IGI*

Archives BL, corresp. with Bliss, Napier, Drummond, Gladstone, Add. MSS 34574, 34616, 34617, 40509, 40510 • Bodl. Oxf., corresp. with James Ingram

Dunhill, Alfred (1872–1959), manufacturer of pipes and tobacco, was born on 30 September 1872 at 2 Church Path, Hornsey, Middlesex, the second son of five children of Henry Dunhill (1842–1901), a master blind-maker, and his wife and cousin, Jane, *née* Styles (1843–1922). Henry Dunhill ran his business from the Euston Road, making among other things, accessories for horse-drawn vehicles. The young Alfred joined the firm when he was fifteen, following his formal education at a private Hampstead

school and by tutors. In 1893 he acquired the business and quickly demonstrated his perspicacity and eye for the main chance by switching emphasis to the needs of the fledgeling motor industry. By the time of his first marriage, to Alice Stapleton (1873/4–1945) on 15 June 1895, he had established a separate business, Dunhill's Motorities, selling everything but the motor to early enthusiasts of the sport. Five years later he set up the Discount Motor Car Company, selling his accessories through mail order. However, Dunhill was determined to capture a good corner of the market and made the decision to tap its top end by forgoing mail order and entering the world of retail sales. In 1902 he opened his first shop in Conduit Street, Mayfair, selling clothing and accessories to both chauffeurs and their employers. The days of draughty driving offered wide scope for Dunhill's creative talents and indeed it was the chance idea of a 'windshield pipe', designed to protect sportsmen from the dangers of flying sparks, that was to herald his entry into the crowded world of the tobacco trade. The patent application for this unique pipe in 1904 prompted him to open his first tobacconist shop in Duke Street, St James's, in 1907. It was evident from the choice of location that Dunhill was intent on offering the very best to a select clientele. His shop, more redolent of a gentleman's club, offered all manner of pleasures for the discerning smoker: individual blends of exotic tobaccos and a whole array of smokers' requisites combined to create a heady mix of opulence and preserve.

By 1910 Dunhill had taken additional premises in Duke Street to accommodate more comfortably the thirteen employees engaged in cigarette manufacturing. The expansion of the business was enhanced further when Dunhill's youngest brother, Herbert, and his eldest son, Alfred, joined him in 1912, followed by his second son, Vernon, in the following year. The war provided the company with its real opportunity to prosper—not only to exploit the mail-order business but to change the image of the smoker, from simperer to decent, home-loving soldier, evoking memories of home and hearth with a flick of the match.

However, it is the pipe that has enjoyed the closest and most enduring association with the name Dunhill. His 1924 monograph, *The Pipe Book*, reveals an encyclopaedic knowledge of the history of the pipe as well as claims to its long-standing appeal. The self-seasoned briar root, used for the manufacture of all top-rate pipes, was hailed by Dunhill as the ideal pipe material, and although briar pipes sold by the company were nearly twice as expensive as any others available there was never a shortage of customers.

The post-war period witnessed both expansion and the commissioning of fresh products. The company always ensured its products were covered by patent and trade mark, a policy prosecuted with vigour from the outset. The early 1920s saw the wholesale and export side of the business move to Notting Hill Gate, close to the pipe and cigarette division located at Campden Hill Road. In 1921 the firm received its first royal warrant, as tobacconist to

Edward, prince of Wales; it enjoyed his loyal custom even during his years in exile. The 1920s also saw the opening of shops in New York, Toronto, and Paris as well as a branch in the City of London to serve the appreciative businessman.

The inter-war years were also a time for innovation and invention. The Unique lighter, a product that Dunhill and his brother had much interest in developing, proved a vast improvement on the undependable match and sold in thousands. This pocket version was followed by a variety of table models and joined a long list of other original ideas, including the somewhat bizarre Lite-up handbag for ladies who needed to see its contents in the dark.

Dunhill's decision to chair his final meeting of the company on 5 February 1929 was precipitated by personal circumstances. Having placed the firm on a steady course, he felt able to leave his son Alfred in charge. He left his wife and journeyed to Worthing to join his mistress of long standing, Vera Mildred Wright (b. 1902/3), who changed her name to his by deed poll. Together they enjoyed their autumnal years, yachting, fishing, and motoring around the south coast. He married Vera on 28 March 1945, shortly after the death of his wife. He died at Hopedene Nursing Home, Wordsworth Road, Worthing on 2 January 1959, and was cremated at Golders Green crematorium. His wife survived him.   BARBARA TROMPETER

Sources M. Balfour, *Alfred Dunhill: one hundred years and more* (1992) · *WWW* · *The Times* (5 Jan 1959), 10 · b. cert. · m. certs. (1895, 1945) · d. cert. · priv. coll.

Archives Alfred Dunhill Museum, London · priv. coll.

Likenesses photographs, repro. in Balfour, *Alfred Dunhill* · photographs, priv. coll. · photographs, Mary Evans Picture Library, London · photographs, Hult. Arch. · photographs, Greater London Photograph Library

Wealth at death £74,117 14s. 1d.: probate, 16 June 1959, *CGPLA Eng. & Wales*

Dunhill, Thomas Frederick (1877–1946), composer and writer, was born on 1 February 1877 at 10 Swiss Terrace, Belsize Road, Hampstead, London, the fourth of five children of Henry Dunhill (1842–1901), a manufacturer of sacks, tarpaulin, and ropes for horse-drawn vehicles, and owner of a small music shop at their home at 10 Swiss Terrace, run by his wife, Jane Styles (1843–1922). Dunhill's elder brother Alfred *Dunhill founded the famous tobacconist company in Piccadilly in 1907, which was later taken over by his younger brother Herbert with great commercial success. Educated first at the North London High School for Boys and then at Kent College, Canterbury (close to their new home at Harbledown), he entered the Royal College of Music in September 1893 to study the piano with Franklin Taylor, counterpoint with James Higgs and W. S. Rockstro, and harmony with Walter Parratt. A year later he began composition with Stanford and he continued to study with him until 1901, during which time he won an open scholarship in composition in 1897. In 1899 he became a piano teacher at Eton College at the invitation of C. H. Lloyd, where he remained until 1908. During this time he was appointed a professor of harmony and counterpoint at the Royal College of Music (from 1905, given up finally in 1922), and he began an active career as an examiner for the Associated Board, not only throughout Britain but also Australia, New Zealand, Jamaica, Canada, and India. Indeed, examining, combined with festival adjudication and lecturing, formed the basis of his income for the rest of his life.

After a number of relationships—among them one with the cellist May Mukle, for whom he wrote his *Capricious Variations on 'Sally in our Alley'* (1910)—he married Mary Penrose Arnold (1886/7–1929) on 4 April 1914. She was the daughter of Edward Arnold the publisher, the great-niece of Matthew Arnold, and the great-granddaughter of Dr Thomas Arnold of Rugby; she died from tuberculosis in 1929, having had two sons and a daughter. At the outbreak of the First World War Dunhill joined the Allied Artists' force before becoming a bandsman with the Irish Guards. After the war was over he resumed his work as examiner, lecturer, and adjudicator and he undertook a substantial number of new duties, including the inspectorship of the Girls' High School Trust, a directorship of the Royal Philharmonic Society, the deanship of the faculty of music of London University, the presidency of the Oxford and Cambridge Musical Club (1938), and work with the Society of Authors and the Performing Right Society; Hugh Allen, the new director of the Royal College of Music, also invited him to teach chamber music in 1919. In 1939 he was invited by Henry Ley to return to Eton, first to teach the piano, and later, in 1942, as a classroom teacher. On 23 December 1942 he married Isabella Simpson Featonby (b. 1902/3), daughter of John Featonby of Scunthorpe. As a music teacher herself she joined her husband at Eton where she taught the piano for many years. Dunhill gave up teaching at Eton in 1945; he died the following year at his mother-in-law's house, 15 Cliff Gardens, Scunthorpe, Lincolnshire, on 13 March. After a funeral at St Lawrence, Frodingham, he was buried at St Bartholomew, Appleby. In recognition of his musical achievements Durham University conferred an honorary DMus on him in 1940, while honorary fellowships were bestowed by the Royal Academy of Music (1938) and the Royal College of Music (1942).

Dunhill initially established his career as a composer of concerted chamber music, namely the quintet for piano trio, horn, and clarinet (1898), the piano quartet (1903), the 'Phantasy' string quartet (1906), the piano quintet (1904), the horn quintet (1905), and 'Phantasy' trio (1911) written for the Cobbett prize. Two violin sonatas were also written of which the second (1916) is arguably his finest work. His preoccupation with chamber music led him to inaugurate the Dunhill concerts (1907–1916) designed to give works by young British composers a second hearing. He also produced two books, *Chamber Music: a Treatise for Students* (1912) and *Mozart's String Quartets* (1927), and he wrote numerous articles for William Cobbett's *Cyclopaedic Survey of Chamber Music* (1930). In recognition of his services to chamber music he was awarded (as the first recipient) the Cobbett chamber music medal in 1924. Among his orchestral works were the *Elegiac Variations* (1919–20) written in memory of Sir Hubert Parry, two late works, the *Triptych* for viola and orchestra (1942) and an overture, *May Time*

(1945) for the Promenade Concerts, and a number of orchestral songs, the finest of which was his setting of W. B. Yeats's 'The Wind among the Reeds' (1909). Most substantial of all, however, was the symphony in A minor (1913–16), first performed in Belgrade in 1922 by the Royal Guard Orchestra in a concert organized by his friends Bratza and Dushko Yovanovitch.

Two other passions—Sullivan's comic operas and Elgar—produced books in 1928 and 1938 respectively. More significantly, Dunhill's enthusiasm for Sullivan and light opera was reflected in a prolific series of works for the stage, including *Princess Una* (1901); the musical fantasy *Frolicsome Hours* (1904); *The Enchanted Garden* (1924), which won a Carnegie award, and two children's operas; *Happy Families* (1933); and *Alicia* (1938). However, the work that brought his name to prominence was *Tantivy Towers* (1930), a satirical discourse on the sport of hunting, composed in collaboration with the writer and (later) politician, A. P. Herbert. Dunhill also enjoyed modest success with his two ballets, *Dick Whittington* (1936) and *Gallimaufry* (1937), the latter of which was performed at the Hamburg State Opera in 1937. JEREMY DIBBLE

Sources D. Dunhill, *Thomas Dunhill: maker of music* (1997) · G. S. K. Butterworth and H. C. Colles, 'Dunhill, Thomas (Frederick)', *New Grove* · b. cert. · m. certs. · d. cert. · *DNB*
Archives priv. coll. | BL, corresp. with League of Dramatists, Add. MS 63374 · BL, corresp. with Society of Authors, Add. MSS 56696–56698 | FILM priv. coll.
Likenesses F. Oxley, drawing, priv. coll. · photograph (as young man), Royal College of Music, London · photographs, priv. coll.
Wealth at death £4794: probate, 23 July 1947, *CGPLA Eng. & Wales*

Dunhill, Sir Thomas Peel (1876–1957), surgeon, was born on 3 December 1876, at Tragowel, Victoria, Australia, the elder of two sons of John Webster Dunhill, overseer on a cattle station, and his wife, Mary Elizabeth, daughter of George Peel, stonemason, of Inverleigh, Victoria. Dunhill's father died of typhoid fever at the age of twenty-six when Thomas was only sixteen months old and before the birth of his brother. Dunhill went to school at Inverleigh; then, when he was twelve, his mother married again and the family moved to Daylesford, near Ballarat, where his stepfather, William Laury, was manager of a goldmine. Dunhill completed his education at the local grammar school, and was then apprenticed to a nearby chemist. He went on to open a chemist's shop at Rochester in northern Victoria, at which point he decided to take up medicine. As soon as he had saved enough money, he became a medical student at the University of Melbourne, where he won a scholarship and obtained first-class honours in several subjects. He took his MB in 1903, was appointed house physician to Henry Maudsley at the Royal Melbourne Hospital, and obtained his MD in 1906. In 1908 he was appointed to the surgical staff of St Vincent's Hospital, Melbourne, and began to develop a special interest in exophthalmic goitre and the surgical treatment of thyroid disease, for which he established an international reputation.

While in Melbourne, Dunhill's contributions to surgery were twofold. By giving patients local anaesthetic instead of chloroform and by removing sufficient of the thyroid gland by gentle dissection, he was able to operate safely on patients with the most severe cases of exophthalmic goitre, even those with heart failure, and restore them to useful active lives. At that time the mortality rate for those treated without surgery was 25 per cent; Dunhill recorded a post-operative mortality rate of 1.5 per cent, in contrast with the rates of 4.5 per cent and 8.1 per cent claimed by famous surgeons in Europe and America. His other contribution was to stress the importance of the surgeon's gaining the confidence of patients before operation, especially if they were frightened and emotionally upset, by himself undertaking the pre-operative treatment and control. The distinction which he attained was due not only to his surgical skill but also to the thought, time, and human sympathy that he expended in his care for each patient.

In 1914 Dunhill joined the Australian Army Medical Corps and served mainly in France, where he became known to and appreciated by his medical colleagues from the United Kingdom. He was three times mentioned in dispatches, became consulting surgeon to the British expeditionary force in 1918 with the rank of colonel, and was appointed CMG in 1919. His return to Australia lasted only a few months, for in 1920 he accepted the invitation of George Gask to become assistant surgeon and assistant director of the newly formed surgical professorial unit at St Bartholomew's Hospital medical college. He quickly impressed his colleagues in London by his skill and energy, and his determination to overcome difficulties and neglect no precaution which could benefit his patients. He was essentially a modest, humble man, who never hesitated to seek advice from anyone who might be helpful. His reputation spread quickly and colleagues from all parts of Britain and from abroad visited him to see him operate and to study his methods. Although the surgical treatment of thyroid disease remained his special interest he was a general surgeon, with a large private practice.

Dunhill did not enjoy formal teaching and found difficulty in publishing his results, but by his example he had a powerful effect on the education of young surgeons and physicians in the inter-war period. His appointment as surgeon to the household of King George V in 1928 was warmly approved and followed by his promotion as surgeon to the king in 1930. In 1939 he became sergeant-surgeon, and in 1952 extra-surgeon. He was appointed KCVO in 1933 and GCVO in 1949.

At the Royal College of Surgeons of England Dunhill was Arris and Gale lecturer in 1931, when he chose as his subject carcinoma of the thyroid gland, and again in 1934, when he lectured on diaphragmatic hernia. In 1950 he was awarded the Cecil Joll prize and in 1951 he delivered the Cecil Joll memorial lecture on the recent history of the surgical treatment of exophthalmic goitre. In 1935 the University of Adelaide awarded him the honorary degree of MD and in 1939 the Royal College of Surgeons of England elected him an honorary fellow.

Dunhill was a short, slim man who gave the impression of nervous tension and of mental and physical energy. An

Australian colleague described him as made of 'stainless steel'. He had a charming smile, made friends easily, and quickly saw the good in his acquaintances, regardless of their social standing. For himself his standards were high and it was not only in his professional work that he sought expert advice wherever he could. Although a keen and successful salmon and trout fisherman he took instruction in order to improve his style and methods. His appreciation of antique furniture, of pictures, and of architecture was also based on the best advice.

In 1914 Dunhill married Edith Florence (d. 1942), daughter of James Affleck and widow of D. G. McKellar. They had no children. He bequeathed his portrait by Sir James Gunn to the Royal Australasian College of Surgeons in Melbourne, of which he was an honorary fellow. He died in Hampstead, London, on 22 December 1957; his home there was Tragowel, North End Avenue, Hampstead.

FRANCIS FRASER, rev.

Sources *The Times* (24 Dec 1957) · J. Peel, 'The early life of Sir Thomas Dunhill', *St Bartholomew's Hospital Journal*, 64 (1960), 306–8 · *Medical Journal of Australia*, 22 (March 1958) · *BMJ* (4 Jan 1958), 43–5 · private information (1971) · personal knowledge (1971)
Archives RCS Eng., case notes, incl. on thyroid patients
Likenesses W. Stoneman, photographs, 1934–52, NPG · J. Gunn, oils, Royal Australasian College of Surgeons, Melbourne, Australia · J. Gunn, oils, St Bartholomew's Hospital, London
Wealth at death £138,163 16s. 11d.: probate, 18 Feb 1958, CGPLA Eng. & Wales

Dunipace. For this title name *see* Spottiswood, Sir Robert, Lord Dunipace (1596–1646).

Dunk, George Montagu, second earl of Halifax (1716–1771), politician, born on 5/6 October 1716, was the only son of George Montagu, first earl of Halifax (c.1684–1739), politician, and his second wife, Lady Mary Lumley (1690–1726), the eldest daughter of Richard Lumley, first earl of Scarbrough. He was educated at Eton College (1725–32) and Trinity College, Cambridge, where he matriculated in 1734. His student days were not wasted, for he earned the reputation of being an 'extremely brilliant' scholar (Cumberland, 99). He succeeded to the earldom of Halifax on his father's death in 1739, when he inherited also the office of ranger of Bushey Park, which he held for life. On 2 July 1741 he married Ann Dunk (1725?–1753), the daughter of William Richards (afterwards Dunk) of Tongues in Hawkhurst, Kent. Richards had inherited the estate of Sir Thomas Dunk, an ironmonger and sheriff of London (1709–10), on condition that he and his heirs took the surname Dunk. His daughter, who was only sixteen at the time of her marriage to Halifax, had a dowry that was allegedly worth £110,000. On his marriage Halifax also took the name of Dunk, which seems to have been a condition of the match, and even signed his name 'Dunk Halifax' thereafter. It was also apparently a condition that he had some connection with commerce, which he fulfilled by becoming a freeman of London. His connection with the City seems to have made him popular with the merchants of London.

Although he was a whig, Halifax was opposed to Walpole and was one of those peers who snubbed the former prime minister when he took his place in the upper house as earl of Orford. He was rewarded for his opposition to the court in 1742 with the post of lord of the bedchamber in the prince of Wales's household, a place which he held until 1744, when he went over to the Pelhams and became master of the buckhounds. After two years in that post he was made chief justice in eyre south of Trent, an office he held until 1748. When the Jacobite rising broke out in 1745 Halifax was one of the noblemen who volunteered to raise a regiment, and was made a colonel on 4 October. 'These new Job Colonels, as they are called' were much criticized for having 'taken advantage of the distress of the Government to fill their own pockets' (Lord Fitzwilliam to Lord Malton, 31 Oct 1745, Wentworth Woodhouse MSS, 1.340). Yet, when Richard Cumberland's father raised two companies of men to enlist in Halifax's regiment, the poet recalled how the earl, 'then high in character and graceful in person, received this tribute of my father's loyalty' (Cumberland, 56). Although Halifax never heard a shot fired in anger, he rose to become a lieutenant-general by 1759.

Meanwhile Halifax had become one of the leading figures in the ministry. On 7 October 1748 he became president of the Board of Trade, and, apart from an interval between June 1756 and October 1757, remained in that office until 21 March 1761. Until his appointment the Board of Trade and Plantations had steadily lost its influence over colonial policy to other agencies of government, notably the secretaries of state for the south. Thus, for example, nominations of colonial governors in North America and the West Indies, which had originally been part of the board's remit when it was established in 1696, had been assumed by the secretary's office since the 1720s. Halifax was determined to retrieve for the board the direction of colonial affairs, especially in America, which it had lost. To achieve this he wished to become a member of the cabinet as president, but though the duke of Newcastle attempted to persuade the king to admit him the request was refused, apparently as a result of the duke of Bedford's advising against it. Bedford, who had previously been Halifax's patron, objected to his rapprochement with the Pelhams and warned George II that it would be detrimental to the royal prerogative to allow the authority of the secretary over the colonies to be ceded to the president of the Board of Trade. Nevertheless Halifax did succeed in appropriating some of the powers assumed by the secretaries. Thus in March 1752 an order in council placed the nominations of colonial governors in the hands of the board.

Halifax injected a new dynamism into the Board of Trade's activities. Cumberland, whom he appointed to be his private confidential secretary, noted that he wrote all his own dispatches. Halifax attempted to reclaim powers which had slipped to the colonial assemblies in the era of 'salutary neglect'. Not for nothing was he referred to as 'the Father of the Colonies'. He even tried to obtain a separate secretariat for the colonies, which would have given him a seat in the cabinet, an issue on which he resigned from the presidency of the Board of Trade in 1756 when the attempt failed. In 1757 he at last obtained entry to cabinet meetings, but the outbreak of the Seven Years' War meant that he was unable to implement schemes to assert ministerial authority over the American colonies. The only lasting impact he had on them was that his name was perpetuated in the town of Halifax, Nova Scotia. When such schemes as he had suggested were implemented after the war he was no longer president, and others, notably George Grenville, were held responsible for them and their catastrophic consequence. But they owed their inspiration to his example, as Charles Townshend, who served under him at the board, acknowledged.

Halifax was appointed lord lieutenant of Ireland in 1761 and arrived in Dublin in October. Despite there being serious unrest in Ireland that year, with the rising of the 'Whiteboys' in Munster, Halifax proved to be 'vastly liked by the inhabitants' (Walpole, 10.335). His popularity was enhanced by his declining to accept an increase in his allowance from £12,000 to £16,000 voted by the Dublin parliament in February 1762, though he accepted it for his successor. This was a particularly altruistic sacrifice, as during his year in Ireland he spent about £20,000. It led to his being praised by John Langhorne in 'The Viceroy' (1762):

> Oh for the muse of Milton, to record
> The honours of that day, when fully conven'd
> Hibernia's senate with one voice proclaim'd
> A nation's high applause; when long opprest
> With wealth-consuming war, their eager love
> Advanc'd the princely dignity's support,
> While Halifax presided! O, belov'd
> By every muse, grace of the polished court,
> The peasant's guardian, then what pleasure felt
> Thy liberal bosom! Not the low delight
> Of fortune's added gifts, greatly declin'd;
> No; 'twas the supreme bliss that fills the breast
> Of conscious virtue, happy to behold
> Her cares successful in a nation's joy.

The poem failed to mention that Halifax had tried to get the nation 'opprest with wealth-consuming war' to increase its military establishment from 12,000 to 18,000 men, but had abandoned this plan when he sensed that the Dublin parliament would resist the measure. His main agent in the Irish legislature was William Gerald Hamilton, who had served on the Board of Trade under him and whom he took to Ireland as his chief secretary. He was known as 'single speech Hamilton' for a contribution in the British House of Commons, but as member of the Irish parliament he proposed a bill to allow Catholics to raise six regiments to serve under the king of Portugal. Although it had Halifax's backing, the measure was also defeated. Halifax and Hamilton did, however, contrive to get a generous supply bill passed.

When in June 1762 Halifax became first lord of the Admiralty he was permitted to combine it with the lord lieutenancy for a year, until April 1763. By September 1762, however, he had been appointed as secretary of state for the north, and in September 1763 he moved to the southern secretaryship. It was as secretary of state for the north that he became embroiled with John Wilkes. The forty-fifth number of Wilkes's paper the *North Briton* contained a scarcely veiled attack on the king for the speech he had made to parliament commending the peace of Paris of 1763. The decision was made to prosecute him for seditious libel, and Halifax issued a warrant for the arrest of the author, printer, and publishers of the paper, without naming Wilkes. Such general warrants had been routinely used by previous secretaries, though they rested on a dubious legal basis. Ultimately they derived from the Licensing Act passed under Charles II to control the press, but this had lapsed in 1695. Wilkes therefore challenged their validity and brought an action against Wood, an under-secretary in Halifax's office, for damages in the court of common pleas. He won and was awarded £1000. Halifax himself escaped a similar action brought by Wilkes by legal chicanery—'all his mazes of essoigns, privileges, and fines, ordinary and extraordinary' (Grenville and Grenville, 2.427)—when Wilkes was declared an outlaw and therefore could not sue him. But after the outlawry was reversed in 1768 Wilkes successfully sued the former secretary, and in 1769 he was awarded £4000 damages.

By then Halifax was out of office, having been dismissed on the fall of Grenville's ministry in 1765. He had been approached to join the Rockingham administration but had refused on principle. He objected to the repeal of the Stamp Act, claiming that 'it is not the Stamp Act that is opposed but the Authority of this Legislature' (Simmons and Thomas, 2.336). In January 1770 he accepted the office of lord privy seal from his nephew Lord North, and in 1771 he became secretary of state again. It seems clear, though, that his mental powers were much decayed, and that 'the spring of his mind was gone' (Cumberland, 185). 'Had I been in his situation and of his age', observed George III, 'I should have preferred his motto, *otium cum dignitate*' (*Correspondence of George III*, 2.207). His private situation was by then quite precarious. His wife, with whom he 'lived in great domestic harmony' (Cumberland, 100), had died in 1753. He had contrived to spend her fortune on buildings, elections, and a favourite mistress. He was 'supposed to have injured his fortune by building' (Walpole, 10.335), and spent a great deal on refurbishing his house at Horton in Northamptonshire. He reputedly laid out £150,000 on an election in Northampton in 1768. Although the sum was certainly wildly exaggerated, the contest clearly had cost a staggering sum and led Halifax to give up his electoral interest in the borough. 'My cousin has turned all his pleasure-ground into tillage', wrote George Montagu to Horace Walpole on 27 August 1769, 'which cost so much at Horton: but his election cost more, and his singing woman more still, that lays in his cold bosom and freezes it against all the family' (ibid., 10.287). The woman in question was Anna Maria *Falkner (*d.* 1796/7), the niece of the Dublin publisher George Falkner. She had married William Donaldson, who had abandoned her. She then, in the late 1750s, became Halifax's mistress, and he built a house for her at Hampton Court Green. This was perhaps the house which George Montagu referred to when he marvelled at Halifax's resigning from the Board of Trade and giving up his salary, which was in fact £2300: 'Three thousand a year when one is building a fine house goes a long way towards paying the workmen's bills' (ibid., 9.213). About 1760 Halifax proposed marriage to Mary Ann Drury, heir to £50,000, which would have recouped his financial losses. But 'to most people's surprise, but much to his honour, when matters were far advanced, he wrote to the lady to let her know of an amour he was then engaged in with another person, which attachment he could not break off' (ibid., 10.335). The attachment was to Anna Maria, and as she was a singer in Drury Lane theatre, in the district frequented by prostitutes and known as the hundreds of Drury, the *bon mot* was that 'the hundreds of Drury have got the better of the thousands of Drury' (ibid., 35.302). The couple had a daughter, Anna Maria Montagu. Halifax had no legitimate sons, and his only legitimate surviving daughter, Elizabeth, married John Montagu, fifth earl of Sandwich.

Halifax died at Horton, Northamptonshire, on 8 June 1771, of jaundice, and was buried at Horton. Walpole was convinced that he had died of drink. He himself was ambivalent towards Halifax, expressing both praise and condemnation over the years. Perhaps his most fitting comment was made to George Montagu in 1757, when he wrote:

> I always had a good opinion of your cousin, and I am not apt to throw about my esteem lightly. He has ever behaved with sense, and dignity, and this country has more obligations to him than to most men living. (Walpole, 9.214)

Richard Cumberland, who 'saw him in his last illness, when his constitution was an absolute wreck' (Cumberland, 185), was 'persuaded he was formed to be a good man, he might also have been a great one' (ibid., 287).

W. A. SPECK

Sources Walpole, *Corr.* · R. Cumberland, *Memoirs of Richard Cumberland written by himself* (1806) · *The Grenville papers: being the correspondence of Richard Grenville … and … George Grenville*, ed. W. J. Smith, 4 vols. (1852–3) · R. C. Simmons and P. D. G. Thomas, eds., *Proceedings and debates of the British parliaments respecting North America, 1754–1783*, 6 vols. (1982–7) · T. C. Barrow, *Trade and empire: the British customs service in colonial America, 1660–1775* (1967) · F. G. James, *Ireland in the empire, 1688–1770* (1973) · J. Langhorne, *Poetical works*, 2 vols. (1804) · *DNB* · Sheffield City Libraries, Wentworth Woodhouse MSS · *The correspondence of King George the Third from 1760 to December 1783*, ed. J. Fortescue, 6 vols. (1927–8) · GEC, *Peerage*
Archives BL, corresp. with George Grenville · BL, letters to first Lord Hardwicke, Add. MSS 35591–35909 · BL, corresp. with Lord Holdernesse, e.g. MSS 3441, 3490 · BL, corresp. with duke of Newcastle, Add. MSS 32692–33072 · Bodl. Oxf., corresp. with first earl of Guilford · NMM, corresp. with Lord Sandwich · priv. coll., corresp. with Lord Bute · priv. coll., letters to James Oswald · U. Mich., Clements L., corresp. with Thomas Gage
Likenesses attrib. D. Gardner, group portrait, gouache, *c.*1765–1767 (after H. D. Hamilton, *Lord Halifax and his secretaries*), NPG · S. Wheatly, mezzotint, BM; repro. in Dunk, *Answer to the Dublin House of Commons* (1762)
Wealth at death apparently bankrupt; mansion at Stansted had to be sold: *Memoirs of Richard Cumberland*, 287

Dunkarton, Robert (*c.*1744–1811x17), engraver and portrait painter, was born in London about 1744. He was a pupil of the mezzotint engraver William Pether and was awarded a premium by the Society for the Encouragement of Arts in 1762. Initially he produced portraits in crayons, and he exhibited nine times at the Royal Academy from 1774 to 1779. In 1775 he published a print after one of his own portraits, but it was as a mezzotint engraver after the work of others that he made his name, working for a wide range of publishers and in a number of areas, including portraits, old master paintings, landscapes, and botanical subjects.

Perhaps the most impressive facet of Dunkarton's work consists of the mezzotint portraits he produced between 1770 and 1811, many on a large scale. J. C. Smith lists forty-five major prints after the most important portrait painters of the day, including John Opie, Nathaniel Dance, William Beechey, and Benjamin West. Some of the most striking were produced after John Singleton Copley's works, among them *Henry Addington* (1799) and *George John Spencer* (1801), which were published by Copley himself. Dunkarton worked for numerous publishers, including John and Josiah Boydell and Robert Sayer, but throughout his life he also published on his own behalf—for example, mezzotints after William Beechey and Arthur William Devis. As well as single sheets, Dunkarton produced numerous smaller works for the book trade, such as the fifty-two subjects for Samuel Woodburn's *Portraits of Illustrious Characters* (1810–15).

In addition Dunkarton produced figure subjects and works after the old masters. Among the former are genre scenes after William Redmore Bigg, fancy pictures after Sir Joshua Reynolds, and histories after Copley and William Hogarth. Prints after the old masters include portraits after Van Dyck and, most impressively, a series of large mezzotints after Guercino's *Life of Joseph*, produced for the Boydells between 1782 and 1784. Among the most attractive of Dunkarton's works were the botanical subjects he produced, particularly those issued in colours. Towards the end of his life he was employed by J. M. W. Turner to provide the mezzotint ground for five of the plates for his *Liber Studiorum*, and these were published in 1811 and 1812. Examples of his work are in the British Museum and the Victoria and Albert Museum, London. Every aspect of Dunkarton's private life remains shadowy, and even the year of his death, variously given as 1811 and 1817, remains conjectural.

GREG SMITH

Sources J. C. Smith, *British mezzotinto portraits*, 1 (1878), 221–37 · Bryan, *Painters* (1903–5) · W. G. Rawlinson, *Turner's Liber Studiorum: a description and a catalogue*, 2nd edn (1906) · Graves, *RA exhibitors* · I. Mackenzie, *British prints: dictionary and price guide* (1987), 97

Dunkellin. For this title name *see* Burgh, Ulick Canning de, Lord Dunkellin (1827–1867) [*see under* Burgh, Ulick John de, first marquess of Clanricarde (1802–1874)].

Dunkerley, Elsie Jeanette [*pseud.* Elsie Oxenham] (1880–1960), author, was born on 25 November 1880 at Southport, Lancashire, the first of the six children of William Arthur Dunkerley (1852–1941), a journalist and novelist, and his wife, Marjorie *née* Anderson (*d.* 1925). Elsie's father wrote under the name John Oxenham: his novels, mainly with religious themes, proved so popular that he became largely identified with his pseudonym, and Elsie used Oxenham as her own *nom de plume*. Her family was religiously inclined and closely knit. She and her three sisters and two brothers shared their father's love of books and enthusiastically read the children's magazines which he brought home, as well as the large family library of biographies, classics, and travel books. A studious child, both at home and in the private day-schools which she attended, Elsie liked to read several books a week, which no doubt stimulated her desire to write but possibly exacerbated the poor eyesight from which she suffered throughout her life.

As a young woman Elsie worked as secretary to John Oxenham. He was a devoted father who had taken his children from their suburban home in Ealing, to places and events of interest in London and also to the countryside, particularly to Buckinghamshire, for which Elsie was to develop a strong and lasting affection. She eventually set her most celebrated series, the Abbey books, in that county, frequently describing the beauties of its extensive beech woods and picturesque villages. The Abbey itself was a transplanted fictional version of the ruins of the fifteenth-century Cistercian Cleeve Abbey, which had entranced Elsie on a holiday visit to Somerset.

Another major and long-standing influence on Elsie's life and work, discovered during her years at Ealing, was English folk-dancing, which she not only performed but taught. The American Camp Fire movement also inspired her with its both practical and romantic emphasis on country traditions, woodcraft, and social responsibility. She became a Camp Fire guardian in Ealing and later in Worthing, Sussex, to which the Dunkerley family moved in 1922.

Few of Elsie's books for girls came strictly into the school-story category. Her first novels, published from 1907, had historical themes. Some school tales followed but her work really became popular when *Girls of the Hamlet Club* appeared in 1914. This heralded the start of the 40-book Abbey series, written over almost a fifty-year period, and still avidly sought by many adult collectors today. As well as harnessing the appeal of the ancient abbey, Camp Fire, and country dance, these books featured the May queen rituals which involved colourful symbolism and dressing-up. Like all of Elsie's books, their portrayal of characters and relationships had a seriousness which was unusual in the girls' story genre.

Elsie continued to produce books (almost ninety in all) throughout her life. She remained in the Worthing area, always close to her three sisters, until she died there, unmarried, on 9 January 1960 in Marlposts Nursing Home, 1 Parkfield Road, where, suffering from severe spinal problems, she had spent her last two years.

MARY CADOGAN

Sources M. Godfrey, *Elsie Jeanette Oxenham and her books* (privately printed, London, 1970–79) · M. Cadogan and P. Craig, *You're a brick, Angela!* (1976) · M. Cadogan, 'E. J. Oxenham', *Twentieth century children's writers*, ed. D. L. Kirkpatrick (1978) · R. Auchmuty, *A world of girls* (1992) · CGPLA Eng. & Wales (1960) · private information (2004) **Wealth at death** £5223 18s. 6d.: administration with will, 28 April 1960, CGPLA Eng. & Wales

Dunkin, Alfred John (1812–1879), printer and antiquary, the only son of John *Dunkin (1782–1846) and his wife, Ann (d. 1865), daughter of William Chapman, a civil engineer, was born at Islington, London, on 9 August 1812. He was given a good education, which included a period at the military college at Vendôme, France. In 1831 he entered his father's printing and stationery business at Bromley, Kent, and in 1837 moved with him to Dartford, where he continued as a printer and wholesale stationer until his death; later in life he opened a London branch at 140 Queen Victoria Street.

Dunkin was introduced to archaeological and antiquarian matters by his father, whose modest short history of Bromley duly acknowledged its sources, something the son was less eager to do. John Dunkin's *History of Dartford* (1844), while it may be based on collections made by the father, shows signs of having been put together by the son, consisting as it does of random items of information without an overall plan.

Alfred Dunkin wrote a number of articles on antiquarian subjects for the *Dover Chronicle*, some of which were reprinted in small booklets, in very short runs. In 1853 he started his own antiquarian journal, which he called *The Archaeological Mine*, and which came out at irregular intervals over some ten years. This included contributions from other writers, but most of the contents were put together by Dunkin in his usual ragbag style, and printed with his habitual love of frequent headings, often in black-letter type. *The Archaeological Mine* was intended to contain a new history of Kent 'on the plan of Hasted', but while this was frequently advertised, only very small portions of it ever appeared here. Three volumes of Dunkin's *History of Kent*, two bound together, were eventually published in a somewhat careless manner, the second without a title-page, between 1854 and 1856. The work was never completed and is little more than a repository of antiquarian jottings: it is repetitive and contains errors of fact.

Dunkin had received an education which gave him considerable fluency in languages. This enabled him to publish some transcriptions of old Latin documents—although without translations—and to attend archaeological congresses abroad, which he clearly took much pleasure in doing. He belonged to numerous archaeological societies, and was among the first members of the British Archaeological Association, to which, in its early days, he gave some assistance as a printer. Despite his enthusiasm for all things antiquarian, Dunkin's work is of little value, apart from the occasional description of the contemporary scene.

Dunkin died unmarried in London at the house of an old nurse at 110 Stamford Street, Blackfriars Road, on 30 January 1879, after being seized with bronchitis while travelling in Berkshire in severe winter conditions. He was buried in Dartford cemetery on 4 February.

SHIRLEY BURGOYNE BLACK

Sources *Dartford and West Kent Advertiser* (1 Feb 1879) · *Dartford and West Kent Advertiser* (8 Feb 1879) · *Dartford Chronicle* (8 Feb 1879) · centre catalogue, CKS · CGPLA Eng. & Wales (1879)

Archives CKS, corresp., newspaper cuttings, notes, etc. relating to fifth congress of British Archaeological Society · County Museum, Aylesbury, Buckinghamshire Archaeological Society, notes · Reading Local Studies Library · Worcs. RO, collections, notes, extracts, typescripts, etc. relating to history of Worcestershire | Dorchester Reference Library, notes, press cuttings, pictures, and other papers for a history of Dorset · Essex RO, collections mainly relating to ecclesiastical history of Essex · Suffolk RO, Ipswich, notes, collections, and papers for a history of Suffolk

Likenesses J. Penstone, mixed engraving (after photograph by Bright, c.1840), NPG

Wealth at death under £3000: administration with will, 26 Feb 1879, CGPLA Eng. & Wales

Dunkin, Edwin (1821–1898), astronomer, was born at 10 Paul's Terrace, Truro, Cornwall, on 19 August 1821, the son of William Dunkin (d. 1838), a computer, or mathematical calculator, on the *Nautical Almanac*, and his wife, Mary Elizabeth Wise, the daughter of a Redruth surgeon. He was always deeply proud of his old Cornish ancestry, and, after receiving an elementary education in Truro, it was with great regret that he accompanied his parents on their reluctant move to London in 1832, following the reorganization of the *Nautical Almanac* office and the abolition of provincial computers, which made it necessary for his father to work in the almanac's London office. In London he attended Wellington House Academy, Hampstead. In July 1837 Dunkin and his younger brother were sent to M. Liborel's school at Guînes, near Calais, where he no doubt acquired the spoken French which was to be so useful in his later life as an astronomer. The death of his father in the summer of 1838 caused him to be recalled to London to find employment. Although his father had warned him of lack of prospects for a mathematical computer, he abandoned the idea of following his maternal relatives into a medical career, and entered the Royal Greenwich Observatory. At Greenwich he was taken on by George Airy, the astronomer royal, to complete the reduction of outstanding Greenwich observations. His autobiography records the arduous twelve-hour days through which the young computers were expected to stay at their desks, where they 'might not even munch a biscuit' (*Monthly Notices of the Royal Astronomical Society*, 59, 1898–9, 222), and where his abilities quickly impressed Airy. In 1840 he was promoted into the observatory's newly founded magnetic and meteorological department, and in 1845 he became a permanent member of the observatory staff. On 4 April 1848 he married Maria Hadlow of Peckham, the daughter of Joseph Hadlow, a stockbroker. One child of the marriage, Edwin Hadlow Wise Dunkin, survived his parents.

Dunkin was pre-eminently a practical astronomer and mathematical calculator, and his dependability and meticulous accuracy led to his being placed in charge of a number of painstaking physical investigations at Greenwich. These included the adjustment and error quantification of new Greenwich instruments, such as the lunar altazimuth (1847) and the transit circle (1850), the conveyance of chronometers, and the expedition to Norway to observe the total eclipse in 1851. He was also employed by

Airy to act as his reliable man on the spot in a number of extra-Greenwich enterprises: among them were the gravitational pendulum experiments at Harton colliery, South Shields (1854), and the telegraphic longitude determinations of the Brussels (1853) and Paris (1854) observatories, where his ability to communicate on easy terms with Quetelet, Faye, and other continental astronomers stood him in good stead. Upon Airy's retirement in 1881 Dunkin was promoted to chief assistant, or deputy astronomer royal, which post he held until his own retirement in 1884.

Perhaps by way of relief from his fastidious work at the Greenwich observatory, Dunkin was a highly sociable figure. He was elected to the Royal Astronomical Society (RAS) in 1845, served on its council, and in 1884 was elected president. He was delighted, in 1868, to be elected to the RAS Dining Club, and in 1880 became the club president. He was elected FRS in 1876, and later served on its council. Although he resided in London for his entire adult life, he always maintained his Cornish associations, naming his Blackheath villa Kenwyn after the village near Truro, and in 1890 and 1891 he served as president of the Royal Institution of Cornwall, where he discussed astronomical matters in his two presidential addresses. Dunkin was a prolific writer and popular communicator of astronomy; in addition to his professional scientific papers he produced numerous articles for the *Leisure Hour* and other periodicals. Perhaps his most famous work was *The Midnight Sky* (1869), with its detailed charts of the sky visible from London, all of which had been computed by Dunkin himself. Dunkin died on 26 November 1898, at Brook Hospital, Kidbrook, after a short illness. For forty-six years he did much of the work that kept the Greenwich observatory running on a practical daily and nightly basis.

ALLAN CHAPMAN

Sources *Monthly Notices of the Royal Astronomical Society*, 59 (1898–9), 221–5 · W. E., *PRS*, 75 (1905), 53–6 · *Nature*, 59 (1898–9), 131 · *Journal of the British Astronomical Association*, 8 (1897–8), 79–80 · private information (2004) · E. Dunkin, 'Autobiography', RAS, Add. MS 55 · d. cert.

Archives NMM, Greenwich, Royal Observatory · RAS, autobiographical notes; letters to Royal Astronomical Society · RS

Dunkin, John (1782–1846), topographer, the son of John Dunkin (d. 1823) of Bicester, Oxfordshire, and his wife, Elizabeth, widow of John Telford and daughter of Thomas and Johanna Timms, was born at Bicester on 16 May 1782. While attending the local free school under James Jones, he suffered a severe accident and for many years it was feared he would remain disabled for life. While recovering he tried his hand at verse but contrived also to pick up some knowledge of history and archaeology. At the age of twenty he was apprenticed to a carpenter or house decorator at Stony Stratford, whom he left to take up employment in Oxford. At twenty-three he was in London, working for the clerk of works at Kensington Palace.

On 11 December 1809, at St Mary's, Islington, Dunkin married Ann, daughter of William Chapman, a civil engineer from Lincolnshire. They had a son, Alfred John *Dunkin, and a daughter, Ellen Elizabeth (d. 1890); neither child married. Ann Dunkin died at Dartford on 12 March 1865, aged seventy-seven.

Dunkin took up printing, served an apprenticeship in London, and set up at the age of thirty as a bookseller, stationer, and printer in Bromley, Kent. Here he published his first topographical work, in part a compilation from *Outlines of the History and Antiquities of Bromley in Kent* (1815) by Philipot, Hasted, and Lysons, with an appendix by A. J. Kempe on the antiquities of Holwood Hill. It was followed by *The history and antiquities of Bicester ... to which is added an inquiry into the history of Alchester, a city of the Dobuni*, in two parts (1816). Published at 17s. in an edition of 250 copies, the Bicester history attracted the attention of Sir Gregory Turner, a local proprietor. In 1819 Turner encouraged Dunkin to work up the extensive collections Dunkin had made for *The History and Antiquities of the Hundreds of Bullingdon and Ploughley*, which was eventually published in two quarto volumes (1823). The work (limited to 100 copies, of which 70 were for sale at 5 guineas) is based on thorough topographical investigation, and draws on Dunkin's superintendence of excavations at Ambrosden and Bicester.

In 1837 Dunkin moved to Dartford, where, with his son, he set up a bookshop at 13 High Street, and started to build a printing establishment. Shortly afterwards he opened a branch business at Gravesend. In 1844 he published his *History and Antiquities of Dartford*. From then on he occupied himself in arranging the materials he had accumulated for the histories of Oxfordshire and Kent. Dunkin, who was an original member of the British Archaeological Association, died on 22 December 1846, and by his own desire was buried on the eastern side of the lich-gate of St Edmund's cemetery, Dartford, as near as possible to the ancient burial-ground of Noviomagus which he had described in his last book. A brass was erected to his memory in that part of Dartford parish church which is now occupied by the organ. Dunkin's collections were presented to the Guildhall Library by his daughter in 1886; since 1954 those relating to Oxfordshire have been in the Bodleian Library, Oxford.

GORDON GOODWIN, rev. ALAN BELL

Sources E. R. Massey, 'Some reminiscences of John Dunkin', *Oxford Archaeological Society Report* (1901), 20–24 [draws on MS autobiographical notebook, now untraced] · *GM*, 2nd ser., 27 (1847), 320–22 · S. K. Keyes, *Dartford: some historical notes* (1933), 10, 191, 334–44 [incl. biography and portrait] · d. cert. · *Dartford Chronicle* (8 Feb 1879) [report of memorial brass]
Archives Bodl. Oxf., collections for Oxfordshire · Bodl. Oxf., corresp. · Bodl. Oxf., draft history for the hundreds of Bullingdon and Ploughley · Bodl. Oxf., draft of the history of the Roman station at Alchester for Dunkin's published work · Bromley Central Library, outlines of the history and antiquities of Bromley · CKS, bills · GL · S. Antiquaries, Lond., corresp. relating to the first report of the British Archaeological Association
Likenesses I. J. Penstone (after photograph by Beard), repro. in J. Dunkin, *The history and antiquities of Dartford* (1844), frontispiece · portrait, repro. in *GM*, 2nd ser., 27 (1847)

Dunkin, William (1706/7–1765), poet, was born in Ireland, the son of Patrick Dunkin. Nothing is recorded of his early life until he was left to the charge of Trinity College, Dublin (aged eighteen), by an aunt who bequeathed her property to the college with the condition that it should provide for his education and advancement in life. He graduated BA in 1725, MA in 1732, and DD in 1744. However, his reputation for fluent scholarship was vitiated by ebullient high spirits, a recollection of which is found in *Techrethyrambeia* (1728), a Latin mock epic which describes riotous and belated Trinity undergraduates attempting to talk their way past Paddy Murphy, an egregiously opinionated college porter. This poem was republished in Patrick Delany's periodical *The Tribune* (1729) and translated into English by Joseph Cowper (1730). Dunkin's verse satire on the London literary scene, *The Poet's Prayer*, appeared in 1734. Swift admired his verse; after an introduction was effected by his cousin, Martha Whiteway, he became Dunkin's patron and was able sometimes to save his protégé from the worst consequences of his imprudence (for example, his assistance in a notorious elopement).

Dunkin was ordained by the archbishop of Cashel in 1735, but an unfortunate marriage marred his clerical career, and Swift's strenuous attempt in 1739 to procure the living of Coleraine for him was unsuccessful. At that time Dunkin was teaching at St Michael-le-Pole, Dublin. In August 1746, through the good offices of Lord Chesterfield, he became master of Portora Royal School, Enniskillen, a post he held until his death on 24 November 1765. Two volumes of his *Select Poetical Works* appeared in 1769–70; his *Poetical Works* were published in two volumes (1774).

Dunkin was regarded by Jonathan Swift as 'a Man of Genius, the best Poet we have [in Ireland]' (Swift, letter to John Barber, 17 Jan 1738), and was remembered by Deane Swift (1707–1783), with whom he 'spent many a jovial evening', as 'a man of genuine, true wit, and a delightful companion' (Nichols, *Illustrations*, 5.384). He wrote pleasing complimentary odes, epistles, and eclogues, but his vigorous, witty, and lively comic poems, such as 'The Parson's Revels' have more lasting appeal. Dunkin's best verse manifests an outrageous sense of fun as well as sharp wit; it shows an acute ear for patois and pungent dialogue, together with fine technical control. The fact that he made alternative versions of some of his longer poems in Greek and in Latin bears witness to the compendious learning which he bore so lightly. At his best Dunkin 'approaches more nearly to Swift's style than that of any contemporary' (*Poems of Swift*, ed. H. Williams, 1937, 1.318). His picture of Swift in old age, in a verse epistle to Robert Nugent, indeed bears comparison with Swift's own *Verses on the Death of Dr. Swift*. His *Vindication of the Libel on Dr. Delany* was formerly thought to be by Swift himself; his English translation of Swift's 'Carberiae rupes' is regularly printed (attributed correctly to Dunkin) in Swift's *Works*.

EDWIN CANNAN, rev. TONY BAREHAM

Sources J. C. Day, 'William Dunkin, "Best poet in the kingdom"?', MA diss., National University of Ireland, 1978 · *The correspondence of Jonathan Swift*, ed. H. Williams, 4–5 (1965) · *The works of Jonathan Swift*, ed. W. Scott, 19 vols. (1814) · MS records, Portora Royal School, Enniskillen · Burtchaell & Sadleir, *Alum. Dubl.*, 2nd edn ·

Nichols, *Illustrations*, 5.384 · Nichols, *Lit. anecdotes*, vol. 2 · *Letters written by the late Jonathan Swift*, ed. D. Swift (1768) · *GM*, 1st ser., 35 (1765), 590 · D. F. Foxon, ed., *English verse, 1701–1750: a catalogue of separately printed poems with notes on contemporary collected editions*, 2 vols. (1975)

Dunleath. For this title name *see* Mulholland, John, first Baron Dunleath (1819–1895).

Dunlop, Alexander (1684–1747), university teacher, was born in the North American colony of Carolina, the son of William *Dunlop (1653/4–1700) and his wife, Sarah Carstairs, a cousin who was the sister of William *Carstares (1649–1715), a leading politician in Scotland under William III. His younger brother was William *Dunlop (1692–1720). Alexander's family formed part of the exiled covenanting diaspora in the colonies, and he went to Glasgow when William III appointed his father principal of Glasgow University in 1690.

Elected professor of Greek in 1704, through his uncle's influence, Dunlop helped to manage university affairs on behalf of the progressive party in the faculty. He recovered money from the Equivalent to compensate for his father's considerable university investment losses in the Darien adventure. He and other professors were suspended when they attempted to extend their rights in the long-running disputes over college and university professorial rights and privileges.

Having favoured university reforms early in his career, Dunlop used his rights to protect his income in later years. As his sight failed he secured his professorial income and house, and by 1746 had sold his chair to his successor, James Moor. He was regarded as a good teacher and scholar, and impressed the Enlightenment philosopher Francis Hutcheson while he was Dunlop's pupil. His method of teaching Greek was highly admired and his Greek grammar (2nd edn, 1731) was in general use in Scottish schools for many years. He died in Glasgow on 27 April 1747.   J. M. RIGG, rev. CAMPBELL F. LLOYD

Sources *Glasgow Journal* (27 April 1747) · C. Innes, ed., *Munimenta alme Universitatis Glasguensis / Records of the University of Glasgow from its foundation till 1727*, 4 vols., Maitland Club, 72 (1854) · J. Coutts, *A history of the University of Glasgow* (1909) · J. D. Mackie, *The University of Glasgow, 1451–1951: a short history* (1954) · Anderson, *Scot. nat.*
Archives NL Scot., corresp. and papers

Dunlop, Alexander Colquhoun-Stirling-Murray- (1798–1870), lawyer and politician, was born in Keppoch, Dunbartonshire, on 27 December 1798, the son of Alexander Dunlop (*b.* 1766), of Keppoch, and his second wife, Margaret Colquhoun, of Kenmure, Lanarkshire, eldest daughter of William Colquhoun. Dunlop's half-brother was William *Dunlop (1792–1848), military physician. Dunlop's father was one of the founders and for a time the manager of the Renfrewshire Bank, the headquarters of which were in Greenock, the town with which Dunlop was to be particularly associated in his later political career.

Dunlop was educated at Greenock grammar school and at the University of Edinburgh, where he was a member and president of the Speculative Society. He was called to the bar in 1820. In these early years of his career, together with another advocate, Patrick Shaw, he took up the reporting of the decisions of the court of session in what became known as 'Shaw's and Dunlop's reports'. Dunlop was also initially interested in the Scottish poor law and in the late 1820s and early 1830s several editions of his work on this subject appeared, to the extent that these became regarded as the standard work. This specialization was reflected in his legal practice and led him on to an interest in church questions. Partly because of a weak constitution and partly as a result of the enmities his church work was to create among the legal establishment at Parliament House, Dunlop was employed mainly as a consulting advocate on these mostly poor-law-related cases.

In church matters Dunlop concerned himself with the controversy relating to the law of patronage. He was a firm supporter of that party, led by Thomas Chalmers and later known as the non-intrusionists, which wished to limit the power of patrons to appoint ministers to Church of Scotland parishes. In 1830 Dunlop was elected to the general assembly of the Church of Scotland as a representative elder for the presbytery of Lochcarron in Ross-shire. He was to carry out this function in both church and, later, Free Church assemblies, until he declined election in 1869. Dunlop thus arrived on the national stage just as the evangelical party was moving to a position of dominance in the church. He became an active member of various church societies, including the Church Law Society and the Anti-Patronage Society, and by 1834 he was editor of the *Presbyterian Review*, the journal of the evangelicals and non-intrusionists.

Dunlop was to play a leading role in most of the controversies in the 'ten years' conflict' which resulted in the Disruption of the Church of Scotland in 1843. He acted as counsel for the non-intrusionists and the presbytery of Auchterarder in what became a test case (heard in 1838 and 1839) on the legality of the Veto Act. By this measure the non-intrusionists had sought to restrict the power of patrons to present nominees to vacant parishes by making it conditional on a measure of popular assent. This was a subject close to Dunlop's heart with his interest in the restoration of the power of eldership and the ordinary parochial lay element, in particular in the Church of Scotland. Dunlop went on to act for the non-intrusionists in other cases brought before the court of session by their opponents in the moderate party of the church, usually in an unpaid capacity. He was also the author in the same cause of *An Answer to the Dean of Faculty's Letter to the Lord Chancellor* (1839), a reply to a pamphlet by John Hope which had attacked the Veto Act and the non-intrusionist leadership in the church. This impressed W. E. Gladstone to the extent that he wrote to Sir James Graham to say that right was apparently not all on the moderate side of the question. Dunlop was also the author of the *Claim of Right*, which was adopted by the 1842 general assembly of the Church of Scotland as an assertion of its spiritual independence. In all these actions Dunlop followed the consistent line that there was no need for a dispute with the civil courts about spiritual independence because such liberties had already been granted to the Church of Scotland. He claimed that the civil power was now trying to take them away illegally. Dunlop was also the principal author of *Protest and Deed of Demission* and appears to have exercised a moderating influence on Thomas Chalmers in the question of the procedure adopted by the non-intrusionists on the day of the Disruption itself in 1843. He was described by Henry Cockburn as the 'purest of enthusiasts' (*Journal of Henry Cockburn*, 1.326) in the sense that his devotion to the non-intrusionist and Free Church cause resulted in sacrifices, both financial—through generous contributions to the sustentation fund—and in terms of professional advancement. Dunlop was certainly not the fanatic the contemporary press sometimes depicted him to be. He has been credited with persuading Chalmers to avoid any public wrangling before the seceders walked out of the Church of Scotland assembly. A similar moderating influence would have been useful in the late 1830s when the tory-leaning Chalmers failed to see the importance of building bridges to the whig government. By 1840, however, Dunlop was active in this matter to the extent that, together with Robert Buchanan, he was lobbying the Melbourne ministry for legislation on the Scottish church question.

After the Disruption Dunlop became legal adviser to the Free Church, a position he held for the rest of his life. He refused to take any salary to avoid any imputation that his former services had been given out of personal interest. On 18 July 1844 he married Eliza Esther (*c.*1818–1902), only child of John Murray, East India merchant, of Ainslie Place, Edinburgh. They had four sons and four daughters, including the women's activist Anna *Lindsay. On the death of his father-in-law in 1849 he altered his name to Murray-Dunlop. Subsequently, in 1866, on succeeding to the estate of his cousin, William Colquhoun-Stirling of Law and Edinbarnet, he took the name of Colquhoun-Stirling-Murray-Dunlop.

The other major strand in Dunlop's life was his parliamentary career. He was active on the whig side in Dunbartonshire in the 1832 election. A disagreement in the whig committee led to Dunlop fighting a duel with James Colquhoun, from which both emerged unhurt. In 1845 and 1847 he contested, unsuccessfully, the representation of Greenock. With his obvious Free-Church sympathies he was unable, because of old pre-Disruption antagonisms, to unite the other dissenting voters in the constituency against Walter Baine, a whig who received support from the established church. In 1852, this time against a protectionist, he was successful, and he went on to represent the constituency until he retired in 1868.

In parliament Dunlop was particularly associated with several measures passed on Scottish reformatories and industrial schools, with proposals in the mid-1850s to restrict irregular 'Gretna Green' marriages, and with legislation passed in 1855 to facilitate the building of working-class housing in Scotland. His public impact was hindered by a weak voice and a hesitating manner, but these belied a truly independent spirit, which at times drove him to oppose the government of which he was otherwise a supporter. His refusal to support Palmerston over the *Arrow* affair in 1857 was thought at the time to have cost him his seat. In 1861 Dunlop tried to effect a committee inquiry into the charge that dispatches written in 1839 by Sir Alexander Burnes, the British envoy at the Afghan court, had, when presented to parliament, been made to express opinions contrary to those which Sir Alexander held. It was claimed that this had been done to help the then government, of which Palmerston was the foreign secretary, to justify its launching the Anglo-Afghan War. Palmerston was saved from defeat by Disraeli who argued that the matter was now too old to reopen.

After his resignation from parliament at the general election of 1868 on the grounds of ill health, Dunlop spent most of his time at Corsock House, on his estate in Kirkcudbrightshire. He died there on 1 September 1870 and was buried in the Free Church graveyard in Corsock. His widow died on 14 July 1902.

Dunlop's significance undoubtedly lies in the work he did for the Free Church. As Cockburn says: 'The generous devotion with which he has given himself to this cause has retarded, and will probably arrest, the success of his very considerable professional talent and learning' (*Journal of Henry Cockburn*, 1.326). Together with his refusal to accept government or professional office in case it compromised his independence, this explains why the man, judged by Cockburn to be superior to both Thomas Chalmers and Robert Candlish 'in everything except impressive public exhibition' (ibid., 2.40), was and should be so particularly associated with the Free Church to the virtual exclusion of his other achievements.

GORDON F. MILLAR

Sources *The Scotsman* (3 Sept 1870) · *Glasgow Herald* (3 Sept 1870) · *The Daily Review* (3 Sept 1870) · *Disruption worthies: a memorial of 1843* (1876), 251–8 · *Journal of Henry Cockburn: being a continuation of the 'Memorials of his time', 1831–1854*, 1 (1874), 321, 323–7, 338–41; 2 (1874), 39–40, 70–71, 206 · Burke, *Gen. GB* (1875) · S. J. Brown, *Thomas Chalmers and the godly commonwealth in Scotland* (1982), 230, 262–6, 328 · G. I. T. Machin, *Politics and the churches in Great Britain, 1832 to 1868* (1977), 123, 133–4 · G. W. T. Omond, *The lord advocates of Scotland, second series, 1834–1880* (1914), 71–5 · F. J. Grant, ed., *The Faculty of Advocates in Scotland, 1532–1943*, Scottish RS, 145 (1944), 64 · S. P. Walker, *The Faculty of Advocates, 1800–1986* (1987), 49 · *Hansard 3* (1861), 162.37–96 · A. C. Cheyne, ed., *The practical and the pious: essays on Thomas Chalmers (1780–1847)* (1985), 104–5, 107 · S. J. Brown and M. Fry, eds., *Scotland in the age of the Disruption* (1993), 18 · *Glasgow Herald* (7 Sept 1870) · WWBMP, vol. 1

Archives NA Scot., letters to second Lord Panmure · NA Scot., letters to Andrew Rutherford · NL Scot., letters to Andrew Rutherford · NRA Scotland, priv. coll., letters to Lord Moncrieff · Orkney Archives, Kirkwall, letters to W. A. Thomson and J. R. Omond · U. St Andr., corresp. with J. Forbes

Wealth at death £5040 2*s.* 3*d.*: inventory, 17 Feb 1871, NA Scot., SC 70/1/151/703 · £1107 5*s.* 7*d.*—Bank of England stock: NA Scot., SC 70/1/151/717

Dunlop, Sir Derrick Melville (1902–1980), physician, was born in Edinburgh on 3 April 1902, the only son and younger child of George Henry Melville Dunlop, MD, FRCP (Edin.), a physician in Edinburgh, and his wife, Margaret Boog Scott. He was educated at the Edinburgh Academy, at Brasenose College, Oxford, where he obtained a third class in natural science (physiology) in 1923, and

Edinburgh University, where he graduated MB, ChB in 1926, MD in 1927, MRCP in 1929, and FRCP (Edin.) in 1932. He was houseman to Edwin Matthew.

Dunlop spent a short time as a morning-suited, top-hatted, general practitioner in London, but he hated it and returned to the University of Edinburgh to pursue an academic career as a lecturer in therapeutics and an assistant in the tuberculosis department. He was a superb teacher and students flocked to hear him even before 1936, when he became professor of therapeutics and consultant physician at the Royal Infirmary. At that time the chemical revolution in therapeutics had scarcely begun, and Dunlop's role was that of a polished interpreter of existing knowledge through his lectures and writing. He collaborated closely with Stanley Davidson and they were editors with John W. McNee of the well-known *Textbook of Medical Treatment* (1939 and many subsequent editions).

Dunlop was a keen territorial soldier and he always claimed that it was only septicaemia, caused by the bite of a ferret on his estate at Bavelaw Castle, that prevented him from being posted to Singapore and being imprisoned by the Japanese. After the war he resumed his teaching and clinical work in Edinburgh and his reputation, already high, grew steadily greater. In 1948 he became FRCP and was elected FRSE. In the same year he became chairman of the British Pharmacopoeia Commission, a post he held until 1958. He was in great demand as a lecturer and in 1951 travelled widely in the Antipodes as Sims British Commonwealth travelling professor. He delivered the Lumleian lecture at the Royal College of Physicians of London in 1954, on the complications of diabetes. He was knighted in 1960 and appointed physician to the queen in Scotland in 1961.

Dunlop was an elegant figure with a remarkable presence, a fine resonant voice, and an impeccable delivery. His lectures and after-dinner speeches were masterpieces of timing and gesture. They appeared to be quite spontaneous but it was said that he rehearsed them before a full-length mirror at his home at Bavelaw Castle. His Harveian oration at the tricentenary dinner at the College of Physicians in 1957 was considered by some the most memorable address in the history of the Edinburgh college.

In 1962 at the age of sixty Dunlop retired from his chair at Edinburgh University, but his greatest contributions were yet to come. The thalidomide disaster had led to great public concern about drug safety and the lack of official procedures for reviewing safety before drugs were marketed. In 1964 in the aftermath of this tragedy Dunlop was asked to set up the committee on safety of drugs. He proceeded with remarkable speed, tact, and sagacity, and quickly assembled a talented academic committee supported by a small but able band of professional officers and civil servants from the Department of Health. His powers of persuasion enabled him to convince the pharmaceutical industry to collaborate fully with the 'Dunlop committee', though at that time it had no statutory powers. Under his chairmanship the committee set up a new voluntary system of reporting adverse drug reactions, by which doctors could record on 'yellow cards'—pre-addressed and stamped fold-over yellow postcards—brief details of suspected drug toxicity. This system and a similar system in Sweden became the most successful systems in the world for reporting adverse drug reactions and led to the detection of a number of important toxic effects of drugs. A notable success was the demonstration of a relationship between the oestrogen dose in the combined oral contraceptive pill and the risk of thrombosis and embolism in blood vessels. In 1969, when the committee on safety of drugs acquired statutory powers and became the committee on safety of medicines under the wing of the Medicines Commission, Dunlop became the first chairman of the commission, a post he held until 1971. He continued his contacts with the pharmaceutical industry and was for a time a director of Winthrop Laboratories.

Dunlop received many honours including the fellowship of the American College of Physicians, honorary fellowships from Brasenose College, Oxford (1968), and the Royal College of Physicians of Edinburgh (1972), and honorary doctorates from Birmingham (1967), Bradford (1970), Edinburgh (1967), and the National University of Ireland (1968). Despite his formidable reputation and imposing exterior he remained a kindly and liberal-minded man who did much to help younger members of the medical profession. He had fire in his belly, but he used his power with discrimination and tact.

On 17 March 1936 Dunlop married Marjorie, eldest daughter of Henry Edward Richardson, writer to the signet, of Broadshaw, Harburn, West Lothian. They had a son and a daughter. Dunlop died in Edinburgh on 19 June 1980. The Winthrop Foundation created an annual travelling fellowship in clinical pharmacology and therapeutics as a memorial to him.   C. T. DOLLERY, *rev.*

Sources *BMJ* (5 July 1980), 66 · private information (1986) · personal knowledge (1986)
Archives U. Edin. L., Lothian Health Services Archive, corresp. and papers

Dunlop [*née* Wallace], **Frances Anna** (1730–1815), letter writer and friend of Robert Burns, was born on 16 April 1730 at Craigie House, Wallacetown, near Ayr, the second child of Sir Thomas Wallace (1702–1770x77), advocate, of Craigie, and Lady Eleanora Agnew (1706–1761) of Lochryan. Her brother, Thomas, a guardsman, died in 1756, aged twenty-seven, and was buried in Westminster Abbey. Her reverence for her father and for her inheritance as a Wallace, descended from Sir Richard Wallace of Riccarton, cousin of Sir William Wallace, made the loss of the 'old ruinous Castle of Craigie', through her eldest son Thomas's mismanagement, one of the more grievous and unforgivable 'vexations' in her life (letters to Burns, March 1788, 12 May 1794, Wallace, 1.81, 2.274). Upon her mother's death, Lochryan became hers, while her father married Antonia Dunlop, known later as the dowager Lady Wallace of Craigie. In 1748 Frances Anna Wallace married John Dunlop of Dunlop (1707–1785), much her senior, by family tradition in a runaway match from Dunskey House. They had thirteen children, three of whom

Frances Anna Dunlop (1730–1815), by A. C.

died in infancy, the remaining ten becoming, next to the 'improvement of [her] morals' and the 'pleasures of [her] mind', her dominant interest (letters to Burns, 6 April and 30 April 1791, Wallace, 2.142–9).

Mrs Dunlop's disaffection with Thomas, exacerbated by her husband's death a year before, resulted in a 'violent fever' (letter to Burns, 3 [or 23] May 1791) which put her mind in a frame to welcome Robert Burns's Kilmarnock *Poems*, in 1786. Her reading led her to initiate a correspondence with Burns; her 'very life', she attested, thereafter acquired that 'bouquet' of friendship which was to give comfort and meaning to her final years (letters, 25 June 1793, 12 June 1794, Wallace, 2.247, 276). Burns was ever reminded of the importance to her of their mutual discovery—she of the only true 'patriot Bard' (letter, 19 Oct 1789, Wallace, 2.8), he of a patroness to whom he could apply for a 'good word' for himself or an acquaintance.

Burns visited Mrs Dunlop at least five times between 1787 and 1792. His perceived sarcasms or neglect of her she could never understand, but typically forgave. His letters became almost her 'sole personal pleasure' (letter, 4 June 1788, Wallace, 2.97). Already in 1786 she found herself objecting to his 'unhappy' phrasing and later to any notion which 'outrages decency' (letter, 30 Dec 1786); of more serious consequence, however, were their political differences. Mrs Dunlop, two of whose daughters had married French royalist refugees, castigated Burns for his sympathy towards revolutionary elements in France, having made known her sentiments on the French nobility as

early as 1791. Burns nevertheless valued his correspondence with Mrs Dunlop, even if he did not take her literary advice, and was dismayed when she, tired of reading of his support for radical causes, ended their correspondence in the summer of 1795. However, she relented after receiving a letter from Burns written a few days before his death and sent him an amicable response.

Mrs Dunlop read Voltaire, Necker, and Paine, as well as Sir John Moore's *Zeluco* and Samuel Bourn on original sin. Her mind was restless to resolve matters of experimental philosophy, even if Burns might find them 'tiresome and ridiculous' (her letter to him, 25 Jan 1792, Wallace, 2.185). Above all, in its 'airy fancy', it loved Hoole's Tasso and 'that glorious stanza', 'The cotter's Saturday night' (letter, 12 July 1791, Wallace, 2.166). She died at home at Dunlop House, Dunlop, Ayrshire, on 24 May 1815.

J. C. STEWART-ROBERTSON

Sources *Robert Burns and Mrs Dunlop: correspondence now published in full for the first time; with elucidations*, ed. W. Wallace, 1st edn, 2 vols. (1898) • J. C. Ewing, 'Burns–Dunlop correspondence: unpublished letters', *The Burns Chronicle* (1904), 67–75 • *The letters of Robert Burns*, ed. J. de Lancey Ferguson, 2 vols. (1931) • *The works of Robert Burns*, ed. the Ettrick Shepherd [J. Hogg] and W. Motherwell, 3 (1835) • *The complete letters of Robert Burns*, ed. J. A. Mackay (1987) • M. Lindsay, *The Burns encyclopedia*, rev. 3rd edn (1980) • J. de Lancey Ferguson, *Pride and passion: Robert Burns, 1759–1796* (1964) • *The complete writings of Robert Burns, with essay on Burns's life, genius, and achievement by, and with an introduction by, John Buchan*, ed. W. E. Henley, 10 vols. (1926) • *The letters of Robert Burns*, ed. F. Allen, 1: *1779–1887: with autobiographical letter and common-place book* (1927) • *The works of Robert Burns*, ed. C. Annandale, 5 vols. (1888) [esp. vol. 4] • D. Daiches, *Robert Burns* (1957) • M. Lindsay, *Robert Burns the man, his work, the legend* (1954–71) • A. Dent, *Burns in his time* (1966) • D. A. Low, ed., *Robert Burns: the critical heritage* (1974) • *The letters of Robert Burns*, ed. J. de Lancey Ferguson, 2nd edn, ed. G. Ross Roy, 2 vols. (1985) • bap. reg. Scot.
Archives Morgan L., Lochryan MSS
Likenesses G. Mosman, portrait, 1747, repro. in *Robert Burns and Mrs. Dunlop*, ed. Wallace • portrait, after 1747, repro. in *Complete letters of Robert Burns*, ed. MacKay, facing p. 192 • J. Edgar, group portrait, wash drawing, c.1854 (*Robert Burns at an evening party of Lord Monboddo's*, 1786), Scot. NPG • A. C., watercolour drawing, Scot. NPG [*see illus.*] • H. Robinson, engraving (after unknown portrait), NL Scot.
Wealth at death £800—in promissory notes with Messrs Carrick, Brown, & Co., Glasgow: NA Scot., CC 9/7/82, 463–4; Ewing, 'Burns–Dunlop correspondence

Dunlop, James (1759–1832), army officer, born on 19 June 1759, was the fifth son of John Dunlop (d. 1785), laird of that ilk in Ayrshire, and his wife, Frances Anna Wallace *Dunlop (1730–1815), last surviving daughter of Sir Thomas Wallace, fifth baronet, of Craigie, Ayrshire. He was enfeoffed of the Dunlop estate in 1784 on the resignation of his father, his only remaining older brother, Sir Thomas, having already succeeded to the Craigie estate under the name of Wallace. Before this, in January 1778, James Dunlop had been appointed ensign in the old 82nd (Hamilton) foot, raised in the lowlands at that time at the cost of the duke of Hamilton. Dunlop accompanied the regiment to Nova Scotia and obtained his lieutenancy in 1779. In the spring of that year he went with the flank companies to New York and was wrecked on the coast of New Jersey, when four-fifths of the company to which he belonged were drowned and the rest made prisoners by the Americans. Having been exchanged, Dunlop accompanied part of the 80th foot from New York to Virginia and was actively engaged there. When the mouth of Chesapeake Bay was seized by two French frigates, he was dispatched with the news to Charlestown, South Carolina, arriving there in April 1781. After this he joined a detachment under Major James Craig at Wilmington, North Carolina, and commanded a troop of mounted infantry acting as dragoons. After Charles Cornwallis's surrender at Yorktown, Virginia, on 19 October 1781, the troops at Wilmington were withdrawn to Charlestown and Dunlop, who meanwhile had purchased a company in his own regiment, the 82nd, rejoined it at Halifax, Nova Scotia, where he served until the peace of Versailles in 1783, when the regiment was ordered home. A leak caused the transport to run for Antigua, in the West Indies, where the troops landed and served until 1784, at which time the regiment was disbanded at Edinburgh and Dunlop put on half pay.

In 1787, having raised men for a company in the 77th foot, one of the four king's regiments raised at that time at the expense of the East India Company, Dunlop was brought on full pay in that regiment, accompanied it to Bombay, and served under Lord Cornwallis in the campaign against Tipu Sahib in 1791. In 1794 he became deputy paymaster-general of king's troops at Bombay, and later, military secretary to the governor of Bombay. That year he also became brevet major, which promotion did not appear in orders in India until two years later. He became major in the 77th in September, and lieutenant-colonel in December 1795. When the latter promotion was announced in orders about twelve months after date, he resigned his staff appointments, joined his regiment, and commanded a field force against a refractory raja in Malabar, defeating three detachments—one of them 2000 strong—sent out against him. After this he commanded at Cochin. On the outbreak of the Anglo-Mysore War he was appointed to a European brigade in General Stewart's division and commanded it in the action at Seedaseer on 6 March, and at the capture of Seringapatam on 4 May 1799, where he led the left column of assault (the right column being led by David Baird) and received a very severe tulwar wound from which he never entirely recovered. He was subsequently employed against the hill forts in the Kanara country, and soon after, in 1800, he returned to England. On 20 July 1802 he married Julia, daughter of Hugh Baillie of Monkton, Ayrshire; they had three sons and two daughters.

On the renewal of the war with France in 1803, Dunlop was ordered to take command of a royal garrison battalion in Guernsey in the Channel Islands, which was composed of recruiting detachments and recruits of king's regiments serving in India. In 1804 he exchanged from the 77th foot to the 59th, then stationed on the coast of Kent, and in 1805 he became brigadier-general and was appointed to a brigade in Cornwall. Afterwards he was transferred to the eastern district and for a time commanded a Highland brigade at Colchester. He became a major-general on 25 July 1810 and in October was appointed to

the staff of the duke of Wellington's army in the Peninsula, which he joined at Torres Vedras in November of the same year. He was appointed to a brigade in the 5th division under General Leith, which took part in the pursuit of the French to Santarém. On Leith's departure after the return of the division to Torres Vedras, Dunlop assumed command. At the head of the division he joined Wellington between Leiria and Pombal in March 1811 and commanded it throughout the ensuing campaign, including at the battle of Fuentes d'Oñoro on 5 May 1811, with the exception of a period of ten days when the command devolved on Sir William Erskine. When the division went into winter quarters at Guarda, Dunlop obtained leave of absence and did not rejoin the peninsular army. He was made lieutenant-general in 1814 and colonel of the 75th foot in 1827. He was MP for the stewartry of Kirkcudbright, where part of his estate lay, in three successive parliaments from 1812 to 1826, when he was narrowly defeated. He largely supported the government, and in 1813 voted against Christian missions to India. He died at Southwick, Hampshire, on 30 March 1832. His son, John Dunlop (1806–1839) MP received a baronetcy in 1838.

H. M. CHICHESTER, rev. ROGER T. STEARN

Sources GM, 1st ser., 102/1 (1832), 640 · R. G. Thorne, 'Dunlop, James', HoP, Commons · J. Paterson, History of the county of Ayr: with a genealogical account of the families of Ayrshire, 2 (1852), 46–8 · J. Philippart, ed., The royal military calendar, 3rd edn, 3 (1820) · P. Moon, The British conquest and dominion of India (1989) · A. J. Guy, ed., The road to Waterloo: the British army and the struggle against revolutionary and Napoleonic France, 1793–1815 (1990) · R. Muir, Britain and the defeat of Napoleon, 1807–1815 (1996) · S. Conway, The War of American Independence, 1775–1783 (1995)

Dunlop, James (1793–1848), astronomer, was born on 31 October 1793 in Dalry, Ayrshire, the fourth of the seven children of John Dunlop (1760–1819), a weaver, and his wife, Janet Boyle (d. 1830). He attended an elementary school in Dalry and a night school in Beith run by a Mr Gardner. At the age of fourteen he left home to work in a tweed factory belonging to his cousin, a Mr Faulds, but he later returned to handloom weaving in Dalry. On 14 June 1816, in Kilwinning, he married his cousin Jean Service; they had no children. Dunlop soon became known as an amateur astronomer and telescope maker. He made the acquaintance of Sir Thomas Makdougall Brisbane, bt, and in 1821 was invited, with his wife, to New South Wales to be an assistant, with Charles Rümker, of Sir Thomas's observatory at Parramatta. In fact Brisbane, as governor of the colony, had little time for astronomy, and the assistants did all the work, using the instruments brought from Brisbane's observatory near Largs in Ayrshire. Their first success was the recovery on 2 June 1822 of the comet Encke on its first predicted return and close to its anticipated position. Dunlop inferred axial rotation from changes in the configuration of the tail and observed an occultation of the star η Eridani by the comet.

Rümker departed on 16 June 1823 following a disagreement with Brisbane, leaving Dunlop in sole charge, and when Brisbane returned to Europe in 1825 Dunlop chose to remain in the colony to continue exploring its little-known skies. From his house, with his own 9 foot reflector and the 46 inch equatorial from Largs fitted with micrometers, he surveyed the sky from the pole to -30° declination. The results were embodied in *A catalogue of nebulae and clusters of stars in the southern hemisphere, observed at Paramatta in New South Wales*, presented to the Royal Society by John F. W. Herschel and read on 20 December 1827. Some of the 629 objects were illustrated with sketches. Herschel praised Dunlop's qualities as an observer at the bestowal of the Astronomical Society's gold medal on him on 8 February 1828. However, Herschel's subsequent re-examination of the objects from the Cape with more powerful instruments revealed that only 211 of Dunlop's 'nebulae' were genuine, and he concluded that the fault lay in the insufficient light-grasp or defining power of his instrument. In some star atlases the designation 'Δ' (Dunlop) is retained for such objects, as well as the NGC number. By February 1826 Dunlop had also made 40,000 observations for the *Brisbane Catalogue* of 7385 stars, whose polar distances were satisfactory but instrumental errors showed up in the right ascensions. On moonlit nights Dunlop had also undertaken places of 254 double stars, of which twenty-nine were micrometrically measured in separation and position angle. These were imparted to the *Memoirs* of the Astronomical Society in the form of a letter to Brisbane with the title 'Approximate places of double stars in the southern hemisphere'. Some have not been re-identified.

Brisbane returned to Scotland in 1826 and erected another observatory on his estate at Makerstoun, near Kelso. Dunlop joined him the following April, to take charge. Several observations were published by Brisbane, Dunlop, and their assistants John Alan Broun and John Welsh. In 1827–9 Dunlop made a series of magnetic observations throughout Scotland at Brisbane's expense, published by the Royal Society of Edinburgh in 1830.

Rümker, who had returned to Parramatta, resigned in 1829, and Dunlop was appointed director of the Parramatta observatory by the New South Wales government at a salary of £300. He took up duties in 1831 only to find the place in a dilapidated condition. He discovered two small comets, on 30 September 1833 and 19 March 1834, determined the relative magnitudes of 400 southern stars with a double-image eyepiece, and made observations of moon-culminating stars, eclipses of the Jovian satellites, and occultations, all sent to Brisbane for publication. He was now struggling against ill health. According to R. Bhathal and G. White, the polar explorer James Clark Ross called in at Parramatta to check his chronometer, but the ailing Dunlop called to his dog to 'attend to the English gentleman' (Bhathal and White, 21). Ross was offended and complained to the Admiralty about the state of the observatory. A commission of inquiry under the naval hydrographer, Captain Philip Parker King, found the building almost totally destroyed by white ants. It was closed in 1847 and demolished, and the instruments were packed away. Dunlop retired in 1842 to his estate at Boora Boora, Brisbane Water, and died there of urinary calculus on 22 September 1848. He was buried on the 25th in the Anglican churchyard at Kincumber, Brisbane; his widow, who survived another eleven years, placed a memorial tablet in the foyer.

Dunlop was of medium height, slim, with a swarthy complexion and dark piercing eyes. He smoked, took snuff, always wore the same coat, and hated ceremony. He was an eccentric and peculiar man, but kind and hospitable. He was elected fellow of the Astronomical Society in 1828 and of the Royal Society of Edinburgh in 1832. He received medals from the king of Denmark (1833) and from the Royal Institute of France (1835), of which he was a corresponding member.   DAVID GAVINE

Sources J. Service, *Thir notandums: being the literary recreations of Laird Canticarl … to which is appended a biographical sketch of James Dunlop* (1890) • H. Wood, 'Dunlop, James', *AusDB*, vol. 1 • P. Serle, *Dictionary of Australian biography*, 2 vols. (1949) • R. Bhathal and G. White, *Under the southern cross* (1991) • *The Observatory*, 3 (1880), 614 • *1000 famous Australians* (1978) • *DNB* • *The record of the Royal Society of London*, 4th edn (1940) • RS
Archives RAS, observations • RS, observations • State Library of New South Wales, Sydney, observations and memoranda
Likenesses drawing, repro. in Bhathal and White, *Under the Southern Cross*, 20

Dunlop, John (1755–1820), songwriter, was born on 3 September 1755, the youngest son of Provost Colin Dunlop of Carmyle, in the parish of Old Monkland, Lanarkshire, and of his wife, Martha Bogle. He began life as a merchant, and was lord provost of Glasgow in 1796. He lived at Rosebank, near Glasgow, a property which he planted and beautified. He was appointed collector of customs at Bo'ness, and later moved to Port Glasgow.

An active-minded man, Dunlop was 'a merchant, a sportsman, a mayor, a collector, squire, captain and poet, politician and factor'. His humour and social qualities made him much sought after. He sang well and wrote songs, some of which show a graceful lyrical faculty and were very popular. 'Oh dinna ask me gin I lo'e ye' is perhaps the best known, and, with 'Here's to the year that's awa', is often included in collections of Scottish poetry. Dunlop was also known as a writer of monumental and other inscriptions. He was a leading member of the convivial Hodge Podge Club in Glasgow, for which some of his verses were composed. His emblem in the club was a hogshead, but 'as jolly a cask as ere loaded the ground' (Strang).

In 1818 Dunlop edited for a son of Sir James and Lady Frances Steuart some letters they had received from Lady Mary Wortley Montagu, *Original letters from the Right Hon. Lady Mary W. Montagu to Sir James and Lady Frances Steuart*, later reprinted by Lord Wharncliffe. He printed for private circulation ten copies of two volumes of his occasional pieces (*Poems on Several Occasions*, 1817–19), and his son, John Colin *Dunlop (d. 1842), the author of the *History of Fiction*, edited a volume of his poems in 1836 (*Poems on Several Occasions from 1793 to 1816*) of which only fifty copies were printed. He died at Port Glasgow on 4 September 1820, aged sixty-five.

                          H. R. TEDDER, *rev.* S. R. J. BAUDRY

Sources G. Stewart, *Curiosities of Glasgow citizenship* (1881), 201–2 • J. Martin, *Bibliographical catalogue of books privately printed*, 2nd edn

(1854), 232, 243, 463 • J. Dennistoun, ed., *The Coltness collections, MDCVIII–MDCCCXL*, Maitland Club, [58] (1842), 310, 383, 388 • 'Letters to Lady Steuart and G. Chalmers, November 1804', BL, Add. MS 22901, fols. 205, 211 • J. Strang, *Glasgow and its clubs*, rev. edn (1857), 43–6, 50, 53 • *Edinburgh Magazine and Literary Miscellany*, 86 (1820), 383 • IGI • bap. reg. Scot.

Archives Mitchell L., Glas., corresp. | NA Scot., letters to Lord Melville • NL Scot., letters to Henry Dundas

Likenesses H. Raeburn, oils, Art Gallery and Museum, Glasgow

Dunlop, John Boyd (1840–1921), inventor of the pneumatic tyre, was born on 5 February 1840 at Dreghorn, Ayrshire, the son of a farmer, John Dunlop, and his wife, Agnes, *née* Boyd. As a boy he attended the local parish school and, being considered too delicate for farm work, was allowed to continue his studies at Irvine's academy, Edinburgh. Reared in a farming atmosphere, it was natural that he should be interested in domestic animals and later he studied veterinary surgery so successfully that at the age of nineteen he secured his diploma. For eight years he worked at his profession in Edinburgh, and in 1867 migrated to Belfast, where he established a practice in Gloucester Street. His personal and professional qualities brought success, and within twenty years the practice was one of the largest in Ireland. In 1871 he married Margaret, daughter of James Stevenson, a farmer. They had a son, John, and a daughter, Jean.

The invention which made Dunlop's name famous was devised in October 1887. His son John, then nine years of age, who had a tricycle fitted with solid rubber tyres, complained of being jarred as he rode over the rough granite blocks with which the streets were paved. Dunlop's interest was aroused by the problem. He obtained a disc of wood and, being skilled at working in rubber, constructed an air tube and laid it round the periphery, fastening it down by a covering of linen tacked to the wood. He tested this arrangement against one of the tricycle wheels by throwing the two along the cobbles of a long courtyard, and the enormously greater resilience and liveliness of the air-tyred disc was at once obvious. Developing the idea further, Dunlop made two rims of wood, fastened air tubes and covers to them, and fixed them over the existing tyres of the rear wheels of his son's machine. A trial of this device in February 1888 having proved eminently successful, a new tricycle frame was ordered, for which wheels with pneumatic tyres were built and fitted. A demonstration before several Belfast businessmen met with approval, and on 23 July 1888, Dunlop lodged his first application for a provisional patent. The patent was finally granted on 7 December.

After exhaustive tests on a bicycle, Dunlop began to procure from Edinburgh tyres made to his specification and, in conjunction with Messrs Edlin & Co., of Belfast, who built the tricycle, he put on the market machines complete with pneumatic tyres. A racing bicycle was also built to the order of W. Hume, captain of a local cycling club, who rode it at a local sports meeting on 18 May 1889 and easily beat a number of superior riders mounted on solid-tyred cycles. Among the defeated riders were the sons of

John Boyd Dunlop (1840–1921), by unknown photographer

(William) Harvey Du Cros, then president of the Irish Cyclists' Association, who, being impressed with the possibilities of the new tyre, made the acquaintance of the inventor. Eventually, late in 1889, the two men refloated the business of Booth Brothers, cycle and agricultural implement agents, of Dublin, as the Pneumatic Tyre and Booth's Cycle Agency. Dunlop, who had been on the point of retiring from his practice, made over his patent to Harvey Du Cros for £300 and took 3000 £1 shares in the company, the £25,000 capital of which was not at first fully subscribed. In 1892 Dunlop removed to Dublin. Contemporary photographs depict him as a strongly built man with a patriarchal white beard.

Dunlop continued to play an important part in the business for several years, but was overshadowed by Du Cros, whose ability helped to guide the company through many struggles. It was found that the pneumatic principle had already been patented in 1846 by Robert William Thompson, a fact which invalidated the Dunlop patent. The company had, however, secured valuable complementary patents for rims, valves, and fixing methods, and after a brief fight with the short-lived cushion tyre, and much litigation, it prospered, and in time pneumatic tyres achieved worldwide popularity. The pneumatic tyre revolutionized cycling, rapidly growing in popularity after the introduction of J. K. Starley's 'safety' bicycle in 1885, and later contributing greatly to the development of the motor car. Dunlop himself did not profit greatly from the success of his invention—after his death his estate was valued at a mere £9867 gross—and took no further part in its development after the original company was sold in 1896 for £3 million to the financier, Ernest Terah Hooley, who refloated it for £5 million. The Dunlop company, especially Arthur *Du Cros, who was somewhat gullible, suffered from association with various dubious financiers, including Hooley. Eventually it became the Dunlop Rubber Company Ltd, with a huge capital and many subsidiary companies. The choice of name was a recognition of how closely the pneumatic tyre was associated with Dunlop in the public mind.

Dunlop lived quietly at Balls Bridge, near Dublin, his only business interest being in the local drapery establishment of Todd, Burns & Co. He died at his home on 23 October 1921. His daughter, Jean McClintock, published some of her father's reminiscences as *The History of the Pneumatic Tyre* (1923).   B. W. BEST, rev. TREVOR I. WILLIAMS

Sources J. McClintock, *The history of the pneumatic tyre* (1923) · G. Jones, 'Dunlop, John Boyd', *DBB* · *The Times* (25 Oct 1921) · *Irish Times* (25 Oct 1921)
Archives LMA, Dunlop Group
Likenesses oils, c.1904 (after photograph by Lafayette), Dunlop Ltd, London · photograph, repro. in W. H. Beable, *Romance of great businesses*, 2 vols. (1926) · photograph, repro. in Jones, 'Dunlop, John Boyd' · photographs, Dunlop Ltd, London [*see illus.*]
Wealth at death £9687 6s. 0d.: probate, 1921, Dublin

Dunlop, John Colin (d. 1842), writer on literature, was the son of John *Dunlop (1755–1820) of Rosebank, Glasgow, a merchant and song writer and lord provost of Glasgow. Studious and retiring in disposition, the younger Dunlop was educated at Glasgow high school and attended Edinburgh University (1803–5). He was admitted an advocate in 1807, but was only nominally at the bar. The first edition of his *History of Fiction* was published in three volumes at Edinburgh in 1814. In an article in the *Edinburgh Review* (November 1814, 38–58) Jeffrey complained about the omission of reference to metrical fiction and the author's narrow and unphilosophical views. The *Quarterly Review* (July 1815, 384–408) considered the work executed on 'a defective plan, in what we incline to think rather a superficial manner'. These strictures are noted in the preface to the second edition of 1816, which the author claims to have improved and enlarged. Some of Dunlop's opinions are obsolete, but he was a conscientious critic. The oriental and modern sections are the weakest. The chapters on romances of chivalry are good, as are those on Italian novelists. The plots are well summarized, and the book is written in a clear and agreeable style. A German translation by Felix Liebrecht appeared in 1851.

Dunlop was appointed sheriff-depute of Renfrewshire in 1816, an office he retained until his death. In 1823 he produced the first two volumes of a *History of Roman Literature*, which is notable for useful abstracts of the works under consideration and illustrations drawn from modern European literatures. *Memoirs of Spain* (1834), deals with the period from 1621 to 1700. In 1836 he printed for private circulation fifty copies of the *Poems* of his father, John Dunlop. His last production was a volume of translations from the Latin anthology (1838), which gave rise to

accusations of plagiarism and negligence (*Blackwood*, April 1838, 521–64).

Dunlop was well read in the Greek and Latin classics, and in the literatures of France, Germany, Italy, and Spain. Reputedly amiable and a good conversationalist, his physical presence was in marked contrast to that of his robust and jovial father. Henry Cockburn recalled of him:

People sometimes wondered how so feeble and so retired a creature could venture as a penal magistrate among the strong sailors of Greenock or the illfed rebels of precarious Paisley; but he did his duty among them very well … In appearance he was exceedingly like a little, old, gray cuddy—a nice kindly body, with a clear, soft Scotch voice … Everybody loved Dunlop; and, with the single exception of a relation who was always trying to swindle him, there was no one whom Dunlop did not love. (*Journal of Henry Cockburn*, 1. 310–11)

Dunlop died in Edinburgh on 26 January 1842.
          H. R. TEDDER, rev. DOUGLAS BROWN

Sources H. R. Tedder and M. Kerney, 'Romance', *Encyclopaedia Britannica*, 9th edn (1875–89) · *Journal of Henry Cockburn: being a continuation of the 'Memorials of his time', 1831–1854*, 2 vols. (1874) · W. Hazlitt, *EdinR*, 24 (1814–15), 38–58 · review, *QR*, 13 (1815), 384–408 · 'The Latin anthology [pt 1]', *Blackwood*, 43 (1838), 521–64 · *N&Q*, 5th ser., 4 (1875), 308, 376, 435 · *N&Q*, 5th ser., 12 (1879), 356

Dunlop, Marion Wallace- (1864–1942), suffragist and artist, was born on 22 December 1864 at Leys Castle, Inverness, in Scotland, the daughter of Robert Henry Wallace-Dunlop, of the Bengal civil service, and his wife, Lucy Dawson. Two of her sisters, Madeline and Rosalind Wallace-Dunlop, wrote *Timely Retreat, or, A Year in Bengal before the Mutinies* (1858), which became a best-seller. Her father, who had been decorated for distinguished service in the Indian mutiny, retired from India in the year of her birth. Although she lived most of her life in London, she did not forget her Scottish origins, describing herself as 'a direct descendant of the mother of William Wallace' (*Votes for Women*, 2 July 1909). Indeed, the large house that her father built in what is now Montpellier Road, Ealing, was named Ellerslie after Wallace's birthplace. She herself was called after the patriot's wife.

Marion Wallace-Dunlop studied at the Slade School of Fine Art and exhibited at the Royal Academy in 1903 (when she also exhibited a painting at the Royal Glasgow Institute of the Fine Arts), and in 1905 and 1906. Her paintings were also exhibited in Paris. She illustrated in art nouveau style two books, *Fairies, Elves, and Flower Babies* and *The Magic Fruit Garden*, both published in 1899.

From 1906 to 1913 Wallace-Dunlop was a member of the Fabian Women's Group. She was involved in the suffrage movement from 1900, when she subscribed to the Central Society for Women's Suffrage, but militancy made an immediate appeal to her, and from 1908 she was active in the Women's Social and Political Union (WSPU). She was arrested and imprisoned in Holloway for the first time in July 1908 for 'obstruction' and again in November of that year for leading a deputation to the House of Commons. In June 1909 she stencilled the following extract from the Bill of Rights on the wall of St Stephen's Hall in the Palace

Marion Wallace-Dunlop (1864–1942), by unknown photographer, 1909

of Westminster: 'It is the right of the subject to petition the King, and all commitments and prosecution for such petitions are illegal' (Rosen, 118). Back in Holloway prison she went on hunger strike, an entirely independent action that was then taken up by the WSPU as future policy. After ninety-one hours of fasting she was released.

At that time (5 July) Frederick Pethick-Lawrence wrote to Marion Wallace-Dunlop: 'Nothing has moved me so much—stirred me to the depths of my being—as your heroic action' (Rosen, 120). In common with a number of other suffragettes, Marion became a vegetarian. In 1910 and 1911 she helped to design many of the spectacular WSPU processions. In November 1911 she helped to organize a window-smashing campaign and was imprisoned for her own part in this. In her entry for the *Women's Who's Who* in 1913, under 'Recreations' she recorded: 'No time for them—till the vote is won.' Nevertheless, early in 1918 she was visited by Mary Sheepshanks, who observed her leading an idyllic pastoral life in the countryside:

> we found her in a delicious cottage with a little chicken and goat farm, an adopted baby of 18 months, and a perfectly lovely young girl who did some bare foot dancing for us in the barn; we finished up with home made honey.
> (M. Sheepshanks to C. Marshall, 7 April 1918, box 23, Catherine Marshall papers, Cumbria AS)

In 1928 Wallace-Dunlop was a pallbearer at Emmeline Pankhurst's funeral, and for a time after that she took care of Mrs Pankhurst's adopted daughter, Mary, in her magnificent Elizabethan house at Peaslake, Surrey. She died on 12 September 1942 at the Mount Alvernia Nursing Home, Guildford.   LEAH LENEMAN

Sources E. Crawford, *The women's suffrage movement: a reference guide, 1866–1928* (1999) • A. J. R., ed., *The suffrage annual and women's who's who* (1913) • London Museum, Suffragette Fellowship Collection • *Votes for Women* (15 Oct 1908) • *Votes for Women* (2 July 1909) • *Votes for Women* (16 July 1909) • A. Rosen, *Rise up, women! The militant campaign of the Women's Social and Political Union, 1903–1914* (1974); repr. (1993) • b. cert. • d. cert. • E. S. Pankhurst, *The suffragette movement: an intimate account of persons and ideals* (1931) • S. Houfe, *The dictionary of 19th century British book illustrators and caricaturists*, rev. edn (1996) • C. Lytten, *Prisons and prisoners* (1914) • R. E. D. Sketchley, *English book-illustration of to-day* (1903) • L. Tickner, *The spectacle of women: imagery of the suffrage campaign, 1907–14* (1987) • M. MacKenzie, *Shoulder to shoulder* (1975) • J. G. Dunlop, *The Dunlops of Dunlop* (1939) • *CGPLA Eng. & Wales* (1942) • M. Sheepshanks to C. Marshall, 7 April 1918, Cumbria AS, Carlisle, Marshall Papers, box 23

Likenesses photograph, 1909, Museum of London, Nurse Pine collection [*see illus.*] • photographs, Museum of London, Suffragette Fellowship collection • photographs, repro. in C. Pankhurst, *Unshackled* (1959) • photographs, repro. in B. M. W. Dobbie, *A nest of suffragettes in Somerset* (1979) • photographs, repro. in Tickner, *The spectacle of women*

Wealth at death £5905 3s. 7d.: probate, 19 Dec 1942, *CGPLA Eng. & Wales*

Dunlop, William (1653/4–1700), university principal, was the eldest son of Alexander Dunlop (1620/21–1667), minister of Paisley, Renfrewshire, and his second wife, Elizabeth (1627–1722), daughter of William Mure of Glanderstoun. After the Restoration both Dunlop's parents suffered imprisonment by the Scottish privy council on account of their sympathy with the covenanter party. Dunlop was probably educated at the University of Edinburgh, where a William Dunlop graduated in 1671. The Dunlop family's close connections with some of the more prominent presbyterians probably explain his post as a tutor to the family of Lord Cochrane, supervising the education of the future second earl of Dundonald and his brother. In 1678 Dunlop was summoned before the privy council to answer the charge of being an unlicensed tutor, and Dundonald was forced to remove him from his post. Before the battle of Bothwell Bridge in 1679 Dunlop was responsible in part for the 'declaration of the oppressed Protestants now in arms in Scotland' (Story, *Carstares*, 55), which was adopted by the moderate presbyterians. Following Bothwell Bridge, Dunlop may have taken refuge in the Netherlands.

Before July 1681 Dunlop married his cousin Sarah (*bap.* 1650, *d.* 1733), daughter of John Carstairs (1623–1686), minister of St Mungo's, Glasgow. They had three sons, one of whom predeceased his father. John Carstairs said of Dunlop and his own son, William *Carstares (1649–1715), 'they will be aye plotting and plodding till they plod the heads off themselves' (Dunlop, *Dunlops*, 124–5). With the position of the presbyterians deteriorating in Scotland, Dunlop made preparations to join a colonial venture in Carolina. On 20 July 1684 John Erskine heard Dunlop preach, noting 'he was not ordained. He preached well, and was otherways accomplished' (*Journal*, ed. Macleod, 71). He was the only preacher who set sail the following day from the River Clyde in the company of Erskine's brother, Lord Cardross, and a group of covenanters on board the *Carolina Merchant*. The ship arrived at Charles Town, Carolina, on 2 October 1684, and the colonists set out to establish a settlement at Stuart's Town, 12 miles from the mouth of the Port Royal River. Dunlop served as the chaplain of this community, as well as a major in its militia, and in 1685 he attended the provincial assembly. In August 1686 Stuart's Town was broken up by a Spanish raid. Dunlop remained in South Carolina, serving on a committee appointed in 1687 to consider whether the colony's constitution should be modified. In June 1687 a group of friends sent him a letter asking him to return to Scotland in the wake of the declaration of indulgence.

The date of Dunlop's departure from Carolina is unknown, but he was in London in October 1689, probably returning to Scotland in January 1690. Through the patronage of Dundonald he was offered the ministry of Ochiltree, and later that of Paisley, but declined both posts. In July he was involved in thwarting the Jacobite plot of Sir James Montgomerie, fourth baronet, of Skelmorlie. By November 1690 there was some heavy lobbying in his favour for the post of principal of Glasgow University, and on 11 December 1690 he was duly inducted into office. He was ordained as a minister in Glasgow, but without a charge, and on 21 September 1691 he was made a burgess and guild-brethren of Glasgow. His influential brother-in-law, William Carstares, procured for him the post of historiographer royal for Scotland in 1693 at a salary of £50 per annum, and he also received £1200 funds to assist the four Scottish universities. In 1694 he was commissioned by the general assembly of the kirk to congratulate the king on his return from the continent that autumn and to be a member of the delegation of the general assembly sent to justify the actions of the commissioners sent to settle the church in the north of Scotland. He was thus on hand in London to present to the king the address of condolence on the death of Queen Mary in January 1695. Dunlop was a director of the Darien Company, in which he invested personally £1000 in the initial Glasgow subscription of March 1696, and in which the university also had funds invested. In September 1697 he was named along with Robert Blackwood to examine William Paterson concerning the embezzlement of company funds entrusted by Paterson to James Smith, an investigation which resulted in Paterson being exonerated of any illegality, but stripped of office in the company.

Dunlop died in Glasgow on 8 March 1700. Robert Wodrow lamented 'in losing him we have lost one of the greatest antiquaries this nation ever produced' (Wodrow, 60), although his only published work to survive is an account of Renfrewshire published by the Maitland Club. He was survived by his wife, who received a pension of £60. In 1726 she petitioned Edinburgh council about the erection of a family monument; she died in 1733, her testament being registered the following year. Dunlop's surviving sons, Alexander *Dunlop (1684–1747) and William

*Dunlop (1692–1720), became respectively professor of Greek at Glasgow and professor of church history at Edinburgh. W. G. BLAIKIE, *rev.* STUART HANDLEY

Sources *Fasti Scot.*, new edn, 7.396; 3.164, 168 · G. P. Insh, 'The *Carolina Merchant*: advice of arrival', *SHR*, 25 (1927–8), 98–108 · E. McCrady, *The history of South Carolina under the proprietory government, 1670–1719* (1897) · Chambers, *Scots.* (1855) · R. H. Story, *William Carstares: a character and career of the revolutionary epoch (1649–1715)* (1874) · *Early letters of Robert Wodrow, 1698–1709*, ed. L. W. Sharp, Scottish History Society, 3rd ser., 24 (1937) · *Journal of the Hon. John Erskine of Carnock*, ed. W. Macleod, Scottish History Society, 14 (1893), 71 · J. H. Burton, ed., *The Darien papers*, Bannatyne Club, 90 (1849) · W. H. L. Melville, ed., *Leven and Melville papers: letters and state papers chiefly addressed to George, earl of Melville … 1689–1691*, Bannatyne Club, 77 (1843) · J. R. Anderson, ed., *The burgesses and guild brethren of Glasgow, 1573–1750*, Scottish RS, 56 (1925), 225 · *IGI* [High Church, Glasgow, parish register] · F. J. Grant, ed., *The commissariat record of Glasgow: register of testaments, 1547–1800*, Scottish RS, 7 (1901) · *CSP dom.*, 1700–02, 5 · R. H. Story, 'Letters from Darien', *Transactions of the Glasgow Archaeological Society*, new ser., 4 (1900–03), 207–25 · J. G. Dunlop, *The Dunlops of Dunlop: and of Auchenskaith, Keppoch, and Gairbraid* (1939) · J. G. Dunlop, ed., *Letters and journals, 1663–1889* (1953)
Archives NL Scot., corresp. and papers · NL Scot., family corresp. and papers · U. Edin. L., corresp. and papers · U. Glas. L., papers
Likenesses portrait, repro. in Dunlop, *Dunlops of Dunlop*, 128

Dunlop, William (1692–1720), university teacher, was born in Glasgow, the younger son of William *Dunlop (1653/4–1700), principal of Glasgow University, and his wife, Sarah Carstairs, a cousin. His elder brother was Alexander *Dunlop (1684–1747). Educated at Edinburgh, Glasgow, and Utrecht universities, he was licensed to preach by the presbytery of Edinburgh in 1714. Within six months he had been appointed to the chair of divinity and church history at Edinburgh University by George I, probably on the recommendation of his uncle William Carstares, principal of the university. While such nepotism was a common feature of university appointments Dunlop was seen to have 'proved himself well worthy of it'. Regarded as an eloquent preacher, he also displayed an interest in church organization. Criticisms of his main work on the confession of faith in the Church of Scotland demonstrate the division in the church over the Toleration Act of 1712. As a member of the post-1688 Presbyterian élite Dunlop was typical in his pragmatic acceptance of pluralism in religious adherence. His development of this progressive position was cut short by his early death, at the age of twenty-eight, in 1720. Two volumes of his sermons were published posthumously.

W. G. BLAIKIE, *rev.* CAMPBELL F. LLOYD

Sources 'Memoir', W. Dunlop, *Sermons preached on several subjects and occasions*, 2 vols. (1722) · Anderson, *Scot. nat.* · A. Grant, *The story of the University of Edinburgh during its first three hundred years*, 2 vols. (1884) · A. Bower, *The history of the University of Edinburgh*, 3 vols. (1817–30)
Archives NL Scot., papers

Dunlop, William [*pseud.* a Backwoodsman] (1792–1848), surgeon and pioneer in Canada, was born in Greenock, Renfrewshire, on 19 November 1792, the youngest of the three sons of Alexander Dunlop (1766–1840), banker, of

William Dunlop (1792–1848), by Daniel Maclise, 1833

Keppoch House, Dunbartonshire, and his wife, Janet Graham (1769–1795). He was educated in Greenock and from 1806 studied medicine at Glasgow University and then London University. He always styled himself MD, but appears not to have taken his degree. He passed his army medical examinations in 1812, and the following year was appointed assistant surgeon to the 89th regiment of foot, with whom he served in Upper Canada in the Anglo-American War. He enjoyed the war but not army life in peacetime, and retired on half pay in 1817 to go to Calcutta, where he edited a tory newspaper in opposition to James Silk Buckingham's *Calcutta Journal*; later he went to the Bay of Bengal, where unsuccessful efforts to rid an island of tigers to turn it into a resort left him with the nickname Tiger. In 1820 he returned to Scotland to recover from fever, and contributed a series of sketches about India to *Blackwood's Edinburgh Magazine*. After turning his hand to lecturing on medical jurisprudence in Edinburgh, he went in 1824 to London to edit the *British Press*, and founded *The Telescope*, which survived for a year.

In 1826 Dunlop was taken on by the Canada Company as warden of the woods and forests, to inspect the company's lands and to monitor settlement. He performed this task with considerable enjoyment, roaming round the countryside, devising often impractical and grandiose schemes for the company's advancement, attracting notice to himself, stirring up controversy in the press, and getting himself appointed commissioner of the peace. In 1832 he published a book under the pseudonym a Backwoodsman. Masquerading as *Statistical Sketches of Upper Canada*, this alleged guide for immigrants was in fact a collection of jolly anecdotes and aphorisms. While he could

play the fool in print, he was also astute and able, as witnessed in his successful defence of the Canada Company before the house of assembly in 1835.

In the disturbances of 1837 Dunlop enjoyed himself raising a militia (The Bloody Useless), but after equipping it from the company's stores, he fell out with its directors and resigned in 1838. The company and he had suited each other in the pioneering phase of settlement, but as it became more conventional, Dunlop proved too exuberant and idiosyncratic. He was elected for Huron to the house of assembly in the interest of the anti-company Colbornites in 1841 and 1844. He proved a moderate tory, whose speeches were 'frequently more notable for their humour than their grasp of the issues' (*DCB*, 262). In 1846 he became superintendent of the Lachine Canal. The following year the *Literary Garland* of Montreal published his humorous and colourful 'Recollections of the American War', which has come to be seen as his best work, although it attracted little attention at the time. He died, unmarried, on 29 June 1848 at Côté-St Paul, near Montreal, where he lived, and was buried first in Hamilton and later in Goderich, Upper Canada, which he had helped to lay out in his Canada Company days.

The success of Dunlop's writings depended on his conscious cultivation of himself as comic hero, and this also left a legacy of tales and legends of his feats, adventures, and practical jokes which long outlived him, and formed an important part of the backwoodsman myth.

ELIZABETH BAIGENT

Sources C. F. Klinck, ed., *William 'Tiger' Dunlop: 'Blackwoodian backwoodsman'* [1958] · G. Draper and R. Hall, 'Dunlop, William', *DCB*, vol. 7 · W. H. Graham, *Tiger Dunlop* (1962) · R. Lizars and K. Lizars, *In the days of the Canada Company* (1896) · R. Lizars and K. Lizars, *Humours of '37* (1897) · F. S. L. Ford, *William Dunlop* (1931) · W. Dunlop, *Recollections* (1898) [introduction by A. H. U. Colquhoun] · D. E. Draper, 'Tiger: a study of the legend of William Dunlop', PhD diss., University of Ontario, 1980 · A. Dunlop, *Dunlop of that ilk* (1898) · J. G. Dunlop, *The Dunlops of Dunlop* (1939)
Likenesses D. Maclise, pencil and watercolour drawing, 1833, NPG [*see illus.*]

Dunlop, William Joseph [Joey] (1952–2000), racing motor cyclist, was born on 25 February 1952 in Ballymoney, co. Antrim, the eldest son and second of the seven children of William Dunlop, motor mechanic, and his wife, May. He attended Ballymoney high school, but 'didn't bother much with education' (*The Independent*). As a youth he had an ambition to join the army, but that changed when, at sixteen, he bought his first motor cycle, a 250 cc BSA. From then he financed his passion for motor cycling by working in various jobs, including as a diesel fitter, lorry driver, steel erector, and roofer, and latterly as the publican of the Railway inn in Ballymoney. On 22 September 1972 he married his childhood sweetheart, Linda Robinson. They had three daughters and two sons.

Motor cycle racing in Ireland evolved differently from that on the UK mainland. Since the middle of the twentieth century motor cycle racing on the mainland had been conducted almost exclusively on purpose-built tracks whose safety had been continuously improved. This was known as 'short circuit' racing, as opposed to road racing, in which public roads were closed off to create a temporary circuit. Although there were short circuits there, Ireland had a long tradition of road racing, especially in the north. In road racing there was very little protection for riders, who raced at immense speed on bumpy back roads, on the limit of control, past trees, walls, telegraph poles, traffic islands, and houses. Deaths and serious injuries were regrettably common.

Joey Dunlop raced successfully on the short circuits, but it was in road racing that he shone. He began racing in 1969, on a 192 cc Triumph Tiger Cub which he had bought for £50, fired with enthusiasm after seeing local rider Mervyn Robinson racing. Robinson became Dunlop's brother-in-law, and along with Frank Kennedy they formed a triumvirate of Irish road racers known as the 'Armoy armada'. Dunlop came close to quitting motor cycle racing when Robinson was killed in a racing accident in 1980. Kennedy also predeceased Dunlop in a racing accident. Dunlop was seriously injured in crashes in 1989 and 1998, and his brother Robert was seriously injured in a racing accident in 1994.

It was not until 1976 that Dunlop became a regular winner in Irish events. His road racing experience stood him in good stead when he entered the Tourist Trophy (TT) races on the Isle of Man. The TT circuit is a public road circuit, 37.73 miles long and tremendously fast. After 1976 the Manx course was deemed too dangerous for use in the motor cycle grand prix world championship, and it was thought that this would spell the end of the TT races. In fact they became the focal point of a week-long festival of motor cycling, attracting 40,000 or more riders to the island every year, and in a series of heroic rides Dunlop won their hearts. He won the Jubilee TT in 1977, the first of twenty-six TT races he won in the years until his death. The next most prolific TT winner, Mike Hailwood, reckoned almost universally to be one of the most talented motor cycle racers ever, won fourteen. Among many other successes, Dunlop won the North-West 200 thirteen times and the Ulster grand prix twenty-four times: these were the most prestigious of the Irish road races. Altogether he won more than 160 road races in Britain and Ireland, and numerous others elsewhere. In 1982 he won the first of five consecutive motor cycle Formula One world championships.

It was not the number of his wins which endeared Dunlop to racing fans, but his modesty and his evident love of the sport. He was a shy man of few words, and he rarely gave interviews, although he was always happy to spend time with the fans. He never accepted the trappings of fame, and he shunned the limelight. He always worked on his own machine, even when it was the latest high-tech equipment from the Honda factory (whose motor bikes he raced from 1983). The fans knew he was one of their own, and perhaps it was this which led to his nickname: 'Yer Maun'. In 2000, at the age of forty-eight and against men many years his junior, he won three of the most prestigious TT races. It was a prodigious feat. His average speed for the 175 mile Formula 1 race was 121 m.p.h.

Dunlop was appointed MBE in 1985 for his services to motor cycling, and OBE in 1995 in recognition of his single-handed van trips, twice to Bosnia and once each to Albania and Romania, to distribute food and other aid he had collected for the needy. For this latter work he became all the more respected by the people of Ireland, and by motor cycling fans all over the world. He once polled more than 60 per cent of the votes cast in an Irish Sportsman of the Year competition. In 1993 he was given the freedom of Ballymoney.

It was Dunlop's love of the sport which kept him racing into his forty-ninth year, and which in summer 2000 led him to Tallinn, Estonia. He drove alone with his bikes in the back of a van to race on the road circuit there. He had won two races and on 2 July was leading a third when he crashed and was killed instantly. Five days later 50,000 people attended his funeral at Garryduff Presbyterian Church, which was broadcast live on Irish national television, and at which government ministers from London, Belfast, and Dublin were present. It was a state funeral in all but name. He was survived by his wife, Linda, and their five children.   ALASTAIR KINROY

Sources M. McDiarmid, *Joey Dunlop: his authorised biography* (2001) · *The Times* (3 July 2000) · *The Guardian* (4 July 2000) · *The Independent* (4 July 2000) · www.iomtt.com/joeydunlop, Dec 2001
Likenesses photograph, repro. in McDiarmid, *Joey Dunlop* · photograph, repro. in *The Guardian* · photograph, repro. in *The Independent*
Wealth at death £180,000: administration, 7 Sept 2000, *CGPLA NIre*

Dunmore. For this title name *see* Murray, Charles, first earl of Dunmore (1661–1710); Murray, John, second earl of Dunmore (1685–1752); Murray, John, fourth earl of Dunmore (1730/31–1809); Murray, Catherine, countess of Dunmore (1814–1886); Murray, Charles Adolphus, seventh earl of Dunmore (1841–1907).

Dunn. For this title name *see* Aitken, Marcia Anastasia, Lady Beaverbrook [Marcia Anastasia Dunn, Lady Dunn] (1909–1994) [*see under* Aitken, William Maxwell, first Baron Beaverbrook (1879–1964)].

Dunn, Henry (1801–1878), educationist, was born on 22 January 1801 at Nottingham, the eldest son of Jonathan Dunn (1771–1859), printer, bookseller, and city councillor, and his wife, Elizabeth Barnett (1774–1803), who died during Dunn's infancy. His father remarried and had a large second family. At fourteen Dunn was apprenticed to his father but he worked for a time in east London at a lace warehouse. As a youth he attended the Castle Gate Independent Chapel in Nottingham but later joined another Congregational chapel in spite of his father's disapproval. In 1826 he married Euphemia Birrell (1800–1879); they had no children.

After a brief stay at Borough Road, Southwark, 'learning the system' Dunn, accompanied by his wife, was sent in 1827 to a monitorial school in Guatemala. Opposition by the Catholic clergy, however, obliged him to return home. In 1830 the British and Foreign School Society (BFSS) gave him the post of superintendent at Borough Road and soon afterwards he was appointed secretary. 'A stern advocate of Truth', Dunn's zeal was displayed at the training institution which, as he informed the parliamentary committee on the state of education in 1834, was the key to the success of all the society's activities. Conditions for the young men selected for training were vigorous. 'Our object is to keep them incessantly employed from five in the morning till nine or ten at night', he explained. As secretary it was Dunn's duty to edit the society's *Reports* and to appoint agents to visit and inspect British schools throughout the country. The demand for the society's teaching manual stimulated Dunn to the publication of his *Popular Education, or, The Normal School Manual* which went into eleven editions. In 1840 he collaborated with John Crossley, master of the Borough Road model school, in a series of graduated *Lesson Books* which was widely used in British schools at home and abroad.

The years following Dunn's appointment as secretary saw much debate on the future role of elementary education. Dunn, who gave evidence in 1838 to the select committee on education of the poorer classes, was opposed to a state system of education, believing that it would fall under the control of the Anglican clergy. Yet in spite of his adherence to the voluntary principle, he supported the system of state grants first established in 1833, believing that without financial aid, the schools and colleges of the British and Foreign School Society would be at a serious disadvantage. This led in 1847 to a dispute between Dunn and the Congregational board, many of whose members were opposed to all state aid.

Another quarrel occurred with the Unitarians who accused the British Society of disregarding the principle of non-sectarian biblical instruction. Prominent Unitarians withdrew their subscriptions, forbade the use of the Dunn and Crossley *Lesson Books* in their schools, and took the dispute to court. Dunn was accused of misrepresentation and there were calls for his resignation. Dunn charged the Unitarians with inculcating atheism and of trying to take over the society. In 1855, however, he revealed that he was considering resignation on health grounds and a year later he handed over the secretaryship. He was aware of lukewarm support for his views among some prominent members of the British Society.

After his resignation as secretary, Dunn served on the BFSS committee, heading a protest in August 1861 against the revised code regulating government grants to elementary schools. He brought out a new edition of his teaching manual and published several books on religious topics. The latter, written mainly from a Congregationalist viewpoint, were published in six volumes under the pseudonym Delta. In 1870 he moved from Blackheath to 7 Holland Road, Brighton, where he died from a stroke on 16 March 1878; he was buried at Norwood cemetery in London. Henry Dunn did much to establish the authority of the British and Foreign School Society during the earlier years of its existence.   G. F. BARTLE

Sources Boase, *Mod. Eng. biog.* · G. F. Bartle, 'Henry Dunn and the secretaryship of the British and Foreign School Society', *Journal of Educational Administration and History*, 18 (1986), 13–22 · G. F. Bartle,

A history of Borough Road College (1976) · *CGPLA Eng. & Wales* (1878) · d. cert. · parish records, Notts. Arch. · private information (2004) **Archives** Brunel University, West London Institute, British and Foreign School Society archives **Wealth at death** under £25,000: probate, 3 April 1878, *CGPLA Eng. & Wales*

Dunn, Sir James Hamet, first baronet (1874–1956), financier, was born on 29 October 1874, in Bathurst, New Brunswick, Canada, only child of Robert Dunn (1846–1875), boatbuilder, and his wife, Elizabeth Abrahams (d. 1918), daughter of John Joudrey. He was educated at St Luke's School, Bathurst, and in 1895–8 studied law at Dalhousie University, Halifax. He was called to the bar of Nova Scotia and North-West Territories in 1898 and to the bar of Quebec in 1901. The following year he bought a seat on the Montreal stock exchange where he swiftly made a fortune.

In 1905 Dunn moved to London, where he established the merchant bank of Dunn, Fischer. He was a wily and opportunistic financier, who often puffed his stocks through corrupt journalists and misleading prospectuses. The Brazilian Traction, Light and Power Company (in 1912) was the most prominent of many Canadian-incorporated foreign utility companies which he floated to British investors through tightly controlled syndicates. His successes were checked in 1913 by the disappearance of his partner C. Louis Fischer, leaving large debts.

Dunn turned to commodity trading, and during the 1914–18 war was involved with the British government in securing nickel supplies from Norway. He had previously cultivated the prime minister, H. H. Asquith, lending his Rolls-Royce car and hoping for a baronetcy; this was finally gazetted in 1920, ostensibly in recognition of his Norwegian services, but in reality because of contributions to the Lloyd George political fund. He is depicted in *Sunflower*, a novel of the 1920s by Rebecca West, as Sir Jack Murphy, 'a verminous little shyster' whose baronetcy is scandalous (209).

During the 1920s Dunn worked with a controversial Belgian financier, Alfred Loewenstein, in promoting, by the technique of stock pyramiding, a series of electrical and artificial fibres trusts, notably the Société Internationale d'Énergie Hydro-Électrique (Sidro) and British Celanese. This activity was terminated by Loewenstein's mysterious death in 1928. Dunn continued to underwrite industrial flotations, and together with Sir Hugo Cunliffe-Owen and Lord Trent bought Boot's the chemists from American control in 1933. In 1935 Dunn took charge of the Algoma Steel Corporation in Canada (gaining full control in 1944). In two decades he transformed the company by vertical integration and strong management from a nearly bankrupt concern into Canada's second largest primary steel maker. He also diversified Algoma into iron-ore mining and other lucrative activities. As a result he left an estate in Canada worth nearly C$70 million. His successes with Algoma finally vested him with the semblance of respectability, and in Canada he received honorary degrees from several universities and was made an honorary king's counsel in 1949.

Dunn married, in 1901, Gertrude Paterson (d. 1957), daughter of Herbert Molesworth Price, timber merchant, of Quebec; they had one son and four daughters. Immediately after their divorce in 1926, Dunn married Irene Clarice Douglas (1898–1977), daughter of Henry William Richards, mill owner, and divorced wife of the eleventh marquess of Queensberry; they had one daughter. This marriage was dissolved in 1942, and on 7 June the same year he married his former secretary, Marcia Anastasia (1909–1994) [see Aitken, Marcia Anastasia, under Aitken, William Maxwell], daughter of John Christoforides, and afterwards wife of his friend and biographer Max Aitken, Lord Beaverbrook.

Dunn had a thin build, vivid blue eyes, sharp features, and a mouth like a trap. Implacable in enforcing his own interests, he could be irascible, callous, obdurate, impulsive, and demanding. Sir Robert Bruce Lockhart in 1947 described him as 'the meanest and hardest man in the world' (Diaries, 2.618). A lavish and even charming host with sybaritic tastes, he was a munificent art collector, who commissioned thirteen portraits of himself, including one by Dalí, in which he was portrayed in the character of Caesar Augustus. His foibles (such as his insistence on having his shoelaces ironed) amused his friends. He hated solitude, was a food faddist, hypochondriacal, and prone to neurotic fears. Dunn died of heart failure, on 1 January 1956, at Dayspring, on Passamaquoddy Bay, near St Andrews, New Brunswick, his ashes being buried in the grounds there, under a favourite tree.

RICHARD DAVENPORT-HINES

Sources Lord Beaverbrook [M. Aitken], Courage: the story of Sir James Dunn (1961) · R. West, Sunflower (1986) · The diaries of Sir Robert Bruce Lockhart, ed. K. Young, 2 (1980), 618 · B. Cartland, The isthmus years (1943) · B. Cartland, The years of opportunity (1947) · H. H. Asquith: letters to Venetia Stanley, ed. M. Brock and E. Brock (1982) · My dear Max: the letters of Brendan Bracken to Lord Beaverbrook, 1925–1958, ed. R. Cockett (1990) · G. P. Marchildon, Profits and politics: Beaverbrook and the gilded age of Canadian finance (1997) · A. Chisholm and M. Davie, Beaverbrook: a life (1992) · Lady Dunn, The ballad of a Bathurst boy, 1874–1956 (1956) · The Times (2 Jan 1956) · R. Michie, 'Dunn, Fischer & Co. in the City of London, 1906–14', Business History, 30 (1988), 195–219
Archives NA Canada | HLRO, Beaverbrook MSS
Likenesses H. Mann, oils, 1916 · A. John, oils, 1925–35 · W. Sickert, oils, 1930–39 · G. Brockhurst, oils, 1940 · H. Carr, oils, 1947 · E. Greene, oils, 1947 · S. Dalí, oils, 1948–55 (as Caesar Augustus), repro. in Beaverbrook, Courage, frontispiece · S. Dalí, oils, 1948–55 · A. Jongers, oils
Wealth at death under C$65,825,000: Beaverbrook, Courage

Dunn, John Robert (1833–1895), chief in the Zulu kingdom, was born, it is believed, at Port Alfred, Cape Colony, the son of Robert Newton Dunn, a Scottish emigrant, and his second wife, Ann Biggar. The family moved to Natal, where the young John Dunn lived on the borders of the colonial frontier, making use of his shooting and riding skills to trade and hunt. He traded in the neighbouring Zulu kingdom, and became known to the heir to the Zulu throne, Cetshwayo, the son of King Mpande kaSenzangakhona. In 1858 he moved to the Zulu kingdom to act as the prince's secretary and adviser. In recognition of this,

Dunn was awarded territory in the south-east of the kingdom along the coast between the Thugela and Mhlatuze Rivers, where he set himself up as a Zulu chief. He also traded, hunted, supplied African labour to Natal, and ran guns into Zululand with the assistance of Natal merchant houses. He exploited his transitional status within colonial and African society with ruthless skill. Using the wealth he accumulated to build up his chieftainship within Zululand, he acquired large herds of cattle, built a number of homesteads, and took, to the lasting scandalized fascination of observers, forty-eight wives from the families of his Zulu neighbours. These wives were in addition to Catherine Pierce, the daughter of Robert Dunn's assistant, Frank Pierce, and a Cape Malay woman, whom John Dunn had taken with him to Zululand.

Dunn fled the Zulu kingdom when it was invaded by the British in 1879, and became an intelligence officer in the British forces. After the defeat of the Zulu army and the exile of King Cetshwayo, Dunn was awarded a huge territory in the south of the kingdom. This he attempted to rule with energy and efficiency, thereby incurring the wrath of his erstwhile benefactor and his former Zulu supporters, who saw him as a traitor. His rule there was described by W. R. Ludlow in his Zululand and Cetewayo (1882); Lord Kimberley, the colonial secretary, commented after reading it: 'Dunn has feathered his nest but the stories put about by the Cetewayo party against him are … mostly untrue' (Gladstone, Diaries, 10.316–17). However, in 1883 the British withdrew Dunn's appointment as the dominant chief in the south of the country. Dunn's protests achieved little, and he died an embittered man on 5 August 1895.

JEFF GUY

Sources C. Ballard, John Dunn: the white chief of Zululand (1985) · T. J. R. Botha, 'Dunn, John Robert', DSAB · J. Guy, The destruction of the Zulu kingdom (1979) · Gladstone, Diaries

Dunn, Marcia Anastasia. See Aitken, Marcia Anastasia, Lady Beaverbrook (1909–1994), under Aitken, William Maxwell, first Baron Beaverbrook (1879–1964).

Dunn, Robert (1799–1877), general practitioner and psychologist, about whose early life little is known, studied in London at Guy's and St Thomas's hospitals, and became a licentiate of the Society of Apothecaries in 1825. He was made a member of the Royal College of Surgeons in 1828 and a fellow in 1852, and he was a fellow of the Royal Medical and Chirurgical Society, the Obstetrical Society, the Ethnological Society, and the Medical Society of London. He was also treasurer of the metropolitan branch of the British Medical Association. Dunn practised in Norfolk Street, the Strand, London, first at no. 15 and then at no. 31. From 1863 his practice was called Dunn & Son. Dunn published a large number of medical cases with post-mortem reports before undertaking his psychological works.

Dunn was one of several early and mid-nineteenth-century medical figures attracted to considering psychological issues in relation to physiology. Hearnshaw (1964) identified him as a member of the informal 'school' associated with W. B. Carpenter. His Medical Psychology (1863), reprinted from the British Medical Journal, urged colleagues to address the psychological aspects of disease—both to illuminate the physical bases of psychological functioning and to enhance diagnosis. He drew eclectically on the most diverse authorities and incorporated material from his 'Case of hemiplegia' (*The Lancet*, 1850), and his 'Essay on physiological psychology' (*Journal of Psychological Medicine*, 1858). Dunn's special interests lay in language, hallucinations (and kindred phenomena), and sleep. Numerous case histories relating to these (and to the effects of alcohol) were included in the book. While holding that in this life mental phenomena manifested themselves through the nervous apparatus (especially the brain) Dunn remained a mind–body dualist. He identified three successively developed levels of conscious functioning: sensory, perceptive, and intellectual, each served by a 'distinct nervous organic instrumentality'. His position is transitional between those of Benjamin Brodie and Henry Holland, for example, and the stance to come in the impending wave of evolutionism. Dunn was apparently then unaware of Paul Broca's discovery in 1861 of the speech area of the brain.

While maintaining an interest in speech pathologies ('Loss of Speech', *BMJ*, 1868), Dunn then ventured into ethnology with 'Some observations on the psychological differences which exist among the typical races of mankind' (*Ethnological Transactions*, 1865), and 'Ethnic psychology' (*Journal of the Anthropological Institution*, 1874), largely a recycling of the previous article. While affirming that the genus *Homo* was one, Dunn believed that differences in cerebral organization between the races underlay their psychological differences, and he urged more research into this. Although side-stepping evolution, he accepted a progressive hierarchy from 'negro', via 'Malay', 'American Indian', and 'Mongolian', to 'Caucasian'. These texts exhibit the ethnocentrism and racial stereotyping characteristic of contemporary 'scientific racism' but they also strongly affirm a sense of 'common humanity'. During the American Civil War, Dunn's membership of the Ethnological Society of London identified him with the antislavery camp—against the pro-South, Anthropological Society of London, formed in 1863. Indeed, Dunn cited innate 'African' docility as evidence against fears regarding the consequences of abolition. Rather than reflecting personal racism, Dunn's position stemmed from his uncritical acceptance of physiological accounts of race differences in skull shape, brain size and brain form, which in turn were reinforced by a belief in the broad truth of phrenology.

Dunn's influence is difficult to gauge; his publications were few and his psychological work was soon overshadowed by that of more eminent contemporaries such as Alexander Bain; moreover, his views on racial brain-differences have long been discredited. Dunn, who had at least two sons, died at his address at 31 Norfolk Street, the Strand, London, on 4 November 1877.

GRAHAM RICHARDS

Sources DNB · CGPLA Eng. & Wales (1877) · *London Medical Directory* (1845) · *London and Provincial Medical Directory* (1863) · *BMJ* (10 Nov 1877), 673 · L. S. Hearnshaw, *A short history of British psychology, 1840–1940* (1964) · d. cert.

Archives Wellcome L. | NL Scot., corresp. with George Combe

Likenesses G. B. Black, lithograph, BM

Wealth at death under £12,000: probate, 7 Dec 1877, *CGPLA Eng. & Wales*

Dunn, Samuel (*bap.* 1723, *d.* 1794), teacher of mathematics and navigation, was born in Crediton, Devon, and baptized there on 7 February 1723, the son of John (*d.* 1744) and Alice Dunn. Nothing is known of his own education, which gave him a competence in mathematics, but by the age of nineteen he was keeping his own school and teaching writing, accounts, navigation, and other mathematical sciences. This building was destroyed in the fire which swept through Crediton in August 1743 and Dunn then taught in a school installed in the Old Church House until December 1751, when he went to London.

There Dunn taught in different schools and gave private lessons. He first caught public attention as the inventor of the 'universal planispheres, or terrestrial and celestial globes in plano, an economical method of teaching spherical geometry without the expense of purchasing actual globes'. His book *The Description and Use of the Universal Planispheres* (1759) was the first of a stream of textbooks which provided his students with all aspects of mathematics and navigation, both theoretical and practical. In 1758 Dunn became master of an academy at Ormond House, Paradise Row, Chelsea, where there was a good observatory from which he observed a comet in January 1760 and the transit of Venus in 1761. This and other astronomical news was communicated in his nine letters to the Royal Society, where he was a frequent visitor, though never elected a fellow. He married in 1763 a Mrs Harrison, keeper of a girls' school at Brompton Park, Kensington, but discovered only after the marriage that she was heavily in debt, which then devolved on him. He considered declaring himself bankrupt, but before the matter was resolved she left him.

Dunn continued to live at Brompton Park, reverting to private teaching. In July 1764 he was in Paris, though the length and purpose of his visit is not known. When the *Nautical Almanac* was introduced (for the year 1767) the board of longitude ruled that all ships' masters appointed henceforth had to have a certificate of competence, and until 1771 Dunn was among the teachers authorized to sign these certificates. Dunn was similarly involved with the East India Company as a recognized teacher, and from the 1770s he prepared charts for far eastern waters. In *A New Variation Atlas* (1776), and *A New Epitome of Practical Navigation, or, Guide to the Indian Seas* (1777), dedicated to the company, Dunn introduced an original solution to the double-altitude problem. Where the approximate latitude was known two observations were to be taken of the sun's altitude, and the time elapsed between observations noted; calculations following Dunn's formula then yielded the true latitude. This solution was a remarkable discovery and later formed the basis of the 'trial and error' method for finding longitude. It also led towards position-line navigation. In 1780 he succeeded William Herbert as editor of the *New Directory for the East Indies* and in 1787 the East India Company's hydrographer, Alexander Dalrymple, made plates of his charts available so that Dunn could group and print them for the sixth edition of the *Directory*.

Dunn also sought to improve instruments for navigation and cartography. An angular micrometer which he demonstrated to the Royal Society in May 1761 was made for him by the firm of Heath and Wing in the Strand, and his pantograph, described in *The Theory and Use of the Pantographer* (1774), was made by their successor, Thomas Newman. In 1768 he showed to the board of longitude models of a sextant for taking large angles, for which he was awarded £20. The instrument maker Jesse Ramsden was asked to construct them, with a recommendation that the instrument should be tested by an expedition going to the Arctic regions to observe the 1679 transit of Venus. Dunn himself was invited by the astronomer royal to observe the transit from the Royal Observatory, Greenwich, in the evening of 3 June.

Not all Dunn's proposals to the board of longitude met with approval. His method of finding the longitude of ports and another for drawing magnetic isolines at sea were rejected, for example. His *Theory and Practice of Longitude at Sea* (1786), dedicated to the Company of Merchants, was however ahead of its time. Watches were still rare in his day and the method matured only after his death.

From 1774 Dunn was residing at 6 Clement's Inn, Westminster, and in July 1777 he was at 8 Maiden Lane, Covent Garden, but by September 1780 he was at 1 Boar's Head Court, Fleet Street, where he died in January 1794. He was buried at St Dunstan-in-the-West on 23 January. His bequests, mainly to family members, included a sum to endow a master to teach all aspects of mathematics and navigation to six boys at Bowden Hill School, which was later known as 'Dunn's school'. On 10–14 April 1794 Sothebys sold his books and maps in 1000 lots, many of which were bought by Dalrymple, followed by eighty lots of his instruments, and several hundred of his own books in sheets. GORDON GOODWIN, *rev.* ANITA McCONNELL

Sources C. Cotter, *A history of nautical astronomy* (1968) · D. Howse, *Nevil Maskelyne: the seaman's astronomer* (1989) · *A catalogue of the valuable library and mathematical instruments, &c., of Mr Samuel Dunn* (1794) [sale catalogue, Leigh and Sotheby, London, 10–14 April 1794] · minutes of the Board of Longitude, CUL, RGO 14/2, 5 · Nichols, *Illustrations*, 4.545 · BL, Add. MS 4305, fols. 88–9; Add. MS 28536, fol. 241 · T. W. Venn, 'Crediton als Critton als Kirton and herabouts', 2 vols., 1957, Society of Genealogists, 2.203–4 · will, PRO, PROB 11/1240, sig. 16 · parish register, Devon RO [baptism]

Dunn, Samuel (1798–1882), Free Church Methodist minister and religious journalist, was born at Mevagissey in Cornwall on 13 February 1798. His father, James Dunn, the master of a small trading vessel, met John Wesley in 1768 and became a class leader; with his crew he protected Adam Clarke from the fury of a mob in Guernsey in 1786. James died at Mevagissey on 8 August 1842, aged eighty-eight. Samuel received his education at Truro under Edward Budd, later the editor of the *West Briton*. In 1819 he became a Wesleyan Methodist minister and, after three

years of probation at St Austell, Kingsbridge, and Pembroke, volunteered for service as the first Wesleyan missionary to the Shetland Islands, where he was under the jurisdiction of Adam Clarke. While there he wrote a series of articles describing the Orkney and Shetland islands and kept a journal, not published until 1976. He married Ann Callum, *née* Morrison, in April 1825. He was afterwards stationed at Newcastle, Rochdale, Manchester, Sheffield, Tadcaster, Edinburgh, Camborne, Dudley, Halifax, and Nottingham successively, until his expulsion from the connexion in 1849. Dunn was a prolific writer of hymns, biographies (of James Dixon, 1832; John Fletcher, 1837; and Richard Treffrey, 1842), and polemical works. He wrote against atheism, popery, Socinianism, and Unitarianism, and in defence of Methodism. He was also a contributor to many theological magazines and reviews.

Until 1847 Dunn continued in harmony with the Wesleyan Methodists, but at that date he was accused of having, with James Everett and William Griffith jun., taken part in the publication of the Fly Sheets. These pamphlets advocated reforms in the Wesleyan governing body, reflected critically on the proceedings of the conference and its committees, and complained of the personal ambition of Jabez Bunting and Robert Newton, two of the past presidents of conference. What part the three ministers had taken, if any, in the Fly Sheets has never been discovered as, on being questioned with others on the matter, they declined to reply. In 1849, however, Dunn commenced the publication of a monthly magazine, the *Wesley Banner and Revival Record*, which, following the example set by the Fly Sheets, continuously pointed out the errors of Wesleyan Methodism and suggested reforms. At a conference held at Manchester in 1849 the three ministers were asked to discontinue the *Wesley Banner*, and to give up attacking Methodism. They, however, refused to make any promises and were expelled on 25 July. Their expulsion gave them a wide popularity and many meetings of sympathy with them were held. These expulsions were very damaging to the Wesleyan Methodist Connexion, as between 1850 and 1855 more than 100,000 members were lost, and it was not until 1855 that it began to recover from this disruption. The literature connected with these events is very extensive, and the interest taken in the matter was so general that in a short time 20,000 copies of a small pamphlet entitled *Remarks on the expulsion of the Rev. Messrs. Everett, Dunn, and Griffith. By the Rev. William Horton* were sold. Dunn subsequently led a very peaceful life. For some time he itinerated and preached in the pulpits of various denominations. From 1855 to 1864 he lived at Camborne in Cornwall, where he ministered to the Free Church Methodists, the denomination formed from the schism. He compiled a hymn book, *Hymns for Pastor and People* (1862), for their use. Having written numerous articles in many American publications and serving as a minister of the New York East Conference of the Methodist Episcopal church from 1865 to 1868 he was created a DD of one of the American universities. He retired to England and died at 2 St James's Road, St Mary Usk, Hastings, on 24 January 1882. G. C. BOASE, *rev.* TIM MACQUIBAN

Sources *Samuel Dunn's Shetland and Orkney journal, 1822–1825*, ed. H. R. Bowes (1976) • G. C. Boase, *Collectanea Cornubiensia: a collection of biographical and topographical notes relating to the county of Cornwall* (1890) • R. E. Davies, A. R. George, and G. Rupp, eds., *A history of the Methodist church in Great Britain*, 2 (1978) • N. B. Harmon, ed., *The encyclopedia of world Methodism*, 2 vols. (1974) • *ILN* (15 Sept 1849), 187–8 • *West Briton* (26 Sept 1851), 5 • *CGPLA Eng. & Wales* (1882)
Archives JRL • University of Manchester, diary of Shetland Islands mission circuit
Likenesses attrib. H. Anelay, oils, Methodist Publishing House, London • W. H. Egleton, stipple (after attrib. H. Anelay), NPG • wood-engraving, BM; repro. in *ILN*, 187–8
Wealth at death £3031 13s. 9d.: probate, 25 Feb 1882, *CGPLA Eng. & Wales*

Dunn, William (1770–1849), cotton manufacturer, was born at Gartclash, in the parish of Kirkintilloch, Dunbartonshire, Scotland, in October 1770. The identity of his parents is not known. He was educated partly at the parish school and partly at the neighbouring village of Campsie. Before he was eighteen he was left an orphan, with four brothers and a sister dependent on him for support. Dunn had already shown an aptitude for making mechanical contrivances and, in his first employment, with a cotton spinner named Waddington, at Stockingfield, near Glasgow, he learned iron turning and machine making. Three or four years later he was in Black and Hastie's works at Bridge of Weir, Renfrewshire, from which he went to Pollokshaws, Glasgow, to the factories of John Monteith. About 1800, having acquired a few hundred pounds by the sale of his patrimony of Gartclash, he resolved to start in business for himself, and accordingly opened a manufactory of machines in High John Street, Glasgow. In or about 1802 he bought a small spinning mill in Tobago Street, Calton, Glasgow, and in 1808 he purchased the Duntocher mill, some 7 miles distant from that city.

Under Dunn's auspices Duntocher, which had before hardly deserved the name of a village, became a thriving and populous place. Before he acquired the mill there were fewer than 150 hands employed there; at his death they numbered about 2000. A few years later he purchased from the Faifley Spinning Company the Faifley mill, which stood about a mile distant from the other. In 1813 he became the proprietor of the Dalnotter ironworks, which had been used for slitting and rolling iron and for making implements of husbandry; and after greatly enlarging the two mills he already owned, he was encouraged by the rapid increase of his business to build upon the site of these ironworks the Milton mill, the foundation of which was laid in 1821, and which was destroyed by fire twenty-five years later. Finally, in 1831 the Hardgate mill was built in the same neighbourhood. All these mills, lying near to each other, were exclusively applied to the spinning and weaving of cotton. Dunn became a large purchaser of land in the neighbourhood of his works, and ultimately his estates extended upwards of 2 miles along the banks of the Clyde, and about 3 miles along the banks of the canal. Upon this property, 1200 acres of which were farmed by himself, he employed more than 250 men. The annual wages which he paid in this parish alone totalled

£35,000. Dunn died, apparently unmarried, at Mountblow, Dunbartonshire, on 13 March 1849, leaving property worth £500,000.

GORDON GOODWIN, *rev.* ANITA MCCONNELL

Sources Anderson, *Scot. nat.*, 109–10
Wealth at death £88,004 13s. 8d.: confirmation, 1849, Scotland

Dunne [Donne], **Gabriel** (*c.*1490–1558), abbot of Buckfast, was one of four surviving children of Angel Donne, grocer and alderman of London (*d.* 1506), and therefore belonged to a leading city family. His father's will of 1505 describes Gabriel as a monk and implies that he was still an adolescent, since it provides a sum of £10 to finance his education at a university. He was probably already a member of the Cistercian abbey of Stratford Langthorne, Essex, to which he belonged by 1517, and whence he proceeded to the order's college of St Bernard, Oxford. There he supplicated for the degree of BTh on 26 October 1521, on the ground of having studied logic, philosophy, and theology for twelve years, a course of instruction that may have begun at Stratford. On 28 March 1530 he matriculated at the University of Louvain, perhaps in order to earn a doctorate in theology, but it is not certain that he received such a degree, although the London writer Henry Machyn refers to him as a doctor at the time of his death.

In May 1535, when Dunne was still living in Louvain, the English cleric Henry Phillips succeeded in decoying the Bible translator, William Tyndale, from Antwerp into the hands of the authorities in the Netherlands, an event that led to Tyndale's execution. In the following month Dunne left Louvain to become abbot of the Cistercian abbey of Buckfast, Devon, thanks to the patronage of Thomas Cromwell. These events caused nineteenth-century historians to portray Dunne as Phillips's active confederate in the betrayal of Tyndale, and to interpret his abbacy as a reward for his service, but the evidence to support such conjectures is lacking. Thomas Theobald, who wrote from Antwerp on 31 July 1535 to his godfather Archbishop Cranmer, does indeed say that Phillips and Dunne lived in the same house in Louvain. He also states that Phillips told him that Dunne was his sole confidant in the plot, but that was merely Phillips's assertion. Phillips was hostile to Henry VIII and fearful of Cromwell, whereas Dunne enjoyed Cromwell's favour, making it unlikely that they took part in a joint plot, and Dunne's promotion to Buckfast is as plausibly ascribable to his learning and London connections. He had good relations with Cromwell in later years. In 1535 Cromwell paid him £100, and two years later Dunne sent a present of fish to Cromwell by sea, but it was captured by a Breton privateer. There was eventually a marriage between Dunne's niece Frances Mirfin and Cromwell's nephew Richard Williams, alias Cromwell.

Dunne and his fellow monks surrendered Buckfast Abbey to Henry VIII on 25 February 1539, and he received the generous pension of £120 a year. He subsequently settled in London and pursued a career as a secular priest, becoming a canon of St Paul's Cathedral and prebendary of Mapesbury in 1541; rector of Stepney, Middlesex, in 1544, on the presentation of Richard Williams; and rector of Langtree, Devon, in 1549, on that of his brother-in-law, Sir Thomas Dennys. In the latter year Cranmer appointed him 'keeper of the spiritualities' (the acting head) of the diocese of London, following the deprivation of Edmund Bonner as bishop. His death took place on 5 December 1558, and he was buried three days later before the high altar of St Paul's Cathedral, beneath a tombstone inscribed with eight lines of Latin verse. He died as a man of some property, including the advowson of Grantham church, Lincolnshire, and gave generously to charities in his will, dated 5 February 1558. He bequeathed to his former college of St Bernard, recently refounded as St John's College, such of his books as his executors should approve; forty-five volumes were later delivered to St John's, including works of classical literature and theology. The residue of his goods was willed to provide dowries for poor maidens and support for poor scholars and students, especially those intending to become priests. One of his executors, Henry Harvey, used £120 from this source to found a scholarship at Trinity Hall, Cambridge, and to hold a commemoration on St Nicholas's day in memory of Dunne's death. Dunne's will also made bequests to provide silver plate for the high altar of St Paul's Cathedral, an iron railing to fence off the laity from the sanctuary, and an altar or monument commemorating the Archangel Gabriel's salutation to the Virgin Mary. This suggests that he took a close interest in the restoration of the cathedral to Catholic worship under Mary Tudor, and that he died an adherent of the faith in which he had spent the greater part of his life.

NICHOLAS ORME

Sources Emden, *Oxf.*, 4.179 · will, PRO, PROB 11/15, fols. 103r–104v · will, PRO, PROB 11/42Afol. 122r–v; 143 [Gabriel Dunne], fols. 453r–454r · J. Foxe, *Actes and monuments*, 6th edn, 2 (1610), 983–4 non-mentio [no mention of Dunne implies non-involvement with Tyndale] · *LP Henry VIII*, 8, no. 1151 · W. Dugdale, *The history of St Paul's Cathedral in London*, new edn, ed. H. Ellis (1818), 45 · *The diary of Henry Machyn, citizen and merchant-taylor of London, from AD 1550 to AD 1563*, ed. J. G. Nichols, CS, 42 (1848), 181 · W. H. Stevenson and H. E. Salter, *The early history of St John's College, Oxford*, OHS, new ser., 1 (1939), 122–3 · N. Orme, 'The last abbott of Buckfast', *Reports and Transactions of the Devonshire Association*, 133 (2001), 97–107
Wealth at death fairly well-to-do: will, PRO, PROB 11/143, fols. 453r–454r

Dunne, John William (1875–1949), writer on philosophy, was born in south Africa, the elder son among the three children of General Sir John Hart Dunne KCB of Cartron, co. Roscommon, and his wife, Julia Elizabeth, daughter of William R. Chapman of Whitby, Yorkshire. He was brought up in south Africa, and at the age of six had a serious accident which confined him to bed for three years. He read a great deal as a child and later said that he read Euclid as easily as an adult reads a novel. At seventeen he became a pupil on a farm. After serving with the imperial yeomanry in the Second South African War he became an aeronautical engineer, using his observation of seabirds in flight to design a revolutionary type of monoplane with swept-back wings. The War Office was sufficiently impressed to employ him, with a view to the production of a prototype, in 1906, but the model was not accepted.

Dunne would have been forgotten—except, perhaps, by fly-fishermen, for his first book was a beginners' guide to the art of the dry fly—if *An Experiment with Time* (1927) had not enjoyed an immediate and lasting success. In it he described a succession of his dreams over a period of thirty years which seemed to show glimpses of the future, and provided a theory of time to account for them. Among those who were impressed was H. G. Wells, who found the book 'fantastically interesting'. It was widely praised, even in *Nature*, which might have been sceptical. A suggestion that Dunne threw out caught many a reader's fancy: anybody, he argued, could obtain the same results as he had simply by having a pad and a pencil beside the bed and writing down remembered dreams immediately on waking up.

'Dunne dreams' became common colloquial usage for dreams foreshadowing future experiences. His 'serialism', however, the theory he provided to account for them, failed to convince scientists that it fused with the new physics. Dunne himself went out of his way to insist that his theory was free from any occult taint, but *An Experiment with Time*, revised and expanded in 1934, was to remain in print for over half a century and, ironically, it won the reputation of doing more to convince the general public of the reality of clairvoyance, in the form of precognition, than all the labours of the psychical researchers whom Dunne so mistrusted.

Dunne belonged to 'the military section of Britain's old upper class', as J. B. Priestley, who based *Time and the Conways* (1937) on his interpretation of Dunne's theory, was to recall; 'he looked and behaved like the old regular officer type crossed with a mathematician and an engineer'. He was also 'as far removed from any suggestion of the seer as it was possible to imagine' (Priestley, 99, 244–61).

In 1928 Dunne married Cicely Marion Violet Joan, daughter of Geoffrey Cecil Twistleton-Wykeham-Fiennes, eighteenth Baron Saye and Sele, of Broughton Castle, Banbury, Oxfordshire. They had one son and one daughter. Dunne died on 24 August 1949 in Tracey House Nursing Home, Banbury.

BRIAN INGLIS, rev.

Sources J. B. Priestley, *Man and time* (1964), 99, 244–61 · *The Times* (27 Aug 1949) · *The Times* (29 Aug 1949), 7b · private information (1993) · CGPLA Eng. & Wales (1950) · d. cert.
Archives BL, corresp. with Society of Authors, Add. MS 63237
Wealth at death £6485 3s. 10d.: probate, 25 Feb 1950, CGPLA Eng. & Wales

Dunne, Sir Laurence Rivers (1893–1970), magistrate, was born on 4 October 1893 at 22 Seymour Street, Marylebone, London, the younger son of Arthur Mountjoy Dunne (1859–1947) and his wife, Alice Sidney (1869/70–1945), daughter of Sir John Lambert, general superintendent of the Bengal police's operations for the suppression of thuggee and dacoity, and subsequently police commissioner of Calcutta. Dunne's father was an Irishman who became one of the leading barristers in late nineteenth-century Calcutta; after returning to Britain, he specialized in Indian appeals before the judicial committee of the privy council, and took silk in 1917. Laurence Dunne's elder brother Arthur was killed in action at Hargicourt on 2 July

1917. Dunne himself was educated at Eton College (1906–12) and Magdalen College, Oxford (1912–14; BA, 1921). Among other sporting achievements he won cups for shooting at Eton and was a half-blue in the shooting eight at Oxford. He served in the 60th rifles in Flanders, Salonica, and Trans-Caucasia (1914–19); in 1918 he received a general staff appointment and was gazetted brevet-major. Thrice mentioned in dispatches, he was awarded the MC. On 18 January 1922 Dunne married Armorel (1890–1967), eldest daughter of Colonel Herman Le Roy-Lewis, formerly British military attaché in Paris. Her first marriage in 1911 to the soldier and spy Richard *Meinertzhagen had collapsed during the honeymoon because of her advanced views on sexual fidelity. The Dunnes had a son, Timothy Laurence Leroy Dunne, who was killed in action at Cassino on his twenty-first birthday, 23 May 1944, and a daughter, who predeceased her parents.

Dunne, who was called to the bar by the Inner Temple (1922), was a pupil of J. D. Casswell, the notable criminal defender. This association continued for many years: it was Casswell who led Dunne in the trial of Charlotte Bryant, a Dorset prostitute who was convicted in 1936 on dubious evidence of murdering her husband with arsenic. Dunne amassed a large common-law practice, mainly on the western circuit, and acquired a dominant position at Wiltshire quarter sessions (of which his father was for many years second chairman). He was a sound lawyer who thought clearly and pleaded succinctly. In court his manner was relaxed, civil, but never obsequious. His prose was elegant, terse, and authoritative. A man of conventional good looks, with a soldierly bearing, who was convivial in male company and commanded a store of legal anecdotes, he was popular both on the western circuit and at the Garrick Club. Fly-fishing was his absorbing interest; he seemed to prefer the company of trout to jurors, witnesses, or even judges.

Dunne became a metropolitan magistrate in 1936, and sat at Marylebone until 1941, when he was transferred to Bow Street. Wartime emergencies added to his responsibilities. Bow Street was the sole magistrates' court for cases involving fugitive offenders, children taken abroad, and so on, and thus became responsible for many decisions to intern enemy or suspect aliens. This was difficult work, but it was not in Dunne's nature to hesitate or repine.

Dunne's judgement was displayed at its best in the aftermath of a civilian catastrophe. On 3 March 1943 panic erupted at the air raid shelter in Bethnal Green underground station. As air raid sirens wailed, crowds hurrying into the station were further alarmed by a salvo of rockets fired from a nearby anti-aircraft battery. Their surge into the shelter caused sudden, severe pressure on those already descending the murky stairway into the station. A woman stumbled, and other people fell, with their weight pressing on those below. Within fifteen seconds the stairway was converted into a charnel house of immoveable and interlaced bodies five or six deep. 173 people were suffocated. Outside the station, meanwhile, a disorderly mob of between 150 and 200 became frantic. Dunne, who was asked by Herbert Morrison, the home secretary, to investigate this tragedy, proved characteristically expeditious and decisive; he examined eighty witnesses in little more than a fortnight, and tendered his report by 23 March. Although protesters in the East End demanded a public inquiry, Dunne interviewed witnesses *in camera* so as to minimize public demoralization. He reported on defects in the shelter's structure, lighting, and supervision, and rebuked responsible officials, but concluded that structural faults were subsidiary causes of the catastrophe. 'This disaster was caused by a number of people losing their self-control at a particularly unfortunate place and time', he concluded (PRO, HO 45/25221, Dunne's report, paragraph 62(a); Dunne, *Tragedy*, 60). Morrison's decision to defer the report's publication raised a local outcry, and caused complications when litigation over the accident was launched in 1944. The report was belatedly published in 1945.

As a sequel to the Bethnal Green inquiry Dunne was appointed in December 1951 to inquire into a recent explosion while a petrol tanker was discharging its load at a Bristol garage, in which a dozen people had been killed. His report published in 1952 concluded that the garage's proprietor 'was either abysmally ignorant about the nature and properties of petroleum spirit or utterly and almost inconceivably reckless' (*The Times*, 25 April 1952, 3c).

Previously, in January 1948, it had been announced that Dunne was to succeed Sir Bertrand Watson, the chief metropolitan magistrate, on his retirement in April. When Watson died in February, however, during his lunchtime adjournment at the Garrick Club, Dunne was swiftly installed as his successor at Bow Street. In June 1948 he was knighted, and elected a bencher of the Inner Temple. As chief metropolitan magistrate he was stringent, crisp, and confident in court; criticism from either journalists or appeal courts remained indifferent to him.

This office brought considerable influence. Dunne had been in the same chambers as Rayner Goddard, lord chief justice since 1946, whom he much admired, and rejoiced in the appointment of his friend Sir David Maxwell Fyfe (afterwards Lord Kilmuir) as home secretary in 1951. Like them he was a significant force among the traditionalists who believed in penal retribution. The distemper of dishonesty that spread over Britain during the late 1940s perturbed him. This was the heyday of the 'spiv' supplying the black market and of the 'wide boy' evading austerity measures. The number of indictable offences in Britain had almost doubled from 266,265 in 1937 to 522,684 by 1948. This crime wave Dunne attributed to a breakdown in national discipline, lax personal morality, and weak parenting. He believed not only in the enforcement of law, but in self-control and moral duty. He warned that short prison sentences lacked deterrent power, and opposed the abolition of capital punishment. In a speech (21 March 1950) he called for the reintroduction of birching for juvenile offenders, and urged that the National Health Service's expenditure on spectacles, false teeth, and wigs should be diverted to fund sports clubs and playing fields where urban youths could work off their energy, gain self-respect, and learn sportsmanship (*The Times*, 22 March 1950, 6b).

Dunne submitted a memorandum describing gambling as a growing 'social evil' to the royal commission on betting, lotteries and gaming in 1949. He urged that, 'quite apart from moral and ethical considerations', gambling wasted money and manpower; but he felt that attempts to enforce laws against street betting were futile, and deprecated repressive legislation on the subject. 'It must be to the national benefit to discontinue football pool betting, and to close all dog-tracks, whose only excuse for existence is to provide ... the poorer classes with practically infinite opportunities for betting' (minutes of evidence, 176–7). In oral testimony he described gaming machines as 'bad things, because they encourage juveniles to waste time and money'. Funfairs were similarly 'a pernicious influence' because 'you get a lot of people wasting time there' (ibid., question 2420, 178). It was a core conviction of Dunne's that, as he wrote in 1955, 'the old saying, "Satan finds some mischief yet for idle hands to do", is as true now as when it was first spoken' (PRO, HO 345/7, document CHP/5).

In 1954 Dunne gave robust evidence to the departmental committee on homosexuality and prostitution chaired by John Wolfenden. He opposed any alleviation in the criminal penalties on homosexuality.

> This aberration is on the increase, and ... is admitted by all, save addicts, to be an evil. To countenance homosexual practices in private is playing with fire. Appetites are progressive, and a homosexual sated with practices with adults, without hindrance, will be far more likely to tempt a jaded appetite with youth. A great deal of encouragement is already given to these perverts by unthinking people who affect to find something funny and not reprehensible in their conduct.

He stigmatized West End urinals as 'plague spots', male prostitutes as 'the lowest of the low', and their clients as 'male harpies'. He abominated 'the homosexual community' in London. 'The perverts in mass are even more noisome than singly. They often wear articles of feminine clothing, answer to feminine names, and use the filthiest of language and innuendo.' However, he was 'happy to say that the old unholy traffic between soldiers of the Guards and Household Cavalry and perverts in the Royal Parks' was no longer 'a public scandal'. This was because the ranks no longer wore tight overalls off duty: 'battle dress or khaki serge lacks the aphrodisiac appeal of the old walking out dress' (PRO, HO 345/7, document CHP/5). He was less hostile to 'these funny girls who turn up in the West End, and who throng Piccadilly Circus' (PRO, HO 345/14, Dunne's oral evidence, 4 Oct 1955). 'There will always be a demand for opportunities for fornication, and that demand will create a supply' of prostitutes, he felt. 'It is a marvel to me how many of the almost grotesque figures can succeed in seducing any sane male into physical contact: I suppose that drink and a dark street supply the answer.' Dunne considered that 'ponces' were 'not necessarily malevolent, oppressive or coercive', but deplored that 'undesirables' from the colonies and dominions could not be deported for pimping. 'A very large number of men engaged in exploiting vice over here are of Mediterranean, African or East or West Indian origin', he wrote. 'The position deteriorates from day-to-day with the influx of the multitudes of coloured men now invading this country with a view to permanent residence here' (PRO, HO 345/7, document CHP/5). Dunne urged several home secretaries to repeal the Statute of Westminster and reform citizenship laws so that miscreant British passport holders of Maltese, Caribbean, and other origins could be punished by deportation.

Dunne's grandfather had served in the Bengal police for thirty-four years, and the grandson remained a staunch upholder of the English police force. On 17 November 1955, after reading a *Daily Mail* article on corruption at Savile Row police station, Dunne went on his own initiative to Scotland Yard, where he consulted the commissioner of Metropolitan Police. On the following day, speaking from the bench, he and three other Bow Street colleagues made a widely reported denunciation of the report and affirmed their belief in police probity. This action was widely criticized for compromising the impartiality of his court. Like most members of the bar, Sir George Coldstream of the Lord Chancellor's Department regarded Dunne's statement as 'a most egregious error' (PRO, LCO 2/5728, minute of 21 Nov 1955), but felt personally sympathetic. 'With his "Henry Fielding" background and outlook, one can understand Dunne's point of view' (ibid., Coldstream to Kilmuir, minute of 24 Nov 1955). Sir Frank Newsam of the Home Office advised that 'in view of the impeccable motives which are always attributable to Dunne's actions ... he ought to be let down lightly' (ibid., Coldstream to Kilmuir, 2 Dec 1955). Dunne's friend Kilmuir, by now lord chancellor, issued the gentlest of rebukes.

In addition to his metropolitan duties, Dunne was deputy chairman of Berkshire quarter sessions from 1945, and subsequently chairman (1964–6). He drew on his Berkshire experiences in his evidence to the interdepartmental committee on the business of the criminal courts chaired by Sir Geoffrey Streatfield (1958). His evidence reaffirmed that he regarded 'buggery of any kind ... as a particularly grave crime' (PRO, HO 326/128, memorandum of 6 Nov 1958).

Dunne had six months' sick leave in 1954–5, but after convalescence in New Zealand returned to serve as chief metropolitan magistrate until his retirement on 18 April 1960. He died of heart failure on 30 June 1970 at the Grosvenor Hotel, High Street, Stockbridge, Hampshire. His funeral was at All Saints' Church, South Ascot, on 7 July 1970.   RICHARD DAVENPORT-HINES

Sources *The Times* (2 July 1970) · [L. R. Dunne], *Tragedy at Bethnal Green: report of an inquiry into the accident at Bethnal Green tube shelter* (1999) · PRO, HO 345/7, document CHP/5 · Dunne's oral testimony to Wolfenden committee, 4 Oct 1955, PRO, HO 345/14 · PRO, LCO 2/5728 · *Spectator* (25 Nov 1955), 705 · PRO, HO 45/25221 · R. Davenport-Hines, *Sex, death and punishment* (1990) · 'Royal commission on betting, lotteries and gaming', *Parl. papers* (1950–51), 8.625, Cmnd 8190 [see also minutes of evidence, 17 Nov 1949] · b. cert.

Archives PRO, HO 45/25121, HO 345/7, HO 345/14, HO 326/128 · PRO, LCO 2/5728 · PRO, MH 102/2030
Likenesses photograph, repro. in *The Times*
Wealth at death £467,980: probate, 19 Aug 1970, *CGPLA Eng. & Wales*

Dunne [*married names* Clairmonte, Golding Bright], **Mary Chavelita** [*pseud.* George Egerton] (1859–1945), writer, was born on 14 December 1859 in Melbourne, Australia, the eldest of the six children of Captain John Joseph Dunne (1837–1910) and Isobel George (1833–1875). Her father was descended from a noble Irish family, and her mother was Welsh. Her family moved to Dublin when Dunne was eleven years old. Known as 'Chav', she was close to her father. He had a weakness for gambling, and could not hold down a job: the family was always in debt. Dunne was raised as a Roman Catholic, but became disenchanted by the religious hypocrisy of the Irish priesthood. On her mother's death in 1875 she was sent to school in Germany. She returned to Ireland two years later to look after her brothers and sisters, but in 1884 left for America to find work. Conditions were very hard, and the dreams and real-life stories of the working women she met in boarding houses in New York and London later provided material for many of her fictional characters.

In London in 1887 Mary Dunne became companion to Mrs Whyte-Melville, the wife of Henry Peter Higginson. She began an affair with Higginson and they eloped to Slottnaes Park, Langesund, Norway, where they lived until Higginson's death in 1889. He left her an income of £220 a year, nearly all of which she spent on supporting her family. She learned Norwegian and read many of the new writers, such as Ibsen, Strindberg, and Björnsen, who greatly influenced her own brand of realism. In 1890 she met and fell in love with Knut Pedersen, who became known as the writer Knut Hamsun (1859–1952). He gave her the confidence to write subjectively about the female experience, writing that later earned her much critical praise and controversy. She translated his novel *Sult* as *Hunger* (1899).

In England in 1891 Mary Dunne met Egerton Tertius Clairmonte (*d.* 1901) and, attracted by his adventurous nature, she married him, although he was practically a stranger to her. Originally from Nova Scotia, he had been a gold prospector and an agent for a diamond mine in South Africa. Similar in many ways to her father, he was also hopeless with money. The couple rented a cottage in Millstreet, co. Cork, but she complained to her father that she was starting to vegetate. They returned in 1893 to London, where she wrote six stories in ten days. *Keynotes* (1893), which she dedicated to Pedersen, was an instant hit, selling over 6000 copies. It was her first and biggest success, written under the name of George Egerton, as a compliment, she said, to her mother and her husband. She was primarily a short-story writer and her realistic style and pessimistic tone lent themselves brilliantly to the form. In many ways she anticipated the modern short story. Only a woman, she wrote, could explore 'the *terra incognita* of herself, as she knew herself to be, not as man liked to imagine her—in a word to give herself away, as man had

given himself away in his writings' (Egerton, 57). Although her work was associated with 'new woman' fiction, she was embarrassed by the connection and was opposed to the women's suffrage movement.

As George Egerton, Mary Clairmonte wrote four more volumes of short stories: *Discords* (1894); *Symphonies* (1896); *Fantasias* (1897); and *Flies in Amber* (1905). Her stories also appeared in the aesthetic literary periodical *The Yellow Book*. She had one son, George Clairmonte, born in 1895, who was killed in the First World War. Two years after George's birth her marriage to Clairmonte ended when she discovered he had made a young girl pregnant, but true to her reputation for unconventionality, she offered the girl money and some of George's outgrown clothes for the baby. She applied for divorce in 1900, and Egerton Clairmonte died less than one year later. She travelled to Norway, where she fell in love with a man fifteen years her junior; her collected love letters to him were published as *Rosa Amorosa* in 1901. He rejected her, but within four months of her return to England she accepted a proposal from Reginald Golding Bright (1874?–1941), also fifteen years younger than her, and they were married on 11 July 1901. He was a dull conversationalist, but was ambitious, reliable, and kind. He later became famous as a drama critic and as a theatrical agent for writers such as George Bernard Shaw.

Mary Golding Bright was considered 'very attractive' (May, 129) and a 'brilliant talker', 'small and fragile' with 'strikingly large and luminous eyes' (*The Times*, 13 Aug 1945). She had many admirers, though her wit could often be caustic and she did not enjoy small talk. She suffered from hypochondria, complaining of pains and minor illnesses throughout her life. By the turn of the century her best writing years were already behind her. The public's taste for 'new woman' fiction, which examined gender roles and issues of sexuality, declined after the trial of Oscar Wilde in 1895, and her audience disappeared. The popular demand for short stories also fell, and, as she could not write novels, she attempted to write plays, without much success.

Reginald Golding Bright died in 1941. His business had been hit by the closure of the West End theatres at the beginning of the Second World War and Mary Golding Bright was left with very little money. She sold her furniture and books and moved into a boarding house and then a hotel in Bayswater. After suffering what may have been a mild stroke she moved into a nursing home in Crawley, Sussex, and died there on 12 August 1945.

ALISON CHARLTON

Sources T. de V. White, *A leaf from the 'Yellow Book'* (1958) · J. L. May, *John Lane and the nineties* (1936) · G. Egerton, 'A keynote to "Keynotes"', in J. Gawsworth [T. I. Fytton Armstrong], *Ten contemporaries: notes toward their definitive bibliography* [1933] · K. L. Mix, *A study in yellow: the Yellow Book and its contributors* (1960) · W. V. Harris, 'Egerton: forgotten realist', *Victorian Newsletter* (1968), 31–5 · *The Times* (13 Aug 1945)
Archives NL Ire., corresp. and papers | Boston University, Mugar Memorial Library, Terence de Vere White collection · Princeton University, New Jersey, O'Connell collection

Likenesses E. A. Walton, charcoal and wash drawing, c.1894, NG Ire.; repro. in *Yellow Book*, 5 (April 1895) · photograph, c.1899, repro. in White, *A leaf from the 'Yellow Book'*, frontispiece

Dunnell, Mary (*fl.* 1807–1813), evangelist, was noteworthy as the first female preacher of the camp meeting community, before the establishment of Primitive Methodism. Nothing is known of her background, and she first came to notice in 1807. She had intended to attend the Norton camp meeting (23–5 August) in Staffordshire, but had been diverted to nearby Tunstall to take the superintendent preacher's appointments, in defiance of the Wesleyan Methodist conference resolution (1803) prohibiting women preachers. This diversion was evidently intended to prevent her from attending the camp meeting, as just a few weeks later she was forbidden from entering the same pulpit. John Smith and James Steele, both Tunstall Wesleyans, were so incensed by this that they determined to have a meeting in Smith's kitchen, so that Dunnell could preach there. Hugh Bourne, one of the founders of the emergent Primitive Methodism, obtained a bishop's licence from Lichfield, and preachings were arranged for Friday evenings.

When, after a preaching trip of several weeks in Cheshire and Lancashire, Bourne returned to Bemersley in January 1810 he found that his brother, James, and William Allcock had engaged Dunnell to help in the missionary work in north Staffordshire. He was initially unhappy about this, but eventually became convinced of Dunnell's usefulness. She worked in Bemersley, Norton, and Standley, and preached at the Rumsor camp meeting on 3 June 1810. After her success there the Primitive Methodists were invited into Derbyshire, and arrangements were made for Dunnell to go, with Hugh Bourne following later.

The mission centred around Darley Moor, Osmanton, and Rodsley, and on 30 June Bourne returned to Rumsor, leaving Dunnell to continue the work. When he visited the area again in November 1810 he found the societies doing well, in spite of much persecution. The mission was reinforced by the arrival in February 1811 of James Crawfoot, William Clowes, and James Bourne's wife, together with her servant, Hannah Mountford (who later married James Crawfoot). Dunnell exchanged appointments with William Allcock, and went to Rumsor for a while before returning to the Derbyshire mission. In June 1811, when Hugh Bourne visited the mission again, he found that Dunnell had become subject to visions. She told him that she saw in a vision that Clowes and Allcock had fallen away, and Bourne, very upset, left immediately to go to them in Staffordshire. It is implied that she acted thus in order to get Bourne away from the Derbyshire mission so that she could claim it for herself. At first the people in the Derbyshire mission were unaware that Dunnell was separating them from the Primitive Methodists, and that they were regarded by outsiders as 'Mrs Dunnell's people', but by October 1811 there had been complaints about Dunnell, and declarations that the members of the Derbyshire mission had no wish to be separated from the camp meeting community. Hugh Bourne was called upon to put

the record straight, and was distressed to find that his confidence had been misplaced.

By the end of 1811 Bourne had become concerned about Dunnell's personal life, and made efforts to check the marriage registers relating to her at Macclesfield and Derby, by which he discovered that 'now she appears to have three husbands living at once!' (Walford, 346). The societies were very annoyed with him for exposing Dunnell in order to extricate them from her clutches, and he left the mission for a time. Recovery was slow, but in March 1813 he recorded that membership in Boyleston, Derbyshire, had risen to thirty. Nothing further is heard of Dunnell in Primitive Methodist, or indeed any other, circles. For a brief while she was a highly successful, if erratic, figure in popular revivalism.

E. DOROTHY GRAHAM

Sources J. Walford, *Life and labours of … Hugh Bourne*, 2 vols. (1855) · H. B. Kendall, *The origin and history of the Primitive Methodist church*, 1 [n.d., c.1906] · E. D. Graham, *Chosen by God: a list of the female travelling preachers of early Primitive Methodism* (1989) · E. D. Graham, 'Chosen by God: the female itinerants of early Primitive Methodism', PhD diss., U. Birm., 1987
Archives JRL, Methodist Archives and Research Centre, Bourne MSS

Dunnett, Sir Alastair MacTavish (1908–1998), journalist and newspaper editor, was born on 26 December 1908 at 1 Overton Terrace, Kilmacolm, Renfrewshire. He was the second of three children of David Sinclair Dunnett (1877–1958), a baker and later an insurance agent, and Isabella (1881–1956), daughter of Alexander MacTavish, a master mariner from Loch Fyne, Argyll. The Dunnett family was of Caithness stock, but David Dunnett came south to Glasgow to find work. He served an apprenticeship in the bakery trade before emigrating briefly to America with his wife and first son, George, in the hope of finding a job in the hotel trade in Denver. When this failed to materialize, he returned in time for his second son, Alastair, to be born in Scotland. They had one other child, a daughter, Doris.

Alastair Dunnett was educated at Overnewton public school and Hillhead high school in Glasgow, finishing his formal education at fifteen. The family was not well off, and Dunnett paid his own fees for five years at Hillhead through winning bursaries. His early childhood was governed by regular attendance at church and by strict discipline at home. In his autobiography, *Among Friends* (1984), he recalled the punishment he and his brother regularly received:

> Both parents hammered and pounded us frequently with hands and fists and belts. This never seemed to be for grave sins like cheek or disobedience. It was unknown for us to attempt such defiance. We were punished for mistakes and accidents.

However, in the same memoir he also spoke warmly of his father, who had never fully recovered from injuries sustained in the Ibrox football stadium disaster of 1901, but who went on to take spare-time classes for students of the bakery trade, studied languages, and became a practised public speaker and debater. From his mother, a Gaelic speaker, Dunnett acquired an encyclopaedic knowledge of Gaelic songs. An inveterate walker and climber, he came to know the highlands of Scotland intimately.

Dunnett's ambition had always been to go into journalism, but his first job, in 1925, was with the Commercial Bank of Scotland, where he qualified as a member of the Institute of Bankers, winning the institute's annual essay competition on the subject 'The art of investment'. Although he impressed the bank's general manager John Erskine, later Lord Erskine of Rerrick, the last governor of Northern Ireland, and was promoted to the head office in Edinburgh, he left in 1933 to join his lifelong friend Seumas Adam, with whom he founded a weekly magazine for boys called *The Claymore*. Its aim was to reflect Scotland as 'the land of adventure' and it was full of accounts of the outdoor life, which Dunnett himself, as a former boy scout, relished. The publication folded after a year, and Dunnett and Adam decided to create their own adventure by embarking on a journey round the Hebrides in two collapsible canvas canoes, later described in his book *Quest by Canoe* (1950). In 1935 he joined the *Glasgow Weekly Herald* as a feature writer, and the following year produced the northern edition of the Glasgow daily newspaper, *The Bulletin*, before joining the *Daily Record* as art editor.

During the war Dunnett was seconded as chief press officer to the influential secretary of state for Scotland, Tom Johnston, whom he later described as 'the greatest man I have ever known', and from whom he acquired a vision for a resourceful, self-sufficient, and modernizing Scotland. On 17 September 1946 he married Dorothy Halliday (1923–2001), who was working on the staff of the Scottish Office: a promising singer and portrait painter, she later took up writing, and, as Dorothy Dunnett, became a successful and prolific author of historical fiction. They had two sons, Ninian and Mungo. That same year Dunnett was asked to return to edit *The Record*, which he did for nine years, assembling a lively team of journalists and photographers and establishing its position as Scotland's leading popular newspaper. In 1956 he was invited by the Canadian media tycoon Roy Thomson, who had recently acquired *The Scotsman*, to become its editor. He ran it for sixteen years, increasing its circulation from 54,000 to nearly 80,000 and transforming it into a paper for the modern era. In 1959 it was named the best designed newspaper in Britain. He put news instead of advertisements on the front page, began a Saturday section, and recruited an eclectic group of writers and reporters who made their mark far beyond the borders of Scotland. He believed that the editor should get out and about, and rarely spoke to fewer than forty meetings a year. As a passionate Scot himself, with an intimate knowledge of the country, he committed the paper to campaigning for the Scottish interest, whether promoting the arts, tourism, business, or industry. This meant, perhaps inevitably, that *The Scotsman* was not, under his editorship, an investigative paper that made a practice of challenging Scottish institutions, but it did allow for the publication of a wide range of opinions, particularly on its letters page, which became one of the liveliest and most provocative in any British newspaper. He was approached three times to edit

national newspapers in London, but preferred to stay with *The Scotsman*. As he wrote once, 'If we don't speak for Scotland, nobody will' (*Among Friends*, 149).

Dunnett believed strongly in the notion of a separate government for Scotland during a period when this must have seemed a distant dream. At times he seemed to veer towards support for outright independence, but in the end he stuck with the idea of a united kingdom, preferring the vision of a federalist Britain, with each country represented by its own parliament. He described his ideal as 'a Scotland engaged in a new and rich partnership, on equal terms again, doing the best for ourselves here at home and setting free the abounding talents and the spirit of the Scot in his own place' (*Among Friends*, 227). He lived to see the referendum of 1997, which ushered in the new Scottish parliament he had championed for so long.

In 1962 Dunnett was asked to become managing director of The Scotsman Publications, a job he combined with his editorship for eight years; he was succeeded by his deputy, Eric Mackay, in 1972. In 1975 he was invited by Lord Thomson to become chairman of Thomson Scottish Petroleum, and he played a key role in helping to establish the oil terminal at Flotta in Orkney. He was governor of the Pitlochry Festival Theatre (1958–84); a member of the Scottish Tourist Board (1956–69), the Press Council (1959–62), the National Trust for Scotland (1962–9), the council of the Commonwealth Press Union (1964–78), the court of Edinburgh University (1964–6), and the Edinburgh Festival Council (1967–80); and a director of Scottish Television (1975–9). He was made an honorary LLD by Strathclyde University, and knighted in 1995. In addition to his autobiography he wrote two plays which were produced in Glasgow and London, and four works of fiction. His books on Scotland included *Land of Scotch* (1953), *The Donaldson Line* (1960), and *The Scottish Highlands* (1988).

Dunnett died in Liberton Hospital, Edinburgh on 2 September 1998, aged eighty-nine. After a funeral service at Canongate Kirk, Edinburgh, he was cremated at Warriston crematorium.   MAGNUS LINKLATER

Sources A. Dunnett, *Among friends* (1984) · *The Scotsman* (3 Sept 1998) · *The Scotsman* (8 Sept 1998) · *The Independent* (4 Sept 1998) · *The Times* (3 Sept 1998) · WW (1998) · *The glorious privilege: the history of the Scotsman* (1967) · *Daily Telegraph* (4 Sept 1998) · b. cert. · m. cert. · d. cert. · personal knowledge (2004) · private information (2004)
Archives NL Scot., corresp. and papers
Likenesses photograph, repro. in *The Scotsman* · photograph, repro. in *The Independent* · photograph, repro. in *The Times* · photographs, The Scotsman Publications Ltd

Dunnett, Sir (Ludovic) James [Ned] **(1914–1997)**, civil servant, was born in India on 12 February 1914, the second son and second of the four children of Sir James Macdonald Dunnett (1877–1953) of the Indian Civil Service, and his wife, Annie (d. 1951), youngest daughter of William Sangster. His father had a distinguished career in India, and was reforms commissioner of the government of India from 1930 to 1936. Ned Dunnett, as he was known, spent much of his youth with two aunts in Edinburgh. He attended Edinburgh Academy from 1920 to 1932. He

Sir (Ludovic) James Dunnett (1914–1997), by Elliott & Fry, 1951

proved a distinguished pupil both academically and ath-letically. He was dux of the school in his last year and excelled at rugby. From the academy he went to University College, Oxford, where he gained a second class in clas-sical moderations in 1934 and a second in Greats in 1936.

In 1936 Dunnett passed well up the list into the adminis-trative class of the home civil service and joined the Air Ministry. A year later he became private secretary to Sir Arthur Street, permanent under-secretary of state throughout the Second World War. Dunnett spent seven years as private secretary. Street had a tremendous cap-acity for hard work and was a demanding master as well as an exemplar, from whom Dunnett learned much. On 27 August 1943 Dunnett married Olga Adair (1909/10–1980), daughter of Samuel Adair, civil servant. There were no children of the marriage.

In 1945 Dunnett moved to the Ministry of Civil Avi-ation—a new department. He was promoted to under-secretary at thirty-four, and at thirty-nine became a dep-uty secretary in the Ministry of Supply. In the first minis-try he was deeply involved in the rapid expansion of international civil aviation. When he moved on, his pri-mary responsibility was for the research, development, and the procurement of weapons for the separate service ministries. This was a period of steeply rising costs, and the service ministries were generally hostile to the separ-ate Ministry of Supply. He was appointed CMG in 1948 and CB in 1957.

In 1959 Dunnett became permanent secretary of the Ministry of Transport, with the extrovert Ernest Marples

as his minister, trying to solve Britain's increasing traffic problems and deal with the diminishing British merchant fleet. He was promoted KCB in 1960. In 1962 he moved to the Ministry of Labour. Incomes policy and the need to improve industrial relations were major national issues. Earlier in his career Dunnett had established good rela-tions with many industrial and trade union leaders. He was a breath of fresh air in the Ministry of Labour, which too often in the past had contented itself by accepting solutions agreed upon by unions and employers. Dunnett took a more interventionist view. During his term some major changes were enacted covering contracts of employment, the training board system, and redundancy payments. He retained a lifelong interest in industrial relations.

Dunnett was a natural choice to become permanent under-secretary of state for defence in 1966. The three ser-vice departments had by then become constitutionally one, under one secretary of state. Nevertheless, the change remained more theoretical than practical. Dunnett wished to produce an organization that would work effectively on defence as a whole rather than on indi-vidual services. To bring this about he set up the headquar-ters organization committee. Old attitudes and loyalties change slowly and die hard, and his success was limited. Moreover, Britain was lurching from one economic crisis to another and defence reviews and cuts were the order of the day. Inter-service rivalry was intense and there were difficult relations with some allies, not least when eco-nomic factors forced a decision to withdraw from east of Suez. To this was added Dunnett's appointment to the Ful-ton committee, set up in February 1966 to review the civil service. Reporting in June 1968, the committee made his workload virtually impossible. Moreover, he did not enjoy a happy home life and his consumption of alcohol was high. Dunnett had privately hoped to become permanent secretary of the newly created civil service department and head of the home civil service. It was not to be. Never-theless, he did produce a more coherent Ministry of Defence before he retired in 1974, and from 1972 the pro-curement executive brought together the research, devel-opment, and procurement functions for all three services. He was promoted GCB in 1969.

Dunnett was a permanent secretary for fifteen years in three different departments. Although he was a shy man, on occasion appearing awkward and ill at ease, many who worked for him stood in considerable awe of him. He had a formidable presence, and was good at asking penetrat-ing questions and at synthesizing the ideas of others. His instincts and actions consistently favoured reorganiza-tion and change. He did not suffer fools gladly and saw himself as a manager. He enjoyed watching both rugby and football and was a very good golfer. He knew many people outside the civil service, not least trade union and business leaders.

Dunnett was a visiting fellow of Nuffield College, Oxford, from 1964 to 1972. He was an active member of the Social Science Research Council from 1977 to 1982; chair-man of the International Maritime Industries Forum from

1976 to 1979; and president of the Institute of Manpower Studies from 1977 to 1988. He was a trustee of the Charities Aid Foundation from 1974 to 1988. In his later years his eyesight began to fail him, which he found frustrating. His first wife having died in 1980, on 24 March 1984 he married Clarisse, Lady Grover, widow of Sir Anthony Charles Grover, chairman of Lloyd's register of shipping (1963–73), and daughter of Bëla Feher, banker. His second marriage was happy, and thanks to his wife he moved in more artistic circles. He died in London of heart failure at St Mary's Hospital, Praed Street, on 30 December 1997, and his remains were cremated on 9 January 1998. He was survived by his wife, Clarisse.   FRANK COOPER

Sources *The Times* (6 Jan 1998) · *The Scotsman* (13 July 1998) · Lord Hunt of Tanworth, address, Westminster Abbey, 23 March 1998 · *WWW* · Burke, *Peerage* · personal knowledge (2004) · private information (2004) · m. cert. [Olga Adair] · m. cert. [Clarisse, Lady Grover] · d. cert.
Archives King's Lond., Liddell Hart C.
Likenesses Elliott & Fry, photograph, 1951, NPG [*see illus.*] · photograph, repro. in *The Times* · photographs, Gov. Art Coll.
Wealth at death under £180,000: probate, 10 Feb 1998, *CGPLA Eng. & Wales*

Dunning, John, first Baron Ashburton (1731–1783), barrister and politician, was born at Ashburton, Devon, on 18 October 1731, the second but only surviving son of John Dunning (1699/1700–1780), an attorney from Ashburton, and his wife, Agnes Judsham. He was educated at the local grammar school before entering his father's office. Dunning retained throughout his life a strong Devon accent and an affection for his native county. He was admitted to the Middle Temple in May 1752, where he associated with Lloyd Kenyon and John Horne Tooke. Called to the bar in July 1756, he practised on the western circuit, at first without great success. His earnings for 1757 were reported as 13 guineas, but by 1761 this sum had risen to £184 15s. 0d. At first he concentrated on disputed election returns, which guaranteed a modest income at every general election, and before the election of 1768 he told Kenyon that he had fifty-three retainers. However, by the 1770s he could ask £300 for an appearance.

Dunning's breakthrough is attributed, in Holliday's *Life of Lord Mansfield*, to John Glynn being taken ill and handing over his cases to Dunning. But Dunning's eventual success was always very probable, despite his own persistent ill health and bronchial trouble, since he was hardworking and gifted. In 1762 he drew up a defence of the East India Company in its dispute with the Dutch East India Company, and in 1764 he was credited with *A Letter to Proprietors of East India Stock on the Subject of Lord Clive's Jaghire*. Dunning's involvement with East Indian affairs brought him into contact with Lord Shelburne, with whom he remained on terms of close friendship and political collaboration for the rest of his life. Horace Walpole believed that Dunning was also the author of *An Inquiry into the Doctrine Concerning Libels, Warrants etc.*, which attracted much attention in 1764. Though Dunning's authorship is doubtful, Walpole praised it as 'the finest piece written for liberty since Lord Somers', adding 'said to be written by one Dunning, a lawyer lately started up, who

John Dunning, first Baron Ashburton (1731–1783), by Francesco Bartolozzi, pubd 1790 (after Sir Joshua Reynolds, 1782)

makes a great noise' (Walpole, *Corr.*, 38.474). Dunning also took part with Glynn in the countless legal actions arising out of the Wilkes case in 1763. In *Leach* v. *Money* in 1765 he won a triumph over Charles Yorke, obtaining for Dryden Leach confirmation of £400 damages against John Money and two other government messengers for trespass and wrongful imprisonment in their hunt for no. 45 of the *North Briton*. The same year he was offered a seat in parliament by the Rockingham administration, and he wrote to Shelburne that 'Your Lordship's wishes will determine mine' (Drummond, 367). Shelburne was cautiously encouraging, but nothing came of it, perhaps because Dunning doubted the stability of the ministry, perhaps because he did not wish to jeopardize the very considerable earnings he was now making in the courts. But the following year he was appointed recorder of Bristol, a post he held for the rest of his life.

In the event, Dunning's entry into the Commons was not long postponed. The marquess of Rockingham's ministry was replaced by one headed by the duke of Grafton, with Lord Chatham as the driving force and Shelburne as a secretary of state. In January 1768, when the solicitor-general, Edward Willes, was appointed a judge of king's bench, Dunning was brought in to replace him. The parliament had nearly run its course and Shelburne arranged for Dunning to be returned, without opposition, for Calne at the general election. In other respects the timing was awkward for Dunning. The ministry was already in poor shape, with Chatham out of action with a mysterious illness and Shelburne at odds with his colleagues. Moreover the Wilkes affair, in which Dunning had taken so prominent a part, was about to reignite when that irrepressible man was returned to parliament for Middlesex at the general election. The question whether Wilkes should be expelled from the Commons became the most pressing issue facing the government, and was one on which Dunning differed from most of his colleagues, save Lord Chancellor Camden.

These considerations cast a shadow over Dunning's début in the house. He attended a meeting of ministers to decide what action should be taken against Wilkes and was presumably uneasy at the decision to recommend expulsion. In autumn 1768, before the new parliament met, his position worsened because first Chatham and then Shelburne resigned. Dunning discussed his own position with Isaac Barré, Shelburne's leading spokesman in the lower house, but was persuaded by Camden to continue. In November 1768, when the house met, he intervened to defend Camden from attack by Edmund Burke and George Grenville, but his silence over Wilkes put him at a great disadvantage. Richard Rigby reported to Bedford that he had performed 'not with such abilities as I think promise to make him so great a figure in the House as he does at the bar' (Drummond) and Horace Walpole agreed that 'his fame did not rise in proportion to the celebrity he had attained at the bar' (Walpole, *Memoirs*, 3.145). His interventions during 1769 were comparatively few and left his colleagues, particularly Lord North, complaining that their solicitor-general did not pull his weight. It was a relief when, in January 1770, Camden resigned and Dunning could join him by moving into opposition; he spoke against the government in the debate of 9 January 1770.

Dunning had not enjoyed his brief spell in office and confided to Lord Kenyon that 'he did not know whether he should ever take employment again' (Brown, 288). But he was a useful recruit to opposition, and on 19 March 1770 he defended the London petitioners in a long speech, described by the reporter as 'one of the finest pieces of argument and eloquence ever heard' (Cobbett, *Parl. hist.*, 16, 1770, 898). His reward was the freedom of the City of London, presented in a gold box. Despite another protracted bout of ill health in 1772, when his life was despaired of, he spoke regularly in the Commons and could take care of himself. Burke, who praised Dunning's performance time after time, noted in February 1771 that he had given 'a good dressing' to a group of macaronies intent on baiting him (*Correspondence*, 2.199). He was a persistent critic of the ministry's policy towards America: in the set-piece debate of 2 May 1774 on American policy, Dunning led for the opposition in a two-hour speech, condemning the bill to suspend the government of Massachusetts Bay as part of 'a system of tyranny'; he later denounced the Quebec Bill as 'destructive of every principle of freedom' (Cobbett, *Parl. hist.*, 17, 1771–4, 1300, 1359). He was deeply committed to religious liberty, calling the need to subscribe to the Thirty-Nine Articles 'palpably ridiculous' (ibid., 294), and in 1778 he seconded Savile's bill for concessions to Catholics, believing the penal laws

'a disgrace to humanity' (ibid., 19, 1777–8, 1140). His language was often forthright, and sometimes extreme. In spring 1775 he insisted that the colonists were not in a state of rebellion and denounced North's conciliation proposals as 'futile and treacherous' (ibid., 18, 1774–7, 338); in December 1775 he insisted that the American Prohibitory Bill was making war 'on those devoted people' (ibid., 1032). In November 1775 he warned the house that the militia could become 'a monster' (ibid., 848), employed to crush critics of the government at home, and later he drew a lurid picture of England cowed by French Canadians, Russian and German mercenaries, and Irish papists.

A series of high-profile legal cases also kept Dunning's name before the public. In 1769 he was successful in the Douglas case; in 1772 he took part in the Somerset case, on the losing side; in 1775 he helped to prosecute the duchess of Kingston for bigamy; in 1777 he advised Horne Tooke, accused of seditious libel; and in 1779 he represented Admiral Keppel, a whig hero, in his quasi-political court martial. The trial of the duchess was attended by most of the fashionable world. Horace Walpole thought Dunning had been very severe on the defendant; Boswell admired his 'shrewdness and vivacity' (*Boswell: The Ominous Years, 1774–1776*, ed. C. Ryskamp and F. A. Pottle, 1963, 339); and Hannah More, in a letter to her sister, left a graphic description of Dunning in action: 'Dunning's manner is insufferably bad, coughing and spitting at every three words, but his sense and his expression pointed to the last degree' (H. More, *Letters*, ed. R. B. Johnson, 1925, 42). Despite his disadvantages, which included an ungainly figure, he was imposing. Chatham, introduced to him in December 1770, found him 'another being from any I have known of the profession ... he is the law itself' (*Correspondence of William Pitt*, 4.41).

The disasters of the American war slowly brought the opposition back into play. In spring 1778 there were negotiations for a government of national unity, to include Chatham and Shelburne, with Dunning pencilled in for attorney-general. When the negotiations foundered, North still hoped to acquire Dunning. But he was unlikely to move without Shelburne, and North's majorities began to shrink. Dunning became involved in the association campaign for economical reform in the winter of 1779–80, which gave the opposition fresh heart. On 14 February 1780 Barré carried a motion for a committee of accounts, which North did not resist, and a week later his call for a list of pensions, which Dunning strongly supported, was lost by only two votes, by 188 to 186. Dunning took the opportunity to declare his own disinterestedness: 'he had no wish for any share in the salvage' (Cobbett, *Parl. hist.*, 21, 1780–81, 90). On 6 April 1780 Dunning had the greatest triumph of his political career when he carried by 233 votes to 215 his famous resolution 'that the influence of the crown has increased, is increasing and ought to be diminished' (ibid., 347). He followed it with a second resolution that the house was competent to investigate and remedy abuses. After a moment of panic, North rallied strongly. A follow-up resolution on 10 April, identifying thirteen places to be made incompatible with a seat in the house, was carried by only two votes, and the king, monitoring events from above, noted that, had five government supporters not arrived late, 'the strange resolution would have been rejected' (*Correspondence of George III*, 5.41–2). Their support seeping away, Dunning and his allies made a false move. On 24 April he asked the Commons to petition the king not to dissolve parliament before grievances had been redressed. His opponents retorted that this undermined the royal prerogative, and he went down to defeat by 254 votes to 203, much to the king's satisfaction. Dunning told the house, with some petulance, that he would give himself no more trouble in the matter.

In fact, Dunning soon recovered his nerve, and he continued to work closely with the association. But the Gordon riots in June 1780 gave a stay of execution to North's ministry. On 31 March 1780, in the midst of this excitement, Dunning married, at the age of forty-eight. His wife, Elizabeth (1744–1809), the daughter of John Baring and Elizabeth Vowler, was a Devon woman and the sister of John Baring (1730–1816), a banker and MP for Exeter. Dunning carried his new brother-in-law over at once into the ranks of opposition: 'Mr Baring was a friend', wrote John Robinson, the government's whip, mournfully, 'until Mr Dunning married his sister' (Drummond).

When North at last resigned in March 1782 it was not easy to know how to reward Dunning. A newly married man, with one young son and another on its way, in declining health and anxious to retain his lucrative practice, he did not want government business: 'I have a perfect dread of office of any sort', he wrote to Shelburne (*Life*, ed. Fitzmaurice, 2.134–5). His obvious line of advance was the lord chancellorship, but Rockingham was committed to obtaining it for Sir Fletcher Norton, a former speaker, and rather than strain the fragile unity of the victors the post went to the existing holder, Lord Thurlow. An alternative was to promote Dunning to the chief justiceship of king's bench, but Lord Mansfield showed no hurry to retire. In April 1782 Dunning was raised to the peerage as Baron Ashburton, taking his title from his native town, and became chancellor of the duchy of Lancaster, which gave him some but not overwhelming business in the Palatinate court. As compensation for his loss of earnings, he took a pension of £4000 per annum, to the scorn of his political opponents, who noted his change of heart from the austerity of his views in opposition. A member of the inner cabinet, he worked closely with Shelburne, staying with him after the ministerial split which followed Rockingham's death. He became something of a favourite with the king and was employed in a number of political negotiations. In 1783 he advised George III not to abdicate but to accept the Fox–North coalition for the time being. Dunning's health was failing and his eyesight deteriorating. He went out of office when Shelburne resigned in the spring of 1783 and by the autumn was a dying man. Nathaniel Wraxall recorded that in July 1783, going home to Devon, he stayed at an inn at Bagshot, where he found his old legal and political adversary James Wallace in no better shape: 'they were carried into the same apartment, laid down on two sofas as nearly opposite, and remained together for a long time in conversation' (*Historical and Posthumous Memoirs*, 3.130). Dunning died on 18 August 1783 at the age of fifty-one at Exmouth and was buried in the parish church at Ashburton. He was succeeded by his second and only surviving son, Richard Barré Dunning (1782–1823).

In the event, the man confidently identified by Chatham and many others as a future lord chancellor failed to attain such high office. But of Dunning's great distinction as a lawyer there is no doubt. The obituary in the *Gentleman's Magazine* referred, not purely conventionally, to his 'amazing powers' (*GM*, 1st ser., 53/2, 1783, 717). Shelburne wrote that 'all parties allowed him to be at the head of the bar … The only doubt was whether he excelled most at equity or common law. There was none as to anybody's coming up to him in either' (*Life*, ed. Fitzmaurice, 3.453–8).   JOHN CANNON

Sources M. M. Drummond, 'Baring, John', HoP, *Commons, 1754–90* · Cobbett, *Parl. hist.*, vols. 16–19, 21 · *Life of William, earl of Shelburne … with extracts from his papers and correspondence*, ed. E. G. P. Fitzmaurice, 3 vols. (1875–6) · GEC, *Peerage* · *The historical and the posthumous memoirs of Sir Nathaniel William Wraxall, 1772–1784*, ed. H. B. Wheatley, 5 vols. (1884) · *Correspondence of William Pitt, earl of Chatham*, ed. W. S. Taylor and J. H. Pringle, 4 vols. (1838–40) · *The correspondence of King George the Third from 1760 to December 1783*, ed. J. Fortescue, 6 vols. (1927–8) · Walpole, *Corr.* · *The correspondence of Edmund Burke*, ed. T. W. Copeland and others, 10 vols. (1958–78) · P. Brown, *The Chathamites* (1967) · H. Walpole, *Memoirs of the reign of King George the Third*, ed. G. F. R. Barker, 4 vols. (1894) · *The Grenville papers: being the correspondence of Richard Grenville … and … George Grenville*, ed. W. J. Smith, 4 vols. (1852–3) · J. Burrow, *Reports of cases*, 5 vols. (1771–80), vol. 3 · Holdsworth, *Eng. law* · G. T. Kenyon, *Life of Lord Justice Kenyon* (1873) · *Autobiography and political correspondence of Augustus Henry, third duke of Grafton*, ed. W. R. Anson (1898) · *GM*, 1st ser., 53 (1783), 717–18 · R. Gore Brown, *Chancellor Thurlow: life and times of an eighteenth-century lawyer* (1953) · C. Wyvill, ed., *Political papers*, 6 vols. [1794–1804] · H. Roscoe, *Lives of eminent lawyers* (1830) · H. Walpole, *Journal of the reign of King George the Third*, ed. Dr Doran, 2 vols. (1859) · H. Cavendish, *Diaries of the unpublished parliament, 1768–74*, 2 vols. (1841) · Boswell, *Life* · *The works of Jeremy Bentham*, ed. J. Bowring, 11 vols. (1838–43); repr. (1962) · J. Holliday, *Life of Lord Mansfield* (1797) · *The autobiography and correspondence of Mary Granville, Mrs Delany*, ed. Lady Llanover, 1st ser., 3 vols. (1861); 2nd ser., 3 vols. (1862) · *The manuscripts of Lord Kenyon*, HMC, 35 (1894) · J. Brooke, *The Chatham administration* (1956) · J. Parkes and H. Merivale, *Memoirs of Sir Philip Francis*, 2 vols. (1867) · *Works of Sir William Jones*, ed. A. M. Jones, 6 vols. (1799) · J. Norris, *Shelburne and reform* (1963) · A. Stephens, *Memoir of John Horne Tooke*, 2 vols. (1813) · State trials

Archives NRA, priv. coll., letters to Lord Shelburne · V&A NAL, letters to Barré

Likenesses studio of Reynolds, oils, 1768–73, NPG · Reynolds, oils, 1774, NPG · C. Bretherton junior, caricature, 1782, BM · J. Downman, chalk drawing, 1782, BM · double portrait, 1782 (with his sister or wife), priv. coll. · J. Reynolds, double portrait, oils, c.1782–1783 (with Lady Ashburton), Tate collection · J. Sayers, caricature, etching, 1783, BM, NPG · Reynolds, group portrait, 1788–9, priv. coll. · F. Bartolozzi, stipple, pubd 1790 (after J. Reynolds, 1782), AM Oxf., BM, NPG [*see illus.*] · J. Ward, group portrait, mezzotint (after J. Reynolds), BM · portraits, repro. in M. D. George, ed., *Catalogue of political and personal satires*, 5: *1771–1783* (1935)

Dunning, Thomas Joseph (1799–1873), trade unionist, was born in London in 1799, but nothing else is known about his early life. He learned the trade of bookbinder, a small trade that participated in the great nineteenth-century expansion of printing and publishing and which, despite the growth of mass production and the mechanization of some stages of production, remained a skilled occupation.

In 1820 Dunning joined the London Consolidated Society of Journeymen Bookbinders, and he quickly became a leading member of lodge no. 5. Elected to the society's committee in the late 1830s, he came to the fore in the great industrial dispute in 1839, writing a number of the society's addresses on the struggle. His desire for an agreement with the employers was opposed by the majority, however, and he resigned from the committee, only to become one of the negotiators of the final settlement. He then led the reorganization of the society, with the merger of the different lodges into a unitary London Consolidated Lodge of Journeymen Bookbinders, which for a brief while also joined the new national union, with Dunning as chief secretary until London was forced to leave.

Dunning's condemnation of wasteful celebrations and strikes, and domineering and sometimes unscrupulous behaviour at meetings led to many attacks on him in the 1840s, culminating in a purge and schism in 1850, leaving him the unchallenged ruler thenceforth. He was also a leading figure in wider movements among the London trades, such as a campaign around 1830 against machinery and orthodox political economy, in connection with which he wrote in *The Advocate, or, Artizans' and Labourers' Friend*. He helped to establish *The Charter* newspaper in 1839, to which he contributed, and also campaigned in support of the London stonemasons' strike of 1841–2. He was active in the formation of the National Association of United Trades in 1845, though he soon led his society out of it, and campaigned in the early 1850s in support of the prosecuted Wolverhampton tin-plate workers and the Preston strike, and over the Friendly Societies' Bill of 1855. He was also a good singer and musician, and took part in activities to help the blind.

In 1850 Dunning persuaded his society to establish the *Bookbinders' Trade Circular*, which he edited for over twenty years. He was also examined in 1856 by a select committee of the House of Commons on arbitration of labour disputes, and in the 1860s produced a number of pamphlets on trade unionism, and papers to the National Association for the Promotion of Social Science, being the sole trade union member of its committee that in 1860 produced an influential report on trade unions and disputes. His most famous work was his pamphlet *Trades Unions and Strikes: their Philosophy and Intention* (1860).

In the 1860s Dunning was one of the most prestigious trade unionists in London, but he led his society out of the London Trades Council, which he regarded as too political, and he joined with George *Potter (1832–1893) in his quarrel with that body, his criticisms of the Amalgamated Society of Engineers as a mere benefit society, and campaigns for reform of the master and servant law and arbitration, though he was sceptical over positive legislation in favour of working men because of the social bias of parliament and law courts. He also contributed to Potter's *Bee-Hive* newspaper. Although he was a member of Potter's London Working Men's Association, he had little interest in parliamentary reform, and his conviction of the inferiority of black people led him to oppose the campaigns in support of the north in the American Civil War and against the conduct of the governor of Jamaica. In 1869 he was prominent in the Labour Representation League.

In 1870 Dunning was leader of an amalgamated committee of the three London bookbinders' societies, but a street accident in 1871 left him partially paralysed and he had to resign as secretary of his society, though he remained editor of the *Circular* until his death from 'apoplexy' on 23 December 1873 at his home, 65 Napier Street, Hoxton New Town. He was buried in Abney Park cemetery. His wife Susannah, whom he had married on 28 June 1824, survived him. As head of a strong trade society for thirty years he was an influential figure in the London trade union world, but he is not easy to classify. He was a trade union reformer who induced his society to cease meeting in public houses and to establish a library and a journal conducted by him, which discussed general trade union and economic questions. While being a constant advocate of conciliation with employers and a Chartist who opposed trade society involvement in political questions and campaigns to secure legal status for trade unions, he nevertheless opposed the new amalgamated forms of trade unionism and the 'junta', and publicly justified strikes.

IORWERTH PROTHERO

Sources *The Bee-Hive* (8 Nov 1873) • S. Coltham and J. Saville, 'Dunning, Thomas Joseph', *DLB*, vol. 2 • E. Howe and J. Child, *The Society of London Bookbinders, 1780–1951* (1952) • S. J. Webb and B. P. Webb, *The history of trade unionism, 1666–1920* (1920) • d. cert. • IGI
Wealth at death under £100: probate, 16 Jan 1874, CGPLA Eng. & Wales

Dunphie, Charles James [*pseuds.* Melopoyn, Rambler] (1820–1908), art critic and writer, was born at Rathdowney House, Rathdowney, Queen's county, Ireland, on 4 November 1820, the elder son of Michael Dunphy, merchant, and his wife, Kate Woodroffe. Dunphie was admitted to Trinity College, Dublin, in 1836 and afterwards studied medicine at King's College Hospital, London. However, he then turned to literature and journalism. He was on the staff of *The Times* for some years. On 31 March 1853 he married Jane, daughter of Luke Miller, governor of Ilford prison; they had two sons and a daughter.

At the outbreak of the Crimean War in 1853 Dunphie was offered the job of *Times* special correspondent in the Crimea, but he turned it down because of his recent marriage, and William Howard Russell went in his place. During the war he was one of the founders of the *Patriotic Fund Journal* (1854–5), a weekly literary magazine, to which he also contributed prose and verse under the pseudonym Melopoyn.

In 1856 Dunphie left *The Times* to become art and theatre critic to the *Morning Post*, where he remained for more than fifty years, until his death, although from 1895 onwards he wrote only about art. He also contributed poems to the *Cornhill Magazine* and to *Belgravia*, and wrote essays for *The Observer* (signed Rambler) and the *Sunday*

Times. His Greek and Latin poems were much admired by Gladstone. Collected volumes of his essays appeared entitled *Wildfire: a Collection of Erratic Essays* (1876), *Sweet Sleep* (1879), *The Chameleon: Fugitive Pieces on many-Coloured Matters* (1888), and *Free Lance: Tiltings in many Lists* (1880).

Dunphie died at his home, 54 Finchley Road, London, on 7 July 1908, and was buried at Putney Vale cemetery, after a service at the church of Our Lady, Grove Road, on 10 July.

A. F. SIEVEKING, *rev.* ANNE PIMLOTT BAKER

Sources Burtchaell & Sadleir, *Alum. Dubl.*, 2nd edn · *The Times* (10 July 1908) · *Morning Post* (Sept 7) [NF] · *Morning Post* (9 July 1908) · *CGPLA Eng. & Wales* (1908)
Wealth at death £4642 4s. 2d.: administration, 24 July 1908, *CGPLA Eng. & Wales*

Dunraven and Mount Earl. For this title name *see* Quin, Edwin Richard Windham Wyndham-, third earl of Dunraven and Mount Earl (1812–1871); Quin, Windham Thomas Wyndham-, fourth earl of Dunraven and Mount Earl (1841–1926).

Dunrossil. For this title name *see* Morrison, William Shepherd, first Viscount Dunrossil (1893–1961); Morrison, John William, second Viscount Dunrossil (1926–2000).

Duns, John (1820–1909), United Free Church of Scotland minister and university professor, was born in Duns, Berwickshire, on 11 July 1820, son of William Duns and Sarah Allan. He was educated locally before entering Edinburgh University to study medicine. The events that culminated in the Disruption of the Church of Scotland inspired him to abandon medicine in favour of the ministry. The Free Church of Scotland licensed him to preach in 1843 and in the following year he was ordained minister of the Free Church, Torphichen, West Lothian. Duns married, on 12 June 1844, Margaret Monteith. The proceeds of her successful, if anonymous, activity as a novelist were applied to the reduction of the congregation's debt.

While he was at Torphichen, Duns encountered Sir James Young Simpson, whose paternal home was in nearby Bathgate, and they developed a friendship based on their shared interest in antiquarian subjects. Duns also developed an interest in geology. In 1854 he published a *Memoir of the Late Rev Samuel Martin*, of Bathgate, and in 1857 he acted as editor of the *North British Review*. He edited John Fleming's *The Lithology of Edinburgh* (1859), to which he also contributed a memoir. His most substantial work was the two-volume *Biblical Natural Science* (1863–6), which was issued in twenty-four parts at 2s. per part. The work was heavily illustrated with woodcuts and engraved plates. Another work, *Science and Christian Thought*, appeared in 1866. In 1873 he published his *Memoir of Sir J. Y. Simpson, Bart*.

In May 1864 Duns was appointed to succeed John Fleming (1785–1857) in the chair of natural science at New College, Edinburgh. At first, this was no more than a lectureship, and the long delay in replacing Fleming reflected the division of opinion in the church as to the appropriateness of retaining such a subject in a theological college. However, in December 1869 fresh endowments were forthcoming to restore the full professorship. Despite his long tenure and his undoubted learning Duns was never an especially influential figure in his church. Perhaps this was because, as an obituary observed, 'it was for his College that he principally lived. Assembly and Presbytery saw little of him, nor did he take any part in ecclesiastical debate, unattracted thereby and perhaps overconscious of a certain hesitancy in speech' (*Missionary Record*, 106). The sentiment was echoed by Alexander Martin in a tribute delivered to Edinburgh United Free Presbytery: 'The New College never had a greater friend, never a servant who loved her better or gave himself more unweariedly to the promotion of all her varied interests' (*The Scotsman*, 3 Feb 1909).

Duns published a number of scholarly papers arising from his scientific and antiquarian interests, and he contributed greatly to the museums of New College and the Society of Antiquaries of Scotland. He was elected a fellow of the Royal Society of Edinburgh in 1859 (vice-president, 1899–1903) and fellow of the Society of Antiquaries of Scotland in 1875 (vice-president, 1878). Duns was also president of the Royal Physical Society, Edinburgh, in 1868 and Rhind lecturer in archaeology in 1890. Duns's long service at New College ended with his retirement in 1903; thereafter he resided at Hilderley, North Berwick, East Lothian, where he died on 1 February 1909. He was buried in the parish graveyard there on 3 February.

LIONEL ALEXANDER RITCHIE

Sources *Missionary Record of the United Free Church of Scotland*, 10/99 (March 1909), 105–6 · *The Scotsman* (2 Feb 1909) · *The Scotsman* (3 Feb 1909) · *WWW* · H. Watt, *New College, Edinburgh: a centenary history* (1946), 53–7, 248–9 · *DSCHT* · W. Ewing, ed., *Annals of the Free Church of Scotland, 1843–1900*, 1 (1914), 54 · J. A. Lamb, ed., *The fasti of the United Free Church of Scotland, 1900–1929* (1956), 576
Likenesses portrait, repro. in *Missionary Record*, 9/99, 105
Wealth at death £245 16s. 2d.: confirmation, 26 March 1909, *CCI*

Dunsany. For this title name *see* Plunket, Patrick, ninth Baron Dunsany (1594/5–1668×70); Plunkett, Edward John Moreton Drax, eighteenth Baron Dunsany (1878–1957).

Dunsford, Martin (1744–1807), serge maker and antiquary, was born on 2 February 1744 in Tiverton, Devon, the eldest son of Martin Dunsford (1711–1763), serge maker, and his wife, Anne Stone (*d.* 1798). He was taught at home by his father until he was eight, when he was sent to Blundell's free grammar school, in Tiverton. At thirteen he entered his father's business.

When his father died in 1763 Dunsford had to support his family as well as run the family business. The American War of Independence dealt a heavy blow to the Devon cloth trade, and between 1773 and 1777 Dunsford travelled widely in Europe, seeking to establish additional trading connections. He kept journals of his travels; he expressed deep hostility to the 'impolitic war' in later publications. On 28 January 1780 he married his cousin Ann (1758–1782), only daughter of Samuel Violl, surgeon, and his wife, Elizabeth, of Moretonhampstead. Their first child, a son, was born in 1780 but did not survive infancy. A daughter, Elizabeth, was born on 19 August 1782; Ann Dunsford, however, died of influenza soon afterwards, on 8 October, and her daughter two months later. All three were buried in a newly built family vault outside the south front of St Peter's, Tiverton.

By this time Dunsford had been elected church warden, despite the fact that he came from a dissenting family and that he was a Unitarian; he also held the offices of portreeve and overseer of the poor. At a time when the corporation was all but administratively defunct he was able to use these offices to exercise considerable influence within the town in opposition to that of the Ryder family, who controlled the parliamentary interest of the corporation and whose agent was the town clerk, Beavis Wood. Dunsford's election as church warden had been opposed by both the corporation and the Ryder interest, who repeatedly attempted to interfere in the performance of his duties, which he performed very conscientiously, finding them a means to distract him from his personal misfortunes. He promoted interdenominational Sunday schools and the introduction of free seating in the parish church. He was at the centre of a reforming circle within Tiverton, which was based at his house, Villa Franca. In 1781 he drew up a petition for the right of free election, signed by 491 men, which was presented by James Townsend, MP for Calne. In his capacity as church warden Dunsford was also responsible for making the returns of parochial charities in response to the government inquiry of 1786. This alerted him to the fact that significant bequests and benefactions intended for the poor had gone astray; his inquiries led him to research the history of Tiverton, as did his attempts to prove that the corporation had usurped what had formerly been a householder franchise.

Dunsford's explicit advocacy of political and religious reform and his concern for the fortunes of the poor run through the work for which he is now best known: *Historical Memoirs of Tiverton* (1790), dedicated to 'all the virtuous and industrious poor of Tiverton'. He made use of an earlier history by John Blundell (1712) and collections by Thomas Westcott and William Hewett, as well as his own extensive reading; he was a founder member of the Tiverton Book Club and Reading Society. Despite the history's obvious political agenda, which went against the usual model of topographical literature, it was favourably received by the *Gentleman's Magazine* and has proved a valuable resource for subsequent historians, particularly in the account of the serge manufactories. His only other publication was *Miscellaneous Observations during Two Tours in the South Western Part of England* (1800), which showed the same interest in the lives of the labouring sort and the nature of the economy, and was rather more muted in its political and religious comment.

During the war with France the Devon cloth trade suffered particularly badly, and Dunsford experienced serious losses in his mercantile and manufacturing businesses, which led to his bankruptcy in 1802. This reinforced his hostility to war and to William Pitt's government. In 1795 he placed an advertisement, addressed to all the inhabitants of Tiverton, in which he described the destructive effects of the French wars on trade in the town. A meeting was subsequently held in the town hall at which Dunsford moved an address to the king for peace; this was opposed by the clergy and the corporation.

On 17 December 1802 Dunsford married Maria, daughter of John and Mary Sheckell, in St Botolph without Bishopsgate, London. He suffered periods of ill health from 1780, and after 1800 his health deteriorated further and he was bedridden for much of the time. He died at Tiverton on 13 March 1807 and was buried in the family vault in St Peter's. R. H. SWEET

Sources E. L. Dunsford, 'The autobiography of Martin Dunsford', *Transactions of the Devonshire Association*, 36 (1904), 218–25 · M. Dunsford, 'Memoirs of the Dunsford family', West Country Studies Library, SX 929.2./DUN. [manuscript] · *GM*, 1st ser., 62 (1792), 926–7 · *GM*, 1st ser., 77 (1807), 380 · F. G. S. Hardy, *The history of Tiverton* (1847) · J. Browne, ed., *Georgian Tiverton: political memoranda of Beavis Wood* (1986) · E. J. Musgrove, *Tiverton Gazette* (1951) · R. H. Sweet, *The writing of urban histories in eighteenth-century England* (1997)

Archives Exeter Central Library, Westcountry Studies Library, family memoirs

Dunsheath [*née* Houchen], **Cissie Providence** [Joyce] **(1902–1976)**, mountaineer and traveller, was born on 8 November 1902 at 32 Onley Street, Heigham, near Norwich, the daughter of Charles Houchen, an accident insurance clerk, and his wife, Gertrude Providence, *née* Balls. She took a degree in modern languages at Bedford College, London, in 1924, and entered the teaching profession. In later life she acquired A-level Russian and, in her sixties, a BSc. Her climbing career began in the Lake District and she had a long association with the Girl Guides, whom she took to camps in Britain and abroad. She married on 24 August 1938 a widower, Percy Dunsheath (1886–1979), a distinguished electrical engineer, whom she had met while on a skiing holiday in Austria. They settled thereafter at St Paul, Abinger Hammer, Surrey.

Percy Dunsheath's career took him to numerous international conferences, and Joyce (as she was always known) was able to accompany him and to share a climbing holiday when the conference ended. She had already travelled in Europe and had been to Australia and New Zealand before her marriage; in 1946–7 and again in 1953 they were able to revisit Australia, and to climb together in New Zealand's South Island. In 1955 she organized a four-woman expedition to the Himalayas; unable to afford the air fare, she and a colleague set out in April 1956 to drive the 9000 miles across Europe and Asia, a journey no less adventurous than the eventual exploration and climbs. In return for a contribution of £500 from the Everest Foundation she proposed to map the Bara Shigri Glacier, largely a blank space on the Indian Ordnance Survey map. The expedition was blessed by fine weather and successful in its aims, the glacier being surveyed and numerous surrounding peaks climbed. On her return Joyce and her husband laboured to reduce her plane table observations and photographs to a map.

In 1956 Joyce Dunsheath was elected fellow of the Royal Geographical Society and she served on the society's library and maps committee from 1965 until her death. In

1957, when Percy Dunsheath, then president of the International Electrotechnical Commission, was arranging a conference in Moscow, the Russians invited Joyce to accompany him and then to join a small Russian party climbing in the western and central Caucasus and walking in Svanetia, Georgia. This entire region had been closed since the Bolshevik Revolution. The first peaks were climbed in July, and in October they reached the summit of Mount Alborz. On her return Joyce was given a warm welcome by the press, along the lines of 'Only lady in the party, Surrey housewife scales Europe's highest mountain'. In 1961 she climbed Damavand, in Afghanistan, an expedition which caused her to write to *The Times*, commenting on the need for medical care in that country and asking why there was no British presence when Russian, Japanese, German, and American goods were conspicuous in the shops and their engineers were busy on the ground.

When Joyce Dunsheath became president of the British Federation of University Women, she was able to include climbs in other regions. She was much in demand as a speaker; on one visit to America she lectured at fourteen places in Canada on her expeditions to the Himalayas and Caucasus. In 1964 she led the first Indian Women's Himalayan Expedition to Mrigthuni, in the Garhwal region. After a meeting in Tokyo she climbed in the Japanese Alps; in 1965 she was invited to join the Iowan Mountain Club on a visit to the Peruvian Andes, and in 1973 she climbed Kilimanjaro and Mount Kenya. She also published three books on her experiences: *Mountains and Memsahibs* (1956), *Guest of the Soviets* (1959), and *Afghan Quest* (1961). Despite her own public appearances, she wrote a forceful letter to *The Times* on 27 March 1974, urging that mountaineering be seen as a sport, not a competition. She warned of the dangers of professionalism, asserting that those who climbed to make a name, or to earn a living by getting money from books and lectures, did not have the right approach. She was an enthusiastic gardener and played the bassoon and flute with a local orchestra. The Dunsheaths were living at Wootton Cottage, Westcott, near Dorking, at the time of Joyce's death in Mount Alvernia Hospital, Guildford, on 30 July 1976.

ANITA McCONNELL

Sources J. Lancaster-Jones, *Alpine Journal*, 84 (1979), 266–7 · *GJ*, 143 (1977), 65 · *The Times* (20 Aug 1956), 11c · *The Times* (22 Oct 1957), 9e · *The Times* (3 Nov 1960), 3d · *The Times* (27 March 1974), 17a · P. Dunsheath, *Nearly ninety* (1975) · J. Dunsheath, 'Climbing in the Caucasus mountains of the USSR, 1957', *GJ*, 124 (1958), 35–40 · b. cert. · m. cert. · d. cert. · *WWW* [Percy Dunsheath]
Wealth at death £65,320: probate, 27 Oct 1976, *CGPLA Eng. & Wales*

Dunsinane. For this title name see Nairne, Sir William, fifth baronet, Lord Dunsinane (*bap.* 1731, *d.* 1811).

Duns Scotus, John (*c.*1265–1308), Franciscan friar and theologian, was born at Duns, in the Scottish borders, some 15 miles west of Berwick.

Life and career Earlier long-held claims for 1274 as the date of his birth and Ireland as his country of origin cannot be sustained, and are no longer accepted. The exact date of his birth, however, remains unknown. The most likely estimate is 1265 or 1266, based upon the earliest reliable dates concerning Duns's life: his entry into the Franciscan order between 1278 and 1279, and his ordination as priest, at Northampton, on 17 March 1291, by Oliver Sutton, bishop of Lincoln (*d.* 1299). Since the minimum age for admission to the order was fifteen, and the minimum age to be ordained priest within the order was twenty-five, Duns could scarcely have been born later than March 1266, although he could in each case have been older than the minimum age. Virtually nothing else is known about his early life or his years as a Franciscan before ordination. The legends surrounding his origins remain simply legends, some given currency by Luke Wadding, the seventeenth-century Franciscan historian, who, as first editor of what were then taken to be the complete works of Duns Scotus (12 vols., Lyons, 1639), was also responsible for the accepted canon of Duns's writings.

Something more is known of Duns's subsequent career, from 1291 to his death at the Franciscan house, in Cologne, in 1308; but the knowledge is only sketchy. Those years, until his departure for Cologne, in 1307, were divided between Oxford, Cambridge, and Paris, studying and teaching at the Franciscan houses and the faculties of theology in the universities there. The precise chronology is uncertain. It seems probable that at the time of his ordination Duns was studying at Oxford, the premier English Franciscan house of studies, and that he remained there until 1293. He was then sent to continue his studies in Paris, where he stayed until 1296 or 1297. Between 1297 and 1300 he was in Cambridge, and between 1300 and 1301 at Oxford. In each of the latter universities he lectured on the *Sentences* of Peter Lombard, the four books of which, covering the main aspects of Christian belief, constituted the basic textbook of the course in theology. Commenting on the *Sentences* was obligatory both for bachelors of theology, as part of the requirements of the course leading to a mastership, or doctorate, in theology, and also for newly graduated masters. That applied equally to members of the religious orders in the theological faculty.

By 1301 or 1302 Duns had become a master of theology at Oxford, having spent the requisite thirteen years studying, first, the liberal arts and then theology. As a religious he would have pursued the liberal arts course, predominantly Aristotle's logical and philosophical works, in his own order's houses of study before proceeding to the course in theology, principally the study of the Bible and the *Sentences*, partly in his order's houses and partly in the university theological faculties, which, like the faculties of the other disciplines, awarded the degrees in the subject. His lectures on the *Sentences* at Cambridge seem to have created a considerable impression. In 1302 he was sent by his superiors to teach at the University of Paris, where he once again lectured on the *Sentences*. He appears already to have commented on three of the four books when he left Oxford. At Paris he began to lecture on the first book for the third time, and in the following year on the fourth book. But he had to return to Oxford, in June 1303, as one of over eighty friars who refused to support the French king, Philippe IV, in his quarrel with the pope, Boniface VIII, over royal taxation of the French clergy.

Duns remained in Oxford for one year, continuing his interrupted lectures on the fourth book of the *Sentences*. In 1304 he was able to resume academic life at Paris, following the settlement of the dispute between king and pope, under Boniface's successor, Benedict XI. In 1305 Duns received the doctor's degree of theology at Paris, and spent from 1306 to 1307 lecturing in the theological faculty. He was transferred to Cologne to teach in the Franciscan house there near the end of 1307. He died on 8 November 1308, from causes unknown, and was buried in the Franciscan church in Cologne. His remains were venerated; and within a few years his doctrines were widely adopted, especially by his order.

Writings Duns's works were exclusively the product of his academic activities of lecturing and disputing. During his comparatively short life he seems never to have left his scholastic milieu, unlike his Franciscan predecessor Bonaventure, or his successor and critic William Ockham (*d.* 1349). In contrast to them, Duns produced no practical or polemical writings; his most scathing denunciations were directed against the doctrine of Averroes (Ibn Rushd) of a single immaterial intellect for all mankind. But, living in the aftermath of the great controversies against the upholders of Averroism at Paris in the 1260s and 1270s, as well as the conflicts of the same period in the theological faculty there between the friars and secular theological masters, Duns was not drawn into any wider struggle, in the way in which Aquinas had been on both those fronts.

The two most striking features of Duns's writings are, first, their unfinished state, and, second, the predominance of his commentaries on the *Sentences* in his *œuvre*. Duns had prepared his own text of his commentary on the *Sentences* for publication (his *Ordinatio*); but his premature death left it incomplete, and in an often confusing state, punctuated by revisions, cancellations, blank spaces waiting to be filled, and additions, sometimes running to pages. Its unfinished form invited attempts to complete it; and were duly made by Duns's pupils and followers, interpolating and amplifying Duns's text with their own or others' reported versions of his lectures (*Reportationes*). Such reports were, however, of varying value, according to the reliability of the reporter; this was a hazard inherent in the *Reportatio* form, which essentially consisted of student lecture notes, and was not confined to Duns's writings. In his case, though, their variability was increased by his different series of lectures on the same books of the *Sentences*, which were often employed undiscriminatingly by his completers to supplement the gaps left in his text, while also adding their own glosses to explain Duns's meaning. Its comprehension was not made easier by Duns's convoluted mode of proceeding. He broke the symmetry of most previous scholastic discussion, where the arguments pro and contra in answer to a question were marshalled from authority and reason, followed by the writer's own conclusions and replies to objections and initial arguments. Instead, Duns would sometimes run one question into another, in a sequence of initial arguments, objections, replies to the objections, counter-objections, and replies, before giving his own reply, in some cases forty folio pages later. By then, even the most attentive reader could have lost the thread.

Problem of authenticity The result of the interventions to bring order to Duns's texts was a mingling of real and pseudo-Duns, perpetuated in the first complete edition of 1639, which printed or reprinted Duns's commentaries from medieval texts without any criterion of authenticity. The edition of 1639 (ed. L. Vivès, 26 vols., repr. 1891–5) remains, pending the completion of the new Vatican edition, under the editorship of the Scotist commission, in Rome, the only comprehensive edition of Duns's works. But it has also perpetuated the misconception, which again came down from the fourteenth century, that Duns produced only two commentaries on the *Sentences*: one at Oxford, his *Opus Oxoniense* or *Ordinatio*; the other, his *Reportatio Parisiensis*, at Paris, without apparent recognition of the difference between an *ordinatio*, as an author's definitive text prepared by him for publication, and bearing his imprimatur, and a *reportatio*, which carried no such authority, and which, in the reports made of Duns's lectures on the *Sentences*, had diverse variants. His early editors accordingly failed to appreciate the divergent status of the two works, or to see his different lecture courses, preserved in the *Reportationes*, as only stages to his final positions in the *Ordinatio*. Understanding of this began only in the later nineteenth century, with the critical study of the manuscript sources, and is embodied in the Vatican edition of Duns's works, the first volume of which appeared in 1950.

The other, and more far-reaching, misconception propagated by the edition of 1639 was the inclusion of almost as many spurious as genuine works under Duns's name: more, if the *Theoremata*, the claims for which as Duns's are far from established, and perhaps the *Questions on 'De anima'*, were not by Duns. That, however, would scarcely alter the balance from being decisively in favour of Duns's own writings, because of the preponderance of his commentaries on the *Sentences*, occupying sixteen of twenty-six volumes in the Vivès reprint of the edition of 1639. That is true also doctrinally: the *Opus Oxoniense*, although unfinished, comes closest to Duns's *summa*, as a synthesis of his system. Nevertheless, size by itself is not the criterion, where significance is concerned; and two of the most significant of the titles ascribed to Duns, *De rerum principio*, definitely not by him, and the *Theoremata*, problematical, would, each in different ways, if accepted as Duns's, entail positing either inconsistency on his part or a change of mind or modification of his doctrines to accommodate them. The last course, applied to *De rerum principio*, treated as genuine, flawed the books on Duns by P. Minges, B. Landry, and C. R. S. Harris.

Despite reputable attempts to assimilate the *Theoremata* to the rest of Duns's outlook, judgement is better suspended: the four known manuscripts of it give no firm evidence that it is by Duns, while, internally, its admission to his proper corpus would involve rewriting too much of Duns's outlook to be completely credible. Although the

Questions on 'De anima' does not pose such problems, external evidence, in remarks made on more than one manuscript, suggests that the questions were in part by followers of Duns Scotus ('Scotuli'), and this work is again better left unutilized in assessing Duns's ideas. The other main works now rejected as inauthentic are a *Speculative Grammar*, commentaries and questions on Aristotle's two *Analytics*, *Physics*, and *Meteorology*, and an exposition and conclusions on the *Metaphysics*. The most important of Duns's own writings, in addition to his commentaries on the *Sentences*, are the *De primo principio*, *Quodlibets*, *Collations*, and *Questions on the 'Metaphysics'* (the first nine of twelve books), the only authentic one of the three on the *Metaphysics* ascribed to Duns. He also wrote commentaries on Aristotle's so-called old logic—*Categories*, *Interpretation*, and *Sophistical Refutations*—together with Porphyry's *Introduction* to the *Categories*. Contrary to past opinions, Duns's logical writings, shorn of the spurious *Speculative Grammar*, were comparatively uninfluential. The *De primo principio* and *Quodlibets*, however, are particularly valuable in clarifying and complementing the commentaries on the *Sentences* as the primary source of Duns's system.

Duns Scotus and the development of scholasticism Duns's system introduced a new, and in many respects final, phase of medieval scholasticism. Together with William Ockham, though from opposed standpoints, he marked the parting of the ways, theologically and philosophically, between the high and later middle ages. Duns has often been regarded as the renewer of Augustinianism, and his thought contraposed to the Aristotelianism of Thomas Aquinas, taken as his main adversary. The first part of that judgement can be accepted with qualifications; the second must be rejected. Duns, as a Franciscan, did follow the Augustinian tradition of his order, albeit to transform many of its features. Neither Aristotelianism nor Aquinas, however, was his primary target, although he criticized both on particular issues. Indeed, compared with his Franciscan predecessors of the previous century, such as Bonaventure, his thought is noticeably more Aristotelian: for example, his denial of inner illumination as the source of certitude, and use of abstraction for knowledge of universals; his rejection of seminal reasons in matter; and his adoption of the notion of the rational soul as man's substantial form, defining him.

What can be said is that, within a few years of his death, Duns became the doctor of the Franciscans, as the counterpart to the Dominicans' designation in 1314 of Thomas Aquinas as official doctor of their order. The two theologians thereby came to stand for rival allegiances; but these were institutional rather than intellectual, and in both cases posthumous. That is not to deny the very real differences between the outlooks of the two thinkers; and to a considerable degree they can be profitably measured against one another, provided that Scotism (named from Duns's sobriquet) is not seen as a direct riposte to Thomism. There is plenty to indicate that Duns's primary opponents were among his own contemporaries or immediate predecessors, notably Henri de Gand (*d.* 1293), in the

generation after Aquinas, and following the condemnations of the doctrines associated with so-called Latin Averroism at Paris in the 1270s.

Duns bears witness to the changed intellectual climate of the last two decades of the thirteenth century, which largely resulted from those condemnations. The latter were pre-eminently a theological reaction against the naturalistic and cosmic determinism associated with Aristotelian and Arabian philosophy, especially as pursued in the arts faculty of the University of Paris: notably the tendency to treat God as a remote mover, not directly involved with the world as either creator or providence; and to posit instead an eternal universe governed by a hierarchy of intelligences and heavenly bodies, to which mankind, together with everything else in the world, was subject. As interpreted in the condemned propositions, whose veracity is by no means certain, that led to the denial of the world's temporal creation, and of human free will or independent intellectual understanding, or, indeed, an individual immortal soul.

The use of metaphysics At the same time the implication, however unjust, of pagan philosophy in those profanities led to a distancing of theology from philosophy. That entailed a narrowing of the range both of theological truths knowable by human reason and experience, and of natural certainty. For, in reaffirming belief in God's sovereignty as creator, as well as man's freedom from all forms of astral and natural necessity, a new emphasis was put upon the contingency of creation in being the work of God's untrammelled will. He could therefore have done otherwise than he had decreed; hence no knowledge which was of created existence was necessary knowledge, since it lacked inherent necessity. The contingency of the universe, as God's creation, simultaneously put no limits upon its possibilities—other than would involve God in self-contradiction, a theological impossibility—while setting limits upon the attainment of natural certainty.

Duns shared these emphases and indeed was instrumental in defining them. He largely inaugurated a new critical demarcation of the boundaries between philosophy and theology, and of the criteria governing each, not only in relation to one another, but also the main contents of each. In the process, he reformulated many of the traditional questions, introducing a range of concepts and distinctions which largely formed the point of departure for his successors, above all Ockham. Fundamental to his outlook was the use of metaphysics as the basis both of philosophical knowledge and of theological truths accessible to natural reason, in particular those concerning God. In opposition to Aquinas, who took the first object of the human intellect to be the species, or form, in things, representing their true nature, Duns made being, or existence, itself the first object of understanding, in virtue of what he called a twofold primacy of commonness, or universality, as included in everything else, and virtuality, as contained in something else which does include being. Together, being therefore extended to everything, created and uncreated. Thus conceived, being was a transcendental reality, going beyond the physical order, and its ten categories, and so belonged to the realm of metaphysics; and the being that was its subject was simply being as such, a common nature shared by whatever is, regardless of its actual existence.

Univocal being Of itself, the common nature of being was, like every nature, neither individual nor universal, but simply what it was as a nature, a doctrine that Duns adopted from Avicenna, using his same example of the nature of a horse, which was solely that of horse, before it was a universal concept in the mind or an individual horse existing outside the mind, the only way in which actual things can exist in the world. The concept that denotes it must therefore be a universal concept of being at the ultimate level of abstraction, removed from all actual existence, because, for Duns, as by this time for the majority of his contemporaries, knowledge came through experience of sensible things. Hence the concept of being, like all concepts, was abstracted from sensible experience; it accordingly could give man no knowledge of immaterial existence; and the only way in which the latter could be included in a concept of being was to make the notion of being apply indifferently to everything that can exist, or, as Duns expressed it, everything to which existence is not contradictory. Such a concept was univocal in having one and the same sense for whatever could be conceived without contradiction, including God, of whose existence man could have no direct experience naturally.

The properties of being and their application to God In that capacity, as a term universally predicable of all that is, regardless of what it is, the notion of being functions as a logical term, denuded of all content. Duns was the first to employ it in that role to provide knowledge of God. He did so, though, on the basis of metaphysics, by distinguishing the properties of being, and so introducing the very distinctions eschewed by univocity, above all between infinite and finite being, the primary modes of being, containing all the others. To demonstrate God's existence metaphysically was, for Duns, to demonstrate the existence of an infinite being. He did that by drawing on the other properties belonging to being as an irreducible common nature. The first two were the conjunctive attributes, of one, good and true, convertible with being, and the disjunctives, such as finite/infinite, and necessary/contingent, only one of which could apply to a particular being, but together covered all being. Their significance for Duns was that the higher member of a disjunction could be inferred from the lower, which was knowable from experience, but not the converse. Thus the necessary could be known from the contingent, but not the other way round. Duns followed Bonaventure in employing that procedure in his proofs of God.

Finally, there were the pure or unqualified perfections, which could be attributed to God, denuded of all imperfection, including the conjunctives and the superior members of the disjunctions. Their full import was to be seen in their application to knowledge of God and his existence. They provided the main supports of a natural theology, in affording natural evidence of supernatural truths. Such knowledge, theology for man, was to be distinguished from theology in itself, which was not attainable in man's present natural state. The difference was between knowing necessary truths as objects of belief, but without understanding them, and understanding them in their own light, not available to man in this life. Theology, however, was not a science, in Aristotle's sense of necessary and certain knowledge, concerning God's external actions, because they were contingent, as in the example of the incarnation. Theology, for Duns, was a practical, as opposed to a speculative, science, providing a norm for man's salutary conduct. He did not deny the certainty of its truths but rather their self-evidence or deducibility in man's present state. In that he was followed by most of his successors. Metaphysics gave only a posteriori truths about God, through his effects; but they were the closest that man could come to forming concepts of God and proving his existence, naturally, namely, in terms derived from the properties of being. Thus it could be proved that God was a first necessary being; but not that he was a Trinity, which was a matter of faith and the preserve of theology.

The existence of God Duns made a univocal concept of being the foundation of his proofs of God's existence, precisely because the same concept of being could be affirmed indifferently of God and everything created; without it, said Duns, there could not be any knowledge by man of God. In adopting univocity Duns broke with the previous reliance upon analogy between God and creatures to demonstrate God's existence, and removed consideration of God beyond the realm of physical existence, the province of physics, concerned primarily with movement. He expressly sided in that preference with Avicenna (Ibn Sina), against Averroes, who had looked to physics in Aristotle's proofs for a first unmoved mover, a path also followed by Aquinas. To prove God as first mover of everything in the universe was to confine him within the universe; God would then be a physical cause who does not transcend the physical order, which is what happens with Aristotle's proof. To conceive God as a first being, on the other hand, was superior to conceiving him as a first mover, as well as nobler, because a first being could give existence to another, as opposed merely to imparting movement.

Metaphysics also provided more attributes to describe God. Duns's proofs made use of the disjunctive co-ordinates of necessary versus contingent being to show that there must be a first being, along the lines of Avicenna's earlier proof, including the same term, first, to describe God, since what was only contingent or possible must owe its existence to some other cause, which must itself be necessary, and so uncaused. Otherwise, if that cause were itself only possible, it would in turn be caused by a further cause; and unless there was a first uncaused cause there would be an infinite regress, which was impossible, because, if everything was simply possible, nothing would exist in the first place to bring anything else into being. The first necessary being must therefore be eternally in being. Duns regarded the contingent as an immediate indemonstrable fact of existence; if therefore the contingent was possible, the necessary, on which the contingent depends, was possible and must then exist, since what is necessary cannot not exist or cease to exist. A further feature of Duns's proof is that, in order to overcome the objection that to begin from the contingent would not provide the necessary premises required for a necessary demonstration, he started from the possible, namely, that something could be produced, rather than from its actual contingent existence as an effect. The use of the mode of possibility to escape contingency was adopted in turn by Ockham, and represented a further new development.

Duns's proofs received their final form in *De primo principio*; both there and in the *Opus Oxoniense* they were among the most elaborate of the middle ages, and included the distinction between essentially and accidentally ordered causes to establish the impossibility of an infinite regress in an essential order, namely, where all the causes must coexist: the case in the relation of a first necessary cause to a chain of possible causes, which not only owed their existence to the first cause, but their immediate conservation. Having established the necessity of a first cause Duns then proved that the first must be triply first, as efficient, final, and most eminently perfect cause. It must also be infinite, as the most perfect mode of being. Duns followed Henri de Gand in giving a new positive meaning to infinity as a divine perfection; but he went further in treating it as the supreme perfection, containing virtually all the other divine perfections, as intrinsic to God's being, rather than as a further attribute superadded to it. Hence to prove the existence of an infinite being was to prove the existence of a perfect being with all the defining perfections of infinite power, infinite knowledge, and the other divine attributes that could be inferred by natural reason, as opposed to those that could only be known theologically, as a matter of faith, such as omnipotence.

The foundations of knowledge Duns's break with analogy for knowledge of God enabled him to dispense with the traditional Franciscan reliance upon the Augustinian doctrine of inner illumination to bring certainty, through the mind's possession of immutable truths. Aquinas had already dispensed with that doctrine by adopting Aristotelian abstraction for all human knowledge. Duns's approach was more diverse. He accepted abstraction for knowledge of universals; but he also remained true to Franciscan tradition in upholding direct intellectual cognition of singulars. Together, they provided certain knowledge, in opposition to Henri de Gand's claims for inner illumination as the only source of certainty and knowledge of God, in face of the unreliability of sensible knowledge. Duns did, however, concede that the human mind is moved by the influence of the eternal ideas of things in God, enabling man to know genuine truths, even though they were from the mind's own powers.

Duns introduced the distinction between abstractive and intuitive knowledge as the foundation of all naturally attainable knowledge. They each represented simple, non-discursive, cognition of the same object; they therefore differed not in what was known but in how it was known. Abstractive knowledge was of a nature or species formed by the mind of an object perceived by the senses, and was indifferent to whether or not the object existed outside the mind. Intuitive knowledge was direct knowledge of an object's existence, without reference to its nature. Abstractive and intuitive cognition were accordingly distinguished by the presence or absence of the object of cognition, as respectively the conceptual and existential facets of the same nature. Each therefore underwent a change from its earlier associations, in being subordinated to a nature or essence which was in itself indifferent to either, and preceded each mode of cognition. In Duns's version of abstraction, the intellect did not disengage the universal from a sensible image of a singular object in the imagination, as it did in Aristotle's original meaning; both were already contained in the common nature of which they were aspects: the singular in its existence outside the mind; the universal exclusively as a mental concept. From that standpoint Duns was less of a realist, in its medieval connotation of upholding the reality of universals, than the adherents of Aristotle's doctrine, such as Aquinas, were.

That is still more apparent over Duns's conception of intuitive cognition, which for the first time allowed the intellect direct contact with a material object without any mediating species or image. His grounds were, that what the less perfect power—the senses—could do, the more perfect—the intellect—could do, and more perfectly. Duns thus overthrew the Aristotelian axiom, which had been at the base of the doctrine of abstraction, that the senses know only singulars, and the intellect only universals, since it would demean the intellect, as immaterial, to be acted upon by what was material. That view was accompanied by the belief that knowledge of universals was superior to individual knowledge, on the Platonic assumption that intelligibility resides in immaterial forms. In rejecting it, and instead making singular knowledge the most perfect knowledge, and intuitive knowledge, as knowledge of singular existence, more perfect than abstractive knowledge, Duns turned that tradition on its head. Following his Franciscan predecessors, he gave a more direct and active role to the intellect, involved from the outset equally in individual and universal knowledge. There was no precognitive stage belonging to the senses, as in the Aristotelian and Thomist theory of abstraction. In Duns's case, however, that was not only because of the intellect's own powers, but also because a common nature was the primary object of intellectual cognition, although its knowledge originated with a sensible species of a singular. In man's present state, however, he could not know singularity in itself; merely the existence that accompanies singularity in the external world. Abstractive knowledge thus provided the first clear cognition of an object's nature.

Duns's conception of abstractive and intuitive cognition was to have far-reaching consequences, especially with Ockham and his successors. It had two further accompaniments. One was the primacy of common natures, already mentioned, in which essences were the constituents of being, with no distinction between essence and existence, the validity of which distinction Duns categorically denied. The other was the rejection of matter as the principle of individuation. The belief that it was such a principle underlay the Aristotelian notion of abstraction, of mentally separating an intelligible form from the sensible individual thing in which it was embodied and encountered by the senses. Matter, for Duns, had its own identity, with its own form, which in man was the form of his body, again in opposition to Aristotelian and Thomist doctrine, of matter as pure potentiality, which was actualized as the component of individual things by its conjunction with a form. Instead Duns posited an ultimate individuating difference, called, in the *Reportatio Parisiensis*, 'thisness' (*haecceitas*), which was from the form, but was not the same as the form or matter or their composite. It was among Duns's most impalpable notions; it implies that a thing has thisness in virtue of existing, as the ultimate reality of being. It was given great prominence by his followers.

The formal distinction As a distinct reality, an ultimate difference, although inseparable from a form, was a pre-eminent example of a formal distinction within the same thing; this, perhaps more than anything else, was the hallmark of subsequent Scotism. The role of the formal distinction was protean: in God, between the three persons of the Trinity, and between his essence and his attributes; in man, between the soul and its powers; in metaphysics, between being and the other transcendentals; and universally between a common nature or form, which was less than a numerical unity, and its ultimate, or contracting, difference, which made it this individual nature, as a real numerical unity. As with many of Duns's concepts, the formal distinction did not originate with him, but went back to the twelfth-century theologian Gilbert de la Porrée, who used it to reconcile triunity in God with his indivisibility. But Duns gave it his own connotation and applied it wherever the mind discerned distinct formalities or essences within the same object, whether material or immaterial, such as the sensitive and intellective powers in man's soul or the perfections in God; they were formally distinct in not being formally the same.

In that sense, their non-identity was founded in the thing and preceded the mind's recognition. A formal distinction was therefore stronger than a merely mental or a virtual distinction. But it was weaker than a real distinction, because no actual distinction was involved; ontologically the formalities remained inseparable from their subject, like the humanity in Socrates or the colour in white; and in every being there was a plurality of forms, but only one subject. From that perspective, Duns's formal distinction was no more than a sustained extension of the traditional Franciscan doctrine of a plurality of forms in things, with at least two in man, one for his soul and one for his body. The difference was that for Duns there could be formal distinctions wherever there was not identity. Even more than a plurality of forms, the formal distinction provided a metaphysical reference for our concepts, guaranteeing their objectivity. Duns took that tendency to the furthest degree. He thus multiplied the diversities of being to correspond to the diversity of concepts of it, rather than posit a discrepancy between them, as Ockham did.

Divine ideas Duns's conception of divine ideas was intimately related to the pre-eminence of formalities. For forms had their source in divine ideas, as the archetypes of the forms of all possible beings. To that extent, divine ideas shared in the greater definition given to forms in Duns's system. But they were also more clearly subordinated in God to the divine intellect, as the outcome of its intellection, and not the means through which it knew all possible beings, which would have been to subordinate God's intellect to divine ideas, the mistake of some of his predecessors. In that aspect divine ideas were logically posterior to God's intellect as objects of his knowledge. They had no other existence.

Duns depicted their generation in a series of hypothetical instants in God, in which he first knew his own essence and then the essences of all possible creatures. The ideas thus engendered were identical with his essence, and so participated in his infinity, necessity, and eternity; but the infinity of possible essences, of which they were the ideas, was finite, contingent, and could only exist in time. It was in deciding which should be realized as actual beings that the divine will entered. The intervention of God's will represented the shift from the necessity in God to the contingency of what was outside him. The earlier view of Duns's supposed voluntarism in relation to divine ideas does not arise. Nor does it in any respect of God's nature. And it only holds for creation in the theologically trivial sense, common to all believers, that his will is its free and contingent cause, but not in any arbitrary manner, as the unqualified exercise of will for its own sake—another misconstruction of voluntarism.

For Duns, no less than for any other medieval theologian, God's will was 'really, perfectly and identically' his essence, and only formally distinct, as his other attributes were. Logically, in God as in rational creatures, knowing preceded willing; and whatever he willed was rational, as it was good and just. Hence his will was itself the reason why it willed; there was no other explanation. Not voluntarism, but contingency, was the operative term. It precluded any natural understanding of God's actions; for, in being contingent, they could not be deduced by necessary demonstrations. Otherwise they would have been necessary. It was in that emphasis upon the contingency of God's will that Duns was distinctive. It led him to apply it at once to natural phenomena, moral laws, and the economy of grace and salvation.

The contingency of the divine will That widespread application was another feature of Duns's outlook. It was sometimes accompanied by the use of the distinction between

God's absolute power, denoting his omnipotence taken in itself, and his ordained power, representing his decrees for this world. Although not in the sustained manner of Ockham and his contemporaries, Duns was among the first to utilize the distinction to exhibit the contingency of the present dispensation by invoking God's absolute power to have superseded the laws ordinarily governing it, for example, allowing matter to exist without being joined to a form. But, for Duns, God's power to have done otherwise was equally true independently of God's absolute power, which tended to be directed to the existing order, rather than possible alternative dispensations.

Thus, in ethics, beyond the immutable obligation to love God above all, and never to hate or dishonour him, enshrined in the first two commandments, actions not related to love or hate of God were not of themselves morally good or bad, but were so because he had willed them to be one or other. He could therefore have willed other commandments than the secondary ones of the Decalogue, which would have been no less good and just and rational, in coming from his will: permitted murder, say, as he had when he commanded Abraham to sacrifice Isaac, or polygamy, as he did among the patriarchs, to increase numbers, or dispensed from the need for private property, obviating the crime of theft. That did not detract from the naturally good actions of natural law; but they only became morally good as well in conformity to divine commands or prohibitions, like those included in the commandments, or if they were in accord with right reason. The juxtaposition of the two appears to leave Duns's ethical doctrines hovering between traditionally inviolable moral laws, from which there could be no dispensation, and their implication in the inherent contingency of everything created, from which only the obligation to love God above all remained unalterable: a juxtaposition in which Duns was to be followed by Ockham, as he was over the dispensability of created grace in God's reward of meritorious actions.

This third area of contingency was to become the focus of the interplay between God's absolute and ordained power, and was one of Duns's most potent legacies to the later middle ages. According to Duns, God, by his present dispensation, had made the infusion of grace into an individual's soul the condition of his acceptance for eternal life. Acceptance by God was therefore the end and came before the award of grace, as the means. God could accordingly, by his absolute power, achieve the end by directly rewarding the meritorious act of will, which, ordinarily, an individual performed in conjunction with grace, on the standard ground that what God ordinarily did through second causes, he could do directly, where no contradiction was entailed. In this case, grace was merely a secondary agent dependent on the prior agency of the will, which was correspondingly independent of grace; otherwise it would not be free. What, then, was ontologically separable, but actually joined, God could separate. The subsequent debate came to be between the competing claims of grace and free will for primacy in acts of merit,

in which the charges of Pelagianism and semi-Pelagianism, made against the Scotist and later Ockhamist view, have too often been mistakenly accepted even until the present. In fact, that view was the opposite of Pelagianism, as Duns himself maintained. The issue was not the human will's freedom to transcend its natural powers and elicit God's reward: the heresy of Pelagius. It was God's freedom to will how his will should be done: a divine, not a human, view.

Human and divine will That leads to the final feature of Duns's thought, his doctrine of the human will and its relation to God's will. He was true to Franciscan tradition—and in opposition to Thomism—in making man's will superior to his intellect. But Duns went further in seeing human free will as alone undetermined to act in a specific manner, the proper meaning of will. It could choose to love or hate what was good or bad, to act or not to act, where the intellect must assent to what was true, and was not a free power. Where the intellect understood, the will loved; its supreme end was happiness, to be found alone in love of God. But, in contrast to the Thomist final end of knowledge of God, which necessitated love of him, for Duns the will's act of love was freely elicited. Although its actions were preceded by knowledge, the will was able to command the intellect not to assent to false propositions; and, as the superior power, its actions were nobler and its sins correspondingly more heinous.

That seemingly libertarian position was firmly qualified by Duns's conception of God's future knowledge of free will's actions. There, also, Duns brought a new challenge to the hitherto accepted view that God knew everything, past, present, and future, determined and freely caused, in the same eternal instant. Hence there was no conflict between his omniscience and free future actions yet to be, because, strictly speaking, there was no future knowledge in God. In effect the problem was dissolved. In reply, Duns first denied that God's knowledge of future events was the same as that of present and past events, because whereas he could know what was present or past as actually existing or having actually been, he could not know as actual what was not yet in being. Second, Duns reaffirmed that the cause of the existence of everything outside God was his will, not his knowledge. Therefore, he could only know anything actually as the result of his willing, including the future actions of free will. The will's decisions were therefore the medium of his future knowledge, once again, though, not as arbitrary or irrational decrees, but on the basis of preceding knowledge. And far from God's willing necessitating the human will's willing, God's will as supremely free was the source of all contingency and freedom among creatures, and pre-eminently of human free will.

Duns's concept of God's future knowledge helped to inaugurate one of the other major theological controversies of the fourteenth century, that over future contingents. There, as in the disputes over created grace, and in his system as a whole, he gave a new direction to later scholastic thought and Catholic theology, which continued beyond the middle ages.

Influence and reputation Although Duns, in contrast to Aquinas, was not recognized as official doctor of his order until 1633, when the heyday of scholasticism was well past, his doctrines were in effect adopted by the Franciscans, within a few years of his death. They were set in sharper relief by the challenge to them from William Ockham in the two decades after Duns's death, a challenge that lasted for the next two centuries. Ockham was also a Franciscan; but his outlook was almost totally opposed to Duns's, as it was to much of preceding scholasticism. Scotism and Ockhamism were the two predominant schools of thought for the rest of the fourteenth century, becoming in the fifteenth century associated with the so-called old and new ways respectively. By then, Scotism, as the old way, was joined by the revived schools of Thomism and Albertism. Scotism was particularly strong at Oxford in the fifteenth century. But with the Reformation, and the growth of humanism in the sixteenth century, all the different branches of scholasticism came under attack. Scotism was particularly a target of ridicule for its fine distinctions; 'Dunsmen' or 'Dunses' were derided as pedants and hair-splitters; and, perversely, the word 'dunce' became associated with blockheads and dullards, the meaning that it has kept. While Scotism, with the rest of scholasticism, was banished from the new protestant countries, it flowered in the Catholic countries of the Counter-Reformation, especially Spain, during the sixteenth and seventeenth centuries, with Scotist chairs established in the principal universities.

The expansion of Scotism was accompanied by a remarkable growth in the Franciscan order, the main support of Scotism, in the seventeenth century; but Scotism also had many followers outside the order, notably among the Augustinians and Jesuits. The official adoption of Scotism by the Franciscans, in 1633, and the publication of the complete edition of Duns's works, in 1639, by Luke Wadding, himself a Franciscan, gave a further stimulus to the spread of Scotism. At the same time writings on the Virgin Mary reached their zenith in the seventeenth century; and Duns's teaching on Marian doctrine became more generally recognized. He was the first schoolman to deny that Mary had been born in original sin. He thereby went against 150 years of scholastic thinking; and for the next 250 years support for his interpretation was largely confined within his own order. It declined during the eighteenth century and early nineteenth century, with the decline of scholasticism. He was, however, finally vindicated in 1854 with the publication by Pope Pius IX of a papal bull declaring the Virgin's immaculate conception.

Although Duns was never officially associated with the doctrine, he was widely known as the Marian Doctor, in addition to his contemporary title of the Subtle Doctor. He was also included among the blessed in his own order; and in 1904 he was confirmed as an object of veneration, from a process dating from 1710. With the revival of scholasticism and of the history of scholasticism in the second half of the nineteenth century, interest in Duns revived, and

has continued to increase as his outlook has become better known. His emphasis upon the immediacy of the individual and individual knowledge, in contrast to the Thomist emphasis upon their universality, attracted Gerard Manley Hopkins, for whom he was 'of realty the rarèst-veinèd traveller' (Hopkins, 156). Scotism now appears as the main scholastic alternative system to Thomism. But its full import awaits the complete publication of Duns's writings.   GORDON LEFF

Sources J. Duns Scotus, *Opera omnia*, ed. L. Wadding and others, 12 vols. (Lyon, 1639); new edn, 26 vols. (Paris, 1891–5) · *Ioannis Duns Scoti opera omnia*, ed. C. Balic and others (Vatican City, 1950–) · J. K. Ryan and B. M. Bonansea, eds., *John Duns Scotus, 1265–1965* (1965) · C. Balic, *John Duns Scotus* (1966) · E. Bettoni, *Duns Scotus* (1961) · F. C. Copleston, *A history of philosophy* (1966), 2: *Mediaeval philosophy: Augustine to Scotus* (1966) · E. Gilson, *Jean Duns Scot* (1952) · E. Gilson, *History of Christian philosophy in the middle ages* (1955) · D. C. Langston, *God's willing knowledge* (1986) · P. Vignaux, *Justification et prédestination au XIVe siècle* (1934); repr. (1981) · H. Schwamm, *Das göttliche Vorherwissen bei Duns Scotus und seinen ersten Anhängern* (Innsbruck, 1934) · W. Dettloff, *Die Lehre von der Acceptatio divina bei Johannes Duns Scotus* (Werl, Westfalia, 1954) · S. J. Day, *Intuitive cognition* (1947) · A. B. Wolter, *The transcendentals and their function in the metaphysics of Duns Scotus* (1946) · G. Leff, *The dissolution of the medieval outlook* (1976) · P. Minges, *J. D. Scoti doctrina philosophica et theologica*, 2 vols. (1908) · C. R. S. Harris, *Duns Scotus*, 2 vols. (1927) · B. Landry, *La philosophie de Duns Scot* (1922) · *The poetical works of Gerard Manley Hopkins*, ed. N. H. Mackenzie (1990) · Emden, *Oxf.*, 1.607–10
Likenesses illuminated initial, 14th cent., repro. in *The new Catholic encyclopaedia*, vol. 4, 1102 · J. Faber senior, mezzotint (after unknown artist), BM

Dunstable, John. *See* Dunstaple, John (*d.* 1453).

Dunstall, John (*d.* 1693), etcher, 'lived in the Strand, [and was] a small professor & teacher of drawing' (Vertue, *Note books*, 2.49). In his will, proved in 1693, Dunstall called himself 'schoolmaster'; this document refers also to his wife, Margaret, who survived him. Two signed drawings by him are in the British Museum, while the rest of his surviving work consists of etchings, many made in series. The earliest is *A Book of Birds Sitting on Sprigs*, which was advertised in Peter Stent's catalogue of 1654 (it can be identified through a later reprint by Henry Overton). In 1661 he produced additions for Stent's editions of the second and third *Booke of Flowers Fruicts Beastes Birds and Flies*, originally published by George Humble in the 1630s. About 1662 he etched a double portrait of Charles II and Catherine of Braganza, and in 1675 a set of six festoons. He also made some portraits intended for use as book illustrations and a set of five views of Chichester.

Dunstall's largest single group of sixty-four plates was made as an aid to his teaching; they are found uniquely in his manuscript treatise 'The art of delineation or drawing in 6 books', now in the British Library, which can be dated to the early 1690s from portraits of William and Mary bound into it. It contains twelve sets of four or eight plates of geometry, parts of the body, trees, houses, flowers, and fruit, all with titles in Greek, Latin, and English. The plates carry various addresses, which show that Dunstall lived in Blackfriars, then moved to London House Yard, Ludgate Street, near St Paul's, and finally returned to Blackfriars. On 31 August 1693 his library was advertised for sale in the

London Gazette, 'consisting of choice books in Divinity, History, Architecture, Perspective, Eng. & Lat., in all volumes; Also his Curious Collection of Prints and Drawings, by the best Masters, with his Mathematical Instruments, Graving and Etching Tools, &c.'.   ANTONY GRIFFITHS

Sources E. Croft-Murray and P. H. Hulton, eds., *Catalogue of British drawings*, 1 (1960), 301–4 · A. Globe, *Peter Stent, London printseller circa 1642–1665: being a catalogue raisonné of his engraved prints and books* (1985), catalogue nos. 518, 523–31 · R. A. Gerard, 'De Passe and early English natural history printmaking', *Print Quarterly*, 14 (1997), 174–9 · Vertue, *Note books*, 2.49 · will, proved 1693, PRO
Archives BL, Sloane MS, 5244

Dunstan [St Dunstan] (*d.* **988**), archbishop of Canterbury, was one of the principal ecclesiastical figures in the tenth-century English church: a scholar of very considerable learning, a vigorous proponent of Benedictine monasticism, a stately and revered churchman, he presided over the Anglo-Saxon church at a crucial period of intellectual and disciplinary renewal.

The sources and their problems Not surprisingly, given that Dunstan was the archbishop of Canterbury and the figurehead of English Christendom, he has often been given personal credit for reforming accomplishments which are now known to be the work of others, and particularly of his colleagues Æthelwold, bishop of Winchester (*d.* 984), and Oswald, bishop of Worcester and archbishop of York (*d.* 992). Dunstan's own contribution must nevertheless have been considerable, even if its outlines are today often blurred and indistinct. Part of the difficulty of assessing Dunstan's career lies in the nature of the sources: for his early life (up to the period of his exile in Ghent in the mid-950s) there is the informative life of St Dunstan, written near the turn of the tenth century (between 995 and 1004) by a secular cleric (known only by the first letter of his name, B.) who had evidently been a member of Dunstan's household in the 940s and early 950s. The difficulty with B.'s evidence, however, is that he was writing at Liège, without access to written Anglo-Saxon records, and furthermore was writing some fifty years after his own employment with Dunstan.

For Dunstan's later life, in particular his tenancy of the archbishopric of Canterbury, B.'s work is silent, and although Dunstan is frequently mentioned by contemporary sources such as the Anglo-Saxon Chronicle and the life of St Æthelwold by Wulfstan of Winchester, there is no reliable narrative source for this period of his life. Dunstan is also the subject of an early eleventh-century life (set out in the form of liturgical lessons) by a continental author, Adelard of Ghent, who was writing at the invitation of Ælfheah, archbishop of Canterbury from 1005 to 1012, who had apparently supplied him with information from Canterbury tradition. (This tradition is often in disagreement with B.'s life, and in any event contains no information on the period of Dunstan's archbishopric.) Furthermore, the later English hagiographers of Dunstan, namely Osbern and Eadmer of Canterbury, and William of Malmesbury, derive their accounts of Dunstan's earlier years from source's such as B's life; although they provide valuable accounts of posthumous miracles effected by the

Dunstan [St Dunstan] (*d.* **988**), drawing [kneeling before Christ]

saint, they are of very limited value in assessing Dunstan's career. The result is that although the broad outlines of Dunstan's life are clear, the details must frequently be a matter of unverifiable conjecture.

Early life and parentage The date of Dunstan's birth is unknown. B. states that Dunstan *oritur* as a *strenuus puer* in Wessex in the days of King Æthelstan (*r.* 924–39). If *oritur* here means 'emerged', 'appeared on the scene' (the primary sense of Latin *orior*), then, given that the term *puer* in medieval Latin (following a scheme set out by Isidore of Seville) referred broadly to a youth aged between seven and fourteen, Dunstan may have been born some time around 910, and subsequently appeared on the Wessex scene at the beginning of Æthelstan's reign. If, on the other hand, *oritur* means 'was born', as Osbern took it to mean, then a chronological difficulty arises. An independent source, Wulfstan of Winchester in his life of St Æthelwold (chaps. 7–8), states that both Dunstan and Æthelwold were ordained as priests by Ælfheah, bishop of Winchester from 934 to 951, at the request of King Æthelstan (hence before Æthelstan's death on 27 October 939). The canonical age for ordination was thirty; if Dunstan was indeed 'born' (*oritur*) in the days of King Æthelstan, hence after 924, he can have been no more than fifteen at the time of his ordination as priest. It seems more reasonable, therefore, to take B.'s expression *oritur* to mean 'appeared on the scene', and to hypothesize that, if Dunstan was ordained at the canonical age of thirty before the death of

Æthelstan, he must have been born in 909 or earlier. But it must be remembered that B. was writing in Liège, far from access to Anglo-Saxon written records, and may have been unable to remember or discover the name of Æthelstan's predecessor, and hence plumped—erroneously—for Æthelstan's reign as the most likely time of Dunstan's birth.

More credence can be given to the hagiographer's statement that Dunstan's parents lived in the vicinity of Glastonbury and were named Heorstan and Cynethryth; regrettably, however, he says nothing about them. The name Heorstan is an uncommon one, and it is therefore possible that the Heorstan who was Dunstan's father is identical with a man of that name who witnessed a charter of Æthelstan dated between 925 and 933 (*AS chart.*, S 1417). In this document the witness Heorstan is not qualified by any title: the fact that the document is attested by various *ministri* or royal thegns, in combination with the fact that this name is not encountered in any other charter of Edward the Elder or Æthelstan, may suggest that Heorstan was a person of lowly social standing. On the other hand, B. also says that Dunstan had a brother, very possibly an elder brother, named Wulfric (chap. 18), and that this Wulfric had acted as reeve (*praepositus*)—in effect a sort of estates bursar—of Glastonbury's landed wealth during the early period of Dunstan's abbacy. It is probable that Dunstan's brother is identical with the Wulfric who, during the 940s, received from kings Edmund and Eadred substantial lands in Wiltshire and Surrey (recorded in a series of charters: *AS chart.*, S 472, 473, 504, 530, 541, 551), some of which Wulfric subsequently bequeathed to Glastonbury. This Wulfric also witnesses various royal charters, but does not appear to attest after 951 (the matter is complicated by the fact that the name Wulfric is a common one, and that there was at least one other wealthy thegn named Wulfric at this time). In any case, the wealth and pre-eminence of Dunstan's brother Wulfric implies that the family had considerable financial resources, whatever the social standing of Heorstan.

Family connections Dunstan may have owed his appointment as abbot of Glastonbury, and his standing at court, to his elder brother, but he was well connected in other ways. He appears to have been related to several high-ranking ecclesiastics. Ælfheah 'the Bald' (so called, perhaps, because he was a tonsured monk), the bishop of Winchester, is said by B. to have been a *propinquus* ('relative'), and Cynesige, the bishop of Lichfield who like Dunstan was driven into exile by King Eadwig in 956, is said by B. to have been Dunstan's *consanguineus* ('blood relative'). Adelard of Ghent says that Athelm (Æthelhelm), successively bishop of Wells and archbishop of Canterbury, was Dunstan's uncle (*patruus*), and that it was Athelm who presented Dunstan to King Æthelstan. Adelard presumably derived this information from his Canterbury sources. Unfortunately, it cannot be confirmed, since it is not mentioned by B., and so must be treated cautiously. But a relationship with a former bishop of Wells, given the proximity of Wells to Glastonbury, cannot be regarded as out of the question. In any event, these family connections must

have helped to promote Dunstan's career. However they are to be estimated, the crucial point is that it was Bishop Ælfheah, certainly a relative, who ordained Dunstan priest.

Dunstan was also, on B.'s evidence, well connected to various aristocratic ladies. According to B., one such noble woman, the niece of King Æthelstan, had in her widowhood taken up residence near the church of Glastonbury (chap. 10), and welcomed the young Dunstan into her household as a spiritual adviser (this woman is not named by B.; she is possibly, but not certainly, identical with the Æthelflæd referred to as a most noble and devout matron in the previous chapter). B. also adds that Dunstan comforted the woman both on religious grounds as well as on grounds of kinship (*causa propinquitatis*), which seems to imply that Dunstan was related, however distantly, to the royal family. Dunstan was on hand to attend her final illness, and since B. describes her as 'exceptionally wealthy', it is likely that some of this was put to Glastonbury's advantage. Similarly, B. reports (chap. 12) Dunstan's companionship with another noblewoman named Æthelwynn, who is not, however, recorded in any other source.

As the scion of a family whose principal estates lay in the vicinity of Glastonbury, it is not surprising that Dunstan should have received his early schooling at the abbey there. There is very little information on the status of the abbey during the early tenth century, but it was presumably of modest extent, for as a boy Dunstan (according to B., chap. 3) had a vision of the greater buildings he was subsequently to construct there. It was nevertheless a centre of pilgrimage for Irish pilgrims (because, according to B., St Patrick 'the Elder' was buried there), and it was from their books, among others, that Dunstan received his early training. Unfortunately none of these books—or indeed any book of this period from Glastonbury—survives, and Dunstan's few Latin writings show no trace of Irish learning. It is perhaps more reasonable to assume that Dunstan's early studies were primarily devoted to the holy scriptures, as B. says. In any event there is no doubt that he was a gifted scholar from his youth onwards. Through his youthful promise, as also through his family connections, Dunstan came to the attention of King Æthelstan, and became a member of the royal court. At Æthelstan's urging, Dunstan was ordained priest and professed as a monk by his kinsman, Bishop Ælfheah. But Dunstan's membership of the royal court was short-lived: his self-righteous piety so aroused the envy and enmity of his colleagues there (including some of his own kinsmen) that he was thrown into a muddy pool and was lucky to escape with his life.

Abbot of Glastonbury King Æthelstan died on 27 October 939, and was succeeded by his brother Edmund (r. 939–46). Dunstan was at first welcomed by the new king as a member of his court; but, according once again to B.'s account, Dunstan's malicious enemies prevailed upon the king, with the result that Dunstan was stripped of his rank and expelled from court. Miraculously, as B. tells the story, King Edmund was hunting near Cheddar Gorge and while chasing a stag he came perilously close to the precipice, but was somehow saved. He attributed this salvation to Dunstan, and straightway appointed Dunstan as abbot of Glastonbury. The king's motive in appointing Dunstan to Glastonbury may simply have been a device to remove from his immediate household a notorious nuisance (Dunstan in any case never appears to witness royal charters of Edmund), but it had very important consequences. The precise date of the appointment is not known: Abbot Dunstan is named as the beneficiary of a charter dated 940, granting an estate at Christian Malford, Wiltshire (*AS chart.*, S 466); however, the charter is not preserved in its original form (it is found solely in fourteenth-century cartulary copies), and since it is not inventoried in the eleventh-century *Liber terrarum* of Glastonbury, there is an abiding suspicion that Dunstan's name may have been added to the charter by a later forger. Leaving aside the Christian Malford charter, Dunstan next appears as a witness to a charter of King Edmund in 946 (S 509). The most that can safely be said is that Dunstan was appointed abbot of Glastonbury during the reign of Edmund, hence between 940 and 946. In any case, the appointment had momentous consequences for the history of tenth-century England, for it was at Glastonbury that the ideals of the Benedictine reform movement were nurtured and articulated.

Dunstan was joined at Glastonbury by Æthelwold, who was professed as monk by Dunstan, and who matched Dunstan in learning and reforming zeal. When Æthelwold left Glastonbury about 953 to establish a reformed Benedictine house at Abingdon, he was able to take with him three young Glastonbury monks (Osgar, Foldbriht, and Frithegar), who were to help establish the pattern of strict Benedictine observance first at Abingdon and subsequently at Winchester, whither they accompanied Æthelwold on his appointment to the vacant bishopric in 963. According to Wulfstan, it was at Glastonbury that Æthelwold learned from Dunstan his (very considerable) skill in grammar and metrics, and various evidence suggests that during the 940s and early 950s the two scholars spent a period of prolonged study that was to establish the parameters of later tenth-century English learning, not only in respect of texts such as the rule of St Benedict (with its accompanying commentaries), but also the works of authors such as Aldhelm, from whom the Glastonbury students learned the ostentatious 'hermeneutic' style of Latin composition which characterizes (for example) Æthelwold's preface to the *Regularis concordia*. It was also at this time that reconstruction of the abbey at Glastonbury was undertaken on a significant scale; according to William of Malmesbury, Dunstan amplified the ancient church (constructed, on Malmesbury's testimony, by King Ine) by adding a tower as well as various *porticus* or side-chapels.

King Edmund was murdered on 26 May 946 and was succeeded by his younger brother Eadred. In contrast to Edmund's deep reserve regarding Dunstan, Eadred was his ardent supporter, and Dunstan once again found a privileged place at court as one of the king's principal advisers. According to B., Eadred also entrusted Dunstan with the safe-keeping of a substantial proportion of his royal treasure. Dunstan's role at Eadred's court is reflected in the fact that he figures prominently among the ecclesiastical witnesses to Eadred's charters, witnessing in second place up to 951 (*AS chart.*, S 556, 557), and then in first place for the rest of the reign (S 553, 555, 559, 571). Dunstan was also the beneficiary of two surviving royal land-grants: at Pucklechurch, Gloucestershire (S 553), and at Badbury, Wiltshire (S 568); and in King Eadred's will (S 1515), Dunstan is named as the beneficiary of £200, 'to be kept at Glastonbury for the people of Somerset and Devon'. These were clearly propitious times for Dunstan; yet, oddly perhaps, when in 952 or 953 Æthelgar, the bishop of Crediton, died, Eadred tried—with the influential help of the dowager queen Eadgifu—to persuade Dunstan to accept the vacant bishopric, Dunstan refused the offer on the grounds that he was not yet fit to assume such high office.

Exile When Eadred died on 23 November 955, he was succeeded by his nephew Eadwig (the son of King Edmund), who was then a youth in his early teens. As B. relates, the young Eadwig promptly fell into the clutches of an aristocratic lady named Æthelgifu and her wanton daughter Ælfgifu. On the day of his coronation, the king spent his time carousing with the two women rather than solemnly attending the coronation feast with his councillors. At the prompting of Archbishop Oda of Canterbury, Dunstan and his kinsman Cynesige, then bishop of Lichfield, retrieved the king from the women's embraces and marched him back to the coronation feast. Dunstan also took the opportunity to berate the women for their foolishness, an act which earned their immediate hatred. Due to their influence over the king, Dunstan was promptly forced into exile, and he left England almost at once for Ghent, probably in or soon after February 956.

B's account of this episode is lurid and exciting, but it is likely that it masks or distorts the political reality. Dunstan's personality was one which very frequently excited suspicion and envy. At the time of King Eadred's death, Dunstan alone of the king's councillors failed to attend the dying king to render account of the royal treasure which had been entrusted to him at Glastonbury: an unfortunate failure which may of itself have aroused suspicion. Furthermore, Eadred's will made no mention of Eadwig, but granted most of his personal fortune to his mother, the dowager queen Eadgifu, who had been on intimate enough terms with Dunstan to have been used as an intermediary when the king was trying to persuade Dunstan to accept the vacant bishopric of Crediton. The suspicion may have arisen among Eadwig's followers that Eadred's fortune was being retained for the use of his brother Edgar, whom some magnates were trying to promote at Eadwig's expense, and that Dunstan was implicitly involved in these machinations. In the event, Eadgifu was deprived by Eadwig of her estates. Among Eadwig's party, the 'wanton woman' Ælfgifu was in fact a member of the highest Wessex nobility and a sister of Ealdorman Æthelweard. She subsequently married Eadwig. Her family's land was held in the same area of Wessex in which Dunstan's family estates lay, and there must be a possibility that the rivalry with Ælfgifu's family was an ancient one, and the real reason for Dunstan's enforced exile.

Dunstan passed his exile in Ghent at the monastery of St Peter (called Blandinium in Latin after the hill on which it is sited, Mont Blandigny). B. apparently knew little about the exile, but Adelard, who was himself a monk of St Peter's, reports that Dunstan was offered protection and support by Arnulf (I), count of Flanders (d. 965). It is not clear why Dunstan should have chosen Ghent, but it is worth recalling that Arnulf's mother was Ælfthryth, daughter of King Alfred and wife of Baudouin (II), count of Flanders (as related in the prologue of Ealdorman Æthelweard's *Chronicon*), and that there may have been a link of some sort between the Wessex nobility and the comital house of Flanders.

Dunstan presumably spent his time at Ghent in study; in particular it is likely that he investigated the monastic customs of St Peter's, which had recently been rebuilt by Count Arnulf, and which was then regulated by the reformed Lotharingian monasticism of Abbot Gerhard of Brogne. The abbot of St Peter's at this time was one Womar (abbot 953–81), who subsequently visited England, perhaps at Dunstan's invitation, and is commemorated in the *Liber vitae* of the New Minster, Winchester, among the monks of the Old Minster. Womar may therefore have been one of the monks from Ghent who offered advice to Æthelwold when he was drawing up the *Regularis concordia* and whose contribution is explicitly acknowledged in the prologue to that work. Even after his return from exile, Dunstan remained in close contact with Ghent: Womar's successor as abbot of St Peter's, Wido (abbot 981–6), wrote to Dunstan to ask for financial aid to relieve a famine caused by crop failure, and Count Arnulf (II) (d. 988) wrote to renew friendly contact with Dunstan, and to ask Dunstan to promote a pact of peace and friendship between himself and the English king.

Archbishop of Canterbury Dunstan spent some two years in Ghent. By the autumn of 957, the political climate in England had changed radically. In that year Eadwig's younger brother Edgar was made king of England north of the Thames, and the dowager Queen Eadgifu (Edgar's grandmother) had had her land restored. Perhaps through Eadgifu's intercession, or that of Æthelwold, who had acted as the young Edgar's tutor, Dunstan was recalled to England. On B.'s testimony, Dunstan was appointed to the see of Worcester on the death of Bishop Cenwald (28 June, probably in 958), and was shortly thereafter given the see of London, which had been vacated by Byrhthelm (a supporter of Eadwig) who was translated to Wells. B.'s chronology may not be wholly reliable on this point: it seems more likely that Byrhthelm was translated to Wells once the kingdom was divided in 957, hence that Dunstan was first appointed to London, and then held Worcester in plurality after the death of Cenwald. However, Eadwig himself died on 5 October 959, and the kingdom was reunited under Edgar.

By now the young King Edgar was Dunstan's firm supporter, and his support began to tell straightaway. Byrhthelm had been translated in the same year from Wells to the vacant archbishopric of Canterbury, but he was deposed by the king and permitted to return to Wells, whereupon Dunstan was installed as archbishop of Canterbury before the end of 959. And although Dunstan was obliged to resign the sees of London and Worcester, he apparently regained personal control over Glastonbury after Eadwig's death. He appears to have retained—uncanonically—the abbacy of Glastonbury for some time after his appointment to Canterbury (how long is unclear: the succession of Glastonbury's abbots at this time is bedevilled by problems, and no abbot of Glastonbury is indisputably attested until Sigeric in 974 or 975). He remained archbishop until his death in 988.

Upon election, Dunstan in 960 travelled to Rome, where on 21 September he received the pallium from the pope as a symbol of his metropolitan authority. A copy of the written papal privilege which accompanied the grant of the pallium by Pope John XII (r. 955–64) is preserved in a surviving book which belonged to Dunstan, the so-called Sherborne pontifical or, more accurately perhaps, the pontifical of St Dunstan (now Paris, Bibliothèque Nationale, Lat. MS 943), and is a unique surviving English example of a document of this sort. On his return from Rome (late 960 or early 961) Dunstan set about restoring the English episcopacy, beginning with the two sees he had held in plurality. On his advice, Archbishop Oda's nephew Oswald, who had recently returned to England from a period of study in Fleury, was appointed to Worcester in 961, and hence to a position where his knowledge of continental monasticism could be put to good effect. The vacancy at London was filled in the same year by one Ælfstan.

Unfortunately, at roughly this time, the two narrative sources for Dunstan's life—B. and Adelard of Ghent—cease to supply first-hand information, so that the achievements of Dunstan's archiepiscopate must be largely a matter of speculation. There is no doubt, for example, that he was an active member of the king's council, for he witnesses virtually every charter issued by kings Edgar, Edward, and Æthelred up to his death in 988. His continuous presence makes it impossible to determine, say, his attitude to the murder of Edward and the accession of Æthelred; he would have crowned King Æthelred, and would presumably have been involved in the translation of Edward's relics from Wareham to Shaftesbury in 980, though no historical source says so explicitly. By the same token, there is no record of his attitude or policy towards the so-called 'anti-monastic' reaction which followed the death of King Edgar, and involved appropriations by Ealdorman Ælfhere of various monasteries in Mercia which had been granted to the church by Edgar. His outrage at these appropriations can be guessed, but is not a matter of record.

Patron of monasticism From his earliest days at Glastonbury Dunstan had been an advocate of Benedictine monasticism, and it was he who, on the occasion of receiving his pallium, had secured papal authority for the expulsion of the secular clerics from the Old Minster, Winchester, which took place on 20 February 964, at Æthelwold's instigation and with the support of King Edgar. The papal privilege, in the name of Pope John XII and addressed to Edgar (datable to the period immediately before November 963) states that permission had been sought by the king 'per fratrem et coepiscopum nostrum Dunstanum ab hac apostolica sede' ('through our brother and co-bishop Dunstan, from this apostolic see'; *Councils & Synods*, vol. 1, ed. D. Whitelock, M. Brett, and C. N. L. Brooke, 2 vols., 1981, 1.111). So although Dunstan did not personally take part in the expulsion, it was he who had secured the papal authority which made it possible. By the same token, it was not Dunstan himself but rather Æthelwold who compiled the *Regularis concordia*, the customary which stipulates monastic observance for reformed English Benedictine houses and which was issued after the Council of Winchester in 973. Dunstan is specifically named in the prologue as having laid down certain stipulations regarding the behaviour of monks towards cloistered nuns. His interest in promoting monasticism is undoubted, and there may therefore be some truth in Osbern's report that he founded—or, better perhaps, endowed—five monasteries from his own patrimony (according to Eadmer, the same patrimony which he had inherited from the noblewoman 'Ælfgifu': perhaps an error by Eadmer caused by careless reading of B.'s text). But, as in the case of most post-conquest tradition concerning Dunstan, it is impossible to verify such statements.

Such evidence as there is indicates that Malmesbury may have been one of the monasteries which Dunstan endowed: in his life of Dunstan, William of Malmesbury—who was in a position to acquire evidence at first hand—reports that Dunstan expelled from Malmesbury the clerics who had been installed there by King Eadwig, and restored the monastery to its former glory. Dunstan also donated to the monastery various ecclesiastical furniture (some of which bore inscriptions which he had composed himself: see below), and was responsible for the translation there of St Aldhelm. Another such monastery may have been Westminster. Again William of Malmesbury, in his *Gesta pontificum*, reports that Dunstan, when he was bishop of London, and hence in 959, appointed one Wulfsige to be abbot of the monastery of St Peter at Westminster (and this report is confirmed by Sulcard, writing between 1076 and 1085), and instituted twelve monks there. Malmesbury's statement appears to be confirmed by a charter (*AS chart.*, S 670), considered by students of diplomatic to have an authentic basis, which records a grant by King Edgar to Dunstan and to St Peter's, Westminster, datable probably to 959; but the matter is problematical because this Abbot Wulfsige cannot be identified with confidence.

Scholarly achievement Of Dunstan's standing as a scholar there can be no doubt, though the number of his surviving writings is modest. He is known as the author of an acrostic poem of thirty-six lines bearing as the telestich

the legend INDIGNVM ABBATEM DVNSTANVM CHRISTE RESPECTES ('May you deign to look, O Christ, on Your unworthy abbot Dunstan'), which fixes the poem's composition to the period of Dunstan's abbacy. It is one of the most difficult Latin poems surviving from pre-conquest England, and reveals not only that Dunstan was a skilled versifier, but that he had enough knowledge of Greek to employ several unusual Grecisms, and enough confidence in Latin to coin new words and to frame them in syntax so complex as at times to be nearly indecipherable. He also composed a number of shorter poems, including three distichs designed to be inscribed on ecclesiastical objects which he had donated to Malmesbury (an organ, a holy-water stoup, and a bell), as well as a distich in the so-called St Dunstan's classbook accompanying a drawing of Christ with Dunstan himself kneeling in prayer at his feet:

> Dunstanum memet clemens, rogo, Christe, tuere,
> Tenarias me non sinas sorbsisse procellas
> ('I ask you, merciful Christ, that you watch over me, Dunstan, that you not allow the Taenarian storms to swallow me')

The reference to the 'Taenarian storms' reveals at the least that Dunstan had studied Statius's *Thebaid*, a text which was not widely known in Anglo-Saxon England.

B. describes Dunstan's skill in various artistic media, including (in addition to writing and poetic composition) lyre playing, painting, and embroidery. No witness to his skill in embroidery survives, but it has often been thought that the line drawing showing the kneeling Dunstan praying to Christ (and accompanied by the aforementioned distich) in the manuscript known as St Dunstan's classbook (now Bodl. Oxf., MS Auct. F.4.32), was drawn by his own hand. In any case, to judge from the distich, the manuscript belonged at some point to Dunstan. In its present form the manuscript is composite, consisting of four parts. Of these, three are likely to have been together when the manuscript was owned by Dunstan: part I (fols. 2–9, a copy of Eutyches, *De verbo*, written in Brittany in the mid-ninth century); part III (fols. 19–36, a computistical and liturgical compilation entitled *Liber commonei*, written in Wales in the first half of the ninth century); and part IV (fols. 37–47, Ovid, *Ars amatoria*, book I, similarly written in Wales in the late ninth or early tenth century). The whole is prefaced by a single leaf or frontispiece containing the Dunstan drawing. On the assumption that the manuscript was owned by Dunstan, it is possible that various additions and corrections which it contains are in his handwriting.

In this connection it is interesting that there survives an original single-sheet charter of 949 recording a grant by King Eadred of Reculver Minster to Canterbury (*AS chart.*, S 546); the charter is witnessed by Dunstan, who describes himself as *indignus abbas*—exactly as in the acrostic poem—and who claims that he drafted and wrote the charter with his own fingers ('dictitando conposui et propriis digitorum articulis perscripsi'). The script is a distinctive form of Anglo-Saxon Square minuscule, and is very similar to the script which accompanies the line drawing of Christ and Dunstan on the frontispiece of St Dunstan's classbook: it is, very probably, Dunstan's own handwriting. From B. it is also known that Dunstan used to 'correct mistakes in books, as soon as he could see the earliest light of dawn' (Stubbs, 49). In theory, Dunstan's handwriting may be identifiable as annotations in surviving Anglo-Saxon books (though it should be borne in mind that, during his two years in Ghent, his script probably underwent the influence of continental Caroline script, and may differ, therefore, from the script of the Reculver charter).

Palaeographers do not always agree about the identity of scribal performances, but the following manuscripts have been claimed by a consensus of palaeographical opinion to contain Dunstan's annotations and corrections: Cambridge, University Library, MS Ee.2.4 (Smaragdus, *Commentarius in regulam sancti Benedicti*); London, Lambeth Palace Library, MS 237 (Augustine, *Enchiridion*); Oxford, Bodleian Library, MS Douce 140 (Primasius, *Commentarius in Apocalypsim*), MS Hatton 20 (Caesarius, *Expositio in Apocalypsim*), and MS Rawlinson C.697 (Aldhelm, *Carmen de virginitate* and *Enigmata*); and Vatican City, Biblioteca Apostolica Vaticana, MS Lat. 3363 (Boethius, *De consolatione philosophiae*). These identifications will continue to be the subject of debate among palaeographers; but if some (or all) can be accepted, they throw important light on Dunstan's scholarly interests and on the books he had read most closely. Light may also be thrown on his personality by books which can be demonstrated to have been owned by him or to have been written under his supervision (though they do not contain his handwriting), such as the aforementioned pontifical of St Dunstan (Paris, Bibliothèque Nationale, MS Lat. 943), or the so-called Bosworth psalter (BL, Add. MS 37517), which contains a liturgical calendar, a copy of the Gallican psalter, and a copy of the 'new hymnal', as revised in the ninth century. It is a reasonable assumption that Dunstan used these two books while performing liturgical rites.

There is no doubt that Dunstan was regarded by his contemporaries as a venerable and outstanding scholar. A small group of anonymous letters and poems addressed to him during the period of his archbishopric praise his learning in effusive terms (for example, those beginning 'Multiplices grates tibi sint', 'Auge potens speculans speculator', and 'Dunstan amande vale'). A letter addressed to Dunstan from Lantfred of Fleury, who had spent a number of years at the Old Minster, Winchester, begs Dunstan to return a copy of a biblical commentary by Florus, the deacon of Lyon, because the library at Fleury has been destroyed by fire. During his brief stay in England (985–7), Abbo of Fleury consulted Dunstan about the career of Edmund, king and martyr (*d.* 869), and was told a story concerning Edmund which Dunstan claimed to have heard from an old man at Æthelstan's court, who had been one of Edmund's retainers at the time of his martyrdom and who was at Æthelstan's court when Dunstan was there in his youth; Abbo reciprocated by dedicating his *Passio sancti Eadmundi* to Dunstan. Abbo also composed two acrostic poems in honour of Dunstan. The poems are preserved in Byrhtferth's life of St Oswald and contain exuberant praise of Dunstan's justice and generosity: possibly Abbo was aware that Dunstan himself had composed verse in acrostic form; he was in any event well aware of the archbishop's standing as a scholar.

Character, death, and commemoration Because of the nature of the sources, Dunstan's character poses problems for the modern historian. On the one hand, sources contemporary with the period of his archbishopric (such as Wulfstan of Winchester's life of St Æthelwold and *Narratio metrica de sancto Swithuno*) view him as a venerable, indeed angelic, white-haired figure, admirable above all for his learning, generosity, and justice. But this kindly figure sits ill with the frantic and possessed zealot sketched by B. from first-hand experience of an earlier period of Dunstan's life. At that time, apparently, Dunstan was easily capable of inspiring hatred and envy on a grand scale, as witness the anecdote related by B. of Dunstan being thrown into a duck-pond by his colleagues at Æthelstan's court, and his banishment from England by King Eadwig. Throughout his life he was excessively prone to visions, which at times gave him the appearance of a madman, as in the stories told by B. of Dunstan being pursued by the devil in the shape of a bear, or swinging his staff at ever-present demons and disturbing the sleep of his monks by whacking the walls of the cloister with it. Nevertheless, there is no doubt that he inspired the admiration of his royal patrons, particularly kings Eadred and Edgar, and the unswerving loyalty of his followers and protégés, such as Bishop Æthelwold. He is regarded by modern historians as a great statesman; it is only unfortunate that there is so little first-hand evidence of this alleged statesmanship in action.

Although Dunstan may have attracted envy and enmity during his lifetime, after his death on 19 May 988 he quickly became one of the most widely venerated English saints. Immediately after his death his name was entered in liturgical calendars (it is found in every surviving calendar written after 988) and added to litanies of the saints, especially those originating in Canterbury, where he was buried. Within a few years of his death, mass sets and benedictions were composed and are found in missals and benedictionals from the beginning of the eleventh century; and at this time too Adelard was invited by Archbishop Ælfheah to compose twelve lections (with responsories) for recitation on the saint's feast day. A hymn (beginning 'Ave, Dunstane, presulum') was also composed, probably early in the eleventh century. With these various liturgical compositions, St Dunstan could be commemorated publicly in mass and office, as well as in private devotions. In the ecclesiastical ordinance issued between 1020 and 1022 and known as Cnut I, King Cnut commanded that St Dunstan's feast on 19 May be observed all over England (c. 17.1); but, to judge from surviving liturgical books, such observance was already universal, and the king was probably simply ratifying a *de facto* situation.

Hagiography pertaining to St Dunstan also burgeoned almost from the date of his death. When the English priest B., then living in Liège, learned of Dunstan's death, he composed his life (drawing largely on memories of his own service in Dunstan's household) and sent it to Ælfric, archbishop of Canterbury, in the hope of attracting patronage; within a few years of B.'s life being received at Canterbury, the abbot of St Augustine's, one Wulfric, had sent a copy of it to the great Abbo (d. 1004), then abbot of Fleury, with the request that Abbo turn it into verse. In the second half of the eleventh century, the Canterbury hagiographers Osbern and Eadmer provided extensive accounts of the miracles accomplished by St Dunstan; and in the early twelfth century, William of Malmesbury also composed a life of St Dunstan. In the late thirteenth century an anonymous vernacular poet from the vicinity of Worcester included a Middle English verse life of Dunstan, consisting of some 206 lines, in the work known as the south English legendary; and in the mid-fourteenth century, lives of Dunstan were included by John Grandison, bishop of Exeter from 1327 to 1369, in his *Legenda sanctorum*, and by John Tynemouth (d. 1349?) in his vast *Sanctilogium Angliae, Hiberniae et Walliae*. In spite of the fact that so little is known of Dunstan's activities as archbishop of Canterbury, he became in subsequent centuries one of the most venerated of all Anglo-Saxon saints.

MICHAEL LAPIDGE

Sources W. Stubbs, ed., *Memorials of St Dunstan, archbishop of Canterbury*, Rolls Series, 63 (1874) · *The life of St Æthelwold / Wulfstan of Winchester*, ed. M. Lapidge and M. Winterbottom, OMT (1991) · T. Symons, ed. and trans., *Regularis concordia Anglicae nationis monachorum sanctimonialiumque / The monastic agreement of the monks and nuns of the English nation* (1953) · R. W. Hunt, ed., *St Dunstan's classbook from Glastonbury* (1961) · N. Brooks, *The early history of the church of Canterbury: Christ Church from 597 to 1066* (1984) · N. Ramsay, M. Sparks, and T. Tatton-Brown, eds., *St Dunstan: his life, times and cult* (1992) · M. Lapidge, 'St Dunstan's Latin poetry', *Anglia*, 98 (1980), 101–6 · M. Lapidge, 'The hermeneutic style in tenth-century Anglo-Latin literature', *Anglo-Saxon England*, 4 (1975), 67–111 · *Willelmi Malmesbiriensis monachi de gestis pontificum Anglorum libri quinque*, ed. N. E. S. A. Hamilton, Rolls Series, 52 (1870) · G. R. Wieland, ed., *The Canterbury hymnal: edited from British Library MS Additional 37517*, Toronto Medieval Latin Texts, 12 (1982)

Likenesses drawing, BL, Royal MS 10 A.xiii · drawing, Bodl. Oxf., MS Auct. F.4.32, fol. 1r [*see illus.*] · group portrait, drawing, BL, Cotton MS Tiberius A.iii, frontispiece; repro. in J. Backhouse, D. H. Turner, and L. Webster, eds., *The golden age of Anglo-Saxon art* (1984), 49

Dunstan, Albert Ernest (1878–1964), research chemist and petroleum technologist, was born on 25 January 1878 at 69 Washington Road, Sheffield, the only son of Arthur Dunstan (d. 1896), a workshop manager, and Mary Ann Wainwright (d. 1897). His father was shop manager for an old-established firm (Edward Greaves & Son) which manufactured cabinet cases and fitted containers for fine cutlery. Dunstan had four sisters, all younger than himself. He was educated in Sheffield, first at Sharrow Lane board school and then, from the age of twelve, at the Royal Grammar School.

In 1895 Dunstan gained a scholarship for intending teachers from the College of Preceptors and for the next two years he combined studies at Firth College with teaching at a preparatory school. Initially a keen classics scholar, he now turned his interest to science, but the death of his parents meant that by 1897 continued education had to yield priority to earning a living. Thus in April 1898 he took up an appointment as junior master at Clifton House School, Eastbourne. In October 1900 he was able to resume his studies, this time at the Royal College of Science in London, and these resulted in a BSc degree. This was followed by a teaching appointment at Dame Alice Owen's School, Islington.

In 1905 Dunstan obtained the post of lecturer in chemistry and physics at the newly built East Ham Technical College and secondary day school. Here he took advantage of good laboratory facilities to explore what was becoming a major interest, namely viscosity. His first paper on the viscosity of liquids had in fact already been published in the *Transactions* of the Chemical Society in 1904. By 1910 he had written several chemistry textbooks and his output of published papers on viscosity had risen to over twenty. In addition, despite his busy teaching schedule at East Ham both during the day and in the evenings, he carried out experimental work on viscosity at University College, London, under Professor Trouton. This led to a DSc in 1910. In 1911 Dunstan married one of his students, Louisa Cleaverley (d. 1963). They had a daughter and a son, Bernard, an artist and member of the Royal Academy.

By early 1913 the refinery at Abadan of the young Anglo-Persian Oil Company (to become Anglo-Iranian Oil in 1937, and British Petroleum in 1954) was in full operation. A prime function of this refinery was to supply fuel oil to the British navy, but it was soon found that the Admiralty fuel oil made from Persian crude could sometimes undergo an increase in viscosity in ships' bunkers. This often meant handling problems under cold weather conditions, as in the North Sea, and was a matter of much concern to the navy, especially following the outbreak of war in 1914. The Admiralty therefore asked their specialist adviser on petroleum matters, Sir Boverton Redwood, for expert assistance in view of his proven knowledge of viscosity phenomena; Dunstan was recommended early in 1915 as the man to tackle the problem. Dunstan took with him Dr F. B. Thole, one of his teaching colleagues, and these two, initially working for the Admiralty, soon officially joined Anglo-Persian, carrying out their investigations in the laboratories at East Ham. They also worked on other interests of Anglo-Persian—for example the refining of motor spirit and kerosene from Persian crude, and the potential manufacture of toluene (for TNT) from petroleum. This latter interest was studied by Dunstan through his activities at a large experimental plant at Thameshaven.

In November 1916 Dunstan was asked by his directors to go out to Persia. He accepted with alacrity, and once there he made a study of refinery operations at Abadan and visited the oilfield at Maidan-i-Naftun. He returned to Britain in April 1917 and reported to Charles Greenway, chairman of Anglo-Persian, that the company possessed a crude oil of vast potentialities, but that little was yet known of its actual composition. The result of this meeting was an instruction to set up a research organization coupled with the offer of the post of research chemist (at a salary of £750 per annum).

A research laboratory was established in September 1917 at Meadhurst, a dilapidated Georgian mansion in Sunbury-on-Thames. This building had a large cellar (initially flooded), which was converted, despite wartime shortages, into a laboratory. Thus was established, with Dunstan and Thole as the only staff, the nucleus of what was later to become the vast Sunbury Research Centre of British Petroleum. In 1919 adjacent land was purchased for the erection of a properly designed new laboratory block complete with workshops, a canteen, and other amenities. Occupation of these new buildings began in 1921, and with the extra space and staff available Dunstan was able adequately to carry out research into the chemistry of crude oil.

One legacy from the war was a shortage of liquid fuels and Dunstan became a chemical adviser to a committee on the production of oil from cannel coal and allied minerals which had been set up by the Institution of Petroleum Technologists (later the Institute of Petroleum) in 1918. In 1921 he visited an experimental plant at Rheinau in Germany, to examine the possibility of producing oil from coal using a high-pressure hydrogenation process developed by Bergius.

During the early 1920s many investigations were in progress at Sunbury, priority being given to processes for the desulphurization of light distillate fractions, one using sodium hypochlorite as the reagent, and the other using selective adsorption over bauxite. These processes were successfully brought into operation during 1921 and 1922 at Abadan and at the company's new refinery at Llandarcy, near Swansea. Many other petroleum products such as fuel oil, lubricating oil, diesel oil, and aviation spirit were investigated by Dunstan and his team, and the decisions concerning which projects to work on were largely taken by Dunstan himself, without interference from head office. Dunstan also developed an intense interest in cracking processes, and was sent to Detroit in 1922 to study an American cracking process (Ramage process). This became the start of a long programme of work on cracking reactions at Sunbury, which by 1924 had led to the development of a new cracking process, the 'A-D-H' process, named after the individuals concerned, Auld, Dunstan, and Herring.

In the autumn of 1924 Dunstan was transferred to head office in London as chief chemist of the company, with overall responsibility for laboratory matters not only at Sunbury but also in the Persian oilfield, and at the Abadan and Llandarcy refineries. He was already a member of the Institution of Petroleum Technologists, and indeed had been elected in 1919 to its council, on which he remained until 1958—a record period. He became vice-president of the institution for the period 1928–9, and president for the sessions 1929–30 and 1930–31. He was also honorary editor of its publications, a duty which he undertook for twenty-five years. In 1938 he was awarded the institute's Redwood medal for his outstanding services to petroleum technology.

Over the years Dunstan participated with similar energy in the affairs of many other learned societies, and his offices included being the chairman of the education committee of the Royal Institute of Chemistry, a member of council of the Chemical Society and of the Society of Chemical Industry, treasurer of the Chemical Council, a member of council of the Institute of Fuel, a member of the Faraday Society, president of the British Association of Chemists, and a member of the parliamentary and scientific committee of the House of Commons. He was also associated with various government departmental committees: he was a member of the fuel efficiency committee and chaired both the liquid fuel committee and the creosote-pitch committee of the Ministry of Fuel and Power; he was a member of the Home Office committee on smoke screens and of the mixtures committee of the petroleum warfare department; he was a board member of HM fuel research station; and he was a general council member of the British Standards Institution. Furthermore he maintained close contact with many universities.

Dunstan travelled widely, on company business, on lecture tours, and to attend international conferences such as the World Power Conference in Berlin in 1930 and the World Petroleum Congress in London in 1933 (for which he was a convenor of papers). He had many valuable friends among outstanding petroleum technologists in America, and in 1929 the American Society for Testing Materials (ASTM) elected him chairman of the ASTM committee for testing petroleum and its products—a tribute to his continuing efforts to promote co-operation between the ASTM and the Institute of Petroleum in developing standardized test procedures for use on both sides of the Atlantic. In all such activities Dunstan assumed the role of unofficial ambassador not only for his company but also for the petroleum industry as a whole, both nationally and internationally. His drive, enthusiasm, and breezy, extrovert manner endeared him to all he met.

Dunstan retired from Anglo-Iranian Oil at the end of 1946 with some 35 patents to his name and over 120 technical papers, as well as several textbooks. Perhaps his greatest achievement in regard to publications was as managing editor for the four massive volumes of *The Science of Petroleum*, published in 1938 and followed by three parts of a fifth volume during the period 1950–55. He spent his latter years in a house in Cambridge. His wife died in 1963, and he died in the following year, on 6 January 1964, at Addenbrooke's Hospital, Cambridge. On 22 September 1965 a new four-storey laboratory block housing 130 staff was formally opened at the Sunbury Research Centre. This new building was named the Dunstan Laboratory, a fitting memorial to the man who had made it all possible.   JOHN HOOPER

Sources A. E. Dunstan, 'Do you remember?', personal memoir, c.1955, BP Archive, University of Warwick · W. H. T. and G. S., 'Albert Ernest Dunstan, 1878–1964', *Journal of the Institute of Petroleum*, 50 (1964), 81–2 · R. W. Ferrier, *The history of the British Petroleum Company*, 1: *The developing years, 1901–1932* (1982) · J. H. D. Hooper, 'A history of BP research' (to 1973), BP Archive, University of Warwick • A. E. Dunstan and D. A. Howes, 'The story of Sunbury', *Naft magazine* (April 1946), 2–5 • A. E. Dunstan, 'First annual report of research department, 1917', BP Archive, University of Warwick • A. E. Dunstan, 'Fourth annual report of research department, 1920', BP Archive, University of Warwick • H. Longhurst, *Adventures in oil: the story of British Petroleum* (1959) • private information (2004)

Archives University of Warwick, BP Archive

Likenesses B. Dunstan, portrait, BP Research Centre, Sunbury-on-Thames

Wealth at death £15,785: probate, 6 March 1964, *CGPLA Eng. & Wales*

Dunstan, Jeffrey (1759?–1797), hawker and 'mayor of Garrett', was a foundling reared in the parish workhouse of St Dunstan-in-the-East, in the City of London. At the age of twelve he was apprenticed to a greengrocer, but he ran away to Birmingham, where he worked in the factories. The heavy labour probably added to his deformities, for as an adult he had knock knees, a large head, and grew to a height of only 4 feet. He returned to London in 1776 and, whether formally married or not, he had two daughters, Polly and Nancy. His chief occupation was buying old wigs; his extraordinary appearance and his droll way of clapping his hands to his mouth and crying his wares always attracted a crowd of people, and this popularity led to his election as 'mayor of Garrett' in 1785, on the death of 'Sir' John Harper.

The custom of the Garrett elections came about following encroachments on Garrett Common, situated between Wandsworth and Tooting, in Surrey. The inhabitants formed an association for the protection of their rights, the head of this association being known as the mayor of Garrett. The mayor was chosen after every general election. These mock elections soon became extremely popular, offering the possibility of a joyful and indeed riotous public holiday for the many thousands who congregated on the common. The most eccentric characters were brought forward as candidates, and it provided an opportunity for political satire in one of Samuel Foote's most successful dramatizations, *The Mayor of Garratt*, in 1763.

'Sir' Jeffrey Dunstan's deformed figure was widely caricatured, but he was a lively and popular wit, and was re-elected at three successive elections, being ousted in 1796 by 'Sir' Harry Dimsdale, a muffin-seller and tinware dealer. He designed his own armorial, bearing four wigs, with a tankard as a crest. An attempt was made to bring Dunstan onto the stage at the Haymarket Theatre, in the part of Dr Last. But, as Charles Lamb's 'Reminiscence of Sir Jeffery Dunstan' relates, despite tutoring from either Foote or David Garrick, 'Sir Jeffery failed … and made nothing of his part, till the hisses of the house at last in very kindness dismissed him from the boards' (Hone, 2, col. 844).

In 1797, after a heavy bout of drinking, Dunstan died. Friends saved his corpse from body-snatchers, and he was buried in the churchyard of St Mary, Whitechapel.

G. F. R. Barker, *rev.* Anita McConnell

Jeffrey Dunstan (1759?–1797), by T. Wilkes, pubd 1794

Sources A. Shaw, *The mayor of Garratt*, Wandsworth Historical Cameos, 1 (1980) • J. Brewer, 'Theater and counter-theater in Georgian politics: the mock elections at Garrat', *Radical History Review*, 22 (1980), 7–40 • H. Lemoine and J. Caulfield, *The eccentric magazine, or, Lives and portraits of remarkable persons*, 2 vols. (1812–13) • R. Malcolm, ed., *Curiosities of biography, or, Memoirs of wonderful and extraordinary characters* (1855) • *GM*, 1st ser., 51 (1781), 304 • W. Hone, *The Every-day Book and Table Book*, 2 vols. (1826)

Likenesses coloured etching, pubd 1779, BP • T. Wilkes, etching, BM, NPG; repro. in *Wonderful Magazine and Marvellous Chronicle* (1794) [*see illus.*]

Dunstan, Sir Wyndham Rowland (1861–1949), chemist and director of the Imperial Institute, was born at Chester on 24 May 1861, the elder son of John Dunstan, constable and governor of Chester Castle, and his wife, Catherine, daughter of (Philip) Cipriani Hambley *Potter, principal of the Royal Academy of Music.

Dunstan was educated at Bedford School and abroad. In 1879 he was appointed assistant to Theophilus Redwood, professor of chemistry in the Pharmaceutical Society's School of Pharmacy, and later was demonstrator in the chemical laboratories; he succeeded Redwood in 1886. Meantime he was made a demonstrator in the University of Oxford's chemical laboratories in 1884 and a year later university lecturer on chemistry in relation to medicine. From 1892 to 1900 he was lecturer on chemistry in St Thomas's Hospital medical school. In 1896 he became director of the scientific and technical department of the Imperial Institute and he succeeded Sir F. A. Abel as its director in 1903, retaining this appointment until he retired in 1924.

Dunstan was an excellent teacher and his lectures were attractive in diction and style. At the Imperial Institute his driving power, clear foresight, and organizing ability helped develop that organization to the greatest extent possible within its rather meagre financial resources.

During his period at the School of Pharmacy Dunstan's research work lay in pharmaceutical chemistry and dealt with such matters as the quality of chemical compounds used in medicine and with the development of methods for the standardization of preparations of such potent drugs as nux vomica and belladonna. In 1887 the Pharmaceutical Society's research laboratory was inaugurated with Dunstan as director, and there important work was done on various drugs including the alkyl nitrites, and an investigation was started on the alkaloids of monkshood (*Aconitum napellus*) which was later extended to a series of Indian aconites when Dunstan moved to the Imperial Institute. The institute had been founded to investigate and publicize new or little-known mineral and vegetable resources of the countries of the empire. Dunstan set to work to fulfil this programme, which required a considerable increase of trained staff, made possible with grants from various public bodies and other donors. After 1900, when the building was taken over by the government, development of the institute's work attracted increasing official interest. A detailed report of 1923 illustrated the remarkable volume and range of the work done and was a tribute to the success of the institute under Dunstan.

The results of investigations into imperial resources were published in official reports, such as those on the mineral surveys which Dunstan helped establish in Ceylon, Nigeria, and Nyasaland. From 1903 further reports and articles were published in the quarterly *Bulletin of the Imperial Institute*.

Dunstan was also interested in the teaching of science and in philosophy; the first led to his service as secretary with the British Association committee on this subject, and the second to his connection with the foundation of the Aristotelian Society, of which he was a vice-president and editor of its *Proceedings*. He was elected FRS in 1893 and was a member of the council in 1905–7. As president of the International Association of Tropical Agriculture, he presided over the third international congress in London in 1914, and he was president of the chemistry section of the British Association meeting at York in 1906. He was successively member of council, secretary, and a vice-president of the Chemical Society, served on the council of the Royal Geographical Society (1916), and was a corresponding member of the Institut Égyptien. He received the honorary degrees of MA from Oxford in 1888 and of LLD from Aberdeen in 1904. He was also a commander of the order of Leopold of Belgium, and was appointed CMG in 1913 and KCMG in 1924.

On 7 August 1886 Dunstan married Emilie Fordyce (1860/61–1893), daughter of George Francis Maclean. She died in 1893, leaving a son and a daughter, and on 14 August 1900 Dunstan married Violet Mary Claudia (*b.* 1876), daughter of Frederick Stephen Archibald Hanbury-Tracy, MP and son of the second Baron Sudeley. She survived her husband with a second daughter. Dunstan died at 10 Clarence Crescent, Windsor, Berkshire, on 20 April 1949.   T. A. HENRY, *rev.*

Sources T. A. Henry, *Obits. FRS*, 7 (1950–51), 63–81 · T. A. Henry, *JCS* (1950), 1022–6 · 'Report on the operations of the Imperial Institute', *Bulletin of the Imperial Institute*, 21 (1923) · private information (1959) · personal knowledge (1959) · *Colonial Office List* (1936) · J. Foster, *Oxford men and their colleges* (1893) · m. cert., 1886 · m. cert., 1900 · d. cert.
Archives CUL, corresp. with Lord Hardinge
Likenesses W. Stoneman, photograph, 1933, NPG · C. Forbes, portrait, Chemical Society, Burlington House, London
Wealth at death £31,882 12*s.* 1*d.*: probate, 13 Aug 1949, *CGPLA Eng. & Wales*

Dunstanville, de. For this title name *see* Basset, Francis, Baron de Dunstanville and Baron Basset (1757–1835).

Dunstanville, de, family (*per. c.*1090–*c.*1292), gentry, was a landholding family with interests in Wiltshire, Shropshire, Sussex, Cornwall, and Oxfordshire. The family, whose members make their first appearance in the late 1090s, probably originated from Dénestanville (Seine-Maritime) in Normandy. Walter de Dunstanville, his brother Robert, and son Adam witnessed an act of William II, while Robert attested three acts of Arnulf de *Montgomery (*d.* 1118x22), and it is these links with the Montgomery family that probably account for the family's later holdings in Sussex and Shropshire. Before 1114 **Adeliza de Insula** [de Dunstanville] (*fl.* 1114–1130) gave land in Wiltshire to Tewkesbury Abbey for her husband, **Reginald de Dunstanville** (*fl.* 1114); they were probably the parents of Reginald de Dunstanville and his sister Gundreda who appear in the Wiltshire section of the pipe roll for 1130. Much of the Wiltshire property afterwards held by the family had been listed in Domesday Book as that of Humphrey de Insula, which suggests that Adeliza de Insula was Humphrey's daughter and a figure of some importance, and an Adeliza de Dunstanville appears as security for a debt in the roll of 1130.

*Reginald, earl of Cornwall (*d.* 1175), is given the toponym of Dunstanville by Orderic Vitalis and, although his relationship to the family is nowhere made explicit, Dunstanvilles, particularly the clerk, Hugh, and another **Robert de Dunstanville** (*d.* 1166/7), were often in his entourage. The connection with Earl Reginald introduced the Dunstanvilles into the Empress Matilda's circle and an **Alan** [i] **de Dunstanville** (*fl.* 1141) witnessed a charter given by her in 1141. Robert de Dunstanville witnessed acts both of the empress and of her son, the future Henry II, attesting one royal act as the king's *dapifer* ('steward'). In the mid-1150s he was given the revenues of Heytesbury, Wiltshire (£40 annually), and from about 1160 received the revenues of Colyton in Devon (£20 annually).

When Robert died his property was inherited by his nephew **Walter** [i] **de Dunstanville** (*d. c.*1195), the son of his (probably older) brother Alan [i]. Walter [i] and his brother **Alan** [ii] **de Dunstanville** (*d.* before 1199) confirmed Robert's grant of land to Monkton Farleigh Priory before 1169, but the younger Alan's interests lay chiefly in

Oxfordshire. He farmed the honour of Earl Giffard from 1180 and married Muriel de Langetot (*b.* 1155), daughter of Geoffrey fitz William, who had himself administered the Giffard honour, securing her property at Shiplake, Oxfordshire. Alan [ii] also held property in Cornwall. His eldest son, Walter, died before 1206 when a second son, **Alan [iii] de Dunstanville** (*d.* after 1216), took control of the Cornish property. Alan [iii] died childless, as did his brother, Geoffrey (*d.* 1234), and the Oxfordshire branch of the Dunstanvilles then failed, the estates descending to the heirs of Alan's and Muriel's daughters.

When Walter [i] inherited the Wiltshire holdings of his uncle Robert he already held lands in Shropshire and Sussex, inherited from his father, Alan [i], and his Wiltshire interests were to be yet further increased by the estates of the senior branch of the family, after the death of Reginald, earl of Cornwall. Walter [i] attested acts of Henry II and later those of King John, but he was not as conspicuous at the royal court as his uncle Robert had been. Links with another family in royal service had been fostered when his sister Adeliza de Dunstanville [**Adeliza Basset** (*d.* in or after 1210)] married Thomas *Basset (*d. c.*1182). Although Walter received some signs of favour from Richard I, his lands and those of a number of his associates were forfeited in 1194, the year in which Richard returned from captivity, suggesting that they may have been involved in Prince John's disloyalty. Walter [i] had apparently taken the cross, but died before he could set out.

A long minority followed when the property was held on behalf of Walter [i]'s son, **Walter [ii] de Dunstanville** (*c.*1192–1241), by a series of custodians, including William Brewer (*d.* 1244) and Walter [ii]'s cousins, Gilbert and Thomas Basset, and serious inroads were made on the lands of the family. Walter attained his majority about 1213 and was summoned to the king's expedition to Poitou in 1214. He was among those who rebelled against King John in 1215, but was quickly restored to favour under Henry III. He fought in the campaigns against the Welsh in the late 1220s and joined the king's expedition to France in 1230. His marriage to Petronilla, daughter of William Fitzalan, brought the family the manor of Isleham, Cambridgeshire, and did something to revive its fortunes.

In 1242 Walter [ii]'s son, **Sir Walter [iii] de Dunstanville** (*b.* after 1212, *d.* 1270), joined Henry III's expedition to Gascony and fought the Welsh in the campaigns of the mid-1240s and 1250s. His service to the royal cause at the battle of Lewes was less distinguished, although the king later pardoned him for running away and in May 1265 made him constable of Salisbury Castle. Walter [iii] was a benefactor of the Cistercian house at Stanley in Wiltshire, to which he gave the services from lands in Costow in Wroughton, Wiltshire. His death on 14 January 1270 ended the direct Dunstanville line. His son, who was probably also called Walter, had died in 1246 and his heir was therefore his daughter, Petronilla [**Petronilla de la Mare** (*b.* 1248, *d.* in or before 1292)]. She married first Robert de Montfort (*d.* 1274) and second John de la Mare (*d.*

1313), and left as her heir William de Montfort, who disposed of most of his interests in the Dunstanville lands by sale.

The Dunstanvilles were a family of middling wealth, whose title was never more elevated than a knighthood. Their interests spread through southern England and the marches, and indicate what such a family might achieve through marriages and access to royal patronage. The family extended its interests beyond Wiltshire through their links with the Montgomery family and built on the advantageous marriage that brought them the lands of Humphrey de Insula. Younger sons of the family had successful careers as royal servants and established their own landed holdings, which by accidents of inheritance were sometimes consolidated into the main branch of the family. In the thirteenth century the Dunstanvilles played an important role in their localities, but were not significant figures at the royal court. KATHLEEN THOMPSON

Sources R. W. Eyton, *Antiquities of Shropshire*, 12 vols. (1854–60), vol. 2, pp. 268–304 • W. Farrer, *Honours and knights' fees* (1923–5), vol. 3, pp. 37–41 • *Pipe rolls*, 2 John, 162–3 • [W. Illingworth], ed., *Rotuli hundredorum temp. Hen. III et Edw. I*, 2 vols., RC (1812–18) • T. D. Hardy, ed., *Rotuli chartarum in Turri Londinensi asservati*, RC, 36 (1837) • *Chancery records* • H. C. M. Lyte and others, eds., *Liber feodorum: the book of fees*, 3 vols. (1920–31) • H. Hall, ed., *The Red Book of the Exchequer*, 3 vols., Rolls Series, 99 (1896) • L. F. Salzman, ed., *The chartulary of the Priory of St Pancras of Lewes*, 2 vols., Sussex RS, 38, 40 (1932–4) • J. L. Kirby, ed., *Hungerford cartulary*, Wilts RS, 49 (1993) • *CIPM*, 1, no. 625 • K. Thompson, 'Affairs of state: the illegitimate children of Henry I', *Journal of Medieval History*, 29 (2003)
Wealth at death £122 14*s.* 1*d.*—for landed property; Walter [iii] de Dunstanville • 35 marks—for advowsons in Wiltshire in 1270; Walter [iii] de Dunstanville: Kirby, ed., *Hungerford cartulary*, no. 625; *CIPM*

Dunstanville, Alan de (*fl.* 1141). *See under* Dunstanville, de, family (*per. c.*1090–*c.*1292).

Dunstanville, Alan de (*d.* before **1199**). *See under* Dunstanville, de, family (*per. c.*1090–*c.*1292).

Dunstanville, Alan de (*d.* after **1216**). *See under* Dunstanville, de, family (*per. c.*1090–*c.*1292).

Dunstanville, Reginald de (*fl. c.***1114**). *See under* Dunstanville, de, family (*per. c.*1090–*c.*1292).

Dunstanville, Robert de (*d.* **1166/7**). *See under* Dunstanville, de, family (*per. c.*1090–*c.*1292).

Dunstanville, Walter de (*d. c.***1195**). *See under* Dunstanville, de, family (*per. c.*1090–*c.*1292).

Dunstanville, Walter de (*c.*1192–1241). *See under* Dunstanville, de, family (*per. c.*1090–*c.*1292).

Dunstanville, Sir Walter de (*b.* after **1212**, *d.* **1270**). *See under* Dunstanville, de, family (*per. c.*1090–*c.*1292).

Dunstaple [Dunstable], **John** (*d.* **1453**), composer, is of unknown origins, though his family presumably took its name from Dunstable in Bedfordshire, to which spelling modern scholarship has often adapted his name, despite the contemporary preponderance of 'p', including in his autograph signature. Nothing certain is known of his date of birth or early career, but his earliest works are datable to the decade 1410–20. It has often been suggested that he entered the service of John, duke of Bedford, perhaps while Bedford was regent of France, after 1422. One fascicle of an astronomical treatise bears the note of ownership 'Iste libellus pertinebat Johanni Dunstaple cum [quondam?] duci Bedfordie musico' (Cambridge, St John's College, MS 162), that is, musician to John, duke of Bedford. Until 1432 Bedford owned the advowson of St Stephen Walbrook, London, where Dunstaple was buried, and presumably resided (he held rents in the parish from at least 1445). But grants to Dunstaple of land in Normandy, the first of them in 1437 of former Bedford lands, constitute the sole and indirect archival corroboration that he was ever in the duke's service. These grants may, however, give substance to the theory that Dunstaple travelled abroad.

A more secure connection is with the dowager queen Joan, widow of Henry IV, whose gifts and payments to Dunstaple span the period 1427–36, and probably continued until her death in 1437. But there is no doubt that he entered the service of Humphrey, duke of Gloucester, since a document of 5 July 1438 describes him as the duke's servant and domestic familiar. It may be significant that in the early 1440s the rector of St Stephen Walbrook was a former chaplain of Duke Humphrey. Dunstaple must also have spent time at St Albans, whose abbot, John Wheathampstead, would probably compose one, or perhaps even two, obituaries for him. Wheathampstead in his turn was closely associated with Duke Humphrey and Queen Joan, and with Italian humanist circles, and all four seem to have had a strong interest in music, mathematics, and astrology. Humphrey's connection with Leonello d'Este, marquess of Ferrara, may account for the presence of so much of Dunstaple's music (including his two St Albans-related motets, on St Alban and St Germanus) in a Ferrarese manuscript, MS Modena α. X.1.11. With princely associations came personal wealth. Tax records for 1436 indicate that Dunstaple had an income that year of £24 from property in Cambridgeshire, Essex, and London, and a large annuity of £80 from Queen Joan. Other records of a man bearing his name who was a gentleman in Cambridgeshire in 1436, and the owner of the Hertfordshire manor of Broadfield in 1449, may be plausibly associated with the composer. Lay status (as gentleman or esquire) may have excluded him from service as a chaplain, but is not incompatible with these unclassified manifestations of royal patronage.

Dunstaple was the most eminent of an influential group of English composers active in the first half of the fifteenth century. His earliest datable works are two isorhythmic motets, *Veni sancte/Veni sancte/Veni creator* (*Complete Works*, 32), for Pentecost, and *Preco preheminencie/ Precursor/Inter natos* (*Complete Works*, 29), for John the Baptist. Henry V and Emperor Sigismund attended a ceremony in Canterbury Cathedral on 21 August 1416, celebrating the treaty of Canterbury and English victories in France, and the chronicle attributed to Thomas Elmham includes these two motets in a list of the six performed on this occasion. The date is surprisingly early, and the first of

the two motets is the only work of Dunstaple's present in the Old Hall manuscript, which was probably compiled for Thomas, duke of Clarence, killed in battle in 1421; it appears there as an addendum, perhaps implying that Dunstaple was newly known as a composer.

Over seventy compositions bear Dunstaple's name, a few with conflicting or disputed attributions, including the famous song 'O rosa bella', which is almost certainly by John Bedyngham. Nearly all his works are mass music and motets, and they survive mainly in continental manuscripts, in northern Italy or Germany. Many English sources have been destroyed, often considered obsolete long before the Reformation, though new copies and new pieces continue to emerge from discoveries of isolated leaves—most recently two pieces in another royal manuscript, now dismembered, one of which is a hitherto unknown canonic Gloria ascribed to Dunstaple. A five-part setting of the Marian antiphon *Gaude flore virginali* by 'Dunstable' has been lost from the Eton choirbook, but at least one incomplete setting could have been that piece. His surviving music is mostly in three parts, some in four, originally intended for all-vocal (if not fully texted) performance.

Half of Dunstaple's output consists of settings of movements from the ordinary of the mass. Some of these are or were linked into groups or cycles built on a common tenor, treated with varying degrees of strictness, a technique pioneered by English composers of his generation. Twelve polytextual isorhythmic motets are all on sacred subjects; two (mentioned above) were written by 1416, and another, for St Albans, probably in 1426, but they lack internal topical indications. Most of his other works are settings of liturgical texts in a song-like style for one texted and two accompanying voices. His name also appears attached to a tetrachordal tenor appended to two copies of a treatise on music theory.

Dunstaple died in London on 24 December 1453, and was buried in St Stephen Walbrook. If women bearing his surname in the parish were relations, then he was probably married. If so, other suggested clerical or monastic identities would be eliminated, including John Dunstapylle, canon of Hereford from 1419 to 1440, a Benedictine at St Albans, and an Augustinian canon at Dunstable Priory. The date of his death is recorded in an epitaph, which was reinstated in the church—destroyed in the great fire of 1666—in 1904, in a version adapted from Anthony Munday's transcription in a late edition of Stowe's *Survey of London* (1618 and subsequent editions). It may have been the work of John Wheathampstead, likewise a second epitaph reported by John Weever in his *Antient Funerall Monuments* (1631). From these epitaphs, the second of which likens him to Miccalus, Ptolemy, and Atlas, we learn that Dunstaple was esteemed as a mathematician and astronomer as well as a musician. Of three non-music manuscripts naming him, the most important (Cambridge, Emmanuel College, MS 70) contains mostly astrological works, some of them bearing his scribal signature, and one of them also containing a series of good astrological drawings that may be in his hand. His astronomical calculations (Bodl. Oxf., MS Laud misc. 674) show high competence, but no particular originality, and though he made copies of treatises, he is not known to have been the author of any. As a composer, however, Dunstaple was internationally recognized during his lifetime and long after his death. He was hailed as the chief exponent of a sweet new English style and, indeed, as the founder of a new musical age. He was referred to—usually with approval—by such contemporary and later writers as Martin le Franc (c.1440), Tinctoris (1477), an anonymous Seville writer of c.1480, Gafurius (1496), Crétin (in his lament on the death of Ockeghem, c.1497), Eloi d'Amerval (1508), Spataro (1529, mentioning the motets *Veni* and *Preco*), Sebald Heyden (1540), and Thomas Morley (1597).

MARGARET BENT

Sources *John Dunstable: complete works*, ed. M. F. Bukofzer, Musica Britannica, 8 (1953); 2nd edn, rev. M. Bent, I. Bent, and B. Trowell (1970) · C. Maclean, 'The Dunstable inscription in London', *Sammelbände der Internationalen Musikgesellschaft*, 11 (1910), 232–49 · M. Bent, *Dunstaple*, Oxford Studies of Composers, 17 (1981) · A. Wathey, 'Dunstable in France', *Music and Letters*, 67 (1986), 1–36 · B. Trowell, 'Proportion in the music of Dunstable', *Proceedings of the Royal Musical Association*, 105 (1978–9), 100–41 · M. Bent, 'A new canonic Gloria and the changing profile of Dunstable', *Plainsong and Medieval Music*, 5 (1996) · M. Bukofzer, 'John Dunstable: a quincentenary report', *Musical Quarterly*, 40 (1954), 29–49 · M. Bent and I. Bent, 'Dufay, Dunstable, Plummer: a new source', *Journal of the American Musicological Society*, 22 (1969), 394–424 · D. R. Howlett, 'A possible date for a Dunstable motet', *Music Review*, 36 (1975), 81–4 · J. Stell and A. Wathey, 'New light on the biography of John Dunstable?', *Music and Letters*, 62 (1981), 60–63 · M. Bent, 'Dunstable, John', *New Grove* · D. Fallows, 'Dunstable, Bedyngham and *O rosa bella*', *Journal of Musicology*, 12 (1994), 287–305 · J. Weever, *Antient funerall monuments* (1631) · J. Stow, *A survay of London*, ed. A. M. [A. Munday], rev. edn (1618)
Archives Bäyerische Staatsbibliothek, Munich · BL, MS Laud misc. 674 · Civico Museo Bibliografico Musicale, Bologna · Emmanuel College, Cambridge, MS 70 · Museo Diocesano, Trent · Museo Nazionale, Trent · Seminario Maggiore, Aosta · St John Cam., MS 162 · University Library, Bologna

Dunster, Charles (1750–1816), Church of England clergyman and writer, was the only son of the Revd Charles Dunster (d. 1750), prebendary of Grimston in Salisbury Cathedral. He was admitted at Oriel College, Oxford, as a commoner in 1767, took his BA degree in late 1770, migrated to Balliol College in early 1771, and to Trinity College in 1773. He became an MA in 1775. Dunster took holy orders and was instituted in 1776 to the rectories of Oddingley (the gift of Lord Foley) and Naunton Beauchamp (by the crown), both in Worcestershire. In 1789 he was nominated as rector of Petworth in Sussex by Lord Egremont, instituted 23 March. It was a profitable living and Dunster had no incentive to move again. He held the rectory of Petworth until his death.

Dunster was a prolific writer and a competent scholar with poetic tastes. He published in 1785 *The Frogs: a Comedy*, translated from Aristophanes, and in 1791 an edition of John Philips's poem *Cider*, 'with notes provincial and explanatory, including the present most approved method of making cyder in Herefordshire'. Dunster had a

strong interest in Milton: he produced an annotated edition of *Paradise Regained* in 1795 and followed it in 1800 with a book that tried to argue Milton owed much to the poet and translator Joshua Sylvester. This was *Considerations on Milton's Early Reading and the Prima Stamina of his Paradise Lost*.

Thereafter Dunster confined himself to the study of sacred subjects in line with his 'disposition favourable to the cause of Religion and Virtue' (*GM*) and he took a combative position in the emerging subject of modern biblical scholarship. Herbert Marsh's translation of J. D. Michaelis's *Lectures on the New Testament* (1793–1801) had suggested that the gospels of Matthew and John, being eyewitness testimonies, were to be regarded as more reliable than those of Mark and Luke. This line was a striking departure from the conventional view that all biblical writings possessed an absolute authority. Dunster was particularly interested in the question of which gospel was first published and, in response to Marsh, he argued that St Luke should be seen as the companion of Cleophas and, as such, was probably an eyewitness to the events recorded in his gospel. His *Discursory Observations on the Evidence that St. Matthew's Gospel was the First Written* (1806) showed how much he had been influenced by J. Macknight's *Harmony of the Gospels* in arguing that Luke had written first. Dunster's work on different aspects of the gospels, under the name of 'a Country clergyman', appeared as a compendium in *Tracts on St. Luke's Gospel* (1813); however, his efforts did not capture the consent of learned opinion at large.

Dunster also produced *A letter to the right reverend the lord bishop of London on a passage in the gospel of St. Matthew* (1804)—arguing on the basis of Matthew 26: 24 that 'the truly pure, humble, immaculate Christian, is destined in his future state of glory, to be an angel …' (24)—and *A Synopsis of the First Three Gospels* (1812) on related topics. The mildly polemical side of Dunster's Christianity also found expression in his *A Letter on the Two Last Petitions of the Lord's Prayer* (1807) and *A Letter on the Incontrovertible Truth of Christianity* (2nd edn, 1808). His *Psalms and Hymns Adapted for the Use of a Parochial Church* (1812) reflected his lifelong interest in the practicalities of Anglican worship. Dunster died in April 1816 and was buried in the churchyard at Petworth on 24 April 1816. He never married.

NIGEL ASTON

Sources *GM*, 1st ser., 86/1 (1816), 472 · Foster, *Alum. Oxon.* · *Fasti Angl., 1541–1857*, [Salisbury] · Nichols, *Lit. anecdotes*, 9.326 · M. Walsh, *Shakespeare, Milton and eighteenth-century literary editing: the beginnings of interpretative scholarship* (1998)
Archives BL, notes relative to Milton's poems, Add. MSS 33602–33607 | W. Sussex RO, Petworth House archives, PHA 90, 9381; Ep I/3/9; PAR 149 1/5/1

Dunster, Henry (*bap.* 1609, *d.* 1659), minister and college principal in America, was baptized on 26 November 1609 at Bury, Lancashire, the fifth child of Henry Dunster (c.1580–1646), yeoman, and his first wife, Isabel (d. 1644). Dunster was educated at Magdalene College, Cambridge, where he graduated BA in 1631 and MA in 1634 and was ordained. He was influenced by the preaching of William Perkins and Thomas Goodwin, and when he returned to

Bury as curate and schoolmaster he was a committed puritan reformer and was intolerant of Laudian regulations. Inspired by the belief that the New England community was built on biblical premises, he emigrated to Massachusetts, arriving in Boston in the summer of 1640. He married on 22 June 1641 Elizabeth (d. 1643), née Harris, widow of the Revd Joseph Glover, who had died on the voyage from England. She brought with her a printing press, intending to print religious material for the conversion of the Indians. There were no children of this marriage, and after her death Dunster married in 1644 Elizabeth Atkinson (d. 1690), with whom he had five children.

Shortly after his arrival in Massachusetts Dunster was elected president of Harvard College. The college had been shaken by the dismissal of Nathaniel Eaton, whose harsh regime had attracted universal disapproval. Dunster shaped Harvard after the model of the English Cambridge colleges: he introduced the study of oriental languages and required students to attend services in Thomas Shepard's Cambridge church; candidates for the MA had publicly to defend a thesis. Though his own college career was undistinguished, under his guidance Harvard achieved international respect, while Dunster himself established a wide reputation as a Hebrew scholar. His expertise in that language led to his involvement in the composition of the *Bay Psalm Book*. Dunster supported efforts to educate Native Americans, and among the college buildings for which he was responsible was the Indian College, where it was hoped that natives would be educated for the ministry.

Dunster came to believe that there was no scriptural justification for infant baptism. He was forced to resign as college president in October 1654, when he refused to present his son for baptism and would not agree to keep his opposition to infant baptism to himself. Some of his former students had migrated to England and Ireland to aid the cause of religious reformation, and through their recommendation Henry Cromwell and the Irish council invited him to go to Ireland. He declined and, after a brief stay in Charlestown, settled in Scituate, in Plymouth Colony, where he ministered until his death on 27 February 1659. His friend Thomas Shepard regarded him as 'a man pious, painful, and fit to teach, and very fit to lay the foundations of the domesticall affairs of the College, whom God hath much honored and blessed' (McGiffert, 71).

FRANCIS J. BREMER

Sources S. E. Morison, *The tercentennial history of Harvard College and University, 1636–1936*, 1: *The founding of Harvard College* (1935) · M. R. McCarl, 'Dunster, Henry', *ANB* · M. McGiffert, ed., *God's plot: puritan spirituality in Thomas Shepard's Cambridge*, rev. edn (1994) · F. J. Bremer, *Shaping New Englands: puritan clergymen in seventeenth-century England and New England* (1994) · C. K. Shipton, *Sibley's Harvard graduates: biographical sketches of graduates of Harvard University*, 17 vols. (1873–1975), vol. 1 · J. Savage, *A genealogical dictionary of the first settlers of New England*, 4 vols. (1860–62) · J. Chaplin, *The life of Henry Dunster* (1872)
Archives Harvard U., MSS · Massachusetts Historical Society, Boston, notebook · New England Historic Genealogical Society, Boston, Massachusetts, conversion narrative in the Cambridge church

Dunster, Samuel (1675–1754), Church of England clergyman and classical scholar, was born at Westminster in September 1675, the son of James Dunster, who came from Somerset. He was educated at Merchant Taylors' School from 12 March 1688, and then at Westminster School. He matriculated from Trinity College, Cambridge, in 1693, from where he graduated BA in 1697, MA in 1700, and BD and DD in 1713. Ordained priest at Fulham in 1700, he was at St James's, Piccadilly, in 1705, and acted as chaplain to Charles, Viscount Maynard, before 1708. In that year he preached a sermon on the civil and sacred importance of popular education before a 'feast' for Merchant Taylors' old boys. Printed under the title *Wisdom and Understanding the Glory and Excellency of Human Nature*, it reached its third edition before the year was out. In 1710 he published *The Considerations of Drexilius upon Eternity, Made English from the Latin*, which also appeared in several editions, up until the final revision of 1844, edited with a preface by H. P. Dunster.

Dunster was a high-churchman and probably had non-juring sympathies; he was closely involved with the Manchester Jacobites, who were to provide the largest English regiment during the 1745 rising. However, a clue to the ambivalence of Dunster's politics is found in his service in 1712 as chaplain to Charles Talbot, earl, later duke, of Shrewsbury, who was in communication with the Jacobite court. In 1716 Dunster published his translation of *A Panegyrick on … King George* by Charles Ludolph, baron de Danckelman. The panegyric, with a preface attacking those who 'under a pretended Zeal for the *Church*, have join'd with Papists' during the 1715 Jacobite rising, was dedicated to Talbot's old friend Lord Somers. Both Talbot, who became lord chamberlain to the new king, and Dunster were anxious to prove their loyalty during the Hanoverian succession.

In 1716 Dunster was presented to the rectory of Chinnor, Oxfordshire. His continued favour under the Hanoverians is evidenced by his rapid promotion to the vicarage of Paddington, and the prebends that he collected at Salisbury (1717) and Lincoln cathedrals (1720). This was despite his dreary and verbose preaching. In 1716 Lady Mary Cowper complained of 'an intolerable dull sermon' given by Dunster at court (*Diary*, 100).

Dunster's career as a poet was similarly uninspired. His earliest verse is included in the *Lacrymae Cantabrigienses in obitum seren. reginae Mariae* (1694–5). He is credited by the editors of Whitaker's *History of Whalley* (4th edn, 2.426) with the authorship of *Anglia rediviva, being a full description of all the shires, cities, principal towns and rivers in England* (1699). His principal publication in verse was an annotated edition of *The Satyrs and Epistles of Horace, done into English* (1710). A second edition, with the addition of the 'Art of Poetry', came out in 1717, with the translator's portrait. The fourth edition is dated 1729. This dull version exposed him to the taunts of the satirists of his day, among whom was Dr T. Francklin, who wrote:

O'er Tibur's swan the muses wept in vain,
And mourn'd their Bard by cruel Dunster slain.

In 1722 he succeeded to the valuable vicarage of Rochdale,

where he died in July 1754, aged seventy-eight. He was buried on 22 July in Rochdale churchyard, near his wife and daughter who had predeceased him. His son, Charles Dunster (*d.* 1750), who had succeeded him in 1748 as prebendary of Grimston in Salisbury Cathedral, was the father of Charles *Dunster (1750–1816).

C. W. SUTTON, rev. PATRICK BULLARD

Sources Venn, *Alum. Cant.* • F. R. Raines, *The vicars of Rochdale*, ed. H. H. Howorth, 2 vols., Chetham Society, new ser., 1–2 (1883), 144 • T. D. Whitaker, *An history of the original parish of Whalley*, rev. J. G. Nichols and P. A. Lyons, 4th edn, 2 (1876), 426 • *Diary of Mary, Countess Cowper*, ed. [S. Cowper] (1864) • PRO, PROB 11/810, fols. 372r–372v • Nichols, *Lit. anecdotes*, 8.463 • C. J. Robinson, ed., *A register of the scholars admitted into Merchant Taylors' School, from AD 1562 to 1874*, 1 (1882), 30 • *Fasti Angl.* (Hardy), vol. 3

Likenesses M. Vandergucht, line engraving, NPG • portrait, repro. in *The Satires and Epistles of Horace*, trans. S. Dunster, 2nd edn (1712), frontispiece

Dunsterville, Edward (1796–1873), naval officer and hydrographer, son of Edward Dunsterville, shipowner, was born at Penryn in Cornwall on 2 December 1796. He entered the navy on 17 July 1812 as a first-class volunteer on board the sloop *Brisk*, on the north coast of Spain, was present in the night attack made in August 1813 on the fortress of San Sebastian, and became a midshipman on 26 September 1813. As a midshipman and an able seaman he served until 18 November 1815, when on the reduction of the fleet he was discharged. Afterwards he was employed as second and chief officer in the merchant service. However, on 9 September 1824 he passed an examination at Trinity House for a master in the navy, and was appointed second master of HMS *Valorous*. As master of the *Bustard*, he was stationed in the West Indies, where he made many useful observations, which were recorded at the Admiralty; afterwards, in England, he passed examinations and received certificates of his practical knowledge as a pilot. On 25 March 1833 he became master of the surveying vessel *Thunderer*, with orders to complete the survey of the Mosquito Coast, Central America, and he held that post until 27 November 1835, when he was invalided from the effects of fifteen years on the West India station. He took part in the operations of 1840 on the coast of Syria, on board the *Cambridge*, and assisted in blockading the Egyptian fleet at Alexandria.

On 19 April 1842 Dunsterville became one of the hydrographer's assistants at the Admiralty in Whitehall, where he remained until 31 March 1870, when he was superannuated, aged seventy-three, on two-thirds of his salary, namely £400 per annum. During his twenty-eight years at the Admiralty he had to attend to the issuing of charts to the fleet, to keep an account of the printing, mounting, and issue of charts and books, to report to the hydrographer on questions of pilotage, and to prepare catalogues of charts and the annual lighthouse lists. Of the latter he revised and saw through the press 102 volumes on the lights and lighthouses throughout the world. In 1860 he produced the *Admiralty Catalogue of Charts, Plans, Views, and Sailing Directions*. He also brought out a revised edition of James Horsburgh's *The Indian Directory, or, Directory for Sailing to and from the East Indies* (2 vols., 1859). Dunsterville

died at his home, 32 St Augustine's Road, Camden New Town, London, on 11 March 1873. He had been twice married, and was survived by his wife, Juliana, and children.

G. C. BOASE, rev. ANDREW LAMBERT

Sources O'Byrne, *Naval biog. dict.* • Boase, *Mod. Eng. biog.* • E. Dunsterville, *The servitude of Commander E. Dunsterville* (1871) • *CGPLA Eng. & Wales* (1873)

Wealth at death under £4000: resworn probate, June 1873, *CGPLA Eng. & Wales*

Dunsterville, Lionel Charles (1865–1946), army officer and literary prototype, was born on 9 November 1865 in Lausanne, Switzerland, the son of Lieutenant-General Lionel D'Arcy Dunsterville (1830–1912) of the Indian army. The family moved to Jersey and then to the Isle of Wight, and Dunsterville was brought up by his older sisters as his mother was an invalid: 'I needed a strong hand, and I got five pair of strong hand. Bless them' (Dunsterville, *Stalky's Reminiscences*, 16). He was then sent to Woolwich under the care of an officer's widow, with whom he remained for five years.

In 1875, about the time his mother died, Dunsterville began to attend the United Services College at Westward Ho! in Devon, where he was to be a studymate and boon companion of the young Rudyard Kipling. 'I was in the passive condition of a bundle of Chinese fire-crackers to which his fertile brain eagerly applied the torch' (Dunsterville, *Stalky's Reminiscences*, 26), Dunsterville later recalled. He is too modest by half; before Kipling's arrival in 1878 the young squib had been thoroughly bullied, had failed in an attempt to run away to sea, and had almost blown himself up with gunpowder. With the advent of Kipling and George Charles Beresford, Dunsterville and his two cronies read and lolled out of bounds in a hut in the furze-bushes, smoked cigars Dunsterville had helped smuggle into England from the continent, and hatched plots against those who had 'incurred our odium'. The result was his 'incorporation' into Kipling's *Stalky & Co.* (1899), perhaps Dunsterville's most lasting claim to fame. In later life he noted that

> [n]o amount of explanation could convince the public that Stalky is a character of pure fiction and I frequently have to undergo a severe examination on the details of exploits which are purely imaginary. Certainly the episodes narrated are very much like things that did happen fifty years ago in the old college at Westward Ho! And it is certain that Kipling, Beresford and myself shared a study and were generally at war with masters and boys who incurred our dislike. Our various plots were often highly ingenious and often hugely successful. From this solid foundation arises the noble structure of 'Stalky & Co'. (*New York Times*)

Dunsterville subsequently passed the army examination and attended the Royal Military College, Sandhurst, from 1883 to 1884. He was posted to the Royal Sussex regiment in Malta, where he received numerous mess fines, and then to Egypt, where he was almost arrested for gambling debts. Ordered to India, Dunsterville transferred to the 24th Punjab regiment and subsequently to the 20th. While he became acclimatized to Indian army life, it is clear that his exuberant tendencies remained; on one occasion when asked to suggest a new march-past tune,

Lionel Charles Dunsterville (1865–1946), by George Charles Beresford, 1923

he offered 'The Man that Broke the Bank at Monte Carlo'. He admits to having 'acquired some renown as a singer of somewhat vulgar music-hall songs' (Dunsterville, *Stalky's Reminiscences*, 106), and on another occasion was accused of having stolen a horse and trap. Bitten by a mad dog in 1891, Dunsterville was sent to Paris for treatment by Louis Pasteur and also began a lifelong friendship with the archaeologist and explorer Sir Aurel Stein. In 1894–5 Dunsterville took part in the Waziristan campaign before coming down with rheumatic fever (a native friend wished to sew him up in the skin of a dead sheep for ten days, but was overruled).

Subsequently Dunsterville visited Germany and Russia to learn and perfect these languages: 'it took me some better time to learn the "song" wherein resides the spirit of the language' (Dunsterville, *Stalky's Reminiscences*, 149). Throughout his career Dunsterville possessed both an ease with people and a facility for foreign languages. A friend noted that

> 'Stalky' spoke Russian like a Slav. In Peking (Beijing) he was the only Englishman who could converse easily with representatives of the different powers in their own tongue. In his command of Pushtu and all the patois of the Northwest Frontier, he is second to none. And he can interpret what is in the hearts of strange people as well as what is on their lips. (*New York Times*)

On 9 November 1897 he married Margaret Emily, the daughter of Colonel W. Keyworth of Bishopsteignton, Devon, whom he had met while in Wiesbaden.

Dunsterville returned with his wife to India, where they hopscotched across the country according to his orders, moving on no fewer than five occasions.

It was at this time that Dunsterville published his own newspaper, *The Jhansi Herald*: it was 'not a financial success … but the unlimited opportunity it gave me of libeling my friends amply compensated me for the money I lost by it' (Dunsterville, *Stalky's Reminiscences*, 171). In 1900 he and his unit were ordered to China to help suppress the Boxer uprising. He vividly describes the effects of halting a company in hobnailed boots on the ice, playing early morning music for the Royal Navy (the officers of the *Algerian* threatened to open fire if the noise did not cease at once), and 'capturing' towns whose cannon had red rags hanging out of their muzzles: '[t]his was done to make us believe that these were flames coming out of the muzzles of the guns and it was hoped that we would retire under the impression that the guns were firing at us' (ibid., 187). In 1902 the Dunstervilles' first son was born before he and his wife received orders back to India. The family visited England in 1903—he almost dying of malaria on the passage—and returned to India, after a continental tour, in late 1904. Dunsterville continued his session there until early 1914, a daughter being born in 1911.

At the outbreak of the First World War Dunsterville was appointed a train-conducting officer in France—and later wrote an amusing account of being shunted in cattle trucks, with cheeses and sides of bacon, as well as the passengers, being hurled in the air. A year later he assumed the command of Jhelium brigade in India, and he saw action for the next two years on the north-west frontier. A Sikh poet memorialized at least some of his achievements here, but Dunsterville was unable to obtain a copy as the gentleman in question was also a shopkeeper who had copied his verses on the back of his customers' bills! Early in 1918 Dunsterville was appointed head of a mission to Tiflis, Georgia, involving the reorganization of revolutionary troops using a core group of officers and NCOs pulled from various fronts to oppose the Turkish push towards Baku's oilfields and the Caucasus. However, 'Dunster force' was understaffed and undersupplied at best, and had no real impact. The Russian General Baratov is alleged to have commented '"Dunsterforce"! … I know Dunster all right, but where is the *Force*?' (Dunsterville, *Stalky's Reminiscences*, 239). Indeed one of Dunsterville's officers improvised 'a very fine armoured car out of a Ford van and some tissue-paper … [A]s no one was allowed near enough to poke their fingers through the "armour", it terrorized the whole countryside' (ibid., 278).

After the war Dunsterville participated in many activities, including the founding of the Kipling Society—about which Kipling rather unfairly commented, 'How would *you* like to be turned into an anatomical specimen, before you were dead, and shown upon a table, once a quarter?' Dunsterville wrote a number of fascinating volumes of memoirs, including *The Adventures of Dunsterforce* (1920), *Stalky's Reminiscences* (1928), and *Stalky Settles Down* (1932). He was also the author of such fictional works as

And Obey (1925) and *More Yarns* (1931). He died at Camelot, Barton Hill Road, St Mary Church, Torquay, on 18 March 1946.   SAMUEL PYEATT MENEFEE

Sources L. C. Dunsterville, *The adventures of Dunsterforce* (1920) · L. C. Dunsterville, *Stalky's reminiscences* (1928) · L. C. Dunsterville, *Stalky settles down* (1932) · *CGPLA Eng. & Wales* (1946) · m. cert. · d. cert. · *WWW* · private information (2004) [*New York Times*]
Archives BL, corresp. with Society of Authors, Add. MS 63238 · Bodl. Oxf., letters to Sir Aurel Stein · CUL, letters to his sister May and papers · U. Sussex, corresp. and papers incl. letters from Rudyard Kipling | FILM IWM FVA, actuality footage · IWM FVA, documentary footage
Likenesses G. C. Beresford, photograph, 1923, NPG [*see illus.*] · W. Stoneman, photograph, 1937, NPG · H. Coster, photographs, NPG
Wealth at death £1233 12s. 4d.: probate, 19 June 1946, *CGPLA Eng. & Wales*

Dunthorn, William (d. 1490), common clerk of London, was unusual among holders of this office in apparently not having received his training in one of the city clerkships, and in being a graduate — of Peterhouse, Cambridge, where he was admitted MA in the mid-1450s. Only one of his predecessors, Richard Barnett (1438–1446), is known to have attended a university. Senior proctor in 1457–8, Dunthorn left in 1461 to take up his appointment in London, arriving in the city less than a fortnight after his election on 2 October. The city had taken nearly two months to decide whom to appoint, ignoring the rival candidature of a sheriff's clerk, Robert Osbarn, despite the fact that he had secured a letter of recommendation from Edward IV. The reason for this was that the previous common clerk, Roger Tonge (alias Spicer), had been dismissed in disgrace for his 'great offences and rebellions against the King which he had many times committed' (CLRO, journal 6, photograph 502). Tonge may possibly have been guilty of revealing the court of aldermen's secret discussions, or other sensitive civic material, for, five months after his arrival, Dunthorn was given sole authority to allow access to the mayor's court records and city custumals. At the same time he was granted the right to remove unsatisfactory clerks at will, and the following May he took over custody and control of access to the chamber records as well; none of his predecessors seems to have enjoyed such authority.

In general, the city was evidently well satisfied with Dunthorn's services. In 1467 he was granted, in addition to his £10 annual fee and his customary reward of £3 6s. 8d., £6 13s. 4d. a year for as long as he remained in office, in recognition of his good services. On 5 April 1475 the king instructed the exchequer to exchange five old tallies with a face value of £172 16s. for new ones, the tallies having been given to Dunthorn in recognition of the costs he had incurred in the defence of the city against Thomas Fauconberg's rebels in 1471, and 'for all his efforts day by day' (PRO, E404/76/1/5). He was granted a further £6 13s. 4d. a year in July 1486. Dunthorn was also given, on 28 November 1474, three tallies assigned against the Sandwich customs, worth £115 3s. 3d. These were to pay for the production of a new custumal which became known as the *liber*

Dunthorn. It is a finely written and illuminated book, containing copies of the city's charters and extracts from the civic records and earlier custumals, as well as up-to-date examples of actions taken by the city authorities in accordance with those customs and privileges. None the less it was its early fifteenth-century predecessor, the *liber albus* of the common clerk John Carpenter, which continued to be the favoured reference book, having to be copied out anew in the sixteenth century because:

> The book that once was white is white no more,
> Made black with grease, and thumb'd its pages o'er.
> (*liber albus*, B(1))

Two considerations probably made the *liber Dunthorn* less useful than the older work: its showiness, and the fact that Carpenter had been unable to complete his work in the way intended, and so had ended it with a calendar of and index to the various sources he had used or discovered.

Little is known about Dunthorn's background. At the time of his death he was living in the parish of St Alban, Wood Street, and was buried in that church. His wife's name was Elizabeth, and they had daughters called Letitia and Joan. Letitia's husband, William Norborough, a grocer, was a common councillor, and may have been related to the mayor's sergeant of that name. Dunthorn bought lands in Essex for £60 in 1473, and since his unmarried daughter, who was entitled to half of one-third of her father's moveable wealth by the custom of London, received a legacy of £67, his personal wealth at death probably amounted to £400–£500. He would have been admitted to the freedom of the city *ex officio* on appointment, but was granted admission to the Mercers' Company in 1463. He may have belonged to Gray's Inn, as he was associated with a number of its fellows, but, if so, it was an honorary admission.

As to Dunthorn's personality, the editor of the city's letter-books judged him a pompous pedant. Certainly he rid the city's records, for some years at least, of the English which had been creeping in under his predecessor. The fact that there were some wholesale changes made to the administration during the 1490s, after his death, including the division of the records of the court of aldermen and common council into two separate series, perhaps suggests that he was, at least in his latter years, a brake upon change. His epitaph offered a kindlier judgement on him, however:

> nullique secundus
> Moribus ingenio, studio …
> pius ipse modestus,
> Longanimus, solers, patiens, super omnia gratus …
> ('second to none
> in manners, intellect, learning
> … he was god-fearing, modest,
> Forbearing, clever, patient, agreeable above all')
> (Stow, 308)

Dunthorn died in 1490, some time between 18 February, the date of his testament, and 10 June, when it was proved, and probably in late February or early March, since his successor was elected on 9 March.   P. TUCKER

Sources CLRO, journals, 6–9 · will, PRO, PROB 11/8, sig. 34 · B. R. Masters, 'The town clerk', *Guildhall Miscellany*, 3 (1969–71), 55–74 ·

Emden, *Cam.* • PRO, feet of fines (Essex), CP 25 • PRO, Exchequer, Exchequer of Receipt, warrants for issues, E 404 • L. Lyell and F. D. Watney, eds., *Acts of court of the Mercers' Company, 1453–1527* (1936) • J. Stow, *The survey of London*, ed. A. M. [A. Munday] and others, rev. edn (1633) • *Liber albus*, ed. H. T. Riley (1861) • E. W. Ives, *The common lawyers of pre-Reformation England* (1983) • R. R. Sharpe, ed., *Calendar of letter-books preserved in the archives of the corporation of the City of London*, [12 vols.] (1899–1912), vol. L • Emden, *Oxf.*

Wealth at death £400–£500; incl. 100 marks (minimum value of chattels); £60 (purchase price of household effects and land): will, PRO, PROB, 11/8; PRO, Feet of Fines (Essex), CP25

Dunthorne, James (*c.*1730–1815). *See under* Dunthorne, John (*bap.* 1770, *d.* 1844).

Dunthorne, James (*c.*1758–*c.*1794). *See under* Dunthorne, John (*bap.* 1770, *d.* 1844).

Dunthorne, John (*bap.* 1770, *d.* 1844), artist and early mentor of John Constable, was baptized on 11 February 1770 in Great Whelnetham, Suffolk, the eldest of four children of James Dunthorne (*c.*1725–1792) and his second wife, Ann Mingay (*c.*1750–1832), who were married by licence on 20 October 1769. Nothing is known of James's occupation, but by 1782 the family was living in Hadleigh, Suffolk. Nor is anything known of John's education and early life until his marriage in East Bergholt, Suffolk, on 5 September 1793 to Hannah Bird (*née* Oxley?), the widow of a local plumber and glazier. Several years older than Dunthorne, Hannah Bird (1757/8–1819) had arranged to take him in, according to John Constable's mother, 'from an advertisement, without a change of raiment or a shilling in his pocket & marry him—put him in possession of her house, furniture, [and] trade' (*Constable's Correspondence*, 1.115). However unorthodox his entry into marriage and his trade, Dunthorne worked successfully as a plumber, glazier, and painter in East Bergholt throughout his life, occasionally serving as the village constable. His historical importance, however, stems not from his occupational activities but from his connections with Constable, first chronicled in C. R. Leslie's *Memoirs* of the artist (1843).

Dunthorne lived in and conducted his business from a house and shop adjacent to the Constable home and owned by Constable's father. Although his social status precluded a formal relationship with the family, Dunthorne established a close friendship with Constable, based on their shared interest in open-air landscape painting. That Dunthorne was an amateur is clear from the only painting definitely attributable to him, *Flatford Lock* (1814; Colchester and Essex Museum); but his skills were sufficiently developed to bring him employment in the less exalted sphere of inn signs and funeral hatchments and to lead to his being asked to help restore a historic seventeenth-century perspectival wall-painting in St Mary's Church, Hadleigh (*Constable's Correspondence*, 2.31; see Pigot, 47). Dunthorne's devotion to outdoor sketching and his practical knowledge of the materials and techniques of oil painting were a crucial source of encouragement and tuition for Constable who, prior to his move to London in 1799, was receiving little of either from anyone else. Dunthorne was subsequently the recipient of several

of Constable's most revealing letters in which the struggling young artist not only shared his seminal thoughts and feelings about landscape painting (*Constable's Correspondence*, 1.101 and 2.21–36), but expressed his deep attachment to Dunthorne, whom he included among 'those whose love and friendship I most value' (ibid., 2.33). Dunthorne's interests extended outside those typically associated with a village plumber: he constructed an artist's lay figure, a model of a post windmill (Wilcox, 61), and a cello. Despite the intimacy which had existed between Dunthorne and Constable, the friendship was summarily altered in 1816 after several years of pressure from the latter's family and future wife. Constable had advised Dunthorne about his 'perverse and evil ways' (*Constable's Correspondence*, 2.171), but whether these were religious, political, or social is not known. The friendship was later resumed. Dunthorne outlived his wife and four children and died in East Bergholt of cancer on 13 October 1844. According to an obituary, 'he was a man of great ability, and of undoubted integrity; he was highly respected, and his departure sincerely regretted' (*Ipswich Journal*, 19 Oct 1844). A sale of his effects included a remarkable collection of scientific books, optical and musical instruments, paintings, drawings, and prints (ibid., 2 Nov 1844). He left his estate, including two cottages, to his twin granddaughters and was buried on 19 October at St Mary's Church, East Bergholt, with his third child, **John Dunthorne** (1798–1832), artist and picture restorer, whose life was also intimately tied to Constable's. Dunthorne, born on 19 April 1798 and baptized on 3 June, showed an early aptitude for art and in his teens was already assisting Constable during the artist's visits to East Bergholt, ultimately joining him in London as his assistant in 1824. It is difficult to determine the exact nature and extent of Dunthorne's subsequent work on Constable's canvases, but his presence in the studio has complicated matters for Constable scholars (Fleming-Williams and Parris, 195–204; Cove, 508). Responsible for the preliminary stages of Constable's studio paintings and for occasional replicas, Dunthorne is also known to have painted his own versions of Constable compositions (*Salisbury Cathedral*, Fitzwilliam Museum, Cambridge); and it is possible that paintings formerly attributed to Constable should be re-attributed to him (*A Wooded Stream*, priv. coll.; reproduced in Fleming-Williams and Parris, 199). That he absorbed much of Constable's style and outlook is evident from a review of one of his paintings exhibited at the Royal Academy, a review that mirrors very closely those of Constable himself: 'a *Landscape after a Shower* … is a peculiar picture, remarkably true to nature. … To have painted this picture, the artist must have been a very close observer of natural effects' (*New Monthly Magazine*, pt III, 1 June 1828, 225). Dunthorne exhibited at the Royal Academy between 1827 and 1832 and at the British Institution; he was a successful picture-cleaner and restorer and was highly praised for his restoration of a Reynolds portrait, a commission gained through the recommendation of Sir Thomas Lawrence (*Literary Gazette*, 22 Aug 1829, 554). Having suffered severe bouts of dropsy in July 1832 (*Constable's Correspondence*,

3.74), Dunthorne returned to East Bergholt where he died from heart disease on 2 November 1832 and was buried on 9 November. 'His loss makes a gap that cannot be filled up with me in this world', Constable reported to a friend (ibid., 3.81). A few of his paintings are scattered in various collections: the Colchester and Essex Museum; the Fitzwilliam Museum, Cambridge; the Yale Center for British Art, New Haven; and the Ipswich Museum Services, which owns a self-portrait and a drawing.

Two other artists named Dunthorne (mistakenly identified in the *Dictionary of National Biography* and in the standard references as John) lived and worked in Colchester and may have been distantly related to the East Bergholt Dunthornes. **James Dunthorne** (*c*.1730–1815), portrait and miniature painter and map-maker, was apprenticed to Joshua Kirby in 1745 for £25. He was also possibly the topographer responsible for several drawings of historic Essex buildings and tessellated pavements reproduced in various antiquarian publications in the 1760s and 1770s. James Dunthorne had nonconformist and whig connections and may have been related to John Dunthorne, a dissenting pastor in Colchester. He and his wife Elizabeth had nine children, the eldest of whom, **James Dunthorne** (*c*.1758–*c*.1794), painter and surveyor, was known as the Colchester Hogarth and exhibited several genre scenes at the Royal Academy between 1783 and 1792. Works by both father and son are in the Colchester and Essex Museum and in the British Museum, department of prints and drawings. An exhibition devoted to all four Dunthornes was held in Colchester in 1937.

JUDY CROSBY IVY

Sources *John Constable's correspondence*, ed. R. B. Beckett, 6 vols., Suffolk RS, 4, 6, 8, 10–12 (1962–8) · C. R. Leslie, *Memoirs of the life of John Constable* (1843); rev. 2nd edn (1845) · I. Fleming-Williams and L. Parris, *The discovery of Constable* (1984) · S. Cove, 'Constable's oil painting materials and techniques', *Constable*, ed. L. Parris and I. Fleming-Williams (1991), 493–529 · T. Wilcox, *The romantic windmill* (1993) · W. G. Benham, 'The Dunthornes of Colchester', *Essex Review*, 10 (1901), 27–35 and 116 · H. Pigot, *Hadleigh* (1860) · I. Fleming-Williams, 'John Dunthorne's *Flatford lock*', *The Connoisseur*, 184 (Dec 1973), 290–91 · will, PRO, PROB 11/2015, sig. 286 · administration, 26 Nov 1832, PRO, PROB 6/208, fol. 244r [John Dunthorne jun.] · Colchester Museum Service, Resource Centre [three files on the Dunthornes] · *Ipswich Journal* (19 Oct 1844) · *Suffolk Chronicle* (10 Nov 1832) · *Ipswich Journal* (10 Nov 1832) · *Ipswich Journal* (2 Nov 1844) · *Colchester Gazette* (6 Jan 1816) · J. Cooper, ed., *History of the county of Essex*, 9 (1994), 340 · S. D'Cruze, *Our time in God's hands: religion and the middling sort in eighteenth century Colchester* (1991) · F. W. Steer and others, *Dictionary of land surveyors and local map-makers of Great Britain and Ireland, 1530–1850*, ed. P. Eden, 2nd edn, ed. S. Bendall, 2 vols. (1997)

Archives priv. coll., cello · priv. coll., model of a post windmill **Likenesses** J. Constable, pencil sketch, 1813, V&A · J. Dunthorne, self-portrait, oils, 1828? (John Dunthorne), Ipswich Museum Services

Wealth at death two properties; books, optical and musical instruments, plus paintings, drawings, and prints: will, PRO, PROB 11/2015, sig. 286; *Ipswich Journal* (2 Nov 1844) [estate sale announcement]

Dunthorne, John (1798–1832). *See under* Dunthorne, John (*bap.* 1770, *d.* 1844).

Dunthorne, Richard (1711–1775), astronomer and surveyor, was born at Ramsey, Huntingdonshire, where his father was a gardener. His progress at the free grammar school in Ramsey caught the attention of Dr Roger Long, master of Pembroke College, Cambridge, who employed him at Pembroke College as his servant. There Dunthorne was able to continue his mathematical and other studies until he was considered qualified to manage a preparatory school for the university at Coggeshall, Essex. Long, however, soon recalled him to Cambridge as his personal assistant, and to serve as butler of his college, a lifetime appointment. In 1746 he married Elizabeth Hill (1714/15–1789) of Huntingdon.

Dunthorne helped Long to construct his great sphere, 18 feet in diameter, within which several persons sat to watch, as the sphere rotated, the simulated movements of heavenly bodies across the night sky. On Long's death, in 1770, Dunthorne found himself named as executor and charged with the task of completing Long's major book on astronomy, but he achieved only a rough draft of the concluding historical section.

Dunthorne himself had two astronomical interests which he could pursue in his study. After consulting numerous ancient records of eclipses, he wrote in support of Edmond Halley's assertion that the moon's motion round the earth was accelerating. He also examined ancient descriptions of comets in order to identify their subsequent appearances, a task in which he was understandably less successful. His letters on these subjects were conveyed to the Royal Society by the Revd Charles Mason, Woodwardian professor, and by Long, and published in the *Philosophical Transactions*. Dunthorne also observed the transit of Venus on 3 June 1769.

In 1754 Dunthorne was elected deputy surveyor to the Middle and South levels of the Bedford Level corporation, and he was thereafter re-elected annually. He conducted a survey of the fens; the locks on the Cam, near Chesterton, were built under his direction, and he left a volume of observations for a map of Cambridgeshire, apparently never drawn up. In 1771 he was supervising a map of the River Orwell and district, and in 1773 he directed Henry Hogben's survey of the River Stour in Kent, with a view to modifying its channel to prevent flooding. Dunthorne suffered a stroke in 1773, but submitted his report on the Stour in September 1774. It was hoped that he would recover sufficiently to attend the Easter session of the House of Commons when the necessary legislation would be debated, but his death intervened. The Stour survey was concluded in 1775 by Murdoch McKenzie.

Dunthorne was esteemed for his integrity and kindliness. He never forgot his humble relatives and assisted some of the younger ones to find employment. He had a taste for art and did his own drawings. His fine astronomical instruments were bequeathed to the observatory of St John's College. He died at Cambridge on 3 March 1775; both he and his wife, who died on 8 January 1789, were buried at St Benedict's Church.

A. M. CLERKE, *rev.* ANITA McCONNELL

Sources C. H. Cooper, 'On Richard Dunthorne, astronomer, engineer and antiquarian artist', *Antiquarian Communications of the Cambridge Antiquarian Society*, 2 (1864), 331–5 · *Cambridge Chronicle and Journal* (11 March 1775) · R. Long, *Astronomy, in five books*, 2 (1764), iii–v, and unpaginated 'advertisment' · BL, Add. MS 5867, fol. 56 · BL, Add. MS 5489, fols. 105–7 · BL, Add. MS 35,680, fol. 298 · R. Grant, *History of physical astronomy, from the earliest ages to the middle of the nineteenth century* (1852), 60–61 · R. T. Gunter, *Early science in Cambridge* (1937), 169–71
Archives MHS Oxf., letters to Samuel Rouse

Dunton, John (1659–1732), bookseller, was born on 4 May 1659 at Grafham, Huntingdonshire, the only child of the Revd John Dunton (1628–1676) and Lydia, *née* Carter (*d.* 1659). His father, grandfather, and great-grandfather, also called John, had all been Anglican ministers. His mother died shortly after he was born, and her grieving husband went to Ireland to take up the position of chaplain to Sir Henry Ingoldsby, leaving his young son under the tutelage of his brother-in-law, William Readings, at Dungrove, near Chesham. The boy's father returned in 1663 and became rector of Aston Clinton, Buckinghamshire. He remarried, and he and his second wife, Mary Lake, had four children: Sarah, Mary, Elizabeth, and Lake Dunton. The Revd John Dunton hoped that his eldest son would follow the family tradition and enter the church, but young John showed no aptitude for study. As a child he experienced 'a strange Kind of Aversion' to learning, finding it 'too difficult and unpleasant' (Dunton, *Life*, 9). His father realized that the boy would never make a scholar, and sent him to London at the age of fifteen to be apprenticed to the eminent Presbyterian bookseller Thomas Parkhurst. Dunton himself was a lifelong Anglican, although he had close personal and professional links with nonconformists throughout his career. His apprenticeship to Parkhurst began on 7 December 1674. His master was a fair and generous man, but Dunton was negligent in his work, distracted by politics and love. Together with Joshua Evans, Dunton rallied the whig apprentices, and raised a petition of 30,000 signatures which was presented to the lord mayor in September 1681. He held a 'funeral' to celebrate the end of his apprenticeship with 100 of his friends, and was awarded the freedom of the Stationers' Company on 5 December 1681.

At first, Dunton rented part of a shop at The Poultry near the Royal Exchange. He recalled how '*Hackney-Authors* began to ply me with *Specimens*, as earnestly, and with as much Passion and Concern, as the *Watermen* do *Passengers* with *Oars* and *Scullers*' (Dunton, *Life*, 70). His first publishing ventures in 1681 were *The Lord's Last Sufferings* by Doolittle, Jay's *Daniel in the den* (which drew a parallel between the biblical story and the trial of Lord Shaftesbury), and a funeral sermon by John Shower. Dunton's early success in business led him to consider marriage. After two months' courtship, he married on 3 August 1682 Elizabeth Annesley, the daughter of the eminent nonconformist minister Dr Samuel *Annesley. She called him Philaret, he called her Iris, and for him their marriage was 'the greatest happiness I have as yet met with in this life' (ibid., 74–6). Elizabeth's sister composed a pen-portrait of Dunton at the time of his marriage:

Philaret is of a middle Stature; his Hair black and curled, his Eye-brows Black and indifferently even, Eyes almost Black, quick and full of Spirit, his Nose rises a little in the Middle, his Lips red and soft; the whole Composure of his Face, tho' it is not so Beautiful as some are, is yet render'd amiable by a chearful sprightly Air.   (ibid., 82)

The only surviving image of the bookseller is an engraving by Vandergucht, the frontispiece to *Athenianism* (1710).

Dunton claimed to have published over 600 titles during his career, although fewer than 200 titles have been traced (Parks, 43). The core of his business consisted of devotional works and sermons, together with political works, chapbooks, 'practical books', and miscellanies, including eleven periodicals (ibid., 45). Notable early successes included Richard Baxter's *Directions to the Unconverted* (1682); a collection by Samuel Annesley, the *Continuation of Morning-Exercise Questions* (1683); and *Maggots, or, Poems on Several Occasions* (1685) by his brother-in-law, Samuel Wesley, father of John and Charles, the founders of Methodism. In 1685 Monmouth's rebellion, put a 'damp upon trade', and Dunton was held liable for a sister-in-law's debts, having acted as her creditor. He resolved to go to America to claim £500 that was owed to him there. He took his apprentice Samuel Palmer and a cargo of books, and sailed for Boston, Massachusetts, on 2 November 1685, arriving on 27 January 1686. He spent his time in the colony visiting local booksellers, clergymen, and dignitaries, met Increase and Cotton Mather, and sold books to students at Harvard. At Roxbury, John Eliot presented him with twelve 'Indian' bibles. Dunton departed for England on 5 July 1686, and arrived one month later to find that his sister-in-law's creditors still required satisfaction. He remained in hiding for ten months, venturing out only once, disguised as a woman (Dunton, *Life*, 197). In early 1687 he went for a 'ramble' in the Low Countries, where he met Monmouth's supporters in exile. He travelled as far as Cologne and Mainz, before returning to England in November 1688. During this time Elizabeth managed the warehouse successfully on her own, thereby proving that she had more business acumen than her husband (Parks, 37). Their shop at the sign of the Black Raven in The Poultry reopened, and Dunton started to print whig propaganda, including *The Bloody Assizes* (1689), an account of those who had suffered under Judge Jeffreys, which sold 6000 copies. In 1691 Dunton wrote the *Voyage Round the World*, an account of the rambling adventures of Don Kainophilus, a precursor of Sterne's *Tristram Shandy*.

In May 1691, inspired by an idea for a new type of periodical, Dunton began to publish his most successful project of all, the *Athenian Gazette, or, Casuistical Mercury*. Readers were invited to send their queries on any subject to an anonymous club of self-styled learned men who met at Smith's coffee house, the 'Athenian Society'. The club was in fact made up of Dunton, Wesley, and a third brother-in-law, Richard Sault, with Dr John Norris making occasional contributions. The periodical was highly successful, sustaining an unusually long print run of nearly seven years, and spawning many imitators, including Daniel Defoe's *Review*. Jonathan Swift wrote an *Ode to the Athenian Society* (which he later regretted) and Charles Gildon composed a *History of the Athenian Society* (1692). In 1692 Dunton published several serialized miscellanies, including the *Compleat Library* by Richard Wolley. Dunton recalled that 'the World now smil'd on me': in the same year, on 7 November 1692, he was elected to the livery of the Stationers' Company, and dined in the presence of the lord mayor (Dunton, *Life*, 279). In 1693 he printed the *Second spira* by Sault, an account of the providential death of an atheist at Westminster, which went through five editions, but caused Dunton much embarrassment when its authenticity was questioned. Queen Mary licensed Dunton to print a translation of the *History of the Famous Edict of Nantes* in two volumes (1693–4), and he promoted her moral crusade by publishing *Proposals for a National Reformation of Manners* (1694). His serialized accounts of conversations with prostitutes, the *Night-Walker, or, Evening Rambles in Search after Lewd Women* (1696), were a more ambiguous contribution to the campaign, in view of their scurrilous content. Dunton was the first bookseller to realize the market potential among female readers: the *Athenian Mercury* appealed to 'all men and both Sexes', and his *Ladies Dictionary* (1694) was produced as a 'General Entertainment for the Fair Sex'. The poet Elizabeth Singer Rowe contributed to the *Athenian Mercury*, and Dunton published her *Poems on Several Occasions* in 1696. In the same year, he printed *Pegasus*, the first example of a newspaper with features.

At the height of his prosperity Dunton began to suffer from kidney problems, and in 1694 he moved from The Poultry to smaller premises in Jewen Street. In November 1696 Elizabeth Dunton fell ill; she died seven months later on 28 May 1697. Grief-stricken, Dunton scaled down his operations and ceased publishing the *Athenian Mercury*. Without her restraint upon his 'rambling', his business began to fail. Dunton remarried somewhat hastily on 23 October that year; his second wife was Sarah Nicholas (Valeria). He was attracted primarily, it seems, by her mother's money. Jane Nicholas of St Albans was a wealthy widow, but refused to give her son-in-law a penny. The marriage was a disaster, and the couple soon separated. Dunton's bitterness towards his mother-in-law was exorcised through a series of pamphlets, such as *An Essay, Proving we Shall Know our Friends in Heaven* (1698). In 1698 he made a trip to Ireland to try and recoup his losses, the subject of *The Dublin Scuffle* (1699). In the years after 1700 Dunton was increasingly troubled with ill health, and relied upon landladies and female friends to nurse him. He did not have any children, but referred in his will to his friend Isabella Edwards as 'my adopted daughter' (Dunton, will). His business in ruins, Dunton resorted to hack writing and selling his copyrights to make a living. In 1705 he published his *Life and Errors of John Dunton, Citizen of London* (1705), one of the earliest examples of autobiography in English, which provides a wealth of information about prominent figures in the London book trade. It was, however, a commercial failure. Andrew Bell edited and reprinted the *Athenian Mercury* in four volumes as the *Athenian Oracle*, in 1703, 1704, and 1710. Dunton was

encouraged to revive his 'question' projects, producing spin-offs such as *The Athenian Spy* (1704). He ruined what remained of his reputation, however, with scurrilous, 'abusive scribblings', and public attacks centring upon his personal grievances, such as his *Whipping-Post, or, A Satyr upon Every Body* (1706). In his final years ill health and financial ruin unhinged his mental state. His decline was also marked by pitiful appeals to George I for recognition for loyal service to the crown. Dunton experienced spells in the Fleet prison, and in 1711 he left less than £600 in his will, although the actual size of his estate at his death is unknown. Dunton continued to write until 1728; his final work of any note was *Neck or Nothing* (1713), a reply to Sir Robert Walpole's *Short History of Parliament* (Parks, 168). John Dunton died in London on 24 November 1732. His will gave instructions for him to be buried with his beloved Elizabeth in the nonconformist cemetery at Bunhill Fields.

Dunton is chiefly remembered as one of the most prominent London booksellers of the 1690s, an innovative if somewhat eccentric figure, who made a significant contribution to whig propaganda in the decade after the revolution of 1688. His search after novelties led him to experiment with new literary forms, and his influence may be traced in the rise of the eighteenth-century periodical.

HELEN BERRY

Sources J. Dunton, *The life and errors of John Dunton … written by himself* (1705) • S. Parks, *John Dunton and the English book trade* (1976) • will, 1711, PRO, PROB 11/657, fol. 82 • J. Dunton, personal MSS, Bodl. Oxf., MS Rawl. D. 72 • G. D. McEwen, *The oracle of the coffee house* (1972) • M. Mascuch, *Origins of the individualist self* (1996) • A. Hall, 'References to the Black Raven in Arber's term catalogues, 1681–95', *N&Q*, 161 (1931), 169 • P. M. Hill, *Two Augustan booksellers: John Dunton and Edmund Curll*, University of Kansas Library Series, 3 (1958) • B. Hammond, *Professional imaginative writing in England, 1640–1740: 'Hackney for bread'* (1997) • D. F. McKenzie, ed., *Stationers' Company apprentices*, [2]: *1641–1700* (1974)
Archives Bodl. Oxf., corresp. and business MSS, MSS Rawl.
Likenesses M. Vandergucht, line engraving (after F. Knight), NPG; repro. in McEwen, *Oracle of the coffee house*
Wealth at death under £600 legacies in 1711: will, PRO, PROB 11/657, fol. 82; Parks, *John Dunton*, 166

Dunton, (Walter) Theodore Watts- (1832–1914), writer and poet, was born on 12 October 1832, the eldest child of John King Watts, solicitor, of St Ives, Huntingdonshire, who was well known for his scientific attainments. He added to his surname that of his mother, Susannah Dunton, in 1896. At school in Cambridge he devoted himself to literature, science, and life in the open air. While working in his father's office he wrote articles which were published in the *Cambridge Chronicle*. After becoming a solicitor he practised for a while in London. His gifts as a friend, conversationalist, and man of business facilitated his connections with the pre-Raphaelite group of poets and artists, to which he was introduced by his brother Alfred, also a solicitor practising in London. 'Watts the worldling', as J. M. Whistler called him, was a familiar figure at London literary gatherings such as those of the poet John Westland Marston. He gave up the legal profession in order to devote himself to literary criticism, writing first for *The Examiner* under William Minto in 1874. Two years

(Walter) Theodore Watts-Dunton (1832–1914), by Dante Gabriel Rossetti, 1874

later he began writing for *The Athenaeum*, where for the rest of the century he enjoyed a great, anonymous reputation.

In *The Athenaeum* Watts-Dunton printed several poems about Gypsy life. His interest in Gypsy lore was first sparked by his meeting with George Borrow in 1872. Another friend, Francis Hindes Groome, was also knowledgeable about Gypsies. The publication of Watts-Dunton's Gypsy poems, with additions, as *The Coming of Love, and other Poems* made a stir in 1897. Contemporary critics felt that the large and adventurous design of the verses overreached his talent. However, he had a great success in 1898 with *Aylwin*, a novel kept back for many years and originally called *The Renascence of Wonder*. This phrase formed the basis of his critical doctrines, intended as a protest against materialism and pessimism. *Aylwin* dealt with the same characters as *The Coming of Love* and revealed a gift for romance and scenery, with an interest in mysticism. Although striking in plot and detail, the book has flat passages which show that the author, a good judge of style, was not a great stylist. The same criticism can be applied to his *Athenaeum* articles, which he himself described as 'too formless to have other than an ephemeral life'. They were very widely admired, but their reputed profundity was exaggerated. What he lacked in style, however, he made up for in critical judgement; he was one of the first to applaud George Meredith's verse, and many young authors owed much to his encouragement. His best critical work is thought to be his essay on poetry in the *Encyclopaedia Britannica* (9th edn, 1885). A. C.

Swinburne maintained that this essay demonstrated that Watts-Dunton was 'the first critic of our time, perhaps the largest-minded and surest-sighted of any age' (Douglas, 1).

Watts-Dunton, however, is perhaps best-known for his literary friendships. He proved a steady friend and practical adviser to Dante Gabriel Rossetti in the poet's declining years. More important was his relationship with Algernon Charles Swinburne, whom he had met during his time in London and for whom by the 1870s he was acting in effect as a literary agent. Swinburne called Watts-Dunton 'one of the best friends I ever had—or any one else ever had, for that matter' (*Swinburne Letters*, 3.238). The death of Swinburne's father in 1877 and the subsequent sale of the family estate led to a decline in the poet's health, accompanied by bouts of depression, loneliness, and alcoholism. With Lady Jane Swinburne's approval and financial support, in 1879 Watts-Dunton took control of the situation, taking Swinburne to live with him at The Pines, his house at 11 Putney Hill, Putney, London. He managed to convince Swinburne to give up drinking and encouraged him in regular work and sleep habits, and he took charge of all his business matters. They continued to live together until Swinburne's death in 1909, and although the devoted and tactful control of Watts-Dunton prolonged Swinburne's life, some contemporaries viewed the living arrangement as less than ideal, observing that it involved a definite loss of the poet's independence in material life and critical judgement. Edmund Gosse, in his 1917 biography of Swinburne, presents Watts-Dunton as a kind of benign domestic tyrant, stifling Swinburne's creativity, and Watts-Dunton's wife wrote *The Home Life of Swinburne* (1922) largely in response to Gosse's portrayal. Max Beerbohm's fine essay, 'No. 2 The Pines' (printed in *And Even Now*, 1920), gives perhaps the best contemporary impression of the arrangement, and twentieth-century critics such as J. O. Jordan have attempted to present a more balanced view of the relationship.

On 29 November 1905 Watts-Dunton had married Clara Jane, the youngest daughter of Gustav A. Reich, merchant, of East India Avenue, London, but this did not change the quiet, ordered life at The Pines. The couple had no children. He died at The Pines on 6 June 1914 and was survived by his wife. Watts-Dunton had, throughout his life, 'protested against the jealousies and personalities of modern literary life. He lived for his friends, read endlessly, put off, polished, and altered his own compositions. The variety of his interests dissipated his energies. He had great kindliness, a good sense of fun, but little humour, and throughout his long life remained a boy in his eagerness for the latest discovery in letters or science' (*DNB*).

MEGAN A. STEPHAN

Sources *DNB* • T. St E. Hake and A. Compton-Rickett, *The life and letters of Theodore Watts-Dunton*, 2 vols. (1916) • J. Douglas, *Theodore Watts-Dunton: poet, critic, novelist* (1904) • E. Gosse, *The life of Algernon Charles Swinburne* (1917) • C. Watts-Dunton, *The home life of Swinburne* (1922) • J. O. Jordan, 'Closer than a brother: Swinburne and Watts-Dunton', *Mothering the mind: twelve studies of writers and their silent partners*, ed. R. Perry and M. W. Brownley (1984) • *The Swinburne letters*, ed. C. Y. Lang, 6 vols. (1959–62) • M. Panter-Downes, *At The*

Pines: Swinburne and Watts-Dunton in Putney (1971) • M. A. de Ford, 'Watts-Dunton, (Walter) Theodore', *British authors of the nineteenth century*, ed. S. J. Kunitz and H. Haycraft (1936), 647–8 • M. Beerbohm, *And even now* (1920) • m. cert. • d. cert. • personal knowledge (1927) [DNB]

Archives BL, corresp. and papers; corresp., Add. MSS 45297, 70627–70628 • King's School, Canterbury, MS introduction and notes for edition of Borrow's *Romany Rye* • PRO NIre., corresp. • Rutgers University, New Brunswick, New Jersey, letterbooks | BL, letters to J. R. Brown, Add. MSS 42712–42713 • Bodl. Oxf., letters to Dante Gabriel Rossetti • Ches. & Chester ALSS, letters to Lady Leighton-Warren • Ransom HRC, corresp. with John Lane • U. Leeds, Brotherton L., corresp. with Edmund Gosse • U. Leeds, Brotherton L., letters to Francis H. Groome • U. Leeds, Brotherton L., letters to Henry Arthur Jones • U. Leeds, Brotherton L., letters to Clement Shorter • U. Leeds, Brotherton L., letters to Algernon Charles Swinburne • U. Leeds, Brotherton L., letters to T. J. Wise

Likenesses portrait, *c.*1841, repro. in Hake and Compton-Rickett, *Life and letters*, following p. 32 • D. G. Rossetti, pastel drawing, 1874, NPG [*see illus.*] • H. T. Dunn, watercolour drawing, 1882, NPG • M. Beerbohm, caricature, AM Oxf.; repro. in Panter-Downes, *At The Pines*, frontispiece • C. Watts-Dunton?, portrait, repro. in Hake and Compton-Rickett, *Life and letters*, frontispiece • photograph, repro. in Panter-Downes, *At The Pines*, facing p. 57 • portrait (after painting by H. B. Norris), repro. in Douglas, *Theodore Watts-Dunton*, frontispiece • portrait, repro. in de Ford, 'Watts-Dunton', 647–8

Wealth at death £22,934 6*s.* 10*d.*: probate, 24 Oct 1914, *CGPLA Eng. & Wales*

Du Parcq, Herbert, Baron Du Parcq (1880–1949), judge, was born in St Helier, Jersey, on 5 August 1880, the only child of Clement Pixley Du Parcq, a bookseller, stationer, and printer in St Helier whose family had been long established in the island, and his wife, Sophia Thoreau, who was related to the American author and naturalist Henry David Thoreau. He attended Victoria College, Jersey, before winning an open scholarship in classics to Exeter College, Oxford, where he obtained a first class in classical moderations in 1901 and a second class in *literae humaniores* in 1903. Elected to King Charles I senior scholarship at Jesus College, Oxford, in 1904, he obtained a BCL in 1908. He also became secretary and treasurer of the union and was president in Michaelmas 1902. In later years he became an honorary fellow of both Exeter and Jesus colleges in 1935 and an honorary LLD of Birmingham University in 1947.

Du Parcq was called to the bar (Middle Temple) in 1906 and admitted to the Jersey bar the same year. He practised on the western circuit. On 8 September 1911 he married Lucy, daughter of John Renouf, a merchant, of St Helier. They had one son and two daughters. His wife assisted him in the research for a biography of David Lloyd George, published in four volumes (1911–13) and still regarded as one of the best accounts of the subject, though for reasons which remain obscure Du Parcq avoided reference either to it or to Lloyd George later in his career (Grigg, 303–4).

Du Parcq took silk in 1926, and became recorder of Portsmouth in 1928 and recorder of Bristol and judge of the Bristol Tolzey court in the following year. In 1931 he became a bencher of his inn and was a member of the general council of the bar from 1928 to 1932. He also became a member of the Council of Legal Education in 1933 and chairman of that body from December 1947 until

his death. In 1938 he delivered a paper, 'The place of criminal law in legal education', published in the *Journal of the Society of Public Teachers of Law*. At the bar he acquired a large and varied practice and in spring 1931 was commissioner of assize of the northern circuit.

In 1931 Du Parcq was appointed to a Home Office committee on persistent offenders. A year later the home secretary, Herbert Samuel, asked him to inquire into disturbances which had occurred at Dartmoor prison on 24 January 1932. His report drew attention to the risks involved in placing dangerous prisoners in such an isolated prison, where difficulties in obtaining staff, and indeed in obtaining reinforcements in case of trouble with inmates, might be encountered. More generally, his report provided no comfort for those who considered that the state had gone soft on offenders. The disturbances at Dartmoor were attributed to a group of hardened criminals who would not in any case have responded to humane treatment which would benefit others. In the same year he was appointed to the king's bench, obtaining the customary knighthood, and judicial promotion was not long delayed. Thus in 1938 he became a privy councillor and lord justice of appeal and in 1946 became a law lord as Baron Du Parcq of Grouville, replacing Lord Goddard, who became lord chief justice.

As a trial judge Du Parcq was patient and courteous to counsel and litigants, while at the same time exercising firm control over the proceedings. As an appellate judge, particularly in the House of Lords, he deviated from the norm (Stevens, 375). Thus he could refer in his writings to the need for certainty in the law and to the importance of settled rules—that is, to the views corresponding with the theory of substantive legal formalism, which perceives judges as interpreters rather than as creators of law (see his Holdsworth Club lecture of 1948, *Aspects of the Law*). On the other hand, he 'opposed the splitting of legal hairs as well as logic for logic's sake' (Stevens, 375–6). He was in fact driven by the pursuit of justice and by the recognition that general rules might require adaptation to individual circumstances. While principles were necessary, they should not be interpreted so narrowly that injustice ensued.

Broadly speaking, Du Parcq believed that judges should appreciate that the law should operate so as to be understood and approved by the general public. The case involving the cyclist who, during the wartime blackout, had collided with a shelter which the defendant local authority had neither lit nor painted (and which denied it was thereby negligent) perhaps fell into that category; two lords justices dismissed the cyclist's claim for damages, but Du Parcq supported it (see *Fox v. Newcastle upon Tyne corporation*, 1941, where Du Parcq's dissent was later approved by the Court of Appeal in *Fisher v. Ruislip–Northwood urban district council and Middlesex County Council*, 1945). He strongly believed that judicial interpretation should be informed by a genuine view, rather than a supposition, of what parliament intended in enacting legislative provisions. Thus he favoured the inclusion of statements of intent in legislation. In common law cases, he pursued his conception of justice by reasoning that to follow an unwelcome precedent in the instant case would be 'to mistake an exception for the rule' (*Mackintosh* v. *Gerrard*, 1947). Perhaps reflecting the spirit of lords Atkin and Wright, he also tended to construe the law relating to industrial accidents in a manner which would benefit workers, for example, in his restrictive approach to contributory negligence (*Grant* v. *Sun Shipping Co.*, 1948).

When the Germans occupied the Channel Islands in the summer of 1940 Du Parcq acted as chairman of the Channel Islands refugees' committee, with Charles Thomas Le Quesne, another Jerseyman, as his deputy. Its work was completed some five years later. To raise the morale of the refugees he travelled widely to visit them, took part in the negotiations for the dispatch of a Red Cross vessel to the islands, and made three appeals for funds on the BBC's *The Week's Good Cause* programme. Other war work included conducting an inquiry into inter-services radio communications and co-operation in 1942. But perhaps his most delicate assignment came immediately after the liberation of the Channel Islands in 1945, when he was asked by the Home Office to investigate the record, *vis-à-vis* the German occupiers, of the island governments. 'It was to be a secret and extremely tactful inquiry' (Bunting, 305) which would include within its scope the actions and role of the bailiffs (the heads of government) of Jersey and Guernsey. On the allegation that the island governments had assisted the German occupation to deport 2200 Channel Islanders to Germany in 1942 and 1943, Du Parcq noted that 'a strong case can be made for the view that the local authorities should have refused to give any assistance in the performance of this violation of international law' (ibid.). He expected the actions of the bailiff of Guernsey, Victor Carey, to be brought before the prime minister before honours were conferred. Carey had described allied soldiers as enemy forces and had offered rewards for information identifying those chalking 'V' signs on the islands. None the less, Du Parcq later told Sir Frank Newsam at the Home Office, after a visit to the islands, that local resentment was not directed against the governments but against individuals who had worked for the Germans, against farmers who sold them food, and against informers. This subsequent explanation conveniently took the heat away from the allegations regarding collaboration by the island governments and, despite Du Parcq's earlier admonition, Carey received his knighthood.

In the post-war period Du Parcq declined the invitation to sit as the British judge at the Nuremberg war crimes trial (Sir Geoffrey Lawrence was appointed instead), but he was appointed to chair the royal commission on justices of the peace which reported in 1948. Justices were now adjudicating on what would by then be considered as middle-class offences such as motoring and wartime regulation offences, as well as continuing to police the working class. The majority none the less acknowledged that the political loyalties of candidates for the magistracy

remained a legitimate albeit not a decisive factor in making appointments, a view favoured by the Labour government at the time, and indeed subsequently. The proper training of magistrates, however, was important. Thus *ex officio* members of the bench (generally district council chairmen, mayors, and, usually for one year after termination of civic office, ex-mayors) were to be pruned in favour of trained, even if amateur and unpaid, magistrates. In the event only former mayors were removed, probably because the more radical step would have weakened Labour representation on the bench.

Du Parcq's three years in the House of Lords before his death were too short a period in which to establish a strong reputation as an enlightened refashioner, in the pursuit of justice for the common man or woman, of legal doctrines. However, there are sufficient examples of his flexible approach to precedent and to legal principle to suggest that he might have stood comparison, in the fullness of time, with the great inter-war and wartime appellate judges lords Atkin and Wright. Legal formalism of the variety associated with Lord Simonds was not his leitmotif. His contribution to public administration was progressive—he was reputedly a Liberal (Stevens, 356)—though his discussions with Newsam regarding the issue of collaboration by Channel Islands government officials contain more than a hint of seeking to avoid the dire legal consequences, for members of the establishment, of his initial inquiries after the liberation.

In 1945 Du Parcq became a member of the Permanent Court of Arbitration at The Hague. He was 'a fine and accomplished speaker with a pleasant voice and delivery, uniting charm of manner with grace and neatness of diction' (*DNB*). He spoke in House of Lords debates on legal matters. He died at 20 Devonshire Place, London, on 27 April 1949. His wife survived him.   G. R. RUBIN

Sources *The Times* (28 April 1949) · *DNB* · R. Stevens, *Law and politics: the House of Lords as a judicial body, 1800–1976* (1979) · M. Bunting, *The model occupation: the Channel Islands under German rule, 1940–1945* (1995) · G. Rose, *The struggle for penal reform* (1961) · P. Polden, *Guide to the records of the lord chancellor's department* (1988) · inquiries by Lord Justice Du Parcq into inter-services radio communications/co-operation, 1942, PRO, CAB 120/70; CAB 125/1 · J. Grigg, *The young Lloyd George* (1973); repr. (1990) · F. L. M. Corbet and others, *A biographical dictionary of Jersey*, [2] (1998) · *CGPLA Eng. & Wales* (1949) · H. Shawcross, *Life sentence: the memoirs of Lord Shawcross* (1995)
Likenesses W. Stoneman, photographs, 1932–43, NPG
Wealth at death £35,573 13s. 8d.: probate, 14 July 1949, *CGPLA Eng. & Wales*

Dupont, Gainsborough (*bap.* **1754**, *d.* **1797**), painter and mezzotint engraver, was baptized at St Peter's, Sudbury, on 28 April 1754, the third of the five children of Philip Dupont (*c.*1722–1788), carpenter, and his wife, Sarah (*bap.* 1715, *d.* 1795), daughter of John Gainsborough and his wife, Mary Burrough. He was a nephew of the painter Thomas *Gainsborough, to whom he was apprenticed in Bath on 14 January 1772. He moved to London with his uncle two years later; on 6 March 1775 he entered the Royal Academy Schools, and thereafter became his uncle's studio assistant. During the first fifteen years of his career documented work is rare, but James Northcote states that uncle and nephew worked together all night on the dress in the portrait of Queen Charlotte (1781; Royal Collection), and according to a letter from Gainsborough of 29 November 1784 Dupont painted a copy of John Vanderbank's portrait of Queen Caroline for the earl of Sandwich (Huntington town hall). He made mezzotints after his uncle's portraits, the earliest known being *Sir Richard Perryn*, published in December 1779. He also painted small-scale copies of his uncle's portraits and fancy pictures, either as a preparation for future prints or as a means of keeping a record of those which Gainsborough painted in the 1780s; examples are in the Cincinnati Art Museum, Ohio; the Metropolitan Museum of Art, New York; the National Gallery of Art, Washington, DC; and Gainsborough's House, Sudbury, Suffolk.

After his uncle's death on 2 August 1788, Dupont continued to work from his studio at Schomberg House until 1793, when he moved to 17 Grafton Street, Fitzroy Square. The similarity between his work and that of his uncle's in both drawings and paintings has often created problems of attribution; his signed portrait *J. Phillips* (1789; priv. coll.), for example, is especially close in style. However, he was able to turn this to his advantage and provide the market with Gainsboroughesque works into the 1790s. Versions of the 1781 portraits of George III and Queen Charlotte, from which he made a very popular pair of mezzotints in 1790, and likenesses of William Pitt based on Gainsborough's prototype must have provided financial security after the latter's death. Despite his 'diffidence and modesty' (Hayes, *Landscapes*, 187) he made original portraits of royalty, and from 1790 exhibited both landscapes and portraits at the Royal Academy. Among his most successful portraits are *John Clementson* (exh. 1792; Gainsborough's House, Sudbury) and *Sir James Sanderson* (exh. 1793). The colouring of his landscapes are more acidic than those of Gainsborough and have been described by John Hayes as idiosyncratic (ibid., 191). Nevertheless canvasses in the Brooklyn Museum, New York; Lady Lever Art Gallery, Port Sunlight; and Gainsborough's House, Sudbury, withstand comparisons with those of his contemporaries. Arguably his most original contribution to landscape is a series of oil sketches, examples of which are in the Huntington Library, San Marino, California; the Yale Center for British Art, New Haven, Connecticut; and Gainsborough's House, Sudbury.

By 1793 Dupont's style had become more personal, and he embarked on two important portrait commissions. Thomas Harris (d. 1820), proprietor of the Covent Garden Theatre, commissioned him to paint a series of theatrical portraits that were completed by 1795 and included *John Quick as Spado* (exh. RA, 1794) and *Alexander Pope as Hamlet*. A number of these works were later acquired by the Garrick Club, London. The Corporation of Trinity House commissioned an immense group portrait, known as 'The Great Court Painting' (1793–5), commemorating the approval of the designs for a new Trinity House and showing the elder brethren with the architect, Samuel Wyatt.

After a short illness Dupont died on 4 January 1797 at his home, 17 Grafton Street, London, and was buried beside his uncle at St Anne's, Kew.   HUGH BELSEY

Sources J. Hayes, 'The Trinity House group portrait', *Burlington Magazine*, 106 (1964), 309–16 • J. Hayes, 'Thomas Harris, Gainsborough Dupont and the Theatrical Gallery', *Connoisseur*, 179, 221–7 • J. Hayes, 'The drawings of Gainsborough Dupont', *Master Drawings*, 3/3 (1965), 243–56 • J. Hayes, *The landscapes of Thomas Gainsborough*, 2 vols. (1982), 187–236 • H. Belsey, *Gainsborough's family*, 20, 34–7 [exhibition catalogue, Gainsborough's House, Sudbury, 1988] • W. T. Whitley, *Thomas Gainsborough* (1915) • H. Belsey, *Gainsborough at Gainsborough's House* (2002) [exhibition catalogue, Sudbury and London]

Likenesses T. Gainsborough, oils, c.1772–1774, Memphis Brooks Museum of Art, Tennessee • T. Gainsborough, oils, c.1772–1775, Tate collection • T. Gainsborough, chalk and watercolour drawing, 1775, V&A • G. Dupont, self-portrait, oils, c.1780; Christies, 29 Jan 1954, lot 128 • T. Gainsborough, oils, Mansfield College, Oxford

Duport, James (1606–1679), dean of Peterborough and college head, was born in the master's lodge of Jesus College, Cambridge, the son of John *Duport (d. 1617/18), master of Jesus College, and Rachel (d. 1618), the daughter of Richard *Cox, bishop of Ely. Educated at Westminster School by John Wilson, he matriculated as a pensioner from Trinity College, Cambridge, in Michaelmas 1622, and was elected a Westminster scholar there the following year. At Trinity his tutor was Robert Hitch, later dean of York. He graduated BA in January 1627 and was elected a fellow of the college the following October. He proceeded MA in May 1630, and in the same year was ordained a priest.

A man of diminutive stature and possessed of a good sense of humour and some wit, Duport was elected *praevaricator* (commencement jester) for 1631, and delivered a humorous and elegant speech on alchemy. In 1637 (the year he received the degree of BD) he published at the university press *Threnothriambos, sive, Liber Job Graeco carmine redditus*, a Homeric paraphrase of the book of Job, with a facing-page Latin prose translation, which established him as a scholar and poet (the work was republished in 1653). In 1639 Duport was elected regius professor of Greek at Cambridge, a position which Trinity College would not allow him to assume unless he resigned his fellowship. Duport refused on the grounds that the accompanying salary of £40 was insufficient to live upon; the master and senior fellows of the college eventually relented, allowing him to retain both his fellowship and his students. He further supplemented his income by accepting the offer of the prebend of Langford Ecclesia and the archdeaconry of Stow, both in the diocese of Lincoln; collated to both on 14 August 1641, he resigned both preferments on 12 November to become prebendary of Leighton Buzzard in the same diocese.

Duport's royalist sympathies lend credence to the *Dictionary of National Biography*'s claim that he was ejected from his prebendal stall in 1643; however, he remained in Cambridge, giving public lectures on the *Characters* of Theophrastus, and it has been argued that Duport would not have been elected by the heads of houses as Lady Margaret preacher in 1646 had he been a non-subscriber to the solemn league and covenant of 1643. This appointment required him to deliver at least six sermons a year in the dioceses of London, Ely, and Lincoln. In 1646 he published another volume of biblical paraphrase in Greek, this time covering the Song of Solomon, Proverbs, and Ecclesiastes. His relinquishment of the professorship in 1654 has also been a matter for debate. The accepted view that he was ejected by the commissioners for reforming the university after refusing to take the engagement oath of 1650–51 has been contested. Rather, it is claimed that while Duport had indeed been ejected for failing to appear to subscribe in August 1650, he must have signed soon afterwards; and, in any case, the engagement was repealed in January 1654. Moreover, one contemporary noted that Duport had simply resigned. Either way, he was succeeded by Ralph Widdrington as Greek professor in December 1654. None the less Duport remained a fellow at Trinity (he was appointed senior fellow in October 1654), and in 1655 he was chosen as vice-master of the college.

Duport was active as a tutor in Trinity for over thirty years: between 1645 and 1659, for example, he was tutor to more than 20 per cent of all the college's students, 180 pupils in all and many of them royalist. In his position as vice-master, in particular, he was able not only to offer a degree of protection to young royalists studying in the university but also to attract well-connected students to the college. His students included Edward Cecil (son of the earl of Salisbury), Henry Puckering, John Knatchbull, Isaac Barrow, John Ray, Francis Willoughby, and two sons of the earl of Bedford. He earned a valuable supplementary income through his tuition, although, as evidenced by the case of Barrow, Duport was not above waiving fees and even offering accommodation to talented but impoverished students. He was particularly active as a patron of Barrow: it has been suggested that Duport extended protection to him as a non-subscriber of the engagement, while John Tillotson, later archbishop of Canterbury, claimed that Duport had recommended Barrow to replace him as the regius professor of Greek in 1654.

While at Trinity Duport drew up a set of 'Rules to be observed by young pupils and schollers in the university'. As one of 'the fullest and most revealing statements of the objectives of undergraduate studies … for early-modern Cambridge', they reveal how important the role of the tutor was in educating the young, shaping their characters, and encouraging them in religion (Cunich and others, 149). The rules ranged from what to read (most notable was the recommendation of George Herbert's 'divine and heavenly' poems as second only to the Bible) to appropriate behaviour and dress (ibid., 148).

The precise nature of the education Duport offered has been the subject of considerable controversy. To some it appears—on the basis of urgings to 'follow not Ramus in logic nor Lipsius in Latin, but Aristotle in one and Tully [Cicero] in the other' ('Rules')—to have been traditional and old-fashioned, emphasizing the importance of university disputations and scorning new learning and philosophy: a demonstration of how behind the times Cambridge was. Others contest this by arguing that Duport's chief concern was the fate of languages and *literare humaniores*, which he considered to be relatively more important than science and mathematics. According to this interpretation Duport feared that Ramism and the new science, when taken to extremes, were inherently philistine in their import. He was not, however, a slave to Aristotle. Instead, he recommended the best authors in every subject and the use of the critical faculties. He also acknowledged the worth of the new science and mathematics, and he encouraged interested students to be tutored by experts such as Barrow. Duport's own 2000-strong library contained very few scholastic texts, but did hold large numbers of classical, linguistic, and literary items along with some modern scientific books (purchased after the Restoration). It thus seems that the latter interpretation is the more persuasive.

Throughout the interregnum Duport had continued to protest against changes in religion: a sermon in St Paul's Cathedral, London, in which he objected to the profanation of the cathedral, led to his being barred from that pulpit. On 20 May 1660, with Charles II shortly to arrive in England as the restored monarch, he was once again invited to preach at St Paul's, with the consequent sermon, published as *Evangelical Politie, or, A Gospel Conversation* (1660), heralding the return of the national church. The Restoration also marked a new stage in Duport's religious and educational career. Confirmed as prebendary of Leighton Buzzard and as Lady Margaret preacher (an appointment he kept until 1665), he was made a doctor of divinity at Cambridge and a royal chaplain in 1660; four years later he was installed as dean of Peterborough. He was briefly restored to the professorship of Greek in 1660 in place of Widdrington, but resigned it in favour of his former pupil Barrow. That same year Duport published his most famous work, *Homeri poetarum omnium seculorum facilè principis gnomologia* (more commonly known as *Homeri gnomologia*), which illuminated a comprehensive collection of Homeric aphorisms with extensive quotations from the Bible and other classical texts. The following year the fellows of Corpus Christi College, Cambridge, were thwarted in their attempt to elect Duport as master by the royal appointment of Peter Gunning. In 1668 Duport was elected as master of Magdalene College, Cambridge, a position he held until his death, and in the same year he became rector of Boxworth, Cambridgeshire. For 1669–70 he served a term as vice-chancellor of the university, while about 1672 he became the absentee rector of Aston Flamville and Burbage, Leicestershire; his family's ancestral links with Leicestershire perhaps account for the latter appointment.

According to the modern historians of Magdalene College Duport was 'an effective and conscientious Master, who left his mark on every aspect of the College's life' (Cunich and others, 150). His tenure oversaw a period of renovation and expansion in the college, with Duport himself personally contributing both plate and an organ to the chapel. An accomplished Latin and Greek poet—who 'broke into verse on the slightest provocation'—Duport also encouraged a classical literary revival in the college, best exemplified by the significant number of Magadalene poets who contributed to the published collections of university poetry during this time (Sandys, 349). Duport published his own collection of poems in 1676 as *Musae subsecivae*, dedicated to the duke of Monmouth, chancellor of the university. While it did not contain Duport's contribution to the Cambridge anthology *Oliva pacis* of 1654 that had celebrated Cromwell's peace with the Netherlands, the collection of 1676 did 'reveal a man of enormous breadth of reading … an interest in "metaphysical" verse, and a genuine if donnish playfulness' (Cunich and others, 147–8).

Duport died and was buried in July 1679; according to the monument in Peterborough Cathedral he died on 17 July, but the burial registers indicate that he was buried on 16 July. Trinity College benefited more than Magdalene—the former received the bulk of Duport's library and the larger bequests—but Magdalene did receive £100 towards new buildings and the endowment of four scholarships. Duport also left a £10 annuity to Peterborough grammar school. His manuscript lectures on Theophrastus's *Characters* were not published until 1712.   ROSEMARY O'DAY

Sources M. Feingold, 'Isaac Barrow: divine, scholar, mathematician', *Before Newton: the life and times of Isaac Barrow*, ed. M. Feingold (1990), 1–104 • G. M. Trevelyan, ed., 'Undergraduate life under the protectorate', *Cambridge Review*, 64 (1943), 328–30 • H. Kearney, *Scholars and gentlemen* (1970) • M. H. Curtis, *Oxford and Cambridge in transition, 1558–1642* (1959) • 'Rules to be observed by young people and schollers in the university', Trinity Cam., MS O.104.33, pp. 1–15 • J. E. Sandys, *A history of classical scholarship*, 2 (1908), 349–50 • *Fasti Angl., 1541–1857*, [Lincoln] • *Fasti Angl., 1541–1857*, [Bristol] • *Fasti Angl., 1541–1857*, [Bristol] • *Fasti Angl., 1541–1857*, [Bristol] • *Fasti Angl., 1541–1857*, [Bristol] • J. Twigg, *The University of Cambridge and the English Revolution, 1625–1688* (1990) • P. Cunich and others, *A history of Magdalene College, Cambridge, 1428–1988* (1994) • Venn, *Alum. Cant.* • *Walker rev.* • M. Feingold, 'Reversal of fortunes: the displacement of cultural hegemony from the Netherlands to England in the seventeenth and early eighteenth centuries', *The world of William and Mary: Anglo-Dutch perspectives on the revolution of 1688–89*, ed. D. Hoak and M. Feingold (1996), 234–61 • D. K. Money, *The English Horace: Anthony Alsop and the tradition of British Latin verse* (1998) • will, PRO, 11/31 [John Duport, father]

Duport, John (d. 1617/18), biblical scholar and college head, was born in Sheepshed, Leicestershire, the eldest son of Thomas Duport and his wife, Cornelia Norton of Kent. Originally descended from a Normandy family, the Duports had been substantial landholders at Sheepshed since the early fifteenth century. Having matriculated as a pensioner from Jesus College, Cambridge, in 1564, Duport remained there for most of his life. In 1570 he graduated bachelor of arts, master of arts in 1573, and doctor of divinity in 1590. He was a fellow of the college between 1574 and 1582, serving as a university proctor in 1580/81. In 1577 he became a deacon and was ordained priest three years later. It is likely that he gave up his fellowship in order to marry Rachel (d. 1618), the daughter of Richard *Cox, bishop of Ely. In 1578 he was master of the free school in Wotton under Edge, Gloucestershire, and subsequently he benefited from several livings: as rector of Harlton,

Cambridgeshire, in 1580–84; of Medbourne and of Husband's Bosworth in Leicestershire; and of Fulham, Middlesex, from 1583 until his death. He was also precentor of St Paul's, in 1585–1617, and a prebendary of Ely between 1609 and 1617.

Duport's mastership of Jesus College, from 1590 until his death, was comparatively lengthy and stable, and he can be identified as one of the several moderate puritans who headed Cambridge colleges during this period. While master he served as the university's vice-chancellor four times: unusually, for two consecutive years in 1593–5, when he oversaw the university's initial condemnation of William Barrett's anti-Calvinist assertions of 1595; and again in 1601/2 and 1609/10. He was also one of the translators of the Apocrypha for the Authorized Version of the Bible. He was survived by seven children, for whom he was able to make substantial provision in his will. Two of his three sons were to be educated at Cambridge, the younger of whom (James *Duport) went on to become an eminent scholar, while his second son was to be bound apprentice for £100 in London. The three unmarried of his four daughters were allocated portions of £200. He was also a benefactor to his college, with a bequest of the perpetual advowson of the church of Harlton. His will, of which his 'most deere and welbeloved wife' was sole executor, was dated 21 October 1617, and was proved in the prerogative court of Canterbury on 19 February 1618. Duport died of ill health about Christmas 1617.

ALEXANDRA SHEPARD

Sources J. Nichols, *The history and antiquities of the county of Leicester*, 3/2 (1804) • P. Lake, *Moderate puritans and the Elizabethan church* (1982) • H. C. Porter, *Reformation and reaction in Tudor Cambridge* (1958) • J. B. Mullinger, *The University of Cambridge*, 2 (1884) • A. Gray and F. Brittain, *A history of Jesus College, Cambridge*, rev. edn (1979) • A. W. Pollard, ed., *Records of the English Bible: the documents relating to the translation and publication of the Bible in English, 1525–1611* (1911) • Venn, *Alum. Cant.* • T. Fuller, *The worthies of England*, ed. J. Freeman, abridged edn (1952) • A. Chalmers, ed., *The general biographical dictionary*, new edn, 32 vols. (1812–17) • PRO, PROB 11/131

Wealth at death £200 portions for six of seven children: will, PRO, PROB 11/131

Duppa, Baldwin Francis (1801–1840), educationist, born at Hollingbourne, Kent, was the eldest son in the family of four sons and five daughters of Baldwin Duppa Duppa (1763–1847), a landowner, and his wife, Mary (d. 1837), daughter of Major-General Gladwin of Stubbing Court, Derbyshire. He was educated at Winchester College and matriculated in 1821 from Brasenose College, Oxford, where he obtained third-class honours in classics in 1824, but did not graduate. In November 1823 he was admitted at Lincoln's Inn, and was called to the bar on 7 June 1833. On 12 September 1826 he married Catherine, daughter and coheir of Philip Darell, of Calehill, Kent. The marriage produced three sons and three daughters.

Duppa became agent in England for the Swiss educationist P. E. von Fellenberg, whose estate schools at Hofwyl in Switzerland had attracted the attention of many observers, including Lord Brougham and Lady Byron. Fellenberg's ideas for creating social harmony through the moral and religious education of the peasantry may have exercised a particular appeal to Duppa following the risings of the agricultural labourers in Kent in October 1830; the Duppa family seat at Hollingbourne was situated in a region which experienced severe outbreaks of unrest. In 1831 he produced an account of the condition of the labouring classes in the south of England, followed in 1834 by *The education of the peasantry in England and what it ought to be, with an account of the establishment at Hofwyl*. Duppa moved in whig-radical circles, belonging to the Society for the Diffusion of Useful Knowledge and the London Statistical Society, for which he helped to organize a social survey of Marylebone (1836). He was most prominent as the honorary secretary and a prime mover with Thomas Wyse and W. E. Hickson in the Central Society of Education, a pressure group founded in 1836 to collect information about educational provision and to promote a secular, state-assisted national system in England following the Irish precedent. Its activities were frequently denounced by Anglicans and orthodox dissenters in the existing school societies. Duppa contributed to the society's publications articles on: 'Industrial schools for the peasantry' (1837), which advocated practical training for children destined to be agricultural labourers; Lord Brougham's Education Bill (1838), in which he advocated a secular system; and 'County colleges of education' (1839), in which he drew upon European developments to illustrate the importance of rural schools as a means of transmitting knowledge of new agricultural methods to tenant farmers. His evidence to the select committee on Irish education (1838) described Fellenberg's schools at Hofwyl, which were attended by his eldest son, Baldwin Francis Duppa (1828–1873). Duppa died at Penzance, Cornwall, on 5 January 1840.   M. C. CURTHOYS

Sources Burke, *Gen. GB* • Foster, *Alum. Oxon.* • W. P. Baildon, ed., *The records of the Honorable Society of Lincoln's Inn: admissions*, 2 vols. (1896) • *GM*, 1st ser., 96/2 (1826), 365 • *GM*, 2nd ser., 13 (1840), 218 • [C. B. Heberden], ed., *Brasenose College register, 1509–1909*, 2 vols., OHS, 55 (1909) • R. Brent, *Liberal Anglican politics: whiggery, religion, and reform, 1830–1841* (1987) • R. Ely, *In search of the Central Society of Education*, Educational Administration and History Monographs, 12 (1982) • W. A. C. Stewart and W. P. McCann, *The educational innovators*, 2 vols. (1967–8)
Archives NL Scot., George Combe MSS

Duppa, Brian (1588–1662), bishop of Winchester, was born at Lewisham, Kent, on 10 March 1588, the son of Jeffrey Duppa, identified by Anthony Wood as the then vicar of Lewisham, but more recently as the 'gentleman' living in Lewisham who was purveyor of the buttery to Elizabeth I and king's brewer to James I; his mother was Lucrece Marshall or Maresall. He was educated at Westminster School, where he was taught Hebrew by the then dean of Westminster, Lancelot Andrewes. He was elected student of Christ Church, Oxford, in May 1605, graduated BA in 1609, was elected fellow of All Souls in 1612, proceeded MA in 1614, and then for some years travelled in France and Spain. On his return he was elected junior proctor in 1619, and he proceeded BD and DD in July 1625; by then he was also chaplain to the prince palatine. Like other churchmen of his day Duppa enjoyed reading and writing poetry.

Brian Duppa (1588–1662), by John Michael Wright, 1660–62

He composed a nonsense verse entitled 'Come good fiddle', and a florid epitaph on Henry Boling (BL, Sloane MS 1446, fol. 27; Add. MS 22602, fol. 31).

According to a near-contemporary account 'the comeliness of his presence, the gentleness of his carriage, and the variety and smoothness of his learning' (BL, Lansdowne MS 986, fol. 11) brought Duppa to the notice of Edward Sackville, fourth earl of Dorset, who made him his chaplain and gave him the two Sussex livings of Hailsham, in 1625, and Withyham, in 1627. In 1626 Duppa was also appointed vicar of Westham near Pevensey. On 23 November that year he married Jane, daughter of Nicholas Killingtree of Longham, Norfolk; his surviving letters show that this was an extremely happy marriage, although childless. In 1628 Dorset recommended Duppa to the duke of Buckingham for the post of dean of Christ Church. As dean he altered the interior of the cathedral and, though not a typical Laudian, supported the election of William Laud as chancellor of the university in 1630. Duppa himself served as vice-chancellor in 1632 and 1633, and in 1634 became prebendary and chancellor of Salisbury. He entertained Charles I on his visit to Oxford in 1636, and in 1638, on the recommendation of Archbishop Laud, was appointed tutor to the young prince of Wales and duke of York, which brought him into close contact with services in the royal chapel. The prince of Wales's governor, William Cavendish, duke of Newcastle, urged the future king to emulate Duppa as both a perfect gentleman and a scholar who wore his learning lightly. Duppa's general standing is revealed in the fact that he was the editor of *Jonsonus virbius* (1638), a collection of poems on the death of Ben Jonson by thirty 'friends of the Muses'.

In May 1638 Duppa was elevated to the see of Chichester and instituted to the valuable Sussex rectory of Petworth, held in commendam. As bishop he tended to follow in the steps of his predecessor, Richard Mountague, as can be seen in his *Articles to be Inquired of throughout the Diocese of Chichester* (1638). But he was one of those moderate churchmen not too closely associated with Laud who were named to fill episcopal vacancies in 1641: in December he was translated to Salisbury. When the bishops were barred from the Lords he withdrew from London and spent much of the next few years with his royal charges or their father, to whose cause he donated £850 in 1642–3. A letter from Duppa at York, 'with part of my charge, till we are sent for', was intercepted in August 1642 and published anonymously as *Two Letters* (1642), and Duppa was almost certainly the real author of *Prince Charles his Gracious Resolution Concerning the Present Affaires of this Kingdome* (Oxford, 1642), in which the prince of Wales was depicted as urging Charles to show clemency to captured officers and to reach a 'speedy accommodation with Parliament'. Also attributed to Duppa, although published anonymously, are *A Prayer of Thanksgiving for his Majesties Late Victory over the Rebels [at Naseby]* (1643); *Two prayers, one for the safety of his majesties person, the other for the preservation of this university and city of Oxford* (1644); and *Private Formes of Prayer, Fit for these Sad Times* (Oxford, 1645). In 1648 Duppa published under his own name, through the royalist publisher Richard Royston, two sermons whose style is reminiscent of his old mentor, Lancelot Andrewes: *Angels Rejoicing for Sinners Repenting*, in which he urged his listeners to begin their repentance now; and *The Soules Soliloquie: and, a Conference with Conscience*, delivered on 25 October before the king, then a prisoner on the Isle of Wight. Duppa was now close to Charles, who told his eldest son to submit to his mother in all points save that of religion, for which he was to trust entirely to the bishop of Salisbury. Charles gave Duppa his Bible, which in 1652 he passed on to his dear friend Sir Justinian Isham, whose heirs still, at the beginning of the twenty-first century, possess it.

From Charles's execution to the Restoration, Duppa lived in a house bought by Isham at Richmond, Surrey, and protected himself 'as the tortoise doth, by not going out of my shell' (*Correspondence*, xxv–xxvii, 52). But he was far from inactive. He performed prayer-book services, confirmed, married, visited the sick, ordained priests and deacons (including a future archbishop, Thomas Tenison), and variously prepared and revised the devotional works that were published in 1660 and posthumously. He also kept in touch with leading lay royalists and with a number of ejected clergy, discussing the state of the church. Most notably, he maintained a clandestine correspondence with Gilbert Sheldon, Henry Hammond, and others on 'the business of the Church'—the campaign to preserve the episcopal succession. Duppa was seen by Sir Edward Hyde (later earl of Clarendon) as the axis around which efforts should be made to persuade the surviving bishops to consecrate new bishops in 1655 and 1659, and again in 1660. On 29 May 1660 Duppa was one of four surviving bishops who, in episcopal dress, publicly greeted Charles

II on his entry into London; on 7 July he was made lord almoner. But Charles was moving cautiously on the ecclesiastical settlement, and on 11 August Duppa told Sheldon how worried he was that the presbyterians might persuade the king to reject episcopacy altogether. However, on 28 August Duppa's translation to Winchester was the first of a series of royal nominations, and on 28 October Duppa deputized for the aged Juxon as chief consecrator of five new bishops in Westminster Abbey. He had already been actively leasing out episcopal properties at Salisbury before his move to Winchester in October, and at the latter (relying on some pre-war officials and his own relations appointed to other diocesan posts) was soon collecting substantial revenues. But receipts of at least £50,000 at Winchester were balanced by remitting £30,000 to his tenants and spending £16,000 on acts of charity, not least giving generous support to the almshouses in Richmond set up by his father and older brother before the wars.

Duppa made his will on 4 February 1662, and after providing for his wife, nephew, and other relatives, gave large sums to the cathedrals and colleges with which he had been associated. He died at Richmond on 26 March 1662, having been visited the day before by Charles II, who on his knees begged his mentor's blessing. The bishop's body lay in state in York House in the Strand, and was buried in Westminster Abbey on 24 April; the funeral sermon was preached by a very old friend, Henry King, bishop of Chichester. A monument in the north aisle of the abbey was erected by his widow.

In addition to the publications cited above Duppa has been credited with the 'author's life' prefixed to John Spottiswood's *The History of the Church and State of Scotland* (1655), but the implication in the preface that the biographer was a Scot, and the initials D. M. at the end of the biography, militate against this. Works that may be more safely attributed to Duppa are *A Guide for the Penitent*—'a model drawn up for the help of a devout soul wounded with sin'—published by Richard Royston, the king's printer, in 1660, 1664, and 1674; and *Holy Rules and Helps to Devotion, both in Prayer and Practice*—'written by … Bryan Duppa, late Lord Bishop of Winton, in the time of his sequestration'. The latter was first published in 1673 but had reached its eighth edition by 1707, and was revived again in the nineteenth century. It reflects Duppa's admiration for the early church as a model of devotion, but also his median position between the high Laudians and the anti-Laudians, and his reputation as a 'man of exemplary piety, eminent candor, humility and meekness, and of so clear a character that he left not the least spot upon his life or function' (*Biographia Britannica*, 3.1824).

IAN GREEN

Sources *The correspondence of Bishop Brian Duppa and Sir Justinian Isham, 1650–1660*, ed. G. Isham, Northamptonshire RS, 17 (1951) · Wood, *Ath. Oxon.*, new edn, 3.541–4 · *Biographia Britannica, or, The lives of the most eminent persons who have flourished in Great Britain and Ireland*, 7 vols. (1747–66), vol. 3, pp. 1823–5 · Bodl. Oxf., MSS Tanner 49, fol. 17; 51, fol. 159; 52, fols. 41, 93–5, 105–8, 206–7, 210–11; 53, fol. 230; 140, fols. 39–88; 141, fol. 101 · BL, Lansdowne MS 986, fols. 11, 17, 22 · N. Tyacke, *Anti-Calvinists: the rise of English Arminianism, c.1590–1640* (1987), 206–7 · J. Davies, *The Caroline captivity of the* *church: Charles I and the remoulding of Anglicanism, 1625–1641* (1992), 99, 195, 219, 274 · R. S. Bosher, *The making of the Restoration settlement: the influence of the Laudians, 1649–1662* (1951) · I. M. Green, *The re-establishment of the Church of England, 1660–1663* (1978), 29, 81–2, 91–2, 103–4, 106, 118–20, 125, 255–6 · K. Fincham, 'Oxford and the early Stuart polity', *Hist. U. Oxf.* 4: *17th-cent. Oxf.*, 179–210, esp. 199, 201, 208–9 · will, PRO, PROB 11/308, sig. 73 · *IGI* · *DNB*

Archives BL, letters, poems etc. | Northants. RO, corresp. with Sir Justinian Isham

Likenesses J. M. Wright, oils, 1660–62, Christ Church Oxf. [*see illus.*] · H. Howard, portrait, 18th cent. (after J. M. Wright), Christ Church Oxf. · H. Cheere, bust, All Souls Oxf. · R. White, engraving (after J. M. Wright), repro. in B. Duppa, *Holy rules and helps to devotion, both in prayer and practice* (1673) · oils, Christ Church Oxf.

Wealth at death left money for wife, nephew, and other relatives, plus large sums to cathedrals and colleges with which he had been associated: will, PRO, PROB 11/308, sig. 73

Duppa, Richard (*bap.* 1768, *d.* 1831), writer and draughtsman, was baptized on 28 February 1768 at Culmington, Shropshire, the son of William Duppa and his wife, Susannah. In 1796 Duppa set out with the intention of making a grand tour, arriving in Rome in the spring of 1797. Most of his time was spent around Naples, however. Later, in Rome, where he lodged with two matrons, his fellow painter William Artaud noted that 'with these fair dames, each pressing with her rosy finger his brawny arm, the Platonic Duppa nightly perambulates the purlieus of Trinita dei Monti' (Ingamells, 322). His letters to Joseph Farington included accounts of English artists then in Rome; he published, in 1799, *A Journal of the most Remarkable Occurrences that Took Place in Rome*. In his late thirties, Duppa matriculated at Trinity College, Oxford, on 9 November 1807; became a student of the Middle Temple on 7 February 1810; graduated LLB at Trinity Hall, Cambridge, in 1814; wrote largely on botanical, artistic, and political topics; was elected a fellow of the Society of Antiquaries; and died in Lincoln's Inn, London, on 11 July 1831. A relative of the same name died at Cheney Longville, Shropshire, on the previous 25 February, while high sheriff of Radnorshire. An elder brother, John Wood Duppa (1762–1840), was rector of Puddlestone, Herefordshire.

Duppa's chief works included *A Brief Account of the Subversion of the Papal Government in 1798* (1799; 3rd edn, 1807); *A Selection of Twelve Heads from the Last Judgment of Michael Angelo* (1801); *Heads from the Fresco Pictures of Raffaele in the Vatican* (1802); *Memoirs of a Literary and Political Character—Richard Glover (1712–1785)*, whom Duppa seeks to identify with Junius (1803); *The Life and Literary Works of Michael Angelo Buonarotti, with his Poetry and Letters* (1806, with fifty etched plates; 2nd edn, 1807; 3rd edn, 1816; reissued in Bohn's European Library, 1846; and in Bohn's Illustrated Library, 1869); *The Life of Raffaele Sanzio da Urbino* (1816); *Outlines of Michael Angelo's Works, with Plans of St Peter's, Rome* (1816); and *Miscellaneous Observations on the Continent* (1825; reissued in 1828 as *Travels in Italy, Sicily, and the Lipari Islands*). *Dr. Johnson's Diary of a Journey into North Wales in 1774* was first printed and elaborately edited by Duppa in 1816 with Mrs Piozzi's help (incorporated in a late edition of J. W. Croker's edition of Boswell's *Life of Johnson*). Duppa also published several works on botany and issued pamphlets on literary copyright (1813), on Junius (1814), and on the

price of corn (1815), besides many classical schoolbooks. His library was sold by Evans of Pall Mall on 3–7 September 1831. Duppa's correspondence and notes for the years 1810–12 are in Herefordshire Record Office.

[ANON.], *rev.* ANNETTE PEACH

Sources J. Ingamells, ed., *A dictionary of British and Irish travellers in Italy, 1701–1800* (1997) · *IGI* · *GM*, 1st ser., 101/2 (1831), 567

Archives Herefs. RO, corresp. and notes

Likenesses C. Turner, mezzotint, pubd 1819 (after H. Edridge), BM, NPG

Dupré, August (1835–1907), analytical chemist, was born on 6 September 1835 at Mainz, Germany, the second son of J. F. Dupré, merchant, and his wife, J. A. Schafer (*d.* 1835) of Frankfurt. Both father and mother were of Huguenot descent. Between 1843 and 1845 the family lived in England, at Warrington, before returning to Germany to settle in Giessen. There and at Darmstadt, Dupré received his early schooling. In 1854 he and his elder brother, Friedrich Wilhelm (*d.* 1908), entered the University of Giessen. Both studied chemistry, primarily with Heinrich Will but also with Liebig. Later in the same year they proceeded to Heidelberg University, where they continued their chemical studies with Bunsen and Kirchhoff, and the following year, both having taken their PhDs at Heidelberg, they moved to London. Dupré obtained a position as assistant to William Odling, then demonstrator of practical chemistry at Guy's Hospital medical school, and Friedrich became lecturer in chemistry and toxicology at Westminster Hospital medical school. When Friedrich resigned the post in 1863 to return to the continent, where he became prominent in mining, his brother succeeded him; he held the post from 1864 until 1897. From 1874 to 1901 he was lecturer in toxicology at the London School of Medicine for Women. In 1866 he became a naturalized British subject, and in 1876 he married Florence Marie, daughter of H. T. Robberds of Manchester. The couple later had four sons and a daughter.

Dupré's main scientific work was as a consultant chemical analyst to various units of local and central government. From 1871 on he was regularly called upon by the medical department of the Local Government Board to analyse waters suspected of transmitting epidemic diseases. This was the context of his most important work. As it became clear, about 1880, that the units of disease transmission were biological, not chemical, entities, Dupré sought a means of demonstrating the presence of bacteria in water, and recognized, in a series of three reports to the Local Government Board, that the oxidation of organic matter in water was an indication of bacterial activity. As a consultant to the Metropolitan Board of Works, then under legal pressure to end the sewage contamination of the Thames estuary, Dupré advised in 1883–5 that the same process, the controlled oxidation by bacteria of decomposable substances, might be made the basis of a process of sewage treatment. W. J. Dibdin, chemist to the Metropolitan Board of Works, carried out a series of experiments initiated by Dupré, which led in the early 1890s to the development of the contact filter, one of the first successful forms of biological sewage treatment.

Dupré was also, along with Sir Frederick Abel, one of the leading British experts on explosives. From 1873 on he served as consulting chemist to the explosives inspectorate of the Home Office. In 1888 he was nominated a member of the War Office explosives committee, of which Abel was chairman, and in 1906 he became a member of the ordnance research board. During thirty-six years he examined 'nearly four hundred entirely new explosives imported into England, as to safety. He had often to evolve original methods of analysis or of testing for safety, and therein especially rendered important services' (Hake, 2272). In 1883 he was responsible for stabilizing a large quantity of nitroglycerine that a Fenian bomber had secretly manufactured in central Birmingham, probably saving that city from a catastrophic explosion.

Dupré was also a leader of the first generation of public analysts, serving as Westminster public analyst from 1873 to 1901. As second president of the Society of Public Analysts in 1877–8, Dupré helped to reunite the society after a difficult episode of conflict over methods and intraprofessional relations during which it almost collapsed. More than half of his fifty scientific papers dealt with aspects of food and drug analysis. An astute oenologist, Dupré also published, with Dr J. L. W. Thudichum, another German chemist practising in London, a treatise on the origin, nature, and varieties of wine (1872). With his assistant, Dr H. Wilson Hake, he wrote a textbook, *A Short Manual of Inorganic Chemistry* (1886; 3rd edn, 1901). Clear and forthright, well-read in many areas of practical chemistry, Dupré was much in demand as an expert witness.

Dupré was elected a fellow of the Chemical Society in 1860, and served on the council (1871–5). He was an original member of the Institute of Chemistry (1877), and a member of the first and four later councils. He was an original member of the Society of Chemical Industry, and served on its council (1894–7). Dupré was elected FRS on 3 June 1875. He died at his home, Mount Edgcumbe, Sutton, Surrey on 15 July 1907, and was buried at Benhilton, Sutton. He was survived by his wife.

CHRISTOPHER HAMLIN

Sources H. Wilson Hake, *PRS*, 80A (1907–8), xiv–xviii · O. Hehner, *The Analyst*, 32 (1907), 313–16 · H. Wilson Hake, *JCS*, 93 (1908), 2269–75 · C. Hamlin, *What becomes of pollution? Adversary science and the controversy on the self-purification of rivers in Britain, 1850–1900* (1987) · C. Hamlin, *A science of impurity: water analysis in nineteenth century Britain* (1990) · R. C. Chirnside and J. H. Hamence, *The 'practising chemists': a history of the Society for Analytical Chemistry, 1874–1974* (1974) · *WWW* · *Catalogue of scientific papers*, Royal Society · O. Guttmann, 'Cantor lectures: twenty years' progress in explosives', *Journal of the Royal Society of Arts*, 57 (1908–9), 113–20 · S. Rideal, *Sewage and the bacterial purification of sewage*, 2nd edn (1901), 17–89 · *Chemical News* (1855–1907) · *DNB* · *CGPLA Eng. & Wales* (1907)

Archives ICL · LMA · RS

Likenesses Mayall & Co., photogravure, repro. in Hehner, *The Analyst*, 312

Wealth at death £1639 12s. 3d.: administration with will, 21 Sept 1907, *CGPLA Eng. & Wales*

Dupré, Desmond John (1916–1974), lutenist and guitarist, was born on 19 December 1916 at 101 Dartmouth Road, Brondesbury, London, the younger son and third child in the family of two sons and two daughters of Frederick Harold Dupré, analytical chemist, and his wife, Ruth Clarkson, a violinist. He was educated at Merchant Taylors' School, London, and won a scholarship to St John's College, Oxford, in 1936, graduating with a first in chemistry in 1940. A conscientious objector, he spent the war as a research chemist in the Glaxo laboratories, where he worked on penicillin. Dupré had always wanted to be a professional musician, and he studied the cello at the Royal College of Music (1946–8). He was taught there by Ivor James and Herbert Howells. When he became interested in early instrumental music he turned to the guitar, which he had played since he was a child, in order to play the lute repertory, and he also taught himself to play the viol. For a few months in 1946 he gave guitar lessons to the thirteen-year-old Julian Bream. On 27 June 1949 he married Catherine Lane Poole (*b.* 1926/7), daughter of Austin Lane Poole, medieval historian and president of St John's College, Oxford, from 1947 to 1957; she later worked as a novelist and painter. They had three sons and two daughters.

In 1948 Dupré joined the Boyd Neel Orchestra, a chamber orchestra, as a cellist, but he left in 1949 to devote himself to the guitar after he had begun to work with the counter-tenor Alfred *Deller (1912–1979), who too was embarking on a career as a soloist. At first he played the lute parts of the Dowland lute-songs on the guitar, and when in 1948 Deller formed the Amphion Ensemble (which became the Deller Consort in 1950), Dupré was one of the instrumentalists, playing the guitar and viola da gamba. He did not confine himself to Elizabethan music: for example, in June 1950 he joined members of the Boyd Neel Orchestra in a performance of Schubert's quartet for guitar and strings. He played an important part in the revival of interest in early music and especially in the restoration of the lute, an instrument that had disappeared from the end of the eighteenth century until Arnold Dolmetsch began to make and play lutes at the beginning of the twentieth century. After Dolmetsch's death in 1940, the only professional lutenist in England was Diana Poulton, a former pupil, and it was the discovery of the English lute-song repertory, at a time when the BBC Third Programme was bringing such little-known music to a wider audience, that helped to spearhead the revival. In 1951 Dupré asked Maurice Vincent to make him a lute and taught himself to play it in time to accompany Deller on 28 May 1951 at one of a series of recitals of English song at the Wigmore Hall, London, as part of the Festival of Britain. He and Deller gave recitals all over the country, including favourite Dowland lute-songs such as 'I saw my lady weep', 'Can she excuse my wrongs', and 'Come away sweet love', and the programme always included lute solos such as fantasias by Dowland: Dupré made skilful arrangements of all the songs and solos for their performances. In April 1953 he took part in a series of nine programmes of English lute music on the BBC Third Programme, organized by Thurston Dart: in these he also played the viola da gamba with Diana Poulton, and the cittern with Julian Bream. He made the first of his many recordings with Deller in 1950, performing two Dowland songs, 'Fine knacks for ladies' and 'In darkness let me dwell', and their first long-playing record was *Shakespearean Songs and Lute Solos* in 1955. After his death Deller wrote: 'It is impossible for me to imagine how my career would have developed without his scholarly help and superb gifts as an accompanist'.

Dupré was also performing regularly on the viola da gamba. In 1948 he played in the first London performance of Monteverdi's *The Coronation of Poppea*, at Morley College (with Deller singing the role of Ottone), and he would often include viola da gamba pieces in his recitals with Deller. In performances of Bach's St John passion, he frequently played both the lute solo accompanying the bass aria 'Betrachte, meine Seele' and the obbligato viola da gamba part accompanying the alto in 'Es ist vollbracht', and he gave the first of many performances of the viola da gamba part in Monteverdi's *Vespers* at King's College, Cambridge, in July 1951 as part of the Festival of Britain. He played the tenor viol in the London Consort of Viols from 1951, playing in three concerts in the Wigmore Hall series 'Music by English composers, 1300–1750' in the summer of 1951. Dupré continued to perform on the guitar, sometimes including modern pieces in his concerts, and in 1955 played in a programme of contemporary music at the Royal Festival Hall which included the first English performance of Stravinsky's songs for soprano, flute, guitar, and harp.

Dupré continued to perform and record with Deller for the rest of his life, touring the world with the Deller Consort and teaching at the Deller Academy, Deller's summer school in Provence, but he formed lasting partnerships with other artists as well, most notably Thurston Dart, with whom he first played in 1949. The two men performed and recorded Bach's sonatas for viola da gamba and harpsichord (BWV 1027–9) and Dart's reconstruction of Handel's concerto for lute and harp op. 4 no. 6. In the late 1960s he accompanied the tenor Robert Tear, performed Italian music with Musica Reservata, played in the Julian Bream Consort, and at Glyndebourne, in 1967, played the lute and the chitarrone in performances of Cavalli's *Ormindo*. He also played the incidental music for many radio plays, first broadcasting on 13 June 1949 with Julian Bream with music for two guitars for Lorca's *Blood Wedding*.

Dupré taught regularly at Morley College and Goldsmiths' College, London: his pupils included the American lutenist Hopkinson Smith. He was the first president of the Lute Society (founded in 1956), from 1965 to 1973. Dupré died suddenly on 16 August 1974 in the Kent and Sussex Hospital, Tunbridge Wells, Kent, following a heart attack while travelling to join Alfred Deller's summer school in Provence.   ANNE PIMLOTT BAKER

Sources A. Deller, 'Desmond Dupré', *Early Music*, 3/1 (Jan 1975); repr. *Lute Society Journal*, 16 (1974) · M. Hardwick and M. Hardwick, *Alfred Deller: a singularity of voice* (1968) · A. Sillery and V. Sillery, eds., *St John's College biographical register, 1919–1975* (1978), 141 · *New Grove*, 2nd edn · private information (2004) [widow and son] · S. W. Button, *Julian Bream: the foundations of a musical career* (1997), 26–8 · d. cert.

Archives FILM BBC Sound Archive | SOUND BL NSA
Likenesses photograph, priv. coll.
Wealth at death £26,583: probate, 3 Sept 1975, *CGPLA Eng. & Wales*

Du Pré, Jacqueline Mary (1945–1987), cellist, was born at 165 Banbury Road, Oxford, on 26 January 1945, the younger daughter and the second of the three children of Derek du Pré, a financial writer and editor, and Iris Maud, *née* Greep, a pianist and composer of music for children, who taught at the Royal Academy of Music. The family name has Jersey origins. Jacqueline's precocious musical gifts were quickly recognized by her mother. She received her first cello at four, after hearing the instrument on a BBC *Children's Hour* programme, and at five began to have lessons with Alison Dalrymple at Herbert Walenn's London Cello School. Iris du Pré further stimulated her daughter's passion for the cello by composing little pieces for her, later published as a collection under the title *Songs for my Cello and me*. By the age of six, when she first played in public, Jacqueline was acknowledged as the school's star pupil, combining an extraordinarily acute musical ear with an innate power of communication.

In 1955, when she was ten, Jacqueline was accepted as a pupil by the famous cellist and teacher William Pleeth, with whom she remained for the next seven years. In the following year she won the first Suggia gift, an international cello prize financed by the legacy of the Portuguese cellist Guilhermina Suggia. In his letter of recommendation to the adjudicating panel, chaired by John Barbirolli, Pleeth wrote that his pupil was 'the most outstanding cellistic and musical talent that I have met so far, to which she adds incredible maturity of mind. I am of the opinion that she will have a great career' (Easton, 42). Barbirolli later said that he recognized Jacqueline as the winner from the moment she started playing. She was offered £175 a year to finance her tuition, with the proviso that she did four hours' practice a day. This in turn entailed a special arrangement with her school, Croydon high school, whereby she was excused from certain subjects. Three years later, just before her fifteenth birthday, her parents removed her from school and continued her education at home. By then a career as a cellist looked assured.

In January 1958 Jacqueline made her first appearance on television in a 'young people's concert', playing the first movement of the Lalo concerto. In April that year she again performed on television, this time in the company of her sister Hilary, a talented flautist. As Pleeth's pupil she had become a student at the Guildhall School of Music in London, where she swept up all the available prizes, including the 1960 gold medal. In that same year she also won the Queen's prize, open to British instrumentalists under the age of thirty. Yehudi Menuhin, the chairman of the jury, an important figure in Jacqueline's artistic life over the next few years, later recalled the elation she created 'with the excitement of her own joy and intoxication with the music' (*Daily Telegraph*, 2 March 1960).

In the summer of 1960 Jacqueline took part in Pablo Casals's masterclasses in Zermatt, performing Saint-

Saëns's A minor cello concerto at the final students' concert. Then, on 1 March 1961, shortly after receiving her first Stradivarius cello as a gift from a godmother, she gave her début recital at the Wigmore Hall in London—a traditional rite of passage for an aspiring professional soloist. The critics were virtually unanimous in their enthusiasm. Martin Cooper, in the *Daily Telegraph*, praised her 'ability to carry through a phrase to its very end' and 'the vigorous strength of her rhythms'. 'Here is a young player', he wrote, 'whose technical accomplishments have not prevented her from being wholly committed to whatever she plays—this is one of the first essentials of a great player' (*Daily Telegraph*, 2 March 1961).

Her Wigmore Hall début effectively launched Jacqueline's career. She was immediately signed up by London's most prestigious agency, Ibbs and Tillett, and received numerous offers of concerts and broadcasts. She made her first radio recording in March 1961, performing pieces by Handel, de Falla, and Mendelssohn. Her first major orchestral date followed a year later, when she appeared with the BBC Symphony Orchestra at London's Royal Festival Hall in the work with which she was to become most closely identified: the Elgar cello concerto, which she had studied since the age of thirteen and had already performed with the Ernest Read senior orchestra in December 1959. In August 1962 she sealed her association with the Elgar when she played it at her Promenade Concerts début. By popular demand she returned to the Proms for four seasons in succession to play the same concerto, each time with Sir Malcolm Sargent. At this period she also formed a sonata duo with George Malcolm and played in chamber recitals with Yehudi and Hephzibah Menuhin. Jacqueline spent the autumn and winter of 1962–3 in Paris, studying with Paul Tortelier; and although the experience was a mixed success (their forceful artistic personalities were not ideally compatible), the French cellist described her as a phenomenon 'who stands out not only for the radiance of her playing, but for her personal radiance as well' (P. Tortelier and D. Blum, *Paul Tortelier: a Self-Portrait*, 1984, 213).

By now a star, Jacqueline formed another duo, with the pianist Stephen Bishop (later Kovacevich), in October 1964; the fruits of their collaboration include a memorable recording of Beethoven's A major and D major cello sonatas. In 1965 she toured the USA and Canada with the BBC Symphony Orchestra, scoring triumphs with her performances of the Elgar concerto in the Carnegie Hall, New York, and elsewhere. The critic in the *New York Herald Tribune* (15 May 1965) compared her to Casals and Mstislav Rostropovich, and wondered at the variety and quality of tone 'that could be likened to a hand moving alternately from velvet to silk to damask'. By the end of the tour she had sealed her reputation in North America.

The years from 1965 to 1970 marked the zenith of Jacqueline du Pré's career as one of the most exciting and charismatic performers of the day. No contemporary cellist, save perhaps Rostropovich, possessed a more opulent tone, or played with such impassioned, elemental force—an impression enhanced by her trademark swaying and hair-tossing on the concert platform. During these years she recorded much of her repertory, most famously the Elgar concerto with Barbirolli, which became an instant best-seller on its release in December 1965 and has remained so ever since. However, her rapid rise to fame had taken its toll; and amid intensive, joyous activity there were periods when she felt listless and dispirited. In January 1966 she took time off from public performance to study in Moscow with Rostropovich, who introduced her to the Britten cello sonata and works by Shostakovich and Prokofiev. From Moscow she wrote to Yehudi Menuhin:

> Over the past two years I have felt extremely lost with my work and generally fatigued by it. Now, under Rostropovich's tuition, I am finding a new freshness in it, and the old desire to go ahead with what I love so deeply is returning. (*DNB*)

At the end of 1966 Jacqueline was introduced to the Argentine-born Israeli pianist and conductor Daniel Barenboim (b. 1942). Their mutual attraction was immediate, and in April 1967 news broke of their engagement. Jacqueline (who had converted to Judaism) and Daniel were married in Jerusalem on 15 June, during the Six Day War. For the next four years the most glamorous couple in the classical music world often performed and recorded together, either as a duo (notably in the Beethoven and Brahms cello sonatas) or with Jacqueline as soloist and Daniel as conductor. The exuberance and spontaneity of their performances, their uncanny intuitive understanding, and their palpable joy in making music together made a profound impression on audiences wherever they played. They were also frequently joined in concert by the young American violinist Pinchas Zukerman, with whom they recorded the complete Beethoven piano trios. In April 1968 Jacqueline premièred Alexander Goehr's *Romanza* for cello and orchestra, which had been written for her. Otherwise her repertory, while extensive, was essentially conservative, stretching from Bach and Haydn (whose concertos she played with unapologetic subjective expressiveness) to Elgar, Delius, and, on rare occasions, Prokofiev and Shostakovich.

In March 1969, in the midst of an intensive international touring schedule, Jacqueline suffered from a strange bout of numbness which, with hindsight, can be seen as an early manifestation of multiple sclerosis. From this period onwards her playing, while often brilliant and moving, became less reliable. During a tour of the USA in the autumn of 1969, for instance, critics complained of mannerism, distortion, and faulty intonation. Attacks of numbness recurred, and she began to suffer increasingly from fatigue. At the end of 1970, after a demanding tour of the USA, it was clear that Jacqueline was suffering from physical and emotional exhaustion. By now her marriage, too, was under strain. On the brink of a nervous breakdown, she spent several months early in 1971 with her sister Hilary and her husband Christopher (Kiffer) Finzi, first at their farmhouse in Berkshire, then at their mountain home in southern France. Jacqueline became increasingly dependent on her brother-in-law, and during the French holiday they became lovers—an episode made notorious in Amand Tucker's film *Hilary and Jackie* of 1998, based on the book *A Genius in the Family* (1997) by Hilary and her brother Piers du Pré. This revealed the vibrant, sunny Jacqueline of popular perception to have been an altogether more complex figure: depressive, intensely vulnerable, and often unable to cope with the burden of celebrity. Hilary later justified her husband's behaviour as a means of helping her sister through a profound crisis—almost as a form of therapy. Within a year, though, Jacqueline had come to regard her brother-in-law as a man 'who wielded his authority in a manipulative way and who had taken advantage of a woman in a distraught state' (Wilson, 382).

Further alarming signs of Jacqueline's encroaching illness appeared in May 1971 when she cancelled the remainder of a tour of the USA after a performance of the Dvořák B minor cello concerto in California. The official reason was that she was suffering from tenosynovitis, an inflammation of the wrist tendon. She recovered sufficiently by the end of the year to record the Chopin and Franck cello sonatas with Barenboim—her last appearance in a recording studio. By now reconciled with her husband, she gave chamber concerts with Zukerman and Barenboim in Israel and Edinburgh during the summer of 1972, arousing hopes of a permanent recovery. Then in February 1973 she made her concerto 'comeback', playing the Elgar at two concerts in the Royal Festival Hall. Some musicians in the audience noted her problems with bow control, and a tendency to exaggeration, as if to compensate for her technical difficulties. But her vision and powers of communication were, if anything, more intense than ever. The violinist Rodney Friend wrote of her performance: 'I have never before or since experienced such absolute giving in music, without any trace of artificiality or superficiality. The pain and suffering in her playing were almost tangible, and it is something for which there is no explanation' (Wilson, 397).

Immediately after what were to be her last London concerts, Jacqueline embarked on her final tour of the USA. With increasing difficulty she managed three performances of the Brahms 'double' concerto (with Zukerman) in New York, but had to cancel a fourth. As Zukerman put it, 'she simply didn't have the energy to play any more'. The press reported that the sudden cancellation was due to a disorder of the nerve endings. After extensive tests multiple sclerosis was finally diagnosed in October 1973.

At first Jacqueline hoped to return to a normal life and even resume her concert career. But it soon became obvious that she would never play in public again. After a period of lethargy and acute depression, her spirits revived, and she started to play again at home with friends (including her one-time teacher William Pleeth), teach, and attend concerts. Though largely confined to a wheelchair from 1976, she gave acclaimed public masterclasses, two of which were televised in 1979. In the same year she was the narrator in Barenboim's recording of *Peter and the Wolf*. After her enforced withdrawal from the concert platform she was appointed OBE (1976) and received numerous honours, including the 'musician of the year' award of the Incorporated Society of Musicians (1980) and honorary doctorates from several British universities. From 1981 her condition deteriorated rapidly; one of the few pleasures of her last years was listening to her own recordings. She died at her home, Flat 28, 36–8 Chepstow Villas, Kensington, London, on 19 October 1987, and was buried at the Jewish cemetery in Golders Green two days later. Her husband survived her. In his funeral address Rabbi Friedlander recalled Jacqueline's courageous words after the onset of her illness: 'I was so fortunate to have achieved everything while I was young. I have recorded the full repertoire … I have no regrets' (*The Times*, 22 Oct 1987).

Among all the many tributes paid to Jacqueline du Pré's art, it was perhaps Christopher Nupen, director of the television film *Jacqueline* (1967), who most movingly and truthfully encapsulated her genius:

> The confidence and sure-footedness in her phrasing which gave her such freedom; her ability to respond to the moment and her apparent total lack of inhibition; these are the qualities that she seems to share more with musicians of the past than the present. And there is something else, a miraculous combination of apparently contradictory qualities. She had the ability to phrase with such natural conviction as to give you the impression that it really should not be done in any other way, and at the same time to make you catch your breath with surprise and delight at an unexpected sound or turn in the phrase. All so natural that it could not be otherwise and yet so surprising that life could suddenly take on a new dimension for a few seconds. (Wordsworth, 111–12)

RICHARD WIGMORE

Sources DNB · C. Easton, *Jacqueline du Pré* (1989) · W. Wordsworth, ed., *Jacqueline du Pré: impressions* (1983) · H. du Pré and P. du Pré, *A genius in the family* (1997) · E. Wilson, *Jacqueline du Pré* (1998) · *WWW* · private information (2004) · b. cert. · d. cert.
Likenesses photographs, 1962–80, Hult. Arch. · photograph, repro. in *The Times* (6 Nov 1993)
Wealth at death under £70,000: probate, 8 May 1988, *CGPLA Eng. & Wales*

Dupuis, Thomas Sanders (1733–1796), musician, was the third son (and fourth child) of John Dupuis and his wife, Susannah, whose maiden name may have been Hadnock. John Dupuis, who was descended from a Huguenot family which emigrated from France to England, is said to have held some appointment at court, and Thomas was born in England, probably in London, on 5 November 1733. He was brought up as a chorister in the Chapel Royal under Bernard Gates and John Travers. Gates made his former pupil a residuary legatee in his will of 1772, granting him (or his descendants) the estate in North Aston, Oxfordshire, to which he had retired, should Gates's nephew lack issue. It seems that the Dupuis family never actually came to benefit from this provision, but Dupuis erected a memorial to his teacher in the church there. On 3 December 1758 he was elected a member of the Royal Society of Musicians. His first substantial publication was a set of six keyboard concertos (1760), the subscription list of which suggests he had good social connections. He is described in 1763 as a harpsichord teacher, and by 1773 at the latest he was organist of the Charlotte Street Chapel. On 24 March 1779 Dupuis was elected an organist and composer to the Chapel Royal, following the death of William Boyce, and he was one of the assistant directors of the 1784 Handel commemoration in Westminster Abbey. On 26 June 1790 he obtained the degrees of BMus and DMus by accumulation at Oxford, and in the same year, together with his lifelong friend Samuel Arnold and others, he inaugurated the Graduates' Meeting, a society with musical and convivial interests. Joseph Haydn, himself an Oxford DMus, occasionally attended their meetings during his visits to London. Haydn was also impressed by Dupuis's extemporary organ playing, describing him in his notebook as a great organist.

Dupuis's compositions were conservative and unremarkable, being characterized by Charles Burney as 'not very rich or original'. Songs, glees, and keyboard works (often designed for teaching purposes) were included in his published output during his lifetime, and his pupil, John Spencer, issued a three-volume collection of his sacred music posthumously in 1797. Dupuis married Martha Skelton of Fulham at St George's, Hanover Square, on 16 July 1765. She predeceased him, and they had three sons, Thomas Skelton (1766–1795), who took holy orders and wrote texts for some of his father's works, George (died an infant in 1767), and Charles (1770–1824). Dupuis died 'of an overdose of opium' (Highfill, Burnim & Langhans, *BDA*) at his house, King's Row, 4 Park Lane, London, on 17 July 1796, and was buried on 24 July in the west cloister of Westminster Abbey. His obituary in the *Gentleman's Magazine* described him as 'distinguished for good sense, knowledge of mankind, integrity, and benevolence' (*GM*, 66, 1796, 621–2).   PETER WARD JONES

Sources H. Wagner, 'Huguenot refugee family of Dupuis', *Miscellanea Genealogica et Heraldica*, new ser., 3 (1880), 249–51 · J. L. Chester, ed., *The marriage, baptismal, and burial registers of the collegiate church or abbey of St Peter, Westminster*, Harleian Society, 10 (1876) · *GM*, 1st ser., 66 (1796), 621–2 · J. W. Callcott, 'Account of the Graduates' Meeting', BL, Add. MS 27693, fols. 6–36 · R. R. Kidd, 'Dupuis, Thomas Sanders', *New Grove* [incl. work list] · P. A. Scholes, *The great Dr Burney: his life, his travels, his works, his family and his friends*, 2 vols. (1948) · *The collected correspondence and London notebooks of Joseph Haydn*, ed. H. C. Robbins Landon (1959) · [C. Burney], 'Dupuis', in A. Rees and others, *The cyclopaedia, or, Universal dictionary of arts, sciences, and literature*, 45 vols. (1819–20) · T. Mortimer, *The universal director* (1763) · Highfill, Burnim & Langhans, *BDA* · J. H. Chapman, ed., *The register book of marriages belonging to the parish of St George, Hanover Square*, 1, Harleian Society, 11 (1886)
Likenesses C. Turner, mezzotint, pubd 1797 (after J. Russell), BM, NPG; repro. in T. S. Dupuis, *Cathedral music*, rev. J. Spencer [1797] · J. Russell, oils, priv. coll. · mezzotint, NPG
Wealth at death see will, detailed in Chester, ed., *Marriage, baptismal, and burial registers*, 457; Highfill, Burnim & Langhans, *BDA*

Durand, David (1680–1763), Reformed minister and historian, was born at Sommières in Languedoc and studied for the ministry at Basel. Thence he went to the Netherlands, and accompanied a corps of French refugees to Spain. Taken prisoner at the battle of Almanza in 1707, he would have been burnt alive by some peasants but for the intervention of the duke of Berwick. He was sent to France, but succeeded in escaping to Switzerland, ultimately finding his way back to the Netherlands, where he became a pastor at Rotterdam and gained the friendship of Pierre Bayle. He left the Netherlands for London in 1711, and was successively pastor of the conformist French churches in St Martin's Lane and the Savoy, later Les Grecs. He became a fellow of the Royal Society in 1728.

Durand was a voluminous author and translator. Among his works, all in French, are a history of the sixteenth century (1725–9) and, more influentially, a continuation of Paul Rapin's *History of England* (1734). Written for foreign consumption, it was, for a generation, 'the standard history of England' (Trevor-Roper, 14). Durand also wrote a history of painting in antiquity (1725) and *Histoire naturelle de l'or et de l'argent, extraite de Pline le naturaliste* (1729), which contains a lumbering imitation of *Paradise Lost* in French verse. He never married and died on 16 January 1763.   F. T. MARZIALS, *rev.* GEOFFREY TREASURE

Sources D. C. A. Agnew, *Protestant exiles from France, chiefly in the reign of Louis XIV, or, The Huguenot refugees and their descendants in Great Britain and Ireland*, 3rd edn, 2 (1886), 214–16 · T. Murdoch, ed., *The quiet conquest: the Huguenots, 1685–1985* (1985), 150 [exhibition catalogue, Museum of London, 15 May – 31 Oct 1985] · H. Trevor-Roper, 'A Huguenot historian: Paul Rapin', *Huguenots in Britain and their French background, 1550–1800*, ed. I. Scouloudi (1987), 3–19 · S. Beuzeville, biographical notice, in D. Durand, *La vie de J. J. Ostervald* (1778) · *GM*, 1st ser., 33 (1763), 46

Durand, Sir Henry Marion (1812–1871), army and political officer in India, was born on 6 November 1812 at Coulandon, France. The *Life* (1883) by his son gave neither Durand's father's nor his mother's name. However, Durand was apparently the illegitimate son of Lieutenant-Colonel Henry *Percy (1785–1825), a prisoner of war in France from 1812 to 1814, and Jeanne Durand; in 1827 Durand told the authorities at Addiscombe College that his mother was living in Paris. He maintained contact with the Percys (the sixth duke of Northumberland was his executor) and their family influence allegedly helped his career. His putative paternity was known to contemporaries: one Anglo-Indian periodical referred to 'his half avowed, half allowed connection with Duke Smithson of Northumberland' (*Friend of India and Statesman*, 17 June 1879). He was raised by his guardian, John Deans (of 48 Connaught Terrace, Edgware Road, London), and Mrs Deans, who treated him kindly.

Education and early years in India Durand was educated at Leicester School and at Mr Carmalt's school, Putney, where the pupils included George Canning. He attended Addiscombe College from 1827 to 1828, winning seven prizes and the sword for good conduct. In June 1828, though under the usual minimum age of sixteen, he was commissioned second-lieutenant in the Bengal Engineers, then he completed the usual training at Chatham. He sailed for India in October 1829 in company with Alexander Duff, the missionary, was shipwrecked off the Cape of Good Hope, and reached Calcutta in May 1830. He was attached to the public works department, and in 1832 was

Sir Henry Marion Durand (1812–1871), by unknown engraver, pubd 1883

sent to the irrigation branch in the North-Western Provinces.

Afghanistan In 1838 Lord Auckland, impressed by his local knowledge, proposed to appoint him secretary of the sudder board of revenue. However, Durand chose to join the 1839 invasion of Afghanistan. He was with Sir John Keane's column which in July reached the crucial fortress of Ghazni. Keane had left behind his heavy artillery. On 23 July Durand, assisted by Sergeant Robertson and Indian sappers, under fire, blew open the Kabul gate and so enabled the capture of Ghazni. At Kabul in August 1839 he was appointed by the envoy, William Macnaghten, engineer to Shah Shuja's government. He argued unsuccessfully that the troops should be stationed in the Bala Hissar citadel. He disagreed with Sir Alexander Burnes over not being sent on an expedition and resigned, which probably saved his life. He reached British India in January 1840, and spent most of 1840 at Mussooree preparing maps and reports of the recent campaign.

In spring 1841 Durand went on leave to England. According to his son he was always 'rather inclined to look on the dark side of life' (Durand, *Life*, 1.68). Bitter, resentful, and believing his Afghanistan services had been unjustly ignored, he considered going to Oxford and entering the church, but decided against it. Through Lord Fitzroy Somerset, who had known his father, Durand became acquainted with Lord Ellenborough who, appointed governor-general of India, took Durand as his aide-de-camp then appointed him to his lucrative (about £4000 p.a.) private secretaryship. They arrived in February 1842.

Marriage On 28 March 1843 at Meerut Durand married Anne (Annie), third daughter of Major-General Sir John McCaskill, a divisional commander in the 1842 Afghan campaign. Their children included Henry Mortimer *Durand (1850–1924), who wrote his father's *Life*. In June Durand was promoted captain. He accompanied Ellenborough on the Gwalior campaign, and was with him at the battle of Maharajpur.

Burmese days In 1844 Lord Hardinge, allegedly influenced by Percy family interest, appointed Durand commissioner of Tenasserim, Burma, replacing his friend George Broadfoot. Durand continued reforms begun by Broadfoot. His opposition to corruption and his forest-law punishment of an influential timber interest provoked its, and colluding officials', hostility and attacks in the Calcutta Anglo-Indian press, where Durand was denounced as the 'Jeffreys of India'. In 1846 Sir Herbert Maddock, acting president of the council and hostile to Durand, recalled him. His friend and defender Alexander Duff wrote, 'I never knew a more decided case of victimizing' (Durand, *Life*, 1.101). For Durand it was 'the commencement of a long course of disappointment and supersession which embittered the rest of his life' (ibid., 92). Hardinge, on his return, tried to make amends by offering the chief engineership at Lahore, but Durand indignantly went to England, arriving in March 1847, and appealed to the court of directors. His having been Ellenborough's secretary was prejudicial to him, and he did not gain redress. He began a history of the Anglo-Afghan War, which he never completed, and which his son H. M. Durand published in 1879.

The Second Anglo-Sikh War Durand returned to India in December 1848, during the Anglo-Sikh War, and joined the commander-in-chief, Lord Gough, at Ramnagar. Durand was at the battles of Chilianwala and Gujrat on the staff of Brigadier-General Colin Campbell, who in his dispatch praised Durand's assistance: Durand was promoted brevet major. After the campaign he was disappointed at not receiving a civil appointment equal to the Tenasserim commissionership. His early secretaryship apparently had raised his self-estimation and career expectations which, disappointed, turned to bitterness. Identified with Ellenborough, he shared his unpopularity, while his own proud, combative character and strong partialities brought him into conflict with others and retarded his career. After refusing several minor appointments he accepted the post of assistant political agent at Gwalior, from which he was soon transferred to a similar post at Bhopal. He remained there until the end of 1853, inspiring its ruler, the Sikandar Begam, with pro-British sentiment, which had good results during the mutiny. He also contributed articles to the *Calcutta Review*, including attacks on East India Company jobbery and demands for administrative reform.

Durand, indignant at continued neglect, resigned his Bhopal post and went to England, arriving in January 1854, but failed to gain employment there and in January 1856 returned to India. Seeing no chance of political employment, in April he became inspecting engineer of the presidency circle. He was promoted brevet lieutenant-colonel.

The mutiny In March 1857 Lord Canning, impressed by Durand's abilities, appointed him acting governor-general's agent in charge of the central India agency at Indore, capital of the Maratha state of Maharaja Tukoji Rao Holkar, while Sir Robert Hamilton was away on sick leave: an important post. Durand started in April, and chose to have little contact with Holkar. After a tense period as mutiny spread, in late June many of the troops at Indore mutinied. After little fighting, on 1 July Durand suddenly withdrew with the British and a few loyal sepoys, unpursued by the mutineers, to Hoshangabad and, on 2 August, to Mhow, where he was joined by British reinforcements. His brave wife, pregnant during the forced marches under burning sun, at Mhow succumbed to fever and died on 28 August, aged thirty-five; her baby had predeceased her. After the rains Durand, who made 'a strange guy of himself by putting on a black cap cover for his wife's death' (Hibbert, 377), from October to December commanded the Malwa column of British and Indian troops which defeated rebel forces in central India, capturing Dhar and Mandasor. This Malwa campaign, like others in 1857, included ruthless reprisals: prisoners shot and houses burned. In December he returned to Indore, and Hamilton replaced him. For his services Durand was appointed CB—but resented not being created KCB—and a brevet colonelcy. Canning wrote in a minute (July 1859) that Durand's conduct showed foresight and sound judgement, and that with only a small reliable force he had saved British interests in central India until support arrived. Nevertheless Durand's relations with Maharaja Holkar and his withdrawal from Indore were criticized then and later, notably in J. W. Kaye's *History of the Sepoy War*, though defended by his son in his *Life* and elsewhere. The central government's refusal to reward Holkar for his conduct during the mutiny was long controversial, with Holkar's advocates alleging Durand had made him a scapegoat and unjustly influenced the government against him.

Political life and marriage In 1858 Canning appointed Durand to collect information for Indian army reorganization, then sent him to England to tell the royal commission the Indian government's views. From January 1859 he was a member of the Council of India, and for the next two years he remained in England unsuccessfully advocating a local European army in India and opposing the new 'staff corps'. In autumn 1859 he married Emily Augusta, daughter of C. B. Allnut of Shrewsbury and widow of the Revd Henry Stedman Polehampton, chaplain at Lucknow during the mutiny. Durand and she had two sons who were blind, and a daughter who died aged two. His wife died on 29 March 1905.

In 1861 Canning appointed Durand Indian foreign secretary, which he continued until 1865: 'the unprecedented appointment of a military officer to this place displeased Civilians' (*The Times*, 7). His policies included reasserting British dominance over the princely states. He quarrelled with the viceroys Lord Elgin and Sir John Lawrence, and was disappointed the latter did not appoint him lieutenant-governor of the Punjab. From May 1865 until 1870 he was military member of the governor-general's council, the Indian counterpart of a war minister. He opposed reorganization of the Madras army on the irregular system, established a torpedo (mine defence) committee, and tried to make India militarily 'self-reliant'. He advocated re-establishing an Indian navy, again quarrelled with Lawrence, and in 1867 wanted command of the Abyssinian expedition but was again disappointed. In 1867 he was promoted major-general and made KCSI.

Death and character In May 1870 Lord Mayo appointed Durand lieutenant-governor of the Punjab, arguably 'an office second in importance only to the Viceroyalty itself' (*The Times*, 7). Touring the frontier, on 31 December 1870 at dusk he rode on an elephant to visit the town of Tank. His howdah was crushed against the roof of the gateway and he was thrown to the ground, his head striking a wall. He died on 1 January 1871, and was buried three days later at Dera Ismail Khan.

Tall, burly, and imposing, Durand was a brave soldier and a capable, if arguably sometimes unwise, administrator, though arguably limited by lack of imagination. Ambitious, proud, masterful, combative, resentful, with strong opinions strongly expressed, sometimes haughty in tone, he was repeatedly in conflict with superior officials: 'in opposition almost all his life' (Durand, *Life*, 1.413). He told his children his life had been hard and bitter, and, repeatedly disappointed, he saw it as largely unsuccessful: he had longed to command an army. Durand was controversial. Critics alleged he was overbearing, imperious, intolerant, and convinced of his own infallibility. Yet Alexander Duff admired his 'great talents, linked with high-toned Christian principle, unbending rectitude and pure patriotic unselfish motives' (Smith, 2.485), and after his death he was much praised: *The Times* called him India's ablest trained statesman and one of the most energetic of her administrators.   ROGER T. STEARN

Sources H. M. Durand, *The life of Major-General Sir Henry Marion Durand*, 1 (1883) • SOAS, Henry Mortimer Durand MSS • V. C. P. Hodson, *List of officers of the Bengal army, 1758–1834*, 2 (1928) • *The Times* (6 Jan 1871) • Bodl. Oxf., MSS Henry Mortimer Durand • E. W. C. Sanders, *The military engineer in India*, 1, 2 (1933–5) • East India Company military seminary, Addiscombe, cadet papers, BL OIOC • *ILN* (14 Jan 1871) • H. M. Vibart, *Addiscombe: its heroes and men of note* (1894) • P. Macrory, *Signal catastrophe: the story of a disastrous retreat from Kabul, 1842* (1966); repr. as *Kabul catastrophe* (1986) • C. Hibbert, *The great mutiny, India, 1857* (1978); repr. (1980) • H. M. Durand, *The First Afghan War and its causes* (1879) • J. W. Kaye, *A history of the Sepoy War in India, 1857–1858*, 3 vols. (1864–76) • G. Smith, *The life of Alexander Duff*, 2 vols. (1879) • Burke, *Peerage* • R. T. Stearn, 'Sir Henry Marion Durand, 1812–1871', *Soldiers of the Queen*, 85 (1996), 10–15

Archives Bodl. Oxf., corresp. and papers • SOAS, extracts from his letters, journals, dispatches, and papers | BL OIOC, letters to Lord Elgin, MS Eur. F 83 • BL OIOC, letters to Lord Elphinstone, MS Eur. F 87–89 • CUL, corresp. with Lord Mayo • NRA Scotland, priv. coll., letters to duke of Argyll • PRO, corresp. with Lord Ellenborough, PRO 30/12

Likenesses engraving, repro. in Durand, *Life of Major-General Sir Henry Marion Durand*, frontispiece [*see illus.*] • engraving, repro. in

The Graphic, 3 (1871), 88 · oils, royal engineers, Gordon barracks, Chatham, Kent · photograph (after a painting?), repro. in Sanders, *The military engineer in India*, 2 (1935), facing p. 332

Wealth at death under £9000: probate, 23 June 1871, *CGPLA Eng. & Wales*

Sir (Henry) Mortimer Durand (1850–1924), by George Charles Beresford, c.1902

Durand, Sir (Henry) Mortimer (1850–1924), administrator in India and diplomatist, was born at Sehore, Bhopal state, India, on 14 February 1850, the second son of General Sir Henry Marion *Durand (1812–1871) and his first wife, Anne, daughter of Major-General Sir John McCaskill. After being educated at Blackheath proprietary school, London, and at Eton House, Tonbridge, he passed into the Indian Civil Service in 1870. Two years later he was called to the bar by Lincoln's Inn. He reached India early in 1873 and, after serving in Bengal for eighteen months, was appointed attaché in the foreign department of the government of India. Proficient in languages, he rose rapidly in the political department, serving under Alfred Lyall in Rajputana, and as political secretary to Sir Frederick Roberts in Afghanistan in 1879–80. In 1875 he married Ella Rebe (*d.* 1913), daughter of Teignmouth Sandys of the Bengal civil service; they had a son and a daughter. During the Second Afghan War, Durand was shut up with Roberts's force in the Shahpur cantonment, and assisted his brother-in-law Sir Charles Metcalfe MacGeorge in recapturing some guns from the enemy. He was mentioned in dispatches for conspicuous gallantry and was awarded the Anglo-Afghan War medal with two clasps.

On his return to Calcutta, Durand rejoined the foreign department, and soon rose to be its head. He enjoyed the confidence of the viceroy, Lord Dufferin (whom he accompanied to Mandalay in 1886), and of his successor, Lord Lansdowne. In 1886 he organized association football in Simla, as an exercise in promoting good relations between all classes, and presented a trophy for an annual competition. He exercised a powerful influence on frontier policy, on the settlement with Russia after the Panjdeh incident of 1885, on the annexation of Upper Burma, and on the negotiations with Amir Abdur Rahman, which led up to the final settlement of the boundaries between Afghanistan and Russia on one side, and Afghanistan, India, and Persia on the other. The amir eventually agreed to receive a mission under Durand in 1893, and accepted the 'Durand line', which was subsequently demarcated, dividing tribes under British political control from those under Afghan influence for the entire length of the frontier zone from Chitral in the extreme north to Sistan in the south. The amir agreed to evacuate the districts held by him north of the Oxus River in exchange for the districts lying south of it. He also promised not to interfere with the frontier tribes and consented to a definition and demarcation of the Indo-Afghan frontier by a joint commission wherever practicable and desirable. He retained Aswar and the Birwal tract, but renounced his claims to the rest of Waziri territory, Dewar and Chageh. In return, the government of India withdrew all restrictions on the amir's purchase and import of ammunition, promised assistance in arms and ammunition, and increased his annual subsidy from Rs 1.2 million to Rs 1.8 million. A

northern border had already been secured for the amir, which marked a definite barrier against Russia's advance, and prepared the way for the Anglo-Russian agreement of 1907 and the Anglo-Russian alliance in the First World War. Durand also planned and carried through the establishment of the imperial service troops of the Indian princes, whereby 26,000 trained men were added to the number of combatants sent from India in the First World War.

Durand was created KCIE in 1889 and KCSI in 1894, after his return from Kabul. That year Lord Rosebery offered him the post of minister-plenipotentiary at Tehran, and he retired prematurely from the Indian Civil Service. He remained in Persia from 1894 to 1900, but in spite of his many good qualities and his exceptional ability in the Persian language, he was not particularly successful, largely because he could not persuade the British government to support a substantial loan requested by the shah's government. He handled the difficult situation which arose from the assassination of Shah Nasir al-Din with good judgement, and made useful suggestions for the establishment of British consulates at important Persian centres, which were later implemented; but his manners were stiff, he was hardly on speaking terms with any of the Persian ministers, and his whole work was obstructed by dominant Russian authority, which contrasted sharply with dwindling British influence.

On being promoted ambassador at Madrid in 1900, Durand received the GCMG, and in 1901 he was made a privy councillor. He was liked and respected in Spain, and Spanish feeling towards Britain improved during his term of office. In 1903 the Washington embassy fell unexpectedly vacant, and Lansdowne, now foreign secretary, offered the post to Durand, who accepted with alacrity. Despite his enthusiasm for the post and his strong admiration for the president, Theodore Roosevelt, Durand was temperamentally unsuited to America: he was not a professional diplomat, was stiff and unyielding in upholding British and Canadian claims, and his deeply rooted patriotism made him very sensitive to criticisms of British methods and ideas. Moreover, both Roosevelt and his senior adviser, Senator Cabot Lodge, had been disgruntled at Durand's appointment when they had hoped for their personal friend, Sir Cecil Spring-Rice. Roosevelt, too, was very annoyed by the refusal of A. J. Balfour's government to advise Japan to 'be reasonable' in the negotiations with Russia in 1905. In 1905 Durand was recalled, to his own surprise, on grounds that his temperament prevented him from keeping in personal touch with the American president and foreign secretary, and that consequently the British embassy was placed at a considerable disadvantage. No hope of a further appointment was held out to him.

Deeply hurt, Durand returned to England in 1906. He was offered and refused the governorship of Bombay, and in 1910 unsuccessfully contested Plymouth as a Conservative. He retired into private life, pursuing literary interests. He edited his father's *History of the Afghan War* (1879), and in 1883 published a biography of his father. His other works included novels, biographies of Sir Alfred Lyall (1913) and Sir George White (1915), and *The Thirteenth Hussars in the Great War* (1921). He served as a director of the Royal Asiatic Society from 1911 to 1919 and as president of the Central Asian Society from 1914 to 1917. During the First World War he was a vigorous recruiter in the west of England, and served as chairman of a committee to review exemptions from military service. Durand died on 8 June 1924 at Polden, Minehead, Somerset, where he was buried.   H. V. LOVETT, *rev.* S. GOPAL

Sources P. Sykes, *The life of Sir Mortimer Durand* (1926) · *The life of Abdur Rahman, amir of Afghanistan*, ed. and trans. M. Khan, 2 vols. (1900) · S. Gopal, *British policy in India, 1858–1905* (1965) · Burke, *Peerage*
Archives BL OIOC, letter-books, corresp., and papers, MS Eur. D 727 · Bodl. Oxf., corresp. and papers · SOAS, corresp. and papers | BL OIOC, corresp. with Sir Alfred Lyall, MS Eur. F 132 · Bodl. Oxf., corresp. with Lord Kimberley; corresp. with Sir Stein Aurel · CUL, corresp. with Lord Hardinge and Lord Salisbury · NAM, letter to Earl Roberts · PRO, corresp. with Lord Cromer, FO 633
Likenesses G. C. Beresford, photograph, c.1902, NPG [see illus.] · W. T. Smith, oils, 1904, NPG · G. C. Beresford, photographs, NPG · D. Deane, oils, Gov. Art Coll. · Spy [L. Ward], cartoon, chromolithograph, NPG; repro. in *VF* (12 May 1904)
Wealth at death £3779 17s. 2d.: probate, 29 July 1924, CGPLA Eng. & Wales

Durant [Durance], **John** (bap. 1620, d. 1689), Independent divine, was baptized on 8 February 1620, the son of Thomas Durant and his wife, Katherine, of Bodmin, Cornwall; his father was mayor of Bodmin in 1641 and 1653. Durant's younger brother, William Durant (1621–1681), was also an Independent minister. John Durant, whose paternal uncle, Ralph Durant, was a London haberdasher, was apprenticed to a London soap-boiler, which his enemies never let him forget. Thomas Edwards, presbyterian hammer of the sectarians, remarked on the ambition 'of a Washing-Ball maker to become such a rare man' (Edwards, 150). Durant may have spent time at Pembroke College, Oxford, and had knowledge of Latin, Greek, and Hebrew. Influenced by the prominent London Independent minister John Goodwin, Durant started preaching in

1641. His sermons caused him, along with three other London preachers, to be summoned before the House of Commons that year, although he did not appear. In 1642 he preached aboard ships of the parliamentarian navy. Through the influence of the earl of Warwick, Durant in 1643 was appointed to the lecturership of St Peter's, Sandwich, where his radical preaching, publicly hoping that King Charles would be bound in chains of iron, attracted a following. In 1646 he was called to lead an Independent congregation in Canterbury, where he spent the rest of his pastoral career, retaining his Wednesday lecturership in Sandwich for some years.

The 1650s, the golden age of Independency, were the high point of Durant's career. A leader of East Kent Independency, included in the Kent committee for scandalous ministers in 1654, Durant prospered, with a lecturership of £100 annually beginning in 1646 and an augmentation of another £100 annually by 1656. Ralph Durant died in 1653, and Thomas Durant renounced his inheritance in favour of John. Durant strongly supported the Commonwealth government and particularly the navy. He published *The spiritual seaman, or, A manual for mariners, being a short tract comprehending the principal heads of the Christian religion, handled in allusion to the seaman's compass and observations* (1655) and his Canterbury congregation supplied three lay preachers to the fleet—Josias Nichols, Arthur Norwood, and James Norwood. Durant's rule over his congregation was contested, notably by opponents of his millenarian beliefs, but he maintained it, also becoming one of the six preachers of Canterbury Cathedral. An engraving of Durant in 1650 shows a plump man with shoulder-length hair, moustache, and goatee. Durant's publications, many of which originated as sermons, show him as a practical divine rather than a theologian, specializing in consoling despairing believers. *Sips of Sweetnesse, or, Consolation for Weak Believers* (1649) went through three editions, and *Comfort and Counsell for Dejected Souls* (1651) through four.

Durant's marriage to Mary (d. 1701) seems to have been happy. There was one son, John, and four daughters, Mary, Grace (who married Jacob Wraight, mayor of Canterbury, 1681–2), Elizabeth, and Renovata, so called because she was born after her sister Mary's death in 1659. Grieved by Mary's death, Durant preached and published *Altum silentium, or, Silence the duty of saints under every sad providence, a sermon preached after the death of a daughter by her father* (1659). Although Durant's works were published under that name, he is referred to by Edwards and in the Canterbury Cathedral register as Durance.

Durant's career soured after the Restoration, although he initially took a quietist position strikingly at odds with his earlier fiery sermons. His last original publication, *A Cluster of Grapes*, appeared in 1660. Driven from the cathedral and his church, Durant established a conventicle in Canterbury by 1663, and on 2 April 1672 was licensed to preach as a congregationalist at Almnery Hall in Longport outside Canterbury. About 1678, following the withdrawal of the declaration of indulgence, Durant fled to the Netherlands, returning to Canterbury late in James II's reign, possibly following James's indulgence. He died early in 1689 in Canterbury and was buried in the church of St George, Canterbury, on 27 February 1689.

WILLIAM E. BURNS

Sources M. V. Jones, 'The divine Durant: a seventeenth-century independent', *Archaeologia Cantiana*, 83 (1968), 193–203 · *Calamy rev.* · Wing, *STC* · T. Edwards, *Gangraena, or, A catalogue and discovery of many of the errours, heresies, blasphemies and pernicious practices of the sectaries of this time*, 2 (1646) · B. Capp, *Cromwell's navy: the fleet and the English revolution, 1648–1660* (1989) · R. S. Acheson, 'Sion's saint: John Turner of Sutton Valence', *Archaeologia Cantiana*, 99 (1983), 183–97 · R. Hovenden, ed., *The register booke of christeninges, marriages, and burialls within the precinct of the cathedrall and metropoliticall church of Christe of Canterburie*, Harleian Society, register section, 2 (1878) · J. Maclean, *The parochial and family history of the deanery of Trigg Minor in the county of Cornwall*, 1 (1873)

Likenesses engraving, repro. in J. Durant, *The salvation of the saints by the appearances of Christ* (1653), frontispiece

Wealth at death widow left a personalty of £300 when she died in 1701: *Calamy rev.*

Durant, Susan Durant (1827–1873), sculptor, was born in Stamford Hill, Middlesex, on 8 July 1827, the second daughter of George Durant (1784–1872), silkbroker, and his wife, Mary Dugdale (*fl.* 1788–1861), both of whom were from Devon. Susan Durant became interested in sculpture when spending a winter in Rome with her parents as a young girl, and decided to adopt it as a profession. She studied with the French sculptor Baron Henri de Triqueti (1804–1874), remaining his pupil and assistant throughout her life, making frequent trips to his Paris studio though maintaining an independent studio in London. In 1847 Durant received the Society of Art's prestigious silver Isis medal for an original portrait bust in plaster. This may have been one of two she exhibited in the Royal Academy that year; she subsequently exhibited almost every year until her death.

From her large social circle in London Durant obtained a clientele for commissions and models for portraits, usually in marble, such as *George Grote*, the historian, whose wife campaigned for women's rights (exh. RA, 1863; University College, London). Often her subject was the active woman, for example, *Harriet Beecher Stowe* (exh. RA, 1857; plaster version, Castle Howard; marble, Harriet Beecher Stowe Center, Hartford, Connecticut) and *Ruth* (exh. RA, 1869; priv. coll. France). Her early neo-classical works, for example her self-portrait (exh. RA, 1853), reflecting her Roman studies, gave way to a more naturalistic style influenced by Triqueti, sometimes incorporating his polychromatic marble inlay technique, as in *Nina Lehmann* (1871; priv. coll.). She exhibited two 'ideal' subjects in the Great Exhibition of 1851, and lent *Robin Hood* (exh. RA, 1856; Society of Female Artists, 1858) to the 1857 Art Treasures Exhibition in Manchester.

In 1866 a contemporary described Durant as 'a tall and very comely young woman … with rounded limbs … flashing face and massive rippling chestnut hair … superbly drest [in Paris fashions presumably] … full of graceful fun' (Dunford, 89). Charismatic, at ease in society, she charmed all her clients, especially the ageing Grote, and certainly her master, Triqueti. She had a private income but chose to conduct her career on a professional basis to avoid accusations of amateurism and to enhance her status as an artist. She ran her elderly father's household, even from Paris. She supported women's access to the vote, education, and the professions. In 1863 she was the only woman out of fourteen sculptors commissioned by the corporation of London to execute figures from English literature for the Mansion House. Her *Faithful Shepherdess* (exh. RA, 1863) earned her £500, was compared favourably with entries by her male competitors, and was 'the first important commission for a public work of sculpture given to a lady in this country' (*ILN*, 1863, 587).

Soon afterwards Triqueti introduced Durant into the royal circle and she received a succession of commissions from Queen Victoria including high-relief marble medallions of the queen, Prince Albert, and their children for the Albert Chapel, Windsor Castle (exh. RA, 1866–9; plaster and marble versions, Royal Collection, Osborne; bronze reductions, NPG). Durant worked regularly at Windsor, Osborne, and Potsdam, and taught Princess Louise sculpture, becoming a royal favourite. She captured naturalistic details of hair, features, and costume and enjoyed a facility for achieving a likeness which was recognized by contemporary critics and appreciated by the queen and her family. Durant's most important commission was that from Queen Victoria for a monument to King Leopold of the Belgians for St George's Chapel, Windsor. This monument of the recumbent king with his hand resting on a lion, and behind him two low-relief angels holding the shields of England and Belgium was installed to the queen's satisfaction and to critical acclaim in 1867, but removed in 1879 to the recently renamed Leopold Room in Christ Church, Esher.

At the height of her career, and having completed a further portrait of Queen Victoria for the Inner Temple (exh. RA, 1872), Durant was struck down by ill health. She died of pleurisy on 1 January 1873, in Paris, and was buried in Père Lachaise cemetery. She was unmarried. Her early death was regretted by her royal clients and many friends, some of whose unfinished portraits remained in her studio. One, *Dr Elizabeth Garrett Anderson*, formed her last Royal Academy exhibit that year. Susan Durant left provision in her will for an infant, Henry Paul Harvey Durant, who was her child by Triqueti.

ANDREA GARRIHY

Sources *Art Journal*, 35 (1873), 80 · S. H. Hurtado, 'Durant, Susan (D)', *Dictionary of women artists*, ed. D. Gaze (1997), 479–81 · P. Dunford, *A biographical dictionary of women artists in Europe and America since 1850* (1990), 88–9 · Royal Arch., Durant papers, RA VIC/Add x2/1–212 · 'Mrs Beecher-Stowe: bust in marble sculptured by Miss S. Durant', *ILN* (18 July 1857), 53–4 · *ILN* (30 May 1863), 587 · 'Art in Scotland and the provinces', *Art Journal*, 28 (1866), 285 · C. A. H. Crosse, 'Susan Durant, the sculptor', *The Queen* (17 Jan 1873) · Graves, *RA exhibitors* · W. Rossetti, 'Art exibitions in London', *Fine Arts Quarterly Review* (1863), 337 · M. L. Clarke, *The leisured scholar, George Grote* (1962) · R. Gunnis, *Dictionary of British sculptors, 1660–1851* (1953); new edn (1968) · C. Yeldham, *Women artists in nineteenth-century France and England*, 2 vols. (1984) · parish register, Tottenham, 1 Aug 1827 [baptism] · private information (2004) [Sylvia Allen]

Archives Courtauld Inst., photographs · Royal Arch., MSS

Likenesses S. Durant, self-portrait, priv. coll. · attrib. Taylor, engraving, Royal Collection · photograph, Royal Collection

Wealth at death in easy circumstances; left £1000 for sister, £100 between four trustees, and the rest for the care and education of infant Henry Paul Harvey Durant: *The Times* (7 May 1873); *Weekly Budget* (15 Feb 1873); RA VIC/Add x2/203 and reverse of /207

Duras, Louis, second earl of Feversham (1641–1709),

soldier and diplomat, was born at Duras, Guyenne, France, the sixth and youngest son of Guy Aldonce de Durfort, marquis de Duras, and his wife, Elizabeth, daughter of Henri de la Tour d'Auvergne, duc de Bouillon and marshal of France. He was well connected in the French nobility, being the brother of the dukes of Duras and Lorge. His French title was marquis de Blanquefort.

Duras moved to England in the early 1660s and entered the service of the duke of York. If Gramont is correct, in 1662 he became lieutenant of York's bodyguard. Although of 'very little certain estate' (Childs, 32), Duras was the nephew of Marshal Turenne, whom York greatly admired, and this clearly paved the way into royal service. In February 1665 he was recorded as dancing in a court masque, and he was named as captain of the duke of York's troop of Life Guards on 24 June 1665. He was naturalized by act of parliament in October 1665.

Duras continued to be a follower of the duke of York, serving from 1667 as keeper of the privy purse and colonel of the duke's troop of Horse Guards (29 June 1667). In 1672 he was in France 'about making conditions to carry over an English regiment of horse' (*Correspondence of the Family of Hatton*, ed. E. M. Thompson, CS, new ser., 22, 1878, 1.83) for service against the Dutch. On 29 January 1673 he was created Baron Duras of Holdenby, named after the Northamptonshire estate which the duke of York had sold to him. In 1673–4 he was a captain of a troop of horse in the French service. In the House of Lords Duras was a follower of the court, supporting the non-resisting test in 1675. By marriage articles dated 28 March 1675 he married Mary (*d.* 1677), eldest daughter and coheir of Sir George *Sondes KB, of Lees Court, Kent. This was quite a catch considering that Duras had only £700 per annum in land, although he had another £2000 from his offices. When Sondes was created earl of Feversham on 8 April 1676 the title was granted with a remainder to his son-in-law Duras. Mary Duras predeceased her father, dying on 1 January 1677, and Duras duly succeeded his father-in-law as second earl of Feversham on 16 April 1677. The new earl had to fight a chancery case over the life interest in his wife's Kentish estates worth £3000 per annum, following a challenge from his sister-in-law, Catherine Sondes, who in July 1677 had married the earl of Rockingham. After losing the chancery suit Feversham appealed to the House of Lords, which reversed the decision in his favour in July 1678.

Meanwhile, Feversham's activity as a diplomat was increasing. In April 1677, when the earl of Sunderland was sent by Charles II on a mission to Calais to compliment Louis XIV, Feversham was sent on behalf of the duke of York. Following the marriage of Prince William of Orange to Princess Mary, Feversham was dispatched to Paris as a special ambassador to Louis XIV, obtaining an audience in mid-November 1677, in which he outlined peace proposals from Charles II and William. On 19 February 1678

he was named as captain and colonel of the King's's dragoons, and he served in Flanders as lieutenant-general and second in command to the duke of Monmouth. In July 1678 he undertook a secret mission to Flanders 'to know what the designs of the confederates were, particularly those on this side the Meuse, in order to carry on a war in case the treaty break off' (BL, Add. MS 25119, fols. 35–6).

On 26 January 1679 Feversham's 'skull was almost broken' (Luttrell, 1.7–8) by falling timber while he was attempting to construct a firebreak in Temple Lane, but he was trepanned, and recovered. The exile of the duke of York in March 1679 saw him remain in England as one of the advocates of the duke's recall, and he advised James to return when the king fell ill in August. In December 1679 Feversham was named as master of the horse to Queen Catherine of Braganza, an event marking the start of a long period in her service. He became her lord chamberlain in September 1680 and continued in that post until her death in 1705. He voted against the Exclusion Bill in November 1680, and his influence with James led to hostile attacks on him in the Lords on 21 December 1680 and in the Commons on 7 January 1681. On the latter occasion the Commons voted to address the king to remove him from his public offices on the grounds that he was 'a promoter of popery and the French interest; and a dangerous enemy to the king and kingdom' (*JHC*, 9.702). Following Charles II's dismissal of the third Exclusion Parliament, Feversham was active in obtaining addresses of support for the king. In August 1682 he was sent to congratulate Louis XIV on the birth of his grandchild, the duke of Burgundy. In November 1682 he became an extra gentleman of the bedchamber. Feversham was present at the deathbed of Charles II, one of only two protestants allowed to remain in the room when the king was received into the Catholic church.

The accession of James II saw Feversham appointed to the privy council, and on 16 May he became a gentleman of the bedchamber. He commanded the royal forces which defeated Monmouth's rebels at Sedgemoor on 6 July 1685. He was duly rewarded with the Garter on 30 July 1685, being installed on 25 August, and also receiving command of the first troop of Life Guards. Others, the duke of Buckingham in particular, were quick to make fun of Feversham, who on the morning of the battle of Sedgemoor had been caught in bed. Burnet thought that his military appointment had courted disaster: 'he was an honest, brave, and good natured man, but weak to a degree not easily to be conceived … He had no parties abroad. He got no intelligence and was almost surprised' (*Bishop Burnet's History*, 3.50). In May 1686 and again in the summer of 1687 Feversham sought the hand of Lady Margaret Cavendish, daughter of Henry Cavendish, duke of Newcastle. Despite his reputed income of £8000 the match did not take place, falling foul of a quarrel between Newcastle and his duchess, and of concerns over Feversham's lack of a landed estate. In November 1687 he was listed as likely to support the repeal of the Test Act and penal laws. He was a sworn witness to the birth of James, prince of Wales, in 1688.

Feversham remained loyal to James II, being appointed lord lieutenant of Kent in October 1688. He was in command of the royal army that advanced to Salisbury to meet the invading army of William of Orange in November 1688, although he was reported to be in favour of negotiation rather than a resort to arms. Under orders from James II not to resist 'a foreign army and a poisoned nation', on 10 December 1688 Feversham disbanded the army, much to the anger of Prince William. Upon his return to London, Feversham was able to ensure the protection of a fearful Queen Catherine, trapped in Somerset House. Following the capture of King James in Kent, Feversham was dispatched by the peers meeting in London on 13 December to go to his assistance, whereupon James sent him on the 16th with a message to William, who promptly arrested Feversham for not having a pass, a technicality employed in order to pressurize James into fleeing for a second time. Feversham was released on 1 January 1689 at the request of the queen dowager. In the convention called to settle the kingdom Feversham supported the proposal for a regency on 29 January 1689, and voted on 4 and 6 February against the throne being vacant. He continued to attend the Lords, voting against moves to favour Titus Oates in May and July 1689.

In June 1690 Feversham took responsibility for the fact that the queen dowager's protestant chaplains had stopped praying for the king and queen. The departure of Queen Catherine for her native Portugal in March 1692 left Feversham in charge of her interests in England, including her household at Somerset House, leading him to be known as the 'king-dowager'. Feversham's close relationship with James II caused the government some alarm, particularly when invasion threatened in May 1692, but Feversham refused to exile himself to the Netherlands, standing on his privilege as a peer. He continued to support the opposition in parliament, supporting place legislation and the reform of treason trials. Feversham's name appears on lists of those peers refusing the voluntary association on 27 February 1696, but he may have signed after being assured that the term 'pretended' did not refer to the facts of the birth of the prince of Wales. He opposed the Fenwick attainder bill in November 1696, once more voting against the court. The queen dowager was responsible for his appointment in October 1698 as master of St Katharine's Hospital, a post worth at least £700 per annum. In June 1701 he supported the impeachment of the former whig ministers.

The accession of Queen Anne saw Feversham embroiled in the controversy in the 1702–3 session over a clause exempting Prince George from a provision under the Act of Settlement which would ban naturalized subjects from sitting in the Lords. Feversham and others feared that the specific exemption would be used to bar pre-Hanoverian lords, but the judges ruled otherwise. Also in the 1702–3 session Feversham absented himself from the division over the Occasional Conformity Bill.

Feversham died from 'gout in his stomach' (Luttrell, 6.428) in London on 8 April 1709, and was buried in the French chapel at the Savoy on the Strand on the 28th. His original will, made on 18 July 1701, instructed that he be buried in Westminster Abbey, and that his estates be sold and divided between his niece Charlotte de Bourbon (Mademoiselle de Mauleuse), her brother Arnaud de Bourbon (marquis de Mirement), and his nephew Frederick William de la Rochefoucoult, earl of Lifford. However, in a codicil shortly before he died, Feversham, on account of 'having at present much less money than I had heretofore' (will), left Lifford only £2000. Feversham's declaration of relative poverty may well be true for following his death the duke of Marlborough recorded that Feversham had owed three years on his mortgage, and that he had tried to purchase his estate two years before. In the event, Feversham was reburied in Westminster Abbey on 21 March 1740, together with his niece and nephew Charlotte and Arnaud de Bourbon.   STUART HANDLEY

Sources GEC, *Peerage* · will, PRO, PROB 11/506, fols. 20v–23r · J. C. R. Childs, *Nobles, gentlemen and the profession of arms in Restoration Britain, 1660–1688: a biographical dictionary of British army officers on foreign service* (1987), 32 · J. L. Chester, ed., *The marriage, baptismal, and burial registers of the collegiate church or abbey of St Peter, Westminster*, Harleian Society, 10 (1876), 355–6 · R. Beddard, ed., *A kingdom without a king: the journal of the provisional government in the revolution of 1688* (1988) · W. A. Shaw, ed., *Letters of denization and acts of naturalization for aliens in England and Ireland, 1603–1700*, Huguenot Society of London, 18 (1911), 96 · *Bishop Burnet's History*, 2.469; 3.49–50 · N. Luttrell, *A brief historical relation of state affairs from September 1678 to April 1714*, 6 vols. (1857) · *Lord Nottingham's chancery cases*, ed. D. E. C. Yale, 2, SeldS, 79 (1961) · H. Horwitz, *Parliament, policy and politics in the reign of William III* (1977), 175 · G. M. Bell, *A handlist of British diplomatic representatives, 1509–1688*, Royal Historical Society Guides and Handbooks, 16 (1990), 123–4 · D. H. Hosford, 'The peerage and the Test Act', *BIHR*, 42 (1969), 116–20, esp. 119 · E. Cruickshanks, D. Hayton, and C. Jones, 'Divisions in the House of Lords on the transfer of the crown and other issues, 1689–94', *BIHR*, 53 (1980), 56–87

Archives BL, letters to first marquess of Halifax · W. Yorks. AS, Leeds, letters to Sir John Reresby

Likenesses I. Beckett, mezzotint (after J. Riley), BM, NPG

Wealth at death see will, PRO, PROB 11/506, fols. 20v–23r

D'Urban, Sir Benjamin (1777–1849), army officer and colonial governor, was born on 16 February 1777 at Halesworth, Suffolk, the youngest and only surviving son of the local doctor, John D'Urban, and his wife, Elizabeth Gooch, daughter of a surgeon. He entered the army as a cornet in the 2nd dragoon guards in 1793. He was promoted lieutenant in March, and captain on 2 July 1794, in which year he accompanied his regiment to the Netherlands, where he served during the retreat from Holland, and in Westphalia. In 1795 he exchanged into the 29th dragoons in order to accompany Sir Ralph Abercromby to the West Indies, and served under him in fever-stricken San Domingo in 1796. In April 1797 he returned to England in command of the sickly remnant of his regiment. He married Anna (d. 1843), daughter of William and Mary Wilcocks of Norwich, on 7 August. Also in that year he exchanged into the 20th dragoons, and acted as aide-de-camp to Major-General the earl of Pembroke, commanding at Plymouth until May 1799. In July 1799 he accompanied Major-General St John to Jamaica as aide-de-camp, but returned in November of that year on being promoted major into the Warwickshire fencibles.

efforts, and served in that capacity throughout the Peninsular War without once going on leave. He was successively promoted brigadier-general and major-general in the Portuguese army, and colonel in the British army on 4 June 1813. He distinguished himself at the battles of Medellin in 1809 and Salamanca in 1812, but his Portuguese cavalry suffered a reverse at Majalahonda, which thenceforth made him a cautious commander, not least in the Cape Frontier War of 1834–5. He was with Beresford at all the great battles of the Peninsular War, and at its close was made KCB and a knight of the Tower and Sword, and received a gold cross and five clasps for the nine pitched battles and sieges at which he had been present, namely Busaco, Albuera, Badajoz, Salamanca, Vitoria, the Pyrenees, the Nivelle, the Nive, and Toulouse. He remained in Portugal after the end of the war until April 1816, when he was summoned to England and appointed colonel of the Royal Staff Corps and deputy quartermaster-general at the Horse Guards. He was made a KCH in 1818, and promoted major-general on 12 August 1819.

In 1820 D'Urban was made governor of Antigua, and in 1824 was transferred to Demerara and Essiquibo—settlements which he tactfully and ably helped to combine with Berbice in 1831 to form British Guiana, of which he then became first governor. In 1829 he was made colonel of the 51st regiment, and, after returning to England, was appointed in 1833 governor and commander-in-chief of the Cape of Good Hope.

At the Cape, D'Urban presided over the emancipation of slaves in 1834, the institution of the legislative council, the establishment of municipal government, and prosecution of the Cape Frontier War (1834–5). But his extension of the frontier and his policy of undermining the chiefly structure of Xhosa society in his new province of Queen Adelaide of 1835 were disapproved in London on financial and humanitarian grounds. These differences led to his dismissal in May 1837, though he was only replaced in January 1838. He remained retired at the Cape until 1846. During this retirement his wife died, on 23 August 1843, at Wynberg, near Cape Town. Together, they had had at least two daughters and a son, William James D'Urban.

D'Urban's governorship was also marked by the great trek of Boers from the eastern districts towards Port Natal in 1836–8. This led to Britain's growing interest in the port and to its final occupation after D'Urban's dismissal. But the port was then given his name as a mark of his popularity among the white colonial community: Durban remains the capital of Natal.

In 1837 D'Urban was promoted lieutenant-general and in 1840 was made a GCB. In January 1847 he was recalled from retirement to command the forces in Canada. During this time they were used to check the Elgin riots. D'Urban died at Montreal on 25 May 1849, aged seventy-two. His remains were buried in the old military cemetery, Papineau Avenue, Montreal, and moved in July 1944 to the Field of Honour, Pointe Claire, Montreal, where there is a monument to his memory.

H. M. STEPHENS, *rev.* JOHN BENYON

Sir Benjamin D'Urban (1777–1849), by Thomas Mogford

D'Urban went on half pay in April 1800, and joined the Royal Military College, where officers were instructed in staff duties and the higher branches of the military profession. He was appointed major in the 25th light dragoons, but still continued at the Royal Military College, where his proficiency was so great that he was in 1803 appointed superintendent of the junior department of the college. He then exchanged into the 89th regiment and was promoted lieutenant-colonel by brevet on 1 January 1805. He gave up his position at the college in June 1805 to serve abroad, in Hanover. There followed several promotions and various staff appointments, which particularly involved establishing a system of communication by means of semaphore between Dublin and the ports of the southern and south-western districts of Ireland. In November 1807 he was appointed assistant quartermaster-general at Dublin, but was afterwards transferred to the Curragh, when Sir David Baird was in command there.

D'Urban accompanied Baird to the Peninsula in the same capacity, but was immediately detached to the force left under Sir John Cradock in the neighbourhood of Lisbon. He served under Sir Robert Wilson in the Lusitanian legion in Castile and Estremadura until April 1809, when Major-General William Beresford arrived to organize the Portuguese army. Beresford knew of D'Urban's high reputation as a staff officer, so he was immediately selected to fill the important post of quartermaster-general under the new arrangements, with the rank of colonel in the Portuguese army. He most ably seconded Beresford's

Sources *The Peninsular journal of Major-General Sir Benjamin D'Urban ... 1808–1817*, ed. I. J. Rousseau (1930) • J. C. S. Lancaster, *The governorship of Sir Benjamin D'Urban at the Cape of Good Hope, 1834–1838*, Archives Year Book for South African History, 54/2 (1991) • *GM*, 2nd ser., 32 (1849), 647 • *Graham's Town Journal* (1 Sept 1849) • C. W. C. Oman, *A history of the Peninsular War*, 1–5 (1902–14) • W. M. MacMillan, *Bantu, Boer and Briton: the making of the South African native problem*, rev. edn (1963) • J. S. Galbraith, *Reluctant empire: British policy on the South African frontier, 1834–1854* (1963) • *The autobiography of Lieutenant-General Sir Harry Smith*, ed. G. C. Moore-Smith, [2nd edn] (1903) • A. K. Fryer, *The government of the Cape of Good Hope, 1825–1854*, Archives Year Book for South African History, 27/1 (1964) • K. S. Hunt, *The development of municipal government in the eastern province of the Cape of Good Hope*, Archives Year Book for South African History, 24 (1961) • G. E. Cory, *The rise of South Africa*, 5 vols. (1910–30) • C. P. Stacey, *Canada and the British army, 1846–1871* (1936) • D. E. R. Carnac, *Hawk's eye* (1966) • M. Nuttall, 'D'Urban, Sir Benjamin', *DSAB*

Archives Cape Archives Depot, corresp. and papers • priv. coll., corresp., journals, papers • Rhodes University, Grahamstown, South Africa, Cory Library for Historical Research, corresp. and papers | Derbys. RO, letters to Sir Robert Wilmot-Horton • NAM, letters to William Warre • priv. coll., corresp. with Lord Cathcart • PRO, 154, 165–7, CO 48/162 *et seq.*, CO 537/145

Likenesses T. Mogford, portrait, NPG [*see illus.*] • marble bust, Durban Municipal Buildings, Palm Court • portrait, National Library of South Africa, Cape Town, portrait collection • portrait, Château de Ramezay, Montreal • portrait, repro. in Cory, *Rise of South Africa*, 3 • portraits, Cape Archives, Elliott collection • steel engraving (after bust), repro. in Napier, *Excursions in Southern Africa*, 1 (1850)

Evan Frank Mottram Durbin (1906–1948), by Bassano, 1947

Durbin, Evan Frank Mottram (1906–1948), economist and politician, was born at the manse, Westcroft, Bideford, Devon, on 1 March 1906, the son and last child of the Revd Frank Durbin, a Baptist minister in Devon, and his wife, Mary Louisa Mellor, the daughter of William Mottram, a well-known Congregationalist minister and temperance campaigner. Durbin was educated at elementary schools in Plympton and Exmouth, Heles School, Exeter, and Taunton School, winning an open scholarship at New College, Oxford. From 1924 he read zoology, but laboratory work failed to inspire him and he took a second-class degree in 1927. He then transferred to modern Greats and completed a first-class degree in philosophy, politics, and economics in 1929. With the support of his economics tutor, Lionel Robbins, Durbin was awarded the Ricardo scholarship in 1929 to study underconsumptionist theories at University College, London. In autumn 1930 he was appointed to a lectureship in economics at the London School of Economics (LSE), where he remained until 1940.

The Labour Party and economic planning Durbin's nonconformist background provided the foundation for his later work. His strict but loving upbringing imparted to him a confidence and frankness that blended humility with conviction in all his work. Although his faith ebbed during his undergraduate years, like many future Labour politicians he first learned the art of public speaking as a local Baptist preacher. His political interests were evident from the outset at Oxford, where he was active in both the union and the Oxford University Labour Club, serving as chairman of the latter in 1927. He also made many friends at Oxford who shaped his later work. He was introduced there to Reginald Bassett, G. D. H. Cole, and Margaret Cole, and he met Hugh Gaitskell in 1926 when both men were working on behalf of the miners during the general strike, initiating a lifelong friendship and political association.

Durbin established his credentials as an economist in the early 1930s with a series of books and articles on contemporary economic conditions, including *Purchasing Power and Trade Depression* (1933), *Socialist Credit Policy* (1933; revised 1935), and *The Problem of Credit Policy* (1935), but in its abstract form economics never captured his imagination. He saw instead the role that economists could play in developing a democratic socialist society. The aftermath of the Labour government's defeat in 1931 provided ideal circumstances for Durbin's ideas to become influential in the Labour Party. He was a prominent member of both the New Fabian Research Bureau and the XYZ Club, groups of left-wing intellectuals committed to finding new directions for socialism and economic policy. Through these groups he worked closely with other young economists such as Douglas Jay, James Meade, and Colin Clark to revise Labour's programme in the light of new economic research. The results were evident in the party's growing commitment to economic planning in the late 1930s, paving the way for the introduction of centralized controls during the Second World War and the continuation of a commitment to planning in the postwar Labour government.

By the mid-1930s Durbin had become committed to economic planning as the most effective means to achieve socialist ends. He believed that a fully planned economy was a precondition for socialism, and his work was increasingly directed towards implementing this idea. But those who knew him best observed that he was a man of conviction who possessed a great deal of what Gaitskell termed 'moral courage'. He was not afraid to take an unpopular line and his ideas often set him apart from the labour movement at this time. In particular, he emphasized the affinities between Soviet communism and European fascism, insisting that both Germany and Russia were dictatorships characterized by similar types of cruelties and injustices against their people. He pointed to the Russians' brutal treatment of kulaks, for example, and likened it to the mass persecution of German Jews. To compare communism to fascism in this way was brave at a time when Soviet-style communism enjoyed much support among prominent British socialists such as Harold Laski, John Strachey, and Sidney and Beatrice Webb. Durbin insisted, however, that communism, just as much as fascism, was incompatible with the commitment to democracy, social justice, and personal freedom that lay at the heart of British socialism. The defence of these values was central to Durbin's anti-Marxism, and his views both set him apart in the 1930s and early 1940s, and proved to be highly influential long after his death.

Durbin diverged from his colleagues in other ways as well. Almost alone among his friends, he endorsed the Munich agreement in 1938. His support for Chamberlain originated not in pacifism, but—like so many of his ideas—in patriotism, because he was convinced that Britain did not yet have the strength to fight. Foreshadowing the frustrations of the Labour government in the late 1940s, he also insisted upon the need for trade unions to recognize the community's interests in efforts to plan the economy, especially in areas such as wage controls. While many other economists in the Labour Party were eager to evaluate Keynes's ideas in a socialist context, Durbin found Keynes's indifference to the moral claims of socialism unacceptable and distrusted his liberal roots. Finally, he was critical of Jay's and Hugh Dalton's economic criteria for socialism when economic theory, for Durbin, was primarily a vehicle to convey social and ethical imperatives within a socialist society.

Durbin believed strongly that economics should not be studied in isolation. His most original ideas were informed by broad reading in psychology, psychoanalysis, sociology, history, and political science, and the combination of these fields with his economic research resulted in a formulation of democratic socialism that was both distinctive and influential. Durbin joined a study group on psychoanalysis and he urged greater communication and co-operation among social scientists. His work focused increasingly on evaluating the relationship between economics, psychology, and equality, which he believed to be central to the realization of a socialist society. He criticized economists' reluctance to depart from their belief in the unproven benefits of inequality, and he exhorted the profession to reconsider the ethical implications of the assumption that inequality promoted a more efficient economic system. The clearest example of his wide-ranging interests was *Personal Aggressiveness and War* (1939), which he wrote with the child psychologist John Bowlby. Here Durbin argued that new research into the origins of aggressive behaviour among animals and children by, among others, Solly Zuckerman and Susan Isaacs, might be used to understand and ultimately to prevent the tendency among adults to wage war.

Democratic socialism and the Second World War   These ideas not only reflected the anxieties of the time, but also formed the core of Durbin's most complete and influential work, *The Politics of Democratic Socialism* (1940). Composed against the background of impending war, the book explored the potential for the emergence of a society based upon the twin principles of social democracy and economic planning. Drawing on his research with Bowlby, as well as Freudian concepts such as repression, projection, and transference, Durbin devoted the first section of the book to a discussion of the need for changes in the social and educational environment of children to encourage a preference for co-operation over aggression. Echoing R. H. Tawney, Durbin argued that economic relations had a direct bearing on social relations. Therefore, while he still believed that socialism was impossible without a fully planned economy, he was convinced that socialist societies must be founded around institutions that both met common needs and emphasized the importance of healthy group relations.

In subsequent sections of *The Politics of Democratic Socialism*, Durbin went on to address alternatives to socialism, outlining the weaknesses of contemporary capitalism and offering a rigorous critique of the internal inconsistencies of Marxism that anticipated Anthony Crosland's similarly clear rejection of an episodic transition to socialism in *The Future of Socialism* (1956). Durbin rejected, in particular, the idea of a universal historical dialectic that excluded all but economic factors. He observed that other variables such as nationality, government, social relationships, and religion were ignored by Marxists in their pursuit of a growing conflict between two distinct classes. 'It is not so,' Durbin countered. 'We are more complicated than the Marxists have us believe' (*Politics of Democratic Socialism*, 1940, 182–3). He concluded the book (which was subtitled 'An essay on social policy') with arguments for the achievement of a democratic socialist society through the Labour Party's programme. He returned repeatedly to the centrality of democracy, the foundation on which he based his certainty that socialism was possible in Britain without revolution. Throughout *The Politics of Democratic Socialism*, Durbin both drew upon and reinforced the indigenous British tradition of democratic socialism. He presented a blend of ideas influenced by ethical socialism in the tradition of Tawney, by the Fabian interest in efficiency, by liberalism, and by advances in economic thought since 1931. It was therefore fitting that when Durbin dedicated the book 'to my friends', he included among them Bassett, Gaitskell, Michael Postan, and Tawney.

In 1940 the war intervened directly in Durbin's career when he was assigned to the economic section of the war cabinet secretariat. Although he had eagerly volunteered for wartime work, he was unhappy at giving up his teaching and research at the LSE and he soon found that he disliked the civil service. In October 1942, however, he was appointed personal assistant to the deputy prime minister, Clement Attlee, a position he held for three years. This civil service experience expanded his practical knowledge of government and reinforced for him the critical role of economists and social scientists in the negotiation of a new relationship between state and citizen, both in wartime and under the post-war Labour government.

The war presented Durbin with an opportunity to put into practice his commitment to using force against those who could not be swayed by reason. While serving in the wartime government, he completed his most compelling and accessible work, a short, intensely patriotic tract entitled *What have we to defend?* (1942). This little book drew on his earlier writing to explore the connection between British socialism and national identity, and to evaluate the potential for economic and social change offered by the war. It was a more impassioned and less technical work than Durbin's earlier writing. Like George Orwell in *The Lion and the Unicorn* (1941), Durbin argued that nationalism and socialism were not antithetical. He believed that patriotic socialists were not defending the British social order, but rather protecting British values against external aggression. He also identified the threat of forces operating within Britain. He found four 'national faults' at work: economic inequality, social inequality, disregard for national heritage, and lack of imagination. He urged the British people to dream of a better world, a strong and safe society free from poverty, unemployment, and class divisions. 'This society does not yet exist', Durbin concluded, 'but only because we do not see it' (*What have we to defend?*, 34).

Election to parliament, death, and legacy   In July 1945 Durbin was elected Labour MP for the north London constituency of Edmonton with a majority of 19,069. He had earlier stood unsuccessfully as Labour candidate in East Grinstead and Gillingham, Kent, in 1931 and 1935 respectively. In government he was frustrated by the slow progress of his career. He served as parliamentary private secretary to the chancellor of the exchequer, Dalton, until March 1947, when he was appointed parliamentary secretary to the minister of works, Charles Key. These roles slowed but did not interrupt Durbin's writing, and he continued to comment upon contemporary issues and engage directly with the government's critics, most notably his former LSE colleague, Friedrich Hayek.

Durbin was no dry intellectual. Married on 29 July 1932 to (Alice) Marjorie (*b.* 1909/10), the daughter of Charles Ernest Green, a teacher, he thrived on family life, enjoying the company of his wife and their three children, two daughters and one son. His openness and capacity for enjoyment attracted a wide circle of friends, among them historians, sociologists, and political scientists. He loved the countryside and the cinema, enjoyed playing racquet sports (though with little skill), and had a passion for

detective stories. He once remarked to his friend Gaitskell, 'The three greatest pleasures in my life are food, sleep and sex' (Gaitskell, 13).

Durbin drowned on 3 September 1948 off the coast of Cornwall at Strangles Beach, Crackington Haven, near Bude, after rescuing one of his daughters and another child in dangerous surf. A memorial service was held at St Margaret's, Westminster, at which Tawney gave an address, and he was buried in New College, Oxford. Durbin's premature death robbed the Labour Party of a man of considerable intellectual rigour, economic expertise, and moral conviction. At the time of his death, Durbin was working on a companion to *The Politics of Democratic Socialism*, provisionally entitled 'The economics of democratic socialism', which built on his post-war concerns about the efficient working of a planned economy, labour relations, nationalized industries, and the steps still required to take Britain from a managed capitalist economy to a fully socialist society. Draft chapters of this work are preserved with Durbin's papers at the LSE, and eleven of his most influential articles were posthumously reprinted as *Problems of Economic Planning* (1949).

Subsequent generations of British socialists and social democrats have continued to be influenced by Durbin's ideas. His legacy has been particularly apparent in two periods: first, during the difficulties that beset the Labour Party in opposition throughout the 1950s; and second, in the founding of the Social Democratic Party (SDP) in 1981. In the 1950s Durbin's mantle was inherited by his close friend Gaitskell, who succeeded Clement Attlee as Labour leader in 1955. Gaitskell and his supporters looked to Durbin as a 'revisionist' ally against leftwing 'fundamentalists' in the party whose definition of socialism placed greater emphasis upon the expansion of public control through the nationalization of major industries. Like Durbin, Gaitskell argued that nationalization was a means, and not an end, of socialism, and he therefore supported a far-reaching review of Labour's policies that recommended alternative methods of control. The most prominent theorist of 'revisionism' in this period, Crosland, also clearly felt an affinity with Durbin, whom he had met in the 1940s. Crosland envisioned a 'Durbin–Crosland front' in democratic socialism (22 April 1941, Crosland MSS, BLPES, 3/26/i), not only agreeing with Durbin that capitalism had shown itself to be capable of significant reforms, but also sharing Durbin's deep antipathy towards Marxism and his commitment to the distinctly British ethical and democratic socialist traditions.

Durbin has also provided a link to the SDP, whose founders have claimed an intellectual lineage from the Gaitskellite 'revisionists.' Bill Rodgers, in particular, was strongly influenced and deeply moved by Durbin's work, and he greatly admired Durbin's conviction that force should be used to defend socialist values if all else failed. For the SDP, Durbin's writing in the 1930s provided a model for a successful fight against the left within the Labour Party, together with a clear rejection of totalitarianism, pacifism, and, by extension, unilateralism. More importantly, Durbin provided a cogent demonstration of

Marxism's internal contradictions and the weakness of Marx within the British social democratic tradition.

Durbin's status as a 'revisionist' should not, however, be overstated. In many respects, Durbin's ideas did not fit the Gaitskellite mould that the SDP admired. Durbin developed his ideas in the 1930s and his major post-war work was unfinished at the time of his death. Nevertheless it is clear that after the war he remained firmly committed to nationalization, economic planning, and controls. Although Durbin recommended flexibility in Labour's policies, his priority was the economic and social management of an expanded public sector, and he had none of Crosland's later confidence in the potential of reformed capitalism. Durbin's anti-Marxism and his commitment to democracy and freedom were attractive to 'revisionists', and subsequently to the SDP, but these general aims are found within a broader tradition of British social democracy, while the substance of Durbin's policy ideas locates him less clearly among 'revisionists'. Throughout his life Durbin placed great emphasis on remaining a man of the left, not only a social democrat, but also a democratic socialist.   CATHERINE ELLIS

Sources H. T. N. Gaitskell, foreword, in E. F. M. Durbin, *The politics of democratic socialism* (1954) · E. H. Phelps-Brown, 'Evan Durbin, 1906–1948', *Economica*, 18 (1951), 91–5 · S. Brooke, 'Evan Durbin: reassessing a labour "Revisionist"', *Twentieth-Century British History*, 7 (1996), 27–52 · E. Durbin, *New Jerusalems: the labour party and the economics of democratic socialism* (1985) · *The Times* (4 Sept 1948); (6 Sept 1948); (8 Sept 1948); (16 Sept 1948); (17 Sept 1948); (20 Sept 1948) · *WWW*, 1941–50 · E. F. M. Durbin, *Problems of economic planning: papers on planning and economics* (1949) [foreword by C. R. Attlee] · S. Brooke, 'Problems of "socialist planning": Evan Durbin and the labour government of 1945', *HJ*, 34 (1991), 687–702 · S. Brooke, 'Revisionists and fundamentalists: the labour party and economic policy during the Second World War', *HJ*, 32 (1989), 157–175 · private information (2004) · b. cert. · m. cert. · d. cert. · *CGPLA Eng. & Wales* (1948)
Archives BLPES, corresp. and papers | BL PES, corresp. with the editors of the *Economic Journal* · Brasenose College, Oxford, Colin Clark papers, corresp. · UCL, H. T. N. Gaitskell papers, corresp.
Likenesses Bassano, photograph, 1947, NPG [*see illus.*]
Wealth at death £11,008 17s.: probate, 20 Oct 1948, *CGPLA Eng. & Wales*

Durel, John [Jean] (1625–1683), Church of England clergyman and apologist, was born in St Helier, Jersey, and baptized at the town church on 18 May 1625, the son of Jean le Vavaseur dit Durel and his wife, Susanne (*d.* in or after 1680), daughter of Nicolas Effard, rector of St Saviour's, Jersey. He matriculated from St Alban Hall, Oxford, on 27 November 1640, aged fifteen, but in the autumn of 1642 left for France. He proceeded MA from the Sylvanian College at Caen, Normandy, on 8 July 1644, his thesis being published as *Theoremata philosophiae rationalis, moralis, naturalis et supernaturalis* (1644). After completing a BD thesis on 4 March 1647 at the Huguenot academy at Saumur he returned to Jersey, where he became chaplain to its bailiff and lieutenant-governor, Sir George Carteret, at Elizabeth Castle. In March 1651 he was also acting rector of St Ouen.

Until this point Durel had exercised his ministry within the established church in Jersey by virtue of his French

theological training. However, while in Paris as an envoy from Carteret to the exiled Charles II, through the offices of John Cosin, who was or became a friend, he obtained episcopal ordination at the hands of the exiled bishop of Galloway, Thomas Sydserff. John Evelyn, who was present in Sir Richard Browne's chapel on 5 June 1651, Whit Sunday, recorded that Durel and Daniel Brevint (another Jersey man), significantly 'in their surplices', were made deacons and priests simultaneously, 'in regard of the necessitie of the times' (Evelyn, 3.8–9). Following the fall of Jersey to the parliamentarian forces that autumn, Durel went to St Malo, Brittany, and then, in a move which was to have further significance for those francophone clergy who later argued for the congruence of the Church of England and continental Reformed churches, he was called to serve the protestant church at Caen in the place of the celebrated Samuel Bochart. Like Philippe le Couteur (also of Jersey) and Brevint, Durel (as he later explained) was accepted by Huguenot ministers on condition 'only to conform to their Rites and Ceremonies, and Orders of their Church, for the Time we should live amongst them' (Kennett, 395–6). From about 1654 or 1655 he was chaplain in Guyenne to the duc de la Force. In both places Durel was evidently a member of the provincial synod.

In Normandy Durel met Jean-Maximilien de Baux, seigneur de l'Angle (1590–1674), whose political and ecclesiological views matched his own. In April 1660 de l'Angle, or perhaps his son, Samuel de l'Angle (1622–1693), also a minister at Rouen, published *A Letter Evidencing the Kings Stedfastnesse in the Protestant Religion*, a refutation of rumours that Charles had converted to Catholicism, but an affirmation of his right to do so and an assertion that it made no difference to the desirability of the Restoration. Soon after Durel himself seems to have been offered the choice of the rectories of St Helier or St Mary, Jersey, but preferred to go to London to advance the cause of a French protestant episcopal church. By March 1661 he was well established as minister of the French congregation at Westminster, originally set up under Jean Despagne. On 10 March Charles II announced his intention to pension Durel and to permit the congregation to meet in the chapel at the Savoy Palace, the residence of the bishop of London, 'provided they submit to the Church of England, use the Book of Common Prayer in French, present the names of their intended ministers to him for approval, and have them instituted by the bishop of London' (*CSP dom.*, 1660–61, 529). Durel hastily arranged a reprinting of Pierre Delaune's 1616 French translation of the prayer book; eagerly snapped up by de la Force's daughter the princesse de Turenne and others both in France and England, it rapidly sold out. The French church at Threadneedle Street expressed its concern at the establishment of this rival to their authority, but some Reformed leaders abroad offered congratulations: de l'Angle wrote to Durel in May that he 'rejoyced very much at the establishment of the Anglico-Gallicane church that the king your soveraigne hath made' (Durel, 70).

With the Savoy conference to determine the future of

the English church and liturgy still to be formally concluded the Savoy Chapel was inaugurated on 14 July 1661. Durel took advantage of a distinguished congregation, which included the duke and duchess of Ormond, the dowager countess of Derby, and the earls of Stafford, Newcastle, and Devonshire, to deliver an apology not just for his own francophone community, but for the traditional Anglican order. His *Sermon prononcé en l'église françoise* (1661), issued later as *The Liturgy of the Church of England Asserted* (1662) and dedicated to the duke of Ormond, denounced contention and affirmed both the Church of England's affinity with continental protestant practice and the pre-eminence of her liturgy. Once the 1662 settlement had been enacted Durel argued that nonconformists were alone among Reformed Christians in refusing to recognize its legitimacy. *A View of the Government and Public Worship of God in the Reformed Churches beyond the Seas* (1662), dedicated to the earl of Clarendon, examined the churches of Scotland, Geneva, Switzerland, France, the Netherlands, Germany, Poland, Bohemia, Hungary, Transylvania, and Lithuania (the preface to whose prayer book it printed) in an attempt to prove to presbyterians the universality of practices they condemned in England; Calvin, after all, was 'no enemy of episcopacy' (p. 161). Letters of endorsement of the Anglican settlement from eminent Reformed ministers abroad were liberally quoted.

On 6 October 1662 the king licensed Durel's monopoly of printing the French prayer book. A revised text, completed before 1665, retained much of Delaune's original, but incorporated changes embodied in the Act of Uniformity and Durel's translation of the Thirty-Nine Articles; it was published eight times between 1666 and 1695. Further apologetics followed in *Sanctae ecclesiae Anglicanae schismaticorum criminationes* (1669), dedicated to Charles II, and its second edition, *Historia rituum sanctae ecclesiae Anglicanae* (1672). Louis du Moulin and Richard Baxter discussed several schemes to answer Durel, but his sustained anti-nonconformist stance finally drew fire from Henry Hickman, ejected fellow of Magdalen College, Oxford, who in *Bonasus vulpans* (1672) accused Durel of 'jumbling together' (p. 30) foreign liturgies and presenting a distorted picture of practice in Scotland and abroad. Durel, Hickman argued, breached the Act of Uniformity in permitting non-episcopally ordained preachers in his church, and had himself received rather questionable ordination from a Scottish bishop. In *Nonconformists Vindicated* (1679) Hickman also cast scorn on his ecclesiastical background in Jersey.

However, Durel enjoyed continued royal favour. On 21 September 1664 he married de l'Angle's daughter Marie (later Mary) at the Temple of Quevilly in Rouen. Like his brothers-in-law, Jean-Maximilien de l'Angle the younger (d. 1724), who had joined him at the Savoy in 1661 and who crowned a series of rectories in Kent with a Canterbury prebend in 1678, and Samuel de l'Angle, who arrived in England in 1683 and was promptly made a prebendary of Westminster, Durel gained rapid preferment. As early as 25 October 1661 the king recommended him for the reversion of a sinecure in the diocese of Winchester held by

Bishop Sydserff. In 1662 he became a royal chaplain, and he gained prebends at Salisbury (installed 1 April 1663), Windsor (11 February 1664), and Durham (1 July 1668). On 28 February 1670 he was created DD at Oxford. In 1677 he became dean of Windsor (and thereby of Wolverhampton) and on 14 September of that year rector of Haseley, Oxfordshire. Anthony Wood reckoned that he was in line for a bishopric.

Durel drew up his will at Haseley on 1 April 1680 professing 'the Protestant Religion by law established in the Church of England, the best constituted in my judgement of all the reformed churches' (will, PRO, PROB 11/373, sig. 82), but consistent with his Gallican beliefs he desired to be buried according to the protestant rites pertaining in whichever country he happened to die. Apart from modest bequests to the poor and to the 'quire men of Windsor Chappell' (ibid.) his estate was to go first to his wife and executor, to whose skills in financial management he paid tribute, and then to their only son, Henry, not yet of age. A codicil dated from Paris in August 1681 revealed Durel to be 'on the way to Bourbon whether I am sent for my health', but he eventually died in England on 8 June 1683, and was buried four days later in St George's Chapel, Windsor. Mary Durel, who is sometimes credited as the translator into French of Richard Allestree's(?) *The Whole Duty of Man*, died in 1700 and was buried on 12 August at St Margaret's, Westminster. Her son, Henry, became an aide-de-camp to the duke of Marlborough.

VIVIENNE LARMINIE

Sources E. Haag and E. Haag, *La France protestante*, 10 vols. (Paris, 1846–59), vol. 1, pp. 54–7; 2nd edn, 6 vols. (Paris, 1877–88), vol. 5, p. 1031 • W. Kennett, *A register and chronicle ecclesiastical and civil* (1728), 395–6 • G. R. Balleine, *A biographical dictionary of Jersey*, [1] [1948], 460–62 • D. N. Griffiths, 'Translations of the English prayer book', *Proceedings of the Huguenot Society*, 22 (1970–76), 90–114 • G. B. Beeman, 'Notes on the sites and history of the French churches in London', *Proceedings of the Huguenot Society*, 8 (1905–8), 20 • Foster, *Alum. Oxon.* • Wood, *Ath. Oxon.*, new edn, 3.87–94 • Wood, *Ath. Oxon.*: *Fasti* (1820), 317 • *CSP dom.*, 1660–64 • will, PRO, PROB 11/373, sig. 82 • Evelyn, *Diary*, 3.8–9; 4.15, 106, 164, 318 • *Fasti Angl.*, 1541–1857, [Salisbury], 22 • *Fasti Angl.* (Hardy), 3.312 • W. J. Oldfield, 'Index to the clergy whose ordination, institution, resignation, licence or death is recorded in the diocesan registers of the diocese of Oxford ... 1542–1908', 1915, Bodl. Oxf., MS Top. Oxon. c. 250 • S. Doyle, 'La messe trouvée dans l'escriture: a new attribution', *Proceedings of the Huguenot Society*, 24 (1983–8), 457–8 • R. Whelan, 'Points of view: Benjamin de Daillon, William Moreton and the Portarlington affair', *Proceedings of the Huguenot Society*, 26 (1994–7), 463–89, esp. 475, 478, 487–8 • *Calendar of the correspondence of Richard Baxter*, ed. N. H. Keeble and G. F. Nuttall, 2 vols. (1991), 781, 785, 796, 1028, 1039, 1068 • Wing, *STC* • J. Durel, *A view of the government and public worship of God in the Reformed churches beyond the seas* (1662)

Durell, Clement Vavasor (1882–1968), mathematics teacher and textbook writer, was born on 6 June 1882 at the rectory, Fulbourn, near Cambridge, the son of John Vavasor Durell (1837–1923), rector of Fulbourn, and his wife, Ellen Annie Carlyon. Educated at Felsted School, he entered Clare College, Cambridge, in 1900, was seventh wrangler in 1903, and, in 1904, gained a first class in part two of the mathematics tripos (which was soon to become part three in the major reform of 1907).

Durell started teaching at Gresham's School, Holt, but

moved in 1905 to Winchester College, where he was appointed senior mathematical master in 1910; he remained there until his retirement. He served in the First World War as a lieutenant in the Royal Garrison Artillery and was mentioned in dispatches. Back at Winchester College, Durell became a housemaster in 1920. He fulfilled his duties at Chernocke House until 1927, but not with great success. He was a naturally shy and rather austere person, who had grown up in a family with four older brothers, and he never married. Through his textbook writing, however, he soon extended his influence on the teaching of mathematics far beyond the confines of Winchester College.

Through his leadership, organization, and growing reputation, Durell did much to raise the status of mathematics at Winchester College. As early as 1900 he had joined the Mathematical Association, an influential organization involving secondary school and university teachers, and he became a life member. Before the First World War he became actively involved in the association's committee work and report production, and contributed articles on pedagogy to its journal, the *Mathematical Gazette*. His first textbook, *Elementary Problem Papers*, was published by Arnold in 1906, but his scope and influence became unrivalled between the wars through his work for the Mathematical Association's publisher, G. Bell & Sons.

Durell's textbook production grew rapidly from 1920 and within fifteen years his publisher was able to claim, in a special 32-page catalogue of his works: 'There can indeed be few secondary schools in the English-speaking world in which some at least of Mr Durell's books are not now employed in the teaching of mathematics' (Bell, *Modern Mathematical Textbooks*, 1). The list included twenty different titles, many available in separate volumes or parts, covering all the branches of school mathematics: arithmetic, algebra, geometry, trigonometry, calculus, and mechanics. The level ranged from introductory work for the aspiring school certificate pupil to advanced work for the university scholarship candidate. Exceptionally, he also produced one book on the pedagogy of algebra, *The Teaching of Elementary Algebra* (1931), and one work of popularization, *Readable Relativity* (1926).

Durell's genius for exposition contributed to his success, and he continually improved and updated his textbooks in response to practical experience, the views of teachers, and the recommendations in the reports of the Mathematical Association. In geometry teaching, however, he joined a committee of the Incorporated Association of Assistant Masters and openly criticized the Mathematical Association's authoritative report of 1923 for its pedagogical élitism and impracticability. He kept in close touch with the Mathematical Association's work through fruitful textbook-writing partnerships with teachers from other leading public schools—C. O. Tuckey (Charterhouse), A. W. Siddons (Harrow), R. C. Fawdry (Clifton College), G. W. Palmer (Christ's Hospital), and R. M. Wright (Eton College). In the writing of more advanced textbooks he also enjoyed a long and productive association with Alan Robson of Marlborough College, a leading figure in the Mathematical Association.

Durell's early commercial success was helped by an expanding market for secondary school textbooks, which continued to grow on an international scale in the period of educational reconstruction after the Second World War. His *General Arithmetic*, first published in 1936, became an outstanding best seller and was still included in Bell and Hyman's list fifty years later, along with his mathematical tables and textbooks in geometry and general mathematics. The post-war shift towards general mathematical textbooks—as opposed to textbooks on the separate branches—was initially resisted by Durell but he was persuaded to produce a new series, in four volumes from 1946, which again proved a major success.

Late in Durell's career he renewed his active involvement with the Mathematical Association by acting as secretary of the committee which produced a major report on higher geometry for schools (1953). He was described by another committee member as 'an indefatigable [*sic*] worker, producing numerous drafts, and a courteous though persistent critic of anything he thought loose or inconsistent in the efforts of others' (Maxwell, 313).

On his retirement from Winchester College Durell moved to 73 North Lane, East Preston, Sussex, where he was accompanied by a housekeeper, a gardener, and large dogs. Golf was, at one time, a chief recreation, and, in his old age, he escaped from English winters to the climates of Madeira and, latterly, South Africa, where he died on 10 December 1968.   MICHAEL H. PRICE

Sources E. A. Maxwell, *Mathematical Gazette*, 53 (1969), 312–13 · G. Bell & Sons, *Modern mathematical textbooks: C. V. Durell* (1934) · *The schoolmasters' yearbook and directory* (1932), 231 · Venn, *Alum. Cant.* · private information (2004) · M. H. Price, *Mathematics for the multitude? A history of the Mathematical Association* (1994) · J. P. Sabben-Clare, *Winchester College* (1981) · Bell and Hyman, *Mathematics catalogue* (1986) · b. cert. · *CGPLA Eng. & Wales* (1970)

Likenesses photograph, repro. in Bell & Sons, *Modern mathematical textbooks*, cover

Wealth at death £200,098—in England: South African probate, 1970, sealed in England, 1970, *CGPLA Eng. & Wales*

Durell, David (1728–1775), biblical scholar, the son of Thomas Durell, a gentleman, was born in Jersey. He matriculated at Pembroke College, Oxford, in 1747, graduating BA in 1750 and proceeding MA in 1753, and afterwards became a fellow, and eventually in 1757 principal, of Hertford College, Oxford. He became BD (23 April 1760) and DD (14 January 1764). The only ecclesiastical preferments he held were the vicarage of Ticehurst in Sussex and a prebend of Canterbury Cathedral, to which he was appointed on 27 January 1767.

Durell became an Old Testament scholar. In 1763 he published *Three dissertations: on the character of the patriarch Abraham; on the principal objections made to the Mosaic institution, and duration of that institution*. His edition, *The Hebrew text of the parallel prophecies of Jacob and Moses relating to the twelve tribes, with a translation and notes and the various lectures of near forty MSS* (1763), with an 'Appendix containing four dissertations on points connected with the subjects of these prophecies', was severely handled by critics, as was his *Critical Remarks on the Books of Job, Proverbs, Psalms, Ecclesiastes, and Canticles* (1772). Considerable extracts from his works were included in the second edition of Andrew Kippis's *Biographia Britannica* (1778). From one of these it appears that he was an ardent advocate of a new translation of the Bible which was to be an improvement on the Authorized Version of 1611.

Durell had lent money for the building of the Oxford market, the interest of which, amounting to £20 a year, he appointed half to be given to the principal of Hertford College, and the other half to the two senior fellows, with the condition that if there should be but one senior fellow, he should receive one-third of the sum and the principal two-thirds. He served the office of vice-chancellor of the University of Oxford from 1765 to 1768, owing this appointment to the chancellor, the earl of Lichfield, whose gesture to Durell was a belated reciprocation for the support of the whig colleges at the time of his own election in 1762. His tenure of office was memorable principally for the expulsion of six students from St Edmund Hall in 1768 for attending unauthorized prayer meetings, a case attracting national attention which Durell handled resolutely. He died at Oxford on 19 October 1775, aged forty-seven.   NICHOLAS POCOCK, *rev.* RICHARD SHARP

Sources Foster, *Alum. Oxon.* · *GM*, 1st ser., 45 (1775), 502 · S. G. Hamilton, *Hertford College* (1903), 86–92 · *Hist. U. Oxf.* 5: *18th-cent. Oxf.*, 154, 165
Archives LPL, philological remarks on the prophets, MS 2580

D'Urfey, Thomas (1653?–1723), playwright and writer, was probably born in Exeter, the son of Severinus Durfey, who may have been a descendant of French protestant migrants (and who was a grandnephew of Honoré d'Urfé, the author of *L'Astrée*, 1607, Sir Richard Steele stated), and Frances Marmion (*d.* 1702), a gentlewoman of Huntingdonshire (the inference that she was related to Shackerley Marmion, the dramatist, is unfounded). Still less is known with certainty of Thomas's education, but it is probable that he did not go to university.

Early years and success at court D'Urfey claimed that he had been intended for the law, but the inns of court have no record of his admission; indeed, a number of contemporary records attest to his serving a scrivener's apprenticeship. What is known is that by 1676 he had moved to London, where he began to pursue a literary career. His first play, *The Siege of Memphis* (1676), a weak imitation of John Dryden's heroic style, was not a success. His career took off in November of the same year with the production at the Dorset Garden of his first comedy, *Madam Fickle* (published 1677). Attending the theatre were Charles II and James Butler, duke of Ormond, who introduced the playwright to the king. D'Urfey was so confused, and so conscious of his stammer, from which he suffered for years, that he said nothing. The stutter disappeared when D'Urfey was singing (or swearing—which he did frequently), however, and it was through his talent for composing and singing witty songs that he became one of the king's intimates; his resonant baritone voice, impudent, vulgar wit, and good-natured willingness to play the buffoon suited the temper of the court. King Charles was

Thomas D'Urfey (1653?–1723), by John Vandergucht

present at three of the first five performances of *A Fond Husband* (1677), an extremely successful bawdy romp which held the stage for days, was frequently revived, and which went through three seventeenth-century editions, and later attended the third performance of *The Royalist* (1681; published 1682), the author's benefit. He even stood shoulder to shoulder with the writer in their rendition of 'Advice to the City'—'a famous *Song*', D'Urfey's subtitle recalls, 'so remarkable, that I had the Honour to Sing it with King *Charles* at *Windsor*; He holding one part of the Paper with Me' (D'Urfey, *Pills*, 1.246).

Having secured an entrée to the court, D'Urfey was cushioned a little from the failure of several of the plays he rattled off in the subsequent decade. These included *Trick for Trick* (1678), little more than a revival of John Fletcher's *Monsieur Thomas* (1615); *Squire Oldsapp* (1678; published 1679); *The Virtuous Wife* (1679; published 1680); *Sir Barnaby Whigg* (1681); *The Injur'd Princess* (1682); *A Common-Wealth of Women* (1685; published 1686), which was adapted from Fletcher's *The Sea Voyage* (1622) and the text of which D'Urfey dedicated to Christopher Monck, second duke of Albemarle, at whose Essex seat, New Hall, the playwright was a welcome guest; and *A Fool's Preferment* (1688), a comedy which, adapting Fletcher's collaborative work *The Noble Gentleman* (1626), is one of D'Urfey's best plays, a tightly constructed tale of middle-class social climbing set against a contemporary rage for gambling. Political events inclined D'Urfey to verse satire as well. *Butler's Ghost, or, Hudibras the Fourth Part* (1682), a sympathetic continuation of Samuel Butler's celebrated burlesque, and *Scandalum magnatum* (1682), inspired by the manner and form of Dryden's *Absalom and Achitophel* (1681) and *The Medall* (1682), both aimed at the position Shaftesbury and the whigs took during the exclusion crisis. Despite his efforts in this regard, and notwithstanding the many songs, panegyrics, and dedications he addressed to the new king, D'Urfey failed to ingratiate himself with James II.

In 1688 Ormond and Albemarle died and the revolution ousted the tory patrons on whom D'Urfey had depended for his livelihood. He turned briefly to education, spending the summer of 1689 as a singing-teacher at Josias Priest's boarding-school for girls in Chelsea, 'a position', his twentieth-century editor notes darkly, 'for which he must have been morally very unfit' (*Songs*, 11). *Momus Ridens* (1690–91), a facetious versified digest of national and international news which ran to twenty weekly issues, was a further money-making venture. As soon as he was assured of the success of William's *coup d'état*, however, D'Urfey pledged himself to the whigs, producing birthday odes and songs for William and Mary, and satirizing those opposed to the new dispensation (nonconformists, nonjurors, and Jacobites among them) in a series of anonymous poems. He was also taken up by several new whiggish patrons. Charles Montague, the sponsor of Joseph Addison, William Congreve, and Matthew Prior, presented D'Urfey to Queen Mary, and Sir Charles Sedley introduced him to Philip Sydney, third earl of Leicester, at whose London home, and at Penshurst, the Sydneys' seat in Kent, he became a frequent visitor.

It was during the reign of William and Mary that D'Urfey enjoyed his greatest dramatic triumphs. *Love for Money, or, The Boarding School* (1691) was a sentimental comedy which anticipates the manner of Colley Cibber and Steele, and whose satire of identifiable characters, drawn from his memories of Priest's establishment at Chelsea, excited a deal of comment. It was his most popular play and remained in the repertoire as an aristocratic or royal request piece throughout his life. Much of D'Urfey's success in this and contemporaneous works can be attributed to his efforts to integrate his writing with the musical interludes which were a feature of all the drama of the period. *The Fool Turn'd Critick* (1676; published 1678), for example, an early lampoon of would-be wits, was the first English play to be published with the musical accompaniments to its songs incorporated in the text. Developments in publishing acknowledged theatrical innovation. D'Urfey was particular in collaborating with composers who were able to furnish his songs with dramatically appropriate settings, airs suited to the lyric, the context, and the character singing. He worked with nearly forty writers of music, including John Blow, John Eccles, Thomas Farmer, Jeremiah Clarke, and Samuel Akeroyde, but chief among their number was his close friend Henry Purcell. *The Marriage-Hater Match'd* (1692), a highly successful farce which Charles Gildon praised, includes no fewer than six songs set by Purcell. D'Urfey also enjoyed success with *Bussy D'Ambois* (1691), his revision of George Chapman's tragedy (1607); *The Richmond Heiress* (1693), a comparative failure when first acted, as Dryden attests (the lyrical second act apart, 'The rest was woefull stuff, & concluded with Catcalls' he told William Walsh; *The Letters of*

John Dryden, ed. C. E. Ward, 1942, 53), but which was revived to applause in a shorter, less satirical version later that same year; and the first two parts of *The Comical History of Don Quixote* (1694), a loosely constructed and episodic musical comedy, or comic semi-opera, which played to packed houses and great acclaim.

The Collier controversy For a few years during the last decade of the seventeenth century D'Urfey enjoyed the heights of success. It did not last. The third part of his Cervantes trilogy (1695; published 1696), with musical settings by Purcell (who died suddenly in 1695), suffered from the upheavals caused by an actors' rebellion, a failure for which the playwright blamed the indifferent singing and dancing of the company, the incompetent stage management of the Dorset Garden, and the bloody-mindedness of one part of the audience. 'A Wife for any Man', a comedy acted in 1696 or 1697, was no more successful; the text appears never to have been printed (although some of the incidental music survives). *Cinthia and Endimion* (1696; published 1697), an opera written perhaps as much as a decade earlier, and *The Intrigues at Versailles* (1697) were both modestly received. Most damagingly of all, D'Urfey became involved in the Collier controversy. In *A Short View of the Immorality and Profaneness of the English Stage* (1698), the Revd Jeremy Collier took D'Urfey, and others, to task for profanity, abuse of the clergy, and a lack of modesty, charges the playwright countered in his preface to the text of *The Campaigners* (1698), a play which failed to win over Drury Lane. As a result, D'Urfey and Congreve, and the publisher Jacob Tonson, were indicted by the justices of Middlesex on 12 May 1698 on the grounds of obscenity.

The case does not appear to have gone to trial. Collier's strictures had a deadening effect on the repertory, however, and none of the plays D'Urfey wrote after the affair was as popular as his earlier work. These included *The Famous History of the Rise and Fall of Massaniello* (1699–1700), in two parts, bombastic tragedies which 'out-Seneca Seneca' (Vaughn, 345) but which have also attracted critical praise for the ambition of their scenes of music and ballet; *The Bath* (1701); *The Old Mode and the New* (1703); and *Wonders in the Sun* (1706), a lengthy, expensive, spectacular failure whose third night clashed disastrously with the opening of Farquhar's *The Recruiting Officer*. The thirteen tales in prose and verse which appear in *Tales Tragical and Comical* (1704), *Stories Moral and Comical* (1706; 1707), and *New Operas* (1721), inspired by Dryden's *Fables Ancient and Modern* (1700), were a departure. They draw on a wide variety of European sources, and are set in as wide a variety of metres, but are of no great literary merit. Borne on the profusion of loyal songs and odes he continued to write, however, D'Urfey was still able to rely on a favourable reception at court. Queen Anne once gave him 50 guineas, it is said, for singing a composition which ridiculed the heir to the throne, the aged Electress Sophia:

The crown's far too weighty
For shoulders of eighty;
She could not sustain such a trophy;
Her hand, too, already
Has grown so unsteady

She can't hold a scepter;
So Providence kept her
Away.—Poor old Dowager Sophy.
(*Songs*, 25)

The song was suppressed when Sophia's son succeeded as George I.

Final years and reputation The king was unmoved by D'Urfey's flurry of welcoming odes, but support was to be found from the prince and princess of Wales, and from Addison and Steele, who organized, and, in the pages of *The Guardian* and *The Lover*, extensively promoted, benefit nights for the dramatist. In his final decade D'Urfey lived in straitened circumstances, but William Bromley, speaker of the House of Commons, who employed him as singing-master for his daughter; Lionel Cranfield Sackville, the seventh earl and first duke of Dorset, a dissipated young man who often entertained D'Urfey at Knole, his magnificent estate in Kent; and Philip, duke of Wharton, another young man of great wealth and low taste, continued to provide for, and, from time to time, accommodated, the writer. D'Urfey spent much of his final years gathering his remaining lyrics; 350 of these (from a total of over 500) appeared in the first two volumes of Jacob Tonson's edition of Henry Playford's and John Young's ongoing collection, *Wit and Mirth, or, Pills to Purge Melancholy* (1719–20). The publication of *New Operas* also allowed D'Urfey to print the texts of three unstaged works, *The Two Queens of Brentford*, a burlesque opera written about 1714; *The Grecian Heroine*, a tragedy; and *Ariadne*, an opera which incorporates virtually every genre of lyric he had explored in fifty years of composition.

In appearance and manner D'Urfey, who never married, was fiercely unprepossessing, but he cultivated a name-dropping, gentlemanly vanity, enjoying pretensions to fashionable society (after 1683 he Gallicized his surname with a non-paternal apostrophe to mark his supposed aristocratic French origins), while suffering from an inability to live within his means. He also had an egregiously high opinion of his literary worth, remaining resilient in adversity (he was apt to condemn detractors, competitors, and audiences in the dedicatory epistles to his plays and their epilogues) and complacent in success. He even entertained hopes of being appointed poet laureate (a position which went to his rival Thomas Shadwell) and hired a page to attend him when he travelled in public to appear sufficiently dignified for the office. His career did not, however, answer his ambitions. D'Urfey was a prolific writer, as his thirty-two plays (all but ten of them comedies), and his many occasional panegyrics, obsequies, and odes, and collections of verse, published at regular intervals, attest. His characteristic style of frenetic town farce, relying heavily on character-types (the rake, the fop, the jilt, and so on), complex plots, and the contrived situations of intrigue comedy (disguise, mistaken identity, eavesdropping, and the like), interspersed with well-placed songs typically performed by actors rather than professional singers, was calculated to entertain; many of his plays, moreover, glance at metropolitan scandal and theatrical gossip: *Madam Fickle*, for example, alludes to the

earl of Rochester's instigation of, and presumed abdication of responsibility for, a fatal brawl at Epsom Wells. Few of his plays have been critically valued, but a number were undoubtedly popular and, in literary-historical terms, his fondness for the humour characters and gulling scenes of Jonsonian comedy, his mediation between the romantic-Gothic description of Spenser's and Milton's poetry and the extravagant melancholy of the graveyard school of the later eighteenth century, and his anticipation of the sentimental comedy of the early eighteenth century all merit attention.

D'Urfey was also strikingly self-possessed. 'The Town may da-da-damn me for a Poet, [...] but they si-si-sing my Songs for all that', he is reported to have observed (*The Fourth and Last Volume of the Works of Mr Thomas Brown*, 1715, 117). As he well knew, his real skill lay in songwriting. D'Urfey went further than any contemporary both in writing for the abilities of individual performers (including William Mountfort, Anne Bracegirdle, and Thomas Doggett) and in making his songs not only fit the action of the play but also advance it, expansions of speech which develop character or emphasize ideas. His range encompassed political ballads and satires; coarse and lively country songs, under which may be included his dialect and sporting songs (D'Urfey was well known as an angler); and courtly lyrics, his most conventional work. Removed from their theatrical context, moreover, they remained remarkably popular (some still being sung in the nineteenth and twentieth centuries), enjoyed by labourers and the gentry and nobility alike. 'I have not quoted one Latin Author since I came down', Alexander Pope told Henry Cromwell, writing from the seclusion of Windsor Forest, 'but have learn'd without book a Song of Mr Tho: Durfey's, who is your only Poet of tolerable Reputation in this Country'. 'Dares any one despise Him', he continues, 'who has made so many men Drink?' (*The Correspondence of Alexander Pope*, ed. G. Sherburn, 5 vols., 1956, 1.81). Among D'Urfey's many literary friends an amused disdain for his writerly achievements was tempered by a fondness for the man; and to his audiences and readers, his long and varied career afforded a deal of topical and racy entertainment set to tunefully memorable song.

D'Urfey died on 26 February 1723 and was buried the same day in St James's, Piccadilly, at the time the most fashionable church in the capital, at the duke of Dorset's expense. He was about seventy.

JONATHAN PRITCHARD

Sources *The songs of Thomas D'Urfey*, ed. C. L. Day (1933) • C. Kephart, 'Thomas Durfey (1653–1723)', *Restoration and eighteenth-century dramatists: first series*, ed. P. R. Backscheider, DLitB, 80 (1989), 81–93 • W. Van Lennep and others, eds., *The London stage, 1660–1800*, 5 pts in 11 vols. (1960–68) • J. A. Vaughn, '"Persevering, unexhausted Bard": Tom D'Urfey', *Quarterly Journal of Speech*, 53 (1967), [342]–8 • G. Langbaine, *An account of the English dramatick poets* (1691), 179–85 • T. D'Urfey, ed., *Wit and mirth, or, Pills to purge melancholy*, introd. C. L. Day, 6 vols. in 3 (1959) • R. Steele and others, *The Guardian*, ed. J. C. Stephens (1982), nos. 29 (14 April 1713), 67 (28 May 1713), 82 (15 June 1713) • C. L. Day, 'Pills to purge melancholy', *Review of English Studies*, 8 (1932), 177–84 • C. L. Day, 'A lost play by D'Urfey', *Modern Language Notes*, 49 (1934), 332–4 • K. E. Robinson, 'A glance at Rochester in Thomas Durfey's *Madam Fickle*', *N&Q*, 220

(1975), 264–5 • P. Holland, 'Durfey's revisions of *The Richmond heiress* (1693)', *Archiv für das Studium der neueren Sprachen und Literaturen*, 216 (1979), 116–20 • C. A. Price, 'Music as drama', *The London Theatre World, 1660–1800*, ed. R. L. Hume (1980), 210–35 • C. B. Graham, 'The Jonsonian tradition in the comedies of D'Urfey', *Modern Language Quarterly*, 8 (1947), 47–52 • W. Lee Ustick, 'Tom D'Urfey and the graveyard', *Modern Philology*, 36 (1938–9), 303–6
Likenesses J. Vandergucht, oils, Knole, Kent [*see illus.*] • G. Vertue, line engraving (after E. Gouge), repro. in D'Urfey, ed., *Wit and mirth*

Durham. For this title name *see* Lambton, John George, first earl of Durham (1792–1840).

Durham, (Mary) Edith (1863–1944), traveller and anthropologist, was born in London on 8 December 1863, the eldest of nine children (three girls and six boys) of Arthur Edward Durham (1834–1895), senior consulting surgeon of Guy's Hospital, and his wife, Mary, daughter of William Ellis, an economist colleague of John Stuart Mill. A brother, Herbert, worked with Ronald Ross on malaria research, and a sister, Frances Hermia *Durham, was the first woman assistant secretary in the civil service.

After attending Bedford College (1878–82) Edith Durham decided to become an artist, and trained at the Royal Academy Schools. She illustrated the reptiles volume of the Cambridge Natural History, and one of her London scenes is in the Guildhall Gallery.

Following an illness, and dismayed at the prospect of remaining a home-bound spinster, Edith Durham began, when already nearly forty, to travel rough in the then hardly visited Balkans, and she described her experiences in a series of vivid and forthright books. While doing relief work after the Macedonian insurrection of 1903, she found that cash in transit was entrusted to Albanians. Intrigued, she made a series of forays on horseback into the trackless tribal areas of northern Albania, and quickly became the champion of the mountaineers, whose lands were coveted by neighbouring nations. As a woman she evoked in her hosts a protective courtesy, mingled with astonishment. Unable to imagine anyone travelling for pleasure, or out of curiosity, they assumed that the king of England must have sent her to discover and redress their grievances. Overarching local events was the terminal collapse of the Ottoman empire. Almost alone, she rightly interpreted the situation as a conflict less of religious faiths than of nationalities, with overlapping claims based on transitory periods of medieval greatness. The Albanians, as a predominantly Muslim people, were at a disadvantage compared with their Christian neighbours, despite their keen sense of nationality and their ethnic links with the indigenous Illyrians of pre-classical times.

Edith Durham sought to redress the balance in dispatches for *The Times* and the *Manchester Guardian* and through indefatigable lobbying in Whitehall and elsewhere. Aubrey Herbert, with whom she founded an Anglo-Albanian association, said that 'she restored Albania to the memory of Europe'. In Albania she was known as the queen of the mountaineers, and streets there have

remained named after her through all changes of regime.

Edith Durham's studies of Balkan ethnography led to gifts of artefacts to the British Museum, the Pitt Rivers Museum in Oxford, and elsewhere, and she wrote a pioneering book on the subject *Some Tribal Origins, Laws and Customs of the Balkans* (1928). She gave her collection of folk costume to the Bankfield Museum, Halifax, and her photographs and sketches to the Royal Anthropological Institute, of which she was a council member and the first woman vice-president. She died in London on 15 November 1944. She was unmarried.

HARRY HODGKINSON, *rev.*

Sources M. E. Durham, *Through the lands of the Serb* (1904) • M. E. Durham, *The burden of the Balkans* (1905) • M. E. Durham, *High Albania* (1909); repr. with introduction by J. Hodgson (1985) • M. E. Durham, *The struggle for Scutari* (1914) • M. E. Durham, *The Serajevo crime* (1925) • *Man*, 44 (1944), 47–8 • M. FitzHerbert, *The man who was Greenmantle: a biography of Aubrey Herbert* (1983) • personal knowledge (1993)
Archives Calderdale Museum and Arts, Halifax, diaries • Royal Anthropological Institute, London, sketches, corresp., papers, photos, journals, and notebooks | BLPES, corresp. with E. D. Morel • Bodl. Oxf., corresp. with J. L. Myres • U. Leeds, Brotherton L., corresp. with Sir E. Boyle
Wealth at death £14,494 13s. 8d.: probate, 29 Jan 1945, CGPLA Eng. & Wales

Durham, Frances Hermia (1873–1948), civil servant, was born at Aldwick, Pagham, Sussex, on 15 August 1873, the youngest of the nine children of Arthur Edward Durham (1834–1895), a surgeon at Guy's Hospital, London, and his wife, Mary, *née* Ellis. (Mary) Edith *Durham was her elder sister. She was educated privately in London and Rugby, attended Notting Hill high school, and then studied from 1892 to 1896 at Girton College, Cambridge, where she was a college scholar. She played hockey for Girton. One contemporary recalled her love of a funny story, but also 'how sternly' she once kept a college reading party to its agreed schedule of seven hours' work a day (*Girton Review*, 29). She gained a second class in the historical tripos in 1895, and a second class in part one of the moral science tripos in 1896. After completing her studies she trained in palaeography and spent three years, from 1897 to 1900, in cataloguing private collections of family archives. She was awarded the Alexander medal of the Royal Historical Society in 1898.

On leaving Cambridge Durham also undertook social work with the Women's University Settlement. In 1900 she became co-founder and co-secretary of its Southwark registry and apprenticeship committee. Having gained valuable experience of social and working conditions in London, she was appointed in 1907 as an inspector and organizer of technical classes for women and trade schools under the London county council education committee. She was also a member of the consultative committee at the Board of Education from 1908 to 1913. In 1915 she entered the civil service as chief woman inspector in the insurance and unemployment department of the

Board of Trade. In the following year she transferred to the Ministry of Labour, and in 1918 she was promoted to assistant secretary. During the First World War Durham was 'largely responsible' for the organization of women's services in the army, munitions, and agriculture (*The Times*, 19 Dec 1933, 14e). In 1919 she was appointed CBE in recognition. She afterwards served on the central committee for employment and training of women (1919–35).

After 1916 increasing numbers of women were admitted to the higher grades of the civil service, and Durham and her Girton contemporary Isabel Dickson (1872–1922) were the first to reach the rank of assistant secretary. Women civil servants were not, however, employed on the same terms as men. They enjoyed neither equal pay nor equal opportunities. In 1920 some of them formed the committee of higher women in the civil service, which later became the council of women civil servants. Durham was its first president. A 'fearless advocate' of women's progress in the service, she was nevertheless cautious in her approach, 'always temperate in her judgments, always sure to present the women's case in moderate and judicial language' (*Girton Review*, 27). One contemporary described her as 'statesmanlike' (ibid.).

Determined that women should make their presence felt, Durham led the committee of higher women in organizing a series of highly successful receptions, which were well attended by heads of department and distinguished outsiders. In 1931 she took the chair at a dinner given by the committee to celebrate the findings of Lord Tomlin's royal commission on the civil service. This had concluded that as far as possible all posts should be open to men and women equally. But while the commission openly recognized the prejudice that women civil servants faced, it gave no clear lead on the key issue of equal pay. It also recommended the retention of the rule whereby women civil servants were expected to retire on marriage. When the Tomlin commission was appointed, in November 1929, Durham was one of only three women to hold the rank of assistant secretary or above. She was a survivor of a period of post-war optimism, when it seemed that women were about to make real inroads in the civil service. By the time of her retirement, in 1933, this optimism had dissipated. In 1939 the number of women at the rank of assistant secretary or higher remained what it had been a decade earlier.

In retirement Durham went to live in the house that she had built with her sister, Florence, at Hawkern, on the edge of the village of Otterton, near Budleigh Salterton, south Devon. She was soon co-opted on to Devon county education committee, on which she served from 1934 to 1939. She surprised her colleagues by visiting schools in remote villages and roundly condemning the poor conditions that she found in some of them. Her sister, who too had been at Girton and who had a career in medical research, shared her social concern. Together they took a keen interest 'in the welfare of their own village folk' (*Girton Review*, 28), and battled with landlords and local authorities for basic improvements to cottage dwellings.

During the war they opened their home to soldiers billeted nearby, offering hot baths, cups of tea, and the tranquillity of their garden. Frances Hermia Durham, who remained unmarried, died of heart failure at her home at Hawkern on 18 August 1948. MARK POTTLE

Sources K. T. Butler and H. I. McMorran, eds., *Girton College register, 1869–1946* (1948) · *Girton Review*, 138, Michaelmas (1948) · *The Times* (19 Dec 1933), 14e · *The Times* (20 Aug 1948), 7d · *WWW* · b. cert. · d. cert. · R. K. Kelsall, *Higher civil servants in Britain from 1870 to the present day* (1955) · D. Evans, *Women and the civil service* (1934) · H. Martindale, *Women servants of the state, 1870–1938: a history of women in the civil service* (1938)
Wealth at death £11,592 2s. 6d.: probate, 21 Oct 1948, *CGPLA Eng. & Wales*

Durham, James (1622–1658), Church of Scotland minister, was the son of Alexander Durham, younger brother of James Durham of Pitkerro, Forfarshire, director of the rolls of the exchequer; his mother was Helen, daughter of John Ramsay, archdean of Dunkeld. He studied at the University of St Andrews but left without taking a degree and pursued the life of a country gentleman. Some time afterwards he was converted during a communion season under the preaching of Ephraim Melville, minister of Queensferry, a man he afterwards referred to as 'his father' (Wodrow, 3.105). While he was serving as a captain in the covenanting army during the civil war the eminent Scottish minister David Dickson overheard him exhorting his soldiers concerning their souls. Recognizing his ministerial gifts Dickson told him, 'Go home, Sir, for you seem to be called to another work than this!' (ibid., 3.109). During a subsequent battle a royalist soldier was about to give him a deadly blow but was prevented by his fellow who, mistaking him for a minister, cried, 'Save him, for he is a priest' (ibid., 3.105). In gratitude to God, Durham devoted himself to the ministry.

Durham returned to his studies, entered the University of Glasgow about 1645, and graduated MA on 30 April 1647. With the help of Dickson he was licensed by the presbytery of Irvine on 18 May, and admitted minister of Blackfriars, Glasgow, on 2 December that year. Immediately after his ordination he gave up all rights to Easter Powrie, a family estate to which he had succeeded in 1643. About 1648 he married Anna Durham of Duntarvie. An intellectually gifted and diligent man of great personal piety, he quickly became one of Scotland's leading ministers. In August 1649 he was appointed to sit on the general assembly's powerful standing committee, the commission for the public affairs of the kirk. In 1650 he was called to replace Dickson in the chair of divinity at the University of Glasgow, but was prevented from taking up this charge when he was appointed one of the king's chaplains. The same year he and Dickson published their famous *Sum of Saving Knowledge*, an important work espousing federal theology, which came to be commonly bound with the Westminster confession of faith and catechisms. In September 1651 he was translated to Glasgow High Church, St Mungo's west quarter, where he remained for the rest of his life. His first wife having died Durham married, on 14 December 1653, Margaret Mure (d. c.1692), widow of Zachary Boyd (1585?–1653), a fellow minister in Glasgow.

During the protester–resolutioner controversy that bitterly divided the kirk during the 1650s Durham steered a course of extreme moderation, and on at least four occasions joined with his colleague Robert Blair in attempting to mediate a settlement between the contending parties. Throughout the controversy, however, he devoted the majority of his time to shepherding his flock of some 1500 souls. He regularly preached three times a week, lectured before his sermons, visited the sick, catechized from house to house, met with his session weekly to consult on matters of church discipline, and attended presbytery and synod meetings. In addition he gave daily public lectures every fifth week, undertook daily catechizing before communion seasons, and spent a considerable part of every day in private devotion, prayer, and study. His labours were increased in late 1656, when, by the importunity of some friends, he was persuaded to publish his lectures on the book of Revelation. While he was preparing these lectures for the press he set aside two days a week for fasting and prayer, 'that he might better apprehend the teaching of its spiritual mysteries' (Christie, 'Courtier', 76). At the same time he was weighed down by 'a great burden of continuall preaching', as he assumed the pulpit responsibilities of his absent colleagues, Robert MacWard and Patrick Gillespie.

As a result of his strenuous labours Durham's health gave way in an alarming manner. At the beginning of 1658 he was confined to his room, and by May he was unable to leave his bed. During his last illness he completed his lectures on Revelation, which were published at Edinburgh in late 1658 under the title *A Learned and Complete Commentary upon the Book of Revelation*. At the same time he also wrote an entire treatise on scandal, the last section of which, dictated to an amanuensis from his deathbed, contained an eloquent plea for peace and unity in the Scottish kirk. It was published posthumously at Edinburgh in 1659 under the title, *A Dying Man's Testament to the Church of Scotland*. Durham died at Glasgow on 25 June 1658, in the thirty-sixth year of his age, and was mourned by protesters and resolutioners alike. In the years following his death many of his remaining manuscripts were published, and throughout the next century and a half went through numerous editions. They include, among others, *Clavis Cantici, or, An Exposition of the Song of Solomon* (Edinburgh, 1668), *A Practical Exposition of the Ten Commandments* (London, 1675), *The Unsearchable Riches of Christ* (Glasgow, 1685), and *An Exposition of the Whole Book of Job* (Glasgow, 1759).

K. D. HOLFELDER

Sources R. Wodrow, *Analecta, or, Materials for a history of remarkable providences, mostly relating to Scotch ministers and Christians*, ed. [M. Leishman], 4 vols., Maitland Club, 60 (1842–3), vol. 1, pp. 167–8; vol. 2, pp. 115–16; vol. 3, pp. 104–9 • *The letters and journals of Robert Baillie*, ed. D. Laing, 3 (1842) • *Fasti Scot.*, new edn, 3.456–7 • 'A collection of some memorable things in the author's life', J. Durham, *A dying man's testament* (1659) [prefix] • G. Christie, 'James Durham as courtier and preacher', *Records of the Scottish Church History Society*, 4 (1930–32), 66–80 • G. Christie, 'A bibliography of James Durham:

1622–1658', *Edinburgh Bibliographical Society*, 11 (1912–20), 34–46 • private information (2004)
Archives Dundee Central Library, MS sermons • Free Church of Scotland, Edinburgh, MS sermons • U. Glas. L., sermons on Isaiah | NL Scot., Wodrow collection, letters and MSS

Durham, Joseph (1814–1877), sculptor, was born in London. He was apprenticed to the sculptor John Francis and afterwards worked in the studio of E. H. Baily, and from 1835 he began exhibiting portrait busts and medallions at the Royal Academy. In 1848 he showed a bust of Jenny Lind, the Swedish opera singer (marble version, 1848; Royal College of Music, London), which was a great public success. This was at the time of the 'Lind mania' in England, and *The Athenaeum* recalled seeing 'an enthusiastic medical student take off his hat, and go down on his knees before the sculpture' (*The Athenaeum*, 572). Durham's bust of Queen Victoria (exh. RA, 1856) also became a well-known image, reproduced in several marble versions and engraved in the *Art Journal* (1857). Durham made many other portrait busts, including *W. M. Thackeray* (marble, c.1864; Garrick Club, London), *Field-Marshal Sir George Pollock* (marble, 1870; NPG), and *William Hogarth* (stone, 1874; Leicester Square, London).

In 1858 Durham's model representing Britannia presiding over the four quarters of the globe won first prize in the competition held to select a memorial to the Great Exhibition of 1851. The monument was originally intended for Hyde Park, but after the death of Prince Albert in 1861 it was redesigned with a statue of the prince (in copper electrotype) and unveiled in 1863 in the Royal Horticultural Society's gardens, Kensington. It was transferred to its present site outside the Albert Hall in 1891. Durham's other commemorative statues included *Frank Crossley, MP* (1860; People's Park, Halifax), *George Stephenson* and *Euclid* (both 1867; Oxford University Museum), and, for 6 Burlington Gardens (the former University of London headquarters), *Newton*, *Milton*, *Bentham*, and *Harvey* (all 1869).

Durham was especially noted as a sculptor of genre, or modern-life, works featuring children. His statuettes of boys engaged in British sports (exh. RA, 1864)—including cricketers and boating boys—were issued in bronze editions, and his group *Go to Sleep* (exh. RA, 1861), representing a girl scolding her pet dog, was commissioned in several marble versions. Durham also courted current taste with his 'fancy portraits', an area of work popularized by Victorian painters such as J. E. Millais and W. P. Frith, in which sitters are portrayed in narrative or 'real-life' situations. Examples include *On the Sea Shore: a Portrait of Savile Brinton Crossley* (marble, 1865; Somerleyton Hall, Suffolk) and *Waiting his Innings: a Portrait of Basil Lawrence* (marble, 1866; Guildhall Art Gallery, London), which was an adaptation of the *British Sports* series. Durham also produced a number of 'ideal' works with subjects taken from literary and classical sources, for example, *Hermione* (1858) and *Alastor* (1864) (both marble, Mansion House, London), subjects from Shakespeare and Shelley; *Perdita and Florizel* (marble, 1870; Walker Art Gallery, Liverpool), from

Shakespeare's *The Winter's Tale*; and *The Siren and the Drowned Leander* (marble, exh. RA, 1875).

Durham's portraiture displays a graceful naturalism and a sensitivity of modelling that was at its best in representations of children and female sitters. His statues and ideal works were elegantly composed and rich in the pictorial detailing that characterized British sculpture of the mid-nineteenth century. According to *The Builder*, Durham was 'of a genial and kindly disposition, and very popular with a large circle of friends' (*The Builder*, 3 Nov 1877, 1110), among whom were Samuel Carter Hall, editor of the *Art Journal*, the writer Martin Farquhar Tupper, and members of the Noviomagians, an informal antiquarian society of the time. He was elected a fellow of the Society of Antiquaries of London in 1853 and became an associate of the Royal Academy in 1866. In later life he suffered increasingly from ill health, probably exacerbated by drink. Hall wrote that he was 'another victim to the curse that has consigned so many men of genius to graves before they had done half the work they might have done' (Hall, 2.243). Tupper attributed his 'occasional lapses from sobriety' to an unhappy love affair (Hudson, 162). Durham never married; he died of phthisis on 27 October 1877 at his home, 21 Devonshire Street, Portland Place, London. He was buried at Kensal Green cemetery, London.

MARTIN GREENWOOD

Sources R. Gunnis, *Dictionary of British sculptors, 1660–1851* (1953); new edn (1968) · *The Athenaeum* (3 Nov 1877), 571–2 · *ILN* (9 June 1866), 560 · *Men of the time* (1875), 355–6 · *The Builder*, 35 (1877), 1110 · Graves, *RA exhibitors* · D. Hudson, *Martin Tupper: his rise and fall* (1949), 138–9, 161–4 · M. Stocker, 'Durham, Joseph', *The dictionary of art*, ed. J. Turner (1996) · B. Read, *Victorian sculpture* (1982) · *DNB* · S. C. Hall, *Retrospect of a long life: from 1815 to 1883*, 2 (1883), 242–3 · Redgrave, *Artists* · *The museums area of South Kensington and Westminster*, Survey of London, 38 (1975), 133–6 · *The Builder*, 16 (1858), 103–4, 158, 194, 230–31 · G. Ashton, *Pictures in the Garrick Club*, ed. K. A. Burnim and A. Wilton (1997), 524 · d. cert.

Likenesses J. Robson, oils(?), exh. RA 1844 · E. Lansheer, marble bust(?), exh. RA 1868 · Lock & Whitfield, woodburytype photograph, NPG; repro. in T. Cooper and others, *Men of mark: a gallery of contemporary portraits* · cartes-de-visite, NPG · print, repro. in J. Maas, *The Victorian art world in photographs* (1984) · woodengraving, NPG; repro. in *ILN* (9 June 1866)

Wealth at death under £5000: resworn probate, July 1878, *CGPLA Eng. & Wales*

Durham, Lawrence of (*c.*1110–1154), poet and prior of Durham, was, as he relates in his *Dialogi* (which can be accepted as autobiographical in its circumstantial detail), born at Waltham, Essex; U. Kindermann has suggested a date of 1114, but this is perhaps a little late. Along with his brother, he was educated at the school of Holy Cross Church. From there he went to Durham (which had had close connections with Waltham since the time of Bishop Walcher), and became a monk during the episcopacy of Ranulf Flambard (*d.* 1128). He notes the esteem in which he was held for his poetry and singing, and eventually he became precentor in the monastery; at this time he may have taught Ailred, later of Rievaulx.

Under Bishop Geoffrey (1133–40) Lawrence moved temporarily to the bishop's court as an official of some kind, but returned to the monastery on Geoffrey's death. In 1143

Lawrence of Durham (*c.*1110–1154), illuminated miniature

the monastic tranquillity was disturbed when William Cumin, at the instigation of David, king of Scots (in support of the Empress Matilda), usurped the bishopric; his soldiers took over the monastery, and some of the monks (including Lawrence, it seems) were forced into exile. After military action Cumin was forced to leave in the autumn of 1144, and Lawrence returned to the monastery. All these events are described in his *Dialogi*. By 1147 Lawrence was sub-prior, and became prior in 1149. In 1153 he led a deputation to Rome to seek papal confirmation of the appointment of Hugh du Puiset as bishop of Durham (opposed by Henry Murdac, archbishop of York). On return from the successful mission—on which he obtained a forty-day indulgence for servants of St Cuthbert—Lawrence fell sick in a French town, and died there on 16 or 18 March 1154; some years later his body was returned to Durham for final burial. His death had been foretold by Godric of Finchale (according to Reginald of Coldingham), who told two Lawrences in his presence that neither would return to Durham. Some scholars, from John Leland onwards, confused the poet with this second Lawrence, who became first a monk at St Albans and later abbot of Westminster.

Lawrence of Durham's reputation rests on his extensive writings in verse and prose. He sent his prose life of the Irish St Brigit (printed in the *Vitae sanctorum Hiberniae*) to Ailred, whose father had sent a version (in a 'semibarbarous' state) to Lawrence for revision. His most popular work, widely quoted in extracts, was the *Hypognosticon*. This is a verse epic, in nine books of 4684 hexameters, on the redemption of mankind; it is divided into the periods of natural law (ending at Moses), positive law (ending with Herod), and grace (to the present), and further subdivided into the six ages of the world and into temporal units based on faith (Abraham), hope (Daniel), and charity (Christ). It was based on the Bible and Josephus's *Antiquitates Judaicae* (of which a Latin text was available in Durham, possibly annotated by Lawrence); it is enlivened by many expansions and digressions; the final book, often dismissed (as in the *Dictionary of National Biography*) as 'miscellaneous religious pieces', is in fact a celebration of the benefits of the period of grace. Lawrence notes that his first draft was lost, but he restored it from memory in a month.

Three short poems by Lawrence are extant: *Tempora nec sexum*, a poem on man's fallen nature; *Aura puer mulier*, a rebuke to a friend for his fickleness; and a dramatic re-enactment, in rhythmical verse, of the resurrected Christ's appearance to the disciples. Lawrence also wrote five prose speeches, probably as school exercises to teach forensic oratory, though they seem to deal with real events: *Laurentius pro Laurentio*; *Pro naufragis*; *Pro iuvenibus*; *Invectio in Malgerium*; and *Pro Milone*. These have all been printed by U. Kindermann. The *Consolatio de morte amici* is a prosimetrum closely modelled on Boethius's *Consolatio philosophiae*, in which Lawrence is rebuked by a testy Consolator for his excessive grief.

From a modern point of view, Lawrence's most interesting work is his *Dialogi*, in four books of hexameters. It utilizes Lawrence's personal history and that of Durham as a model for the working of divine grace in human affairs. The first two books describe Lawrence's desolation at the treatment suffered by Durham at the hands of Cumin and his soldiers. The third book, set late in 1144, is about the divine grace that finally persuaded Cumin to desist and repent. The last book is about vice, virtue, God, and heaven. As its name indicates, the *Dialogi* is a series of conversations between three friends, Lawrence and Philip (monks) and Peter (a Breton); despite many classical allusions, they are delivered in an informal style, full of banter, jokes, and personal arguments, showing that God's grace operates not just in ancient history but among ordinary people who behave in ordinary ways.

Lawrence's only other claim to fame is that, because of a diatribe against love (in the *Hypognosticon*), he was chosen as one of the three 'angels' sent to dissuade Gawain from marriage, in the satirical poem *De coniuge non ducenda*, written shortly after 1222.   A. G. RIGG

Sources M. L. Mistretta, ed., 'The "Hypognosticon" of Lawrence of Durham: a preliminary text with an introduction', PhD diss., Fordham University, New York, 1941 · *Dialogi Laurentii Dunelmensis monachi ac prioris*, ed. J. Raine, SurtS, 70 (1880) · U. Kindermann, ed., *Consolatio de morte amici* (1969) · W. W. Heist, ed., *Vitae sanctorum Hiberniae ex codice olim Salmanticensi nunc Bruxellensi*, Subsidia Hagiographica, 28 (Brussels, 1965), 1–37 · A. G. Rigg, *A history of Anglo-Latin literature, 1066–1422* (1992), 54–61 · D. Knowles, C. N. L. Brooke, and V. C. M. London, eds., *The heads of religious houses, England and Wales*, 1: *940–1216* (1972), 43 · U. Kindermann, 'Das Emmausgedicht des Laurentius von Durham', *Mittellateinisches Jahrbuch*, 5 (1968), 79–100 · U. Kindermann, 'Die fünf Reden des Laurentius von Durham', *Mittellateinisches Jahrbuch*, 8 (1973), 108–41 · Gaufridus de Coldingham [Geoffrey of Coldingham], 'De statu ecclesiae Dunhelmensis', in *Historiae Dunelmensis scriptores tres: Gaufridus de Coldingham, Robertus de Graystanes, et Willielmus de Chambre*, ed. J. Raine, SurtS, 9 (1839), 3–31 · Reginald of Durham, *Libellus de vita et miraculis S. Godrici, heremitae de Finchale*, ed. J. Stevenson, SurtS, 20 (1847), 232–3 · A. G. Rigg, ed., *Gawain on marriage: the textual tradition of the 'De coniuge non ducenda'* (1986) · A. Hoste, 'A survey of the unedited work of Lawrence of Durham, with an edition of his letter to Aelred', *Sacris Erudiri*, 11 (1960), 249–65

Likenesses illuminated miniature, U. Durham L., Cosin MS V.iii.l, fol. 22v [*see illus.*]

Durham, Sir Philip Charles Henderson Calderwood

(1763–1845), naval officer, was born Philip Charles Durham, third son of James Durham of Largo in Fife and Polton, Edinburghshire, and his wife, Ann, daughter and heir of Thomas Calderwood of Polton and his wife, Margaret *Calderwood. He entered the navy on 1 May 1777, on board the *Trident*, under the protection of Captain John Elliot. In the following year he went to North America in the *Trident*, where he had the misfortune to come under the command of Captain Molloy, a harsh and tyrannical officer. Under him, and with the ship's company on the verge of mutiny, young Durham's position for the next twelve months was far from pleasant; and in June 1779 he procured his discharge and returned to England, arriving in time to be taken by Captain Elliot into the *Edgar*, in which he was present at the defeat of Langara and the relief of Gibraltar. He remained in the *Edgar* until July 1781, when he was appointed acting lieutenant of the *Victory*, and was selected by Rear-Admiral Kempenfelt to assist with the signals. He continued serving with Kempenfelt during the year, and was present at the capture of a French convoy on 12 December; the following year, still an acting lieutenant, he followed Kempenfelt to the *Royal George*. When she sank at Spithead, on 29 August 1782, Durham was officer of the watch, and, being on deck at the time, was among those saved, though he spent nearly an hour in the water before being picked up by a boat and taken on board the *Victory*. Although the verdict of the court martial was that 'the ship foundered because she was rotten, and a great piece of her bottom fell out', the real cause was incompetent handling by her officers, and Durham must have known the truth. He was moved shortly afterwards from the *Victory* to the *Union* (90 guns). He was present in the *Union* at the relief of Gibraltar by Lord Howe, and in the subsequent encounter with the combined fleet off Cape Spartel. The *Union* was then detached to the West Indies, where, on 26 December, Durham was confirmed in the rank of lieutenant, and appointed to the *Raisonnable* (64 guns), in which he returned to England at the peace of 1783. In the following year he was appointed to the frigate *Unicorn*, under orders for the coast of Africa. His health prevented his sailing in her; and the next two years he spent in France, learning the language and mixing freely in society.

On his return to England, Durham was appointed to the *Salisbury* with Commodore Elliot, then going out as governor of Newfoundland. In 1790 he became Elliot's signal lieutenant in the *Barfleur*, and on 12 November of the same year was promoted to the command of the *Daphne* (20 guns) for a passage to the West Indies; there he was transferred to the sloop *Cygnet*, which he brought home in December 1792. He was immediately afterwards appointed to the *Spitfire* (20 guns), in which he put to sea on 12 February 1793; on the 13th he captured the *Afrique*, a French privateer, the first prize of the French Revolutionary War. He continued cruising with success; on 24 June 1793 he was posted to the frigate *Narcissus*, from which, in October, he was moved to the *Hind*. In the following spring he was sent out to the Mediterranean with convoy, returning a few months later. This homeward convoy numbered 157 ships; Durham's successful guardianship of it was recognized by his appointment (30 October 1794) to the *Anson* (46 guns), one of the largest frigates then in the navy. He commanded her for the next six years, during which time he was present at the action off the Île de Groix and Lorient on 23 June 1795, and was with Sir John Borlase Warren in his expedition to Quiberon Bay in July 1795, and again on the coast of Ireland in September and October 1798. He took part in the defeat and capture of the French squadron off Tory Island on 12 October, a service for which he, together with the other captains present, received the thanks of parliament and a gold medal. On 28 March 1799 Durham married Lady Charlotte Matilda Bruce (d. 1816), only surviving daughter of the earl of Elgin.

In February 1801 Durham was moved into the *Endymion* (40 guns), which was paid off at the peace of Amiens. In April 1803 he was appointed to the *Windsor Castle*, but was presently moved into the *Defiance* (74 guns), in which he took part in Sir Robert Calder's action off Cape Finisterre on 22 July 1805. The ship was then sent home to be refitted, but was hurried out to join Nelson off Cadiz. When Calder was ordered home to be tried for retreating in the face of the enemy, he was permitted to name such captains as he desired for witnesses, who thereupon received leave to accompany him to England; Durham was selected but, finding that his going home was optional, he decided to stay. He thus served at Trafalgar, where he was slightly wounded; being ordered home directly afterwards, he arrived in time to give evidence at Calder's court martial. He was next appointed to the *Renown*, which during 1806 formed part of the Channel Fleet, and for a short time carried Lord St Vincent's flag. Afterwards she was sent to join Collingwood in the Mediterranean, and continued there until 1810, during the latter part of which period Durham wore a broad pennant as a commodore, and on 26 October 1809 was engaged, in company with Rear-Admiral Martin, in the destruction of two French ships, near Cette.

On 31 July 1810 Durham was promoted rear-admiral. During 1811 he commanded a squadron in the North Sea, and had struck his flag only a few days when he was ordered to go to Portsmouth, take command of such ships as he chose, and sail at once in quest of a French squadron that had put to sea from Lorient. The cruise was a short one, for the French returned to port, and Durham, bringing his ships back to Portsmouth, struck his flag. He next had command of a squadron in Basque Roads, and in December 1813 was sent out as commander-in-chief of the Leeward Islands station, with his flag in the *Venerable*. On the outward voyage he cleverly captured two large French frigates, *Alcmène* and *Iphigénie*, on 16 and 20 January 1814. Afterwards he cleared the West Indies of American cruisers; and in June and August 1815 he co-operated in the capture of Martinique and Guadeloupe, at which place the last French flag was struck to Durham, as the first had been. The following year he returned to England. On 2 January 1815 he had been nominated a KCB; he was now created a knight grand cross of the order of Military Merit of France, the only English officer, it is said, who received that distinction. On 16 October 1817 Durham married Anne Isabella, only daughter and heir of Sir John Henderson, bt, of Fordell in Fife. On the occasion of this marriage he took the additional name of Henderson, and afterwards, on succeeding, by the death of his brother in 1840, to the Polton estate, took also the name of Calderwood.

On 12 August 1819 Durham was promoted to the rank of vice-admiral, and on 22 July 1830 to admiral; on 17 November 1830 he was made a GCB. He was MP for Queensborough in 1830 and for Devizes from 1834 to 1836, being forced to relinquish his seat on his appointment, in March 1836, as commander-in-chief at Portsmouth—a post which he held until April 1839. He commanded a squadron off Brighton on Queen Victoria's visit in 1837. Lady Durham died suddenly towards the end of 1844. Shortly after her death, Durham started on a tour abroad, but bronchitis, caught during his winter journey, proved fatal, and he died at Naples on 2 April 1845. He had no children, and his estates passed to his niece, daughter of his brother Thomas, wife of Robert Dundas of Arniston.

Durham was an officer with a long, varied, and largely distinguished career. His good fortune was, perhaps, even more noteworthy than his ability.

J. K. LAUGHTON, rev. ANDREW LAMBERT

Sources NMM, Minto MSS · R. F. Johnson, *The Royal George* (1971) · J. Marshall, *Royal naval biography*, 1 (1823) · O'Byrne, *Naval biog. dict.* · private information (1888) · Burke, *Peerage* · A. Murray, *Memoir of the naval life and services of Admiral Sir P. C. H. C. Durham* (1846)
Archives NA Scot., naval and other corresp. and papers · NL Scot., orders and corresp. · U. Edin. L., corresp. and dispatches | NL Scot., letters to Sir Alexander Cochrane and Sir Thomas Cochrane · NMM, letters to Lord Keith · W. Sussex RO, letters to duke of Richmond
Likenesses F. Grant, oils, *c.*1833, Scot. NPG · J. Wood, oils, *c.*1840, NMM · oils, Painted Hall, Greenwich, London

Durham, Symeon of. *See* Symeon of Durham (*fl. c.*1090–*c.*1128).

Durham, Walter of (d. *c.*1305), painter, was of unknown origins, and nothing is known of his training or background, except that he was a layman and not a monk (unlike William of Westminster, an earlier thirteenth-century royal painter). The suggestion that he owned property in St Albans is probably without foundation. When first recorded, at Westminster late in 1265, he was already styled master, and was responsible for colouring statuary in the palace of Westminster. By December 1266 he was responsible for replacing the murals damaged or destroyed by a fire in 1263 in the king's great chamber at Westminster, later known (from 1307/8) as the Painted Chamber. In the following year Henry III was careful to compensate him for damages and injuries sustained during a riot in the palace, and by 1270 Walter held a serjeanty at Henry's court, and was referred to as *pictor regis*—although the formal post of 'king's painter' which developed in the fourteenth century did not yet exist, Walter fulfilled most of its obligations. The range of his work, on statuary, murals, and woodwork (including, in the 1270s, the queen's barge), was normal for medieval court painters.

The workshop of Walter of Durham, apparently based in London, produced the most important schemes of wall painting executed for the crown in the late thirteenth century, and may also have produced panel painting. Walter continued to work in the chamber and elsewhere in the palace and abbey until the 1270s. In 1289 Edward I recalled him to continue work in the king's great chamber and palace rooms, and his workshop was employed between 1292 and 1297 in the palace, at the house of the archbishop of York at Westminster, and in Westminster Abbey on paintings on the tombs of Henry III and Queen Eleanor of Castile. Walter was also engaged to decorate the heart-tomb of Queen Eleanor at the London Blackfriars, 1291–2. His last documented work was the provision between 1297 and 1300 of a painted and gilded wooden throne, the so-called Coronation Chair, to house the Stone of Scone taken from the Scots by Edward I in 1296, which was placed on a step by the shrine of St Edward in the abbey.

The type of work Walter of Durham was engaged upon may be judged by the watercolour copies of the Painted Chamber murals taken in 1819 (Society of Antiquaries, London), and by the two panels from the chamber's ceiling, datable to *c*.1263–4, which were discovered in 1993 (now in the British Museum, London). His style indicates the growing influence of French Gothic painting, best represented by the Westminster Retable of *c*.1270–90 in Westminster Abbey, which may have been produced by painters in Walter's circle. Walter died *c*.1305. In the 1290s his son Thomas was working with him at Westminster; he may have been identical with the Thomas Westminster recalled in 1307/8 to decorate the palace of Westminster for the coronation of Edward II.   PAUL BINSKI

Sources *Chancery records* · PRO, exchequer, lord treasurer's remembrancer, pipe rolls, E 372 · PRO, exchequer, queen's remembrancer, accounts various, E 101 · [B. Botfield and T. H. Turner?], eds., *Manners and household expenses of England in the thirteenth and fifteenth centuries, illustrated by original records*, Roxburghe Club, 57 (1841), 95–139 · J. Gage Rokewode, 'A Memoir on the Painted Chamber in the Palace of Westminster', *Vetusta Monumenta*, 6 (1885) · W. Page, 'The St Albans school of painting, mural and miniature, pt 1: mural painting', *Archaeologia*, 58 (1902–3), 285–6 · W. R. Lethaby, 'Master Walter of Durham, king's painter', *Burlington Magazine*, 33 (1918), 3–8 · E. W. Tristram, *English medieval wall painting: the thirteenth century* (1950), 1.450–53 · H. M. Colvin, ed., *Building accounts of King Henry III* (1971) · P. Binski, *The Painted Chamber at Westminster*, Society of Antiquaries of London Occasional Papers, new ser., 9 (1986) · P. Binski, *Westminster Abbey and the Plantagenets: kingship and the representation of power, 1200–1400* (1995)

Durham, William of (*d.* 1249), theologian and university benefactor, may have been born at Sedgefield, co. Durham. Nothing otherwise is known of his origins or early life, until he is recorded as a regent master in theology at Paris, at a date between 1220 and 1223. To Matthew Paris, Durham was a famous master, a tribute amply accounted for by the range and sophistication of the questions attributed to him in Douai, Bibliothèque de la Ville, MS 434; these suggest that he also wrote a commentary on Peter Lombard's *Sentences*. Durham was still at Paris in 1229, when, with other English masters, he was forced to leave when the university was dispersed by the secular authorities. But if he returned to England, he soon left again, to become archdeacon of Caux in Normandy, and also to hold the living of Laise, which carried with it a stall in Rouen Cathedral. His position in the diocese came to be such that on 30 March 1236 a majority of the canons elected him archbishop. But the minority appealed against the election to the pope, on grounds that included William's holding the archdeaconry in plurality with Laise, and Durham, perhaps feeling the force of this objection, had by 12 August 1236 declined to accept election.

Instead Durham returned to England, probably to his native county, where in the previous year Bishop Richard Poor had made him a life grant of the episcopal manors of Wearmouth and Ryhope and the town of Sunderland, within which the rectory of Wearmouth was almost certainly comprehended. For this he was to pay a yearly rent of 40 marks. He may well have been intending to settle in the north-east, since in 1237 and 1238 he was given timber by the crown to make beams for the house he was building at Wearmouth. But letters of protection he received in November 1244 may indicate that he was about to go overseas, perhaps to Rome, since he was at some time appointed a papal chaplain. He certainly went abroad in 1248, when he mounted a successful defence at the curia at Lyons of his rights in Wearmouth, which had been challenged by Poor's successor, Bishop Nicholas of Farnham. He set off back to England via Normandy, but died at Rouen between 25 March and 11 May 1249.

Matthew Paris remarked upon Durham's wealth, and alleged that he was greedy to add to it. Be that as it may, Durham became a notable posthumous benefactor to Oxford University. He is not in fact known to have studied at Oxford, though his being owed £20 by Studley Priory, Warwickshire, in 1243 shows that he had contacts with the English midlands. But in his will he bequeathed 310 marks (£206 13s. 4d.) to the university, directing that the money be invested in rents which should provide for ten or more masters studying theology. Two halls were bought, one in 1253 and the other in 1255, and further purchases followed, but when about 1280 a committee of masters was appointed to investigate the uses to which Durham's bequest had been put, it was found that much of the money had either been diverted to the university's own purposes or lent to outsiders, and that the properties acquired as Durham had instructed were bringing in only some £12 per annum. The attempt to implement Durham's bequest which resulted from these inquiries effectively amounted to the foundation of a new college, albeit a very small one, of just four fellows; it was supported by the rents already acquired, and by further purchases paid for with such money from the bequest as could be recovered. Additional statutes were issued in 1292, and these, together with a gradual improvement in its financial position, helped to secure the position of what was to become known as University College.

HENRY SUMMERSON

Sources A. D. M. Cox, 'Who was William of Durham?', *University College Record*, 8 (1980), 115–23 · A. D. M. Cox, 'William of Durham and the archbishopric of Rouen', *University College Record* (1948–9), 11–20 · Emden, *Oxf.*, 1.612–13 · Paris, *Chron.*, vols. 3–5 · H. Anstey, ed., *Munimenta academica*, 2, Rolls Series, 50 (1868), 781 · T. H. Aston and R. Faith, 'The endowments of the university and colleges to circa 1348', *Hist. U. Oxf.* 1: *Early Oxf. schools*, 265–309
Wealth at death approx. 310 marks [£206 13*s*. 4*d*]: Emden, *Oxf.*, 1.613

Durham, William (1610/11–1684), Church of England clergyman, was born at Willersey, Campden, Gloucestershire, the third son of John Durham of Willersey. Generations of the Durham family had lived there and in his will of August 1679 William asked to 'be buried by my Ancestors at Willersey' (PRO, PROB 11/377). He was educated at Henry Sturley's school in Broadway, Worcestershire. In 1626 aged fifteen he entered New Inn Hall, Oxford, where he graduated BA in 1630 and proceeded MA in 1633 and BD in 1650. After graduating he took holy orders and in 1634 became curate to Thomas Bunbury, the rector of St Mary's, Reading.

In 1636 Durham was a contributor to the verse collection *Annalia Dubrensia*, in which the Cotswold games, revived by his Gloucestershire neighbour Robert Dover, were celebrated. Durham 'celebrated the exuberance of youthful pleasures on holy days' (Hutton, 195), though his poem is not, unlike others in the collection, explicitly anti-puritan. By 1642, however, when the civil war broke out, he was a strong puritan and 'an ardent supporter of Parliament' (ibid., 205). Durham went from Reading to London, took the covenant, and was chosen preacher at the Rolls Chapel.

In 1650 Durham was presented to the rich rectory of Tredington, then in Worcestershire. In July 1651 he preached an assize sermon at Warwick, published in 1652 as *Maran-Atha: the Second Advent, or, Christ's Coming to Judgment*. His theme was the mutual dependence of magistrates and ministers, and he called on judges and magistrates to protect ministers against 'Papist, atheist, libertine and sectary'. Durham, as his *Maran-Atha* shows, had ties with the ministers of both Worcestershire and Warwickshire (this was partly due to the fact that Tredington was an island of Worcestershire within the adjacent county). By 1656, however, he had chosen to join the Worcestershire Association rather than the presbyterian Kenilworth classis of

Warwickshire ministers. His 1659 work *A serious exhortation to the necessary duties of families and personal instruction, for the use of Tredington parish* indicates that, like other members of the association, he had implemented Baxterian catechizing and ministerial oversight in his parish. Like most puritan ministers Durham faced a crisis of conscience with the Restoration of 1660. At one point he was preaching at one end of Tredington church, and another minister, appointed by the crown in June 1660, was preaching at the other end. He was rector of Cawston, Norfolk, in 1661–3, but resigned after refusing to conform. He was only persuaded to conform by his close friend Humphrey Henchman, bishop of London. He was presented by Sir Nicholas Crisp to the London rectory of St Mildred, Bread Street, in February 1664.

Durham married in July 1638 Honor Lilley, the daughter of the vicar of Campden, and they had several children. His wife predeceased him; Durham himself died in London on 7 July 1684. He was buried in the ministers' vault at St Mildred. In his will he referred to his 'very great losses by barbarous oppressive wicked men whome God forgive', which presumably occurred in the civil war. To his son William [*see below*] he left 'all my Bookes which escaped the fire … except Thuanus his History and Matthew Poole's *Synopsis* which belong to my son John'. To John he left £50 'to maintaine him in Oxford till he bee Mr of Art and to discharge the expences of his degree' (PRO, PROB 11/377, fols. 24*r*–24*v*). John graduated MA in February 1681. Durham also published a life in 1660 of his cousin Robert *Harris, a famous puritan who was president of Trinity College, Oxford, until his death in 1658.

The younger **William Durham** (1639–1686) was baptized at Campden on 16 April 1639. He was educated at Charterhouse School and at Corpus Christi College, Oxford, from where he matriculated in December 1654, graduating BA in 1657 and proceeding MA in 1661 and BD in 1669. In 1674 he became rector of Letcombe Bassett, Berkshire. He was chaplain to James, duke of Monmouth, while the duke was chancellor of Cambridge University and, on Monmouth's recommendation, he became a Cambridge DD in 1676. He died unmarried on 18 June 1686 at Letcombe Bassett, where he was also buried. His will (PRO, PROB 11/385), dated 4 June 1685, was proved on 2 November 1686. Several of his sermons were published in his lifetime.

C. D. GILBERT

Sources C. Whitfield, *Robert Dover and the Cotswold games: annalia Dubrensia* (1962) · A. Hughes, *Godly reformation and its opponents in Warwickshire, 1640–1662*, Dugdale Society, 35 (1993) · *Calamy rev.* · will, PRO, PROB 11/377, sig. 100 · will, PRO, PROB 11/385/146 [William Durham the younger] · E. Calamy, *A continuation of the account of the ministers … who were ejected and silenced after the Restoration in 1660*, 2 vols. (1727) · R. Hutton, *The rise and fall of merry England: the ritual year, 1400–1700* (1994) · G. F. Nuttall, 'The Worcestershire Association: its membership', *Journal of Ecclesiastical History*, 1 (1950), 197–206 · Wood, *Ath. Oxon.*, new edn · Wood, *Ath. Oxon.: Fasti*, new edn · *N&Q*, 118, 201 · parish register, Tredington, Worcs. RO · parish register, Chipping Camden, Glos. RO · W. Durham, *Maran-Atha: the second advent, or, Christ's coming to judgment* (1652) · Foster, *Alum. Oxon.*
Wealth at death see will, PRO, PROB 11/377, sig. 100

Durham, William (1639–1686). *See under* Durham, William (1610/11–1684).

Durham House group (*act.* 1617–1630), theologians of the Arminian wing of the Church of England, took its name from the London residence in the Strand of the patron of the group, Richard *Neile (1562–1640), bishop of Durham between 1617 and 1628 and later archbishop of York. Neile seems to have kept open house for some of the leading theologians of the day, including William *Laud, John *Buckeridge, John *Cosin, Augustine *Lindsell, Richard *Mountague, Francis *White, and Thomas *Jackson (*bap.* 1578, *d.* 1640). On gaining the see of Durham on 9 October 1617, that which apparently:

> gave him most content was his palace of Durham House … not only because it afforded him convenient room for his own retinue, but because it was large enough to allow sufficient quarters for Buckeridge, Bishop of Rochester, and Laud, Dean of Gloucester, which he enjoyed when he was Bishop of St. Davids also. Some other quarters were reserved for his old servant Dr. Linsell, and others for such learned men of his acquaintance as came from time to time to attend upon him, insomuch as it passed commonly by the name of Durham College. (Heylyn, 74–5)

Richard Neile was the political and practical patron of the Arminian group within the Church of England that took Lancelot *Andrewes and John *Overall as intellectual mentors and sought some return to reverence, dignity, and decorum in worship—lost, they felt, at the Reformation. They opposed the fashionable stress on preaching and reaffirmed their belief in the importance of prayer and the sacraments, which in turn led them to emphasize strict adherence to the Book of Common Prayer. Neile used his influence as a minor favourite of James I to further the careers of those noted above, many of whom served as his domestic chaplains. For some like Richard Mountague, Durham House was a haven to which he had frequent recourse: he signed off one letter in December 1624 with the words, 'God bless and keep you at Durham House, and especially that worthy Bishop the owner of the house, still like himself in his thorough courses for right, though alone and left alone' (*Correspondence of John Cosin*, 34–5). In 1626 he still referred to Neile as the 'only man that stands up to purpose in the gap' (ibid., 61). Mountague's controversial books *A New Gag for an Old Goose* and *Appello Caesarem* were both published with the aid of Neile's chaplains Cosin, Lindsell, and White, all based at Durham House.

Opponents of this group were equally aware of the importance of Neile and Durham House. When a proclamation was issued in June 1626 to quell preaching on controversial matters like predestination, Bishop John Davenant wondered 'how far those of Durham House will stretch the meaning thereof I know not' (*Whole Works of … Ussher*, 15.356). More blatant still, when the consecration of Francis White as bishop of Carlisle was held at Durham House in December 1626, a libel was posted to the door with revealing questions, 'Is an Arminian now made Bishop? And is a consecration translated from Lambeth to Durham House?' (Birch, 1.179–80).

There was nothing unusual in bishops establishing 'teams'—often made up not only of divines, but also civil lawyers and administrators—and Neile had already gathered small groups around him at Westminster, Rochester, Lichfield and Coventry, and Lincoln, whence he was translated in 1617 while on progress to Scotland with James I. Some figures collected in his earlier dioceses moved with him to become members of the Durham House group—well-known people like John Buckeridge, William Laud, and Augustine Lindsell, but also lawyers such as William *Easdall and Edward Liveley (1586–1650, educated at Trinity College, Cambridge), and less well-known relatives like William Neile (1560–1624), Robert *Newell, and Gabriel Clarke (1589–1662, educated at Christ Church, Oxford: BA, 1609; MA, 1612). Of these, Edward Liveley went on to serve as Neile's loyal personal secretary for the rest of his career, Robert Newell elected to stay as archdeacon of Buckingham in the diocese of Lincoln, and Gabriel Clarke reached the pinnacle of his career as archdeacon of Durham in 1620.

It was clear as early as 1611 that Neile enjoyed moving to a diocese with an entourage. He may even have been in William Prynne's mind when the latter wrote scathingly 'that they [bishops] commonly take with them seven other spirits as bad, or more wicked themselves (to wit, Archdeacons, Chancellors, Registers, Appariters, household chaplains, Secretaries and private informers against good men' (Prynne, 9). Easdall, Robert Masters (BCL, All Souls, Oxford, 1590; DCL, 1594; principal of St Alban's Hall, 1599–1603), Newell, and Liveley all followed Neile from Rochester to Lichfield. Others congregated about Neile who did not become part of the later Durham House group, not because they were not able or loyal, but simply because their career paths diverged. In this group should be counted some of Neile's Cambridge associates like Richard Clayton (*d.* 1612, fellow of St John's College, Cambridge, 1577; MA, 1579; DD, 1592; master of Magdalene College, Cambridge, 1595; dean of Peterborough in 1607), Richard *Butler, and fellow royal chaplain Benjamin *Carier (who eventually defected to Rome and who died in 1614). These three were involved closely with Neile in his dealings with the Wightman affair in 1611. In many senses, therefore, the Durham House group had already become established before 1617, and all that was provided then was a larger London residence on the fashionable Strand.

Much of the success of Neile's team-building at Durham House was based on the family atmosphere engendered through his wife, Dorothy, remembered with affection in the wills of Buckeridge and Lindsell, and also through the services of, first, his brother William, who served as household steward between 1617 and his death in 1624, and then of his brother-in-law, William Holmes, who took over that role. John Cosin preached the funeral sermon for the latter's wife in 1623. Cosin was undoubtedly the most famous and controversial figure associated with Durham House, but others like White, Lindsell, and Jackson found it an intellectually stimulating environment in which to live.

Durham House meant different things to different people. It is most commonly associated with theologians operating at court in and around London in the 1620s. But it also had pronounced Durham associations, where figures like Eleazar *Duncon, Francis Burgoyne (d. 1633, educated at Peterhouse, Cambridge: BA, 1582; MA, Jesus College, 1585; fellow of Jesus, 1583–91), Daniel Birkhead (educated at Emmanuel College, Cambridge: BA, 1600; MA from Trinity College, 1603; BD, 1610; DD, 1618), Thomas Astell (c.1600–1658, of Northumberland, educated at Clare College, Cambridge: BA, 1622; MA, 1626; BD, 1634), and Andrew *Perne chiefly operated in the northern environment yet carried out ceremonial changes which became the talk of London in 1628. The practical work of these figures was almost as controversial as that of their better known—and published—colleagues in Neile's circle. Ceremonial associated with the altar, use of candles and incense, strict adherence to liturgy, all aided by the new organ installed by Thomas Dallam, brought Durham into the limelight when in 1628 prebendary Peter Smart published—notably in Edinburgh—an extraordinary attack, *A Sermon Preached in the Cathedral Church of Durham*.

Francis Burgoyne was already established in Durham when Neile arrived, but he spotted his chances well and became archdeacon of Northumberland in 1620, a post he held until his death in 1633. Daniel Birkhead was another who moved into Neile's entourage and was rewarded with a prebend in 1619; he died relatively young—much to the proclaimed grief of Mountague and Cosin—and was buried in the cathedral in 1624. Thomas Astell was the only cleric Neile trusted sufficiently to allow (when still relatively young in his twenties in 1625) to preach throughout the diocese. He eventually followed Neile to York, where he was also one of very few licensed to preach throughout the northern province, was deprived of a prebend of Ripon in 1640, and died in 1658. Andrew Perne was one of those who followed Neile from Lincoln to be allowed to hold the vicarage of Norton and the rectory of Washington *in commendam*, possibly because he was one of Neile's domestic chaplains.

The changes at Durham were presided over after 1620 by the dean, Richard Hunt (d. 1638; educated at Trinity College, Cambridge: BA, 1586; MA, 1589; DD, 1608; dean of Durham, 1620–38), but it is not clear how involved he was in the work of his chapter. At a later date, when Smart drew attention to the divisions within the close, he seems to have tried to mediate. It is important to remember that the Durham House group was not a completely homogeneous one—there were clergy who attached themselves to the house in the Strand, others who sought Neile's patronage in the north, while others simply took their chances as careerists who saw which way the wind was blowing. Like-minded theologians like Samuel Harsnett and John Howson never became members of this particular group whose allegiance to Neile was such a marked characteristic.

One feature of the success of the Durham House group in the north can be glimpsed by the control they took not only over the cathedral and diocese, but also over civil society through their dominance of the bench of justices of the peace. In the parliament of 1621 it was claimed that the clergy now outnumbered the gentry by thirteen to twelve on the Durham commission of the peace. This was a gross exaggeration but Neile's cronies Chancellor Craddock, Birkhead, Burgoyne, Clarke, Blakiston, Ewbank, and Morecroft were certainly more conscientious attenders of meetings than many members of the gentry, and so might well have dominated some sessions.

Although the London group might seem logically to have dissolved on Neile's promotion to Winchester in 1628, when a house in Southwark became available for meetings, it is possible to argue that Durham House had already fulfilled its purpose before that, and that the group was splintering, particularly on Laud's symbolic departure from the house in 1626. On the other hand, Neile's work in recruiting new scholars to the fold continued and people like Benjamin *Lany and Edward Burby (c.1616–1654, educated at Lincoln College, Oxford: BA, 1619; MA, 1622; DD, 1636; prebendary of Winchester, 1630; archdeacon of Winchester, 1631; prebendary of Southwell, 1638; married Neile's niece Frances in 1630) joined the group through Winchester livings.

Durham House itself was a hive of activity, not only because of Neile's company, but also because its central location and size made it an ideal site for diplomatic purposes. In 1610 the house had been used for the ceremony of the creation of knights of Bath. In 1619 the French ambassador stayed there. When it was thought that Prince Charles might be bringing back guests from Spain in 1623, the house was requisitioned to receive them. The French ambassador stayed again in 1624 and serious disputes broke out in 1626 when English Catholics were found to be attending services there under the protection of the ambassador. Neile had to intervene to gain order.

The Durham House group played a vital part in the history of the Church of England in the early seventeenth century. The work of theologians associated with it influenced the nature of the church as it developed in the 1630s under Archbishop William Laud; their work also influenced the Restoration church settlement of the 1660s. Four of Neile's known chaplains went on to become bishops either before or after the Restoration; this in itself is a tribute to the success of this group and his patronage.

ANDREW FOSTER

Sources A. W. Foster, 'A biography of Archbishop Richard Neile (1562–1640)', DPhil diss., U. Oxf., 1978 • N. Tyacke, *Anti-Calvinists: the rise of English Arminianism, c.1590–1640* (1987), chap. 5 • K. Fincham, *Prelate as pastor: the episcopate of James I* (1990) • V. E. Raymer, 'Durham House and the emergence of Laudian piety', PhD diss., Harvard U., 1981 • P. Heylyn, *Cyprianus Anglicus* (1668), 74–5 • *The correspondence of John Cosin D.D., lord bishop of Durham*, ed. [G. Ornsby], SurtS, 52 (1869) • *The whole works of … James Ussher*, ed. C. R. Elrington and J. H. Todd, 17 vols. (1847–64), vol. 15 • Venn, *Alum. Cant.* • Foster, *Alum. Oxon.* • [T. Birch and R. F. Williams], eds., *The court and times of Charles the First*, 1 (1848) • M. James, *Family, lineage, and civil society: a study of society, politics, and mentality in the Durham region, 1500–1640* (1974) • A. Foster, 'The clerical estate revitalized', *The early Stuart church, 1603–1642*, ed. K. Fincham (1993), 139–60 • P. Smart, *A sermon preached in the cathedral church of Durham* (1628) • W. Prynne, *A looking glass for all lordly prelates* (1636), 9 •

D. Marcombe, ed., *The last principality: politics, religion and society in the bishopric of Durham, 1494–1660* (1983)

Durie. For this title name *see* Gibson, Alexander, Lord Durie (*d.* 1644); Gibson, Alexander, Lord Durie (*d.* 1656).

Durie, Andrew (*d.* **1558**), bishop of Galloway, was born probably at Durie, Fife, the son of John Durie of that ilk and his wife, Janet Beaton. He was the nephew of James *Beaton and first cousin of Cardinal David *Beaton, successive archbishops of St Andrews, and the brother of George *Durie, commendator of Dunfermline. Having matriculated at St Andrews in 1511 and subsequently graduated, he was in 1520 presented by James Beaton to be treasurer of the Chapel Royal, Stirling. In 1523 he executed a commission to the lords of council on his uncle's behalf. The period immediately after 1524 was one of power struggle, King James V being then only twelve. When the abbot of Melrose, Robert Beaton (James's brother and Durie's uncle), died about November 1524, James Beaton as chancellor of the realm had Durie nominated as his successor. Other factions contested this, and, despite having Roman provision twice in 1525, Durie did not receive the temporalities of Melrose until December 1526.

Durie's provision required him to take the habit within three months and he thus became the regular abbot of the largest Cistercian monastery in Scotland. At some point he was made Cistercian visitor, but the general chapter of 1530 deposed him for negligence and gave the post to Walter Malynne, abbot of Glenluce, instead. Malynne acted with energy and came into conflict with Durie, whereupon the king asked chapter to replace Malynne. The French abbot of Chaalis who was then appointed also proved energetic and summoned Durie to appear before the general chapter of 1533, but James told chapter that Durie's presence was needed in Scotland. Chapter, however, commissioned Malynne and another abbot to implement the French visitor's enactments. The main issue was the custom at Melrose and its daughter-houses (over which Durie had disciplinary rights and duties) of treating monks' portions and gardens as virtually private property, contrary to Cistercian ideals. In October 1534 the two new visitors issued an ultimatum to Durie and summoned him to the general chapter of 1535, where again he failed to appear. During his abbacy the Melrose community declined from thirty-five to nineteen monks.

As abbot of Melrose Durie played a modest part in public affairs, attending parliament at times, welcoming the occasional important visitor from England, and in 1537 leading a delegation through England to France. In May 1541 the king granted him the temporalities of the bishopric of Galloway and in July nominated him as bishop and his own thirteen-year-old natural son, James, to be commendator of Melrose. Bulls of 22 August provided Durie, according to custom, to hold Tongland Abbey and the Chapel Royal, Stirling, as well as Galloway, and in addition a large annual pension from Melrose (still being paid in 1552).

In the 1540s Durie attended the privy council regularly and was assigned duties by it; in 1543–6 he was an auditor of exchequer. Remaining faithful to the Catholic, pro-French party, he was quite often at St Andrews with his cousin Cardinal Beaton, and in July 1543 he signed a bond supporting him. During the Anglo-Scottish hostilities in 1547 he was in Fife commandeering boats when Inchcolm was occupied by English forces. He attended the provincial church council in 1549 and in 1550 took part in the trial of Adam Wallace for heresy. Durie accompanied the queen mother to France that same year, and seems also to have been in Paris about 1554. On 14 December 1557 he signed the commission for negotiating the queen's marriage with the dauphin. Both as abbot and as bishop, however, he was seriously in arrears with payment of his taxes. John Knox condemned his somewhat coarse humour and loose morals, but no illegitimate child of Durie is recorded. He died in 1558, probably in September, never recovering (according to Knox) from the shock sustained through protestant mob violence in Edinburgh.

MARK DILWORTH

Sources J. Dowden, *The bishops of Scotland … prior to the Reformation*, ed. J. M. Thomson (1912), 373–4 · M. Dilworth, 'Franco-Scottish efforts at monastic reform, 1500–1560', *Records of the Scottish Church History Society*, 25 (1993–5), 204–21 · *APS*, 1424–1567 · J. B. Paul, ed., *Compota thesaurariorum regum Scotorum / Accounts of the lord high treasurer of Scotland*, 6 (1905); 8 (1908) · *Reg. PCS*, 1st ser., vol. 1 · *LP Henry VIII*, vols. 4, 7, 12, 14 · W. M. Brady, *The episcopal succession in England, Scotland, and Ireland, AD 1400 to 1875*, 1 (1876), 1.159, 199 · R. K. Hannay, ed., *Acts of the lords of council in public affairs, 1501–1554* (1932) · M. Livingstone, D. Hay Fleming, and others, eds., *Registrum secreti sigilli regum Scotorum / The register of the privy seal of Scotland*, 1–2 (1908–21) · M. Dilworth, 'Monks and ministers after 1560', *Records of the Scottish Church History Society*, 18 (1972–4), 201–21 · D. Patrick, ed., *Statutes of the Scottish church, 1225–1559*, Scottish History Society, 54 (1907), 85, 134n · W. Macfarlane, *Genealogical collections concerning families in Scotland*, ed. J. T. Clark, 2 vols., Scottish History Society, 33–4 (1900), 7, 23 · J. M. Anderson, ed., *Early records of the University of St Andrews*, Scottish History Society, 3rd ser., 8 (1926), 206 · *CSP Scot., 1547–62* · R. C. Reid, ed., *Wigtownshire charters*, Scottish History Society, 3rd ser., 51 (1960) · *Lettres, instructions et mémoires de Marie Stuart, reine d'Écosse*, ed. A. Labanoff, 7 vols. (1844), vol. 1

Durie, George (*d.* **1577**), administrator and Roman Catholic ecclesiastic, was the youngest of the three sons of John Durie of that ilk and his wife, Janet Beaton; the Duries and Beatons were landed families in Fife. Nothing is known of Durie's early life but he belonged to the second generation of the Beaton hegemony in the church. Archbishop James *Beaton of St Andrews and Abbot Robert Beaton of Melrose were his uncles; his brother Andrew *Durie was abbot of Melrose and later bishop of Galloway; Cardinal David *Beaton was his first cousin; and a later archbishop, James *Beaton, was the cardinal's nephew.

George Durie's early career was marked by pluralism and nepotism. His first appointment, about 1522, was apparently as archdeacon of St Andrews. Even more prestigious was his papal provision on 23 May 1526 to Dunfermline Abbey, held by the archbishop in commendam, though the latter retained all rights and revenues. This was a way of determining future succession to a benefice. As for lesser benefices, in March 1525 Durie was claiming the vicarage of Inchbrayock and by September 1527 he had been given the parsonage of Benholme by the archbishop. In 1531 he paid tax for the churches of Inchbrayock, Moffat, and Linton, and in 1534 he held the parsonage of Strathbrock. Presumably at some point he was ordained priest.

Durie was no stranger to litigation. There were rival claimants for his parishes, and in 1546 the crown petitioned Rome to reconsider its judgment over Strathbrock against Durie. Strife over the archdeaconry began in 1524, when a rival received papal provision. The case came before the privy council in 1529 and was referred in 1535 to the king for adjudication, but a year later Durie had contravened the terms of the agreement. In 1539 he ceded the archdeaconry, now in his firm possession, to his sister's young son, Robert *Pitcairn, retaining the revenues and administration. The king protested in vain to Rome. Although Beaton and Durie signed Dunfermline documents together, relations between them did not remain friendly. In 1533 Durie had been intent on resigning his title to Dunfermline, but in 1538 the lords of council found in Beaton's favour over Durie's non-payment of debts, and a year later Beaton revoked his litigation at Rome against Durie.

James Beaton died in 1539 and was succeeded as archbishop by his nephew David. Durie was now sole superior of Dunfermline, but as commendator, for as archdeacon he remained a secular cleric. For the next twenty years he retained these offices and played a considerable part in public affairs, though by 1547 he was eleven years in arrears with tax payments for the college of justice. He sat in parliament, was a lord of council, and was frequently appointed to committees or commissions. In 1541 he travelled to France on government business, and in 1550 accompanied the queen dowager there. Several times he was auditor of exchequer, and in 1552–5 was keeper of the privy seal. During Queen Mary's minority he corresponded with the governor of the kingdom, and later with the queen regent. He is recorded in 1547–50 as engaged in military matters: advising the rejection of Somerset's overtures before the battle of Pinkie; requisitioning boats to besiege the English forces in Inchcolm; and being commissioned to receive the fort at Inveresk from the French forces. As regards church affairs, Durie took part in the heresy trials of Patrick Hamilton in 1527, of Adam Wallace in 1550, and of Walter Milne in 1558. He was in the group convened by David Beaton in 1539 to combat heresy and attended the provincial church council of 1549. In 1553 he ceded Dunfermline to Pitcairn, retaining the revenues and administration.

At this time Catholics in Scotland were pro-French, and protestants pro-English. Durie remained Catholic and was condemned by protestant writers, in particular for the plan to trick David Beaton's murderers, besieged in St Andrews Castle, into surrender when force was unsuccessful. He was also criticized for his advice before Pinkie, considered to be anti-protestant, and for the execution for treason of John Melville of Raith in 1548.

In 1559–60 Durie was involved in some minor military

movements, but he did not attend the Reformation Parliament of August 1560 and in January 1561 went to France, where he remained for almost ten years. Robert Pitcairn now became archdeacon and commendator in reality, being described specifically as commissary of Durie during his absence abroad. Little is known of Durie's stay in France, but his cousin Archbishop James Beaton of Glasgow resided in Paris as Queen Mary's ambassador. In 1564 Durie was exhorted by the pope to remain faithful to Catholicism, and two years later the queen wanted him to accompany a papal nuncio to Scotland. When Durie returned to Scotland in June 1570, Mary was a prisoner in England but hoped he would be active on her behalf. He was in fact under open arrest at Durie, while Pitcairn was at least a nominal protestant and hostile to Mary and to Durie. By March 1577 Pitcairn had total control of the affairs of the now senile Durie who died in October that year. He is said to have been buried at Dunfermline's western church.

Hardly anything is known of Durie as a person, for the relevant records are legal or formal. He matriculated at St Andrews in 1528 when already abbot of Dunfermline, and was termed master in 1531, which should denote a graduate. Certainly he was educated and competent. His frequent appearance in public records reveal him mostly as a secular official devoted to the crown. As a churchman he exemplified the abuses of pluralism, nepotism, and blatant incelibacy. Being in major orders he could not contract a valid marriage, but his mistress, Katherine Sibbald, lived openly at Craigluscar, just 3 miles from Dunfermline. Two sons, Peter and Henry, received crown legitimation in 1543; another two, George and John, in 1549. In the 1550s the elder two witnessed Dunfermline monastic documents, and they and their mother received grants of monastic land and founded landed families. His two younger sons, John *Durie and George Durie became Jesuits and missionaries in Scotland. Durie's career was marked by an apparent contradiction, in that although it exemplified some of the more reprehensible features of the pre-Reformation church, yet he remained loyal to it, even under adverse conditions. MARK DILWORTH

Sources M. Dilworth, 'Dunfermline, Duries and the Reformation', Records of the Scottish Church History Society, 31 (2001), 37–67 · J. M. Webster, History of Carnock (Fife) (1938) · C. Innes, ed., Registrum de Dunfermelyn, Bannatyne Club, 74 (1842) · contemporary state, church, and local records · J. M. Anderson, ed., Early records of the University of St Andrews, Scottish History Society, 3rd ser., 8 (1926) · J. M. Webster and A. A. M. Duncan, eds., Regality of Dunfermline court book (1953), 192–3

Likenesses portrait (of Durie?), priv. coll.; repro. in Webster, History of Carnock, 326

Durie, John (1537–1600), Church of Scotland minister, was born at Mauchline, Ayrshire. Following his education at Ayr he became a Benedictine monk at the abbey of Dunfermline through the influence of its abbot, his cousin George *Durie. Suspected of heresy after some three years in the abbey, he was tried and condemned to be enclosed until he died, but friends persuaded James Hamilton, third earl of Arran, to obtain his release. This would have occurred in the early 1550s, for his second son, Robert

*Durie (d. 1616), was born in 1555. Durie and his wife, Marion, daughter of Sir John Marjoribanks, provost of Edinburgh, had five other children, Joshua, Simeon, Christian, Elizabeth, and a third daughter.

According to John Spottiswoode, Durie embraced protestantism shortly after the Reformation. After serving as exhorter at Restalrig, outside Edinburgh, from 1563 to 1569, he was minister at nearby Hailes (in the parish of Colinton) before being transferred to Leith in May 1570. Following Queen Mary's deposition in 1567, he worked with James Lawson and Robert Pont to advance the presbyterian cause. Early in 1572 he attended the convention at Leith which established procedures to dispense the revenue of episcopal sees and abbacies, and on 31 July that year he and John Brand led the exiles who supported the king's party on their triumphant return to Edinburgh. By 6 August 1573 he had become minister of St Giles, Edinburgh, with a stipend of 200 merks, which increased to £200 by 1577. At the general assembly in August 1575 Durie, supported by Andrew Melville, questioned whether bishops as constituted in the Church of Scotland were lawful. The assembly decided that the term 'bishop' was acceptable and applied to all ministers, but it rejected dignitaries who functioned as diocesan bishops. In October 1576 the assembly named him to the committee to revise a draft of the Book of Discipline, and four years later it appointed him visitor of Teviotdale.

A bitter opponent of the earl of Morton's regime, Durie urged in October 1580 that no supporter of Morton or Esmé Stewart, earl of Lennox, be elected to the Edinburgh council, and in December he and Walter Balcanquhal were summoned before the privy council for having publicly criticized French courtiers and their Catholic faith. For refusing to provide the council with copies of his sermon, he was briefly incarcerated in Edinburgh Castle. The same month he represented the general assembly at James Melville's installation as principal of New College, St Andrews. Durie and Balcanquhal met Morton before the earl's execution in June 1581 and recorded his reputed confession. In October 1581 he advised the presbytery of Stirling about the excommunication of Robert Montgomerie, the newly appointed archbishop of Glasgow. Durie's relationship with Patrick Adamson, archbishop of St Andrews, was mercurial; he welcomed Adamson into his home in 1581, yet the following year treated him 'maist seveire' before Adamson repented (*Autobiography and Diary of … Melvill*, 128), whereupon Durie embraced him.

For attacking Lennox, criticizing the king for accepting horses from the duc de Guise, and denouncing the archbishop of Glasgow as an apostate in May 1582, Durie was banished from Edinburgh by the privy council in June. Lennox's angry chiefs were reportedly prepared to kill him. Before leaving the city Durie reported to the general assembly, which urged the king to rescind the council's order. Unsuccessful, the assembly included Durie's banishment in a list of grievances presented to the convention of estates in July. In August 1582, the synod of Lothian and the presbytery of Edinburgh dispatched Durie and John Davidson to canvass the lairds of Teviotdale and Lothian for support for the Ruthven lords, heads of a hardline protestant government that had just taken power by a coup. With the latter's permission Durie returned to Edinburgh on 4 September, to be given a triumphant reception by a swelling crowd of up to 2000 people, singing psalm 124, 'Now Israel may Say', with 'a great sound and majestie' (Cowan, 158).

Durie was again in trouble in July 1583, this time for defending the Ruthven coup. After pledging his loyalty to King James he was released, only to be summoned again for the same offence in November and banished from Edinburgh to Montrose. As minister of Montrose he remained active in church affairs, participating in the general assemblies of 1586–8, 1590, 1593, and 1595. Having been given an assistant in 1589, for his service to the church he received a pension of £140 on 7 August 1590. In 1592 the assembly appointed him to report on the activities of Catholics in the Brechin area. Before his death at Montrose on 28 February 1600 he wrote advice for the king and general assembly. James Melville praised his piety and hospitality to ministers and godly barons and gentlemen, but acknowledged that he was 'of small literature' (*Autobiography and Diary of … Melvill*, 78). In Spottiswoode's judgement he was a man of zeal, 'but too credulous … and easily abused by those he trusted' (Spottiswoode, 457). His wife survived him. His sons became ministers—Joshua at Inverkeilor, Forfarshire; Robert at Anstruther, Fife; and Simeon at Arbroath, Forfarshire—and his daughters married clergy—Christian married George Gledstanes, later archbishop of St Andrews; Elizabeth, James Melville; and the third daughter John Dykes, minister of Kilrenny, Fife.

RICHARD L. GREAVES

Sources *Fasti Scot.*, new edn, 1.2, 52, 164, 343; 5.409–10; 8.14, 31, 208 • *The autobiography and diary of Mr James Melvill*, ed. R. Pitcairn, Wodrow Society (1842) • J. Spottiswoode, *The history of the Church of Scotland* (1655) • J. Row, *The history of the Kirk of Scotland, from the year 1558 to August 1637*, ed. D. Laing, Wodrow Society, 4 (1842) • T. Thomson, ed., *Acts and proceedings of the general assemblies of the Kirk of Scotland*, 3 pts, Bannatyne Club, 81 (1839–45) • D. Calderwood, *The true history of the Church of Scotland, from the beginning of the Reformation, unto the end of the reigne of King James VI* (1678) • M. Lynch, *Edinburgh and the Reformation* (1981) • T. M'Crie, *The life of Andrew Melville*, 2nd edn, 2 vols. (1824) • J. Kirk, *Patterns of reform: continuity and change in the Reformation kirk* (1989) • A. R. Macdonald, *The Jacobean kirk, 1567–1625: sovereignty, polity and liturgy* (1998) • M. F. Graham, *The uses of reform: 'Godly discipline' and popular behavior in Scotland and beyond, 1560–1610* (1996) • G. R. Hewitt, *Scotland under Morton, 1572–80* (1982) • F. Bardgett, *Scotland reformed* (1989) • I. B. Cowan, *The Scottish Reformation* (1982)

Durie, John (c.1544–1588), Jesuit, was probably born at Dunfermline in Fife where his father, George *Durie (d. 1577), became abbot; his uncle, Andrew *Durie, was bishop of Galloway, and his older brother George also returned to the Scottish mission as a priest. The third son of his father's liaison with Katherine Sibbald, John Durie was legitimated in 1549. He was educated at Paris and Louvain and entered the Society of Jesus about 1576. After graduating MA (it is not known where) he lived at Collège de Clermont, Paris, and by 1582 he was a priest teaching rhetoric there. In that year his only book appeared, his

Confutation in answer to the *Responses* of William Whitaker, regius professor of divinity at Cambridge and a leading Calvinist, whose work had followed the *Ten Reasons* of Edmund Campion, the Jesuit martyr executed in 1581. The leading Italian Jesuit Antonio Possevino praised Durie highly for learning and eloquence, and he was also described as a simple and humble man though 'exceptionally skilled in the classics' (Chadwick, 67). Durie's *Confutation* was reprinted at Ingoldstadt in 1585.

In July 1585, having left Angers in France, Durie landed in Scotland with another Jesuit, Edmund Hay, and a Roman Catholic political agent, Robert Bruce. Under the protection of John, eighth Lord Maxwell at Dumfries, a sensitive urban centre near the border, Durie ministered against a complex background involving England, Spain, and James VI, whose conversion to Roman Catholicism was sought. Durie regularly received penitents after nightfall. Following a three-day Roman Catholic celebration of Christmas at nearby Lincluden Abbey, Maxwell was banished, early in 1586. When James held court at Dumfries in April 1587, Durie too had left the area. The 'saintly' priest (Shearman, 27) died of consumption in the care of Lady Wood on 20 October 1588 at Balbegno Castle in Kincardineshire. According to his fellow Jesuit Robert Abercrombie, who gave him the last rites, Durie converted 'several sons of the lady of the house' from his deathbed (Forbes-Leith, 205).   ALASDAIR ROBERTS

Sources M. Dilworth, 'Dunfermline, Duries and the Reformation', *Records of the Scottish Church History Society*, 31 (2001), 37–67 • W. Forbes-Leith, ed., *Narratives of Scottish Catholics under Mary Stuart and James VI* (1885) • P. J. Shearman, 'Father Alexander McQuhirrie', *Innes Review*, 6 (1955), 22–45 • H. Chadwick, 'A memoir of Fr Edmund Hay S. I.', *Archivum Historicum Societas Iesu*, 8 (1939), 66–85 • K. Brown, 'The making of a *politique*: the Counter-Reformation and the regional politics of John, eighth Lord Maxwell', *SHR*, 66 (1987), 152–75 • T. G. Law, 'Robert Bruce, conspirator and spy', *Collected essays and reviews of Thomas Graves Law*, ed. P. H. Brown (1904), 313–19

Durie, John. See Dury, John (1596–1680).

Durie, Robert (1555–1616), Church of Scotland minister, was the second son of John *Durie (1537–1600) and his wife, Marion, daughter of Sir John Marjoribanks, provost of Edinburgh. He studied at St Mary's College, St Andrews, and while there he and James Melville tutored Robert Bruce, son of the laird of Airth, in 1583. He later joined Melville, who was also his brother-in-law, at La Rochelle, and in December 1585 accompanied him to Linlithgow, where parliament convened. When Melville accepted the pastorate at Anstruther, Fife, in December 1586, Durie served as his assistant, with responsibility for Anstruther while Melville ministered at Pittenweem and Kilrenny. His friendship with Melville led to his contributing a commendatory sonnet to the former's *Spirituall Propyne*. In 1588 Durie accepted the living at Abercrombie (parish of St Monance), Fife, but on 1 February 1592 he was transferred to Anstruther and granted the portership of the outer port of the abbey of Dunfermline for life. In February 1597 the synod of Fife named him one of the delegates to seek royal approval to postpone an assembly at Perth

until the general assembly had convened at St Andrews in April. By this time he had married Elizabeth Ramsay, with whom he had eight children: Andrew, Eliezer, John (1596–1680), James, Margaret, Nanse, Jean, and Robert (*bap.* 8 March 1607).

For the purpose of founding protestant churches Durie accompanied a group of adventurers to the island of Lewis in the Outer Hebrides in October 1598. In April 1601 the presbytery of St Andrews asked him to return, and a month later the general assembly commissioned him and Robert Pont to visit Orkney and Shetland. Durie then went back to Lewis, but when the adventurers were massacred there in December he escaped and returned to Anstruther. For participating in the general assembly that met in Aberdeen in July 1605, despite a royal ban, Durie was imprisoned in Blackness Castle, Linlithgowshire, later that month. Cited before the privy council on 24 October, ten of the offenders submitted, but Durie and twelve others rejected the council's authority and unsuccessfully requested trial by a general assembly. On 13 November their petition for transportation was also rejected. Tried at Linlithgow on 10 January 1606, they were convicted of treason, but sentencing was deferred until 23 October, when they were banished.

Faced with the death penalty if he returned, Durie sailed from Leith on 7 November 1606. After landing at Bordeaux, he and John Forbes settled at Veere in the Netherlands, where they ministered to Scottish merchants. Occasionally they also preached at the garrison church in Flushing and the Merchant Adventurers' church at Middelburg. The lieutenant-governor, Sir William Browne, who heard Durie preach, found nothing controversial and noted that he prayed zealously for James and his family. Durie even baptized Browne's son. The king, however, ordered that none of his subjects be instructed by such men. Ordered to leave Veere, Durie petitioned James, but Browne held the document until 21 October 1608, when he forwarded it to Viscount Lisle. For a time Durie preached to the English Reformed church in Amsterdam, but held no regular position. In March 1610 the magistrates of Leiden approved his appointment as minister of the English church that shared St Catherine Gasthuis with a Dutch congregation. Six years later Forbes obtained permission for Durie to return to Scotland, but Andrew Melville, with whom Durie corresponded, expressed doubts about the safety of doing so. In any event, Durie died at Leiden in September 1616, and Hugh Goodyear succeeded him as pastor.   RICHARD L. GREAVES

Sources *Fasti Scot.*, new edn, 5.177, 182–3; 7.205, 546; 8.454 • *The autobiography and diary of Mr James Melvill*, ed. R. Pitcairn, Wodrow Society (1842) • D. Calderwood, *The true history of the Church of Scotland, from the beginning of the Reformation, unto the end of the reigne of King James VI* (1678) • J. Spottiswoode, *The history of the Church of Scotland* (1655) • R. Pitcairn, ed., *Ancient criminal trials in Scotland*, 2, Bannatyne Club, 42 (1833), pt 2, pp. 494–50 • J. Forbes, *Certaine records touching the estate of the kirk in the years MDCV & MDCVI*, ed. D. Laing and J. Anderson, Wodrow Society, 19 (1846) • *Report on the manuscripts of Lord De L'Isle and Dudley*, 6 vols., HMC, 77 (1925–66), vol. 4, pp. 23–4, 61 • *Calendar of the manuscripts of the most hon. the marquess of Salisbury*, 20, HMC, 9 (1968), 184 • K. L. Sprunger, *Dutch* *puritanism: a history of the English and Scottish churches of the Nether-lands in the sixteenth and seventeenth centuries* (1982) • T. M'Crie, *The life of Andrew Melville*, 2nd edn, 2 vols. (1824) • M. F. Graham, *The uses of reform: 'Godly discipline' and popular behavior in Scotland and beyond, 1560–1610* (1996) • A. R. Macdonald, *The Jacobean kirk, 1567–1625: sovereignty, polity and liturgy* (1998)

Durkan, John (*c*.1855–*c*.1925x35). *See under* Knock, visionaries of (*act.* 1879).

Durlacher, Sir **Esmond Otho** (1901–1982), stockjobber, was born on 8 October 1901 at Thorpe Satchville, Leicester, the second of three children of Frederick Henry Durlacher (1859–1936), stockjobber, and his wife, Violet, daughter of Sir Reginald Hanson of Thorpe Satchville. The family was of German-Jewish origin, settling in England during the reign of George I. Durlacher had two brothers: the elder, Richard, was killed on board HMS *Indefatigable* at Jutland in May 1916; the younger, (Admiral Sir) Laurence (1902–1986), became deputy chief of naval staff and fifth sea lord.

Durlacher was educated at Repton School and Trinity Hall, Cambridge, but left the university in 1921 without taking a degree. He spent a short time as a cowboy in America, but his real ambition was to follow his brothers into the Royal Navy. The loss of the eldest, however, meant that instead he was required to join the family partnership F. and N. Durlacher, a jobbing firm in the London stock exchange, which had originally been established by his father in 1881. When Durlacher joined in 1923, after a brief apprenticeship with the stockbroker Roger Mortimer & Co., there were four partners and the stock exchange generally was composed of small family partnerships. Jobbers confined themselves to clearly defined segments of the market and depended on the brokers to bring them orders, which still originated overwhelmingly with private clients. Durlacher later recalled that he felt even then that jobbers would have to provide a better service if they were to have a secure future. Outwardly, however, his career followed a conventional path. Despite his reluctance to go into the City, he became a partner and stock exchange member in 1926. His father's early retirement through ill health also made him *de facto* senior partner, although he did not formally assume that position until the former's death in 1936. On 31 December 1930, he married Sheila Jackson, *née* Scott (*b*. 1906), the daughter of Rupert Charles Scott, the earl of Clonmell, with whom he had two sons and a daughter.

Like the rest of his generation, Durlacher's career was interrupted by the war. He served as a member of the intelligence corps attached to Scotland Yard and did ARP duty at night. Outwardly, the stock exchange to which he returned in 1945 had little changed. At best, however, with a Labour government in office and the economy subject to tight controls, the prospect was uncertain. The persistence of high taxation and steady growth of the pension and insurance funds also had profound consequences for patterns of investment and capital accumulation, which became even clearer when the economy recovered in the

1950s. In particular, the size of stock exchange transactions began to increase at precisely the moment that jobbing firms were experiencing difficulty in retaining the capital to finance them.

Durlacher's distinction, together with that of two other senior partners of jobbing firms, Hugh Merriman of Akroyd and Smithers and Lewis Powell of C. D. Pinchin & Co., was to recognize the implications of these trends and, through a combination of foresight and opportunism, adapt the dealing system of the London stock exchange to meet them. In essence, the solution lay in welding the multiplicity of small jobbing firms into larger units which commanded greater capital and crossed several markets. Durlacher's first merger in 1953 with a jobber in the textile and woollen markets more than doubled the partnership and placed it in the first rank of stock exchange firms. Thereafter, its growth until 1965 proceeded through amalgamation with several other firms and was paralleled throughout the stock exchange. In some instances, mergers came about through relationships of long standing; in most, Durlacher simply rescued firms which were already in considerable financial difficulty.

With the absorption of a substantial part of the third-largest industrial jobber, Kitchin Baker Shaw, in 1965, the partnership later known as Durlacher Oldham Mordaunt Godson was the dominant trader in British equity stocks. It had grown to twenty partners, and Durlacher was known in the markets as 'the emperor', the recognized spokesman of the jobbing system at large, and head of a firm which the City editor of *The Times* declared to have 'more extroverts to the square inch than anywhere else in the City' (29 April 1968, 21). In a decade when company mergers and contested corporate takeovers became common occurrences, the firm's considerable dealing capacity also brought Durlacher influence with brokers and company directors. The firm's expansion, however, would have been impossible without a corresponding increase in its capacity to settle bargains, and in 1965 Durlacher was one of the first senior partners of a jobbing firm to order a computer.

Durlacher retired on 14 March 1967 with the firm at the height of its influence and prestige, and shortly to embark on its most ambitious merger of all, a marriage with the gilt-edged jobber Wedd Jefferson, which, under the name Wedd Durlacher, transformed it into the largest stock exchange firm and triggered a series of similar mergers. Durlacher retained his involvement as a consultant, and continued on the board of St George's Hospital, which he had joined in 1944. In 1953, he had also been appointed a governor of the Victoria Hospital for Children, becoming chairman four years later. The two hospitals merged in 1967. In 1972, he was knighted for his charitable work. He was a Conservative and, during Edward Heath's prime ministership, he worked closely with the party chairman, Lord Carrington, and personally raised some £2 million for the party.

Durlacher's first marriage had been dissolved in 1947. He remarried on 30 July 1953; his new wife was Elizabeth Steele, *née* Ensor (*b*. 1915/16). Always immaculately dressed, Durlacher worked and played hard. One of the outstanding senior partners of his generation, he was also an excellent bridge player and an accomplished sportsman who won distinction in several fields. He died at Wootton Fitzpaine Manor, Charmouth, Bridport, Dorset, from cancer, on 28 May 1982. A memorial service was held at St Lawrence Jewry-next-Guildhall in the City on 29 June. BERNARD ATTARD

Sources 'The jobbing system of the London stock exchange: an oral history', BL NSA, interviews 19, 40 · private information (2004) · *The Times* (1 June 1982) · 'Wedd Durlacher Mordaunt & Co.: members of the stock exchange', GL · E. Durlacher, 'Thoughts on retirement', *Stock Exchange Journal*, 11 (1966), 4–5 · *WW* · GL, MS 14,600, vols. 111, 113 · *Members and Firms of the Stock Exchange* [London, Stock Exchange (list of members to 1955)] (1918/19–1972/3) · *The Times* (12 Aug 1965) · *The Times* (29 April 1968) · *The Times* (30 June 1982) · b. cert. · m. certs. · d. cert. · *CGPLA Eng. & Wales* (1982)
Likenesses photographs, GL, *Wedd Durlacher Mordaunt and Co.: members of the stock exchange* · photographs, repro. in Durlacher, 'Thoughts on retirement'
Wealth at death £59,512: probate, 20 July 1982, *CGPLA Eng. & Wales*

Durlacher, Lewis (1792–1864), chiropodist, was born probably in Warwickshire, the son of Solomon Abraham Durlacher (1757–1845), chiropodist and dentist, and his wife, Elizabeth Harris. He learnt the craft of chiropody from his father, in Bath, Somerset. About 1816 Durlacher commenced practice at 22 St James's Street, London. He had the support of several surgeons, including Sir Astley Paston Cooper, which was unusual because chiropody was regarded as a humble, non-medical trade. In 1826 he won the approval of *The Lancet* after he demonstrated his treatment for embedded toenails at the hospital of surgery in Panton Square. From 1823 until his death he was surgeon-chiropodist to the royal household of three successive sovereigns: George IV, William IV, and Victoria. He was presented with a snuff box engraved 'To my friend Lewis Durlacher from William IV'.

Durlacher's book, *A Treatise on Corns, Bunions, the Diseases of Nails, and the General Management of the Feet*, was published in 1845. It had good reviews; the *British and Foreign Medical Review* (19, 1845, 560–1) considered it 'the result obviously of much experience and written in a fair and honest spirit. It is, in fact, the only work on the subject which has any pretensions to scientific accuracy'. An American edition appeared the same year and had considerable influence. The book contained the first description of plantar digital neuroma, and included the best accounts of the embedded toenail and the inward-forming wart. He also developed the use of silver nitrate.

Durlacher tried to establish a free dispensary for people with diseases of the foot. He believed that the public should be protected from empirics either by legislation or by the medical licensing bodies' making the study of diseases of the feet part of the medical curriculum.

Durlacher married Susanna Levi (1798–1874) on 2 January 1820. They had five sons and one daughter. He had a thorough education in scripture and Hebrew literature.

Active in the Jewish community in London, he took a leading part in the affairs of the Western Synagogue. Durlacher died at his home and place of practice, 15 Old Burlington Street, London, on 3 March 1864.

J. C. DAGNALL

Sources W. Seelig, 'Durlacher, four generations of a family in English chiropody', *The Chiropodist*, 11 (1956), 76–83 · J. C. Dagnall, 'A history of chiropody-podiatry and foot care', *British Journal of Chiropody*, 48 (1983), 137–83 · J. C. Dagnall, 'Durlacher and "the nail growing into the flesh"', *British Chiropody Journal*, 27 (1962), 263–7 · J. C. Dagnall, 'The origins of the society of chiropodists and podiatrists and its history, 1945 to 1995', *Journal of British Podiatric Medicine*, 50 (1995), 135–41, 151–6, 174–81 · private information (2004) · d. cert.
Wealth at death under £300: probate, 2 April 1864, *CGPLA Eng. & Wales*

Durnford, Anthony William (1830–1879), army officer, eldest son of General Edward William Durnford, colonel commandant of the Royal Engineers, and Elizabeth Rebecca Langley, was born on 24 May 1830 at Manorhamilton, Leitrim, Ireland. Educated in Ireland, and afterwards at Düsseldorf in Prussia, he entered the Royal Military Academy, Woolwich, in 1846, and obtained a commission as second lieutenant in the Royal Engineers on 27 June 1848. In 1851 he proceeded on foreign service to Trincomalee, Ceylon. On 17 February 1854 he was promoted first lieutenant, and in 1855 he was appointed assistant commissioner of roads and civil engineer to the colony in addition to his military duties. He entered into an early marriage on 15 September 1854 at Trincomalee with Frances Catherine, youngest daughter of Lieutenant-Colonel Tranchell, late of the Ceylon rifle regiment. A daughter, Frances Elizabeth Maria, born in 1857 and to whom Durnford was devoted, outlived both her parents.

On the outbreak of the Crimean War Durnford volunteered for active service, but fever delayed his departure, and it was not until March 1856 that he joined the reserves at Malta, where he served as adjutant to his father, who was in command of the Royal Engineers stationed there. In February 1858 he returned to England and took up duties as an instructor in field work. His marriage, meanwhile, was failing, undermined by the deaths of an infant son on Malta in 1856 and an infant daughter in 1860. Durnford and his wife separated in 1860 and he accepted a posting to Gibraltar. Late in 1864 he sailed for China, intending to serve under Charles Gordon who was reorganizing the Chinese army after putting down the Taiping uprising, but he was invalided home before reaching China. For the next five years he was stationed at Devonport. Though recognized as an energetic and able officer, Durnford was exasperated by his failure to see active service and tried to compensate through physically taxing outdoor activities. Charming and witty, with impeccable manners and high principles, he was also restless and short-tempered, and a compulsive gambler. He was 6 feet tall, slim, and with a neat, upright bearing, and he sported long Dundreary whiskers.

Durnford was posted to Cape Colony in January 1872 and promoted major in July. In May 1873 he was sent to Natal, where he joined the imperial garrison at Fort Napier in

Pietermaritzburg. There he became intimate with the family of the humanitarian Anglican bishop of Natal, John Colenso. He became involved in a close sentimental friendship with Frances Ellen *Colenso [see under Colenso, Harriette Emily], the bishop's 24-year-old second daughter. She idolized him, but Durnford was still married, and there is no evidence to suggest that their relationship was ever other than platonic.

Towards the end of 1873 relations broke down between Langalibalele, chief of the Hlubi who lived in the foothills of the Drakensberg Mountains, and the Natal administration. Rather than suffer punishment for perceived offences against his colonial masters, Langalibalele resolved to lead his people out of Natal by way of the Bushman's river pass into Basutoland. Durnford, with a small force of Natal mounted volunteers and mounted Sotho, was ordered to co-operate with a force of African levies in preventing their departure. During the march, on the night of 2 November 1873, Durnford's horse fell with him, dislocating his shoulder. He fainted from pain and fatigue during the difficult ascent the following day, and had to be carried part of the way. He and his depleted force were at the head of the Bushman's river pass by the morning of 4 November, but the levies failed to make the rendezvous. The bulk of the Hlubi and their cattle had already passed into Basutoland, but Durnford tried to persuade the remaining Hlubi to proceed no further. He attempted an ordered withdrawal rather than risk an armed confrontation, but it rapidly degenerated into a disordered flight. Five of his men were killed before he succeeded in rallying them. He himself was speared in the side and in the left elbow, which severed the nerves and permanently damaged his arm. The expedition had been a discreditable failure. At a court of inquiry in October 1874 much of the evidence was highly critical of Durnford's leadership, though his considerable personal courage was acknowledged.

On 11 December 1873 Durnford was promoted lieutenant-colonel, and between November 1873 and October 1875 he was acting colonial engineer in Natal. It was an unhappy time for him. Already unpopular with the colonists over the Langalibalele expedition, he antagonized them further by championing the cause of the Ngwe (Putili), unjustly punished by the Natal authorities for allegedly aiding the Hlubi. With Bishop Colenso's strong encouragement, he nevertheless succeeded in rehabilitating them. In this controversial undertaking Durnford revealed a tenacious concern for the downtrodden, and showed (as Frances Colenso believed) that his true calling lay in commitment to social issues rather than in the elusive search for military renown. Between May and July 1874 he led an expedition to block the passes over the Drakensberg and, in a further attempt to restore shaken settler morale, in November 1874 began the erection to his own competent design of a stone blockhouse at Estcourt, later named Fort Durnford.

Durnford left Natal in May 1876 in a vain search for a cure for his injured arm, which he kept hidden under his tunic. He was posted in August 1876 to Queenstown in Ireland, before securing his return to Pietermaritzburg in March 1877. Britain was then attempting to bring about a confederation of southern African states, and the high commissioner, Sir Bartle Frere, saw the Zulu kingdom as an impediment that must be removed. Durnford was appointed in February 1878 to sit on a boundary commission meeting at Rorke's Drift to adjudicate in the border dispute between the Transvaal (annexed as a British colony in April 1877) and Zululand. The commission's report, which was completed on 20 June 1878, was favourable to Zulu claims, but its findings were submerged in Frere's inexorable drift to war with Zululand, which finally broke out on 11 January 1879. Durnford's response was ambivalent. While his humanitarian side deprecated a war of aggression against the Zulu, he was nevertheless impatient to satisfy his desire for military success. During August and September 1878 he prepared memoranda for Lord Chelmsford, the British commander, on the raising, organization, and training of African levies and pioneers, helped select suitable invasion points, and completed an essential map of Zululand based on earlier surveys of the territory.

Durnford was promoted colonel in the army on 11 December 1878, and Chelmsford appointed him to the command of no. 2 column of the invading force stationed at Kranskop. It consisted of the three battalions of the 1st regiment Natal native contingent, the Natal native horse, and a rocket battery of artillery. Durnford's popularity with the Natal Africans living towards the Drakensberg meant that his force was rapidly up to strength, and he proved himself a firm, though popular, commander. He remained impulsive, however, and was severely reprimanded by Lord Chelmsford when, without orders, on 14 January he ordered his men to Middle Drift on the Thugela to stop a rumoured Zulu invasion. On 19 January Chelmsford ordered no. 2 column forward to Rorke's Drift in support of no. 3 column, leaving two battalions of the Natal native contingent at Kranskop. Meanwhile, no. 3 column encamped at Isandlwana Mountain. By the early morning of 22 January, Chelmsford and over half of no. 3 column were committed to a reconnaissance in force south-east of Isandlwana in search of the Zulu army, and Chelmsford ordered up Durnford to reinforce the camp at Isandlwana, whose commander, Lieutenant-Colonel Pulleine, had been instructed to act strictly on the defensive. When Durnford arrived in camp at mid-morning he assumed command as the senior officer. He then upset the defensive arrangements by advancing to prevent Chelmsford from being attacked in the rear (as he supposed) by the small decoy Zulu forces he observed, and by requiring Pulleine to move up in his support if required. Durnford's patrols unexpectedly encountered the main Zulu army and provoked it into a premature advance. The strung-out British forces tried to fall back on the camp and consolidate, but the rapidly deploying Zulu succeeded in outflanking their firing line and entered the camp from the rear. The battle ended in desperate hand-to-hand fighting.

Durnford, who had been exhilarated by the fury of battle, rallied the remnants of his men on the right flank of the camp and died the central figure of a knot of brave men. He and his companions lay unburied until May 1879. In October 1879 his body was brought from its grave at Isandlwana and re-interred in the military cemetery at Fort Napier in Pietermaritzburg.

The court of inquiry into the loss of the camp duly attributed most of the blame for the defeat to Durnford's rash conduct. This was hardly surprising since Chelmsford's staff were determined to make Durnford the scapegoat for the disaster. His brother Lieutenant-Colonel Edward Durnford and Frances Colenso endeavoured through their writings and public lobbying to rehabilitate his reputation. They did not wholly succeed. Durnford's heroic death did much to blunt public criticism of him, but there can be little doubt that his actions contributed materially to the disaster at Isandlwana. As Sir Theophilus Shepstone wrote of him, Durnford was 'as plucky as a lion but as imprudent as a child'.

J. P. C. LABAND

Sources R. W. F. Droogleever, *The road to Isandhlwana: Colonel Anthony Durnford in Natal and Zululand, 1873–1879* (1992) • E. C. L. Durnford, ed., *A soldier's life and work in South Africa, 1872 to 1879: a memoir of the late A. W. Durnford* (1882) • P. L. Merrett, 'Frances Ellen Colenso, 1840–1887: her life and times in relation to the Victorian stereotype of the middle class English woman', MA diss., University of Natal, 1980 • E. R. Guest, *Langalibalele: the crisis in Natal, 1873–75* (1975) • J. Mathews, 'Lord Chelmsford: British general in southern Africa, 1878–1879', DLitt et Phil diss., University of South Africa, 1986 • J. P. C. Laband, *Kingdom in crisis: the Zulu response to the British invasion of 1879* (1992) • A. Wylde, *My chief and I* (1880) • E. C. L. Durnford, *Isandhlwana: Lord Chelmsford's statements compared with the evidence* (1880) • R. W. F. Droogleever, 'A figure of controversy: Colonel Anthony Durnford in Natal and Zululand, 1873–1879', DLitt et Phil diss., University of South Africa, 1982 • CGPLA Eng. & Wales (1879)
Archives Royal Engineers Museum, Chatham
Likenesses two photographs, c.1872–1878, Institution of Royal Engineers Library, Chatham • photograph, 1878, Killie Campbell Africana Library, Durban
Wealth at death under £800: administration with will, 5 May 1879, CGPLA Eng. & Wales

Durnford, Richard (1802–1895), bishop of Chichester, eldest son in the family of three sons and three daughters of the Revd Richard Durnford (b. 1765/6) and his wife, Louisa (d. 1864), daughter of John Mount, was born at Sandleford, near Newbury, Berkshire, on 3 November 1802. His childhood was passed at Chilbolton, near Andover, Hampshire, where his father acted as *locum tenens* for the rector, Phineas Pett, canon of Christ Church, Oxford. At the age of eight he was sent to the Revd E. C. James's preparatory school at Epsom, and three years later was taken home by his father to be under his own instruction, with the view of standing for a scholarship at Winchester. Failing election at that school, he stood for a king's scholarship at Eton College, where he was successful in 1814. There he became the pupil of the Revd Charles Yonge, and a favourite with John *Keate, the headmaster. At this time he showed great facility for Latin verse, two specimens of

which are given in *Musae Etonenses*, and he was a contributor to *The Etonian*, edited by W. M. Praed and Walter Blunt. In 1820, while still at Eton, he matriculated at Pembroke College, Oxford, but did not reside at the college, being elected to a demyship at Magdalen College in 1822. He was one of the founders of the Oxford Union (at first styled the Union Debating Society), and was president in its first year (1823) and again in 1825 and 1826. He was a private pupil of James Garbett, and graduated BA in 1826, having obtained first-class honours in the classical school, and MA in 1827. He was elected probationer fellow of Magdalen College in 1827 and full fellow in the following year, and was ordained deacon at Oxford in 1830 and priest in 1831. From 1826 to 1832 he was private tutor at Eton to Edward Harbord, eldest son of Lord Suffield, and spent two years in travel on the continent, where he acquired unusual fluency in French, Italian, and German.

In 1833 Durnford was presented by Lord Suffield to the living of Middleton, Lancashire, but was not inducted until 1 July 1835. His parish was a heavily populated manufacturing district, comprising dispersed communities undergoing the strains of industrialization. Despite having no experience of this type of parochial charge, he managed to exercise a considerable local influence. He was credited with dissuading the textile workers in Middleton from joining the Stalybridge strikers during the great Lancashire strike of August 1842. He gave a high priority to founding church schools, establishing a new national school at Middleton in 1842, which subsequently prospered. His wife, Emma (d. 1884), whom he had married on 6 October 1840, daughter of his former headmaster John Keate, helped to teach in the local Sunday schools. He was concerned to increase the capacity of the churches in the area, abolishing pew rents and building new churches at Thornham, Rhodes, and Parkfield. The old parish church at Middleton was restored during his incumbency. Although he declined to be appointed a justice of the peace, he took a leading part in the secular institutions of his parish, serving as a member of the board of guardians and from 1861 as chairman of the local board with responsibility for roads, gas and water supplies, and drainage. One of the most prominent Anglican clergymen in Lancashire, he was made a rural dean soon after the formation of the Manchester diocese in 1848. He became an honorary canon, archdeacon of Manchester in 1867, and canon residentiary of Manchester Cathedral in 1868.

When James Prince Lee, bishop of Manchester, died in December 1869, Durnford's claims to be his successor were discussed by Gladstone, who, however, selected James Fraser (1818–1885) on the grounds that a younger man was needed. Two months later, in February 1870, the see of Chichester became vacant, and it was offered to and accepted by Durnford. The consecration took place at the Chapel Royal, Whitehall, on 8 May 1870. He had then reached the age of sixty-eight, but he soon proved himself in body and intellect fully equal to his new duties. His episcopate began at a time of particular difficulty; the south coast parishes were hotbeds of party conflict within the church over the ritualism question. The judgment on appeal in the case of John Purchas was an immediate concern. But Durnford, by his impartiality, patience, sympathy, and forbearance, won confidence throughout his diocese. These qualities were clearly shown in his visitation charges of 1871 and 1875, and by the manner in which he conducted the church congress at Brighton in 1874, at a time when controversy over the Public Worship Regulation Act was at its height. A friend of Samuel Wilberforce and W. F. Hook, he was a high-churchman, but no ritualist, disliking the excesses of the Tractarians. He had formed his opinions before the Oxford Movement had begun, and was 'convinced that such theologians as Hooker, Andrewes, Pearson Barrow, Jackson, Sanderson, are our best guides even in these days' (Stephens, 333). In the early days of his episcopate he resuscitated Bishop Otter's Memorial College at Chichester as a training college for schoolmistresses, and revived the theological college in the same city. He also reorganized the Diocesan Association, founded in 1837 to provide additional churches and to promote church schools. He preferred that diocesan conferences should discuss practical subjects of this type rather than controversial questions of principle. He was a strong supporter of the Mothers' Guild in his diocese. He was an important member of the Lambeth conference of bishops in 1888, and, in conjunction with bishops Lightfoot and Stubbs, framed the encyclical letter which was issued by the bishops embodying the principal conclusions of their debates. In 1888 he was elected an honorary fellow of Magdalen College.

Contemporaries found Durnford a delightful and lovable companion. He was an able classical scholar, with a rare knowledge of botany and horticulture, and of natural history generally. Bishop Stubbs said: 'He was, I almost think, the most wonderfully complete person I ever knew, and the same to the last' (Stephens, 365). He had a remarkably robust constitution, continuing his recreations of mountain climbing and walking in the Tyrol into his eighties.

Durnford died at Basel on 14 October 1895, as he was returning from a holiday spent at Caddenabbia, on Lake Como. He was buried at Chichester Cathedral, where an alabaster recumbent effigy to his memory was unveiled on 23 May 1898. A brass with a Latin inscription was placed in Eton College chapel. He was survived by a daughter and two sons, the younger of whom, Walter *Durnford, became provost of King's College, Cambridge.

C. W. SUTTON, *rev.* M. C. CURTHOYS

Sources W. R. W. Stephens, *A memoir of Richard Durnford, DD* (1899) · *Manchester Guardian* (15 Oct 1895) · *The Guardian* (1895), 1551, 1654 · T. Cooper and others, *Men of mark: a gallery of contemporary portraits*, 2 (1877) · Boase, *Mod. Eng. biog.* · M. Smith, *Religion in industrial society* (1994) · *GM*, 2nd ser., 14 (1840), 536
Archives BL, corresp. with W. E. Gladstone, Add. MSS 44425–44762 · LPL, corresp. with Edward Benson · LPL, corresp. with A. C. Tait
Likenesses W. W. Ouless, oils, 1890 · C. A. Tomkins, mezzotint, exh. RA 1892 (after a mezzotint by W. W. Ouless, exh. RA 1890), NPG · A. H. Fry, photograph, 1894, repro. in Stephens, *Memoir of Richard Durnford*, facing p. 353 · Bodley & Garner, alabaster effigy, 1898, Chichester Cathedral · Fradelle, photograph, repro. in Stephens, *Memoir of Richard Durnford*, frontispiece · Lock & Whitfield,

woodburytype photograph, NPG; repro. in T. Cooper, *Men of mark: a gallery of contemporary portraits*, 2 (1877) · cabinet photograph, NPG · portrait, repro. in *ILN* (14 May 1870), 505 · portrait, repro. in *ILN* (19 Oct 1895), 487
Wealth at death £38,076 2s. 4d.: probate, 27 Nov 1895, CGPLA Eng. & Wales

Durnford, Sir Walter (1847–1926), college head, was born on 21 February 1847 at Middleton, Lancashire, the younger son of the Revd Richard *Durnford (1802–1895), rector of Middleton, and afterwards bishop of Chichester, and his wife, Emma (d. 1884), daughter of John *Keate, headmaster of Eton College from 1809 to 1834. Durnford entered Eton in 1859 as an oppidan in a dame's house but was soon elected a king's scholar. In 1865 he was admitted a scholar of King's College, Cambridge, where he obtained a first class (as fourth classic) in the classical tripos of 1869, becoming, on graduation, a fellow of his college in the same year.

In 1870 Durnford returned to Eton as an assistant master under J. J. Hornby and later became a housemaster. He was head of the army class, commanded the volunteer corps, and administered rowing. In 1899 he was compelled by persistent attacks of gout to retire.

As he had never married, Durnford still held his fellowship at King's College under the statutes of 1861, and to King's he returned. He speedily became an important and influential member of many university boards and syndicates, including the council of the senate and the town council. In 1909 he was mayor of Cambridge, and in the same year he became principal of the Cambridge University Day Training College for Elementary Teachers, having eased out Oscar Browning, an antagonist since his Eton days. In 1909 he also became vice-provost of King's, and in 1910 a fellow of Eton. On the outbreak of war in 1914 Durnford threw himself into the task of selecting candidates for commissions; his services during the war were recognized in 1919 when he was created GBE. In 1918 Durnford was elected provost of King's, reinforcing the Eton connection with the college. He held the office until his death, at The Lodge, King's College, Cambridge, on 7 April 1926 at the age of seventy-nine.

Durnford was a man of great sweetness of character, which he masked under a humorous incisiveness of manner. J. H. Clapham remembered him as 'a good scholar of the old school' who viewed the idea of academic research with especial aversion (*Durnford*, 18). He was not without a certain family resemblance to his grandfather, Dr Keate. He was held in particular affection by his pupils at Eton and his undergraduate friends at Cambridge, in whose pursuits (not least those connected with drama) he took a vivid interest, and whom he regularly entertained in vacations at his house at Bembridge, Isle of Wight.

M. R. JAMES, *rev.* M. C. CURTHOYS

Sources *The Times* (8 April 1926) · *Walter Durnford, 1847–1926* (privately printed, 1926) · L. P. Wilkinson, *A century of King's* (1980) · Venn, *Alum. Cant.* · CGPLA Eng. & Wales (1926)
Archives Bodl. Oxf., visitors' book | King's Cam., letters to Oscar Browning; letters to Sir J. T. Sheppard · Suffolk RO, Ipswich, corresp., mainly letters to R. H. White

Sir Walter Durnford (1847–1926), by Sir William Orpen, 1924

Likenesses A. S. Cope, oils, 1914, Eton · W. Orpen, oils, 1924, King's Cam. [*see illus.*] · Spy [L. Ward], caricature, chromolithograph, NPG; repro. in *VF* (4 Dec 1902)
Wealth at death £16,047 12*s.* 6*d.*: probate, 2 June 1926, *CGPLA Eng. & Wales*

Durno, James (1755/6–1795), history painter and copyist, was born in England to a Scottish father, the proprietor of a brewery at Kensington Gravel Pits. According to the archives of San Giovanni in Laterano in Rome, he was twenty-two in 1777. He was trained by Andrea Casali (*c.*1723–1780) and subsequently by Benjamin West, for whom he also worked as a copyist, and entered the Royal Academy Schools on 28 February 1769.

Durno competed for the prizes offered for large-scale history paintings by the Society of Arts, winning 30 guineas for his picture *Margaret of Anjou with the Prince in the Wood Assailed by Robbers* in 1770 and 100 guineas for his picture *Isaac, a Tyrant of Cyprus, and his Daughter, Brought Prisoners before Richard the First* in 1771. In 1769 and 1771 he competed for the Royal Academy's gold medal for history painting, but was unsuccessful on both occasions. Between 1767 and 1773 he exhibited a portrait and a number of historical subject pictures at the Society of Artists. At the beginning of the 1770s Durno worked with John Hamilton Mortimer, Francis Wheatley, and Thomas Jones as part of the team that provided decorations for Lord Melbourne at Brocket Hall, Hertfordshire. His drawings of the period show a frank debt to Mortimer, notably in the highly mannered graphic depiction of *Agrippina and her Children Mourning Germanicus* (*c.*1774; British Museum, London).

Durno left England for Italy in January 1774, and remained in Rome until his death. Between 1777 and 1778 he was living with the sculptor Thomas Banks and his wife

by the piazza Mignanelli, and helped nurse Banks during a severe illness in 1778. In 1779 he executed a large copy of Raphael's *Transfiguration* for which he asked the remarkably high price of £1000. The copy was sold to Frederick Augustus Hervey, fourth earl of Bristol, in 1783, and is now in the National Gallery of Ireland, Dublin. During the 1780s Bristol provided Durno with a number of further commissions for original history paintings. In 1783 Durno entered the competition for the decoration of the doge's palace in Genoa, which was granted to Domenico Tiepolo; Durno's drawings for the commission are in the Berlin Museum. In the late 1780s John Boydell commissioned two pictures for the Shakspeare Gallery, *Falstaff Examining the Recruits* (known from the engraving) and *Falstaff in Disguise, Led out by Mrs Page* (Sir John Soane's Museum, London). The pictures he sent to London received considerable criticism for their stiffness and cold colouring, characteristics said to derive from his long stay on the continent.

Like many other British artists in Italy, Durno was also active as an art dealer, and it was this activity, together with his extensive practice as a copyist, which seems largely to have supported him. Durno died in Rome of a fever on 13 September 1795 following a period of ill health. Farington reported that he had a long association with an Italian woman and had a sixteen-year-old daughter (Farington, *Diary*, 9 Dec 1795). The *Gentleman's Magazine* reported that his funeral was attended by Prince Augustus and a number of noblemen, testifying to his high standing within the British community in Italy.

MARTIN MYRONE

Sources E. Edwards, *Anecdotes of painters* (1808); facs. edn (1970) · J. Ingamells, ed., *A dictionary of British and Irish travellers in Italy, 1701–1800* (1997) · N. L. Pressly, *The Fuseli circle in Rome: early Romantic art of the 1770s* (New Haven, CT, 1979) [exhibition catalogue, Yale U. CBA, 12 Sept – 11 Nov 1979] · *GM*, 1st ser., 66 (1796), 81 · N. Figgis, 'Irish portrait and subject painters in Rome, 1750–1800', *GPA Irish Arts Review Yearbook*, 5 (1988), 125–36 · N. Figgis, 'Raphael's *Transfiguration*: some Irish grand tour associations', *Irish Arts Review Yearbook*, 14 (1998), 53–6 · minutes of the General Assembly/Council minutes, RA · N. Figgis, 'Irish artists and society in eighteenth-century Rome', *Irish Arts Review*, 3/3 (1986), 28–36 · MS minutes of the committee of polite arts, RSA · Farington, *Diary* · P. Dreyer, 'James Durno: Beiträge zu seiner Zeichenkunst und zu seinen Entwürfen für die Ausmalung der Sala Grande in Palazzo Ducale in Genua von 1783', *Jahrbuch der Berliner Museen* (1975), 38–57
Wealth at death see will, Rome State Archives, De Rubels 1795 6371; inventory, Rome State Archives, fondo 30; note capitolini, Ufficio 2, v. 618; notes at Ford Archive, Paul Mellon Centre for Studies in British Art, London

Durrell, Gerald Malcolm (1925–1995), author, naturalist, and animal conservationist, was born in Jamshedpur, India, on 7 January 1925, the fifth and youngest child of Lawrence Samuel Durrell (1884–1928), civil engineer, and his wife, Louisa Florence, *née* Dixie (1886–1964). Lawrence George *Durrell (1912–1990), poet and novelist, was his eldest brother; a second child died in infancy, but another brother and sister survived to adulthood. Following the death of Durrell's father in April 1928, the family uprooted themselves from India and went to England, moving to Bournemouth early in 1931. There Durrell

Gerald Malcolm
Durrell (1925–
1995), by Wolfgang
Suschitzky, 1960

indulged his passion for small creatures of all kinds, announcing to his mother when he was six that he would have his own zoo one day—an ambition he was to pursue with extraordinary single-mindedness. Meanwhile his entire formal education amounted to two terms at a prep school. In 1935 the Durrell family again moved, settling on the Greek paradise island of Corfu. This was perhaps the great defining moment in Durrell's life. There he lived out an idyll of which other children could only dream. In the three books he later wrote about his Corfu childhood— notably *My Family and other Animals* (1956)—he described his forays on foot to look for wildlife, and the impact his pet scorpions and snakes had on the rest of the household. Out of a bevy of eccentric private tutors, two laid the foundations of the man of achievement he became. The first was his brother Lawrence, who instilled in him a passion for language and encouraged him to take his first steps in creative writing. The second was a Corfiot medic, Dr Theo Stephanides, a biologist and polymath, who gave the boy a marvellous grounding in field biology and a broad appreciation of life on earth in all its diversity.

With the onset of the Second World War the Corfu years came to an end and Durrell returned to Bournemouth with his mother. In 1945, after various odd jobs with animals, he became a student keeper at Whipsnade Zoo, where he learned the basics of large animal husbandry and first became aware of the role of man in the extinction of species. At the age of twenty-one he inherited £3000 from his father's legacy. This enabled him to fulfil another ambition—to collect wild animals for zoos. Between 1947 and 1951 he undertook two major collecting expeditions to the British Cameroons and another to British Guiana.

On 26 February 1951 Durrell married Jacqueline Sonia (Jacquie) Rasen (*b.* 1929), a student opera singer, who staunchly encouraged him in the next turn in his life. Jacquie encouraged his zoo ambitions and persuaded him to write his first book, *The Overloaded Ark* (1953), about his first Cameroons expedition, and two further animal books in quick succession—*Three Singles to Adventure* (1954)

and *The Bafut Beagles* (1954). The freshness of these books, their charm, their ebullient humour, their totally new approach to wild animals and wild places, and the vivid, lyrical quality of their descriptive writing ensured their instant success worldwide. Almost overnight Durrell became one of the finest nature writers of the century, an inspiration to millions. Now a fully-fledged professional author, he set off on more collecting expeditions, resulting in further animal travel books including *The Drunken Forest* (1956), set in Argentina and Paraguay, and *Zoo in my Luggage* (1960), featuring one of the great characters of travel literature, Durrell's regal African drinking companion, the legendary Fon of Bafut. But it was his classic evocation of his childhood idyll in Corfu, *My Family and other Animals*, that brought him true fame and fortune.

Durrell had never forgotten his boyhood ambition of founding a zoo of his own. In 1957 he returned from the Cameroons with a large collection of animals that was to form its nucleus. This was later transferred to Jersey, where he had taken a lease on the house and grounds of Les Augrès Manor, Trinity, and was first opened to the public on 29 March 1959 as Jersey Zoo, which has become one of the world's finest small zoos. As a conservationist Durrell was a pioneer a long way ahead of most of the field. He had always intended that Jersey should become a conservation zoo dedicated to the breeding of animals in danger of extinction and their eventual return to the wild. With the founding of the Jersey Wildlife Preservation Trust on 6 July 1963 his life's mission got under way. Within a few years the trust had established breeding groups of many species of endangered mammals, reptiles, and birds, and had begun to return their progeny to the wild. In 1976 Durrell created what he called a mini-university in a manor house adjacent to the zoo to provide intensive training for conservation workers from around the world, so that they could begin the process of saving species in their country of origin—arguably the greatest innovative achievement of his life. By 2000 more than 1000 students from over 100 countries had received training at the International Training Centre. Durrell also established affiliate organizations in the United States and Canada to fund his work, which have since become international organizations in their own right. In 1989 the Durrell Institute of Conservation and Ecology (DICE) was founded at the University of Kent.

For his contributions to animal conservation and animal literature Durrell received many honours. Though he had received virtually no formal education, he was awarded honorary doctorates from the universities of Yale (1977), Durham (1988), and Kent (1989), and among other honours was appointed officer of the Golden Ark by Prince Bernhard in 1981, and OBE in 1982. Over the years the private man became a public figure of international stature. Slim and lissom as a young man, with film star looks and a debonair aura, Durrell rounded out in maturity into a larger than life, bacchanalian figure, endowed with immense charisma and a hilarious sense of humour—but also a proneness to depression and despair. In reality he was a latter-day St Francis confronted with an animal holocaust that St Francis could not have envisaged in his worst nightmare. His struggle to save the animal world was eventually to cost him his health, his happiness, and his marriage.

In 1976 Durrell separated from his first wife. The next year, while on one of his many lecture tours to the USA, he met Lee Wilson McGeorge (b. 1949), a zoology graduate working on a PhD at Duke University, North Carolina. After their marriage in 1979 they travelled the world together, collecting endangered animals for Jersey Zoo, monitoring overseas conservation projects, jointly and singly authoring books (notably *The Amateur Naturalist*, 1982, with sales of several million worldwide), and taking part in many major documentary television series broadcast on networks around the world. In all Durrell wrote and presented more than 175 television documentaries, and wrote forty-two books, published in more than thirty countries. He died in Jersey on 30 January 1995 from complications following a liver transplant. He was survived by his second wife (there were no children of either marriage), who took over the reins as honorary director of the Jersey Wildlife Preservation Trust, later renamed the Durrell Wildlife Conservation Trust in honour of its founder, to help carry on the task of animal conservation at the cutting edge in the twenty-first century.

DOUGLAS BOTTING

Sources D. Botting, *Gerald Durell* (1999) · Jersey Zoo, Gerald Durell Archives · *The Times* (31 Jan 1995) · *The Independent* (31 Jan 1995) · *WWW*, 1991–5
Archives Jersey Zoo, Jersey | CUL, corresp. with Sir Peter Markham Scott · Rice University, Houston, Texas, Woodson Research Center, Julian S. Huxley MSS | FILM BFI NFTVA, 'Gerald Durrell: the man who built the ark', BBC2, 8 Sept 1996 · BFI NFTVA, documentary footage | SOUND BL NSA, oral history interview · BL NSA, performance recordings · BL NSA, recorded lecture (Royal Geographic Society)
Likenesses W. Suschitzky, photograph, 1960, NPG [*see illus.*] · photograph, repro. in *The Times* · photograph, repro. in *The Independent* · photographs, Hult. Arch. · statue, Jersey Zoo

Durrell, Lawrence George

Durrell, Lawrence George (1912–1990), novelist and poet, was born on 27 February 1912 at Jullundur in the Punjab, India, the first of the five children of Lawrence Samuel Durrell (1884–1928), a civil engineer then with the railway system, and his wife, Louisa Florence Dixie (1884–1964), from a family associated with the Thomason College of Civil Engineering at Roorkee. Neither parent had seen England, and many of Durrell's forebears, over half from England, but some protestant Irish on his mother's side, had gone to India before the revolt of 1857–9 as privates or non-commissioned officers in the British army. Durrell emphasized how rooted in India his ancestors were, speaking the local languages and studying Buddhism. Durrell's father became quite successful: his construction firm, Durrell & Co., built much of the Tata iron and steel enterprise in Jamshedpur. This heritage was vital in forming Durrell's outlook: a cosmopolitan, he called himself 'a pure Anglo-Irish-Indian ASH BLOND' (*Durrell–Miller Letters*, 50), but could never identify fully with England, Ireland, or even India.

Lawrence George Durrell (1912–1990), by Mark Gerson, 1968

Early years, education, and first writings During Durrell's early life the family followed his father to various postings. The next child born after Lawrence died in infancy, but two brothers and a sister survived to adulthood. His youngest sibling was Gerald Malcolm *Durrell (1925–1995), who became a noted zoologist and author. After some tutoring by his Irish governess in Kurseong, Durrell spent the years 1921–2 in the primary school at St Joseph's College in Darjeeling, within sight of the Himalayas, and the vast panorama of snowy peaks remained his lifelong metaphor for unattainable beauty. Although baptized at the chapel of St Luke in the Jullundur cantonment, late in his life Durrell considered himself a Buddhist.

In 1923 Durrell sailed with his family for England, where he was left by his parents to continue his schooling for two years at St Olave's and St Saviour's in Southwark and then for one year and a term at St Edmund's College in Canterbury. Durrell dropped out of St Edmund's in December 1927, having completed only the fourth form. He then studied with an army crammer at Cambridge, but did not join the army, and claimed—no corroborating evidence exists—to have repeatedly failed university entrance examinations. On the death of his father, aged forty-three, at Dalhousie in April 1928, his mother moved to England, living successively in south London and Bournemouth. Durrell demanded his patrimony, and on £150 a year he embarked at about the age of eighteen on a bohemian existence in London, convinced that he would become a poet and spending much of his time in the British Museum reading room, while attempting to supplement his income through various stratagems: as estate agent, jazz pianist, and, with the Slade art student Nancy Isobel Myers (1912–1983), studio photographer. Durrell's first book of poems, *Quaint Fragment*, was printed on a friend's hand press in 1931. A year spent in relative seclusion in a Sussex cottage produced Durrell's first work of fiction, *Pied Piper of Lovers*, written as an entry for a first novel prize offered by Cassell. Durrell did not win, but Cassell published his novel, paying an advance of £50. Early in March 1935, having married Nancy Myers on 22 January, the 5 foot 2 Durrell and his tall, slender bride set off for the island of Corfu, where they were soon joined by his mother and siblings. In 1956 Gerald Durrell published his hilarious version of their Corfu adventures, *My Family and other Animals*.

Durrell, who had hated 'Pudding Island', loved Corfu. Inspired by the liberating Greek ambience and an exotic acquaintanceship, he wrote two novels in three years: *Panic Spring* (1937, published under the pseudonym Charles Norden) and *The Black Book* (1938); drafted many of the poems that would form his first collection, *A Private Country*; and initiated a correspondence with Henry Miller that continued until Miller's death in 1980. *The Black Book*, inspired by Miller's *Tropic of Cancer*, but also the novel in which Durrell claimed that he 'first heard the sound of [his] own voice' (preface, *The Black Book*, 1960, 13), attacked both the stultifying 'English death' and Lawrence's *Lady Chatterley's Lover*. T. S. Eliot wrote that the book was 'the first piece of work by a new English writer to give me any hope for the future of prose fiction', praising especially the 'sense of pattern and of organisation of moods' (flyleaf copy, *The Black Book*, 1938). However, he judged that it could not be published unexpurgated in England, so Durrell gave it to the Obelisk Press in Paris. In the modernist *Black Book* Durrell displayed the narrative complexity and linguistic virtuosity that characterized his later novels: the multiple points of view, achieved through diary fragments, letters, and dialogue reported by characters turned narrators; an Elizabethan fascination with the language of trades and sciences; and the tendency to describe scenes in lavish painterly terms.

In 1941 Durrell, Nancy, and their infant daughter, Penelope, fled to Egypt ahead of the German invasion. While in Egypt during the war he composed *Prospero's Cell*, a lyrical account of the life he had lived on Corfu, as well as a teasing suggestion that the island might have been the setting for Shakespeare's *Tempest*. Durrell's book is not travel literature but a 'foreign residence' account, combining a first-person narration and vividly presented characters and events with a palimpsest of history, botany, and folkways. In 1947 he drafted another book in this genre about Rhodes: *Reflections on a Marine Venus*, eventually published in 1953.

Durrell's first volume of poetry to be published by a major press, *A Private Country*, appeared in 1943 with Faber and Faber, where Eliot was his editor. Durrell's best poetry captures the spirit of Greek places:

And the Greek sea's curly head
Keep its calms like tears unshed.
('Bitter Lemons', *Collected Poems*, 1974)

He had a fine ear for lyrical utterance, and there is a flower-like perfection to his best short poems:

… go
mimic your mother's lovely face
('Cradle Song', *Collected Poems*, 1974)

he admonishes Sappho, his daughter with his second wife, Eve. His best sustained sequence is 'Cities, Plains and People' (1946), in which his theme is his evolution as an artist.

The Alexandria Quartet Durrell still thought of himself as a poet forced to write novels to support himself, but in 1945 he sketched out for Eliot his master plan for fiction. He would treat, sequentially, the *agon* (struggle), *pathos* (suffering), and *anagnorisis* (recognition). These three main thrusts would present dislocation, uniting, and acceptance and death. In *The Black Book* Durrell had already described the necessary dislocation of the artist from suffocating England. 'The Book of the Dead'—Durrell's working title for *The Alexandria Quartet*—would show the birth of the artist through suffering and love. The final segment he called provisionally 'The Book of Time', and, true to his plan, *The Revolt of Aphrodite* and *The Avignon Quintet* would purport to vanquish time and death. Durrell's sequence, loosely linked by his major themes, love, art, and death, by geography (the Mediterranean world), and by a few recurring characters, eventually comprised twelve volumes in all and took him almost fifty years to complete. Durrell considered his first two novels outside his master plan, and he placed in the potboiler category two later works of fiction, *The Dark Labyrinth* and *White Eagles over Serbia*.

In Egypt Durrell found employment as public information officer attached to the British embassy, first in Cairo and, from 1942, in Alexandria. His familiarity with a broad spectrum of the polyglot society of the Egyptian cities provided him with material for his *Quartet*. Divorce from Nancy, marriage on 17 February 1947 to the Alexandrian Yvette (Eve) Cohen (*b.* 1918), various press officer jobs in Rhodes, Yugoslavia, and Cyprus, interrupted by a year as director of the British council in Córdoba, Argentina—where he wrote the monograph *A Key to Modern Poetry*—postponed Durrell's start on the *Quartet* until 1955. He completed *Justine*, the first volume of the *Quartet*, on Cyprus in 1956, after his separation from Eve, and wrote the remaining three volumes in Languedoc, where he lived near Nîmes and in Sommières.

The concept in the *Quartet* that perceived truth is relative, dependent on the situation and condition of the observer, was derived by Durrell from Einstein's theory of relativity. Thus, the naïve L. G. Darley, bearer of Durrell's initials and principal narrator of *Justine*, tells the story of Darley's love affair with Justine as he perceived it. In the next volume, *Balthazar*, the eponymous commentator reveals that Justine had really loved another and was using Darley as a decoy. *Mountolive*, the third volume, is a straight third-person narrative in which Justine is shown to have been engaged with her husband in a political conspiracy for which her affairs provided cover. Each of the three versions is 'true' within its own parameters. The final volume, *Clea*, moves the story forward in time and shows the emergence of Darley as an artist, thanks to the lessons in love and narrative 'truth' that he has been given.

The four novels emerged in rapid succession from 1957 to 1960 and elicited wildly divergent but generally favourable reviews, praising or attacking Durrell's luxuriant prose, his highly romantic recreation of Alexandria, and his self-proclaimed use of Einstein. Only with the *Quartet* sales did Durrell begin to live from his writing, but he never became rich. Despite an excellent cast that included Anouk Aimee, Dirk Bogarde, and Michael York, the film based on the *Quartet*, known as *Justine* (1969), was mediocre.

During 1957 Durrell published not only *Justine*, but also *Bitter Lemons*, an analysis of the tragedy of modern Cyprus and his best work in the foreign residence genre; *Esprit de corps*, a series of Wodehousian sketches based on Durrell's days on 'Embassy Row'; and *White Eagles over Serbia*, a thriller directed towards juvenile readers. *Bitter Lemons* gained Durrell a Duff Cooper award.

Durrell's fascination with the Elizabethans led to three verse dramas, *Sappho* (1950), *An Irish Faustus* (1963), and *Acte* (1964), which, despite excellent productions in Hamburg and Edinburgh, did not establish the author's stage reputation: his plays are more notable for the quality of their verse than for dramatic verve.

Later novels and last years Durrell's life was darkened by the death on 1 January 1967 of Claude-Marie Forde, *née* Vincendon (*c*.1926–1967), like Eve an Alexandrian, a secretary and novelist whom he had married on 27 March 1961, and he took up novels again. *The Revolt of Aphrodite* was orginally published as two volumes, *Tunc* (1968) and *Nunquam* (1970), titles derived from Petronius's phrase *aut tunc, aut nunquam* ('it was either then or never'). Ostensibly a comic novel, *Revolt* is Elizabethan and Jacobean in its careful numerological structure and its mix of comic and tragic elements—contrasting with various farcical subplots, the scientist-narrator's son is killed by an elaborate booby trap intended by his father for the head of Merlin's, the multinational firm at the centre of the story. Durrell proved an accurate prophet of the development of the personal computer and of the modern mega-corporations that can exceed nations in wealth and power, but *Revolt* offended many readers who had expected a rewrite of the romantic *Quartet*.

A similar fate befell *The Avignon Quintet*. Eastern in philosophy, the *Quintet* demonstrates the breakdown of the 'discrete ego', and characters exchange traits and are reincarnated. More overtly postmodern than the *Quartet*, the *Quintet* further erodes the distinction between reality and fiction. Characters talk back to their creators, as a pattern of narrators within narrations unfolds. Durrell called his structure a *gigogne*, like the nesting boxes of a Chinese puzzle. A system of fives provides the basic structure: the *quincunx* pattern employed in medieval arboretums, with trees planted like the dots on a five in dominoes, and the five *skandas* of Buddhism—form, sensation, perception, conformation, consciousness. *Monsieur*, the first volume, turns out to be the centre dot on the domino, the 'reality prime' or fiction derived from the 'reality' presented in the other four novels of the *Quintet*. Fives pervade the *Quintet*, as Durrell attacked the 'five M's' that he believed were destroying western society: monotheism, Messianism, monogamy, materialism, *merde*—'The gold bar is the apotheosis of the human turd', he wrote in *Monsieur* (p. 142). Fascinated by the Gnostics, and a convinced Manichean, Durrell saw in 'divine entropy' the running down

of the universe, against which the artist must valiantly throw the creative act, both in love-making and in literature.

Durrell's later years were trouble-filled. His marriage to his fourth wife, Ghislaine de Boysson, a model and actress whom he married in 1973, ended in divorce in 1978; and his daughter Sappho committed suicide in 1985. Although he talked about a major novel to follow the *Quintet*, Durrell was barely able to complete *Caesar's Vast Ghost*, his nonfiction tribute to his beloved Languedoc and to Provence. His relationship with his final companion, Françoise Kestsman, a translator and restaurateur, was turbulent; his laboured breathing was diagnosed as due to emphysema; and he tried with varying degrees of success to stave off his heavy drinking with yoga and acupuncture. He died on 7 November 1990 of a cerebral haemorrhage at his home in Sommières, France, and was buried on 8 November at La Chapelle St Julien, Sommières. After Durrell's death, Sappho's literary executor accused the author of an incestuous relationship with his daughter, on the uncorroborated revelations of 'recalled memory' induced while Sappho was undergoing psychoanalysis. On the basis of present evidence, this accusation should be regarded as unfounded.

The final verdict on Durrell's writing is still open. His readership peaked in the 1960s and declined with the negative reaction to his later fiction, falling further because, especially after his death, many of his titles went out of print. His foreign residence books have become accepted as classics, but he remains underrated as a poet. All this may change as the narrative and technical mastery of his later work becomes acknowledged. *Deus loci*, a Durrell newsletter, was founded in 1977, and it was succeeded by an annual Durrell journal of the same name. The creation of the International Lawrence Durrell Society in 1980 has led to an unbroken series of biennial conferences devoted to Durrell, and the growth in size of these meetings (ninety speakers appeared on the programme for the 2000 conference in Corfu), plus a burgeoning French society, Lawrence Durrell en Languedoc, demonstrate that he still has a considerable following. This scholarly and popular interest suggests that he may well achieve status not merely as an intriguing minor experimenter in fictional relativism, but as an important twentieth-century writer.

I. S. MacNiven

Sources I. S. MacNiven, *Lawrence Durrell: a biography* (1998) • R. Pine, *Lawrence Durrell: the mindscape* (1994) • *The Durrell–Miller letters, 1935–80*, ed. I. S. MacNiven (1988) • L. Durrell, *Spirit of place: letters and essays on travel*, ed. A. G. Thomas (1969) • L. Durrell, *A key to modern poetry* (1952) • *Literary lifelines: The Aldington–Durrell correspondence*, ed. I. S. MacNiven and H. T. Moore (1981) • A. G. Thomas and J. A. Brigham, *Lawrence Durrell: an illustrated checklist* (1983) [periodically updated by Brigham, G. Koger, and I. S. MacNiven in *Deus loci: the Lawrence Durrell Journal*] • I. S. MacNiven and C. Peirce, eds., 'Lawrence Durrell, Parts I and II', *Twentieth Century Literature*, 33/3 (autumn 1987); 33/4 (winter 1987) • G. Bowker, *Through the dark labyrinth: a biography of Lawrence Durrell* (1996) • H. T. Moore, ed., *The world of Lawrence Durrell* (1962) • G. S. Fraser, *Lawrence Durrell: a study* (1968) • J. R. Raper and others, eds., *Lawrence Durrell: comprehending the whole* (1995) • M. H. Begnal, ed., *On miracle ground: essays on the fiction of Lawrence Durrell* (1990) • F. L. Kersnowski, *Into the labyrinth:*

essays on the art of Lawrence Durrell (1989) · A. W. Friedman, *Critical essays on Lawrence Durrell* (1987)

Archives Southern Illinois University, Carbondale · Université de Paris X, Nanterre, France, Bibliothèque Lawrence Durrell | BL, corresp. and MSS incl. MS of *Justine* · BL, letters to Gwyn Williams · Ransom HRC, letters and literary MSS · U. Cal., Los Angeles, literary MSS · University of British Columbia, corresp. and corrected proof of *Balthazar*

Likenesses E. Auerbach, group portrait, photograph, 1962, Hult. Arch. · H. Oloff de Wet, terracotta bust, 1962, Curtis Brown Ltd, London · D. Sim, double portrait, photograph, 1962 (with Henry Miller), Hult. Arch. · T. Disney, photograph, 1968, Hult. Arch. · M. Gerson, photograph, 1968, NPG [*see illus.*] · D. N. Smith, photograph, *c.*1980, Hult. Arch. · B. Robinson, oils, 1982, priv. coll. · A. Springs, photograph, 1984, NPG · C. Freire, photographs, priv. coll. · photographs, Faber & Faber archives, London

Durward, Alan (*d.* 1275), magnate, was the son of Thomas Hostiarius, or Durward. The family name derived from the honorific post of king's usher or doorward held from William the Lion's reign (1165–1214). The original name of the family was de Lundin, from Lundie in Angus. Alan Durward inherited substantial landed interests in the north from his father—they included the lordship of Lundie; a substantial tract of land in Mar based on the castle at Lumphanan, with possibly another at Coull; and land in Mearns, Cluny, and Aberdeenshire. By 1233 Alan was also lord of Urquhart on the western shore of Loch Ness, part of the royal rewards bestowed on the family because of Thomas Durward's role in the suppression of Guthred MacWilliam's rebellion in 1211. Durward's fierce political rivalry with the Comyns in the 1240s and 1250s stemmed from landed rivalry in the north, the Comyns also gaining reward after 1211 with the earldom of Buchan (*c.*1212) and the lordships of Badenoch and Lochaber (*c.*1229).

Durward sought an earldom to break into the forefront of Scottish politics and for a time, from about 1233, held the title earl of Atholl, after Thomas of Galloway. It is not known how he gained this title but it is possible that his right was based on either wardship of the heir or marriage to the heiress, Forueleth. But between 1237 and 1242 the earldom came under the control of the Comyn family through their kinsman Patrick of Atholl (*d.* 1242), son of Countess Isabella and Thomas of Galloway. Durward's claims to the earldom of Mar, deriving from Malcolm of Lundie's marriage to the daughter of Gilchrist, earl of Mar (*c.*1203–1211), was similarly thwarted by the Comyns when William, earl of Mar, of an alternative line of earls, married the daughter of William Comyn, earl of Buchan.

Durward's fortunes changed *c.*1244 when Alexander II, desiring to curb the power of two powerful and clearly defined baronial parties led by Walter Comyn, earl of Menteith (*d.* 1258), and Patrick, earl of Dunbar (*d.* 1248), turned to Durward, as a nobleman outside these groups, to be his chief adviser. Durward took the office of justiciar of Scotia which had been under Comyn control since about 1205. He was the first nobleman to swear on the Scottish king's soul that the terms of the treaty of 1244 with Henry III of England would be kept, and he further entrenched himself in the royal circle by marrying Alexander II's illegitimate daughter, Marjory. After Alexander

II died in 1249, leaving the young Alexander III a minor, Durward continued to head the government. Because of the instability of a minority period, Durward sought to formalize his position, unsuccessfully, by claiming the right to knight the young king before he was enthroned, thus following the precedent set in England in 1216 by William (I) Marshal.

It soon became apparent, between 1249 and 1251, that Durward did not carry enough authority over the Scottish nobility. He had not eclipsed Comyn leadership of this nobility, and an approach by the magnates and clergy to Henry III led to his being replaced by a Comyn-led government in 1251. The pro-Comyn Melrose chronicle accused Durward of seeking the pope's help to legitimize the daughter born to his wife, illegitimate half-sister of Alexander III, in order to strengthen the family's royal connections and make succession to the throne a possibility. Durward was forced into exile and received safe conduct to go to England in July 1252. The next few years demonstrated the strength of Durward's ambition. Like Walter Comyn, he realized the necessity of Henry III's support during the Scottish king's minority. Durward skilfully ingratiated himself with the English king by serving with him on the Gascony campaign in 1253–4 on behalf of the earl of Strathearn; for this he was given £50, commuted in 1257 for the castle and manor of Bolsover, which he held free from tallage until October 1274. More importantly for Durward's Scottish ambitions, he was regarded by 1255 as one of Henry III's 'beloved friends' and given full support in a successful counter-coup against the Comyn government. A new council, comprising fifteen opponents of the Comyns, was appointed for seven years, with Durward reclaiming the vital office of justiciar of Scotia. He then sought to strengthen his power in the north by renewing the family claim to the earldom of Mar—he challenged the legitimacy of the earl of Mar's father and grandfather. But Durward's lack of broad-based support in Scotland, especially within the church, was revealed by his failure both to gain the earldom of Mar and to prevent the consecration of Gamelin (*d.* 1271), chancellor under the Comyn government and their nominee to the see of St Andrews.

The use of strong-arm tactics against the Comyns by the new king's council led the Comyns to seize the young king and queen, as well as the offices of government, in 1257. Durward fled to England, where Henry III organized a safe retreat for him at Norham. Envoys of Henry III brokered a compromise settlement in 1258 with equal representation of Durward and Comyn supporters in a new council of ten. Alan Durward did not, however, hold major office after 1258, the post of justiciar of Scotia remaining firmly under Comyn control. He was still recognized as a leading political figure in Scotland in 1259 when, with the head of the Comyn party, he travelled to England to recover the document of 1255 agreeing to Alexander's minority continuing to 1262 under Henry III's tutelage. And in 1260 he was one of thirteen authorized to take Alexander III's child back to Scotland should the king die during the queen's confinement in England. Durward also appeared prominently in 1264 among the leaders of an expedition, ordered by the king, to the Western Isles. Yet he made infrequent appearance in the royal circle in Scotland in the 1260s, and seems to have faded altogether from the Scottish political scene after 1268. In his later years Durward received greater favours in England, where from 1260 to 1274 he was in regular receipt of gifts from the English king, including privileges in the royal forests and freedom from distraint for any debt.

As a leading player in the political crisis of Alexander III's minority, opinions on Alan Durward's role have varied dramatically. To the pro-Comyn Melrose chronicle, Durward was 'master builder of the whole mischief' (*Melrose Chronicle*, 114) while the anti-Comyn Walter Bower regarded him as 'a generous man extremely vigorous in arms and most faithful to king and kingdom' (Bower, 5.402). Historians have portrayed him as leader of the pro-English party in Scotland but in reality no party in Scotland could afford to oppose Henry III. Alan Durward was more reliant on Henry III to maintain his position in Scotland simply because his support was less broadly based than that of the Comyns. When in government, however, Durward did take an anti-English stance by pressing at the papal curia for Alexander III's being anointed at a coronation ceremony, and by trying to prevent taxes raised in Scotland from being used for Henry III's Sicilian schemes.

Alan Durward died in 1275 and was buried at Coupar Angus Abbey. He was religious patron to Coupar Angus, and also to Lindores and Arbroath abbeys and to the hospital of Kincardine O'Neill. Alan Durward's son, Thomas, witnessed one of his father's charters c.1256, but Durward was survived only by his three daughters, who shared his lands.

ALAN YOUNG

Sources D. E. R. Watt, 'The minority of Alexander III of Scotland', *TRHS*, 5th ser., 21 (1971), 1–23 · A. Young, 'Noble families and political factions in the reign of Alexander III', *Scotland in the reign of Alexander III, 1249–1286*, ed. N. H. Reid (1990), 1–30 · A. A. M. Duncan, *Scotland: the making of the kingdom* (1975), vol. 1 of *The Edinburgh history of Scotland*, ed. G. Donaldson (1965–75) · C. Innes, ed., *Registrum episcopatus Aberdonensis*, 2 vols., Spalding Club, 13–14 (1845) · D. E. Easson, ed., *Charters of the abbey of Coupar-Angus*, 2 vols., Scottish History Society, 3rd ser., 40–41 (1947) · J. Dowden, ed., *Chartulary of the abbey of Lindores*, Scottish History Society, 42 (1903) · *CDS*, vols. 1–5 · W. Bower, *Scotichronicon*, ed. D. E. R. Watt and others, new edn, 9 vols. (1987–98), vol. 5 · G. W. S. Barrow, ed., *Regesta regum Scottorum*, 2 (1971) · A. O. Anderson, ed. and trans., *Early sources of Scottish history, AD 500 to 1286*, 2 vols. (1922) · A. O. Anderson and M. O. Anderson, eds., *The chronicle of Melrose* (1936) · Chancery records · Scots peerage, vol. 5
Archives NA Scot.

Dury [née King], **Dorothy** (c.1613–1664), writer on education, was probably born at Bagot-Rath, Dublin, the daughter of Sir John *King (d. 1637), royal administrator in Ireland, and Catherine (d. 1617), daughter of Robert Drury, nephew of Sir William Drury, the lord deputy of Ireland. Dorothy was one of nine children, her elder brother Robert *King being the inheritor of their father's offices and principal estates at Boyle Castle. The brother to whom she was closest in age, Edward *King, was Milton's 'Lycidas'. Dorothy's educational background remains unclear. Dancing and singing was how she would describe it disparagingly, but she certainly somehow acquired the ability to

write fluent French and read Latin and Greek as well as an abiding interest in educational matters. In 1640 she was complimented by the talented female scholar Anna Maria von Schurman as the first learned lady to come out of England since Lady Jane Grey.

It was probably in the late 1620s that Dorothy married into the Anglo-Irish aristocracy. Through her husband, Arthur Moore (d. 1635), landowner and politician, fifth son of Garret *Moore, first Viscount Moore of Drogheda, Dorothy became an aunt to Katherine *Jones (née Boyle), Lady Ranelagh, and Margaret Clotworthy, the wife of Sir John Clotworthy. She and Moore had two sons, Charles and John. Moore was wealthy (his father had granted him 1000 acres of land at Drumbanagher in co. Armagh in 1609) and fond of drink. Following his death on 9 April 1635 Dorothy moved to London and lived with the natural philosopher and physician Gerard Boate and his wife Katherine in their house at Aldermanbury in 1641. Although she had an apparently ample portion from her former husband's Irish estates, it evaporated after the Irish uprising of that year. In 1650 her second husband complained that she was owed £400 per annum from 1641 onwards and, with the coming of the Cromwellian settlement in Ireland, she eventually gave her rights to her son John Moore. In March 1642 she subscribed £150 for shares in Irish land as an adventurer but in due course she sold these to Katherine Boate.

It was around this time that Dorothy first met the protestant eirenic divine, John *Dury (1596–1680), seeking his assistance in getting her two sons educated with the great Dutch scholar Voetius at Utrecht. It soon became a 'covenant of friendship' in which Dury wrote to her as his 'most sweet & louing freind', hoping that they would 'make each other perfect in the best thinges'. When Dury became chaplain to Princess Mary at The Hague in March 1642 she followed him there with her sons in August 1642. It had already been rumoured in the Netherlands as early as May 1642 that they had been secretly married, gossip that Dury sought to counteract as 'hurtfull to us both as yet; till wee be better knowen here and know how to live together if it should bee Gods will so to dispose matters'. Dorothy wrote to the Dutch envoy in London to scotch any scandal. For the next two years she followed Dury around the towns of the Netherlands, part of the entourage of the exiled queen of Bohemia (whose cause she championed), and was briefly canvassed for the post of governess to Charles I's children back in England in succession to Lady Vere. 'We need persons of hir spirit amongst the women kind which are with our princes' wrote Dury warmly. In The Hague by late autumn 1644, she had epileptic fits and Dury, who resigned his post as royal chaplain, went to look after her. They were married in late February 1645 and the couple returned to England.

Dorothy Dury's talents as a writer appear briefly in this period. In a now lost set of letters to the Dutch divine André Rivet she explored the question of the role of women in the church. In his surviving replies he obliged him to concede that since women had no role in the public ministry of the (protestant) churches, the opportunities for women to 'édifier le corps mystique de Christ' ('edify Christ's mystical body') were limited. She wrote a treatise to Lady Ranelagh on girls' education at about this same time and it is possible that her influence is to be detected in Dury's *The Reformed School* (1649). Their letters to Lady Ranelagh on the covenant of love in marriage were edited and published by their mutual friend Samuel Hartlib in 1645. It is probable that she was among those who met at Lady Ranelagh's residence in Pall Mall in 1645—the nearest equivalent in England to the Parisian aristocratic ladies' intellectual salons of this period.

With the arrival of the Durys' first child in 1649, a boy who died in childhood about 1656, Dorothy stayed in London while John continued his European perambulations. She was afflicted with illness, possibly allied to her pregnancies, and probably had to live on her own inheritance. It seems that she began to sell medical potions, either to support the family or because she was interested in chemical remedies. In 1654 she gave birth to their second child, Dora Katherina, and by 1658 her husband was considering pawning 'some things which are lesse usefull to us' (Turnbull, 287). Following the Restoration, John Dury left England in February 1661 but Dorothy and her daughter remained behind. Dorothy's death was reported in London in June 1664. John Dury died at Kassel, Germany, on 26 September 1680. Henry *Oldenburg, the first joint secretary of the Royal Society, was eventually entrusted with the responsibility for Dora Katherina's welfare. He married her on 13 August 1668. She brought to the marriage a small property in Kent (Wansunt Farm, near Charlton) and a fortune said to be worth (in capital terms) between £1500 and £2000.   M. GREENGRASS

Sources G. H. Turnbull, *Hartlib, Dury and Comenius: gleanings from Hartlib's papers* (1947) · J. Minton Batten, *John Dury advocate of Christian reunion* (1944) · *The correspondence of Henry Oldenburg*, ed. and trans. A. R. Hall and M. B. Hall, 13 vols. (1965–86), vols. 1–2, 6 · 'Madam, Although my former freedom', 1645, BL, E.288(14) · 'Madam, Ever since I had a resolution', 1645, BL, E.288(14*) · K. Bottigheimer, *English money and Irish land: the 'adventurers' in the Cromwellian settlement of Ireland* (1971) · *CSP Ire.*, 1633–47 · J. Dury, *The unchanged, constant and single-hearted peacemaker* (1650) · P. Dibon, ed., *Inventaire de la correspondance d'André Rivet, 1595–1650* (1971) · *The diary and correspondence of Dr John Worthington*, ed. J. Crossley, 1, Chetham Society, 13 (1847), 194 · University of Sheffield, Hartlib papers, 2/5/1A–2B; 2/9/13A–B; 2/10/3A–5; 2/10/42A–B; 3/2/76A–B; 9/11/18B; 21/4A–5; 26/33/4A; 29/5/104
Archives University of Sheffield, Hartlib papers [available in M. Greengrass and M. P. Leslie, *Samuel Hartlib: the complete edition* (1995)]
Wealth at death £1500–£2000; £400 p.a.?: Oldenburg, *Correspondence*, 5.xxiv, xxvi; 6.xxvii; Worthington, *Diary and correspondence*, 194

Dury, Ian Robins (1942–2000), popular singer, songwriter, and actor, was born on 12 May 1942 at 43 Weald Rise, Harrow Weald, Harrow, Middlesex, the only child of William George Dury (d. 1968) and Margaret Cuthbertson (Peggy) Dury, formerly Walker (d. 1995). At the time of his birth, his father—a working-class Londoner—was driving buses for London Transport. In contrast, Ian's mother was the middle-class daughter of a doctor and a housewife, and worked as a health visitor. Born during the blitz, Ian soon moved with his parents to his grandmother's home in Mevagissey, Cornwall. When peace came they moved to a village near Montreux, Switzerland, where his father worked as a chauffeur for the Western European Union. By 1946 his parents' social incompatibility had taken its toll on their marriage; Ian and his mother returned home and moved into a cottage owned by Ian's aunt Betty in Cranham in Essex. This matriarchal, somewhat feminist, household set the tone for his upbringing and shaped his character to lasting effect.

Ian Dury was five when he started at Upminster infants' school, and records at Upminster junior school show that he arrived there for the new term in September 1947. But a terrible twist of fate meant that Ian never attended this school. That summer, he and a friend had been taken by the other boy's mother to Southend-on-Sea for the day, where they swam in an outdoor pool. Within weeks Ian fell ill and was diagnosed with polio, then a scourge in England (between 1947 and 1958 it affected 58,000 people). The indiscriminate nature of the disease saved his friend from infection, but Ian's left side was paralysed and he lived with the scars all his life. As a result, in 1951 he was sent, for better or worse, to Chailey Heritage Craft School in Sussex, a school and hospital for children with a range of disabilities, and one with what would be considered half a century later an extremely tough regime. But Ian's mother, Peggy, was anxious for his educational as well as physical needs to be met, and began contacting schools. He was eventually enrolled at the Royal Grammar School in High Wycombe, Buckinghamshire, but it proved a disastrous choice. Its deep-seated desire for academic excellence and emphasis on traditional values alienated the young disabled boy and he rebelled. He did, however, discover rock and roll at that time, and American jazz musicians such as John Coltrane and Ornette Colman. In Upminster, Essex, where his mother and aunt were now living, he became involved in a skiffle group. He left grammar school with O levels in English language, English literature, and art, and the last became his ticket to a bohemian lifestyle and a new-found happiness. Walthamstow College of Art was a hotbed of talent as the 1960s began to swing, and there Ian rubbed shoulders with Vivian Stanshall, the eccentric genius behind the Bonzo Dog Doo-Dah Band, and the film-maker Peter Greenaway, as well as being taught by the acclaimed artist Peter Blake.

Dury continued to study art after he left Walthamstow, taking up a place at the Royal College of Art in London, where he met his first wife, Elizabeth (Betty) Rathmell (1942–1994), the daughter of two Welsh painters. They each graduated (upper second class) with the diploma of associate of the Royal College of Art in July 1966, settled in a flat near the college, and soon after marrying in 1967 had a daughter, Jemima. Dury started to pick up work as an art lecturer, including a spell at Canterbury College of Art, and socialized extensively with many of his students. The couple moved to Buckinghamshire, where a son, Baxter, was born, but by this time Ian's professional focus lay elsewhere. Along with some of his students and other musician friends, including pianist Russell Hardy, he had started his own group—the memorably named Kilburn and the High Roads. Initially the band made little impact and the personnel changed constantly, but this eccentric ensemble was eventually embraced by the 'pub rock' scene that took off in smoke-filled bars and pub back rooms around London in the early to mid-1970s. An album recorded for Raft, a subsidiary of the American label Warner, came to nothing when Raft was suddenly closed, but in November 1974 the coarse strains of Ian Dury were finally committed to vinyl when 'Rough Kids/Billy Bentley' was released as a single on the Dann label, a subsidiary of Pye. The Kilburns had a cultlike following, but their live reputation did not translate into sales; their album *Handsome*, issued in the following year, sold only about 3000 copies. But while pub rock provided a badly needed platform for bands outside the mainstream to play live, the independent record label Stiff—launched in the summer of 1976—was the perfect home for the maverick recording talents of Ian Dury. He kept company with Elvis Costello, among others, on the Live Stiffs tour of 1977, on which he was the unexpected success; he was a charismatic performer who, far from being daunted by his disability, used it as part of his stage act. During the tour his backing band, the Blockheads, were christened, and his début single 'Sex and Drugs and Rock 'n' Roll', co-written with Chaz Jankel, became a punk anthem. The song's title entered the language, but the record itself did not chart, and neither did the follow-up 'Sweet Gene Vincent', a tribute to the 1950s rocker who had captivated Dury as a child. But the overall impact of the accompanying album, *New Boots and Panties* (1977), was seismic and it inhabited the British album charts for more than ninety weeks.

In common with several acts of the era, Dury preferred singles not to appear on his albums and the following two were no exception. 'What a Waste', an early example of the songwriter's penchant for outlandish rhyme, became his first hit single, reaching number nine, while its successor ensured Ian Dury's place in pop history. 'Hit Me with your Rhythm Stick' mixed quirky, memorable lyrics with a jazz/funk beat and reached number one in January 1979, selling more than 1 million copies. His second album, *Do It Yourself*, was eagerly awaited, but despite extensive touring in the UK and mainland Europe, it was not the commercial success some had expected. Another unique-sounding single recorded during the expedition did strike a chord with the public, however, and maintained his high profile. 'Reasons to be Cheerful (Part 3)'—a fast-paced Cockney version of 'These are a Few of my Favourite Things', set to a dance beat—climbed to number three in August 1979.

Dury's regular songwriting partner, Chaz Jankel, left to pursue a solo career and took no part in the album *Laughter* (1980). He was replaced by guitarist Wilko Johnson, formerly of Doctor Feelgood, who played on the singles 'I Want to be Straight', which made it to number twenty-

two, and 'Sueperman's Big Sister', which peaked at number fifty-one. Having changed labels from Stiff to Polydor, Dury released the reggae-influenced album *Lord Upminster* (1981), which contained his most controversial single 'Spasticus Autisticus', a protest at the attitudes implicit in the United Nations' designation of 1981 as the year of the disabled. It was banned by Radio One and did not chart. Two years later he recorded the album *4,000 Weeks' Holiday* with a new group, the Music Students, and two singles, 'Really Glad you Came' and 'Very Personal'; all of these failed commercially, and he and Polydor parted company. By now he had begun to devote much of his time and creative energies to acting, having made his stage début in a high-speed *Hamlet* and having gone on to appear in the plays *Talk of the Devil* and *Road*. Following his 1984 appearance in the television film *Number One*, he went on to feature in numerous films, including Roman Polanski's *Pirates* (1986); *The Raggedy Rawney* (1989); *The Cook, the Thief, his Wife and her Lover* (1989); *Judge Dredd* (1995); and *The Crow: City of Angels* (1996). In collaboration with Blockheads keyboardist Mickey Gallagher he wrote a musical entitled *Apples*, which enjoyed a run at the Royal Court Theatre in 1989, and the pair also supplied the words and music for *The Joviall Crew* and *The Country Wife*, which were performed by the Royal Shakespeare Company. His television acting credits, meanwhile, included *Skallagrigg* (1994) and *King of the Ghetto* (1986). Ian was invited to fulfil a prestigious ambassadorial role with the United Nations Children's Fund in 1997, travelling to Zambia to take part in a polio immunization programme. The following year he joined up with the singer Robbie Williams on another vaccination mission in Sri Lanka, and was rewarded for his efforts when the United Nations Children's Fund endowed him with the title 'special representative'.

Dury's first marriage had effectively broken up after only a few years and the couple were divorced in 1985. In April 1998 he married again; his second wife was Sophy Jane Tilson, a sculptor, the daughter of the artist Joe Tilson. With her he had two children, Billy and Albert. He had found time to record new material and had been reunited with many of the Blockheads for *The Bus Driver's Prayer and other Stories* (1989). However, it was when the original line-up came together for *Mr Love Pants* (1998) that Dury received the widespread critical acclaim that had eluded him for so long. Despite being diagnosed with cancer in 1995, he continued to play in live shows. He died at his home in Fitzjohn's Avenue, Hampstead, London, on 27 March 2000. His funeral was held on 5 April at Golders Green crematorium, London. A tribute album, *Brand New Boots and Panties*, featuring—among others—Paul McCartney and Robbie Williams, was released in April 2001.   RICHARD BALLS

Sources R. Balls, *Sex and drugs and rock 'n' roll: the life of Ian Dury* (2000) · *The Guardian* (28 March 2000) · *The Independent* (28 March 2000) · *The Times* (28 March 2000) · *Daily Telegraph* (28 March 2000) · www.iandury.co.uk, Nov 2001

Dury, John (1596–1680), preacher and ecumenist, was born in Edinburgh, the fourth child of Robert *Durie (1555–1616), Church of Scotland minister, and his wife, Elizabeth (*née* Ramsey). Following his father's banishment from Scotland in 1606 he moved with his family to the Netherlands, where from 1609 Dury senior was minister to the English and Scottish presbyterians in Leiden.

Early life, 1596–1630 Dury enrolled at Leiden University on 3 August 1611 NS. In 1615 or 1616 he attended the Huguenot academy in Sedan, France, but returned to Leiden and stayed at the Walloon College there from September 1616 to about March 1621. Between 1621 and 1623 he was tutor to the son of the Dutch merchant Barthelemy Panhuysen and toured France with his charge. He is said to have attended Oxford University in 1624. He took his 'proponents examen' (qualifying him for Reformed ordination) at Leiden on 15 October 1624 NS and shortly thereafter became preacher with the clandestine Walloon Reformed church in Roman Catholic Cologne. Finding this church too doctrinaire for his tastes, and suffering a crisis of faith, he resigned in February 1626 and may have returned to Scotland, where his mother was by then again living. By 1627 at least he was in Elbing, Poland, as secretary to James Spens, English ambassador to Sweden, and by 1628 was minister to the English Company of Merchant Adventurers there. Here he made three of the most important contacts of his life: with the English ambassador, Thomas Roe, the Anglo-German intelligencer Samuel Hartlib, and the Moravian educationist Jan Amos Comenius. Roe was to be the first patron of what became for Dury a lifetime of itinerant negotiations in the cause of protestant reunion, while the latter two became Dury's principal allies in prosecuting a shared vision of universal reformation.

Efforts for church unity, 1630–1641 These new contacts did much to confirm Dury in a sense of personal mission to heal the rifts in Christianity, though his background and aptitudes in any case predisposed him to the cause. He had been brought up a religious refugee in Leiden, served a banned protestant community in Cologne, and lived close to the atrocities of the ostensibly religious Thirty Years War. He was, moreover, an instinctive diplomat, an indefatigable traveller, and a gifted linguist with a perfect command of Latin, Dutch, German, and French.

Although presented in many guises, Dury's two basic strategies for Christian reconciliation remained consistent throughout his life. One was the promotion of 'practical divinity', that is, an ethical rather than a doctrinal approach to Christianity, eschewing, as he later described it, the 'gibberidge of Scholastical Divinity' (J. Dury, *Israel's Call to March out of Babylon*, 1646, 48). The other was the establishment of a mutually accepted list of 'fundamental' doctrines on which all sides must agree, clearly distinguished from 'incidentals' on which they might agree to differ. He also set great store by education as a means to inculcate from infancy piety and tolerance, and wrote several works on the subject.

The Merchant Adventurers' operations at Elbing having closed down, Dury moved to England in June or July 1630 with a recommendation from Roe. He tried to interest both church and state in his eirenic proposals but met with a cool response, especially from William Laud, then bishop of London, though some more Calvinistically inclined episcopalians such as Joseph Hall, John Davenant, and William Bedell encouraged him. In July 1631, with funding from Roe, he embarked on a tour of Germany and Poland, gaining audiences with political and ecclesiastical leaders, especially those of Sweden (then occupying large parts of the former two lands). He later claimed to have secured the warm approval of Sweden's King Gustavus Adolphus, but Gustavus was killed in battle in 1632 and Dury met with less encouragement from Chancellor Oxenstierna, his successor as acting head of state. In April 1633 Dury attended the Heilbronn convention of protestant estates. His two-year journey yielded a number of rather noncommittal acknowledgements of his proposals for more meetings and closer co-operation, but no endorsement from Oxenstierna and no more concrete results.

In November 1633 Dury returned to England and tried again to woo Laud, now archbishop of Canterbury, who expressed polite interest to Dury's and Roe's faces but wrote to Robert Anstruther, English representative at the Frankfurt convention of 1634, forbidding him to express official sanction for their schemes. In the vain hope of calming Laudian doubts about his orthodoxy, and of earning a living, Dury was reordained, as a Church of England minister, on 24 February 1634. Laud had promised him a non-residential living in Devon at £120 per annum if he did this, but to the archbishop's alleged surprise that living turned out to be already occupied. (The following year Dury was given the much more modest living of Saxby in Lincolnshire, but he never occupied it, appointing a curate as stand-in and eventually resigning in 1644.)

Despite a chronic lack of funds, Dury attended the Frankfurt convention in September 1634, and then spent some months in the Netherlands before returning to England in February 1635. That July he began a round of negotiations throughout northern Europe which kept him abroad for six years, mainly in the Netherlands until May 1636, Sweden until July 1638, and then northern Germany. He lived mostly on piecemeal (but not inconsiderable) donations supplied or raised by Roe and Hartlib. Roe was in Hamburg as ambassador from 1638 and employed Dury irregularly on state business there, but Dury constantly complained of being distracted by such mundane affairs from his religious mission.

England and the Netherlands, 1641–1649 The reconvening of the English parliament in November 1640 seemed to Hartlib a providential sign that the moment had come to realize his dreams in England, and he sent urgent summonses to both Dury and Comenius to join him there. Dury had done so by March 1641, and after a short visit to the Netherlands returned in September, in which month Comenius also arrived. They presented parliament with a petition, *Englands Thankfulnesse* (1642), probably co-written by Hartlib and Dury, which set out in decidedly millenarian tones three main strategies for founding a New Jerusalem in England. First was a complete overhaul of the education system to imbue piety and exclude doctrinal squabbling, and second the promotion of protestant unity throughout Europe: Comenius and Dury were proposed by name as the ideal men to organize these missions. The third part of the plan was the encouragement of Christian understanding of Judaism through the foundation of a college of Jewish studies, in the interests of encouraging the Jews to convert. Similar ideas, with particular emphasis on educational reform, are set out under Dury's own name in *A Motion Tending to the Publick Good* (1642). Hartlib had many allies in parliament sympathetic to these schemes, such as John Pym and Cheney Culpeper. However, the country's political upheavals proved discouraging, and in May 1642 Dury took up an appointment at The Hague as chaplain to the nine-year-old Princess Mary, Charles I's daughter, who had just been married to William of Orange.

In 1643 Dury was invited to sit on the Westminster assembly of divines, which was supposed to settle the nation's religious differences, but agreed to stay in the service of the Dutch court until a replacement could be found. In May 1644, however, he was allowed to accept the post of minister to the English Merchant Adventurers in Rotterdam, where even by his own account (*A Declaration of John Durie*, 1660, 3–7) his attempts to steer a middle course between the 'puritan' and 'Anglican' factions in the congregation made him thoroughly unpopular with both.

In February 1645 he married his long-standing friend Dorothy Moore (*née* King) (*c.*1613–1664) [*see* Dury, Dorothy]. This seemed an advantageous match for him both socially and financially, but Dorothy's estates were in Ireland and the unrest there made it difficult to obtain any rents from them. In August 1645 Dury resigned from Rotterdam and took his place on the Westminster assembly, of which he became an active member, though serving also as minister at the cathedral church in Winchester. From 1647 to 1649 he was also appointed tutor to the younger royal children (James, Elizabeth, and Henry), who were under the guardianship of the earl of Northumberland. From 1645 Dury was Hartlib's most active second in elaborating and promoting plans for an 'Office of Address', or state-sponsored institution for the advancement and dissemination of learning.

This comparatively settled period saw the production of several of Dury's most important writings. A sermon preached to parliament, *Israel's Call to March out of Babylon* (1646), is effectively another petition for state support and funding for his eirenic mission, which he advertised again in *Considerations Tending to the Happy Accomplishment of Englands Reformation* (1647) and *A Seasonable Discourse* (1649). In *A Peace-Maker without Partialitie and Hypocrisie* (1648) and *The Unchanged, Constant and Single-Hearted Peace-Maker* (1650), he defended his strategies against a growing number of critics. He also wrote *The Reformed School* (1649?), the fullest exposition of his educational ideas, and *The Reformed Librarie-Keeper* (1650): these two are arguably his most interesting and original works.

Commonwealth service, 1649–1660 Despite so many associations with the royal household, Dury promptly endeared himself to the new regime with *Considerations Concerning the Present Engagement* (1649), in which he urged all citizens to sign the oath of allegiance required by the republican government. This change of stance earned him the undying hatred of presbyterians and royalists and embroiled him in a number of polemical exchanges, but helped secure him the post of deputy keeper (under Bulstrode Whitelocke) of what had been the king's library at St James's Palace. He held this post from 1650 to 1660, but, although he did catalogue the collection, his duties were nominal. In 1652 he spent three months accompanying a diplomatic mission to Sweden, and from 1654 to 1657 was continuously abroad, furnished with parliamentary funding and personal recommendations from Cromwell, visiting Switzerland, Germany, and the Netherlands. His wife, who was pregnant when he left, remained in England. His own accounts of these journeys, *A Summarie Account of ... J.D's Former and Latter Negotiation* (1657) and *The Effect of Master Dury's Negotiations* (1657), dwell on the favourable response he claimed was received by his proposals for religious negotiation and reconciliation, and expressly disavow any political role. Parliament's main interest, however, was undoubtedly in his detailed reports of state affairs in the countries he visited.

After Dury's return to England in February 1657, the mounting crises preoccupying parliament led to a steady decline of official interest in his religious proposals, especially after Oliver Cromwell's death in 1658. Upon the restoration of the monarchy he attempted in *A Declaration of John Durie* (1660) to persuade the new regime that he had always remained a royalist at heart but had been forced in the interests of England and protestantism to move with the times. This was a vain hope. He lost his librarianship and his petitions for renewed sanction and funding went unanswered.

Exile and death In February 1661, leaving his family behind and his debts unpaid, Dury left England for good (though initially hoping to return if the political climate changed again). By this time his son, born in 1649, had died. When his wife also died, in 1664, his daughter Dora Katherine (1654–1677) entered the household of Henry *Oldenburg, whom she married in London on 13 August 1668, with her father's consent. Dury moved first to the Netherlands and then to Germany and Switzerland, attending more colloquies and engaging in more negotiations, but to less effect than ever now that he was shorn of official backing. In 1663, however, he was offered accommodation and financial support by Landgravine Hedwig-Sophie of Hesse-Cassel. From this date on Kassel was his base, though he toured northern Europe tirelessly for another eleven years. That he continued to be admitted to a number of protestant colloquies probably reflects respect for his new patroness rather than any real interest. A visit to Berlin in 1668 ended with his being ordered out of the state of Brandenburg by Elector Frederick William. After 1674 he remained in Kassel and devoted himself to writing. In his last works, such as *Brevis disquisitionis de articulis veri Christianismi* (1672), he pared down his proposed list of 'fundamental' doctrines to the ten commandments, the Lord's prayer, and the apostles' creed, and envisaged a reconciliation of the Roman Catholic as well as the protestant churches.

Dury was a prolific (if very verbose and ponderous) writer. Most of his works either set out his plans for religious rapprochement or give detailed accounts—often defensive in tone—of his travels and negotiations to achieve it. He always consciously avoided explicit doctrinal commitment, and his later writings turn increasingly from a historical or political interpretation of biblical prophecies and injunctions to an internalized, pietistic understanding of them. Throughout his career as an ecumenist, however, his efforts were hampered by the mutual suspicions of the camps he sought to reconcile. To many in England and Scotland he seemed to shift allegiance with the political tide between Laudians, presbyterians, episcopalians, and Independents, while in mainland Europe he was suspected of crypto-Calvinism by Lutherans and of crypto-Lutheranism by Calvinists. Opinions still differ as to whether he was a naïve but genuine visionary or a calculating time-server. Perhaps he was something of both. He died at Kassel on 26 September 1680, three years after his daughter's death. Details of his estate and what became of it remain obscure, though in 1668 his daughter's wealth had been estimated by a friend, John Collins, at between £1500 and £2000.

JOHN T. YOUNG

Sources G. H. Turnbull, *Hartlib, Dury and Comenius: gleanings from Hartlib's papers* (1947) • J. M. Batten, *John Dury, advocate of Christian reunion* (1944) • *The Hartlib papers*, ed. J. Crawford and others, 2nd edn (2002) [CD-ROM] • E. G. E. van der Wall, *De mystieke chiliast Petrus Serrarius (1600–1669) en zijn wereld* (1987) • G. Westin, *Negotiations about church unity* (1932) • K. Brauer, *Die Unionstätigkeit John Duries unter dem Protektorat Cromwells* (1907) • *The correspondence of Henry Oldenburg*, ed. and trans. A. R. Hall and M. B. Hall, 1–2 (1965); 5–6 (1968–9) • G. H. M. Posthumus Meyjes, *Geschiedenis van het Waalse College te Leiden, 1606–1699* (1975) • Wood, *Ath. Oxon.: Fasti* (1815), 420–21 • A. Milton, '"The unchanged peacemaker"? John Dury and the politics of irenicism in England, 1628–1643', *Samuel Hartlib and universal reformation: studies in intellectual communication*, ed. M. Greengrass, M. Leslie, and T. Raylor (1994), 95–117 • C. Webster, *Samuel Hartlib and the advancement of learning* (1970) • T. Klähr, 'Johannes Duraeus: sein Leben und seine Schriften über die Erziehungslehre', *Monatshefte der Comenius-Gesellschaft*, 6 (1897), 191–203 • T. H. H. Rae, *John Dury and the royal road to piety* (1998)
Archives HLRO | BL, Add. MSS • BL, Hartlib MSS • BL, Lansdowne MSS • BL, Sloane MSS • Bodl. Oxf., corresp. and papers, Rawl. MS C.911 and Lat. MS th.c.8 • CUL, Add. MS 2658 • DWL, corresp. with Richard Baxter • Ständische Landesbibliothek, Kassel, Hass. MS • Staatsarchiv, Zürich, Dureana MS • Staatsarchiv, Geneva, Livre du Conseil • University of Sheffield, Hartlib MSS • Zentralbibliothek, Zürich, Thesaurus Hottingerianus vol. 29

Du Sautoy, Peter Francis

Du Sautoy, Peter Francis (1912–1995), publisher, was born at 29 Hagley Road, Halesowen, Worcestershire, on 19 February 1912, the son of Edward Frank Du Sautoy, mechanical engineer and brick manufacturer, and his wife, Mabel Emmeline Annie Howse. His father served with distinction in the First World War and became a colonel in the army. He was educated at Uppingham School and Wadham College, Oxford, where he was a senior classical scholar and took a first in Greats. His literary interests were not reflected in any way in his family background.

After a brief spell as a private tutor, and then as an assistant master at Newcastle under Lyme grammar school, he worked in the department of printed books at the British Museum with Angus Wilson in 1935, and then in the city of Oxford education department for three years. On 18 December 1937 he married Phyllis Mary (known as Mollie; b. 1910/11), daughter of Sir Francis Floud. They had two sons. He served with the RAF during the Second World War.

In 1946 Du Sautoy joined the publishers Faber and Faber; his aptitude for administration quickly led to his becoming general manager of the company. The founders and directors of the firm—Geoffrey Faber, Richard de la Mare, and T. S. Eliot, all literary figures and writers in their own right—devolved much of the responsibility for running the business onto him. He was promoted to the board later in the same year, and he took over the development of their activities in the United States, and the rights and contracts portfolios. Although he enjoyed the literary atmosphere of the firm and the meetings of the book committee, he also gave his time to other sides of the Faber list (which provided much of their profits), such as medicine and nursing, so that this shy and fastidious man sometimes found himself at nursing exhibitions, selling books on gynaecology to midwives. During his early years with Faber, he was reticent on policy matters, accepting the decisions of his eminent colleagues. He kept up a voluminous correspondence with authors, but did not try to write creatively himself, observing on occasion that a publisher had to be more of a politician than an artist. But from the beginning he involved himself in editorial work, taking a particular interest in the poetry list, and he succeeded Eliot as poetry editor. When he became vice-chairman of the firm in 1960, and chairman in 1971, he felt more free to decide the character of the house, and to introduce more variety into the catalogue. He expanded the juvenile list, and started Faber Music, which was run by a new generation of musical scholars, notably Donald Mitchell, who brought Benjamin Britten's music to the firm. Du Sautoy commented that the atmosphere of this new branch was akin to the excitement of the early days of Faber in literature.

Du Sautoy was trusted by both writers and publishers, and faithfully carried out his instructions where he was given posthumous responsibility. He destroyed T. S. Eliot's private correspondence after the poet's death, as he had been asked to do, to the great chagrin of Eliot's biographers. He also administered the estates of Ezra Pound and James Joyce, and was involved in textual controversies over the latter. A strong supporter of the net book agreement, which for most of the twentieth century protected publishers and booksellers from competition, thereby ensuring a rich literary culture and enabling slower-selling books to remain longer in print, he gave evidence in 1962 before the restrictive practices court, and was active in many book-trade causes. On behalf of the Publishers' Association he travelled with many delegations to other countries. For these activities he received the OBE in 1964 and the CBE in 1971.

Du Sautoy retired from active participation in the firm in 1975, although he remained chairman until 1977. He was sometimes asked to arbitrate in disputes that arose among other publishers who did not want to go to law. He was eminently fair and imaginative in such matters, and proved that he would have made an excellent judge. He retired to Aldeburgh in Suffolk where he became an active member of the Aldeburgh Festival committee, which enabled him to indulge his taste for music, and brought his talent for decision making once again into play. He chaired conferences and lectures there, and derived great pleasure from the many activities of the festival, which went through a difficult period after Britten's death in 1976: Du Sautoy's firm presence on the board was a major, but under-appreciated, factor in the festival's survival. He also played a part in literary events in Suffolk, and became president of the Ipswich and Suffolk Book League. He died at his home, 31 Lee Road, Aldeburgh, on 17 July 1995, survived by his wife. He left an extensive correspondence and a number of penetrating essays, and a reputation as one of the last of the gentlemen publishers.   JOHN CALDER

Sources *The Independent* (19 July 1995) · *The Times* (20 July 1995) · *WWW, 1991–5* · personal knowledge (2004) · private information (2004) · b. cert. · d. cert. · *CGPLA Eng. & Wales* (1995)
Archives priv. coll. | Bodl. RH, corresp. with Margery Perham · NL Wales, letters to George Ewart Evans
Likenesses M. Gerson, photograph, 1977, repro. in *The Independent* · photograph, repro. in *The Times*
Wealth at death £172,977: probate, 1995, *CGPLA Eng. & Wales*

Duse, Eleonora Giulia Amalia (1858–1924), actress, was born on 3 October 1858 at the Albergo Cannon d'Oro in Vigevano, Lombardy, northern Italy, the daughter of Vincenzo Alessandro Duse (1820–1892), an actor, and his wife, Angelica Cappelletto (*d.* 1875), an actress. Her grandfather Luigi Duse (1792–1854) had been one of the best-known actors of his day, and Eleonora was to become Italy's greatest actress and an international star. From birth she was destined to the standard fate of a *figlia d'arte*—to join her parents on stage and spend her life touring. Her name first appeared on a playbill in 1863 at the Nobile Teatro di Zara, in what is now Zadar in Croatia, playing the part of Cosette in a stage version of Victor Hugo's *Les misérables*. By the age of fourteen, in 1872, she was billed as the company's leading lady, and in the same year she played Juliet in Verona. In the novel *Il fuoco*, which Gabriele D'Annunzio (1863–1938) based on his seven-year affair with Duse, there is a graphic account of the emotional impact of the Verona performance on Duse's life as an actress.

Duse's early years were spent in an atmosphere of financial insecurity and grindingly hard work. As the daughter of one of the founders of the company, she was at least guaranteed leading roles, but the state of the Italian theatre in the mid-nineteenth century was not a healthy one. As the country moved gradually towards political unification, through decades of unrest and civil strife, the problems of the small-scale touring theatre companies increased. There was no room for innovation, little rehearsal time and a huge range of parts to learn. In the

Eleonora Giulia Amalia Duse (1858–1924), by John Singer Sargent, *c.*1893

1850s the leading actress of the age, Adelaide Ristori, whom Duse was to regard as a mentor, set a precedent of touring abroad, demonstrating that the best way for an Italian company to survive was to perform outside Italy. Duse was to follow that precedent, and once she became an established figure in Italy she began the international tours that ended only with her death.

In 1875 Duse's mother died. The company disintegrated, and Duse and her father joined a series of other small companies: the Brunetti–Pezzana troupe for the 1875–6 season, the Dondini–Drago company in 1877, and finally, in 1878, the Ciotti–Belli–Blanes company. After arriving in Naples in 1878, Duse was helped by the great actress Giacinta Pezzana, and had her first success, as Teresa Raquin, in the play of the same name in 1879. In this role she established herself as an actress specializing in the portrayal of psychological realism. Throughout her career she was to choose roles that demanded great internal conflict, which led Ristori to comment that she epitomized modern womanhood, with 'all her complaints of hysteria, anaemia and nerve trouble' (*Le Gauloise*, 26 May 1897, trans. S. Bassnett). Her acting technique, developed early in her career, involved the internalization of characters and close identification with them (in contrast to the grand style of Ristori), with exaggerated gesture and declamatory vocal range. Luigi Rasi, who acted with Duse, comments on her tendency to use distorted facial expressions commonly associated with mental illness in many of her roles, and stresses the neurasthenic quality of her acting. Guido Noccioli, who also toured with Duse, records how carefully she prepared herself for each part. His account of her skilful use of make-up contradicts the myth perpetuated by many critics that she used no make-up at all and relied only on an inner energy. Duse may have been regarded as an almost mystical actress by the end of her career, but she was primarily a craftswoman who knew how to use her body and her voice to maximum effect in a theatre.

The turning point in Duse's career came with her portrayal of Santuzza in Giovanni Verga's *Cavalleria rusticana* in 1884. Her fame spread, and in 1887 she started her own touring company, the Compagnia Drammatica della Città di Roma. Her determination to find new roles for herself and simultaneously to expand the horizons of Italian theatre, which she perceived as too limited, had a major impact on her life. Her two principal love affairs were with Arrigo Boito, the writer, who created a number of roles for her, and with D'Annunzio. She sought out men who could guide her intellectually and professionally, though she does not seem to have been happy with any of them. Her first recorded love affair was with the Neapolitan journalist Martino Cafiero, whom she met in 1879. Despite the absence of any reliable documentation, apart from a few letters to Cafiero which appear to confirm the story, most biographers agree that Duse gave birth to a still-born child fathered by Cafiero. Her close friend the writer Matilde Serao gives an account of this episode, though Duse's only surviving child never confirmed it.

On 7 September 1881 Duse married a fellow actor, Tebaldo Checchi (1844–1918), and their daughter Enrichetta was born on 7 January 1882. Throughout her life Duse adored Enrichetta, though in her determination to provide her daughter with a respectable, stable upbringing she kept the child at a distance from her profession. The marriage with Checchi broke down, and in 1885 Duse began an affair with her leading man, Flavio Andò, during a tour of Latin America. Then in 1887 she began her long relationship with Boito, who wrote a version of *Antony and Cleopatra* for her in 1888. The play was not a success: Duse was better suited to modern roles than to Shakespeare.

In 1893 Duse visited England for the first time, and her season at the Lyric Theatre was a great success. Critics praised her naturalness, and even her less successful Cleopatra received good notices. She returned to London in 1894, and was invited to give a command performance of Goldoni's comedy *La locandiera* at Windsor Castle before Queen Victoria. Following her third visit to London in 1895, Bernard Shaw ranked her playing as greater than that of Sarah Bernhardt. She returned in 1903 and 1904, then for the last time in 1923, when Arthur Symons wrote his study of her acting technique and declared her to be the greatest actress in the world . Although her performance techniques were quite different from those of her English counterparts, and the Italian company structure was unfamiliar, the reception of Duse by London audiences was enthusiastic, and she was probably the most popular European actress of her day.

Duse's stormy relationship with D'Annunzio, which began in 1897 and lasted until 1904, has received disproportionate attention from many critics. D'Annunzio created several roles for her, including the title role of *Francesca da Rimini*, which was staged at enormous personal expense to Duse in Rome in 1901. When the two met, D'Annunzio was eager to establish his credentials as a playwright and Duse was searching for a wider repertory. Both shared a dream of a new, pure Italian theatre, and at the start of their affair it seemed as though they had each found their soulmate. But D'Annunzio's florid dramas were not as successful as he had anticipated, although Duse loyally kept some of them in repertory. D'Annunzio also systematically betrayed Duse, both sexually and professionally, and the end of the affair came after he gave the role of Mila in his biggest success, *La figlia di Iorio*, to Irma Gramatica in 1904.

After the collapse of her hopes of personal happiness and professional success with D'Annunzio, Duse collaborated with Lugné-Pöe in Paris in 1907, and then with Edward Gordon Craig, who designed her production of *Rosmersholm* in 1906. Her first portrayal of an Ibsen protagonist was as Nora in the first Italian production of *A Doll's House* in 1904. For the rest of her life she developed her passion for Ibsen, and among her greatest successes were the title role of *Hedda Gabler* (1898), Ellida Wangel in *The Lady from the Sea* (1907), and Mrs Alving in *Ghosts* (1922). She retired from the theatre abruptly in 1909, following her portrayal of Ellida Wangel, but returned to the stage in the same role in 1921, at the age of sixty-three.

Duse's reasons for leaving the theatre remain unclear; her daughter Enrichetta married in 1909 and moved to England. During her retirement, Duse kept well away from the theatre, though she made her only film, *Cenere* ('Ashes'), and established a library for actresses in Rome in 1914. When her savings ran out, she returned to the stage, despite poor health, and resumed a heavy touring schedule. Her foreign tours had taken her across Europe on numerous occasions, to North and South America, Egypt, and Russia. She toured Italy in 1921 and 1922, though suffering occasional bouts of bronchial pneumonia, then played in London and in Vienna in 1923. In October 1923 she sailed for the United States. After performances in New York, Boston, Baltimore, and Chicago, she agreed to continue, and travelled to New Orleans, Havana, San Francisco, Detroit, and finally Pittsburgh, where she gave her last performance on 5 April 1924. She died of pneumonia in her room at the Hotel Schenley, Pittsburgh, on Easter Monday, 21 April 1924. Her body was transported to New York, where a requiem mass was held, then taken back to Italy. She was buried in the cemetery of Asolo on 12 May following a state funeral.   SUSAN BASSNETT

Sources P. Nardi, ed., *Carteggio D'Annunzio–Duse* (1975) • P. Radice, ed., *Eleonora Duse–Arrigo Boito: lettere d'amore* (1979) • G. Pontiero, *Eleonora Duse: in life and art* (1986) • C. Molinari, *L'attrice divina: Eleonora Duse nel teatro italiano fra i due secoli* (1985) • L. Rasi, *La Duse*, ed. M. Schino (1986) • W. Weaver, *Duse: a biography* (1984) • O. Signorelli, *Eleonora Duse* (1955) • G. Pontiero, *Duse on tour: Guido Noccioli's diaries, 1906–8* (1984) • S. Bassnett, 'Eleonora Duse', in J. Stokes, M. Booth, and S. Bassnett, *Bernhardt, Terry, Duse: the* *actress in her time* (1988) • A. Symons, *Eleonora Duse* (1927) • E. Le Galli-enne, *Eleonora Duse: the mystic in the theatre* (1966) • D. Setti, *La Duse com'era* (1978) • d. cert.

Archives Fondazione Cini, Venice • Fondazione del Vittoriale, Gardone Riviera • Museo del Burcardo, Rome | Biblioteca Museo dell'Attore, Genoa • Museo del Teatro della Scala, Milan • NYPL for the Performing Arts | SOUND BL NSA, documentary recording **Likenesses** J. S. Sargent, portrait, *c.*1893, priv. coll. [*see illus.*] • photographs, repro. in O. Signorelli, *Eleonora Duse*, trans. I. Quigley (1959) • photographs, repro. in G. Guerrieri, ed., *Eleonora Duse exhibition* (1969) [catalogue to exhibition mounted by Gerardo Guerrieri and Pietro Nardi, Teatro La Fenice, Venice] • photographs, repro. in G. Guerrieri, ed., *Eleonora Duse e il suo tempo, 1858–1924* (1974) [catalogue to Duse exhibition at Treviso] • photographs, repro. in G. Guerrieri, ed., *Eleonora Duse: tra storia e leggenda* (1985) [catalogue of exhibition, Asolo] • prints, Harvard TC

Dusgate [Benet], **Thomas** (*d.* 1532), protestant martyr, was born in Cambridge. Nothing is known about his parents and his early years are entirely obscure. He was a scholar of Christ's College and took his bachelor's degree in 1522–3. He was officially a fellow of Corpus Christi College from 1523 to 1525, though he appears to have left the university in 1524. (According to John Foxe, Dusgate was an MA, but there is no record of this). At Cambridge, Dusgate became friends with the evangelical preacher Thomas Bilney, and it was at the university that he became an adherent of the reformed religion. As a fellow of Corpus Christi, Dusgate was also an ordained priest serving the adjoining church of St Benet. According to Ralph Morice, who knew him at Cambridge, Dusgate became 'very moche combered with the concupissence of the fleshe, and stryvyng gretely to suppresse the same, felt hymself to wek to overcom it' (BL, Harleian MS 419, fol. 125r–v). He then went overseas to visit Martin Luther who advised him to leave the priest-hood rather than live in sinful lust. In 1524 Dusgate left Cambridge, and married (his wife's identity is unknown). According to Morice he changed his name to Benet. He went to live in Devon, and for some years kept a school, first at Torrington (in 1524) and then at Exeter in Butcher Row, Smithen Street.

Dusgate moved in Exeter's small evangelical circle, and even wrote a letter comforting one William Strowd when he was imprisoned for heresy. In October 1531 he placed bills on the cathedral doors at various times impugning the veneration of saints, and denouncing the pope as Antichrist. Dusgate was soon detected and imprisoned, although there are conflicting accounts of how this happened. After his arrest Gregory Basset, the warden of the Franciscans and himself a recanted heretic, tried hard to persuade Dusgate to follow his example. But Dusgate refused to submit, and he was tried, and on 22 December 1531, condemned and handed over to the secular power. The sheriff of Devon, Sir Thomas Dennis, would have had the execution take place at Southernhay, but the mayor of Exeter refused permission, and Dusgate was therefore taken to the usual place of execution, Liverydole in Heavitree, about 2 miles from Exeter, and there burnt. This was on either 15 January, or more probably, 10 January 1532.

THOMAS S. FREEMAN

Sources J. Foxe, *The second volume of the ecclesiasticall history, conteyning the acts and monuments of martyrs*, 2nd edn (1570), 1180–

84 • BL, Harleian MS 419, fol. 125r–v [H. Ellis (ed.), *Original letters of eminent literary men*, CS, old ser., 23 (1843), 24] • Exeter city muni-ments, Book 55, fol. 89; calendared in *Report on records of the city of Exeter*, HMC, 73 (1916), 361 • chancery, significations of excommunications, PRO, C 85/82/13 • Venn, *Alum. Cant.* • *DNB*

Dussek, Jan Ladislav (1760–1812), pianist and composer, was born on 12 February 1760 at Čáslav, Bohemia, the son of Jan Dussek (1738–1818) and his wife, Veronika Štěbetová. His parents were both musicians: his father was the organist and elementary school teacher at Čáslav, while his mother was a talented harpist. He studied the piano from the age of five, and at the age of nine was described as 'a very good performer' (Burney, 2.5). Dussek was a chorister at the Minorite church at Iglau in 1772–3, and then attended the Jesuit *Gymnasium* in Kuttenberg from 1774 to 1776. He studied in Prague from 1776 to 1778, first at the New City *Gymnasium* and then briefly at the University of Prague. During the next decade, before his arrival in London in 1789, Dussek found employment as a piano teacher and performer in Malines in the Southern Netherlands, The Hague, Hamburg (where in 1782 he met C. P. E. Bach, from whom he may have received some instruction), at the court of Catherine the Great in St Petersburg, in Lithuania as kapellmeister to Prince Karl Radziwill, and from 1786 to 1789 in Paris, where he was acquainted with both Queen Marie-Antoinette and Napoleon Bonaparte.

Dussek spent ten years in London, from 1789 to 1799, during which time he appeared on London's concert platforms more frequently than any other pianist, capitalizing on London's flourishing concert life; his sixty-six appearances (in which he always performed his own works) were exactly twice the number of those given by his closest rival, Johann Baptist Cramer. The two appear to have been good friends, and Dussek was also on good terms with Muzio Clementi, Joseph Haydn (in London in 1791–2 and 1794–5), and Johann Peter Salomon, at whose concert series he often appeared. His own compositions were much in demand, especially with young performers making their London débuts, and among his pupils was the young André Georges Louis Onslow. On 31 August 1792 he married the seventeen-year-old Sophia Justina Corri (1775–1847) [*see* Dussek, Sophia Justina], an accomplished pianist, singer, and harpist and daughter of the publisher Domenico *Corri [see under Corri family (per. c.*1770–1860)], with whom Dussek established a business partnership. This partnership collapsed in 1799, with Corri gaoled for bankruptcy, and Dussek fled England, never again seeing his wife and daughter. From then until 1804 Dussek was based in Hamburg, also making successful trips to Prague and Čáslav in 1802. From 1804 to 1806, he was based at Magdeburg as kapellmeister to Prince Louis Ferdinand of Prussia, who was not only a leading musical patron but also a composer of some repute. They became close friends, and Dussek accompanied the prince to war in the autumn campaign of 1806. The prince's death at the battle of Saalfeld on 10 October 1806 was to inspire one of Dussek's greatest piano compositions, the *Elégie harmonique sur la mort du Prince Louis Ferdinand de Prusse*, op.

61. During his last years, Dussek worked briefly for Prince Isenburg, a leading Austrian army officer, and from 1807 he was in the employ of the French politician Charles Maurice Talleyrand. He died on 20 March 1812, either at St Germain-en-Laye or in Paris.

Dussek's compositions were almost exclusively written for the piano, and a clear division can be discerned between the easier and more simple sonatas composed for the drawing-room and for domestic music-making (particularly in England) by a rapidly expanding amateur market, and the highly virtuosic and more challenging sonatas and concertos intended for public performance. The latter works were frequently entitled 'grand' and are larger in scale than the former, exploiting a much greater range of pianistic figurations, with dramatic modulations and extensive use of the furthest reaches of the keyboard. Dussek's most prolific years as both a composer and a performing pianist appear to have been his London years. Dussek encouraged the piano manufacturing firm John Broadwood & Sons to increase the compass of the piano from five to six octaves in the early 1790s, and the extent of his dominance of the concert platforms may be reflected in the overt virtuosity and the drama and display of his 'grand' sonatas and concertos, such as the three sonatas op. 35 (1797), the grand sonata 'The Farewell' op. 44 (1800), and the hugely popular 'Military' concerto op. 40 (1798). In these works (and also the *Elégie harmonique* op. 61, 1807, and *Le retour à Paris* op. 64, 1807) Dussek demonstrates a richness of piano sonorities, with dense textures, extensive use of the sustaining pedal, sudden and surprising modulations, and high technical demands, all of which are more characteristic of the piano writing of the mid-nineteenth century than of their period. Dussek was the first to place the piano sideways to the audience, and contemporary accounts of his own performance describe an artist of considerable charisma and allure, much praised for his powers of both expression and execution.

NICHOLAS SALWEY

Sources H. A. Craw, 'A biography and thematic catalogue of the works of J. L. Dussek (1760–1812)', PhD diss., University of Southern California, 1984 [microfilm] • N. Salwey, 'The piano in London concert life', DPhil diss., U. Oxf., in preparation • N. Salwey and S. McVeigh, 'The piano and harpsichord in London's concert life, 1750–1800: a calendar of advertised performances', *A handbook for studies in 18th-century English music*, ed. M. Burden and I. Cholij, 8 (1997), 27–72 • D. Wainwright, *Broadwood by appointment* (1982) • A. Ringer, 'Beethoven and the London pianoforte school', *Musical Quarterly*, 56 (1970), 742–58 • C. Burney, *The present state of music in Germany, the Netherlands, and United Provinces*, 2nd edn, 2 vols. (1775) • E. Blom, 'The prophecies of Dussek', *Classics major and minor* (1958), 88–117

Dussek [*née* Corri; *other married name* Moralt]**, Sophia Justina** [Giustina] (**1775–1847**), singer and composer, was born on 1 May 1775 in Edinburgh, the daughter of Domenico *Corri (1746–1825) [*see under* Corri family], an Italian musician who had settled in Edinburgh in 1771, and Alice, *née* Bacchelli. She first played in public at the age of four. In 1788 the family moved to London, where Corri established himself as a music publisher in Soho, and Sophia took singing lessons from Luigi Marchesi, Viganoni, and Giambattista Cimador. She gave her first public performance as a singer on 15 April 1791 at one of Salomon's concerts, at which she subsequently performed regularly.

On 31 August 1792, at St Anne, Westminster, Sophia married the Bohemian pianist Jan Ladislav *Dussek (1760–1812), and, encouraged by him, became an accomplished pianist and harpist. They took part in the first performance of Haydn's *The Storm*, and Haydn presided at her benefit concert on 29 May 1795. Dussek joined his father-in-law in 1794 to form the publishing firm Corri, Dussek & Co., but when the business ran into debt in 1799 he fled to Hamburg, leaving Corri to serve a prison sentence, and it seems that he never saw his wife or daughter again.

In 1808 Sophia Dussek was engaged for an opera season at the King's Theatre, Haymarket, to perform minor roles and to act as understudy to Angelica Catalani, and she sang the role of Aeneas in Paisiello's *Didone* because of the lack of a suitable male singer. She also wrote a considerable amount of music, much of it published by Corri and Dussek. Her compositions included sonatas for the piano and for the harp, a *German Waltz* for the harp, and *The Duchess of York's Waltz* for piano.

After her husband's death in 1812 Sophia married a viola player, John Alois Moralt. They lived at 8 Winchester Row, Paddington, where she started a piano school. She died in London in 1847.

Her daughter, **Olivia Francisca Buckley** [*née* Dussek] (1799–1847), organist, was taught piano and harp by her mother, and made her first appearance at the Argyle Rooms at the age of eight. She was married to William Richard Buckley, with whom she had ten children. She wrote some piano music and songs and *Musical Truths* (1843). The title-pages of two books of *Fairy Songs and Ballads for the Young* (1846) and a set of *Aesop's Fables* (1847) were designed by George Cruikshank. From 1840 until her death in Kensington, London, on 24 December 1847 she was organist of Kensington parish church.

ANNE PIMLOTT BAKER

Sources H. A. Craw and B. Shaljean, 'Dussek, Sophia (Giustina)', *New Grove*, 2nd edn • W. C. Smith, *The Italian opera and contemporary ballet in London, 1789–1820* (1955) • H. C. Robbins Landon, *The symphonies of Joseph Haydn* (1955), 451, 549 • E. L. Gerber, *Lexikon der Tonkünstler* (1812) • d. cert. [Olivia Buckley]

Dustin, Lydia (d. 1692). *See under* Salem witches and their accusers (*act.* 1692).

Duston [*née* Emerson]**, Hannah** (1657–1736?), captive of American Indians, was born in December 1657 in Haverhill, Massachusetts, one of fifteen children born to Michael Emerson, an English shoemaker and immigrant to the Massachusetts Bay colony, and his wife, Hannah, daughter of an original settler of Ipswich. Her early life and the lives of her parents remain a mystery, leaving Hannah's known history to begin with her marriage to Thomas Duston (d. 1732), originally of Dover, New Hampshire. She married Duston, a bricklayer and farmer in Ipswich, in December 1677 and they settled in a house near

Haverhill. Here Duston earned a reputation as a good citizen, for which he was awarded appointment as constable of Haverhill. They had a long and stable marriage of about fifty-five years and Hannah bore thirteen children. It was at the time of the birth of the twelfth child that she became a celebrity in the puritan colony.

Hannah gave birth, with help from the widow and nurse Mary Neff, in the first days of March 1697. On 15 March American Indians attacked the village and the Duston home. While Thomas Duston was able to escape with most of the children, Hannah, Mary Neff, and the newborn were taken as captives and marched north towards Canada, a distance believed to be about 100 miles. According to Hannah, the Indians killed her baby and warned the remaining captives of the fate awaiting them in Canada. In New Hampshire, Hannah, Mary Neff, and Samuel Lennardson—a young boy captured some months earlier from Worcester—were given to an Indian family. Motivated by fear, a desire for revenge, or both, the three captives murdered their captors, adults and children, took their scalps, and escaped captivity on 30 March 1697.

Hannah Duston's story of her daring escape made her famous in the colony and the scalps earned a considerable reward for the three escapees. She was praised from the pulpit by Cotton Mather, who cast her in the biblical image of Jael, who saved Israel, and blessed her deeds as inspired by prayer. She was also honoured in the home of Judge Samuel Sewell of the general court, and monuments were erected later by her community to commemorate the event. To her contemporaries her feat seemed to deserve such glorification because the colony still felt the reverberations of earlier Indian attacks: she was exonerated on the grounds that the Indians had converted to Catholicism, but her own response to the meaning of her experience is not clear. She apparently did not see in it proof of her own salvation, as she continued to attend Haverhill's First Church, though she did not seek full membership until 1719.

However, those who, later and from outside the community, considered the captivity, murders, and escape viewed Hannah Duston in a different light. Timothy Dwight's account in the early nineteenth century added a caveat for the reader. 'Whether all their sufferings, all the danger of suffering anew, justified this slaughter may probably be questioned by you or some other exact moralist' (Ulrich, 172). Nathaniel Hawthorne's assessment was harsher. Holding female aggression to be contrary to nature, he wrote: 'Would that the bloody old hag had been drowned in crossing Contocook river or that she had sunk over head and ears in a swamp, and been there buried, until summoned forth to confront her victims at the Day of Judgment' (Ulrich, 172).

Hannah Duston, who gave birth to one more child, lived out her life in the close-knit farming community; her stable marriage ended with the death of her husband, Thomas, in 1732. It is presumed that she died in 1736, when her will was filed at Ipswich. She was buried at Haverhill.   CAROL BERKIN

Sources C. Berkin, *First generations: women in colonial America* (1996) · R. B. Caverly, *Heroism of Hannah Duston* (1875) · C. Mather, *Magnalia Christi Americana*, 3rd edn, 7 bks in 2 vols. (1853–5) · R. McHenry, ed., *Famous American women: a biographical dictionary from colonial time to the present* (1980) · A. S. McKinley, 'Duston, Hannah', *ANB* · L. T. Ulrich, *Good wives: images and reality in the lives of women in northern New England* (1982)
Archives New York Historical Society

Dutens, Louis (1730–1812), diplomatist and writer, was born at Tours on 15 January 1730, one of seven children in a Huguenot family. He was educated by his father. An early love affair, one of many which ended more or less unsuccessfully, caused him to leave home for Paris. When his sister was placed in a convent by the archbishop of Tours he realized that his religion made a career in France impossible and he determined to settle in England. There he was received by his uncle, a jeweller who had retired with a large fortune and lived in Leicester Square. After having failed in various endeavours in England he went back to Paris, but soon returned to England to become tutor in the family of a Mr Wyche.

In 1758 Dutens was appointed chaplain to the embassy at Turin, under the Hon. Stuart Mackenzie. He at once took orders in the Church of England and left London for Turin in October. When Mackenzie was summoned to London to become secretary of state for Scotland, he obtained permission for Dutens to remain at Turin as chargé d'affaires. In May 1762 George Pitt (Lord Rivers) was appointed envoy-extraordinary to the court of Turin and Dutens returned to London after a short stay in Paris; in 1763 he obtained a pension of £300 and was again sent as chargé d'affaires to Turin. While there he edited the works of Leibnitz (6 vols., Geneva, 1768) and published a pamphlet attacking the *philosophes* called *Le tocsin* (Paris, 1769) which was later re-edited and also translated into English. About this time, through Mackenzie, he was given the living of Elsdon in Northumberland, worth £800 p.a., by the duke of Northumberland, and went to England in 1766 to take possession of it. On his arrival the king through General Conway gave him £1000 for his services. He never performed any professional duties as a clergyman. The duke continued his patron through life, and in 1768 sent him to travel for four years through Europe with his second son, Lord Algernon Percy. On his return the duke gave him £1000, and Dutens continued to live chiefly with him, going to Alnwick, Spa, and Paris in his company. Dutens remained in France after the duke and duchess had left but in 1776 he returned to England, and was with the duchess of Northumberland at her unexpected and sudden death, after which he went a third time to Italy with Mackenzie. On his return he was persuaded to accompany Lord Mountstuart who had been appointed envoy at Turin but having found the situation unpleasant he left Turin for Bologna, Florence, and Rome. He went to Paris in June 1783, and the next year to London, where he spent most of his time with the duke of Northumberland and Lord Bute. Dutens was again at Spa in 1789 but in 1791 he returned to England where he divided his time between London and Petersham, near Richmond, to the end of his life, mostly with Mackenzie, who left him a legacy of £15,000. He devoted his time to literary correspondence, and his very wide circle of acquaintances inscribed for him copies of their pamphlets of which many were collected into the eighty-nine volumes of 'miscellaneous tracts' bequeathed by Dutens to the Royal Institution. Most of these in turn were sold in 1970. He died in London on 23 May 1812. He had received the title of historiographer to the king, was FRS, and was also associate of the Académie des Inscriptions et Belles-Lettres. That part of his fine library not bequeathed to the Royal Institution was sold at Christies in 1813.

His memoirs were published in 1805, as *Mémoires d'un voyageur qui se repose*. The work had a mixed reception, and Dutens was particularly upset by a review in the 1806 *Edinburgh Review* which described him as 'a dangler in large houses' and 'a worn-out odometer' (Grinke and Rodgers, 3). In addition he wrote numerous other works ranging from poetry, through history, geography, and philosophy, to fine art and fire prevention. Most were published originally in French, but some were translated into English.

H. R. LUARD, *rev.* ELIZABETH BAIGENT

Sources L. Dutens, *Mémoires d'un voyageur qui se repose*, 3 vols. (1806) · *GM*, 1st ser., 82/2 (1812), 197–8, 391–7 · E. Haag and E. Haag, *La France protestante*, 10 vols. (Paris, 1846–59) · *Biographie universelle* · P. Grinke and T. Rodgers, *Pamphlets from the library of Louis Dutens* (1970), catalogue no. 4 [booksellers' catalogue with introduction]
Archives Chatsworth House, Derbyshire, letters to the fifth duke of Devonshire
Likenesses E. Fisher, mezzotint, pubd 1777, BM; repro. in Grinke and Rodgers, *Pamphlets*, cover · attrib. J. Flaxman, Wedgwood medallion, 1787, Wedgwood Museum, Barlaston, Staffordshire · plaster medallion (after J. Tassie), Scot. NPG

(Rajani) Palme Dutt (1896–1974), by Howard Coster, 1943

Dutt, (Rajani) Palme (1896–1974), political leader, was born at Cambridge on 19 June 1896, the younger son (there was also a daughter) of Upendra Krishna Dutt, a Bengali, who had studied medicine in England and established a practice in Cambridge. Dutt's Swedish mother, Anna Palme, made him a distant relative of Olaf Palme, the Swedish prime minister. But it was his father who brought politics into the family household, which became a meeting place for visiting Indian nationalist leaders and leading figures in the British labour movement. Dutt was educated at the Perse School, Cambridge, from 1907, and Balliol College, Oxford, where he won a scholarship and took up residence in the autumn of 1914. His academic record was distinguished; honourable mentions for the Ireland and Craven scholarships in 1915 were followed by a first in classical moderations in 1916. He immediately joined the Independent Labour Party on his arrival at Oxford, opposed the war as a conflict of rival imperialisms, and was imprisoned in 1916 for refusing the draft. The following year he was sent down from Oxford after a meeting of students—convened to discuss 'Socialism and the war'—was broken up by rowdies. He was allowed to return in 1918 to take the final examination of *literae humaniores*, in which he gained a first, having scored fourteen alphas. A short period in teaching followed until, in March 1919, he joined the Labour Research Department, where he remained until the launch of *Labour Monthly* in July 1921.

Dutt graduated to international secretary for the Labour Research Department and served on the Labour Party's advisory committee on international questions for two years. But these positions did not prevent him from becoming a foundation member of the British Communist Party in 1920, which he joined via the National Guilds League, one of the smallest groups fusing to form the new organization. Two years later he drafted the report on organization which sought to 'bolshevize' the infant Communist Party. Further evidence of his importance in the party was provided by his editorships of *Labour Monthly*—which he always claimed as a direct benefaction from Lenin—and, from February 1923, of *Workers' Weekly*.

In 1924 Dutt married the Estonian Bolshevik agent Salme Murrik (1888–1964), with whom he had worked closely since her arrival in Britain in 1920. Together they set up more or less permanent residence in Brussels for the next twelve years. Though officially absent from Britain on health grounds, Dutt continued to involve himself closely in party affairs, intervening in disputes within the leadership circle, editing *Labour Monthly*, and concerning himself with India and the party's colonial responsibilities generally. His *Modern India* (1926) established him as one of the Communist International's experts on the subcontinent, and by 1929 he achieved notoriety there when the prosecution in the Meerut conspiracy trial named him as a leading subversive of British rule. Through all the twists and turns of communist policy in India, Dutt remained the principal conduit of guidance and instruction to the Communist Party of India until his authority faded in the faction-ridden years after independence. Even Nehru—whom he had known since childhood—turned to him for advice on communist policy, and his influence extended far into the Congress left which Nehru led.

In Britain Dutt was better known in the inter-war years for his 'Notes of the month', with which each issue of *Labour Monthly* opened for over fifty years. This journal did more than any other in Britain to promote the Leninist (and Stalinist) positions on imperialism. It found its way, despite bans and proscriptions, to the furthest reaches of the colonial world and succeeded in bringing overseas nationalists, communists, and socialists into the same pages as leaders of the British labour movement. Dutt's own substantial monthly contribution became required reading for anyone who wanted to know the party line on current affairs, and his analyses of events often brilliantly fused historical narrative and theoretical analysis. Many militants obtained their understanding of the modern world and the importance of the anti-imperialist dimension of Leninism from this source. As his most successful books show—books such as *Socialism and the Living Wage* (1927), *Fascism and Social Revolution* (1935), *World Politics* (1936), and *India Today* (1940)—theory for Dutt meant above all Lenin's *Imperialism: the Highest Stage of Capitalism* (1916). Dutt turned his ingenuity to the application of Lenin's conception of the imperialist epoch and this project undoubtedly drew strength from the fact that international crises, world wars, colonial conflicts, and fascist regimes actually dominated the years of his adult life. He was a middle-aged man before the theses of *Imperialism* began to diverge markedly from the movement of world events.

Dutt's expectations at the age of twenty-five—set out with great clarity in the entry 'Communism' which he prepared for the twelfth edition of the *Encyclopaedia Britannica* in 1921—centred on the 'catastrophic condition of capitalism' from which he said the character of the Communist Party derived as an organization, combining the 'strictest internal discipline' and 'an external policy of revolutionary opportunism'. The existence of 'a single ultimate directing centre' (*Encyclopaedia Britannica*, 12th edn, 732–3) for each of these national parties—parties conceived as 'different divisions in a single army'—attracted him enormously. Whereas close exposure to Bolshevik methods led the future Labour MP Ellen Wilkinson to declare in 1919 that 'this is the most ghastly, callous, inhuman machine I have witnessed', Dutt concluded from the same shared experience that 'At last I have found what I have been looking for; socialists who mean business' (Callaghan, 34). His deep conviction was that capitalism meant servitude, social decay, and authoritarianism, and that only an unscrupulous, disciplined, fighting machine of the sort Lenin stood for could overcome it on a world scale.

When the British general strike ended in 1926, Dutt could see only further polarization and sharper conflicts ahead, rather than exhaustion and defeat for the trade unions. Like Harry Pollitt, he soon became an ardent champion of the infamous 'social fascist' analysis of the Sixth World Congress of the Communist International, which depicted capitalism everywhere as a system in terminal crisis and the Communists as the only working-class party opposed to a fascist takeover. When the international leadership imposed this perspective on the British party in 1928 Pollitt became general secretary and Dutt a member of the politburo. For the next three decades these two dominated the Communist Party of Great Britain, with Dutt ever the ideologue and guardian of the international (that is, Moscow) line.

Dutt's last open disagreement with the Communist International also occurred at its sixth world congress, when he opposed the application of its sectarian 'new line' to India and was officially reprimanded for his heterodoxy. If his belief that the communists could go it alone in Britain was evidence of his alienation from that country and his incomprehension of its political culture, his continued advocacy of alliances between communists and nationalists in India was perhaps evidence of a genuine sympathy for the liberation struggle on the subcontinent. Certainly he was an unenthusiastic advocate of communist colonial policy during its phases of unqualified confrontation with erstwhile allies (1928–35; 1948–56). Uncharacteristic silences on Indian affairs marked these phases. His pen flowed again only when the 'class against class' phase ended with the turn to the anti-imperialist popular front in 1935. It was during this period through to the end of the Second World War that he was most influential in Indian politics.

Dutt's loyalty to Moscow was, however, never in doubt, whatever his private misgivings. This was given dramatic proof by his role in the events which saw the British communists perform an abrupt volte-face over the meaning of the Second World War in September 1939. When Stalin instructed the world communist movement to characterize the war as imperialist and unjust on both sides, Pollitt was unable to comply and Dutt took over the general secretaryship (until the Nazi invasion of Russia in June 1941 when Pollitt was reinstated). The acrimonious debate in the central committee which accompanied this transformation revealed a minatory Dutt, outraged by his colleagues' doubts and insisting that communists had 'no sanctum of private opinions' separate from their public expressions of faith. The debates also reveal a man despised by some of his leading colleagues as a political chameleon. Yet when Fenner Brockway encountered him on a train, the day after the party's about-turn had been made public on 8 October 1939, he found a man 'overjoyed that it had returned to the classical line' (Callaghan, 180–88). The truth is that throughout the 1930s Dutt had been more able than Pollitt in depicting the British National Government as having fascist tendencies of its own; he had always invoked the empire as evidence of the British state's slender democratic credentials. Moreover, it was easier for Dutt to adapt than Pollitt or William Gallacher because, unlike them, his sense of belonging to a world party marching in step regardless of nation was seldom disturbed by the pull of local working-class politics. He unsuccessfully stood for parliament as the Communist Party candidate for Birmingham Sparkbrook (1945) and for Woolwich East (1950).

Dutt's cosmopolitanism, erudition, and capacity for subtle logical analysis were always put at the service of the Soviet state and the Communist International. The double crisis of 1956—brought about by Khrushchov's speech to the Twentieth Congress of the Soviet Communist Party and the Soviet invasion of Hungary—illustrated this to the disgust of many former admirers. To the end of his days he remained a Stalinist, stepping down from party office only in 1965. He remained in charge of *Labour Monthly* and re-entered the limelight periodically to defend the crumbling Stalinist order, as in 1968 when he angrily criticized his own party for its disapproval of the Soviet invasion of Czechoslovakia. In 1962 he was made an honorary doctor of history at Moscow University and in 1970 he received the Lenin centenary medal. His best theoretical and historical writing belonged to the period when Lenin's foundation myth for the Communist International—as summarized in *Imperialism* and elaborated by the first four congresses—was most convincing. After the Second World War, Dutt's work lost its spark and depth. Mere apologetics and controversialism took up more of his time. He died in Highgate, London, on 20 December 1974, ten years after Salme and just days after completing his last triumphalist survey of world politics for *Labour Monthly*. His marriage was childless.

In India Dutt's passing was marked by naming the communist centre in New Delhi the R. Palme Dutt Bhawan. The Communist Party of India (Marxist)—with 200,000 members in West Bengal alone—celebrated Dutt's centenary in 1996, by which time the Communist Party of Great Britain had ceased to exist.   JOHN CALLAGHAN

Romesh Chunder Dutt [Rameshchandra Datta] (1848–1909), by unknown photographer

Sources J. Callaghan, *Rajani Palme Dutt: a study in British Stalinism* (1993) · F. Brockway, *Inside the left* (1942) · F. King and G. Matthews, eds., *About turn: the British communist party and the Second World War* (1990) · K. Morgan, *Harry Pollitt* (1993)
Archives BL, memoranda, out-letters, reports, TS articles, etc., CUP 1262 K1–K6 · JRL, Labour History Archive and Study Centre, corresp. and papers incl. logbooks of notes, etc. · Working Class History Library, Salford | JRL, Labour History Archive and Study Centre, corresp. with Harry Pollitt · priv. coll., corresp. with John Strachey · U. Hull, Brynmor Jones L., corresp. with R. Page Arnot | SOUND IWM SA, oral history interview
Likenesses H. Coster, photograph, 1943, NPG [see illus.]
Wealth at death £6478: probate, 25 March 1975, *CGPLA Eng. & Wales*

Dutt, Romesh Chunder [Rameshchandra Datta] (1848–1909), administrator in India and author, son of Ishanchandra and Thakamani Dutt, was born in Calcutta on 13 August 1848. He came from one of the Calcutta families who had prospered through their commercial associations with the British East India Company. His great-grandfather, Nilmani Dutt, was famous for his command of the English language in the latter half of the eighteenth century. His father was a deputy collector, but both his parents died while he was a student at Coolootolla branch school (later known as Hare School). He was then brought up by his younger uncle, Shashichandra, a well-known literary figure of his time who profoundly influenced him. Romesh married, at the age of sixteen, Mohini Basuja (afterwards Matangini Dutt), second daughter of Nabagopal Basu. They had two daughters. While a final-year student at Presidency College, Calcutta, he planned to sail to Britain without the knowledge (and against the wishes) of his orthodox Hindu grandfather, to whom sea voyages were taboo. Eventually he left for Britain in secret in the company of two friends, Bihari Lal Gupta and Surendranath Banerjea, in 1868.

Early career In London, Dutt secured admission to University College and sat for the Indian Civil Service examination in 1871. He stood third in the examination and his two friends, Gupta and Banerjea, were also among the successful candidates. Dutt was called to the bar at the Middle Temple the same year, and also joined the Indian Civil Service as assistant magistrate and collector. In 1883 he was the first Indian to be appointed district magistrate, and after serving in many districts of Bengal was appointed divisional commissioner, first in Burdwan and later in Orissa (1894–5). The Anglo-Indian mouthpiece, *The Englishman*, commented ironically: 'it must be pleasant for the European Civilians who are placed in subordination to the first Native Commissioner in India' (Bandyopadhya, 15).

He took leave, ostensibly for reasons of health, and left for England in January 1897, retiring at the end of the year. Probably the real reason was his dissatisfaction at being passed over in favour of his British juniors for appointments to the secretariat. As he wrote to his brother, 'if Government is not disposed to repose any real trust and confidence in me, I am free to utilise my powers and abilities, such as they are, to the benefit of my country in other ways' (ibid., 17–18).

Dutt decided to stay on in England for some years with the twin objects of pursuing his scholarly ambitions and pressing for reforms in India. The council of University College, London, offered him a non-stipendiary lectureship in Indian history in 1897; the only emolument was the fees which the students paid for joining his class. He lectured mainly on the history, literature, and civilization of the ancient Hindus. He also began his translation of the *Mahabharata* into English verse at this time. His criticisms of government policy had limited impact: in his words, 'they want to shut us out, not because we are critics, but because we are natives, and their policy is rule by Englishmen' (Bandyopadhya, 20–21).

Administration in India In 1899 Dutt was invited to preside over the fifteenth session of the Indian National Congress held at Lucknow. He gave evidence before the police commission in 1902, arguing that the 'inadequate scale of pay … draw[s] to that service … a class of men not fit for their responsibilities, and that we train them in dishonesty by giving them ample powers, and an undue degree of protection when they are detected in wrong-doing'. He presided over the industrial exhibition held in Benares in connection with the twenty-first session of the Congress in 1905. He pointed out in his presidential address the fact that virtually every nation in the world had policies to protect their industries from uncontrolled competition and since Indians had no control over their fiscal legislation, *swadeshi*, or the movement for the exclusive consumption of home manufactures, was the only way out. When the premier literary association of Bengal, Bangiya Sahitya Parishad, was set up in 1894, Dutt was elected its first president.

Dutt accepted the Gaikwar of Baroda's invitation to join the state service as revenue minister in 1904 and worked hard, in his words, 'to initiate progress in all lines, and to make Baroda a richer and a happier State'. He again went to England on leave in 1906, hoping to recover his failing health. But he had little rest because, with the liberal leader Gokhale to help him, he became involved in the agitation against the decision to partition Bengal. His three-volume *Baroda Administration Report*, published when he returned to India later that year, is a testimony to his achievements in that princely state. But he was not happy there. 'I feel I am proving false to my higher pursuits, false to my destiny', he wrote in a letter (Bandyopadhya, 27–8). He again took leave from the state service in July 1907, and was appointed member of the decentralization commission in September that year. He travelled extensively in India in connection with its work and went to England in 1908 with other members of the commission. He had prolonged correspondence with the secretary of state, Lord Morley, during his tenure as member. He urged a measure of moderation in dealing with the extremist threat, and argued against the principle of electorates based on caste and creed which, he felt, would exacerbate relationships between the communities. He pleaded for the abrogation of the partition of Bengal, for it had strengthened the hands of the extremists. One of his strongest recommendations, that the district magistrate should not preside over the district board (an institution of local self-government), was not accepted. He returned to India in June 1909, and was appointed diwan of Baroda. He died in Baroda on 30 November 1909, survived by his wife.

Writings Dutt is best remembered for his literary and scholarly contributions. He first began to publish poems and essays in English in the *Bengal Magazine* (edited by Lal Bihari De) and *Mukherjee's Magazine* under a pen-name, Arcydae (that is, R. C. D.). The leading literary figure of Bengal, Bankim Chatterji, induced him to take up writing in the mother tongue. The novels he wrote in Bengali are reckoned among the classics of Bengali literature: they include four historical novels, *Bangabijeta* (1874), *Madhabikankan* (1877), *Jibanprabhat* (1878), and *Jibansandhya* (1879). The last two are very much in the mould of patriotic novels of the period, one built around the career of Shivaji as a great Hindu hero and the other focused on the last days of Rajput glory, their decline traced to the tradition of vendetta and the consequent internecine conflicts. His two social novels, *Samsar* (2 vols., 1886; rev. edn, 1910; republished after his death under the title *Samsarkatha*) and *Samaj* (n.d.), were reformist in inspiration, and written in support of widow remarriage and inter-caste marriage. Dutt also wrote a large number of essays in the literary periodicals of the day on a wide range of topics relating to ancient Indian history, Sanskrit and Bengali literature, contemporary political and economic issues, and travelogues. Some of his letters were published posthumously in literary journals. In 1879 he published a school textbook in Bengali on the history of India. He also took an important initiative in making the Hindu scriptures accessible to his fellow Bengalis. He edited and translated into Bengali the *Rigveda-samhita* (1885–7), and followed this up with a collaborative effort, entitled *Hindushastra*: published in two volumes, it contained nine parts covering, in original and translation, large segments of the Vedic literature, the epics, *shruti* texts, the eighteen *puranas*, the *Gita*, and the six systems of philosophy. This monumental work, to which he contributed the translations of the Vedic literature, made the Hindu sacred literature available to educated Bengalis for the first time.

Most of Dutt's publications were, however, in English. Of these the first, *Three Years in Europe*, was published anonymously (the author was described simply as a Hindu) in 1872; a Bengali translation was published the following year. Based on extracts from letters he sent from Europe, the book is a remarkably perceptive account of Western social mores of his time, and reflects Dutt's highly advanced ideas. Among other things, he deplored the class values of English society, especially the snobbish adulation of the aristocracy. He was also not impressed with the superficial freedom granted to Victorian women, whose education and accomplishments, in his view, were geared to the sole purpose of catching a husband; emancipation of women, he concluded, would come only with the opening of all careers to women. He compared the conservatism of the English on such matters with Brahmanical orthodoxy.

Later Dutt wrote copiously on Indian history, literature, and contemporary problems, and tried his hand at poetry as well. His study of the Bengali peasantry published in 1874 is an incisive study of their condition from the middle ages onwards: he approved of the permanent settlement of land revenue with the Bengali zamindars, but argued that there should be a similar settlement of rent with the peasants so that they had an incentive for improving cultivation. *The Literature of Bengal*, published in 1877 'with copious extracts from the best writers', was the first serious effort to produce a systematic history of Bengali literature. His other works include *A History of Civilisation in Ancient India* in three volumes (1889–90): based on Sanskrit literature, this work was a remarkable exercise in cultural history. A number of other volumes were devoted to translations from Sanskrit: *Lays of Ancient India* (1894); *Mahabharata* (1899), an abridged translation in verse published with an introduction by Max Müller; *Ramayana* (1900), also an abridged translation in verse; and *Indian Poetry* (1905), selections rendered into English. Two of his Bengali novels, *Samsar* and *Madhabikankan*, were published in English translation as *The Lake of Psalms* (1902) and *The Slave Girl of Agra* (1909) respectively. (*Samsar* was also translated into Gujarati by a family friend). Besides these he published two autobiographical works, *Rambles in India* (1895), an account of his travels from 1871 to 1895, and a volume of poems for private circulation, *Reminiscences of a Workman's Life* (1896).

Dutt's major historical work was his two volumes on the economic history of India under British rule, *The Economic History of British India, a Record, 1757–1837* (1902; 2nd edn, *The Economic History of India under Early English Rule*, 1906) and *India in the Victorian Age: an Economic History* (1904). Taken with the two volumes of his *Speeches and Papers on the Indian Question* (1902), this work encapsulates his perception and analysis of the colonial nexus. As noted above, his scholarly interests developed primarily around the literature and civilization of ancient India and, to a lesser extent, the literature of Bengal. This celebrated *magnum opus* emerged from his public concerns as a moderate nationalist who hoped to alter the conditions of colonial rule through propaganda, debate, and criticism.

Political thought and assessment Dutt belonged to the generation of Indian nationalists whose faith in the beneficence of British rule remained unshaken, though their own experience of it, as observers and collaborators in administration, contradicted many of their assumptions.

Dutt summed up both his persistent faith and his misgivings in a classic passage:

> The Indian Empire will be judged by History as the most superb of human institutions in modern times. But it would be a sad story for future historians to tell that the Empire gave the people of India peace but not prosperity, that the manufacturers lost their industries; that the cultivators were ground down by a heavy and variable taxation which precluded any saving; that the revenues of the country were to a large extent diverted to England; and that recurring and desolating famines swept away millions of the population. (R. C. Dutt, *India under Early English Rule*, 1906, Introduction)

With Major B. D. Basu and Dadabhai Naoroji, Dutt formulated what is now recognized as the classic diagnosis of the Indian economic problem under colonial rule. It emphasized the 'drainage of wealth' from India through home charges payable to Britain and unrequited exports, the absence of protection for India's infant industries, and the negative implications of even the constructive efforts like the railways, which deprived many providers of traditional transport services and facilitated the import of British manufactured goods. Two recurrent themes of India's economic nationalism, drainage of wealth and destruction of Indian handicrafts, traceable to the colonial nexus, can be found in the writings of Dutt and his fellow publicists. The *swadeshi* programme of more militant nationalists owed much to this political economic discourse.

Dutt's exercises in historical analysis of the Indian problem had strong emotional overtones. He commented that at the very time the Delhi durbar of 1903 was celebrated with great pomp, thousands of famine-stricken Indians were living in relief camps. He traced all this misery and maladministration to one basic cause, 'the form and method of an absolute Government—not in touch with the people, and not able to secure their well-being' (Bagchi, 166). He summed up his solution of the problem in two words—'retrenchment' and 'representation'. The first referred to the need for reducing all expenditure inessential for India's needs, especially the heavy military expenditure and the home charges: this would allow, among other things, a reduction in land revenue, which he considered excessive. Secondly, he considered it essential for the success of the administration that Indians should be admitted to some share in decision making. Secretaries of state, ruling without hearing any Indian voice, meant an 'exclusive and distrustful administration' which was necessarily unpopular as well as unsuccessful. 'The oligarchy at Whitehall and the oligarchy at Simla' (ibid., 167) had to be replaced by representative government in which the entire population would have a share. Despite every discouragement, he retained his faith in the methods of persuasion and was deeply worried by the development of extremist politics, especially after the partition of Bengal in 1905. In Baroda, he formed a close friendship with a much younger nationalist, Aurobindo Ghose, who was one of the chief proponents of the new extremism. He conceded in private that the methods of moderation were losing their appeal and the future must lie with the younger leadership. He also spoke with great admiration of a person who inspired the extremists though he had no direct connection with politics, Swami Vivekananda.

Dutt was one of India's great Victorians. His intense seriousness of purpose, public concern, prodigious capacity for hard work, and great scholarship place him firmly in the tradition of Victorian eminence. He was driven by great ambitions—literary and scholarly fame for himself, and an honourable place for India in the community of nations. But all his energy and involvement in public affairs notwithstanding, his personal correspondence makes rather sad reading. One has an impression of loneliness and a sense of failure. He was sceptical about the survival value of his literary labours—the translations from the epics and the economic history excepted. The hopes of progress towards representative government through persuasion were also confounded: extremism in politics, which he abhorred, was taking over. Dutt saw in his own lifetime the failure of the Indian liberals' agenda and, though he never withdrew from his many-sided activities, his last years were overshadowed by a sense of despair.   TAPAN RAYCHAUDHURI

Sources J. N. Gupta, *The life of R. C. Dutt* (1911) • B. Bandyopadhya, *Rameshchandra Datta* (1947) [in Bengali] • S. Banerjea, *A nation in making: being the reminiscences of fifty years in public life* (1925) • M. Bagchi, *Rameshchandra* (1962) [in Bengali]

Archives National Archives of India, New Delhi, corresp. • Nehru Museum, New Delhi

Likenesses photograph, repro. in Gupta, *Life of R. C. Dutt*, frontispiece [*see illus.*] • portrait, National Library of India, Calcutta • portrait, Bangiya Sahitya Parishad, Calcutta, India

Wealth at death £198 10s. 5d.: administration with will, 14 Nov 1910, *CGPLA Eng. & Wales*

Dutton family (*per.* 1522–1743), gentry, arrived in Gloucestershire in the aftermath of the dissolution of the monasteries. **Thomas Dutton** (1507–1581) was a surveyor of monastic lands in the county who acquired the former monastic manor of Sherborne by purchase in March 1552. The son of William Dutton, a younger son of the Duttons of Cheshire, and Agnes, daughter of John Conway of Flint, he attended Brasenose College, Oxford. About 1546 he married Mary Bigge, daughter of Robert Taylor of Westwell, Oxfordshire. She was a widow with several children, and in a subsequent chancery suit brought by two of those children against Thomas, the executor of their grandfather's will, it was alleged that he had obtained 'his whole preferment and advancement and chief living' through their mother (Morgan, 4). Thomas and Mary had one daughter before Mary died at about the time that Thomas acquired Sherborne. He subsequently allied himself to an influential family of London merchants through his marriage to Anne, daughter of Stephen Kirton, a London alderman, Merchant Taylor, and merchant of the staple of Calais. They had two sons and two daughters before Anne's death in 1566. Finally, Thomas made a third marriage, to Margaret, heir of Ralph Johnson, esquire, of London, and widow of John Mayney, esquire, of Biddenden, Kent. Although financially advantageous for Thomas, the marriage was not happy, and in his will dated March 1581 he left his wife nothing but her legal dower:

'the world knoweth she hath deserved no courtesy or to be remembered'. None the less, his marriages to mercantile wealth helped to secure Thomas Dutton's financial position, while the consolidation of his initial landholdings in the county had established his family within the Gloucestershire gentry. At his death on 4 October 1581 he owned the manor, rectory, tithes, and advowson of Sherborne with forty messuages and 3000 acres, thirty-six messuages in Northleach, and twenty messuages in the parish of St Thomas, Oxford.

Thomas was succeeded by his eldest son, **William Dutton** (1561–1618), who matriculated at Hart Hall, Oxford, in 1572. In 1584 William consolidated his family's ties with the city of London by his marriage to Anne, daughter of Sir Ambrose Nicholas, who had been lord mayor in 1576. Her jointure was £3000, and they had seven sons and four daughters, of whom four sons and one daughter outlived their father. William served as sheriff in 1590 and 1601, and under James I he was a deputy lieutenant. The family's status within Gloucestershire society was marked and enhanced by Elizabeth I's visit to Sherborne on her progress in 1592. In the military survey of Gloucestershire compiled in 1608 William Dutton had fourteen named gentlemen and yeomen at Sherborne, nine husbandmen, servants, and two shepherds. He expanded the family's property in Gloucestershire, acquiring the manors of Northleach Forran, Nether Turkdean, Aldsworth, Nether Coberley, Upper Coberley, Nether Hampen, Hinchwicke, and Standish, and the advowsons of Coberley, Standish, and Bourton on the Water. He died on 10 November 1618, and was buried at Sherborne on the following day. By his will he devised his 'great house' at Northleach to charitable uses.

He was succeeded by his son **John Dutton** (1594–1657), who was known as Crump Dutton on account of his hunchback. John graduated BA from Exeter College, Oxford, in 1612 and subsequently attended the Inner Temple. Unlike his father and grandfather he took a wife not from among the daughters of London merchants but from an established gentry family, marrying Elizabeth (1606–1638), daughter of Sir Henry *Baynton of Bromham, Wiltshire [*see under* Baynton family]. He followed his father in becoming a deputy lieutenant, and he represented Gloucestershire in the parliament of 1624–5. Imprisoned in 1627 for opposing the forced loan, he was later active in the opposition to the imposition of ship money. Within two generations the Duttons had moved from being newcomers to a place among the élite of Gloucestershire society. In 1635 John Dutton's wife purchased the wardship and marriage of Thomas *Pope, second earl of Downe, from William Murray, groom of the bedchamber, for £3500. The earl came to live at Sherborne, and in 1638 married Lucy, the younger of John and Elizabeth's two surviving daughters. The marriage was not happy, and the enhanced social status it implied for the Dutton family was overshadowed by the outbreak of civil war. In the contested election for the Short Parliament, John was instrumental in ensuring that Sir Robert Tracy secured the seat for Gloucestershire in the face of puritan opposition, declaring that in the light of the experience 'he would never more trust any man, that wore his hayre shorter then his ears' (PRO, SP 16/448/79). Subsequently John was himself elected to represent Gloucestershire in the Long Parliament; he sat until disabled in January 1644. Like other leaders of the county gentry who had opposed some of the king's extra-parliamentary financial measures, Dutton was disquieted by the growing divisions he witnessed in religion and politics. When the civil war erupted he became a colonel in the royal army and raised troops for the siege of Gloucester, but his physique prevented his taking an active part in the fighting. His daughter Lucy was also an active royalist, entertaining Charles I at her manor house of Coberley in 1643 and 1644.

In the years before the civil war the Duttons were rich enough to be able to establish a younger son firmly within the gentry community of Gloucestershire. John Dutton's younger brother, **Sir Ralph Dutton** (1601–1646), was provided with his own estate at Standish. He was knighted in 1624, served as sheriff in 1630, and was a gentleman of the privy chamber extraordinary to Charles I. Unlike his brother, Sir Ralph continued the family tradition of maintaining close links with the mercantile élite of London through marriage. In 1624 he married Mary, coheir of William Duncomb, a London haberdasher, with the consent of her grandfather Sir Thomas Bennet. A royalist like his brother, in 1642 he appeared at Nottingham with a newly raised regiment of horse, and was subsequently adjutant to the royalist governor of Oxford.

John Dutton was with the king at Oxford, where he was created DCL in November 1642, and was one of the commissioners who drew up the articles of Oxford. A personal friendship with Oliver Cromwell, however, ameliorated the consequences of his allegiance. He compounded for his estate, paying fines of £3434 4s. and £1782, representing property worth about £60,000. Following his brother's death in 1646 he also paid a fine of £952 17s. 1d. upon the sequestration of Sir Ralph's manor of Standish. Despite this he was able to finance an extensive rebuilding of the house at Sherborne in the 1650s. His work was lost when the house was rebuilt in the nineteenth century, but an engraving and drawings show that it had been influenced by the existing structure. Two decades earlier, by contrast, John Dutton had built a lodge of pioneering classical design in a new deer park at Sherborne. Following the death of his first wife in 1638 he married Anne, daughter of John King, bishop of London. They had no children. He died on 14 January 1657 and was buried at Sherborne on 28 February, where the memorial erected by his second wife describes him as a 'Master of a large Fortune And Owner of a Mind Aequall to it Noted for his great Hospitality farr and neer And his charitable Relief of the Poor'. To Anthony Wood he was 'a learned and a prudent man, and as one of the richest, so one of the meekest, men in England' (Wood, *Ath. Oxon.: Fasti*, 2.42).

John Dutton had no male heir and the manor of Sherborne passed by entail to his nephew **William Dutton** (1642–1675), the elder son of Sir Ralph Dutton. Other properties were charged with an annuity of £400 to Elizabeth,

John's elder daughter, who had married George Colt, while the manor of Coberley had been settled on Lucy at the time of her marriage to the earl of Downe. Despite the royalism of his father, uncle, and cousin William had been brought up in London in the household of Oliver Cromwell, where Andrew Marvell was his tutor. His uncle bequeathed the guardianship of his nephew and his estate to Cromwell in his will, expressing the hope that William would marry Cromwell's youngest daughter, Frances. In the event Frances married elsewhere and William acquired as his bride Mary, daughter of Viscount Scudamore and widow of Thomas Russell, esquire, the heir of Sir William Russell, bt, who had £7000 from her first husband. There were no children of the marriage. Following the Restoration the Dutton family resumed their position as one of the pre-eminent families in Gloucestershire. William was a JP and served as sheriff in 1667.

William Dutton died in 1675 and was succeeded by his brother **Sir Ralph Dutton** (*c*.1645–1720/21), who married Grissel, the daughter of Sir Edmund Poole of Kemble, Wiltshire, about 1674. She died in 1678, having borne a daughter. In that year her husband became a baronet, for a payment of £1100. In 1679 he married Mary (1662–1723), the heir of Peter Barwick of London, physician to Charles II, whose marriage portion was £10,000. They had several children, who were all baptized at Westminster. Sir Ralph represented Gloucestershire in parliament in 1679–81 and in 1689–98, when he was aligned with the whigs. In 1705 he stood as a tory and was defeated. He was a JP and deputy lieutenant and served as colonel of the Green regiment of Gloucestershire foot militia. Despite his advantageous second marriage, Sir Ralph came close to ruining his family by his extravagance, particularly his addiction to greyhound coursing. In 1710 he made his estate over to his son and took refuge from his creditors in Ireland, while in 1716 he was obliged to agree to the execution of a special deed to protect his son's marriage settlement. In this deed his liabilities were stated to be nearly £10,000. He was eventually limited to a yearly allowance of £400. He died in Ireland some four years later and his wife died shortly afterwards.

Sir Ralph was succeeded by his only surviving son, **Sir John Dutton**, second baronet (1684–1743), who had been educated at the Middle Temple at the expense of his maternal grandfather. In 1714 he married Mary, heir of Sir Rushout Cullen of Upton, Warwickshire, with a marriage portion of £12,500. She died childless, in 1717. He was a colonel in the same militia regiment as his father, served as a JP, and represented Gloucestershire in parliament in 1727–41 as a whig. In 1728 he married Mary, the daughter of Francis Keck of Great Tew, Oxfordshire, whose marriage portion was £20,000. She also died childless the following year. By his careful management of his estate Sir John was able to repair much of the damage resulting from his father's depredations. Between 1723 and 1730 he undertook a general repair and overhaul of the house at Sherborne, and improved the hunting lodge built by his great-uncle, adding a parlour and bedrooms. He died in 1743 and was buried at Sherborne. His estates passed to his nephew James Lenox Naper of Loughcrew, Meath, on condition that he took the name and arms of Dutton.

The success of the Dutton family in establishing themselves within the Gloucestershire élite depended upon the careful acquisition, consolidation, and management of property combined with the forging and maintenance of ties with the London mercantile élite. The depredations of the second Sir Ralph Dutton might have ruined a family whose fortunes were less firmly established, but by reasserting the family tradition of prudent marriages and careful estate management his son was able to pass a thriving estate to his nephew. JAN BROADWAY

Sources B. Morgan, *Memoirs of the Dutton family of Sherborne, Gloucestershire* (1899) · J. Burke and J. B. Burke, *A genealogical and heraldic history of the extinct and dormant baronetcies of England, Ireland, and Scotland* (1838), 178–9 · W. Williams, *Parliamentary history of Gloucestershire* (1898) · J. M. Roper, *Monumental effigies of Gloucestershire and Bristol* (1931) · J. Smyth, *Men and armour for Gloucestershire* (1980) · 'Gloucestershire justices of the peace', *Gloucestershire Notes and Queries*, 5 (1894), 142–6 · R. Bigland, *Historical, monumental and genealogical collections, relative to the county of Gloucester*, ed. B. Frith, 3 (1992) · *VCH Gloucestershire*, 6.120–27 · J. Maclean and W. C. Heane, eds., *The visitation of the county of Gloucester taken in the year 1623*, Harleian Society, 21 (1885) · HoP, *Commons, 1715–54* · HoP, *Commons, 1660–90* · B. Morgan, *Memoirs of the Duttons of Dutton in Cheshire* (1901), 97–109 · Wood, *Ath. Oxon.: Fasti* (1820) · state papers, domestic, Charles I, PRO, SP 16/448/79
Archives Glos. RO, deeds; estate, family, legal, and manorial papers · Glos. RO, Aldsworth estate map · Glos. RO, estate and personal accounts of Sir John Dutton
Likenesses portrait (William Dutton, 1561–1618), Sherborne Park, Gloucestershire; repro. in Morgan, *Memoirs* · portrait (John Dutton, 1594–1657), Sherborne Park, Gloucestershire; repro. in Morgan, *Memoirs* · portrait (Sir Ralph Dutton, *c*.1645–1720/21), Sherborne Park, Gloucestershire; repro. in Morgan, *Memoirs* · portrait (Sir John Dutton, 1684–1743), Sherborne Park, Gloucestershire; repro. in Morgan, *Memoirs*
Wealth at death compositions after civil war suggest main estate valued at £60,000 and second estate (subsequently reunited with main) valued at £6000; these are probably conservative estimates: Morgan, *Memoirs of the Dutton family*

Dutton [*née* Williams], **Anne** (1691x5–1765), writer and autobiographer, was born in Northampton of devout parents (in 1691/1692 according to her gravestone, in 1695 according to her memoirs). Reared in a religious climate of hyper-Calvinism, increasing missionary zeal, and heightened passion for religious liberty, Anne attended the Independent church at Castle Hill, professing conversion at the age of thirteen and joining the church two years later under the pastorate of John Hunt (1698–1709). She was a vivacious beauty as a young woman and was more apt to speak her mind than to be silent.

After Hunt's death Thomas Tingey became Anne Williams's pastor in 1709, about whom Anne had little positive to say publicly. Because of her dissatisfaction with his ministry, she moved to the open-membership Baptist church in College Lane, Northampton, a church in which membership was granted on profession of faith without the necessity of baptism. It was here, under the ministry of John Moore, that she was baptized and became an active member, enjoying Moore's doctrinal preaching and the 'fat, green pastures' of spiritual nourishment she found there (Whitebrook, 'Life and works', 132).

In 1714 Anne Williams married a man named Cattel, or possibly Coles. The couple moved to London the next year, where she aligned with the Baptist church in Cripplegate that met in Curriers' Hall, to which she 'gave a large and choice account of the work of the Spirit of God upon her soul to the great joy of the church' (Robinson, 53). The church was under the ministry of John Skepp (1715–21), a notable hyper-Calvinist. Except for short periods in which they moved to Warwick and Evershall because of business, the couple lived in London until 1720, when her husband died. Anne then returned to Northampton.

In 1721 Anne Cattel married Benjamin Dutton (1691/2–1747), a lay Baptist preacher, clothier, and draper, who was the youngest of many children of Matthew Dutton (d. 1719). Following the death of her former pastor Skepp in 1721 Anne pressured her husband to move to Wellingborough to be closer to her favourite cleric and spiritual mentor, the Revd William Grant. In 1732 her husband became the pastor of the Baptist church in Great Gransden, Huntingdonshire. Sensing that any call to minister was as much hers as her husband's, Anne debated much over the decision before agreeing to move. The church grew rapidly under their leadership and a new meetinghouse and minister's house were built by 1743. That same year Benjamin travelled to America to solicit funds for the building work at Great Gransden. He had raised sufficient funds by 1747, but on his return home drowned in a shipwreck, leaving Anne a widow again. During the next two decades she focused on her writing.

Anne Dutton's published work, comprising some fifty volumes, includes poetry, theological discourse, hymns, letters, correspondence with such notable religious leaders as John Wesley and George Whitefield, and an autobiography. Attached to the latter is a cogent defence of the right of a woman both to write and to publish. Her autobiography, *A Brief Account of the Gracious Dealings of God with a Poor, Sinful, Unworthy Creature*, was written in three parts. The first two parts, completed in 1743, cover respectively her early years and conversion, and the 'special providences of God', and her opportunities for worship and spiritual training. Part three, written in 1750, describes her published works in lengthy detail, most of which were published under the initials A. D. Among her many theological treatises, three are most important: *A Discourse on Walking with God* (1735), *On God's Act of Adoption* (1737), and *On the Inheritance of the Adopted Sons of God* (n.d.). In these works she argues a Calvinistic view of atonement, thereby aligning herself with Whitefield, and openly criticizes the teachings of evangelists such as Wesley and Ralph Cudworth, the Moravian Brethren, and the Sandemanians. Without children of her own, she regarded her books as her offspring, finding 'divine Kindness in that freedom from worldly encumbrances!' (Robinson, 55). A zealous woman, she was especially eager for her volumes to be well received in America.

In 1764 Anne Dutton began to suffer from a throat condition, possibly cancer, and could no longer swallow food. In the next few months, writing, by her own account, 16–18 hours per day, she finished eight volumes of unpublished letters. By October 1765 she could no longer attend public worship. She died at Great Gransden on Monday 17 November 1765. Her body was interred the following Thursday in the burial-ground of the church of which she had been such a long and useful member. She left sackfuls of letters from England, Wales, Scotland, America, the Netherlands, and elsewhere. She had endowed the church with houses, land, a sum of £25 5s. per annum, and her library of 212 volumes. A tombstone was erected in 1822 by Christopher Goulding, which cited her age at death as seventy-three. A replacement stone was erected in 1887 by James Knight of Southport.

While Anne Dutton was at times vain, pretentious, ambitious, and verbose, these characteristics do not detract from her reputation as perhaps the most theologically capable and influential Baptist woman of her day. As a female writer in an era which did not foster such self-expression, her pioneering spirit served as a role model for other Baptist women, particularly the hymn-writer Ann Steele (1717–1778), to whom Anne bequeathed her Bible. The sheer magnitude of her published corpus, both in diversity of topic and number of correspondents, deserves to be acknowledged as a unique contribution to the English Baptist heritage.

KAREN O'DELL BULLOCK

Sources J. C. Whitebrook, *Anne Dutton: a life and bibliography* (1922) · J. C. Whitebrook, 'The life and works of Mrs. Ann Dutton', *Transactions of the Baptist Historical Society*, 7 (1920–21), 129–46 · H. W. Robinson, *The life and faith of the Baptists* (1946) · W. T. Whitely, *A history of British Baptists* (1923) · J. A. Jones, *A narration of the wonders of grace in six parts, and other writings of Anne Dutton* (1833) · Cripplegate church book, registry of letters, c.1715 and 1718, Regent's Park College, Oxford, Angus Collection · College Lane church book, 18 Aug 1715, Regent's Park College, Oxford, Angus Collection · S. Burder, *Memoirs of eminently pious women of the British empire*, 3 vols. (1815)
Likenesses engraving, repro. in Burder, *Memoirs*

Dutton, Emily Courtier- [*known as* Mrs Charles L. Carson; *performing name* Kittie Claremont] (1862?–1919), theatrical philanthropist, was apparently born in London in 1862. She made her theatrical début under the name of Kittie Claremont in *Le voyage en Chine* at the Garrick Theatre, Whitechapel, and subsequently appeared as Clairette in *La fille de Madame Angot*. *The Theatre* for 1888 noted her performances in the trial of John Lart's *The Monk's Room* (20 December 1887), as Hebe in J. F. Nisbet's *Dorothy Gray* at the Princess's (10 April 1888), and as Dolly Truefitt in C. Lemore's *A Crooked Mile*, in which she was described as 'bright and winning' (*The Theatre*, 1 June 1888, 325). She gave up the professional stage on her marriage to Lionel Courtier-Dutton (1846/7–1901). Courtier-Dutton was the founder and editor of the theatrical weekly *The Stage*; professionally he used the name Charles L. Carson, and Emily adopted the form Mrs Charles L. Carson in her public work. He already had three children, Edith, Lionel, and Ralph, from his first marriage; according to his will, they 'owed more to her loving kindness and honorable [*sic*] affection than they perhaps can ever fully understand'. Once they were old enough to attend boarding-school Mrs Carson returned to the stage, acting in amateur and charity fund-raising performances, for example appearing as Cecilia in F. S. Boas's *The Favourite King* at the Comedy Theatre in 1890.

In November 1891 Mrs Carson founded the Theatrical Ladies' Guild, which organization she served as secretary and treasurer. The charity, uniquely in the history of the British theatre, helped actresses not merely by offering financial support but also through strategic practical assistance: clothes for both daily and professional wear, meal tickets, and blankets were provided for the needy, and children's clothing and medical assistance for pregnant actresses was provided, irrespective of the marital status of the mothers. Mrs Cecil Rayleigh recalled of the founding of the guild that 'Mrs Carson very cleverly exploited our fondness for chatter and afternoon tea by suggesting that we could combine a pleasant afternoon's chat with very useful and very necessary labour for the good of our sisters who were in distress' (*The Stage*, 24 Jan 1901). Mrs Carson was also the founder, secretary, and treasurer of the Theatrical Christmas Dinner Fund, and in 1896 she co-founded with Mrs Clement Scott the Actors' Orphanage. Her husband's death on 2 January 1901 did not interrupt her charitable work. Mrs Carson died at 45 Norton Road, Hove, on 21 March 1919.

KATHARINE COCKIN

Sources J. P. Wearing, *The London stage, 1890–1899: a calendar of plays and players*, 2 vols. (1976) · B. Hunt, ed., *The green room book, or, Who's who on the stage* (1906), 63 · T. C. Davis, *Actresses as working women: their social identity in Victorian culture* (1991), 60–63 · G. B. Ryan, *Stage deaths: a biographical guide to international theatrical obituaries, 1850 to 1990*, 1 (1991), 245 · d. certs. [Emily and Lionel Courtier-Dutton] · wills [Emily and Lionel Courtier-Dutton] · *CGPLA Eng. & Wales* (1919) · *The Stage* (24 Jan 1901) · *The Theatre*, 4th ser., 10–11 (1887–8)
Archives Ellen Terry Memorial Museum, Smallhythe, Kent
Likenesses photographs (of Kittie Claremont?), Theatre Museum, Covent Garden, London, Guy Little collection
Wealth at death £786 16s. 1d.: probate, 16 May 1919, *CGPLA Eng. & Wales*

Dutton, John (1594–1657). *See under* Dutton family (*per.* 1522–1743).

Dutton, Sir John, second baronet (1684–1743). *See under* Dutton family (*per.* 1522–1743).

Dutton, Joseph Everett (1874–1905), pathologist in tropical medicine, was born on 9 September 1874 at New Chester Road, Rock Ferry, Birkenhead, the fifth son of John Dutton, a retired chemist of Brookdale, Banbury, and his wife, Sarah Ellen Moore. After education at King's School, Chester, from January 1888 until May 1892, he entered University College, Liverpool, where he gained the gold medal in anatomy and physiology, and the medal in materia medica in 1895. At Victoria University, Manchester, he won the medal in pathology in 1896, graduated MB CM in 1897, and was elected Holt fellow in pathology. He then acted as house-surgeon and house-physician at the Liverpool Royal Infirmary.

In 1900 Dutton accompanied Henry Annett and Jabez Elliott of Toronto on the third expedition of the Liverpool School of Tropical Medicine to southern and northern Nigeria, to study the life history and surroundings of the mosquito and generally to take measures for the prevention of malaria. *The Report of the Malaria Expedition to Nigeria* (1901) was published in two parts. The first part dealt with anti-malarial sanitation; the other was a monograph on filariasis. In 1901, the same year that he gained the Walter Myers fellowship in tropical medicine, Dutton travelled alone to the Gambia on the sixth expedition of the Liverpool School of Tropical Medicine, and drew up a comprehensive report on the prevention of malaria. During this expedition he identified in the blood of a patient at Bathurst, on the Gambian coast, *Trypanosoma gambiense*, a protozoan belonging to a group of parasites which had hitherto been found only in animals. Dutton's discovery of the first trypanosome in man was an important factor in determining the cause of sleeping sickness, which was afterwards shown by other observers to be due to the same parasite. In addition to *Trypanosoma gambiense*, Dutton also described several other trypanosomes new to science. In 1902 he visited the Senegambia with John L. Todd and drew up a report on sanitation which was presented to the French government; he also published further papers on trypanosomiasis. His last expedition was made to the Congo in charge of the twelfth expedition of the Liverpool School of Tropical Medicine. He started in August 1903, accompanied by Todd and Dr C. Christie. The expedition reached Stanley Falls about the end of 1904 and discovered independently the cause of tick fever in man, a discovery which had been anticipated a few weeks earlier by Ronald Ross and Dr Milne in the Uganda protectorate. Dutton was able to show the transference of the disease from man to monkeys. During the investigation Dutton and Christie contracted the disease. Dutton died of spirillum fever on 27 February 1905 at Kasongo in the Congo territory. His burial was attended by more than 1000 people, many of them Africans whom he had treated. Dutton and Todd's *The Nature of Human Tick-Fever in the Eastern Part of the Congo Free State* was published in the year of Dutton's death.   D'A. POWER, *rev.* MICHAEL BEVAN

Sources *BMJ* (1905), 1020–21 · *The Lancet* (6 May 1905), 1239 · private information (1912) · *Medical Directory* (1899–1900)
Archives U. Lpool, school of tropical medicine, papers · Wellcome L., diaries and papers
Likenesses photomechanical print, Wellcome L.
Wealth at death £2781 3*s.* 3*d.*: resworn probate, 4 Oct 1905, *CGPLA Eng. & Wales*

Dutton, Sir Ralph (1601–1646). *See under* Dutton family (*per.* 1522–1743).

Dutton, Sir Ralph, first baronet (*c.*1645–1720/21). *See under* Dutton family (*per.* 1522–1743).

Dutton, Thomas (1507–1581). *See under* Dutton family (*per.* 1522–1743).

Dutton, William (1561–1618). *See under* Dutton family (*per.* 1522–1743).

Dutton, William (1642–1675). *See under* Dutton family (*per.* 1522–1743).

Duval, Charles Allen (1808–1872), portrait and subject painter, was born in Ireland in 1808. His parentage is

unknown. After a time as a sailor, he settled as an artist in Liverpool, marrying on 1 May 1833 Elizabeth Renney, before moving to Manchester, where he continued to reside for the rest of his life.

Duval exhibited twenty pictures at the Royal Academy between 1836 and 1872, and exhibited regularly in the local exhibitions at Liverpool and Manchester. His portraits were regarded by contemporaries as good likenesses, and have considerable artistic merit, particularly his chalk studies of children. In 1838 he received a commission from Daniel Lee to paint a portrait of the Irish politician Daniel O'Connell, who would only sit for two and a half hours; but the artist had the ability to catch expression and to work quickly, and the result was regarded as a characteristic portrait. He had previously painted a picture containing one hundred portraits of the leading Wesleyans in the United Kingdom, who met in Manchester to celebrate the centenary of Methodism. Among his best-known productions in this branch of art are portraits of the chief members of the Anti-Corn Law League, which were afterwards engraved. He had a large practice in Liverpool and Manchester, and also in London.

Throughout his artistic career Duval never wholly abandoned subject picture painting. One of his first and best-known works in this line is *The Ruined Gamester*, which was purchased and engraved by a Manchester printseller named Dewhurst. It became so popular that a cartoon in *Punch*, caricaturing Sir Robert Peel, was drawn from it, and an etching from the picture and accompanying verses, both by the artist, appeared in the *North of England Magazine* for June 1842. He afterwards exhibited *The Giaour* (1842), *Columbus in Chains* (1855), *The Dedication of Samuel* (1858), *The Morning Walk* (1861), and many others in local exhibitions. He also painted during his later years some sea pieces. All his work was judged by contemporaries to possess great taste and beauty.

Duval, who in his youth hesitated between art and literature, published many papers in the *North of England Magazine*, and in 1863 he published five pamphlets on the American Civil War. He died at Bollin Fee, near Wilmslow, Cheshire, on 14 June 1872, survived by his wife.

ALBERT NICHOLSON, *rev.* PATRICIA MORALES

Sources *Manchester Examiner and Times* (17 June 1872) · *Art-treasures examiner: a record of the art-treasures exhibition, at Manchester, in 1857* · Thieme & Becker, *Allgemeines Lexikon* · Redgrave, *Artists* · Graves, *RA exhibitors* · A. Graves, *A century of loan exhibitions, 1813–1912*, 5 vols. (1913–15) · *CGPLA Eng. & Wales* (1872) · personal knowledge (1888) · d. cert.
Wealth at death under £1500: administration, 8 July 1872, *CGPLA Eng. & Wales*

Du Val, Charles Henry (1846–1889), entertainer, was born at Platt Terrace, Rusholme, Manchester, on 27 October 1846, the youngest child and only son of Irish parents, John Du Val, a schoolmaster, and his wife, Eliza Ann, *née* Murray. He was educated in Manchester and articled to a solicitor, but abandoned the law in 1864 to join Oldham repertory theatre. In 1865 he went to Dublin, where he devised and presented the first version of his one-man show *Odds and Ends*. A handsome man of middle height with brown wavy hair, he had a pleasant tenor voice, danced nimbly, and could mimic any accent: his impersonation of female characters was widely admired. He was adept at political satire and could hold the stage alone for two hours, provoking almost continual laughter. He wrote his own material, words, and music, and toured Ireland and Britain for more than ten years.

On 9 May 1877 Du Val married Mary (Minnie) Dorcas Burke (1848–1914), the daughter of George Courtney Burke, a merchant, of Cork, at Christ Church, Dublin. They had one daughter and a son who died in infancy. Following a serious illness, possibly tuberculosis, Du Val decided to take his show to South Africa, and set sail in November 1879. He was also acting as a special correspondent for the *Weekly Irish Times*. After a season in Cape Town, the Du Vals travelled throughout the country; Minnie, who was pregnant, returned to Ireland from Port Elizabeth. Du Val and his manager continued the tour, reaching Pretoria on 18 November 1880, where they were trapped by the First South African War in the siege of the city until April 1881. Du Val joined the Pretoria Carabiniers and saw service in several engagements; he also edited the *News of the Camp*. After the siege was lifted he completed his tour, and arrived back in Dublin in October 1881. He resumed his performances and also lectured on his experiences in the war. His book *With a Show through Southern Africa* (1882) sold 25,000 copies in the first few weeks.

In April 1883 Du Val made his London début with his one-man show and was engaged for a short season at the Lesser St James's Hall, Piccadilly. It was so successful that he was brought back on 24 September in the Grand Hall, where he gave 431 consecutive performances, seen by more than half a million people. On 7 July 1884 he gave a command performance for the prince and princess of Wales.

Du Val returned to South Africa in July 1885, but finding it deep in depression moved on to Mauritius, Ceylon, and India. In India he was commanded to appear before the nizam of Hyderabad and gave a gala performance for the viceroy on 12 January 1886. On his return home he moved from Dublin to London, where his second season opened on 30 July 1886, at the Prince's Theatre (later the Prince of Wales Theatre) in Coventry Street, Piccadilly. The show closed at the end of January 1887 because Du Val was suffering from laryngitis.

The Du Vals made a third, successful, tour of South Africa in 1888 and went on to Mauritius and Ceylon. Du Val was exhausted and ill on reaching Ceylon and the tour was abandoned. They sailed for home on 13 February 1889. Du Val seemed better, but on the evening of 22 February 1889, during the passage through the Red Sea, he became agitated and ran up on deck, saying he wanted a walk. He was never seen again. His death made headlines in London and South Africa; reports suggesting suicide were denied, but stigma attached itself to his memory. He left a personal estate amounting to over £3000 and was survived by his wife and daughter.   VIVIEN ALLEN

Sources C. H. Du Val, *With a show through southern Africa* (1882) · C. H. Du Val, ed., *News of the camp* (1880–81) · C. H. Du Val, 'Boerland revisited' [unpubd galley proofs] · V. Allen, *Du Val tonight! The story of a showman* (1990) · *Weekly Irish Times* (1881) · *Weekly Irish Times* (1888–9) · *Excalibur* [Cape Town] (7 Dec 1888), 5 · Johannesburg Public Library, Africana Museum · Kimberley Public Library, South Africa · South African Library, Cape Town · private information (2004) · register of deaths at sea

Archives CUL, Royal Commonwealth Society Library, corresp. and papers

Likenesses engraving (after a photograph), repro. in Du Val, *With a show through southern Africa*, frontispiece · photographs, repro. in Du Val, *News of the camp* · photographs, repro. in Allen, *Du Val tonight!* · photographs, priv. coll.

Wealth at death £3835: probate, 8 May 1889, *CGPLA Eng. & Wales*

Duval, Claude (*d.* 1670), highwayman, was born, according to *The Memoires of Monsieur Du Vall* (1670), the fuller of the two biographies which greeted his execution, in 1643 in Domfront, Normandy, the son of Pierre Du Vall, a miller, and his wife, Marguerite de la Roche, a tailor's daughter. However, as the author immediately conceded in a sardonic undercutting typical of the work,

> There are some that confidently averr that he was born in Smock-Alley without Bishopsgate, that his Father was a Cook, and sold boyled Beef and Pottage: But this report is as false, as it is defamatory and malicious … If he had been born there he had been no Frenchman, but if he had not been a Frenchman, 'tis absolutely impossible he should have been so much beloved in his life, and lamented in his death, by the English ladies.   (*Memoires*, 1–2)

The Life of Deval, the other contemporary biography, states no more than that 'Lewis Deval, alias John Brown [two of the other names Duval was known by] was born of French Parents' (*Life*, 3), and this is probably the most that one can say about his birth. *The Memoires*, like Samuel Butler's mock heroic poem, *To the Memory of the most Renowned Du-Vall*, which also appeared shortly after his death, had good satiric reasons for claiming that Duval was not just the son of French parents but French born himself. Both, in a way that *The Life* was not, were extended satires on French manners (and notably on their effect on English womanhood), though *The Life* nevertheless noted his genteel upbringing. *The Memoires*, which became the source for all later accounts of Duval's life, provided plentiful detail to substantiate his reputation as the debonair, gentlemanly highwayman. The legend of Duval's gallantry and elegance may have owed something to an image that he had himself cultivated. But the stories told in *The Memoires* are best read as filtered through the invention and satirical purpose of the author.

According to *The Memoires* Duval left Domfront for Paris in search of employment at fourteen. It claims that he got work running errands at the St Esprit, a tavern-cum-brothel in the English quarter of Faubourg St Germain. Duval then went to England in the service of a 'person of quality' when large numbers of exiled royalists returned home at the restoration of Charles II in 1660 (*Memoires*, 7). *The Life* also claimed that Duval was initially a servant in a socially prestigious household. *The Memoires* further states that Duval's three main extravagances, as a ladies' man, card-sharp, and drinker, led him into highway robbery and he quickly gained a reputation as a gentleman high-wayman *par excellence*, with an eye for the ladies.

In his most famous exploit Duval and four accomplices held up a coach carrying a gentleman, his wife, and a maid. To show that she was unafraid the lady began to play her flageolet, which prompted Duval to ask if he might dance a courante with her upon the heath. The dance over, Duval requested money from her husband for the entertainment, knowing him to have £400. When the husband willingly handed over £100, Duval rewarded his generosity by guaranteeing the party safe passage for the remainder of the journey. *The Memoires* demonstrated that Duval could act more brutishly and the most famous story it told against him was that he snatched a silver suckling bottle from a baby and only returned it to the distressed infant when forced to do so by an accomplice. *The Memoires* juxtaposed these two incidents, with the clear implication that this was what the courtesy of a Frenchman amounted to: fine manners but willing to steal the dummy out of a baby's mouth. Modern retellings suggest that it was an accomplice who stole it and Duval who forced him to return it. He allegedly returned to France for a few months in the late 1660s but found the opportunities for a highwayman more limited there. While in France, according to an early eighteenth-century elaboration by Alexander Smith, he carried out a notable confidence trick. Pretending to be an alchemist who had discovered the substance that would turn base metals into gold he won the trust of his patron in order to find and steal the man's hoarded wealth.

By late 1668 the Duval of the chapbooks and the Duval who can be traced through official records can be seen coming together. As *The Memoires* reported, the *London Gazette* placed him highest on its list of wanted highwaymen. On 23 December 1668 a proclamation offered a reward of £10 (raised the following week to £20) for the capture of twenty-three men, 'highwaymen of one party'; the name of 'Lodowick alias Lewis alias Peter Devall' appeared third on the list (Steele, 1.425). By the time of a repeat proclamation issued on 19 November 1669 'Lewis alias Lodowick alias Claude Deval alias Browne' had indeed moved to the head of the list (Steele, 1.426). The authorities were following other strategies alongside the promise of a reward. In March 1669 Sir William Morton, judge in the court of king's bench, who was later to boast that he had been responsible for the capture of more than a hundred highwaymen, wrote to the king's security chief, Sir Joseph Williamson, to discuss placing a further advertisement against Duval and others in the *London Gazette*: 'I have Emissaryes out against those fellowes', he noted (PRO, SP 29/257, no. 145). *The Life* described the authorities slowly closing in, capturing other members of his gang (and indeed five had been taken in March 1669). Duval was captured by the bailiff of Westminster on the night of Christmas eve 1669—according to *The Memoires* at the Hole-in-the-Wall tavern in Chandos Street, Covent Garden, while he was celebrating a successful hold-up, too drunk to resist. He was committed to Newgate by Morton, where (according to *The Life*) he was accompanied by his wife. 'His

Majesty upon his first being taken … excluded him from all hopes of pardon upon what intercession soever', the *London Gazette* reported (*LondG*, no. 437, 20–24 Jan 1670). The emphasis perhaps lends credence to the account in the 'Memoires' of Duval being visited in prison by large numbers of women, among whom some of the higher ranking ones pleaded with the king for a pardon.

Duval was found guilty of six charges of robbery at his arraignment at the Old Bailey on 17 January 1670 (and the authorities had many more to be proved should they have failed). The lists of witnesses on the back of the surviving indictment include the name of George Witherington or Widdrington, who along with William Dudley was acting as an informer against his former confederates. Duval was hanged at Tyburn on 21 January and in his dying speech, supposedly found on his body after his death, Duval acknowledged his obligation to the 'fair English ladies' (*Memoires*, 14).

The Memoires reported, with a show of scepticism, the story that Duval was laid out in a room draped in black with eight cloaked men keeping vigil at The Tangier tavern in St Giles-in-the-Fields. Appalled that so many thronged to this mock lying-in state, the room was supposedly cleared by the order of the judge 'betwixt whom and the Highway-men there's little love lost'—clearly a reference to Morton (*Memoires*, 13). Duval was, again according to *The Memoires*, given a splendid funeral at St Paul's, Covent Garden, and was buried there beneath a plain white marble stone in the middle aisle which bore an epitaph which began:

> Here lies Du Vall. Reader, if Male thou art
> Look to thy purse: if female, to thy heart.
> (*Memoires*, 16)

Duval remains a figure more of literary invention than of history: the bare verifiable facts of his life to be found in the sparse record provided by the authorities who pursued and hanged him. Whatever its origins in his own behaviour and self-presentation the Duval of pamphlet and ballad (his death produced as well as the two lives and Butler's poem a ballad, *Devol's Last Farewell*) was the creation of particular literary conventions and social concerns. His Frenchness was a matter of ambivalence: it meant fashion and glamour, but it also spoke to anxieties about the corrupting influence of Catholic France at the court of Charles II. On the one hand Du Val was 'that famous artist' who brought to England 'the most gentile methods of following the high-pack, taking a purse alamode, mustering his savage Arabians, and exercising them to perform their parts', as one pamphlet of 1674 described him (Spurr, 90). On the other hand, in 'the Tears that fell from divers Personages of the feminine Sex, that made application for that insipid Highway-man Du Vall', Titus Oates in 1696 discerned a sexual corruption—the taste of 'your fine, but (debauched) ladies' for 'a French Kickshaw'—that stood as a metaphor for the political and cultural corruption that was emanating from France (T. Oates, *Eikon basilike*, 1696, part 1.4). In so doing he was only making more explicit a theme already present in the more genial satire of manners of *The Memoires*.

In death as in life, it remains difficult to align the legend of Duval peddled by the pamphlet accounts with independent documentary evidence. It has been claimed that the stone and epitaph recorded by *The Memoires* were lost in a fire in 1759. However, his name does not appear in the burial registers of St Paul's, Covent Garden, while John Strype's apparently exhaustive list of monuments in the church in his 1720 edition of John Stow's *Survey of London* mentions neither tombstone nor epitaph.

BARBARA WHITE

Sources *The memoires of Monsieur Du Vall: containing the history of his life and death* (1670) · *The life of Deval* (1670) · S. Butler, *To the memory of the most renowned Du-Vall: a pindarick ode* (1671) · *Devol's last farewell: containing an account of many … robberies … with his lamentation on the day of his death* (1670) · *LondG* (20–24 Jan 1670) · R. Steele, ed., *Tudor and Stuart proclamations*, 2 vols. (1910), 425–6 · *CSP dom.*, 1669–70 · letter of Sir William Morton to Sir Joseph Williamson, PRO, SP 29/257 no. 145 · Middlesex gaol delivery roll, January 1670, LMA, MJ/SR/1381 · J. Spurr, *England in the 1670s: 'this masquerading age'* (2000) · H. Evans and M. Evans, *Hero on a stolen horse* (1977) · C. G. Harper, *Half hours with the highwaymen* (1908) · A. Smith, *A complete history of the lives and robberies of the most notorious highwaymen, footpads, shoplifts and cheats*, ed. A. L. Hayward (1926) · J. Strype, *Survey of the cities of London and Westminster*, 2 vols. (1720) · W. H. Hunt, ed., *The registers of St Paul's Church, Covent Garden, London*, 5 vols., Harleian Society, 33–7 (1906–9)

Duval, Lewis (1774–1844), lawyer, was born in Geneva on 11 November 1774, the second son of John Duval of Warnford Court, Throgmorton Street, London, a well-known diamond merchant of Genevese origin, and his wife, Elizabeth Beaufel de Vismes, of The Nowell, York. He matriculated in 1791 at Trinity Hall, Cambridge, and took the degree of LLB in 1796. In 1802 he was elected a fellow of his college. Duval was admitted a student of Lincoln's Inn on 18 June 1793, and on leaving Cambridge he became a pupil of Charles Butler (1750–1832), in whose chambers he remained for more than two years. He then commenced practice as a draftsman and conveyancer, and in the early years of his professional career was much employed by Butler, who had the highest opinion of the talents of his old pupil. Duval was called to the bar on 19 June 1804.

Unlike many eminent conveyancers, Duval owed his rise in the profession entirely to his skill as a chamber practitioner. He never published any legal work, and a hesitation in his speech deterred him from practising in court. After the retirement of Butler, Richard Preston, and F. W. Sanders, Duval became the acknowledged head of his particular branch of learning. Though not an original member of the real property commission, he was subsequently appointed a commissioner, and wrote the greater portion of its second report, which was related entirely to the establishment of a general registry of deeds. As a draftsman Duval to a great extent followed Butler's forms and was greatly admired for the clarity and thoroughness he displayed in his work.

Among Duval's more distinguished pupils were E. B. Sugden, C. H. Bellenden Ker, and Sir Charles Hall, who married Duval's niece and later became a vice-chancellor. Duval died, probably of a heart attack, at St Petersburg House, Bayswater Hill, London, on 11 August 1844, and was buried nearby at St George's Chapel in the Bayswater Road.

G. F. R. BARKER, *rev.* BETH F. WOOD

Sources *Law Review*, 1 (1844–5), 139–44 · *GM*, 2nd ser., 22 (1844), 328 · W. P. Baildon, ed., *The records of the Honorable Society of Lincoln's Inn: admissions*, 2 vols. (1896) · *Annual Register* (1844) · Venn, *Alum. Cant.*

Likenesses G. Hayter, portrait; formerly in possession of his nephew, Mr Lewis Duval, 1888 · Sievier, bust; formerly in possession of his nephew, Mr Lewis Duval, 1888

Wealth at death £44,246 11s. 10d.: probate

Duval, Philip (*d. c.*1709), painter, was born in France, and studied under Charles le Brun. He spent some time in Venice and Verona where 'he studyd his manner of Drawing & Colouring after Titian Tintoret Paul Veroness from where he form'd an agreeable style of painting being a mixt manner of the French Lombard Schools' (Vertue, *Note books*, 1.126). He finally settled in London about 1670. He painted the celebrated Frances Stuart, later duchess of Richmond, posing as Venus in a scene depicting Vulcan giving Venus armour for her son Aeneas. Vertue noted that this was 'dated (on the anvil) 1672 with his name on it' (ibid.). He is said to have had a fascination with 'chemistry', and as a result of spending too much time and money in its pursuit, he neglected his art and his income. He was subsequently supported by the Hon. Robert Boyle, who gave him an annual allowance of £50. Upon his patron's death, Duval descended into poverty and mental derangement. He died *c.*1709, and is believed to have been buried in St Martin-in-the-Fields, London.

L. H. CUST, *rev.* SUSAN COOPER MORGAN

Sources H. Walpole, *Anecdotes of painting in England: with some account of the principal artists*, ed. R. N. Wornum, new edn, 3 vols. (1849); repr. (1862) · Redgrave, *Artists* · E. K. Waterhouse, *The dictionary of British 16th and 17th century painters* (1988) · Bénézit, *Dict.*, 4th edn · Bryan, *Painters* (1886–9) · Vertue, *Note books*, 1.83, 126

Archives Courtauld Inst., photographs, catalogues, cuttings

Duval [Fortuyn], **Robert** (1649–1732), painter and art administrator, was born in The Hague, Holland. Of his parents, nothing is known. He first worked as a pupil of the artist Nicolaes Willingh and subsequently studied and worked in Berlin and at Rome (where he was known as Fortuyn), Venice, and Padua for a total of twelve years. On his return to The Hague he married the daughter of an influential French preacher, Daniel de Marets, who became comptroller-general of the household of the stadholder, William of Orange, later William III of England. It was through Marets that Duval was appointed court painter and keeper and curator of the stadholder's paintings in October 1682. He was responsible for keeping an inventory of William's collection, as well as maintenance and acquisitions of works. Although he produced many paintings and decorative interiors, none of his work survives. A twentieth-century copy of his decoration of the grand staircase at Het Loo, after designs by Daniel Marot, provides an impression of his work.

Duval accompanied William III's pictures to Hampton Court Palace and his biographer, Van Gool, states that he assisted in the cleaning and ordering of the Raphael cartoons there (Leeuwen, 43 n. 16). John Shearman, however, makes no reference to Duval's contribution in his authoritative book on that subject. In England he renewed his friendship with the artist Sir Godfrey Kneller whom he had known in Italy, and each artist's portrait of the other is now in the Academy of Fine Arts at The Hague. The portrait of Duval by Kneller has been dated to about 1697 by J. Douglas Stewart.

On his return to Holland Duval became director of the Draughtsmen's Academy in The Hague, which he had been involved in founding in 1682. He was also a warden, then dean, of the Confrerie Pictura in The Hague. In 1713 he compiled a list now in the Royal Archives, The Hague, of the paintings brought to Holland from England by William III, many of which remain in the Rijksmuseum. He died in The Hague on 22 January 1732.

Robert Duval is sometimes confused with the artist Philip Duval who was no relation. In the *Dictionary of National Biography* article on Robert Duval, Lionel Cust suggests that two engravings of paintings in the gallery of Boyer d'Aguilles, ascribed to Philip Duval, should be given to Robert.   KATHRYN BARRON

Sources E. Buijsen, *Haagse schilders in de Gouden Eeuw: het Hoogsteder Lexicon van alle schilders werkzaam in Den Haag, 1600–1700* (The Hague, 1998), 303 [exhibition catalogue, Haagse Historisch Museum, The Hague, 12 Dec 1998–7 Mar 1999] · B. Brenninkmeyer-De Rooij and others, *Paintings from England: William III and the royal collections*, ed. R. van Leeuwen (1988), 14–15, 34–5, 52–3, 43 nn. 15–17 [exhibition catalogue, Royal Cabinet of Paintings, Mauritshuis, The Hague, 12 Nov 1988 – 29 Jan 1989] · J. B. Descamps, *La vie des peintres flamands, allemands et hollandois*, 3 (Paris, 1760), 172–4 · J. D. Stewart, *Sir Godfrey Kneller and the English baroque portrait* (1983), 9 n. 38, catalogue no. 250, p. 104 · DNB · J. Shearman, *Raphael's cartoons in the collections of her majesty the queen* (1972) · P. J. Mariette, *Cabinet de Monsieur Boyer d'Aguilles* (Aix, 1744), pl. 82, 83
Archives Royal Society, The Hague, Dutch Royal Archives, papers
Likenesses G. Kneller, oils, *c*.1687, Academy of Fine Arts, The Hague

Duval [*née* Dugdale], **Una Harriet Ella Stratford** (1879–1975), suffragette and marriage reformer, was born on 28 January 1879 at Slanmore, Beulah Hill, Upper Norwood, Surrey, the elder daughter and one of five children of Commander Edward Stratford Dugdale, a naval officer, and his wife, Alice Florence Richards. Brought up in a distinguished Warwickshire family, Una was educated in Aberdeen near the family's holiday home in Aboyne and at Cheltenham Ladies' College, finishing her education in Paris and Hanover where she studied singing. Although both her parents supported the women's suffrage struggle, it was during the summer of 1907, when in London for the social season, that Una became involved herself and joined the Women's Social and Political Union (WSPU) after hearing Christabel Pankhurst speak in Hyde Park.

For the next five years Una Dugdale, like many other women of her age and social class, committed herself to the militant suffrage struggle, campaigning for the women's vote in Scotland on speaking tours with Emmeline Pankhurst, helping to arrange social events for the WSPU in London, and engaging in direct action. In 1909 during a WSPU 'raid' on the House of Commons she was arrested in Parliament Square and imprisoned for a month.

In 1911 Una Dugdale met her future husband Victor Diedrichs Duval (1885–1945). Also from a wealthy upper-class family with liberal credentials, Duval had founded the Men's Political Union for Women's Enfranchisement and had been arrested and imprisoned for activism. It was as a result of her refusal to say the words 'I obey' at her marriage ceremony on 13 January 1912 that Una Duval acquired a brief notoriety within the women's movement. Although on the day of the wedding two priests were sent by the archbishop of Canterbury to the Chapel Royal at the Savoy where the service was taking place, the only concession made to their insistence that Una Duval pronounce the words 'I obey' was that the officiating minister read the words out even though they were not repeated. Marriage reform had long been a feminist concern and Duval's standpoint signified a feminist commitment to marriage as an equal partnership based on love and respect rather than subservience and subordination. Later in the year she explained her reasons for departing from convention in her pamphlet *Love and Honour but NOT Obey*.

After the First World War Una Duval appears to have devoted herself to family life, in particular bringing up her two daughters; but she did not encourage them to take up careers. Although she remained committed to preserving the memory of the militant suffrage struggle through membership of the Suffragette Fellowship, of which she was co-founder and was treasurer for many years, there is no evidence of any further active engagement in women's politics. Una Duval died in St Stephen's Hospital, Chelsea, London, on 24 February 1975.

                              CATHERINE BLACKFORD

Sources E. Crawford, *The women's suffrage movement: a reference guide, 1866–1928* (1999) · R. Fulford, *Votes for women* (1957) · *Thanksgiving service for Una Dugdale Duval: 24th April 1975 the Queen's Chapel of Savoy* [pamphlet] · b. cert. · m. cert. · d. cert.
Wealth at death £16,126: probate, 18 June 1975, *CGPLA Eng. & Wales*

Duveen, Sir Joseph Joel (1843–1908), art dealer and benefactor, was born Joel Joseph Duveen at Meppel in the Netherlands on 8 May 1843, the elder son in a family of two sons and two daughters of his wife, Eva (1812–1864), the daughter of Henry van Minden of Zwolle. His grandfather Henry Duveen, who had first settled at Meppel during the Napoleonic wars, was the youngest son of Joseph Duveen of Giessen, army contractor to the king of Saxony. Napoleon's repudiation of the debts of the Saxon forces ruined Henry Duveen, whose twelve sons were then forced to seek their fortunes in different countries.

Duveen left Meppel in 1866 and settled at Hull, where he was originally employed in a firm selling provisions. On 10 February 1869 he married Rosetta, daughter of Abraham Barnett, a pawnbroker of Carr Lane, Hull. She survived him, and together they had a family of ten sons and four daughters. Duveen possessed a good knowledge of Nanking porcelain, then becoming fashionable. Cargo loads of this china had been brought to the Netherlands by the early Dutch traders with China; Duveen purchased large quantities which he shipped to Hull, soon finding a ready market for it in London. In partnership with his younger brother, Henry, he soon secured the chief American trade in oriental porcelain, and in 1877 opened a branch house at Fifth Avenue, New York. They helped to form many fine collections in America, including Henry Garland's superlative cabinet, which they bought back *en bloc* in March 1902, reselling it at once to John Pierpont Morgan. They also played an important role in the formation of significant American collections such as the Taft, Widener, Gould, and Altman collections, expanding thus into the fields of painting and fine art.

In 1879 the brothers built a gallery of fine art next to the Pantheon in Oxford Street, London, and began to take an important share in the trade in decorative arts in the capital, extending their interests in many areas, particularly in that of old tapestry, of which they became the largest purchasers. When Robinson and Fisher vacated their auction rooms at 21 Old Bond Street the Duveens secured these additional premises and built spacious art galleries in the spring of 1894. From 1890 onwards they purchased pictures and were large buyers at the Mulgrave Castle sale of 1890 and at the Murrieta sale, which contained works purchased in Spain, two years later. They purchased the whole of the Hainauer collection of Renaissance *objets d'art* for about £250,000 in June 1906, and in 1907 the Rodolphe Kann collection of pictures and *objets d'art* in Paris, for nearly £0.75 million. By this time, Duveen's son, another Joseph Joel *Duveen, later Baron Duveen (1869–1939), had begun to dominate the firm with his enormous enterprise and ambition.

J. J. Duveen had amassed a large fortune and was generous in his benefactions to English public galleries. Besides dynamic energy and initiative, he possessed an eye for beauty. He was a subscriber to the purchase of Velázquez's *The Toilet of Venus* ('Rokeby Venus') for the National Gallery in 1906. In the same year he presented J. S. Sargent's full-length portrait of Ellen Terry as Lady Macbeth—which he had brought in the Irving sale of 1905 for £1200—to the Tate Gallery, starting the family connection to the gallery maintained so strongly by his son. In May 1908 he undertook the cost of about £35,000 of the new Turner wing of the gallery. He was also associated with the public art gallery in Hull, where he had started his career: his son presented Edward Stott's *The Good Samaritan* to the gallery as a memorial of the connection. Duveen was knighted on 26 June 1908. He died at Hyères in France on 9 November 1908, and was buried in the Jewish cemetery, Willesden.

WILLIAM ROBERTS, rev. HELEN DAVIES

Sources *The Times* (7 Aug 1907) · *The Times* (7 May 1908) · *The Times* (7 Dec 1908) · *Morning Post* (7 Dec 1908) · *The Year's Art* (1908) · A. C. R. Carter, *Let me tell you* (1940) · private information (1912) [family; A. C. R. Carter] · S. N. Behrman, *Duveen* (1952) · J. H. Duveen, *Collection and recollections: a century and a half of art deals* (1935) · J. H. Duveen, *Secrets of an art dealer* (1937) · J. H. Duveen, *The rise of the house of Duveen* (1957) · E. Fowles, *Memoirs of Duveen brothers* (1976) · m. cert.
Likenesses E. Fuchs, oils, 1903, Tate collection, London

Wealth at death £540,409 13s. 7d.: probate, 3 Dec 1908, *CGPLA Eng. & Wales*

Duveen, Joseph Joel, Baron Duveen (1869–1939), art dealer and benefactor, was born at Hull on 14 October 1869, the eldest of the ten sons and four daughters of Sir Joseph Joel *Duveen (1843–1908) and his wife, Rosetta, daughter of Abraham Barnett of Hull. He was educated privately, and at the age of seventeen entered his father's business, which dealt mainly in oriental porcelain, tapestries, furniture, and *objets d'art*. Duveen quickly realized the vast profits to be made by buying great masters in Europe and selling them in America, thus adding enormously to the activities of the family business, which became the most prominent in the British art trade. His intense energy and salesmanship soon made him the world's foremost dealer, and his transactions were on an unprecedented scale; he paid, for instance, £60,900 for George Romney's small portrait of Mrs Bromley Davenport (National Gallery of Art, Washington, DC), £77,700 for Thomas Lawrence's portrait of Mary Moulton Barrett (*Pinkie*; Henry E. Huntington Library and Art Gallery, San Marino, California), and £73,500 for Gainsborough's *Harvest Waggon* (Barber Institute, Birmingham). Apart from purchases at auction, he acquired whole collections at immense sums, including the Hainauer collection of Renaissance *objets d'art* in 1906, and the Rodolphe Kann collection of pictures and *objets d'art* in 1907, both bought when his father Joseph Joel Duveen was still alive. Joseph Duveen went on to purchase the Maurice Kann collection in 1909, the Morgan collection of Chinese porcelain and eighteenth-century furniture, and in 1914, the great Fragonard room now in the Frick Museum in New York. In 1927 he acquired the R. H. Benson collection of Italian paintings for $3 million, in 1930 the Gustav Dreyfus collection of Italian sculpture and bronzes, and in 1936 Lord Hillingdon's collection of Sèvres porcelain and furniture.

A vast number of important paintings passed through Duveen's hands. Frequently he purchased works from aristocratic collections in Britain and Europe to sell to American clients, who included Benjamin Altmann, Jules S. Bache, Henry Clay Frick, Henry E. Huntington, Andrew Mellon, Mrs Hamilton Rice, Samuel H. Kress, and Joseph E. Widener. In 1921 he acquired Gainsborough's portrait of Jonathan Buttall (*The Blue Boy*) from the duke of Westminster and sold it to Henry Huntington. In 1929 he sold the Raphael *Madonna* of 1508 ('The Cowper Madonna'; National Gallery of Art, Washington, DC) to Andrew Mellon for $970,000. In 1937 he bought from Lord Allendale Giorgione's *Adoration of the Shepherds* (National Gallery of Art, Washington, DC). As the family firm had originally specialized in the decorative arts, Duveen wisely made use of the expertise of art historians and museum officials to authenticate the paintings he acquired, and was associated in this respect with Wilhelm von Bode and Bernard Berenson. Through Duveen's agency, many significant European works of art, donated by American collectors, have entered American museums and art galleries.

Duveen's art benefactions in Britain were on a grand scale. He donated Hogarth's *The Graham Children* and

Joseph Joel Duveen, Baron Duveen (1869–1939), by Walter Tittle, 1920s?

Correggio's *Christ Taking Leave of his Mother* to the National Gallery, and John Singer Sargent's study of Mme Gautreau and Augustus John's portrait of Mme Suggia to the Tate Gallery. To the Tate he also gave several galleries to house contemporary non-British paintings, one devoted to the work of Sargent, and in 1937 a new building comprising three large and two smaller galleries for contemporary sculpture. In 1932 he presented a gallery for early Italian pictures to the National Gallery; in 1933 he paid for an extension to the National Portrait Gallery; and he provided the British Museum with a gallery for the Elgin marbles (during the preparation of which the statues were controversially cleaned). He also bore the cost of the decorations at the Wallace Collection and of Rex Whistler's mural decorations at the Tate, and was a generous contributor to the National Art Collections Fund. He founded, financed, and organized the British Artists Exhibitions Organization for the encouragement of lesser known British artists, and in 1931 he endowed a chair for the history of art in London University.

Duveen was a trustee of the Wallace Collection from 1925, of the National Gallery from 1929 to 1936, and of the National Portrait Gallery from 1933. He was an honorary member of the council of the National Art Collections Fund and of the council of the British School at Rome. He was director of the American Institute for Persian Art and Archaeology, New York, a trustee of the Museum of Modern Art, New York, and honorary correspondent of the commissions of ancient and modern art of the Royal Belgium Museum of Fine Art. In 1929 he was presented with the freedom of the city of Hull. He received foreign decorations from France, Belgium, Holland, Serbia, and Hungary. He was knighted in 1919, created a baronet in 1927, and raised to the peerage as Baron Duveen of Millbank, commemorating his long association with the Tate Gallery, in 1933.

Duveen was an overwhelming and extremely persuasive character. A fervent cigarette smoker, he adopted a fake cigarette when illness precluded his maintenance of the habit. On 31 July 1899 he married Elsie, daughter of Sol Salomon, tobacco grower, of New York. She survived him with their only child, a daughter. The peerage therefore became extinct when he died at Claridges Hotel, Brook Street, London, on 25 May 1939.

ALEC MARTIN, *rev.* HELEN DAVIES

Sources *The Times* (26 May 1939) · auction and exhibition catalogues · personal knowledge (1949) · A. C. R. Carter, *Let me tell you* (1940) · S. N. Behrman, *Duveen* (1952) · J. H. Duveen, *Collection and recollections: a century and a half of art deals* (1935) · J. H. Duveen, *Secrets of an art dealer* (1937) · J. H. Duveen, *The rise of the house of Duveen* (1957) · E. Fowles, *Memoirs of Duveen brothers* (1976) · C. Simpson, *The partnership: the secret association of Bernard Berenson and Joseph Duveen* (1987) · F. Spalding, *The Tate: a history* (1998) · W. St Clair, *Lord Elgin and the marbles*, 3rd edn (1998) · *CGPLA Eng. & Wales* (1940) · m. cert.
Archives BL, corresp. with lords D'Abernon and Baldwin, Add. MS 48932 · U. Glas. L., letters to D. S. MacColl
Likenesses W. E. Tittle, pencil drawing, 1920–1929?, NPG [*see illus.*] · G. C. Beresford, photograph, 1930, NPG · W. R. Dick, stone bust, 1933, NPG · J. Lavery, c.1933 (*Opening of the Lord Duveen annex at the National Portrait Gallery*), NPG · J. Lavery, group portrait, oils, c.1937 (*Lord Duveen of Millbank at home*), Ferens Art Gallery, Hull · I. Isaac, oils, NPG · W. Tittle, oils, Guildhall, Hull · D. Wilding, photograph, NPG · photographs, repro. in Duveen, *Rise of the house of Duveen*
Wealth at death £1247 10s. 0d.: probate, 20 April 1940, *CGPLA Eng. & Wales*

DuVerger, Susan [Susan Du Vergeere; *née* Suzanne de La Vallée] (*bap.* 1610, *d.* 1657×9), translator and author, was born in London and baptized at the French Huguenot church in Threadneedle Street on 29 April 1610, the fifth of the five children of Charles and Ester de La Vallée. Nothing is known about her parents other than their names recorded in the baptismal records, or about her early life in London, but at some point before 1633, Suzanne de La Vallée married Jean-Jacques DuVerger. In the early 1630s she gave birth to two daughters: Françoise (*c.*1633) and Suzanne (*c.*1635). There is no more information about their family life.

DuVerger published two English translations of works by the French Catholic bishop Jean-Pierre Camus. In 1639 came *Admirable Events*, her translation of his collection of moralistic prose romance tales, which she dedicated to England's French Catholic queen, Henrietta Maria. Although the title-page gives the author only as S. DuVerger, the Stationers' register for 3 October 1638 lists the author of *Admirable Events* as Susan du Vergeere. In 1641 DuVerger published a second translation of Camus, entitled *Diotrèphe*. The dedicatory letter, to Lady Herbert, Elizabeth Somerset Powis—a zealous and active Catholic aristocrat—is signed simply S. DuVerger, but it refers pointedly to her earlier 'labours in this kind', suggesting that this DuVerger was also the translator of *Admirable Events*.

Susan DuVerger was probably also the author of an original prose work published in 1657, entitled *DuVergers Humble Reflections* with the lengthy subtitle 'Upon some passages of the right honorable the lady marchionesse of Newcastles Olio, or, An appeale from her mes-informed, to her owne better informed judgement'. The *Humble Reflections* is a scholarly defence of monastic life against critical charges made by the prolific author Margaret Cavendish, the marchioness of Newcastle, in her 1655 work *The World's Olio*. Internal evidence suggests that the DuVerger of the title is an English woman. The author writes, in an introductory letter to the duchess, that the *Olio* promotes 'the honour of our nation, and sexe, wherin we have had but few arguments'. Much later in the *Humble Reflections*, DuVerger includes a letter to Margaret Cavendish from a male friend who refers to the author as 'Mrs. DuVerger' and describes her as a 'lover of learning, and a verie vertuoso in antiquities, beyond the rate of a woman'. The *Humble Reflections* is a fascinating book-length letter to Cavendish. As a salvo in a public debate on religion between two educated women, this work is extremely unusual.

All three of DuVerger's published works raise challenging and as yet unanswered questions about her life. The most intriguing of these is why a woman born into a Huguenot family chose to publish works that seem to support Catholic culture and doctrine.

Susan DuVerger seems to have died soon after completing the *Humble Reflections*. In 1659 both her daughters emigrated from France to Quebec and married soon after their arrival. On their marriage records, their mother, listed as 'Suzanne de Laval de Londres, Angleterre', is described as deceased.   JANE COLLINS

Sources P. Schlueter and J. Schlueter, eds., *An encyclopedia of British women writers*, rev. edn (1998) · Arber, *Regs. Stationers*, vol. 5 · R. Jette, *Dictionnaire généalogique des familles du Québec* (1983) · *IGI*

Duwall, Mauritz. *See* MacDougal, Maurice (1603–1655).

Duwes [Dewes], **Giles** [*pseud.* Aegidius de Vadis] (*d.* 1535), musician and royal tutor, was perhaps of Norman origin; the village of Le Vey on the plain of Caen was then called Wez and Latinized as Vadum. One of the many useful foreigners who served Henry VII, Duwes first appears in the Tudor household accounts about the turn of the sixteenth century as a professional musician. His will mentions a wife named 'Jhone' and four children: Henry, Arthur, Gwylliam, and Margaret. Because he named all but one of these children after his royal pupils, they must have been born later than their royal counterparts and probably following his entrance into royal service. Arthur was old enough by 1515 to enter Henry VIII's household as a professional lute player. Giles had therefore probably entered Henry VII's service by the mid-1490s. As 'Luter unto oure derrest Son the duke of Yorke', Duwes was formally a member of Prince Henry's household by November 1501. In the course of music tuition, he bought lute strings for 'the Quene of Scottes lewte' (Princess Margaret) in July 1502 and 'for My Lady Mares lute' in 1507. From 1502 onwards he drew his regular half-yearly salary of 10s. as a lute player from the king's privy purse. At the funeral of Henry VII in 1509 he appears in the household roster as one of three 'Mynstrells of the Chambre'.

Duwes's role as French tutor may have begun informally as a consequence of his music lessons. In his French grammar, *An Introductorie for to Lerne to Rede, to Pronounce, and to Speke French Trewly* (1533?), he recalls that he had already served the Tudor court 'thirty yeres and more' as 'schoolmaster for the French tongue', an observation that seems to date the beginning of his French teaching career to about the turn of the century. He also claims to have taught French to all of Henry VII's children (Arthur, Henry, Margaret, and Mary), as well as to Henry VIII's daughter, Mary, and to Henry Courtenay, the future marquess of Exeter (Duwes, *Introductorie*, 895–6). His career as a French tutor to Prince Arthur probably began in 1500, when the poet Bernard André retired, and it ended with Arthur's departure for Wales (November 1501), where the prince died. During the same period, he must have given Princess Margaret French lessons along with her lute instruction. Soon after she left for Scotland in 1503 Duwes, now described as Prince Henry's 'Master to lute French', had begun to teach both French and lute playing to the new heir apparent, and in that capacity he attended the funeral of Queen Elizabeth. From 1507 on (by which time he would have begun teaching French to both Princess Mary and Henry Courtenay), the household account books routinely identify him as 'Master Giles Luter', the unusual title (no other household musician is so described) apparently referring to his dual role as schoolmaster and entertainer.

From April 1506 a dramatic increase in his salary (from 10s. to 10 marks half yearly) probably represents Duwes's assumption of the royal librarian's duties, in addition to his tutorial and entertainment responsibilities, on the departure of his predecessor, Quentin Poulet. At the accession of Henry VIII, Duwes's position as keeper of the king's library at Richmond was formalized by a patent on 20 September 1509 at annual salary of £10 'during pleasure', and this patent was then renewed on 24 March 1512 'for life' (*LP Henry VIII*, 1(1), 190(27); 1(1), 1123(56)). During his long tenure as keeper of the royal library, Duwes presided over a collection that served both as a working library and as an impressive ornament of the royal estate. In 1521 he composed 'Dialogus inter naturam et filium philosophiae' in the Richmond Library, completing it, he says, on '17 ides July'. An alchemical treatise, it circulated widely both in its original Latin and in a late sixteenth-century English translation. In it, the goddess Natura appears to an earnest, if befuddled, student of philosophy to explain the 'dark riddles, labyrinths, tropes, intricate allegories, metaphors, and shadows' which have nearly discouraged him from the further pursuit of alchemy (BL, Sloane MS 3580B, fol. 186v). In February 1535, a few weeks before Duwes's death, two French visitors drew up a list of 143 of the volumes then in the Richmond Library. Though containing a few English works, the inventory suggests that Duwes oversaw a predominately Latin and French-language collection full of chronicles, history, Latin classics, religion, and theology, together with a few volumes of poetry and romance.

After the accession of Henry VIII, Duwes found that his

old pupil seemed eager to bestow favour and wealth upon him. In 1510 the king appointed him keeper of 'le Prince Warderobe' in the city of London, one of the large warehouses used as a storehouse for the royal household, and also increased his salary to 40s. per month. In 1515 he accepted Duwes's son, Arthur, into his household, initially as a lute player at a monthly salary of 10s. 4d., later as a lute teacher for Henry Fitzroy, duke of Richmond. Through the next twenty-five years there followed numerous gifts, lucrative concessions to import Toulouse woad and Gascon wine, and a licence to keep up to £1000 of the customs duties on his imported or exported goods over a five-year period.

Between 1525 and 1528 Duwes accompanied the Princess Mary as one of her 'gentleman waiters' to the Welsh marches, where he served for the last time in his familiar roles as music teacher and French language tutor. His royal pupil apparently flourished under his supervision, for a French embassy of 1527 reported that she spoke French well, and others remarked upon her mastery of the lute. His *Introductorie* emerged from this experience as a result of an explicit royal command 'to reduce and to put by writtyng' the methods he had used for over thirty years to teach the language to his royal pupils (Duwes, *Introductorie*, 897). In response, he produced a pioneering work on French language pedagogy in two books, a grammar and a series of model dialogues in French and English. The dialogues provide an illuminating, if perhaps idealized, glimpse of court life in Princess Mary's household. In one, he frames a dialogue on the subject of love between the princess and John ap Morgan, the treasurer of her chamber (whom he playfully styles 'her husband adoptif'); in another, he represents Mary as 'crased' for lack of ap Morgan's company. In still others, her almoner teaches her the meaning of the mass or practises speaking French with her in 'the Park of Tewksbury', which Mary visited in September 1526. In several, Duwes excuses his absences from lessons because of sickness, once explicitly the gout. Duwes often represents himself as a philosophical interlocutor, now expounding St Augustine's ideas on peace, now St Isidore's on the nature of the soul. Throughout, he represents himself as a witty and avuncular schoolmaster on mutually affectionate terms with his pupil. He published his *Introductorie* in 1533 or 1534, dedicating it of necessity not only to King Henry and the Lady Mary but also to the new queen, Anne Boleyn. At the same time, as a final expression of royal favour, his wife was appointed to Mary's household as one of her gentlewomen.

By 1534 Duwes's tenure as royal librarian was ending. On 11 March William Tyldysley was granted a patent to establish his right to succeed Duwes in 'the office of Keeper of the King's Library in the manor of Richmond or elsewhere, whenever it shall happen to be vacant' (*LP Henry VIII*, 7, no. 419(11)). Duwes made his will on 20 December 1534, apparently expecting impending death. He thus mentions a series of bequests in the form of 'tokens' which he had already wrapped and labelled and to which he had affixed his seal for the 'knoolege' and

'behooff' of his beneficiaries. He also left a large collection of musical instruments—'clavicordes, virginalles, recordes, regalles'—to his sons Arthur and Gwylliam, but specifically reserved his lute and his 'bookes of musyck and frensshe' for his son Arthur alone. A few months later, on 12 April 1535, Duwes died and a second patent was issued to confirm William Tyldysley's actual possession of the now vacant office. He was buried in the London church of St Olave Upwell, and his will was proved on 24 April 1535. A gift of a 'Frountlet' to a 'maistres Colson sometyme maistres giles' recorded among the Princess Mary's privy purse expenses for January 1538 may suggest that his widow married again after his death.

GORDON KIPLING

Sources accounts of John Heron, treasurer of the chamber, 1 Oct 1495–30 Sept 1497, PRO, E 101/414/6 · accounts of John Heron, treasurer of the chamber, 1 Oct 1497–30 Sept 1499, PRO, E 101/414/16 · accounts of John Heron, treasurer of the chamber, 1 Oct 1499–30 Sept 1502, PRO, E 101/415/3 · accounts of John Heron, treasurer of the chamber, 1 Oct 1502–30 Sept 1505, BL, Add. MS 59899 · accounts of John Heron, treasurer of the chamber, 1 Oct 1505–21 April 1509, PRO, E 36/214 · accounts of John Heron, treasurer of the chamber, 1 May 1509–31 March 1518, BL, Add. MS 21481 · H. C. de Lafontaine, ed., *The king's musick: a transcript of records relating to music and musicians, 1460–1700* [1909] · Æ. de Vadis [G. Duwes], 'Dialogus inter naturam et filium philosophiae', *Theatrum chemicum, praecipuos selectorum auctorum tractatus de chemiae et lapidis philosophici antiquitate, veritate, jure, praestantia, & operationibus*, ed. L. Zetzner, 2 (1659), 85–109 · Æ. de Vadis [G. Duwes], 'A dialogue betwene nature & ye disciple of philosophye', trans. T. Potter (?), 1580, BL, Sloane MS 3580B, fols. 186v–202v · G. Duwes, 'An introductorie for to lerne to rede, to pronounce and to speke French trewly', *L'éclaircissement de la langue française … la grammaire de Gilles Du Guez*, ed. F. Génin (Paris, 1852), 891–1079 · funeral accounts for Queen Elizabeth, wife of Henry VII, PRO, LC 2/1, fols. 46v–78v · *LP Henry VIII* · livery warrant for Giles Duwes, 'Documents subsidiary to accounts of the great wardrobe, 1 October 1502–30 September 1503', PRO, E 101/415/7, item 67 · D. Loades, *Mary Tudor: a life* (1989) · *DNB* · F. Madden, *Privy purse expenses of the Princess Mary, daughter of King Henry the Eighth* (1831) · W. Nagel, *Annalen der englischen Hofmusik*, Monatshefte für Musikgeschichte, 26 (1894) · N. H. Nicolas, ed., *The privy purse expences of King Henry the Eighth* (1827) · N. H. Nicolas, ed., *Privy purse expenses of Elizabeth of York: wardrobe accounts of Edward the Fourth* (1830) · C. Ord, Extracts from John Heron's account books, 1 Oct 1491–21 April 1509, BL, Add. MS 7099 · J. Stow, *A survay of London*, rev. edn (1603); repr. with introduction by C. L. Kingsford as *A survey of London*, 2 vols. (1908); repr. with addns (1971) · W. Streitberger, *Court revels, 1485–1559* (1994) · will, GL, MS 9171/10, fols. 244v–245r
Archives BL, Sloane MSS 3580 B, 3772, 3762, 3661, 1098 · Bodl. Oxf., Ashmole MSS 1487, 1490
Wealth at death left clothing, books, musical instruments, goblets, spoons, and household bric-a-brac: will, GL, MS 9171/10, fols. 244v–245r

Dvořák, Antonín Leopold (1841–1904), composer and conductor, was born on 8 September 1841 in Nelahozeves, to the north of Prague, the eldest of nine children of František Dvořák (1814–1894), musician, butcher, and innkeeper, and his wife, Anna Zdeňková (1820–1882). Recognition of his early musical talent led to his being sent at the age of twelve to Zlonice, where his studies continued under the local organist, Antonín Liehmann. At the age of fifteen he went to Česká Kamenice in North Bohemia, to

Antonín Leopold Dvořák (1841–1904), by unknown photographer, *c*.1890

improve his German prior to entering the Prague organ school in 1857. Dvořák was an excellent pupil, and after graduating in 1859 he embarked on a freelance career in Prague as piano teacher, viola player, and composer.

Although, thanks to the recommendations of Brahms, Dvořák began to have some small recognition outside Bohemia by 1876, it was his subsequent popularity in Great Britain which was to establish him as an international composer and brought him his later invitation to America. This came about through nine visits between 1884 and 1896, supported by special relationships with Henry and Alfred Littleton of the firm of Novello, Ewer & Co., as well the (Royal) Philharmonic Society. On 17 November 1873 Dvořák had married Anna Františka Čermáková. Under the impact of the tragic loss of their first three children between 1876 and 1877, he composed his *Stabat mater* (op. 58; Burghauser 71), and it was this work which first brought him to England. Although a number of his orchestral pieces, including the *Slavonic Dances* (op. 48; B83), piano concerto (op. 33; B63), and symphony no. 6 (op. 60; B112), had been heard in London at the concerts of Hans Richter and August Manns, the discovery by the great British amateur choral societies that Dvořák had written fine choral works increased the interest. In March 1884 Dvořák reached England for the first time, and conducted his *Stabat mater* in the Royal Albert Hall as well as orchestral concerts at the Crystal Palace, both to great public acclaim. His success resulted in immediate

commissions from the Philharmonic Society and the Birmingham and Leeds festivals. In September 1884 he returned to conduct his *Stabat mater* and symphony no. 6 at Worcester, for the Three Choirs festival and the 800th anniversary of the founding of the cathedral.

Dvořák's third visit was in April 1885, to conduct the first performance of his symphony no. 7 (op. 70; B141), commissioned by the Philharmonic Society, at St James's Hall, Piccadilly. In August 1885 he was back with another new work written for Britain, this time conducting the première of his cantata *Svatební košile* (*The Spectre's Bride*) (op. 69; B135) for the Birmingham festival. In October 1886 he conducted another new commission, his oratorio *Svata Ludmilá* (*St Ludmila*) (op. 71; B144), for the Leeds triennial festival, followed by an orchestral concert in Birmingham. While in Birmingham, Dvořák accepted a further commission for a choral work for the 1888 festival, and *The Dream of Gerontius* was suggested. In the event, it was not until 1891 that this commission was completed, and was to be not *Gerontius* but his Requiem (op. 89; B165). While, in the first part of *St Ludmila*, it is possible to trace Dvořák's debt to the English oratorio tradition from Handel, his own influence was to be heard later in some of the major choral works of Stanford and his pupils, as well as Elgar.

The sixth visit was in 1890 for the Philharmonic Society, and in June 1891 Dvořák was made an honorary doctor of music by Cambridge University, proposed by Stanford. As a result he dedicated his new overture, *V přírodě* ('Amid Nature'; op. 91; B168), to the university. Later that year he returned to conduct the première of his Requiem at the Birmingham festival, after which followed his American years (1892–5) as director of the National Conservatory, the direct result of a recommendation by Alfred Littleton. In March 1896 Dvořák came to England for the last time, to conduct the first performance of his cello concerto no. 2 (op. 104; B191), at a Philharmonic Society concert in the Queen's Hall. Thereafter he received further invitations, including a commission for the Cardiff festival. However, his family- and home-loving nature led him to refuse all other inducements to travel; he remained in his beautiful Bohemian surroundings, writing his late great operas and symphonic poems.

From the outset Dvořák was a popular figure in Britain, and thereafter he always felt a great warmth for English audiences. After his first visit he wrote of his astonishing reception and said: 'The English are a good, cordial and music-loving nation, and it is well known that if they are fond of anyone they remain loyal to him. May God grant that this should happen in my case too' (Kuna, 1.400). The modest Dvořák remained amazed at his popularity in England. After the first performance of *St Ludmila* he wrote: 'I confess that I have never seen the artists around me on the platform as well as the audience in such a state of enthusiasm' (Kuna, 2.184). Dvořák died of a pulmonary embolism following influenza at his Prague home, 14 Žitná Ulice, on 1 May 1904. The nation gave him a state funeral and he was buried on 5 May in Slavín at Vyšehrad in Prague, where most of the great figures in Czech history since the nineteenth century lie today.   GRAHAM MELVILLE-MASON

Sources J. Burghauser, *Antonín Dvořák, thematický katalog, bibliografie přehled života a díla* (1960) · J. Clapham, *Antonín Dvořák, musician and craftsman* (1966) · O. Šourek, *Život a dílo Antonína Dvořáka*, 4 vols. (1954–7) · M. Kuna and others, eds., *Antonín Dvořák, korespondence a dokumenty*, 8 vols. (1987–), vols. 1–2 · V. Fischl, 'Dvořák in England', *Proceedings of the Musical Association*, 68 (1941–2), 1–17 · b. cert. · baptismal records · m. cert. · d. cert.
Likenesses photographs, *c.*1877–*c.*1900, priv. coll. · photograph, *c.*1890, Hult. Arch. [*see illus.*]

Dwarris, Sir Fortunatus William Lilley (1786–1860), lawyer and writer, eldest son of William Dwarris of Warwick and Golden Grove, Jamaica, and Sarah, daughter of W. Smith of Southam in Warwickshire, was born in Jamaica on 23 October 1786. He inherited considerable property there, but left the island in infancy. He went to Rugby School in 1801, and in 1804 he entered University College, Oxford, graduating BA in 1808. Having decided on a legal career he was called to the bar at the Middle Temple on 28 June 1811. The same year, on 28 February, he married Alicia, daughter of Robert Brereton, a captain in the army.

Through his connection with Jamaica, Dwarris was appointed in 1822 as one of the commissioners to inquire into the state of the law in the colonies in the West Indies. On the passing of an act based on his report (he being the only surviving commissioner), his services were acknowledged by knighthood, which he received at St James's Palace on 2 May 1838. He was an opponent of slavery, arguing in *The West India Question Plainly Stated* (1828) for an improvement in the condition of the slaves and for the gradual abolition of slavery. His views on these subjects were also set out in a long letter written from Barbados in January 1823 to Samuel Parr (*Works of Samuel Parr*, 25–8).

Dwarris held numerous official appointments. He was a member of the commission for the examination of municipal corporations, a master of the queen's bench, recorder of Newcastle under Lyme, and counsel to the Board of Health. In 1850 he was elected a bencher of the Middle Temple, and in 1859 he was appointed its treasurer, in which capacity he took the chief part in the ceremony of laying the foundation stone of the new library. His *General Treatise on Statutes* (2 vols., 1830–31), compiled with the assistance of his son-in-law, William Amyot, was a comprehensive survey of the history and development of statute law. It had considerable success in Britain and an American edition was produced in 1871.

Dwarris was a fellow of the Royal Society, a fellow of the Society of Antiquaries, a vice-president of the British Archaeological Association, and a member of the Archaeological Institute. In a letter addressed to the fellows of the Society of Antiquaries in 1852, he argued for a reduction in the rate of subscription and for increased energy in the society's operations. He contributed articles to the *Journal of the British Archaeological Association* and *Archaeologia*, and was the author of a number of short plays and stories. In 1850 he published his theory that the letters of Junius were the work of several persons, of whom Sir Philip Francis was the chief.

Dwarris died at 75 Eccleston Square, London, on 20 May 1860; he was buried in Brookwood cemetery, Woking, on 26 May alongside his wife, who had died at the same address on 10 June 1856. Their family consisted of four sons and two daughters.

W. P. COURTNEY, rev. JONATHAN HARRIS

Sources G. A. Solly, ed., *Rugby School register*, rev. edn, 1: *April 1675 – October 1857* (1933), 155 · Foster, *Alum. Oxon.* · *GM*, 3rd ser., 8 (1860), 646 · T. J. Pettigrew, *Journal of the British Archaeological Association*, 17 (1861), 182–3 [memoir] · *Law Times* (2 June 1860), 141 · Allibone, *Dict.* · Holdsworth, *Eng. law*, 1.535 · *The works of Samuel Parr ... with memoirs of his life and writings*, ed. J. Johnstone, 8 vols. (1828), vol. 8, pp. 25–8
Wealth at death under £7000: administration with will, 6 Aug 1860, *CGPLA Eng. & Wales*

Dwelly, Edward [*pseud.* Ewen MacDonald] (1864–1939), lexicographer, was born on 2 February 1864 at 4 Crown Crescent, Twickenham, Middlesex, the son of Thomas Edward Dwelly and his wife, Clara Isabella, *née* Hill. His father worked in Cox's Bank, Charing Cross, London, and Edward began his working career there. But his ambitions did not allow him to stay for long in banking. He was strongly attracted to playing the bagpipes and to learning Scottish Gaelic, and he served in the London Scottish Volunteers, and later in similar units connected with the Argyll and Sutherland and the Seaforth regiments, playing in their pipe bands; by the 1890s he was using the name Ewen MacDonald as one more appropriate for a highland piper.

Dwelly left London in 1891 and took up work with the Ordnance Survey in Scotland. In 1896 he married Mary MacDougall at Doune, Perthshire. She was a native Gaelic speaker. It was about this time that he began to collect Gaelic vocabulary in a systematic way, corresponding with Gaels in many highland areas and recording local usages in a detailed way, as well as information about implements and practices that were already near the end of their lifespan, including a multiplicity of names for an early-morning dram of whisky. He also made extensive use of previously published Gaelic dictionaries.

Later in the 1890s Dwelly returned to England, and settled in the village of Skeete, near Lyminge, in Kent. Here he set up his own hand printing press, did his own compositing, and began to publish small Gaelic almanacs, which appeared from 1901 to 1908. In 1902 he acquired a larger printing press and began to publish his Gaelic dictionary in parts, issued at four-monthly intervals and paid for by subscriptions of 6½*d.* per issue. This appeared in thirty-three parts between 1902 and 1911, under his pseudonym, Ewen MacDonald. In 1904 the family, now with three children, moved to Herne Bay. Bound volumes of the whole dictionary were also published there, using a Gaelic name, Camus-a'-Chorra, for Herne Bay, and emphasizing that the volumes were made with paper produced in Scotland. The dictionary is copiously illustrated, many of the illustrations made by Dwelly, with advice and help from his highland correspondents. No work of this sort can be perfect, and various inaccuracies and faults of emphasis have been identified over the years, but overall it was a remarkable achievement. A revised edition appeared in 1920, with a valuable listing of place names and personal names supplied by Professor W. J. Watson, and the dictionary remained in print throughout the century, published later by Alexander MacLaren & Son in Glasgow, and after 1971 by Gairm Publications, Glasgow.

Dwelly continued to collect Gaelic words and usages after the publication of the dictionary, and these notes were deposited in the National Library of Scotland after his death. In 1991 they were edited and published under the title *Appendix to Dwelly's Gaelic–English Dictionary*, edited by Douglas Clyne. The additions are much more numerous for initial letters A, B, and C, presumably because additions under later letters were being made before 1911.

Having published the dictionary Dwelly turned to investigating and publishing parish records, and about a dozen books appeared in the series Dwelly's Parish Records. Unpublished papers of this kind were deposited at Bristol University, and later passed to the Society of Genealogists. Dwelly seems to have led a life driven by obsession, but he was loyally supported by his wife and family. He was given a civil-list pension, which helped to keep them above the poverty line. He died at Greenside, Kenilworth Road, Fleet, Hampshire, on 25 January 1939, and was survived by his wife.   DERICK S. THOMSON

Sources C. MacLeod, *An Gaidheal*, 34 (1939), 93 · E. MacDonald [E. Dwelly], preface, *A Gaelic dictionary*, 3 vols. (1902–11), iii–vii · E. Dwelly, preface, *The illustrated Gaelic–English dictionary* (1920) · *Appendix to Dwelly's Gaelic–English dictionary*, ed. D. Clyne and D. Thomson (1991) · H. Gough, 'Eideard Dwelly, Eòghan MacDhòmhnaill agus am faclair mòr', *Gairm*, 164 (autumn 1993), 333–5 · b. cert. · d. cert. · *CGPLA Eng. & Wales* (1939)
Archives NL Scot., family and personal papers · priv. coll., family MSS · Society of Genealogists, London, genealogical MSS
Likenesses photograph (aged seventeen), repro. in E. Dwelly, ed., *The illustrated Gaelic-English dictionary*, 10th edn (1988)
Wealth at death £1443 6s. 4d.: administration, 31 March 1939, *CGPLA Eng. & Wales*

Dwight, John (1633x6–1703), chemist and potter, is presumed to have been born at Todenham in Gloucestershire, the second son of a yeoman farmer, George Dwight, and his wife, Joane Greenough (d. 1680), whose marriage took place at Bampton in Oxfordshire on 30 September 1630. By 4 March 1632 they were living at Todenham, where their first son George was baptized, and where it is likely that John also was born. Shortly after 1636 they moved to North Hinksey, Berkshire, where George Dwight senior died in 1670.

Recent research has disproved those romantic myths of a Dutch ancestry promulgated in the late eighteenth century by Daniel Lysons, as well as the entire line of Dwight's ancestors published by Sir Arthur Church in *The Genealogist* in 1910. It is now known that, from comparatively humble origins, Dwight showed such promise that a place was somehow found for him at Oxford, where he studied civil law and chemistry, and where in the later 1650s he was fortunate enough to work in the laboratory of the distinguished scientist Robert Boyle, in company with Robert Hooke. After marriage to Lydia Parker (d. 1709) at St Mary Mounthaw, London, on 23 February 1661, his degree of bachelor of civil law, conferred on 17 December 1661, qualified him for a post as secretary to Brian Walton,

John Dwight (1633x6–1703), by unknown sculptor, c.1673–5

bishop of Chester. Thereafter for ten years his career as a diocesan legal adviser advanced under three successive bishops, notably in 1663–8 when Bishop Hall appointed him successively 'Dean Rurall' of Manchester, joint commissary of Richmond, Yorkshire, and advocate of the consistory court of the diocese of Chester. In November 1669 Dr John Wilkins, who had succeeded to the bishopric on the death of Hall in October 1668, brought a bill of complaint against Dwight which, though unproven, effectively brought to a close his service to the church.

By this time Dwight had developed other interests and was living at Wigan where, as he told Sir John Lowther in March 1698, 'having tryed many experiments he concluded he had the secret of making China Ware. Thereupon he sold his Office, came to London, was encouraged therein by Mr Boyl and Dr Hook' (Weatherill and Edwards, 163). With the money obtained from selling his ecclesiastical posts he was able to obtain a fourteen-year patent on 23 April 1672 to make 'transparent Earthenware commonly known by the names of Porcelane or China and Persian Ware as also … the stone ware vulgarly called Cologne ware' and to settle at Fulham, where he built a pottery near the river (PRO, Patent Rolls, C66/3133).

Initially Dwight attempted to make all the fine ceramic wares imported into England at the time: red stoneware teawares from Yixing, Chinese porcelain, and the brown salt-glazed stoneware bottles and mugs which for the preceding hundred and fifty years had been shipped in vast quantities from the Rhineland by Dutch merchants. The full extent of his ambitions was revealed by chance discoveries at the pottery in the 1860s and excavations undertaken in 1971–9. Besides misfired 'wasters' copying brown Frechen and blue and grey Westerwald stonewares, there were a few fragments of red stoneware, many trial pieces made from an experimental porcelain body, and pieces of the highly accomplished figures which were modelled from his refined stoneware clay about 1673–5. Complete examples of these latter products, including the well-known recumbent bust of his daughter inscribed 'Lydia Dwight dyed March 3 1673', were discovered at the pottery after the death of his last descendant in 1859.

It was, however, the basic brown stonewares that enabled Dwight's pottery to flourish. His boast to a committee at the House of Lords in 1674 that he could make 'as good and as much Cologne ware as would supply England' (*Ninth Report*, HMC, appx, calendar, 32–5, no. 130, extracts), though perhaps premature, was followed by full-scale production in 1675, when he hired the experienced potters Henry Parker and John Stearne. The following year he entered into partnership with Windsor Sandys and, in order to ensure an outlet for all his products, made a three-year agreement to supply the Glass-Sellers' Company which controlled the London pottery trade. This agreement was renewed by Dwight alone in 1677, the year that Dr Plot published his eulogistic account of Dwight's activities.

That the pottery prospered may be inferred from the fact that in 1684, two years before the expiry of his existing patent, Dwight obtained (allegedly for the sum of £100) a further patent for 'white Gorges marbled Porcelane Vessels Statues and Figures and fine stone Gorges and Vessels never before made in England or elsewhere', claiming that he 'hath discovered the mistery of transparent Porcellane and opaccous redd and dark coloured Porcellane or China and Persian wares and the mistery of the Cologne or Stone wares' (PRO, Patent Rolls, C66/3245). No doubt this renewed patent was hastened by Sir Humphry Miller's intentions to set up a stoneware pottery at Oxenheath, Kent, to be managed by Dwight's employee John Stearne.

Apart from a speculative purchase of 500 acres of Pennsylvania in 1685, little is known of Dwight's fortunes after 1684 until he embarked on a series of lawsuits to protect his patent in 1693. The documents surviving from this litigation provide much information about Dwight, his competitors, and the general state of the pottery trade in England at that period. The first to be sued were John Chandler (formerly a 'labourer' at Dwight's pottery), the potters and silversmiths John Philip and David Elers, and the Nottingham stoneware potter John Morley. Later the same year the names of Aaron, Thomas, and Richard Wedgwood of Burslem in Staffordshire were added, and in 1694–5 the London potters Matthew Garner, Luke Talbot, Richard White, and Moses Johnson. In 1697, the year before the expiry of his second patent, Dwight sued the Staffordshire potters Moses Middleton, Cornelius Hamersley, and Joshua Astbury. The results of this legal action were mixed: those London potters unwise enough to make stoneware at Southwark were fined or put out of business, the Elers brothers were compelled to make the patented red stoneware under licence from Dwight, but in the midlands neither John Morley, who admitted making

stoneware, nor the Wedgwood brothers, who denied the accusation, were affected. With the patent about to expire, and Dwight's health deteriorating, the litigation was not pursued further.

By his will written in January 1703, Dwight left his grandson John Dwight £200, his younger son Phillip an income of £100 for three years, his eldest but 'undutifull' son Samuel *Dwight £5, and the residue to his widow, Lydia. He was buried at Fulham (the location now lost) on 13 October 1703, after which the pottery continued under Lydia's management until her death in 1709, when Phillip was left £1100 and £50 per annum for seven years from the profits of the pottery business, and Samuel was left £1000, the house and the pottery. Samuel practised as a physician in Fulham, remaining the owner, if not the manager, of the pottery until his death in 1737.

Dwight's place in the history of ceramics was established only towards the end of the nineteenth century. Although a brief account of Dwight and his role in the Fulham pottery was given in Daniel Lysons's *Environs of London* in 1795, in Staffordshire even Josiah Wedgwood, who took an active interest in the history of his craft, was entirely unaware of his existence. It was only with the death of Charles Edward White, Dwight's last descendant, in 1859 that the experimental pieces, the so-called Dwight heirlooms, were discovered and lent to the 'Special exhibition of works of art on loan at the South Kensington Museum' (1862), with the first accounts of Dwight's life published by Baylis and Chaffers in the *Art Journal* in 1862 and 1865. The discovery of a group of intact 'wasters' during rebuilding of the pottery in 1869, a visit by the great ceramic collector Lady Charlotte Schreiber in 1870 and her finding of two of Dwight's recipe books of 1689–98 at the pottery, and finally the sale of the heirlooms in 1871, when most of the figures and vessels were divided between the British Museum and the South Kensington Museum, secured Dwight's reputation as a great ceramic innovator.

After exhaustive documentary research supported by eight years' excavation at the pottery in the 1970s, it is possible to give a balanced verdict on John Dwight's achievements. If he was not actually the first to make salt-glazed stoneware in Britain, it is certain that he discovered the process by independent experiment, unlike William Killigrew who had employed a German potter to make the material at Southampton as early as 1666, but whose patent application was submitted thirteen days after Dwight's in April 1672. To unravel the process by experiment was no small achievement, since it entailed not only the development of high-firing furnaces, the identification of suitable stoneware clays in England, but also the closely guarded secret method of producing the vapour glaze by throwing rock salt into the kiln at its maximum temperature. Dwight's determination to set new standards of ceramic refinement by 'fritting' and grinding the Dorset clay and Isle of Wight sand of his new stoneware body, his employment of the best available throwers, lathe-turners, and figure-modellers, his invention of new types of decoration including marbling and applied decoration from 'sprig' moulds, together with his ceaseless pursuit of the secret of porcelain, set him apart from all European potters of the seventeenth century. Rather, he may be seen as a precursor of Johann Friedrich Böttger, the Saxon alchemist of Augustus the Strong who discovered the secret of hard-paste Chinese-type porcelain which led to the founding of the Meissen factory in 1710. Whereas the many 'wasters' of experimental porcelain found at the Fulham pottery show that Dwight was unsuccessful in finding the China stone to mix with his China clay, Böttger needed to look no further than his native Saxony for ample supplies of both materials. The elusive China stone was eventually found in Cornwall in 1745 by William Cookworthy.

Like Josiah Wedgwood nearly a hundred years later, Dwight was a serious amateur chemist and numbered many of the foremost scientific thinkers among his circle of friends. In contrast to Wedgwood, he had no training in the potting business, but rather set up his pottery as a speculative venture which would put his successful experiments to practical and lucrative use. The recipe books of 1689–98, with their details of comparatively large sums of money hidden around the pottery, indicate a secretive nature, a character trait which perhaps helped to fuel his suspicions of industrial espionage and his relentless pursuit of those he suspected of infringing his patent rights. Though no great fortune was made by Dwight, none the less the pottery that he founded was worked continuously from 1672 to 1969.

Despite Dwight's efforts to contain it, the secret of fine lathe-turned salt-glazed stoneware spread rapidly from the 1690s, eventually reaching Staffordshire, where by the 1720s it had developed into a major industry: from salt-glaze came creamware, and from creamware came the vast expansion and wealth of the Staffordshire potteries from the late eighteenth century onwards. Dwight's figures, superbly modelled by four unknown sculptors, should be viewed as ceramic sculpture rather than as precursors of the ubiquitous Staffordshire pottery figure. His red stonewares (and those made by the Elers) were not reproduced in Staffordshire until some fifty years later, but his brown salt-glazed stoneware tavern mugs and bottles formed the basis of many highly productive potteries in London, Bristol, Nottingham, and Derbyshire in the eighteenth and nineteenth centuries—of which perhaps the best remembered is Doulton of Lambeth.

ROBIN HILDYARD

Sources D. Haselgrove and J. Murray, eds., 'John Dwight's Fulham pottery, 1672–1978: a collection of documentary sources', *Journal of Ceramic History*, 11 (1979) [whole issue] · D. Haselgrove and J. Murray, eds., 'John Dwight's Fulham pottery, 1672–1978: a collection of documentary sources', *Journal of Ceramic History* [supplement] (1992) · C. Green, *John Dwight's Fulham pottery: excavations, 1971–79* (1999) · R. Edwards, 'London potters, circa 1570–1710', *Journal of Ceramic History*, 6 (1974), 56–9 · M. Bimson, 'John Dwight', *Transactions of the English Ceramic Circle*, 5 (1960–64), 95–109 · L. Weatherill and R. Edwards, 'Pottery making in London and Whitehaven', *Post-Medieval Archaeology*, 5 (1971), 160–81 · D. Gaimster, *German stoneware, 1200–1900* (1997) · A. Oswald, R. G. Hughes, and R. J. C. Hildyard, *English brown stoneware* (1982) · M. S. Tite, M. Bimson, and I. C. Freestone, 'A technological study of Fulham stoneware', *Proceedings of the 24th International Archeometry Symposium* (1986), 95–104 · M. Bimson, 'References to John Dwight in a 17th century manuscript', *Transactions of the English Ceramic Circle*, 4/5 (1959), 10–12 · F. H. Garner, 'Dwight: some contemporary references', *Transactions of the English Ceramic Circle*, 1/5 (1937), 30–37 · A. Esdaile, 'Further notes on John Dwight', *Transactions of the English Ceramic Circle*, 2 (1938–48), 40–47 · R. Plot, *The natural history of Oxford-shire* (1677) · L. F. W. Jewitt, *The ceramic art of Great Britain, from pre-historic times*, 2 vols. (1878) · A. H. Church, *English earthenware* (1911) · *Ninth report*, 2, HMC, 8 (1884), 32–5

Likenesses salt-glazed stoneware bust, *c*.1673–1675, V&A [*see illus.*]

Wealth at death see will, Haselgrove and Murray, eds., 'John Dwight's Fulham pottery', 148–9

Dwight, Samuel (1668–1737), physician, was the son of the potter John *Dwight (*d*. 1703). A brother, Philip, was vicar of Fulham, Middlesex, from 1708 until his death in 1729. Another brother, Edmund, was born in 1676. In July 1687 the father is described as being then of Wigan, Lancashire. Samuel entered Westminster School in 1686, matriculated a commoner of Christ Church, Oxford, in 1687, when eighteen years of age, and as a member of that house proceeded BA in 1691, and MA in 1693. Some verses of his occur among the academical rejoicings on the birth of James II's son in 1688; others are in the collection celebrating the return of William III from Ireland in 1690. He appears to have carried on his father's pottery business. In 1716 he married Margaret Price (*d*. 1750), of Fulham; the pottery descended to their daughter Lydia and her husbands. Dwight was admitted a licentiate of the Royal College of Physicians in 1731. On the title-pages of two of his medical treatises, published respectively in 1725 and 1731, he is represented as a doctor of medicine; but his degree was not recognized by the college. He practised at Fulham, and dying there on 10 November 1737, was buried in the church on 17 November.

Dwight was the author of *De vomitione, ejusque excessu curando, nec non de emeticis medicamentis* (1722); *De hydropibus: deque medicamentis ad eos utilibus expellendos* (1725); and *De febribus symptomaticis … deque earum curatione* (1731). This last work is dedicated to Sir Hans Sloane, whom Dwight was accustomed to consult in cases of more than ordinary difficulty (Dwight to Sloane, 21 Nov 1721, BL, Add. MS 4043, fol. 226). Dwight is sometimes wrongly credited (*GM*, 702) with the inventions in pottery made by his father.   GORDON GOODWIN, rev. MICHAEL BEVAN

Sources Munk, *Roll* · T. Faulkner, *An historical and topographical account of Fulham* (1813), 27 · J. Welch, *The list of the queen's scholars of St Peter's College, Westminster*, ed. [C. B. Phillimore], new edn (1852), 205, 207, 214, 222 · *A catalogue of all graduates … in the University of Oxford, between … 1659 and … 1850* (1851) · BL, Add. MS 4043, fol. 226 · D. Lysons, *Supplement to the first edition of 'The environs of London'* (1811), 150 · C. J. Féret, *Fulham, old and new*, 2 (1900), 46, 52–4 · *GM*, 1st ser., 7 (1737), 702

Dwnn, Lewys [Lewys ap Rhys ab Owain] (*b. c.*1545, *d.* in or after **1616**), Welsh-language poet and herald, was the son of Rhys ab Owain; he took the surname Dwnn from his mother, Katherine, daughter of Rhys Goch Dwnn of Gwestydd, Llanllwchaearn, Montgomeryshire, a descendant of

David Dwnn of Kidwelly, Carmarthenshire, who is said by Lewys Dwnn to have gone to Powys after killing the mayor of Kidwelly. Very little is known of Dwnn's life. He was perhaps born at Betws Cedewain in Montgomeryshire. He married Alice, a daughter and coheir of Maredudd Fain, and they had four sons, including James Dwnn, also a poet and genealogist, and two daughters. He had a traditional bardic training, his tutors, according to a statement believed to have been written by himself, being Hywel ap Syr Mathew (for whom he composed an elegy in 1581), Owain Gwynedd, and Wiliam Llŷn (d. 1580). He states that he had copies of all Wiliam Llŷn's genealogical books and that he had inherited many of those of Hywel ap Syr Mathew (NL Wales, MS 5474A, 78–81).

Dwnn wrote much verse in Welsh, addressed to persons in all parts of Wales, the bulk of which survives in two large manuscripts in his own hand (NL Wales, Peniarth MS 96 and NL Wales, MS 5270B). The earliest dates from 1568 and the latest from 1616. His poetry shows signs of the decline in the quality of the bards' work which had begun in the second half of the sixteenth century. Pedigrees were part of the learning of the bards and his poems contain much detail of his patrons' ancestry, with a few descriptions of coats of arms. His reputation in this domain led to his appointment as deputy herald for all Wales on 3 February 1586 by Robert Cooke, Clarenceux king of arms, and Robert Glover, Somerset herald, acting as marshal for William Flower, Norroy king of arms. This appointment was made at 'the request made unto us by sondry gentlemen of good credit wellwillers unto the Country of Wales' on Lewys's behalf:

> in respecte of his former traveyles thoroughowte the most part of the said Countrey for the atteyninge unto the knowledge of the lynes, pedigrees, and descentes of the chiefest families and kinredes within that principalitie (the bookes and gatheringes wherof we have seene). (Coll. Arms, MS H (Dale), pedigrees 16, pp. 202–3)

Stress was also laid on the importance of his knowledge of the Welsh language.

Flower died between 14 October and 22 November 1588, and Cooke in August 1593. Lewys Dwnn's appointment was not renewed by their successors, so that technically it lapsed in their respective territories when they died; but he continued his visitations for the rest of his life (the last dates in the visitation of south-west Wales being 1613) and still described himself as deputy herald for all Wales under Clarenceux and Norroy kings of arms in 1597. From the surviving manuscripts it appears that the visitation of north-east Wales and some of that of north-west Wales were made before the death of Norroy, and a large part of that of south-west Wales before the death of Clarenceux.

The original manuscripts of Dwnn's visitations of north-west and south-west Wales have survived (NL Wales, Peniarth MS 268 and BL, Egerton MS 2585), together with some twenty pages of that of north-east Wales (NL Wales, MS 13215E). Many of the pedigrees are signed by the head of the family, often with a note of the fee paid for Dwnn's pains. Most of the pedigrees in north-west Wales bear the date and regnal year of the visitation, while in south-west Wales a few bear the date and others indicate only the year. Many of the pedigrees show later additions, citing the year, and some families were visited several times. From references in these manuscripts it is clear that Dwnn visited all parts of Wales. In 1846 S. R. Meyrick published a two-volume edition of Dwnn's visitations, entitled *Heraldic Visitations of Wales and Part of the Marches*. This included the visitations of north-west Wales (from a copy, the original being found only after Meyrick's work had gone to press), south-west Wales, and a copy by George Owen of Henllys (with whom Dwnn was on friendly terms) of that for north-east Wales and Radnorshire (BL, Egerton MS 2586), together with 'a copy of Dwnn's visitation of Montgomeryshire, selected about 1711–12 from the original visitation by John Rhydderch'. This 1846 edition contains a number of errors and omissions, in a few cases of an entire pedigree. A manuscript dating from c.1660 on deposit at the National Library of Wales (NL Wales, minor deposit 138B, pp. 97–100, 141–333) contains a collection of pedigrees of Montgomeryshire families with years (in many cases 1586) and regnal years very similar to those given by Lewys Dwnn, which was probably copied from his Montgomeryshire book. Another manuscript in his hand (Cardiff, Central Library, Cardiff MS 2.36) contains pedigrees of families from all parts of Wales with dates from 1583 to 1612, but it is not a visitation manuscript. In addition Dwnn compiled several heraldic pedigree rolls, one in his own hand, others signed by him. Almost all his pedigrees are written in Welsh (often with an intermixture of English words spelt as if Welsh), except for some of the pedigree rolls, which are in English.

Where Dwnn's work can be tested against record evidence it is found to be very reliable, especially for the later generations. For the earlier parts of the pedigrees he was naturally dependent on earlier writers, and there are some inaccuracies. His work has since been recognized as a most important and authoritative source for Welsh pedigrees and heraldry and is very widely used and trusted.

Lewys Dwnn's date of death and place of burial are not known with any certainty; the last date recorded on his manuscripts is 1616. Although no fewer than five poets addressed *englynion* to him on his appointment as deputy herald, no elegies to him have survived.

MICHAEL SIDDONS

Sources BL, Egerton MS 2585 · NL Wales, Peniarth MS 268 · NL Wales, MS 13215E, 623–52 · BL, Egerton MS 2586 · *Heraldic visitations of Wales and part of the marches … by Lewys Dwnn*, ed. S. R. Meyrick, 2 vols. (1846) · Coll. Arms, MS H (Dale), pedigrees 16, pp. 202–3 · NL Wales, MS 5474A, 78–81 · M. P. Siddons, *The development of Welsh heraldry*, vols. 1–3 (1991–3) · W. G. Harries, 'Moliant Lewys Dwn', *Llên Cymru*, 4 (1956–7), 177–9 · BL, Harleian MS 1973, fol. 51

Dwyer, George Patrick (1908–1987), Roman Catholic archbishop of Birmingham, was born in Manchester on 25 September 1908, the eldest in the family of five sons and two daughters of John William Dwyer, a wholesale egg and potato merchant, and his wife, Jemima (Ima) Chatham. He was educated at St Bede's College, Manchester (1919–26), and was then accepted as a candidate for the priesthood in the diocese of Salford, and sent to study at the Venerable English College, Rome. He soon proved outstanding academically, and was awarded doctorates in philosophy and theology at the Gregorian University, Rome, being ordained priest on 1 November 1932. On his return to England the following year he was sent to Christ's College, Cambridge, where he was Lady Margaret scholar and obtained second classes (division one) in both parts of the modern and medieval languages tripos (1935 and 1937). In 1937 he began a ten-year stint on the staff of St Bede's, Manchester, where he taught French.

While in Rome, Dwyer established a firm friendship with a fellow student three years his senior, John Carmel Heenan, and their names were linked in partnership over nearly fifty years. Some saw Dwyer as following in Heenan's footsteps, yet each achieved greatness in his own right. Possessing complementary talents, they were very different characters: Heenan was a brilliant communicator and preacher; Dwyer was an outstanding theologian and linguist, with a phenomenal memory, and an outspoken clarity of expression, which at times, especially in his younger days, reflected his inability to suffer fools gladly. Yet both had a wide circle of friends and were renowned for great personal kindness towards those less gifted than themselves.

In 1947 Heenan was invited to re-establish the Catholic Missionary Society, a group of diocesan clergy charged with preaching parish missions throughout England and Wales. Heenan promptly chose Dwyer as his principal assistant, and together they organized a general mission nationwide in 1949. When Heenan was appointed bishop of Leeds in 1951, Dwyer was the automatic choice as superior of the Catholic Missionary Society. In this role he showed both leadership and initiative, and established the Catholic Enquiry Centre. He himself wrote the series of pamphlets used to answer postal enquiries about the Catholic faith. The success of this venture owed much to his clear style, human understanding, and sound theology.

In 1957 Heenan was appointed archbishop of Liverpool and Dwyer was named as his successor in Leeds. He was consecrated bishop on 24 September, and set about the task of calming what had become known under Heenan as 'the cruel see'. His episcopal motto *Spe gaudentes* described well his strong and joyful faith. By his energy, zeal, and learning he did much to prepare northern Catholics for their church's call for renewal. When the Second Vatican Council was convened in 1962, Dwyer was elected to the commission for the rule of dioceses, where his polyglot prowess and pastoral common sense proved of great value.

At the end of the council Dwyer was appointed to Birmingham, where he was installed as archbishop on 21 December 1965. Of average height, stocky build, and cheerful expression, he became in later years stout and florid in appearance, yet he was never the Rabelaisian character suggested by his relative Anthony Burgess in the latter's two-volume autobiography, *Little Wilson and Big God: being the First Part of the Confessions of Anthony Burgess*

(1987), *You've had your Time: being the Second Part of the Confessions of Anthony Burgess* (1990). He had a deep, straightforward, and traditional piety, with little sympathy for postconciliar excesses. Yet, when the newly established bishops' conference of England and Wales entrusted to him oversight of the revision of the church's liturgy, he insisted, no matter what his personal feelings, on following each new decree of the church. In the ten years that followed, Dwyer's influence throughout the country steadily increased. He took a firm line in dealing with Irish Republican Army troubles in Birmingham, yet increasingly won the admiration and affection of his priests, to whom he was known as Instant Wisdom. Age added warm compassion and support to the strict disciplinarian. As Heenan suffered a series of heart attacks, Dwyer naturally supplied leadership to the bishops' conference, for which he wrote the widely acclaimed statement on moral questions.

When Heenan died in November 1975, it was inevitable that people should wonder whether once again Dwyer would follow him, this time to Westminster. But he recognized the danger and publicly informed the apostolic delegate that at sixty-seven he felt too old to be considered for the post. But he did not escape entirely. While Archbishop Basil Hume became used to episcopal leadership, Dwyer was elected president of the bishops' conference for a three-year period, the only priest who was not archbishop of Westminster ever to have filled that position. It was after this that his own health began to fail and in 1981, suffering from circulatory problems, he resigned his archdiocese, continuing as apostolic administrator until the appointment of his successor in March 1982. He had honorary degrees from Keele (1979) and Warwick (1980). He lived another five years in retirement at St Paul's Convent, Selly Park, Birmingham, showing exemplary patience as he lost the use of one faculty after another. He died on 17 September 1987 at the Alexian Brothers' nursing home in Manchester. DEREK WORLOCK, *rev.*

Sources personal knowledge (1996) · private information (1996) · *The Times* (18 Sept 1987) · *The Independent* (24 Sept 1987) · **Archives** Birmingham archdiocesan archives, corresp. and papers · **Wealth at death** under £70,000: probate, 14 Oct 1988, *CGPLA Eng. & Wales*

Dwyer, Michael (1772–1825), Irish nationalist, was born in Camara, Glen of Imaal, co. Wicklow, the eldest son of John Dwyer, a tenant farmer, and his wife, Mary, daughter of Charles Byrne of Cullentra, of the same county. He learned to read and write in a small school at Bushfield, near Camara, and in 1784 his family moved to Eadestown, 4 miles away, to a larger farm procured for them with the help of the Emmet family. He grew to be about 6 feet tall and had dark hair and eyes and was a reliable and daring young man.

In mid-1797 Dwyer joined the United Irishmen and by the spring of 1798 was the captain for his parish, Talbotstown. When the rebellion began on 23–4 May he remained in Imaal, inactive, but on 29 May he made his way southwards to join the northern division of the Wexford rebel army; he later participated in the battles at Arklow, Vinegar Hill, Hacketstown, Ballyellis, Ballyraheen, and Ballygullen. He retreated to Glenmalure, at the head of a few hundred men, while the remnant of the rebel army conducted a final campaign in the midlands in early July. He and Joseph Holt led a fierce resistance in the mountains over the next five months until Holt's surrender in November. Dwyer and a handful of men resorted to guerrilla tactics for the next five years. They were in touch with Robert Emmet in 1802 and 1803 but took no direct part in the abortive rebellion of the latter year.

Dwyer finally surrendered in December 1803 and remained in Kilmainham prison for the next year and a half, during which he made a detailed statement concerning his life as a rebel. He had married a young woman he met while on the run, Mary Doyle of Knockandarragh, co. Wicklow, on 16 October 1798, and by the time of his arrest they had several children. She and two of these children accompanied him when he set sail for a life of exile in New South Wales in August 1805. They reached Port Jackson in February 1806 but in the following August the governor, William Blighe, had Dwyer and several other former rebels sent to Norfolk Island, 800 miles into the Pacific, on suspicion of conspiring to revolt. In January 1808 Blighe was replaced and Dwyer returned to New South Wales, and he and his family settled on a 100-acre farm at Liverpool, near Sydney. In 1815 he became constable for the district. He died at Liverpool on 23 August 1825, at the age of fifty-three, probably of dysentery. He was buried at Redfern cemetery, but his body was later moved to Waverley cemetery when Redfern was used as the site for the central railway station. His wife, Mary, died in 1861, at the age of eighty-three. All of the Dwyers' children eventually settled in Australia.   DANIEL J. GAHAN

Sources C. Dickson, *Life of Michael Dwyer* (1944) · C. Dickson, *The Wexford rising in 1798* (1955) · R. R. Madden, *The United Irishmen: their lives and times*, 2nd edn, 4 vols. (1857–60) · *Memoirs of Miles Byrne*, ed. F. Byrne, new edn, 2 vols. (1906) · J. E. Hogan, *The Irish in Australia* (1887) · P. S. Cleary, *Australia's debt to Irish nation-builders* (1933) · K. Sheedy, *Upon the mercy of the government* (1988) · J. T. Campion, *Michael Dwyer* (1907) · J. Holt, *Memoirs* (1838) · G. Cargeeg, *The rebel of Glenmalure* (1988) · O. MacDonagh, *Ireland and Irish-Australia* (1985) · P. O'Farrell, *The Irish in Australia* (1986)
Archives NA Ire., rebellion and state of country papers · TCD, Madden MSS
Likenesses stipple, *c.*1800, NG Ire. · J. Petrie, engraving, *c.*1804 (after his portrait), NG Ire.; repro. in R. Madden, *United Irishmen*, 3rd. ser., 3 vols. (1846) · group portrait, coloured lithograph (*The United Irish patriots of 1798*), NPG

Dyce, Alexander (1798–1869), literary scholar, was born on 30 June 1798 in George Street, Edinburgh, the eldest of the six children of Alexander Dyce (1758–1835), a major, later lieutenant-general, in the Madras infantry of the East India Company, and his wife, Frederica Meredith Mary (1778–1859), daughter of Captain Neil Campbell of Duntroon Castle, Argyll, and sister of General Sir Neil Campbell.

Dyce's parents departed for India the year after his birth, leaving him at Aberdeen in the care of two paternal aunts. He was educated at Edinburgh high school and at Exeter College, Oxford (1816–19), where he took a third in classics. He was also admitted to the Inner Temple in 1818, but he was never called to the bar.

Instead, at his father's insistence, Dyce was ordained as an Anglican priest in 1823, having rejected a career in the East India Company. However, he had already given notice of his true vocation, editing as an undergraduate Swynfen Jervis's *Dictionary of the Language of Shakspeare* (1868), and publishing at Oxford his *Select Translations from the Greek of Quintus Smyrnaeus* (1821). Having served in curacies at Lanteglos, near Fowey, from 1822 to 1824, and at Nayland, Suffolk, from 1824 to 1825, Dyce settled in London, no later than the summer of 1826, to take up the literary life in earnest. Henceforth his clerical duties were confined to occasional weddings. After his father's death, if not before, he was provided with a private income sufficient to support him in his occupation. In May 1829 he leased chambers at 9 Gray's Inn Square, where his quiet bachelor existence amid expanding collections of books and artworks remained undisturbed until 1859 when he was persuaded by his brother Archibald to move to a more spacious residence at 33 Oxford Terrace (Sussex Gardens), Paddington.

Dyce began his London career in fruitful association with William Pickering, a publisher distinguished by his standards of book production and generosity towards his authors. For Pickering he edited the works of William Collins (1827), George Peele (2 vols., 1828; rev. edn, 3 vols., 1829–39), John Webster (4 vols., 1830), Robert Greene (2 vols., 1831), and Christopher Marlowe (3 vols., 1850), an anthology of English sonnets (1833), and the volumes of James Beattie (1831), Alexander Pope (3 vols., 1831), Shakespeare (1832), and Mark Akenside (1835) in the prestigious Aldine Edition of the British Poets. His reputation as a textual scholar was swiftly established and he was chosen by John Murray to complete William Gifford's edition of James Shirley's dramatic works and poems (6 vols., 1833). He acknowledged his debt as a critic to Richard Bentley with an ambitious edition of the latter's works (3 vols., 1836–8) but this was curtailed owing to public indifference; it was followed by an edition of Thomas Middleton (5 vols., 1840).

At this time Dyce became closely involved with the newly emerging literary societies. As a council member of the Camden Society, he edited *Kemps Nine Daies Wonder* (1840). That year he helped to found the Percy and the Shakespeare societies. For the former he edited several volumes in its Early English Poetry series, and for the latter the plays *Timon* (1842) and *Sir Thomas More* (1844).

After this productive phase, including editions of John Skelton (2 vols., 1843) and Beaumont and Fletcher (11 vols., 1843–6), Dyce became absorbed in the controversy surrounding the Shakespearian forgeries of his former friend John Payne Collier. He wrote several critiques which attacked Collier's editions with increasing severity, and in turn endured the assaults of former colleagues convinced of Collier's good faith. Dyce's sense of scholarly outrage and personal betrayal may also have been stimulated by professional rivalry, since he was then engaged on his own edition of Shakespeare (6 vols., 1857; rev. edn, 9 vols., 1864 [1863]–7). This, in its second edition, became widely accepted as the most authoritative text then available. A third edition was completed after his death by John Forster. His last published work was a revision of Gifford's edition of John Ford (3 vols., 1869).

On Dyce's death *The Times* recognized that it was 'a question whether we or certain of our poets of the 16th and 17th centuries are in reality more deeply indebted to his labours' (20 May 1869, 11c). He did much to rescue Shakespeare's precursors and contemporaries from the neglect of the eighteenth century and added considerably to the stock of knowledge of the Elizabethan stage. As a scholar he was distinguished by his erudition, industry, probity, and judgement. Although lacking in originality and apt to sneer at rival commentators, he cleared a pathway through obscurity for later critics and several of his editions, notably those of Shirley, Skelton, and Ford, remain standard texts.

Throughout his life Dyce retained his boyhood enthusiasm for the stage and was a familiar figure in theatrical circles. Nor did his studious habits exclude him from fashionable literary society. He was a regular attender at the breakfast parties of Samuel Rogers where he conscientiously kept notes of the poet's *conversazione*. His *Recollections of the Table-Talk of Samuel Rogers* (1856) was nevertheless strongly criticized for traducing its subject.

There is little on public record concerning Dyce's own reticent personality, save his agreeable manners. Exceptional is the collection of letters to his fellow scholar John Mitford which reveal a worldly man of sardonic humour, contending with frequent illness, depression, and the toil of scholarship: 'My bothering about old dramatists is at an end. I almost believe that their lives, at the very worst, could not have been more painful to them than they have been to me' (V&A, MS L 6027–1975.109, 1850?). They also hint at an early love affair with the poet Euphrasia Fanny Haworth whose *Pine Tree Dell and other Tales* (2 vols., 1827) he had edited; she may also have inspired his pioneering anthology *Specimens of British Poetesses* (1825).

Towards life Dyce held the attitude of a textual scholar, keeping a critical distance and noting with pleasure the idiosyncratic and anecdotal. Much of his leisure was engaged on a translation of the *Deipnosophistai* of Athenaeus, left unfinished at his death. Towards the end of his life he wrote his reminiscences, chiefly of contemporaries. He also kept a diary, since lost. His library of over 14,000 volumes, including many rarities of English, Italian, and classical literature, was bequeathed to the South Kensington Museum, together with his large and various art collection. Valuable for its English watercolours and theatrical portraits, this also contains examples of his own work as a flower painter.

William Carew Hazlitt described Dyce as a 'singularly huge, shambling, awkward, ungainly figure' (Hazlitt, 2.262). In later years he was much stooped and was usually to be seen carrying a cane. During the summer of 1868 he contracted jaundice, symptomatic of the organic liver disease from which he died, after a long confinement, at his home, 33 Oxford Terrace, Paddington, on 15 May 1869. He was buried at Kensal Green cemetery on 22 May.

J. P. HOPSON

Sources *The reminiscences of Alexander Dyce*, ed. R. Schrader (1972) · A. Burton, 'The private life of Alexander Dyce', *Blackwood*, 326 (1979), 398–409 · *Dyce collection: a catalogue of the printed books and manuscripts bequeathed by the Reverend Alexander Dyce*, 2 vols. (1875) · *Dyce collection: a catalogue of the paintings, miniatures, drawings, engravings, rings and miscellaneous objects bequeathed by the Reverend Alexander Dyce* (1874) · R. Renton, *John Forster and his friendships* (1912), 197–203 · *Handbook of the Dyce and Forster collections in the South Kensington Museum* (1880?) · *The Times* (20 May 1869) · W. C. Hazlitt, *Four generations of a literary family*, 2 (1897), 262 · S. Schoenbaum, 'Alexander Dyce', *Shakespeare's lives*, new edn (1991), 309–11 · D. Ganzel, *Fortune and men's eyes: the career of John Payne Collier* (1982) · G. L. Keynes, *William Pickering, publisher: a memoir and a check-list of his publications*, rev. edn (1969) · D. S. Macleod, *Art and the Victorian middle class: money and the making of cultural identity* (1996), 410–11 · *The Register, and Magazine of Biography*, 7/2 (1869), 475–6 · *DNB* · Crockford · d. cert.
Archives V&A NAL, collection of manuscripts and printed books | BL, letters to Philip Bliss and others · Folger, John Payne Collier MSS · Man. CL, Manchester Archives and Local Studies, letters to James Crossley · U. Edin. L., letters to David Laing · U. Edin. L., corresp. with James Halliwell-Phillipps · V&A NAL, letters to John Mitford
Likenesses D. Maclise, sketch, 1844, V&A · C. H. Jeens, line engraving (after photograph facsimile), BM, NPG, V&A · oils (as boy), V&A
Wealth at death under £25,000: probate, 10 June 1869, *CGPLA Eng. & Wales*

Dyce, William

Dyce, William (1806–1864), painter and educationist, the fifth of fourteen children of William Dyce (1770–1836), a lecturer in medicine at Marischal College, was born on 19 September 1806 at 48 Marischal Street, Aberdeen. His mother was Margaret, daughter of James Chalmers of Westburn; both parents were of long-established Aberdeen families and, despite spending most of his career in London, William Dyce remained closely involved with the town of his birth.

Education and early career William Dyce attended Aberdeen grammar school from the age of thirteen and, like his five brothers, completed his education at Marischal College, where he was awarded a masters degree at the early age of seventeen. Following in the footsteps of his father, a distinguished physician and accomplished scientist, he began by studying medicine, but, with parental support, soon turned to theology with the intention of taking orders at Oxford. An increasing enthusiasm for painting occupied his leisure time and early works such as the *Portrait of Sir James M'Grigor* of 1823 (University of Aberdeen) indicate a considerable, if as yet untutored, talent. Dyce overcame his father's disapproval of art as a career by painting, in secret, a grand historical picture, *The Infant Hercules Strangling the Serpents Sent by Juno to Destroy him* (1824; NG Scot.), much influenced by the work of Sir Joshua Reynolds, and transporting it by fishing smack from Aberdeen to London. There he sought the opinion of Sir Thomas Lawrence, president of the Royal Academy, whose warm commendation was enough to persuade the elder Dyce to sanction art as a career for his son.

William Dyce (1806–1864), by John Partridge, 1825

On the basis of drawings made in the exhibition rooms of Alexander Day at the Egyptian Hall, Piccadilly, London, Dyce was admitted as a probationary student at the Royal Academy Schools on 7 July 1825. Soon disillusioned with the academy's teaching, Dyce withdrew suddenly in autumn 1825 in order to travel to Italy with Day, who had become a close friend. Rome seemed to him 'a kind of living poem' (Pointon, 8) and there he developed his artistic skills through life classes at the English academy organized by young British artists with C. L. Eastlake as secretary, and through copying works of Titian and Poussin, as well as classical sculpture. In 1826 he returned to Aberdeen and began his first major work, *Bacchus Nursed by the Nymphs of Nysa*, which was exhibited at the Royal Academy in 1827. Later that year, however, he returned to Rome, perhaps with the intention of meeting his older friend Augustus Wall Callcott, who was honeymooning in Italy. On his first visit to Rome, Dyce had entered the circle of Christian Karl Josias, Freiherr Bunsen, secretary to the Prussian legation for Rome, through whom he might have met the Nazarenes, a community of German painters based in Rome, whose interests in reviving Renaissance art, early religious music, and theology closely mirrored his own developing tastes. There is stronger evidence that Dyce met the German painters in 1828, when their leader, Johann Friedrich Overbeck, saw a *Madonna* painted by Dyce and urged his fellow artists to hurry to the Englishman's studio. According to several accounts, the Germans even subscribed to a fund to purchase the work to avoid Dyce's departure from Rome on pecuniary grounds. The painting does not survive and it is impossible to know whether Dyce had already adopted the hard-edged, flat,

historicizing style, influenced by early Renaissance painting, which characterized his works from the mid-1830s. Despite his inability to speak more than a few words of German, Dyce's career constituted a significant link between British and German art worlds in the mid-nineteenth century.

By 1829 Dyce had returned to Aberdeen and entered a period of uncertainty in which, in addition to portrait painting, he lectured and published on archaeological subjects, wrote an essay, *On the Garments of Jewish Priests*, and, in 1830, won the Blackwell prize for his treatise 'On the relations between the phenomena of electricity and magnetism'. Underpinning all these activities, including his explorations of the natural sciences, was a deep and unwavering Christian faith which eventually found its fullest expression in his art. Dyce settled in Edinburgh in 1830, by which time he was an established portraitist, much in demand for his stylish studies of women and children. At this time he became increasingly interested in naturalistic landscape painting, especially of Scottish highland subjects. He was elected a fellow of the Royal Society of Edinburgh in 1832 and in 1835 an associate of the Royal Scottish Academy. Further travels on the continent in 1832, in the company of the Scottish artist David Scott, produced a number of landscape watercolours. Dyce reached artistic maturity with *The Dead Christ* (1835), in which he distilled the influences of his 'first loves' Perugino, Botticelli, and Raphael; stylized figures are geometrically deployed before a carefully observed landscape. In 1838 he exhibited a *Madonna and Child* at the Royal Academy, one of a series of this subject which made clear Dyce's Anglo-Catholic religious affiliations.

Pedagogical, administrative, and ecclesiological interests Dyce's long involvement with the relationship between art, design, and industry began with his successful participation in a competition organized by the Board of Trade, for the encouragement of manufacture in Scotland, to design a tapestry cartoon. Dyce and Charles Heath Wilson, a fellow Edinburgh artist, approached the board in 1837, proposing to teach two new classes, on colour and form, at the Trustees' Academy, the major school of art and design in Edinburgh. As there were no funds available for the new courses, Dyce and Wilson were retained on a small salary to draw up a scheme for the reorganization of the academy. Their report, addressed to Sir Alexander Machonchie Welwood and published as *Letter to Lord Meadowbank*, appeared in 1837. On the basis of this document Dyce was offered a teaching appointment at the Trustees' Academy. However, so compelling was Dyce's strategy for reform that, when the published letter reached the newly established parliamentary select committee on the arts and their connections with manufactures, Dyce was summoned to London and was soon appointed superintendent of the Government School of Design. Almost immediately after arriving in London in the early summer of 1837, Dyce left for a fact-finding tour embracing Prussia, Bavaria, Saxony, and France. He returned secure in his preference for a workshop system, as practised in Bavaria, in which students were taught specific skills in the branch of design they wished to follow, rather than participating in an academic training in the fine arts based on life drawing and the copying of sculptural casts. This opinion was vehemently contested by the painter Benjamin Robert Haydon, among others, who advocated a fine art training for all students. Dyce occupied the position of superintendent, despite continual controversy and increasing vilification, until his resignation in 1843, at which point he was offered the less gruelling post of inspector of the provincial schools. Although he finally abandoned the schools in 1844 (only to return, briefly and unhappily, in 1848) many of Dyce's concerns and principles were eventually vindicated through the development of the South Kensington Schools of Art, from 1857 under the direction of Sir Henry Cole. Dyce played a minor role in Cole's most spectacular achievement, the Great Exhibition of 1851, serving as a juror and writing a report on 'iron and general hardware'. He also served as a juror, this time for stained glass, at the International Exhibition of 1862. His theoretical concerns were developed during a brief tenure as professor of fine art at King's College, London, in 1844, though his inaugural lecture, *Theory of the Fine Arts*, failed in its over-ambitious attempt to provide a unified aesthetic and scientific theory.

The development of the National Gallery was a lifelong preoccupation. Dyce's report of 1853, *The National Gallery: its Formation and Management*, subsequently published as a letter addressed to Prince Albert, was sufficiently trenchant in its criticisms to warrant the appointment of a select committee to examine the gallery's affairs. In accordance with his art-historical principles, Dyce argued that the collection should provide an overview of the development of art encompassing all periods. His enthusiasm for the art he called 'early Christian' (referring to work of the fourteenth and fifteenth centuries), in which he discerned 'freshness of thought and intention, a vivacity, a gaiety, a vividness of impression' (Dyce, *National Gallery*), was innovatory. In 1854 his selection of seventeen works for the nation from the voluminous collection of Carl Wilhelm August Krüger (1797–1868) was criticized in the *Art Journal*, which adamantly opposed Dyce's taste for early Renaissance art.

Dyce was a genuine polymath, and his breadth of interests inevitably reduced his productivity as a painter. In the late 1830s the religious impulse which had earlier led him toward the church came to dominate his intellectual life. His close friendship and collaboration with the statesman William Ewart Gladstone was based on their shared enthusiasm for the doctrines and aesthetics of high Anglicanism. Although Dyce was close to the future Cardinal Nicholas Wiseman, who had sought him out when in 1833 the artist published a pamphlet, *The Jesuits*, Dyce seems never to have been tempted to abandon the Scottish Episcopal church for Roman Catholicism. His pamphlet *Notes on Shepherds and Sheep* (1851) engaged in a theological controversy with the critic John Ruskin, suggesting that Ruskin's *Notes on the Construction of Sheepfolds* (1851) had not

made specific recommendations about the planning and decoration of churches. Dyce, a keen ecclesiologist, had published learned studies entitled *Notes on the Altar* and *The Form and Manner of Laying the Foundation Stone* in 1843. As the Gothic revival came to affect all aspects of church decoration, such expertise in historical forms of ornament garnered high regard. Dyce became an acknowledged authority not merely on visual matters, but also on church music. A musician of considerable accomplishment, in 1844 he founded the Motett Society for the study of neglected early religious music and described his métier as 'an arranger of Latin music to our English language, and a composer both of simple and of elaborate music of the purest school of ecclesiastical art' (Pointon, 74). His *Non nobis domine* was sung at the Royal Academy dinner in the year of its composition, 1856. In 1843 he prepared *The Order of Daily Service*, a version which initiated the reintroduction of Marbeck's musical setting of communion service.

Artistic maturity and public commissions By his mid-thirties Dyce felt that his administrative and pedagogical activities had undermined his abilities as a painter. In 1843, along with William Etty, he joined the life class of a Mr Taylor in St Martin's Lane, turning attention to the formal, academic virtues which his early departure from the Royal Academy Schools had denied him earlier in his career. His next major painting, *Joash Shooting the Arrow of Deliverance* (1844; Kunsthalle, Hamburg), took its subject from the book of Kings. Bold and powerful in its delineation of the male body, and confident in its deployment of figures within a confined and simplified space, the success of *Joash* clinched his associate membership of the Royal Academy and established Dyce at the front rank of British history painters. Full membership of the Royal Academy followed in 1848.

The remainder of Dyce's life was overshadowed by one vast project: the decoration of the new Palace of Westminster. In 1841 a royal commission under the chairmanship of Prince Albert, with Sir Charles Eastlake as secretary, had been moving toward commissioning decorations for the new building by Charles Barry and A. W. N. Pugin. Following the advice of Peter Cornelius, the Nazarene painter and author of mural schemes in Munich and Berlin, fresco was selected as the appropriate medium, and a competition was held in 1843 to solicit cartoons from British artists. It was at one stage suggested that Cornelius himself should undertake the frescoes, but Ford Madox Brown recorded that Cornelius himself declared 'what need have you of Cornelius to come over to paint your walls when you have got Mr Dyce?' (Hueffer, 36). Overwhelmed by his administrative burdens, Dyce did not enter the competition but in 1844 sent to Westminster Hall a fragment of a fresco, *The Consecration of Archbishop Parker*, on which he was already engaged at Lambeth Palace, but of which nothing remains. Despite adverse criticism of the Lambeth fragment, Dyce was one of the six artists chosen in 1844 to present full-scale cartoons; *The Baptism of King Ethelbert* was duly completed, along with a colour sketch and fresco sample, and the work was commissioned for the central panel above the throne in the House of Lords. Dyce undertook a trip to Germany and Italy to examine examples, respectively, of modern and Renaissance fresco painting. The results of his researches appeared as *Observations on Fresco Painting* (appendix to sixth report of the commission on fine arts, 1846). The tall fresco of *The Baptism of King Ethelbert* (Palace of Westminster, much restored) was unveiled to considerable acclaim in 1846.

Prince Albert played a significant role in Dyce's life from 1844 onwards. The prince consort commissioned a number of artists to execute scenes from Milton's *Comus* for a garden pavilion (des. 1928) at Buckingham Palace. Dyce's contribution, however, was solicited only when William Etty's was judged a failure and removed, causing offence to Dyce's old friend. Work on this scheme was poorly remunerated, and Dyce was forced to rely on a loan of £100 from his friend and patron W. E. Gladstone. Significant royal patronage did follow when Prince Albert purchased a *Madonna* (1845; Royal Collection) which reached back to the world of the Italian 'Primitives' of the fifteenth century: pure and confident in line, the painting is characterized by rich and brilliant colour. In 1846 a further commission from Albert enjoined Dyce to produce a fresco for the staircase at Osborne House on the Isle of Wight. The explicitly patriotic subject, *Neptune Resigning his Empire of the Seas to Britannia*, was suggested by the royal couple; Dyce's response, which uncomfortably mingled a medievalizing crispness of line with a high Renaissance flamboyance of composition, can only be described as partly successful. The prince evidently thought the image 'rather nude; the Queen however said not at all' (C. W. Cope, *Reminiscences*, 1891, 167–8). Albert developed a close relationship with the artist, and it was during this time that the idea of a cycle of frescoes based on Malory's *Morte d'Arthur* emerged. The subject seemed perfect for the romantic, nationalist programme of the new buildings at Westminster. In 1847 Dyce was commissioned to decorate the queen's robing room with an Arthurian fresco cycle; work began, after prolonged discussions, in 1849 and continued at an agonisingly slow pace until Dyce's death. Although the finished frescoes (Palace of Westminster) are now in poor condition, they remain the most important, and the most successful, painted decorations at Westminster. Broadly conceived and honest in homage to the achievements especially of Raphael, they narrate an English epic in a pictorial style well judged to accord with the neo-Gothic architecture of Barry and Pugin.

The robing room commission gained for Dyce an annual salary of £800 for six years, providing sufficient financial security for him to propose marriage to Jane (later known as Jean) Bickerton Brand, daughter of James Brand of Milnathort, Kinross. Their marriage took place on 17 January 1850 at Brixton, Surrey, and the couple moved to The Oaks in Norwood. In 1856 they moved to a modern villa nearby in Leigham Court Road, Streatham, a rural suburb newly accessible by train, which provided a tranquil home for their growing family.

The church of All Saints, Margaret Street, London, funded by Alexander J. R. Beresford Hope, was intended as the model church of the ecclesiologists: Dyce's work there is the pinnacle of his achievement in the field of ecclesiastical decoration. Despite his Westminster commitments, Dyce accepted the commission for a reredos, which he completed between 1858 and 1859 in fresco rather than on the traditional framed wood panels. A study in oils (V&A) indicates the grandeur of Dyce's composition with figures of saints in *trompe-l'œil* architectural niches surmounted by an image of the risen Christ. Characteristically, Dyce debated the iconography intently with Beresford Hope. The fresco had decayed beyond repair in 1908, but in that year a new reredos was created by J. N. Comper, whose oil paintings were closely based on Dyce's designs.

Dyce was also active in other fields of church decoration. Although he collaborated unhappily with a number of leading glass designers during the 1840s and 1850s, he was responsible for only one significant window himself, that of St Paul's, Alnwick, Northumberland. Rather than adopting the flattened and simplified designs which William Morris was to develop from the example of Pugin, Dyce insisted on an elaborately pictorial approach to stained and painted glass, based on the Raphael cartoons (Royal Collection). Dyce's brilliantly orchestrated design was executed, contrary to the artist's wishes, at the royal factory in Munich, and was installed in 1857.

Dyce and the Pre-Raphaelite Brotherhood Dyce's relationship to the Pre-Raphaelite Brotherhood is complex. As a painter committed to religious ideals and to the revival of earlier styles and forms of artistic practice, and as an enthusiast for the medieval and for Arthurian legend, he offered the Pre-Raphaelites a role model. He was personally acquainted with the brothers and became something of a mentor for William Holman Hunt. The linear severity of style which Dyce, in works like *Joash*, shared with the Nazarenes was also a formative influence on the younger men. Furthermore, Dyce was influential in gaining acceptance for the Pre-Raphaelites in their earliest days; he served on the Royal Academy's hanging committee in 1849, the year in which Hunt's *Rienzi* (priv. coll.) and John Everett Millais's *Isabella* (Walker Art Gallery, Liverpool) were selected. The brotherhood owed the decisive critical advocacy of Ruskin to Dyce's intervention: Dyce, Ruskin recalled, 'dragged me literally up to the Millais painting of the Carpenter's Shop … and forced me to look for its merits' (*The Works of John Ruskin*, ed. E. T. Cook and A. Wedderburn, 1903–12, vol. 37, pp. 427–8). Yet the analytical precision of early Pre-Raphaelite painting was also a formative influence on Dyce. A new spirit entered Dyce's easel paintings in the last years of his life, probably as a result of his increasing disillusionment with the medium of fresco. Many of these works, which constitute his finest artistic achievement, were painted on family holidays, and found a ready purchaser in his father-in-law, James Brand. *Titian Preparing to Make his First Essay in Colouring* (1857; Aberdeen Art Gallery) depicts the sixteenth-century artist as a boy surrounded by scrupulously observed plants and flowers providing a riot of natural colour. The work was described by Ruskin as being 'quite up to the high-water mark of Pre-Raphaelitism' (ibid., vol. 14, p. 98). Dyce returned to biblical subject matter with *The Man of Sorrows* (1860; NG Scot.), in which the figure of Christ is portrayed against a vividly detailed landscape of desolate highland country. In *George Herbert at Bemerton* (1861; Guildhall Art Gallery, London) Dyce adopted the Pre-Raphaelite practice of painting on the spot, recording the peaceful English garden of the seventeenth-century divine whose poetry was much admired by the Tractarians. Widely acknowledged as his finest achievement is the evocative landscape *Pegwell Bay, Kent—a Recollection of October 5th, 1858* (1859, Tate Collection). In the foreground a family group collecting shells is made up by Dyce's wife, her two sisters, Grace and Isabella Brand, and one of Dyce's sons; a distant figure with artist's apparel may represent Dyce himself. Donati's comet is visible in the evening sky and the strata of the chalk cliffs add astronomical and geological dimensions to Dyce's meditation on time and memory. As early as 1860 the *Art Journal* recorded, and refuted, the suggestion that this work, already celebrated for its verisimilitude, had been painted from a photograph. Dyce was familiar with photography through his friendship with David Octavius Hill, and used photographic sources on more than one occasion. However, it seems most likely that his painting style in the 1850s was merely influenced by the particularity and vividness of photography.

Character and death Dyce's extraordinary diversity of activities place him among the great polymaths of early Victorian England. Though he could be disputatious, outspoken, and obstinate, he was bound by a commitment to public service and by the unswerving religious conviction indicated by his motto 'In all ways acknowledge Him and He shall direct thy steps' (Pointon, 5). In his own view 'under an aspect of pride almost approaching insolence toward the proud and pretending, my real nature is humble and simple' (ibid., 45). He collapsed at work on the Westminster frescoes in the winter of 1863 and died at Streatham on 14 February 1864 from a chronic liver condition; a memorial brass was erected in St Leonard's Church, of which he had been a warden and where he was buried. A few yards away on Streatham Green can still be seen a drinking fountain erected by the parishioners in his honour in 1862; its neo-Gothic design is by Dyce himself. Dyce's richly varied work, visual and verbal, is mixed in quality but his most successful paintings belong without question among the enduring masterpieces of Victorian art.   TIM BARRINGER

Sources M. Pointon, *William Dyce: a critical biography* (1979) [incl. full bibliography and check-list of works] • J. C. Dafforne, 'William Dyce RA', *Art Journal*, 6 (1860), 293–6 • W. Vaughan, *German Romanticism and English art* (1979) • C. Willesdon, 'Dyce "in camera": new evidence of his working methods', *Burlington Magazine* (Nov 1990), 760–65 • L. Errington, 'Ascetics and sensualists: William Dyce's views on Christian art', *Burlington Magazine* (Aug 1992), 491–7 • A. Staley, *The Pre-Raphaelite landscape* (1973) • W. Dyce, *The National Gallery: its formation and management, addressed by permission to HRH Prince Albert* (1853) • W. Dyce, *Notes on shepherds and sheep* (1851) • W. Dyce, *Theory of the fine arts: an introductory lecture* (1844) • F. M.

Hueffer, *Ford Madox Brown: a record of his life and works* (1896) • m. cert. • d. cert.
Archives Aberdeen Art Gallery, corresp. and papers | BL, corresp. with W. E. Gladstone, Add. MSS 44358–44527, *passim* • LPL, letters to William Scott • NL Scot., letters to J. R. Hope-Scott • V&A NAL, report made to council of School of Design on his return from continent
Likenesses J. Partridge, drawing, 1825, NPG [*see illus.*] • D. Scott, watercolour drawing, 1832, Scot. NPG • C. Christian Vogel, drawing, 1837, Staatliche Kunstsammlungen, Dresden • C. Watkins, carte-de-visite, *c*.1850–1855, repro. in J. Maas, *The Victorian art world in photographs* (1984), 102 • E. G. Papworth, marble bust, exh. RA 1865, Aberdeen Art Gallery • G. G. Adams, sculpture, medallion, *c*.1866, NPG; for the Art Union, 1875 • W. Dyce, self-portrait, oils, Aberdeen Art Gallery • A. Edouart, silhouette, Scot. NPG • J. & C. Watkins, photograph, carte-de-visite, NPG • brass memorial, St Leonard's Church, Streatham, London
Wealth at death under £8000: probate, 30 June 1864, *CGPLA Eng. & Wales*

Dyche, Thomas (*d.* 1722×7), schoolmaster and writer on language, is of unknown origins. He was educated at Ashbourne Free School, Derbyshire, under the Revd William Hardestee, and subsequently took holy orders. He moved to London and in 1708 was keeping a school in Dean Street, Fetter Lane. By this time he had married, for two children of Thomas and Hannah Dyche, John and Hannah, were baptized at St Andrew's, Holborn, in 1709 and 1712. Dyche's wife, named Hannah in his will, may have been the Hannah Bonnel who married Thomas Dyche at St Nicholas's, Rochester, Kent, on 23 July 1700.

At some time after 1710 Dyche became master of the free school at Stratford Bow. By then he had published two useful works on learning Latin and English; *Vocabularium Latiale, or, A Latin Vocabulary* (1707; 14th edn, 1791) was reasonably long-lived, but *A Guide to the English Tongue* (1707; 102nd edn, 1800) was phenomenally successful and continued to be reprinted until 1830. Prefaced by verses by the poet laureate Nahum Tate addressed to 'my ingenious Friend the Author', Dyche's *Guide to the English Tongue* was especially concerned with teaching correct pronunciation, and foreshadowed similar works by Thomas Dilworth, Daniel Fenning, and William Fordyce Mavor. He followed this work with a spelling dictionary, first published in 1723 as *A Dictionary of All the Words Commonly Us'd in the English Language*, that was intended to supplement the *Guide*. Eight editions were published to 1756, and in the text Dyche proposed some spelling reforms to simplify the written language. He began working on a larger English dictionary that would also provide readers with correct spellings rather than derivations or etymologies. This was left unfinished at his death and was completed and published by William Pardon in 1735 as *A New General English Dictionary*, comprising some 20,000 words. It continued to be reprinted throughout the century, and a French version appeared in 1756. Dyche's other works were a translation into English of Phaedrus's fables and an orthodox account of the Anglican communion, *A Companion to the Lord's Table* (1726).

In 1719 Dyche became embroiled in a quarrel with John Ward of Hackney after denouncing in print Ward's embezzlement over the repairs to Dagenham Breach—a wide opening in the Thames wall—which resulted in a lake being closed off from the Thames. Ward successfully sued Dyche for libel and was awarded £300 in damages at the trial on 18 June 1719. Dyche was still living in Stratford Bow when he made his will on 28 March 1722, and had died by 22 December 1727, when the will was proved in favour of his widow, Hannah.

GORDON GOODWIN, *rev.* S. J. SKEDD

Sources will, Dec 1727, GL, MS 9171/65 · J. Green, *Chasing the sun: dictionary-makers and the dictionaries they make* (1997), 194–203 · *N&Q*, 2nd ser., 8 (1859), 249; 3rd ser., 8 (1865), 9; 4th ser., 3 (1869), 395 · W. Robinson, *The history and antiquities of the parish of Hackney, in the county of Middlesex*, 1 (1842), 124 · IGI · R. C. Alston, *A bibliography of the English language from the invention of printing to the year 1800*, 4: *Spelling books* (1967); repr. with corrections (1974), 311–16

Likenesses J. Nutting, engraving (after Fry), repro. in T. Dyche, *A guide to the English tongue* (1707), frontispiece · line engraving, NPG

Dyck, Sir Anthony [*formerly* Antoon] **Van** (1599–1641), painter and etcher, was born on 22 March 1599 at the house Den Berendans (the Dancing Bear) in the Grote Markt in Antwerp, and baptized there the following day in the Onze-Lieve-Vrouwekerk. He was the seventh of the twelve children of Franchois Van Dyck (or Frans van Dijck) the elder (*d.* 1622), a silk merchant, and his second wife, Maria Cuypers, or Cupers (*d.* 1607), whom he married on 6 February 1590, the daughter of Dierick (or Theodorus) Cuypers (*d.* 1584) and Catharina Conincx. Eight of Van Dyck's brothers and sisters lived to be adults: Catharina (*b.* 1590), who married Adriaen Diericx, a notary, on 2 May 1610; Maria (1592–1620), who married Lancelot Lancelots, a merchant, in 1615; Franchois the younger (*b.* 1594), who married Catelijn Kanewers on 8 February 1616; Cornelia (1598–1627) and Susanna (1600–1664), who entered the Béguinage in November 1618 and December 1626 respectively; Anna (*b.* 1601), also known as Gertrudis, who became an Augustinian nun in 1618; Dierick, or Theodoricus or Theodoor (1605–1668), who became a Norbertine canon under the name Waltmannus and from 1640 was a parish priest at Minderhout; and Elisabeth, or Isabella (1606–1658), who became a Béguine in 1628.

Van Dyck's paternal grandfather, also called Anthony (1529–1580), had moved to Den Berendans in December 1579. He made a living as a silk merchant, although he also practised as an artist and had been trained by Jan Ghendrick, alias van Cleve, in 1546, becoming a master of the guild in 1556. Anthony the elder's older brother Peter (*d.* 1581) also trained as an artist, and is recorded in the workshop of Geert Ghendrick in 1552. There appears to have been no artist in the Cuypers family, and the profession of Maria Cuypers's father is not known, although her grandfather Sebastiaan (*d.* 1585) was a schoolmaster.

In December 1599, soon after Van Dyck's birth, the family moved to the Kasteel van Rijsel (Castle of Rijsel) in the Korte Nieuwstraat in Antwerp, and on 7 March 1607 (shortly before Maria Van Dyck died, on 17 April) they bought the adjacent, larger, and more expensive house, the Stadt van Ghent (City of Ghent), in the same street, which even had a bathroom. Their prosperity and tranquillity were not to last. In 1610, for reasons unknown,

Sir Anthony Van Dyck (1599–1641), self-portrait, *c.*1632–3

Jacobmyne de Kueck smashed the windows of the house and threatened to kill Franchois. By 1615 Franchois was in financial difficulties, and on 24 July his sons-in-law Adriaen Diericx and Lancelot Lancelots brought a lawsuit against him. This concerned an inheritance from Catharina Conincx and the late Maria Van Dyck that should have been paid to the latter's under-age children, but was now threatened by Franchois's creditors. He was soon referred to as disgraced, and in 1617 some of his assets were auctioned in the Vrijdagmarkt ('Friday market'). On 3 December 1616 and 13 September 1617 Van Dyck took legal action against his brothers-in-law, attempting to have a commissioner appointed to protect the interests of his younger siblings. The elder children had been in a financial position to marry, but the younger ones had little choice but to take holy orders. On 30 May 1620 the Stadt van Ghent had to be sold and all remaining furniture and fittings auctioned at the Vrijdagmarkt. The good name of this quarrelsome and impoverished family now depended on the young artist.

Apprenticeship and training Van Dyck was apprenticed to Hendrik Van Balen, dean of the Guild of St Luke, as early as 1609. Van Balen was a successful painter of small cabinet pictures, often with mythological subjects, in many of which he contributed the figures while Jan Brueghel the elder or Joos de Momper provided the landscape backgrounds. Little is known about Van Dyck's period of study with Van Balen, although an apprenticeship would normally have lasted three or four years. The earliest dated work by Van Dyck, a *Portrait of a Man Aged Seventy* (Musées Royaux des Beaux-Arts, Brussels), is inscribed 1613. Van Dyck adopted the half-length formats established by earlier Flemish artists such as Peter Pourbus the elder and Willem Key, but worked with a greater variety of touch and focus. Around 1615 Van Dyck set up a studio in a large house, the Dom van Ceulen (Cathedral of Cologne), in the Lange Minderbroedersstraat (now Mutsaertstraat), near the Franciscan convent in Antwerp. This date is supported by Guilliam Verhagen's testimony on 5 September 1660 that a series of pictures of Christ and the apostles had been sold to him from Van Dyck's studio 'forty-four or forty-five years earlier' (Galesloot, 596), at which time Herman Servaes and Justus van Egmont were his assistants. Since Van Dyck's father, Franchois, was in financial difficulties around 1615 the youthful artist must have been earning enough to pay the substantial rent.

Van Dyck and Rubens Peter Paul Rubens had returned to Antwerp from Italy in 1608 and established a highly productive workshop which attracted numerous young and able artists. Van Dyck's presence in this studio was soon noted by contemporaries, and the courtier and diplomat Sir Toby Matthew called him Rubens's 'famous Allievo' (Ruelens and Rooses, 2.262), but it is not known when—or on what basis—the association began, although it could have been as early as 1615. Van Dyck can never have been Rubens's apprentice because he received his basic training from Van Balen, and he must have entered Rubens's workshop as someone who was already skilful enough to paint from the master's designs. An understanding of Van Dyck's career at this point is complicated because he was selling paintings under his own name from his studio, while at the same time working for Rubens and imitating his style with great virtuosity. Van Dyck became a master of the Guild of St Luke on 11 February 1618, but he had received prominent commissions in Antwerp before then, notably *Christ Carrying the Cross*, painted in 1617 for a cycle of fifteen paintings devoted to the mysteries of the rosary in the Sint-Pauluskerk. Van Dyck was paid 150 guilders by the donor, Jan van den Broeck, exactly the same amount as received by Rubens and Jacob Jordaens, who also contributed to the series. But neither early success nor admission to the guild stopped Van Dyck from continuing to work closely with Rubens.

According to Bellori, Rubens gave Van Dyck the job of making detailed drawings after his compositions to be used as models by engravers, part of an ambitious project to spread Rubens's fame and make money. Van Dyck began work around 1617, and during the next few years Rubens obtained print privileges for France (3 July 1619), Brabant (29 July 1619), the Spanish Netherlands (16 January 1620), and Holland (24 February 1620). Most of the engravings after Van Dyck's drawings were made by Lucas Vorsterman and published between 1621 and 1622. Van Dyck also painted study heads on panel that were part of the stock-in-trade of Rubens's workshop; these were not made for a specific commission but could be adapted repeatedly.

Bellori also claimed that Van Dyck painted the eight large cartoons (Liechtenstein collection, Vaduz) for Rubens's tapestry cycle on the life of Decius Mus. The commission was negotiated through Franco Cattaneo, a Genoese merchant, who acted as middleman and signed a contract with the Brussels tapestry weavers Jan Raes and Frans Sweerts on 9 November 1616. Work on the cycle must date from between then and May 1618, when the cartoons were delivered. This was Rubens's first tapestry cycle, and it is indicative that he made the cartoons not on paper (as was usual) but on canvas, in order to provide the weavers with models which were as pictorial as possible.

On 16 February 1661 Gonzales Cocques, Jan Carlo de Witte, and Jan Baptist van Eyck identified the Decius Mus cartoons as designed by Rubens and painted by Van Dyck, but, despite the unanimity of the early sources, his exact contribution has not proved easy to determine.

Around 1619 Van Dyck set himself to emulate a number of subjects that had been painted by Rubens, while at the same time striving to find his own character as an artist. He chose to work with a deliberate roughness and dryness of touch, perhaps consciously rejecting the smoothness of Rubens's handling which he could imitate with such skill. Van Dyck also adopted very different preparatory methods, making numerous compositional drawings which reveal bewildering changes of mind, before moving directly to the canvas without making an oil sketch (no doubt because he was not relying on assistants to do some of the work). For example, his *Samson and Delilah* (Dulwich Picture Gallery, London) both recalls and challenges a work painted by Rubens around 1610 (National Gallery, London), but the result—despite its extraordinary precocity—is awkward, and while Van Dyck's skill at painting surfaces and textures is not in doubt, he found it more difficult to match Rubens in story-telling.

In a letter dated 28 April 1618 Rubens described a painting of *Achilles Discovered among the Daughters of Lycomedes* (Museo del Prado, Madrid) as 'done by the best of my pupils but entirely retouched by my own hand' (Ruelens and Rooses, 2.137). It has been universally accepted that this pupil was Van Dyck. Bellori adds that Van Dyck played a major role in executing many of the large commissions that issued from Rubens's workshop, a view maintained in the older literature, although recent writers have been more cautious. At any rate, the relationship was not one-sided. Van Dyck's most impressive religious work from the period 1618–20, *St Martin Dividing his Cloak*, for the Sint-Martinuskerk, Zaventem (where it remains), was almost certainly a commission which had been passed on to him by Rubens, and he worked from Rubens's oil sketch (priv. coll.). This give and take may have helped keep Van Dyck as Rubens's right-hand man, and ensured his willingness to paint the thirty-nine ceiling paintings (des., 1718) for the side aisles and galleries of the Sint Carolus Borromeuskerk, the Jesuit church in Antwerp, from the older artist's designs. The contract, signed on 29 March 1620, specified that Van Dyck (with some assistance) should carry out the entire work, which Rubens would retouch, and also gave him one of the four side altars to paint at a later date. On 17 July 1620 Francesco Vercellini, then in Antwerp, wrote that Van Dyck was still assisting Rubens, that his work was no less admired, and that he would be unlikely to leave the city because he saw the good fortune that attended Rubens. None the less, Antwerp was not big enough to contain both artists for long.

First visit to England, 1620–1621 Van Dyck arrived in London for the first time shortly before 20 October 1620, when Thomas Locke wrote that he was 'newly come to the towne' (Howarth, 709). It seems that the visit was arranged by John Villiers, first Viscount Purbeck, the brother of George Villiers, marquess (later duke) of Buckingham, the king's favourite. Van Dyck received a payment of £100 from James I in February 1621 for 'speciall service' (Carpenter, 9), but nothing is known about what this covered. Only two works are securely dated to this period: one, *The Continence of Scipio* (Christ Church, Oxford), was recorded in Buckingham's possession in 1635; it is a large history subject which neither of Van Dyck's rivals in London, Paul van Somer and Daniel Mytens, could have attempted. The other is a portrait of *Thomas Howard, Second Earl of Arundel* (Getty Museum, Los Angeles). Arundel was one of the most exceptional collectors of the age, and the quantity and quality of Italian sixteenth-century pictures in his possession far exceeded what Van Dyck had seen in Antwerp. Somewhat precipitately, Van Dyck decided to set out for Italy, and a pass 'to travaile for 8 months' (Carpenter, 10) was obtained for him, with Arundel's assistance, on 28 February 1621. By March he was back in Antwerp (in time for the installation of the Jesuit ceiling), where he painted an outstanding portrait of Rubens's wife, Isabella Brandt (National Gallery, Washington), and pendants of Frans Snyders and his wife, Margaretha de Vos (Frick collection, New York).

Visit to Italy, 1621–1627 Van Dyck left Antwerp on 3 October 1621. By late November he had arrived in Genoa, which was then the most important Italian centre for Flemish artists after Rome. He stayed at the house of the artist and dealer Cornelis de Wael and his brother Lucas, who ran what was virtually a hotel for visiting painters, particularly if they came (like the de Waels) from the Spanish Netherlands. Van Dyck later painted a double portrait of the brothers (Pinacoteca Capitolina, Rome) in thanks for the introduction they provided to a network of art agents and collectors throughout Italy.

During the next few years Van Dyck worked for the great aristocratic families of Genoa—the Adorno, Balbi, Brignole, Doria, Grimaldi, Lomellini, Pallavicino, and Spinola, among others, whose fortunes were derived from mercantile trade, particularly with Spain. Van Dyck was now able to see—for the first time—the portraits that Rubens had painted in Genoa in 1605 and 1606. These provided a model for his own Italian portraits, in which the sitters, sumptuously dressed and elongated in body, are set against architectural backgrounds seen from a low viewpoint so that they appear elegant, powerful, and aloof. Van Dyck's Genoese portraits were generally painted on coarse canvas, prepared with a single layer of brownish-cream ground, over which he worked thinly and quickly.

In February 1622 Van Dyck travelled by boat to Civitavecchia and from there to Rome, where he remained until August. Towards the end of the visit he painted full-length portraits of *Sir Robert Shirley*, the English-born ambassador to the shah of Persia, and his Circassian wife, *Teresia, Lady Shirley* (Petworth House, Sussex), who were in the city between 22 July and 29 August. It may have been during this first visit to Rome that Van Dyck met George Gage, an English art agent and Roman Catholic priest, whose portrait he also painted (National

Gallery, London), and who was helpful in maintaining contact with the English court. In the 1630s Van Dyck dedicated an engraving after one of his works (a *Lamentation*) to Gage with a reference to their cordial dealings in the city. The sketchbook that Van Dyck compiled during his travels in Italy (British Museum, London) reveals that he visited the villas and palaces of the Aldobrandini, Borghese, Farnese, and Ludovisi families in Rome in search of works by Titian (and others), and that he also drew antiquities—as was proper for a pupil of Rubens—including the famous fresco known as *The Aldobrandini Wedding*, now in the Musei Vaticani, and a statue of *Diogenes*, then at the Palazzo Borghese on Ripetta in Rome.

By September 1622 Van Dyck had reached Venice, where he met Aletheia Talbot, countess of Arundel, who had rented the Mocenigo Palace on the Grand Canal. Here he joined a circle which included Titian's relative Tizianello (who published a short biography of the great Venetian painter during this year) and the art agent Daniel Nys, whose name is recorded in Van Dyck's Italian sketchbook. No less important was Van Dyck's association with Lucas van Uffel, a shipowner, arms dealer, and collector, whom he later described as his 'patron and dear friend' (Depauw and Luijten, 240) and whose portrait he painted twice (Metropolitan Museum, New York; Herzog Anton Ulrich-Museum, Brunswick). Given Van Dyck's enthusiasm for Venetian art it is surprising he did not stay longer in the city, but he found little or no patronage there. In the last few months of 1622 or the beginning of 1623 he left Venice with the countess of Arundel to travel to Turin via Mantua and Milan.

Van Dyck returned briefly to Genoa in early 1623, before setting out again for Rome, where he remained from March to October, perhaps stopping in Florence on the way. During his second stay in Rome he enjoyed the protection of Cardinal Guido Bentivoglio—which he may well have needed since, according to Bellori, his fine clothes and retinue of servants inspired envy and loathing among the Netherlandish artists living in the city. However, he found at least one sympathetic contact, the sculptor François Duquesnoy, in the expatriate community associated with the hospice of San Giuliano dei Fiamminghi. Bentivoglio had close ties with the Spanish Netherlands, where he had been papal nuncio between 1607 and 1616; his association with Van Dyck is recorded in a particularly grand full-length portrait (Palazzo Pitti, Florence). It may have been through Bentivoglio that Van Dyck met and painted the young, but dying, cleric Virginio Cesarini (portrait, Hermitage Museum, St Petersburg), a favourite of Maffeo Barberini (who was elected as Pope Urban VIII in August). Despite these contacts, Van Dyck did not obtain any major commissions in Rome. In the last few months of 1623 he returned to Genoa, where he dated two pendant portraits of aristocratic children, *Filippo Cattaneo* and *Maddalena Cattaneo* (National Gallery, Washington). He remained in the city until early in 1624.

Van Dyck next moved to Palermo, possibly at the invitation of Emanuele Filiberto of Savoy, the viceroy, whose portrait in armour he painted (Dulwich Picture Gallery,

London) shortly before the sitter's death on 3 August. Van Dyck reached the city before 19 May 1624, when he drew a witch led from an *auto-da-fé*, and on 12 July he is known to have visited the very elderly painter Sophonisba Anguissola. The timing of his visit was bad, since the plague broke out in Palermo in midsummer and he was trapped in the city when it became quarantined. St Rosalie, whose bones were discovered on 14 July, was invoked as a popular intercessor, and Van Dyck painted several images of her for Sicilian patrons. During this period he is documented as working for Hendrik Dych, a Fleming from Antwerp, who was consul-general of Flanders and the German community in Sicily, in return for 'all the food he [Dych] had given him at his home' (Mendola, 60). Van Dyck painted two *Crucifixions* for Dych, for which he was paid 4 and 6 Sicilian onze respectively. On 22 August 1625 Van Dyck received his most important commission in Palermo, the large altarpiece of *The Madonna of the Rosary* (in which St Rosalie appears) for the oratory of the Compagnia del Rosario, for which he was to receive 260 Neapolitan ducats. Van Dyck left Palermo in September 1625 (perhaps moving on to Naples), no doubt because the plague had abated. The altarpiece was completed in Genoa and shipped by Antonio della Torre to the Rosarians in 1628, who paid for it on 8 April of that year.

It is not known what made Van Dyck leave Italy, unless it was the death of his sister Cornelia on 18 September 1627. He had not been spurred home by the death of his father, Franchois, on 1 December 1622, and he waited as late as 1629 to donate an altarpiece of *Christ on the Cross with St Dominic and St Catherine of Siena* (Koninklijk Museum, Antwerp) to the Dominicanessenklooster in his father's memory. Van Dyck had found it hard to settle in any one city for long and may have realized that he was in danger of becoming a jobbing portraitist, untrained in fresco painting, and blocked by jealous Italian artists from obtaining the most lucrative church commissions.

Return to Antwerp, 1627–1631 Soon after Van Dyck's return to Antwerp he made a will (6 March 1628), asking to be buried near Cornelia in the church of the Begijnhof, where three of his other sisters were nuns. In May he joined the Jesuit lay confraternity of bachelors (Sodaliteit der Meerderjarige Jongmans) for whom he was to paint *The Coronation of St Rosalie* in 1629 for the sum of 300 guilders, and *The Vision of the Blessed Herman Joseph* in 1630 for an even more modest 150 guilders (both Kunsthistorisches Museum, Vienna). This excess of piety set the tone for the next few years, when Van Dyck seized every opportunity to become a painter of devotional images, and he accepted the many commissions for altarpieces that came his way during Rubens's absence from the city in Madrid (1628–9) and London (1629–30). He also contributed to the market for books of pious images, notably the *Vita S Rosaliae virginis Panormitanae pestis patronae iconibus expressa*, published by Cornelis Galle in 1629 with engravings by Philip de Mallery. Van Dyck's religious works appear languid and sentimental by contrast to Rubens's more robust and physical treatments of similar subjects, although even Rubens was to respond to the cloying devotional

tastes of the 1630s. Intimate religious subjects, often taken from the life of the virgin and holy family, suited Van Dyck's abilities far better than heroic scenes of martyrdom, and could be interpreted with gracefulness, domestic charm, and even mild eroticism. Van Dyck was also suited to subjects drawn from Christ's passion, where intense pathos could be suggested through a few half-length figures, as may be seen in the strikingly Venetian *Mocking of Christ* (Art Museum, Princeton), which he also issued as an etching.

Van Dyck's talents as a painter of religious subjects were put to the test when, in 1628, he painted *St Augustine in Ecstasy* for the left aisle of the Sint-Augustinuskerk in Antwerp (for which he was paid 600 guilders by Father Marinus Jansenius), where it faced *The Martyrdom of St Apollonia* by Jordaens in the right aisle, and competed with Rubens's vast *Virgin and child adored by Saints* (all Koninklijk Museum, Antwerp) on the high altar, which cost 3000 guilders. Van Dyck remained on good terms with Rubens, since on 27 May 1628 James Hay, first earl of Carlisle, reported meeting Rubens at 'Monsr Van-digs' (Sainsbury, 119). However, for different reasons, neither Jordaens nor Rubens were Van Dyck's main competitors for religious commissions, and it was Gerard Seghers, master of a highly charged Italianate style, who was a serious rival at this time. This situation is reflected in the fact that, although Van Dyck found plentiful employment, his prices were no higher than those of his contemporaries.

Van Dyck's status after his return to Flanders from Italy is shown by the gift of a golden chain, worth 750 guilders, from the Archduchess Isabella Clara Eugenia in December 1628, shortly after he had painted her portrait. In 1630 he is known to have received a salary of 250 guilders as court painter, although (like Rubens) he resided in Antwerp, not at the Brussels court. Van Dyck also worked for patrons further afield, although his employment was not as international as that of Rubens. In 1630 Van Dyck painted *The Crucifixion* for the brotherhood of the sacred cross in the Sint-Michielskerk in Ghent (still *in situ*), for which he was paid the relatively high price of 800 guilders—a commission that had originally been given for the same fee to Rubens, who got no further than painting an oil sketch (Rockoxhuis, Antwerp). In 1630–31 Van Dyck produced three altarpieces for the minorites of Malines, an impressive decorative scheme containing a *Crucifixion* for the high altar, which has remained in the Sint-Romboutskathedraal, *The Communion of St Bonaventura* (Musée des Beaux-Arts, Caen), and *St Anthony of Padua and the Ass of Rimini* (perhaps the version in Musée des Beaux-Arts, Lille) for the side altars. He received payment of 2000 guilders from Chevalier Jan van der Laen, lord of Schriek and Grootloo. Other commissions came from as far afield as Dendermonde, Kortrijk, and Lille. Antoon Triest, bishop of Ghent, a leading lawyer, art collector, and philanthropist, was among Van Dyck's most influential patrons at this date.

During this period Van Dyck continued to paint numerous portraits, generally of wealthy citizens of Antwerp, but also of aristocrats from the Arenberg, de Croy, de Bois-chot, and Tassis families, among others. These works have a restraint and sobriety very different from those he had painted in Italy. Dated works include the pendants of *Peeter Stevens* and *Anna Wake* (both Mauritshuis, The Hague) of 1627 and 1628 respectively. On 15 April 1628 Van Dyck was commissioned to paint for 2400 guilders a life-size group portrait of twenty-four members of the city council of Brussels, to go in the burgomaster's chamber in the Brussels town hall. Its destruction in 1695 (together with another group portrait painted in 1634-5) has made the work of Van Dyck's second Antwerp period seem more dominated by religious commissions than was in fact the case.

Visit to The Hague, 1631-1632 Van Dyck visited the court of Frederik Hendrik, prince of Orange and stadholder, at The Hague, shortly before July 1631, around which time he painted the young Prince William of Orange (Museum Schloss Mosigkau, Dessau Mosigkau), before he returned in December of the same year. During this second visit Van Dyck presented the stadholder with portraits of the Archduchess Isabella (Musée des Beaux-Arts, Bordeaux) and Marie de' Medici (Jagdschloss Grunewald, Berlin), who had been painted by him during her recent stay in Antwerp, between 4 September and 16 October 1631. Constantijn Huygens, secretary to the stadholder and an eminent scholar, wrote in his diary that the artist painted his likeness (lost) on 28 January 1632, the day when a tree fell on his house.

While at The Hague, Van Dyck was commissioned to paint three-quarter-length portraits of the stadholder (Baltimore Museum of Art) and his wife, Amalia van Solms-Braunfels (priv. coll.). As far as the stadholder was concerned, Van Dyck entirely supplanted Dutch portrait painters such as Michiel Janszoon van Miereveldt and Jan van Ravesteyn. Frederik Hendrik was an avid collector of works by artists from the Southern Netherlands, which he needed in quantity to decorate the *stadhouderlijk kwartier* (stadholder's quarters) in the Binnenhof and the Oude Hof on the Noordeinde at The Hague, as well as his residences at Honselaarsdijk, near Naaldwijk, and Huis ter Nieuwburch at Rijswijk. Although a Calvinist, Frederik Hendrik was not at all bothered by Catholic religious subjects or erotic mythologies, and he commissioned four works taken from ancient and modern literature which Van Dyck treated in a refined and sensuous manner: *Rinaldo and Armida* (Musée du Louvre, Paris), *Venus at the forge of Vulcan* (Staatliche Schlösser, Potsdam-Sanssouci), *Amaryllis and Mirtillo*, and *Achilles among the Daughters of Lycomedes* (both priv. coll.), the last-mentioned being placed in the stadholder's bedroom. This visit encouraged Van Dyck to think that a Catholic artist might have a tolerable existence at a protestant court, but he chose to settle not in The Hague but in London.

Second visit to England, 1632-1634 Van Dyck was reintroduced to the British court by the purchase of his large and spectacular *Rinaldo and Armida* (Baltimore Museum of Art), for which Endymion Porter received £78 from Charles I on 23 March 1630. Despite the success of this subject from Tasso's *Gerusalemme liberata* (which shows Van Dyck working in much the same vein for the Stuarts as for the house of Orange), during the next few years the king and his courtiers were to employ him solely as a painter of portraits. Indeed, there is a tradition that it was Van Dyck's likeness of the court musician and art agent Nicholas Lanier (Kunsthistorisches Museum, Vienna), painted in Antwerp in June 1628, that made the king invite the artist to England.

Van Dyck arrived in London in 1632 and presented Charles I with portraits of Frederik Hendrik, Amalia van Solms (perhaps Museo del Prado, Madrid), Prince William of Orange (Petworth House), the Archduchess Isabella, and Gaston, duc d'Orléans (perhaps Musée Condé, Chantilly), for which he was subsequently reimbursed. Van Dyck was accommodated with Edward Norgate, Windsor herald, who received £45 for the artist's 'diett and lodging' from 2 April to 31 May (PRO, E 403/2751) before a house in Blackfriars was made ready for him. This property was on the waterside and had a garden; it was outside the jurisdiction of the London Painter–Stainers' Company, but within easy reach of the court by boat. Van Dyck was also given rooms at the royal palace of Eltham in Kent. On 5 July he was knighted at St James's Palace and became 'principalle Paynter in Ordinary to their Majesties' (Carpenter, 29). In May 1633 he was granted a substantial pension of £200, which set him above all the other artists employed by Charles I except the medallist Nicolas Briot. It was to commence retrospectively from 25 March but was not paid regularly, a common occurrence at the Stuart court. An order for five years' pension in arrears (£1000) was made on 14 December 1638, but it may never have been honoured.

Van Dyck quickly supplanted Daniel Mytens, his main rival at court. Shortly before 1631 Mytens had painted a double portrait of Charles I and Henrietta Maria (Royal Collection) for the cabinet room at Denmark (Somerset) House, but he was now required to repaint the likeness of the queen using one of Van Dyck's portraits as a model. Even so, the result did not satisfy, and Mytens's work was replaced by an entirely new version by Van Dyck (archiepiscopal castle, Kroměříž). It is hardly surprising that Mytens returned to the Netherlands in 1634.

Immediately after his arrival in London, Van Dyck set to work on the group portrait of *Charles I and Queen Henrietta Maria with their two eldest children, Charles, prince of Wales, and Mary, princess royal* (Royal Collection), since a request for payment was made as early as 15 July 1632 and a privy seal warrant was issued on 8 August, which was paid in September. This work was first known as the 'great piece', reflecting its vast scale and prominent location in the Long Gallery at Whitehall. Although the work echoes earlier Tudor portraits, and includes the crown of state, orb, and sceptre, it presents the royal family with a degree of informality. In several large canvases Van Dyck reinvented Stuart royal iconography through his knowledge of European portraiture, while keeping earlier Tudor precedents in mind. In 1633 he painted *Charles I on Horseback with M. de St Antoine* (Royal Collection), which was placed at the end of the gallery at St James's Palace, where the king must have appeared to advance illusionistically towards the spectator through the painted archway. Van Dyck's last major contribution in this vein, the *Equestrian Portrait of Charles I* (National Gallery, London), is not documented but has been generally dated in the late 1630s, and so falls into his third period of work in England. It shows the king, accompanied only by an equerry, riding across an empty field of campaign, wearing tilting armour with a lance-rest and holding an imperial baton.

Charles I viewed Van Dyck as a modern Titian, and he could have made no greater compliment, since the work of the great Venetian artist was much to the royal taste. Van Dyck was required to paint a replacement for Titian's *Emperor Vitellius* (lost) from the series of Roman emperors, formerly in the Mantuan collection, which was said to have been 'washed away' during transport from Venice to London (Millar, *Van Dyck in England*, 22), as well as carrying out repairs on Titian's *Emperor Galba* from the same series. Van Dyck's own collection contained such outstanding Venetian pictures as Titian's *Vendramin Family* (National Gallery, London) and *Perseus and Andromeda* (Wallace Collection, London). Puget de la Serre, secretary to Marie de' Medici, described the collection as the 'Cabinet de Titien' (Wood, 'Cabinet', 681).

Van Dyck was one of the small number of Flemish Catholics who decided to work in a protestant country, but as a foreign national he was free to attend mass at the queen's chapel or the houses of ambassadors. He could have expected the favour of Henrietta Maria, herself a Catholic, and in 1633 she appointed the artist's brother Theodoor as one of her chaplains, but he returned to Antwerp on 9 March 1634. Surprisingly, Van Dyck appears to have painted only one devotional image for her, *The Holy Family with Dancing Angels* (des.). The king trusted pro-Spanish courtiers with Catholic sympathies, and one of these, the lord treasurer, Richard Weston, first earl of Portland, obtained *The Mystic Marriage of St Catherine* (lost) by Van Dyck as early as 1631, intending to give it to either the king or queen as a new year's gift, although for reasons that are unclear the artist repudiated the work. Bellori claimed that Van Dyck painted some popish religious subjects for the convert Sir Kenelm Digby, but none of these have been traced. In addition Van Dyck was on good terms with Hispanophile courtiers such as Endymion Porter, groom of the bedchamber, who was also an art agent, and the artist depicted himself with Porter in a friendship portrait (Museo del Prado, Madrid). Nevertheless, these contacts were less fruitful than might be expected.

Van Dyck's most important English patrons were puritans or puritan sympathizers. The most voracious of these was Philip, fourth Lord Wharton, who in 1632 (immediately after Van Dyck's arrival) commissioned his portrait in the guise of an arcadian shepherd (National Gallery, Washington). By the end of the decade Wharton owned more than twenty works by the artist (including fourteen full-lengths), more than anyone else at court

apart from the king. Philip Herbert, fourth earl of Pembroke, a fierce opponent of popery, commissioned numerous portraits from Van Dyck and a vast family group (Wilton House, Wiltshire), one of the largest works the artist ever painted, intended for Durham House, Pembroke's London mansion on the Strand. Other generous patrons who were undoubted protestants included Francis Russell, fourth earl of Bedford (often wrongly described as a puritan), and Algernon Percy, tenth earl of Northumberland. Northumberland paid £200 in 1635 for several portraits of himself and his family, and he also commissioned a posthumous likeness of his father, the ninth earl (Petworth House), which was 'done by an old picture' (BL, Egerton MS 1636, fol. 92r). Northumberland remained a collector of Van Dyck's work throughout the 1630s and 1640s, and also bought the two most important paintings by Titian from the artist's collection after his death.

Van Dyck quickly established a lucrative studio practice in London, charging £50 to £60 for a full-length, £30 for a half-length, and £20 for a head and shoulders portrait. The demand for his paintings forced the artist to work at ever increasing speed and to depend more and more on assistants. Some contemporary accounts—such as one supplied by the banker and collector Everhard Jabach—provide an idea of how the workshop operated. Sitters would visit the studio for an hour at a time, so a large number of portraits could be produced simultaneously. Van Dyck would make a compositional drawing from life in black chalk on blue paper, which was then enlarged by an assistant onto the canvas. Only the sitter's head would be painted by Van Dyck directly from life, but this did not mean that patrons were indifferent to quality, and Thomas Wentworth, first earl of Strafford, was insistent that Van Dyck should 'take good paines upon the perfecting [of his portrait] … with his owne pensell' (Millar, 'Strafford', 115). The costume to be represented would be sent to the studio and stand-in models were used by specialist drapery painters. Van Dyck's assistants included Jan van Belcamp, Remigius van Leemput, and George Geldorp, who also catered to the growing hunger for pastiches and copies of Van Dyck's work.

The terms of Van Dyck's court appointment suggest that he was expected to settle in London. He soon had a virtual monopoly of royal portraits, receiving £444 for 'nine pictures of o^r Royall self and most dearest Consort the Queene', according to a privy seal warrant of 7 May 1633 (PRO, E 403/2567), full payment for which was made on 23 May. But it was not until March 1638 that a grant of denizenship was made to Van Dyck 'and to his heires borne in forraine partes' (PRO, SO 3/11). He still owned property in Antwerp and may have travelled abroad more frequently than is recorded. Van Dyck was in Rye, one of the main ports on the south coast, on 27 August 1633, when he inscribed a drawing of the city (Pierpont Morgan Library, New York), and a similar sheet is dated 1634 (Fitzwilliam Museum, Cambridge), when he was *en route* for the Southern Netherlands.

Return to Antwerp and Brussels, 1634–1635 Van Dyck kept an eye on Habsburg patronage. The death of the Archduchess Isabella in December 1633 drew him back to Antwerp, where he was recorded shortly before 28 March 1634. He remained in the Southern Netherlands for a year, returning to London in the spring of 1635. On 14 April 1634 Van Dyck authorized his sister Susanna to administer his property in Antwerp; this suggests that he wanted to put his affairs in order and did not intend remaining in the city. On 16 December he was recorded as resident at 't-Paradijs ('The Paradise') in Brussels, shortly after the arrival of the Cardinal-Infante Ferdinand, with whom he was in contact and whose portrait he painted (Museo del Prado, Madrid).

Van Dyck was occupied mainly in the service of the political and social élite of Flanders at this time. In particular, he worked for the Abbé Cesare Alessandro Scaglia, a professional diplomat for the house of Savoy, a spy (agent '2X' in the ciphers) and art lover whom Van Dyck may have already met in Turin or Brussels. Van Dyck painted a *Lamentation* (Koninklijk Museum, Antwerp) as *predella* for the altar in Scaglia's funerary chapel, dedicated to Our Lady of the Seven Sorrows in the Minderbroederskerk, Antwerp, as well as several portraits of the abbé, who died in 1641 owning seven works by the artist. During this brief period Van Dyck characteristically worked under great pressure on several ambitious commissions, notably the large group of *John, Count of Nassau-Siegen, and his Family* (priv. coll.), an imposing equestrian portrait of *Prince Tommaso Francesco of Savoy-Carignano* (Galleria Sabauda, Turin), who was acting governor of the Spanish Netherlands before the arrival of the cardinal-infante, and a life-size group portrait of seven magistrates with a personification of Justice (des., 1695) for the Schepene Camer in the Brussels town hall, now known only from a preparatory oil sketch in the École des Beaux-Arts, Paris. The works of this date have a distinctive character, as if Van Dyck looked back to the work of his Italian period but now painted with the fluent elegance of his most accomplished English commissions.

Third period in England, 1635–1641 Van Dyck returned to London early in 1635, almost certainly bringing his collection of Italian paintings with him, and a landing stage was constructed at his house in Blackfriars so that the king could visit 'to see his Paintings in the moneths of June and July' (PRO, E 351/3268). On 17 March 1635 Charles I wrote to Gian Lorenzo Bernini in Rome, asking him to carve 'our likeness in marble from a painting which we shall soon send you' (D. Bernini, *Vita del Cavalier Gio. Lorenzo Bernino*, Rome, 1713, 65), referring to the triple portrait which Van Dyck painted for this purpose (Royal Collection), but it was more than two years before the marble bust arrived at Oatlands, on 17 July 1637. Shortly afterwards Van Dyck began work on a group of *The Three Eldest Children of Charles I* (Galleria Sabauda, Turin) to be sent as a gift from Henrietta Maria to her sister Christina, duchess of Savoy. The king was displeased that Van Dyck did not show the children wearing the *tabliers* (aprons) which protected their clothes, and almost transparent lace ones visible in the

picture were added on Henrietta Maria's advice after the portrait arrived at Turin. Van Dyck made a second attempt at this subject (Royal Collection), also datable to 1635, where the prince of Wales is shown wearing breeches and posed like a miniature adult. Van Dyck's largest and most complex group of this kind was *The Five Eldest Children of Charles I* (Royal Collection), which he signed and dated in 1637. Payment of £1200 was ordered 'for certeyne Pictures by him' on 23 February 1637 (PRO, PSO, 2/104), which he received in three instalments between May and December.

In 1638 Van Dyck sent a 'memoir' (Carpenter, 67) to Charles I asking for payment for twenty-five paintings, on which the king marked down the asking price for a number of items. The works listed included 'Le Roi alla ciasse', identifiable as a portrait of the king hunting (Musée du Louvre, Paris), and two portraits of Henrietta Maria (Royal Collection) painted in 1638 with the intention that Bernini would carve a companion bust to the one of the king, although this was never realized. 'Le dessein de Roy et tous le Chevaliers' referred to an oil sketch (priv. coll.) for tapestries of the history and ceremonial of the Order of the Garter, intended for the Whitehall Banqueting House, but never woven. In addition Van Dyck noted that his annual pension of £200 had not been paid for the past five years. Payment was ordered under a privy seal warrant in December, but only £603 for the pictures was paid, in February and March 1639.

The visual character of Van Dyck's English portraits is very different from his earlier work: areas of local colour are brilliant in hue, surfaces are polished, and the handling of paint is extremely fluid. In this period he followed the example of Paolo Veronese by painting on a grey ground, sometimes with a pale brown tint. Van Dyck began to include symbolic details much in the manner of earlier Elizabethan portraits, as in his own *Self-Portrait with a Sunflower* (priv. coll.) and the allegorical *Lady Venetia Digby as Prudence* (Palazzo Reale, Milan). It must have been the sitters themselves who demanded the incorporation of Latin texts, something unknown in Van Dyck's earlier work, as in his portraits of *George Stuart, seigneur d'Aubigny* (NPG) and *Sir John Suckling* (Frick Collection, New York), the former shown in arcadian costume and the latter in Persian dress. Van Dyck introduced a number of new formats into his English portraits, notably the depiction of women wearing timeless robes and gauzy veils in what William Sanderson described as a 'careless romance' (*Graphice*, 1658, 39), often standing in rocky, 'wilderness' settings, as in *Mrs Endymion Porter* (priv. coll.), or, more fashionably dressed, in gardens where they may dip a hand into a fountain or be seen near a large vase, as in *Ann Carr, Countess of Bedford* (priv. coll.). Van Dyck had previously painted married couples together, but in England he introduced a new category of male and female friendship portraits, using a horizontal format where the sitters are depicted seated, as in the much-admired *Thomas Killigrew and (?) William, Lord Crofts* (Royal Collection), which is signed and dated 1638. English patrons were blind to Van Dyck's talent for narrative. But he did paint at least one sensuous and elegant subject from mythology for the crown, the *Cupid and Psyche* now in the royal collection.

The Iconography Van Dyck's series of etched and engraved portraits of famous men and women came to be known in the eighteenth century as the *Iconography*. It followed the precedent of Domenicus Lampsonius's *Pictorum aliquot celebrium Germaniae inferioris effigies* of 1572, and contained more than fifty likenesses of artists and art lovers, but differed from this prototype by including a substantial number of portraits of princes, military leaders, statesmen, and scholars. Van Dyck prepared the series by making chalk or wash drawings, subsequently developed as oil sketches painted in grey, brown, or green oils, which were used as models by the engravers. Most of the drawings were made from life, but the series included posthumous images of Desiderius Erasmus, Jacques Dubroeucq, and Frans Francken the elder. While the drawings are scattered throughout many public and private collections, a large group of about forty of the oil sketches remain together in a private collection.

Work on the series began in Antwerp in the late 1620s, and some epigrams written by Constantijn Huygens show that partial sets were in circulation before 1632. Van Dyck's earliest plates show him etching the faces and leaving much of the remainder to be completed by specialist engravers. The most important and accomplished of these were Lucas Vorsterman and Paulus Pontius, who were responsible for the lion's share of the series. Van Dyck continued work on the project during the 1630s while in England, and in a letter dated 14 August 1636 (but oddly referring to a book published in 1637) he wrote to Franciscus Junius for a Latin motto to be inscribed on the portrait of Kenelm Digby. At this time he used Robert van Voerst to engrave his works (including some of the plates for the *Iconography*), until this printmaker's premature death in October 1636. The *Iconography* engravings were distributed by the Antwerp *constvercooper* (art dealer) and print publisher Martinus van den Enden, to whom the copperplates must have been shipped and with whom the artist would have been in frequent contact. The first identifiable edition with a title-page was published posthumously in 1645 by Gillis Hendricx, a business rival of van den Enden, who obtained the plates from him. The importance of this series was enormous, and it provided a repertory of images that were plundered by portrait painters throughout Europe over the next couple of centuries.

Last years and death Van Dyck's last months showed him in a fever of activity, travelling back and forth between the Southern Netherlands, France, and England. In autumn 1640 he was in Antwerp, where he attended the celebrations of the feast of St Luke by the guild on 18 October, having earlier been elected honorary dean, a distinction granted otherwise only to Rubens. Van Dyck had returned to the city because of Rubens's death on 30 May and the opportunities now open to the artist's successor. The cardinal-infante was keen that Van Dyck, the most brilliant of Rubens's 'disciples', should complete the works that had been commissioned by Philip IV for the Alcázar, Madrid, in 1639 and were now left unfinished, but Van Dyck refused. During this visit he received his last major religious commission, *The Martyrdom of St George*, for the altar of the guild of *jonge voetboog* (young crossbowmen) in Antwerp Cathedral, but this was never completed and is known only through oil sketches (Christ Church, Oxford; Musée Bonnat, Bayonne).

Late in December 1640 Van Dyck left Antwerp for Paris, having heard of plans to decorate the Grand Galerie in the Louvre, a job that was given to Nicolas Poussin—to whom it was even less suited. Despite rumours that Van Dyck was mentally unstable—the cardinal-infante even called him a raving madman—his last works remained highly accomplished. This is evident from the portrait of William II, prince of Orange, with his ten-year-old bride, Princess Mary (Rijksmuseum, Amsterdam), which Van Dyck painted on his return to London in mid-1641. Despite falling ill soon after it was completed, he took the portrait to The Hague and was recorded in Antwerp in October. He was accompanied by his wife, Mary Ruthven (whom he had married on 27 February 1640), a lady-in-waiting to the queen and the daughter of Patrick Ruthven MD, styled Lord Ruthven (d. 1652), and his wife, Elizabeth, *née* Woodford (d. 1624). Her grandfather was William, fourth Lord Ruthven and first earl of Gowrie. She appears to have returned directly to London, while Van Dyck accompanied her only as far as Calais, where he met Louis de Béthune, lieutenant-general of the city, who encouraged him to change his plans and proceed to Paris. He arrived there before November, but, now seriously ill, was forced to turn down a commission to paint 'Monseigneur le Cardinal' (Richelieu); he travelled back to London, where his wife was nearing the end of a pregnancy.

Van Dyck must have known that he was close to death, since he made his will on 4 December. He bequeathed his property in Antwerp to his sister Susanna for the maintenance of his illegitimate daughter Maria Theresia (c.1634/5–1699), and his sister Isabella was to receive 250 guilders a year. His estate in London was to go to his wife and his legitimate daughter, Justiniana, who was born on 1 December. Van Dyck died in Blackfriars, London, on 9 December, the same day as Justiniana's baptism, and was buried on 11 December in the choir of St Paul's Cathedral. His mortal remains and tomb (erected by the king) were destroyed in the great fire of 1666.

Van Dyck's widow (d. 1645) remarried almost immediately, her second husband being Sir Richard Price (d. 1651) of Gogerddan, Cardiganshire, who according to Richard Symonds 'expected much money to pay debts' (BL, Egerton MS 1636, fol. 102r), and it is clear that Justiniana's estate was soon embezzled, many of the pictures from the studio being smuggled abroad by Richard Andrewes (whose father-in-law was the court jeweller Nicasius Russell) or used as collateral against Price's debts. Justiniana married Sir John Baptist Stepney in 1653 (when still a minor); in 1660 the couple travelled to Antwerp, where, on 19 August, they were rebaptized and remarried in the Sint-Jacobskerk according to the rites of the church of

Rome, before returning to London to petition Charles II for the renewal of Van Dyck's pension. They had four children, and two of their daughters, Maria and Priscilla, later became nuns at Hoogstraten. Maria Theresia became the third wife of Gabriël Essers (1621–1685), *drossaard* (bailiff) of Bouchout, on 1 March 1654, in a ceremony conducted by her uncle Theodoor (or Waltmannus) Van Dyck. The couple had five daughters (Theresa Margaretha, Susanna, Maria Barbara, Anna, and Theresa) and three sons (Gabriël, Justo Bartholomeus, and Antoon).

Character and reputation Van Dyck's contemporaries said surprisingly little about his personality, and few letters by him survive. This did not inhibit the creation of a colourful legend, and he was frequently described as narcissistic and volatile. When the haughty Antoon Triest sat for his portrait, he apparently found Van Dyck impertinent and said he was as short in height as his tongue was long and malicious (Weyerman, 1.306–7). In London the artist's liaison with Margaret Lemon attracted comment, and she was said to have tried to bite off the thumb of his painting hand in a fit of jealousy. Van Dyck was certainly a ladies' man, but, unusually for the period, he delayed marriage until late in his relatively short life. He clearly enjoyed worldly success, but his punishing workload seems to have contained an element of self-destruction.

Van Dyck's work had an immediate impact on portrait painting in the Netherlands, as may be seen from the work of Cornelis de Vos in the 1620s and Adriaen Hanneman in the 1640s. His influence was no less in religious and historical subjects; during the 1630s Jan Boeckhorst skilfully imitated Van Dyck's fluid style of brushwork, and in the 1640s Thomas Willeboits Bosschaert and Pieter Thijs adopted the elegance and almost hysterical emotionalism of his figures, both artists finding employment at the court at The Hague, where Van Dyck's talents were sorely missed. In Britain, Van Dyck's impact can be measured by Jonathan Richardson's remark: 'When Van Dyck came hither he brought Face-Painting to us; ever since which time … England has excell'd all the World in that great Branch of the Art' (*An Essay on the Theory of Painting*, 1715, 41). In the eighteenth century artists as different as Sir Joshua Reynolds, Thomas Gainsborough, and Richard Cosway were not only deeply indebted to his example but often depicted their sitters in Van Dyck costume.

Van Dyck's restlessness has made it difficult for historians to write a coherent account of his career, and this has been compounded by the lack of a reliable complete catalogue of his paintings. Van Dyck's role in Rubens's workshop between 1615 and 1620 has attracted a great deal of interest, but his exact contribution remains elusive. In recent years the attribution of the so-called Antwerp sketchbook (priv. coll.), largely copied from a lost pocketbook by Rubens, has proved particularly contentious. On the other hand, the increased attention given to patronage and collecting at the courts of the archduchess at Brussels, the house of Orange at The Hague, and Charles I in London has led to a better understanding of the contexts in which the artist worked.

Despite the adulation given to Van Dyck over the centuries the shadow of Rubens has fallen over his reputation, and his work has been viewed as more facile and worldly and less intellectually rigorous than that of the older artist. Reynolds was in the minority when he praised the altarpieces of the late 1620s, claiming that Van Dyck 'truly had a genius for history-painting, if it had not been taken off by portraits' (Reynolds, 24). Modern attention to the meaning and symbolism of Van Dyck's works has helped revise traditional views of him as an instinctive and unlettered artist. Not least, recent interest in the history of taste and the rise and fall of artistic reputations has opened up the topic of Van Dyck's immense influence over European portraiture, summed up in the words reportedly said by Gainsborough on his deathbed: 'We are all going to heaven, and Van Dyck is of the Company.'

JEREMY WOOD

Sources G. P. Bellori, *Le vite de' pittori, scultori et architetti moderni* (1672) · J. C. Weyerman, *De levens-beschryvingen der Nederlandsche konst-schilders en konst-schilderessen*, 4 vols. (The Hague, 1729–69) · W. H. Carpenter, *Pictorial notices: consisting of a memoir of Sir Anthony Van Dyck* (1844) · W. N. Sainsbury, *Original unpublished papers illustrative of the life of Sir Peter Paul Rubens as an artist and a diplomatist, preserved in H.M. state paper office* (1859) · C. Ruelens and M. Rooses, eds., *Correspondance de Rubens et documents épistolaires concernant sa vie et ses œuvres*, 6 vols. (Anvers, 1887–1909) · L. Galesloot, 'Un procès pour une vente de tableaux attribués à Antoine van Dyck, 1660–1662', *Annales de l'Académie d'Archéologie de Belgique*, 24 (1868), 561–606 · E. Larsen, ed., *La vie, les ouvrages et les élèves de Van Dyck: manuscrit inédit des archives du Louvre par un auteur anonyme* (Brussels, 1975) · C. Baisier, ed., *Antoon Van Dyck anders bekeken over 'registers en contrefeytsels, tronies en copyen' in Antwerpse kerken en kloosters* (1999) · A. K. Wheelock, jun., S. J. Barnes, and J. S. Held, *Anthony van Dyck* (1990) · D. Maufort, 'Notices biographiques sur la lignée d'Antoon van Dyck', *Jaarboek Koninklijk Museum voor Schone Kunsten, Antwerpen* (1999), 111–23 · K. van der Stighelen, 'Young Anthony: archival discoveries relating to Van Dyck's early career', *Van Dyck 350*, ed. S. J. Barnes and A. K. Wheelock, jun. (1994), 17–46 · A. Balis, '"Fatto da un mio discepolo": Rubens's studio practices reviewed', *Rubens and his workshop: the flight of Lot and his family from Sodom*, ed. T. Nakamura (1994), 97–127 · J. R. Martin, *The ceiling paintings for the Jesuit church in Antwerp* (1968) · G. Adriani, *Anton Van Dyck: italienisches Skizzenbuch* (1940) · S. J. Barnes, 'Van Dyck in Italy, 1621–1628', PhD diss., New York University, 1986 · G. Mendola, 'Van Dyck in Sicily', *Van Dyck, 1599–1641*, ed. C. Brown and H. Vlieghe (1999), 58–63 · S. J. Barnes, P. Boccardo, C. Di Fabio, and L. Tagliaferro, eds., *Van Dyck a Genova: grande pittura e collezionismo* (1997) · M. Vaes, 'Le séjour de Van Dyck en Italie (mi-novembre 1621–automne 1627)', *Bulletin de l'Institut historique belge de Rome*, 4 (1924), 163–234 · H. Vlieghe, 'Images of piety and vanity: Van Dyck in the Southern Netherlands, 1627–32, 1634–5, 1640–41', *Van Dyck, 1599–1641*, ed. C. Brown and H. Vlieghe (1999), 65–77 · F. Baudouin, 'Van Dyck in The Hague', *Van Dyck, 1599–1999: conjectures and refutations*, ed. H. Vlieghe (2001), 53–64 · P. van der Ploeg and C. Vermeeren, *Princely patrons: the collection of Frederick Henry of Orange and Amalia of Solms in The Hague* (1997) · D. Howarth, 'The arrival of Van Dyck in England', *Burlington Magazine*, 132 (1990), 709–10 · O. Millar, *The Tudor, Stuart and early Georgian pictures in the collection of her majesty the queen*, 2 vols. (1963) · O. Millar, *Van Dyck in England* (1982) · O. Millar, 'Strafford and Van Dyck', *For Veronica Wedgwood these studies in seventeenth-century history*, ed. R. Ollard and P. Tudor-Craig (1986), 109–23 · O. Millar, 'Philip, Lord Wharton, and his collection of portraits', *Burlington Magazine*, 136 (1994), 517–30 · M. F. S. Hervey, *The life, correspondence and collections of Thomas Howard, earl of Arundel* (1921) · J. Wood, 'Van Dyck and the earl of Northumberland: taste and collecting in Stuart England', *Van Dyck 350*, ed. S. J. Barnes and A. K. Wheelock, jun. (1994), 281–324 · J. Wood, 'Van Dyck: a Catholic artist in protestant England, and the notes on painting compiled by Francis Russell, 4th earl of Bedford', *Van Dyck, 1599–1999: conjectures and refutations*, ed. H. Vlieghe (2001), 167–98 · A. Cifani and F. Monetti, 'New light on the Abbé Scaglia and Van Dyck', *Burlington Magazine*, 134 (1992), 506–14 · C. Depauw and G. Luijten, *Anthony van Dyck as printmaker* (1999) · M. Mauquoy-Hendrickx, *L'Iconographie d'Antoine van Dyck: catalogue raisonné*, rev. 2nd edn, 2 vols. (1991) · J. Wood, 'Van Dyck's "Cabinet de Titien": the contents and dispersal of his collection', *Burlington Magazine*, 132 (1990), 680–95 · F. Baudouin, 'Van Dyck's last religious commission: an altarpiece for Antwerp Cathedral', *Journal of the Warburg and Courtauld Institutes*, 57 (1994), 175–90 · J. Reynolds, *A journey to Flanders and Holland*, ed. H. Mount (1996) · will, 6 March 1628, Stadsarchief, Antwerp, notaris L. de Pieters 944 · J. B. Paul, ed., *The Scots peerage*, 4 (1907), 264–5

Archives Bodl. Oxf., MS Marshall 80 · PRO, E, exchequer of receipt: issue rolls and registers 403/2565–2568, 2607, 2748, 2751–2752, 2756–2757 · PRO, E, exchequer of receipt: warrants for issues 404/154 · PRO, LC, records of the Lord Chamberlain and other officers of the Royal Household 5/132 · PRO, PSO, doquet books, 5/5 · PRO, PSO, doquet books and letters recommendatory 3/9–12 · PRO, PSO, signet and other warrants for the privy seal 2/104 · PRO, SP, Commonwealth Exchequer Papers 28/350/9 · Stadsarchief, Antwerp, purchase and ownership of 'De Stadt van Ghent', Pk 2284; SR 466 · Stadsarchief, Antwerp, Van Dyck's case against Peter van den Broek, 1630, notaris L. de Pieters 945 · Stadsarchief, Antwerp, Van Dyck's lawsuits against Diericx and Lancelots, Pk 708, 709

Likenesses Rubens, portrait, 1614–15, Rubenshuis, Antwerp · A. Van Dyck, self-portrait, oils, *c*.1614–1615, Gemäldegalerie der Akademie, Vienna · A. Van Dyck, self-portrait, *c*.1620–1621, Metropolitan Museum of Art, New York · A. Van Dyck, self-portrait, oils, *c*.1621, State Hermitage Museum, St Petersburg; version, Alte Pinakothek, Munich · oils, *c*.1621 (after A. Van Dyck), NPG · A. Van Dyck, self-portrait, oils, *c*.1632–1633, priv. coll. [*see illus.*] · A. Van Dyck, double portrait, self-portrait, oils, *c*.1633 (with Endymion Porter), Prado, Madrid · J. Neefs, etching (after A. Van Dyck), BM, NPG; repro. in *Centum icones* (1645) · A. Van Dyck, self-portrait (copy of oils, priv. coll.), Berkeley Castle, Gloucestershire · A. Van Dyck, self-portrait, etching, AM Oxf.; Rijksprentenkabinet, Amsterdam · A. Van Dyck, self-portrait, oils, Louvre, Paris

Wealth at death see will, 6 March 1628, Stadsarchief, Antwerp, notaris L. de Pieters 944

Dyer, Sir Edward (1543–1607), courtier and poet, was born in October 1543 at Weston, Somerset, the eldest son of Sir Thomas Dyer (d. 1565) and his first wife, Frances (*née* Darcy), widow of William Thornburgh. Wood states that Edward studied at either Balliol College or Broadgates Hall, Oxford, and travelled abroad thereafter. He was only seventeen, however, when he was admitted to the Inner Temple in 1560.

Dyer came into his inheritance upon his father's death in 1565 and by 1567 had begun his career at court as a member of the earl of Leicester's retinue. A royal export licence dated 12 April 1568 styles him the queen's servant, as he is likewise described in 1570, when Elizabeth appointed him steward of the manor and woods of Woodstock, with the rangership and portership of the park. While Holinshed records that Dyer served with the English forces that successfully besieged Edinburgh Castle in the spring of 1573, this seems to contradict Gilbert Talbot's well-known report of 11 May to his father, the earl of Shrewsbury, that Dyer had only recently recovered from a consumption. Talbot added that Dyer had been in disgrace

with the queen for the past two years, but was now restored to favour, having persuaded Elizabeth that her displeasure had caused his illness.

Dyer inherited a substantial landed income and he received frequent gifts from the crown, yet the costs of life at Elizabeth's court plunged him into a lifelong cycle of borrowing and debt. As early as November 1572 he appealed to Sir Walter Mildmay, chancellor of the exchequer, to postpone the repayment of his debts. He gained an irregular income from the patent granted on 2 May 1573 (renewed 1588, regranted 1601) to search for and profit from concealed lands, that is, privately held lands that legally belonged to the crown. An early benefit of this patent was the grant in fee farm of Sharpham Park and the manor of Strete, Somerset (14 November 1575). Dyer acquired a further source of funds in January 1576, when Elizabeth awarded him the monopoly to license tanners and to pardon infractions of the tanning statute. Finally, the queen lent him £3000 in 1579, a sum he never managed to repay. Early in 1582 a Spanish agent at court described Dyer as 'That bankrupt poltroon' (*CSP for.*, 1581–2, 472); by the end of his life his total indebtedness exceeded £11,000.

As Leicester's protégé, Dyer became closely allied with members of the Dudley and Sidney families, particularly the earl's nephew Philip Sidney and his boyhood friend Fulke Greville. The three formed that 'happy blessed Trinitie' celebrated in one of Sidney's lyrics. They were writing poetry together by the late 1570s when Spenser referred to their 'Aereopagus'. Dyer may have written verse at court during the 1560s, but his earliest datable poem is 'The Songe in the Oke', which he apparently sang before Elizabeth in person during the Woodstock entertainment of September 1575. In his *Choice of Emblemes* (1586) Geoffrey Whitney praised Sidney for reviving English poetry, an honour that Sidney declined in favour of his friend Dyer. The twelve or more extant lyrics that can be attributed to Dyer include love laments that rank among the most popular and influential poems of the Elizabethan age. Even if he did not write the perennial favourite 'My mind to me a kingdom is' (to which the earl of Oxford holds a slightly better claim), Dyer's 'The lowest trees have tops' and 'He that his mirth hath lost' circulated widely in print and manuscript well into the seventeenth century. The latter poem, moreover, inspired imitations and responses by Greville, James VI of Scotland, Sir Francis Drake, and Robert Southwell, among others.

In addition to poetry, Dyer cultivated the broad spectrum of intellectual pursuits associated with the ideal of the Renaissance man. His friendship with Dr John Dee, with whom he shared interests in New World exploration and alchemy, dated back to at least 1566. With Sidney, Dyer studied alchemy under Dee's direction, and as late as 1589 he was advising the countess of Shrewsbury on the medicinal value of gold salts. In dedicating his *Discourse of the Navigation which the Portugales doe Make* to Dyer in 1579 John Frampton characterized his patron as 'a speciall favourer of all good knowledges' (*STC, 1475–1640*, 10529, sig. A2). Dyer was keenly interested in international politics. Sir Amias Paulet, ambassador in Paris, wrote to Dyer in 1577 to apologize for the delay in sending him a copy of Jean Bodin's *La république*, an analysis of French government. In the same year Roger Baynes's dedication of *The Praise of Solitarinesse* to Dyer acknowledged his overall command of foreign languages, albeit the earl of Leicester affirmed only that Dyer understood 'Italian well and the Latin which he somewhat speaketh' (*CSP for.*, *1578*, 530).

Dyer's financial plight did not detract from his reputation as a patron. In addition to Baynes's book and two by Frampton, an unidentified T. N. dedicated to Dyer an early work of utopian fiction, *A Pleasant Dialogue* (1579; *STC*, *1475–1640*, 18335.5). Dyer's friendship with Sidney probably led John Dickenson to choose him as the dedicatee of his pastoral romance *Arisbas* (1594). Dyer also received the dedications of at least five manuscripts, among them Abraham Fraunce's 'Shepheardes Logicke' (BL, Add. MS 34361) and John Florio's 'Giardino de recreatione' (BL, Add. MS 15214).

With Sidney, Dyer subscribed to invest in Frobisher's three voyages in search of gold and the north-west passage (1576–8). He served on the governing commission of the Adventurers of the North-West Passage that eventually handled the company's bankruptcy, for the voyages yielded neither gold nor the fabled passage. Frobisher's failure did not, however, extinguish Dyer's belief that England might yet gain a direct route to the wealth of the East. He met Dee and Sir Francis Walsingham on 18 February 1583 to discuss Captain John Davis's plan to resume the search for the north-west passage. Davis's voyage (1585) enjoyed no more success than Frobisher's ventures, although the name of Cape Dyer in northern Canada remains as a lasting tribute to Dyer from the expedition.

Despite his financial difficulties, Dyer's fellow courtiers respected his good sense and maturity. Sir Nicholas Throckmorton, ambassador to Scotland, had entrusted Dyer with a confidential message to Leicester as early as 1567. Lady Mary Sidney praised 'the wyse, noble Mr. Dyers frendely Counsell' (Collins, 1.66–7), and Paulet's letters to Dyer from France, almost deferential in tone, refer to him 'as one of my best asured frindes' (Bodl. Oxf., MS Rawl. A.331, fol. 123*v*). Dyer's skilful courtiership and sound judgement qualified him for foreign service, the first instance of which occurred in May 1577, when Leicester wrote that Dyer would stand proxy for him at the baptism of William of Orange's daughter. Elizabeth waited until January 1584 to send Dyer on his first official embassy, again to the Netherlands, whence he returned on 28 February, the Dutch having formally agreed to send twenty ships to England's defence in the event of foreign invasion. In spite of the success of his mission, Dyer saw no further service abroad for several years. He remained at court in 1585 when Leicester led an English army to the Netherlands, although he advised the earl at some length on military strategy in a letter of 22 May 1586. A tragic upshot of this English intervention was Sidney's death that October; Dyer served as pallbearer at his friend's

funeral, and with Greville shared in the bequest of all of Sidney's books.

In anticipation of the Spanish Armada, Dyer was again dispatched to the Netherlands in May 1588, apparently to encourage the Dutch to fulfil their promise. In June, however, just weeks before the Armada entered the channel, Dyer left Holland for Prague. He probably bore an informal mandate from the crown to do so, or he would surely have returned home to help England face the regime's most serious external threat. His journey to Bohemia was in any event prompted by the fact that Dee had found patronage and taken up residence there along with his erstwhile protégé Edward Kelley. Kelley had convinced Dee and Emperor Rudolph II that he could turn base metal into gold. In July Dyer visited Dee in Trebona, where he met and conferred with William of Rosenberg, Dee's patron and a high-ranking imperial nobleman. Dyer too was persuaded that Kelley had found the secret of the philosopher's stone; he returned to England in late summer.

That winter Dyer served for the first time in parliament as representative of Somerset. His committee appointments included one for the subsidy and one for the queen's safety. In March the following year Elizabeth proposed sending him as envoy to James VI, but he was instead dispatched on an unspecified mission to the Danish court in November. By February 1590 he had left Denmark on his second embassy to Prague, charged, no doubt, with persuading Kelley to return to England. Dyer went back to London alone, however, on 15 March, and his account of affairs in Bohemia only whetted the government's resolve to repatriate Kelley. By October Dyer was again in Prague, where he undertook months of alchemical experimentation with Kelley, being prompted the while by letters from Burghley, the lord treasurer, to bring Kelley back. Suspicious of Kelley's loyalty and Dyer's intentions, the emperor kept Dyer under house arrest from April to June, forcing Elizabeth to send a special envoy, Thomas Webbe, to negotiate his release. Dyer returned to England with Webbe on 30 July, leaving Kelley to continue the charade in Prague that cost him his life in 1595.

Throughout the 1590s Dyer remained on good terms with Burghley and his son Sir Robert Cecil, despite their rivalry with the earl of Essex, Leicester's stepson and heir to the Dudley–Sidney alliance at court. Dyer again represented Somerset in parliament in 1593; he rejoined the subsidy committee and served as well on committees dealing with recusants and the punishment of rogues. In April 1596 he was knighted as a prerequisite to his appointment as chancellor of the Order of the Garter; significantly, Cecil procured the signet office warrant that conferred this post on Dyer. When Cecil's wife, Elizabeth, died in 1597, Dyer was a pallbearer at her funeral. Cecil intervened thereafter on several occasions to forestall the repayment of Dyer's debts to the crown. In September 1599, however, when Essex defied orders and returned from his military command in Ireland, Dyer showed his endorsement of the earl by dining with him and his party of friends. He was equally supportive of the earl's interests when John Daniel got possession of some compromising letters Essex had written to his wife. Daniel attempted to blackmail the countess, but Dyer was instrumental in both recovering the letters and seeing that Daniel was tried and imprisoned.

Dyer marched in Queen Elizabeth's funeral procession on 28 April 1603 and was present at Windsor on 2 July for Prince Henry's installation as knight of the Garter. But with the accession of James I Dyer lost his offices at Woodstock and apparently retired from court. His name is missing from the one new year's gift roll of James's reign that survives from his lifetime (1605–6), although he is listed on the extant Elizabethan new year's gift accounts of 1578–1603. Dyer never married. He died in Southwark in May 1607 and was buried in St Saviour's, Southwark, on the 11th; administration of his estate was granted to his sister, Margaret. STEVEN W. MAY

Sources R. M. Sargent, *The life and lyrics of Sir Edward Dyer*, 2nd edn (1968) · *CSP for.*, 1578; 1581–2 · S. W. May, *The Elizabethan courtier poets* (1991) · *CPR*, 1566–9, 314; 1569–72, 168–9, 457; 1572–5, 389 · E. Lodge, *Illustrations of British history, biography, and manners*, 2nd edn, 2 (1838), 440 · S. W. May, 'The authorship of "My mind to me a kingdom is"', *Review of English Studies*, new ser., 26 (1975), 385–94 · H. Sydney and others, *Letters and memorials of state*, ed. A. Collins, 1 (1746), 66–7 · T. Birch, *Memoirs of the reign of Queen Elizabeth*, 1 (1754), 46 · *The diaries of John Dee*, ed. E. Fenton (1998) · HoP, *Commons, 1558–1603* · PRO, Signet Office 3/1, fol. 580 · R. Holinshed and others, eds., *The chronicles of England, Scotlande and Irelande*, 2 vols. (1577), 1868 · E. H. Martin, 'History of the Dyer family', 1904, Shrops. RRC [6 vols.] · Wood, *Ath. Oxon.*

Wealth at death £13,000; also debts of over £11,000: Sargent, *Life and lyrics*

Dyer, Elinor Mary Brent- (1894–1969), children's writer, was born on 6 April 1894 at 52 Winchester Street, South Shields, co. Durham, the name on her birth certificate being Gladys Eleanor May Dyer. The elder of the two children of Charles Morris Brent Dyer (1856–1911), a surveyor at Lloyds, and his second wife, Eleanor Watson, *née* Rutherford (1869–1957), she was throughout her life secretive about her background, which was strikingly different from the backgrounds of her fictional heroines. Her childhood home was without garden or inside sanitation, and her parents had separated when she was three—a fact that her mother strove to conceal, representing herself as a widow. She was educated privately at a small local school (1900–12), later attending the City of Leeds Teacher Training College (1915–17). She then worked in a variety of state and private schools; taught, at different times, English, history, Latin, and class-singing, coached hockey and folk-dancing, and ran a Girl Guide company. She also spent a brief period (late 1920s) studying music with Edgar Bainton at the Newcastle Conservatoire. Finally, after five years as a family governess, she founded and ran her own school, the Margaret Roper School (1938–48) in Hereford, where she had settled in 1933.

Despite the many demands on her time, Brent-Dyer published a total of 101 books. Her first, *Gerry Goes to School*, was published in 1922, and her output during the ensuing forty-eight years included, in addition to school stories, family, historical, Girl Guide, adventure, and animal stories, a cookery book, and four educational readers. She also wrote plays (several were performed at local theatres), short stories, numerous unpublished poems, and a romantic novel, *Jean of Storms*. (This story, originally serialized during 1930 in the *Shields Gazette* and rediscovered by chance sixty-five years later, was published in book form in 1996.)

Unquestionably, though, it is Brent-Dyer's Chalet School series of fifty-nine books, with numerous related titles, which has kept her name alive. Not only have the stories been continuously in print since the first book, *The School at the Chalet*, appeared in 1925, but in the late 1990s nearly 100,000 Chalet School paperbacks were still being sold each year. The 1990s also saw the Chalet School feature in broadcasts and university theses, and the growth of fan clubs numbering over 1000 members in fifteen different countries. The continuing popularity of these books about the fictional Chalet School, with its trilingual, international, and interdenominational traditions, may owe something to the attractively described settings (Austria, Guernsey, Herefordshire, Wales, Switzerland), but is due mainly to the author's having created, early in the series, a cast of recognizable characters, who reappear in book after book and gradually achieve a kind of reality for the reader, foremost among them being Joey Bettany/Maynard of the unruly black hair. Joey, when portrayed as an impulsive schoolgirl, frequently in trouble and with plenty of faults to balance her many talents, is convincingly drawn; and, although she later becomes far less credible, the comments expressed over the years in fan mail suggest that interest in Joey has undoubtedly helped the Chalet School to outlive other school stories.

As was common in the genre, the books frequently emphasized religious values, but they are unusual in portraying Roman Catholic girls associating on equal terms with protestants. Brent-Dyer was herself brought up a practising Anglican but converted to Roman Catholicism in 1930, and her stories demonstrate a remarkably ecumenical attitude for the period.

A large, untidy, and heavy-featured woman, described by a former pupil as 'a very eccentric and different sort of person', Brent-Dyer appears to have aroused widely varying reactions in different people. One found her 'occasionally tiresome and exhausting'. Another, 'a deeply kind and generous woman—surprisingly understanding'. All seem agreed that her 'imagination and vitality were amazing'.

Brent-Dyer's final years were spent at 56 Woodlands Road, Redhill, Surrey, where she moved in 1964 to share a house with friends, Phyllis and Sydney Matthewman. Here she died peacefully in her sleep on 20 September 1969. Her grave in Redstone Hill cemetery was marked with a headstone specially commissioned by Chalet School fans during the 1994 celebrations of her centenary, which also saw commemorative plaques erected in South Shields, Hereford, and the Tyrolean village of Pertisau-am-Achensee, where Brent-Dyer had spent the holiday that inspired her Chalet School series.

HELEN McCLELLAND

Sources H. McClelland, *Behind the Chalet School*, 2nd edn (1996) [incl. bibliography] · private information (2004) [family, friends, pupils, publishers] · b. cert. · baptism cert. · d. cert.
Wealth at death £2526: probate, 12 March 1970, *CGPLA Eng. & Wales*

Dyer, Eliphalet (1721–1807), lawyer and revolutionary politician in America, was born on 14 September 1721 at Windham, Connecticut, the second child, and only son, of Colonel Thomas Dyer (*b.* 1694), local political leader and shoemaker, and his wife, Lydia Backus. Born into the local oligarchy, Dyer spent his life seeking the political positions and economic prosperity that would maintain his standing in the community and enhance his reputation as a gentleman. He enrolled in Yale College in 1736, the same year that he made the profession of faith required to join the First Congregational Church in Windham. He graduated in 1740, when he stood ninth in a class of twenty men ranked according to the prominence of their families; he received master's degrees in due course, from Yale in 1743 and Harvard the next year. He settled in Windham and embarked on a career as a farmer, entrepreneur, and lawyer.

As was customary in towns across the colony, voters gave young men of education and social prominence an opportunity to participate in public affairs. Dyer held a succession of town offices beginning in 1743, and on 9 May 1745 married Huldah (*d.* 1800), daughter of Colonel Jabez Bowen of Providence, Rhode Island; they had six children in the next dozen years. In October 1745 his prosperous neighbours elected him captain of the newly organized militia troop of horse, a more prestigious unit than the local foot company. In May 1746 he was admitted to the Connecticut bar and appointed by the general assembly a justice of the peace, an office he would hold for the next sixteen years. Windham voters elected him to the assembly for the first time in May 1747, and returned him sporadically over the next fifteen years until voters from across eastern Connecticut elected him to the council, the upper house of the colony's legislature, in May 1762. In politics as in religion he was a moderate New Light, as supporters of the recent revival of religion called the Great Awakening were called; issues of religion and land speculation divided easterners from westerners, roughly along the line of the Connecticut River.

Dyer began to attract attention beyond Windham as early as May 1753, when the assembly named him major of the regional militia regiment. The assembly thought so highly of his standing with his neighbours that it appointed him colonel of the 3rd regiment that it raised to reinforce the British-American expedition against French-held Crown Point in August 1755, but Dyer had little interest in things martial; he saw no action in 1755, and declined to serve when the assembly offered him a similar appointment in March 1758.

Dyer's true passion was land speculation, because it offered him the chance to live the life of a country gentleman without having to continue in the 'slavish practice' of the law (McCaughey, 309). At Windham in July 1753 he was one of the principal organizers of the Susquehannah

Company, men mainly from eastern Connecticut who sought to revive the colony's long-dormant claims to land in the Susquehannah valley, which is now north-eastern Pennsylvania. Dyer spent the better part of the next twenty years promoting the company's, and his own, interests. In August 1763 he agreed to go to London to attempt to secure imperial recognition of the company's claims, a quest that was ultimately unsuccessful. Dyer, like many prominent colonial travellers, was seduced by the civilization and refinement of the capital, and even accepted a position in the imperial customs service as comptroller of the port of New London.

When Dyer returned home in the fall of 1764 he quickly realized that the new British imperial programme of regulating and directly taxing the colonies was extremely unpopular. Choosing to stand with his native colony against the Stamp Act of 1765, he adjusted the record to backdate his opposition to the stamp tax, served as a low-profile delegate to the anti-Stamp Act congress held at New York in September 1765, relinquished his imperial post in December 1765, and participated in the successful attempt in May 1766 to oust Governor Thomas Fitch, who had sworn to uphold the act as a means of deflecting imperial anger away from Connecticut's charter privileges. Dyer was rewarded by re-election to the council—where he now ranked fifth in seniority among the twelve assistants—and appointment as one of four justices of the superior court, an office he would occupy amid much other public service until May 1793. It was a remarkable political recovery.

Dyer spent the next decade involved with his law practice, his service on the court, and his relentless advocacy of the claims of the Susquehannah Company. His flirtation with imperial office a fading memory, in politics he devoted himself to the cause of justice for the colonies, for example supporting intercolonial efforts to stop importing British goods in early 1769 and lamenting that the defection of New York merchants led to the breakdown of the movement in Connecticut by late 1770. But ambition still burned bright, and Dyer was bitterly disappointed that he was not elected lieutenant-governor in the reshuffle following the death of Governor William Pitkin in October 1769. His undiminished ardour for western lands, a decidedly partisan issue in Connecticut, probably cost him the colony-wide support he needed for election.

As a senior leader whose American patriot principles were not in doubt, Dyer was a good choice to represent the colony at the continental congresses that were convened at Philadelphia in September 1774 and again in May 1775. A firm advocate of intercolonial unity and a vigorous defender of colonial rights, he found that his equally forceful efforts on behalf of the Susquehannah Company diminished his influence with the other delegates. John Adams's assessment in September 1775 seems fair: 'Dyer is long winded and roundabout—obscure and cloudy. Very talkative and very tedious, yet an honest, worthy Man, means and judges well' (*Diary and Autobiography*, 2.173). His Susquehannah liabilities probably explain why the assembly did not reappoint him as a delegate in October 1775; he remained in Philadelphia as a lame duck until late January 1776 because his replacement was late in arriving.

Dyer spent most of 1776 as an active member of the Connecticut council of safety that advised Governor Jonathan Trumbull in the intervals between meetings of the assembly; at Windham he was only a few miles from Trumbull's home in Lebanon. His service on the council seems to have eased the assembly's qualms about his ability to represent the state effectively in congress. In October 1776 it reappointed him a delegate, an honour he turned down for personal reasons; he did not return to congress until June 1777. He spent over half of the next twenty-two months in congress, participating especially in debates on issues of finance and the recruitment and provisioning of the continental army. When he returned to Windham in early April 1779 he continued his public service as a superior court judge and member of the council of safety, most notably in helping to arrange, in an era of rampant inflation, the provisioning of the allied French forces that had arrived in Rhode Island to co-operate with the American army.

Dyer returned to congress in June 1782 on a mission that was both public and personal: the assembly named him, along with Jesse Root and William Samuel Johnson, to defend the state's claims to the Susquehannah lands. When the case came to trial in November the Connecticut agents made the best of an issue that stood to poison co-operation among the states, and lost. On 30 December 1782 the court awarded jurisdiction to Pennsylvania. Connecticut's great speculation in western lands was over.

With the exception of the Susquehannah claims, Dyer had always advocated in congress positions that tended to strengthen the national government. Ultimately that stance proved the undoing of his long political career. Accepting that the states had to pay more of the financial burden of maintaining the national government, especially the continental army, Dyer in March 1783 led the Connecticut delegation in supporting commutation, the conversion of a promise of half pay for life for continental army officers to full pay for five years. Dyer was aware that many people in Connecticut bitterly opposed what they viewed as an unfair gratuity to an élite group at a time of severe financial hardship for all, and, in an unlovely display of political cowardice, tried to shift the blame for his support of commutation to anyone but himself. The voters were not fooled and denied Dyer re-election to the council in May 1783; although the assembly continued to appoint him to the superior court, it did not reappoint him to congress. Windham voters did continue to call on his services, electing him a deputy in May 1784; the assembly named the elder statesman speaker for that session. His law career reached its zenith in the late 1780s. Yale College awarded its distinguished graduate an honorary doctor of laws degree in 1787, and the assembly named him chief judge of the superior court in October 1789 (he served until May 1793). His political career culminated in his election by Windham as a delegate to the state convention to ratify the new federal constitution in January 1789. He apparently had some doubts about parts of the document, but eventually voted to ratify. He supported the new government, although he worried that federal assumption of state debts might prove its financial undoing. Hale and hearty in his last years, he died at Windham on 13 May 1807. His wife predeceased him.

HAROLD E. SELESKY

Sources W. F. Willingham, *Connecticut revolutionary: Eliphalet Dyer* (1976) · G. C. Groce, 'Eliphalet Dyer: Connecticut revolutionist', *The era of the American Revolution*, ed. R. B. Morris (1939) · C. K. Shipton, 'Eliphalet Dyer', *Sibley's Harvard graduates: biographical sketches of those who attended Harvard College*, 10 (1958), 482–93 · H. W. H. Knott, 'Dyer, Eliphalet', *DAB* · F. B. Dexter, 'Eliphalet Dyer', *Biographical sketches of the graduates of Yale College*, 1 (1885) · O. Zeichner, *Connecticut's years of controversy, 1750–1776* (1949) · R. L. Bushman, *From puritan to Yankee: character and the social order in Connecticut, 1690–1765* (1967) · E. P. McCaughey, *From loyalist to founding father: the political odyssey of William Samuel Johnson* (1980) · J. P. Boyd and R. J. Taylor, eds., *Susquehannah Company papers*, 11 vols. (1930–71) · J. H. Trumbull and C. J. Hoadly, eds., *The public records of the colony of Connecticut*, 15 vols. (1850–90), vols. 9–15 · C. J. Hoadly and others, eds., *The public records of the state of Connecticut*, 11 vols. (1894–1967), vols. 1–5 · *Diary and autobiography of John Adams*, ed. L. H. Butterfield and others, 1–4 (1961) · W. C. Ford and others, eds., *Journals of the continental congress, 1774–1789*, 34 vols. (1904–37) · P. H. Smith and others, eds., *Letters of delegates to congress, 1774–1789*, 26 vols. (1976–2000) · *Collections of the Massachusetts Historical Society*, 7th ser., 3 (1902) [*The Trumbull papers*, vol. 4] · C. Isham, ed., *The Deane papers*, 5 vols. (1887–91)
Archives Connecticut State Library, Hartford, Connecticut archive, diary · Hist. Soc. Penn. | Boston PL, Chicago Historical Society, Chamberlain papers · Connecticut Historical Society, general assembly papers · Connecticut Historical Society, William Samuel Johnson papers · Connecticut Historical Society, Jonathan Trumbull papers · Connecticut Historical Society, Joseph Trumbull papers · Connecticut Historical Society, Jeremiah Wadsworth papers · Dartmouth College, Hanover, New Hampshire, Eleazer Wheelock papers · Harvard U., Harvard College Library · L. Cong., Connecticut miscellany · L. Cong., Peter Force transcripts · L. Cong., Jared Ingersoll papers · L. Cong., Jonathan Trumbull papers · L. Cong., William Williams papers · Maine Historical Society, Portland, Fogg collection · Mass. Hist. Soc., Trumbull papers · New York Historical Society, William Williams papers · NYPL, Emmet collection · Yale U., Franklin collection · Yale U., historical manuscripts
Likenesses W. Johnston, oils, Old State House, Hartford, Connecticut
Wealth at death $9000: Windham, Connecticut, probate district records, 1734–1858, Connecticut State Library, Hartford, #1231, 1807

Dyer, George (1755–1841), author and advocate of political reform, was born on 15 March 1755 in east London, the son of John Dyer, a shipwright of Bridewell, London. As a child he attended a charity school, and on 1 July 1762 entered Christ's Hospital, aged seven. Here he was encouraged by Anthony Askew, classicist and physician to the school. Dyer left Christ's Hospital in 1774 as a Grecian—a senior student of classics—and was admitted as a sizar to Emmanuel College, Cambridge. He made a favourable impression on the master of the college, Richard Farmer, and his college rooms were opposite those of William Taylor, later William Wordsworth's teacher at Hawkshead grammar school. Dyer was also acquainted with Gilbert

George Dyer (1755–1841), by Elizabeth Cristall, pubd 1795 (after Joshua Cristall)

Wakefield of Jesus College, Cambridge, an eminent classicist and, in the 1790s, a vociferous reformist. It was Dyer who in 1794 introduced Wakefield to Samuel Taylor Coleridge.

Dyer took his BA in 1778, and the following year was appointed usher (assistant teacher) at Dedham grammar school. Subsequently he preached as a Baptist at Oxford, 'with no very happy results' (Payne, 265), and in June 1782 joined the Baptist school at Northampton run by John Collett Ryland. Dyer's fellow teacher was John Clarke, and the two were rivals for the affection of Ryland's stepdaughter Ann Isabella Stott. Dyer was apparently too timid to declare his feelings, and she married Clarke. The school was bankrupted in 1785, and the following year Ryland founded Enfield Academy, which was attended from 1803 by John Keats. John Clarke's son Charles Cowden Clarke (who encouraged Keats's first poems) recalled 'more than one visit' to the school by Dyer. He describes Dyer's 'eccentric ways, under-toned voice, dab-dab mode of speaking, and absent manner', and also writes of his 'thoroughly noble disposition and generous heart' (Clarke and Clarke, 11–12).

After 1785 Dyer returned to Cambridge as tutor in the family of the Baptist minister Robert Robinson. Dyer, like Robinson, became a Unitarian and was one of the influential circle of Cambridge dissenters which included Robert Tyrwhitt, Benjamin Flower, William Frend, and Robert Hall. Dyer's first pamphlet, *An Inquiry into the Nature of Subscription to the Thirty-Nine Articles* (1789), argued for religious liberty in the university and was circulated among his Cambridge friends.

In 1792 Dyer moved to London. When he first met Coleridge, in August 1794, he was living at Carey Street, Lincoln's Inn Fields. From 1795 he settled at 1 Clifford's Inn, Fleet Street, which was to be his home for the rest of his life. At this time he revisited Christ's Hospital, and Leigh Hunt recalled in his *Autobiography* (1850) that Dyer was a figure of 'wonder' to the pupils 'with his passing through the school-room (where no other person in "town-clothes" ever appeared) to consult books in the library' (Hunt, 1.98). In 1800 Dyer was among the subscribers to Hunt's *Juvenilia*. Dyer was tall and lean, with small dark eyes, and Cowden Clarke describes him as typically dressed in 'the old student's rusty suit of black, threadbare and shining with the shabbiness of neglect [with a] limp wisp of jaconot muslin, yellow with age, round his throat … dusty shoes, and stubbly beard' (Clarke and Clarke, 13).

Dyer swiftly emerged in public affairs in London, a member of the Constitutional Society and active in the cause of parliamentary reform. A second edition of his *Inquiry* was published in 1792 by Joseph Johnson, revised in the light of the French Revolution, which Dyer believed would help to 'humanize the order of society' (*Inquiry*, ix). He predicted that France would become a republic, and risked prosecution for treason when he declared that a republican convention would be 'the most complete form of government' for Britain (ibid., xxiv, 276). Unworldly, eccentric, and afflicted with a stutter, Dyer was nevertheless a vigorous participant in the revolution controversy, and his radical ideals were based firmly in personal experience of poor people's lives. Cowden Clarke recalled that Dyer had at one time lived with 'a wandering tribe of gipsies … to know something of [their] language and habits', and he added, 'beneath [Dyer's] strange bookworm exterior there dwelt a finely tender soul, full of all warmth and sympathy' (Clarke and Clarke, 12).

Dyer's *Complaints of the Poor People of England* (1793) was a thoroughgoing call for reform that drew on Thomas Paine's *Rights of Man* (1791–2). The *Complaints* demonstrated Dyer's skill as a pamphleteer in making the case, from firsthand experience, for practical and compassionate social change:

> in a country where one man possesses three or four magnificent houses, and sixty or eighty thousand a year … while many of the industrious poor can scarcely get the necessaries of life; in such a country, I say, the government must be defective. (*Complaints*, 2nd edn, 1793, 44)

He demanded schools 'accessible to every poor child' (ibid., 17), and urged the reform of taxes, laws, workhouses, prisons, and the 'degraded state of the military profession' (ibid., 44). In his subsequent pamphlet, *A Dissertation on the Theory and Practice of Benevolence* (1795), Dyer (like Coleridge) traced the capacity for 'universal tenderness' in human society from responsiveness to nature (*Dissertation*, 19), and he discussed the treason trials of Thomas Hardy, John Horne Tooke, and John Thelwall.

Between 1792 and 1795 Dyer was an intellectual leader

of the reform movement, one of the most effective and visible of the 'English Jacobins'. He was present when Wordsworth met William Godwin at Frend's house in Buckingham Street, London, on 27 February 1795. He was a helpful and generous London contact for Coleridge and Southey, and was rapturously enthusiastic about their scheme for pantisocracy. Dyer encouraged the publication of their play *The Fall of Robespierre* and distributed copies of it. In May 1796 he helped offset Coleridge's financial losses on his *Watchman* magazine.

Like many contemporaries who welcomed the French Revolution, after 1795 Dyer abandoned active politics for a life of scholarship, journalism, and literature. In 1797 he made a pedestrian tour of Scotland with the natural scientist Arthur Aikin. He contributed widely to journals, and made a modest living as a paid writer for booksellers. In 1802 Dyer was (briefly) tutor to the sons of Charles, third Earl Stanhope, and in 1816 received a small legacy from Stanhope's estate. Charles Cowden Clarke remembered that in 1820, after his father's death, Dyer mentioned his 'youthful attachment for [Clarke's] mother' and enquired 'whether her circumstances were comfortable, because in case, as a widow, she had not been left well off he meant to offer her his hand'. Reassured that all was well with her, Dyer 'never made farther allusion to the subject' (Clarke and Clarke, 13).

Dyer's major publications after the revolutionary era included his *Memoirs of the Life and Writings of Robert Robinson* (1796), which looked back to his time at Cambridge, as did his valuable two-volume *History of the University and Colleges of Cambridge* (1814), and *The Privileges of the University of Cambridge* (1824). His *Four Letters on the English Constitution* (1812), first published as essays in Leigh Hunt's *Reflector* (1811–12), showed he had not abandoned his reformist ideals. Dyer's prolific output as a poet comprised *Poems, Consisting of Odes and Elegies* (1792), *The Poet's Fate* (1797), *Poems* (1801), *Poems and Critical Essays* (1802), and *Poetics* (1812). 'Ode on Liberty' and 'Ode on Peace', published in *Poems* (1792), celebrated the humanitarianism and 'patriot zeal' of his Cambridge friends; his blank verse poem 'To Mr. Arthur Aikin', commemorating their Scottish tour, was published in the *Monthly Magazine* in 1798. While most of Dyer's verse was undistinguished, his critical writings were sometimes bizarre, giving much amusement to friends such as Charles Lamb. In December 1800 Dyer cancelled (and burned) the preface to his poems having discovered, as Lamb reported, 'that in the very first page of said preface he had set out with a principle of criticism fundamentally wrong' (C. Lamb to T. Manning, 27 Dec 1800, *Letters of Charles and Mary Lamb*, 1.263). A footnote to his 1801 collection asserted:'Discrimination is not the *aim* of the present volume. It will be more strictly attended to in the next' (*Poems*, 332). Dyer was more successful as a classical scholar, so much so that his labours for Abraham John Valpy's 141-volume edition of the classics (1819–30) contributed to his blindness in later life.

Poor eyesight may explain why, on leaving Charles Lamb's house one day in 1823, Dyer walked straight into the New River and nearly drowned. Lamb describes his astonishment at Dyer's accident in his essay 'Amicus redivivus'; elsewhere, in 'Oxford in the vacation', Lamb humorously portrays Dyer's bookish researches, 'busy as a moth over some rotten archive'. According to Lamb, he was typically 'very dirty' in appearance: on one occasion Lamb observed that Dyer's 'Nankeen Pantaloons … were absolutely ingrained with the accumulated dirt of ages' (*Letters of Charles and Mary Lamb*, 1.262 and 2.26). On 3 May 1824 Dyer married Honour Mather (1761–1861), whose third husband, a solicitor in chambers opposite Dyer's, had died. With marriage Dyer's domestic circumstances and his appearance improved; now 'affectionately tended', the last years of his life were happy (Clarke and Clarke, 13). He died in Clifford's Inn, London, on 2 March 1841, very shortly after hearing of the death of his old Cambridge associate William Frend. His widow died in May 1861, aged ninety-nine. Dyer's obituary in the *Gentleman's Magazine* (May 1841) drew on his manuscript autobiography, which has since been lost.

NICHOLAS ROE

Sources N. Roe, *The politics of nature* (1992), 17–35 • N. Roe, *Wordsworth and Coleridge: the radical years* (1988) • N. Roe, *John Keats and the culture of dissent* (1997) • M. R. Adams, *Studies in the literary backgrounds of English radicalism* (1947) • C. C. Clarke and M. C. Clarke, *Recollections of writers* (1878), 11–13 • 'George Dyer', *Emmanuel College Magazine*, 15 (1905–6), 194–213 • W. F. Courtney, *Young Charles Lamb, 1775–1802* (1982) • C. Lamb, *'Elia' and 'The last essays of Elia'*, ed. J. Bate (1987) • E. V. Lucas, *The life of Charles Lamb*, 2 vols. (1905) • *The letters of Charles and Mary Lamb*, ed. E. W. Marrs, 3 vols. (1975–8) • E. A. Payne, 'The Baptist connections of George Dyer', *Baptist Quarterly*, 10 (1940–41), 260–67; 11 (1942–5), 237–8 • R. Jarvis, 'Poetry in motion. George Dyer's pedestrian tour', *Wordsworth Circle*, 29/3 (1998), 142–51 • H. Jump, '"Snatch'd out of the fire": Lamb, Coleridge, and George Dyer's cancelled preface', *Charles Lamb Bulletin*, new ser., 58 (1987), 54–67 • L. Hunt, *The autobiography of Leigh Hunt, with reminiscences of friends and contemporaries*, 3 vols. (1850) • S. Butterworth, 'Charles Lamb: some new biographical and other details', *The Bookman*, 60 (1921), 165–70 • *GM*, 2nd ser., 15 (1841), 545

Archives BL, letters, Add. MSS 34369–34370, 34581, 40856, 51828–51843, 52286 • Bodl. Oxf., corresp. • Emmanuel College, Cambridge, corresp. • GL | BL, letters, as sponsor and applicant, to the Royal Literary Fund, loan no. 96 • NL Scot., letters to Robert Anderson • NL Wales, corresp. with Edward Williams

Likenesses E. Cristall, stipple and aquatint, pubd 1795 (after J. Cristall), BM, NPG [*see illus.*] • H. Meyer, oils (in old age), FM Cam.

Dyer, Gilbert (*bap.* **1743**, *d.* **1820**), antiquary and bookseller, was born at Dunstone in the parish of Widecombe in the Moor, Devon, and baptized on 14 September 1743. He was the son of Gilbert Dyer, schoolmaster (*d.* 1809), and his wife, Mary. After assisting his father, he was appointed on 30 June 1767 master of the school for children of freemen of the Corporation of Weavers, Fullers and Shearmen at Tuckers' Hall in Exeter. In 1770 he published *The most General School-Assistant*, a work of practical arithmetic. On 13 July 1772, in Exeter Cathedral, he married Sarah Sayer (*d.* 1788), of the cathedral close. They had two children, including his successor Gilbert, baptized on 9 June 1776. His second wife, Sarah Finnimore (*b.* 1727/8) of Exeter, whom he married on 29 November 1789, died on 24 October 1811.

Dyer continued as schoolmaster until his resignation in

1788, but already by October 1783 he had established a circulating library and bookshop, from which for a short period to November 1785, he accommodated the stock of the Exeter Library Society. From at least 1791 he produced annual catalogues which were highly regarded. Thomas Frognall Dibdin described his two-part catalogue of 1810 with its 19,945 items as having 'never been equalled by that of any provincial bookseller, for the value and singularity of the greater number of volumes described in it' (Dibdin, 629). A contributor to Hone's *Year-Book* remembered 'the erudite maister Dyer, the collector of a circulating library, the choicest and perhaps the most extensive, of any in the whole kingdom, except in the metropolis' (Hone, 1469). Hone himself commented on Dyer's collection of theology as being 'astonishing; it was stacked on manifold shelves to the angle point of the gable of their huge upper warehouse' (ibid.).

Dyer's erudition was displayed in several publications. In 1796 he published anonymously *The Principles of Atheism Proved to be Unfounded, from the Nature of Man*, in which he set out to prove that man 'must have been created, preserved, and instructed by Divine Providence'. In 1805 appeared *A restoration of the ancient modes of bestowing names on the rivers, hills, vallies, plains, and settlements of Britain*, which investigated the Celtic origins of river and other place names in the Exeter region. His *Commentary on Richard of Cirencester, and Antoninus's Itineraries of Britain* was published in 1814 and two years later this and his tract on atheism were reissued with an introduction as *Vulgar Errors Ancient and Modern*. Several of the ideas expressed in this volume had appeared in the *Monthly Magazine* in 1809. His works were admired by contemporaries for their 'considerable industry and research' (Oliver).

Dyer died at Exeter on 19 October 1820 from a fever contracted after a long walk, and was buried six days later in St Martin's churchyard, Exeter. He was succeeded in his bookselling business by his son Gilbert, his circulating library being taken over by Maria Fitze. IAN MAXTED

Sources G. Oliver, 'Biography of Exonians, no. 11', *Trewman's Exeter Flying Post* (1 Feb 1849), 6 · I. Maxted, *The Devon book trades: a biographical dictionary* (1991), 59 · W. Hone, *The yearbook of daily recreation and information* (1832), 1469 · T. F. Dibdin, *Bibliomania, or, Book madness: a bibliographical romance*, 2nd edn, [2 vols.] (1811), 629 · *Alfred, or, A West of England Journal* (24 Oct 1820) · parish register (baptism), Widecombe in the Moor, 14 Sept 1743 · register (marriage), Exeter Cathedral, 13 July 1772 · parish register (marriage), St Martin, Exeter, 29 Nov 1789 · parish register (burial), St Martin, Exeter, 25 Oct 1820
Wealth at death see will, Devon RO, 53/6 Box 94

Dyer, Henry (1848–1918), engineer and educationist, was born on 16 August 1848 at Muirmaden in the parish of Bothwell, Lanarkshire, the son of John Dyer, a foundry labourer born in co. Cork, and Margaret Morton. Dyer attended evening classes at Anderson's University (later Anderson's College), Glasgow, and served his apprenticeship as a student engineer under Thomas Kennedy and A. C. Kirk at James Aitken & Co., Cranstonhill, Glasgow. In 1868 he won a Whitworth exhibition as a 'workman', and then in 1870 a Whitworth scholarship. Early in 1873, newly graduated from the University of Glasgow as a BSc,

he was appointed, at the age of twenty-five, principal of the Imperial College of Engineering in Tokyo. This new institution under the authority of the ministry of public works was designed to train the first generation of modern engineers for the newly opened Japan.

'Dyer's College', as the Imperial College of Engineering was sometimes called in Tokyo at the time, in Toranomon, in central Tokyo, was a remarkable institution, the building and equipment of which were generously funded. Dyer, in consultation with Yozo Yamao, who had lived in Glasgow (1866–8) and had worked in Napier's shipyard on the Clyde and studied at evening courses at Anderson's University, worked out a six-year course during which students alternated practical and theoretical classes. All the teaching was done in English. The first- and second-year courses, which all students attended, included English (language and composition), geography, mathematics, mechanics (theoretical and applied), physics, chemistry, and drawing (geometrical and mechanical). At the beginning of the third year each student chose to specialize in one of six options—civil, mechanical, or telegraph engineering, architecture, chemistry and metallurgy, or mining and engineering.

The students were almost all from the samurai class and engineering as a subject was alien; they found it difficult to comprehend the idea of getting their hands dirty. As William Ayrton, who was later professor of physics at Imperial College, London, but in the 1870s was teaching at the Imperial College of Engineering, noted, 'the Japanese boy is not observant' (*General Report*, 77). Notwithstanding the difficulties, most of the Japanese students were hardworking, enthusiastic, and dedicated.

Dyer left the college, and Japan, in July 1882. The Japanese government was generous in its praise of him, appointed him to the order of the Rising Sun (third class), and made him honorary principal of the college. Times were changing; the Akabane engineering works was to become an Imperial Japanese Navy facility, and in 1886 the college itself was taken out of the hands of the ministry of public works and united with other colleges to become the faculty of engineering of the University of Tokyo, under the ministry of education. On his return to Glasgow, Dyer failed, both in 1883 and in 1886, in attempts to obtain the newly established chair of naval architecture in the University of Glasgow. He remained actively involved in advisory roles at Anderson's College and became an important, if unofficial, confidant and friend of the many Japanese who flocked to Glasgow at this time to study engineering technology in both the university and the college, and practical shipbuilding on the Clyde. From 1901, at Dyer's request, the court of the University of Glasgow agreed that Japanese should qualify as a foreign language for those seeking admission to the university.

In 1874 Henry Dyer married Marie Euphemie Aquart Ferguson (1848–1921). They had four sons, one of whom died four months after birth, and a daughter. In Glasgow Henry Dyer became a prolific writer, first of pamphlets and later of more substantial, wide-ranging works. His first major book was *The Evolution of Industry* (1895). Later his pro-Japanese stance resulted in his writing *Dai Nippon: the Britain of the East* (1905), and also *Japan in World Politics: a Study in International Dynamics* (1909).

Henry Dyer died of pneumonia on 25 September 1918 at his home, 8 Highburgh Terrace, Dowanhill, Glasgow, aged seventy, and was buried at the Glasgow necropolis. He left an estate of over £9000, a fine achievement for the son of an Irish labourer. His main earnings had been in Japan where for nearly a decade he was paid, as principal of the Imperial College of Engineering, the remarkably high salary of ¥660 per month.

It was William John McQuorn Rankine (1820–1872), then professor of engineering at the University of Glasgow, who proposed Henry Dyer to Hirobumi Ito as first principal of the imperial college. Rankine, who believed that 'in theoretical science the question is what are we to think? But in practical science the question is—*what are we to do?*' (Rankine, 8), recommended him as one who could combine theory and practice. Henry Dyer's achievement was the introduction of high quality heuristic engineering education into Japan, a country previously committed to Confucianism and learning by rote. At home in Glasgow, his constant and eloquent advocacy of engineering education as well as his service to the Glasgow school board were highly regarded. He became DSc in 1890, and the University of Glasgow, for his services to education, honoured him with an LLD in 1910. OLIVE CHECKLAND

Sources O. Checkland, *Britain's encounter with Meiji Japan, 1868–1912* (1989) · Mitchell L., Glas., Dyer collection · U. Glas., Dyer material · W. J. M. Rankine, *Manual of applied mechanics* (1858) · *Imperial College of Engineering (Kobu-Dai-Gakko), Tokei: reports by the principal and professors for the period 1873–77* (1877), 77 · d. cert. · General Register Office for Scotland, Edinburgh · private information (2004)
Archives Mitchell L., Glas., lecture notes, papers relating to Glasgow school board · U. Glas., Archives and Business Records Centre · U. Glas. | University of Tokyo, history of the university unit
Likenesses cartoon (with members of Glasgow corporation education committee), repro. in W. M. Haddow, *My seventy years* (1943), 66 · pencil?, repro. in *The Baillie*, 84/2166 (22 April 1914)
Wealth at death £9147 12s. 8d.: confirmation, 24 April 1919, CCI

Dyer, Sir James (1510–1582), judge and law reporter, was born between January and March 1510, the second son of Richard Dyer (*d.* 1523) of Wincanton, Somerset; his mother's surname was Walton. There was an old tradition that he spent some time at Oxford, possibly at Broadgates Hall, and his scholarly tastes are reflected in a more extensive Latin vocabulary than most common lawyers, a love of grammar and philology, the occasional citation of classical authors, and the fact that he left a library of Latin books. But he was destined for the common law, and as a Somerset law student he was naturally entered at Strand Inn, preparatory to joining the Middle Temple about 1530: a destiny confirmed by the family's connection with their neighbour John Fitzjames.

Dyer's clerkship with John Jenour (*d.* 1542), protonotary of the common pleas, equipped him with a mastery of the forms of pleading and he always thereafter exhibited an affection for entries and plea rolls, referring more than once in his reports to the great book of entries compiled by Jenour. His handwriting also bore for the rest of his life the outward signs of a rigorous training in court-hand. The fact that Dyer's law reports seem to begin in Trinity term 1532 fixes that year as the *terminus ad quem* for his commitment to regular attendance in Westminster Hall. His earliest reports make special mention of his activities as counsel in Easter term 1537, by which time he is likely to have been recently called to the bar. Dyer became a bencher of his inn some time in the 1540s, but there is no surviving record of his having delivered a reading before the distinguished exposition of the Statute of Wills which he gave, as a serjeant-elect, in August 1552.

In 1542 Dyer was elected member of parliament for Wells, in Somerset, and he later served for Cambridgeshire, ending his parliamentary career as speaker in the last parliament of Edward VI in March 1553; he referred in his notebook to this last honour, and to his consequent knighthood at Whitehall on 9 April 1553. The reason for changing his constituency had been that in 1547, upon his marriage to Margaret, *née* Abarough (*d.* 1569), widow of Sir Thomas Elyot, he had become seated at Carlton in Cambridgeshire. He served as a justice of the peace for that county from then until his death, even though in 1558 he moved his seat to Great Staughton in the adjacent county of Huntingdon. He also acquired a London house in Cow Lane, near Smithfield, and moved to another, near the Charterhouse, in 1562.

Dyer's summons to the parliament of 1553 was as one of the king's serjeants-at-law, an appointment that he had received immediately upon taking the coif in 1552. Assuming the coif marked not only a new phase in his professional practice, but also the commencement of his judicial career, as a commissioner of assize on the midland circuit. In May 1557 Dyer was appointed a judge of the common pleas, and he was promoted to chief justice in January 1559 when Sir Anthony Browne was removed to a puisne justiceship on religious grounds. He took over a court embroiled in a series of controversies arising from illegal grants of offices to unqualified persons in the time of Mary I. These were soon resolved, though not without an unsavoury taste of court interference. Dyer presided over the common pleas throughout the first half of Elizabeth I's reign. It was a very busy phase in the history of the common-law courts, and Dyer was not opposed to the profitable influx of business. The jurisdiction of his court was seen as an inheritance to be defended, and in 1573 Dyer was moved to complain about procedural delays which drove litigants to seek relief elsewhere: 'This court is debased and lessened, and the Kings Bench doth encrease with such Actions which should be sued here … to the Slander of the court, and to the Detriment and Losse of the Serjeants at the Barr' (Hughes, 51, pl. 73). This remark was prompted by the recent practice of using ejectment to try freehold title, and is perhaps the first recorded comment on the development that doomed the ancient real actions to virtual extinction. Dyer disliked the new practice, and tried unsuccessfully to clog ejectment with some of the old learning of real actions; but he could hardly prevent the action taking root in his court as well. On the other hand, he was implacably opposed to the extension of actions on the case, as tolerated in the other bench, whether as a replacement for older actions or as a vehicle for suits concerning defamatory words. In such matters Dyer did not always carry the court with him, though his caution was to become common pleas orthodoxy in the time of his successor.

The business of the court did increase during Dyer's period of office, and the pressure of work may explain Dyer's aversion both to the discussion in court of questions unconnected with litigation in the common pleas and to the revival of special verdicts, which forced the court to discuss issues of law. On the other hand, there was still a lingering sense that the court should be interested in legal scholarship for its own sake, and it still regarded itself as an open repository of learning. This may account for what the younger generation saw as a cunctatory disposition on Dyer's part, at any rate in his later years. But the old tradition of moving questions and 'doubts' was, like oral 'tentative' pleading, almost at an end.

Though capable of some doctrinal ingenuity, as in his invention of the *scintilla juris* (which provoked a controversy lasting for three centuries), Dyer was not a prominent innovator. His merit lay in bringing to the court the meticulous intellectual discipline and legal learning that is amply reflected in his reports. His love of textual scholarship is obvious. He was familiar with ancient manuscripts and records, some of which he may have worked on personally in the Tower, and some of which he owned personally. Like Sir Edward Coke, he used these old manuscripts as working sources of authority; but he had a less anachronistic sense of history than Coke and on occasion explained institutions with a historian's sense of the past. He seems to have been blessed with a ready memory, and often recollected unpublished precedents in the course of argument. Dyer's court issued the first practice directions for over a century, in 1573. He also revived the practice of charging a jury of attorneys from time to time to investigate malpractice, and his speeches on these occasions contain the first full exposition of professional ethics for that side of the profession.

In Hilary term 1582 Dyer was absent from court on grounds of illness. Even as he lay dying, the Star Chamber had an opportunity to pronounce something like an obituary. A Northamptonshire man had made some foolish remarks about him, and was sentenced to lose both ears, to pay a heavy fine, and to remain in the Fleet until he had obtained Dyer's forgiveness. In the course of their judgment, in February, all the lords of the council commended Dyer for his learning, integrity, and diligence; and it was no doubt intended that a report should reach the old man's ears. On 13 March the chief justice made his last will:

> consideringe with my selff the incertentye of this vaine and transitorie life … and for the avoydinge of discorde and strife, that commonlie I see to ensue after the deathes of suche as dye intestate aboute the trasshe and pelfrye of this wicked worlde.   (PRO, PROB 11/64/28)

He died on 24 March 1582. He was rumoured to have surrendered his office orally just before his death, returning his gold collar of SS to the queen, in the unrealized hope of securing the succession for a former fellow bencher, William Peryam. At the same time Roger Manwood was said to have offered a large consideration for the place, though in the event the queen chose Edmund Anderson. Sir Edward Coke, who must have seen Dyer in court on many occasions, penned a glowing tribute thirty years after his death:

> a judge of profound knowledge and judgment in the laws of the land, and principally in the form of good pleading and true entries of judgments, and of great piety and sincerity, who in his heart abhorred all corruption and deceit; of a bountiful and generous disposition, a patron and preferrer of men learned in the law and expert clerks; of singular assiduity and observation, as appears by his book of reports, all written with his own hand, and of a fine, reverend and venerable countenance and personage.   (Coke, 9.14v–15)

Dyer left no children, his heir, Richard, being the grandson and heir of his elder and only brother, John (d. 1558). He directed in his will that he should be buried at Great Staughton next to his wife, and 'that a grave stone be layde upon her corps and myne there withe oure names and stiles to be engraven with the daies and tymes of our deathes'. A monument in the church there, with Dyer's kneeling effigy in judicial robes and collar of SS, together with the effigies of his wife and great-nephew Richard, was erected early in the following century. The Staughton branch of the family did not flourish. Although Richard's grandson, Lodowick, was created a baronet in 1627, he sold the Great Staughton estate during the interregnum and died a pauper, without surviving issue, about 1670.

In '1585'—actually in January 1586—a volume of law reports was published by Richard Tottell entitled *Ascuns novel cases collectes per le jades tresreverend judge, Mounsieur Jasques Dyer*. The edition was prepared for the press by the reporter's nephews Richard Farwell, the second son of his sister Dorothy, and James Dyer, the fifth son of his elder brother, both young members of the Middle Temple. They had been left the autograph manuscript by the chief justice, together with his other law books, for their private use and without any directions as to publication. However, according to their preface, they had been under pressure from friends, first to lend the reports for copying and then to see them printed. After resisting for two years they were put under further pressure from 'others of greater countenance', perhaps Dyer's successor, Sir Edmund Anderson, and Lord Chancellor Bromley, to whom the first edition was dedicated. The editors claimed that their uncle had intended 'to polish and beautify the said cases with more large arguments', but it is clear that he had not done so and it may be doubted whether he would have approved the publication of his working notes as jotted down in the course of a busy life. The editors' intention was to publish a law book, not a historical record, and they deliberately omitted matter that might upset living persons and 'collaterall and bye causes', such as historical memoranda that were of no forensic value to Tottell's

Elizabethan customers. Doubtless they were under pressure from Tottell to keep the volume to a manageable size. As it was, the edition contained over 1000 entries. It was reprinted in 1592, 1601, 1621, and 1672. A table, composed by Thomas Ashe, was printed in 1588 and separately reprinted in 1600 and 1622.

Despite their present scarcity, these editions must have been produced in quite large print runs, given that Dyer was an essential possession for every law student. Dyer and Plowden probably feature more often than any other printed books in legal commonplaces of the late Elizabethan and Jacobean period, though the impecunious or less industrious student could make use of a printed abridgement of Dyer which appeared within a few years of the first edition and was reprinted in 1595, 1602, and 1620. An abridgement in English, by Sir Thomas Ireland, was printed in 1651. What may be considered a second edition of the reports was published in 1688. It introduced more textual errors than it eliminated, but it was embellished with a large quantity of marginal references, together with quotations from manuscript reports and readings, many of which are now known only from this source. This prodigious labour was attributed by the publishers to 'five or six of the most eminent and learned lawyers that this last age hath bred', though professional tradition in the following century gave the sole credit to Sir George Treby of the Middle Temple. A third edition, of an entirely different character, was undertaken by John Vaillant of the Inner Temple in 1794. This comprised an English translation, generally very accurate and skilful, with added references to some later authorities, a new index and tables of cases, and an introduction with a life of Dyer. Vaillant's edition was reprinted in 1907, and is the version still in most general use. Much of the matter omitted from the printed editions survived in manuscript form, since the autograph remained available for copying until the late seventeenth century, and an edition of some 500 further entries, together with Dyer's circuit notes (the earliest of their kind), was published in 1994.   J. H. BAKER

Sources Reports from the lost notebooks of Sir James Dyer, ed. J. H. Baker, 2 vols., SeldS, 109–10 (1994) [esp. introd. to vol. 109] • HoP, Commons, 1509–58, 2.70–73 • L. W. Abbott, Law reporting in England, 1485–1585 (1973), 158–62 • G. Whetstone, A remembrance of the precious vertues of … Sir James Dier (1816) • J. Dyer, Reports of cases in the reigns of Hen. VIII., Edw. VI., Q. Mary, and Q. Eliz., ed. and trans. J. Vaillant, 3 vols. (1794) • will, PRO, PROB 11/64, sig. 28 • W. Hughes, ed., The third part of the reports of several excellent cases of law collected by William Leonard (1663) • E. Coke, Le neufme part des reports de Sr. Edw. Coke (1613)

Likenesses oils, 1575, NPG • effigy on monument, 1600–40, Great Staughton church, Huntingdonshire • J. Drapentier, line engraving, 1675 (after portrait, 1575), BM, NPG; repro. in R. Farwell and J. Dyer, eds., Les reports des divers select matters and resolutions des reverend judges and sages del ley (1672) • oils (after portrait, 1575), NPG; copy, Exeter College, Oxford • oils (after portrait, 1575), Arbury Hall, Warwickshire

Dyer, John (*bap.* **1699**, *d.* **1757**), poet, was baptized on 13 August 1699 at his birthplace, Llanfynydd, Carmarthenshire, the second of four sons of Robert Dyer (*d.* 1720), attorney-at-law, and his wife, Catherine, daughter of John Cocks of Hinlip, Worcestershire, and his wife, Elizabeth

(*née* Bennet). Dyer's Welsh descent from his father begins with certainty with a David Dyer, mayor of Kidwelly in 1531–2. Llanfynydd is some 5 miles from Llangathen village in the Tywi valley, with its large house and grounds, Aberglasne, owned off and on by Welsh ancestors, 'repurchased' by Dyer's father in 1710 as part of the manor and lordship of Kidwelly, and made famous in the poet's verse.

From a local education, possibly at Queen Elizabeth's Grammar School, Carmarthen, Dyer went to Westminster School probably in 1713 and, despite running away to Windsor in 1714, stayed there long enough to make strong significant friendships with some outstanding future scholars, antiquaries, and civil servants, most of them London-based. Unlike his brothers, he did not go up to Oxford but returned to Aberglasne to study law. At his father's death in 1720 Dyer went to London to practise poetry and study painting, being apprenticed to the portrait painter Jonathan Richardson. An early poem, 'Epistle to a Famous Painter', addresses Richardson as 'Delightful partner of my heart' and, while deploring his own fainter art, 'As yet I but in verse can paint', demonstrates his skill in natural description. In London Dyer enjoyed the stimulation of a Serle's Coffee House circle of young men of artistic and literary ambitions and sufficient money to pursue them; they were lifelong supporters of his works and included Thomas Edwards, Arthur Pond, George Vertue, and Daniel Wray. He also exchanged poems within a more flamboyant and controversial writers' circle, including Aaron Hill, Richard Savage, and Clio (Mrs Martha Fowke Sansom).

Dyer spent over a year, 1724–5, in Italy sketching art and architecture, as a foundation for 'living well' should he choose. From this period derives 'The Ruins of Rome' (1740), a philosophic-moralistic and descriptive poem of 545 lines based on a narrative of his ascent of the Palatine hill. Other remarkable poems, such as 'Written at Ocriculum', were composed in Italy, and he was working at the earlier 'Grongar Hill', descriptive of the ascent to a prospect above his home, Aberglasne. To his mother, in Carmarthenshire, he returned in 1725 to complete 'Grongar Hill' and 'The Country Walk'.

Publication of Dyer's poems started in 1726 with three versions of 'Grongar Hill' in separate miscellanies, as a Pindaric ode and in two versions of octosyllabic couplets; the version usually preferred is that in David Lewis's New Miscellany, which included works by two other Westminster friends, Samuel and John Wesley.

Until 1730 Dyer's time was divided between London and Wales, despite a successful lawsuit in 1727–8 against his brother Robert to secure the inheritance for the three younger brothers under the terms of their father's will. From 1730 to 1738 Dyer was farming for his aunt at Mapleton, near Bromyard, 14 miles from Worcester, where he was much influenced by the elderly Bishop Hough. In 1738 he bought two farms for himself at Higham on the Hill, near Nuneaton; in the same year he married a young widow, Sarah Hawkins, *née* Ensor (1712–1768), of Warwickshire. The first of their four children was born in 1739. In

1741 Dyer was ordained deacon and priest, and he served as rector of Catthorpe, Leicestershire, until 1751. In Leicestershire he started sheep farming and began his major work, *The Fleece*, in four books; the first book of over 700 lines was carried to a London publisher in 1750. In 1751 he was made LLB of Cambridge and moved to livings in Belchford and Coningsby, Lincolnshire, as benefactors wished to remove him from sheep farming so that he could complete *The Fleece* (1757). Its last book reached the publisher in November 1756. Dyer died of consumption at the rectory in Coningsby in December 1757. He was buried in the church there on 15 December.

Only seven of Dyer's paintings are known to survive, although a south Wales landscape shows him continuing into the 1750s; they include a self-portrait of the 1720s. There are sketches from Italy. Manuscript notebooks, commonplace books, letters, and poems survive, mutilated by a nineteenth-century editor, a descendant; and some of his prose work, 'The commercial map of England', started in 1737, is in Durham Cathedral Library.

Dyer was driven in life and writings by a 'desire to do universal good'; this shows in all his poems from that metaphoric landscape for 'sweetly-musing Quiet' and 'joys ... run high', Grongar Hill, to the portrait of the ideal man, 'The Cambro-Briton' (1735), and to *The Fleece*, which celebrates in fine full detail British wool production and world trade. Dr Johnson mocked the subject of *The Fleece*; William Gilpin found Dyer's colouring wrong in his word-painting of the Tywi valley beneath Grongar Hill; but Thomas Gray appreciated Dyer's 'imagination', and Wordsworth in a sonnet recognized the 'living landscape' of *The Fleece*, especially 'those soft scenes thro'' which [his] childhood strayed', and the power of the thrush's song in 'Grongar Hill'. Dyer was a revolutionary, experimental genius in verse in English. In the 1720s he produced the first extended descriptive local poetry, conveying a real sense of place using a musical 'language of men'. And in writing *The Fleece* over fifteen years, he was equally original in developing a more intricately daring wordplay in presenting a great variety of landscapes, threading them with autobiographical narrative and portraits of friends.

BELINDA HUMFREY

Sources J. Dyer, NL Wales, MSS 23294–23297 · *The poetical works of Mark Akenside and John Dyer*, ed. R. A. Willmott (1855) [introduction by W. H. D. Longstaffe] · B. Humfrey, *John Dyer* (1980) · R. M. Williams, *Poet, painter and parson: the life of John Dyer* (1956) · E. Parker, 'A study of John Dyer in the light of new manuscript material', [1938], Bodl. Oxf., MS B. Litt. d. 313 · W. H. D. Longstaffe, 'Notes respecting the life and family of John Dyer, the poet', *The Patrician*, 4 (1847), 7–12, 264–8, 420–26; 5 (1848), 75–81, 218–35 · W. H. D. Longstaffe, 'John Dyer as a painter', *Montgomery (County) Collections, Historical and Archaeological*, 11 (1878), 396–402 · T. Edwards, letters, 1720–56, Bodl. Oxf., MSS 1007–1012 · B. Victor, *Original letters, dramatic pieces, and poems*, 3 vols. (1776) · D. Wray, letters to Philip Yorke, 1740–67, BM, Add. MS 35401 · J. Duncombe, ed., *Letters by several eminent persons deceased*, 3 vols. (1772), vol. 2, pp. 239–43, vol. 3, pp. 107–17 · H. S. Hughes, 'John Dyer and the countess of Hertford', *Modern Philology*, 27 (1929–30)
Archives NL Wales, notebooks, commonplace books, letters, poems, etc., MS 23294 · NL Wales, notes involving draft poems

Likenesses J. Dyer?, self-portrait?, 1726–9, repro. in Humfrey, *John Dyer*; priv. coll. · photograph (after unknown artist), NL Wales

Dyer, Joseph Chessborough (1780–1871), inventor, was born at Stonington Point, Connecticut, USA, on 15 November 1780, the son of Captain Nathaniel Dyer of the Rhode Island navy. Joseph's mother died about a year later and the boy was sent to school at Wickford, Rhode Island, on Narragansett Bay, where his father joined him about 1794. Joseph showed his talent for invention at an early age: by lashing small watertight casks inside the hull, he rendered unsinkable the small boat in which he and his father went on long fishing expeditions. At sixteen, he took employment as a clerk to a French importing merchant named Nancrède, on whose behalf he made frequent journeys to England to visit manufacturers. When Nancrède returned to France, Dyer and a partner bought his business and continued it until 1811, when the import of English goods was prohibited, whereupon he left America for good. He married Ellen (d. 1842), daughter of Somerset Jones, of Gower Street, London, in 1811, and set up house at Camden Town, where they raised three sons. In 1815 Dyer moved briefly to Birmingham, where he and William Tudor founded the *North American Review* in 1815, before settling permanently in Manchester in 1816.

Henceforth Dyer devoted himself to mechanics. He introduced and patented his own ideas as well as those sent to him by American inventors, for whom he acted as agent. These patents covered subjects as diverse as Jacob Perkins's plan for steel-engraving, which Dyer hoped would prove attractive to printers of banknotes, and his own fur-shearing and nail-making machines. Robert Fulton sent him specifications for his steamboat in 1811, but this, like Perkins's project, was difficult to market, and many years passed before either found acceptance. His textile card-making machines were manufactured in his own factory in Manchester. In 1832 he established a machine-making works at Gamaches in France, which was put into the care of his eldest son, Charles.

Dyer was involved in the founding of the *Manchester Guardian* in 1821, and he was a founder and director of the ill-fated Bank of Manchester, which after some years of prosperity came by fraud and neglect to a disastrous end, whereby he lost £98,000. His interest in politics arose after the Peterloo massacre in August 1819, when he became a determined supporter of parliamentary reform and was elected chairman of the Reform League; he also actively supported the Anti-Corn Law League. In 1830 he was a member of a delegation to Paris, taking contributions from Manchester to relieve those wounded in the July revolution, and charged with congratulating Louis-Philippe on his accession. It was claimed that he, as chairman of the Reform League, was instrumental in encouraging the British government to recognize the French king, thus averting the possibility of war with France. He strongly opposed slavery and wrote several pamphlets on the subject.

Joseph Chessborough Dyer (1780–1871), by Edward Scriven (after J. Allen)

The Dyers lived at various town addresses in Manchester until about 1832, when they moved further out to Burnage, where they owned some 16 acres of land. Here Dyer built Burnage Hall, and 'Dyer's Tower', which he intended as a mausoleum for his family, but local residents objected and it was later demolished. He then built Leegate Hall, which was completed in 1840. In 1842 troubles came thick and fast. Ellen died in July, Charles died at Gamaches in November; in October the Bank of Manchester failed, and to meet calls on his shares Joseph sold Leegate Hall, his textile-card factory, and other Manchester property. He and his two sons moved back to Burnage. In 1848 Gamaches succumbed due to another revolution and Joseph again lost heavily. He sold his remaining land and resided alternately with his two sons, who were now married and living at Whaley Bridge and Macclesfield.

Dyer always took a close interest in science, and soon after settling in Manchester he was elected to the Manchester Literary and Philosophical Society. In 1851 he became a vice-president, and remained so until 1868, taking the chair regularly until 1864 when he was almost eighty-four years old. He published numerous papers in its journals and elsewhere. He was described as tall and powerful in his younger days, grown bent in later years. He had a nervous habit of fidgeting with his glasses and spoke slowly and haltingly, never wasting a word. He was never heard to complain about the loss of his once-great fortune.

In 1867 his son Wilson died. Wilson had been a painter, and latterly in business with his father. Joseph went to live with his remaining son Frederick, a novelist and schoolmaster, at Endfield Cottage, Broken Cross, Macclesfield. There, after a lingering illness, he died, penniless, from gastritis and bronchitis on 3 May 1871, and was buried in his wife's grave at the Rusholme Road dissenters' burial-ground, Manchester.

C. W. SUTTON, rev. ANITA MCCONNELL

Sources R. Angus Smith, *Centenary of science in Manchester* (1883), 298 · E. Leigh, *Science of cotton spinning*, 2 (1873), 192 · L. H. Grindon, *Manchester banks and bankers: historical, biographical, and anecdotal* (1877), 296 · *Manchester Literary and Philosophical Society Proceedings*, 3–7 (1864–9) · *Memoirs of the Literary and Philosophical Society of Manchester*, 3rd ser., 2–4 (1865–71) · S. McKenna, 'Joseph Chessborough Dyer, 1780–1871', *Memoirs of the Literary and Philosophical Society of Manchester*, 117 (1974–5), 104–11
Likenesses W. Brockedon, chalk drawing, 1831, NPG · E. Scriven, line print (after J. Allen), BM, NPG [*see illus.*]
Wealth at death under £300: probate, 31 Aug 1871, *CGPLA Eng. & Wales*

Dyer [*née* Barrett], **Mary** (*d.* 1660), Quaker martyr in America, of whom all that is known of her parentage is her maiden name, married William Dyer (*bap.* 1609), a milliner and member of the Fishmongers' Company, probably in St Martin-in-the-Fields, Middlesex, on 27 October 1633. The couple had several children, of whom the eldest, William, was baptized at St Martin-in-the-Fields in October 1634 and buried there only three days later. The second son, William, was born in Massachusetts, where his parents had emigrated, and was baptized into the Boston church on 20 October 1635, one week after his parents had been admitted to its membership. The third, who was still-born and badly misshapen after a breech birth, brought Dyer to notoriety. She was reputed to have given birth to a monster.

The case of Mary Dyer's stillborn child came to light in March 1638, by which time the prophet Anne Hutchinson, both a friend and her midwife, was on trial. When the charge of 'traducing the ministers' was upheld against Hutchinson, Mary Dyer took her friend's hand in court, an action which identified her as a 'Hutchinsonian' or, more pejoratively, an antinomian. Interest in her led John Winthrop to exhume the body of her infant: sensational accounts describe the appearance of the body as part-fish, part-bird, part-beast.

The Dyers, escaping the severity of the puritan authorities, then made their home first in Portsmouth and then in Newport, Rhode Island. William became general recorder of the colony. In 1650 or 1652 Mary returned to England, where she became a Quaker. Her return to Boston, in January or February 1657, was marked by her immediate imprisonment. In 1659 she was banished from Boston, but she was not daunted by the threat of the death penalty should she return. Having returned once more, she appeared in a Boston court alongside her fellow Quakers William Robinson and Marmaduke Stevenson on 20 October 1659. Though the men met their ends on the gallows, Dyer was dramatically reprieved even as she climbed the scaffold. She spent the winter in Rhode Island but, in May 1660, returned once again to Boston. In a letter explaining her actions, an unrepentant Dyer proclaimed the 'Spiritual Wickedness' of the 'Egyptian' court which tried her; comparing herself to Esther, she further states 'to dye is my Gain' (Burrough, 25–7). To the last she protested against the 'unrighteous laws', taking on the mantle of prophet and religious martyr and condemning 'the unrighteous and unjust law of banishment upon pain of death' (Burrough, 29). This time Governor John Endecott ensured that the penalty was carried out; she died 'sweetly and cheerfully' on the gallows on 1 June 1660 (Burrough, 30). Her contemporaries believed that Mary Dyer 'did hang as a flag for them to take example by' (Burrough, 30). But in fact Charles II responded to petitions for less severe religious laws, and she was the last but one Quaker to be hanged in Boston. Today a statue of her, by Sylvia Shaw Judson (1959), stands in the state house grounds, Boston.

CATIE GILL

Sources E. Burrough, *A declaration of the sad and great persecution* (1660) · R. Plimpton, *Mary Dyer* (1994) · J. Winsser, 'Mary Dyer and the "monster" story', *Quaker History*, 79 (1990), 20–34 · H. J. Cadbury, 'Briefer notices', *Bulletin of the Friends' Historical Society*, 38/1 (1949), 49 · P. Mack, *Visionary women: ecstatic prophesy in seventeenth-century England*, new edn (Berkeley, CA, 1994) · E. D. Baltzell, *Puritan Boston and Quaker Philadelphia* (1979) · A. Schrager-Lang, *Prophetic woman* (1987) · M. Bell, G. Parfitt, and S. Shepherd, *A biographical dictionary of English women writers, 1580–1720* (1990) · D. Lovejoy, *Religious enthusiasm in the New World* (1985) · A. J. Worrall, *Quakers in the colonial northeast* (1980) · W. A. Dyer, 'William Dyer, a Rhode Island dissenter—from Lincoln or Somerset?', *Rhode Island Historical Society Collections*, 30 (1937), 9–26 · M. J. Lewis, 'Dyer, Mary', *ANB*

Dyer, Mary. *See* Hodgson, Mary (*bap.* 1673?, *d.* 1719?).

Dyer, Reginald Edward Harry (1864–1927), army officer, was born at Murree, a hill station in the Punjab, India, on 9 October 1864, the youngest son and sixth child of Edward Dyer (*b.* 1831), managing partner of the Murree Brewery Company, and his wife, Mary Passmore of Barnstaple. He was educated first at Bishop Cotton School, Simla, India; entered Midleton College, co. Cork, in 1875; and attended the Royal Military College, Sandhurst (1884–5). On 4 April 1888 Dyer married Anne, daughter of Colonel Edmund Pippon Ommaney, Indian Staff Corps; they had two sons, and a daughter who died in infancy.

Dyer was commissioned a second lieutenant on 28 August 1885 in the Queen's Royal West Surrey regiment. He briefly served in Ireland before joining the 2nd battalion of his regiment in Burma in November 1886. Dyer first saw active service during the Third Anglo-Burmese War before transferring to the Indian army on 30 August 1887. He joined the 39th Bengal native infantry at Cawnpore and then briefly served at Jhansi. In April 1888 Dyer was appointed wing officer with the 29th Punjab infantry, in charge of half the regiment, at Peshawar on the north-west frontier of India. He saw active service during the Black Mountain expedition later that year and the relief of Chitral in 1895. In 1896–7 Dyer attended the Staff College at Camberley, before rejoining the 29th Punjabis at Rawalpindi early the following year. In March 1901 he was appointed a deputy assistant adjutant general for instruction in command of the Garrison School at Chakrata, a post which he held, with other instructional appointments, until 1909, but which was interrupted by his

Reginald Edward Harry Dyer (1864–1927), by Vandyk

briefly seeing active service as an orderly officer during the Waziristan blockade (1901–2), intended to punish the Mahsuds and Wazirs by preventing them from trading with British India. Dyer was promoted major in 1903, and in 1906 was chosen for accelerated promotion.

Dyer returned to regimental service in 1908 as second in command of the 25th Punjabis stationed at Rawalpindi. Following leave in England he was promoted lieutenant-colonel on 25 February 1910 and took command of the regiment which garrisoned Hong Kong between 1912 and 1914. In December 1914 Dyer returned to India and was appointed chief staff officer to Sir Gerald Kitson at Rawalpindi where he was primarily responsible for training new recruits. In February 1916 Dyer was given command of the military operations in south-east Persia, intended to prevent the passage of German missions to Afghanistan and stop tribal raiders attacking British border posts in Baluchistan. Dyer was notably successful in this command and, after returning to India in October, he was created CB the following year for his services, was mentioned in dispatches, and given command of the Jullundur brigade, responsible for recruiting and training replacements for units serving overseas. During the spring of 1917 a serious riding accident incapacitated him for a year and compelled him to return to England. Following a partial recovery he resumed command at Jullundur in April 1918, but was plagued by severe headaches and gradual loss of strength in his lower limbs for the rest of his life.

The Punjab was wracked by serious civil disorder during

the spring of 1919, which Dyer witnessed at first hand. It followed the promulgation of the Rowlatt Act, extending draconian emergency powers into peacetime, and M. K. Gandhi's response of calling for a general strike across India. Unrest quickly spread in April to the Jullundur brigade area. News of the arrest of several nationalist leaders in the city of Amritsar on 10 April 1919 sparked rioting during which a mob attacked and killed five Englishmen, gutted several public buildings, looted two banks, and attacked and left for dead a female missionary. When Dyer arrived on the scene at 9 p.m. the following day, the local deputy commissioner, R. B. Beckett, soon relinquished control into his hands and authorized him to use all necessary force to restore order. Dyer took immediate steps to restore law and order within the city, without reference to higher command, ordering a series of arrests. When Dyer marched a force of British and Indian troops around the city's periphery on 12 April all seemed peaceful, but he then issued a proclamation that banned all movement into and out of the city, imposed a curfew, and forbade public meetings which were to be regarded as unlawful assemblies and dispersed by force of arms if necessary. News of a large unauthorized mass meeting at the Jallianwalla Bagh, a walled enclosure near the Golden Temple with only one exit, reached Dyer the following day after a series of acts of sabotage had been reported in the city.

Dyer marched a force of ninety Gurkha and Baluchi troops into the Jallianwalla Bagh on 13 April 1919 to disperse the unlawful assembly and without warning opened fire upon the estimated 20,000 strong crowd. For 10–15 minutes the firing continued without interruption during which 1,650 rounds were expended, killing an officially estimated 379 and wounding 1,200 men, women, and children. Dyer then immediately withdrew, leaving the dead, dying, and wounded unattended. The massacre at the Jallianwalla Bagh immediately restored law and order in Amritsar and pacified the surrounding area. Further action was taken by Dyer on 19 April when he issued an order that all Indians passing along the street in which the missionary had been attacked were to do so crawling on their hands and knees. Finally he directed that six Indians convicted on a separate charge were to be whipped on the exact spot where the missionary had been attacked. Dyer was immediately given strong support by Sir Michael O'Dwyer, the governor of the Punjab, for his actions in restoring order in Amritsar, and he was made an honorary member of the sect by Sikh religious leaders at the Golden Temple.

Following the outbreak of the Third Anglo-Afghan War in May 1919 Dyer took command of a brigade ordered on active service. Dyer distinguished himself leading the 45th brigade, despite suffering almost continuous physical pain, during operations leading to the relief of the beleaguered fort at Thal in the Kurram valley on 1 June 1919. A superior force of Afghan regulars and tribesmen, led by the Afghan commander-in-chief, were defeated and then pursued back across the Durand line, which marked the boundary between British and Afghan control. For his services during the campaign Dyer was mentioned in dispatches.

News of the Amritsar massacre spread slowly from the Punjab across India and to England, but as it became known it caused widespread revulsion. On 14 October 1919 the government of India appointed a committee, chaired by Lord Hunter, a Scottish judge, to 'investigate the recent disturbances … their causes and the measures to cope with them'. Dyer was summoned as an official witness. During his testimony Dyer allowed himself to be provoked by Indian nationalist lawyers. He averred that he believed martial law was in effect and therefore that he was justified in using whatever force he thought necessary to restore order. Moreover, while giving evidence, frequently tinged with racist comments, he justified his actions in the Jallianwalla Bagh by arguing that he had prevented a general rebellion and that he had wanted to create an impression that would help pacify other parts of India. Finally he stated that if he had been able to get an armoured car into the square he would have opened fire upon the crowd with a machine gun.

The Hunter committee's final report was damning, asserting that Dyer had not in fact been suppressing a rebellion, but was merely dispersing an unlawful assembly. Accordingly he was strongly censured for 'acting out of a mistaken concept of duty' by not giving advance warning before opening fire, continuing firing after the crowd had dispersed, and for not providing medical assistance to the wounded. This indictment led General Sir Charles Monro, the commander-in-chief in India, to revoke Dyer's recent promotion to an officiating divisional command and insist upon his immediate resignation from the Indian army. In March 1920 Dyer resigned despite the fact that he was within only a few months of his age limit for retirement.

The treatment Dyer received from the government of India aroused fierce controversy in Britain and India. Many members of the European community in India felt that Dyer had prevented another Indian Mutiny and that he had been condemned without a properly constituted trial; after all, he had only been a witness before the Hunter committee. The depth of public support was reflected when Dyer returned to England and the *Morning Post* opened a public subscription which collected £26,000. In contrast most Indian public opinion was alienated, and relations with nationalist leaders, who now felt that Britain was indifferent to their political aspirations, were poisoned. Most thought Dyer had been too leniently treated and the Indian National Congress bought the Jallianwalla Bagh as a memorial to the dead and a rallying point for the nationalist movement.

Following his return from India Dyer appealed to the army council, but the British government decided that he had completely failed to act in accord with the principle of minimum force, had inexcusably omitted to give a warning, and had failed in his obvious duty to give succour to the injured, and finally declared that the crawling order was an offence against every canon of civilized behaviour. Crucially Edward Montagu, the secretary of state for

India, also ignored Dyer's appeals for support. His case was debated in the House of Commons which voted against the censure of Dyer, while the House of Lords also deprecated the treatment he had received.

Dyer's health rapidly declined after resigning from the army; he suffered increasingly from arteriosclerosis. In November 1921 he was stricken with paralysis after suffering from a stroke from which he never fully recovered. On 23 July 1927 Dyer died at St Martin's, Long Ashton, near Bristol, after a further severe stroke caused a cerebral haemorrhage. He was cremated at Golders Green, Middlesex. His wife survived him. The controversy surrounding General Dyer and the Amritsar massacre has never abated. The Amritsar massacre became as notorious an event in imperial history as the Peterloo massacre was in British history. Most historians are united in condemnation of his actions and the public support he received in India and England, but some still argue that Dyer's actions averted a bloody uprising in the Punjab, and that his treatment by the British authorities was fundamentally unjust.   T. R. MOREMAN

Sources I. Colvin, *The life of General Dyer* (1929) • *The Times* (25 Oct 1927) • *Indian Army List* • DNB • NAM, Dyer MSS • R. E. H. Dyer, *Raiders of the Sarhad* (1921) • *Despatch by Brigadier General Sir Reginald Edward Harry Dyer, GOC Seistan field force, on the operations against the Damanis* (1st to 24th April 1916) (1916) • G. de S. Barrow, *The life of General Sir Charles Carmichael Monro* (1931) • 'Report of the committee to investigate the disturbances in the Punjab, etc.', *Parl. papers* (1920), 14.19–33, Cmd 681 • H. Fein, *Imperial crime and punishment at Jallianwala Bagh and British judgement* (1977) • C. Shepherd, *Crisis of empire: British reactions to Amritsar* (1992) • A. Draper, *The Amritsar massacre: twilight of the raj* (1988) • CGPLA Eng. & Wales (1927) • A. Swinson, *Six minutes to sunset* (1964) • V. N. Datta, *Jallianwala Bagh* (1969)

Archives NAM, papers, corresp. of his wife | FILM IWM FVA, documentary footage

Likenesses Vandyk, photograph, repro. in Colvin, *Life of General Dyer*, frontispiece • Vandyk, photograph, NPG [*see illus.*]

Wealth at death £11,941 1s. 1d.: probate, 27 Sept 1927, CGPLA Eng. & Wales

Dyer, Samuel (*bap.* 1721, *d.* 1772), translator, the youngest son of Joseph Dyer, a wealthy jeweller in the City of London, and his wife, Mary, was baptized at Old Jewry Presbyterian Church, London, on 4 January 1721. His parents were dissenters and after receiving his initial education at John Ward's school in Tenter Alley, Moorfields, he moved to Philip Doddridge's academy at Northampton. Dyer entered the University of Glasgow in 1741 and studied philosophy under Francis Hutcheson; he afterwards completed his education at Leiden, matriculating on 16 September 1743 and remaining for two years. He returned to England an excellent classical scholar and mathematician, master of French, Italian, German, and Hebrew, and a student of natural philosophy.

Instead of becoming a dissenting minister as his parents might have hoped, Dyer chose to pursue a literary life. His wide erudition and amiable temperament made him welcome in learned circles. He was an original member of the club founded by Samuel Johnson in the winter of 1749 which met weekly at the King's Head in Ivy Lane. Dyer's means were now limited, his father having died and left

his property to his widow and eldest son and daughter. He supplemented his income by tutoring Richard Gough in Greek in 1755 and undertook several translation projects, although, as Sir John Hawkins notes, he only successfully completed the revision of Plutarch's *Lives* published by Tonson in 1758. For this edition he translated the lives of Pericles and Demetrius and revised the whole work, receiving £200 in payment. At Johnson's request Dyer prepared notes for a revised edition of the dictionary, though these were never used. In 1759, through the interest of a friend, Dyer became a commissary in the army in Germany.

On his return to England about 1764, Dyer became the first elected member of the Literary Club which was frequented by Samuel Johnson, Oliver Goldsmith, and Joshua Reynolds. The other members had, according to Bishop Percy, 'such a high opinion of his knowledge and respect for his judgment as to appeal to him constantly, and … his sentence was final' (Prior, 425). Through the club Dyer met Edmund Burke, of whom he became an intimate friend. In 1760 Dyer had been elected a fellow of the Royal Society, and in 1766 he was elevated to the council. By the death of his mother and brother Dyer came into possession of £8000, which he disastrously invested in East India Company stock. About 1770 he also contracted debts to Lord Verney, possibly having invested in annuities on his estate. Dyer suffered an attack of quinsy in autumn 1772, which proved fatal. He died intestate on 15 September, at his home in Castle Street, Leicester Fields, London, and Verney received the residue of his estate. The suggestion that Dyer's financial losses drove him to commit suicide is considered by Malone and others to have been the malicious invention of Hawkins.

Edmund Burke wrote the following notice of Dyer in one of the London papers:

> He was a man of profound and general erudition, and his sagacity and judgment were fully equal to the extent of his learning. His mind was candid, sincere, and benevolent, his friendship disinterested and unalterable. The modest simplicity and sweetness of his manners rendered his conversation as amiable as it was instructive, and endeared him to those few who had the happiness of knowing intimately that valuable and unostentatious man.   (*DNB*)

Johnson referred to his late friend as the 'learned Mr. Dyer' in the 'Life of Watts' and bought a copy of his engraved portrait to hang in a room which he was fitting up with prints (Johnson, *Lives of the English Poets*, 3.308). Dyer's obscurity is partly accounted for in Reynolds's observation that, although Dyer was 'a very judicious and learned Critic, and held in the highest estimation in our Club … not having published anything his name is not much known in the world' (*Letters of Sir Joshua Reynolds*, 140–41).

Dyer's reputation suffered greatly at the hands of Hawkins, whose widely reprinted account of him, first appearing in his 1787 biography of Johnson, asserts that at best Dyer abused his considerable abilities, and at worst he was an atheist and gross sensualist. Hawkins recalled one day finding Dyer 'in a fit of melancholy occasioned by a discovery that he had lost his taste for olives' (Hawkins, 225). No love was lost between Hawkins and Dyer, who had found the former, as Bishop Percy recalled, 'a man of the most mischievous, uncharitable, and malignant disposition' (Prior, 425). Malone, who never knew Dyer, vindicated his character, attributing Hawkins's 'malignant prejudices' to his having quarrelled with Burke: an enmity which was carried 'even to Mr. Burke's friends' (ibid., 419). Further posthumous indignity resulted when the publisher Bell mistakenly affixed Dyer's portrait, engraved from an original painting by Reynolds, to a volume of John Dyer's poems.

Reynolds and Malone both believed Dyer was the author of 'Junius's letters'. Evidence for this is chiefly founded on the fact that immediately after Dyer's death Reynolds entered his rooms in Castle Street and found William Burke destroying a large quantity of manuscript (P. Burke, 68). Although Dyer's death in 1772 does not preclude his having been a co-author of the essays, the suggestion that Dyer was Junius is now not much credited. The burnt manuscripts may have concerned the failed East India stock, investments in which the Burkes were also involved.   CATHERINE DILLE

Sources J. Hawkins, *The life of Samuel Johnson, LL.D.* (1787), 222–32 · J. Prior, *Life of Edmond Malone, editor of Shakespeare* (1860), 419–26 · [E. Burke], *The correspondence of Edmund Burke*, 2, ed. L. S. Sutherland (1960), 334–5 · *The letters of Samuel Johnson*, ed. B. Redford, 3 (1992), 192; 4 (1994), 126 · *The critical and miscellaneous prose works of John Dryden*, ed. E. Malone, 3 vols. (1800), vol. 1, pp. 180–84 [with Malone's MS notes, Bod. MS Malone E. 61] · Boswell, *Life*, 1.28, 190, 363, 478–80; 2.453; 4.10–11; 5.109 · *DNB* · Nichols, *Lit. anecdotes*, 6.266 · E. Peacock, *Index to English speaking students who have graduated at Leyden University* (1883), 32 · W. I. Addison, ed., *The matriculation albums of the University of Glasgow from 1728 to 1858* (1913), 27 · *The record of the Royal Society of London*, 4th edn (1940) · D. Wecter, *Edmund Burke and his kinsmen: a study of the statesman's financial integrity and private relationships* (1939) · *The letters of Junius*, ed. J. Cannon (1978), appx 8, n. 542 · *Letters of Sir Joshua Reynolds*, ed. F. W. Hilles (1929), 140–41 · S. Johnson, *Lives of the English poets*, ed. G. B. Hill, [new edn], 3 (1905), 308 · P. Burke, *Public and domestic life of E. Burke* (1853), 68 · *IGI*
Likenesses G. Marchi, mezzotint, pubd 1773 (after J. Reynolds), BM

Dyer, Thomas Henry (1804–1888), historian, was born on 4 May 1804 in the parish of St Dunstan-in-the-East, London. After being educated privately, he spent his early years in a firm trading in the West Indies, but after the abolition of slavery in 1833 he gave up his commercial interests and devoted himself to literature. He travelled on the continent, and wrote a series of works on the topography, history, and antiquities of Rome, Athens, and Pompeii. He also became a voluminous contributor to William Smith's classical and biographical dictionaries, and to the publications of the Society for the Diffusion of Useful Knowledge. For several years Dyer was engaged in the study of Aeschylus, endeavouring to emend his tragedies and to restore certain lost passages, and in 1841 he published his *Tentamina Aeschylea*. He next took up the study of Calvin, and in 1850 published his *Life of Calvin*. His view of Calvin's character was rather severe, but his work was grounded on original documents. In 1865 Dyer published *A History of the City of Rome*. It was the first attempt in English to give a connected narrative of the rise, progress, and decline of the city. Dyer drew heavily on the works of Papencordt, Gregorovius, and Ampère. His *History of the Kings of Rome* (1868) was preceded by a dissertation on the sources from which the early history of Rome is derived, and took a highly conservative view, in opposition to Niebuhr. Dyer maintained the credibility of the main outlines of the story. His theories were attacked by J. R. Seeley in an edition of the first book of Livy. Dyer replied in an essay entitled *Roma regalis, or, The Newest Phase of an Old Story* (1872), and in *A Plea for Livy* (1873). Dyer spent much time in exploring the ruins of Pompeii, and his narrative of the remains went through several editions. In 1867 he published *Pompeii: its History, Buildings, and Antiquities*, which includes some early photographs of the site. As the outcome of several visits to Athens, Dyer issued in 1873 *Ancient Athens: its History, Topography, and Remains*. The important discoveries made in the city, and especially the excavation of the Dionysiac theatre in 1862, had suggested the preparation of this new dissertation on Athenian topography and antiquities.

Dyer's most substantial work was the *History of Modern Europe*, which originally appeared in 1861–4, in four volumes. It represented the labour of years, and chronicled the period from the fall of Constantinople to the end of the Crimean War. It was a clear and painstaking compilation, but neither memorable in its style, nor influential in its scholarship. A third edition, continued by Arthur Hassall to the end of the nineteenth century, came out in 1901 (6 vols.). Dyer's last work was *On Imitative Beauty* (1882). The University of St Andrews gave him the degree of LLD in 1865. His final years were spent at Bath, where he died at 7 Green Park on 30 January 1888.

G. B. SMITH, *rev.* RICHARD SMAIL

Sources *The Academy* (11 Feb 1888), 97 · *The Athenaeum* (11 Feb 1888), 180 · Boase, *Mod. Eng. biog.* · *CGPLA Eng. & Wales* (1888)
Archives Dorset RO, Strode MSS · U. Reading L., letters to George Bell, publisher
Wealth at death £1681 2s. 11d.: probate, 27 Feb 1888, *CGPLA Eng. & Wales*

Dyer, William (1632/3–1696), clergyman and ejected minister, probably came from the west country: at the time of his death a brother and a sister were living in Tedburn St Mary in Devon, another brother in Chard, Somerset. Nothing is as yet known of his parents or his education.

In 1660 Dyer was curate of Cholesbury in Buckinghamshire, having previously been a preacher at Chesham in the same county. He was ejected from Cholesbury and by July 1662 the living was vacant. On 28 June of the following year its churchwardens reported that Dyer had returned to the parish to preach the Sunday before last, further adding that he was 'to be married to Sara Ward, a rich man's daughter' (*Calamy rev.*, 176). It is not certain whether the marriage took place, although his wife at the time that he made his will thirty-three years later also bore the (very common) Christian name of Sarah.

Described by Edmund Calamy as 'a man of great piety, and a serious fervent preacher' (Palmer, 1.235), Dyer was a popular writer and in 1663 published *A Cabinet of Jewels* and *Christ's Famous Titles* which were described by a later scholar as 'evangelical in tone and akin to much written by Saltmarsh, Dell, and Bunyan' (Greaves & Zaller, *BDBR*, 1.239). *Christ's Famous Titles* contained some radical statements, with Dyer writing, for example, that kings were afraid of the government of Christ in case it should 'un-king them', parliaments 'lest it should usurp their authority', and lawyers 'lest it should take away their gains' (W. Dyer, *Christ's Famous Titles*, 1663, 7).

In 1665 Dyer preached sermons on the plague at St Anne and St Agnes within Aldersgate, in which he attributed the pestilence to God's wrath at the sinfulness of man. These were subsequently published under the title of *Christ's Voice to London* (1666) and along with his earlier works went through many editions. His collected works first appeared in 1668 and there followed a number of later editions. Towards the end of his life he wrote only a few more tracts including *Mount Sion, or, A Draught of that Church* (1689).

Edmund Calamy noted that in later life he 'inclined to the Quakers' (Calamy, *Continuation*, 1.147), a statement which has been questioned and the suggestion made that 'this was probably nothing more than an affinity shared with others (like Dell) who stressed the baptism of the Spirit rather than water' (Greaves & Zaller, *BDBR*, 1.239). However, Dyer is listed in the Society of Friends' London burial register, and following this Joseph Smith, in the nineteenth century, included him in his *Supplement to a Descriptive Catalogue of Friends' Books*.

In his will, made on 1 April 1696, Dyer described himself as a merchant living at The Park in Southwark. The Quaker digest registers record that he died of a 'hectic fever' eight days later, aged sixty-three, and was buried in the Quaker burial-ground at The Park, Southwark. His will reveals his continued interests in the west country, where one man owed him £400, and in Chesham, where he held land. His will makes no mention of any children: his bequests were made to his wife and to his siblings and their families.   CAROLINE L. LEACHMAN

Sources Greaves & Zaller, *BDBR*, 1.239 · E. Calamy, *A continuation of the account of the ministers … who were ejected and silenced after the Restoration in 1660*, 2 vols. (1727), vol. 1, p. 147 · *The nonconformist's memorial … originally written by … Edmund Calamy*, ed. S. Palmer, 1 (1775), 235 · *Calamy rev.*, 175–6 · E. Calamy, ed., *An abridgment of Mr. Baxter's history of his life and times, with an account of the ministers, &c., who were ejected after the Restauration of King Charles II*, 2nd edn, 2 vols. (1713), vol. 2, p. 110 · digest registers of births, marriages, and burials, RS Friends, Lond. · will, PRO, PROB 11/431, sig. 63 · J. Smith, ed., *A descriptive catalogue of Friends' books*, suppl. (1893), 110 · G. Lipscomb, *The history and antiquities of the county of Buckingham*, 4 vols. (1831–47), vol. 3, p. 322
Likenesses line engraving, BM, NPG; repro. in W. Dyer, *Dyer's works* (1668) · portrait, repro. in W. Dyer, *Christ's famous titles* (1663)
Wealth at death legacies totalling £300, as well as farmland and tenements in Chesham, Buckinghamshire; £400 owed to him: will, PRO, PROB 11/431, sig. 63

Dyer, Sir William Turner Thiselton- (1843–1928), botanist, was born on 28 July 1843 at Westminster, the elder son of William George Thiselton Dyer (1812–1868), physician, and his wife, Catherine Jane, daughter of Thomas Firminger, assistant at Greenwich observatory. He attended King's College School and in 1861 entered King's College

Sir William Turner Thiselton-Dyer (1843–1928), by Elliott & Fry

as a medical student. Changing his mind about medicine as a career, he proceeded in 1863 to Christ Church, Oxford, where he graduated in the second class in mathematics two years later. At Oxford he admired the work of C. G. B. Daubeny, Sherardian professor of botany, and, influenced by his friends H. N. Moseley and E. Ray Lankester, he turned to the study of natural science, graduating in the first class in 1867.

From 1868 to 1870 Thiselton-Dyer was professor of natural history at the Royal Agricultural College, Cirencester. He then moved to Dublin as professor of botany at the Royal College of Science, and this was followed in 1872 by his appointment as professor of botany at the Royal Horticultural Society in London. Sir Joseph Hooker, director of the Royal Botanic Gardens at Kew, had recommended him for the London post, and by the close of 1872 Hooker had also employed him part-time at Kew. Significantly, he also became actively involved in T. H. Huxley's recently established summer courses in biology for teachers held under the auspices of the Department of Science and Art at South Kensington. After assisting with the course in 1872 Thiselton-Dyer took charge of all the botanical teaching in 1873, and again in both 1875 and 1876. Teaching was not limited to the flowering plants but included all main plant groups. Key aspects were the adoption of microscopical techniques, continental methods, and the use of living specimens wherever possible. All students gained extended practical experience. During this period Thiselton-Dyer became a guiding influence for a number of students and for those who assisted him as demonstrators. Subsequently he used his position to provide opportunities for S. H. Vines, F. O. Bower, W. Gardiner, D. H. Scott, and H. Marshall Ward, who themselves came to assume leadership roles during the late 1880s and 1890s.

In 1875 Thiselton-Dyer edited A. W. Bennett's translation, as *Textbook of Botany*, of Julius von Sachs's standard work, perhaps the most influential botany text of the period. He also intended to write a practical manual based on his South Kensington courses but due to pressure of administrative duties he passed the task to Bower and Vines. Nevertheless, Thiselton-Dyer's work subsequently formed the basis of practical botanical education in British universities.

By 1875 Sir Joseph Hooker had appointed Thiselton-Dyer as assistant director and on 23 June 1877 he married Hooker's eldest daughter, Harriet Ann. They had one son and one daughter. As assistant director, Thiselton-Dyer looked after the colonial activities of Kew and his achievements included the introduction of rubber trees to Malaya. In view of his laboratory experience, he was also placed in charge of the Jodrell Laboratory at Kew, over which he presided until 1892.

Thiselton-Dyer was appointed director of the Royal Botanic Gardens in 1885 in succession to Hooker, and was responsible for improvements to the gardens, enlargements of the library and herbarium building, and the initiation of a forestry museum. One of his early tasks was the foundation of the *Kew Bulletin* for the exchange of information between Kew and satellite institutions throughout the empire. Thiselton-Dyer continued the systematic work at Kew and edited *Flora Capensis* (1896–1925), *Flora of Tropical Africa* (1897–1913), *Icones plantarum* (1896–1906), and the *Botanical Magazine* (1905–1906). His interest in the geographical distribution of plants and Darwinian theory is demonstrated in an essay contributed to *Darwin and Modern Science*, ed. A. S. Seward (1909). He also continued to champion the cause of botany outside the confines of Kew, inducing the delegates of the Clarendon Press to publish *Annals of Botany* when they were about to drop the proposal. He supported the British Association for the Advancement of Science and was president of the biology section at Bath in 1888 and of the botany section at Ipswich in 1895.

Perceived by some contemporaries at Kew as somewhat autocratic, Thiselton-Dyer was, however, an able administrator with a broad vision of botany. He was a pivotal figure in its rapid development in Britain during the late nineteenth century. He was elected FRS in 1880, created CMG in 1882, CIE in 1892, and KCMG in 1899. On retirement in 1905 he moved to Gloucestershire. He died at his house, The Ferns, Crickley Hill, Witcombe, on 23 December 1928 and was buried at Witcombe on 27 December. His wife survived him.   BERNARD THOMASON

Sources *Bulletin of Miscellaneous Information* [RBG Kew] (1929), 65–75 · F. W. O., *PRS*, 106B (1930), xxiii–xxix · *DNB* · 'Sir W. T. Thiselton-Dyer, K.C.M.G.', *Nature*, 123 (1929), 212–15 · draft biography of W. T. Thiselton-Dyer, RBG Kew · F. O. Bower, *Sixty years of botany in Britain* (1875–1935) (1938), 48–51 · m. cert. · d. cert.

Archives RBG Kew, corresp. and papers | BL, letters to Lord Gladstone, Add. MSS 46055–46056 · BL, corresp. with Alfred Russel Wallace, Add. MSS 46436–46438 · Bodl. Oxf., letters to T. F. Fenwick · Harvard U., Arnold Arboretum, letters to Asa Grey · ICL, letters to Thomas Huxley · Linn. Soc., corresp. with G. J. Romanez · NHM, letters to Albert Gunther and R. W. T. Gunther · Oxf. U. Mus. NH, letters to Sir E. B. Poulton

Likenesses Elliott & Fry, photograph, repro. in Bower, *Sixty years of botany*, facing p. 48 · Elliott & Fry, photograph, RBG Kew [*see illus.*] · photograph, repro. in *Bulletin of Miscellaneous Information*, 3, facing p. 65

Wealth at death £14,280 4s. 11d.: probate, 2 March 1929, *CGPLA Eng. & Wales*

Dyfnwal Moelmud ap Garbanion [Dumngual Moilmut ap Garbaniaun] (*fl. c.*450–470), dynast, is identified in the tenth-century genealogies in BL, Harley MS 3859 as the grandson of Coel Hen and the ancestor of Morcant ap Coledauc, one of the 'men of the north' (the Britons of what became northern England and southern Scotland). The early genealogies in Oxford, Jesus College, MS 20 also identify him in this manner. These are the only references to him that can be regarded as in any sense historical; by the time Geoffrey of Monmouth composed his *Historia regum Britanniae* in 1136, Dyfnwal had become in Welsh tradition a figure of primarily mythological significance.

Geoffrey depicts him as the son of Cloten, king of Cornwall, and a great legislator of the early Britons. After defeating the kings of England, Wales, and Scotland to ascend the throne of the island of Britain 'Dunwallo Molmutius' established the 'Molmutine laws'—said by Geoffrey to have been later translated into Latin by Gildas and into English by King Alfred and to remain in use among the English of his day. That Geoffrey was drawing at least in part on Welsh sources for this story is suggested by the fact that two thirteenth-century law books from Gwynedd (*Llyfr Iorwerth* and *Llyfr Colan*) also identify Dyfnwal as the principal legislator among the Britons before the time of Hywel Dda, and their accounts must be independent of Geoffrey's. These law books identify Dyfnwal's father (named Clydno in NL Wales, Peniarth MS 40) as the earl of Cornwall rather than as the king; they allege his mother (not mentioned in the *Historia regum Britanniae*) to be a daughter of the king of England and his accession to the throne to be the result of inheritance rather than battle; and they name him as the original 'measurer' of the island of Britain and the builder of great roads linking 'Penryn Blathaon' in the north with 'Pen Pengwaed' in Cornwall, and 'Crugyll' in Anglesey with 'Soram' (Sarre) in Kent. The names given these geographical extremes in the law books are paralleled in *Enweu ynys Prydein* ('The names of the island of Britain') and may derive from this text (Bromwich, no. 3, 228–9); Geoffrey's account names four different points and identifies Dyfnwal's son Belinus as the king who constructed these roads.

Dyfnwal appears in later Welsh tradition in a variety of guises. The late triads ascribed to Dyfnwal that are now known to be the work of Iolo Morgannwg, or Edward Williams (1747–1826), call him the 'king of the Welsh' and the 'best lawman who ever was' (Owen, 13/1.34). But whereas

Dyfnwal's laws are said in *Llyfr Iorwerth* to have been abrogated by Hywel Dda, who replaced them by laws of his own, the later triads claim that Hywel confirmed Dyfnwal's legislation. Geoffrey used Dyfnwal to make the point that the English laws of his day were British in origin; the later triads used him to demonstrate the historical continuity of British legal tradition. In the thirteenth century, however, with the conquest of Wales as yet undecided, the need to assert a legal identity separate from that of the English invaders was paramount, and the law of the Britons had thus to give way to the law of the Welsh.   ROBIN CHAPMAN STACEY

Sources P. C. Bartrum, ed., *Early Welsh genealogical tracts* (1966) · P. C. Bartrum, ed., *Welsh genealogies, AD 300–1400*, 8 vols. (1974); suppl. (1980) · *The Historia regum Britannie of Geoffrey of Monmouth*, ed. N. Wright, 1: *Bern, Bürgerbibliothek, MS 568* (1985) · A. R. Wiliam, ed., *Llyfr Iorwerth*, University of Wales History and Law Series, 18 (1960) · D. Jenkins, ed., *Llyfr Colan*, University of Wales History and Law Series, 19 (1963) · A. Owen, ed., *Ancient laws and institutes of Wales* (1841) · R. Bromwich, ed. and trans., *Trioedd ynys Prydein: the Welsh triads* (1961) · H. Lewis, ed., *Brut Dingestow* (1942) · R. Bromwich and D. S. Evans, eds., *Culhwch and Olwen: an edition and study of the oldest Arthurian tale* (1992) · D. Jenkins, *The law of Hywel Dda: law texts from medieval Wales translated and edited* (1986) · M. Curley, *Geoffrey of Monmouth*, Twayne's English Authors Series, 509 (1994)

Dyfrig [St Dyfrig, Dubricius] (*supp. fl. c.*475–*c.*525), holy man and supposed bishop, was founder of the churches of Hentland and Moccas in what is now south-west Herefordshire and in the early middle ages was revered in southeast Wales for his learning and wisdom. By the twelfth century, however, he had been appropriated by the expanding see of Llandaff, and erroneously turned into its first bishop. He is the subject of the *Vita sancti Dubricii* in the Book of Llandaff, which was compiled under Bishop Urban in the early twelfth century and intended to provide the episcopal church with a demonstrable early history. Although this should urge caution, analysis of the content of this life suggests that it is not as much an overtly Llandaff composition as those of Dyfrig's alleged successors Teilo and Oudoceus, and may preserve some traditions relating to the Herefordshire saint. Dyfrig is also noticed in the earlier *Vita sancti Samsonis* (now thought to have been composed *c.*750) and Rhigyfarch's *Vita sancti Davidis* (composed *c.*1090), as well as in a number of twelfth-century lives of other Welsh saints. Some of this later material was employed by Benedict of Gloucester (*fl.* 1150) in his life of Dyfrig, otherwise based on the Llandaff text and preserved in BL, Cotton MS Vespasian A.xiv. The reference in the *Annales Cambriae* for the year 612 to 'Conthigerni obitus et Dibric episcopi' ('the death of Kentigern and of bishop Dyfrig') does not accord with the hagiographical accounts (below) which, if reliable, would suggest he flourished in the late fifth or early sixth century; and consequently the phrase 'et Dibric episcopi' has been regarded by some scholars as a later gloss to Kentigern's obit.

According to his life, Dyfrig was born at Madley and was the son, possibly illegitimate, of Efrddyl, daughter of Peibio, king of Ergyng. This early Welsh kingdom was equivalent to the region of Archenfield in south-west Herefordshire and was probably centred on the old Roman *vicus* of Ariconium. Dyfrig is said to have founded the monastic school at Hentland, 4 miles north-west of Ross-on-Wye, which attracted many disciples to him. Subsequently he relocated to Moccas, near Madley, and eventually retired to Bardsey Island (off the Llŷn peninsula) where he is said to have died. As this basic outline shows, the life has little to do with Llandaff and may reflect at least some aspects of the original Herefordshire saint. A slightly different picture is presented in the first part of the seventh-century life of Samson: here 'papa Dubricius' is frequently mentioned, for example, visiting St Illtud's Monastery at Llantwit Major, Glamorgan, where he ordains Samson, or spending his Lenten retreat on Caldy Island (off the south Pembrokeshire coast), where he is said to have had his own house. (The fragmentary inscription on Caldy once thought to refer to Dubr[icius] is generally no longer identified with the saint.) The Dyfrig of the life of Samson has little in common with the figure in the Book of Llandaff and probably reflects a local veneration at Llantwit of the Herefordshire saint. The notice of Dibric in the *Annales Cambriae*, whether a gloss or not, shows that by the mid-tenth century he was regarded as a saint of some importance in south Wales; and subsequently the idea that he was a 'visiting bishop' became common: he appears in the *Vita sancti Gundleii* in this capacity, and is also said to have consecrated St Leonorius (Lunaire), again at Llantwit. Furthermore, according to Rhigyfarch's *Vita sancti Davidis*, it was Dubricius along with St Deiniol who finally persuaded St David to attend the Synod of Llanddewibrefi (545), possibly indicating the growing importance of these two saints in the north-west and south-east respectively.

Other than the *Vita sancti Dubricii*, the material relating to Dyfrig in the Book of Llandaff is almost entirely the product of the ecclesiastical propaganda underlying that manuscript and has nothing to do with the Herefordshire saint. For example, it is claimed that Dyfrig was ordained archbishop of the whole of 'southern Britain' by saints Germanus of Auxerre and Lupus of Troyes who established his episcopal see at Llandaff. The text proceeds to define the extent of the diocese, which of course equates to that claimed by Bishop Urban in the early twelfth century. Furthermore, the text claims that on 7 May 1120 the relics of Dyfrig were removed from Bardsey Island and translated to Llandaff, where they were ceremonially received on the 23rd of that month—thus physically completing the appropriation of the saint to the interests of Urban and his church. The topographic evidence for the cult of Dyfrig further demonstrates the late date of this appropriation since it is focused on south-west Herefordshire and not Llandaff. The dedications are clustered in Archenfield, including Hentland: for example, he is the eponym of St Devereux in Archenfield, near Kilpeck, and of the former church of Devereux in the parish of Woolhope. There is little trace of his cult in what is now Wales, except for one dedication in Brecknockshire and the holy well Ffynnon Dyfrig, near Llancarfan, Glamorgan. Dyfrig was also the patron of Porlock, on the north Somerset coast. His feast day is 14 November.

DAVID E. THORNTON

Sources J. G. Evans and J. Rhys, eds., *The text of the Book of Llan Dâv reproduced from the Gwysaney manuscript* (1893) · A. W. Wade-Evans, ed. and trans., *Vitae sanctorum Britanniae et genealogiae* (1944) · J. Williams ab Ithel, ed., *Annales Cambriae*, Rolls Series, 20 (1860) · P. Flobert, ed. and trans., *La vie ancienne de Saint Samson de Dol ('Vita sancti Samsonii episcopi Dolensis')* (1997) · *Rhigyfarch's Life of St David*, ed. J. W. James (1967) · G. H. Doble, *Lives of the Welsh saints*, ed. D. S. Evans (1971) · E. G. Bowen, *The settlements of the Celtic saints in Wales*, 2nd edn (1956) · [H. Wharton], ed., *Anglia sacra*, 2 (1691) [prints rest of Benedict of Gloucester's life of Dyfrig, omitting a few miracle stories] · C. Horstman, ed., *Nova legenda Anglie, as collected by John of Tynemouth, J. Capgrave, and others*, 1 (1901), 1 · P. C. Bartrum, ed., *Early Welsh genealogical tracts* (1966)

Dygon [Wyldebore], **John** (*c*.1482–1566?), Benedictine monk and composer, was a nephew of John Dygon, abbot of St Augustine's Abbey, Canterbury, and was himself a monk of St Augustine's in 1505 when he was ordained subdeacon; he occurs as sub-prior in 1521 and prior in 1535. A good example of the pre-dissolution monastic intellectual, he studied in Paris (1520–21) and Louvain (1521–3) with the humanist scholar and philosopher Juan Luis Vives. Moreover, as a practitioner of music he had already supplicated for conferment of the degree of bachelor of music from Oxford University in March 1512. At the dissolution of St Augustine's (30 July 1538) he was awarded as prior (under the name Wyldebore) a generous pension of £13 6s. 8d. per year; in 1556 he was still in receipt of this award, and thus had no need to undertake further formal employment. It appears likely that he was the John Dygon, sometime monk, whose burial in the parish of St Andrew, Canterbury, was recorded in August 1566.

The Canterbury schoolmaster John Twyne recollected Dygon as an educated intellectual, and imagined his participation with Abbot Vokes and Dr Nicholas Wotton in learned discussions of matters antiquarian. More particularly, as 'Joannes Dygonus v[ulg]o Vuylborus' he was the author of the first of two tracts on the complexities of proportional musical notation surviving in a contemporary manuscript (Cambridge, Trinity College, MS o.3.38); he may also have been the author of the second. The seventy-six music examples were his own, even if the text was an abbreviated abstract and adaptation of book 4 of Gaffurius's *Practica musice* (1496). Otherwise, his sole surviving compositions consist of three extracts from a single major work for five or six voices on a text relating to the feast of Easter. The final extract includes examples of the proportional notation explained in Dygon's treatise. The music is a suave and assured exercise in the expansive and non-imitative melismatic polyphony of the 1520s and 1530s.   ROGER BOWERS

Sources Emden, *Oxf.*, 4.182 · Trinity Cam. · R. Hallmark, 'An unknown English treatise of the 16th century', *Journal of the American Musicological Society*, 22 (1969), 273–4 · *Joannis Twini Bolingdunensis, Angli, De rebus Albionicis*, ed. T. Twyne (1590), 6, 8 · W. Urry, *Christopher Marlowe and Canterbury*, ed. A. Butcher (1988), 9, 148 · J. Hawkins, *A general history of the science and practice of music*, new edn, 3 vols. (1853); repr. in 2 vols. (1963), 356–8 · R. Bray,

'British Library, R. M. 24 d 2, John Baldwin's commonplace book: an index and commentary', *Royal Musical Association Research Chronicle*, 12 (1974), 137–51, esp. 138, 145 · F. A. Gasquet, *The eve of the Reformation*, 3rd edn (1900), 40–41

Dyke, Daniel (*d.* 1614), Church of England clergyman, was the son of **William Dyke** (*d.* 1608), a puritan stormy petrel whose repeated brushes with the ecclesiastical authorities took him from Great Yarmouth to Coggeshall in Essex, St Michael's at St Albans, and, finally, to Hemel Hempstead. Bishop John Aylmer of London pursued Dyke relentlessly, but he was sheltered and supported by Lady Anne Bacon, who deployed some heavy artillery in his defence: her brother-in-law, Lord Burghley, her son, Anthony Bacon, and the earl of Essex, who secured him the safe living of Hemel Hempstead, just inside the diocese of Lincoln. There he was the neighbour of the famous puritan divine Thomas Wilcox, who shared some of the same patrons who would be enjoyed by Daniel Dyke and his brother Jeremiah *Dyke. Jeremiah was baptized at Coggeshall in 1584, his siblings Nathaniel, Elizabeth, Solomon, and Joseph at Hemel Hempstead, between 1594 and 1601. Daniel was probably the eldest son, perhaps born about 1580. He matriculated at St John's College, Cambridge, *c*.1593, and proceeded BA in 1595/6, and MA in 1599 from Sidney Sussex College, where he became a fellow in 1606, at about the time that he took his BD. His MA was incorporated at Oxford in 1602.

Very little is known of Daniel Dyke's relatively brief clerical career. There is no evidence that he married, which may suggest that he was never beneficed. His patrons were Lord and Lady Harington of Exton; their son, the second Lord Harington, Dyke's contemporary at Sidney Sussex and a close friend of Prince Henry; and his sister Lucy Harington, countess of Bedford and great patron of the Jacobean poets. From Dyke's *Two Treatises* (posthumously published, 1618), consisting of an exposition of the epistle of Paul to Philemon and 'The schoole of affliction', it appears that he served as chaplain to the Haringtons at Coombe Abbey near Coventry, where Princess Elizabeth was brought up between 1603 and 1608, and perhaps after that at Kew, where the Haringtons remained in charge of the princess's own household. He was involved in the dramatic escape of Harington and his royal charge to Coventry on 7 November 1605, and he dedicated to Princess Elizabeth his thanksgiving sermon for deliverance from the Gunpowder Plot, describing himself as 'a daily eye-witness' of her virtues in *Certaine Comfortable Sermons upon the 124 Psalme*, published in 1616 but entered with the Stationers in 1606.

All Dyke's written works were published posthumously by his brother Jeremiah Dyke, vicar of Epping, and in the strongly elegiac atmosphere created by the deaths, all within little more than a year, of Prince Henry, the first and second lords Harington, and Dyke himself (in 1614). In a dedicatory epistle to *The Mystery of Selfe-Deceiving* (1615) Jeremiah Dyke referred to the two lords Harington as 'glorified saints', and imagined the second lord 'singing heavenly Halleluiahs in the presence of the Lord'. *The Mystery*, a work much admired by Thomas Fuller, and in 1636 published in French in Geneva, and *Two Treatises* (1618) were both dedicated to the countess of Bedford; another collection, entitled *Two Treatises, the one of Repentance, the other of Christs Temptations* (1616), to her sister-in-law, Lady Harington. In the 1630s Jeremiah Dyke published, with dedications to his own patrons, two volumes of his brother's collected *Works*. According to Jeremiah, Daniel kept a spiritual diary in which he recorded, every night, the sins of that day, on the sabbath the faults of the preceding week, and at the end of every month he surveyed 'the whole moneths transgressions', a habit which he seems to have shared with the second Lord Harington. 'The truth is, the world was not worthy of him' (Dyke, *The Mystery*, epistle).

The Dykes were a clerical dynasty. Jeremiah's son, another Daniel *Dyke, named for his uncle, was rector of Great Hadham, Hertfordshire, Oliver Cromwell's chaplain, and one of the triers for the approval of ministers, dying as a Baptist in 1688. Nothing better illustrates the growing respectability of Jacobean puritanism than the careers of the second-generation Dykes. So many 'gadded' to Jeremiah's lectures at Epping, which in his father's days was a crime which had driven him out of St Albans, that a new chapel had to be built and consecrated, with full episcopal approval, to accommodate the crowds. When he made his will in 1639, Jeremiah Dyke disposed of £600 or £700 in money and goods.   PATRICK COLLINSON

Sources P. Collinson, *The Elizabethan puritan movement* (1967); pbk edn (1990) · W. Urwick, *Nonconformity in Hertfordshire* (1884) · Venn, *Alum. Cant.*, 1/2.79 · *The workes of that late reverende divine D. Dike* (1635) · *The second and last part of the workes of D. Dyke* (1633) · D. Dyke, *Certaine comfortable sermons upon the 124 Psalme* (1616) · D. Dyke, *The mystery of selfe-deceiving* (1615) · J. H. Wiffen, *Historical memoirs of the house of Russell*, 2 (1833) · B. Winstone, ed., *Two sermons preached in 1622 & 1628 by the Rev. Jeremiah Dyke, vicar of Epping* (1896) · 'Harington, John, first Baron Harington of Exton', *DNB* · 'Harington, John, second Baron Harington of Exton', *DNB* · will, LMA, DL/C/340, fol. 128r (x19/5)

Dyke, Daniel (1614–1688), General Baptist minister, was born on 21 January 1614 in Epping, Essex, the son of Jeremy (or Jeremiah) *Dyke (*bap.* 1584, *d.* 1639), vicar of Epping, and reputedly 'a good old puritan' (Calamy, 1.370), and his wife, Mary Haggar, daughter of Oliver Haggar of London. Indeed, Daniel was born into a strong clerical dynasty of puritans. His grandfather William had been a contentious preacher at St Albans, his uncle Daniel Dyke was the author of pious works, and his brother Jeremiah, rector of Great Parndon in Essex, was a presbyterian minister in the 1640s. Apparently educated privately in the country, Dyke matriculated at Emmanuel College, Cambridge, in 1629, where he remained until taking his MA degree in 1636. He seems to have been ordained about this date.

In 1636 Dyke was appointed vicar of Eastwick, Hertfordshire. In 1640 he edited and published his father's sermons as *Divers Select Sermons*. Dyke became rector of St Mathew's, Friday Street, London, in 1645, but apparently on account of poor health resumed his living at Eastwick

the following year. On 16 October 1649 he married Elizabeth Manning (*d.* 1678) at St Helen's, Bishopsgate, London; the couple went on to have at least two daughters. Renowned for his erudition and pastoral oratory, he was appointed by parliament to replace the Anglican rector of Much Hadham (also known as Great Hadham or Hadham Magna), Hertfordshire, about 1650.

By this time Dyke had firmly embraced General Baptist principles, and he subsequently held a number of offices within the interregnum state. He became chaplain-in-ordinary to Oliver Cromwell in 1651, and in 1653–4 was one of just three professed Baptists appointed to the board of triers for the approval of ministers. He was assistant to the Hertfordshire commission in 1654, and the following year served on a committee addressing the Jewish question; in 1656 he was a member of the committee for relieving protestants in Piedmont.

Dyke anticipated the persecution of nonconformists upon the Restoration and, although urged by his friends to conform, resigned his living in 1660; this action, for Baptist historians, clearly evidenced his 'great integrity and faithfulness to his conscience' (Crosby, 1.356). Despite his voluntary resignation, Dyke is listed in Calamy's catalogue of ministers forcibly silenced and ejected by, or immediately before, the 1662 Act of Uniformity (Calamy, 1.370).

Dyke's precise whereabouts for the next eight years are uncertain, although he preached as often as possible and, despite the frequent issuing of writs against him, seems to have suffered no more than the most cursory imprisonment. In 1668, following a year of probationary preaching, Dyke was elected joint elder with William Kiffin to a Baptist congregation at Devonshire Square, London; he continued in this office until his death in 1688.

During this period Dyke wrote the recommendatory epistle to Nehemiah Coxe's *Vindiciae veritatis, or, A confutation of … the heresies and gross errors asserted by Thomas Collier* (1677); he also allegedly contributed to some writings by Thomas Hicks and Hanserd Knollys. At some point after Elizabeth's death in 1678, Dyke married Margaret, a woman of whom no further details survive. Dyke appears to have been resident for the last twenty years of his life in the parish of St Giles Cripplegate, London, and was interred in the dissenters' burial-ground in Bunhill Fields. In his will, made on 12 January 1683 and proved on 11 September 1688, he left to his second wife £360 to be put out at interest for her maintenance, their household goods, and a collection of plate and books. Upon her death, this estate was to be equally divided between his two married daughters (after £100 had been paid to the husband of the younger of them as part of his promised marriage portion).

Early accounts of Dyke's life are unanimous in characterizing him as an articulate man of exceptional integrity. Such a view is indeed borne out by the many appointments and responsibilities which he enjoyed during the interregnum and his voluntary resignation upon the Restoration. Although he was clearly involved in the editing, and perhaps composition, of a number of printed Baptist works, he published nothing of his own accord: this, by his daughter's account, was due to his 'mean opinion' of his own substantial abilities (Crosby, 1.358).

A. C. BICKLEY, rev. BETH LYNCH

Sources Calamy rev. • The nonconformist's memorial … originally written by … Edmund Calamy, ed. S. Palmer, 2 (1775) • Venn, Alum. Cant., 1/2 • T. Crosby, The history of the English Baptists, from the Reformation to the beginning of the reign of King George I, 4 vols. (1738–40) • E. Calamy, A continuation of the account of the ministers … who were ejected and silenced after the Restoration in 1660, 2 vols. (1727), vol. 1 • R. Clutterbuck, ed., The history and antiquities of the county of Hertford, 3 (1827) • J. E. Cussans, History of Hertfordshire, 1 (1870) • Greaves & Zaller, BDBR • W. Wilson, The history and antiquities of the dissenting churches and meeting houses in London, Westminster and Southwark, 4 vols. (1808–14), vol. 1 • J. Ivimey, A history of the English Baptists, 4 vols. (1811–30) • CSP dom., 1655–6 • Wing, STC • W. Urwick, Nonconformity in Hertfordshire (1884) • will, PRO, PROB 11/392, sig. 116
Wealth at death £360; plus household goods, books, and plate: will, PRO, PROB 11/392, sig. 116

Dyke, Jeremiah (bap. **1584**, d. **1639**), Church of England clergyman, was baptized at Coggeshall, Essex, on 13 October 1584, son of William *Dyke (d. 1608) [see under Dyke, Daniel], the preacher there and (younger?) brother of Daniel *Dyke (d. 1614). He was admitted as a sizar to Emmanuel College, Cambridge, on 28 May 1598 and migrated to Sidney Sussex College in October of the same year. He graduated BA in 1602, proceeded MA in 1605, and was a fellow of his college. During 1609 he was rector of Toft, Cambridgeshire, but soon moved, on being presented the same year by Sir Moyle Finch to the living of Epping, Essex. In or before 1611 Dyke married Mary, daughter of Oliver Haggar of London. They had three surviving children, Jeremiah (bap. 24 Nov 1611), Daniel *Dyke (1614–1688), and Elizabeth (bap. 19 Feb 1617).

Dyke remained at Epping for the rest of his life. His long ministerial career was accompanied by a number of successful publications which had their origins in his preaching there, although his A Counterpoyson Against Covetousness (1619) had been delivered at Paul's Cross. His printed works were mainly concerned with matters of practical divinity rather than with theological or polemical controversy, demonstrated by such works as The Mischiefe and Miserie of Scandals both Taken and Given (1631) and The Right Receiving of and Rooting in Christ (1640). His most successful work was Good Conscience, which ran into six editions between 1623 and 1635. This work took its place in a tradition of protestant and puritan writing about conscience which can be traced back to the works of Richard Greenham and William Perkins in the reign of Elizabeth. Like that of other ministers of his time Dyke's work tended towards the more exhaustive, academic, and analytical style of Perkins while retaining the sense of pastoral urgency to be found in both Greenham and Perkins. His concern for plainness in preaching and writing was explicitly articulated in a sermon reflecting on the contemporary ministry published as A Caveat for Archippus (1619): Dyke noted in this that 'some affect such craggie scholasticall disquisitions, as are fitter for the Chaire then for the Pulpit' and that 'our language is now grown so learned, that a man may Clerum in English, and may so speake his own language, that he may be a barbarian to the men of his own language' (pp. 22–3). As well as his own works Dyke was also instrumental in the publication of those of his brother Daniel, author of the influential Mystery of Self-Deceiving (1614).

There is little direct evidence of Dyke's attitude to the controversies surrounding church ceremonial and doctrine which were current during his career. Epping was subject solely to the authority of the bishop of London, and given that throughout his time there Dyke seems to have escaped suspension, some degree of conformity in ceremonies must be assumed. His most explicit statement on such matters was made on 5 April 1628 in A Sermon Preached at the Publicke Fast. to the Commons House of Parliament (1628), where he noted a series of ominous signs of recent years such as a comet, heavy tides, and an earthquake. The most significant sign of all was the discovery of a copy of John Frith's Preparation to the Crosse in the belly of a fish in Cambridge. For Dyke all this added up to the likelihood that God was about to strike a sinful nation, and he was clear as to the main sources of this newly virulent sinfulness: 'so we may see the goings of God … What else meanes the spread, and growth of Popery and Idolatry? What else means the departure of our old Truth in the increase of Arminianisme?' (J. Dyke, A Sermon Preached at the Publicke Fast, 1628, 25). His sermon earned him the gift of a silver tankard from the House of Commons.

In November 1629 Dyke was among the forty-nine Essex ministers who signed a petition to Bishop William Laud of London on behalf of Thomas Hooker, lecturer at Chelmsford, who had been brought before the Star Chamber on charges of nonconformity. It is probable that he observed the ecclesiastical changes of the 1630s with great discomfort, even if he did not choose to take a stand that might result in the loss of his ministry. His 1636 treatise concerning the Lord's supper, The Worthy Communicant, is entirely unmarked by the ceremonial emphasis of Laud and his supporters, concentrating instead on the place of the sacrament in the spiritual development of the communicant in faith and repentance, a focus which once again owed much to earlier divines of a puritan hue like Greenham, John Dod, and Robert Cleaver.

His first wife having died, on 12 February 1637 Dyke married Joyce Fenner. He died in 1639 and was buried in Epping on 9 April 1639. Several of his works were subsequently brought to press by his sons. One such piece, The Right Receiving and Rooting in Christ (1640), contains a warm tribute from Jeremiah Dyke the younger to his father, commending his 'indefatigabilitie in his labours', his 'inoffensive life', and a preaching manner which took pains 'that always mens sinnes, not their persons, were the objects of his hottest thunder-bolts' (A12r–v).

JASON YIANNIKKOU

Sources Two sermons preached in 1622 and 1628, by the Rev. Jeremiah Dyke, ed. B. Winstone (1896) • T. W. Davids, Annals of evangelical nonconformity in Essex (1863), 108, 157 • Venn, Alum. Cant. • IGI • T. Webster, Godly clergy in early Stuart England: the Caroline puritan movement,

c.1620–1643 (1997) • W. Hunt, *The puritan moment: the coming of revolution in an English county* (1983)
Wealth at death £560; plus goods: *Two sermons*, ed. Winstone

Dyke, William (*d.* 1608). *See under* Dyke, Daniel (*d.* 1614).

Dyke, Sir William Hart, seventh baronet (1837–1931), politician, was born at East Hall, Orpington, Kent, on 7 August 1837, the second son of Sir Percyvall Hart Dyke, sixth baronet (*d.* 1875), of Lullingstone Castle, Eynsford, Kent, and his wife, Elizabeth, youngest daughter of John Wells of Bickley Park, Kent, tory MP for Maidstone (1820–30), and niece of William *Wells (1768–1847). He was educated at Harrow School and Christ Church, Oxford, where he graduated MA in 1864.

At Oxford Dyke (or Hart Dyke, as he was often known) was the most famous rackets player of his day. He played for four years against Cambridge, and won every match, both doubles and singles. In 1862, at Woolwich, he easily beat Francis Erwood, the professional and holder of the world championship. To him was due the starting of the public schools' rackets championship. He was very fond of real tennis and kept up the game at Prince's Club, Knightsbridge, until he was well past his seventieth year. 'Though never quite first class … [he] was a good player of attractive style' (Noel and Clark, 1.26). He was also one of the originators of lawn tennis. In 1873, a year before Major W. C. Wingfield took out a patent for 'Sphairistike', Dyke and two friends laid out a court at Lullingstone Castle and played one of the early recorded games (though the credit for the game's origination lies with Wingfield).

Although Dyke wished to enter the navy, he acquiesced in his father's desire that he should go into parliament. He was elected Conservative member for West Kent in 1865 and represented Mid Kent from 1868 to 1885. Before the general election of 1885 he was candidate for the Medway division, regarded as a safe seat, but he was asked to contest the Dartford division, considered a probable Liberal seat, and was returned at the head of the poll; and he sat for Dartford until the Liberal revival of 1906, when he was defeated and retired from parliament into private life. In 1868 he was appointed a whip and in 1874 he was promoted to be chief whip as patronage secretary to the Treasury. In this capacity, known as Billy Dyke, he had to manage the delicate balance between the powers of the whips' office and the influence of the National Union of Conservative Associations. Though there were clashes with John Gorst, Dyke maintained party equanimity. He was sworn of the privy council in 1880.

In Salisbury's minority government of 1885–8, Dyke was appointed chief secretary for Ireland and sworn of the Irish privy council. He made little impression on Irish affairs, the Land Purchase Act of 1885 being the work chiefly of lords Ashbourne and Carnarvon. On 16 January 1886 Dyke resigned as Irish secretary, for no clear reason (Cooke and Vincent, 303). He was not immediately a member of Salisbury's next government, but was appointed vice-president of the committee of council on education (1887–92). He established a reputation as an efficient and conscientious administrator and was partly responsible

for the code of 1890 which was the first step in the abolition of the system of 'payment by results'. During its passage through the House of Commons he was in charge of the Free Education Bill in 1891. He did not return to office with the tories in 1895.

Dyke, who succeeded his father as baronet in 1875, spent practically his whole life in Kent, being alderman of the county council as well as deputy lieutenant. He married in 1870 Lady Emily Caroline (*d.* 1931), elder daughter of John William Montagu, seventh earl of Sandwich. They had three sons, the two elder of whom predeceased their father, the second in infancy, and three daughters. Dyke died at his seat, Lullingstone Castle, on 3 July 1931 in his ninety-fourth year, and was succeeded by his youngest son, Oliver Hamilton Augustus (1885–1969). His wife died on 8 August the same year.

E. I. CARLYLE, *rev.* H. C. G. MATTHEW

Sources *The Times* (4 July 1931) • R. Shannon, *The age of Disraeli, 1868–1881: the rise of tory democracy* (1992) • A. B. Cooke and J. Vincent, *The governing passion: cabinet government and party politics in Britain, 1885–86* (1974) • G. Sutherland, *Policy-making in elementary education, 1870–1895* (1973) • E. B. Noel and J. O. M. Clark, *A history of tennis*, 2 vols. (1924) • private information (2004) • Burke, *Peerage* (1999)
Archives Bodl. Oxf., corresp. with Benjamin Disraeli • CKS, letters to Aretas Akers-Douglas • Mitchell L., Glas., Glasgow City Archives, letters to Sir William Stirling-Maxwell • Mitchell L., Glas., Strathclyde Regional Archives, Stirling MSS • W. Yorks. AS, Leeds, letters to Rowland Winn
Likenesses Ape [C. Pellegrini], caricature, chromolithograph, NPG; repro. in *VF* (4 Sept 1875) • G. W. Baldrey, oils, Hughenden, Buckinghamshire • Maull & Fox, photograph, NPG; repro. in *Our conservative and unionist statesmen*, 2 (1896–7) • wood-engraving, NPG; repro. in *ILN* (7 Dec 1867)
Wealth at death £79,112 5*s.* 9*d.*: probate, 1 Oct 1931, *CGPLA Eng. & Wales* • £100,000: further grant, 8 Dec 1931, *CGPLA Eng. & Wales*

Dyke [*née* Bond], **(Millicent) Zoë, Lady Dyke** (1896–1975), pioneer of British sericulture, was born on 6 February 1896 at 9 Manor Road, Leyton, Essex, the daughter of Barnabas Mayston Bond, medical practitioner, and his wife, Eliza Josephine Luxon. She was the youngest of four children. The family moved to Westwood, Poole, Dorset, where at the age of four Zoë developed a passion for keeping silkworms, an activity that she continued despite a subsequent move to Brook Green, Hammersmith, London. She attended a succession of local schools before entering St Paul's Girls' School. In 1912 she went to the Collège des jeunes filles, Saumur, France, but immediately before the First World War she returned to London to work for an insurance company. In response to her mother's illness her parents moved after the war to France, leaving Zoë to live on her own in London.

On 29 July 1922 Zoë Bond married Oliver Hamilton Augustus Hart Dyke (1885–1969). He was a modest, rather self-effacing man, in contrast to his charismatic father, Sir William Hart *Dyke (*d.* 1931), a noted Victorian politician involved in drawing up the rules of lawn tennis. Unlike most members of the aristocracy Oliver Dyke had pursued a profession, qualifying as an engineer. His family's ancestral home was Lullingstone Castle, Eynsford, Kent, a property mentioned in the Domesday Book and owned by the Hart family since 1351. When the Hart family died out, in 1738 Dame Anne Hart married Sir Thomas Dyke, of Horeham, and established the tradition that all males received the forename Hart.

Zoë and Oliver Dyke had three children: Derek, William, and Rosemary. Following the death of his father in 1931 Oliver Dyke succeeded to the title of eighth baronet, of Horeham, Sussex, and to the estate. Zoë's revived interest in sericulture led to silkworms being produced in the attic at Lullingstone, with a reeling machine made by her husband separating the filatures. Their activities rapidly became famous, and Queen Mary made an official visit to their silk farm on 25 June 1936. By this time Zoë was a leading expert on the British silk industry, organizing talks and demonstrations of the latest developments in silkworm production that were taking place at Lullingstone Castle. As a result she was awarded a silver medal by the Royal Society of Arts.

During the Second World War Lullingstone was requisitioned by the services and turned into a decoy fighter station, which necessitated the construction of underground shelters. With her spinning activities in abeyance Zoë concentrated on breeding for stock purposes only, and helped to run a small market garden while her husband resumed his career as a mechanical engineer, working for Vickers Armstrong, Dartford, before becoming works manager at Heston Aircraft Company, Slough. Their marriage was dissolved in 1944. In the following year Oliver Dyke married Mildred Turnor Berens, widow of Cecil Berens, and daughter of James Blackwood. At the end of the war silk production was resumed at Lullingstone with the establishment of a limited company in 1946, of which Oliver Dyke was for a few months a director. He then moved to London to run a small machine shop, before selling it and relocating to Hampshire.

Lullingstone Silk Farm rapidly regained its pre-war position as a Mecca for leading experts of Britain's silk industry and students of sericulture from all over the world, including thousands of eager children and countless foreign visitors. In 1949 Zoë's book *So Spins the Silkworm* was published. Dedicated to Queen Mary, who had shown a keen personal interest in the silk enterprise with its royal and ancient history, it contains autobiographical reminiscences together with a detailed account of the history of silk and the development of the silk farm at Lullingstone. The text omits any reference to the Dykes' divorce, merely pointing out that Sir Oliver continued to assist with the company until other work led to his resignation in 1946. Zoë also published *Silk Farm* (1948?), a book intended for children, with drawings illustrating the rearing of silkworms and the reeling of silk at Lullingstone Castle. The publication of these texts heralded the high point of her popularity and reputation as the silk empress of Britain, and Lullingstone silk was used for the coronation robes of Elizabeth II.

In 1952 Sir Oliver and Mildred moved back to the Bothy Cottage at Lullingstone before taking up residence at the castle in 1956. Zoë moved the business to Ayot House, Ayot St Lawrence, Hertfordshire, but it was a mere shadow of the large, internationally famous and commercial concern that she had run at Lullingstone. Her former husband and his wife devoted their energies to restoring the castle to its former glory; he developed it as a tourist attraction in its own right, while playing down its earlier association with the silk industry. Zoë eventually relinquished her business activities in Hertfordshire and returned to Kent, where illness compelled her to move to Kimberley Nursing Home, Herne Bay. She became a prolific reader, borrowing as many as eight books from the library at any one time. She died at the nursing home on 12 February 1975.

JOHN MARTIN

Sources M. Dyke, *So spins the silkworm* (1949) • *WWW* [Sir Oliver Hamilton Augustus Hart Dyke] • Burke, *Peerage* • *The Times* (10 July 1969); (14 Feb 1975), 18h • *Sevenoaks Chronicle* (20 Feb 1975) • *Dartford Chronicle* (18 July 1969); (1 Aug 1969); (20 Feb 1975) • b. cert. • m. cert. • d. cert.
Likenesses A. Beauchamp, photograph, repro. in Dyke, *So spins the silkworm*, pl. II • photograph (aged six), repro. in Dyke, *So spins the silkworm*, facing p. 6 • photograph, repro. in Dyke, *So spins the silkworm*, facing p. 121
Wealth at death £2690: probate, 15 May 1975, *CGPLA Eng. & Wales*

Dykes, John Bacchus (1823–1876), composer and Church of England clergyman, was born on 10 March 1823 at Kingston upon Hull, the son of William Hey Dykes, banker, of Hull, and grandson of the Revd Thomas *Dykes, incumbent of St John's Church, Hull. His appreciation of music was evident from an early age: when ten years old he played the organ in his grandfather's church. Shortly after 1840 his father moved to Wakefield, where Dykes attended the proprietary school until October 1843, when he entered St Catharine's College, Cambridge. There he distinguished himself as an amateur musician; together with William Thomson he founded the University Musical Society, and at early concerts his performances of comic songs were a popular feature. He graduated senior optime in January 1847, and in the same year was ordained deacon to the curacy of Malton, Yorkshire. In 1849 he was appointed minor canon and then precentor of Durham Cathedral. The University of Durham conferred on him the honorary DMus degree in 1861. On 25 July 1850 he married Susannah Thomlinson Kingston, daughter of George Kingston; they had two sons and four daughters.

In 1862 Dykes was appointed vicar of St Oswald's, Durham. During his fourteen years there his engaging personality and pastoral devotion won him great influence, but his high-churchmanship involved him in prolonged and trying disputes with his low-church bishop. Dykes needed two curates for the work of his parish, but the bishop refused to license them unless a pledge was given that they would not wear coloured stoles, burn incense, or turn their backs on the congregation during the celebration of communion. Dykes refused to give such a pledge, and appealed to the court of the queen's bench for a mandamus requiring the bishop to issue his licence without any such special declaration; in the end he lost the case, and was left to deal with the large parish on his own. The stress was too great for him: his mental and physical health broke down and he suffered some kind of stroke in 1874. Though at times he rallied, he never regained his strength and died at Ticehurst, Sussex, on 22 January 1876. He was buried in the churchyard of St Oswald's on 28 January. His wife and six children were left almost unprovided for, but the bishop of Durham inaugurated a memorial fund which raised £10,000.

While Dykes was distinguished as a preacher and writer on liturgics, he is best known for his hymn tunes, most of which appeared in *Hymns Ancient and Modern* (1861) and Chope's *Congregational Hymn and Tune Book* (1862); many of his tunes were still popular more than a century later. He had an extraordinary facility for mirroring natural musical speech through rhythmically repeated notes and rising accompaniment—a technique derived from opera. He was also fond of naming tunes after notable persons and places in northern England, such as 'Rivaulx', 'St Aelred', 'St Oswald', and 'St Godric'. He wrote nearly 300 hymn tunes, as well as services and anthems.

W. B. SQUIRE, rev. LEON LITVACK

Sources J. T. Fowler, *Life and letters of John Bacchus Dykes* (1897) · E. Routley, 'Victorian hymn composers II: John Bacchus Dykes, 1823–1876', *Hymn Society Bulletin*, 44 (July 1948), 1–8; 46 (Jan 1949), 71–5 · A. Hutchings, 'J. B. Dykes: amateur or professional?', *Hymn Society Bulletin*, 138 (Jan 1977), 209–15 · M. Frost, ed., *Historical companion to 'Hymns ancient and modern'* (1962) · J. I. Jones and others, *The Baptist hymn book companion*, ed. H. Martin (1962) · J. Moffatt and M. Patrick, eds., *Handbook to the church hymnary, with supplement*, 2nd edn (1935) · K. L. Parry, ed., *Companion to 'Congregational praise'* (1953) · [J. B. Dykes], 'In memoriam J. B. Dykes', *Literary Churchman*, 22 (1876), 63–6; pubd separately (1876) · m. cert.
Likenesses photograph, Hymns Ancient and Modern Ltd, St Mary's Works, St Mary's Plain, Norwich · process block print, BM
Wealth at death under £1000: administration, 21 Feb 1876, CGPLA Eng. & Wales

Dykes, Thomas (1761–1847), Church of England clergyman, was born on 21 December 1761 at Ipswich, the son of Philip Dykes, a merchant, and his wife, Mary Jarvis. After attending a boarding-school at a village in the neighbourhood he entered his father's business. An illness, however, led him to turn his mind to religion. After taking the advice of the Revd Joseph Milner of Hull he entered Magdalene College, Cambridge, as a fellow commoner in 1785, and graduated in 1788. He was ordained the same year, and became curate of Cottingham, near Hull. On 13 March 1789 he married Mary, the daughter of William Hey, a well-known surgeon of Leeds. They had three children: two sons and a daughter. In October 1789 Dykes became curate of Barwick in Elmet. However, he was now bent upon supplying the want of churches in Hull by building a new church at his own cost in the parish of the Holy Trinity. In spite of the opposition of the corporation, who were the patrons of the living, he obtained the sanction of the archbishop of York. The new church, St John's, opened in 1792 with Dykes as the first incumbent. Though a popular preacher he never realized from his pew rents the amount invested in the building; the deficiency, over £500, was eventually raised by private subscription. Two hundred

sittings were added to the church in 1803, and the steeple was built at the same time.

Dykes was an active and vigorous evangelical clergyman who exerted over a long period considerable influence in Hull. It was chiefly through his exertions that the female prison was built in 1812. His greatest aim, however, was to increase the number of churches in the town. Christ's Church, founded in 1821, and St James's Church, founded in 1829, were offshoots of St John's. Dykes promoted the erection of the Mariners' church as well as St Stephen's and St Paul's, and supported the enlargement of Drypool church. In 1833 Dykes became master of the Charterhouse at Hull, and took up residence there. In the following year he was presented to the vicarage of North Ferriby, where he engaged a curate to perform the duties. Dykes continued to discharge his duties at St John's until about eighteen months before his death on 23 August 1847 at Newland, Hull. He was buried in the vault under St John's Church.

During his long ministry Dykes had followed in the footsteps of Joseph Milner, who had laid the foundations of the evangelical revival in Hull. Dykes was a moderate Calvinist; his sermons were characteristically moving and persuasive. He was a tory in politics and emphatically opposed Catholic emancipation. Dykes published several occasional sermons, and a further selection of his sermons was published posthumously.

L. C. SANDERS, rev. I. T. FOSTER

Sources J. King, *Memoir of the Rev. Thomas Dykes, LLB, incumbent of St John's Church, Hull: with copious extracts from his correspondence* (1849) · *Christian Observer* (1848), 211–13, 346–53 · *GM*, 2nd ser., 28 (1847), 545–6 · Venn, *Alum. Cant.* · *Record* (30 Aug 1847) · T. Dykes, correspondence, Hull Central Library · R. V. Taylor, ed., *The biographia Leodiensis, or, Biographical sketches of the worthies of Leeds* (1865) · private information (2004) [archivist, Ipswich Central Library]
Likenesses W. D. Keyworth, bust, 1840, St John's Church, Hull · R. J. Lane, lithograph, 1847, NPG

Dymock, Cressy (*fl.* 1629–1660), agriculturist, was possibly the son of Sir Thomas Dymocke, from the Lincolnshire/Nottinghamshire borders, but little is known of his background. He entered Gray's Inn on 3 August 1629. Surviving poetry in the British Library suggests a ready pen and naïve wit. Dymock attributed his commitment to agrarian reform to Samuel Hartlib, whom he met about 1648. In the early 1650s he became one of Hartlib's most loyal admirers, promoting machines for setting corn and grinding, rabbit-farming schemes, and intensive husbandry, mostly known only through Hartlib's papers. He appreciated the weaknesses of contemporary agrarian production and tackled them with mechanical and other innovations. He understood that intensive husbandry involved a planned farming environment. His layout of an ideal farm, which Hartlib published as *A Discoverie for … Setting Out of Land* (1653), deplored the 'Want of Enclosure'. At the same time, Dymock was particularly proud of his 'universal engine', the 'wedding of strength and tyme' which was advertised in print in 1651. Dymock also contributed to Hartlib's other agrarian publications.

Dymock was not a landowner and finding a suitable

location and backers for his schemes proved problematic—the nearest he came to success was in 1653 at Wadworth, near Doncaster, on a cousin's farm. His mechanical drill and roller worked well but the labourers proved 'extremely Churlish', a problem he had anticipated in his proposed 'Colledge of Husbandrye', reflecting the utilitarian educational notions of Hartlib's circle. By the Restoration, however, Dymock was poor. His claim 'to the office of [king's] Champion' in the forthcoming coronation (an office to which he believed his family had ancient rights) was disappointed and he apparently died shortly thereafter.   M. GREENGRASS

Sources *The Hartlib papers*, ed. J. Crawford and others (1995) [CD-ROM] · [C. Dymock], *An invention of engines of motion …* (1651) · [C. Dymock], *An essay for the advancement of husbandry-learning …* (1651) · [C. Dymock], *The reformed husband-man …* (1651) · [C. Dymock], *A discoverie for division or setting out of land …* (1653) · C. Webster, *The great instauration: science, medicine and reform, 1626–1660* (1975) · J. Thirsk, 'Plough and pen: agricultural writers in the seventeenth century', *Social relations and ideas: essays in honour of R H Hilton*, ed. T. H. Aston and others (1983), 295–318 · H. Dircks, *Hartlib* (1865) · Foster, *Alum. Oxon.*

Archives BL, Egerton MS 2623 · University of Sheffield, Hartlib MSS

Wealth at death in poverty; 'having sold and pawn'd all things that would yield money … the last went for 10s which being gone, I knewe not how to support or supply my selfe': University of Sheffield, Hartlib MSS, HP 65/22/4A Dymock-Hartlib

Dymock, Roger. *See* Dymoke, Roger (*fl.* 1370–*c.*1400).

Dymocke [Dymock], **James** (*d.* 1718×25), Roman Catholic priest, was the younger son of a collateral branch of the Dymocke family of Scrivelsby, Lincolnshire. Having been sent abroad as a youth he was educated and ordained, possibly at the English College at Lisbon, and completed his studies at the English seminary in Paris. From there he returned to England as a missionary priest, slipping back into the country at some point in the 1660s and serving as the chaplain to the duke of Norfolk's household. It was to the duke and his family that Dymocke dedicated his first published work, *Le vice ridiculé* (1671), which attempted to provide a guide for Roman Catholics to a seemly and a charitable life, while highlighting the dangers which might befall everyone from soldiers and sailors to the poor and the young. Astrologers, usurers, libertines, and swaggering 'gallants' came under particular censure from his pen.

Dymocke had close connections with the Portuguese embassy in London, seeking refuge there in times of trouble and making use of it in order to smuggle books and correspondence in and out of the country. He enjoyed the patronage and friendship of the ambassador, Don Francisco De Millo, and it is possible that he even served as his personal chaplain during the mid-1670s. In 1676 his most significant work, *The Great Sacrifice of the New Law, Expounded by the Figures of the Old*, was privately published and became an instant best-seller, running through eight editions in only eleven years. The book provided a comprehensive English translation of the mass and vigorously defended the doctrine of transubstantiation. By the time it had reached its eighth edition in 1687, *The Great Sacrifice* was being sold openly on the streets of London and had been thoroughly revised and expanded in order to include the mass for the dead. Taking advantage of the fresh climate of religious toleration and royal favour shown to Roman Catholics following the accession of James II, Dymocke's activities became far less covert in the mid-1680s. In 1686 the secular clergy had acquired the use of the Fishmongers' Hall in Lime Street, London, and set about converting the building into a chapel at very considerable expense. The Revd Andrew Giffard (alias Jonathan Cole) took charge of the new mission and Dymocke was appointed as his assistant. A third priest, the Revd Christopher Tootell, joined them shortly afterwards. Unfortunately, a power struggle took place between the conflicting groups of religious and secular Catholic priests gathered around the court at Whitehall, and within six months of its opening the chapel was removed from the charge of Giffard and Dymocke and entrusted instead to Robert Petre and the Society of Jesus. Dymocke was removed to another mission but the revolution of 1688–9, and the enormous popular backlash against Catholicism which followed in its wake, caused him to flee for his life from the City mobs and to seek refuge in exile in France.

Controversy surrounds Dymocke's later life. Dodd, in his standard history, tells us that Dymocke was 'afterwards … made prior of St. Arnoul, near Chartres … with another small benefice' (Dodd, 3.481). However, this is not possible. There was no priory of that name near Chartres and no evidence that Dymocke ever took monastic orders. Moreover, his holding of a benefice would be entirely incompatible with such a position. What does seem likely is that he retired to one of the monasteries close to the village of St Arnoul-des-Bois which lie some 16–17 kilometres from Chartres, and received the courtesy title of prior under a grant from the French crown. This was almost certainly obtained through the influence of James II and Mary of Modena, and would have done much to supplement his small existing benefice, enabling him to live out his last years with a measure of security and comfort. Dodd (whose real name was Hugh Tootell) recalled that Dymocke 'was still alive in 1718, a very old man' (Dodd, 3.481), while Dodd's uncle, Christopher Tootell, writing in the spring of 1725, sadly noted that he himself was now the last survivor of the three secular priests who had officiated at the Lime Street Chapel (Shipley, vii). Therefore, it is certain that Dymocke passed away—in relative obscurity—at some unknown point between 1718 and the early months of 1725. He was remembered as a lively individual, 'a person of great reading and curiosity' (Dodd, 3.481), and left behind him—in addition to his other works—a geographical history and a manuscript edition of a miscellaneous dictionary, neither of which appears to be still extant.   JOHN CALLOW

Sources J. D. [J. Dymock], *The great sacrifice of the new law, expounded by the figures of the old* (1676); 4th edn (1685); rev. 8th edn (1687); ed. O. Shipley (1890) · C. Dodd [H. Tootell], *The church history*

of England, from the year 1500, to the year 1688, 3 (1742) • J. Dymock, *Le vice ridiculé* (Louvain, 1671) • Gillow, *Lit. biog. hist.*, vol. 2 • G. Anstruther, *The seminary priests*, 3 (1976) • J. Bossy, *The English Catholic community, 1570–1850* (1975) • O. Shipley, preface, in J. D. [J. Dymock], *The great sacrifice*, ed. O. Shipley (1890)

Archives Hunt. L., MS vol. on nature, arts, and sciences

Dymoke [Dymmok] **family** (*per. c.*1340–*c.*1580), king's champions, claimed their right to that office through their tenure of Scrivelsby, Lincolnshire. The family's first successful claimant was **Sir John** [ii] **Dymoke** (*d.* 1381), son of John [i] Dymoke and Felicia Harevill. He married Margaret, daughter of Thomas Ludlow, who inherited Scrivelsby from her grandmother Joan, the youngest daughter of Philip Marmion.

In 1355 Dymoke was pardoned at the request of Edward, the Black Prince, for receiving John Ludlow, indicted for two deaths. A member of John of Gaunt's Lancastrian affinity from at least 1369, he was paid an annuity of 20 marks in 1370–72. Sir John was appointed to peace commissions in 1364, 1368, 1371, 1375, and 1377 and represented Lincolnshire in the parliaments of 1372, 1373, and 1377. Dymoke served on commissions of oyer and terminer, array, and walls and ditches within the county and he (or his father) was briefly escheator for Lincolnshire, Northamptonshire, and Rutland from January to November 1341. In 1376 during a two-year term as escheator for Lincolnshire (1375–7) he took legal action through an oyer and terminer commission against those who, he alleged, had assaulted him and tried to prevent him from exercising his duties.

Sir John asserted the right to act as king's champion before the coronation of Richard II in 1377. A rival claimant, Baldwin Freville, however, alleged the right to perform the same service through his tenure of Tamworth Castle. The respective positions were based on claims initiated at Edward III's coronation in 1327 and devolved from the property ownership of a common ancestor, Philip *Marmion (*d.* 1291). There is no direct evidence, though, that Marmion had performed the service himself or was a descendant of the champions to the dukes of Normandy, nor that Scrivelsby or Tamworth were linked to champion service. Nevertheless, in 1327 Henry Hillary, then tenant of Scrivelsby and second husband of Marmion's youngest daughter, claimed that the manor was held by grand serjeanty directly from the king and that the tenant had the duty on coronation day of providing a well-armed knight on horseback to prove in combat, if necessary, that the king crowned on that day was the true and rightful heir of the kingdom. Hillary's claim was challenged by Alexander Freville, whose wife, one of Marmion's granddaughters, had inherited Tamworth. In the event, Edward III declined both offers, but Hillary, who petitioned that his proffer be recorded and consideration taken of his expenses, was granted his fee.

The parties' contentions of 1377 were duly placed before the court of claims. On the basis of better records and evidence, the lord steward, the duke of Lancaster, found in favour of Dymoke. Edward III and the Black Prince were also said to have frequently asserted Dymoke's right. Baldwin Freville was given the opportunity of a further hearing if within a time limit set by the court he could provide the necessary evidence. In default of his appearance he would be forever excluded and Dymoke would perform in the right of his wife. Freville failed to appear at the appointed time. The Frevilles resurrected their claim for the coronation of Henry IV, but the court was not convinced.

Sir John died about April 1381. Margaret presented their son Thomas [i] Dymoke (*d.* 1422) to act as champion in 1399, though Henry IV was supposedly overheard to say, 'If need be, Sir Thomas, I shall personally relieve you of this task' (*Chronicle of Adam Usk*, 73). Sir Thomas also performed the service at Henry V's coronation, and his son, Sir Philip Dymoke (*d.* 1455), at that of Henry VI.

Sir Thomas [ii] **Dymoke** (*d.* 1470), the son of Sir Philip, married Margaret, daughter and coheir of Leo *Welles, Baron Welles (*c.*1406–1461). Thomas [ii] was knighted at the battle of Northampton on 9 July 1460 and later acted as champion at the coronation of Edward IV. In December 1461 he was granted for the life of Elizabeth, wife of William Tailboys, a third of all the manors and lands of which that rebel was seised. Three months later Dymoke (with John Denham and Thomas Burgh) received a further grant for the life of the same Elizabeth of lands in Lincolnshire and Durham. Sir Thomas [ii] was appointed to the peace commission in Lindsey in 1463 and 1467. During the unsettled period marking the Wars of the Roses, he became embroiled in a competition for local dominance between his brother-in-law, Richard *Welles, Lord Welles [see under Welles, Leo], and Thomas Burgh, Edward IV's master of horse. In this private feud Burgh's manor at Gainsborough was attacked and destroyed, causing the king to summon the ringleaders to appear before him at Westminster in March 1470. Dymoke and Welles dutifully obeyed, but were sent on to Huntingdon where Edward had marched as a result of a fresh outbreak of violence. The leader of the new rebellion appeared to be Welles's son, Robert, who was hailed as the 'great captain of the commons of Lincolnshire'. Dymoke and Welles were pardoned on 6 March, but Welles was forced to demand his son's immediate submission to the king's forces under threat that Dymoke and he would be put to death. The exhortation obviously failed as both men were summarily executed at Stamford on 12 March. On 25 April 1470 an order was issued to seize all the lands and possessions of the rebels. If Sir Thomas was identical with the Thomas Dymoke of Horncastle, merchant, to whom a pardon was granted four months later, hopes of remission were dashed when the political tide turned again, for in December 1471 Scrivelsby, Horncastle, and the other Dymoke estates were granted to Richard, duke of Gloucester.

Sir Robert [i] **Dymoke** (*c.*1461–1545), Sir Thomas [ii]'s heir, married Anne, daughter of John Sparrow of London. Robert's eventful minority included in May 1471 an order to arrest him and his mother. The following year his custody and wardship were entrusted to Robert Radcliffe. Dymoke was given licence to inherit his father's lands and those of Robert Waterton in 1482. Account of the former (which in addition to Scrivelsby included the Lincolnshire manors of Coningsby, Thornton, Donington, and Horncastle among others) was to be rendered after an inquiry in 1483 into the possessions of named rebels. In 1485 he requested an exemplification that any act of forfeiture should not extend to Waterton's lands.

Dymoke was knighted on 5 July 1483 before Richard III's coronation, at which he first performed his duties as king's champion. It is recorded that at the second course of the banquet Dymoke rode into the hall and proclaimed that he would fight anyone who dared to say that Richard was not the lawful king. The whole hall was silent, but Dymoke having thrown down his gauntlet, the company cried out 'King Richard'. This happened three times. Sir Robert was then brought a cup of wine covered and when he had drunk, he cast out the remaining wine and departed with the cup (BL, Add. MS 6113, fol. 22). He later acted as champion at the coronations of Henry VII (1485) and Henry VIII (1509).

Sir Robert [i] Dymoke was appointed sheriff of Lincolnshire in 1484, 1502, and 1509 and became mayor of Boston in 1520. From 1486 he served on many administrative and judicial commissions within the county including peace commissions for Lindsey (1486–1507, 1520–32, and 1539). He was made a banneret in 1512 and served as treasurer of the rearward in Henry VIII's invasion of France in 1513. Henry appointed him treasurer of the captured city of Tournai, a post he occupied until 1515. In 1522 Dymoke provided the sum of £200 towards the king's expenses for regaining the French crown. For at least eight years (1527–35) he was chancellor to the queen's household, though he is also described as Katherine of Aragon's 'almoner and receiver' and 'queen's chamberlain' under Anne Boleyn. During the Lincolnshire rebellion of 1536 the rebels came to fetch Sir Robert from Scrivelsby together with his sons Edward, the current sheriff, and Arthur. Although a banner depicting the family arms was used at the rebels' head, the family's conduct, like that of the other leading gentry caught up in the revolt, attracted suspicion but no punishment from the king.

Sir Robert died on 15 April 1545. His will dated 1543 desired his son Edward [i] to appoint two discreet and honest priests and one poor man for five years to say mass daily in the church at Scrivelsby and pray for the souls of Robert, his wife, and his parents.

Sir Edward [i] Dymoke (d. 1567), who married Anne, daughter of George Tailboys, Baron Kyme, was the champion at the coronations of Edward VI, Mary, and Elizabeth. His son, **Robert** [ii] **Dymoke** (d. 1580), married Bridget, daughter of Edward Fiennes de *Clinton, first earl of Lincoln (1512–1585), and of Elizabeth *Blount, and had at least four sons, Edward [ii], Robert [iii], Nicholas, and Tailboys *Dymoke. Robert [ii], who suffered from a paralysis in later life, may have died in prison as a result of his unyielding recusancy. He was buried at Scrivelsby on 26 September 1580.   A. J. MUSSON

Sources *Chancery records* · GEC, *Peerage*, new edn, vol. 8 · S. Lodge, *Scrivelsby, home of the champions* (1893) · A. F. Sutton and P. W. Hammond, eds., *The coronation of Richard III: the extant documents* (1983) · L. G. W. Legg, *English coronation records* (1925) · J. H. Round, *King's serjeants and officers of state* (1937) · J. G. Nicholls, ed., 'Chronicle of the rebellion in Lincolnshire, 1470', *Camden miscellany, I*, CS, 39 (1847) [Sir Thomas Dymoke] · R. L. Storey, 'Lincolnshire and the Wars of the Roses', *Nottingham Medieval Studies*, 14 (1970), 64–83 · HoP, *Commons, 1509–58*, vol. 2 · S. J. Gunn, 'Peers, commons and gentry in the Lincolnshire revolt of 1536', *Past and Present*, 123 (1989) · S. Walker, *The Lancastrian affinity, 1361–1399* (1990) · C. G. Cruickshank, *The English occupation of Tournai, 1513–1516* (1971) · R. Challoner, *Memoirs of missionary priests*, ed. J. H. Pollen, rev. edn (1924) · W. C. Metcalf, *A book of knights, Henry VI–Charles II* (1885) · C. F. R. Palmer, *History of the baronial family of Marmion* (1875) · *The chronicle of Adam Usk, 1377–1421*, ed. and trans. C. Given-Wilson, OMT (1997) · A. Hughes, *List of sheriffs for England and Wales: from the earliest times to AD 1831*, PRO (1898) · A. C. Wood, *List of escheators for England and Wales* (1971) [from typescript at the PRO, 1932 and 1949] · *Return of … members of parliament, 1213–1876* (1878), vol. 1
Archives armour in royal collections

Dymoke, Sir Henry, baronet (1801–1865), king's champion, eldest son of John Dymoke (1764–1828), rector of Scrivelsby and prebendary of Lincoln, and his wife, Amelia Jane Alice, *née* Elphinston (d. 1856), was born on 5 March 1801 at Scrivelsby, Lincolnshire. He was distinguished solely by representing his father (who deemed the office incompatible with that of a clergyman) as hereditary king's champion at the banquet in Westminster Hall following the coronation of George IV on 19 July 1821, the last occasion on which the champion appeared. He was created a baronet in 1841 as recompense for the champion being dispensed with at subsequent coronations.

Dymoke married, on 14 January 1823, Emma (d. 1884), second daughter of William Pearce of Weasenham Hall, Norfolk, and they had an only daughter. He died at 8 Portman Square, London, on 28 April 1865, when the baronetcy became extinct; Scrivelsby passed to his brother.

K. D. REYNOLDS

Sources Burke, *Gen. GB* (1914) · Boase, *Mod. Eng. biog.* · *DNB* · M. Girouard, *The return to Camelot: chivalry and the English gentleman* (1981)
Likenesses portrait (as champion at George IV's banquet), repro. in C. Lloyd, *The Royal Collection* (1992)
Wealth at death under £18,000: resworn double probate, Sept 1865, *CGPLA Eng. & Wales*

Dymoke, Sir John (d. 1381). See under Dymoke family (*per. c.*1340–*c.*1580).

Dymoke, Sir Robert (*c.*1461–1545). See under Dymoke family (*per. c.*1340–*c.*1580).

Dymoke, Robert (d. 1580). See under Dymoke family (*per. c.*1340–*c.*1580).

Dymoke [Dymock], **Roger** (*fl.* 1370–*c.*1400), prior of Boston and theologian, was the son of Sir John Dymoke of Scrivelsby, Lindsey, Lincolnshire, and Margaret, daughter of Sir Thomas Ludlow and widow of Sir Henry Hilary. By September 1370 he was a friar of the Chelmsford Dominican convent, moving to the Langley convent in December of the same year. By 1379 he was prior of the Boston convent, as is clear from the inquiry into a break-in at the house that year. At some point he studied at Oxford, and by 1396 was doctor of theology; in the same year he was regent at the London convent. He preached before Richard II on Whitsunday 1391. In the autumn of 1397 a royal licence was given to allow Dymoke to go unhindered abroad, a licence that followed a previous writ preventing Dymoke's passage on the understanding that the journey might be prejudicial to king and people; following inquiry and sureties from William Waltham, a canon of York, and Hugh Bavent of Norfolk, that writ was cancelled. The only later evidence for Dymoke is the legacy of a cope and habit from his fellow Dominican William Bottlesham, bishop of Rochester, who died in February 1400.

Dymoke's most celebrated action was the composition of the *Liber contra xii errores et hereses Lollardorum*, almost certainly in 1395. During the parliament that sat from 27 January to 15 February 1395 the Lollards had caused the posting of the twelve conclusions on the doors of Westminster Hall and, according to the chronicler Thomas Walsingham, also on the doors of St Paul's Cathedral and possibly of Westminster Abbey; though probably not formally presented in parliament, they were seen by contemporaries, particularly since they were posted in English, as an attempt to arouse the support of those attending and of the populace. The series of conclusions present Wycliffite positions on the eucharist, confession, the temporalities and secular powers of the clergy, the religious orders, images, and pilgrimages; Wyclif is mentioned as the Doctor Evangelicus and his *Trialogus* quoted. Dymoke set himself to answer these, and it is in his *Liber* alone that the English text survives. He translated the conclusions into Latin, and produced arguments against each of them in turn; he quoted a number of earlier authorities, at greatest length Aquinas.

Dymoke's refutation, despite its evasiveness on some of the Lollard charges, shows some insight into the implications of the wording of the conclusions, and awareness of at least one other text in which those conclusions had been expanded. The dedicatory epistle addressed Richard II, looking to the king to put down those who had advanced such views; the copy that survives as Cambridge, Trinity Hall, MS 17 was, in view of its decoration with the arms and white hart badge of Richard and a miniature of the king enthroned, the copy presented to the king on his return from Ireland in May 1395. Three other copies survive (now CUL, MS Ii.4.13, Bodl. Oxf., MS Lat. theol. e.30, and Paris, Bibliothèque Nationale, MS Lat. 3381), and a fourth was destroyed in the Cotton Library fire of 1731 (MS Otho C.xvi); John Leland knew copies at Crowland Abbey and Wells Cathedral, John Bale two more at Glastonbury Abbey and Eton College; John Carpenter, common clerk to the city of London, owned one at his death in 1442.　　　　ANNE HUDSON

Sources R. Dymoke, *Liber contra xii errores et hereses Lollardorum*, ed. H. S. Cronin (1922) · [T. Netter], *Fasciculi zizaniorum magistri Johannis Wyclif cum tritico*, ed. W. W. Shirley, Rolls Series, 5 (1858), 360–69 · *Thomae Walsingham, quondam monachi S. Albani, historia Anglicana*, ed. H. T. Riley, 2 vols., pt 1 of *Chronica monasterii S. Albani*, Rolls Series, 28 (1863–4), vol. 2, p. 216 · *The chronicle of Adam Usk, 1377–1421*, ed. and trans. C. Given-Wilson, OMT (1997), 72–4 · *CPR, 1377–81*, 421 · exchequer, king's remembrancer, accounts various, PRO, E101/402/5, fol. 26v · Bale, *Cat.*, 1.513–14 · Bale, *Index*, 401 · *Joannis*

Lelandi antiquarii de rebus Britannicis collectanea, ed. T. Hearne, [3rd edn], 6 vols. (1774), vol. 3, p. 30 · T. Brewer, ed., *Memoir of the life and times of John Carpenter, town clerk of London, in the reigns of Henry V and Henry VI* (1856), 139

Archives Bodl. Oxf., MS Lat. theol. e.30 · CUL, MS Ii.4.13 · Paris, Bibliothèque Nationale, MS Lat. 3381 · Trinity Hall, Cambridge, MS 17

Dymoke, Tailboys [*pseud.* Thomas Cutwode] (*bap.* **1561**, *d.* **1602/3**), poet, was baptized on 6 February 1561, at Kyme in Lincolnshire, the son of Sir Robert *Dymoke (*d.* 1580) [*see under* Dymoke family], landowner, and Bridget, eldest daughter and coheir of Edward, Lord Clinton (later earl of Lincoln). He was entered at Lincoln's Inn on 26 May 1584.

Dymoke and his brother Sir Edward were engaged in a bitter feud with their uncle, Henry Clinton, earl of Lincoln. In the autumn of 1590 the earl brought an accusation against the Dymokes that they had written a slanderous poem about him and his relatives. Dymoke's brother-in-law admitted that he had heard the poem and Dymoke's brother John said that he once had a copy of it and had read it to his family. Dymoke himself did not give evidence. The poem, titled 'Faunus his Four Poetical Furies', is not extant.

In 1599 Dymoke published *Caltha poetarum, or, The Bumble Bee*, an allegorical poem of 187 seven-line stanzas, under the pseudonym Thomas Cutwode. The pseudonym was derived from a translation of Dymoke's first name—the French *taille-bois* meaning 'cut wood'. The identification of Cutwode and Dymoke was first made by Leslie Hotson in 1938. The text opens with a poem by G. C., stating that *Caltha* is to be decoded, and real people to be matched to the allegorical figures. Few contemporaries can now be extracted from this obscure tale of a bumble-bee (Dymoke himself) who is in love with a marigold (one of Elizabeth's maids of honour) and metamorphosed into the figure of Musaeus at the court of Diana (Elizabeth). It has been suggested that Samuel Daniel was meant by the figure of Musaeus (Hotson, 62), and the two had spent time together in 1592, when Daniel was living with his then patron, Sir Edward Dymoke. In Dymoke's preface to *Caltha*, titled 'To the Conceited Poets of our Age', Daniel is one of four modern poets mentioned with admiration, alongside Sidney, Spenser, and Tasso. On 1 July 1599 the archbishop of Canterbury and the bishop of London ordered the Stationers' Company to burn a number of satires, epigrams, and licentious poems. *Caltha* was included in the list, although for some reason, *Caltha* and the satires of Joseph Hall were spared the flames.

In a bill of complaints dated 23 November 1601 the earl of Lincoln laid a number of charges against the Dymoke brothers. Tailboys had been overheard making slanderous statements against the earl in the street and scurrilous verses by him had been pinned on a maypole; the Dymoke brothers were also charged with riot and unlawful assembly (the result of a drunken clash in Coningsby) and 'for contriving and acting a stage play ... containing scurrilous and slanderous matter' (O'Conor, 108–9). The play in question was 'The Death of the Lord of Kyme', written by Dymoke, and staged in August 1601 at the maypole in

Kyme. Dymoke took the principal role of Lord Kyme himself and was carried off by the Devil at the play's end. Afterwards one John Craddock came on, dressed as a priest, and delivered a mock sermon on the death of 'their lord', written by Tailboys and Edward Dymoke some time before, and recycled for this occasion.

By January 1602 a number of the actors in this performance had been subpoenaed. Dymoke, described by the earl as 'a Common contriver and publisher of infamous pamphelites and libells' and 'a man of verie disordered and a most dysolute behaviour and condicion', gave his evidence on 7 December 1602 (O'Conor, 109). He denied that he had 'counterfeited' his uncle in the play and claimed that the play had been a regular part of the May game festivities. The case was eventually decided in the earl's favour, with severe penalties handed out to those involved. Dymoke, however, escaped the judgment. In February 1603 he was referred to as 'now deceased'; it is not known how or when he died.   ELERI LARKUM

Sources L. Hotson, 'Marigold of the poets', *Essays by Divers Hands, being the Transactions of the Royal Society of Literature of the United Kingdom*, new ser., 17 (1938), 47–68 · N. J. O'Conor, *Godes peace and the queenes* (1934) · *IGI* · W. P. Baildon, ed., *The records of the Honorable Society of Lincoln's Inn: admissions*, 2 vols. (1896) · Burke, *Gen. GB* (1952) · GEC, *Peerage*

Dymoke, Sir Thomas (d. 1470). *See under* Dymoke family (*per. c.*1340–*c.*1580).

Dymond, Jonathan (1796–1828), Quaker moralist and peace advocate, was born on 19 December 1796 at Bridge House, Bridge Street, Exeter, the fifth child of the five sons and two daughters of John Dymond (1761–1838) and his wife, Olive Hitchcock (1761–1840). His family belonged to the Society of Friends, of which both his parents were ministers. He was probably educated at a Quaker academy kept by Thomas Davis at Milverton, Somerset, before joining his father's linen drapery business. On 3 July 1822 he married Anna (1798–1849), daughter of John and Sarah Wilkey of Plymouth; they had a son and a daughter.

In 1823 Dymond published anonymously *An Enquiry into the accordancy of War with the Principles of Christianity*, based on papers he had delivered to a family essay society known as the Iscan Budget. It passed through several editions, and was also published in the United States. He founded an auxiliary peace society at Exeter in 1825, and was for four years on the committee of the Peace Society, though he did not attend its meetings. In 1825 he published a Peace Society tract called *Observations on the applicability of the pacific principles of the New Testament to the conduct of states*, which was also reprinted several times. His chief book, *Essays on the Principles of Morality* (1829), was published posthumously. Favourably reviewed by Southey in the *Quarterly Review* for January 1831, it was an exposition of ethical theories, and attacked utilitarianism as the foundation of moral obligation, which, he argued, derived solely from the 'immediate communication of the will of God'. It was more devoted to the application

than to the theory of moral principles, and attacked duelling, war, and the lax morality of professions and trades. It passed through many editions and was used by the University of London as the textbook in a special subject for its MA in moral philosophy. In 1870 Joseph Pease of Darlington had the book translated into Spanish. A critique of religious establishments entitled *The Church and the Clergy* appeared posthumously in 1832. Various extracts from Dymond's works were separately reprinted.

In 1826 Dymond contracted a disease of the throat, which developed into pulmonary tuberculosis. For twenty months he could communicate only in writing. He died at Bridge House, Exeter, on 6 May 1828, and was buried in the Quaker burial-ground there.

LESLIE STEPHEN, *rev.* K. D. REYNOLDS

Sources C. W. Dymond, *Memoir, letters and poems of Jonathan Dymond* (1907) · *Biographical catalogue: being an account of the lives of Friends and others whose portraits are in the London Friends' Institute*, Society of Friends (1888) · *Annual Monitor* (1829), 13 · E. Isichei, *Victorian Quakers* (1970)
Likenesses J. Bird, 1823, repro. in Dymond, *Memoir, letters and poems*, frontispiece · J. B Forrest, engraving, 1844, repro. in J. Dymond, *Essays on the principles of morality*, New York edn (1834) · T. O. Barlow, engraving, 1852, repro. in J. Dymond, *Essays on the principles of morality*, London edn (1829) · engraving, 1888, Friends' Institute, London

Dympna [St Dympna] (*fl.* late 6th–early 7th cent.), martyr, is the patron saint of the town of Geel in Belgium, where she is invoked against insanity. Dympna and her counsellor, the priest Gerebern, are both supposed to have been buried in Geel. Fragments of their presumed sarcophagi still exist in the church of St Dympna there, and seem to belong to a pre-Romanesque period, possibly as early as the seventh or eighth centuries. When the relics were translated in the thirteenth century, a tile of ninth- or tenth-century date was found in one sarcophagus which bore the inscription *diph//na*. Her cult was famous by the tenth century, when pilgrims from Xanten are said to have tried in vain to steal her relics, but could take only those of Gerebern, which are now venerated at Sonsbeck, near Xanten, as a remedy against gout and fevers.

The translation of Dympna's relics prompted the production of her extant life, and a set of miracles, written by Pierre, canon of St Aubert at Cambrai, at the request of Guido, bishop of Cambrai (r. 1238–47). According to the life, Dympna was the daughter of an Irish pagan king living at the end of the sixth century. Her mother died when she was still a child and she secretly received a Christian baptism and education. Her father, discovering in his grown-up daughter all the virtues of her late mother, fell in love with her and decided to marry her. Dympna escaped and left Ireland in the company of Gerebern, made for the continent, and found refuge at Geel, where they settled in a cave. Her irate father, however, followed their trail, discovered them, and killed Gerebern. He proposed once more to his daughter and, when she refused, murdered her too. The story has no historical value—the invention of the cults of Irish saints was in vogue on the continent from the eighth century onwards—but it does contain important literary and folkloric motifs which can also be detected in fairy tales like *Peau d'âne*.

Since Dympna's perverted father was regarded as a lunatic, she was invoked to cure insanity. Following its discovery in the thirteenth century, the tile from her sarcophagus was hung around the necks of the mentally ill in the hope of curing them. On Dympna's feast day of 15 May the healthy participated in a general pilgrimage for the prevention of mental disease. This and other rituals proved so popular that Geel became, and has remained, something of a sanatorium, especially renowned for its practice of allowing the mentally ill to live with the town's inhabitants.

Iconographical representations surviving from the fifteenth century onwards sometimes show Dympna in the cave where she took refuge, but more often depict her standing, spear in hand, and bringing down the devil.

NATHALIE STALMANS

Sources *Bibliotheca hagiographica latina antiquae et mediae aetatis*, 1 (Brussels, 1898), 2352–5 · L. van der Essen, *Étude critique et littéraire sur les vitae des saints mérovingiens de l'ancienne Belgique* (1906), 313–20 · F. Heuckenkamp, *Die heilige Dymphna* (1887) · H. Delehaye, *Les légendes hagiographiques*, 3rd edn (1927), 9, 99, 148–9 · K. Künstle, *Ikonographie der christlichen Kunst*, 2 (1926), 190–92 · L. Réau, *Iconographie de l'art chrétien*, 3/1 (1958), 407–8 · L. Gougaud, *Les saints irlandais hors d'Irlande étudiés dans le culte et dans la dévotion traditionnelle* (1936), 78–80 · Pierre of St Aubert, Cambrai, *Vita* · E. H. J. Reusens, *Éléments d'archéologie chrétienne*, 1 (Paris, 1885), 204 **Likenesses** H. von Tongheren, votive stone, 1448, Church S. Dympna, Geel · G. van der Weyden and R. van der Weyden, eight paintings, 1505 (about Dympna's life), Baron Van der Elst Collection · J. van Wave, engraving on altar, 1515, Church S. Dympna, Geel · G. Seghers, painting, Pinac, Munich, Germany · painting, Church of Beguine, St Zeruiden, Belgium · reliquary, Church S. Dympna, Geel · tile, repro. in Reusens, *Éléments d'archéologie chrétienne*, vol. 1, p. 204

Dynevor. For this title name *see* Trevor, George Rice Rice-, fourth Baron Dynevor (1795–1869).

Dynham, John, Baron Dynham (*c.*1433–1501), administrator, was the son and heir of Sir John Dynham and his wife, Elizabeth, the sister and heir of John Arches. At Nutwell in Devon since at least 1122 and patrons of Hartland Abbey, the Dynhams were a leading family of gentry in the county. There were five successive Sir John Dynhams: Lord Dynham's grandfather, who died in 1428, left a widow who survived until 1465; his father's widow occupied Nutwell itself until her death in 1496. Thus John, Lord Dynham, who was twenty-four and more when he entered his father's lands in 1458, held his whole ancestral estate only very briefly: some compensation was afforded by his first marriage in 1467 to the widowed Elizabeth Ratcliffe (*née* Fitzwalter), whose heir was her son from her previous marriage.

Quite how Dynham was connected with the Yorkist earls is unclear. In 1459 he accompanied them to Devon, where they may have stayed at his mother's house at Nutwell, and it was he who purchased them the balinger for £40 that carried them first to Guernsey and thence to Calais. He was attainted with them at the Coventry parliament of 1459. From Calais he led two successful raids against the king's forces at Sandwich in 1460, capturing Lord Rivers on the first and being wounded on the second. Following the Yorkist victory he was appointed sheriff of Devon and, in November, chancellor of Ireland. He fought for Edward IV at Towton, was a member of the new king's household by July 1461, and was granted the custody of the lands of the widowed Elizabeth Fulford. However, Dynham's rewards came slowly and contrast sharply with those of Humphrey Stafford of Southwick, earl of Devon. Whereas Stafford's interests spanned all five south-western counties and he rapidly monopolized royal office and succeeded to the pre-eminence of the Courtenays, Dynham's importance was essentially within Devon and he had some limited interests in Cornwall. It is significant that all four of his sisters married into families prominent only in Devon and Cornwall, two of them baronial: lords Fitzwarine and Zouche, Sir John Carew and Sir Thomas Arundel of Lanherne. Dynham was granted eight Hungerford manors in 1464, but was unable to make his title good and had to content himself with a £100 annuity. His summons to parliament as Lord Dynham of Cardenham on 28 February 1467 was unaccompanied by any other grant. Following Stafford's execution in 1469 he became steward of all his lands and keeper of the forests of Exmoor and Neroche for life, but the Courtenay lands were granted in turn to the Marquess Montagu (1470) and George, duke of Clarence (1471), who was resident at Tiverton Castle and politically active in Devon for part of each year. The Courtenay lands were kept in royal hands after Clarence's death in 1478.

Dynham was a member of the royal council in London during Warwick's coup in the summer and of Edward's great council in the autumn of 1469. He was ordered to act against the rebels the following March when, however, he inadvertently helped them. Dynham and the other commissioners were besieged in Exeter by the Courtenays of Bocannoc, perhaps before the king's commission arrived, and were relieved by Warwick and Clarence. It may have been at this time that Clarence extorted money from him, for which he was compensated with an annuity of £100 on the duke's fall. In 1471 Dynham was one of the commissioners who fined those who had rebelled with Thomas Neville, the Bastard of Fauconberg, in Kent. In 1475 he was commander of the fleet during Edward IV's Picquigny campaign and he was sworn as a royal councillor with a further annuity of £100. In 1480 he was granted the former Courtenay manor of Thorne. Already Lord Hastings's lieutenant at Calais in 1483, Dynham was retained as such by Richard III and was not promoted to the captaincy of Calais. Even though his west country importance was recognized by his appointment as chief forester of Dartmoor, steward of Bradninch, and the chief steward and surveyor of the duchy of Cornwall, it was not he but Sir Richard Ratcliffe and others who secured the major grants of forfeited lands in the west country. Offices and annuities he had secured, but the family patrimony was little changed.

While Dynham did not betray King Richard, he evidently had better connections with Henry VII, most probably through Robert Willoughby, steward of the king's household, who was created Lord Willoughby de Broke. Dynham married Willoughby's sister Elizabeth in or after 1485. His brother-in-law Lord Zouche had been attainted and his sister therefore impoverished, so in 1488 Dynham was one of those granted 100 marks a year on her behalf. However, Dynham was not to be the king's man in the west country, but instead a royal minister and courtier. Elected knight of the Garter before 23 April 1487, he was appointed treasurer of England on 14 July 1486 and remained in office until his death. He was a frequent commissioner not just in Devon but elsewhere: indeed in 1497 he was one of those commissioned to act as constable and marshal of England for the trial of the rebel James, Lord Audley, who was duly executed. Henceforth, it seems, he was occupied continually at the exchequer at Westminster and resided for convenience at his house at Lambeth. It was there that his only two children died: George (b. before 1470) in 1487 and Philippa in 1485; both were buried at Lambeth church. It was there also that he died on 28 January 1501. He was buried two days later at the London Greyfriars. At his death he possessed a great stock of plate. As his three younger brothers Charles, Roger, and the clerk Oliver had also died childless, Dynham was the last of his line: his lands were divided among the families of his four sisters. A bastard son, Thomas, was endowed with land in Buckinghamshire.   MICHAEL HICKS

Sources R. P. Chope, 'The last of the Dynhams', *Report and Transactions of the Devonshire Association*, 50 (1918), 431–92 · Chancery records · M. A. Hicks, 'False, fleeting, perjur'd Clarence': George, duke of Clarence, 1449–78 (1980) · J. Warkworth, *A chronicle of the first thirteen years of the reign of King Edward the Fourth*, ed. J. O. Halliwell, CS, old ser., 10 (1839) · J. Gairdner, ed., *The historical collections of a citizen of London in the fifteenth century*, CS, new ser., 17 (1876) · J. Prince, *Danmonii orientales illustres, or, The worthies of Devon* (1701) · A. H. Thomas and I. D. Thornley, eds., *The great chronicle of London* (1938) · C. L. Kingsford, ed., *Chronicles of London* (1913), 233 · GEC, *Peerage*

Dyos, Harold James [Jim] **(1921–1978)**, historian, was born at 16 Lady Margaret Road, Kentish Town, London, on 21 February 1921, the middle son of Charles Alfred Dyos, dye works manager, and his wife, Lilian Maud Violet King. After childhood in Clapham he moved to north London and left school at fifteen when his father lost his job. All three sons were achievers: his elder brother became a Lloyds underwriter and his younger brother a JP and headmaster of a large school in Sunderland. Jim held office jobs in several firms, and while working as a commercial clerk for the National Cash Register Company met Olive Marjorie Steel (1919/20–1995), the daughter of Arthur Benjamin Steel, a house painter. They married at Paddington register office on 16 April 1942, and their daughter Linda was born on 13 May 1946. He served in the Royal Artillery, and was a bombardier on marriage, but rose to the rank of captain, and later viewed the 1940s as one of the happiest periods in his life. The televised fly-past at Churchill's funeral ceremonies in 1965 moved him to tears.

Dyos seized the wartime opportunity of part-time study through a correspondence college, and in 1946 entered the London School of Economics for a BSc degree in economics, before graduating with upper second-class honours in 1949. His PhD thesis (1952) on the suburban development of Victorian south London, supervised by H. L. Beales, was a labour of love—stuffed with plates, diagrams, maps, and statistical appendices. At Leicester he became lecturer in economic history in 1952, reader in urban history in 1964, and Britain's first professor of urban history in 1971. With Jack Simmons pioneering transport history and W. G. Hoskins refining local history, Leicester was intellectually congenial, nor did Dyos shirk administrative responsibilities there. Yet in his academic work he did not embrace provinciality; he identified with London, the subject of his first book: *Victorian Suburb: a Study of the Growth of Camberwell* (1961). A prolific author from 1953 onwards, he approached the book through a stream of academic articles published in the 1950s on the history of transport and housing. He had long been fascinated by topography and maps, and tucked a map into the back of his *Victorian Suburb*. His interest in transport history culminated in collaboration with D. H. Aldcroft on the pioneering synthesis *British Transport: an Economic Survey from the Seventeenth Century to the Twentieth* (1969; 2nd edn, 1974).

'I have been lucky enough to catch one of the biggest breakers to have risen in Modern History since the war', Dyos observed in his inaugural lecture, *Urbanity and Suburbanity* (1973). The demand for urban history had been primed by the two-volume *History of Birmingham* (1952), by Conrad Gill and Asa Briggs, and by Briggs's *Victorian Cities* (1963). The 1960s were an exciting decade for British social historians, when it still seemed adventurous to carry scholarly British history beyond 1832. It was exhilarating, too, to find the sub-discipline breaking out in all directions from its earlier confines in local, economic, and labour history. Social historians were learning much from adjacent disciplines: from literature to social anthropology, from economics to urban sociology and demography. Should urban history concentrate on comparative analysis or on what was unique to each city? Should it cling to economic history, focus on geography, or risk the subjectivities of preoccupation with architecture, art, and literature? What was the role of the computer and the tape recorder? Such questions seemed worth asking, especially as funds and energy then sufficed for every flower to bloom. The times demanded an academic entrepreneur of the best sort who could get people round a table, and in Dyos they found him.

Dyos was an undogmatic, unsectarian bridge-builder: between academic disciplines, between colleagues, between professional and amateur historians, between academic life and the general public, between the brash, self-confident, slum-clearing present of the 1960s and the rapidly disappearing urban past. His rich empiricism, informed by a strong sense of place, combined with his continuing desire to ensure that the reader perceived 'what it all felt like' in a vanishing past; hence his refusal to see quantification as a panacea. Nor did Dyos ever succumb to the contrary temptation: antiquarianism; comparison, generalization, and explanation were his objectives. His publications grew less empirical, more speculative, and increasingly collaborative. Energetic, enthusiastic, intellectually receptive, sociable, and ever on the watch for new talent, he organized the first meeting of what became the urban history group at Sheffield in 1962. British urban history was united and driven forward by the cyclostyled *Urban History Newsletter* which he launched in 1963 and for many years edited and largely wrote himself. By 1974 it had become a full-blown academic journal, the *Urban History Yearbook*, though Dyos's *Newsletter* persisted as a sort of enlarged occasional epistle to friends.

Conferences, collaboration, and communication were integral to the centralized yet permissive voluntarism over which Dyos presided. The ground was consolidated in the tightly organized and highly professional interdisciplinary conference at Leicester, whose tape-recorded proceedings he edited and published in 1968 as *The Study of Urban History*. By then he had already embarked on a second big collaborative project, launched from a conference at Bloomington, Indiana, in 1967: the huge, amply illustrated and eclectic two-volume *The Victorian City: Images and Realities* (1973), which he edited with Michael Wolff and dedicated to Beales. It attracted no fewer than thirty-eight essays from forty authors, willing victims of Dyos's constructive but firm editorial discipline, marshalled as though for a military operation. Here was the two-volume bible for what by the 1970s had become a worldwide crusade for urban history, a cornucopia displaying its range and potential.

For all this intellectual sociability there was a price to pay. Dyos's later publications were less firmly based on empirical research, and he made only slow progress with bringing his *Victorian Suburb* forward to the present with his projected trilogy. Nor was the price paid solely intellectual. His scholarly life had never been plain sailing. His thesis refers to Olive, 'without whose unselfishness it would never have been completed', and his *Victorian Suburb* is dedicated to Olive 'with love and gratitude'. She was a staunch mainstay: listening to his drafts, over whose phrasing he struggled endlessly; providing him with a stable working background; but above all, boosting his self-confidence.

Outwardly ebullient and assured, somewhat larger than life, Dyos at home was intensely private, obsessively hardworking, and acutely aware of gaps in his early education. He had disliked being classified as an economic historian, and his promotion to reader in urban history in 1964 at last located him correctly. A striving meritocrat could have responded to his pinched background with indignant radical protest, but instead Dyos showed a 'Victorian' eagerness for self-improvement and metropolitan social acceptance. He enjoyed surrounding himself with antiques; in his fifties he relished his growing contacts and public recognition, as well as his selection to succeed Sir Nikolaus Pevsner as chairman of the Victorian Society

in 1976. In his last days he seemed hyperactive, and on 22 August 1978 he died at Leicester General Hospital from a stroke. For urban history, and for the academic colleagues to whom he had always been so generous, it was tragic that he should have died at the height of his powers.

BRIAN HARRISON

Sources D. Reeder, 'H. J. Dyos: an appreciation', *Urban History Yearbook* (1979), 4–10 · *The Times* (24 Aug 1978), 12 · *The Times* (8 Sept 1978), 16 · B. M. Stave, 'A conversation with H. J. Dyos: urban history in Great Britain', *Journal of Urban History*, 5/4 (Aug 1979), 469–500 · F. Sheppard, 'Professor H. J. Dyos', *London Journal*, 4 (1978), 155–7 · private information (2004) [Linda Dyos, daughter] · b. cert. · m. cert. · d. cert.
Likenesses photographs, priv. coll. · portrait, repro. in H. J. Dyos, *Exploring the urban past*, ed. D. Cannadine and D. Reeder (1982)
Wealth at death £17,771: administration with will, 7 March 1979, *CGPLA Eng. & Wales*

Dyott, William (1761–1847), army officer, born on 17 April 1761, was the second son of Richard Dyott (1723–1787) of Freeford Hall, near Lichfield, Staffordshire—the head of a family there since Elizabeth I's reign, many members of which were Lichfield MPs—and his wife, Katherine, daughter of Thomas Herrick of Knighton, Leicestershire. He was educated at private schools (Clifford's in Lichfield, and then Price's), Ashbourne grammar school in Derbyshire—which he later described as 'such a school as fitted youth for no pursuit in life beyond a retail shop-board' (*Dyott's Diary*, 1.xi)—and at Nottingham. In 1781, for four months, he attended a private military college, Locke's academy, near London.

Dyott entered the army as an ensign in the 4th (King's Own) regiment on 14 March 1781, was promoted lieutenant on 9 May 1782, and was placed on half pay in late 1783. In February 1785 he rejoined his regiment in Ireland as adjutant, and in 1787 he accompanied it to Nova Scotia, where he met Prince William (later William IV), then commanding the *Andromeda*. The prince became his personal friend, and they played practical jokes and drank together. Dyott was promoted captain on 25 April 1793, and in June 1793 he returned to England to take up the post of aide-de-camp to Major-General Hotham, commanding the Plymouth district. He purchased a majority in the 103rd (Bristol) regiment on 19 May 1794, and, after acting as brigade major in the western district, was promoted lieutenant-colonel on 18 February 1795. After two exchanges he took command of the 25th regiment in November 1795, when under orders for the West Indies, and after being driven back by 'Christian's storm' he reached Barbados in February 1796. He served at the capture of Grenada but soon had to return to England because of ill health. He was appointed assistant adjutant-general for the south-western district in 1799, promoted colonel on 1 January 1800, and appointed aide-de-camp to George III in 1801: his duties, which he took up in 1804, included accompanying members of the royal family to the theatre, and playing cards with the queen and princesses.

In 1801 Dyott was given command of a brigade in the army in Egypt, and he arrived there in July, at which time he was appointed to George Ludlow's division before Alexandria. He commanded his brigade in the action of 22 August which led to the capture of Alexandria, and following the peace of Amiens on 27 March 1802 he returned to England. In 1803 he was appointed to command a brigade in the West Indies, and after commanding at Waterford and Dublin was transferred to the English staff and commanded in Sussex until his promotion to major-general on 25 April 1808. In December 1808 he was appointed to command a brigade in Spain, but never sailed, and in July 1809 he took command of a brigade, of the 6th, 50th, and 91st regiments, in the unsuccessful Walcheren expedition in the Netherlands. His brigade was attached to the marquess of Huntly's division, which occupied the island of South Beveland, and owing to the return of many of his superior officers he acted as second in command there for a month, from September to October 1809, when he returned to England. He never again went on active service, but commanded at Lichfield from August 1810 until promotion to lieutenant-general on 4 June 1813. In 1811 he commanded a force of 15th dragoons and Berkshire militia to suppress Luddism in Nottingham. In 1813 he succeeded to the family estates on the death of his brother, and after the death in 1826 of his brother's widow he resided at Freeford Hall. He was made colonel of the 63rd regiment in 1825, and general on 22 July 1830.

On 11 January 1806, at Dublin, Dyott had married Eleanor, daughter of Samuel Thompson of Green Mount, co. Antrim; they had two sons and a daughter. In 1813 his wife became ill, diagnosed as suffering from disease of the spine, and in 1814 she wanted to separate from him. He attempted a reconciliation, but in September 1814 she eloped with a Mr Dunne, and Dyott never saw her again. In 1815 he divorced her by act of parliament. She died in London in December 1841 and was buried in the new Highgate cemetery.

As a country landowner Dyott was much concerned with agricultural pursuits and politics, and was an active JP and deputy lieutenant. Robert Peel was his neighbour and friend. Dyott was a 'Tory of the old school' (*Dyott's Diary*, 1.xxi) and in 1819, after the Peterloo massacre, joined other tory landowners in calling for more yeomanry and for town armed associations against popular unrest. He opposed Roman Catholic emancipation, parliamentary reform—breaking with his neighbour and close friend the marquess of Anglesey over the latter's support for the Reform Bill—slave emancipation, corn-law repeal, and, initially, railways.

Following a bout of influenza, Dyott died at Freeford Hall on 7 May 1847 and, in keeping with ancient family custom, was buried by torchlight in the vault of St Mary's Church, Lichfield, on the night of 14 May. From 1781 to 1845 he had kept a journal, which filled sixteen volumes of various sizes. Extracts from this, edited by Reginald W. Jeffery, were published as *Dyott's Diary, 1781–1845* (2 vols., 1907).   H. M. STEPHENS, *rev.* ROGER T. STEARN

Sources *Dyott's diary, 1781–1845*, ed. R. W. Jeffery, 2 vols. (1907) • *GM*, 2nd ser., 28 (1847) • Burke, *Gen. GB* (1914) • J. Philippart, ed., *The royal military calendar*, 3 vols. (1815–16) • N. Gash, *Sir Robert Peel: the life of Sir Robert Peel after 1830*, new edn (1986) • Marquess of Anglesey [G. C. H. V. Paget], *One-leg: the life and letters of Henry William Paget, first marquess of Anglesey* (1961) • T. C. W. Blanning, *The French revolutionary wars, 1787–1802* (1996) • R. Muir, *Britain and the defeat of Napoleon, 1807–1815* (1996)
Archives King's Own Scottish Borderers Regimental Museum, Berwick upon Tweed, letter-book • Staffs. RO, military and personal corresp. and papers • Surrey HC, corresp. relating to shooting rights | BL, corresp. with Sir Robert Peel, Add. MSS 40389–40542 • NRA Scotland, priv. coll., letters to George Callander

Dysart. For this title name *see* Murray, William, first earl of Dysart (*d.* 1655); Murray, Elizabeth, duchess of Lauderdale and *suo jure* countess of Dysart (*bap.* 1626, *d.* 1698).

Dyson, Charles (1788–1860), Church of England clergyman and university teacher, is thought to have been born at Acton, Middlesex. He was the grandson of Jeremiah *Dyson (1722?–1776) and the son of a clerk of the House of Commons, also Jeremiah Dyson (*d.* 1835). He first attended a private school at Southampton, and in 1804 was elected a scholar of Corpus Christi College, Oxford, where he became close friends with John Keble, Thomas Arnold, and John Coleridge. To them he was 'a great authority … as to the world without and the statesmen whose speeches he sometimes heard', while his 'remarkable love for historical and geographical research, and his proficiency in it, with his clear judgment, quiet humour, and mildness in communicating information made him peculiarly attractive to Arnold' (Stanley, 13). He took his BA degree with a second class in 1808, and became an MA in 1812.

Early on, Dyson had married a cousin, Elizabeth. They had no children. From 1812 to 1816 he held the Rawlinsonian professorship of Old English at the university. The post was then a sinecure and his first, 'admirable', lecture was also his last (Coleridge, 37). Having been ordained deacon in 1816, Dyson became successively the incumbent of Nunburnholme in Yorkshire (1818–28), of Nazeing in Essex (1828–36), and finally, through the patronage of Dowager Lady Mildmay, of Dogmersfield, near Winchfield, Hampshire, from 1836 to his death. At this last parish, at his own expense, he built a rectory and, with his sister, a fine new church. He was an admirable parish priest, a delightful host, and a man of deep learning, though he never published. He contributed four poems, under the signature of D., to *Days and Seasons, or, Church Poems for the Year* (1845). For many years his health was delicate. He died at his rectory on 24 April 1860. His wife, Elizabeth, and his sister survived him.

L. C. SANDERS, *rev.* JOHN D. HAIGH

Sources J. T. Coleridge, *A memoir of the Rev. John Keble*, 3rd edn (1870), 19, 35–46, 74, 146–8, 245–6, 464–5 • *The Guardian* (2 May 1860), 389, cols. 2–3 • A. P. Stanley, *The life and correspondence of Thomas Arnold … of Rugby School*, 2 vols. (1844), 13 • Boase, *Mod. Eng. biog.* • Crockford (1858) • *The honours register of the University of Oxford: completed to 1883* (1883) • Foster, *Alum. Oxon.* • CGPLA Eng. & Wales (1860)
Archives Bodl. Oxf., corresp. with Sir John Taylor Coleridge and John Keble
Wealth at death under £9000: probate, 8 June 1860, CGPLA Eng. & Wales

Dyson, Sir Frank Watson (1868–1939), astronomer, was born at the Baptist manse in Measham, near Ashby-de-la-Zouch, Derbyshire, on 8 January 1868, the eldest child in a family of four sons and three daughters of Watson Dyson (1837–1904), a Baptist minister, and his wife, Frances (1839–1909), the daughter of James Dodwell, a farmer of Long Crendon, Buckinghamshire, and his wife, Deborah. After early schooling in Nottinghamshire, Dyson moved with his family to Yorkshire, where he attended Heath grammar school in Halifax. He won scholarships first to Bradford grammar school and then to Trinity College, Cambridge. He was second wrangler in the mathematical tripos in 1889. In 1891 he became first Smith's prizeman and was elected a fellow of his college, and the following year he was awarded an Isaac Newton studentship to carry out research in astronomy.

The *International Astrographic Catalogue* In 1894 Dyson was offered by the astronomer royal, William Christie, the post of chief assistant at the Royal Greenwich Observatory. He accepted with alacrity, as this enabled him to marry Caroline (Carrie) Bisset (1867–1937), the daughter of Palomen Best MB JP of Louth, Lincolnshire. They had two sons and six daughters. Though he had little prior experience of instrumentation, he threw himself into the work of practical astronomy with considerable enthusiasm. Christie had committed the Greenwich observatory to an international project involving photography of specified regions of the sky, followed by measurement of the positions of the stars recorded. Dyson's first major task was to take charge of the Greenwich share in this *International Astrographic Catalogue*. By 1909 the Greenwich observatory was the only one of the participating institutions to have completed its allotted programme of observation, measurement, and publication. This work brought home to Dyson the need to improve knowledge of stellar motions. He therefore undertook with one of the assistants, William Grasset Thackeray, a new reduction of observations of more than 4000 circumpolar stars made between 1806 and 1819 by Stephen Groombridge. Combining the reduced data with new observations extended knowledge of stellar motions to considerably fainter stars than hitherto. In 1906 Arthur Stanley Eddington, who had just been appointed to Greenwich, used this new information to confirm the proposal by the Dutch astronomer Jacobus Cornelius Kapteyn that stars had preferred directions of motion in space.

In the same year Dyson moved to Edinburgh to take up the posts of astronomer royal for Scotland and regius professor of astronomy at the university. His most important work there continued to be on stellar positions and motions. He reached agreement with staff at Perth observatory in Australia to help with measuring and reducing the photographs of the southern sky they were taking for the *International Astrographic Catalogue*. He also countered criticisms of Kapteyn's work by showing that preferential directions of motion were exhibited by stars with large proper motions, where observational errors were less important.

Sir Frank Watson Dyson (1868–1939), by Walter Stoneman, 1919

Astronomer royal On Christie's retirement in 1910, Dyson was appointed ninth astronomer royal. He is the only person to have been successively astronomer royal for Scotland and astronomer royal. As one of his first projects he turned again to the stars observed for the *International Astrographic Catalogue*, but now concentrated on the measurement of their parallax to try and determine stellar distances. By the time he retired some 500 parallaxes had been determined at Greenwich—an important addition to the existing total. He also initiated studies into determining stellar magnitudes and colours on a systematic basis, as well as continuing the tradition of meridian observations at Greenwich. However, his most important initiative related to his interest in solar eclipses.

In 1896, and again in 1898, Christie was away for several months on eclipse expeditions. This gave Dyson early experience in the running of a national observatory. The first solar eclipse Dyson observed was from Portugal in 1900, and the weather was fine. This began a remarkable run of six eclipse expeditions in which he was officially involved, where the conditions were good enough to make observations. Dyson developed a special interest in eclipse spectroscopy. At his first two eclipses he obtained some of the best observations of coronal lines up to that time. He fully realized the need for innovation in eclipse work. At the 1927 eclipse, visible from northern England, he helped organize the first use of colour film and of making photographs from an aircraft. The results of this continuing interest in eclipses were later summarized in a book published in 1937, *Eclipses of the Sun and Moon*, which was written in conjunction with Richard van der Riet Woolley, later eleventh astronomer royal.

In 1917 Dyson pointed out that Einstein's recently propounded general theory of relativity could be subjected to an observational test at the solar eclipse due in 1919. The theory predicted that stars seen near the eclipsed sun would appear to be shifted in position by a small, but measurable, amount. Dyson's proposal came at a difficult moment during the First World War, but the necessary preparations were made, and after the war the observations were obtained. When Dyson presented the results to a joint meeting of the Royal Society and the Royal Astronomical Society at the end of 1919, demonstrating that the data favoured Einstein's predictions, it was recognized both within science and outside that a major turning point in scientific thought had been reached.

Time measurement The Greenwich observatory had always been involved in time measurement, and this became one of Dyson's particular concerns. Under his guidance the observatory introduced a Shortt free-pendulum clock for its time service from 1924 onwards. At about the same time he was approached by John Reith, who asked that the Greenwich observatory should provide time signals to the public via the British Broadcasting Corporation. It was Dyson who ultimately decided to adopt the system of six pips, with the sixth denoting the hour. This 'Greenwich time signal' was transmitted worldwide for the benefit of shipping from 1927. Dyson was for many years president of the British Horological Institute, which awarded him its gold medal in 1928. He was also twice master of the Clockmakers' Company.

When Dyson took over from Christie, he decided that it had become essential to update the observatory's magnetic equipment. A new building was erected to house the equipment, and Dyson, working in collaboration with his chief assistant, Sydney Chapman, overhauled the recording and publication of magnetic data. After the First World War the growth of electrification of suburban rail services made magnetic measurements at Greenwich increasingly difficult. Dyson therefore decided to move the magnetic equipment to Abinger, near Leith Hill, in Surrey. (Not long after Dyson's retirement it became necessary to move it again, this time to Devon.)

Dyson had to work hard to keep the Greenwich observatory running during the First World War, when many of the staff joined the armed forces. After the war he played a major role in reconstituting international scientific co-operation via the International Research Council and, especially, via the formation of the International Astronomical Union (of which he was president from 1928 to 1932). He was president of the Royal Astronomical Society from 1911 to 1913 and of the British Astronomical Association from 1916 to 1918. He played an important role in the former body by ensuring that members of the new discipline of geophysics continued to be members along with the astronomers. Dyson was elected to the Royal Society in 1901, and was awarded its royal medal in 1921. He was later awarded the Bruce gold medal of the Astronomical

Society of the Pacific (1922) and the gold medal of the Royal Astronomical Society (1925). He received honorary degrees from a number of universities, including Cambridge and Edinburgh, and was foreign or corresponding member of various academies. He was knighted in 1915 and appointed KBE in 1926.

Dyson was due to retire in 1928 at the age of sixty, but he was asked to continue for another five years until 1933. In 1931 William Johnson Yapp, a wealthy manufacturer, offered to present the Greenwich observatory with a new telescope, in commemoration of Dyson's work. The 36 inch reflector came into use at Greenwich the year after Dyson retired.

Dyson was a man who combined charm with common sense. He retained his religious belief throughout his life, along with liberal views in politics. He died on board ship, on the *Ascanius*, on 25 May 1939, while returning from a visit to Australia, and was buried at sea on the same day.

A. J. MEADOWS

Sources M. Wilson, *Ninth astronomer royal* (1951) • A. S. Eddington, *Obits. FRS*, 3 (1939–41), 159–72 • A. J. Meadows, *Greenwich observatory: the story of Britain's oldest scientific institution*, 2: *Recent history (1836–1975)* (1975) • H. A. Brück, *The story of astronomy in Edinburgh from its beginnings until 1975* (1983) • W. H. McCrea, *Royal Greenwich Observatory: an historical review* (1975)
Archives CUL, corresp. and papers • RAS, letters to Royal Astronomical Society, London • Royal Observatory Library, Edinburgh, corresp. and papers | California Institute of Technology, Pasadena, archives, corresp. with G. E. Hale
Likenesses W. Stoneman, photograph, 1919, NPG [see illus.] • photograph, repro. in Jones, *Obits. FRS* • photographs, repro. in Wilson, *Ninth astronomer royal* • photographs, RAS
Wealth at death £4331 6s. 7d.: resworn probate, 27 July 1939, CGPLA Eng. & Wales

Dyson, Sir George (1883–1964), composer and music administrator, was born at 4 Schofield's Court, off Crossley Terrace, Halifax, Yorkshire, on 28 May 1883. He was the eldest of the three children of John William Dyson, blacksmith, and his wife, Alice Greenwood, a weaver. Dyson's father was also organist and choirmaster at the local Baptist church, though later Dyson remembered, 'neither of my parents could play more than a halting hymn-tune. But they both sang in amateur choirs, were interested listeners, and therefore proud and pleased when I showed promise' (Dyson, *Fiddling*, 71). Dyson played the piano and composed from an early age and when only thirteen became a church organist. At sixteen he became a fellow of the Royal College of Organists, and in 1900 he won an open scholarship to the Royal College of Music (RCM) where he became a composition student of Sir Charles Villiers Stanford.

Little of Dyson's early music survives, though a setting of Psalm 89 written at the age of eleven and a cello sonata in A major dated 19 January 1904 came to light in 2001, and were deposited at the Royal College of Music. In 1904 Dyson was awarded the Mendelssohn scholarship, which enabled him to spend three years abroad, mainly in Italy but also including time in Austria and Germany. Centred on Florence and Rome, he became a protégé of Clara Gigliucci, the fourth daughter of Vincent Novello. In Rome he wrote a rhapsody for string quartet, which fifteen years later was published as the first of three when submitted to the UK Carnegie Trust's publishing competition. In Vienna and Berlin he met some of the leading musicians of the day, and visited Richard Strauss at his home. While in Dresden in 1907 he wrote the choral evening service in D, which remains one of his best-known works. A three-movement symphonic poem, *Siena*, thrice heard at the Queen's Hall, London, and conducted by Arthur Nikisch in May 1909, is now lost. On Sir Hubert Parry's recommendation Dyson was appointed director of music at the Royal Naval College, Osborne, in 1908, and he moved to Marlborough College in 1911. The second and third rhapsodies were written during these appointments, in 1912 and 1908 respectively.

Dyson enlisted in the Royal Fusiliers in 1914, and as the brigade grenadier officer, 99th infantry brigade, he published a sixteen-page training pamphlet on grenade warfare for which he became celebrated. Shell-shocked, he was invalided home in 1916. On 17 November 1917 he married Mildred Lucy (1880–1975), daughter of Frederick Walter Atkey, a London solicitor. They had a son and a daughter. In 1917 he was awarded the Oxford degree of DMus. After a long convalescence he was commissioned in the RAF, where he organized military bands. In this role he completed the piano sketch of Sir Henry Walford Davies's *RAF March Past*, adding the trio tune and scoring it. Dyson's earliest surviving orchestral work, *Won't you Look out of your Window* (later renamed *Children's Suite, after Walter de la Mare*), was heard at the Promenade Concerts in 1925.

In 1921 Dyson became a composition professor at the Royal College of Music, the year in which he was also appointed music master at Wellington College. In 1924 he moved to Winchester College as director of music, and there the various strands of his mature career as a composer developed. His students at both institutions later recalled his inspirational teaching. In 1937 he succeeded Sir Hugh Allen as director of the Royal College of Music. He was to play an important role in transforming the college into:

> a small, tough, high-quality school for the training of professional musicians. He had an astringent style and brought the college to high professional and international repute … His ability for administration and financial acumen were outstanding and his innovations in government grants, buildings, syllabuses, and pensions proved of lasting benefit. (*DNB*)

He managed to keep the college functioning throughout the blitz, being knighted in 1941. Dyson retired in 1952, and enjoyed a considerable creative Indian summer thereafter.

In his autobiography Dyson characterizes himself as a kapellmeister, writing, 'my repute is that of a good technician … not markedly original. I am familiar with modern idioms, but they are outside the vocabulary of what I want to say' (Dyson, *Fiddling*, 19). But he evolved a personal and immediately recognizable tonal idiom, albeit one derived from the diatonic style of Parry. He wrote tuneful, vigorous music—successful because of its strong invention—

including many partsongs and short choral works, among them music for both the 1937 coronation service (*O Praise God in his Holiness*) and that in 1953 (*Confortare*).

In 1928 Dyson completed a major work for chorus and orchestra, *In Honour of the City*, which established his reputation—at a time of far-reaching modernist developments—as an approachable composer in the same mould as Parry and Elgar. This was followed by his most celebrated work, *The Canterbury Pilgrims*, first performed at Winchester on 19 March 1931 with leading soloists of the day, though with local choral and orchestral forces, conducted by the composer. This sequence of thirteen vivid character pieces after Chaucer was popular for over thirty years, but after Dyson's death it was long neglected until brought to wider notice by Richard Hickox's recording in 1996.

In the 1930s Dyson wrote four extended scores for the Three Choirs festivals, three choral and one orchestral, starting with *St Paul's Voyage to Melita* for performance at Hereford (1933). For the Leeds festival in 1934 he wrote his rhythmic and percussive choral *tour-de-force*, *The Blacksmiths*. For the festival at Worcester in 1935 came *Nebuchadnezzar*; the *Prelude, Fantasy and Chaconne* for cello and orchestra for Hereford followed in 1936. His most ambitious score, *Quo vadis?*, a large-scale suite of five extended choral movements, was a casualty of the cancelled 1939 Three Choirs festival. Its first part was first performed in London in April 1945, but the complete work had to wait for the festival at Hereford in 1949, and was not widely taken up.

By the late 1930s Dyson's reputation as a composer was at its peak, and he went on to complete two large-scale orchestral works, the symphony in G (1937) and the violin concerto (1942), the latter championed by Albert Sammons, but neither became established in the repertory, and until their recordings in the 1990s, despite being published, they were little known. Later came the concert overture *At the Tabard Inn*, based on themes from *The Canterbury Pilgrims*. Three concertos for strings, the *Concerto leggiero* for piano and strings, the *Concerto da camera*, and the *Concerto da chiesa*, completed his orchestral output.

Dyson's later works included a number of organ pieces, but were dominated by further choral music. *Sweet Thames Run Softly* (1954), a lyrical setting of words by Edmund Spenser for baritone, chorus, and orchestra, was in a Delius-like idiom out of date in the mid-1950s, but regarded fifty years later as a timeless evocation, perfectly caught. *A Christmas Garland* (1959) and *A Spring Garland* (1957) were typical chains of lyrical settings. In one of his last extended works, *Agincourt* (1955), with familiar words from Shakespeare's *Henry V*, Dyson looked back thirty years to *In Honour of the City* with choral writing of undiminished vibrancy and freshness. It was followed by *Hierusalem* (1956), a setting of words by St Augustine, in which he achieved a radiant mysticism.

After the First World War Dyson lectured on new music, soon publishing a series of four articles entitled 'The texture of modern music' (*Music & Letters*, 1923), which were incorporated into his influential book *The New Music*, published the following year. Remarkably precise in expression, the book remained in print for over twenty years. Ultimately his aesthetic was a traditional one: at one point he confessed, 'My difficulty is that I cannot find a logical definition of atonality'. Dyson subsequently published *The Progress of Music* (London, 1932) and a collection of autobiographical essays, *Fiddling while Rome Burns* (London, 1954).

With striking blue eyes, Dyson had a great sense of humour. Over and above his professional commitments he was a great supporter of amateur music-making, and was a patron of the Winchester Music Club and festival. In 1935 he became the first president of the National Federation of Music Societies. Dyson loved living in Winchester—where he was made a freeman—but was also a tenacious hill-walker. He died at his home, 1 St James Terrace, Winchester, on 28 September 1964.

The revival of Sir George Dyson's music was started by Christopher Palmer, who published *George Dyson: a Centenary Appreciation* (1984) and *Dyson's Delight* (1989), a selection of Dyson's uncollected articles and talks on music, and also promoted the first modern recordings. The Sir George Dyson Trust was established in 1998.

LEWIS FOREMAN

Sources C. Palmer, *George Dyson: man and music* (1996) · G. Dyson, *Fiddling while Rome burns: a musician's apology* (1954) · G. Dyson, *The new music*, 2nd edn (1926) · *Dyson's delight: an anthology of Sir George Dyson's writings and talks on music*, ed. C. Palmer (1989) · *DNB* · papers of the Sir George Dyson Trust, priv. coll. · b. cert. · m. cert. · d. cert.
Archives King's AC Cam., letters to Oscar Browning
Likenesses group portrait, photograph, 1943, Hult. Arch. · W. Stoneman, two photographs, 1943–53, NPG · E. Marks, plaster bust, 1948, Royal College of Music, London · A. Devas, oils, 1952, Royal College of Music, London
Wealth at death £17,348: probate, 24 Nov 1964, *CGPLA Eng. & Wales*

Dyson, Humfrey (*d.* 1633), book collector, was probably the son of Christopher Dyson (*d.* 1609), wax chandler of the parish of St Alban, Wood Street, London, and his wife, Mary. He was practising as a notary public by 1609, when he witnessed Christopher's will, and continued to do so until shortly before his death, drawing up wills and other documents. He was a citizen of London, as a member of the Wax Chandlers' Company, from 1603, and married Elizabeth, daughter of Thomas *Speght (*fl.* 1566–1602), the editor of Geoffrey Chaucer and John Lydgate.

Dyson is notable chiefly for the enormous library he amassed. No catalogue of the library is known, apart from six notebooks (All Souls College, Oxford, MS 117) listing in order of date of publication those books 'touching as well the State Ecclesiasticall as Temporall of the Realme of England': in 1631 these alone totalled nearly 1100. He also owned a large number of works of Elizabethan and Jacobean literature; in some instances his is now the unique surviving copy. Nearly all the extant printed proclamations of Queen Elizabeth I's reign belong to the seven sets, each of which he collected together, bound, and provided with its own specially printed title-page (1618). Dyson

printed nothing else, but he collaborated in the 1633 revision of John Stow's *Survey of London*—an edition that included many copies of acts of parliament and of the common council of London.

Dyson died between 7 January 1633, when he made his will, as a parishioner of St Olave Jewry, London, and 28 February 1633, when it was proved. In it he made monetary bequests to his four daughters and two sons, allowed the use of his professional papers to his apprentices, and gave a two-volume book of statutes to 'my noble friend Sir William Paddy … to be by him put and given to the library of St John's College in Oxford'. He directed simply that his other books be sold by William Jumper; a great many of them were acquired by Richard Smith (*d.* 1675) and were dispersed when his library was sold in 1682. Thomas Baker wrote: 'There are Books (chiefly in old English) almost in every Library that have belong'd to H. Dyson, with his Name upon them' (Hearne, 7.369). NIGEL RAMSAY

Sources R. L. Steele, 'Humphrey Dyson', *The Library*, 3rd ser., 1 (1910), 144–51 · W. A. Jackson, 'Humphrey Dyson and his collections of Elizabethan proclamations', *Harvard Library Bulletin*, 1 (1947), 76–89 · W. A. Jackson, *Records of a bibliographer*, ed. W. H. Bond (1967), 135–41 · T. Hearne, *Collections*, 7.369 · H. R. Woudhuysen, *Sir Philip Sidney and the circulation of manuscripts, 1558–1640* (1996), 177–80
Archives All Souls Oxf., notebooks, MS 117 · BL, collection of laws and ordinances relating to London, Add. MS 36761

Dyson, Jeremiah (1722?–1776), clerk of the House of Commons and politician, was the eldest son of Jeremiah Dyson of Bartholomew Close, London, from whom in 1730 he inherited extensive estates in Hertfordshire, Buckinghamshire, and Bedfordshire. Horace Walpole's description of his father as 'a tailor' therefore smacks of snobbery. The diarist also recalled that young Dyson was 'a staunch republican' (Walpole, 1.316–17). No evidence survives on his political radicalism, but in religion he was a dissenter, and so was educated at Edinburgh and Leiden universities. A man of unblemished private life, in June 1756 he married Dorothy (1735?–1769), the daughter of his cousin Ely Dyson; they had three sons and four daughters before her death on 16 December 1769. Dyson was called to the bar at Lincoln's Inn in 1746, and, clearly not a man tempted into idleness by his inheritance, then embarked on two successive if interrelated careers.

In February 1748 Dyson paid £6000 to Nicholas Hardinge to succeed him as clerk of the House of Commons, having previously served under him in a junior post. He used his wealth not only to subsidize his friend Mark Akenside, a physician and poet, but also to establish new standards of probity in the conduct of his office. No longer would appointments in his gift be for sale, nor did he sell the clerkship itself on relinquishing it in 1762: these changes proved to be morally binding on his successors. From 1749, moreover, he shared his fees for engrossing legislation with the three engrossing clerks. John Hatsell was so grateful for being granted the post of clerk assistant in 1760 without having to pay an anticipated fee of £3000 that he dedicated to Dyson his famous *Precedents* of parliamentary procedure, and later, when clerk himself, appointed Dyson's son and heir, Jeremiah, as clerk assistant in 1797 and deputy clerk in 1814.

Dyson introduced greater efficiency as well as probity into the clerical organization of the House of Commons. When he came to office the printing of the *Commons Journal*, hitherto in manuscript, had just commenced under his predecessor. Dyson reorganized the new *Journal* office, and so accelerated the printing of the backlog, undertaking personal responsibility for the volumes from 1741, that he virtually completed the catching-up process. In 1763, a year after his resignation, it was possible for the house to begin sessional payments for current volumes. It was also under him that in 1751 a system of calculating fees chargeable on private bills was finally worked out. And it was Dyson who persuaded the Treasury to build, at a cost of some £3000, a clerk's house on the Westminster site between 1758 and 1760.

Being clerk to the House of Commons was a demanding task. It was Dyson's duty to sit at the table when the house was in session, to offer procedural guidance as required. Expertise in all ways of the house was the main requirement in a clerk, and Dyson was acknowledged to excel in this respect; though no direct evidence on the point has come to light, he was probably the author of the only contemporary manual of procedure (since published as the *Liverpool Tractate*, in 1937). While it was the clerk assistant who took notes of the house's proceedings, the clerk was responsible for the compilation of the daily *Votes*, which were printed immediately, and the sessional *Journal*. Outside the chamber of the house the clerk was responsible for an administrative department, comprising four offices respectively for committees, engrossing, fees, and the *Journal*, containing altogether twelve clerks and numerous writing clerks. Dyson never enjoyed good health, and Walpole thought that the chief reason why he gave up the clerkship in 1762: 'Being of an unhealthy complexion, and very fretful temper, he had quitted his laborious task' (Walpole, 1.317).

Another motive may have been a more congenial political atmosphere after the accession of George III in 1760. Dyson seems to have had influential contacts at the new court, for the appointment of his friend Akenside as physician to the queen in 1761 was attributed to Dyson, and he himself was appointed a secretary to the Treasury in May 1762 when the king's favourite Lord Bute became prime minister, before resigning his clerkship in August and being brought into parliament in December 1762 for a government-controlled seat at Yarmouth, on the Isle of Wight. Walpole had had fourteen years as an MP to appreciate Dyson's talents as clerk:

> In that employment he had comported himself with singular decency and intelligence. In truth his parts were excellent: he was quick, subtle, shrewd, clear both in conception and delivery, and was master of argumentative eloquence, though void of every ornamental part of it. (Walpole, 1.317)

Dyson now began his second career as a politician. He had already shown himself to be an able administrator,

and Bute's successor, George Grenville, lauded his competence, integrity, and knowledge in Treasury business. Ill health caused him to give up the post of Treasury secretary in April 1764, when he was appointed a lord of trade. Never out of office, whatever the changeover of ministers, he moved in 1768 to the Treasury board, and finally, in March 1774, he was given a lucrative court office as cofferer of the household, with appointment to the privy council. In 1768 he moved to another government seat at the borough of Weymouth and Melcombe Regis. Such an expert on procedure was too valuable a counter in the parliamentary game for any ministry to part with. Dyson's debating weapons were his knowledge of appropriate precedents and his deployment of such procedural devices as the previous question, which blocked awkward opposition motions by avoiding a direct vote. In the 1760s he even corrected Speaker Cust on procedural points, but in the 1770s the more formidable Speaker Norton would not brook such behaviour.

Every ministry in turn relied on Dyson, as when, during the first Rockingham administration (1765–6), the attorney-general, Charles Yorke, wrote on 1 January 1766 about a paper by the chancellor of the exchequer, William Dowdeswell: 'If Dyson is well disposed, I would settle it with him in two or three hours, as conversant in the forms of Parliament and wording questions for the House' (BL, Add. MS 35430, fol. 25). But Dyson disapproved of that ministry's American policy, and harassed it by parliamentary sniping. After the debate of 24 February 1766 the Treasury lord George Onslow commented to William Pitt: 'Mr. Dyson acted with his usual Parliamentary sagacity, and endeavoured to embarrass us all he could' (*Correspondence of William Pitt*, 2.394–5). At the end of the parliamentary session the exasperated prime minister asked George III to dismiss him, but it was the administration that went. Every other ministry enjoyed Dyson's full support.

No MP had played such a role before. Dyson's predecessor as clerk, Nicholas Hardinge, was a failure as a parliamentarian. But Dyson, as Walpole observed, was 'excellently useful from his parts and great knowledge of Parliamentary business, to all who employed him' (Walpole, 1.317). Even before he entered the house, apprehension about his expertise was the reason Henry Legge gave for refusing to lead the Commons opposition in 1762. 'That he shall have nobody with him', so the duke of Newcastle reported to the duke of Devonshire, 'That if he had Mr. Dyson, who is perfectly acquainted with the rules of business, and forms of the House of Commons, he could do something' (BL, Add. MS 32945, fols. 280–81). Dyson soon won notoriety among opposition MPs by never deciding points of order against government, and he was adept at all forms of parliamentary obstruction. He made hundreds of such interventions in debate, so much so that on 26 January 1769 the opposition MP Isaac Barré provoked an outburst of laughter by comparing him with Mungo, an overworked black slave in the comic opera *The Padlock*, by Isaac Bickerstaff and Charles Dibdin; the nickname Mungo stuck to Dyson for the rest of his life. Dyson was especially useful to the ministry of the duke of Grafton in the Middlesex election controversy of 1768–70, his value being underlined by the debate of 25 January 1770. Nursing a grievance of inadequate reward, Dyson was deliberately absent from the chamber when an opposition motion was found impossible to reject on principle and, since the house was in committee, could not be evaded by the usual devices. Confusion prevailed on the Treasury bench as Dyson refused three requests to attend, but in the end he rescued the ministry by suggesting words for a destructive amendment that nullified the original motion. This episode spurred Grafton to obtain for Dyson, before his own resignation, an Irish pension of £1000 a year for his life and those of his three sons. This itself became a *cause célèbre* because it broke an earlier promise to cease granting such pensions to the Irish parliament, which refused to vote the necessary finance: not until November 1775 did the pension come into effect, after the British Treasury had authorized its payment.

Dyson's behaviour soon caused him to forfeit the goodwill of the house he had acquired as their clerk. He annoyed all those whom he tied up in procedural knots. He seemed to lack political principle by supporting different ministers in turn, being 'slippery to his friends as fast as they fell', noted Walpole, who also remembered that his dogmatic behaviour made MPs recall 'he had once been their servant' (Walpole, 1.317). His odium extended beyond the house, for during the 1771 controversy over newspaper reporting Barré drew the attention of the house to a press reference to 'Jeremiah Weymouth, the d——n of this country' (BL, Egerton MS 226, fols. 28–32), sarcastically moving that no such person was an MP. Many MPs must have relished Edmund Burke's pointed reference to Dyson on 25 February 1774: 'There are persons in this world, whose whole soul is a previous question, and whose whole life is the question of the adjournment' (BL, Egerton MS 252, fol. 212).

In the early 1770s Dyson became less prominent in the Commons as his health deteriorated, and because the prime minister, Lord North, was himself an expert parliamentarian. The bestowal of a court office in 1774 may have been an acknowledgement of his failing physical condition. In the autumn he suffered a stroke, which contemporaries called palsy, and though he was elected in October 1774 for another government seat, at Horsham, his political career was over. He died on 16 September 1776, and was buried at Stoke church, near Guildford, where he had purchased an estate in 1765. His political unpopularity among opponents of government often caused him to be mocked in contemporary cartoons, notably 'Alas! poor Mungo' after the loss of his Irish pension in 1771. Yet as a man he was much respected and liked by those who knew him personally, and his social life had a cultural dimension. The novelist Samuel Richardson was among Dyson's friends, and in 1772 he arranged for the publication of the collected poems of Mark Akenside, who had died in 1770, bequeathing Dyson his entire estate.

PETER D. G. THOMAS

Sources P. D. G. Thomas, *The House of Commons in the eighteenth century* (1971) • O. C. Williams, *The clerical organization of the House of Commons, 1661–1850* (1954) • parliamentary diary of Henry Cavendish, 1768–74, BL, Egerton MSS 215–263, 3711 • H. Walpole, *Memoirs of the reign of King George the Third*, ed. G. F. R. Barker, 4 vols. (1894) • HoP, *Commons* • *Correspondence of William Pitt, earl of Chatham*, ed. W. S. Taylor and J. H. Pringle, 4 vols. (1838–40) • *The Liverpool tractate: an eighteenth-century manual on the procedure of the House of Commons*, ed. C. Strateman (1937) • BL, Newcastle MSS, Add. MS 32945 • BL, Hardwicke MSS, Add. MS 35430

Archives BL, Egerton MSS • BL, Hardwicke MSS • BL, Newcastle MSS

Dyson [*married name* Thomas], **(Barbara) Ruth** (1917–1997), keyboard player, was born on 28 March 1917 at 5 St Mark's Square, St Pancras, London, the only child of Ernest Andrews Dyson (1884–1979), a doctor, from Sheffield, then serving as captain in the Royal Army Medical Corps, and his wife, Minnie, *née* Cornish, sister of Dr Sidney Cornish, a general practitioner in Dorking, Surrey, and—after the First World War—Dr Dyson's partner. She spent her childhood and most of her adult life in Dorking. She was educated at home, and in 1935 entered the Royal College of Music, where she studied the piano with Angus Morrison, the violin with W. H. Reed, and harmony with Herbert Howells.

At the Royal College Dyson was inspired by Kathleen Long's playing of Arne's sonata no. 3 on the piano, and became interested in the collection of old keyboard instruments in the college museum. She first played the harpsichord and clavichord at the Dorking home of the musicologist Susanne (Susi) Jeans, and she acquired a spinet, made by Robert Goble, a former assistant of Arnold Dolmetsch. On 15 November 1941 she made her Wigmore Hall début on the piano, with the London Women's String Orchestra; her programme included the concerto no. 5 in G minor by Thomas Arne, a composer whose work she was to perform often on the harpsichord. During the Second World War she taught music to children at the War Evacuation Day Nursery in Dorking; her settings of poems written by Rose Fyleman for the children were later published as *Playgames* (1955). She worked for the Red Cross at Dorking General Hospital as an auxiliary nurse, and toured hospitals, army camps, and factories for the Council for the Encouragement of Music and the Arts (CEMA) as part of the Le Fèvre Piano Quartet.

After the war Dyson developed a career both as a harpsichordist and a pianist, playing concertos with many of the leading orchestras. As a harpsichordist she specialized in the English baroque repertory, especially the works of John Blow, while several contemporary English composers writing for early keyboard instruments, including Alan Ridout, dedicated works to her. Her collection of instruments grew to include a clavichord by Thomas Goff, virginals by Derek Adlam, and a double harpsichord by Michael Johnson.

On 2 May 1964 Dyson married Edward Eastaway Thomas (1918–1996), a research officer with the joint intelligence bureau until 1970 and one of the team that produced *British Intelligence in the Second World War* (1971–88). He was the son of Julian Thomas, government auditor, and a nephew of the poet Edward Thomas. Through her husband Dyson acquired a stepson and a stepdaughter. She taught at the Royal College of Music from 1961, and in 1964 she was appointed professor of harpsichord and piano, and lecturer in the history of early keyboard instruments, reflecting the growing enthusiasm for the harpsichord; her pupils included Robert Woolley and Melvyn Tan. She became a fellow of the Royal College of Music in 1980, and continued to teach there until 1987, writing the entry on the history of the piano for the *New Oxford Companion to Music* (1983).

Dyson toured extensively for the British Council, giving many recitals in Europe, mainly of English music; she lectured in fluent German to the Telemann Society in Hamburg in 1963 and in French to the world forum of the harpsichord in Paris in 1976, and she represented the United Kingdom as an adjudicator at the Bruges International Festival in 1972. She also made many recordings for the BBC archives on instruments from the Victoria and Albert Museum, the Colt clavier collection, and the Royal College of Music museum of instruments, while on her own modern instruments she recorded the complete works of Herbert Howells for the clavichord, to celebrate his ninetieth birthday in 1982. In the 1980s and 1990s she made recordings with the singer and harpsichordist Peter Medhurst, including an album of Schubert songs recorded at the Colt collection and *For Two to Play* (1988), a recording of all the double-harpsichord works written up to the time of Mozart. She continued to give recitals with Peter Medhurst until the year of her death. To mark her long association with the BBC a seventieth-birthday recital, *Dyson's Delight*, was broadcast in 1987.

Dyson also played an important part in the musical life of Surrey. Ralph Vaughan Williams was her father's patient, and as a girl she often took part in haymaking and tea parties organized by 'Uncle Ralph'. At the age of five she participated in one of the first children's days in the Leith Hill Musical Festival, founded in 1905 as a competitive festival for local choirs and conducted by Vaughan Williams every year until 1953; she traced her love of Bach to hearing Harold Samuel play on that occasion. Her father was a member of the committee from 1930 and chief hall steward from 1944 to 1960, and she herself helped informally as one of the 'nymphs' before the war. She was a member of the committee from 1946 to 1962 and from 1977 to 1979, before her election as a vice-president in 1981. Vaughan Williams was a very important influence in her development as a musician. For many years after the war she played among the second violins in the festival orchestra, serving as orchestra librarian from 1948 to 1960, and from 1968 to 1995 she played the harpsichord continuo in the annual performances of Bach's St Matthew passion given by members of the participating choirs. Her final appearance at the Leith Hill festival was in 1995, when she played Walter Leigh's concertino for harpsichord and strings in one of the evening concerts. She also became a friend of the Dolmetsch family, appearing regularly at the Haslemere festival from 1979 and as a tutor at the Dolmetsch summer schools.

Much loved by her wide circle of friends and colleagues, Ruth Dyson was very hard working and very professional.

She died, of a heart attack, at the Royal Surrey County Hospital, Guildford, Surrey, on the final day of the 1997 Dolmetsch summer school, 16 August. Survived by her stepson and stepdaughter, she was buried at St Martin's Church, Dorking. She left her library and most of her instruments to the Royal College of Music.

ANNE PIMLOTT BAKER

Sources A. A. Gordon Clark, ed., *Leith Hill Musical Festival, 1905–1955* (1955) · B. Tucker, ed., *And choirs singing: an account of the Leith Hill Musical Festival, 1905–1985* (1985) · J. Day, *Vaughan Williams*, 3rd edn (1998), 29 · C. Holland, *Dorking people* (1984), 41 · *The Times* (23 Aug 1997) · *The Independent* (19 Aug 1997) · *The Guardian* (27 Aug 1997) · *Harpsichord and Fortepiano*, 6/2 (Nov 1997) · archives, Leith Hill Musical Festival · museum archives, Museum of Royal College of Music · *New Grove*, 2nd edn · private information (2004) [stepson; former colleagues] · b. cert. · m. cert. · d. cert.
Archives Royal College of Music, London, papers | priv. coll., archives of the Leith Hill Musical Festival · Surrey HC, archives of Leith Hill Musical Festival | SOUND BL NSA, *Dyson's delight*, NSA ref: B1878/1 · BBC Archive recordings
Likenesses photograph, 1970–74, repro. in *The Independent* · photograph, repro. in *The Guardian*
Wealth at death £1,294,613: probate, 18 Feb 1998, *CGPLA Eng. & Wales*

Dyson, William Henry [Will; *pseud.* Emu] (1880–1938), cartoonist and printmaker, was born in Gillies Street, Alfredton, Ballarat, county Grenville, Victoria, Australia, on 3 September 1880, the ninth of the eleven children of George Arthur Dyson (1839?–1923), of London, a goldminer and traveller in dry goods, and his wife, Jane (1842–1930), daughter of Ambrose Mayall, cotton spinner, of Ashton under Lyne, Lancashire. Following the family's move to South Melbourne, Dyson's brief education was at Albert Park state school, when his family received financial support from his elder brother, Edward (Ted) Dyson (1865–1931), who later became a successful author and prolific journalist but who was then working in his uncle's printing and stationery business. At the age of sixteen, self-taught, he began his professional career as a caricaturist and soon attracted national attention in the Sydney *Bulletin* and the *Lone Hand*. In 1903 he took over from his elder brother Ambrose, also a cartoonist, on the Adelaide *Critic*, contributing coloured caricatures. His work became more widely known in Australia through his illustrations to his brother Edward's book *Fact'ry 'ands* (1906). The poet Hugh McCrae described Dyson as:

> young and good looking, with eyes full of brightness, and flushed cheeks, while he said something not to be missed, smilingly, out of the corner of his mouth. Tightly fitting clothes emphasized the sinuous lines of his body; and, instead of a collar, he wore a black silk scarf wound many times round his throat. (McRae, 17)

In time the scarf was replaced by a tie; the stocky body was covered by ample, pinstripe, suits; but the mockery, humour, and, particularly, the discontent remained. This 'tough, sardonic man' (Palmer, 213) married Ruby Lindsay (1887–1919), a much praised black and white illustrator, at the Methodist church, Creswick, Victoria, on 30 September 1909. Ruby (who used the pseudonym Ruby Lind) was the sister of Norman Lindsay, then Dyson's closest friend, a controversial Australian artist and writer. Dyson and

Lindsay shared digs for a time. They also explored the streets of Melbourne together, discussing draughtsmanship, the depiction of character, Plato and Nietzsche, magazine editors, and sex. They shared a large circle of like-minded friends and acquaintances, including Norman Lindsay's brothers Percy, Lionel, and Reg, who were also artists and occasional cartoonists. Dyson did not often sketch outdoors except when pursuing a subject for a *Bulletin* caricature. Photographic and film references were rare in the early years of the century and in a smaller, more parochial world caricaturists usually drew their subjects from life, trailing them through streets, theatres, and restaurants. In May 1909 an exhibition of Dyson's caricatures had been held at Furlong's Studios in the Royal Arcade, Melbourne.

In 1910 Dyson and his wife moved to London, where he was first published in Northcliffe's *Weekly Dispatch*. Caricatures, under the pseudonym Emu, drawn in the *Vanity Fair* manner—Thomas Beecham and Sir Herbert Beerbohm Tree were among his subjects—appeared in *Vanity Fair's* rival, *The World*. A. R. Orage, editor of the *New Age*, a new, close, influential friend, began publishing his literary cartoons in 1913.

The Dysons' only child, Elizabeth Jane (Betty), was born in 1911. The following year Dyson joined the radical *Daily Herald* as political cartoonist at £5 a week. Influenced by Lindsay's brilliant penmanship and by the cartoonists of *Simplicissimus*, his draughtsmanship quickly matured. 'There was a savage penetration about these drawings that fascinated the London intellectual world' (Palmer, 214). In the most biting political cartoons since James Gillray (1757–1815) he attacked not only capitalism but also the Trades Union Congress and others on the left who, in his view, toadied to capital: strong stuff provoking outrage from all quarters. Two best-selling collections of his cartoons were published in 1913 and 1914. Throughout his career he fought hard for his independence and for his beliefs, which developed from syndicalism to guild socialism to, finally, social credit.

During the First World War Dyson abandoned socialism for patriotism, reaching his widest popularity with the publication of *Kultur Cartoons* (1915), a savage indictment of German militarism. The drawings were also exhibited at the Leicester Galleries in London to critical and public acclaim. From 1917 he served as an official war artist with the Australian Imperial Force in France and was several times wounded.

Australia at War, a collection of reportorial war drawings, each accompanied by a finely written commentary by the artist, was published in 1918. In his introduction G. K. Chesterton observed: 'through all the rags and equipment that Dyson draws can be traced the lines of a sort of nakedness like that of the dead on the Last Day'. Although not a commercial success, *Australia at War* was later assessed by William Moore, a distinguished Australian art critic: 'The distinction of the text and the quality of the drawing make this book the most valuable individual Australian volume to come out of the war' (*The Story of Australian Art*, 2, 1934, 54).

Dyson's most famous cartoon was published on 17 May 1919. Three weeks after the draft treaty of Versailles had been presented to the Germans he drew a small child, labelled '1940 Class', weeping unseen behind a pillar while Clemenceau, accompanied by Lloyd George, Vittorio Emmanuele Orlando, and Woodrow Wilson, remarks, 'Curious! I seem to hear a child weeping'. This prescient idea, foretelling the Second World War, was reproduced many times in many countries and as the war approached it gave the artist further posthumous fame.

That year Ruby died of influenza at their home at 30 Glebe Place, Chelsea, London, a victim of the post-war worldwide epidemic. Her death was the central tragedy in Dyson's life and served to strengthen his long-held belief that all things were decreed by fate to suffer unhappy endings. His marriage to the strong-willed Ruby had held his pessimism in abeyance but on her death it returned and remained. His grief was expressed in *Poems: in Memory of a Wife* (1919). He never remarried.

After the war Dyson rejoined the *Daily Herald* but, unhappy there, resigned in 1921; he briefly joined the post-Horatio Bottomley *John Bull* where his work seemed dated and out of touch. He subsequently produced some literary cartoons for J. C. Squire's *London Mercury*. Experiments on film with animated models brought acclaim from, among others, the *Daily Mail*, whose anonymous critic wrote of 'the creation of a new art'. Dyson, he added, was 'on the threshold of immortality', but the artist's money ran out, the experiment was abandoned, and the film was presumed lost.

In 1925, broke, Dyson reluctantly returned to Australia to draw for Melbourne *Punch* and the Melbourne *Herald*. Frustrated by his editors, and dissatisfied with his work and with himself, he sought new means of expression: painting and, more successfully, etching. His several *London Mercury* series were recycled into the novel form of satirical dry-points which, on leaving Australia for good, he took to the United States where, in 1930, the first of several acclaimed exhibitions was held. Ironically, the Bloated Capitalist, once the cartoonist's adversary, was now his best customer. In the same year a similar, successful exhibition, held at St George's Gallery, London, also drew lavish praise, though one perceptive critic noted that Dyson occasionally roasted an old chestnut (the result of rewarming old ideas, perhaps) (T. W. Earp, 'Our intellectuals', *New Statesman*, 36, 15 Nov 1930, 176). The depression killed this flourishing market.

In 1930 Dyson, a much changed artist, returned to England to a much changed, less radical *Daily Herald*. Friends found him 'tired, like a man who had run a long and exhausting race and wonders if the effort has been worth while' (Hetherington, 194). He found time to write *Artist among the Bankers* (1933), a serious work embracing the theory of social credit which he expounded with a wit lacking in intellectual rigour. A contemporary critic, John Lewis, described him as tilting at 'the wind-mills of high finance' ('Don Quixote the second', *Plebs*, 26, 1934, 90).

Occasionally Dyson's old brilliance asserted itself but

his later work for the *Daily Herald* generally lacked the passion and energy with which, between 1912 and 1919, he had so violently and effectively uncovered 'the bone and structure of capitalist society' (Brailsford, *Daily Herald*, 22 Jan 1938). Dyson died of heart failure on 21 January 1938 at his home, 8 Netherton Grove, Chelsea, London, and was buried on 26 January in Hendon Park cemetery, London. Examples of his work, including about 500 *Daily Herald* cartoons, are in the Centre for the Study of Cartoons and Caricature, University of Kent at Canterbury, and at the Australian War Memorial, Canberra, Australia.

JOHN JENSEN

Sources V. Palmer, *Will Dyson*, Meanjin Quarterly, 8/4 (1949), 213–23 · *DNB* · J. Jensen, 'Curious! I seem to hear a child weeping!': Will Dyson', *20th Century Studies*, 13–14 (1975), 36–55 · H. R. Westwood, *Modern caricaturists* (1932) · V. Lindesay, *The inked-in image* (1970) · R. McMullin, *Will Dyson: cartoonist, etcher and Australia's finest war artist* (1984) · J. Jensen, *Will Dyson, 1880–1938: cartoons, caricatures, drawings and satirical portraits … 'A sort of bird of freedom'* (1996) [exhibition catalogue, Australia House, London] · H. McRae, *Story book only* (1948) · J. Hetherington, *Norman Lindsay: the embattled Olympian* (1973) · N. H. Brailsford, *Daily Herald* (22 Jan 1938) · private information (2004) · V. Lindesay, 'Dyson, William Henry', *AusDB*, vol. 8 · b. cert. · d. cert. · A. McCulloch, *Encyclopedia of Australian art* (1981) · d. cert. [Ruby Dyson]
Archives Mitchell L., NSW · priv. coll., Chanteau collection, drawings and prints, artist's own archive · University of Kent, Canterbury, Centre for the Study of Cartoons and Caricature | Australian War Memorial, Canberra, C. E. W. Bean MSS · Mitchell L., NSW, A. G. Stephens MSS · NL Aus., V. & N. Palmer MSS · State Library of Victoria, Melbourne, E. Dyson MSS · State Library of Victoria, Melbourne, W. Dyson MSS · State Library of Victoria, Melbourne, Lindsay MSS
Likenesses L. Lindsay, photograph, c.1908, University of Sydney, Rare Book and Special Collections Library · W. H. Dyson, self-portrait, chalk drawing, repro. in *Everyman* [London] (26 Nov 1931) · R. Lind, drawing, repro. in *TP's Weekly* (20 Feb 1915) · D. Lindsay, group photograph, repro. in Jensen, *'A sort of bird of freedom'* · portraits, repro. in L. Lindsay, *Comedy of life: an autobiography* (1967) · portraits, repro. in Hetherington, *Norman Lindsay* · portraits, repro. in McMullin, *Will Dyson*
Wealth at death £7655 19s. 10d.: probate, 24 May 1938, CGPLA Eng. & Wales

Dyve, Sir Lewis (1599–1669), royalist army officer, was born on 3 November 1599, at Bromham Hall, Bedfordshire, the first son of John Dyve of Bromham, Bedfordshire (knighted in 1603), and his second wife, Beatrice Walcot (1574?–1658), daughter of Charles Walcot of Walcot, Shropshire. His father died in 1607, and on 31 May 1609 his mother married Sir John *Digby (later first earl of Bristol) of Sherborne Castle, Dorset. Dyve was therefore in due course the elder half-brother of the sons of that marriage, George *Digby and John Digby.

Courtier and MP Dyve matriculated at Oxford (his college is not known) on 21 February 1614. He was knighted at Whitehall on 19 April 1620. His stepfather was a privy councillor, who headed important embassies to Vienna and Madrid. Dyve stayed in the Spanish embassy (and there met a Dorset neighbour, Sir John *Strangways, another rich and accomplished gentleman) and gained a good knowledge of the language. As well as completing his education he was involved in street brawls, on one occasion along with Sir Kenelm Digby, the noted alchemist.

Dyve's acquaintance with Strangways was sealed by his marriage to Sir John's daughter, Howarda (d. 1646), on 14 August 1624. She was the widow of another prominent county landowner, Edward Rogers. Wealthy in his own right, with property in at least five counties, Dyve was thus linked to a powerful political network of Dorset families, which occupied leading roles in the shire. He was elected MP for Bridport in 1625 and 1626. His critical stance in these parliaments towards the court and Buckingham was no doubt influenced by their harsh treatment of his stepfather following the failure of the Spanish match. Along with his father-in-law and half-brother George Digby he was detained at the end of the 1626 Parliament for 'stirring up … disaffection', but he was returned for another Dorset seat, Weymouth and Melcombe Regis, in 1628 (*Life and Letters*, 9–10). There is no record of his speaking in this parliament. He lived at homes in Dorset and London, where four sons and three daughters were born.

Dyve's relationship with the wealthy Strangways family involved financial and diplomatic activity abroad. He, Sir John Strangways, and another associate, Sir Edward Stradling, were accused in 1637 of the illegal export of gold and silver. He showed some expertise and interest in precious metals and coinage later. With his Digby relations, Henry Jermyn (the queen's leading courtier), Stradling, and others he developed property in Covent Garden, and became an early resident of this newly fashionable district. Several of his associates, like Kenelm Digby, were Catholics. Clearly an adventurous, combative, and fearless young man he frequented pleasure gardens, gaming houses, and theatres, and participated in various affrays as he had in Spain. He fought or assisted at several duels, including that of his half-brother George and the courtier William Crofts in the winter of 1634–5.

Dyve's reputation as a brawler on the verge of the court, an illicit projector and a possible papist, hindered his election to the parliaments of 1640. He failed to win one of the Bedfordshire county seats at a by-election in December 1640, despite pocketing the writ itself at a critical moment. He kept in close touch with his Dorset kinsmen in the House of Commons, however, and, like them, moved from an anti- to a pro-court position in 1641. He was instrumental in publishing George Digby's attack on the attainder of Strafford, and was a marked man thereafter. Briefly imprisoned by the Commons, and unsuccessfully proposed by Digby in his absence for the post of lieutenant of the Tower, he joined the royal court at York in April 1642. A plot to seize Hull misfired and he fled to the Netherlands to assist the queen in raising men and arms. It was there that he and Digby first made close contact with Prince Rupert.

The first civil war Dyve was back in July, when he was named one of the commissioners of array for Bedfordshire (where he was a JP), and attempted to seize arms stored at Bedford. He narrowly escaped arrest at his house at Bromham, which was soon plundered by his great political rival and neighbour, Sir Samuel Luke MP, of Cople Hall. With the raising of the royalist army in August he was given command of a troop of horse and a regiment of foot, largely recruited in Yorkshire and Lincolnshire. He fought at the head of his troop, alongside Rupert, at the first major skirmish of the war, Powick Bridge, in September 1642, and was wounded. He was present at the battle of Edgehill on 23 October. When the army settled into winter quarters he was made governor of Abingdon, which served as the headquarters of Rupert and the cavalry. His troop was part of the prince's own regiment. Dyve accompanied the marching army on campaign in the summer of 1643.

Following the first battle of Newbury, and the promotion of George Digby to one of the secretaryships, he was ordered to lead an expedition into Northamptonshire and Bedfordshire, to extend the royal quarters and impede parliamentarian supply lines. He was able to drive in the outposts of the local enemy commander, Luke, plunder his house, and seize Newport Pagnell. But 'a mistake of orders' from court led to its abandonment (Clarendon, *Hist. rebellion*, 3.232). He returned to Abingdon for the winter, where he struggled to keep the garrison from starving.

Dyve was again with Rupert at the start of the new campaigning season, taking part in the prince's relief of Newark in March 1644. With the decision to abandon Abingdon in May, Dyve and his regiment were released to join the main army in its successful pursuit of Essex into Cornwall. But as a valuable and well-connected courtier–diplomat he did not remain continuously with his unit. In June he was employed to carry dispatches from Oxford to Rupert. Later in the year he was commissioned major-general in Dorset, and made his stepfather's house, Sherborne Castle, his headquarters. With the powerful aid of the Strangways connection, as well as the Digbys, he quickly mobilized the local cavaliers. He provided local intelligence to the new royalist high command in the west at Bristol. But though busy as an active regional commander his diplomatic skills were not forgotten: in May 1645 he was mentioned as a possible candidate to lead an embassy to Turkey or Spain.

Imprisonments and escapes In the last stages of the war Dyve conducted raids into enemy quarters within reach of Sherborne. He was severely wounded in an attack on Dorchester, and had a 'lame legg' thereafter (*Life and Letters*, 141). He briefly recaptured the strategic port of Weymouth, assisted by his old political contacts there, but lost it again when Lord Goring failed to aid him in good time (February–March 1645). He tried to win over the strong Clubmen movement in Dorset, but the appearance of the conquering New Model Army settled matters, and Sherborne was surrendered on 15 August 1645. Many prominent Dorset cavaliers, including his own family members, his wife, his uncle Sir John Walcot, and Strangways in-laws, were comprised in the articles of surrender.

Dyve himself was too important and intransigent to be allowed to make his peace with parliament. He had been excepted from pardon earlier, and was now charged with high treason. With his brother-in-law Sir Giles Strangways he appeared before the House of Commons. Showing contempt for their authority, he was sent to the Tower of London. He remained there for two years. One of his fellow prisoners was John Lilburne, and during 1647 he was able to keep the king informed, by coded letter, of the political intrigues centred on the Leveller leader, and to offer his own advice. He tried to persuade Lilburne that Cromwell and the grandees were about to make a private treaty with the king. Both he and Lilburne exaggerated their own importance, and misinterpreted the fast-moving events of this revolutionary year, but Dyve's letter-book is valuable evidence of the relations between the London Levellers and the New Model Army.

During this long captivity Dyve's family suffered. His wife died in childbirth on 24 February 1646, and his debts mounted: he had spent a fortune in the king's cause (£164,000 according to one contemporary historian) and his estates were forfeit to the state. He and his children were granted only a small living allowance. 'Dives [is] now pauper', gloated one London newspaper (*Life and Letters*, 79). He was removed to the king's bench (debtors') prison. But this gave him a chance to make the first of his many escapes from custody (15 January 1648). He joined the forces raised for the king in Scotland, fought at Preston and was taken prisoner. Held by the army in Whitehall, while they dealt with the king, he managed to escape again (this time in a spectacular leap down through a privy into the Thames) on the night following Charles's execution, 30 January 1649.

Dyve now made his way to Ireland to serve the marquess of Ormond. Breaking his journey at the Isle of Man, he took the opportunity to issue, with Sir Marmaduke Langdale, *A Declaration of the Noble Knights* (1649). This printed declaration in defence of the governor there, the earl of Derby, showed Dyve's skill with his pen in propaganda matters. In Ireland he fought with the English royalist forces at the unsuccessful siege of Dublin and in their dogged resistance to the advance of Cromwell's army in Munster. He left Ireland for The Hague with a letter from Ormond to the king, in June 1650, and published a perceptive and detailed narrative of the campaign, which praises Ormond and is critical of Lord Inchequin. This led to a prolonged controversy at the exiled royal court (Dyve, *Letter … New-Castle*, 1650).

Exile and return Dyve joined his Digby relatives in Paris. George Digby had been appointed by Mazarin commander of part of the French forces guarding the north-eastern approaches to Paris, and he made Dyve governor of a stronghold there (1652). He was mainly employed, however, as Digby's man of business at the French court, protecting his interests, lobbying for his pay, and, on his own behalf, seeking promotion. His task was made more difficult by the disorders in Paris connected with the second *fronde*, and the unpopularity of the exiled English court there. In 1655–7 he was active as a commander with the French forces in Piedmont, but he was often ill and penniless. His main associates at this time were the foreign mercenaries, like himself, in French pay. Politically, like Digby, he was counted one of the Louvre group around the queen mother, Henrietta Maria, and Lord Jermyn.

With the restoration of the king he returned to England. Much of his property had been disposed of by the state. His father-in-law, Sir John Strangways, had purchased some in 1652, and Dyve gave Bromham to his eldest son, Francis. He resided at a smaller estate at Combe Hay in Somerset. Still closely associated with the court he promoted schemes for reform of the Royal Mint, travelled abroad with Jermyn, and regaled old friends with accounts, highly coloured, of his many escapes. 'A great gamester in his time', he could do no more now than 'sit and look on' at the gaming tables, Pepys observed (Pepys, *Diary*, 8.566, 9.3). He died at Combe Hay on 17 April 1669, and was buried in the church, where there is a monumental inscription. Three sons and one daughter survived him.

Dyve was described, in a wanted notice after one of his escapes, as 'of a middle size, and hath a flaxen hair' (*Life and Letters*, 92). A portrait exists. He was a figure of some importance in the politics of the court, before, during, and after the civil war, and as a soldier, diplomat, and propagandist; but will be better remembered for his hair-raising escapades. His story was sufficiently romantic to be the subject of a 'fanciful' historical novel in the 1930s. His 'able pen' embroidered what were already tall tales. On Dyve's recounting his adventures to fellow exile John Evelyn in 1651, the diarist concluded that 'This Knight was indeede a valiant Gent: but not a little given to romance, when he spake of himselfe' (Evelyn, *Diary*, 3.40, see also 49–50).   IAN ROY

Sources *The life and letters of Sir Lewis Dyve, 1599–1669*, ed. H. G. Tibbutt, Bedfordshire Historical RS, 27 (1948) • 'The Tower of London letter-book of Sir Lewis Dyve, 1646–47', ed. H. G. Tibbutt, *Bedfordshire Historical Record Society*, 38 (1958), 49–96 • W. M. Harvey, *History of the hundred of Willey* (1872–8) • *Memoirs of Prince Rupert and the cavaliers including their private correspondence*, ed. E. Warburton, 3 vols. (1849) • Clarendon, *Hist. rebellion* • A. R. Bayley, *The great civil war in Dorset, 1642–1660* (1910) • L. Dyve, *A letter from Sir Lewis Dyve to the lord marquis of New-Castle* (1650) • L. Dyve, *A letter from Sir Lewis Dyve … to a gentleman … in London* (1648) • L. Dyve and M. Langdale, *A declaration of the noble knights* (1649) • J. Rushworth, *Historical collections*, 5 pts in 8 vols. (1659–1701) • *Calendar of the Clarendon state papers preserved in the Bodleian Library*, 1: *To Jan 1649*, ed. O. Ogle and W. H. Bliss (1872); 2: *1649–1654*, ed. W. D. Macray (1869), vols. 1 and 2 • *CSP dom., 1625–62* • D. Lloyd, *Memoires of the lives … of those … personages that suffered … for the protestant religion* (1668) • will, PRO, PROB 11/329, sig. 53 • M. A. E. Green, ed., *Calendar of the proceedings of the committee for advance of money, 1642–1656*, 3 vols., PRO (1888) • M. A. E. Green, ed., *Calendar of the proceedings of the committee for compounding … 1643–1660*, 5 vols., PRO (1889–92) • *VCH Bedfordshire*, vol. 3 • R. Lee, *Law and society in the time of Charles I: Bedfordshire and the civil war*, Bedfordshire Historical RS, 65 (1986)
Archives Beds. & Luton ARS, copies of letters written as a prisoner in the Tower • BL, letters, Add. MSS 18980–18981, *passim* | BL, Rupert corresp., letters • PRO, Digby transcripts, letters
Likenesses P. Audinet, line engraving, BM • engraving (after portrait; known to be in family possession, 1948), BM • repro. in *Life and letters*, ed. Tibbutt, frontispiece

Wealth at death lost £164,000 (incl. loss of rents) for loyalty to king: Lloyd, *Memoires of the lives*, 691; Green, ed., *Calendar of … advance of money*, 1451; Green, ed., *Calendar of compounding*, 1303–8; will, PRO, PROB 11/329, sig. 53 • owned five to six manors in Bedfordshire: *VCH Bedfordshire*, vol. 3, p. 45; Lee, *Law and society in the time of Charles I*

E—. For certain Anglo-Saxon names beginning E— (for example, Ethelred, Ethelstan, Ethelwine) *see under* Æ— (Æthelred, Æthelstan, Æthelwine).

Ea—. For certain Anglo-Saxon names beginning Ea— (generally those that have a modern English form: for example, Eadgar, Eadward) *see under* the modern form (Edgar, Edward).

Eachard, John [*pseud.* T. B.] (*bap.* **1637**, *d.* **1697**), college head, was baptized on 26 January 1637 at St Peter's Church, Yoxford, Suffolk, the eldest son of Laurence Eachard, vicar of Yoxford, and his wife, Mary (*d.* 1700). The Eachards were an old East Anglian family and several were clergymen. Laurence Eachard was sequestered after charges were laid against him in 1650, but restored in 1660. Having entered St Catharine's College, Cambridge, as a sizar on 10 May 1653, John Eachard matriculated in 1654, held a Gostlin scholarship about 1655, and graduated BA in 1657. He became a fellow in 1658 and proceeded MA in 1660.

All Eachard's published works appeared between 1670 and 1673. His first and best-known, written as a letter to 'R. L.' and signed 'T. B.', is *The Grounds and Occasions of the Contempt of the Clergy and Religion Enquired into* (1670). This dealt with two serious concerns of his, education and emoluments, in the witty style between jest and earnest that delighted contemporary readers. As Anthony Wood observed in 1672, 'People [are] taken with fooleries, plays, poems, buffooning and drolling books; Ihhard's "Contempt of the clergy", Marvill's "Rehearsall Transprosed", Butler's "Hudibras"' (2.240). The outlandish similes and perverse deductions, supposedly quoted from sermons, are especially memorable, and the controlled modulation of tone throughout the tract anticipates the manner of Swift. Inevitably there were responses: he ridiculed one, *An Answer to a Letter of Enquiry* (1671), in *Some Observations upon the Answer* (1671); the others he dealt with in 'Five letters from the author of … Contempt of the Clergy' (1672). Swift mocked Eachard's answerers, 'whose Memory if he had not kept alive by his Replies, it would now be utterly unknown that he were ever answered at all' (*Prose Writings*, 1.4).

'Five letters' is appended to Eachard's *Mr Hobb's State of Nature Considered, in a Dialogue between Philautus and Timothy* (1672). Here the elderly philosopher is 'tormented … with buffoony' (*Life and Times of Anthony Wood*, 4.472). Philautus (Hobbes) is a megalomaniac know-all afflicted by the fear and selfishness Hobbes saw in human nature. Timothy, by contrast, has intelligence, common sense, and good humour. The colloquial language of both speakers makes the discussion lively and concrete—the same technique as employed in *Contempt of the Clergy*. Dryden, in his 'Life of Lucian', ranks Eachard with Erasmus and Fontenelle as modern exponents of the Lucianic dialogue: by this method, Dryden writes, he 'has more baffled the Philosopher of *Malmsbury*, than those who assaulted him with the blunt, heavy Arguments, drawn from Orthodox Divinity' (*Works*, vol. 20, ed. W. Maurer, 1989, 221–2). Eachard's continuation of the dialogue, *Some Opinions of Mr. Hobbs Considered* (1673), was less popular; unlike his other works it was not reprinted in the seventeenth century.

One more publication is plausibly attributed to Eachard: *Moon-Shine, or, The Restauration of Jews-Trumps and Bagpipes* by J. Achard (1672), is an answer to Robert Wild's pamphlet supporting Charles II's declaration of indulgence. It was reprinted in *Dr. Eachard's Works*, part 2 (1697), and there is also internal evidence. An answer to Martin Clifford's *Treatise of Humane Reason* (1674), entitled tentatively 'How to write a book that can't be answer'd', remains a fragmentary draft (Cambridge, St Catharine's College MS XL/14, fols. 41–68). Towards the end of his life Eachard 'revised and corrected' translations by the young Laurence Echard of Terence (1694) and, probably, of Plautus (1694); some notes among his papers suggest a further volume of Plautus was projected (Cambridge, St Catharine's College, MS XL/12[b]).

Eachard received his DD by royal mandamus after his election in 1675 to the mastership of St Catharine's College. His major achievement in this office was the rebuilding of the hall, which he both planned and supervised. He was energetic and resourceful in securing donations, and also in arranging loans; by the time of his death he was personally responsible for £603 borrowed from his family and friends. He displayed his own coat of arms on a stained-glass window in the master's lodge.

When Eachard was master he still tutored undergraduates, sometimes as many as twelve freshmen. He wanted to associate good schools with the hall by means of close scholarships and bye-fellowships; he proposed Eton College and Merchant Taylors' School, and between 1675 and 1680 he negotiated, in the end unsuccessfully, with King Edward's School, Birmingham. His correspondence shows him dealing with various problems in the hall, including in 1680 and 1681 a highway robbery by two undergraduates and in 1691 the voiding of two non-jurors' fellowships. In 1687 the university refused Alban Francis, a Benedictine monk, the master's degree to which James II wanted him admitted without an oath; Eachard was one of the senate's eight nominees who subsequently appeared with the vice-chancellor before the ecclesiastical commission, where they were roundly abused by Jeffreys, the lord chancellor. In 1696 Eachard, then vice-chancellor, as he had been in the year 1679/80, collected subscriptions for the establishment in Cambridge of the university press. He also made a university loan of £950 to St Catharine's College's building fund and took personal responsibility for its repayment.

In the course of his career Eachard also held a variety of livings. He was rector of Widdington, Essex, between 1681 and 1684, and of Dennington, Suffolk, between 1683 and 1697. Between 1684 and 1697 he also held the sinecure rectory of Llanynys, Denbighshire. He died, probably at St Catharine's College, after a 'lingering sickness' (Eachard MS XL/28), on 7 July 1697, and was buried in the antechapel there on 14 July. He had never married. The loans he had negotiated for the college from family and friends occasioned extensive correspondence, and helped delay until 1719 the probate of his will. Eachard was said to have no talent for serious discourse. Thomas Baker, the antiquary, 'went to St. Mary's with great Expectation to hear him preach, but was never more disappointed' (BL, Add. MS 5813, fol. 223v). Swift noted: 'I have known men happy enough at ridicule, who upon grave subjects were perfectly stupid; of which Dr. *Echard* … was a great instance' (*Prose Writings*, 4.301). Eachard is aptly described as a 'curious blend of hardheadedness and generosity' (Mason, 47)—a relentless fund-raiser who also gave liberally to beggars.
HUGH DE QUEHEN

Sources Venn, *Alum. Cant.* · St Catharine's College, Cambridge, Eachard MSS, XL/12, XL/14, XL/28 · St Catharine's College, Cambridge, MS MEMB/Beversham, MS F9/Buddle · W. H. S. Jones [W. H. Samuel], *A history of St Catharine's College, once Catharine Hall, Cambridge* (1936) · W. H. S. Jones, *St Catharine's College, Cambridge* (1951) · E. Mason, 'The life and works of John Eachard', PhD diss., U. Lond., 1967 · *The life and times of Anthony Wood*, ed. A. Clark, 2, OHS, 21 (1892) · *The prose writings of Jonathan Swift*, ed. H. Davis and others, 14 vols. (1939–68) · E. E. Rich, ed., *St Catharine's College, Cambridge, 1473–1973: a volume of essays to commemorate the quincentenary of the foundation of the college* (1973) · *State trials*, 11.1315–40 · parish register (baptism), Yoxford, Suffolk RO, 26 Jan 1637 · BL, Add. MS 5813 [Thomas Baker] · *CSP dom.*, 1675–6, 492 · *Walker rev.*

Archives St Catharine's College, Cambridge, MSS

Wealth at death over £1000; brother chief beneficiary: *The State of St Katharine's Hall in Cambridge*, Cath. MS XL/28; will

Eadbald (*d.* 640), king of Kent, was the son and successor of *Æthelberht I (*d.* 616?), the first Anglo-Saxon king to accept Christianity, and his wife, *Bertha (Ætheburgh) (*b. c.*565, *d.* in or after 601). Eadbald was still an unbaptized pagan at the time of his accession in 616, and he scandalized Archbishop Laurence and the other Italian missionaries by marrying his stepmother, an action condoned by Germanic custom but anathema to the Christian church; Bede observes with some satisfaction that as a punishment Eadbald was 'afflicted by frequent fits of madness and possessed by an unclean spirit' (Bede, *Hist. eccl.*, 2.5). Discouraged by Eadbald's attitude and by a simultaneous pagan backlash in Essex, the missionaries made preparations to leave England. But Laurence's departure was forestalled by a painful vision in which St Peter scourged him for leaving his flock. He confronted the king with the highly visible marks of this holy visitation, whereupon Eadbald repented, gave up his unlawful wife, accepted the Christian faith and was baptized, and thereafter supported the missionaries' activities.

Bede notes that Eadbald was less powerful than his father, and was unable to coerce the East Saxons into once more accepting Christianity. Nevertheless, he may have enjoyed a measure of control over London, for the Crondall hoard (datable to *c.*650) contains a single gold coin bearing a name which may be his (Auduarld) and which was probably struck by a London moneyer; this is a highly unusual find, for Southumbrian coins do not otherwise carry the names of kings until the eighth century.

Eadbald died in 640 and was buried in the church dedicated to St Mary which he had built in the precincts of the monastery of St Peter and St Paul (later St Augustine's) in Canterbury. There it was remembered that he had died on 22 January; an alternative date of 20 January appears in an early set of annals from Salzburg. Eadbald's wife, who was named Ymme or Emma, died in 642 and was buried beside him. The monastery's sources claim that she was the daughter of a Frankish king, but it has been suggested that her father may have been Erchinoald, the mayor of the palace in the Frankish kingdom of Neustria (an earlier suggestion that he was King Theudebert II of Austrasia arose from confusion between Eadbald and Adaloald, king of the Lombards). Eadbald was succeeded by his son *Eorcenberht. Hagiographical sources supply the names of two further offspring of Eadbald: a son named Eormenred (father of Æbba, who founded Minster in Thanet), and a daughter named Eanswith, the first abbess of the minster at Folkestone. Two diplomas in Eadbald's name are extant, but both are spurious.   S. E. KELLY

Sources Bede, *Hist. eccl.*, 2.5–6, 9–11; 3.8; 5.24 • N. Brooks, *The early history of the church of Canterbury: Christ Church from 597 to 1066* (1984), 63–4, 100–02 • D. W. Rollason, *The Mildrith legend: a study in early medieval hagiography in England* (1982) • P. Grierson and M. Blackburn, *Medieval European coinage: with a catalogue of the coins in the Fitzwilliam Museum, Cambridge*, 1: *The early middle ages (5th–10th centuries)* (1986), 158, 161–2 • I. Wood, *The Merovingian kingdoms, 450–751* (1994), 177 • K. H. Krüger, *Königsgrabkirchen der Franken, Angelsachsen, und Langobarden* (Munich, 1971), 264–87 • *William Thorne's chronicle of St Augustine's Abbey, Canterbury*, trans. A. H. Davis (1934), 20 • 'Annales juvavenses majores', Annals of Salzburg, [*Annales et chronica aevi Carolini*], ed. G. H. Pertz, MGH Scriptores [folio], 1 (Stuttgart, 1826), 87, s.a. 640 • F. M. Stenton, *Anglo-Saxon England*, 3rd edn (1971), 61, 112–13 • P. H. Blair, 'The letters of Pope Boniface V and the mission of Paulinus to Northumbria', *England before the conquest: studies in primary sources presented to Dorothy Whitelock*, ed. P. Clemoes and K. Hughes (1971), 5–13, at 7–8

Eadberht [Eadbert] (d. **698**), bishop of Lindisfarne, succeeded Cuthbert as bishop about a year after the latter's resignation early in 687. The intervening period was a time of great trouble for Lindisfarne, when the see was administered by Wilfrid, lately restored to the bishopric of York. Eadberht, however, brought peace to the community, of which he may well have been a member.

Bede, who is the only authority, speaks highly of Eadberht, describing him as a man of great spiritual power, learned in the scriptures, and ardent in almsgiving. He was evidently given to ascetic observance in imitation of Cuthbert, and spent the penitential seasons of Advent and Lent in solitude at the spot on the coast to which Cuthbert himself used to retreat before his withdrawal to Farne. Eadberht's only known acts as bishop were to replace the thatched roof of the abbatial church of St Peter with lead, and to authorize in 698 the elevation to a new shrine of Cuthbert's miracle-working and imperishable remains, an event of great significance for the community. Eadberht himself died on 6 May 698, within two months of the elevation, and was buried in the grave originally occupied by Cuthbert, a signal honour and one which presumably reflected the affection in which he was held by his community.

Eadberht's relics were removed from Lindisfarne with those of Cuthbert in the early ninth century and accompanied the monastic community on its wanderings until the monks finally settled in Durham. His cult was undoubtedly early: Alcuin ascribed a miracle to his prayers, and his feast day (6 May) is included in the ninth-century Old English martyrology.   ALAN THACKER

Sources Bede, *Hist. eccl.* • Alcuin, 'Carmina', *Poetae Latini aevi Carolini*, ed. E. Dümmler, MGH Poetae Latini Medii Aevi, 1 (Berlin, 1881) • G. Kotzor, ed., *Das altenglische Martyrologium*, Bayerische Akademie der Wissenschaften, Phi.-Hist. Klasse, Neue Forschung, 88 (1981)

Eadberht [Eadbert] (d. **768**), king of Northumbria, was a cousin of his predecessor *Ceolwulf who abdicated in his favour in 737. Like Ceolwulf, Eadberht descended from the collateral Northumbrian royal line of Ocga, son of the Ida who became the first Bernician king of the Northumbrians in 547. His reign was not free from dynastic strife arising from this, for there was opposition to him from Offa, son of the former King Aldfrith (d. 704/5), and thus a descendant of the main royal line of the seventh century, that is via Ida's son Æthelric. In 750 this prince sought sanctuary at the tomb of St Cuthbert on Lindisfarne, but was forcibly removed by Eadberht following a siege of Lindisfarne, events no doubt connected with Eadberht's arrest of Cynewulf, bishop of Lindisfarne, in the same year. Alcuin (d. 804), who regarded Eadberht's reign in conjunction with that of his brother *Ecgberht as bishop and then archbishop of York (732?–766), as being prosperous, harmonious, and militarily successful, may have exaggerated these qualities. That the king's relations with the church were not uniformly smooth is shown by a letter addressed to him and Ecgberht by Pope Paul I and accusing him of alienating three monasteries in favour of a certain Moll, perhaps the future king Æthelwold Moll. Moreover, although the continuation of Bede's *Historia ecclesiastica gentis Anglorum* mentions under the year 750 a successful conquest of the plain of Kyle in south-western Scotland and of other lands, not all Eadberht's campaigns had such a happy outcome. According to the same source, his kingdom was devastated by Æthelbald, king of the Mercians, in 740 while he was engaged in fighting the Picts; and the Northumbrian annals recount the near total destruction of his army in 756 (the correct date may be 755), even though, in alliance with King Óengus of the Picts, he had just conducted a successful campaign against the Britons of Dumbarton. Eadberht's reign is notable for the minting of a silver coinage, partly in his own name, partly in the names of both himself and his brother Archbishop Ecgberht; this was the first to have been minted in Northumbria since the reign of Aldfrith and was superior in fineness to that of southern England at the time. According to Symeon of Durham, he received gifts from Pippin, king of the Franks. Eadberht abdicated in 758 in favour of his son *Oswulf, and received the tonsure, probably at York, where he died on 19 August 768 and was buried with his brother in St Peter's Minster.

DAVID ROLLASON

Sources Bede, *Hist. eccl.* · Symeon of Durham, *Opera* · Alcuin, *The bishops, kings, and saints of York*, ed. and trans. P. Godman, OMT (1982) · Symeon of Durham, *Libellus de exordio atque procursu istius, hoc est Dunhelmensis, ecclesie / Tract on the origins and progress of this the church of Durham*, ed. and trans. D. W. Rollason, OMT (2000) · A. W. Haddan and W. Stubbs, eds., *Councils and ecclesiastical documents relating to Great Britain and Ireland*, 3 (1871), 394–6 · J. J. North, *English hammered coinage*, 3rd edn, 1: *Early Anglo-Saxon to Henry III, c.600–1272* (1994) · D. P. Kirby, *The earliest English kings* (1991) · *ASC*, s.a. 768 (texts A, E)

Eadberht I (*d.* 748). *See under Æthelberht II (d. 762).*

Eadberht II (*fl.* 762–763). *See under Æthelberht II (d. 762).*

Eadberht [Eadbert, Odberht] **Præn** (*fl.* 796–798), king of Kent, came to power by taking advantage of the turmoil that followed the death of King Offa in 796. Since *c.*785 Offa had treated Kent as a province of the Mercian kingdom and had probably killed or driven out anyone with hereditary claims to the throne. Eadberht's name suggests that he had some connection with the ancient Kentish dynasty, which was represented in the earlier part of the century by Eadberht I (*r.* 725–62) and Eadberht II (*r.* 762–*c.*764). In a papal letter of 798 he is denounced as a renegade priest and he is probably to be identified with the exiled priest Odberht (a continental spelling for Eadberht) who was harboured by Charlemagne and sent by him to Rome, in the teeth of Offa's displeasure; he may have been forcibly tonsured on the orders of the Mercian king, with the aim of disqualifying him from kingship. Having established himself as an independent king in 796, conceivably with Charlemagne's help, Eadberht had coins struck in his name by the Canterbury moneyers, some of whom had previously worked for Offa. He also drove out the Mercian archbishop of Canterbury, Æthelheard, and may have sacked his seat at Christ Church (where the early archives seem to have been destroyed at about this time). Eadberht's downfall came in 798 when the Mercian succession crisis had been resolved, and the new king, Cenwulf, was in a position to reannex the wealthy kingdom of Kent. Eadberht was captured and taken to Mercia in chains; there he was blinded and his hands cut off (as a priest he could not be killed). Later medieval sources claim that he was imprisoned in the monastery at Winchcombe and finally released in 811, on the day that the abbey church was dedicated.

S. E. KELLY

Sources *ASC*, s. a. 796, 798 · N. Brooks, *The early history of the church of Canterbury: Christ Church from 597 to 1066* (1984), 114, 121–5 · E. Dümmler, ed., *Epistolae Karolini aevi*, MGH Epistolae [quarto], 4 (Berlin, 1895), no. 100; trans. as 'Letter of Charles the great to Offa, king of Mercia, 796', *English historical documents*, 1, ed. D. Whitelock (1955), no. 197 · W. de G. Birch, ed., *Cartularium Saxonicum*, 1 (1885), no. 288; trans. in *English Historical Documents*, 1 (1955), no. 205 · *Willelmi Malmesbiriensis monachi de gestis regum Anglorum*, ed. W. Stubbs, 2 vols., Rolls Series (1887–9), vol. 1, pp. 94–5 · Symeon of Durham, *Opera*, 1.59 · P. Grierson and M. Blackburn, *Medieval European coinage: with a catalogue of the coins in the Fitzwilliam Museum, Cambridge*, 1: *The early middle ages (5th–10th centuries)* (1986), 281, 283–6, 288

Eadbert. *See* Eadberht (*d.* 698); Eadberht (*d.* 768); Eadberht Præn (*fl.* 796–798).

Eadburga. *See* Eadburh (*fl.* *c.*716–*c.*746); Eadburh (*d.* 751); Eadburh (*fl.* 789–802); Eadburh (921×4–951×3).

Eadburh [St Eadburh, Eadburga] (*d.* 751), abbess of Thanet, succeeded St Mildrith, who died at some time after 733, the probable date of the latest charter in which she appears. Eadburh played an important role in promoting the cult of her predecessor, whom she had translated to a new church dedicated to Sts Peter and Paul which she founded in the monastery of Thanet. The church was in existence by 748, when it is referred to in a charter in which King Æthelbald of Mercia granted to Eadburh half the toll due on a ship. Thomas Elmham places Eadburh's death in 751, and, according to some manuscripts associated with St Mildrith, it occurred on 13 December. She was subsequently venerated as a saint, but at the monastery of Lyminge rather than Thanet. Her saintliness and burial at Lyminge is first referred to in a charter of 804 whose recipient, Selethryth, seems to have been abbess of both Lyminge and Thanet in the late eighth and early ninth centuries. In 1085 Eadburh's remains were apparently translated from Lyminge by Lanfranc to his new foundation of St Gregory's Priory in Canterbury.

It is often stated that Eadburh of Thanet was the Eadburh whom Leoba named as her teacher in a letter to Boniface; but as Leoba's biographer gives no indication that she left Wessex for Kent, it is more reasonable to assume that Leoba's teacher was also associated with the foundation of Wimborne. It is not impossible that Eadburh of Thanet was the abbess who received three letters from Boniface and one from Lull, but nor is there anything to support the identification and Boniface's correspondent might be thought more likely to be the West Saxon *Eadburh (*fl.* *c.*716–*c.*746). Nor can Eadburh, a diminutive form of whose name is Bugga, be identified with the Kentish abbess *Bugga with whom Boniface corresponded, since the full name of the latter was Hæaburh.

BARBARA YORKE

Sources *AS chart.*, S 86, 87, 91, 160 · D. W. Rollason, *The Mildrith legend: a study in early medieval hagiography in England* (1982) · [Rudolf of Fulda], 'Vita Leobae abbatissae Biscofesheimensis auctore Rudolfo Fuldensi', [*Supplementa tomorum I–XII, pars III*], ed. G. Waitz, MGH Scriptores [folio], 15/1 (Stuttgart, 1887), 118–31

Eadburh [Eadburga] (*fl.* *c.*716–*c.*746), abbess (probably of Wimborne), first appears in the historical record as the recipient of a letter from Boniface, written while he was still known by the Anglo-Saxon name of Wynfrith, recounting at her request the recent vision of a monk at Much Wenlock. The letter can be dated to 716–19. Three further letters survive from Boniface to Eadburh, written after he was established in Germany and she had been appointed abbess, and one to her from Lull while he was a deacon; the date range for these letters has been estimated as *c.*735–746. In one of his letters Boniface commissions Eadburh to copy the epistles of St Peter in gold, and there are other general references to books that she had supplied to the mission, as well as clothing. It is usually assumed that she is the Eadburh whom Leoba identified, in a letter to her kinsman Boniface, as her teacher; this evidence makes it unlikely that the Eadburh who was Boniface's correspondent was the same person as the *Eadburh (d. 751) who was abbess of Thanet. Leoba's biographer Rudolf of Fulda makes no reference to Leoba's studying in Kent and implies that she remained at Wimborne until she joined Boniface in Germany. It is also unlikely in the political climate of the first half of the eighth century that a nun would be sent from Wessex to Kent. It would appear then that Eadburh was at one time in charge of the education of the nuns at Wimborne. The form of address in Boniface's letters suggests that Eadburh had been appointed abbess by about the middle of the 730s. The natural assumption is that she was abbess of Wimborne, but the identification is not completely certain because it is not known when Abbess Tetta ceased to be in charge of the foundation, and Leoba's biographer Rudolf implies that Tetta was still abbess when Leoba left for Germany, an event which cannot be closely dated but which is also likely to belong to the mid-730s, though it could be as late as 748. The recognition of Eadburh as West Saxon is important for an appreciation of standards of learning and literacy in the West Saxon church in the first half of the eighth century, and among its nuns in particular. The reference to the epistles written in gold is especially valuable as no surviving manuscript of this calibre has yet been identified as coming from a West Saxon foundation. BARBARA YORKE

Sources M. Tangl, ed., *Die Briefe des heiligen Bonifatius und Lullus*, MGH Epistolae Selectae, 1 (Berlin, 1916), nos. 10, 29–30, 35, 65, 70 · [Rudolf of Fulda], 'Vita Leobae abbatissae Biscofesheimensis auctore Rudolfo Fuldensi', [*Supplementa tomorum I–XII, pars III*], ed. G. Waitz, MGH Scriptores [folio], 15/1 (Stuttgart, 1887), 118–31 · P. Sims-Williams, *Religion and literature in western England, 600–800* (1990), 243–72 · B. Yorke, 'The Bonifacian mission and female religious in Wessex', *Early Medieval Europe*, 7 (1998), 145–72

Eadburh [Eadburga] (*fl.* 789–802), queen of the West Saxons, consort of King Beorhtric, was the daughter of *Offa (d. 796), king of the Mercians, and his wife *Cynethryth (*fl. c.*770–798). In 789 she became the wife of *Beorhtric (d. 802), who ruled Wessex from 787; no offspring are recorded. Beorhtric's future successor Ecgberht was exiled in 789 by Offa, and spent three years in Francia. Beorhtric supported Offa 'because he had his daughter as his *cwen*' (*ASC*, s.a. 839). The rest of Eadburh's story is told by Asser in chapters 13–15 of his life of Alfred. Independently supporting contemporary Frankish evidence that the West Saxons later in the ninth century refused to let their kings have queens, Asser claims to have 'heard often … from the truth-telling Alfred' that Eadburh's 'wickedness' explained 'this perverse custom' (*Life of Alfred*, chap. 13).

Once married, Eadburh had acquired 'power [*potestas*] over almost the whole kingdom. She began to live tyrannically, like her father, and … to accuse to the king everyone she could, and so to deprive them deceitfully of either

life or power'. Intending to poison 'a young man particularly dear to the king', she accidentally poisoned her husband (*Life of Alfred*, chap. 14). Two possibly authentic charters of 801 show Eadburh as *regina*; one was also attested by Ealdorman Worr. The Anglo-Saxon Chronicle (s.a. 802) records the deaths of Beorhtric and Worr (perhaps identifiable with the 'young man particularly dear'), then Ecgberht's accession. Asser says Eadburh, taking 'innumerable treasures', fled to Charlemagne's court and offered gifts. Charlemagne told her to choose between himself and his son. Eadburh:

> foolishly replying without thinking, said: '… I choose your son because he's younger than you.' Charlemagne, grinning, replied: 'if you had chosen me, you would have had my son. Now … you'll have neither.' He did, however, give her a large convent. (*Life of Alfred*, chap. 15)

But she 'fornicated with a man of her own people, was … expelled from the convent on Charles's orders, and ended her days miserably … begging in Pavia, as we have heard from many who saw her' (ibid.).

Royal convents in Francia, ruled by royally appointed abbesses, were political and religious centres but hardly ascetic establishments. From Anglo-Saxon England many women went as pilgrims to Italy and some stayed there, like Alfred's own sister, buried at Pavia in 888. The *Liber vitae* (confraternity book) of the convent of San Salvatore, Brescia, shows high-born English men and women visiting in the 850s, including, almost certainly, Alfred and his retinue. An entry dating to between 825 and 850 in the Reichenau *Liber vitae* shows an 'Eadburg', abbess of a large Lombard convent. Eadburh's story thus acquires verisimilitude (and Asser's life plausibility). It justified, but may also have explained, the downgrading of subsequent West Saxon kings' wives. Further, Eadburh's blackening discredited those whom Ecgberht and his line supplanted. JANET L. NELSON

Sources *Alfred the Great: Asser's Life of King Alfred and other contemporary sources*, ed. and trans. S. Keynes and M. Lapidge (1983) · *ASC*, s.a. 789, 802, 839 · P. A. Stafford, 'The king's wife in Wessex, 800–1066', *Past and Present*, 91 (1981), 3–27 · A. P. Smyth, *Alfred the Great* (1995) · S. Keynes, 'Anglo-Saxon entries in the *Liber vitae* of Brescia', *Alfred the Wise: studies in honour of Janet Bately*, ed. J. Roberts and J. L. Nelson (1997), 99–119

Eadburh [St Eadburh, Eadburga] (921x4–951x3), Benedictine nun, was a daughter of King *Edward the Elder and his third wife, *Eadgifu. She entered Nunnaminster, Winchester, which had been founded by her grandmother Queen Ealhswith, at the age of three and remained there until her death in her thirtieth year on 15 June. The main source for her is the Latin life, written by Osbert of Clare in the early twelfth century though probably drawing upon earlier written materials which were utilized by other post-conquest writers such as William of Malmesbury and the anonymous author of a Middle English life. Her activities were concentrated within the confines of Nunnaminster and her claims to sanctity rested on her charity and humility, manifested in such incidents as her rising in the night secretly to clean the shoes of the other sisters or to pray at the nearby church of St Peter, Colebrook Street. Her presence was important for increasing the wealth and endowments of Nunnaminster, and an estate at All Cannings, Wiltshire, which is said to have been obtained from King Edward by her intercession (though her probable dates suggest she would have been too young to do this in person), was one of Nunnaminster's major possessions in Domesday Book. However, an estate at Droxford, Hampshire, granted to her by her half-brother King Æthelstan did not remain in the nunnery's possession; the charter recording the grant is the only record of her outside hagiographical tradition.

Eadburh's recognition as a saint allowed her patronage on behalf of Nunnaminster to continue after her death. The translation of her body on 18 July from the nunnery cemetery to burial by the high altar in the church cannot be dated precisely, but is likely to have occurred in the 960s. Probably in the following decade, her remains were transferred to a silver shrine, with Bishop Æthelwold of Winchester (d. 984) officiating. The occasion of the second translation was probably the rebuilding of the original timber church of Nunnaminster in stone, as revealed by modern excavations. Her cult seems to have enjoyed considerable popularity in Winchester in the later Saxon period and there seems to have been some rivalry with that of Swithun. Pershore Abbey subsequently claimed that it had purchased some of Eadburh's relics from an abbess of Nunnaminster in the late tenth or the eleventh century. But it is possible that the St Eadburh culted at Pershore and at Bicester Priory, which also claimed to possess relics of her, may in fact have been an earlier Mercian saint, or saints, of the same name, who by the twelfth century had become confused with the better-known Eadburh of Nunnaminster. BARBARA YORKE

Sources S. J. Ridyard, *The royal saints of Anglo-Saxon England*, Cambridge Studies in Medieval Life and Thought, 4th ser., 9 (1988) · L. Braswell, 'St Eadburga of Winchester: a study of her cult, AD 950–1500, with an edition of the fourteenth-century Middle English and Latin lives', *Mediaeval Studies*, 33 (1971), 292–333 · M. A. Meyer, 'Patronage of the West Saxon royal nunneries in late Anglo-Saxon England', *Revue Bénédictine*, 91 (1981), 332–58 · AS chart., S 446 · G. Scobie and K. Qualmann, *Nunnaminster: a Saxon and medieval community of nuns* (1993) · B. Yorke, *Nunneries and the Anglo-Saxon royal houses* (2003)

Eade, Charles Stanley (1903–1964), journalist, was born on 10 June 1903, at 100 Grove Green Road, Leytonstone, London, the son of Arthur Eade, an auctioneer, and his wife, Alice Steadman. He left school at the age of fourteen to join the editorial staff of the *Daily Chronicle*, and also worked on *Lloyd's Weekly News*, until he moved to the *Daily Herald* in 1919. He first worked for the Rothermere press in 1922, when he began writing for the *Daily Mirror*, founded by Alfred Harmsworth in 1903, remaining there until 1930, while also working for the *Sunday Pictorial*, another Rothermere title, between 1922 and 1924, and *The Observer* from 1926 to 1930. He became the proprietor of the *East Ham Echo and South Essex Mail* in 1928. After travelling abroad for two years, he was briefly sports editor and later deputy editor of the *Sunday Express*, belonging to Rothermere's rival, Lord Beaverbrook, and then worked for Allied Newspapers as deputy editor of the *Sunday Graphic* (1933–6), and deputy editor of the *Daily Sketch* (1936–8). He also did sports commentaries on the radio (1932–8). In 1941 Eade married Vera Manwaring: they had one son and two daughters.

Eade was appointed editor of the *Sunday Dispatch*, another Rothermere paper, in 1938, and remained there until 1957, except for the later years of the Second World War, when he was public relations adviser to Admiral Lord Mountbatten, supreme allied commander in south-east Asia, and from 1943 to 1944 he organized newspaper and radio services for allied troops in India, Burma, and Ceylon. In 1953, in an effort to improve the circulation of the *Sunday Dispatch* in the face of competition from Beaverbrook's *Sunday Express*, Eade selected the American best-selling historical novel *Forever Amber* (1944), by Kathleen Winsor, for serialization in the paper. Despite Randolph Churchill's attack on the *Sunday Dispatch* for publishing what Churchill regarded as pornography, Eade succeeded in adding 400,000 to the circulation figures, and continued to publish more of the same kind of material. However, later in the 1950s the *Sunday Dispatch* began to lose money, and in 1961 Rothermere closed it down and sold the title to Beaverbrook Newspapers.

During the war Eade edited five volumes of the war speeches of Winston Churchill to the House of Commons, publishing one a year beginning with *The Widening Struggle* (1942) and ending with *Victory* (1946). After the war he compiled Churchill's *Secret Session Speeches* (1946), speeches made to the House of Commons in secret session between 1940 and 1942. There were five major speeches that had not been recorded, even for official purposes, and after the House of Commons agreed in December 1945 that they need no longer be kept secret, Churchill passed his notes to Eade, giving him authority to publish them. The first of these speeches was made on 20 June 1940, when Churchill told parliament that if Hitler failed to invade Britain, he had lost the war. On 17 September 1940 he gave details of how parliament would carry on sitting despite the air raids; on 25 June 1941 he reported on the grave shipping losses in the Atlantic; he spoke to the Commons on 23 April 1942 after the fall of Singapore, and on 10 December 1942 explained the reasons for recognizing Admiral Darlan as the French leader in north Africa. This was followed by *Churchill by his Contemporaries* (1953), edited by Eade, a series of short articles by people who had known and worked with Churchill, including Eisenhower.

Eade was a director of Associated Newspapers from 1947, a member of the Press Council from 1956 to 1957, and from 1961, and he sat on the council of the Commonwealth Press Union. He died on 27 August 1964 at his home, Bleak House, Broadstairs, Kent, and was buried on 1 September. ANNE PIMLOTT BAKER

Sources *The Times* (28 Aug 1964) · WW · W. Churchill, *Secret session speeches*, ed. C. Eade (1946) · b. cert. · d. cert.

Archives CAC Cam., corresp., diary, and papers relating to Winston Churchill | CUL, corresp. with Sir Samuel Hoare
Likenesses photograph, repro. in *The Times*

Eadfrith [Eadfrid] (*d.* 721?), bishop of Lindisfarne, was very probably a monk and scribe at Lindisfarne before he became bishop. He is celebrated as the scribe and painter of the Lindisfarne gospels, produced in honour of St Cuthbert, probably about the time of the saint's translation in 698. The attribution rests on a tenth-century colophon to the gospels, almost certainly based upon reliable tradition.

The gospels, the script and decoration of which are undoubtedly the work of a single hand, show that Eadfrith was an extremely accomplished calligrapher and a brilliant artist, highly trained in native Insular majuscule but also well acquainted with culturally wide-ranging, above all Italian, scholarship and painterly techniques. The advanced nature of his learning is indicated by his use of an 'Italo-Northumbrian' gospel text and layout, newly adopted at Wearmouth–Jarrow, and in his case evidently copied from a gospel book written in or near Naples in the early sixth century. Eadfrith's sophisticated and eclectic tastes as a painter are demonstrated most clearly by the refined carpet pages, which arguably exhibit Coptic influence, and by the classicizing evangelist portraits, which stand four-square in a Mediterranean tradition, and, with their Greek superscriptions, derive perhaps ultimately from Byzantine prototypes. Elsewhere, his lavish use of zoomorphic and geometric decorative motifs on initials and incipits owes more to Celtic and Germanic models. Nothing is known of how Eadfrith acquired these skills, but his accomplishment is such that he must not only have been trained in a well established native school but also further instructed in southern Italy or by a master trained there.

The Lindisfarne gospels, which probably took at least two years of full-time work to produce, can scarcely have been written after Eadfrith was bishop. If, as was believed by the twelfth century, he was the immediate successor of Eadberht, he presumably became bishop in 698 and hence had almost certainly finished the gospels by then. As bishop, he clearly promoted the Cuthbertine cult with notable enthusiasm. Between 699 and 705 he commissioned a life of the saint from a member of his own community, a work which later ('some years before' 725) he authorized Bede to revise, extend, and rewrite, probably in order to bring Cuthbert's merits to the attention of a wider readership. He was also responsible for the restoration of Cuthbert's hermitage on Farne, in the time of Felgild, Cuthbert's second successor on the island.

Eadfrith's only other recorded act was to give advice and instruction to Eanmund, founder of the unlocated monastery celebrated in Æthelwulf's early ninth-century poem *De abbatibus*, and to cause him to add an ordained teacher to his community. The bishop may also have sent thither Ultan, an Irish priest and famous scribe, established there while Eanmund was still abbot.

In the twelfth century it was recorded that Eadfrith died in 721. He was apparently buried in the abbey church of St Peter, Lindisfarne, and was sufficiently revered for his remains to be taken with those of Cuthbert and other saints, probably when the community finally deserted Lindisfarne in 875. In 995 his remains were taken to Durham, where he was eventually commemorated with the other early bishops of Lindisfarne on 4 June.

ALAN THACKER

Sources *Evangelium quattuor codex Lindisfarnensis*, 2 vols. (Olten and Lausanne, 1956–60) • B. Colgrave, ed., *Two lives of St Cuthbert* (1940) • Æthelwulf, *De abbatibus*, ed. A. Campbell (1967) • Symeon of Durham, *Opera*, vol. 1 • John of Worcester, *Chron.*, vol. 2 • G. Henderson, *From Durrow to Kells: the Insular gospel books* (1987)
Archives BL, Cotton MS Nero D.iv

Eadgifu (*d.* in or after 951), queen of the West Franks, consort of Charles III, was born in Wessex, the daughter of *Edward the Elder, king of the Anglo-Saxons (*d.* 924), and his second wife, Ælfflæd, and thus half-sister of *Æthelstan, king of England (*r.* 924–39). Between 917 and 919 Eadgifu married King Charles III (879–929), nicknamed Simplex ('the Straightforward', commonly but misleadingly translated as 'the Simple') of the West Franks, after the death of his first wife, with whom he had six daughters. Some time between late April and September 921, Eadgifu gave birth to a son, Louis (IV), later king of West Francia from 936 to 954 and nicknamed Transmarinus ('From-over-the-Sea', 'd'Outremer'). Widowed in 929, in 951 she married Count Heribert of Soissons, lay abbot of St Médard, Soissons. She died in Soissons on 26 December in an unknown year.

Eadgifu's career, barely mentioned in Anglo-Saxon sources, is relatively well documented in West Frankish ones. King Charles dowered her with the royal estate of Tusey on the Meuse in Lotharingia, an apt sign of his ambitions in that region. Although Eadgifu produced the long-hoped-for son, Charles's regime collapsed soon afterwards. After his deposition and imprisonment by rebel aristocrats in July 923, and the succession of Rudolf (*r.* 923–36), Eadgifu struggled to secure her son's literal as well as political survival, and probably also, on her own account, to retain her dower. Little Louis was sent for protection 'to his uncle King Athelstan because of the hostility of Hugh [duke of Francia] and Herbert [Heribert (II), count of Vermandois]' (Richer, 2.1). Louis's departure may have occurred, as usually assumed, in 923, but perhaps happened only after Charles's death in October 929. Eadgifu is generally said to have 'taken' Louis, but Folcuin, writing *c.*960, while mentioning that 'she too had suffered many persecutions at this time', clearly states that she 'sent her son to the English' (Folcuin, chap. 101). Eadgifu apparently preferred to stay in West Francia. She may have played some role in Duke Hugh's marriage to her full-sister Eadhild in 926, splitting the alliance between Hugh and Heribert. Another full-sister, Eadgyth, married Otto, son of the East Frankish king Henry, in late 929 or early 930, perhaps to cement a 'legitimist' alliance following Charles's death and Louis's arrival at Æthelstan's court. This could provide a plausible context for the transfer of the so-called Gandersheim gospels, a manuscript of Metz provenance, from West to East Francia, and for the addition on the last leaf of an inscription in Anglo-Saxon square minuscule: 'Eadgifu regina :- æthelstan rex angulsaxonum et mercianorum :-'. Charles's supplanter, Rudolf, died childless in January 936. Some months later, the recall of Louis to Francia 'from over the sea … by Hugh and the other magnates' (Richer, 2.4) certainly attested Æthelstan's influence but probably also the efforts of Eadgifu and her sister. In 937, as part of a successful attempt to throw off Hugh's 'guardianship', Louis gave his mother charge of the key royal stronghold of Laon, and of the rich convent of Notre Dame there. He thus acknowledged as well as enhanced Eadgifu's political importance. Eadgifu also received, perhaps at this time, the palace of Attigny.

Louis's marriage with Gerberga, sister of Otto I, in 939 did not apparently alter Eadgifu's position at Laon. But when Louis was captured by the Normans in 946, it was Gerberga (not, *pace* Whitelock, Eadgifu) who wrote to 'King Edmund of the English' (Richer, 2.49), Eadgifu's half-brother, to beg his intervention. In 951:

> without her son's knowledge, his mother Queen Eadgifu married Count Heribert (III), son of Heribert (II), and after leaving Laon was taken home by him. The king was furious, entered Laon with Queen Gerberga, took away from his mother estates [*predia*] and the royal palace and bestowed these on his wife.   (Richer, 2.101)

Flodoard clarifies: Eadgifu left Laon 'escorted by the men of Heribert and of his brother Adalbert' (Flodoard, s.a. 951), before marrying Heribert; and Gerberga then got Notre Dame, Laon, while Louis himself kept Attigny. Both Flodoard and Richer suggest that Eadgifu took the initiative in this alliance. As lay abbot of St Médard, Heribert gave many of this rich monastery's lands and revenues to Eadgifu as dower. Although now in her mid-forties, she may have hoped for more offspring. There is no record of her alive after 951. When she died, Heribert saw to her burial at St Médard, where in the mid-seventeenth century her barely legible tomb epitaph was deciphered by Jean Mabillon. Heribert died between 980 and 984, leaving no children.

Eadgifu's first, royal, marriage, together with her sisters' marriages, showed the new involvement of Anglo-Saxon rulers in the dynastic alliances of the late Carolingian world, and hence the new standing of Alfred's descendants. Eadgifu's second marriage, to an ambitious young noble, was her response to increasing marginalization at the hands of her son and powerful daughter-in-law: it signalled the special prestige that association with the dowager-queen conferred, yet it was no *mésalliance*, for the Vermandois family could boast, like Louis, descent in the male line from Charlemagne. Threatened with political extinction at Laon, Eadgifu preferred, understandably, to live out her days with Heribert at Soissons.

JANET L. NELSON

Sources L. C. Bethmann, 'Witgeri Genealogia Arnulfi comitis', [*Chronica et annales aevi Salici*], ed. G. H. Pertz, MGH Scriptores [folio], 9 (Stuttgart, 1851), 302–4 • Flodoard, *Annales (916–966)*, ed. P. Lauer (1905) • Folcuin [Folcwinus], 'Gesta Abbatum Sithiensium', ed. O. Holder-Egger, [*Supplementa tomorum I–XII, pars*

I], ed. G. Waitz, MGH Scriptores [folio], 13 (Hanover, 1881), 607–35, 607–34 • Richer of St Rémi, *Historiarum libri IV*, ed. and trans. R. Latouche, 2nd edn (1964) • *English historical documents*, 1, ed. D. Whitelock (1955) • J. Mabillon, *Vetera analecta*, new edn (Paris, 1723), 377–8 • A. Eckel, *Charles le Simple* (1899) • P. Lauer, *Le règne de Louis IV d'Outremer* (1900) • R. L. Poole, 'The alpine son-in-law of Edward the Elder', *EngHR*, 26 (1911), 310–17; repr. in R. L. Poole, *Studies in chronology and history*, ed. A. L. Poole (1934) • J. Verdon, 'Les femmes et la politique en France au Xe siècle', *Economies et sociétés au moyen âge: mélanges offerts à Edouard Perroy* (1973), 108–19 • P. Stafford, *Queens, concubines and dowagers: the king's wife in the early middle ages* (1983) • S. Keynes, 'King Athelstan's books', *Learning and literature in Anglo-Saxon England: studies presented to Peter Clemoes on the occasion of his sixty-fifth birthday*, ed. M. Lapidge and H. Gneuss (1985), 143–201 • E. Freise, 'Die "Genealogia Arnulfi comitis" des Priesters Witger', *Frühmittelalterliche Studien*, 23 (1989), 203–47

Eadgifu (*b.* in or before **904**, *d.* in or after **966**), queen of the Anglo-Saxons, consort of Edward the Elder, was the daughter of Sigehelm, a Kentish ealdorman killed at the battle of the Holme in 903. She was the wife of King *Edward the Elder and the mother of two kings, *Edmund and *Eadred, and of two daughters, *Eadburh, who became a nun at Winchester and was venerated as a saint, and Eadgifu.

Edward married Eadgifu *c.*919; she was his third wife. When he died in 924, it was the sons of earlier marriages who came to the throne and Eadgifu disappears from court. By 939, however, all her stepsons were dead, apparently without offspring, and Eadgifu's sons now reigned in turn. Her triumphant return to court is signalled in her prominence in the witness lists of charters; during the reign of Edmund, the king, his mother, and his brother appear almost as a triumvirate. Eadgifu's influence remained great when her second son, Eadred, came to the throne in 946: indications from charter witness lists that her power waned slightly after 952 may simply reflect the special nature of these ('Dunstan B') charters. The death of Eadred in 955 saw another turn in Eadgifu's fortunes. In the course of the ensuing struggle for the throne between her grandsons, she was first deprived of all her lands by the eldest of them, *Eadwig, who became king, and later restored by the younger, *Edgar, after he came to the throne of Wessex in 959. These shifts suggest she may herself have taken sides in this struggle, probably against Eadwig. Her future was at stake; the marriage of Eadwig to *Ælfgifu threatened Eadgifu's position at court and required that her landed endowment be given to the new queen. Although she recovered some lands, and Edgar made generous gifts to his grandmother, his own marriages meant that her days as a queen were over. She was rarely at court after 959 and probably lived in religious retirement. Her last appearance has a typically familial context, at the great gathering of the royal family in 966, attested in the witness list of Edgar's charter for the refoundation of New Minster, Winchester. The presence of the elderly dowager queen added to the demonstration of family unity at such a potentially divisive moment. Eadgifu probably died and was buried at Winchester but the date is unknown.

Eadgifu is remembered as a friend and ally of saintly churchmen; she persuaded Æthelwold to remain in England and she tried to get a bishopric for Dunstan. In one grant by Eadred to his mother, she is described as 'famosa famula Dei' ('celebrated handmaid of God'; *AS chart.*, S 562). This secondary supportive role is a cliché of saints' lives and only a partial picture. Eadgifu's wide interest in the foundation and endowment of churches—she was remembered as a benefactor at Christ Church, Canterbury—and in land acquisition, particularly in eastern England, show a queen actively involved in the extension of West Saxon power. Such an extension was the motive for her marriage, since she was a wealthy woman. Her father had left his 'ancestral inheritance' at Cooling and 'Osterland' in Kent to her: Cooling had been given a century earlier by Cenwulf, king of the Mercians, to his thegn Eadwulf, perhaps one of Sigehelm's forebears (*AS chart.*, S 1211, 163). Farleigh, Kent, which Sigehelm received from King Alfred (*AS chart.*, S 350), also passed through Eadgifu's hands (*AS chart.*, S 1212). The augmentation of her wealth by her sons and grandsons is further testimony to her involvement in royal rule. Eadred, for example, gave her land at Felpham, Sussex, during his lifetime and bequeathed to her the royal vills at Amesbury, Wiltshire, Basing, Hampshire, and Wantage, Berkshire, and all his booklands in Surrey, Sussex, and Kent. She may even have acted as a sort of regent in Kent, where the will of one thegn (*AS chart.*, S 1511) was apparently arranged before her, in company with Oda, archbishop of Canterbury (and so between 941 and 958). Eadgifu's political career, its peaks and vicissitudes, were shaped by dynastic politics. She is an example of the potential power, and of the accompanying vulnerability, such politics meant for an early medieval queen.   PAULINE STAFFORD

Sources C. Hart, 'Two queens of England', *Ampleforth Journal*, 82 (1977), 10–15, 54 · F. E. Harmer, ed., *Select English historical documents of the ninth and tenth centuries* (1914) · M. A. Meyer, 'Women and the tenth century English monastic reform', *Revue Bénédictine*, 87 (1977), 34–61 · A. Campbell, ed. and trans., *Encomium Emmae reginae*, CS, 3rd ser., 72 (1949), 62–5 · P. A. Stafford, 'The king's wife in Wessex, 800–1066', *Past and Present*, 91 (1981), 3–27 · D. N. Dumville, *Wessex and England from Alfred to Edgar* (1992) · *The life of St Æthelwold / Wulfstan of Winchester*, ed. M. Lapidge and M. Winterbottom, OMT (1991) · W. Stubbs, ed., *Memorials of St Dunstan, archbishop of Canterbury*, Rolls Series, 63 (1874) · J. A. Robinson, *The times of Saint Dunstan* (1923) · N. Ramsay, M. Sparks, and T. Tatton-Brown, eds., *St Dunstan: his life, times and cult* (1992) · M. A. Meyer, 'The queen's "demesne" in later Anglo-Saxon England', *The culture of Christendom* (1993), 75–113 · *AS chart.*, S 350; 562; 1211; 163; 1212; 1511

Eadgifu [Eddeua] **the Fair** [the Rich] (*fl.* **1066**), magnate, held over 270 hides of land (or the equivalent) on the eve of the conquest, making her one of the richest English magnates at that time and giving rise to her alternative name of Eadgifu the Rich. Most of her estates lay in Cambridgeshire, but she also held property in Buckinghamshire, Hertfordshire, Essex, and Suffolk, and men whose lands were tributary to other magnates took her as their lord. Her estates passed after 1066 to Ralph de Gael. It has been suggested that Eadgifu was his mother, and wife to Ralph the Staller, but the Anglo-Saxon Chronicle specifically says that Ralph de Gael's mother was a Breton. One of Eadgifu's manors was Mentmore, in Buckinghamshire, and she might be the widow (or perhaps daughter) of Leofwine of Mentmore, whom the Domesday Book mentions in passing.

It has also been suggested that Eadgifu was the first wife (or mistress) of Harold Godwineson [see Harold II]. The chronicle of Waltham Abbey, of which Harold was patron, describes how his body was identified on the field of Hastings by his former concubine, Eadgyth Swanneshals ('Edith Swanneck'). Although Eadgifu and Eadgyth are different names, the forms (Eddeua and Eddid or Edied respectively) are sometimes confused, and the abbey of St Benet of Hulme, Norfolk, which had close connections with Harold, remembered an Eadgifu Swanneshals among its patrons. An unnamed concubine of Harold's held property in Canterbury, but this need not be Eadgifu the Fair; he probably had more than one.

Domesday Book gives some indications of a connection between Eadgifu the Fair and Harold: she held a manor in the vill of Harkstead, Suffolk, land which was attached to Harold's manor of Brightlingsea, Essex; and some of the Suffolk lands held by her men were tributary to Harold's manor of East Bergholt. Moreover, when Earl Ralph de Gael forfeited his property in 1075, most of Eadgifu's land went to Count Alan Rufus (Alan the Red), lord of Richmond, Yorkshire, who in 1093 carried off Gunnhild, Harold's daughter, from Wilton. When Count Alan died soon afterwards, Gunnhild became the mistress of his brother and heir, Alan Niger (Alan the Black), though Archbishop Anselm attempted to dissuade her. If Gunnhild was the child of Harold's first wife, and if the identification of that wife with Eadgifu the Fair is accepted, then she was the heir of Eadgifu, whose lands Alan Rufus held. It is odd that Gunnhild was not taken to Denmark by her grandmother Gytha along with her sister, the younger Gytha, in 1068; but Gunnhild apparently suffered from a tumour of the eyes, healed by Wulfstan of Worcester (*d.* 1095), which might explain why she was left at Wilton.

ANN WILLIAMS

Sources A. Farley, ed., *Domesday Book*, 2 vols. (1783), 1.134, 136v, 137, 140v, 141v, 146v, 148v, 152, 189v, 193v, 195v, 196v, 198, 198v, 199v, 200, 200v, 201, 201v; 2.7v, 35, 35v, 284v, 285, 295, 296, 397, 410, 430v, 431 · P. A. Clarke, *The English nobility under Edward the Confessor* (1994) · E. Searle, 'Women and the legitimization of succession at the Norman conquest', *Anglo-Norman Studies*, 3 (1980), 159–70, 226–9 · L. Watkiss and M. Chibnall, eds. and trans., *The Waltham chronicle: an account of the discovery of our holy cross at Montacute and its conveyance to Waltham*, OMT (1994) · *Chronica Johannis de Oxenedes*, ed. H. Ellis, Rolls Series, 13 (1859) · C. R. Hart, *The early charters of eastern England* (1966) · R. W. Southern, *Saint Anselm and his biographer: a study of monastic life and thought, 1059–c.1130* (1963) · *The Vita Wulfstani of William of Malmesbury*, ed. R. R. Darlington, CS, 3rd ser., 40 (1928) · C. P. Lewis, 'The formation of the honor of Chester, 1066–1100', *Journal of the Chester Archaeological Society*, 71 (1991), 37–68 [G. Barraclough issue, *The earldom of Chester and its charters*, ed. A. T. Thacker]

Eadgyth. See Edith (*d.* 1075).

Eadie, John (1813/14–1876), biblical scholar, was born at Alva, Stirlingshire, on 9 May 1813 or 1814, the only surviving child of his father's second marriage at nearly seventy years of age. Eadie was a lively child who showed a talent for languages at school and a remarkable memory. He was said at one time to have known the whole of Milton's *Paradise Lost* by heart. He went to the University of Glasgow, where he did well in several classes; but his lack of money meant that he was not able to pay for tuition. He took on a good deal of temperance lecturing, however, for which he became well known. In his theological classes his preference lay with studies affording some scope for investigation and discovery. Thus he found dogmatics much less interesting than exegetics. He was licensed as a preacher with the United Secession church in 1835. His mother, who lay dying as he preached his first sermon, had exercised a profound religious influence on him, which deepened at her death. She was a strong-minded woman who was well read in the popular theology of Scotland and deeply imbued with its spirit.

Within a few weeks of being licensed, Eadie was chosen minister of the Cambridge Street United Secession congregation, Glasgow. Although he had no previous experience of working as a city minister, the congregation flourished under his charge. After 1847, when the United Secession church had joined with the Relief Synod to form the United Presbyterian church, he and some of his congregation moved in 1863 to Lansdowne Church on the city outskirts. This was a large and influential congregation, with whom he remained connected until his death, combining his ministerial duties with his academic appointments.

In 1838–9 Eadie taught the Hebrew class in Anderson's University, Glasgow. Then in 1843, having temporarily taught the biblical literature class in the United Secession Divinity Hall (later the United Presbyterian Divinity Hall), he was appointed professor of biblical literature by the Associate Synod. In 1847 his title changed to that of professor of humanities and evidences. In 1844 he received the degree of LLD from the University of Glasgow, and in 1850 that of DD from the University of St Andrews. In 1857 he was appointed moderator of synod, the highest court in the United Presbyterian church.

Eadie first visited Europe in 1846 to investigate the short-lived reformation movement on the borders of the duchy of Posen, which arose out of exhibitions of the 'holy coat'.

As his professorship was essentially an honorary post, Eadie was in a position that allowed him to concentrate much of his academic energy on publishing. His interest lay in editing and writing both popular and specialist works. He began by editing a magazine, the *Voluntary Church Magazine*, and contributing articles to the *North British Review*, the *Eclectic Review*, and the *Journal of Sacred Literature*. The founder of the last, John Kitto, was the subject of a biography written by Eadie that was published in 1857. He was in charge of the ecclesiastical section of Mackenzie's *Dictionary of Universal Biography*, and contributed many articles to it. He had earlier edited Cruden's *Concordance* (1839), which became popular. He also edited a *Biblical*

Cyclopaedia (1848), a condensed *Bible Dictionary*, *An Analytical Concordance to the Holy Scriptures* (1856), and an *Ecclesiastical Encyclopaedia* (1861).

Eadie's interest in St Paul and his commitment to Pauline theology were also reflected in his published work. In 1859 he produced an exposition of Paul's sermons as found in the Acts of the Apostles which he called *Paul the Preacher*. From his largely self-taught knowledge of Greek, he was able to produce commentaries on the Greek text of five Pauline epistles: Ephesians, Colossians, Philippians, Galatians, and Thessalonians. Bishop Ellicott, the chairman of the New Testament Revision Company, which Eadie later joined, judged that Eadie's exegesis was superior to his grammatical work, although Eadie pointed out that, like other students of Greek in Scotland, his knowledge of the language had suffered through his having had to work as a city priest rather than being able to lead the life of an academic.

In 1869 Eadie went to Egypt and the Holy Land with some friends, and was able to verify many geographical and other points on which he had speculated in some of his books. In 1873 he received a commission from the synod of the United Presbyterian church to visit the United States, and continue to build good relations between his church and American Presbyterians.

As early as 1867 symptoms of heart disease had become manifest. In 1872 these symptoms returned in an aggravated form. But it was not possible to persuade Eadie to take the rest that he required.

In 1876 Eadie published *The English Bible: an external and critical history of various English translations of scripture; with remarks on the need of revising the English New Testament* (2 vols.). His interest in the movement for a revision of the Authorized Version, combined with the attention engendered by his commentaries and a popular family bible he had edited (1851), led to his being invited to join the newly formed New Testament Revision Company, as one of the non-Anglican members. Although one of the more reserved members, he was held in great esteem by the chairman and other colleagues. His last illness was in 1876; he died in Glasgow on 3 June of that year, survived by his wife, Mary (*née* Horne). The enormous number of letters of sympathy and statement from public bodies which followed attested to the esteem and affection in which he was held. Eadie used to say that there were three things he was fond of—bairns, birds, and books. After his death some friends tried to buy his library for the church when Thomas Biggart of Dalry purchased it for £2000, presented it to the synod, and installed it in the United Presbyterian College, under the name of the Eadie Library.

JOANNA HAWKE

Sources J. Brown, *Life of John Eadie* [1878] • [Glasgow newspapers] (4 June 1876) • J. F. Waller, ed., *The imperial dictionary of universal biography*, 3 vols. (1857–63) • Irving, *Scots.* • J. Eadie, *Biblical cyclopaedia* (1857) • J. Smith, *Our Scottish clergy*, 1st ser. (1848), 95–102 • Boase, *Mod. Eng. biog.* • *CCI* (1876)

Likenesses J. Fergus, photograph, repro. in *Dublin University Magazine*, 88/525 (Sept 1876), facing p. 276

Wealth at death £51,265 14s. 10d.: confirmation, 14 Aug 1876, CCI

Eadmer [Edmer] **of Canterbury** (b. c.1060, d. in or after 1126), Benedictine monk and historian, was born to English parents, and entered Christ Church, Canterbury, as an oblate. As a child he witnessed the sudden destruction of the cathedral during the fire of 1067; he took special care afterwards to commit to memory the plan of the old church and the locations of its relics. His recollections as an old man of these childhood memories provide historians with a surprisingly detailed portrait of the Anglo-Saxon building. In 1093 the newly elected Archbishop *Anselm made Eadmer a member of his household and keeper of his chapel. He became as a result Anselm's constant companion, witnessing his disputes with William II and Henry I, and accompanying him during the two exiles that resulted from those disputes. While in exile Eadmer visited European ecclesiastical centres such as Cluny, Lyons, and Rome. Together with Anselm he saw the Normans of southern Italy besiege Capua and met their leader, Roger of Apulia. He also attended two important ecclesiastical councils, at Bari in 1098 and at the Vatican in 1099. Even in the midst of such dazzling spectacle, however, his thoughts never strayed far from England. His most exhilarating moment at the Vatican Council, for example, came when he realized that the bishop of Benevento's cope had been a gift to the Beneventan church from Canterbury's Archbishop Æthelnoth (d. 1038).

During this period of exile Eadmer began an unusual two-part biography of Anselm. In one part, the *Historia novorum*, he described the archbishop's public life. In the other, the *Vita S. Anselmi*, he provided a record of Anselm's private conversation. Both works are particularly remarkable for their use of recorded speech, chiefly from Anselm but also from other fascinating personalities, such as William Rufus. Anselm learned of the biography about the year 1100. After initially approving it, the archbishop changed his mind and ordered that the manuscripts be destroyed. Eadmer obeyed, but preserved an extra copy of his notes.

When Eadmer finally completed the project, it had lost its initial sense of intimacy. The *Historia novorum*, in particular, began to use official correspondence instead of conversation to advance its narrative. Eadmer further transformed his conception of the books when he expanded them some years later. To the *Vita S. Anselmi* he attached a collection of posthumous miracles, making the work more closely resemble standard hagiography. To the *Historia novorum* he added two more books which detailed the efforts of Anselm's successor, Ralph d'Escures (d. 1122), to preserve Canterbury's primacy over York. Originally, Eadmer had kept both works side by side in his manuscript, where he preserved all his writings (Cambridge, Corpus Christi College, MS 371). In their new form, however, the books proved too bulky to occupy the same space and, in a decision symbolic of the breakdown in the project's original unity, Eadmer separated the historical chronicle from the saint's life. An autograph of the revised version survives in another manuscript (Cambridge, Corpus Christi College, MS 452).

Comparable to the zeal with which Eadmer defended Anselm's legacy was the thoroughness with which he documented the Anglo-Saxon past in lives of a series of Canterbury saints. He wrote accounts of major figures, such as Wilfrid (d. 709), Oda (d. 959), and Dunstan (d. 988), and of the obscure eighth-century Archbishop Bregowine (d. 765). He also produced a life of St Oswald (d. 992), probably at the request of friends at Worcester. Worcester, like Canterbury, was an important centre for historical thought in post-conquest England. Eadmer specifically consulted a monk there named Nicholas about politics during the life of St Dunstan and about the primacy of Canterbury over Scotland.

Behind Eadmer's devotion to Anglo-Saxon culture was a belief that England's Norman conquerors were destroying it. Even Archbishop Lanfranc (d. 1089), whom Eadmer admired, comes under criticism in the *Vita S. Anselmi* because of his apparent disrespect for Anglo-Saxon saints. Eadmer particularly resented the archbishop's decision to place most of the church's relics above the north transept of his newly rebuilt cathedral, and hence outside the daily liturgical life of the monks. Shortly after Lanfranc's death Eadmer and his friend Osbern are described as surreptitiously climbing the spiral staircase that led to the relic depository, in order to investigate its contents. In his *Breviloquium* of the life of St Wilfrid, written in the early years of Anselm's archiepiscopate, he describes a monk's vision on St Wilfrid's day in which angels interrupted their own liturgical ceremony at Christ Church to ascend the staircase and pray before Wilfrid's remains. The vision both celebrated and justified the relics' translation back into the main body of the church. One of his theological tracts, 'On the memory of saints', is largely an argument for the necessity of physical proximity to relics during the performance of liturgy. Eadmer undoubtedly misinterpreted Lanfranc's intentions, but because the English monk did so closely associate veneration for relics with the Anglo-Saxon world, the arrangement of the post-conquest cathedral must have seemed to him a direct attack upon his heritage.

Outside their literary context, Eadmer's crusades for his church and its history were unsuccessful. In 1116 he set off on another journey to Rome with Anselm's successor, Archbishop Ralph, in order to battle against York over the primacy of the English church. The mission ended in failure, and Eadmer abandoned it early, returning to Canterbury late in 1118 or early in 1119. Then in 1120 Alexander I, king of Scots, offered Eadmer the bishopric of St Andrews. St Andrews was attempting to establish its independence, with that of the whole Scottish church, of York, which had claimed metropolitan rights there since 1070. Eadmer's solution—to profess obedience to Christ Church—pleased no one, and by 1121 he had returned his episcopal ring and staff and departed, still unconsecrated, for Canterbury. With characteristic pride he observed that 'he would not in exchange for all of Scotland deny himself a monk of Canterbury' (*Historia novorum*, 284).

The date of Eadmer's death is unknown, but it was probably in or a little after 1126. At Christ Church he occupied his final years with the composition of increasingly idiosyncratic theological treatises. In the most influential of them—it came to be attributed to Anselm because of a similarity in argumentative methods—he justified through reason the celebration of the feast of the Immaculate Conception of the Blessed Virgin. This tract was in reality another aspect of Eadmer's campaign to preserve Anglo-Saxon culture. Christians used to celebrate the feast of the Immaculate Conception, he writes, but stopped recently after certain seemingly knowledgeable men had led its observance into contempt.

Perhaps most revealing of these final writings, however, is a letter Eadmer wrote to the church of Glastonbury. In the 1120s Glastonbury claimed that some of its monks had stolen St Dunstan's relics from Christ Church in 1012. Dunstan was Canterbury's most important saint, and the supposed theft must have seemed to Eadmer to undermine most of his life's work. His letter is noteworthy for its use of historical reasoning in order to dismantle Glastonbury's pretensions, but is more remarkable for the tone of moral outrage that characterizes its rhetoric. Even if the claim were true, he writes, then those 'who had been made guardians of the sacred relics, violated the womb of the mother whom they had set out to protect. They robbed her of her heart. They plundered, they ravaged, they stole away her entrails' (Stubbs, 414). With the battle over the primacy lost, and a foreign culture still dominating England, Eadmer filled his letter with all the outrage of a lifetime of frustrated local ambition and wounded national pride.   J. C. RUBENSTEIN

Sources Eadmer, *The life of St Anselm, archbishop of Canterbury*, ed. and trans. R. W. Southern, 2nd edn, OMT (1972) • *Eadmeri Historia novorum in Anglia*, ed. M. Rule, Rolls Series, 81 (1884) • R. W. Southern, *Saint Anselm and his biographer: a study of monastic life and thought, 1059–c.1130* (1963) • W. Stubbs, ed., *Memorials of St Dunstan, archbishop of Canterbury*, Rolls Series, 63 (1874), 162–249, 412–25 • A. Wilmart, 'Edmeri Cantuariensis Cantoris nova opuscula de sanctorum veneratione et obsecratione', *Revue des sciences religieuses*, 15 (1935), 184–219, 354–79 • [Nicolaus Wigorniensis], 'Epistola ad Eadmerum Wigorniensis', *Patrologia Latina*, 159 (1854), 234–6 [letter of Nicholas to Eadmer, on the position of the Scottish church in relation to Canterbury and York] • *Hugh the Chanter: the history of the church of York, 1066–1127*, ed. and trans. C. Johnson, rev. edn, rev. M. Brett, C. N. L. Brooke, and M. Winterbottom, OMT (1990) • Symeon of Durham, *Opera*, 2.3–283 • M. Gibson, 'Normans and Angevins, 1070–1220', *A history of Canterbury Cathedral, 598–1982*, ed. P. Collinson and others (1995), 38–68 • D. L. Bethell, 'English Black monks and episcopal elections in the 1120s', *EngHR*, 84 (1969), 673–98 • R. Gem, 'The significance of the eleventh-century rebuilding of Christ Church and St Augustine's, Canterbury, in the development of Romanesque architecture', *Medieval art and architecture at Canterbury before 1220*, ed. N. Coldstream and P. Draper, British Archaeological Association Conference Transactions [1979], 5 (1982), 1–19 • H. M. Taylor, 'The Anglo-Saxon cathedral church at Canterbury', *Archaeological Journal*, 126 (1969), 101–30 • A. Wilmart, 'Les reliques de Saint Ouen à Cantorbéry', *Analecta Bollandiana*, 51 (1933), 285–92 • N. R. Ker, ed., 'Un nouveau fragment des miracles de S. Ouen à Cantorbéry', *Analecta Bollandiana*, 64 (1946), 50–53 • R. W. Southern, *Saint Anselm: a portrait in a landscape* (1990) • CCC Cam., MS 371 • CCC Cam., MS 452 • J. C. Rubenstein, 'The post-
conquest hagiography of Christ Church, Canterbury', MPhil diss., U. Oxf., 1991
Archives CCC Cam., MSS 371, 452

Eadnoth the Staller (*d.* 1068), landowner and administrator, is addressed in a writ of Edward the Confessor, relating to Hampshire and dated between 1053 and 1066 (*AS chart.*, S 1129); his attestation is also found on two spurious charters for 1065 and he was probably at the beginning of his career in the 1060s. Stallers were members of the royal household and Eadnoth is elsewhere identified as the Confessor's steward; he seems also to have served as a royal justice. He continued in the service of Harold II and then of William I until he was killed in 1068 at Bleadon at the head of a force defending Somerset against an invasion by the sons of Harold. His estates, in Berkshire, Wiltshire, Dorset, Somerset, Devon, and Gloucestershire, passed to Hugh d'Avranches, earl of Chester. He may have held some 65 hides of land in all, but there is some doubt as to whether he should be identified with another of Earl Hugh's predecessors, Alnoth the Staller. The names are distinct, but Alnoth could represent Old English Ealdnoth, and the Domesday scribe occasionally confuses the name elements Eald- and Ead-; alternatively Alnoth and Eadnoth may have been brothers. Eadnoth has been identified as the father of Harding son of Eadnoth, who by 1086 was a substantial landowner in Somerset, probably by virtue of service to the king; he was a royal justice in the time of William II and was still living in the early 1120s. Harding's Somerset lands went to his son, Nicholas of Meriott; another son was *Robert fitz Harding, the Bristol burgess and founder of the second house of Berkeley.

ANN WILLIAMS

Sources ASC, s.a. 1067 • John of Worcester, *Chron.* • R. B. Patterson, 'Robert fitz Harding of Bristol: profile of an early Angevin burgess–baron patrician and his family's urban involvement', *Haskins Society Journal*, 1 (1989), 109–22 • A. Williams, *The English and the Norman conquest* (1995) • C. P. Lewis, 'The formation of the honor of Chester, 1066–1100', *Journal of the Chester Archaeological Society*, 71 (1991), 37–68 [G. Barraclough issue, *The earldom of Chester and its charters*, ed. A. T. Thacker] • P. A. Clarke, *The English nobility under Edward the Confessor* (1994) • S. Keynes, 'Regenbald the chancellor (sic)', *ANS*, 10 (1988) • F. E. Harmer, ed., *Anglo-Saxon writs* (1952) • *AS chart.*, S 1129

Eadred [Edred] (*d.* 955), king of England, was the younger son of *Edward the Elder (*d.* 924) and his third wife, *Eadgifu (*d.* in or after 966). Eadred succeeded his elder brother, *Edmund, who was murdered on 26 May 946. He was consecrated at Kingston upon Thames on 16 August 946, by Oda, archbishop of Canterbury; his coronation was attended by Hwyel Dda ('the Good'), king of south Wales, with his brothers Morgan and Cadwgan, and by four earls bearing the Scandinavian names Orm, Morcar, Grim, and Coll (*AS chart.*, S 520).

The struggle for the north Eadred stepped into the same pre-eminence among the rulers in Britain which his brother, Edmund, had inherited from their half-brother *Æthelstan (*d.* 939) but (like Edmund) he had to fight to retain it. It is unfortunate that all the chroniclers of this

Eadred (d. 955), coin

period wrote after the event, and doubly unfortunate that they often contradict both each other and the surviving charters which are the only strictly contemporary source. It seems, however, that Eadred's authority over the kingdom of York was challenged both by Olaf Sihtricson (called Cuarán, 'sandal', in Gaelic), king of Dublin (d. 981), who had ruled (briefly) in York in Edmund's time, and by the Norwegian prince Erik Bloodaxe. The position was complicated by the presence within the kingdom of York of rival factions, one of them led by Wulfstan, archbishop of York, and by the rivalry between the Anglo-Scandinavian rulers of York and the English of Northumbria beyond the Tyne, led by Osulf of Bamburgh, a supporter (when it suited him) of the West Saxon kings.

Olaf Sihtricson seems to have established himself at York in 947, possibly with Eadred's approval, or at least his acquiescence; Olaf was, after all, King Edmund's godson, and it is noticeable that his coins followed the designs of those issued by English kings, whereas Erik's issues include a sword type, like that used by the viking rulers of the early 920s. Olaf's expulsion, by the Northumbrians themselves, is recorded in the E version of the Anglo-Saxon Chronicle under 952, but the true date is likely to be 949. Five of the eleven charters issued by Eadred in 949 and 950 describe him as 'king of the English, Northumbrians, pagans and Britons' (or variants thereof), and three of the five are attested both by Osulf of Bamburgh and by a group of earls with Scandinavian names who appear for the first time since 947. It seems clear, then, that Eadred had direct control of York in these years, and that the formal submission to Eadred on the part of Archbishop Wulfstan and the Northumbrian magnates, recorded in the D version of the chronicle under the year 947, should probably also be dated to 949. Soon, however, 'they were false to it all, both pledge and oaths as well' (ASC, s.a. 947, text D), and accepted Erik as king.

The advent of Erik presented a serious threat to West Saxon power in the north. Eadred's response was a punitive raid on Northumbria, in which 'the glorious minster' built by St Wilfrid at Ripon was burnt down. As the English returned southward, the army of York overtook the rearguard at Castleford and 'made a great slaughter there'; but when the enraged king threatened to return in force to Northumbria and 'destroy it utterly', the Northumbrians (or at least those associated with Archbishop Wulfstan) abandoned Erik and paid compensation to Eadred for their actions (ASC, s.a. 948, text D). The date of the expedition is disputed; the D text of the chronicle gives 948, but the Historia regum (compiled, from earlier materials, in the early twelfth century) has 950. Moreover, the church of Ripon was closely associated with the archbishopric, and its spoliation may reflect the king's displeasure with Archbishop Wulfstan; if so, the whole campaign may have taken place in 952, when (according to the D text) Wulfstan was arrested on the king's orders and deprived of the archbishopric. Wulfstan was later reinstated, but his successor at York was Oscytel, bishop of Dorchester-on-Thames (d. 971), who was appointed by Eadred. It was probably at this point that the relics of St Wilfrid (d. 709) were seized and brought south to be enshrined at Canterbury, where the Life of Wilfrid of Stephen of Ripon was later rewritten by the Frankish scholar Frithegod of Canterbury. The appropriation of such important cults was one of the means employed by the West Saxon kings to fasten their authority on conquered territories; the removal of the relics both identified the new rulers with the cults of the regions and weakened the local centres of allegiance around which resistance might form.

The D text of the Anglo-Saxon Chronicle and the Historia regum agree that the Northumbrians submitted to Eadred after the defeat at Castleford, and it was perhaps at this point that Erik Bloodaxe was ousted from the kingship, for the Historia regum adds that it was in 952 that 'the kings of the Northumbrians came to an end, and henceforward the province was administered by earls' (English Historical Documents, 1, ed. D. Whitelocke, 1955, no. 3). The circumstances of Erik's death (which probably occurred in 954) are related by the thirteenth-century historian, Roger of Wendover, who, however, had access to earlier material. Wendover names the actual slayer as Earl Maccus (Magnus), but says that Erik was betrayed by Earl Osulf of Bamburgh. Some colour to this is given by the site of the killing, at Stainmore, on the frontier of Osulf's territory, where the Roman road to Carlisle crosses the Pennines; and by the fact that it was Osulf whom Eadred chose as earl of Northumbria after the ending of the independent kingdom of York.

Government and administration   Eadred's counsellors were, by and large, the men who had advised his brother, Edmund and, in some cases, his half-brother Æthelstan, which made for a certain continuity in policy and practice over the three reigns. Among the greater counsellors,

Oda, archbishop of Canterbury, was particularly prominent; under Eadred's will (*AS chart.*, S 1515) he received a personal bequest of 240 gold mancuses (£30 of silver pennies). Oda was a professed monk, closely connected with the reformed house of Fleury-sur-Loire, and a leading figure in the movement to reform the English church. In contrast Ælfsige, whom Eadred appointed bishop of Winchester in 951, was a married man with a son. Among the laymen, the leading figure was still Æthelstan Half-King, ealdorman of East Anglia, who was first promoted by King Æthelstan. He was another champion of ecclesiastical reform and it is significant that his wife, Ælfwynn, was foster mother to Eadred's nephew *Edgar, the younger son of Edmund and Ælfgifu. Æthelstan Half-King was also a close friend of Dunstan, abbot of Glastonbury, who attests several of Eadred's charters in the period between 949 and 955; his brother Wulfric, already favoured by Edmund, received further grants of land from Eadred. Dunstan was one of the churchmen entrusted with the king's treasures, including his landbooks (the charters which constituted his title-deeds), to be kept 'in the security of his monastery' (Stubbs, 29). He seems to have had a hand in the production of royal charters for Eadred and his successors. He himself may have written Eadred's charter of 949, granting Reculver to Christ Church, Canterbury (*AS chart.*, S 546), and the group of royal diplomas now known as the 'Dunstan B' charters, written for various beneficiaries in the period between 951 and 975, seem to have been produced by someone who had been trained at Glastonbury under Dunstan and who remained there after Dunstan himself had moved on. Another influential churchman was Cenwald, bishop of Worcester, who was perhaps responsible for the series of alliterative charters produced in the 940s and 950s.

The queen mother, Eadgifu, was another important member of Eadred's court and council. Her father was the Kentish ealdorman Sigehelm, killed at the battle of the Holme in 903, and Eadgifu was a considerable landowner in Kent before her marriage to King Edward the Elder. These Kentish interests continued: she witnessed the will of a Kentish thegn in company with Archbishop Oda and therefore between 941 and 958 (*AS chart.*, S 1511), and was remembered as a benefactor of Christ Church, Canterbury. Her importance in her son's life is shown by his bequests to her, consisting of the royal vills of Amesbury, Wiltshire, Basing, Hampshire, and Wantage, Berkshire, and 'all the booklands which I have in Surrey, Sussex and Kent, and all those which she has previously had'; the latter presumably included the estate at Felpham, Sussex, which Eadred had given his mother, described as *famosa famula Dei* ('a celebrated handmaid of God'), in 953 (*AS chart.*, S 562).

Among the men promoted by Eadred himself, two are worthy of especial notice. In 951, the king gave land in Buckland, Somerset, to his kinsman *Ælfhere, later ealdorman of Mercia. This is Ælfhere's first appearance in the surviving sources, though his brother Ælfheah had received lands from both Æthelstan and Edmund. Their family's power was soon to rival that of the 'Half-King'

himself. The other newcomer is equally significant. Towards the end of his reign, the king's mother, Eadgifu, persuaded him to give the royal vill of Abingdon to Æthelwold, then a monk at Glastonbury under Dunstan. Æthelwold transformed the secular minster at Abingdon into a regular Benedictine house. A great feast was held to celebrate the foundation of the new church, at which the mead flowed like water, and the Northumbrian guests, 'after their usual fashion', got spectacularly drunk (*Vita S. Æthelwoldi, Chron. Abingdon*, 2.258). Whether the king enjoyed it is doubtful. Towards the end of his life Eadred was seriously ill of the malady which eventually killed him. Dunstan's first biographer, who had been in his household and was in a position to have attended him on his visits to court, describes how Eadred was unable to swallow his food, and was reduced to sucking the juice out of it and spitting what remained back onto his plate, 'a nasty practice that turned the stomachs of the thegns who dined with him' (Stubbs, 31). As if this was not enough, he may also have been lame or disabled, for the eleventh-century writer, Hermann of Bury, claims that he suffered a weakness of the feet (Arnold, 1.29).

The king's household A charter issued on the date of the king's coronation in 946 (*AS chart.*, S 520) grants land at Warkton, Northamptonshire, to the Mercian thegn Wulfric, described as *pedisequus* (sometimes appearing as *sequipedus*), which, like the later 'staller', denotes someone in especially close attendance on the king. Eadred's will reveals a little about the hierarchy of royal counsellors and the composition of the king's household. The largest personal bequests, as already described, are the extensive lands bequeathed to his mother, followed by the 240 gold mancuses left to Archbishop Oda. Each bishop and each ealdorman received 120 gold mancuses (£15 of silver pennies). Each *discþegn*, *hræglþegn*, and *biriele* received 80 mancuses of gold (£10 of silver pennies). These are the main household officials: the *discþegn* (*dapifer*, seneschal) was responsible for the provisioning of the king's household with food; the *biriele* (*pincerna*, butler) for the provision of drink; and the *hræglþegn* (*burþegn*, *camerarius*, chamberlain) oversaw the king's personal possessions. The chaplains in charge of the king's relics (his *haligdom*, which could include documents of various kinds, including royal charters), each received 50 gold mancuses and £5 of silver pennies (equivalent to £11¼ of silver pennies). His other priests received £5 of pennies each, and each steward (*stigweard*) and lesser official, lay or ecclesiastic, received 30 gold mancuses (£3¾ of silver pennies).

Eadred's legacy Although Eadred is remembered as the king who oversaw the final incorporation of the viking kingdom of York into the kingdom of the English, this was probably not apparent at the time and his will reveals the uncertainty and sense of danger still felt in the middle of the tenth century. Eadred left £1600 of silver 'for the redemption of his soul and for the good of his people, that they may be able to purchase for themselves relief from want and from the heathen army if they [have] need' (*AS chart.*, S 1515). The money was entrusted to four leading churchmen: Archbishop Oda, who received £400 for the people of Kent, Surrey, Sussex, and Berkshire; Ælfsige, bishop of Winchester, who got £200 for Hampshire and £100 apiece for Wiltshire and Dorset, plus £200 for the episcopal see itself or 'for whichever shire may need it' (ibid.); Dunstan, who got £200 to keep at Glastonbury for the people of Somerset and Devon; and Oscytel, bishop of Dorchester-on-Thames, who got £400 for the Mercians (the West Saxon bias in the royal government is still strongly marked). In addition gold to the weight of 2000 mancuses (equivalent to £250 pounds of silver pennies) was to be coined into mancuses (1 mancus = 30*d*.) and divided between the archbishop, Bishop Ælfsige, and Bishop Oscytel 'and they are to distribute them throughout the bishoprics for the sake of God and for the redemption of my soul' (ibid.).

Eadred's bequests to his household have already been mentioned. His ecclesiastical benefactions were largely to the Winchester houses: the Old Minster was left three estates in Wiltshire, at Downton, Damerham, and Calne; the New Minster received Wherwell, Andover, and Kingsclere, Hampshire; and Nunnaminster got Shalbourne and Bradford, Wiltshire, and Thatcham, Berkshire. Nunnaminster also received £30 of silver, as did the other royal nunneries at Wilton and Shaftesbury. Twelve almsmen were to be appointed on each estate (and on the others mentioned in the will) to pray for the king's soul, and their successors likewise 'so long as Christianity endures' (*AS chart.*, S 1515). Eadred also left two golden crosses, two golden-hilted swords, and £400 to 'the foundation wherein he desires that his body shall rest' (ibid.); he does not specify which it is to be, but in the event he was buried in the Old Minster, Winchester.

Eadred was clearly an able and even energetic king, hampered by debility and (at the last) by a serious illness which brought about his early death, aged not much above thirty, on 23 November 955 at Frome in Somerset. Perhaps because of his physical weakness, he never married, and his heirs were his nephews, *Eadwig and Edgar, the sons of his brother, Edmund. ANN WILLIAMS

Sources ASC, s.a. 955 [text A]; s.a. 946, 955, 971 [text C]; s.a. 946, 947, 948, 952, 954, 955 [text D]; s. a. 948, 949, 952, 954 [text E] • *AS chart.*, S 163, 350, 516–580, 1211, 1212, 1511, 1515 • John of Worcester, *Chron.* • P. Sawyer, 'The last Scandinavian rulers of York', *Northern History*, 31 (1995), 39–44 • A. Campbell, 'Two notes on the Norse kingdoms in Northumbria', *EngHR*, 57 (1942), 85–97, esp. 91–7 • A. P. Smyth, *Scandinavian York and Dublin: the history of two related Viking kingdoms*, 2 (1979) • N. Brooks, 'The career of St Dunstan', *St Dunstan: his life, times and cult*, ed. N. Ramsay, M. Sparks, and T. Tatton-Brown (1992), 1–23 • D. Whitelock, 'The dealings of the kings of England with Northumbria in the 10th and 11th centuries', *The Anglo-Saxons: studies in some aspects of their history and culture presented to Bruce Dickins*, ed. P. Clemoes (1959), 70–88 • F. M. Stenton, *Anglo-Saxon England*, 3rd edn (1971) • B., 'Vita sancti Dunstani', *Memorials of Saint Dunstan, archbishop of Canterbury*, ed. W. Stubbs, Rolls Series, 63 (1874), 3–52 • C. R. Hart, 'Æthelstan "Half-King" and his family', *Anglo-Saxon England*, 2 (1973), 115–44 • D. Rollason, 'Relic-cults as an instrument of royal policy, *c*.900–*c*.1050', *Anglo-Saxon England*, 15 (1986), 91–103 • A. Thacker, 'Æthelwold and Abingdon', *Bislop Æthelwold: his career and influence*, ed. B. Yorke (1988), 433–64 • S. Keynes, 'The "Dunstan B" charters', *Anglo-Saxon England*, 23 (1994), 165–93 • C. R. Hart, *The early charters of northern England and the north midlands* (1975), 371–4 • S. Keynes, *The diplomas of Æthelred II, 'the Unready', 978–1016* (1980), 158–61 • N. Brooks, *The early history of the church of Canterbury: Christ Church from 597 to 1066* (1984), 205, 222–37, 250 • M. Lapidge, 'B and the Vita s Dunstani', *St Dunstan: his life, times and cult*, ed. N. Ramsay, M. Sparks, and T. Tatton-Brown (1992), 247–59 • C. E. Blunt, B. H. I. H. Stewart, and C. S. S. Lyon, *Coinage in tenth-century England: from Edward the Elder to Edgar's reform* (1989) • D. Hill, *An atlas of Anglo-Saxon England* (1981) • T. Arnold, ed., *Memorials of St Edmund's Abbey*, 1, Rolls Series, 96 (1890), 29

Likenesses coin, BM [*see illus.*]

Eadric (*d.* 686). *See under* Hlothhere (*d.* 685).

Eadric of Laxfield (*d.* in or after 1066?), magnate, was one of the major landholders before 1066. All that is known of him comes from Little Domesday, the return of the Domesday commissioners for the East Anglian circuit, which reveals that he had held some 123 carucates of land in Suffolk and Norfolk. He had also attracted the commendation of large numbers of lesser thegns and free men; just how many it is impossible to say, since most of them are unnamed, but a minimum of eighty-two named individuals can be identified. Little Domesday also records the outlawry of Eadric at some time in Edward the Confessor's reign, though unfortunately the reason is unspecified. His lands were confiscated by the king and his men sought other lords. When he was subsequently pardoned and reinstated, Edward issued a writ permitting Eadric's men to return to their allegiance, if their lord wished it (*Domesday Book*, 2.310v–311). This was the cause of several disputes after 1066, when Eadric's lands were redistributed among the incoming Normans. In theory, commendation had no bearing on the ownership of the commended man's land, but many post-conquest lords appropriated the estates of men commended to their predecessors as well as those belonging to the predecessors themselves. Indeed it seems that many lesser thegns and free men, deprived of the support of their dead or dispossessed lords, actively sought the protection of those who had supplanted them; and, moreover, brought their lands with them, even if those lands had formed part of a manor belonging to a landowner other than the former lord. Thus the land of Stanwine at Heveningham was claimed by Robert Malet because Stanwine had once been commended to his predecessor, Eadric of Laxfield, even though the tenement in question was attached to the manor of Peasenhall, held by Northmann, the predecessor of Roger (I) Bigod; and Stanwine himself offered to prove that he had still been commended to Eadric on the day of King Edward's death, even though the local hundred jury testified that he was at that time the man of Earl Harold (*Domesday Book*, 2.313, 332).

Eadric's name is one of the commonest in eleventh-century England, and only where Little Domesday gives him the distinctive toponymic from his estate at Laxfield in Suffolk (or refers to him as the antecessor of Robert Malet) can he be securely identified. For this reason the identification of Eadric of Laxfield with Eadric Cecus (Eadric the Blind), whom Domesday records as a king's thegn in Wiltshire, must be regarded as dubious; especially as it seems unlikely that Eadric of Laxfield was living in 1086. Most of his land had passed either to William Malet, who was killed in 1071, and thence to his son Robert, or (in Norfolk) to Ralph de Gael, exiled in 1076, and thence to the king (Happisburgh and probably Eaton) or to Roger Bigod (Sutton). All these men were in royal service, either as sheriffs of Suffolk or (in Ralph's case) as earl of East Anglia, and this pattern of distribution suggests that Eadric had died in or soon after 1066 and that his lands had been taken into the king's hand and used to endow the local royal officials.   ANN WILLIAMS

Sources A. Farley, ed., *Domesday Book*, 2 vols. (1783) • P. A. Clarke, *The English nobility under Edward the Confessor* (1994) • D. C. Douglas, ed., *Feudal documents from the abbey of Bury St Edmunds*, British Academy, Records of Social and Economic History, 8 (1932) • J. A. Green, *English sheriffs to 1154* (1990)

Eadric [Edric] **Streona** (*d.* 1017), magnate, was the son of a certain Æthelric, also called Leofwine; the name of his mother is not known.

Origins and historical character Eadric's family would appear to have had interests in Shropshire and Herefordshire, and may have originated in the vicinity of Shrewsbury. Much was made in the early twelfth century of Eadric's low birth, and of his ability to gain advancement by his skill in speech and by his effrontery. A Worcester chronicler names his brothers as Brihtric, Ælfric, Goda, Æthelwine, Æthelweard, and Æthelmær, of whom the last is said (probably mistakenly) to have been 'father of Wulfnoth, father of Godwine, ealdorman of the West Saxons' (John of Worcester, *Chron.*, s.a. 1007, leaving a blank space between Ælfric and Goda, as if for the name of another brother). Thegns bearing these names occur among the witnesses to the charters issued in the name of King *Æthelred II in the late tenth and early eleventh centuries. It is striking that the thegns in question occur quite often in groups of two or three, which might be interpreted as evidence that they were members of the same family. On this basis, Eadric's father, Æthelric, can be identified (tentatively) as a thegn who attended court from the late 980s onwards, and who was accompanied from the mid-990s onwards by one or more of his sons (not including Ælfric); and if only to judge from the witness lists, it may be that the name of the other brother was Æthelnoth. Eadric himself is first identifiable in the witness lists, with his father, in 1002 and members of his family seem to have been present at court in some strength in 1004–5; there are no lists for 1006, but Eadric occurs in first place among the thegns in 1007 (*AS chart.*, S 916, for St Albans Abbey), in which year he was appointed ealdorman of Mercia. It may have been in 1007, or thereabouts, that Eadric married Eadgyth, daughter of King Æthelred, reflecting or accounting for his sudden rise to prominence, for John of Worcester implies that the marriage had taken place by 1009.

Eadric Streona came to acquire a reputation second to none for his complicity in numerous acts of subterfuge, treachery, and murder, and it seems remarkable under these circumstances that he should have been entrusted with high office by three successive kings (Æthelred, Edmund Ironside, and Cnut). There is a wealth of information on Eadric in eleventh- and twelfth-century sources, to the extent that one might suppose that he became the subject of an oral saga, of which parts are preserved in each source. While the temptation is to assemble all the references and so to produce a single composite account, it is important to admit the possibility that elements of the story developed independently of each other, and to maintain a distinction between the portrayal of Eadric in each source.

Eadric Streona in the Anglo-Saxon Chronicle Eadric's reputation as a traitor to the English cause, and as a murderer of his political opponents, is already pronounced in the account of Æthelred's reign written perhaps by a Londoner, *c.*1017, and incorporated in certain recensions of the Anglo-Saxon Chronicle (texts C, D, E, and F). It is apparent that there were major upheavals at court in the first half of 1006, as a result of which Ælfhelm, a member of a prominent Mercian family who held office as ealdorman of southern Northumbria, was killed and his two sons, Wulfheah and Ufegeat, blinded. The chronicler does not, however, impute complicity in these events to any one person in particular. In July of the same year, the course of viking activity in England took a sudden turn for the worse, with the arrival of 'the great fleet' at Sandwich, probably led by a certain Tostig. The army did great damage wherever it went, but left the country in 1007 with a payment of £36,000. According to the chronicler, it was at this point that Eadric was appointed 'ealdorman over the kingdom of the Mercians' (*ASC*, texts C, D, E). So, while the domestic upheavals in 1006 may have signified the emergence of a new faction at court, it was not until the immediate aftermath of a viking invasion, in the following year, that the king chose to make an appointment which itself represented a significant reform in the administrative or military structure of the kingdom. Another viking army, led by Thorkill the Tall, was active in England from 1009 until 1012, with devastating effect. It was during this period that Eadric seems to have risen to great prominence in the kingdom (symbolized by his primacy among the king's ealdormen), and to have started to earn his reputation for undermining the best efforts of the English to resist the Danish invaders. In 1009 the whole people was ready to attack the army, 'but it was hindered by Ealdorman Eadric, then as it always was' (*ASC*, texts C, D, E), reflecting the chronicler's awareness of his further activity in 1015–16. In 1012, 'Ealdorman Eadric and all the chief councillors of England, ecclesiastical and lay, came to London before Easter … and they stayed there until the tribute [*gafol*], namely 48,000 pounds, was all paid after Easter' (*ASC*, texts C, D, E). It may have been at about this time that Æthelric, bishop of Sherborne, was obliged to sell an estate at Corscombe, Dorset, to Eadric, 'on account of the attacks and injuries of the wicked Danes', as if the bishop had not been able to raise sufficient funds to pay Sherborne's share of the tribute, and as if Eadric was ready to take advantage of his predicament; some years later, a certain Wulfgar bought the land from Eadric and restored it to the abbey (*AS chart.*, S 933, dated 1014). It was at about the same time that Eadric seems to have been active across the border in Wales: according to a set of

Welsh annals, 'Menevia [St David's, Dyfed] was ravaged by the Saxons, namely Edrich and Ubrich' (*Annales Cambriae*, 22), apparently in 1011–12.

It is not clear what part Eadric played in the events of 1013, which led to the acceptance of Swein Forkbeard as full king, and it is even possible that he gained some credit for holding out as others succumbed. Following Swein's death on 3 February 1014, King Æthelred returned to England from his brief exile in Normandy. The atheling *Æthelstan resumed his position as prospective heir to his ailing father, and following Æthelstan's death, on 25 June 1014, his younger brother Edmund Ironside [see Edmund II] was obliged, in effect, to assume the same role. Matters seem to have come to a head at a 'great assembly' convened at Oxford in the opening months of 1015: 'and there Ealdorman Eadric betrayed Sigeferth and Morcar, the chief thegns belonging to the Seven Boroughs: he enticed them into his chamber, and they were basely killed inside it' (*ASC*, texts C, D, E). King Æthelred seized their estates and ordered that Sigeferth's widow be taken to Malmesbury; whereupon Edmund took her against the king's will, married her, himself took possession of Sigeferth's and Morcar's estates in the east midlands, 'and the people all submitted to him' (*ASC*, texts C, D, E). It is possible to interpret this turn of events in several different ways. It could be that Edmund, with the help of his associates Sigeferth and Morcar, was known to be making a bid for the throne (fearing that he might be losing ground to Æthelred's children with his second wife, Emma), and that Eadric took what action he could in 1015 to protect the king's position. It is also possible that Eadric was the instrument by which the king punished Sigeferth and Morcar for submitting to Swein in 1013. It could be, on the other hand, that Eadric was jealous of the influence which Sigeferth and Morcar were coming to enjoy in court circles, in as much as they represented the interests of an entrenched midlands aristocracy and were associated by marriage with the family of Wulfric Spot and Ealdorman Ælfhelm, and that in 1015 he resorted to foul means in order to dispose of two of his main political rivals. Whatever the case, Edmund Ironside seems to have been prompted by Eadric's treacherous behaviour to take a firm stand against him, and against the influence which he exercised over the king, by establishing a position of power for himself in the east midlands. The sudden and unexpected appearance of Cnut, at Sandwich, and his invasion of Wessex (while the king lay ill at Cosham), turned the drama into a crisis. Eadric wished to betray Edmund himself, having decided (it seems) that his political future lay in service to Cnut, and in the event took forty ships from the king and defected to the Danish side. In 1016 Cnut and Eadric were active initially in Warwickshire. Edmund, and Uhtred, earl of Northumbria, responded not by engaging the enemy directly but by taking their forces into Staffordshire, Shropshire, and Cheshire, ravaging the land from which Eadric might have hoped to draw further resources and support. Soon afterwards, Uhtred and the Northumbrians were forced to submit to Cnut; 'and nevertheless he was killed by the advice of

Ealdorman Eadric' (*ASC*, text C, though not in texts D and E), perhaps in revenge for Uhtred's activities in Mercian territory, or in order to dispose of one who might have remained a threat to the security of Cnut's interests in the north. Interestingly, the author of the tract *De obsessione Dunelmi*, writing much later in the eleventh century, places the death of Uhtred in the context of a far more elaborate tale of Northumbrian politics, having no discernible connection with Eadric.

Following the death of King Æthelred, on 23 April 1016, Edmund Ironside fought a series of five battles against the Danish invaders, across the breadth of southern England. The first was at Penselwood (near Gillingham, Dorset), and the second was at Sherston (near Malmesbury, Wiltshire). The chronicler states explicitly that Ealdorman Eadric and a certain Ælfmær Darling were on the Danish side at Sherston; and much would be made, subsequently, of Eadric's disgraceful attempt on this occasion to deceive the English into thinking that their king was dead. The third battle was at London and the fourth at Otford in Kent, both represented by the chronicler as victories for the English. At this point Ealdorman Eadric came to meet the king, at Aylesford in Kent, and seems to have been accepted back onto the English side; as the chronicler remarked (with hindsight), 'No greater folly [*unræd*] was ever agreed to [*ge red*] than that was' (*ASC*, texts C, D, E). The fifth battle took place at 'Assandun' (which may be identified with Ashingdon, in Essex) on 18 October 1016, with predictable results. 'Then Ealdorman Eadric did as he had often done before: he was the first to start the flight with the Magonsæte, and thus betrayed his liege lord and all the people of England' (*ASC*, texts C, D, E). Cnut pursued Edmund into Gloucestershire and the two leaders came to terms at Alney (an island in the Severn, near Deerhurst). 'Then Ealdorman Eadric and the councillors who were there advised that the kings should be reconciled, and they exchanged hostages' (*ASC*, texts C, D, E). King Edmund died on 30 November 1016, in circumstances which remain obscure, and Cnut succeeded to all the kingdom of England. Initially, Cnut rewarded Eadric for his services by appointing him ealdorman of Mercia; but it was not long before the ealdorman was seen to have outlived his usefulness to the new regime, and in 1017 he was killed.

Eadric Streona in later sources It is apparent that the chronicler was not alone in his estimation of the decisive role played by Eadric Streona in undermining English resistance to the Danes. The author of the *Encomium Emmae*, writing in 1041–2 (and not aware, it seems, of the account of the period in the Anglo-Saxon Chronicle), provides a hopelessly garbled version of the events of 1015–17, from which it is difficult to salvage much more than a general impression of Eadric's reputation for treacherous behaviour. The encomiast represents Eadric as King Edmund's principal supporter at London, displaying awareness of his importance, and that he was for a while on Edmund's side, but transferring a situation which obtained in the summer of 1016 back to the winter of 1015–16. The encomiast states further that Eadric was instrumental in precipitating the flight of the English at the battle of 'Assandun', citing his supposed words ('Let us flee, oh comrades …') and alleging that he was at the time in cahoots with the Danes (*Encomium*, 2.9). The encomiast also attributes to Eadric a speech extolling the advantages of taking flight in the face of an overwhelming enemy force, and urging a partition of the kingdom between Edmund and Cnut. It is clear, however, that even from the Anglo-Danish point of view Eadric was a traitor who received his just deserts. He was beheaded by Earl Erik of Hlathir, on the king's orders, at London in 1017, 'so that retainers [*milites*] may learn from this example to be faithful, not faithless, to their kings' (*Encomium*, 2.15).

Eadric's credentials as the villain of the piece were thus well enough established before the Norman conquest, and his role in the history of England well defined before the Anglo-Norman historians took over in the late eleventh and early twelfth centuries. One has to bear in mind, however, that a man's posthumous reputation was determined by those who happened to have occasion to write about him, and not necessarily by those who might have been counted among his friends. Eadric's roots lay in Shropshire, and it may be that his primary association (as at the battle of 'Assandun') was with the Magonsæte (the people of Herefordshire and Shropshire); his brother Ælfric was the father of Eadric Silvaticus, also known as *Eadric the Wild, whose interests lay in the same part of the country. No tradition of Eadric Streona survives from this area. Yet while Eadric the Wild was renowned at Worcester for his spirited resistance to the Normans, his uncle Eadric Streona was reviled there as an enemy of the church. The Worcester tradition was transmitted in two roughly contemporary sources. One is a short history of some Worcester Cathedral priory estates compiled in the late eleventh century and preserved in Hemming's cartulary; this source, which stresses Eadric's power, describing him as one who has been set up over the whole kingdom of the English and held dominion as if a sub-king, also contains the first instance of Eadric's byname Streona, 'the Grasper'. The other consists of material assembled by the Worcester monk Florence, now subsumed into John of Worcester's twelfth-century chronicle and also used in the 1120s by William of Malmesbury. The Worcester chronicle records, for example, that Eadric was deeply implicated in the killing of Ealdorman Ælfhelm which had prepared the way for his own advancement in 1007; that, at the battle of Sherston in 1016, Eadric cut off the head of a certain Osmær, who was similar in appearance to Edmund, and held it aloft, shouting that their king was dead; and more concretely, that he was killed in London at Christmas 1017 and that Cnut ordered his body to be thrown over the city wall and left unburied. The Worcester tradition differs from the Anglo-Saxon Chronicle in not accusing Eadric of any involvement in the death of Earl Uhtred, in placing his opportunistic return to the English side before, not after, the events in London, and in giving a more damaging account of Eadric's meeting with Edmund at Aylesford. William of Malmesbury made

effective, if sometimes imaginative, use both of information from his version of the Anglo-Saxon Chronicle and of some of the Worcester material. It is often difficult to judge the historicity of these augmentations of the legend. The most substantial addition Malmesbury made to his main sources has the effect of implicating Eadric in the death of King Edmund. Hermann, monk of Bury St Edmunds, had alluded to a similar story in his late eleventh-century *Liber de miraculis sancti Edmundi*; and Malmesbury himself reports the story as if it had come to him separately from the rest of his material on Eadric. Henry of Huntingdon, making his own use of a version of the Anglo-Saxon Chronicle and of some of the material found at Worcester and in William of Malmesbury's *Gesta regum*, gives an interesting version of the story of Eadric's exhortation to the English to take flight, here transferred from the battle of Sherston (when Eadric was on the Danish side) to the battle of 'Assandun' (when he was back on the English side), and thereby stressing Eadric's complicity in the final defeat of the English.

It is unlikely that any of the new material found in the stories of Eadric that were adapted by later generations of historians has any basis in actual eleventh-century events. An extended tale of Eadric's death was told in Gaimar's mid-twelfth-century *L'Estoire des Engleis*. In the first half of the thirteenth century, Roger of Wendover related Eadric's murder of Gunnhild (sister of King Swein) and her husband and son. By stating that Eadric accompanied Queen Emma and the athelings to Normandy in 1013, Wendover hints that Eadric was aligned with Æthelred's children with Emma, against those with his first wife, Ælfgifu, but it would be hazardous to pursue the point. Tales of Eadric spread to Iceland in the thirteenth century: Snorri Sturluson knew him as 'Heinrekr strjóna', murderer of King Edmund (*Óláfs Saga Helga*), and he appears in *Knytlinga saga* and *Jómsvíkinga saga*. It remains unclear whether tales of Eadric were transmitted as part of an oral cycle, or by means of written text.

Reputation The composite picture of Eadric Streona which emerges from the sources adduced above is one of a man accused of complicity in an extraordinary assortment of politically motivated crimes: the killing of Gunnhild and Pallig (1002); the killing of Ealdorman Ælfhelm (1006); the killing of Sigeferth and Morcar (1015); the killing of Earl Uhtred (1016); the killing of Edmund Ironside (1016); and the elimination of the surviving athelings (1016–17). In addition, Eadric is said to have hindered the English army in 1009 and is known to have defected to the Danes in 1015; he tried to betray the English when fighting on the Danish side at the battle of Sherston (1016), and he precipitated the flight which led to the defeat of the English at the battle of 'Assandun' (1016). The question arises: was Eadric really so comprehensively and irredeemably wicked, and is he rightly regarded as the principal cause of the disastrous outcome of King Æthelred's reign? It might be argued that he is the proverbial much-maligned figure long overdue for rehabilitation: that he was no more than the instrument by which Æthelred achieved his political purposes, in an age when such purposes were often accomplished by murder, outlawry, and exile; that he was a leader whose actions were misunderstood or misrepresented by chroniclers whose natural sympathies and loyalties lay elsewhere; that it was a matter of rivalry between one faction and another, determined by family ties, local loyalties, or political interests; that his motive in 1015 had been to protect Æthelred, and Queen Emma and her children, from the ambitions of Edmund Ironside; and that when this failed, he was left with little alternative but to give his support to the Danish invader, and thereafter to watch his own back. No doubt Eadric Streona had good reasons of his own for acting as he did. It is, however, the record of his actions in 1016 which condemns him as a traitor to the English cause, and which leads to the suspicion that his reputation as an unscrupulous operator in the interests of self-advancement is most thoroughly deserved.   SIMON KEYNES

Sources ASC · English historical documents, 1, ed. D. Whitelock (1955) · AS chart., S 916, 933 · Hemingi chartularium ecclesiæ Wigorniensis, ed. T. Hearne, 1 (1723), 280–81 · William of Malmesbury, Gesta regum Anglorum / The history of the English kings, ed. and trans. R. A. B. Mynors, R. M. Thomson, and M. Winterbottom, 2 vols., OMT (1998–9), vol. 1, pp. 274, 300, 314–20 · John of Worcester, Chron., 2.456–504 · Henry, archdeacon of Huntingdon, Historia Anglorum, ed. D. E. Greenway, OMT (1996), 344–62 · Orderic Vitalis, Eccl. hist., 2.194 · L'estoire des Engleis by Geffrei Gaimar, ed. A. Bell, Anglo-Norman Texts, 14–16 (1960) · W. Map, De nugis curialium / Courtiers' trifles, ed. and trans. M. R. James, rev. C. N. L. Brooke and R. A. B. Mynors, OMT (1983), 428–9 · J. Williams ab Ithel, ed., Annales Cambriae, Rolls Series, 20 (1860) · F. M. Stenton, Anglo-Saxon England, 3rd edn (1971), 381–2, 388–9, 394, 398–9 · S. Keynes, The diplomas of King Æthelred 'The Unready' (978–1016): a study in their use as historical evidence, Cambridge Studies in Medieval Life and Thought, 3rd ser., 13 (1980), 211–14 · P. Stafford, 'The reign of Æthelred II: a study in the limitations on royal policy and action', Ethelred the Unready: papers from the millenary conference [Oxford 1978], ed. D. Hill (1978), 15–46 · S. Keynes, 'A tale of two kings: Alfred the Great and Æthelred the Unready', TRHS, 5th ser., 36 (1986), 195–217, esp. 213–17 · J. Whybra, A lost English county: Winchcombeshire in the tenth and eleventh centuries (1990), 114–25 · A. Williams, 'The spoliation of Worcester', Anglo-Norman Studies, 19 (1996), 383–408, esp. 385 · C. E. Wright, The cultivation of saga in Anglo-Saxon England (1939), 142–3, 178–82, 183–92, 198–213 · R. M. Wilson, The lost literature of medieval England, 2nd edn (1970), 52–4 · A. Campbell, ed. and trans., Encomium Emmae reginae, CS, 3rd ser., 72 (1949); repr. with introduction by S. Keynes, CS, Classic Reprints, 4 (1998) [suppl. introduction by S. Keynes, Camden Classic Reprints, 4 (1998)]

Eadric [Edric] **the Wild** [Eadric Cild] (fl. **1067–1072**), magnate, was a son of Ælfric, brother (or perhaps nephew) of *Eadric Streona (d. 1017). He held land in Herefordshire, but most of his estates lay in Shropshire, where he and his kinsman Siward, son of Æthelgar (Eadric Streona's grandson), were the richest lay magnates below the rank of earl. He may have submitted to William the Conqueror at Barking in January 1067, but by the summer of that year he had fallen out with Richard Scrob and the Norman garrison at Hereford, and, in alliance with Bleddyn ap Cynfyn of Gwynedd, ravaged the shire 'as far as the bridge over the River Lugg' (John of Worcester, Chron., s.a. 1067). Perhaps he had legitimate cause, for no action seems to have been taken against him on this occasion.

In 1069 the northern magnates rebelled against the king and the thegns of Mercia took advantage of the situation to launch their own assault on Shrewsbury, where Roger de Montgomery had built his castle in the previous year. The only leader named is Eadric the Wild, once more in alliance with Bleddyn ap Cynfyn. With the men of Chester, they took the town of Shrewsbury but failed to capture the castle. They advanced to Stafford, but were met by a detachment of the royal army, led by the king in person, and driven back to Chester. In February 1070, after quelling the northerners, William led his men across the Pennines and ravaged the northern shires of Mercia, including Shropshire. Eadric himself, however, was pardoned, and accompanied the royal army which campaigned in Scotland in 1072.

Eadric seems to have lost much of his land, but is probably identifiable with Eadric, son of Ælfric, who held two estates from Much Wenlock Priory. He might also be Eadric of Hindlip, Worcestershire, who in the 1070s and 1080s appeared on behalf of Bishop Wulfstan of Worcester (d. 1095) in a lawsuit against the abbot of Evesham. This Eadric had once been commander of the bishop's military contingent and steersman of the ship he owed to the king's service, but after 1066 he had become the man of Robert the Lotharingian, bishop of Hereford; and in 1085–6 an Eadric of Wenlock (presumably the Eadric, son of Ælfric, who appears as Much Wenlock's tenant) attests charters of Bishop Robert and of Roger de Montgomery, earl of Shrewsbury. Moreover, Walter Map alleges that Eadric the Wild held land of the bishop of Hereford, at Lydbury North, Shropshire, which was given to the episcopal church by his son Alnoth when he was cured of paralysis at the shrine of St Æthelberht. Walter also records the legend of Eadric's fairy bride, a variant of a well-known folk-tale.

In 1086, Eadric's cousin Siward still held some of his land as the tenant of Roger de Lacy, Osbern fitz Richard Scrob, and Earl Roger de Montgomery, and it is possible that Eadric also continued to hold some estates as the tenant of Ralph de Mortimer; these lands were later held by the Savage family, whose name suggests that Eadric Salvage might be their ancestor. It has also been suggested that the name Wild (Silvaticus) arose from Eadric's participation in the northern rebellion; Orderic Vitalis has a passage on 'wild men' (silvatici) who lived rough in the woods to toughen themselves up for resistance to the king (Ordericus Vitalis, Eccl. hist., 2.216–18). In fact the by-name Wild is not particularly unusual; it was borne, for instance, by Wulfwig Wilde and Oswig Silvagius the priest, two of the minor tenants in pre-conquest Kent.   ANN WILLIAMS

Sources ASC, s.a. 1067 [text D] · A. Farley, ed., Domesday Book, 2 vols. (1783), 1.13, 183v, 252v, 253v, 254, 256, 256v, 257, 258v, 260 · John of Worcester, Chron. · W. Map, De nugis curialium / Courtiers' trifles, ed. and trans. M. R. James, rev. C. N. L. Brooke and R. A. B. Mynors, OMT (1983) · V. H. Galbraith, 'An episcopal land-grant of 1085', EngHR, 44 (1929), 353–72 · J. F. A. Mason, 'Eadric of Bayston', Transactions of the Shropshire Archaeological Society, 55 (1954–6), 112–18 · S. Reynolds, 'Eadric silvaticus and the English resistance', BIHR, 54 (1981), 102–5 · A. Williams, The English and the Norman conquest (1995) · C. P. Lewis, 'An introduction to the Shropshire Domesday',

The Shropshire Domesday, ed. A. Williams and R. W. H. Erskine (1990) · C. P. Lewis, 'An introduction to the Herefordshire Domesday', *The Herefordshire Domesday*, ed. A. Williams and R. W. H. Erskine (1988) · E. Mason, *St Wulfstan of Worcester, c.1008–1095* (1990) · J. Morris, ed., *Domesday Book: a survey of the counties of England*, 38 vols. (1983–92), vol. 25 [Shropshire] · *Hemingi chartularium ecclesiæ Wigorniensis*, ed. T. Hearne, 2 vols. (1723) · Ordericus Vitalis, *Eccl. hist.*, vol. 2

Eadsige (*d.* 1050), archbishop of Canterbury, was one of Cnut's royal priests, who became a monk of Christ Church, Canterbury, *c.*1030. According to a later charter, Cnut granted Folkestone to Christ Church in order to obtain Eadsige's admission, stipulating that he should have the land for his lifetime. Eadsige was suffragan bishop in Kent in 1035, and is said to have had his see at the church of St Martin, Canterbury. He succeeded Archbishop Æthelnoth in 1038, and in 1040 fetched his pall from Rome. He may have crowned Harthacnut, and certainly crowned Edward the Confessor on 3 April 1043, delivering an exhortation to the king and the people. Soon after the accession of Edward, Eadsige became ill and was unable to perform the duties of his office. According to the Anglo-Saxon Chronicle, fearing that someone inappropriate might beg or buy the archbishopric, he secretly obtained the permission of the king and Earl Godwine to appoint Siward, abbot of Abingdon, as his coadjutor . Siward was consecrated in 1044, although it is uncertain from which see he took his title, and he attests charters until 1046 as archbishop, as bishop, or as abbot. William of Malmesbury says that Siward was ungrateful and kept Eadsige short of food during his illness, for which he was deprived of the succession to Canterbury and had to console himself with the bishopric of Rochester. This story evidently arose from Malmesbury's confusion involving another Siward, bishop of Rochester from 1058 to 1075, and was undoubtedly fabricated to account for the apparent discrepancy in dates and the failure of the suffragan to succeed to the archiepiscopal see as Eadsige had done. Siward's retirement was really caused by ill health; he went back to Abingdon and died there, within eight weeks, on 23 October 1048.

It seems probable that Eadsige recovered from his sickness in 1046, when he again attests a charter as archbishop (Siward using the title of bishop) and that he resumed the government of his entire see on the retirement of Siward, with Godwine, bishop of St Martin's, as his suffragan. Eadsige died on 29 October 1050. His relations with Christ Church may have been strained, as he seems to have been responsible for the alienation of Canterbury lands, probably through leases, to Earl Godwine and his family. This perhaps accounts for some element of William of Malmesbury's story and Eadsige's own bequests to the rival house, St Augustine's.

WILLIAM HUNT, *rev.* MARY FRANCES SMITH

Sources N. Brooks, *The early history of the church of Canterbury: Christ Church from 597 to 1066* (1984) · *ASC*, s.a. 1038, 1042, 1043, 1046, 1047 [text E] · *Willelmi Malmesbiriensis monachi de gestis pontificum Anglorum libri quinque*, ed. N. E. S. A. Hamilton, Rolls Series, 52 (1870) · William of Malmesbury, *Gesta regum Anglorum / The history of the English kings*, ed. and trans. R. A. B. Mynors, R. M. Thomson, and M. Winterbottom, 2 vols., OMT (1998–9) · John of Worcester, *Chron.* · J. Stevenson, ed., *Chronicon monasterii de Abingdon*, 2 vols., Rolls Series, 2 (1858) · *AS chart.*, S 967, 981, 1404 · R. Twysden, ed., *Historiæ Anglicanæ scriptores X* (1652) · [H. Wharton], ed., *Anglia sacra*, 2 vols. (1691)

Eadwig [Edwy] (*c.*940–959), king of England, was the elder son of *Edmund, king of England (*d.* 946), and of Ælfgifu (of Shaftesbury; *d.* 944), and thus a grandson of King *Edward the Elder. He was born *c.*940, and came to the throne following the death of his uncle *Eadred, king of England, on 23 November 955. Eadwig has acquired a reputation as a debaucher, an opponent of monasticism, a despoiler of the church, and an incompetent ruler, which derives from the account of him in the earliest life of St Dunstan, written *c.*1000, and from later sources which elaborate the same themes. It is the case, however, that Eadwig quarrelled with Dunstan, and sent him into exile; and it may be doubted whether a life of the saint would provide impartial evidence for the life of the king.

Early life, accession, and coronation Eadwig does not make any impression on the historical record in the 940s and in the early 950s. The charters issued during the early 940s, in the name of King Edmund, are attested by the king's mother, Queen Eadgifu (widow of Edward the Elder), and by his brother Eadred, perhaps with the implication that his wife, Queen Ælfgifu, and the athelings Eadwig and *Edgar were not in regular attendance at court. The charters issued in the later 940s and early 950s, in the name of King Eadred, are often attested by Eadgifu, but it is not until 955 that Eadwig and Edgar make their first appearances in authentic texts. By this stage in Eadred's reign, the four most important people in the realm, apart from the king, were arguably Queen Eadgifu herself, Æthelstan Half-King, the ealdorman of East Anglia whose family also held extensive estates in Wessex and Mercia, Oda, archbishop of Canterbury (941–58), and Dunstan, abbot of Glastonbury (*c.*940–56). Their importance was probably increased by King Eadred's ill health, remarked upon by the author of the life of St Dunstan and expressed by the king's epithet, 'Debilis Pedibus' ('the Weak-in-the-Feet'). It is known that Eadred had entrusted Abbot Dunstan, at Glastonbury, with the safe-keeping of the best of the royal treasures, and there is also reason to believe that he had entrusted Dunstan with responsibilities which extended to the production of charters in the king's name.

Eadwig was a young man about fifteen years old when he succeeded his uncle in late November 955, and seems to have been determined from the outset to establish his own independence of action. The position of Ealdorman Æthelstan Half-King, north of the River Thames and in eastern England, was effectively impregnable, although the fact that the king made a number of new appointments in 956, in precisely those areas where Æthelstan was dominant, suggests that he had it in mind to institute some different arrangements. Soon after his accession, Eadwig deprived his grandmother Queen Eadgifu of all her possessions. Eadred had made generous provision for her in his will and Eadgifu herself seems to have regarded his death as an event which led to proceedings as the result of which she was 'despoiled of all her property' (*AS chart.*, S 1211); the author of the life of St Dunstan also alludes to her discomfiture, without further explanation. The story of the king's quarrel with Archbishop Oda and Abbot Dunstan, on the occasion of his coronation at Kingston, in Surrey, probably towards the end of January 956, is first told in the same life. At a banquet on the day following the coronation ceremony, Eadwig left the assembled company in order to debauch himself with a certain woman of noble birth, and her daughter, said to be 'a girl of ripe age'; Dunstan, and his kinsman Cynesige, bishop of Lichfield, were dispatched by Archbishop Oda to induce Eadwig to return to the coronation feast; and Dunstan was obliged to use force in order to achieve their purpose. Not surprisingly, the firm action aroused the resentment of Eadwig and the two women. At the instigation of the mother, called Æthelgifu, Abbot Dunstan was deprived of his status, and of his possessions, and was driven into exile.

The tale of Eadwig and the two women, as told about forty years after the event, is the kind of story which enlivens a period always in need of enlivenment, quite apart from its significance as the earliest circumstantial account of the ceremonial attending a royal coronation. There is no reason to believe, however, that the author of the life of St Dunstan was necessarily correct in the construction that he chose to put upon these events. It is known that in 956 King Eadwig was married to a woman called *Ælfgifu, daughter of a woman called Æthelgifu (*AS chart.*, S 1292; also named in the *Liber vitae* of the New Minster, Winchester), and that in 957 or 958 Archbishop Oda separated Eadwig and Ælfgifu 'because they were too closely related' (*ASC*, s.a. 958, text D); and it is a reasonable presumption that these are the two women who feature in the life of St Dunstan. Ælfgifu has been identified further as the testatrix of a will (*AS chart.*, S 1484), and on that basis as the sister of a certain Æthelweard, who has himself been identified as the person of that name appointed ealdorman of the western provinces *c.*977, and best known as the author of the Latin chronicle which bears his name. Since Æthelweard the chronicler is known to have been descended from Æthelred I, king of the West Saxons (*r.* 865–71), this identification would have the effect of making his putative sister Ælfgifu a member of a dispossessed branch of the royal family, and King Eadwig's third cousin once removed. Unfortunately, there do not seem to be any compelling or decisive grounds for presuming that the testatrix was Eadwig's wife, or indeed that the testatrix's brother Æthelweard was Æthelweard the chronicler. The simple fact remains, however, that in 956 King Eadwig wished to marry a woman who must already have been known to be within the prohibited degrees of consanguinity. It is possible, therefore, that Archbishop Oda objected to the marriage, as a matter of ecclesiastical law; that Abbot Dunstan, and Bishop Cynesige, were prevailed upon to press the case; and that initially Eadwig was able to have his way. It would not have been the first time that a marriage took place within the prohibited degrees, even though the objection was

known at the time of the marriage; and well might the biographer of St Dunstan have chosen to represent it, in retrospect, as an occasion of sinfulness and debauchery. It is apparent, however, that other stories about Eadwig's amorous affairs were in circulation. In the account of Archbishop Oda which forms the first part of Byrhtferth's life of St Oswald (written *c.*1000), and which should be authoritative on a matter concerning a prelate who was St Oswald's uncle, it is related how King Eadwig was enamoured of a woman who was below his wife in rank, and eloped with her; whereupon Oda intervened, and managed to induce the king to mend his ways (*Vita S. Oswaldi*, i.2). In view of the obvious discrepancies, the possibility must exist that stories about Eadwig and his women became confused and conflated.

Domestic politics An exceptionally large number of charters survives from King Eadwig's brief reign (about ninety in all), and it is this very substantial body of evidence which provides the basis for a more balanced judgement of the king. Knowledge of Eadwig's activities in the first full year of his reign depends on the detailed and systematic analysis of over sixty charters, themselves representing perhaps only a small proportion of the total number of charters issued in 956. There would appear to have been four main occasions during the year on which the charters were produced—the first possibly at the end of January (at about the time of the king's coronation), the second around 13 February, the third at some indeterminate point thereafter, and the fourth around 29 November—and it is apparent that the charters were drawn up on each occasion by a single agency, probably a central writing office or royal secretariat within the king's household. The extraordinary profusion of charters issued in 956 was not, therefore, a matter of any failure on the part of the king's government to maintain control of this aspect of royal activity. It is not easy, however, to judge the significance of the phenomenon, and besides, it is unlikely that a single explanation would suffice to account for the evidence as a whole. In view of the king's later reputation, and in view of the fact that the majority of the charters are in favour of laymen, it may be that some land was appropriated by the king from the church; but it is difficult to show in more than a few cases that the land concerned had once been church property, and at Abingdon Abbey, at least, Eadwig was remembered as a benefactor. It is often presumed that the king was simply alienating large amounts of royal property, in a desperate attempt to buy support for himself; but, again, this cannot be substantiated in any detail. It may be, on the other hand, that Eadwig was intent upon raising money in the short term by the sale of privileges (allowing favoured landholders to have particular estates converted from folkland, on which food rents and customary services were imposed, into bookland which was exempt from such public burdens), and that to this end he relaxed normal constraints on a procedure which in the longer term would diminish the revenues due to the king.

It is noteworthy, however, that a substantial proportion of the estates which were the subject of royal charters in

956–7 had been the subject of royal charters in the previous twenty years or so; and, since a charter might normally be expected to serve as a title deed for longer than a single generation, it may be that something more sinister or irregular was afoot. Eadwig had seized the opportunity soon after his accession to escape from the influence of at least two of those who had been particularly close to his late uncle Eadred, not least, perhaps, in order to secure his interest in the royal treasures and estates which might otherwise have passed out of his control. The author of the life of St Dunstan also refers more generally to those whom Eadwig 'had caused to be plundered by an unjust judgement' (*Vita S. Dunstani*, chap. 24). This may indicate that in 956 land was taken from certain men for no good reason, and either retained by the king, or redistributed (or more likely sold) to those who happened to enjoy the king's favour, or to those who were manipulating the king and persuading him to act in their interests at the expense of others. One might not expect a landholder to surrender a charter which served as the title deed to an estate which was appropriated from him; but it is possible that in some cases the appropriation was effected by legal procedure, and not simply by force, and that in such cases earlier title deeds passed into the hands of the authorities, and were passed on to the new owner, accompanied by a fresh title deed drawn up in respect of the estate at the same time. It may be concluded that the extraordinary burst of charter production in 956 need not have had anything to do with the wholesale appropriation of church property, or with the reckless alienation of royal demesne, and that in many cases it may have reflected factional activity of the kind which must often have enlivened a king's dealings with his thegns. The charters cast a potentially revealing light on domestic affairs within the kingdom, as members of the land- and office-holding élites jostled for reward, advancement, and influence. They reveal that Eadwig made some important appointments, especially to offices in the royal household, duly reflected by detectable changes in the attestations of the thegns. At a higher level of the secular hierarchy, three of those appointed to ealdordoms by Eadwig began to attest charters at different stages during the course of the year: Ælfhere, made responsible for some part of Mercia, first appears in charters of 'group one'; Æthelwold, son of Æthelstan Half-King and made responsible for some part of East Anglia, first appears in 'group three'; and Byrhtnoth, ealdorman of Essex, first appears in 'group four'. It would be hazardous to reduce domestic affairs to the promotion of one kin group at the expense of others. The ties which linked the royal and noble families in the tenth century were complex, and are now often irrecoverable, but doubtless friendships, relationships, and rivalries would have affected the course of domestic politics in many different ways.

Division of the kingdom The profusion of charters issued in 956 does not redound well to Eadwig's credit, and it may be no coincidence that the king's independence of action was soon checked. In 957 or 958 Archbishop Oda separated Eadwig from Ælfgifu; the objection of close relationship must have been known at the time of the marriage, but now Oda was able to get his way. Perhaps more significantly, the kingdom of the English was divided in the summer of 957 between Eadwig (in the south) and his younger brother Edgar (to the north), with the River Thames separating their respective realms. This development is represented in the life of St Dunstan as an expression of internal dissension: the king 'was wholly deserted by the northern people, being despised because he acted foolishly in the government committed to him, ruining with vain hatred the shrewd and wise, and admitting with loving zeal the ignorant and those like himself' (*Vita S. Dunstani*, chap. 24). Later sources, elaborating the basic account, represent the division of the kingdom more unequivocally as the outcome of rebellion against Eadwig. It is conceivable, under such circumstances, that this division reflected dissatisfaction north of the Thames with King Eadwig's regime, or that there were those in high places who disapproved of his actions and wished to provide Edgar with a base from which he might have better prospects of succeeding his elder brother. It is possible, on the other hand, that the division of the kingdom in 957 did not involve the degree of internal discord which 'rebellion' normally implies. The charters of the period 957–9 show in some detail what the division entailed, and convey the impression that it was a partition of the kingdom made with the agreement of all parties, or (in other words) the outcome of a peaceful political settlement. The alignment of individual office-holders with Eadwig or Edgar was not determined by complex personal loyalties; rather, all the bishops and ealdormen whose areas of responsibility lay south of the Thames remained with Eadwig, and those whose areas of responsibility lay north of the Thames joined Edgar's court (including several men who had received advancement under Eadwig, and who might therefore be expected to have remained with him had the matter been one of individual choice). The royal styles used in Eadwig's charters issued after the division are relatively restrained, implying that he recognized that the division imposed some limitation on the geographical extent of his authority. The division may, indeed, have proceeded from factors other than dissatisfaction with Eadwig's regime. If only to judge from his nickname, Æthelstan Half-King had accumulated a degree or extent of power in the 930s and 940s which put him second only to the king; and since he would appear (at least on one interpretation of the evidence) to have given up his position as ealdorman and to have retired to Glastonbury at precisely the time of the division, it may be that by 957 Æthelstan felt that the moment had come for him to hand over his responsibilities. There would have been no presumption at this stage in the tenth century that political unification was something necessary and desirable for its own sake, and it may always have been intended that Edgar (who was, significantly, fostered with Ealdorman Æthelstan's family) should one day share the burden of kingship with his brother. It is possible, at the same time, that Eadwig's activities had brought matters to a head. Eadwig seems none the less to have retained some kind of overall authority, to judge from the fact that his coins were the only currency throughout England in 957–9; no coins were issued in Edgar's name until after his brother's death.

Death and reputation Very little is known of Eadwig's activities between the division of the kingdom in the summer of 957 and his death on 1 October 959. A certain Ælfric was appointed an ealdorman in the south-east in 957, but seems to have died in the following year. More significantly, Ælfheah, brother of Ealdorman Ælfhere, was appointed an ealdorman in Wessex in 959, putting one brother in each court. Eadwig was buried at the New Minster, Winchester, a church founded by his grandfather in 901 and intimately connected with the royal establishment; and by his death the kingdom of the English was reunited under the rule of his younger brother. There were some office-holders (like Byrhthelm, archbishop of Canterbury) who were quickly replaced under the new dispensation, and others (like the thegn Wulfric Cufing) who soon recovered their lost estates. More generally, however, it is notable that the royal courts which had been distinct from each other for over two years were now reconstituted as one.

Opinions of the late king remained controversial. To Æthelwold, bishop of Winchester (963–84), it seemed that Eadwig 'had through the ignorance of childhood dispersed his kingdom and divided its unity, and also distributed the lands of the holy churches to rapacious strangers' (*English Historical Documents*, 1, no. 238). For his part, the chronicler Æthelweard, who may or may not have been Eadwig's brother-in-law, remarked that 'for his great beauty he got the nickname *Pancali* ['All-Fair'] from the common people' (*Chronicle of Æthelweard*, 4.8). Æthelweard added that Eadwig 'held the kingdom for four years, and deserved to be loved', perhaps implying that Eadwig's overall authority was continuous from November 955 to October 959, and implying at the same time that he was not as well loved as one who knew him thought he should have been. It was, however, the hostile treatment of Eadwig in the life of St Dunstan and in the life of St Oswald which effectively determined the king's subsequent reputation. The later lives of St Dunstan by Osbern (*c*.1090) and Eadmer (*c*.1100), as well as Eadmer's life of St Oda, represent early stages in a process of deterioration. William of Malmesbury describes Eadwig as 'a wanton youth', who 'misused his personal beauty in lascivious behaviour', and depicts him as a determined oppressor of the monastic order (Malmesbury, 2.147). John of Worcester states that Eadwig 'was abandoned by the Mercians and the Northumbrians with contempt' (John of Worcester, *Chron.*, 405). Henry of Huntingdon, on the other hand, describes Eadwig as 'the praiseworthy possessor of the regalia of the kingdom', whose 'prosperous and promising start was cut off by premature death' (Huntingdon, *Historia Anglorum*, OMT, v.23), perhaps for lack of any information to any other effect.

The legendary history of Eadwig burst upon a wider public in the second half of the eighteenth century, inspiring artists prepared to indulge the developing taste for history painting, and providing material for a number of plays based loosely on the king's amorous affairs. One of the drawings made by Samuel Wale in the early 1760s, and first published as an engraved illustration to Thomas Mortimer's *New History of England* (1764–6), is entitled 'The Insolent Behaviour of Dunstan to King Edwy on the Day of his Coronation Feast'. Thomas Sedgwick Whalley's play *Edwy and Edilda*, first published in 1779, was followed by Thomas Warwick's *Edwy: a Dramatic Poem* (1784) and Frances Burney's *Edwy and Elgiva* (1788). In 1786 William Bromley exhibited *The Insolence of Dunstan to King Edwy* at the Royal Academy; and when William Hamilton was commissioned to produce a painting for Robert Bowyer's 'Historic Gallery', in 1791, he chose as his subject *Edwig and Elgiva*, showing Abbot Dunstan, assisted by Archbishop Oda, attempting to prise the king away from the beauteous Ælfgifu. Other artists known to have been moved by the tale of Eadwig include William Dyce, *St Dunstan Separating Edwy and Elgiva* (1839), Richard Dadd, *Elgiva the Queen of Edwy in Banishment* (1840), and Thomas Roods, *The mother of Elgiva, Edwy's queen, interceding with Odo, archbishop of Canterbury, on behalf of her daughter* (1846). SIMON KEYNES

Sources AS chart., S 581–666, 1211, 1292, 1484 • B., 'Vita sancti Dunstani', *Memorials of Saint Dunstan, archbishop of Canterbury*, ed. W. Stubbs, Rolls Series, 63 (1874), 3–52 • B., *Vita s. Dunstani*, ed. and trans. M. Lapidge and M. Winterbottom [forthcoming] • [Byrhtferth of Ramsey], 'Vita sancti Oswaldi auctore anonymo', *The historians of the church of York and its archbishops*, ed. J. Raine, 1, Rolls Series, 71 (1879), 399–475 • Byrhtferth, *Vita s. Oswaldi*, ed. and trans. M. Lapidge [forthcoming] • D. Whitelock, M. Brett, and C. N. L. Brooke, eds., *Councils and synods with other documents relating to the English church, 871–1204*, 1 (1981), no. 33, pp. 142–54 • *The chronicle of Æthelweard*, ed. and trans. A. Campbell (1962) • ASC, s.a. 955–959 • *English historical documents*, 1, ed. D. Whitelock (1955) • D. Whitelock, ed. and trans., *Anglo-Saxon wills* (1930), pp. 20–23, no. 8 • F. E. Harmer, ed., *Select English historical documents of the ninth and tenth centuries* (1914), 37–8, 66–8 (no. 23) • Eadmer, 'Vita Odonis, archiepiscopi Cantuariensis', *Anglia sacra*, ed. [H. Wharton], 2 (1691), 78–87 • William of Malmesbury, *Gesta regum Anglorum / The history of the English kings*, ed. and trans. R. A. B. Mynors, R. M. Thomson, and M. Winterbottom, 2 vols., OMT (1998–9) • John of Worcester, *Chron.*, vol. 2 • Henry, archdeacon of Huntingdon, *Historia Anglorum*, ed. D. E. Greenway, OMT (1996) • F. M. Stenton, *Anglo-Saxon England*, 3rd edn (1971), 364–7 • C. E. Blunt, B. H. I. H. Stewart, and C. S. S. Lyon, *Coinage in tenth-century England: from Edward the Elder to Edgar's reform* (1989), 146–56, 278–80 • B. Yorke, 'Æthelwold and the politics of the tenth century', *Bishop Æthelwold: his career and influence*, ed. B. Yorke (1988), 65–88 • S. Keynes, *The diplomas of King Æthelred 'The Unready' (978–1016): a study in their use as historical evidence*, Cambridge Studies in Medieval Life and Thought, 3rd ser., 13 (1980), 48–69 • S. Keynes, 'The "Dunstan B" charters', *Anglo-Saxon England*, 23 (1994), 165–93 • S. Keynes, 'England, 900–1016', *The new Cambridge medieval history*, 3, ed. T. Reuter (1999), 456–84 • S. Keynes, *An atlas of attestations in Anglo-Saxon charters, c.670–1066* (2002)

Likenesses coins (stylized portraits), repro. in Blunt, Stewart, and Lyon, *Coinage* (1989)

Eadwig [Eadui] **Basan** (*fl. c*.1020), Benedictine monk and scribe, is identified by himself in the gospel book Hanover, Kestner Museum, MS W. M. XXIa, 36, in which he added a colophon to the end of John's gospel: 'Do not disdain, Father, to pour forth a prayer for the scribe. The monk Eadwig, with the surname Basan, wrote this book.

Eadwig Basan (*fl. c.*1020), miniature [prostrate before St Benedict]

May long-lasting health be his. Farewell servant of God, n[ame], and be mindful of me.' His hand has been recognized in a further three gospel books or lectionaries, three psalters, and four charters, and it is on this corpus of material that knowledge of him rests. Eadwig wrote all of the Hanover gospels (often called the 'Eadwig [or Eadui] gospels'), the Grimbald gospels (BL, Add. MS 34890), and the gospel lectionary, Florence, Biblioteca Medicea Laurenziana, MS Plut. XVII, 20; he also contributed a single page to the York gospels (York Minster, Add. MS 1). He wrote the entirety of a psalter (BL, Arundel MS 155) in its original form, datable to between 1012 and 1023, contributed four quires to the Harley 603 psalter, and added a supplementary quire to an eighth-century psalter (BL, Cotton Vespasian MS A.i). His four charters are: a grant by Cnut to Ælfstan, archbishop of Canterbury, dated 1018 (BL, Stowe Ch., no. 38); Cnut's confirmation of the privileges of Christ Church, Canterbury, granted between 1017 and 1020, which was added to the de luxe gospel book, BL, Royal MS 1 D.ix; a wide-ranging privilege for Christ Church, which was added to a gospel book presented to that house by King Æthelstan (BL, Cotton Tiberius MS A.ii) and which is a forgery; and a transcript of the confirmation made at the Council of 'Clofesho' (716) of liberties granted to Kentish houses by King Wihtred (BL, Stowe Ch., no. 2).

The dated and datable specimens of Eadwig's work place his *floruit* late in the second and early in the third decade of the eleventh century. He describes himself in his colophon as a monk; and the content of the charters, along with the affiliations of some of his manuscripts, indicate that he was a member of the community of

Christ Church, Canterbury. Whether all his scribal work was accomplished there is an open and probably insoluble question, but it is clear that some of his manuscripts were distributed soon after being written. A striking feature of Eadwig's extant *œuvre* is the high status of many of the projects on which he worked. He added particularly important charters to prestigious books and he wrote or contributed to a series of de luxe manuscripts. Consequently, it is likely that he held a high position in the Christ Church scriptorium in the generation after the viking sack of Canterbury in 1011. It is possible that he was an illuminator as well as a scribe, and it has also been suggested that he was personally responsible for drafting the forged refoundation charter. Certainty is, however, elusive on both points.

Eadwig wrote a highly distinctive English Caroline minuscule script of generous dimensions. Its matrix is rectilinear, but the curving strokes are carefully rounded; ascenders terminate in wedge-like serifs, while minims are finished with horizontal feet. The overall effect is neat and easily legible. Eadwig's vernacular script is also neat, and his style of writing seems to represent a turning point in the history of English script. In simple terms, his Caroline hand united the rotundity that characterized Winchester work of the later tenth century with the rectilinearity that distinguished Canterbury writing of the same period. His monumental display capitals likewise integrated rounded forms into the rectilinear Canterbury tradition, while he provided Old English script with a more regular matrix. The resulting script types were to prove remarkably popular and much English writing of the mid- and later eleventh century echoes the forms of which Eadwig was the most skilful, albeit not the earliest, exponent. Whether this was a direct result of his personal influence is unclear.   RICHARD GAMESON

Sources BL, Add. MS 34890 · BL, Arundel MS 155 · BL, Cotton Vespasian MS A.i · BL, Royal MS 1 D.ix · BL, Stowe Ch., nos. 2, 38 · T. A. M. Bishop, *English Caroline minuscule* (1971) · N. Barker, ed., *The York gospels*, Roxburghe Club (1986) · R. W. Pfaff, 'Eadui Basan: scriptorum princeps', *England in the eleventh century* [Harlaxton 1990], ed. C. Hicks (1992), 267–83 · D. N. Dumville, *English Caroline script and monastic history* (1993) · gospel book, Kestner Museum, Hanover, W. M. XXIa, 36
Archives Biblioteca Medicea Laurenziana, Florence, MS Plut. XVII, 20 · BL, Add. MS 34890 · BL, Arundel MS 155 · BL, Cotton Tiberius MS A.ii · BL, Cotton Vespasian MS A.i · BL, Harley MS 603 · BL, Royal MS 1 D.ix · BL, Stowe Ch., nos. 2, 38 · Kestner Museum, Hanover, W. M. XXIa, 36 · York Minster, Add. MS 1
Likenesses miniature, BL, Arundel MS 155, fol. 133*r* [*see illus.*]

Eadwine [St Eadwine, Edwin] (*c.*586–633), king of Northumbria, was the son of *Ælla, king of Deira, and the fifth of the seven overkings named by Bede. His life, as recorded in vivid and detailed anecdotes by both Bede and the author of the Whitby life of St Gregory, has many of the attributes of a heroic legend.

Exile, return, and expansion of power Eadwine was a prince of the ruling family of the Deirans, whose kingdom stretched from the Humber to the Tees, but when his father Ælla died, *c.*597 according to one calculation, or 588 to another, he was probably considered too young to rule, and the control of Deira passed to Æthelric, who may have been his uncle. About 604 Æthelfrith, the powerful ruler of Bernicia (the northern part of Northumbria, stretching from the Tees to beyond the Tweed), seized power in Deira and cemented his conquest by marrying Eadwine's sister Acha. As an obvious future contender for the Deiran kingdom, Eadwine's life was not safe in Northumbria, and his early years were spent in perilous wanderings in exile among those courts, whether British or English, who were currently at war with the powerful Bernician kings of Northumbria.

When still a youth, if the accounts of later tradition are to be believed, Eadwine seems to have been in exile among the western Britons, perhaps at the court of Cadfan of Gwynedd. He later found refuge with one of the Mercian kings, Cearl, and married Cearl's daughter Coenburh, with whom he had two sons, Osfrith and Eadfrith; but as King Æthelfrith of Northumbria pushed his conquests further south and west, Eadwine sought a stronger and more distanced protector, Rædwald, king of the East Angles, a ruler as powerful in his area as Æthelfrith was in his. It was perhaps because of the wider struggle for supremacy between these two, rather than the loyalty of a host to a guest, that Rædwald refused to be intimidated by Æthelfrith's repeated threats in an attempt to secure Eadwine's death. In 616 Æthelfrith, having defeated the army of the king of Powys at Chester, was ready to fill the vacuum left by the recent death of Æthelberht of Kent, the third of the Anglo-Saxon *bretwaldas* or overkings, but the East Anglian king pre-empted this. Rædwald swiftly raised an army against the unprepared Æthelfrith, defeated and killed him at the River Idle, and put Eadwine on the Northumbrian throne, thus securing a grateful client on his northern flank. This special relationship between Northumbria and East Anglia lasted into the next generation, even after Rædwald's death and the ascendancy of Eadwine.

Eadwine's first power base was his dynastic province of Deira, but essentially he ruled over the same territory as his Bernician predecessor, and indeed he subdued the British West more effectively by conquering the independent kingdom of Elmet, and occupying the islands of Man and Anglesey. For the first time Anglo-Saxon authority in Northumbria stretched from sea to sea. He extended his lordship and tribute-taking directly over the people of Lindsey, and perhaps less effectively over all the southern kingdoms except Kent. The resentment felt by the southern rulers towards Eadwine's growing power is well illustrated by the legendary story of how Cwichelm, a West Saxon king, sent an agent 'to deprive King Eadwine of his kingdom and his life' (Bede, *Hist. eccl.*, 2.9).

The assassin entered the king's hall under the pretence of delivering a message, and, while speaking, drew from under his cloak a poisoned dagger and made a rush at the king. In Bede's words:

> Lilla, a most devoted thegn, saw this, but not having a shield in his hand to protect the king from death, he quickly interposed his own body to receive the blow. His enemy thrust the weapon with such force that he killed the thegn

and wounded the king as well through his dead body. (Bede, *Hist. eccl.*, 2.9)

Eadwine, when healed of his wound, took his revenge in a punitive campaign against those who had organized the assassination attempt, thus, in the time-honoured manner of pagan Germanic society, rewarding the unquestioning loyalty of his follower by taking up the blood-feud. It was hard to exchange the fiercely satisfying revenges and blood-feuds for the meeker forgiveness of one's enemies that Christianity demanded.

Conversion to Christianity About 624 Eadwine had obtained as his second wife a Kentish princess, Æthelburh (d. 647), a Christian, whose family agreed to the marriage only if Eadwine respected her religion and agreed to consider conversion himself. Despite this and the pressure brought by Æthelburh's chaplain, Bishop Paulinus, Eadwine did not easily become the first non-Kentish ruler to embrace the new faith. On the night of the assassination attempt the queen gave birth to a daughter, and in thanksgiving Eadwine allowed Paulinus to baptize her, 'the first of the Northumbrian race to be baptized, together with eleven members of his household' (Bede, *Hist. eccl.*, 2.9), but agreed to renounce the idols of his own religion only after his punitive campaign against the West Saxons. When he returned he no longer worshipped his idols but, as Bede said, 'made it his business, as opportunity occurred, to learn the faith systematically from the venerable Bishop Paulinus' (ibid.). This account of Paulinus's instruction is supported by the account in chapter 15 of the life of Gregory the Great, but despite letters from Pope Boniface V to himself and his wife, Eadwine still spent long hours deliberating privately what he ought to do and which religion to follow.

Bede's account of the struggle of the king with his own doubts, and of the opinions voiced in public debate by his pagan high priest and one of his counsellors, may present a higher moral tone and more artistry in articulation than existed in reality, but clearly Eadwine was an intelligent and thoughtful man, who must have weighed the implications, both political and personal, of his conversion, and it is unquestionable also that the public debate provided some of the most memorable prose in Bede's *Historia ecclesiastica gentis Anglorum*. The chief of the king's priests, Coifi, noted that the worship of the heathen gods he had followed so zealously held no virtue nor profit:

> None of your followers has devoted himself more earnestly than I have to the worship of our gods, but nevertheless there are many who receive greater benefits and honour from you than I do, and are more successful in all their undertakings. If the gods had any power they would have helped me more readily. (Bede, *Hist. eccl.*, 2.13)

Consequently he urged acceptance if the new doctrines seemed 'better and more powerful' (ibid.), and later Eadwine skilfully led him to offer to profane his own shrines and to destroy the idols.

Another of the king's thegns is reported as urging acceptance of the new religion because it took away the vulnerability and dark uncertainty that surrounds the earthly life of man:

This is how the present life on earth, King, appears to me in comparison with that time which is unknown to us. You are sitting feasting with your ealdormen and thegns in the winter time; the fire is burning on the hearth in the middle of the hall, and all inside is warm, while outside the wintry storms of rain and snow are raging; and a sparrow flies swiftly through the hall. It enters in at one door and quickly flies out through the other. For the few moments it is inside, the storm and wintry tempest cannot touch it, but after the briefest moment of calm, it flits from your sight, out of the wintry storm and into it again. So this life of man appears but for a moment; what follows or indeed what went before we know not at all. If the new doctrine brings us more certain information it seems right that we should accept it. (Bede, *Hist. eccl.*, 2.13)

So in 627, the eleventh year of his reign, King Eadwine, with members of his family, all the nobles of his race, and a vast number of the common people, was baptized in the church of St Peter in York, and this was followed by mass baptisms and conversions throughout Bernicia and Deira. Whether indeed Eadwine had been baptized before, in his youthful exile among the West Britons, remains an unsolved mystery. The facts given above are common to Bede and the author of the Whitby life of Gregory, but later Celtic sources, the *Historia Brittonum* and the *Annales Cambriae*, claim that Eadwine was baptized by Rhun, son of Urien, the famous king of Rheged. Although these texts are less authoritative than Bede, it remains at least a possibility that Eadwine was baptized and then lapsed, as did several other Anglo-Saxon kings. Eadwine encouraged the conversion of his satellite kingdoms also: Paulinus baptized in Lindsey; Eorpwald, the king of East Anglia, was baptized; and despite his continuing close links with Kent, Eadwine seems to have embarked on a policy to establish a separate northern province for the Anglo-Saxon church, as Pope Gregory had intended when he launched the Augustinian mission.

Kingship Eadwine's second marriage had given him enhanced status and contacts: his children were related to the Frankish king; Pope Boniface wrote to him and his wife and sent high status diplomatic gifts; and his baptism in the Roman city of York emphasized a link with the Roman past, as did his solemn progress with standards between the main centres of his kingdoms. The excavation of his 'palace' complex at Yeavering, Northumberland, has revealed not only a fort and an impressive series of timber halls, but also a remarkable triangular structure designed along the lines of a Roman amphitheatre, apparently for public assemblies.

It is possible that Eadwine had picked up his ideas of how a ruler should behave, maintaining a sort of consular state, from his contacts in Kent and East Anglia, but it is also possible that he wished to ally himself with those elements in Northumbria which still hankered after a Roman past and probably still claimed 'Roman' descent. Indeed many of those who flocked to be baptized by Paulinus may have been descended from Christian Roman Britons. The Bernician royal family, whose members fled into exile during Eadwine's reign, went for protection to the Irish of Dalriada, and it is conceivable that Eadwine

deliberately cultivated 'Roman' mores to distinguish himself from the more 'Celtic' court style of the Bernicians.

Eadwine's seventeen years of rule were remembered as a secure and peaceful period in Northumbria, in which, 'as the proverb still runs, a woman with a new-born child could walk throughout the island from sea to sea and take no harm' (Bede, *Hist. eccl.*, 2.16). He also provided public amenities which, although a product of their times, may have been reminiscent of the civic benefits of Roman rule. 'The king cared so much for the good of his people that where he had noticed clear springs near the highway, he caused stakes to be set up and bronze drinking cups to be hung on them for the refreshment of travellers' (ibid.). These were probably like the bronze hanging bowls found in Anglo-Saxon graves.

Death and collapse of Northumbrian kingdom Yet the precocious achievements of Eadwine's reign, which had been cemented by firm alliances with the two most cosmopolitan Anglo-Saxon kingdoms of Kent and East Anglia, and grounded in the faith and traditions of late Roman Britain, were not proof against the volatile politics of the seventh century. Eorpwald, king of the East Angles, was killed by a pagan soon after his conversion, perhaps *c*.630, and this removal of an ally must have constituted a threat to Eadwine's power in the midlands. Here the small tribes had begun to coalesce into a powerful new Mercian kingdom under the leadership of one of their royal family, Penda, and no doubt the British kings of Wales were watching for any signs of weakness in the ruler they had once sheltered, but who later raided deep into their territory and formed other alliances.

In 633 Cadwallon ap Cadfan, king of Gwynned, launched an invasion into Eadwine's territory, and was joined by Penda with his army. On 12 October a fierce battle was fought on the borders of Mercia and Northumbria, on the plain called Hæthfelth—Hatfield Chase—and Eadwine was killed and his whole army either slain or scattered. One of his sons died beside him, while the other deserted to Penda (who later killed him). Bernicia and Deira fell apart into two separate kingdoms again, and although for a short time Eadwine's cousin Osric continued the fight against Cadwallon, in the following summer Cadwallon surprised Osric's troops and killed the Deiran leader. In order to try to save something of the Deiran royal succession in this time of confusion and disaster, one of Eadwine's thegns, Bass, took by sea to Kent a group consisting of the queen, Æthelburh, Bishop Paulinus, Eadwine's daughter *Eanflæd, his son Uscfrea, and his grandson Yffi. Later the queen sent these two small boys to the protection of King Dagobert in Francia. Both children died there in infancy and the Deiran royal house was extinguished.

Ruler, saint, and hero Eadwine's reign was a striking interlude of Deiran supremacy in the run of power of the Bernician kings, but many of his achievements were precocious and not deeply rooted. His posture as one of the barbarian heirs to Roman traditions and power was one shared by other continental Germanic rulers attempting to create new states. But their attempts were not proof against the new conditions which prevailed, and were not followed through. If Eadwine had had longer to consolidate his sponsorship of Christianity, then York might have attained the status of a metropolitan see, as Pope Gregory intended, a century earlier than it did. But Paulinus's missionary journeys were made as part of the royal progress through the kingdoms, and there was insufficient manpower to follow up his preaching and mass baptisms by establishing permanent mission stations, as was done by monks from Iona in the next generation.

After the fatal battle, Eadwine was buried at the royal monastery of Whitby (the St Denis of the Deiran royal family), where subsequently there was a valiant attempt to create a martyr cult for him; and to a certain extent this succeeded, though papal approval was given only by Gregory XIII in the late sixteenth century. But despite his fundamental role in fostering the introduction of Christianity to the Northumbrians, it is as the Germanic hero depicted by Bede that Eadwine was truly remembered. Bede's artistic account of his life—a youth passed in wandering in perilous exile, a sudden rise to the position of a successful war leader of his people, then the peaceful rule of a powerful king, shattered when he dies defending his territory against overwhelming odds—has the classic shape of heroic poetry. ROSEMARY CRAMP

Sources Bede, *Hist. eccl.* • B. Colgrave, ed. and trans., *The earliest life of Gregory the Great … by an anonymous monk of Whitby* (1968) • *ASC*, s.a. 601, 626, 627, 633 [text E] • Nennius, 'British history' and 'The Welsh annals', ed. and trans. J. Morris (1980) • N. K. Chadwick, 'The conversion of Northumbria: a comparison of sources', *Celt and Saxon: studies in the early British border*, ed. N. K. Chadwick (1963), 138–66 • D. N. Dumville, 'The Anglian collection of royal genealogies and regnal lists', *Anglo-Saxon England*, 5 (1976), 23–50 • D. P. Kirby, *The earliest English kings* (1991) • B. Hope-Taylor, *Yeavering: an Anglo-British centre of early Northumbria* (1977)

Eadwine, earl of Mercia (d. 1071). *See under Ælfgar, earl of Mercia (d. 1062?).*

Eady, Charles Swinfen, first Baron Swinfen (1851–1919), judge, was born at Chertsey on 31 July 1851, the second son of George John Eady, surgeon, of Chertsey, and his wife, Laura Maria, daughter of Richard Smith, physician, of Chertsey. He was tutored at home before going to London University where he took his LLB in 1874. In 1873 he was articled to a solicitor by the name of Jenkins in Chertsey. He was admitted a solicitor in 1874 but soon decided to go to the bar. He was admitted as student of the Inner Temple in 1876 and was called to the bar in 1879. He read as a pupil in the chambers of Herbert Cozens-Hardy. Eady's experience as a solicitor gave him confidence, and he quickly built up a good practice on the Chancery side. In 1894 he married Blanche Maude, the younger daughter of Sydney Williams Lee, of Dereham, Putney Hill; they had a son and two daughters.

In 1893, Eady became queen's counsel in the court of Mr Justice North when Cozens-Hardy left. For the next six years he had the largest practice after Mr Justice North. His arguments, although a little prolix, were lucid and learned, and he was always in command of the facts of his cases. In 1901 he was selected by Lord Halsbury to fill the Chancery judgeship left vacant through Cozens-Hardy's promotion to the Court of Appeal. In the same year he was knighted.

In 1913, on the resignation of Sir George Farwell, Eady was promoted to the Court of Appeal and created a privy councillor. Though not a great judge, in the Court of Appeal he was an effective lawyer of common-law as well as chancery cases. After the death of Lord Justice Kennedy in 1915, he often presided in the second Court of Appeal, and in May 1918, on Cozens-Hardy's resignation, was selected to succeed him as master of the rolls.

In 1919 Eady was created Baron Swinfen of Chertsey. But his health soon began to fail, and after the Easter sittings of 1919 he was too ill to resume his duties. He resigned in the autumn and died a few weeks later on 15 November 1919 at his London house, 23 Hyde Park Gardens.

DAVID DAVIES, rev. HUGH MOONEY

Sources *The Times* (17 Nov 1919) • *Law Journal* (22 Nov 1919), 427 • *CGPLA Eng. & Wales* (1920)
Likenesses W. Stoneman, photograph, 1917, NPG • Elliott & Fry, cabinet photograph, NPG • J. S. Lucas, portrait, repro. in *Exhibition of the Royal Academy* (1901), 109 • J. S. Lucas, portrait, repro. in *Exhibition of the Royal Academy* (1901), 61 • Spy [L. Ward], caricature, chromolithograph, NPG; repro. in *VF*, 34 (13 Feb 1902)
Wealth at death £192,192 0s. 8d.: probate, 14 Jan 1920, *CGPLA Eng. & Wales*

Eady, Eric Thomas (1915–1966), meteorologist, was born on 5 September 1915 at 51 Devonshire Road, Ealing, London, the elder child and only son of Thomas Christopher Eady, civil servant with the Post Office, and his wife, Charlotte Anderton. He was educated at Ealing county grammar school, where he was awarded a state scholarship and a minor open scholarship to Christ's College, Cambridge, where he graduated as a senior optime in part two of the mathematical tripos in 1935. After short periods as a lecturer in mathematics at King Alfred's Teacher Training College in Winchester and as a technical researcher in aircraft vibration for De Havilland, he joined the Meteorological Office as a technical officer in 1938, where he served as a weather forecaster in fighter and reconnaissance groups. Following commission as flight lieutenant in the Royal Air Force Volunteer Reserve he specialized in upper-air analysis and forecasting for bomber groups. His last posting was to Lagos, Nigeria, before he was demobilized in February 1946.

Eady had spent much of his spare time working on a theory for the formation of atmospheric depressions and decided to devote all his time to it; he resigned from the Meteorological Office to become a graduate student at Imperial College. He was not accepted into the department of meteorology but registered as a student in the department of mathematics, where he wrote a doctoral thesis, 'The theory of development in dynamical meteorology'.

The novelty and importance of his work were appreciated even before he was awarded the PhD degree in 1948. He proceeded rapidly from research student to lecturer and then to reader in dynamical climatology (in the department of meteorology) by 1949. In that year he married Marjorie, daughter of Edgar Currie, formerly a warehouse foreman for a removals firm, but incapacitated during the First World War. There were no children.

Eady was invited to discuss his work at leading meteorological institutes round the world. Since then the 'Eady problem' has become a classical reference in the subject— J. G. Charney, the leading American worker in the same field, acknowledged that Eady's treatment was exceptional, being more comprehensible and more physically realistic than his own seminal contribution. However, Eady published little of his work, even though he wrote, as he spoke, fluently and well (talking with him was one of the pleasures of life). He continually broadened his professional interests to include the ocean, the earth's core, motions in the atmospheres of planets, the theory of fluids, biophysics, and biochemistry. Eventually he became depressed by the sheer difficulty of his subject, by the realization that he was not, as he put it, going to be able to build a cathedral. He isolated himself more and more from his friends and colleagues; he died, after an overdose of painkillers, at the Royal County Hospital, Guildford, on 26 March 1966.   H. CHARNOCK, rev.

Sources H. Charnock and others, *Quarterly Journal of the Royal Meteorological Society*, 92 (1966), 591–2 · private information (1993) · personal knowledge (1993) · *CGPLA Eng. & Wales* (1966)
Wealth at death £8090: probate, 14 June 1966, *CGPLA Eng. & Wales*

Eady, Sir (Crawfurd) Wilfrid Griffin (1890–1962), civil servant, was born on 27 September 1890 in Argentina, the elder son of George Griffin Eady, a railway engineer, and his wife, Lilian Armstrong, the daughter of General John Millar. He was educated at Clifton College, Bristol, and Jesus College, Cambridge, where he graduated with first-class classical honours in 1912.

Eady entered the home civil service in 1913 and served initially in the India Office and Home Office. On 3 April 1915 he married Elizabeth Margaret (1885/6–1969), the daughter of Max Laistner, with whom he had two sons and was to enjoy much happiness. His poor eyesight precluded him from wartime military service. In 1917 he was promoted to the department of foreign trade and then to the newly formed Ministry of Labour, where he was private secretary successively to the permanent secretary and the minister. It was in this relatively junior ministry that, confronted with the human consequences of mass unemployment during the next twenty-one years, he was encouraged both to question current orthodoxies and to develop the necessary administrative skills to implement radical new policies. This was a challenge to which, like many colleagues including Sir Horace Wilson and Sir Alan Barlow, he had the ability and ambition to respond. It also led him, like them, to a senior position within the Treasury.

Eady's radical views were advanced by his membership of the Romney Street Group of left-wing public figures of which Tom Jones, the deputy secretary of the cabinet, was a leading member, and it was through him that Eady came to draft Baldwin's controversial speech to the Peace Society just before the 1935 election. Within the ministry he was among the first to appreciate the structural problems of British industry and the ineffectiveness of orthodox economic policy. Economic recovery, he argued, required systematic industrial investment which government alone, either directly or indirectly, could ensure, and, although he opposed Keynes's ambitious public works programmes, his subsequent attempts to stimulate investment were appreciated by industrialists for displaying an exceptional 'keenness to achieve something practical' (*Lancashire and Whitehall*, 14).

It was in social policy, however, that Eady principally made his mark. As secretary of the Industrial Transference Board in 1928, the first major attempt to transfer the unemployed from the depressed regions, he was identified by the head of the civil service, Sir Warren Fisher, as a man of 'real quality' for his knowledge, sympathy, resourcefulness, and resolution (Baldwin MSS, 12/410). Then, having played an increasingly forthright role in the controversial and protracted reform of unemployment relief, he became, in 1934, secretary to the Unemployment Assistance Board. This was a semi-autonomous body charged, for the first time anywhere in the world, to provide a national system of standardized unemployment relief. Like many later executive agencies its constitutional position was somewhat anomalous and its resources inadequate. This led to an immediate crisis, with public demonstrations, the suspension of the initial benefit rates, and endless political machinations. However, as Robert Armstrong wrote in the *Dictionary of National Biography*, Eady was 'at his best with something specific to organize and administer, which engaged his energy, his constructive powers, and his skills in negotiation and handling people'. His ever willingness to consult with both claimants and staff, and his determination to provide a humane and flexible service which precluded any return to poor-law deterrence, quickly restored the board's morale and public reputation.

Eady's administrative achievements led to his transfer in 1938 to the Home Office as under-secretary to effect, amid some acrimony and personal ill health, a much needed revision of air-raid precautions. He then moved to the board of customs and excise as deputy chairman in 1940 to oversee the introduction of purchase tax, becoming chairman in the same year. Two years later he was appointed joint second secretary of the Treasury in charge of overseas and home finance. He remained in this post until his retirement in 1952, although he was relieved of responsibility for overseas finance in 1948.

In this post Eady was at the heart of revolutionary changes in fiscal, monetary, and international economic policy, such as the adoption of Keynesian demand management, the nationalization of the Bank of England, and the creation of the International Monetary Fund. He was also involved in major crises, including the renegotiation of the Anglo-American loan in 1946 and the suspension of sterling convertibility in 1947. He looked back on the period—and especially on his working with Keynes—as the most exciting part of his life. Labour politicians at the time and historians since, however, have been critical of his conservative influence, and economists were at times scathing of his technical competence. His conservatism was most apparent in relation to the Beveridge report, where he opposed the two major principles of universality and adequacy of benefit on the traditional Treasury grounds of the danger of non-compliance and cost. He similarly worked with Sir Hubert Henderson during the drafting of the 1944 employment policy white paper to qualify the acceptance of Keynesian demand management techniques, so that the final document was rightly described as an 'antiphon between Keynes and Eady' (*War Diary of Hugh Dalton*, 742). His opposition, based on his own inter-war experiences, again reflected traditional Treasury concerns about the political dangers of an unbalanced budget and the inability of macroeconomic policy to resolve structural, microeconomic problems. In the light of the later questioning of universalism and Keynesianism, both sets of reservations might be said to have had some justification.

Eady's limited command of the technicalities of economic policy was less justifiable. He famously admitted that for him, as for most officials, dealing with principles of Keynesianism was 'a voyage into the stratosphere' (*Collected Writings of John Maynard Keynes*, 27.371). On monetary policy Lionel Robbins exposed his shortcomings in a notorious footnote (Robbins, 89) and Robert Hall wondered whether he was 'slightly gaga' (*Hall Diaries*, 104). His ability to grasp technical detail in less theoretical policy areas, however, was demonstrated by his successfully handling a series of extremely complex negotiations—particularly regarding trade with Argentina, India, and Egypt—and during the convertibility crisis when he was the senior negotiator in Washington. Moreover he had an understanding, which economic advisers themselves often lacked, of political and practical policy constraints.

Eady was a small, ebullient man with an impish wit and an unflagging consideration for others. After 1942 his public career may have reflected some of the limitations of a generalist administrator in a rapidly changing and increasingly specialist world. Acceptance of the editorship of *The Observer*, which was then offered him, might have been advisable. However, he was an ambitious man. The Unemployment Assistance Board, according to Whitehall folklore, had had to be created for 'the poor and Eady'. Consequently he relished promotion to the Treasury. Despite his heavy commitments there, however, he continued to pursue a wide range of personal interests. His introduction of the voluntary 'Eady' levy on British cinema exhibitors to help finance British film production reflected his own creative past, which had seen the production of one of his plays (*The Widow Maker*) in London's West End in the 1920s. Between 1944 and 1955 he was also principal of the Working Men's College in London—a foundation established by the Christian socialists in 1854 to bring liberal education and a spirit of collegiality to those excluded from university.

Eady was appointed CMG in 1932, CB in 1934, KBE in 1942, and GCMG in 1948; in retirement his business and artistic interests were reflected by directorships in two steel companies, the Old Vic Trust, the Glyndebourne Arts Trust, and the National Film Institute. He died at the Victoria Hospital, Lewes, Sussex, near his home, Hill Farm House, Rodmell, on 9 January 1962.   RODNEY LOWE

Sources *The Times* (10 Jan 1962) • *The Times* (16 Jan 1962) • *DNB* • R. Lowe, *Adjusting to democracy: the role of the ministry of labour in British politics, 1916–1939* (1986) • G. C. Peden, *The treasury and British public policy, 1906–1959* (2000) • T. Jones, *A diary with letters, 1931–1950* (1954) • *Lancashire and Whitehall: the diary of Sir Raymond Streat*, ed. M. Dupree, 1 (1987) • *The collected writings of John Maynard Keynes*, ed. D. Moggridge and E. Johnson, 27 (1980) • *The Robert Hall diaries, 1947–53*, ed. A. Cairncross, 1 (1989) • *The Second World War diary of Hugh Dalton, 1940–1945*, ed. B. Pimlott (1986) • L. Robbins, *Political economy: past and present* (1976) • Violet Markham MSS, London School of Economics • NL Wales, Thomas Jones papers • Baldwin MSS, CUL • private information (2004) • Burke, *Peerage* (1959) • *WWW* • CGPLA Eng. & Wales (1962) • m. cert.

Archives King's Cam., corresp. with John Maynard Keynes • London School of Economics, Violet Markham MSS • NL Wales, corresp. with Thomas Jones • PRO, LAB 2/1215/ED 48401; T 237/241 (employment policy); T 237/51 (Beveridge) | FILM BFI NFTVA, news footage

Likenesses P. Ranos, portrait, Working Men's College, St Pancras, London

Wealth at death £18,135 15s. 2d.: probate, 20 Feb 1962, *CGPLA Eng. & Wales*

Eager, John (1782–1853?), organist and composer, was born on 15 August 1782 in Norwich, where his father, after retiring as a public servant, became a musical instrument maker and organ builder. His father taught him the rudiments of music, and his progress was such that at the age of twelve he attracted the notice of the duke of Dorset, an amateur violinist, who took him to his seat at Knowle as a page. There he continued and improved his education in the fine library and learned the violin. Towards the end of the century his patron's mental health deteriorated, and Eager, for whose support no provision had been made, established himself in Yarmouth as a violinist and music teacher. Soon afterwards he married a Miss Barnby, a wealthy lady, and in October 1803, on the death of John Roope, was appointed organist to the corporation of Yarmouth.

In 1814 J. B. Logier patented his chiroplast, or 'hand-director' mechanism, an invention for holding the hands in a proper position while playing at the keyboard, and his system of teaching was taken up with enthusiasm by Eager. Despite the controversy caused by the new method (and Eager came in for his full share of criticism in the Norfolk papers and elsewhere), Eager gradually convinced a considerable number of people of the usefulness of the system, which, in addition to the use of the chiroplast, helped to teach the fundamentals of harmony rapidly and thoroughly. The system also involved group piano teaching, and as many as twelve or more pupils were required to play simultaneously on as many pianos. Eager opened an academy for music and dancing at the assembly rooms, Norwich, assisted by his two daughters, and public examinations were held in due course in order to convince the audience of the value of the method. After the second of these Eager published *A brief account, with accompanying examples, of what was actually done at the second examination of Mr Eager's pupils in music, educated upon Mr Logier's system. ... June 18, 1819 ... addressed to Major Peter Hawker.* The appendix to the account includes letters written to, but not published in, the *Norwich Mercury* and the *Norfolk Chronicle* by those who considered that the opinions expressed by those papers were unfair. The negative publicity does not appear to have harmed Eager's reputation, and ten years later he was praised by J. Chambers in his *A General History of Norfolk* (1829). He then held the post of organist to the corporation.

In 1833 Eager left Norwich for Edinburgh, where he resided until his death some twenty years later. He separated from his wife, with whom he had two daughters (who became Mrs Bridgman and Mrs Lowe), before moving north. Having obtained a Scottish divorce about 1839, he married a Miss Lowe, the sister of his second daughter's husband. One of his pupils was his grandson, F. W. Bridgman. He also taught the royal children at Balmoral for a time. His compositions include a piano sonata and some songs and glees of little importance. He died in Edinburgh, probably on 1 June 1853.

J. A. F. MAITLAND, rev. DAVID J. GOLBY

Sources J. C. Kassler, *The science of music in Britain, 1714–1830: a catalogue of writings, lectures, and inventions*, 1 (1979), 303–5 • W. H. Husk, 'Eager, John', Grove, *Dict. mus.* (1954), 2.850 • [J. Chambers], *A general history of the county of Norfolk*, 2 vols. (1829) • private information (1888)

Eagles, Fanny Elizabeth (1836–1907), Church of England deaconess, was born on 10 December 1836 in Bedford, the youngest of the three children of Ezra Eagles (1804–1865), solicitor, coroner, and clerk of the peace, and his wife, Elizabeth Halfhead (c.1804–1866). Fanny survived both her brothers, the eldest, Ezra, dying in 1862 and her younger brother, Edward, in 1900. Fanny, being a delicate baby, was baptized privately, and was later received at St Peter's Church, Bedford. Her family was staunchly Anglican in a town which had strong nonconformist connections.

Nothing has been recorded of Fanny Eagles's early life except her confirmation at St Mary's, Bedford, by Bishop Thomas Turton of Ely in 1860. After the death of her father in 1865 and her mother in 1866, she decided to enter an Anglican sisterhood. As a member of St Paul's Church, Bedford, she had been influenced by the Revd John Donne and his successor, the Revd Michael Ferrebee Sadler, vicar since 1864. Sadler was a Tractarian who, as well as restoring the church building and introducing daily services, became a national figure within the Tractarian movement. It was he who dissuaded Fanny Eagles from joining a sisterhood and persuaded her to stay in Bedford and serve the poor there.

Initially, Fanny Eagles went to King's College Hospital, London, to train in nursing, and thence to St Peter's Home in Brompton Square to experience life in an Anglican sisterhood. But it was as a deaconess that she chose to fulfil her vocation, and on 5 February 1869 (seven years after the admission of the first Anglican deaconess) she was admitted in the palace chapel at Ely by Bishop Harold Browne in

the presence of a few friends. She then returned to Bedford to work among the poor in St Paul's parish, using her home, St Loyes, together with a stable loft in Allhallows Lane. She founded the Ely Deaconess Institution at St Loyes but this body grew very slowly. In 1870 two deaconesses were admitted but numbers never exceeded more than half a dozen (the last died in 1934). Habited like religious sisters and living in a community bound by a rule, it was very difficult to distinguish them from Sisters of Mercy. They were always known as 'sister', which added to the confusion, and in the nonconformist environment of Bedford they encountered much prejudice.

At first the deaconesses ran Sunday schools, night schools for men and boys, guilds for young girls, and women's meetings. But in the winter of 1871–2 Bedford was struck by a smallpox epidemic. Together with Harry Hocken, curate of St Paul's, Sister Fanny went into the homes of the sick to comfort and minister. They worked day and night for three months, often going where no other ministers would venture, and they frequently had to put the dead bodies into their coffins. A few months later their work was attacked by the minister of the Bunyan Meeting and dismissed as 'mimicries of the black veil and other monastic mummeries' (*Bedford Times and Independent*, 28 May 1872). Despite these difficulties Sister Fanny was described as 'always cheerful, almost indeed exuberant in spirit and with a keen sense of humour' (*Bedfordshire Mercury*).

The work grew steadily and was assisted by the gift of a substantial house in Bromham Road, Bedford, provided by Anthony Gibbs of Bristol who had heard of her heroism in the epidemic. In 1881 the deaconess community moved from St Loyes to Bromham Road and soon afterwards Sister Fanny took in a homeless orphan girl. From this small beginning grew St Etheldreda's Home, which cared for about twenty children. In 1890 the home was extended by the addition of a chapel and refectory, and in 1907 the neighbouring house was acquired.

Sister Fanny died peacefully at St Etheldreda's on 7 March 1907, having been seriously ill for some time. Her funeral took place at St Paul's on 11 March in the presence of a large congregation, including many poor people, and was followed by interment in the family plot at Ampthill. She was described as a 'gentle, good woman' (*Bedfordshire Mercury*) whose work would long be remembered, and indeed St Etheldreda's Home continued until 1983. A friend wrote that 'Sr Fanny belonged to the same School as Harriet Monsell, Mother Susan (of St Peter's Community), Pusey and Keble' (*A Short Memoir*, 25). Sister Fanny was a pioneer of women's ministry at a time when both deaconesses and religious sisters were new in the Anglican church.

VALERIE BONHAM

Sources *Bedfordshire Mercury* (15 March 1907) • P. Bell, *Sister Fanny Eagles and St Etheldreda's* (1983) • *Sister Fanny: a short memoir and an appeal by two associates* (1907?) • E. R. Desert, 'The influence of the Oxford Movement on the parish of St Paul's, Bedford, from the 1860s to the turn of the century', MA diss., Leicester University, 1993

Archives Beds. & Luton ARS, St Etheldreda's Home MSS

Eagles, John (1783–1855), art critic and poet, was born in Bristol and baptized there on 8 November 1783 in the parish of St Augustine, the second of the two children, and only son, of Thomas *Eagles (*bap.* 1746, *d.* 1812), merchant and classical scholar, and his wife, Charlotte Maria Tyndale (*d.* 1814). He was descended from a family which had held estates in Monmouthshire for several centuries. He was taught by the Revd Samuel Seyer at the Royal Fort School in Bristol before entering Winchester College in 1797. After leaving Winchester in 1802 he went to Italy, intending to become a landscape painter, attempting to copy the styles of Gaspard Poussin and Salvator Rosa. He narrowly escaped death when sketching on a tier of the Colosseum at Rome. In 1823 he published six etchings in the style of Poussin.

Eagles eventually decided to enter the church; he matriculated from Wadham College, Oxford, in 1808, taking a BA in 1812 and an MA in 1818. He was appointed curate of St Nicholas Church, Bristol, and in 1822 he moved to Halberton in Devon, where he remained for twelve years. For the last five years of his time in Devon the wit Sydney Smith was his rector. In 1834 he moved to the curacy of Winford, near Bristol, and then to Kinnersley in Herefordshire. After his retirement in 1841 he moved back to Bristol.

Eagles edited *The Journal of Llewellin Penrose, a Seaman* (1815), a partially autobiographical work by William Williams, whom Eagles's father had helped. From 1831 until within a few months of his death Eagles was a contributor to *Blackwood's Magazine*, a periodical whose narrow conservatism accorded with his own stance in both politics and art. His contributions were mainly on art, and the best of these were contained in a series of papers entitled 'The sketcher', which appeared in the magazine from 1833 to 1835. These were collected and published as a book in 1856. Another miscellaneous volume, entitled *Essays Contributed to 'Blackwood's Magazine'*, came out in 1857.

Eagles also wrote poetry, and many of his poems were published in 'The sketcher'. His friend John Mathew Gutch made a selection from these and others of his poems, original or translated, and fifty copies were privately printed, after his death, as *A Garland of Roses* (1857). The volume contained a poem which had appeared at intervals in the columns of *Felix Farley's Bristol Journal* (then under Gutch's editorship) and which had been written to expose the abuses which had existed for years in several public bodies in Bristol, especially in the corporation. These rhymes, enlarged and translated with notes and some humorous designs, were published as *Felix Farley, Rhymes, Latin and English, by Themaninthemoon* (1826). Eagles also published *The Bristol Riots* (1832), a response to local disturbances over the Reform Bill. A volume entitled *Sonnets*, edited by another friend, Zoë King, appeared posthumously, in 1858.

Eagles died at King's Parade, Clifton, Bristol, on 8 November 1855, and was survived by a large family. He left in manuscript translations of the first two books of the *Odyssey* and of five cantos of the *Orlando Furioso*.

GORDON GOODWIN, *rev.* ANNE PIMLOTT BAKER

Sources *GM*, 2nd ser., 44 (1855), 661–2 • J. M. Gutch, 'Preface and reminiscences', in J. Eagles, *A garland of roses* (1857) • Boase, *Mod. Eng. biog.* • Foster, *Alum. Oxon.* • *Wellesley index*
Archives Bristol RO, literary and artistic MSS, corresp. | BL, letters to G. Cumberland, Add. MSS 36511–36513 • NL Scot., corresp. with *Blackwood's* and poems
Likenesses N. Branwhite, crayon • J. Curnock, oils

Eagles, Thomas (*bap.* 1746, *d.* 1812), classical scholar and merchant, was baptized in the parish of Temple Holy Cross, Bristol, on 28 April 1746. He was descended on his father's side from a family which had resided in Temple parish for nearly two centuries; his mother (*née* Perkins), originally came from Monmouthshire. On 16 September 1757 he entered Winchester College, where he showed signs of becoming an excellent classical scholar. However, the death of his benefactor obliged him to give up all thoughts of making the church his profession, as his father desired. Accordingly he left Winchester on 18 January 1762 and returned to Bristol, where he eventually prospered as a merchant. From 1809 until his death he was collector of the customs at Bristol. He married Charlotte Maria Tyndale (*d.* 1814); they had several children including John *Eagles, art critic and poet. Throughout his life Eagles cherished a love for the classics and in 1811 he was elected a fellow of the Society of Antiquaries. He left a translation of part of Athenaeus, which, under the title of *Collections from the Deipnosophists, or, Banquet of the Gods*, was announced for publication in the *Gentleman's Magazine* (January 1813). It never appeared, but through the care of his son *Selections* from the first two books, with notes, were published anonymously in volumes three and four of *Blackwood's Magazine* (1818–19). Eagles contributed to a periodical essay, *The Crier*, which ran intermittently between 1785 and 1802. The title which appeared on page four of *Felix Farley's Bristol Journal* was perhaps the first attempt to support a periodical essay in a provincial English town. In 1807 Eagles attempted unsuccessfully to commence a series of papers to be called *The Ghost*. He took a warm interest in the Rowley and Chatterton controversy, on which he left some dissertations.

Eagles's other talents included painting and music. He died at Clifton on 28 October 1812 and was survived by his wife, who died on 20 February 1814. One of Eagles's many acts of quiet benevolence was beautifully commemorated by his son in an essay, 'The Beggar's Legacy', contributed to *Blackwood's Magazine* in March 1855. A selection from his correspondence with a young acquaintance, R. D. Woodforde, between 1787 and 1791, was published by the latter in 1818.

GORDON GOODWIN, *rev.* PHILIP CARTER

Sources *GM*, 1st ser., 82/2 (1812), 498, 589–90 • *GM*, 1st ser., 84/1 (1814), 411 • J. Eagles, 'Reminiscences', *A garland of roses*, ed. J. M. Gutch (1857) • PRO, PROB 11/1542, fols. 218v–221r
Archives Bristol RO, literary MSS, commonplace books

Ealdgyth [Aldgyth] (*fl. c.*1057–1066), queen of England, consort of Harold II, was the daughter of *Ælfgar, earl of Mercia (*d.* 1062?), and probably of his wife, Ælfgifu; she was sister of *Eadwine, earl of Mercia [*see under* Ælfgar, earl of Mercia (*d.* 1062?)], and *Morcar, earl of Northumbria. According to William of Jumièges, Ealdgyth was very beautiful. Her first marriage was to her father's ally, *Gruffudd ap Llywelyn (*d.* 1063), king of Gwynedd from 1039 and ruler of all Wales after 1055. This marriage probably took place *c.*1057, the year in which Ælfgar succeeded his father *Leofric as earl of Mercia. Ealdgyth appears to have brought with her into the marriage a small amount of property in England, although the only certain holding is an estate at Binley, Warwickshire. She and Gruffudd had at least one child, a daughter, Nest, who married the Herefordshire border lord, *Osbern fitz Richard [*see under* Richard Scrob], through whose hands ownership of Binley passed before 1086. Ealdgyth was widowed in 1063, when an expedition into Wales by Earl Harold Godwineson (1022–1066) [*see* Harold II] provoked the murder of Gruffudd.

At some point after this, Harold proposed to marry Ealdgyth. His motivation for this was almost certainly political, aimed not only at securing the support of the Mercian house for himself in his royal ambitions, but also at weakening the links between that same house and the rulers of north Wales. It is not certain when this second marriage occurred, or whether Harold married Ealdgyth before or after his election as king; however, it had certainly taken place before the Norman invasion in 1066. At the time of Harold's death at Hastings, Ealdgyth was in London, whence her brothers Eadwine and Morcar took her to Chester for protection. Her fate after this is not known. It seems likely that her marriage to Harold was childless, although it is not impossible that she was the mother of his son Harold.   K. L. MAUND

Sources Ordericus Vitalis, *Eccl. hist.*, 2.120, 183 · *The Gesta Normannorum ducum of William of Jumièges, Orderic Vitalis, and Robert of Torigni*, ed. and trans. E. M. C. van Houts, 2 vols., OMT (1992–5) · John of Worcester, *Chron.* · B. Hudson, 'The family of Harold Godwinsson and the Irish Sea province', *Journal of the Royal Society of Antiquaries of Ireland*, 109 (1979), 92–100 · A. Farley, ed., *Domesday Book*, 2 vols. (1783), fol. 238d · K. L. Maund, *Ireland, Wales, and England in the eleventh century* (1991), 66, 68–9, 137–40, 208

Ealdred (*fl.* 757–777). *See under* Hwicce, kings of the (*act. c.*670–*c.*780).

Ealdred (*d.* 933?), leader of the Northumbrians, was the son of Eadulf and lord of Bamburgh. He was the most important Anglo-Saxon in Northumbria during the early tenth century, a time of renewed viking activity, and the last representative of an independent Anglo-Saxon royal family in the north. His father, Eadulf, is styled king of the north Saxons by the tenth-century record embedded in the Irish annals of Ulster, while the contemporary *Historia de sancto Cuthberto* describes him as *princeps*. Ealdred, like his father before him, was prominent in efforts to unite Northumbria with the other English-ruled regions; the *Historia de sancto Cuthberto* claims that he was as beloved by Edward the Elder as his father had been by Alfred the Great.

Ealdred succeeded his father in 913, after the murder of Eadulf by an Eadred, son of Rixinc. Eadred led an invasion against Eadulf, killed him, and seized his wife before retiring south of the River Tyne to the sanctuary of the lands of St Cuthbert, where he resided for three years before dying in a battle fought against the vikings in 916. Ealdred came to power at the time when three vikings—Ragnall, Sihtric, and Guthfrith—began a campaign to bring Northumbria under their control. At the same time they were establishing themselves in south-eastern Ireland and taking control of the Irish Sea. Some time between 914 and 916 Ragnall attacked eastern Britain and occupied the lands of Ealdred, who fled north and sought aid from the Scottish king Constantine II. Seeking assistance from a Scottish rather than an English prince may not have been eccentric: Constantine had a son named Idulb, the Gaelic rendering of Eadulf, which suggests that the Scottish royal family and the dynasty of Bamburgh were allied by marriage. This alliance proved unable to halt the vikings and 'through some unknown sin', according to the *Historia de sancto Cuthberto*, Constantine and Ealdred were defeated in the battle of Corbridge. Constantine redeemed himself in a later battle when the Scots fought the vikings to a draw in 918. The death of Ragnall in 920 or 921 brought to Britain a less formidable opponent in his kinsman Sihtric, who ruled Northumbria until his death in 927. Ealdred remained powerful, however, and the contemporary version of the Anglo-Saxon Chronicle notes that he submitted to King Edward the Elder in 924, together with all the Northumbrians: English, Danes, and Norwegians. After the death of Sihtric Northumbria was annexed by Edward's son Æthelstan (*d.* 939) and Ealdred submitted to him. Ealdred then disappears from the chronicle record, but reappears as a witness to several charters issued at the court of Æthelstan in 931 or 932. Those charters were all issued in the south of England, suggesting that Ealdred was in constant attendance on the royal court during that time. The absence of Ealdred from later documents suggests that he might have died in the year 933.

Little is known of Ealdred's family, although he had a brother named Uhtred who survived the battle of Corbridge. Ealdred was probably the father of Oswulf, who later ruled in Northumbria under King Eadred (*d.* 955). Oswulf engineered the downfall of Erik Bloodaxe (*d.* 954), the last king of an independent Northumbria, so that the kingdom could be annexed by Eadred. Oswulf was a witness to several royal charters where he is identified as 'high-reeve of Bamburgh'.   BENJAMIN T. HUDSON

Sources J. Earle, ed., *Two of the Saxon chronicles parallel with supplementary extracts from the others*, rev. C. Plummer, 2 vols. (1892–9) · 'Historia de sancto Cuthberto', Symeon of Durham, *Opera*, vol. 1 · W. de G. Birch, ed., *Cartularium Saxonicum*, 4 vols. (1885–99) · *The chronicle of Æthelweard*, ed. and trans. A. Campbell (1962) · A. Campbell, 'Two notes on the Norse kingdoms in Northumbria', *EngHR*, 57 (1942), 85–97 · D. Whitelock, 'The dealings of the kings of England with Northumbria in the 10th and 11th centuries', *The Anglo-Saxons: studies in some aspects of their history and culture presented to Bruce Dickins*, ed. P. Clemoes (1959), 70–88 · F. T. Wainwright, 'The battles of Corbridge', *Saga Book of the Viking Society*, 13 (1950), 156–73 · R. Vaughan, ed., 'The chronicle attributed to John of Wallingford', *Camden miscellany, XXI*, CS, 3rd ser., 90 (1958) · F. M. Stenton, *Anglo-Saxon England*, 3rd edn (1971) · *Ann. Ulster* · *AS chart.*, S 396

Ealdred [Aldred] (*d.* 1069), archbishop of York, may have come originally from the west country, although little is known of his background. Since his career progressed, both ecclesiastically and politically, in the footsteps of Lyfing, bishop of St Germans, of Crediton, and of Worcester, it is likely that they were kinsmen. If so, Ealdred would also have been related to Brihtwald, bishop of St Germans (*d. c.*1027).

Early career Like Lyfing, Ealdred began his career as a monk at Winchester and followed Lyfing as abbot of Tavistock in 1027 when the latter was elevated to the see of Worcester. Ealdred retained a lifelong interest in Tavistock, where Lyfing was buried, and is named as the previous holder of two estates held by the abbey in 1086. Lyfing had been a great benefactor to Tavistock and it is possible that Ealdred's estates were part of their family holding. By 1044 Ealdred was witnessing royal charters as bishop, probably as suffragan to Lyfing, whom Ealdred succeeded after his death on 23 March 1046. In July 1049 Ealdred, with the men of Herefordshire and Gloucestershire, was called upon to repel an invasion force of Irish and Welsh. However, they were taken by surprise in the early hours of 29 July and Ealdred narrowly escaped with his life. In April 1050 he and Bishop Hermann of Ramsbury visited Rome on an errand of Edward the Confessor, most probably to seek dispensation for the removal of the see of Crediton to Exeter; according to later and possibly unreliable sources it was to secure the king's release from a vow of pilgrimage made before his accession. The E version of the Anglo-Saxon Chronicle says the two bishops were sent to a great synod, probably the Easter Synod which began on 29 April. Returning the same year, Ealdred reconciled Earl Swein Godwinsson with the king and brought him back from Flanders. In 1051 almost the entire Godwine family was exiled and Edward sent Ealdred with troops to intercept Earl Harold Godwinsson as he fled, but, according to the Anglo-Saxon Chronicle, 'they could not or would not' (text D, s.a. 1052). Undoubtedly, the events of 1051 and Ealdred's known partisanship with the Godwines caused him to be passed over as the successor to Ælfric Puttoc at York in favour of the king's chaplain, Cynesige. However, with the return of the Godwines the following year, it was not long before Ealdred's fortunes were restored. This was aided, perhaps, by his appointing Godric, son of Godman the king's chaplain, to the abbacy of Winchcombe in 1054. Ealdred consecrated Godric on 17 July, having held the abbey himself since the death of Abbot Godwin in 1053. Later in 1054, the king sent him to Germany to arrange the return from Hungary of Edward the Exile, son of Edmund Ironside. He was received with honour by Archbishop Hermann of Cologne and Emperor Henry III and remained there for a year, being presented, among other gifts, with a psalter and sacramentary sent there by Cnut. Ealdred later presented these books to his prior and successor at Worcester, Wulfstan. While he was in Germany,

Ealdred gave permission to Bishop Leofwine of Lichfield to consecrate the rebuilt church of Evesham on 10 October in his stead.

On his return in 1055, possibly as a reward for his diplomatic success in Germany, Ealdred was entrusted with the diocese of Ramsbury after Bishop Hermann's resignation and departure from England, until his return in 1058.

On 12 April 1056, Ealdred dedicated a chapel built by Earl Odda at Deerhurst in memory of his brother, Ælfric, who had died three years earlier. Two months later, on 16 June, Leofgar, bishop of Hereford, was killed fighting against the Welsh at the battle of Glasbury-on-Wye and Ealdred was called upon, with the earls Leofric and Harold, to negotiate peace terms with King Gruffudd of north Wales. The successful outcome of these talks resulted in Ealdred being rewarded with the vacant see of Hereford.

Travels abroad In 1058 Ealdred consecrated the abbey church of St Peter in Gloucester, which he had rebuilt from its foundations. He maintained his influence over the abbey by installing a kinsman, Wilstan, a monk of Worcester, as abbot and retaining several estates belonging to the abbey under his control. These estates remained under the jurisdiction of the archbishop of York long after Ealdred's death. Following the consecration of St Peter's, Ealdred travelled by way of Hungary to Jerusalem 'in such state as none had done before him' (*ASC*, text D, s.a. 1058). Ealdred's visit to Hungary may have been to arrange for Edward the Exile's family (which included his son Edgar Ætheling) to be brought to England, as Edward had died soon after his arrival in England in 1057. While Ealdred was in Jerusalem he gave a gold chalice worth 5 marks to the church of the Holy Sepulchre. He was elected archbishop of York on Christmas day 1060, and gave up the see of Hereford, while intending to hold York and Worcester in plurality like earlier archbishops, including St Oswald. In 1061, accompanied by Earl Tostig Godwinsson, he went to Rome to receive his pallium, but was denied it and deprived of episcopal rank by Pope Nicholas II because his transference from one see to another was against church law. However, he and Earl Tostig were robbed by brigands on their way home and forced to return to Rome, where Nicholas reinstated Ealdred and gave him the pallium, while insisting that he give up Worcester. Papal legates were with Ealdred in England in 1062 to see this implemented, and on 8 September at York he consecrated Wulfstan bishop of Worcester.

Crowning monarchs Ealdred's known support of the Godwine family suggests that it was he who crowned Harold Godwinsson on 6 January 1066, contrary to the scene portrayed in the Bayeux tapestry. After Harold's death at Hastings, he joined with the earls Eadwine and Morcar in promoting the succession of Edgar Ætheling, but on the earls' withdrawal, Ealdred was among the English leaders who submitted to the Normans at Berkhamsted. He accompanied Duke William to London and crowned him king at Westminster on Christmas day 1066; but not, according to the Anglo-Saxon Chronicle, before he exacted a promise 'that he would rule this people as well as any king before him best did' (*ASC*, text D, s.a. 1066). On 11 May 1068 Ealdred also crowned William's queen, Matilda.

Diocesan disputes The evidence for Ealdred's tenure of Worcester is overshadowed by the later veneration accorded to St Wulfstan. However, three out of the four leases issued by Ealdred survive in the original and he is said to have made several grants of land to the monks. After his elevation to York, it is clear that Ealdred was reluctant to release his hold over Worcester and intended Wulfstan to act as his suffragan. The life of Wulfstan suggests that this desire governed Ealdred's choice of the more malleable Wulfstan as his successor rather than the 'worldly' Æthelwig, abbot of Evesham. The life tells that, initially, Ealdred withheld all but seven of Worcester's estates from Wulfstan and that Wulfstan was able to regain all but twelve vills after lengthy negotiation. Indeed, Wulfstan was only able to obtain full control of his dioceses after litigation against Ealdred's successor at York, Thomas of Bayeux. In fact, Thomas, as Ealdred's heir, claimed jurisdiction over the whole diocese of Worcester. There is evidence in Domesday to suggest that the division of Worcester's lands between the bishop and the cathedral clergy reflects, in part, the original alienation by Ealdred. It was Ealdred, rather than Wulfstan, who took out lawsuits, both before and after 1066, to reclaim Worcester estates from unlawful tenants, and when the building of the castle by the Norman sheriff, Urse d'Abetot, encroached upon the cathedral's cemetery, it was Ealdred who, it is said, uttered the famous words 'Hattest thu Urs, have thu Godes kurs' (*De gestis pontificum*, 253).

For two years Ealdred simultaneously held the dioceses of Worcester, Ramsbury, and Hereford without censure. No sources survive to illustrate his guardianship of Ramsbury. However, while bishop of Hereford, he was able to ensure the protection of the lands of the monks of St Æthelbriht, Hereford, by royal writ.

Archbishop of York As archbishop of York, Ealdred was active within his archdiocese, building refectories for the communities at York and Southwell, completing the building of a refectory and dormitory begun by his predecessor, and erecting a presbytery at Beverley. The church at Beverley was decorated with paintings and given a bronze, silver, and gold pulpit and crucifix in the German style. Ealdred also commissioned Folcard, a continental monk under his protection, to write a life of St John of Beverley. His building works were part of an attempt to introduce a more regular life to the chapters of these churches, apparently inspired by his observations in Cologne. He also gave lands to them and had those of Beverley protected by royal writs. Folcard recounts 'that during the time of Ealdred the church of York shed its former backwardness and, inspired by Ealdred's teaching, grew to handsome maturity' (Raine, 1.241).

There is also evidence to suggest that Ealdred pursued the claims of his predecessors to jurisdiction over the see of Dorchester and the old diocese of Lindsey. A bull of Pope Nicholas dated 3 May 1061 states that Wulfsige of Dorchester is to hold his see free from the control of the archbishops of York, both past and future. Due to the paucity of northern sources, Ealdred's role in this dispute is shadowy. However, it would appear that he attempted to extend York's interests within Wulfsige's diocese through the purchase of estates, including several from Ulf son of Topi, who appears as a Lincolnshire tenant in Domesday. Distrust of Ealdred's intentions towards the see of Dorchester may well have influenced the pope's refusal to accept readily Ealdred's candidature for York and it is clear that the bull issued in Wulfsige's favour was made while Ealdred was in Rome. Just as Thomas of Bayeux, at York, laid claim, as Ealdred's heir, to the bishopric of Worcester and his estates in Gloucester, so he was also to be more vociferous in his attempts to acquire control over the see of Dorchester.

Ealdred and the Anglo-Saxon Chronicle Much more is known about Ealdred than most Anglo-Saxon churchmen, partly because both the D version of the Anglo-Saxon Chronicle and the chronicle of John of Worcester were written in his former dioceses not long after his death. He is, in fact, probably the most prominent non-royal individual in the entire D text. The particular interests of this version, in Scotland and the north, with the west midlands until 1061–2 but in the north alone thereafter, parallel Ealdred's career as bishop of Worcester and archbishop of York. The parallel is so close as to suggest that the D text was compiled largely from sources associated closely with Ealdred. It is no surprise, then, that the D text, as well as John of Worcester and Folcard, speaks well of him, and William of Poitiers thought him 'wise, good and eloquent' (Poitiers, *Histoire*, 221). The Worcester sources, including the hagiographical life of Wulfstan, have presented a picture of Ealdred as one whose major concerns were not with holy matters but with secular affairs, and as such his reputation is coloured by comparison with Wulfstan, whose canonization was sought as early as 1118.

However, the anonymous chronicle of the archbishops of York tells how Ealdred, influenced by his travels, instigated liturgical reform 'which he subsequently caused to be observed in the churches of England' (Raine, 1.345). He is thought to have been responsible for the introduction of a copy of the *Pontificale Romano-Germanicum* into England, on which the composition of the third coronation ordo is based. Ealdred is considered to have composed the ordo, or at the very least instigated its composition, for the coronations of Harold Godwinsson and William I.

Death Ealdred was the most widely travelled bishop of the Anglo-Saxon age and appears to have been a skilled diplomat earning the respect of both Anglo-Saxon and Norman contemporaries. There is a York tradition that just before his death he admonished William the Conqueror for the imposition of harsh taxes, contrary to his coronation oath. It is said that the king sent messengers to appease the archbishop but they arrived three days too late. Ealdred died at York on 11 September 1069, and was buried there.   M. K. LAWSON, *rev.* VANESSA KING

Sources *ASC*, s.a. 1047, 1050, 1052, 1054–68 [text D] · John of Worcester, *Chron.* · F. Barlow, ed. and trans., *The life of King Edward who rests at Westminster* (1962) · *The Vita Wulfstani of William of Malmesbury*, ed. R. R. Darlington, CS, 3rd ser., 40 (1928) · A. Farley, ed., *Domesday Book*, 2 vols. (1783) · W. of Poitiers [Gulielmus Pictariensis], *Histoire de Guillaume le Conquérant*, ed. R. Foreville (1952) · F. E. Harmer, ed., *Anglo-Saxon writs* (1952) · J. Raine, ed., *The historians of the church of York and its archbishops*, 3 vols., Rolls Series, 71 (1879–94) · J. M. Cooper, *The last four Anglo-Saxon archbishops of York* (1970) · F. Barlow, *The English church, 1000–1066: a history of the later Anglo-Saxon church*, 2nd edn (1979) · J. L. Nelson, 'The rites of the Conqueror', *Anglo-Norman Studies*, 4 (1981), 117–32, 210–21 · M. Lapidge, *Anglo-Latin literature: 900–1066* (1993) · *Willelmi Malmesbiriensis monachi de gestis pontificum Anglorum libri quinque*, ed. N. E. S. A. Hamilton, Rolls Series, 52 (1870) · P. Wermald, *How do we know so much about Anglo-Saxon Deerhurst?* (1993) · V. King, 'Ealdred, archbishop of York: the Worcester years', ed. C. Harper-Bill, *Anglo-Norman Studies*, 18 (1995)

Ealdwulf (*fl. c.*760). *See under* South Saxons, kings of the (*act.* 477–772).

Ealdwulf [Aldulf] (*d.* 1002), archbishop of York, is best known for his long association with Peterborough Abbey. Most of what is known about him derives from traditions recorded at Peterborough in the twelfth century in the E version of the Anglo-Saxon Chronicle and by Hugh Candidus. According to Hugh, Ealdwulf was King Edgar's lay chancellor and accidentally suffocated his son as the child slept between his drunken parents. He was about to seek absolution in Rome when he was persuaded by his godfather, Bishop Æthelwold, to make amends by rebuilding Peterborough Abbey. Ealdwulf became a monk at Peterborough, then abbot, and set about endowing the abbey, both personally and by attracting the benefaction of Edgar and his magnates. The supposed refoundation date for Peterborough of 963 is probably too early, however, and it is unlikely to have been refounded until the early 970s, with Ealdwulf's appointment coming up to ten years later. He remained abbot until his appointment in 992 to the archbishopric of York, and held the bishopric of Worcester in plurality, as was common. He was perhaps not consecrated archbishop immediately and until 996 attested charters as either bishop of Worcester or as archbishop-elect. On 15 April 1002 he presided over the translation of the body of his predecessor, St Oswald, at Worcester. Ealdwulf died less than a month later, on 6 May 1002, and was buried at Worcester.

WILLIAM HUNT, *rev.* MARY FRANCES SMITH

Sources C. R. Hart, *The early charters of northern England and the north midlands* (1975) · *The chronicle of Hugh Candidus, a monk of Peterborough*, ed. W. T. Mellows (1949) · *ASC*, s.a. 963, 992, 1002 [text E] · John of Worcester, *Chron.* · J. Raine, ed., *The historians of the church of York and its archbishops*, 3 vols., Rolls Series, 71 (1879–94) · *Codex Diplomaticus aevi Saxonici*, ed. J. M. Kemble, 6 vols. (1839–48) · *Willelmi Malmesbiriensis monachi de gestis pontificum Anglorum libri quinque*, ed. N. E. S. A. Hamilton, Rolls Series, 52 (1870)

Eales, Mary (*d.* 1717/18?), cookery writer and confectioner, is known almost exclusively through the texts published under her name. No details of her birth or parentage are known and it is only on the title-page to *Mrs. Mary Eales's Receipts*, published in 1718, that the nature and achievements of her career are suggested. Here she is described as

'confectioner to her late majesty Queen Anne', while the title-page to a later, slightly modified edition of this text, entitled *The Complete Confectioner, or, The Art of Candying and Preserving in its Utmost Perfection* (1733), suggests that the by then 'late ingenious Mrs Eales' served both William III and his successor. Unfortunately there is no record in the lord steward's accounts of a Mary Eales's being employed as a confectioner in the royal household during Queen Anne's reign (although the position of first confectioner was held by a woman, one Elizabeth Stephens, in 1702).

It is clear nevertheless that Mary Eales was, as commended by her publishers, an 'exquisite artist' in her field (*Complete Confectioner*, sig. A1r), and that her recipes for sweetmeats, candied fruits, creams, and preserves were in great demand. The publishers of the 1733 volume describe how the few printed copies of the earlier volume, derived from a manuscript of recipes which Eales had put together for a few readers 'of prime quality', sold immediately at an enormous premium, while manuscript copies of the recipes were purchased for 'five guineas' apiece (ibid., sig. A1v). This may of course be advertising rhetoric, but Mrs Eales's recipes must have been in wide circulation in manuscript form for several years before 1718. The recipes in the manuscript collection of Elizabeth Sloane (daughter of Sir Hans Sloane), dated internally to 1711, are noted as being 'a copy from Mrs Eales book' (BL, Add. MS 29,739, fol. 61r); the recipes in Sloane's manuscript are, almost verbatim, those published in the 1733 text. If more evidence were needed of Eales's contemporary popularity the ledgers of Charles Ackers, who printed *The Complete Confectioner*, record that 2000 copies were prepared—a substantial edition indeed for any book, fiction or non-fiction, in this period.

It is not clear whether Eales assumed her married title or was indeed married. If she is the Mary Eales who was buried at St Paul's, Covent Garden, on 11 January 1718, for whose estate administration was granted to Elizabeth Eales on 21 November 1718, the indications are that she did marry and bear children. Indeed it may have been with her family that she passed what her publishers term a 'retirement [of] … some years' (*Complete Confectioner*, sig. A1v) prior to her death, and prior to the publication of the volumes in which her confectionery skills and her name were both celebrated and perpetuated.

S. M. PENNELL

Sources [M. Eales], *The complete confectioner, or, The art of candying and preserving in its utmost perfection* (1733) · *Mrs Mary Eales's receipts: confectioner to her late majesty Queen Anne* (1718) · E. Sloane, recipe collection, 1711, BL, Add. MS 29739 · D. F. McKenzie and J. C. Ross, eds., *A ledger of Charles Ackers, printer of the London Magazine* (1968), 254 · 'An establishment of the yearly charge of diet in Queen Anne's household', 1702, BL, Add. MS 30232 · warrant book of the lord steward [of the royal household], 1702–14, PRO, LS 13/259 · warrant book of royal appointments [to the royal household], 1702–14, PRO, LS 13/258 · PRO, PROB 6/94, fol. 218v · W. H. Hunt, ed., *The registers of St Paul's Church, Covent Garden, London*, 4, Harleian Society, register section, 36 (1908), 250

Ealhmund [St Ealhmund] (*d.* 800), prince and martyr, is the subject of a *passio* (account of martyrdom) preserved only in the fourteenth-century manuscript in the Gotha Forschungsbibliothek (MS I.81). This text, which is utterly unreliable, presents him as the son of Aldfrith, king of Northumbria, and himself king after the murder of King Osred in 716. After emphasizing his religious inclinations, it describes how he journeyed to what is now Wiltshire to protect some lands he had there against enemies, how the men of Wiltshire were attacked by Æthelmund, ealdorman of Mercia, and how Ealhmund, having failed to mediate a peace, fought on the side of the Wiltshire men and lost his life in assisting them to victory at Kempsford. This account is historically valueless and seems to be based on the 800 entry in the chronicle of John of Worcester, which describes the battle of Kempsford (as in the Anglo-Saxon Chronicle), which was indeed fought between the men of Wiltshire and Ealdorman Æthelmund, but which did not involve Ealhmund. The latter's death in 800, however, is recorded at the end of the same annal in John's chronicle, and it appears that the author of the *passio* has conflated this with the preceding account in order to provide Ealhmund with a spurious history involving the battle, which he has in addition misdated to 822.

The true history of Ealhmund is given, insofar as it can be known, in what is almost certainly a reliable annal for 800 in the *Historia regum*, which states: 'Some say that Ealhmund, son of King Alchred, was apprehended by King Eardwulf's guards and on his orders was killed along with those who had fled with him' (Symeon of Durham, *Opera*, 2.63). Ealhmund was thus the son of a former king, *Alhred (*fl.* 765–774) [*see under* Oswulf], and the brother of another, *Osred II, expelled in 790. He would no doubt have been a threat to Eardwulf, who was of another line, and this adequately explains his killing. According to what is probably the ninth-century section of an early eleventh-century list of saints' resting places, *Secgan be þam godes sanctum þe on Engla lande ærost reston* ('Concerning God's saints who formerly rested in England'), however, his remains were enshrined at Derby. The *passio* also mentions the translation of his remains from the place of his death (Lilleshall in Shropshire) to Derby, and this information about the localities of his subsequent cult is likely to be reliable. The principal church of Derby was dedicated to him and preserves an impressive late Saxon coffin lid which may possibly come from his shrine. Veneration of him as a royal saint who suffered a violent death is paralleled by that of other saints of this date such as Cynehelm and Wigstan, but it is not easy to explain why he should have been venerated in Mercia. The explanation may lie in the war between Eardwulf and King Cenwulf of Mercia in 801, fought because Eardwulf accused Cenwulf of sheltering his enemies, among whom Ealhmund was no doubt numbered. Tension between the kings continued, for Pope Leo III (*r.* 795–816) blamed Cenwulf for the expulsion of Eardwulf from his kingdom in 807–8. In these circumstances, the Mercian kings may have had an incentive to foster Ealhmund's cult at what was probably the royal church of Derby, as a means of advertising and commemorating Eardwulf's guilt in Ealhmund's murder.

DAVID ROLLASON

Sources P. Grosjean, ed., 'De codice hagiographico Gothano', *Analecta Bollandiana*, 58 (1940), 90–103, 177–204 [appx], esp. 178–83 [Ealhmundi passio] · D. W. Rollason, 'The cults of murdered royal saints in Anglo-Saxon England', *Anglo-Saxon England*, 11 (1983), 1–22 · Symeon of Durham, *Opera*, vol. 2 · F. Liebermann, *Die Heiligen Englands* (1889) · ASC, s.a. 800 [texts D, E] · John of Worcester, *Chron.*

Ealhmund (*fl.* **784**). *See under* Æthelberht II (d. 762).

Ealhswith (d. **902**), consort of Alfred, king of the West Saxons from 871 and of the Anglo-Saxons from 886, was the daughter of Æthelred Mucel, ealdorman of the 'Gaini' (presumably an old tribal group of the Mercians), and his wife, Eadburh, who, according to Alfred's biographer Asser, was a member of the Mercian royal family. She had a brother, an ealdorman named Æthelwulf, whose appearance in a charter of 897 confirms the siblings' Mercian royal pedigree (AS chart., S 1442). In 868 she married *Alfred (848/9–899), at that time apparently regarded as 'heir-apparent' to his brother *Æthelred, king of the West Saxons (r. 865–71). The Mucel who appears in two charters of that year in company with West Saxon dignitaries was probably her father (AS chart., S 340 and 1201).

In marked and curious contrast to her husband, the best-attested of all the Anglo-Saxon kings, Ealhswith is very obscure in the sources. Asser never names her explicitly, and, in accordance with what he says was the West Saxon custom of the time, she was apparently never called 'queen'; nor does she appear as a witness to any of Alfred's extant charters. The couple had three daughters and two sons who survived into adulthood. Their first-born child, *Æthelflæd (d. 918), married *Æthelred (d. 911), ealdorman and ruler of the Mercians from at least 883. Another daughter, Æthelgifu, was made abbess of his own foundation of Shaftesbury by her father. *Ælfthryth married Baudouin (II), count of Flanders, at some time after 893. Of the two sons, *Edward (the Elder) (d. 924) succeeded his father as king of the Anglo-Saxons. The youngest child, Æthelweard, was well educated at the royal court, received generous provision in his father's will, attested several of his brother's charters, and died on 16 October, probably in 920.

It was probably on her own initiative, and perhaps after Alfred's death in 899, that Ealhswith founded the convent of St Mary at Winchester, usually called Nunnaminster. The bounds of her land in Winchester, which survive in a tenth-century addition to an earlier prayer book which came into Nunnaminster's possession, probably describe the site of the foundation, to the east of Edward's New Minster, founded in 901. The New Minster's *Liber vitae*, compiled c.1030, describes her as Nunnaminster's builder. Construction was probably not completed until c.908, if the tower which (according to the chronicler Æthelweard) Archbishop Plegmund then dedicated belonged to Nunnaminster.

In his will (AS chart., S 1507), Alfred left to his wife the highly symbolic bequest of three key estates: Edington (Wiltshire), the site of one great victory over the vikings; Lambourn (Berkshire), at or near the site of another—Ashdown; and Wantage (Berkshire), his birthplace. These were all part of Alfred's 'bookland', which, in order to ensure that they remained in the king's family, could be purchased by any of his male kin during Ealhswith's lifetime, and would pass to his direct male descendants on her death: all three were still royal estates in the tenth century. Ealhswith died on 5 December 902, and was buried, with Alfred, by their son Edward, in the newly consecrated New Minster, Winchester. She is commemorated in two manuscripts of an early tenth-century metrical calendar as 'the true and dear lady of the English' (McGurk, 110), finally but posthumously sharing the honour so recently won by her husband.   MARIOS COSTAMBEYS

Sources Alfred the Great: Asser's Life of King Alfred and other contemporary sources, ed. and trans. S. Keynes and M. Lapidge (1983) · M. Biddle and D. J. Keene, 'Winchester in the eleventh and twelfth centuries', Winchester in the early middle ages: an edition and discussion of the Winton Domesday, ed. M. Biddle, Winchester Studies, 1 (1976), 241–448 · S. J. Ridyard, The royal saints of Anglo-Saxon England, Cambridge Studies in Medieval Life and Thought, 4th ser., 9 (1988) · S. Keynes, ed., The Liber vitae of the New Minster and Hyde Abbey, Winchester (Copenhagen, 1996) · AS chart., S 340, 1201, 1442, 1507, 1560 · P. McGurk, 'The metrical calendar of Hampson: a new edition', Analecta Bollandiana, 104 (1986), 79–125

Eames, John (1686–1744), Independent layman and tutor, was born on 2 February 1686, the son of John Eames (b. 1645), of Berkhamsted, Hertfordshire. Like his father, he was educated at the Merchant Taylors' School in London, from 1696 to 1702. His intent was to enter the ministry, but following training he found that he was totally unsuited to preaching. He is supposed to have preached but once. 'There was a great defect in his organs of speech, and his pronunciation was exceedingly harsh, uncouth and disagreeable … so that he quit the pulpit entirely' (Wilson, 2.73). He readily turned to learning and teaching. His opportunity came in 1712 when Thomas Ridgley became theological tutor at the Congregational Fund Academy in Tenter Alley, Moorfields, and Eames was appointed assistant tutor with responsibilities for teaching classics and science.

Eames soon gained a high reputation for his knowledge of classical literature, mathematics, and the sciences. His contact with Sir Isaac Newton led to his election as a fellow of the Royal Society in 1724. His contribution to the work of the society consisted of comments on moving bodies, hydraulics, and magnets. He contributed, with John Martyn, to an abridgement of the society's Philosophical Transactions (10 vols., 1731–56). Apart from an edition of Isaac Watts's treatise on geography and astronomy of 1726, that was dedicated to Eames, this is his only known publication, although notes taken of his lectures were later used by tutors in various academies. He is said to have been the first to introduce anatomy into the curriculum of a dissenting academy. Although reticent and unassuming, Eames attracted to his lectures the best students, some of the most distinguished ever to enter a nonconformist academy, including Richard Price, Philip Furneaux, and Samuel Morton Savage. Thomas Secker, later archbishop of Canterbury, attended his lectures during 1716–17 when he was considering medicine as a profession. Eames's outlook was liberal, as is demonstrated by the part he played in the debate with two Roman Catholic priests held in March 1735 in conjunction with Samuel Chandler and Jeremiah Hunt. He was most unusual in being a layman in a tutoring role customarily held by a dissenting minister.

When Ridgley died in 1734 Eames succeeded him as theological tutor, with Joseph Densham, one of his pupils, taking over his previous duties. Eames, who was unmarried, was devoted to his task. He died very suddenly on 29 June 1744 in Coleman Street, in St Stephen's parish, City of London, and was buried in Bunhill Fields burial-ground. '"What a change", said Dr Isaac Watts, … "did Mr Eames experience!—but a few hours between his lecturing to his pupils, and his hearing the lectures of angels"' (Monthly Magazine, April 1803, 242). Densham declined to take over the tutorship so the Moorfields academy closed; the students and Eames's books and apparatus (bequeathed to the Congregational Fund Board) passed to David Jennings's new academy at Wapping.

ALEXANDER GORDON, rev. ALAN RUSTON

Sources W. Wilson, The history and antiquities of the dissenting churches and meeting houses in London, Westminster and Southwark, 4 vols. (1808–14), vol. 2, pp. 73–4 · Monthly Magazine, 15 (1803), 241–2 · Mrs E. P. Hart, ed., Merchant Taylors' School register, 1561–1934, 2 vols. (1936) · personal record, RS · A. Kippis and others, eds., Biographia Britannica, or, The lives of the most eminent persons who have flourished in Great Britain and Ireland, 2nd edn, 1 (1778), 175 · J. A. Jones, ed., Bunhill memorials (1849), 340 · C. E. Surman, index to dissenting ministers, DWL, card E.13 · H. McLachlan, English education under the Test Acts: being the history of the nonconformist academies, 1662–1820 (1931), 118–19 · D. Bogue and J. Bennett, History of the dissenters, from the revolution in 1688, to … 1808, 2nd edn, 2 vols. (1833), 216–17 · D. O. Thomas, Richard Price, 1723–1791 (1976), 13–15
Archives BL, 'Mechanica', Add. MS 58842 · BL, 'Anthropology, or lectures on man', Add. MS 60351
Wealth at death under £600: will, PRO, PROB 11/733, sig. 146

Eanbald (I) (d. 796), archbishop of York, had a career which was undoubtedly of considerable importance but which is notably poorly documented. The early northern annals preserved in the Historia regum and the Anglo-Saxon Chronicle give the dates of his archiepiscopate and of councils and consecrations of bishops which occurred during it; what other information there is is preserved in Alcuin's letters and in lines 1515–32 of his Versus de patribus regibus et sanctis Euboricensis ecclesiae ('Verses on the Fathers, Kings and Saints of the Church of York'), and in the record of a synod held by two papal legates in 786 (Dümmler, no. 3). A pupil (discipulus) of Archbishop Ælberht, Eanbald had been appointed archbishop before the latter's death, probably in July 777 or 778, and as Ælberht's 'associate bishop' (Alcuin, ll. 1518, 1565) he collaborated with Alcuin in building the church of the Beneficent Wisdom (Alma Sophia) in York. Alcuin described Eanbald after his death as his 'father and brother and most faithful of friends' (Dümmler, no. 112).

When Ælberht died in 779 or 780, King Ælfwald of the Northumbrians sent Alcuin to Rome to obtain the pallium from Pope Hadrian I, and this was duly received and Eanbald consecrated in the same year. According to Alcuin, Ælberht had assigned to his successor the 'government of the church, treasure, lands, and money', reserving the library for the direction of Alcuin himself (Alcuin, ll. 1531–5). The northern annals record Eanbald consecrating Ealdwulf, bishop of Mayo, at Corbridge, Northumbria, in 786 and Badwulf, bishop of Whithorn, at an unidentified place called 'Hearrahalh' in 790. His archiepiscopate was notable for a resurgence in the practice of holding ecclesiastical synods, which took place at sites which are unidentified but presumed to be in Northumbria: at 'Acleah' in 782 and 788, and at 'Pincanhalh' in 787. Eanbald presumably presided over these, but in 786 he received the papal legates George of Ostia and Theophylact of Todi when they came to Northumbria, and, along with King Ælfwald of the Northumbrians, he was present at the synod they held there. This was concerned, among other things, with condemning regicide, for Eanbald's archiepiscopate fell in a notable period of political instability in Northumbria, seen especially in the murders of King Ælfwald in 788 and King Æthelred I in 796, and Alcuin referred to the hostility he had faced from kings and princes (Dümmler, no. 232). No information is available about the precise circumstances of that hostility, but the view of regicide taken by the synod referred to above cannot have been welcome to all the various claimants to the Northumbrian kingship. After Æthelred's death, a 'patrician' called Osbald ruled for twenty-seven days, following which Eanbald, assisted by other bishops, undertook the consecration at St Peter's (York Minster) of a new king, Eardwulf. The record in the northern annals as preserved in the *Historia regum* states that he was 'consecrated' (Symeon of Durham, *Opera*, 2.58), suggesting that this was a religiously inspired ceremony, possibly involving anointing with holy oil in a way comparable to Carolingian royal inaugurations, and possibly inspired by the 786 council, one chapter of which referred to the king as the 'anointed of the Lord' (*christus Domini*). How far the form of the ceremony was Eanbald's initiative is not known. Eanbald died on 10 August 796 at an unidentified monastery called 'Ætlæte', and his body was taken in a great procession to York Minster to be buried.

DAVID ROLLASON

Sources Symeon of Durham, *Opera* • Alcuin, *The bishops, kings, and saints of York*, ed. and trans. P. Godman, OMT (1982) • J. Earle, ed., *Two of the Saxon chronicles parallel with supplementary extracts from the others*, rev. C. Plummer, 2 vols. (1892–9) • C. Cubitt, *Anglo-Saxon church councils, c.650–c.850* (1995) • E. Dümmler, ed., *Epistolae Karolini aevi*, MGH Epistolae [quarto], 4 (Berlin, 1895)

Eanbald (II) (*fl.* 796–803), archbishop of York, is known from the early northern annals preserved in the *Historia regum* and the Anglo-Saxon Chronicle and from Alcuin's letters. The former do not extend beyond 806 at the latest, and their last reference to Eanbald (II) is for the year 798 relating to a synod at an unidentified location called 'Pincanhalh'. That Eanbald was still archbishop on 11 June 803 is attested by Symeon of Durham's *Libellus de exordio atque procursu istius, hoc est Dunhelmensis, ecclesie*, which describes him as consecrating Bishop Ecgberht of Lindisfarne eleven years after the ravaging of that church in 793. Coins were also struck in his name, and numismatic opinion dates them to as late as *c.*830–35, suggesting that his

pontificate may have been much longer than is attested by the historical sources. There was evidently anxiety at York that there would be interference, possibly from the king of the Northumbrians, in Eanbald (II)'s appointment, for Eanbald himself had in 794 or 795 carried a letter to Alcuin, then so highly placed in relationship to Charlemagne, which may possibly have been connected with a letter written by Alcuin shortly afterwards to Eanbald (I), stressing that, should he resign his post, his successor should be elected by the church of York itself (Dümmler, nos. 43–4). The haste with which Eanbald (II) was consecrated at Sockburn, in modern co. Durham, on 15 August 796 (his predecessor, Eanbald (I), had died only on the 10th) suggests the same thing, as does the forcefulness with which Alcuin requested Pope Leo III to send Eanbald the pallium (Dümmler, no. 125).

Like Eanbald (I), the new archbishop convened a synod at the unidentified site of 'Pincanhalh', in 798, the outline of the canons of which is noted in the northern annals preserved in the *Historia regum* (Symeon of Durham, *Opera*, 2.59–60, §59). According to these, the synod dealt with the observation of Easter, ecclesiastical and secular law which had been established in former times, and with the church's needs and the augmenting of the service due to it. According to an immediately subsequent passage in the *Historia regum* (ibid., 2.61 §60), which may, however, be a later interpolation, by Eanbald's command, the synod recited the faith of the five ecumenical councils as had been set out by Archbishop Theodore at the Synod of Hatfield in 679 (described by Bede, in his *Historia ecclesiastica gentis Anglorum*, bk 4, chap. 17) in response to the heresy of Monophysitism. Alcuin's letters show Eanbald as one of his pupils at York, and as having visited him on the continent in 795. They also hint at the involvement of the archbishop in political turmoil in Northumbria: one suggests that Eanbald maintained too large a retinue of soldiers, another that he was experiencing difficulties as a result of giving shelter to the enemies of the king, who was King Eardwulf of the Northumbrians. Dated to 801, the second of these letters may be related in some way to Eardwulf's attack on King Cenwulf of the Mercians, who had allegedly also been sheltering his enemies, but certainty is impossible.   DAVID ROLLASON

Sources Symeon of Durham, *Opera* • J. Earle, ed., *Two of the Saxon chronicles parallel with supplementary extracts from the others*, rev. C. Plummer, 2 vols. (1892–9) • E. Dümmler, ed., *Epistolae Karolini aevi*, MGH Epistolae [quarto], 4 (Berlin, 1895) • Symeon of Durham, *Libellus de exordio atque procursu istius, hoc est Dunhelmensis, ecclesie / Tract on the origins and progress of this the church of Durham*, ed. and trans. D. W. Rollason, OMT (2000) • C. Cubitt, *Anglo-Saxon church councils, c.650–c.850* (1995) • J. J. North, *English hammered coinage*, 3rd edn, 1: *Early Anglo-Saxon to Henry III, c.600–1272* (1994)

Eanberht (*fl.* 757–759). *See under* Hwicce, kings of the (*act. c.*670–*c.*780).

Eanflæd [St Eanflæd] (*b.* 626, *d.* after 685), queen in Northumbria, consort of King Oswiu, was the daughter of *Eadwine (*d.* 633), king in Northumbria, and his wife, the Kentish princess Æthelburh (*d.* 647). Born on Easter eve (19

April) 626, she was baptized by Bishop Paulinus at Pentecost (8 June) and was, according to Bede, the first Northumbrian to receive that sacrament. It is possible, however, that (as British sources report) she was first baptized in a British rite by King Rhun of Rheged, who may also have baptized her father. After Eadwine's defeat and death at the battle of Hatfield Chase in 633, she was taken by Paulinus, together with her mother and other members of the king's family, to Kent, where she remained until brought back to Northumbria to marry King *Oswiu, in or shortly after 642.

The marriage effected the union of the ruling dynasties of the two Northumbrian provinces, those of the Deiran Eadwine and the Bernician Oswiu. Almost certainly it reflected Oswiu's intention to retain his brother *Oswald's hard-won control over Deira. If so it was, initially at least, a failure. By 644 Deira was ruled by Eanflæd's kinsman *Oswine, whom Oswiu caused to be murdered in 651. The crime evidently caused a crisis within the royal family, and at Eanflæd's request Oswiu in atonement founded the monastery of Gilling, the first abbot of which was Oswine's kinsman Trumhere.

The queen clearly cut a figure at Oswiu's court. In the late 640s, when the young aristocrat Wilfrid was sent thither, he was presented to Eanflæd by his father's friends and placed by her in the monastery of Lindisfarne, under the tutelage of one of Oswiu's former companions. A few years later Eanflæd sent him to her kinsman, King *Eorcenberht of Kent. Eanflæd clearly valued her Kentish background: she maintained a Kentish chaplain, Romanus, and adhered firmly to the method of calculating the date of Easter established in Kent by the Roman mission, a decision which meant that from time to time she celebrated Easter separately from her husband, who adhered to the Irish reckoning followed at Lindisfarne. Very probably she also ensured that the Roman Easter was observed at Gilling.

In 664 the Easter issue was resolved in Rome's favour, at a synod held at the royal foundation of Whitby, where Eanflæd's kinswoman *Hild was abbess, and her young daughter *Ælfflæd a nun. Significantly, the principal spokesman for the Roman party was Eanflæd's former protégé, Wilfrid. By then Wilfrid was closely associated with Oswiu's son and heir, *Alchfrith, but he also maintained contacts with Gilling from which he obtained monks for his new monastery of Ripon. It may be that Eanflæd herself played some part in forging those links.

With the mysterious disappearance shortly after 664 of Alchfrith, who was Oswiu's son by an earlier wife, the children of Eanflæd move into the limelight. Almost certainly the new heir, *Ecgfrith, was her son. Nothing more is known, however, of Eanflæd herself until after Oswiu's death in 670, when she apparently entered the monastery of Strensall–Whitby. There she assisted her daughter Ælfflæd as abbess after Hild's death in 680, and took an active part in the translation of the remains of her father, Eadwine, to the monastery. She died some time after 685 and was buried at Whitby, by then the family mausoleum.

Eanflæd is not known to have been the object of a pre-conquest cult. By the twelfth century, however, the queen's name was inscribed on one of the two 'pyramids' which stood near the old conventual church at Glastonbury, evidence, William of Malmesbury believed, that her corporeal remains had been translated thither. In late calendars Eanflæd's feast day occurs on 24 November.

ALAN THACKER

Sources Bede, *Hist. eccl.* • B. Colgrave, ed. and trans., *The earliest life of Gregory the Great … by an anonymous monk of Whitby* (1968) • William of Malmesbury, *Gesta regum Anglorum* / *The history of the English kings*, ed. and trans. R. A. B. Mynors, R. M. Thomson, and M. Winterbottom, 2 vols., OMT (1998–9) • William of Malmesbury, *The early history of Glastonbury*, ed. J. Scott (1981) • K. H. Jackson, 'On the northern British section in Nennius', *Celt and Saxon: studies in the early British border*, ed. N. K. Chadwick (1963), 20–62 • C. Phythian-Adams, *Land of the Cumbrians: a study in British provincial origins, AD 400–1120* (1996)

Eanfrith (*fl. c.*670). *See under* Hwicce, kings of the (*act. c.*670–c.780).

Eanhere (*fl. c.*670). *See under* Hwicce, kings of the (*act. c.*670–c.780).

Eanmund (*fl.* 763–764). *See under* Æthelberht II (*d.* 762).

Eanred (*fl. c.*830–c.854). *See under* Eardwulf (*fl.* 796–c.830).

Earbery, Matthias (1690–1740), writer and nonjuring Church of England clergyman, was born on 11 July 1690 in Hoveton St Peter, Norfolk, the son of the Revd Matthias Earbery (*d.* 1735), vicar of Hoveton and Neatished. Matthias Earbery the elder had sworn allegiance to William and Mary only 'as a conquered person'. In 1695 he was presented by Charles Finch, fourth earl of Winchilsea, to the mastership of Wye grammar school in Kent, though retaining his livings. He published in 1697 an answer to Spinoza's *Tractatus theologico politicus*, entitled *Deism Examin'd and Confuted*. He also published *A review of the bishop of Bangor's* [Hoadly's] *sermon* from Neatished (1718). In 1730 he became rector of Barsham in Suffolk, where he died in 1735.

Matthias Earbery the younger was educated by his father before entering St John's College, Cambridge, then noted for its nonjuring sympathies. He was ordained to a curacy in Kent, where he became a friend of Thomas Brett. On 18 November 1715 he was received by George Hickes into the nonjuring communion, and became minister to a congregation in Holborn. In June 1716 he signed the petition which began the 'usages' controversy; he soon changed his opinion, however, and fiercely attacked Brett and the 'usagers' in *Reflections upon Modern Fanaticism* (1720).

Earbery's views on the rights of hereditary monarchy and episcopacy were those of Charles Leslie, whom he admired, but Earbery had none of Leslie's wit or power of reasoning: his numerous works are largely made up of quantities of historical narrative, related with a strong ideological bias, often laced with personal abuse. In 1717 *The History of the Clemency of our English Monarchs*, contrasting the treatment of the rebels after the battle of Preston with the leniency of previous reigns, was seized by the government. Earbery escaped to France, and published a second edition, complete with a portrait of himself, in 1720. He was arrested in London in 1723 for seditious libel, and again in 1732 for attacks on Sir Robert Walpole (later first earl of Orford) and King George II in the *Royal Oak Journal*. His targets ranged from the 'filth of Bangorianism' to John Wyclif, Gilbert Burnet, and Sir John Oldcastle.

Earbery lived apparently by his writing, which accounts perhaps for his translation of Thomas Burnet's notoriously heterodox *State of the Dead* (1727). He died, apparently unmarried, at 'a gentleman's house in Yorkshire' on 3 October 1740, leaving no account of some £350 subscribed to a projected edition of his works.

JOHN FINDON, *rev.*

Sources parish registers, Hoveton St Peter, Norfolk · Bodl. Oxf., MSS Rawl. C. 735, D. 367, D. 1254 · Bodl. Oxf., MSS Eng. th. C35, C40 · Bodl. Oxf., MS Carte 114 · *Remarks and collections of Thomas Hearne*, ed. C. E. Doble and others, 11 vols., OHS, 2, 7, 13, 34, 42–3, 48, 50, 65, 67, 72 (1885–1921) · H. Broxap, *The later nonjurors* (1924) · J. H. Overton, *The nonjurors: their lives, principles, and writings* (1902)

Likenesses portrait, repro. in M. Earbery, *The history of the clemency of our English monarchs*, 2nd edn (1720)

Earconwald [St Earconwald, Erkenwald] (*d.* **693**), abbot of Chertsey and bishop of the East Saxons, was the brother of Æthelburh of Barking. Nothing is reliably known of Earconwald (the preferred seventh/eighth-century spelling), beyond what Bede records, passing references by the biographer of Wilfrid, and a correspondent of Boniface, and what can be deduced from the charters and legislation associated with him. His princely origin (if any) lay not in the East Anglian/Lindsey dynasty fabricated by his later lives, but perhaps in that of Kent: the name Æthelburh and the Earcon- prefix recur among Kentish royalty, as with King Earconberht (*r.* 640–64) and his daughter, Earcongota, a nun at the Frankish abbey of Faremoutier-en-Brie. Earconwald indeed shared the name of Erchinoald, Earconberht's grandfather and mayor of the Neustrian palace in Francia.

Earconwald was made bishop in London by Theodore when the archbishop divided the see of Mercia in 675 or 676. He had previously founded Chertsey under the auspices of King Ecgberht of Kent (*r.* 664–73) and was its abbot *c.*664–693; this is attested in a charter of Frithuwald, sub-king of Surrey for King Wulfhere of Mercia (*r.* 658–74), which hugely increased the abbey's holdings (not least with a stretch of river frontage 'at the port of London'). Then, or later, he founded Barking for his sister; it was a house for both nuns and monks of a type familiar in seventh-century Francia, and Bede took his description of it from a *libellus* that was possibly modelled on an account of Faremoutier. Its charters include an 'original' in the name of Hodilred, kinsman of the East Saxon king, which enlarges its estates; this serves partially to validate otherwise questionable documents where Earconwald himself reviews Barking's endowment by a series of kings, East Saxon, West Saxon, and Mercian, and claims that the whole had been put under papal protection on his visit to Rome in 677 or 678 (though extant papal charters for St Paul's and Chertsey are certainly bogus). In addition, it can

be shown that formulas in these charters resurface not only in later documents from the London diocese but also in grants by early kings of Wessex (one, Cædwalla, a Barking benefactor); they include a proem on the value of putting 'synodal statutes' in writing 'because of the uncertainty of future times'. Earconwald's advice was invoked by King Ine of Wessex in promulgating his 'statutes' (that is, law code, 688–94), so he may have been instrumental in disseminating a trend-setting series of formulas throughout southern England.

Bede implies that Earconwald died in 693 and his reference to miracles worked by splinters of the horse-litter in which the bishop travelled when ill must have helped to perpetuate his cult in the later Anglo-Saxon period, when his 30th April obit features in several calendars. More importantly, it must have commended him to post-conquest bishops of London looking for a more inspiring patron than Mellitus, who had founded the see only to be ignominiously expelled by a contumaciously pagan king. Earconwald was thus translated to a shrine east of the high altar of St Paul's Cathedral on 14th November 1148, a move which stimulated an earlier bishop's nephew to write a life and account of miracles: they form the basis of the life included in the *Nova Legenda Angliae* and printed by the Bollandists. It is these sources (of value solely for their own time of course) which say that Earconwald was born at 'Stallington' (possibly Stallingborough) in Lindsey, son of its king, 'Offa'; that Hildelith, identified by Bede as Æthelburh's successor at Barking, was *de transmarinis partibus* ('from regions across the sea'); and that possession of the saint's body was contested between the canons of St Paul's, the monks of Chertsey, and the nuns of Barking (where he was said to have actually died): the parting of the swollen River Lea resolved the dispute in favour of St Paul's.

The cult of Earconwald was boosted again in and after 1386 by Bishop Robert Braybrooke; his efforts may have inspired indirectly the composition of an alliterative Middle English poem, conceivably by the *Gawain* poet, in which Earconwald procures salvation for a judge who was just but unbaptized. The theme of the good pagan was an abiding medieval concern, and a poet of *c.*1400 could have made Earconwald his hero because London was where one would look for judges (if not virtuous ones). Earconwald's importance is thus a matter of two distinct parts. In his own time, he was a clerical counterpart of the very highly born aristocrats who sought service and patronage with the most generous royal lords; the monopoly control of London by Mercian kings after the 730s meant that he was the last Anglo-Saxon bishop in London who could do this. From the twelfth century, he was London's equivalent to Swithun at Winchester or John of Beverley in Yorkshire: the capital's nearest to a native patron saint.

PATRICK WORMALD

Sources Bede, *Hist. eccl.*, 4.6–11 · E. Stephanus, *The life of Bishop Wilfrid*, ed. and trans. B. Colgrave (1927), 86–7 · M. Tangl, ed., *Die Briefe des heiligen Bonifatius und Lullus*, MGH Epistolae Selectae, 1 (Berlin, 1916), no. 36 · *AS chart.*, S 1165, 1171, 1246, 1248 · F. Liebermann, ed., 'Laws of Ine', *Die Gesetze der Angelsachsen*, 1 (Halle, 1898), 88–9 ·

W. Dugdale, *The history of St Paul's Cathedral in London*, new edn, ed. H. Ellis (1818), 289–91 · C. Horstman, ed., *Nova legenda Anglie, as collected by John of Tynemouth, J. Capgrave, and others*, 1 (1901), 391–405 · *Acta sanctorum: Aprilis*, 3 (Antwerp, 1675), 780–87 · W. Stubbs, 'Saint Erkenwald', *Dictionary of Christian biography*, ed. W. Smith and H. Wace, 4 vols. (1877–87), 2.177–9 · D. Whitelock, *Some Anglo-Saxon bishops of London* (1975), 6–10 · P. Wormald, *Bede and the conversion of England: the charter evidence* (1984?), 9–11 · I. N. Wood, 'Ripon, Francia, and the Franks' casket in the early middle ages', *Northern History*, 26 (1990), 1–19, esp. 14–15 · *Saint Erkenwald*, ed. C. Peterson (1977), 1–23, 35–51, 62–4 · *Saint Erkenwald*, ed. R. Morse (1975)

Archives BL, Cotton MS Tiberius E1, fols. 116v–121r · BL, Harley MS 2250 · Bodl. Oxf., MS Tanner 15, fols. 232v–243r · CCC Cam., MS 161, fols. 31r–44r

Likenesses miniature, letter patent of Henry VII

Eardley [*formerly* Smith], **Sir Culling Eardley**, **third baronet** (1805–1863), religious campaigner, was born on 21 April 1805 in Lower Grosvenor Street, London, the only son of Sir Culling Smith, second baronet (1768–1829), and his wife Charlotte Elizabeth (*d.* 15 Sept 1826), second daughter and coheir of Sampson, Lord Eardley. He was of French Huguenot descent on his father's side, and his maternal great-grandfather was Sampson Gideon, the Jewish financier. Smith, as he was surnamed until he changed his name to Eardley by royal licence on 14 May 1847 (when he inherited the Eardley estates), was educated at Eton College and at Oriel College, Oxford. He passed his BA examinations in 1827, but for conscientious reasons never took his degree. After leaving Oxford he became a convinced evangelical. He succeeded to the baronetcy on his father's death on 30 June 1829, and on 29 February 1832 he married Isabella (*d.* 1 May 1860), fourth daughter of Thomas William Carr, of Eshott, Northumberland; they had one son and two daughters.

Smith initially appears to have cherished political ambitions, but sat only briefly in parliament, representing Pontefract from 1830 to 1831. During the 1830s he took a strong interest in the reform of the poor laws. His political affinities were Liberal, but his primary allegiance was defined by his protestant evangelical religious principles. He unsuccessfully sought re-election for Pontefract at the general election of 1837.

In the meantime Smith was finding his true vocation as a lay leader of interdenominational and international evangelicalism. Although he had been born and brought up in the Church of England and professed to adhere to its essential doctrines, he believed that it had been corrupted by its connection with the state. He thus became in effect a Congregationalist, though he never formally changed denomination and he continued to attend Anglican evangelical services. In 1839 he was elected chairman and treasurer of the Evangelical Voluntary Church Association, which campaigned for disestablishment while eschewing aggressive political tactics. It was dissolved in 1844. In 1845 Smith assumed a high-profile role as chairman of the Anti-Maynooth Committee and Conference which agitated unsuccessfully against Sir Robert Peel's endowment of the Irish Catholic seminary.

Smith's overriding conviction that all true Christians should be united led him in 1845–6 to be a prime mover in the foundation of the Evangelical Alliance and to become

Sir Culling Eardley Eardley, third baronet (1805–1863), by George Sanders, pubd 1865 (after W. Roeting)

the chairman of its council. Initially he sought to further the alliance's objectives by domestic political means, standing unsuccessfully as a Liberal candidate for Edinburgh in 1846 (opposing Macaulay on account of the latter's support for the Maynooth grant) and in the West Riding of Yorkshire in 1848, consistently refusing to bribe voters. Increasingly, however, his energies became centred on the alliance's endeavours to promote religious liberty abroad, campaigning for the release of prisoners of conscience such as, in 1852, the Tuscan protestants Francesco and Rosa Madiai. He was notably consistent in his opposition to all forms of religious persecution: thus he was instrumental in the abolition of penal laws against Roman Catholics in Sweden in 1858, and in 1859 campaigned for the liberty of Edgar Mortara, an Italian Jewish child. Eardley was an energetic and visionary leader who during the 1850s acquired considerable prestige and influence as a European religious statesman, with contacts who included Garibaldi, Bunsen, and Frederick William IV of Prussia.

Eardley's other religious activities included service as treasurer of the London Missionary Society from 1844 to 1863, and of the fund established to relieve the Lebanese Christians after the 1861 massacres. He also took a strong interest in the condition of the Jews, which reflected his maternal family connections. He laboured hard to improve relations between the Church of England and nonconformity through his friendships with prominent evangelical Anglicans. He gave active support, however, to those who felt themselves excluded from their parish churches by ritualist practices, notably through his sponsorship of the construction in 1850–53 of Furrough Cross Church, Babbacombe, in defiance of the local vicar and of Bishop Phillpotts of Exeter. He also built All Saints' Church, Belvedere, on his estate at Erith in Kent, and in 1854 published his own version of the Book of Common Prayer for use there, with slight modifications to remove material offensive to nonconformists. His hope was that the church would be used for worship by Christians of all denominations.

Eardley was a very wealthy man who inherited Bedwell Park, Hertfordshire, from his father, and in 1847 Belvedere, together with a fine collection of paintings, and the Eardley estates, from his cousin, Lord Saye and Sele. He lived at Bedwell for most of his life, although he resided at Belvedere from 1848 to 1858, and for a period in the late 1840s and 1850s he also kept a house at Frognel, Torquay. His health declined in his last years, but the immediate cause of his death, which took place at Bedwell Park on 21 May 1863, was an adverse reaction to re-vaccination against smallpox. He was succeeded as baronet by his only son, Eardley Gideon Culling Eardley (1838–1875), at whose death the baronetcy became extinct.   JOHN WOLFFE

Sources DNB · *The Record* [magazine of Oriel College, Oxford] (22 May 1863) · *Evangelical Christendom*, 17 (1863), 257–60 · C. E. Eardley, *The rights of the laity in the universities* (1856) · J. Wolffe, *The protestant crusade in Great Britain, 1829–1860* (1991) · W. H. Mackintosh, *Disestablishment and liberation: the movement for the separation of the Anglican church from state control* (1972) · D. M. Lewis, ed., *The Blackwell dictionary of evangelical biography, 1730–1860*, 2 vols. (1995) · Burke, *Peerage* (1907) · *Dod's Peerage* (1858) · *GM*, 1st ser., 99/2 (1829), 176 · *The Times* (22 May 1863) · *GM*, 3rd ser., 8 (1860), 643

Archives Herts. ALS, corresp. and papers | BL, letters to Sir Robert Peel and others

Likenesses G. Sanders, mezzotint, pubd 1865 (after W. Roeting), BM, AM Oxf. [*see illus.*]

Wealth at death under £45,000: probate, 31 July 1863, *CGPLA Eng. & Wales*

Eardley, Joan Kathleen Harding (1921–1963), painter, born on 18 May 1921 on her father's dairy farm near Horsham, Sussex, was the elder of the two daughters of Captain William Edwin Eardley (1887–1929) and Irene Helen Morrison (1891–1991), who had met when he was stationed in Glasgow's Maryhill barracks during the First World War. When Joan was seven her father, who had suffered from gas poisoning, committed suicide, forcing his widow to join her mother at Blackheath, London, where Joan and her sister spent their schooldays. Her talent for drawing was always evident, so that on leaving St Helen's School in Blackheath in 1938 she enrolled at Goldsmiths' College, London. But that course was very soon interrupted when the family moved to Blanefield, near Glasgow, in order to escape the threat of bombing in London. In January 1940 she was accepted for the four-year diploma course in drawing and painting at the Glasgow School of Art, where her good fortune was to be taught by the charismatic but singularly undidactic painter Hugh Adam Crawford. She was a prize-winning front runner at

Joan Kathleen Harding Eardley (1921–1963), by Audrey, Lady Walker [painting on the clifftop at Catterline]

the school during each of her years there, but immediately after gaining her diploma, and throughout 1944, her studies were interrupted by her chosen brand of 'war work', which amounted to camouflaging the hulls of boats at a small local shipyard. It was at that point that her first important work, a painting of some of her workmates which she called *The Mixer Men*, was hung on the line at the Royal Glasgow Institute of the Fine Arts. In 1947, after having attempted to live and work in London for a year, she spent several months at Hospitalfield House, near Arbroath, Angus, then a summer art school for post-diploma students where another influential senior, James Cowie, was warden. After that summer in Arbroath she returned to Glasgow for a session of post-diploma study which, in its turn, led to a year of travel in Italy and France financed by scholarships from the Glasgow School of Art and the Royal Scottish Academy.

Among the influences absorbed during Joan Eardley's Glasgow School of Art years were the monumental life drawings of Henry Moore, the intense colour clashes of André Derain and the Fauves, and, by no means least, the work of Vincent Van Gogh which Glasgow experienced at first hand in a major exhibition of his work shown at the Glasgow Art Gallery and Museum in 1948. It is surely not accidental that Van Gogh's influence, so evident in the drawings which she brought back from France and Italy, coincided with the onset of her creative maturity. In Italy, in particular—where, as well as potent landscape studies, she made numerous drawings of peasants at work in their natural surroundings (Giotto and Masaccio were her declared favourites among the old masters)—it began to be obvious that direct stimulus through the eye was for her a necessary starting point for emotional expression. As her later life was to prove, her affinity with Van Gogh went deeper than the deliberately simple existence of hardships and denials which they had in common. Hers, too, was a lifelong struggle to convey in line and coloured pigments the unusual power of her response to visual and sensual experience. Back at home in Scotland, where she eventually rented a glass-roofed studio in Glasgow's Townhead, this remained her aim, whether she was drawing and painting the surprisingly colourful street life— the dark Victorian tenements, the derelict shop-fronts with their peeling paint, and the cheerful, demonstrative urchins who gathered around her studio—or struggling to express an exceptionally acute response to the power of the North Sea at Catterline, the cliff-top fishing village south of Stonehaven in Kincardineshire. From the mid-1950s she spent the major part of each year at Catterline, and it was there that she sensed deep roots—justifiably so, since her maternal grandfather was a native of Aberdeenshire. Sturdy, with short dark hair and black eyes, she remained essentially a country girl.

All her life Joan Eardley drew incessantly, but more as visual 'feeding' than as the basis for future paintings. Around Catterline, in summer and winter, and even in the wildest storms, she painted on the spot: on the shore, on the cliff-top, and not least in the wonderfully fertile hinterland of summer fields. There, too, some of her best work was done in the chill of midwinter, on the stubblefields bleak with snow against fiery red skies. Increasing illness (a long-neglected breast cancer which eventually killed her) seemed merely to heighten her determination to continue working at full throttle. Her late canvases, not least the large seascapes in which she seems intent on conveying, above all, her sense of oneness with the elements, are among her finest and most moving works. It is interesting that a photograph of Eardley showing her working on a very large canvas on the rocky Catterline foreshore on a wild winter afternoon is eerily reminiscent of a late nineteenth-century camera image of her well-known Scottish predecessor William McTaggart, painting the Atlantic Ocean from the beach at Machrihanish on the Kintyre peninsula.

Joan Eardley had discovered and fallen in love with Catterline at first sight in 1952. She first worked from borrowed lodgings, but after several visits she acquired a primitive studio cottage, 1 The Row, a tiny two-room shack without even running water, at the southernmost end of the village. Eventually, when her paintings began to find buyers in Edinburgh and London, she bought a slightly larger and at least more habitable home at 18 The Row while still retaining the other cottage as a store and a favourite place to set up her easel. However, Glasgow was by no means forsaken: she kept her roof-top studio to the end, returning again and again to re-create on paper or canvas the colourful, raucous, insouciant young life on her doorstep, drawing more and more obviously on

abstract expressionist influences—Willem De Kooning in particular. In the Glasgow subjects, as at Catterline even in the wildest seascapes, she never completely 'lost the image', however; with Eardley all influences—Van Gogh, Derain, De Kooning, even at one stage Nicolas de Staël— were swiftly subsumed in her own individual style.

From the autumn of 1948, when her travelling scholarship exhibition was shown at the Glasgow School of Art, Joan Eardley's admirers began to grow in number. Her work became widely known in Scotland and her paintings were regularly hung in the major open Scottish exhibitions as well as in solo shows at Aitken Dott's Scottish Gallery in Edinburgh. Never interested or involved in the official business of the art societies, she had none the less been a professional member of the Society of Scottish Artists since 1948 and accepted associateship of the Royal Scottish Academy a few years later. (Full membership in the academy came in 1963, the year of her death.) By the early 1950s she was being invited to exhibit with some of her southern contemporaries in London galleries and before long her work was being seen regularly at Roland Browse and Delbanco. Joan Eardley died too soon for general acceptance as a major British artist; during her short working life her paintings attracted less serious assessment furth of Scotland than they deserved. But it was the art critic Eric Newton of the *Manchester Guardian* who perceived her quality. After seeing her final London exhibition in 1961, he wrote:

> Only in an occasional Goya do I remember the translation of small children into paint mixed so inseparably with warmhearted self-identification with the inner life of the child. And only in Turner's seapaintings does one find oneself so involved with the skies and winds that hang over the uneasy tumult of the waves. (*The Guardian*, 1 June 1961)

Joan Eardley died, unmarried, on 16 August 1963 in the hospital at Killearn, Stirlingshire; after her cremation the ashes were scattered on the shore at Catterline. Her works are in the Tate collection and the Scottish National Gallery of Modern Art, Edinburgh, as well as in several university collections and municipal galleries in a number of British cities, including Glasgow, Edinburgh, Aberdeen, Dundee, Birmingham, and Huddersfield. CORDELIA OLIVER

Sources personal knowledge (2004) · private information (2004) · W. Buchanan, *Joan Eardley*, Modern Scottish Painters, 5 (1976) · C. Oliver, *Joan Eardley, RSA* (1988) · *CCI* (1963)
Archives NG Scot., papers | NL Scot., corresp. with Audrey Walker | FILM Templar Film Studios, 'Maxwell, Eardley, Philipson' [1963]
Likenesses A. Walker, photographs, priv. coll. [*see illus.*]
Wealth at death £19,881 14s. 0d.: confirmation, 11 Oct 1963, NA Scot., SC 5/41/102/21045–8

Eardwulf (d. in or before **762**). *See under* Æthelberht II (d. 762).

Eardwulf (*fl.* 796–*c*.830), king of Northumbria, was recalled from exile after the deposition of King Osbald in 796 and was inaugurated as king in York Minster on 26 May. Nothing is known of his parentage apart from the name of his father, also Eardwulf or, in one source, the erroneous 'Earulf'. But he had evidently been involved in royal affairs, for the northern annals record how in 790 he was arrested by King Æthelred I of the Northumbrians and put to death outside the gates of Ripon Minster. The monks took his body into the church, where during the night he was found to be living. This alleged miracle, which is alluded to in a letter of Alcuin addressed to the king, may have resulted in his being regarded as a saint, for a list of saints' resting-places records his sepulture as a saint at Breedon on the Hill, Leicestershire, where the church is still dedicated to him.

Eardwulf's reign was a troubled one. In 798 he defeated a revolt led by Ealdorman Wada, one of the murderers of Æthelred I in 796, who may have had the support of the exiled Osbald (if a letter of Alcuin to the latter belongs to 798 and was intended to dissuade him from joining the revolt). The rebels were defeated and put to flight at Billington Moor near Whalley on 2 April. In 799 an ealdorman called Moll, possibly a descendant of the former king Æthelwold Moll (*fl.* 759–765), was put to death at the king's urgent order; and in 800 Ealhmund, said by some to have been son of the former king Alhred (*fl.* 765–774), was seized and put to death by Eardwulf's guards. Nor were the king's relations with the church smooth. Alcuin accused him of sin, and in particular of putting aside his wife and publicly taking a concubine. Moreover, it appears from another letter of Alcuin that Eanbald (II), archbishop of York, had received and protected the king's enemies, while seizing the lands of others, so that he found it advisable to go about with a large armed force. Mercia too was hostile. Eardwulf's victim Ealhmund was buried at Derby and there venerated as a saint; and in 801 the king led an army against Cenwulf, king of the Mercians, allegedly because the latter had received his enemies. This campaign was followed by a peace accord between the two kingdoms. The northern recension of the Anglo-Saxon Chronicle (text D), however, records Eardwulf's expulsion in 806 and this date is probably to be preferred to that of 808 given by other sources. According to Roger of Wendover (*d.* 1236) and the twelfth-century *De primo Saxonum aduentu*, he was succeeded by a certain Ælfwald II, who reigned for two years, but about whom nothing is known. The northern annals come to an end after 806 and the historical record for ninth-century Northumbrian kings is late and exiguous. Although the fact is not mentioned in any English sources, the royal Frankish annals state that in 808 Eardwulf was restored to his kingdom by envoys of the pope and the emperor Charlemagne, and this is corroborated by papal correspondence.

Roger of Wendover gives 810 as the beginning of the reign of Eardwulf's successor as king of the Northumbrians **Eanred** (*fl. c.*830–*c.*854), whose reign is presented as extending to 840 (or 841 by Symeon of Durham). The dates are likely to be very unreliable, however, especially as they pay no regard to the second reign of Eardwulf. Numismatic evidence, including a silver penny of Eanred in a hoard at Trewhiddle, Cornwall, which on stylistic grounds appears to be no earlier than *c.*850, suggests a radically revised chronology. According to this, Eardwulf's second reign would last as late as *c.*830, with Eanred ruling into the 850s, perhaps down to *c.*854. His successor, **Æthelred II** (*fl. c.*854–*c.*862), would then have reigned in Northumbria until *c.*862 (not 840–48 as according to Roger of Wendover or 841–9 as according to Symeon of Durham). Wendover alone describes a usurpation (dated by him to 844, but by numismatic evidence to *c.*858) by **Rædwulf** (*d. c.*858), who was killed in the same year by vikings at Elvet (modern co. Durham), so that Æthelred was able to resume his reign. Wendover asserts further that Æthelred's reign ended when he was killed, but no details are known. He was succeeded by Osberht.

DAVID ROLLASON

Sources Symeon of Durham, *Opera* · E. Dümmler, ed., *Epistolae Karolini aevi*, MGH Epistolae [quarto], 4 (Berlin, 1895) · Symeon of Durham, *Libellus de exordio atque procursu istius, hoc est Dunhelmensis, ecclesie / Tract on the origins and progress of this the church of Durham*, ed. and trans. D. W. Rollason, OMT (2000) · E. Classen and F. E. Harmer, eds., *An Anglo-Saxon chronicle from British Museum, Cotton MS Tiberius B. IV* (1926) · *Rogeri de Wendover chronica, sive, Flores historiarum*, ed. H. O. Coxe, 4 vols., EHS (1841–2) · D. W. Rollason, 'The cults of murdered royal saints in Anglo-Saxon England', *Anglo-Saxon England*, 11 (1983), 1–22 · F. Kurze, ed., *Annales regni Francorum*, MGH Scriptores Rerum Germanicarum, [6] (Hanover, 1895) · H. E. Pagan, 'Northumbrian numismatic chronology in the ninth century', *British Numismatic Journal*, 38 (1969), 1–15 · P. Grierson and M. Blackburn, *Medieval European coinage: with a catalogue of the coins in the Fitzwilliam Museum, Cambridge*, 1: *The early middle ages (5th–10th centuries)* (1986) · D. P. Kirby, *The earliest English kings* (1991)

Earl, George Samuel Windsor (1813–1865), colonist and geographer, the son of a veteran sea captain and shipowner, Percy Earl (1771–1827), and his second wife, Elizabeth, *née* Sharp (1778/9–1874), was born at Hampstead, Middlesex, on 10 February 1813. His brief formal education was at the Revd John Stephenson's school at Orpington and at Dr Alexander Jamieson's Wyke House Academy until his father's death in June 1827. Later that year, aged fourteen, he made a voyage to India as midshipman on the *Lady Holland*, returning to England in March 1829. In August of that year he took ship for Swan River Colony on the *Egyptian* with the intention of becoming a farmer with his elder brother, William Percy, who arrived later with four indentured servants and some sheep.

Finding that the 200 acres allocated to him on the lower Swan were unsuitable, Earl spent some time exploring the coast before going south to Augusta. There he was employed as clerk to the resident, Captain John Molloy, and was assigned town land. In February 1832 he sailed 150 miles in an open boat to Fremantle to seek relief supplies for the struggling settlement. Deciding that there was no future for him in the colony, he took ship in August for Batavia (Jakarta), learning the Malay language and the rudiments of navigation while on board. During the next two years he served as chief officer on trading voyages to the Malay states and Thailand as well as ports in Java, becoming proficient in Bugis, Bajau, and Macassarese. In March 1834, on behalf of some Singapore Chinese merchants, he took an 80 ton schooner, the *Stamford*, with a cargo of opium, tea, and iron to the west Borneo port of Singkawang in the hope of breaking the Dutch trade embargo. During this time he visited the Chinese gold-mining *gongsi* (co-operative autonomous community) at Montrado.

On returning to England in early 1835, when he was still only twenty-one, Earl became involved in agitation for a British settlement in northern Australia. Elected as a fellow of the Royal Asiatic Society after an address to its members, his authority on the area was further strengthened by his pamphlet *Observations on the Commercial and Agricultural Capabilities of the North Coast of New Holland* (1836) and his book, *The Eastern Seas* (1837). This important work also described north-western Borneo in detail for the first time, and led to the visit there by James Brooke in 1839. Indeed, it seems likely that Brooke asked him to join his party. Instead, in late 1837 Earl was appointed linguist and draughtsman with the north Australia expedition under Sir J. J. Gordon Bremer. From October 1838 he was based at the garrison settlement of Port Essington, which he had advocated as a 'second Singapore', to tap the trade of eastern Indonesia. In 1844 he was appointed crown lands commissioner and police magistrate. During his five years at Port Essington he made several voyages to the islands to the north to obtain supplies. He also developed a knowledge of the Aboriginal peoples of the Cobourg peninsula.

Suffering from malaria and dysentery, Earl returned to England on leave in September 1844 and completed *Enterprise in Tropical Australia* (1846), a historical account of the Port Essington settlement with chapters on the climate, flora, and fauna of northern Australia and the prospects of growing cotton there using Asian labour. While in London he met, and later married on 4 April 1846, sixteen-year-old Clara, daughter of the Waterloo veteran and historian Captain William *Siborne of the Royal Military Asylum at Chelsea. He also gave a lecture to the Royal Geographical Society on the Aboriginal peoples of northern Australia. Later that year he and Clara sailed to Sydney to settle the affairs of his brother, who had drowned at sea in April *en route* for Port Essington. After the birth of their only child, Elisabeth Christiana, in Sydney in the following year they travelled via Hong Kong to Singapore, where Earl was admitted as a law agent in April 1849. He also contributed articles on a wide range of subjects to the lawyer and antiquary J. F. Logan's *Journal of the Indian Archipelago* and began work on a major ethnographical undertaking. *Native Races of the Indian Archipelago: the Papuans* was published in London in 1853, where he spent the years 1852–4 in poor health but cheered by his election as one of the first corresponding members of the Ethnological Society. In 1853 he became involved in a public controversy with Sir Roderick Murchison as to who first anticipated the discovery of gold in New South Wales in 1851. This brought him to the attention of the engineer and antiquary Hyde Clarke, and to a spell as agent on the New South Wales and Victoria goldfields for the Berdan Pan, a gold ore processing machine patented by the American inventor Colonel Hiram Berdan. When this failed to make his fortune, he returned with his family to Singapore in mid-1855.

Appointed magistrate and third assistant resident councillor for Singapore in 1857, Earl then took Thomas

Braddell's place in Penang for a year as senior assistant resident councillor before moving to Province Wellesley on the mainland to a similar post. In early 1864, while visiting Adelaide with his wife and daughter for the latter's marriage to the Anglo-Irish merchant William Alt, he influenced the South Australian government in its choice of Adam Bay, near the mouth of the Adelaide River, as the site for the capital of its newly acquired Northern Territory. Earl spent his remaining years as resident councillor and police magistrate in Penang and Province Wellesley. Retaining his keen interest in northern Australia, in 1863 he published *A Handbook for Colonists in Tropical Australia*. Despite deteriorating health, he offered to lead a rescue party when the first South Australian expedition to Adam Bay was a failure. He died of dysentery on 9 August 1865 when about to return to England, and was buried at Penang the following day. There is a monument to him there and also an Earl family commemorative stone at St John's, Hampstead. An imperialist in the tradition of Dalrymple and Raffles, Earl was a gifted hydrographer, geographer, linguist, and ethnographer, and an effective publicist in the cause of northern Australian settlement. He coined the term 'Indonesia' in the context of linguistic groupings.   R. H. W. REECE

Sources C. A. Gibson-Hill, 'George Samuel Windsor Earl', *Journal of the Malayan Branch of the Royal Asiatic Society*, 32/1 (1959), 105–53 · B. Reece, 'The Australasian career of George Windsor Earl', *Journal of the Malaysian Branch of the Royal Asiatic Society*, 65/2 (1992), 39–67 · R. Jones, 'Out of the shadows: George Windsor Earl in Western Australia', *Indonesia Circle*, 64 (1994), 265–78 · R. Jones, 'George Windsor Earl and "Indonesia"', *Indonesia Circle*, 7 (1975), 12–14 · R. Jones, 'George Windsor Earl and "Indonesia"', *Indonesia Circle*, 8 (1975), 4–12 · G. W. Earl, *The Eastern seas* (1837); repr. with an introduction by C. M. Turnbull (1971) · private information (2004) · Record Office of Western Australia · RGS · National Archives of Singapore · South Australian Archives · NL Aus., Alt MSS · *South Australian Register* (27 Nov 1865) · Mitchell L., NSW, Earl family MSS · parish register (baptism), 13 July 1813, St John, Hampstead · m. cert. · yard burial records, St John's church, Hampstead

Archives Mitchell L., NSW · National Archives of Singapore · RGS | NL Aus., Elisabeth Alt MSS

Likenesses photograph, NPG

Wealth at death two life insurance policies combined value 10,000 East India Company's rupees

Earle, Erasmus (*bap.* 1590, *d.* 1667), lawyer and politician, was baptized on 20 September 1590 at Sall, Norfolk, the only son of Thomas Earle (1563–1605) and his first wife, Anne (1567–1598), daughter of Arthur Fountaine of Sall. Educated at Norwich grammar school he matriculated as a pensioner from Peterhouse, Cambridge, in 1609. Earle resolved to study law, first at Furnival's and then (from 16 April 1611) at Lincoln's Inn, where he was called to the bar in 1618. On 25 February 1617 he married his beloved cousin Frances Fountaine (1592–1671), daughter of James Fountaine, with whom he had four sons and two daughters. Aided by his East Anglian connections, Earle's career advanced steadily. Steward for Sir Julius Caesar's Norfolk manors by 1626, he became standing counsel to Sir Henry Bedingfield in 1635. Another significant client was Walter Long, an MP arrested after the 1629 dissolution and offered release on security for good behaviour. Earle's arguments prevailed, but Long, discovering that none of his imprisoned colleagues had complied, tried to revoke his bond, alleging 'weak counsel' (Birch, 30–31). From 1633 to 1634 Earle was a pensioner of Lincoln's; in 1635 he attained heraldic arms, while 1636 found him a bencher of his inn. By 1641 he was recorder of Thetford and a Norfolk JP.

In the civil war Earle supported parliament—at first reluctantly. Censured in October 1642 for failing to contribute financially, he was a reliable committee man by 1644, when Norwich appointed him one of its counsel. In 1645 he served as joint secretary, with John Thurloe, to the English commissioners at the Uxbridge negotiations. On 4 January 1647 Norwich elected Earle to the Commons. There he was moderately active, handling legal matters and such local problems as parish amalgamation, the 'distractions and differences' occasioned by the excise, and the Norwich riots of April 1648 (*JHC*, 5.249). On 12 October 1648 parliament raised him to the degree of serjeant-at-law; in December he presided over the rioters' trial. Revolution did not alter his custom of residing in London for the legal terms and in Norfolk outside them. Although he re-entered the house in February 1649, his infrequent attendance thereafter exasperated fellow burgess Thomas Atkin, who accused him of pursuing 'his great advantage'—law practice—at his constituency's expense (Atkin, fol. 162). Despite these allegations, Norwich honoured Earle with the offices of steward (1648–50) and recorder (1649–60). Yet Atkin's complaints were justified. Entrusted with bills for regulating Norwich weavers and relieving creditors, Earle failed to report either; he did chair five sessions of the grand committee on the bill for a new representative in November 1651, but disappears from the journal after January 1652. Thus his direct contribution to the Commonwealth was negligible.

The mid-1650s saw Earle's emergence as leading counsel to the protectorate. Now 'His Highness Serjeant-at-law', he not only delivered opinions on various topics but was junior assize judge for the northern circuit in the summers of 1656 and 1657 (PRO, C181/6/253). Service to the Cromwells did not diminish his standing when the republic returned. In May–June 1659 Earle resumed his seat and indolent legislative habits, heeding neither importunate constituents nor orders to report bills. That summer, having abandoned initial objections to the prescribed engagement of loyalty, he became sole judge on the midland circuit, and did not revisit the house until the new year. Confirmed as Commonwealth's serjeant-at-law in January 1660, he was twice named to committees after the secluded members' readmission. The Long Parliament's final dissolution in March terminated his undistinguished parliamentary career. At the Restoration, Earle obtained the king's pardon. Although deprived of the Norwich recordership and denied judicial promotion, he remained a serjeant and Norfolk JP. His legal practice still prospered—in old age he had 'almost a monopoly' of the eastern circuit, and was reputedly 'very covetous' (North, 53). He invested his gains in land, acquiring seven Norfolk

manors. Earle died at his home, Heydon Hall on 7 September 1667 and was buried in the parish church at Heydon. An able lawyer with considerable local influence, Erasmus Earle was the typical conformist, proclaiming no principles but serving himself under all regimes.

RUTH E. MAYERS

Sources PRO, C231/5/431, 489 · PRO, C181/6 · PRO, C181/7 · T. Atkin, letters to Norwich corporation 1646–50, BL, Add. MS 22620 · *JHC*, 2 (1640–42); 5–7 (1648–59) · *The manuscripts of the earl of Westmorland*, HMC, 13 (1885); repr. (1906) · *CSP dom., 1651; 1657–9* · W. Parsons, *Salle* (1937) · R. North, *The lives of … Francis North … Dudley North … and … John North*, ed. A. Jessopp, 1 (1890); repr. as *The lives of the Norths* (1972) · [T. Birch and R. F. Williams], eds., *The court and times of Charles the First*, 2 (1848) · J. T. Irons, *Seventeenth century Norwich* (1979) · [B. Whitelocke], *Memorials of the English affairs* (1682) · H. Le Strange, *Norfolk official lists* (1890) · F. Blomefield and C. Parkin, *An essay towards a topographical history of the county of Norfolk*, [2nd edn], 11 vols. (1805–10), vol. 6 · *The Genealogist*, new ser., 14 (1897–8), 244 · *DNB* · Venn, *Alum. Cant.*
Archives Hereford Public Library, Boycott MSS
Wealth at death see will, PRO PROB 11/325, fols. 256–66

Earle, Giles (*c*.1678–1758), politician and wit, was born about 1678 at the family residence, Eastcourt House, Crudwell, near Malmesbury, Wiltshire, the sixth son of Sir Thomas Earle MP, a merchant and mayor of Bristol, and his wife, Elizabeth Ellinor Jackson. He was educated at the Middle Temple from 1692, before joining the army, in which he rose to the rank of colonel, and for twenty years was attached to John, the second duke of Argyll. During the course of his military career, he married Elizabeth, the daughter of Sir William Rawlinson, knight and serjeant-at-law, and the widow of William Lowther of Westmorland (license granted 20 May 1702). They had two children, Eleanor and William Rawlinson (*b*. 1703). The History of Parliament records a second wife, Margaret, about whom there are no details.

Earle was returned in 1715 as the whig MP for Chippenham and began his political career as a government supporter speaking in favour of the Septennial Bill in 1716. He lost his commission in the following year after voting against the government but, through his flattery of the prince of Wales and his alleged mistress Mrs Howard, became groom of the prince's bedchamber in 1718. He held this post until 1720, when, following public arguments between the prince and his father, he resigned to serve under Argyll as clerk-comptroller of the king's household.

In 1722 Earle was elected MP for Malmesbury and emerged as an active speaker in the Commons. In 1727 he was appointed chairman of the elections committee, and in the following year he became a commissioner of Irish revenue. His political conduct in the 1720s and 1730s earned him a reputation as a man of little principle who was prepared to do Robert Walpole's bidding, regardless of the task. Certainly his chairmanship of the election committee, which he held until 1741, and his appointment as a lord of the Treasury in 1737, owed much to his popularity with the prime minister. His covetous disposition and his witticisms, often directed at the Scots, also made him unpopular with many writers, including Horace Walpole and Lord Chesterfield. Two dialogues between 'G——s E——e and B——b D——n' (Earle and George Bubb Doddington) were published in 1741 and 1743; the first, written by Sir Charles Hanbury Williams, conveyed a 'lively image of Earle's style and sentiments'. Both essays reveal the shameless political conduct of this pair of intriguers. Lady Mary Wortley Montagu took an equally dim view, describing Earle as 'a facetious gentleman, vulgarly called Tom Earle. … His toast is always "God bless you, whatever becomes of me."'

Earle's unpopularity eventually ended his political career. In the contest for the chairmanship of the committee of privileges and elections, held in December 1741, he was challenged by a candidate, George Lee, put up by the anti-Walpole faction. The sentiments of Earle's opponents were made clear by Chesterfield, who stated that

> the court generally proposes some servile and shameless tool of theirs to be chairman of the committee of privileges and elections. Why should not we therefore pick out some whig of a fair character and with personal connections to oppose the ministerial nominee?

Earle lost the election by four votes, a result that was interpreted as a criticism of his sponsor, Walpole. He continued to support the government after Walpole's fall, but lost the seat of Malmesbury in 1747.

Earle died at his home, Eastcourt House, Crudwell, on 20 August 1758, aged eighty, and was buried in Crudwell church. His son by his first marriage, William Rawlinson Earle, also served as MP for Malmesbury, sitting alongside his father between 1727 and 1747. He died in 1774, aged seventy-two, and was buried near his sister in the vault of his grandfather at Hendon, Middlesex.

PHILIP CARTER

Sources E. Cruickshanks, 'Earle, Giles', HoP, *Commons* · Walpole, *Corr.*, vol. 17 · *The letters of Philip Dormer Stanhope, fourth earl of Chesterfield*, ed. B. Dobrée, 6 vols. (1932), vol. 2 · *The complete letters of Lady Mary Wortley Montagu*, ed. R. Halsband, 3 (1967) · John, Lord Hervey, *Some materials towards memoirs of the reign of King George II*, ed. R. Sedgwick, new edn, 3 vols. (1952) · *The works of Charles Hanbury Williams*, 3 vols. (1822) · GM, 1st ser., 28 (1758), 396 · J. L. Chester and G. J. Armytage, eds., *Allegations for marriage licences issued by the bishop of London*, 2, Harleian Society, 26 (1887), 328 · DNB

Earle, Henry (1789–1838), surgeon, third son of Sir James *Earle (1755–1817) and grandson (through his mother) of Percivall *Pott, both of whom were surgeons; he was born on 28 June 1789 in Hanover Square, London. Apprenticed to his father at the age of sixteen, he became a member of the Royal College of Surgeons in 1808. He was then appointed house surgeon at St Bartholomew's Hospital and was elected assistant surgeon in 1815; in 1827 he succeeded John Abernethy as surgeon. In 1811 he began private practice as a surgeon. He was married and was survived by his wife and their two daughters and six sons. He lived in George Street, Hanover Square, London.

Earle published twelve papers in *Medico-Chirurgical Transactions* (1812–35), and two in *Philosophical Transactions* (1821–2). His book *Practical Observations in Surgery* (1823) has a detailed account of fracture of the neck of the femur and accurately describes the different kinds of such fractures

along with the characteristic clinical features (pain in the hip, and sudden and complete loss of function with retraction and external rotation of the leg). He noted that it was much more common in the old and more common in women than men, and that the femur could be fractured by a twist of the leg or a slight stumble as well as by a blow or heavy fall. He crossed swords with Astley Cooper, who said that such fractures never healed; Earle claimed that they could heal spontaneously, provided they were inside the joint capsule, and the evidence he adduced suggests that he was right. He invented a bed for cases of fracture of the legs (described and illustrated in *Practical Observations*), taking care that the design should not be too expensive to make, nor beyond the skill of a carpenter.

In 1813 Earle won the Jacksonian prize at the Royal College of Surgeons for an essay on the diseases and injuries of nerves and he was made professor of anatomy and surgery there in 1833. He was president of the Royal Medical and Chirurgical Society (1835–7) and surgeon-extraordinary to Queen Victoria (1837).

Earle was short and said to be somewhat arrogant—*The Lancet* called him the 'cock sparrow' (*Lancet*, 255). He worked hard, and was trusted by friends and patients. He died at home, of an inflammatory sore throat, on 18 January 1838, and was buried at Chiswick.

NORMAN MOORE, rev. JEAN LOUDON

Sources *British and Foreign Medical Review*, 5 (1838), 627–8 · *London Medical Gazette*, new ser., 1 (1837–8), 665, 824, 864, 943 · GM, 2nd ser., 9 (1838), 329 · *The Lancet* (14 Nov 1829), 255–8 · *Transactions of the Provincial Medical and Surgical Association*, 8 (1840), 280–81
Wealth at death left family comfortably provided for: *British and Foreign Medical Review*, 627–8

Earle, Jabez (1673×6–1768), Presbyterian minister, was probably a native of Yorkshire but little is known with certainty about his early years, including the year of his birth. He was trained for the ministry by Thomas Brand and John Ker at Bishop's Hall Academy, Bethnal Green, Middlesex, where he appears to have been a student from 1691 to 1692. On leaving the academy he became a tutor and chaplain in the family of Sir Thomas Roberts at Glassenbury, near Cranbrook, Kent. He was ordained in 1699 at St Albans, and in the same year he was appointed assistant to Thomas Reynolds at the King's Weigh House Presbyterian chapel, Eastcheap, London.

In 1706 Earle accepted an invitation to become pastor of the Presbyterian congregation in Drury Lane, Westminster. Two years later, together with five other nonconformist ministers, William Harris, Benjamin Grosvenor, Thomas Reynolds, John Newman, and Thomas Bradbury, he began a course of Friday evening lectures at the Weigh House, on institutionalized religious worship. Among the subjects discussed were prayer, singing, 'hearing the word', and reading the scriptures. These sermons were afterwards published in four small volumes. Earle's ministry at Drury Lane proved popular and the size of the congregation increased, although this was in part due to a secession from the congregation of Daniel Burgess at New Court, Carey Street. As a consequence the congregation was obliged to move, about 1709, to a new and larger meeting-house in Hanover Street, Long Acre, where an assistant pastor was appointed to share the burden of ministerial duties. During Earle's ministry some distinguished preachers, including Benjamin Hollis, John Allen, Samuel Morton Savage, and Rice Harris, were to occupy this position.

From 1706 to 1768 Earle was a member of the Presbyterian Fund board, and in 1723 he was elected a trustee of Dr Williams's Charity. The degree of DD was conferred on him on 21 August 1728 by Edinburgh University, and shortly afterwards, on 23 December, he was awarded the same degree by King's College, Aberdeen. In June 1730 he was chosen as one of the Tuesday lecturers at Salters' Hall, a post which he held until his death. At the end of 1734 he accepted an invitation, together with several other eminent nonconformist ministers, including Jeremiah Hunt and Josiah Bayes, to deliver a course of lectures at Salters' Hall against Roman Catholicism. Each minister agreed to preach a set of sermons on the 'main principles and errors, doctrines and practices of the Church of Rome, to guard Protestants against the efforts of its emissaries' (Toulmin, 1.xi); Earle's chosen subject was 'the popish doctrine of purgatory'. For a time in the 1720s Earle was also chaplain to Archibald Douglas, first duke of Douglas.

Earle had the energy and enthusiasm to perform all these duties effectively and efficiently. He was a good preacher and well respected by his fellow ministers. To what extent he deviated from orthodox Calvinism is not clear. Although he voted with the subscribers at Salters' Hall in 1719 he is said to have disowned his subscription by 1725, and his involvement with the Bagweel Papers (1716–18) indicates that he was liberal in doctrine by that time.

Earle was a prolific writer and author of numerous publications. His first published work was *Sermon to the Societies for the Reformation of Manners*, delivered at Salters' Hall on 26 July 1704 and published in the same year. His most enduring work was *A Treatise on the Sacraments* (1707), which was reprinted several times and even translated into Gaelic in 1827. Also well received was his *Sacred Poems*, dedicated to Mrs Susanna Langford and published in 1726. He translated into Latin some of Dr Williams's works, and published anonymously in 1729 a small collection of Latin verse, entitled *Unbritii cantiani poemata*. Between 1704 and 1735 he published over twenty single sermons in addition to those already mentioned. He was also one of the authors of the Bagweel Papers, or *The Occasional Papers*, as they were also known. These essays, which were issued monthly between 1716 and 1718 and were later published in three volumes, made an important contribution to the theological development of English Presbyterianism as they stressed the importance of personal judgement in matters of doctrine. Philip Doddridge, an admirer of much of Earle's work, describes his style as 'judicious, pathetic and very laconic' (Allibone, *Dict.*, 1.538).

Earle was also a classical scholar of some repute. When ninety years of age he could quote with great fluency a hundred verses or more from Homer, Virgil, Horace, Juvenal, and other classical authors. His friendly disposition and cheerfulness 'never deserted him to his last breath'

(Jeremy, 123), but whether this geniality prevailed in his domestic life is questionable; he married three times and lived 'inharmoniously with each of his wives', whom he called 'the world, the flesh and the devil' (ibid.). During his long life Earle never experienced a moment's ill health and, though blind for some years, he preached to the last Sunday of his life. His age at his death, in London on 29 May 1768, is uncertain; several sources give it as ninety-two but both Jeremy and an obituary notice in the *Gentleman's Magazine* maintain that he died aged ninety-four.   M. J. MERCER

Sources DNB · W. Wilson, *The history and antiquities of the dissenting churches and meeting houses in London, Westminster and Southwark*, 4 vols. (1808–14), vols. 1–3 · C. Surman, index, DWL · W. D. Jeremy, *The Presbyterian Fund and Dr Daniel Williams's Trust* (1885) · *Protestant Dissenter's Magazine*, 6 (1799) · *GM*, 1st ser., 38 (1768), 246 · A. Chalmers, ed., *The general biographical dictionary*, new edn, 32 vols. (1812–17) · Allibone, *Dict.* · J. Toulmin, 'Memoir of D. Neal', in D. Neal, *Neal's history of the puritans*, rev. E. Parsons, 1 (1811), xi · A. Gordon, ed., *Freedom after ejection: a review (1690–1692) of presbyterian and congregational nonconformity in England and Wales* (1917), 4, 256 · C. G. Bolam and others, *The English presbyterians: from Elizabethan puritanism to modern Unitarianism* (1968), 155, 164 · J. Earle, 'De sacrarum scripturarum detorsione', 1732, DWL, MS 24.34
Archives DWL

Earle, Sir James (1755–1817), surgeon, was born in London and received his medical education at St Bartholomew's Hospital. He was elected assistant surgeon to the hospital in 1770. From 1776 to 1784, as Stafford Crane, one of the surgeons, was unable to operate, Earle performed one-third of the operations at the hospital. After a two-week courtship he married the daughter of Percivall *Pott (1714–1788), then surgeon to St Bartholomew's Hospital; their third son, Henry *Earle (1789–1838), became surgeon to the same hospital. Earle was elected surgeon on 22 May 1784, and held that office for thirty-one years, resigning in 1815. He lived in Hanover Square, London, was appointed surgeon-extraordinary to George III in 1786, and was celebrated for his operating skills. In 1807, when master of the Royal College of Surgeons, he was knighted by the king. Earle wrote the memoir of Percivall Pott prefixed to the three-volume edition of Pott's works, published in 1790, and a life of another colleague, William Austin, prefixed to an essay on lithotomy. Both are written in a simple, lucid style, which is also found in his surgical writings, and which was probably acquired from his study of the methods of thought and the writings of his father-in-law. Earle was famous for his skill in lithotomy, and introduced an improvement in the treatment of hydrocele. His writings include *A Treatise on the Hydrocele* (1791, with additions in 1793, 1796, and 1805), *Practical Observations on the Operation for Stone* (1793), *A New Method of Operation for Cataract* (1801), and *Letter on Fractures of the Lower Limbs* (1807). He died in 1817.   NORMAN MOORE, rev. MICHAEL BEVAN

Sources *GM*, 1st ser., 56 (1786) · S. C. Lawrence, *Charitable knowledge: hospital pupils and practitioners in eighteenth-century London* (1996) · Z. Cope, *The Royal College of Surgeons of England: a history* (1959) · MS Journal of St Bartholomew's Hospital
Archives Devon RO, executorship accounts, estate

Earle, John (1598×1601–1665), bishop of Salisbury and character writer, was born at York, the son of Thomas Earle or Earles, registrar of the archbishop's court in the city. He matriculated, 'aged eighteen' (Foster, *Alum. Oxon.*), from Christ Church, Oxford, on 4 June 1619, but may have been two or three years older and may have already spent some time at the university, and was probably thus also the John Earle who graduated BA from Merton on 8 July and who became a fellow there the same year. He proceeded MA in 1624.

Earle's first known work is a poem on the death in 1616 of Francis Beaumont the dramatist, subsequently published in *Poems by Francis Beaumont, Gent.* (1640). He also wrote lines on the return of Prince Charles from his jaunt to the Spanish court in 1623, a short poem on Sir John Burroughs, who was killed in the unsuccessful August 1626 expedition to the Île de Rhé, and, while a fellow of the college, a Latin poem, 'Hortus Mertonensis', first printed in John Aubrey's *Natural History and Antiquities of the County of Surrey* (5 vols., 1718–19, 4.167–71). Earle's *Microcosmographie, or, A Peece of the World Discovered in Essayes and Characters* was published anonymously by Edward Blount in 1628, but was soon known to be Earle's work. The craze for characters—pithy, ironic, pen portraits of social or moral types, often with a didactic moral purpose—began with Isaac Casaubon's translations of the Greek characters of Theophrastus in the 1590s. Sir Thomas Overbury and Joseph Hall made notable contributions to the genre, but Earle's book was immensely popular and went through many editions in the seventeenth, eighteenth, and nineteenth centuries, in the course of which the original fifty-four characters were augmented to seventy-eight.

In 1630 Earle wrote a short poem on the death of William Herbert, third earl of Pembroke, elder brother of Philip, fourth earl and chancellor of Oxford University. The following year he served as a university proctor, and about that time he also became the chancellor's chaplain, a position which brought him a lodging at court. At an unknown date he married Bridget and may have been the John Earles who married Bregit Dixye on 7 October 1637 at St Mary Magdalen, Old Fish Street, London. In 1639 Pembroke presented him to the rectory of Bishopston, Wiltshire, in succession to William Chillingworth.

During the 1630s Earle was one of those in the habit of meeting at Lord Falkland's house. 'He would frequently profess', wrote the earl of Clarendon, 'that he had got more useful learning by his conversation at Tew than he had at Oxford'. In his rose-tinted account of the circle at Great Tew, Clarendon described Earle's conversation as 'so pleasant and delightful, and so very facetious, that no man's company was more desired and more loved' (Hyde, *Selections*, 38). The king also formed a high opinion of him, and appointed him tutor to the prince of Wales in succession to Brian Duppa when the latter became bishop of Salisbury in 1641. On 20 November the previous year Earle had proceeded DD at Oxford.

In 1643 Earle was nominated to the Westminster assembly, but the nature of his views on the Church of England did not permit him to attend. On 10 February

John Earle (1598×1601–1665), by unknown artist, c.1660

1644 he was elected chancellor of Salisbury Cathedral but soon afterwards, as a malignant, he was deprived both of this appointment and of the living of Bishopston. His wife, Bridget, petitioned in 1646 for the fifth of the living's profits which was allowed to the wives and families of sequestered ministers. After pressure from the committee for plundered ministers the Wiltshire county committee let the rectory for a year at £280, of which Mrs Earle was to receive a fifth.

Earle went into exile in the later 1640s and continued to occupy himself with translations into Latin. His edition of Richard Hooker's *The Laws of Ecclesiastical Politie* was written chiefly at Cologne, but although believed by Isaac Walton to be nearly finished in 1665, was, according to a letter to Thomas Hearne, 'utterly destroyed by prodigious heedlessness and carelessness' (Wood, *Ath. Oxon.*, 3.718); his edition of *Eikon basilike* was published in 1649. On 27 June 1647 he married John Evelyn and Mary Browne at Sir Richard Browne's chapel in Paris, and Evelyn reports Earle's presence in the city again in 1649. During the period of Charles II's expedition in Scotland, Earle, with George Morley, future bishop of Winchester, appears to have lived in the house of Sir Charles Cotterell at Antwerp. From 1651 he was at the royal court in exile in Paris, attending Charles as chaplain and clerk of the closet. That year he and fellow chaplain John Cosin debated with Father Coniers to reclaim Thomas Keightley for protestantism. When Evelyn heard Earle preach against the vicious life of the exiled cavaliers that September, 'the discourse was so passionate, that few could abstaine from tears'. However, these were also difficult years. Charles often lacked funds to pay Earle and Cosin. Earle often had to cope alone and seems to have relied on gifts from friends and possibly from his wife, who travelled between England and her husband on the continent.

Following the Restoration, Earle was preferred in June 1660 to the deanery of Westminster, as had been planned as early as July the previous year. On 25 March 1661 he was nominated as a commissioner to review the prayer book, on 28 March he preached at court, and on 23 April he assisted at the coronation. He was one of the commissioners at the Savoy conference, but seems to have taken little part, if any: Richard Baxter noted that he 'never came' (*Reliquiae Baxterianae*, 3.364). The suggestion that, together with Gilbert Sheldon and George Morley, Earle formed a committee to vet ecclesiastical appointments and so shape the restored Church of England is no longer given credence by historians. Despite his initial refusal of the office, on 30 November 1662 he was consecrated bishop of Worcester in succession to John Gauden, and on 28 September 1663, on the promotion of Humphrey Henchman to the see of London, he was translated to Salisbury.

Earle was described by his contemporaries as a gentle individual: his friend Clarendon asserted that he was without enemies; another 'deare friend', John Evelyn claimed that Bishop Earle was 'universaly beloved for his gentle & sweet disposition', and that he was 'a most humble, meeke, but cherefull man, an excellent schol[a]r & rare preacher' (Evelyn, 3.265, 345–6). Others concurred. Richard Baxter called him 'a mild and quiet man' (*Reliquiae Baxterianae*, 2.381). Yet, as with so many churchmen of a similar temperament, a reputation for leniency and moderation towards dissent has been foisted on Earle by subsequent writers with very little evidence. In June 1662 Earle wrote a conciliatory letter to Richard Baxter after Baxter explained why he had abruptly refused to wear a tippet when preaching before Charles II on 22 July 1660. Earle wrote that while he could not agree with Baxter 'in some particulars, yett I cannot but esteem [you] for your personal worth & abilityes' and, perhaps taken with the politeness, Baxter seems to have written in the margin 'O that they were all such!' (Keeble and Nuttall, letters 702, 703, and 625 n. 1). Other than this, there is little evidence of his attitude: White Kennett claimed that Bishop Earle followed Henchman's example and did not trouble Salisbury's nonconformists; Earle probably had a part in a 1663 government inspired attempt to ease the scruples of the nonconformist clergy about conforming while simultaneously closing loopholes in the Act of Uniformity. There seems no ground for the sweeping claims of Gilbert Burnet, who was not in England at the time, and others that Earle was opposed to the first Conventicle Act and the Five Mile Act. These assertions seem to have originated in the partisan tracts of Edward Pearse in the 1680s and to have been further amplified by Edmund Calamy.

Whatever his views on nonconformity Earle probably had little opportunity to act upon them since his health was already failing: he sought help from the waters of Bath and Barnet, and wrote in 1663 to Clarendon that 'though your Lordship I trust may live many summers yet, I that am now in my 65th yeare and under all these infirmityes look upon every month as a yeare and every yeare as an age' (Ollard, 252). But the end, when it came, seems to have been swift. In October 1665 parliament met at Oxford to escape the plague then in London. Earle had rooms in University College and here he took to his bed. On 15 November, in the presence of Bishop Henchman of London, Earle indicated that his wife was to have all his property.

The bishop died between 7 and 8 p.m. on 17 November 1665, and was buried with much state on 25 November. The cortège gathered in the Convocation House where Dr South, the university orator, spoke, then processed to St Mary's where John Dolben preached on 'being dead he yet speaketh', and thence proceeded to Merton College chapel for anthems, prayers, a speech, and the interment. Earle's grave was near the high altar, and in the north-east corner of the chapel a monument was erected to him with a highly laudatory Latin inscription.   JOHN SPURR

Sources *Walker rev.*, 372 · Wood, *Ath. Oxon.*, new edn · Wood, *Ath. Oxon.: Fasti*, new edn · Foster, *Alum. Oxon.* · *The life and times of Anthony Wood*, ed. A. Clark, 5 vols., OHS, 19, 21, 26, 30, 40 (1891–1900) · *Calendar of the correspondence of Richard Baxter*, ed. N. H. Keeble and G. F. Nuttall, 2 vols. (1991) · E. Hyde, earl of Clarendon, *Selections from 'The history of the rebellion' and 'The life by himself'*, new edn, ed. G. Huehns (1978) · R. S. Bosher, *The making of the Restoration settlement: the influence of the Laudians, 1649–1662* (1951) · W. Kennett, *A register and chronicle ecclesiastical and civil* (1728) · *Fasti Angl.* (Hardy) · Evelyn, *Diary* · P. Barwick, *The life of … Dr John Barwick*, ed. and trans. H. Bedford (1724) · *Reliquiae Baxterianae, or, Mr Richard Baxter's narrative of the most memorable passages of his life and times*, ed. M. Sylvester, 1 vol. in 3 pts (1696) · *Burnet's History of my own time*, ed. O. Airy, new edn, 2 vols. (1897–1900) · I. M. Green, *The re-establishment of the Church of England, 1660–1663* (1978) · P. Seaward, *The Cavalier Parliament and the reconstruction of the old regime, 1661–1667* (1988) · R. Ollard, *Clarendon and his friends* (1987) · *Calendar of the Clarendon state papers preserved in the Bodleian Library*, 4: *1657–1660*, ed. F. J. Routledge (1932) · E. Cardwell, *A history of conferences and other proceedings connected with the revision of the Book of Common Prayer* (1840) · T. Fowler, 'Earle's *Microcosmographie* from the Hunter MSS in Durham Cathedral', *N&Q*, 4th ser., 8 (1871), 363, 411, 475, 508; 9 (1872), 33 · J. Earle, *The autograph manuscript of 'Microcosmographie'* (1966) · E. Calamy, ed., *An abridgement of Mr. Baxter's history of his life and times, with an account of the ministers, &c., who were ejected after the Restoration of King Charles II*, 2nd edn, 2 vols. (1713), vol. 1, p. 174 · [E. Pearse], *The conformists plea for the nonconformist*, 2nd edn (1681), 35, 61 · *Reg. Oxf.*, 2/1–4 · J. Aubrey, *The natural history and antiquities of the county of Surrey*, 5 vols. (1718–19) · will, PRO, PROB 11/318, fol. 406r · Thurloe, *State papers*, 2.427 · Bodl. Oxf., MS Tanner 48, fol. 46; MS Add. C. 302, fol. 234 · DNB · IGI
Likenesses oils, *c.*1660, NPG [see illus.]

Earle, John (1749–1818), Roman Catholic priest, was born in London on 31 December 1749, the son of Tobit (or Tobias) Earle and his wife, Elizabeth, *née* Hutton, and was baptized on 4 January 1750 by William Errington. He entered the English College, Douai, on 11 November 1770. On 17 August 1774 he left Douai to explore his vocation as a Carthusian, but decided not to proceed and returned on 8 November. He took the college oath in 1777, and was ordained priest at Arras on 18 December 1779. He taught at Douai until he left for the English mission on 5 February 1784. Earle officiated at Brockhampton, Hampshire, from 1784 to 1787. In 1788 he was assistant priest at the Bavarian embassy chapel, Warwick Street, London, and from 1789 was assistant priest at the Spanish embassy chapel, Spanish Place, Dorset Street; he became head chaplain there in 1792.

Earle's first published work was *Gratitude*, a poem composed to commemorate the Catholic Relief Act of 1791. This was followed in 1799 by *Remarks on the prefaces prefixed to the first and second volumes of a work entitled the holy Bible; or the books accepted sacred by Jews and Christians*. This edition of the Bible, translated and with commentaries by the Catholic priest and biblical scholar Alexander Geddes, had excited widespread controversy. Earle rejected Geddes's conclusion that much of the Pentateuch was mythological and argued for the historical veracity of the early books of the Bible, citing the continuity of tradition from Seth to Abraham to Moses. He also accused Geddes of reducing Moses to no more than a talented creative thinker without especial divine insight. He further suggested that Geddes was tainted by French revolutionary ideology. Earle's work pleased Bishop John Douglass, vicar apostolic of the London district, who bought fifty copies to be distributed to his clergy.

Earle died at Spanish Place, Dorset Street, London, on 15 May 1818, and was buried at St Pancras churchyard on 22 May 1818.   MATTHEW KILBURN

Sources R. C. Fuller, *Alexander Geddes, 1737–1802: a pioneer of biblical criticism* (1984) • G. Anstruther, *The seminary priests*, 4 (1977) • P. R. Harris, ed., *Douai College documents, 1639–1794*, Catholic RS, 63 (1972) • Gillow, *Lit. biog. hist.*, 2.151 • J. S. Hansom, ed., obituaries from the *Laity's directory, 1773–1839*, *Obituaries*, ed. R. Stanfield, J. S. Hansom, and J. H. Matthews, Catholic RS, 12 (1913), 16–231, esp. 138 • *DNB* • F. Blom and others, *English Catholic books, 1701–1800: a bibliography* (1996)

Earle, John (1824–1903), philologist, was born on 29 January 1824 at Elston, in the parish of Churchstowe near Kingsbridge, south Devon, the only son of John Earle, a small landed proprietor who cultivated his own property, and his wife, Anne Hamlyn. Their other child, a daughter, Mary, married George Buckle, afterwards canon of Wells, and was mother of George Earle Buckle, editor of *The Times*. John Earle received his earliest education in the house of Orlando Manley, then incumbent of Plymstock, and then attended Plymouth new grammar school. He spent the year 1840–41 at the grammar school of Kingsbridge, and matriculated at Magdalen Hall, Oxford, in October 1841; he graduated BA in 1845 with a first class in *literae humaniores*. He then devoted his studies to 'the sources of English Philology' (*A Word for the Mother Tongue*, 1876, 4). In 1848 he won a fellowship at Oriel College, then one of the chief distinctions in the university. In 1849 he proceeded MA, was ordained deacon, and was elected to the professorship of Old English then tenable for five years only. At the time the chair was little more than an elegant sinecure, but Earle brought it into the academic mainstream before his retirement in 1854, and assiduously pursued his Anglo-Saxon studies. (The chair was occupied from 1858 to 1876 by Dr Joseph Bosworth.) Meanwhile in 1852 he became tutor of Oriel in succession to his future brother-in-law, George Buckle. In 1857 he was ordained priest and presented by his college to the rectory

of Swanswick, near Bath, which he retained until his death.

On 19 August 1863 Earle married Jane (*d.* 1911), daughter of George Rolleston, vicar of Maltby, and sister of George Rolleston, Linacre professor of anatomy at Oxford. They had three sons and four daughters. His second daughter, Beatrice Anne Earle, married her first cousin, Mr George Earle Buckle. In 1871 Earle was appointed to the prebend of Wanstrow in Wells Cathedral, and from 1873 to 1877 he was rural dean of Bath.

In 1876 Earle was re-elected professor of Old English by convocation; his competitor was Thomas Arnold. The tenure of this chair had then been made permanent, and he held the post for the rest of his life. His inaugural lecture, *A Word for the Mother Tongue*, was one of many published pleas for the inclusion in the university curriculum of English philological study.

Earle was an industrious writer, and combined devotion to research with a power of popularizing its fruits. His earliest published work was *Gloucester Fragments: Legends of St. Swithun and Sancta Maria Aegyptiaca* (1861). In 1865 appeared *Two of the Saxon chronicles parallel, with supplementary extracts from the others*, edited with introduction, notes, and a glossarial index. This was in many ways his most important work, and was the first attempt to give a rational and connected account of the growth of the chronicle, and the relations of the different manuscripts. It was recast by C. Plummer in two volumes (1892–9). In 1866 appeared both *A Book for the Beginner in Anglo-Saxon* (4th edn, 1902) and *The Philology of the English Tongue* (5th edn, 1892). The latter volume was Earle's most popular work: it largely helped to popularize the results of the new science of comparative philology as applied to the English language. With the later developments of comparative philology Earle hardly kept pace. He was always more interested in tracing the development of language as an instrument of thought, and in analysing the various elements that had contributed to the formation of English, than in purely philological science.

Apart from English philology, Earle was an efficient Italian scholar. He wrote an introduction to C. L. Shadwell's translation of Dante's *Purgatorio* (1892) and a remarkable essay on Dante's *Vita nuova* in the *Quarterly Review* (1896). His varied intellectual interests are also shown in his other publications, which include two books on the city of Bath (1864, 1895); *English Plant Names* (1880); various works on Old English literature, including the masterly *Deeds of Beowulf* (1892); works on English prose and grammar; and a study entitled *The Psalter of 1539* (1894).

Earle died on 31 January 1903, at 84 Banbury Road, Oxford, and was buried in Holywell cemetery. A brass tablet was erected to his memory in Swanswick church.

CHARLES PLUMMER, rev. JOHN D. HAIGH

Sources personal knowledge (1912) • private information (1912) • *Oxford Magazine* (4 Feb 1903), 182, 186 • *Oxford Magazine* (11 Feb 1903), 202, 205–206 • *The Times* (2 Feb 1903), 7b • *Men and women of the time* (1899) • Crockford (1874) • Foster, *Alum. Oxon.* • *CGPLA Eng. & Wales* (1903) • m. cert.

Wealth at death £6173 19s. 2d.: probate, 17 June 1903, *CGPLA Eng. & Wales*

Earle, Sir Lionel (1866–1948), civil servant, was born in London on 1 February 1866, the second son of Captain Charles William Earle, rifle brigade, and his wife, (Maria) Theresa [see Earle, (Maria) Theresa (1836–1925)], daughter of Edward Ernest Villiers, younger brother of the fourth earl of Clarendon. Her sister married the first earl of Lytton.

Educated at Marlborough College and then sent abroad to learn languages, Earle studied at Göttingen and the Sorbonne, at which time he seems to have contemplated medicine as his future career. He went up to Merton College, Oxford, but did not take a degree and, after attempting unsuccessfully to enter the diplomatic service, he accepted in 1898 a post as assistant secretary to the royal commission on the Paris Exhibition. He served as acting second secretary at the Paris embassy in 1900. In 1902–3 he was private secretary to Lord Dudley, lord lieutenant of Ireland, and in 1907 private secretary to the lord president of the council, Lord Crewe, whom he followed to the Colonial Office shortly afterwards as principal private secretary. When Lewis Harcourt succeeded Crewe in 1910, Earle continued to serve in the same capacity for the next two years. In 1912 Asquith appointed him permanent secretary to the office of works where he remained until his retirement in 1933.

Although his appointment caused some surprise, Earle held the post with considerable success. Affable, although somewhat distant in manner, handsome, and well connected, he had many social contacts and was able to give valuable assistance to successive governments, particularly in artistic matters where his cultured mind and good taste found adequate scope. In his day the office of works was small and the staff few, and Earle's experience as a man of the world supplemented the departmental knowledge of his officials. It was especially due to his efforts that the Royal Fine Arts Commission was established in 1924, and he gave that body active support. He also helped to develop government hospitality, until then somewhat haphazard, on liberal and dignified lines. Earle took special interest in the royal parks in London, which he regarded as 'the most humanizing influences in this great city of ours' (The Times, 12 March 1948, 7e), and his tenure of office was notable for improvements in layout and the display of rare and beautiful plants. In the field of public memorials and statues he also did valuable work. No statue could be erected in London in any public place without the authority of the office of works, and in the spate of memorials and statues which followed the First World War Earle's influence was invariably exerted to bring about the selection of suitable sculptors and the allocation of appropriate sites.

In the more humdrum work of providing accommodation for government staffs Earle was less interested. He was inclined to chafe at the restrictions of estimates procedure and public accounting; but his tact and common sense, together with the gift of knowing where to go for advice, remedied a somewhat impulsive judgement. He was popular with his staff and respected by them. In his retirement he continued to work for the advancement of British horticulture and he was chairman of the shrubs and flowers advisory committee in 1934. He also took a leading part in the coronation planting committee, which initiated many plans for decorating town and countryside in commemoration of the coronation in 1953. He was a member of the royal commission on national museums and galleries (1927–30), a trustee of the Wallace Collection, and chairman of the Ancient Monuments Board for England.

Earle was appointed CMG. (1901), CB (1911), KCB (1916), KCVO (1921), and GCVO (1933). In 1926 he married Betty Strachey, daughter of William Edward Marriott and Mrs Lindsay Jopling, and granddaughter of Sir John Strachey. The marriage was dissolved in 1937 and there were no children. He died in St George's Hospital, London, on 10 March 1948. His recollections, *Turn over the Page*, appeared in 1935.   ERIC DE NORMANN, rev. MARK POTTLE

Sources personal knowledge (1959) · private information (1959) · The Times (12 March 1948) · The Times (7 April 1948)
Archives NL Scot., corresp. about Scottish Regimental Museum | Bodl. Oxf., corresp. with Herbert Asquith · Bodl. Oxf., corresp. with Lewis Harcourt
Likenesses W. Stoneman, photograph, 1917, NPG · W. Rothenstein, chalk drawing, 1933, Gov. Art Coll. · W. Rothenstein, chalk and pastel drawing, priv. coll. · bronze head, Gov. Art Coll. · photograph, repro. in L. Earle, Turn over the page (1935) · photograph, NPG
Wealth at death £82,873 1s. 9d.: probate, 12 July 1948, CGPLA Eng. & Wales

Earle, Ralph Anstruther (1835–1879), civil servant, was born at Edinburgh, second son of Charles Earle (1798–1880) of Everton, Lancashire, and his wife, Emily, daughter of Primrose Maxwell of Tuppendence, Kent. He was educated at Harrow School (1849–54), but instead of continuing to Cambridge in 1854 he became, through his Liberal connections, unpaid attaché to the British embassy in Paris.

In 1855 or 1856 Earle met Benjamin Disraeli. He scented personal opportunity in Disraeli's plans to bring down the Liberal government, and turned coat to become his 'mole' at the embassy. Until the Conservative return to power in 1858, Earle fed confidential government information, anonymously and via other undercover agents, to Disraeli ('Aunty') in London. Disraeli used this inside knowledge to attack Palmerston's foreign policy, and it contributed to his decision to oppose the 1858 Conspiracy Bill which defeated Palmerston.

Earle then became Disraeli's private secretary (1858–66), 'only 23, but a man in matured thought and power of observation' (Disraeli to Mrs Brydges Willyams, 20 May 1859, Disraeli, vol. 7). Handsome and clever, he managed correspondence, interviews, and patronage; drafted speeches and memoranda; maintained newspaper liaison; and advised on parliamentary tactics—all despite absences at German spas for his health. As confidential clerk, he undertook secret missions to Napoleon III in 1858 and 1860, the second a highly unpatriotic incitement to defy the British government. He was snobbish and vindictive, particularly towards his former chief, Cowley: 'if we cannot reward friends, it is something … to punish enemies' (Earle to Disraeli, 1 June 1857). His shady financial affairs included dealings with railways and short-lived companies. A brief period as Conservative MP for Berwick (May–August 1859) ended abruptly in his resignation, and led to charges of collusion that also implicated Disraeli and prompted the resignation of the Conservative Party election manager, Philip Rose.

Earle was Conservative MP for Maldon (1865–8), but his most substantial political contribution was as negotiator in 1866 with Liberals disaffected over political reform; they eventually assisted the Conservative return to power. Possibly, however, he overreached in his promises, and the Liberals' expectations of coalition temporarily jeopardized Disraeli's position as house leader in Derby's new government in 1866. Disraeli appointed him secretary of the poor-law board, but withdrew from their former confidential association. After a bitter quarrel (probably over further promotion) in March 1867, Earle resigned, and in April foolishly made a speech sniping at Disraeli. 'I am not', Disraeli remarked, 'so much surprised at Ralph's want of political morality, but I am surprised at his want of political sagacity' (Disraeli to Lord Spencer, Henderson, 286). Earle's display of disloyalty ended his political career, and he retired to profiteering in Turkish Railways. In 1877 he attempted to convert to Roman Catholicism but was prevented by his brother Charles; he successfully converted two days before his death, which took place on 10 June 1879 at Soden, Nassau, Germany, where he was buried. Earle's activities do not reflect well on either him or Disraeli, but they give an insight into the hidden infrastructure of Victorian politics and into Disraeli's unofficial intelligence network.   MARY S. MILLAR

Sources R. Earle, letter to Benjamin Disraeli, Bodl. Oxf., Hughenden MSS B/XX/E, fols. 1–422 · G. B. Henderson, 'Disraeli and Palmerston', *Crimean War diplomacy, and other historical essays* (1947), 249–66 · G. B. Henderson, 'Ralph Anstruther Earle', *Crimean War diplomacy, and other historical essays* (1947), 267–89 · *Benjamin Disraeli letters*, ed. J. A. W. Gunn and others (1982–), vols. 6–7 · G. E. Buckle, *The life of Benjamin Disraeli*, 4 (1916) · R. Blake, *Disraeli* (1966) · M. Cowling, 'Disraeli, Derby and fusion, 1865–1866', *HJ*, 8 (1965), 31–71 · W. Fraser, *Disraeli and his day* (1891) · *ILN* (28 June 1879) · *The Times* (13 June 1879) · *The Times* (14 June 1879) · *Annual Register* (1879) · *The diary of Gathorne Hardy, later Lord Cranbrook, 1866–1892: political selections*, ed. N. E. Johnson (1981) · H. D. Wolff, *Rambling recollections*, 1 (1908) · S. Bradford, *Disraeli* (1982) · Boase, *Mod. Eng. biog.* · Venn, *Alum. Cant.*

Archives Bodl. Oxf., corresp. with Benjamin Disraeli · Bodl. Oxf., Hughenden MSS, B/XX/E, fols. 1–422 · Som. ARS, letters to Sir William Jolliffe

Wealth at death under £50,000: resworn probate, Oct 1879, *CGPLA Eng. & Wales*

Earle [*née* Villiers], **(Maria) Theresa** [*known as* Mrs C. W. Earle] (**1836–1925**), horticulturist, was born at 45 Cambridge Terrace, London, on 8 June 1836, the eldest daughter of Edward Ernest Villiers (1806–1843), younger brother of the fourth earl of Clarendon, and his wife, Elizabeth Charlotte (1807–1890), *née* Liddell, fifth daughter of the first Baron Ravensworth (second creation). She was educated by governesses, while the family divided its time

(Maria) Theresa Earle (1836–1925), by unknown photographer

between London and Grove Mill House, Hertfordshire, and, in the 1850s, wintered in France or Italy. She was presented at court in 1854, and in 1856 declined an invitation to serve as maid of honour to Queen Victoria, thus earning the family epithet Radical Theresa.

The Villiers family moved in literary and artistic circles, with Henry Taylor and George Frederick Watts notable acquaintances. Theresa aspired to become an artist, won the encouragement of Ruskin, and received an award from the South Kensington School in 1856. In 1857, while in Florence, she met Captain Charles William Earle (*c.*1828–1897), son of William Earle of Liverpool; they became engaged in 1863, after his return from military service in India, and were married in St Paul's, Knightsbridge, on 14 April 1864. The following year Earle was appointed a director of the Belgrave Mansions Company; in 1869 he was elected managing director of the Australasian Telegraph Company, and followed this with a series of other telegraphic directorships. The Earles had three children: Sydney (1865), Lionel (1866), and Maxwell (1871).

In 1878–9 Earle inherited the estates of his brothers, depriving Mrs Earle of what she had considered her two vocations in life: to nurse her husband and to be what she called a good 'poor man's' wife. (Her younger sisters became countess of Lytton and Baroness Loch by their marriages.) The Earles continued their artistic connections, becoming friends of Burne-Jones, Oscar Wilde, George Eliot, and the Rossettis.

In 1879 the Earles took a new house at 5 Bryanston Square, and soon after a small country house, Woodlands, in Cobham, Surrey, a house with a 2 acre garden which Mrs Earle described as 'a small piece of flat ground surrounding an ordinary suburban house'. Here she developed a garden which was much admired by her social circle, comprising a terrace with tubbed plants, beds and borders of hardy plants, and a kitchen garden in which culinary herbs were given prominence. In the 1890s she advised a German friend, Mme De Grunelius, about furnishing a country house near Frankfurt, and was urged by her to write her advice down. With encouragement and contributions from her niece Constance Lytton she compiled a book, arranged according to the months of the year, of reflective essays on gardening and household matters. It was published by Smith Elder in 1897 under the title *Pot-Pourri from a Surrey Garden*. Shortly after its publication, on 8 June 1897, her husband was killed in a road accident.

The book became an instant success; it was favourably reviewed in the gardening press, bought by fashionable society because of her social connections, and recommended by Dean Samuel Reynolds Hole in the *Nineteenth Century* with the words 'Buy it'. Within two years the book had been through ten editions, mostly simple reprints, although an appendix on Japanese flower arranging by Constance Lytton was added in the eighth edition. While not the first book of its genre—contemporary reviewers singled out Henry Arthur Bright's *A Year in a Lancashire Garden* (1879) as its predecessor—it was by far the most successful, and formed the model for the first books of Gertrude Jekyll a few years later. Mrs Earle modified the formula only slightly for two subsequent works, which, together with her first, form a trilogy: *More Pot-Pourri from a Surrey Garden* (1899) and *A Third Pot-Pourri* (1903).

In the years after her husband's death, Mrs Earle travelled in Germany and Italy, developed friendships with Gertrude Jekyll and younger gardeners such as Ethel Case, and collaborated with the latter on two gardening books: *Gardening for the Ignorant* (1912) and *Pot-Pourri Mixed by Two* (1914). She also wrote two books of autobiography and family history: *Letters to Young and Old* (1906) and *Memoirs and Memories* (1911). In 1905 she wrote the chapter on spring in the anthology *Garden Colour*, illustrated by Margaret Waterfield.

Mrs Earle died at Woodlands on 27 February 1925. Her son, Sir Lionel *Earle (1866–1948), as permanent secretary of the office of works (1912–33), followed his mother's example by his promotion of horticulture in the royal parks.   BRENT ELLIOTT

Sources Mrs C. W. Earle, *Memoirs and memories* (1911) • *Mrs Earle's pot-pourri*, ed. A. Jones (1982) • D. MacLeod, *Down-to-earth women* (1982) • T. Clark, 'Mrs C. W. Earle (1836–1925), a reappraisal of her work', *Garden History*, 8/2 (1980), 75–83 • *Gardeners' Chronicle*, 3rd ser., 77 (1925), 174 • *Botanical Exchange Club Report* (1925), 846–7 • S. Festing, 'A patient gleaner', *The Garden*, 103 (1978), 412–14 • B. Massingham, *A century of gardeners* (1982) • B. Massingham, 'Some nineteenth-century English gardens', *Huntia*, 84/2 (1982), 93–102 • d. cert.

Likenesses H. West, photograph, 1908, repro. in Earle, *Memoirs and memories* • photograph, NPG [*see illus.*]

Wealth at death £3028 10s. 6d.: probate, 16 April 1925, CGPLA Eng. & Wales

Earle, William (1833–1885), army officer, third son of Sir Hardman Earle (1792–1877) of Allerton Tower, Woolton, Lancashire, a Liverpool merchant who was created a baronet in 1869, and his wife, Mary (d. 1850), daughter of William Langton of Kirkham, Lancashire, was born at Liverpool on 18 May 1833. Reportedly educated at Winchester, he was commissioned ensign in the 49th regiment on 17 October 1851, and promoted lieutenant on 6 June 1854. In 1854 he accompanied the 49th to the Crimea, where it formed part of Pennefather's brigade in the 2nd division under Sir De Lacy Evans. He served with the 49th throughout the war, and was at the battle of the Alma, the repulse of the Russian sortie on 26 October, the battle of Inkerman, and the attack on the Redan on 18 June 1855. He received the Mejidiye (fifth class). On 16 February 1855 he had been promoted captain, and at the end of the war in 1856 he exchanged into the Grenadier Guards as lieutenant and captain. On 28 April 1863 he was promoted captain and lieutenant-colonel, and on 21 July 1864 he married Mary, second daughter of General Sir William John *Codrington; she survived her husband.

Earle found no difficulty in getting plenty of staff employment, and was assistant military secretary to General Sir W. J. Codrington, governor of Gibraltar, from 1859 to 1860. He was brigade major in Nova Scotia in 1862 and 1863, and military secretary to General Sir C. H. Doyle, commanding in North America, from 1865 to 1872. On 20 May 1868 he was promoted colonel, and in 1872 he accompanied Lord Northbrook to India as a military secretary; he remained such until 1876, when he returned with Northbrook and was made a CSI (7 March 1876). In 1878 he became a major in the Grenadier Guards, and on 31 October 1880 was promoted major-general; he was at once appointed to command at Shorncliffe, from which he was transferred in 1881 to command the 2nd infantry brigade at Aldershot. In 1882 Earle was sent to Egypt, and commanded the Alexandria garrison and the base and lines of communication during Wolseley's Tell al-Kebir campaign. He was made a CB, and awarded by the khedive the Mejidiye (second class). He remained in command at Alexandria until the end of 1884.

In 1884, when appointments for the Gordon relief expedition were considered, Wolseley wanted the more experienced and better-known Buller as his subordinate commander, but was overruled by the duke of Cambridge who wanted Earle, who was senior to Buller. Wolseley liked Earle, an old friend, but believed that, though 'a very good officer', he was untried and would 'never rise to the position of commander' (Preston, 6–7), inspire troops, and get the best from them. However, during the campaign—though Evelyn Wood alleged Earle was fit only to be a sergeant-major—Wolseley wrote, on 11 December 1884, that Earle was 'the most businesslike & reliable man I have on the Line of Commns.—I wish he had been at its head instead of dear puzzle-headed Evelyn Wood' (ibid., 85).

After the army had concentrated at Korti, Wolseley dispatched the 'desert column' under Sir Herbert Stewart across the desert towards Khartoum, while he sent the 'river column' up the Nile under Earle, with Colonel Henry Brackenbury as chief of the staff. Earle's column was not expected to reach Khartoum until after Stewart's, and one of the principal reasons of its dispatch was to punish those who had murdered Colonel J. D. H. Stewart and Frank Power on their way from Khartoum in the previous year. This was accomplished, and the murderers' village burnt. A few days later Earle attacked a strong force of Mahdists at Kirbekan on 10 February 1885. The enemy position was carried successfully by a flanking movement and rear attack, suggested by Butler. After the main battle, the British were mopping up remaining Mahdists when Earle was shot through the head and died within minutes. He was initially buried near Kirbekan. Following news of the fall of Khartoum, Brackenbury, who succeeded Earle, brought back his column, and also brought back Earle's body, which was sent to England and buried at Allerton, Liverpool. A statue by C. B. Birch was erected at Liverpool. His old friend Sir William Butler wrote, 'Earle was a man of very fine character' (*Butler: an autobiography*, 301).

H. M. STEPHENS, *rev.* ROGER T. STEARN

Sources *The Times* (16 Feb 1885) • *Hart's Army List* • H. Brackenbury, *The River Column* (1885) • *Sir William Butler: an autobiography*, ed. E. Butler (1911) • *In relief of Gordon: Lord Wolseley's campaign journal of the Khartoum relief expedition, 1884–1885*, ed. A. Preston (1967) • J. Symons, *England's pride: the story of the Gordon relief expedition* (1965) • B. Bond, ed., *Victorian military campaigns* (1967) • *Dod's Peerage* (1878) • Boase, *Mod. Eng. biog.* • J. B. Wainewright, ed., *Winchester College, 1836–1906: a register* (1907) • Walford, *County families*
Likenesses C. B. Birch, bronze statue, *c.*1886, St George's Hall, Liverpool • engraving, repro. in *ILN* (21 Feb 1885), 200 • photograph, NPG • portrait (after a photograph by Mayall), NPG
Wealth at death £103,344 1s. 3d.: administration with will, 16 July 1885, *CGPLA Eng. & Wales*

Earle, William Benson (1740–1796), philanthropist, eldest son of Harry Benson Earle, was born at Shaftesbury, Dorset, in 1740, but spent his life at Salisbury. He was a descendant of William Benson (1682–1754). He was educated first at the school in the close at Salisbury Cathedral, then as a commoner at Winchester College, and then at Merton College, Oxford, from where he matriculated in 1758, and graduated BA in 1761 and MA in 1764. He made the grand tour of the continent (1765–7), and having returned published some minor descriptions of his travels in periodicals. On the death of his father in 1776 Earle succeeded to an ample fortune. In 1786 he published a new edition of Bishop John Earle's *Microcosmographie*, first published anonymously in 1628. He was an excellent musician, who actively promoted music in Salisbury and composed several glees as well as a Sanctus and a Kyrie, both of which were occasionally performed in Salisbury Cathedral into the nineteenth century. He died at his home in the close, Salisbury, on 21 March 1796 and was buried at the parish church of Newton Toney on 30 March alongside other family members. He bequeathed large sums to various learned and charitable institutions, especially those in Salisbury and other parts of the west country.

THOMPSON COOPER, *rev.* ELIZABETH BAIGENT

Sources *GM*, 1st ser., 66 (1796), 353–4 • Foster, *Alum. Oxon.* • *GM*, 1st ser., 65 (1795), 95 • R. Benson and H. Hatcher, *Old and New Sarum or Salisbury*, 2 vols. (1843)
Likenesses W. Evans, stipple (after W. Hoare), BM, NPG

Earley, John (II) of (*c.*1173–1229), administrator and follower of William (I) Marshal, was the son of William of Earley, a royal chamberlain, and Ascelina or Aziria, daughter of Ralph de l'Isle. The surname is derived from Earley Whiteknights, Berkshire, which was in the family's hands from the time of John (I) of Earley, John (II) of Earley's grandfather. William of Earley died soon after Christmas 1181 leaving his lands and heir in royal wardship. John (II) of Earley first appears in 1188 in a skirmish at Montmirail in Anjou as squire to William *Marshal, then a leading courtier. It is probable that John had been recently granted in wardship to the Marshal, and would have remained as such until he came of age. This occurred early in 1194, the year he first answered for the farm of the hundred of North Petherton, indicating a probable birth date *c.*1173. He married before 1195 a certain Sibyl, and had two sons, John (III) (*d.* 1231) and Henry (*d.* 1271); there was also a daughter, whose name is unknown, who was the mother of Henry de Brehull.

The relationship with the Marshal defined Earley's political life. He remained devoted to the older man's service after he had come into his substantial inheritance: several manors in Berkshire, together with other lands and the aforementioned hundred in Somerset. He appears frequently in the *Histoire de Guillaume le Maréchal*, the verse history of William Marshal's life, and the attestations of the Marshal's charters also indicate John's constant attendance on him. Earley comes into prominence in the *Histoire* during the Marshal's difficulties with King John over his Irish estates. He went to Leinster in early spring 1207 as a member of the Marshal's military household. When the Marshal was recalled to England in September 1207, he was left (reluctantly) as seneschal of Osraige (Ossory) and Uí Chennselaig, to defend the Marshal's embattled interests there against the justiciar, Meiler fitz Henry. In January 1208 Earley and his colleagues left in Ireland defied a royal order to return to England (at Earley's insistence); as a result Earley had his lands confiscated by the king's officers. The problem between the king and the Marshal was resolved in March 1208, when Earley's lands were returned. John probably remained with the Marshal in Ireland for most of the period of his exile there until 1212; he witnessed many of the Marshal's charters from this period. In 1210 Earley acted as one of two hostages for the Marshal's conduct and was held briefly in Nottingham Castle. In 1213, in the new atmosphere of good relations between his master and the king, he was named a royal marshal (probably an error in the *Histoire* for the royal chamberlainship John had been claiming since at least 1210) and given custody of William Marshal's elder sons, who had long been kept at court as security for their father. John was then dispatched to Ireland with instructions that the Marshal go to England to assist the king.

It would seem that John was thereafter constantly with his master during the events of the barons' war and the minority of Henry III. In 1216 he is said to have counselled the Marshal not to accept the keeping of England during the minority of Henry III because he was concerned for the Marshal's health. He had grants of wardship and other favours during the minority. He attended the Marshal in his death chamber at Caversham constantly from mid-March to mid-May 1219, except when sent in haste to Chepstow (where his son was acting as his deputy in the seneschalcy of Netherwent) to get the silk palls the Marshal required for his bier. After the Marshal's death John acted as one of the executors of his last testament. He is specifically named as one of the promoters of the verse history which commemorated the Marshal's life, although there is no evidence that he composed it, as has been asserted. The link between John and the Marshals continued under the younger William Marshal, second earl, until John's own death which occurred before May in 1229.　　　DAVID CROUCH

Sources E. H. Bates, *Cartularies of Muchelney and Athelney abbeys* (1899) • F. W. Weaver, ed., *Buckland cartulary* (1909) • H. Hall, ed., *The Red Book of the Exchequer*, 3 vols., Rolls Series, 99 (1896) • P. Meyer, ed., *L'histoire de Guillaume le Maréchal*, 3 vols. (Paris, 1891–1901) • *Curia regis rolls preserved in the Public Record Office* (1922–) • T. D. Hardy, ed., *Rotuli litterarum clausarum*, 2 vols., RC (1833–4) • D. Crouch, *William Marshal* (1990) • C. Roberts, ed., *Excerpta è rotulis finium in Turri Londinensi asservatis, Henrico Tertio rege, AD 1216–1272*, 1, RC, 32 (1835), 184

Earlom, Richard (1743–1822). *See under* Boydell, John, engravers (*act.* 1760–1804).

Early, Charles (1824–1912), blanket manufacturer, was born on 29 December 1824 at West End, Witney, Oxfordshire, the eighth child and youngest son in the family of four sons and five daughters of John Early (1783–1862), blanket maker, and his wife, Elizabeth (Betsy), *née* Waine (1782–1864). He was sent away to boarding-school in Oxford at a young age, before being apprenticed to his father to learn blanket weaving in 1839, the last apprentice bound with the Witney Company of Blanket Weavers. After finishing his apprenticeship he went to London to work for his uncle, Thomas Early, who had a clothing business. There he met, and in 1848 married, Sarah (1824–1906), daughter of John Vanner of Stamford Hill, Stoke Newington. John Vanner was one of the founders of the City Bank and the Star Life Insurance Company and was descended from Huguenot silk weavers in Spitalfields. They had two sons, who became partners in the family firm, and one daughter.

Shortly after his marriage Charles Early returned to Witney to take charge of the family business, John Early & Co., which was in difficulties, and in 1851 one of their patterned blankets won a bronze medal at the Great Exhibition. His father took him into partnership in 1851, the firm becoming John and Charles Early & Co., one of several blanket-manufacturing firms in Witney owned by members of the Early family. There had been weaving in Witney since before the Norman conquest, and a flourishing blanket-making industry had developed along the River Windrush, using wool from Cotswold sheep. The founder of the firm, Thomas Early (1655–1733), was the first master of the Blanket Company between 1711 and 1712. A cottage industry in the eighteenth century, blanket making was moving into mills by the early nineteenth century. The introduction of Kay's 'fly shuttle' in Witney in the early 1800s meant that only one weaver was needed to work the hand loom, and by 1838 John Early & Co. employed seventy weavers, working in two mills a mile apart.

Following John Early's death in 1862 the firm became Charles Early & Co. in 1864. Charles Early continued the firm's expansion and modernization, always keeping abreast of the latest innovations. He had already installed his first self-acting spinning mule at New Mill in 1853, and from 1860 onwards he introduced power looms at Witney Mill. He built a large new warehouse at Newland, where he lived and had his office, in 1881–2, and by the end of the century he owned three mills and had taken over Edward Early & Son, concentrating the blanket manufacturing at Witney Mill. He remained head of the firm until 1910, when it became a private limited company, with his elder son, Charles William Early, as chairman, and he continued to play a part in the business until early in 1911.

Charles Early was one of the blanket manufacturers who brought a successful legal action in 1908–9, limiting the description 'Witney blankets' to blankets made in Witney, so that rival blankets made in the West Riding of Yorkshire could no longer be called 'Witney' blankets. By then Witney blankets were famous: a Witney blanket was soft and loosely woven, containing mainly merino wool.

A Wesleyan Methodist, Early became a local preacher in 1848, and he preached on the Witney circuit for the rest of his life; he also held all the offices open to laymen in the Wesleyan church. He was a member of the first Wesleyan conference open to lay representatives, in 1878. A teetotaller and temperance reformer, he managed to turn the New Inn in Witney into a temperance hotel. Although a JP from 1890, Early did not take much part in public life in Witney, but he was one of the promoters and first directors of the Witney Railway Company, later taken over by the Great Western Railway Company.

Charles Early died on 17 May 1912 at his home, Newland House, Harcourt Street, Witney. He was buried at Witney cemetery on 21 May. A new organ for the Wesleyan church in Witney was donated by the family in his memory in 1919.　　　ANNE PIMLOTT BAKER

Sources A. Plummer and R. E. Early, *The blanket makers, 1669–1969: a history of Charles Early and Marriott (Witney) Ltd* (1969) • C. Gott and J. Gott, *The book of Witney*, rev. edn (1994) • *Witney Gazette* (18 May 1912) • *Witney Gazette* (25 May 1912) • *CGPLA Eng. & Wales* (1912)
Archives Oxon. RO, Oxfordshire Archives
Likenesses oils, after 1880, Oxfordshire County Museums • Hudson and Kearns, photograph, 1897, Oxfordshire Archives, County Hall, Oxford • photograph, 1909, Oxfordshire Archives, County Hall, Oxford • photograph, 1964, Oxfordshire Archives, County

Hall, Oxford; repro. in Gott and Gott, *Book of Witney*, 61 · photograph (with his sons), Oxfordshire Archives, County Hall, Oxford **Wealth at death** £80,668 0s. 8d.: probate, 19 June 1912, CGPLA Eng. & Wales

Earnshaw, Lawrence (1707?–1767), mechanic and clockmaker, was born at Mottram in Longendale, Cheshire, the son of a weaver, probably John Earnshaw (*b.* 1653?), who married Lidia Johnson in 1693. After a short training with his father and four years apprenticed to a brother as a tailor, he served a seven-year apprenticeship to Samuel Kinder, a woollen manufacturer of Hyde Green in Staley. Following this, he spent just one month with a Stockport clockmaker called Shepley (probably John Shepley), continuing as a clockmaker thereafter. He seems to have been talented with mechanisms of all kinds; he made musical instruments, sundials, and optical instruments, and he was a bell-founder and worker in various metals. Other intellectual activities included teaching music, and studying chemistry, metallurgy, and mathematics; he was also a gifted engraver, painter, and gilder. About 1753, fourteen years before Richard Arkwright, he invented a machine to spin and reel cotton in one operation, which he showed to some neighbours, but then decided to destroy on the grounds that its use might deprive the poor of employment. He was a friend of the great engineer James Brindley and during the construction of the Bridgewater Canal they often met for long discussions on technical and scientific matters. Earnshaw's greatest achievement was a series of complex astronomical clocks, designed and built by him over many years. He made about four of these, one of which was sold to Lord Bute for £150, and afterwards became the property of Lord Lonsdale. The mechanism of one passed into the care of the University of Exeter's science department, and another, complete with its elaborate mahogany case, was preserved at the Henry Ford Museum at Dearborn, Michigan, USA.

Despite his great local fame as a mechanic, Earnshaw's earnings were small, and he remained poor throughout his life. He was married to Mary Lees (1711–1755) on 22 January 1734 or 1735; they had five children—Lawrence, Joshua, John, Mary, and Lydia. His difficulties were increased by his wife's being bedridden for many years, and by his own disability in the latter part of his life. For most of his life he was teetotal. According to his contemporary J. Holt,

> Upon a first approach, his manner and general aspect were unmeaning; his countenance, far from exhibiting the marks of superiority, was rather that of a man possessed of weak intellects. It was curious enough to observe what a difference of feature was exhibited when he displayed his abilities in animated conversation. (Holt, 1165)

Earnshaw died on 12 May 1767, aged about sixty, and was buried in a common grave in Mottram. A hundred years later a monument was erected in his memory by public subscription in Mottram churchyard. Its inauguration was marked by a public procession on 10 April 1868.

JONATHAN BETTS

Sources J. Beckwith, letter, *GM*, 1st ser., 57 (1787), 665–6 · J. Holt, letter, *GM*, 1st ser., 57 (1787), 1165–7, 1200 · J. Butterworth, *History and description of the towns and parishes of Stockport, Ashton-under-Lyne,* *Mottram-Longendale and Glossop* (1827), 200–10 · J. J. Hall, *Horological Journal*, 74 (1932) · J. J. Hall, *Horological Journal*, 75 (1932–3) · J. J. Hall, *The Watch and Clockmaker*, 7/77 (1934) · W. Chadwick, 'Reminiscences of Mottram and its people', *Ashton Reporter* (16 March 1867); (25 March 1867); (11 April 1868) · M. Nevell, *People who made Tameside* (1994), 26–8, 114 · M. Duckworth, 'Lawrence Earnshaw: a remarkable clockmaker', *Journal of the British Astronomical Association*, 78 (1967–8), 22–7 · M. Duckworth, 'Lawrence Earnshaw: a remarkable clockmaker', *Journal of the British Astronomical Association*, 80 (1969–70), 40–45 · J. Aikin, *A description of the country from thirty to forty miles round Manchester* (1795), 466–8 · R. B. Rolinson, *Longendale: historical and descriptive sketches of the two parishes of Mottram and Glossop* (1863), 11–12 · J. P. Earwaker, *East Cheshire: past and present, or, A history of the hundred of Macclesfield*, 2 (1880), 124, 136–7, 149–50 · G. Ormerod, *The history of the county palatine and city of Chester*, 2nd edn, ed. T. Helsby, 3 (1882), 857, 872 · T. Middleton, *Annals of Hyde and district* (1899), 311–12 · parish register (marriage), Mottram in Longendale, Cheshire, 1734/5 · *Ashton Reporter* (23 May 1867)
Wealth at death £19 16s. 2d.: will and inventory, Ches. & Chester ALSS, WS 1767

Earnshaw, Thomas (1749–1829), maker of watches and chronometers, was born on 4 February 1749 at Ashton under Lyne, Lancashire. At the age of fourteen he was apprenticed to the watchmaker William Hughes of 119 High Holborn in London and on 27 March 1769, one year before his apprenticeship ended and falsely claiming to be over twenty-one years, he married Lydia Theakston (*d.* 1801) at St James's Church, Piccadilly. Lydia and Thomas had four children: Manasseh William (*bap.* 1770), James (*bap.* 1771), Thomas (*bap.* 1774), and Elizabeth Ann (*b.* 1781).

Once out of his apprenticeship Earnshaw worked for the trade and quickly gained a reputation as a first-rate workman, although he made little money. By 1774 the family had moved from Clerkenwell, where they lived at Portpool Lane and then Saffron Street, to Battle Bridge, St Pancras. In order to escape his creditors, Earnshaw was obliged to abscond from there to Dublin, where he probably worked for the watchmaker John Crosthwaite. In December he returned, was admitted to the Fleet debtors' prison and in the following months was enabled to reach solvency again.

In the next few years Earnshaw learned the specialist trades of escapement making and watch jewelling and in 1780 turned his attention to improving marine timekeepers. After John Harrison's pioneering work in this field, the London watchmaker John Arnold had been virtually alone during the 1770s in simplifying and perfecting Harrison's very complex designs. Now Earnshaw arrived on the scene and, almost at a stroke, finalized the form of escapement (the 'spring detent') and the form of compensation balance which were to be used in the standard marine chronometer thereafter. Unfortunately he showed his new design of escapement to Arnold's friends, whereupon Arnold patented a variation of the idea as his own in 1782 and used it from then on.

Earnshaw patented his original invention through a sponsor, the watchmaker Thomas Wright, in 1783 and only allowed other watchmakers to use his design if they paid a fee of 1 guinea and stamped the watch 'Wright's Patent'. In later years, in his 1808 *Longitude, an Appeal to the*

Public, Earnshaw himself admitted he was 'naturally of an irritable habit'; after Arnold's deception he seems to have become paranoid about the intentions of his horological peers. Over the next twenty-five years his bitterness caused almost the whole trade to turn against him. His outspoken condemnation of people he disliked and his naïve and blunt manner prevented any question of social advancement and his eventual business success came about despite his demeanour rather than because of it.

On 1 July 1789 Earnshaw was introduced to Nevil Maskelyne, astronomer royal at Greenwich, who tested an Earnshaw chronometer for six weeks and encouraged Earnshaw to continue making them. So impressed was Maskelyne with his work that, over the next few years, Earnshaw received orders to repair clocks at the observatory and was commissioned to make a regulator for the new observatory at Armagh in Ireland. The watchmaker Earnshaw demurred (in his *Longitude* he put it that he 'never had made a clock, and did not know how many wheels were in one') but he produced one of the finest regulators ever to have been created. It is still at the observatory at Armagh. Earnshaw's master, William Hughes, who had married Earnshaw's sister Mary in 1785, died in November 1792 and Earnshaw succeeded to the business at 119 High Holborn, although his home, by this time, was in Belmont Row in Kennington. Once Earnshaw had his own retail premises he signed his work with his own name, selling high-quality clocks, watches, and chronometers, and with an increasing demand for relatively inexpensive marine chronometers his business at last began to prosper.

Unlike Arnold, who continued to modify his designs, Earnshaw formulated a standard plan for the mechanism of his marine and pocket chronometers which he adhered to for virtually the whole of his career, and it was almost certainly he who established the supply of batches of standard rough movements for marine chronometers from Lancashire. These were then made up by specialist self-employed workmen on behalf of finishers and retailers like Earnshaw, for sale in the London trade, as had been the custom in watchmaking for many years. Earnshaw's accounts, preserved in the archives of Hoare's Bank in London, contain many references to his payments to workmen of all kinds for their contributions to his chronometer manufacturing business. By 1798 Earnshaw was sufficiently prosperous to have his portrait painted by Martin Archer-Shee and this was exhibited at the Royal Academy that year. In 1801 Lydia Earnshaw died and he moved from Belmont Row to a large villa, Greenford Hall, Greenford, Middlesex, which was his principal residence for the rest of his life.

From the beginning of the 1790s Earnshaw was in regular contact with the board of longitude, sending timekeepers for trial at the observatory. He often petitioned the board for prize money, usually with his characteristic candour and occasionally with quite startling impertinence. After several years of tests and deliberations, during which time he was given £200 for two of his trial chronometers and an award of £500, the board finally decided, on 6 December 1804, to award him a prize of £3000 on condition that he disclose the nature of his invention to its satisfaction.

The vexed question of priority of invention between Earnshaw and John Arnold (especially that of the spring detent escapement) had been investigated; unfortunately this had come to no firm conclusions, but the subject of recognition for Arnold (who had died in 1799) and an award for his son John Roger had thus arisen, and it was agreed that the younger Arnold be given the same award as Earnshaw, on the same conditions, a decision which infuriated the latter. At this point board member Sir Joseph Banks (president of the Royal Society) assumed the position of implacable opponent to Earnshaw and, with his fellow Arnold-supporter Alexander Dalrymple (hydrographer to the Royal Navy), did all he could to prevent Earnshaw's reward, causing dissension within the board. In March 1804 Banks had published his *Protest Against a Vote … Granting to Mr Earnshaw a Reward*, prompting Nevil Maskelyne to publish *Arguments for Giving a Reward to Mr Earnshaw*. It was proposed by the board that models of the two escapements be provided and that descriptions and drawings be printed and circulated among other notable watchmakers for comment. After having to pulp the first edition in April 1805, owing to vitriolic remarks in Earnshaw's description, the new, expurgated edition was circulated among Earnshaw's peers with predictable results. Almost no one was prepared to support him and some comments were more personal than professional. Nevertheless, the final edition, entitled *Explanations of Timekeepers Constructed by Mr John Arnold and Mr Thomas Earnshaw* was published in March 1806 and both parties received their awards, minus moneys already granted. Dissatisfied with his lot, Earnshaw published a broadsheet and put a similar notice, stating his case, in the *Morning Chronicle* (4 February 1806) and *The Times* (13 February 1806), prompting Dalrymple to publish his *Longitude, a Full Answer*, bitterly denying Earnshaw's allegations.

Earnshaw's notices were deemed by Banks to be personally libellous and he demanded the board sue on his behalf. When this was tactfully refused he announced he would prosecute privately, but appears to have dropped the case soon after. Earnshaw informed the board that he intended to petition parliament for further reward and in 1808, when his petition was due to be considered, he published *Longitude, an Appeal to the Public*, telling the whole story and forming what is virtually a small autobiography. His petition was unsuccessful, as was another in the following year, after which he appears to have reluctantly accepted the situation. About 1815 he seems to have retired from running the business, handing over to his son Thomas, who continued in business at 119 High Holborn until 1854. On 11 March 1820 Earnshaw married Rachel Walton at St George's, Bloomsbury. Although Earnshaw maintained Greenford Hall until his death, he also leased a house in Chenies Street, Bedford Square, London, which is where he died, aged eighty, on 1 March 1829. He was buried at St Giles-in-the-Fields, Bloomsbury, on 8 March.   JONATHAN BETTS

Sources T. Earnshaw, *Longitude, an appeal to the public* (1808) • R. T. Gould, *The marine chronometer: its history and development* (1923) • J. Banks, *Protest against a vote of the board of longitude granting to Mr Earnshaw a reward* (1804) • N. Maskelyne, *Arguments for giving a reward to Mr Earnshaw* (1804) • A. Dalrymple, *Longitude, a full answer* (1806) • V. Mercer, *John Arnold & Son, chronometer makers, 1762–1843* (1972) • ledgers, Hoare's Bank, London • *GM*, 1st ser., 99/1 (1829), 283 • parish register (burials), 8/3/1829, St Giles-in-the-Fields, London

Archives CUL, RGO Board of Longitude MSS • Hoare's Bank, London, business and personal bank accounts

Likenesses M. A. Shee, oils, 1798, Sci. Mus. • M. A. Shee, oils, *c.*1810, NMM • oils, 1861 (after M. A. Shee, 1798), Sci. Mus. • S. Bellin, engraving (after M. A. Shee, 1798)

Wealth at death £14,000: PRO, death duty registers, IR 26/1193

Earp, Thomas (1830–1910), maltster and politician, was born on 7 May 1830 at Muskham Grange, Muskham, near Newark-on-Trent, Nottinghamshire, the only son of William Earp, gardener at Muskham Grange, and his wife, Sarah, daughter of James Taylor. Shortly after Thomas's birth, the family moved to Osmaston Hall, near Derby. Thomas Earp was educated at the village school, where his many talents were soon evident. By the age of ten, he led the choir at Osmaston church and was a proficient violinist. Through the patronage of the vicar, he progressed to the Traffic Street School, Derby, and thence to Derby Diocesan (later Grammar) School. However, the opportunity to train for clerical orders was refused.

At the age of sixteen Earp began his career as junior clerk with the Newark wine and spirits merchant and maltster, George Harvey. Within two years, he had replaced the firm's Manchester malt agent and was soon managing the rapidly expanding malting business. In conjunction with Joseph Richardson and W. Slater, he also leased the town's Trent Brewery and in 1862–80 was a partner in the brewing enterprise, Richardson, Earp, and Slater. In 1872 he became a partner in Harvey and Earp. When George Harvey died eight years later, the firm was amalgamated with the neighbouring business of William Gilstrap to form the most prestigious malting enterprise in Britain. Earp relinquished his brewing interests, and remained as managing partner of Gilstrap, Earp & Co. until his retirement in 1905.

Earp was a man of tremendous energy, whose ambitions were equally realized in politics and civic life. Indeed, there are few more representative examples of a self-made Victorian businessman and politician. A staunch Liberal, he was a town councillor from 1864 until his death forty-six years later, alderman from 1889 until 1910, and mayor in 1869 and 1891–2. He was also a member of Nottinghamshire's county council on its formation in 1889. First returned as MP for Newark in 1874, he represented the town for eleven years. In the Commons he worked and voted with the extreme radicals, counting Joseph Chamberlain, Sir Charles Dilke, and the famous temperance reformer, Sir Wilfred Lawson, among his closest political allies. When in 1885 Newark lost its separate representation, despite requests to stand for Peckham, Canterbury and Grantham, Earp opted to fight the Newark division, but was soundly beaten.

According to his obituarist, no man influenced the course of events in Newark during this period more than Earp. An 'advocate and initiator of new forces' (*Newark Advertiser*, 23 Feb 1910), he was a relentless, if controversial, reformer. He resigned from the county council after failing to establish the county asylum at Newark and, a proponent of a national system of free education and opposed to sectarianism, he took his reforming zeal to the newly created school board. He was also instrumental in the town's purchase and modernization of the local waterworks, erection of the new workhouse, and acquisition of the market tolls from the duke of Newcastle. His interests were widespread: a JP, commissioner of the River Trent Navigation, and secretary of the Newark Agricultural Society, he served on the museum, library, and infirmary and workhouse committees. He was vice-president of the Newark School of Science and Art and, as chairman of the governors, donated £10,000 towards modernizing the historic Magnus School.

Earp married Martha (*d.* 1888), daughter of Thomas Weightman of Langford, in 1855. There were no children. He was survived by his second wife, Mary Rowland Wade, the daughter of Charles Wade of Skegsby, Nottinghamshire, and their son, Thomas. Following a severe attack of bronchitis, Earp died on 17 February 1910, at his home, White House, Millgate, Newark-on-Trent, and was buried at Newark cemetery on 22 February.

CHRISTINE CLARK

Sources *Newark Advertiser* (23 Feb 1910) • WWBMP • partnership deeds, Notts. Arch., DDH 154/318, 178/27 • P. Stephens, *Newark: the magic of malt* (1993)

Likenesses W. H. Cubley, oils, 1879, priv. coll. • H. Knight, oils, 1903, Newark council chamber • Robinson, photograph, repro. in *Newark Advertiser*

Wealth at death £69,214 16s. 4d.: resworn probate, 2 May 1910, CGPLA Eng. & Wales

Earwaker, John Parsons (1847–1895), antiquary, son of John Earwaker, a Manchester merchant, and Louisa, his wife, was born at Cheetham Hill, Manchester, on 22 April 1847. Educated first at a private school at Alderley Edge, Cheshire, he afterwards went to a school in Germany, and subsequently studied at Owens College, Manchester, where he took prizes in natural science. From there he went to Pembroke College, Cambridge, but then obtained a postmastership at Merton College, Oxford; he matriculated there in November 1868, graduated BA in 1872, and proceeded MA in 1876. He originally intended to read for the bar and in 1869 entered at the Middle Temple but was never called. He remained at Oxford until 1874 and his early studies were in the direction of zoology and geology; but he soon became more interested in historical and antiquarian studies. He was elected honorary secretary of the Oxford Archaeological Society, and acted as deputy keeper of the Ashmolean Museum in 1873–4. In January 1873 he was elected FSA. On 1 June 1875 he married Juliet, daughter of John Bergman of Bruton, Somerset. They had three sons and three daughters. After their marriage the couple lived at Withington, near Manchester, but in 1881 moved to Osborne House, Pen-sarn, near Abergele, Denbighshire. Earwaker served as chairman of the Abergele

John Parsons Earwaker (1847–1895), by unknown photographer

local board and was an active member of the local community.

Earwaker was a professional freelance antiquarian and historian who was 'largely employed by public and private bodies in the investigation of their muniments'. In April 1875 he began the publication in the *Manchester Courier* of a series of 'Local gleanings relating to Lancashire and Cheshire', which was continued until January 1878. There followed a succession of important works. His *East Cheshire, Past and Present, or, A History of the Hundred of Macclesfield*, published in two volumes in 1877 and 1881, shows the author's grasp and lucid arrangement of facts, and his thoroughness in proving every statement by reference to original authorities. In 1882 Manchester corporation engaged Earwaker as editor for the *Court Leet Records of the Manor of Manchester*, ranging from 1552 to 1846. The records were published, with full annotation, in twelve volumes between 1884 and 1890, and were supplemented by *The Constables' Accounts of the Manor of Manchester, from 1612 to 1647 and from 1743 to 1776*, published in 1891–2.

Earwaker was unusual among his contemporaries in having a special interest in municipal, parochial, and other administrative records, rather than those mainly concerned with genealogy, manorial descents, and topography, and his work on the town history of the northwest is perhaps his most important legacy. He also indexed the Cheshire and Lancashire probate records held at Chester for 1545–1760. The indexes, published by the Record Society of Lancashire and Cheshire, have not yet been superseded for Lancashire.

Earwaker was a founder and honorary secretary of the Record Society of Lancashire and Cheshire, and a member of the councils of the Chetham Society, the Historic Society of Lancashire and Cheshire, the Chester Archaeological Society, and the Lancashire and Cheshire Antiquarian Society. He contributed numerous articles to the journals of these societies. He died on 29 January 1895 at Osborne House and was buried in the old churchyard of Abergele. He was survived by his wife. His large library of printed books and manuscripts, including a vast number of transcripts of original documents, was divided after his death. The Cheshire portion was purchased by the duke of Westminster, and presented by him to the Chester Museum; it is now owned by the Chester Archaeological Society. The Lancashire portion was acquired by William Farrer of Marton, near Skipton.

C. W. SUTTON, *rev.* ALAN G. CROSBY

Sources *Journal of the Architectural, Archaeological, and Historic Society for the County and City of Chester and North Wales*, new ser., 5 (1895), 317 · *Transactions of the Historic Society of Lancashire and Cheshire*, 47 (1895), 259 · *Manchester Guardian* (31 Jan 1895) · Foster, *Alum. Oxon.* · catalogue of Earwaker MSS, Chester Archaeological Society · *CGPLA Eng. & Wales* (1895)

Archives Ches. & Chester ALSS, antiquarian collections, corresp., etc. · Ches. & Chester ALSS, corresp. and papers relating to Leigh family papers · Derby Local Studies Library, items relating to Derbyshire from Constable's accounts of the manor of Manchester · JRL, corresp. and papers relating to Bromley Davenport muniments · JRL, index to High Legh deeds · Man. CL, Manchester Archives and Local Studies, corresp.; notes and papers · NL Scot., corresp. and papers relating to the *Black Prince's sword* · NL Wales, notes and papers | Ches. & Chester ALSS, Farrer MSS · Man. CL, Manchester Archives and Local Studies, letters to R. D. Radcliffe

Likenesses photograph, repro. in *Transactions of the Lancashire and Cheshire Antiquarian Society*, 13 (1895), 143 [*see illus.*]

Wealth at death £1381 16s. 0d.: administration, 15 March 1895, *CGPLA Eng. & Wales*

Easdall, William (*d.* 1643), civil lawyer, was born of unknown parents in Westminster. He was educated at Trinity Hall, Cambridge, and started his working career acting as an attorney collecting rents for Westminster Abbey, although there is no record of his appointment. Leases reveal that Easdall acted as an attorney for Richard Neile in Rochester diocese in 1610, in which year he also performed the duties of a personal secretary and carried out a survey of the diocese of Coventry and Lichfield for Neile, prior to the latter's becoming bishop of that see. It was after Neile's move to Lincoln in 1614, the year that Easdall graduated LLB from Cambridge, that Easdall's career really blossomed. In June 1616 he was appointed commissary to the bishop for the archdeaconries of Lincoln and Stow and official of the archdeacon of Buckingham (who happened to be Neile's half-brother, Robert Newell). Easdall remained on close terms with Neile, but 1617 witnessed a parting of their ways as Neile moved to Durham. In 1620 Easdall proceeded LLD, and in 1623 submitted a request to join Doctors' Commons, although he does not appear to have started paying dues until 1624.

From that date Easdall occupied various prominent positions in the northern province. It may have been in recognition of a shift of interests that he surrendered the office of porter of Westminster Abbey close. From 1624 to 1632 he occupied, through the patronage of Archbishop Toby Matthew, the important post of commissary of the exchequer and prerogative court of York. He also shared the chancellorship of York—with Matthew Dodsworth (1624–7), Edward Mainwaring (1627–37), and George Riddell (1637–40). It is perhaps ironic that Easdall was appointed, additionally, chancellor of the diocese of Durham in 1627 just as Neile was leaving for Winchester, but they were reunited when he retired from that post to devote all his efforts to York in 1632 on Neile's appointment as archbishop. By this date Easdall had also become a commissioner for causes ecclesiastical in the province of York.

Easdall served as a justice of the peace for Yorkshire between 1629 and 1632. Once described as a 'typical Caroline bureaucrat of the school of Wentworth and of "Thorough"' (Marchant, *Church under the Law*, 48), Easdall was much more than that. As a loyal friend of Richard Neile—acting as godfather to the latter's grandchildren—Easdall deserves great credit for the success of the campaigns which were initiated throughout the province of York in the 1630s. It was he who masterminded the metropolitical visitation of 1632–3; he personally ensured that it was one of the most successful in living memory, both in its effect on the lives of clergy and laity and in its production of revenue for the archbishop, and that the campaign to restore churches initiated at that visitation was sustained throughout the province through the work of the chancery court to which his roving inspectors reported. Easdall's reports to Neile serve as key evidence of diocesan administration in the 1630s and indicate that Easdall was as committed as his episcopal master to the programme to promote the 'beauty of holiness'. Easdall died in York in December 1643 and was buried on 16 December in York Minster. An administration of his goods was entered on 22 February 1644 and finalized on 2 May. He left everything, apart from an earlier gift of £20 for Peterhouse Chapel, to his daughter Barbara, his wife, whose name is unknown, having apparently died.   ANDREW FOSTER

Sources R. Marchant, *The puritans and the church courts in the diocese of York, 1560–1642* (1960) · R. A. Marchant, *The church under the law: justice, administration and discipline in the diocese of York, 1560–1640* (1969) · B. P. Levack, *The civil lawyers in England, 1603–1641* (1973) · Venn, *Alum. Cant.* · Borth. Inst., R VII PR 108, administrations fol. 260 · A. Foster, 'The function of a bishop: the career of Richard Neile, 1562–1640', *Continuity and change: personnel and administration of the Church of England, 1500–1642*, ed. R. O'Day and F. Heal (1976), 33–54 · A. W. Foster, 'A biography of Archbishop Richard Neile (1562–1640)', DPhil diss., U. Oxf., 1978 · A. Foster, 'Church policies of the 1630s', *Conflict in early Stuart England*, ed. R. Cust and A. Hughes (1989), 193–223 · K. Fincham, *Prelate as pastor: the episcopate of James I* (1990) · Rochester diocesan records · Lichfield and Coventry diocesan records · Lincoln diocesan records · Durham diocesan records · York diocesan records · Westminster Abbey records · G. D. Squibb, *Doctors' Commons: a history of the College of Advocates and Doctors of Law* (1977)

Easmon, McCormack Charles Farrell (1890–1972), medical practitioner in Sierra Leone, was born in Accra, on the Gold Coast, on 11 April 1890. His was a distinguished Sierra Leone Krio (Creole) family descended from one of the original Nova Scotian settlers and also from an Irishman,

John McCormack, a pioneer in the export timber trade, long resident in Freetown, after whom Easmon was named. His father, John Farrell Easmon (1856–1900), qualified as a doctor in 1879, did important original research into blackwater fever, and from 1893 to 1897 was chief medical officer in the Gold Coast. His mother, Annette Kathleen, *née* Smith (1870–1951), also belonged to a prominent Freetown family: five of her siblings either were or married Krio doctors.

When his father died in 1900 Easmon was brought by his mother to Freetown and then to London, where she settled with her sister Mrs Casely-Hayford. He was educated at Colet Court School, London (1901–3), and Epsom College (1903–7), where he won two scholarships to St Mary's Hospital, London. He qualified BS in 1911, and in 1912 (by which time he was resident medical officer at Huntingdon County Hospital) MB, MRCS, and LRCP.

Easmon applied for a post in the West African Medical Service (WAMS) but was turned down; the service, founded in 1902, excluded anyone of African or Indian descent. Instead he was offered employment in Sierra Leone in a separate service, as a 'native medical officer' on a lower salary scale and junior in rank to any member of the WAMS. Having raised this discriminatory provision in parliament to no avail, he accepted, and—despite his future efforts to have the regulations altered, and his taking an MD (the first African to do so) in 1925—he retained the status that put him under the orders of the most junior white doctor until he retired. Similarly with the outbreak of war in 1914 he was excluded from commissioned rank, which was reserved for those 'of pure European parentage'. He was, however (presumably to avoid the public outcry that refusing him a commission would have caused in Freetown), sent unobtrusively on duty to the Cameroons with the ungazetted rank of temporary lieutenant, and served in the campaign there (1914–15), making him almost the only African to have served as a British officer in the First World War.

Easmon was chiefly stationed in Freetown until 1934, when as a result of his again protesting against WAMS regulations he was deliberately posted to the protectorate, where he completed his service, serving in every station. Here and in Freetown his skills (particularly as an obstetrician) and his courteous, considerate manner gained MCF, as he was generally known, affection and respect. He became interested in the local cultures, especially in the weaving of cotton 'country cloths', and arranged a substantial display of them for the British Empire Exhibition of 1924, writing a comprehensive brochure to accompany it. In 1945 he reached the service age limit and retired, but continued to work as a temporary medical officer. In 1954 he was awarded an OBE.

When Sierra Leone became independent in 1961 the first prime minister was Sir Milton Margai, a former medical colleague whom Easmon had protected against discrimination in his early years. Margai rewarded his integrity and ability with various government appointments, notably as first director of the Sierra Leone National Bank. But his chief interest now was in his country's history. He was first chairman of the monuments and relics commission, and contributed useful articles to the locally published *Sierra Leone Studies*, including an important contribution on Sierra Leone doctors. Above all he was largely responsible for founding the Sierra Leone National Museum, an imaginatively arranged small museum accessibly sited in the heart of Freetown, which in its heyday was said to attract more daily visitors than any museum in the world.

Easmon married Enid Winifred Shorunkeh-Sawyerr (d. 1999), of another leading Krio family; their son Professor Charles Easmon continued the family medical tradition with a distinguished medical career in London. In 1969, on a visit to England, Easmon fell ill, and remained an invalid for the rest of his life, which was passed in Croydon, where his wife was living; on 2 May 1972, at their home—10 Beech House Road—he suffered a stroke, and died. He was buried in Bawdon Hill cemetery, Croydon.

CHRISTOPHER FYFE

Sources *The encyclopaedia Africana dictionary of national biography*, vol. 2 (Sierra Leone, Zaire, 1979) · PRO, CO 267/550, 551, 646 · M. C. F. Easmon, *Sierra Leone country cloths* (1924) · M. C. F. Easmon, 'Sierra Leone doctors', *Sierra Leone Studies*, new ser., 6 (1956), 81–96 · A. M. Cromwell, *The life and times of Adelaide Smith Casely Hayford* (1986) · private information (2004) [family]
Likenesses photograph, repro. in *Encyclopaedia Africana*, 62
Wealth at death £4025: probate, 1972, *CGPLA Eng. & Wales*

Eason, Ursula Vernon (1910–1993), broadcaster and broadcasting executive, was born on 19 August 1910 in Streatham, London, the fifth of six children of Edward Eason, auctioneer and surveyor, and his wife, Aisling (Nancy), *née* Bruton (d. 1967), from a well-known Gloucester family of auctioneers. She was educated at Mount Nod School, Streatham, and University College, London, where she took a good degree in English. After a secretarial course she worked for nine months at the Times Book Club as secretary to the assistant manager.

Eason had always loved the theatre and enjoyed acting, so she applied to the BBC, where she was interviewed by John Reith. In an interview report she was described as 'a practical, sensible, nice-looking 23-year-old' (*The Independent*, 15 Jan 1994) and she was offered a post in 1934 as children's hour organizer in Belfast, where she stayed for eighteen years. There she became a producer and head of the children's hour unit. She took part in the programmes as Auntie Phoebe and was also responsible for all gramophone transmissions from Belfast. In spite of her attempts to return to London she remained based in Belfast, and when many male staff left for war service she was made acting programme director, planning and producing all the output from BBC Northern Ireland. After the war she had become so indispensable that it was not until 1952 that she was transferred to London and the growing television service.

Eason was attached first to television talks, then to the film unit, and in 1953 to children's programmes. In 1955 she became assistant head of the department and stayed in the same post until she retired in 1970. Her knowledge of the BBC and her dedication to public service made her invaluable to the producers and to the four heads under whom she served: Freda Lingstrom, Owen Reed, Doreen Stephens, and Monica Sims. A more selfish or ambitious person might have resented the people who were promoted over her head but she supported them all loyally. Her wisdom was greatly appreciated and was influential in maintaining the high standards that she felt children deserved. She loved and respected the audience and encouraged young producers to recognize their responsibility to respond to the individual needs of children at different stages of development.

Eason had some hearing difficulties herself and was particularly concerned for deaf children. In 1953 she created a monthly programme, *For Deaf Children*, with the co-operation of the Royal National Institute for the Deaf (RNID). In 1964, with the imaginative contribution of the producer Patrick Dowling, she introduced the weekly series *Vision On*. This was directed to the whole audience, not solely to deaf children, and was one of the first truly visual programmes, not depending on words for comprehension. Original cartoons, mime, dance, drama, drawing, and painting drew on all the techniques available at the time. The programme won the top prize for the best children's programme at the Prix Jeunesse. The presenter was Pat Keysell, who used sign language and later was a founder of the British Theatre of the Deaf. Some teachers objected to signing, but with the support of the RNID and the National Deaf Children's Society it later became familiar to audiences in many theatres. *Vision On* invited children to send in their art work, stimulated by the creations of the artist Tony Hart, who displayed selections each week from the thousands entered. The shoestring budget for the programme led to many experimental forms of animation, including the plasticene man, Morph, who was the forerunner of Wallace and Gromit of the Aardmann Studios in Bristol.

Humour was essential in a department steeped in different theories of child psychology and arguments between idealistic producers. It was Eason's throaty chuckle that could produce a calmer sense of proportion. Her well-founded good taste and experience informed her judgement of programmes and of people. Thus she dismissed the saccharine sweetness of a French puppet series but recognized its potential value, if given an astringent sound track. *The Magic Roundabout*, with commentary by Eric Thompson, subsequently became one of the series best loved by both adults and children, and a cult on building sites and in university common rooms. In purchasing American series she rejected violence and bad language or any assumptions in which villains were shown as black people or foreigners.

Eason's tall, handsome appearance and modestly diffident manner could camouflage her keen intellect and firm moral outlook; her retirement robbed the BBC of a distinguished public servant. In private life she enjoyed family gatherings at her beautiful Georgian house on Kew Green, travelling in India and the Middle East, and working for charities and deaf people. She died in Kew on

Christmas day 1993, a few years after the onset of Alzheimer's disease, and was cremated at Mortlake. She never married. MONICA SIMS

Sources *The Independent* (15 Jan 1994) · personal knowledge (2004) · private information (2004) [Ann Comper, niece] · *CGPLA Eng. & Wales* (1994)
Likenesses photograph, repro. in *The Independent*
Wealth at death £156,976: probate, 14 March 1994, *CGPLA Eng. & Wales*

East, Sir Alfred Edward (1844–1913), landscape painter, was born at Kettering, Northamptonshire, on 15 December 1844, the youngest son of Benjamin East, a boot and shoe manufacturer, and his wife, Elizabeth Wright. He was educated at Kettering grammar school. At the time of his marriage on 16 September 1874 to Sarah Annie Heath (b. 1849/50), the daughter of an inspector of works at High Wycombe, Buckinghamshire, East was working as a commercial traveller; however, by the following year he had enrolled in the Government School of Art in Glasgow. By 1880 East was studying at the École des Beaux-Arts and at the atelier Julian in Paris, working at Barbizon and along the Seine valley during his summer vacations. It was on these expeditions that East established his affection for landscape painting and his earliest work betrays the influence of French *plein-air* painting. He exhibited for the first time at the Royal Academy in 1883, a French landscape entitled *A Dewy Morning*. He returned briefly to Glasgow about 1883 before settling in London. By 1886 East was showing classic English landscapes such as *By Tranquil Waters* and had established a regular exhibiting pattern which was maintained for the rest of his life. During the late eighties and nineties he worked successively in Cornwall, Worcestershire, Suffolk, and the Wye valley. While his large landscapes were popular at the academy it was a cityscape entitled *The New Neighbourhood* (watercolour, 1887; oil version, 1905; priv. coll.) that drew East to the attention of French critics when it was awarded a gold medal at the Universal Exhibition in Paris in 1889. This dramatic depiction of the construction of new villas at Hampstead struck a chord with other artists and writers who were also recording the incursion of the city into the countryside at this period.

However, by the time this success was achieved, East's life had changed dramatically as a result of a commission from the Fine Art Society to visit Japan and paint scenes of Japanese life. While he later recognized that he had painted Japan 'from the European point of view' (East, 'On sketching from nature', 98) his pictures of landscapes, gardens, and village life around Tokyo and Kyoto charmed British critics. Pictures such as *Dawn on the Sacred Mountain* (1889; Fine Art Society, London), for all their obvious echoes of Hokusai, typify the Westerners' approach to the Japanese landscape. Although East followed this expedition with regular trips to France, Spain, and Italy, on which he executed majestic views often recalling the work of Claude and Richard Wilson, it was widely recognized by contemporary commentators that East was 'born to paint' the English landscape (Wedmore, 141). His poetic sense of the countryside is best expressed in *A Haunt of*

Ancient Peace (1897; Hungarian National Gallery, Budapest), a picture that draws its title from Tennyson, and which depicts an English traveller returning to an abandoned manor house at twilight. At a time of distant imperial adventures, East envisioned an essential England.

During the early years of the twentieth century East acquired a reputation as a teacher and published widely his views on landscape painting and the methods by which those working in oil and watercolour should record nature. His books, *The Art of Landscape Painting in Oil Colour* and *Brush and Pencil Notes in Landscape*, were published in 1906 and 1914 respectively. East became president of the Royal Society of British Artists in 1906. Knighted in 1910, he was elected Royal Academician in the year of his death by which time he had established the Alfred East Gallery in his home town of Kettering. He died on 28 September 1913 at 67 Belsize Park, Hampstead, and was survived by his wife.

TANCRED BORENIUS, rev. KENNETH McCONKEY

Sources A. East, *The art of landscape painting in oil colour* (1906) · A. East, *Brush and pencil notes in landscape* (1914) · A. East, 'The art and practise of monotyping in colour', *Representative art of our time*, ed. C. Holme (1903), 51–4 · A. East, 'On sketching from nature: a few words to students', *The Studio*, 37 (1906), 97–103 · A. East, 'The art of the painter-etcher: etching from nature', *The Studio*, 40 (1907), 278–85 · A. East, 'Introduction', *Sketching grounds: a special number of The Studio*, ed. C. Holme (1909), 1–3 · A. East, 'Tintern and the Wye as a sketching ground', *The Studio*, 50 (1910), 141–7 · A. East, *A British artist in Meiji Japan*, ed. H. Cortazzi (1991) · W. Armstrong, 'Alfred East', *Magazine of Art*, 18 (1894–5), 81–8 · F. Wedmore, 'The work of Alfred East, RI', *The Studio*, 7 (1896), 133–42 · 'Modern British etchers: Alfred East', *Magazine of Art*, 28 (1903–4), 381–4 · F. Newbolt, 'The etchings of Alfred East', *The Studio*, 34 (1905), 124–37 · C. Marriott, 'The watercolours of Sir Alfred East', *The Studio*, 56 (1912), 259–68 · E. Gosse, 'Prefatory note', *Memorial exhibition of the work of the late Sir Alfred East* (1914) [exhibition catalogue, Leicester Galleries, London, Feb 1914] · M. Currie, *Sir Alfred East: the forgotten genius* (1978) [exhibition catalogue, Roy Miles Fine Paintings, London, 24 Oct – 24 Nov 1978] · P. Skipwith, 'An enlightened artist in Japan', *Country Life*, 175 (1984), 24–5 · K. McConkey, *Haunts of ancient peace: landscapes by Sir Alfred East* (privately printed, Kettering, 1988) [exhibition catalogue, Alfred East Memorial Gallery, Kettering, 30 July–10 Aug 1988] · b. cert. · m. cert. · d. cert. · *CGPLA Eng. & Wales* (1913)
Archives Richmond Local Studies Library, London, letters to Douglas Sladen
Likenesses B. Stone, photograph, 1899, Birm. CL · A. East, self-portrait, oils, c.1910, Alfred East Memorial Gallery, Kettering · A. East, self-portrait, oils, 1912, Uffizi Gallery, Florence · G. Beresford, photographs, NPG · F. Brangwyn, oils, NPG · Elliott & Fry, photographs, NPG · P. A. de Laszlo, portrait
Wealth at death £14,416 5s. 11d.: probate, 24 Dec 1913, *CGPLA Eng. & Wales*

East, Sir Cecil James (1837–1908), army officer, born at Herne Hill, Surrey, on 10 July 1837, was the son of Charles James East, merchant, of London, and his wife, Eliza Frederica Bowman. After private education he entered the army on 18 August 1854 as ensign in the 82nd regiment, and became lieutenant on 5 June 1855. He served with his regiment in the Crimea from 2 September 1855, and was present at the siege and fall of Sevastopol. He later served during the Indian mutiny in 1857 and was severely wounded at Cawnpore on 26 November 1857. In 1863 he married Jane Catharine (*d.* 1871), eldest daughter of Charles Chase Smith MD, of Bury St Edmunds, and they had a son and a daughter.

Promoted captain on 17 November 1863, East joined the 41st regiment, and served as assistant quartermaster-general with the Chittagong column of the Lushai expeditionary force in 1871–2; he was mentioned in dispatches, received the thanks of the governor-general in council, and in 1872 was promoted brevet major. In 1875 he married Frances Elizabeth, daughter of Revd Arthur Mogg of Chilcompton, Somerset, and widow of Edward H. Watts; they had one daughter.

Through the latter part of the Anglo-Zulu War, East was deputy adjutant and quartermaster-general. He was present at Ulundi, and was promoted brevet colonel. During the Third Anglo-Burmese War in 1886–7 he commanded the 1st brigade after the capture of Mandalay and was mentioned in dispatches, being made CB on 1 July 1887. From 1883 to 1888 he commanded a second-class district in Bengal and Burma, and a first-class district in Madras from 1889 to 1893, having been made major-general on 23 January 1889. After leaving India in 1893, he was until 1898 governor of the Royal Military College, Sandhurst. He was made KCB on 22 June 1897. He became lieutenant-general on 28 May 1896, and general in 1902, retiring in 1903. After 1898 he resided at Fairhaven, Winchester, where he died on 14 March 1908, survived by his wife. He was buried at King's Worthy in Hampshire.

H. M. Vibart, *rev.* James Falkner

Sources *The Times* (16 March 1908) · *Army List* · *Hart's Army List* · *LondG* (21 June 1872) · *LondG* (21 Aug 1879) · *LondG* (2 Sept 1887) · C. R. Dod, *The peerage, baronetage and knightage of Great Britain and Ireland* (1907)
Likenesses photograph, repro. in *Navy and Army Illustrated* (12 Nov 1897)
Wealth at death £9777 19s. 2d.: probate, 7 April 1908, *CGPLA Eng. & Wales*

East, Edward (*bap.* 1602, *d.* 1696), clock- and watchmaker, was born in Southill, Bedfordshire, and baptized there on 22 August 1602, the second of seven children born to John East and his wife, Martha, *née* Newsam. East was apprenticed to Richard Rogers in the Goldsmiths' Company on 27 March 1618 and made free on 8 February 1628. Of his three surviving brothers, John (*b.* 1600), James (*b.* 1607), and Jeremy (*b.* 1610), were all similarly apprenticed to goldsmiths; subsequently John and James traded as London goldsmiths and Jeremy became a clockmaker. His only surviving sister, Angelett (*b.* 1605), married Robert Greene, a Fleet Street ironmonger.

East's early years were probably spent in the service of Edmund Bull, 'citizen and blacksmith', one of the most celebrated clock- and watchmakers of that period. On 8 August 1627, East married Ann (*bap.* 1609), Bull's daughter, at St Nicholas Cole Abbey, London. In 1628, he took over the workshop of the clockmaker Anthony Risbye, an apprentice of Bull's uncle Randolph, on the corner of Ram Alley and Fleet Street. By the time of his wife's death in 1654 the couple had had sixteen children. In February 1656 East married Sarah Powell, a widow, with whom he

had a further six children. At least eleven of his children survived into adulthood.

Before the founding of the Clockmakers' Company, clockmakers were freemen of several companies, primarily the Goldsmiths and Blacksmiths. In addition, numbers of foreign makers had set up businesses within London but outside the control of the livery companies. Two petitions to James I for the founding of a Clockmakers' Company, in 1622 and 1630, demonstrated the need for more rigorous controls over London clock and watch manufacture. On the founding of the company in 1631, East, who was made free by redemption, held the office of assistant, a token of his important role in its establishment. In later years he was master, first in 1645 and again in 1652. He also held offices in the Goldsmiths' Company: fourth, third, second, and prime warden in 1657, 1662, 1663, and 1671 respectively.

On Bull's death in 1644, East entered into a dispute with his son, John Bull, over the property once leased to Risbye. This dispute, which probably concerned one of the main workshops in Bull's business, lasted at least twelve years and was finally resolved in East's favour. In November 1660 East was appointed clockmaker to Charles II. The quantity and value of deeds in East's name point to him being a very successful businessman and the number and excellence of extant pieces demonstrate him as a prolific and superior maker. Examples of his work entered the collections of the British Museum, Victoria and Albert Museum, and other institutions throughout the world. Towards the end of his life in 1693, East placed £100 in trust to pay to five freemen of the Clockmakers' Company or their widows 20s. annually.

East's apprentices bound in the Clockmakers' Company were Walter Gibbs (1639), Thomas Wolverstone (1643), Robert Hanslap (1646), Edward Wagstaffe (1650), John East (his nephew) and Henry Jones in 1654, Adam Pearce (1657), and Benjamin Jones and Richard Bellinger in 1676. In the Goldsmiths' Company he bound his brother Jeremy in 1627, Benjamin Cawcott (1631), Robert Cotchett (1636), James Bell (1638), and Edmund Bull, his nephew, in 1657.

East spent most of his working life in Fleet Street but in 1667, following the great fire, moved to the Church ward of St Clement Danes. In 1674, he moved to the Strand near the Haymarket, and about 1687 made a final move to Hampton, where he died in 1696.   Valerie Finch

Sources A. Finch and V. Finch, 'Edmund Bull and Edward East: family connections in seventeenth-century London clockmaking', *Antiquarian Horology and the Proceedings of the Antiquarian Horological Society* · A. Finch and V. Finch, 'Edmund Bull and Edward East: family connections in seventeenth-century London clockmaking', *Proceedings of the Antiquarian Horological Society* · parish register (baptism), Southill, Bedfordshire, 22 Aug 1602 · parish register (baptism), St Dunstan-in-the-West, 1609 [Ann Bull] · parish register, St Nicholas Cole Abbey, London, 8 Aug 1627 [marriage] · parish register (marriage), St Dunstan-in-the-West, Feb 1656 · PRO, PROB 11/436, fol. 29
Archives BL, clocks, watches, longcase clocks, etc. · GL, Clockmakers' Company Museum, clocks, watches, longcase clocks, etc. · V&A, clocks, watches, longcase clocks, etc.

East, Sir Edward Hyde, first baronet (1764–1847), judge in India and legal writer, was born in Jamaica on 9 September 1764, the son of Edward East of Whitehall, Jamaica, and Amy, daughter of James Hall of Jamaica. His great-grandfather Captain John East had taken part in the conquest of Jamaica, and obtained the sugar plantations there on which the family's fortunes were based. East was educated at Harrow School from about 1776, before going on to Magdalen College, Oxford, where he matriculated in 1782, and to the Inner Temple where he was admitted in 1781. He was called to the bar in 1786, and afterwards practised on the western circuit. On 23 December 1786 he married Jane Isabella (d. 27 Jan 1844), daughter of Joseph Chaplin Hankey of East Bergholt, Suffolk; they had a son, Sir James Buller *East, second baronet (1789–1878), and a daughter, Anna Eliza. From 1792 to 1796 East sat in parliament for Great Bedwyn on the interest of the first earl of Ailesbury. He supported the Pitt administration, and regularly spoke in defence of the interests of West Indian planters. In parliament he attempted to form a political club to further this end, and out-of-doors, he was a lifelong stalwart of the West Indian planters' committee. After 1796 he resumed his professional activities. From 1785 he had co-edited the *Term Reports in the Court of King's Bench* with Charles Durnford, the first such reports to be published. From 1800 to 1812 he shouldered this editorial burden alone: according to one near contemporary reviewer, the indispensability of the resulting volumes was 'too well known to render comment necessary' (Allibone, *Dict.*). Of his other legal publications, the most important was *Pleas of the Crown, or, A General Treatise on the Principles and Practice of Criminal Law* (1803), which won immediate authority, and contemporary critical plaudits for its 'accuracy, neatness and conciseness; a classical performance of its kind' (ibid.).

In 1813 East was made chief justice of Bengal, a post to which he had aspired for several years, and was knighted (26 February) before setting sail for India. According to his son, who accompanied him, he was active in promoting progressive changes in the Indian legal system, though his attempts to curtail the use of diplock courts were substantially frustrated by the reluctance of many settlers to serve on juries. He was vice-president of the Calcutta School Book Society, and was an active promoter of the Hindu College founded in 1816, though contemporary claims that he was actually instrumental in its foundation have since been disputed. On his departure he was presented with an address commending him for the disinterested performance of his duties, and a statue of him (by Chantrey) was financed by public subscription. A memoir of a judicial colleague, published in 1907, commended East as 'one of the ablest and most independent of Calcutta judges' (Drewitt, 36). His ten-year stint, however, was not free of mishap: in March 1819 his son-in-law James William Croft was fined and banished for the seduction of one Louisa Comberbatch, an episode which apparently led to calls in London for East's resignation. He felt slighted when, on his return, he was not appointed to the

Sir Edward Hyde East, first baronet (1764–1847), by G. B. Black (after George Chinnery)

privy council; he was, however, made a baronet on 25 April 1823.

By this time East had been re-elected to parliament at a by-election for Winchester (18 February 1823), which he represented until 1831. Like the other remnants of the Grenvillite parliamentary squad, he voted in general with the tory ministries of Lord Liverpool and the duke of Wellington. He was a supporter of Catholic relief. For his parliamentary patron, the fat and feckless duke of Buckingham and Chandos, he also performed the thankless task of auditor. Buckingham's finances were a disaster area, but East's were scarcely better, as the fall in the price of sugar and the hardening of public opinion against slavery had transformed his West Indian estates into an economic and political liability. It was thus by necessity that he enjoyed a busy retirement after he left parliament, having voted against the first draft of the Reform Bill as a parting shot. Lord Chancellor Brougham then finally gratified his wish for a seat on the privy council, and named him to its judicial committee in 1833; East was evidently glad enough of the work, although, at the age of sixty-six, he had begged to be reappointed to his Bengal posting. His shifts of address, to Minchenden House, Southgate, Middlesex, in July 1832, and from thence to Sherwood House, Battersea, Surrey, bespoke a need to conserve resources.

East died on 8 January 1847 at his home, Sherwood House, Battersea, in circumstances of sufficient doubt to merit a coroner's inquest, which ruled that his death had resulted from 'sanguineous apoplexy, induced solely from natural causes'. He was buried in Kensal Green cemetery, Middlesex. His personal estate of less than £3000 was exhausted before the bequests specified in his will could be paid. In India, East's chief legacy was in the field of education: his role in the foundation of the Hindu College may have been exaggerated, but the encouragement he gave to its founders effectively constituted a significant repudiation of Christian missionary zeal. His legal writings have proved robust: *Pleas of the Crown* was reprinted in 1972, with an introduction that noted that his termly reports 'achieved a standard of accuracy and scholarship which has never been bettered' (East, viii).

H. J. SPENCER

Sources E. H. East, *Pleas of the crown, or, A general treatise on the principles and practice of criminal law*, ed. P. R. Glazebrook (1972) · M. H. Port and R. G. Thorne, 'East, Edward Hyde', HoP, *Commons, 1790–1820* · H. J. Spencer, 'East, Edward Hyde', HoP, *Commons, 1820–32* [draft] · M. A. Laird, *Missionaries and education in Bengal, 1793–1837* (1972) · R. C. Majurinder, 'The Hindu College', *Journal of Asiatic Society of Bengal*, 21/1 (1955), 39–51 · N. L. Basak, 'Origin and role of the Calcutta Book Society', *Bengal Past and Present*, 78 (1959), 30–69 · U. Lond., Institute of Commonwealth Studies, West India Committee archives, M915 · BL OIOC, MS Eur. A. 145, fol. 1 · BL, Add. MS 40538, fols. 35, 37, 43, 49, 53 · J. J. Sack, *The Grenvillites* (1979) · GM, 2nd ser., 27 (1847), 422–3 · *The Times* (15 Nov 1819) · *The Times* (13 Jan 1847) · DNB · W. S. Seton-Karr and H. D. Sandeman, eds., *Selections from the Calcutta Gazettes*, 5 vols. (1864–9), vol. 5 · F. D. Drewitt, *Bombay in the days of George IV: memoirs of Sir Edward West* (1907) · PRO, IR26/1770/266
Archives BL OIOC, MS Eur. A 145, fol. 1 · Inner Temple, London, notes on cases, Misc. MSS 96–97 | BL, letters to C. P. Yorke, Add. MS 45038 · Hunt. L., letters to Grenville family · U. Lond., Institute of Commonwealth Studies, West India Committee archives, M915
Likenesses F. Chantrey, marble statue, *c*.1829, Supreme Court, Calcutta · G. B. Black, lithograph (after G. Chinnery), NPG [*see illus.*] · F. Chantrey, pencil drawing, NPG
Wealth at death under £3000: PRO, death duty registers, IR 26/1770/266

East, Sir James Buller, second baronet (1789–1878), barrister, only son of Sir Edward Hyde *East (1764–1847), judge, and his wife, Jane Isabella, daughter of Mr Joseph Chaplin Hankey of Old Hall, East Bergholt, Suffolk, was born in Bloomsbury, London, on 1 February 1789. He was educated at Harrow School and at Christ Church, Oxford, where he graduated BA in 1810 and MA in 1824, and was created a DCL on 13 June 1834. He was called to the bar of the Inner Temple on 5 February 1813, became a bencher of his inn on 15 January 1856, and was made a reader in 1869. He was married on 27 June 1822 to Caroline Eliza (1794–1870), second daughter of James Henry Leigh and the Hon. Julia Twiselton Fiennes, daughter of Lord Saye and Sele.

East succeeded his father as second baronet on 8 January 1847. As a liberal conservative he replaced his father as MP for Winchester, sitting from 30 July 1831 to 3 December 1832, when he was defeated, and then from 10 January 1835 to 10 February 1864, when he accepted Chiltern Hundreds. He was a JP and deputy lieutenant for Gloucestershire, and a magistrate for Oxfordshire. He died at his home, Bourton House, near Moreton in Marsh, Gloucestershire, on 19 November 1878, leaving no heir. The baronetcy, which had been created in 1823, became extinct.

G. C. BOASE, rev. BETH F. WOOD

Sources *Law Times* (30 Nov 1878), 88 · *The Times* (25 Nov 1878), 9 · WWBMP · R. B. Mosse, *The parliamentary guide* (1836) · Boase, *Mod. Eng. biog.* · J. E. Martin, ed., *Masters of the bench of the Hon. Society of the Inner Temple, 1450–1883, and masters of the Temple, 1540–1883* (1883) · Foster, *Alum. Oxon.* · *Annual Register* (1878)
Archives Bodl. Oxf., Phillipps-Robinson MSS, corresp. with Sir Thomas Phillipps · Devon RO, letters to Sir Thomas Acland and others · Hunt. L., letters to Grenville family
Likenesses F. C. Lewis, stipple (after J. Slater; Grillion's Club series), BM
Wealth at death under £70,000: probate, 13 Jan 1879, CGPLA Eng. & Wales

East, Michael (*c*.1580–1648), composer, was the nephew of the music printer Thomas *East and, according to John Hawkins, possibly a brother of John Est, a barber known for his skill as a viol player. The first record of him is his madrigal 'Hence, stars, too dim of light', composed for and published in Thomas Morley's *Triumphes of Oriana* (1601). By sending in his contribution late he inadvertently secured for his piece a prime position on the opening pages of this important anthology. He was granted the degree of MusB at Cambridge in 1606. By this time he may have been employed at Ely House, Holborn, from where he dated the preface to his second set of compositions. The link with Ely House may imply an early connection with the Hatton family, for it was the home of Lady Hatton, and it is possible that East worked for her. Certainly he was associated with the family in later years, as he dedicated his 1638 publication to Sir Christopher Hatton. East became a lay clerk at Ely Cathedral in the spring of 1609 but, on the evidence of the cathedral accounts, served there only intermittently—for little more than eighteen months at most in the first instance and again, for just a term, in 1614—presumably because of his commitments in London.

By 1618 East was master of the choristers at Lichfield Cathedral, the first holder of that post who can be named. He was not also organist, however: about 1630 young Elias Ashmole, the future antiquary, was a chorister at the cathedral, and he later recalled that 'Mr Michael East ... was my tutor for song and Mr Henry Hinde, organist of the Cathedral ... taught me on the virginals and organ' (Shaw, 147). East remained in office at the cathedral probably until 1644, when the civil war brought an end to sung services, and he stayed at Lichfield for the rest of his life.

East was one of the most published composers of the first half of the seventeenth century, and his seven sets of music were all issued during his lifetime. However, he is remarkable more for the range of vocal and instrumental genres in which he wrote than for the quality of his work. In the eighteenth century Charles Burney apparently struggled to reconcile East's good fortune in print with his moderate talent, concluding rather sneeringly that the sheer amount of East's music, 'either from the constancy of the public, or the barrenness of the composers [of the period], was sufficient to give him the reputation of great fertility' (Burney, *Hist. mus.*, 2.114). In the assessment of modern scholars East was a capable composer who wrote some attractive works, though his lack of originality (he often reset old madrigal texts and sometimes recycled musical ideas) has been criticized, and his poor contrapuntal technique is a notable flaw.

The first two sets of compositions (1604, 1606) are collections of madrigals for three to five voices, and demonstrate an enthusiasm for the secular Italian idiom that marked East's sacred works too. Books 3 (1610) and 4 (1618) also contain madrigals, but there are sacred anthems and consort songs as well, and a group of fancies for viols in the 1610 set may reflect the interests of musicians at Ely Cathedral at that time. The fifth set (1618) contains three-part pieces with titles but without words, possibly derived from texted originals and here expressly intended for performance by either instrumentalists or textless singers. Book 6 (1624) has almost all sacred vocal music—consort songs and mainly verse anthems—and book 7 (1638) is a collection of instrumental pieces, some of them, 'that may be as well Sung as Plaid', similar to those in book 5.

East's church music, like that of other minor composers of the period, generally emulated and thereby helped to preserve the Anglican style of William Byrd and Orlando Gibbons. The favourable impression gained by John Williams, bishop of Lincoln, on hearing some of East's anthems was such that he granted the composer an annuity, in gratitude for which East dedicated to him his sixth set. This set includes the anthem 'As they departed', commissioned in 1620 by the authorities at St John's College, Oxford, and seemingly heard at Oxford by East himself. The reconstitution of the church repertory in the early years of the Restoration depended on the revival of much music from before the civil war, including East's. Three of his anthems, as well as his burial service, are included in cathedral partbooks that were in use at Lichfield after 1660, and the text of his full anthem 'O clap your hands' is in James Clifford's collection *The Divine Services and Anthems* (1663). East's will, dated 7 January 1648, mentions that he was then still living in the cathedral close at Lichfield, and it is presumed that he died at Lichfield. He was married to Dorothy, and they had a daughter, Mary Hamersly, a son, Michael, and a grandson, also Michael (*b*. 1645/6). His wife was still alive when he wrote his will, which was proved on 9 May 1648.   PETER LYNAN

Sources H. W. Shaw, *The succession of organists of the Chapel Royal and the cathedrals of England and Wales from c.1538* (1991), 146–7 • *New Grove*, 2nd edn • Burney, *Hist. mus.*, new edn, 2.114 • J. Hawkins, *A general history of the science and practice of music*, new edn, 3 vols. (1853); repr. in 2 vols. (1963), vol. 2, p. 570 • P. Le Huray, *Music and the Reformation in England, 1549–1660* (1967); repr. with corrections (1978) • I. Spink, *Restoration cathedral music, 1660–1714* (1995)

East, Sir (William) Norwood (1872–1953), forensic psychiatrist and criminologist, was born in London on 24 December 1872, the tenth of twelve children of William Quartermaine East and his wife, Charlotte Isabella Bateman. His father was proprietor of the Queen's Hotel, St Martin's-le-Grand, one time sheriff of London, and deputy lieutenant for London and Middlesex. The family lived at Epsom. East was educated at King's College School and King's College, London. He studied medicine at Guy's Hospital, qualifying MRCS and LRCP in 1897, MB in 1898 and MD (London) in 1901. On 3 February 1900 he married Selina, only daughter of Alfred Triggs; they had a daughter, Joan, who married Dr John Stuart Knox, deputy superintendent at Broadmoor Hospital, Crowthorne, Berkshire.

After various house staff appointments at Guy's, and residencies in mental hospitals, East joined the prison medical service in 1899. Posted to Portland as deputy medical officer, he moved subsequently to Brixton, Liverpool, and Manchester prisons, and then returned to Brixton as senior medical officer in the early 1920s. His approach to forensic psychiatry might be characterized as pragmatic, straightforward, unequivocal, and unsentimental, but East also displayed considerable ease and acuity in dealing with theoretical issues in lectures and publications. This approach was strongly influenced in his early years by the prison commissioner, Dr Treadwell, and the governor of Holloway prison and one-time medical officer of Brixton, Dr James Scott.

In 1924 East was appointed medical inspector of HM prisons in England and Wales and in 1930 commissioner of prisons and director of the convict prisons medical service. He was also appointed inspector of retreats under the Inebriates Acts. As a prison commissioner East was instrumental in the provision of an up-to-date operating theatre at Wormwood Scrubs. He also established a nursing service with state registered nurses to deal with women prisoners, a scheme that was extended later to include men's prisons where there was a large hospital section. East also served on departmental committees on prison diet and persistent offenders.

East gained a formidable reputation both as a prison service administrator and as an expert witness, appearing regularly at the Old Bailey and at assizes in the home counties. He also won respect among colleagues for his humane and sympathetic treatment of prisoners and for being a prodigiously hard worker, regarded as strict but fair with juniors. He was a great critic of what he saw as a previous lack of commitment in forensic psychiatry to research and experimentation, and emphasized the need to balance official duties with scientific and therapeutic endeavour. East was also one of the doctors appointed by the home secretary to inquire into the mental state of prisoners who had received capital sentences.

In the 1920s East was appointed lecturer on criminology and forensic psychiatry at the Maudsley Hospital's Institute of Psychiatry, lecturing for over thirty years on crime and insanity as part of the course for the diploma of psychological medicine. In addition, he lectured on crime and mental deficiency within courses on mental deficiency for medical practitioners, jointly organized by the university extension board and the Central Association for Mental Welfare. East served as president of the Medico-Legal Society (1945–7, having been a member since 1914) and of the Society for the Study of Inebriety and Drug Addiction (1940–45), and was chairman of the psychiatric section of the Royal Society of Medicine (1943). He was a corresponding member of various medico-legal societies abroad.

After retiring from active work in 1938, East briefly

returned to the prison service, being reappointed prison commissioner for seven months during the wartime secondment of his successor in 1940–41. He continued to lecture in forensic psychiatry at the Maudsley and to fulfil his responsibilities regarding prisoners with capital sentences, also remaining a regular attender of conferences. Latterly he also became special consultant to the Royal Navy.

East was a prolific writer, and produced a number of important books. His début in print was an article on the physical and moral sensibility of the criminal (1901). His first book was *An Introduction to Forensic Psychiatry in the Criminal Courts* (1927), a practical textbook for medical practitioners inexperienced in giving forensic testimony. Based partly on the lectures he had delivered at the Maudsley, as well as on his London University lectures, it was also founded on East's own extensive experience as a forensic witness over many years and was illustrated with numerous cases. It was unusual in focusing on milder and more problematic cases, in order to emphasize the difficulties of evaluating criminal responsibility. This was followed by *Medical Aspects of Crime* (1936). An investigation East conducted in collaboration with Dr W. H. de Bargue Hubert was published as the *Psychological Treatment of Crime* (1939); it emphasized the value of the psychological treatment of criminals (although confined to male offenders), and led its authors to recommend the inauguration of a special institution under the Prison Commission not only for psychopathic and other disturbed adults, but also for disturbed borstal boys. Their proposal for an institution primarily for research but also with facilities for treatment was, however, not to be realized until well after East's death, with the opening of Grendon, Buckinghamshire, in 1962. *The Adolescent Criminal* (1942) was the outcome of a medico-sociological study of 4000 male adolescents, undertaken and published by East in collaboration with the medical statistician Percy Stocks and the prison medical officer H. T. P. Young. It was heavily reliant on the contacts made and histories ascertained by an army of women visitors and the examinations conducted by numerous other prison medical officers at Wormwood Scrubs boys' prison. It focused on the causes of delinquency among adolescents. This work, and a number of others East conducted, including an examination of 1000 cases of attempted suicide and a survey of criminals' susceptibility to atmospheric changes, testify to his thorough and analytical approach to scientific research in forensic psychiatry. East's penultimate book, reprising his broad, interdisciplinary approach to criminology, was *The Roots of Crime* (1954), a book he edited but which was published posthumously, and included his article 'Legal and medical advances in criminology'. Later in his career, East became recognized as especially knowledgeable with regard to sexual offenders, publishing a number of studies on the subject, although his final publication, *Sexual Offenders* (1955), was mostly rehashed material and was perhaps already outdated when it appeared. Some of these books were largely compilations of some of the numerous articles East published in contemporary medical journals.

Typical was *Society and the Criminal* (1949), a collection of essays East described as 'some of the stepping stones over which I have travelled towards a better understanding of crime and criminals' (p. 1).

East was an early and continuing sympathizer with eugenics, contributing a number of articles to the *Eugenics Review* and delivering the 1946 Galton lecture. He was a particularly regular contributor to the *Journal of Mental Science* and the *Medico-Legal Journal*, but also wrote articles for *Brain*, the *British Journal of Medical Psychology*, *The Lancet*, and the *BMJ*. East's work continued to be cited in later studies and in standard textbooks of forensic psychiatry for many years.

Besides his medical duties and interests, East was a keen fisherman, gardener, and walker. He was also a committed freemason. He was knighted in 1947 in recognition of his services to criminal psychology. East died at his home, Rhododendrons, which was close by Broadmoor Hospital at Crowthorne, on 30 October 1953, having given his last course of Maudsley lectures just five months earlier. He was survived by his wife and daughter.

JONATHAN ANDREWS

Sources *The Lancet* (7 Nov 1953), 996–7 · *BMJ* (7 Nov 1953), 1050–51 · *Medico-Legal Journal*, 21 (1953), 110 · R. R. Trail, ed., *Lives of the fellows of the Royal College of Physicians of London continued to 1965* (1968), 114 · *DNB* · *CGPLA Eng. & Wales* (1953) · m. cert.
Likenesses W. Stoneman, photograph, 1947, NPG · W. Stoneman, photograph, RCP Lond. · photo, repro. in *Medico-Legal & Criminological Review*, 14/1 (Jan–June 1946), facing p. 1 · photograph, repro. in *BMJ*, 1050
Wealth at death £5396 6s. 8d.: probate, 31 Dec 1953, *CGPLA Eng. & Wales*

East, Thomas (1540–1608), printer, was born in Swavesey, Cambridge, the oldest son of Thomas East (d. c.1593). Suggestions that East had an Italian ancestry and that he was father of the composer Michael *East have been discounted; he was the composer's uncle. East's wife, Lucretia East, née Hassell (c.1555–1629), was one of several daughters of a prominent London pewterer. East adopted her nephew, Thomas Snodham, whom he bound as an apprentice in 1595 and freed in 1602, as son and heir. Lucretia and Snodham participated extensively in East's business affairs during his lifetime, and both printed music books after his death.

On 6 December 1565 East was granted his freedom from London's Stationers' Company. In 1567 he was located in Fleet Street; the following year he was in Bread Street. From 1571 to 1575 he lived at London Wall, and from 1577 to 1588 he was resident by Paul's Wharf. During these years he worked most often as a trade printer and bookseller: he published relatively few works himself, but they included popular titles by John Lyly and Edmund Spenser, and a lengthy series of English translations of Spanish romances. About 1577 he signed a petition opposing monopolistic privileges of the book trade; like many of his fellow signatories, East would later exploit the protections of the same patents he had once opposed. In 1583 and 1586 he was noted as operating one printing press.

In 1587 East's career took a turn that eventually brought him great distinction. Although he continued to do general trade printing and some independent publishing, this was soon completely overshadowed by his emerging speciality in music. Soon after Thomas Vautrollier's death in 1587, East acquired his fount of music type and in or after 1588 he settled permanently at Aldersgate Street, near St Paul's. At his main residence he displayed the sign of a black horse, the family crest; much later he set up two additional shops in locations nearby.

The music trade of East's London was a divided enterprise. John Day, the prominent stationer and music printer, was successful above all with his editions of metrical psalters with music produced under auspices of a patent of monopoly granted in 1559. This grant was the key to Day's power, but the queen characteristically ignored it when she bestowed a twenty-one-year patent in 1575 for all music printing, printed music paper, and music importation on Thomas Tallis and William Byrd, the finest English musicians of their respective generations. After Day's death in 1584, his son Richard obtained a similar patent to his father's. Less powerful than John Day, the younger Day allowed a group of stationers, known as 'the assigns of Richard Day', to actually run the enterprise. East was not a member of this group but he did acquire some printing materials from Richard Day, including a distinctive set of type initials.

The first work to be published by Tallis and Byrd under the terms of their patent, their magnificent 1575 *Cantiones ... sacrae*, met with profound neglect in the market place; however, in 1587 Byrd entrusted a set of pieces with much more market appeal to East's new music-press. East is rightly acclaimed for his careful music editing and his fidelity to the intentions of his author–musicians, but an equally notable accomplishment of his was entrepreneurial, and he treated the overlapping royal grants as an economic opportunity. Taking advantage of the tension between the two music monopolies, East nurtured both sides of the music field. Overall he promoted 'popular' as well as 'cultivated' styles, and helped to bring out a new vitality in both.

In 1587 East entered Byrd's *Psalmes, Sonets & Songs* in the Stationers' register, and soon thereafter he produced three separate editions of the volume that he dated, and probably also printed, in 1588. Byrd apparently knew of the vogue for singing Italianate madrigals a cappella, for he added texts to his consort songs for voices and viols to conform to this performance style. The composer meticulously edited his music at East's press. In 1588 East also produced the *Musica transalpina*, the first printed collection of Italian madrigals with texts translated into English. This volume featured the lighter madrigal styles that were emulated by the great school of Elizabethan madrigalists, many of whom also had their own works printed at East's press. East printed most of the subsequent collections of 'Englished' Italian madrigals of this era too, including the sequel edition of *Musica transalpina* in 1597 and the anthologies edited by Thomas Watson and Thomas Morley.

Byrd and East pursued more individualized goals for music printing after 1588. Typical of the Elizabethan courtier, Byrd used the monopoly to promote his own accomplishments and those of his friends and students. More intriguingly, he used the music press as a vehicle to serve his fellow dissident Catholics. As Byrd's assign, East printed two collections of Byrd's Latin-texted *Cantiones sacrae* (1589 and 1591) that contained texts for Byrd's co-religionists. Then East printed music for the Catholic liturgy itself: Byrd's mass ordinaries for three, four, and five voices (c.1593–5) and the two volumes of Byrd's *Gradualia* with mass propers (1605 and 1607). East took the precaution of printing the mass ordinaries anonymously, but they still drew him dangerously close to illicit activities. During a second printing of the three- and four-voiced masses c.1600, two of East's apprentices discovered an alleged Jesuit conspiracy at East's house, and they quickly reported it to the privy council. Copies of Byrd's masses were no doubt near the scene, but neither Byrd nor East was arrested. The recusants involved were interrogated, imprisoned, and tortured.

From the start, East used Byrd's privilege as a means to circumvent Day's psalter-with-music monopoly. At first East limited himself to relatively inconspicuous selections of psalm settings included in editions of English songbooks. In 1591, however, he brought out William Daman's books, which were a clear commercial threat as they 'contain[ed] all the tunes of David's psalms: as they are ordinarily sung in the church: most excellently ... composed into 4 parts' (*Former Booke of the Musicke of M. William Damon*). A year later East published his own famous *Whole Booke of Psalmes with Notes to Sing them*, featuring four-part settings by ten prominent composers. It was East's greatest triumph. He brought out new editions in 1594 and 1604, and the book was paid the ultimate backhanded compliment when pirated by a rival music publisher, William Barley, in 1599.

In 1596 Byrd's patent expired, and East encountered a new kind of competitor in Thomas Morley. The latter had already monopolized East's press in the mid-1590s, publishing his own volumes of English- and Italian-texted canzonets and other light madrigals. Between 1596 and 1598, however, Morley purposely selected music printers other than East as he exploited the market for Italianate music and capitalized on a flourishing market for books of English lute songs. Once he obtained a music monopoly like Byrd's in 1598, Morley also set his sights on the lucrative psalters with music. Byrd had allowed East to trade these popular books, but Morley openly competed with members of the Stationers' Company for the sole rights to control them.

During the gap between Byrd's and Morley's music monopolies, East revealed his true commitment to the music field. Almost immediately after Byrd's patent ended, for copyright purposes East registered at the Stationers' Company the music books he had printed earlier. He then reprinted several of them surreptitiously, disguising the actual date by printing them with the date of the original edition. This 'hidden edition' format was one East resorted to each time it was unclear who owned the music monopoly, and it was a technique continued by his heir.

East also invited an aspiring group of youthful composers to his press at this time, including John Wilbye and Thomas Weelkes. At the time Morley had the more illustrious clientele, but music history suggests East chose wisely among the tyros.

After 1600 Morley regularly selected East for various music printing assignments, which included John Dowland's *Second Booke of Songs* (1600) and Morley's famous collection of madrigals in the *Triumphs of Oriana* (1601, reprinted c.1605). The former work was to cause an extensive court battle with one-time music publisher George Eastland over East's alleged breach of contract. The court records are especially useful for offering rare evidence of early music pricing and editing processes. The publishing history of the *Triumphs* has been a source of scholarly confusion, with some claiming that the first edition was suppressed by the queen; all evidence suggests, however, that the second printing was simply a hidden edition. The book was popular enough to inspire East to reprint the collection during a gap in music monopoly ownership after the queen's death.

After Morley died in 1602, East enjoyed an era of free trade in the music field that lasted until 1606. At this point Barley and East came to legal blows. This was not, as often thought, a dispute over who owned the music monopoly: the litigation actually concerned copyright procedures and, specifically, whether Barley could interfere with the rights to music books that East had already registered. On 25 June 1606 the Stationers' Company court, of which East had been a member since June 1603, decided that when he reprinted these volumes, East must compensate Barley. Yet, the court also held that East's registrations were valid copyrights, and they instructed Barley 'not [to] intermeddle with the printinge of any of them' (Jackson, 19). East subsequently printed music as 'the assign of William Barley'. Upon his death which took place between 5 February and 8 April 1608, East left an estate of £482 8s. 3d. and his interest in leases for three properties equipped with presses and printing materials.

JEREMY L. SMITH

Sources D. W. Krummel, *English music printing, 1553–1700* (1975) · J. L. Smith, 'The hidden editions of Thomas East', *Notes*, 53 (1997), 1059–91 · F. Keymer, 'Thomas East, citizen & stationer of London: the reconstruction of a Tudor family using public records', *PROphile*, 11/1 (2000), 3–10 · J. L. Smith, *Thomas East and music publishing in Renaissance Britain* (New York, 2002) · M. Miller, 'London music printing, c.1570–c.1649', PhD diss., U. Lond., 1969 · G. D. Johnson, 'William Barley, "Publisher & Seller of Bookes", 1591–1614', *The Library*, 6th ser., 11 (1989), 10–44 · R. R. Steele, *The earliest English music printing: a description and bibliography of English printed music to the close of the sixteenth century* (1903) · W. A. Jackson, ed., *Records of the court of the Stationers' Company, 1602 to 1640* (1957) · will, GL, MS 9052 3B, fol. 61 · will, PRO, PROB 11/156/61 · deposition, *East v. East*, PRO, C24/170 · Ely Consistory Administration, Cambs. AS, Cambridge, EDR G2/20, fol. 12v · *STC, 1475–1640* · Arber, *Regs. Stationers*

Wealth at death £482 8s. 3d.: will, PRO, PROB 11/156/61

East Anglia. For this title name *see* Thorkell the Tall, earl of East Anglia (*fl.* 1009–1023); Gyrth, earl of East Anglia (*d.* 1066); Ralph the Staller, earl of East Anglia (*d.* 1068×70).

Eastcott, Richard (*bap.* 1744, *d.* 1828), writer on music and Church of England clergyman, was baptized on 22 November 1744 at Launceston, Cornwall, the son of Sandford Eastcott. He matriculated at Oriel College, Oxford, on 9 July 1764. He does not seem to have taken a degree, but was at some point ordained. He devoted his life to musical circles in Devon. About 1775 the young John Davy (1763–1824), who became a well-known songwriter, was introduced to him by James Carrington, rector of Upton Helions, and after hearing him play the piano Eastcott recommended that Davy be taught by a cathedral organist; Davy was later articled to William Jackson of Exeter (1730–1803), organist of Exeter Cathedral.

Eastcott is known mainly for his *Sketches of the origin, progress, and effects of music, with an account of the ancient bards and minstrels*, published in Bath in 1793. This shows the influence of Sir John Hawkins's five-volume *General History of the Science and Practice of Music* (1776) and Charles Burney's *History of Music* (1776–89), the earliest histories of music published in England. Eastcott wrote that he intended the book for the education of 'young ladies' learning music at 'public academies' (p. iv). In the chapter on 'the use and abuse of Church Music', Eastcott deplores the low standard of singing by the choirs in country churches, and agrees with Burney that the way in which the music is performed is more likely to drive Christians out of the church than to draw pagans in. He says that if he were in charge of the music in a parish church he would never allow any choral music in more than two parts, in order that the words could be heard: taking as one of his examples the six-part anthem 'Lift up your heads, O ye gates' by Orlando Gibbons, he complains that the words and music form 'a most unnatural connection' (p. 190). The book was so successful that it ran to a second edition in the same year.

A composer himself, Eastcott advertised his works *The harmony of the muses* (a collection of songs) and *Six sonatas for the piano forte* at the end of *Sketches*, and he also published *Poetical essays* (1788), a book of poems, printed in Exeter.

At the time of his death, which was reported in the *Gentleman's Magazine* for December 1828, Eastcott was chaplain of Livery Dale, Devon, under the patronage of John Rolle, Baron Rolle of Stevenstone. His will was proved on 8 December 1828 by his widow, 'Fanny otherwise Frances Eastcott' (will, PRO, PROB 11/1749, fol. 11v). He was survived by his sons Edwin and Richard, his daughters 'Mrs King' of Fitzray Square, London, and Fanny, and 'Mr Withers of Rathbone Place London Druggist', husband of a deceased daughter (ibid.).

ANNE PIMLOTT BAKER

Sources Grove, *Dict. mus.* (1878–90) · Brown & Stratton, *Brit. mus.*, 134 · *Monthly Review*, 13 (1794), 45–50 · *DNB* · Foster, *Alum. Oxon.* · *GM*, 1st ser., 98/2 (1828), 647 · *IGI* · will, PRO, PROB 11/1749, sig. 702

Easter Kennet. For this title name *see* Hay, Alexander, of Easter Kennet, Lord Easter Kennet (*d.* 1594).

Eastfield, Sir William (*d.* 1446), merchant and mayor of London, first appears in the records in 1419 as a mercer. He was probably the son of William Eastfield of Tickhill,

Yorkshire, since in 1435 he acquired from Joan, widow of William Eastfield of Tickhill, the lands of her husband in Yorkshire, Nottinghamshire, and Derbyshire. On 28 September 1420 he was appointed one of the collectors of tunnage and poundage at London (a position he held until at least 1427), and in the same year he was one of those nominated to hear differences which had arisen within the London Cutlers' Company. In 1422 he was elected sheriff of London, and already in that year was the object of complaints of harassment by Hanseatic merchants, which earned him a royal order to desist. In 1425 he became one of the wardens of the Mercers' Company, and in the following year was appointed one of the collectors of the wool subsidy at London. An alderman from 1423 until his death, by 1429, when he was elected mayor, he can be regarded as having reached the summit of London society. Eastfield was married twice: Juliana, presumably his first wife, was living in October 1437; his second wife was Alice.

Eastfield's greatest prominence, however, resulted from his position as a stapler—a wool exporter—which brought him into connection with royal finance. On 20 December 1430 he was promised repayment from clerical subsidies as one of a group of staplers, he being the only one named, who had lent the crown £2333 6s. 8d. On 24 April 1431 he was promised repayment from clerical subsidies as one of a consortium of eight men who had lent the crown 4000 marks. In 1435, together with Hamo Sutton and Hugh Dyke, he was promised repayment of a loan of 8000 marks, with preference as an exporter over others. This was an important instance of the crown's trying to break through the restrictive arrangements of the staple, and presumably Eastfield's participation made him a favourite with court and exchequer. He was responsible for loans of £1000 in 1440–41, £1000 in 1443, £500 in 1444–5, and £4800 in 1445. He was in fact the biggest individual lender to the crown during the 1440s. He was appointed one of the collectors of the tax imposed on landed property in January 1436. Less is known about him in the period 1436–9, but he then leapt back into prominence, to be regarded in his later years as someone to be favoured: member of parliament for London in 1439 and again in 1441, he was knighted in 1439. He was granted £40 a year from the issues of London and Middlesex in March 1443, and £10 a year from Lincolnshire in May 1444. In July 1443 he received a licence to hunt in the royal parks in Essex and Middlesex. In 1442 and 1444 he was mentioned as mayor of the staple of Westminster. Between 1442 and 1444 he was one of the royal emissaries who negotiated with representatives of Holland, Zeeland, and Friesland over trade disputes. In 1445 there is mention of a necklace which the king had bought from him.

Eastfield died shortly before 13 May 1446; both his wives were deceased by July 1444. His will mentions a daughter Margaret, married to John Bohun. It also contains very considerable bequests to the London poor, to several religious orders, and to the repair of the bridge at Wallingford, and also a bequest of £100 towards the maintenance of London highways. It shows him concerned to contribute to water conduits, especially at Aldermanbury, and in this respect he was remembered by Stow, particularly for piping water into the city from as far away as Paddington. He was also an important patron of the church of St Mary Aldermanbury, partially rebuilding it, adding a steeple, and founding a chantry at the altar of St George. He also gave a chalice to the church, and was himself buried there. The 'chapelayn for Maister Estfelde' was mentioned in the acts of court of the Mercers' Company as late as 1525.   GEORGE HOLMES

Sources A. B. Beaven, ed., *The aldermen of the City of London, temp. Henry III–[1912]*, 2 vols. (1908–13) · R. R. Sharpe, ed., *Calendar of wills proved and enrolled in the court of husting, London, AD 1258 – AD 1688*, 2 vols. (1889–90) · L. Lyell and F. D. Watney, eds., *Acts of court of the Mercers' Company, 1453–1527* (1936) · A. B. Steel, *The receipt of the exchequer, 1377–1485* (1954) · S. L. Thrupp, *The merchant class of medieval London, 1300–1500* (1948) · *Chancery records* · A. H. Thomas and P. E. Jones, eds., *Calendar of plea and memoranda rolls preserved among the archives of the corporation of the City of London at the Guildhall*, 6 vols. (1926–61) · R. R. Sharpe, ed., *Calendar of letter-books preserved in the archives of the corporation of the City of London*, [12 vols.] (1899–1912) · E. Power and M. Postan, *Studies in English trade in the fifteenth century* (1933) · J. Stow, *A survay of London*, rev. edn (1603); repr. with introduction by C. L. Kingsford as *A survey of London*, 2 vols. (1908); repr. with addns (1971)
Archives PRO, exchequer

Easthope, Sir John, baronet (1784–1865), politician and journalist, was born at Tewkesbury on 29 October 1784, the eldest son of Thomas Easthope and his wife, Elizabeth, daughter of John Leaver of Overbury, Worcestershire. He was originally a clerk in a provincial bank, and went to London to seek his fortune. In 1818, in partnership with Mr Allen, he became a member of the stock exchange and engaged in a series of speculations by which in the course of a few years he is said to have realized upwards of £150,000. He was a magistrate for Middlesex and Surrey, chairman of the London and South-Western Railway Company, a director of the Canada Land Company, and chairman of the Mexican Mining Company. He unsuccessfully contested St Albans as a Liberal on 9 June 1821, but was elected and sat for that borough from 1826 to 1830. In 1831 he was returned for Banbury; he contested Southampton and Lewes without success in 1835, but sat for Leicester from 1837 until 1847 when he retired from parliamentary life after contesting Bridgnorth unsuccessfully. Easthope was a fluent speaker in the Commons, confining himself to mercantile subjects. He purchased the ailing Liberal newspaper, the *Morning Chronicle*, from William Innell Clement in 1834 for £16,500, and sold his interest in the paper on his retirement from parliament in 1847. On 24 August 1841 he was created a baronet by Lord Melbourne, as a reward for his adherence to the Liberal Party, and for his advocacy of a war policy in connection with the potential conflict between Egyptian and Turkish interests in the Levant.

Easthope married, first, on 4 August 1807, Ann, daughter of Jacob Stokes of Leopard House, Worcester; second, on 19 September 1843 Elizabeth (d. 1865), eldest daughter of Colonel A. Skyring RA, and widow of Major John Longley RA. They had a son who died unmarried and three daughters; the baronetcy thus became extinct when Sir John died at his home, Fir Grove, Weybridge, Surrey, on 11 December 1865.   G. C. BOASE, *rev.* ANITA MCCONNELL

Sources *GM*, 4th ser., 1 (1866), 128; repr. in F. D. Barrows and D. B. Mock, *A dictionary of obituaries of modern British radicals* (1989), 135–6 · J. Sedgwick, *Letters addressed to … Lord Granville Somerset … F. Lewis … and … H. Goulburn, on the … proceedings connected with the … dissolution of the late Board of Stamps: with an address to the British public containing strictures on the conduct of Sir J. Easthope, as proprietor of the Morning Chronicle* (1845) · *The Times* (14 Dec 1865), 9 · [J. Grant], *Portraits of public characters*, 1 (1841), 76–86
Archives Bodl. Oxf., letters to Benjamin Disraeli · Duke U., Perkins L., corresp. and papers · UCL, corresp. with Sir Edwin Chadwick
Likenesses G. B. Black, lithograph (after J. Holmes), BM
Wealth at death under £30,000 in England: probate, 27 Jan 1866, *CGPLA Eng. & Wales*

Eastlake, Sir Charles Lock (1793–1865), painter and art administrator, was born at Plymouth on 17 November 1793, the fourth son of George Eastlake (*d.* 1820), judge-advocate and solicitor to the Admiralty, and his wife, Mary (*d.* 1823), daughter of Samuel Pierce of Exeter and step-daughter of the Revd Charles Lock.

Education and artistic training   Small in stature and very studious, Eastlake attended the grammar schools at Plymouth and Plympton, began French with a tutor, and had his first drawing lessons from Samuel Prout. Restless at Plympton, he was sent off to Charterhouse in the autumn of 1808. In December, however, he informed his father that he had decided to become a historical painter and wished to begin artistic studies at once.

With paternal consent, Eastlake began work in London as the first pupil of B. R. Haydon, a fellow townsman; in March 1809, on Haydon's advice, he entered the Royal Academy Schools. In 1810 the Society of Arts awarded him a silver medal, and the banker Jeremiah Harman gave him his first commission, fulfilled in 1812 with *The Raising of Jairus' Daughter*. In 1814, after a brief excursion to France, he finished *Brutus Exhorting the Romans to Revenge the Death of Lucretia* (Williamson Art Gallery and Museum, Birkenhead). He returned to France for the first eleven weeks of 1815 and saw in Paris in the Musée Napoléon paintings looted from continental collections. Like other alert contemporaries, he found that the juxtaposition of many works never before seen together quickened in him a curiosity about the historical development of art and a new breadth of taste. In July, seeing Bonaparte himself a captive on the *Bellerophon* in Plymouth Sound, he drew a sketch and then painted two portraits, of which the larger (National Maritime Museum, Greenwich) was purchased by five Plymouth gentlemen for 1000 guineas. This extraordinary success enabled the aspiring young painter to realize his dream of visiting Italy.

Years in Rome   Eastlake arrived in Rome on 24 November 1816 and resided there for fourteen years, visiting England only in 1820, after his father's death, and in 1828. Rome gave him more than a university could have offered: a studio at piazza Mignanelli 12, access to longed-for scenes, opportunities to travel, and the company of remarkable friends. The duchess of Devonshire gave him several

Sir Charles Lock Eastlake (1793–1865), by John Prescott Knight, exh. RA 1857

commissions; Sir George Beaumont, Sir Humphry Davy, and Samuel Rogers came to Rome as visitors; Sir Thomas Lawrence and J. M. W. Turner worked in Eastlake's studio. Younger artists formed an English academy with Eastlake as secretary, and his German friend Carl Bunsen provided a connection with the Nazarene painters and with J. D. Passavant, a rising historian of art.

Travelling south of Rome in 1817 with Seymour Kirkup, Eastlake felt a new passion for landscape; and in 1818, with Charles Barry and two other friends, he journeyed to Greece, then to Malta and Sicily, sketching indefatigably. At Rome the demand for Italian and Greek scenes proved so great that Eastlake needed, he said in 1819, ten hands. That summer he sojourned in the Apennines with Captain Thomas Graham and his wife, Maria, who later became Lady Callcott and the author of an important description (1835) of Giotto's frescoes in the Arena Chapel in Padua. For Maria Graham's *Three Months in the Mountains East of Rome* (1820), Eastlake prepared six illustrations, including the frontispiece, 'Costume of the Brigands'. Nine subsequent paintings of brigands attracted attention in England: eight shown at the British Institution (1823–5), six engraved in mezzotint, and three transmuted as tableaux in J. R. Planché's play *The Brigand* (1829).

Eastlake's first paintings exhibited at the Royal Academy were three views of Rome, shown in 1823. His works of the later 1820s included *The Champion* (exh. British Institution, 1825; City Museum and Art Gallery, Birmingham), *The Spartan Isadas* (exh. RA, 1827; priv. coll.), *Pilgrims Arriving in Sight of Rome* (exh. RA, 1828; priv. coll.), and *Lord*

Byron's 'Dream' (exh. RA, 1829; Tate collection). In 1824 Eastlake had become a member of the Athenaeum and in 1827 an associate of the Royal Academy, the first elected *in absentia*. Returning to Rome in 1828 after his visit to England, he travelled for nearly three months in Flanders, the Netherlands, Germany, and northern Italy, studying masterworks in the galleries and buying books. He developed a keen interest in early Netherlandish and Italian painting, and he formed at Berlin a lasting friendship with G. F. Waagen, later director of the Royal Gallery.

Return to London In 1830, elevated to full status as a Royal Academician, Eastlake returned to London and settled in Upper Fitzroy Street. At the academy he deposited his diploma picture, *Hagar and Ishmael*, and in 1831 he exhibited there *Head of a Greek Girl: Haidee* (Tate collection). He continued to favour Greek and Italian subjects: *Greek Fugitives* (exh. RA, 1833; Benaki Museum, Athens), *The Escape of the Carrara Family* (exh. RA, 1834; repetition, 1849; Tate collection), *Gaston de Foix before the Battle of Ravenna* (exh. RA, 1838), repetitions and variations of *Pilgrims* for several eminent patrons, and 'fancy portraits' of charming young Englishwomen in Italian costume. The 'Archbishop'—so W. M. Thackeray placed Eastlake in the hierarchy of British artists—painted also two scenes from the New Testament: *Christ Blessing Little Children* (exh. RA, 1839; Manchester City Galleries) and *Christ Weeping over Jerusalem* (exh. RA, 1841; repetitions, 1846 and 1855; Tate collection and the Art Gallery and Museum, Glasgow).

In 1840, recently elected a fellow of the Royal Society, Eastlake published *Goethe's Theory of Colours*, a translation of *Die Geschichte der Farbenlehre*, with extensive notes. The work so interested Turner that he scribbled marginalia in his copy. In the *Quarterly Review* of June 1840 Eastlake expressed admiration for Passavant's principles in *Rafael von Urbino*; and his translation of F. T. Kugler on the Italian schools of painting (1842) not only won Kugler as a grateful ally but also gave to English art lovers the book to be carried in Italy together with the indispensable Murray. John Murray—publisher of Eastlake's books as well as of the *Quarterly* and the guidebooks—became a very good friend.

Administrating arts: at the Palace of Westminster and the National Gallery Eastlake moved permanently to 7 Fitzroy Square in 1842. With appointments as secretary of the Fine Arts Commission (1841) and keeper of the National Gallery (1843), he now began an additional career. The commission, proposed by Sir Robert Peel and established in 1841 with Prince Albert as president, bore responsibility for the interior decoration of the new Palace of Westminster, designed by Eastlake's friend Charles Barry. The charge called for encouragement of British art and for consideration of fresco as the appropriate medium. Working harmoniously with the prince and the commissioners, Eastlake arranged the competitions for artists and the exhibitions of cartoons in Westminster Hall, wrote hundreds of letters to painters and sculptors, sought guidance from Nazarene fresco painters whom he had met in Rome, and watched attentively the progress of the British artists assigned to work in the new palace. These included Daniel Maclise, William Dyce, C. W. Cope, and E. M. Ward. The work dragged on into the 1860s, delayed by problems that included inadequate knowledge of fresco, damp walls causing some of the frescoes to disintegrate, changes in the artists' assignments, and a few artists who were dilatory or otherwise required diplomatic treatment. But Eastlake, and Prince Albert until he died in 1861, showed constant resolve and tact; and all involved in the enterprise deserve to be remembered for what they accomplished.

As keeper of the National Gallery, selected by Peel in 1843, Eastlake lasted four difficult years. He tended the collection; he might, on request, advise the trustees, who had responsibility *ex officio* but, lacking an annual grant for acquisitions, had to apply to the Treasury for funds whenever a suitable painting turned up in a London sale. As a result, the gallery lost several pictures to readier or higher bidders. Critics blamed Eastlake rather than the trustees, and considered him responsible also for questionable purchases. John Ruskin scolded him for buying another Guido Reni; J. Morris Moore (Verax) attacked him for buying the so-called 'Bad Holbein' (now known as *A Man with a Skull*) and the *Boar Hunt* of Velázquez (now entitled *Philip IV Hunting Wild Boar*). In 1844 the first cleaning of pictures in the gallery attracted little notice, but the next, in 1846, aroused Ruskin and Verax, a most persistent gadfly, to protest vehemently. Eastlake decided to resign but withheld his letter, while his defenders rallied, until November 1847.

Now painting relatively little, Eastlake enhanced his reputation as connoisseur and scholar with the first volumes of his impressively learned *Materials for a History of Oil Painting* (1847) and his *Contributions to the Literature of the Fine Arts* (1848), a compilation of articles, notes, and reports.

Marriage and presidency of the Royal Academy On 9 April 1849, in Edinburgh, Eastlake married Elizabeth Rigby [see Eastlake, Elizabeth (1809–1893)], a spirited forty-year-old Norwich bluestocking, translator of Passavant's *Kunstreise durch England* (1836), author of *A Residence on the Shores of the Baltic* (1841), reviewer of *Vanity Fair* and *Jane Eyre* for the *Quarterly Review* (December 1848), and a friend of the Murrays. On 4 November 1850 Eastlake was elected president of the Royal Academy. *Ex officio* he became a trustee of the National Gallery. On 13 November he was knighted by the queen at Windsor.

The Eastlakes were swept into the whirl of London social, cultural, and intellectual life, mixing with lords and ladies, clerics and scientists, writers and artists. Waagen and Passavant came and stayed in Fitzroy Square. Eastlake served in 1851 as a commissioner of the Great Exhibition, which opened on 1 May. On 4 June Lady Eastlake bore their only child, who was stillborn. She immersed herself in work on the second edition of Kugler (1851) and, late in 1852, undertook to translate the work by Waagen as *Treasures of Art in Great Britain* (1854). In 1853 the Photographic Society elected Eastlake as its first president, and the University of Oxford bestowed on him the degree of DCL, saluting incidentally his *conjugem clarissimam*. Lady Eastlake, inches taller than her husband, was sometimes known less diplomatically as 'Lago Maggiore'.

As president of the Royal Academy, Eastlake was precisely the person that almost all his colleagues wanted—a respected painter and a gentleman who could go anywhere and talk with anybody. For fifteen years he presided over the academy's affairs (including the first admission of women to the schools) with intelligence, patience, and tact, if not with dazzling innovativeness. The Eastlakes invited academicians to quasi-familial dinners, and Sir Charles delivered consistently 'admirable' discourses to students in the schools. In 1863, as the first witness before the commission inquiring into the Royal Academy's relations with art, artists, and the public, he answered 902 questions, many touching upon charges of clubby illiberality and self-protective taste-making; he received thanks for his candid and able testimony.

Director of the National Gallery As a trustee of the National Gallery, Eastlake could watch developments and sometimes offer advice based on experience. From 1847 to 1850 nothing had been purchased, and the quest for pictures had begun to shift from England to the continent; in 1852 the trustees' agent effected in Paris the first foreign purchase, Titian's *Tribute Money*. That summer the Eastlakes made their first continental journey together and saw their friend Waagen in Berlin.

Another picture-cleaning in the National Gallery soon reawakened the ire of Morris Moore, supported now by Francis Wemyss Charteris MP (later Lord Elcho by courtesy and earl of Wemyss). Responding to these and other critics, the house appointed a select committee on the National Gallery which listened in 1853 to testimony focused largely on dubious acquisitions and ill-defined administrative responsibilities. To clarify the situation, Eastlake (who answered 1156 questions) suggested an annual Treasury grant for purchases and the appointment of a managing triumvirate—a director in full charge but reporting to the trustees, a keeper to look after the collection, and a travelling agent to survey pictures that might become available abroad. This proposal drew strong support.

But in 1854 the National Gallery drifted into near chaos. At several meetings the trustees failed to muster a quorum. Not the trustees but the chancellor of the exchequer, W. E. Gladstone, masterminded the purchase of sixty-four German pictures, of which only seventeen proved acceptable. The keeper, Thomas Uwins, aged seventy-two, neared the end of his tether. A rumour spread: Waagen would be summoned from Berlin to impose order. But the man preferred by the queen, Prince Albert, and the prime minister, Lord Aberdeen, was Eastlake. On 2 July 1855 he was officially appointed first director of the National Gallery, with R. N. Wornum, who had catalogued the collection, as keeper and Otto Mündler, a knowledgeable and astute Bavarian, as travelling agent.

In August, Eastlake and Mündler began their first continental picture hunt, mainly in Italy, with a Treasury allowance of £3000. Lady Eastlake accompanied her husband. The seekers encountered difficulties: doubtful attributions, unthinkable asking prices, unwillingness to divide collections by selling only the finest specimens, disputed ownership, and Tuscan law prohibiting exportation of Tuscan property. Eventually Eastlake and Mündler surmounted obstacles and bought twenty pictures, among them a Mantegna *Madonna and Child* and Giovanni Bellini's *Madonna of the Pomegranate*. The total outlay doubled the allowance. Owing largely to Mündler's protracted efforts under Eastlake's direction, the National Gallery acquired in 1856 the 'Melzi Perugino', an important altarpiece, and in 1857—*annus mirabilis*—forty-two Italian paintings, including Madonnas by Margarito and Duccio, Uccello's *Battle of San Romano*, Pollaiuolo's *St Sebastian*, and Paolo Veronese's *Family of Darius before Alexander*. These extraordinary acquisitions failed to silence Lord Elcho and Morris Moore, however, and in July 1858 the house stopped Mündler's salary.

With Lady Eastlake, the director resumed his annual journeys abroad but made fewer notable foreign purchases—in 1860 Fra Angelico's *Christ Glorified in the Court of Heaven* and Bronzino's *Venus, Cupid, and Time*, in 1862 Crivelli's *Madonna delle rondine*. Among the paintings acquired in England were Piero della Francesca's *Baptism of Christ* in 1861, Giovanni Bellini's *Agony in the Garden* in 1863, and the 'Garvagh Raphael', *Madonna and Child with St. John*, in 1865. In the years since 1855 the National Gallery had purchased 175 pictures—138 Italian, thirty Netherlandish and German, seven British, and Eastlake, together with Wornum, had coped with routines and crises. Eastlake, always conscientiously avoiding any conflict of interest, had also added to his private collection.

Death and conclusion In August 1865 the Eastlakes left for Italy, where Sir Charles developed violent inflammation of the lungs. He died at Pisa on Christmas eve 1865. Buried first on 27 December 1865 at the protestant cemetery at Florence, he was reinterred more ceremoniously at Kensal Green, London, on 18 January 1866. In retrospect, all his earlier career appears to have prepared him uniquely for his years at the National Gallery. No Englishman of his time knew more about art; none could match his combination of experience, aesthetic judgement, historical knowledge, and *savoir-faire*. In experience, he was painter, connoisseur, and administrator; in habits of research, inquisitive and disciplined; in outlook, not insular but European. He was sixty-two when he took office as the first director of the National Gallery. Setting a brilliant example of intellectual strength and honourable service, he made the National Gallery great.

In 1861 Eastlake had given to the National Gallery an *Annunciation* by Filippo Lippi; in 1867 Lady Eastlake offered at the original prices, as her husband had wished, fifteen other paintings that he had bought privately since 1855. Nine were accepted at that time. All told, twenty-five pictures from Eastlake's collection have entered the gallery, and his art library and notebooks are preserved there, as is

Mündler's diary. Lady Eastlake completed in 1869 the second volume of her husband's *Materials for a History of Oil Painting* and wrote the memoir published in 1870 with the second series of his *Contributions to the Literature of the Fine Arts*. Eastlake's nephew and namesake, historian of the Gothic revival, succeeded Wornum as keeper of the National Gallery in 1878.   DAVID ROBERTSON

Sources Lady Eastlake [E. Eastlake], 'Memoir of Sir Charles Eastlake', in C. L. Eastlake, *Contributions to the literature of the fine arts*, 2nd ser. (1870) · *Journals and correspondence of Lady Eastlake*, ed. C. E. Smith, 2 vols. (1895) · D. Robertson, *Sir Charles Eastlake and the Victorian art world* (1978) · *DNB* · 'Select committee on … the National Gallery', *Parl. papers* (1852–3), vol. 35, no. 867 · *Report of the director of the National Gallery* (1856–65) · *The travel diaries of Otto Mündler, 1855–1858*, ed. C. T. Dowd, 51 (1985) [whole vol.] · C. Holmes and C. H. C. Baker, *The making of the National Gallery, 1824–1924* (1924) · 'Royal commission to inquire into … the Royal Academy', *Parl. papers* (1863), 27.1, no. 3205; 27.587, no. 3205-I · S. C. Hutchison, *The history of the Royal Academy, 1768–1986*, 2nd edn (1986) · 'Fine arts commission: report', *Parl. papers* (1842), 25.105–52, no. 412; (1843), 29.197–268, no. 499; (1844), 31.169–226, no. 585; (1845), 27.151–68, no. 671; (1846), 24.253–308, nos. 685, 749; (1847), 33.267–88, no. 862; (1849), 22.349–58, no. 1060; (1850), 23.329–36, no. 1180; (1854), 19.441–56, no. 1829; (1857–8), 24.201–12, no. 2425; (1861), 32.213–38, no. 2806; (1863), 16.317–28, no. 3141 [reports 1–13] · T. S. R. Boase, 'The decoration of the new Palace of Westminster, 1841–1863', *Journal of the Warburg and Courtauld Institutes*, 17 (1954), 319–58

Archives BL, corresp., RP 3236, 3336 [photocopies] · National Gallery, London, notebooks and art library · Plymouth City Museum and Art Gallery, letters from Rome · RIBA BAL, note and sketchbook made in Rome · V&A NAL, corresp. | BL, corresp. with W. E. Gladstone, Add. MSS 44374–44589 · BL, letters to Sir A. H. Layard, Add. MSS 38984–38991 · BL, corresp. with Sir Robert Peel, Add. MSS 40432–40600 · Bodl. Oxf., corresp. with John Callcott Horsley · CUL, letters to Joseph Bonomi · John Murray, London, archives, letters to John Murray · JRL, letters to Joseph Severn · National Gallery, London, Otto Mündler's diary · National Gallery, London, corresp. with Ralph Nicholson Wornum · NRA, priv. coll., corresp. with Lord Wemyss · RA, minutes of council and general assembly · RA, corresp. with Thomas Lawrence · V&A NAL, corresp. mainly as secretary of Fine Arts Commission

Likenesses attrib. J. Hayter, ink and pencil drawing, 1814, BM · G. Hayter, double portrait, pencil and wash drawing, 1816 (with S. Kirkup), BM · J. Partridge, pencil drawing, 1825, NPG; repro. in Robertson, *Sir Charles Eastlake*, fig. 2 · W. Brockedon, chalk drawing, 1828, NPG · C. C. Vogel, drawing, 1834, Staatliche Kunstsammlungen, Dresden · J. Gibson, marble bust, 1840–49, NPG · T. Bridgford, drawing, c.1844, Royal Hibernian Academy, Dublin · D. Huntington, oils, exh. RA 1852, New York Historical Society; repro. in J. Steegman, *Consort of taste* (1956), pl. 15 · J. P. Knight, oils, exh. RA 1857, RA [*see illus.*] · C. B. Birch, pencil drawings, c.1858/9, NPG · T. Bridgford, pencil drawing, c.1858, NPG · C. W. Cope, pen-and-ink caricature, c.1862, NPG · Caldesi, Blandford & Co., carte de visite, NPG · G. Partridge, group portrait (*The fine arts commissioners, 1846*), NPG · A. H. Ritchie, marble bust, City Museum and Art Gallery, Plymouth

Wealth at death under £40,000: probate, 10 May 1866, *CGPLA Eng. & Wales*

Eastlake, Charles Locke (1833–1906), museum keeper, was born on 11 March 1833 in Plymouth, the fourth son of George Eastlake (*b.* 1785), who was Admiralty law agent and deputy judge-advocate of the fleet in that town (an office held by the Eastlakes for many generations). His uncle was Sir Charles Lock *Eastlake (1793–1865), president of the Royal Academy and director of the National

Gallery. The elder Charles Eastlake took a personal interest in his young nephew, devoting every weekend to him, and in 1846 placed him at Westminster School where two years later he became a queen's scholar. Throughout his life Eastlake maintained an interest in the school and in later years was invited to join the governing body.

Showing a taste for architecture, Eastlake became a pupil of Philip Hardwick, and in 1853 entered the Royal Academy Schools. There, a year later, he gained a silver medal for architectural drawings; he exhibited two designs at the academy in 1855–6. On 1 October 1856 he married Eliza (*d.* 1911), youngest daughter of George Bailey. Soon after, having developed some skill in watercolours, he gave up architectural work and toured Europe for three years studying painting and sculpture. It was during this time that he acquired his taste for the Gothic style which became a lifelong passion.

On his return to England, Eastlake became a freelance journalist, contributing to a number of leading publications, including the *Nineteenth Century*, the *Cornhill Magazine*, *Building News*, and the *London Review*. Although he continued to write throughout his life, these early years when he 'used to sit up half the night writing for the press' (Eastlake, *Gothic Revival*, 18) were his most prolific. Between 1859 and 1862, as Jack Easel or Our Roving Correspondent, he contributed twenty-eight articles to *Punch* on a variety of artistic and social topics at home and abroad, and according to the author of the history of *Punch*, M. H. Spielmann, 'their note was lively enough to cause his papers to be looked forward to by *Punch*'s readers' (Spielmann, 362).

Interior decoration and industrial design were the aspects of his career for which Eastlake obtained popular recognition. In 1868 (based on a series of controversial articles originally published in *The Queen*) he published his first and best-known book, *Hints on Household Taste, in Furniture, Upholstery and other Details*. In this text he criticized the two most popular sub-styles of the day, the rococo and the Renaissance revival, and declared himself in favour of 'simplicity, rectangularity, and honest craftsmanship' (Eastlake, *Gothic Revival*, 19). The book was intended to show readers how to 'furnish their houses picturesquely, without ignoring modern notions of comfort and convenience' (Eastlake, *Hints on Household Taste*, vii), and had a considerable effect in preparing the way for the improvement of furniture design and applied art. In the United States, Eastlake's ideas were particularly popular and a new word was coined: a house furnished in improved taste was said to be 'Eastlaked' (Eastlake, *Gothic Revival*, 19). Several pieces of Eastlake-inspired furniture can now be found in the Hudson River Museum in New York. The book reached its fourth London edition in 1887. The sixth American edition was published in 1881.

In 1866 Eastlake gained his first administrative post, as secretary of the Royal Institute of British Architects. He conducted his duties punctiliously and was remembered as a man of 'courtesy and refined manners' (*The Builder*, 24 Nov 1906) who 'never missed a meeting' (Eastlake, *Gothic*

Revival, 19). He resigned in 1878, following his appointment by Lord Beaconsfield as keeper and secretary of the National Gallery. He performed the duties of his new post with efficiency until 1898. During this period he opened several rooms to exhibit Turner's sketches and watercolour drawings, improved the situation and accommodation for art students and copyists, and had many of the paintings placed under glass to protect them from the polluted London atmosphere. Perhaps his most notable achievement, however, was to rearrange and classify all the paintings, displaying them for the first time not as a 'miscellaneous chronological assortment' but according to 'scholastic subdivision' (Eastlake, 'Picture hanging', 821), under the different schools to which they belonged.

Eastlake was greatly disappointed that he did not succeed Sir Frederic Burton, who retired in 1894, as director of the gallery. The post then fell to Sir Edward Poynter. Eastlake retired four years later and described his keepership of the National Gallery as the 'most congenial occupation of his life' (Eastlake, 'Administration of the National Gallery', 946). He maintained an affection for the gallery for the rest of his life and donated one of his own paintings by Herman Saftleven to the collection in 1906.

Throughout his life Eastlake had continued to write. His second book, *A History of the Gothic Revival in England*, which retains much validity as a work of reference, was published in 1872. In 1876 he issued lectures on decorative art and art workmanship which he had delivered at the Social Science Congress. A series of illustrated notes on the principal pictures in foreign galleries dealt with the Brera Gallery in Milan (1883), the Louvre in Paris (1883), the Alte Pinakothek in Munich (1884), and the Accademia in Venice (1888). Following his disappointment at not becoming director of the National Gallery, he turned to anecdote and published *Our Square and Circle*, 'a nostalgic autobiographical sketch of wit and charm' (Eastlake, *Gothic Revival*, 22), in 1895.

For the duration of his retirement Eastlake lived with his wife in Leinster Square, Bayswater. They had no children. Eastlake spent his time in his library indulging in his favourite pastimes: reading and writing. He died at his home, 41 Leinster Square, Bayswater, London, on 20 November 1906, and was buried in Kensal Green cemetery.

      F. W. GIBSON, rev. CHARLOTTE L. BRUNSKILL

Sources C. L. Eastlake, ed., *A history of the Gothic revival* (1970) • D. Robertson, *Sir Charles Eastlake and the Victorian art world* (1978) • C. L. Eastlake, 'The chiefs of our national museums: the National Gallery, Mr C. L. Eastlake', *Art Journal*, ne ser., 11 (1891), 120–22 • B. L. Scherr, 'The Gothicist, shades of Charles Locke Eastlake', *The Connoisseur* (July 1983), 75–9 • *The Builder* (24 Nov 1906) • C. L. Eastlake, 'Picture hanging at the National Gallery', *Nineteenth Century*, 22 (1887), 817–26 • C. L. Eastlake, 'The administration of the National Gallery: a retrospect', *Nineteenth Century and After*, 54 (1903), 926–46 • C. L. Eastlake, *Hints on household taste in furniture, upholstery and other details*, 3rd edn (1872) • M. H. Spielmann, *The history of 'Punch'* (1895) • *Art Journal* (1907), 31 • NGI board minutes, vols. 5–7, 1871–1907, National Gallery, London, archives • letters from Eastlake, 1862–95, Punch Library, London, archive of *Punch* magazine, contributors' files, 1859–1862 • register, 1825–90, RA, Royal Academy Schools • letters to Council, 1866–85, RIBA BAL, manuscripts and archives collection • d. cert.

Archives RIBA BAL, sketchbook | *Punch* Library, London, archive of Punch magazine, contributors' files, letters • BL, letters to Sir A. H. Layard, Add. MSS 39036–39098, *passim* • National Gallery, London, NGI board minutes, vols. 5–7 • RA, Royal Academy Schools register, 414 • RIBA BAL, letters to council • Ruskin Gallery, Sheffield, Ruskin Gallery Collection of the Guild of St George (code: 969), letters to John Ruskin

Likenesses S. Fox, oils; formerly in possession of Mrs Eastlake

Wealth at death £15,082 6s. 3d.: probate, 14 Dec 1906, *CGPLA Eng. & Wales*

Eastlake [*née* Rigby], **Elizabeth**, Lady Eastlake (1809–1893), journalist and writer on art, was born in Norwich, Norfolk, on 17 November 1809, the third child and second daughter of Dr Edward *Rigby (1747–1821), physician, and his second wife, Anne (1777–1872), daughter of William Palgrave of Yarmouth. Elizabeth Rigby was one of their twelve children.

Childhood and education, 1809–1827 Both family connections and the region of her birth placed Elizabeth Rigby at the centre of impressive intellectual and social connections. Her father, who came from Lancashire, had been a pupil of Joseph Priestley; he moved to Norwich in 1762 to study medicine with Dr Norgate. A friend of Edward Jenner, he brought vaccination to Norwich but was not just a gynaecologist and obstetrician, but also a classical scholar, social reformer, and an expert on agricultural matters. He had important friends and his children had the advantage of 'mixing freely with such visitors' (*Journals*, 1.5). Norwich, where Elizabeth Rigby passed her childhood, was pivotal in the development of middle-class dissenting and liberal intellectual circles in the south of England. Through her father she was connected to leading Norwich families, such as the Taylors, the Meadows, and the Martineaus; relatives on this side of the family included Henry Reeve, political writer for *The Times*, Lucie Duff-Gordon, the travel writer, and Sir William Edward Parry, the Arctic explorer. Her connections were equally impressive on her mother's side. Her mother's sister was married to Dawson Turner, the botanist, antiquary, and patron of John Sell Cotman, and Elizabeth's relations through this marriage included Francis Palgrave, the historian.

Elizabeth Rigby early showed a love of art: she began drawing when she was eight, and left some 2000 specimens of her work. Her father brought in masters to teach his daughters French, geography, Italian, and arithmetic, and he encouraged them to read widely, a habit Elizabeth never lost. After his death in 1821 his widow moved to Framingham Earl, where the family had a small estate. Here the children seem only to have had a French governess, and Elizabeth Rigby was 'now permitted to educate herself' (*Journals*, 1.5).

Travel and early writing career, 1827–1842 In 1827 Elizabeth Rigby had typhoid fever: her family took her to Heidelberg and Switzerland to recuperate, a two-year visit which acted as a catalyst for her writing career. She began learning German, and translated and published J. P. Passavant's essay on English art collections as *Tour of a German Artist in*

England (1836); this début performance was apparently followed by the publication of a short story for *Fraser's Magazine*, 'My Aunt in a Salt Mine', which has proved difficult to trace. Despite this promising start to authorship, she still seems to have hoped for an artistic career as well: her portraits were praised by E. T. Daniell, and in July 1832 she moved to London, where she spent a year studying literature and art in the British Museum and the National Gallery. She became a pupil of Henry Sass, who held art classes for ladies in Bloomsbury.

Travel soon claimed Elizabeth Rigby's attention again: in 1835, she returned to Germany, and subsequently wrote an article on Goethe for the *Foreign Quarterly*. Then, in October 1838, she travelled to Russia, and spent a year and a half there, staying mainly in Estonia with a married sister who owned both a country estate and a town house in Reval (Tallinn). Her letters home during this prolonged stay were published in 1841 by John Murray, to whom she was introduced by Henry Reeve. *A Residence on the Shores of the Baltic* (1841) is a very readable travel book, which reflects her enquiring mind: she describes everything from the high-society events of St Petersburg (where she stayed on her way to and from Estonia) to Baltic marriage customs, from the impact of Russian government in Estonia to a duty-free shopping spree in Helsinki. The manuscript was read by J. G. Lockhart (who may have later developed a *tendre* for her), and he asked her to write for the *Quarterly Review*, of which he was editor. Although she claimed that 'my pen has never been a favourite implement with me; the pencil is the child of my heart' (*Journals*, 1.10), a career as a professional writer was becoming increasingly appealing. Her first article in the *Quarterly Review* appeared in March 1842: it discussed three travellers' accounts of Russia. She was the first woman to write regularly for the *Review*. A flow of articles followed, including reviews of recent evangelical novels (May 1843) and—appropriately enough—travel books by women writers (June 1845), which were judged as much on the feminine and domestic characters of their writers as their intrinsic value as *aperçus* into the cultures of other countries. *Livonian Tales*, a collection of three stories, based on her Baltic experiences, was published by Murray in 1846.

Edinburgh years, 1842–1849 In October 1842 Anne Rigby sold her Framingham estate and moved her family to Edinburgh. There Elizabeth Rigby's connections with Murray and Lockhart secured the entrée into intellectual circles which included individuals such as Lord Jeffrey, Professor Wilson, Sir William Drysdale, and D. O. Hill, who photographed her. She clearly established herself, her nephew commenting that she was 'A strikingly handsome, imperial-looking woman, of commanding figure'— she was 5 feet 11 inches tall—who 'had the additional attraction of great conversational powers' (*Journals*, 1.30). Hill's and Adamson's photograph of 1844–5 largely confirms the physical side of this description: rather more striking than handsome, Elizabeth Rigby was unusually tall and commanding. As for her powers of conversation, these were supported by wide-ranging reading—her diary in the early 1840s records books by Robert Southey, Walter

Scott (an old favourite), W. E. Gladstone, Francis Bacon, Maria Edgeworth, and Sarah Tytler—while she also took a lively interest in contemporary events such as the Disruption in 1843.

Tours continued too. Some were near home: in summer 1843 the Rigby family stayed in the highlands at Dunoon, where Elizabeth admired the scenery but not so much the highlanders themselves. But some trips took her further afield: early in 1844, for instance, she stayed in London with the Murrays and met literary and artistic lions, including Thomas Carlyle, George Borrow, J. M. W. Turner, and Agnes Strickland. In 1846 she repeated the visit, going to the Royal Academy exhibition, where she admired the works of Etty, Landseer, Turner, and Eastlake. Eastlake took her into dinner at a party on 19 May, and she found him 'most refined and amiable' (*Journals*, 1.187). Elizabeth Rigby also continued to visit the continent. In 1844 she again visited her married sisters in Estonia, travelling back through Stockholm, and in 1845 she spent two months in Germany. Two *Quarterly Review* articles resulted from this latter trip—one on modern German paintings (March 1846) and one on the cathedral of Cologne (September 1846). In 1848 she again visited Germany for two months, meeting Passavant in Frankfurt.

In October 1848 Elizabeth Rigby began her most famous *Quarterly Review* article of all, the review of *Vanity Fair* and *Jane Eyre* which was published in December that year. While the article delighted in Becky Sharp's amoral wickedness, it condemned *Jane Eyre* as 'an anti-Christian composition … a murmuring against God's appointment' and described its heroine as 'the personification of an unregenerate and undisciplined spirit' (*QR*, 84, Dec 1848, 173–4, 171). Nevertheless Rigby (somewhat uneasily) acknowledged the power of the novel, commenting that it was 'a very remarkable book: we have no remembrance of another combining such genuine power with such horrid taste' (ibid., 163). Some of her criticisms—for instance, of the unrealistic dialogue of the lady visitors to Thornfield—are well made. The most curious feature of all remains Rigby's famously inaccurate identification of the author as a man. This was made on the basis of errors in details about dress and cuisine which (she argued) no woman would have made, an insight which—as she was herself writing as a man—she was obliged to attribute to an imaginary female friend.

Marriage and London society In February 1846 Elizabeth Rigby commented in her diary that in civilized countries it was no wonder that many women remained single: there were many compensations, and spinsters did not attract the opprobrium which was their lot elsewhere. Despite this heartening reflection, in her fortieth year she became engaged to Charles Lock *Eastlake (1793–1865); they were married in Edinburgh on 9 April 1849, and three weeks later began their London life together in 7 Fitzroy Square. The match was a good one, in both senses of the word (although without children—their only child was born dead in June 1851). Eastlake, who was knighted in 1850, was a painter more distinguished for his broad knowledge of the history of art and his pivotal role in the London art world than for his artistic output.

Lady Eastlake quickly became part of London society. In the first few years of her marriage she attended a round of concerts and dinners, mixing with individuals as varied as Lady Lovelace (Byron's daughter), Lady Marion Alford (an expert on needlework), the mathematician Charles Babbage, the historian Macaulay, the antediluvian Misses Berry, Charles Dickens, Thomas Carlyle, the philanthropist Angela Burdett-Coutts, and the notorious Caroline Norton. In 1851, following Eastlake's election as president of the Royal Academy, the Eastlakes held a series of dinners for artists; guests included both Landseers, the Chalons, Charles Cope, David Roberts, and William Dyce. These dinners included foreign visitors on occasion: in May and June 1850 both Passavant and Gustav Friedrich Waagen, director of the Royal Gallery in Berlin, came to stay with the Eastlakes. Lady Eastlake attended all major social and cultural events, including the opening of the Great Exhibition and the funeral of the duke of Wellington in November 1852; in that year she also apparently made an appearance at Turner's deathbed.

In 1854 Lady Eastlake was involved in a minor social scandal, when she found herself confidante to Effie Ruskin, in her attempt to annul her marriage with John Ruskin. She had met the couple in 1850, and never seems to have warmed to John Ruskin. She certainly did not admire his art criticism: her review of volumes 2 and 3 of *Modern Painters* (which appeared in the *Quarterly Review* of March 1856) roundly condemned his work as 'morbid and diseased', characterized by 'active thought, brilliant style, wrong reasoning, false statements, and unmannerly language' (*QR*, 98, March 1856, 402, 387). Lady Eastlake never abated her dislike of Ruskin himself: as late as February 1870, having heard Ruskin address the Royal Institution, she commented acidly in a letter to A. H. Layard that the lecture was 'a brilliant, ridiculous, and interesting performance' (*Journals*, 2.214).

Continental connections, 1852–1865 In autumn 1852 Lady Eastlake visited the continent with her husband, as she was to do every year afterwards until his death, except for 1853 and 1856. These trips had as their final destination Italy, but *en route* the Eastlakes would visit France, Belgium, Germany, Austria, and Switzerland; in 1859 they even visited Spain. These tours greatly enriched Lady Eastlake's art-historical knowledge, teaching her a wide appreciation of continental art and architecture. The tour of 1852 was typical of these journeys. In this year the Eastlakes visited Bruges, Ghent, Antwerp, Berlin, Dresden, Vienna, Prague, and Venice.

The tour of 1855 was equally impressive, and illustrates the Eastlakes' involvement in purchases for the National Gallery. It began in Paris, where they saw the Universal Exhibition in the Palais des Beaux-Arts. They travelled on to Strasbourg, Karlsruhe, and then Switzerland, where Lady Eastlake admired the honesty and cleanliness of the people. Then they went on to Bergamo, Milan, Parma, Modena, and Carrara, before reaching Tuscany. They arrived in Lucca, and visited Pisa before spending a week

or so in Florence. Lady Eastlake reflected on the Italians' neglect of their artworks, and on her own growing fondness for early Italian art: she wrote that 'I am now fairly bitten with all the true pre-Raphaelites' (*Journals*, 2.76). The tour continued to Ferrara and Venice, before they returned to London.

Publications, 1849–1865 After her marriage Elizabeth Eastlake remained a prolific writer, often collaborating to some extent with her husband. She continued to popularize German art-historical research among British readers with the publication in 1851 of *Handbook of the History of Painting, Part I: The Italian Schools*, her translation of the second edition of F. T. Kugler's original, a work which her husband had translated originally in 1842. In October 1852 she began a translation of G. F. Waagen's monumental work, published as *Treasures of Art in Great Britain* (1854). For her next book she was required to do more than translate: in 1860 the pioneering woman art historian Anna Jameson died, and Lady Eastlake was asked to complete her *History of Our Lord*, a study of the iconography of Christ. She finished the book in 1863, having effectively maintained Jameson's feminist approach, and it was published in 1864. Lady Eastlake continued to contribute frequently to the *Quarterly Review* in the 1850s and early 1860s, writing articles on subjects as diverse as the Crystal Palace (March 1855) and photography (April 1857). This last article—besides accurately summarizing the history of photography—intelligently discussed its relationship to art.

Widowhood and later years In August 1865 the Eastlakes set off as usual on their continental tour; however, Charles Eastlake was already unwell, and he died in Pisa on 24 December. Although grief-stricken, Lady Eastlake faced her bereavement with her characteristic resilience, writing *Fellowship: Letters Addressed to my Sister Mourners* (1868), a sensible but rather moving book of advice which reflected her conventional but deep Anglican piety. She also increasingly cultivated her circle of friends, among whom the most stalwart was Austen Henry Layard, the archaeologist, who advised her to write the memoir of her husband which was published in 1870. She also became close to Harriet Grote, the former muse of the utilitarians, and wrote an appreciative memoir of her (1880). Dean and Lady Augusta Stanley and the illustrator Eleanor Vere Boyle were also close friends, as too the curious Mme Mohl.

Lady Eastlake retained her interest in travel and continental art: in September 1871 she toured Germany, the focus of her visit being the Holbein exhibition then in Dresden. She visited Paris in the following spring, and in autumn 1873 Scotland, staying at Lochgilphead at Sir John Orde's. Her most ambitious tour was in 1877, when she spent half the year in Venice, publishing 'Venice defended' in the *Edinburgh Review* for July 1877. In 1878 she returned to the Baltic provinces and St Petersburg.

At home Lady Eastlake often visited exhibitions, including those of Fred Walker and George Pinwell (1876). In February 1883 she visited the Rossetti exhibition in Savile

Row, London, and described the paintings to her nephew as 'horrors', without a single merit' (*Journals*, 2.277). Current affairs also attracted her attention. Her political sympathies had always been Conservative, and this tendency increased with age: she developed a dislike for Gladstone as vehement as that of Queen Victoria. She opposed compulsory elementary education, but took a more moderate line on women's suffrage:

> it is simply a matter of sense and consistency. Low as the qualification is now, it is still a property-, not a sex-qualification; and if women can hold property, then *that* should give them the vote.   (ibid., 2.283-4)

Later publications, 1865–1893 In a letter to Layard in December 1873 Lady Eastlake wrote that 'I lack spirit for company, and find work a more congenial filler up of my days than any amusement' (*Journals*, 2.233). This is certainly borne out by her publications in the last decades of her life. She continued to write for the *Quarterly Review* on topics including reform of the British Museum (with Harriet Grote; January 1868), the dangers of drink (October 1875), and women's education (July 1878). However, the majority of her art-historical articles appeared in the *Edinburgh Review* between 1872 and 1883: on Leonardo da Vinci, Michelangelo, Titian, and Raphael. These articles—together with one on Dürer in the *Quarterly Review*—appeared as *Five Great Painters* (1883). She also published a memoir of her friend the sculptor John Gibson, in 1870, and re-edited her translation of Kugler, the *Handbook of Italian Art*, 'importing into it all Cavalcaselle's latest information' (ibid., 2.214). In 1880 she published her edition of her father's letters, written while he was detained in Paris during the French Revolution.

Death and assessment From the late 1870s Elizabeth Eastlake increasingly suffered from rheumatism. However, she faced advancing age with humour, content to read interesting books as she became more confined to her room and missing only exhibitions and dinner parties. In August 1893 she became seriously ill with breathlessness and died on 2 October 1893 at her home, 7 Fitzroy Square, London. She was buried in Kensal Green cemetery on 6 October 1893.

Elizabeth Eastlake is best known for her extraordinary—and apparently contradictory—interventions in the lives of Charlotte Brontë and the Ruskins: historians of women can find much to ponder in the extremes of religious conventionality and liberal-minded feminist sympathy reflected in these two episodes—as too in the nature of the intellectual exchange between herself and her husband, which has recently been the subject of scholarly debate. But her long career as a journalist and a writer on art and art history is ultimately more significant. With Harriet Martineau and Frances Power Cobbe, she was a pioneer of female journalism; like women such as Maria Callcott, Anna Jameson, Lady Dilke, and Julia Cartwright, she played an important role in the development of nineteenth-century art criticism and history.

Elizabeth Eastlake's writing on art comes as a sensible if uninspired counterfoil in the age of Ruskin: she rejected literary approaches to art, stressing its autonomy, and she had little truck with the Romantic idea that art reflected the moral condition of society. Although at times there is little in her analysis of paintings that would surprise Sir Joshua Reynolds, she played an important role in the development of new standards in connoisseurship, reading and digesting new scholarship by Crowe, Cavalcaselle, and Giovanni Morelli. With her husband she was an important figure in the revival of interest in the Italian primitives. Her appreciation of artworks was eclectic, within the boundaries of better-known European artworks: she wrote with perception about more than six centuries of art. She had 'a readiness to appreciate, what was, at any given time, generally considered to be somewhat beyond the average range of approval' wrote Francis Haskell, somewhat unkindly (*Rediscoveries in Taste*, 1976, 20); her own view was that 'my heart is large, and catholicism in art is everything' (*Journals*, 2.266).

ROSEMARY MITCHELL

Sources *Journals and correspondence of Lady Eastlake*, ed. C. E. Smith, 2 vols. (1895) • D. Robertson, *Sir Charles Eastlake and the Victorian art world* (1978) • M. Locchead, *Elizabeth Rigby, Lady Eastlake* (1961) • E. Rigby, *A residence on the shores of the Baltic* (1841) • A. M. Ernstrom, '"Equally lenders and borrowers in turn": the working and married lives of the Eastlakes', *Art History*, 15 (1992), 470–85 • M. Lutyens, *Millais and the Ruskins* (1967) • C. R. Sherman and A. M. Holcomb, *Women as interpreters of the visual arts, 1820–1979* (1981) • *Wellesley index* • G. Paston, *At John Murray's: records of a literary circle, 1843–1892* (1932) • W. S. Johnson, 'The bride of literature: Ruskin, the Eastlakes and mid-Victorian theories of art', *Victorian Newsletter*, 26 (autumn 1964), 23–8 • *CGPLA Eng. & Wales* (1894)

Archives AM Oxf., MSS • John Murray, London, MSS • V&A NAL, corresp. | BL, corresp., mainly with Sir A. H. Layard • Holborn Library, London, Camden Local Studies and Archives Centre, letters to Mrs Acton Tindal and others • NL Scot., letters to William Blackwood & Sons • NRA, priv. coll., letters to Hannah Brightwen • U. Nott. L., corresp. with R. L. Brown • University of North Carolina Library, Chapel Hill, letters to Sir William Boxall [copies in National Gallery]

Likenesses D. O. Hill, calotype, 1844–5, repro. in Robertson, *Sir Charles Eastlake*, 105 • D. O. Hill, calotype, 1844–5, NPG; repro. in Ernstrom, '"Equally lenders"', 472 • W. Boxall, chalk drawing, *c.*1850, AM Oxf. • W. Boxall, oils, 1854, repro. in Smith, ed., *Journals and correspondence*, frontispiece • Ferrier, woodcut (after photograph by J. & C. Watkins), NPG; repro. in *Lady's Own Paper* (9 March 1867) • D. O. Hill and R. Adamson, photographs, NPG • C. Smyth, watercolour miniature, NPG • lithograph, NPG

Wealth at death £27,945: probate, Aug 1894, *CGPLA Eng. & Wales*

Eastmead, William (d. 1847?), Congregational minister, was pastor at Kirkby Moorside, Yorkshire, between 1813 and 1826, when he moved to Hull. In 1814 he published *Observations on Human Life*. In 1821 William Buckland (1784–1856) discovered a cave at nearby Kirkland containing the remains of several species of animal long extinct in England, which he was to use to support the theory of catastrophic geology; shortly afterwards Eastmead made a proposal to publish, by subscription, a 'memoir of the hyena's den lately discovered at Kirkdale' (*BL cat.*). This work was published in 1824, dedicated to Francis Wrangham, archdeacon of Cleveland, as *Historia Rievallensis: containing the history of Kirkby Moorside, and an account of the most important places in its vicinity; To which is prefixed a dissertation* *on the animal remains and other curious phenomena in the recently discovered cave at Kirkdale.* Eastmead died about 1847.   THOMPSON COOPER, *rev.* K. D. REYNOLDS

Sources review, *Evangelical Magazine*, 18 (1810), 170 • *Evangelical Magazine and Missionary Chronicle*, 23 (1815), 547 • *N&Q*, 3rd ser., 4 (1863), 186–7, 258 • P. J. Bowler, *The Fontana history of the environmental sciences* (1992)

Easton, Adam (*c.*1330–1397), Benedictine monk, scholar, and ecclesiastic, was presumably a native of the village of Easton 6 miles north-west of Norwich. He became a monk of Norwich Cathedral priory, and there are some grounds for believing that the young novice found his religious community there 'a centre of lively theological controversy' (Pantin, *English Church*, 177). By 1352–3 Easton had already been sent to study at Gloucester College, Oxford, where he was soon—at a remarkably early stage of his career—noted for his skills as a preacher. On at least one occasion between *c.*1357 and 1363 he was temporarily recalled to his mother house in order to denounce the errors of the Norwich friars. On the evidence of Easton's own later writings, he was presumably already elaborating the antimendicant teachings of Richard Fitzralph (*d.* 1360), and so demonstrating his ability to engage in the most controversial intellectual issues of the age. By the early 1360s his fellow Benedictine scholars at Oxford regarded Easton as their most academically promising colleague; and in 1363–4 he became a doctor of theology after demonstrating his scholastic skills with a carefully prepared *determinatio*. He remained at Oxford at least long enough to be academic superior (*prior studentium*) of Gloucester College in September 1366.

When Easton eventually left Oxford, it was not for a secluded monastic life at Norwich Cathedral (which he probably revisited only rarely, if at all, during the last thirty years of his life), but for the greater and more dangerous opportunities of residence at the papal curia. So unusual a change of career can only have been due to the influence of a still more senior black monk, Simon Langham, who in November 1368 resigned the archbishopric of Canterbury to become a cardinal of the Holy See. Easton was already at Avignon by May 1368, when he was sent as an envoy to Edward III by Pope Urban V (*r.* 1362–70), and he was obviously an ideal companion for a new English Benedictine cardinal at the papal court. He probably accompanied Langham to Avignon in early 1369, apparently acted as one of his secretaries thereafter, and finally served as one of the cardinal's executors on his death in 1376. Easton's precise movements and responsibilities during the closing years of the Avignon papacy are often obscure, but he certainly served as a proctor at the curia for the English Benedictine chapters. In November 1376 he wrote from Avignon to the abbot of Westminster asking for copies of John Wyclif's writings 'against our order' as well as his *libellus* 'concerning royal power' (Pantin, *Documents Illustrating the … Black Monks*, 3.76–7). Easton and his fellow Benedictines at the curia were quick to appreciate the dangerous implications of Wyclif's teachings, and by 22 May 1377 Tolstanus (probably a garbled form of Easton's name) and his 'black dogs' (as they were soon to

be castigated by the heretic himself) had persuaded Gregory XI (*r.* 1370–78) to issue the first full-scale papal denunciation of Wyclif's most heinous conclusions. Easton's determination to expose Wyclif's errors emerges quite as clearly from what seems to have been his longest and most encyclopaedic work, the *Defensorium ecclesiasticae potestatis*. Although only the prologue and the first of its six books now survive (*Defensorium ecclesiasticae potestatis*, Vatican City, Biblioteca Apostolica Vaticana, MS Vat. lat. 4116), it is evident that Easton's original purpose had been to defend the superiority of the pope against the criticisms of William Ockham (*d.* 1349), Marsilio de Padua, and Jean de Jandun; but by the time he had completed the *Defensorium* in 1378–81, Wyclif had become the 'notable doctor' whose attacks on the authority of the church alarmed him most of all.

Easton dedicated his *Defensorium* to the 'monarch of the world', Urban VI (*r.* 1378–89), at whose fateful election as supreme pontiff in Rome on 8 April 1378 he had himself been present. In the course of a conversation held on the following day Easton prophesied that Urban's election should be highly popular in England because it would emancipate so many wealthy benefices from the acquisitive appetites of the French clergy. Only a few months later, and partly for that very reason, Christendom was in a state of schism; and henceforward Easton's career was to be inseparably linked to the ever changing political fortunes of the Urbanist papacy he and his king were committed to support. At first his rewards were spectacular enough. On 21 December 1381 Urban created Easton cardinal-priest of Santa Cecilia in Trastevere; and in the following March Easton, who was henceforward often known simply as the Cardinal of England, was provided to the deanery of York, the most wealthy non-episcopal benefice in England. But three years later the fortunes of the new cardinal were completely reversed. On 11 January 1385 he and five other cardinals were arrested and tortured at Nocera in Umbria by the notoriously unstable Urban VI, on the grounds that they had launched a conspiracy against him. Whether Easton himself ever did much more than complain of Urban's excessive arrogance is now impossible to determine. However, after being deprived of his cardinalate and deanery of York, he was almost put to death, despite the protests of the English government and the presidents of the black monks' provincial chapter. Only after Boniface IX succeeded Urban VI in late 1389 was Easton set at liberty again. On 18 December of that year Boniface reinstated him as cardinal; and in the next few years Easton received a series of papal provisions—not always effective—to a bewildering variety of benefices, ranging from the archdeaconry of Shetland and Orkney (1391) to the precentorship of Lisbon Cathedral (1390). By the 1390s the available evidence suggests that the elderly Cardinalis Angliae was no longer much involved in the detailed conduct of Anglo-papal relations; and it was as a venerable man of learning that he was to be most remembered at the curia he had served so long, when in 1397 (on 15 September according to his epitaph) he died at Rome. He was buried in his titular church, where his imposing tomb still displays the leopards and lilies of England and France.

Few of the many works attributed to Easton by John Bale and others have yet been identified, if indeed they survive at all. One of his most remarkable accomplishments was his proficiency in Hebrew, which he learnt with the help of a Jewish scholar at Avignon. Easton allegedly produced nothing less than a complete translation of the Old Testament (except the psalter) from Hebrew into Latin, a copy of which still survived in early sixteenth-century England. However the surviving first book of the *Defensorium*, with its discussion of the issues of divine and human lordship as adumbrated by Fitzralph as well as its more traditional defence of papal superiority, was the outcome of twenty years of study and probably represents Easton's learning at its most characteristic. As an Urbanist cardinal he was apparently careful not to engage himself directly in the strident new polemical debates stimulated by the papal schism; and his later writings ranged widely from anti-heretical treatises to a liturgical office in honour of the Blessed Virgin Mary. Less conventional was his elaborate and highly sympathetic defence of the rule of St Bridget of Sweden (whom he had probably met at the curia before her death in 1373), which Easton presented to Boniface IX in the early 1390s. Not surprisingly, the cardinal's own library was a very large one; survivals from it include a Hebrew dictionary, the *Policraticus* of John of Salisbury, and an illuminated copy of Fitzralph's *De pauperie Salvatoris*. Easton bequeathed no less than 228 of his books to his former monastery, where in 1407 they at last arrived (packed in six barrels) as a final memorial to his old community of the most celebrated of all the alumni of Norwich Cathedral priory.   R. B. DOBSON

Sources L. J. Macfarlane, 'The life and works of Adam Easton OSB', PhD diss., U. Lond., 1955 · W. A. Pantin, 'The *Defensorium* of Adam Easton', *EngHR*, 51 (1936), 675–80 · W. A. Pantin, *The English church in the fourteenth century* (1955) · D. Knowles [M. C. Knowles], *The religious orders in England*, 2 (1955), 56–8 · L. Macfarlane, 'An English account of the election of Urban VI, 1378', *BIHR*, 26 (1953), 75–85 · *Hist. U. Oxf.* 2: *Late med. Oxf.*, 183, 201–6 · W. A. Pantin, ed., *Documents illustrating the activities of … the English black monks, 1215–1540*, 3 vols., CS, 3rd ser., 45, 47, 54 (1931–7) · Bale, *Cat.*, 1.516–17 · Emden, *Oxf.* · M. Harvey, 'John Whethamstede, the pope, and the general council', *The church in pre-Reformation society: essays in honour of F. R. H. Du Boulay*, ed. C. M. Barron and C. Harper-Bill (1985), 108–22 · H. C. Beeching and M. R. James, 'The library of the cathedral church of Norwich', *Norfolk Archaeology*, 19 (1915–17), 67–116 · L. C. Hector and B. F. Harvey, eds. and trans., *The Westminster chronicle, 1381–1394*, OMT (1982), 106, 410–11 · *Thomae Walsingham, quondam monachi S. Albani, historia Anglicana*, ed. H. T. Riley, 2 vols., pt 1 of *Chronica monasterii S. Albani*, Rolls Series, 28 (1863–4), vol. 2, pp. 122–3, 197 · H. B. Workman, *John Wyclif*, 2 vols. (1926), vol. 1, pp. 101, 129, 183; vol. 2, pp. 72, 124, 422 · G. Holmes, *The Good Parliament* (1975), 146, 167, 174 · E. Perroy, *L'Angleterre et le grand schisme d'occident* (Paris, 1933) · J. Greatrex, 'Monk students from Norwich Cathedral priory at Oxford and Cambridge, c. 1300–1530', *EngHR*, 106 (1991), 555–83 · N. P. Tanner, *The church in late medieval Norwich, 1370–1532* (1984)

Archives Biblioteca Apostolica Vaticana, Vatican City, MS Vat. lat. 4116 · Bodl. Oxf., MS Hamilton 7

Likenesses tomb effigy, St Cecilia Church, Trastevere, Rome

Easton, Hugh Ray (1906–1965), stained-glass artist, was born in London on 26 November 1906, the son of Frank Easton, medical practitioner, and his wife, Alice Muriel, daughter of William Howland. Easton was educated at Wellington College, Berkshire, and studied languages at the University of Tours. He later studied art in France and Italy. He learnt the craft of stained glass from the Guildford firm of Blacking and set up his first studio in Cambridge. During the Second World War he was naval adviser to the censorship division of the Ministry of Information with rank of commander RNVR. After the war he constructed a studio from a partly bombed house in Hampstead. He then settled at 6a Holbein Place. Most of his windows were made at The Studio, 4 High Street, Harpenden, Hertfordshire, run by Robert L. Hendra and Geoffrey F. Harper.

Easton designed the stained glass (1943–7) for the Battle of Britain Chapel in Westminster Abbey, arranging the heraldic elements (the RAF squadron badges) in an unusually dramatic way and successfully mixing these with references to loss and sacrifice using a pictorial device that he referred to as 'visions'. In one window, for example, a young airman kneels before the radiant figure of Christ. On a similar theme, a new window was completed (1949) for the front hall of the Rolls-Royce factory in Derby. Here before a background of Rolls-Royce workshops a young pilot in battledress stands on the three bladed spinner of an airscrew. Above him a golden eagle flies against the sun.

Stylistically Easton's work derives from Sir Ninian Comper and his pupil Christopher Webb with whom Easton was on 'weekly visiting' terms at Webb's Orchard House Studio in St Albans. Easton described his working methods as starting with 'the roughest of small drawings' (Armitage, 188–9) from which he gradually developed the definitive full-sized drawing which would be taken to Hendra and Harper for fabrication. 'Although I painted my earliest windows myself, I soon found that if one was fortunate enough to discover an artist who could paint and interpret one's drawings, a far greater technical mastery was achieved' (ibid.).

Peter Ryall, an employee in the studio, remembered Easton as tall, slim, and 'approachable and very friendly'. Brian Thomas wrote of his 'accomplished social manner' (*DNB*). Easton was a popular designer of memorial windows (about 250) which were much in demand during the post-war years and it is undoubtedly his stained-glass figure of the young airman that remains one of the defining images of those days. Easton died of cancer on 15 August 1965 at the King Edward VII Hospital for Officers, London.   CAROLINE SWASH

Sources *The Times* (16 Aug 1965) · E. L. Armitage, *Stained glass: history, technology and practice* (1959) · Westminster Abbey Muniment Room and Library, MSS relating to the Battle of Britain Chapel · Westminster Abbey Muniment Room and Library, Peers MSS · 'Unveiling of a window', *Rolls Royce commemorative brochure*, 11 Jan 1949, Rolls Royce plc, Derby · *Journal of the British Society of Master Glass Painters*, 14 (1964) · *CGPLA Eng. & Wales* (1965) · *DNB* · personal knowledge (1981) [*DNB*] · private information (1981, 2004) [P. Ryall, F. Sheat]

Archives V&A NAL, diaries, artwork, publications, and photographs
Likenesses photograph, 1949, repro. in 'Unveiling of a window'
Wealth at death £53,506: administration, 4 Nov 1965, CGPLA Eng. & Wales

Easton, Sir James Alfred [Jack] (1908–1990), air force officer and intelligence officer, was born in Winchester on 11 February 1908, the youngest in the family of two sons and five daughters of William Coryndon Easton, chemist and botanist, and his wife, Alice Summers. He was educated at Peter Symonds School, Winchester. He passed into the Royal Air Force College at Cranwell in 1926, and was commissioned into the RAF in 1928. He held a series of flying appointments, including a spell in biplanes co-operating with the army on the north-west frontier of India (1929–32) and duties in Egypt (1934–6). He was also increasingly regarded as an able young officer with a promising future. In 1937 he was posted to Canada as RAF armament liaison officer with the Canadian national ministry of defence (1937–9). There he met and married in 1939 Anna Mary (d. 1977), daughter of Lieutenant-Colonel John Andrew McKenna, of the Royal Canadian Engineers, from Ottawa. Not only was it a very happy marriage, but it had a strong influence on his subsequent career. They had a son and a daughter.

Jack Easton returned to England early in 1940, having been mentioned in dispatches that year, and was posted to the intelligence department at the Air Ministry. He gradually concentrated on the problem of technical innovations introduced by the Luftwaffe, particularly in the field of navigational aids and radar. In 1943 he became an air commodore, and was director of the intelligence (research) department at the Air Ministry. He represented the RAF's interests on Winston Churchill's Crossbow committee, whose function was to consider all means of countering the threat of the V1 flying bomb and the V2 rockets. He also became involved in the allocation of RAF aircraft for the clandestine dropping of agents into north-west Europe. All this brought him increasingly in touch with organizations and individuals outside the Air Ministry, including the Special Operations Executive and MI6, where he worked closely with the gifted young Professor R. V. Jones. His clear mind, considerable administrative ability, cool temperament, and gift for getting the best out of different groups with differing vested interests, made him an increasingly respected figure in the intelligence world.

Immediately after the Second World War, Easton was guided towards MI6, for which he had excellent qualifications. Sir Stewart Menzies, the chief of the service at that time, was glad to accept him. When Menzies retired in 1951, and Major-General John A. Sinclair took over as 'C' or head of the service, Easton was appointed his deputy, with the clear understanding that he would eventually take over.

Easton made a substantial contribution towards rationalizing and uniting a service that had developed too fast in the war. Within the service he was liked and trusted. His one possible weakness was that, except for North America

and Australia, foreign politics did not greatly interest him. When the treachery of H. A. R. (Kim) Philby, Guy Burgess, and Donald Maclean was discovered in 1951, Easton was one of those whose minds remained calm and objective at a time when Whitehall in general, and the Foreign Office in particular, wrung their hands. He decided in the summer of 1951, after a careful review of the evidence, that Philby was guilty. It was in this context that he first worked closely with Dick White of MI5. He dealt with the Americans pragmatically over the case. He understood the clear distinction in Britain between a firm belief in guilt and the many difficult security problems involved in an open trial in a public court before a British jury. The fact that the Philby case did not destroy relations between MI6 and the CIA for very long was partly due to Easton's calm pragmatism.

For the next few years Easton worked closely with Sinclair. However, the world was changing and the influence of the armed services in Whitehall was gradually declining. The year 1956 was a climacteric, with the twentieth party congress in Moscow, the disaster and folly of the Suez affair, the Commander Lionel Crabbe incident, and the Soviet invasion of Hungary. The Crabbe case, in which Easton was in no way involved, was in itself of little importance and did not upset the Russians. But time and chance turned it into a political and governmental time bomb, and it was used as a reason for dismissing Sinclair. Dick White, the head of MI5, was appointed to replace him late in 1956. Easton served him loyally, and with grace, as his deputy, but he was told that the succession would not be his; he was not prepared to accept this. That he did not become chief of MI6, as planned, was not due to any failure on his part, but was the result of an inevitable switch of power in Whitehall from the armed forces to the Cabinet Office and the Foreign Office.

In 1958 Easton was offered a respectable job as consul-general in Detroit, Michigan. His wife had many friends in the area, and he accepted the post without outward bitterness. He was for ten years a popular consul-general there. On his retirement in 1968 he decided to remain in the area which he had found so congenial. He became a much respected member of various Detroit-based industrial concerns, and a convivial golfing companion at the Grosse Pointe country club. In 1988 he caused a sensation when he publicly discussed the Kim Philby affair with the author Anthony Cave Brown before the latter's biography of Sir Stewart Menzies was published (*The Secret Servant*, 1988). In 1980 he married Jane, widow of William H. Walker, of Detroit, and daughter of Dr Joseph Stanley Leszynski, surgeon, also of Detroit.

Easton was neat, slim, dark, and conventionally dressed. He was appointed an officer of the American Legion of Merit in 1945, CBE in 1945, CB in 1952, and KCMG in 1956. He died on 19 October 1990 at Grosse Pointe, Michigan.   JOHN BRUCE LOCKHART, rev.

Sources *The Times* (23 Oct 1990) · *WWW* · personal knowledge (1996) · private information (1996) · CGPLA Eng. & Wales (1991)
Wealth at death £172,780—effects in England: probate, 11 July 1991, CGPLA Eng. & Wales

Eastry, Henry (*d.* 1331), prior of Christ Church, Canterbury, was born to unknown parents, probably in the village of Eastry, Kent, as his name indicates. While still a young man he entered the Benedictine priory of Christ Church, Canterbury. Over the next few years he gained considerable administrative experience, serving first as a member of the household of Archbishop Robert Kilwardby (*d.* 1279), and later as warden of the priory's Essex manors and as treasurer for two terms. In 1285 he was elected prior after the resignation of the incompetent Thomas of Ringmere, and he remained in charge for the next forty-six years. Finding the priory heavily in debt he drew up a plan for reducing household expenses and delegated a greater measure of control, especially for the collection of arrears, to the monk–wardens of the priory estates.

By the 1290s the priory's financial base was secure enough to enable Eastry to invest in the local land market and, after the expulsion of the Jews, to acquire the former Jewish tenements in the city of Canterbury. But the election of Archbishop Robert Winchelsey (*d.* 1313), in 1293, and the outbreak of war with France and Scotland in 1294 and 1296 respectively, imposed new strains on the priory's resources. In early 1297 the monks' support of Winchelsey in his struggle with the crown caused them to be temporarily driven out of their house and they had to watch their grain rot in their granary. Eastry, however, reduced expenses, spending scarcely anything on the purchase of land and rents, or rebuilding, and halving the convent's expenditure on wine and grain. Later high grain prices, at a time of excellent harvests, allowed the treasurers to build up a substantial surplus. By the end of 1299 the priory had nearly one year's revenue in hand.

This surplus revenue financed agricultural improvement and extensive rebuilding at both a local and central level. Under Eastry's direction the priory poured substantial sums into increasing the size of sheep flocks and cow herds. In addition, on some manors, the liberal application of marl made possible an extension of the area under wheat. The priory also invested in the construction of new wind-, water-, and fulling mills. The building of sea walls helped to protect its marsh manors from flooding. On the manors themselves new barns, halls, and chapels were erected, and in the house at Canterbury Eastry renovated the choir and chapter house, as well as the prior's own apartments. During the first thirty-seven years of his rule, he was said to have spent no less than £839 on 'new works' within the cathedral precincts. In the area of urban investment Eastry exploited opportunities more intensively than anyone before him. He increased the priory's rents within the city of Canterbury by building nine stone shops in the Burgate, and by purchasing other property. He also built fourteen new shops at the priory's London property of Southwark. These achievements are recorded in a magnificent collection of documents—correspondence, registers, a memorandum book, and innumerable local accounts.

Within the convent, Eastry had difficulties keeping the monks within the strict confines of the Benedictine rule. Winchelsey, after his first visitation in 1298, complained that brothers were living too well, wearing silks and rich furs, and eating too much meat. A few years later, he complained that the monks had been given permission to leave the monastery and wandered round the countryside on the pretext of making pilgrimages. In the 1320s Archbishop Walter Reynolds (*d.* 1327) reiterated these complaints, stressing that the monks should be spending more time in their celebration of divine office. Finally, towards the end of his life, Eastry's authority was challenged by a small group of discontented monks, who sent letters and a list of grievances to both the archbishop and the pope. It is not clear how widespread their support was. In 1317 Eastry publicly cleared himself of charges of abstracting and secreting letters destined for the chapter and for failing to pay a promised pension. In the 1320s the accusations surfaced again, and Eastry sequestered their suspected author, Robert Aledon, for several years. His charges appear to have been totally unfounded.

So far as national affairs were concerned, Eastry attended several royal parliaments and ecclesiastical conventions. During the political unrest of Edward II's reign Eastry sought to restore tranquillity to the realm. He co-operated with Archbishop Reynolds and they wrote to each other constantly. In the years 1325–7 they were greatly concerned about the rumours of a French invasion and the possibility of open strife between Edward II and Queen Isabella. Both prelates were anxious not to antagonize either party, but their pleas for order, at a time of political violence and uncertainty, went unheeded. Nor was Eastry any more successful in maintaining peace at home. In his treatment of others he could be haughty, dictatorial, and overbearing. His tenants at Sandwich were ousted from their houses, and at one point the citizens of Canterbury rose in revolt and threatened to blockade the monks. None the less, he did succeed in maintaining the rights of the convent, and on his death in April 1331 he left the priory a considerable estate of books, vestments, plate, and horses. He was buried in Canterbury Cathedral.

MAVIS E. MATE

Sources Eastry correspondence, Canterbury Cathedral, archives · CUL, MS Ee.5.31 · BL, MS Cotton Galba E.iv · T. L. Hogan, 'The memorandum book of Henry de Eastry, Prior of Christ Church, Canterbury', PhD diss., U. Lond., 1966 · J. B. Sheppard, ed., *Literae Cantuarienses: the letter books of the monastery of Christ Church, Canterbury*, 1, Rolls Series, 85 (1887)

Archives BL, MS Cotton Galba E.iv · Canterbury Cathedral, archives, corresp. · CUL, MS Ee.5.31

Likenesses effigy, Canterbury Cathedral

East Saxons, kings of the (*act.* late 6th cent.–*c.*820), rulers in the area of modern Essex and London, traced their descent from Sledd, who must have flourished in the late sixth century. He was married to Ricula, sister of King *Æthelberht of Kent, and their son **Sæberht** (*d.* 616/17) recognized the overlordship of his uncle. At the instigation of Æthelberht, Sæberht was converted to Christianity in 604, and Mellitus, one of the second wave of Italian missionaries dispatched by Pope Gregory to Kent, was appointed the first bishop of the East Saxons. It was Æthelberht, not Sæberht, who was remembered as the founder of St Paul's in London for Mellitus's episcopal seat, although London was apparently regarded as part of East Saxon territory. When Sæberht died in or soon after 616, he was succeeded by his three sons, two of whom (as is known from the East Saxon genealogies) were called **Seaxred** (*d.* in or after 617) and **Sæward** (*d.* in or after 617). The sons had not been converted to Christianity, and expelled Mellitus when, according to Bede, he would not allow them to have some of his communion bread. Mellitus was obliged to return to Kent. The brothers were killed not long after in battle with the Gewisse, which Bede saw as just punishment for their rejection of the true faith. Little is known of their successor **Sigeberht I** [*called* Sigeberht Parvus] (*fl.* 626), though he too seems to have been a pagan. However, the next king, **Sigeberht II** [*called* Sigeberht Sanctus] (*fl. c.*653), who was probably the son of King Sæward, was converted through the influence of his overlord, King Oswiu of Northumbria, and was baptized *c.*653 by Bishop Finan on a Northumbrian royal estate near Hadrian's Wall. As a result of Oswiu's intervention, Cedd (who had been trained at Lindisfarne) was dispatched to become the second bishop of the East Saxons. However, Sigeberht's change in religion was not approved by all his court, and he was murdered by two brothers (who were also his kinsmen) on the grounds that by being too willing to spread Christian forgiveness to his enemies, he was not sufficiently honouring his supporters. His successor **Swithhelm** (*d.* 663) was the son of Seaxbald, who is otherwise unknown. He too came to the throne a pagan, but was baptized by Cedd in the East Anglian royal palace at Rendlesham with King Æthelwold of the East Angles as his sponsor.

On Swithhelm's death in 663, two kings succeeded jointly to the throne—**Sigehere** (*fl.* 663–664), who was probably the son of Sigeberht Sanctus, and **Sæbbi** (*d.* 693/4), the son of King Seaxred. They seem to have divided the kingdom between them. Sigehere and his portion of the East Saxon people reverted to paganism after the outbreak of the great plague of 664, and incurred the wrath of their overlord King Wulfhere of the Mercians, who seems to have interpreted rejection of Christianity as rejection of his own authority. Jaruman, bishop of the Mercians, was dispatched to restore the true religion. Sæbbi, in contrast, appears to have been an enthusiastic convert who considered renouncing his throne to become a monk, earning the comment from Bede 'that a man of his disposition ought to have been a bishop rather than a king' (Bede, *Hist. eccl.*, 4.11). In the end Sæbbi became a monk only when he fell ill shortly before his death in 693 or 694. He was buried in St Paul's, in a stone sarcophagus which apparently miraculously lengthened in order to accommodate the king's body. He was subsequently regarded as a saint.

Although Sigehere does not seem to have had the same inclinations as his co-ruler, a cult did develop around his wife, *Osgyth (Osyth), the founder of a nunnery at Chich, Essex. Charters surviving from the time of Sigehere and Sæbbi reveal that there were other sub-kings of the East Saxons during their reigns who may have had charge of

dependent territories. The area that is now Surrey was sporadically under East Saxon control in the late seventh century, and Sigehere's wife was reputedly the daughter of Frithuwald, who had been a Mercian under-king of the province. The East Saxons also attempted to extend their control into west Kent. Sigehere may have ruled there briefly, perhaps in collaboration with Cædwalla of Wessex (*r.* 685–8). Sæbbi's son Swæfheard was more successful and ruled as king of part of Kent for a number of years (687/8–692x4), until Wihtred, who had shared rule with him, gained complete control. However, in spite of these successes charter attestations suggest that Sigehere and Sæbbi generally recognized Mercian overlordship, apart possibly from a brief interlude of West Saxon authority during the reign of Cædwalla. Sigehere probably predeceased Sæbbi and when the latter died he was succeeded by his two sons **Sigeheard** (*fl.* 693/4) and **Swæfred** (*fl.* 693/4). Not much is known of these two kings, though Sigeheard was a patron of St Paul's and Swæfred founder of a double monastery at Nazeing, Essex. They became embroiled in serious, but unspecified, conflicts with Ine of Wessex in the early eighth century, which the bishops of the two kingdoms attempted to resolve through mediation. The dispute is the subject of the earliest surviving original letter in Europe, from Waldhere, bishop of the East Saxons, to Berhtwald, archbishop of Canterbury. Also exercising some kind of royal authority during their reign was **Offa** (*fl.* 709), the son of Sigehere and Osgyth, whose name marks a departure from the use of names beginning with 'S' which otherwise seems to have been rigidly adhered to by male members of the royal house. Offa abdicated and left for Rome in 709 with Cenred who had formerly been king of the Mercians and overlord of Sigeheard and Swæfred.

It is not known when Sigeheard and Swæfred ceased to rule, and their eighth-century successors are shadowy figures. Attested rulers include: **Swæfbert** (*d.* 738); **Selered** (*d.* 746), a descendant of a brother of Sæberht; **Swithred** (*fl. c.*746), grandson of King Sigeheard; and **Sigeric** (*d.* in or after 798), son of Selered, who abdicated in 798. Mercian overlordship continued, and Æthelbald and Offa detached London and the surrounding Middle Saxon province from East Saxon control. However, the East Saxon rulers seem to have retained their regalian rights in Essex and issued their own *sceatta* coinage. The last independent East Saxon ruler was probably **Sigered** (*fl.* 811), son of Sigeric, who was ruling in 811, though recognizing Mercian supremacy. Sigered may have been expelled in 825 when the East Saxons surrendered to Ecgberht of Wessex and became a West Saxon dependency. Even after the West Saxon takeover, there is a surviving reference to a Sigeric styled king of the East Saxons in the entourage of King Wiglaf of the Mercians.

BARBARA YORKE

Sources Bede, *Hist. eccl.* · AS chart., esp. S 10–14, 64–5, 165, 168, 170, 1246, 1783–91 · C. R. Hart, *The early charters of eastern England* (1966) · S. E. Kelly, ed., *Charters of St Augustine's Abbey, Canterbury, and Minster-in-Thanet*, Anglo-Saxon Charters, 4 (1995), nos. 40–43, pp. 139–53, 195–203 · L. Webster and J. Backhouse, eds., *The making of England: Anglo-Saxon art and culture, AD 600–900* (1991), 30 · B. A. E. Yorke, 'The kingdom of the East Saxons', *Anglo-Saxon England*, 14 (1985), 1–36 ·

K. Bascombe, 'Two charters of King Suebred of Essex', *An Essex tribute: essays presented to Frederick G. Emmison*, ed. K. Neale (1987), 85–96 • B. A. E. Yorke, *Kings and kingdoms of early Anglo-Saxon England* (1990) • *English historical documents*, 1, ed. D. Whitelock (1955), 729–30 • Symeon of Durham, *Opera* • *ASC*, s.a. 798 [text F]

Eastwick, Edward Backhouse (1814–1883), orientalist and diplomatist, was born on 13 March 1814 at Warfield, Berkshire, one of three sons of Captain Robert William Eastwick of Brompton, Middlesex, and his wife, Lucy, daughter of John King. His family had a long history of service with the East India Company, of which his brother became a director. Eastwick was educated at Charterhouse and at Balliol and Merton colleges, Oxford, matriculating in 1832. In 1836, at the age of twenty-two, he joined the Bombay infantry as a cadet, but his proficiency in oriental languages soon caused him to move from the military to the civil profession, and procured him political employment in Kathiawar and Sind. Ill health compelled him to return to Europe, and he spent some time at Frankfurt busily engaged in linguistic study. In September 1845 the East India Company appointed him to the post of professor of Urdu at East India College, their public school at Haileybury. He remained in this position until the abolition of the college in 1857. From 1851 to 1857 he was also the college librarian. In 1847 he married Rosina Jane, daughter of James Hunter of Hapton House, Argyll. There was at least one child from the marriage, Robert William Egerton Eastwick.

In 1859, Eastwick was appointed assistant political secretary at the India Office. His thoughts at this time turned towards the bar, and in 1860 he was called to the Middle Temple, but it does not appear that he practised. In the same year he left England as secretary of legation to the court of Persia, where he remained for three years. In 1864 he was named one of the commissioners for arranging a Venezuelan loan, and worked again for the same commission in 1867. In 1866 he became private secretary to Robert Cecil, Lord Cranborne (later marquess of Salisbury), secretary of state for India between July 1866 and March 1867. On 6 November 1866 he was awarded the companionship of the Bath. For six years from 1868 to 1874 he sat in the House of Commons as the Conservative member for Penryn and Falmouth. He was defeated in 1874; money losses then enforced his retirement, and he devoted himself to literary work. He was created an honorary master of arts at Oxford in 1875. He died at Ventnor, Isle of Wight, on 16 July 1883, and was survived by his wife.

Eastwick was an industrious writer, and some of his books are valuable. His best-known works are his translations from the Persian of Sa'di's *Gulistan* (*The Rose Garden*) and Kashifi's *Anvar-i Suhaili* (*The Light of Canopus*), which was dedicated to Queen Victoria and was better received than *Gulistan*. Between 1859 and 1883, he wrote several interesting handbooks on various cities of India. Eastwick also edited or prefaced a good many books by Indian scholars, as well as publishing the Persian text of the *Gulistan*, and editing *Genesis* in Dakhani for the Bible Society. He wrote several accounts of his experiences when working in Persia and Venezuela, including *Journal of a Diplomate's Three Years' Residence in Persia* (2 vols., 1864) and *Venezuela, or, Sketches of Life in a South American Republic* (2nd edn, 1868), which was written for *All the Year Round* at Dickens's request. Eastwick also contributed to the eighth edition of the *Encyclopaedia Britannica*, as well as to literary journals.   STANLEY LANE-POOLE, *rev.* PARVIN LOLOI

Sources *The Athenaeum* (21 July 1883), 81 • *The Times* (18 July 1883) • *BL cat.* • Foster, *Alum. Oxon.* • Boase, *Mod. Eng. biog.* • F. C. Danvers and others, *Memorials of old Haileybury College* (1894), 192–4 • *WWBMP* • Ward, *Men of the reign* • C. E. Buckland, *Dictionary of Indian biography* (1906) • Colvin, *Archs.* • *CGPLA Eng. & Wales* (1883)

Archives BL OIOC, corresp. and papers, MS Eur. A 27–28, C 31, E 144–147, F 18/1 | Bodl. Oxf., letters to Benjamin Disraeli • PRO, letters to Sir Henry Pottinger, FO 705

Wealth at death £635 13s. 3d.: probate, 13 Aug 1883, *CGPLA Eng. & Wales*

Eastwood, Sir Eric (1910–1981), physicist and electrical engineer, was born on 12 March 1910 at Rochdale, Lancashire, the youngest in the family of five sons and one daughter of George Eastwood, who worked in cotton mills, and his wife, Eda Brooks. He was educated at Oldham municipal secondary school and Manchester University where, in 1931, he came top of the class list for BSc honours in physics. He was awarded a two-year grant for research but, after working for one year on spectroscopy for his MSc degree, he moved to the department of education and gained its diploma in 1933. In that year he was awarded a further grant for research at Cambridge. He was admitted to Christ's College and worked in the department of physical chemistry to gain his PhD in 1935.

At this stage Eastwood intended to become a schoolmaster and he taught with success at King's School in Taunton, Somerset, Runcorn grammar school, Cheshire, and Liverpool Collegiate. In 1937 he married Edith, daughter of Harry Butterworth, an engineer. They had two sons, who both became engineers. In 1941 he volunteered for service with the Royal Air Force. Commissioned in the education branch, he was soon transferred to 60 Group, which was responsible for the operation and maintenance of radar stations. Initially he worked on the calibration of a station to take account of the topographical features of the surrounding country. Submission of a detailed theoretical report on the influence of atmospheric refraction on the performance of the station led to his promotion and later to transfer to 60 Group headquarters as squadron leader in charge of calibration of all RAF radar stations in the United Kingdom. For this work he was mentioned in dispatches.

After release from the RAF in 1946 Eastwood joined the research laboratories of the English Electric Company. He was placed in charge of the physics department, with a major commitment to the development of wartime radar for civilian purposes. When the English Electric Company acquired the Marconi Wireless Telegraph Company in 1947 the radar work was moved to the Marconi laboratories at Great Baddow, Chelmsford, Essex, to which Eastwood went as deputy director of research in 1948; he became director in 1954. During this period, in his own time and with the help of some colleagues, he carried out extensive scientific research on the migration of birds, using the high power Marconi radar transmitter, to which he had access. This work was published in *Radar Ornithology* (1967). From 1952 to 1968 he was director of research for the whole of the English Electric Company and, when the company merged with the General Electric Company in 1968, he became director of research for the combined group. But he was not happy in this post and in 1972 he retired and went back to the Marconi laboratories as chief scientist, a post which he held until shortly before his death.

Eastwood was a good committee man and his services were in great demand. Among many bodies which profited from his advice, often as committee chairman, were the Electronics Research Council, the Appleton Laboratory, and the Defence Scientific Advisory Council. He devoted much time to the Institution of Electrical Engineers and became its president in 1972–3. He was appointed CBE in 1962 and knighted in 1973. He was awarded honorary degrees by Exeter, Cranfield, Aston, City, Heriot-Watt, and Loughborough universities and medals by the Royal Aeronautical Society, the Institute of Physics, and the Institution of Civil Engineers. He was elected FRS in 1968 and honorary fellow of the Institution of Electrical Engineers in 1979.

Eastwood was a kind and gentle person who would nevertheless defend strongly any cause in which he believed. His early years had been spent in a happy and close-knit family, though his father was sometimes out of work and moves to different towns in search of employment were not unknown. A love of music was handed down from the father, a skilled violinist, to the children, several of whom played musical instruments. Eric Eastwood himself joined the family band as a cellist and later learned to play the flute. The love of music remained with him throughout his life; he had a good voice and often sang in choirs. In his early years he had been a regular attender at Sunday morning church and afternoon Bible class. To this may be ascribed his absolute integrity in later life—and his habit of producing apt biblical quotations at unexpected moments. Eastwood died on 6 October 1981 at his home, 5 The Ryefield, Little Baddow, Chelmsford.

CHARLES OATLEY, *rev.*

Sources F. E. Jones, *Memoirs FRS*, 29 (1983), 177–95 · personal knowledge (1990) · *CGPLA Eng. & Wales* (1982)
Archives CAC Cam., corresp. and papers relating to radar
Wealth at death £33,553: probate, 17 Feb 1982, *CGPLA Eng. & Wales*

Eastwood, Jonathan (*bap.* 1823, *d.* 1864), topographer, was baptized at Horbury, Wakefield, on 23 November 1823, the son of John Eastwood and his wife Frances Hepworth. He was educated at Uppingham School and at St John's College, Cambridge, where, after obtaining both classical and mathematical honours, he graduated BA in 1846 and proceeded MA in 1849. He was ordained deacon in 1847 and priest in 1848, and was appointed curate of Ecclesfield, Yorkshire. His time there produced his *History of the Parish of Ecclesfield in the County of York* (1862). In 1854, before its publication, he had moved to be curate of Eckington,

Derbyshire, and from 1862 he was vicar of Hope, Staffordshire. He published scriptural notes in the *Monthly Paper*, a periodical for Sunday schools. With Dr William Aldis Wright he worked these up and they were published as *The Bible Word-Book* (1866), with a second edition, in Wright's name only, in 1881. Eastwood was also an indefatigable reader for the early stages of the English dictionary planned by the Philological Society (eventually the *Oxford English Dictionary*). The date of his marriage and the name of his wife, a daughter of William Frederick Dixon of Page Hall, Ecclesfield, are not known. They had at least one son, Charles Edmund Eastwood, who survived him. Eastwood died at St Leonards, Sussex, on 5 July 1864.

H. C. G. MATTHEW

Sources *GM*, 3rd ser., 17 (1864), 254 · Venn, *Alum. Cant.* · *The Oxford English dictionary*, ed. J. A. Simpson and E. S. C. Weiner, 2nd edn, 1 (1989), xxxvii [list of principal readers] · Crockford (1864)
Wealth at death under £3000: probate, 31 Aug 1864, *CGPLA Eng. & Wales*

Easty, Mary (*d.* 1692). *See under* Salem witches and their accusers (*act.* 1692).

Eata [St Eata] (*d.* 685/6), bishop of Hexham, is known almost entirely from Bede's *Historia ecclesiastica gentis Anglorum* and life of St Cuthbert. One of twelve English boys trained by Bishop Áedán at Lindisfarne, by 651 he had become abbot of Melrose, where the celebrated spiritual director Boisil was prior and Cuthbert became one of his monks. In the late 650s he was invited by Alhfrith, son of King Oswiu, to rule the monastery which he had just lavishly endowed at Ripon, and came thither bringing Cuthbert as his guest master. He was soon, however, displaced by Alhfrith's protégé Wilfrid, and returned with Cuthbert to Melrose.

Eata accepted the decision of the Synod of Whitby (664) against the Columban Irish customs, which he had hitherto observed. Shortly afterwards, he was made abbot of Lindisfarne, at the request of the retiring bishop, Colman. He seems, however, to have retained the abbacy of Melrose, where Cuthbert succeeded Boisil as prior. Later, probably in the 670s, Eata brought this favoured disciple to Lindisfarne to hold the same office.

In 678 Eata was made bishop of the Bernician see, created from the subdivision of the great Northumbrian diocese, hitherto ruled by Wilfrid. Initially, his diocesan seat was at either Hexham or Lindisfarne, perhaps both. In 681, however, it was fixed exclusively at Lindisfarne, after a further subdivision of the see and the establishment of a new bishop at Hexham. In 685 or 686, after Cuthbert's consecration to the see of Hexham, Eata was prevailed upon to exchange sees. He died at Hexham shortly afterwards, of dysentery, and according to later tradition was buried to the south of the sacristy. A small chapel was built over his tomb, and at an uncertain date his remains were elevated and translated to a shrine inside the abbatial church.

Gentle, straightforward, and greatly revered, Eata was a man of genuine and eirenic spirituality and a discerning patron, who promoted men accounted exceptionally holy. He was evidently a peacemaker, chosen to heal the wounds of the defeated monks at Lindisfarne in 664, and of the followers of Wilfrid at Hexham in 678. He seems to have been well-fitted for such sensitive appointments and to have left fond memories in both communities.

Although remembered as a holy man when Bede was writing in the early eighth century, it is not clear when Eata became the object of a formal cult. His translation perhaps occurred in the mid-eleventh century, and by 1075 he was titular of the church at Atcham in Shropshire. A twelfth-century life, based almost entirely on Bede, tells of his appearance in a vision in 1113 to frustrate the attempts of Archbishop Thomas (II) to translate his remains to York. His feast day was 26 October.

ALAN THACKER

Sources Bede, *Hist. eccl.* · B. Colgrave, ed. and trans., *Two lives of Saint Cuthbert* (1940) · *Venerabilis Baedae opera historica*, ed. C. Plummer, 2 vols. (1896) · J. Raine, ed., 'Vita Oswini regis deirorum', *Miscellanea biographica*, SurtS, 8 (1838), 1–59 · Ordericus Vitalis, *Eccl. hist.* · J. Raine, ed., *The priory of Hexham*, 2 vols., SurtS, 44, 46 (1864–5) · G. Bonner, D. Rollason, and C. Stancliffe, eds., *St Cuthbert, his cult and his community* (1989)

Eaton [*née* Waldie]**, Charlotte Anne** (1788–1859), writer, was born on 28 September 1788, the second of the three daughters of George Waldie of Hendersyde Park, Roxburghshire, and his wife, Ann, *née* Ormston, eldest daughter of Jonathan Ormston of Newcastle upon Tyne. Charlotte also had two brothers, and her elder sister Maria Jane married Richard John *Griffith (1784–1878), the distinguished geologist and valuator. Little is known about Charlotte's education but at a young age she began to write a novel in the Gothic style, 'At Home and Abroad', which she abandoned in 1814 because of similarities to Maria Edgeworth's *Patronage*. She published a letter in the *Monthly Magazine* (2, 1814) addressing the points of resemblance.

In June 1815 Charlotte visited Brussels, the hastily established headquarters of Wellington's army, via Bruges and Ghent with her brother John and sister Jane [*see below*]. They were evacuated to Antwerp because of the rapid French advance, and visited the battlefield at Waterloo before returning to England after six weeks away. Charlotte wrote an account of the battle published first as 'Circumstantial detail' by 'a Near Observer' in *The Battle of Waterloo* (1815) which was accompanied by panoramic sketches by Jane Waldie. In 1816 Charlotte and Jane met John in France and continued with him to Italy. In 1817, while she was still in Italy, Charlotte's family published a more extended account based on her own experiences in *Narrative of a Residence in Belgium, During the Campaign of 1815, and of a Visit to the Field of Waterloo. By an Englishwoman*. It was noted for its liveliness and its unflinching account of the horror of the battle, vestiges of which were still very much in evidence when Charlotte visited Waterloo:

> the effluvia which arose from [the grave pits], even beneath the open canopy of heaven, was horrible; and the pure west wind of summer, as it passed us, seemed pestiferous, so deadly was the smell that in many places pervaded the field. (pp. 270–71)

It was also a staunchly patriotic piece of writing, which revelled in 'English greatness and glory', and was considered one of the best contemporary accounts by a non-military writer.

Charlotte Waldie was in Italy until 1818, and in 1820 she anonymously published the very popular and acclaimed *Rome in the Nineteenth Century*, which remained in her lifetime the definitive guide to the city. On 22 August 1822 she married Stephen Eaton, a banker, of Ketton Hall, Stamford, Rutland. They had two sons and two daughters. Charlotte Eaton anonymously published *Continental Adventures* in 1826, which integrated factual travel writing with 'a fictitious story and imaginary characters', and in 1831 revised and published her early *At Home and Abroad*. After her husband's death on 25 September 1834 Eaton revised *Narrative of a Residence in Belgium* as *The Days of Battle, or, Quatre Bras and Waterloo; by an Englishwoman Resident in Brussels in June 1815* (1853) prior to her own death from breast cancer at 17 Hanover Square, London, on 28 April 1859. A further edition of the *Narrative* was issued in 1888 as *Waterloo Days*.

Jane Watts [*née* Waldie] (1793–1826), artist and author, showed a taste for painting at an early age, and studied under Alexander Nasmyth. She painted many pictures, mostly landscapes inspired by the scenery surrounding her home in Roxburghshire. The result of her travels with her sister Charlotte was *Sketches Descriptive of Italy in 1816–17; with a Brief Account of Travels in Various Parts of France and Switzerland* (1820). In 1819 she exhibited *The Temple at Paestum* at Somerset House. On 20 October 1820 she married Captain (later Rear-Admiral) George Augustus Watts of Langton Grange, Staindrop, Darlington. After losing her only child, she died at Langton Grange on 6 July 1826.

CLARE L. TAYLOR

Sources E. Bell, introduction, in C. A. Eaton, *Waterloo days: the narrative of an Englishwoman resident in Brussels in June, 1815* (1888) · [C. A. Eaton], *At home and abroad, or, Memoirs of Emily de Cardonell* (1831), preface · *DNB* · J. Robinson, *Wayward women: a guide to women travellers* (1990) · Blain, Clements & Grundy, *Feminist comp.* · d. cert.
Archives Yale U., Beinecke L., journal of a tour through France
Likenesses Yellowlees, portrait, 1824; formerly at Hendersyde Park, 1859 · Edmonstone, portrait, 1828; formerly at Hendersyde Park, 1859 · Thompson of Edinburgh, miniature (aged eighteen)

Eaton, Daniel Isaac (*bap.* 1753, *d.* 1814), radical writer and publisher, was baptized in the parish of St Katharine Coleman, London, on 7 January 1753, the eldest of three children and only son of Daniel Eaton (*c.*1728–*c.*1805), a prosperous stationer, and his wife, Anna. After six years at boarding-school and several years at the English College at St Omer in France, on 5 February 1767 young Daniel was bound apprentice at Stationers' Hall in London, becoming a freeman and liveryman on 1 March 1774. On 16 October 1777 he married Sussana Maria Greene, with whom he had three children: Henry (1778–1802), Sussana (*b.* 1779), and John (*b.* 1792).

After employment as a paper maker at Guildford, Surrey (*c.*1778), Eaton returned to London, working as parchment maker at Deptford (*c.*1784), establishing a stationer's shop at Hoxton (1786), and then moving to 81 Bishopsgate

Daniel Isaac Eaton (*bap.* 1753, *d.* 1814), by William Sharp, pubd 1794 (after Lemuel Francis Abbott)

Eaton (under the pseudonym Antitype) wrote and published the extravagantly ironic *The Pernicious Effects of Printing upon Society, Exposed* (1794). When in May 1794 the Pitt administration arrested sixteen radical leaders, he was a prime target. He managed to evade arrest, however, and defiantly offered the prisoners moral and financial support, firing a steady salvo of pamphlets against the government from his press. Along with pamphlets he published several weekly journals. *Political Classics* (August 1794 to February 1795) reprinted works by Sydney, Rousseau, and More. *The Tribune* (March 1795 to April 1796) comprised selections from Thelwall's lectures. *The Philanthropist* (43 numbers, March 1795 to January 1796), Eaton's second miscellany of comment and opinion, continued many of the political themes and literary devices of *Politics for the People*, emphasizing social and economic issues.

On several occasions Eaton stepped forward and published pamphlets that other printers considered too dangerous to handle. His enterprise and daring were rewarded when on 4 December 1795 Thomas Paine authorized him to publish the only official London edition of *The Age of Reason, Part the Second*. To the end of his life Eaton continued to be a major publisher of Paine's works. When in 1795 the Treasonable and Seditious Practices Act and the Seditious Meetings Act restrained liberal political journals and mass meetings of reform societies, Eaton countered with *An Appeal to the Public on the Two Despotic Bills* (1796). Fluent in French, he also began translating and publishing works of French rationalistic thought: Volney's *The Law of Nature, or, Catechism of French Citizens* (1796); Helvetius's *The True Sense and Meaning of the System of Nature* (1810); Freret's *A Preservative Against Religious Prejudices* and *The Moseiade* (both 1812).

Tried *in absentia* for publishing Pigott's *Political Dictionary* and Iliff's *A Summary of the Duties of Citizenship* (both 1795) and convicted (1796), Eaton went into hiding while his wife and family maintained the business, issuing several scathing pamphlets in late 1796 and 1797. In exile near Philadelphia (1797–1800) Eaton tried to resume his stationer's trade, vending works brought from England, but the yellow fever epidemic of 1797 and the American government's alien and sedition laws (1798) strangled his business. A consignment of his books valued at nearly £3000 was lost at sea, and in 1801 he slipped quietly back into England.

In 1803 Eaton established a stationer's shop at Stratford-on-Green, east London, but on 6 November was declared bankrupt. Arrested on the old 1796 charges and found guilty, he was sentenced to fifteen months' solitary confinement and £2800-worth of his books packed for the American market were publicly burnt. His furniture and personal goods were seized until he paid £286 to redeem them. Released from gaol on 4 February 1805, Eaton resolved to desist from political publishing. For the next five years he worked with his son John making and selling Eaton's Anti-Scorbutic Soap, from a formula learned in America.

In 1810, again financially solvent, Eaton founded at 8 Cornhill Street, London, the *Ratiocinatory, or, Magazine for*

Street (1792). Though raised, married, and buried in the Church of England, Eaton early in life became a sceptic, later a deist and freethinker. A reformer, and stern critic of the Pitt administration, he published his first known political pamphlet, Parkinson's *The Budget of the People*, in 1792, and became active in the *London Corresponding Society. Reacting to Burke's reference to the lower classes as 'a swinish multitude', Eaton became their champion. Twice prosecuted in 1793 for publishing libellous pamphlets, he was twice released when juries refused to convict.

In the same year, having acquired his own press, Eaton launched *Hog's Wash, or, A Salmagundy for Swine*, a weekly designed to spread political enlightenment among the masses. Partly original items, partly excerpts, enlivened by satire, irony, humour, and verse, it was immediately successful. Renamed *Politics for the People*, it ran for sixty numbers (September 1793 to March 1795). Through its pages—as through his pamphlets—Eaton consistently advocated universal manhood suffrage, annual parliaments, peace among nations, education of the poor, and unfettered discussion of politics and religion. When in the eighth number (16 November 1793) he published two items attacking monarchy (one comparing the king to a cruel, tyrannical gamecock), Eaton was prosecuted for seditious libel but acquitted on both counts. He triumphantly adopted the imprint: 'Printed by D. I. Eaton at the Cock and Swine, No. 74, Newgate Street.' The London Corresponding Society caused silver medals to be struck commemorating his acquittal. His shop became a gathering place for reformers and radicals.

Resisting government's attempts to control the press,

Truths and Good Sense and soon after moved it to another shop at 3 Ave Maria Lane. He resumed publishing controversial pamphlets, including Paine's *The Age of Reason, Part the Third* (1811). Convicted for printing this work (15 May 1812), he was sentenced to eighteen months in Newgate and to stand in the pillory once within a month. His appearance in the pillory (26 May) was a triumph. Instead of pelting him with stones and rubbish, the crowd cheered him and offered him food. In the public press the Hunt brothers, Shelley, and others defended him. In gaol, though forced to appeal for donations, he wrote and published *Extortions and Abuses of Newgate* (1813), and soon afterward a parliamentary committee was named to investigate conditions in London prisons.

On his release in November 1813, Eaton was immediately prosecuted for publishing an anonymous translation of Baron d'Holbach's *Ecce homo! or, A Critical Inquiry into the History of Jesus Christ* (1813), but charges were dropped when Eaton revealed the identity of the translator, George Houston.

Aged, ill, impoverished, and by now estranged from his wife and children (possibly as a result of the marital infidelity charged by William Cobbett in a 1799 pamphlet), Eaton retired to his sister's house at 220 Union Row in Deptford, London, where he died on 22 August 1814 of a gallstone infection. He was buried on 27 August in St Nicholas's churchyard at Deptford.

Eaton's enduring legacy lies in his publishing—despite unending official harassment—of liberal, progressive thought in politics and religion. An advocate by word and deed for freedom of expression, Eaton was hailed as late as 1883 by J. M. Wheeler as 'one of the many sturdy champions to whose courageous labors and sufferings we owe the right of a Free Press' (Wheeler). In 1974 *Daniel Isaac Eaton and Thomas Paine: Five Tracts, 1793–1812* was printed in New York, and reprints of *Politics for the People* and *The Pernicious Effects of Printing upon Society, Exposed* appeared respectively in 1968 and in 1985.

DANIEL LAWRENCE McCUE JR.

Sources *The trial of Mr. Daniel Isaac Eaton, for publishing the third and last part of Paine's Age of Reason* (1812), 23, 68–9 · T. Paine, *The age of reason, part the second* (1796) [Paine's prefatory letter] · D. McCue, 'Daniel Isaac Eaton and *Politics for the People*', PhD diss., Columbia University, 1974 · M. Davis, 'Daniel Isaac Eaton', *British reform writers, 1789–1832*, ed. G. Kelly and E. Applegate, DLitB, 158 (1996), 94–102 · *State trials*, 22.753–83, 785–822; 23.1013–54; 31.927–58 · D. McCue, 'The pamphleteer Pitt's government couldn't silence', *Eighteenth-Century Life*, 5 (1978–9), 38–49 · J. M. Wheeler, Foreword, in *Shelley on blasphemy, being his letter to Lord Ellenborough ...* (1883) · Peter Porcupine [W. Cobbett], *Remarks on the explanation, lately published by Dr. Priestley, respecting the intercepted letters of his friend and disciple, John H. Stone* (1799), 21 n. · N. Freret, preface, *A preservative against religious prejudices*, trans. Eaton (1812) · 'Freemen's book 29 Sept. 1751–5 July 1796', Stationers' Company, London [under 1 March 1774]

Likenesses R. Newton, caricatures, 1793, repro. in *English cartoons and satirical prints, 1320–1832*, microfilm 2167, reel 11, prints 7801, 8620-A · W. Sharp, line engraving, pubd 1794 (after L. F. Abbott), NPG [*see illus.*] · black and white portrait, repro. in *The trial of Mr. Daniel Isaac Eaton*, frontispiece · pencil drawing, BM · stipple and line engraving, BM; repro. in *The trial of Mr. Daniel Isaac Eaton*

Wealth at death very little: Freret, preface, *A preservative*

Eaton, Herbert Francis, third Baron Cheylesmore (1848–1925), army officer, was born in London on 25 January 1848, the third son of Henry William Eaton, created in 1887 Baron Cheylesmore, of Cheylesmore, Coventry, and his wife, Charlotte Gorham, daughter of Thomas Leader Harman of New Orleans. Eaton was educated at Eton College, and joined the Grenadier Guards in 1867. All his life the welfare of the guards was of primary concern to him. He commanded the 2nd battalion from 1890 to 1894, taking it to Bermuda for a year in 1890, following insubordination in the battalion. He retired as a major-general in 1899, after commanding the regiment, but without any active service. He returned to military work during the First World War as president of courts martial in espionage and other cases, and as chairman of various boards; he was also commandant of the National Rifle Association's School of Musketry at Bisley. He succeeded his brother, William Meriton *Eaton (1843–1902), in the barony in 1902. He was created CVO in 1905, KCVO in 1909, KCMG in 1919, and GBE in 1925.

He married on 14 July 1892 Elizabeth Richardson (d. 1945), daughter of Francis Ormond French, of New York, and they had two sons. As a boy Eaton shot at Wimbledon for Eton in 1866, and he always retained a great interest in rifle shooting; he was closely associated with the National Rifle Association, and joined its council in 1899. He was its chairman from 1903 until his death, and was enthusiastic in developing rifle shooting overseas and among the boys of the empire. Under his chairmanship Bisley developed into the main shooting centre in the empire, and produced expert marksmen, who, formed into a school of musketry, were important in training instructors for the new armies raised during the First World War.

Eaton was extensively involved in public life: with the volunteers and territorials, with ex-service and other charities, and in local government—first on Westminster council then on the London county council, of which he was chairman in 1912–13. In 1887 he was unsuccessful Conservative candidate at Coventry. Dignified, courteous, considerate, and experienced, he was an ideal chairman. He was widely popular, and by his brother officers was affectionately nicknamed Brown.

Eaton formed a large collection of military medals, and in 1897 published *Naval and Military Medals of Great Britain*. He lived mainly in London, but at one time rented Hughenden Manor, and resided later at Cooper's Hill. He died at the Cottage Hospital, Englefield Green, Egham, on 29 July 1925 from injuries received in a motor accident, and was succeeded in the barony by his elder son, Francis Ormond Henry (1893–1974). COTTESLOE, *rev.* JAMES FALKNER

Sources *The Times* (30 July 1925) · *Army List* · *National Rifle Association Journal* (Aug 1925) · Burke, *Peerage*

Likenesses V. Rousseau, statue, Westminster Embankment, London · Spy [L. Ward], caricature, chromolithograph, NPG; repro. in *VF* (3 Oct 1891) · W. H., cartoon, chromolithograph, NPG; repro. in *VF* (17 July 1912) · photograph, repro. in *Household Brigade Magazine* (Jan 1899)

Wealth at death £98,850 7s. 4d.: probate, 26 Nov 1925, *CGPLA Eng. & Wales*

Eaton, John (1574/5–1630/31), Church of England clergyman, was born in Kent. At some point during his youth he was tutored by the minister and writer Ephraim Pagitt. On 26 June 1590, aged fifteen, he matriculated from Trinity College, Oxford, where he became the first recipient of the newly founded Blount exhibition. He graduated BA on 16 February 1596 and proceeded MA on 7 July 1603, by which time he had been ordained. After holding several curacies, including one under Robert Wright at St Catharine Coleman, London, Eaton became vicar of Wickham Market, Suffolk, about 1604.

Here Eaton developed a new style of divinity—focusing on the overwhelming power of God's free grace and the uselessness of the law in man's salvation—which challenged many of the central assumptions of mainstream puritan religiosity. At the core of his new style of divinity was the claim that as a consequence of Christ's all-sufficient sacrifice, God could see no sin in those who had been justified. To use Eaton's own favoured phrase, as in his *The Honey-Combe of Free Justification* (1642), these true believers were taken to be clothed with 'the wedding garment of Christs perfect righteousnesse' (Eaton, *Honey-Combe*, 1–2), such that God no longer beheld their iniquities. These ideas, which were widely deemed to be antinomian, quickly brought him into conflict with his fellow ministers and the ecclesiastical authorities.

In 1614 Eaton was disciplined for a sermon preached at a clerical synod in Norwich, and in 1615 the Suffolk minister Peter Gunter published an attack on his doctrinal innovations, *A sermon preached in the countie of Suffolk … for the discoverie and confutation of certaine strange, pernicious, and hereticall positions*. Eaton apparently continued to disseminate his ideas unabated, for in 1619 he was tried before the high commission and deprived of his living as 'an incorrigible divulger of errors and false opinions' (*CSP dom.*, 1619–23, 41). Archbishop George Abbot later remarked that the court had found him 'soe ignorant, and … soe simple, that we thought fitt to send him to Westminster Schoole and Paule's Schoole to be instructed' (Gardiner, 320) before allowing him to return to the ministry as a curate. These rehabilitative efforts failed, however, and Eaton soon fell back to his old ways.

By 1621 Eaton was in London, where he married, by licence dated 26 December that year, Anne Crosman, widow of the Ipswich curate Thomas Crosman, who may possibly have been Eaton's second wife. At this point, he began actively to disseminate his ideas from the pulpit, in conference, and through a series of unpublished manuscripts, which circulated widely in the 1620s and 1630s. Through these efforts he won a considerable lay following (sometimes dubbed Eatonists by their enemies). In short time he found himself spearheading an increasingly visible antinomian 'movement' in the capital, which soon attracted other dissident ministers, including John Traske, Robert Towne, Samuel Prettie, John Emersone, and the young Thomas Hodges. All of these men appear to have shared Eaton's dissatisfaction with the 'legalistic' mode of divinity promoted by puritan preachers, and unsurprisingly the group soon fell into heated conflicts with their godly counterparts in London. These controversies quickly spilled over into the church courts, resulting in the prosecution of several well-known antinomian ministers and lay people before the high commission beginning in 1629. Eaton was spared the same fate only by death, which appears to have overtaken him some time between August 1630 and July 1631 (by which latter date he was without question dead).

This did not, however, signal the end of Eaton's influence. In the wake of his death one of his followers, the Suffolk vicar John Eachard, hailed him as a new St Paul, and exhorted his fellow antinomians to take courage from the various persecutions and imprisonments that Eaton had patiently endured during his lifetime. At the same time, Eaton's admirers in London attempted to secure the unlicensed publication of his manuscripts, which had been adjudged heterodox by the church authorities. In 1632 Eaton's widow, Susan, whom he had married at an unknown date following the death of his wife Anne, was called before the high commission for her efforts to publish his magnum opus, 'The honey-combe of free justification'; when she refused to hand over her manuscript copies she was gaoled for several months. Meanwhile, Eaton's puritan enemies tried to close the breaches that had been opened by their antinomian critics, publishing several books of polemic designed to undermine their opponents. These included Henry Burton's *The Law and the Gospell Reconciled* (1631), which refuted Eaton's writings and opinions (although without mentioning him by name). When ecclesiastical censorship collapsed in the early 1640s Eaton's followers quickly moved to publish his work, which appeared as *The Honey-Combe of Free Justification* (1642) and the *Discovery of the most Dangerous Dead Faith* (1642). These books exerted considerable influence within the cacophonous religious scene of the English civil wars and interregnum, contributing to the evolution of sectarianism. Likewise, the antinomian community that Eaton had helped to create became a breeding-ground for religious and political radicals of all stripes.

DAVID R. COMO

Sources D. R. Como, 'Puritans and heretics: the emergence of an antinomian underground in early Stuart England', PhD diss., Princeton University, 1999 · T. D. Bozeman, 'The glory of the "third time": John Eaton as contra-puritan', *Journal of Ecclesiastical History*, 47 (1996), 638–54 · J. Eaton, *The honey-combe of free justification* (1642) · J. Eaton, *Discovery of the most dangerous dead faith* (1642) · P. Gunter, *A sermon preached in the countie of Suffolk* (1615) · *DNB* · *CSP dom.*, 1619–23 · S. R. Gardiner, *Reports of cases in the courts of star chamber and high commission*, CS, 39 (1886) · Foster, *Alum. Oxon.* · E. Pagitt, *Heresiography, or, A description of the hereticks and sectaries sprang up in these latter times* (1662) · J. L. Chester and G. J. Armytage, eds., *Allegations for marriage licences issued by the bishop of London*, 2, Harleian Society, 26 (1887) · PRO, SP 16/520/80

Eaton, Nathaniel (*bap. c.*1610, *d.* **1674**), college head and clergyman, was baptized in Great Budworth, Cheshire, one of seven sons of the Revd Richard Eaton, vicar of Great Budworth and Trinity Church, Coventry, and his wife, Elizabeth. Nathaniel attended Westminster School and then matriculated pensioner at Trinity College, Cambridge, in 1630. He left before receiving a degree and stayed for a time with his brother Theophilus in London. Having obtained a licence to travel, he journeyed to the Netherlands, where he studied briefly under William Ames at the University of Franeker. While in the Netherlands he published a thesis setting out the sabbatarian views of various theologians. He returned to England after 1634 and became a schoolmaster, teaching briefly in two separate places.

In June 1637 Nathaniel, accompanied by his first wife, Elizabeth (d. 1640), and his brothers Theophilus *Eaton and Samuel *Eaton, arrived in New England. He lived initially in Charlestown, across the river from Boston, but soon settled in Newtown, soon to be renamed Cambridge, where the colony had established a college with a bequest of John Harvard. Eaton was invited to head the new school, and he took up that position in the autumn of 1638. It is possible that he lobbied for the position since he evidently provided the college overseers, including John Winthrop, with copies of his work on the sabbath. Thomas Hooker, who had known Eaton in the Netherlands, had doubts about him, but Hooker had moved to Connecticut and his advice was disregarded. Eaton was a respected scholar and he got the college off to a good academic start. Among the 'many scholars, the sons of gentlemen and others of best note in the country' (*Journal of John Winthrop*, 310) who began their Harvard studies under Eaton was George Downing. He also named, fenced, and planted Harvard Yard. But his regime at Harvard was a very harsh one; along with his wife he cheated the students by providing them with inadequate and poorquality food and drink with the funds allocated to him for that purpose. By Elizabeth Eaton's own admission the students were provided with no beef, sour bread, and no beer between meals and little at them. More seriously, he repeatedly and excessively employed corporal punishment on the students. In the later judgement of Cotton Mather, 'though his avarice was notorious ... yet his cruelty was more scandalous than his avarice' (Mather, 4.126).

One year after assuming the leadership of Harvard (the title 'president' was not yet employed) Eaton was brought before the general court of the colony to answer charges regarding his maladministration. The incident that precipitated this confrontation was his cudgelling a college usher with a walnut staff while the victim was held by two servants. During the course of the proceedings the full range of charges against him emerged. Questioned about reports that he often inflicted twenty or thirty stripes on students and would not cease until they told him what he wished, he responded that 'he had this rule, that he would not give over correcting till he had reduced the party to his will' (*Journal of John Winthrop*, 303). On 9 September 1639 the court fined him and removed him as head of the college. He was also ordered to answer for his behaviour to the Cambridge church, but before his church trial he fled the colony, travelling first to New Hampshire and then taking ship for Virginia. Subsequent examination of the college affairs revealed that Eaton had both embezzled funds and run up unpaid debts in excess of £1000.

Eaton had little success in Virginia. Having settled on the colony's eastern shore, where there was a strong puritan presence, he served as an assistant to the rector of Hungar's parish in Northampton county. He sent for his wife and children to join him, but all, except his eldest son, who had remained at Cambridge, were lost at sea. In or after 1640 Eaton married Anne Graves, daughter of a local planter, but he abandoned her by 1646 when he was forced by reports of dissolute personal behaviour to leave the colony and return to England. According to the Massachusetts governor, Winthrop, Eaton was while in Virginia given up 'to extreme pride and sensuality, being usually drunken, as the custom there is' (*Journal of John Winthrop*, 343).

Eaton next appeared on the continent, where he received doctorates in philosophy and medicine at the University of Padua in 1647. His commencement oration was published. He then returned once again to England. His activities over the next decade are unknown, but following the Restoration he conformed to the Church of England and was appointed vicar of Bishop's Castle in Shropshire. In 1661 he published a series of epigrammatic poems on church festivals, *De fastis Anglicis*. In 1669 the earl of Bath gave him the living of the rectory of Bideford, Devon. He married for a third time during the 1660s; his wife's name was Mary.

There is no evidence that Eaton was employed as a teacher after his Harvard experience, but he continued to exhibit some of the traits that had caused his downfall in Massachusetts. In 1665 and again in 1674 he was arrested for debt. On the first occasion he attempted to escape his predicament by perjury and bribery. On the latter occasion he was incarcerated in king's bench prison, Southwark, where he died that same year.

GORDON GOODWIN, *rev.* FRANCIS J. BREMER

Sources S. E. Morison, *The founding of Harvard College* (Cambridge, MA, 1935) • S. S. Cohen, 'Eaton, Nathaniel', *ANB* • *The journal of John Winthrop, 1630–1649*, ed. R. S. Dunn, J. Savage, and L. Yeandle (1996) • C. Mather, *Magnalia Christi Americana*, 7 bks in 1 vol. (1702) • F. J. Bremer, *Shaping New Englands: puritan clergymen in seventeenth-century England and New England* (1994) • J. L. Sibley, *Biographical sketches of graduates of Harvard University*, 1 (1873) • J. Savage, *A genealogical dictionary of the first settlers of New England*, 4 vols. (1860–62) **Archives** Harvard U.

Eaton, Peter (1914–1993), bookseller, was born Peter Eton at 8 York Gate, London, on 24 January 1914. His father is unknown, but his mother was (Elizabeth) Maria Eton, who later married George Papp and lived in Hungary. Peter was advertised in the *Nursing Times* for fostering, and was brought up by John William Atkinson, electrical engineer, and his wife, Catherine Elizabeth Atkinson of 37 Haslam Street, Rochdale. For several years Peter's mother wrote confused and emotional letters to Mrs Atkinson which showed concern for the boy's welfare and education. In these she referred to Peter's father as 'in no way a reliable man', and to the fact that Peter 'has ... Scotch and Irish and Hungarian blood in his veins' (private information). The Atkinsons adopted Peter on 25 April 1928, and in 1933 George Papp wrote to terminate the correspondence.

It was in Rochdale that Peter acquired his soft Lancashire accent and assumed the name Peter Eaton Atkinson. Asthma and the Atkinsons' poverty blighted his childhood, and he later described himself in campaigning literature as having been 'brought up … in the slums of Lancashire'. Sunday school was an important influence, but his day school is unknown, and he left at fourteen to work for a Rochdale printer. Also about this time he attended art school, developing there his skill at painting and his lifelong interest in it as a collector. Promoted at sixteen from errand boy to machine minder, he took up a three-year printing apprenticeship, and joined the Typographical Association.

Catherine Atkinson died aged sixty-six on 12 January 1931, and her husband not long afterwards, and Peter then lived briefly and not very happily with their son George and his wife. An unusual career of self-help and self-improvement followed—unusual in that it diverged from the conventional Victorian pattern because it contained elements of what can only be described as an anti-career, whose details he did not conceal in later life. Studying at the Municipal School of Technology, Manchester, for two days a week, he was (according to his *Who's Who* entry) 'expelled', and did not complete his apprenticeship. None the less, self-education was taking place as he browsed in lunch hours among the books for sale at Shude Hill market in Manchester. He was also picking up socialist ideas, but of the Methodist rather than Marxist variety.

A second ingredient of the self-help career—the search for opportunity through a move to London—also featured: at twenty he walked there, and in later years liked to describe how the price of lodging at a Church Army hostel was to cut up firewood until his hands bled. He took several low-grade jobs, but also dabbled in bookselling, helped to found the Domestic Workers' Union, joined the Labour Party, and in 1937 the Peace Pledge Union, by which time he was living at 103 Hereford Road, Paddington. On 27 August 1940 a tribunal of three unanimously accepted his status as a conscientious objector, requiring him to work full-time on air-raid precautions work or on the land. He worked full-time for the London rescue squad from 1939 to 1946, occasionally also helping with bomb disposal.

Dealing in books on Saturday afternoons from 1945 at what was then Portobello Road's only bookstall, Atkinson soon found that this brought in more than his entire weekday income from the rescue squad. At this point luck gave a twist to his self-help career, for the late 1940s were a time when the book shortage invigorated the secondhand book market, and when the contents of many large houses were being cleared; in Kensington many of their occupants were selling off interesting collections. He had soon raised enough to rent his own premises and eventually moved up to a shop in Church Street, Kensington, where he got to know many interesting customers, some of them prominent figures on the left. From there he moved his shop to Notting Hill Gate, and thence in 1957 to Holland Park Avenue, by which time he was attending five or six auctions a week and networking widely among well-to-do owners of private libraries but also among sharp-eyed dustmen and rag-and-bone men.

Atkinson's family life also diverged from a conventional self-help pattern of respectability: his first marriage, on 31 May 1943, to Edith Laura (Ann) Wilkinson (*b.* 1916/17), telephonist, and daughter of Albert Wilkinson, tug boat operator, was dissolved shortly thereafter. With Valerie Carruthers he then had two sons, the elder of whom was named Russell, after Bertrand Russell. On 28 June 1948 he changed his name by deed poll to Peter Eaton, and on 23 February 1952 he married his second wife, Margaret Taylor (*b.* 1930/31), daughter of Henry Gordon Taylor, accountant, and his wife, Liliane Robinson. They later adopted two daughters, Ruth and Diana. Margaret Eaton looked after the firm's accounts, which freed up Peter's entrepreneurial flair, a quality more frequently combined with socialist belief than is often supposed. Eaton's consistently socialist commitment had no Fabian puritanical or gradualist component, and he stood at least three times without success as a Labour candidate for Kensington borough council. These were anyway no-hope contests, and as he hated committee work he would have been horrified to win. Politically he was a rationalistic and lifelong idealist who lacked the temperament which organizes sympathetic opinion: his was the principled stand from the floor which gave a headache to the organizers of many a meeting.

Yet in the book trade Peter Eaton was always a step ahead. This was partly because the autodidact's wide and rather indiscriminate reading made him knowledgeable about what was contained in the shrewdly purchased books that he sold, and he was well able to build up subject-based book collections in a scholarly way. These he sold to libraries overseas at a time when the foundation of many new universities boosted worldwide demand for out-of-print books. Among the beneficiaries were the Toike Library in Hitotsubashi University, Japan, for his collection on the co-operative movement; Riverside University, California, for his Marie Stopes collection; and the University of Ife, Nigeria, for his collection of books on the study of soil. His secondhand bookselling business boomed in the 1960s and 1970s, enabling him to travel widely on business at home and overseas. In acquiring Pre-Raphaelite paintings, too, he ran ahead of fashion, buying them just because he liked them; but at a time of rapid inflation, owning things was coincidentally prudent.

In 1975 Eaton moved into purpose-built premises designed by Rick Mather a few doors away from his Holland Park shop. In 1969 he and his wife had also acquired Lilies, a seventy-roomed dilapidated country mansion in Weedon, near Aylesbury, which in subsequent years they gradually restored. 'It was a crazy thing to do', he later recalled, 'but all I was concerned about was somewhere to put the books' (*The Bookdealer*). As events turned out, it was financially not crazy at all, but Eaton was no mere money-maker, and often gave away prize discoveries to suitable institutions. Feminist in outlook, he published with Marilyn Warnick in 1977 a fifty-nine-page indexed checklist of Marie Stopes's writings which grew out of listing items he had collected and sold. He also published *A History of Lilies*, a booklet which had gone into three editions by 1993; it discussed not only the house and its history, but also some of the treasures he had collected there.

Eaton's life centred increasingly on Lilies in his last years, and the Holland Park shop was let. From the hospitable lunch table that was central to social life at Lilies, family talk ranged widely over a host of subjects, and many visiting scholars, customers, and friends were entertained there. President of the Private Libraries Association from 1989 to 1992, Eaton was influential in the book trade, and influential, too, on those who got to know him. Tall, casually dressed, with hinged double-layered spectacles on a high forehead, and with unusually long earlobes, he was a prize individualist and breaker of rules and conventions. Inquisitive, argumentative, plain-speaking, and provocative, he listed his recreations in *Who's Who* as 'taking the dog for a walk' and 'watching my wife play tennis'. He was fond, too, of music, with an avant-garde taste for Mahler, and always said that the book for his desert island would be the *Dictionary of National Biography*. Heart problems from the late 1980s, however, forced him to sell parts of the Lilies estate, and he died of heart disease at Lilies on 23 October 1993. He was survived by his wife, Margaret, their two adopted daughters, and his two sons from his relationship with Valerie Carruthers.   BRIAN HARRISON

Sources *The Bookdealer* (March 1991) · *The Guardian* (28 Oct 1993) · *The Independent* (30 Oct 1993) · P. Minet, 'Book chat', *Antiquarian Book Monthly* (Dec 1993), 38–9 · C. Jordan, interview, *Profile* programme, BBC World Service · *WWW* · private information (2004) · baptism certificate · adoption certificate · m. certs. · d. cert. · *CGPLA Eng. & Wales* (1993)
Archives priv. coll. | SOUND priv. coll.
Likenesses photograph, repro. in *The Guardian* · photograph, repro. in *The Independent*
Wealth at death under £125,000: probate, 20 Dec 1993, *CGPLA Eng. & Wales*

Eaton, Samuel (*d.* 1665), Independent minister and religious controversialist, was probably the third son of Richard Eaton (*d.* 1616/17), vicar of Great Budworth, Cheshire, and his wife, Elizabeth; Theophilus *Eaton (1590–1658) and Nathaniel *Eaton were his brothers. He was educated locally and subsequently entered Magdalene College, Cambridge, in 1621, graduating BA in 1625. He was ordained deacon and then priest at Peterborough on 18 and 19 December that year and proceeded MA in 1628.

While at Cambridge, Eaton acquired the godly principles that directed an itinerant life punctuated by controversy. In 1628 he was appointed rector of the parish of West Kirby, Cheshire, but immediately found himself in trouble with the authorities. On 31 July 1629 he was presented for unlicensed preaching and administering to sitting communicants at Bromborough, Cheshire. On 22 February 1630 he married his first wife, Ellen Holford of Davenham, Cheshire. Later that year he was presented again, 'for delivering in his sermon upon Easter Tuesday last that the first and second lesson and the reading of the homilies was nothing available nor to be esteemed of' (Richardson, 40). After further irregularities he was suspended from his

living in 1632, but he continued to preach and to attend exercises with like-minded clergy in Cheshire. In 1634 he decided to leave England and sailed for the United Provinces, settling at first in Amsterdam, where he 'joined with others in a Congregational way' (Sprunger, 119). He soon established a small gathered church at Amsterdam, but was disciplined by the Amsterdam classis for holding unlawful conventicles. During 1635 or 1636 he retreated to the English Reformed church at Rotterdam but, ultimately disillusioned, returned to West Kirby in 1636.

Upon his return Eaton was horrified to learn that for failing to appear before the high commission in 1634 to answer his earlier offences he had incurred fines amounting in total to £1550. The severity of his punishment, together with the promise of a freer religious climate in America, doubtless contributed to his decision to sail with his brother Theophilus and several other ministers to New England in 1637. After settling in New Haven, Eaton preached regularly at Harvard University, but became estranged from others who wished to restrict public offices solely to members of the New Haven church. Subsequently good fortune came his way when, on 29 August 1640, he received a grant of land at Toboket near New Haven. Late in 1640 he sailed for England, probably to gather a party to settle his new lands, but also to protect his living at West Kirby, which the high commission wished to distrain in lieu of his unpaid fines.

Eaton returned to a transformed political climate and, after the opening of the Long Parliament in November 1640, wasted no time in contributing to evolving debates concerning church government. In his widely distributed *Remonstrance Against Presbytery* (1641), the Cheshire landowner Sir Thomas Aston detailed two sermons delivered by Eaton during 1641 which attacked both the prayer book and the episcopacy while advocating congregationalist church government. Yet Eaton's criticism of the Church of England was considered moderate compared to others within Cheshire. In August 1641 it was reported that 'the New England Mr. Eaton and Mr. Holford preached at Barrow … but Eaton was modest in comparison of Holford, whoe railed most damnably against all church government as it is established' (*CSP dom.*, 1641–3, 77).

Following the outbreak of the civil wars, however, Eaton seized the opportunity to construct a congregationalist gathered church that encouraged lay participation and did not discriminate against non-church members. In early 1643 he became closely associated with the prominent Cheshire parliamentarian Colonel Robert Duckenfield, who installed him as minister to the chapel at Dukinfield. Subsequently Eaton, together with his friend Timothy Taylor, established a thriving church which gained both local and national notoriety. Between 1645, with the appearance of *A Defence of Sundry Positions*, and 1647 the two entered into a bitter printed dispute over the future of church government with the Lancashire minister Richard Hollingworth, a prominent figure in the Manchester presbyterian classis founded in early 1647. In 1646 the presbyterian heresiographer Thomas Edwards also decried the success of the Cheshire Independents in his *Gangraena*. By the end of the first civil war in 1646, however, Eaton was convinced that the new millennium was at hand, and urged the Cheshire parliamentarian commander Sir William Brereton to complete the work of further reformation.

After 1646 Eaton actively promoted the cause of congregationalist government, publishing, in response to Edwards, *A Just Apologie for the Church of Duckinfield* (1647). He became chaplain to the garrison at Chester, and ministered to the congregationalist church there until his resignation in 1648. In July 1648 he refused to sign the attestation of presbyterian ministers in Cheshire, and in 1650 published a spirited rebuttal of the oath of allegiance and national covenant, which represented a response to the engagement enacted by parliament on 2 January 1650. He also preached in both London and Scotland, and during the 1650s spoke regularly at Stockport and Macclesfield. At Dukinfield, Eaton remained a popular figure during the interregnum, although there were frequent disagreements with various lay members of his church. In June 1651 the committee for plundered ministers granted him an annual stipend of £40, and in 1654 two Stockport citizens petitioned unsuccessfully for this to be increased. In 1658, however, Eaton was maliciously accused of embezzling funds at Dukinfield, although the charges were later dismissed.

Eaton had become alarmed by the diversity of opinions which evolved after 1649. During 1650 and 1651 he published three refutations of the work of John Knowles, who denied the divinity of Jesus Christ. When, in 1654, some Cheshire Quakers posted nineteen written questions at a place where Eaton was due to preach, he responded with *The Quakers Confuted*, an impassioned condemnation of their position. On the other hand, throughout the 1640s and 1650s Eaton remained on friendly terms with several Lancashire and Cheshire presbyterians, including Adam Martindale, John Angier, and Henry Newcome. In 1654 he worked with the newly established Cheshire commission for the ejection of 'ignorant, scandalous, insufficient or negligent ministers' alongside other presbyterian and Independent divines. He also continued to enjoy the patronage of Sir William Brereton, and eventually received land in co. Tipperary, Ireland, valued at £120 in 1654. Eaton collaborated with others in bringing to press *Several Works of John Murcot* (1657), whose life in Cheshire and Ireland the editors described. In the late 1650s he enthusiastically contributed to an emerging agreement between presbyterians and Independents, which was effectively ruined when Cheshire presbyterians supported the abortive rising of Sir George Booth in August 1659.

Following the Restoration in 1660 Eaton continued to preach, but came under increasing pressure from the Cheshire authorities. He was effectively silenced by the Act of Uniformity in 1662, but conversed with Henry Newcome about a petition supporting ejected ministers. Thereafter the nonconformist minister Oliver Heywood noted that Eaton was 'several times brought into trouble and imprisoned' and became gravely ill (*Oliver Heywood*, 5.509). In his final years Eaton attended the church of his long-time friend John Angier at Denton, Lancashire. At an unknown date his first wife had died, and he married Alice (*d.* 1681), daughter of Thomas Leigh of Irby, Lancashire. He died at Bredbury, Cheshire, on 9 January 1665, and was buried at Denton on 12 January. Eaton had remained a tolerant Independent even in death. His will, proved on 12 July 1665, defiantly bequeathed £50 to twenty-one recently ejected presbyterian and Independent ministers and a further £100 'to all such poor ministers as are put by their places and are in a distressed condition ... and ... other distressed saints' (Earwaker, 2.33–4).

S. J. GUSCOTT

Sources *Calamy rev.*, 178 · J. P. Earwaker, *East Cheshire: past and present, or, A history of the hundred of Macclesfield*, 2 (1880), 27–34 · R. C. Richardson, *Puritanism in north-west England: a regional study of the diocese of Chester to 1642* (1972) · *The diary of the Rev. Henry Newcome, from September 30, 1661, to September 29, 1663*, ed. T. Heywood, Chetham Society, 18 (1849), 52–3 · *The life of Adam Martindale*, ed. R. Parkinson, Chetham Society, 4 (1845) · K. L. Sprunger, *Dutch puritanism: a history of English and Scottish churches of the Netherlands in the sixteenth and seventeenth centuries* (1982), 119–20 · *CSP dom.*, 1641–3, 77; 1654, 293 · J. S. Morrill, 'Puritanism and the church in the diocese of Chester', *Northern History*, 8 (1973), 145–55 · *The whole works of the Rev. Oliver Heywood ... with memoirs of his life*, ed. R. Slate and W. Vint, 5 (1826), 509 · W. F. Irvine, ed., *Marriage licences granted within the archdeaconry of Chester in the diocese of Chester*, 3, Lancashire and Cheshire RS, 57 (1909), 178 · W. A. Shaw, ed., *Minutes of the committee for the relief of plundered ministers and of the trustees for the maintenance of ministers ... 1643–1660*, 2 vols., Lancashire and Cheshire RS, 28, 34 (1893–6) · K. S. Bottigheimer, *English money and Irish land* (1971), 153–4 · J. S. Morrill, *Cheshire, 1630–1660: county government and society during the English revolution* (1974) · *DNB* · Venn, *Alum. Cant.*

Wealth at death £50 to twenty-one ejected ministers and £100 to other 'distressed saints': will, proved at Chester 12 July 1665, Lancs. RO, WC6 Chester Wills Act Book, 1661–7; Earwaker, *East Cheshire*, vol. 2, pp. 33–4

Eaton, Theophilus (1590–1658), merchant and colonial governor, was born in Stony Stratford, Buckinghamshire, the eldest of the seven sons of Richard Eaton (1562/3–1616/17), clergyman, and his wife, Elizabeth. After attending school in Coventry, about 1604 he started a seven-year apprenticeship in the wool trade in London. After completing his tenure of service he joined the Eastland Company, which by its charter of 1579 was granted a monopoly on the Baltic commerce. Eaton rose to the rank of deputy governor in the company and became the commercial agent in Denmark between James I and Christian IV of Denmark. While living in Denmark he married in 1622 Grace Hiller (*d.* 1626). After her death, in 1627 he married Anne (*d.* 1659), widow of David Yale and daughter of George Lloyd, bishop of Chester. Eaton had a total of six children from the two marriages.

After leaving Denmark, Eaton settled in the London parish of St Stephen, Coleman Street, where he renewed his childhood friendship with John Davenport, the controversial puritan minister. Together they supported the development of New England, becoming members of the Massachusetts Bay Company. In 1637 they moved to Massachusetts but, finding the colony in the midst of religious and social controversy, set out to start their own settlement on the north shore of Long Island Sound. On 24 November 1638 Eaton and Davenport agreed to a treaty with the Quinnipiac Indians. In exchange for protection and 'Twelve Coates of english trucking cloath, Twelve Alcumy spoones, Twelve Hatchetts, twelve hoes, two dozen of knives, twlve porengers and four Cases of french kives and sizers' the American Indians at the conference handed over rights to virtually all their lands (small plots and hunting rights were retained; Calder, 53). This was the first of a series of purchases on similar terms which shaped the New Haven colony. In 1643 the towns of New Haven, Branford, Guildford, Milford, Stamford, and Southwold joined together to form the colony.

Eaton's wealth and political experience made him the obvious candidate for governor, and he was duly chosen in 1643 and held that post until his death. The colony did not prosper. There were regular economic setbacks, and pressure from surrounding Dutch settlements made life precarious and expansion difficult. Moreover, the religious controversy that Eaton and Davenport avoided in Massachusetts followed them. Eaton's wife Anne was among the victims of a series of excommunications that encompassed other leading members of the community, including the colony's first schoolmaster. Having at some point adopted an opposition to infant baptism, Anne increasingly withdrew from services when the sacrament was administered. Eventually she stopped attending altogether. She was publicly admonished on 14 July 1644, and over a period of nine months failed to convince church elders that she had sufficiently repented. On 21 April 1645 she was excommunicated by a unanimous vote.

Eaton nevertheless attempted to prolong the colony's independent survival. He contributed to its law code with *New Haven's Settling in New England* (1656), which maintained the governmental outline of the Mosaic-inspired code of John Cotton but drew heavily on the Massachusetts code of 1648. Most notably it denied trial by jury. In an effort to protect the colony from New Netherland, which claimed territory on its outlying settlements, Eaton strove to seek mutual protection from neighbouring English colonies. This began in 1643 with the establishment of the United Colonies of New England, or, as it was more commonly known, the New England Confederation. He presided over the annual meeting of the body when it came to New Haven on rotation every five years from 1646.

Eaton died in New Haven on 8 January 1658 while still in office. His wife survived him but, never happily settled in the colony, left shortly after his death and returned to England where she died in 1659. Ironically, it was after her grandson Elihu Yale, a staunch Anglican, that the college in New Haven was named. The colony was ultimately absorbed into Connecticut in 1665.

TROY O. BICKHAM

Sources I. M. Calder, *The New Haven colony* (1934) · R. W. Roetger, 'Eaton, Theophilus', *ANB* · E. E. Atwater, *History of the colony of New Haven to its absorption into Connecticut* (1881) · J. T. Main, *Society and economy in colonial Connecticut* (1985) · H. E. Selesky, *War and society in colonial Connecticut* (1990) · S. Peters, *A general history of Connecticut: from its first settlement under George Fenwick, esq. to its latest period of amity with Great Britain; including a description of the country, and many curious and interesting anecdotes. To which is added, an appendix, wherein new and the true sources of the present rebellion in America are pointed out; together with the particular part taken by the people of Connecticut in its promotion* (1782) · DNB

Archives Connecticut Historical Society, Hartford, papers · Connecticut State Library, Hartford, papers · New Haven Colony Historical Society, Connecticut, papers

Eaton, William Meriton, second Baron Cheylesmore (1843–1902), mezzotint collector, was the second son in a family of three sons and two daughters of Henry William Eaton, first Baron Cheylesmore (d. 1891), and his wife, Charlotte Gorham (d. 1877), daughter of Thomas Leader Harman of New Orleans. He was born at 9 Gloucester Place, Regent's Park, London, on 15 January 1843. His father, who founded the prosperous firm of H. W. Eaton & Son, silk brokers, represented Coventry in parliament as a Conservative from 1865 to 1880 and from 1881 to 1887, and was raised to the peerage at Queen Victoria's jubilee in 1887. He was an authority on fine arts and an enthusiastic collector of contemporary paintings; among his treasures was Edwin Landseer's *Monarch of the Glen* (priv. coll.), which, at the sale of his collection at Christies on 7 May 1892, fetched 6900 guineas, and Paul Delaroche's *The Execution of Lady Jane Grey* (bequeathed to the National Gallery, London, by the second baron).

After education at Eton College, William entered his father's firm and subsequently became partner. He took little part in the business, however, and from 1866 onwards devoted himself to politics in the Conservative interest with little success. He failed in his attempts to enter parliament for Macclesfield in 1868, 1874, and 1880.

Like his father, Eaton had artistic tastes. In 1869 he started a collection of British portrait engravings, evidently working closely with John Chaloner Smith whose catalogue of British portrait mezzotints was published from 1878 to 1885. Although Eaton's collection was fully representative, only a small percentage of it was in the choicest condition. The prints at his home at Prince's Gate, London, comprised the finest private mezzotint collection ever formed; it was especially rich in eighteenth-century prints after Joshua Reynolds, George Romney, and their contemporaries. Thirty-nine of Eaton's mezzotints, including the valuable *Miranda*, engraved by W. Ward, after John Hoppner, which he had bought from Herbert Percy Horne for £40, were shown at the exhibition in 1902 of English mezzotint portraits (1750–1830) of the Burlington Fine Arts Club, of whose committee Eaton was a member. Eaton succeeded his father as second Baron Cheylesmore in 1891, and died, unmarried, at his residence, 16 Prince's Gate, on 10 July 1902. He was buried at Highgate cemetery. He was succeeded in the peerage by his younger brother, Herbert Francis *Eaton (1848–1925), to whom passed his collection of mezzotints other than portraits. Nearly 8000 mezzotint portraits and 2675 portraits of Queen Victoria and her family were bequeathed to the British Museum, where 641 prints were exhibited from 1905 to 1910. The acquisition almost doubled the museum's holdings of mezzotints.

W. B. OWEN, *rev.* SHEILA O'CONNELL

Sources *The Times* (11–12 July 1902) · *The Times* (5 Aug 1902) · *Daily Telegraph* (7 July 1905) · J. Frankau, 'Lord Cheylesmore's mezzotints', *The Connoisseur*, 2 (1902), 3–13 · S. O'Connell, 'William, 2nd Baron Cheylesmore (1843–1902) and the taste for mezzotints', *Landmarks in print collecting: connoisseurs and donors at the British Museum since 1753*, ed. A. Griffiths (British Museum Press, 1996), 134–58 [exhibition catalogue, Museum of Fine Arts, Houston, TX, 1996, and elsewhere] · F. O'Donoghue, *Guide to an exhibition of mezzotint engravings, chiefly from the Cheylesmore collection* (1905) [exhibition catalogue, BM] · *English mezzotint portraits* (1902) [exhibition catalogue, Burlington Fine Arts Club, London, 1902] · 'Manuscript catalogue of Cheylesmore collection', thirty notebooks, BM, department of prints and drawings · report to trustees, 6 Dec 1902, BM, department of prints and drawings · report to trustees, 6 Feb 1903, BM, department of prints and drawings · S. Colvin, letters to third Baron Cheylesmore, 26–8 Aug 1902, BM, department of prints and drawings [copies] · Burke, *Peerage* · d. cert.

Archives BM, department of prints and drawings, MS catalogue of collection, press mark Vv.1.11–40

Likenesses photograph, BM

Wealth at death £51,737 7s. 0d.: probate, 23 Oct 1902, CGPLA Eng. & Wales

Ebba. *See Æbbe (d. 683?).*

Ebba (*supp. fl. 870*). *See under Æbbe (d. 683?).*

Ebbutt, Norman (1894–1968), journalist, was born at 6 Victoria House, South Lambeth Road, London, on 26 January 1894, the elder son of William Arthur Ebbutt, journalist on the staff of the *Morning Leader* and later on the *Daily News* and *News Chronicle*, and his wife, Blanche Berry. He was educated at Willaston School, Nantwich, Cheshire, which he left in 1909. He spent the next few years in Berlin, Barcelona, and St Petersburg to learn languages. Before going to Russia he worked in Paris for a while in 1911 as assistant correspondent of the *Daily News*. In 1914 he joined *The Times* in London, but in November of that year he became a lieutenant in the Royal Naval Volunteer Reserve and served mainly in the Atlantic patrol and on the North American station. In 1918 he married Louise Ingram, daughter of W. I. Crockett, of Henderson, Kentucky, with whom he had a son and a daughter.

After the war Ebbutt returned to work in the foreign department of *The Times*, and in 1925 he was sent to Berlin to be assistant correspondent under H. G. Daniels. At the beginning of 1927 Ebbutt became chief correspondent in Germany. As an ardent democrat he had much sympathy for the fragile Weimar republic and was on friendly terms with some of its leading representatives. He was especially close to Chancellor Brüning, whom he greatly admired and whose futile efforts to manage the German state crisis he tried to support by favourable news coverage.

Because of his excellent knowledge of German affairs and his long-standing contacts Ebbutt was better able than most of his fellow correspondents to cope with the serious restrictions on news gathering imposed immediately after Hitler became chancellor on 30 January 1933. As Hitler consolidated his power Ebbutt reported events with deep seriousness and dispassionate accuracy. He had a special sense for the latent antagonisms hidden behind the seemingly monolithic façade of the Führer state.

In one field Ebbutt's dispatches were particularly full and reliable: for more than four years he recorded the disputes within the German protestant church and the growing tensions between confessing Christians and the Nazi regime in precise detail. This was due to a unique source close to the inner ranks of the German protestant church leadership. In February 1933 Ebbutt had been introduced by the former chancellor Brüning to Dr Horst Michael, a trained historian, who was prepared to undertake the risky job of a confidential contact in order to keep the outside world informed about what was going to happen in Germany. As a member of the Berlin brethren council of the confessing church Michael had access to inside news about the church conflict but could also provide authentic material on other aspects of Nazi policy, such as massive rearmament. This co-operation between Michael and the Berlin office of *The Times*, which lasted until March 1939, did much to make the London paper one of the most important sources of serious information about Nazi Germany.

Given the sensitivity of Hitler's regime to unfavourable press coverage it is no wonder that Ebbutt's candid reports were a thorn in the side of the Nazis. Repeatedly the Berlin correspondent of *The Times* endured hostile and depreciating attacks in German papers. In August 1937 the German government used the expulsion of three Nazi journalists from Britain for reasons of espionage as a pretext to require the withdrawal of Ebbutt. When *The Times* did not comply, Ebbutt was served with an expulsion order. On 21 August he left Berlin, seen off at the station by a large gathering of his colleagues. The extent to which he had become *persona non grata* in the eyes of the Nazi regime is shown by the fact that Goebbels himself instigated the momentous sanction against the renowned correspondent.

Ebbutt's expulsion is indeed the weightiest argument against the common charge that his dispatches were constantly toned down by the editorial team of *The Times*. From 1935 at the latest the responsible editors, Geoffrey Dawson, and his deputy, Robert Barrington-Ward, were firmly set on a course of appeasement and accordingly tried to avoid too much critical comment on Nazi Germany. But despite Dawson's self-damaging remark in a private letter to H. G. Daniels of 23 May 1937 that he did his utmost 'to keep out of the paper anything that might hurt their [German] susceptibilities' (*DNB*), there is no positive evidence for a systematic suppression of news. The disagreements between Ebbutt and the London office of *The Times* that survive on the record related to matters of style and length (his dispatches were sometimes late, often exceeded the promised length, and could be convoluted in their expression) and do not indicate censorship for political reasons. On the other hand Ebbutt had good reasons for his complaint that the half-hearted support he got from his London superiors did not facilitate his difficult task in the capital of the Third Reich.

The extreme strain of Ebbutt's time in Berlin contributed much to his physical breakdown a month after his expulsion, when he suffered a severe stroke which left him heavily paralysed, with speech impaired, for the next thirty-one years. His first marriage ended in divorce, and on 14 October 1942 he married Gladys Olive Cayford Holms, (*b.* 1894/5), the divorced wife of Charles Russell Holms and daughter of Frank William Apps, colonial broker. Ebbutt's companion from Berlin days, she nursed him throughout his long illness.

The impact of Ebbutt's work on German affairs came from the cumulative force of his reporting. He was scrupulously careful to avoid over-simplification, and assuming too much when evidence was only tentative. His lengthy and sometimes over-elaborate dispatches were not always easy reading, but they stand as models of accurate reporting and honest interpretation of the news. Ebbutt's widely acknowledged experience as a foreign correspondent, his complete honesty of mind, and his high conception of his professional duties fully justify the characterization as 'one of the foremost journalists of all time' (Woods and Bishop, 293). He had few relaxations, but those who knew him recalled that he was at his easiest when presiding night after night at a Berlin restaurant table where he and other British and American correspondents used to gather to exchange news and views on developments in Germany: 'At such times he could sit back: a man squarely built, looking out quizzically and expectantly through his thick spectacles, striking matches as he repeatedly lit his pipe, smiling delightedly when anyone made a telling point in discussion' (*DNB*). Ebbutt died at his home, Flat 4, Stedham Hall, Midhurst, Sussex, on 17 October 1968.   MARKUS HUTTNER

Sources DNB · *The Times* (19 Oct 1968) · M. Huttner, *Britische Presse und nationalsozialistischer Kirchenkampf* (1995) · F. McDonough, 'The Times, Norman Ebbutt and the Nazis, 1927–37', *Journal of Contemporary History*, 27 (1992), 407–24 · O. Woods and J. Bishop, *The story of The Times: bicentenary edition, 1785–1985* (1985) · I. McDonald, *The history of The Times*, 5 (1984) · [S. Morison and others], *The history of The Times*, 4/2 (1952) · F. R. Gannon, *The British press and Germany, 1936–1939* (1971) · D. McLachlan, *In the chair: Barrington-Ward of The Times, 1927–1948* (1971) · M. Dodd, *Through embassy eyes* (1939) · W. L. Shirer, *Berlin diary: the journal of a foreign correspondent, 1934–1941* (1941) · MSS relating to Ebbutt, News Int. RO, The Times archive · b. cert. · m. cert. [Norman Ebbutt and Gladys Olive Cayford Holms] · d. cert. · CGPLA Eng. & Wales (1969)
Archives News Int. RO, papers
Likenesses group portrait, photograph, 1933 (with von Neurath and Goebbels), repro. in P. Stoop, '"Licht in ein dunkles Zimmer bringen …?": Ausländische Korrespondenten in Berlin 1933 bis 1939', *Jahrbuch des Landesarchivs Berlin* (1988), 86 · photograph, before 1937, repro. in Dodd, *Through embassy eyes*, following p. 182 · photograph, repro. in *The Times* (19 Oct 1968)
Wealth at death £436: administration with will, 4 June 1969, CGPLA Eng. & Wales

Ebdon, Thomas (*bap.* 1738, *d.* 1811), organist and composer, was baptized in the parish church of St Oswald in the suburbs of Durham on 30 July 1738, the third of seven children of Thomas Ebdon (1709–1795), shoemaker, and his wife, Margaret (1705–1793), daughter of John Kay, the city's bellman. His younger brother, Christopher Ebdon, became an architect and county bridge surveyor. In 1748, at the age of nine, Ebdon was admitted as a chorister in Durham Cathedral, where his uncle, Robert, had been sworn as an almsman in 1736; his father was similarly

sworn in 1763. Ebdon became a supernumerary singing man in the choir in 1755 and was admitted as a full member in 1761. He must have been an adept musical pupil for when James Heseltine, who had been cathedral organist since 1711, died in 1763 Ebdon temporarily filled the vacancy for a few months and was then appointed organist and master of the choristers by Dean Spencer Cowper, against the advice of the other prebendaries in residence. His appointment was confirmed in the following year. On 10 January 1765 he married Elizabeth Miller (*bap.* 1735, *d.* 1771) at St Nicholas Church, Durham. They had five children of whom three survived infancy, a son who became a naval officer, and two daughters. His wife died in childbirth in January 1771.

The choir consisted of ten singing boys and ten lay clerks, most of whom had risen like Ebdon from among the ranks of the choristers. His contemporaries in the choir included the brothers William and Stephen Paxton, later to make a name for themselves in London as cellists. Their father, Robert Paxton, was a lay clerk and a prime mover along with the composer John Garth in the organization of fashionable subscription concerts in Durham. Ebdon inherited the role of director, initially with Garth, and the series of concerts alternated between two venues during the winter months for many years. Eventually Ebdon acquired the lease of the assembly room and took up residence there.

Among those recruited to the choir from outside Durham several, including Edward Meredith, John Friend, and William Evance, made a name for themselves as soloists in the north-east and further afield. One of Ebdon's pupils, Ralph Banks, became organist of Rochester Cathedral. For a time Ebdon organized concerts in Newcastle upon Tyne as well as Durham but as he grew older he gradually withdrew from such activities, closing down his assembly room in 1793, although the concerts and assemblies continued under other auspices. He died in Durham on 23 September 1811. His two unmarried daughters, Elizabeth and Mary, lived on in the city, sharing a cottage on the banks of the Wear, at first with the diminutive Count Boruwlaski, until their deaths in 1839 and 1851 respectively.

Of the school of Charles Avison, Ebdon was a prolific composer of anthems, glees for three voices, and harpsichord sonatas and concertos, and he published two volumes of music for the use of the Durham choir in 1788 and 1810.   C. D. WATKINSON

Sources parish register, Durham, St Nicholas, Durham RO, 1 June 1735 [baptism] · parish register, Durham, St Nicholas, Durham RO, 10 January 1765 [marriage] · abstracts of chapter minutes, 2, 1726–1829, Durham Cath. CL · Wood's pedigrees, Newcastle Central Library, local studies library, 68 Ebdon · *Newcastle Courant* (1763–1811) · *Letters of Spencer Cowper, dean of Durham, 1746–74*, ed. E. Hughes, SurtS, 165 (1956) · B. Crosby, *Durham Cathedral choristers and their masters* (1980) · B. Crosby, *A catalogue of Durham Cathedral music manuscripts* (1986) · J. H. Hinde, 'Public amusements in Newcastle', *Archaeologia Aeliana*, new ser., 4 (1860), 229–48, esp. 241–5 · R. Hird and J. Lancelot, *Durham Cathedral organs* (1991) · T. M. Heron, *Boruwlaski: the little count* (1986) · H. W. Shaw, *The succession of organists of the Chapel Royal and the cathedrals of England and Wales from c.1538* (1991) ·

H. D. Johnstone and R. Fiske, eds., *Music in Britain: the eighteenth century* (1990), vol. 4 of *The Blackwell history of music in Britain*, ed. I. Spink (1988–95) • P. Barrett, *Barchester: English cathedral life in the nineteenth century* (1993)

Ebers, John (c.1785–1858), bookseller and opera manager, was born in London, the son of German parents. At some time between 1808 and 1811 he took over from his father a fashionable bookshop in Old Bond Street (at no. 33, then no. 23, ultimately no. 27), already established in 1805. Besides selling books (still luxury articles at that time) and running a circulating library, such bookshops were letting agencies, night by night or for the season, for opera boxes owned by rich people who did not choose to attend; hence London theatre ticket agencies were long known as 'libraries'. The Ebers family also lent money to the managers of the Italian Opera at the King's Theatre (before 1813 to William Taylor, then to his successor Edmund Waters); as security they received some of the boxes the manager had at his disposal. After Waters had fled the country in August 1820, leaving the orchestra unpaid, Ebers's interests led him to take over the theatre's management. Some of the boxholders he dealt with pressed him to do so; a committee of five noblemen both assisted and, as an alternative focus of authority, hampered him.

The early 1820s, a period of agrarian depression, were difficult years for opera managers, whose audiences drew much of their income from land. In his first three seasons (1821–3) Ebers lost more than £7000, £5000, and £9000. After his first year he agreed to pay the new leaseholder of the King's Theatre, the banker Edward Chambers, a rent of £10,000 for two years; he was ultimately (1826) to pay £15,000 a year. In his seemingly accurate account, *Seven Years of the King's Theatre* (1828), Ebers acknowledged that these sums were hopelessly uneconomic for an opera management to bear when it enjoyed no subsidy. His motive for assenting to them seems to have been in part vanity—the satisfaction of dealing on apparently equal terms with aristocrats and famous artists.

These early seasons were dominated by the works of Mozart and Rossini, with the fashion for Rossini beginning to turn into a craze. The singers were distinguished—Violante Camporesi, Giuseppina Ronzi, Laure Cinti, Rosalbina Caradori, and Manuel García among them. Works new to London included Rossini's *La gazza ladra*, *Il turco in Italia*, and *Mosè in Egitto* (renamed, to placate the censor, *Pietro l'eremita*). In 1824 Ebers, tired of losses, sublet to the agent G. B. Benelli, who brought Rossini himself, Rossini's wife, the soprano Isabella Colbran (well past her best), and the great dramatic singer Giuditta Pasta. Rossini's operas dominated the season, among them his latest, *Zelmira*; he began another, *Ugo, conte di Parigi* (in part based on earlier work), but, before it could be put on, heavy losses caused Benelli to flee the country, leaving the company partly unpaid; Benelli also sued Ebers in chancery. The score of *Ugo* disappeared.

Ebers, in any case liable for some of Benelli's debts, took over again for the 1825–7 seasons, the first of which was, to begin with, held in the Little Theatre in the Haymarket while the King's Theatre underwent repair. These seasons were again dominated by Rossini's works and, among the singers, by Pasta, who performed her standard, much admired repertory (Mayr's Medea, Zingarelli's Juliet, Paisiello's Nina, Rossini's Tancredi, Semiramide, and Desdemona). Other artists were, in 1825, the young Maria García (later Malibran) and G. B. Velluti—last of the great castrati, and a curiosity—in Meyerbeer's vehicle for him, *Il crociato in Egitto*; and, in 1827, the great bass Filippo Galli. Continuing losses (of over £6000 and £7000 in 1825–6) owed more to the excessive rent than to the general economic situation, though the bursting of the 1826 financial bubble led to the abrupt cutting short of the 1827 season by Ebers's bankruptcy.

Ebers then wrote and published his account of his management. In it he gave precise and, so far as is known, accurate figures for salaries and expenses; the book was relatively free of boasting and disingenuousness, unlike other writings by opera impresarios. He blamed his failure on his initial ignorance, on the rent, and on the lack of a government subsidy on continental lines; subsidy, he recognized, was against English habits. The answer, he thought, might be management by a body of proprietors under an act of parliament. It is hard to tell from the book, or from the often partisan criticism of the time, how far Ebers was to blame. The stage directors he engaged—William Ayrton, then, for a time, Angelo Petracchi, a former manager of La Scala, then Ayrton again—were well practised, his singers, with some exceptions, of high repute, his productions more careful than those of his predecessors; but his lack of theatrical experience may have told.

Bankruptcy did not prevent Ebers from carrying on the bookselling and ticket agency business, which remained in the family until 1863. Nothing, however, is known of his wife or children. He died on 8 December 1858 at 18 Notting Hill Terrace, Kensington.   JOHN ROSSELLI

Sources J. Ebers, *Seven years of the King's Theatre* (1828) • D. Nalbach, *The King's Theatre, 1704–1867* (1972) • R. Edgcumbe, *Musical reminiscences, containing an account of the Italian opera in England from 1773*, 4th edn (1834), 181, *passim* • A. Porter, 'A lost opera by Rossini', *Music and Letters*, 45 (1964), 39–44 • *DNB* • *London Directory* (1805–63) • *The diaries of William Charles Macready, 1833–1851*, ed. W. Toynbee, 2 vols. (1912)

Ebert, Carl [Anton Charles] (1887–1980), actor and opera director, was born on 20 February 1887 in Berlin, the eldest child of Count Potulicky, a Prussian government official in Berlin, who was Polish, and his wife, Mary Collins, who was Irish. He was legally adopted by Wilhelm and Maria Ebert of Berlin. Customarily known as Carl, Ebert was educated at Friedrich Werder'sche Oberrealschule, Berlin, and then at Max Reinhardt's School of Dramatic Art, Berlin. After a short spell as a clerk in a private bank to help support his foster parents he embarked on an acting career. He was accepted, even as a student, by Max Reinhardt for a number of important roles in productions at the Deutsches Theatre, Berlin, which was under Reinhardt's direction. He then joined the Frankfurt-am-Main Drama Theatre and in the seven years up to 1922 played most of the major roles in that theatre. He joined the

Berlin State Drama Theatre in 1922 and continued his career as one of Germany's leading actors until 1927.

In 1919 Ebert had founded the Frankfurt Drama College and in 1925 he became director of the Berlin Academy of Music and Drama with the title of professor. In 1927 he became the first actor to be appointed Generalintendant of the Hessische Landestheater in Darmstadt where until 1931 he had the opportunity of practising his ideas on modernizing attitudes and methods in opera production. In 1931 he was appointed to the post of Intendant of the Staedtische Oper, Berlin.

When the Nazis took power in Germany, Ebert decided, despite the offer of an enhanced position in the Berlin theatre, to build a new career abroad. He settled with his family in Switzerland. His first major assignment was as director of the opening production of the first Maggio Musicale in Florence (1933). Subsequently he directed in the major opera houses of the world, including La Scala, Metropolitan Opera, Vienna State Opera, Teatro Colon Buenos Aires, and at the Salzburg Festival, among others.

In 1934 Ebert was invited by John Christie and his wife, Audrey, to join with them and Fritz Busch to help to launch the Glyndebourne Opera. He accepted the appointment as Glyndebourne's artistic director, a position he held until 1959. During this period he directed almost every production mounted by Glyndebourne both in the festivals there and in the first Edinburgh festivals of 1947 to 1955. His productions initially concentrated on the operas of Mozart, but soon embraced a wide variety of repertory extending from the British premier of Verdi's *Macbeth* and of Stravinsky's *The Rake's Progress* (the world première of which he had in 1952 directed in Venice) through the works of Strauss, Rossini, Debussy, Gluck, and Donizetti. His collaboration with Busch immediately gave Glyndebourne the hallmark of artistic excellence which established its reputation as a festival of international importance. His subsequent work with a variety of conductors, in particular Vittorio Gui in the 1950s, maintained Glyndebourne's position at the forefront of operatic enterprise. Perhaps his greatest contribution to British opera was to establish it as a *Gesamtkunst*—an artistic synthesis—of music and theatre, giving dramatic credibility in the production of opera in a way that had been previously absent. Glyndebourne's artistic foundations and its policy of operation were to a major extent established by Ebert and Busch, and the weight of their contribution played a vital part in Glyndebourne's early years and as a heritage for its continued success after Ebert's final production there in 1962.

During the Second World War, Ebert 'fathered' Turkish opera and drama, having from 1936 advised Kemal Atatürk on the establishment of the Turkish national opera and theatre companies and helped to establish music and drama academies there.

In 1948 Ebert created the opera department of the University of Southern California, Los Angeles, the success of which resulted in the establishment of a new professional company, the Guild Opera Company of Los Angeles. At this time he obtained American citizenship. In 1954 he

accepted an invitation to resume his pre-war position at the Staedtische Oper (later renamed the Deutsche Oper), Berlin. In 1961 he supervised the rebuilding and directed the opening production of the new opera house in Berlin.

Among Ebert's honours were: honorary doctorate of music, Edinburgh University (1954); honorary doctorate of fine arts, University of Southern California (1955); the Ernst Reuter plaque of the city of Berlin (1957); a knighthood of the Dannebrog order of Denmark (1959); Grosses Verdienstkreuz mit Stern, Germany (1959); Grosse Ehrenzeichen for services to Mozart, Austria (1959); honorary CBE (1960); and grande médaille d'argent de la ville de Paris (1961).

Ebert was a man of majestic appearance, powerfully built, with in later years a mane of white hair. He was a man of considerable resolve, displaying on occasions a fiery temperament, but more often than not exercising a considerable amount of persuasive charm.

In 1912 Ebert married Lucie Karoline Friederike, daughter of Oskar Splisgarth, electrical engineer. They had one daughter, who became a prominent German actress and died in 1946, and one son, Peter, theatre producer and administrator, who was awarded an honorary DMus of St Andrews University in 1979. This marriage was dissolved in 1923 and in 1924 he married Gertrude Eck (*d.* 1979). Of the second marriage there were two daughters and one son. Ebert died in Santa Monica, California, on 14 May 1980. GEORGE CHRISTIE, *rev.*

Sources *The Times* (16 May 1980) · *The Times* (22 May 1980) · *The Times* (28 May 1980) · personal knowledge (1986)
Archives FILM BFI NFTVA, performance footage

Eborard. *See* Everard (*d.* 1147).

Eborius (*fl.* 314), bishop of Eburacum (York), held a see centred on an important legionary and civilian town, where fourth-century Christianity has been attested by material remains. He is mentioned in history only as one of the three bishops from Britain who attended the Council of Arelate (Arles) in August 314. The council was convoked by the emperor Constantine to represent all the provinces in the prefecture of the Gauls (Gaul, the Rhineland, Britain, Spain and Tangier) to meet at Arelate under the presidency of Marinus, bishop of Arelate. Its main object was to adjudicate between Caecilianus and Donatus as to who was rightful bishop of Carthago (Carthage). Having decided that right lay with Caecilianus and that his opponents were 'madmen', the council agreed a number of disciplinary canons, which were transmitted with a covering letter to Pope Silvester. The canons included a decision that Easter should be celebrated on a single day throughout the world, and another that rejected the north African practice of rebaptizing converts from heresies, if these had been baptized in the name of the Trinity.

Eborius's British colleagues at Arelate were, 'Restitutus de civitate Londinensi' and 'Adelfius de civitate colonia Londinensium'. This latter could be either Lindum (Lincoln) or Camulodunum (Colchester), and appears to have been the senior see, as its bishop was accompanied by a presbyter and a deacon. The presence of the three bishops at Arelate indicates that the church in Britain was organized on the same hierarchical lines as on the continent, and also that the bishoprics were centred on urban communities. The suggestion has been made by J. C. Mann that as there were four provinces in Roman Britain, it could be expected that there were four bishops, and not just three, whose sees would be located in the provincial capitals. This does not seem unreasonable.

In the first half of the fourth century, the British episcopate supported Athanasius and with other western churches resisted the emperor Constantius II's attempt to remove him from the see of Alexandria. Hilary of Poitiers wrote on this dispute in 360 and referred to support from the church in Britain for Athanasius (*Patrologia Latina*, 10, col. 479). The previous year, British bishops had attended the Council of Ariminum (Rimini) with more than 400 of their western colleagues. Near the end of the century, Sulpicius Severus records that three accepted their return expenses and use of the imperial post from Constantius. Their plea of poverty was accepted by their western colleagues who had refused any favours from the Arianizing emperor.

The similarity of the names Eborius and Eburacum could raise the suspicion that the former derived from the latter, but Ivor was a common Welsh name, easily Latinized into Eborius. The *Annales Cambriae*, under the year 501, reads: 'Episcopus Ebur pausat in Christo' ('Bishop Ebur rests in Christ'); Manuscript B reads 'Ywor' for 'Ebur'. No memorial of Eborius survives.   W. H. C. FREND

Sources J. Gaudemet, *Conciles Gaulois du IVe siècle*, Sources Chrétiennes (1977) • [Hilarius of Poitiers], *Hilarii Pictaviensis Liber de synodis, Sancti Hilarii Pictariensis Episcopi Opera omnia*, 10 (1845) • Sulpicius Severus, 'Chronicon', *Sulpicii Severi libri qui supersunt*, ed. C. Halm (Vienna, 1866) • J. C. Mann, 'The administration of Roman Britain', *Antiquity*, 35 (1961), 316–20 • W. H. C. Frend, 'Ecclesia Britannica: prelude or dead end?', *Journal of Ecclesiastical History*, 30 (1979), 129–44 • J. Williams ab Ithel, ed., *Annales Cambriae*, Rolls Series, 20 (1860), 3, *s.a.* 501

Ebsworth, Joseph (1788–1868), playwright and musician, the elder son of Joseph and Isabella Ebsworth, was born at Islington, London, on 10 October 1788, and was in early life apprenticed to a watch-jeweller named Cornwall. He was a talented watch-mender and was later chosen to reconstruct the watch of the prince regent. Having a rich baritone voice, he joined the operatic company at Covent Garden immediately after fulfilling his indentures, and soon turned to playwriting. He also acted in melodrama, and became secretary to D. E. Morris, of the Haymarket. On 22 June 1817 he married Mary Emma Fairbrother (1794–1881) [*see* Ebsworth, Mary Emma], the eldest daughter of Robert Fairbrother, a member of the Glovers' Company. The couple settled at 3 Gray's Walk, Lambeth, where five of their children, including Joseph Woodfall *Ebsworth, were born. In 1822 Ebsworth made his first journey to Scotland. Soon after 1826 he and his family moved from London to Edinburgh, where he held an engagement at the Theatre Royal, as actor and prompter, with his lifelong

friend William Henry Murray, the brother of Harriet Siddons.

Ebsworth became gradually established as a teacher of music and singing, and accepted the position of leader of the choir at St Stephen's Church, Edinburgh, which caused him to abandon acting. He continued to write and to translate innumerable successful dramas, which were popular in London and the provinces. Many of these were printed, and a few reprinted more than once. His rise to fame began in London with the production of *The Two Prisoners of Lyons, or, The Duplicate Keys* (1824), probably the earliest English adaptation of *Robert Macaire*, from the French of Benjamin's *St Amant and Paulyanthe*; *Adelaide, or, The Fatal Seduction*, translated from Pixérécourt, performed at the Coburg Theatre; and *The Rival Valets* (1825) and *Rosalie, or, The Bohemian Mother* (1828), both performed at the Haymarket. By the time *Rouge et noir, or, Whigs and Widows* was first acted at the Adelphi, Edinburgh, in 1841, he was equally well known in the Scottish theatre, for which he had written *Tam o'Shanter, or, Auld Alloway's Haunted Kirk* (a dramatization of the poem by Robert Burns) as early as 1824.

In 1828 Ebsworth opened an 'English and foreign dramatic library and caricature repository' at 23 Elm Row, at the head of Leith Walk, Edinburgh, and for fifteen years maintained it successfully as a supplier of periodical literature. His vocal and instrumental concerts at the Hopetoun Rooms, Queen Street, were continued annually from 1830 until 1868, the year of his death. His various 'entertainments' were modelled on those of Charles Dibdin, whom he admired. He was for forty years a teacher of music, not only to private pupils, but at such public institutions as the Merchant Maidens' Hospital, Watson's, and the normal school, and enjoyed universal esteem. He was an accomplished linguist, in modern languages and in dead languages such as Hebrew and Sanskrit; he left voluminous compilations of Egyptian hieroglyphics and astrological documents from every available source. He was also an amateur artist and his musical compositions were considered singularly sweet and effective. He published *A Short Introduction to Vocal Music* and several large collections of psalm and hymn tunes, doxologies, sanctuses, and dismissions, many composed expressly for St Stephen's Church, and for his lifelong friend William Muir. As librarian of the Harmonist Society, Edinburgh, he showed rare knowledge of musical literature; his own manuscript and printed collections were unsurpassed in Scotland.

Ebsworth was remarkable for a playful humour and warm affections. He had a vast fund of anecdote, theatrical and literary, and an ungrudging hospitality. He was often pressed to write his memoirs, but firmly resisted this request, and when he died his widow faithfully destroyed all his private correspondence. Of his five children born in Scotland, three died young and two sons survived. News of the sudden death in Australia of his son Charles (*b.* 24 Oct 1833) reached him in the summer of 1868. The shock of this bereavement was partly responsible for his own death 'by an apoplectic seizure', three weeks later, on

23 June 1868, at his home, 4 Montgomery Street, Edinburgh. He was buried at the Dean cemetery, Edinburgh, at the feet of David Scott RSA. On the following Sunday his own music was played and sung in churches of all denominations in Edinburgh.

J. W. EBSWORTH, rev. NILANJANA BANERJI

Sources Adams, *Drama* · *Edinburgh Evening Courant* (24 June 1868) · *Edinburgh Weekly Review* (27 June 1868) · *The Scotsman* (24 June 1868) · personal knowledge (1888)
Likenesses J. W. Ebsworth, watercolour drawing, 1848, Scot. NPG

Ebsworth, Joseph Woodfall (1824–1908), literary editor and artist, was born on 2 September 1824 at 3 Gray's Walk, Lambeth, London, the younger son (of thirteen children) of Joseph *Ebsworth (1788–1868), playwright and musician, and his wife, Mary Emma *Ebsworth, *née* Fairbrother (1794–1881), also a playwright. In 1828 the family moved to Edinburgh, where Joseph's father established a bookshop.

Ebsworth began his career as a practical artist and art teacher: having entered the Trustees' Academy Art School in Edinburgh at fourteen, in 1848 he became chief artist to Faulkner Brothers, lithographers, in Manchester, but soon returned to Scotland to a teaching post at Glasgow School of Design. In 1849 and 1850 he exhibited at the Scottish Academy.

Ebsworth was admitted as a freemason in Edinburgh in July 1852 and was for two years senior warden of his lodge, where he met the novelist G. J. Whyte-Melville. In July 1853 he started on a solitary walking tour through central Europe and Italy, returning to Edinburgh in 1854. Between 1854 and 1860 he wrote for the press, including, in 1859, an article on Emily Brontë (Francis, 315–17). While working on the *Dumfries Herald* he came to know George Gilfillan, the literary editor, who helped him secure lecturing assignments on literary topics. Gilfillan wrote, oddly, of his 'nice, fluent, discriminatory, though somewhat dim and divisive talk' (*George Gilfillan: Letters and Journals*, ed. R. A. Watson and E. S. Watson, 1892, 226).

At this point Ebsworth's plans changed radically. The impassioned outpourings in a letter from an unidentified lady (priv. coll.) suggest a broken engagement, and in 1860 he departed for St John's College, Cambridge, where he took his BA in 1864 and MA in 1867. On 31 July 1864 he was ordained deacon at York; he was curate of Market Weighton in Yorkshire in 1864–5. On 29 May 1865 he married Margaret (d. 1906), eldest daughter of William Blore, rector of Goodmanham, East Riding of Yorkshire. In 1868 he was ordained priest at Ripon.

After three further curacies in and near Bradford, Ebsworth left the north for good in January 1871. Until 1894 he served as vicar of Molash near Ashford, Kent, a poor parish. In a letter to the Icelandic scholar Vigfusson he described himself as being 'choir-master, clerk, sexton, pastor, parish church-warden and sole paymaster' (Bodl. Oxf., MS Eng. misc. d. 131, fols. 236–7), but he devoted most of his time to literary work at home and to research in the British Museum. Only now did his literary talents begin to find their fullest expression, though he had previously

Joseph Woodfall Ebsworth (1824–1908), by Maull & Fox, c.1892–3

published at Edinburgh a curiously hybrid work, blending prose and verse. *Karl's Legacy* (2 vols., 1867) seems to derive from his continental experiences, partly fantasy, in which the College of Nirgends, where Karl is professor, is the 'Inner-home or Dreamland Rest, carried within ourselves' (2.301), partly a collection of essays and poems including a chapter entitled 'Among Gypsies'. (In 1903 he wrote that he had acquired 'much of the Romany Lingo, gathered from Borrow and others', which made him 'free of every Gipsy tent wherever [he] roved' (Francis, 296–7). His *Literary Essays and Poems* of 1868, mentioned in the *Dictionary of National Biography*, has not been traced.

Ebsworth's true métier was as an editor. Working on the love poetry and popular street balladry of the seventeenth century, some of it of a racy bawdiness not quite consonant with his clerical profession, in 1875 he published new editions of *The Westminster Drolleries* of 1671 and 1672, and *The Merry Drolleries* of 1661 and 1670, followed in 1876 by *The Choyce Drolleries* of 1656. He became one of the ablest and most energetic supporters of the Ballad Society, which had been founded in 1868, editing a number of works for the society. A man of deep affections and fierce antipathies, he corresponded over many years with friends such as Bertram Dobell, the bookseller, and John Payne Collier. His antipathies included Leslie Stephen, with whom he quarrelled about 1889, as we learn from a lively letter to Sir Sidney Lee (Bodl. Oxf., MS Eng. misc. d. 176, fols. 365–6). He had made several contributions to the *Dictionary of National Biography*, edited by Stephen, running from A to G of the alphabet, his last accepted contribution being his article on Gilfillan. His article on Grimaldi came to grief through disagreement over articles he was not invited to write, and the association ceased. Another antipathy was towards Frederick James Furnivall, founder of the Early English Text Society among many others, whom he described in the same letter as 'the notorious pensioner Furnivallus Furioso'.

Editions Ebsworth saw through the press included *The Bagford Ballads* from the British Museum (2 parts, 1876–8), together with the *Amanda Group of Bagford Poems* (1880). A major unpublished work seems to have disappeared from view: in his preface to *The Bagford Ballads* (1876) he refers to 'some future day, if we ever print that *Ebsworthian Catalogue of every known Song and Ballad*, issued before the year 1801 … On this voluminous and far-advanced Catalogue we have been working quietly, during recent years, without help from anybody' (lix). Alongside work on the massive *Kentish Garland* (2 vols., 1881–2), which he edited with Julia H. L. de Vaynes, he had already, from 1879 onwards, embarked on his main labour for the Ballad Society, the completion of its edition of the Roxburghe collection of ballads in the British Museum. The first three volumes (1869–79) had been edited by William Chappell, and Ebsworth published six further volumes between 1883 and 1899, classifying some 1400 pieces under historical and other headings, such as *Early Legendary Ballads* (1888), *Robin Hood Ballads* (1896), and *Restoration Ballads* (1899). Ebsworth freshly transcribed the texts, supplied exhaustive introductions, notes, and indexes, and grappled with recalcitrant printers. He characteristically introduced verses of his own, as prelude and envoi, and produced his own woodcuts after the original illustrations. A staunch supporter of the Stuart cause and hater of puritanism, he enlivened his editorial comments with scornful references to political and religious views from which he dissented: 'We have never scrupled to express our abhorrence of the foolish and cruel acts performed, or the intolerable nonsense talked and written, by the class that arrogated to themselves, as a proud distinction, the name of Protestants' (Ebsworth, *The Bagford Ballads*, iii–iv). But despite editorial eccentricities he was a meticulous scholar and made an invaluable contribution to the history of English ballad literature. He was elected a fellow of the Society of Antiquaries in 1881.

In 1894 Ebsworth retired from Molash vicarage to live privately at Ashford, where his wife, to whom he had been devoted, died on 18 April 1906. They had no children. A letter to J. R. Tutin (priv. coll.) describes his grief at losing her and his despair at the sale of his library in 1907. He died at his home, The Priory, Sackville Crescent, Godington Road, Ashford, only fourteen months later, probably of heart failure, on Whitsunday, 7 June 1908, and was buried in the same grave as his wife in Ashford cemetery, on 11 June 1908.   ANN MARGARET RIDLER

Sources J. C. Francis, *Notes by the way, with memoirs of Joseph Knight and the Rev. Joseph Woodfall Ebsworth, editor of the Ballad Society's publications* (1909) [incl. bibliography] · Venn, *Alum. Cant.* · Crockford (1908) · private information (2004) [A. Freeman] · J. W. Ebsworth, ed., *The Bagford ballads*, 2 vols. (1876–8), preface · Bodl. Oxf., MSS Dobell d. 2–3 · J. W. Ebsworth to J. R. Tutin, 16 July 1907, priv. coll. · letter to F. G. Stephens, Bodl. Oxf., MS Don. e. 82, fols. 134–5 · letter to Vigfusson, Bodl. Oxf., MS Eng. misc. d. 131, fols. 236–7 · *Catalogue of the valuable library of the Revd. J. Woodfall Ebsworth … which will be sold by auction by Messrs Puttick & Simpson Thursday Feb 28th & following day, 1907* [sale catalogue] · *The Times* (9 June 1908) · d. cert.

Archives Bodl. Oxf., corresp. with Bertram Dobell, d. 2–3 · LPL, letters to A. C. Tait

Likenesses T. Duncan, oils, 1853 · portrait, 1873, repro. in Francis, *Notes by the way* · Maull & Fox, photograph, c.1892–1893, repro. in Francis, *Notes by the way*, following p. 286 [*see illus.*]

Ebsworth [*née* Fairbrother], **Mary Emma** (1794–1881), playwright and translator, was born on 2 September 1794 in London, the eldest daughter of Robert Fairbrother (1769–1841), actor and popular entertainer, and his wife, Mary Bailey, the daughter of the actor Joseph Grimaldi's sometime landlady. Her early life is mostly unrecorded but was influenced strongly by both parents. From her mother, who had been raised in a convent at St Omer in French Flanders, she learned fluent French, which enabled her to translate such books as the popular romance *Masaniello*. Her father was a performer and general factotum for Richard Brinsley Sheridan at the Theatre Royal, Drury Lane, London, where apparently Mary Emma performed as a child actress during the 1807/8 season. She was again in Drury Lane's chorus and its *corps de ballet* during the 1817/18 season when she met her future husband, Joseph *Ebsworth (1788–1868), a member of the theatre's chorus since 1812. They married on 22 June 1817 and lived at 3 Gray's Walk, Lambeth, London, where the first five of their ten surviving children were born. (The remainder were born in Scotland.) Their eldest daughter, Emilie Marguerite (1818–1899), married the comedian Samuel Houghton Cowell (1820–1864), a union which produced the theatrical dynasty which included Sydney Cowell (1846–1925), Florence Cowell (1852–1926), and Sydney Fairbrother.

In 1826 Mary Emma Ebsworth joined her husband in Edinburgh where, in 1822, he had restarted his career as an actor and prompter at William Henry Murray's Theatre Royal. They both joined the company at the Caledonian Theatre, playing leading roles in J. B. Buckstone's *Luke the Labourer* in 1826. However, their prominence and promise dissipated quickly and they were merely minor members of the companies at the Theatre Royal and the Adelphi (formerly the Caledonian). Nevertheless Mary Emma Ebsworth attracted attention each Christmas (until the 1832/3 season) when 'she played Columbine in the pantomime, wearing the decorous long skirts then fashionable for harlequinades' (*Cowells in America*, xv).

Mary Emma Ebsworth also collaborated with her husband on his translations and numerous plays. In her own right she wrote several plays which were issued in John Cumberland's acting drama and by her brother, the theatrical publisher Samuel Glover Fairbrother. One of her earliest melodramas, *The Two Brothers of Pisa*, a translation of *Le délateur* by Charles Nodier and Isidore-Justin-Séverin Taylor, and with music by T. Hughes, was performed at the Royal Coburg on 7 January 1822 (published 1828). The production featured T. P. Cooke, the celebrated melodramatic actor, which probably accounted for the 'enthusiastic applause' it received (playbill, Harvard Theatre Collection). It now appears a typically thin and overwritten melodrama in which, for example, a bloody dagger becomes an 'ensanguined poniard'. Mary Emma Ebsworth's 'petite drama' in one act, *Payable at Sight, or, The Chaste Salute*, was performed at the Surrey Theatre in London on 23 October 1834. It is a comedy of romantic entanglements caused by inconsequential misunderstandings which are resolved satisfactorily. George Daniel's introduction to the published script called it a lively piece 'not a little indebted to the humorous acting of Charley Hill [as a valet], that fails not to attract a good audience, and is always seen with pleasure' (Daniel, 7). Other notable, but unpublished, plays included *Ass's Skin*, and *The Sculptor of Florence*, regarded by some contemporaries as her best work.

Mary Emma Ebsworth placed great importance on her family life. Her son the ballad editor and Anglican clergyman Joseph Woodfall *Ebsworth (1824–1908) declared that 'She was of a most retiring and unselfish nature, loving a private life with the constant care of her children and of her parents' (*DNB*). Her marriage of fifty-one years was shattered by her husband's death in 1868, itself brought on by news of the sudden death of their son Charles Ebsworth (*b.* 1833) in Australia. Mary Emma Ebsworth survived her husband for thirteen years and outlived all but three of her children. She returned to London in 1879 and died of a stroke and exhaustion, surrounded by her surviving family, at her home, 57 Boyson Road, Walworth, Surrey, on 13 October 1881. She was buried on 19 October at Norwood cemetery, London.

J. P. WEARING

Sources *DNB* · J. C. Francis, *Notes by the way* (1909) · *The Cowells in America: being the diary of Mrs Sam Cowell during her husband's concert tour in the years 1860–1861*, ed. M. W. Disher (1934) · Highfill, Burnim & Langhans, *BDA*, 5.138–40 [Robert Fairbrother] · *The Athenaeum* (22 Oct 1881), 537 · J. Parker, ed., *Who's who in the theatre*, 10th edn (1947), 1504, 1525 · G. Daniel, 'Introduction', in M. E. Ebsworth, *Payable at sight, or, The chaste salute* · d. cert.

Ebury. For this title name *see* Grosvenor, Robert, first Baron Ebury (1801–1893).

Eccardt, John Giles (*d.* 1779), portrait painter, was born in Germany and is said to have moved to England at an early age, possibly with the French portrait painter J. B. Van Loo. No other details of his early life are known. In London he was assistant to Van Loo, and may also have been his pupil, but when his master left Britain in October 1742, leaving portraits 'unfinished to be dressed by his Men', Eccardt and another assistant, Root, 'remain here and sett up for themselves' (Vertue, *Note books*, 3.110).

Working in partnership Eccardt and Root met with some success in the portrait business, Root painting the draperies and Eccardt the faces of the sitters who were attracted by the painters' continued use of Van Loo's style. However, it is not known how long the two continued in partnership. Eccardt's rise as a fashionable portrait painter can be gauged from his move in October 1746 from Bow Street, Covent Garden, via Carnaby Market, to his master's former lodgings in Covent Garden. About that time he married Susannah, daughter of Duhamel, a watchmaker; they had one son, Jacob, baptized in July 1748 at St Paul's, Covent Garden, and a daughter, also Susannah (*bap.* May 1752).

Eccardt specialized in small-scale portraits, including at least twenty-six for his most important patron, Horace Walpole, fourth earl of Orford, painted between *c.*1746 and 1754. Typically measuring 15 inches x 12 inches, Eccardt's portraits remained heavily indebted to his former master, although he was capable of adapting his style to that required by his patrons. He painted in the manner of Rubens, Van Dyck, and Watteau, and made copies after not only Van Loo but also Holbein and Sir Peter Lely, for example *Elizabeth, Countess of Grammont* (NPG). Eccardt painted Walpole on a number of occasions, including the famous portrait of 1754 (NPG), which hung with six others by Eccardt in the blue bedroom at Walpole's residence, Strawberry Hill; other subjects in this group included the poet Thomas Gray and the writer and artist Richard Bentley (both NPG). Dressed in rich blue velvet and delicately painted lace, Walpole's facial features are closely observed. This delicate and detailed painting is typical of Eccardt, as is the emphasis on the sitter's hands; both features are typical of French painting and of the style promoted by Van Loo.

Walpole's admiration for Eccardt went further than simple patronage; he wrote a poem, 'The Beauties: an Epistle to Mr Eckardt the Painter' (composed for Lady Caroline Fox and published without his consent in September 1746) and though Walpole only footnoted Eccardt in his *Anecdotes of Painters* he listed him in his manuscript 'Book of materials' as among the principal painters in London. By 1761 Eccardt was living in Joshua Reynolds's old house, 5 Great Newport Street, from where he exhibited at the Society of Artists that year and again in 1768. A few of his works were engraved, including *Conyers Middleton* and *Margaret 'Peg' Woffington*, both reproduced in mezzotint by John Faber jun. (both NPG). In 1770 he sold his collection at auction and retired to Paradise Row, Chelsea, where he died in 1779. His will was proved on 20 October 1779; in it he left his son £2000 and his leasehold house in Henrietta Street, Covent Garden. A number of portraits by Eccardt are in the collection of the National Portrait Gallery, London.

L. H. CUST, rev. DEBORAH GRAHAM-VERNON

Sources J. G. C. Collins Baker, biography of Eccardt, NPG, Heinz Archive and Library, Eccardt file · Waterhouse, *18c painters* · Vertue, *Note books*, 3.110, 127, 132 · P. Toynbee, *Strawberry Hill accounts* (1927) · will, PRO, PROB 11/1057, sig. 411 · H. Walpole, *Fugitive verses* (1931)

Wealth at death left son £2000 and leasehold house: will, PRO, PROB 11/1057, sig. 411

Eccles, Charlotte O'Conor (1864/5–1911), journalist and novelist, was born in Roscommon, Ireland, the elder surviving daughter of Alexander O'Conor-Eccles of Ballinagard, near Roscommon. She was educated in Catholic convents at Upton Hall, near Birkenhead, and in Paris and Germany. Her European education was probably the source of her good knowledge of continental languages. A lecturer in Ireland for the board of agriculture and technical instruction, she was particularly interested in housing for the poor.

On taking up residence in London, probably in late 1890 or early 1891, Charlotte O'Conor Eccles sought work as a newspaper journalist, which she preferred to work on magazines, which she felt to be irregular and precarious. She had previous newspaper experience in Dublin, helping to sub-edit an evening newspaper, for which she undertook translations from American, Australian, French, and German periodicals, corrected proof, did general reporting, and conducted a ladies' column. Her article 'The experience of a woman journalist' (Eccles) describes vividly the difficulty she encountered in finding employment. In it she commented 'One is horribly handicapped in being a woman'. Her first big break came when she was hired by the London office of the *New York Herald*, where she was put on the staff at a salary of 3 guineas per week. The *Herald* had a short life (2 February 1889 to 31 May 1891); she worked during the last six months of its existence and gained valuable experience. Thereafter, as she mastered the technicalities of the London newspaper world, she worked variously as sub-editor of a woman's paper, for weeklies, as London correspondent to provincial papers, and as a freelance. Other articles identified as hers include 'Irish housekeeping and customs in the last century' (*Blackwood's Edinburgh Magazine*, December 1888), 'A royal elopement' (*Dublin Review*, 3rd ser., no. 48, 1890, 302–18), and 'Hospital where plague broke out' (*Nineteenth Century*, no. 272, 1899, 591–602). Others have yet to be identified.

As a novelist Charlotte O'Conor Eccles published *The Rejuvenation of Mrs Semaphore* (1897), using the pseudonym Hal Godfrey, and *The Matrimonial Lottery* (1906). She translated from the Polish a novel by Henryk Sienkiewicz, a Nobel laureate, which was published in America in 1899 as *Peasants of the West* and in England as *Aliens of the West* (1904). She was a fellow of the Institute of Journalists and a member of the Writers', Lyceum, and Ladies' Park clubs in London. She died unmarried on 14 June 1911, at the age of forty-six at her home, 139A Alexandra Road, St John's Wood, London, of cerebral thrombosis.

ROSEMARY T. VAN ARSDEL

Sources WWW · d. cert. · *Wellesley index* · C. O'Conor Eccles, 'The experiences of a woman journalist', *Blackwood*, 153 (1893), 830–38

Eccles, David McAdam, first Viscount Eccles (1904–1999), businessman and politician, was born on 18 September 1904 at 124 Harley Street, London, the third of four sons and the fourth of five children of William McAdam Eccles (1867–1946), surgeon, and his wife, Anna Coralie

Anstie (1870–1930), who came from a family of tobacco manufacturers in Devizes.

Education and early career Both Eccles's parents seem to have been rather withdrawn and preoccupied by religion. William Eccles, who never smoked, drank, or swore, and banned his wife from attending the theatre during the first ten years of their marriage, 'practised a severe Presbyterianism which subdued our pleasures', as his son put it (Eccles, *By Safe Hand*, 9). In view of his evident capacity to enjoy life, this upbringing imposed obvious strains on the young David, and he developed a habit of speaking out and disregarding convention which remained with him throughout life. Surprisingly, his father never spoke to his children about religion, nor did he have them baptized. Consequently, at Winchester College, Eccles at thirteen came under pressure to be baptized and confirmed, which he resisted with the acquiescence of the headmaster, Monty Rendall. However, he spent much of his life attempting to define his religious convictions, eventually becoming an adherent of the Church of England. He published his thoughts in *Half Way to Faith* (1966) and *Life and Politics: a Moral Diagnosis* (1967), almost as though trying to justify himself in the face of parental disapproval.

From Winchester, Eccles went on to read philosophy, politics, and economics at New College, Oxford, where he was taught by Lionel Robbins. There he managed to pay off his debts by buying and selling books. What began as an expedient turned him into an enthusiastic collector of antiquarian books, paintings, and sculpture throughout his life. Soon after graduating with a second-class degree in 1926 he was offered employment in the City. For once his father showed an urgent interest in his son, recommending the professions and arguing forcibly against going into business. Despite this, Eccles became a manager of Central Mining and Investment, which specialized in Spanish railways, and he quickly prospered as a businessman. On 10 October 1928 he married the Hon. Sybil Frances Dawson (1904–1977), eldest daughter of the royal physician, Bertrand Edward *Dawson, Viscount Dawson of Penn, who was a neighbour. Their marriage, he claimed later, broke all the rules: 'Sybil and I were as equal, and wanted to be as equal, as any man or woman could be.' (Eccles, *By Safe Hand*, 10). They signified this by incorporating the name Dawson into the names of each of their children: John (*b*. 1931), Simon (*b*. 1934), and Polly (*b*. 1937). The family lived in Montagu Square in London and established a country home at Chute in Wiltshire.

War service On the outbreak of the Second World War in 1939 Sybil Eccles took the children off to Wiltshire while Eccles himself began work for the Ministry of Economic Warfare; from 1940 to 1942 he was posted to Madrid and Lisbon as adviser to the British ambassador. His chief object, which on his own admission he accomplished by extensive bribery, was to keep Spanish mineral supplies and Portuguese wolfram, an ingredient in steel making, out of German hands. A minor duty involved keeping in touch with the duke and duchess of Windsor, aiming to curtail their Nazi sympathies; he dismissed the duke as 'pretty fifth column' and the duchess as 'a very vulgar woman' (Eccles, *By Safe Hand*, 139). Unhappily the prolonged separation from Sybil led Eccles into an affair which by 1942 threatened his marriage. In June of that year, however, he 'took the decision to stop trying to love two people' and applied to return to England (ibid., 12). His marriage was restored, and from 1942 to 1943 he worked in the Ministry of Production, where he co-ordinated the Anglo-American munitions programme. This experience led to a radical change in his career.

Conservative MP Up to this time Eccles had apparently not contemplated taking up politics. However, by chance he was in the presence of Churchill when news arrived that the Conservative member for Chippenham in Wiltshire had died. Encouraged by the prime minister, he stood in the by-election of 1943 and managed to retain the seat at the general election two years later. He adjusted easily to the House of Commons, and during the next six years gained valuable experience as a front-bench speaker on economics. As a result, by 1951 he stood out as a rising man on the Conservative benches. Despite his dour, Scots background, he seemed a cultivated, faintly aristocratic figure, though his involvement with the world of art made him suspect to colleagues who lived for nothing but politics. Moreover, his undoubted elegance and good looks won him the nickname 'Smarty Boots', which to his rivals also reflected his smugness and excessive confidence in his own abilities. Lacking the sense of discipline engendered by a lengthy party apprenticeship, he never learned to curb his natural tendency to speak out, and he handicapped himself by letting slip tactless remarks which seemed to betray a high opinion of himself.

None the less, during the 1950s Eccles was well placed to rise in a party whose leadership was dominated by consensus politics. The legacy of his father's belief in service to others and the experience of the inter-war depression helped to place him on the liberal wing of Conservatism. 'I've been a capitalist and made quite a lot of money,' he once remarked, 'but I didn't like it' (*The Guardian*). He conceded that nationalization was sometimes necessary, and he collaborated with R. A. Butler over *The Industrial Charter* (1947). In 1951 he published his own *Forward from the Industrial Charter* and urged fellow tories to represent those who created wealth rather than those who inherited it. But when he reportedly claimed in 1950 to have taken over the intellectual leadership of the Conservative Party he played into the hands of his rivals and critics. During the crucial general election of 1951 he unwisely called for cuts in the social services.

Cabinet minister When the Conservatives returned to office Churchill, perhaps fearing the rivalry between Eccles and Butler, the new chancellor, confined Eccles to the lowly post of minister of works. Yet the irrepressible Eccles managed to steal the limelight in his role as stage manager of the coronation in 1953. In a typical off-the-cuff comment he described it as 'show-business' and the queen as the 'perfect leading lady', language which attracted criticism in the deferential mood of the 1950s. None the less, in 1953 he was knighted KCVO for his efforts and stood in line for promotion.

Eccles's opportunity came with the resignation of Florence Horsbrugh as education minister in 1954. A strong and imaginative minister, as Horsbrugh's successor Eccles fought the Treasury for extra resources and promoted education as an economic investment, an idea which later came to be almost universally accepted. Over the next three years the economy programme that had undermined his predecessor was cancelled. Eccles improved grants for university students and created a hierarchy of colleges culminating in the new colleges of advanced technology; he accepted the principle of comprehensive schools; he also reopened negotiations with teachers over their pensions, forcing them to contribute more to the scheme, thereby provoking the derisive cry 'Shekels not Eccles'. Despite the controversy, during his two terms from 1954 to 1957 and 1959 to 1962, Eccles emerged as the major architect of the post-war expansion of education in Britain.

His success gave Eccles a strong claim on the economic post he had always wanted in the crisis following the resignation of Sir Anthony Eden. In 1957 the new premier, Harold Macmillan, whom he greatly admired, sent him to the Board of Trade. In this role he worked energetically to help businessmen to increase exports. Though an enthusiast for the Common Market, he promoted the idea of a wide free-trade area incorporating western Europe, North America, and south Asia. Unfortunately he clouded his reputation by committing several indiscretions, notably the revelation that the government planned to reduce the cinema tax, which caused shares in cinemas to soar in value. The prime minister stood by him but sent him back to education after the general election of 1959. Backed by additional funding, Eccles continued his earlier work, managing to reduce class sizes, raise the qualifications of teachers, and ensure that all students who qualified for university places by obtaining two A levels received local authority grants. He also initiated the CSE examinations and the Curriculum Study Group, which later became the Schools Council. Eventually, however, he began to run up against the deteriorating economic situation, which generated a controversy with teachers over the failure to implement a national pay award.

Eccles's criticism of Selwyn Lloyd's budget in 1962 led Macmillan to suspect him of plotting a dramatic departure from the government and a bid for the leadership. Since he had never cultivated a following, this seems unlikely. However, the suspicion contributed to the decisive check to Eccles's career in July 1962 when he became an unintended victim of the collapsing popularity of the Conservative government. Attempting to rejuvenate the cabinet's image by sacking a third of his ministers, Macmillan summoned Eccles to Downing Street to offer him a further spell at the Board of Trade. Sensing the prime minister's weakness, Eccles overplayed his hand, declining the offer and reportedly insisting, 'It's the

Exchequer or nothing'. Though well qualified and possessing the flair required by a chancellor, he was too independent and risky a candidate for the prime minister. Macmillan, increasingly stressed by his dwindling popularity, promptly let him go. Eccles claimed he had been 'sacked with less notice than a housemaid' (*Daily Telegraph*). When he resigned his seat Macmillan added to the insult by granting him a peerage as a mere baron, with the title Baron Eccles (1962).

Business and the British Library Eccles enjoyed a sufficiently wide range of business and cultural interests to be able to adjust easily to life beyond the cabinet. He now devoted more time to collecting works of art and taking holidays abroad. In 1963 he was appointed a trustee of the British Museum. During the next eight years he also returned to his business career as a director of Courtaulds and later as chairman of West Cumberland Silk Mills. In 1964 Sir Alec Douglas Home raised him to the viscountcy as first Viscount Eccles.

Somewhat to the general surprise, Eccles's political career was resuscitated following Edward Heath's victory in the general election of 1970. Officially paymaster-general, he was in effect minister for the arts, a role in which he achieved an enduring success despite becoming embroiled in controversy over the introduction of charges for museum entry. He took the initiative in separating the library at the British Museum from the museum itself and combining it with the National Central Library and the National Lending Library for Science and Technology to create the British Library. He resigned in 1973 to become the first chairman of the British Library board (until 1978). After initially opposing the transfer of the reference library from Bloomsbury, he accepted the case for a new building on a site adjacent to St Pancras Station. The active support he had given to craftsmanship, especially pottery, was recognized when he was appointed president of the World Craft Council from 1974 to 1978. He became a Companion of Honour in 1984.

Sybil Eccles had died in 1977, but on 26 September 1984, aged eighty, Eccles married again. His new wife, Mary Morley Gapo Hyde (*b.* 1912/13) of Four Oaks Farm, Somerville, New Jersey, widow of Donald Hyde, was an authority on Samuel Johnson and fully shared his passion for books. Together they helped to establish the Centre for American Studies at the British Library. In this way Eccles maintained his interests well into old age, dividing his time between his home in England and his wife's farm in New Jersey. It was at Four Oaks Farm that he died on 24 February 1999. After his cremation his ashes were taken home and scattered at Dean Farm in Upper Chute, Wiltshire. A memorial service was held at St Margaret's, Westminster, on 8 June 1999. He was survived by his second wife, Mary, and by the three children of his first marriage. He was succeeded in the viscountcy by his elder son, John Dawson Eccles, general manager of the Commonwealth Development Corporation (1985–94) and chairman of Courtaulds Textiles (from 1995), whose wife, Diana (*b.* 1933), a director of Tyne Tees Television (1986–94), J. Sainsbury (1986–95),

and the Yorkshire Electricity Group (1990–97), had been elevated to the peerage as Baroness Eccles of Moulton in 1990.   MARTIN PUGH

Sources *Daily Telegraph* (26 Feb 1999) · *The Times* (27 Feb 1999) · *The Guardian* (27 Feb 1999) · *The Independent* (1 March 1999) · Viscount Eccles, *By safe hand: letters of Sybil and David Eccles, 1939–42* (1983) · Viscount Eccles, *Life and politics: a moral diagnosis* (1967) · Viscount Eccles, *Half way to faith* (1966) · A. Horne, *Macmillan*, 2: *1957–1986* (1989) · Burke, *Peerage* · WWW · private information (2004) [son] · b. cert. · m. certs.
Archives NRA, priv. coll. · Wilts. & Swindon RO, constituency papers | Bodl. Oxf., corresp. with L. G. Curtis · Bodl. Oxf., letters to Jack Lambert · CAC Cam., corresp. with Sir E. L. Spears
Likenesses photograph, 1951, repro. in *The Times* · photographs, 1952–61, Hult. Arch. · photograph, 1954, repro. in *The Independent* · photograph, 1959, repro. in *Daily Telegraph* · N. Colvin, pen-and-ink drawing, NPG · Frink, sculpture, priv. coll. · Frink, sculpture, BL · E. Sargeant, priv. coll. · photograph, repro. in *The Guardian*
Wealth at death £2,427,345: probate, 11 June 1999, *CGPLA Eng. & Wales*

Eccles, Henry. *See* Leech, Humphrey (1571–1629).

Eccles, Henry (*bap.* 1682?), violinist and composer, was born probably in London during the last quarter of the seventeenth century, and was possibly the son of Solomon Eccles (possibly but not certainly the musician who died in 1710) and his wife, Rebeka, baptized at St Bride, Fleet Street, London, on 28 February 1682. The details of the subject of this article and those of the related Henry Eccles (sometimes called Eagles) the elder (*c.*1645?–1711), who was possibly his cousin, have often been confused. The more famous John Eccles was the son of the older Henry and definitely not the present subject's brother as is often claimed, and references to the Henry Eccles in the king's musick concern the older man.

The first reference to Henry Eccles junior, as he was known, dates from 2 January 1705, when he performed several Italian violin sonatas at his benefit held at Mr Hill's dancing room in Crosby Square, Bishopsgate Street. He was also writing and publishing songs about this time and contributed a prelude to *Select Preludes & Voluntarys for the Violin* (1705). He may have been the same person as an Ecles at the Queen's Theatre in 1706 and a violinist named Echel or Igl at the same theatre during the period 1710–11. The next appearance that can be cited with any certainty concerns a benefit concert given for Eccles on 15 May 1713 in the Stationers' Hall, in the presence of the duke d'Aumont, 'Embassador extraordinary from France' (Laurie). Eccles is described as 'Musician to his Grace' on this occasion, and it is likely that he returned to France with the duke's party later that year. Details of any performing activities in France prior to the London concert are unknown. It was, however, in Paris that he published, in 1720 and 1723, two volumes of *Sonates à violon seul et la basse*. These works owe far more to the Italian than the French style. In fact, of the twelve sonatas in the first volume, eighteen movements are taken from Giuseppe Valentini's *Allettamenti per camera* op. 8 and one movement from Bonporti's *Invezioni* op. 10. The second set may, in time, reveal similar plagiaristic tendencies.

The next information on Eccles comes, via Sir John Hawkins, from his brother Thomas (*c*.1672–*c*.1745) (also an excellent violinist and pupil of Henry, although apparently hampered by alcoholism). The brother claimed about 1735 that Henry was serving the king of France, but this evidence appears unreliable and uncorroborated. The details of Henry's death are unknown.

DAVID J. GOLBY

Sources M. Laurie, 'Eccles, Henry (ii)', *New Grove* · Highfill, Burnim & Langhans, *BDA*

Eccles, Isaac-Ambrose (1736?–1809), literary scholar, possibly born on 10 January 1736 in Dublin, was the eldest of the four sons of Hugh Eccles, of Cronroe, co. Wicklow, and his wife, Elizabeth, only daughter of Isaac Ambrose, clerk of the House of Commons of Ireland, after whom Isaac-Ambrose Eccles was named. He was related to John Baker *Holroyd, first earl of Sheffield, on his mother's side. Eccles was educated at Trinity College, Dublin, and embarked on the grand tour, visiting France and Italy. Ill health forced his return home, and he settled at his seat, Cronroe, co. Wicklow. About 1763 he married Grace, eldest daughter of Thomas Ball, of Urker, co. Armagh, and Sea Park, co. Wicklow; they had three sons and three daughters.

Eccles was an eminent drama critic, and published editions of several of Shakespeare's plays. He felt that the dramas had suffered in their structure from the ignorance or carelessness of earlier editors, so produced editions in which he transposed such scenes as appeared to him wrongly placed. These plays are: *Cymbeline* (1793), *King Lear* (1793), and *Merchant of Venice* (1805). They contained notes and illustrations, besides critical and historical essays. The *Cymbeline* volume contained a version of the ninth tale of Boccaccio's *Decameron*. Eccles also prepared an edition of *As You Like It*, but it was never published. Eccles died in 1809, at an advanced age, at his seat at Cronroe, co. Wicklow, Ireland.

A. P. WOOLRICH

Sources Burke, *Gen. GB* · *DNB* · D. E. Baker, *Biographia dramatica, or, A companion to the playhouse*, rev. I. Reed, new edn, rev. S. Jones, 3 vols. in 4 (1812) · R. A. Ryan, *Biographical dictionary of the worthies of Ireland* (1819) · J. Watkins, *The universal biographical dictionary*, new edn (1821) · Allibone, *Dict.* · A. J. Webb, *A compendium of Irish biography* (1878) · Adams, *Drama*
Archives TCD, letters to J. C. Walker, MS 1461

Eccles, John (*c*.1668–1735), composer, was probably born in London. He was the only son of the musician Henry Eccles (sometimes known as Eagles) the elder (*c*.1645?–1711), not the son of the eccentric Solomon Eccles the elder as has often been stated. He probably received musical instruction from members of his family, and published some songs in 1691. Two years later he established himself as a theatre composer, composing for the United Company at Drury Lane, where he enjoyed great success, especially with the actress–singer Anne Bracegirdle. He wrote many successful songs for her and composed music for at least fifteen plays during this period. On 22 June 1694 he was appointed (probably as a violinist) to the king's band, although he did not receive a salary (£40 a year plus livery) until 1696, when he replaced Thomas Tollett and became one of the king's twenty-four musicians-in-ordinary.

Eccles, Mrs Bracegirdle, and other principal actors had severed themselves from Rich's United Company in 1695. They set up a new company in competition with Drury Lane at Lincoln's Inn Fields, under the direction of Thomas Betterton and with Eccles as musical director. He provided music and songs for plays, masques, a dramatic opera, *Rinaldo and Armida* (1698), and additional instrumental music for the first professional performance of Henry Purcell's *Dido and Aeneas* in 1700.

Following the death of Nicholas Staggins in 1700, Eccles was appointed master of the king's musick on 30 June, earning £300 a year and providing music for new year, birthday, and other odes. Still active in the theatre, he made a setting of Motteux's *Acis and Galatea* (*c*.1700, now lost) which became very successful. More importantly, in March 1701 his music for William Congreve's *The Judgment of Paris* was heard at the Dorset Garden Theatre as part of the important and now famous contest devised to encourage the progress of English opera. Eccles came only second to the young John Weldon, but his setting was popular and, unlike Weldon's, was published in full score. Eccles and Congreve collaborated again and produced an ode for St Cecilia's day in 1701, and Eccles contributed to *A Collection of Lessons and Aires for the Harpsichord or Spinnett* in 1702.

The most important theatrical works that Eccles then produced were associated with the new theatre in the Haymarket, the new home of the Lincoln's Inn Fields company, where he was music director and John Vanbrugh and Congreve were joint managers. Vocal music for the semi-opera *The British Enchanters* by George Granville, Baron Lansdowne (Haymarket, February 1706), was followed by *Semele*, completed in 1707 but not performed until 1972 (a new critical edition appeared in 2000). Written with prevailing trends in mind, *Semele* is a highly effective setting of Congreve's libretto (used by Handel in 1744) and attempts to fuse elements of the English masque and Italian opera into a native form. Unfortunately, its delayed completion and abandonment put paid to any chance of establishing a national English opera and offering some resistance to the ascendancy of the Italian genre. Consequently, Eccles, the foremost composer for the Restoration theatre in the wake of Henry Purcell, followed Congreve and Anne Bracegirdle and withdrew from the operatic scene.

In 1710 Eccles settled at Hampton Wick, Kingston upon Thames, where he spent his days angling. He did, however, continue to compose for the court until his death (in 1715–16 he was paid £22 for compositions for new year's day and the king's birthday). During the early eighteenth century many of his songs were printed individually and in collections, and his works featured in volumes of *Theatre Musick* (1698–1700). Some songs and instrumental music are available in modern editions. He died at Hampton Wick on 12 January 1735. His will, dated 30 July 1728 and proved on 13 January 1735, provided his three daughters, Ann, Bridget, and Mary, with only 1s. each. His estate went to his servant Sarah Gainor, and a codicil (27 December 1734) provided an additional £30 for wages due. The parish registers of St Giles-in-the-Fields, if indeed relevant to the subject, suggest that Eccles's wife's name was Ann and that they also had another daughter, Eleanor, and a son, Henry-Thomas, who was born before both Bridget and Eleanor.   DAVID J. GOLBY

Sources S. Lincoln, 'Eccles (4)', *New Grove*, 2nd edn [incl. work list] · C. Price, 'Eccles, John', *The new Grove dictionary of opera*, ed. S. Sadie, 2 (1992), 5–6 · Highfill, Burnim & Langhans, *BDA* · *GM*, 1st ser., 5 (1735), 51 · C. Price, 'Judgment of Paris, The', *The new Grove dictionary of opera*, ed. S. Sadie, 2 (1992), 924–5 · C. Price, 'Semele (i)', *The new Grove dictionary of opera*, ed. S. Sadie, 4 (1992), 305 · H. D. Johnstone and R. Fiske, eds., *Music in Britain: the eighteenth century* (1990), vol. 4 of *The Blackwell history of music in Britain*, ed. I. Spink (1988–95), 98–101, 106–8
Wealth at death bequests: Lincoln, 'Eccles (4)'; Highfill, Burnim & Langhans, *BDA*

Eccles, Sir **John Carew** (1903–1997), neurophysiologist, was born on 27 January 1903 in Melbourne, Australia, the eldest of two children of William James Eccles (1866–1947), schoolteacher, and his wife, Mary, *née* Carew (1869–1952), also a schoolteacher. Roman Catholic by upbringing, he attended Warrnambool high school, Victoria, from 1915 to 1919, and then studied science and mathematics at Melbourne high school from 1919 to 1920. He won a scholarship to university, shared the Victoria state geometry prize, and entered Melbourne University in 1920 to read medicine. Top of his class, he won various clinical prizes, gained a blue for pole-vaulting, and graduated in 1925. Thereafter he devoted himself to laboratory research; for seventy years of distinguished scientific life he was a 'wanderer' (he likened himself to Odysseus), repeatedly re-creating his academic and laboratory base camp in a different part of the world and sallying forth to meetings and to lecture.

As a medical student Eccles became enthralled by the problem of the relationship between the brain and the mind, concluding that scientific study of the specialized junction between nerve cells (the synapse) should provide vital clues to understanding. After graduating and working briefly in hospital he pursued this goal by winning a Rhodes scholarship in 1925 and working under Sir Charles Sherrington; he took his finals in Oxford in physiology (in which he obtained a first) before starting research in 1927. On 3 July 1928 he married Irene Frances Mary Miller (*b.* 1904), daughter of Herbert Miller, a farmer; she was a devout Catholic, and their family eventually grew to five daughters and four sons.

For the rest of his life Eccles threw his tremendous energies into experimenting on the nervous system and philosophizing about its relation to the mind, with the balance gradually shifting towards the latter. Within two years he completed his doctoral thesis and eliminated a serious artefact from the optical myograph, Sherrington's long-favoured tool for studying reflex action. Eccles thereafter published nineteen books (twelve as sole author) and

Sir John Carew Eccles (1903–1997), by unknown photographer

more than 500 scientific papers, and he established laboratories in six different cities in three continents. He was knighted (1958) and shared a Nobel prize (1963), and became a legendary figure loaded with honours. During fourteen golden years at the Australian National University in Canberra (1952–66) his laboratory was a Mecca, unrivalled in neuroscience, attracting a remarkable proportion of the world's up-and-coming neurophysiologists from twenty countries to collaborate with him and expand their experience. A generation became his avowed disciples; but, as he fully acknowledged, they gave as much as they received, partly through their dedicated labour but equally through their scientific insight. Moreover, without the expert electronic and engineering assistance he so successfully recruited and enthused, his scientific life would have faltered. Jack or Synaptic Jack, as he was sometimes called, was born to lead. He had warm charisma, vigour, and forcefulness in debate with unrivalled enthusiasm, and was a tireless experimentalist working far into the night. He was a prolific writer, with direct rather than subtle thinking, and some found him overpowering and egotistical and reacted against him and his tendency to dogmatic simplification.

Eccles spent ten further formative years in Oxford as junior research fellow (1927–32) and Staines medical research fellow (1932–4) at Exeter College, fellow and tutor of Magdalen College, and university lecturer in physiology (1934–7), working latterly on synapses in the peripheral sympathetic ganglia. He became the European protagonist of the view that transmission from one nerve cell to the next was produced by the spread of electric current, rather than by the liberation of a chemical transmitter as time has proved correct. He repeatedly argued his case in public with energy and skill, and his distinguished pharmacological opponents, without following the details, were driven to acknowledge that their case remained unproven and progressively to improve the quality of their evidence. Nevertheless, unsettled by the aftermath of Sherrington's retirement and the prospect of war, Eccles went home in 1937 to a relatively unimportant post in Sydney, but with the opportunity to devote himself largely to research, as director of the Kanematsu Institute, responsible also for overseeing routine hospital pathology. He built a research laboratory and recruited two European refugees (Bernard Katz and Stephen Kuffler), who both became world leaders in their field, definitively establishing that the 'synaptic' transmission from nerve to muscle was indeed chemical. Eccles's views on the synapse itself remained unchanged, however. In 1941, aged thirty-eight, his contributions sufficed for his election to the Royal Society; he was awarded its royal medal in 1962.

Eccles's plans for expanding research in Sydney were frustrated, so in 1944 he took the professorship in physiology at the University of Otago and moved to Dunedin, New Zealand, where he remained until 1951. Teaching became his first priority, with systematic lectures and practicals covering the whole of physiology, but he also rapidly developed a laboratory, recruited colleagues and students to study the synapses in the spinal cord, and continued to defend electrical transmission. Thus he was poised to exploit the American invention (in 1949) of a micro-electrode suitable for studying synaptic transmission by recording from inside rather than outside the neurone. This was rapidly achieved, with incredible technical virtuosity, and immediately destroyed the electrical hypothesis by virtue of the findings for inhibitory synaptic action (the inverse of excitation). A lesser scientist might have mounted a futile rearguard action, but Eccles simply switched sides and proceeded to analyse the detailed mechanisms. His work led to his receiving the Nobel prize, which he shared along with Sir Alan Hodgkin and Sir Andrew Huxley. He remained unperturbed on abandoning his brainchild because of his enduring friendship with the philosopher Karl Popper, who encouraged him that science only evolved through the creative formulation of hypotheses sufficiently rigorously formulated to be tested to destruction (later they jointly wrote *The Self and its Brain*, 1977). Subsequently, however, he defended a losing view on the role of dendrites until it lost all credibility. Over the years Eccles wrote four classic books centred around his evolving findings about synaptic transmission. His ultimate goal remained unchanged, with the first work called *The Neurophysiological Basis of Mind* (1953), but in the laboratory he was absorbed in the excitement of experimentation.

On moving to pure research at the Australian National University, Canberra, in 1952, the pace accelerated and Eccles also involved himself in wider affairs, becoming president of the Australian Academy of Sciences (1957–61). Almost everything that could be done on the spinal cord with the new techniques was done, and new lines were progressively opened up, including the pattern of connectivity between various neurones and the long-term neural regulation of the muscle biochemistry affecting its speed of contraction. Aided by various collaborators with the requisite experience, Eccles then shifted his attention to higher parts of the nervous system, unravelling a mass of detail on the synaptic behaviour and connectivity of various neurones. The cerebellum was studied particularly thoroughly leading to a book entitled *The Cerebellum as a Neuronal Machine* (1967), co-authored with his neurophysiologist pupil Masao Ito from Japan and his histologist friend János Szentágothai from Hungary; the book emphasized the cerebellum's machine-like properties and Eccles kept returning to this idea over the years. Interestingly, his experimental programme was divorced from his continuing philosophical preoccupation with the mind–brain problem, since the cerebellum regulates muscle contraction without contributing to consciousness, and he did not move on to study the cerebral cortex. Perhaps he became a prisoner of the techniques and mode of thinking that he had developed so successfully for the spinal cord. He always worked on anaesthetized animals and may have felt that the synapse itself still held the clue, and that he was too old to move over to recording from cortical neurones in conscious animals, as became widespread in his later years. Eccles's drive continued unabated, however, and with retirement looming he moved to the USA in 1966 to set up new laboratories. In 1968 his marriage to his first wife, Irene, was dissolved; he became estranged from his large family, and he married on 27 April 1968 Helena Táboříková (*b.* 1925), daughter of Karel and Anežka Tábořík, a much younger Czech neuroscientist who collaborated closely with him from 1966 onwards.

Eccles's next laboratory, at the Institute of Biomedical Sciences of the American Medical Foundation in Chicago (1966–8), was unhappy and foundered in recrimination. The State University of New York at Buffalo then provided a haven where he delighted in continued experimentation (1968–75), but without major new achievement. Writing beckoned, and at the age of seventy-two he retired voluntarily with his reprints to Contra, in the Italian part of Switzerland. He remained active for nearly twenty further years, during which he travelled and lectured widely, wrote four further books, and co-authored another five, including in 1979 a life of his mentor Sherrington. Eccles's concerns became largely philosophical, and being a lifelong dualist and believer in God he satisfied his early ambition by hypothesizing about how the mind might influence the brain via the synapse. His last book was *How the Self Controls the Brain* (1994), but neurophysiologists had more practical concerns, and most philosophers were likewise uninterested. Eccles died near Locarno, Switzerland, on 2 May 1997, and was survived by his second wife. He is remembered for his contributions to the backbone of mechanistic neuroscience.

PETER B. C. MATTHEWS

Sources D. R. Curtis and P. Anderson, *Memoirs FRS*, 47 (2001), 159–87 · J. C. Eccles, 'My scientific odyssey', *Annual Reviews of Physiology*, 39 (1977), 1–18 · J. C. Eccles, 'Under the spell of the synapse', *The neurosciences: paths of discovery*, ed. F. G. Worden, J. P. Swazey, and G. Adelman (1975), 158–79 · J. C. Eccles, 'From electrical to chemical transmission in the central nervous system', *Notes and Records of the Royal Society*, 30 (1975–6), 219–30 · B. Katz, 'Reminiscences of a physiologist, 50 years after', *Journal of Physiology*, 370 (1986), 1–12 · J. Jack and S. Redman, 'Introduction', *The theoretical foundation of dendritic function*, ed. I. Segev, J. Rinzel, and G. M. Shepherd (1995), 27–33 · WWW · personal knowledge (2004) · *The Times* (14 May 1997) · *The Independent* (17 May 1997) · m. cert. · WW
Archives CAC Cam., corresp. with A. V. Hill
Likenesses photograph, 1963, Hult. Arch. · photograph, repro. in *The Times* · photograph, repro. in *The Independent* · photograph, repro. in Eccles, 'My scientific odyssey' · photograph, repro. in Curtis and Anderson, *Memoirs FRS* · photograph, repro. in *Experimental Brain Research*, 116 (1997), 1 · photograph, NL Aus. [*see illus.*]

Eccles, Sir Josiah (1897–1967), engineer and industrialist, was born in northern Ireland on 29 July 1897, the son of Johnston and Mary Anne Eccles. Nothing is known of his schooling but he had begun to study engineering at Queen's University, Belfast, when the First World War began. Eccles left his studies for active service and, in 1917, he was awarded the Military Medal. When peace came he returned to the university, completing his studies in 1922 when he took a BSc in engineering with first-class honours. From 1922 to 1928 he worked with the Metropolitan-Vickers Electrical Company, where he specialized in outside construction work. In 1928 he was elected an associate member of the Institution of Electrical Engineers, becoming a full member ten years later.

From 1928 until 1944 Eccles worked for the electrical department of Edinburgh corporation, first as senior technical assistant and then successively as construction engineer, generating engineer, and deputy engineer; in 1940 he was appointed engineer and manager of the department. He married Katherine Lillie Gillah, daughter of Alfred Summerson, a solicitor, in 1930; they had three children, a son and two daughters.

In 1944 Eccles was appointed Liverpool's city electrical engineer and when the Labour government nationalized the electricity supply industry, he was involved in planning as a member of the organizing committee of the British Electricity Authority (BEA), the industry's new centralized governing body. He was the natural choice for the chairmanship of the newly created Merseyside and North Wales Electricity Board. In the six years he held the position he was concerned with the amalgamation of the distribution operations of a number of formerly independent corporate and municipally owned undertakings. He was appointed CBE in 1950.

Eccles's primary interest, however, had always been in electricity generation, which was the responsibility of the BEA in London; he therefore welcomed the offer that came in 1954 to succeed Sir John Hacking as deputy chairman of the BEA. In his three years with the authority Eccles made his most significant contribution to the generation side through his support for the development of much larger and more thermally efficient sets, hitherto rejected by the more conservatively minded engineers at the BEA. He encouraged F. H. S. (Stanley) Brown, who had worked with him at Liverpool and who became, shortly after Eccles arrived at the BEA, its generation design engineer, to introduce the larger sets into the power station construction programme for the late 1950s and early 1960s. This took the British industry, for a time, into the technological vanguard in Europe. In 1956 Eccles played a major part in securing the appointment of Brown as BEA's chief engineer.

By then the authority was being pressed by the government to expand the nuclear power programme. Eccles opposed this on the grounds that it was neither feasible nor economic and although events were to prove that his views were correct, the rest of his career in the industry was blighted. In 1957 the industry was reorganized and the Central Electricity Generating Board (CEGB) created; the appointment of a nuclear engineer, Christopher Hinton, as its chairman not only bypassed Eccles (who refused to be Hinton's deputy) but also signalled the government's intention to press ahead with the construction of the Magnox nuclear-powered stations. Eccles became deputy chairman of the Electricity Council, also created by the reorganization, and was knighted. In 1961 Eccles was a member of the McKenzie committee on the organization of electricity supply in Scotland, whose recommendations for centralization were rejected, on political rather than economic grounds. Eccles retired from the deputy chairmanship of the Electricity Council in 1961.

Jack Eccles (as he was always known) combined his professionalism as an engineer with a shrewd commercial sense and a willingness to consider new ideas in both engineering and business not always characteristic of senior men in the industry. It was his misfortune that those qualities were not always appreciated by a government with its own agenda for the electricity supply industry and the power to impose its decisions on the nationalized industry. Throughout his life Eccles played an active role in the Institution of Electrical Engineers, as a member of its council from 1945 and serving as its president in 1954. He was made an honorary fellow in 1967. He also participated in several other industry organizations, including the Incorporated Municipal Electrical Association, the British Electrical Development Association, and the British Electrical Power Convention. He wrote many articles on both engineering and management matters in the electricity supply industry. He died at his home, 21 Sandy Lodge Road, Moor Park, Rickmansworth, Hertfordshire, on 14 October 1967.

JUDY SLINN

Sources L. Hannah, 'Eccles, Sir Josiah', *DBB* · WWW · *The Times* (16 Oct 1967), 12 · L. Hannah, *Engineers, managers, and politicians: the first fifteen years of nationalised electricity supply in Britain* (1982)
Wealth at death £15,831: probate, 1968, *CGPLA Eng. & Wales*

Eccles, Solomon (1617?–1682), musician and Quaker missionary, was probably baptized on 14 September 1617 at Hatfield, Hertfordshire, the son of Solomon Eccles. His father was a musician, but little else is known of Eccles's early life. He appears to have lived at Spitalfields for most of his life; his first wife was Elizabeth (d. 1665).

Early in his life Eccles was a musician, and taught both the virginals and viol, bringing in an annual income of about £130. In his later tract against music, *A Musick-Lector* (1667), Eccles recounted his religious journey through a series of groups during this period: the Anglicans, presbyterians, and Independents, followed by the Baptists 'about the year 1642', after which he described himself as an antinomian, before finally becoming a Quaker before or by 1659 (Eccles, *Musick-Lector*, 9). At this point he began to question his profession: 'when truth came, I was not able to stand before it, the Lord did thunder grievously against this practise … it was nothing but vanity, and vexed the good spirit of God'. He lamented that 'it was hard to flesh and blood to give it up, for it was not only my livelihood, but my life was in it' (ibid., 10). After his convincement he sold all his books and instruments and became a tailor, considering this a harmless trade. However, 'the voice of the Lord' urged him to buy back his instruments and then burn them upon Tower Hill as a testimony against his former profession, but he was prevented by a crowd. Instead, he 'was forced to stamp upon them, and break them to pieces', which sorely grieved him as his father, grandfather, and great-grandfather before him had all been musicians (ibid., 12).

From this time onwards Eccles felt called to testify by signs in the manner of Old Testament prophets, a practice common to some other early Quakers, although it died out in the later seventeenth century. In his broadside *Signes are from the Lord* (1663) the first episode occurred in 1659 'when I was made to go into *Calamy's Steeple-House*', for which he was imprisoned for eight months. Further episodes followed throughout the 1660s, often leading to his imprisonment. In 1662 he was arrested following an interruption of morning service at St Mary Aldermanbury, while the following year he was prosecuted for preaching at a meeting at Tanner's End near Edmonton. In 1665 he was arrested on the orders of the duke of Albemarle for attending an unlawful meeting and refusing to pay a fine, while in 1667 he was imprisoned in Gloucester gaol for refusing to take oaths. He was particularly noted for processing naked with a bowl of fire and brimstone on his head. Not only did he attend each of the Bartholomew fairs in such a manner between 1660 and 1663 in protest at the 'filthy tricks upon stages, with fools and monsters, in ugly shapes, to draw the minds of people from the Lord', but he also made similar appearances during the plague year (Eccles, *Signes*). Defoe later described Eccles as an 'Enthusiast' who 'went about denouncing of judgement upon the city in a frightful manner' (Defoe, 120). Defoe claimed that Eccles's wife, who died on 24 July 1665, was a victim of the plague; however, Quaker evidence suggests she died from dropsy. Two years later, on 29 July 1667, Pepys observed a naked Eccles at Westminster Hall ('only

very civilly tied about the privities to avoid scandal'), bearing a bowl of fire and brimstone on his head and crying 'Repent! Repent!' (Latham, 814). A year later Pepys saw Eccles again, this time covered in excrement, and it was presumably this episode that prompted the Quakers' famous adversary Lodowick Muggleton, in *The Answer to William Penn* (1673), to describe Eccles as 'a wild boar, his bristles were all off his back, and he was so besmeared and daubed with his own dung that his flesh could hardly be seen' (Braithwaite, 245).

In 1668 Eccles published *The Quakers Challenge*, in which he dared Baptists, presbyterians, Independents, Catholics, and others to fast for a week without food, water, or sleep; anyone who survived this 'fiery trial' could be 'counted a worshipper of the true God' (p. 2). The next year he travelled to Ireland with fellow Quakers William Penn, John Wilkinson, and John Banks, where he processed naked through Galway, bearing fire and brimstone and urging repentance. Eccles and his companions were later sent to prison, but Eccles was free by 1670, when his naked appearance in Cork led to flogging, imprisonment, and expulsion. In 1671 Eccles was one of the Friends who accompanied George Fox to the West Indies, and was instrumental in organizing Quakerism in Barbados and Jamaica; Fox noted that Eccles fasted for seven days on the voyage. Eccles pressed on into New England, where he was arrested at a meeting in Boston in 1672 and banished. He returned to Barbados in 1680, only to be imprisoned and expelled for expressing 'blasphemous and seditious words' about the 'three persons in the Godhead' (Besse, 2.325). However, he was apparently still in the colony on 30 May 1681, when he provided a written testimony of regret following his 'angry' prediction of the death of the Quaker separatist John Story a year earlier, an apparent prophesy which had been seized upon by the anti-Quaker writer Thomas Crisp in his *Babel's Builders Unmasking themselves* (1681) (Crisp, 8). This was not the first time Eccles had troubled the mainstream Quaker movement: in November 1674 a manuscript, 'The soul saveing principle', which he had presented to the second day morning meeting for approval ahead of publication, was declared 'not safe to be published'; six years later in January 1681 another work, 'Entitled to the Jewes', was also 'laid aside' (Morning meeting book, 1.3, 39).

Eccles had remarried on 16 October 1673, his second wife being Anne Butcher. However, she seems to have been dead by the time Eccles drew up his will on 29 December 1681, as he makes no mention of her nor any children. Describing himself as a chandler in Stepney, Eccles left various sums of money to Quaker friends, including Leonard Fell and James Lancaster, and appointed the leading Friend George Whitehead as one of his executors, which suggests he remained on good terms with Friends in spite of his ideas and actions which must have caused some embarrassment to the movement. He died at Spitalfields on 2 January 1682, probably aged about sixty-five, and was buried at Chequer Alley. In *Signes are from the Lord* Eccles had claimed that he had 'strove much, and besought the Lord, that this going naked might be taken from me, before ever I went a Sign at all'. Muggleton described him as

> very giddy in the head, as if he were frenzy in the brain; for he could live with less food than any of the wild beasts in the wilderness, being much given to fasting, which made his head to totter and joggle, and his eyes dazzle and his brains to hang loose,

while a contemporary who knew him well judged Eccles as possessing 'great zeal; and though in some respect he might by it have been transported a little too far, yet he gave proofs of a sincere heart' (Braithwaite, 245–6; Sewel, 491).

Eccles has been often confused with the composer and musician Solomon Eccles (1640x1650–1710), who was possibly a nephew. John Eccles (c.1668–1735), also a musician and composer, was not Eccles's son as has been previously thought.   CAROLINE L. LEACHMAN

Sources S. Eccles, *A musick-lector* (1667) · J. Besse, *A collection of the sufferings of the people called Quakers*, 2 vols. (1753) · S. Eccles, *Signes are from the Lord* (1663) · *The journal of George Fox*, ed. N. Penney, 2 (1911) · W. Sewel, *The history of the rise, increase, and progress of the Christian people called Quakers* (1725) · J. Hawkins, *A general history of the science and practice of music*, new edn, 2 (1853) · A. Chalmers, ed., *The general biographical dictionary*, new edn, 13 (1814) · Quaker digest registers, RS Friends, Lond. · J. Smith, ed., *A descriptive catalogue of Friends' books*, 1 (1867) · R. L. Greaves, *God's other children: protestant nonconformists and the emergence of denominational churches in Ireland, 1660–1700* (1997) · R. Latham, ed., *The shorter Pepys* (1987) · D. Defoe, *A journal of the plague year* (1722) · A. Davies, *The Quakers in English society, 1655–1725* (2000) · 'Dictionary of Quaker biography', RS Friends, Lond. [card index] · R. L. Greaves, *Dublin's merchant-Quaker: Anthony Sharp and the community of Friends, 1643–1707* (1998) · morning meeting book, 1673–92, RS Friends, Lond., vol. 1 · IGI · M. Laurie, 'Eccles, Solomon (i)', *New Grove* · W. C. Braithwaite, *The second period of Quakerism* (1919); 2nd edn, ed. H. J. Cadbury (1961) · S. Crisp, *A Babylonish opposer of truth* (1681) · will, Essex RO, D/AER 24/59 (1682)

Archives RS Friends, Lond., Portfolio MSS, 31/59, 17/2 | BL, Egerton MS 3020, fols. 61, 62 · RS Friends, Lond., Robson MSS

Wealth at death left money to family and Quaker friends: will, 1682, Essex RO, D/AER 24/59

Eccles, William Henry (1875–1966), physicist and engineer, was born on 23 August 1875 at 2 Buccluch St, Barrow in Furness, Lancashire, the son of Charles Eccles, a blacksmith and later an engineer, and his wife, Annabella Todd. In later life Eccles said that it was in his father's workshop that he had learned about designing metal structures. He was educated privately and in 1894 went as a national scholar to the Royal College of Science, South Kensington. In 1897 he graduated BSc with first-class honours in physics and he became a demonstrator in the physics department. In 1899 he was appointed as one of Marconi's assistants, working on his pioneering transatlantic wireless signalling. He left the Marconi Company in 1900 to become head of the mathematics and physics department of the South Western Polytechnic, Chelsea. In 1901 he also became DSc (London). In 1912 he was appointed to a readership in graphic statics (structural engineering design) at University College, London. This interest in structural design, particularly of masts for wireless transmitters, continued throughout his career. On the death of Silvanus Thompson in 1916 he was appointed professor of applied

physics and electrical engineering at the City and Guilds College, Finsbury.

During Eccles's working life wireless developed into widely used commercial radio and public broadcasting. Throughout this time Eccles was in close contact with nearly every aspect of the subject, as researcher, writer of articles and textbooks, influential member of advisory committees and learned societies, and expert witness. For many years he was the leading (and almost the only) independent physicist working in the field of radio science.

His early research concentrated on the behaviour of the coherer which was used in certain early wireless receivers to bring waves into phase. It consisted of a loose aggregate of small metal particles contained in an insulating tube; normally it had a fairly high resistance, but if a radio frequency voltage was momentarily applied to it, the particles cohered together and it became a good conductor. However, consistent results were difficult to obtain, and many theories were put forward to explain its behaviour. Eccles developed experimental methods which gave reliable results, and suggested a theory to account for them. Also, in conjunction with A. J. Mackower, he developed a type of quenched spark gap transmitter, which sought to overcome the problem of transmission on two frequencies which dogged earlier spark gap transmitters. Eccles next turned his attention to the thermionic triode, the development of which was encouraged by military-sponsored research in the First World War. Eccles was one of the first to represent its action algebraically in terms of the self- and mutual conductances of its electrodes. He pioneered its use in circuits, several of which he developed with F. W. Jordan. One of the most ingenious of these produced rectangular waveforms of relatively low frequency; known as the Eccles–Jordan (rigger relay or 'flip-flop') circuit, it was later one of the first to be used for counting pulses. It long remained an essential computer component, and has been described as the first digital electronic circuit.

In 1902 Oliver Heaviside had postulated the existence of an upper atmospheric layer to explain Marconi's successful transmission of signals across the Atlantic over the intervening curvature of the earth. In 1912 Eccles showed in detail how this Heaviside layer could result from ionization of the upper atmosphere. To do this he had to study how wireless waves travel over large distances; however, commercial wireless transmissions were too scarce and too irregular to provide enough data. Instead, he made measurements on naturally occurring atmospheric radio waves radiated by lightning flashes. Although incomplete, his theory paved the way for those more detailed explanations which were provided in the 1920s by Edward Appleton and others.

As one of the few independent scientists with a knowledge of wireless, Eccles's expert advice was widely sought. He did important work during the war as adviser to the War Office, the army council, the air force wireless technical committee, and the Admiralty. He was the honorary secretary of the conjoint board of scientific societies whose report led to the formation of the Department of Scientific and Industrial Research in 1916. The rapid post-war development of wireless gave rise to major issues of organization and politics, including the role of amateurs in transmitting and receiving, the relative functions of private industry and government, the most appropriate method for transmission across the proposed imperial wireless chain, and the organization of public broadcasting. Until 1926, when he retired to become a consulting engineer, Eccles was deeply involved in attempting to resolve these questions.

One of Eccles's most significant roles was as chairman of the committee which in 1926 examined the BBC's proposals for regional broadcasting. The plan faced opposition from the Post Office and a large section of the wireless trade on the grounds that the proposed broadcasts might interfere with other wireless users such as the armed forces. The Eccles committee unanimously endorsed the BBC's scheme, considerably strengthening its hand as it sought to reach more listeners. From his retirement in 1926 until 1958 Eccles was retained by EMI as a technical adviser on recording, broadcasts, and patents, and as an expert witness, a role in which he was unusually effective.

In 1926–7 Eccles was president of the Institution of Electrical Engineers; earlier, in 1919, he had been active in arranging for the establishment of its wireless section, of which he was the first chairman. He was president of the Physical Society from 1928 to 1930 and in 1929 he served as first president of the Institute of Physics, which represented the professional activities inappropriate to the Physical Society's remit. A lifelong involvement in amateur wireless led in 1923 to his presidency of the Wireless Society of London, later the Radio Society of Great Britain. Eccles was elected a fellow of the Royal Society in 1921, an honorary president of Union Radio Scientifique Internationale in 1934, and a fellow of Imperial College in the same year. Those who worked with Eccles recalled particularly his friendship, his courtesy, and the trouble he took to familiarize himself with technical matters. His adherence to Quaker beliefs may have contributed to his reluctance to patent his inventions. On 4 January 1924 Eccles married his secretary, Nellie Florence Paterson (b. 1894/5), the daughter of Robert Henry Paterson, a railway clerk; they had no children. Eccles died at the Randolph Hotel, Beaumont Street, Oxford, on 29 April 1966, and was cremated at Oxford crematorium on 3 May. His wife survived him.   J. A. RATCLIFFE, rev. TIM PROCTER

Sources J. A. Ratcliffe, Memoirs FRS, 17 (1971), 195–214 • 'The indefatigable Dr. Eccles', Wireless World (Sept 1965), 436 • curriculum vitae, correspondence file, GL, City and Guilds Institute MSS • 'Pioneers: 46, W. H. Eccles, 1875–1966, the first physicist of wireless', Electronics World and Wireless World (Oct 1990), 908–10 • A. Briggs, The history of broadcasting in the United Kingdom, 2 (1965) • W. A. Atherton, From compass to computer (1984) • Electronics and Power (Oct 1966), 365 • Nature (9 July 1966), 129 • Wireless World (June 1966), 281 • b. cert. • m. cert. • d. cert. • private information (2004) • election certificate, RS • CGPLA Eng. & Wales (1966)
Archives GL, corresp. City and Guilds of London Institute

Likenesses photograph, Inst. EE • photograph, repro. in Ratcliffe, Memoirs FRS, facing p. 195
Wealth at death £11,737: probate, 19 July 1966, CGPLA Eng. & Wales

Eccleston, Thomas (1659–1743), Jesuit, was the only son of Henry Eccleston (d. 1665) of Eccleston Hall, Prescot, Lancashire, and his wife, Eleanor, daughter of Robert Blundell of Ince Blundell, Lancashire, and nephew of Thomas Eccleston (1643–1698), also a Jesuit. He was educated in the English College, St Omer, leaving in 1677, and continued his studies for two years (1677–9) in the English College, Rome. He spent a short time in France before returning to England to take over the Eccleston estate, his father having died in 1665.

In 1689 Eccleston was with James II's Irish army serving as a captain of horse under Colonel J. Parker. In 1691, while in Ireland, probably at Dublin, he was engaged in a duel, with fatal consequences for his opponent, George Cony. He received a royal pardon from William and Mary in 1693 for the killing of Cony. Being seized with remorse and determined to enter the religious state, he entered the Jesuit noviciate at St Andrea, Rome, in 1697, and continued his studies at Liège. He was ordained in 1703 and returned to England. He served in Yorkshire from 1705 to 1714, taking the Jesuit vows in 1712, and for some time was chaplain to the Bar Convent, York. He then served in the Middlesex district before going to the Petre family at Ingatestone, Essex, about 1724.

His estate, registered in 1717 as worth an annual rental of some £340, was reported to the commissioners of the exchequer by the former Catholic priest Hitchmough as 'being used for superstitious uses' (for the benefit of the Jesuits). As a consequence the estate was confiscated and the eighty-year old Eleanor Eccleston was made homeless. Eccleston successfully regained his property, and in 1725 entailed it to his cousin John Gorsuch, and then to his godson and cousin Basil Thomas Scarisbrick, who both took the name of Eccleston. His treatise, The Way to Happiness, was published in 1726.

Eccleston remained with the Petres until 1729, when he accompanied them to the continent, going first to Liège and in 1731 to St Omer. He stayed at St Omer for the remainder of his life, acting as rector from August 1731 to September 1737. He died on 30 December 1743.

THOMPSON COOPER, rev. M. PANIKKAR

Sources G. Holt, The English Jesuits, 1650–1829: a biographical dictionary, Catholic RS, 70 (1984) • H. Foley, ed., Records of the English province of the Society of Jesus, 2 (1875), 582; 5 (1879), 348; 6 (1880), 426; 7 (1882–3), 220 • Gillow, Lit. biog. hist. • A. de Backer and others, Bibliothèque de la Compagnie de Jésus, new edn, 3, ed. C. Sommervogel (Brussels, 1892), 322 • C. Dalton, ed., English army lists and commission registers, 1661–1714, 2 (1894); repr. (1960), 179 • Scarisbrick Hall documents, Lancs. RO, MS DD Sc. • R. S. France, ed., The register of estates of Lancashire papists, 1717–1788, Lancashire and Cheshire RS, 108 (1960), 117–25 • E. E. Estcourt and J. O. Payne, eds., The English Catholic nonjurors of 1715 (1885), 17 • VCH Lancashire, 3.365 • J. O. Payne, ed., Records of the English Catholics of 1715 (1889), 149 • S. Foster, The Catholic church in Ingatestone (1982), 43–4 • F. Blom, English Roman Catholic books, 1701–1800 (1996), 961
Archives Lancs. RO, papers incl. family papers, MS DD Sc.

Likenesses portrait; formerly at Eccleston Hall in 1888 (possibly at Scarisbrick Hall after 1888

Wealth at death estates valued at £340 p.a.

Ecclestone, Alan (1904–1992), Church of England clergy-man and communist activist, was born on 3 June 1904 at 233 Princes Road, Stoke-on-Trent, the second of the two children of George Henry Ecclestone (1867–1942), a pot-tery designer, and his wife, Emily Florence, *née* Heath (1872–1945). A scholarship to Newcastle high school set him on the road to Cambridge, while his English teacher introduced him to the Catholic Crusade, a radical form of Christian socialism headed by Conrad Noel. At St Cathar-ine's, Cambridge, to which he went in 1922, he read his-tory and English, gaining brilliant firsts in both in 1925. After a year's schoolteaching he was offered a lectureship in English at Durham, where he taught from 1927 to 1930. At the same time he began teaching courses for the Work-ers' Educational Association, a commitment he kept up for the rest of his working life. A desire to change rather than simply interpret events led him to leave university life and seek Anglican ordination. He trained at Wells—an experience, he later said, designed to break one's spirit. He served a two-year curacy in Carlisle before moving to Barrow in 1934. On 17 July of the same year he married Delia Abraham (1902–1982), the youngest and most radical of the children of C. T. Abraham, the bishop of Derby. Delia, a teacher, shared both her husband's faith and his politics. A stormy but completely committed relationship was at the heart of much of Ecclestone's later thought on prayer. The couple had three children.

In 1936 Ecclestone obtained his first living in Frizington, a Cumberland mining village where unemployment was high and poverty severe. Here he began to develop Cath-olic Crusade ideas, attempting to reorient church life around a weekly meeting where every facet of human life was up for discussion. Through a networking leaflet called *The Leap* he sought to extend this idea throughout the area. These activities brought him to the attention of the bishop of Sheffield, Lesley Hunter, who asked him to come to Darnall, an inner city parish in the heart of the Sheffield steel-making district. Ecclestone moved there in 1942, and stayed there for the rest of his working life, until 1969. Here he at once began what was by now called the 'parish meeting'. Politics, both national and local, were always high on the agenda, but so were art, literature, his-tory, and theology.

Although initially a supporter of the Attlee government of 1945, Ecclestone soon felt that it had reneged on its elec-tion commitments and had ceased to be socialist. He therefore joined the Communist Party in April 1948, fol-lowed by Delia two weeks later. The two remained faithful party members throughout the traumas caused by the invasions of Hungary (1956) and Czechoslovakia (1968). Ecclestone became a well-known party speaker and cam-paigned tirelessly on behalf of the Soviet-inspired Peace Conference. His activity here was instrumental in the choice of Sheffield as the venue for the second World Peace Conference in 1950, opened by a speech from Picasso. The hostility of the Labour government led to the

Alan Ecclestone (1904–1992), by unknown photographer, *c.*1960

refusal of visas for many delegates, including Shostako-vich, Pablo Neruda, and Paul Robeson, and the conference shifted, after three days, to Warsaw, with Ecclestone in train. In 1955 he headed a delegation to Tashkent and in the 1960s he stood six times as Communist candidate for Darnall ward, losing his deposit each time. This activity scandalized even progressive bishops such as George Bell and made promotion, and even a change of parish, impos-sible. For most church people his stand seemed morally grotesque. Ecclestone always insisted, however, that the church was guilty of crimes equally as great as those of the party, and believed that commitment to a person, place, calling, or principle should not be lightly revoked. In the late 1960s he was a prominent member of the Christian Marxist dialogue then taking place throughout Europe. When he finally left the party, he almost instantly regret-ted his decision.

Throughout his years in Sheffield, Ecclestone continued to teach for the Workers' Educational Association, mostly in English and history, and no class ever failed. In the par-ish he was an innovator liturgically, anticipating many later developments in his services for marriage, baptism, and the eucharist. After retirement in 1969 he settled down to write, and the first of his major books, *Yes to God* (1975), won the Collins religious book prize. The book put the concept of prayer onto a completely new footing, understanding it as part of the fabric of human response to sexuality, art, literature, and politics. It was one of the truly creative works of spirituality of the twentieth century. None of the later books had the same success, although *The Night Sky of the Lord* (1980), a book about Christian responses to the holocaust, won appreciation especially from the Jewish community. These books and his earlier reputation made him a much sought-after speaker at retreats and conferences.

Delia died after a long illness in 1982. Ecclestone's home at Gosforth, Cumberland, remained a place of pilgrimage for students and seekers of all kinds; there they were met with a mixture of warm hospitality and relentless questioning. He died in London on 14 December 1992 after a series of strokes, and was buried in Gosforth on the 19th. As the primary exemplar of the union of *mystique* and *politique* in twentieth-century Anglicanism he remains a seminal figure, but it is likely that he will be remembered chiefly for his work on prayer.   T. J. GORRINGE

Sources T. J. Gorringe, *Alan Ecclestone: priest as revolutionary* (1994) • R. Groves, *Conrad Noel and the Thaxted movement* (1967) • personal knowledge (2004) • private information (2004) [family] • *The Times* (17 Dec 1992) • *The Independent* (16 Dec 1992) • *CGPLA Eng. & Wales* (1993)

Archives Sheffield Central Library, personal MSS | FILM BBC WAC, televised talk, 1992 • Christmas Day broadcast, with David McClellan, Channel 4/BBC, June 1992 • broadcast on faith and politics, with David McClellan, Channel 4/BBC, June 1992

Likenesses photograph, c.1960, priv. coll. [*see illus.*] • photograph, 1966, repro. in Gorringe, *Alan Ecclestone*, frontispiece • photograph, repro. in *The Times* • photograph, repro. in *The Independent* • photographs, repro. in *Church Times* (19 June 1992)

Wealth at death under £125,000: probate, 23 Feb 1993, *CGPLA Eng. & Wales*

Ecclestone, William (d. c.1624), actor, may have been the son, born about 1591 and one of six children, of John Ecclestone (d. 1604), a merchant tailor of London. If this is correct his mother, Mary Barret, had married his father in 1586 at St Olave, Hart Street, but Ecclestone was probably brought up in the parish of St Martin Outwich, where his father died in 1604. He attended the Merchant Taylors' School between 1599 and 1604, where he may well have been one of the boy players supervised by the headmaster, William Hayne. Ecclestone is believed to have been one of the Children of the Queen's Revels along with Nathan Field and Joseph Taylor. He is mentioned in Henslowe's papers when these players joined with the Lady Elizabeth's Company in 1612–13 (Gurr, 58). Before this amalgamation, however, Ecclestone joined the company of actors of whom Shakespeare was a member, who worked under the patronage of James I, playing at both the Blackfriars and Globe theatres.

Ecclestone is known to have acted in Jonson's *The Alchemist*, performed about 1610, as Kastril, the 21-year-old heir from out of town who so wants to be an 'angry boy' (Riddell, 290–91). He performed in the same writer's *Catiline* in 1611, but by 29 August 1611 had left the King's Men and joined the Lady Elizabeth's Company at Henslowe's Fortune Theatre. He played in *The Honest Man's Fortune* there in 1613, but later that year he rejoined the King's Men, appearing on the actor-list of John Fletcher's *Bonduca*

that was performed by them in 1613–14. Ecclestone was still a member of the king's company in 1619. His name occurs as an actor on the list of 'Principall Actors' for Shakespeare's plays printed in the preliminaries of the first folio of 1623 as well as many of the lists given in the Beaumont and Fletcher folio of 1679. These include *The Mad Lover* (1616), *The Loyal Subject* (1618), *The Humorous Lieutenant* (1619?), *The Laws of Candy* (1619?), *The Custom of the Country* (1619–21), *The Island Princess* (1619–21), *Women Pleased* (1619–21), *The Little French Lawyer* (1619–22), *The Sea Voyage* (1622), and *The Spanish Curate* (1622). He is known to have been living in 1623, when he was released from a debt in the will of a fellow actor, Nicholas Tooley. He was not, however, in the company lists of 1625.

     EVA GRIFFITH

Sources M. Eccles, 'Elizabethan actors, II: E–J', *N&Q*, 236 (1991), 454–61 • Mrs E. P. Hart, ed., *Merchant Taylors' School register, 1561–1934*, 1 (1936), vol. 1 • F. W. M. Draper, *Four centuries of Merchant Taylors' School, 1561–1961* (1962) • A. Gurr, *The Shakespearean stage, 1574–1642*, 3rd edn (1992) • J. A. Riddell, 'Some actors in Ben Jonson's plays', *Shakespeare Studies*, 5, 285–98 • G. E. Bentley, *The Jacobean and Caroline stage*, 7 vols. (1941–68), vol. 2, pp. 429–31 • E. Nungezer, *A dictionary of actors* (1929), 127 • E. A. J. Honigmann and S. Brock, eds., *Playhouse wills, 1558–1642: an edition of wills by Shakespeare and his contemporaries in the London theatre* (1993), 125 • *DNB*

Ecgberht [St Ecgberht, Egbert] (639–729), church reformer and holy man, was an Anglo-Saxon nobleman, almost certainly Northumbrian, who was in Ireland in 664 when he contracted the great plague of that year. Like many Englishmen he was there to study and perhaps to acquaint himself better with the monastic way of life. Thinking of his past sins he vowed that if he recovered, he would remain in voluntary exile as a 'pilgrim' (*peregrinus*), that is, he would never return to his homeland of Britain and would lead a life of penitential prayer and fasting. At this time he was twenty-five; he recovered, became a priest, and lived to be ninety. He is one of the most famous 'pilgrims' of the early middle ages. Bede was particularly interested in him because, after 664 (the year of the Synod of Whitby, where the Easter issue was debated, the synod so fully and vehemently described by Bede from the Roman point of view), he saw Ecgberht's life work as bringing the Ionans and the Picts round from the Columban to the Roman discipline of calculating the date of Easter, which the Irish at the synod had refused to accept. Adomnán, abbot of Iona from 679 to 704, became converted to the Roman way when on an extended visit to Northumbria in the mid-680s; but while he brought round a number of Irish monasteries (presumably of the Ionan connection), he could not win over Iona itself before his death. That was left for Ecgberht to achieve, under Abbot Dúnchad, about 716, after which he remained at Iona for the last thirteen years of his life and was buried there. Bede was particularly impressed that he died on Easter Sunday 729 after celebrating mass; it was 24 April, whereas under previous Ionan rules 21 April would have been the latest possible date for Easter.

Ecgberht's monastic base in Ireland was Rath Melsigi, now plausibly identified with Clonmelsh in co. Carlow. This Irish centre of Anglo-Saxon influence reciprocated by having in its turn a considerable influence on Northumbrian culture. Three factors contributed particularly to Ecgberht's effectiveness. First was his sanctity. Bede refers to his zeal in teaching, his authority to reprove, his goodness in giving away what he had received from the rich, as well as to his humility, meekness, continence, simplicity, and justice. These are terms very similar to those in which he described Áedán and no doubt are in a sense stock terms; but they are not necessarily untrue for that and would help to explain Ecgberht's impact on a world which may have been harsh but valued such qualities all the more for that. Second was the high standing which the *peregrinus* had come to hold in Irish society by the late seventh century, despite the ascetic aim of *peregrinatio* being renunciation of the world. Irish law tracts called such a person 'exile of God', and gave him a status similar to that of bishop, or chief poet, or even of some kings: 'the *peregrinus* might have renounced the world, but the power which he held prevented the world from renouncing him' (Charles-Edwards, 53). Anthropologists know the moral authority often attached to strangerhood. Third, his very high and wide connections in the insular world were important. Unsuccessful his warnings may have been in deterring King Ecgfrith of Northumbria from his attack on Ireland in 684, but they assume his right to warn. It has been strongly suggested also that he was an influence behind the approach of King Nechtan of the Picts, *c*.709, to Ceolfrith, abbot of Wearmouth-Jarrow, when Nechtan wished to adopt the Roman Easter. Ecgberht worked among the Picts as well as the Irish (exile from Britain, practically speaking, in his case seems to have meant from the Anglo-Saxon parts of Britain). It is known that Cuthbert, as prior of Melrose (664–*c*.678), had made a journey to the *Niduari* Picts; it is also known that in the 680s Ecgberht had connections with Melrose and that relations between Melrose and Wearmouth-Jarrow were close. Here, then, there appears to be a network of connections to which Ecgberht was integral. Moreover, Ecgberht also knew Bishop Curitan, an Irishman and missionary to the Picts whose principal church was apparently Rosemarkie; and the two were together in 697 at the Synod of Birr, where they both acted as guarantors of Adomnán's 'Law of the Innocents'. Curitan (who may also have been called Boniface) was also a Romanizing influence among the Picts.

Dimly perceptible is the fact that Ecgberht, while never again after 664 living among the English, was also a central figure to the whole missionary effort of the early Anglo-Saxon church; its missionary character is present to a remarkable degree from the start. About 688 he intended to work as a missionary among the pagan Frisians and Saxons on the continent, but was warned against doing so by the dream of a monk of Melrose. Bede tells the story vividly of how Ecgberht was eventually, though reluctantly, forced to take this warning seriously and to accept that his work lay in establishing the Roman Easter and unity of church discipline among the Irish and the Picts. His place in the Frisian mission, however, was taken by one of his English companions at Rath Melsigi, Wihtberht; and when Wihtberht's mission there was unsuccessful, Ecgberht sent the famous Willibrord, another Northumbrian nobleman, who had been in exile with Ecgberht in Ireland for twelve years and who was successful, becoming the first bishop of Utrecht. Willibrord had previously been a pupil at Ripon of Wilfrid, the greatest of all seventh-century English missionaries. Wilfrid was some five years the senior of Ecgberht and likewise a Northumbrian nobleman; the implied connection between Ecgberht and Wilfrid is reinforced by their common zeal to establish the Roman Easter. The two Hewalds, also English in exile in Ireland, who met an early martyrdom when they went to preach Christianity to the continental Saxons, also appear to have been associates of Ecgberht. Moreover, Ecgberht recounted a vision (probably his own) in which he had seen the soul of Ceadda (Chad) carried up to heaven—Ceadda, the bishop of the Mercians, whose preaching of the gospel from place to place Bede so admired. Thus, although Ecgberht's long working life was spent in voluntary exile from the English, and although he never even became a bishop, he exercised a profound influence on the character of the early Anglo-Saxon church.   HENRY MAYR-HARTING

Sources Bede, *Hist. eccl.*, 3.27; 4.3, 26; 5.9–10, 15, 21–2 • H. Mayr-Harting, *The coming of Christianity to Anglo-Saxon England* (1972) • H. Mayr-Harting, 'Saint Wilfrid in Sussex', *Studies in Sussex church history*, ed. M. J. Kitch (1981), 1–17 • T. M. Charles-Edwards, 'The social background to Irish *peregrinatio*', *Celtica*, 11 (1976), 43–59 • D. P. Kirby, 'Bede and the Pictish church', *Innes Review*, 24 (1973), 6–25 • D. O'Croinin, 'Rath Melsigi, Willibrord, and the earliest Echternach manuscripts', *Peritia*, 3 (1984), 17–49

Ecgberht [Egbert] (*d.* 766), archbishop of York, was the first metropolitan at York, receiving the pallium from Pope Gregory III in 735. It has been argued that Bede wrote his *Historia ecclesiastica* (completed in 731) in part to prepare the ground for a northern metropolitan see to parallel Canterbury in the south (and with its co-operation), in accordance with Pope Gregory I's scheme for the ecclesiastical organization of Britain. Ecgberht was the son of Eata, a descendant of Ida, by tradition the founder of the Bernician dynasty in Northumbria. He was thus of royal descent and his brother was *Eadberht, king of Northumbria. He visited Rome with another brother, Ecgred (who died there), was ordained deacon, and returned to Britain to become a determined propagator of Roman liturgical books. He is said in the life of Alcuin to have been a pupil of Bede, though whether he was taught by Bede in his youth, or was merely an avid student of Bede's writings, as Alcuin meant when he called Bede his own master, is not clear. That he was at least the latter is shown by two letters of St Boniface to him requesting copies of Bede's works.

Although the precise date at which it began is unclear, it was early in his pontificate, in 734, that Ecgberht received a famous letter from Bede (nearing his end), admonishing him on his office. Bishops were so keen on their revenues that dioceses were kept too large to admit of regular pastoral visits to out-of-the-way places; establishments masqueraded as monasteries (for the sake of land-holding and inheritance advantages) which had nothing to do with a monastic way of life; Ecgberht should study Pope Gregory the Great's celebrated *Pastoral Care*. How far Ecgberht followed all this advice is unknown. Doubtless he studied the *Pastoral Care* and took his duties as bishop seriously, but there is no sign of his ever dividing his own unwieldy diocese. A letter of Pope Paul I to him and Eadberht, accusing them of removing three monasteries from Forthred, a religious abbot who had appealed to the pope, and giving them to his secular brother, Moll, would raise a question as to whether their monastic policy too was always truly Bedan; though in his *Dialogus*, Ecgberht stresses the religious interests of monasteries in the choice of superior, and Rome may not have been a better vantage point than York from which to make such judgements.

Where Ecgberht was in accord with Bede's advice was in his choice of company and his aim to form priests and other teachers to instruct the laity, for he must be credited with founding the school at York. In his poem on the church of York, written probably in the early 790s, Alcuin praises Ecgberht especially as an outstanding teacher ('egregius doctor'; Godman, line 1260), a consecrator of upright ministers of the altar, and a teacher of singing. 'These were fortunate times for the people of Northumbria', he continues, 'ruled over in harmony by king and bishop, the one ruling the church, the other the business of the realm' (Godman, lines 1277–9). As the leader of Charlemagne's court school at Aachen who had himself been educated at York, Alcuin seems to look back here to York as a prototype court school. In his poem Alcuin also gives an impressive picture of the York library (which would not outlast the viking raids except in its influence on Carolingian Europe); its range of classical and theological authors was wide. Alcuin attributes the build-up of this library mainly to Ecgberht's successor, Ælberht, but with his knowledge of Roman books and his proven supply of books to St Boniface about 750, it is inconceivable that Ecgberht did not have a large hand in its beginnings.

Ecgberht was of great note in his own day as a canon lawyer, following in this as in the York school the footsteps of Archbishop Theodore of Canterbury (d. 690). When, in 746 or 747, St Boniface sent Ecgberht from the continent a copy of his letter of reproach to King Æthelbald of Mercia, he did so not only to make it an all-English responsibility (a West Saxon upbraiding a Mercian king with the backing of a weighty Northumbrian), but also and expressly because he wanted Ecgberht's advice and help in matters relating to ecclesiastical laws and decrees. The archbishop's reputation in this respect is attested by the penitential (that is, treatise on prescribed penances for various sins) which passed under his name. Even though Ecgberht had the pastoral authority to issue such a work (unlike Bede who cannot have compiled the penitential attributed to him), it is certain that many of the prescriptions in the latter part of this penitential were added on the continent, and it is not certain how much of the earlier part, if any, is Ecgberht's work. The scope of the compilation is less than that of its famous precursor,

the penitential of Archbishop Theodore, but the prologue goes beyond Theodore in offering instruction for the priest, which sounds true to the known Ecgberht. Perhaps the reason why 'Ecgberht' dealt more cursorily than Theodore with homicide for instance (obviously a vital subject in such a society), was because the former relied more on secular law or custom here. In any case, the earliest (late eighth-century) manuscript of the work already attributes it to Ecgberht, and the very attribution highlights his canonistic reputation. Ecgberht's *Dialogus ecclesiasticae institutionis*, on the other hand, is generally considered authentic. The object of this work, cast in question and answer form, is nothing less than to fix the clerical order into society. Secular law codes such as that of Ine of Wessex (r. 688–94) assumed that to some extent the clergy would have their own laws. Ecgberht deals with such matters as priests moving from one diocese to another, monks involved in crime, priests and deacons as witnesses to people's last words about their property, the value of clerical oaths in court, impediments to holy orders and deposition from them, and wergilds of clergy in relation to those of lay people. It is an example of the benefits of fraternal co-operation in Northumbria, for much of it could have been given little effect without royal support. It also describes, as if factually, the importance that had come to be attached to penitential practice and the taking of the eucharist (another point on which Bede had admonished Ecgberht) among the English.

Ecgberht died in York on 19 November 766 and was buried in York Minster. In his building on the work of Archbishop Theodore, especially in his legal and educational efforts, he must be regarded as one of the great architects of the English church in the eighth century.

HENRY MAYR-HARTING

Sources Bede, *The ecclesiastical history of the English people*, ed. J. McClure and R. Collins (1994) [Eng. trans. of *Historiam ecclesiasticam gentis Anglorum*] · Bede, *Historia ecclesiastica gentis Anglorum*, ed. C. Plummer, 3 vols. (1896), vol. 1 · Symeon of Durham, *Libellus de exordio atque procursu istius, hoc est Dunhelmensis, ecclesie / Tract on the origins and progress of this the church of Durham*, ed. and trans. D. W. Rollason, OMT (2000) · Alcuinus, 'Beati Flacci Alcuini Vita', *Patrologia Latina*, 100 (1851), 93B · Alcuin, *The bishops, kings, and saints of York*, ed. and trans. P. Godman, OMT (1982) · M. Tangl, ed., *Die Briefe des heiligen Bonifatius und Lullus*, MGH Epistolae Selectae, 1 (Berlin, 1916) · *English historical documents*, 1, ed. D. Whitelock (1955), nos. 170, 179, 184 · A. W. Haddan and W. Stubbs, eds., *Councils and ecclesiastical documents relating to Great Britain and Ireland*, 3 (1871) · A. J. Frantzen, *The literature of penance in Anglo-Saxon England* (1983) · W. Goffart, *The narrators of barbarian history* (1988) · Symeon of Durham, *Opera*, vol. 1

Ecgberht [Egbert] (d. 839), king of the West Saxons, became king in 802 and ruled Wessex for thirty-seven years and seven months. During the latter part of his reign he extended the territory under his authority to include Kent, Surrey, Essex, and Sussex, and he founded a dynasty which continued to rule this area (and later the whole of England) for the best part of two and a half centuries. The descent of the modern British royal family can be traced back to this dynasty.

Acquisition of the kingship, 802 Ecgberht appears to have gained power in Wessex by conquest. The Anglo-Saxon Chronicle states that his predecessor, King Beorhtric (*d.* 802), helped Offa (*d.* 796), king of the Mercians and Beorhtric's father-in-law, to drive Ecgberht into exile in Francia some years earlier. It is therefore unlikely that Ecgberht was Beorhtric's designated successor. The chronicle also records that Beorhtric and one of his leading men, Ealdorman Worr, died on the same day, which suggests that they died by violence, and upheavals in Wessex at this time are attested by a battle between the men of what is now Wiltshire and an invading army of the Hwicce which occurred simultaneously with Beorhtric's death. The coinage which had begun to be minted in Wessex came to an abrupt halt. And a story incorporated into Asser's life of Alfred told how Beorhtric's queen, Eadburh, took countless treasures and fled the country: precisely what she could be expected to have done on the violent overthrow of her husband. Less plausible parts of the story of Eadburh, including the allegation that she poisoned her husband, may have originated as rumours spread by Ecgberht in order to strengthen his own (presumably precarious) position by discrediting his predecessor's regime and in particular his widow, who, if she had sons, remained a potential threat.

West Saxon or Kentish origins? Ecgberht's origins have been the subject of controversy among modern scholars. Since he became king of the West Saxons, and his family claimed West Saxon descent, it has not unnaturally been assumed in the past that he was by origin a West Saxon and some scholars still take this view. Alternatively, however, there is some reason to believe that he may have been from Kent. The genealogy drawn up in the name of his son, *Æthelwulf (*d.* 858), begins by stating that Æthelwulf was the son of Ecgberht, the son of Ealhmund, and it is quite possible that the genealogy is to be relied upon this far. A chronicler working at Christ Church, Canterbury, in the late eleventh or early twelfth century identified Ealhmund, the father of Ecgberht, with *Ealhmund (*fl.* 784) [*see under* Æthelberht II], king in Kent, whose reign is attested by a charter of between 765 and about 785. If the family were West Saxon, it is difficult to see why Ealhmund should have sought power in Kent, thereby embroiling himself quite unnecessarily with Offa, who was mounting determined attacks on Kent both before and after Ealhmund's reign. If the family were Kentish, then Ealhmund's position is perfectly natural, and there is no great difficulty in accounting for Ecgberht's: by 802 the native Kentish rulers had been wholly dispossessed, so it is not surprising that a Kentish ætheling should turn up elsewhere, while the evidence that Ecgberht gained power by conquest precludes any necessity to assume that he had any prior support within Wessex. In the years since the reign in Kent of his putative father, Ealhmund, he may well have operated as an independent war leader (like the West Saxon Cædwalla, or St Guthlac, earlier), with his own following of fighting men at whose head he achieved his successful coup in Wessex.

The Anglo-Saxon Chronicle, recording Ecgberht's annexation of south-east England in the 820s, asserts that the people of Kent, Surrey, Essex, and Sussex submitted to him because they had been forced away from his kinsmen. This appears to be a plain statement that Ecgberht's family were rulers in the south-east, dispossessed by the Mercian kings. Further evidence is provided by the chronicle's statement that when Offa and Beorhtric expelled Ecgberht (between 789 and 796), Beorhtric helped Offa because he had married Offa's daughter. Evidently Beorhtric had no personal quarrel with Ecgberht, so Ecgberht cannot at this time have been perceived as a possible claimant to the West Saxon kingship. Offa was the one who wanted rid of him, and the most likely reason for this is that Ecgberht was a potential contender for the throne in Kent.

The claim in Æthelwulf's genealogy of a West Saxon descent for Æthelwulf and his father is no evidence for the truth of this assertion. It would have been extraordinary if the family had not claimed descent from Cerdic, as West Saxon kings traditionally did. It may well be that the genealogy was drawn up during Ecgberht's reign as part of his attempts to legitimize his dynasty and secure the peaceful succession of his son.

Campaigns against the Cornish Virtually the only recorded actions of Ecgberht during his first twenty years as king are campaigns against the Cornish. The earliest such expedition noted by the Anglo-Saxon Chronicle is dated 815, when Ecgberht is said to have ravaged Cornwall from east to west. But the thirteenth-century historian Roger of Wendover, possibly drawing on sources now lost, records campaigns in 809, when Ecgberht attacked and subdued the Cornish with heavy losses on both sides; in 810, when Ecgberht subdued the Cornish again and compelled them to pay tribute (a dubious detail, perhaps added by Roger); and in 811, when he ravaged Cornwall from north to south. Bearing in mind that a journey from the extreme north of Cornwall to the extreme south and one from the extreme east to the extreme west would both traverse the length of the peninsula, Roger's third entry sounds like a different record of the campaign mentioned in the Anglo-Saxon Chronicle; but unfortunately it is impossible to deduce the correct date, nor can the dates or details of any of these campaigns be absolutely relied upon.

More precise information is contained in an unusual charter-dating clause (*AS chart.*, S 273), which states that the first draft of the charter was made at 'Creodantreow' on 19 August 825 during military service when Ecgberht moved against the Britons (that is, the Cornish). According to the Anglo-Saxon Chronicle, the men of Devon fought the Cornish in the same year, but the outcome is not stated. It is possible that the men of Devon, led by their ealdorman, were defeated and that Ecgberht then mounted a further campaign to retrieve the situation.

Rivalry with the Mercians and annexation of south-eastern England The same year there occurred the second major turning point of Ecgberht's career, when he defeated King Beornwulf of the Mercians in a battle at Wroughton, in what is now Wiltshire. The East Anglians, also in conflict with Mercia, appealed to Ecgberht for 'peace and protection', which should probably be interpreted as a wish for an alliance against the common enemy. Whether Ecgberht was able to give them any assistance is unknown, but Beornwulf was killed in battle against the East Anglians, probably in 826. It may have been after his death that Ecgberht sent an army to Kent, under the leadership of his son, Æthelwulf, Ealhstan, bishop of Sherborne, and Ealdorman Wulfheard; there they drove out the Mercian sub-king Baldred (*fl.* 823–827) and took control. There is no record of a battle and the Anglo-Saxon Chronicle states that the former kingdoms of Kent, Surrey, Essex, and Sussex, subject in recent years to Mercian control, now submitted to Ecgberht. This process may in fact have been more difficult and time-consuming than the chronicle suggests, and it is probable that Sussex was not annexed until 827. In Kent the coinage of Archbishop Wulfred was terminated and coins were struck in Ecgberht's name; the series of Mercian grants to Wulfred ended; and Ecgberht seized an estate which Baldred had given to Christ Church at the time of his flight.

In 829 there was another battle between the West Saxons and the Mercians and Ecgberht defeated King Wiglaf (*fl.* 827–840). This seems to have been a more comprehensive victory than the earlier one, reducing Mercia to total disarray. Ecgberht was apparently in control of Mercian territory for some time, as he is assigned a one-year reign in a Mercian king-list and issued coins as king of the Mercians from the London mint. Moreover, he was able to raid as far north as Northumbria and compel the Northumbrians to submit to him. The Anglo-Saxon Chronicle states, probably with some exaggeration, that at this time Ecgberht controlled everything south of the Humber, and describes him as *bretwalda*, adding his name to Bede's list of overlords.

Ecgberht's immense conquest could not be maintained and within a year or two Wiglaf had recovered his kingdom and begun to issue charters. But no coins of Wiglaf can be securely dated to his second reign and no coins were minted at London between the 830s and *c*.843; nor does it appear that Mercian power in the south-east was restored. There Ecgberht remained in control, ruling Kent in a style very different from that of the earlier Mercian overlords. The Mercians had issued charters relating to Kentish affairs from councils held in Mercia. Ecgberht, however, held councils in Kent itself, and involved the Kentish nobility in the affairs of the province. While the Mercians presumably regarded Kent as conquered territory from which wealth could be creamed off and taken home to Mercia, it is tempting to see in Ecgberht's rather different approach, the attitude of a man for whom Kent was home.

Direct rule of the extensive territory brought together by his successive conquests must have presented many problems, and by 830 Ecgberht had appointed his son as king in Kent, whereupon Æthelwulf presumably took over much of the work and responsibility relating to Kentish affairs, enabling Ecgberht to devote more time to Wessex. Unfortunately there is very little evidence for Wessex during the 830s. Surviving charters, other than those concerning Kent, are very few for the whole reign, and in most cases have been altered by later generations, so that they afford only a few glimpses of Ecgberht's life as king of the West Saxons.

Charters, patronage, and coinage Ecgberht's earliest recorded grant dates from 824, when he gave land on the River Meon in what is now Hampshire to Wulfheard, who was an ealdorman, probably of that area. Another charter, spurious as it stands but possibly recording a genuine transaction, mentions a grant to the layman Burhheard of land at Alton Priors, Wiltshire, in 826. On 26 December 833 Ecgberht was at the royal vill at Dorchester and confirmed arrangements relating to estates in Dorset and Devon, the inheritance of three sisters. The land in Devon was at Dartington, no further west than Crediton (where there is evidence for West Saxon control much earlier), but a long way south of it, and one of the sisters went to live there, which tends to imply that the West Saxons were effectively in power in this area at this time, probably as a result of Ecgberht's earlier Cornish campaigns. The majority of coins in Ecgberht's name were minted in Kent, mostly at Canterbury between 825 and 839, with a smaller number produced at Rochester. In the 830s, however, coins were struck for Ecgberht in Wessex, probably at Southampton, then an important centre of trade.

The Council of Kingston, 838 In 838 Ecgberht held a council at Kingston in Surrey, attended by his son, Æthelwulf, the archbishop of Canterbury, Ceolnoth (*d*. 870), who had succeeded to his see in 833, and numerous other prominent men. The report of the conclusions of this council is of unimpeachable authenticity, but of such poor Latinity that it is difficult to interpret. It appears that Ecgberht and Æthelwulf restored to Archbishop Ceolnoth the estate at 'Malling' (probably East Malling, Kent, or South Malling, Sussex) which the West Saxons had seized on their first arrival in Kent. In return Ceolnoth ceded to the West Saxon kings that control over the estates of the Kentish minsters which Archbishop Wulfred had fought for so long to deny to the Mercian kings. The grant of 'Malling' was made on condition that Ecgberht and his heirs should henceforth enjoy the firm and unshakeable friendship of the archbishop, his community, and his successors, and the provisions regarding the Kentish minsters are followed by further reference to the perpetual peace which was to obtain between the parties. It has been calculated that the estates of the Kentish minsters added up to a quarter of the land in Kent, so the Kingston agreement gave Ecgberht control over very considerable wealth. However, Ecgberht had already been king of the West Saxons for thirty-six years, and had been active politically for at least six years before that, and he must have been very much aware at this time that the future belonged to his descendants. Both the material wealth and the archbishop's reiterated promise of eternal friendship served to strengthen the position of Æthelwulf and his sons, and it seems likely that the future of the dynasty was Ecgberht's chief concern at this meeting. It may well be that Æthelwulf was formally anointed as king on this occasion, just as Offa's son, Ecgfrith, had been consecrated as king in his father's lifetime as part of Offa's strenuous efforts to ensure his succession. It has been convincingly argued that the earliest surviving English liturgy for king-making, which incorporates provision for the anointing of the king, dates from no later than the first half of the ninth century. Moreover, Kingston was by the early tenth century the place where West Saxon kings were crowned.

Advent of the vikings and death Ceolnoth's motive both for ceding control of the estates and promising to support the West Saxon dynasty was probably fear of viking attacks, which by this time posed a serious, recurring threat. The archbishop probably recognized that an effective defence was only likely to be achieved by the West Saxon kings. Ecgberht had fought the Danes at Carhampton, on the Somerset coast in 836, apparently unsuccessfully, as the vikings are said to have retained possession of the battlefield. However, two years later, in the same year as the Council of Kingston, he defeated a coalition of vikings and Cornishmen at Hingston Down, west of the Tamar, in Cornwall. In 839 Ecgberht died, leaving his property to the male side of his family. Æthelwulf succeeded as king of the West Saxons. HEATHER EDWARDS

Sources ASC, s.a. 784 [text F], 802, 815, 825, 829, 830, 836, 838, 839, 855 [texts A, E] · AS chart., S 271, 272, 273, 274, 277, 278, 279, 280, 281, 282, 283, 286, 323, 1438, 1623 · Alfred the Great: Asser's Life of King Alfred and other contemporary sources, ed. and trans. S. Keynes and M. Lapidge (1983) · Rogeri de Wendover chronica, sive, Flores historiarum, ed. H. O. Coxe, 4 vols., EHS (1841–2) · N. Brooks, The early history of the church of Canterbury: Christ Church from 597 to 1066 (1984) · S. Keynes, 'The control of Kent in the ninth century', Early Medieval Europe, 2 (1993), 111–32 · P. Wormald, 'The ninth century', The Anglo-Saxons, ed. J. Campbell (1982), 132–57 · A. Scharer, 'The writing of history at King Alfred's court', Early Medieval Europe, 5 (1996), 177–206 · J. L. Nelson, Politics and ritual in early medieval Europe (1986) · H. Edwards, The charters of the early West Saxon kingdom (1988) · H. Pagan, 'Coinage in southern England, 796–874', Anglo-Saxon monetary history: essays in memory of Michael Dolley, ed. M. A. S. Blackburn (1986), 45–65 · English historical documents, 1, ed. D. Whitelock (1955) · P. A. Stafford, 'The king's wife in Wessex, 800–1066', Past and Present, 91 (1981), 3–27 · P. Grierson and M. Blackburn, Medieval European coinage: with a catalogue of the coins in the Fitzwilliam Museum, Cambridge, 1: The early middle ages (5th–10th centuries) (1986) · D. N. Dumville, Wessex and England from Alfred to Edgar (1992)

Ecgberht I (d. 673). See under Eorcenberht (d. 664).

Ecgberht II (fl. 765–779). See under Æthelberht II (d. 762).

Ecgburh [Ecgburg] (fl. c.717), Benedictine nun, is known from her one extant letter, sent to the West Saxon missionary Boniface in Germany between 716 and 718 and preserved in his collected correspondence. 'No day unrolls nor night slips by without some recollection of your teaching. Therefore believe me, as God is my witness, I embrace you with the noblest kind of love' (Tangl, no. 13). Although Ecgburh describes herself as 'the least' of Boniface's pupils, her educational attainment is revealed by her allusions to Virgil and Jerome. She laments that her sister Wehtburh is in prison in Rome, and declares that

Boniface has been her spiritual brother since the cruel death of her blood brother Oshere. Her letter includes a postscript by a certain Ealdbeorht, who was later to add a similar postscript to a letter by Tyccea, probably the abbot of that name who (as abbot probably of Glastonbury) in 757 attested a charter of Æthelbald of Mercia, probably in favour of the monastery of Malmesbury. This western orientation supports the suggestion that Ecgburh's brother Oshere was *Oshere, king of the Hwicce [see under Hwicce, kings of the (act. c.670–c.780)], the alleged founder of the see of Worcester in 679, who had probably died (or retired) in the 690s or soon after, and certainly by 709. Ecgburh may be the same person as the abbess of Gloucester called Eadburh in later sources, according to which she succeeded Abbess Cyneburh (d. after 704), the sister of King Osric (Oshere's predecessor), and was the widow of Wulfhere, king of Mercia (d. 674/5). This Ecgburh was buried at St Peter's, Gloucester. The names Ecgburh (or Ecgburg) and Eadburh (or Eadburg) were distinct, but the latter appears as a corruption of the former, as in the case of Ecgburg (miswritten Eadburg), sister of Ælfwald, king of the East Angles (d. 749). (The identification of the East Anglian Ecgburg with Boniface's correspondent is unlikely.) PATRICK SIMS-WILLIAMS

Sources M. Tangl, ed., Die Briefe des heiligen Bonifatius und Lullus, MGH Epistolae Selectae, 1 (Berlin, 1916) · P. Sims-Williams, Religion and literature in western England, 600–800 (1990) · The English correspondence of Saint Boniface, trans. E. Kylie (1911) · The letters of Saint Boniface, trans. E. Emerton (1940)

Ecgfrith (645/6–685), king of Northumbria, was the elder son of *Oswiu (611/12–670), king in Northumbria, and his wife, *Eanflæd (b. 626, d. after 685), daughter of King *Eadwine of Northumbria. Born in 645 or, less probably, in 646, he is first heard of in 655, at the time of the battle of the Winwæd between the Mercians and the Northumbrians, when he was a hostage with Queen Cynewise of Mercia. He became king after his father's death in February 670.

Ecgfrith's reign was marked by his generous endowment of the Northumbrian church, by his bitter quarrel with its most flamboyant leader, Wilfrid, bishop of York, and by a militancy towards neighbouring peoples, the Mercians, the Picts, and the Irish, which eventually brought him disaster. His reputation as 'a venerable and most pious king'—the words of Bede ('Historia abbatum', 364)—rested chiefly on his friendship with Benedict Biscop, Oswiu's former thegn turned monk, and with the ascetic Cuthbert. His provision of 70 hides of land for Benedict's new foundation in Wearmouth in 674 and a further 40 hides for his parallel foundation in Jarrow in 681 associated him with the two houses, which were to become preeminent in Northumbrian monastic culture and scholarship. He was equally generous to Cuthbert, pressing him to accept the bishopric of Lindisfarne in 685 and granting him and his church land in Cartmel and Carlisle in the north-west and in Crayke in the Vale of York.

With Wilfrid, who had a sharper sense of his own worth than either Benedict or Cuthbert, Ecgfrith's relations were more difficult. Initially his friend and patron, and present when Wilfrid's splendid new church in Ripon was consecrated between 671 and 678, he later fell out with him, for two main reasons. The first concerned Ecgfrith's wife. He had married, probably in 660, *Æthelthryth, daughter of Anna, king of the East Angles, and widow of Tondbehrt, *princeps* of the South Gyrwe. Despite her previous marriage, Æthelthryth had always lived as a virgin and was determined to remain one, retiring altogether to live as a nun in Coldingham about 672. Wilfrid seems to have been her spiritual adviser: she had endowed his new monastery in Hexham, he had veiled her on her entry to religion, and Ecgfrith had reportedly offered Wilfrid land and wealth in order to get him to persuade the queen to live as his wife. Frustrated dynastically as well as sexually, Ecgfrith is likely to have blamed Wilfrid for Æthelthryth's contumacy. Secondly, Wilfrid was excessively powerful. His huge diocese, covering not only Northumbria itself but also the tributary territories of the Picts and the Irish colonies in western Scotland, his riches, and the numbers of his monasteries and his followers, made him very much a prince bishop. In 678 Ecgfrith, urged on by his second wife, Iurminburg, expelled Wilfrid from his see and divided it in two, with a new bishop in Hexham as well as York. Archbishop Theodore of Canterbury confirmed these changes, which fell in neatly with his own plans to break up unmanageably large tribal dioceses. Wilfrid appealed to Rome and secured a papal judgment in his favour; but vainly. On his return in 680 he was deprived of his relics by Iurminburg, imprisoned for nine months by Ecgfrith, and then expelled for a second time from the kingdom.

It gave Stephen of Ripon, Wilfrid's biographer, some satisfaction to point out that Ecgfrith's partnership with Wilfrid coincided with the king's years of military success and that his failures followed from their differences. Before 675 he had defeated Wulfhere of Mercia, bringing the kingdom of Lindsey (the north of modern Lincolnshire) and possibly a larger part of Mercia under his direct rule: his presence at the Synod of Hertford in 672 may be a mark of this temporary overlordship. About the same time he defeated the Picts in battle. But in 679 he himself was defeated by Æthelred of Mercia at the battle of the Trent, where Ecgfrith's brother Ælfwine was killed. Lindsey was lost and the Humber restored as Northumbria's southern frontier. The main threat now came from the north and west: from the Picts and their allies the Irish, with whom *Aldfrith, Ecgfrith's half-brother, may also have been in alliance. Aldfrith's exile in Irish territory, and his relationship through his mother with the Uí Néill, the most powerful of the Irish tribes, partly explains the successful attack by Ecgfrith on the Uí Néill lands in Ireland in 684. In the following year he invaded Pictish territory, where he was defeated and killed at Nechtansmere (now identified as Dunnichen Moss, near Forfar) on 20 May 685. The battle was a turning point in Northumbrian fortunes. The Picts and the Irish of western Scotland recovered their independence, the Forth was probably re-established as Northumbria's northern frontier, and

the bishopric at Abercorn on its southern shore, established by Ecgfrith for the Picts, was abandoned.

Ecgfrith has suffered historically by comparison with Eadwine, *Oswald, and Oswiu, his great Northumbrian predecessors, and by reason of his final failure in the north. Like his predecessors, he was both a barbarian warlord and (as Stephen of Ripon admitted) 'a most Christian king' (*Life of Bishop Wilfrid*, 37). Although he lacked the control over the southern kingdoms which might have put him on Bede's famous list of kings holding *imperium* in the south, he remained a formidable ruler, with the resources to endow the church lavishly and to raise the navy which must have been necessary for his invasion of Ireland. Deprived after Nechtansmere of the land and tribute from the Picts and Irish which probably underlay such power, Northumbria is likely to have been a poorer as well as a less dominant kingdom. J. R. MADDICOTT

Sources Bede, *Hist. eccl.* • E. Stephanus, *The life of Bishop Wilfrid*, ed. and trans. B. Colgrave (1927) • B. Colgrave, ed., *Two lives of St Cuthbert* (1940) • 'Historia abbatum auctore Baeda', *Venerabilis Baedae opera historica*, ed. C. Plummer, 1 (1896), 364–87

Ecgfrith (*d.* **796**). *See under* Offa (*d.* 796).

Ecgwine [St Ecgwine] (*d.* **717**?), bishop of Worcester, is a figure of whom almost nothing is known. He is not mentioned by Bede or in the Anglo-Saxon Chronicle. The early twelfth-century historian John of Worcester recorded that Ecgwine succeeded Oftfor as the third bishop of Worcester in 692; that a few years later he began to construct the monastery known as Evesham; and that he died on 30 December 717. The sources of John's information are unknown, and even the bare facts which he records are not beyond suspicion (it is uncertain, for example, that Oftfor died in 692; he may have died some years later, perhaps between 693 and 699). Ecgwine's name is recorded in the witness lists of seven charters issued between 692 and 717 (but not outside these dates), and he is named as beneficiary, on Evesham's behalf, of three others. Although none of these charters is authentic in its present form (and several are manifest forgeries), some seem to have an authentic basis, and may be considered broadly trustworthy. Depending on how much reliance one wishes to place on these various charters (and omitting the manifestly spurious ones), they reveal Ecgwine as an active promoter of Evesham's interests, building up a substantial endowment from royal and lay patronage, including estates at Ombersley, Stratford upon Avon, Abbots Morton, Oldberrow, and Droitwich. Ecgwine's last datable act as bishop was his appearance at the council of 'Clofesho' in July 716.

It was approximately three centuries later that the first life of Ecgwine was composed (*c.*1016) by Byrhtferth, a monk of Ramsey who may at the time have been resident at Evesham. By the early eleventh century all memory of Ecgwine had passed away, and there was very little documentary record of his bishopric. In order to compose his *Vita sancti Ecgwini* Byrhtferth was obliged to resort to hagiographical fiction. The life is set out in four parts, corresponding to the four ages of man, and Ecgwine is described proceeding through the seven ecclesiastical grades and then being appointed bishop of Worcester in the days of King Æthelred of the Mercians (675–704). As a result of his stern preaching to the people of his diocese (Byrhtferth puts the text of Bede's *De die judicii* into Ecgwine's mouth), Ecgwine was forced by the people to leave his see and go to Rome. Before setting off, he shackled himself and threw the key to his shackles into the River Avon; when he reached Rome, one of his companions caught a fish in the Tiber which miraculously was found to contain the key to the shackles (Byrhtferth has here adapted an international folk-tale widely attested in western literature from Herodotus onwards). When he returned home, Ecgwine founded the monastery of Evesham on a site revealed to him in a vision; he subsequently went to Rome with kings Offa of the East Saxons and Coenred of the Mercians (whose trip is described by Bede, though Ecgwine is nowhere mentioned) in order to secure a papal privilege for his foundation. On his return, the privilege was endorsed at a synod (otherwise unrecorded) at Alcester under the presidency of Archbishop Berhtwald (d. 731). Byrhtferth takes the opportunity here to list some of the estates in Evesham's endowment, including Stratford and Twyford; his source for this information was apparently charters preserved at Evesham, spurious or otherwise. The life closes with various miracles which took place at tenth-century Evesham through the divine agency of St Ecgwine.

Byrhtferth's account of Ecgwine's life is largely fiction, but it served as the basis for all subsequent hagiography, including a life by Dominic of Evesham written *c.*1100, an anonymous recension of Dominic's life compiled in the early twelfth century and known as the Digby-Gotha recension, and a further recension of Dominic's text by Thomas of Marlborough (d. 1236) in the early thirteenth century. A Middle English verse life of St Ecgwine is included in the popular south English legendary, produced at Worcester between 1270 and 1285. These various works supply no further information about the historical Ecgwine, but give some indication of the extent to which his cult had grown, particularly at Evesham and in its environs. From the eleventh century onwards, St Ecgwine's deposition is recorded in liturgical calendars (particularly from Evesham and Worcester) against 30 December, and his name is frequently invoked in litanies of the saints.   MICHAEL LAPIDGE

Sources John of Worcester, *Chron.* • AS chart., S 22, 64, 75, 78, 79, 80, 81, 97, 102, 1175, 1252 • Byrhtferth of Ramsey, *The lives of Oswald and Ecgwine*, ed. M. Lapidge [forthcoming] • M. Lapidge, 'Byrhtferth and the *Vita S. Ecgwini*', *Mediaeval Studies*, 41 (1979), 331–53 • M. Lapidge, 'The medieval hagiography of St Ecgwine', *Vale of Evesham Historical Society Research Papers*, 6 (1977), 77–93 • M. Lapidge, 'The Digby-Gotha recension of the life of St Ecgwine', *Vale of Evesham Historical Society Research Papers*, 7 (1979), 39–55 • 'Dominic of Evesham, *Vita S. Ecgwini episcopi et confessoris*', ed. M. Lapidge, *Analecta Bollandiana*, 96 (1978), 65–104

Echard, Laurence (*bap.* **1672**, *d.* **1730**), historian, was baptized at Barsham, Suffolk, on 23 March 1672, the eldest of three sons of the Revd Thomas Echard (d. 1693) and his

wife, Sarah Ox. He was educated at Christ's College, Cambridge, where he graduated BA in 1691 and remained until he took his MA in 1695. While a student he produced an astonishing list of publications: *An Exact Description of Ireland* (1691), *A Description of Flanders* (1691), *The Compleat Compendium of Geography* (1691), *Plautus' Comedies* (1694), *Terence's Comedies Made English* (1694), *The Gazetteer's or Newspaperman's Interpreter* (1695), and *The Roman history from the building of the city to the perfect settlement of the empire by Augustus* (1695). The three geographical works and the 'gazetteer' capitalized on the many wars in progress at the time (over the English succession, the League of Augsburg, and against the Ottomans). Echard claimed that he was encouraged to produce the compendium by none other than Sir Isaac Newton. It was dedicated to Dr John Covel, master of Christ's, and went through at least eight editions. The gazetteer reached at least seventeen editions by 1751 and was translated into French, Italian, Spanish, and Polish. The translation of Plautus was described by Echard himself as 'scrupulously nice', but Thomas Cooke called it 'very injudicious and grossly low and vulgar' (*Mr Cooke's Edition and Translation of the Comedys of Plautus*, 1746, 53). It was claimed a century later that the translation of Terence gave his works 'a buffoonery not their own' (J. Granger, *Biographical History of England*, 1806, 3.106), but more recently Robert Graves ascribed to it 'fascinating vigour' (*Comedies of Terence*, ed. R. Graves, 1963, ix), and no fewer than nine editions appeared by 1741. The most important work of this early period, however, was the Roman history, the first in English, dedicated to the lord keeper of the great seal, Sir John Sommers, which attained ten editions by 1734 and was twice issued in French. The work was designed to be 'particularly useful to young Students and Gentlemen' (preface). There was, as one would expect, a heavy emphasis on moralizing, following the Sallustian model. It is a smooth narrative, without clash of sources, although Echard revealed an interesting preference for Greek sources over Livy, who was declared 'a little too verbose and circumstantial' (ibid.). Echard's political interpretations were conservative: blame the tribunes. He was, in general, an apologist for Roman imperialism, save for the obliteration of Carthage. He was under the spell of Caesar, and then of Octavian-Augustus. Strangely, he used only literary sources, neglecting inscriptions, coins, and archaeological evidence. G. Cornewall Lewis grouped Echard among the 'unenquiring and uncritical' (*Enquiry into the Credibility of the Early Roman History*, 2 vols., 1855, 1.4). In an age of raging Pyrrhonism, Echard was certainly very conservative. Yet his history held the field in English until Hooke (1738) and Ferguson (1783). A continuation of it was the first imperial inspiration of the young Gibbon.

Echard was ordained priest at Norwich on 2 May 1696, and obtained the livings of Welton-le-Wold and South Elkington, both in Lincolnshire. In April 1697 in Lincoln Cathedral he was made prebendary of Louth, which he remained until his death, and became chaplain to Bishop James Gardiner, a position he held until 1705. He resided at Louth for more than twenty years. On 14 August 1697 he married Jane Potter, daughter of the Revd Potter; she died in August 1704 after only seven years of marriage. On 14 April 1707 Echard married Justina Wooley. There were no children of either marriage. Echard's highest ecclesiastical post was conferred on 16 August 1712, when he became archdeacon of Stowe; he held the post until his death.

Echard's writing continued unabated. The most important works are an abridgement of Ralegh's *History of the World* (1700), *A general ecclesiastical history from the nativity of our blessed Saviour to the first establishment of Christianity* (1702), *The history of England from the first entrance of Julius Caesar and the Romans to the end of the reign of James I* (1707), *The Classical Geographical Dictionary* (1715), and the *History of England*, volumes 2–3 (1718), continuing the story to William and Mary. The ecclesiastical history was dedicated to Queen Anne, and celebrated the peace of Rijswick, but the preface complained of his absence from libraries, his many duties, and private troubles. He stated candidly that he had borrowed freely (notably from Cave and Dupin), 'for in matters of Plagiary I shall always study my Reader's profit before my own Reputation'. Despite its lack of originality it attained a seventh edition by 1729. Echard's history of England was the first to be written by a single author. The first volume, from Caesar to James I, was dedicated to the duke of Ormond, the second and third, reaching 1688, to George I (by which time Ormond had been impeached). The permission for the royal dedication was obtained by William Wake, archbishop of Canterbury, and Joseph Addison, and Echard was rewarded with £300. He finally accomplished what historians had been calling for since the end of the previous century; the previous *Compleat History of England* (1706) had been the work of nine hands (including Camden, Bacon, and Milton). Echard's aims were 'Truth and Fidelity ... Perspicacity and Elevation, Diversion and Instruction' and he argued that the historian's task was to 'enlarge [the reader's] mind'. Most importantly, he claimed to be of no party but the truth. He pleased nobody, especially not nonconformists, Catholics, radical whigs, or Jacobites, and his *History* was attacked by the Presbyterian Edmund Calamy (*A Letter to Archdeacon Echard*, 1718) and the whig John Oldmixon (*The Critical History of England*, 1724). The Jacobite Thomas Hearne declared it 'a most roguish, Whiggish Thing', 'vile', 'to get preferment and to ingratiate himself' (*Remains of Thomas Hearne*, 1966, 194, 411). Mark Noble saw the explanation: 'his History of the Revolution keeps a very quiet place upon the shelf of a library. Charles I was the idol of his idolatry before, William III after the Revolution' (Noble, 1.34). After being indulgent to the Stuarts, Echard called the revolution an 'inestimable Deliverance', and gave large play to Providence. The most famous page of all, however, was the description of Cromwell's interview with the Devil in September 1651 (*History of England*, 2.713)—which he declared not worth expunging or vindicating! Despite all this, Echard's history remained the standard one until replaced by Hume (who does not seem to mention him) and Macaulay (who cites him frequently). More recently he has been complimented for his 'vital

imagination' (B. Dobree, *English Literature in the Eighteenth Century*, 1959, 383) and for citations from original authorities (D. Douglas, *English Scholars, 1660–1730*, 1951, 134).

In February 1718 Echard was elected a fellow of the Society of Antiquaries. In 1722 George I presented him with the livings of Rundelsham, Sudborne, and Alford in Suffolk but by this time his health was failing. The last eight years of his life were spent in continual ill health, and he wrote no more. He was, in fact, on his way to Scarborough to take the waters when he died at Lincoln on 16 August 1730. He was buried there in St Mary Magdalen on 19 or 29 August; no monument survives.

Echard deserves to be remembered as a pathbreaking historian, albeit of second rank, in two very different fields: the Roman republic and the history of England. He is a sound representative of the great scholarly activity of the Anglican clergy before the transfer of the historical profession to the universities. There is no physical description of Echard, but his portrait (now in Christ's College) by the leading portraitist of his day, Sir Godfrey Kneller, shows a conventional churchman of the time, seemingly of plump build and satisfied disposition.

R. T. RIDLEY

Sources R. Goulding, *Laurence Echard* (1927) · Venn, *Alum. Cant.* · J. Peile, *Biographical register of Christ's College, 1505–1905, and of the earlier foundation, God's House, 1448–1505*, ed. [J. A. Venn], 1 (1910) · M. Noble, 'The lives of the fellows of the Society of Antiquarians in London', 1818, S. Antiquaries, Lond. · *European Magazine and London Review*, 49 (1806), 418–19 · D. Stephan, 'Laurence Echard—whig historian', *HJ*, 32 (1989), 843–66 · R. T. Ridley, 'The forgotten historian: Laurence Echard and the first history of the Roman republic', *Ancient Society* [Leuven], 27 (1996), 277–315 · *DNB* · R. E. G. Cole, ed., *Speculum dioeceseos Lincolniensis sub episcopis Gul: Wake et Edm: Gibson, AD 1705–1723*, Lincoln RS, 4 (1913), 45, 138

Archives BL, letters and MSS

Likenesses G. Vertue, line engraving, 1719, BM, NPG; repro. in L. Echard, *The history of England*, 2 vols. (1720) · G. Kneller, oils, Christ's College, Cambridge

Echion. *See* Chatfield, Edward (1800–1839).

Echlin [*née* Bellingham], **Elizabeth, Lady Echlin** (*bap.* 1704, *d.* 1782), author, was baptized on 6 March 1704 at Rufford, Lancashire, the elder of the two daughters of William Bellingham (*c.*1660–1718), son of James and Elizabeth Bellingham of Levens, Westmorland, and his wife, Elizabeth, daughter of William Spencer of Ashton, Lancashire, and widow of Robert Hesketh (*d.* 1697), of Rufford. The Bellinghams were a prominent landed family, but the estate inherited by Elizabeth's father in 1693 had been squandered by his elder brother Alan (1656–1693), and Levens Hall, the Bellingham home for over a century, had been sold. Called to the bar in 1686, William Bellingham seems to have practised law for a while, but his marriage of 1703 restored his fortunes and provided the Rufford home in which his two daughters and coheirs were raised with their half-sister, Elizabeth Hesketh (1694–1776), the future countess of Derby. Decades later the younger daughter, Dorothy *Bradshaigh, had Elizabeth in mind when describing 'a sister, that, before [the age of twenty], read divinity … lectured me for saying short prayers, and talked like a sage old woman' (Barbauld, 6.112).

The air of religiosity did not impede Elizabeth's marriage in 1727 to Sir Robert Echlin, second baronet (1699–1757), an Irishman of Scots descent, and for the next thirty years Lady Echlin lived at Rush House, the family estate (previously owned by the dukes of Ormond) in north-east co. Dublin. She also resided for periods in Dublin itself, but at some distance from a fashionable society in which, by her own account, she was thought uncouth, methodistical, and 'a strange, old-fashioned, humdrum creature' (Barbauld, 5.40). Her two sons, Henry and Robert, died young, but her daughter Elizabeth survived to marry, in 1747, Francis Palmer of Palmerston, co. Mayo, into whose family the Rush estate eventually passed. Little trace of the scenes described in her letters now survives: the house was devastated by fire in the following century, and its grandiose Victorian successor, Kenure House, was demolished in 1973. A coastal grotto or 'shell house' built by Lady Echlin in 1755–6, and engraved with verses composed for the occasion by the novelist Samuel Richardson, is marked on Rocque's 1759 map of co. Dublin, and has recently been discovered in use as a cattle pen.

It is from her association with Richardson, begun in 1753 through the grudging offices of Lady Bradshaigh, that Lady Echlin's reputation now derives. Until Richardson's death in 1761 the two corresponded regularly on subjects including the alternative ending to *Clarissa* which Lady Echlin seems to have written at her sister's Lancashire house in the winter of 1748–9 (when the novel's final instalment was published), and which she at last sent to Richardson six years later. Several of her letters, including picturesque accounts of Villa Russa (Rush House) and Rock-savage (the grotto), appeared in Barbauld's *Correspondence of Samuel Richardson* (1804), but the alternative ending remained unpublished until 1982. Presented with an odd mixture of self-deprecation and assertiveness—the ending is 'a jumble of ill-connected thoughts … badly told', but sets right the original 'in several material points, which I presume to think faulty' (E. Echlin, 174, 172)—it is a providentialist attempt to evade the tragic logic of *Clarissa*, written in the sentimental mode of the early Sarah Fielding, but lightened by comic touches. The novel's two protagonists still die, but Clarissa's rape is averted and Lovelace turns penitent; Bella marries 'a dirty, stinking, cross-leg'd prick-louse' named Mr Cabbage (ibid., 162–3).

Sir Robert Echlin died on 13 May 1757 and was buried at nearby Lusk, where his tomb bears a memorial inscription adapted by Lady Echlin from Pope's epitaphs on Mrs Corbett and Elijah Fenton. From 1759 Lady Echlin lived mainly in England. A year later she was still describing herself to Richardson (whom she had yet to meet) as 'the most unfashionable plain country body you can imagine' (Barbauld, 5.100), but the unflattering picture presented by Barbauld's selections and character sketch of 1804 was contested in the *Gentleman's Magazine* by Lady Echlin's granddaughter Elizabeth Budworth (née Palmer), who stressed her polite accomplishments, charitable works, and religious orthodoxy. At the time of her death she was

living at Bellingham Lodge, on the edge of Lady Bradshaigh's Lancashire estate, Haigh Hall. She was interred in the Bradshaigh family vault at All Saints, Wigan, on 9 July 1782.   THOMAS KEYMER

Sources T. C. D. Eaves and B. D. Kimpel, *Samuel Richardson: a biography* (1971) • *The correspondence of Samuel Richardson*, ed. A. L. Barbauld, 6 vols. (1804) • V&A NAL, Forster Library, Richardson papers • parish register, Croston, Lancashire, 1704 [birth] • parish register, All Saints, Wigan, Lancashire, 1782 [burial] • *Selected letters of Samuel Richardson*, ed. J. Carroll (1964) • *GM*, 1st ser., 53 (1783) • *GM*, 1st ser., 74 (1804), 899–900 • *GM*, 1st ser., 83/2 (1813), 307 • *VCH Lancashire* • L. Naylor, 'Bellingham, Alan', HoP, *Commons*, 1.617–18 • J. R. Echlin, *Genealogical memoirs of the Echlin family*, 2nd edn (privately printed, Edinburgh, [1882]) • E. Echlin, *An alternative ending to Richardson's 'Clarissa'*, ed. D. Daphinoff (1982) • A. D. Bagot, *Levens Hall* [1963] • GEC, *Peerage* • Burke, *Peerage* (1840) • J. Foster, ed., *Pedigrees recorded at the herald's visitations of the counties of Cumberland and Westmorland* (1891) [c.1891] • J. Nicolson and R. Burn, *The history and antiquities of the counties of Westmorland and Cumberland*, 2 vols. (1777) • W. P. Baildon, ed., *The records of the Honorable Society of Lincoln's Inn: admissions*, 2 vols. (1896) • A. L. Reade, 'Samuel Richardson and his family circle [pt 4]', *N&Q*, 12th ser., 11 (1922), 383–6 • J. Todd, ed., *A dictionary of British and American women writers, 1660–1800* (1984) • memorial inscription, tomb of Sir Robert Echlin, co. Dublin, Lusk • private information (2004) [E. A. Coyle, chairman, Skerries Local History Society] • M. Bence-Joyce, *A guide to Irish country houses* (1988) • *Evening Press* (3 June 1963) • *Irish Times* (8 Dec 1972)

Echlin, Robert (1576–1635), Church of Ireland bishop of Down and Connor, was the second of three sons of Henry Echlin, laird of Pittadro in Fife (who was in Edinburgh Castle during the famous siege of 1573), and Grizel, daughter of Robert Colvile of Cleish, Kinross. He studied at the University of St Andrews, where in May 1596 he received the degree of MA. In 1601 he was inducted by the presbytery of Dunfermline in the Second Congregation of Inverkeithing, on the coast of his native county. Not much is known of his ministry here. John Forbes mentioned that on 9 January 1606 Echlin visited the ministers imprisoned at Blackness, and on 22 September of that year the Scottish council obtained a £1000 caution from James Wode of Dunune when it ordered Andrew Wode 'not to harm' Echlin (*Reg. PCS*, 7.654). During his incumbency of Inverkeithing, Echlin married Jane, daughter of James Seton of Latrisse. They had two sons, John and Hugh, and four daughters.

On 4 March 1613 Echlin was appointed to the bishopric of Down and Connor, and on 18 May was made a free denizen of Ireland. That month he also attended the Irish parliament. According to George Crawfurd, it was the king himself who ordered the appointment on the grounds of the 'merit' of Echlin's father (Crawfurd, 14). Several Scots were appointed to Ulster bishoprics at this time, as many of their countrymen were settling in the province. Echlin succeeded another Scot, James Dundas, who was appointed in June 1612 but died within a year of his appointment. The property of the diocese had been much depleted when Dundas acquired it, and he worsened rather than improved the situation during his short tenure. Therefore Echlin went to discuss the 'decayed state of his diocese' with the king, who in July 1616 ordered the lord deputy to set up a commission to examine the matter and to restore to the bishop 'all lands detained from the said bishopric, or fraudulently granted away' (*CSP Ire.*, 1615–25, 129–30). Echlin, however, by the end of his life, was also being accused of alienating church property. He received permission in 1618 to hold *in commendam* the precentorship of his cathedral 'by reason of the great waste which had been made in the revenues of the see', exchanging it for the treasurership in the following year (Cotton, 3.261). A return of the state of his diocese, which he drew up in 1622, is preserved among the manuscripts of Trinity College, Dublin.

The main interest of Echlin's life arises from his connection with the Scottish nonconformist ministers of the north of Ireland, the first of whom, Edward Brice, settled in co. Antrim almost contemporaneously with the bishop's arrival, and was, along with other nonconformist clergy of that day, received and acknowledged by the bishop, who in 1619 gave him the prebend of Kilroot. In 1623 another of their number, Robert Blair, arrived in the country. According to his account, although he plainly apprised the bishop of his aversion both to episcopacy and the prayer book, Echlin kindly said:

> I hear good of you, and will impose no conditions on you; I am old, and can teach you ceremonies, and you can teach me substance. Only I must ordain you, else neither I nor you can answer the law, nor brook the land.

Blair answered that such an ordination would be against his principles, to which Echlin replied:

> whatever you account of Episcopacy, yet I know you account a presbytery to have divine warrant; will you not receive ordination from Mr. Cunningham and the adjacent brethren, and let me come in among them in no other relation than a presbyter?

Blair concurred, and in this way he was ordained (*Life of Robert Blair*, 58–9).

Blair asserted that Echlin began to turn against the nonconformist ministers in 1626, initially in a covert way, but by 1631 openly. This hostility may have been less his own policy than one thrust upon him. In September 1631 the dean of Down, Henry Leslie, wrote to a minister in Edinburgh reporting that, though the bishop opposed such ministers, he was too weak in dealing with them, and he asked his correspondent to report the matter to William Laud. By that time Echlin had begun proceedings to depose Blair and John Livingston, another minister with similar attitudes, but they delayed the process, first by leaving Ireland without licence, and subsequently by gaining the support of Archbishop Ussher. In April 1632 Echlin went to Dublin to defend himself against the charge of leniency, where, contrary to Blair's account, he claimed that the minister had shown no sign of nonconformity when ordained. Blair appealed to the king, but by 1634, after an open debate between him and Echlin, the latter finally succeeded in deposing the two ministers. Nevertheless, in 1635, after the bishop's death, Laud stated that he believed that Echlin had not acted out of conviction, but in order to save his reputation. Blair, on his part,

claimed, on the basis of a report from the attending physician at Echlin's death, that he died with a guilty conscience. Echlin died on 17 July 1635 at The Abbacy, a house which he had built for himself at Ardquin, near Portaferry, co. Down, and was buried at Ballyphilip close by.

THOMAS HAMILTON, *rev.* M. PERCEVAL-MAXWELL

Sources J. R. Echlin, *Genealogical memoirs of the Echlin family*, 2nd edn (privately printed, Edinburgh, [1882]) · G. Crawfurd, *Memoirs of the ancient familie of the Echlins of Pittadro, in the county of Fyfe, in Scotland, now transplanted to Ireland* (1747) · *The life of Mr Robert Blair ... containing his autobiography*, ed. T. M'Crie, Wodrow Society, 11 (1848) · H. Cotton, *Fasti ecclesiae Hibernicae*, 3 (1849) · *CSP Ire.*, 1611–47 · J. S. Reid and W. D. Killen, *History of the Presbyterian church in Ireland*, new edn, 1 (1867) · *Report on the manuscripts of the late Reginald Rawdon Hastings*, 4 vols., HMC, 78 (1928–47), vol. 4 · J. Forbes, *Certaine records touching the estate of the kirk in the years MDCV & MDCVI*, ed. D. Laing and J. Anderson, Wodrow Society, 19 (1846) · *The works of the most reverend father in God, William Laud*, ed. J. Bliss and W. Scott, 7 vols. (1847–60), vols. 2–3 · *Fasti Scot.*, new edn, vol. 5 · *Reg. PCS*, 1st ser., vol. 7 · M. Perceval-Maxwell, *Scottish migration to Ulster in the reign of James I* (1973)

Wealth at death see est. at £400–£500 p.a. in 1635: Sept 1629, *CSP Ire.*, 1625–32, 481; Aug 1635, Hastings MSS, 4.69

Eckenstein, Lina Dorina Johanna (1857–1931), feminist polymath and cultural historian, was born on 23 September 1857 at 17 St George's Villas, Islington, London, the daughter of Frederick Gottlieb Eckenstein, a German businessman, and his wife, Julie Amalie Antonia Helmke. No trace of her education in England has been found, so it is likely that she was educated in Germany and Switzerland; it is improbable that she acquired her proficiency in French, German, and Italian, classical and medieval Latin, Middle High German, Middle English, and classical and medieval European history entirely unaided. In 1881 she was living at her parents' home in Islington.

The first reference to Lina Eckenstein's activities is found in the manuscript record made by her friend Maria Sharpe of her time with the Men and Women's Club (1885–9). The club had been founded by Karl Pearson for a few 'middle class radical-liberals, socialists and feminists ... to talk about sex' (Walkowitz, 57). In 1888 Eckenstein, whose membership of the club was supported by Olive Schreiner, presented papers entitled 'Sexual relations among the Romans' and 'Sexual relations during the Reformation period in Switzerland', having already taken up a feminist stance the previous year in the club's discussions on state regulation of prostitution. In 1889 she accompanied Maria Sharpe on a pilgrimage to Ibsen's Norway.

Herself a 'new woman', strong-faced as well as 'strong-minded', Lina Eckenstein is an illuminating example of what the new woman did next—once she was no longer 'new'. First she earned a little money teaching, translating, proof-reading, indexing, and being a research assistant to more eminent male scholars while she herself researched and wrote her ambitious cultural study *Woman under monasticism: chapters on saint-lore and convent life, 500–1500 AD*, published by Cambridge University Press in 1896. Citing a vast range of translated materials from medieval

France, Sweden, Britain, and Germany, she postulated that the 'right to self-development and social responsibility which the woman of to-day so persistently asks for, is in many ways analogous to the right which the convent secured to womankind a thousand years ago' (preface), while also appreciating that it was, eventually, to be in the lands of the Reformation 'that the modern movement for women's education [arose]' (conclusion).

In the late 1890s Lina Eckenstein became German governess to Margery Corbett, later Dame Margery Corbett Ashby, who became her lifelong friend as well as a leading suffragist and Liberal advocate of disarmament. In 1902 Eckenstein published her detailed account of the life and art of Albrecht Dürer and *Through the Casentino*, a record of her tramp, knapsack on back, through the upper valley of the Arno. During 1903 to 1906 she was occupied in the startlingly different world of Egyptology, as she joined Flinders Petrie and his wife Hilda—another close friend—on several important archaeological digs. She 'took charge of the registration, mending and storing of objects and helped in the general running of the camp' at Abydos, Sethos, Saqqara, El Shatt, and Serabit (Drower, 268). At one testing moment, when village hooligans were reported to be out to destroy the excavation in the dark, 'Miss Eckenstein, always enterprising … joined hands and danced with a great variety of fancy steps all the way from the camp to the dig' with Hilda Petrie and Margaret Murray in the moonlight to scare away the men (Murray, 116). At the age of forty-eight she rode with Hilda Petrie and an Egyptian desert tracker on camel-back to Sinai, across rough mountain country and red sandstone gorges, armed with whip, revolver, and water bottle. Eckenstein later turned her archaeology into historical and imaginative reconstruction in her article 'The moon cult in Sinai' (1911), *A History of Sinai* (1921), and her strange fable of Moses's youth under the pharaohs, *Tutankh-aten* (1924). Fifty years before the Opies' authoritative work, she published her pioneering *Comparative Studies in Nursery Rhymes* (1906), triggered by her sight of a cult scene in the temple of King Sety that seemed to anticipate 'The Death and Burial of Cock Robin' 3000 years later.

Between 1908 and 1910 Eckenstein's antiquarian work gave way to the contemporary struggle for equal citizenship, as she contributed articles for the Women's Franchise League and gave public lectures on the history of the changing status of women. In 1920, at the International Women's Suffrage Alliance congress at Geneva, she helped Margery Corbett Ashby with translation of the congress proceedings from and into English, French, German, and Italian. She was interested that the international women's movement should still be urging the endowment of motherhood and the abolition of state regulation of vice—questions discussed over thirty years earlier in the Men and Women's Club.

Despite suffering from ill health, Lina Eckenstein continued to be intellectually vigorous to the end. She wrote the drafts of two works published posthumously—*A Spell of Words: Studies in Language Bearing on Custom* (1932) and *The*

Women of Early Christianity (1935) about the first women disciples, including 'those who cut off their hair and, assuming the garb of a man, went forth devoting themselves to the cure of bodies and souls' (p. xiv). Herself a lifelong sceptic, she focused on the contribution made by Christianity to humanism and feminism. She died from coma and exhaustion, together with chronic cystitis, at her home, The Cell, Little Hampden, Great Missenden, Buckinghamshire, on 4 May 1931. She was unmarried. Her friend from the Men and Women's Club days, the pioneering doctor Ethel Williams, wrote of her: 'It is easy for the feminist movement to appraise what it owes to its executive and political leaders; it is more difficult to realize what it owes to its scholars and philosophers' (*Woman's Leader*). SYBIL OLDFIELD

Sources E. Williams, *Woman's Leader* (29 May 1931) · M. Sharpe [M. Pearson], autobiography, c.1890, UCL, Pearson MSS, 10/1 · J. Walkowitz, 'Science, feminism and romance: the Men and Women's Club, 1885–1889', *History Workshop Journal*, 21 (1986), 36–59 · M. Drower, *Flinders Petrie: a life in archaeology* (1995) · H. Petrie, 'On camel-back in Sinai', *The Queen* (25 Nov 1905) · M. Murray, *My first hundred years* (1963) · b. cert. · census returns, 1881 · d. cert.
Archives UCL, Pearson and Sharpe papers, MSS and rare books
Likenesses photographs, 1865–1920, UCL, Pearson Papers
Wealth at death £9499 6s. 5d.: probate, 15 July 1931, CGPLA Eng. & Wales

Eckersley, Peter Pendleton (1892–1963), broadcasting engineer, was born on 6 January 1892 in Puebla, Mexico, the third son, and the third and youngest child, of (William) Alfred Eckersley, a railway engineer, and his wife, Rachel, daughter of Thomas Henry *Huxley, physiologist. Eckersley's elder brother was the physicist and engineer Thomas Lydwell *Eckersley. Educated at Bedales School, he was apprenticed with the Manchester firm of Mather and Platt before entering Manchester Municipal College of Technology in 1912. He graduated with a certificate of electrical engineering in 1915, and on 17 March 1917 married Stella (b. 1894/5), daughter of Julian Charles Grove, tea merchant, son of Sir George Grove, writer on music; they had two sons and one daughter.

Peter had become interested in wireless and the work of Marconi while at Bedales, and he served with the Royal Flying Corps as a wireless equipment officer from 1915 to 1918, mainly in Egypt and at Salonika, and was then sent to the Wireless Experimental Station at Biggin Hill. In 1919 he joined Marconi's Wireless Telegraph Company as head of the experimental section of its designs department. He worked at Writtle, near Chelmsford, where he was the leader of an able, if unconventional, team that provided regular transmissions of programmes for radio amateurs at the request of the Radio Society of Great Britain.

A lively and energetic character, enjoying publicity and recognized by his contemporaries as a 'personality', Eckersley did more than any other person to lay the technical foundation of broadcasting in Britain. In 1923 he was hired personally by John Reith as chief engineer of the recently formed British Broadcasting Company, staying in the post until 1929, by which time it had become a public corporation. Eckersley was fully in charge of the 'spreading of the service', and of converting his own idea of a regional plan for radio transmission into a reality. He was highly successful, both in negotiating behind the scenes with the Post Office and in informing and interesting listeners in the implications for them—such as a choice of programmes—of developing communications technology. He also played a prominent part in the first international meetings on wavelength allocation and in the preparations for empire broadcasting.

The high point of Eckersley's BBC career was the opening in 1929 of the first dual transmitter high-power station in Brookman's Park, north of London. It had been conceived of in 1927, but by the time of its delayed opening, Eckersley had been compelled to leave the corporation, after a painful divorce earlier in 1929. The parting with Reith, who was temperamentally completely different from him and who had been a friend as well as a colleague, was difficult for both men. On resigning from the BBC Eckersley received a gratuity, and stayed on as a consultant until the beginning of October 1929. He also had lucrative consultancies with the Marconi Company and His Master's Voice, part of the Radio Corporation of America. Despite these political and financial difficulties, Eckersley continued throughout the 1930s to develop his often original ideas on communications technology, regarding himself as 'an inventor of mechanisms to serve ideas'. Although never attracted by television, he was fascinated by the possibilities of cable broadcasting. In 1931 he was one of the founders of Rediffusion; the company name was suggested by him. In 1932 Eckersley went briefly to Australia to advise on the setting up of a national broadcasting organization. He was also interested in radio advertising. Some of his ideas were set out in his only book, *The Power behind the Microphone* (1941), which also charted, albeit selectively, his own experience.

Eckersley's second wife, whom he married on 25 October 1930, was Frances Dorothy (b. 1894), divorced wife of Edward Thomas Clark and daughter of Lieutenant-Colonel Arthur James Stephen, a member of the distinguished Stephen family. The new marriage had political, and later ideological, overtones. Eckersley joined Oswald Mosley's new party in 1931, and from 1935 they spent each summer holiday in Germany where they admired the progress that Germany was making under national socialism. When war was declared in 1939 Dorothy and the son of her first marriage remained in Germany, where they earned a living broadcasting in English on German radio the bulletins prepared for them. Eckersley himself blamed Britain for declaring war in 1939 and for opposing Hitler, and British intelligence kept a sizeable dossier on him. He had declared himself bankrupt in 1939.

Eckersley's war-time years were frustrating—he called them 'shabby'—even when his security problems became less serious, and on one occasion he attempted suicide. Yet he remained innovatory in his attitudes to radio and set out to exploit his 'talking telephone'. In 1943 he joined with Belgian and Polish colleagues in exile to devise a long-wave public service European radio network. 'Electromagnetic waves know no frontiers', they explained. 'Broadcasting symbolises through the ether the unity of nations.'

His last bachelor years after 1945 were more tranquil. He protected Dorothy when, having been arrested by the British army, she was brought back to London in 1945 to face trial and imprisonment in Holloway, but the marriage had long been dead. By 1961 the BBC was beginning to acknowledge the major contribution he had made to its early history; Eckersley was photographed with Reith and Hugh Greene, then BBC director-general, at the Institution of Electrical Engineers, on the occasion of the publication of the first volume of the corporation's history. His last journey was to try to market his talking telephone in the Cameroons. He died at the West London Hospital, Hammersmith, on 18 March 1963, leaving just enough money to pay his outstanding debts.

ASA BRIGGS, *rev.*

Sources A. Briggs, *The history of broadcasting in the United Kingdom*, 1–2 (1961–5); [rev. edn] (1995) · *WWW* · *The Times* (19 March 1963), 15c · J. H. Badley, *The Times* (22 March 1963), 15e · *The Times* (2 Nov 1945), 2c · *The Times* (10 Nov 1945), 2c · *The Times* (15 Nov 1945), 2c · m. certs. · d. cert.
Likenesses group portrait, photograph, *c.*1924, Hult. Arch. · O. Edis, photograph (as a young man), NPG
Wealth at death £1378 13s. 4d.: probate, 27 May 1963, *CGPLA Eng. & Wales*

Eckersley, Thomas [Tom] (1914–1997), poster artist and design teacher, was born on 30 September 1914, in Newton-le-Willows, and baptized at Lowton, Lancashire, the younger son of John Eckersley (1886–1950), Methodist minister, and his wife, Eunice Hilton (1888–1958). He was educated at Lord's College, Bolton, and then went at his mother's suggestion to Salford School of Art, where his diligence won him the Heywood medal for best student. He next took the risky step of setting off for London with his fellow student Eric Lombers, intending to find whatever work could be got by offering their ideas to advertising agencies such as W. S. Crawford and to firms such as Austin Reed, Shell, and London Transport. The gamble paid off: poster jobs from these important sources came their way and they established themselves as freelance partners, signing their joint work 'Eckersley-Lombers'. In 1935 he married Daisy Brown, *née* Mudge (1918–1986), a young Sunday school teacher whom he had met at a prayer meeting in the Euston Road within hours of his first arriving in London, when she was only seventeen; they had three sons.

The war separated Eckersley and Lombers. Eckersley worked in the RAF first as a cartographer and then in its publicity unit, managing improbably to do his work from home. This wartime work included posters for the Post Office and one for the Ministry of Food, of an elephant eating lettuce over the slogan 'Don't forget—green vegetables keep you fit'. After the war Eckersley resumed the busy but undramatic life of a freelance artist. He did not follow the French studio practice of his hero A. M.

Cassandre, who worked surrounded by studio apprentices; apart from his early working partnership with Lombers, only briefly revived after the war, he worked alone. He was a natural loner: an artist-craftsman reliant on his own skills and ideas rather than on the resources and back-up of a team, avoiding the wider responsibilities eagerly shouldered by later generations of designers who joined forces to form blockbuster-scale design groups in order to tackle more complicated but also duller corporate work. He was also single-minded in sticking to his last: throughout his life, apart from some early illustrations for the *Radio Times* and two children's books about animals, one of them written by his first wife, he designed only posters. He was apparently not even much interested in drawing and painting, or indeed in typography, outside the needs of a poster. But his poster work was clever, resourceful, ingenious, and recognizable. The work, like the man, had a certain innocence, a childlike simplicity: nothing in it was fraught, sinister, or deep; and at his chosen job he was a star.

Eckersley's ideas were simple, straightforward, throughout his life. For Gillette the heads of two goats nose-to-nose, one bearded and the other clean-shaven; another poster in the series shows a couple of pandas, one bristly. For the more ambitious *Scientists Prefer Shell* a chemist's flask and beaker against a cross-section of rock strata, a fluffy cloud, four distant planets. For an anti-leprosy poster, the silhouette of a black child's head with the continents brain-like within the cranium. Because the ideas behind Eckersley's posters were themselves so simple, one hardly notices how basic were his techniques compared with those of his close contemporaries. Unlike F. H. K. Henrion he used almost no photographs; unlike Abram Games no virtuoso airbrush; unlike Hans Schleger (Zero), some of whose posters are virtually easel paintings, no perspective and no third dimension, no recession, and no depth. Eckersley preferred areas of flat colour, often little more than silhouettes, their hard edges softened if necessary by stippling with a stencil brush. The images were not pictorial—they were too simplified for that—but they were bold and realistic but quickly recognizable: a child would understand what they meant straight away.

This spare graphic manner worked as well with an abstract idea—a diagram or a symbol—as with a pictorial one. In Eckersley's poster for the extension of the underground to Heathrow, where the horizontal bar of the London Transport symbol doubles as part of the tube map, two famous earlier graphic icons are combined into one. His best posters have become classics, collectors' pieces. Yet his most widely seen design, made for a less ephemeral purpose than the others, has survived him to this day, as the Concorde platform panels at Heathrow underground station.

Eckersley's work was individual and always what is currently called 'accessible'—meaning comprehensible and intelligible to a wide public. This early work occasionally had a sweetness and a humour which some find engaging, others sentimental and even cloying: on an early poster for winter-grade Shell, a warmly jacketed scottie dog trots fetchingly along beside a walking pair of gumboots. This winsome quality might have endeared him to people when he was struggling to gain recognition but it has not worn as well as his later clarity. Later, as he grew more experienced, the posters grew starker and more economical. In all of them there was a skilful balance between image and space: the artist skilfully left plenty of empty space so that they never looked crowded or filled-up like a well-stocked drawer. The typography too was spare and simple, though the artist, more intent on the image than the words, is said on occasion to have let a friend cope with the task of laying the text out.

But while the ideas were simple and even austere, the colours—while always appropriate—were subtle and even sensuous. For a London Transport Museum poster, a steam locomotive is seen head-on, its smokestack, boiler, and buffers reduced to flat geometrical silhouettes in black and blue-grey, their starkness relieved by a rectangle of paler colours overlaid quite arbitrarily over the red footplate. For the Imperial War Museum, the camouflaged head of a soldier, the grey-green profile beneath a black helmet covered with leaves of four different and beautiful greens, all in flat hard-edged colours against a white background.

Eckersley's work is rooted in a popular poster tradition that in his youth must have seemed set to go on for ever: in the posters of Toulouse-Lautrec and the Beggarstaffs, in his more recent predecessors Tom Purvis (*Skegness is so Bracing*), in John Gilroy (*Guinness for Strength*), and in his two great contemporary heroes, the Parisian Cassandre and the American visitor Edward McKnight Kauffer. The war brought its new influx of cosmopolitan talents, such people as Hans Schleger, George Him, Henri Henrion, to startle and enrich the native scene; and Eckersley, not merely English but northern provincial at that, made friends with these newcomers, gained new horizons from the shake-up, and built on it in the public-spirited and united atmosphere of the war years.

After the war, however, although Eckersley remained busy and in demand, the climate for posters and their designers began to change. Until then, poster printers had little truck with photography; poster designs, even of photographs themselves, had been laboriously redrawn by hand by lithography artists. But on the poster hoardings of the 1950s, well-printed colour photographs, well art-directed and laid out, began to replace drawn or painted images and to achieve the kind of vigour and brilliance that had previously been exclusively the poster artists' preserve. At the same time, the primacy of the hoardings was giving way as commercial television began to supplant posters as the most conspicuous advertising medium. And advertising itself was changing: under new and supposedly harder-nosed commercial pressures, even a trail-blazing firm like Shell lost its old confidence and distinction, ditching its splendid pre-war painted posters in favour of comic photographs of television 'personalities'. From this point on, designers could still produce good posters on demand but hardly anyone could any longer specialize in them; and while a resilient artist like Eckersley could still hang on to some tough commercial clients like Gillette and Guinness, more of his work was now for more limited and lower-profile public service purposes: for road safety, for the Royal Society for the Prevention of Accidents, worthy but earnest causes lightly tinged with piety. He remained a big fish but in a rapidly shrinking pond.

At this point Eckersley, like many other good designers, turned to teaching. For twenty years he was head of the department of design at the London College of Printing at the Elephant and Castle, always as much a school of design as of printing. He was a teacher of the amiable kind: much loved, skilled, and dedicated, shrewd enough to pick good assistants, his example as influential as his advice. One of his more touching posters, made for a show of his students' work, shows a flower bud bursting. Though he could be sharp with lazy students who sought refuge in design clichés, he was remembered with respect and affection by his ex-students and his staff, many of whom became well-known designers themselves. His second marriage, in 1966, was to the painter Mary Kessell (d. 1983), who had served as a war artist and had been badly shaken by having to make drawings of the German death camps in 1945. She had also had a close and extended association lasting twelve years with Kenneth Clark, a relationship of which Clark later made no mention. Public spiritedly, Eckersley served also on the National Council for Academic Awards, where he was brought up short by unfamiliar concepts: 'intellectual rigour—what's that?' But he did not let teaching submerge his own work, believing that any teacher worth his salt had to go on designing too, and in 1976 he took early retirement so as to pursue his own work full-time. This included some striking posters for the World Wildlife Fund and for UNICEF.

Eckersley's posters never lacked admirers, being both generally popular and also respected by his peers. He was appointed OBE in 1948, elected a member of AGI (Alliance Graphique Internationale) in 1952, and an RDI (Royal Designer for Industry) in 1963; in 1990 he was awarded the Chartered Society of Designers' medal. His work was widely and internationally reproduced, written up, and exhibited; there were notable retrospective exhibitions at the London Transport Museum in 1986 and at the London Institute in 1997, and in 1981 at the British Gallery at Yale University.

In appearance Eckersley was gentle, in manner uncomplicated, diffident, and unassertive, though he could be fierce in defence of aspects of design he cared about. He was not an intellectual, or politically minded; his main outside interest was in cricket and his pleasure was in his friends. His personal life was full and happy. His last studio and flat were in Belsize Park Gardens, Hampstead; photographs show him in this studio against a background of posters, in tweeds or a pullover, his face long and narrow, his expression thoughtful and placid, serious but not anxious, determined and quietly confident rather than triumphantly assertive.

Eckersley's last years were clouded by the onset of Alzheimer's disease, but despite a failing memory he remained sociable and communicative and fond of the company of women, if increasingly vague as to who precisely they were. He died of pneumonia in London on 4 August 1997 and was cremated on 12 August 1997 at Finchley crematorium. He was survived by two of his three sons. Eckersley was the last full-time British poster designer. Over a long working life he created a sustained series of posters, simple and straightforward, equally effective whether for commercial or public service clients, yet always recognizably his own. These posters, popular, clean, and economical in design, in touch with the trends then current, neither flamboyant nor assertively avant-garde, were among the best of their time. He survived even as the demand for good posters withered, to become the last in the line of distinguished poster artists to devote himself exclusively to this now vanished skill.

David Gentleman

Sources F. H. K. Henrion, *AGI annals: Alliance graphique internationale, 1952–1987* (Zürich and Tokyo, 1989) · K. Cato, ed., *First choice: the world's leading graphic designers select the best of their work* (Tokyo, 1989) · R. de Harak, ed., *Posters by members of the Alliance Graphique Internationale, 1960–1985* (New York, 1985) · *Tom Eckersley, OBE, RDI, AGI: his graphic work* (London College of Printing, 1994) · personal knowledge (2004) · private information (2004)
Archives IWM · London College of Printing, London · London Transport Museum · Museum of Modern Art, New York · RSA, Archive of Royal Designers for Industry · V&A
Likenesses G. DeRose, oils · portraits; exh. London College of Printing, *c.*1962 ('Homage to Tom' exhibition)

Eckersley, Thomas Lydwell (1886–1959), theoretical physicist and engineer, was born at 4 Marlborough Place, Marylebone, London, on 27 December 1886, the second son of (William) Alfred Eckersley, a railway engineer, and his wife, Rachel, a daughter of T. H. *Huxley, in whose house Eckersley was born. He was educated at Bedales School between the ages of eleven and fifteen, after which he went, rather younger than most undergraduates, to University College, London, where he obtained third-class honours in engineering (1908). He then worked at the National Physical Laboratory until 1910, when he went to Trinity College, Cambridge, to read mathematics. In 1911 he was listed as being successful in part two of the tripos, but as an 'advanced student' he was not eligible for the award of a class. In 1912, after the statutory lapse of one year, he took his BA. He then spent some time in the Cavendish Laboratory but, after an unsuccessful attempt to gain a Trinity fellowship, he left Cambridge and joined the Egyptian government survey as an inspector (1913–14). When war started he took a commission in the Royal Engineers and worked on problems of wireless telegraphy. By the time the war ended he had acquired a deep interest in problems of radio wave propagation and in 1919 he joined Marconi's Wireless Telegraph Company, Ltd, as a theoretical research engineer. The remainder of his career was spent with this company.

On 14 April 1920 he married Eva Amelia, daughter of Barry *Pain, the author; they had one son and two daughters.

Although Eckersley studied engineering at London University and worked on experimental problems at the National Physical Laboratory and in the Cavendish Laboratory, he came to realize that his real interest was in theoretical work; that was where he found that he could make original contributions, first during the war and later with the Marconi Company. While serving with the wireless intelligence branch of the Royal Engineers in Egypt and Salonika he was concerned with the problem of locating enemy radio stations by measuring the direction of arrival of the waves which they radiated. In this work he came to realize that waves reflected downwards from the Heaviside layer could interfere with the proper behaviour of the direction-finding equipment, and he started to consider the mechanism of these reflections. It was problems of this kind which occupied most of his attention for the rest of his life.

He developed his ideas in a number of well-known papers presented mainly to the Institution of Electrical Engineers. In particular he showed how to evaluate the details of the reflection by a 'phase integral' method, and he emphasized the importance of waves scattered by irregularities in the ionosphere. He read widely in many branches of mathematical physics, and much of his work on radio waves was closely parallel to similar work being done in a rapidly developing field. The title of one of his papers, 'On the connection between the ray theory of electric waves and dynamics', shows how he drew on his wide knowledge of physical theory to discuss wave propagation in terms of other concepts.

Although Eckersley was predominantly a theoretician, he led and inspired a small team of experimental workers, and he was delighted to take part in observations with them at all times of day or night. If a line of research was not going well it was his habit to say 'Let's try a damn fool experiment' and he was frequently rewarded with some new insight into the mechanism of radio wave propagation.

Eckersley's ability was widely recognized. He was a much valued member of the Union Radio Scientifique Internationale and of the Comité Consultative Internationale de Radio, whose assemblies he attended regularly. He was elected FRS in 1938, and was awarded the Faraday medal of the Institution of Electrical Engineers in 1951. For each of his major papers in the *Proceedings* of the institution he received a premium. His advice was of importance to the Marconi Company, particularly in the development of their direction-finding apparatus and their long-distance short-wave communication links.

Eckersley had such originality that he tended to see his theories in his own way and never troubled to relate them to other people's ways of thought. If one looks back at Eckersley's work it is a matter of surprise that some of it, particularly that concerned with direction-finding errors and with the scattering of radio waves from the ionosphere, should have been so little appreciated when it was written. If he had taken more pains to make his work readable by others who were thinking about the same problems, it is probable that it would have been better appreciated during his lifetime.

When Eckersley retired from the Marconi Company in 1946 he was already suffering from multiple sclerosis and, although he continued, as a consultant to the company, to do theoretical work at his home, Weatheroak, Danbury, in Essex, the disease pursued its inevitable course and in his later years he was almost completely helpless. He died at Manor House, Danbury, on 15 February 1959. His elder brother, Roger Huxley Eckersley, who was director of programmes (1924–30), assistant controller (1930–39), and chief censor (1939–45) of the BBC, had died in 1955. His younger brother, Peter Pendleton *Eckersley, who died in 1963, was chief engineer to the BBC from 1923 to 1929.

J. A. RATCLIFFE, *rev.*

Sources J. A. Ratcliffe, *Memoirs FRS*, 5 (1959), 69–74 · *Nature*, 184 (1959), 149 · personal knowledge (1971) [J. A. Ratcliffe] · private information (1971) [J. A. Ratcliffe] · *The Engineer* (20 Feb 1959), 301 · *Engineering* (27 Feb 1959), 260 · *ILN* (28 Feb 1959), 353 · *The Times* (17 Feb 1959), 12d
Archives Inst. EE, notebooks
Likenesses W. Stoneman, photograph, 1938, NPG · photograph?, repro. in Ratcliffe, *Memoirs FRS* · photograph?, repro. in *Engineering* · photograph?, repro. in *ILN*
Wealth at death £10,749 11s. 10d.: probate, 23 Sept 1959, *CGPLA Eng. & Wales*

Eckford, Henry (1775–1832), naval architect and shipbuilder, was born on 12 March 1775 at Kilwinning, in Ayrshire, Scotland, the son of John Eckford and his wife, Janet Black. At the age of sixteen, in 1791, he went to Canada and began to study the principles and practice of ship design in the Quebec yard of his uncle John Black. After five years he moved to New York where he soon found work in a shipyard. He married, on 13 April 1799, Marion, daughter of Joseph and Miriam Bedell, and in the following year set up his own shipyard.

Eckford's ships came to be known for their strength and speed, and after the outbreak of war in 1812 he built a number of notable US Navy warships, being appointed naval constructor at the Brooklyn navy yard in 1817. He resigned three years later and resumed work in his own yard, building the *Robert Fulton* which made the first successful seagoing voyage by steam power from New York to New Orleans and Havana in 1822. He became interested in politics and made some influential friends, two of whom married his daughters. In 1825 the failure of an insurance company lost him much of his fortune, and three years later personal tragedy followed when three of his children died. The last ship he built was a corvette in which he sailed to Europe in 1831. The ship was bought by the sultan of Turkey who put Eckford in charge of the imperial naval shipyard, but in the following year he fell ill and died at Constantinople, on 12 November 1832. His body was returned to the United States in a barrel of spirits.

RONALD M. BIRSE

Sources W. B. Shaw, 'Eckford, Henry', *DAB* · R. Turner and S. L. Goulden, eds., *Great engineers and pioneers in technology*, 1 (1981)
Likenesses portrait, Long Island Historical Society · portrait, NYPL, New York; repro. in Turner and Goulden, eds., *Great engineers and pioneers*

Ecroyd, William Farrer (1827–1915), worsted manufacturer and politician, was born on 14 July 1827, at Lomeshaye, near Burnley, Lancashire, the first of the four children of William Ecroyd (1796–1876), worsted spinner, and his second wife, Margaret (1797–1835), the eldest daughter of William Farrer, a farmer at Wythmoor, Kendal, and his wife, Mary. Yeomen in origin (their ancestry was traced back to the fourteenth century by Ecroyd's second son, the historian William *Farrer), the Ecroyds became members of the Society of Friends in the 1680s. They added further small estates to their existing property in the early eighteenth century, and in 1747 set up the worsted spinning and weaving firm at Edgend, moving in 1780 to Lomeshaye, where the family was to continue to run the firm until 1933.

Educated at Lower Bank Academy, Blackburn, Ecroyd went on in 1837 to the Quaker Ackworth School before joining the family firm in 1841. Having learned the trade under his father, a good-humoured, fat, and communicative mill owner, Ecroyd was made a partner in 1849. This was a period of rapid growth and prosperity for the firm, as it extended its manufacturing capacity to over 3000 looms, and its workforce to about 1250. By the 1860s, it was one of the few remaining houses producing soft woollen fabrics in 150 varieties for the home and foreign trade. Imbued with a strong religious sense of the stewardship of wealth, Ecroyd was involved in a wide range of activities designed to improve the condition of the workpeople and to mollify the embittered industrial relations which had marked north-east Lancashire in the early 1850s. He ensured that the Lomeshaye mills were equipped with healthy, well ventilated rooms and provided dining-rooms, a sick club, a mill library, and half-time schools. He was widely esteemed not only for his business sense but his upright conduct, fair dealing with the workforce, and unselfish actions. However, Ecroyd's broadening theological vision, derived from Kingsley, Maurice, and Arnold, increasingly separated him from his father and from the narrow tenets of the Quakers, which he now believed inhibited the proper Christian endeavours of employers. In 1851 Ecroyd had married, within the Society of Friends, Mary (d. 1867), daughter of Thomas Backhouse of York, a railway and bank director with strong botanical interests; they had three sons and six daughters. Following his second marriage in 1869 to the Baptist Anna Maria (1831–1913), daughter of another local employer George Foster (once a partner of Cobden and a strong free trader), Ecroyd and his wife continued to attend Quaker meetings but he was to renounce formally his membership of the Society of Friends following his father's death.

Having abandoned his family's Quakerism, Ecroyd also abandoned its Liberalism, standing unsuccessfully for parliament in 1874 as Conservative candidate for Carlisle, upholding in politics the Church of England principles which he had now embraced. He also spoke widely on behalf of denominational education and served on the executive of the National Educational Union from 1875 to 1879. His political views, however, were to move in less conventional directions by the later 1870s, when the worsted industry began to suffer more than most from the impact of foreign, especially French, competition. Ecroyd, a member of the Anti-Corn Law League as a youth and a keen reader of political economy, now became one of the more thoughtful critics of free trade and the most articulate exponent of the alternative creed of 'fair trade'. In 1879 he composed its leading tract, *The Policy of Self-Help*, arguing that Britain's policy of free trade would only be reciprocated by other nations if Britain herself imposed import duties both on foreign wheat and manufactured imports. At the same time, free imports from the colonies would strengthen the empire (on the federal model of the United States) and help prevent Britain's decline to the rank of third-rate power.

Ecroyd stood unsuccessfully on this platform ('Ecroydism' as his opponent Lord Hartington called it) in North-East Lancashire in 1880 but won a dramatic by-election victory at Preston in 1881. 'Fair trade' was now at its peak and, with several spokesmen in the House of Commons, was able to bring considerable pressure to bear during the unsuccessful renegotiation of the Anglo-French commercial (Cobden) treaty of 1880–82. Ecroyd did not defend Preston in 1885 (on grounds of ill health) but did unsuccessfully oppose Hartington in the Rossendale division of Lancashire. He was not to stand again but in 1885 he was appointed by Lord Salisbury to the royal commission on the depression in trade and industry, which provided the most effective outlet for the 'fair trade' analysis of the British economy in the later nineteenth century. Ecroyd himself dropped from the forefront of this movement after 1886 but its central strands were to be taken up by Chamberlain, with Ecroyd's warm encouragement and approval, in his advocacy of tariff reform in 1903. Ecroyd was ready to campaign locally for tariff reform and reputedly wrote several tariff reform pamphlets.

After 1886 Ecroyd moved back from the national scene to the family firm, and increasingly to the Herefordshire estate at Credenhill which he had acquired in 1880. There he devoted himself to agriculture but also to replicating in the countryside the paternalism he had first practised in the town, erecting model dwellings and new schools, taking over the patronage of and restoring the local church, rebuilding the parsonage, and aiding the Revd Charles Henry Bulmer in his campaign against the adulteration of cider. Yet Ecroyd still spent much time in Lancashire, and at his estate at Whitbarrow in Westmorland. Having overseen the reconstruction of the family firm on limited liability lines in 1896, he remained nominally its chairman until his death, but increasingly withdrew from its affairs. By the standards of its time, it was now only a modestly sized enterprise and Ecroyd's own fortune probably owed more to prudent speculation in overseas railways than to his industrial shareholdings. In 1896 he commemorated over fifty years' service with a retirement address on the duties of employers (*A Few Words to the Workers at Lomeshaye Mills*, 1896), with the factory evoked more as a site of moral training than of profit-making. His own practice of such duties had been exemplary, not only within his factory but in his providing the adjoining town of Nelson with schools, a new Anglican church (St Mary's) in 1884, and generous support of Burnley Hospital. He also acted as JP in both Lancashire and Herefordshire and was deputy lieutenant of Herefordshire.

An invalid in later years, Ecroyd died at Credenhill on 9 November 1915, and was buried there on 11 November. Between the 1850s and 1880s he had been a frequent traveller in Europe, and in England, a keen admirer of natural beauty, much influenced by Wordsworth. Ecroyd's own interest in history (he believed his name was derived from the Mercian King Croyda, also providing the derivation of Credenhill, which itself abutted Offa's Dyke) was taken up by his sons, while his eldest son Thomas Backhouse Ecroyd (1857–1945) took over the declining firm. Part of the Credenhill estate later became home to the Special Air Service.   A. C. Howe

Sources *Nelson Leader* (12 Nov 1915) · *Nelson Leader* (19 Nov 1915) · *Hereford Times* (13 Nov 1915) · B. H. Brown, *The tariff reform movement in Great Britain, 1881–1895* (1943) · Man. CL, Farrer MSS · D. Puseley, *The commercial companion* (1858) · *Annual Monitor* (1917) · private information (2004) · William Ecroyd & Sons Ltd, PRO, BT31/31441/47811 · *Hansard* · *Fair Trader* (31 Dec 1887) [special issue with portrait] · *The Times* (10 Nov 1915) · *WW* · Burke, *Gen. GB* · *CGPLA Eng. & Wales* (1916)
Archives Lancs. RO, Badgery deposit, business MSS · Man. CL, Farrer MSS and transcripts, family MSS
Likenesses group portrait, repro. in *Fair Trader* · oils, priv. coll. · photograph, repro. in *Nelson Leader* (12 Nov 1915)
Wealth at death £179,199 7s. 2d.: probate, 22 Jan 1916, *CGPLA Eng. & Wales*

Ecton, John (*d.* 1730), ecclesiastical administrator, was a native of Winchester. By 1711 he was deputy remembrancer of first fruits in the office of Queen Anne's bounty when he published *Liber valorum et decimarum; being an account of the valuations and yearly tenths of all such ecclesiastical benefices in England and Wales as now stand chargeable with the payment of first-fruits and tenths.* Seven subsequent editions of this work appeared between 1723 and 1796, the best of which were the 1754 edition, *Thesaurus rerum ecclesiasticarum*, and the 1763 edition annotated by Browne Willis. In 1786 the antiquary John Bacon made a few additions, changed the title to *Liber regis*, and published it as entirely his own work, an action denounced as an 'unexampled specimen of the grossest plagiarism' (Nichols, *Lit. anecdotes*, 9.6). Ecton became a key adviser to the governors of the bounty, who appointed him the first receiver of tenths in 1717. He published an account of their administration of the bounty from 1704 to 1718, and 'a continuation to Christmas, 1720', which contained a defence of the governors' slow progress in making augmentation grants, appeared in 1721.

A good antiquary and musician, Ecton was elected FSA on 29 March 1723 and was admitted in November 1723. He died at Turnham Green, Middlesex, on 20 August 1730. His will, dated 7 July 1730, in which he asked to be buried in Winchester Cathedral, was proved at London on 8 September 1730 by his widow, Dorothea Ecton. He appears to have left no surviving children and he bequeathed all his 'manuscript bookes, papers, and collections' to his wife

and Dr Edward Butler, vice-chancellor of Oxford University, with the request that those likely to prove useful might be published. He left his collection of music and musical instruments to James Kent, the church composer. His library was sold in 1735.

GORDON GOODWIN, *rev.* P. R. N. CARTER

Sources G. F. A. Best, *Temporal pillars: Queen Anne's bounty, the ecclesiastical commissioners, and the Church of England* (1964) · A. Savidge, *The foundation and early years of Queen Anne's bounty* (1955) · [B. Bandinel and P. Bliss], eds., *A catalogue of the books relating to British topography, and Saxon and northern literature, bequeathed to the Bodleian Library* (1814) · J. Bacon, *Liber regis, vel, Thesaurus rerum ecclesiasticarum* (1786) · Nichols, *Lit. anecdotes*
Archives BL, transcription of *Taxatio bonorum ecclesiasticorum Angliae*, incl. notes, St MS 118 · Magd. Oxf., view of ecclesiastical benefices | PRO, Queen Anne's bounty

Edalji, Shapurji (1841/2–1918), Church of England clergyman and victim of racial harassment, was born in India in late 1841 or early 1842, son of Doralji Edalji, a Parsi merchant. After converting to Anglican Christianity, he was admitted to Free Kirk College, Bombay (1864). A man of his name published a Gujarati/English dictionary (1863), a lecture to the Bombay Dialect Society (1864), and a Gujarati grammar (1867). In 1866 Edalji proceeded to St Augustine's College, Canterbury, and in 1869 received his first curacy at Burford. Afterwards he was curate at Holy Trinity, Oxford (1869–70), in Lancashire parishes at Farnworth and Toxteth (1870–72, 1874–5), St Levan, Cornwall (1873–4), and Bromley St Leonard (1875–6). On 17 June 1874 Edalji married Charlotte Elizabeth Stuart (1842–1924), daughter of Thompson Stoneham, vicar of Ketley, Shropshire. They had two sons and one daughter (Maud Evelyn, who died unmarried in 1961).

G. A. Selwyn, when bishop of Lichfield, appointed Edalji in 1876 as vicar of Great Wyrley, Staffordshire, where he continued as incumbent until his death. Collieries and agriculture provided the chief employment of this parish. An amiable, devoted clergyman, he published his *Lectures on St Paul's Epistles to the Galatians* in 1879. His misfortunes began when he was pestered by anonymous letters written by a servant (1888). During 1892–5 bogus advertisements were inserted in his name in newspapers, rubbish was strewn on his lawn, and detectives, solicitors, tradesmen, and fellow clergy were sent mischievous or vicious missives over his forged signature: an 'evil business', as he wrote, pursued by a hidden antagonist 'to gratify his own desire for fun or revenge' (*The Times*, 16 Aug 1895, 12c). Local police (especially Staffordshire's chief constable, the Hon. George Anson) improbably convinced themselves that the vicar's elder son, George Ernest Thompson Edalji (*b.* 1876), was the miscreant. The Edaljis were not again disturbed until 1903. During that year sixteen sheep, cattle, or horses were horribly mutilated in Edalji's district. Anonymous letters denounced Edalji junior, then working as a solicitor, who was tried (October 1903) at Staffordshire quarter sessions before an ignorant county justice on charges of wounding a horse on the night of 17 August and of having sent a letter to a local policeman threatening to murder him. The case arrayed against young Edalji was preposterous. As an astigmatic myopic he was incapable of complicated nocturnal excursions; the vicarage was surrounded on the night of 17 August by a cordon of men through which he could not have penetrated; apparently incriminating dirty razors found in a police search of the vicarage were stained with rust, not blood; putatively incriminating mud found on his clothes and boots did not come from the field where the horse was slaughtered; horse hairs which police claimed to have found on his coat were probably threads; his father's sworn oath that they had slept the night in the same room behind a locked door was disregarded. After George Edalji was condemned to seven years' penal servitude, his family was brutally baited.

Shapurji Edalji battled for three years against an intransigent Home Office. Eventually his son was freed from prison with his career ruined (October 1906). The case was taken up by Arthur Conan Doyle, who published a series of cogent investigative articles in the *Daily Telegraph*, and by Sir George Lewis as part of his campaign for a court of criminal appeal. A Home Office departmental committee exonerated Edalji from the wounding, although implausibly adhering to the theory that he had written anonymous letters; the home secretary, Herbert Gladstone, thereupon granted a free pardon, though in grudging terms, and without compensation (May 1907). The long persecution of the Edaljis, Anson's hostility, the misconduct of police inquiries, the extravagance of local rumour-mongering, the injustice of the trial, and the Home Office attitude were all attributable, in differing degrees, to grievous racial bigotry.

Having been blind for some months, Edalji died five weeks after suffering a cerebral haemorrhage, on 23 May 1918, at Great Wyrley vicarage, and was buried in his parish churchyard.   RICHARD DAVENPORT-HINES

Sources A. C. Doyle, *The case of Mr George Edalji* (1907) · 'The Edalji case and the home office', *The Spectator* (26 Jan 1907), 131–2 · *The Times* (16 Aug 1895) · *The Times* (21–4 Oct 1903) · *The Times* (18 May 1904) · *The Times* (2 June 1904) · *The Times* (13 Oct 1905) · *The Times* (1906–7) · report of home office departmental committee on papers relating to the case of George Edalji (session 1907, Cd 3503), PRO · m. cert. · d. cert. · Crockford · census returns, 1881, 1901
Archives LPL
Wealth at death £147 19s. 1d.: administration, 2 July 1918, CGPLA Eng. & Wales

Eddington, Sir Arthur Stanley (1882–1944), theoretical physicist and astrophysicist, was born on 28 December 1882 in Kendal, Westmorland, the second child of Arthur Henry Eddington (d. 1884) and his wife, Sarah Ann Shout of Darlington, whose family was of Dutch origin. Both came from traditional Quaker families. His father, a Somerset man, was headmaster and proprietor of Stramongate, the Friends' school in Kendal, where John Dalton the chemist had taught a century earlier.

Education and early work in astronomy Before Eddington was two his father died of typhoid and he, his mother, and his sister Winifred, who was six, moved to Weston-super-Mare. He early showed his unusual interest in numbers by learning the twenty-four times table. In Weston he attended Brynyclyn School and won a Somerset county

Sir Arthur Stanley Eddington (1882–1944), by Elliott & Fry, 1942

scholarship so that at fifteen he entered Manchester University. His course consisted of a general year followed by three years of physics under Arthur Schuster and mathematics under Horace Lamb. Eddington consciously modelled his own elegant prose style upon that of Lamb. When he graduated from Manchester with first-class honours, an entrance scholarship (later changed to a major scholarship) enabled him to enter Trinity College, Cambridge, in 1902 to read mathematics. In 1904 he was senior wrangler in part one of the mathematical tripos and in the following year was placed in the first division of the first class in part two.

Eddington returned to Cambridge in the autumn of 1905 to earn his living as a mathematical coach, but early in 1906, aged twenty-four and a year before his first published paper, moved to Greenwich as chief assistant to the astronomer royal, in place of Frank Dyson who became the astronomer royal of Scotland. Some of the work was observational but he also had time to carry out a theoretical investigation of the motion of stars. When the apparent stellar motions caused by the earth's rotation have been allowed for, the much smaller proper motions remain. The Dutch astronomer Jacobus Kapteyn had found in 1904 that the proper motions evidenced two 'star streams'; Eddington greatly extended Kapteyn's work and used his results as successful bases for a Smith's prize essay and a Trinity fellowship dissertation. He was an obvious choice to fill the Plumian chair of astronomy in Cambridge when Sir George Darwin retired in 1913. When Sir Robert Ball died in the following year it was decided to join the directorship of the observatory to the Plumian chair, so Eddington, with his mother and his sister, took up residence at the observatory, where he was to stay for the rest of his life. In that year he published his first book *Stellar Movements and the Structure of the Universe*, and he was also elected to the Royal Society. The book marks an end to his contributions to that particular field for he realized that the Kapteyn–Eddington explanation was less elegant than an alternative put forward by Karl Schwarzschild.

Stellar research Research underlying two of Eddington's three major claims to fame began in 1916. His interest in the stars had turned to their internal structure and their heat-producing mechanism. He had been stimulated by wanting to understand the energy process that would explain the specific property of one class of stars, the Cepheid variables, the discovery of which allowed astronomers to set up a scale of distance. Their distinctive property was that their intrinsic brightness was fixed by the period of variation. In 1914 Harlow Shapley at Harvard proposed that the variability might be due to periodic pulsations, a vague hypothesis because of lack of knowledge of the internal structure of stars. Eddington seized upon the challenge, and developed a theory which accounted for many Cepheid characteristics. It was generally accepted that in some way all stars produced their heat deep inside and it reached the surface by convection. Eddington realized that radiation, not convection, played the major role. It was the radiation pressure which prevented the star from collapsing under its own weight. With some further assumptions and a huge amount of laborious computation, Eddington was able to explain the empirical link between the period of a Cepheid and its absolute magnitude. He then derived, and in March 1924 announced, the 'mass–luminosity relation'. He then calculated the central temperature of stars, and so hypothesized that the source of the stars' energy was the burning of hydrogen into helium. This has since proved to be the case. These results, collected and published as *The Internal Constitution of the Stars* (1926), were a major contribution to the problem of stellar evolution, and elevated Eddington into the front rank of international astrophysicists.

The second of Eddington's major innovations of 1916 had a more lasting effect on his life. He was by then secretary to the Royal Astronomical Society and William de Sitter in the Netherlands sent him a copy of Einstein's new theory of gravitation, 'general relativity'. The special theory of relativity of 1905 had caused relatively little excitement in Cambridge, and Eddington had not thought about it. Now he became very interested in both of Einstein's theories, and expounded clearly for the first time in England what had seemed to be difficult mathematics. His report was later expanded into *The Mathematical Theory of Relativity* (1923).

Verifying Einstein Events in the outside world now impinged on Eddington's essentially intellectual existence. At thirty-four he was eligible to be conscripted, although as a Quaker he would have refused to serve. However after Gallipoli the scientific establishment felt

the need to safeguard post-war science against the loss of its best workers: the solar eclipse of May 1919 would provide an exceptional opportunity to test one of the predictions of Einstein's bold new theory of gravitation which challenged Newton's laws (Einstein predicted that starlight grazing the sun during total eclipse would be deflected by an amount significantly larger than the Newtonian value) and it was natural to choose Eddington to prepare two expeditions, and lead one. Overcoming difficulties at the end of the war, his successful photographic observation from Principe in the Gulf of Guinea was 'dramatic verification of Einstein's esoteric theory' (Gingerich, 282), shot the latter to fame, and overnight made Eddington a public figure. Like his rival Sir James Jeans he became a personality mentioned in the pages of *Punch*, and, following Jeans, he wrote highly successful popular scientific books. The best of them is perhaps *The Nature of the Physical World* (1928), while *Space, Time and Gravitation* (1920) was immensely important as the authoritative popularization of Einstein's theory. Brilliant, confident, generous to his students but brutal in debate, during the 1920s Eddington clashed with Jeans and latterly Milne at the Royal Astronomical Society but never bore grudges. In 1935 at the society he ridiculed the young Cambridge graduate S. Chandrasekhar who used quantum mechanics to calculate stellar collapse; Chandrasekhar was later proved right.

In two other, more subtle ways, general relativity affected Eddington's intellectual development. He already saw clearly that Einstein's theory had two distinct parts: first, a general and scarcely improvable formulation of what any possible relativistic gravitational theory should be, based on the 'tensor calculus'; second, a specific set of field equations for which the arguments were much weaker. Eddington attached importance to his alternative way of seeing the Einstein field equations as a mere definition of the absence of matter. This pushed him into the ontological position of seeing matter, not as substance, but as a construction. He was led in turn to thinking deeply about the nature of physical theory and to concluding that its results were not intrinsic results about the external world but were about the measurements that were made of the world. This was the first stage of an intellectual programme which dominated most of the rest of his life, though he was not able to carry it through. He perceived the basis of natural philosophy as epistemology.

The second subtle influence of relativity was a little more technical. Eddington's exposition of relativity, even more than Einstein's, relied heavily on the ability of the tensor calculus to generate in a mechanical way relativistically legitimate forms of mathematical theory. In common with other physicists and most mathematicians he also believed that, conversely, all legitimate forms were produced in this way and he stated as much in his book. It had become for him part of the scarcely corrigible general part of the theory. Since the turn of the century, general relativity had been only one of the two basic but inconsistent advances in physics. The other, quantum mechanics, which dealt with the very small, had advanced rapidly but without much attention from Eddington. Then in 1928 Paul Dirac, a young theoretical physicist, constructed an equation describing the electron in order to put right some of the defects of quantum mechanics in spectroscopy. It was relativistically legitimate and yet was not producible by the tensor calculus mechanism. Eddington was amazed and concerned.

Unified field theory, 1928–1944 Eddington's work in reaction to this discovery was his third major claim to fame, and in the long run probably his most enduring. It occupied nearly all his working time until his death in 1944. He began by thinking that something had mysteriously slipped through the net. The solution to the mystery, in his view, was Dirac's use of an unusual algebraic structure and Eddington set about elaborating this structure. His initial view was that quantum mechanics was a subtheory of some elaborate structure that would arise from general relativity by incorporating the Dirac algebra. The suggestion of a unified theory of which general relativity and quantum mechanics would be special cases was at first received with interest and approval by the international community, for the schism in physics was widely regarded with horror. The analogy would be the way in which James Clerk Maxwell had united the disparate theories of magnetism and electricity in the nineteenth century.

Maxwell's unification had led to the theoretical determination of a physical constant, the speed of light, in terms of the electric and magnetic properties of the medium. So here, for Eddington, the unification would be expected to yield theoretical values of some of the numerical physical constants which had by now been discovered. Principal among these were the 'fine-structure constant' whose inverse is now measured to be 137.0360 and the ratio of the masses of the proton and the electron (now 1836.1527). Eddington began to publish his first speculations in that direction in an inadequate form in 1928. He related the inverse fine-structure constant with the 136 terms in his elaboration of the Dirac algebra. A more satisfactory presentation and a suggestion giving the mass-ratio within one per cent followed in 1932 and 1933. His international reputation sank rapidly. Of the most eminent theoretical physicists, only Erwin Schrödinger made a serious attempt to come to terms with Eddington's arguments. The generally held but mistaken opinion was that Eddington held the absurd belief that these measured constants could be determined from no physics at all. In fact, he was happy to borrow all kinds of qualitative results from physics but he saw the numerical constants as being part of what he had believed since 1919 to be epistemically based. They were structural parameters and the whole determination was seen as an investigation of physics as structure. There was no inherent impossibility in such an argument, and it is Eddington's lasting claim to fame to have pointed out its possibility.

There remains the question of the extent to which Eddington carried out the construction of the theory satisfactorily. The answer is rather complicated. By 1933 Eddington believed that he had satisfactorily determined four fundamental constants. His publications of these results had not produced much adverse criticism—he had become too eminent a figure for that—but the silence of his colleagues was even more significant. For the second time the pressures of the outside world intruded into his intellectual isolation. He saw clearly that the advent of Hitler made war very likely. He felt the need to get the theory into finished form before disaster struck, even if his usual polished style was beyond achievement. The result was *The Relativity Theory of Protons and Electrons* (1936), a book which none the less provides the best description of his later ideas.

Eddington had by now seen that his earlier search for a unified theory in which general relativity and quantum mechanics were special cases was doomed to failure because the two theories started from wholly different concepts. His new point of view was to allow general relativity and quantum mechanics their independent approaches and to search for physical problems, of which there might be very few, to which both approaches were applicable. It would now be the agreement between predicted numerical values in the two theories which would yield the numerical values of physical constants. Eddington's chosen problem was a very simplified cosmological model—the 'Einstein universe'—the discussion of which was well known in general relativity. It cannot be said that his corresponding discussion in quantum mechanics is clear or satisfactory.

The adverse criticism engendered by *Protons and Electrons* drove Eddington further into isolation. His critics held that he had not succeeded in his approach, probably because it was impossible. He could have taken on the second point successfully but instead he ignored it and concentrated on the first. For eight years he laboured on his *Fundamental Theory*, posthumously published in 1946, in which many more physical constants were determined. It is difficult not to see the hand of the successful popular science writer in its beautifully written failures to provide cast-iron proofs. Eddington's speculative imagination may be reminiscent of science fiction but must be seen in the light of his overriding and correct conviction that quantum mechanics was failing to provide any imaginative picture of the origin of discreteness which it introduced. Any inadequately formulated ideas pointing in the right direction were hugely exciting and more valuable to him and his readers than mathematically consistent theories going the wrong way. In *Fundamental Theory* the 'rigid field convention' was central to these attempts. It enabled quantum conditions to be isolated from the classical background. This and his earlier 1936 book, as well as his realization of the possibility of a structural theory in physics, remain his most important contributions.

Eddington was elected to the Royal Society in 1914, was awarded a royal medal in 1928, knighted in 1930, and appointed to the Order of Merit in 1938. He was president of the Royal Astronomical Society in 1921–3, of both the Physical Society and the Mathematical Association in 1930–32 and of the International Astronomical Union from 1938 until he died. He never married; he died from cancer in the Evelyn Nursing Home, Cambridge, on 22 November 1944. Eddington was a member of the Society of Friends throughout his life, and his religious beliefs shaped what he regarded as his most important scientific work. While it may seem that in searching for unified fields, and asserting the primacy of mind or conscious-ness over quantum uncertainty 'his religion led him into scientific dead-ends' (Batten, 268), those cross-disciplinary problems continue to occupy the best minds decades later.

C. W. KILMISTER

Sources A. V. Douglas, *Arthur Stanley Eddington* (1956) · *The Times* (23 Nov 1944) · H. C. Plummer, *Obits. FRS*, 5 (1945–8), 113–25 · *DNB* · N. B. Slater, *The development and meaning of Eddington's fundamental theory* (1957) · private information (2004) [T. Bastin] · S. Chandra-sekhar, *Eddington, the most distinguished astrophysicist of his time* (1983) · A. H. Batten, 'A most rare vision: Eddington's thinking on the relation between science and religion', *Quarterly Journal of the Royal Astronomical Society*, 35 (1994), 249–70 · *History of the Royal Astro-nomical Society, 2: 1920–1980*, ed. R. J. Tayler (1987), 54–5 · O. Ging-erich, *The great Copernicus chase and other adventures in astronomical history* (1992), 282 · H. S. Hogg, 'Variable stars', *Astrophysics and twentieth-century astronomy to 1950*, ed. O. Gingerich (1984), 73–89, esp. 84–6 · *CGPLA Eng. & Wales* (1945)

Archives ETH Bibliothek, Zürich, corresp. with H. Weyl · Hebrew University, Jerusalem, corresp. with Albert Einstein · ICL, corresp. with Herbert Dingle · Nuffield Oxf., corresp. with Lord Cherwell · Queen's University, Kingston, Ontario, corresp. and papers · RS, letters to Sir Joseph Larmor · Trinity Cam., papers · U. Cam., Insti-tute of Astronomy, papers

Likenesses W. Stoneman, two photographs, 1925–38, NPG · W. Rothenstein, chalk drawing, c.1928–1929, NPG · A. John, chalk drawing, 1933, Trinity Cam. · H. Coster, photographs, 1936, NPG · photograph, 1939, Hult. Arch. · Elliott & Fry, photograph, 1942, NPG [*see illus.*] · H. Carter, photograph, Central Office of Informa-tion, London · photograph, RAS

Wealth at death £47,237 1s. 10d.: probate, 8 March 1945, *CGPLA Eng. & Wales*

Paul Clark Eddington (1927–1995), by Johnny Boylan, 1990

Eddington, Paul Clark (1927–1995), actor, was born on 18 June 1927 at 174 Sutherland Avenue, Paddington, London, the son of Albert Clark Eddington, a decorative artist, and his wife, Frances Clark Eddington, *née* Frances Mary Roberts. He was brought up in St John's Wood, London. His father, a Quaker related to the Quaker Clark family of Somerset shoemakers, was an addictive gambler who had emotional problems after serving in the trenches in the First World War. His mother, a Roman Catholic, was a rad-ical thinker and hostess to artists and intellectuals. Eddington was brought up as a Catholic and was educated at the Holy Child Convent, Cavendish Square, London, but when his parents' marriage ended his mother sent him to board at the Friends' school at Sibford Ferris, Oxfordshire. He remained a Quaker for the rest of his life. Leaving school at seventeen with no ambition but to do something artistic, he became a window dresser at a Birmingham store and an amateur actor. In 1944 he joined the Enter-tainments National Service Association at the garrison theatre, Colchester, but he acted only briefly for the troops before it was discovered that he was a registered conscientious objector and he was dismissed. After the war he spent over ten years at the repertory theatres in Birmingham, Sheffield, and Ipswich, with a year at the Royal Academy of Dramatic Art in 1951. On 28 April 1952

he married (Vida) Patricia Scott (*b.* 1929/30), an actress whom he had met in the wings at Sheffield repertory the-atre. She was the daughter of Jonathan Joseph Scott, a police officer. They had three sons and one daughter.

After several years in television Eddington made his West End début as the Rabbi in *The Tenth Man* (1961). He joined the Bristol Old Vic as leading man in 1962. In trans-fers to London he was seen as Prince Andrei in *War and Peace* (Old Vic and Phoenix, 1962–3), a sexually obliging psychiatrist in Iris Murdoch's *A Severed Head* (Criterion, 1963; New York, 1964), and Benjamin Disraeli in *A Portrait of the Queen* (Vaudeville, 1965). Other roles at Bristol included Ibsen's Brand, Brutus in *Julius Caesar*, Henry II in Anouilh's *Becket*, Parolles in *All's Well that Ends Well*, and Biedermann in Frisch's *The Fire Raisers*.

Still unambitious by nature but with a growing family to support, Eddington—who had long been familiar with the labour exchange—once considered giving up the the-atre for a job as salesman with an oil company, but in 1966, as Captain Doleful in the musical comedy *Jorrocks* (New), he won the Clarence Derwent award as the season's best supporting actor. This led to another West End musical comedy, but it was Alan Bennett's musical satire *Forty Years On* (Apollo, 1968) that brought better luck. As a nervous young housemaster trying to impress John Gielgud's haughty headmaster, Eddington learned not only the technical value of keeping still on stage but he also learned how much he had in common with Gielgud: once, in their mutual desire not to upstage the other, the two actors nearly fell into the orchestra pit. It was a feature of Eddington's later career that he thrived in some of Gielgud's finest roles. After the headmaster in a revival of *Forty Years On* (Chichester and Haymarket, 1984), Eddington shone as Spooner in Harold Pinter's *No Man's Land* (Almeida and Comedy, 1993), though he did not smoke, as Gielgud had in imitation of W. H. Auden, on whom the part was based. Eddington also proved an affecting Harry in David Storey's *Home* (Wyndham's, 1995). Although he wanted to cover his baldness, caused by medical treatment for a skin disease, with a straw hat, the author persuaded him not to. It was his last stage performance.

It was, however, on television that Eddington achieved renown for his light touch and expert sense of understated comedy. He was the henpecked husband of Penelope Keith's snobbish Margo in *The Good Life* (1975–9), and a wily but naïve Jim Hacker MP in *Yes, Minister* and its sequel, *Yes, Prime Minister*, which ran through the 1980s. It was while watching Alan Ayckbourn's suburban comedy *Absurd Person Singular* (Criterion and Vaudeville, 1974), that a television producer took a shine to Eddington's diffident style, with his slight stoop, wary eyes, and drawn cheeks. Eddington was at heart a more serious-minded actor than his light touch on television might indicate; at this time he had just played James Tyrone in *Long Day's Journey into Night* and Osborne in *Journey's End* for the Bristol Old Vic, and whenever he could he evaded typecasting with surprising success. As the cruel and drooling husband George in Edward Albee's *Who's Afraid of Virginia Woolf?* (National, 1981) and as the pathetic old classics master in Terence Rattigan's *The Browning Version* (Theatre Royal, Bristol, and Royalty, London, 1984), Eddington's command of the stage was emotionally complex and deep. His moral philosopher in Tom Stoppard's *Jumpers* (Aldwych, 1985), his exuberant Sir Hartley Courtly in Boucicault's *London Assurance* (Chichester, 1989), and his Orgon in Molière's *Tartuffe* (Playhouse, 1991) were further evidence of his power, range, and technique.

Eddington's role as the embattled Jim Hacker MP (and later as prime minister) brought him fame, and sometimes also embarrassment. He was happy to have been one of the few non-politicians to address Westminster's lobby correspondents—he was appointed CBE in 1987— but he could only smile wrily at the frequency with which the red carpet was rolled out for him on his travels, as if he had political influence: breakfast with the prime minister of Norway and an invitation to address a general election rally in Australia were only two examples. While the party allegiance of the character Hacker was never proclaimed, he was assumed to be right-wing, whereas Eddington himself belonged to the left. When he was asked by 10 Downing Street to pose for publicity pictures with the prime minister, Margaret Thatcher, he replied: 'To put it bluntly, she needs us more than we need her' (*The Times*, 7 Nov 1995). As a governor of the Bristol Old Vic Theatre trust, Eddington declared that he would never act there again until the company declined a tobacco company's grants. A

former campaigner against nuclear arms and the chairman of the International Committee for Artists' Freedom—which raised funds for dissident theatre groups— Eddington also strove in vain for the admission of women as members of the Garrick Club.

During his illness, which was not identified until the mid-1980s as a form of skin cancer, mycosis fungoides, Eddington resolved that his health should not interfere with his acting. His Justice Shallow in *Henry IV* for BBC television was shown shortly before he died in London on 4 November 1995. His memoirs, *So Far, so Good*, were published the previous month. His wife and four children survived him.   ERIC SHORTER

Sources *Who's who in the theatre*, various edns · P. Barnes, *A companion to post-war British theatre* (1986) · P. Eddington, *So far, so good* (1995) · *The Times* (7 Nov 1995) · *The Independent* (7 Nov 1995) · *WWW, 1991–5* · b. cert. · m. cert. · *CGPLA Eng. & Wales* (1996)
Likenesses J. Boylan, photograph, 1990, Rex Features Ltd, London [*see illus.*] · photograph, repro. in *The Times* · photograph, repro. in *The Independent* · portrait, repro. in M. Joseph, *Who's who on TV* (1982)
Wealth at death £239,214: probate, 22 April 1996, *CGPLA Eng. & Wales*

Eddis, Eden Upton (1812–1901), portrait painter, was born on 9 May 1812 in Newington Green, Middlesex, the eldest son of Eden Eddis, a clerk at Somerset House, and his wife, Clementia, *née* Parker. His grandfather, William Eddis, was secretary to Sir Robert Eden, governor of Maryland. Eddis was baptized in the Union Independent Church in Islington on 13 June. He was taught to draw at the school run by Henry Sass in Charlotte Street, Bloomsbury, before being admitted to the Royal Academy Schools on 8 December 1828, where he won a silver medal in 1831. He had to leave the Royal Academy after his father's early death, and as a young man travelled extensively round the continent in the company of his friend, the watercolour painter James Holland.

Eddis first exhibited at the Royal Academy in 1834, and he showed 130 pictures there during the next fifty years. Some of his early works became very popular, including *Naomi and her Daughter-in-Law* (exh. RA, 1843), *The Raising of the Daughter of Jairus* (exh. RA, 1844), and two paintings, *The Sisters* (exh. RA, 1848), inspired by 'Bereavement', a poem by John Keble. Eddis became a successful portrait painter, and most of his Royal Academy exhibits were portraits, including *Archbishop of Armagh* (1838), *Viscount Ebrington, Lord Lieutenant of Ireland* (1839), *Thomas Babington Macaulay* (1850), *Samuel Jones Loyd, First Lord Overstone* (1851), *J. B. Sumner, Archbishop of Canterbury* (1851; Lambeth Palace), and *Charles Blomfield, Bishop of London* (1851). A number of his sitters were schoolmasters, including Dr George Mortimer, headmaster of the City of London School (Guildhall Library and Art Gallery, London), the master of Marlborough College (exh. RA, 1854), and the master of Alleyne's College, Dulwich (exh. RA, 1867). He particularly liked painting the portraits of children, and one of his most popular works, frequently reproduced, was *Going to Work* (exh. RA, 1869), of a child, Florence Halford, on the beach. He was also known for his portraits in chalk.

In 1883, when Eddis began to go deaf, he gave up painting professionally, and moved from his home in Harley Street, London, to Shalford, near Guildford, Surrey. There he continued to paint until his death, on 7 April 1901, at Shalford, where he was also buried. His wife, Elisabeth, *née* Brown, had already died. He left one son and one daughter. His oil painting of the novelist Theodore Edward Hook (*c*.1839), and a chalk drawing of the sculptor Sir Francis Chantrey (exh. RA, 1838), are in the National Portrait Gallery.   ANNE PIMLOTT BAKER

Sources Wood, *Vic. painters*, 3rd edn • Graves, *RA exhibitors* • K. K. Yung, *National Portrait Gallery: complete illustrated catalogue, 1856–1979*, ed. M. Pettman (1981) • S. C. Hutchison, 'The Royal Academy Schools, 1768–1830', *Walpole Society*, 38 (1960–62), 123–91 • B. Stewart and M. Cutten, *The dictionary of portrait painters in Britain up to 1920* (1997) • J. Johnson and A. Greutzner, *The dictionary of British artists, 1880–1940* (1976), vol. 5 of *Dictionary of British art* • *The Times* (10 April 1901) • *IGI* • R. Ormond, *Early Victorian portraits*, 2 vols. (1973) • *DNB*

Likenesses W. Hodgson, pencil, 1891, NPG • photograph, repro. in *ILN* (1901)

Wealth at death £15,737 10s. 2d.: probate, 18 May 1901, *CGPLA Eng. & Wales*

Eddisbury. For this title name *see* Stanley, Edward John, second Baron Stanley of Alderley and first Baron Eddisbury (1802–1869); Stanley, Henry Edward John, third Baron Stanley of Alderley and second Baron Eddisbury (1827–1903); Stanley, Edward Lyulph, fourth Baron Sheffield, fourth Baron Stanley of Alderley, and third Baron Eddisbury (1839–1925).

Ede, Harold Stanley [Jim] (1895–1990), museum curator and art collector, was born on 7 April 1895 in Penarth, Glamorgan, the younger son and second of three children of Edward Hornby Ede (1862–1940), solicitor, of Penarth, and his wife, Mildred Mary Furley (1866–1953), sometime schoolteacher, only daughter of Joseph Blanch, Methodist minister. At the Leys School, Cambridge (1909–12), where he began a lifelong friendship with Donald *Winnicott, he developed an interest in early Italian art which had burgeoned on a trip to Paris as a fourteen-year-old. He retained this passion throughout his life, and in 1926 published *Florentine Drawings of the Quattrocento*.

Ede was a somewhat rebellious child who enjoyed reverie and nature rather than academic discipline. In his unpublished memoir he described himself as an effeminate young man. As he grew older he placed particular value on male friendships. However, he enjoyed the company of his maternal grandmother and of his aunt Maud, a painter whom he visited in Paris. He gained a passion for reading from his mother and his father was a bibliophile.

Leaving the Leys early Ede began to train as a painter at Newlyn and then Edinburgh College of Art before war service interrupted his studies. In 1914 he joined the 6th battalion (pioneers) of the South Wales Borderers. He served as a lieutenant in France, was invalided back, and was posted to Cambridge (officer cadet battalion), and then India, where he suffered serious illness for several months. He returned via Alexandria, which he described as the first place in which he felt at home. Earlier generations of his family had lived around the Mediterranean.

In 1919 Ede enrolled at the Slade School of Fine Art; he left in March 1921 to become the photographer's assistant at the National Gallery and then, in 1922, an assistant at the Tate Gallery. During his fourteen years at the Tate (1922–36) Ede established close contacts with avant-garde artists in Paris but served under a director, J. B. Manson, who was unable to recognize his talents. Had his friendships with Picasso, Braque, Chagall, Brancusi, Miró, and others been exploited, the Tate could have had an unrivalled collection of early twentieth-century art. Similarly his friendships with younger British artists such as Ben Nicholson and Winifred Nicholson, Barbara Hepworth, Henry Moore, David Jones, and Christopher Wood were also ignored.

Ede met the Nicholsons in 1923, and it was they who kindled his interest in contemporary art. Others whom he acknowledged as important influences on his life were Gertrude Harris (widow of Frederick Leverton Harris), Lady Ottoline Morrell, Helen Sutherland, and T. E. Lawrence, with whom he regularly corresponded. Indeed, correspondence was a central activity in Ede's life. On 6 January 1921 Ede married Helen (1894–1977), daughter of Otto Schlapp, professor of German at the University of Edinburgh. Scottish by birth, Helen began to call him Jim, a name which he was to adopt for the remainder of his life. Together they had two daughters. Within two years Ede acquired 1 Elm Row, Hampstead, with the help of his father, and there he and his wife entertained relentlessly, creating something of a salon for artists, collectors, and dignitaries. Ede was a collector of people as much as of art.

In 1926 Ede discovered the work of the sculptor Henri Gaudier-Brzeska (1819–1915), when his estate was offered to the Tate, but there was little enthusiasm for his work. After persuading a number of collectors to purchase sculptures and drawings, Ede was given permission to acquire the remainder. From that year onwards he championed the cause of Gaudier-Brzeska by publishing books—*A Life of Gaudier-Brzeska* (1930), republished as *Savage Messiah* (1931)—and making generous gifts to museums, notably the Tate Gallery, the Musée des Beaux-Arts in Orléans (1959), and the Musée National d'Art Moderne in Paris (1967). He was nominated chevalier (1959) and officer (1967) of the Légion d'honneur.

In October 1936 Ede, a leading contender to be the next director, resigned from the Tate on grounds of ill health, unable to work further with Manson. Supporting himself by American lecture tours, and with financial aid from his father, he and his family moved to Tangier. He spent the Second World War years in Tangier, North America, and England.

The Edes sold their house in 1952, and acquired a large, old farmhouse in the Loire valley. They returned to England in 1956, and in 1957 purchased a row of four derelict, seventeenth-century cottages in Cambridge. Ede converted them into a single dwelling and named it Kettle's Yard. Here he arranged his by then considerable collection of works of art, some given to him by his mother, who had purchased them on his advice, in a manner which would make modern art not merely approachable but alive, combining his twentieth-century enthusiasms with his love of artefacts and materials from the past. Works of art by Ben Nicholson and Brancusi would sit alongside antique country furniture, ancient stones, flints, and amphora. Old floorboards, tiles, and windows salvaged from demolished buildings found a natural home in a building which harmonized the modernist spirit of the 1930s with the experience of living in north Africa. A respect for light and space was the hub of Ede's vision. The house was infused with the spirituality which formed the core of his and his wife's life. They kept open house every afternoon and those fortunate to be there at closing time were invited to tea. In 1966 Ede gave Kettle's Yard to the University of Cambridge. He also endowed a student travel fund. Ede remained in residence until 1973, when he and his wife moved to Edinburgh. She died in 1977. He maintained links with the curators of Kettle's Yard and published a book on it, *A Way of Life* (1984).

Although Ede was confirmed in the Church of England in the 1960s, his belief in God was unbound by the strictures of any one denomination or by his early Methodist formation. He believed in God's all-pervasiveness and Kettle's Yard was for him a manifestation of God. Determination, obstinacy, and a sense of rightness, mixed with a twinkling charm, were important traits of his character. His own description of David Jones best encapsulates him: 'Someone with a strange force which comes, not out of the strength of his body, but from the strength of his intention.' He died in Edinburgh on 15 March 1990 and his ashes were interred at St Peter's Church, Cambridge.

JEREMY LEWISON, *rev.*

Sources H. S. Ede, unpublished memoir, priv. coll. · personal knowledge (1996) · private information (1996) · *The Times* (17 March 1990) · *The Times* (28 March 1990) · *The Independent* (23 March 1990) · *The Independent* (2 April 1990) · *Kettle's Yard and its artists* (1995) · J. Lewison, *Kettle's Yard: an illustrated guide* (1980) · J. Ede, *A way of life* (1984)

Archives Kettle's Yard, Cambridge, corresp. and papers | Ransom HRC, corresp. with T. E. Lawrence · Tate collection, letters to Ben Nicholson

Ede, James Chuter Chuter-, Baron Chuter-Ede (1882–1965), politician and educationist, was born on 11 September 1882 at Epsom, Surrey, the son of James Ede, a grocer, and his wife, Agnes Mary Chuter. He had one sister. In common with many lower-middle-class shopkeepers in the late Victorian period, Ede's father was firmly attached to religious nonconformity (in the shape of Unitarianism) and to political radicalism, in the form of Gladstone's Liberal Party. In addition to sustaining these concerns, he also inherited from his parents a passion for education and learning. Later in his career he would often be introduced as someone who started life as a teacher. To this he would add the corrective that he began as a pupil, and had been on the side of the underdog ever since.

From his local elementary school (Epsom national schools), Ede progressed to Dorking high school, and then to Battersea Pupil Teachers' Centre, and eventually to

James Chuter Chuter-Ede, Baron Chuter-Ede (1882–1965), by Howard Coster, 1945

Christ's College, Cambridge, where he studied natural science. But lack of money meant he had to leave Cambridge before securing a degree, and he returned to his native Surrey, where he became an assistant master at a council elementary school in Mortlake. Increasingly, however, his energies were directed towards public service and political activity, which in the eyes of his parents were inseparable from their religious convictions.

Ede's political career began to take shape in the Edwardian period. As a forthright critic of contemporary teaching conditions (he was placed in charge of classes of up to seventy pupils), he became active within the National Union of Teachers and was the youngest member elected to the post of president of the Surrey County Teachers' Association. He also became active in local politics. In 1908 he was elected to Epsom urban district council, where he was an assiduous attender—missing only four meetings over the next six years—and where he made no attempt to hide his pronounced Liberal views, which he developed as secretary and agent of the local association. In the summer of 1914 he was elected as Epsom's representative on Surrey county council, but the further advancement of his career was delayed by the outbreak of the First World War.

The war proved to be an important watershed in Ede's life, both personally and politically. He served in the front line with the east Surreys and the Royal Engineers, reaching the rank of sergeant, and while home on leave in 1917 he married Lilian Mary Stephens Williams (*d.* 1948), the daughter of Richard Williams, a Plymouth doctor. She was herself a teacher in Surrey and became a member of the county council. He also abandoned the Liberal Party in favour of the emerging labour movement, believing it had become a more effective representative of the cause of the underdog. At the 1918 general election he was heavily defeated when he stood as the Labour candidate for Epsom.

In the early 1920s Ede concentrated on establishing himself as a county councillor, and in March 1923 he was returned to parliament after defeating the Conservative minister of health, Sir Arthur Griffith-Boscawen, by the margin of 800 votes in a fiercely contested by-election at Mitcham. In the House of Commons he was quickly recognized as a knowledgeable speaker with a dry sense of humour. But in a general election held later in 1923 Ede was narrowly beaten in Mitcham, and suffered the same fate in a further contest a year later; his entry into national politics had been impressive but short-lived.

In 1929 Ede secured a narrow victory at South Shields—a seat which had returned a Liberal MP at every election since the 1832 Reform Act—this time by a mere forty votes. He was privately critical of the inability of Ramsay MacDonald's Labour government to tackle mounting unemployment, but voted against the administration only once in parliament, conscious of the party's precarious position in office. Like many colleagues, he was soundly defeated at the election which followed the formation of the National Government in 1931.

In spite of this set-back, the 1930s witnessed a consolidation of Ede's political career. In 1933 he became chairman of Surrey county council and in 1935 he won a handsome victory at South Shields—the constituency he represented without further interruption until 1964. At last, in his mid-fifties, his talents received recognition within the Parliamentary Labour Party, and in 1939 he was appointed to a vacancy on the opposition front bench.

At the time of the formation of Winston Churchill's wartime coalition in May 1940, Ede was appointed as parliamentary secretary at the Board of Education, serving after 1941 under the Conservative minister R. A. Butler. During his five years at the board, Ede played a central role in preparing plans for reform, culminating in the passage of the 1944 Education Act, which introduced compulsory secondary schooling for all children over eleven in the state sector. His expertise was invaluable: in setting out the nonconformist case while devising a settlement for the vexed issue of religious education; in negotiating with the teaching profession; in preparing for a reorganization of local education authorities; and in liaising with Labour MPs.

When later asked what he regarded as his main contribution to the socialist cause, Ede pointed with great pride to his part in drafting the Education Bill and ensuring its passage through parliament. Wartime reform was later much criticized as local authorities, using the flexibility offered by the act, developed prestigious grammar schools alongside the markedly inferior secondary modern schools in which most children found themselves. In time Ede concurred with the growing view in Labour ranks that continuing inequality could only be remedied by the introduction of a single form of comprehensive education for all children over the age of eleven. But his admiration for the 1944 act remained undiminished. During the war years there were few, either in the Labour Party or the educational world, who questioned the assumption that 'parity of esteem' between various types of secondary school was attainable. He regarded secondary education for all—in whatever form—as a great improvement on pre-1939 provision, and nothing could detract from securing a settlement for church schools that had eluded policy makers since the turn of the century. Ede's attachment to the cause of educational reform was such that at one point in the war he rejected the prime minister's offer of promotion to another department. This was an action, he noted ironically, that gave him the distinction of being the only man to turn down a move from the Board of Education.

Ede's administrative ability, and his association with the successful passage of the Education Act, ensured his promotion to cabinet rank in the Labour government elected at the end of the war in 1945. The new prime minister, Clement Attlee, saw him as a natural choice for the Home Office, combining long experience of local government with knowledge of the judiciary as a magistrate. As home secretary for the next six years he was responsible for a large body of legislation, including measures on deprived children, police pensions, reform of magistrates' courts, and changes to the licensing laws. The most controversial problem he encountered came during the passage of the Criminal Justice Act in 1948, when he argued against a Commons motion calling for the abolition of capital punishment for an experimental period of five years. The Commons rejected his advice by a small majority. The issue was only defused, temporarily, by agreeing to establish a royal commission on the working of the death penalty.

Ede was also criticized for his handling of electoral boundary changes, which were said to have assisted the Conservative recovery at the 1950 general election. But on the whole he was considered a fair-minded and efficient home secretary, and the esteem in which he was held by members of all parties was one factor behind his appointment as leader of the House of Commons for a brief period before Attlee's government lost office in 1951.

Ede remained an influential figure in Labour politics for several years to come, though successive Conservative election victories in the 1950s afforded him no opportunity of a return to high office. When he eventually left the front bench, he was able to take up the seat in the house traditionally reserved for the opposition spokesman of highest standing. In 1964 he ended his connection with South Shields, changed his name by deed poll to Chuter-Ede, and went to the upper chamber as a life peer with the title Lord Chuter-Ede of Epsom.

Although overshadowed by more powerful personalities at the top of the Labour hierarchy, Ede had been a respected party figure for over two decades. Close colleagues were struck by his tolerance, humour, and deep commitment to what he called the good old causes of freedom and social justice. Those who knew him less well found him to carry the aura of an austere schoolmaster, especially after the death of his wife in 1948. They were a devoted couple and he was much affected by the loss. There were no children.

The public issue which overshadowed Ede's later life was that of the death penalty. Growing evidence emerged in the mid-1950s that a serious miscarriage of justice had taken place in the case of Timothy John Evans, who had been sentenced to death for murder during Ede's term as home secretary. Ede maintained that he could not have granted a reprieve to Evans on the basis of the evidence available to him at the time, and in this he was supported by official inquiries. But his anguish over the case encouraged him to revise his view of capital punishment.

In old age Ede campaigned for the abolition of the death penalty and for a posthumous free pardon in the case of Evans, whose remains he argued should be transferred from prison to family relatives. This was to be the last struggle of a liberal nonconformist of the old school. After suffering from a fall, Chuter-Ede was admitted to a nursing home, Wilmor Lodge, Epsom Road, Ewell, Surrey, where he died on 11 November 1965—one day after the remains of Evans had been transferred from prison.

KEVIN JEFFERYS

Sources *Labour and the wartime coalition: from the diaries of James Chuter Ede, 1941–1945*, ed. K. Jefferys (1987) · *DNB* · *The Times* (12 Nov 1965) · K. O. Morgan, *Labour in power, 1945–1951* (1984) · K. Jefferys, 'R. A. Butler, the board of education and the 1944 Education Act', *History*, new ser., 69 (1984), 415–31 · M. Barber, *The making of the 1944 Education Act* (1994) · R. Barker, *Education and politics, 1900–1951: a study of the labour party* (1972)
Archives BBC WAC, papers relating to broadcasting · BL, diaries, Add. MSS 59690–59703 · Labour History Archive and Study Centre, Manchester, corresp. · PRO, private office papers relating to education · Surrey HC, corresp. and papers; photographs, scrapbooks, and research notes | Bodl. Oxf., corresp. with Clement Attlee · CUL, corresp. with Sir Samuel Hoare
Likenesses W. Stoneman, photograph, 1941, NPG · H. Coster, photograph, 1945, NPG [*see illus.*] · photograph, 1945, Hult. Arch. · H. Coster, photographs, NPG · photographs, Surrey HC
Wealth at death £7702: probate, 23 Feb 1966, *CGPLA Eng. & Wales*

Edelman, (Israel) Maurice (1911–1975), politician and novelist, was born on 2 March 1911 at Cardiff, the third of five children (two sons and three daughters, one of whom died in childhood) of Joshua Edelman and his wife, Esther Solomon, who had emigrated from eastern Europe in 1904, in the wake of pogroms at the turn of the century. His father, a painter and photographer who had studied art in Berlin, was an early socialist and member of the local labour party. His indigent background was a spur to Maurice Edelman, who secured an exhibition from Cardiff high school to Trinity College, Cambridge, and also gained a state scholarship, a rare achievement in Wales at that time. He obtained a first class in part one of the modern and medieval languages tripos in 1930 and a second class (division one) in part two in 1932. Later in life he was

(Israel) Maurice Edelman (1911–1975), by Mark Gerson, 1959

an accomplished linguist, fluent in French, Italian, German, and Russian.

Going down in a year of economic slump, Edelman sought employment in London and for a time gave French lessons. In the following year he met and married Matilda (Tilli), daughter of Harry Yager, a timber merchant and furniture manufacturer. Edelman was endowed with singular good looks, natural charm, and a mellifluous voice, and his marriage provided him with a secure anchorage. It proved a happy union and his wife played a notable part in his subsequent career. They had two daughters.

For some years Edelman worked in his father-in-law's business. This took him to Scandinavia and to Russia, and he perfected his command of Russian. In 1938, amid condemnation in Britain of the state trials and executions in the USSR, Edelman published *GPU Justice*, an account of the experiences of Peter Kleist, a German engineer working in Russia who had been accused of espionage and briefly imprisoned while undergoing investigation by the GPU. Kleist denied that torture was used and asserted that those who confessed in the show trials were *de facto* guilty, arguing that Stalin's purges were necessary in the face of the fascist threat; Edelman presented Kleist's testimony as destroying 'the more fantastic' of the 'inventions' circulating in the West about the inhumanity of the Soviet state police's treatment of political prisoners (Edelman, *GPU Justice*, 7). Like many on the British left, Edelman's romanticization of the Soviet Union reached its apogee once Russia was engaged in the war against Nazism and in 1942 he wrote a Penguin special, *How Russia Prepared*—described as, by his later standards, a 'dreadfully uncritical eulogy' of the Soviet system (*The Times*, 15 Dec 1975). In

1941 Victor Gollancz's Left Book Club published his critique of British capitalism during the war, *Production for Victory, not Profit!*

Between 1941 and 1944 Edelman was a war correspondent for *Picture Post* and followed the campaigns in north Africa, Italy, and, after D-day, France. He was a gifted journalist, and his articles were graphic and politically astute. De Gaulle was his wartime hero, and throughout his life he was a leading francophile. He was made an officer of the Légion d'honneur in 1960. Towards the end of the war his Penguin Special *France: the Birth of the Fourth Republic* (1944) received much acclaim.

At the general election in 1945 Edelman, who had been almost fortuitously selected as a candidate, was elected Labour MP for Coventry West, which he represented until 1950. From 1950 to February 1974 he represented Coventry North; and from February 1974 to his death in December 1975, Coventry North West. Edelman seemed an obvious candidate for office and few in 1945 would have believed that he would remain a back-bencher for the next thirty years. A courageous and independent-minded man, he was an effective and hard-working parliamentarian. He opposed on moral grounds the manufacture of the hydrogen bomb, and in the 1960s defended the British aircraft and motor industries against job losses: he helped to save the Concorde project from being scrapped. He was strongly in favour of European union and was a delegate to the consultative assembly of the Council of Europe (1949–51 and 1965–70) and chairman of the socialist group in the Western European Union (1968–70). His fluency in French made him a well-known figure in continental politics and he held numerous Anglo-French parliamentary group positions.

Edelman also exposed the enormous profits made by pharmaceutical companies from the sale of brand-name drugs and was in the forefront of the campaign for polio vaccination of children. Towards the end of his career he felt growing concern about the spread of commercial influence on governments, campaigned for a register of ministers' interests, and also saw the need to regulate quangos. But in spite of his hard work and his many talents he failed to win the favour of party leaders or build for himself a strong base in the parliamentary party or trade union movement. In September 1956 he shared his frustration with his friend and colleague Richard Crossman: 'If only I could speak as well as I can write, I would make a real impression in politics'. Crossman replied: 'You can speak as well as you can write, but the trouble is that what you say doesn't matter unless you represent something or have some votes behind you' (*Backbench Diaries*, 512). On this hard political reality Edelman's hopes of office foundered.

Edelman, who had little interest in money, revealed a rare versatility in the arts: he loved to write, paint, and play the balalaika, and sang melodiously. His writing covered a wide spectrum—from the serious political works which grew from his experience as a war correspondent to articles, plays, biographies, and novels mainly on political themes and many of them bestsellers.

He wrote a weekly column in the *New Statesman* and also contributed articles to the mass-circulation newspapers. His journalistic activities, though, had the potential to compromise him with his party and in March 1968 there was an angry exchange with Harold Wilson, during which the latter accused Edelman of serving the *Daily Express* better than his own government. *Who Goes Home* (1953), his second novel, was widely read and, like other later novels, was published in several languages. *A Call on Kuprin* (1959), set in Moscow, showed a prophetic sense of the perils for MPs abroad trapped in compromising situations. It enjoyed a successful Broadway run in 1961. One of the novels, *The Minister* (1961), was reissued in 1994. But he will be best remembered for his last two novels which were authentic portrayals of Disraeli, with whom Edelman felt a special affinity. *Disraeli in Love* (1972) and *Disraeli Rising* (1975) have a lasting quality. The planned third volume was never completed. His deep research and understanding of the man and his period was apparent to leading historians. In 1972 Edelman, imbued with the Disraelian tradition, leased a wing of Hughenden Manor, Disraeli's country house in Buckinghamshire, from the National Trust.

The diversity of Edelman's talents did not detract from his political ambitions, nor did his considerable literary success compensate for his disappointment in not attaining office. He manifested a degree of resentment at being passed over by Wilson, but this did not lessen his attachment to his party, which in later years he feared would be infiltrated by extremists. By then he had 'long since ceased to be enamoured of the left, or Russia', and as president of the Anglo-Jewish Association made strong protests about Soviet treatment of the Jews (*The Times*, 15 Dec 1975). He died suddenly of an embolism on 14 December 1975, at the Brompton Hospital, London, on his return from a parliamentary visit to India.

NEVILLE SANDELSON, *rev.* MARK POTTLE

Sources private information (1986) · personal knowledge (1986) · *The Times* (15 Dec 1975) · F. W. S. Craig, *British parliamentary election results, 1918–1949*, rev. edn (1977) · F. W. S. Craig, *British parliamentary election results, 1950–1970* (1971) · *WWBMP*, vol. 4 · *The diary of Hugh Gaitskell, 1945–1956*, ed. P. M. Williams (1983) · *The backbench diaries of Richard Crossman*, ed. J. Morgan (1981) · R. H. S. Crossman, *The diaries of a cabinet minister*, 3 vols. (1975–7) · *CGPLA Eng. & Wales* (1978)

Archives U. Warwick Mod. RC, diaries, constituency files, papers · U. Warwick Mod. RC, political corresp. |FILM BFI NFTVA, party political footage |SOUND BL NSA, current affairs recording · BL NSA, oral history interview

Likenesses H. Magee, double portrait, photograph, 1943 (with Al Wykes), Hult. Arch. · H. Magee, group portrait, photograph, 1945 (*Team spirit in Coventry*), Hult. Arch. · M. Gerson, photograph, 1959, NPG [*see illus.*]

Wealth at death £60,669: probate, 17 March 1976, *CGPLA Eng. & Wales*

Edelsten, Sir John Hereward (1891–1966), naval officer, was born on 12 May 1891 at Fir Lodge, Village Road, Bush Hill Park, Enfield, the third son of John Jackson Edelsten, a tea broker, and his wife, Jessica Gooding. He entered the Royal Naval College, Osborne, in 1904, under the then new Selborne scheme and after passing on to Dartmouth two years later joined his first ship, the battleship *Hibernia*, as a

Sir John Hereward Edelsten (1891–1966), by Elliott & Fry, 1952

midshipman in September 1908. His relatively poor performance at the colleges reflected a certain slowness of manner which caused one of his superiors to describe him as 'thick headed' (ADM 196/53, fol. 103). Good service at sea in the armoured cruiser *Natal* and battleship *London*, however, led to the report in August 1911 that he 'promises well' (ibid.).

Edelsten became a sub-lieutenant in 1911 and embarked on courses ashore that at that time included engine-room training. He was promoted lieutenant at the end of 1913 while serving as executive officer of the large destroyer *Swift*. By this time he was being assessed much more highly as 'very intelligent … will make exceptionally good officer' (ADM 196/53). It was also noted that Edelsten handled men well. He joined the light cruiser *Yarmouth* in March 1914 and served in her in the Grand Fleet until the end of 1917. A request to specialize in signals led to a signals course in which Edelsten did so well that he was recommended for duty as a flag lieutenant. As such he served Admiral Sir Thomas Hurt, commander-in-chief, South America station, from 1919 to 1921, and at the end of 1921 Edelsten became a lieutenant-commander. At his request he took the war staff course at Greenwich in 1921–2 and then joined *Delhi* as a staff officer to Rear-Admiral Sir Hubert Brand, commanding the 1st light cruiser squadron. The squadron visited the Baltic and Edelsten earned their lordships commendation for his work compiling the intelligence reports resulting from the cruise. The squadron also took part in the empire world cruise in 1923–4. Edelsten next interspersed short courses with service in

the recommissioned reserve cruisers *Carysfort* on trooping duties and *Comus* in the Atlantic before his potential as a staff officer—'splendid qualities of leadership and influence, very tactful' (ibid.)—led to his promotion to commander at the end of 1926 and nomination to represent the navy on the army's staff course at Camberley the following year. Edelsten next taught on the staff course at Greenwich from 1928 to 1930, when he joined the cruiser *London* to serve in her for two years. On 14 December 1926 he married, at Holy Trinity, Brompton, Frances Anne Hoile, daughter of H. V. Masefield. They had no children.

Edelsten seems to have been chosen for higher things and was promoted captain on 30 June 1933. He was also sent on a number of courses in 1933–4, including that at the Imperial Defence College. Edelsten then commissioned the new light cruiser *Galatea* in 1935 before taking up the Admiralty staff appointment of deputy director of plans at a key time, the beginning of 1938. He was still in this appointment when war broke out in 1939 but went back to sea on active service in the cruiser *Shropshire* in March 1940, serving on trade protection duties in the south Atlantic and Indian oceans. In 1940–41 he was senior naval officer in the operations against Italian Somaliland.

At the Admiralty, Edelsten had attracted the favourable attention of the then deputy chief of naval staff, Sir Andrew Cunningham, who had been appointed commander-in-chief, Mediterranean, in 1939. In March 1941 Cunningham lost his trusted chief of staff, Rear-Admiral Sir Algernon Willis, and needed an able staff officer to take his place. After some disagreement with Sir Dudley Pound, the first sea lord, he insisted on Edelsten. As Cunningham later wrote, he had 'marked him down as a very fine officer', knew that Pound's predecessor as first sea lord, Sir Roger Backhouse, 'had had the highest opinion of this officer', and felt that 'no better man could have been found' to replace Willis (Cunningham, 324). The position brought the rank of commodore, first class.

Edelsten went to sea in March before he actually relieved Willis to gain experience and this happened to be the sortie that culminated in the battle of Matapan. From the flagship *Warspite* Edelsten was the first to spot the Italian cruiser *Zara* and *Fiume* leading directly to their rapid destruction. Edelsten remained as chief of staff to the commander-in-chief, Mediterranean, until the end of 1942, having been promoted rear-admiral in February. In June he was mentioned in dispatches 'for outstanding zeal, patience and cheerfulness and for never failing to set an example of wholehearted devotion to duty without which the traditions of the Royal Navy could not have been upheld' (ADM 196/53, fol. 103).

Edelsten returned to London for the hardly less exacting task of assistant chief of naval staff with membership of the Board of Admiralty and special responsibility for anti-U-boat warfare and trade defence. The battle of the Atlantic reached its climax in 1943 under Edelsten's direction. He began to serve his old master again when Cunningham replaced Pound in October 1943 and the first sea lord's support helped him in the following year to gain the post of rear-admiral, destroyers, in the new British Pacific Fleet

(BPF). This was a remarkable expression of confidence in a staff officer by a destroyer man and a recognition of the nature of the duties required from a rear-admiral (D) in the context of the late war when all Edelsten's tact would be required for Anglo-American relations and his organizational ability for the logistical demands of the destroyer flotillas in the huge Pacific theatre.

Edelsten was promoted vice-admiral shortly after the war ended and in October 1945 was briefly appointed flag officer commanding the 1st battle squadron and the western area BPF. At the end of the year as the battleships went home he moved to command the 4th cruiser squadron but his staff skills were soon required back at the Admiralty, being first used from late 1946 as an adviser to the deputy chief of naval staff and then in being appointed back to the board as vice-chief of naval staff in 1947. He became a full admiral in February 1949 and was appointed as commander-in-chief, Mediterranean, the following year. Edelsten's diplomatic skills were at a premium in the early uncertain days of NATO in the Mediterranean, as they were in his next and last position as commander-in-chief, Portsmouth, from 1952 to 1954, when he was the first NATO commander-in-chief, channel. He was designated the next commander-in-chief, Home Fleet, but plans changed and Edelsten was placed on the retired list on 24 November 1954. In retirement he was made rear-admiral of the United Kingdom in 1955 and vice-admiral of the United Kingdom and lieutenant of the Admiralty in 1962.

Edelsten was made CBE in September 1941 for his services off Somaliland. He was appointed CB in the king's birthday honours in June 1944 and received his knighthood as KCB in June 1946. He was promoted GCB in January 1953. Edelsten's services to the allied cause throughout the war were marked by appointment to the American Legion of Merit in the degree of commander in June 1946 and he was promoted in this order in 1954 in recognition of his later services to NATO. In 1947 he also received the cross of the grand order of the Phoenix with swords from the king of the Hellenes. In May 1953 he was appointed first and principal aide-de-camp to the queen, and was made a knight grand cross in the Royal Victorian Order in the coronation honours of that year. Admiral Sir John Edelsten died on 10 February 1966 at Westlands, Longmoor Road, Liphook, Bramshott, Hampshire. He was survived by his wife.   ERIC J. GROVE

Sources PRO, ADM 196/53, fol. 103 [naval service record of Admiral Sir J. H. Edelsten] · *WWW, 1961–70* · A. Cunningham [first Viscount Cunningham], *A sailor's odyssey: the autobiography of admiral of the fleet, Viscount Cunningham of Hyndhope* (1951) · b. cert. · d. cert.

Archives CAC Cam., corresp. and papers · Royal Naval Museum, diaries while midshipman on HMS *Hibernia*, HMS *Natal*, and HMS *London* | BL, Cunningham MSS · PRO, Admiralty MSS (ADM) | FILM IWM FVA, actuality footage

Likenesses Elliott & Fry, photograph, 1952, NPG [*see illus.*]

Wealth at death £8651: probate, 8 June 1966, *CGPLA Eng. & Wales*

Edema, Gerard [Gerardus] (*b. c.*1652, *d.* in or before 1707), landscape painter, was born either in Friesland or in Amsterdam. He may have been the Gerard Edema who was baptized on 13 June 1656 in Amsterdam, the second son out of the four children of Hercules Edema (*b.* 1616) and his wife, Marijke, *née* Rotgans (*b.* 1619), though this has not been established conclusively. He was apprenticed to Allart van Everdingen (1621–1675), landscape painter, in Amsterdam. Edema travelled extensively: to Norway, to Newfoundland and New York, and also to Surinam. Gerard is probably the Nicholas Edema who painted insects and plants in Surinam. He is said to have settled in England about 1670. His arrival coincided with a burgeoning in the popularity of decorative landscape painting, and his pictures were set as overdoors or mantlepieces into the panelling of English country houses such as Althorp and Drayton House in Northamptonshire. Lord Radnor, the duke of Schomberg, and Lord Ranelagh also owned a number of his paintings, although these collections have long been dispersed.

Van Everdingen painted from nature and helped introduce a vogue for dramatic Scandinavian scenes. Edema also chose to portray wild prospects with mountain storms, cliffs and waterfalls, winding rivers and fallen trees. At Chatsworth there are three paintings by him, one an enormous *Mountainous Landscape with Devastated Fir Trees*, which presages the Romantic movement. Lionel Cust wrote, 'their strange and awe-inspiring character earned him the name of "the Salvator Rosa of the North"' (*DNB*). But the mood of other paintings is sometimes tempered by a quieter, less moralistic tone, the landscape a perfect emerald under a cool refreshing light, as in two scenes of waterfalls which more suitably decorate a bedchamber at Drayton. There is little evidence in his pictures of the cultivation of man, though small human figures take their properly diminutive place in their sometimes daunting natural surroundings. These figures were apparently often painted in by Jan Wyck, and Edema is also said to have collaborated over seascapes with William Van der Velde the younger. His occasional topographical views include several of Plymouth which he made at Mount Edgcumbe when he was, together with Van der Velde and Wyck, a guest of the amateur artist Sir Richard Edgcumbe.

Edema never received denization, and does not appear to have married. He died before 13 April 1707 when two of his creditors applied for administration of his estate, in Richmond, Surrey. There he had at least twice painted views of the Thames from the top of Richmond Hill (one is in the Royal Collection, together with *The Weir*). Buckeridge stated that 'His too great intemperance shortened his days' (Buckeridge, 370).   KATHARINE GIBSON

Sources [B. Buckeridge], 'An essay towards an English school', in R. de Piles, *The art of painting, with the lives and characters of above 300 of the most eminent painters*, 3rd edn (1754), 354–439; facs. edn (1969), esp. 370 · H. V. S. Ogden and M. S. Ogden, *English taste in landscape in the seventeenth century* (1955), 121–3, 149, 155 · O. Millar, *The Tudor, Stuart and early Georgian pictures in the collection of her majesty the queen*, 2 vols. (1963), vol. 1, p.26; vol. 2, cat. nos. 434–7 · E. Waterhouse, *Painting in Britain, 1530–1790*, 4th edn (1978), 154 · H. Walpole, *Anecdotes of painting in England: with some account of the principal artists*, ed. R. N. Wornum, new edn, 3 vols. (1888), vol. 2, p. 132 ·

DNB • Vertue, *Note books*, 1.131–2; 4.29; 5.48, 50 • *IGI* • administration, PRO, PROB 6/83, fol. 195*r*

Eden, (Robert) Anthony, first earl of Avon (1897–1977), prime minister, was born at Windlestone Hall, Ferryhill, co. Durham, on 12 June 1897. He was the third of the four sons, and the fourth of the five surviving children, of Sir William *Eden (1849–1915), seventh baronet of the first creation (1672) and fifth baronet of the second (1776), whose estates in co. Durham and Northumberland extended to some 8000 acres marching with each other. Speculation that Eden could actually have been the son of George Wyndham, the Victorian statesman and man of letters, to whom he bore a striking physical resemblance, is inaccurate, as Wyndham was in South Africa at the time of Eden's conception. Eden's mother was Sybil Frances (1867–1945), daughter of Sir William *Grey, a great-niece of the second Earl Grey, prime minister from 1830 to 1834, and a kinsman of one of her son's predecessors as foreign secretary, Sir Edward Grey. Alec Douglas-Home, prime minister (1963–4), was also a distant collateral through the Grey line. Eden thus had both landowning and political threads in his lineage, though his upbringing in Durham gave him an insight into domestic issues that placed him firmly in the tory paternalist 'one nation' tradition.

Early years and education Eden was a sensitive child, who had a somewhat lonely upbringing at Windlestone Hall. His father was an irascible and distant figure, though Eden's aesthetic sensibility, not to mention his sometimes short temper, was inherited from his father, who was an amateur painter of renown and a noted collector of art. From his mother, a renowned society beauty, not over-cautious in financial matters, he inherited charm and his handsome bearing. His closest relationships within the family circle, however, were with his elder sister, Marjorie, ten years his senior, who was a protective shield against the unpredictable whims of his sometimes eccentric parents, and with his younger brother, Nicholas, three years his junior, to whom he was devoted. A vivid portrait of life at Windlestone is contained in the memoir *Tribulations of a Baronet* (1933), written by his second brother, Sir Timothy Eden. Eden learned French and German at an early age, and was later able to converse fluently with his political counterparts in private; however, he never negotiated in a foreign language but always through an interpreter, thereby avoiding the embarrassment and ambiguity suffered by some twentieth-century prime ministers who had an exaggerated confidence in their linguistic abilities.

Eden's education was the traditional one of the landed class. After private tuition at Windlestone, in April 1907 he joined his brother Timothy as a boarder at Sandroyd School in Cobham, an established nursery for Eton College. Even as a young boy he followed keenly the consequences of Lloyd George's 'people's budget' of 1909, women's suffrage (which he supported), and the growing home-rule crisis in Ireland. He entered Eton College in the Lent half of 1911. To the surprise of his father, for whom religion was a closed book, he won the Brinckman divinity

(Robert) Anthony Eden, first earl of Avon (1897–1977), by Philippe Halsman, 1955

prize, though his main enthusiasms were for languages and modern history. His sporting interests centred on the river and on individual sports such as fives, at which he also proved proficient. He was rowing on the Thames when he heard of the assassination of Archduke Ferdinand at Sarajevo in June 1914. The shadow of war hung over his last year at Eton, as each Sunday the lists of the latest casualties, many known personally to him, were read out in chapel, including his eldest brother, John, killed in France with the 12th lancers on 17 October 1914. His second brother, Timothy, in Germany when war broke out, was imprisoned for two years in a prison camp outside Berlin. For Eden, already an enthusiastic and accomplished Shakespearian, the saying that sorrows come not as single spies was never more evident than when he heard of the death of his father, after a long illness, on 20 February 1915.

Military service in the First World War On leaving Eton, Eden enlisted with the 21st battalion, the yeoman rifles, of the King's Royal Rifle Corps, on 29 September 1915. He saw active service for the first time at Ploegsteert Wood in May 1916. Shortly after arriving in France, Eden heard the devastating news that his youngest brother, Nicholas, a midshipman on HMS *Indefatigable*, had been killed at the age of sixteen at the battle of Jutland. He experienced some of the most bitter fighting in the trenches of the western front. In June 1917 he was awarded the Military Cross for his selfless rescue of his wounded sergeant under fire at Ploegsteert. His last posting was in the British lines at La

Fère on the River Oise in March 1918 at the time of the Ludendorff spring offensive. On 26 May 1918 he was promoted brigade major in the 198th infantry brigade, at the age of twenty the youngest in the British army.

Eden's upbringing and gentlemanly reticence meant that he rarely referred to his formative experiences during the First World War, but its effects were profound, convincing him in the 1930s that a resolution and steadfastness in the face of the dictators was the policy best able to prevent the tragedy of a further world war. Only with the publication of his memoir *Another World, 1897–1917* in 1976, the year before his death, did many first fully realize the intensity of these formative experiences for him, though even then he stressed the camaraderie in adversity as an enduring theme.

Oxford and political apprenticeship After demobilization with the rank of captain on 13 June 1919, the day after his twenty-second birthday, Eden returned to Windlestone to contemplate his future career. Even the beauties of the park were not inseparable from his memories of the war, and he wondered if he 'could ever again see them free from the memory of those other shell-torn trees and ravaged fields with their torn wire and heaped and silent bodies' (Avon MSS, AP 7/25/19). He had no prospect of inheriting either the baronetcy or, after his mother's litigious dealings with moneylenders, what little money remained, and until the publication of his memoirs in the 1960s finance was a continuing concern. One aristocratic lady to whom he was attracted even declined interest in him because he was not an eldest son with prospects.

Eden's first thought on demobilization had been to seek a diplomatic career, but he feared this would be a slow-track world, 'forever handing round teacups in Teheran' (Eden, *Memoirs*, 1.4). Nevertheless, he felt that a knowledge of Eastern languages would be invaluable in any future political career, and in the autumn of 1919 he entered Christ Church, Oxford, to read oriental languages, specializing in Persian and Arabic. He obtained first-class honours in 1922. The Middle East was thereafter one of his main areas of interest. Unusually for a putative politician Eden took no interest in the Oxford Union, but along with Lord David Cecil and Henry (Chips) Channon founded the Uffizi Society in November 1920. As president Eden invited many of the leading artistic figures of the day, such as Augustus John and Roger Fry, to speak. Eden's own scholarly paper for the Uffizi on Cezanne, privately printed, was long remembered for its far-sighted appreciation of the artist's innovations. In 1921, while on vacation in Munich, Eden bought a Constable for £200, the beginning of a lifelong enthusiasm for collecting. He also made shrewd purchases of paintings by Degas, Braque, and Picasso, as 'an amateur of the arts, who if circumstances had been different might have been a painter' (D. Sutton, 'A statesman's collection', *Apollo*, June 1969).

At the general election of November 1922 Eden stood in the Conservative interest in the Labour stronghold of Spennymoor in his home county—a valuable, if forlorn, apprenticeship. Eden's opportunity to enter parliament came the following year at Warwick and Leamington, a seat he was to retain for the next thirty-four years. Lord Willoughby de Broke, the local Conservative Association chairman and a veteran of the House of Lords crisis of 1911, recommended Eden to his executive committee because of Eden's knowledge of unemployment questions from his earlier campaign in Spennymoor. The election attracted wide attention owing to the unconventional socialist candidature of Frances, countess of Warwick, mother-in-law of Eden's sister, Marjorie, who toured the constituency in a carriage drawn by four milk-white steeds, and was mistaken by many voters as an advertisement for *The Garden of Allah* at the Leamington Playhouse. Initially a by-election, the contest at Warwick and Leamington was subsumed into the general election of 6 December 1923 after the Conservative prime minister, Stanley Baldwin, had sought an unexpected, and unsuccessful, mandate for his protectionist policy. Eden won a majority of over 5000.

On the afternoon of 5 November 1923, during a lull in the campaign, Eden married Beatrice Helen Beckett (1905–1957), also related to Frances, countess of Warwick, and daughter of Sir Gervase Beckett, baronet (created 1921). They were to have three sons, Simon (*b.* 1924), Robert (*b.* 1928), who survived for only fifteen minutes, and Nicholas (*b.* 1930), named in memory of Eden's younger brother.

Eden's father-in-law, a prominent banker and chairman of the *Yorkshire Post*, a Conservative newspaper of influence in the north of England, was to be of inestimable value to Eden in his early political career. Through Beckett he gained a source of supplementary income and a forum, as a contributor to the *Yorkshire Post*, of articles, many on foreign policy, following his empire tour of 1925. Eden's first book, *Places in the Sun* (1926), with an admiring preface from Stanley Baldwin, was a collection of these articles for the *Yorkshire Post*. For his part, Eden always remembered Baldwin's advice to him as young back-bencher—never to underestimate the Labour Party opposite. 'You may have had better educational advantages, do not presume upon that, they know more about unemployment insurance than you' (Eden, *Memoirs*, 1.5). He was also influenced in his early years in parliament by the Conservative MP Noel Skelton, who emphasized the importance of 'a property-owning democracy'.

Eden's own assertive maiden speech in the House of Commons on 19 February 1924, in support of Sir Samuel Hoare, stressed the importance of strong air defences and was critical of Labour pacifism. With the return of a Conservative government in October 1924, he became an unpaid parliamentary private secretary to Godfrey Locker Lampson, under-secretary at the Home Office. But his interests were increasingly on defence and foreign policy, and in July 1926 Eden was appointed parliamentary private secretary to Sir Austen Chamberlain, the foreign secretary, then at the height of his reputation after the Locarno treaty of 1925. This decisive promotion conditioned much of Eden's later thinking, and he learned at first hand from Sir Austen Chamberlain how the Foreign Office operated. Like his mentor, Eden believed that the best way to keep the peace in Europe was to remain on good terms with France, at a time when many in the Conservative Party were impatient of such views, favouring *rapprochement* with Germany. With Chamberlain's illness and absence in 1928 Eden achieved unexpected autonomy and was widely regarded as a potential foreign secretary.

In May 1929 Ramsay MacDonald formed a minority government, and Eden, on the left of his party and a supporter of Baldwin during his 1930 leadership difficulties, seized his opportunity in opposition to address the question of the future direction of Conservative philosophy. Eden dined weekly with a group of like-minded progressive tories, which included Noel Skelton, William Ormsby-Gore, Walter Elliot, W. S. Morrison, and Oliver Stanley. Eden, with his film-star looks, was already in the early 1930s the glass of fashion and the mould of form, cutting a dashing figure in his immaculate suits and Homburgs, soon known as the Eden hat. (Together with the duke of Wellington, he was thus one of only two British prime ministers to have given his name eponymously to an article of clothing or footwear.) His outward image, cultivated at this time in the popular press as the Beau Brummel of British politics (even his London residence was Beau Brummel's former house in Chesterfield Street), disguised a deeper seriousness, often denied by his critics in Westminster, who were envious of his swift ascent. His diligent work behind the scenes at Conservative associations, speaking on the need for the party in an age of mass enfranchisement (completed by Baldwin's government in 1928), to enable all workers to become capitalists through industrial co-partnership schemes, did not make the headlines. Eden consolidated his reputation as a coming man with speeches on defence and overseas policy, especially on League of Nations affairs.

National Government minister The short-lived Labour government came to an end with the financial crisis of August 1931. When Ramsay MacDonald formed a national coalition government, both Baldwin and Austen Chamberlain pressed Eden's claims with the new foreign secretary, Rufus Isaacs, first marquess of Reading, and Eden was appointed under-secretary of state at the Foreign Office. As Reading was in the upper house, Eden was prominent as the Foreign Office's lone representative in the Commons, particularly over the Manchurian crisis in September. After the general election on 27 October 1931, Sir John Simon became foreign secretary. Eden's relationship with his new political master was complex, and soon one of disillusionment. As a relatively junior figure in the political hierarchy, Eden was exasperated by Simon's unwillingness to get to grips with the pragmatic details of international diplomacy, especially at the World Disarmament Conference in Geneva between 1932 and 1934. But this proved Eden's opportunity, and he swiftly became established as a respected British presence on the international scene. On 31 December 1933 Eden was promoted to the post of lord privy seal.

With the collapse of the disarmament conference in Geneva and Germany's withdrawal from the League of Nations, Eden now became a roving ambassador for the Foreign Office, and in the next fourteen months was to become the first Western politician to meet Hitler, Mussolini, and Stalin. He derived different impressions of all three, regarding Mussolini and Stalin as the most sinister. At his meeting with Hitler, the two men found that they had been serving on opposite banks of the River Oise in 1918, and Hitler was more keen on military reminiscences than the 'Memorandum on disarmament' Eden had brought for discussion. Eden was wary of Hitler's easy charm, which the Führer turned on at will, but he made a more favourable impression than Mussolini, whom Eden regarded as a complete gangster with dreadful table manners to boot. In Moscow in March 1935, Eden was most struck by the intense cruelty of Stalin's face; at a time when many of his domestic political opponents had a rose-tinted view of Russia, Eden never forgot that he was dealing with a tyrannical state.

Following the assassination in October 1934 of King Alexander of Yugoslavia and the French foreign minister, Louis Barthou, Eden acted as a mediator for the League of Nations in the ensuing Balkan crisis. The acceptance of Eden's proposals, which prevented another 'Sarajevo', owed much to his patient diplomacy and added greatly to his international reputation. Owing to severe heart strain in April 1935, exacerbated by a turbulent flight home from Czechoslovakia, he was unable to attend the Anglo-French-Italian conference at Stresa that month. As a result Ramsay MacDonald, on the verge of retirement as prime minister, reluctantly headed the British delegation. Eden had little confidence in Simon's ability as foreign secretary to address the question either of Germany's expansionist aims or Mussolini's ambitions towards Emperor Haile Selassie's Abyssinia. Privately, he agreed with the former deputy cabinet secretary Thomas Jones that 'MacDonald and Simon funked talking straight out to Mussolini because they wanted his support in Europe' (T. Jones, *A Diary with Letters, 1931–1950*, 1954, 187).

In the National Government reshuffle in June 1935 following MacDonald's retirement, Eden entered the cabinet for the first time as minister for League of Nations affairs (without portfolio), an awkwardly worded title that overcame the law officers' objections about the minister without portfolio actually having a designated special responsibility. Sir Samuel Hoare, the secretary of state for India, had been appointed foreign secretary, and Eden was deeply pessimistic about these dyarchical arrangements. Hoare stated that there was no League of Nations department, yet Robert Cecil, Viscount Cranborne, one of Eden's closest friends, was appointed parliamentary undersecretary, and questions were submitted specifically to Eden in the House of Commons, a practice Hoare resisted. Further disagreements with Hoare followed over negotiations with Mussolini, after the invasion on 4 October 1935 of Abyssinia, a fellow member of the League of Nations.

First term as foreign secretary In December 1935 public opinion brought about Hoare's resignation following the Hoare–Laval pact, which ceded substantial parts of Abyssinia to Mussolini. He was replaced as foreign secretary by

Eden on 22 December 1935. Eden was not the automatic choice as Hoare's successor, and for a while Baldwin shrank from the decision. But after rejecting Eden's own suggestions of Sir Austen Chamberlain and Lord Halifax as possible replacements, Baldwin ended a bizarre conversation by saying 'It looks as if it will have to be you' (Eden, *Memoirs*, 1.316). With this far from ringing endorsement Eden assumed the high office with which his name was forever to be associated. He was the youngest foreign secretary since Lord Granville in 1851 and, apart from Sir Edward Grey, he was to be the longest serving foreign secretary of the twentieth century. At the age of thirty-eight, Eden was now the crown prince of the Conservative Party, though, as he was to observe, this was 'a position not necessarily enviable in politics' (Eden, *Full Circle*, 266).

Eden became foreign secretary at a critical time in international relations. Mussolini was established in Abyssinia, Hitler was shortly to tighten his grip on the demilitarized Rhineland, and in the Far East the Japanese planned further advances through China. All three countries were potential enemies of Great Britain and, although Eden did not regard Europe and the Far East as separate problems, he was more hopeful of Anglo-American co-operation against Japan than in conflicts nearer to home, a hope not fulfilled by the Brussels Conference of 1937 and the disregard shown by the Japanese government to the polite diplomatic appeals of Mr Cordell Hull.

Also on the agenda in Brussels was the Spanish Civil War, which had broken out in July 1936 and was to continue until March 1939. Eden agreed with the duke of Wellington that there was no European country in which foreigners could interfere with so little advantage as Spain, and his main aim, outlined in October 1936 at the Conservative Party conference in Llandudno, was one of non-intervention, but not indifference. His main concerns were to keep Italian intervention at bay and to maintain British freedom of commerce in the Mediterranean. He was helped in this aim by Leon Blum, the new French prime minister, who proposed a wider non-intervention agreement, with Anglo-French solidarity at its core. Eden described this policy in the House of Commons on 29 October 1936 as 'an improvised safety-curtain' (*Hansard 5C*, vol. 316, p. 51) and the best means of limiting the risks of war. But it came at the cost of any reconstruction of the Stresa front and a brake on Germany's expansionist plans. An earlier attempt by Eden to establish oil sanctions against Italy in February 1936 was opposed by Pierre Flandin, the new French foreign minister. To Flandin's confident assertion that sanctions would not work, Eden replied that it was difficult, in that case, to understand why Mussolini was so exercised about the prospect. When Hitler occupied the demilitarized zone of the Rhineland in March 1936 both dictators had achieved their immediate aims. In retrospect Eden considered this failure to treat the occupation as a *casus belli* a grave mistake, though at the time he had believed that it was in Britain's interest to conclude with Germany 'as far reaching and enduring a settlement as possible whilst Herr Hitler is in the mood to do so' (Eden, *Memoirs*, 1.345).

November 1936 saw the establishment of the Rome–Berlin axis, and the anti-Comintern pact between Germany and Japan to oppose international communism. Not all agreed with Eden that this posed the greatest threat to Russia. But when Italy joined the anti-Comintern pact a year later and left the League of Nations, Count Ciano, the Italian foreign minister, confided to his diary that the pact was 'unmistakably anti-British' (Count Ciano, *Ciano's Diary, 1937–38*, 1952, 27).

Eden's concerns at this time were not solely in the international arena. When he became foreign secretary Sir Warren Fisher, head of the home civil service, made it clear he wished ambassadorial appointments to be submitted through him to the prime minister. Eden flatly refused to comply, stating that his constitutional duties in this matter were to serve the monarch, not a civil servant. In the battle of wills, Eden eventually prevailed, but at the avoidable expense for a man of his temperament of much emotional energy. He was reassured when Baldwin told him that any cabinet of twenty members contained only one who wanted to be minister of labour, but that there would always be nineteen who thought they could be foreign secretary. Indeed five former foreign secretaries remained in parliament in 1935, and although one of them, Lord Reading, died in late December, Eden was initially conscious of the scrutiny of his predecessors.

Eden's diplomatic successes in 1936 reassured many who would have preferred a more senior figure in the Foreign Office. On 20 July his contribution at the Montreux convention, over the delicate question of the passage of warships through the Dardanelles, and in a manner acceptable to Turkey, improved relations between the two countries and had concomitant benefits for the allies during the early years of the Second World War. Even one of Eden's severest critics has written that the convention 'constituted one of the most enduring and valuable, if generally underrated, of his achievements' (Carlton, 97). The Anglo-Egyptian treaty of friendship and alliance, signed in the Locarno Room at the Foreign Office on 26 August 1936, was also important in the next decade. The international character of the Suez Canal was confirmed, the demands for Egyptian independence recognized, and British troops guaranteed a base in the Suez Canal Zone for twenty years. When the treaty was renegotiated in 1954, it proved the prelude to the Suez crisis two years later.

When Neville Chamberlain succeeded Stanley Baldwin as prime minister in May 1937, Eden initially welcomed the prospect of a more pro-active Downing Street involvement in foreign affairs, especially as Chamberlain shared his view that war with Germany could be avoided through rearmament and collective security backed by the League of Nations. 'I entirely agree that we must make every effort to come to terms with Germany', wrote Eden to Chamberlain on 31 January 1938 (PRO, PREM 1/276). Eden's popularity and prestige also served a useful purpose for Chamberlain in that it reinforced the isolation of Winston

Churchill on the back benches. But Chamberlain's belief that Mussolini could be wooed as a friend of Britain, or that his friendship was even worth having, was regarded by Eden with profound mistrust, as was Chamberlain's increasing reliance at this time on his personal adviser, Sir Horace Wilson. Eden found that he no longer enjoyed the easy rapport that had existed with Baldwin, and an unhappy time ensued, with disagreements on Chamberlain's whole approach and attitude to the conduct of foreign policy. 'I fear the difference between Anthony and me is more fundamental than he realises', wrote Chamberlain. 'At bottom he is really dead against making terms with the dictators' (N. Chamberlain to H. Chamberlain, 15 Oct 1938, Neville Chamberlain papers, Birmingham University Library, NC 18/1/1073). As a result Chamberlain bypassed Eden, whom he saw as a hindrance to his wish for Anglo-Italian rapprochement, writing in his diary of a letter to Mussolini, after a private meeting with Count Grandi, the Italian ambassador in London, in July 1937, 'I did not show my letter to the Foreign Secretary, for I had the feeling that he would object to it' (K. Feiling, *The Life of Neville Chamberlain*, 1946, 330).

Objections from Eden did arise over Halifax's proposed visit to Berlin in November 1937 for talks with Goering. When Eden, who was ill at the time, learned that Halifax would in fact also be travelling on to Berchtesgaden to see Hitler, he felt this 'pursuit' of the Führer gave entirely the wrong signals. Halifax's visit went ahead, but the main political consequence of the episode was the replacement on 1 January 1938 of the increasingly anti-Germanic Sir Robert Vansittart as permanent under-secretary at the Foreign Office by Sir Alexander Cadogan. In a curious sideways move Vansittart became chief diplomatic adviser to his majesty's government, and Chamberlain and Eden still seemed in outward accord. Eden's relationship with Cadogan over the next eighteen years was to be an important thread in his career. 'I don't think any Secretary of State I served', Cadogan later wrote of Eden, 'excelled him in finesse, or as a negotiator, or in knowledge of foreign affairs' (A. Cadogan, *The Diaries of Sir Alexander Cadogan, 1938–45*, ed. D. Dilks, 1971, 345).

Resignation, February 1938 The seeds of Eden's eventual break with Chamberlain can be traced back to the Nyon Conference of September 1937 over the protection of Mediterranean shipping routes against piracy, a success that Chamberlain thought had been secured at the expense of Anglo-Italian relations. 'Even if our relations with Italy could be much improved', Eden argued in cabinet, 'it would make very little, if any, difference to our military preparations' (cabinet minutes, 8 Sept 1938, PRO, CAB 23/89). Chamberlain's personal diplomacy, and the ill-advised and unofficial interventions in Italy of his sister-in-law, Dame Ivy Chamberlain (Sir Austen's widow), who was received by Mussolini in the Palazzo Venezia in Rome and who had 'talks' with Count Ciano, the Italian foreign minister, in February 1938, placed Eden in what he described as 'a most difficult position' (Eden, *Memoirs*, 1.573). Although the prime minister apologized and promised to curb his sister-in-law's activities, he was privately delighted that progress was being made with Mussolini and Ciano.

The fundamental disagreements about the conduct of foreign policy came to a head over the Roosevelt initiative of 12 January 1938. While Eden was on holiday abroad, the president had sent Chamberlain secret details of a plan by his assistant secretary of state, Sumner Welles, to call an international conference in Washington, with a deadline of 17 January for acceptance of the invitation by Britain, so that the proposal could be presented as a *fait accompli* to smaller nations. Sir Ronald Lindsay, the British ambassador in Washington, recommended a quick acceptance, but Chamberlain would not commit the British government. Warned by Cadogan of these developments, Eden returned post-haste from the south of France and tried in vain to reverse Chamberlain's response. In a furious confrontation with Chamberlain, Eden pointed out that the choice was between Anglo-American co-operation or a dubious piecemeal settlement with an untrustworthy Mussolini over *de jure* recognition of the Italian position in Abyssinia. As with the earlier struggle with Warren Fisher, Eden prevailed, but it proved a hollow victory. Roosevelt's initiative lapsed after Eden had left the government, prompting speculation in some quarters that the president's hidden agenda had been support for Chamberlain in his difficulties with Eden. The issue of Mussolini's 'volunteers' in the Spanish Civil War, and Ciano's insistence that the British should go to Rome for talks on the issue, was the final straw that drove Eden to resignation on 20 February 1938, together with Cranborne and J. P. L. Thomas, his parliamentary private secretary. Cranborne and Thomas were to prove enduring pillars of support throughout the sometimes lonely phases of Eden's career. 'Why should we go to Rome?', wrote Thomas later of these dramatic events, outlining Eden's position.

We were not the debtors in this affair. We were the creditors. It was not we who had broken our word and damaged our reputation. It was Italy. If she wanted good relations with us, let her come to London. (MS cilc. coll. 61, Cilcennin papers)

Halifax succeeded Eden at the Foreign Office, a sign of Chamberlain's determination to control policy.

In a muted resignation speech, on 21 February 1938, Eden said 'There are occasions when strong political convictions must override all other considerations' (*Hansard 5C*, vol. 332, p. 42). His resignation has been compared to that of Lord Randolph Churchill, but the circumstances were quite different: Eden's aim was not to bring down the Chamberlain government or to manoeuvre himself into 10 Downing Street. The government had decided on a broad policy which he could not recommend to the House of Commons or the country, and he thus felt he had no option but to resign. The delicacy of the situation meant that he could not fully reveal the background to his decision, and this led to charges, from within the Conservative ranks as well as from the Labour Party, of wounded vanity or hidden ambition. The government whips' office even referred disparagingly to his followers after his resignation as 'the Glamour Boys'.

Reactions covered the whole gamut. Count Ciano was

relieved that Eden had gone, 'for an Eden Cabinet', he wrote in his diary, 'would have as its first aim the fight against the dictatorships—Mussolini's first' (Count Ciano, *Ciano's Diary, 1937–38*, 1952, 78). In a famous passage in his war memoirs, published in 1948, by which time Eden was his deputy, Churchill wrote,

> There seemed one strong young figure standing up against long, dismal, drawling tides of drift and surrender, or wrong measurements and feeble impulses. He seemed at this moment to embody the life-hope of the British nation. … Now he was gone.   (W. S. Churchill, *The Gathering Storm*, 1948, 257)

One consequence of this later romanticized picture was that it reinforced the tendency to see the pre-war appeasement debate in personal terms, the Municheers versus the Churchillians. Was one for 'The Coroner' (Neville Chamberlain) or against him? The issues were more complex than that, and not all who were sceptical of Chamberlain's strategy were in alliance with Chartwell. Eden disagreed with Churchill over the relative threats posed by Hitler and Mussolini, and in the immediate pre-war era they were not natural political allies. Eden was willing to admit his own mistakes, especially the appointment in April 1937 of Sir Nevile Henderson to the embassy in Berlin, the one occasion when he did not see the candidate personally before a new mission. For his part, Churchill was disappointed that Eden, despite his following among the 'Glamour Boys', was not more of a focus for criticism of the Chamberlain government, especially after the Munich agreement of September 1938. But there was a sense of constraint about Eden, who did not see what purpose would be served by such action. By his conciliatory speech in the Munich debate he left the door open for his eventual return to government.

Rehabilitation, 1938–1940 Eden's resignation brought him international recognition, but his first, and uncontroversial, speech was to his constituents in Warwick and Leamington. Chamberlain and Halifax thanked Eden and had no complaints when he visited America in December 1938, where he was treated more like visiting royalty and received at the White House by Roosevelt and Sumner Welles. As war became ever more inevitable during 1939, Eden (at the age of forty-two) joined the London rangers, a motor battalion of the King's Royal Rifle Corps. The news of the German–Soviet pact reached him while in camp with the King's Royal Rifle Corps at Beaulieu. On 29 August, Churchill and Eden were photographed walking to the House of Commons for the recall of parliament amid demands for their recall to high office. 'If we are to have an inner War Cabinet', ran the accompanying caption when the photograph was published, 'it is difficult to see how either of them can be left out of it' (*The Tatler*, 6 Sept 1939).

On 3 September, when war was declared, Eden accepted office in the National Government as dominions secretary. Churchill returned to the Admiralty, but unlike Eden as a member of the war cabinet. Although Eden was disappointed with the division of the spoils, he regarded it as his patriotic duty to serve. He dealt efficiently with a myriad of problems in his spell at the Dominions Office, not least the intractable question of Éire, still technically a dominion, which had declared itself to be neutral. In February 1940 Eden flew to Cairo and personally met Australian and New Zealand troops on their arrival at Suez. He always retained a special affection for New Zealand among Commonwealth countries. While in Egypt, Eden bore a message from George VI to the young King Farouk of Egypt. 'Unhappily', reported Eden to the king, 'there is no Egyptian [Lord] Melbourne to guide and warn', a warning of prophetic irony in the light of later events.

In May 1940 Chamberlain fell from power and was replaced by Churchill as prime minister. For the Municheers this was an unmitigated disaster. 'The good clean tradition of English politics', said R. A. Butler, 'had been sold to the greatest adventurer of modern political history' (J. Colville, *The Fringes of Power: Downing Street Diaries, 1939–1955*, 1985, 122). Churchill's arrival in Downing Street was to prove the turning point of Eden's career. As the new war secretary, Eden moved closer to the executive decision-making process, although still not a member of the war cabinet. However, he impinged on the public consciousness more than some of his nominally more senior colleagues. On 14 May he made a radio broadcast appealing for able-bodied men to join the Local Defence Volunteers, a cabinet initiative that became part of the folk memory of the war, through Robb Wilton's contemporary radio sketch, 'The day I joined the Home Guard'. (Eden's broadcast was later used at the outset of the film version made in 1971 of the television comedy series *Dad's Army*.) On 25 May, Eden overruled General Sir Edmund Ironside in his wish to withdraw the British brigade from the defence of Calais. As a result of this decision, which Eden described as one of the most painful of the war, as it involved the fate of a battalion of the King's Royal Rifle Corps, two German divisions were held up and the evacuation of the British expeditionary force from Dunkirk made possible. With the fall of France in June, Eden had the first of many battles of will with Churchill on the conduct of the war. He was opposed to the French prime minister's conclusion of a separate peace with Germany, and defended the positions of Sir John Dill, the chief of the Imperial General Staff, and Sir Archibald Wavell, commander-in-chief Middle East, whose quiet integrity he much admired, against Churchillian impatience that could have led to their premature replacements.

On 6 October 1940 Eden undertook an important mission to Cairo in which he assessed at first hand the situation in Egypt and north Africa. He believed that allied defence of Egypt was the paramount priority and resisted, albeit unsuccessfully, Churchill's determination to divert troops to Greece to counter Mussolini's offensive. From Cairo he went on to Palestine and Transjordan, before returning to London, where he informed Churchill of the secret plans for operation Compass in the western desert, launched on 9 December. The success of Eden's Middle East mission was the prelude to his return on 22 December to the post of foreign secretary.

Churchill's wartime foreign secretary Churchill had long wanted Eden beside him as foreign secretary, not least because it would deliver 'centrist' support, but, even in 1940, had to wait for the propitious moment. With the retirement of Neville Chamberlain from the post of lord president of the council on 3 October, a few weeks before his death, Churchill had suggested to Halifax that he might assume the office of lord president, with Eden succeeding him at the Foreign Office. Not surprisingly, Halifax was unenthusiastic and the matter lapsed. On the unexpected death of Lord Lothian, the British ambassador in Washington, on 12 December, Churchill was not to be deflected a second time, and the eventual outcome of some tortuous negotiations was Halifax's reluctant acceptance of the Washington embassy. Eden now entered the war cabinet. Only Clement Attlee, the Labour Party leader, was to serve longer in the central councils of the war as one of Churchill's principal lieutenants. Looking back on their five years together, Attlee told Eden that their unique function had been to put a curb on Churchill's wilder schemes and, when necessary, to give him unpalatable advice. Eden's second term as foreign secretary (December 1940–July 1945) was arguably the most productive phase of his career, though the complex situation in the eastern Mediterranean in early 1941 proved an inauspicious beginning.

As at the Montreux Conference in 1936, Eden believed that Turkey was the key to the tangled web. His unresolved hope was to see Turkey in a triple alliance with Greece and Yugoslavia. In a reversal of his earlier position, he hoped to stiffen Turkish and Yugoslavian resistance to German expansion in the Balkans by a military presence in Greece, even though this would mean diverting some of Wavell's forces at Benghazi. As a member of the cabinet defence committee Eden was party to the decision on 10 February 1941 to send troops and materials to Greece, and went with Lieutenant-General Sir John Dill, with plenipotentiary powers, on a two-month mission to Cairo and Ankara. The failure of the subsequent Greek expedition was a grievous set-back, with ramifications in north Africa, where Rommel's Afrika Korps made rapid counter-offensives. Eden's discomfiture, when defending the decision to help Greece in a speech in the House of Commons on 6 May, gave private satisfaction to Chamberlain's dwindling band of supporters in parliament; though in the larger context, the time and energy expended by Hitler in invading Yugoslavia and Greece diverted his resources in the next crucial stage of an increasingly global conflict.

On 22 June 1941 Hitler invaded Russia. Eden, who was staying at Chequers when the news broke, fully backed Churchill's unilateral decision to treat the Russians as partners in the struggle against Hitler. Eden's experience of the Soviets went back to his pre-war talks with Stalin and Maysky in 1935. Eden assured the Russians of Britain's continued determination to resist Hitler, and on 12 July concluded an Anglo-Soviet agreement on mutual support, a prelude to his broader negotiations with Stalin in December. Eden began his journey to Moscow on 7 December 1941, the very day of the Japanese attack on

Pearl Harbor that brought the Americans into the war, in the company of Oliver Harvey, his former Foreign Office private secretary, whom he had reappointed to the post. For three years Harvey was to be a valued sounding board and support for Eden, accompanying him on three occasions to Moscow, on this first occasion with the Germans only 19 miles from the Russian capital.

Stalin was at his most intractable in these negotiations, demanding recognition of Soviet Russia's 1941 frontiers. Only when Eden pointed out that such concessions were not in his gift, but needed further consideration by the cabinet, the dominions, and the United States, now in common cause with the allies, did Stalin relent. Eden was keener for Stalin to extend Soviet efforts eastwards against the Japanese to relieve British forces in their desperate struggle. On his return to Britain he argued, albeit unsuccessfully, in cabinet on 1 January 1942 that Stalin, whom he believed to be more the heir of Peter the Great than Lenin, should be accommodated regarding the 1941 frontiers, apart from Poland.

Eden's attitude to the other great member of the alliance was more equivocal, and he agreed with Harold Macmillan that the great mistake in dealing with the Americans was to regard them as Anglo-Saxons. He was wary of the price the Americans might eventually exact from Britain for their help and support. As co-operation with Roosevelt was at the centre of Churchill's strategy, relations between the prime minister and his foreign secretary were more complex than has often been acknowledged. Both personalities had an element of the 'prima donna', and although there was a symbiotic basis to their alliance, the shadow of Churchill's presence lay over Eden for the rest of his career, not always to his benefit.

However much they may have disagreed, Eden remained loyal to his political chief (while others openly criticized him at the time of the fall of Tobruk) and did not plan, as has sometimes been suggested, to oust Churchill from the premiership in February 1942. Nevertheless Churchill, in reshuffling the government team that month, retained the Ministry of Defence, which Eden had wished to see devolved elsewhere, making Attlee deputy prime minister and Sir Stafford Cripps leader of the House of Commons. But this was for the immediate future. Churchill had told Eden on 30 September 1940 that he would be his eventual successor, a promise reiterated on 11 November 1941. On 16 June 1942 Churchill went further, formally recommending to George VI that, in the event of his death on his forthcoming journey to Washington, the king should summon Eden, 'who is in my mind the outstanding Minister in the largest political party in the House of Commons and in the National Government' (W. Churchill to George VI, 16 June 1942, Royal Archives, Windsor, RA PS GVI C 069/17). The tragedy of Eden's career was that he had to wait thirteen years for that opportunity.

On 22 November 1942 Eden was made leader of the House of Commons, an almost insupportable burden in addition to his duties in the war cabinet, on the defence committee, and in running the Foreign Office. Inevitably he was diverted from the central concerns of foreign policy, and did not attend the Casablanca Conference with Churchill and Roosevelt in January 1943. Later he attended the first Quebec Conference (August 1943), the first Cairo Conference (November 1943), Tehran (November 1943), the second Cairo Conference (December 1943), and the second Quebec Conference (September 1944). At this last conference he had a public disagreement with Churchill over the merits of the Morgenthau plan for the de-industrialization of post-war Germany.

Other disagreements with Churchill came over Anglo-French relations, in particular the question of de Gaulle's National Committee of Free France, to which Eden had given limited recognition in September 1941 (without diplomatic representation) as a focus for the Free French cause. Churchill's indifference was partly caused by his wish to follow Roosevelt, whose mistrust of de Gaulle knew no bounds. Controversies also followed over de Gaulle's broadcasts from London. It was not until June 1943 that the newly constituted French Committee of National Liberation was recognized as a government in waiting. Eden now believed that the best way to contain Germany was by building up France, as he believed that, although the Bear's manners were improving, it was not in Britain's interest to share the cage alone with the Soviets. Also, he was aiming to include France within a European counterbalance to American influence. Eden's support for France was not forgotten by de Gaulle, and after the war Eden was widely regarded as 'the one British statesman for whom France had ever felt any tenderness' (M. Bromberger and S. Bromberger, *Secrets of Suez*, 1957, 160).

In 1942 Eden took the lease on a seventeenth-century house at Binderton, near Chichester, which became a haven of repose for the next decade, and where he could indulge his enthusiasm for gardening and tennis. He loved to take walks in the neighbouring Sussex countryside and, as a connoisseur of good food and wine, kept a hospitable table for his many visitors from the political, military, and artistic worlds. When finance permitted, Eden, with a shrewd eye for a bargain, continued to build up his distinctive collection of modern paintings. He read widely, including French and Persian literature in the original, and eighteenth-century English novels, particularly Smollett. His favourite author, however, remained Shakespeare, and one of his after-dinner recreations was to have readings from the plays with his wife and sons. At Binderton he also found the time to reflect on the post-war settlements, and in December 1942 first raised the prospect of a new world organization to replace the discredited League of Nations. After discussions with Ernest Bevin, Eden was responsible for the white paper *Proposals for the Reform of the Foreign Service* (January 1943), which Bevin implemented when he succeeded Eden as foreign secretary after the war.

When Churchill suggested that Eden might become viceroy of India in April 1943, Eden was torn between his wish to finish the work of the war and the temptation to hold the greatest of imperial offices at a crucial time for the subcontinent. But doubts were raised. Oliver Harvey told Eden that his absence 'would have catastrophic consequences on the future peace' (22 April 1943, *The War Diaries of Oliver Harvey, 1941–1945*, ed. J. Harvey, 1978, 247). George VI was also unwilling to see his foreign secretary depart, not least because of his restraining influence on Churchill; and Baldwin, whom Eden consulted, rightly pointed out that no viceroy had ever returned to take up the premiership, though this was not Eden's primary consideration in declining the office.

Eden believed, with General James Wolfe, that 'war is an option of difficulties' (*Hansard 5C*, vol. 371, p. 733). Never was this more true than in the latter stages of the conflict. The war cabinet's decision in July 1944 to accede to Stalin's request for repatriation of captured Russian soldiers in German uniforms may, in the complex *Realpolitik* then obtaining, have saved Greece from being devoured in the communist maw, but it came at a fearful moral price. The famous 'percentage agreement' meeting in Moscow in October 1944 (code-named Tolstoy) ordained the degree of influence Russia and Britain should have over the Balkan states, 90 per cent of Greece coming under the United Kingdom in accord with America. In complex negotiations with his Russian opposite number, Molotov, Eden haggled over the percentages for Bulgaria and Hungary. But Churchill's view, as expressed to his doctor, Lord Moran, was that 'The Foreign Secretary could be obstinate, he must be told that there is only one course open to us—to make friends with Stalin' (9 Oct 1944, Moran, *Winston Churchill: the Struggle for Survival, 1940–1945*, 1968, 215). By the time of the Yalta Conference (code-named Argonaut) in January 1945, Britain, cast in the minor role of a Lepidus in the three-fold world dominated by Stalin and Roosevelt, could do little in the persons of Churchill and Eden as Poland, the country for which Britain went to war in September 1939, was abandoned to its fate. Despite the success of his personal initiative with Stalin on a future Soviet withdrawal from Iran, overall Eden took the gloomiest view of Russian behaviour at Yalta and was dismayed by evidence of Roosevelt's fading powers.

Roosevelt died on 12 April 1945. Churchill asked Eden to represent Great Britain at the funeral in Washington. Again the British were cast in a minor role. 'No word of greeting or thanks from anyone', recorded the countess of Athlone, the wife of the governor-general of Canada; 'when one thinks Eden had flown the Atlantic to be present and show the sympathy of the British Gov: and also that of the King of England' (countess of Athlone to Queen Mary, 16 April 1945, Royal Archives, Windsor Castle, RA GV/CC 53/1381). Eden was heartened by Truman's bearing and humility as the new president, and believed that he would prove a loyal collaborator. From Washington, Eden went on to the San Francisco Conference, the inaugural meeting of the United Nations, which began on 25 April and continued for two months, by which time the war in Europe was over and Britain was in the throes of its first general election for ten years.

The next weeks were to be the low point of Eden's life. In 15 June his mother died, and Eden, laid up with illness at

Binderton, was unable to attend her funeral at Windlestone, and was confined to Sussex during the election campaign. Shortly before leaving for the Potsdam Conference, Eden heard that his eldest son, Simon, a pilot officer with the RAF in Burma, was missing. He specifically arranged that this news should not be made public in the press, as the general election campaign was under way and he did not wish to seek any sympathetic advantage. It was not for four weeks that the news of Simon's death was confirmed, on 20 July. Eden's bearing at the function and dinner that day at Sans Souci were long remembered by those present.

Simon's death was also the last act of Eden's increasingly fragile marriage. Beatrice had spent much of the latter part of the war in Paris and in 1946 left him to live in America. Her interest in politics had always been minimal and the burdens of war had taken a heavy toll. Their separation had an air of inevitability about it, and the marriage was dissolved in 1950. Divorce was, even in the immediate post-war era, a disqualifying social solecism for advancement in many professions, and Churchill discreetly protected Eden from the difficulties of his new situation, not least from the Church of England under the leadership of Geoffrey Fisher, when overt and implicit criticisms were made of him (foreshadowed in an article in 1952 in the *Church Times*) as the first divorced person to become prime minister.

Within a week of Simon's death the declaration of the election results (delayed for three weeks to allow counting of postal votes) confirmed a Labour landslide, a result not entirely unexpected to Eden. In marked contrast to Churchill, he had made a temperate contribution to the Conservatives' programme of election broadcasts, and he was in no doubt that the Conservatives would now have to adapt to the changed social climate. On leaving office he declined the offer of the Order of the Garter. Ernest Bevin, a figure Eden regarded as the best of Labour's men, became foreign secretary, and Eden fostered a bipartisan approach, particularly over Bevin's difficulties with the Labour Party's pro-Soviet lobby. Oliver Stanley, one of Eden's pre-war dining group, when the party was last in opposition, even praised Ernest Bevin for having shown 'the importance of being … Anthony' (N. Fisher, *Harold Macmillan: a Biography*, 1982, 127). Later, Eden's bust in the Foreign Office was placed at the foot of the grand staircase facing that of Ernest Bevin on the half-landing; two figures from very different traditions, they were united by their trust and belief in the indomitable spirit of the British people in adversity, which as fellow members of the war cabinet they had done so much to uphold and sustain.

Rebuilding the Conservatives in opposition Apart from brief interludes, Eden had been in office for the greater part of two decades. The enforced spell of opposition gave him a much needed chance to recharge his political and personal batteries, although he was considered as a candidate for the post of first secretary-general of the United Nations until Russia, as one of the permanent members of the Security Council, opted for the Norwegian Trygve Lie, an oblique tribute to Eden's lack of compliance towards the Soviets. As Churchill's main political activity came in important overseas speeches, such as that on the 'iron curtain' at Fulton in March 1946, and in Strasbourg and Zürich on European concerns, Eden was, in effect, acting leader of the opposition for much of this period. Again, he did not see entirely eye to eye with Churchill on the cold war or the future integration of Europe. He was frankly impatient for the succession, and was not alone in the Conservative Party in thinking that Churchill should step aside.

At the first post-war Conservative conference at Blackpool in October 1946 Eden returned in a key-note speech to his first concern, that of domestic policy. He realized that this was the area in which the old-style Conservative Party was deficient, and he worked tirelessly in support of the efforts of the new party chairman, Lord Woolton, to modernize the party's finance, philosophy, and organization. Housing was one of the issues on which he concentrated. However, his most influential and educative contribution was on the need for the improvement of industrial relations, through share ownership, employee participation, and profit sharing, ideas which found expression in the party's *Industrial Charter* of 1947. He had worked with the young Reginald Maudling, a future chancellor of the exchequer, then in the Conservative Research Department, on reviving Noel Skelton's pre-war call for 'a property-owning democracy'. The success of this initiative, which was to be the centrepiece of Eden's electoral programme in May 1955, led to Oliver Stanley's quip that the party, once Eton and Magdalen in its education, was now 'Eden and Maudling' in its philosophy. Eden later felt that his specific contributions to post-war Conservative renewal had been underestimated. When R. A. Butler was given credit in some quarters for the 'property-owning democracy', Eden, who had made it the subject of his 1946 conference speech, commented that 'Rab of course had about as much to do with that quotation as he had with the battle of Agincourt' (Lord Avon to Robert Carr, 11 April 1972, Avon papers, AP 33/6).

Bevin continued to consult Eden, notably over the proposed Marshall plan in June 1947 on American economic aid for Europe. Eden also gave Bevin every support over the Korean War from June 1950, important after the Labour government's majority had been reduced to eight seats at the general election of February 1950. However, on 26 June Eden led for the opposition—some Conservatives felt not forcefully enough—in a censure motion on the Labour government's hostility to the Schuman plan for combining the coal and steel industries of Germany and France, and eventually other nations (which under Labour was not to include Britain), into a supra-national 'high authority'.

When Bevin, a dying man, was replaced as foreign secretary in March 1951 by Herbert Morrison, Eden's criticisms of the government's tepid response to Dr Mussadeq's nationalization of the Anglo-Iranian Oil Company's refineries at Abadan that April were uninhibited. In retrospect, the Abadan crisis can be seen as the first few preliminary notes of the last tragic movement of Eden's career. His stance was motivated by concern for Britain's economic interests through maintenance of Middle Eastern oil supplies, unlike some Conservatives, who saw the crisis as an opportunity to show personal vindictiveness towards Morrison. Eden's links with Morrison went back to the early 1940s in the national coalition (he felt a camaraderie towards most members of the old war cabinet), and he was later to regard Morrison's failure to win the Labour Party leadership in December 1955 as a national misfortune. When Attlee called a general election for 25 October 1951, Eden made history during the campaign by appearing in the first televised election broadcast in Britain, a carefully scripted exercise, pre-rehearsed with a deferential interviewer, Leslie Mitchell.

Return to the Foreign Office The Conservatives won the election with a majority of seventeen seats. Like a man returning home, Eden became foreign secretary for the third time, and his private secretary, Evelyn Shuckburgh, recorded that when Eden made his first appearance at the United Nations in Paris in November, foreign ministers and diplomats crowded up to welcome him on every side, everyone 'feeling that a new era had begun for Europe and for the cause of peace' (E. Shuckburgh, *Descent to Suez: Diaries, 1951–56*, ed. J. Charmley, 1986, 13).

A new era was also about to begin for Eden in his private life. In August 1952 he married Clarissa Anne Spencer-Churchill (*b.* 1920), the daughter of Major John Strange Spencer-Churchill, and the niece of the prime minister. It proved a serenely happy marriage that brought Eden a calm contentment after his years of loneliness, and devoted care in his illnesses, both before and after his retirement. His first major illness in April 1953 nearly ended his life after a failed operation to remove gallstones, when his bile duct was accidentally cut. A lifesaving operation in Boston in May 1953 largely rectified the earlier damage, but Eden, wary of Churchill's enthusiasm for summitry, spent much of the summer recuperating. If he had been in harness he could well have succeeded to the premiership in June after Churchill suffered a major stroke, but Churchill, who had taken over the Foreign Office in Eden's absence, made a remarkable recovery.

At the Margate Conference in October 1953 Eden spoke of his concept of foreign policy as Britain at the centre of the 'three circles' of the United States, the Commonwealth, and Europe. With East–West cold war relations at a critical stage, the problem facing Eden was how to maintain Britain's world role with the reduced economic resources then available, and at a time of changing political priorities in the international arena. America was increasingly concerned with keeping abreast of Russia, not least in the arms race; following India and Pakistan's independence in 1947, Commonwealth countries were now more willing to follow their own political and economic agendas (in 1951 Britain was excluded from the ANZUS treaty between America, Australia, and New Zealand); and the nascent Schuman plan was to have unforeseen repercussions for the idea of an integrated Europe.

In a speech at Columbia University on 11 January 1952 Eden said that for Britain to join such a European federation was 'something which we know, in our bones, we cannot do', and on the European question he was always concerned 'that the British people should know where they are going before they wake up and find themselves where they do not want to be' (earl of Avon to Viscount Chandos, 12 Oct 1962, Avon papers, AP 23/17/62A). Nevertheless, many of Eden's successes at this time came on European issues. He continued Labour's policy of association with, but not full membership of, the European Coal and Steel Community and the European Defence Community (EDC), as he wanted no erosion of sovereign rights or Commonwealth links. In 1954, following French intransigency, he saved the EDC, and with it the North Atlantic Treaty Organisation, from collapse virtually single-handedly. The settlement of the tortuous Trieste question in 1954 also owed much to his diplomatic skills through the rapport he established with Marshal Tito, for Eden the acceptable face of communism. The Austrian peace treaty was also signed in May 1955, shortly after Eden became prime minister, his skill in co-ordinating the efforts of the Western powers in Paris having done much to bring the Soviets to the negotiating table.

Further afield major problems included the continuing Anglo-Iranian oil crisis; King Farouk's abrogation of the 1936 Anglo-Egyptian treaty that allowed British troops in the canal zone; the unresolved Korean War; and the threat to world peace over the growing conflict in Indo-China. With the election of Dwight D. Eisenhower as United States president in November 1952, Eden's opposite number in Washington became John Foster Dulles, a man he regarded as 'a preacher in a world of politics' (Eden, *Full Circle*, 64), and with whom he was to have a complex and sometimes stormy relationship over the next five years. Dulles's help in overthrowing Mussadeq in August 1953, which temporarily solved the Iranian imbroglio, was not, however, an accurate clue to his future attitude to the Egyptian question, now endangered by terrorist attacks on British troops and punitive reprisals, after King Farouk's overthrow in July 1952 in a military coup, and the eventual rise to power of Colonel Nasser. After meeting Nasser in Cairo in 1953, Dulles believed that Egypt would not join any Western anti-Russian alliance until the British had withdrawn from the canal base. In June 1954 Churchill and Eden had talks in Washington at which the United States government gave a tacit understanding that through economic aid to Egypt they would provide an incentive for any agreement with Egypt to be made and kept on acceptable terms. The ensuing Suez Base agreement, signed in October 1954, preparing the way for a phased withdrawal of British troops, led to a considerable schism in the Conservative Party between those who believed that the nuclear age had made the base redundant, and the 'Suez Group', led by Captain Charles Waterhouse, who thought it a dangerous sell-out. Churchill's private sympathies were with this latter group, and when asked to speak at a back-benchers' 1922 committee meeting that promised to be particularly critical of Eden's policy, replied 'I'm not sure I'm on our side' (Thorpe, 211).

At Eden's only meeting with Nasser (at the British embassy in Cairo in February 1955), Egyptian opposition to the recent Turco-Iraqi defence pact in the northern tier of Middle Eastern states was clear. But for Eden such an agreement was some compensation for the failure, because of Egyptian hostility, to establish a Middle East defence organization and a vital defensive pro-Western buffer alongside Russia's southern boundaries. On 5 April 1955, Eden's last day as foreign secretary, Britain, alone among the Western powers, formally joined the Baghdad pact, a move not reinforced by equivalent American action. Eden was greatly frustrated by Dulles's equivocations, after Washington's earlier enthusiasm for the unity of this defensive northern tier.

Eden made significant contributions to the North Korean armistice in 1953 and the arrangements for the exchange of prisoners. But his greatest achievement in these years, and indeed the diplomatic triumph of what became known as his *annus mirabilis*, came at the Geneva Conference of 1954 with the settlement of the Indo-China War, 'the last example', the historian of the conference has written, 'of an independent British policy exercising significant influence in the resolution of a major international crisis' (J. Cable, *The Geneva Conference of 1954 on Indochina*, 1986, 3). Eden was one of the joint chairmen and the key figure in this two-month conference, attended by the foreign ministers of France, America (Dulles initially, but for the majority of the time General Walter Bedell Smith, with whom Eden forged a productive relationship), Russia, and communist China. French involvement in Indo-China was ended, and a ceasefire line was established on the 17° N parallel latitude between North and South Vietnam. Following the Geneva Conference, Eden was a key figure in the establishment of the South East Asia Treaty Organisation on 8 September, providing for collective defence in a volatile area. Eden's prestige and authority were now at their height. Like his first mentor, Sir Austen Chamberlain on his return from Locarno, Eden accepted the Order of the Garter, which he had declined in 1945, the honour being conferred upon him by the queen at Windsor on 20 October 1954.

However, there was still no indication of when Churchill might retire. His eightieth birthday on 30 November 1954 was felt by many Conservatives to be a suitable moment, but not by the prime minister. By the spring of 1955 there was considerable underlying tension at cabinet meetings, graphically recorded in Harold Macmillan's diaries, about the failure of Churchill to hand on responsibility to Eden. An election was due by October 1956, and Eden, not unreasonably, wanted time to make his own impact on the electorate as the head of a new administration. But the situation in early 1955 was complex, and historical opinion is divided between those who believe that Churchill stayed on to allow Eden time to recover fully his former strength, something his achievements in 1954 had

amply demonstrated, and those who felt he stayed on for exactly the opposite reason, rather as Attlee's delayed retirement later that same year dealt a grievous blow to Morrison's hopes of succeeding him as Labour leader. On 5 April 1955, amid a newspaper strike, Churchill finally relinquished power, and Eden became prime minister the next day. The crown prince had at last ascended the throne.

Premiership before Suez Eden's long years as deputy leader had contributed to his irascibility, his inability at times to delegate, and his touchiness in the face of criticism, characteristics that were to become more apparent in Downing Street. His appearances at the dispatch box were marked more by formality than spontaneity. Nevertheless, Eden's premiership began in an atmosphere of goodwill and optimism, though the newspaper strike was soon to be followed by industrial unrest among the London busmen and dockworkers. Although the Conservatives had a lead of only 4 per cent in the opinion polls, Eden, after much soul-searching in the weeks before taking over, believed that he should take an early opportunity of seeking a fresh mandate from the electorate, and nine days after becoming prime minister he announced a general election for 26 May. As he had waited so long for his inheritance, this was an act of considerable political bravery, but the omens were good. The Labour Party in his Warwick and Leamington constituency even considered whether it would be 'unpatriotic' to field a candidate against him. Eden's decision was vindicated when the Conservatives, after a quiet campaign during which Eden emphasized the theme of the 'property-owning democracy', won by sixty seats, the first peacetime occasion on which an incumbent administration had increased its majority since 1900. For the last time in the century, the Conservatives won an absolute majority of the seats, and even more remarkably votes, in Scotland, where Eden had been greeted with enthusiasm, even while canvassing in the poorer parts of the great cities.

With such a decisive victory, Eden should arguably have rebuilt the cabinet in his own mould there and then. R. A. Butler, whose spring budget on 19 April with £135 million of tax reliefs had contributed to the Conservatives' electoral victory, was an exhausted man after nearly four years at the Treasury, and had also recently suffered the loss of his wife after a long and harrowing illness. Economic problems now crowded the domestic agenda. A major strike on the railways led Eden to declare a state of emergency. There was also concern over the effect the prolonged dock strike was having on the balance of payments deficit. Domestic inflation led to Butler imposing a July credit squeeze, but the pound, now in effect convertible, remained under pressure, and wages outstripped productivity. Eden, with misplaced kindness, shrank from replacing him as chancellor, and when Butler was forced to increase purchase tax, taking back most of the earlier reliefs, in the so-called 'pots and pans' Budget on 26 October, the damage to both the government and Butler's reputation for fiscal competence was grievous.

Eden's choice of Harold Macmillan to replace him as foreign secretary on 7 April also did not work out for the best. Macmillan, three and a half years older than Eden, had covert ambitions for the premiership, and their relationship over issues in Eden's acknowledged field of expertise was not an easy one. With hindsight, Eden felt he should have followed his first instinct to appoint Lord Salisbury, a preference set aside owing to Salisbury's membership of the upper house, not a consideration that was to inhibit Macmillan himself five years later when he appointed Lord Home to the post, or Margaret Thatcher in 1979 with the appointment of Lord Carrington. When the first reshuffle came belatedly in December 1955, Macmillan succeeded Butler at the Treasury, though significantly in his exchange of letters, and with doubtful constitutional propriety, Macmillan wanted it acknowledged that this should be seen as a step towards the premiership, not away from it. Butler became lord privy seal and leader of the House of Commons. The standing of the two main rivals for Eden's own position had subtly changed.

Selwyn Lloyd became the new foreign secretary. Eden had much admired Lloyd's work in opposition and had asked for him as minister of state at the Foreign Office in October 1951. Lloyd's ascent through the Conservative ranks had thereafter been swift, including a spell as secretary of state for defence. In the remaining thirteen months of Eden's premiership, Lloyd, together with Lord Home, who had replaced Lord Swinton as Commonwealth secretary, showed unswerving loyalty to his political chief, not something that could be said of all Eden's cabinet colleagues.

When Hugh Gaitskell became Labour leader in December, British politics moved into a new era. Press criticisms became less inhibited. To some extent, Churchill and Attlee had been above criticism, but both Eden and, eventually, Gaitskell were 'fair game' for a new breed of journalist, epitomized above all by Randolph Churchill, the former prime minister's son, whose vitriolic outbursts against his cousin's husband in the *Evening Standard* owed much to a deep-seated psychological feeling that he had been replaced as his father's favoured son by an outside political heir. Eden had a thin skin when it came to press criticism, and on 14 January 1956 responded in a speech at Bradford which fuelled the fire. William Clark, Eden's press secretary, was even instructed to put out a statement that the prime minister did not intend to resign.

Despite the industrial unrest in the early part of 1955, Eden's premiership was dominated by foreign affairs. On 10 June 1955, a fortnight after the election, the six countries of the European Coal and Steel Community met at the Messina Conference in Sicily, a crucial stage in the development of the European movement. For pro-Europeans, particularly in retrospect Macmillan, Britain's failure to accept an invitation to Messina was the great missed opportunity of the Eden government, the long-term effects of which were to be more significant than the ramifications of Suez, though Macmillan was in agreement with cabinet decisions at the time. Macmillan and Eden were also to be at odds in 1955 over Project Alpha, a

complex redistributive land scheme for ending the Arab–Israeli deadlock, which eventually faltered, though Eden felt that both Macmillan and Evelyn Shuckburgh, now head of the Middle East department, had gone ahead of instructions on this and other matters relating to the Baghdad pact. In July 1955, at a five-day conference in Geneva on the future of Germany, Eden met for the first time the new Russian leaders, Bulganin and Khrushchov, who accepted Eden's invitation to visit Britain in the spring of 1956, a visit bedevilled by the episode of Commander Crabb, a frogman who disappeared while on espionage activities under Russian vessels in Portsmouth harbour. Eden's fury with MI6, the foreign intelligence agency, which had sanctioned the operation, knew no bounds, and he appointed Sir Dick White, head of MI5, the domestic counter-intelligence agency, as its new head. Embarrassing security matters had also been raised in November 1955 when, under protection of parliamentary privilege, Kim Philby had been named as the 'third man', who had tipped off Donald Maclean and Guy Burgess before their defection to Russia in 1951. Eden's first concern was to avoid any censure of Herbert Morrison, foreign secretary in 1951, but in the debate he also made it clear that he would not head a government that assumed that a man was guilty before he had been so proven in a court of law. At a time when McCarthyism had only recently been discredited by a senate motion of censure in America, Eden's stance received widespread cross-party support.

But the Middle East was to prove the cauldron. Despite British withdrawal from the canal zone, Nasser waged a continuous propaganda war against Britain and pro-British countries in the Middle East, such as Iraq and Jordan. After the withdrawal, Cyprus had become for Britain the vital Mediterranean base, but its viability was threatened by the outbreak of EOKA terrorist activity over self-determination. Following an inconsequential London Conference in September 1955, Eden asked Sir John Harding to become governor of Cyprus, confident that Harding's experience in Malaya and Kenya would make him uniquely qualified to control the demand for union with Greece (*enosis*), under its leader, Archbishop Makarios, whom Eden had deported to the Seychelles.

On 27 September 1955 Nasser announced his $80 million Russian arms deal, handled through the Czechoslovak government. By this means the Soviets consolidated their infiltration into the Middle East, with obvious consequences for the stability of the Baghdad pact, which Eden sought to strengthen in December by trying to persuade King Hussein to bring Jordan into membership. Egyptian propaganda reprisals were swift. Jordan swiftly fell into chaos, and Hussein's own position was under threat. On 1 March 1956 King Hussein dismissed General Sir John Bagot Glubb (Glubb Pasha), the British commander of the Arab Legion, an action Eden was convinced was inspired by Nasser. Selwyn Lloyd, on a Middle East tour, was dining with Nasser when he heard news of Glubb's dismissal. To Lloyd's incredulity, Nasser congratulated Britain, in the person of its foreign secretary, for having arranged the dismissal of Glubb as a means of improving relations between Britain and Egypt. Lloyd telegrammed London with news that Nasser was not responsible, but for Eden the die was cast, and Nasser, in his mind, was the new Mussolini. The two men were now on an irrevocable collison course. The catalyst came with the American withdrawal on 19 July 1956 of the offer of financial help for the Aswan High Dam, a policy Dulles referred to as 'withering on the vine', as consequentially British aid would also lapse. On 26 July, in an impassioned speech in Alexandria, Nasser announced that he had nationalized the Suez Canal.

Suez crisis The Suez crisis was for the generation of the 1950s what Munich had been for that of the 1930s, dividing families and crossing party lines. Conventional wisdom has it that there was a 'right' and a 'wrong' side in both crises, and that Eden was in the former category in the 1930s and the latter in the 1950s, but this is a simplified view of political and economic situations of overwhelming intractability. Nasser's nationalization of the Suez Canal in July 1956 was above all an economic threat to Britain and France. In the days before North Sea oil, the canal was a vital conduit for western Europe, and Dulles's statement that 'a way had to be found to make Nasser disgorge' (Kyle, 160) was one fully shared by Eden and Guy Mollet, the French prime minister. 'It is all very familiar', said Gaitskell, the leader of the opposition in the Commons on 2 August. 'It is exactly the same that we encountered from Mussolini and Hitler in those years before the war' (*Hansard 5C*, vol. 557, p. 1613). This seeming unanimity, in a crisis that was to last over five months, was short-lived. Eden and Mollet were always convinced that as a last resort force would have to be used, with or without United Nations backing, to make Nasser 'disgorge', and this was the agreed cabinet line on 27 July 1956, at which an Egypt committee was established to formulate the plans for putting that policy into effect. Bipartisan support was not achieved, and a rebarbative element entered into the relationship between Eden and Gaitskell.

Three further complicating factors became apparent in the months ahead. Lord Mountbatten, first sea lord, whose responsibility it was to undertake the logistical preparations for seaborne operations to take the canal zone, was, in his own words, 'violently against' the operation (*The Life and Times of Lord Mountbatten*, 12 pt ITV television series, 1969), and he made these reservations known at Buckingham Palace. Second, the American government was increasingly preoccupied with preparations for the presidential election in November, what William Clark called 'the quadrennial winter of the western world' (William Clark papers, Bodl. Oxf., MS Eng. 4814). As a result, American priorities were never those of the British or French governments, and the abiding lesson of Suez, as regards the 'special relationship', was that tacit American support is not enough; a more formal understanding, as in the Falklands War of 1982, was to prove an essential constituent of any punitive military action. In this respect, Suez confirmed that Britain was no longer one of the 'big three' nations of Yalta or Potsdam. Third, Eden did not have the backing of a united cabinet, and leaks made their

way to Archbishop Fisher at Lambeth Palace, who became a consistent critic of government policy in the House of Lords. The role of Macmillan, in particular, was to become increasingly shadowy, and the famous remark of Harold Wilson, shadow chancellor of the exchequer, that Macmillan was 'first in, first out' (A. Horne, *Macmillan, 1894–1956: Volume one of the Official Biography*, 1988, 441) by no means gives full expression to the complexities of Macmillan's role. As early as 16 November, Macmillan was describing himself to Winthrop Aldrich, the American ambassador in London, as 'Eden's deputy', and was clearly preparing the ground to be regarded as the only viable successor to the prime minister.

The chronology of the Suez crisis has about it the inexorable momentum of a Greek tragedy. The first London Conference of twenty-two countries, from 16 to 23 August, provided a formula (the eighteen nations proposals) for a new convention that gave Egypt a place on the board of a mixed operating company for the canal and increased revenues. The mission of Sir Robert Menzies, Australian prime minister, to Cairo (3–9 September) to seek Egyptian reaction to these proposals was effectively scuppered by Eisenhower's comment on 5 September that the United States was 'determined to exhaust every feasible method of peaceful settlement' (PRO, FO 371/119126/JE142111/1339), an undercutting of his position that Menzies remembered for the rest of his life. Dulles's suggestion for an alternative basis for negotiation, to counter Eden's wish to take the matter to the Security Council of the United Nations, was the creation of Suez Canal Users' Association (SCUA), which led to the second London Conference (19–21 September). In a news conference on 2 October, however, Dulles stated 'There is talk about "the teeth" being pulled out of it [SCUA]. There were never "teeth" in it, if that means the use of force' (Kyle, 273). For Eden this was the last straw, compounded by the Russian veto on the eighteen powers plan at the United Nations on 13 October. As the Conservative Party gathered for its annual conference at Llandudno, the crisis moved onto a new level.

On 14 October a French delegation outlined to Eden at Chequers what became known as 'the plan', whereby the Israelis were to be invited to launch an attack on Egypt across the Sinai peninsula, after which the French and British would intervene to separate the combatants and regain the canal. For Eden this was the *casus belli* for which he had been waiting, and in conditions of great secrecy Selwyn Lloyd met the French and Israelis at a villa at Sèvres, outside Paris, on 22 October. Eden made it clear to Lloyd before he went that any British involvement in such a plan must not be regarded as a response to a request from Israel. The Sèvres protocol was signed on 24 October, and its essentials presented to cabinet the following day. Reactions were mixed on both sides; some were extremely enthusiastic, others hesitant, but as the doubters included junior figures such as Derick Heathcoat Amory, who carried little political weight, the cabinet, including Macmillan and Butler, agreed to 'the plan'. Accordingly, on 29 October Israeli forces entered Egypt, and British and French action to separate the combatants began. The next day, as arranged, Eden delivered his ultimatum, which was rejected by Egypt. On 5 November, the day before the American presidential election, British and French paratroopers landed at Port Said, and the next day the main amphibious forces succeeded in capturing 23 miles of the canal. Hostile reactions from the United States, the United Nations, and the Soviet Union, then engaged in its simultaneous invasion of Hungary, led within twenty-four hours to a humiliating ceasefire. The key factor in the decision was economic. Macmillan told the cabinet on 6 November, in terms which are now known to be disingenuous in their degree of pessimism, of the run on sterling reserves (he told the cabinet of £100 million lost reserves in the first week of November, when the true figure was £31.7 million) and American treasury pressures to end the hostilities. Faced with this information, Eden had no option but to call a halt. Churchill summed up the mood for many when he said of the Suez operation, 'I would never have dared, and if I had dared, I would never have dared stop' (M. Gilbert, *Never Despair: Winston S. Churchill, 1945–1965*, 1988, 1222).

Public opinion polls, though narrowly in favour of Eden's action, showed a divided Britain. The atmosphere in the House of Commons was so poisonous that the speaker had suspended the sitting on 1 November to allow tempers to cool. Two junior ministers, Edward Boyle and Anthony Nutting, minister of state, who had negotiated the final stages of the Anglo-Egyptian agreement of 1954, later resigned. By this stage rumours of collusion were already circulating in the House of Commons, and when the session resumed the Conservative back-bench MP for the Wrekin, William Yates, asked directly about whether Britain had been engaged in an 'international conspiracy' (*Hansard 5C*, vol. 558, p. 1716).

Evasiveness over collusion was one of the persistent charges levelled at Eden in the years ahead, especially as his last statement in the House of Commons on 20 December was a denial of foreknowledge that Israel would attack Egypt. Such charges fail to acknowledge the *Realpolitik* of international diplomacy. Robert Blake wrote:

> There must have been a great deal of *suppressio veri* principally of course in connection with the charge of 'collusion'. No one of sense will regard such falsehoods in a particularly serious light. The motive was the honourable one of averting further trouble in the Middle East, and this was a serious consideration for many years after the event. (R. Blake, *British Prime Ministers in the Twentieth Century*, vol. 2: *Churchill to Callaghan*, ed. J. P. Mackintosh, 1978, 112–13)

On 19 November Downing Street announced that Eden was cancelling his engagements owing to ill health. Two days later it was announced that, on medical advice, Eden would be travelling to Jamaica to recuperate. The Edens stayed at Goldeneye, the remotely situated home of Ian Fleming, while back in Britain R. A. Butler was left in charge of the government, an arrangement that actually allowed Macmillan more scope to prepare his dispositions for the future. When Eden returned on 14 December it was to a dispirited party. Further medical opinion left him no option but to resign.

Eden resigned as prime minister on 9 January 1957. In a farewell audience, he gave no formal advice to the queen as to his successor, whom he assumed would inevitably be Macmillan, but on 11 January, in a dictated note for his biographer, he recorded that the queen had given him the opportunity during the audience 'to signify that my own debt to Mr Butler while I have been Prime Minister was very real' (Eden, note of 11 Jan 1957, Avon papers, AP 20/33/12A). On the night that Macmillan became prime minister, Butler received (in the words of his official biographer) 'a very touching letter from Clarissa Eden which, without being explicit, managed to convey the impression that the choice made by the Palace owed nothing to any recommendation offered by the outgoing Prime Minister' (A. Howard, *Rab: the Life of R. A. Butler*, 1987, 248n.). Eden declined the queen's gracious offer of an earldom, as in 1945 he had declined the offer of the Garter from her father, George VI. He resigned his seat at Warwick and Leamington, and on 18 January sailed with his wife to New Zealand, which he had first visited in 1925 at the outset of his parliamentary career.

Selwyn Lloyd recorded of Suez that 'whatever was done then, was done in what was genuinely believed to be the national interest' (Selwyn Lloyd papers, SELO 237 (3)). Unfortunately, this did not guarantee a successful outcome. Eden's policy had four main aims: first, to secure the Suez Canal; second and consequentially, to ensure continuity of oil supplies; third, to remove Nasser; and fourth, to keep the Russians out of the Middle East. The immediate consequence of the crisis was that the Suez Canal was blocked, oil supplies were interrupted, Nasser's position as the leader of Arab nationalism was strengthened, and the way was left open for Russian intrusion into the Middle East. It was a truly tragic end to his premiership, and one that came to assume a disproportionate importance in any assessment of his career. 'Men's evil manners live in brass', wrote Shakespeare; 'their virtues we write in water' (*Henry VIII*, IV.ii, 45–6). So, for too long, it was to prove with Eden.

Nutting was to claim (in 1967) that Suez had given Britain 'No end of a lesson'. But few were agreed as to what that lesson might be. The final dispatch of Sir Charles Keightley, commander-in-chief of the allied forces, gives a better clue than most:

> The one overriding lesson of the Suez operations is that world opinion is now an absolute principle of war and must be treated as such. However successful the pure military options may be they will fail in their object unless national, Commonwealth and Western world opinion is sufficiently on our side.   (PRO, AIR 8/1940)

Retirement, honours, and reputation Eden lived for twenty years, almost to the day, after leaving Downing Street. His first priority on returning from convalescence in New Zealand was to prepare his memoirs, which appeared in three volumes between 1960 and 1965. A talented team of researchers helped him work through his voluminous Foreign Office archives over the years in his various homes in Wiltshire. Brendan Bracken was foremost among those who advised him as to the commercial aspects of this venture, and a lucrative publishing deal with the Times Publishing Company Ltd removed the financial uncertainties of his earlier years.

Eden was a fierce defender of his reputation in retirement and could prove litigious towards unwary historians. His memoirs, skilfully documented, show his preoccupations over foreign policy at a time when domestic policy was becoming increasingly important as Britain's place in the world order diminished. At the insistence of his publishers, Eden wrote the volume on his premiership, *Full Circle* (1960), first. The disadvantage of this was that his account of Suez, in particular, was superseded by fuller accounts in due course. *Facing the Dictators* (1962) and *The Reckoning* (1965) have stood the test of time as essential sources for an understanding of the politics of the 1930s and 1940s. In the last year of his life Eden published *Another World, 1897–1917*, the story of his youth, which has taken its place as one of the classic accounts of the First World War.

On 26 July 1961, the fifth anniversary of Nasser's nationalization of the Suez Canal, Eden took his seat in the House of Lords as the first earl of Avon. Although he spoke from time to time, his influence in the days of the Macmillan hegemony was much reduced. However, when Macmillan sacked seven cabinet members in the 'night of the long knives' in July 1962, including Selwyn Lloyd, then chancellor of the exchequer, Eden went out of his way at a Young Conservative rally at Leamington Spa on 26 July to say that he felt that his former foreign secretary had been 'harshly treated'.

Many honours came Eden's way. He had honorary degrees from thirteen universities and was elected an honorary student (fellow) of Christ Church, Oxford, in 1941. From 1945 to 1973 he was an unusually active chancellor of Birmingham University, where his extensive private archive now resides in the Avon Room in the university library. He was an honorary bencher of the Middle Temple (1952), and an honorary member of the Salters' Company (1946) and of the Fishmongers' Company (1955). He was an elder of Trinity House (1953) and an honorary fellow of the Royal Institute of British Architects (1955). Eden was a trustee of the National Gallery from 1935 to 1949. He was an honorary colonel of the Queen's Westminster King's Royal Rifle Corps (1952–60) and of the Queen's Royal Rifles (1960–62). He was an honorary commodore of 500 (County Kent) squadron RAF (1943–57). From 1958 to 1966 he was an enthusiastic president of the Royal Shakespeare Theatre and a loyal supporter of the company's productions in Stratford and London, returning in old age to the English poet who meant most to him and whose insights into human nature he so admired.

An abiding interest and enthusiasm for Eden in his retirement was his pedigree herd of Hereford cattle, one of which, Avon Priam, won first prize at the Royal Highland Show. Over a period of six years he travelled to warmer climes in the winter months, owning successively homes in Bequia and Barbados in the West Indies, and it was in December 1976, while staying with Averell Harriman at Hobe Sound in Florida, that he fell seriously ill. The

prime minister, James Callaghan, arranged that he should be flown home to Wiltshire in an RAF plane. Eden died at his home at Alvediston Manor, Alvediston, Wiltshire, on 14 January 1977, and was buried three days later in the churchyard at St Mary's Church, Alvediston. A memorial service was held at Westminster Abbey. He was succeeded as second earl of Avon by his son, Nicholas, who died in 1984, when the title became extinct.

Eden's standing has been more than usually prone to the swings of modish fashion. Perhaps overpraised in his pre-war days, not least by the gilded pen of Winston Churchill, he was unfairly treated at the time of his spell as the unluckiest of twentieth-century prime ministers. Since Eden's death a more sober perspective has been evident. The fascination of his career remains undimmed, and an unusually large number of biographies and studies has appeared over the years. Until Suez, Eden was always more highly regarded by those outside his own party than in it; for a time the obloquy after Suez crossed party lines. His critics felt that Eden had lived too much under the shadow of his past attitudes, and that in drawing a false analogy between Hitler and Nasser had attempted to solve the Suez crisis by tactics mistakenly influenced by his earlier experience of Munich. But a quarter of a century after his death, Eden was increasingly recognized as a serious and patriotic figure who worked under the most appalling pressure for nearly three decades at the front line of British and world politics.   D. R. Thorpe

Sources U. Birm., Avon MSS · A. Eden, earl of Avon, *The Eden memoirs*, 3 vols. (1960–65) · Earl of Avon [R. A. Eden], *Another world, 1897–1917* (1976) · D. R. Thorpe, *Eden: the life and times of Anthony Eden first earl of Avon, 1897–1977* (2003) · R. R. James, *Anthony Eden* (1986) · D. Carlton, *Anthony Eden: a biography* (1981) · D. Dutton, *Anthony Eden: a life and reputation* (1997) · V. Rothwell, *Anthony Eden: a political biography, 1931–1957* (1992) · K. Kyle, *Suez* (1991) · CAC Cam., Selwyn Lloyd papers · D. R. Thorpe, *Selwyn Lloyd* (1989) · R. Lamb, *The failure of the Eden government* (1987) · J. Ramsden, *The age of Churchill and Eden, 1940–1957* (1995) · priv. coll., countess of Avon papers · CAC Cam., Churchill papers · Bodl. Oxf., MSS Stockton · Hatfield House, fifth marquess of Salisbury papers · Carmarthenshire RO, Cilcennin papers (J. P. L. Thomas)

Archives U. Birm., corresp. and papers · Warks. CRO, letters from the front | BL, corresp. with Lord Cecil, Add. MS 51083 · BL, corresp. with P. V. Emrys Evans, Add. MS 58242 · BL, corresp. with Lord Keyes · Bodl. Oxf., corresp. with Clement Attlee · Bodl. Oxf., corresp. with Arthur Mann · Bodl. Oxf., corresp. with Lord Monckton · Bodl. Oxf., corresp. with Gilbert Murray · Bodl. Oxf., corresp. with Lord Simon · Bodl. Oxf., Stockton Papers · Bodl. Oxf., corresp. with Lord Woolton · Bodl. RH, corresp. with Sir R. R. Welensky and some papers · Borth. Inst., corresp. with Lord Halifax · CAC Cam., corresp. with Patrick Buchan-Hepburn · CAC Cam., Churchill papers · CAC Cam., corresp. with Duff Cooper · CAC Cam., corresp. with Sir Henry Page Croft · CAC Cam., corresp. with Lord Halifax [copies] · CAC Cam., Selwyn Lloyd MSS · CAC Cam., corresp. with Oliver Lyttelton · CAC Cam., corresp. with Sir Eric Phipps · CAC Cam., corresp. with Sir Edward Spears · CAC Cam., corresp. of him and his wife with Lady Spencer-Churchill · CAC Cam., corresp. with Baron Strang · CUL, corresp. with Sir Samuel Hoare · Cumbria AS, Carlisle, letters to Lord Howard of Penrith · Hatfield House, Hertfordshire, fifth marquess of Salisbury MSS · HLRO, corresp. with Lord Beaverbrook · King's Lond., Liddell Hart C., corresp. with Sir B. H. Liddell Hart · NA Scot., corresp. with Lord

Lothian · NL Wales, corresp. with Desmond Donnelly · Nuffield Oxf., corresp. with Lord Cherwell · PRO, Foreign Office papers, FO 800/750–851 · Tate collection, corresp. with Lord Clark | FILM BFI NFTVA, *Twentieth century*, 27 Dec 1964 · BFI NFTVA, *Suez*, BBC2, 23 Oct 1996 · BFI NFTVA, *Alan Clark's history of the tory party*, BBC2, 21 Sept 1997 · BFI NFTVA, *Reputations*, BBC2, 6 June 2000 · BFI NFTVA, current affairs footage · BFI NFTVA, news footage · BFI NFTVA, party political footage · BFI NFTVA, propaganda film footage (ministry of information) | SOUND BL NSA, 'Case history: Sir Anthony Eden', BBC Radio 4, 1998, H10 110/1 · BL NSA, 'Dining with … Anthony', B4 764/03 · BL NSA, documentary recordings · BL NSA, news recordings · IWM SA, 'Personalities of the twentieth century', 21 Feb 1938, 3539 · IWM SA, oral history interviews · IWM SA, recorded talk

Likenesses E. Kapp, lithographic chalk drawing, 1935, NPG · W. Stoneman, three photographs, 1942–50, NPG · P. Halsman, photograph, 1955, NPG [*see illus.*] · W. Coldstream, oils, 1961, Christ Church Oxf. · D. Hill, drawing, *c*.1965, NPG · R. Noakes, bust, 1994, Gov. Art Coll. · C. Beaton, photograph, NPG · D. Levine, ink caricature, NPG · D. Low, three pencil caricatures, NPG · M. Yevonde, photograph, NPG

Wealth at death £92,900: probate, 17 March 1977, *CGPLA Eng. & Wales*

Eden, Sir Ashley (1831–1887), administrator in India, third son of Robert John *Eden (1799–1870), third Baron Auckland and bishop of Bath and Wells, and his wife, Mary (*d*. 1872), eldest daughter of Francis Edward Hart of Alderwasley, Derbyshire, was born at Hertingfordbury, Hertfordshire, on 13 November 1831. His father was a brother of George *Eden, earl of Auckland and governor-general of India. Eden was educated at Rugby School and Winchester College and, from 1849 until 1851, the East India Company's college at Haileybury.

He arrived in Bengal in 1852 and was posted as assistant to the magistrate and collector of Rajshahi. In 1855 he was appointed assistant to the special commissioner for suppressing the Santal rebellion and afterwards became the first deputy commissioner of the Santal parganas, in which post he successfully advocated the exemption of 'primitive tribes' such as the Santals from regulation government and laid the basis for the paternalistic style of government by which India's indigenous peoples would in future be ruled.

In 1856 Eden took medical leave in Mauritius and returned with such graphic reports of the abuse of Indian labourers there that emigration to the colony was briefly suspended. In 1857–9 as magistrate of Barasat he highlighted abuses in the indigo cultivation system and in 1860 gave evidence before the indigo commission of planters imposing unprofitable and often fraudulent contracts on peasant cultivators. From 1862 until 1871 he was secretary to the government of Bengal and an *ex officio* member of Bengal's legislative council.

In 1861 Eden was appointed special envoy to Sikkim and, backed by an army, wrung from the maharaja a treaty guaranteeing free trade and the cessation of raids into British territory. In 1863 he was sent on a similar mission to Bhutan but without the same military support and he found himself taken virtual prisoner by the Bhutanese and forced to sign a treaty humiliating to the British. The

insult was amply repaid when Britain went to war against Bhutan in November 1864.

In 1871 Eden was the first civilian to be appointed chief commissioner of British Burma, and in January 1877 he became lieutenant-governor of Bengal. His reputation for being 'too friendly with the natives' initially worried Calcutta's European community, but Eden was no sentimental liberal. He backed Lytton's Vernacular Press Act of 1868 and watered down Ripon's factory legislation. Eden himself said that he had no policy beyond that of providing good government and in this aim he was more fortunate than most. His term was free from famine, and a run of good harvests, added to the devolution of financial control to the provinces, enabled him to invest in roads, railways, canals, hospitals, and schools. A fervent advocate of public works, he considered parsimony in this area a dereliction of duty. He was acclaimed as one of Bengal's most successful governors, and upon his retirement in 1882 received a warm send-off from both Europeans and Bengalis. His friendships with leading Bengali intellectuals, such as Krishnadas Pal and Bhudev Mukhopadhyay, had earned him a rare respect among Bengal's educated élite. A statue was raised in Dalhousie Square, Calcutta, by public subscription, and Eden Hospital was founded in his memory.

Eden was made CIE and KCSI in 1878. In 1882 he returned to England to become a member of the Council of India. He had married on 13 August 1861 Eva Maria (*d*. 1877), daughter of Vice-Admiral Rowland Money CB, and widow firstly of H. E. M. Palmer and secondly of J. M. Bellew, but had no children. He died at his home, 31 Sackville Street, London, on 9 July 1887 and was buried at Armthorpe, near Doncaster.

H. M. STEPHENS, *rev.* KATHERINE PRIOR

Sources C. E. Buckland, *Bengal under the lieutenant-governors*, 2 (1901) · K. P. Dey, *Sketch of the official career of the hon'ble Ashley Eden* (Calcutta, 1877) · Burke, *Peerage* (1970) · *Charivari's album* (1875) · T. Raychaudhuri, *Europe reconsidered: perceptions of the West in nineteenth century Bengal* (1988) · S. Gopal, *British policy in India, 1858–1905* (1965) · BL OIOC, Haileybury MSS · J. B. Wainewright, ed., *Winchester College, 1836–1906: a register* (1907) · G. A. Solly, ed., *Rugby School register*, rev. edn, 1: *April 1675 – October 1857* (1933) · E. Kilmurray, *Dictionary of British portraiture*, 3 (1981) · F. C. Danvers and others, *Memorials of old Haileybury College* (1894)

Archives BL, Bruce MSS · BL, corresp. with William Muir, Add. MS 43999 · BL, Ripon MSS · BL OIOC, letters to Sir E. B. Sladen, MS Eur. E 290 · CUL, corresp. with Lord Mayo · Herts. ALS, letters to earl of Lytton

Likenesses Boehm, marble statue, *c*.1877, Dalhousie Square, Calcutta · J. H. Walker, oils, exh. RA 1883, Chamber of Commerce, Calcutta · Isca, coloured lithograph, repro. in *Charivari's Album* · photograph, repro. in Dey, *Sketch of the career* [photograph in BL OIOC copy] · photogravure (after photograph by Bourne & Shepherd), repro. in Buckland, *Bengal under the lieutenant-governors*, facing p. 688

Wealth at death £12,914 17s. 2d.: probate, 11 Nov 1887, *CGPLA Eng. & Wales*

Eden, Charles (1673–1722), colonial governor, was born in co. Durham, of uncertain parentage but probably a member of the prominent Eden family of West Auckland. Little is known of Eden before his appointment in 1713 to succeed Edward Hyde as the proprietary governor of North Carolina. He arrived in that colony in the following year and was sworn in before the North Carolina provincial council on 28 May 1714. At some point after his arrival he married Penelope Golland, a widow with two children. Eden enjoyed personal prosperity from the appointment. As the proprietors' representative, he had rights to substantial lands, and in 1718 he became the last person to be made a landgrave—a Carolina aristocratic title—which entitled him to further territory. The following year he bought property on the Chowan River in what became Bertie county and there he built his plantation, Eden House.

Eden's tenure as governor was generally marked with success. He took control of a sparsely populated colony that was recovering from a lethal, but successful, general war with the Tuscarora Indians (1711–13) and Cary's uprising (1711), which had erupted in North Carolina over issues involving religious dissenters' rights. He worked to revise the colony's legal code and to encourage overseas trade. A devout member of the Church of England, in early 1715 he became a vestryman of St Paul's Church in the colony's capital (renamed Edenton after his death). He corresponded regularly with the evangelical wing of the Church of England and the Society for the Propagation of the Gospel in London from whom he requested missionaries, ministers, and school teachers, and warned that lack of action would hand over the colony to the Quakers. Nevertheless he also protected the rights of dissenters in the colony.

The greatest controversy attached to Eden was a possible association with Edward Teach, the notorious pirate Blackbeard. Pirates had long operated on the southern coasts of North America, using the colonies' harbours to refit their vessels, hide, and rest. By the time Eden took office, the British government had changed its generally tolerant policy towards pirates, necessary during the previous decades of war, to an aggressive drive to clear its commercial waterways. While the neighbouring colonies of Virginia and South Carolina mounted campaigns to thwart the pirates, Eden remained suspiciously inactive. Further questions were asked when a letter from Tobias Knight, the secretary of the governor's council, declaring Eden's desire to meet with Blackbeard was found on the pirate's dead body. Captured cargo stored by Teach in Knight's barn certainly further implicated the colony's secretary, but the evidence against Eden is inconclusive. The colony's proprietors cleared him after an investigation, but rumours persisted despite Eden's attempts to silence his critics in the colony through a series of arrests.

Eden died in office on 26 March 1722, at his home. He had no surviving children of his own, and his chief beneficiary was his friend and the secretary of the governor's council, John Lovick. Eden made no provision for his stepdaughter, Penelope, probably the result of his dispute with her husband, William Maude; however, she ultimately became mistress of Eden House when she married Lovick several years later. Eden was buried at his plantation, his tombstone carrying the crest of the Edens of West Auckland, co. Durham. His remains were moved to St Paul's churchyard, Edenton, in 1889.

TROY O. BICKHAM

Sources J. D. Nash, 'Eden, Charles', *Dictionary of North Carolina biography*, ed. W. S. Powell (1986), 2.134 • C. D. Clowse, 'Eden, Charles', *ANB* • A. Ashe, ed., *Biographical history of North Carolina: from colonial times to the present*, 1 (1905) • H. T. Lefler and W. S. Powell, *Colonial North Carolina: a history* (1973) • W. L. Saunders and W. Clark, eds., *The colonial records of North Carolina*, 30 vols. (1886–1907), vols. 2 • S. C. Hughson, *The Carolina pirates and colonial commerce, 1670–1740* (1894) • H. F. Rankin, *The pirates of North Carolina* (1960) • R. E. Lee, *Blackbeard the pirate: a reappraisal of his life and times* (1974)
Wealth at death substantial landholdings and many slaves: Nash, 'Eden, Charles'

Eden, Charles Page (1807–1885), author, born at Whitehall, St George's, near Bristol, on 13 March 1807, was third son and youngest but one of the eight children of Thomas Eden (*c.*1751–1809), curate of St George's, Bristol, and his wife, Ann (*d.* 1846), daughter of the Revd Charles Page of Northleach, Gloucestershire. Thomas Eden died when Charles was an infant, leaving a widow and young family in poverty. Charles was educated at a day school at Bristol, and at the Royal Institution School in Liverpool. Afterwards he was teacher for a time in a private school run by his cousin, the Revd John Charles Prince, and at Michaelmas 1825 went to Oxford as a Bible clerk at Oriel College. He was appointed to this office by the provost, Edward Copleston, and afterwards spoke of it as 'a position calculated to guard him from idleness and expense' (Burgon, 402). He graduated BA with a first class in classics in 1829, and in the two following years gained the prizes for the Ellerton theological essay and the chancellor's English essay. In April 1832, after two failures, he was elected a fellow of his college, which was still one of the highest honours in the university. After his ordination (deacon 1833 and priest 1834), he held several university and college offices, and in October 1843 succeeded J. H. Newman as vicar of St Mary's, Oxford. In March 1850 he was presented by his college to the vicarage of Aberford, near Leeds, which he retained until his death, and where on 16 November 1852 he married Isabella Jane, a daughter of the Revd James Landon, his predecessor. He was elected proctor three times in the convocation of the province of York (1869, 1874, 1880), and in 1870 was preferred by the archbishop to the prebendal stall of Riccall, whence he was popularly called Canon Eden.

Eden produced for the Library of Anglo-Catholic Theology editions of Peter Gunning's *Paschal or Lent Fast* (1845) and of Lancelot Andrewes's *Pattern of Catechistical Doctrine* (1846); his major publication was a new edition of Jeremy Taylor's works, which appeared in ten volumes, 1847–54. In 1855 Eden published a volume of sixteen *Sermons Preached at St Mary's in Oxford*, the first of which had been privately printed in 1840 under the title of *Early Prayer*, and had excited much attention in the university from its tone of earnest and practical piety. To the Tracts for the Times he contributed no. 32, *On the Standing Ordinances of Religion*

(1834), but was never a prominent member of the Tractarian party, though in his theological opinions he was more inclined to that school than to any other in the Anglican church. In 1835 he produced a pamphlet defending the subscription to the Thirty-Nine Articles as a condition of admission to Oxford. Contemporaries considered that certain peculiarities of manner, more than temper, prevented his being appreciated so much as his abilities, learning, and piety deserved. Eden died at Aberford vicarage, Yorkshire, on 14 December 1885, leaving a widow, two sons, and two daughters. He was buried in Aberford churchyard.   W. A. GREENHILL, *rev.* M. C. CURTHOYS

Sources J. W. Burgon, *Lives of twelve good men*, new edn (1891), 402–21 • *Manchester Guardian* (16 Dec 1885) • *Oxford University Herald* (26 Dec 1885) • G. C. Richards and C. L. Shadwell, *The provosts and fellows of Oriel College, Oxford* (1922) • *GM*, 2nd ser., 39 (1853), 194 • Boase, *Mod. Eng. biog.*

Archives Oriel College, Oxford, commonplace book and corresp.

Likenesses photograph, repro. in Burgon, *Lives of twelve good men*, facing p. 402

Wealth at death £14,458 1s. 5d.: probate, 22 May 1886, *CGPLA Eng. & Wales*

Eden, Emily (1797–1869), writer, was born on 3 March 1797 at Old Palace Yard, Westminster, the twelfth of fourteen children of William *Eden, first Baron Auckland (1744–1814), diplomatist, and his wife, Eleanor Elliot (1758–1818), daughter of Sir Gilbert *Elliot (1722–1777). The Edens were influential and active members of the whig aristocracy, and Emily grew up in a household at the centre of early nineteenth-century political and cultural life. She was from her adolescence a sharp-eyed and sharp-tongued observer of that world: in one of her earliest surviving letters, written when she was seventeen, she tells a sister of the betrothal of Annabella Milbanke, a family friend, adding drily that Miss Milbanke 'does not seem to be acting with her usual good sense' in looking for marital bliss with Lord Byron (*Miss Eden's Letters*, 7).

After her mother's death in 1818 Emily and her sister Frances established a household with their brother George *Eden, Lord Auckland (1784–1849), in London, and in 1827 at Ham House near Richmond, where Emily worked on a novel. Eden's young womanhood, as described in her letters, seems to have involved a round of social gatherings and country house visits with the literary and political élite of the day. On a visit to Lord Lansdowne in 1826, for example, she was entertained by the poet Thomas Moore: 'here the last three days, singing like a little angel' (*Miss Eden's Letters*, 110). Several years later she was charmed by Talleyrand, whom she met in London. She also became a friend of Lord Melbourne, briefly prompting some gossipy speculation that they might marry. Inevitably she took a personal interest in the era's politics—'the triumph of one's enemies is always an ugly business', she wrote gloomily after Wellington was invited to form a government in 1828 (ibid., 156)—but, as she demonstrates in her fiction, she was also able to observe political jockeying for position with detached amusement.

Politics entered Eden's life most dramatically when her

Emily Eden (1797–1869), by Simon Jacques Rochard, 1835

brother George was appointed governor-general of India in 1835. He was unmarried, and Eden and Frances accompanied him to Calcutta, where they arrived in March 1836 and carried out the official duties of the governor's lady, with Emily, the elder, assuming chief responsibility. Eden had dreaded the appointment; in 1834, when it was first raised as a serious possibility, she exclaimed that she would prefer Botany Bay to Calcutta: '[t]here is a decent climate to begin with, and the fun of a little felony first' (*Miss Eden's Letters*, 245). She chose to leave England none the less because she was devoted to her brother, whom she could not bear to think of being 'alone in this country [India]—for any earthly consideration' (*Letters from India*, 2.41). She initially found life in India thoroughly unpleasant, and her first letters home are filled with complaints about the heat and the insects, as well as with intense expressions of homesickness. The stateliness and parade of viceregal life were also something of a shock; in one early letter to England, she reports that on their first visit to their villa outside Calcutta they travelled with a party of sixteen, accompanied by more than four hundred servants: '[S]uch a simple way of going to pass two nights in the country', she noted ironically (ibid., 1.98). Her correspondence presents a picture of enervating luxury—there were servants to fan her all night, to carry her upstairs if she was tired, even to attend to her lapdog—and an almost claustrophobic boredom as she spent the hot season in darkened rooms behind dampened blinds. None the less, by her second year there she was growing reconciled to her new life, writing with characteristic dryness that 'the pain of being indolent is no longer very irksome, I am ashamed to say' (ibid., 2.41).

The monotony of her Calcutta life was also broken by an extended tour of north-western India between October 1837 and February 1840. The governor-general's party spent April to October in 1838 and 1839 at Simla, which Eden proclaimed the 'best part of India' (*Up the Country*, 125). Her travels during these two years formed the basis of what became perhaps her best-known book, *Up the Country*, which was drawn from a series of letters to one of her sisters. Eden's dry, ironic style and eye for memorable detail ensures that the letters are more than a simple enumeration of marvels. While she presents vivid large-scale pictures of state travel in the company of 12,000 people, she is also attentive to such relatively mundane matters as silk gowns ruined by the custom of pouring attar of roses on the hands of visitors and the difficulties of painting a portrait of the new Queen Victoria, whom nobody in their party had seen, for an official present for the maharaja Ranjit Singh. Eden, who was a talented amateur painter as well as a writer, occupied herself with sketching, in addition to carrying out her official duties, leaving a visual as well as a verbal record of her travels in India. Despite the generally light tone of the letters, however, the Edens were in India during troubled times. They travelled from Calcutta during a year of devastating famine, and Eden was deeply shocked by the suffering she witnessed as they passed through the Cawnpore region early in 1838. That year also saw the build-up to the first Anglo-Afghan War, a disaster that seriously damaged Lord Auckland's reputation as governor-general. Eden's last letters from India, written after the return to Calcutta, are filled with anxious comments on the 'distressing and incomprehensible' news from Kabul (*Letters from India*, 2.284).

In 1842 the Edens returned to England, where Emily Eden spent the rest of her life. In 1849 she was devastated by the deaths of both Lord Auckland and her sister Frances. Nearly a year after Auckland's death, she wrote to a friend that her final parting from him 'is so burnt in on my mind' that she still found herself 'living it all dreamily over again' (*Miss Eden's Letters*, 381). She had by that time published *Portraits of the People and Princes of India* (1844), a collection of her accomplished lithographs. She read widely all her life and seems to have had some thoughts of a literary career long before she published her fiction: 'I wish I could write like Mrs. Hannah More, and have money enough to build myself a Barley Wood', she wrote rather wistfully to a friend in 1834 (ibid., 243). Her admiration for More did not mean that her taste in literature was limited to improving works; she was delighted by Thomas Moore's life of Byron, finding it fascinating precisely because she thought it 'a wicked book', one that made her 'glad [Byron] lived, else we should not have had his *Life* to read' (ibid., 209). She also immensely admired Jane Austen, whose writing influenced her own fiction. *The Semi-Detached House*, Eden's second novel, was published anonymously in 1859 with the help of her lifelong friend Lady Theresa Lewis, who negotiated Eden's

terms—no less than £300 and early publication—with Richard Bentley, the publisher. In this lively satirical novel, the pregnant heroine Lady Blanche Chester, whose husband has been posted abroad, shares the middle-class home of the Hopkinsons with the *nouveau riche* Baron Sampson and his wife. Blanche revises her class prejudices after experiencing the warmth of the Hopkinson family. It was enough of a success to encourage Eden to publish, the following year, *The Semi-Attached Couple*, a novel centred on a materially fortunate, but unhappily married, couple. Drawing on her knowledge of political characters, it was originally written shortly before the passage of the first Reform Bill in 1829. Both novels share Austen's focus on the domestic lives of young women, although Eden's characters move in somewhat higher social circles than Austen's, and Eden relies on melodrama (near-fatal fevers, financial skullduggery) to advance her plots in a way that Austen seldom did. Eden's relatively short publishing career was then rounded off by *Up the Country* (1866) and by the posthumous publication of other letters from India, edited by her niece Eleanor Eden, in 1872. Emily Eden died on 5 August 1869 at Fountain House, 5 Upper Hill Street, Richmond, and was buried in the Eden family vault in Beckenham, Kent. According to her great-niece Violet Dickinson, who edited another collection of Eden's letters published in 1919, her household had 'remained a centre of political interest' (*Miss Eden's Letters*, x) even through Eden's final years of invalidism.

PAM PERKINS

Sources *Miss Eden's letters*, ed. V. Dickinson (1919) • E. Eden, *Letters from India*, 2 vols. (1872) • E. Eden, *Up the country: letters from India* (1983) • E. Eden, *The semi-attached couple and the semi-detached house* (1982) • I. Dunbar, *Golden interlude: the Edens in India, 1836–1842* (1955) • Burke, *Peerage* (1917) • C. A. Bayly, ed., *The raj: India and the British, 1600–1947* (1990) [exhibition catalogue, NPG, 19 Oct 1990 – 17 March 1991] • *DNB* • *CGPLA Eng. & Wales* (1869) • d. cert.
Archives BL, letters • Trinity Cam., letters | NL Scot., letters to second earl of Minto • U. Durham L., letters to Elizabeth Mary Copley • U. Durham L., letters to Maria, Lady Grey • UCL, letters to Lord Brougham
Likenesses S. J. Rochard, watercolour and pencil, 1835, NPG [see illus.]
Wealth at death under £25,000: probate, 21 Oct 1869, *CGPLA Eng. & Wales*

Eden, Sir Frederick Morton, second baronet (1766–1809), insurance company manager and writer on the state of the poor, was born at Ashtead, Surrey, the eldest son of Sir Robert Eden (created a baronet in 1776), governor of Maryland, and grandson of Sir Robert Eden, third baronet, of West Auckland. On his father's death in 1784 he succeeded as second baronet. William Eden, first Baron Auckland, was his uncle. His mother was Caroline Calvert, sister and coheir of the sixth Lord Baltimore. He matriculated at Christ Church, Oxford, in April 1783, where he was nominated to a studentship, graduating BA in 1787 and proceeding MA in 1789. He vacated his studentship on his marriage in January 1792 to Anne (d. 1808), the only daughter and heir of James Paul Smith of New Bond Street, London. The rest of his life seems to have been spent in the insurance business, and in social and economic investigations. He was one of the founders and chairman of the Globe Insurance Company, and died at the office of the company in Pall Mall, London, on 14 November 1809, aged forty-three. He was buried at Ealing parish church. He left five sons and two daughters: the eldest son, Sir Frederick, third baronet, was killed at New Orleans on 24 December 1814; the second, Sir William, succeeded his brother as fourth baronet; the third was Robert *Eden, bishop of Moray.

Eden's chief claim to fame rests on his authorship of his descriptively titled *The state of the poor, or, An history of the labouring classes in England from the conquest to the present period; in which are particularly considered their domestic economy with respect to diet, dress, fuel, and habitation; and the various plans which, from time to time, have been proposed and adopted for the relief of the poor etc* (3 vols., 1797). This ambitious privately financed inquiry was begun during the period of acute grain scarcity in 1794–5, and was a pioneering piece of social investigation based on a set of 'queries' posed by the author and pursued by himself with the help of 'a few respectable clergymen' and an investigator who spent a year visiting parishes throughout England. Although the work was valued at the time, as it has been by social and economic historians since, for its information on living standards, it was written from a perspective that reveals Eden's general adherence to Adam Smith's system of natural liberty in economic affairs; this led Karl Marx to claim that Eden was the only eighteenth-century disciple of Smith to produce a work of any significance. Eden should be described as an enlightened philanthropist with considerable practical knowledge of poor-law administration, friendly societies, and the insurance principle. He was judiciously unfavourable to legislative provision and government regulation in the Smithian manner, placing his faith in the self-improvement motive while remaining unconvinced by Smith's opinions on the adverse effects of the settlement laws and the social drawbacks associated with the division of labour. Enclosure of commons was advocated on grounds of its value to employment and general agricultural improvement, and the permanent value of the poor laws was questioned. In this respect Eden anticipated T. R. Malthus's opposition to the allowance system in his first *Essay on Population* (1798), but retained a pro-populationist position of the kind that Malthus was to bring into doubt. Eden also anticipated the first decennial population census in 1801 by bringing out his own *Estimate of the Number of Inhabitants of Great Britain and Ireland* in the previous year, undershooting the census by just under 5 million.

Eden wrote two pamphlets on economic questions connected with the Napoleonic wars, *Eight Letters on the Peace; and on the Commerce and Manufactures of Great Britain and Ireland* (1802) and an *Address on the Maritime Rights of Great Britain* (1808), advising on the effects on British trade of war. Making use of his preference for self-help through insurance, he wrote *Observations on friendly societies, for the maintenance of the industrious classes, during sickness, infirmity and old age and other exigencies* (1801) and *On the Policy and Expediency of Granting Insurance Charters* (1806). His correspondence with Jeremy Bentham over various interests they had in common, where rivalry (between Bentham's schemes for 'annuity notes' and 'frugality banks' and Eden's efforts to obtain a charter for the Globe Insurance Company) turned into friendship, reveals a similar concern for practical philanthropy. As further indication of this trait Eden wrote *Porto-Bello, or, A Plan for the Improvement of the Port and City of London* (1798), and was responsible for a proposal to create a London Fire Brigade on the lines of the *corps des sapeurs-pompiers* in Paris.

The catalogue of Eden's library, which he compiled and published in 1806, contains nearly 8000 entries and reveals a cultivated and scholarly mind. This is confirmed by the anonymous Latin epic which he published in the same year, *Brontes: a Cento to the Memory of the Late Viscount Nelson*, and by a poem entitled 'The Vision', in which he satirized his friend Jonathan Boucher's devotion to etymological researches, later attempting to have the results of these researches published as a supplement to Dr Johnson's dictionary.   DONALD WINCH

Sources GM, 1st ser., 79 (1809), 1178 · *The correspondence of Jeremy Bentham*, ed. T. Sprigge and others, [11 vols.] (1968–), in *The collected works of Jeremy Bentham*, vols. 6, 7 · J. R. Poynter, *Society and pauperism: English ideas on poor relief, 1795–1834* (1969) · B. E. Supple, *The Royal Exchange Assurance: a history of British insurance, 1720–1970* (1970) · Foster, *Alum. Oxon.* · C. Walford, *The insurance cyclopaedia*, 6 vols. (1871–80)

Archives BL, Add. MSS 33542–33544, 34454–34457, 43702 · GL, committee of insurance and the treasury committee of the Globe Insurance Company · Harvard U., Houghton L., 'Epsom, a vision' | E. Sussex RO, Boucher MSS · Williamsburg College of William and Mary, Virginia, corresp. with Jonathan Boucher

Eden, George, earl of Auckland (1784–1849), politician and governor-general of India, was born at Eden Farm, near Beckenham in Kent, on 25 August 1784, the second son of William *Eden, first Baron Auckland (1744–1814), and his wife, Eleanor (1758–1818), daughter of Sir Gilbert *Elliot, of Minto, Roxburghshire, third baronet. He had three brothers and eight sisters. He was educated at Eton College (1796–1801) and at Christ Church, Oxford, where he matriculated in 1802, and graduated BA in 1806 and MA in 1808. He entered Lincoln's Inn in 1806, was called to the bar in 1809, and practised as a barrister, but was drawn into politics in 1810 when his elder brother, William Eden, was drowned in the Thames. George succeeded to William's seat in the House of Commons for the borough of New Woodstock. In parliament he gravitated towards the whig opposition. In 1814, on the death of his father, he entered the House of Lords as the second Baron Auckland. Although thought to be rather shy and reserved, he and his sisters Emily *Eden and Fanny, who kept house with him, became esteemed members of whig society.

In the whig administration of 1830 Auckland was given the mastership of the Royal Mint and the presidency of the Board of Trade. At the Board of Trade he began to reveal the talents for assiduous application and orderly administration that were to mark his whole career, but a contemporary verdict was that 'the real business of the

George Eden, earl of Auckland (1784–1849), by Simon Jacques Rochard, c.1835–6

department' was left to Poulett Thomson, a very vigorous vice-president (Brown, 16). In 1834, after an upheaval in the government, Auckland was made first lord of the Admiralty. The appointment was widely criticized: Auckland's 'unpopular manners, his want of talent for public speaking and of distinction as a public man caused everyone to cry out against it' (Aspinall, 381). Auckland himself was diffident about his promotion: 'I have no turn for great elevation and am not very confident of myself' (Maxwell, 2.83–4), but he was regarded as a success at the Admiralty and was made GCB. In 1835 the whig government decided to cancel the appointment of Lord Heytesbury as governor-general of India made by the short-lived tory administration and to choose Auckland instead. His need for financial security clearly induced Auckland to accept, even though he and his sisters were thought to be very unhappy at the prospect of a long exile. At the Board of Trade, Auckland estimated his income at £2800 a year in office and £1500 out of office: the governor-general of India was paid a salary of £25,000.

On his arrival in Calcutta in March 1836 Auckland immediately made a good impression. T. B. Macaulay was not surprised at 'the sensible manly w[ay] in which he looks at every subject—the liberality of his views, his industry, and the extent of his information', but he found that Auckland had overcome his awkwardness in company, showing 'a simplicity and bonhomie', 'a readiness to be amused' and 'a general courtesy' that made him very popular (*Letters of Thomas Babington Macaulay*, 3.189). He was never, however, to master his inability to speak in

public. He replaced Lord William Bentinck, who had been a strong-willed reforming governor-general. Warned by his ministerial colleagues at home that he should not follow Bentinck's example and 'rush into reforms' without prior permission from Britain, Auckland complained that this was asking 'the Governor General not to govern', but his own inclination was to be cautious. He summed up his objectives as, 'rather to seek the gradual introduction of administrative reforms, than to aim at sweeping changes of principle and of system' (Sinha, 313). He proceeded cautiously in implementing Bentinck's policies of legal reform and of favouring education in English at the expense of support for learning in classical Indian languages. He hoped to be able to put the finances of the government of India back into surplus.

Auckland spent over two years of his governorship, from the end of 1837 to the beginning of 1840, away from Calcutta on an extended tour into northern India. He was of course accompanied by his sisters, Emily later publishing an engaging account of their travels as *Up the Country* in 1866. On his tour the governor-general negotiated directly with some of the rulers of states subordinate to British India or on its frontiers. He visited Lahore, the capital of the Sikh state of the Punjab, in the winter of 1838.

The problems of the north-western frontier were to draw Auckland into sanctioning a British intervention into Afghanistan which ended in military catastrophe and the discrediting of his governor-generalship. British interest in Afghanistan was aroused by the extension of Russian influence into central Asia and Persia. An Afghan regime favourable to Britain would be a barrier to further Russian penetration towards India. In 1838 Auckland decided that Britain should intervene to bring about such a regime. Dost Muhammad, actually in control at Kabul, was to be displaced by British troops in favour of the long deposed Shah Shuja, who promised be a firm ally of the British. Auckland evidently believed that resolute action was needed, not only to ward off a Russian threat, but also to reassure Indian allies and deter potential Indian enemies elsewhere. The invasion was successful. Auckland was fully supported by the British government and created earl of Auckland on 21 December 1839 as a reward. But the quick withdrawal that Auckland had hoped for proved to be impossible. Shah Shuja's continuation in power depended on British troops. The British kept 10,000 men in Afghanistan while trying to run the government through an envoy and British agents. The cost of operations in Afghanistan together with the dispatch of an expeditionary force to China in 1840 for the First Anglo-Chinese War pushed the Indian budget into deficit. No funds could be spared for the improvements which Auckland had hoped to introduce. In November 1841 there was a rising in Kabul. The British envoy, Sir William Macnaghten, was murdered, and the British force retreating to India was completely destroyed. Auckland saw 'the plans of public good and public security upon which I had staked so much ... all broken down under circumstances of horror and disaster of which history has few parallels'

(Auckland to Hobhouse, 18 Feb 1842, BL, Add. MS 37707, fol. 187). If he cannot be directly blamed for the final military disaster, he still bears full responsibility for having sanctioned a commitment to the hazardous project of trying to impose a regime on Afghanistan. Ministers at home were urging firm action on him and he could be reasonably sure that they would support him, but the decision was his.

Auckland was replaced by Lord Ellenborough, nominee of a new Conservative government, and returned to Britain in August 1842. The rest of his career was by no means an anticlimax: in 1846, when the whigs regained power, he was again appointed first lord of the Admiralty, again proved that he was an administrator of the highest calibre, and won 'the golden opinions of the service' (Lambert, 51). He is credited with having reformed the Admiralty to enable it effectively to conduct the Crimean War a few years later.

Auckland was suddenly struck with 'a fit of apoplexy' on his return from shooting and died on 1 January 1849 at Lady Harriet Baring's house, The Grange, Alresford, Hampshire. He was buried five days later at Beckenham. He never married and the earldom became extinct; the barony of Auckland passed to his brother Robert John *Eden.   P. J. MARSHALL

Sources M. E. Yapp, *Strategies of British India: Britain, Iran and Afghanistan, 1798–1850* (1980) · J. A. Norris, *The First Afghan War, 1838–1842* (1967) · D. P. Sinha, *Some aspects of British social and administrative policy in India during the administration of Lord Auckland* (1969) · A. D. Lambert, *The last sailing battlefleet: maintaining naval mastery, 1815–1850* (1991) · E. Eden, *Up the country*, [new edn] (1983) · R. G. Thorn, 'Eden, Hon. George', HoP, *Commons* · *The Greville memoirs*, ed. H. Reeve, new edn, 8 vols. (1888) · L. Brown, *The board of trade and the free-trade movement, 1830–42* (1958) · *The letters of Thomas Babington Macaulay*, ed. T. Pinney, 6 vols. (1974–81) · A. Aspinall, ed., *Three early nineteenth-century diaries* (1952) [extracts from Le Marchant, E. J. Littleton, Baron Hatherton, and E. Law, earl of Ellenborough] · H. E. Maxwell, *Life and letters of George William Frederick, fourth earl of Clarendon*, 2 vols. (1913) · GEC, *Peerage* · BL, Auckland MSS, Add. MS 37707
Archives BL, Auckland MSS · BL, corresp. and papers, Add. MSS 29475, 34459–34460, 37689–37718, 45730, 46491, 46519, 47075 · BL, corresp. and papers, Eg MS 2427 · BL OIOC, home misc. series, corresp. relating to India · McGill University, Montreal, McLennan Library, corresp., minutes, and dispatches [copies] | Beds. & Luton ARS, letters and memoranda addressed to Earl de Grey · BL, corresp. with Lord Broughton, Add. MSS 36473–36474, 47227–47228 · BL, corresp. with Sir Charles Napier, Add. MSS 40022–40023, 40040–40041 · BL, corresp. with Sir Robert Peel, Add. MSS 40367–40598 *passim* · BL OIOC, corresp. with Sir George Russell Clerk, MS Eur D 538 · BL OIOC, corresp. with Lord Elphinstone, MS Eur F 87–89 · BL OIOC, corresp. with J. C. Hobhouse, MS Eur F 213 · BL OIOC, letters to George Lyall, MS Eur D 1165 · BL OIOC, corresp. with Sir John McNeill, MS Eur D 1165 · Borth. Inst., letters to Sir Charles Wood · CKS, Hardinge MSS · Harvard U., Houghton L., letters to Sir John Bowring · Lincs. Arch., corresp. with Sir Henry Fane [copies] · Lpool RO, letters to Lord Stanley · NAM, letters to Jasper Nicolls · NL Scot., letters to Lord Minto · NMM, letters to Sir Charles Napier · NMM, letters to Sir William Parker · PRO, corresp. with Henry Pottinger, FO 705 · PRO, corresp. with Lord John Russell, PRO 30/22 · RS, letters to Sir John Henschel · U. Durham L., letters to second Earl Grey · U. Durham L., letters to third Earl Grey · U. Hull, Brynmor Jones L., letters to Sir Charles Hotham · U. Nott. L., corresp. with duke of Portland · U. Southampton L., Broadlands MSS · U. Southampton L., corresp. with Lord Palmerston · UCL, letters to the SDUK · W. Sussex RO, letters to duke of Richmond
Likenesses S. J. Rochard, portrait, *c.*1835–1836, NPG [*see illus.*] · J. Thomson, lithograph, pubd 1850 (after L. Dickinson), NPG · G. Hayter, group portrait, oils (*The trial of Queen Caroline, 1820*), NPG · G. Stodart, stipple (after L. Dickinson), NPG
Wealth at death £70,000: will, PRO, PROB 8/342

Eden, Henry (1797–1888), naval officer, fourth son of Thomas Eden, deputy auditor of Greenwich Hospital, and cousin of George Eden, first earl of Auckland, entered the navy in 1811 on board the *Acasta*, in which he served on the North American station until August 1815. He was shortly afterwards appointed to the frigate *Alceste*, commanded by Captain Murray Maxwell, which sailed from Spithead in February 1816, carrying Lord Amherst as ambassador to China. The *Alceste* was wrecked in the Gaspar Strait on 18 February 1817, and Eden, with the others from her, returned to England in a merchant ship. In October he was made lieutenant and, after two years in the *Liffey* on the coast of Portugal, was in June 1820 appointed flag-lieutenant to his brother-in-law Sir Graham Moore, commander-in-chief in the Mediterranean. In October 1821 he was promoted to command the *Chanticleer*, from which, in July 1822, he was moved to the *Martin*, and was employed for the next two years on the coast of Greece during the Greek revolution. In April 1827 he was advanced to post rank, and from 1832 to 1835 commanded the frigate *Conway* on the home station, and afterwards off South America. From 1839 to 1842 he served as flag-captain to Sir Graham Moore, commander-in-chief at Plymouth, and in May 1844 was appointed to the *Collingwood*, fitting for the Pacific as flagship of Sir George Francis Seymour. His health, however, obliged him to resign before the ship sailed, and he had no further service afloat.

From 1846 to 1848 Eden was private secretary to his cousin Lord Auckland, then first lord of the Admiralty. In 1849 he married Elizabeth Harriet Georgina Beresford, daughter of Lieutenant-General Lord George Beresford, who later inherited Gillingham Hall in Norfolk from her aunt Miss Schutz. There were no children. From 1848 to 1853 Eden served as a junior naval superintendent of Woolwich Dockyard. In 1854 he was temporary superintendent at Devonport, and he was lord of the Admiralty from 1855 to 1858. He became rear-admiral on 7 August 1854, vice-admiral on 11 February 1861, and admiral on 16 September 1864; but after his retirement from the board, where the name of Eden had long been a potent spell, he had no active connection with the navy. In his retirement he lived for the most part at Gillingham Hall and served as a magistrate. He died on 30 January 1888 at his house in Eaton Square, London.

Eden proved himself to be a capable administrator, as his long posting at Woolwich, then the home of steam engineering in the navy, demonstrated. He transferred these skills to the Admiralty as a junior lord under Sir Charles Wood. It was there that he made his contribution.

His early career was made by his political and family connections, and his failure to serve in command afloat suggests that he was not cut out for the responsibility of high office: he was a colourless man who left little to show for his life. J. K. LAUGHTON, *rev.* ANDREW LAMBERT

Sources O'Byrne, *Naval biog. dict.* · *Annual Register* (1888) · *The Times* (2 Feb 1888), 10b · *CGPLA Eng. & Wales* (1889)
Wealth at death £68,895 6s. 6d.: resworn probate, May 1889, *CGPLA Eng. & Wales*

Eden, Morton, first Baron Henley (1752–1830), diplomat, was born at West Auckland, co. Durham, on 8 July 1752, fifth and youngest surviving son, with three daughters, of Sir Robert Eden, third baronet (c.1716–1755), of West Auckland, and his wife, Mary (d. 1794), daughter of William Davison of Beamish. He was educated at Eton College (1761–70), matriculated from Christ Church, Oxford, on 13 July 1770, took no degree, and at the age of twenty-four entered upon a diplomatic career. Appointed minister-plenipotentiary to the electoral court of Bavaria, and minister at the Diet of Regensburg on 10 October 1776, he soon gave such satisfaction in his office that in February 1779 he was transferred to Copenhagen as envoy-extraordinary. In 1783 he returned to England and married, on 7 August, Lady Elizabeth Henley (1757–1821), fifth daughter of Robert *Henley, first earl of Northington, and Jane Huband. Lady Elizabeth was coheir to her brother Robert *Henley, the second and last earl, who died in 1786.

Eden proceeded to Dresden as envoy-extraordinary and was advanced to the dignity of minister-plenipotentiary, continuing in his post until 1791. At the instigation of his elder brother, William *Eden, the mentor of his career, he was appointed before the close of the year envoy-extraordinary and minister-plenipotentiary at the court of Berlin. He was nominated a knight of the Bath on 16 December 1791 and, at the special request of George III, was publicly invested with the insignia of the order by the king of Prussia on 1 January 1792. In February he very readily proceeded to Vienna as ambassador to the emperor of Austria for a year, and on 12 November 1794 he was sworn in a privy councillor, and, after reluctantly agreeing to be dispatched to Madrid as ambassador-extraordinary, he was reappointed envoy-extraordinary to Vienna to negotiate the war loan to the emperor. He remained in the Austrian capital for five years. On his retirement from the public service, with a pension of £2000 a year, he was created a peer of Ireland under the title of Baron Henley of Chardstock, Dorset, on 9 November 1799.

Abandoning the expatriate life he had grown accustomed to, he settled in England, though often changing abode. He became a fellow of the Royal Society (1800), was an affectionate observer of royal family life while living near Windsor, and was a wry spectator of the political scene, in which his main attachments were to his brother William and his former patron at the Foreign Office, Lord Grenville. He was instituted GCB in January 1815. He died on 6 December 1830 while visiting Gumley Hall, Leicestershire, and was buried on the 13th at Watford, Northamptonshire. He had three surviving sons and one daughter.

His eldest son, Frederick, had died in 1823, and his second son, Robert *Henley (formerly Eden), succeeded to the title as second Baron Henley.

G. B. SMITH, *rev.* ROLAND THORNE

Sources D. B. Horn, ed., *British diplomatic representatives, 1689–1789*, CS, 3rd ser., 46 (1932) · S. T. Bindoff and others, eds., *British diplomatic representatives, 1789–1852*, CS, 3rd ser., 50 (1934) · *The journal and correspondence of William, Lord Auckland*, ed. [G. Hogge], 4 vols. (1861–2) · *The manuscripts of J. B. Fortescue*, 10 vols., HMC, 30 (1892–1927), esp. vols. 2–3 · GEC, *Peerage*, new edn, 6.435 · GM, 1st ser., 101/1 (1831), 81 · *Annual Register* (1830) · *The later correspondence of George III*, ed. A. Aspinall, 5 vols. (1962–70), vol. 2, p. 1152; vol. 4, p. 2870 · *Selections from the letters and correspondence of Sir James Bland Burges*, ed. J. Hutton (1885), 191 · R. A. Austen-Leigh, ed., *The Eton College register, 1753–1790* (1921), 174 · Foster, *Alum. Oxon.* · *Boyle's Court Guide* (1805–29) · PRO, estate duty register, IR 26/1259, fol. 32 · IGI · Burke, *Peerage*
Archives Foreign Office, London, Foreign Office dispatches · Northants. RO, corresp. and papers · priv. coll., travel journal · PRO, letter-book and corresp., FO353 · Woburn Abbey, dispatches and MSS | Bedford estate office, London, Adair MSS · Beds. & Luton ARS, corresp. with Lord Grantham · BL, corresp. with Lord Auckland, letters and papers, Add. MSS 34412–34460 · BL, Fortescue MSS · BL, corresp. with Lord Grenville, Add. MSS 34436, 34440–34451, 34453, 36814, 59018 · BL, corresp. with Sir Robert Keith, Add. MSS 35511–35544, *passim* · BL, corresp. with Sir Arthur Paget, Add. MS 48394 · Bodl. Oxf., corresp. with Sir James Bland Burges · Hants. RO, corresp. with William Wickham · Hunt. L., letters to Grenville family · NA Scot., corresp. with Lord Melville · NL Scot., letters to Hugh Elliot · NL Scot., corresp. with Sir Robert Liston · NL Scot., corresp. with Lord Lynedoch · Suffolk RO, Ipswich, letters to Alexander Stratton · U. Edin., corresp. with Grimr Thorkelin
Wealth at death under £45,000: PRO, death duty registers, IR 26/1259, fol. 32

Eden, Richard (c.1520–1576), translator, was born into a family of East Anglian cloth merchants and clerics, possibly in Herefordshire. His father was George Eden, a cloth merchant. He attended Christ's College, Cambridge (1534–7) (probably intending to take holy orders), and subsequently Queen's College, graduating BA in 1538 and MA in 1544. He was taught by Sir Thomas Smith when he became professor of civil law in 1542, and Smith's enthusiasm for colonial projects undoubtedly had a shaping influence on Eden's career. Eden held a minor position in the treasury (1544–6), presumably as a protégé of Smith. He married in 1547, and had twelve children in the next fourteen years, all of whom survived into adulthood, as Eden noted in 1573. Through Smith, Eden would have associated with some of the most innovative scientific and literary figures of the mid-Tudor period, including John Cheke and Roger Ascham.

Eden also began to acquire a reputation as a chemist, and was offered the position of distiller of waters in the royal household, although the post was offered to someone else after Henry VIII died in January 1548. Manuscript evidence suggests that he was also becoming interested in alchemy (Bodl. Oxf., Savile MS 18). In the late 1540s and early 1550s Eden was employed by Richard Whalley, a prominent Nottinghamshire gentleman who held public office—at a salary of £20 per annum, plus board for himself, his wife, and a servant—to work in a laboratory searching for the secret of turning base metal into gold.

Whalley was frequently imprisoned and was accused of plotting to restore the duke of Somerset; he and Eden fell out badly in 1551, the experiment having proved, not surprisingly, unsuccessful.

In 1552 Eden became a secretary to Sir William Cecil. Cecil probably wanted to employ a scholar with scientific interests to work on the voyages that he was planning to open up the Far East to European trade, all part of the grand plans of the new protector, the earl of Northumberland, who wanted England to be able to challenge Spain's global empire. Northumberland was keen to have works produced that would help encourage such enterprise and it was undoubtedly under his direction that Eden produced his first major work, *A Treatyse of the Newe India* (1553), a translation of part of book five of Sebastian Muenster's *Cosmographia*.

When Edward VI died in 1553 Eden was placed in a difficult position, as his father and uncle had taken part in the attempt to establish Northumberland's daughter-in-law, Lady Jane Grey, as queen instead of Mary. Nevertheless, Eden appears to have affirmed loyalty to the new sovereign, and to have prospered materially. His most important work, a translation of considerable portions of Pietro Martire d'Anghiera's *De orbe novo decades*, Gonzalo Oviedo's *Natural hystoria de las Indias*, and other works, was entitled *The Decades of the Newe Worlde or West India* (1555). The translation contains elaborate prefatory material extravagantly praising Spanish heroism in the Americas and urging the English to unite with and copy their European imperial forebears. Eden was appointed to a prominent position in the treasury: as he later noted, he obtained this post through the support of Spanish nobles at court. Nevertheless, his religion came under suspicion of heresy towards the end of 1555 and he had to surrender his office.

Eden's movements are not recorded in the next few years. He visited the explorer Sebastian Cabot, who had been involved in the practical side of Northumberland's plans for overseas exploration, on his deathbed in 1557. As clerk of the council in the Star Chamber in 1559 he received 5 yards of scarlet for Elizabeth's coronation. The same year he revised Thomas Gemini's abbreviation of Vesalius's *De humani corporis fabrica* and in 1561 he translated Martin Cortes's *Breve compendio de la sphaera y de la arte de navigar* as *The Arte of Navigation*, the first English manual of navigation, to which is appended descriptions of mathematical instruments, possibly by Eden himself. Now a widower, he was employed in 1562 by Jean de Ferrieres, vidame (chief lay officer) of the bishop of Chartres, as a travelling companion and secretary. He remained in Ferrieres's service until 1572, travelling extensively in France and Germany and conducting a series of chemical experiments, about which he wrote to Sir Thomas Smith in 1572. Eden managed to flee from Paris just before the massacre of St Bartholomew's day and he returned to London in September 1572.

Lacking employment and income, Eden unsuccessfully petitioned the queen to make him a poor knight of Windsor, submitting a *curriculum vitae* which is the source for much of the information about his life (reprinted in Arber, xlv–xlvi). In 1574 he produced an English version of John Taisnier's *De natura magnetis*, which, because of his death and that of his printer, Richard Jugge, did not appear until 1579, together with his translation *The Arte of Navigation*. The last work Eden translated was Ludovico de Varthema's *Itinerario*, a semi-fictionalized account of his travels in the east in 1503. Eden died in 1576 and Richard Willes revised the work, which was published in 1577 entitled *The History of Travayle*.

Eden's importance as a translator and promoter of colonial projects and ideas makes him a key figure in the intellectual life of sixteenth-century England. His work had a major influence on that of Richard Hakluyt, and was reprinted in Hakluyt's *Principal Navigations, Voyages, Traffiques and Discoveries of the English Nation* (1589, 1598, 1600).   ANDREW HADFIELD

Sources D. Gwyn, 'Richard Eden: cosmographer and alchemist', *Sixteenth-Century Journal*, 15 (1984), 13–34 · E. Arber, ed., *The first three English books on America* (privately printed, Birmingham, 1885) · Venn, *Alum. Cant.* · A. Hadfield, *Literature, travel, and colonial writing in the English Renaissance, 1545–1625* (1998) · *STC, 1475–1640* · *CPR, 1553–4* · *DNB* · C. J. Kitching, 'Alchemy in the reign of Edward VI: an episode in the careers of Richard Whalley and Richard Eden', *BIHR*, 44 (1971), 308–15 · E. G. R. Taylor, *Tudor geography, 1485–1583* (1930) · H. Marchitello, 'Recent studies in Tudor and early Stuart travel writing', *English Literary Renaissance*, 29 (1999) · R. Hakluyt, *The principal navigations, voyages, traffiques and discoveries of the English nation*, 2nd edn, 3 vols. (1598–1600); repr. 12 vols., Hakluyt Society, extra ser., 1–12 (1903–5) · private information (2004) [C. S. Bayne] · *CSP dom.*, 1547–80

Archives PRO, 70.146.446/12.98.32 · PRO, SP 46/8, fols. 164–8 | BL, Lansdowne MS 101. art. 5 · Bodl. Oxf., MS Savile 18

Eden, Sir Robert, first baronet (1741–1784), army officer and colonial governor, was born on 14 September 1741 in Durham, the second son of Sir Robert Eden, third baronet (*c*.1712–1755), of West Auckland, MP, and his wife, Mary (*c*.1720–1794), daughter of William Davison of Beamish, co. Durham. Eden was one of eight children, having four brothers and three sisters.

Two years after the death of his father Eden obtained, in February 1757 at the age of sixteen, an army commission in the Royal Regiment of Artillery. In May 1758 he was promoted to the rank of ensign in the Coldstream regiment of foot guards, and in July 1760 was posted with the regiment's 2nd battalion to Germany for active service in the Seven Years' War. At the war's conclusion Eden returned with his regiment to London in September 1762, having achieved the rank of captain.

Within a few years of his return, on 26 April 1765 Eden married the Hon. Caroline Calvert, daughter of Charles, fifth Baron Baltimore (1699–1751), and his wife, Mary (*d*. 1748), daughter of Sir Theodore Janssen (*c*.1658–1748) and his wife, Williamsa (*d*. 1731). Caroline's brother Frederick (1732–1771) was the sixth Baron Baltimore at the time of her marriage. Within three years Eden's marriage brought him the governorship of Maryland, the proprietary colony ruled by the Calverts.

The official letter informing the incumbent governor, Horatio Sharpe, of the appointment of Eden as his successor ascribed the decision to Baltimore's 'partiality for his

Sir Robert Eden, first baronet (1741–1784), by Charles Willson Peale, 1775 [replica]

In recognition of his service as governor, George III created Eden a baronet in October 1776. A parliamentary act of 1781 awarded Eden and his wife £17,500 as settlement of litigation over the proprietorship of Maryland, and Eden was also awarded a pension by the government. At the conclusion of hostilities Eden returned to Maryland in 1783 with Henry Harford, the illegitimate son of Frederick, sixth Baron Baltimore, and the inheritor of the proprietorship, who hoped to gain compensation for his confiscated property. Eden and Harford stayed with Dr Upton Scott while in Annapolis, and it was at Scott's home that Eden died on 2 September 1784 of 'dropsy'. He was buried in St Margaret's parish church, Anne Arundel county, but his body was reinterred in St Anne's churchyard in Annapolis in 1926.   JEAN B. RUSSO

Sources E. C. Papenfuse and others, eds., *A biographical dictionary of the Maryland legislature, 1635–1789*, 1 (1979) [pt of the Maryland State Archives biography project] · B. C. Steiner, *Life and administration of Sir Robert Eden* (1898) · R. R. Beirne, 'Portrait of a colonial governor: Robert Eden, I—his entrance', *Maryland Historical Magazine*, 45 (1950), 153–75 · R. R. Beirne, 'Portrait of a colonial governor: Robert Eden, II—his exit', *Maryland Historical Magazine*, 45 (1950), 294–311 · 'Correspondence of Governor Robert Eden', *Maryland Historical Magazine* (1907), 1–13, 66–7, 97–110, 227–44, 293–309 · A. C. Land, *Colonial Maryland: a history* (1981)
Archives Maryland Hall of Records, Annapolis, papers
Likenesses C. W. Peale, miniature, 1775, priv. coll. [*see illus.*] · F. MacKubin, oils, 1914 (after C. W. Peale, 1755), Annapolis, Maryland
Wealth at death personal property appraised by general assembly at £2745 15s. 0d.; income at death at least £800 from British government pension: Papenfuse and others, eds., *A biographical dictionary*

sister', 'the merit of his brother-in-law to himself', and 'the solicitations of relatives' (Steiner, 11). Sharpe had served the proprietor well but competence was no match for kinship. Eden resigned his army commission on 14 July 1768 and arrived in Maryland on 5 June 1769, with his wife and two sons. The following year saw the birth of the couple's third and last child.

Eden's affable nature quickly won him many friends among the colony's social and political élite. A leader of Annapolis society during his tenure, Eden supported the touring theatrical companies that visited the city; became an honorary member of the Homony Club, a gathering place for young gentlemen of wealth and position; owned a stable of horses that he raced in the fall season; and took part in the rounds of visiting that occurred in town and at rural plantations.

The early years of Eden's administration were marked by only one serious dispute with the legislature, concerning the related issues of the power to set the fees charged by government officials and the amount of tobacco collected per poll for support of the Church of England clergy. Not until 1773 did the assembly finally resolve the issues, passing an act setting the clerical poll tax at the previous rate and allowing to stand the fee proclamation Eden had issued in November 1770, after proroguing the assembly, as it too continued the old rates.

Eden was less successful, however, when the crisis in relations between colonists and crown came to a head during his governorship. Although he retained the good will of his Maryland subjects, he was unable to reconcile the colonists to continued parliamentary rule despite his best efforts to act as a buffer between the two sides. Eden succeeded in remaining in Maryland as nominal governor until June 1776, but his effective authority had ended two years earlier when the first extra-legal Maryland convention assembled in June 1774. 'He [had] survived without being able to prevail' (Land, 309). Finally, in May 1776, Maryland's sixth convention resolved 'that the Publick quiet and safety … require that [Eden] leave the Province and that he is at full liberty to depart peaceably with all his effects' (Beirne, 173). On 26 June he sailed for England on HMS *Fowey*, his wife and children having departed earlier.

Eden, Robert (1804–1886), Scottish Episcopal bishop of Moray, Ross, and Caithness, the third son of Sir Frederick Morton *Eden, second baronet (1766–1809), and his wife, Anne (*d.* 1808), daughter and heir of James Paul Smith of New Bond Street, London, was born on 2 September 1804. He was educated at Westminster School and Christ Church, Oxford (1823–6). He achieved a third class in classics in 1826 and graduated BA in 1827 and MA in 1829. In 1827 he married Emma (*d.* 1880), third daughter of Justice Allan Park; they had five sons and five daughters. Ordained deacon and priest by the bishop of Gloucester in 1828, he served successively the curacies of Weston-sub-Edge in Gloucestershire, and Messing and Peldon in Essex, and became rector of Leigh, Essex, in 1837. An energetic incumbent, Eden's ministry revealed high-church principles, and a commitment to overseas missions and elementary education. When Bishop David Low resigned the see of Moray and Ross, Eden was elected his successor; he was consecrated at St Paul's Church, Edinburgh, on 9 March 1851, receiving a DD from Cambridge on his elevation. He made a great personal sacrifice in accepting a see in the poor Scottish Episcopal church, relinquishing a comfortable English living worth approximately £600 a year for a position of no more than £150 with no episcopal residence. His pro-cathedral was in fact a small cottage, fitted up as a mission chapel, on the bank of the River Ness. However, during his tenure he quadrupled the income of the see, founded the beautiful cathedral of St Andrew in

Inverness, and was mainly instrumental in securing a residence for his successor. Dignified and firm in character, he was a capable but not brilliant preacher. A close friend of Archbishop Charles Longley and bishops Blomfield, Selwyn, Hamilton, and Samuel Wilberforce, with whom he was at school, his English contacts proved useful to his influence in Scotland.

In 1862 Eden was elected primus of the Scottish Episcopal church, in succession to Bishop Charles Terrot. As primus he was active in the long-standing campaign to remove the disabilities of Scottish Episcopalian orders in the ministry of the Church of England. A concern for relations with Eastern Orthodoxy came to a head in 1866 when he visited Russia, publishing *Impressions of a Recent Visit to Russia* (1866) about the trip, followed by a pamphlet on advocating intercommunion between Anglicanism and Orthodoxy (1867). His other works were tracts, sermons, and addresses. Eden's enlistment of Archbishop Longley to take part in the foundation of Inverness Cathedral in 1866, with the consequent official recognition of the unity between the Episcopal church and the Church of England, created a small controversy with some in England and Scotland who feared the erosion of the constitutional principle of established religion. Although an Englishman, in Scotland Eden became conscious and supportive of the native Episcopalian tradition, upholding the use of the Scottish communion office, and the importance of the episcopate in relations with the established church which, nevertheless, remained cordial during his years as bishop.

It was probably in the government and administration of the Scottish Episcopal church that Eden's greatest gifts were exercised. This competence became important in a church that was increasing in its geographic spread, its membership, and its social outreach during the later nineteenth century. A long-standing supporter of lay involvement in church government, Eden's support was instrumental in 1876 in remodelling the whole financial structure of the Episcopal church to include the laity in its decision making. The issue created a high degree of interest and division among Episcopalian laity and large meetings of its members were held in Edinburgh. The Church Society, the creation of the popular Dean Edward Ramsay, was increasingly unable to meet the needs of church extension. A small group of reformers aimed at replacing this society by an organization which should represent every congregation but those who had been generous supporters of the Church Society were opposed to this. Eden's support for the reformers in this divided issue, his moderation in the debates, and his excellent knowledge of business directly contributed to the creation of a new financial body, known as the Representative Church Council.

Eden's good humour and love of jokes were distasteful to some older, stricter Episcopalians, but his confident leadership inspired numbers of his clergy to feel more assured. He was a little out of his theological depth in the doctrinal controversies which divided nineteenth-century Scottish Episcopalians. Politically he remained an uncompromising tory. In his final years he became too ill and paralysed to fulfil his episcopal duties and a coadjutor-bishop was consecrated in 1885, but he continued as primus until his death. He died peacefully on the evening of 26 August 1886 at his official residence, Edencourt, in Inverness, and was buried at Tomnahurich cemetery on 1 September.   ROWAN STRONG

Sources J. Archibald, *The historic episcopate in the Columban church* (1893) • J. Wordsworth, *The episcopate of Charles Wordsworth, bishop of St Andrews* (1899) • R. Strong, *Alexander Forbes of Brechin* (1995) • M. Lochhead, *Episcopal Scotland in the nineteenth century* (1966) • Burke, *Peerage* • Foster, *Alum. Oxon.* • *CCI* (1887)
Archives Bodl. Oxf., diary • NRA, priv. coll. | BL, corresp. with W. E. Gladstone, Add. MSS 44368–44450 • LPL, corresp. with C. Blomfield • LPL, corresp. with A. C. Tait • LPL, letters to Frederick Anthony White • University of Dundee, letters to Alexander Forbes • W. Sussex RO, letters to duke of Richmond
Likenesses S. Cousins, mezzotint (after G. Richmond), BM, NPG
Wealth at death £7625 13s. 6d.: confirmation, 20 June 1887, *CCI*

Eden, Robert Henley. *See* Henley, Robert, second Baron Henley (1789–1841).

Eden, Robert John, third Baron Auckland (1799–1870), bishop of Bath and Wells, third son of William *Eden, first Baron Auckland (1744–1814), and his wife, Eleanor (1758–1818), youngest daughter of Sir Gilbert Elliot, third baronet, was born at Eden Farm, Beckenham, Kent, on 10 July 1799. He was sent to Eton College in 1814 and in 1817 entered Magdalene College, Cambridge, where he proceeded MA in 1819, and BD and DD in 1847. Ordained in 1822, he was rector of Eyam, Derbyshire, from 1823 to 1825. He married on 15 September 1825 Mary (d. 1872), eldest daughter of Francis Edward Hurt of Alderwasley, Derbyshire. From 1825 to 1835 he was rector of Hertingfordbury, Hertfordshire, and was vicar of Battersea from 1835 to 1847. He was chaplain to William IV from 1831 to 1837, and chaplain to Queen Victoria from 1837 to 1847.

A liberal in politics, Eden was, on Lord John Russell's recommendation, consecrated bishop of Sodor and Man on 23 May 1847, and installed at Castletown on 29 June. On the death (1 January 1849) of his elder brother, George *Eden, earl of Auckland, who was unmarried, he became third Baron Auckland. He was translated on 2 June 1854 to the see of Bath and Wells, which he held until his resignation on 6 September 1869. He died at the palace, Wells, on 25 April 1870, and was buried in the Palm churchyard, near the cathedral, on 29 April. Eden was considered moderate in his views, but inclining to the high-church school. His published charges as bishop of Bath and Wells (1855, 1858, and 1861) included a denunciation (1861) of *Essays and Reviews*. He also edited the journal and correspondence of his father (1860). The third son in his family of five sons and five daughters was Sir Ashley *Eden.

G. C. BOASE, *rev.* M. C. CURTHOYS

Sources *ILN* (7 May 1870), 489–90 • *The Times* (27 April 1870), 12 • *Bath Chronicle* (28 April 1870), 6 • *Bath Chronicle* (5 May 1870), 7 • *The Greville memoirs*, ed. H. Reeve, pt 1, vol. 1 (1874), 131, 151; pt 1, vol. 2 (1874), 86 • GEC, *Peerage* • Boase, *Mod. Eng. biog.* • Venn, *Alum. Cant.*
Archives LPL, corresp. with A. C. Tait
Likenesses portrait, *c.*1870, repro. in *ILN*

Wealth at death under £100,000: resworn probate, Dec 1870, *CGPLA Eng. & Wales*

Eden, Thomas (*d.* 1645), civil lawyer, the second son of Richard Eden, gentleman, of South Hanningfield, Essex, and Margaret, daughter of Christopher Payton of Bury St Edmunds, Suffolk, was born near Sudbury, Suffolk. His grandfather Richard Eden was doctor of laws and principal of Sudbury School. Thomas attended Sudbury School and was admitted as a scholar at Trinity Hall, Cambridge, in December 1596. Three years later he was elected a fellow, and in 1600 he received the degree of LLB. Soon afterwards he became reader in civil law at Trinity Hall, and in 1613 he succeeded Clement Corbett as professor of civil law at Gresham College in London. Eden held his disputation for the doctorate in civil law at Cambridge in the presence of James I in 1614 and was created LLD the following year. He was admitted as an advocate of the court of arches on 17 October 1614 and became a member of Doctors' Commons on 4 November 1615.

Eden resided both in London, where he was active in the ecclesiastical courts, and at the University of Cambridge, where he served as master of Trinity Hall from 1626 to 1643. In 1633 he completed an extensive manuscript commentary on the last title of the *Digest*, *De regulis juris* (Bodl. Oxf., MS Tanner 422; Trinity Hall, Cambridge, MS 27). Eden combined his duties at Trinity Hall with service as the official to the archdeacon of Sudbury in 1621, as master in chancery from 1625 until 1640, and as the chancellor of Ely diocese from 1630 until 1641. He also acted as commissary for Westminster, Bury St Edmunds, and Sudbury, and between 1633 and 1641 he served on the court of high commission. In these positions Eden was often called upon to support the policies of Archbishop Laud and Bishop Matthew Wren in the maintenance of ecclesiastical conformity. In 1640 articles were drafted against Eden for presenting those who refused to bow at the name of Jesus, for fining those who attended a second sermon on Sunday, and for moving communion tables from the body of the church (Bodl. Oxf., MS Tanner 65, fols. 4–5).

Eden served as MP for the University of Cambridge in the parliaments of 1626, 1628, and 1640. He defended the appointment of Buckingham as chancellor of the university in 1626, and in 1628 he resisted efforts to restrict the jurisdiction of the University of Cambridge and to regulate its affairs. In 1636, however, he defended the jurisdiction of the bishop of Ely and the archbishop of Canterbury over scholars at the university. In the Long Parliament Eden's position regarding ecclesiastical politics underwent an apparent shift. He was originally included in the articles of impeachment against Laud for his role in the high commission's prosecution of John Bastwick. The house did not press this prosecution, however, and Eden contributed heavily to the parliamentary cause, lending the house £1000 in 1641 and contributing £500 to the Irish campaign. He signed the protestation of 3 May 1641 and took the solemn league and covenant in 1643. Eden thus became one of the few members of Doctors' Commons to support parliament during the civil war. In 1644 he cited international law in supporting the cause of free trade,

and in the following year he was appointed to the parliamentary committee to manage the affairs of the admiralty. He died in London on 18 July 1645 and was buried on 2 August at Trinity Hall, Cambridge, where a mural monument was installed in his memory. Having never married, Eden willed considerable sums to each of his two nieces and to various institutions, including Trinity Hall.

BRIAN P. LEVACK

Sources B. P. Levack, *The civil lawyers in England, 1603–1641* (1973) · *DNB* · J. Ward, *The lives of the professors of Gresham College* (1740) · Keeler, *Long Parliament* · articles against Eden, Bodl. Oxf., MS Tanner 65, fols. 4–5 · *CSP dom.*, *1640–41* · W. B. Bidwell and M. Jansson, eds., *Proceedings in parliament, 1626*, 4 vols. (1991–6) · R. C. Johnson and others, eds., *Commons debates, 1628*, 6 vols. (1977–83) · M. B. Rex, *University representation in England, 1604–1690* (1954) · G. D. Squibb, *Doctors' Commons: a history of the College of Advocates and Doctors of Law* (1977) · R. H. Helmholz, *Roman canon law in the Church of England* (1990) · Eden to Sir John Lambe, PRO, SP 16/313/49 · Venn, *Alum. Cant.*, 1/2.227
Archives Trinity Hall, Cambridge | Bodl. Oxf., Tanner MS 422
Wealth at death over £10,000—incl. £4000 each to two nieces: 1 July 1645, will, PRO, PROB 11/193, sig. 96

Eden, William, first Baron Auckland (1744–1814), penal reformer and diplomatist, was born on 3 April 1744, the third son of Sir Robert Eden, third baronet (*d.* 1755), landowner, of Windlestone Hall, West Auckland, co. Durham, and Mary (*d.* 1794), daughter of William Davison of Beamish in the same county. Eden was educated at Durham School (1755–8) and Eton College (1758–62) before going up to Christ Church, Oxford, in 1762. Here he was profoundly influenced by the lectures of William Blackstone, who has been credited with steering Eden away from the church and towards the law as a prospective career (Bolton, 31). He gained his BA in 1765 and that same year was admitted to the Middle Temple to read for the bar, to which he was called in 1768.

Eden began to practise on the northern circuit but the practice of law was less to his liking than the philosophy of jurisprudence and his most significant achievement in his legal career was the publication of *The Principles of Penal Law* (1771). Influenced chiefly by Blackstone and Beccaria, but also by Puffendorf and Montesquieu among others, Eden argued for a relativist and historicist view of the law, which he regarded not as fixed but as evolutionary (Bolton, 32). If the law was not immutable then this clearly opened up the possibility for reform and in the pages of *The Principles* Eden advocated a reduction in the number of capital offences in English law and for a reformatory rather than a punitive basis for punishment in general, singling out notoriously harsh examples of legislation, such as the game laws, for particular condemnation. In the second edition of *The Principles* (also 1771) Eden proposed that the criminal law should be codified by legal experts.

Partly through the impact made by *The Principles* and partly through the influence of his friend Alexander Wedderburn, Eden obtained the post of under-secretary to the secretary of state for the northern department, Lord Suffolk, in 1772. This marked the beginning of Eden's career as a 'man of business', a career which would always see

William Eden, first Baron Auckland (1744–1814), by Sir Thomas Lawrence, 1792

him more comfortable as an administrator, whether at home or abroad, than as a party politician, a role into which he only really threw himself with gusto during the perfervid atmosphere of 1783–5, following the fall of the Fox–North coalition and the installation of William Pitt the younger as prime minister by George III. More immediately, Eden's appointment as Suffolk's under-secretary provided him with the opportunity to put some of his ideas about penal and legal reform into practice. The outbreak of war with America in 1775 removed the thirteen colonies as potential recipients of transported British criminals and Eden attempted to find a solution to the problem of the prisoners left rotting in the hulks on the Thames by this development. In 1774 he had been returned to parliament as MP for New Woodstock on the interest of the fourth duke of Marlborough and this allowed him to attempt to introduce two related bills in the Commons to deal with the problem of the hulks. The first, the Hulks Bill, was intended to regulate the housing of convicts on the hulks and to allow for the employment of convicts on projects such as clearing the Thames; it became law in May 1776. The second, the Penitentiary Bill, which proposed a system of penitentiaries around the country, did not, however, make it to the statute book. An attempt to revive it, the Hard Labour Bill of 1778, also failed, but a Penitentiary Act supported by Eden was passed in 1779.

At the same time as he was closely involved with these projects of penal reform Eden's political and administrative career began to take off. His industry as an under-secretary brought him a promotion to the Board of Trade

in March 1776 and attracted the increasing admiration of the first lord of the Treasury, Lord North. On 26 September 1776 Eden married Eleanor Elliot (1758–1818), the youngest daughter of Sir Gilbert *Elliot, third baronet (1722–1777), politician, and Agnes Dalrymple Murray Kynynmourd. Two years later, in 1778, North appointed Eden to be one of the five-man commission for conciliation with America, which was led by Eden's old Oxford friend the fifth earl of Carlisle. The commission was a failure both publicly, in so far as it failed to conciliate the rebellious colonists, and also in personal terms for Eden who found, on his return from America in 1779, that it had not advanced his career to the degree he had hoped. It did, however, lead Eden into print again with his *Four Letters to the Earl of Carlisle* (1779) in which he defended, among other things, the ministry's policy of negotiating with the Americans. When Carlisle was appointed lord lieutenant of Ireland in 1780 Eden accompanied him as chief secretary, being returned also to the Irish House of Commons for Dungannon. In Ireland he developed an expertise in commercial matters and was involved in the foundation of the Bank of Ireland.

Upon the fall of Lord North's ministry in April 1782 Eden found himself out of office. He did not actively oppose the short-lived successor ministry of Rockingham, but when Rockingham died and was succeeded by Shelburne, Eden became a strong advocate for a junction between the forces of North and the Rockinghamites (led now by Charles James Fox) as he felt it would provide the only viable ministry in the long term. Disappointingly for Eden, when the Fox–North coalition took office in 1783 he received only a sinecure, the vice-treasurership of Ireland, but he was sworn of the privy council and sat on important parliamentary committees. The fall of the Fox–North coalition in December 1783 precipitated Eden into the most active phase of his career as a party politician. In particular he was a moving force behind the defeat of Pitt's propositions for freer trade with Ireland in 1785. None the less Pitt survived and Eden soon became convinced that any administrative future he had was dependent on a *rapprochement* with Pitt. Eden duly approached Pitt in September 1785 and after two months of negotiations they were reconciled. Pitt had initially thought of Eden as a potential speaker of the House of Commons but eventually decided, in December 1785, to send him as an envoy to negotiate a commercial treaty with France, a task which particularly suited Eden's expertise in matters of finance and commerce. This step inaugurated the most important and successful phase of Eden's career.

Under the terms of the treaty of Versailles (1783), which had formalized the end of the American War of Independence, Britain had committed herself to negotiate a commercial treaty with France. The British, however, were markedly reluctant to fulfil their treaty obligations in this matter and it took a combination of French diplomatic and commercial pressure to persuade Pitt to agree to negotiations in 1785. The negotiations had already begun, in an albeit desultory way, prior to Eden's appointment with the dispatch of George Crawfurd to Paris in September 1784, but it was only with the replacement of Crawfurd by Eden that the process assumed any meaningful shape. Once appointed in December 1785 Eden immediately threw himself into an assiduous process of information-gathering prior to his departure for France in March 1786. After a surprisingly speedy set of preliminary negotiations Eden was able to forward to London on 17 April 1786 a French *projet* which advocated the principle of 'reciprocity and mutual convenience' (Ehrman, *The Younger Pitt*, 1.487) but left the details of what this might involve to be settled at a later date. For the British ministers, however, this was an unacceptable method for transacting the negotiations: they wanted the details to be in the initial agreement. The British government thus responded in late May with its own declaration which, while agreeing to most favoured nation status as a basis for negotiation, insisted that specific duties must be considered in the agreement. This last point was effectively conceded by the French *contre-declaration* of 16 June 1786. Eden was dismayed, therefore, by the month-long delay in the British reply to the *contre-declaration* which was not sent until 18 July 1786, but he then set about, with great industry and skill, concluding the details of the final treaty, which was signed at Versailles on 26 September 1786. Eden's success in bringing this process to fruition was augmented by two further agreements with the French. In January 1787 a supplementary convention on commercial matters was signed and in February 1787 he began a series of negotiations intended to resolve the outstanding disputes between the British and French East India companies. This latter set of negotiations was concluded on 30 August 1787. Despite this series of triumphs, however, these years were not without their setbacks for Eden. Indeed, the very success of Eden's negotiations with the French had aroused suspicions among some politicians and diplomats (such as, for example, John Harris, later Lord Malmesbury, and even the foreign secretary himself, Lord Carmarthen) that Eden was rather too francophile in his outlook. This became clear during the crisis over the United Provinces in 1787 when it was felt that Eden, in the absence of the official ambassador to Paris, Lord Dorset, was not representing the British position accurately enough, particularly in regard to British willingness to resort to arms to prevent French intervention in the United Provinces. As a consequence William Grenville, later Lord Grenville, was dispatched to Paris to conduct negotiations with the French which helped to secure the British diplomatic triumph of preventing French intervention, thus leaving the Prussians free to invade the United Provinces and restore the stadholder to his rights.

In 1788 Eden was sent to Madrid as ambassador in an attempt to resurrect the commercial negotiations with Spain which had foundered, but he did not meet with the success that had attended his efforts in France and nothing of substance had been agreed by the time he left Spain in the summer of 1789. Eden, having been raised to the Irish peerage as Baron Auckland on 18 November 1789,

then embarked upon the last phase of his diplomatic career, his period as ambassador to The Hague (1789–93) during the turbulent opening years of the French Revolution and the ensuing Revolutionary Wars. During the Nootka Sound crisis of 1790, in which Britain threatened to go to war with Spain over territorial disputes on the Pacific coast of North America, Auckland prevailed upon the Dutch to provide material assistance to Britain in the form of a naval squadron. In the Ochakov crisis of 1791, however, in which Britain again threatened to go to war, this time with Russia, Auckland was more sceptical about British sabre-rattling, fearing that a general European war would make the French Revolution less easy to contain. The impact of events in France had indeed turned Auckland away from his earlier francophilia, and having initially advocated a negotiated solution to the growing European crisis consequent upon the outbreak of war between France and Austria he recognized that Britain was bound to defend the infringement of Dutch treaty rights by the French opening of the River Scheldt to navigation, the issue which led to the outbreak of hostilities between Britain and France in February 1793. Although involved in the early events of the French Revolutionary Wars, such as the conference of British, Prussian, Austrian, and Dutch ambassadors and generals at Antwerp in April 1793 following the retreat of the French from the Netherlands, Auckland's diplomatic career came quickly to a close. In May 1793 he retired from the diplomatic service and returned to England, being raised to the British peerage as Baron Auckland of West Auckland.

Following the end of his diplomatic career Auckland remained a political figure of some significance. He was still close to Pitt, and his public pronouncements were often regarded as reflecting the thinking of the prime minister. For example, in late 1795 Auckland published *Some Remarks on the Apparent Circumstances of the War in the Fourth Week of October 1795*, in which he implicitly argued for a negotiated settlement with France upon the basis of the *status quo ante bellum*. Auckland sent a copy of the pamphlet to Edmund Burke, who was outraged at what he saw as a veiled announcement of the ministry's intention to negotiate with what he regarded as the illegitimate government of France. Auckland's pamphlet thus proved the immediate inspiration for Burke's *Letters on a Regicide Peace* (1796–7), the first of which to be written, although published as the *Fourth Letter*, was a point-by-point attempt to refute Auckland's arguments. Pitt was indeed so close to Auckland and his family at this time that he came very near to marrying Auckland's daughter Eleanor Eden (1777–1851) in 1796–7 only to break off his dalliance suddenly and mysteriously, for reasons which are not fully understood to this day. Although this episode curtailed the social relationship between Auckland and Pitt they remained politically close. In 1798 Auckland was appointed by Pitt to the position of joint postmaster-general and he was one of Pitt's closest advisers on the prospective union with Ireland in the years 1798–1800. In 1801, however, Auckland broke with Pitt by opposing Pitt's plan to accompany the Act of Union with a measure of Catholic emancipation and he was rumoured to have been partly behind George III's opposition to such a measure, opposition which led Pitt to resign. Auckland remained in office under Pitt's successor, Henry Addington, but was dismissed when Pitt returned in 1804. In 1806–7 Auckland was the president of the Board of Trade in the ministry of all the talents, his last major period in public office. Upon the fall of the talents he followed Grenville into opposition. Auckland's final years were blighted by the apparent suicide of his eldest son, and his intended political heir, William Frederick Eden (1782–1810), who, having disappeared from his home in January 1810 was found a month later drowned in the Thames. Auckland and his wife had a total of twelve children who included, in addition to William Frederick and Eleanor already noted, George *Eden (1784–1849), Auckland's heir and later governor-general of India, Robert John *Eden (1799–1870), who succeeded his brother as third Baron Auckland, and the novelist Emily *Eden (1797–1869). On 28 May 1814 at his home, Eden Farm, Beckenham, Kent, Auckland was 'suddenly seized with a spasm whilst at breakfast with his family, and instantly expired' (GM). STEPHEN M. LEE

Sources The journal and correspondence of William, Lord Auckland, ed. [G. Hogge], 4 vols. (1861–2) · G. C. Bolton, 'William Eden and the convicts, 1771–1787', Australian Journal of Politics and History, 26 (1980), 30–44 · J. Ehrman, The younger Pitt, 3 vols. (1969–96) · J. Ehrman, The British government and commercial negotiations with Europe, 1783–1793 (1962) · J. Black, British foreign policy in an age of revolutions, 1783–1793 (1994) · I. R. Christie, 'Eden, William', HoP, Commons, 1754–90 · R. G. Thorne, 'Eden, William', HoP, Commons, 1790–1820 · G. C. Bolton and B. E. Kennedy, 'William Eden and the treaty of Mauritius, 1786–7', HJ, 16 (1973), 681–96 · J. Holland Rose, 'The missions of William Grenville to The Hague and Versailles in 1787', EngHR, 24 (1909), 278–95 · GM, 1st ser., 84/1 (1814), 629 · The writings and speeches of Edmund Burke, ed. P. Langford, 9/1–2: The revolutionary war, 1794–1797, and Ireland, ed. R. B. McDowell (1991), 19–21 · The correspondence of Edmund Burke, 8, ed. R. B. McDowell (1969), 333–5 · C. C. O'Brian, The great melody: a thematic biography and commented anthology of Edmund Burke (1992), 543–52 · DNB

Archives BL, corresp. and papers, Add. MSS 29475, 34412–34471, 45728–45730, 46490–46491, 46519, 54328, 59704 · Duke U., Perkins L., letters | BL, letters to Francis Drake, Add. MS 46822 · BL, corresp. with Lord Grenville, Add. MSS 36814, 58919–58927, 59070–59072, 69046 · BL, corresp. with Lord Holland, Add. MS 51532 · BL, letters to Sir Robert Keith and Lord Hardwicke, Add. MSS 35504–35743, passim · BL, corresp. with fifth duke of Leeds, Add. MSS 28059–28066 · BL, corresp. with first earl of Liverpool, Add. MSS 38209–38236, 38307–38311, 38458, 38471–38472, passim · BL, letters to Lord Sheffield, Add. MS 61980 · BL, letters to Lord Wellesley, Add. MSS 37282, 37308–37309 · BL, corresp. with William Windham, Add. MSS 37876, 37885, 37887 · Bodl. Oxf., corresp. with Sir James Burges · Bucks. RLSS, letters to Lord Hobart · Castle Howard, Yorkshire, letters to fifth earl of Carlisle · Ches. & Chester ALSS, letters to Lord Sheffield · CKS, corresp. with third duke of Dorset · Devon RO, corresp. with first Viscount Sidmouth · Hants. RO, corresp. with William Wickham · Hunt. L., letters to Grenville family · NL Scot., corresp. with Robert Liston · NL Scot., letters to Lord Minto · NMM, letters to Sir Richard Keats · NMM, letters to earl of Sandwich · NRA Scotland, priv. coll., corresp. with Joseph Ewart · PRO, corresp. with F. J. Jackson, FO 353 · PRO, letters to William Pitt, PRO 30/8 · PRO NIre., corresp. with Lord Castlereagh · Sheff. Arch., corresp. with Edmund Burke · Suffolk RO, Ipswich, letters to Alexander Straton · U. Durham L., letters to second Earl Grey · U. Mich., Clements L., letters to Lord George Germain

Likenesses J. Sayers, caricature, etching, pubd 1785, BM, NPG · E. G. Mountstephen, wedgwood medallion, c.1789, BM · T. Lawrence, oils, 1792, Christ Church Oxf. [see illus.] · H. Edridge, watercolour drawing, 1809, NPG · J. Brown, stipple and line engraving, pubd 1860 (after N. Dance), NPG

Eden, Sir William, seventh baronet and fifth baronet (1849–1915), sportsman and artist, was born at Windlestone Hall, co. Durham, on 4 April 1849, the second son of Sir William Eden, sixth baronet and fourth baronet (1803–1873), and his wife, Elfrida Susanna Harriet, daughter of Colonel William Iremonger of Wherwell Priory, Hampshire. William was one of eleven children, of whom six died during their father's lifetime, the death of the eldest son making him heir to the baronetcies and the estate of Windlestone. Windlestone Hall, a neo-classical mansion of the 1830s designed by Bononi, stood amid 8000 acres.

After an education at Eton College, William Eden joined the army, serving as an ensign in the 28th regiment and as a lieutenant in the 8th hussars. On his father's death in 1873 he resigned his commission and, after some months spent yachting in the Mediterranean, settled into the life of a landed gentleman.

Eden appeared the epitome of the sporting squire. A handsome man with red cheeks, blue eyes, and a reddish-brown beard, he was over 6 feet tall and very strong. He was a magnificent athlete who excelled at a range of sports: he could hold his own with the best professional boxers of his day and was a friend of Bombardier Billy Wells, who often stayed with him; he was a fine horseman, who won many steeplechases on horses he had trained himself, and was a legendary master of the South Durham hounds (1878–81; 1884–90); and he was one of the best shots in England. He punctuated the sporting seasons with visits to London, where he frequented music-halls and was a member of the Turf, the Coaching Club, the Travellers', and White's, and indulged a taste for travel, spending nine months abroad in 1877 and journeying through India, China, and Japan during 1882. As a magistrate in co. Durham, he was known as 'Old Seven and Sixpence' or 'the Bloody Baronet' (James, 14).

There was another side to Eden, an aesthetic sensibility, which found expression in his accomplished watercolours, his love of gardening, his pride in the beauty of his house and fine collection of paintings, and his association with the aristocratic aesthetes the Souls. There was little that was harmonious in his nature, and the aesthetic side warred with and exacerbated, rather than complemented, his athleticism, making him a bored sportsman and a militant aesthete. As he grew older, the world's failure to correspond to his ideals drove him to furious rages and the debased taste of humanity confirmed his atheism—for how could a God have made such a botch of things?

Eden's marriage to Sybil Frances Grey, daughter of Sir William *Grey, governor of Jamaica and grandson of the first Earl Grey, on 20 July 1886 was an expression of his taste, for she was a noted society beauty. It was not a happy marriage, though there were five sons (one dying at birth)

Sir William Eden, seventh baronet and fifth baronet (1849–1915), by Prince Paulo Troubetzkoy

and a daughter. Sir William's incandescent rages could be stimulated by many things, such as a boy whistling in the street or a dog barking, and, as these things included children, he made a less than perfect father.

Sir William's great pride in his wife's beauty was the occasion of his having to take the artist James McNeill Whistler to court when the artist, having received from the baronet less for a small oil painting of Lady Sybil than he thought proper, kept the cheque and refused to hand over the painting. Whistler's obsession with the case resulted in his book *The Baronet and the Butterfly* (1899). That Eden was a serious and a talented artist is undeniable. He exhibited at almost every exhibition of the New English Art Club between 1896 and 1909, and had work shown at the Paris Salon and at the London galleries favoured by those painters influenced by the French impressionists and post-impressionists. The paintings he collected by Corot, Degas, Renoir, Fantin-Latour, Whistler, and Sickert testify to his avant-garde taste.

During the last two decades of his life Eden and his wife lived largely separate lives. Matrimonial relations were not made easier by Lady Eden's impulsive and foolish generosity, which nearly brought financial ruin on the family, and by her infatuation with George Wyndham (1863–1913), the Conservative politician and man of letters. Sir William was consoled by his close friendship with Lady Londonderry. His last years were marked by ill health, but he spent much time in London in a flat adjoining the Cavendish Hotel in Duke Street, where he was well looked after by his valet, Woolger, and the owner of the hotel, the

redoubtable Rosa Lewis. He died there on 20 February 1915 and was buried at Windlestone on 24 February, survived by his wife. His eldest son, Lieutenant John Eden (*b.* 1888), with whom he had quarrelled, having been killed in action the previous year, he was succeeded by his second son, Timothy Calvert (1893–1963). His third son was (Robert) Anthony *Eden (1897–1977), prime minister.

A. W. PURDUE

Sources T. Eden, *The tribulations of a baronet* (1933) · L. Wilkes, *The aesthetic obsession: a portrait of Sir William Eden bt* (1985) · J. M. Whistler, *The baronet and the butterfly* (1899) · A. Eden, *Another world* (1976) · R. R. James, *Anthony Eden* (1986) · D. Carlton, *Anthony Eden: a biography* (1981) · *The Times* (22 Feb 1915) · S. Weintraub, *Whistler: a biography* (1974), 406–21 · *Newcastle Daily Journal* (25 Feb 1915) · Burke, *Peerage* · Walford, *County families*

Likenesses portrait, 1881, Hult. Arch. · M. Beerbohm, cartoon, repro. in Eden, *Tribulations of a baronet* · P. Troubetzkoy, photograph, NPG [*see illus.*]

Wealth at death £71,570 3s. 3d.: probate, 6 Aug 1915, CGPLA Eng. & Wales

Eder, (Montague) David (1865–1936), psychoanalyst, was born on 12 August 1865 at 19 Euston Square, London, the eldest of the four children of David Martin Eder, shipping merchant, and his second wife, Esther Burnstein, formerly Soloman. His parents were both Jewish. Eder was educated in London, Belgium, and Germany and then at University College, London, obtaining his BSc in 1891 and completing his medical degree in 1895. He obtained a doctorate in medicine from the University of Bogota in 1898. He was married twice. His first wife was Florence Mary Murray (*b.* 1864/5), daughter of the late Captain Stephen Murray of the Indian army; they married on 3 November 1894. After her death he married, on 20 October 1909, Edith Clara Guest (1874/5–1944/1945?), the divorced wife of Leslie (later Lord) Haden Guest, and daughter of the late Maximilian Low, stockbroker. Neither marriage produced children, although there were two stepchildren, Stephen and Richard Guest, by his second marriage.

From 1897 to 1905, prior to working as a doctor and psychoanalyst in England, Eder travelled widely, earning his living as a doctor in South Africa and South America; he also practised intermittently in poor, industrial areas of England. On his return to England from Bolivia in 1905 Eder joined the council of the Jewish Territorial Organisation and was sent by them to Cyrenaica, north Africa, in 1908.

Eder was a significant figure in the early history of psychoanalysis: he was, according to Freud, the first doctor in England to practise psychoanalysis; he used Freud's ideas in his writings from 1908, and was a founder member of the London Psycho-Analytical Society (established in 1913), acting as its first secretary. His presentation to the British Medical Association in 1911 has been acknowledged as the first public contribution to clinical psychoanalysis in England. However, despite these important early contributions to the development of English psychoanalysis there has been little recognition of Eder's place in its history. There are two main reasons for this oversight.

First, although his interest in and devotion to psychoanalysis began early in his career and continued throughout his life, he also made serious commitments to other causes, most notably Zionism and socialism. As a consequence his time was not wholly given over to the pursuit of a psychoanalytic career. Second, his attitude to psychoanalysis was not doctrinaire: in the early years he drew on the work of both Freud and Jung. This open-minded approach was not popular with Ernest Jones, the president of the London Psycho-Analytical Society and Freud's most loyal supporter. Jones's distrust of Eder seems to have been a crucial factor in the decision, taken by Jones, to disband the London Psycho-Analytical Society in 1915 and reform it in February 1919 as a purely Freudian organization. By the early 1920s Eder had changed his mind about the usefulness of Jung's ideas and went into Freudian analysis with Sándor Ferenczi in Budapest. However, Ernest Jones remained suspicious of Eder, going so far as to dispute Freud's claim that Eder had been the first English doctor to practise psychoanalysis.

Eder's work with children, first at a clinic in Poplar, and then with Margaret McMillan in Deptford, informed his early writings on psychoanalysis. He wrote *Child Study*, in collaboration with his second wife, and in 1910 he founded and became joint editor of the educational journal *School Hygiene*. His concern for disadvantaged members of society was given political shape through his membership in the late 1890s of the Independent Labour Party, the Bloomsbury Socialist League, and the Fabian Society. Eder's interest in socialism led him to consider the problems of family and childhood and he used this knowledge to add weight to his proposals for a state programme of assistance for mothers. In 1908, when there was very little public knowledge about psychoanalysis, and one year prior to the publication of Freud's work in an English edition, Eder published a twopenny pamphlet entitled *The Endowment of Motherhood* in which he used Freud's ideas about repression to call for social reform based on a recognition of the importance of instinctual drives. Citing Freud's ideas about the harmful effects of repression, he argued that 'until civilised people recognise the dangers they court by pretending to conform to a super-imposed morality, we shall not establish a civilisation founded upon a decent and dignified attitude towards ourselves' (M. D. Eder, *The Endowment of Motherhood*, 1908, v).

Eder was not afraid to air his views, despite their controversial nature: it is alleged that the chairman and audience of nine walked out of the British Medical Association meeting mentioned above, at which Eder presented his paper 'A case of obsession and hysteria treated by the Freud psycho-analytic method'. Eder worked as a doctor during the First World War, serving as a temporary captain in the Royal Army Medical Corps. He was appointed medical officer in charge of the psycho-neurological department in Malta, and his book, *War-Shock* (1917), took a radical stance regarding the treatment of soldiers, calling for a psychotherapeutic approach to the phenomenon now known as shell-shock. However, this being Eder, the

book was open-minded in its approach, acknowledging the value of hypnotism, suggestion, and psychoanalysis.

Eder was a keen popularizer of psychoanalysis. He was a regular contributor to the *New Age*, a radical literary journal, working for them as an editorial consultant from 1907 until 1915. He wrote innumerable papers about psychoanalysis and these were published in medical, educational, and psychoanalytical journals. He translated both Freud (*On Dreams*, 1914) and Jung (*Studies in Word Association*, 1918).

In 1918 Eder was appointed chief residential Zionist agent in Palestine under the Balfour declaration. He lived in Palestine from 1918 until 1922, when he returned to London, and where he continued to work for the Zionist cause, while at the same time pursuing his medical and psychoanalytical career. Eder died from a coronary thrombosis on 30 March 1936 at his home, 6 Brendon House, Great Woodstock Street, London. His wife survived him.

Eder, described by Hobman as 'burly and strong' in physique, yet 'kind, sardonic and sagacious' in character, is spoken of with great fondness in the biographical memoir prepared after his death. These views are confirmed by Freud, who commented that 'one's heart warmed at the thought of him' (Hobman, 18–21). According to other contributors Eder was a passionate and authoritative man, gentle with children, yet fearless in his opinions. Although Jewish by birth, and a Zionist by conviction, he took, on the whole, an atheistic approach to life. He corresponded with George Bernard Shaw and was friends with Dorothy Richardson, Rebecca West, and D. H. Lawrence. His second wife's sister was the psychoanalyst Barbara Low. Eder's life was shaped by his interest in new ideas and his desire to play an active part in bringing about a fairer society; the insights he gained from psychoanalysis, and the contributions he made to it, worked in tandem with his interests in education, sex reform, feminism, socialism, and Zionism, to produce a man who held strong views, but who was not afraid to learn from others.

S. ELLESLEY

Sources J. B. Hobman, ed., *David Eder: memoirs of a modern pioneer* (1945) · J. Carswell, *The exile: a life of Ivy Litvinov* (1983) · V. Brome, *Ernest Jones: Freud's alter ego* (1982) · E. Jones, *Free associations: memories of a psycho-analyst* (1959) · R. A. Paskauskas, 'Freud's break with Jung: the crucial role of Ernest Jones', *Free Associations*, no. 11 (1988), 7–34 · C. Steedman, *Childhood, culture and class in Britain: Margaret McMillan, 1860–1931* (1990) · *The complete correspondence of Sigmund Freud and Ernest Jones, 1908–1939*, ed. R. A. Paskauskas (1993) · b. cert. · m. certs. · d. cert. · *CGPLA Eng. & Wales* (1936) · *WWW, 1929–40*

Archives Central Zionist Archives, Jerusalem, papers

Likenesses Elliott & Fry Ltd, photograph, repro. in Hobman, ed., *David Eder*, inside cover

Wealth at death £2325 17s. 4d.: probate, 24 June 1936, *CGPLA Eng. & Wales*

Edern Dafod Aur (*fl. 13th–15th cent.*), grammarian, is of very uncertain identity. Edern is a not uncommon personal name; the incorrect Edeyrn first appears in 1621. *Dosbarth Edern Dafod Aur*, a brief discussion attributed to him of the letters of the alphabet and of word-formations, is found in some five manuscripts dating from *c.*1588 to the early seventeenth century. Apparently a late composition, the text is, nevertheless, found either prefixed to or in association with other bardic grammars in these manuscripts and appears therefore to have been accepted as genuine by the scribes and antiquaries who wrote them. Since it sometimes preceded the medieval grammar attributed to *Einion Offeiriad (d. 1353?) in the manuscripts it was almost inevitable that Edern's authorship should be claimed for both texts or the assumption made that his work was somehow based on the latter. Einion's grammar was published under the editorship of John Williams ab Ithel in 1856 from a manuscript copy by Edward Williams, 'Iolo Morganwg' (d. 1826), who had, in his usual fashion, elaborated the misunderstood statement of attribution to Edern. John Williams therefore gave it the title *Dosparth Edeyrn Davod Aur* with the result that Edern himself gained a more assured place in literary history than the evidence warranted. Sir John Morris-Jones believed that the text was a sixteenth-century forgery and that the name Edern Dafod Aur (the epithet means 'Golden-Tongued') was created as a calque upon Herodian Chrysostom (that is, Dion Chrysostom the rhetorician) to give it spurious authority. But a contemporary elegy to the poet and bardic teacher Tudur Aled who died in 1526 praises him as excelling even 'the method of Edern Dafod Aur', suggesting that Edern's reputation as a bardic grammarian was well established and that the particular text associated with his name may have been compiled at least in the previous century. The floruit of 1280 given to him by Dr John Davies in his Dictionary of 1632 may be no more than an educated guess. However, that the late medieval Welsh poets had grammars, which are now lost, besides that of Einion Offeiriad is suggested by references to a thirteenth-century grammarian and poet, Cnepyn Gwerthrynion. Edern may be another traditional bardic teacher whose name, though not necessarily whose work, has been preserved. BRYNLEY F. ROBERTS

Sources J. Morris-Jones, 'Dosbarth Edern Dafod Aur', *Transactions of the Honourable Society of Cymmrodorion* (1923–4), 1–28

Edersheim, Alfred (1825–1889), biblical scholar, was born in Vienna of Jewish parents on 7 March 1825. His father, Marcus Edersheim, a banker and a man of culture and wealth, had come originally from the Netherlands, and his mother was Stéphanie, *née* Beifuss, of a well-known Frankfurt family. Edersheim was a bright child, and as English was spoken at home he became fluent at an early age. He was educated at a local *Gymnasium* and also at a Hebrew school, and in 1841 he entered as a student at the University of Vienna. However, his father suffered financial ruin before the completion of his university education, and he was thrown on his own resources.

Edersheim next journeyed to Pest, in Hungary, where he supported himself by giving language lessons and met Dr John Duncan (1796–1870) and other Presbyterian ministers, who were acting at the time as chaplains to the Scottish labourers engaged in constructing the bridge over the Danube. Under their influence Edersheim converted to Christianity, and later he accompanied Duncan

on his return to Scotland. Edersheim then studied Christian theology both in Edinburgh and also (under Hengstenberg, Neander, and others) in Berlin, and in 1846 he became a Presbyterian minister. Shortly afterwards he travelled abroad, and for a year he preached as a missionary both to ethnic Jews and to Germans living in Jassy in Romania. He also met there his first wife, Mary Broomfield, whom he married in 1848 after returning to Scotland.

Edersheim was particularly skilled in preaching; the incumbent at a large church in Aberdeen, he was soon appointed minister of the free church in Old Aberdeen, where he remained for twelve years. During this time he translated several philosophical and theological works from German to English, including *Historical Development of Speculative Philosophy, from Kant to Hegel* (1854), *History of the Old Covenant* (1859), *History of the Christian Church* (1860), and *Theological and Homiletical Commentary on the Gospel of St Matthew* (1861). He also wrote *History of the Jewish Nation from the Fall of Jerusalem to the Reign of Constantine the Great* (1856), and he contributed learned articles to the *Athenaeum* and other periodicals.

In the winter of 1860–61 poor health led Edersheim to move to Torquay, where his first wife died. He subsequently married Sophia, *née* Hancock. Through his influence, the Presbyterian church of St Andrew was built at Torquay, and he became its first minister. In 1872 his failing health prompted him to retire from active work and to devote himself to writing. He therefore resigned his charge at Torquay and moved to Bournemouth. In 1874 he published *The Temple: its Ministry and Services at the Time of Jesus Christ*. Through his work he met and became friends with Dr George Williams, theologian, and thanks to his influence Edersheim took orders in the Church of England in 1875. From 1876 to 1882 he worked in the parish of Loders, near Bridport, in Dorset. Here he wrote his most important work, *The Life and Times of Jesus the Messiah* (2 vols., 1883), arguably lacking in critical acumen but encyclopaedic in its range of information; he also used his personal knowledge of both Judaism and Christianity to write a fluent and engaging essay.

In 1880 Edersheim was appointed Warburtonian lecturer at Lincoln's Inn in London, an office which he held for four years. In 1882 he moved from Loders to Oxford where he had been granted an MA *honoris causa* the previous year. He had also been awarded honorary degrees from Kiel (PhD) and Vienna, Berlin, Giessen, and New College, Edinburgh (DD). In 1884–5 he was select preacher to the University of Oxford, and from 1886 to 1888 and 1888 to 1890 he was Grinfield lecturer on the Septuagint. In 1885 his Warburtonian lectures appeared, entitled *Prophecy and History in Relation to the Messiah*. Soon afterwards he wrote, with the co-operation of D. S. Margoliouth, a commentary on Ecclesiasticus for the Speaker's Commentary on the Apocrypha (1888). His next project was to be a work on *The Life and Writings of St Paul*; he had already written the opening chapters when he fell suddenly ill and died, on 16 March 1889, at Menton, France, where he had been spending the winter on account of his health.

Edersheim was remembered fondly for his tolerance and good humour, as well as for his skills as a preacher and writer. His daughter Ella wrote a short memoir of his life which was published as a foreword to Edersheim's *Tohu-Va-Vohu* ('Without form and void', 1890).

S. R. DRIVER, *rev.* SINÉAD AGNEW

Sources A. Edersheim, *Tohu-va-vohu / Without form and void: a collection of fragmentary thoughts and criticisms*, ed. E. Edersheim (1890), vii–xxxii · *The Guardian* (27 March 1889), 474 · P. Schaff and S. M. Jackson, *Encyclopedia of living divines and Christian workers of all denominations in Europe and America: being a supplement to Schaff-Herzog encyclopedia of religious knowledge* (1887) · Allibone, *Dict.* · F. L. Cross, ed., *The Oxford dictionary of the Christian church*, 2nd edn, ed. A. E. Livingstone (1974); repr. (1983), 444
Likenesses print (after a photograph by Debenham & Co.), repro. in Edersheim, ed., *Tohu-va-vohu*, frontispiece
Wealth at death £9828 8s. 10d.: probate, 2 May 1889, *CGPLA Eng. & Wales*

Edes [Eades], **Richard** (*bap.* 1554, *d.* 1604), dean of Worcester, was baptized at Newport, Isle of Wight, on 23 January 1554, the eldest son of Lawrence Edes (*d.* 1585/6) and Alice James of Newport (*d.* 1599/1600); the archivist and physician John James and the librarian Thomas James were his cousins, the sons of Alice's brother Richard. Educated at Westminster School, Richard Edes was elected in 1571 student of Christ Church, Oxford, where he graduated BA on 17 December 1574 and proceeded MA on 2 May 1578. Having taken orders about this time, he became, according to Wood, 'a most noted and celebrated preacher' (Wood, *Ath. Oxon.*, 1.749). Elected university proctor on 10 April 1583, he proceeded BTh on 6 July 1584 and DTh on 6 July 1590. In 1584 he was presented by its then patron, Hugh Mansfield, to the prebend of Yetminster Prima in Salisbury Cathedral, being installed on 31 July. On 10 February 1586 he was installed as canon of the fourth prebend in Christ Church Cathedral, Oxford, having been presented by the queen to the next vacant prebend in 1582. In 1587 he became rector of Freshwater, Isle of Wight.

According to Wood, Edes spent his younger years 'in poetical fancies and composing of plays (mostly tragedies)'. He was the reputed author of *Julius Caesar*, a tragedy acted at Christ Church in 1582. When his close friend Tobie Matthew was about to move from Oxford to Durham early in 1584, Edes:

> intended to have him on his way thither for one day's journey; but so betrayed were they by the sweetness of each others company, and their own friendship, that he not only brought him to Durham, but for a pleasant penance wrote their whole journey in Latin verse, entitled 'Iter Boreale', several copies of which did afterwards fly abroad. (Wood, *Ath. Oxon.*, 1.749–50)

A copy survives in Bodl. Oxf., MS Rawl. B. 223, folios 1–16. Other verses by Edes are in the British Library and the Bodleian.

Edes married Margaret, daughter of Herbert Westfaling, bishop of Hereford; no doubt it was through his father-in-law's influence that he became prebendary of Preston in Hereford Cathedral on 17 January 1590, and treasurer of the cathedral on 22 August 1596. He was also a chaplain to the queen, and a frequent court preacher; in 1603 he declared before James I that his was an office 'to the which for some yeares I have ben employed in this Court, under the religious reigne of the peerelesse Queene of the world, my many waies most gratious ladie and mistris' (McCullough, 105). His position at court, along with those of two of his kinsmen, both also from Newport, Isle of Wight, prompted the queen to comment upon them to Lady Walsingham that:

> one was for her sowle viz Dr Eades, the sonn of a clothier who dwelt att the corner howse in the Beastemarket; he was Rector of Freschwater and Deane of Worcester and Chaplayne in Ordinarye; the other for her bodye—viz Dr James, her Phisition in Ordinarye and one that daylie redd to her; his father lived at the corner howse to the west of the Fischmarket; the third Mr Thomas Fleminge—for her goodes; his father was a mercier in Nuport and lived at the corner howse tourninge into the Cornmarket; the 3 were cosens germain.

Sir John Oglander, who records her remarks, goes on to attribute their promotion to 'Sir Francis Walsinghame having married theyre counterywoman, the widowe of Sir Rychard Woorseley, and the Earle of Essex theyre dawghter' (*Oglander Memoirs*, 102–3). The relationship helps to explain the repeated efforts made by Essex in 1595 and early 1596 to have Edes promoted dean of Christ Church in succession to William James; but he encountered strenuous opposition from Lord Buckhurst, the chancellor of the university, who at first proposed Peter Lillie and then, probably with Whitgift's backing, Thomas Ravis, the successful candidate. On 19 August 1596, however, Edes was made treasurer of Christ Church, and on 19 June 1597 dean of Worcester. He was presented to the rectory of Upton upon Severn, Worcestershire, on 21 December 1598.

Edes remained a royal chaplain and court preacher under James I, and in 1604 was one of the scholars appointed to produce a new version of the English Bible, being a member of the Oxford group responsible for the four gospels, the Acts of the Apostles, and the book of Revelation. But he died at Worcester before he could start work, on 19 November 1604, and was buried in the cathedral, in the chapel at the east end of the choir. His monument, erected by his widow with a punning verse epitaph in the form of a dialogue between the monument (Lapis) and a traveller meditating among the tombs (Viator), now stands in the nave. Collections of his sermons were published in 1604 and 1626. His picture was placed with those of other noted churchmen and scholars in the school gallery at Oxford, and also in the frieze in the top floor gallery of the Bodleian Library. No doubt he owes his place in the latter in part to his own munificence, having given £13 6s. 8d. to the library in 1601, but still more to the fact of the frieze's having been devised by his own first cousin Thomas James, then Bodley's librarian.

GORDON GOODWIN, *rev.* TOM BEAUMONT JAMES

Sources parish register, Newport, Isle of Wight [baptism] · *The Oglander memoirs*, ed. W. H. Long (1888) · T. B. James, unpublished lecture to the Friends of the Bodleian Library, Oxford, priv. coll. · will, PRO, PROB 11/95, sig. 4 [Alice Edes] · Wood, *Ath. Oxon.*, new edn, 1.749–50 · Foster, *Alum. Oxon.*, 1500–1714, 2.452 · *Fasti Angl., 1541–1857*, [Salisbury] · *Fasti Angl., 1541–1857*, [Bristol] · *Fasti Angl.*

(Hardy) • T. Nash, *Collections for the history of Worcestershire*, 2 vols. (1781–2) • A. Wood, *The history and antiquities of the University of Oxford*, ed. J. Gutch, 2 vols. in 3 pts (1792–6) • P. E. McCullough, *Sermons at court: politics and religion in Elizabethan and Jacobean preaching* (1998) [incl. CD-ROM] • *Calendar of the manuscripts of the most hon. the marquis of Salisbury*, 6, HMC, 9 (1895)
Likenesses E. Harding, stipple, BM, NPG; repro. in F. G. Waldron, *The Biographical Mirror*, 3 vols. (1795–1810) • monument, Worcester Cathedral • portrait; known to be in the school gallery, Oxford, in 1888 • portrait; known to be at Bodl. Oxf. in 1888

Edgar [*called* Edgar Pacificus] (943/4–975), king of England, was the younger son of King *Edmund (920/21–946) and his first wife, Ælfgifu. His mother, who died in 944, was venerated as a saint at Shaftesbury, a house connected with her mother Wynflæd (*d. c.*950), a 'religious woman' or vowess (*AS chart.*, S 485). Edmund's second wife, Æthelflæd of Damerham, survived him, subsequently marrying Æthelstan Rota ('the Cheerful'), ealdorman of south-east Mercia. She seems to have had no part in the rearing of her stepsons, who were brought up by their paternal uncle, King *Eadred (*r.* 946–55), but her brother-in-law *Byrhtnoth was made ealdorman of Essex by *Eadwig, Edgar's elder brother.

Eadred, who was unmarried, entrusted the infant Edgar to the care of Ælfwynn (*d.* 986), wife of *Æthelstan Half-King, ealdorman of East Anglia. Another influence on Edgar's childhood was his paternal grandmother *Eadgifu, widow of King *Edward the Elder. It was she who, in 954, persuaded Eadred to give the royal vill of Abingdon to Bishop Æthelwold, who refounded its church as a Benedictine house, and it was there that Edgar was educated. Those most concerned with Edgar's upbringing were thus adherents of the Benedictine reform movement, which perhaps explains why that movement came to fruition during his reign. As a result, Edgar received lavish praise from its exponents, notably his old tutor, Æthelwold, and, in the next generation, Wulfstan, archbishop of York (*d.* 1023), who composed a poem in his honour, incorporated into the Anglo-Saxon Chronicle (text D, s.a. 959).

Yet Edgar remains an enigmatic figure. The Anglo-Saxon Chronicle has but ten entries for his reign, and most of the other contemporary and near-contemporary sources relate not so much to the king as to the Benedictine reformers and their affairs. It was this lack of material which led Sir Frank Stenton to characterize Edgar's reign as 'singularly devoid of recorded incident' (Stenton, *Anglo-Saxon England*, 368). In such circumstances it is tempting to flesh out the chronicle's story by drawing upon the accounts of twelfth- and thirteenth-century historians, but their additional material is often mere embroidery, based on the legends and stories which accumulated around the bare names of historical characters. Given these problems it is impossible to write a continuous history of Edgar's reign, and only a few of the better-documented aspects can be discussed with profit.

Succession to the kingdom Edgar attained his majority in 957, in which year he became king of the Mercians. This is presented by the biographer of St Dunstan as a coup against King Eadwig, and even Æthelwold, who was more

Edgar (943/4–975), manuscript drawing [centre, with Æthelwold (left) and Dunstan (right)]

sympathetic to Eadwig, complains that he 'dispersed the kingdom and divided its unity' (*English Historical Documents*, 1.847). On the other hand, the chronicler Æthelweard (*d.* 998?), Eadwig's brother-in-law, claims that he 'held the kingdom continuously for four years' (*Chronicle of Æthelweard*, 55), and throughout the period Eadwig used the title 'king of the English', while Edgar remained only 'king of the Mercians' (and occasionally of the Northumbrians also).

The only hint of a difference of opinion between the brothers is their treatment of Dunstan, expelled by Eadwig, but welcomed home by Edgar to receive the Mercian bishoprics of London and Worcester, and it may be that the division of 957 was simply a recognition of Edgar's position as his brother's heir. Indeed the D version of the Anglo-Saxon Chronicle says that he became king of the Mercians in 955, at the same time that Eadwig became king of the West Saxons, and he is called *regulus* in a Mercian charter, albeit of uncertain authenticity, of 956 (*AS chart.*, S 633). An agreed partition is also suggested by the fact that the ecclesiastics and lay magnates who attest the charters of the respective kings divide on a geographical, not a factional basis. Moreover, when Edgar succeeded to the kingship on the death of Eadwig (1 October 959), he retained most of the men whom Eadwig had promoted; only Brihthelm, archbishop-elect of Canterbury, was ousted in favour of Dunstan. It is particularly noteworthy that Edgar appears to have been on good terms with his brother's widow, Ælfgifu, who is described as his kins-woman in the charters recording his grants to her (*AS chart.*, S 737–8), and whose brother, the chronicler Æthelweard, was promoted to the ealdordom of the western shires, perhaps in 973.

The royal court One of the dominant influences at Edgar's court was his old tutor Æthelwold, elevated in 963 to the bishopric of Winchester. Æthelwold was a close friend of *Ælfthryth, widow of Ealdorman Æthelwold of East Anglia, whom Edgar married in 964 or 965. Little is known of Edgar's first wife, Æthelflæd Eneda, save that she was the mother of his eldest son, *Edward the Martyr, and it is not certain that he was actually married to *Wulfthryth, the mother of his daughter, *Edith, both of whom were later venerated as saints; the king's devotion to the Benedictine reform movement should not be taken as evidence of high personal morals. In contrast to Edgar's earlier consorts, Ælfthryth emerges as a force to be reckoned with, and her family were favoured by the king; her father, *Ordgar, was made ealdorman of Devon by Edgar, and her brother Ordwulf became one of the most influential advisers to her younger son, *Æthelred II. She was also connected with the family of *Ælfhere, ealdorman of Mercia (*d.* 983); his eldest brother, *Ælfheah, ealdorman of Hampshire [*see under* Ælfhere], seems to have been the godfather of one of her children, perhaps the elder son, Edmund, who died in 971.

All the major figures of the Benedictine movement were favoured by Edgar. Dunstan was promoted to the archbishopric of Canterbury at Brihthelm's expense, receiving the pallium on 21 September 960, and in 971 Oswald became archbishop of York, without relinquishing the bishopric of Worcester which he had received in 962. He was closely associated with *Æthelwine, Edgar's foster brother, the youngest son of Æthelstan Half-King, whom Edgar appointed to the ealdordom of East Anglia on the death of his elder brother, Æthelwold. Oswald and Æthelwine were associated in the refoundation of Ramsey as a Benedictine community, and Oswald was responsible for the foundation of a monastic church (St Mary's) at Worcester, a house for the training of monks at Westbury-on-Trym, Gloucestershire, and (with Ealdorman Æthelweard) the refoundation of the abbey of Pershore in Worcestershire. Æthelwold is most famous for his expulsion of the monks from the Old Minster at Winchester, but he concentrated his attention on the eastern shires, founding or refounding the houses of Peterborough, Ely, Crowland, and Thorney. Edgar's surviving charters show the extent of the massive transfer of land into the hands of the reformed monasteries in this period, a transfer which was the cause of much dispute when the king's hand was withdrawn.

Law and administration Four of the surviving Old English law codes have been attributed to Edgar, but I Edgar, also known as the hundred ordinance, omits the name of the issuing king and may belong to the time of Eadred. It describes the operation of the court belonging to the hundred, which, by the late Old English period, functioned as a subdivision of the shire. Even the most privileged landowners (and their men) were bound to attend the courts of the shire and hundred, and their emergence as units of judicial, fiscal, and military organization testify to the growing powers of the West Saxon kings. It is difficult, however, to say precisely how and when the English shires were created. All the West Saxon shires are recorded by the ninth century, but it was only after the expansion of Wessex in the tenth century that the shires of midland England were established and the process may not have been complete until the eleventh century, when most of them are named for the first time. The individual hundreds cannot logically predate the shires to which they belong, though they may, of course, have been created out of already existing units. The hundred ordinance thus describes an institution which had been taking shape for some time and was to develop further in the future. It refers back to earlier legislation promulgated by Edgar's father, Edmund, and some of the expedients it describes were already in place in the times of *Æthelstan and Edward the Elder.

The two codes known as II and III Edgar probably represent a single act of legislation, promulgated at Andover. The date is uncertain, but III Edgar refers back to the hundred ordinance. Ecclesiastical matters are the concern of II Edgar, notably the payment of church dues, whether tithe, churchscot, or Peter's Pence; as with the hundred ordinance, reference is made to a previously existing code (*domboc*), possibly that of *Alfred. The code II Edgar is particularly noteworthy for its testimony to the building by secular magnates of 'estate-churches', which impinged on the rights of tithe and burial dues enjoyed by the old minster churches. Eventually the estate churches (or at least some of them) were to form the basis for the parishes of the later middle ages.

Matters of secular interest appear in the second part of the code, III Edgar. Its main concerns are the accessibility of justice, the prevention of unjust judgments (a perennial theme), and the establishment of surety (*borh*). Its final clause is an attempt to standardize weights and measures and includes the command that 'one coinage is to be current throughout all the king's dominion [*anweald*], and no man is to refuse it' (*English Historical Documents*, 1.397). This was not the first such decree (Æthelstan had made a similar stipulation) but modern opinion agrees that Edgar's reforms set a new standard for the production of a uniform coinage throughout England, at least south of the Tees.

The code which has attracted the greatest attention is IV Edgar, issued at 'Wihtbordesstan', probably in the early 970s. Interest has focused on the code's recognition of Danish legal particularism: the Danes are to have 'such good laws as they best decide on', and Edgar is said to have made this concession 'because of your loyalty, which you have always shown me'. The identity of the 'Danes' in question is made clear towards the end of the code, when the king commands that 'Earl Oslac and all the host [*here*] who dwell in his aldormanry are to give their support that this may be enforced' (*English Historical Documents*, 1.400). There is a striking contrast between this language and the instructions to the ealdormen Ælfhere and Æthelwine, in west Mercia and East Anglia respectively, who are simply told to distribute the copies of the decrees which will be sent them. The 'Danes' whose customs were to be respected were the inhabitants of the former kingdom of York, now incorporated into the ealdordom of Northumbria, over which Oslac presided. But the legal integrity of the former kingdom was limited; IV Edgar legislates specifically for 'all the nation, whether Englishmen, Danes or Britons, in every province of my dominion' (*English Historical Documents*, 1.399).

The assimilation of Danish York must have been one of the major priorities in the 950s and 960s. It was probably in this period that the short-lived 'confederacy of the Five Boroughs' (Lincoln, Stamford, Nottingham, Derby, and Leicester) was established as a regional system of defence for the southern provinces of the old kingdom, though whether this was the work of Eadred or of Edgar is debatable. By the early eleventh century the confederacy had been abandoned and the region had been shired on the West Saxon pattern, but Yorkshire and the north midlands are distinguished from southern England by a common administrative structure; each shire is divided not into hundreds but into wapentakes, and each wapentake was further divided into units known confusingly as 'hundreds' or 'small hundreds'. The different names, however, describe the same thing; the functions of the wapentake and its court are identical to those of the hundred, and the 'small hundreds' are comparable to the tithings of the south, groups of men mutually responsible for each other before the law.

The meeting at Chester, 973 In 973, according to the Anglo-Saxon Chronicle, Edgar was consecrated king on 11 May (Pentecost), at Bath. Debate has centred on the reasons for the delay in crowning the king and alternative explanations have been advanced; that Edgar waited until he was thirty, the canonical age for consecration to the episcopate, or that the ceremony in 973 was a second consecration, symbolizing Edgar's attainment of 'imperial' rule over all the nations of Britain. Reservations have been expressed in respect of both solutions: all versions of the chronicle make it clear that Edgar was twenty-nine (in his thirtieth year) at the time of the ceremony, and there are no indications of any territorial expansion which might enhance Edgar's authority in the years leading up to 973. Perhaps the most remarkable thing about Edgar's consecration is that the chronicle troubles to record it; it does not mention the consecrations of Alfred, Edward the Elder, Æthelstan (though his consecration at Kingston, Surrey, is recorded by the Mercian register), Edmund, Eadred, or Eadwig. Moreover it records the consecrations of only three of Edgar's successors, Æthelred II, Edward the Confessor, and Harold II.

The fact that the earliest versions of the Anglo-Saxon Chronicle (the A and B texts) record the consecration in alliterative verse suggests that there was something unusual about the 973 ceremony. Some indication of what that might be is supplied by the D and E texts (representing the 'northern recension' of the chronicle text). Both record that immediately after his coronation, Edgar 'took his whole naval force [*sciphere*] to Chester, and six kings came to meet him, and all gave him pledges that they would be his allies on sea and on land' (*ASC*, s.a. 972, texts D and E). Ælfric of Eynsham has a more nearly contemporary reference to what seems to be the same event, though without place or date: 'And all the kings who were in this island, Cumbrians and Scots, came to Edgar, once eight kings on one day, and they all submitted to Edgar's direction' (*English Historical Documents*, 1.853).

Like Ælfric, the twelfth-century historian John of Worcester has eight kings, rather than the six of the Anglo-Saxon Chronicle, but unlike Ælfric he goes on to name them: Kynath, king of Scots; Malcolm, king of the Cumbrians; Maccus, 'king of many isles'; Dufnal; Siferth; Huuual; Iacob; and Iuchil. William of Malmesbury has a similar though not identical list, and the names of the first three kings are also recorded in an early twelfth-century Durham compilation. Stenton believed it unlikely that John of Worcester's list of kings could be mere invention, since there was no 'glaring anachronism' and most of those named could be identified as contemporaries of Edgar: Kenneth II of Scotland (*r.* 971–95), Malcolm of Strathclyde (*r.* 975–97), Maccus Haroldson, king of the Sudreys (Man and the Hebrides), who was killed *c.*977, Iago (Iacob) ab Idwal Foel of Gwynedd (*r.* 950–79), and Hywel ab Idwal Ieuaf (*r.* 979–85), his nephew and eventual supplanter. In addition Iuchil (Iudethil in William of Malmesbury's version) might represent an Englishman's attempt at the name Idwal, borne by one of Iago's brothers, Idwal Fychan (*d.* 980). It is true that Malcolm's father Donald did not die until 975, in Rome, but he might already have relinquished power to his son, especially if he is to be identified (as Stenton suggested) with the Dufnal (Dunmail, Donald) of John of Worcester's list. Stenton concluded that 'no Anglo-Norman writer, inventing a list of names with which to garnish an ancient annal, could have come as close as this to fact or probability' (Stenton, *Anglo-Saxon England*, 369–70).

William of Malmesbury's account of the meeting differs from that of John of Worcester both in detail (Maccus, for instance, appears as 'prince of the pirates') and in context, for he gives no indication of place or date, and does not associate it with his description of Edgar's consecration. These differences suggest that the two chroniclers were using a common source, rather than copying from each other. Since both are known to have used the archives of Christ Church, Canterbury, it may be significant that seven of John of Worcester's kings, excepting only Hywel ab Idwal Ieuaf, attest a spurious charter of Edgar, restoring rights in the port of Sandwich to Christ Church, Canterbury (*AS chart.*, S 808). The charter is undated, but was issued on Whit Sunday (Pentecost), at Bath: the day and place at least of Edgar's consecration. It is undoubtedly a forgery and the context is probably the long-running dispute between Christ Church and St Augustine's, Canterbury, over the port of Sandwich, a dispute which was particularly virulent between 1116 and 1127, when both John of Worcester and William of Malmesbury were engaged upon their respective histories. It has been assumed that the charter's attestations are based on John of Worcester's description of the rowing on the Dee but it is equally possible that the reverse is true, or at least that the compiler of the charter used the same source as did John of Worcester and William of Malmesbury.

What that source might be is another matter. The attestations of two kings, Siferth and Iacob (Iago ab Idwal of Gwynedd), are also found in a genuine charter of Eadred dating from 955 (*AS chart.*, S 566), preserved at Peterborough Abbey, a house which had connections with Canterbury, but not apparently with Worcester or Malmesbury. The charter's draftsmen, however, may have been associated with Worcester, and the Siferth who appears there cannot have been at Chester in 973, for, as the Anglo-Saxon Chronicle records, he committed suicide in 962. It may be (as Ælfric of Eynsham indeed implies) that Edgar received approaches from a number of other kings, at various times in his reign, and that the list which appears in John of Worcester and elsewhere has simply conflated the names of all those known to have been involved in negotiations with Edgar at whatever date.

That some particularly important meeting took place at Chester in the summer of 973 is not in doubt, but its significance needs close examination. Any West Saxon account of a meeting between Edgar and the other kings of Britain would present the English ruler as the dominant figure. It is noticeable that whereas the Anglo-Saxon Chronicle suggests no more than that the kings made a treaty with Edgar (*trywsodon*), Ælfric's language implies that they did homage (*gebugon*) to him. It is this aspect of the event which is emphasized by the twelfth-century historians who used and interpreted the chronicle texts; Henry of Huntingdon, for instance, says that the six kings 'pledged the loyalty that was owed to him [Edgar] as lord, to serve him … according to his overlordship' (Huntingdon, *Historia Anglorum* (OMT), 13), and John of Worcester, who demotes the kings to *subreguli*, also makes them swear fealty as well as co-operation.

It is from John of Worcester that there comes the celebrated description of how the 'subkings' rowed Edgar on the Dee:

> with them, on a certain day, he boarded a skiff; having set them to the oars, and having taken the helm himself, he skilfully steered it through the course of the river Dee and, with a crowd of ealdormen and nobles following in a similar boat, sailed from the palace to the monastery of St John the Baptist, where, when he had prayed, he returned with the same pomp to the palace. As he was entering it, he is reported to have declared to his nobles at length that each of his successors would be able to boast that he was king of the English, and would enjoy the pomp of such honour with so many kings at his command. (John of Worcester, *Chron.*, 2.424–5)

John of Worcester is the source of most subsequent accounts of this incident, depicted on a commemorative 4½p stamp issued in 1974 by the Isle of Man, one of whose kings was (allegedly) among the oarsmen. William of Malmesbury merely says that the eight kings were 'exhibited … on the Dee in triumph' (*De gestis regum*, 1.165); like Ælfric, Malmesbury gives neither the date nor the occasion of the incident.

The attempts of successive Norman kings to impose their suzerainty on Scotland gave twelfth-century English commentators 'a vested interest in rewriting Anglo-Scottish history in a way that showed the Dark-Age Scottish realm as a client kingdom of Wessex' (Smyth, 237), and the same could be said of their presentation of the Welsh princes. A glance at the events immediately preceding the meeting at Chester may serve to show it in a rather different light.

To take the Welsh princes first, the *Annales Cambriae* record that in 967 'the English laid waste the kingdom [*regionem*] of the sons of Idwal [Foel]', and the *Brut y tywysogyon* adds that the English were led by Ælfhere. No English source mentions this incursion into Gwynedd, but any English expedition into Welsh territory in 967 was likely to have been commanded by Ælfhere, ealdorman of Mercia from 956 to 983; he is duly recorded in 983 as the ally of Hywel ab Idwal Ieuaf against Einion ab Owain of Brycheiniog. In the late 960s Gwynedd was also experiencing internal dissension; it was in 969 that Ieuaf ab Idwal was imprisoned by his brother Iago. Furthermore, the *Annales Cambriae* record a raid on Môn (Anglesey) in 971, perpetrated by 'the son of Harold' (named as Maccus by the *Brut y tywysogyon*), and a second attack in 972 by Godfrey, son of Harold, resulted in the subjection of the island. Finally, in 973, the *Annales Cambriae* record 'a great gathering of ships at Chester by Edgar, king of the Saxons' (*Annales Cambriae*, s.a. 973). If John of Worcester is to be believed, this gathering was attended both by Maccus, 'king of the islands' (Man and the Hebrides), and by the princes of Gwynedd: was one of its purposes to negotiate a truce between them, and between both parties and the English king?

Something similar may lie behind the presence of the Scots and Cumbrians at Chester in 973. Again the starting point is an English incursion, this one recorded in the Anglo-Saxon Chronicle, which reports that Thored Gunnar's son ravaged Westmorland in 966. No context is given, and Stenton believed that Thored's raid was no more than 'an act of private violence' (Stenton, 'Preconquest Westmorland', 219). It could, however, be argued that Thored's action was an attempt to stem the southward advance of the Strathclyde rulers. They and their Scottish overlords had been encroaching upon the formerly English lands west of the Pennines, an encroachment demonstrated in 971, when Kenneth II began his reign with a plundering raid across Cumbria which reached as far east as Stainmore and as far south as the Chester Dee. The Scots kings also had their eyes on Bernicia east of the Pennines, governed in the 960s and 970s by Oslac, as earl of Northumbria, and Eadulf Yvelcild of

Bamburgh, whose son had been captured by Kenneth in a raid of 972.

By the 970s, the build-up of pressure on the northern frontiers of his kingdom demanded from Edgar some kind of diplomatic, if not military solution. Seen in this context, the meeting of 973 looks less like an imperial durbar than a conference of the 'great powers' to sort out their numerous interlocking disagreements. It may have been on this occasion, rather than in 975, that Edgar 'ceded' Lothian (northern Bernicia) to Kenneth of Scotland, though the area had probably been in Scots hands by the 950s, and any agreement between Edgar and Kenneth probably represents a mutual recognition by the kings of their respective spheres of influence. The choice of Chester as a meeting place may have been influenced by its position as the chief centre for trade between England and viking Dublin; which may in turn help to explain the choice of Bath, convenient for the Severn estuary and the sea route around Wales, as the site for Edgar's elaborate consecration (or reconsecration). For the most striking thing about the Chester meeting, noticed by the *Annales Cambriae* as well as the Anglo-Saxon Chronicle, is the demonstration of English sea-power. If Edgar had an edge over the other rulers in Britain, it was not so much as an imperial overlord, but as the possessor of a fleet strong enough to enforce obedience.

Defence of the realm The encomium on Edgar which is incorporated into the annal for 975 in the D and E texts of the Anglo-Saxon Chronicle claims that 'nor was there fleet so proud nor host so strong that it got itself prey in England' (*ASC*, s.a. 975, texts D and E) during his reign, a claim echoed by Ælfric the Homilist's statement that 'no fleet was ever heard of except of our own people who held this land' (*English Historical Documents*, 1.853). Great claims were made for Edgar's sea-power by the twelfth-century historians. John of Worcester attributes to him a fleet of 3600 ships which were assembled every year after Easter, 1200 on the east coast, 1200 on the west, and 1200 on the north, so that the king could circumnavigate the island (clockwise) each summer, in a show of force 'for the defence of his kingdom against foreigners and to train himself and his men in military exercises'. William of Malmesbury has a similar account (though without the numbers) and the thirteenth-century historian Roger of Wendover added a fourth fleet, bringing the total number of ships to 4800.

The exaggeration of later commentators may be set aside, but it is easy to believe that Edgar had a substantial fleet at his disposal. It may have been in his time that the foundations were laid for the naval organization evident from the reign of his son Æthelred II. The *Leges Henrici primi*, a twelfth-century legal tract, alleges that the English shires were divided into shipsokes (*sipessocna*), and though the term is not used in any pre-conquest source, its statement has been linked with the entry for 1008 in the Anglo-Saxon Chronicle, when 'the king [Æthelred II] ordered that ships should be built unremittingly over all England, namely a warship from 310 hides' (*ASC*, s.a. 1008, text C). There are problems with the interpretation of this annal, but it is generally taken to relate to the 300-hide ship-

providing units recorded elsewhere, notably in a contemporary letter of Æthelric, bishop of Sherborne (*AS chart.*, S 1383). How widespread such units were is uncertain; the five possible examples which are known are all connected with important religious houses.

The best-documented shipsoke is the triple hundred of Oswaldslow, Worcestershire, attached to the bishopric of Worcester; a second triple hundred in the same shire, which certainly owed ship service by 1066, belonged to Pershore Abbey. The charter which fathers the creation of Oswaldslow upon Edgar (*AS chart.*, S 731) is a twelfth-century forgery, and Edgar's charter of 972 (*AS chart.*, S 786), which restores its land to the refounded abbey of Pershore, is also spurious. Nevertheless, it can be argued that Edgar was responsible for the creation of both triple hundreds. Pershore's triple hundred cannot logically predate its refoundation as a Benedictine abbey in the late tenth century; and since it seems that the reformed community collapsed almost immediately, reviving only in the 1020s (and then briefly), it is difficult not to believe that its endowment could have been acquired only at the moment of its refoundation, probably in Edgar's reign. Moreover, neither Pershore's triple hundred nor Oswaldslow was territorially discrete, each consisting rather of a scatter of lands belonging to the religious house in question and interpenetrating each other to an extent which suggests that they were created at the same time. If Pershore's triple hundred dates to Edgar's time, so also must Oswaldslow.

Edgar's fleet may have been drawn from other sources than the English shires. In his panegyric upon Edgar mentioned above, Archbishop Wulfstan tempers his praise with one complaint: 'Yet he did one ill-deed too greatly: he loved evil foreign customs and brought too firmly heathen manners within this land, and attracted foreigners and enticed harmful people to this country' (*ASC*, s.a. 959, text D). Wulfstan can scarcely be speaking of the continental churchmen who visited England during Edgar's reign. William of Malmesbury, amplifying Wulfstan's words, specifies Saxons (Germans), Flemings, and Danes, from whom the English learnt, respectively, ferocity, effeminacy, and drunkenness, in none of which they had indulged heretofore. Malmesbury may well have been thinking of his own times rather than the tenth century, but Wulfstan's reference to 'heathen manners' suggests men of Scandinavian origin. It is probable that, like Alfred before him, Edgar was hiring viking stipendiaries and their ships, an expedient which was to be used by his son also.

Edgar's legacy In his account of Edgar's annual circumnavigations, John of Worcester adds that the king was accustomed to make similar perambulations by land, 'through all the English provinces' in winter and spring, in order to establish 'justice' (*iustitia*). It seems that Edgar's arm was not only long but also heavy; certainly the faction-fighting and other disturbances which marked the brief reign of his elder son, Edward the Martyr, suggest the sudden loosening of a tight and masterful grip. Edgar was only thirty-one or thirty-two when he died, on 8

July 975, and his death was perhaps unexpected. He was buried at Glastonbury Abbey. The vicissitudes which befell his younger son, Æthelred II, coupled with the plaudits of the reformers whom Edgar had patronized, ensured that his reign came to symbolize a golden age of peace and plenty, exemplified by the epithet Pacificus, which first appears in the twelfth-century chronicle of John of Worcester; whether things were so comfortable for those who lived through it probably depended upon the point of view.   ANN WILLIAMS

Sources ASC, s.a. 955–75 · John of Worcester, Chron. · J. Williams ab Ithel, ed., Annales Cambriae, Rolls Series, 20 (1860) · T. Jones, ed. and trans., Brut y tywysogyon, or, The chronicle of the princes: Peniarth MS 20 (1952), 8–10 · M. O. Anderson, Kings and kingship in early Scotland (1973), 252 · F. M. Stenton, Anglo-Saxon England, 3rd edn (1971), 364–71 · D. Roffe, 'The origins of Derbyshire', Derbyshire Archaeological Journal, 106 (1986), 102–22 · A. P. Smyth, Warlords and holy men: Scotland, AD 80–1000 (1984) · G. W. S. Barrow, The kingdom of the Scots: government, church and society from the eleventh to the fourteenth century (1973), 148–61 · J. E. Lloyd, A history of Wales from the earliest times to the Edwardian conquest, 3rd edn, 1 (1939); repr. (1948), 350–51 · N. Hooper, 'Some observations on the navy in late Anglo-Saxon England', Studies in medieval history presented to R. Allen Brown, ed. C. Harper-Bill, C. J. Holdsworth, and J. L. Nelson (1989), 203–13 · B. Yorke, 'Æthelwold and the politics of the tenth century', Bishop Æthelwold: his career and influence, ed. B. Yorke (1988), 65–88 · Ælfric's Lives of saints, ed. W. W. Skeat, 1, EETS, 82 (1885), 468–9 · F. M. Stenton, 'Pre-conquest Westmorland', Preparatory to 'Anglo-Saxon England': being the collected papers of Frank Merry Stenton, ed. D. M. Stenton (1970), 218–23 · A. J. Robertson, ed., The laws of the kings of England from Edmund to Henry I (1926), 16–39, 299–310 · F. Liebermann, ed., Die Gesetze der Angelsachsen, 1 (Halle, 1898), 192–215 · Willelmi Malmesbiriensis monachi de gestis regum Anglorum, ed. W. Stubbs, 2 vols., Rolls Series (1887–9), vol. 1, p. 165 · Symeon of Durham, 'De primo Saxonum adventu libellus', Symeonis Dunelmensis opera et collectanea, ed. H. Hinde, SurtS, 51 (1868), 203 · A. O. Anderson, ed. and trans., Early sources of Scottish history, AD 500 to 1286, 2 vols. (1922); repr. with corrections (1990) · Henry, archdeacon of Huntingdon, Historia Anglorum, ed. D. E. Greenway, OMT (1996) · [Roger of Wendover], Rogeri de Wendover chronica, sive, Flores historiarum, ed. H. O. Coxe, EHS, 1 (1841), s.a. 975 · F. E. Harmer, ed., Anglo-Saxon writs (1952), 266–70 · R. H. M. Dolley and D. M. Metcalf, 'The reform of the English coinage under Edgar', Anglo-Saxon coins: studies presented to F. M. Stenton, ed. R. H. M. Dolley (1961), 136–68 · N. Lund, 'King Edgar and the Danelaw', Medieval Scandinavia, 9 (1976), 181–95 · O. Fenger, 'The Danelaw and Danish law', Scandinavian Studies in Law, 16 (1972), 85–96 · W. H. Stevenson, 'The great commendation to King Edgar in 973', EngHR, 13 (1898), 505–7 · A. Williams, 'An introduction to the Worcestershire Domesday', The Worcestershire Domesday, ed. A. Williams and R. W. H. Erskine (1988), 1–31, esp. 13–18 · B. O'Brien, 'Forgery and the literacy of the early common law', Albion, 27 (1995), 1–18 · P. H. Sawyer, From Roman Britain to Norman England (1978), 127–8 · The chronicle of Æthelweard, ed. and trans. A. Campbell (1962) · English historical documents, 1, ed. D. Whitelock (1955)
Likenesses manuscript drawing, 966 (charter of Edgar to the New Minster, Winchester), BL · manuscript drawing, BL, Cotton MS Tiberius A.iii, fol. 2v [see illus.] · manuscript drawing, BL, Cotton MS Vespasian A.viii, fol. 2v · silver penny, BM

Edgar (late 1070s?–1107), king of Scots, was probably the fourth son of *Malcolm III (d. 1093) and his second wife, *Margaret (d. 1093), and was probably born in the late 1070s. He was named after his mother's ancestor, Edgar, king of England, and may have been the son who brought to her news of the death of his father and oldest brother, Edward, after their defeat at Alnwick on 13 November 1093. After his mother's death and the accession of his uncle *Donald III he presumably fled to England. He was probably the Edgar who left his cross on the charter of his half-brother *Duncan II to St Cuthbert in 1094, and would be expelled again at the restoration of Donald in November 1094. At Norham in 1095, calling himself 'Edgar, son of Malcolm king of Scots, possessing the land of Lothian and the kingdom of Scotland by the gift of my lord William, king of the English and by paternal heritage' (Lawrie, no. 15), he made an extensive grant to St Cuthbert of the twelve-vill shires of Berwick and Coldingham; the charter (known only from later copies) apparently bore the cross 'of King Edgar', a circumstance which has weighed against its authenticity, but a genuine charter of King William II confirmed the grant.

Edgar would recover the kingdom only with English help, given in 1097, when his uncle *Edgar Ætheling invaded Scotland, defeated Donald in battle, and set up Edgar as king, in fealty to William Rufus; it seems likely that Edgar's older brother Edmund, ally of Donald III, was still alive, but was imprisoned. The following year, Magnus, king of Norway, sailed to Orkney, Man, and Anglesey, where, according to saga evidence, instead of making war on Scotland, he negotiated with King Malcolm a peace whereby he kept all the islands to the west of Scotland, adding Kintyre to this by being dragged across the isthmus of Tarbert in his ship; Malcolm is conveniently taken by historians to mean Edgar, and the kingdom of the Isles is given its origins in this event. But it may be doubted if any king of Scotland had drawn tribute from the Western Isles.

In 1099 Edgar attended a crown-wearing of Rufus and carried the king's sword; but he also secured the release of Robert, son of Godwin of Winchester, to whom he had given an estate in Lothian, and who had been arrested by the men of Ranulph Flambard, bishop of Durham, apparently for seeking to build a castle on his estate. Edgar deprived the bishop of the shire of Berwick, though Durham thereafter retained Coldingham, where a dependent priory was established forty years later. Although he did not attend the opening of Cuthbert's tomb in 1104, he added to the saint's endowment Swinton in Berwickshire, formerly the possession of a native landowner, with twenty-four cattle and burdened its inhabitants with an annual payment of half a merk of silver; in his gift of the waste of Ednam to Thor the Long, he helped Thor to stock the land. Such fragments suggest that Berwickshire had suffered serious devastation, either in the time of Malcolm III or from Bishop Ranulph. The see of St Andrews, and possibly also Glasgow, remained vacant during his reign, but he gave Portmoak in Kinross-shire to the Culdees of Loch Leven, and a shire on the northern shore of the Firth of Forth to the Benedictine priory of Dunfermline, founded by his mother, whither the archbishop of Canterbury sent monks at his request; probably Edgar was reviving the priory after collapse under Donald III. His attitude to the church remains somewhat enigmatic, and was perhaps as conventional as that of Henry I.

Edgar evidently had no say in the removal of his sister

Edith (or Matilda) from a nunnery and her marriage to Henry I on 11 November 1100, nor in Henry's decision to marry their sister Mary to Eustace, count of Boulogne, after she had been rejected by the count of Mortain. His seal, single-faced, shows strongly the influence of that of Edward the Confessor, but his surviving writ and charters are Anglo-Norman in form and phraseology. They were grants to St Cuthbert; four originals survive and one in a copy, but only one has witnesses, all with native Anglo-Saxon or Anglo-Norse names, and it must be concluded that despite the circumstances of his accession, Edgar did not stimulate an Anglo-Norman migration to Scotland. He did, however, give to Muirchertach, king of Munster, a very large animal, variously translated as camel and elephant, which was presumably brought back from the east by a participant in the first crusade (1098–9), in which Scots, including Robert, son of Godwin, participated.

In his will Edgar instructed that a substantial appanage in Strathclyde and Teviotdale be given to his youngest brother, *David; it is possible that this, or some of it, was enjoyed by their intermediate brother, *Alexander I, during Edgar's lifetime. It is usually said that he never married: no wife is known and no children are hinted at. He was described by Ailred of Rievaulx as 'sweet and lovable, employing no tyranny, no harshness, no greed against his people, but ruling his subjects with the greatest charity and benevolence' (Anderson, *Scottish Annals*, 128). He died at Edinburgh in 1107, possibly on 15 January, more probably on the 8th, and was buried in Dunfermline Abbey. He was succeeded by his brother Alexander I.

A. A. M. DUNCAN

Sources A. O. Anderson, ed., *Scottish annals from English chroniclers, AD 500 to 1286* (1908), 118–28 · A. O. Anderson, ed. and trans., *Early sources of Scottish history, AD 500 to 1286*, 2 (1922), 99–141 · A. C. Lawrie, ed., *Early Scottish charters prior to AD 1153* (1905), 12–19 · A. A. M. Duncan, *Scotland: the making of the kingdom* (1975), vol. 1 of *The Edinburgh history of Scotland*, ed. G. Donaldson (1965–75), 126–8 · G. W. S. Barrow, *The kingdom of the Scots: government, church and society from the eleventh to the fourteenth century* (1973), 167–8 · A. H. Dunbar, *Scottish kings*, 2nd edn (1906) · A. A. M. Duncan, 'Yes, the earliest Scottish charters', *SHR*, 78 (1999), 1–38
Archives Durham Cath. CL
Likenesses seal, U. Durham L., dean and chapter archives, Misc. Ch. 556, 557, 558

Edgar Ætheling (*b.* 1052?, *d.* in or after 1125), prince, was the son of *Edward Ætheling (*d.* 1057) and grandson of *Edmund II; in 1066 he was the only candidate for the throne who could trace his descent from an English king. Subsequently, he was involved in failed rebellions against William I, before he successfully adapted to Norman rule.

Birth in exile, return to England, and the Norman conquest Edgar was born before 1057, perhaps in 1052, and probably in Hungary, where his father Edward Ætheling finally found refuge from Cnut's attempts to eliminate him. His mother, Agatha, was kinswoman of a German emperor, either Henry II or Henry III. Edgar's two sisters, *Margaret and *Christina, were apparently younger. Edward Ætheling was brought to England in 1057, with his family, presumably to be heir to the throne. He died almost immediately. Allegations that Earl Harold had him poisoned are

not only unfounded, but assume that he had already determined to seize the throne, and fail to explain why Edgar was not also removed. According to the *Leges Edwardi Confessoris* ('Laws of Edward the Confessor'), the young Edgar was given the designation 'ætheling', meaning 'throneworthy', by the king, his great-uncle *Edward the Confessor. He appears in the *Liber vitae* of the New Minster at Winchester, *c.*1060, as Edgar *clito* (the Latin equivalent of *ætheling*). Since Edgar was not the son of a king, this was apparently a political statement by the childless King Edward concerning the succession. However, the early sources agree that when Edward died on 4 or 5 January 1066, he had passed over Edgar by bequeathing the kingdom to Earl Harold. Although some leading nobles may have wished to crown him, political reality told against Edgar. While his youth was not in itself decisive, he had no powerful kin to promote him and to resist Earl Harold, the dominant figure in English politics and the most powerful man in the kingdom. The initial opposition of the brothers Eadwine and Morcar, earls of Mercia and Northumbria, was a consequence of their own ambition rather than concern for Edgar's legitimacy, and they were won over by Bishop Wulfstan of Worcester.

Harold's death at the battle of Hastings (14 October 1066) did not cause the surviving English leaders to submit. In London, Archbishop Ealdred of York and the citizens wished to have Edgar as king 'as was his proper due by birth' (*ASC*, s.a. 1066, text D), according to a version of the Anglo-Saxon Chronicle which displays a marked interest in the Ætheling and his family. There is some evidence that Edgar's claim was taken seriously outside London. The abbot of Peterborough died soon after Hastings and the monks chose as his successor Brand, sending him to Edgar for confirmation 'because the local people expected that he would be king, and the ætheling gladly gave assent to it' (*ASC*, s.a. 1066, text E). At first 'Edwin and Morcar promised him that they would fight on his side; but always the more it ought to have been forward the more it got behind' (*ASC*, s.a. 1066, text D). Edgar was not crowned, and without the backing of the two most significant surviving earls his cause was hopeless. In early December he submitted to William of Normandy at Berkhamsted, together with several bishops and earls. In spring 1067 Edgar was among the leading Englishmen taken to Normandy with King William to ensure security, and he presumably returned with the king in December. He was awarded land and honours, and was treated as one of William's dearest companions, at least according to William of Poitiers, a writer whose intention was to flatter his master the king (*Gesta Guillelmi*, 238). Whether or not this is true, what is most striking about William's treatment of Edgar is that he allowed him both life and freedom, in stark contrast to Cnut's behaviour towards the English royal family after his conquest of England in 1016.

Rebellion In 1068 Edgar with his mother and sisters quit England for the court of King *Malcolm III of Scotland. This may have been connected with the short-lived northern revolt of that summer, although a well-informed writer believed their original destination to have been

Hungary (Ailred of Rievaulx, cols. 734–5). Edgar certainly was involved in the great northern rebellion of 1069–70. Early in 1069 he was at the head of the Northumbrian rebels who entered York, and following their defeat by William he fled to Scotland. In the late summer a large Danish fleet arrived in the Humber. Edgar and other northern nobles returned to lead a Northumbrian army which 'rejoicing exceedingly' (ASC, s.a. 1069, text D) captured the Norman castle in York and killed its garrison. During the winter, when the Danish fleet sheltered in the marshy Humber, Edgar narrowly avoided capture when he raided into Lincolnshire with one ship. Meanwhile William systematically and brutally crushed northern resistance. In spring 1070 the Danish king Swein brought a fresh fleet to the Humber, and it was believed he would conquer England. Indeed, throughout the rebellion there is no indication that the intention was to make Edgar king. Swein soon concluded an agreement with William, leaving the English rebels in the lurch, and once more Edgar withdrew to Scotland. It was probably in 1070 that his sister Margaret reluctantly married King Malcolm. Although Edgar resisted his advances, 'he dared not do anything else, because they had come into his control' (ASC, s.a. 1067, text D). Edgar played no part in the last English rebellion at Ely in 1071–2. He was probably expelled from Scotland as a consequence of William I's invasion in 1072, and by 1074 he was in Flanders. He returned to Scotland in that year, then the French king offered him the castle of Montreuil as a base from which 'he could do daily harm to those who were not his friends', that is, the Normans (ASC, s.a. 1074, text D). But he was shipwrecked on the way and regained Scotland with difficulty.

Friendship with Robert Curthose and William Rufus This phase of Edgar's career, as a rebel, was coming to a close. Following his brother-in-law's advice, he submitted to William I and was established at his court, keeping out of the 1075 rebellion. William of Malmesbury, writing in 1125, bitterly criticized Edgar's behaviour, 'remaining at court for many years, silently sunk into contempt through his indolence, or more mildly speaking, his simplicity'. He alleges that Edgar gave up his daily stipend of a pound of silver in return for a single horse (De gestis regum, 2.310). Domesday Book reveals that Edgar held two estates in Hertfordshire, at Barkway and Hormead, in 1086. It was presumably during these years that he struck up a friendship with the king's eldest son, Robert Curthose, for the two were later described as 'virtually foster brothers' (Ordericus Vitalis, Eccl. hist., 5.273). Nothing further is known of Edgar until 1086, when he left William I's court, 'because he did not have much honour from him' (ASC, s.a. 1085, text E), and led two hundred knights to Apulia, another land under Norman rule. Although nothing is known of what Edgar did there, it is remarkable evidence of his adaptation to Norman life that he apparently chose knight errantry in preference to joining his sister in Scotland. Edgar then went to Normandy where Robert, duke since 1087, gave him land and favour. In 1091 William Rufus, now King William II, invaded Normandy and, according to the terms reached with his brother Robert,

Edgar was expelled. William perhaps feared the propaganda value Robert could gain from having the Anglo-Saxon claimant to the throne with him. But his vindictiveness benefited him little. Edgar went to Scotland and incited Malcolm to invade England; William led a costly expedition north; and finally, an agreement was brokered between the two kings by Robert and Edgar, who together left for Normandy on 23 December.

Subsequently, Edgar won William II's trust. In 1093 William employed him to escort Malcolm to his court. In the same year Malcolm was killed and Margaret died, Donald Bane became king, and an anti-Norman reaction occurred in Scotland. William II recognized Edgar Ætheling's nephew *Edgar as king of Scotland (late 1094 or 1095) and both Edgars campaigned with William against the rebellious earl of Northumbria, Robert de Mowbray, in 1095. Edgar Ætheling became his nephews' guardian, and late in 1097 he 'went with an army, with the king's support, into Scotland, and conquered the country in a severe battle' (ASC, s.a. 1097, text E), making his nephew Edgar king before returning to England. However, his relations with William II after 1093 were not universally smooth. According to John Fordun, a late fourteenth-century Scottish chronicler, Edgar was accused by Ordgar, an English knight, of plotting against William, and forced to defend himself by judicial combat. His successful champion was another English knight, Godwine of Winchester. Despite the late date of the story, it is probably true in outline. Edgar's tenant for his two estates in 1086 was named Godwine, and a Robert, son of Godwine, was associated with Edgar in 1097 and later.

Crusade In the next phase of his career Edgar became a crusader. According to Orderic Vitalis, he was with an English fleet which arrived at Latakia in the Levant in June 1098. He took the place under his protection and then transferred it to Robert Curthose. There are difficulties with this version. Edgar was occupied in Scotland in October 1097, and would have found it difficult to join a fleet which must already have set sail. No other sources record his participation in the first crusade, and another authority places his visit to the Holy Land in 1102, when he was accompanied by Robert, son of Godwine, who was captured by the Egyptians and martyred (De gestis regum, 2.310). It is possible that Edgar visited the Holy Land twice, or stayed there for several years: the sources do not permit certainty on the matter. Nevertheless, he returned by way of the Byzantine and German emperors, who treated him with respect and wished him to remain with them. However, 'he gave up everything through regard to his native soil' (ibid.) and returned to England out of a 'foolish desire' (ibid.) to breathe his native air. Edgar's final recorded action was in 1106. He left England to fight on the losing side at the battle of Tinchebrai, for Robert Curthose against Henry I. The fate of the two friends was very different: Robert was imprisoned until his death in 1134, while Edgar was soon released. Henry I had married Edgar's niece *Matilda as soon as he became king in 1100, so his

Anglo-Saxon royal descent represented no further challenge.

Character and last years The barest outline of Edgar's life has to be pieced together from a variety of sources, which makes it difficult to assess his character and actions. William of Malmesbury's harsh criticism has been given above, and Orderic Vitalis summed up Edgar as 'handsome in appearance, eloquent, generous and nobly born … but indolent too' (Ordericus Vitalis, *Eccl. hist.*, 5.270–72). Both were Anglo-Normans writing in the first half of the twelfth century, but it is questionable whether either knew as much about him as is now known. A modern writer has described him as lacking 'any quality of leadership' and as an 'ineffectual claimant', adding that 'William could safely pardon him as often as he rebelled; he was more dangerous to his own side than to his enemies' (Chibnall, 18–19). Certainly, Edgar lacked the force of personality to impose himself upon events in the period between 1066 and 1074, although he was handicapped by political isolation in 1066 and the disunity of the English leaders. His actions from 1086 to 1102 suggest that he did have some qualities of leadership, but it must be admitted that his decision to back Robert in 1106, so obviously a loser, seems characteristic.

Edgar's death occurred without record. William of Malmesbury wrote in 1125, 'he now grows old in the country in privacy and quiet' (*De gestis regum*, 2.310). The pipe rolls record an Edgar Adeling in Northumberland in 1158 and 1167. He is unlikely to be the subject of this memoir, who would have been at least 110 by 1167. It is possible that he was a descendant of Edgar Ætheling, although no marriage, other liaison, or children are recorded. Since 1071 he had been a political irrelevance. Perhaps the true interest of his career is how an Anglo-Saxon prince was treated by, and adapted to, the new political dispensation following the Norman conquest.   NICHOLAS HOOPER

Sources N. Hooper, 'Edgar the Ætheling: Anglo-Saxon prince, rebel and crusader', *Anglo-Saxon England*, 14 (1985), 197–214 • *ASC*, s.a. 1066–7, 1069, 1075 [text D]; s.a. 1066, 1067, 1069, 1074, 1085, 1091, 1093, 1097, 1106 [text E] • *Willelmi Malmesbiriensis monachi de gestis regum Anglorum*, ed. W. Stubbs, 2 vols., Rolls Series (1887–9), vol. 2 • Ordericus Vitalis, *Eccl. hist.*, vol. 5 • Aelredus Rievallensis [Ailred of Rievaulx], 'Genealogia regum Anglorum', *Patrologia Latina*, 195 (1855), 711–38, esp. 733–5 • F. Liebermann, ed., 'Leges Edwardi Confessoris', *Die Gesetze der Angelsachsen*, 1 (1903), 665, para. 35, 1c • *The Gesta Guillelmi of William of Poitiers*, ed. and trans. R. H. C. Davis and M. Chibnall, OMT (1998) • M. Chibnall, *Anglo-Norman England, 1066–1166* (1986) • S. Keynes, ed., *The Liber vitae of the New Minster and Hyde Abbey, Winchester* (Copenhagen, 1996)

Edgar, James (1688–1764), secretary to James Francis Edward Stuart, was born at Keithock, Forfarshire, on 13 July 1688, the fifth of seven sons of David Edgar (1650?–1722) of Keithock, a farmer, and his second wife, Elizabeth, *née* Guthrie, of St Vigeans. Despite his large Forfarshire family and its modest income, Edgar was well connected to prominent Scots Jacobites. Godson of the earl of Panmure, Edgar served in the rising of 1715 as clerk to Brigadier John Hay of Cromlix (later ennobled as the Jacobite earl of Inverness), Lord Mar's brother-in-law. Edgar proudly reminded correspondents he was 'amongst the

first' (Tayler and Tayler, 1715, 39) to join Mar when the Jacobite standard was raised at Braemar. Widely reputed for his integrity and amiable nature, Edgar escaped Scotland after the rising's collapse by supposedly evading capture in borrowed farmer's clothes, which he later took pains to return to their rightful owner.

Edgar was counted among other Jacobite refugees at Avignon in late 1716, and had proceeded to Italy by 1717. Here he resided as loyal servant and private secretary to James Francis Edward Stuart, the Pretender, for the next four decades in a relationship characterized by mutual devotion and the utmost confidence. Although Edgar's education is something of a mystery, his facility as a writer is evident throughout the Stuart papers in the Royal Archives at Windsor. His neat, tight script maximized available space on each page. The sheer magnitude of his involvement in Jacobite correspondence is overwhelming. By the later 1720s he had assumed increased responsibility for correspondence into and out of the Jacobite court, often composing the bulk of a letter's content while James attached a signature and occasionally added a few comments. Edgar thus responded to countless requests from impoverished supporters and former agents, as well as all manner of queries and advice for achieving a restoration and other subjects.

After 1732 Edgar not only wrote but also signed many letters for James. By 1740 the overwhelming majority of the letters dispatched by the exiled Stuart court were Edgar's. It is difficult to assess the extent and impact of his advice to James as the Jacobite cause proceeded to languish. His responsibilities included attending to minutiae such as court financial arrangements in Rome and abroad, and the upbringing of James's sons. Edgar also supplies some of the most vivid accounts of a youthful Bonnie Prince Charlie, with whom he developed an affinity in the aftermath of the Jacobite rising of 1745. Often thrust into an intermediary role in efforts to reconcile James and his wayward son, the alienated, self-destructive Charles relied upon Edgar as his own confidant after 1750.

Edgar's esteem and unflagging loyalty were recognized with his presentation of an engraved silver snuff-box as a token of James's appreciation. Amid faction, jealousy, government bribery, and his supporters' defection, James made no appointment as Jacobite secretary of state after 1732. Thus Edgar, who was on cordial terms with nearly every one of the Jacobites' supporters and who was deemed 'too unobtrusive to excite' (Haile, 346) such passions, assumed the *de facto* position. He was commissioned clerk of Scotland's 'Councils, Registers, and Rolls' in 1759. Edgar finally received the seals of office as secretary of state in 1763, yet retained them only briefly, for following a long illness he succumbed to a stroke on 24 September 1764 at Rome. His replacement was Andrew Lumisden, a relative who had served as his own assistant since 1750.

The principal manuscript collection for Edgar's career is the literally thousands of autograph letters and other assorted documents found in the Stuart papers. Edgar's diligent organization of the voluminous correspondence received in Rome and his painstaking care in making duplicates and translations were both instrumental in enriching this corpus of material for posterity. Far more than a mere secretary, Edgar's influence pervades the Stuart papers after 1730 and has enabled historians to formulate a clear and instructive picture of the decline of Jacobitism. LAWRENCE B. SMITH

Sources Royal Arch., Stuart papers · H. Tayler, ed., *Jacobite epilogue* (1941) · *Calendar of the Stuart papers belonging to his majesty the king, preserved at Windsor Castle*, 7 vols., HMC, 56 (1902–23) · *The Jacobite peerage*, facsimile edn (1964) · A. Tayler and H. Tayler, *1715: the story of the rising* (1936) · A. Tayler and H. Tayler, eds., *The Stuart papers at Windsor* (1939) · M. Haile, *James Francis Edward, the Old Chevalier* (1907) · C. S. Terry, ed., *The Jacobites and the union* (1922) · F. J. McLynn, *Charles Edward Stuart: a tragedy in many acts* (1988) · D. Dobson, *The Jacobites of Angus, 1689–1746* (1997) · G. Hay, *History of Arbroath to the present time, with notices of the civil and ecclesiastical affairs of the neighbouring district*, 2nd edn (1899) · G. H. Jones, *The main stream of Jacobitism* (1954) · R. W. Twigge, 'Jacobite papers at Avignon', *SHR*, 9 (1911–12), 60–75 · C. Petrie, *The Jacobite movement*, 2 vols. (1948–50) · BL, Add. MS 39923 · NL Scot., Forbes of Culloden MSS 2964–70, 2980 · H. Tayler, ed., *The Jacobite court at Rome in 1719*, Scottish History Society, 3rd ser., 31 (1938) · B. Bevan, *King James the third of England: a study of kingship in exile* (1967) · P. Miller, *James* (1971) · NL Scot., Blaikie MS 291
Archives BL, Add. MS 39913 | NL Scot., Walter Blaikie collection · NL Scot., Forbes of Culloden MSS · Royal Arch., Stuart MSS
Likenesses portrait, Scot. NPG

Edgar, James (*d.* 1799). *See under* Poker Club (*act.* 1762–1784).

Edgar, John (1798–1866), minister of the United Secession church and philanthropist, was born at Ballykine, co. Down, a few months before the battle of Ballynahinch (12–13 June 1798), the son of Revd Samuel Edgar (1766–1826), minister of the Burgher congregation of Ballynahinch, and his wife, Elizabeth McKee. He attended his father's local academy, the University of Glasgow, and the Belfast Academical Institution, and for a time he supported himself by teaching. In 1818 the Burgher synod, to which the Edgars adhered, coalesced with the even more strictly Calvinist Anti-Burgher synod to form the Secession synod, which remained aloof from the more moderate, numerous and affluent General Synod of Ulster. On 14 November 1820 John Edgar was ordained as minister of a poor and struggling Belfast congregation of Seceders for which, by means of a tour of Britain, he raised the funds to build a meeting-house in Alfred Place. In 1826 he was elected to succeed his late father as the Secession synod's professor of theology in the Belfast Academical Institution. Although neither the Alfred Place pulpit nor the professorship alone would have provided a comfortable living, Edgar resourcefully built a remarkable career as a philanthropic and religious leader upon the simultaneous tenure of these two posts. On 24 September 1828 he married Susanna, daughter of Thomas Grimshaw, a merchant of Whitehouse; they had a number of children.

Edgar was active in various Belfast charitable endeavours, including the Ulster Religious Tract and Book Society, the Belfast Anti-Slavery Society, the Ulster Female Penitentiary, the Destitute Sick Society, the Belfast Town Mission, and the Society for Promoting the Education of the Deaf and Dumb and the Blind. His impact was felt beyond the north of Ireland between 1829 and 1834 when, despite an unprepossessing personal appearance, his colourful and effective platform manner and his forcefully written pamphlets made him the leading advocate in Ireland of the temperance movement. He played an important role in transmitting to Britain the temperance enthusiasm which had arisen in the 'Second Great Awakening' in America. Ultimately, however, his stubborn refusal on biblical grounds to endorse teetotalism isolated him from the mainstream of the temperance movement. He turned to other causes after 1840, when the Secession synod merged with the general synod (which had extruded its non-subscribing minority in 1829) to form the general assembly on the basis of unqualified subscription to the Westminster confession.

When Edgar was elected moderator of the general assembly in 1842, the 200th anniversary of the first Irish presbytery, he launched a bicentenary fund to support a home mission programme for the evangelization of Roman Catholic Ireland, and over the next decade the promotion of that enterprise claimed much of his considerable energy. His thinking about the relationship of his communion to Catholicism was brought into sharp focus by the famine of 1845–51, which many contemporaries tended to explain in providential terms. Policy makers often saw the potato failure as God's provision of an opportunity to change Irish economic behaviour; some evangelicals saw in it divine punishment of Catholics and of the state's concessions to Catholicism. In contrast to such confident assessments of the Almighty's intentions, Edgar referred to it as 'an awfully mysterious Providence' (Killen, 212). He bluntly rejected the 'species of heartless philosophy current which says this calamity will, in the end, be good for Ireland, because it will cure the Irish of their laziness' (ibid., 209) and gave priority to saving 'the perishing body' (ibid., 217) over the work of saving souls in the catastrophic circumstances.

Edgar made an eloquent plea for support of the mission to Catholics in 'A cry from Connaught', published in the *Missionary Herald* for November 1846, and subsequently as a pamphlet of which 26,000 copies were circulated. This initiative arose out of the conjuncture of the failure of the 1846 potato harvest with his inspection tour of the general assembly's Irish schools. In those schools Irish speakers were taught, usually by Roman Catholic teachers, to read the Bible in Irish, a mission technique which accorded with Edgar's conviction that merely reading the scriptures would lead some students to grasp the saving truths of the gospel (as understood by Presbyterians). In the 'Cry' he proposes a mission strategy based on the voluntary character of attendance at those schools, his perception of religious insights on the part of some of their pupils, and his observation of the dignity of sufferers from the harvest failure and of their responses to his own acts of kindness. He believed that such a strategy could avoid sectarian controversy and the 'bribery' which had so often been imputed to the Church of Ireland's 'Second Reformation' conversion efforts over the preceding generation. The concrete results of Edgar's initiatives included the collection and disbursement of perhaps £20,000 in famine relief and the creation of the Belfast Ladies' Relief Association for Connaught, which for several years maintained a number of industrial schools in which young women received training in knitting and embroidery along with scriptural instruction. Edgar's confidence in the Irish schools, however, was misplaced, and by 1852 he was writing of 'withering disappointments arising from the baseness of those who made professions only to deceive' (Magee, 25).

An increase in the parliamentary provision for the general assembly's theological professorships (tenured from 1853 in Assembly's College, now Union Theological College, Belfast) enabled Edgar to resign his pastoral charge in 1848. He received a DD from Hamilton College in 1836 and an LLD from the University of the City of New York in 1860. His original contributions to theology, however, were slight: a posthumous edition of his *Select Works* (1868) consists mainly of speeches and tracts promoting the various social causes to which he devoted his career, the most 'theological' being perhaps his 'The intoxicating drinks of the Hebrews'. His real achievements were as promoter of a style of social Christianity within a rigidly confessional tradition. He died of a throat polyp and other respiratory difficulties on 26 August 1866 at the home of Hugh Moore at Rathgar, Dublin, and was buried in Belfast on 29 August. His wife survived him.

DAVID W. MILLER

Sources W. D. Killen, *Memoir of John Edgar, DD, LLD* (1867) · J. Edgar, *Select works of John Edgar, DD, LLD* (1868) · E. Malcolm, '*Ireland sober, Ireland free': drink and temperance in nineteenth-century Ireland* (1986) · A. Jordan, *Who cared? Charity in Victorian and Edwardian Belfast* [1993] · H. Magee, *Fifty years in 'The Irish mission'* (1905?) · D. Stewart, *The Seceders in Ireland with annals of their congregations* (1950) · J. M'Connell, *Presbyterianism in Belfast* (1912) · J. Jamieson, *The history of the Royal Belfast Academical Institution, 1810–1960* (1959, [1960])

Likenesses photograph?, *c*.1830 (after oil portrait?), repro. in Stewart, *Seceders in Ireland*, 204 · H. Adlard, engraving, *c*.1850, repro. in Killen, *Memoir of John Edgar*, frontispiece

Wealth at death £4000: probate, 9 Oct 1866, *CGPLA Ire.*

Edgar, John George (1827/8–1864), children's author and magazine editor, was born at Hutton, Berwickshire, the fourth son of the Revd John Edgar, who represented the ancient family of Edgar of Wedderlie, which had long been settled in Westruther in Berwickshire. Most nineteenth-century sources give 1834 as his date of birth, but this appears to have been a mistake (according to his death certificate and Hannay, 174). Edgar was educated at Coldstream School under Richard Henderson and the Latin he acquired there was a great value to his literary career, enabling him to read medieval documents. In 1843, probably aged sixteen, he entered a commercial house in Liverpool; he went out to the West Indies from 1846 to 1848, then returned to Liverpool, where he continued in commerce from 1848 to 1852, when he went to live in London and devoted himself to literature.

Edgar concentrated upon history and biography and wrote in a simple and elegant style for the young; his first book for children was *The Boyhood of Great Men* (1853). He became a major contributor to Beeton's *Boy's Own Magazine* and the first editor of *Every Boy's Magazine*, to which he subsequently contributed regularly. Many of his full-length stories such as *Cressy and Poictiers* (1865) first appeared in serial form in these magazines.

Edgar specialized in writing about the manners and events of the Middle Ages, and possessed extensive knowledge of early English and Scottish history and a minute knowledge of border traditions and topography. He also wrote political leaders from time to time which were remarkable for their sarcasm and satire and esteemed by London journalists. In his historical works, much influenced by Sir Walter Scott and delighting in chivalry and battles, he kept close to his original sources such as Froissart. In *Cressy and Poictiers*, one of his most popular books, he used the device (later perfected by G. A. Henty) of attaching his fictitious hero to a real historical character, in this case the Black Prince. In just over a decade he wrote sixteen books intended mainly for young readers, and although he contributed to other magazines and occasionally wrote political pieces, he was 'rather a writer of books than a journalist. He studied his subjects for their own sake, and then made what literary use he could of them' (Hannay, 175). He had a fine if conservative historical sense; in his description of Runnymede, for example, he made plain that the barons were fighting for their own selfish ends. Yet a characteristically Victorian penchant for the 'great men' school of history was well represented in such works as *The Heroes of England* (1858), in which he gave a robust account of heroes 'who added to the national greatness' (Thwaite, 211).

Edgar's books were well reviewed when they appeared, *Footprints of Famous Men* (1854) being praised for its 'clear and pleasing style' by the *Daily News*; its biographies were described as 'not too short to be amusing' by *The Examiner*, which considered that 'as thousands of boys thirst for greatness, which is acquired by ones and tens, there will be thousands glad to read a book like this'. On the other hand Thwaite, in a retrospective judgement, found 'His tendency to use old-world language rather heavily is a handicap but it does not obscure the vigour of his spirited scenes of action' (Thwaite, 176). His work attracted astonished tributes by contemporaries for his acquaintance with such sources as Roger of Wendover, Matthew Paris, Walter of Coventry, and Ralph of Coggeshall, and his style, according to Hannay, seemed 'uniformly excellent … it is singularly clear, masculine, and free from every trace of literary impurity or fashionable affectation'. He did not write down to his young audience and, for example, in 'The True Story of the Man in the Iron Mask', which appeared in *Every Boy's Annual* (1863), the level of writing was adult, fluent, and straightforward. The fact that Everyman's Library published editions of *Cressy and Poictiers* in 1906 and *Runnymede and Lincoln Fair* in 1908, more than forty years after his death, is a sufficient tribute to the value of his work.

Edgar was described by contemporaries as an enthusiastic Conservative. He worked without rest for weeks at a time when writing a book, with tobacco and tea as his main sources of sustenance. It was as a result of such a spell of work that he suffered congestion of the brain and died in his mid-thirties after a brief illness. He had little use for the literary life and was indifferent to advancement in it, while being profoundly tory in his beliefs and attached to feudal traditions which, according to Hannay, he supported 'with fearless and eccentric eloquence'. He died at 30 Thornhill Square, Islington West, London, on 15 April 1864, at the age of thirty-six and was buried on 19 April at Highgate cemetery. GUY ARNOLD

Sources J. Hannay, *Characters and criticisms* (1865) • L. K. Hughes, introduction, in J. G. Edgar, *Runnymede and Lincoln Fair: a story of the great charter* (1908) • E. Rhys, introduction, in J. G. Edgar, *Cressy and Poictiers, or, The story of the Black Prince's page*, ed. [S. O. Beeton] (1906) • *GM*, 3rd ser., 16 (1864) • M. F. Thwaite, *From primer to pleasure in reading*, 2nd edn (1972) • Allibone, *Dict.* • H. Carpenter and M. Prichard, *The Oxford companion to children's literature* (1984) • d. cert.

Archives BL

Edgcumbe, George, first earl of Mount Edgcumbe (1720–1795), naval officer, was born on 3 March 1720 and baptized on 5 May 1721 at St Martin-in-the-Fields, London. He was the third son of Richard *Edgcumbe, first Baron Edgcumbe (*bap.* 1680, *d.* 1758), politician, and Matilda (1698/9–1721), daughter of Sir Henry *Furnese, first baronet, of Waldershare, Kent, and Matilda Vernon. It appears that George (appointed on 14 August 1733), was one of the first eight scholars of the Royal Naval Academy at Portsmouth. However, he received no credit for this when he passed for lieutenant on 4 October 1739, having by then served nearly four years in the *York*, followed by short periods in several other ships. On the following day he was appointed third lieutenant of the *Superbe*, bound for the Mediterranean, where he continued to serve, before moving to the *Nassau* and then being made commander in the bomb-vessel *Terrible* early in 1743. He left her on being appointed captain of the *Kennington* on 19 August 1744, and commanded her in the Mediterranean until 1745, when he was advanced to the *Salisbury* (50 guns) on the home station. In her he remained until the peace of 1748. From 1746 to 1761 Edgcumbe was MP for Fowey in Cornwall, though he rarely attended the house and appears never to have spoken.

Edgcumbe went to the Mediterranean in 1751 as senior officer first in the *Monmouth*, and the following year in the *Deptford* (50 guns). He was still in her and with his small squadron at Minorca, when the French invaded the island on 19 April 1756. He hastily landed the marines and as many of the seamen as could be spared, and sailed the next day for Gibraltar, before the French had taken any measures to block the harbour. At Gibraltar he was joined by Admiral John Byng, by whom he was ordered to move into the *Lancaster* (66 guns). In the battle off Cape Mola on 20 May 1756 the *Lancaster* was one of the ships in the van, under Rear-Admiral Temple West, which did get into action; being unsupported he suffered severely. Edgcumbe made two prizes in 1757. In 1758, still in the *Lancaster*, he was in the fleet under Edward Boscawen at the siege of Louisbourg.

On his return to England, with the dispatches announcing this success, Edgcumbe was appointed to the *Hero* (74 guns), in which he took part in the blockade of Brest during the long summer of 1759, and in the crowning battle of Quiberon Bay (20 November). He continued in the *Hero* attached to the Grand Fleet under Admiral Sir Edward Hawke or Admiral Edward Boscawen, until, on the death of his brother, Richard *Edgcumbe, second Baron Edgcumbe, on 10 May 1761, he succeeded to the title as third baron; and on 18 June he was appointed lord lieutenant of Cornwall. On 16 August that year he married Emma (1729–1807), the only daughter of John Gilbert, archbishop of York; the couple had one child, Richard *Edgcumbe, who later inherited his father's title. George Edgcumbe was promoted rear-admiral on 21 October 1762, was treasurer of the household (1765–6), and from 1766 to 1770 was commander-in-chief at Plymouth. On 24 October 1770 he was advanced to vice-admiral, and in 1773 he again held the chief command at Plymouth, whence in June he went round to Spithead and commanded in the second post when George III reviewed the fleet. He held no further appointment afloat, though on 29 January 1778 he was advanced to the rank of admiral. On 17 February 1781 he was created Viscount Mount Edgcumbe and Valletort, in compensation, it was said, for the damage caused to the woods of the family seat, Mount Edgcumbe, in strengthening the fortifications of Plymouth. From 1771 to 1773 and from 1784 to 1793 he was one of the vice-treasurers of Ireland; and between 1773 and 1782 he was captain of the band of gentlemen pensioners. On 31 August 1789 he was created earl of Mount Edgcumbe. He died on 4 February 1795 at his house in Grosvenor Street, London. He was survived by his wife who died on 26 December 1807. Edgcumbe was evidently regarded as a capable commander and, with some interest in his favour, received continuous employment, though in his later career he was clearly a local grandee. However, his will indicates that he did not regard his financial position as strong, and this possibly explains the number of posts he acquired.

J. K. LAUGHTON, rev. A. W. H. PEARSALL

Sources GEC, *Peerage* • [earl of Bristol], *Augustus Hervey's journal*, ed. D. Erskine (1953) • J. S. Corbett, *England in the Seven Years' War: a study in combined strategy*, 2 vols. (1907) • J. Charnock, ed., *Biographia navalis*, 5 (1797), 293 • R. Beatson, *Naval and military memoirs of Great Britain*, 3 vols. (1790) • 'Memoir of the public services of the late George Edgcumbe', *Naval Chronicle*, 22 (1809), 177–88 • *GM*, 1st ser., 65 (1795), 174 • M. M. Drummond, 'Edgcombe, George', HoP, *Commons, 1754–90* • letters, PRO, ADM 1/383 • muster books, PRO, ADM 36/4207 *Terrible*; 4741 *York* • passing certificate, PRO, ADM 107/3, p. 346 • others, PRO, ADM 6/427 (academy) • PRO, MSS, ADM

Archives BL, letters to Lord and Lady Camelford, Add. MS 69307 • BL, corresp. with duke of Newcastle, Add. MSS 32919–32989; 33072

Likenesses J. Reynolds, oils, 1749, NMM • J. Reynolds, oils, *c.*1755–1756, Exeter City Museum • J. Reynolds, oils, 1758, Mount Edgcumbe, Cornwall • J. Reynolds, oils, exh. 1761, Mount Edgcumbe, Cornwall • S. W. Reynolds, mezzotint, pubd 1820 (after J. Reynolds), BM, NPG • S. W. Reynolds, mezzotint, pubd 1838 (after J. Reynolds), BM, NPG • J. Reynolds, oils, NG Ire. • J. Singleton Copley, group portrait, oils (*The collapse of the earl of Chatham in the House* of Lords, 7 July 1778), Tate collection • portrait, repro. in *Naval Chronicle*

Wealth at death extensive estates; two houses (Mount Edgcumbe and London)

Edgcumbe, Sir Peter (1477–1539). *See under* Edgcumbe, Sir Richard (c.1443–1489).

Edgcumbe [Edgecombe]**, Sir Richard** (c.1443–1489), administrator, was the son of Piers Edgcumbe of Cotehele in Calstock, Cornwall, and Elizabeth, daughter of Richard Holland. In the parliament of 1467–8 he represented the borough of Tavistock, and in the same year was appointed escheator for the counties of Devon and Cornwall. He was a determined Lancastrian, and in 1471 his lands were taken into the hands of the restored king, Edward IV, but though he was pardoned on 8 April 1472, he was not won over by the king's leniency. Put on a number of commissions for Cornwall in 1473–4, and appointed a justice of the peace for the county in 1474–5, he nevertheless joined in the rebellion against Richard III of 1483. After its suppression a commission was appointed to try him for treason, but he escaped to Brittany and joined Henry Tudor; he was pardoned again on 26 January 1484.

Edgcumbe landed with Henry Tudor in 1485, served at Bosworth, was knighted after the battle, and was soon rewarded for his loyalty to the Lancastrian cause. He was appointed controller of the royal household, a knight of the body, and, on 20 September 1485, a chamberlain of the exchequer for life, but this appointment appears to have been superseded nine days later by that of Sir Richard Guildford. Edgcumbe nevertheless became a member of the royal council, escheator and feodary of the duchy of Cornwall, constable of Launceston Castle, a justice of the peace for Cornwall again, and steward of the earldom of March. He was further rewarded with a grant of the lands of John, Lord Zouche, which included Totnes Castle, and those of Sir Henry Trenowth and Francis, Lord Lovell, some seven manors in all, as well as other offices. Before the end of 1485, as one of the witnesses to the inquiry that led to the dispensation for the king's marriage to Elizabeth of York, Edgcumbe stated that he was then forty-two years of age. He himself married Jane, daughter of Thomas Tremayne of Collacombe Barton in Lamerton, Devon.

In 1485 Edgcumbe was also a commissioner to receive the allegiance of people from parts of Devon, and in 1487 he was sheriff of the county. On 16 June of that year he came to the king's support at the battle of Stoke, and in November he was sent on a diplomatic mission to Scotland. In 1488 Henry VII sent him to Ireland to establish royal authority there. Paid £300 for his expenses, he landed at Kinsale with a small force of perhaps 500 men, with authority to receive oaths of allegiance, grant pardons and give safe conducts. A detailed account of this expedition, possibly written by Edgcumbe himself, survives in the British Library (BL, Cotton MS Titus B.xi, fols. 332–77; calendared in *Collins Peerage*, 5.309–15). His final service to Henry VII was an embassy to the duchess of Brittany in the following year, but he did not complete this

mission, for he died on 8 September 1489 at Morlaix, and was buried in the Dominican church there. His will, mainly concerned with the payment of his debts, was dated at Penryn on 14 June 1489, presumably before he embarked, and proved on 29 April 1492.

Sir Peter Edgcumbe (1477–1539), son and heir of Sir Richard and his wife, Jane, was a student of Lincoln's Inn, London, in 1488, and aged only twelve at his father's death in 1489. As well as Cotehele, he inherited the castle, manor, and borough of Totnes, along with the manors of Bodrigan, Tregrehan, and Tremodret in Cornwall, and holdings in Huish, Loddiswell, and North Molton in Devon. On 24 February 1497 he had licence to enter his father's lands without proving his age. He was already a squire of the king's body, holding his father's offices of escheator and feodary of the duchy of Cornwall and constable of Launceston Castle. Knighted in 1494, he was sheriff of Devon four times between 1494 and 1522, and of Cornwall four times between 1498 and 1534; he was knight of the shire for Cornwall in 1515 and 1529. In 1513 he took part in the battle of the Spurs and was present at the Field of Cloth of Gold in 1520. By his marriage, to Jane, daughter and heir of James Derneford, and widow of Charles Dynham of Nutwell, Devon, he greatly enlarged his holdings, securing the manors of West Stonehouse in Devon and Rame in Cornwall. There were three sons and three daughters of this marriage. Jane died before 1525, by when Edgcumbe had made a second marriage, to Catherine, daughter of Sir John St John of Bletsoe and widow of Sir Gruffudd ap Rhys of Carmarthen. He died on 14 August 1539, and his will, dated 3 March 1530, was proved on 15 September 1539. J. L. KIRBY

Sources Chancery records • W. Campbell, ed., *Materials for a history of the reign of Henry VII*, 2 vols., Rolls Series, 60 (1873–7) • *LP Henry VIII*, vols. 1–14 • BL, Cotton MS Titus B.xi, fols. 332–77 • Rymer, *Foedera*, 2nd edn, 2.348, 355–7 • S. B. Chrimes, *Henry VII* (1972), 259–60 • *CEPR letters*, 14.20 • *Collins peerage of England: genealogical, biographical and historical*, ed. E. Brydges, 9 vols. (1812), vol. 5, pp. 306–21 • J. M. Currin, 'Henry VII and the treaty of Redon', *History*, new ser., 81 (1996), 343–58 • R. Polwhele, *The history of Cornwall*, 7 vols. (1803–8); repr. with additions (1816), vol. 4, pp. 47, 49 • *Report of the Deputy Keeper of the Public Records*, 9 (1848), appx 2, esp. 110 • T. Westcote, *A view of Devonshire in MDCXXX, with a pedigree of most of its gentry*, ed. G. Oliver and P. Jones (1845), 494 • R. Carew, *The survey of Cornwall* (1602), pt 2, p. 114 • *HoP, Commons* • J. D. Mackie, *The earlier Tudors, 1485–1558* (1952) • *CIPM, Henry VII*, 1, no. 536 • A. Hughes, *List of sheriffs for England and Wales: from the earliest times to AD 1831*, PRO (1898); repr. (New York, 1963), 9 • *List of escheators*, list and index soc., no. 72 • will, PRO, PROB 11/9, sig. 11

Archives BL, Cotton MS Titus B.xi, fols. 332–77

Edgcumbe, Sir Richard (1499–1562), landowner and member of parliament, was the eldest son of Sir Peter *Edgcumbe (1477–1539) [see under Edgcumbe, Sir Richard] of Cotehele, Cornwall, and his first wife, Jane (d. before 1525), daughter and heir of James Derneford of Stonehouse and Ramm, Devon, and widow of Charles Dynham of Nutwell, Devon. According to his grandson, Richard *Carew, who wrote an account of Edgcumbe entitled *A Friendly Remembrance of Sir Richard Edgcomb*, he 'spent some part of his youth at Oxford' (Carew, 165–6). About 1516 he married Elizabeth, daughter of Sir John Arundell of Lanherne, Cornwall, but they had no children. A year later, Edgcumbe entered Lincoln's Inn with his brother, John. On his admission he was excused attendance for six vacations. His first wife having died, in 1535 he married Elizabeth, daughter of John Tregian of Golden, Cornwall, with whom he had four sons and four daughters. On his father's death in 1539, his friend and patron John, Lord Russell, asked Cromwell for prompt livery of his inheritance, but it was not obtained until after Cromwell's execution nearly a year later.

Edgcumbe was elected MP for Cornwall in 1542, possibly with the help of Arundell, and was knighted with other shire members at the opening of parliament on 16 January. He sat again in 1547, but was allowed home during the fourth session, on 2 March 1552, because someone had died at his lodgings, raising fears of infection. As one of the principal landowners in Devon, Edgcumbe played an important part in local affairs: he was JP for Devon and Cornwall from 1532 until his death; steward of Plymouth from about 1539 until his death; and sheriff of Devon in 1543–4. In the 1540s he was involved in the suppression of piracy and the erection of coastal forts, especially near Plymouth. In 1548 he raised men to restore order at Helston, Cornwall, following the very nasty riot there in which William Body was killed. Edgcumbe's involvement so far from home may seem surprising, but it has been argued that:

> The gentry had no hold over the far west and called on Edgecombe, as one of the principal Devon gentry, to come to their aid. He collected men from the parishes in the east of the county on his way. (Fletcher, 41)

It is therefore strange that Edgcumbe played no part in suppressing the western rebellion in the following year. He may have been constrained by social sympathies. It has been pointed out that 'the rebellion was (thus) aimed principally against gentlemen while also being led mainly by gentlemen' (Speight, 10). In this Edgcumbe could have been influenced by Sir John Arundell of Lanherne, who was also a religious conservative. They had several links: Arundell's brother, Thomas, had been admitted to Lincoln's Inn on the same day, 2 February 1517, as Edgcumbe and his brother; furthermore Edgcumbe had married Arundell's daughter, while Arundell married Edgcumbe's sister. Arundell's cousin, Humphrey Arundell, was a leader of the first uprising at Bodmin, which was only about 12 miles from Arundell's property and sphere of influence at St Mawgan in Pyder. Arundell himself later ignored a request from Russell to raise a force and was eventually sent to the Tower, because he was suspected of complicity in the rising. His brother, Thomas, was executed in 1552 for plotting to support the duke of Somerset.

Helen Speight has suggested that the rebellion was not dealt with promptly by the gentry because there was a gap in the chain of command and communication, and because Somerset was preoccupied with Scotland. Furthermore, Lord Russell, who had become the dominant magnate in the south-west in the 1530s, was effectively an absentee landlord who regarded the court as his natural milieu and failed to establish a local affinity through his extensive patronage. On top of that, the gentry were deeply divided over agrarian, fiscal, and particularly religious, issues and there was bitter rivalry between old established families, like the Edgcumbes, and newcomers, like the Grenvilles and Godolphins, particularly over commissions of the peace.

For whatever reason, Edgcumbe played only a small part in national affairs thereafter. He never sat for parliament again. He was sheriff of Devon in 1552–3 and Cornwall in 1555–6. In January 1554 he was instructed to oppose Sir Peter Carew's rising, and in July that year he entertained the admirals of the fleet escorting Philip of Spain to Southampton at the house he had just built, Mount Edgcumbe, formerly Stonehouse, on the Tamar estuary. On the fall of Calais in 1558 he mustered the Cornish militia for its relief. In 1559, following the accession of Elizabeth, he was one of the commissioners who conducted the royal visitation of the diocese of Exeter.

Richard Carew said that Edgcumbe was popularly known as 'the good old man of the castle', valued for his generosity to friends and servants (Carew, 165–6). His impartiality as a justice and his Christian observance in doing good for evil made him one of the most respected figures in the south-west. He earned a reputation as a poet, though none of the poems seems to have survived. He was also was a skilled letter writer and a deeply religious man who kept a chaplain in his house. At an unknown date he married again; his third wife was Winifred, daughter of Sir William Essex of Lambourn, Berkshire; they had no children. She was not mentioned when he made his will in 1560, though he provided for his servants and his children. A rich man, he left £400 to his eldest son, Peter, with which to sue out his livery, and made him his executor. Edgcumbe died on 1 February 1562, probably at Mount Edgcumbe, and was buried in Maker church, where a plain stone slab long marked his grave.

PATRICIA HYDE

Sources HoP, Commons, 1509–58, 2.83–4 · Collins peerage of England: genealogical, biographical and historical, ed. E. Brydges, 9 vols. (1812), vol. 5, pp. 320–28 · J. L. Vivian and H. H. Drake, eds., The visitation of the county of Cornwall in the year 1620, Harleian Society, 9 (1874), 4, 63–5, 141–2 · W. H. Edgcumbe, Records of the Edgcumbe family (1888) · A. Fletcher, Tudor rebellions, 3rd edn (1983) · J. G. Nichols, ed., The chronicle of Queen Jane, and of two years of Queen Mary, CS, old ser., 48 (1850) · will, PRO, PROB 11/45, sig. 12 · APC, 1542–47; 1556–58 · R. Carew, The survey of Cornwall (1602); facs. edn (1969) · CPR, 1553 · A. L. Rowse, Tudor Cornwall: portrait of a society, new edn (1969) · LP Henry VIII, vols. 5–21 · W. P. Baildon, ed., The records of the Honorable Society of Lincoln's Inn: the black books, 1 (1897), 182 · CSP dom., 1547–80 · H. Speight, 'Local government and the south-western rebellion of 1549', Southern History, 18 (1996), 1–23
Wealth at death considerable: will, PRO, PROB 11/45, sig. 12

Edgcumbe, Richard, first Baron Edgcumbe (*bap.* 1680, *d.* 1758), politician, was born at Mount Edgcumbe in Cornwall, near Plymouth, and baptized on 23 April 1680. He was the third but only surviving son of Sir Richard

Edgcumbe, MP for Cornwall, and Lady Anne Montagu (*b*. 1653), the daughter of the first earl of Sandwich. He entered Trinity College, Cambridge, on 25 May 1697, where he wrote some elegant Latin verses on the occasion of William III's return to England; he received an MA in 1698. In June 1701 he became MP for Cornwall; in December 1701 he was returned for St Germans and in 1702 for Plympton Erle, which he represented until 1734. On 12 March 1715 he married Matilda (*d*. 1721), the daughter of Sir Henry Furnese, bt, MP, of Waldershore, Kent, and his wife, Matilda, the daughter of Sir Thomas Vernon.

On 22 June 1716 Edgcumbe was made a lord of the Treasury. He followed his 'most intimate friend' Robert Walpole into opposition in 1717 and was rewarded for his loyalty by regaining his place on the Treasury board on 11 June 1720. On 9 March the following year his wife died, aged twenty-two. On 3 April 1724, with Hugh Boscawen, Viscount Falmouth, Edgcumbe accepted the offices of vice-treasurer, receiver-general, treasurer of war, and paymaster-general of his majesty's revenues in Ireland, worth £3000 a year. He remained a loyal supporter of Walpole, and was used by Carteret as a go-between in his attempt to improve relations with the prime minister in 1725. During the 1727 election campaign he managed the Cornish boroughs for the government, and he became chief government manager in Cornwall just before the 1734 election, when he was returned as MP for Lostwithiel. His success in 1734 was not matched in 1741. At this election the Walpole administration, partly as a result of Edgcumbe's lack of political judgement, suffered the unprecedented loss of the Cornish boroughs. Edgcumbe was returned to represent Plympton Erle, but on 20 April 1742, dismissed from his office by William Pulteney, he was made Baron Edgcumbe of Mount Edgcumbe.

In December 1743 Edgcumbe was appointed chancellor of the duchy of Lancaster and the following January was made lord lieutenant of Cornwall and a member of the privy council on the instructions of George II. According to Lord Hervey's memoirs, Edgcumbe's popularity with the king was because he was even shorter than the diminutive monarch. On the outbreak of the Jacobite rising of 1745 Edgcumbe was one of the twelve noblemen who were commissioned to raise an infantry regiment, and he was promoted from colonel to major-general in February 1755. On 24 January 1758, having resigned the office of chancellor of the duchy of Lancaster, he was appointed warden of the king's forests beyond Trent. Despite his close political relationship with Walpole, he was judged by Horace Walpole to be 'one of the honestest and steadiest men in the world'. He died on 22 November 1758, and was succeeded by his eldest son, Richard *Edgcumbe.

L. C. SANDERS, *rev.* PHILIP CARTER

Sources E. Cruickshanks, 'Edgcumbe, Richard', HoP, *Commons* · GEC, *Peerage*, new edn, vol. 2 · *GM*, 1st ser., 28 (1758), 557 · R. Ollard, *Cromwell's earl: a life of Edward Mountagu, 1st earl of Sandwich* (1994) · Venn, *Alum. Cant.*

Archives BL, corresp. with duke of Newcastle, Add. MSS 32697–32869

Likenesses S. W. Reynolds, mezzotint, pubd 1825 (after J. Reynolds), BM

Edgcumbe, Richard, second Baron Edgcumbe (1716–1761), politician, second son of Richard *Edgcumbe, the first baron (*bap*. 1680, *d*. 1758), and his wife, Matilda, and brother of George *Edgcumbe, first earl of Mount Edgcumbe, was born on 2 August 1716 and baptized at St Martin-in-the-Fields, London, ten days later. Educated at Eton College between 1725 and 1732, he then entered the army, and ultimately rose to the rank of major-general, but saw little service. He represented the borough of Plympton from 1742 to 1747, of Lostwithiel from November 1747 to 1754, and of Penryn from 1754 to 1758. In 1754 he was appointed lord of trade and in December 1755 he was appointed a lord of the Admiralty, but resigned his seat on that board in November 1756 on being constituted comptroller of his majesty's household, when he was also sworn of the privy council. (His accounts for 1759–60 are in the British Library, Add. MS 29266.) In 1758 he succeeded as second baron on the death of his father, and on 23 February 1759 he was constituted lord lieutenant and *custos rotulorum* of the county of Cornwall. With his mistress, Mrs Ann Franks, or Day, he had four children, and he later made Horace Walpole her trustee. The relationship was the subject of a dull satire entitled *An Epistle from the Hon. R[ichard] E[dgcumbe] to his Dear Nanny [Day]*, said to be by Charles Jones, and published in 1752 by R. Sim, near St Paul's. Mrs Day subsequently became Lady Fenouilhet, and her portrait by Reynolds, painted in 1760, was in the possession of Lord Northbrook. Edgcumbe took another mistress, whose identity is unknown other than by her nickname, the Kitten, but the liaison does not appear to have brought him much happiness.

Dick Edgcumbe, as he was invariably known, was a close friend of Horace Walpole, George Selwyn, and Gilly Williams, and is frequently mentioned in Horace Walpole's letters. An inveterate gambler, Edgcumbe regularly lost 20 guineas a day at White's Club. His financial affairs became so disastrous that Henry Pelham (a fellow member of White's) arranged for him to receive a secret service pension of £500 a year. In 1746 Colonel Charles Russell wrote of Edgcumbe and his friends: 'I never sup with them because they keep bad hours' (GEC, *Peerage*).

Of his poetry all that remain are two sets of verses, 'The Fable of the Ass, Nightingale, and Kid', and an 'Ode to Health', preserved in *The New Foundling Hospital for Wit* (6, 1786, 107–10). They are of little merit, though they gained Edgcumbe a notice in Walpole's *Catalogue of the Royal and Noble Authors* (T. Park's edition, 1806, 4.242–3). He was also an accomplished draughtsman, and designed a clever coat of arms for the 'Old and Young Club' at Arthur's, which was purchased at the sale at Strawberry Hill by Arthur's Clubhouse; it has since disappeared. It was engraved by Grignon. Edgcumbe also painted a portrait of the convict Mary Squires. He was among the first to recognize the talent of Joshua Reynolds, who painted for Horace Walpole a group of Selwyn, Edgcumbe, and Williams, entitled *Conversation*, which was purchased at the Strawberry Hill sale by Henry Labouchere, Lord Taunton. Edgcumbe's services to art are also recognized in Müntz's dedication to him of his treatise 'Encaustic, or, Count Caylus's method of painting in the manner of the ancients'. Edgcumbe suffered from dropsy and died on 10 May 1761; he was buried at Maker, Cornwall; his family seat had been at Mount Edgcumbe, Cornwall. His brother George succeeded to the title.

L. C. SANDERS, rev. MICHAEL BEVAN

Sources GEC, *Peerage* · HoP, *Commons, 1715–54* · GM, 1st ser., 31 (1761), 237 · Walpole, *Corr.*, vol. 9
Archives BL, corresp. with Lord Holland, Add. MS 51403 · BL, corresp. with duke of Newcastle, Add. MSS 32885–32918 *passim*
Likenesses J. Reynolds, oils, *c*.1748, Mount Edgcumbe, Cornwall · J. Reynolds, group portrait, oils, 1759–61 (*A conversation piece*), City Museum and Art Gallery, Bristol; *see illus. in* Williams, George James (1719–1805) · J. Reynolds, oils, exh. 1760, Mount Edgcumbe, Cornwall · W. Reynolds, mezzotint, pubd 1823 (after J. Reynolds), BM

Edgcumbe, Richard, second earl of Mount Edgcumbe (1764–1839), writer on opera, was born on 13 September 1764, the only child of George *Edgcumbe, first earl of Mount Edgcumbe (1720–1795), naval officer, and his wife, Emma (1729–1807), the only child of John *Gilbert, archbishop of York. He matriculated at Christ Church, Oxford, in 1781, and was awarded a DCL in 1793. On 21 February 1789 he married Lady Sophia (1768–1806), the third daughter of John *Hobart, second earl of Buckinghamshire. They had three sons and two daughters. As Viscount Valletort Edgcumbe was MP for Fowey as a tory from 1786 to 1795, when he succeeded to the earldom. He also followed his father in the office of lord lieutenant of Cornwall. In March 1808 he was appointed captain of the band of gentlemen pensioners, and was sworn of the privy council. He held the captaincy until 1812.

Edgcumbe was an enthusiastic amateur actor and musician, and wrote an opera, *Zenobia*, which had one performance, on 22 May 1800 at the King's Theatre, Haymarket. One of the male parts was written for a soprano, and Mme Banti sang in this performance. He was also the author of *Musical reminiscences of an old amateur; chiefly respecting the Italian opera in England … from 1793 to 1823*. Originally written for private circulation, it was published anonymously in 1825, and ran to two more editions under his own name. The final edition, which appeared in 1834, included a description of the Handel festival at Westminster Abbey. In this Edgcumbe comments on the decline in the standard of singing during the previous fifty years. Mount Edgcumbe died on 26 September 1839 in Richmond, Surrey, and was buried in Petersham churchyard. He was succeeded by his second son, Ernest Augustus, as his eldest son had died unmarried in 1818.

ANNE PIMLOTT BAKER

Sources W. C. Smith, *The Italian opera and contemporary ballet in London* (1955) · Burke, *Peerage* · Foster, *Alum. Oxon.* · GEC, *Peerage* · GM, 2nd ser., 12 (1839), 540
Archives Cornwall RO, family MSS
Likenesses J. Zoffany, group portrait, oils, 1772–8 (*The tribuna of the Uffizi*), Royal Collection · J. Reynolds, oils, exh. RA 1774, Mount Edgcumbe, Cornwall · J. Jones, group portrait, mezzotint, pubd 1788 (as Young Clackitt in *The guardian*; after *Marlborough theatricals* by J. Roberts), BM, NPG · S. W. Reynolds, engraving (after J. Reynolds), repro. in S. W. Reynolds, *Engravings*, vol. 2, pl. 55

Edge, Sir John (1841–1926), judge in India, was born on 28 July 1841 at Clonbrock, Queen's county, Ireland, the only child of Benjamin Booker Edge JP (1810–1887), of Clonbrock, and his wife, Esther Anne (*d*. 1879), only child of Thomas Allen, of the Park, co. Wicklow. The family, which claimed descent from Edwin, a Saxon thane, of the manor of Edge, Malpas, Cheshire, had settled in Ireland in Stuart times. Like his father before him, Benjamin Edge possessed qualifications as a mining engineer, unusual among the Irish gentry then, and worked coalmines in Queen's county and elsewhere.

John Edge was educated by a private tutor, and from March 1858 at Trinity College, Dublin (BA and LLB, 1861), where he was a silver medallist (ethics, logics, and metaphysics). He was called to the Irish bar by the King's Inns, Dublin, in 1864, and to the English bar by the Middle Temple in 1866, and went on the northern and north-eastern circuits. On 18 September 1867 Edge married Laura, youngest daughter of Thomas Loughborough, solicitor, of Selwood Lodge, Tulse Hill, Surrey; they had one son and four daughters.

In 1886 Edge took silk, and was appointed chief justice of the high court of judicature for the North-Western Provinces of India at Allahabad, being knighted on appointment. As chief justice it was Edge's good fortune to preside over an exceptionally strong court, several of his colleagues being men of marked ability. But he quickly showed himself worthy to be their leader. An example of his quality was the judgment in *Bhagwansingh* v. *Bhagwansingh* (1895), in which he held that the adoption of certain near relatives is not invalid in Hindu law. In the appeal from this decision which came before the privy council in 1898, Lord Hobhouse, although differing from his conclusions, complimented Edge on the 'elaborate fullness' of his judgment, and it remained worthy of study. In fact, although the law was subsequently settled in the opposite sense, the general opinion of scholars inclined to Edge's view, and it was found necessary to engraft on the prohibition laid down by Lord Hobhouse a large body of customary exceptions.

In addition to his judicial work Edge found scope for his administrative ability. On his initiative the rules and orders of the high court were codified. From 1887 to 1893 he was the first vice-chancellor of the new University of Allahabad and did much to guide it. His services were recognized by an honorary doctorate in laws. In 1896 he was chairman of the famine relief committee in the great famine that year.

Retiring from the chief justiceship in 1898, Edge was appointed in January 1899 judicial member of the Council of India, being elected at the same time to the bench of the Middle Temple, where he subsequently served as treasurer (1919). His duties on the Council of India were not onerous, and he was a member of the royal commission on the war in South Africa (1902) and served on the committee of inquiry into the case of Adolph Beck (1905), who had been convicted for an offence of which he was

Sir John Edge (1841–1926), by Walter Stoneman, 1924

subsequently proved not guilty. The report of this committee helped to secure the establishment in 1907 of the court of criminal appeal.

Edge retired from the Council of India in 1908, and in January 1909 was sworn of the privy council and appointed a member of the judicial committee. From 1916 until his retirement in May 1926, two months before his eighty-fifth birthday, he was constant in the hearing of Indian appeals. He maintained his reputation for care and thoroughness, and the tribute to him by the lord chancellor Viscount Cave in moving the second reading of the Judicial Committee Bill in 1923 was well deserved. In the case of *Arumilli* v. *Subharayadu* (1921), though loyally accepting the decision in *Bhagwansingh* v. *Bhagwansingh*, Edge had the satisfaction of pointing out limitations to the principles laid down by Lord Hobhouse. His judgments remained to the last models of clear and cogent reasoning; but towards the end of his career his knowledge of the lacunae in the law occasionally tempted him into elaborate *obiter dicta* intended to settle doubtful points which did not really arise in the case before him.

Of quiet and unassuming presence, Edge was a man of wide interests. When chief justice of Allahabad he was notably hospitable. He was proficient with rod, rifle, and gun, and was a keen alpinist. In freemasonry he held high rank. He was an enthusiastic volunteer in the Inns of Court Rifles during his early days at the bar and later in India, where (as lieutenant-colonel) he commanded a battalion of the Allahabad rifle volunteers and was honorary aide-de-camp to the viceroy. For many years his hobby was

genealogy; he bequeathed four stout volumes on his own family to the William Salt Library at Stafford. He survived his retirement barely two months, dying suddenly at his house, 123 Oakwood Court, Kensington, London, on 30 July 1926.   S. V. FitzGerald, *rev.* Roger T. Stearn

Sources The Times (2 Aug 1926) · *Indian Law Reports, Allahabad series* (1886–98) · *Law Reports: Indian appeals*, 39–53 (1912–26) · Burke, *Gen. GB* (1908) · private information (1937) · *WWW* · Burke, *Peerage* (1894) · Burke, *Peerage* (1924) · Walford, *County families* (1919) · *Debrett's Peerage* (1924) · Burke, *Gen. Ire.* (1904) · Burke, *Gen. Ire.* (1912) · Burtchaell & Sadleir, *Alum. Dubl.*, 2nd edn · *CGPLA Eng. & Wales* (1926)

Archives BL, genealogical notes on the Edge family, Add. MS 39563 · BL OIOC, minute on council reform in India, MS Eur. D 573 · Chetham's Library, Manchester, genealogical notes, MUN A.7.22–23 | Bodl. Oxf., corresp. with Lord Kimberley, MSS Eng. a 2013–2014, 62047–62049, c 3933–4514, d 2439–2492, e 2790–2797

Likenesses W. Stoneman, photograph, 1924, NPG [*see illus.*]

Wealth at death £1006 15s. 6d.: probate, 7 Oct 1926, *CGPLA Eng. & Wales*

Edge, Selwyn Francis (1868–1940), motor car entrepreneur and racing driver, was born in Concord, Sydney, New South Wales, on 29 March 1868, the son of Alexander Ernest Edge and his wife, Annie Charlotte Sharp. In 1871 he was taken to Britain, where he attended Belvedere House College, Upper Norwood, London. He was originally intended for a career in the army but his success as a racing cyclist—he won the Westerham Hill climb on a safety bicycle at the age of nineteen—helped to launch his career in the cycle and, later, the motor car trades. He was employed by the Rudge Cycle Company and the New Howe Company (cycle makers), the latter as general manager, before moving to the Dunlop Tyre Company. In 1900 Edge formed the British Motor Traction Company, a reconstruction of Harry J. Lawson's British Motor Syndicate (1895), which had sought to control the industry through its ownership of motor vehicle patents. This attempt to continue the Lawson monopoly scheme failed when challenged at law in 1901 by Charles Friswell of the Automobile Mutual Protection Association.

Edge was more successful in his relationship with Montague Napier, whom he met when they were both members of the Bath Road (cycle) club. By 1899 Napier was attempting to revive the fortunes of the engineering business of D. Napier & Son and it was Edge who persuaded him to diversify into motor car manufacture. Edge was a businessman rather than an engineer, though he did acquire a technical knowledge of motor vehicles through his association with Lawson. This helped him to contribute to the success of Napier cars, which for a time dominated the luxury market, but the publicity value of his achievements on the motor racetrack was perhaps of greater significance. Edge marketed Napier cars, firstly through the Motor Vehicle Company and then through S. F. Edge (1907) Ltd. After selling his majority holding in the latter to Napiers in 1912, on condition that he stayed out of the motor trade for seven years, Edge concentrated upon his agricultural interests in Sussex, where he bred pedigree pigs. He became known for his pioneering application of mechanical traction to farming, and for a short

Selwyn Francis Edge (1868–1940), by London Stereoscopic Co.

period during the First World War served as controller of the agricultural machinery department at the Ministry of Munitions. He returned to the motor industry in 1921 with the A. C. (Acedes) car but the venture was not a success and the company finally collapsed in 1929.

Edge was perhaps best-known among motoring enthusiasts for his exploits on the racetrack. His first race, on a De Dion tricycle, the Paris–Bordeaux event of 1899, ended in failure when he was forced to retire. In 1901 Edge attempted to gain European recognition driving a 50 hp vehicle of more than 17 litres' capacity, but was unsuccessful in both the Paris–Bordeaux and Paris–Berlin events. However, in the following year he drove a smaller-engined Napier car to victory in the Gordon Bennett cup, a first for Britain, and a source of great interest within the motoring community as a whole. He was unable to repeat his success in the 1903 race, held in Ireland, finishing last in his 80 hp Napier. He gave technical advice for the construction of Brooklands, the world's first purpose-built racing circuit, and provided the initial entertainment when it was opened in 1907 by driving for 1581 miles over twenty-four hours at an average speed of 65.9 m.p.h. During the following two seasons Napier cars achieved considerable success at Brooklands, but thereafter Edge effectively withdrew from racing. He did, however, return to Brooklands in 1922 to break his earlier 24-hour record driving a 30/40 hp 6-cylinder Spyker. He also enjoyed some success in motor boat racing.

Edge was one of the first members of the Royal Automobile Club and was actively involved in its affairs over many years. However, his relationship with club officials was somewhat ambivalent. To begin with, he was an ardent critic of the organization's exclusive membership policy, though conversely in 1915 he was equally opposed to a reduction in the entrance and subscription fees designed to allow the club to expand its membership. He also helped to found the Automobile Association in 1905, which was set up with the aim of defeating speed traps. He wrote *My Motoring Reminiscences*, which was published in 1934.

Edge was said to be able, confident, and self-centred, with handsome features and a prominent tumescent moustache. His first marriage, in 1892, was to Eleanor Rose, daughter of John Sharp, warehouseman, of Forest Hill. After her death he married in 1917 Myra Caroline, daughter of John Martin, 'gentleman', with whom he had two daughters. Edge died at the Princess Alice Hospital, Eastbourne, on 12 February 1940. His wife survived him.

DAVID THOMS

Sources P. Brendon, *The motoring century: the story of the Royal Automobile Club* (1997) · *DNB* · W. J. Reader, 'Edge, Selwyn Francis', *DBB* · K. Richardson and C. N. O'Gallagher, *The British motor industry, 1896–1939* (1977) · G. N. Georgano, ed., *The encyclopaedia of motor sport* (1971) · S. F. Edge, *My motoring reminiscences* (1934) · C. H. Wilson and W. Reader, *Men and machines: a history of D. Napier and Son, Engineers, Ltd, 1808–1958* (1958) · *CGPLA Eng. & Wales* (1940)
Archives Veteran Car Club of Great Britain, Ashwell, Hertfordshire, albums of cuttings, photographs, etc. | British Motor Industry Heritage Trust, Gaydon, Warwickshire, letters to F. R. Simms · LUL, F. R. Simms MSS · Veteran Car Club of Great Britain, Ashwell, Hertfordshire, letters to F. R. Simms
Likenesses London Stereoscopic Co., photograph, NPG [*see illus.*] · photograph, repro. in Brendon, *Motoring century*, 27 · photographs, repro. in Edge, *My motoring reminiscences*
Wealth at death £398 17s. 7d.: probate, 23 May 1940, *CGPLA Eng. & Wales*

Edgell, Beatrice (1871–1948), psychologist, was born on 26 October 1871 in Church Street, Tewkesbury, Gloucestershire, the youngest daughter of Edward Higginson Edgell, a bank manager, and his wife, Sarah Ann, *née* Buckle. She attended Notting Hill High School for Girls, London, and the University College of Wales, Aberystwyth, obtaining in 1894 a BA with second-class honours in mental and moral science awarded by the University of London. She earned a BA with first-class honours from London in 1897, followed by a BA (first-class honours), and then an MA, from the University of Wales during the following two years. She also obtained a PhD from Würzburg, in 1901, and a DLitt in 1924 from the University of Wales. In 1897 Edgell was appointed lecturer in philosophy and head of the department of mental and moral science (renamed the department of philosophy and psychology in 1906) at Bedford College for Women in the University of London, holding the latter post until her retirement in 1933. She became reader in psychology in 1913, professor of psychology in 1927 (attracting much newspaper attention as the first female holder of a chair in psychology), and, on her retirement, emeritus professor of psychology. Edgell held many other appointments in the college and the University of London, including a time as a member of senate (1906–11) and external examiner in psychology (1913–19).

The turn of the century was a period of intellectual discovery for Edgell, since the academic year 1900–01 saw her in Oswald Külpe's psychological laboratory at Würzburg working on experimental studies of the 'higher mental functions'. That she retained an interest in this area for all her professional life is indicated by her well received *Theories of Memory* (1924) and her presidential address to the Aristotelian Society in 1930 on the topic of 'Images'. Indeed, her cross-disciplinary interests in experimental psychology and philosophy meant that she was equally at home as president from 1929 to 1932 of the British Psychological Society (of which she had been an active member almost from its inception), as she was as president of the Mind Association in 1927, and (in 1932) of section J (psychology) of the British Association for the Advancement of Science. She was also the first female president of each of these four organizations.

It is, however, as a teacher and standard-bearer for psychology, not least within her college and the University of London, that Edgell is best remembered. An anecdote from 1933 records the response to the enquiry, 'What did Miss X get?' as an indignant 'Get? Why a first, of course. Miss Edgell's students always do.' She was by all accounts a conscientious and painstaking teacher who cared deeply about the education, welfare, and future careers of her students. Colleagues and former students alike spoke of her personal qualities, such as her kindness and generosity, her diplomatic skills, and sense of humour, as well as paying tribute to her considerable intellectual achievements. Her practical approach to teaching led to two successful textbooks. *Mental Life* (1926) was especially designed for social science students at Bedford College, while *Ethical Problems* (1929) was meant primarily for nurses and social workers—professions in which she took a special interest. Edgell was also successful in building up the laboratory and lecturing facilities serving psychology within Bedford College, although it was not until the college moved to its spacious Regent's Park site in 1913 that her more ambitious teaching and research plans were realized.

After her retirement, Edgell worked in a child guidance clinic and acted as a teacher and examiner in psychology for the nursing profession. Her brief history of the British Psychological Society (1947) is notable as much for its personal and candid reminiscences of the early years of the society as it is for the quality of its easy scholarship; it is perhaps typical that she made no mention of her own part in shaping the society during this period. Edgell died from cancer on 10 August 1948 in the Ash Priors Nursing Home, Pittville Circus, Cheltenham, Gloucestershire. Her funeral service was held in Tewkesbury Abbey on 13 August 1948, after which she was cremated and her ashes buried. She was unmarried.   P. LOVIE and A. D. LOVIE

Sources private information (2004) · E. R. Valentine, *Psychology at Bedford College, London, 1849–1985* (1997) · E. R. Valentine, 'Beatrice Edgell: an appreciation', *British Journal of Psychology*, 92 (2001), 23–36 · *British Journal of Psychology*, 39 (1948–9), 120–22 · *The Times* (12–13 Aug 1948) · WWW · b. cert. · d. cert. · *CGPLA Eng. & Wales* (1948)

Likenesses photograph, 1933, Bedford College, London · photograph, 1933, repro. in *British Journal of Psychology*, 39, facing p. 121
Wealth at death £26,441 16s. 6d.: probate, 18 Nov 1948, *CGPLA Eng. & Wales*

Edgeworth, Francis Ysidro (1845–1926), economist and statistician, was born on 8 February 1845 at Edgeworthstown in co. Longford, the fifth and last son of Francis Beaufort Edgeworth (1809–1846), and his wife, Rosa Florentina (1815–1864), daughter of General Antonio Eroles, an exile from the absolutist Spain of Ferdinand VII. Reflecting this Spanish inheritance, an elder brother was baptized Antonio Eroles and Edgeworth himself Ysidro Francis, a form that he used sometimes even as an adult. Alfred Marshall, considering the amalgam of friendliness and reserve in Edgeworth's character, used to say that 'Francis is a charming fellow, but you must be careful with Ysidro' (Keynes, 152).

The educationist Richard Lovell *Edgeworth (1744–1817) was Francis Ysidro Edgeworth's grandfather, the novelist Maria Edgeworth (1768–1849) his aunt—remembered by him as a 'very plain old lady with a delightful face' (Butler and Butler, 244)—and the poet Thomas Lovell Beddoes (1803–1849) his cousin. R. L. Edgeworth's eldest child Richard ran away to sea and then to South Carolina, where he had three sons and died, disinherited, long before his father. Death and infertility so drastically reduced the number of the other male heirs that when Antonio died in 1911 his brother Francis Ysidro, fifth son of a sixth son and the youngest grandson, inherited the Edgeworthstown estate. Francis Ysidro's death from pneumonia in Oxford on 13 February 1926 thus brought to an end (at least outside America) the male line begun so energetically by his grandfather, whose twenty-two children by four wives over forty-eight years included seven sons who survived infancy.

Edgeworth's father had an unremarkable career, its last years spent administering the estate. Edgeworth himself, only twenty months old when his father died, was brought up at home and educated there by tutors. He entered Trinity College, Dublin, in 1862 and read classics with considerable success, but without taking a degree transferred to Oxford in 1867, originally to Magdalen Hall and then to Balliol, where in 1869 he obtained a first class in *literae humaniores*. Thereafter he moved to London, where he lived in two small rented rooms at 5 Mount Vernon, Hampstead, and studied law and mathematics. Specializing in commercial law, he was called to the bar at the Inner Temple in 1877 but never practised. The direction of Edgeworth's informal but serious mathematical studies was perhaps affected by the example of the mathematician William Rowan Hamilton, who had known him (as Frank) and had also been a great friend of his father.

Almost certainly those early London years were financed by subventions from home, which allowed him, in 1871, to join the recently founded Savile Club; a year later Antonio also joined. An honorary secretary of the club from 1878 to 1881, Edgeworth obviously enjoyed and profited from its friendly intellectual atmosphere. His fellow members Henry Sidgwick and the psychologist James

Francis Ysidro Edgeworth (1845–1926), by Walter Stoneman, 1917

Sully were strong influences on his first book, *New and Old Methods of Ethics*, published at his own expense in 1877 and never reprinted. Its chief aim was to reformulate Sidgwick's utilitarian ethics in the light of Fechnerian psychophysics and the calculus of variations, of which Edgeworth 'already showed a confident and creative mastery' (Stigler, 'Francis Ysidro Edgeworth', 290). The resulting 'exact utilitarianism' is in many ways superior to the version that appeared later in *Mind* (1879), though the latter is the source for most critical discussion of Edgeworth's utilitarianism. The literary style of the book is extraordinary, faithfully reflecting its author's character: 'his courtesy, his caution, his shrewdness, his wit, his subtlety, his learning, his reserve—all are there full-grown' (Keynes, 145).

Edgeworth belonged to the Sunday Tramps, an informal group organized in 1879 by Leslie Stephen (another member of the Savile), whose purpose was to spend each Sunday striding briskly up and down the home counties (Maitland, 357–61, 500; Sully, 302–11). Physically strong, and active well into his seventies, Edgeworth also liked to climb, cycle, golf, sail, and swim in icy water. To judge from photographs his physical appearance owed more to Spain than to Ireland. Indeed, suitably attired, he could well have been a nobleman in a canvas by El Greco, though the usual look of veneration might have been missing; 'Music appealed to him little, and the Church not much more' (Bonar, 653). Apparently it was aversion to risk rather than to women that led him to remain single.

Before her marriage Beatrice Potter (Webb) was 'half-heartedly courted by a middle-aged economist named Edgeworth' (MacKenzie and MacKenzie, 134), and his writings throughout a long life betray a *tendresse* for that formidable woman.

In 1879 Edgeworth became in effect an apprentice in economic theory to his friend and neighbour William Stanley Jevons. Starting from scratch, he learned economics so well and so fast that in 1881 he published his masterpiece *Mathematical Psychics*. Although its reviewers Jevons and Marshall praised the book, neither showed any understanding of the profound 'economical calculus' that is its heart, a positive analysis of exchange in both market and non-market settings. In the latter, the possibility of coalitions between the various parties to the exchange poses severe and quite novel analytical difficulties, but even so Edgeworth was able to reach deep and highly non-intuitive theorems about relations between non-market and market exchange.

The general incomprehension of what *Mathematical Psychics* is all about continued for eighty years, owing in part to the mistaken belief that, because the normative analysis of its 'hedonical calculus' (reprinted from *Mind*, 1879) is so nakedly and unacceptably utilitarian, the positive analysis of its 'economical calculus' must also depend critically on the same fragile assumptions of cardinal measurability and interpersonal comparability of utility. It was not until the coming of game theory, whose concept of 'core' corresponds to the 'final settlements' of the economical calculus, that Edgeworth's supreme originality was fully recognized (in the work of M. Shubik and H. Scarf; there is analogy here to Hamiltonian dynamics, which also had to wait eighty years until the advent of quantum mechanics brought full understanding).

Its difficult mathematics and its ornamented style also help to explain why *Mathematical Psychics* was misjudged for so long. A few readers were enchanted by 'the strange but charming amalgam of poetry and pedantry, science and art, wit and learning of which he had the secret' (Keynes, 146), but more of them were bewildered and some (the more literal-minded) enraged. This did not prevent economists from borrowing, for their own purposes, much of the theoretical machinery devised especially for the economical calculus. Such standard tools as general utility functions, indifference curves, offer curves, and contract curves all originated there, as did the essential assumption that preferences be convex. Moreover, Edgeworth's definition of settlement fully anticipated the eponymous invention, some twenty years later, of the famous concept of Pareto optimum.

For whatever reasons (and one can think of several), soon after *Mathematical Psychics* appeared Edgeworth changed course completely, and in 1883 began the series of papers that were to make him 'the leading theorist of mathematical statistics of the latter half of the 19th century' (Stigler, 'Edgeworth as statistician', 98). He set himself

to do at last what had been talked about and assumed possible for over a century, but had never been accomplished: adapt the statistical methods of the theory of errors to the quantification of uncertainty in the social, particularly economic, sciences. (Stigler, 'Francis Ysidro Edgeworth', 295)

In this he succeeded brilliantly, but, as with his economics, his achievements were consistently underrated for many years. Only after 1975 did sympathetic criticism by Stephen Stigler and others lead to proper evaluation of Edgeworth's contributions, which culminated in 1996 in three large volumes (ed. C. R. McCann) which reprint nearly all his papers on statistics and probability.

From 1883 to 1888 all of Edgeworth's originality was directed to statistical theory and its applications to such topics as banking and index numbers, but in those years he also took the time to expand greatly his reading in economics, especially in classical and contemporary economic theory. His flood of publications and swiftly growing reputation lifted him in 1888 from the margins of academic life to a professorship in political economy at King's College, London, then in 1890 to its Tooke chair. In early 1891 he was appointed Drummond professor of political economy at Oxford, tenable at All Souls, and he continued thus—though with singularly little success as a teacher—until becoming emeritus in 1922. Spartan rooms in that college, and the same bare *pied-à-terre* at Hampstead, were his homes for the rest of his life.

Edgeworth received several academic honours: he was twice president of section F of the British Association (1889, 1922), president of the Royal Statistical Society (1912), and fellow of the British Academy, and was made an honorary DCL by the University of Durham. His most conspicuous honour was his editorship of the *Economic Journal*. He became its first editor in 1890 and served until 1911, and resigned to become chairman of the editorial board when J. M. Keynes became editor. Keynes being busy at Versailles, in 1919 Edgeworth came back to serve alongside him as joint editor of the journal for the next seven years; 'his fellow-editor received a final letter from him about its business after the news of his death' (Keynes, 140).

Edgeworth was a prolific writer. In the absence of a definitive bibliography, a preliminary count, treating his several multipart papers as separate items, yields a total of more than 500 books, articles, essays, and book reviews. He wrote only four books (at 150 pages *Mathematical Psychics* is much the longest) but over 200 book reviews. After 1890 even his articles on economic theory (as distinct from statistics) tended to take review form, being extended commentaries on the work of his contemporaries around the world. 'There was no other economist, of his period, who read so much of what was appearing, in many countries and in many languages' (Hicks, 164). Often, as in his major papers on distribution, international trade, monopoly, returns to scale, and taxation, his analysis was brilliant, original, penetrating, subtle, and instructive; but it remained commentary none the less. At the invitation of the Royal Economic Society, in 1925 he gathered many of these economic articles and reviews together, in some

cases with editorial amendments, in his three-volume *Papers Relating to Political Economy*.

Edgeworth has always been regarded as an exceptionally distinguished 'all-rounder', making major contributions to both economic and statistical theory to a degree that no one else, with the possible exception of Harold Hotelling, has ever approached. Since 1960, however, serious reappraisal of the depth and subtlety of those contributions to each discipline has shown decisively that he was indeed one of the truly great economists of his time, and one of its greatest statisticians. PETER NEWMAN

Sources J. M. Keynes, 'Francis Ysidro Edgeworth, 1845–1926', *Economic Journal*, 36 (1926), 140–53 • P. Newman, 'Edgeworth, Francis Ysidro', *The new Palgrave: a dictionary of economics*, ed. J. Eatwell, M. Milgate, and P. Newman (1987) • S. Stigler, 'Francis Ysidro Edgeworth, statistician', *Journal of the Royal Statistical Society: series A*, 141 (1978), 287–322 • S. Stigler, 'Edgeworth as statistician', *The new Palgrave: a dictionary of economics*, ed. J. Eatwell, M. Milgate, and P. Newman (1987) • M. Shubik, 'Edgeworth market games', *Contributions to the Theory of Games*, ed. A. W. Tucker and R. D. Luce, 4 (1959), 267–78 • H. Scarf, 'An analysis of markets with a large number of participants', *Recent advances in game theory* [Princeton, NJ 1961] (1962), 127–55 • H. J. Butler and H. E. Butler, *The 'Black book of Edgeworthstown' and other Edgeworth memories, 1585–1817* (1927) • J. Bonar, 'Memories of F. Y. Edgeworth', *Economic Journal*, 36 (1926), 647–53 • N. MacKenzie and J. MacKenzie, *The Fabians* (1977) • S. M. Stigler, *The history of statistics* (1986) • J. R. Hicks, 'Francis Ysidro Edgeworth', *Economists and the Irish economy*, ed. A. E. Murphy (1984), 157–74 • F. W. Maitland, *The life and letters of Leslie Stephen* (1906) • J. Sully, *My life and friends: a psychologist's memories* [1918] • *The Savile Club, 1868–1923* (1923)

Archives BLPES, corresp. and papers relating to Royal Economic Society • priv. coll., personal MSS, photographs etc. | BLPES, letters to Edwin Cannan • BLPES, corresp. with Alfred Marshall • Col. U., Rare Book and Manuscript Library, letters to Edwin Seligman • King's AC Cam., letters to John Maynard Keynes • UCL, letters to Sir Francis Galton • UCL, corresp. with Karl Pearson • University of Toronto, letters to James Mavor

Likenesses photograph, 1892, All Souls Oxf. • Elliott & Fry, photograph, 1906, repro. in Bonar, 'Memories of F. Y. Edgeworth' • W. Stoneman, photograph, 1917, NPG [*see illus.*]

Wealth at death £8609 2s. 1d.: resworn probate, 10 April 1926, *CGPLA Eng. & Wales* • £1374 15s. 5d.: probate, 20 Oct 1926, *CGPLA Éire*

Edgeworth [*later* Edgeworth de Firmont], **Henry Essex** (1745–1807), Roman Catholic priest and confessor to Louis XVI, was the second son, in a family of eight children (four of whom died in infancy), of the Revd Robert Edgeworth, rector of Edgeworthstown, co. Longford, and his wife, a granddaughter of Archbishop James *Ussher. When Henry was about four years old his parents became Roman Catholics and moved to Toulouse in France, where he was educated by the Jesuits. On his father's death and the return of his elder brother, Robert, to Ireland in 1769, he moved to Paris and trained for the priesthood while resident at the Collège des Trente-Trois. He assumed the name de Firmont, from the paternal estate of Firmount, near Edgeworthstown. After his ordination he lived at the Séminaire des Missions Etrangères in the rue du Bac, but instead of going on the foreign missions or accepting a see in Ireland he remained resident in Paris, acquiring a reputation for piety and as a good pastor and director, especially among the Paris Irish. The French Revolution gave

Henry Essex Edgeworth (1745–1807), by Anthony Cardon, pubd 1800 (after Augustin de Saint-Aubin)

delicate Edgeworth described as 'the land of ice' (Woodgate, 216). Mittau, in the Baltic duchy of Courland, later became part of modern Latvia. In 1800 Edgeworth was sent to St Petersburg with the order of the Holy Spirit for the tsar, who settled a pension of 200 ducats on him. In 1806, following the loss of his Irish estate, Edgeworth was given a pension by the British government. Among the offers he refused was the presidency of St Patrick's College, Maynooth.

Edgeworth died from a fever, contracted from attending French prisoners at Mittau, on 22 May 1807. He was nursed by Louis XVI's daughter, the duchesse d'Angoulême, rescued from the Temple in 1795, and the Latin epitaph on his tomb at Mittau was written by Louis XVIII. At the Restoration a marble group of Louis XVI and Edgeworth by François-Joseph Bosio formed the centrepiece of the Chapelle Expiatoire in Paris, which was built to the designs of Charles Percier and Pierre-Léonard Fontaine between 1815 and 1826 as a restored Bourbon memorial to Louis XVI and the 'martyrs' of the revolution.

DOMINIC AIDAN BELLENGER

Sources *DNB* · M. V. Woodgate, *The Abbé Edgeworth* (1945) · V. M. Montagu, *The Abbé Edgeworth and his friends* (1913) · C. S. Edgeworth, *Memoirs of the Abbé Edgeworth: containing his narrative of the last hours of Louis XVI* (1815) · L. Swords, *The green cockade: the Irish in the French Revolution, 1789–1815* (1989) · D. A. Bellenger, *The French exiled clergy in the British Isles after 1789* (1986) · P. Mansel, *The court of France, 1789–1830* (1988)

Likenesses A. Cardon, stipple, pubd 1800 (after A. de Saint-Aubin), BM, NPG [*see illus.*] · sculpture, Chapelle Expiatoire, Paris

him a prominence which he would probably not otherwise have attained.

The revolution rapidly took on an anti-clerical character and, although at risk, Edgeworth's nationality allowed him a freedom of movement and an active ministry denied to his French colleagues, and it is said that on St Patrick's day, 17 March 1791, he became confessor to Madame Elisabeth, sister of King Louis XVI. He was also appointed vicar-general of the archdiocese of Paris by the exiled Archbishop Antoine-Eléonore-Léon Le Clerc de Juigné (1728–1811). The Princess Elisabeth recommended Edgeworth's services to Louis XVI, and Edgeworth, in lay dress, attended the king, following his trial and death sentence, on the eve of his execution, which was set for 21 January 1793. He heard the king's confession, celebrated mass, and gave him communion at the Temple, where the king was imprisoned, travelled with him to the execution in the mayor of Paris's carriage, and attended the king on the scaffold. When the king's hands were tied Edgeworth told Louis, 'Sire, I see the last insult only one more resemblance between your majesty and the God who is about to be your recompense' (*DNB*). Edgeworth had no recollection of his legendary final commendation, 'Fils de Saint Louis, montez au Ciel' (ibid.), but by his presence at the king's death, literally drenched in the royal blood, he became part of royalist propaganda and counter-revolutionary mythology.

Edgeworth remained in hiding in Paris until August 1796, when he went, briefly, to England. His first royal patron, Madame Elisabeth, had been executed on 10 May 1794. He became confessor to the émigré Louis XVIII, his iconic presence giving the king a special legitimacy, and lived with his household as chaplain at Mittau, which the

Edgeworth, Maria (1768–1849), novelist and educationist, was born on 1 January 1768 at Black Bourton, Oxfordshire, the eldest daughter and third child of Richard Lovell *Edgeworth (1744–1817), inventor and educationist, and his first wife, Anna Maria Elers (1743–1773). The year of her birth was long given as 1767, but the revised date has been generally accepted. Her place of birth was the home of her maternal grandfather, Paul Elers, a person of limited financial acumen. Her mother died when Maria was six shortly after the birth of a child who did not survive. Her father was married a further three times, first to Honora Sneyd in 1773.

Family and early life The Edgeworths were Irish landowners, with property in co. Longford. Richard Lovell Edgeworth inherited a neglectful attitude to the estate and, prior to 1782, spent little time at Edgeworthstown (formerly Mastrim). No fewer than eight members of the family sat in the Irish House of Commons between 1661 and 1800, but only Richard Lovell Edgeworth among them has any claim to political reputation. The family's return in 1782 was in part prompted by the Enlightenment views of English midlands industrialists and philanthropists with whom he associated, but it coincided with a campaign for constitutional reform of the Irish parliament in its relations with Britain. The title-page of Maria Edgeworth's most famous novel, *Castle Rackrent* (1800), describes it as 'taken from the manners of the Irish squires, before the year 1782', a date with great domestic

Maria Edgeworth
(1768–1849), by
Richard Beard, 1841

and political significance for the anonymous author and her family.

The 1780s in Ireland were dominated by a self-congratulating House of Commons which had extracted major concessions from London in the context of the American crisis. The political scene was frequently theatrical, and rival reformers contended for leadership. Among disputed issues was the Catholic question, with some arguing for a near complete relaxation of the penal laws. The Edgeworths were conspicuously lax in their religious practice. But, at the Volunteer Convention of November 1783, Richard Lovell Edgeworth pulled back from radical reform, realizing (as many gentry delegates did) that their material interests might not be best served by an extension of the franchise and reform of land tenure. Maria Edgeworth herself was proud of his role, exaggerating it at the time, but tended to downplay it when she wrote about him after his death.

Maria Edgeworth's childhood was unhappy: she was neglected by her father, who was too much involved with his new wife, and she was deemed to be a difficult child. With the collapse of the health of her stepmother Honora Sneyd in 1775, Maria was dispatched to Mrs Lattafière's school in Derby, where she entertained her fellow pupils with her story-telling in the dormitories, and later in 1780 to Mrs Devis's flashier establishment in Upper Wimpole Street, London. Diminutive in height, she was subjected to stretching, being held by the head with her feet off the ground. A better, if still uncomfortable, experience came when she spent extended periods with her father's friend the Rousseauesque Thomas Day at Anningsley in Surrey. He encouraged her education and stimulated self-respect in an anxious girl. In 1781 he also nearly blinded her by applying tar water to cure eye disease.

Richard Lovell Edgeworth was both libidinous and abstracted. He used the term 'your present mother' to describe young Edgeworth's surrogate parent, as if to emphasize the temporary or serial nature of the appointment: after Honora's death in 1780 he married her sister Elizabeth. The threat to Maria's sight late in 1781 brought

the girl more to his attention, though he still recommended arithmetic because it 'requires no attention of the eyes' (M. Butler, 76). He later encouraged her in her reading, although he disapproved of her reading novels, and set her to translate Mme de Genlis's *Adèle et Théodore* (which was recalled before publication in 1783). The removal to Edgeworthstown in June 1782 renewed the bond between father and daughter, leading to a formidable intellectual partnership of which she was the more able and nimble mind. The house, which was her permanent home for the rest of her life, was unremarkable, the estate in a condition of mismanagement. From the outset Edgeworth accompanied her father on tours of the property and acted as rent clerk at the twice yearly gale days. This practical experience of estate business, which brought her into direct contact with tenants, is reflected in the detail and colour of her novels dealing with Ireland, notably *Castle Rackrent* (1800), *Ennui* (1809), *The absentee* (1812), and *Ormond* (1817).

Early writings: education and collaboration During this time Edgeworth's domestic role was expanding, as she became responsible for the education of her younger half-siblings: thirteen of them were educated at home. She experimented with various teaching techniques, and documented the children's progress. The reprehensible conduct of her eldest brother Richard (1764–1796), who had entered the navy, increased the sense of her being deputy and heir apparent.

Concern for the young was a theme which early took root in Edgeworthstown House. In 1788–9 Edgeworth's father entertained his household of adults and children with an invented oral saga about a large family, generally referred to as 'The Freeman Family'. Maria Edgeworth sought to commit these performances to paper, checking details with her father as they toured the estate. Her first version was completed by the end of 1790.

The saga developed into Edgeworth's longest novel, *Patronage*, and though the final version did not appear until 1814, a rough draft was complete by early 1791, and a revision of the whole accomplished between November 1793 and the following May. As the ultimate dénouement of the published novel (set almost entirely in England) involves a repercussion of the Irish rising of 1798, this dimension of the work may be assigned to Edgeworth's taking the manuscript with her to England in 1799. Consideration of *Patronage* raises two interrelated and intractable problems—how much Edgeworth as a writer was influenced by her father, and the extent to which some of her work originated far earlier than dates of publication would suggest. For example, the *Essays on practical education* (1798), which Edgeworth and her father jointly wrote, is echoed in the heavily didactic and moralizing *Patronage*. The fact that she defended the education of women in *Letters for literary ladies* (1795) and tutored her brother Henry suggests independence of paternal dominance, though her public references to her father were later decidedly loyal. *Letters for literary ladies* was a retort to Thomas Day, who had strong objections to women publishing. In the following year she published *The parent's assistant*, the first evidence of her concern to write for children, and further stories for the young were published in her *Early lessons* in 1801.

Independence: *Castle Rackrent* In 1791 tuberculosis (not a newcomer to the household) struck one of the Edgeworth children and Richard Lovell Edgeworth took him to England in search of treatment. During this first period of Edgeworth's extended separation from her father, she turned to an aunt, Margaret Ruxton (1746–1830), for emotional support. It was to her that Edgeworth recounted the verbal antics of John Langan, a steward at Edgeworthstown, and he became in time the fictional narrator of *Castle Rackrent*. Mrs Ruxton's preferred reading was literary, and she provided a counterbalance to her brother's predominantly scientific interests. Although the publication of *Castle Rackrent* in 1800 coincided with the union debates, its origins lie in 1792 and a very brief period in early 1795 when William Wentworth Fitzwilliam (second earl Fitzwilliam) as lord lieutenant promised drastic reform of the Irish administration. The novel's oscillations between verbal antic and brute fact reflect the disappointed optimism in liberal circles. The onset of greater violence in 1797 and especially in 1798 further affected its evolution.

In February 1798 Richard Lovell Edgeworth entered the Irish House of Commons. On 31 May he married for the last time. Before summer was out, the family was forced to flee Edgeworthstown as a French invasionary army moved eastward towards Dublin. Later returning with her family, Maria Edgeworth found the house relatively undisturbed, despite her father's having to seek refuge in Longford town. The battlefield at which the French were finally defeated (8 September) lay close to Edgeworth property. Her immediate reaction as a writer was to disinter the Langan narrative (in October 1798) and to bring it closer to its final state as *Castle Rackrent* (January 1800).

Castle Rackrent was published in London by Joseph Johnson, a radical whom the Edgeworths once visited in prison. Edgeworth's loyalty to Johnson, and to his successors after his death in 1809, only partly explains her studied indifference to Irish outlets (none the less the work was quickly published in pirated editions in Dublin). Her father spoke in favour of, and voted against, the union between Britain and Ireland, but Edgeworth's attitude to the measure is not extensively recorded. The family welcomed better prospects for Irish commerce but deplored British corruption. Thady Quirk's fictional narrative in *Castle Rackrent* concludes with an editorial note about the union. Its final cryptic sentences read 'Did the Warwickshire militia, who were chiefly artisans, teach the Irish to drink beer? or did they learn from the Irish to drink whiskey?' Apart from occasional brief tours, the family displayed no wish to abandon Ireland after 1800.

Public and private life, 1802–1830 In November 1802 Edgeworth and her father visited Paris, where they were well received as the authors of *Practical Education*. While there, Edgeworth received an unexpected proposal of marriage from a Swedish courtier, Abraham Niclas Clewberg-Edelcrantz, who shared her father's scientific interests.

Though her father appears to have been tolerant of the notion, Maria Edgeworth refused the offer and both parties remained unmarried. Reticent on personal matters, she none the less referred to the Swede as 'one who was once dear to me' (Edgeworth to various family members, 27 Nov 1817)—this less than six months after her father's death. The episode of 1802 constitutes virtually the only instance of intimate emotion intruding from a source outside the family circle, despite the extent of her growing fame and her success in London and Parisian society.

At this time Edgeworth was exploring questions of nationality, gender, and the authorial profession. In the advertisement to *Belinda* (1802) she questioned the form of the novel itself:

> The following work is offered to the public as a Moral Tale— the author not wishing to acknowledge a Novel … so much folly, errour and vice are disseminated in books classed under this denomination, that it is hoped the wish to assume another title will be attributed to feelings that are laudable, and not fastidious.

Her *Essay on Irish Bulls* (1802) manipulates professed authorship in a brilliant fashion, as the 'narrator' is successively English, Irish, singular, plural, and so on. Her fictions focused sharply on women tended to prefer English settings, and her treatment of Irish women veered towards the satirical (Mrs Rafferty, for instance, in *The absentee*) or the sentimental (Ellinor in *Ennui*). She commented in a notebook on the absurdity of a woman wishing to be a lawyer. To Lord Grey she declared in 1832 that 'facts are of no sex', while preparing for the last of her novels which take a woman's name as title, *Helen* (1834). Beginning with *Belinda* Edgeworth had encountered resistance to her frank treatment of female characters and the vicissitudes they could endure, and *The modern Griselda* (1805) was written without her father's knowing. Both series of *Tales of fashionable life* (1809 and 1812)—whose longest tale was 'The Absentee'—feature stories in which a woman's life is the predominant theme. *Leonora* (1806) may be a lesser performance.

Partly as a consequence of timely excursions to London from co. Longford, Edgeworth's fiction was reviewed widely. Between 1804 and 1820 Francis Jeffrey contributed six anonymous notices of her work in the whiggish *Edinburgh Review* of which he was editor, to which should be added Sydney Smith's review of *Patronage* in the same organ. Less predictably, John Wilson Croker wrote favourably of *Tales of fashionable life* (2nd ser.) but harshly of the *Memoirs of Richard Lovell Edgeworth* in the tory *Quarterly Review*. Lesser magazines also noted her work, which vied with that of Jane Austen in certain areas of critical esteem. Edgeworth was also well rewarded for her work, receiving £1050 for *Tales of fashionable life* (2nd ser.), and becoming the most commercially successful novelist of her age. She received numerous private endorsements and congratulations, counting Jeremy Bentham, Sir Humphrey Davy, Etienne Dumont, David Ricardo, and Walter Scott among her friends and admirers. From Scott's description of her it seems that her appearance matched her vivacity, good sense, and friendliness. There was, however, a vein of opinion which regarded her as too didactic and moralistic in the fiction: *triste utilité* was a phrase of Madame de Staël's which stung the novelist. In May 1820 she conversed with Talleyrand in the British ambassador's Paris home. In 1825 Scott and J. G. Lockhart visited her at Edgeworthstown.

Scott was by far the most important reader of her work. He was prompted by *The absentee* to unearth his incomplete manuscript of what became *Waverley* in 1814. Indirectly, Edgeworth helped to launch the historical novel across Europe, even if her own contribution to the genre was limited to *Ormond*. What she demonstrated was a means of relating one cultural tradition to another, whether across a long passage of time or in a tense contemporary setting (the stories of émigrés, for instance). Scott's public acknowledgement of the debt came in the collected edition of his works (1829–33), when Edgeworth's star seemed to have waned.

The family's strong interest in pre-revolutionary French society and thought is reflected in *Ormond* (1817), a novel which Edgeworth wrote in haste as her father was dying. The novel counterbalances its scenes of fashionable Parisian society (drawn from Edgeworth's own experiences over forty years previously) with primitivistic settings on the west coast of Ireland, and appeared in tandem with *Harrington*, a fiction of English life in which Edgeworth sought to make amends for an antisemitic passage in *The absentee*. These were her last novels for adults for sixteen years. The desire to complete *Ormond* for her father was followed by her completion of his *Memoirs* three years after his death in 1817, the second volume being entirely her work.

Later work After her father's death Edgeworth moved towards a more conservative attitude towards Irish politics and the possibilities of local reform, and resumed writing for children with, for example, *Rosamond, a sequel* (1821). Deteriorating economic and social conditions in Ireland of the 1820s laid the ground for a retrenchment of her thinking. The rise of Daniel O'Connell and the politicization of many Catholic clergy alarmed her, and she viewed the activities of individual priests virtually as insubordination. Catholic emancipation in 1829 and the Reform Act of 1832 sank a double ditch between the world she had been brought up in and a new Ireland of which she was only superficially aware. In 1833 Gaelic translations (by Tomás Ó Fianachtaigh) of *Forgive and forget* and *Rosanna* were published in Belfast and Dublin.

On 3 October 1833 a party set out from Edgeworthstown heading westwards into Connemara by way of Athlone. This was Edgeworth's first extended encounter with the west of Ireland. Her account of the trip was published in 1950, edited from letters which she wrote home. It confirms her preference for people and events over landscape and setting, and the experience did not inspire any further fiction. Her last full-length novel, *Helen*, was set among English middle-class folk. In a significant departure from her other novels, the story was focused not on a didactic theme, but on a dramatic situation and the relationships between three main characters. 'I have been reproached for making *my moral* in some stories too prominent', she wrote to her publisher J. G. Lockhart, 'I am sensible of the inconvenience of this both to reader and writer & have taken much pains to avoid it in *Helen*' (Edgeworth to J. G. Lockhart, 12 May 1833). At Lockhart's suggestion the novel was published by Bentley, a younger firm than those with whom Edgeworth had been associated; an American edition was in circulation by the end of August 1834, and a German translation by Christmas. Earlier in the year Edgeworth had declared 'it is impossible to draw Ireland as she now is in a book of fiction—realities are too strong', though by November her position had softened ('the scene of the next story I write, if ever I do write again shall be in Ireland' (Edgeworth to Rachel Mordecai Lazarus, 10 Nov 1834).

In the event, only *Orlandino* (published Edinburgh, 1848) extended her range. This temperance story was sold to 'earn a little money for our parish poor' at the end of the great famine (Slade, 203). Her endorsement of Father Theobald Mathew, the pioneer of total abstemption among Ireland's Catholics, should be weighed against her determination 'to excite the people to work for good wages, and not, by feeding gratis, to make beggars of them, and ungrateful beggars, as the case may be'. Her father's practice of 1782 in the management of Edgeworthstown was steadily maintained in the face of demographic catastrophe.

When Sir William Rowan Hamilton was elected president of the Royal Irish Academy in 1837, he sought Edgeworth's advice on the advancement of polite literature in Ireland. Her lengthy reply (Edgeworth to W. Hamilton, 6 Jan 1838, Royal Irish Academy, 24.F.23.2) recommended the admission of women to the academy's evening parties, among other reforms. She was elected an honorary member of the academy on 13 June 1842 (Royal Irish Academy minutes, 2.258), her kinswoman Louisa Beaufort having preceded her as a member.

At the end of the famine, Edgeworth was over eighty though she still addressed her third stepmother, Frances Beaufort (one year her junior), as 'Mother'. With other bereavements, she lost a favourite stepsister Fanny (1799–1848), and was increasingly deprived of company of her own age. In spring 1849 she paid a visit to relatives at Trim, co. Meath. Safely back home at Edgeworthstown House she complained of heart pains, and died quite suddenly on 22 May in the house to which she had come from England nearly seventy years earlier. She was buried in the churchyard of St John's, Edgeworthstown.

Afterlife Maria Edgeworth is unrivalled among Irish women as an intellectual, working both as a literary writer and (in the broad sense) as an educationist. Her practice of textual allusion was at once dense and deft, and her reading exceptionally broad. *Patronage* (1814), her longest and most complex novel, draws on a wide range of sources, including seventeenth-century English political intrigue and the philosophical quest for a universal language. The list of her publications testifies to almost uninterrupted endeavour over a quarter of a century, followed by a period (1818 onwards) in which she oversaw two multi-volume collections of her work, and later re-engaged with fiction. Though the 1830s saw a renewal of literary publication in Ireland, Edgeworth remained aloof: in April 1834 the *Dublin University Magazine* lamented her indifference to 'anything like revealed religion'—an old complaint revived at a time of increasing sectarian conflict. Nevertheless, her influence on younger writers, for instance the Banim brothers and Charles James Lever, is obvious. Anthony Trollope's first two novels are written clearly in an Edgeworthian mode. Less obviously so, the debt owed by William Makepeace Thackeray to her hero-less social novels has been remarked on. The influence of *The absentee* can be traced down to J. G. Farrell's *Troubles* (1970), though the 'troubles' of 1969 onwards have led to some hostility towards Edgeworth as an allegedly 'colonial' writer.

Edgeworth's contemporary fame was greater perhaps in England than in Ireland. *Tales and miscellaneous pieces* appeared in fourteen volumes in 1825, but the texts of some items (notably *Patronage*) were unsatisfactory. A better *Tales and novels* succeeded in eighteen monthly volumes (1832–3), over which she exercised more control. The Victorian period saw several reissued 'collected' editions, most notably that edited by Anne Thackeray Ritchie. In Ireland the rise of cultural nationalism with W. B. Yeats and others led to an eclipse of her reputation, though *Castle Rackrent* has been almost continuously in print. (A Soviet Russian edition appeared in 1972.) Feminist publishing houses, followed by Oxford University Press and Penguin, issued a number of the novels in the late twentieth century. The latest effort at a collected edition was published by Pickering and Chatto, and by 1999 eight volumes had appeared.

The great bulk of Edgeworth correspondence awaits publication. The nineteenth-century selections are unreliable, though *Lettres intimes de Maria Edgeworth pendant ses voyages en Belgique, en France, en Suisse, et en Angleterre en 1802, 1820 et 1821* (Paris, 1896) deserves attention, not least because it provided a model when Lady Colvin came to publish her selections in the 1970s. The result is that few of the multitudinous letters written from Edgeworthstown House have been edited for publication.

W. J. McCormack

Sources *Life of William Allen with selections from his correspondence* (1847) • H. J. Butler and H. E. Butler, *The 'Black book of Edgeworthstown' and other Edgeworth memories, 1585–1817* (1927) • A. Romilly, ed., *Romilly–Edgeworth letters, 1813–1818* (1936) • B. Coolidge Slade, *Maria Edgeworth, 1767–1849: a bibliographical tribute* (1937) • H. Edgeworth Butler, ed., *Maria Edgeworth: tour in Connemara and the Martins of Ballinahinch* (1950) • M. Hurst, *Maria Edgeworth and the public scene: intellect, fine feeling, and landlordism in the age of reform* (1969) • *Maria Edgeworth: letters from England, 1813–1844*, ed. C. Colvin (1971) • M. Butler, *Maria Edgeworth: a literary biography* (1972) • *The education of the heart: the correspondence of Rachel Mordecai Lazarus and Maria Edgeworth*, ed. E. E. MacDonald (Chapel Hill, NC, 1977) • C. Colvin, ed., *Maria Edgeworth in France and Switzerland: selections from the Edgeworth family letters* (1979) • W. J. McCormack, *Ascendancy and tradition in Anglo-Irish literature from 1789 to 1939* (1985)
Archives Bodl. Oxf., corresp., literary MSS, and papers • Hunt. L., letters • NL Ire., family and other corresp., account book, notebooks • TCD, letters • Yale U., Beinecke L., papers | Beds. & Luton

ARS, corresp. with Elizabeth Whitbread • Birr Castle, co. Offaly, letters to Lawrence Parsons, second earl of Rosse • BL, corresp. with Sir Robert Peel, Add. MSS 40423-40603, *passim* • Bodl. Oxf., letters mainly to Mary Somerville • Bristol RO, letters to Zoe King and papers • Denbighshire RO, Ruthin, letters to John Brinkley and Esther Brinkley • Derbys. RO, letters to Fanny Strutt and corresp. with Edward Strutt • Derbys. RO, letters to Sir R. J. Wilmot-Horton • FM Cam., letters to William Strutt • Lincs. Arch., letters to George Elers • LPL, letters to Archbishop Howley • NL Ire., letters to Mary Leadbeater • NL Ire., corresp. with T. Spring-Rice • NL Scot., corresp. with Archibald Constable • NL Scot., corresp. with J. G. Lockhart • NL Scot., corresp. with Sir Walter Scott • NRA Scotland, priv. coll., letters to John Swinton • PRO NIre., corresp. with John Foster • RCS Eng., letters to Joanna Baillie and Agnes Baillie • RS, corresp. with Sir John Herschel • TCD, corresp. with Sir Philip Crampton • TCD, corresp. with W. R. Hamilton • TCD, letters to marquess of Lansdowne • U. Birm. L., letters to J. E. Moilliot, banker • U. Nott. L., corresp. with the countess of Charleville • Yale U., Beinecke L., letters mainly to Mary Leadbeater
Likenesses group portrait, lithograph, 19th cent. (after crayon drawing by A. Buck, 1787), NG Ire. • F. Mackenzie, line and stipple engraving, pubd 1808 (after W. M. Craig), BM, NPG • pencil drawing, *c.*1819–1821, NPG • F. Mackenzie, line and stipple engraving, 1822 (after W. M. Craig), NG Ire. • R. Beard, daguerreotype, 1841, NPG [*see illus.*] • M. P. Edgeworth, calotype print, 1846–7, NPG • stipple, 1873 (after A. Chappel), NG Ire.

Edgeworth, Michael Pakenham (1812–1881), botanist and East India Company servant, was born on 24 May 1812 at Edgeworthstown, co. Longford, Ireland, the youngest in a family of two sons and four daughters of Richard Lovell *Edgeworth (1744–1817), educationist and improver, and his fourth wife, Frances Anne Beaufort (d. 1865), daughter of the Revd Daniel Augustus *Beaufort. He was half-brother to Maria *Edgeworth, the novelist. In September 1823 he entered Charterhouse School and in 1827 moved to Edinburgh where in the following year he matriculated at Edinburgh University. There he began the study of oriental languages, and acquired his grounding in botany under Professor Robert Graham. After a distinguished career at the East India College, Haileybury (1829–30), he was appointed writer to the East India Company (30 April 1831), arriving in India on 14 September of that year. There he held a series of administrative and judicial posts at Ambala, Muzaffarnagar, and afterwards at Saharanpur. In February 1842 he returned home on leave. He was elected a fellow of the Linnean Society, and in February 1846 married Christina (d. 1881), daughter of Dr Hugh Macpherson of King's College, Aberdeen. They had two daughters, one of whom (Christina) died in infancy in 1848. On his return to India in 1846 he took advantage of a stop for coaling at Aden to look about for plants. He published the results in the *Journal of the Asiatic Society of Bengal* (16, 1847, 1211) under the title 'Two hours' herborization at Aden'. Of the forty species he collected in that short period, no fewer than eleven were new to science.

Edgeworth was stationed at Banda until 1850, when he was chosen as one of the five commissioners for the settlement of the Punjab, first at Multan, and afterwards at Jullundur. However, his Indian career was finally cut short by sunstroke and he retired in 1859. On his return to England he lived in London, but died suddenly while on the island of Eigg, on 30 July 1881.

Edgeworth published thirteen papers on botany, climatology, and travels in the *Journal of the Asiatic Society of Bengal* between 1834 and 1853. He also contributed to the *Transactions* and *Journal* of the Linnean Society, provided a section on Indian *Caryophyllaceae* in J. D. Hooker's *Flora of British India* (1872–97), and published a volume on pollen in 1878 (2nd edn, 1879). He was an early experimenter in the applications of photographic techniques to botany, working in the field as early as 1839. He later made a number of daguerreotypes and photogenic drawings, but few have survived.   B. D. JACKSON, *rev.* ANDREW GROUT

Sources *Proceedings of the Linnean Society of London* (1883), 63 · *Journal of Botany, British and Foreign*, 19 (1881), 288 · Dodwell [E. Dodwell] and Miles [J. S. Miles], eds., *Alphabetical list of the Honourable East India Company's Bengal civil servants, from the year 1780 to the year 1838* (1839) · A. C. Fox-Davies, *Landed gentry of Ireland*, new edn (1912) · F. C. Danvers and others, *Memorials of old Haileybury College* (1894), 397 · I. H. Burkill, 'Chapters on the history of botany in India II: the advances', *Journal of the Bombay Natural History Society*, 54 (1956), 42–86 · E. Blatter, 'Flora of Aden', *Records of the Botanical Survey of India*, 7 (1914–16), 5–6 · Desmond, *Botanists*, rev. edn · Boase, *Mod. Eng. biog.* · *CGPLA Eng. & Wales* (1881) · G. Smith, *Disciples of light: photographs in the Brewster album* (1990) · private information (2004)

Archives Bodl. Oxf., Indian Institute, corresp., journals, and papers | Falconer Museum, Forres, corresp. with Hugh Falconer · Moray District Libraries RO, Forres, Falconer MSS

Likenesses portrait, Hunt Botanical Library, Pittsburgh

Wealth at death £9767 13s.: probate, 5 Oct 1881, *CGPLA Eng. & Wales*

Richard Lovell Edgeworth (1744–1817), by Horace Hone, 1785

Edgeworth, Richard Lovell (1744–1817), educational writer and engineer, was born on 31 May 1744 in Pierrepont Street, Bath, the only surviving son of Richard Edgeworth (1701–1769), a middling Irish country gentleman, whose family had been settled in co. Longford since the seventeenth century, and his wife, Rachel Jane Lovell (*d.* 1764). The main source for his life is a lively autobiography, to which a sequel was written by his daughter, the novelist Maria *Edgeworth.

Education, marriage, and early scientific activity As a child of seven, on a visit to Dublin, Edgeworth was shown an orrery and other scientific equipment which aroused in him a permanent interest in mechanics. In 1752 he spent a year at Dr Lydiat's school in Warwick. After this he went to schools in Drogheda and Longford. He subsequently passed six dissipated months at Trinity College, Dublin, but access to Lord Longford's library at Pakenham Hall and his mother's interest in John Locke's writings on education converted him to more intellectual occupations.

In October 1761 Edgeworth's father sent him to Corpus Christi College, Oxford, chosen because an old friend, Paul Elers, lived nearby at Black Bourton. Elers forwarded Richard Lovell's academic studies, and the latter found time for his hobby of mechanics, making friends with Thomas Hornsby, who interested him in astronomy and horology. While an undergraduate he made a camera obscura and a clock, and sent to the Society of Arts two letters on agricultural vehicles. He also flirted with Elers's daughter Anna Maria (1743–1773) and felt himself 'insensibly entangled so completely that he could not find any

honourable means of extrication' (Edgeworth and Edgeworth, *Memoirs*, 1.97). In 1763 they eloped to Scotland. On 21 February 1764 his father had the pair remarried by licence in Black Bourton church. A son, Richard, was born on 29 May 1764. The couple spent most of the next year at Edgeworthstown, in co. Longford, Ireland. Edgeworth read some law, made an orrery, and designed vehicles. In the autumn they returned to England with a small allowance. Edgeworth rented a small house at Hare Hatch, Berkshire, travelling intermittently to London to study law and visit his wife's Blake relations. There he met Sir Francis Blake Delaval, a leader of London's fashionable gambling world. Edgeworth made a bet with Lord March on the time of arrival in London of racing news and announced that he had better means of communication than mounted messengers. The bet was therefore aborted: he had meant to use a primitive semaphore telegraph, an idea he revived many years later.

Delaval's influence was counterbalanced by that of Thomas Day, a neighbour and an awkward young radical; though Day was a complete contrast to the seemingly frivolous Edgeworth, the two shared a youthful enthusiasm for Rousseau, whose recent *Émile* provided a programme for educating Edgeworth's son, Richard. Edgeworth set up a workshop at Hare Hatch, where he made various inventions, including a carriage propelled by the wind and another on an idea of Erasmus Darwin of Lichfield. Darwin introduced him to the informal group of people interested in the application of science to industry, later known as the Lunar Society of Birmingham, of whose early days Edgeworth provides the first coherent account. Among its best-known members were James Watt and Matthew Boulton, James Keir, John Whitehurst, Joseph Priestley, and Josiah Wedgwood. About 1770, besides some co-operative work on Watt's steam engine, Edgeworth did research on the definition of horsepower and took out a patent for a 'Portable railway or artificial road to move along with any carriage to which it is attached' (patent no. 21, close roll 10 Geo. III, 15). This is thought to have been a prototype of a track-laying vehicle. In 1767 and 1769 the Society of Arts awarded him their silver and gold medals for diverse inventions, including an ingenious 'waywiser'. In London James Keir introduced him to the distinguished scientists meeting at Young Slaughter's Coffee House in St Martin's Lane, chaired by John Hunter and including Sir Joseph Banks and John Smeaton.

The attractions of Lichfield had included Anna Seward, the poetess. She had a beautiful ward, Honora Sneyd (1751–1780), with whom Edgeworth fell deeply in love. To avoid an entanglement, he fled to France in 1771, accompanied by his son and by Thomas Day. They travelled to Lyon, where they were later joined by his wife. Here he designed machinery for land reclamation on the River Rhône. A winter spate delayed operations and Anna Maria, escorted by Day, returned to England for her confinement. In March 1773 she died in childbed and Edgeworth was obliged to go home. On arrival he found that Honora Sneyd was still single, and they were married in Lichfield Cathedral on 17 July 1773.

The study of education In 1769, on the death of his father, Edgeworth had inherited the family estate at Edgeworthstown, whose management now required his attention. In Ireland he and Honora spent two or three years in 'untired felicity', putting things in order and painfully learning about children's upbringing. The two elder children, Richard and Maria, were sent to school in England. Later Richard Lovell, his wife, and the younger children (Anna Maria's daughters Emmeline and Anna, and babies Honora and Lovell from his second marriage) returned to England, where he rented a house at Northchurch, Hertfordshire, and occupied himself with horology and the beginnings of a substantial study on education. He and his wife set out to provide experiments and facts, not the many theories so abundantly published by others. From 1776 or 1778 they kept a 'register' of the children's progress. Edgeworth also began research for *A Rational Primer* (1799). Together they projected a small three-volume work, to be entitled *Practical Education*, of which only volume two was printed anonymously (1780), but not published. It was to give 'such pictures of real life, as may make a Child wish to put himself in place of the characters intended to excite his emulation' (*Practical Education*, iv). About 1778 Honora became incurably ill with tuberculosis and the family moved to Beighterton, near Shifnal, to be attended by Dr Darwin. There she died in April 1780. She had advised her deeply distressed husband to remarry, recommending to him her sister Elizabeth Sneyd (1753–1797). Though legal at the time, marriage to a deceased wife's sister could, and did, cause lasting scandal. Matthew Boulton advised

removal to a parish where they were less well known so that no one would oppose the banns. The couple were eventually married on Christmas day 1780 at St Andrew's, Holborn. Edgeworth rejected Boulton's plan to set up in industry, and after spending the summer in Cheshire he and his wife moved briefly to lodgings in London, where Sir Joseph Banks sponsored his election as a fellow of the Royal Society.

Ireland Edgeworth and his wife then followed the plan agreed earlier with Honora: they went to Ireland to manage their estate, to educate their children, and to make some return to the country whence they drew their income. On his arrival in June 1782, when the Volunteers were at the height of their success, Edgeworth, a novice in Irish politics, published a radical address urging the co. Longford Volunteers to seize the moment to petition the Irish House of Commons for further reform, especially on Catholic emancipation. Abroad, Edgeworth had been a friend both of the populist and volatile Frederick Augustus Hervey, bishop of Derry, and of Lord Charlemont, the moderate law-abiding Volunteer commander-in-chief, with whom he was probably more in agreement. At the end of his life he claimed to have played some part in preventing the bishop from ill-advisedly inciting the Volunteers, armed and uniformed, to march to the House of Commons with their petition. Politics, however, were never a major concern to a man whose primary interest was in education.

Edgeworth had now to turn to his own affairs and the upbringing of his family. He found Edgeworthstown a scene of dilapidation and waste, ill-managed by unreliable agents. He took direct control, insisting that all rents should be paid to himself, on conditions agreed with himself. He rode around with his teenage daughter Maria, teaching her accounting, valuing the land, and getting to know the tenants. Long leases were no longer to be granted, nor tenancies divided; he would allow tenants to profit by their improvements and they might keep in hand a year's rent.

More satisfying, Edgeworth could now concentrate on the family's education. Honora Edgeworth's 'register' was continued by her sister Elizabeth and afterwards by Maria. To vary the more scientific kind of training which he gave to some of the family, especially to his eldest daughter and to the brilliant Honora, he introduced more imaginative literature and the writing of stories. Thomas Day's moralistic *Sandford and Merton* began to be published as children's reading matter in 1783, and Edgeworth himself amused his family with a serial, 'The Freeman Family'. Maria Edgeworth's own short stories did not come out until 1796 as *The Parent's Assistant*. In 1790 Edgeworth's daughter Honora died, like her mother, of tuberculosis, and shortly afterwards her brother Lovell showed signs of the same disease. Edgeworth and his wife took Lovell to England for medical treatment, the family settling at Clifton Spa. Here in 1791–2 Maria, who had continued to maintain the 'register', took the initiative in completing *Practical Education* with her father.

At the end of 1793 the family went back to Ireland,

alarmed by exaggerated accounts of local unrest. In the following year a French invasion was rumoured, and Edgeworth revived his old schemes for a telegraph. After much procrastination by government officials all were rejected, although at the time of Emmet's insurrection in 1803 they were looked at again. A number of signalling stations were then erected from Dublin to Galway under the supervision of Edgeworth's brother-in-law Francis Beaufort RN, and efforts were made to train signallers. The experiment was a failure: the weather was bad and the code of signals far too difficult for the semi-literate workmen.

In 1796 Edgeworth stood unsuccessfully for the Irish House of Commons in a county by-election; a neighbour commented that with his intelligence and independence he would have made an excellent MP. However, in 1798 Lord Granard offered him the borough of St Johnstown. Both he and his patron favoured the Union in principle but voted against it, disgusted at the measures used to secure it.

In 1797 Elizabeth Edgeworth died after a long illness. She left six young children and a large household to be looked after. Edgeworth was fortunate to find an admirable successor in Frances Anne Beaufort (1769–1867), eldest daughter of Daniel Augustus Beaufort, the Irish topographer. They were married on 31 May 1798 and had six children. On their journey home the county of Longford seemed quiet, but towards autumn Edgeworth found it necessary to raise a corps of infantry, whose non-sectarian character gave offence in protestant circles. Arms failed to reach it, and at the beginning of September the family and the corps had to take refuge in Longford. Their own home was, in fact, spared by the rebels, but later in Longford they were only just saved from lynching by the arrival of the army.

Practical Education (1788) In the middle of this eventful year (1798) Joseph Johnson announced the publication of Edgeworth's *Practical Education* (2 vols.). This became his best-known work, a scheme for the educational upbringing of children within the family almost from birth to the time when they reached the contemporary standard of a university. Education at the time was limited in scope, with long lessons and parrot-fashion learning without well-arranged associations of subject. The Edgeworths advocated that for the very young the lessons should avoid drudgery and, if the child appeared bored, they should be cut to between four and five minutes. It is not possible to apportion credit between the 'partner' authors, father and daughter, but the lively chapters 'Toys' and 'Tasks' well display the attraction of their joint work. Broadly, Edgeworth gave very clear instructions on the teaching of the more down-to-earth subjects (such as reading and arithmetic), while Maria dealt with the less technical (including 'Taste and imagination' and 'Memory and invention'). More than half was written by Maria Edgeworth, but the project, dating back to the 1770s, owed as much to her father. The most spirited section demonstrates Edgeworth's experimental system, with selections from the children's questions and answers, derived from

the family 'registers'. These 'conversation lessons' show Edgeworth's skill as a teacher, for example when the children are led to reinvent a component of a steam engine by asking them suitable questions.

The book was read and abused quite often, but a second edition ('by Maria and R. L. Edgeworth') was published in 1801 and was much translated abroad. People complained persistently at the absence of religious education in the book, to which the authors steadily replied that this was the parents' business; they themselves were members of the established church and they explicitly disavowed the design of laying down a system of education founded upon morality exclusive of religion.

Practical Education perhaps received more attention on the continent than at home. After the peace of Amiens it was their Swiss translator, Marc Auguste Pictet, who urged the Edgeworths to visit France, promising them introductions to French intellectual society. Edgeworth, his wife, and his daughters Maria and Charlotte reached Paris at the end of October 1802, and the next day they were visited by François Delessert. The salons of the Delesserts attracted the top ranks of industry and banking as well as members of the Institut, to the meetings of which Edgeworth went as a fellow of the Royal Society. He became a member of the Société pour l'encouragement de l'industrie nationale. These encounters were probably the high points of the French visit. Literary figures they met included Mme de Genlis, Jean-François de La Harpe, and André Morellet. The family were much enjoying themselves when Edgeworth, without warning, was ordered to quit Paris. This was thought to be due to his distant relationship to the Abbé Henry Edgeworth de Firmont, who had attended Louis XVI on the scaffold. The order was quickly withdrawn, but Edgeworth thought it wise to watch for signs of war, and the family crossed the channel at the beginning of March 1803, in time to avoid internment.

Later works In 1811 Sir John Sinclair consulted Edgeworth about the evidence presented to a commission on broad wheels to decide whether cylindrical or conical wheels were the more damaging to road surfaces. This led Edgeworth to publish in 1813 *An Essay on the Construction of Roads and Carriages*, which became popular as a practical manual. This included a description of a road-building system similar to that later associated with the name of McAdam. Three years earlier the Edgeworths followed *Practical Education* with *Professional Education* (1808) which bore Richard's name on the title page, but was largely conceived and written by his daughter. She was worried that it might attract criticism if it were known that a woman had so large a part in it. Maria's reputation as a novelist was at its height with the publication of *Tales of Fashionable Life* in 1809–12. In the spring of 1813 Edgeworth spent six weeks in London with his wife and daughter. They were immediately overwhelmed with invitations, some from old friends, but many primarily to meet 'society'. Probably they most enjoyed meeting scientists such as Sir Humphry Davy, his wife, Lady Davy, and the guests at Mrs Marcet's salon. Edgeworth went to an educational meeting with the followers of Andrew Bell and Joseph Lancaster, and received a welcome compliment for his part in the last report of the Irish board of education. Despite letters home filled with grand names, Edgeworth clearly did not make a wholly happy impression. He got in the way of those wishing to talk to a speechlessly shy daughter and bored the wits who did not care for mechanics or education.

Edgeworth had a highly inventive mind and wrote many articles on scientific and mechanical ideas. One of the last was a description (*Nicholson's Journal*, December 1811) of a prefabricated spire he designed for Edgeworthstown church. It was 50 feet high, with a frame of iron bars held together by horizontal diaphragms. The whole was slated and painted to look like stone. It was put in position in July 1811 before a considerable crowd, and despite a heavy storm in the night remained unmoved. It stood until 1935.

In 1814 Edgeworth's health began to fail, but in the next two or three years, although seriously ill, he managed to go through a last series of wheel-carriage experiments for the Dublin Society. He died at Edgeworthstown House on 13 June 1817. He left instructions that his coffin should be entirely plain and should be carried, without a hearse, by his own labourers. He was buried in St John's Church, Edgeworthstown, where his monument is a small marble tablet, recording only his name and the dates of his birth and death. Out of a total of twenty-two children, thirteen—including Maria, his heir, Lovell, and the botanist and civil servant (Michael) Pakenham *Edgeworth—survived him.

Edgeworth was a man of boundless energy, both physical and intellectual. In youth an accomplished dancer, at sixty he could still demonstrate his agility by jumping over a dining-room table. Too miscellaneously inventive to become a major figure in either science or manufacture, he was the co-author of an educational manual which enjoyed an international reputation, especially in France, and in the British Isles still remained in use in the latter part of the nineteenth century.

CHRISTINA EDGEWORTH COLVIN

Sources R. L. Edgeworth and M. Edgeworth, *Memoirs of Richard Lovell Edgeworth*, 2nd edn, 1 (1821) · R. L. Edgeworth and M. Edgeworth, *Memoirs of Richard Lovell Edgeworth*, 2nd edn, 2 (1821) · R. L. Edgeworth and M. Edgeworth, *Practical education*, 2 vols. (1798) · Mrs Edgeworth [F. A. Edgeworth], *A memoir of Maria Edgeworth*, 3 vols. (privately printed, London, 1867) · M. Butler, *Maria Edgeworth: a literary biography* (1972) · R. E. Schofield, *The Lunar Society of Birmingham* (1963) [incl. bibliography of R. L. E.'s writings] · D. Clarke, *The ingenious Mr. Edgeworth* (1965) · D. Hudson and K. W. Luckhurst, *The Royal Society of Arts, 1754–1954* (1954) · B. C. Slade, *Maria Edgeworth, 1767–1849: a bibliographical tribute* (1937) [inc. some by R. L. E.] · H. J. Butler and H. E. Butler, *The 'Black book of Edgeworthstown' and other Edgeworth memories, 1585–1817* (1927) · A. Friendly, *Beaufort of the Admiralty* (1977) · *Maria Edgeworth: letters from England, 1813–1844*, ed. C. Colvin (1971) · *Maria Edgeworth in France and Switzerland: selections from the Edgeworth family letters*, ed. C. Colvin (1979)

Archives Bodl. Oxf., corresp. and literary papers · Bodl. Oxf., MSS incl. letters and literary and educational material · Hunt. L., letters · NL Ire., memoir and family corresp. · NL Ire., MSS · NL Scot., commonplace books | Birm. CA, letters to Matthew Boulton · Derbys. RO, letters to Joseph Strutt · PRO NIre., corresp. with John Foster · U. Nott. L., letters to countess of Charleville

Likenesses P. D. Hamilton, oils, *c*.1783, NG Ire. · H. Hone, miniature, 1785, NPG [*see illus.*] · A. Buck, lithograph, 1787 (*The Edgeworth family*; after crayon drawing, 1787), repro. in Butler, *Maria Edgeworth*; priv. coll. · J. Henning, paste medallion, 1803, Scot. NPG · A. Buck, watercolour, repro. in Butler and Butler, *Black book of Edgeworthstown*; priv. coll. · J. Comerford, chalk and watercolour drawing, NG Ire. · H. D. Hamilton, oils, NG Ire.; repro. in Edgeworth, *Memoirs of Richard Lowell Edgeworth*

Edgeworth, Roger (*c*.1488–1559/60), Church of England clergyman and religious controversialist, was born at Holt Castle within the marches of Wales in the county of Denbigh and the diocese of Chester. Nothing is known of his parents, who 'set me to schole in youth' (Wilson, 155), but he was possibly the eldest of three brothers. From one brother, John, were descended the educational writer Richard Lovell, and his daughter, the novelist Maria Edgeworth.

In the volume upon which Edgeworth's reputation rests, *Sermons Very Fruitfull, Godly and Learned* (1557), he thanks 'my bringer vp & exhibitoure' (Wilson, 155), William Smyth, bishop of Coventry and Lichfield from 1493. In 1501 Smyth founded Banbury grammar school, where Edgeworth was taught by John Stanbridge, subsequently becoming Smyth's exhibitioner at Oriel College, Oxford, *c*.1503 when the bishop was chancellor of Oxford University and visitor of Oriel and Lincoln colleges. After determining BA, Edgeworth was on 8 November 1508 elected the first incumbent of a fellowship of Oriel which Smyth had founded, holding it until 1519. Ordained to all three orders in 1512, he became college chaplain in that year and treasurer in 1513. He proceeded MA on 6 February 1512, was admitted BTh on 13 October 1519, and became DTh on 2 July 1526, having already acquired a reputation as a university preacher.

Edgeworth's use in the *Sermons* of the humanist methods of biblical exegesis, *secundum ordinem textus*, a colloquial preaching style, and vernacular preaching aids such as Heywood's *Proverbs*, and Erasmus's *Adagia*, indicates his affinity with the school of Colet and Erasmus, and the collection reflects that school's impact on Tudor homiletics. As fellow of Eton College in 1518 and precentor from 1520/21, Edgeworth may have sided with the master, Robert Aldridge, an advocate of the new learning, and the grammarian William Horman, another fellow, in the dispute over the teaching of Latin to schoolboys known as the 'grammarians' war'. In 1521 he was presented by Eton to the living of Christchurch in Monmouthshire, and between 1523 and 1528 he was vicar of Chalfont St Peter's in Buckinghamshire. From 1525 until his resignation in 1528 he was prior of the Guild of Kalendars in Bristol. Apart from brief absences, he remained in the west country for the rest of his life.

Until the end of Henry VIII's reign, Edgeworth consolidated his reputation as a theologian and preacher and increased his livings through service to the crown and political friendships. Following his attendance in 1529 at the legatine court convened in the London Blackfriars to debate Henry VIII's divorce, he was instituted to the prebends of Slape in Salisbury, Warminster-alias-Luxville in Bath and Wells (both by 1535), the rectory of Brandesburton in Holderness, Yorkshire (until 1556), and by April 1536 he was a canon residentiary of Wells Cathedral. Edgeworth represented the Wells chapter in its dealings with Thomas Cromwell at a time when Bishop John Clerk was following a policy of propitiating the vicegerent with cathedral treasure, grants, and concessions. Edgeworth's friendship with the bishop's brother, Thomas Clerk, a powerful friend of Cromwell, and also his role as arbitrator in local disputes, underline his prominence in diocesan affairs.

His attendances at convocation in 1539, 1540, and 1545 indicate that Edgeworth moved increasingly among the 'conservative Henricians', a group which included bishops Edmund Bonner, Stephen Gardiner, and Cuthbert Tunstall. In 1540 he served on a committee of twenty-five bishops and clergymen appointed to formulate true doctrine and ceremonies; their deliberations were published in the third Henrician formulary, the King's Book of 1543. He was rewarded with the prebend of the second stall in Bristol Cathedral by the charter of erection of 4 June 1542, and in 1543 with his appointment as royal chaplain and admission to the vicarage of St Cuthbert's, Wells. In the years which followed he preached a sequence of twenty sermons on St Peter's first epistle in Bristol Cathedral.

Edgeworth valiantly defended the religious conservatism of Henry VIII's last years against radical protestantism in the west country, and was associated with traditionalist opposition to Hugh Latimer, bishop of Worcester from 1535 to 1539, and his 'light' preachers:

> I preached at Redcliffe crosse in the good and worshipfull citie of Bristow ... although I was interrupted many yeares by the confederacie of Hughe Lathamer, then aspiringe to a bisshopriche and after being bishop of worce[s]ter, and ordinary of the greatest part of the sayd Bristow, and infecting the whole. (Wilson, 96)

The Edwardian years were turbulent. The Wells chapter divided in mixed opposition to Bishop William Barlow, who handed over most of the episcopal endowment to Protector Somerset. Edgeworth himself suffered forcible silencing and imprisonment: 'I have invehied ernestlie and oft in my sermons in disputacions and reasoninge with the protestauntes, untill I have be put to silence either by general prohibitions to preache, or by name, or by captivitie and imprisonment' (ibid., 95). That William Turner, a protestant appointed dean of Wells in 1551, attacked Edgeworth as 'the greatest wolfe in Welles' (Turner, sig. D8), on account of his multiple benefices, confirms the strength of the latter's opposition.

Following the accession of Mary I and the appointment of the Catholic Gilbert Bourne as bishop, Edgeworth was collated in 1554 to the chancellorship of Wells, vacant by the deprivation of the protestant John Taylor, alias Cardmaker. He also received the rectory of Kingsbury in Wells. Although he investigated cases of suspected heresy, witchcraft, and clerical marriage, Edgeworth is not associated with any burnings in the diocese. At the Elizabethan

settlement in 1559 he resigned out of conscience both St Cuthbert's and the chancellorship, and probably would have also resigned his prebends at Salisbury and Bristol, had he not died, probably from influenza, between 24 December 1559, when he made his will, and 17 January 1560. He requested burial before the choir door in Wells Cathedral, but nothing survives to mark the spot. His will, proved on 11 June, reveals his affluence: beneficiaries include his brother John's family; his cousin Richard, student at Oriel College; his nephew Edward, later Anglican bishop of Down in Ireland; Wells and Salisbury cathedrals, and his former parish church, Christchurch in Monmouthshire. To Oriel College he left his copies of St John Chrysostom and St Ambrose, to Thomas Jury, a fellow canon of Wells and his executor, the works of St Gregory.

Edgeworth's *Sermons*, published to endorse the Marian church's provision of officially approved instruction in Catholicism, reveals the limited defence of many practices after the Henrician Reformation. Image worship and purgatory are tentatively explained and Edgeworth directs his polemic at the protestant preachers, 'greene Diuines' whose readings of scripture bring the vocation into disrepute, who murder a merchant, and encourage children to play with discarded images, calling them 'ydolls'. His sermons on the creed (1546) and on ceremonies (*c*.1548) are authoritative formulations of belief and ritual just before Cranmer's liturgical changes, while his Edwardian sermons stridently condemn priestly marriages, iconoclasm, and the new order of communion.

Edgeworth's preaching styles reflect the pressure of Reformation controversies, so that his *Sermons* occupies a midpoint of Tudor homiletic prose, between the florid Marian style and the unadorned styles of Latimer and Cranmer. Conventional devotional images, biblical *exempla*, and an authoritative style convey pre-Reformation piety; this is juxtaposed against the accent of contemporary religious discord, evident in native speech rhythms, homely diction, and first-recorded idioms and proverbs such as 'to kepe a low saile', and 'beatinge the bulkes with theyr heeles' (Wilson, 333, 358). In religious terms Edgeworth was a moderate Catholic who became outspoken when occasion permitted; as his contribution to the King's Book demonstrates, he conformed to the Henrician settlement of the 1540s. His principled stand against protestantism proves that this conformity was severely tested. If he benefited financially during the Edwardian confiscations and as an absentee and pluralist, this was not unusual in his circle. Like his friend Stephen Gardiner, Edgeworth was one of those conservative Henricians for whom caution and compromise meant survival. His *Sermons*, balancing the demands of pragmatic preaching with the assertion of ecclesiastical authority, records the turbulent years of 1535 to 1553 and the commitment of those who aimed to preserve Henrician Catholicism.

JANET M. WILSON

Sources R. Edgeworth, *Sermons very fruitfull, godly and learned* (1557) • '*Sermons very fruitfull, godly and learned' by Roger Edgeworth: preaching in the Reformation, c.1535–c. 1553*, ed. J. Wilson (1993) •

Emden, *Oxf.*, 4.184 • will, 1559, PRO, PROB 11/43, sig. 34 [pubd as appx 2 in J. Wilson, ed., *Sermons very fruitfull* (1993)] • Bodl. Oxf., MS Rawl. D. 831, C. 1558–1560 • *DNB* • C. Lloyd, ed., *Formularies of faith put forward by authority in the reign of Henry VIII* (1856) • G. Burnet, *The history of the Reformation of the Church of England*, rev. N. Pocock, new edn, 4 (1865), vol. 4 • W. Turner, *The huntyng of the romyshe vuolfe* (1555?), sig. D8 • J. W. Blench, *Preaching in England in the late fifteenth and sixteenth centuries* (1964) • C. Field, *The province of Canterbury and the Elizabethan settlement of religion* (1973) • *Calendar of the manuscripts of the dean and chapter of Wells*, 2, HMC, 12 (1914)

Archives Bodl. Oxf., MS Rawl. D. 831 • MS Bodl. James 29 (1620–1638)

Wealth at death left 40s. each to Wells and Salisbury cathedrals and Christchurch (Wales); 40s. each to sister-in-law, nieces, nephew; also plate; £10 to cousin Richard; £10 to nephew Edward; copies of works of St John Chrysostom and St Ambrose to Oriel College, Oxford; copies of works of St Gregory to executor; bequests to choir and priests for prayers and saying psalter at his burial; considerable income; earned £100 p.a. as canon of Wells and another £11 6s. 8d. as prebend of Warminster-alias-Luxville (resigned 1554), but rectory of Kingsbury (1554) was valued at £40 5s. p.a.; continued to receive £20 p.a. as prebend of Salisbury and £20 as canon of Bristol cathedral; living of Christchurch, Monmouthshire, was £23 5s. 7d. gross (vacated 1554); rectory of Brandesburton, Holderness, Yorkshire, was £24 14s. 4d; the living of St Cuthbert (St Andrew's in Wells) was £33 13s. 6d.: will, PRO, PROB 11/43, sig. 34

Edgson, (Walter) Stanley (1893–1950), commercial property developer, was born in 1893. Nothing else is known about his life until he began his estate agency career with the practice of Rawlins and Culver, moving to the commercial chartered surveyors Hillier and Parker, based in the West End, prior to the First World War. He joined the Middlesex yeomanry as a territorial in 1912 and was commissioned to the Royal Field Artillery in June 1915, serving in France from 1915 until 1918. He was wounded on the Somme, and retired in 1918 with the rank of major. On returning to Hillier and Parker following the war he was made a partner.

Following its merger with the shops agency May and Rowden in 1912, the renamed Hillier, Parker, May, and Rowden grew to dominate commercial estate agency during the inter-war years. Edgson took charge of Hillier Parker's London and home counties business, becoming an eminent authority on the City and West End property markets, while Hillier Parker's other leading light, Douglas Overall, took charge of the provincial markets. During this period of rapid suburban expansion many new shopping centres were established along London's growing arterial road network. Edgson played an important part in these developments, assisting retailers in finding appropriate sites for new stores and bringing together shopping parade developers and the multiple retailers which were essential to the success of their projects.

Edgson was also directly involved in the commercial property market, establishing Central Commercial Properties in 1929. This specialized in London area high street shops, the section of the property market with which he was particularly well acquainted. Overall and Edgson became joint senior partners of Hillier Parker in 1937, by which time the latter had married; he and his wife, Nellie,

had two sons and a daughter. His son Peter was also to become a senior partner of Hillier Parker.

Edward Erdman, another of the leading commercial chartered surveyors of this period, recalled Stanley Edgson as a dynamic personality and first class auctioneer, who was the main driving force behind Hillier Parker's spectacular success during the inter-war years (Erdman, 4). As an auctioneer he was well known for his rich turn of phrase, such as 'the pleasure of offering from this rostrum' (*Daily Express*). He won the Penfold gold medal of the Royal Institution of Chartered Surveyors and was also an active member of the Chartered Auctioneers and Estate Agents Institute, serving on its council for many years, including a period as senior vice-president.

Edgson's non-business interests included local politics; in 1925 he became a member of Westminster city council and in 1941 he became mayor of Westminster. As vice-chairman of the council's civil defence committee he was closely involved in dealing with the effects of the blitz. In 1945 he stood, unsuccessfully, as a Conservative candidate for Balham and Tooting. He remained active in Westminster city council until his death.

Edgson retired in 1947 and in the following years devoted much of his energy to raising funds for a new estate management department at the University of Cambridge. He died suddenly at Sunset Lodge Hotel, Montego Bay, Jamaica, on 18 February 1950, and was survived by his wife. 　　　　　　　　　　　　　　　　PETER SCOTT

Sources E. L. Erdman, *People and property* (1982) • O. Marriott, *The property boom* (1967) • *West London Press* (3 March 1950) • 'Going, going, still going', *Daily Express* (28 July 1938) • private information (1985) • *CGPLA Eng. & Wales* (1950)

Wealth at death £121,526 7s. 4d.: probate, 24 July 1950, *CGPLA Eng. & Wales*

Edguard, David. *See* Edwardes, David (1502?–1542).

Edgware Bess. *See* Lyon, Elizabeth (*fl.* 1722–1726).

Edgware Road Murderer, the. *See* Greenacre, James (1785–1837).

Edinburgh. For this title name *see* Alfred, Prince, duke of Edinburgh (1844–1900).

Edinburgh Seven (*act.* 1869–1873), a group of women who attempted to gain professional qualifications in medicine from the University of Edinburgh, were led by Sophia Jex-*Blake (1840–1912). The '*Septem contra Edinam*', as Jex-Blake sometimes styled them, were the core of the small band of women who battled, ultimately unsuccessfully, to obtain medical degrees from Edinburgh University between 1869 and 1873. In 1869 the indomitable Jex-Blake sought access to medical classes in Edinburgh University at a time when all routes to medical education in Britain appeared to be closed to women. Her initial application was accepted by the medical faculty but was overruled by the university court on the grounds that mixed classes were unacceptable and special classes for one woman impracticable, a ruling that intimated that special classes might be possible for a group of women. Jex-Blake advertised in *The Scotsman* and other newspapers for likeminded women to join her.

The first to do so was **Isabel Jane Thorne** (1833/4–1910), wife of Joseph Thorne, a tea merchant, and already mother of four children. Although born in London, Mrs Thorne had spent her early married life in Shanghai, and partly as a result of the death there of one of her own children, had become convinced of the need for women, especially in China and India, to have women doctors for themselves and their children. Her husband fully supported her attempts to obtain a medical training. On their return to England about 1868 Mrs Thorne, who had attended Queen's College in London, began taking classes at the Female Medical College in London, opened in 1864 to provide midwifery training for women.

The next to join Jex-Blake was (Mary) Edith Pechey, later Pechey-*Phipson (1845–1908), daughter of William Pechey, an Essex clergyman. She had been indentured to Elizabeth Garrett, later Garrett Anderson, then the only practising woman doctor with her name on the medical register. Pechey had hoped to take the examinations of the Society of Apothecaries via apprenticeship, the route Garrett had taken, but which the society then closed. The third to join Jex-Blake was another former student from the Female Medical College, Matilda Chaplin, later Chaplin *Ayrton (1846–1883). Helen Evans [**Helen de Lacy Evans Russel** (*b.* 1833/4)], daughter of Henry Carter, a soldier, was born in Athy, Ireland, and was the prematurely white-haired widow of a cavalry officer named Evans; she made the fifth of the group of women who were permitted to enrol as matriculated students at Edinburgh University in October 1869, the first women to do so in a British university.

The five women were soon joined by Mary Anderson [**Mary Adamson Anderson Marshall** (1837–1910)] and Emily Bovell [**Emily Bovell Sturge** (1840–1885)]. Mary Adamson Anderson, the daughter of the Revd Alexander Anderson (*d.* 1884) and his wife, Mary Gavin Mann of Boyndie, Banffshire, was born at Boyndie on 17 January 1837. James George Skelton Anderson (*d.* 1907), who married Elizabeth Garrett in 1871, was her brother. These were the Edinburgh Seven, specifically the group in whose names a petition for admission to clinical instruction at Edinburgh Royal Infirmary was submitted in 1870. They were not the only women to matriculate to study medicine at Edinburgh in 1869 and 1870. But they were the first and were all committed to qualifying in medicine from the outset, whereas some of the other female matriculants had probably enrolled as partial students in a gesture of solidarity.

By the end of 1871 the seven were engaged in increasingly bitter public disputes with opponents of medical women holding powerful positions in the university and Edinburgh Royal Infirmary. But their progress was also threatened by the marriages of three of them, leading to their withdrawal (albeit temporarily in two cases) from the struggle to study medicine. Evans married Alexander *Russel (1814–1876), editor of *The Scotsman* and staunch supporter of the women medical students, on 3 November 1871. Russel was a widower with two children and he and Evans had two children of their own before his sudden death on 18 July 1876. On 5 October 1871 Anderson married Claud Marshall (*b.* 1820/21), a solicitor from Greenock, and son of Claud Marshall, sheriff substitute of Renfrewshire, but he died within two months of their marriage; her newborn son died in 1872. On 21 December 1871 Matilda Chaplin married physicist William *Ayrton (1847–1908), moving to Tokyo in 1873 on his appointment to the Imperial Engineering College.

Despite these losses to matrimony, the battle of the remaining four and some new female entrants continued in Edinburgh. But in June 1873 the women's legal action seeking declaration of their right to graduate from Edinburgh University was finally lost. The court of sessions upheld the appeal by the university senate against an earlier judgment on the grounds that the university's original admission of women in 1869 had been *ultra vires*, that is, beyond its powers. Some of the women students, including Jex-Blake, Thorne, Bovell, and Pechey stayed on in Edinburgh for several months taking such extramural classes as they could but with no hope of graduation.

The campaign then shifted to London and was fought on two fronts: parliamentary action to resolve the legal barriers to women's access to medical qualifications, and the foundation, largely through Jex-Blake and Thorne's efforts, of the London School of Medicine for Women (LSMW). Of fourteen pupils enrolled when the LSMW opened in the autumn of 1874 twelve had been students in Edinburgh, including Jex-Blake, Thorne, Pechey, and the now-widowed Anderson Marshall of the seven. They were later joined by Bovell, who shortly afterwards married Dr William Allen Sturge, an honorary physician at the Royal Free Hospital, where the women students received clinical instruction. Sturge was to prove a strong supporter of medical women in general as well as of his wife's career despite this damaging his own professional prospects. Ayrton also took classes at the LSMW on her return from Japan in 1877.

So six of the seven came together at the LSMW, providing much of its female leadership in its early years. Jex-Blake acted as unofficial secretary between 1874 and 1877. She and Pechey, Thorne (and her husband), and Bovell Sturge (and her husband) were all members of the school's executive committee or governing body during much of its first decade. In 1877 Isabel Thorne agreed to become the school's officially appointed honorary secretary to avoid overt controversy over Jex-Blake's nomination for the post. Given Thorne's family commitments this meant that she abandoned her medical studies permanently. It was Thorne's tact and diplomacy that steered the initially precarious school to a firmer foundation until her retirement in 1908 when she was succeeded as honorary secretary by her daughter, the surgeon May Thorne.

The remaining five all obtained medical qualifications, taking European medical degrees, some of which had been opened to women while all British qualifications remained closed. Jex-Blake and Pechey passed their MD examinations in Bern in 1877. Bovell Sturge took her MD in Paris in 1877, and Marshall and Chaplin Ayrton did so in 1879. All but Bovell Sturge also obtained the licence of the King and Queen's College of Physicians in Ireland, a registerable qualification opened to women following an enabling act of 1876 which empowered medical corporations and universities to admit women if they so chose.

The subsequent and successful medical careers of Jex-Blake, in Edinburgh, and Pechey, mainly in India, and the much briefer one of Chaplin Ayrton are described in their individual entries. Bovell Sturge's London based medical career was also to be brief. She was appointed assistant physician in place of Frances Hoggan at Garrett Anderson's New Hospital for Women in London in 1878. But from 1881 ill health forced her to winter in Nice and she died there from tuberculosis on 2 April 1885. Marshall also set up in practice in London and was senior physician at her sister-in-law's New Hospital for many years. In 1895 she moved to Cannes because of ill health, returning to England just before her death on 8 August 1910 at 1 Rickmansworth Road, Watford. She was buried at Woking on 12 August 1910. Thorne died at her home, 148 Harley Street, Marylebone, London, on 7 October 1910 and was cremated four days later. Her ashes were interred at Southover churchyard, Lewes.

The Edinburgh Seven were brought together by their shared aim of gaining a training in medicine. They did not deliberately seek confrontation with Edinburgh University, let alone their central role in a major public controversy, the founding of a new medical school, and the passage of primary legislation in 1876 which enabled medical examining bodies to admit women if they chose. But the opposition and formal defeat they experienced in Edinburgh hardened their personal resolve to complete their training on behalf of all women as well as for themselves. That five of the seven did so and at least began professional careers is testimony to their determination and paved the way for others. There were clear differences of temperament and preferred strategy, particularly between the impetuous Jex-Blake and the more diplomatic Thorne, but the personal friendships of Jex-Blake, Pechey-Phipson, and Thorne survived Jex-Blake's severance of her ties with the London School of Medicine for Women. These three in particular, through the medical schools and women-run hospitals they were associated with, were to be key figures in the small network of first generation medical women. They proved that professional success was possible and fostered opportunities for those who sought to follow them.   M. A. ELSTON

Sources M. A. Elston, 'Women doctors in the British health service: a sociological study of their careers and opportunities', PhD diss., U. Leeds, 1986 · J. Manton, *Elizabeth Garrett Anderson* (1965) · S. Roberts, *Sophia Jex-Blake: a woman pioneer in nineteenth century medical reform* (1993) · M. Todd [G. Travers], *Sophia Jex-Blake* (1918) · J. Bradley, A. Crowther, and M. Dupree, 'Mobility and selection in Scottish university medical education, 1858–1886', *Medical History*, 40 (1996), 1–24 · *BMJ* (11 Aug 1883) [Matilda Chaplin Ayrton] · E. Orme, *Englishwoman's Review*, 14 (5 Aug 1883), 343–50 [Matilda Chaplin Ayrton] · *The Times* (11 Oct 1910) [Isabel Jane Thorne] · *The Times* (12 Aug 1910) [Mary Adamson Anderson Marshall] · *BMJ* (20 Aug 1910) [Mary Adamson Anderson Marshall] · matriculation records database, Edinburgh University medical school, U. Glas., Wellcome Unit for the History of Medicine · archives, Royal Free Hospital School of Medicine, London · archives, Medical Women's Federation · E. Lutzker, *Edith Pechey-Phipson, MD: the story of England's foremost pioneering woman doctor* (1973) · bap. reg. Scot. [Mary Adamson Anderson Marshall] · b. cert. [Mary Edith Pechey Phipson] · m. cert. [Helen de Lacy Evans Russel] · m. cert. [Mary Adamson Anderson Marshall] · d. cert. [Mary Adamson Anderson Marshall] · d. cert. [Mary Edith Pechey-Phipson] · d. cert. [Alexander Russel] · d. cert. [Emily Bovell Sturge] · d. cert. [Isabel Jane Thorne] · *Englishwoman's Review*, 16 (1885), 239 [Emily Bovell Sturge] · m. cert. [Matilda Chaplin]

Likenesses photograph, *c*.1890 (Isabel Thorne), Royal Free Hospital School of Medicine Archives

Wealth at death £7060 3*s*. 4*d*.—Isabel Jane Thorne: probate, 16 Nov 1910, CGPLA Eng. & Wales · £2816 6*s*. 7*d*.—Emily Bovell Sturge: probate, 1885, CGPLA Eng. & Wales

Edington, Thomas (1742–1811), ironmaster and merchant, about whose early life little is known, joined the Carron Company about March 1764 as a travelling salesman. Apart from selling Carron's products, Edington served as the eyes and ears of the company in other ironworking districts. Carron had purchased Cramond ironworks on 21 December 1759, and Edington became its manager in February 1765. Cramond was engaged on rolling and slitting bar iron, and Edington applied to its operations the lessons he had learned at Bedlington slit mill (1764) and at Ambrose Crowley's Winlaton works (1766).

The key to Edington's later career was his association with the Cadell family. William Cadell (1708–1777), of Prestonpans and Cockenzie, shipmaster, merchant, and industrialist, was a founding partner at Carron, and his son, also William (1737–1819), became general manager. In October 1770 the Cadells exchanged their Carron shareholding for the Cramond works; Edington had clearly impressed them with his technical knowledge and business skills and remained as manager. This alliance was firmly cemented when Edington married, on 13 November 1772, Christian Cadell, daughter of William senior; they had nine children. During this time Edington also became 'joint proprietor' of Cramond.

Edington improved and extended Cramond ironworks, adding a furnace for producing steel (possibly the first in Scotland). Initially, the main products were hoops for wine and spirit casks, handle iron to be fitted to cast-iron products at local foundries, pan plates for the saltworks of the Forth, and, most importantly, rod iron for nails (300 tons being produced annually in the 1770s), sold to the nailers of Fife and Stirling and exported by Glasgow merchants. In the 1780s a wider product range included spades and shovels, plough socs, files, and a great variety of nails.

Cramond ironworks depended upon imported Swedish and Russian bar iron, which rose in price, thereby encouraging the younger William Cadell and Edington to seek cheaper supplies by investing in blast furnaces and associated bar-iron plants. The first venture was the Clyde ironworks, which became Edington's responsibility. A contract of copartnery (19 December 1786) specified a capital of £6000, split into twenty-four shares, of which Edington took eighteen (£4500) while the resident partner, John Mackenzie of Strathgarve (Ross-shire), had six (£1500). On 7 April 1787 Edington transferred six shares to William Archibald Cadell (1775–1855), but these were controlled by his father, William. This syndicate was also involved at Omoa ironworks through John Mackenzie.

Clyde was built under Edington's supervision on 600 acres of the Carmyle estate near Glasgow. This ironworks was dependent upon local supplies of coal and ironstone, under the control of James Dunlop (1741–1816) of Garnkirk who contracted to supply Edington with 20,000 tons of coal annually, but his bankruptcy (1793) led Cadell and Edington to open new coal seams with Dunlop's agreement (1795). Meanwhile, John Mackenzie's death (2 December 1788) caused Edington to move from Cramond to Glasgow. However, he retained his minority shareholding (⁸⁄₂₈) in a capital valuation which increased from £13,286 in 1772 to £30,148 in 1792.

Three malleable-iron companies—Smithfield, Dalnottar, and Cramond—formed a partnership in 1787 to exploit Ayrshire minerals at Muirkirk ironworks. Muirkirk became a major source of bar iron for Cramond, but like Clyde it was heavily engaged in armaments production during the French wars. Gradually, Edington withdrew his investments in Clyde, Muirkirk, and Cramond and turned to engineering and foundry work; and about 1797 he opened the very successful Phoenix foundry in partnership with two of his sons, James and Thomas.

In association with members of the Cadell family, Thomas Edington played a key role in the development of a coke-fired iron industry in Scotland on a large scale in the last two decades of the eighteenth century. A member of the Church of Scotland and a trustee of Anderson's Institution for scientific education, Edington, and his sons James and Thomas, also joined the Glasgow Highland Society (1809). Edington died in Glasgow in May 1811. His heir was not one of his sons in the iron business but Lieutenant John Edington of the 12th regiment of dragoons.

JOHN BUTT

Sources P. Cadell, *The iron mills at Cramond* (1973) · B. C. Skinner, *The Cramond ironworks* (1965) · J. Sinclair, *Statistical account of Scotland*, 7 (1793), 386–8 · J. R. Hume and J. Butt, 'Muirkirk, 1786–1802: the creation of a Scottish industrial community', *SHR*, 45 (1966), 160–83 · Cadell of Grange muniments, NL Scot., Acc. 5381 · Members of the Glasgow Highland Society, Mitchell L., Glas., C 311729 · Service of heirs, NA Scot., C22/105 · register of deeds, NA Scot., DAL, vol. 312, May–Aug 1811 · Cramond kirk session records, NA Scot. · Melville Castle muniments, NA Scot., GD 51/6/1010 · *Edington v. Hamilton*, 1793, NA Scot., court of session papers · *Clyde Ironworks v. Dunlop*, 1805, NA Scot., court of session papers · *Edington v. Herriott*, 1806, NA Scot., court of session papers · R. H. Campbell, *Carron Company* (1961)

Archives NA Scot., court of session papers, *Clyde Ironworks v. Dunlop* (1805) · NA Scot., court of session papers, *Edington v. Hamilton* (1793) · NA Scot., court of session papers, *Edington v. Herriott* (1806) · NL Scot., Cadell of Grange muniments, Acc. 5381

Edington, William (*d.* 1366), administrator and bishop of Winchester, was the son of Roger and Amice of Edington near Westbury, Wiltshire. Claims that he was educated at

William Edington (*d.* 1366), tomb effigy

Oxford have no substance, and he was never given an academic title in contemporary records. However, he was first taken up by Gilbert Middleton, a long-term royal counsellor and highly influential administrator in the Winchester diocese, who was chancellor of the university from 1320, so Edington will have been familiar with Oxford. Middleton was also a lifelong friend and colleague of Edington's diocesan, Bishop Adam Orleton, who took him into his service after the former's death in 1331. The bishop collated him to the rectory of Cheriton, Hampshire, on 26 August 1335, and from 28 March 1335 to 1346 Edington was master of St Cross Hospital in Winchester, which was a demanding post. Principally, however, he was proving his abilities in the bishop's own administration, but even from 1335 he was also designated as a king's clerk.

Orleton was a strong supporter of the young Edward III in the king's early years, especially in his conflict with his own chief officers of state in 1340. He made the king aware of Edington's ability, if Middleton had not already, and agreed to his transfer into full-time service with the crown after this latest crisis. On 26 March 1341 Edington was a receiver for the recent parliamentary subsidy south of Trent. On 25 November 1341 he was named keeper of the wardrobe, at a time when Edward was obstinately determined to keep his vast war expenditure flexibly under household control. In this capacity, Edington played an important role in organizing and financing the campaigns into Scotland in 1341–2 and Brittany in 1342–3. Preferments were commensurate: on 18 February 1341 he was presented by the king to the prebend of Leighton Manor (Lincoln). By 2 May 1344 he also held the prebend of Netheravon (Salisbury), and by 28 March 1345 that of Putston Major (Hereford).

Edington's performance had impressed the king. The still young Edward III had had dreadful relationships with his early great officers, especially as he turned his country into a war-state; he changed them frequently. Now he found his own men, retained them in office for long spells, and was well rewarded by their fresh minds. On 12 April 1344 Edington became treasurer of the realm and was to serve until 29 November 1356, the longest tenure since William of Ely (1196–1215) and before John, Lord Dynham

(1486–1501). On 9 December 1345 he was papally provided at the king's request to the see of Winchester, on the death of Orleton. It was easily the richest see in England, and was customarily reckoned to have only the archbishopric of Milan as its equal in all Catholic Christendom. It was, besides, his own native diocese, potentially a huge loan-finance resource for the crown, and Edward III in his emerging pomp was never to hesitate in demanding the greatest bishoprics in his realm for his principal officers: 'Tout's bishops', as they would become known in tribute to the great Manchester historian of English administration and government in this period. On 27 July the monks of Winchester had elected one of their number, John Devenish, who can scarcely have hoped to succeed but was an obstacle; he was rebuked by the crown, but had to be bought off by papal provision to the abbacy of St Augustine's, Canterbury (overruling the monks' own choice there). Edington secured his temporalities on 15 February 1346, and was consecrated without pomp at Otford, Kent, an archiepiscopal manor, on 14 May.

The king's lengthy retention of Edington as treasurer bore witness to his satisfaction with the bishop's work, which was indeed outstanding. He was remembered (at least by the St Albans chronicler, Thomas Walsingham) as distinctly more dedicated to the king's benefit than to consideration for people at large, but the contemporary writer John Reading (a monk of Westminster, but as his name shows, connected with Edington's diocese) preferred to see him as someone whose ability and hard work had at least put crown finances onto a professional footing, and saved the realm from arbitrary extortion. The latter judgement has stood up far better to inspection of the record evidence.

Edington inherited huge royal debts and a public loss of confidence, especially because the king had resorted to loans and then defaulted on them. The king would not diminish his war ambitions in the late 1340s, which left the financial position in continuing crisis, but at least Edington persuaded him to rationalize the costs. Meanwhile he was implementing longer-term strategies. An acute shortage of silver led to the reduction of the weight of the coinage four times between 1344 and 1351, and by 19 per cent altogether. This process, in which Edington was closely involved, caused severe difficulties for those who used the smallest coins, and in 1352 Edward III responded to anxiety by promising that future changes would only be made in parliament. No more were found necessary until 1412. To reconcile opinion further at no cost to the king, in the following year Edington helped develop the scheme to use money raised through the Statute of Labourers to subsidize ordinary taxation. Behind the scenes Edington achieved fundamental changes. Between 1344 and 1353 he overhauled the internal methods of bookkeeping in his department. In that last year he dealt very severely with two of his clerks who had mislaid tallies worth £2500. Meantime, although the exchequer was formally only an audit body, the bishop stretched this authority to develop means of overseeing cash flows

across the whole government. Poacher turned gamekeeper, he contrived from 1348 to have exchequer officials appointed to senior household offices, so that even these jealously guarded areas could be included by 1355 in the unprecedented overall accounts and budgets of the crown's income, cash flow, and expenditure which he was now producing.

On 27 November 1356 Edward III, at his peak after the great victory at Poitiers, promoted Edington to be chancellor, an office he held until 21 February 1363. The bishop was well recognized as the most influential of the king's circle of administrators, and especially as the author of the sea change that had persuaded the different departments of state and the household to work together more flexibly. In character, then, he caused his chancery to work more closely with the office of the privy seal. Whether it was the peace with France, or the ageing and retirement of the king and of his principal officers from the great years, such enhanced direction and attitude in administration would quickly fall away, since they were based on no institutional reform. Meantime, he was closely involved in negotiating the treaty of Calais of 1360, but without ever being seen as a political arbiter. Indeed, only once (in 1348, when accompanying the king to conclude a treaty with the count of Flanders) had he ever been required to desert his desk. Edington retired from office in 1363, perhaps through declining stamina, and certainly because, with peace in France and resurgent revenues (not least through his own characteristic closer audit and eventual reclaiming of direct control of customs duties for the exchequer), the king could afford to let him go.

Edington had inevitably been a gross absentee from his diocese, although he had made efforts to visit it when he could, and had always known how to use its resources for nepotism on a scale unusual even at that time. While chancellor he had been willing to take a bribe. His register is a testimony to seeking no trouble and finding none. He embarked on the funding of the great restoration, eventually replacement, of the nave of Winchester Cathedral, although he did not get much beyond the west front. He completely rebuilt the church at his birthplace, first as collegiate (1351), then as a house of *bonshommes* (a passing fashion with the king and his family which found no popularity) for a dean and twelve clerks in 1358.

Even after he retired Edington retained the king's gratitude. On 10 May 1366 Edward had the monks of Canterbury elect him as archbishop. It is possible that this was only intended as a warm compliment, because Edington at once declined on the grounds of failing health, and neither his age nor his background made him an obvious candidate, even under Edward, who alone would have regarded him as any candidate at all. Nor indeed had he been offering a polite excuse for his refusal. He made his will at Bishop's Waltham on 11 September 1366. There were bequests to the three chief officers of state, to the bishop of Salisbury, and to five old associates in the king's service, individual payments to 128 servants, and bequests for prayers to sixteen monasteries and all the friaries in

Winchester, Salisbury, Oxford, and London. It is the meticulous but depressingly soulless summation of someone with a career instead of a life. Edington died on 7 October at Bishop's Waltham. He was buried in the magnificent chantry chapel he had built at the head of the cathedral nave. His effigy, therefore, was presumably much to his liking. The residue of his estate had been left to continue the rebuilding of the cathedral, but his successor in both Winchester and eminence in the administration of the realm, William Wykeham, secured the diversion of £2000 of it to repair alleged dilapidations in the properties of the see. Such may have been all too true. Edington had had very sharp talents but a narrow range, with little evidence of broader intellectual or cultural imagination. His birthplace, his burial place, and dedication to the administrative role that had taken him from small beginnings to great offices in church and realm were all that filled his mind. This suited Edward III, an autocrat given to off-the-cuff policy making, very well. R. G. DAVIES

Sources Emden, *Oxf.*, 1.629–30 · R. G. Davies, 'William Edington', *Lexikon des Mittelalters*, 3 (1986), 1577 · W. M. Ormrod, *The reign of Edward III* (1990) · Tout, *Admin. hist.*, vols. 3–4 · *Registrum Simonis Langham, Cantuariensis archiepiscopi*, ed. A. C. Wood, CYS, 53 (1956), 318–24 (will) · P. Spufford, *Money and its use in medieval Europe* (1988), 316–18 · S. F. Hockey, ed., *The register of William Edington, bishop of Winchester, 1346–1366*, 2 vols., Hampshire RS, 7–8 (1986–7) · T. F. Kirby, ed., *Wykeham's register*, 2, Hampshire RS, 11 (1899), 151–6
Archives Winchester Cathedral, register
Likenesses tomb effigy, Winchester Cathedral [*see illus.*]
Wealth at death very wealthy

Edis [*married name* Galsworthy], **(Mary) Olive** (1876–1955), photographer, was born on 3 September 1876 at 22 Wimpole Street, London, the home of her parents, Mary, *née* Murray (1853–1931), from Aberdeen, and Arthur Wellesley Edis FRCP (1840–1893), obstetrician and gynaecologist. In 1880 her twin sisters, Emmeline and Katherine, were born, and these three girls completed the family. Olive went to Baker Street high school, London; the Cliff boarding-school, Eastbourne; and King's College, London. However, when she was seventeen her father died unexpectedly and she had to earn her own living. Her aunt Caroline, daughter of Surgeon-General John Murray (1809–1898), a well-known photographer in India, had already given her a camera and she had photographed Caroline successfully. It was, as she wrote on the back 'My very first attempt at a portrait which turned my fate in 1900' (print, NPG).

Self-taught and determined, Olive made a studio at the top of 34 Colville Terrace, Notting Hill, a large flat on three floors to which she, her mother, and her sisters had moved. By 1905 she also had, with Katherine, a smaller studio—again with living space—in Church Street, Sheringham, a popular middle-class seaside resort in Norfolk. Other studios appeared briefly, in Cromer and in Farnham, Surrey, but Sheringham and Colville Terrace were Olive Edis's work places for almost all her working life, and long after Katherine's marriage and departure in 1907. In Sheringham she started with local postcard views but soon turned to portraits, both studio and 'at home', of local and visiting celebrities, and also of the photogenic but notoriously camera-shy Norfolk fishermen. This latter achievement highlights her persuasive persistence, but sometimes she overpainted the images with oils. In London she took mainly portraits, pursuing well-known people to sit for her. She commuted regularly between the two studios in her tiny car, burdened with heavy glass plates and often with punctures. In Sheringham two local women assisted with processing.

By 1912 Olive Edis had become one of the first women to use autochromes (introduced in 1907), responding sensitively to their rich colours and inventing her own viewer. She won a medal with an autochrome, *Portrait Study*, at the Royal Photographic Society's 1913 exhibition, became a fellow of the society the next year, and exhibited regularly for many years. In 1918 the Imperial War Museum commissioned her to record war work by the British women's services in France and Flanders. As the only official woman photographer, and with a specially designed uniform, she travelled 2000 wintry miles in March 1919, testing her stamina, ingenuity, and three cameras to the limit, and brought back unique and poignant pictures. Many are still in the museum's collection with the diary that she kept. One shows six WAACs at Étaples in 1919, tending rows of war graves bearing temporary numbered wooden crosses, a bleak, snow-covered and wooded hill in the background. In 1920 she was commissioned to make 'colour plates ... of the Rockies' for the Canadian Pacific Railway, and she extended her travels to visit Washington, DC, and to learn to film. The commissioned photographs were exhibited in London later, but sadly none has been traced.

On 27 June 1928 Olive married Edwin Henry Galsworthy, solicitor, a cousin of the writer John Galsworthy. Now she became known as Olive Edis-Galsworthy, and Edwin moved into the Colville Terrace flat. After her mother's death Olive and her husband moved to 32 Ladbroke Square. She gave up the Church Street studio in Sheringham and moved to South Street, where she built a replica studio in the garden, although after her marriage she carried out fewer commissions. Following her husband's death in 1948 she annotated some of her best portraits and presented them to the National Portrait Gallery. She also made a scrapbook 'to hold some autographs and some notes of interesting days' (Edis, MS scrapbook, priv. coll.). Her exhibition in Cambridge in February 1920 included a representative sample of her work: portraits of six members of the royal family, various generals, bishops, university dignitaries, politicians, and titled people that were reasonably flattering and reassuringly conventional representations. Her style, with or without colour, showed great naturalism and changed very little over the years; her favourite medium was the 10 inch by 8 inch platinotype, with its velvety, deep-brown effect, used with natural light wherever possible.

Olive Edis-Galsworthy died on 28 December 1955 at her Ladbroke Square flat. She was cremated at Golders Green

on 2 January 1956 and her ashes interred in the Wey-
bourne Road cemetery, Sheringham, beside her husband,
on 5 January.   SHIRLEY NEALE

Sources archival material, incl. photographs, NPG, Heinz Archive and Library · archival material, incl. photographs, IWM · arch-
ive information, Museum of Local History, Sheringham, Norfolk ·
The lady's who's who: who's who for British women … 1938–9 (1939) ·
J. Carmichael, 'Olive Edis: museum photographer in France and
Belgium, March 1919', *Imperial War Museum Review*, 4 (Sept 1989), 4–
11 · V. Williams, *The other observers: women photographers in Britain,
1900 to the present* (1986) · S. Neale, 'Olive Edis (1876–1955)', *History of
Photography*, 16 (1992), 371–8 · S. Neale, 'Olive Edis, autochromist',
History of Photography, 18 (1994), 150–53 · J. Stanley, 'Marketable
maidens', *Women's Art Magazine*, 59 (1994), 45–6 · private informa-
tion (2004) · b. cert. · d. cert. · *CGPLA Eng. & Wales* (1956) · *BMJ* · *East-
ern Daily Press* (29 Dec 1955) · *Eastern Daily Press* (13 Jan 1956) ·
S. Neale, 'Arthur Wellesley Edis (1840–1893), obstetrician and
gynaecologist', *Journal of Medical Biography*, 4 (1996), 200–07
Archives IWM, prints, negatives, and diary
Likenesses O. Edis, self-portraits, photographs, NPG · photo-
graphs, priv. coll. · portrait, IWM · portrait, Sheringham Museum,
Norfolk
Wealth at death £15,681 19s. 11d.: probate, 25 April 1956, *CGPLA
Eng. & Wales*

Edis, Sir Robert William (1839–1927), architect, was born
on 13 June 1839 at Huntingdon, the eldest son of Robert
Edis, printer and bookseller, and his wife, Emma, *née*
Elkin. He was educated at the Brewers' Company School,
Aldenham, Hertfordshire. He was articled to the architects W. G. Habershon and Edward Habershon, and was
head assistant to Anthony Salvin. Edis joined the Architectural Association in 1859 and applied successfully for the
associateship of the Royal Institute of British Architects in
1862, before becoming a fellow of the institute in 1867. On
10 July 1862 he married at the Scotch National Church, St
Martin-in-the-Fields, Middlesex, Elsie Jane (1838/9–1897),
daughter of James Anton, parliamentary agent, with
whom he had five daughters. In his early years Edis moved
with the artistic élite of architecture: he was friendly with
Edward Godwin and travelled with William Burges to visit
Philip Webb's Red House, Bexleyheath, Kent, in 1862. He
commenced practice in 1863; his early work included
warehouses in Southwark Street and Paul's Wharf, in a
Gothic style, and one of the early schools for the London
school board, the Joseph Lancaster School in Harper Road,
off New Kent Road (1872–3), an early example of the
Queen Anne style.

Architecturally, Edis was a popularizer rather than an
innovator, whose work reflected the tendencies of his
time. He is associated primarily with the Queen Anne
style of the 1870s and 1880s: the Boscombe Spa Hotel,
Bournemouth (1873), and London houses at 94 Bond Street
(1878), 10 Fleet Street (1885), 59–61 Brook Street, (*c*.1884),
and 114 Mount Street (1892), were all designed in brick and
terracotta with Dutch gables. The Grand Central Hotel,
222 Marylebone Road, London (1897–9), was a prominent
late example of this style. In the 1890s several of Edis's
buildings reflected the turn towards Italian Renaissance
in English architecture: for example, 101–4 Piccadilly,
built as the Badminton and Junior Constitutional Clubs
(1890–91). The ballroom and other additions made by Edis

Sir Robert William Edis (1839–1927), by Olive Edis

to Sandringham House, Norfolk, for the prince of Wales in
1883 were in a Jacobean style.

In 1860 Edis joined the newly formed Artists' Rifles volunteer rifle club; he was its colonel in 1883–1902, and used
this title in his professional life as well as bringing many
architectural students into the volunteer movement. He
was a strikingly handsome figure, sporting luxurious
moustaches and proud of his military uniforms. He
designed a drill hall in Duke's Road, Euston Road (1889).
He was president of the Architectural Association (1865–
7), and assisted in its consolidation. He was a member of
the Arts Club, the Foreign Architectural Book Society, and
the Westminster and Keystone lodge no. 10 of the freemasons.

Edis delivered the Cantor lectures at the Royal Society of
Arts in 1880, published in 1881 as *Decoration and Furniture of
Town Houses*. This was a practical and accessible guide to
Queen Anne and 'aesthetic' taste, and it influenced the
diffusion of these movements to the middle class, modifying their more extreme aspects. Edis also published
Healthy Furniture and Decoration at the time of the International Health Exhibition in 1884. He was interested in
various aspects of practical reform in the design of buildings, including fireproof construction, after he had witnessed the burning of Paris in 1871 while on service with
the volunteers.

In 1894 Edis bought the Old Hall, Ormesby St Margaret,

Norfolk, to which he retired. In 1919 he was knighted 'for services rendered in connection with war'. He died at the Old Hall on 23 June 1927.   ALAN POWERS

Sources S. Neale, 'An architect presents arms', *Country Life*, 168 (1985), 1570–73 • S. Neale, 'Robert William Edis 1839–1927: decorator and furnisher', *Victorian Society Annual* (1985–6) • J. Lever, 'Edis, Robert William', *The dictionary of art*, ed. J. Turner (1996) • *Dir. Brit. archs.* • R. W. Edis, *Decoration and furniture of town houses* (1881) • R. W. Edis, *Healthy furniture and decoration* (1884) • J. M. Crook, *William Burges and the high Victorian dream* (1931) • *The Builder* (1 July 1927), 26 • *The Architect and Building News* (1 July 1927), 25 • b. cert. • m. cert. • d. cert. • CGPLA Eng. & Wales (1927) • *Debrett's Peerage* (1924) • *The Times* (25 June 1927)

Likenesses O. Edis, photograph, NPG [*see illus.*] • photographs, RIBA BAL

Wealth at death £68,315 17s. 2d.: probate, 1927

Edisbury, Kenrick (*d.* 1638), naval administrator, was the son and heir of Robert Wilkinson, alias Edisbury (*d.* 1610), of Marchwiel, Denbighshire, and Jane, daughter of Kenrick ap Howel, also of Marchwiel, and his wife, Rose Stanley. No record of his birth or baptism survives, and though a deposition of 1608 suggests that he was born about 1577/1578 another of 1626 indicates that the date may have been about 1584/1585. By May 1604 he had entered the service of the corrupt surveyor of the navy Sir John Trevor, who, like Edisbury, hailed originally from Denbighshire. In that month he witnessed a bond on Trevor's behalf and by August 1606 he was acting as Trevor's chief clerk. In July 1608 he bought the keepership of Chatham's stores from the previous incumbent for £100. Close association with Trevor perhaps inevitably coloured Edisbury's behaviour, and during the course of the 1608–9 inquiry into the navy he was accused of misappropriating stores and receiving kickbacks. No action was taken against the malefactors exposed by the inquiry, however, and consequently he went unpunished. In November 1609 he was appointed a deputy governor of the Chatham Chest, a fund for disabled seamen, having previously served as its clerk, with responsibility for collecting rents. In the following April he became deputy governor of the Sir John Hawkins' Hospital, Chatham, a position which required him to keep detailed accounts. He continued in naval administration despite Trevor's resignation in 1611, attaining the position of clerk of the survey by April 1616, and some time before 1619 he penned a little-known treatise on the navy, which has been misdated to 1630. Its underlying purpose was to establish its author's credentials as a reformer, even if this entailed condemning many of the practices, such as the buying and selling of offices, in which he himself had formerly indulged. The tract evidently served its function, for in May 1618 Edisbury resigned his position at the Hawkins' Hospital to become shortly thereafter paymaster of the navy under the newly appointed treasurer, Sir William Russell. In November Edisbury was also made an assistant to the admiralty, the last man ever to be appointed to this obsolete office, which carried with it an annual salary of £20 and no duties. He nevertheless remained ambitious for further promotion and unsuccessfully pursued a reversion to the clerkship of the navy, the most junior position on the navy board, despite having condemned the award of reversionary grants in his treatise.

Edisbury's promising naval career was suddenly thrown into jeopardy in March 1627 by the resignation of Russell, whose successor as treasurer, Sir Sackville Crowe, installed one of his own servants as paymaster. Crowe's shortcomings, however, helped pave the way for Edisbury's return to naval administration. In June 1628 he was appointed deputy treasurer at Portsmouth after secretary of state Sir John Coke, who had been put in charge of naval preparations there for the relief of La Rochelle, complained that Crowe would not provide him with clerical support. Edisbury acquitted himself so well in this service that, when the fleet returned to Portsmouth from France in November, he was unofficially permitted to resume his former duties as paymaster. His stock was now rising fast, unlike that of the navy board, whose members were widely perceived to be indolent, ineffectual, and incompetent. In late November, for example, the admiralty secretary canvassed Edisbury's view after the navy's surveyor advised against grounding a particular ship. A few weeks earlier Edisbury had advertised his abilities by submitting on his own initiative a short paper on the work needed to prevent the navy's vessels from decaying over the remaining winter months. By January 1629 the admiralty commissioners were so impressed with Edisbury that they promoted him assistant to the navy board, with responsibility for paying off mariners, backdating his appointment to the previous June, and in this capacity he worked alongside the official paymaster, John Harpur. Edisbury was again called upon to fill an administrative gap after Sir Sackville Crowe was suspended for suspected malfeasance in June 1629. During the period of Crowe's suspension, Edisbury and the navy's comptroller were jointly authorized to perform the treasurer's functions. Although Crowe returned to active duty in July, his shortcomings were now too plain to ignore, and in the following January the treasurership was again conferred on Sir William Russell, who immediately reinstated Edisbury as paymaster.

Edisbury's second term as paymaster was of short duration. In December 1632 he was appointed surveyor following the resignation of Sir Thomas Aylesbury, thereby achieving membership of the navy board, which he had long coveted. He undoubtedly owed his appointment in large part to Sir John Coke. Now an admiralty commissioner, Coke received glowing testimony of Edisbury's abilities in September 1632 from his protégé Sir Kenelm Digby: 'he studyeth continually how to contrive and mould things for the King's best advantage, and his thoughts are ever upon this subject, and in a word he hath no other business or recreation'. Pronounced 'honest and upright' by Digby, Edisbury rapidly demonstrated a degree of energy and dedication to business unequalled by his colleagues on the navy board, which he proceeded to dominate, although as late as September 1633 he encountered distrust from the leading admiralty commissioner, Lord Treasurer Portland. Within months of taking office, he revealed that three of his fellow officers, plus a number of other dockyard officials, had sold junk rope without admiralty authorization, while in February 1634 he exposed the widespread practice of embezzling wood-chips. His term as surveyor was also marked by the reinstitution of the practice of holding detailed, three-yearly inspections of the navy's stores and ships. Yet for all his energy and professionalism Edisbury, like his predecessors, was not a trained shipwright and so lacked the expertise to oversee shipbuilding and repair. In 1634 he failed to detect that the newly built *Unicorn* was so badly designed that she would prove unseaworthy without substantial modification, while that same year he ignored the advice of several shipwrights to remove from the navy's ships all sheathing more than seven years old to allow their caulking to be renewed. In consequence, the *Assurance*, which had not been re-sheathed in twenty-five years, proved so leaky in 1636 that she had to be withdrawn from the second ship money fleet. These failings aside, however, Edisbury was unquestionably the most competent and dedicated member of the navy board in the 1630s.

Edisbury's official salary was insufficient to meet the costs of his office, even allowing for his fee as an admiralty assistant. Nevertheless, throughout the 1620s and 1630s he bought up a substantial landed estate in north Wales. How he found the money to do so is unclear, but had he attempted to accrue a personal fortune by corrupt practice he would not long have escaped detection by his backer, the incorruptible and eagle-eyed Sir John Coke. His wealth was almost certainly derived from the property acquired at his marriage about 1605 to Marie Harding, alias Peters, the daughter and heir of a Rochester inn-keeper; from the lands he inherited from his father in 1610; from the profits of leases held of the Hawkins' Hospital; and from his income as feodary, surveyor, and receiver of the court of wards for Denbighshire, an office he acquired in January 1628.

Edisbury, whose residence alternated between Chatham, Deptford, and London, died in lodgings belonging to the navy at Chatham on 27 August 1638. His death was not preceded by a lengthy period of illness, though the effects of a fall from a ship in 1618 had proved long lasting. By the terms of his will, drawn up one week before his death, Edisbury appointed as his executors his wife, Marie, and their eldest son, John, to whom he bequeathed his landed estate. No provision was made in the will for Edisbury's younger son Richard. A monument in Edisbury's memory stands near the west door of St Mary's, Chatham, where he was buried. There was no lack of competitors to succeed Edisbury as surveyor, despite the smallness of his official salary. The successful candidate was William Batten, who once teased Pepys with the story that Pepys's chamber in Chatham was haunted by Edisbury's ghost.

ANDREW THRUSH

Sources PRO, SP 14 and 16 · A. P. McGowan, ed., *The Jacobean commissions of enquiry, 1608 and 1618*, Navy RS, 116 (1971) · navy treasurer's declared accounts, PRO, E351 · Edisbury MSS, Denbighshire RO · *Report on the papers of the Erddig estate, 16th–20th century* (Clwyd RO, 1975) · W. Berry, *County genealogies: pedigrees of the families in the county of Kent* (1830), 339 · A. N. Palmer, *A history of the town and parish of Wrexham*, 5 (1903), 225–6 · Sir John Hawkins' Hospital, Chatham, minute book · Medway Archives and Local Studies Centre, Rochester, Kent, Chatham Chest records, item 131 · Edisbury's treatise on the navy, misdated 1630, Longleat House, Wiltshire, Coventry MSS, vol. 117, fols. 1–21 · Edisbury's 'State of the navy', undated, but almost certainly written in mid-November 1628, Society of Antiquaries, Burlington House, vol. 203 ter., fol. 9 · petition for an increase in his salary, 1635, NMM, REC/1/62 · R. F. Dell, ed., *The Glynde Place archives: a catalogue* (1964), 57 · PRO, PROB 11/178, fol. 62r–v · J. Thorpe, ed., *Registrum Roffense, or, A collection of antient records, charters and instruments … illustrating the ecclesiastical history and antiquities of the diocese and cathedral church of Rochester* (1769), 733 · will, CKS, DRb/PW19 [Edward Harding *alias* Peters] · BL, Add. MS 9311, fol. 9v · Pepys, *Diary*, 2.68 · *DWB* · *CSP dom.*

Archives Denbighshire RO, Ruthin, MSS · Erddig Hall, Denbighshire, MSS

Likenesses bust, St Mary's Church, Chatham

Wealth at death substantial landed estate in north Wales

Edith [St Edith, Eadgyth] (961x4–984x7), nun, was a daughter of King *Edgar and the noblewoman *Wulfthryth, and was born in the royal vill at Kemsing, Kent. When her mother retired from secular life to become abbess of Wilton, Edith also entered the foundation and remained there until her death at the age of twenty-three. The main source for her is the life written by Goscelin between 1078 and 1087. Goscelin seems to have served at one point as chaplain to the Wilton nuns and drew upon oral and written traditions preserved there about the saint, as well as having firsthand knowledge of buildings and relics associated with her, such as her clothes' chest which had been miraculously preserved during a fire. Goscelin concentrates his justification of Edith's sanctity on her humility and rejection of her worldly status, which was manifested, for instance, in the wearing of a hair shirt and in the no doubt apocryphal story of her refusal of the English throne on the death of Edward the Martyr (978). However, in spite of these claims it is clear that Edith and Wilton did enjoy special advantages and wealth because of her royal birth. Edgar was responsible for the appointment to Wilton of two foreign chaplains, Radbod of Rheims and Benno of Trier, to oversee his daughter's education. Edith used her own wealth to build an *oratorium* dedicated to St Denis where she was to be buried. The church was of timber, but with lavish fittings of gold and semiprecious stones and decorated with a cycle of wall-paintings executed by Benno. Confirmation of Edith's royal status and independent wealth comes from the survival of her personal seal, which was subsequently used as the conventual seal of the abbey; on it she is described as 'royal sister'. Goscelin praises Edith for her skills in music, calligraphy, painting, and embroidery and had seen an alb embroidered by her in gold, jewels, and pearls, in which Edith had depicted herself as a suppliant at the feet of Christ.

Edith died on 16 September; the exact year is not known, but it must have fallen between 984 and 987. Her translation occurred on 3 November, thirteen years after her death, and seems to have been enthusiastically promoted by her half-brother King *Æthelred; the king and his uncle Ordulf were among those to whom Edith appeared demanding that her sainthood be recognized. Subsequent royal patrons included Cnut, who claimed

Edith had intervened to save him during a storm at sea and who provided a golden shrine for her body, decorated with scenes from the New Testament, and Queen Edith, the daughter of Earl Godwine and wife of Edward the Confessor, who had been educated at Wilton. Edith as saint proved a formidable defender of the rights of Wilton and of her own remains. Cures were effected among the Wilton nuns and humbler visitors from the locality and further abroad, such as the epileptic dancers from Colebeck who had wandered through Europe looking for a cure. Edith's cult was modestly represented in only five preconquest calendars, but remained significant for Wilton throughout the middle ages. BARBARA YORKE

Sources A. Wilmart, 'La légende de Ste Édith en prose et vers par le moine Goscelin', *Analecta Bollandiana*, 56 (1938), 5–101, 265–307 · S. J. Ridyard, *The royal saints of Anglo-Saxon England*, Cambridge Studies in Medieval Life and Thought, 4th ser., 9 (1988) · B. A. E. Yorke, 'The legitimacy of St Edith', *Haskins Society Journal*, 11 (2003), 97–113 · T. A. Heslop, 'English seals from the mid ninth century to 1100', *Journal of the British Archaeological Association*, 133 (1980), 1–16 · C. R. Dodwell, *Anglo-Saxon art: a new perspective* (1982)

Edith [Eadgyth] (d. **1075**), queen of England, consort of Edward the Confessor, was the eldest daughter of *Godwine, earl of Wessex (d. 1053), and his wife, *Gytha (fl. c.1022–1068) [see under Godwine]. Since she was married to *Edward (d. 1066) on 23 January 1045, she was probably born no later than 1027. Much of what is known about her comes from the *Vita Ædwardi regis*, which she commissioned. The first book (originally written in 1065–6) was conceived as a history of her own family, later recast and continued as a life of her husband. Naturally it gives a sympathetic portrait of the queen, who is praised for her physical beauty, piety, literary accomplishments, artistic skill (especially in embroidery), care for the king, efficient management of his household, and influence as his counsellor.

Edith was Edward's crowned queen, but their marriage was intended to cement the friendship between the king and her father; and when king and earl fell out in 1051, Edward repudiated his wife, perhaps because she was—and remained—childless. Both the Anglo-Saxon Chronicle and John of Worcester allege that the king deprived her of her possessions and imprisoned her at the abbey of Wherwell, ruled by his (unnamed) sister; the life of King Edward softens her treatment by sending her to Wilton, where she had been reared and educated, 'with royal honours and an imperial retinue' (*Life of King Edward*, 23). Whatever the truth of the matter, it was Godwine's successful return from exile in 1052 which forced Edward to reinstate Edith and restore her possessions. The queen's dower included property in Exeter and lands in Rutland, and she shared in the customary renders paid to the king. By 1066 Edith held lands worth £400, some of which must have been inherited from her father. She also had charge of the king's great-nephew Harold, son of Ralph, earl of Hereford, and at least some of his property.

As well as running the king's household, the queen supported her own, four members of which attest a memorandum of 1072 in company with their lady: the Wiltshire landowner Harding *pincerna* of Wilton, the queen's butler (*AS chart.*, S 1036, 1042); the rich thegn Wulfweard White, who had also been in the service of Queen Emma; Wulfweard's son-in-law, Æthelsige, the steward, whose marriage Edith herself arranged; and Ælfweald, the chamberlain. Edith's steward Godwine attests a charter of 1062 (*AS chart.*, S 1036) and her waiting-woman (*cameraria*) Matilda married Ælfweard, a Worcestershire thegn. Not all her servants were satisfactory: in William I's reign she asked the hundred court of Wedmore for judgment against Wudumann, who kept her horses at Mark, Somerset, for withholding six years' rent (*AS chart.*, S 1241). Her known chaplains are Ælfgar, a tenant of Peterborough Abbey, and the Lotharingian Walter, made bishop of Hereford in 1060.

The life of King Edward stresses Edith's piety. At Wilton, where she had been brought up, she replaced the wooden church with a stone building. It was dedicated in the summer of 1065 by Hermann, bishop of Ramsbury, and, through the queen's influence, of Sherborne as well. Since Edith was holding the episcopal manor of Sherborne in 1066, there may have been a price for her support. Giso, bishop of Wells, acknowledged the queen's help in securing the endowments of his see. Edith persuaded Edward to grant Wedmore, and herself leased Milverton, Somerset, to the bishop; after the conquest she added land at Mark. She also endowed St John's, Lewes, with land in Sussex and gave Lewknor, Oxfordshire, to Abingdon Abbey. Other religious houses remembered her less kindly. The monks of Evesham alleged that she had the relics of many monasteries assembled at Gloucester, so that she could pick the best for herself; their own relics of St Odulf narrowly escaped such a fate through the saint's miraculous intervention. Leofric, abbot of Peterborough from 1052 until 1066, laid out 36 gold marks (£216) to redeem three estates coveted by Edith, who also seized the property bequeathed to Peterborough by Archbishop Cynesige, consisting of a gospel book, £300 worth of treasure, and the manor of Tinwell. Edith was clearly a woman of strong character. When Gervin, abbot of St Riquier, at Ponthieu, who was visiting Edward's court, rejected her kiss of greeting, the king had to reprove her for taking, and showing, offence; she subsequently accepted the rebuff, presented Gervin with a richly embroidered cope, and tried to persuade the English churchmen (who did not object to the custom) not to kiss women.

In the closing years of Edward's reign, Edith seems to have become embroiled in the rivalry between her brothers, Harold [see Harold II] and *Tostig. She and Harold were instrumental in Tostig's appointment as earl of Northumbria in 1055, but in the autumn of 1065, the northerners rebelled against him and elected Morcar, Earl Eadwine's brother, in his place. King Edward wanted to attack the rebels in force, but Earl Harold, who was probably already married to Ealdgyth, the sister of Eadwine and Morcar, negotiated terms which resulted in the confirmation of Morcar as earl, the restoration of customary law in the north, and Tostig's departure in dudgeon for

Flanders. The queen was devastated by this turn of events, against which her advice could not prevail.

The life of King Edward throws the blame on the northern thegns, whose violence and brigandage Tostig had suppressed, and on Eadwine of Mercia and his brother Morcar. The Anglo-Saxon Chronicle is much more critical, reporting accusations of misgovernment by Tostig; these are elaborated by John of Worcester, who records Tostig's murder of two northern thegns under a truce and alleges that Edith herself had engineered the murder of Gospatric (son of Uhtred of Bamburgh) in 1064. Some colour to this is provided by William of Malmesbury's remark that Edith knew too well the 'mutinous disposition' of the northerners (*De gestis regum*, 2.331); and Gospatric's nephew, Osulf, was made earl of Bamburgh by Morcar in 1065.

It is possible that Tostig's fall provoked a rift between Edith and Harold. The life of Edward reports (though professing scepticism) Tostig's public accusation that Harold himself had been encouraging the northerners; and the earl must be placed among those who 'did not so much divert the king from his desire to march [against the rebels] as wrongfully and against his will desert him' (*Life of King Edward*, 53). Conversely, the Anglo-Saxon Chronicle hints darkly at a conspiracy against Harold. Edith's role in Harold's brief reign is impossible to establish. On the Bayeux tapestry she is shown sitting at the foot of Edward's deathbed, a scene also described in the life of Edward, which reports (ambiguously) the king's commendation of the kingdom to Harold. William of Poitiers, however, alleges that Edith hated Harold and worked to secure William's accession, and the *Carmen de Hastingae proelio* relates that she advised the citizens of Winchester to submit to the duke after the battle of Hastings. Certainly she retained much of her land in the Conqueror's reign. She may have lived at Wilton, where, on 28 February 1072, she attested a sale of land to Giso of Wells, but is more often found at Winchester. She visited and consoled the deposed Archbishop Stigand, urging him to eat properly and take care of himself. At Easter 1071 she attended the consecration of Walcher, bishop of Durham, allegedly foretelling his murder. She died at Winchester, on 18 December 1075, and was buried beside her husband in Westminster Abbey.   ANN WILLIAMS

Sources ASC, s.a. 1044, 1052, 1065 [text C]; s.a. 1051, 1065, 1075 [text D]; s.a. 1045, 1051, 1052, 1075 [text E] · F. Barlow, ed. and trans., *The life of King Edward who rests at Westminster* (1962) · D. A. E. Pelteret, *Catalogue of English post-conquest vernacular documents* (1990) · F. E. Harmer, ed., *Anglo-Saxon writs* (1952) · F. Barlow, *Edward the Confessor* (1955) · K. E. Cutler, 'Edith, queen of England, 1045–1066', *Mediaeval Studies*, 35 (1973), 222–31 · P. Stafford, *Queens, concubines and dowagers: the king's wife in the early middle ages* (1983) · P. Stafford, *Queen Emma and Queen Edith: queenship and women's power in eleventh-century England* (1997) · John of Worcester, *Chron.*, vol. 2 · Guillaume de Poitiers [Gulielmus Pictaviensis], *Histoire de Guillaume le Conquérant / Gesta Gulielmus ducis Normannorum et regis Anglorum*, ed. R. Foreville (Paris, 1952) · *The Carmen de Hastingae proelio of Guy, bishop of Amiens*, ed. C. Morton and H. Muntz, OMT (1972) · T. J. Oleson, *The witenagemot in the reign of Edward the Confessor* (1955) · A. Williams, *The English and the Norman conquest* (1995) · A. Farley, ed., *Domesday Book*, 2 vols. (1783), 1.21v, 43v, 63v, 77,

100, 129v, 153v, 293v, 294, 336v; 2.290 · *AS chart.*, S 1036, 1042, 1476 · *Willelmi Malmesbiriensis monachi de gestis regum Anglorum*, ed. W. Stubbs, 2 vols., Rolls Series (1887–9) · *Willelmi Malmesbiriensis monachi de gestis pontificum Anglorum libri quinque*, ed. N. E. S. A. Hamilton, Rolls Series, 52 (1870) · Hariulf, *Chronique de l'abbaye de Saint-Riquier*, ed. F. Lot (1894) · 'A brief history of the bishoprick of Somerset from its foundation to the year 1174', *Ecclesiastical documents*, CS, 8 (1840) · J. Stevenson, ed., *Chronicon monasterii de Abingdon*, 2 vols., Rolls Series, 2 (1858) · W. D. Macray, ed., *Chronicon abbatiae de Evesham, ad annum 1418*, Rolls Series, 29 (1863) · W. D. Macray, ed., *Chronicon abbatiae Rameseiensis a saec. x usque ad an. circiter 1200*, Rolls Series, 83 (1886) · *The chronicle of Hugh Candidus, a monk of Peterborough*, ed. W. T. Mellows (1949) · C. R. Hart, *The early charters of eastern England* (1966) · D. Hill, *An atlas of Anglo-Saxon England* (1981) · T. D. Cain, 'An introduction to the Rutland Domesday', *The Northamptonshire and Rutland Domesday*, ed. A. Williams and R. W. H. Erskine (1987) · R. Fleming, *Kings and lords in conquest England* (1991)

Edith, Mother. *See* Langridge, Edith (1864–1959).

Edlin [Edlyn], **Richard** (1631–1677), astrologer, was born on 29 September 1631 near St Albans. He practised in London from the late 1650s, announcing his availability each day between nine and five for the astrological judgement of diseases, nativities, and horary questions; he also offered tuition in astrology and shorthand. All this, he promised, was 'without the least prejudice to (or derogation from) the principles of our Christian faith' (Bodl. Oxf., MS Ashmole 436, fol. 110v).

Edlin was particularly interested in conjunctions, and published two substantial astrological tracts on this theme. In *Observationes astrologicae* (1659), where he described himself as a student in the mathematical and physical sciences, he discussed the probable effects of the conjunction of Saturn and Mars in 1658. Reviewing earlier conjunctions he linked Penruddock's royalist uprising in 1655 with the conjunction of the preceding year. The tract was dedicated to the marquess of Dorchester, as a patron of 'the sublime sciences' though Edlin admitted they were strangers. His friends the astrologers John Deacon and John Gadbury supplied commendatory verses, and he referred to the mathematician Thomas Streete as another friend. *Prae-Nuncius sydereus* (1664), dedicated to Elias Ashmole, considered the conjunction of Saturn and Jupiter in 1663. The earlier conjunctions in 1603 and 1623, he argued, had been marked by outbreaks of plague and by new monarchs ascending the English throne. In analysing the likely short-term and long-term effects of the recent conjunction Edlin predicted a great plague before the end of 1665 and a great fire in 1666. These prophecies were soon fulfilled, and his triumph was hailed by George Parker in 1692 as conclusive vindication of judicial astrology, a claim repeated by Tycho Wing as late as 1744. Edlin was not always so successful; he had also predicted the likely death of the king of Spain in 1666 and promised twenty years of peace, honour, and tranquillity for England.

Little is known of Edlin's personal life. In 1659 he was living at Sugar Loaf Court, at the end of Tenter Alley near Little Moorfields. By 1664 he had moved to Bishopsgate Street. His wife, whose name is unknown, had died at Christmas 1676. He died on 19 February 1677 (another source gives the month as January), only two weeks after telling a visitor that his astrological chart showed he would recover and live for several more years. Though he was dismissed in the *Dictionary of National Biography* as 'a more than ordinarily illiterate knave', Edlin won the friendship of some of the leading contemporary practitioners; his *Prae-Nuncius sydereus* contains brief commendations by George Wharton, John Booker, and William Lilly, all of whom are praised in the text.

BERNARD CAPP

Sources Bodl. Oxf., MSS Ashmole 426, fol. 292v; 436, fol. 78; 436, fol. 110v • J. Partridge, *Flagitiosus mercurius flagellatus, or, The whipper whipped* (1697) • B. S. Capp, *Astrology and the popular press: English almanacs, 1500–1800* (1979) • BL, Sloane MS 1120, fol. 2 • *DNB*
Archives BL, Sloane MS 1120

Edmond [Edmonds], **Sir William** (*d.* 1606), army officer in the Dutch service, was a native of Stirling where his father was a baker, probably the 'William Edmen, baxter' recorded as a juror in 1598 and later as a bailie of the town (Renwick, *Extracts*, 89, 96). At an early age he is said to have 'run away … to the Low Countries' (Sibbald, 40), joining the many Scots who had found employment in the army of the emerging Dutch republic, and he was commissioned there on 10 June 1589 as a captain of cavalry. In 1596 troops under his command suffered severe losses in a surprise encounter with Count Hendrik van den Bergh near Nijmegen, a setback which the Italian commander, Lodovico Melzo, attributed to inadequate reconnaissance on Edmond's part. But in the following three years he distinguished himself in successful actions at Turnhout, Grol, and Zevenaar, in the last of which he took Count Bucquoy prisoner. The Dutch captain-general, Count Maurice of Nassau, considered him 'the ablest of the Scottish captains' (Ferguson, 178n.); and when Alexander Murray was killed in action during the defence of Bommel, Edmond was promoted on 11 June 1599 to succeed him as colonel commanding the first Scottish infantry regiment in the Netherlands.

After winter service in Gueldres, Edmond fought in the Flanders campaign of June to July 1600, joining Count Ernst Casimir of Nassau in a brave but doomed attempt to stop the enemy's advance towards Nieuwpoort: their encounter with the Spanish army at Leffinge on the morning of 2 July 1600 (a few hours before the battle of Nieuwpoort) left 600 of his men dead, and was commemorated in a print inscribed to Edmond by Floris Balthasarz van Berckenrode. Briefly in Scotland from late July—it was probably about this time that he was knighted—he returned to the Low Countries in October 1600 with 800 new recruits whom he commanded in the defence of Ostend, in Luxembourg, and on the Waal. In 1604 he was in correspondence with Henry, prince of Wales, about a suit of armour to be made in Holland for the prince. But before he could complete this commission, Edmond died of head wounds received on 3 September 1606 during the defence of Rheinberg. The armour was eventually sent over by his widow, Agneta Berck.

Honoured by his contemporaries as a 'valiant gentleman' who had achieved military command by merit

rather than birth (Peacham, 15), Edmond was also remembered as a benefactor who provided generously for the repair of the almshouse at Stirling 'and for the maintenance of certain poor to be admitted therein' (Renwick, *Charters*, 109). He was succeeded in the Dutch service by his son Thomas Edmond, commissioned as a captain of infantry in 1617 and of cavalry in 1625.   HUGH DUNTHORNE

Sources J. Ferguson, ed., *Papers illustrating the history of the Scots brigade in the service of the United Netherlands, 1572–1782*, 1, Scottish History Society, 32 (1899) • F. J. G. ten Raa and F. de Bas, eds., *Het staatsche leger, 1568–1795*, 2 (Breda, 1913) • R. Renwick, ed., *Charters and other documents relating to the royal burgh of Stirling, 1124–1705* (1884) • R. Renwick, ed., *Extracts from the records of the royal burgh of Stirling, AD 1519–1666* (1887) • R. Sibbald, *Sibbald's history and description of Stirlingshire: ancient and modern* (1707); repr. (1892) • H. Peacham, *The compleat gentleman* (1615) • A. E. C. Simoni, 'John Wodroephe's *Spared houres*', *Studies in seventeenth-century English literature, history and bibliography: Festschrift for Prof. T. A. Birrell*, ed. G. A. M. Janssens and F. G. A. M. Aarts (1984), 211–32 • L. Melzo, *Regole militari del Cavalier Melzo sopra il governo e servitio della cavalleria* (1611), 56–8 • *CSP Scot.*, *1596–1603*, 637, 703–4 • *DNB* • H. Dunthorne, 'Scots in the wars of the Low Countries, 1572–1648', *Scotland and the Low Countries, 1124–1994*, ed. G. G. Simpson (1996), 104–21 • J. L. Motley, *History of the United Netherlands*, 4 (1904), 1–61 • T. Birch, ed., *The life of Henry, prince of Wales* (1760), 41–3 • J. Mac Lean, *De huwelijksintekeningen van Schotse militairen in Nederland, 1574–1665* (1976)
Archives BL, corresp. with Henry, prince of Wales, Harleian MS 7007, fols. 31, 37, 119
Likenesses F. B. van Berckenrode, print (battle of Leffinge 2 July 1600 NS; with a Latin inscription to Edmond), University of Leiden, Prentenkabinet; repro. in Simoni, 'John Wodroephe's *Spared houres*', 224

Edmondes, Sir Clement (1567/8?–1622), government official, was born in Shropshire, probably at Shrawardine, though the identity of his parents is not known. He entered All Souls College, Oxford, in 1585 as a clerk or chorister, and matriculated as a yeoman's son on 8 July 1586, aged nineteen. He graduated BA in 1589, proceeded MA in 1593, and was made a fellow of All Souls in 1589. On his marriage in 1598 he was described as being thirty. This evidence suggests that he was born in 1567 or 1568, although his monumental inscription gives his age in 1622 as fifty-eight, suggesting a birth date about 1564. His marriage was to Mary Clerk, daughter of Robert Clerk of Grafton, Northamptonshire, and attendant upon Lady Stafford. Edmondes was described as of St Alfege's parish in the City of London, where the marriage took place. His wife survived him, as did three children, Charles, Mary, and Elizabeth. In 1599 he was living in one of the parks belonging to Castle Hedingham manor and may have held a position with the earl of Oxford or another member of the de Vere family.

The conduct of war was prominent among Edmondes's interests. He urged the necessity for soldiers to read about and discuss the practice of their profession, to supplement their practical experience. He was encouraged by Sir John Scott to undertake an explanatory study of Caesar's *Commentaries*, published in 1600 as *Observations, upon the Five First Bookes of Caesar's Commentaries* and followed in the same year by *Observations on the Sixth and Seventh Books*.

Edmondes explained that the work was directed at English soldiers and he supplemented his comments on Roman military practice with observations on contemporary campaigns, including those of the English forces in France and the war in Ireland, as well as the battle of Dreux of 1562 between the royal army and protestant forces in France. He also discussed the question of how to deal with an invasion of England, whether to oppose an invading army at the coast or to withdraw and offer battle later. His preference was to fortify the coast of Kent and oppose a landing. As well as military matters, he included an explanation of the causes of tides. The *Observations* was dedicated to Sir Francis Vere, as his 'honourable friend'. Edmondes was present at the battle of Nieuwpoort in 1600 and was privy to the discussions of the English and Dutch commanders. He reported that Vere drew upon an example from Caesar's *Commentaries* when advising Prince Maurice on the tactics he should employ. Vere chose Edmondes to carry to the privy council his dispatch describing the battle. It is unclear whether Edmondes undertook any further campaigning. Indeed, Thomas Fuller regarded him as an example of an author who achieved 'perfection of theory' in writing on military matters without having practical experience.

In May 1601 Edmondes became assistant to the remembrancer of the City of London, Dr Giles Fletcher, receiving half the fee. In July 1605, on Fletcher's resignation, he was appointed remembrancer at an annual salary of £100. Despite his duties with the City he was able to maintain his interest in military affairs. In an edition of the *Observations* published in 1604, dedicated to Prince Henry, he included comments on the battle of Nieuwpoort and referred to the sieges of Ostend (1601–4) and Grave, in Brabant (1602). He also included a treatise on contemporary tactics, 'The maner of our moderne training, or, Tacticke practise', a slightly altered version of which was issued in 1642 as *A Few Words to the Trained Bands and Souldiers of London Citie in these Perilous Times*. A further edition of the *Observations*, published in 1609, was again dedicated to Prince Henry and had epigrams by William Camden, Samuel Daniel, Joshua Sylvester, and Ben Jonson.

Edmondes's existing contacts with the court were enhanced during his tenure of the post of remembrancer. In 1608 he was responsible for preparing the assurance made by the king for loans made to him by the City, for which he was paid £113 13s. 4d. On 13 August 1609 he was appointed one of the four clerks to the privy council, for life. On his subsequent resignation of the post of remembrancer the City presented him with 40 angels for a velvet cloak. He was made muster master-general for life on 4 October 1613. He was also granted the reversion of the post of muster master of the cautionary town of Brill, in Zeeland, but had not obtained it before the town was surrendered to the states general in 1616. He received a compensatory payment of £400 from the crown. He was knighted on 29 September 1617.

Edmondes's duties as clerk to the council included a diplomatic mission to the United Provinces in 1615, investigating the possibility of concerting the British and Dutch enterprises in the East India trade. Accompanied by Robert Middleton and Maurice Abbot he left on 29 December 1614 and returned about 5 May 1615, receiving £300 for the assignment. An inquisitive envoy, he compiled an account of the country, 'The politia of the United Provinces' (Exeter College, Oxford, MS 105; Bodl. Oxf., MS Tanner 216). This wide-ranging account includes descriptions of the constitution, the system of taxation, the armed forces, the economy, and religion, drawing attention to the degree of religious toleration, which, he feared, could lead to 'destruction and confusion'. He also described the dress and deportment of Dutch men and women, and commented on their enthusiasm for collecting pictures and flowers.

In 1618 Edmondes was required to investigate the state of the drainage of the fens and reconcile the differing views among the commissioners of sewers. He attended a meeting of the commissioners at Huntingdon and spent a week carrying out a survey of the channels. His report to the privy council described the condition of the various waterways and touched on the disputes between those living around the fenland and those in the adjacent uplands regarding their contributions to the cost of scouring the channels. He recommended that the commissioners enforce their decrees and begin work to clear the outfalls of the rivers Nene and Welland. He was given 'two pieces of 44s.' by the mayor of Exeter in 1620 to expedite a matter before the council. He was also accused by Nicholas Leate, the deputy of the Levant Company, of being suborned by the Spanish merchants and accepting a bribe of £50 to favour them over those trading to Turkey, in the allocation of the share of the levy for financing an expedition against the North African pirates.

In 1620 Edmondes presented the Bodleian Library with a pentagonal pillar of alabaster, faced with pilasters of the five orders. Used to display models of the five geometrical solids, it may have been designed as a teaching aid for the Savilian professor of geometry, a post established in 1619. Edmondes was chosen MP for Oxford University in 1621. He apparently took no part in debates, but was appointed a member of the council's committee on trade, established in November 1621.

Edmondes was promoted to the post of secretary of state but before he could take up his duties he died of an apoplexy, on 13 October 1622, at his house in St Martin-in-the-Fields. He was buried in the church of Sts Peter and Paul, at Preston Deanery, near Northampton, having acquired the manor of Preston in 1620. An alabaster monument, since destroyed, was placed on the north wall of the chancel and a small brass plate with an effigy of Edmondes in an ornamental suit of armour was fixed on a slab in the chancel floor. The inscription on his wall monument described him as 'worthily esteemed excellent in his own vocatione, and in the art militarie' (Bridges, 1.382). Anthony Wood wrote that 'He was a learned person, was generally skill'd in all arts and sciences, and famous as well for military, as for politic affairs, and therefore esteemed by all an ornament to his degree and profession' (Wood, *Ath. Oxon.*, 3rd edn, 2.322).   STEPHEN PORTER

Sources DNB · APC, 1618–19, 292–9 · D. D. Hebb, *Piracy and the English government, 1616–1642* (1994), 39–40 · J. Bridges, *The history and antiquities of Northamptonshire*, ed. P. Whalley, 1 (1791), 382 · Wood, *Ath. Oxon.*, new edn, 2.322–3 · PRO, PROB/11/140/92, fols. 243–4 · H. C. Darby, *The draining of the fens*, 2nd edn (1956); repr. (1968), 36–8 · J. Newman, 'The architectural setting', *Hist. U. Oxf.* 4: *17th-cent. Oxf.*, 135–77 · G. M. Bell, *A handlist of British diplomatic representatives, 1509–1688*, Royal Historical Society Guides and Handbooks, 16 (1990), 195 · J. Nichols, *The progresses, processions, and magnificent festivities of King James I, his royal consort, family and court*, 3 (1828), 259, 437 · W. Notestein, F. H. Relf, and H. Simpson, eds., *Commons debates, 1621*, 3 (1935), 415

Likenesses attrib. M. van Mierevelt or D. Mytens, portrait, Corporation of London · line print, BM; repro. in C. Edmondes, *Observations upon Caesar's Commentaries* (1604) · monumental brass, church of Sts Peter and Paul, Preston Deanery, Northamptonshire

Edmondes, Sir Thomas (d. 1639), diplomat, was born in Plymouth, Devon, the fifth son of Thomas Edmondes of Fowey, Cornwall, head customer of Plymouth, and his wife, Joan, daughter of Anthony Delabere of Sherborne, Dorset. His father, who came from a relatively obscure west country family, was mayor of Plymouth in 1582, but it is possible that he was also, as Anthony Wood states, employed in some way at court and that he had brought his son with him at an early age. Lord Burghley praised a Thomas Edmondes for having carried out an 'office of trust' in 1585 (W. Murdin, *A Collection of State Papers*, 1759, 545). Francis Walsingham employed the younger Thomas Edmondes too and he became secretary to Sir Henry Unton during his embassy to France of 1591–2. When Unton returned to England in June 1592 Edmondes remained as the English chargé d'affaires at a diet of 20s. p.a. (later raised to 30s. on 1 April 1594) until April 1596. He returned to England briefly in the early months of 1594 (January to May), which meant that he missed Henri IV's entry into Paris in March. Even his modest remuneration was irregularly paid and he complained in a ciphered letter to an unknown party in May 1593 that he lived 'as the Camellions doe by the ayre. If they doe not shortlie revoke me, I protest … I will lay the key under the doore and goe without leave' (Butler, 80). He was reduced to surviving on advances of £2000—and then a further £200 from Ottiwell Smith.

These years gave Edmondes an unparalleled knowledge of regional France. Following Henri IV's army took him to most of the provinces and their capitals north of the Loire. He gained firsthand experience of military affairs, concerning not only the English expeditionary forces in Brittany and Normandy but also the levying and retaining of German mercenary forces that were vital to the French king's strategic efforts to win back the French kingdom from the Catholic League. He also became the most acute observer of the delicate politics of the French court. He reported shrewdly on the danger of a Catholic 'tiers parti' (third way) to rival Henri IV's claim to the throne in 1592. He already knew of 'that metamorphosis' (the king's decision to abjure the protestant faith) at Mantes on 26 April 1593 (Butler, 67). His dry sense of humour captured the shifts and turns in the peace process between Henri IV and the aristocratic leaders of the league who (as he said in June 1593) 'do play mockhollydaie' (Butler, 82).

During these years in France, Edmondes wrote frequently to the earl of Essex. If he sought rewards from the latter, however, it was Burghley that he acknowledged as his master in November 1595. This was the moment when Sir Henry Unton arrived as resident ambassador at the French court. Edmondes reverted to being secretary to the resident and his letters to the earl abruptly ceased. This led one of the earl's supporters to call him a 'mere Judas' and 'more corrupt than any Jesuit' (*Salisbury MSS*, 5.429). But Edmondes did not entirely trust Essex and was reported as saying that 'the Earl would spoil everything and ruin himself, as being much more proper for throwing a court into disorder, than contributing to its order' (Birch, *Memoirs*, 1.345, 2.392). On 17 May 1596 he was rewarded by the queen with the secretaryship for the French tongue and a salary of £66 13s. 4d. Shortly thereafter he was recalled to London, although he returned to France for two further special embassies in late March, and then again in early May 1597 in connection with possible English assistance to the French king during the siege of Amiens.

These were the prelude to Edmondes's second major stay as English agent (from late May 1598 chargé d'affaires) in Paris, which lasted from September 1597 through to Sir Henry Neville's arrival as resident ambassador in May 1599. It was thanks to his careful dealings that the vicomte de Turenne and the hotter heads of the French protestant movement were encouraged to reach an accommodation with the French king rather than enlist foreign support and destabilize the war-torn kingdom. The greatest diplomatic challenge of his career so far, however, was about to begin with the preparations for the conference at Boulogne. Since Archduke Albert of the Netherlands was unwilling to send peace commissioners to England, Elizabeth dispatched Edmondes in December 1599 as the first English representative to the Brussels court since the Dutch rising. During this special embassy he met the archduke on 9 January, and returned for a second time in March, meeting the archduke again, on 22 March, for an audience which established the basis for the Boulogne conference between representatives of the archduke, France, and England. Edmondes went directly to Boulogne as one of the English commissioners, staying there until the French king came to Calais in August 1601. The attempts to end the long war with Spain there foundered on questions of precedence and diplomatic misunderstandings with the French. But Edmondes had already earned the praises of the French king, Henri IV, the grudging respect of the French secretary of state, Villeroy, and the fulsome tribute of his successor, Henry Neville. 'I should be very ungrateful if I should not yield a true testimony unto this gentleman', he wrote to Elizabeth I, '[about] his knowledge of the affairs of this state, which I assure your Majesty to be very exquisite' (Sawyer, 1.44). The queen recognized his exceptional talents in appointing him clerk to the privy council during the Boulogne peace conference and he returned to France briefly as a special ambassador in June 1602 to argue the case for better treatment of English merchants there.

In between his diplomatic missions Edmondes sat in parliament and married his first wife. He was the MP for Chippenham, Wiltshire, in 1597 at the instigation of Sir Walter Mildmay, but was replaced by a proxy when he left on embassy before he was able to take up his seat. In May 1601, according to John Chamberlain, Edmondes married Magdalen (d. 1614), daughter and coheir of Sir John Wood, clerk of the signet. That year it was probably a combination of the recommendation of Henry Neville and the support of Sir Robert Cecil that ensured his nomination as MP for the borough of Liskeard, Cornwall, by Jonathan Trelawny, its steward. Cecil, with the earl of Shrewsbury, stood godfather to Edmondes's only son, Henry, born in July 1602. In the first Stuart parliament of 1604 Edmondes was MP for Wilton, Wiltshire. He became a well-known figure among a circle of men of business meeting in the Mermaid tavern in London, who included John Chamberlain and Ralph Winwood. His diplomatic experience was, however, regularly put to use over the next decade and he and Winwood were the most skilful diplomats the early Stuart court had at its command. He was among the very first knights dubbed by James I on 20 May 1603.

Following the English peace with Spain in August 1604 Edmondes became, for the first time in his career, a full resident ambassador, this time at the Brussels court, taking up his post in November 1604 and remaining at the archduke's court until September 1609. He trained his successor, William Trumbull the elder, who served as his secretary, and later replaced him in the embassy. With the Spanish Netherlands still at war with the Dutch his greatest diplomatic task consisted in acting as a mediator when possibilities for peace were being explored. In many respects his greatest achievement was his role supporting Winwood in The Hague and securing the twelve years' truce (the treaty of Antwerp) that was signed on 29 January 1609. But he had numerous other issues to handle, of which that of the earl of Tyrone was potentially the most explosive. The Spanish Netherlands proved a safe haven for Catholic exiles from various quarters in north-west Europe and the earl of Tyrone's flight to Brussels in 1607 led to Edmondes's immediate demands that he be sent back to England. The archduke refused—although Edmondes's diplomatic efforts would ensure that he was quietly hustled out of the Low Countries before the year was out. Edmondes's relations with the archduke and archduchess were such that when his elder daughter, Isabella, was born in Brussels in November 1607 the archduchess, whose name she was given, was her godmother.

Back in London in autumn 1609 Edmondes was already rumoured as the replacement for Sir George Carew, the resident ambassador in Paris who retired in October of that year. In practice, however, it was not until April 1610 that he was assigned once more as ambassador ordinary to the court of Henri IV. He arrived in Paris on (or around) 24 May to a court mourning the king's assassination less than two weeks previously and fearing a renewal of France's

internal strife. Edmondes shared these anxieties throughout the next seven years at the French court. Some of his efforts to mediate between the protestant aristocracy and the French crown were misinterpreted by the regent, Marie de Medici, who felt that he exceeded his authority. However, once again Edmondes expressed through his family his close links with his royal hosts. His daughter Louisa, born in Paris in 1611, was baptized on 15 September with the young King Louis XIII as her godfather and the regent as her godmother. Edmondes was a major player in marriage negotiations, first between the elector palatine and Princess Elizabeth, and then between Prince Henry and Louis XIII's sister, Princess Christina. When the regent heard of the death of Prince Henry (6 November 1612), he immediately proposed that Prince Charles act as his substitute. Edmondes suppressed the proposal as unbecoming in its haste and his action won James I's endorsement. The match occupied Edmondes for much of 1613–14, although it eventually came to nothing. In 1613 it is said that he undertook a private journey to Rome in order to obtain proof from the papal archives as to England's right to precede Castile in diplomatic arrangements at Paris. He returned to England from February to June 1614 and again from December 1616 to May 1617 and, finding the passive stance of James I in foreign affairs increasingly irksome, he sought his release from December 1613 onwards. 'It hath always been our custom to seek still to put off the time and never to endeavour the preventing of mischiefs till they be fallen upon us', he wrote, with a wealth of experience to draw on, adding 'which maketh that afterwards they are not either at all to be remedied, or at the least not without great difficulty' (*Downshire MSS*, 3.128–9). Some time in 1614 his wife died in Paris. In January 1617, while back in London, he co-operated with his old friend Ralph Winwood in planning with Scanafissi, the Savoyard envoy, that Sir Walter Ralegh should attack Genoa in the interest of Savoy and against Spain, under cover of an expedition to seek for gold in Guiana. Just before his execution in 1618 Ralegh named Edmondes among those who had a hand in the business and only Edmondes's well-attested and prudent loyalty assisted him in escaping major embarrassment from the affair.

James I, doubtless on the recommendation of Winwood, made Edmondes the controller of his household on 21 December 1617 and admitted him of the privy council the following day. A year later, on 19 January 1618, he became treasurer of the royal household and, in 1620, he enjoyed the reversion of the clerkship of the crown in the king's bench. He served in all the Stuart parliaments of the 1620s, being elected MP for both Dorchester and Bewdley in December 1620 (he chose to sit for the latter), Chichester in February 1624, and Oxford University on 16 April 1625. He was re-elected at Oxford on 23 March 1626, but the return was declared void. He was elected for Penryn, Cornwall, on 3 March 1628. He was a frequent spokesman in the house on behalf of both James I and, more controversially, Charles I. In March 1628 he proposed the appointment of Sir John Finch as speaker and sought to protect him from the taunts of his opponents. His last diplomatic engagements involved a visit to Paris as ambassador-extraordinary, dispatched in late May 1629 to ratify a new peace treaty between France and England (on 6 July 1629).

On 11 September 1626 Edmondes married the sixty-year-old Sara (1566–1629), daughter of James Harington of Exton, Rutland, widow first of Francis Hastings, Lord Hastings, and then of Edward la Zouche, eleventh Baron Zouche, but she died three years later and was buried on 3 October 1629. From 1630 Edmondes lived in retirement at Albyns, near Romford, Essex, a manor inherited from his first wife; Inigo Jones had built him a country mansion there. His son is said to have been a knight of the Bath, but he suffered as an alcoholic and died in 1635. In March 1636 Louisa married one of her father's servants, but her sister Mary married Robert Mildmay; among their sons were Henry and Benjamin Mildmay, successively barons Fitzwalter. Edmondes died on 20 September 1639, leaving his daughters as coheirs. Known as a 'little man' to his contemporaries because of his short stature, his diplomatic correspondence testifies to his clarity, capacity, and concision, but betrays no deep ambition beyond loyal service.

M. GREENGRASS

Sources G. G. Butler, ed., *The Edmondes papers: a selection from the correspondence of Sir Thomas Edmondes, envoy from Queen Elizabeth at the French court* (1913) · *Calendar of the manuscripts of the most hon. the marquis of Salisbury*, 24 vols., HMC, 9 (1883–1976), esp. vols. 4–5 · R. B. Wernham, ed., *List and analysis of state papers, foreign series, Elizabeth I*, 5–6 (1989–93) · E. Sawyer, ed., *Memorials of affairs of state*, 2 vols. (1725) · T. Birch, *Memoirs of the reign of Queen Elizabeth*, 2 vols. (1754) · T. Birch, ed., *Historical view of the negotiations between the courts of England, France and Brussels from the year 1572 to 1617* (1749) · *The letters of John Chamberlain*, ed. N. E. McClure, 2 vols. (1939) · T. E. Hartley, ed., *Proceedings in the parliaments of Elizabeth I*, 3 vols. (1995), vol. 2, pp. 75–6 · *Report on the manuscripts of the marquis of Downshire*, 6 vols. in 7, HMC, 75 (1924–95) · *The correspondence of Sir Henry Unton, knt: ambassador from Queen Elizabeth to Henry IV, king of France*, ed. J. Stevenson (1847), 333 · BL, Stowe MS 166, fols. 17 ff.; MS 167, fols. 163–7, 179; MS 171, fols. 202–18; MS 179, fols. 24ff. · G. M. Bell, *A handlist of British diplomatic representatives, 1509–1688*, Royal Historical Society Guides and Handbooks, 16 (1990), 99 · PRO, SP 77/7, fols. 133–46; SP 77/8, fols. 204–5; SP 78/39, fols. 237–9; SP 78/56, fols. 101–14, 196–7, 354–5; SP 78/84, fols. 100–13, 128–149 · BL, Cotton MS Galba B. i., fols. 296–9 · S. P. Anderson, 'The elder William Trumbull', *British Library Journal*, 19/2 (1993), 115–32 [a biographical sketch] · GEC, *Peerage* · DNB · Foster, *Marriage licences*, p. 441

Archives BL, Add. MS 5664 · BL, corresp. and state papers, Stowe MSS 166–177 · NYPL, letters and dispatches [transcripts] · University of Chicago Library, letters relating to his embassy to Paris | BL, letters to J. Caesar, Add. MS 12504 · BL, Cotton MS, Calig. E.ix · BL, Cotton MSS, diplomatic papers, etc. · BL, letter to C. Hatton, Add. MS 29550 · BL, letters to Lord Hay and Secretary Winwood, Egerton MS 2592 · BL, letters to M. Du Plessis, Add. MS 21406 · BL, corresp. with William Trumbull, Add. MSS 72288, 72334–72338, 72343 · CKS, dispatches from Brussels to earl of Salisbury · HMC, Cowper, vol. 2 · HMC, Salisbury, letter-book, etc., vol. 18 · PRO, SP 78/28–36; 78/39; 40–43; 45; 56–57; 84–86 (France series); SP 77/6–8 (Netherlands series) · Staffs. RO, report on religious toleration in France

Likenesses D. Mytens, oils, *c*.1620, NPG; on loan to Montacute House, Somerset

Edmonds, Enid Flora Balint- (1903–1994). *See under* Balint, Michael Maurice (1896–1970).

Edmonds, Sir James Edward (1861–1956), military historian, was born in Baker Street, London, on 25 December 1861, the son of James Edmonds, master jeweller, and his wife, Frances Amelia Bowler. He went as a day boy to King's College School, London, then still in the east wing of Somerset House, and astonished masters by the extent, maturity, and exactitude of his knowledge. He was wont to relate that he learned languages at the breakfast table at home. In after life he could extract what he wanted from any European language and a number of eastern ones, although he could not write an idiomatic letter in any foreign language except German. He passed first into the Royal Military Academy, Woolwich, and the most experienced examiners were unable to recall any year in which he would not have done so. As a matter of course he passed out first after winning the sword awarded for the best gentleman cadet, the Pollock medal, and other prizes. In 1881 he was gazetted to the Royal Engineers, specializing in submarine mining, then treated as a task which the Royal Navy could not be expected to undertake.

In 1885, after long anxiety about the possibility that Russia might walk into Hong Kong without warning, it was decided to reinforce the colony with two companies of engineers of which one, the 33rd, was Edmonds's. His criticism of the situation was blistering. The reinforcement of two companies reached the scene in one case eight strong, in the other about thirty. The non-starters were either sick, permanent invalids, or on attachment from which they had not been liberated in time to catch the boat. Edmonds found that the numerous rock pillars just below the surface in Hong Kong harbour were uncharted and consequently often grazed by ships, once in a while causing a serious accident. He set about demolition by trailing a rail between two longboats and lowering a diver to fix a gun-cotton necklace on the peak.

Three months' sick leave in Japan was followed by a leisurely return home in 1888 by way of the United States. In 1890 Edmonds became instructor in fortification at the Royal Military Academy, where he spent six happy years and made use of the long vacations to travel and learn more languages, including Russian. In 1895 he entered the staff college, once again first, and in that year he married Hilda Margaret Ion (d. 1921), daughter of the Revd Matthew Wood; they had one daughter. His conversation became more stimulating and impressive than ever. Among those who enjoyed it were Douglas Haig, of whom he heard an instructor predict that he could become commander-in-chief, Aylmer Haldane, and E. H. H. Allenby. His verdict on Allenby was that it was impossible to hammer anything into his head, an error typical of Edmonds's worst side.

In 1899 Edmonds was appointed to the intelligence division under Sir John Ardagh, with whom in 1901 he went to South Africa, at the request of the Foreign Office, to advise Lord Kitchener on questions of international law. Lord Milner next borrowed him (1902–4) in the task of establishing peace. Back at home in 1904, Edmonds resumed work at the War Office in the intelligence division and was put in charge of a section formed to follow the Russo-Japanese war. He was promoted in 1907 to take charge of MO5 (counter-espionage, later known as MI5). It was Edmonds who in 1908 definitely convinced the secretary of state for war, R. B. Haldane, of the size, efficiency, and complexity of the German espionage network in Britain.

In 1911 Edmonds, who had reached the rank of colonel in 1909, was appointed GSO1 of the 4th division. His divisional commander, Thomas Snow, a formidable and irascible man, gave him his complete confidence and at an early stage said to him 'I provide the ginger and you provide the brains.' This was very much to Edmonds's taste, and if ever he spoke with excessive pride it was of his achievement in the training of the 4th division for the war, the summit of his career, although fatal to his personal ambitions. During the retreat from Mons he broke down from insufficient food, lack of sleep, and strain. The engineer-in-chief stretched out an arm to him from general headquarters, where he remained for the rest of the war, in the latter part of it as deputy engineer-in-chief. He was regularly consulted by Haig and regarded as a mentor on the general staff side and every branch of his own corps, which in its turn could afford him greater knowledge of transportation problems than those who had to undertake the tasks.

In 1919 Edmonds retired with the honorary rank of brigadier-general and was appointed director of the historical section, military branch, committee of imperial defence. His task was to direct; all narratives were to be written by historians; but finding the first choice unsatisfactory, Edmonds himself took over the main field, the western front, and sowed and reaped it to the end. He was altogether too patient with failures, although delighted to be able to say that he sacked three lieutenant-generals in quick succession. He has been blamed for tardiness in producing the history, but his resources were minimal by comparison with those accorded to the historians of the Second World War. The first virtue of his style was compression, the second lucidity; but it was attractive to a minority only and came to be regarded as dull. A feature of the method, not new, but brought to perfection, was the combination of material from British records with those of foes and allies with equal care, whereas many famous predecessors had left the second and third as pale as ghosts. He was allowed to establish liaison with his German opposite number and treated him with complete candour. He found Berlin equally reliable and disinclined to make propaganda, a practice which only began after Hitler's ascent to power. It may indeed be said that Edmonds revolutionized the very principles on which the history of campaigns and battles had hitherto been compiled in Britain. His humour as chief was mordant, but when he denounced one person as a crook, another as a drunkard, and a third as utterly incompetent, he was nine-tenths of the time playing an elaborate game. Part of the vast stock of *boutades* took the form of letters which were treasured by recipients. Some turned up finally as evidence for theories which he would have repudiated: for instance, the belittlement of Haig.

Edmonds was gifted with a prodigious memory. He never forgot the sciences learned in youth and kept up with them throughout his life. The originality of his reflections and his skill in engineering earned for him the sobriquet of Archimedes, which amused him and with which he frequently signed letters to the press. A history of the American Civil War (1905), in collaboration with his brother-in-law W. B. Wood, ran through a number of editions and became an official textbook in the United States. He collaborated also with L. F. L. Oppenheim in the official manual *Land Warfare* (1912), an exposition of the laws and usages of war on land. After his retirement in 1949 he wrote *A Short History of World War I* (1951). Coming from an author almost ninety years of age, it naturally showed signs of wear and tear, but it is none the less a highly useful and creditable vade-mecum.

Edmonds was the happiest of individuals and never felt the slightest regret that he had not risen to a rank befitting his talents. As a soldier he was intellectually brilliant and in both theory and technical knowledge the outstanding figure of his generation; yet he could not be regarded as complete master of his profession or as having to reproach fortune for failure in attaining that status. He was over-sensitive, shy, inclined to be uncertain in emergency, and lacking in that sustained energy, carried almost to the point of harshness and sometimes beyond it, which has marked great soldiers and without which powers of command are generally limited.

Edmonds was appointed CB in 1911, CMG in 1916, and knighted in 1928. He received the honorary degree of DLitt from the University of Oxford in 1935. He retired to Brecon House, Long Street, Sherborne, Dorset, and died there on 2 August 1956.

CYRIL FALLS, *rev.* H. C. G. MATTHEW

Sources E. E. B. M., 'Brigadier-General Sir James Edmonds', *Royal Engineers Journal*, new ser., 70 (1956), 395–8 · *The Times* (7 Aug 1956) · *The Times* (10 Aug 1956)

Archives King's Lond., Liddell Hart C., corresp. and papers incl. those relating to historical interests · Royal Engineers Museum, Gillingham, military papers | CAC Cam., corresp. with Sir E. L. Spears · King's Lond., Liddell Hart C., corresp. with Sir B. H. Liddell Hart

Likenesses W. Stoneman, photograph, 1919, NPG

Wealth at death £551 4s. 2d.: probate, 27 Nov 1956, CGPLA Eng. & Wales

Edmonds, Richard (1801–1886), antiquary and geologist, was born on 18 September 1801 in Penzance, Cornwall, the eldest son of Richard Edmonds (1774–1860), attorney, of Penzance, and his wife, Elizabeth Rowe (1770–1840). His elder brother was the political economist Thomas Rowe *Edmonds. He was educated at Penzance grammar school and, from 1816, at Helston grammar school. He was articled as an attorney with his father in 1818; he qualified in 1823 and practised in Penzance until 1825. In the latter year he moved to Redruth, and returned to Penzance in 1836.

Much interested in local customs and natural history,

Edmonds wrote a number of papers for the Penzance Natural History and Antiquarian Society (founded in 1839), which were later revised and collected in a volume entitled *The Land's End District: its Antiquities, Natural History, Natural Phenomena, and Scenery* (1862). In 1832 Edmonds sent papers on 'Meteors observed in Cornwall' and 'The ancient church discovered in Perranzabuloe' to the *Literary Gazette* and the *London and Edinburgh Philosophical Magazine*, and subsequently made other contributions to these journals on antiquarian and geological subjects. He was corresponding secretary for Cornwall of the Cambrian Archaeological Society. He made careful enquiries of the evidence for Phoenician commerce, for Roman rule, and Celtic civilization in the western peninsula of Cornwall. He collected many interesting facts, but his further research was weak.

Edmonds became a member of the Royal Geological Society of Cornwall in 1814, and made geological observations in Mount's Bay, especially on the sandbanks between Penzance and Marazion and the submerged forests of that shore. He read eleven papers on such topics to the society between 1843 and 1869 (all published in the society's *Transactions*), and also sent his observations to the Royal Irish Academy, the British Association for the Advancement of Science, the *Gentleman's Magazine*, the *Philosophical Magazine*, and the *Journal of the Royal Institution of Cornwall*. On 5 July 1843 disturbance of the sea was observed in Mount's Bay. Edmonds carefully recorded the phenomenon as observed by him at Penzance, in a paper to the Royal Geological Society of Cornwall, 'An account of an extraordinary movement of the sea in Cornwall, in July 1843, with notices of similar movements in previous years, and also of earthquakes which have occurred in Cornwall' (1846). He collected accounts of analogous phenomena on the Cornish coast, and in subsequent years several examples of similar alternate ebbings and flowings of the sea were recorded by him and others.

Edmonds was singularly modest and timid, even to the point of confusion in stating his views. Notwithstanding this he collected considerable information about earthquakes, and believed that he had traced a connection between the abnormal tides of the Atlantic and the small earthquake shocks sometimes felt in Cornwall; his ideas reflect the uncertainty of knowledge at that time about the causes of earthquakes. He was also interested in writing poetry, and he contributed forty-four hymns to *Hymns for the Principal Festivals of the Church and other Occasions* (1857). There is no record that Edmonds was married. He left Cornwall to live in Plymouth about 1861, and died there at his home, 9 Clarendon Terrace, North Road, on 12 March 1886.   ROBERT HUNT, *rev.* DENISE CROOK

Sources Boase & Courtney, *Bibl. Corn.* · R. Edmonds, 'An account of an extraordinary movement of the sea in Cornwall, in July 1843, with notices of similar movements in previous years, and also of earthquakes which have occurred in Cornwall', *Transactions of the Royal Geological Society of Cornwall*, 6 (1846), 111–21 · M. D. Stephens and G. W. Roderick, 'Science training for the nineteenth century English amateur: the Penzance Natural History and Antiquarian Society', *Annals of Science*, 27 (1971), 135–41

Wealth at death £1249 12*s.* 3*d.*: probate, 12 May 1886, *CGPLA Eng. & Wales*

Edmonds [*née* Dickie], **Rosemary Lilian** (1905–1998), translator, was born on 20 October 1905 at Clifton, Coldfall Avenue, Muswell Hill, Middlesex, the daughter of Walter Herbert Dickie, a private secretary, and his wife, Lilian Worthington. After her schooling at St Paul's Girls' School, she spent some time at the Sorbonne in Paris studying French. In 1927 she married James Edmonds; their marriage was subsequently dissolved.

During the Second World War, Rosemary Edmonds worked as multilingual translator to General de Gaulle at his Free French headquarters in London. She was appointed (in 1940) at the insistence of Winston Churchill and the British government on having a native English speaker as de Gaulle's official translator. De Gaulle, who had wanted an all-French staff, had been obliged to compromise, although during the time she spent working for him in London, Edmonds remained the only non-French person on his staff.

After the liberation, at de Gaulle's request, Edmonds returned to Paris with him, continuing to work as a translator on his staff. He personally paid for her to take Russian courses at the Sorbonne. She greatly admired de Gaulle and respected the way he had treated her; she recalled, for instance, how he had been careful to arrange for her to be compensated for the British taxes on her earnings, in order to ensure that she remained on an equivalent salary to her untaxed French colleagues. She was soon forced to resign her post, however, in order to retain her British citizenship.

Back in London, Edmonds was approached by E. V. Rieu, founder editor of the series Penguin Classics. Rieu set her to work on a translation of Tolstoy's *Anna Karenina* (which she preferred to call *Anna Karenin*) in 1950; this work, which took her three years, helped to establish her as one of the country's foremost translators of Russian literature. Rieu immediately followed this up with a commission for a translation of *War and Peace*, which appeared in 1957.

These were followed by several other translations of Tolstoy; this very prolific period produced *The Death of Ivan Ilyich*, *The Cossacks*, and *Happy Ever After* (1960), *Childhood, Boyhood, Youth* (1964), and *Resurrection* (1966), as well as several works by other Russian writers including Pushkin (*Queen of Spades, and other Stories*, 1962), Turgenev (*Fathers and Sons*, 1965), and Gogol (*Divine Liturgy*, 1960).

Tolstoy, whom she called both 'a prophet' and 'a moralist', was, for Edmonds the greatest humanist: '[His] subject is humanity', she wrote in her introduction to *War and Peace*; 'Tolstoy does not contrive: he records, recoiling from nothing'. Her translations of Tolstoy are today considered among the most successful in English, and her work has made a substantial difference to how he has subsequently been read in the English-speaking world. At the time of her death her Tolstoy translations had sold over four million copies.

During her time in Paris, Rosemary Edmonds had met the Archimandrite Sophrony; it was this acquaintance which introduced her to Russian Orthodox spirituality, of which she remained a fascinated student until the end of her life—she even, with Sophrony's help, became proficient in Old Church Slavonic. Her interest in the religion extended to helping Sophrony establish an Orthodox monastery community in England (near Maldon, Essex) in 1959. Both before and after her work for the Penguin Classics, Edmonds produced translations of Sophrony's writings about his mentor Father Silouan in *The Monk of Mount Athos* (1973) and *Wisdom from Mount Athos* (1974). She spent much of the later part of her life researching Old Church Slavonic texts, and brought together Old Church Slavonic service books with their corresponding Greek texts to produce a translation of the Orthodox Church liturgy, which was published by the Oxford University Press in 1982.

Throughout her life Rosemary Edmonds was an advocate for numerous charitable causes of all kinds. In 1979 she was awarded the freedom of the City of London, considering it a great honour, though she was essentially an intensely private person, with just a small circle of close friends. She reserved her devotion mainly for her work, which she continued almost full-time into the last years of her long life.

She died of Parkinson's disease on 26 July 1998 at a nursing home, Joan Bartlett House, 3 Beatrice Place, Marloes Road, in Kensington, London.   DANIEL HAHN

Sources b. cert. · d. cert. · *The Independent* (14 Aug 1998) · *Daily Telegraph* (22 Aug 1998) · private information (2004) · *CGPLA Eng. & Wales* (1998)

Likenesses photograph, repro. in *Daily Telegraph*

Wealth at death £621,369: probate, 10 Dec 1998, *CGPLA Eng. & Wales*

Edmonds, Thomas Rowe (1803–1889), actuary and political economist, was born on 20 June 1803 in Penzance, the third of seven children of Richard Edmonds (1774–1860), solicitor, and town clerk of Marazion, Cornwall, and his wife, Elizabeth (1770–1840), daughter of Thomas Nicholas and his wife, Mary Rowe. He was the brother of Richard *Edmonds, the antiquary and geologist. Edmonds attended Cornwall School, Penzance, and Trinity College, Cambridge, where he took his BA in 1826. He settled in London and in 1832 became actuary to the Legal and General Life Assurance Society, a position he held until his retirement in 1866.

Recent scholars have paid little attention to Edmonds, and then almost exclusively with reference to his first book, *Practical moral and political economy, or, The government, religion, and institutions most conducive to individual happiness and to national power* (1828). This work offers a critique of early industrial capitalism characteristic of Ricardian socialism. Some scholars have found in it anticipations of Karl Marx's theory of surplus value and the conception of capitalism as a historical stage to be succeeded by a more communal stage, which Edmonds called the 'social system'. Like others of his generation who proposed improving the lives of the working class by changing institutions, Edmonds felt obliged to respond to Thomas Malthus. In his *Enquiry into the principles of population, exhibiting a system of regulations for the poor; designed immediately to lessen, and finally to remove, the evils which have hitherto pressed upon the labouring classes of society* (1832) Edmonds rejected Malthusian pessimism about social reform and tried to show instead that at each stage of human history, human misery is the result of ignorance and of poor government, both remediable conditions. In commercial nations poverty is mainly due to the unequal distribution of property and to the utter dependence of workers on their masters. Nevertheless, Edmonds acknowledged that in a nation like Britain a surplus of labour depressed the income of workers. The best solution to the problem of poverty was to eliminate that labour surplus. This was to be done mainly by promoting emigration to the colonies and by encouraging the working class to delay or forgo marriage. An improving standard of living and rising expectations were the best guarantee that the latter would happen. Changes in the poor law, public encouragement for workers to become independent producers or manufacturers, public patronage of the arts, cultivation of wastelands, the encouragement of investment in life insurance, education, and moral reform all have a place in his plan.

In 1832 Edmonds also published *Life tables founded upon the discovery of a numerical law, regulating the existence of every human being, illustrated by a new theory of the causes producing health and longevity*, a book in which he announced the discovery of a mathematical law describing how human mortality changed in geometrical series during three periods of life. It also presented three theoretical or model life tables constructed using his law of mortality. Nearly three decades later Edmonds was involved in a dispute in the *Assurance Magazine* (1859–61) over his claim that his law was different from the one Benjamin Gompertz had published in the *Philosophical Transactions* in 1825. While his critics were right about his mathematics, Edmonds can claim originality for his theoretical tables, which he demonstrated corresponded to the best available life tables constructed on vital experience, and for his discussion of the uses to which they could be put. He elaborated these applications in a series of twenty articles in *The Lancet*, fifteen of these in the years 1835–9, in two articles in the *British Medical Almanack* (1835–6), and in a further article in the *Actuary Magazine* (1855) showing how his methods could be used to study mortality differences between population groups, to measure the sanitary condition of a population, and to study the relationship between mortality and morbidity. Edmonds's publications in the 1830s influenced William Farr, who designed the national system of vital statistics at the general registrar office.

About the time of his retirement Edmonds published three articles in the *Philosophical Magazine*, one on a new formula for the law of mortality and two others describing in mathematical terms the behaviour of saturated steam. He was elected a fellow of the Statistical Society of London in 1836 and served as a member of its committee on vital statistics. He gave important testimony to the parliamentary select committee on assurance associations in May 1853. He was proposed for the fellowship of the Royal Society on several occasions but never succeeded in gaining election.

Little is known about Edmonds's personal life. He married Elizabeth Elspith Ruddack on 12 July 1833 and had at least two children. His eldest son, Frederic Bernard Edmonds, achieved some notice as a natural philosopher. During his retirement Edmonds continued to live in London. Although well-known in his prime, for the last twenty-five years of his life he seems to have been totally forgotten; he received none of the usual notices on his death. He died at 72 Portsdown Road, Maida Vale, on 6 March 1889. JOHN M. EYLER

Sources J. E. King, 'Utopian or scientific? A reconsideration of the Ricardian socialists', *History of Political Economy*, 15 (1983), 345–73 · M. Perelman, 'Edmonds, Ricardo, and what might have been', *Science and Society*, 44 (1980), 82–5 · E. Nolte, 'Thomas Hopkins und T. R. Edmonds—Zwei Vergessene "Ricardische Sozialisten"? Zugleich ein Beitrag zur Begriffsklärung', *International Review of Social History*, 26 (1981), 66–91 · J. M. Eyler, *Victorian social medicine: the ideas and methods of William Farr* (1979) · C. Walford, *The insurance cyclopaedia*, 6 vols. (1871–80) [see also Edmonds's (T. R.) "mean" mort. table] · G. C. Boase, *Collectanea Cornubiensia: a collection of biographical and topographical notes relating to the county of Cornwall* (1890) · D. E. C. Eversley, *Social theories of fertility and the Malthusian debate* (1959), 43–4, 74–5, 108 · C. H. Driver, 'A forgotten sociologist', *Journal of Adult Education*, 3 (1929), 134–54 · M. Beer, *A history of British socialism*, 1 (1919) · D. H. Driver, 'Thomas Rowe Edmonds', *Encyclopaedia of the social sciences*, ed. E. R. A. Seligman and A. Johnson, 3 (1937), 399 · d. cert. · CGPLA Eng. & Wales (1889)
Wealth at death £14,666 4s. 4d.: probate, 21 March 1889, CGPLA Eng. & Wales

Edmonds, Sir William. *See* Edmond, Sir William (*d.* 1606).

Edmondson, George (1798–1863), educationist, was born in Lancaster on 8 September 1798, the son of John and Jane Edmondson, trunk manufacturers. His parents were Quakers, and he spent his early years entirely among Quakers, and always belonged to the Society. He had a gift for mechanical invention, shared by his brother Thomas *Edmondson. They were both educated at Ackworth School, Yorkshire, of which John Fothergill was a leading supporter. Fothergill proposed that pupils of both sexes should be taught a trade. Little was done to realize his views, but Ackworth was a better English middle-class school than existed elsewhere in the country at the time. Edmondson left at the age of fourteen. He wished to be a teacher, and was apprenticed to William Singleton, the reading master of the Ackworth School, who had opened a boarding-school in a large house at Broomhall, near Sheffield. Singleton was a humane man who objected to the use of the rod. Edmondson learned bookbinding under him, and carried out all the bookbinding the school needed. A well-known Friend, Daniel Wheeler, taught Edmondson agriculture.

In 1814 Alexander I of Russia visited England. He was much impressed by the Quakers, and in 1817 invited Wheeler to superintend some agricultural institutions in Russia. On Singleton's suggestion, Edmondson joined the party as tutor to Wheeler's children and assistant in the work. He lived in Russia until 1820, when he returned to England to marry Anne Singleton, the daughter of his old schoolmaster. He returned with his wife to Okhta, near St Petersburg, where they were living at the time of the flood in 1824. In the course of the following year the whole of the bog land around the capital was brought into cultivation. After seven years' residence in Russia, Edmondson returned to England, although the tsar made him handsome offers to remain, tempting him with 1000 acres of unreclaimed land at Shoosharry, which Edmondson declined, because the only dwelling available while work was being carried out would have been unhealthy for his family. He returned to England less rich than he might have been had he not scrupled to accept bribes, but equipped with a good conversational knowledge of the Russian language.

In England, Edmondson opened a school at Blackburn in 1825, and, in 1841, one at Tulketh Hall, near Preston, which was so popular that he had to refuse numerous pupils. In 1847 he became head of the school at Queenwood Hall, near Stockbridge, Hampshire, founded by the followers of Robert Owen but taken over by the Society of Friends in 1846. There 800 acres of land enabled him to add agriculture to the subjects taught in his school, and he was able to carry out his great aim of establishing a science and technical school. His genius lay more in organization than teaching, and under his headmastership the school became very well-equipped. He had a carpenter's and a blacksmith's shop as well as a printing-office, in which a monthly periodical was issued, edited, and at one time set up by the boys. He had several editions of Henry Bradshaw's *Railway Time Tables* among his school books, in which the boys were examined in finding routes. John Tyndall, Archer Hirst, Dr H. Debus FRS, and Edward Frankland were among the teachers. One of the earliest pupils at Queenwood was Henry Fawcett. The school went into decline after about 1855 but continued until Edmondson's death.

Like Pestalozzi, Edmondson had the power of influencing those about him through his own enthusiasm, and did much to introduce a new system of education. He was one of the original promoters of the College of Preceptors, founded in 1846, and was in advance of his fellow private schoolmasters in the importance he attached to practical instruction. He was largely assisted by his wife, who, in the opinion of many, had a superior intellect to his own. Their daughter, Jane, dedicated an account of *Quaker Pioneers in Russia* (1902) to their memory. Edmondson died, after one day's illness, on 15 May 1863, at Queenwood, and was buried in the burial-ground of the Society of Friends at Southampton. People of all shades of opinion came together to show their regard for his ability, usefulness, and integrity.

G. J. HOLYOAKE, *rev.* M. C. CURTHOYS

Sources Boase, *Mod. Eng. biog.* · J. Benson, *From the Lune to the Neva* (1879) · *Letters of Prof. J. Tyndall, Dr John Yeats, and C. Wilmore* (1888) · D. Thompson, 'Queenwood College, Hampshire: a mid-nineteenth century experiment in science teaching', *Annals of Science*, 11 (1955), 246–54
Wealth at death under £5000: probate, 9 July 1863, CGPLA Eng. & Wales

Edmondson, Henry (1606/7–1659), schoolmaster, was born in Cumberland. He matriculated at Queen's College, Oxford, on 10 May 1622, aged fifteen, graduated BA on 30

June 1627 and MA on 30 June 1630, and was elected fellow of his college. He became usher of Tonbridge School, Kent, under Nicholas Grey, and in 1655, on the death of Thomas Widdowes, was appointed by Queen's College to the post of master of the endowed free school of Northleach, Gloucestershire, where he remained for the rest of his life.

Edmondson wrote and published mainly on educational topics and language teaching. A manuscript work, 'Incruenta contentio sive bellum rationale', dated 1 January 1647, is dedicated to Sir Charles Worsley. His most famous work was *Lingua Linguarum: the Naturall Language of Languages* (1655 and 1658), and as Democritus Secundus he published *Comes facundus in via: the fellow-traveller through city and country among students and scholars … with short stories*. He was buried in the church at Northleach on 15 July 1659, leaving behind him a reputation as a highly efficient schoolmaster. His *Homonyma et synonyma linguae Latinae* appeared posthumously in 1661.

SIDNEY LEE, rev. S. E. MEALOR

Sources *Reg. Oxf.*, vol. 2/2 • Wood, *Ath. Oxon.*, new edn, 3.475 • Wood, *Ath. Oxon.: Fasti* (1815), 426, 456 • S. Rivington, *The history of Tonbridge School*, 4th edn (1925) • Foster, *Alum. Oxon.*

Edmondson, Joseph (*bap.* **1732**, *d.* **1786**), herald and coach-painter, was baptized on 6 February 1732 at St Andrew's, Holborn, London, the first of five children of Benjamin Edmondson (*d.* before 1771?) and his wife, Elizabeth (*d.* 1771). Of humble origins, he was originally apprenticed as a barber. He later became a heraldic artist, emblazoning arms on coaches, which presumably led to his interest in heraldry; by 1763 he was coach-painter to Queen Charlotte. Some time after 1759 he bought the great manuscript collection of peers' pedigrees known as the *Baronagium genealogicum*, very probably compiled by Simon Segar, great-grandson of Sir William Segar, Garter king of arms. His proposal to update and publish this work engendered the rivalry of the heralds at the College of Arms, who resolved to produce their own peerage genealogies. Their attempt fell through and in 1764 Edmondson began the publication of his *Baronagium*. It was originally published in numbers, and when completed sold for 25 guineas. It was followed by a sixth volume of subsequent creations. It brought him to the attention of the nobility, many of whom asked him to compile or revise their pedigrees.

On 21 January 1764, thanks to the support of the new deputy earl marshal, Lord Suffolk, Edmondson was created Mowbray herald of arms extraordinary, although he continued his successful coach-painting business until his death. His brother officers, especially Stephen Martin Leake, Garter, regarded him as an ignorant and low 'mechanic', and only reluctantly did they now allow him, as an extraordinary herald and not a member of the college, access to their records and collections. During the 1760s he repeatedly upset the college by attempting to provide heraldic supporters or arms for individuals, although he had no right to act in this capacity. On one occasion, in 1768, he presented a memorial at the secretary of state's office for the king's warrant to authorize a person based in Jamaica the right to bear arms claiming this was *extra regnum* and, therefore, outside the provinces of the kings of arms. Had he shown more tact and discretion towards the heralds he might have fulfilled his hopes of becoming an officer of the college.

In 1764 Edmondson also published his small tract *Tables of Precedency*, and in 1766 his *Historical and Genealogical Account of the Noble Family of Greville*, dedicated to Francis Greville, earl of Warwick, appeared. It was followed ten years later by his *Companion to the Peerage of Great Britain and Ireland*. In 1780 he produced his most famous work, *A Complete Body of Heraldry*, in two volumes, for which he went to great lengths to acquire the subscription of members of the royal family and a host of the higher aristocracy. This comprehensive work included an alphabet of 50,000 coats of arms and owed much to the 'Officers of arms', an unpublished manuscript by John Anstis the elder, Garter, which Edmondson had bought but sadly did not acknowledge. In the compilation of the first volume, as in his *Baronagium*, he was greatly helped by Sir Joseph Ayloffe. In 1785, a year before his death, his last work, *The Present Peerages … the Plates of Arms Revised by Joseph Edmondson*, appeared in eight volumes. His manuscript papers include 'An alphabet of arms with the arms in trick', 'A proposal for the institution of an order of merit, with drawings' (BL, Add. MS 6330, fol. 32), 'Papers relating to the institution of the Order of St Patrick, 1783' (BL, Add. MS 14410, fol. 10), and 'Pedigrees of families of Great Britain, 1784–86' (BL, Add. MS 19819).

Edmondson was not a scholar by training, but he copied entire pedigrees from the college records, despite deliberate interruptions from the heralds, and was elected an FSA on 15 May 1770. He was also made deputy to Sir Thomas Grey Cullum, Bath king of arms. His works are clearly impressive. He was enthusiastic and enterprising, and he realized the immense value of the unpublished manuscripts of Segar and Anstis. But he was also pushy and intrusive. Leake thought of him as a sycophant, who turned to aristocratic patrons such as Lord Warwick when in need of support. He was disliked by his brother officers for his low origins and for encroaching on their prerogatives. He was, however, almost revered by the Revd Mark Noble in his *History of the College of Arms* (1805), for his industry, research, and rise in station, although it is doubtful whether Noble realized Edmondson's reliance on Anstis's material.

Edmondson lived in Warwick Street, Golden Square, Westminster, London, where he died on 17 February 1786. He was buried in the cemetery of St James's, Piccadilly. Because of his extravagant lifestyle he was unable to leave any considerable property. His will, dated 31 January 1781, makes no mention of his wife, who may have been named Elizabeth and who probably died before 1781. It refers to his two sons, Philip (*b.* 1756?), who continued the coach-painting business, and John, and to his two married daughters. When Edmondson's mother died in 1771 she had made her second son, Benjamin, her heir, leaving to Joseph just 1 guinea to buy a ring and 'a rust handled knife and fork (being a piece of antiquity that he has taken a liking to)' (Elizabeth Edmondson's will). Edmondson's library was sold in 1788 and the College of Arms bought thirty-two books and seventeen of his manuscripts. The British Library holds a printed catalogue of his library, including a collection of manuscripts sold 26–28 June 1786.   ADRIAN AILES

Sources A. Wagner, *Heralds of England: a history of the office and College of Arms* (1967) · W. H. Godfrey, A. Wagner, and H. Stanford London, *The College of Arms, Queen Victoria Street* (1963) · M. Noble, *A history of the College of Arms* (1805) · Coll. Arms, Leake MSS, vols. 45, 65–6 · T. Moule, *Bibliotheca heraldica Magnae Britanniae* (privately printed, London, 1822) · will, PRO, PROB 11/1139, fols. 384v–385 · Elizabeth Edmondson's will, PRO, PROB 11/969, fols. 151v–152 · parish register, Holborn, St Andrew's, GL · parish register, St George's, Hanover Square, City Westm. AC · W. T. Lowndes, *The bibliographer's manual of English literature*, ed. H. G. Bohn, [new edn], 6 vols. (1864) · Nichols, *Lit. anecdotes* · *GM*, 1st ser., 56 (1786) · J. C. Smith, *British mezzotinto portraits*, 4/2 (1884)

Archives BL, extracts from Edmondson's works, Add. MS 6331, fol. 69 · BL, MSS relating to the institution of the order of St Patrick, Add. MS 14410, fol. 10 · BL, pedigrees of families of Great Britain, Add. MS 19819 · BL, proposal for the institution of an order of merit, Add. MS 6330, fol. 32 · Coll. Arms, collection of heraldic MSS, incl. Simon Segar's 'Baronagium genealogicum' | Bodl. Oxf., corresp. with J. C. Brooke

Likenesses F. Bartolozzi, line engraving, 1780 (after unknown artist), repro. in J. Edmondson, *A complete body of heraldry*, 1 (1780), frontispiece · J. Jones, mezzotint (after portrait by T. Beach, pubd 1787), BM · copy (after J. Jones?), Coll. Arms

Edmondson, Thomas (1792–1851), inventor of ticket-printing machinery, was born at Lancaster on 30 June 1792. The son of Quaker parents, John and Jane Edmondson, trunk manufacturers, he was a brother of George *Edmondson. He was educated at Ackworth School, Yorkshire, a Quaker institution. In his youth he displayed great aptitude for mechanical invention; and his mother, seeing that he could never be kept out of mischief, taught him knitting to keep him quiet and useful. He became a journeyman cabinet-maker with the firm of Gillows & Co. in Lancaster. While there he made several improvements in cabinet-making implements, and invented a mechanism by which women could churn butter and rock a cradle at the same time. Thoroughness in manufacture, completeness in detail, and adaptability to the work required were points on which he was conscientious. He became a businessman but although a Friend he was not successful. He entered into partnership in Carlisle; the firm became bankrupt. He nevertheless paid all his creditors when he was able to.

Edmondson became a railway clerk at a small station at Milton, afterwards called Brampton, about 14 miles from Carlisle, on the Newcastle and Carlisle Railway. Having to fill up paper tickets for each passenger, he found the writing irksome as well as time-consuming. It occurred to him in 1837 that the work might be done by a machine, and tickets be printed on one uniform system. When he afterwards showed his family the spot in a Northumberland field where his invention occurred to him, he used to say that it came into his mind complete in its whole scope and all its details. Out of it grew the railway clearing house, which was of great advantage in saving time and trouble.

Blaylock, a Dublin watchmaker, helped to carry out Edmondson's idea. The first machine used at the Dublin office needed very few repairs in five years, and never needed more until the sheer wearing away of the brasswork necessitated replacement. The Manchester and Leeds Railway first adopted Edmondson's invention, and employed him at Oldham Road for a time. The checking machine was also his invention, as well as the dating press.

Edmondson's greatest debt was to William Muir, a skilled engineer, to whom he was introduced by Joseph Whitworth in April 1836. Edmondson needed a metallurgist and engineer to give practical expression to his ideas. When both acquired premises in Millers Lane, Salford, in June 1836, Edmondson occupied the top floor as a ticket-printing office while the rest of the building was used by Muir for the manufacture of Edmondson's ticket-printing, dating, and other machines. The ticket-printing machine was subsequently greatly improved, and while the original feature of printing one ticket at a time was maintained, its general completeness and efficiency were materially increased by James Carson. Edmondson took out two patents. He recouped his expenses by charging railway companies a fee based on their length of track, a railway 30 miles long paying £15 a year for a licence to print its tickets.

Edmondson died on 22 June 1851. His wife was named Rachel; nothing else is known of her, save that they had at least one son and one daughter. He worked out his invention with skill and patience, enjoyed its honours with modesty, and dispensed its fruits with generosity.

G. J. HOLYOAKE, *rev.* PHILIP S. BAGWELL

Sources R. Smiles, *Brief memoir of the late William Muir, mechanical engineer of London and Manchester* (1888) · J. B. Edmondson, 'To whom are we indebted for the railway ticket system?', *English Mechanic and World of Science* (2 Aug 1875); pubd separately (1878) · P. H. Emden, *Quakers in commerce: a record of business achievement* (1939) · R. S. Gardiner, *History of the railroad ticket* (1938) · W. J. Wyse, *Fare and ticket systems: the key to success or failure in rail transport*, Walter Gratwicke Memorial Lecture (1980) · P. S. Bagwell, *The railway clearing house* (1968) · Thomas Edmondson MSS, JRL

Archives Friends House, Euston Road, London · JRL

Edmondston, Arthur (1776?–1841). *See under* Edmondston, Laurence (1795–1879).

Edmondston, Laurence (1795–1879), ornithologist and physician, was born in Lerwick, Shetland, the youngest son of Laurence Edmondston, a surgeon in that town, and Mary Saunderson. His mother hailed from Buness on the fiord of Baltasound in the northernmost of the Shetland Islands, Unst, to which the children were taken on extended visits. There had been naturalists in the family for generations and the rich bird life of that region early captivated the boy and his brother Thomas, and turned them to collecting the eggs and skins of the different kinds.

When fourteen Edmondston shot an unfamiliar gull at Buness which was not in any of the few books available to him. Suspecting it was new to science, he set about studying its habits, but twelve years were to pass before he had sufficient knowledge to publish a description of it and by then he had been anticipated by Temminck. Nevertheless, it proved to have been the first British record of the glaucous gull, *Larus hyperboreus*. By the time he published his description, he had managed to claim two more, still rarer, Arctic visitors to Baltasound for the British list: the Iceland gull, *L. glaucoides*, and the ivory gull, *Pagophila eburnea*. Yet another of his Shetland discoveries was the snowy owl, *Nyctea scandiaca*.

Edmondston's knowledge of birds was greatly expanded through residence on the continent, where he was employed as agent for a London merchant house (and no doubt realized the flair for languages which was to give him a command of most of those of the western half of Europe). A commercial career, however, increasingly sat ill with his scientific bent, and in 1820 he took himself off to Edinburgh University to follow his father and eldest brother and train as a doctor. An adult student with so much expertise to offer proved a windfall for Edinburgh's Wernerian Natural History Society and few numbers of its journal at that time were without at least one scholarly paper from him.

Edmondston qualified and married Elisabeth (d. 1868?), only daughter of Robert Macbraird, of Edinburgh, and eldest grandchild of David Johnston (1734–1824). In 1824 the couple returned to Edmondston's family roots and settled in Unst, where he practised as its only doctor. His brother Thomas had already gone to live there as its laird and a maiden aunt was a neighbour also. Despite acquiring an MD in 1830, Edmondston was never to be tempted away for the professional advancement he could readily have had elsewhere, and although his wife's permanent disablement following a serious accident served as an additional anchor, his attachment to Unst was too profound to bear shifting. The calls on his skills as a physician, while demanding, gave many opportunities for studying birds in between visiting patients, and when at home there were more birds to be watched in the trees and shrubs which he had planted in great variety, an eventual wooded oasis in that otherwise bare landscape which attracted many bird species not previously known in Shetland. Latterly averse to shooting, as a further means of enticing birds to come close he followed the then unusual practice of putting out food for them.

Edmondston also studied the behaviour of insects and of spiders (in which he was particularly interested), and in the fields attached to his house did much agricultural experimenting, passing on seed to fellow islanders to encourage them to grow cereal varieties and other crops better suited to the local conditions. Necessarily self-sufficient professionally, he was an accomplished chemist as well. Tirelessly hospitable to visiting naturalists, and with a wide circle of them as correspondents, he nevertheless published little in later years, content to leave that to his sons, who included the naturalist Thomas *Edmondston (1825–1846), nephew, and son-in-law (Henry Linckmyer Saxby MD); many of his records

reached print in the latter's posthumous *The Birds of Shetland* (1874). One of his five daughters similarly shared and carried on his interest in local antiquities and folklore.

Edmondston died on 7 March 1879 at Halligarth, Buness, the house in which he had lived for nearly fifty years, and was buried at Baltasound cemetery next to his first wife. He was survived by his second wife, Penelope (*née* Hamilton). His brother, **Arthur Edmondston** (1776?–1841), was the eldest son. He followed his father into medicine, entered the army, and served in Egypt. On his return to Shetland, he took over his father's practice. He was known as a skilful physician, and became an authority on diseases of the eye, publishing two treatises on the subject (1802 and 1806). His *View of the Ancient and Present State of the Zetland Islands* (2 vols., 1809) is an important source of information on early nineteenth-century Shetland and includes a complete list of fauna as known up to that time. He died unmarried in 1841. D. E. ALLEN

Sources B. Edmondston and J. M. E. Saxby, *The home of a naturalist*, 2nd edn (1888) · 'The home of a naturalist (in memoriam)', *Chambers's Journal* (11 Feb 1882), 89–92 · J. R. Tudor, *The Orkneys and Shetlands: their past and present state* (1883), 558–61 · L. Edmondston, *Memoirs of the Wernerian Natural History Society* (1820–24) [series of papers] · W. MacGillivray, *A history of British birds*, 5 (1852) · W. MacGillivray, 'Description, characters, and synonyms of the different species of the genus *Larus*', *Memoirs of the Wernerian Natural History Society*, 5 (1824), 247–76 · H. L. Saxby, *Birds of Shetland*, ed. S. H. Saxby (1874) · *DNB* · parish register (deaths), 14/3/1879, Unst, Shetland · J. Laughton Johnston, *A naturalist's Shetland* (1999)
Likenesses photograph, repro. in Edmondston and Saxby, *Home of a naturalist*, frontispiece · photograph, repro. in J. Laughton Johnston, *A naturalist's Shetland* (1999), 259
Wealth at death £209 12s. 4d.: confirmation, 16 Oct 1879, *CCI*

Edmondston, Thomas (1825–1846), botanist, was born at the home of his uncle at Buness in Unst, the most northerly of the Shetland Islands, on 20 September 1825, the elder son of Laurence *Edmondston (1795–1879), medical practitioner, and his first wife, Elisabeth Macbraird (d. 1868?), a journalist. The family, long established in Shetland, had a strong tradition of scholarly recreations, exemplified in his father by a keenness for ornithology in particular. Even so, Edmondston was startlingly precocious in displaying a similar bent, driven by a restlessly enquiring mind and gifted with a prodigious memory. Fortunate to have an area of outstanding botanical interest almost on his doorstep, his attention early became drawn to the local flora. At the age of only eleven he compiled a remarkably competent catalogue of the plants of Unst, listing 174 of these by their Latin names; he had identified them from the standard unillustrated handbook of the period. Edmondston's catalogue was published two years later by William Dawson Hooker, a family friend, in the second edition of his *Notes on Norway* (1839). It included mention of what was subsequently recognized as an endemic chickweed and named *Cerastium edmondstonii* in his honour (subsequently, and more correctly, *C. nigrescens* subsp. *nigrescens*). In 1837 Dr Gilbert McNab, a visiting botanist, had spotted in Edmondston's herbarium what turned out to be Arctic sandwort, *Arenaria norvegica* subsp.

norvegica, which was not to be detected elsewhere in Britain for another half-century. In 1838 Edmondston similarly impressed two further Edinburgh visitors, Professor Goodsir and Edward Forbes, accompanying them to some of the neighbouring islands. Following their departure, he made a three-week tour of his own of Shetland. The further, lengthier botanical list that resulted from this appeared in the *Annals and Magazine of Natural History* in 1841, when he was still only fifteen. Four years later his fieldwork culminated in a small book, *A Flora of Shetland*. Arranged on an idiosyncratic blend of the Linnaean and natural systems, this does not stand up well to the adult standards by which his work by then has to be judged; there are many unaccountable omissions and much over-generalizing from an experience mainly limited to Unst.

Edinburgh had meanwhile beckoned. On a visit there in 1840 with his mother Edmondston had made further useful contacts—and seen full-grown trees for the first time. When the next year he entered the university to study medicine, his reputation as Britain's most promising young botanist had preceded him and the Botanical Society of Edinburgh lost no time in recruiting him as its assistant secretary. Lecturing engagements in the vacations followed, first in Shetland's main town, Lerwick, then further afield, in Forres and Elgin. While botanizing in the eastern highlands in 1844 he encountered H. C. Watson, with whom he sheltered for a night in a shepherd's shieling. Watson was at that time seeking a new curator for the Edinburgh Society's London rival, but Edmondston saw his future in Scotland and was not to be lured south.

That autumn Edmondston settled in Aberdeen to attend lectures at the university, only to be elected the following January, while still only nineteen, to the professorship of botany and natural history in Anderson's College at Glasgow (forerunner of the University of Strathclyde). Before he had time to begin his lectures in that post, however, he accepted an offer through Edward Forbes to serve as naturalist on the frigate HMS *Herald*, which had been ordered to the Pacific and Californian coast. After sailing round Cape Horn and touching at several ports northwards, the *Herald* visited the Galápagos Islands and then returned to the coast of Peru, dropping anchor in Sua Bay, near the River Esmeraldos. The next day, 24 January 1846, a boat was sent ashore, but as the party was re-embarking a rifle was accidentally discharged and the ball passed through Edmondston's head, killing him instantly. He was buried on shore the following day.

This tragic loss at the start of what seemed set to be a brilliant career was mourned internationally. Berthold Seemann, who published an obituary of him in German in his journal *Bonplandia*, named a genus of tropical American plants *Edmonstonia* in his memory (though this proved to have been described already and the name disappeared into synonymy). A mollusc was also named after him.

D. E. ALLEN

Sources *The young Shetlander … being life and letters of Thomas Edmondston*, ed. E. Edmondston (1868) [biography by his mother] · R. K. Brummitt and others, 'The history and nomenclature of

Thomas Edmondston's endemic Shetland *Cerastium*', *Watsonia*, 16 (1987), 291–7 · W. Scott and R. Palmer, *Flowering plants and ferns of the Shetland islands* (1987), 57–8 · C. F. A. Saxby, ed., *A flora of Shetland*, 2nd edn (1903), 11–34 · *Bonplandia* (1853), 4–5

Archives NHM, notes for his flora · Shetland Archives, Lerwick, papers

Likenesses photograph, repro. in Saxby, *Flora of Shetland*

Edmonstone, Sir Archibald, third baronet (1795–1871), writer, the eldest son of Sir Charles Edmonstone of Duntreath, Stirlingshire, second baronet, and his first wife, Emma, fifth daughter of Richard Wilbraham Bootle of Rode Hall, Cheshire, and sister of Edward Bootle Wilbraham, first Baron Skelmersdale, was born at 32 Great Russell Street, Bloomsbury, London, on 12 March 1795. He entered Eton College in 1808 and moved in 1812 to Christ Church, Oxford, where he proceeded BA on 29 November 1816. In 1819 he went to Egypt, publishing *A Journey to Two of the Oases of Upper Egypt* in 1822. At the death of his father, on 1 April 1821, he succeeded to the baronetcy, and unsuccessfully contested his father's constituency of Stirlingshire on 24 May 1821. He married, on 10 October 1832, his cousin Emma, third daughter of Randle Wilbraham of Rode Hall, Cheshire; they had three daughters, who all died in infancy. Edmonstone was the author of several works, mainly devotional but also two tragic plays and a family history. He died at 34 Wilton Place, Belgrave Square, London, on 13 March 1871 and was succeeded by his half-brother.

G. C. BOASE, *rev.* ELIZABETH BAIGENT

Sources *The Times* (18 March 1871), 4 · *ILN* (1 April 1871), 322 · *ILN* (29 April 1871), 427 · Burke, *Peerage* · Boase, *Mod. Eng. biog.*

Archives NL Scot., letters | BL, corresp. with W. E. Gladstone, Add. MSS 44362–44371 · Falkirk Museums History Research Centre, letters to William Forbes

Wealth at death under £3000: probate, June 1873, *CGPLA Eng. & Wales* (1871)

Edmonstone, Sir George Frederick (1813–1864), administrator in India, fourth son of Neil Benjamin *Edmonstone (1765–1841), member of the supreme council in India, and his wife, Charlotte Anne Friell, was born in Calcutta on 11 April 1813. His father, who was a director of the East India Company, gave him a nomination to the Indian Civil Service; Edmonstone entered the East India College, Haileybury, in 1829, and proceeded to Bengal in 1831. After acting as assistant collector at Gorakhpur and Ghazipur, he became deputy collector at Saharanpur in 1837. At the close of the First Anglo-Sikh War in 1846 he was appointed to the important post of commissioner and superintendent of the Cis-Sutlej states. He subsequently became financial commissioner of the Punjab in 1853. In 1856 he was selected by Lord Canning to succeed Sir H. M. Elliot as secretary in the foreign department, the same position which his father had filled under Lord Wellesley. His tenure of office coincided with the Indian mutiny of 1857. How far Edmonstone influenced Canning during these years can never be satisfactorily ascertained, but he was at least the official mouthpiece of the governor-general, and every important dispatch and proclamation, including the famous one by which the land of Oudh was confiscated, was drawn up and signed by him.

In January 1859 Lord Canning appointed Edmonstone lieutenant-governor of the North-Western Provinces, with his headquarters at Allahabad, instead of Agra as before the mutiny, and with his government shorn of the divisions of Delhi and Hissar, which were transferred to the Punjab. With the exception of Oudh, these provinces had suffered most severely during the uprising, and Edmonstone directed his activities to restoring the efficiency of the administration. He also helped create the new government of the Central Provinces, and he endeavoured, with limited success, to find a place in the Indian administration for the local landholders. In 1863 he left India, and on his return to England was created a KCB. He died on 24 September 1864, at Effingham Hill, Effingham, Surrey. His wife, Anne Farly (b. 1826), daughter of Thomas Jacob Turner and his wife, Eliza Rachel Lowe, died in 1859. They had two sons and a daughter. At Haileybury College, the new public school that succeeded the East India Company's college, the six houses were named after six distinguished Indian civil servants, of whom Edmonstone was one. H. M. STEPHENS, rev. THOMAS R. METCALF

Sources T. R. Metcalf, *The aftermath of revolt: India, 1857–1870* (1964) · J. W. Kaye, *A history of the Sepoy War in India, 1857–1858*, 3 vols. (1864–76) · *CGPLA Eng. & Wales* (1864) · BL OIOC
Archives W. Yorks. AS, Leeds, letters to Lord Canning
Wealth at death under £25,000: administration, 12 Nov 1864, *CGPLA Eng. & Wales*

Edmonstone, Neil Benjamin (1765–1841), East India Company servant, was born on 6 December 1765, the fifth and youngest son of Sir Archibald Edmonstone, first baronet (d. 1807), of Duntreath, and his first wife, Susanna Mary Harenc. His father was MP for Dunbartonshire (1761–80 and 1790–96) and the Ayr burghs (1780–90), and was created a baronet in 1774. Edmonstone was admitted to the East India Company as a writer, and reached Calcutta in 1783. He soon gained entry to the secretariat: he was made deputy Persian translator by Lord Cornwallis in 1789, and Persian translator by Sir John Shore in 1794, and in 1798 he was appointed by Lord Mornington (later Lord Wellesley) as his private secretary. In that capacity, in 1799, he accompanied the governor-general to Madras and took part in the campaign which crushed Tipu Sultan. One great concern, at this time, was the presence of French officers within the armies of princely states; documents found in Tipu's palace, which Edmonstone translated and published, served to show how real this danger was, and served also to justify the British attack. Promoted on 1 January 1801 to the post of secretary of the government of India's secret and political department, Edmonstone was made responsible for the planning of relations with all princely states. As such, he played an important part in forming strategies which led to the subduing of the Maratha confederacy led by the peshwa. The 'Wellesley policy' of assuring company hegemony in India by means of a system of 'subsidiary alliances' can be attributed to Edmonstone, though he remained discreetly in the background. In 1803 Edmonstone married Charlotte Anne, daughter of Peter Friell.

Edmonstone continued in his post after the departure of Lord Wellesley in 1805. Lord Cornwallis, upon his return to India that year, did not survive long enough to counteract the imperial system which had been constructed; Edmonstone was able, therefore, to reinforce the system he had done so much to initiate. After the interregnum of Sir George Barlow and the arrival of Lord Minto as governor-general in 1807, Edmonstone's powerful influence became, if anything, even stronger. Again, as in the days of Lord Wellesley, he acted as the governor-general's private secretary, and in this capacity he soon gained as much influence over policy as he had possessed before. On 30 October 1809 he became chief secretary to the government of India; and, on 30 October 1812, he succeeded his colleague and friend James Lumsden as member of the supreme council at Calcutta. By the end of his five-year term, when he retired from India, the company's 'paramountcy' over India was nearly complete. His thirty-four years of service in India were crowned, soon after his return to England, by election to the East India Company's court of directors. In this capacity he continued to act until his death, which occurred at his residence, 49 Portland Place, London, on 4 May 1841. In his *Lives of Indian Officers* (1867), J. W. Kaye described him as 'the ubiquitous Edmonstone, one of the most valuable officials and far-seeing statesmen which the Indian civil service has ever produced'. The most distinguished of his family of five sons and six daughters was his fourth son, Sir George Frederick *Edmonstone, who became Lord Canning's foreign secretary, and lieutenant-governor of the North-Western Provinces after the mutiny of 1857–8.

ROBERT ERIC FRYKENBERG

Sources J. W. Kaye, *Lives of Indian officers*, new edn, 2 vols. (1904) · H. H. Dodwell and Miles, *Indian civilians* (1939) · *The despatches, minutes and correspondence of the Marquess Wellesley … during his administration in India*, ed. M. Martin, 5 vols. (1836–40) · *The Wellesley papers: the life and correspondence of Richard Colley Wellesley, Marquess Wellesley*, ed. [L. S. Benjamin], 2 vols. (1914) · Burke, *Peerage* · C. E. Buckland, *Dictionary of Indian biography* (1906) · DNB
Archives BL, official corresp., Add. MSS 13546–13773 · BL OIOC, home misc. series, corresp. and papers · Cleveland Public Library, corresp. and papers · CUL, corresp. and papers · U. Cam., Centre of South Asian Studies, corresp. and papers | BL OIOC, corresp. with East India Co. officials, MS Eur. F 128 · Bodl. Oxf., corresp. with Charles Russell and Sir Henry Russell · NL Scot., letters to first earl of Minto
Likenesses M. Gauci, lithograph (after W. Bradley), probably BM, NPG

Edmonstone, Robert (1794–1834), painter, was born at Kelso, Roxburghshire, one of the three sons and four daughters of 'highly respectable parents' (*GM*, 213). The identity of his parents remains obscure, though in his will Edmonstone mentions 'dear Bella, my stepmother'. He was bound apprentice to a watchmaker. Having shown an interest in painting from an early age he was sent by his father to Edinburgh, where he enrolled at the Trustees' Academy. His drawings attracted much attention; he was patronized by Sir Abraham Hume, bt, and settled in London in 1818, when he exhibited some portraits at the Royal Academy. After studying with G. H. Harlow he attended the Royal Academy Schools, but does not appear to have registered there as a student. In 1821 he exhibited at the

Royal Scottish Academy *Jemmy the Showman* from his address in London at 9 Charles Street, Cavendish Square; this work, depicting an Edinburgh character, was later engraved.

Edmonstone subsequently travelled in Italy. In 1824 he exhibited at the Royal Scottish Academy a portrait of Major Gordon, giving both his London and Edinburgh addresses, the latter at North David Street; in 1825 his address was given as 26 Frederick Street, Edinburgh. Between 1824 and 1829 he was painting chiefly portraits, but also figurative and historical pictures, in London, where he lived between 1827 and 1833 at 63 Upper Charlotte Street. He was elected an honorary member of the Royal Scottish Academy in 1829. In 1830 he exhibited at the Royal Academy *Italian Boys Playing at Cards*. He paid a second visit to Italy in 1831–2, and painted *Venetian Carriers* and the *Ceremony of Kissing the Chains of St Peter*, which was exhibited at the British Institution in 1833 when he lived at 2 Greek Street, Soho, London. He exhibited in all fifty-eight pictures at the Royal Academy, British Institution, and Suffolk Street exhibitions before 1834. A severe attack of fever at Rome in 1832, combined with overwork, permanently injured his health. He returned to London, but found himself so enfeebled that he went to Kelso, where he died on 21 September 1834. In his will Edmonstone requested that all his letters and papers be burnt. His last pictures were *The White Mouse*, exhibited at Suffolk Street in 1834, and *Children of Sir E. Cust*, exhibited at the Royal Academy. His *Hurdy Gurdy Player* (exh. Royal Scottish Academy, 1830) was exhibited in 1863 with two of his other works at an exhibition at the academy of the work of deceased and living Scottish artists. Two delightful pictures by Edmonstone of the Cust children were auctioned at Christies (8 June 1995, lots 34 and 35). He was very good at painting children, and his portraits were popular and noted for their 'fine tone of colouring' (*GM*, 214), but he sought fame as a painter of imaginative subjects and as a student of Correggio. At his death he left 'nearly completed' two pictures of Italian subjects commissioned by Lord Morpeth and Robert Vernon (ibid.). He showed great promise.   [ANON.], *rev.* ANNETTE PEACH

Sources DNB · W. D. McKay and F. Rinder, *The Royal Scottish Academy, 1826–1916* (1917); repr. (1975) · P. J. M. McEwan, *Dictionary of Scottish art and architecture* (1994) · will, PRO, PROB 11/1840, sig. 682 · artist's notes, NPG, Heinz Archive and Library · *GM*, 2nd ser., 3 (1835), 213–14 · Redgrave, *Artists* · R. Brydall, *Art in Scotland, its origin and progress* (1889)

Edmund [St Edmund] (*d.* 869), king of the East Angles, was venerated as a saint soon after his death at the hands of vikings. According to numismatic evidence, Edmund succeeded King Æthelweard. The number of coins issued in Edmund's name indicates that he reigned for several years, but the only fact known about him from contemporary writings is in the Anglo-Saxon Chronicle, which records under 870: 'In this year the raiding [Danish] army took up winter quarters at Thetford. And that winter King Edmund fought against them, and the Danes had the victory, and killed the king and conquered all the land.' Since the Anglo-Saxon Chronicle seems to begin the year on 24

September this dates Edmund's death to 869. The annal could mean that Edmund fell in battle. That is how Asser interpreted it in his life of King Alfred, composed *c*.890. He writes: 'Edmund, king of the East Angles, fought fiercely against the army, but alas! the heathens triumphed beyond measure, and he and a great part of his men were killed' (*Life of Alfred*, chap. 33).

Oswald, king of Northumbria, was venerated as a martyr because he died fighting the heathen. Possibly Edmund won his claim to martyrdom for the same reason. The earliest evidence for his sanctification is a memorial coinage inscribed 'Scē Eadmund Rex' widely current in the Danelaw within a generation of his death, until *c*.930. A comparatively late source, the so-called annals of St Neots compiled in Bury St Edmunds Abbey between *c*.1120 and *c*.1140, states, on no known authority, that Edmund began to reign on Christmas day 855, at the age of fourteen, and was consecrated by Hunberht, bishop of East Anglia, on Christmas day 856, 'with much joy and very great honour in the royal vill of Burna' (*Annals of St Neots*, s.a. 856). The place is identified as Bures, about 18 miles south of Bury St Edmunds.

The earliest hagiography, the root from which St Edmund's later legend grew, is the *Passio sancti Eadmundi* by Abbo of Fleury, written during his visit to Ramsey, 985–7. In the prologue Abbo claims Dunstan as his authority. He states that Dunstan heard the story when at the court of King Æthelstan: a very old man, who asserted that he was Edmund's armour bearer on the day he died, had told the story to the king in Dunstan's presence. The story as related by Abbo has clearly received much hagiographical embellishment. As Dorothy Whitelock observed 'it may always be a matter of opinion just how far [Abbo] represents the actual facts told by the armour-bearer' (Whitelock, 'Fact and fiction', 219). Abbo's objective was to depict a king worthy of veneration and his portrait of Edmund is an idealized one which is paralleled in hagiographies of other saints. He represents him as a perfect, peace-loving Christian ruler who chose martyrdom rather than to cause the shedding of Christian blood. This description accords ill with the picture conjured up by the Anglo-Saxon Chronicle and Asser, of a warrior king in a bloody battlefield. Abbo's account of the martyrdom itself is a patchwork of hagiographical topoi. He explicitly compares Edmund's sufferings with those of Christ and St Sebastian: Edmund was mocked and scourged like Christ, and tied to a tree and shot at with arrows like St Sebastian, until he bristled 'like a prickly hedgehog or a spiny thistle' (Abbo of Fleury, § 10.19–21). Finally, his lacerated body was unbound and he was beheaded.

Some of Abbo's statements could well be true. He asserts that Edmund was 'of noble birth' which is probable, but he is more likely to have been of ancient Anglian rather than ancient Saxon stock, as Abbo claims. Abbo names the viking leaders who invaded East Anglia in 869 as Hinguar and Hubba. Although Hubba is unidentified, Hinguar was probably Ivarr the Boneless, whose death the Anglo-Saxon Chronicle records under 878. When attacked, Edmund was in a vill called 'Haegilisdun' or

'Haeglesdun' (Haegel's *dun*, meaning hill). Dorothy White-lock identified this as Hellesdon in the outskirts of Norwich. More recently Hellesden, the name of a field near Bury St Edmunds, has been suggested. However, etymologically the name Hellesdon is closer to Abbo's spelling which has -*dun* for its last element. The termination -*den* of Hellesden has a different meaning. Abbo dates the martyrdom to 20 November, which could be right.

There is no credible information about the fate of Edmund's body after his death. Abbo's story of its loss and recovery is a product of a creative imagination inspired by incidents in other hagiographies. Abbo relates that the Danes left the body at the place of martyrdom but threw the head into brambles in the wood at 'Haeglesdun'. Later, Christians found the body and searched for the head. They made a noise meanwhile by signalling to each other with horns and pipes, but one party went to a silent part of the wood, calling '"Where are you?" and marvellous to relate … the head replied in their native tongue, "Here, here, here"'. The head was found guarded between the paws of a wolf 'of terrible appearance' (Abbo of Fleury, § 12.41–3). The wolf followed the Christians as they carried the head to the body for burial, before retreating again into the wood. The Christians fitted the head on to the body, buried the whole, and built a simple chapel over the grave.

Abbo's account of the body's later history combines fact and fiction. He relates that after many years a very large wooden church 'of wonderful workmanship' was built at the royal vill of Beadericesworth (the later Bury St Edmunds), to which the body was translated 'with great glory'. Moreover, he asserts that the body was incorrupt; the only sign of martyrdom was 'a thin red crease around the neck, like a scarlet thread', as testified by a woman called Oswyn who tended the shrine 'a little before' Abbo's time. Every Maundy Thursday Oswyn trimmed the body's hair and nails, putting the parings in a receptacle which 'to this day lies on the altar' (Abbo of Fleury, § 14.15–21). The church was given rich treasures and eight thieves tried to break in, to rob the shrine; they were miraculously paralysed and captured. Theodred, 'bishop of the province', condemned them and had them hanged. Later, Theodred repented this breach of canon law, since clerics were forbidden to pass the death sentence. After due penance he verified Edmund's incorruption: he opened the coffin, washed the body, clothed it in garments 'of the best' and replaced it in a wooden coffin. The *De miraculis sancti Eadmundi* attributed to Hermann the archdeacon, composed *c*.1100, adds two details to Abbo's account. He names Edmund's first burial-place as 'Sutton'. But this is such a common place name that identification is hazardous. Possibly the name entered the St Edmund legend because of conflation with the legend of St Æthelberht, the king of the East Angles who was murdered at 'Sutton', probably Sutton Walls near Hereford, in 794. Hermann also asserts that the translation to Beadericesworth took place in Æthelstan's reign, perhaps reasoning from the prominence of Æthelstan in Abbo's prologue.

Despite the hagiographical details, the general drift of the legend told by Abbo is true. Relics believed to be those of St Edmund were at Beadericesworth, in a church served by clerics, before the mid-tenth century. The Theodred of Abbo's narrative must be Theodred, bishop of London (909×26–951×3), who bequeathed his estates at Nowton, Horningsheath, Ickworth, and Whepstead, all near Beadericesworth, 'to St Edmund's church, as the property of God's community' (Whitelock, *Anglo-Saxon Wills*, no. 1). Numerous royal and other benefactions to St Edmund's church at Beadericesworth soon followed. It is most unlikely that any woman was ever custodian of St Edmund's shrine: reliable evidence shows that it was served first by clerics and then, from 1020, by monks. However, among the relics listed by Henry VIII's commissioners in 1538 were 'the paring of S. Edmundes naylles' (Wright, 85). And there certainly was a recognizably human body in the coffin when the coffin was opened by, according to Hermann, Leofstan, abbot of Bury St Edmunds from 1044 to 1065, and then, as Jocelin of Brakelond relates in detail, by Samson, abbot of Bury St Edmunds from 1182 to 1211, in 1198.

Before the end of the twelfth century the abbey of Bury St Edmunds had become one of the richest and most highly privileged monasteries in England. It owed much of its success to the cult of St Edmund and to the hagiographers who fostered it. Besides recording St Edmund's miracles they embellished his life story, creating a detailed and romantic legend, a piece of attractive literature but not sober history.   ANTONIA GRANSDEN

Sources Abbo of Fleury, *Passio sancti Eadmundi, Three lives of English saints*, ed. M. Winterbottom (1972), 67–87 · D. Whitelock, 'Fact and fiction in the legend of St Edmund', *Proceedings of the Suffolk Institute of Archaeology*, 31 (1967–9), 217–33 · A. Gransden, 'The *Passio sancti Eadmundi* by Abbo of Fleury', *Revue Bénédictine*, 105 (1995), 20–78 · Hermann the Archdeacon, 'De miraculis Sancti Eadmundi', *Memorials of St Edmund's Abbey*, ed. T. Arnold, 1, Rolls Series, 96 (1890), 26–92 · S. J. Ridyard, *The royal saints of Anglo-Saxon England*, Cambridge Studies in Medieval Life and Thought, 4th ser., 9 (1988) · C. E. Blunt, 'The St Edmund memorial coinage', *Proceedings of the Suffolk Institute of Archaeology*, 31 (1967–9), 234–55 · H. A. Grueber, *Handbook of the coins of Great Britain and Ireland in the British Museum*, rev. J. P. C. Kent and others, 2nd edn (1970), xvi–xvii, 11, 13 · D. Dumville and M. Lapidge, eds., *The annals of St Neots, with Vita prima sancti Neoti* (1985), vol. 17 of *The Anglo-Saxon Chronicle*, ed. D. Dumville and S. Keynes (1983–), xiii, lxxii, 1–107 · *ASC*, s.a. 870 · *Alfred the Great: Asser's Life of King Alfred and other contemporary sources*, ed. and trans. S. Keynes and M. Lapidge (1983), 78 · S. E. West, 'A new site for the martyrdom of St Edmund?', *Proceedings of the Suffolk Institute of Archaeology and History*, 35 (1981–4), 223 · A. Gransden, 'The composition and authorship of the *De miraculis sancti Eadmundi* attributed to "Hermann the Archdeacon"', *Journal of Medieval Latin*, 5 (1995), 1–52 · D. Whitelock, ed. and trans., *Anglo-Saxon wills* (1930), no. 1 · A. Gransden, 'The alleged incorruption of the body of St Edmund, king and martyr', *Antiquaries Journal*, 74 (1994), 135–68 · T. Wright, ed., *Three chapters of letters relating to the suppression of monasteries*, CS, 26 (1843) · *AS chart.*, S 1526
Likenesses manuscript illumination, 12th cent. (cycle of his life), Morgan L., MS 736

Edmund [*called* Edmund Crouchback], **first earl of Lancaster and first earl of Leicester** (**1245–1296**), prince, second son of *Henry III (1207–1272) and his queen, *Eleanor of Provence (d. 1291), daughter and coheir of Raymond-Berengar, count of Provence, was born on 16 January 1245, probably at the royal palace of Westminster.

Birth Edmund had one elder brother, the future *Edward I, three sisters, one of whom was *Margaret, who married Alexander III of Scotland, and possibly a further four younger brothers who did not survive infancy, but the number of children born to Henry and Eleanor remains very uncertain. His father was evidently delighted at the news of Edmund's birth: he offered an embroidered chasuble at the high altar of Westminster Abbey on the day of his birth; and he joyfully wrote to inform the abbot of Bury St Edmunds of the event, since Edmund was named after the martyred king of the East Angles, and this, according to Henry himself, at the abbot's suggestion, although the king probably needed little persuasion since Edmund was one of his favourite saints. The king also paid for an embroidered cope of samite offered by Eleanor at her purification, when the royal chapel rendered the *Christus vincit* before the queen, and for another cope used on the occasion of Edmund's baptism. Before the birth, as Eleanor's confinement drew near, Henry had also instructed that 1000 candles be placed around the shrine of St Thomas at Canterbury, and another 1000 in the church of St Augustine, Canterbury, for the preservation of Eleanor's health and for her safe delivery. He had also arranged for the antiphon of St Edmund to be chanted for Eleanor while she was in labour. Few births in the later middle ages are so well documented.

Childhood and the kingdom of Sicily Knowledge of Edmund's childhood is sparse, but the surviving evidence indicates that his upbringing was entirely typical for a boy of his rank in the mid-thirteenth century. From at least October 1246 he was living in Windsor Castle with his elder siblings, and the royal records occasionally reveal the purchase of dishes, saucers, cups, robes, and other items for Edmund and the other children. He was put in the care of Aymon Thurbert, constable of Windsor and keeper of the king's children, and from Aymon, or others deputed to the task, he presumably learned his letters, his horsemanship, and the other accomplishments expected of a Plantagenet prince. By 1255–6, at the latest, a distinct household had been assigned to him: Aymon Thurbert is now described as Edmund's own knight, and two named yeomen attached to the prince are mentioned in the records. Whether he travelled much beyond Windsor in his early years is unknown, but in May 1254 he accompanied his mother and Edward to Gascony and stayed there until December.

It was at Bordeaux, on 30 October, that the grant of the principality of Capua was made in his name to his great-uncle, Thomas of Savoy. This was in consequence of the most important event concerning Edmund in his childhood, his designation as the future king of Sicily. Following the deposition in 1245 of the Hohenstaufen emperor, Frederick II, from his various thrones, Pope Innocent IV duly offered the kingdom of Sicily, a papal fief, to Charles d'Anjou, brother of Louis IX of France, and Richard, earl of Cornwall, brother of Henry III, in 1252. Charles, who later became king of Sicily, was preoccupied with other, pressing business at the time, and Richard of Cornwall could not be persuaded to accept the papal offer, despite his brother's best efforts. Henry, however, was determined to grasp the opportunity and began to negotiate with Innocent IV in favour of his second son. On 6 March 1254 Alberto di Parma, the papal nuncio in England, formally offered the Sicilian throne to Edmund, and the grant was confirmed by Innocent on 14 May. On 25 May Henry ordered that a great seal be made for Edmund as king of Sicily. The terms of the grant were clarified in the further confirmation of 9 April 1255 by Pope Alexander IV: Sicily was to be held by liege homage from the pope in return for 2000 ounces of gold per annum and the service of 300 knights for three months when required; Henry III was to render homage in Edmund's name, to be repeated by Edmund when he reached the age of fifteen years; and Henry was required to pay the huge sum of 135,541 marks (£90,360) to reimburse the papacy for the money that it had already expended in seeking to oust Manfred, Frederick II's son, from the kingdom. The contract was agreed and the papal nuncio invested Edmund with Sicily on 18 October 1255.

That Henry was entirely serious in his intention of

Edmund, first earl of Lancaster and first earl of Leicester (1245–1296), tomb effigy

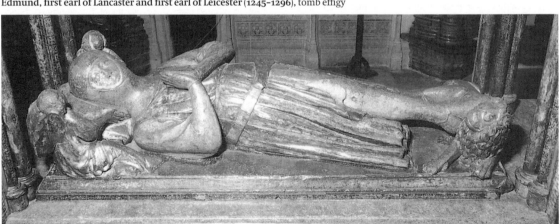

establishing Edmund in Sicily and extending Plantagenet power into the Mediterranean is further suggested by the negotiations conducted in 1256 concerning the proposal that Edmund marry Plaisance, queen of Cyprus, regent of the kingdom, and that the heir, Hugues, later King Hugues II, marry Henry III's daughter Beatrice. Concurrently, a marriage alliance with Manfred was also being given consideration at the English court: Edmund would marry his daughter and Manfred would resign Sicily to his putative son-in-law when the union occurred. Neither proposal came to anything, however, and Sicily never came into Edmund's possession. First, Henry was unable to raise the money required from his English subjects, who bitterly opposed the plan, despite his persistent efforts to persuade them to grant him a subsidy. (These included his parading of Edmund, presented in Apulian dress, before the English magnates at the Lent parliament of 1257.) Second, Manfred proved to be far too strong; he had himself crowned king of Sicily in August 1258 in full contempt of the papacy. And third, the entire matter of Plantagenet involvement with Sicily became subsumed in the wider set of English political issues that led to the provisions of Oxford (June–July 1258) and baronial attempts to control the king. Not surprisingly, the baronial council implemented in accordance with the provisions soon sought from the pope alterations to the conditions of the Sicilian offer which Alexander IV was never likely to grant. On 18 December 1258, in consequence, the pope rescinded the offer unless the previous conditions and terms were met. Henry persevered despite this, presumably with Edmund's full approval. In March 1261 Edmund even ordered his Sicilian subjects to prepare for his reception in the kingdom in person, and intermittent negotiations, reflecting the changing political situation in England, continued until Pope Urban IV definitively cancelled the grant and absolved Henry and Edmund of all their obligations in respect of Sicily on 28 July 1263. By then Urban had offered Sicily to Charles d'Anjou who, now free of other encumbrances, proceeded to wrest the kingdom from Manfred and Conradin, the last of the Hohenstaufens, in the years 1266–8.

The barons' wars Between 1258 and 1265 Edmund, like his father and brother, was largely preoccupied with events closer to home. He was in France with Henry between November 1259 and April 1260 and gave the formal consent required of him to his father's renunciation of claims to Normandy, Anjou, Maine, and Touraine, in the treaty of Paris concluded on 3 December 1259. He was in France again with Henry in the summer of 1262, returning to England in September to convalesce after he became very ill. He was then appointed captain of the king's forces in England, an honorific position, in response to the threats of Llywelyn ap Gruffudd, prince of north Wales, and instructed by Henry to allow no parliaments to be held while the king was absent abroad. With the real prospect of civil war looming in England, he was appointed to keep the key castle of Dover in June 1263, but on Henry's surrender to Simon de Montfort in July he was forced to relinquish it, although he initially resisted commands to do so.

Soon afterwards, it would seem, he left again for France with his mother and supported her in her attempts to raise mercenaries in Flanders and elsewhere to invade England on behalf of King Henry. The two did not return until after the battle of Evesham (4 August 1265). In the long period of political turbulence that followed Edmund seems to have played only a limited role, most notably in the summer of 1266 when he was stationed with a force at Warwick with the responsibility of checking the depredations committed by the political irreconcilables (the so-called 'disinherited') based in Kenilworth Castle. This he successfully did in advance of the establishment of the comprehensive siege of Kenilworth (25 June – 14 December 1266), during which he commanded one of the four royalist battalions involved. Shortly after the capitulation of the defenders the king granted the castle to him. Then, in February 1267, he was sent with Robert Walerand to treat for peace with Llywelyn ap Gruffudd, and their negotiations contributed to the treaty of Montgomery, agreed on 25 September 1267.

Foundations of the duchy of Lancaster Edmund is probably most significant, historically, for his accumulation of the vast estates that came to form the core of the later duchy of Lancaster. The process began on 26 October 1265, when Henry III granted him the honour and borough of Leicester and all the lands previously held by Simon de Montfort, earl of Leicester, although there was no formal grant of the earldom (Edmund was styled earl of Leicester from January 1267). On 28 June 1266 he was granted the castles and lands forfeited by the rebellious earl of Derby, Robert de Ferrers, followed on 12 July by the grant of the honour of Derby. Earl Robert had the right to seek to regain them according to the terms of the dictum of Kenilworth (30 October 1266), but despite later legal process against Edmund in 1270 and 1274, especially following an unpleasant piece of legal chicanery on the part of Edmund and his brother Edward in 1269, Ferrers recovered only a few properties for himself and his heirs. Edmund received many other grants from his father in the years 1265–8, including Builth, Kidwelly, and Shireburn castles, and the castles and counties of Cardigan and Carmarthen (exchanged for other properties in November 1279), but the most important grant was undoubtedly that of 30 June 1267, whereby he received the honour, county, town, and castle of Lancaster, and all royal demesne land in Lancashire, effectively becoming earl of Lancaster, along with the great lordships of the 'Three Castles' (Grosmont, Skenfrith, and Whitecastle) and Monmouth, and certain other properties including Newcastle under Lyme and the honour and castle of Pickering, although he only used the title earl of Lancaster from December 1276. He had, moreover, hoped to secure the lordships of Holderness and the Isle of Wight, along with the earldom of Devon, when he married his first wife, Avelina de Forz, heir to those estates, on 8 or 9 April 1269. However, her childless death on 11 November 1274 disqualified Edmund from inheriting them, and they passed to others. Nevertheless the immense wealth and power that he had come to enjoy in so short a space of time is revealed by the inquisition into the extent of his lands taken on Edmund's death, for comparatively little was added after 1267. In 1296 he held property in 632 separate locations distributed through twenty-five counties of England and in Wales, and concentrated in Derbyshire, Lancashire, Lincolnshire, Leicestershire, Staffordshire, Northamptonshire, and south Wales. These properties comprised a total of 263 ⅓ knights' fees along with fourteen castles, including some of the most important in the land. This huge endowment, the reward for his unwavering political support of his father in the 1260s, and partly, perhaps, intended as compensation for his failure to secure Sicily, was worth some £4500 per annum, making him one of the very greatest English landed magnates of the later thirteenth century. It was Edmund, too, who acquired the palace of Savoy on the Strand, London, originally the house of his maternal uncle, Peter of *Savoy, this famous property duly passing into the possession of the later dukes of Lancaster.

Crusade After the pacification of England following the end of the barons' wars Edmund turned his mind towards the crusade. Henry III's crusading vow of 1250 still remained unfulfilled, and in 1268 Pope Clement IV authorized Ottobuono, his legate in England, to pay Edmund an appropriate sum from moneys raised for the crusade in England if Edmund vicariously fulfilled his father's vow. This scheme was rapidly abandoned, however, since Edward was determined to go on crusade himself. The two brothers, along with many others, took their crusading vows at the parliament held at Northampton in June 1268, and ultimately it was Edward who carried Henry's cross to the East in 1270. Edmund, meanwhile, had agreed to serve Edward on crusade, contracting to provide 100 knights, himself included, for one year's service in return for 10,000 marks and shipping. Edmund planned carefully for his crusade and left England in February or March 1271, appointing his mother, Eleanor of Provence, as his general attorney with very extensive powers, and having taken a number of measures to raise the liquid funds he required. Nevertheless he was hard pressed financially during his brief stay in the Holy Land (August 1271 – May 1272) and was obliged to borrow money from creditors in Acre, while his mother raised further sums for him at home.

Little is known of Edmund's activities in the Holy Land, but his expedition seems to have earned him the nickname Crouchback (crossed back), and for the remainder of his life there existed almost continuously the very real prospect that he would go on crusade again. As early as December 1276 Edward I empowered his envoys to the papal court to bind himself or Edmund to set out on the next general passage to the Holy Land. It was clearly Edward's intention that Edmund should lead an English crusade on his behalf, for demands upon him at home militated against Edward's own participation, and he persisted with this plan in the following years, dispatching embassies to both Nicholas III and Martin IV in August 1280, April 1281, and January 1282 and persuading the archbishops of Canterbury and York to lobby the papal court concurrently. Edmund was very warmly recommended as a prospective crusade leader in the letters that resulted, but a succession of popes remained unmoved since it was Edward's leadership of the proposed new crusade that they fervently sought. After prolonged negotiations Edward himself took the cross again in June 1287, and Edmund almost certainly followed his lead at the same time. Reference to his second crusading vow occurs in a papal bull of November 1289, but it apparently remained unfulfilled at the time of Edmund's death in 1296.

Service to Edward I in Wales Edmund's preparedness to co-operate with Edward's plans for a crusade is altogether typical of the close relationship that they enjoyed. Only rarely did the brothers clash. Their most serious quarrel occurred in 1274 when Edmund seems to have boycotted Edward's coronation on 19 August. This followed rejection of Edmund's claim to carry the great sword Curtana in the ceremony, a claim probably based on his tenure of the stewardship of England, granted to him for life on 9 May 1269. But the quarrel was soon resolved and on the following day Edmund renounced all claim to the stewardship for himself and his heirs, before Edward granted it to him again for life in February 1275. During 1275 the brothers were again in dispute, over moneys granted towards their crusading expenses by Henry III and the papacy, but again the issue quickly subsided. Later clashes were similarly of little import, and it is Edmund's loyalty and service to his king and brother which are the hallmarks of his career at home and abroad just as they typified his conduct during their father's lifetime.

It is scarcely surprising that Edmund played a significant role in Edward I's Welsh wars, especially considering his interests as one of the more important marcher lords. Following the rapid deterioration in relations between Edward and Llywelyn ap Gruffudd, Edmund was summoned on 12 December 1276 to Worcester, the main mustering point for the English feudal host, which was ordered to assemble there on 1 July 1277. He commanded one of the armies engaged in the war of 1277, operating from his lordship of Carmarthen, and advanced northwards to Llanbadarn, arriving there by 25 July. Edmund at once ordered the construction of a new castle, the future Aberystwyth, before returning to England on 20 September having disbanded the field army and left Roger de Molis to oversee the completion of the new castle. In the second Welsh war of 1282–3 he again commanded an army in south Wales, but it is not the case, as is sometimes stated, that he was directly responsible for the capture and execution of Llywelyn, near Builth, on 11 December 1282. Welsh resistance finally came to an end following the capture of Dafydd ap Gruffudd in June 1283, and Edmund was one of those summoned at Michaelmas 1283 to the parliament at Shrewsbury, where Dafydd's gruesome death was decided. Finally Edmund served during the operations to quash the uprising led by Madog ap Llywelyn in 1294–5. He spent most of his time in Wales during the months from November 1294 to May 1295.

Power and diplomacy in France Edmund served his brother well enough in a military capacity, but perhaps of greater value was his service as an intermediary and diplomat in the context of the difficult and frequently fraught relations that existed between the French and English kings in the last decades of the thirteenth century. His capacity to act thus stemmed, first, from his birth and position, for he was the cousin of Philippe III and Philippe IV of France as well as brother to Edward I, and, second, from his marriage to Blanche of Artois (d. 1302), which took place between 18 December 1275 and 18 January 1276. His second wife, daughter of Robert (I), count of Artois (d. 1250), was the widow of Henri, king of Navarre (d. 1274), and by virtue of their union Edmund governed the great French fief of Champagne for eight years on Blanche's behalf before the heir, her daughter Jeanne de Navarre, married Philippe IV in 1284. Edmund was accordingly granted the courtesy title of count of Champagne and Brie, before Philippe IV bought out his residual rights and interests for a considerable sum after his marriage to Jeanne. Even after this Edmund continued to hold various lands in the Île-de-France on Blanche's behalf, notably Beaufort and Nogent-sur-Marne. During the years 1276–8 and 1281–2 he was regularly travelling between England and Champagne, and he visited Navarre at least once, in 1276, but he took only a limited interest in the affairs of Champagne, his most significant action being his personal quelling of the insurrection at Provins in January 1280, when the townsmen rose in revolt to protest against the severity of financial burdens imposed on them. Nevertheless his frequent presence in France, his position in French society, and his personal ties, directly and through Blanche of Artois, to the Capetian court meant that he was very useful to Edward I diplomatically. In particular, he was engaged in negotiations with Philippe III in 1279 concerning Edward's claims to Agenais and Quercy, and the claims of Eleanor of Castile, Edward's queen, to the county of Ponthieu. (In 1291 he was appointed lieutenant of Ponthieu to hold on behalf of Prince Edward, the future Edward II, until he came of age.) But most important was his part in the Anglo-French diplomacy that preceded the war of 1294–8. In particular, Edward sent him on an embassy to Philippe IV in early 1294 with the intention of settling the differences between the two kings over the question of jurisdictional rights over, and in, Aquitaine and over the trouble that had flared up between sailors of Normandy and Gascony culminating in the sack of La Rochelle in May 1293. Edward was eager to avoid war, and Edmund and his advisers were instructed to treat for peace with Philippe. The result was the so-called 'secret treaty' negotiated in February 1294, which sought to resolve the tensions stemming from the English king's position as duke of Aquitaine. But as a result of Philippe's duplicity and bad faith, or of Edmund's lack of caution and naïvety, or of the influence of the powerful anti-Plantagenet faction at the French court at the time, the 'secret treaty' was not implemented and in May 1294 Aquitaine was confiscated. Edmund renounced his own homage to Philippe and returned to England with Blanche of Artois.

French war, death, and assessment From the very beginning of the war that followed Edward clearly intended to rely heavily upon his brother. As early as 1 June 1294 Edward wrote to inform the magnates of Gascony that Edmund was being sent to win back the duchy from the French, but the Welsh war of 1294–5 intervened, and then Edmund fell ill. It was not until January 1296 that Edmund, accompanied by Henry de Lacy, earl of Lincoln, finally sailed at the head of a considerable force to reinforce the troops previously raised locally in south-west France and those earlier dispatched from England. The expedition achieved little, however. After sailing up the Gironde to Bourg and Blaye, Edmund collected what forces he could and advanced on Bordeaux in late March, but the occupying French forces had had time to prepare and the city proved impregnable. A few English soldiers did manage to force an entry, but the gates were closed behind them and they were taken. It seems that an attempt was then made to bribe some citizens into handing the city over to the English, but this was discovered. With money running short, and, in the knowledge of the approach of a large French force, Edmund raised the siege and moved to Bayonne. He fell ill about Whitsun and died on 5 June 1296 at Bayonne. He had instructed that his body was not to be buried until his debts had been paid, so the body was embalmed and kept by the Franciscans of Bayonne until it was shipped back to England in 1297 and honourably buried by Edward I in Westminster Abbey. Edmund's elaborately carved tomb survives, fittingly, next to Edward's own. His first wife, Avelina, is also buried there, her small canopied tomb surviving on the north side of the presbytery. With his second wife, Blanche, who survived him, Edmund had three sons, *Thomas, *Henry, and John, and one daughter.

Little is known for certain of Edmund's character. He was conventionally pious; he was a major patron and possibly the initial founder of the Franciscan priory at Preston, Lancashire, and of the Dominican house at Leicester; he also assisted his wife Blanche in establishing the house of the nuns of the order of St Clare outside Aldgate, London, in 1293. Given his remarkable wealth, however, his ecclesiastical patronage appears otherwise to have been restricted to a few houses and limited in its substance. In 1270, probably in connection with his crusade preparations, he granted the manor of Bere Regis to the nuns of Tarrant. In 1278 Merton College, Oxford, was granted the advowson of Embledon. He granted 20s. per annum in 1285 for a lamp at Finchale Priory and 6s. 8d. to Monmouth Priory in 1289 for the same purpose. Burscough Priory was given a market in 1286, and at some point between 1267 and Edmund's death Ware Priory was granted the sum of £9 per annum. Edmund's most significant commitment seems to have been to the cause of the Holy Land, judging by his involvement with the crusading movement during the last twenty-five years of his life. He appears to have been a competent soldier and commander, though no more than that, and was plainly trusted by his father and brother in military matters. His most notable trait was his consistent loyalty to them both. More than conventional sentiment lies behind the words chosen by Edward when he wrote to ask his leading churchmen for prayers on behalf of Edmund's soul following his death. He spoke of him as

> Edmund, our dearest and only brother, who was always devoted and faithful to us and to the affairs of our realm, and in whom valour and many gifts of grace shone forth … whose loss has devastated us and our whole realm. (Rymer, *Foedera*, 4th edn)

SIMON LLOYD

Sources *Chancery records* · PRO · Rymer, *Foedera*, new edn · *Ann. mon.* · *CEPR letters*, vol. 1 · R. Somerville, *History of the duchy of Lancaster, 1265–1603* (1953) · W. E. Rhodes, 'Edmund, earl of Lancaster', *EngHR*, 10 (1895), 19–40, 209–37 · J. R. Maddicott, *Thomas of Lancaster, 1307–1322: a study in the reign of Edward II* (1970) · M. Vale, *The Angevin legacy and the Hundred Years War, 1250–1340* (1990) · H. d'Arbois de Jubainville, *Histoire des ducs et des comtes de Champagne*, 6 (Paris, 1866) · H. R. Luard, ed., *Flores historiarum*, 3 vols., Rolls Series, 95 (1890), vol. 2, p. 286 · *Calendar of the liberate rolls*, 2, PRO (1930)
Likenesses tomb effigy, Westminster Abbey, London [*see illus.*]

Edmund [Edmund of Woodstock], **first earl of Kent** (1301–1330), magnate, was the sixth son of *Edward I (1239–1307) and the second from Edward's second marriage, to *Margaret (1279?–1318), daughter of Philippe III, king of France (d. 1285). He was born on 5 August 1301 at Woodstock, the half-brother of *Edward II (1284–1327) and the younger brother of *Thomas of Brotherton, earl of Norfolk (d. 1338).

The young courtier Edward I sought to provide for his youngest son's future by promising in 1306 to find him lands worth 7000 marks a year within two years, and just before he died augmented his original grant by 1000 marks. Unfortunately, he did not identify the property that would constitute this endowment, though he had apparently intended to give either Edmund or his brother Thomas the earldom of Cornwall. Edward I's failure to make the grant before his death gave Edward II the opportunity to create his friend Piers Gaveston earl instead. Edward partially honoured his father's promise, however, by granting Edmund various manors in 1315, and further lands to the value of 2000 marks in 1319. In October 1320 Edmund was summoned to attend parliament for the first time, as Edmund of Woodstock, and the following year, on 26 July, Edward II named him earl of Kent, girded him with the sword of the county, and granted him additional assets to support his new title.

During these years Edmund gradually became embroiled in national politics, and proved to be a strong supporter of his half-brother and the latter's courtiers. With Edward II's permission, he joined other magnates in witnessing the treaty of Leake in 1318. Edmund led an embassy, which also included Hugh Despenser the elder and Bartholomew Badlesmere, to Paris and then to Avignon to confer with Pope John XXII in the spring of 1320. Their mission was overtly to secure the see of Lincoln for Henry Burghersh, Badlesmere's nephew, but they were also there to persuade the pope to release Edward II from his oath to uphold the ordinances. On their way back from Avignon they met Edward outside Paris at Amiens.

Involvement in civil war Now a major figure at court, Edmund took a leading part in the suppression of the contrariants' uprising against the court in 1321–2. The Despensers had aroused the hatred of the nobles, and opposition to them became so widespread that it even attracted Sir Bartholomew Badlesmere, steward of the household. Enraged by Badlesmere's betrayal, Edward now turned against his former friend. On 16 June 1321 he appointed Edmund to be keeper of Kent, constable of Dover Castle, and warden of the Cinque Ports, abruptly replacing Badlesmere. In creating Edmund earl of Kent on 26 July, Edward hoped further to undermine Badlesmere's power in that county, and took another step in that direction when on 26 September he named Edmund keeper of Tonbridge Castle, again in place of Badlesmere. In the previous July Edmund had attended the parliament that banished the Despensers, but later claimed that he had been forced to give his consent to their exile. By autumn, the political situation had changed dramatically. In October Edmund responded to Edward's summons to besiege Leeds Castle in Kent, which was in Badlesmere's custody, and in November he sat on the royal council that annulled the judgment against the Despensers. On the eve of fighting between the king and the contrariants, Edward ordered Edmund, among others, to raise men-at-arms and infantry to serve the king. He was with the royal army as it pursued the contrariants in the Welsh marches, and then turned northward against Thomas of Lancaster. Edmund was one of the magnates who, on 11 March 1322, counselled Edward to declare the rebels traitors and move against them with all force. Edward then dispatched Edmund and John de Warenne (d. 1347) to seize Pontefract. After Lancaster was captured at the battle of Boroughbridge on 17 March, he was taken to York and then to Pontefract, where a tribunal of seven magnates, including Edmund, condemned him to death on 22 March 1322. Although they had been defeated, the contrariants continued to cause problems. Maurice Berkeley, who had been captured and imprisoned in Wallingford Castle, managed to overwhelm his captors and seize the castle. In January 1323, therefore, Edward sent Edmund and the elder Despenser to help restore order and retake the castle. They seized Berkeley at once, and did not scruple to ignore ecclesiastical sanctuary when some of the rebels took refuge in a chapel in the castle.

Edmund was amply rewarded for his loyalty. At the end of March Edward granted him extensive holdings in Wales forfeited by Roger Mortimer of Wigmore. He was appointed sheriff of Rutland, an office he held until 1326, and in July Edward gave him custody of the castle of Oakham during pleasure. In 1323 Edmund was made responsible for arresting and charging the adherents of the rebel Robert Ewer, and that September he was licensed to told a tournament at Northampton.

Service in Scotland and France After triumphing over his opponents Edward turned his attention to Scotland. In 1322 Edmund served as one of the leaders in the Scottish campaign of August and September; he was present when the retreating English were routed by the Scots at Old Byland on 14 October, and accompanied the king on his flight to York. Because of the fears of a further invasion by the Scots, Edward ordered Edmund and other lords to raise as many soldiers as possible and to lead them to York in December. In February 1323 Edward named Edmund as his lieutenant in Scotland, and also as lieutenant in the northern counties bordering Scotland in place of Andrew Harclay, who was charged with treason, and later appointed him one of the judges to pass judgment on Harclay. Edmund was also active arraying forces from Cumberland, Westmorland, and Lancashire to fight in Scotland, and he himself was summoned to serve as well as to make additional preparations for a new campaign. On 30 May he was present with the king and council when relations between England and Scotland were deliberated, resulting in a truce that was intended to last thirteen years. In August, after Roger Mortimer escaped from the Tower of London, Edmund was one of the magnates ordered to arrest him.

Trouble had also been brewing in France, which would occupy Edmund for the next few years. The French demanded that Edward II perform homage for Gascony by Easter 1324, while in Gascony itself a dispute between the priory at St Sardos and the English over the construction of another *bastide* on English territory had led to violence in October 1323. The French summoned English officials to answer for their outrages, including the hanging of a French official, and when they failed to appear Charles IV moved to confiscate the duchy in the spring of 1324. In April Edward sent Edmund and the archbishop of Dublin to inquire into the affair and argue his case, but the mission failed. Edward appointed Edmund his lieutenant of Gascony on 20 July 1324, and sent him to defend the duchy. Charles quickly overran most of the Agenais, where Edmund had managed to make himself unpopular because of his unreasonable exactions, and then besieged him in La Réole. Edmund held out until 22 September, but was forced to surrender and make a six-month truce to prevent his being overwhelmed. He remained in Gascony, however, and in April 1325 Edward instructed him to rally the Gascons in advance of the arrival of a large company of reinforcements, to be led by John de Warenne.

The revolution against Edward II Edward himself had hesitated to leave England for fear that in his absence enemies of his court might move against him, so in March 1325 he sent Queen Isabella to France to negotiate with her brother, Charles. They quickly agreed to a truce, which was ratified by Edward in June, and the French eventually agreed to accept the homage of Edward's eldest son in his place. The young Edward departed for France and performed homage on 24 September. Towards the end of 1325 Edmund found time to marry Margaret (d. 1349), the sister of Thomas *Wake, Lord Wake of Liddell (d. 1349), and widow of John Comyn of Badenoch (d. 1314).

At some point about this time Edmund, who would appear to have come to share the general resentment at the Despensers' control of government, joined Isabella and Edward in Paris. Fearful of their plotting, Edward II ordered them all back to England. When Edmund refused, Edward confiscated his lands in March 1326, along with those of the others around Isabella. Edmund was with the queen and her company at the betrothal of the young Edward and Philippa of Hainault in Hainault. In August he participated in the invasion of England led by Isabella and Mortimer, which landed on estates belonging to his brother Thomas, who, with Henry of Lancaster, immediately joined the rebels. Edmund and Thomas were both present at the baronial council in Bristol on 26 October, which declared that Edward would be keeper of the realm in his father's absence. The two brothers also sat on the tribunal that condemned the elder Despenser to death and later in November participated in the trial of the younger Despenser; and they were among the nobles summoned to the first parliament of the new regime. They both attended the coronation of the young king, and were named to the regency council, headed by Henry of Lancaster, to supervise Edward III.

Edmund profited at first from his support of Isabella. Shortly after Edward III's coronation he received various lands including property of the earl of Arundel (also executed in 1326) and the two Despensers. He received other Despenser lands in 1328. In addition, some of his followers received land and other favours from the king at his request. During the early stages of the new reign, Edmund was frequently at court, attesting charters and witnessing the transfer of the great seal. He also served in other capacities. In 1327 he was appointed to be one of the captains of the marches of Scotland, and served as a supervisor of the peace commissions in Suffolk with his brother Thomas. In 1329 he was in Gascony on royal business.

Downfall and death Yet Edmund's commitment to the new regime was not as profound as these honours and activities suggest, presumably as a result of misgivings over the growing predominance of Roger Mortimer. In the autumn of 1328 Edmund, his brother Thomas, and Edmund's brother-in-law Thomas Wake joined Henry of Lancaster in the latter's opposition to Mortimer and Isabella. They gathered in London with other dissident magnates and prelates at the beginning of December, and became part of a confederation aimed at reforming the kingdom. Edmund's opposition was only lukewarm, however, and he and his brother soon rejoined the king, causing the rebellion to collapse. Yet thereafter he was not welcome at court either. Although he had witnessed charters sporadically but regularly in the year leading up to the rebellion, he disappears from the witness lists after January 1329. Nevertheless, in January 1330 he and Thomas performed the ceremonial function of accompanying Philippa on the way to her coronation from London to Westminster.

By this time, however, Edmund had become entangled in a more dangerous enterprise. Duped into believing that his brother Edward II was still alive and in captivity, Edmund entertained a plot to release him, and plans for invasion and insurrection were brought to him by a number of clerics and adventurers, some with ties to the Despensers. News of the conspiracy became widespread, and Edmund was indicted in parliament in March 1330 and condemned to death. On 19 March he was executed outside the walls of Winchester Castle in shameful circumstances—nobody could be found willing to put to death a man so eminent, and he was kept waiting all day until the evening, when a common criminal was induced to behead him. His body was buried at first in the Franciscan church in Winchester, but in 1331 was removed to Westminster Abbey. Among those accused of adhering to Edmund was his brother-in-law Thomas Wake, who forfeited his lands and had to flee the realm for a time. Later in that year, when Roger Mortimer was tried in parliament, it was revealed that he and his henchmen had had a hand in persuading Edmund that his brother was alive. Edward III formally pardoned Edmund in the same parliament. Edmund's son, another Edmund, then about four years old, inherited his father's lands and title, which, when the younger Edmund died on 5 October 1331, passed to the latter's brother John. John died childless in 1352, and the earldom passed successively to Thomas *Holland, earl of Kent (d. 1360), and to *Edward the Black Prince, the husbands of John's sister *Joan. Edmund's widow, Margaret, died on 29 September 1349.

Although the chronicler Henry Blaneford called him mighty among great men, Edmund did not have a good reputation during his brief life, something his political waverings can have done nothing to remedy. There was widespread resentment, too, at the conduct of his household, which was apt to plunder the countryside through which it passed, paying little or nothing for what it seized. Consequently there were few who mourned when Edmund came to his sordid end.   SCOTT L. WAUGH

Sources GEC, *Peerage*, new edn, 7.142–8 · F. Palgrave, ed., *The parliamentary writs and writs of military summons*, 2 vols. in 4 (1827–34) · *RotP*, vols. 1–2 · *Chancery records* · Rymer, *Foedera*, new edn, vol. 4 · P. Chaplais, ed., *The War of Saint-Sardos (1323–1325): Gascon correspondence and diplomatic documents*, CS, 3rd ser., 87 (1954) · *Chronica monasterii de Melsa, a fundatione usque ad annum 1396, auctore Thoma de Burton*, ed. E. A. Bond, 3 vols., Rolls Series, 43 (1866–8) · *Chronicon Henrici Knighton, vel Cnitthon, monachi Leycestrensis*, ed. J. R. Lumby, 2 vols., Rolls Series, 92 (1889–95) · *Adae Murimuth continuatio chronicarum. Robertus de Avesbury de gestis mirabilibus regis Edwardi tertii*, ed. E. M. Thompson, Rolls Series, 93 (1889) · *Chronicon Galfridi le Baker de Swynebroke*, ed. E. M. Thompson (1889) · W. Stubbs, ed., *Chronicles of the reigns of Edward I and Edward II*, 2 vols., Rolls Series, 76 (1882–3), esp. *Annales Paulini, Gesta Edwardi de Carnarvon, Vita et mors Edward II* · *Johannis de Trokelowe et Henrici de Blaneforde … chronica et annales*, ed. H. T. Riley, pt 3 of *Chronica monasterii S. Albani*, Rolls Series, 28 (1866) · *Thomae Walsingham, quondam monachi S. Albani, historia Anglicana*, ed. H. T. Riley, 2 vols., pt 1 of *Chronica monasterii S. Albani*, Rolls Series, 28 (1863–4), vol. 1 · H. R. Luard, ed., *Flores historiarum*, 3 vols., Rolls Series, 95 (1890), vol. 3 · N. Denholm-Young, ed. and trans., *Vita Edwardi secundi* (1957) · M. Prestwich, *Edward I* (1988), 131 · N. Fryde, *The tyranny and fall of Edward II, 1321–1326* (1979), 48, 58, 60, 131, 136, 142, 143, 144, 179, 182, 194, 204, 206, 208, 217, 222, 236–7 · J. R. Maddicott, *Thomas of Lancaster, 1307–1322: a study in the reign of Edward II* (1970), 5, 23, 71, 255, 293, 310, 312 · J. R. S. Phillips, *Aymer de Valence, earl of Pembroke, 1307–1324: baronial politics in the reign of Edward II* (1972), 11, 19, 172, 192, 208, 219, 221, 224–6, 228, 232, 284 · R. Nicholson, *Edward III and the Scots: the formative years of a military career, 1327–1335* (1965), 13, 22–4, 62–3, 106 · M. Vale, *The Angevin legacy and the Hundred Years War, 1250–1340* (1990), 232–42 · Tout, *Admin. hist.*, 1.256–7; 2.302 (n. 2); 3.4, 5 (n. 2), 14, 24, 28–9, 43, 95 (n. 3), 189; 4.78, 446

Edmund [Edmund of Langley], **first duke of York** (1341–1402), prince, was the fifth (but fourth surviving) son of *Edward III, king of England, and *Philippa of Hainault, daughter of William, count of Hainault and Holland.

Birth and early life Edmund was born on 5 June 1341 at his father's manor of Kings Langley in Hertfordshire. According to Walsingham he was baptized by the abbot of St Albans. The abbot and the earls of Arundel and Surrey were his godfathers. John de Warenne, earl of Surrey, died in 1347 and bequeathed his young godson a glass goblet decorated with gilded silver and standing on a tripod. The earl died without an heir male and the king granted Edmund his lands north of the Trent. These lay predominantly in Yorkshire, and included the castle and lordship of Conisbrough; the bulk of the inheritance, however, went to Edmund's other godfather, the earl of Arundel. Edmund's first experience of war came in 1359, when he accompanied his father on the unsuccessful Rheims campaign. Edward III had intended to take Rheims and have himself crowned king of France, but he was compelled to abandon his siege of the city and in the following year he concluded the treaty of Brétigny with France: Edmund was one of the witnesses to the treaty. In 1361 (probably on 23 April) he became a knight of the Garter. In the Michaelmas parliament of 1362 Edward, wishing to honour his three younger sons who were now all of age, created *Lionel of Antwerp, duke of Clarence, *John of Gaunt duke of Lancaster, and Edmund earl of Cambridge. He was granted an annuity of 1000 marks to maintain his estate as earl, but only gradually over the following years was this annuity converted into grants of land. He received the lordship of Tynedale in 1375 (though at his death in 1402 the lordship was said to be worth nothing because of damage inflicted by the Scots) and in 1377 he was granted the castle and manor of Fotheringhay in Northamptonshire. He also received the castles and manors of Stamford and Grantham in Lincolnshire, but despite these grants he remained poorly endowed by comparison with his peers who were not of royal blood.

Negotiations for marriage A more substantial endowment at home might have come from a marriage to an English heiress, but Edward III had other plans for his son. In the early 1360s Edward hoped to negotiate a marriage between Edmund and Margaret, daughter and heir of Louis de Mâle, count of Flanders. Edward III stood to gain substantially from such a marriage. Not only would Flanders move firmly into the English political and diplomatic orbit, but Edmund would become, by marriage, lord of a large appanage on France's northern and eastern borders that would include not just Flanders but the counties of Artois, Burgundy, Nevers, and Rethel, to which Margaret was also heir. A 'northern Aquitaine' would thus be created, in which English influence would be dominant. It is not surprising, therefore, that Charles V of France vigorously opposed the marriage, putting forward as his own candidate his brother Philip, duke of Burgundy.

Negotiations between England and Flanders opened in February 1362, and with the co-operation of Margaret's father they moved forward to a successful conclusion. On 19 October 1364 a marriage treaty was agreed between the two rulers. However, Edmund and Margaret were related within the forbidden degrees, and a papal dispensation was therefore necessary if the marriage was to proceed. This gave Charles V an opportunity to put pressure on the papal curia at Avignon to refuse the dispensation; the pope, Urban V, himself a Frenchman, gave way; the dispensation was refused, and the marriage negotiations were finally abandoned in 1369.

Even before the Flemish marriage proposal collapsed Edward III had begun to look elsewhere for a marriage for Edmund. In 1366 he opened negotiations for a marriage between either Lionel, duke of Clarence, or Edmund, and Violante, daughter of Gian Galeazzo Visconti, the ruler of Milan. Lionel was Edward's preferred candidate for this marriage, which was celebrated in Milan in May 1368. By 1370, however, the focus of Edward's dynastic and diplomatic ambitions had turned to the Iberian peninsula. In 1371 John of Gaunt had married, as his second wife, Constanza, elder daughter of Pedro the Cruel, king of Castile, and his mistress Maria de Padilla. Pedro regarded Constanza and her younger sister Isabella as his heirs, and, by his marriage to Constanza, Gaunt acquired a claim to the throne of Castile, which was to preoccupy him particularly between 1385 and 1389. **Isabella of Castile** (1355–1392) was married to Edmund a few months later, on 11 July 1372, at Wallingford, becoming countess of Cambridge and later duchess of York. The purpose of the marriage was to reinforce the dynastic link between England and Castile and to ensure that both Pedro's heirs were married into the English royal line.

There is little doubt that, in marrying Isabella, Edmund was simply carrying out his father's instructions. His apparent willingness to do so (in contrast, it seems, to his eldest brother Edward, the Black Prince) has contributed powerfully to the impression of feebleness of character and idleness of disposition which modern historians have identified in Edmund. There is some contemporary warrant for such opinions. Froissart described Edmund as 'mol et simple et paisible' ('indolent, guileless, and peaceable'), and Sir Richard Stury apparently told Froissart during his visit to England in 1395 that Edmund preferred a life of ease, spending his time with his new wife, Joan of Kent, whom Stury described as 'a beautiful young lady' (*Œuvres*, 15.163). The later chronicler John Hardyng struck a similar note, saying that:

> When all the lords to councell and parlyament
> Went, he wolde to hunte and also to hawekyng.
> (*Chronicle*, ed. Ellis, 340)

Edmund's conduct of the only military expedition for which he was responsible, to Portugal in 1381, suggests a lack of capacity for military command, and although Richard II (not necessarily a good judge of character) twice appointed him keeper of the realm (in 1394–5 and in 1399), his defection to Henry Bolingbroke in July 1399 suggests a lack of firmness of purpose. Perhaps contemporary judgements on his character were correct.

Isabella seems to have found him boring. A more spirited woman than her sister Constanza, she became the subject of various scandals at court. She is said to have had an affair with Richard II's half-brother John Holland, earl of Huntingdon (*d.* 1400), and Walsingham described her as a worldly and sensual woman, although he goes on to say that she repented and reformed before her death, which took place on 23 December 1392 when she was only thirty-seven. She was buried in the church of the Friars Preachers at Kings Langley in Hertfordshire. In her will she made no legacy to her husband; apart from a few bequests of jewellery, the residue of her estate was left to Richard II in the hope that he would grant her younger son *Richard, earl of Cambridge (*d.* 1415), who was the king's godson, an annuity of 500 marks for life. The king later issued letters patent giving effect to her wishes. In view of her reputation another of her bequests is not without irony: she left a book of vices and virtues to one of her executors, Sir Lewis Clifford.

Military career Although Edmund showed no great enthusiasm or aptitude for war, he took part in several of the expeditions which England sent to France in the 1370s. He accompanied his eldest brother, the Black Prince, on the expedition to Spain in 1367 which culminated in the victory at Nájera. In 1369 he brought a retinue of 400 men-at-arms and 400 archers to serve with John Hastings, earl of Pembroke, on campaign in Brittany and Angoulême, and in the following year he first joined Pembroke again on an expedition to relieve the fortress of Belle Perche and then accompanied the Black Prince on the campaign which resulted in the siege and sack of Limoges. In 1372 he engaged to serve with Edward III in a proposed expedition to France, but although the expedition put to sea it had to turn back after a few weeks and was then abandoned. By 1374 Brittany had become the main focus of English military activity: on 1 August Edmund, together with Edmund Mortimer, earl of March, and Lord Despenser, sealed indentures for an expedition which would, it was hoped, relieve Brest and Bécherel in Brittany and St Sauveur-le-Vicomte in the Cotentin, which were hard-pressed by the French. The expedition did not sail, however, until 25 April in the following year. It took St Pol de Léon and laid siege to Quimperlé, but the truce agreed at Bruges on 27 June put an end to military operations, and the expedition returned home with its leaders disappointed and out of pocket. Edward III now expected Edmund to substitute diplomacy for war, and on 1 September 1375 appointed him as a commissioner to negotiate with France in the continuing talks at Bruges.

In none of these expeditions did Edmund hold sole command, and there is no suggestion in the chronicles that he had acquitted himself with great distinction. While serving with the Black Prince, however, he acquired some experience of campaigning in Spain, and when Iberian affairs once again came to the fore in 1380 John of Gaunt proposed that he should lead an expedition to Portugal which would join the Portuguese in an attack on Castile. The Anglo-Portuguese alliance of 1373 was renewed, and Edmund's eldest son Edward (b. 1373) was betrothed to Beatriz, daughter of Fernando, king of Portugal. Edmund's expedition sailed from Plymouth in July 1381; his lieutenants were mainly associates of Gaunt with previous experience of the Iberian peninsula; many of the troops, however, were Castilians loyal to Gaunt, and Gascons. The modern historian of the campaign has observed that 'the feeble Edmund of Cambridge was the worst possible leader to command so heterogeneous an army' (Russell, 303). Little went right on the expedition; the marriage between Edward and Beatriz was solemnized, but Edmund's irresoluteness and Fernando's deviousness led to the English army staying in camp at Vila Viçosa, close to the Castilian border, over the winter. Some elements in the army mutinied, partly perhaps through boredom but mainly because they had not been paid. In the spring of 1382 it seemed that they might at last see some action, but Fernando was under pressure to make peace with Castile, and an agreement was concluded in August. Edmund now had to extricate himself and his army as best he could, and he arrived back in England in October 1382 to a hostile reception and owing his troops much of their pay. In a final humiliation the pope annulled the marriage between Edward and Beatriz, because both were under age, and Fernando married Beatriz to Juan I of Castile. Gaunt was asked to help to discharge Edmund's debts, but he refused, and even insisted in his will that his executors should not contribute towards them. When Gaunt renounced his right to the Castilian throne in the treaty of Bayonne of 1388, any right that Edmund might also have had by virtue of his marriage to Isabella seems to have gone by default, for it is not mentioned in the treaty. None the less, personal relations between the two brothers seem to have remained cordial during these years.

Edmund has been severely criticized by modern historians for the failure of the Portuguese expedition. It is true that he showed little initiative or enterprise as a leader; but the expedition was essentially a Lancastrian idea, intended to further Gaunt's ambitions in Castile, and Fernando's deviousness in negotiating with Castile behind Edmund's back put him in an almost impossible position. The débâcle in Portugal suggests not so much that Edmund was incompetent, but that once again he had allowed his family to use him in the furtherance of their political and diplomatic schemes.

Edmund's political role in Richard II's reign Edmund never again led a military expedition overseas, but he joined Richard II's expedition to Scotland in 1385, and on 6 August, 'at the king's entry into Scotland', he was created duke of York and given an annuity of £1000 (*RotP*, 3.205). Neither this annuity nor his earlier annuity as earl of Cambridge were ever fully replaced by grants of landed property, and he evidently had difficulty in obtaining payment of his annuities. In 1380, for example, he had had to sue at the exchequer for payment of the annuity of 500 marks granted to him at the beginning of Richard II's reign. He

was granted lands in Wiltshire in 1387, and the reversion of the honour of Rayleigh in Essex in 1391, but like his younger brother *Thomas, duke of Gloucester, he remained dependent on exchequer annuities for part of his income for the rest of his life.

Despite Edmund's lack of an appropriate territorial endowment and the difficulties he encountered in obtaining payment of his annuities, he did not show the hostility to the king and his courtiers which Gloucester developed in these years: perhaps this is further evidence of his 'mol et paisible' character. In his loyalty to the crown he resembled his elder brother Gaunt rather than Gloucester, but his indolence and limited ability probably explain why he played only a minor part in government until 1386. He was appointed constable of Dover Castle and warden of the Cinque Ports on 12 June 1376 and held office until 1 February 1381. During that time he was also justice of the peace in Kent, as might have been expected, but otherwise he held few commissions of the peace until the last years of Richard II's reign. On 28 September 1385 he was appointed justice of Chester, but within two months he had sought and obtained power to appoint someone else to do the job on his behalf. He surrendered the post on 8 September 1387 and was replaced by Richard's favourite, Robert de Vere.

Edmund was a member of the commission of government which was established in the parliament of October 1386, and in the autumn of the following year, as relations between Richard and Gloucester deteriorated, he attempted a moderating role. After the victory of the lords appellant at Radcot Bridge in December 1387, Edmund, together with the earl of Northumberland and three bishops, sought to mediate between the king and the appellants, though without success. In the Merciless Parliament of February 1388 he was appointed to the committee set up by the appellants to examine the charges against Sir Nicholas Brembre; the committee reported that it could find nothing in his conduct which justified his death. Later in the same parliament Richard nominated Edmund and Sir John Cobham to appear before the Commons and plead for Sir Simon Burley's life, again unsuccessfully. Edmund may have been ineffective, but he was loyal and moderate in his political stance, and in the violence of his dispute with the duke of Gloucester over Burley's life showed for once an independence of mind. In the calmer political atmosphere of the early 1390s he attended the council frequently, and in 1391 he and Gaunt were appointed to conduct negotiations at Amiens for peace with France, though perhaps he owed his place to his status rather than to his ability.

Confident of his loyalty, Richard appointed Edmund keeper of the realm during his absence in Ireland from October 1394 to May 1395, and he was again appointed keeper for six weeks in the autumn of 1396 when Richard went to France for his marriage to Isabella, daughter of Charles VI. As political tension rose again in 1397, Edmund remained loyal to Richard. Froissart suggests that Gloucester discussed his opposition to Richard II's plans for peace with France with him, but had little respect for his opinions. The author of the *Chronicque de la traison et mort de Richart deux roy Dengleterre* stated that Edmund was one of the nobles whom Gloucester and his fellow conspirators intended to arrest and imprison in 1397, but neither Froissart nor the author of the *Traison* are reliable witnesses: the evidence for a conspiracy by Gloucester and others against the king in 1397 is virtually non-existent.

In the parliament of September 1397, when Gloucester, Arundel, and Warwick were arraigned for treason, Richard evidently regarded Edmund as loyal. He was given licence to come to parliament with 100 men-at-arms and 200 archers 'for the comfort of the king' (*CPR, 1396–9*, p. 192), but his part in the proceedings of the parliament seems to have been little more than formal. Trusting in his loyalty, Richard now gave him a greatly enhanced role as a justice of the peace, appointing him to the commission in Cambridgeshire, Northamptonshire, Essex, Norfolk, the West Riding of Yorkshire, and the Holland and Kesteven divisions of Lincolnshire. His son Edward, however, was more closely identified with the court, and was created duke of Aumale during the parliament. Perhaps Edward's standing at court served to protect Edmund from the conspiracies which now seemed to be aimed at his brother Gaunt, and when Richard set off for Ireland again on 1 June 1399 Edmund was once again appointed keeper of the realm.

Edmund's role in the invasion of Bolingbroke and deposition of Richard II Henry Bolingbroke began his preparations to invade England as soon as he was satisfied that Richard had landed in Ireland. Edmund got wind of his movements by 28 June, and assumed at that stage that Henry intended to take Calais as a base for his invasion of England. He summoned shire levies from the south-east to muster at Ware and prepare to defend the realm against invasion, but about 1 July Henry landed in Yorkshire and Edmund now tried to raise a full-scale army to oppose him. He summoned those of the king's knights and esquires who were still in England; the shire levies from the southern counties answered his appeal, and so did a number of magnates, including John Beaufort, marquess of Dorset, and the earls of Suffolk and Wiltshire. His hastily assembled army numbered perhaps 3000; yet in the event he offered no resistance to Henry. At Berkeley on 27 July he went over to Henry; he rode with him to Bristol, and according to Walsingham used his authority as keeper of the realm to demand the city's surrender to Henry.

Edmund's defection ensured that resistance to Henry would be no more than sporadic and localized. He had a sizeable army at his back, yet chose not to fight his invading nephew. Some historians have argued that this too shows his incompetence and irresoluteness, and that in the final crisis of his reign Richard had entrusted his realm to the wrong man. Edmund faced, however, a formidable opponent. Supporters from the north had been rallying to Henry since he landed, and he had been joined by the retinues of the earls of Northumberland and Westmorland, Northumberland's son Henry Percy (Hotspur), and the lords Willoughby, Ros, and Greystoke. Some of

Edmund's troops had deserted well before he met Henry at Berkeley, while the best troops in his army were those commanded by John Beaufort, Henry's half-brother. It is possible furthermore that Edmund himself, for all his previous loyalty to Richard, had some sympathy with the exiled and disinherited Henry Bolingbroke. There is no evidence that his castles at Wakefield and Conisbrough in Yorkshire offered any resistance to Henry, and Doncaster, where Henry rallied his troops before marching south, was one of his possessions.

Edmund did not, however, play any part in the events leading to Richard's capture and imprisonment in the Tower of London. His part in the deposition proceedings was formal, although he and the two archbishops conducted Henry to the throne after his claim to the crown had been accepted by the assembly that met on 30 September 1399. He gave his support to the new Lancastrian regime, and was appropriately rewarded by Henry IV. His possession of the castle and lordship of Rising in Norfolk was confirmed, he was granted the lordship of the Isle of Axholme in Lincolnshire, and received preference at the exchequer for the payment of his annuities assigned on the wool customs. He attended court and witnessed charters, but his political career was now drawing to its close.

Final years, death, and progeny If the author of the *Traison* is to be believed, Edmund's last important act was to relay to the king the report of a conspiracy against Henry in January 1400 that Edmund had received from his son Edward, who was probably implicated in the early stages of the plot. Edmund's action enabled Henry to move swiftly to frustrate the conspiracy. His loyalty to the new regime, as to the old regime before the events of 1399, remained firm. He made his will on 25 November 1400, at Kings Langley, where he died on 1 August 1402 and was buried beside his first wife in the church of the Friars Preachers. His second wife, *Joan (d. 1434) [see under Willoughby family (per. c.1300–1523)], daughter of Thomas Holland, earl of Kent, whom he had married about 1393, survived until 1434. He had two sons and a daughter from his first marriage: *Edward, earl of Rutland, who inherited the dukedom of York on his father's death and was killed at Agincourt in 1415; Richard, who was created earl of Cambridge in 1414 and was executed the following year for his involvement in the Southampton conspiracy against Henry V; and Constance [see Despenser, Constance, Lady Despenser (c.1375–1416)], who married Thomas, Lord Despenser, killed in 1400 for his involvement in the January plot against Henry IV that her elder brother had betrayed to their father. He had no children with his second wife.   ANTHONY TUCK

Sources *Calendar of the charter rolls*, 6 vols., PRO (1903–27) • *CClR* • *CIPM* • *CPR* • *Gesta abbatum monasterii Sancti Albani, a Thoma Walsingham*, ed. H. T. Riley, 3 vols., pt 4 of *Chronica monasterii S. Albani*, Rolls Series, 28 (1867–9) • 'Annales Ricardi secundi', *Johannis de Trokelowe et Henrici de Blaneforde … chronica et annales*, ed. H. T. Riley, pt 3 of *Chronica monasterii S. Albani*, Rolls Series, 28 (1866), 155–280 • C. Given-Wilson, ed. and trans., *Chronicles of the revolution, 1397–1400: the reign of Richard II* (1993) • *The chronicle of John Hardyng*, ed. H. Ellis (1812) • *Œuvres de Froissart: chroniques*, ed. K. de Lettenhove, 25 vols. (Brussels, 1867–77) • [J. Nichols], ed., *A collection of … wills …*

of … every branch of the blood royal (1780) • N. H. Nicolas, ed., Testamenta vetusta: being illustrations from wills, 1 (1826) • [J. Raine], ed., Testamenta Eboracensia, 3, SurtS, 45 (1865) • B. Williams, ed., Chronique de la traison et mort de Richart Deux, roy Dengleterre, EHS, 9 (1846) • M. H. Dodds, ed., A history of Northumberland, 15 (1940) • C. Given-Wilson, The royal household and the king's affinity: service, politics and finance in England, 1360–1413 (1986) • D. Biggs, 'A wrong whom conscience and kindred bid me to right: a reassessment of Edmund Langley, duke of York, and the usurpation of Henry IV', Albion, 26 (1994), 253–72 • A. Goodman, John of Gaunt: the exercise of princely power in fourteenth-century Europe (1992) • G. Holmes, The Good Parliament (1975) • M. Jones, Ducal Brittany, 1364–1399 (1970) • J. L. Kirby, Henry IV (1970) • J. J. N. Palmer and B. Powell, eds., The treaty of Bayonne (1388) with the preliminary treaties of Trancoso (1387) (1988) • J. E. Powell, 'A king's tomb', History Today, 15 (1965), 713–17 • T. B. Pugh, Henry V and the Southampton plot of 1415, Southampton RS, 30 (1988) • P. E. Russell, The English intervention in Spain and Portugal in the time of Edward III and Richard II (1955) • A. Tuck, Richard II and the English nobility (1973) • R. Vaughan, Philip the bold (1962) • GEC, Peerage • N. Saul, Richard II (1997)

Archives PRO, government records
Likenesses effigy on tomb of Edward III, c.1377–1380, Westminster Abbey, London

Edmund I (920/21–946), coin

Edmund I (920/21–946), king of England, was the elder son of *Edward the Elder (d. 924) and his third wife, *Eadgifu (d. in or after 966), daughter of the Kentish ealdorman, Sigehelm (d. 903). Since he was eighteen years old at his succession in 939, he was born in 920 or 921. He had one full brother, *Eadred (d. 955), and two full sisters, *Eadgifu (d. in or after 951), who married Louis of Aquitaine, and *Eadburh (d. 951x3), who became a nun at Winchester. Edmund grew up at the court of his half-brother *Æthelstan (r. 924–39). He fought beside Æthelstan at the battle of 'Brunanburh' in 937 and was perhaps already his half-brother's intended heir; certainly he succeeded to the kingship immediately on Æthelstan's death on 27 October 939. It was probably then that he married his first wife, Ælfgifu, for their second son, *Edgar (d. 975), was born in 943. Ælfgifu died in 944 and was buried at Shaftesbury, where she was soon venerated as a saint. Edmund then married Æthelflæd of Damerham (d. after 991) (AS chart., S 513, 1494), daughter of Ælfgar, later ealdorman of Essex from 946 to 951; the king gave him a sword finely embellished with gold and silver, which Ælfgar later presented to King Eadred (AS chart., S 1483).

The struggle for the north Æthelstan was the first of the West Saxon kings to rule the whole of England, including York, and his overlordship was acknowledged by the Northumbrians of Bamburgh and by the rulers of Wales, Cornwall, Scotland, and Strathclyde. Edmund inherited his half-brother's realm, but had to fight hard to retain it; much of his short reign was occupied in struggling against the viking rulers of Dublin for control of the north-east midlands and the kingdom of York. Æthelstan's dominance had been based on military force and his own formidable reputation and his death encouraged the York vikings to acknowledge Olaf Guthfrithson of Dublin as king. Olaf was in England by the end of 939. He clearly had ambitions to recreate the York–Dublin axis destroyed by Æthelstan; among the coins struck for him at York, one series bears the figure of a raven, recalling the

'Raven banner' captured by the English from the brother of his great-grandfather, Ivarr (ASC, s.a. 878).

Olaf also aimed to recover the southern territories of the kingdom of York, overrun by Edward the Elder and Æthelflæd of Mercia. In 940 he led his armies as far south as Northampton, and, being repulsed there, turned north-west to the old Mercian royal centre at Tamworth. The town was taken by storm, with much loss on both sides. It is clear that in order to campaign so far into Mercia, Olaf must already have overrun the old Danish strongholds to the north-east, and indeed it was at Leicester that he was overtaken by King Edmund's army. Edmund besieged Leicester, but there was no decisive engagement. Instead a truce was made, in which the north-east midlands, so laboriously won, were conceded to Olaf.

The agreement at Leicester was brokered, on the English side, by Oda, archbishop of Canterbury, and, for the Danes, by Wulfstan (d. 956), archbishop of York. Earlier archbishops of York had come to terms with the York vikings, which is presumably why Æthelstan had taken some trouble to engage their support, notably by the grant of Amounderness in 934 (AS chart., S 407). Wulfstan himself had been consecrated at Æthelstan's court, but ceases to attest his charters after 935, for reasons which can only be guessed at. Though secure in York itself, Olaf had enemies to the north as well as the south; in 941 he launched an expedition to Lothian, in the course of which the church of St Balthere at Tyninghame was burnt down, and in the same year the men of York raided Lindisfarne, within sight of Bamburgh, the main residence of the high-reeve Osulf, ruler of northern Northumbria.

The recovery of the north midlands Olaf Guthfrithson's death in 941 allowed Edmund to retrieve his position. In 942 he recaptured the lost territories in the north-east midlands, and even went further, for he succeeded in detaching Lincoln and its dependent territory, Lindsey, from the control of the York kings. The Anglo-Saxon

Chronicle, which breaks into alliterative verse at this point, presents Edmund's conquests as a 'redemption' of the Danes in these regions, hitherto 'subjected by force under the Norsemen, for a long time in bonds of captivity to the heathens' (*ASC*, s.a. 942, text C). Whether contemporaries saw the matter in these terms is debatable; the chronicle is not contemporary for this period, and the 'redemption' poem was probably not composed before the late 950s. It cannot therefore be taken as evidence that the Five Boroughs (Lincoln, Stamford, Nottingham, Derby, and Leicester) existed at that time as an organized confederacy, nor that the shires later dependent on these boroughs had already been formed. In 942 the territory of Nottingham probably consisted only of the valley of the Trent, perhaps including Derby, with the rest of the later shire dependent upon a borough at Blyth or possibly Tickhill; likewise, the southern parts of what was to become Lincolnshire (Kesteven and Holland) were probably dependent upon Stamford. It was only after the English conquest that the Five Boroughs were organized as an administrative unit, probably in the 950s or 960s.

What arrangements Edmund himself made are unknown, but in 942 he granted substantial estates in what was to become Derbyshire to Wulfsige the Black (*AS chart.*, S 479, 484, 1606). Wulfsige was probably related to a powerful north Mercian kindred, that of the lady Wulfrun, who is the only captive taken by Olaf at Tamworth in 940 to be mentioned by name in the Anglo-Saxon Chronicle; she later established the minster at Wolverhampton (*AS chart.*, S 1380), and her son Wulfric Spot founded Burton Abbey (*AS chart.*, S 1536). Edmund was continuing a policy of endowing nobles friendly to the West Saxon line with lands—and therefore an interest in retaining them—in the Danelaw; Edward the Elder had earlier given lands at Hope and Ashwell, Derbyshire, to Uhtred, son of Eadulf of Bamburgh, which were confirmed by Æthelstan (*AS chart.*, S 397).

The recovery of York Olaf Guthfrithson was succeeded at York by his cousin, Olaf Sihtricson, called Cuarán ('Sandal') by the Irish. In 943 this latter Olaf accepted baptism, with Edmund as his godfather, an act which suggests some acceptance, albeit temporary, of West Saxon suzerainty. Although the sources for this period are both late and fragmentary, it is clear that Olaf had rivals within York itself. Olaf Guthfrithson's brother, Ragnall, was at York by 943, and later in the same year he also accepted baptism under Edmund's sponsorship. Both Olaf and Ragnall issued coinages at York, as did a certain Sihtric, who is otherwise unknown. The coins of all three share common designs, also used for Olaf Guthfrithson, which may suggest some kind of joint authority. Whatever the circumstances, Edmund was able to expel both Olaf and Ragnall in 944. Æthelweard the Chronicler, writing in the late tenth century, attributes their expulsion to Archbishop Wulfstan and 'the ealdorman of the Mercians', who must, in the context, be Æthelmund, appointed by Edmund in 940, who probably held authority in north-west Mercia. It was Edmund himself, however, who ravaged Cumbria in 945 and had the sons of King Dunmail of Strathclyde

blinded. The Anglo-Saxon Chronicle says he then 'gave' Strathclyde to Malcolm I, king of Scots, in return for an undertaking to defend the area 'on sea and on land' (*ASC*, s.a. 945), which probably means he acknowledged Malcolm's overlordship of the area in return for some kind of alliance against the vikings of Dublin. It was perhaps in the course of these campaigns that the relics of St Áedán and other saints from the Northumbrian 'golden age' were brought south to Glastonbury, for William of Malmesbury attributes their enshrinement there to Edmund.

England and Europe Æthelstan's half-sisters had married into the leading royal and princely families of Europe, and his court had been open to churchmen and scholars from Ireland, Brittany, Wales, and both eastern and western Francia. Edmund's court was dominated by the men who had advised his half-brother, notably Ælfheah the Bald, bishop of Winchester, Oda, bishop of Ramsbury, whom Edmund made archbishop of Canterbury, and Æthelstan Half-King, ealdorman of East Anglia. It is, therefore, not surprising that Edmund inherited not only his half-brother's hegemony, but also many of his interests and policies. Like Æthelstan, he maintained contact with his brother-in-law, the emperor Otto I (*d.* 973), and the two of them supported the Frankish king Louis d'Outremer (*d.* 954), nephew of them both and Otto's brother-in-law, against his domestic enemies in 946. It was to Edmund also that the clergy of St Bertin (at St Omer in what was later Flanders) fled in 944 when their house was forcibly reformed by Gerhard of Brogne. The king gave them the secular minster at Bath as a refuge. He also helped the Gaelic churchman Catroe on his journey from Scotland to the continent in the early 940s. It was probably in Edmund's reign also that Archbishop Oda recruited the Frankish scholar Fredegaud (Anglicized as Frithegod) to his household.

Ecclesiastical reform Edmund's translation of Bishop Oda from Ramsbury to Canterbury in 941 had important implications for the reform of the English church. Like Ælfheah the Bald of Winchester, Oda was a professed monk, who had served Æthelstan as counsellor and ambassador, and who had close contacts with the reform movement on the continent (especially at Fleury). His role in arranging the truce between Edmund and Olaf Guthfrithson in 940 has already been mentioned, and his hand has been detected in Edmund's first law-code, promulgated at an Easter synod held in London. It is largely concerned with ecclesiastical discipline and the collection of church dues, themes continued in Archbishop Oda's constitutions, which date from the years between 942 and 946.

Another sign of revival in the English church at this time is the number of noblewomen who chose the religious life, either as professed nuns or, more commonly, as vowesses living on their own estates, often close to ecclesiastical communities. Two of those who received grants from Edmund are the nun Ælfgyth, patron of Wilton Abbey, and the 'religious woman' Wynflæd, who was associated with Shaftesbury, and was perhaps the mother of

Edmund's first wife, Ælfgifu. Both houses were royal foundations, much patronized by the West Saxon kings.

It was also Edmund who gave the royal vill of Glastonbury, with its church and appurtenant estates, to Dunstan, then a protégé of Ælfheah the Bald. Much has been made of this act, since Glastonbury was the first of the old minsters to be 'reformed' as a Benedictine house. It has to be said, however, that at least one of Dunstan's monks (Æthelwold, later bishop of Winchester) found the observance too lax, and sought a stricter discipline elsewhere. Dunstan's earliest biographer, 'B', says that he was placed by Edmund among the 'royal magnates and palace officials' (Stubbs, *Memorials*, 21) but made enemies and was expelled. Edmund had a change of heart only after his miraculous escape from death in a hunting accident near the Cheddar Gorge: the stag he was pursuing plunged over the edge of the chasm, followed by Edmund's hunting-dogs, and the king pulled up his horse on the edge of the precipice, only just in time to avoid the same fate (ibid., 23–4). In fact Dunstan seems not to have had much influence at Edmund's court, and his fame lay in the future. Although his brother Wulfric was given valuable estates (*AS chart.*, S 472–3, 504) and attests Edmund's charters in a prominent position among the thegns, Dunstan himself does not appear as a witness, and it was probably only towards the end of his reign that Edmund appointed him as abbot of Glastonbury.

Secular government In the field of royal government, the formulation of Edmund's surviving charters follows developments already in train in Æthelstan's time, and suggests the continuing existence of a group of royal scribes, trained to produce charters and constituting a royal secretariat. Edmund also continued his half-brother's legislative tradition. Three codes in his name survive, beginning with the ecclesiastical legislation mentioned above. His second code is concerned with the need to maintain 'peace and concord'; the king and his counsellors are said to be 'greatly distressed by the manifold illegal deeds of violence which are in our midst' (Robertson, 8–9). The code is largely an attempt to regulate and control the blood-feud. It prohibits attacks on any except the actual slayer, and any assault which violates the sanctuary of a church or a royal manor house. The king's agents are charged to prevent feuding by overseeing the process of mediation between the kin of the slain and the slayer, which produces the compensatory payment of wergeld; this is the clearest statement of how the feud and the wergeld actually worked in practice. The second code also contains the earliest recorded reference to *hamsocn*, the crime of attacking a man in his own house. *Hamsocn* is equated with *mundbryce* (breach of the king's protection or peace) and its judgment is reserved to the king. The penalty is stipulated as loss of all the offender's property, 'and it shall be for the king to decide whether his life shall be preserved' (ibid., 10–11).

Edmund's third code was issued at Colyton, Devon, perhaps in 945. This too is concerned with public order, and especially with the punishment of theft, in particular cattle rustling. The first clause commands that all should swear a general oath of fidelity to the king. The terms of the oath, taken on relics, are recited: to 'be faithful to King Edmund, even as it behoves a man to be faithful to his lord, without any dispute or dissension, openly or in secret, favouring what he favours and discountenancing what he discountenances' (Robertson, 12–13). The terminology should be compared with the tenth-century tract on how hold-oaths (oaths of fidelity) should be sworn, and illustrates that 'tendency to associate kingship with personal lordship' (Abels, 84) already visible in the legislation promulgated by Edmund's father and half-brother. Local communities are also important; all, both nobles and commoners, are commanded to unite and seize thieves, dead or alive, and co-operate in the tracking of stolen cattle; those who refuse to help or who hinder the process of law are to be fined. Lordship also plays its part: lords are to take responsibility for their followers, and stand surety for them, whether commended men, household dependants, or holders of lands attached to their estates; they are not to harbour fugitives or to accept the service of those whom the law is pursuing. In both the second code and the Colyton legislation, the functions of the four pillars of medieval society, kingship, lordship, family, and neighbourhood, are clearly evident.

Edmund's achievement In view of Edmund's measures against violence, it is ironic that he was killed in a brawl, at the royal vill of Pucklechurch, Gloucestershire. 'It is well-known how he ended his life, that Leofa stabbed him', says the Anglo-Saxon Chronicle (*ASC*, text D, s.a. 946), and John of Worcester adds that Edmund had intervened to save the life of his seneschal whom Leofa, a convicted outlaw, had attacked (John of Worcester, *Chron.*, 398–9).

Edmund was killed on 26 May 946 (St Augustine's day) and was buried by Dunstan at Glastonbury. It is clear that he was an energetic and forceful ruler, who, but for his early death (he was no more than twenty-five), 'might have been remembered as one of the more remarkable of Anglo-Saxon kings' (Dumville, 184). His widow, Æthelflæd, later married the ealdorman Æthelstan Rota; her family history can be traced in the wills of her father, Ælfgar, her sister Ælfflæd, wife and widow of Ealdorman Byrhtnoth who was killed at Maldon in 991, and Æthelflæd herself. Edmund was also survived by his two sons with Ælfgifu, *Eadwig and Edgar; but, since Edgar was only three years old and Eadwig no more than five or six, the kingship passed to Edmund's brother, Eadred.

ANN WILLIAMS

Sources *ASC*, s.a. 937, 940, 942, 943, 944, 945, 946 [text C]; s.a. 941, 943, 946 [text D]; s.a. 940, 942, 948 [text E] • *AS chart.*, S 397, 407, 459–515, 1380, 1483, 1494, 1536, 1606 • A. J. Robertson, ed., *The laws of the kings of England from Edmund to Henry I* (1926) • F. Liebermann, ed., *Die Gesetze der Angelsachsen*, 3 vols. in 4 (Halle, 1898–1916) • *The chronicle of Æthelweard*, ed. and trans. A. Campbell (1962) • B., 'Vita sancti Dunstani', *Memorials of Saint Dunstan, archbishop of Canterbury*, ed. W. Stubbs, Rolls Series, 63 (1874), 3–52 • John of Worcester, *Chron.* • Symeon of Durham, *Opera*, vol. 2 • W. Stubbs, ed., *Select charters and other illustrations of English constitutional history*, 9th edn (1913) • C. R. Hart, *The early charters of northern England and the north midlands* (1975) • P. H. Sawyer, ed., *Charters of Burton Abbey*, Anglo-

Saxon Charters, 2 (1979) • C. E. Blunt, B. H. I. H. Stewart, and C. S. S. Lyon, *Coinage in tenth-century England: from Edward the Elder to Edgar's reform* (1989) • A. P. Smyth, *Scandinavian York and Dublin: the history of two related Viking kingdoms*, 2 (1979) • D. N. Dumville, 'Learning and the church in the England of King Edmund I, 939–46', *Wessex and England from Alfred to Edgar* (1992), 173–84 • R. Abels, *Lordship and military obligation in Anglo-Saxon England* (1988) • D. Roffe, 'The origins of Derbyshire', *Derbyshire Archaeological Journal*, 106 (1986), 102–22 • N. Brooks, 'The career of St Dunstan', *St Dunstan: his life, times and cult*, ed. N. Ramsay, M. Sparks, and T. Tatton-Brown (1992), 1–23 • N. Brooks, *The early history of the church of Canterbury: Christ Church from 597 to 1066* (1984) • G. Owen, 'Wynflæd's wardrobe', *Anglo-Saxon England*, 8 (1979), 195–222 • R. V. Coleman, 'Domestic peace and public order in Anglo-Saxon law', *The Anglo-Saxons: synthesis and achievement*, ed. D. Woods and D. A. E. Pelteret (1985), 45–61 • C. R. Hart, 'The ealdordom of Essex', *An Essex tribute: essays presented to Frederick G. Emmison*, ed. K. Neale (1987), 57–73 [repr. in C. R. Hart, *The Danelaw* (1992), 115–40] • M. Lapidge, 'A Frankish scholar in tenth-century England: Frithegod of Canterbury / Fredegaud of Brioude', *Anglo-Saxon England*, 17 (1988), 45–65 • D. Hill, *An atlas of Anglo-Saxon England* (1981)
Likenesses coin, BM [*see illus.*]

Edmund II [*known as* Edmund Ironside] (*d.* 1016), king of England, was the son of *Æthelred II, the Unready (*c*.966x8–1016), and his first wife, Ælfgifu, according to Ailred of Rievaulx the daughter of Earl Thored of Northumbria (according to John of Worcester, however, her father was an otherwise unknown Ealdorman Æthelberht). The *Liber vitae* of New Minster, Winchester, places Edmund second in a list of six of Æthelred's sons, but their appearances from 993 onwards among the witnesses of royal charters show that he was really the third, being preceded by Æthelstan and Ecgberht, and followed by Eadred, Eadwig, and Edgar, and then by Æthelred's sons with his second wife, *Emma of Normandy, *Edward the Confessor and *Alfred Ætheling. In two charters, of 1014 and 1015, he heads the princes, Ecgberht last appearing in 1005, Edgar in 1008, and Æthelstan in 1013. In a document of between 1007 and 1014, witnessed by members of Edmund's household, the church of Sherborne leased him land at Holcombe Rogus, Devon, for his lifetime in return for £20; while the will of his brother Æthelstan of 1014 or 1015 gave him a sword which had belonged to King Offa of Mercia, a sword with a pitted hilt, a blade, a silver-coated trumpet, and estates in East Anglia and at Peacesdele (perhaps Pegsdon, Bedfordshire).

The life of Edward the Confessor, written fifty years later, claims that when Emma was pregnant with him all Englishmen swore to accept a boy child as king; if so, such ambitions probably caused friction with her stepsons, and in 1015, following the murder of the Danelaw thegns Sigeferth and Morcar by Eadric Streona, ealdorman of Mercia, Edmund took Sigeferth's widow, Ealdgyth, from Malmesbury against Æthelred's will, married her, and received the submission of the people of the Five Boroughs (Derby, Leicester, Lincoln, Nottingham, and Stamford). Simultaneously, Cnut of Denmark arrived off Kent, intent on conquering England. Perhaps assisted by his mother's and wife's links with the midlands and north, Edmund raised an army late in 1015, but Eadric and his Mercians joined the West Saxons in submitting to Cnut. The first army assembled by Edmund in 1016 dispersed when Æthelred

did not appear to lead it, and the second achieved little when he did. Edmund and Earl Uhtred of Northumbria then ravaged Staffordshire, Shropshire, and Cheshire (perhaps to put pressure on Eadric); but when Cnut occupied Yorkshire, Uhtred returned to Northumbria, submitted, and was executed, while Edmund went to London. Æthelred died there on 23 April and the citizens, and such national councillors as were present, chose and probably crowned Edmund as king.

Edmund then proceeded to Wessex where the people submitted to him, fighting inconclusive battles against the Danes and their English allies at Penselwood, Somerset, and Sherston, Wiltshire, the latter probably on 25 June. He subsequently forced another Danish army to abandon its siege of London, and defeated it after crossing the Thames at Brentford. They renewed the siege when he went to Wessex to raise further troops, but these relieved the city again, overcame the Danes at Otford, and pursued Cnut into Kent. Here Ealdorman Eadric went over to Edmund, while the Scandinavians crossed the Thames into Essex and ravaged in Mercia. After Edmund had 'collected all the English nation for the fifth time' (*ASC*, s.a. 1016) he was defeated by Cnut on 18 October at 'Assandun' (probably Ashdon or Ashingdon, Essex), where Eadric and his men fled and the English suffered heavy losses.

The twelfth-century Anglo-Norman poet Gaimar tells how Edmund took the sister of a Welsh king as consort and received Welsh support in his campaigns. This latter point, at least, is apparently confirmed by allusions to Welsh troops in two contemporary sources: the German chronicler Thietmar of Merseburg's report of events in England in 1016; and the poem *Liðsmannaflokkr* ('Song of the men of the host'), composed by one of Cnut's men, which refers to their blows falling upon Welsh armour. A poem about Cnut, Ottar the Black's *Knútsdrápa*, says that 'Assandun' was followed by a battle at Danaskógar (perhaps the Forest of Dean), and this may explain why Edmund and Cnut eventually made peace at Alney in Gloucestershire. They divided the country, Cnut accepting a promised payment to his army and taking Mercia and probably Northumbria, while Edmund received Wessex. The Anglo-Saxon Chronicle records his death shortly thereafter, on 30 November 1016 (a twelfth-century Ely calendar gives 29 November), at London according to most later chroniclers. His infant sons, *Edward Ætheling and Edmund, left England shortly after Cnut took sole control. Although Edmund's demise was obviously convenient for his enemies, the scanty contemporary sources do not suggest foul play, and exhaustion or the effects of a battle wound might seem adequate explanation. Nevertheless, by the 1070s the German chronicler Adam of Bremen was stating that he was poisoned, while twelfth-century writers tell much wilder tales, which doubtless owe more to folklore than history. Some have him pierced from below, at Eadric of Mercia's behest, when seated on a toilet; Gaimar reports that an arrow was fired up into him from a toilet.

The Anglo-Saxon Chronicle questions Edmund's political acumen in taking Eadric Streona of Mercia back into favour before the battle of 'Assandun', but little is known of Edmund's government. No coin bearing his name has survived. A charter giving land in Suffolk to Thorney Abbey in return for help in this life and the next was probably issued before April 1016, as Edmund calls himself simply 'son of the king'. A second text gives to New Minster, Winchester, estates in Northamptonshire which had belonged to Sigeferth, the first husband of Edmund's wife, Ealdgyth, for the salvation of all three, while a grant of Cnut from 1018 claims to confirm to Bishop Burhwold of Cornwall land which King Edmund had exchanged with him. Fragments these may be, but they are enough to hint that Edmund's activities extended beyond the military matters which are his chief claim to fame.

Although not recorded by the Anglo-Saxon Chronicle until 1057, his sobriquet, Ironside, may well be contemporary. The chronicle reports that he was so called 'because of his valour' (ASC, s.a. 1057, text D). The intensity of his struggle against the Danes in 1016 is known to have been matched in pre-conquest history only by the campaigns of Alfred in 871, and contrasts markedly with Æthelred's failure to offer adequate resistance, despite having at his disposal the powerful and sophisticated Anglo-Saxon administrative system built up during the tenth century. Edmund's initial difficulty in persuading his countrymen to fight indicates the poor state of their morale late in his father's reign, while his subsequent success in raising one army after another suggests that there was little the matter with the organs of government once under competent leadership. Probably a highly determined, skilled, and indeed inspiring leader of men, he may also have drawn, at least within Wessex, on deep wells of loyalty to the native royal family. It is noteworthy that, despite his links with the midlands and north, it was Wessex that he took in the division of 1016 and that he was buried, along with his grandfather *Edgar, at Glastonbury Abbey. Cnut, who seemingly wished to stress the brotherhood established between them (according to John of Worcester) when they made peace, later visited the tomb on the anniversary of Edmund's death and laid a cloak decorated with peacocks upon it—probably (as the peacock symbolized the resurrection of the flesh) to assist his salvation.

M. K. LAWSON

Sources ASC, s.a. 1015, 1016, 1057 [(texts C, D, E)] · AS chart., S 947, 948, 951, 1422, 1503 · S. Keynes, ed., The Liber vitae of the New Minster and Hyde Abbey, Winchester (Copenhagen, 1996) · Thietmar of Merseburg, Chronicon, ed. R. Holtzmann (1955), 446–9 · F. Barlow, ed. and trans., The life of King Edward who rests at Westminster, 2nd edn, OMT (1992), 12 · Adam of Bremen, Gesta, ed. B. Schmeidler (1917), 114 · John of Worcester, Chron. · Aelredus Rievallensis [Ailred of Rievaulx], 'Genealogia regum Anglorum', Patrologia Latina, 195 (1855), 741 · L'estoire des Engleis by Geffrei Gaimar, ed. A. Bell, Anglo-Norman Texts, 14–16 (1960), 130, 134 · Willelmi Malmesbiriensis monachi de gestis regum Anglorum, ed. W. Stubbs, 2 vols., Rolls Series (1887–9) · English historical documents, 1, ed. D. Whitelock (1955) · E. A. Freeman, The history of the Norman conquest of England, 2nd edn, 6 vols. (1870–79), 2.694–8 · S. D. Keynes, The diplomas of King Æthelred 'the Unready', 978–1016 (1980) · R. Poole, 'Skaldic verse and Anglo-Saxon history: some aspects of the period 1009–1016', Speculum, 62 (1987), 281–3, 292–8 · M. K. Lawson, Cnut: the Danes in England in the early eleventh century (1993)

Edmund of Almain, second earl of Cornwall (1249–1300), magnate, was born at his father's castle of Berkhamsted on 26 December 1249, as the second and only surviving son of *Richard, first earl of Cornwall (1209–1272), brother of *Henry III, and his wife Sanchia (d. 1261), daughter of Raymond-Berengar, count of Provence, and sister of Henry III's queen, *Eleanor. He was baptized by his mother's uncle, Boniface of *Savoy, archbishop of Canterbury, and named Edmund in honour of St Edmund of Abingdon, Boniface's predecessor as archbishop.

Early life and inheritance By a previous marriage, Richard of Cornwall already had one surviving son, *Henry of Almain (that is, Germany), Edmund's senior by fourteen years, and originally destined to inherit his father's lands and titles. As a result, Edmund's earliest years are somewhat obscure, and it is noteworthy that he was neither knighted nor married until the surprisingly advanced age of twenty-two. In 1257 he accompanied his father and mother on their initial expedition into Germany, following Richard's election as king and claimant to the Holy Roman empire. He returned to England with Richard and Sanchia in January 1259, and in 1264, following his father's capture by the barons at the battle of Lewes, was held prisoner together with Richard at Kenilworth Castle, being released in September 1265. From August 1268 until August 1269 he was in Germany with his father, and there, according to a semi-mythical account written many years later, is said to have acquired a relic of the blood of Jesus Christ, which had previously belonged to the emperor Charlemagne and which had been stored among the imperial regalia in the castle of the Trifels in the Rhineland. Part of this relic he is said to have bestowed upon the monks of his father's foundation at Hailes Abbey in Gloucestershire, following a splendid ceremony in September 1270.

By October 1269 Edmund was already in possession of the manor of Alderley in Gloucestershire, and in February 1271 set out to join the crusade of his cousin, the Lord *Edward, eldest son of Henry III. He sailed in the company of Edward's younger brother, *Edmund, earl of Lancaster. However, hearing abroad of the death of Henry of Almain, murdered at Viterbo in March 1271, Edmund was forbidden by the king to proceed further, and returned to England, much to the relief of his aged father, Earl Richard. Following Richard's own death, on 2 April 1272, Edmund was recognized as his heir, swearing homage to the king for his father's vast estates on or shortly before 1 May. In July 1272, for a payment of 3500 marks, he acquired a four-year lease of the town and lordship of Leicester from his cousin Edmund, earl of Lancaster, still absent on crusade. On 6 October 1272 he was married in the chapel of Ruislip to Margaret, sister of Gilbert de Clare, earl of Gloucester and Hertford, and a week later, on 13 October, the feast of St Edward the Confessor, he was knighted at Westminster by Henry III in the company of fifty other English and foreign nobles. On the same occasion he was invested with his father's title and honours as earl of Cornwall. Richard's claim to the throne of Germany and the title Holy Roman emperor lapsed with his death. None the less,

Edmund continued to commemorate his father's memory by styling himself Edmund of Almain, or 'Edmund earl of Cornwall, son of Richard the king of Germany', in many of his charters and letters.

Service to Edward I With the death of Henry III in November 1272, Edmund assumed a role within the governing council in England, pending the return of Edward I from crusade. In November 1272 he was among those councillors who wrote to inform the new king of Henry III's death. For much of this time he was engaged in the execution of his father's will, and began to loan some of his vast wealth to prominent courtiers: the first of many such transactions in which he was to become involved. He travelled to France in June 1273 to meet Edward I, and at Paris, in August, acknowledged repayment of 2000 of the 3000 marks already owed to him by the king. He attended Edward's coronation at Westminster on 19 August 1274, and in the summer of 1277 joined the king's expedition to Wales with fourteen of his knights, the largest military contingent brought by any of the king's supporters. In September 1278 he was present when the king of Scots did homage to Edward I, and in 1279 he was appointed, together with Thomas, bishop of Hereford, and the bishop of Worcester, to the regency council set to govern England when the king and queen crossed to France to take possession of the county of Ponthieu. In the same year he loaned the king 3000 marks to assist with a recoinage. In May 1280 he himself crossed overseas with the abbot of Colchester, and in the following month, through the mediation of Queen Eleanor and Robert Burnell, bishop of Bath, settled a long-standing dispute with the bishop of Exeter over their rival jurisdictions, for which, at one time, he had been placed under ecclesiastical sentence.

From April 1282 until Christmas 1284, while the king campaigned in Wales, Edmund served as his lieutenant in the government of England, intervening in the collection of a clerical subsidy towards the proposed crusade, ensuring the transport of the exchequer rolls to Shrewsbury in August 1282, representing the king at a clerical convocation held at Northampton in January 1283, and in his own right receiving custody of several valuable wardships and estates, including the heir and lands of Baldwin Wake for which he fined in the massive sum of 7000 marks. Once again, from 13 May 1286 until 12 August 1289, when King Edward crossed overseas to impose order in Gascony and to mediate in the bitter dispute between the kings of Aragon and Sicily, Edmund served as regent in England. Shortly after his appointment, in June 1287, the Welsh prince Rhys ap Maredudd of Dryslwyn seized the castle of Llandovery. Edmund suppressed the ensuing rebellion with an elaborate campaign against the Welsh, capturing Dryslwyn in September but thereafter being unable to effect the captivity of Rhys, who escaped into hiding. The costs of this campaign were met by loans from Italian merchants of some £10,000. In June 1289, despite having co-operated with the earl of Gloucester in the suppression of Rhys's rebellion, Edmund intervened in a dispute on the Welsh marches between the earls of Hereford and

Gloucester, forbidding the earl of Gloucester to build a castle on disputed land at Morlais in Brecknockshire. Elsewhere, the period of the king's absence was marked by violent disturbances and perhaps by corrupt misgovernment. Certainly, after the king's return in 1289, it was considered expedient to institute inquiries into wrongdoing in central and local government, resulting in the disgrace of several leading judges and exchequer officials, and the collection of nearly £20,000 in fines to the financially astute Edward. Edmund, however, appears to have been entirely immune from this inquiry, obtaining retrospective pardon for all forest offences committed during the king's absence, and being permitted to answer by proxy for any complaints against his administration in Cornwall.

In September 1289 Edmund attended the translation of the relics of St Frithuswith at Oxford, and in the same year miracles began to be reported at the chapel which in 1288 the earl had caused to be built on the site of the birth of his patron saint, Edmund, at Abingdon. In the king's parliament held at Westminster Hall in April 1290, Edmund was served with a writ obtained by Bogo de Clare, a kinsman of his wife, demanding his attendance in the court of the archbishop of Canterbury. For this, one of the earliest reported breaches of what would later be termed parliamentary privilege, the archbishop was fined the enormous sum of £10,000. The king spent the Christmas festivities of 1290 at Edmund's manor of Ashridge in Hertfordshire, and there held a parliament where the business of Scotland was discussed. By this time Edmund's loans to the crown, including a sum of £4000 advanced in 1290, were coming to play an essential role in royal finance. In May 1292 Edmund's treasurer, Roger of Drayton, was murdered while processing to parliament at Westminster, apparently in revenge for his harsh treatment of the mother of one of his murderers, put in the stocks at Berkhamsted. The murderers fled to sanctuary, and thence travelled to Dover where they abjured the realm.

Edmund was regularly summoned to parliament throughout the 1290s, served as a frequent witness to the king's charters, and continued to advance major loans to the king and his courtiers, including the bishop of Durham, Antony (I) Bek, who was loaned £4000 repayable from the issues of the manor of Howden. Prisoners sent south from the king's Scottish campaign in May 1296 were entrusted to his charge at the castles of Wallingford and Berkhamsted. In the same year the king is said to have commanded the removal of Edmund's treasure from Berkhamsted to London, perhaps in anticipation of the time when Edmund's estate would escheat to the crown. In 1297 he was summoned to Gascony, and was therefore absent from England for much of the ensuing political crisis between king and barons. In the same year, he pledged the entire output of his tin mines in Devon and Cornwall in repayment of 7000 marks of the king's debts to the men of Bayonne, and served as one of the councillors of the king's son Edward, set to govern in the absence of Edward I, responsible for the settlement of disputes between the king and the earls of Hereford and Norfolk. The crown debt to Edmund already stood at £6500 by 1299 when the king borrowed a further 2000 marks, repayable from the profits of the vacant archbishopric of York.

Death and legacy Summoned to send knights to the Scottish campaign early in 1299, in May summoned to attend in person at York by 2 August, and in December 1299 to attend at Carlisle the following June, Edmund appears to have compounded for his service, offering 1000 marks to be excused attendance. In July 1297 he had been granted licence to make a will. His physical infirmity is already referred to in a summons of December 1298, and by 1300 he was fatally ill. The exact date of his death, which took place at Ashridge, is unknown, but fell before 25 September 1300 when the king ordered the celebration of exequies for the late earl. On the following day the royal escheators were ordered to take possession of his lands. His heart and flesh were interred at Ashridge in the presence of Edward the king's son, and on 23 March 1301 his bones were laid to rest at the abbey of Hailes in Gloucestershire, in the presence of the king himself. He left no children to succeed him, and as a result, his estate passed entire to the king, save for dower set aside for his widow. Thereafter the earldom and later duchy of Cornwall was to form a major crown apanage, granted in 1307 to Edward II's favourite Piers Gaveston (d. 1312), and in 1328 to John of Eltham, younger son of Edward II. The unhappy state of Edmund's marriage to Margaret de Clare explains his disputes with her kinsmen, the earl of Gloucester and Bogo de Clare. In January 1285 Margaret was expecting a child, but the baby was either stillborn or died in infancy. Thereafter, relations between husband and wife deteriorated, and by 1289 their marriage was subject to papal and archiepiscopal investigation. Edmund's refusal to cohabit with Margaret led to a sentence of excommunication from Archbishop Pecham in 1290, and eventually to an official separation in 1294. In February of that year Edmund settled £800 of land upon Margaret for the term of her life. In return, and perhaps somewhat reluctantly, Margaret took vows of chastity to last until Edmund's death. She died, without remarrying, in 1312.

Wealth and religious patronage Although appointed on at least two occasions to serve as regent in the absence of Edward I, Edmund makes surprisingly little impact upon the records of political history. As a royal counsellor, and above all as the source of massive loans to the crown, he was none the less a powerful figure at court. His death, and the descent of his vast estate to the king, came at a crucial moment, propping up the king's finances amid the expense of the Scottish wars, above and beyond the more than £18,000 which, during his lifetime, Edmund had loaned to the crown. As the son and heir of Richard of Cornwall, Edmund had inherited manors, lands, and jurisdictions in some twenty-five counties of England, concentrated upon the great honours of Berkhamsted in Hertfordshire, Eye in East Anglia, Oakham in Rutland, Knaresborough in Yorkshire, Beckley in Oxfordshire, and Wallingford in Berkshire, and the estate formerly held by Richard's mother, *Isabella of Angoulême, including the towns of Chichester, Exeter, and Malmesbury. Above all, he possessed the earldom of Cornwall with its mines and its control over eight and one-third of the county's nine hundreds. Besides the Cornish stannaries, which he held from the time of his accession, from 1278 he was also granted the farm of the tin mines of Devon, and from the early 1270s for the remainder of his life accounted as sheriff for the counties of Cornwall and Rutland. The income from these various sources, totalling roughly £8000 a year, ensured Edmund's pre-eminence as the richest lay baron in England after the king.

Perhaps surprisingly, and despite his extensive credit transactions, Edmund spent relatively little of his income on purchasing new land. Given the acrimonious nature of his marriage to Margaret de Clare, and the failure of this union to produce an heir, it may be that Edmund devoted a disproportionate amount of his wealth to the patronage of the religious, deliberately disposing of large tracts of land which would otherwise have escheated at his death. Something of the exceptional lavishness of his religious devotions can be gauged from his possession of a great gold cross valued at £237 and set with 160 precious stones, which he wished to be sold after his death so that the proceeds of the sale might be divided between the Franciscan, Dominican, Carmelite, and Augustinian friars. His will left money to pay for 100 knights to serve for a year against the infidel, presumably in an attempt to reconquer the lost crusader states. As a patron of religion he rebuilt and greatly augmented the endowment of Hailes Abbey in Gloucestershire, originally founded by his father, but seriously damaged by a fire in 1271. Interpreting the terms of his father's will in a most liberal sense, he founded and endowed a Cistercian abbey at Rewley near Oxford, subsequently the centre for Cistercian studies at the Oxford schools. Again, following in his father's footsteps, he made major benefactions to the Trinitarian friars of Knaresborough, guardians of the shrine of St Robert of Knaresborough. To the collegiate chapel of St Nicholas at Wallingford he gave rents worth £40 a year, and there were further awards to more than a dozen abbeys, priories, hermitages, and churches, of several different religious orders including the Cistercians, the Carthusians, the templars, the hospitallers, and several orders of friars. In his own right and following a vision, in 1288 Edmund founded and built a chapel at Abingdon on the site of the birthplace of St Edmund, and in 1291 he founded a house and chantry for the Trinitarian friars at Oxford.

The greatest of his foundations was at Ashridge in Hertfordshire, intended to house a portion of the holy blood which Edmund had acquired in Germany in 1268–9, completed in 1285 and placed under the care of secular priests later recognized as an independent order of English Augustinian Bonshommes, endowed with more than a dozen of the earl's manors and churches. Besides his well-attested interest in the relic of Christ's blood, shared between Hailes and Ashridge, Edmund clearly felt a particular devotion for the English saints, including not only his patron, St Edmund of Abingdon, but St Frithuswith of Oxford, St Robert of Knaresborough, and the saintly bishops Robert Grosseteste of Lincoln and Thomas of Hereford. In 1286 he wrote to Pope Honorius IV in support of an unsuccessful attempt to obtain the canonization of Grosseteste, testifying to the miracles that had occurred at the bishop's tomb in Lincoln Cathedral. As part of the canonization process for Thomas of Hereford in 1307, various witnesses testified to Edmund's relations with the bishop: to Edmund's foundation of an oratory at Hambleden in Buckinghamshire at Thomas's birthplace, to his possession of Thomas's hair shirt which had defied destruction by fire after the bishop's death, and to Edmund's presence at Wallingford at Pentecost 1281, when a flock of more than thirty crows, doves, and starlings appeared outside the glass windows of the earl's chapel and remained there throughout Thomas's recitation of the hymn *Veni Creator Spiritus*. According to St Thomas's successor as bishop of Hereford, Richard Swinfield, Edmund declared that he had even greater faith in the blessing and prayers of Thomas than in those of St Augustine of Canterbury, evangelist to the English. Thomas's heart was duly buried by Edmund in the shrine of his new college at Ashridge, and it was through Edmund's intercession in 1283 that burial was obtained for the bishop's body at Hereford.

NICHOLAS VINCENT

Sources Chancery and exchequer rolls · *Ann. mon.* · *Matthaei Parisiensis, monachi Sancti Albani, Historia Anglorum, sive … Historia minor*, ed. F. Madden, 3 vols., Rolls Series, 44 (1886–9) · T. Stapleton, ed., *De antiquis legibus liber: cronica majorum et vicecomitum Londoniarum*, CS, 34 (1846) · L. M. Midgley, ed., *Ministers' accounts of the earldom of Cornwall, 1296–1297*, 2 vols., CS, 3rd ser., 66, 68 (1942–5) · *Registrum epistolarum fratris Johannis Peckham, archiepiscopi Cantuariensis*, ed. C. T. Martin, 3 vols., Rolls Series, 77 (1882–5) · *Registrum Roberti Winchelsey, Cantuariensis archiepiscopi, AD 1294–1313*, ed. R. Graham, 2 vols., CYS, 51–2 (1952–6) · *Registrum Johannis de Pontissara, episcopi Wyntoniensis AD MCCLXXXII–MCCCIV*, ed. C. Deedes, 2 vols., CYS, 19, 30 (1915–24) · *Acta sanctorum: October*, 1 (Antwerp, 1765), 539–705 [the canonization process of St Thomas of Hereford, with additional, unpubd material in Paris, Bibliothèque Nationale, MS Latin 5373A] · *The chronicle of Walter of Guisborough*, ed. H. Rothwell, CS, 3rd ser., 89 (1957) · M. Prestwich, *Edward I* (1988) · N. Denholm-Young, *Richard of Cornwall* (1947) · N. Vincent, *The holy blood: King Henry III and the blood relics of Westminster and Hailes* (New York, 2001) · H. J. Todd, *The history of the college of Bonhommes, at Ashridge, in the county of Buckingham* (1823) · R. E. G. Cole, 'Proceedings relative to the canonization of Robert Grosseteste bishop of Lincoln', *Associated Architectural Societies' Reports and Papers*, 33/1 (1915) · M. Jancey, ed., *St Thomas Cantilupe, bishop of Hereford: essays in his honour* (1982) · M. Altschul, *A baronial family in medieval England: the Clares, 1217–1314* (1965) · D. L. Douie, *Archbishop Pecham* (1952) · earldom of Cornwall cartulary, PRO, E36/57 · Exchequer Liber A, PRO, E36/274 · S. Raban, 'The land market and the aristocracy in the thirteenth century', *Tradition and change: essays in honour of Marjorie Chibnall*, ed. D. Greenway, C. Holdsworth, and J. Sayers (1985) · P. L. Hull, ed., *The caption of seisin of the duchy of Cornwall, 1337*, Devon and Cornwall RS, 17 (1971)
Likenesses seal
Wealth at death very wealthy

Edmund of Langley. *See* Edmund, first duke of York (1341–1402).

Edmund of St Joseph. *See* Loop, George (1648–1716).

Edmunds, John (*d.* in or before 1544), college head, graduated BA at Cambridge in 1504/5 and MA in 1508; nothing is known of his early life or parents. He became a fellow of St John's in 1516 and took his BTh in 1516/17. Between 1517 and 1522 he was a fellow of Jesus College. It has wrongly been asserted that he was prebendary of Brondesbury (St Paul's) from 1510 and chancellor of St Paul's between 1517 and 1530, but this was John Edmonds, fellow and bursar of Lincoln College, Oxford, who was probably also the man of that name who was vicar of Harmondsworth, Middlesex, between 1511 and 1515. John Edmunds of Jesus College, Cambridge, was awarded his doctorate of theology in 1519/20 and was appointed Lady Margaret preacher in 1521. By May 1530 he was in possession of the vicarage of Aldbourne in Wiltshire. The chief sphere of his activity, however, was Cambridge. In 1522 he was elected master of Peterhouse, and was also that year appointed as vice-chancellor of the university. Edmunds held his mastership for over two decades until 1544, and was repeatedly elected (in the academic years 1522, 1527, 1528, 1533, 1540, and 1541) as vice-chancellor, an indication of his high reputation and influence in the university.

When Henry VIII sought the views of Cambridge University upon the legality of his marriage to Katherine of Aragon, Edmunds was certainly anxious to accommodate him. In February 1530 Gardiner and Fox wrote to the king assuring him that in this regard 'we found much towardness, goodwill and diligence in the vice-chancellor and Dr Edmunds, being as studious to serve your grace as we could wish or desire' (Burnet, 4.130). After Chancellor Buckmaster visited court to present the university's judgment, he reported to Edmunds that 'The King willed me to send unto you, and to give you word of his pleasure in the said question' (ibid., 6.32–5). Edmunds was one of the compilers of *The Institution of a Christian Man*, issued in 1537 as a guide to the doctrine of the Church of England and usually known as the Bishops' Book. He was also a signatory of 'A declaration of the functions and divine institution of bishops', issued in 1537/8. Confirmation, he thought, was 'not a sacrament of the new law, instituted by Christ by any expressed word in holy Scripture, but only by tradition of the fathers'; it contained 'no promise of spiritual grace', but by it 'is received strength to fight against the spiritual enemies' (Strype, 1/2.353).

Strype reported that Edmunds married the sister-in-law of a Cambridge bedel, John Mere, and concealed it from the authorities, which has been taken as indicating considerable commitment to the cause of church reformation. The couple had a son, also named John, who was taken into the service of John Perne, was made butler of Peterhouse, acquired the profitable post of vintner to the university, and later adopted his father's name. Walker, the historian of Peterhouse, thought that no son of the master would have needed to seek the patronage of Perne, and doubted this account of his paternity. But the simplest explanation is that John Mere was illegitimate, conceived in the days when clerical marriage was forbidden. However that may be, after his election as mayor of Cambridge, Mere alias Edmunds appears to have refused to take the university's part in the continuing squabbles with the town, and had the temerity to impound hogs belonging to the bailiff of Jesus College. Such ingratitude aroused the high indignation of the university authorities, who discommoned him in 1587.

John Edmunds senior did not live to see this. He had continued to profit from appointments in the church and university. On 31 October 1538 he was installed in the chancellorship of Salisbury Cathedral, with its attached prebend of Brixworth. He held this position until his death, which occurred before the collation of his successor on 19 October 1544. Edmunds left money to St John's College, and to Salisbury Cathedral he bequeathed a cope worth £5. A brother Thomas is remembered in his will, and money provided for repairing the church at Braintree. The case for his commitment to religious reform is further weakened by Edmunds's anxiety that his father's 'dirge and masse' be regularly observed. John Edmunds requested burial at St Mary-the-Less, Cambridge.

STEPHEN WRIGHT

Sources T. A. Walker, *Peterhouse* (1906) · T. A. Walker, *A biographical register of Peterhouse men*, 2 vols. (1927–30) · Emden, *Oxf.*, vol. 4 · Venn, *Alum. Cant.* · Cooper, *Ath. Cantab.* · will, PRO, PROB 11/30, sig. 21 · J. Strype, *Ecclesiastical memorials*, 3 vols. (1822) · G. Burnet, *The history of the Reformation of the Church of England*, rev. N. Pocock, new edn, 7 vols. (1865) · *Fasti Angl., 1541–1857*, [Salisbury], 10
Wealth at death approx. £250: will, PRO, PROB 11/30, sig. 21

Edmundson, William (1627–1712), Quaker leader, was baptized on 4 October 1627 at Little Musgrave, Westmorland, the youngest of the six children of John Edmundson (*d.* 1635), yeoman, and his wife, Grace (*d.* 1632). Orphaned around the age of eight, Edmundson was thereafter raised by a strict maternal uncle, who eventually apprenticed him to a joiner and carpenter in York. After joining the New Model Army, Edmundson went to Scotland with Cromwell and subsequently participated in the battle of Worcester and the siege of the Isle of Man. While quartered near Chesterfield, Derbyshire, he learned of the Quakers. After further military service in Scotland, he left the army in 1652 and shortly thereafter married Margaret Stanford (*c.*1630–1691), daughter of Thomas Stanford of Derbyshire. The Edmundsons had seven children, two of whom were named Hindrance and Tryal. Shortly after the marriage, Edmundson, following his brother's advice, moved to Ireland, intending to settle at Waterford but going to Antrim when his brother's army unit was dispatched to Ulster. Having established himself as a shopkeeper, Edmundson returned to England in 1653 or early 1654 to purchase additional wares, and while there was 'convinced' to become a Friend by James Nayler. After relocating to Lurgan, co. Armagh, in the spring of 1654, Edmundson founded the first settled Quaker meeting in Ireland. When John Tiffin came to Ireland the same year, he stayed with Edmundson at Lurgan, the first of numerous visiting Quakers to do so over the years. The two men travelled to various towns in Ulster, including Belfast, preaching in market places and at fairs. In 1655 Edmundson went to England to meet George Fox, who urged him to consult Edward Burrough and Francis Howgill in southern Ireland.

When he returned to Ireland, Edmundson resumed his travels to visit Friends and win converts, a pattern he followed the rest of his life. With Richard Cleaton he visited Coleraine and Londonderry before being imprisoned at Armagh. Following his release, he decided around 1656 to relinquish his shopkeeping and become a farmer in order to provide a clearer testimony against tithes; the change provided him with more freedom to travel. Edmundson leased a farm in co. Cavan from Lieutenant-Colonel Nicholas Kempson, Edmund Ludlow's brother-in-law. At Belturbet, Edmundson was briefly detained and put in the stocks, and at Cavan he was held in a dungeon for fourteen weeks before being released at the assizes after acknowledging the legitimacy of government and 'wholesome' laws. When Kempson refused to renew their leases in 1659, Edmundson and other Quakers moved to the Mountmellick area in Queen's county; the Edmundsons settled on a farm at Rosenallis. Viewing himself as God's threshing instrument to rebuke the immoral, Edmundson frequently visited the 'thick dull sottish people' of Ulster (Swarthmore MS 4/77). He was incarcerated at Strabane and, after denouncing actors, at Londonderry. Imprisoned at Maryborough in 1661, he obtained the sheriff's permission to go to Dublin and petition the lords justices to liberate gaoled Friends. As he visited meetings, he discovered that some Quakers were still in prison for refusing to pay gaolers' fees. He returned to Dublin and persuaded the earl of Mountrath to order their release in August. However, efforts to repress Quakers continued; Edmundson had four cows worth £12–£13 seized and was fined £7 at Cavan for refusing to remove his hat at the assizes. When George Clapham, minister at Mountmellick, persuaded millers not to grind the Quakers' corn, Edmundson successfully protested to the privy council in 1669, but Clapham retaliated by confiscating Edmundson's cheese in lieu of church rates and having him imprisoned. Mountrath again interceded for Edmundson, leading to the quashing of the indictment at the assizes. Undaunted, Clapham had Edmundson arrested for attending a conventicle and refusing to pay church rates (for which a mare worth £3 10s. was seized). When Edmundson appealed to the privy council, it ruled the prosecutions illegal. He continued his public testifying, for which he was again incarcerated at Armagh, but at Londonderry he was permitted to address Bishop Robert Mossom and his clergy in the prelate's residence.

When George Fox came to Ireland in May 1669, he helped to establish the half-yearly meeting and better organize men's and women's meetings. 'I was much eased by [this]', Edmundson acknowledged, 'for I had a great Concern in those Things, which had lain heavy upon my Spirit for several Years' (W. Edmundson, 59). He accompanied Fox on at least part of his three-month journey through Ireland, and later in the year he participated in several meetings with William Penn. As a leading Friend, Edmundson affixed his name in 1669 to the indenture for the Bride Street property on which the Quakers built a meeting-house in Dublin. With Fox and ten others, Edmundson left in August 1641 for a visit to America. After stops in Barbados, Antigua, Nevis, and Jamaica, Edmundson went to Maryland, Virginia, Carolina, and New York. In Jamaica he wrote *A Letter of Examination* (1672), warning the clergy of God's impending judgment. At Fox's urging, Edmundson went to New England, where he, John Burnyeat, and John Stubbs answered Roger Williams's challenge to debate fourteen propositions denouncing Quaker tenets. Held on 9, 10, and 12 August at Newport, Rhode Island, and on the 17th at Providence, the debate was acerbic. Williams directed most of his wrath against Edmundson, 'a flash of wit, a Face of Brass, and a Tongue set on fire from the Hell of Lyes and Fury' (R. Williams, *George Fox Digg'd out of his Burrowes*, 1676, 57). Edmundson dismissed Williams as a 'bitter old Man' baffled by the Quakers' arguments (W. Edmundson, 74). Edmundson later published an account of the debate in *A Narration of a Conference* (1676). From Providence, Edmundson travelled to Boston before returning to Ireland, whence he sent a report of his trip to Margaret Fell in November 1672. He went back to America in 1675, 'convincing' African slaves in the West Indies, debating with Seventh Day Baptists in Connecticut, opposing Ranters in Long Island and East Jersey, and ranging from Carolina to Massachusetts. He returned to Ireland via London, where he attended the yearly meeting in 1677. A third trip to the West Indies, where he spent seven months, followed in 1683–4.

As his ministry in Ireland continued, Edmundson wrote an epistle in May 1680 counselling Friends not to be married by professional clergy and urging Quaker parents to disinherit children who wed non-Friends; thousands of copies were distributed in ensuing years. In 1682 Clapham's vicar had Edmundson cited in the bishop's court for refusing to pay tithes; Edmundson was excommunicated and imprisoned for approximately twenty weeks until Viscount Ely interceded. Bishop William Moreton released Edmundson after the latter argued that the Henrician act under which he had been incarcerated did not apply to those whose objections to tithes were conscientious.

Following the accession of James II, Edmundson was briefly incarcerated in the Marshalsea, Dublin, but by 1687 he was one of nineteen Friends who had access to the earl of Tyrconnell. With the leading Dublin merchant and Quaker Anthony Sharp and six others, he petitioned Tyrconnell in May for redress of Quaker grievances, and in July, after James issued a declaration of indulgence, Edmundson and others drafted an address of thanksgiving and loyalty. When war erupted, dragoons were quartered in Edmundson's house, prompting an appeal to Tyrconnell that resulted in the gaoling of troops who had misbehaved. As Friends suffered during the war, Edmundson met with James several times to protest at their maltreatment. Following the battle of the Boyne, retreating Irish troops plundered his house several times. When William's forces arrived, Edmundson aided Irish civilians. Rapparees burned his house in December 1690,

taking him and two sons prisoner and threatening to execute them; instead they were imprisoned at Athlone. After being stripped by rapparees, Edmundson's wife, wearing only shoes, walked 2 miles seeking help. Weakened by her ordeal, she died on 15 July 1691 and was buried in Dublin.

In the meantime, Edmundson had resumed his travels, visiting Ulster in 1691. Penn sent him a copy of *Some Proposals for a Second Settlement* (1690) in January, asking him to distribute copies to potential emigrants. Edmundson was at the yearly meeting in London when his wife died. On his return to Ireland he repaired his house, where he lived alone with Tryal, the other children having left. During the ensuing years he travelled extensively throughout Ireland and England. In 1695 he and other Quakers appealed to MPs in Dublin not to pass an act for the recovery of tithes in temporal courts, and the following year he met with a lord justice, several MPs, and the chancellor to express his objections. Between 1696 and 1698 Edmundson was estranged from Sharp, possibly because Edmundson had denounced the sort of 'great Trading' in which Sharp engaged. On 1 December 1697 Edmundson wed Mary Strangman (*c*.1648–1732), widow of Joshua Strangman, at Mountmellick. As persecution abated, he worried about complacency and materialism in the movement; his postscript to an epistle in September 1698 reminded Friends of their first principles and practices. In the 1690s and early 1700s he also helped lead the Irish Quaker opposition to the affirmation, a simple declaration which many Quakers deemed essentially an oath. In 1700 he reviewed the documents that Thomas Wight subsequently edited and published as *A History of the Rise and Progress of … Quakers in Ireland*. The following year, Edmundson wrote *An Epistle Containing Wholesome Advice and Counsel to All Friends*, cautioning them against all superfluity. Although a 'raging Distemper' threatened his life in the spring of 1704, he continued his travels until May 1712, when he attended the half-yearly meeting in Dublin. Following his death at Rosenallis, Queen's county, on 31 August 1712, he was buried at Tineel, near Rosenallis. The inventory for the probate of his estate listed personal property (excluding house and land) worth £33 5s. 4d. A portly man with a big voice, according to Roger Williams, Edmundson belonged to the first generation of rustic Quakers, unlike the more polished Penn and Sharp. Wight, who appropriately recognized Edmundson as the principal figure in Quakerism's spread throughout Ireland, attributed his success to the 'dread and awfulness upon his spirit' when he prayed (Wight, 199).

RICHARD L. GREAVES

Sources W. Edmundson, *A journal of the life, travels, sufferings and labour of love*, 2nd edn (1774) • T. Wight, *A history of the rise and progress of the people called Quakers, in Ireland, from the year 1653 to 1700*, rev. J. Rutty, 4th edn (1811) • F. Edmundson, 'William Edmundson, 1627–1712, "the Great Hammer of Ireland": some new and little-known memorabilia', *Bulletin of the Friends' Historical Association*, 42 (spring 1953), 3–12 • R. L. Greaves, *Dublin's merchant–Quaker: Anthony Sharp and the community of Friends, 1643–1707* (1998) • R. L. Greaves, *God's other children: protestant nonconformists and the emergence of denominational churches in Ireland* (1997) • *The journal of George Fox*, ed. N. Penney, 2 vols. (1911) • *The papers of William Penn*, ed. M. M. Dunn,

R. S. Dunn, and others, 1–2 (1981–2); 4 (1987) • 'Dictionary of Quaker biography', RS Friends, Lond. [card index] • L. R. Camp, 'Roger Williams vs. "The Upstarts": the Rhode Island debates of 1672', *Quaker History*, 52 (1963), 69–76 • minutes of the Half-Yearly National Meeting, Ireland, Religious Society of Friends, Dublin • minutes of the Leinster Provincial Meeting, Religious Society of Friends, Dublin • 'Record of Friends travelling in Ireland, 1656–1765 [pt 1]', *Journal of the Friends' Historical Society*, 10 (1913), 157–80 • RS Friends, Lond., Swarthmore papers

Archives RS Friends, Lond., letters | Religious Society of Friends, Dublin, minutes of the half-yearly national meeting, Ireland • Religious Society of Friends, Dublin, minutes of the Leinster provincial meeting • Religious Society of Friends, Dublin, minutes of Mountmellick meeting • Religious Society of Friends, Dublin, Mountmellick records of suffering • RS Friends, Lond., Barclay MSS • RS Friends, Lond., Swarthmore MSS

Wealth at death £33 5s. 4d.—personal goods: Edmundson, 'William Edmundson', 12

Ednyfed Fychan (d. 1246). *See under* Tudor family, forebears of (*per.* c.1215–1404).

Édouard, Henry. *See* Henryson, Edward (1522–c.1590).

Edouin, Willie [*real name* William Frederick Bryer] (1846–1908), actor, was born at Brighton on 1 January 1846, the son of John Edwin Bryer, a dancing master, and his wife, Sarah Elizabeth May. He was the youngest of a family of five enterprising children, all of whom took to the stage when they were young. Willie first appeared in public in the summer of 1852 (with two sisters and others) in the juvenile troupe the Living Marionettes, at the Théâtre des Variétés, Linwood Gallery, Leicester Square, in farces, *ballets d'action*, and extravaganzas. At Christmas in 1852 and 1854 the Edouin children acted in pantomimes at the Strand Theatre. In 1857 'the Celebrated Edouin Family' were taken by their parents on a prolonged tour of Australia, India, China, and Japan. In 1863, after the disbandment of the troupe, Willie and his sister Rose (afterwards Mrs G. B. Lewis, of the Maidan Theatre, Calcutta) were both members of Fawcett's stock company at the Princess's Theatre, Melbourne, playing in burlesque. Later Willie made a long stay in California.

On 2 June 1870 Edouin made his first appearance in New York, at Bryant's Minstrel Hall, as Mr Murphy in *Handy Andy*. Shortly afterwards he began a notable association with Lydia Thompson, playing with her burlesque troupe at Wood's Museum, New York, in October and November. In the company was Alice Atherton (1854–1899), whom Edouin subsequently married. At Wallack's Theatre, New York, in August 1871 he was first seen in his droll impersonation of Washee-Washee the Chinaman in H. B. Farnie's burlesque *Bluebeard*. It was in this character that he made his first adult appearance in London, at the Charing Cross Theatre on 19 September 1874. In 1877 he returned with the Lydia Thompson troupe to New York, where pantomime or burlesque largely occupied him for the next six years.

In September 1884 Edouin made his first experiment in London management, in partnership with Lionel Brough, by opening Toole's Theatre with Harry Paulton's *The Babes, or, Whines from the Wood*, which, with himself and his wife in the principal characters, ran for 100 nights. In August

1886 he played a six-week season at the Comedy, as Carraway Bones in Mark Melford's farcical comedy *Turned Up*, which proved so successful that he transferred it, under his own management, to the Royalty Theatre, where it ran for more than 100 nights. In February 1888 Edouin began his first managerial period at the Strand by producing *Katti, the Family Help*, with himself and his wife in the principal characters. On 13 June 1889, at the Prince of Wales's Theatre, he proved very successful as Nathaniel Glover (an amiable caricature of Sir Augustus Harris) in *Our Flat*. A fortnight later he transferred the play to the Opera Comique, under his own management, where it had a run of close on 600 nights. During 1891 and 1893 Edouin resumed management of the Strand, and appeared there in light pieces suiting his idiosyncrasy. On 18 June 1894 he had a congenial part in Jeremiah Grubb in Melford's *The Jerry Builder*, a farcical comedy in which, as Mattie Pollard, his daughter May made a promising début. In February 1897 he won great success at the Prince of Wales's with his quaint embodiment of Hilarius in *La Poupée*.

On 4 February 1899 Edouin's wife, who had long acted with him, died, and the following year he went to America for a brief period. In June 1901 he created Samuel Twanks in *The Silver Slipper* at the Lyric. He then performed in sketches in South Africa. On his return he originated the role of Hoggenheimer in *The Girl from Kay's* at the Apollo (15 November 1902). Afterwards his acting showed a serious falling off, notably in *The Little Michus* at Daly's in April 1905. In 1906 he toured the leading provincial halls, and in 1907 he played in vaudeville in the United States, but developed symptoms of mental failure. He returned home, and died at 19 Bedford Court Mansions, London, on 14 April 1908. He was buried at Kensal Green cemetery. Two daughters survived him. In parts of grotesquerie and whim Edouin was an admirable comedian. As a manager he showed little business aptitude, however; he made large sums of money but left only £821.

[ANON.], rev. NILANJANA BANERJI

Sources *Daily Telegraph* (15 April 1908) • B. Hunt, ed., *The green room book, or, Who's who on the stage* (1906) • J. Parker, ed., *The green room book, or, Who's who on the stage* (1907) • Adams, *Drama* • *Players of the day* (1902) • *Theatrical Journal* (1852) • *Theatrical Journal* (1854) • ILN (1852) • T. A. Brown, *A history of the New York stage from the first performance in 1732 to 1901*, 3 vols. (1903) • W. Archer, *The theatrical 'World' of 1894* (1895) • P. Hartnoll, ed., *The Oxford companion to the theatre* (1951); 2nd edn (1957); 3rd edn (1967) • E. Reid and H. Compton, eds., *The dramatic peerage* [1891] • CGPLA Eng. & Wales (1908) • d. cert. • personal knowledge (1912)

Likenesses lithographs, Harvard TC • pencil and watercolour sketch, NPG • photograph, repro. in *Daily Telegraph* • portrait, repro. in *Players of the day*

Wealth at death £821 11s. 9d.: probate, 4 June 1908, CGPLA Eng. & Wales

Edred. *See* Eadred (d. 955).

Edric Streona. *See* Eadric Streona (d. 1017).

Edrich, William John [Bill] (1916–1986), cricketer, was born on 26 March 1916 in Lingwood, Norfolk, the second

William John [Bill] **Edrich** (1916–1986), by unknown photographer, 1937

son and second child in the family of four sons and a daughter of William Archer Edrich, tenant farmer, and his wife, Edith Mattocks, originally of Cumbrian farming stock, whose family had moved to Norfolk. Educated at Bracondale School, Norwich, where his cricketing prowess soon became evident, Bill Edrich was a member of a noted family of cricketers, which was able to field an entire eleven under the family name. His three brothers— Geoffrey, Eric, and Brian—all played first-class cricket, while his cousin John Hugh Edrich MBE was to be a well-known Surrey and England batsman.

After several successful seasons with Norfolk in the minor counties championship, Edrich was advised to seek an engagement with Middlesex. He qualified for Middlesex and lived in London, playing variously for the Marylebone Cricket Club and Norfolk. He made his first-class début for the minor counties in 1934, and such was his progress that, in his first full season for Middlesex in 1937, he scored more than 2000 runs, and was chosen to accompany the third Baron Tennyson's tour of India the following winter. In spite of several failures, he retained his test place, and in South Africa in the winter of 1938–9 he scored a match-saving 219 at Durban. In 1938 he managed the unusual feat of 1000 runs before the end of May. During the Second World War he served as a pilot with 21 squadron, Coastal Command, rising from flight lieutenant to acting squadron-leader, and his bravery was rewarded with the DFC (1941).

Returning to the cricketing fray in 1946, Edrich eventually regained his England place—his test career was always dogged by selectors' inconsistencies—and in 1947 he changed status from professional to amateur. The year 1947 proved to be his greatest. In partnership with the mercurial Denis *Compton, he broke many records, and Middlesex and England flourished accordingly. In that summer he made 3539 runs, including 12 centuries, and averaged 80.43. He captained Middlesex from 1951 to 1957, initially in harness with Denis Compton, and, after his retirement from first-class cricket in 1959, played for his native Norfolk until 1971.

In his 571 games in first-class cricket, Edrich scored 36,965 runs, including 86 centuries, with an average of 42.39. His highest score was 269 not out, against Northamptonshire in 1947. He also took 479 wickets and 529 catches, and made a solitary stumping. In 39 test matches he scored 2440 runs for an average of 40, and took 41 wickets.

Edrich approached his cricketing duties with much the same fervour with which he tackled his romantic ventures. Gusto and valour were his watchwords. As a batsman, he was a courageous player of quick bowling, relishing the hook and the pull-drive, and dealing plainly and authoritatively with much that he faced. As a bowler, he rushed intrepidly into the attack, hurling the ball awkwardly at often startled opponents. He was a most effective fielder, initially in the out-field, but mainly in the slips. Above all, he was, in cricket as in his domestic life, abundantly cheery and optimistic. A Robert Bruce among cricketers, he was ever ready to try again. A very popular sportsman, he was only a little short of the highest rank of cricketers, and his fame was very much bound up with his sparkling relationship with Denis Compton. The sports journalist R. C. Robertson-Glasgow wrote that, while Compton was poetry, Edrich was 'prose, robust and clear'. Edrich was short, dark, and keen-eyed, with brisk, lithe movements. A man of ardent amorous energies, he was married five times, each for relatively short periods. His first four marriages ended in divorce, and his fifth wife outlived him briefly. His first marriage, in 1936, was to Betty, typist, daughter of Sydney William Hobbs, railway official. The marriage ended in divorce in 1944 and in the same year he married Marion, an officer in the Women's Auxiliary Air Force, the divorced wife of Edward Reginald Fish and daughter of Albert Ernest Forster, works manager. They were divorced in 1948, and in 1949 he married Jessy Shaw, the divorced wife of Harold Tetley and daughter of Hubert Gomersall, building society manager. They had one son and the marriage ended with divorce in 1960. In the same year he married Brenda Valerie Terry, insurance consultant, whose previous marriage had been dissolved, the daughter of Constant Wells Ponder, medical practitioner. They had one son; the marriage ended with divorce in 1973. His fifth and final marriage, in 1983, was to Mary Elizabeth Somerville, hairdresser, whose previous marriage had been dissolved, daughter of Frederick Vincent Wesson, sales manager. Edrich died in Chesham as the result of a fall down the stairs at home, following a St

George's day celebration, just after midnight on 24 April 1986. A grandstand at Lord's cricket ground is named after him, matching one for Denis Compton.

ERIC MIDWINTER, rev.

Sources R. Barker, *The cricketing family Edrich* (1975) • A. Hill, *Bill Edrich, a biography* (1994) • *Wisden* (1948) • *Wisden* (1987) • *CGPLA Eng. & Wales* (1986)
Likenesses photographs, 1937–58, Hult. Arch. [*see illus.*]
Wealth at death under £40,000: probate, 22 July 1986, *CGPLA Eng. & Wales*

Edridge, Henry (1768–1821), portrait painter and landscape draughtsman, was born at Paddington, Middlesex, in August 1768, and baptized in St James's, Paddington, on 3 October 1768, the son of Henry Edridge, a tradesman in St James's and his wife, Sarah, *née* Brett. He was educated by his mother and at a school in Acton, before being apprenticed at fifteen to the mezzotint engraver William Pether. Edridge acquired an eye for detail in this meticulous work; he was also given permission to study his master's other work as a miniaturist. He attended the Royal Academy Schools from 1784 and his copies after the works of Reynolds were much admired by Sir Joshua. He married Ann in 1789 and at the same time set up in London on his own at 14 Church Street, Soho, and then at 5 Old Compton Street. He was in business at 10 Dufour's Place from 1790 to 1799, when his reputation was being established, and also worked from a cottage he had purchased at Hanwell, Middlesex. In 1789 Edridge had become acquainted with the landscape watercolourist Thomas Hearne, and went sketching with him, adopting a little of his style and technique. Through Hearne he met Dr Thomas Monro and after 1794 attended Monro's unofficial drawing school at Adelphi Terrace in company with J. M. W. Turner and Thomas Girtin. But Edridge was already becoming well known for a style of portraiture that combined the delicacy of miniature painting with breadth of draughtsmanship and also included landscape. His earliest (anonymous) biographer stated:

> It was only of late years that he made those elaborately high-finished pictures on paper, uniting the depth and richness of oil paintings with the freedom and freshness of watercolours, and of which there is perhaps scarcely a nobleman's family in England without some specimens. (*Georgian Era*)

It was not strictly true that these watercolour full-lengths were late works: he had been engaged on them since 1790 but perfected them from 1805 to 1810, when he exhibited almost 200 at the Royal Academy. Edridge drew his subject in soft lead pencil, applying watercolour with a miniaturist's technique of stippling, principally to the face and hands, but using some washes or body colour to enrich the drapery. His meticulous pencil lines, occasionally strengthened by pen, give his figures a posed appearance, but the accuracy of dress and detail is remarkable. An accomplished landscape draughtsman, Edridge used trees, especially silver birches, to enliven the background, and details of a house or a terrace to set the figure in a topographical context. The outline and the drapery of his sitters exactly suited the neo-classical mood of the time.

Joseph Farington gave some indication of Edridge's popularity when he noted in his diary on 30 December 1805 that he was invited to Windsor in 1805, 'where he is employed in making a set of drawings of the Princesses to be presented by them to the Queen—He is now established at the Equerry's table' (Farington, *Diary*, 7.2667). Edridge aimed to paint individual portraits of families as he moved from house to house in his fashionable circle. But his rarer group portraits, for example, *Unknown Gentleman with Children* (V&A) or *The Vere Poulett Family* (Cecil Higgins Art Gallery, Bedford), are equally finished productions, often showing the family's interests as painters, musicians, antiquaries, or sportsmen. They seldom include more than three figures. In August 1802 he was at Merton, Surrey, with Sir William and Lady Hamilton, drawing Lord Nelson's portrait; in February 1805 he made a portrait of William Pitt, and in June 1809 William Wilberforce sat to him. He was patronized by such leaders of taste as Sir George Beaumont and Sir John Leicester. On 30 March 1806 Farington recorded that Edridge was able to raise his charge for a full-length portrait drawing from 15 to 20 guineas (ibid., 2706). Neither did he neglect his landscape work, often in pen outline with very sensitive rendering of architecture and great virtuosity in detailing carving and stone. He made several trips abroad at the end of his life, notably to Normandy in 1818 or 1819, and to Paris in 1820, when he specialized in views of the great Gothic churches.

Edridge was quiet and well mannered, and of gentlemanly appearance. A portrait drawing of Edridge by Thomas Monro, formerly in the Panzer collection (reproduced in Houfe) shows a heavy-jowled man of middle age with an aquiline nose, side whiskers, and a good head of hair. Edridge was very anxious to be elected to the Royal Academy, but Farington noted on 18 June 1808 that, as he was a watercolourist, Thomas Lawrence did not consider Edridge in a line to be admitted (Farington, *Diary*, 9.3299). He was eventually elected an associate of the Royal Academy in 1820, possibly on the strength of his Normandy landscapes.

Edridge died of heart disease at his home, 65 Margaret Street, London, on 23 April 1821 and was buried on 30 April at Bushey parish church, Hertfordshire. He left a fortune of £12,000 to his widow and executors. Examples of Edridge's work may be found in the National Portrait Gallery, the British Museum (including three sketch-books), and the Victoria and Albert Museum, London; the Ashmolean Museum, Oxford; the Fitzwilliam Museum, Cambridge; Birmingham City Art Gallery; the Laing Art Gallery, Newcastle; and Saltram, Devon. SIMON HOUFE

Sources [Clarke], *The Georgian era: memoirs of the most eminent persons*, 4 (1834), 496 • Farington, *Diary* • S. Houfe, 'Henry Edridge, 1769–1821: a neoclassical portraitist', *Antique Collector*, 43 (1972), 211–16 • M. Hardie, *Water-colour painting in Britain*, ed. D. Snelgrove, J. Mayne, and B. Taylor, 3: *The Victorian period* (1968), 2–4 • I. O. Williams, *Early English watercolours and some cognate drawings by artists born not later than 1785* (1952), 208–9 • *IGI*
Likenesses T. Monro, portrait, repro. in Houfe, 'Henry Edridge, 1769–1821: a neoclassical portraitist'

Wealth at death £12,000; excl. home at Hanwell, Middlesex: will, PRO

Edward [*called* Edward the Elder] (**870s?–924**), king of the Anglo-Saxons, was probably born in the 870s (he was the second child of a marriage of 868, and led troops in battle in 893). He was the son of *Alfred, king of the Anglo-Saxons (848/9–899), and *Ealhswith (*d.* 902), a Mercian noblewoman. He had a younger brother, Æthelweard, and three sisters: *Æthelflæd, 'Lady of the Mercians', who married *Æthelred, ealdorman of Mercia, *Ælfthryth, who married Baudouin (II), count of Flanders, and Æthelgifu, who became abbess of Shaftesbury. Edward's byname, the Elder, first appears at the end of the tenth century (in Wulfstan's life of St Æthelwold), probably to distinguish him from the later King Edward the Martyr (*d.* 978).

Family Edward was married three times and had fourteen children. Four of his sons were king after him, and five of his daughters married into continental noble or royal houses. He was first married in the 890s and his wife Ecgwynn (*fl. c.*893–900) was the mother of King *Æthelstan (*d.* 939) and of a daughter, Edith, who married Sihtric (*d.* 927), the Norse king of York, in 926. Almost nothing is known about Ecgwynn: even her name is recorded only in post-conquest sources, and it has been argued that she was a concubine rather than a wife. The near-contemporary Hrotsvitha of Gandersheim notes that Ecgwynn's status was lower than that of one of Edward's later wives, but as she was praising the child of one of these later wives this is inconclusive. Whether justified or not, stories do seem to have circulated about the legitimacy of the union: by the twelfth century Ecgwynn could be seen both as a noble woman and as a beautiful shepherd's daughter who bore Edward an illegitimate child.

Whatever Ecgwynn's precise status, by 901 Edward had married Ælfflæd, daughter of Æthelhelm, ealdorman of Wessex. If the second English coronation ordo, accompanied by an ordo for the anointing of a queen, is correctly attributed to Edward, it may be that he was married to Ælfflæd by the time of his coronation on 8 June 900. Ælfflæd was the mother of Ælfweard, who succeeded as king on Edward's death on 17 July 924 but died himself under a month later, and of Eadwine, who was drowned at sea in 933. Ælfflæd also bore six daughters. Two were religious—a nun, Eadflæd, and a lay recluse, Æthelhild. Four married into great continental houses—Eadgifu, who married Charles the Simple, king of the Franks, between 916 and 919; Eadhild, who married Hugh the Great, duke of the Franks, in 926; Eadgyth (Edith), who married the future German emperor Otto I in 929 or 930; and Ælfgifu, who accompanied Eadgyth to Germany so that Otto would have a choice of brides, and married another continental prince there.

By 920 Edward had married for a third time; this wife was *Eadgifu (*d.* in or after 966), daughter of Sigehelm, ealdorman of Kent. The date is fixed by the fact that their son *Edmund, later king of England (*r.* 939–46), was born in 920 or 921. Eadgifu was also the mother of *Eadred,

who became king of England on his brother's death (*r.* 946–55), of *Eadburh, a nun at Winchester, and of *Eadgifu, who married Louis of Aquitaine. Edward's wife Eadgifu outlived both her husband and her sons, witnessing the charters of her grandson King *Edgar (*r.* 957×9–75).

A post-conquest text, William of Malmesbury's *De antiquitate Glastonie ecclesiae*, raises the possibility that Ælfflæd as well as Eadgifu was still alive after Edward's death. If this could be confirmed from other sources, it would mean that Edward divorced Ælfflæd some time before his marriage to Eadgifu. Unfortunately the *De antiquitate* is the only source for this information, and as the work contains many historical errors, being more concerned with Glastonbury estates than with wider events, it cannot be relied upon.

Edward in Alfred's reign Sources from Alfred's reign say little about his eldest son, Edward. The Anglo-Saxon Chronicle does not mention Edward until after his father's death in 899. Asser's life of King Alfred mentions Edward among Alfred's other children, and calls him an obedient son to Alfred, one who treats others with humility, friendliness, and gentleness, and one who has a good liberal education, having learned the psalms, books in English, and especially English poems. Another side of Edward's activities, not found in Asser or the chronicle, appears in Æthelweard's Latin translation of a lost version of the chronicle: here Edward appears in 893 conducting a campaign throughout southern England and leading a successful attack against the Danes at Farnham. The absence of references to Edward and the battle at Farnham in surviving Old English versions of the chronicle may suggest that in the 890s there were separate pro-Alfred and pro-Edward versions, just as in the eleventh century there were pro- and anti-Godwine versions.

Edward first appears in Alfred's charters in two forged documents, whose witness lists, if genuine, date from between 871 and 877, but these cannot be relied upon. His first certain appearance is in 892 (*AS chart.*, S 348), where he witnesses as *filius regis* ('king's son'). He witnesses three more undated charters the same way, but in 898 he witnesses one of Alfred's charters (S 350) as *rex*. Unfortunately both the Anglo-Saxon Chronicle and Æthelweard's Latin version are blank for the last two years of Alfred's reign, so the narrative sources offer no explanation of what had happened. Since the charter dealt with land in Kent and since Alfred's will bequeathed to Edward all his bookland there, it may be that Alfred had established his eldest son as sub-king of Kent, as his father, Æthelwulf, and grandfather, Ecgberht, had done. While Ecgberht and Æthelwulf established their sons in Kent from the beginning of their reigns (or, in Ecgberht's case, from his conquest of Kent), Alfred appointed Edward only towards the end of his reign, which may suggest that the move was more a recognition of Edward's popularity, seen clearly in Æthelweard's description of the 893 battle, than a part of Alfred's intended policy. The preamble to Alfred's will, in which he belabours the point that all his father's inheritance is his by right (and no one could justly claim that he had cheated his nephews), shows that Alfred understood the importance of not dividing an inheritance; it may further indicate that Alfred would not have named his son sub-king of Kent unless there were pressing reasons to do so. It has even been suggested that Alfred's title in the charter, 'King of the Saxons', instead of his more usual 'King of the Anglo-Saxons', shows Alfred claiming a more limited authority than he did in the 880s and earlier 890s, perhaps under threat from Edward. This is probably going too far: based on its formulation the charter is a local Rochester product rather than one emanating from the king's circle, so the style more likely reflects a Kentish indifference to Alfred's wider authority than a diminishing of that authority.

Alfred's death and Æthelwold's revolt Alfred died on 26 October 899 and Edward succeeded to the kingdom. Immediately Æthelwold, one of Alfred's nephews (son of Alfred's older brother *Æthelred I), rebelled and seized Wimborne, where his father was buried, and Christchurch, and prepared to hold them against all comers. Edward brought an army to Badbury, near Wimborne, but Æthelwold stayed within Wimborne with his men and a nun he had kidnapped, saying that he would live there or die there. The stage seemed set for Edward and Æthelwold to recreate the tale of Cynewulf and Cyneheard, that eighth-century set piece of battle to the death between royal kinsmen and their loyal retainers immortalized in the Anglo-Saxon Chronicle, but Æthelwold chose the less heroic if more pragmatic course of riding away in the night. He escaped to the Danes in Northumbria, who swore allegiance to him and took him as their king: some Northumbrian coins with the name Alvaldus (Æthelwold) survive from this period. In the autumn of 901 Æthelwold came with a fleet into Essex; a year later he induced the East Anglian Danes to break the peace and with an army harried Mercia as far as Cricklade in what is now Wiltshire. When Æthelwold crossed the Thames into Wessex to raid Braydon (also in modern Wiltshire), King Edward gathered his army and harried Danish-held Essex and East Anglia. He then tried to stage an orderly withdrawal, but the men of Kent lingered, the Danish army overtook them, and on 13 December 902 the battle of 'the Holme' (unidentified) was fought, resulting in the deaths of, among others, Æthelwold the pretender and his allies Eohric, the Danish king of East Anglia, and an atheling, Brihtsige (probably Mercian, as his name alliterates with those of the Mercian kings).

Reconquest of the southern Danelaw Nothing is reported of hostilities between the English and the Danes after the battle of 'the Holme' and before 906. That there were conflicts is suggested by the peace which Edward made with the East Anglian and Northumbrian Danes in that year; one manuscript of the Anglo-Saxon Chronicle says he made peace 'from necessity', a formula which suggests he had to pay the vikings to cease ravaging. A cryptic note from 907 that Chester was restored suggests more fighting in that year.

The first clear instance of renewed fighting came in 909, when Edward sent an army of West Saxons and Mercians into Northumbria, where it ravaged for five weeks. The following year the Northumbrian Danes descended on Mercia, and the army of the West Saxons and Mercians overtook them at Wednesfield, near Tettenhall, and killed a great many of them, including two or three kings and, according to the chronicle, 'many thousands of men' (*ASC*, s.a. 911, text D). After this defeat the Northumbrian Danes stayed north of the Humber, which allowed Edward and his Mercian allies, his sister Æthelflæd and her husband, Ealdorman Æthelred, to concentrate on the Danish armies to the south, in East Anglia and the territory of the Five Boroughs (Leicester, Lincoln, Nottingham, Stamford, and Derby).

An important part of Edward's efforts against the Danes, as it had been of Alfred's, was the construction of fortresses to restrict the freedom of movement of the invading armies. The restoration of Chester in 907 has already been noted. In November 911 Edward ordered a fort built at Hertford, blocking the southward advance of Danes from Bedford and Cambridge; in the summer of 912 he took his army to Maldon in Essex and camped there while a fort was built at Witham, blocking the westward advance of Danes from Colchester, and a second fort was built at Hertford. This made London relatively secure to attacks from the north and east, and many of the English in Essex who had been under Danish rule submitted to Edward instead. Also in 912 Æthelflæd built a fortress at Bridgnorth, blocking a crossing of the Severn recently used by the Danes, and another at 'Scergeat'.

Edward's advance paused in 913 and 914. In 913 the main text of the Anglo-Saxon Chronicle records only local raids, though Æthelflæd's fortress building continued, at Tamworth and Stafford, to shore up the north-eastern border of English Mercia against the Danish armies in the Five Boroughs. In 914 a viking army came from Brittany and ravaged the Severn estuary, but was eventually defeated by the armies of Hereford and Gloucester, which besieged it, extracting hostages and a promise to leave. Edward kept the English army stationed on the south side of the estuary: wisely, since the vikings twice broke their oaths and stole ashore. They were repelled both times and in the autumn, when they were growing very short of food, sailed to Ireland. In the meantime Æthelflæd had built forts at Eddisbury, to stop invaders raiding into northern Mercia from the Mersey, and at Warwick, as another barrier on the border between English Mercia and the Five Boroughs.

Between late 914 and 918 Edward advanced until he held all the land south of the Humber. In November 914 he went to Buckingham and built two fortresses, one either side of the river, and the Danish Earl Thurcetel submitted to him, as did many of the Danes of Northampton and Bedford, where Edward had a fort built. In 915 Æthelflæd built a fort at Chirbury on the Welsh border, another at 'Weardburh', and a third at Runcorn, which, like that at Eddisbury, would block access to the north of Mercia from the Mersey.

In 916 Edward built a fortress at Maldon, near Witham

and so another bulwark against the Danes of Colchester. In the same year Earl Thurcetel and his men left for Francia. In Mercia, an Abbot Ecgberht was killed, presumably by the Welsh, since Æthelflæd retaliated by sending an army into Wales. Her fort at Chirbury may therefore have been built as part of ongoing hostilities between the English and the Welsh that are otherwise unrecorded.

By April 917 Edward had ordered a fort built at Towcester, to block the southern advance of Danes from Northampton. Within a month he ordered another, at 'Wigingamere'. That summer the Danes of Northampton and Leicester and 'north of these places' stormed Towcester but were repelled, though afterwards this army made a successful raid on a less well-protected area. Meanwhile, the Danish army of Huntingdon and East Anglia built a fortress at Tempsford, some 10 miles south of Huntingdon which they abandoned because Tempsford was closer to the English border. The Danes of Tempsford attacked the nearby English garrison of Bedford, but were put to flight. Another Danish army, from East Anglia, Essex, and Mercia, besieged the fort at 'Wigingamere', but they too were defeated. The system of fortifications put together by Edward and Æthelflæd was showing its worth: the Danes were attacked from two fronts, Edward's armies preventing any southward advance from the Five Boroughs and advancing eastward into East Anglia, while Æthelflæd took Derby, one of the Five Boroughs, to which siege many Danes may have been diverted. Towards the end of the summer, a great English host besieged the Danish fort of Tempsford and took it, killing the last Danish king of East Anglia.

In the autumn of 917 the English took Colchester. An army of East Anglian Danes (probably fragmenting, with their king and many other nobles dead) besieged the English fort at Maldon, but they were put to flight and many of them were killed. Edward went back north to Towcester and built a stone wall around the fort there, which show of strength probably convinced Earl Thurferth and the Danes of nearby Northampton to submit. The army then took the fort at Huntingdon and repaired it, and all those who survived in the area submitted to Edward. Before the end of 917 Edward went to Colchester and repaired that fortress, and many people in East Anglia and Essex who had been ruled by the Danes submitted, as did the Danish armies of East Anglia and of Cambridge.

The year 917, therefore, saw the submission of all the Danish armies south of the Humber, except for those of Leicester, Stamford, Nottingham, and Lincoln (four of the Five Boroughs). Æthelflæd peacefully obtained the submission of the borough of Leicester, and also pledges from the Northumbrians of York in 918, but she died shortly afterwards, at Tamworth, on 12 June. Edward, meanwhile, having taken his army to Stamford and built a fortress south of the river, received the surrender of that borough. When he heard of Æthelflæd's death, he occupied Tamworth and received the oaths of the Mercians, as well as of the Welsh. He then returned to the Five Boroughs, taking Nottingham and ordering the fort to be manned by both English and Danes. The concluding words of the Anglo-Saxon Chronicle for 918, 'And all the people who had settled in Mercia, both Danish and English, submitted to him', suggest that the last of the Five Boroughs with a Danish force, Lincoln, also submitted to Edward at this time.

'Father and lord' of the north The peaceful submission of Leicester and York to Æthelflæd in 918 look odd in the context of the Anglo-Saxon Chronicle, especially as the Northumbrian Danes had not been threatened by the English since the battle of Wednesfield in 910. But the chronicle is chiefly concerned with the south of England. What it overlooks, and what must be reconstructed from Irish annals and the works of Symeon of Durham, is the advent of Norse vikings in the north in the second decade of the tenth century. About 914 Ragnall seized the lands of Ealdred of Bamburgh: the English Northumbrians allied themselves with the Scots, but Ragnall defeated their combined armies at Corbridge on the Tyne. It was doubtless in response to Ragnall that Æthelflæd built the two forts near the mouth of the Mersey in 914 and 915. Ragnall's actions cannot be traced for the next few years, but in 918 he won another battle at Corbridge, probably against another combined English and Scottish army. It is uncertain whether the people of York at this time were English or Danes or whether they were already a mixed people, but in submitting to Æthelflæd they showed a pragmatic political sense seen again in the middle of the tenth century as they chose between Eadred and Erik Bloodaxe.

It seems that the people of York did not renew their oaths to Edward after Æthelflæd's death. At any rate, Edward did not prevent Ragnall from taking York in 919: some Northumbrian coins survive bearing Ragnall's name. Edward took a Mercian army to Thelwall, built a third fort there near the mouth of the Mersey, and sent another Mercian army to occupy and repair the fort of Manchester in Northumbria. The order of events in 919 and 920 is uncertain, but it may only have been when another Norse viking, Sihtric, invaded north-west Mercia in 920 and destroyed Davenport (in what is now Cheshire) that Edward began his final move against the north. Before midsummer of 920 he had ordered a second fortress built at Nottingham, and he went from there into the Peak District, where he had a fort built at Bakewell. It is uncertain whether this was followed by any combat between the English and the Norse: the chronicle simply reports that after the building of the fortress at Bakewell, the king of the Scots, and Ragnall, and all of those who lived in Northumbria, English and Danish and Norse, and also the Welsh of Strathclyde, chose Edward as their 'father and lord'.

Although the north had in some sense submitted to Edward, it seems unlikely that he had any direct control beyond the Humber. The only entry in the Anglo-Saxon Chronicle in the last four years of Edward's reign notes that he built a fortress at Cledemutha (probably the mouth of the Clwyd, in north Wales, not far from the cluster of forts at the mouth of the Mersey), suggesting that the Norse vikings were still a threat. Although Ragnall died in 920 or 921, his cousin Sihtric took over as king of York, and some coins survive in Sihtric's name. Further, it is likely that these were minted in Lincoln rather than York, which suggests that Sihtric's York absorbed Lincoln in the last four years of Edward's reign, or even that Lincoln was not part of the general submission of Mercians to Edward in 918.

Edward and the Mercians Since Ealdorman Æthelred of Mercia had acknowledged the overlordship of King Alfred in 883 or earlier (*AS chart.*, S 218), Alfred, and Edward after him, had held a rulership over both the West Saxons and the Mercians which is reflected in a change in the royal style used in their charters. Alfred adopted the style 'king of the Anglo-Saxons' rather than 'king of the West Saxons', and this style continued in use through the reign of his son Edward and into the beginning of the reign of his grandson Æthelstan. Edward's lordship over Mercia is also evident in his command of a joint army of West Saxons and Mercians in 909 and 910, and in the fact that, though they governed Mercia, Æthelred and Æthelflæd did not normally issue their own charters, but appeared as subordinates in charters of Edward. Coins were minted in Wessex and western Mercia and, in the last ten years of the reign, in the reconquered Danelaw, in the name of Edward rather than Æthelred or Æthelflæd.

A charter (*AS chart.*, S 221) of Æthelred and Æthelflæd, which gives the lord and lady of the Mercians grander styles than usual, and does not mention Edward, may indicate an attempt at Mercian independence in 901. This was also the time of Æthelwold's revolt against Edward, which might have encouraged the Mercians to make their own bid for freedom. Mercia was certainly fully under Edward's control by 903, however, when Æthelflæd and Æthelred are explicitly said to hold the governance of the Mercians under the authority of Edward (S 367).

Æthelred died in 911, and Æthelflæd took over as sole governor of the Mercians. In the same year Edward assumed direct control of London and Oxford and their surrounding areas. This has been seen as an encroachment on Mercian territory, but as the evidence of charters and coins makes clear, all of English Wessex and Mercia was already under Edward's overall jurisdiction. And in terms of the campaigns of Edward and Æthelflæd over the next several years, in which Edward concentrated on the southern Danes of Essex and East Anglia while Æthelflæd built fortresses mostly against the northern Danes of the Five Boroughs, it made sense for the lands that Edward was defending to be under his immediate control.

On 12 June 918 Æthelflæd died. Edward, who was in the process of reducing one of the Five Boroughs, went immediately to Tamworth and 'occupied' it, and all the Mercians who had been subject to Æthelflæd submitted to him. This seems at first glance an unnecessarily martial transfer of power. Although it has been suggested that it was the Danish threat that had kept the kingdom of the Anglo-Saxons together, and that, with that threat removed, the Mercians would rather have chosen a ruler from their own people, the Norse in Northumbria still posed a significant danger to Mercia. It is also possible, since Æthelflæd had taken two of the Five Boroughs,

Derby and Leicester, that Edward's move was designed to secure the loyalty not of the English Mercians, but of the Danish Mercians. The submission of the Welsh to Edward immediately after the capture of Tamworth suggests that the show of force may not have been to impress the Danes alone.

Two further events in 918 relate to the Mercians, and perhaps also to each other. The main annals of the Anglo-Saxon Chronicle note that after Edward reduced Nottingham, all of the Mercians, both Danish and English, submitted to him. This appears to be a second submission, after the first submission of all the Mercians at Tamworth in the summer. Given that two of the Five Boroughs were still in hostile Danish hands at the time of the first submission, there would need to be a 'second' submission at least for these areas when they finally fell. The Mercian annals of the Anglo-Saxon Chronicle also record that in December 918 Ælfwyn, the daughter of Æthelflæd and Æthelred, 'was deprived of all authority in Mercia and taken into Wessex' (*ASC*, s.a. 919, text C). There was clearly a feeling that whether Edward enjoyed overall authority or not, the Mercians expected to retain their own governor. It is possible that the second submission of the Mercians in 918 should be associated with Edward's removal of Ælfwyn and establishment of his own direct control. This is not the impression given by the main annals of the chronicle, which have Edward receiving the second submission after reducing Nottingham. But this is another case where different versions of the chronicle come from very different viewpoints. The 'main' version in the 910s is very much a West Saxon version and records only Edward's achievements, describing none of Æthelflæd's vital fortress building against the Five Boroughs, the Northumbrian vikings, or the Welsh, and simply noting her death. In this context it is not at all surprising that Ælfwyn, and whatever aspirations the Mercians may have had for her continuing governorship, go unrecorded by the West Saxon annalist.

Nor does any charter evidence survive to shed light on the nature of Ælfwyn's authority in Mercia, if any, and on the position in the conflict of Edward's son Æthelstan, normally assumed to have been brought up at Æthelflæd's court. Unfortunately, the last charters of Edward are dated 909 and the series does not resume until Æthelstan's reign. There are two charters of Æthelflæd from about 914 and 915 (S 224, 225), one of them witnessed by Ælfwyn, but otherwise Ælfwyn makes no appearance in the records.

There is no reference to Edward's relations with the Mercians in the narrative sources between 919, when he was in command of Mercian armies, and 924, when William of Malmesbury records a Mercian revolt at Chester. It may be that lingering Mercian resentment of Edward's summary treatment of Ælfwyn helped to inspire the revolt. A more pragmatic reason, though it cannot be dated precisely to Edward's reign, might be the reorganization of western Mercia into shires, which may have taken place in the last five years of the reign. The first evidence of the new Mercian shires comes in a reference to Cheshire in 980: the boundaries of the new shires run roughshod over the ancient divisions of Mercia. Such a rearrangement would probably have caused at least as much resentment in the tenth as it did in the twentieth century. Edward, having just conquered the Danes south of the Humber, is unlikely to have worried about the unrest of the English Mercians, and it is plausible that the rearrangement of the Mercian shires closely followed his assertion of direct control over Mercia in 918. It is equally plausible that this action would result in revolts, such as the one that apparently led to Edward's death on 17 July 924, at Farndon, near Chester. Contemporary sources record no further details, but William of Malmesbury, in his *Gesta regum*, records that he died a few days after quelling a combined Mercian and Welsh revolt at Chester.

Edward's New Minster Edward was buried at the New Minster, Winchester, a monastery he himself had founded in 901. The New Minster was just beside the Old Minster, built by the West Saxons in the mid-seventh century, and one of the purposes of the new and more spacious church was probably to be a visual symbol of the wider horizons of the new kings of the Anglo-Saxons. It also served as a royal mausoleum in the first twenty-five years of its existence, housing not only Edward himself but both his parents, Alfred and Ealhswith, his younger brother Æthelweard, and his son Ælfweard. The house did not retain this role after the accession of Edward's son Æthelstan, who was buried at Malmesbury and who, in any case, after he took full control of Northumbria in 927, played in an even wider arena than his father and grandfather. But, for that first twenty-five years, the New Minster stood as a symbol of Edward's dream and achievement of a united England of Angles and Saxons south of the Humber.

SEAN MILLER

Sources *ASC*, s.a. 901–924 · *AS chart.*, S 221, 223–5, 348, 350, 358–85 · *Alfred the Great: Asser's Life of King Alfred and other contemporary sources*, ed. and trans. S. Keynes and M. Lapidge (1983) · Hrotsvitha, 'Gesta Ottonis', *Hrotsvithae opera*, ed. P. von Winterfeld, MGH Scriptores Rerum Germanicarum, [34] (Berlin, 1902) · *The chronicle of Æthelweard*, ed. and trans. A. Campbell (1962) · John of Worcester, *Chron.* · *Willelmi Malmesbiriensis monachi de gestis regum Anglorum*, ed. W. Stubbs, 2 vols., Rolls Series (1887–9) · *The early history of Glastonbury: an edition, translation, and study of William of Malmesbury's De antiquitate Glastonie ecclesie*, ed. J. Scott (1981) · Symeon of Durham, *Opera* · A. Campbell, 'Two notes on the Norse kingdoms in Northumbria', *EngHR*, 57 (1942), 85–97, esp. 85–91 · C. E. Blunt, B. H. I. H. Stewart, and C. S. S. Lyon, *Coinage in tenth-century England: from Edward the Elder to Edgar's reform* (1989) · S. Keynes, 'The West Saxon charters of King Æthelwulf and his sons', *EngHR*, 109 (1994), 1109–49 · J. L. Nelson, 'The second English ordo', *Politics and ritual in early medieval Europe* (1986), 361–74 · J. L. Nelson, 'Reconstructing a royal family: reflections on Alfred, from Asser', *People and places in northern Europe, 500–1600: essays in honour of Peter Hayes Sawyer*, ed. I. Wood and N. Lund, [another edn] (1991), 47–66 · A. P. Smyth, *Scandinavian York and Dublin: the history of two related Viking kingdoms*, 2 vols. (1975–9) · P. A. Stafford, 'The king's wife in Wessex, 800–1066', *Past and Present*, 91 (1981), 3–27 · F. M. Stenton, *Anglo-Saxon England*, 3rd edn (1971) · F. T. Wainwright, 'The submission to Edward the Elder', *History*, new ser., 37 (1952), 114–30 · *The life of St Æthelwold / Wulfstan of Winchester*, ed. M. Lapidge and M. Winterbottom, OMT (1991) · New Minster *Liber vitae*, Stowe 944

Likenesses coins, repro. in Blunt, Stewart, and Lyon, *Coinage in tenth-century England*, pl. 1–6 · silver penny, BM

Edward [St Edward; *called* Edward the Martyr] (*c.*962–978), king of England, was the son of *Edgar, who died on 8 July 975.

Parentage and legitimacy Nothing is known of the cause of Edgar's death, nor is there any secure information about his wishes concerning the succession. He left at least three children, of whom Edward, the eldest surviving son, was of doubtful legitimacy. Contemporary sources are silent as to the identity of Edward's mother and later accounts are contradictory; such ambiguity may point to an early attempt to conceal a youthful indiscretion by Edgar. Osbern of Canterbury, writing in the 1080s, mistakenly claimed that Edward's mother was a nun of Wilton. But it is most likely that a late insertion into John of Worcester's chronicle (completed 1140) is correct in identifying his mother as Æthelflæd Eneda ('the white duck'), daughter of an ealdorman, Ordmær, who once held an estate at Hatfield, which he exchanged with the ealdorman Æthelstan Half-King for lands in Devon. Edgar's relationship with Æthelflæd is likely to have developed some time after his accession as king of all the English in October 959 at the age of sixteen. Edward was probably born *c.*962. His mother disappeared from the scene soon afterwards; she may have died in childbirth. The identity of his foster mother is not known.

A little later, Edgar formed a second known union, with *Wulfthryth. Edgar and Wulfthryth had a daughter *Edith (Eadgyth), who eventually, like her mother, became abbess of Wilton. Some time after Edith's birth, Edgar married *Ælfthryth, a daughter of the powerful Devonshire thegn *Ordgar (d. 971), who thereupon became ealdorman of the western shires, and the widow of Æthelwold, ealdorman of East Anglia, the eldest son of Æthelstan Half-King. The marriage was blessed by the church and Ælfthryth was crowned and anointed queen. Edgar and Ælfthryth appear to have had two sons: Edmund, who seems to have been regarded as the legitimate heir until his death in 971, and Æthelred, who was born in 968 [see Æthelred II]. Edward first appears in history as a witness to the foundation charter of the New Minster, Winchester, dated 966, in which he is listed immediately below his younger stepbrother Edmund.

Struggle for the succession On Edgar's death, the principal contestants for the kingdom were Edward, aged about thirteen and probably illegitimate, and Æthelred, undoubtedly legitimate but aged no more than nine, and probably six or seven. Youth prevented either son from putting forward his own claim: the arguments were conducted by those already placed in positions of power during Edgar's reign. With the removal of the firm, perhaps overbearing, rule of Edgar, the issue of the succession mingled with a release of the tension that had built up among the aristocracy, especially concerning ecclesiastical lands and the related issue of church reform. Edgar had favoured monasteries which pursued the new, rigorous, ideals of ecclesiastical reform. His extensive grants to

Edward [St Edward; Edward the Martyr] (*c*.962–978), coin

Initially, the allegiance of the English kingdom may have divided along lines familiar enough in disputes throughout the previous century: the south and west were for Edward, the north and the east for Æthelred. Byrhtferth, who wrote the earliest and best surviving account in his life of Oswald, claims that a state bordering on civil war very quickly developed. As the conflict continued, individuals changed their positions, if not their loyalties. Although his hagiographers are largely silent on his last years, Archbishop Dunstan seems to have demonstrated little support for the monastic foundations of his fellow reformer Bishop Æthelwold after Edgar's death, perhaps indicating an estrangement between the two. But Dunstan's political influence waned after Edward's accession, though he continued to be venerated as a religious leader. The violent reaction which Edward's brief reign witnessed against the expansion of the reformed monasteries may also have led other supporters of reform to regret their initial backing for the king.

Byrhtferth claims that some nobles were opposed to Edward because of his hot temper, which caused terror even within his own household, and draws a contrast with the easy-going temperament of the young Æthelred. It is highly unlikely, however, that Edward's character influenced the succession, and Byrhtferth's statement conflicts with that of Osbern, who remarks on the general good opinion that men had of him.

Kingship Edward died too young to have had much influence on government on his own account, and political affairs remained firmly in the hands of Ealdorman Ælfhere. Edward's power base seems to have been very restricted when compared with that of his father. The chancery's control over the issue of royal diplomas came to an end. The three surviving authentic charters of the reign all concern land in Wessex; two of them were written at Crediton, where the king had been educated. He failed to achieve any impact on England north of the Thames, and it is doubtful how far his authority was maintained in the Danelaw, or even in English Mercia beyond Ælfhere's ealdordom. Winchester's monopoly on the cutting and issuing of coin dies was also broken, and fresh die-cutting centres were set up (under whose authority is not clear) at Lincoln and York. It is notable that in the region of the Five Boroughs (particularly at Lincoln and Stamford), Edward's coinage was executed to a standard lower than that of his father.

Murder and sainthood Edward himself seems to have harboured no ill feeling towards his stepmother, Ælfthryth, to whom he is said to have confirmed the gift of jurisdiction over the whole of Dorset as part of his father's dower. Ælfthryth established herself, together with her surviving son, Æthelred, on a large estate centred on a natural defensive mound dominating the gap of Corfe in the Purbeck hills. Here the succession was finally decided on 18 March 978. The only detailed account of the event is that of Byrhtferth's life of Oswald, which expands an earlier version that Byrhtferth had included in a Latin chronicle

such houses represented a redefinition of piety that disrupted aristocratic families' traditional networks of religious patronage. His death therefore provoked attacks on the property of the reformed monasteries. Religious differences became entangled with personal rivalries among a powerful group of protagonists whose influence in the kingdom depended on the outcome of the disputed succession. Naturally, Æthelred's claim was advanced by his mother, Ælfthryth. She appears to have gained the support of Æthelwold, bishop of Winchester, and also of Æthelwine, ealdorman of East Anglia, to whose brother she had previously been married, and of Byrhtnoth, ealdorman of Essex (who by then probably also had responsibility for much of the northern Danelaw). Crucially, however, Edward was chosen by the archbishop of Canterbury, Dunstan, who crowned him.

Dunstan's action was approved of by Ælfhere of western Mercia, the most powerful of the ealdormen, who probably also held the ealdordom of central Wessex at that time. If Byrhtferth of Ramsey is correct, for some years before Edgar's death Edward was fostered by Ælfhere's protégé Sideman, bishop of Crediton. Edward's crowning may also have been supported by Oswald, archbishop of York. It must, however, have dismayed Dunstan's friends, Æthelwine and Byrhtnoth. The presence of supporters of church reform in both factions indicates that the conflict between them depended as much on issues of land ownership and local power as on ecclesiastical legitimacy. Adherents of both Edward and Æthelred can be seen appropriating, or recovering, monastic lands: for example, Æthelwine regained land from the abbey of Ely, while Ælfhere concentrated his attack on Oswald's foundations in the Severn valley, notwithstanding the possibility that the archbishop was a supporter of Edward. The families of both Æthelwine and Ælfhere had already vied for political control of the territories of the old West Saxon kingdom.

surviving, in altered form, in the chronicle of John of Worcester. Travelling to visit his stepbrother, Edward arrived at Corfe early in the evening, accompanied by a small retinue. He was met at the gates of Ælfthryth's residence by her retainers, who dragged him from his horse and murdered him, before burying his body unceremoniously nearby (perhaps at Wareham), 'at the house of a certain unimportant person' (*English Historical Documents*, 1.842).

Ælfthryth's son Æthelred, much too young to have been involved personally in the murder, was the sole candidate for the succession, though he faced a long wait before the kingdom was formally entrusted to him. What negotiations took place during the interregnum can only be the subject of speculation. Nearly a year later, Ealdorman Ælfhere rode to Corfe and disinterred Edward's body. After staying for a few days at Wareham he carried it for burial to the nunnery of Shaftesbury, where Edward soon came to be venerated as a saint and martyr. With Edward now safely at rest in a sanctuary where his bones could be honoured, Æthelred was consecrated king by Archbishop Dunstan on 4 May 979.

Regicide was a crime particularly condemned by the monastic reformers, for whom the anointed monarch was regarded as God's representative on earth; yet, as Byrhtferth remarked some thirty years later, the perpetrators escaped punishment. Edward's murder was undoubtedly very convenient for the hard-pressed reformers, though it is an exaggeration to say that it saved Benedictine monasticism in England, and there is no evidence that a conspiracy of prominent reformers was responsible. The sources allow the finger of suspicion to point at only one person: Ælfthryth was on the spot and above all others stood to gain from the deed. It is impossible to exculpate her from all knowledge of the crime. At the very least, as holder of the local jurisdiction, she should have ensured that the murderers were brought to justice, but they remained scot free. Forty years later, Archbishop Wulfstan of York blamed her and her followers unequivocally, and took the trouble to insert his powerful denunciation into the precursor of the D text of the Anglo-Saxon Chronicle. At the time, however, political reality demanded that her position remain inviolate. She was allowed to retain possession of her extensive estates and subsequently she fostered Æthelstan, the eldest of Æthelred's numerous progeny.

Whether it was designed to compose the disputes of Edward's reign or to promote his own status, there is little doubt that Æthelred himself was the most important champion of his half-brother's cult. Edward's *passio* (account of martyrdom), written in the late eleventh or early twelfth century, which seems to be the earliest source that attaches to him the epithet 'the Martyr', ascribes to Æthelred the initiative for a second translation of Edward's relics at Shaftesbury in 1001, traditionally dated 20 June. Contemporary sources confirm this picture: a grant by Æthelred in favour of Shaftesbury in 1001 states that the gift is being made to God and to 'his saint, my brother Edward, whom, drenched with his own blood, the Lord has seen fit to magnify in our time through many

miracles' (*AS chart.*, S 899; trans. Ridyard, 156). A clause included in the extant text of the law-code V Æthelred, though it may be a later interpolation, includes the provision that the feast of St Edward be observed throughout England on 18 March. William of Malmesbury (d. *c*.1142) noted that some of his relics had been distributed to Leominster and Abingdon. A proper of the mass for Edward is included in the missal of Robert of Jumièges, written before 1023.   CYRIL HART

Sources [Byrhtferth of Ramsey], 'Vita sancti Oswaldi auctore anonymo', *The historians of the church of York and its archbishops*, ed. J. Raine, 1, Rolls Series, 71 (1879), 399–475 · C. Fell, ed., *Edward, king and martyr* (1971) · *ASC*, s.a. 965–978 · S. J. Ridyard, *The royal saints of Anglo-Saxon England*, Cambridge Studies in Medieval Life and Thought, 4th ser., 9 (1988) · S. Keynes, *The diplomas of King Æthelred 'The Unready' (978–1016): a study in their use as historical evidence*, Cambridge Studies in Medieval Life and Thought, 3rd ser., 13 (1980) · C. R. Hart, 'Edward the Martyr', *The early charters of northern England and the north midlands* (1975) · D. N. Dumville, 'The Ætheling: a study in Anglo-Saxon constitutional history', *Anglo-Saxon England*, 8 (1979), 1–33 · C. Hart, *The Danelaw* (1992) · P. Stafford, *Unification and conquest: a political and social history of England in the tenth and eleventh centuries* (1989) · D. J. V. Fisher, 'The antimonastic reaction in the reign of Edward the Martyr', *Cambridge Historical Journal*, 10 (1950–52), 254–70 · John of Worcester, *Chron.* · *AS chart.*, S 745, 828–832, 899, 937, 1485 · *English historical documents*, 1, ed. D. Whitelock (1955) · *Willelmi Malmesbiriensis monachi de gestis pontificum Anglorum libri quinque*, ed. N. E. S. A. Hamilton, Rolls Series, 52 (1870) · F. E. Warren, ed., *The Leofric missal* (1883) · Osbern of Canterbury, 'Vita Sancti Dunstani', *Memorials of St Dunstan, archbishop of Canterbury*, ed. W. Stubbs, Rolls Series, 63 (1874), 68–164
Likenesses coin, BM [*see illus.*]

Edward [St Edward; *known as* Edward the Confessor] (1003×5–1066), king of England, known as 'the Confessor' after his canonization in 1161, was born between 1003 and 1005 at Islip, near Oxford. He was the seventh son of King *Æthelred II, but the first from his father's second marriage, to *Emma, sister of Richard (II), duke of Normandy. A younger full brother, *Alfred, died unmarried in 1036 or 1037 and a sister, Godgifu, who married Drogo, count of the Vexin, and, after his death in 1035, *Eustace (II), count of Boulogne, may likewise have predeceased Edward. Although the ambitious Emma indubitably had high ambitions for these children, and her marriage contract may have stipulated that her issue should have precedence over the king's existing offspring, Edward's eventual acquisition of the crown was, indeed, 'miraculous'.

Background and youth, 1003–1043 The son of a warrior king, Edward's youth was conditioned by warfare. The kingdom had become the target for viking raids, colonization and, in the end, conquest. And Æthelred's marriage to Emma, designed to secure the support of established Scandinavian raiders and settlers against the new wave, in the event only added an even more lethal Norman involvement to the Norwegian and Danish interest in England. It was an age of military heroes, such as the vikings Olaf Tryggvason and Thorkill Hávi (the Tall) and the English *Edmund Ironside, Edward's half-brother. And, although neither Æthelred nor Edward was quite in that class, they were of that world and culture. The warfare and political instability were particularly dangerous for the nobility; and in the struggle for survival bravery was not always the most useful quality.

Edward's early years are not well recorded. It was not until the close of his relatively successful reign and, even more, after a movement had developed to get him recognized as a saint, that monastic writers began to take an interest. In 1065–7 an anonymous author, probably a monk of St Omer, wrote an account of Edward's life for his widow, Queen Edith, designed, it would seem, to advance the claims of her family to provide a successor to the childless king. This *Vita Ædwardi regis*, although it was to serve as the basis for the hagiographical legend, is, in its earliest form, almost completely free from hagiography and has some historical value. But, unfortunately, the author was probably both ignorant of and uninterested in his subject's 'viking' background. The legend itself, since it has little historical basis, is completely unhelpful. And not much trust can be put in the few references to Edward's youth in later chronicles composed during or after the canonization process. Among these is the claim in the twelfth-century Ely chronicle that Edward's parents gave him as a child to the monastery to be educated as a monk. Even if there is a grain of truth in this story—and it was produced to validate a relic and a charter—Edward did not become a monk, never had a reputation for literacy, and in his lifestyle would seem to have been that of a typical member of the rustic nobility.

In the first eight years of Edward's life viking pressure intensified. Between 1006 and 1012 much of southern England was ravaged and in 1013 the king of Denmark, Swein Forkbeard, accompanied by his younger son, *Cnut, invaded in person. In the autumn Queen Emma, followed by her children and then her husband, fled to her brother's court in Normandy. When Swein died unexpectedly in February 1014 Æthelred sent Edward with ambassadors to England to negotiate for his return to the throne.

While the crown was disputed severally by Æthelred, his sons from his first marriage, led by Edmund Ironside, and Cnut, Edward, according to Scandinavian saga, fought at Edmund's side with conspicuous bravery. When Æthelred died on 23 April 1016 and Edmund on 30 November, Cnut took possession of the whole kingdom. Edward returned to his mother, brother, and sister and was to remain in exile for twenty-five years. Emma, however, had no taste for the sidelines, and represented a potential source of legitimacy for the new, Danish, king of England. In July 1017 she returned to England to marry Cnut, who had already 'married' Ælfgifu of Northampton with whom he had children, including Harold Harefoot. Emma gave her new husband a son, *Harthacnut, and a daughter, Gunnhild, later Queen Kunigund of Germany.

Edward's resentment at his mother's neglect of his interests (although it could be argued that she did her best in the circumstances) was long-lasting. And, although the duke, her brother, and his successors up to, and including, William the Bastard, maintained and protected the athelings, the Norman court was divided in its sympathy. It is, therefore, likely that Edward, whose sister was soon at Mantes in the Vexin and had many other relatives in north-west France, moved around. To judge by his behaviour when king, he would have lived like any other nobleman, engaged in hunting if not in war; and, although he did not marry while in exile, this was probably simply because he lacked an estate and good expectations. An ambiguous sexual orientation and a late marriage were not unusual among the aristocracy. But the ecclesiastical legend of a vow of celibacy is obviously absurd. In 1035 Edward's prospects took a turn for the better. On 12 November Cnut died in England and his empire, comprising England, Denmark, Norway, and part of Sweden, collapsed. Harthacnut, on whom Emma doted, was in Denmark defending the Scandinavian lands against Magnus

Edward [St Edward; Edward the Confessor] (1003x5–1066), embroidery (Bayeux Tapestry) [seated, centre]

of Norway, and his mother was unable to sustain his claim to the English throne against the growing popularity of her stepson, Harold Harefoot. She had to appeal to her English sons. Probably in 1036 first Edward and then Alfred crossed the channel. Edward, according to Norman sources, sailed up the Solent, presumably in order to join his mother on her dower lands at Winchester, won a battle near Southampton, and returned to Normandy with the booty. Evidently he was intercepted and driven out. Alfred sailed from Wissant or Boulogne, was captured by Earl Godwine near Guildford, handed over to Harold Harefoot, and blinded in order to destroy his king-worthiness. He did not survive this treatment and a brief cult of the 'martyr' appeared at Ely Abbey where he was buried.

In 1038 Harold expelled Emma, who took refuge at Bruges in order to await Harthacnut's arrival. In the meantime, according to her own story (*Encomium Emmae Reginae*), Edward, when summoned to meet her, disclaimed interest in the throne. However that may be, Harthacnut was the only one who could mount a military invasion. In 1039 he arrived in Flanders with ten ships and looked round for more. On 17 March 1040 Harold died opportunely and in June Emma and her favourite son crossed unopposed with sixty ships and recovered their inheritance. Next year Edward, presumably by invitation, joined them, and seems to have been appointed joint king. Then, on 8 June 1042, Harthacnut died, like Harold apparently childless. Once again the English crown was there for the taking. Although Swein Estrithson (of Denmark), Harthacnut's cousin, considered himself a claimant, and although it was rumoured that Emma thought of Magnus of Norway, *Godwine of Wessex (perhaps the most powerful of the English earls, an Englishman married to a Dane) opted for Edward. On Easter day (3 April) 1043 this atheling of Anglo-Norman stock was crowned at Winchester, where both Cnut and Harthacnut were buried, by the archbishops of Canterbury and York. Death had served him well. The survivor began to rule at an age, at least thirty-eight, that no recent English king, save his father, had even reached; and he was to rule with some success for almost twenty-three years.

The struggle for power, 1043–1051 Edward started from a position of unusual weakness. He followed two insecure rulers, the sons of a usurper. Loyalty to the house of Cerdic had been eroded by a new Scandinavian aristocracy. The ancestral province of Wessex was ruled by Godwine, an Englishman but one of Cnut's new men. The royal demesne was doubtless diminished. After twenty-five years in exile, he returned as a stranger. That he was able to restore the traditional strong monarchy proves his mettle. In his first years as king he showed that he was a vigorous and ambitious man, a true son of the impetuous Æthelred and the formidable Emma. The famous description of him near the beginning of *Vita*, illustrated on the Bayeux tapestry—rosy cheeks, milky white hair and beard, and long translucent fingers—is a stereotype for a good old man, appropriate for 1065–6. It should not be applied to his middle age, still less to his youth. The anonymous author also considered him of outstanding

height and, in his anger, as terrible as a lion. His career proves that he enjoyed a strong constitution and good health.

Edward's main initial tasks—and to some extent they were standing problems—were to establish his authority over the English nobility and church and to withstand threats from external enemies. Of the three great provincial earls, Godwine of Wessex, Siward of Northumbria, and Leofric of Mercia, only the last was a scion of a family which had served Æthelred. Most of the bishops and abbots had likewise been appointed by Cnut. But the church, committed to peace and authority, looked for a strong and just ruler, especially one untainted by Scandinavian heathenism. And the earls, although probably slower to rally to Edward, had no good reason to reject him. The most independent, Siward, a Dane, had his eye on Scotland. Godwine had decided to take Edward under his wing. The first indication of Edward's accommodation with the earls is their riding together on 16 November 1043 from Gloucester to Winchester in order to punish Emma. She was deprived of her possessions and her adviser, Stigand, recently made bishop of East Anglia, was likewise disseised. It was an admonitory gesture; and both were soon readmitted to the royal favour. In the course of the next few years Edward punished some other members of the nobility and he must also have paid for allegiance by gifts of land and office.

He repaid one great debt on 23 January 1045 by marrying *Edith (Eadgyth), the daughter of Earl Godwine and his wife, *Gytha [*see under* Godwine], Cnut's former sister-in-law. Edith, from the highest Anglo-Danish nobility and no more than twenty-five at the time, was, on political grounds, eminently suitable. She was also, according to *Vita*, a paragon of all the virtues. Beautiful and intelligent, educated in the fashionable nunnery at Wilton, she was highly literate, spoke several languages, and practised many arts. In addition, she was modest, religious, and chaste. When queen, she became devoted to her husband's comfort and image. Edward, accustomed to the lifestyle of a bachelor knight, was, apparently, uninterested in royal splendour. But when Edith had fitted him out with embroidered garments adorned with gold and jewels, he shone like Solomon in all his glory. His walking stick was encrusted with gold and gems and even his saddle and horse-trappings were hung with little beasts and birds fashioned out of gold. His throne was resplendent in a hall strewn with precious carpets from Spain. Edith was also a wise counsellor, but always behind the scenes. Presumably, unlike Emma, she never pushed herself forward. In these several activities, her encomiast remarks, 'she seemed more like a daughter than a wife, not so much a spouse as a good mother' (Barlow, *Life*, 24). The hagiographers subsequently read a great deal into these words. They became, indeed, the text on which the whole case for Edward's sanctity was based. It may be that in *Vita* there is a subtext. Edith was at least fifteen, and possibly twenty, years younger than Edward; and she adored her father. But the marriage was intended to secure the dynasty by producing sons; no contemporary even hinted at unusual features; and there is no evidence for any overt anxiety over the couple's childlessness before 1051. It was by no means an unusual occurrence.

There is an amusing glimpse of the couple, accompanied by Emma, on a visit to Abingdon Abbey, probably not long after the marriage. Edith, because she was a sophisticated lady, was surprised to find the children taking lunch in the refectory at an unfashionable early hour and having only bread to eat. She drew Edward's attention to their plight and asked him if he would provide some revenue so that, as a result of their attendance at this 'banquet', the boys could be better fed. Her husband replied with a laugh that he would be only too pleased to give something if only someone would provide him with a bit of property he could give away. And when his wife said that she had just acquired a village and would be delighted if Edward would consent to its gift, he agreed that it was a splendid idea. But not all observers viewed her so favourably. To some, she seemed a scheming and venal woman; the monasteries came to fear her passion for collecting relics; and she was even suspected of procuring the assassination of enemies of her family. Her own kin certainly did well out of her royal marriage. In 1043 her eldest brother, *Swein, was given an earldom in the west midlands, and, shortly afterwards, *Harold, the next in line, one covering East Anglia, Cambridgeshire, Essex, and Middlesex. When Beorn Estrithson, her Danish cousin, was, in 1045, made earl of the territory lying between that of Harold and of Swein, the family ruled, subordinately, all the kingdom south of the Humber except for Leofric's Mercia, Siward of Northumbria's outpost at Northampton, and, by 1050, Ralph of Mantes's small marcher earldom of Hereford. This last was the only piece to fall to Edward's side, although, since Beorn was also Emma's nephew from her marriage to Cnut, his allegiance was uncertain. Indeed, his primary loyalty may have been to his brother, Swein Estrithson, king of Denmark, Harthacnut's replacement.

Since the royal demesne was scattered unequally through the southern earldoms Edward had no great power base. Nor was his private household a source of strength. His remembered early companions are a rather miscellaneous group: one kinsman, Ralph of Mantes, one Norman abbot, Robert Champart of Jumièges, and two clerks educated in Lotharingia, Herman and Leofric, the last probably an expatriate from Cornwall. Besides Edith's *femme de chambre* named Matilda, the Normans in the household are almost invisible. Two Bretons, Ralph the Staller and Robert fitz Wimarc, received small grants of land. Such a group of servants offered no threat to the old order except through intrigue and influence over their master. But they became unpopular.

There was, however, one sphere in which Edward was able to exercise the king's traditional rights—the church. He appointed to the bishoprics and royal abbeys and, as in Capetian France, royalist bishops and abbots served as some counterweight to the earls. Different interests clashed whenever a vacancy occurred. There were local concerns and a curial perspective, and rivalry between the monastic and the clerical orders. But there can be little doubt that Edward and his closest advisers normally had their way. They had a strong bias against a local connection. For example, in 1051 the election to Canterbury of Æthelric, a Christ Church monk and a kinsman of Earl Godwine, was refused. And although Edward appointed as a whole about equal numbers of monks and royal clerks to bishoprics, clerks tended to get the richer and more important sees. The situation between 1051 and 1057 when there were only four monk-bishops may be thought to be Edward's ideal. Moreover, it was through royal clerks that most foreigners, especially reforming 'Germans', entered the episcopate. The only foreign monk promoted, admittedly to the two most important sees, London in 1044 and Canterbury in 1051, was Robert of Jumièges. The history of the monasteries during the reign is extremely obscure. But since the rule produced by the great tenth-century monastic reformers, the *Regularis concordia*, exalted the role of the king and queen in order to check the power of local 'tyrants', it is likely that Edward and Edith exercised their rights over and within at least the royal abbeys and nunneries, and that these in general were centres not only of English patriotism but also of a royalist cult. The royal bounty also attracted visitors from foreign, mostly Norman, abbeys to the English court; and some modest gifts of land, for example to Fécamp, have been interpreted, probably wrongly, as providing future bridgeheads for a Norman invasion. A sporadic intercourse with the papal curia has, similarly, been attributed to Edward's continental leanings. But the causes were largely Stigand's irregular position at Canterbury, the memory, on both sides, of an ancient special relationship, and the popularity of pilgrimages.

Even more, perhaps, than ecclesiastical affairs, the kingdom's security and foreign policy were under the king's personal control. His youthful adventures had given him a wide first-hand knowledge of princely courts and dynastic business; and the political insecurity in northern Europe made successful diplomacy a necessity. Edward was determined not to go on his travels again. According to *Vita*, he was not without important friends at his accession, for the emperor and all the rulers of 'Gaul' sent congratulatory embassies after his coronation. Named are Edward's brother-in-law, the German emperor Heinrich III, Henri I of France, called, probably erroneously, 'another close kinsman', and an unnamed king of the Danes. If this was Swein Estrithson, who 'submitted himself to Edward as a son' (Barlow, *Life*, 16), it was because Denmark was being conquered by Magnus of Norway and wanted English help. Swein also, like Magnus, had claims of various kinds on the English throne and seems even to have believed that Edward regarded him as his heir. Edward, however, was no lover of vikings. In 1044 he banished Cnut's niece, Gunnhild, and her children and in 1046 Osgod Clapa, a Danish landholder in the eastern shires. In 1044 and 1045, fearing an invasion by Magnus, he took command of the fleet at Sandwich. But in 1047, although Swein was in desperate straits, Edward refused Godwine's demand that he should be sent aid; and it was only Magnus's death on 25 October which saved Swein and also England from attack.

Harald Hardrada became king of Norway; but it was not until 25 September 1066 that he met his death at Stamford Bridge on the River Derwent. All the same, in 1048 a viking fleet of twenty-five ships, commanded by the otherwise unknown pirates Lothen and Yrling, sailed from Flanders and raided some south-east ports, including Sandwich and Thanet, and perhaps the Isle of Wight.

Flanders and Normandy were the traditional forward bases for the vikings against England. Normandy, since Emma's marriages, had been less welcoming, but Flanders under Count Baudouin (V) (1034–1067) seems to have been open to all enemies of the kingdom. The basic purpose of every prince's foreign policy was to make and keep friends. Since most of the princes in northern Gaul were, as a result, interrelated, foreign relations were a complicated business. In the furtherance of his basic policy, the containment of Flanders, Edward could count on the emperor, Eustache (II), count of Boulogne (his brother-in-law), and Walter (III), count of the Vexin (his nephew). But Henri I of France, although generally friendly, was also Baudouin's brother-in-law and, until 1052, the protector of William, duke of Normandy, who, about 1051, married Baudouin's daughter. When Baudouin in 1047 joined in the Lotharingian rebellion against the emperor, Edward and Swein of Denmark, at the emperor's instigation, in 1049 mobilized their fleets against the rebel and risked the resentment of Henri of France and William. Osgod Clapa, whom Edward had banished in 1046, also arrived in Flanders with twenty-nine ships and promptly raided Essex. Moreover, into this already complicated situation intruded Swein, Earl Godwine's eldest son, the former earl who had been banished in 1047 and replaced by Ralph of Mantes for having abducted the abbess of Leominster. He too returned from Denmark with some ships and, when pardoned by Edward, went off and at Dartmouth murdered his cousin Earl Beorn. He then sailed for Bruges and was given asylum by Baudouin. But after all this excitement 1050 was a peaceful year. In mid-Lent the royal council decided to pay off nine of the fourteen foreign ships which Edward had kept as a standing navy and to offer only a one-year contract to the rest. Even more imprudently, it would appear, the king once more, probably under pressure from his wife's family, pardoned Earl Swein. He was, however, coming to believe that he had become strong enough to cut this family down to size.

The mid-term crisis, 1051–1052 A basic theme in *Vita* is that the English kingdom and Edward were preserved by the efforts of Godwine's family. The author describes the earl as an able, cautious, and popular provincial governor, an English patriot, who was well supported in his aims by his daughter, the queen, and four of his sons, Harold, *Tostig, *Gyrth, and *Leofwine. It was only because of some evil counsellors, particularly Robert of Jumièges, that Edward sometimes disregarded Godwine's wise advice and in 1051 tried to destroy the whole family. This is a biased, although tenable, thesis. It disregards, however, Edward's inevitable dislike of the constraints on his freedom of action. He had to live in Godwine's earldom and with the earl's agent, the queen. By 1051 Edward needed only the opportunity to kick over the traces.

A series of events led to a showdown. In the spring Edward promoted his favourite, Robert of Jumièges, from London to Canterbury, and the new archbishop claimed that Godwine was in unlawful possession of some archiepiscopal estates. Then, it seems, on his way to Rome for the *pallium*, he negotiated an alliance between Edward and William, duke of Normandy, who at the age of about twenty-three was still attempting to marry Matilda of Flanders. As good relations between the two courts, essential for England's safety, were long-standing, their confirmation would seem harmful to no one, unless, as Norman apologists for William's conquest of England, writing long after the event, and *ex parte*, maintained, Edward at this juncture made William his heir. But, even if this is true, its importance should not be exaggerated. Childlessness gave Edward a diplomatic asset which, it seems, he dangled not a few times in order to make a friend or punish those claimants who were out of favour. At the beginning of September, Edward's brother-in-law, Eustache of Boulogne, visited him on unstated, but probably family, business, and an affray at Dover, caused by his men, had serious repercussions. Edward ordered Godwine as earl of Kent to punish the burgesses, and, when Godwine refused, the king, urged on by Eustache, Robert of Jumièges, and some other Frenchmen, summoned his council and army to meet at Gloucester on 7 September. Earl Ralph, his nephew, brought up his troops, while earls Leofric and Siward sent urgently for theirs. On the other side, Godwine's sons Swein and Harold ordered their vassals to assemble at Beverstone, south of Gloucester. Godwine demanded the surrender of Eustache and perhaps of the French garrisons established by Ralph in Herefordshire. Archbishop Robert accused Godwine of conspiring to kill the king, just as he had killed his brother Alfred in 1036.

Although tempers were rising fast, neither side was eager to fight; and, with Edward standing firm, his position steadily improved, to such an extent that intermediaries were able to arrange that the earl should stand trial, presumably on a charge of treason, in a council summoned to London for 21 September. It would also seem that Godwine and Swein each gave as hostage a son, who were later to be found in Normandy. As the two armies moved on parallel routes to London, Godwine's began to disintegrate. Edward arbitrarily outlawed Swein, for whom there could have been little general sympathy, and by the time Godwine reached his manor of Southwark he was in no position to fight. When Bishop Stigand of Winchester conveyed to him Edward's grim jest that the earl could have his peace and pardon only when he restored to him his brother Alfred and his companions alive and with all their possessions intact, Godwine and his family split up and fled. Godwine, Gytha, Swein, and Tostig embarked at Bosham for Flanders. Harold and Leofwine sailed from Bristol to Ireland in a ship which had been prepared for Swein. The king's court pronounced sentences of outlawry on them all. Edward distributed some of their shires among his supporters and kept some for himself. And Edith was sent to a nunnery, either Wherwell or Wilton, while the archbishop advocated her divorce. One English chronicler believed that 'earl' William (of Normandy) visited Edward's court, and it has been suggested that Edward then promised William the succession.

Edward took measures to prevent the outlaws from returning by force. In the summer of 1052 he appointed earls Ralph and Odda to command a fleet at Sandwich. The one had profited from Swein's expulsion in 1047, the other by Godwine's in 1051. Edward also put all local coastal forces on the alert. The Somerset *fyrd* repulsed Harold and Leofwine's attempt to provision their nine ships at Porlock on their way to rendezvous with their father in the English Channel. And Godwine's first sortie from the River Yser in June was harried by the royal fleet and then driven back by westerly gales to Flanders. But the king's ships also were dispersed and local forces offered little resistance to both sets of invaders when, in August, they resumed their attempt to link up. From Portland Bill in Dorset the combined navies sailed east, receiving a welcome and recruits from several ports as they progressed to North Foreland and the Thames estuary. Meanwhile Edward had decided to base himself in London, and, as in 1051, summoned reinforcements. By the middle of August he had a land army, some fifty ships, and five earls under his command.

Godwine's fleet reached London on 14 September and was allowed by the sympathetic citizens to set up camp on the south bank of the Thames beyond London Bridge. When it became clear that Godwine was prepared to use force, the royalists began to cave in. The Frenchmen, who feared Godwine's vengeance, fought their way out of the East Gate and fled. Among the fugitives were Archbishop Robert and bishops Ulf of Dorchester and William of London. Earls Leofric and Siward gave the king no support. Once again Bishop Stigand was the go-between. Edward raged at his loss of authority but had to submit. On 15 September Godwine and Harold, with a suitable escort, went ashore to attend a large meeting of the king's council held outside London, perhaps at Westminster. Godwine declared his and Harold's innocence of all the crimes with which they had been charged. They were then inlawed and restored both to the king's favour and to all their former offices and possessions, while Edith was brought back to court. Conversely, all those Frenchmen who had brought false charges and caused the trouble were outlawed. But there were no excesses. Stigand, a prelate probably acceptable to all parties, replaced Robert at Canterbury, but retained Winchester, at first no doubt as insurance. The disturbance had rid the kingdom of some disruptive elements and sobered down the survivors.

The 'rule of Solomon', 1052–1066 According to *Vita Ædwardi regis* (Barlow, *Life*, 6, 18), Edward's reign, like Solomon's after the martial David's, was soon a time of peace, a golden age. In the last thirteen years of the reign death, as usual, worked in Edward's favour. His mother died on 6 March 1052, his brother-in-law, Swein, on 29 September at Constantinople while returning from a pilgrimage to Jerusalem, and his father-in-law, Godwine, at the royal court on 15 April 1053. Harold succeeded to the earldom of Wessex; and East Anglia, which he vacated, was returned to Ælfgar, Earl Leofric's son. The resulting balance between the provincial governors could not, however, be maintained for long. When Siward of Northumbria died in 1055 his heir, Waltheof, was too young for such a dangerous command and it was decided that the queen's younger brother, Tostig, should be substituted. As at the same time Ælfgar was banished temporarily, he had probably coveted the appointment. Part of his earldom was then given to Gyrth, the third surviving son of Godwine. Tostig, seemingly Edith's favourite brother, had married Judith of Flanders in 1051. The author of *Vita* regarded him as more pious than Harold, but also more erratic. When in 1057 earls Leofric and Ralph died, the house of Godwine advanced even further. Although Ælfgar was allowed to succeed to Mercia, Gyrth took over the whole of East Anglia, the fourth brother, Leofwine, was given a new earldom made up of the south-eastern shires, and Harold took Ralph's earldom as compensation. Hence the Godwinesons controlled subordinately the whole of England except for Mercia. Edward cannot be regarded as the architect of this scheme. But he seems to have got on well with the four brothers and been content to leave government at comital level to them. As the author of *Vita* maintained, with Harold driving off the foe from the south and Tostig scaring him off from the north, Edward could live free from cares.

The king's retirement from active military command after 1052 was not due to a serious reduction in his physical or mental vigour. He continued to hunt indefatigably, his temperament remained bellicose, and he was not completely under his wife's thumb. He and his advisers were also, traditionally, imperially minded. As his obituary poem in the Anglo-Saxon Chronicle claims, Edward ruled over the Welsh, Britons, Scots, Angles, and Saxons. He was king over the whole of Britain. In practice, his powers over Welsh princes and Scottish kings were limited and intermittent. While vikings looted Wales, Scotland, and Ireland, English interference in Wales was usually in response to Welsh plundering raids, whereas in Scotland it was to intervene in dynastic disputes. In 1054, on Edward's instructions, Siward invaded Scotland, defeated King Macbeth in a battle north of the Tay in Perthshire and put on the throne Duncan's son, Malcolm (III) Canmore. In 1057 Malcolm killed Macbeth in battle. Although Malcolm visited Edward's court at Gloucester in 1059, he was never a subservient vassal; indeed, he began to aim to annex Northumbria. Wales, however, was closer to the English heartlands. After 1047 Earl Ralph developed Herefordshire as a marcher earldom defended by castles and cavalry. In 1053 Edward ordered the assassination of Rhys ap Rhydderch, prince of south Wales, because of his raids across the border, and the victim's head was duly delivered to him. In 1055 Gruffudd ap Llywelyn, prince of north Wales, extended his rule over the whole area, and since he became the natural ally of the discontented Ælfgar of Mercia, Edward was determined to destroy him. On the earl's death in 1062 the king allowed his young son, Eadwine, to succeed, but also took the opportunity to bring Gruffudd to account. After Christmas Harold invaded north Wales and almost captured the prince at Rhuddlan. And in the spring Tostig tried his hand in the north while Harold sailed with a fleet from Bristol. They obtained the submission of most of the Welsh nobles and, on 5 August, Gruffudd was killed by his own men. His head and the ornaments of his ship were surrendered to Harold who delivered them in person to Edward. Without its charismatic leader Wales again fragmented, and Edward and Harold imposed vassalage on a number of princes. It was a great triumph for the king and his commanders.

The royal government was also effective in domestic affairs. Because of Edward's canonization his treatment of the English church is especially interesting. His appointment of Stigand to Canterbury after the expulsion of Robert of Jumièges, his toleration of Stigand's pluralism and failure to obtain a generally recognized pallium, his creation of other 'empires' for marcher-bishops, and his and Edith's probable acceptance of gifts from candidates for bishoprics and abbacies are evidence of a worldly attitude. But in general Edward's appointments were respectable, some of his bishops were reformers and one, Wulfstan of Worcester, was later canonized. Perhaps increasingly as he aged, he took an interest in his monasteries and he rebuilt Westminster Abbey on a scale almost without parallel north of the Alps; the church is shown in all its glory on the Bayeux tapestry. Edward also features in legend as a law-giver, and the *Laga Eadwardi* ('Laws of Edward') were, indeed, often invoked in the post-conquest period. But the reference was to the corpus of Old-English law, of which Cnut was the latest codifier. All the same, the period from 1052 to 1065 was clearly an oasis of peace and prosperity. If Edward suspended the collection of the land-tax, 'danegeld', in 1050–51, when he paid off the standing fleet, it could not have been for long, for the taxation system was in full working order after 1066. But, even if royal taxation was heavy, there is much to suggest that the kingdom was in this period prosperous, with trade, internal and foreign, lively and the towns and countryside in good heart.

The one unsolved, and seemingly insoluble, problem was the succession to the throne. Edith could not have been more than forty-six when widowed; but it must have been generally accepted after 1052 that, whatever the reason, the couple would remain childless. If Edward had, indeed, in 1051 promised William of Normandy the succession, this engagement remained dormant until at least 1064. In 1054 Bishop Ealdred of Worcester visited the emperor Heinrich III in search of the only surviving English atheling who could be considered Edward's heir. Edmund Ironside's son, *Edward Ætheling (also known as Edward the Exile), had married Agatha, a German-Hungarian princess, and obtained a distinguished post at the Magyar court. In 1054 the pair had three children, Margaret, Christina, and *Edgar Ætheling. In 1057 the exile arrived in England, only to die almost immediately. The

children were brought up at the royal court; but as Edgar was apparently no more than five years old at the time, it is uncertain how the king and queen regarded their grandnephew. The other, even more enigmatic, move to be reported—but not until after the Norman conquest—was Harold's mission to William's court in, perhaps, 1064 or 1065. If William of Jumièges and later Norman writers are to be trusted, the purpose was to confirm Edward's bequest. But whether the queen's family would have colluded in a policy which would seem to be fatal to their own interests, is a moot point. The position of Scandinavian pretenders, such as Edith's nephew, Swein of Denmark, was peripheral, for they lacked any support in England.

The author of *Vita* believed that the queen and her four brothers had made a pact whereby they would work together and, it would seem, perpetuate in some form their position after Edward's death. But in 1065 Harold and Tostig quarrelled. In August a Welsh prince attacked Portskewett, near Chepstow, which Harold had recently restored and fortified. And in October, while Tostig was hunting with the king in Wiltshire, a rebellion in Northumbria, actively supported by Eadwine and his brother, Morcar of Mercia, and, according to Tostig, by Harold, was completely successful. One cause was Tostig's severe government; the rebels demanded his replacement by Morcar; and, to the fury of the king and queen, neither Harold nor anyone else would fight to restore the unpopular earl. In the following year Harold, when king, is found hand-in-glove with the two Mercian earls and married to their sister. In 1065, as in 1052, Edward had to sanction the banishment of a friend. Tostig and his family took refuge in his wife's country, Flanders.

This humiliation probably caused Edward's death. He seems to have suffered a series of strokes. He was unable to attend the dedication of his new church at Westminster on 28 December and he died at the royal palace at Westminster on 4 or 5 January 1066. His last words were variously reported by several untrustworthy sources; but not even the Norman writers claim that he mentioned William. It is likely that he entrusted the kingdom to Edith and Harold, who were both in attendance. He was buried before the high altar in Westminster Abbey on 6 January; and on the same day, in the abbey, Harold was crowned king.

Conclusion: reputation and cult   Edward's obituary notice, a poem, in the Anglo-Saxon Chronicle is an unqualified encomium. He lived in royal splendour, blithely courageous, a ruler of heroes, lavish with his riches, the master and protector of a wide empire. He was a good man, wise and strong in counsel. At his death he consigned the kingdom to a suitable successor. Angels led his righteous soul to heaven. And so might he have been regarded by posterity had Harold succeeded in holding on to his valuable bequest. Instead, Edward began to be viewed, on the one hand, as a physical and political weakling, and, on the other, in compensation, as unworldly and pious. The ultimate conflation of the two produced a bloodless creature which completely misrepresents the energetic, sometimes ruthless, sometimes rash, resourceful prince, who was not only a great survivor but also a great conservator.

The cult of St Edward the Confessor was a product substantially of the twelfth and thirteenth centuries. Some 'miraculous' cures seem to have occurred at his tomb shortly after his burial, as had happened with his grandfather, King *Edgar in 975 and his brother, Alfred, in 1036 or 1037. And, later, he was credited with some cures during his lifetime, including one of a young woman who was suffering from scrofulous glands of the neck, a disease which became known as the king's evil. In 1102 Gilbert Crispin, abbot of Westminster, had the grave opened and the corpse inspected by, among others, Gundulf, bishop of Rochester, an indication of either a continuing or a renewed interest in Edward, which, apparently, the seniors discouraged as both unseemly and politically subversive. But it was the subsequent championship of Edward's claim to sanctity by a Westminster monk, Osbert de Clare, and the saint's life he composed before 1138, which converted a rather thin popular interest into a movement supported by the English church and monarchy. The first attempt, in Stephen's reign, by the abbey to secure the canonization was shelved by the prudent Pope Innocent II. In 1160, however, a new abbot, Laurence, supported by a new king, Henry II, and seemingly the entire English hierarchy, petitioned the newly recognized Pope Alexander III; and the pope, threatened by a rival and grateful for English support, on the strength of Osbert's book of miracles and a decent set of testimonials, issued the necessary bull on 7 February 1161. Edward was to be inscribed in the catalogue of saints and numbered among the holy confessors.

Edward never became a very popular saint in England or elsewhere. But he was valued by the medieval English monarchy. Henry II's grandson, Henry III, was one of his most ardent worshippers. He rebuilt Westminster Abbey, had a splendid new tomb constructed to which the saint was translated on 13 October 1269, and named his eldest son and successor after the Confessor. He seems also to have been the first English king to have regularly 'touched' for the king's evil, a custom which probably owed something to the miracle attributed to the Confessor, even if more to the virtue claimed by the Capetian kings of France, most immediately by St Louis. In England the practice continued until the accession of the Hanoverian George I in 1714. Thus Edward cast a long shadow. It was, however, but a pale and distorted image of a robust historical figure.   FRANK BARLOW

Sources ASC · F. Barlow, ed. and trans., *The life of King Edward who rests at Westminster*, 2nd edn, OMT (1992) · A. Campbell, ed. and trans., *Encomium Emmae reginae*, CS, 3rd ser., 72 (1949) · F. Barlow, *Edward the Confessor*, 2nd edn (1979) · John of Worcester, *Chron.* · F. E. Harmer, ed., *Anglo-Saxon writs* (1952) · AS chart., S 998–1162 · *Willelmi Malmesbiriensis monachi de gestis regum Anglorum*, ed. W. Stubbs, 2 vols., Rolls Series (1887–9) · *Magistri Adam Bremensis gesta Hammaburgensis ecclesiae pontificum*, ed. B. Schmeidler, 3rd edn, MGH Scriptores Rerum Germanicarum, [2] (Hanover, 1917) · *The Gesta Normannorum ducum of William of Jumièges, Orderic Vitalis, and Robert of Torigni*, ed. and trans. E. M. C. van Houts, 2 vols., OMT

(1992–5) · *The Gesta Guillelmi of William of Poitiers*, ed. and trans. R. H. C. Davis and M. Chibnall, OMT (1998) · 'La vie de S. Édouard le Confesseur par Osbert de Clare', ed. M. Bloch, *Analecta Bollandiana*, 41 (1923), 5–131 · F. Barlow, *The English church, 1000–1066: a history of the later Anglo-Saxon church*, 2nd edn (1979) · E. A. Freeman, *The history of the Norman conquest of England*, 2nd edn, 6 vols. (1870–79), vol. 2 · S. Körner, *The battle of Hastings, England, and Europe, 1035–1066* (1964) · T. J. Oleson, 'Edward the Confessor in history', *Proceedings and Transactions of the Royal Society of Canada*, 3rd ser., 52 (1959), section 2, pp. 27–35

Likenesses attrib. Theodoric, silver pennies, *c.*1065, NPG · coin, BM · coins, repro. in Barlow, *Edward the Confessor*, pl. 10 · drawing (with his mother and Harthacnut), BL, 'Encomium Emmae reginae', Add. MS 33241, fol. 1*v*; *see illus. in Emma* (*d.* 1052) · embroidery (Bayeux Tapestry), Bayeux, France [*see illus.*] · manuscript, BL, Royal MS 20A. II, fol. 5 · polychrome carving, Westminster Abbey, London · stained-glass window, All Souls Oxf. · statue, Canterbury Cathedral · wax seal, BM

Edward [Edward of Woodstock; *known as* the Black Prince], **prince of Wales and of Aquitaine** (1330–1376), heir to the English throne and military commander, was the eldest son of *Edward III (1312–1377) and *Philippa of Hainault (1310?–1369).

Early years Edward was born at the royal palace at Woodstock on 15 June 1330. From his birth he was regarded as the future earl of Chester, and in 1331 the revenues of Chester were assigned to his mother for his maintenance. He was a year old when a marriage alliance was proposed, involving his betrothal to the daughter of the king of France. He was created earl of Chester on 18 March 1333, and on the death of the king's brother *John of Eltham in 1336 was given the revenues of the earldom of Cornwall (which included some valuable manors outside Cornwall itself); on 9 February 1337 he was created duke of Cornwall. He was very early present at court occasions, and by the age of seven he had been equipped with a complete suit of armour. In 1340 he is reported as having lost money gambling with John Chandos (*d.* 1370); he also lost the substantial sum of 37s. to his mother. Little is known about his formal education; Holinshed and Stow claim that the celebrated schoolman Walter Burley, who died in 1343, was his tutor, but no evidence survives.

Guardian of England, 1338–1346 Edward's first official appearance was probably when, in late 1337, as his father's representative, he met the two cardinals who had come to negotiate a settlement of the quarrel between England and France, and escorted them into London. With his father's departure for Flanders in July 1338 Edward was named *custos Angliae*, an office he was to hold again in 1340 and 1342. In the course of his guardianship of the realm he incurred 'great charges which it behoved the keeper of the realm to support' (*CPR, 1345–8*, 72), and £1000 was provided in August 1340 towards these costs. But he was also a pawn in his father's diplomatic attempts to forge an anti-French alliance. In May 1339 John, duke of Brabant, was promised that Edward would marry his daughter Margaret. This proposed match was regarded as likely as late as April 1345, when the king wrote again to Clement VI seeking the necessary dispensation.

From 1340 onwards Edward took an active part in public life. When Edward III sailed to Flanders on the voyage that

Edward, prince of Wales and of Aquitaine (1330–1376), tomb effigy

led to the naval battle at Sluys, the prince was rowed out to the royal ship before the king's departure from the Orwell estuary, and he left his own messengers along the coast to glean any news of the king's fortunes. During the summer he remained close to London, until his father's dramatic return in November. After 1343 he was regarded as old enough to accompany his father on expeditions abroad. At this time he was also created prince of Wales, like his grandfather before him, in the parliament that began at Westminster on 28 April 1343. However, he never visited Wales, which was not central to his interests: by contrast, he was frequently in Cornwall, which was the real source of his revenues. The following January he attended the great feast at Windsor at which his father solemnly swore that he would found a round table like that of King Arthur. This scheme, however, was interrupted by the renewal of war with France in 1345. The prince's first journey abroad was to Flanders, in his father's company, where the king hoped to open a new campaign. But when the Flemish civic leader Jacob van Artevelde was assassinated on 17 July, the English contingent returned home at once. Plans for a major expedition to France were now based on the two royal armies already in Gascony and Brittany, and were postponed until the next year: the fleet did not finally depart until July 1346. Meanwhile the prince was authorized to make his will; he also went on pilgrimage to

Walsingham and to Thomas Becket's shrine at Canterbury.

The Crécy campaign, 1346–1347 The king's original intention when the fleet left the Isle of Wight on 11 July may have been to make for Gascony. However, a westerly wind took the ships safely to Normandy, where the army landed unopposed at La Hogue. At midday the following day, the king knighted Edward to mark the beginning of his career as a soldier. The prince at once exercised his right to make other knights. In the march across Normandy the vanguard was nominally under his command, and usually quartered separately from the king's division, about 2 or 3 miles apart. The prince's division played an important part in the capture of Caen on 26 July; the actual command was in the hands of the earls of Warwick and Northampton. The following month, as his company passed Beauvais:

> the prince of Wales and his division stayed longer than they should have done before the town; and indeed he dearly wanted to obtain permission for his men to attack from his father the king. But he did not dare carry it out, for the king told him that he was likely to meet the enemy shortly, and he did not want to lose any men in such an attack.
> (Cambridge, Corpus Christi College, MS 370, fol. 105)

This may reflect a personal whim: Warwick and Northampton were still clearly in charge. The French forces caught up with the English army on the north bank of the Somme, and the king selected a site just north of the forest of Crécy to give battle.

The English forces were drawn up in defensive order, with archers and two divisions in the front, and the king's division forming the reserve; the prince was in the centre of his men, with his household knights and the two earls, and his standard was carried by Sir Richard Fitzsimon. The brunt of the fighting fell on the prince's men. Some reports state that the duke of Alençon, who led the first charge, beat down the prince's standard just before he was killed: the prince was in the thick of the fight from the outset. The second French charge penetrated into the centre of the division, and the prince was in considerable personal danger. Exactly what happened is not clear: the prince was said to have been forced to his knees, and to have been captured for a few moments by the count of Hainault, from whom he was rescued by Sir Richard Fitzsimon, who had to lower his banner—normally a serious offence against discipline—in order to defend the prince. The king sent twenty knights, led by Thomas Hatfield (d. 1381), bishop of Durham, to rescue the prince. However, when they reached him, he and his companions were resting, leaning on their swords, having repulsed the French attack. Enemy onslaughts continued until nightfall, at which point the French king withdrew, leaving the English in command of the field. It was only with the defeat of a further body of French troops the next day that victory was deemed secure.

Edward's courage in his first major engagement in the field clearly impressed his contemporaries, and quickly became the stuff of legend. The story that the messenger sent to the king at the moment of crisis was turned back by him with the words 'Let the boy win his spurs' was current by the time Froissart came to write his account of the battle, probably after the prince's death; but it is not found in his source, the chronicle of Jean le Bel. It was at Crécy that the prince won a new device. King John of Bohemia, one of the great chivalric figures of the age, had insisted on being led into battle, despite his blindness, and he and his entourage had been killed fighting the prince's men. To honour his memory the prince adopted his badge of an ostrich feather, shown singly in the early years; later princes of Wales bore triple feathers as their badge. Despite this glorious beginning, when the king asked the prince afterwards what he thought of going into battle, the latter, according to a Hainault chronicler, 'said nothing and was ashamed' (K. de Lettenhove, *Récits d'un Bourgeois de Valenciennes*, 234).

Edward remained with his father throughout the rest of the campaign, including the siege of Calais, where he may have been ill, as his physician, William Blackwater, was requested to attend the prince urgently. After the fall of Calais, on 3 August 1347, he and his father did not return to England until early November, by which time a year's truce had been negotiated.

The Order of the Garter, 1348–1354 Edward now turned to the chivalric pastimes that were the normal occupation of young noblemen: his father, unlike most contemporary monarchs, was also an enthusiast for tournaments, and the two often fought at the same events. The prince was actively involved in the foundation of the Order of the Garter, which brought together the inner circle of the king's military commanders in France, who were also his companions in the lists. Some of the earliest records of its existence come from the prince's wardrobe accounts: in December 1348 the prince's wardrobe keeper bought twenty-four garters, given to the knights at some unspecified later date. And in St George's Chapel at Windsor, the home of the order, one of the sets of facing stalls was designated as the king's side, the other being the prince's. The reason for the foundation is now generally accepted as having been political, reflected in the choice of heraldry and motto: the gold and blue of France is combined with words that refer to Edward's claim to France: 'Shame on him who thinks evil of it.' The romantic origin invented for the Garter in later years seems to have no basis in reality. The order celebrated the English triumph at Crécy, and cemented the companionship of king, prince, and nobles, who hoped to lead the English armies that would make good the king's claim to France. The choice of the garter itself may possibly have originated in a tournament badge; it had the practical advantage that it could be worn outside armour.

Tournaments certainly figured largely in court life in 1348, and both the royal accounts and those of Edward show lavish expenditure on such occasions. Neither the king nor the prince was averse to display, a vital attribute of a popular monarchy in the fourteenth century, and the prince's purchases of jewels and plate were very substantial: the chivalric virtue of largesse is certainly evident in his new year gifts at this period. Yet although the prince's style of living was intended to impress, it does not seem to have been excessive.

At the advent of the black death the king and Edward stayed away from London, retreating to their country manors. In October they were both at Hereford when a Genoese mercenary in English pay, Amerigo of Pavia, sent letters to the king revealing a French plot to take Calais by treachery. The king and the prince with a small group of knights left at once for Calais, where an ambush was laid, for which the king and the prince were said to have concealed themselves and their knights behind a false wall for three days. The ruse succeeded, and the king and thirty knights pursued the retreating French, capturing the French commander, Geoffroi de Charny. The episode reveals an enthusiasm for small-scale warfare very much in keeping with the individual chivalric ethos of this period, but having little to do with serious military strategy.

The truce with France was still current when warfare was renewed at sea in the summer of 1350. English plans for an Anglo-Castilian marriage alliance involving Edward's sister Joan lapsed with her death in 1348, and the French seized the opportunity to encourage the Castilians to send a large fleet to harass Gascon, Breton, and English shipping. In response to these attacks the English ships assembled at Sandwich in late July, and in mid-August the Castilian fleet was reported to be off Winchelsea. The king and prince embarked on 28 August, and the next evening the two fleets engaged. Although numbers were roughly equal, the Castilian ships were much higher, and presented a formidable obstacle to English attempts to board them. According to Froissart both the king and the prince had to fight their way onto Spanish ships because their own were sinking. It was a fiercely contested battle, and ended with the retreat of half the Spanish ships, the remainder being in English hands. The king made much of the victory, which came to be known as 'les Espagnols sur Mer', and the new coinage of 1351 reflected his claim to be 'king of the sea', showing him standing in a ship, crowned and armed.

Administration and finance Edward did not see action again until 1355. By now his household was an independent entity, and he spent considerable time on his estates from which most of his resources were derived—at his death they had an estimated yearly value of £9982. They were based upon four substantial but largely self-sufficient units of lordship, in Cornwall, Chester, Wales, and Aquitaine. Unity came through his council, an amorphous body with no specific constitution, which directed his business, and through a number of household institutions—wardrobe, great wardrobe, chamber— whose position in the management of the prince's finances was eclipsed, though by no means entirely supplanted, by the creation of an exchequer in 1343/4, set up at Westminster close to the king's exchequer. Orders were authenticated by the prince's privy seal—he had no great seal—supplemented by local seals for Wales, Chester, and Aquitaine. The workings of the system can be seen principally in the volumes of the prince's register which have survived. The prince's need for money was considerable, and not only to finance a princely lifestyle. He also had to be able to pay his own servants and retainers—in 1369 (admittedly the year when war in France recommenced, when such costs were likely to be high) he spent no less than £1537 on annuities. Not surprisingly his lordship could be oppressive, and it is clear that his officials missed no opportunity for maintaining and extending their master's rights. The pressure they exerted in the Welsh marches in the late 1340s and early 1350s was such as to prompt resistance by the lords of the region, and led to the king's intervening against his son.

Only in time of war did Edward's household function as a military headquarters organization, on a parallel with the king's household. It did not constitute a politicized system, or a shadow government, not least because it shared some of its personnel with that of the central government. The prince's financial officers, both central and local, had often been king's clerks; one such was Peter Gildesburgh, who became the first (and only) keeper of the prince's exchequer. Others passed from the prince's service to the king's, or served both men simultaneously; Peter Lacy, the receiver-general and keeper of the prince's wardrobe, retained both offices when he became the keeper of the king's privy seal in 1367. John Fordham (d. 1425), a confidential servant of the prince in the latter's last years, became keeper of Richard II's privy seal and bishop successively of Durham and Ely. But few of the prince's officials, unlike the king's, rose to bishoprics, or gained great estates. Sir John Wingfield, his steward, grew rich in the prince's service, and John Harewell and William Spridlington too became bishops, but these were exceptions.

Berkhamsted, Sonning, and Byfleet were among the prince's residences near London, but he also went to Cheshire and Cornwall. Cheshire was the subject of a major visitation in the summer of 1353, because there had been unrest and the local administration needed reform. On 15 August records note that he dined at Chester with the local nobles, and the next day hunted near Shotwich; but this was primarily a business visit, and its effect was to increase dramatically the prince's revenue from the county. The following summer he went to Cornwall, having spent Christmas as usual at Berkhamsted. The difficulties in Cornwall were less easily resolved than those in Cheshire, because of the remoteness and relative poverty of the county.

The expedition to Aquitaine, 1355 By the autumn of 1354 it was clear that the series of truces with France would shortly end, and the prince spent the next months at Berkhamsted, keeping in touch with his father's court. He made a pilgrimage to Walsingham in the autumn of 1354, and, with the king, to various shrines in the spring of 1355. On the new campaign the prince was to be given his own theatre of operations, in Gascony, where Henry, duke of Lancaster, had been active in 1345–51, with considerable success. Since 1351 the French had gained the upper hand: Jean II had shrewdly appointed a local Gascon lord, Jean d'Armagnac, as his lieutenant, and the English adherents

in Gascony had come to London in the spring of 1355 to ask for help in the face of a deteriorating situation. One of them, Jean de Grailly, captal de Buch, a knight of the Garter, had suggested that it would boost morale if the prince were to come to Aquitaine, and the prince himself was enthusiastic: he 'prayed the king to grant him leave to be the first to pass beyond the sea' (*Register of Edward the Black Prince*, 2.77). At the same time the duke of Lancaster was to go to Normandy with an army.

The organization of the expedition was largely carried out by Edward's household officers. The prince's entourage consisted of Suffolk, Warwick, Oxford, and Salisbury, Sir Reginald Cobham and Sir John Lisle, and a group of highly experienced knights who were also close personal friends: Sir John Chandos, Sir Bartholomew Burghersh the younger, Sir Nigel Loring, and Sir James Audley. Of this group, all except the earl of Oxford were knights of the Garter. In formal terms the prince went as the king's lieutenant in Aquitaine, with full powers to administer the English territories there, and with a wider brief than the duke of Lancaster had had in the 1340s. He also had a military contract of service, which made provision for a major campaign, and for such events as the capture of 'the head of the war' (that is, the French commander) and the prince's own possible capture. In the latter event Lancaster was to abandon the Normandy campaign and come to his rescue.

By the time Edward left in early September, King Charles of Navarre, from whom the English had hoped for support in Normandy, had been reconciled with King Jean, and Lancaster's expedition was scaled down. The prince's army was now the focus of English hopes, and when he landed at Bordeaux on 20 September, all the great lords who supported the English cause were assembled to meet him. The plan of campaign had probably already been prepared; after only a fortnight the army set out, on 5 October. The target was to be the lands of Jean d'Armagnac. Once the expedition crossed into enemy territory on 10 October it moved in three columns, spreading out in order to live off the land. Three days later the prince had a narrow escape when fire broke out in the newly captured town of Monclar, where he was lodging. For the rest of the campaign, he insisted on sleeping in tents pitched in the open countryside. A fortnight was spent ravaging Jean d'Armagnac's lands, and the army then headed towards Toulouse, in an attempt to draw out Armagnac, who was in the city with a considerable army. But the French strategy was evidently defensive, and precautions had been taken against just such a raid as the prince's. The prince, unable to mount a full-scale siege of the city, decided to take the bold step of bypassing it, even though it would leave an enemy army on his line of retreat to Bordeaux.

Edward's entry into Languedoc was an unexpected move, and the local towns were ill prepared. The prince was able to inflict considerable damage, and to raise substantial ransoms. He seized and burnt the town of Carcassonne, but was unable to take the citadel. On 8 November he reached the furthest point of his march, at Narbonne on the Mediterranean shore, where once again the town was taken despite fierce resistance, but the castle held out. Scouts sent to nearby towns reported that hasty defences were being thrown up. Rather than risk further fighting, and hearing that Jean d'Armagnac had emerged from his headquarters at Toulouse, the prince turned back on 10 November: the army had been on the march for only a month, but had achieved its primary object. The prince now had hopes of drawing Jean d'Armagnac into battle, but Armagnac initially eluded him; so the prince avoided Toulouse, turning south instead. The French troops came within 6 miles of the rearguard on 19 November, and for the next week there were rumours of an imminent French attack as the army moved back through Armagnac's lands to the border of English Aquitaine.

On 27 November the prince was back in friendly territory, and on 2 December the expedition closed with a council of war at La Réole. The raid had been a classic exercise in *guerre guerroyante* (warfare as conducted principally through raiding, pillage, and destruction), and in the view of the prince's steward Sir John Wingfield it had done substantial damage to the enemy's resources. If the prince's other objective had been to draw the French into battle, he had failed in this respect; but some of his movements seem to imply attempts to evade the enemy. He had certainly won a propaganda victory, making his opponent seem hesitant: one story had it that the constable of France, Jacques de Bourbon, had quarrelled with Armagnac, because the latter refused to attack the English army.

The battle of Poitiers, 1356 Edward spent December 1355 in Bordeaux, while his captains carried out raids along the Garonne and Dordogne rivers, and captured Périgueux. His household acted as the nerve centre of operations, and there were attempts to enlist the help of the count of Foix and the king of Aragon. In January Edward moved to Libourne, where he remained until March. He learnt that the king was proposing to invade Picardy, but reinforcements were to be sent to Gascony and to Brittany. These did not arrive until 19 June; six weeks later the prince's army assembled at Bergerac, and it set out on 4 August. By this time the plans for Lancaster and Edward III had changed: Charles of Navarre was once more in dispute with Jean II, but Lancaster landed in Normandy with a force too small to give battle. Jean was therefore free to march south to engage the prince, who himself marched north towards Bourges, partly to meet the French king and partly to try to effect a junction with Lancaster's forces. From 30 August to 4 September the prince besieged Romorantin, and eventually took it. He then marched up the Loire, hoping to draw the French out of Tours and defeat them before crossing to join Lancaster. At this point the main French army came into play, having left Orléans on 8 September. The traditional view that the prince was avoiding an engagement in the manoeuvres that followed has been challenged by recent historians, who have interpreted his movements as designed to secure an advantageous position in which to fight. Some of the prince's

actions—such as the two-day halt at Châtellerault 'waiting to know more certainly' about the French king (Riley, 287)—bear this out, but many other incidents imply the pursuit by the French of a retreating English army.

At all events, the French and English forces came into contact east of Poitiers; skirmishes ensued and on Sunday 18 September 1356 Edward drew up his men at Nouaillé, 5 miles south of the city. However, Cardinal Talleyrand de Périgord, who had earlier tried to arrange a truce, obtained a day's grace for talks. The two sides both later claimed that the delay had been to their disadvantage; the French had brought up reinforcements, while the English had improved their defensive position. The talks failed; Jean, confident of victory, would settle for nothing less than the prince's complete surrender. It seems that the prince again offered a truce on the morning of 19 September, but nothing came of this, and the first manoeuvre of the battle was made at about 8 a.m.

The interpretation of the tactics used by Edward at Poitiers depends to a great extent on the view of his overall position. If he was indeed positively seeking battle, the opening moves are difficult to explain. Warwick, with the baggage train, moved downhill and away from the French army; if this was a flanking move, why was the baggage train involved? It looks more like an attempt to see if a covering rearguard action could be fought while the army escaped. The French planned, on the advice of Sir William Douglas, a Scottish knight in French service, that the main body of knights was to fight dismounted, and the cavalry were to break through the English line and disperse the archers. But the two French commanders, Clermont and Audrehem, quarrelled early in the battle and led separate cavalry attacks on the two wings; both of them were outflanked by small bodies of archers, who caused disproportionate damage to the horses, killing Clermont and many others as a result.

So the French force moved forward to find the English centre intact; but despite this the archers made little impression on the armoured infantry, which made its way slowly uphill, hindered by heavy armour. The two armies were soon engaged in hand-to-hand combat. Edward was in the centre of the line, and Warwick's men had regrouped with the prince's battalion: the only reserves were 400 horsemen. The attack by the first French battalion was driven off, and, in the confusion, the knights of the dauphin, Charles, duke of Normandy, rode off to Chauvigny with him. Perhaps because of this, the second battalion, seized by an inexplicable panic, retreated from the field. This left the French king's battalion to attack alone. Realizing this, the prince and his advisers now committed their reserve, under Jean de Grailly, to make a wide flanking movement and take the enemy in the rear, while the prince and his men mounted in order to counterattack. Despite bitter resistance from the French, in which many knights were killed, the charge downhill against soldiers unused to fighting on foot succeeded, and King Jean himself was captured.

The main reason for the English success seems to have been good communications and swift and well-judged responses to a changing situation: the English army had campaigned as a body for much of the previous year, while the French army had barely gathered once during the march from Orléans, travelling in separate units and moving erratically. The quarrel between Clermont and Audrehem contrasts with the close collaboration of the English captains. Again, the English ability to remount at the end of the battle and deliver an effective charge argues a good standard of discipline. The prince seems to have had the same genuine qualities of leadership that both his father and great-grandfather Edward I had displayed in the field.

The aftermath of the battle was even more dramatic than that of Crécy. The capture of the French king had transformed the political situation, and some of the Gascon lords who fell into English hands decided it was time to change sides, notably Guichard d'Angle, seneschal of Poitou. The main business, however, was to convey King Jean safely to captivity in England. Froissart paints an idealistic picture of the prince's chivalric behaviour, describing how he refused to sit at table with the French king, but instead served him, and tried to cheer him by praising his prowess, saying he 'had outdone his own greatest knights' (*Chroniques*, 5.63–4). The story is probably apocryphal, because Geoffrey Baker, whose information may have come from someone in the prince's household, has a rather different version (*Chronicon Galfridi le Baker*, 53–4). According to him, the prince was about to sit down to dine with the king, when word was brought that Sir James Audley had been found on the battlefield, seriously wounded, and had been carried to the prince's tent. The prince went to him at once, excusing himself to the king for leaving him during dinner. This reflects equally well on the prince, but lacks the high chivalric tone that Froissart seeks to depict.

The profits of victory, 1356–1359 Edward and his army returned to Libourne by steady marches, arriving on 1 October. When suitable accommodation had been made ready, the prince and King Jean moved to Bordeaux. Just after Christmas negotiations for a truce with the French began; it took nearly three months to reach agreement that there would be no renewal of warfare until Easter 1359. The prince then set out for England with his royal captive, reaching Plymouth in early May. The prince made his solemn entry into London in late May; the account in the Anonimalle chronicle makes this one of the earliest formal occasions of this kind of which a record survives. There was a great procession of the city guilds, while the conduits ran with wine; only the French king struck a sombre note, dressed in a black robe.

Edward's prestige was now at its height, and his followers were suitably rewarded for their part in the campaign: Sir James Audley received a huge annuity of £400. He and Sir John Chandos were both given grants of 600 gold crowns, while his chamberlain, Sir Nigel Loring, received an annuity of £83 6s. 8d. But overall, even though the revenue from the campaign had been substantial, the prince's generosity meant that he himself was little better off,

since any ransom for Jean II, 'the head of the war', had specifically been reserved to the king at the outset of the campaign.

Edward now turned to the relaxations of peacetime, notably a series of tournaments, beginning with jousts at Smithfield at which his father and his two royal captives, Jean II and David of Scotland, were present. At Christmas there was a torchlit tournament at Bristol by night, and the Garter feast at Windsor in 1358 was marked by another great gathering. The prince gave over £100 to heralds and minstrels, as well as lavish quantities of armour to his friends. Expenditure on a grand scale was not limited to entertainment: when the prince visited Cheshire in August 1358, he returned by way of Vale Royal Abbey, for which his great-grandfather had commissioned a new church in 1277, which was still incomplete, and the prince now had plans drawn up which would have made it larger than any other comparable building in England, at a cost of £860. But although work began at once, a great gale in 1360 blew down the columns of the nave, and the church was never completed.

Meanwhile Jean II had formally agreed the terms of his ransom in May 1358, but ratification by the dauphin and his council had not materialized by 1 November. Edward III had made it a condition of the agreement that the terms should be executed promptly, and he now told the French that the war would be renewed. The expedition which left in late 1359 was the largest ever to leave England at one time, totalling 12,000 men. He and the prince went on a series of pilgrimages before going to Sandwich on 16 September to embark. The prince's retinue consisted of 7 bannerets, 136 knights, 443 squires, and 900 mounted archers, and several of the knights who had fought at Poitiers accompanied him.

The Rheims campaign and the making of peace, 1359–1360 The army disembarked in October 1359, late in the campaigning season, and found a more organized resistance than they had expected. Edward III's avowed objective was Rheims, where he intended to be crowned king of France. As a result, the dauphin was able to organize local forces who delayed the English progress; stores were destroyed or brought into towns. The three wings of the army, under the king, Edward, and the duke of Lancaster, had to march 30 miles apart in order to find sufficient supplies. This caused problems in keeping in touch, and the army assembled outside St Quentin to reorganize its methods of communication. But the blockade of Rheims proved ineffective and the scarcity of supplies in midwinter forced the army to move on, its main objective unachieved.

Soon afterwards the prince separated his men from the main body of the army, and moved to Auxerre; but this was a well-fortified area, and the troops suffered from raids mounted from the local castles. After a month, during which a ransom was exacted from the Burgundians for not invading the duchy, Edward moved on with the rest of the army. This was the only independent action by the prince in what proved to be a fruitless campaign. By April 1360 there were no obvious military targets, the army was weary, and Edward turned to negotiations. A treaty was at last agreed at Brétigny in May; Edward was to have Aquitaine as a sovereign state; the French king's ransom was reduced to 3 million francs. The details were to be settled at Calais, in a conference to begin on 15 July.

As soon as agreement was reached, the English army moved towards home: Edward sealed a copy of the preliminary treaty at a village in the Seine valley on 15 May; three days later he and his father landed at Rye. A month later he escorted Jean II to Dover, stopping at Thomas Becket's shrine at Canterbury on the way. The conference at Calais was delayed, and it was only on 24 August that the prince left England. The business proved difficult, and agreement was not reached until the end of October, with many reservations on both sides. On 26 October Jean II, Prince Edward, and the dauphin swore to observe the treaty at the church of St Mary in Boulogne, and peace was finally made.

Prince of Aquitaine, 1360–1367 Once the treaty was fully in force, the English were to rule Aquitaine as a sovereign state, independent of France. Edward was the obvious choice to lead the English government there; plans for the appointment were made during the summer of 1361, but the formal announcement was delayed until July 1362.

Edward was now over thirty, and still unmarried, despite the numerous proposed alliances involving his marriage. His natural son, Sir Roger *Clarendon, had already been born. In the summer of 1361 he became engaged to his cousin *Joan, countess of Kent (c.1328–1385), a choice that seems to have been entirely unpolitical and personal. The French chroniclers reported faintly scurrilous stories about the prince's wooing: and Joan had a reputation both as one of the great beauties of the realm and as a cause for scandal. She had been brought up in Queen Philippa's household, and had exchanged vows with Sir Thomas Holland in an informal marriage when she was about fifteen. But a match was arranged for her with William Montagu, the young earl of Salisbury, and, in Holland's absence in Prussia, she was married to the earl. Holland reclaimed his bride only after a dramatic series of hearings in the papal court.

Holland died in December 1360: during the early summer of 1361 Edward's esquire Nicholas Bond was sent to Avignon to obtain the necessary dispensation, which was granted on 8 September. The marriage took place on 10 October at Windsor, in the presence of the king and queen. One chronicler records that 'the match greatly surprised many people' (*Polychronicon*, 8.360), and in diplomatic terms it removed one of the principal English weapons for making alliances; furthermore, no heir to the throne had married into the English nobility since the Norman conquest. But rumours of a rift between the prince and his father because of the marriage, or his 'exile' to Aquitaine as a result, seem to be without foundation.

Edward spent much of the following summer at Kennington in Kent, where his manor was being rebuilt by Henry Yevele, the greatest master mason of the age: the hall was probably brought into use at this time. His household, enlarged by the princess's retinue and her three children, was now on a considerable scale; in addition, he spent substantial sums on clothes and jewellery, since Joan evidently shared the prince's tastes.

On 19 July the prince did homage to Edward III for the principality of Aquitaine. He was to rule a virtually independent state, paying 1 ounce of gold annually to the king in token of his sovereignty. Aquitaine was also to be financially self-supporting, a bold move in view of the costs incurred each year since 1356: but if the principality was at peace, and the revenues of lordship all came to the prince, it must have seemed a feasible arrangement. The principality reached from Poitiers in the north to Bayonne on the Atlantic coast, and inland to Auch, Montauban, and Rodez in the Rouergue.

Edward seems to have intended to cross to Aquitaine in the autumn of 1362, but delays and bad weather meant that he was still at Restormel in Cornwall in January: the prince and princess finally embarked on 9 June, and arrived at Bordeaux on 29 June. The first action required was the taking of homage from the Gascon nobles: this began at Bordeaux on 9 July and continued until the following April. The journey took the prince as far as Poitiers, Périgueux, Saintes, and Agen, where he spent Christmas. The operation in general went smoothly, apart from an altercation over whether the clergy should also swear homage, as they would have done in England.

The administration of Aquitaine was largely in the hands of Edward's entourage, though John Harewell, constable of Bordeaux, was a professional administrator from the royal service. Soon after his arrival the prince had to raise a hearth tax, traditionally the main source of revenue for the rulers of Aquitaine: but it was set at a very high rate, 25 sous per hearth, and there was disaffection over this, one or two areas refusing to pay. Charles V, playing on incidents like this, and on pro-French feeling among some of the local lords, set about creating difficulties for the prince. Edward, like his father, was not a natural intriguer, and his skill in leadership was confined to the battlefield. Until the transfer of lands and other provisions were executed, the treaty of Brétigny did not take full effect, and the English sovereignty in Aquitaine could be disputed.

What now counted was the support of those lords who were hostile to the general settlement, and who valued their independence. Edward's style of government was not calculated to win them over. His taste for luxury and an autocratic manner—he seems to have been at ease only with a circle of close friends—meant that he appeared spendthrift and unresponsive. In cleverer hands the display on occasions such as the baptism of his eldest son, Edward, in March 1365 at Angoulême could have been turned to good effect, to show the natives of Aquitaine that they now had their own sovereign; there were 154 lords, 706 knights, and (reputedly) 18,000 horses stabled at the prince's expense, and over £400 was spent on candles alone. That he aspired to sovereign status is confirmed by his gold coinage of 1364, similar to that of the French crown, which shows the prince standing under a Gothic porch.

The Spanish campaign, 1367 Meanwhile the French had achieved another diplomatic coup. After the Anglo-Castilian hostilities of the 1350s the Castilians had changed sides, and an alliance negotiated in 1362 with King Pedro the Cruel had been signed just before the prince's departure for Aquitaine. In 1365 the pretender to the Castilian throne, Pedro's illegitimate half-brother Enrique da Trastamara, enlisted the aid of the French general Bertrand du Guesclin and seized the throne of Castile in June 1366. Pedro's appeal to the English, under the terms of the treaty of 1362, was answered with positive and rapid action. Edward was suspicious of his ally, however, and an elaborate agreement was drawn up at a meeting with Pedro at Capbreton near Bayonne at the end of July, before the prince formally agreed to assist; the negotiations were complicated by the need to ensure free passage through Navarre, whose king, Charles, extracted the maximum payment for his consent. In the end the concessions in the document sealed at Libourne on 23 September included the surrender of the Castilian north coast to the English, and were so extensive that Pedro, already unpopular because of his efficient but despotic rule, was put in an untenable position.

Despite an attempt by Charles of Navarre to go back on his agreement, which lulled Trastamara into a false sense of security, Edward was able to set out from Bordeaux early in 1367. He had first to get his army across the Pyrenees in winter: despite 'great cold, snow and frost' (*Vie du Prince Noir*, ll. 2304–6) the journey was accomplished, and by the end of February the English army was at Pamplona, the capital of Navarre. Charles of Navarre was with them, but on 11 March arranged to be captured by the French, yet again securing himself against all possible outcomes. With Navarre again in uncertain hands, the prince kept to the north Spanish coast in order to be sure of communications by sea with Aquitaine. When he came up against Trastamara near Vitoria, the latter avoided a direct encounter. The Castilians caused severe casualties among Sir Hugh Calveley's men in a night ambush, nearly surprised the main army, and attacked an outlying troop of 400 men-at-arms and archers under Sir Thomas Felton (*d.* 1381), whom they either killed or captured. This reverse was followed by bad weather and difficulties of supply, while Trastamara shadowed the prince's army.

But at the beginning of April Trastamara seems to have changed tactics, perhaps judging that Edward's army was now an easy target; he was also troubled by desertions, and felt that he must strike quickly. The armies finally met on 3 April, at Navarrete near Nájera. The prince managed to surprise the Castilians by a night march which meant that he appeared on their flank instead of attacking their prepared position across a stream from his camp. The battle was fought largely on foot: some of Trastamara's horsemen deserted before the battle, and his two wings, also composed of cavalry, fled at the first English onslaught, leaving the Castilian vanguard to fight on alone. Despite Trastamara's personal courage they were overwhelmed,

and the majority either killed or captured; among the latter were the French commanders, du Guesclin and Audrehem. Audrehem, who had not paid his ransom after being taken prisoner at Poitiers, had been released on parole, having sworn not to fight against the prince until his debt was paid. The prince threatened to execute him as a traitor, but Audrehem pointed out that he was not fighting the prince, but his employer, Pedro of Castile. The point was a fair one; and the prince was soon to discover the difficulties of a mercenary's life. For the moment the prince wrote to Joan, in one of his few surviving personal letters, to report his victory, and moved to Burgos, where he was quartered in the royal monastery of Las Huelgas. Here the cost of the campaign was calculated: the sum—2,720,000 gold florins—was nearly as much as King Jean's ransom, and the prince held no security for payment. Castile was much poorer than France and the price was clearly impossible. Nor was he dealing with a trustworthy character: at the ceremony at which the deeds were exchanged the prince felt the need for a massive English armed presence to guarantee his safety.

Although Pedro seems to have made a genuine attempt to raise money, he was not in a strong position in his own kingdom, and Edward grew increasingly dissatisfied with the results, negotiating a secret alliance with Aragon in July. The heat of summer brought epidemics in the unfamiliar climate, probably malaria and dysentery, and the prince himself was gravely ill. His continued presence in Castile was achieving nothing, and in August the English army retraced its steps through Navarre and across the Pyrenees to Bayonne, where it was formally disbanded. Early in September the prince returned to Bordeaux, where he was met by Joan and his elder son, Edward; his second son, Richard of Bordeaux (afterwards *Richard II), had been born just before the campaign started.

The last years, 1367–1376 The victory at Nájera was a hollow one: by the end of 1367 Enrique was back in Castile. Nor had the political situation in Gascony improved: although Charles V himself stuck scrupulously to the terms of the treaty of Brétigny, he encouraged others to disturb the peace, in the hope that Edward would respond with repression. In this he succeeded, and from 1367 onwards the prince's relationship with the great Gascon lords rapidly deteriorated. Gaston Phébus of Foix had defied the prince's demands for homage for Béarn; now the lords who had accompanied him to Spain had cause for complaint, because despite the military victory they had returned empty-handed. The prince may indeed have been relying on the financial success of the expedition to solve some of his problems. Arnaud-Amanieu d'Albret was owed a pension of £1000 p.a., now ten years in arrears, and the prince was trying to extract repayment of a loan from Jean d'Armagnac. To make matters worse, the prince's only option was to raise a hearth tax to fund the financial deficit. At an assembly of the estates of Gascony in January 1368 at Angoulême he asked for the tax to be paid at the rate of 24*d.* But what was traditionally an occasional levy was to become annual. Although he was granted the tax, the assembly drew up a charter of rights, which the prince had to confirm. Edward was trying to impose a central administration on an area that had long been governed from a distance, and was used to local customs rather than central authority. Even his father the king reproved him for introducing 'novelties' into the administration. At the end of June, Albret and Armagnac signed an understanding with Charles V. Charles gave Armagnac money to clear his debts with the prince, and paid Albret the arrears of his pension. Armagnac furthermore appealed to Paris over the hearth tax, reopening the question of ultimate sovereignty over Aquitaine, given that the provisions of the treaty of Brétigny remained unfulfilled.

Edward's handling of matters was now in question at Westminster as well as Paris, and although he defended himself bluntly to Westminster in a letter of 7 December 1368, he had to face a formal summons to appear at Paris over the hearth tax. This was tantamount to admitting that the treaty of Brétigny was now a dead letter, and the English reaction was to prepare for war. The prince himself, throughout this period, had been suffering from repeated attacks of what was probably dysentery, and much of the work was left to his officials. They were unable to prevent mass defections to the French cause, and in the spring a full-scale French campaign to seize the easternmost part of Aquitaine developed. The loss of Sir James Audley and Sir John Chandos in the months that followed dealt a serious blow to English morale: both had been among the prince's closest companions.

The following summer Edward himself took to the field. He had travelled little in the previous two years, and may well have been in a litter. His objective was Limoges, whose lord bishop had surrendered to the French a month earlier. The English took only five days to seize the city. Froissart paints a black picture of their ensuing actions, claiming that they massacred the inhabitants; he regards this as a stain on the prince's character, and attributes it to his sense of betrayal at the hands of the bishop. Local historians, however, contradict this account, showing only that the numbers of casualties correspond to the likely numbers of the garrison: there is no firm evidence for any killing of civilians, though the city was systematically devastated. Tactically, however, this was not sufficient to frighten other cities into submission.

During the campaign the prince's eldest son, Edward, had died at Angoulême, and Edward's own health was now so poor that he sailed for England in January. His father was elderly, and also in poor health. On 5 November 1372 Guy, Lord Brian (d. 1390), as the prince's spokesman, surrendered to the king the deeds for Aquitaine, ostensibly because the revenues were insufficient to pay for the administration. But the real reason—the prince's illness—was obvious, even though there were hopes that he might recover and provide the good governance that was so eagerly sought. There are glimpses of Edward at work on government business, but his limited range of movements—he was rarely more than 50 miles from London—argues that his sickness continued to be debilitating. At the so-called Good Parliament of 1376 he and the king attended the opening ceremony in late April, but the business of the parliament was left to John of Gaunt.

The following month Edward's illness became critical: contemporary reports describe his piety in the face of death, attesting a religious faith that may have been more than conventional. He had a particular devotion to the Trinity, and a lead badge survives which shows him worshipping the Trinity. He is recorded as going on pilgrimage before major campaigns. His relations with the Lollards in the last years of the reign are obscure, since the only accounts come from partisan sources. Walsingham makes a dubious claim that he refused to see Sir Richard Stury, one of the most prominent Lollard knights, on his deathbed. On the eve of Trinity Sunday 7 June 1376 he made his will at Westminster Palace, and the following day he died.

Edward's will stipulated that he should be buried at Canterbury, where he had founded two chantry chapels after his marriage, and on 5 October the funeral procession passed through the city; the hearse was preceded by two war-horses with his arms of war and arms of peace, the latter being the ostrich feathers he had adopted after the battle of Crécy.

Appearance and reputation Something of Edward's appearance can be gathered from the effigy on his tomb in the Trinity Chapel at Canterbury Cathedral, one of the best known of medieval monuments, and from miniatures and paintings: the most graphic is the depiction of the prince and his father in the initial of the deed creating him prince of Aquitaine. He seems to have been tall and strongly built, with the characteristic long Plantagenet face, best seen in Edward III's funeral effigy at Westminster. A similar image appears on the lead badge already described, and in the drawings of the lost murals in St Stephen's Chapel, Westminster.

Edward's reputation has always been that of a heroic figure: the spectacular victories at Crécy, Poitiers, and Nájera have eclipsed his failure in Aquitaine, and he played relatively little part in English politics. His weaknesses—perhaps the result of his precocious triumphs—seem to have been an autocratic manner and an insensitive love of luxury, but these were soon to fade into insignificance beside the behaviour of his son in the following decades. Edward has attracted relatively little attention from serious historians, but figures largely in popular history. The first historian to attempt a serious assessment of his career was Joshua Barnes in his *History of Edward III* (1688); military historians have of course treated him as a major figure, but neither his household nor his period of government in Gascony has been fully studied. Even his sobriquet, the Black Prince, which is not found until the Tudor period, is as obscure as his character; it has been variously attributed to his black armour and to French hatred of him. Rightly or wrongly, it is Froissart's depiction of him that has fired the imagination of succeeding centuries, for whom he embodies a golden age of English military feats and of chivalry.

RICHARD BARBER

Sources *La vie du Prince Noir by Chandos herald*, ed. D. B. Tyson (1975) · Cuvelier, *La chanson de Bertrand du Guesclin*, ed. J.-C. Faucon,

3 vols. (Toulouse, 1990–91) • P. Lopez de Ayala, *Crónicas de los reyes de Castilla*, ed. C. Rosell, 3 vols. (Madrid, 1875–8); repr. (1953) • *Chroniques de J. Froissart*, ed. S. Luce and others, 15 vols. (Paris, 1869–1975) • *Chronicon Galfridi le Baker de Swynebroke*, ed. E. M. Thompson (1889) • *Knighton's chronicle, 1337–1396*, ed. and trans. G. H. Martin, OMT (1995) [Lat. orig., *Chronica de eventibus Angliae a tempore regis Edgari usque mortem regis Ricardi Secundi*, with parallel Eng. text] • *Chronica monasterii de Melsa, a fundatione usque ad annum 1396, auctore Thoma de Burton*, ed. E. A. Bond, 3 vols., Rolls Series, 43 (1866–8) • *Adae Murimuth continuatio chronicarum. Robertus de Avesbury de gestis mirabilibus regis Edwardi tertii*, ed. E. M. Thompson, Rolls Series, 93 (1889) • *CPR, 1330–76*, esp. 1345–8 • *CCIR, 1327–76* • C. L. Kingsford, ed., *Chronicles of London* (1905) • *Polychronicon Ranulphi Higden monachi Cestrensis*, ed. C. Babington and J. R. Lumby, 9 vols., Rolls Series, 41 (1865–86), vol. 8 • H. T. Riley, ed., *Memorials of London and London life in the XIIIth, XIVth, and XVth centuries* (1868) • K. de Lettenhove, ed., *Récits d'un bourgeois de Valenciennes* (1877) • M. C. B. Dawes, ed., *Register of Edward, the Black Prince*, 4 vols., PRO (1930–33) • N. H. Nicolas, ed., *Testamenta vetusta: being illustrations from wills*, 1 (1826) • Rymer, *Foedera*, new edn • G. Wrottesley, *Crécy and Calais* (1897); repr. (1898) • J. Moisant, *Le Prince Noir en Aquitaine* (Paris, 1894) • R. Barber, *Edward, prince of Wales and Aquitaine: a biography of the Black Prince* (1978) • R. Barber, ed. and trans., *The life and campaigns of the Black Prince: from contemporary letters, diaries and chronicles* (1979) • G. F. Beltz, *Memorials of the most noble order of the Garter* (1841) • H. J. Hewitt, *The Black Prince's expedition of 1355–1357* (1958) • J. Vale, *Edward III and chivalry: chivalric society and its context, 1270–1350* (1982) • K. P. Wentersdorf, 'The clandestine marriages of the Fair Maid of Kent', *Journal of Medieval History*, 5 (1979), 203–32 • C. J. Rogers, 'Edward III and the dialectics of strategy, 1327–1360', *TRHS*, 6th ser., 4 (1994), 83–102 • C. Given-Wilson, *The English nobility in the late middle ages* (1987) • Tout, *Admin. hist.*, vol. 5 • R. R. Davies, *Lordship and society in the march of Wales, 1282–1400* (1978), 269–73 • S. L. Waugh, *England in the reign of Edward III* (1991), 132 • [T. Walsingham], *Chronicon Angliae, ab anno Domini 1328 usque ad annum 1388*, ed. E. M. Thompson, Rolls Series, 64 (1874), 88 • PRO, E30/180, E403/460

Likenesses double portrait, miniature, 1362? (with his father) • coins, BM • electrotype, NPG • gilt-copper tomb effigy, Canterbury Cathedral [*see illus.*] • lead seal • miniatures and paintings • portrait, repro. in J. Alexander and P. Binski, eds., *Age of chivalry: art of Plantagenet England, 1200–1400* (1987), 478 [exhibition catalogue, Royal Academy of Arts, London] • portrait, LUL, MS I, fol. 3*v*

Wealth at death est. £9982 p.a. from lands: Given-Wilson, *English nobility*, 190 n.31

Edward [Edward of Langley, Edward of York], **second duke of York** (*c*.1373–1415), magnate, the eldest son of *Edmund (1341–1402), the fifth son of *Edward III, and Isabella of Castile (*d*. 1393), second daughter of Pedro the Cruel (*r*. 1350–69) and his mistress Maria de Padilla, was probably born, like his father, at Langley, Hertfordshire. The Monk of Evesham styles him Edward of Langley. The appellation Edward of Norwich ('de norwik') is probably a misreading of 'd'everwick' (of York), the appellation regularly used during his father's lifetime. His father's inquisition post mortem suggests that Edward was born *c*.1375, but as this would make him only two years old when he was knighted at the coronation of his cousin, Richard II, in 1377, most authorities have preferred to date his birth to 1373, the year after his parents' marriage.

Favourite of Richard II Edward's closeness to the king was apparent by 1390. Numerous royal grants were made at his instance, and on 25 February he was made earl of Rutland. In 1392 he was a member of the royal council. He accompanied Richard on the Irish campaign of 1394–5, and led a number of successful forays. During the campaign he is called earl of Cork, a title he had probably been granted before the army left England and which he continued to use for the rest of his life. In the next few years Rutland emerged as the leading member of the circle of intimates that the king was creating around himself. He was involved in the king's diplomacy in France and the empire. After the death of Queen Anne in 1394 he was one of the three feoffees of her estates (the others being the archbishop of York and the bishop of Salisbury)—a role which allowed him control of a significant amount of patronage. His other gains from royal favour were extensive, including the office of admiral of England, the reversion of the constableship of the Tower of London (which he finally received in October 1397), and the offices of constable of Dover and warden of the Cinque Ports (11 September 1396). His wealth and his status as the king's intended brother-in-law (see below) were reflected in his plans to build a new house outside Temple Bar in 1397, although apparently nothing came of the scheme.

In 1397 Rutland played a leading role in the arrest and trial of the duke of Gloucester and the earls of Warwick and Arundel. In Henry IV's first parliament he was also to be accused of urging Gloucester's subsequent murder, a claim that evidently commanded contemporary belief, although he vehemently denied it. He was given a major share of the forfeitures that followed, including Arundel's lordship of Clun, Shropshire, and Gloucester's lordship of Burstwick in Holderness, Yorkshire. In September 1397 he was made duke of Aumale and succeeded Gloucester as constable of England. As constable he presided over Richard's extension of the jurisdiction of the court of chivalry to include treason and other offences touching the king's dignity. On 10 February 1398, as part of Richard's policy of extending his power in the north of England, Aumale was appointed warden of the west march towards Scotland.

The usurpation of Henry IV Jean Creton considered that there was no man alive whom Richard loved better. For him (and French opinion in general) Aumale was the Judas who deliberately betrayed his king in 1399. Edward may well have been made uneasy by the exile of his cousin Henry Bolingbroke in 1398, and by the seizure of the Lancastrian inheritance following the death of John of Gaunt, duke of Lancaster. He later claimed that he had not drawn any of the revenues from the great block of duchy of Lancaster lands which had been put in his custody. But there is no evidence that he was conspiring with Bolingbroke, or that there was a treacherous motive behind his advice, when news of Bolingbroke's invasion reached Richard II during his expedition to Ireland of 1399, that John Montagu, earl of Salisbury, be sent immediately to north Wales, while Richard gathered the rest of his forces. Indeed, the advice was arguably sound, since Montagu was able to raise 4000 men, although he was then unable to hold them together long enough for the king to join him. Richard landed in south Wales, and there, inexplicably, left Aumale and most of his men and pressed northwards. Aumale's subsequent movements are unknown, although he was reputedly attacked as he made his way through Wales. He is next reported, by Creton, in the delegation sent by Bolingbroke to Richard at Flint, wearing Henry's livery. During the meeting Aumale 'said nothing to the king, but kept at as great a distance as he could from him' (Webb, 158).

The first parliament of Henry IV saw a spectacular expression of animosity against Richard's former allies, particularly against Aumale, who, according to Thomas Walsingham, came close to being lynched. Henry resisted demands for the death penalty and restricted their punishment to the resumption of the titles and rewards granted to them since 1397. The process of confiscation had in fact already begun: Aumale had lost the constableship by the time Creton saw him at Flint; he had surrendered the constableship of the Tower of London on 31 August, and Burstwick had been granted to the earl of Northumberland on 12 September.

These losses were substantial, but Rutland (as he now became again), with several of Richard's other allies, did receive marks of favour from Henry after parliament rose. In Rutland's case these included confirmation of his custody of the Channel Islands and of his possession of the Isle of Wight, and the strategic significance of these grants suggests that Henry was confident of his cousin's loyalty. That confidence was probably not misplaced. By the end of the year a group of Richard's former favourites were planning to seize and murder the king and his sons under colour of a tournament to be held at Windsor on twelfth night. According to the *Chronicque de la traïson et mort de Richart Deux, roy Dengleterre*, Rutland was among the conspirators, but betrayed it to the king, and this version has been generally accepted, although the author of the *Eulogium historiarum sive temporis* (ed. F. S. Haydon, Rolls Series, 9, 1858) describes the rising and its betrayal with no reference to the earl at all. The *Traïson* leaves open whether Rutland's betrayal was deliberate, but the evident confidence subsequently placed in his cousin by Henry seems incompatible with any genuine commitment to the conspiracy. Certainly Rutland collaborated in the process of repressing the rebellion, and was rewarded with the restoration of the lordship of Oakham, Rutland, in tail male.

Servant of the Lancastrian kings In October 1400 Henry IV made Rutland keeper of north Wales with the supervision of all the castles there during pleasure, a significant mark of confidence in him given the unrest in the region. On 5 July in the following year the earl was made Henry's lieutenant in Aquitaine in response to a petition from the archbishop of Bordeaux, who described the earl as the man closest to the king after the king's sons. He remained based in Bordeaux throughout the following year, but had yielded the office by May 1403. He had by then succeeded to the duchy of York, following the death of his father on 1 August 1402.

On his return to England Edward became involved in the Welsh campaign of autumn 1403 and on 15 October was appointed lieutenant of south Wales. Initially the appointment was for one year, but on 12 November York

indented to serve for three years from 29 November. The appointment was not a happy one for the duke. The king's inability to meet the cost of the war left York in desperate financial straits. He was still owed substantial sums for his service in Guyenne, although £8000 of the debt had been cancelled in return for the grant, in May 1403, of the wardship and marriage of his nephew Richard Despenser. By June 1404 he had already sold or pledged his plate and faced the prospect of mortgaging his land to pay his troops.

In this situation York's loyalty may have wavered. In February 1405 his sister Constance, Lady Despenser, accused him of involvement in a plot against the crown. After an initial denial York conceded that he had known of the conspiracy and was imprisoned at Pevensey. After seventeen weeks he petitioned for release on the grounds of his 'trouble and heaviness' but it was not until October that there were signs of his return to favour. His land was restored on 8 December, and its issues nine days later. By November 1406 he was sufficiently trusted to be made constable of the Tower—an office he had not held since Richard II's deposition. He also remained active in Wales. In December 1407 the prince of Wales went out of his way to praise the duke's efforts to parliament. York, he said

> had served and laboured in such a way as to support and embolden all the other members of the company, as if he had been the poorest gentleman in the realm wishing to serve him in order to win honour and renown. (*RotP*, 3.611–12)

In spite of his military links with the prince, York apparently sided with Henry IV in the dispute over foreign policy that opened up between father and son late in the reign. In 1412 he accompanied Henry IV's second son, Thomas, on the campaign to aid the Armagnacs against the Burgundians. He may have returned to England briefly after the death of Henry IV on 20 March 1413, but in June 1413 he was preparing to go to the defence of Aquitaine. In August he was in Paris, discussing the possibility of a marriage between Henry V and Catherine of Valois. He returned to England late in October, but remained involved in the English end of the diplomacy which filled the months before Henry's invasion of France in 1415.

Death and reputation The army's departure, early in August, was overshadowed by the discovery of a conspiracy headed by Edward's brother Richard, earl of Cambridge, but there is no suggestion that York himself was involved. The duke was present at the siege of Harfleur, where he made his will on 17 August, describing himself as 'of all sinners the most wretched and guilty' (*Register of Henry Chichele*, 2.64). He commanded the van on the march through northern France, and was killed on 25 October at Agincourt, where he commanded the right wing of the English army. Accounts of his death differ, one tradition ascribing it to a head wound, another (later followed by John Leland) blaming it on 'much heat and pressing'. His bones were brought back to England and interred, as he had wished, under the step to the choir in the church of Fotheringhay, Northamptonshire, where he had established a college of priests. The present monument was erected on the orders of Queen Elizabeth, after the choir had fallen derelict.

For most later writers Edward's career is tainted by suggestions of treachery, and the numerous occasions in the reign of Henry IV when his loyalty was publicly stressed suggest that contemporaries, too, felt that he had a reputation to live down. But he was evidently a man of considerable ability. Richard II reputedly considered resigning the crown to him, as 'the most able, wise and powerful man that he could think of' (Given-Wilson, 211), and the chronicler of Godstowe regarded him as a 'second Solomon' (Hearne, 242). He carried heavy responsibilities under three kings, apparently with success. On two occasions he took on major office when the previous holder had felt unable to continue, replacing Somerset in south Wales in 1403 and Bedford as warden of the east march in September 1414. He also gave serious attention to his office of master of the king's game. He was an authority on hunting, and particularly, it seems, on hunting-dogs. His *Master of Game*, dedicated to the prince of Wales, translated the *Livre du chasse* of Gaston Phébus, count of Foix, with the addition of several extra chapters of his own.

Family life Edward did not marry until late in Richard's reign. He had been betrothed to Beatriz of Portugal on 29 August 1381, as part of an Anglo-Portuguese alliance against Castile; but in the following year Portugal and Castile came to terms, and Beatriz was betrothed instead to a son of Juan I of Castile. As Edward rose in Richard's favour, the king seems to have taken over the job of finding him a suitable bride. During the first Irish campaign Richard suggested a marriage between Rutland and a sister-in-law of Giangaleazzo Visconti of Milan (r. 1378–1402). At the same time he was exploring the possibility of marrying him to one of the three kinswomen of Charles VI of France who had been proposed as suitable wives for Richard himself. The most serious proposal, however, was that Rutland should marry Jeanne, the younger sister of Isabelle de Valois, for whose hand Richard was negotiating from July 1395, in spite of Jeanne's earlier betrothal to Pierre de Montfort. On the strength of the proposed match Edward was referred to in English sources as the king's brother—a title used as late as April 1399, although by then the plan had fallen through and Edward had married (by October 1398) Philippa Mohun, the third (not, as is usually claimed, the second) daughter of John Mohun of Dunster (d. 1375) and Joan Burghersh (d. 1404). It was a surprising marriage for someone who must have been the most eligible aristocratic bachelor of his day. Philippa would bring him none of the Mohun land, her mother having sold the reversion to Elizabeth Lutterell. Philippa's date of birth is unknown, but she is likely to have been some twenty years older than Edward. She had had children by neither of her previous husbands (Walter Fitzwalter and John Golafre), and although York apparently had hopes of an heir in 1401, this marriage too was childless and York's heir was his nephew, Richard. Philippa outlived York, apparently spending her widowhood in Carisbrooke Castle. She died on 17 July 1431, and was buried in the chapel of St Nicholas in Westminster Abbey, where her monument survives.

According to William Worcester, Edward also had a mistress, who subsequently married the Charlton killed at Verneuil in 1424. This seems to have been Walter Charlton of Wiltshire. His first wife, Elizabeth, had died in 1414, and by his death he had remarried. His new wife's name was Joan; she outlived him and is presumably the woman Worcester had in mind; but she cannot be identified further.

ROSEMARY HORROX

Sources Chancery records · GEC, *Peerage* · *RotP*, vol. 3 · *CEPR letters*, vols. 4–6 · Rymer, *Foedera*, 1st edn · [J. Creton], 'Translation of a French metrical history of the deposition of King Richard the Second … with a copy of the original', ed. and trans. J. Webb, *Archaeologia*, 20 (1824), 1–423 · B. Williams, ed., *Chronicque de la traïson et mort de Richart Deux, roy Dengleterre*, EHS, 9 (1846) · C. Given-Wilson, ed. and trans., *Chronicles of the revolution, 1397–1400: the reign of Richard II* (1993) · L. Bellaguet, ed. and trans., *Chronique du religieux de Saint Denys*, 6 vols. (Paris, 1839–52) · T. Hearne, *Anonymi chronicon Godstovianum*, in *Guilielmi Roperi Vita D. Thomae Mori*, ed. T. Hearne (1716) · M. D. Legge, ed., *Anglo-Norman letters and petitions from All Souls MS 182*, Anglo-Norman Texts, 3 (1941) · *The diplomatic correspondence of Richard II*, ed. E. Perroy, CS, 3rd ser., 48 (1933) · E. F. Jacob, ed., *The register of Henry Chichele, archbishop of Canterbury, 1414–1443*, 4 vols., CYS, 42, 45–7 (1937–47) · *The itinerary of John Leland in or about the years 1535–1543*, ed. L. Toulmin Smith, 11 pts in 5 vols. (1906–10) · *Itineraries [of] William Worcestre*, ed. J. H. Harvey, OMT (1969) · N. H. Nicolas, ed., *Proceedings and ordinances of the privy council of England*, 7 vols., RC, 26 (1834–7), vols. 1–2 · W. A. B. Grohman and F. B. Grohman, 'The Master of Game' by Edward second duke of York (1904) · E. Curtis, ed., *Richard II in Ireland, 1394–1395, and submissions of the Irish chiefs* (1927) · D. Johnston, 'Richard II's departure from Ireland, July 1399', *EngHR*, 98 (1983), 785–805 · J. Sherborne, 'Richard II's return to Wales, July 1399', *Welsh History Review / Cylchgrawn Hanes Cymru*, 7 (1974–5), 389–402 · P. E. Russell, *The English intervention in Spain and Portugal in the time of Edward III and Richard II* (1955) · J. J. N. Palmer, *England, France and Christendom, 1377–99* (1972) · M. G. A. Vale, *English Gascony, 1399–1453: a study of war, government and politics during the later stages of the Hundred Years' War* (1970) · J. H. Wylie, *History of England under Henry the Fourth*, 4 vols. (1884–98) · J. H. Wylie and W. T. Waugh, eds., *The reign of Henry the Fifth*, 3 vols. (1914–29) · N. H. Nicolas, *History of the battle of Agincourt*, 2nd edn (1832) · H. C. Maxwell-Lyte, *A history of Dunster*, 2 vols. (1909) · A. Tuck, *Richard II and the English nobility* (1973)

Archives Northants. RO

Edward [Edward of Westminster], **prince of Wales** (1453–1471), was born at Westminster on 13 October 1453, the only son of *Henry VI (1421–1471) and his queen, *Margaret of Anjou (1430–1482), at a time of political crisis arising from King Henry's mental collapse. According to a report in January 1454, 'at the Princes comyng to Wyndesore, the Duc of Buk' toke hym in his armes and presented hym to the Kyng in godely wise, besechyng the Kyng to blisse hym; and the Kyng yave no maner answere' (*Paston Letters*, 2.295–6). Duke of Cornwall from birth, Edward was created prince of Wales and earl of Chester, and this was confirmed in parliament on 15 March 1454. When the duke of York became protector on 28 March, the terms of his appointment safeguarded the prince's position: York's commission would last during the king's pleasure or until Edward reached years of discretion. Meanwhile, provision was made for Edward's household, which was limited to thirty-nine persons.

Henry VI recovered his faculties about Christmas 1454, and on 30 December Margaret presented the prince to him again:

> the Queen came to hym, and brought my Lord Prynce with her. And then he askid what the Princes name was, and the Queen told him Edward; and than he hild up his hands and thankid God therof. And he said he never knew til that tyme.
> (*Paston Letters*, 3.13)

Although the birth of an heir did nothing either to improve the effectiveness and popularity of Henry VI's government, or to reduce political tension, Edward's rights continued to be protected. Arrangements were made on 12 November 1456 for his household to have £1000 per annum from the revenues of his patrimony until he reached the age of eight, and for him to reside with the king until he was fourteen. He was brought up by his mother, often in the midlands or Cheshire; rumours that Henry VI was not his father were doubtless politically inspired. On 28 January 1457 a council was appointed for him and it administered his patrimony; inevitably its affairs were largely directed by the queen. An attempt to arrange a marriage for him in the autumn of 1458, with a Valois or Burgundian princess, came to nothing. The prince's affinity under Margaret's control assisted Lancastrian dominance of the midlands in the late 1450s, and it turned out in Edward's livery at Bloreheath on 23 September 1459. Margaret and Edward were present at the Coventry parliament in November 1459 when the Yorkists were attainted: the Lords in parliament acknowledged the prince as their prospective king, but rumours that Margaret was trying to persuade Henry VI to abdicate in favour of Edward were probably far-fetched. In the early months of 1460, Edward was nominally placed on commissions to secure Wales and Cheshire.

The accord of 25 October 1460 between Henry VI, captured at the battle of Northampton on 10 July, and the duke of York disinherited Edward as heir to the throne in favour of York himself, who secured a grant of the prince's patrimony: the principality of Wales, the county of Chester, and the duchy of Cornwall, valued at 10,000 marks per annum. Edward's council was doubtless responsible for the protest which was sent under the prince's signature to the city of London, denouncing York, asserting Edward's rights, and vowing to release Henry VI. Margaret and Edward also appealed to the Scots for aid. At Lincluden Abbey on 5 January 1461, the queen regent, Mary of Gueldres, agreed to help them in return for Berwick, and negotiations opened for a marriage between Edward and Mary, James III's sister. Thus fortified, Margaret marched south, taking Edward with her; her army wore the prince's livery. At St Albans on 17 February 1461 Warwick was defeated; Henry VI was reunited with his wife and son, and he knighted Edward on the battlefield. The prince wielded authority for the first time: he knighted others who had distinguished themselves in the field, and the next day he pronounced judgment on Sir Thomas Kyriell and Lord Bonville before their execution on the queen's orders. But rather than try to enter London, the Lancastrian army retired northwards, and at Towton

on 29 March it was routed by the new king, *Edward IV. Henry, Margaret, and their son quickly fled to Scotland. On 16 December 1461, in Edward IV's first parliament, Margaret and Edward were attainted.

During the next ten years, Edward grew up a fugitive or an exile in his mother's company. Margaret tirelessly sought allies in Scotland and France in order to reinstate Henry VI and secure her son's inheritance, with little success at first. Late in 1462 she left Northumberland with her son for Bruges to appeal to the duke of Burgundy, who provided money to enable them to join Margaret's father, René of Anjou, in Lorraine. In August 1463 Margaret and Edward travelled to Flanders in an attempt to prevent a *rapprochement* between France, Burgundy, and Edward IV. From September 1463 to 1470 Prince Edward lived at René's castle of Koeur, near St Mihiel-en-Bar, with a small court of refugee Lancastrians. They plotted with fellow fugitives and tried to rally support from kinsmen like Alfonso V of Portugal; Edward himself signed letters of appeal. During this time, too, the prince suffered childhood illnesses that required the services of René's doctors, and, as part of Margaret's strategy, there were proposals of marriage, including, in January 1468, to Marguerite, Louis XI's daughter. However, in 1470 Edward IV's differences with Richard *Neville, earl of Warwick, and the duke of Clarence led to an accommodation between Margaret and Warwick. On 25 July 1470 these former enemies met at Angers, and during their negotiations it was proposed that Prince Edward should marry Warwick's younger daughter, *Anne (1456–1485); in return, the earl would strive to restore the Lancastrians to power in England. The betrothal took place at Angers, and Anne was placed in Margaret's charge pending the marriage, which took place at Amboise, probably on 13 December, after Warwick had landed in England.

Contemporaries found Edward a spirited boy. In 1467 the Milanese ambassador in France reported that he 'already talks of nothing but cutting off heads or making war, as if he had everything in his hands or was the god of battle or the peaceful occupant of that [English] throne' (*CSP Milan*, 1385–1618, 1.117). Sir John Fortescue, who as a fellow exile would have known him well, commented that 'as soon as he became grown up, [he] gave himself over entirely to martial exercises; and, seated on fierce and half-tamed steeds urged on by his spurs, he often delighted in attacking and assaulting the young companions attending him' (Fortescue, *De laudibus*, 2–3). The contrast with the pacific Henry VI could not have been more marked, and indeed, Edward's mentors were aware that, should he return to England, his government must be an improvement on his father's. George Ashby, a former signet clerk of both Henry VI and Queen Margaret, may have addressed to Edward his book of advice, 'On the active policy of a prince'. Fortescue was on hand to produce guidance in rulership. The scene was set for his return to England.

But although Warwick and Clarence soon put Edward IV to flight, the Lancastrian army was delayed in its return to England, and only landed at Weymouth on 14 April 1471, the day on which Warwick was defeated and killed at Barnet by the returning King Edward. Marching via Exeter and Bristol, Prince Edward and his forces reached Tewkesbury on 3 May. Edward IV encamped at Cheltenham the same evening. The battle next day was a disaster for the house of Lancaster. The prince was in nominal command of the centre of the army, advised by Sir John Langstrother, prior of the hospitallers in England, and Lord Wenlock, both of whom died at Tewkesbury. Opinions differ as to Edward's fate: he was most likely killed while fleeing to the town, possibly appealing for succour to Clarence who had deserted the Lancastrians for his brother, Edward IV; stories of his capture and defiance before the king, whose lords allegedly slew him on the spot, were told first by continental and later by Tudor writers, culminating in Shakespeare (*3 Henry VI*, v.v). He received honourable burial in the nearby abbey. His widow, Anne Neville, married Richard, duke of Gloucester, a year later, on 12 July 1472.

Prince Edward's birth had made reconciliation between Henry VI and his critics more difficult. As the sole Lancastrian heir, Edward in dying sealed his father's fate: a prisoner in the Tower of London since 1465, Henry was put to death as soon as Edward IV reached London after Tewkesbury (21–2 May). Margaret of Anjou was captured after the battle, and was returned to Louis XI's custody in 1476.

R. A. GRIFFITHS

Sources *Chancery records* · *The Paston letters, AD 1422–1509*, ed. J. Gairdner, new edn, 6 vols. (1904) · J. Fortescue, *De laudibus legum Anglie*, ed. and trans. S. B. Chrimes (1942) · J. S. Davies, ed., *An English chronicle of the reigns of Richard II, Henry IV, Henry V, and Henry VI*, CS, 64 (1856) · J. Fortescue, *The governance of England*, ed. C. Plummer (1885) · M. L. Kekewich and others, eds., *The politics of fifteenth-century England: John Vale's book* (1995) · J. Bruce, ed., *Historie of the arrivall of Edward IV in England, and the finall recoverye of his kingdomes from Henry VI*, CS, 1 (1838) · *RotP*, vol. 5 · *CSP Milan* · P. W. Hammond, *The battles of Barnet and Tewkesbury* (1990) · C. L. Kingsford, *English historical literature in the fifteenth century* (1913), 376–7 [The Tewkesbury Chronicle] · C. E. Dumont, *Histoire de la ville de Saint-Mihiel*, 2 vols. (1860–62)
Likenesses J. Rous, portrait, Coll. Arms, Rous Roll · portrait (at the battle of Tewkesbury), University of Ghent Library, Netherlands

Edward [Edward of Middleham], **prince of Wales** (1474×6–1484), was the first-born and probably only son of Richard, duke of Gloucester (the future *Richard III), and his wife, *Anne Neville (1456–1485). While the place of his birth is recorded by John Rous (*d.* 1492), its date is not. Although the latter is usually attributed to 1474, the Tewkesbury chronicle records the birth of an unnamed son at Middleham in 1476. While this might be a reference to a second son, also born at Middleham, who died at birth, it might be a reference to the birth of Edward himself. There is, indeed, no reliable firsthand authority for an earlier birth date. Edward's nurse, Isabel Burgh, was later rewarded by Richard with a generous annuity from the revenues of Middleham. In February 1478 Edward was created earl of Salisbury.

Nothing more is known of Edward until the momentous summer of 1483 when his father became king. He spent most of that summer at Middleham. A schedule of

the receiver of the lordship's expenses, settled on 25 September, reveals visits to Coverham, Fountains, and Jervaulx abbeys, Tadcaster, Wetherby, and 'Kyppes' (probably Kippax), the purchase of a primer for him, and the payment of a fool for his entertainment. It would appear that he set off on 22 August to meet his father at Pontefract, travelling via York and riding in a chariot with two guards 'rynning on fote by side' (Horrox and Hammond, 2.25).

The child Edward was made nominal lieutenant of Ireland on 19 July, but more significantly was created prince of Wales on 24 August. It would seem that his father's decision to invest him at York on 8 September was made late, for only on 31 August, at the end of his progress to the north, did the king send to London for the regalia and robes for the occasion. The ceremony began with a solemn mass performed in York Minster, not by Archbishop Thomas Rotherham (*d.* 1500) but by Bishop William Dudley of Durham (*d.* 1483), after which the king, queen, and prince processed, crowned, through the streets of York to the archbishop's palace, where the king invested his son. After his investiture it seems that Edward returned to Middleham or to another of the king's Yorkshire castles. He was formally declared heir apparent to the throne in parliament in February 1484. More unusually, and a reflection of his father's sense of insecurity, the lords and principal members of the royal household were also called together in the palace of Westminster to swear an oath of allegiance to the prince, in the event of the king's demise.

But this precaution was in vain, for by the end of March 1484 the prince was dead. The news reached his father and mother at Nottingham, where, the author of the Crowland continuation wrote, 'you might have seen [them] almost out of their minds for a long time when faced with sudden grief' (Pronay and Cox, 171). The elaborate but badly worn alabaster effigy of a young man, in civilian dress, in the north chapel of St Helen's Church, Sheriff Hutton, might be his tomb. However, it has also been argued, from the heraldic detail recorded in the seventeenth century by Roger Dodsworth, that the effigy is more likely to represent a son of Richard Neville, earl of Salisbury (*d.* 1460). Moreover Rous records a report that he had been buried at Middleham. Edward's place of burial, like his date of birth, is uncertain. Apart from a conventional encomium in the charter of creation as prince of Wales, praising his noble character and singular gifts, nothing is known of his character. It is likely that, after his investiture, Richard III intended to establish the prince's household as the focus of the royal administration of the north, just as Edward IV had deployed the household of his heir for the same purpose in Wales. In July 1484, at the end of an extended visit to Yorkshire, the king formally established the first council of the north, styled the king's household, which appears to have been a continuation of the prince's household without the prince.

A. J. POLLARD

Sources R. Horrox and P. W. Hammond, eds., *British Library Harleian manuscript 433*, 2 (1980) · P. W. Hammond, *Edward of Middleham, prince of Wales* (1973) · N. Pronay and J. Cox, eds., *The Crowland* *chronicle continuations, 1459–1486* (1986) · M. A. Hicks, 'One prince or two? The family of Richard III', *The Ricardian*, 9 (1991–3), 467–8 [incl. details of *Tewkesbury Chronicle*] · A. J. Pollard, *North-eastern England during the Wars of the Roses: lay society, war and politics, 1450–1500* (1990)

Likenesses representation, BL, Beauchamp pageant · representation, BL, Rous roll

Edward, styled earl of Warwick (1475–1499), potential claimant to the English throne, was the first and only surviving son of *George, duke of Clarence (1449–1478), and Isabel, daughter and coheir of Richard *Neville, earl of Salisbury and Warwick. He was born on 21 or 25 February 1475 at Warwick Castle. Edward IV was among his godparents and ordered that he be called earl of Warwick from the time of his baptism. His older surviving sister was Margaret [*see* Pole, Margaret], who was to be restored to the earldom of Salisbury in 1513, but she was executed in 1541, as a possible threat to the Tudor succession. His younger brother Richard died in infancy, his mother having died soon after Richard's birth, and it was Clarence's high-handed use of the law to punish two of his servants for their alleged murder of these two that was one of the immediate causes of the duke's fall. On his father's attainder in February 1478, Edward's lands, consisting essentially of the Warwick earldom as it stood at Clarence's death, were taken into royal custody. This was officially for his minority only, and he was indeed subsequently on occasion referred to as earl of Warwick. In practice, however, the attainder was never reversed and, although he was of full age in 1496, and could well have been given at least partial livery earlier, the lands remained with the crown under successive kings until his death, and both the lands and Clarence's west midland affinity were effectively absorbed into the growing crown estate and affinity. Edward himself was placed in the wardship of Thomas Grey, marquess of Dorset, in 1481.

Edward's only appearance on the political stage was under Richard III, when he was present at the coronation in July 1483 and was knighted at the investiture of Richard's son as prince of Wales at York the following September. Thereafter he was kept in some sort of custody at Sheriff Hutton, one of Richard's principal northern residences, though he does seem to have been associated, albeit nominally, with the prince of Wales's council in the north, and may even have been heir apparent to the throne for a while on the prince's death in 1484. Richard is said eventually to have named John de la Pole, earl of Lincoln, as heir, and, whether formally named or not, he was undoubtedly preferred over Warwick. This was almost certainly because of the dangers of drawing attention to the fact that Edward had a better claim to the throne than Richard himself. In 1485 Henry VII was quick to remove Edward, now the obvious Yorkist claimant, from Sheriff Hutton to the Tower of London and there he remained, except for an appearance at St Paul's in 1487 designed to make public the fraudulence of Lambert Simnel's attempt to impersonate him. There followed other plots focused on Edward, now clearly seen as the main Yorkist rival to Henry VII. Finally, in 1499, the Yorkist pretender Perkin

Warbeck, who had been placed in the Tower in 1498, was alleged to have plotted to free himself and Edward, and the latter was accused of conspiracy to depose the king. In November both were tried and executed; Edward met his death at Tower Hill on the 28th. This double execution may simply have been a precondition for the marriage of Prince Arthur to Katherine of Aragon, which finally occurred in 1501. Edward was buried at Bisham Abbey, the burial place of the Montagu earls of Salisbury, from whom his mother was descended. CHRISTINE CARPENTER

Sources Dugdale, *Monasticon*, 2.64 · *Report of the Deputy Keeper of the Public Records*, 3 (1842), appx 2, pp. 216–18 · C. L. Kingsford, ed., *Chronicles of London* (1905), 227–8, 331 · Chancery records · C. Carpenter, *Locality and polity: a study of Warwickshire landed society, 1401–1499* (1992) · J. Rous, *Historia Regum*, ed. T. Hearne, 2nd edn (1745), 217–18 · *Thys rol was laburd and finished by Master John Rows of Warrewyk*, ed. W. Courthope (1859); repr. as *The Rous roll* (1980), no. 60 · *The Anglica historia of Polydore Vergil, AD 1485–1537*, ed. and trans. D. Hay, CS, 3rd ser., 74 (1950) · A. Raine, ed., *York civic records*, 1, Yorkshire Archaeological Society, 98 (1939), 116 · M. A. Hicks, 'False, fleeting, perjur'd Clarence': George, duke of Clarence, 1449–78 (1980), 137–40 · J. Gairdner, ed., *Letters and papers illustrative of the reigns of Richard III and Henry VII*, 2 vols., Rolls Series, 24 (1861–3) · A. F. Pollard, ed., *The reign of Henry VII from contemporary sources*, 1 (1913), 1.84–7

Archives PRO, duchy of Lancaster and minister's accounts classes, accounts of Clarence estates · PRO, chancery rolls, estate officer appointments

Likenesses drawing, repro. in Rous, *Rous Roll*

Edward, Prince, duke of Kent and Strathearn (1767–1820), the fourth son of *George III (1738–1820) and Queen *Charlotte (1744–1818), was born on 2 November 1767 at Buckingham House, London. After an up-and-down career in the army, he became the father of Queen Victoria.

Prince Edward's preceptor from 1780 to 1785 was John Fisher, a future bishop of Salisbury and an amateur artist. The young prince was taught etching by Alexander Cozens, and also shared in his family's enthusiasm for music. In 1783 he was the first prince to be appointed a knight of the new Order of St Patrick. George III intended that all his younger sons should spend a large proportion of their lives in Germany, and in 1785 Edward was sent to Lüneburg in his father's electorate of Hanover, where he joined the garrison as a cadet in the Hanoverian foot guards. Under his governor, Lieutenant-Colonel George von Wangenheim, he studied German, law, history, religion, classics, and artillery. Wangenheim, a stingy bully, allowed Edward only 1½ guineas a week pocket money out of £6000 a year for maintenance, leading Edward to acquire lifelong habits of indebtedness. While in Geneva, Edward fathered at least two natural children including Edward Schencker *Scheener. Edward was gazetted brevet colonel in the British army in 1786, in which year he moved to Hanover and was appointed a knight of the Garter. George III also allowed him the pay of a colonel in the Hanoverian foot guards, but it was again directed through Wangenheim and Edward saw little of it, borrowing money to support his cherished regimental band. From 1788 to 1790 he concluded his education at Geneva. He accepted the command of the Royal Fusiliers (7th foot) in April 1789, but at the same time declined the same rank in the Hanoverian foot guards, perhaps a sign that he was

Prince Edward, duke of Kent and Strathearn (1767–1820), by Sir William Beechey, 1818

tired of living in Europe. In January 1790 he returned home without leave but, after a brief meeting with his furious father, was virtually banished to Gibraltar, where he served in the garrison as an ordinary officer. While at Gibraltar he imported from Marseilles Thérèse-Bernardine Mongenet (1760–1830) to be his 'chanteuse' and long-term mistress. Known as Madame de Saint-Laurent, she probably used the forename Julie. She was the daughter of Jean Mongenet (b. 1726), a highway engineer from Besançon, and his wife, Claudine, née Pussot (1734?–1805). She devoted herself to Edward for nearly twenty-eight years before she was set aside. Although evidence suggests that they had no children, many families in Canada have claimed descent from the couple. Edward also had at least two illegitimate children: Adelaide Victoire Auguste (b. 1789, d. in or after 1832), whose mother was Adelaide Dubus (d. 1789), who died in childbirth, and Edward Schencker *Scheener (1789–1853), whose mother was Anne Gabrielle Alexandrine Moré.

Edward's disciplinarian excesses (perhaps learned from Wangenheim) caused his removal in 1791 to Canada. In August that year he took up residence with his regiment in Quebec City, where his presence, and that of the regimental band, dramatically enhanced social life. Edward was the first member of the royal family to reside in North America for a prolonged period (his elder brother, the future *William IV, had visited Nova Scotia in 1788) and in Quebec City became the focus—probably sometimes an organizing one—of assemblies, subscription concerts, and theatrical performances. He attended to his regimental duties, was promoted major-general on 2 October 1793,

and seized the opportunity to shine, serving successfully in the West Indies campaign to reduce Martinique and St Lucia in 1794. On his way to the West Indies, Edward became the first prince to visit the United States since independence, travelling through Boston and New York. Following the campaign he was mentioned in dispatches and received the thanks of parliament. His father refused his request to return home, and instead he was stationed in Halifax, Nova Scotia. There he attempted to maintain the standards of social life he had established in Quebec and entertained himself by making alterations to the house and grounds he rented from the governor of Nova Scotia, Sir John Wentworth. Edward was promoted lieutenant-general on 12 January 1796, but only when he suffered a fall from his horse was he permitted to leave Nova Scotia for Britain, landing at Plymouth on 15 November 1798. His North American career is remembered in the name of Prince Edward Island, adopted in 1799.

Edward's career peaked in 1799. As well as being created duke of Kent and Strathearn on 24 April, he received the thanks of parliament and an income of £12,000, was gazetted general on 10 May, and in July was appointed commander-in-chief of British forces in North America, although he only held that post until 1800. Two years later he met with disaster. He was appointed governor of Gibraltar on 27 March 1802, with specific orders to restore discipline to the drunken garrison, but his severity provoked a mutiny which he suppressed by shooting three ringleaders. Recalled in May 1803 and refused permission to return for an inquiry, he learned instead that the garrison had returned to their old licentious ways. He was promoted field marshal on 5 September 1805, but three days after his thirty-eighth birthday (5 November 1805) the duke accepted the *reductio ad absurdum* of his career: he was made keeper and paler of Hampton Court. He settled at Castle Hill Lodge, Ealing.

On the domestic front the prospect brightened with the duke's new life in England, which put him in touch with his niece Princess *Charlotte Augusta (1796–1817), heir apparent, and her suitor, Prince Leopold of Saxe-Coburg-Saalfeld, whose successful courtship Edward assisted. They in turn urged him to marry Leopold's sister *Victoria Mary Louisa of Saxe-Coburg-Saalfeld (1786–1861), the widow since 1814 of Emich Charles, prince of Leiningen, and the mother of a young son and daughter. Edward's courtship, kept secret from Madame de Saint-Laurent, nevertheless hung fire. Suddenly the whole scene changed.

Edward had moved to Brussels in 1815, not to participate in the battle of Waterloo but to economize. In 1817 Princess Charlotte died in childbirth, and parliament backed a marriage marathon of unmarried princes to safeguard the succession. Madame de Saint-Laurent was distressed but accepted the separation with dignity and left Brussels for Paris; she was cared for by General William Knollys (whose son William was appointed comptroller to the future King Edward VII by Queen Victoria when Prince Albert died), and died in Paris on 8 August 1830. Edward married Victoria at Coburg on 29 May 1818 (Lutheran rite) and at Kew Palace on 13 July. They visited Victoria's mother, the duchess of Coburg, who thought Edward was 'embarrassed' at falling like a 'bomb' into their family circle (Coburg diary, Royal Archives). The bridal pair were striking: he tall, heavily built, blue-eyed, with dyed brown whiskers; she brown-eyed and black-ringletted. They lived mainly in Amorbach Castle, Leiningen, Victoria's dower house, until late in Victoria's pregnancy, when Edward rushed her back to Kensington Palace for the birth of their daughter, (Alexandrina) *Victoria, the future queen, on 24 May 1819.

Money and creditors were still the duke's problem. Bishop Fisher of Salisbury advised him to holiday in Devon—cheap and healthy. But the duke caught cold in the icy cathedral on the way there. He died of pneumonia in Woolbrook Cottage, Sidmouth, Devon, on 23 January 1820 and was buried in a giant coffin nearly 7½ feet long in St George's Chapel, Windsor, on 11 February.

The duke had been intensely proud of his infant daughter and would tell his friends to look at her well, for she would be queen of England. Queen Victoria herself managed to be proud of her father. Having read her mother's diary after her death, she wrote: 'All these notes show how very much She & my beloved Father loved each other!' (Royal Archives Y 106/14). Lord Melbourne said her father was as agreeable as George IV and more 'posé' than William IV, without his talkativeness; 'from all what [sic] I heard', Victoria added in her journal of 1 August 1838, 'he was the best of all'.

Edward combined character defects with charm and abilities. His sisters called him Joseph Surface, Oliver Goldsmith's hypocrite. Though a martinet, he was the first to abandon flogging and introduced the first regimental school. Wellington rated him a first-class speaker. Sir Matthew Wood, the radical mayor of London, was his trustee—and the unruly Queen Caroline's spokesman.

George Hardinge, a Welsh judge, emphasized Edward's friendliness and popularity with servants. This tribute seems to contradict his known unpopularity with the army rank and file. The answer may be that the duke drew a distinction between correct military and civilian behaviour. He showed an interest in Robert Owen's social experiments. He supported literary, Bible, and anti-slavery societies and voted for Catholic emancipation. And he performed his own duties with every bit as much rigour as he demanded of others.

ELIZABETH LONGFORD

Sources Duchess of Coburg, diary, Royal Arch., Kent papers • M. Gillen, *The prince and his lady* (1970) • E. Longford, *Victoria RI* (1964) • R. Fulford, *Royal dukes* (1933) • *Annual Register* (1820) • Tunbridge Wells Library, General Knollys MSS • P. H. Stanhope, *Notes of conversations with the duke of Wellington, 1831–1851* (1888); repr. with introduction by E. Longford (1998) • J. Roberts, *Royal artists: from Mary queen of Scots to the present day* (1987) • *DNB* • Queen Victoria, journal, Royal Arch. • F. A. Hall, 'A prince's sojourn in eighteenth-century Canada', *Studies in Eighteenth-Century Culture*, 19 (1989), 247–66 • GEC, *Peerage*, new edn • *The later correspondence of George III*, ed. A. Aspinall, 5 vols. (1962–70) • D. M. Potts and W. T. W. Potts, *Queen Victoria's gene* (1995)

Archives LMA, deeds, financial and London estate papers • Royal Arch. | BL, corresp. with Sir James Willoughby Gordon, Add. MSS 49475 • BL, corresp. with Lord Grenville, Add. MSS 58868 • BL, corresp. with Lord Holland, Add. MS 51524 • BL, corresp. with Prince Lieven, Add. MSS 47287–47290 • BL, corresp. with earl of Liverpool, Add. MSS 38190, 38259–38323, 38564 *passim* • Bucks. RLSS, corresp. with Sir William Fremantle • CKS, corresp. with Lord Camden • CKS, letters to William Knollys • Devon RO, corresp. with Lord Sidmouth • Hunt. L., letters to Lord Moira • Morgan L., letters to Sir James Murray-Pulteney • NA Scot., letters to Sir Alexander Pope • NL Scot., corresp. with Sir Alexander Cochrane • PRO, letters to Lord Cornwallis, PRO 30/11 • PRO, letters to William Pitt, PRO 30/8 • Royal Arch., letters to George III • Royal Military Academy Library, Sandhurst, letters to Gaspard Le Marchant • Southampton City Archives, letters to J. G. Smyth • Staffs. RO, letters to Lord Dartmouth • U. Durham L., corresp. with Earl Grey • University of New Brunswick, letters to William Edmeston

Likenesses J. Zoffany, group portrait, oils, 1770 (*George III, Queen Charlotte, and their six eldest children*), Royal Collection • B. West, double portrait, oils, 1778 (with Prince William), Royal Collection • B. West, group portrait, oils, 1779 (*Queen Charlotte with her children*), Royal Collection • T. Gainsborough, oils, 1782, National Collection • T. Gainsborough, oils, *c.*1786–1788, YCBA • S. Weaver, oils, 1796, Nova Scotia Legislature Library; repro. in Gillen, *The prince and his lady*, frontispiece • J. Hoppner, oils, in or after 1799 (in uniform with Garter ribbon), Royal Collection • H. Edridge, pencil and wash drawing, 1802, Windsor Castle • W. Beechey, oils, 1814, Fishmongers' Hall, London • J. Bacon jun., marble bust, 1818, Royal Collection • W. Beechey, oils, 1818, NPG [*see illus.*] • G. Dawe, two portraits, oils, 1818, Royal Collection; copies at Broadlands and at Kent House, Quebec • P. Turnerelli, marble bust, 1820, Royal Collection • P. Turnerelli, marble bust, 1820, Scot. NPG • Gahagan, bronze statue, 1823, Park Crescent, Portland Place, London • Francis, marble bust, 1832, Freemasons' Hall, London • attrib. F. Cotes, oils (as Cupid in landscape), Royal Collection • J. Downman, drawing, Royal Collection • H. Edridge, drawing, Royal Collection • Fry, engraving (after Gahagan), repro. in *European Magazine* • H. D. Hamilton, drawing, Royal Collection • F. X. Winterhalter, oils, Royal Collection

Wealth at death under £80,000: *Annual Register*, 681–91

Edward, prince of Saxe-Weimar (1823–1902), army officer, was the eldest son of Bernard, duke of Saxe-Weimar-Eisenach (1792–1862), and his wife, Princess Ida (1794–1852), daughter of George, duke of Saxe-Meiningen. His father was the younger son of Charles Augustus, grand duke of Saxe-Weimar. His mother was younger sister of Princess (afterwards Queen) Adelaide, wife of the duke of Clarence, later William IV. His parents were frequent visitors to the Clarences' residence in Bushey Park, and there he was born on 11 October 1823 and named William Augustus Edward. Brought up chiefly in England by Queen Adelaide, the young prince was one of Queen Victoria's playfellows and was always on affectionate terms with her and her family. Another of his childhood associates, Prince George, second duke of Cambridge, became one of his closest friends. Having been naturalized, he passed through the Royal Military College, Sandhurst, and entered the army as an ensign on 1 June 1841. His long career was wholly with the British army. Originally attached to the 67th regiment, he soon transferred as ensign and lieutenant to the Grenadier Guards, became captain on 19 May 1846, and was adjutant from November 1850 to December 1851.

Prince Edward accompanied the 3rd battalion to the Crimea, where he served with distinction as major (brevet major 20 June 1854) at Alma, Balaklava, and the siege of

Sevastopol. He was wounded in the leg in the trenches on 19 October and was mentioned in dispatches. At Inkerman, Prince Edward, on picket duty with his company at quarter-guard point, successfully repelled the Russian attack on the British flank. On 15 June 1855 he was appointed aide-de-camp to Lord Raglan, and three days later engaged in the desperate but unsuccessful attack on the Malakhov and the Redan. For his services he received the CB, the Légion d'honneur, and the Mejidiye (fourth class). He was appointed brevet colonel and aide-de-camp to Queen Victoria on 5 October 1855, and retained the position until 22 February 1869, when he was promoted major-general.

From 1 April 1870 to 31 July 1876 Prince Edward commanded the home district. On 6 July 1877 he became lieutenant-general, and from 1 October 1878 until 30 April 1881 he commanded the southern district (Portsmouth). In 1878 he was appointed colonel of the 10th (North Lincolnshire) regiment, and on 14 November 1879 became general. From October 1885 to September 1890 he commanded the forces in Ireland. On 24 May 1881 he was made KCB, and on 21 June 1887 GCB. From 1888 he was colonel-in-chief of the 1st Life Guards, and as such was gold stick-in-waiting to the queen. He retired on 11 October 1890. On 22 June 1897 Queen Victoria made him a field marshal; he was also created a knight of St Patrick in 1890, and on 8 March 1901 GCVO.

On 27 November 1851 Prince Edward had married, in London, Lady Augusta Katherine (d. 1904), second daughter of Charles Gordon-*Lennox, fifth duke of Richmond and Lennox. They had no children. The marriage was morganatic and his wife was given in Germany the title countess of Dornburg; in 1866 by royal decree she was granted the title of princess in Great Britain. Prince Edward died at his home, 16 Portland Place, on 16 November 1902, and was buried in Chichester Cathedral.

H. M. VIBART, *rev.* JAMES FALKNER

Sources *The Times* (17 Nov 1902) • *Army and Navy Gazette* (22 Nov 1902) • *Army List* • *Hart's Army List* • A. W. Kinglake, *The invasion of the Crimea*, 8 vols. (1863–87) • E. Sheppard, *The duke of Cambridge* (1906) • W. Verner, *The military life of H.R.H. George, duke of Cambridge*, 2 vols. (1905) • C. Kinloch-Cooke, *Life of the duchess of Teck*, 2 vols. (1900) • Burke, *Peerage* • *LondG* (7 Nov 1854)

Likenesses J. Slater, pencil and wash drawing, 1832, Royal Collection • Ape [C. Pellegrini], lithograph, 1872, NPG • photograph, *c.*1900, Royal Collection; repro. in duke of Connaught's album • photograph, 1902, repro. in *Navy and Army Illustrated* • Ape [C. Pellegrini], lithograph, NPG; repro. in *VF* (30 Oct 1875) • G. Hayter, group portrait, oils (*The christening of HRH Edward, prince of Wales, 1842*), Royal Collection • F. Marks, oils (after a portrait in possession of duke of Richmond, 1912), Goodwood House, West Sussex

Edward, **duke of Windsor**. *See* Edward VIII (1894–1972).

Edward I (1239–1307), king of England and lord of Ireland, and duke of Aquitaine, was born at Westminster on the night of 17–18 June 1239, the eldest son of *Henry III (1207–1272) and *Eleanor of Provence (*c.*1223–1291).

Childhood and youth, 1239–1258 Widespread delight at the news of Edward's birth was tempered when the king made it known that he expected gifts from his subjects. 'God gave us this child, but the king is selling him to us'

Edward I (1239–1307), manuscript illumination

was one comment (Prestwich, *Edward I*, 4). The name Edward was chosen by the king, who was devoted to the cult of Edward the Confessor. The boy was soon given his own household, and provided with companions, of whom the most notable was his cousin Henry of Almain (d. 1271), son of Richard, earl of Cornwall (1209–1272). Letters from the king demonstrate a fatherly concern: in 1242 he expressed worry that Edward and the other children had no good wine to drink, and the sheriff of Gloucester was ordered to send him a regular supply of lampreys. Hugh Giffard was the first to be given charge of the young Edward; in 1246 Bartholomew Pecche took his place. There were serious concerns about the boy's health in 1246, 1247, and 1251, but he grew up to be strong and healthy. Little is known of his education, but by seventeen he was skilled enough in arms to take part in a tournament at Blythe. As heir to the throne he was known simply as 'Dominus Edwardus', the Lord Edward. There was no question of his being crowned king during his father's lifetime, in the way that Henry II had his eldest son elevated to kingly status in 1170.

In 1254 alarm at the possibility of a Castilian invasion of Gascony led to the plan for Edward's marriage to *Eleanor of Castile (1241–1290). Alfonso X was anxious that his son-in-law should receive a substantial endowment of land, and Edward, who was given Gascony, Ireland, the earldom of Chester, major estates in Wales, Bristol, Stamford, and Grantham, gained some measure of independence. Yet it was not until 1256 that orders were given for Edward's seal to replace Henry's in Ireland, and even then the king occasionally countermanded his son's orders. There were more significant disagreements between the king and Edward over policy in Gascony, the former following a policy of reconciliation, the latter giving his firm backing to one faction in Bordeaux, the Soler family. In Wales policies of Anglicization pursued by Edward's officials, notably Geoffrey Langley, provoked rebellion in 1256, and an ineffective royal campaign in the north of the country in the following year. At this period Edward's income was probably in the region of £6000 a year; that this was insufficient is indicated by his sale of the wardship of Robert Ferrers for 6000 marks, and a loan he obtained from the archbishop of Canterbury of £1000.

Politically, from 1254 until 1257, Edward was under the influence of the powerful court faction of the Savoyards, relatives of his mother, Eleanor of Provence, of whom the most notable was Peter of Savoy. In 1258, however, he linked his cause to that of the Lusignans, the Poitevin half-brothers of the king. Stamford and Grantham were handed over to one of them, William de Valence, in return for a loan. Edward planned to make Geoffrey de Lusignan seneschal of Gascony, and his brother Guy keeper of Oléron and the Channel Islands. Given the extreme unpopularity of the Lusignans, this was a dangerous line for Edward to take, and it is not surprising that the veteran chronicler Matthew Paris viewed the prospect of his succeeding one day to the throne with no enthusiasm at all.

The baronial reform movement, 1258–1264 Edward's role in the difficult period of baronial reform and rebellion was understandably ambivalent, for the man who emerged as the most formidable opposition leader was his uncle by marriage, Simon de Montfort. When the crisis first erupted in 1258 Edward initially, with considerable reluctance, swore to accept what should be decided. When a reform scheme was drawn up at the Oxford parliament in May 1258, Edward made his attitude very plain, by giving public support to the Lusignans. Four councillors, John de Balliol, Roger de Mohaut, John de Grey, and Stephen Longespée, were then appointed to curb Edward, the first two being baronial supporters, the latter experienced officials who had served him previously. As the success of the reformers became increasingly apparent, so Edward's attitude softened. He began to build up a new following, which included his cousin Henry of Almain, John, Earl Warenne (d. 1304), Roger Clifford, Roger Leyburn, Hamon L'Estrange, and others, men who were to play very significant roles later in Edward's career. In March 1259 Edward entered into a formal alliance with Richard de Clare, earl of Gloucester, one of the leading reformers. One possible reason for this is that Edward was anxious to have the support of at least one of those about to negotiate peace terms with the French, for it was important that his interests in Gascony should be safeguarded. In October 1259 an appeal was made directly to Edward and Gloucester by a body

calling itself the 'community of the bachelors of England'. The complaint was that the king had done all he had been asked to do, while the baronial reformers had not acted. Edward's response was that he had been initially reluctant to swear to the oath demanded of him at Oxford, but that he was now ready to stand by it. He was ready, indeed, to die in the cause of the community of the realm. Various interpretations of this incident have been proposed, but it seems likely that Edward was indeed enthusiastic about the cause of reform. On 15 October he issued letters announcing that he had sworn to do all in his power to support Simon de Montfort, and that he was committed to support the baronial enterprise. Montfort, it should be noted, had quarrelled with Gloucester, and was the man most likely to carry influence in the negotiations with the French. Edward may have been motivated by idealistic concepts, but there was hard political sense to his alignments in this difficult period.

From November 1259 until April 1260 Henry III was in France for the peace negotiations. Edward used his father's absence to make a bid for independence, and Henry at least was persuaded that his son was plotting to depose him. Edward was certainly in dispute with the earl of Gloucester. On the king's return to England Henry initially refused to see Edward, but reconciliation was achieved by the earl of Cornwall and the archbishop of Canterbury. Edward and Gloucester's dispute was to be settled by arbitration. Roger Leyburn and Roger Clifford were removed from the respective commands of Bristol and the 'Three Castles' (Grosmont, Skenfrith, and Whitecastle) in south Wales to which Edward had appointed them. Edward himself was sent abroad, to take part in tournaments, but returned briefly in the autumn after allegedly failing to distinguish himself. In November he went back to France, and made common cause once more with the Lusignans.

When Edward arrived in England again, in the spring of 1261, it seems probable that he once more briefly changed sides, uniting with Montfort and Gloucester. If so, he was soon brought back to his father's cause, and in July went to Gascony, where he achieved some success in bringing order to an unruly province. Early in 1262 he came back to England, to face a crisis in his own private affairs. Roger Leyburn was accused and found guilty of misappropriating Edward's funds, a move that alienated Edward from the group of young English magnates, headed by Henry of Almain, Earl Warenne, and Roger Clifford, who had provided him with significant backing. To prevent further financial mismanagement Edward handed the bulk of his lands over to his father, receiving in exchange the receipts of the English Jewry for a three-year period. Once again Edward, presumably in some disgrace, was sent away to amuse himself in tournaments in France, and returned to England early in 1263.

A fresh problem faced Edward in the spring of 1263. *Llywelyn ap Gruffudd had taken advantage of the confused political situation in England to extend his power in Wales and the marches. Edward led a campaign against him in April and May, but although he had the support of

Llywelyn's brother *Dafydd ap Gruffudd, the expedition achieved little. In England Henry III's situation deteriorated; Simon de Montfort had left England in 1261, but returned in the spring of 1263, determined to re-establish the baronial reform movement. The death of the earl of Gloucester in 1262 made it easier for him to assert his dominance. Edward was by now staunchly royalist. He went to Bristol, where the conduct of his men caused the townspeople to besiege him in the castle. Only when the bishop of Worcester organized a truce could he escape. Provocatively, he garrisoned Windsor Castle with foreign mercenary knights. Lack of money was a major problem, which he remedied in part by the forcible seizure of funds deposited for safe keeping in the New Temple in London. On 16 July Henry III accepted the baronial terms, but Edward continued to resist. In August he re-established links with his former supporters, notably Henry of Almain, Earl Warenne, and Roger Leyburn, and abandoned his unpopular use of foreign mercenaries. Attempts to reach a settlement in parliament in October failed, and Edward withdrew, seizing Windsor Castle, which his men had surrendered earlier. Lengthy negotiations eventually produced agreement that the dispute between the king and his opponents should be settled by the arbitration of the French king, Louis IX. Edward went with his father to Amiens for the discussions, which in January 1264 predictably yielded a firm justification for the royalist position.

The civil war, 1264–1267 The mise of Amiens was the prelude not to peace, but to civil war. The initial outbreak was in the Welsh marches. At Gloucester Edward displayed his lack of good faith; he forced an entry to the town, but when a relieving force under Robert Ferrers, earl of Derby, appeared, he agreed to a truce. Once Ferrers had departed, Edward ignored the terms of the agreement, and pillaged the town. In April the conflict moved to Northampton, where Edward played a leading role in the assault on the town where Montfort's son Simon had gathered baronial forces. Edward then pursued his quarrel with Ferrers, capturing Tutbury Castle and ravaging the earl's lands. Despite the scale of royalist success, London remained staunchly baronial, and a royal campaign to secure the south-east was countered by the Montfortian forces when they advanced on the royalists encamped at Lewes. Battle was joined on 14 May 1264. Edward, in command of the cavalry on the right, charged the Londoners to great effect, routing them. Unfortunately he did not control his troops effectively, and by the time he had regrouped them after a lengthy pursuit, the main battle was lost. Following negotiations during the night Edward and his cousin Henry of Almain gave themselves up as hostages, not to be released until a final settlement was achieved.

Edward's imprisonment lasted until March 1265. He then agreed to accept the scheme of government introduced by Montfort, and handed over Bristol as a pledge that he would keep his word. Five royal castles were to be transferred to Edward, who would then entrust them to Montfort for five years as a further guarantee. Nor was he fully free; close surveillance was the order of the day. At the end of May he went riding with his escort, and succeeded in making his escape, fleeing from Hereford to Roger Mortimer's castle of Wigmore. He joined forces with the young earl of Gloucester, Gilbert de Clare (d. 1295), who had quarrelled with Simon de Montfort earlier in the year. Men soon flocked to Edward's standard; there was growing alarm at the increasingly autocratic attitude taken by Montfort. The marcher lords were quick to make common cause with Edward, and Earl Warenne and William de Valence rapidly joined him. Worcester fell without a fight, and the Gloucester garrison soon surrendered. Simon de Montfort looked to Llywelyn of Wales for support, and made a formal alliance with him on 19 June. By breaking the bridges across the Severn the royalists cut Montfort off from potential support. Meanwhile the younger Simon de Montfort marched north from his siege of Pevensey to Kenilworth, where he was surprised by Edward's troops who had made a swift night march from Worcester. The elder Montfort marched to Evesham, hoping to join forces with his son. On 4 August battle was joined. Montfort was completely outmanoeuvred before the battle, and the defensive formation of his troops was not strong enough to resist Edward's and Gloucester's men. Montfort and his eldest son, Henry, were killed, along with many of their supporters. The campaign had been a triumph for Edward, though how far he had personally masterminded it is not apparent from the sources.

The battle of Evesham did not mark the conclusion of the civil war. The political mood of the victors was not one of reconciliation, and late in the year Edward campaigned against the younger Simon de Montfort and other rebels who had taken refuge in the Isle of Axholme in Lincolnshire, coming to terms with them at Christmas 1265. A campaign together with Roger Leyburn against the Cinque Ports followed, with success achieved by 25 March. A mopping-up operation in Hampshire saw Edward engage a notable rebel knight, Adam Gurdun, in single combat. The romantic story was that Edward was so impressed with Gurdun's courage that he gave him his lands back, and regarded him with great favour. The reality was that he was given to the queen as a prisoner, and made to buy his lands back at a heavy price.

The major military operation against the rebels was the siege of Kenilworth, though it was not until May 1266 that Edward himself joined the royalist forces engaged in a complex and expensive operation there. Nor does it appear that he played any significant part in the negotiations that led to the promulgation of the dictum of Kenilworth at the end of October. This set out the principles by which former rebels were allowed to repurchase their lands, and was not enough to persuade the Kenilworth garrison to surrender; they held out, cold and hungry, until mid-December. Edward, meanwhile, had gone north to deal with John de Vescy, who had rebelled in protest at the policy of confiscation of lands adopted by the royalists. He had to pay 3700 marks to redeem his lands, but bore Edward no ill will, and became in time one of his most loyal associates. The one remaining problem was the continued resistance of John d'Eyville, which became acute in April 1267 when the earl of Gloucester joined forces with him and marched on London. Gloucester, who had done so much to secure Edward's success in 1265, had received little recognition for his services, and there was a real danger that civil war would break out again on a big scale. Negotiations, however, were successful, and Gloucester left London. The government adopted a more conciliatory line toward the former rebels, and Edward reduced the final rebel redoubt in the Isle of Ely with little difficulty. The summer was dry, making it easy to advance through the fens, and on 11 July the rebels surrendered.

The settlement of England, 1267–1270 Important steps were taken in the autumn of 1267 to secure the royalist position. On 29 September the treaty of Montgomery was agreed with Llywelyn ap Gruffudd. The English recognized him as prince of Wales, and as the feudal lord of all other Welsh princes with the sole exception of Maredudd ap Rhys of Ystrad Tywi, who owed homage directly to Henry III. The lands of the Four Cantrefs in the north were conceded to Llywelyn. Edward had earlier handed over important interests in Wales to his brother *Edmund (1245–1296), to whom he granted Cardigan and Carmarthen in 1265. Edward therefore had largely abandoned his interests in Wales; although he gave his consent to the treaty of Montgomery, it is hard to imagine that he did so very willingly. In November 1267 the Statute of Marlborough was issued. This lengthy series of legal measures continued in many respects the work of legislative reform begun by the king's opponents in 1259, and in many ways it anticipated the legal reforms of Edward's reign, though it is not clear that he took any part in the debates which must have taken place about the measures.

It is, indeed, difficult to determine what Edward's role was in the years following the pacification of England. In some respects his behaviour did not seem statesmanlike. His relations with the earl of Gloucester remained stormy; the two men were in dispute over the ownership of Bristol, while decisions Edward made in 1269 when hearing disputes between the marcher lords and Llywelyn of Wales antagonized the earl. In 1269 he was involved in the harsh treatment of his former ward Robert Ferrers, earl of Derby. Ferrers was forced to acknowledge a huge debt of £50,000 to Edward's brother Edmund, in return for his release from captivity. Inevitably, the money could not be found, and Edmund acquired the bulk of Ferrers's estates. Edward undoubtedly took a leading part in the discussions in the royal council, but the only measures that can be clearly associated with him were one for the holding of tournaments, and another dealing with debts owed to Jewish moneylenders. He received some major grants, which gave him the custody of London, seven royal castles, and eight counties, but this was presumably in order to pay off the debts he must have incurred in his military operations, rather than as a means of giving him added political authority. The evidence does not suggest that he played a dominant political role in all areas. Until 1268 the papal legate Ottobuono had played a leading role

in the affairs of state, and after that Edward's concerns were increasingly directed towards his planned crusade.

Edward had a hard political apprenticeship. He had found it difficult to balance the various pressures that were placed upon him, and it is not surprising that he gained a reputation for unreliability as a result of his various changes of side since 1258. One contemporary saw him as on the one hand a *leo*, a brave lion, proud and fierce; and on the other as a *pard*, a leopard, inconsistent and unreliable, a man who made promises when in difficulties and then broke them when it suited him. The ambivalence in his character was very clear in this period of his life; such traits may have been less obvious later, but they did not leave him.

Edward on crusade, 1270–1274 The papal legate Ottobuono was ordered to preach the crusade in the autumn of 1266, as part of a campaign throughout Europe. Louis IX decided to participate, and took the cross with his sons in March 1267. There was little initial support in England, and this was not to be a movement buoyed up by popular enthusiasm. The important step was taken in 1268 at Northampton, when Edward, his brother Edmund, Henry of Almain, Earl Warenne, the earl of Gloucester, William de Valence, and others agreed to go on crusade. It is not obvious why Edward himself took the cross. His father had done so in 1250, and in 1268 Henry III probably still hoped to go to the East. Should he not do so, it was his second son Edmund, not Edward, who was seen by the pope as an acceptable substitute. The papal view was that the situation in England demanded Edward's presence there. Edward, however, was undoubtedly enthusiastic about the crusading cause, and perhaps welcomed the opportunity to leave England and its problems. He may also have felt honour-bound to go: if the king of France's sons were setting out for the East, so should the king of England's.

The core of Edward's expedition was provided by his own household. In July 1270 contracts were made with eighteen men to provide a total of 225 knights. The force was largely composed of men who had fought on the royalist side in the civil war; only for a few former rebels did the crusade provide a means of gaining royal favour. The earl of Gloucester was one opponent of Edward who did take the cross, but he became increasingly reluctant to go. Richard of Cornwall had to negotiate an agreement between him and Edward at the Easter parliament in 1270, which provided that the earl should follow Edward to the East within six months. In the event he did not do so, Welsh attacks on his lands providing him with an excuse. The expedition that set off in the summer of 1270 was, by any standards, a small one. Recruitment for the crusade had not been easy, nor was its financing. Louis IX provided a loan of about £17,500 in 1269, while lengthy discussions in a series of parliaments eventually led to the grant of a tax of a twentieth in 1270.

Edward's forces arrived at the crusading port of Aigues-Mortes on the southern French coast at the end of September 1270, long after the main expedition had departed for Tunis. When Edward's small fleet reached Tunis, it was to discover that the French king had died of dysentery in August, and that his successor was also stricken. Charles of Anjou had entered into negotiations with the Tunisian emir, and reached agreement on 1 November. An indignant Edward had to accept the decision of the crusade leaders to sail for Sicily, with the intention of going on to the East in the spring. He was the only one to stick to the plan, sailing from Sicily early in May 1271, and revictualling his troops in Cyprus. On 9 May he landed at Acre. English sources suggest that had he not arrived, the port would have been lost to the mameluke leader, Baibars, but Arab sources do not suggest that Baibars intended any major assault. When Baibars rode up to the walls, Edward was in no position to take any action against his vastly superior forces. Late in June the English force finally made a sortie, to St Georges-de-Lebeyne, about 15 miles from Acre. Heat and food poisoning took their toll of the troops, and little was achieved. In November a further raid took place under Edward's command, this time with the support of a good many local nobles and members of the military orders. Qaqun, 40 miles from Acre, was the target, and an enemy force of some numbers but little strength was defeated, but the citadel itself was not taken. It was clear that little could be achieved, and in May 1272 Hugues III, king of Cyprus and titular king of Jerusalem, agreed a ten-year truce with Baibars. Edward was angry at this, and remained in the East until 24 September 1272, perhaps in the hope that further military action might be possible. His return to the West may also have been delayed because of the after-effects of the most celebrated incident of his crusade. In June 1272 a Muslim assassin attempted to kill him with a poisoned dagger. Edward kicked him, seized his knife, and slew him; but he was himself wounded in the arm. The master of the Temple provided a remedy, which failed; the wound began to putrefy. Eventually an English doctor cured Edward, by cutting away the decaying flesh. The classic story is, of course, that Eleanor of Castile devotedly sucked the poison from the wound. The same tale is told of Edward's close Savoyard friend Otto de Grandson; neither account has contemporary support.

Edward returned from the East to southern Italy, where he heard news of the death of his father, Henry III. He did not, as might have been expected, hasten to England for his coronation. His journey through Italy was leisurely; he then made an important visit to Savoy, and engaged in a tournament at Châlons-sur-Marne, which turned more violent than was proper for such an occasion. He did homage for his French lands to Philippe III of France at Paris, where he stayed in late July and early August, and then, instead of directing his journey to England, went to Gascony, where there was serious news of the rebellion of Gaston de Béarn. Not until 2 August 1274 did Edward finally return to England.

Crusading and diplomacy, 1274–1291 Edward undoubtedly enhanced his reputation by taking part in the crusade. He distinguished himself by persisting longer in an obviously futile cause than any of the other leaders who set out in 1270. His diplomatic efforts to win Mongol support failed,

his military efforts were mere pinpricks to the mamelukes. The expedition was marked by a curious mixture of over-ambition and a full awareness of the limitations of the resources available. In the military sense Edward showed himself to be suitably cautious; in financial terms he displayed less realism. The crusade had proved an extremely expensive venture. The money raised before the expedition proved sufficient only until Edward arrived at Acre. Thereafter he borrowed funds from Italian merchants and others. The company of the Riccardi of Lucca lent him over £22,000 for the period from his landing in Sicily in 1272 until his return to England. In all, the crusade probably cost £100,000 or more.

Edward hoped to be able to go on crusade once more, and was to take the cross again in 1287. His role in European diplomacy in the first half of his reign was directed at the prevention of conflict, so as to make this possible. The dispute between the Angevins ruling in Naples and the kingdom of Aragon was a major obstacle to the European peace that was needed if a major crusade was to be mounted. Edward hoped to act as a peacemaker in the 1280s in this dispute. In 1283 he even made available his city of Bordeaux as the venue for single combat to settle the issue between Charles of Anjou and Peter of Aragon, but the engagement never took place. In 1286 Edward was successful in brokering a truce between France and Aragon, and two years later he provided money and hostages to Peter of Aragon so as to secure the release of the Angevin Charles of Salerno. Edward was a major figure in the European politics of this period, but in the end his peacemaking efforts were in vain. He had planned marriage alliances with Navarre, Aragon, and the Habsburg dynasty, but all failed, and it was only the marriage of his daughter Margaret to the duke of Brabant's heir, John, that was carried through in 1290. Charles of Salerno's release was secured, but at great cost and without securing lasting peace between Aragon and the Angevins. Edward hoped for a grand alliance between the forces of the West and those of the Mongols in the East, but this was too ambitious an idea, and came to naught. The city of Acre fell in 1291, and though Edward still dreamed of going on crusade, nothing came of his hopes.

The government of England, 1274–1290 Edward's first concern on his return to England in 1274 was of course his coronation, which took place on 19 August. There was some dispute with his brother Edmund over the role the latter was entitled to play in his position as steward of England; there was also a problem over the perennial argument between the archbishops of Canterbury and York, which resulted in the latter's exclusion from the ceremony. Otherwise, the coronation went smoothly, with celebrations on a truly exceptional scale.

The coronation over, Edward could give his attentions to the affairs of his realm. The first task, after some changes of personnel, which included the appointment of Edward's close associate Robert Burnell (d. 1292) as chancellor, was to conduct a major inquiry into the state of the realm. On 11 October 1274 commissioners were appointed to inquire into a wide range of matters, the prime purpose being to discover what rights and lands had been lost by the crown. By March of the following year the process of investigation was complete. Only some of the returns, known as the hundred rolls, survive, but they are sufficient to show the immense scale of the inquiry. Jurors often found it hard to know whether or not royal rights had been usurped by magnates; they found it much easier to tell tales about official wrongdoings. The scale of the returns was such that it was hard for the government to make much use of them; the Dunstable annalist cynically commented that no good came of the inquiry. There were no judicial commissions set up to hear the complaints against royal and private officials that were brought up. Yet many of the issues raised in the hundred rolls were the subject of legislation in the first Statute of Westminster, promulgated in the April parliament of 1275, though it is not clear that the clauses of the statute were directly based on the huge mass of material in the hundred rolls.

Edward I's statutes are one of the great achievements of the reign. The sweep of the legislation was extensive, and the majority of the statutes were not dedicated to a single topic, but covered a range of matters. They were not the work of a single legislator, and many clauses had their origins in specific issues that had arisen in the courts. The most important of the statutes were: Westminster I (1275); Gloucester (1278); Mortmain (1279); Acton Burnell (1283); Westminster II (1285); Winchester (1285); Merchants (1285); *Quia emptores* (1290); *Quo warranto* (1290).

Land tenure was one important theme in the legislation. The first clause of Westminster I, *De donis conditionalibus*, was designed to meet the grievance of those who found that even if they made gifts of lands on precise conditions, these were often flouted. Family settlements were the major issue here. *Quia emptores* ensured that if feudal tenants disposed of lands the new holder would enter into the same feudal relationship with the lord as the former holder. Much was done to clarify relations between lords and tenants, providing protection for tenants against unjust distraint, and giving lords ways of dealing with recalcitrant tenants. Landlords were provided by Westminster II with new methods of dealing with fraudulent bailiffs. The question of the grant of lands to the church was dealt with in what was perhaps the most political of the statutes, Mortmain. In the course of a dispute with Archbishop Pecham the king forbade the grant of lands to the church without royal licence, a measure that reiterated a clause of the provisions of Westminster of 1259.

The question of debt was the subject of the Statute of Acton Burnell, which was revised in the Statute of Merchants. Merchants were provided with a new mechanism for the registration of debt. If a debt was not paid off promptly, the debtor was threatened with prison, and eventually with handing over his lands to his creditor. The Statute of Winchester dealt with the maintenance of law and order, updating earlier provisions setting out the military equipment all free men should possess (necessary if they were to prevent crime), and making local hundreds responsible for bringing forward indictments. Arrangements were outlined for watch and ward in towns and cities; roads were to be widened, so that there should be no undergrowth nearby in which highway robbers might lurk.

It is impossible that so major a programme of legal change should have been carried out without the active encouragement of the king himself, but evidence for Edward's own involvement in the statutes is hard to find. It is unlikely that he was much concerned in the detailed work of drafting the new measures; that was a task for the experts. Much of the drive for change, however, must have been due to the king, and his experiences of the baronial reform movement of the late 1250s and early 1260s surely help to explain his determination to improve the way in which the law operated.

The church and the bench The appointment of John Pecham to the see of Canterbury in 1279 was followed by a series of arguments between king and primate. Proposals for ecclesiastical reform set out by Pecham at Reading in 1279 directly attacked royal officials, and threatened royal rights. The archbishop was forced to retreat in parliament in the autumn of that year, but in 1280 a massive list of clerical grievances was presented in parliament. Pecham continued his practice of excommunicating royal officials, and another church council, at Lambeth in 1281, continued the work of reform. Pecham sent a long letter to Edward, stressing the king's obligation to bring English practices into line with the rest of Christendom. Further clerical grievances were put forward in 1285. From the crown's point of view it was claimed that church courts in the see of Norwich had overstepped their proper bounds in over 150 cases. But in the next year Edward issued a conciliatory writ, *Circumspecte agatis*, ordering Richard of Boyland, the justice active in the bishopric of Norwich, to act with due circumspection towards the clergy. Edward's readiness to compromise was probably because he wanted to avoid troubles while he was abroad in Gascony. In taking this course he displayed statesmanlike good sense.

Edward clearly did not believe that the country could be ruled well in his absence, and his return from Gascony in 1289 was followed by a major purge of judges and officials. The first scandal was that Thomas Weyland, chief justice of the common pleas, had protected two of his men who had committed murder. He was forced out of sanctuary by blockade, and driven into exile. A commission was set up to hear complaints against royal officials, and eventually some 1000 men were charged with a wide range of offences. The greatest to be brought down was Ralph Hengham, chief justice of the king's bench. The fact that Edward accepted fines from most of those convicted won him little favour with the chroniclers. A sad blow to Edward at this time was the death of his beloved queen, Eleanor, on 28 November 1290, and there were other deaths that transformed the character of the administration: those of the treasurer, John Kirkby, in 1290, and the chancellor, Robert Burnell, in 1292. A new generation of officials would dominate the policies of the 1290s, the most difficult decade of Edward's reign.

The conquest of Wales, 1274–1284 In 1267 Edward had abandoned most of his interests in Wales, but when he returned to England from crusade in 1274 Welsh affairs soon came to the fore. The Welsh prince Llywelyn ap Gruffudd had taken advantage of the political troubles in England in the 1260s; he failed to appreciate how the situation had changed by the 1270s. He refused to do homage to Edward I, invaded English territory, began building a threatening new castle at Dolforwyn, and planned to marry Simon de Montfort's daughter Eleanor. His own brother Dafydd, and the powerful Welsh magnate Gruffudd ap Gwenwynwyn, found his ambitions unacceptable, and took refuge at the English court. War became unavoidable, and in the autumn of 1276 Edward I decided to act. In the summer of the following year a great royal host, over 15,000 strong, advanced from Chester along the coast of north Wales to Deganwy. Naval support was essential, and ships were used to take English troops to Anglesey, where they reaped the grain harvest, so reducing Llywelyn's capacity to resist. No major fighting took place; Llywelyn appreciated the overwhelming strength of Edward's army, and came to terms in the treaty of Aberconwy. The Four Cantrefs, originally granted to Edward in 1254 but regained by the Welsh in 1267, were handed over to the English. Llywelyn's political authority was severely curtailed; he was in future to receive homage only from the lords of Snowdonia, not of all Wales. A massive war indemnity of £50,000 was imposed, though not in practice collected.

War broke out again in 1282. The imposition of English jurisdiction caused much discontent in Wales. Llywelyn ap Gruffudd had been involved in a complex and humiliating legal dispute over the cantref of Arwystli with his former enemy Gruffudd ap Gwenwynwyn. Llywelyn's appeal to Welsh law stressed the threat that Edward I presented to the very identity of the Welsh people. Llywelyn's brother Dafydd, ill-rewarded by Edward for his part in the first Welsh war, made the first move in 1282, attacking Hawarden Castle on 21 April. Concerted attacks soon came on other English castles. Edward was quick to respond, making plans at a council at Devizes in April. The overall strategy was similar to that of the first Welsh war, with a major royal campaign in the north, and operations on a smaller scale by other commanders in the marches and the south. Logistical planning was on an impressive scale; the king even called on his overseas dominions of Ireland, Gascony, and Ponthieu for aid, and arrangements were made to link Anglesey to the Welsh mainland by a great pontoon bridge. By the autumn of 1282 Llywelyn's heartland of Snowdonia was threatened on all sides, notably by the royal army, which had advanced from Chester, and by a force under Luke de Tany, which had established itself in Anglesey. At this stage Archbishop John Pecham attempted to negotiate a settlement. Luke de Tany, disobeying orders, tried to take advantage of the peace negotiations by advancing across the bridge from Anglesey to the mainland. He was ambushed and killed; his force suffered heavy losses. The setback was no more than that. Edward's determination was hardened, and Llywelyn attempted to break out of the stranglehold in which he had been placed. A bold move into mid-Wales led to disaster. He was lured into a trap at Irfon Bridge, and was killed in battle. The war was continued by his brother Dafydd, but to little real effect. Castell y Bere, the last Welsh stronghold, surrendered in April 1283, and in June Dafydd himself was captured by men of his own nationality and handed over to the English for execution at Shrewsbury as a traitor.

The victory of 1283 was followed by a full-scale English settlement. The Statute of Wales of 1284 extended the English system of administration, and new counties of Flint, Anglesey, Merioneth, and Caernarfon were created with the full institutional complexity of sheriffs, county courts, and coroners, though at the local level of the commote it proved impossible to reconstruct local government on a purely English pattern. Welsh land law was not eradicated, but English criminal law was instituted for all major felonies. The settlement was limited to those areas of Wales under direct royal control, and did not extend to the marcher lordships. It was not therefore comprehensive, but it was statesmanlike. The policy adopted toward the Welsh aristocracy was less admirable. Disinheritance was on a huge scale. Llywelyn's dynasty was destroyed, and other Welsh princely families lost their lands. New lordships were created for Edward's followers, such as Bromfield and Yale for John, Earl Warenne, and Denbigh for the earl of Lincoln.

The consolidation of English rule in Wales, 1284–1295 The conquest was symbolized in physical terms by a most elaborate and ambitious castle-building programme. The first Welsh war had been followed by the building of new castles at Flint, Rhuddlan, Builth, and Aberystwyth; to these were now added Conwy, Caernarfon, and Harlech, with works also taking place at Cricieth. Edward looked to Savoy for expertise in castle building after his first Welsh campaign, perhaps because he did not want to divert his English masons from their work on the Tower of London. The man chiefly responsible for the Welsh castles was James St George; his selection was indicative of Edward's skill in choosing the right man for a job. With him came a number of other Savoyard experts, masons, and carpenters, though the bulk of the workmen were of course recruited in England. Details of window design, of scaffolding structure, and even the measurements of the latrine chutes prove the connection between these castles in Wales and those in Savoy. The castles were not built to a standard pattern; where the site allowed, concentric lines of defence added to the strength of round towers and massive curtain walls. Twin D-shaped towers formed the gatehouses at Rhuddlan, Harlech, and elsewhere. At Conwy and Caernarfon the exigencies of the site demanded not a concentric plan, but an elongated twin bailey. At the latter Master James abandoned his usual style and built a magnificent structure with polygonal towers and dark stripes of masonry decorating the walls. This echoed the

Theodosian walls of Constantinople, for Edward, in a romantic gesture, wanted to express in the building a traditional Welsh legend that the father of the emperor Constantine was buried at Caernarfon. Three eagles on the great Eagle tower emphasized imperial ambitions, as well as perhaps providing a further symbol of the link with Savoy.

Along with the castles went new towns. Flint, Aberystwyth, and Rhuddlan were creations after the first Welsh war; Caernarfon, Conwy, and Harlech after the second. Cricieth and Bere were Anglicized. In the new lordships new boroughs were set up at Holt, Denbigh, and Ruthin. The intention was that these towns should be peopled by Englishmen, brought in on very favourable terms.

Conclusive as the conquest of 1283 had been, rebellion still broke out in 1287 and 1294. In 1287 Rhys ap Maredudd, lord of Dryslwyn, a man who had been loyal to the English in 1277 and 1282, rebelled. He was furious at the way he had been treated by English officials and considered that he had been humiliated, rather than rewarded, by Edward. As in other cases, Edward was very conscious of his own rights, but unsympathetic to the feelings of others; he had rebuked Rhys publicly for taking seisin of lands granted to him before formal investiture had taken place. Rhys's rebellion took place while the king was in Gascony. The regency government had little difficulty in putting it down, capturing Dryslwyn in September, though not its lord. Rhys then took Newcastle Emlyn, but after it fell in January 1288 he was left a fugitive and an outlaw until finally captured and executed in 1292.

Far more serious than Rhys's localized rising was the rebellion of 1294. The imposition of an English-style tax of a fifteenth in 1292, in addition to the generally oppressive English administration, provided the background. The outbreak of war with France provided an obvious opportunity for rebellion. The main leader was Madog ap Llywelyn, a man distantly related to the princely family of Gwynedd. This was a widespread, popular, and national uprising, which took the English completely by surprise. With the exception of Caernarfon, which was only half-completed, the new royal castles held out, but many baronial strongholds fell to a concerted series of assaults. Edward's response was to adopt once more the strategy that had served him so well in the past. The royal army advanced from Chester, while baronial forces operated in south and mid-Wales. Over 30,000 men in all were employed in the various operations. The campaign was not without its problems. Edward himself was for a time besieged in Conwy, with supplies running short during the winter months. But in March 1295 a force under the earl of Warwick defeated Madog and his men at Maes Moydog, near Oswestry, and although Madog himself was not captured in the fight, the rebellion began to collapse. The king was able to go on a triumphant tour of a defeated country. Hostages were taken to England, and heavy fines imposed on Welsh communities. One new castle was built, at Beaumaris in Anglesey. The overall lines of the settlement of 1284 were maintained, though the revolt certainly meant that English officials viewed the Welsh

with increased suspicion. 'Welshmen are Welshmen, and you need to understand them properly', wrote one in 1296 (Prestwich, *Edward I*, 231). The rebellion had been a major embarrassment to Edward. It had diverted his attention from the French war at a significant moment, and had cost him some £55,000.

Fiscal reform, 1275–1289 Financial problems at the start of Edward's reign were acute, for there was a heavy debt resulting from the crusading expedition. Major measures were taken in 1275 to put the crown's finances on a secure basis. In the April parliament a customs duty was negotiated of 6s. 8d. on every sack of wool exported. There were some precedents for this. Edward had imposed a levy on imports and exports by foreign merchants in 1266, which was used as a means to repay the Riccardi bankers of Lucca for their loans, but the bankers were undoubtedly anxious for a more secure and lucrative form of repayment. The profitability of a levy of 10s. a sack taken from merchants who had disobeyed an embargo on wool exports to Flanders imposed in 1273, pointed the way forward. The new customs duties agreed in 1275 yielded some £10,000 a year. This was still not sufficient, and in the October parliament of 1275 a tax of a fifteenth, assessed on a valuation of moveable goods, was granted. This was assessed at over £81,000. Measures were also taken to improve the efficiency of the financial organization. New procedures for the exchequer were set out, and three officials were appointed to take charge of royal demesne lands. This was a radical scheme; it foundered upon the resistance of the sheriffs, and was abandoned after three years. The pattern for the future financial structure of Edward's government was largely set in 1275. Customs duties provided good security for loans from Italian bankers, while grants of taxation were an essential supplement to the ordinary revenues of the crown. One missing element was that there was no grant of taxation from the clergy in 1275; that was remedied in 1279, when the province of Canterbury agreed to pay a fifteenth for three years, and in 1280 when the province of York agreed to a tenth for two years. Clerical taxes were a valuable resource throughout the reign.

Reform of the currency was a further part of the overall financial reforms. Edward decided on a recoinage early in 1279. Large numbers of foreign workmen were recruited; provincial mints, long closed, were reopened. The new currency was issued at a slightly lower standard than the old, though since much of the coin in circulation was heavily worn and clipped, the new money was in practice much superior to the old. By 1281 silver to the value of at least £500,000 had been minted, and the mints remained active for the rest of the decade. The reminting was thoroughly successful, although in 1300 it proved necessary to take action against low-quality foreign imitation sterlings that had come into the country in considerable numbers.

War inevitably required additional financial resources, though the first Welsh campaign, in 1277, did not see a request made to the laity for a tax, perhaps because it was too soon after the grant of 1275, and because the expedition was not particularly costly. The second Welsh war, of

1282–3, was a different matter. The Welsh rising came too suddenly for a parliament to be summoned, and initially loans were raised from urban communities, totalling about £16,500. This was not enough, and regional assemblies were called to meet in York and Northampton in January 1283, resulting in the grant of a tax of a thirtieth. The Riccardi played a major role in financing the war, and about £20,000 was collected in forced loans from other Italian companies. The experience of the problems involved in financing the war led to a further attempt to reform exchequer administration. The Statute of Rhuddlan of 1284 simplified bookkeeping, clearing the large number of unrecoverable old debts from the pipe rolls of the exchequer. But an estimate of crown revenue still made depressing reading. As a result commissioners were sent round the country to inquire into debts owed to the crown, and the exchequer court was ordered to limit itself to cases involving the king and his officials. The campaign to recover debts was, of course, unpopular, and it achieved little, though in more general terms the overhaul of the financial administration did result in some clear gains.

Financial problems and taxation, 1290–1307 When Edward returned from Gascony in 1289, he faced new financial problems in England, initially because of the expenses incurred during his stay abroad. In the April parliament of 1290 he obtained permission to levy a feudal aid, a tax to which he was entitled by custom on the occasion of the marriage of his daughter Joan to the earl of Gloucester. This, however, was unlikely to raise much money, and the plan was shelved. In its place, knights of the shire were summoned to Westminster for 15 July, to give their consent to a tax of a fifteenth. The contemporary view was clear: the tax was granted in return for the expulsion of the Jews from England in that year. The assessment was over £116,000. In addition, the clergy were asked for taxes, and tenths were duly granted by both provinces. The tax placed Edward in a strong financial position in the early 1290s; the outbreak of war with France in 1294, followed by a major Welsh rebellion in the same year, and a campaign in Scotland in 1296, put a very different complexion on affairs. To make matters more difficult, the Riccardi company, which had played such an important part in the finances of the first part of the reign, with the crown incurring an aggregate debt to it of £392,000 in all, was effectively bankrupted.

Demands for taxes on moveable goods resulted in successive grants in parliament in 1294, 1295, and 1296, though with each tax the level of assessment fell sharply. The attempt to impose a further tax, of an eighth, in 1297, foundered on political opposition, though in the autumn it was replaced by a properly granted ninth. The clergy proved less obliging than the laity. In 1294 a half was demanded from them, by threatening them with outlawry. In 1295 a tenth was granted, but in 1296, at Bury St Edmunds, Archbishop Robert Winchelsey used the papal bull *Clericis laicos* as a means of postponing an answer to the king's request for a further tax. The bull forbade the payment of taxes by the church to the lay power, a device

intended by Pope Boniface VIII to hasten the end of the Anglo-French war. Early in 1297 Edward, faced by Winchelsey's refusal to grant a tax, duly outlawed the clergy, and collected in fines what they would have paid in taxation.

Trade offered further possibilities for raising money. The initial plan in 1294 was for a seizure of all the wool in England; this would then be exported by the crown at a substantial profit. The merchants protested, and a scheme whereby an additional duty of 40s., known as the maltote, was paid on each sack of wool exported, replaced the seizure. In 1297, however, a new seizure of wool was ordered at Easter. This yielded little, and a further order for the taking of 8000 sacks of wool was issued in August. Both additional customs duties and wool seizures, or prises, were abandoned in the autumn following protests. In his final years, Edward had to rely on what had become traditional sources of income. A tax of a fifteenth was granted in 1301, and one of a thirtieth and a twentieth in 1306. It proved possible in 1303 to negotiate an additional duty of 3s. 4d. on each woolsack exported by foreign merchants. Taxes, ostensibly for crusade purposes, were imposed on the clergy by the papacy, and the proceeds shared with the crown. Such resources were not adequate to meet the needs of the crown, heightened as they were by the Scottish war. Loans from the Italian company of the Frescobaldi were of considerable assistance to Edward, but many men owed money by the crown went unpaid. By the end of the reign the debt probably stood at some £200,000.

Gascony Gascony was important to Edward, perhaps in part because it was there that he had his first real taste of independent power in 1254–5. He visited it twice, and perhaps three times, in the early 1260s, and it was to Gascony, not England, that he first directed his attention on his return from crusade in 1274. The main reason was to bring the powerful and rebellious magnate Gaston de Béarn to heel. It had been intended that Gaston should accompany Edward on crusade, and the marriage of his daughter to Henry of Almain had been meant to reinforce his links with the English crown. Henry, however, was murdered at Viterbo in 1271, and Gaston refused to appear in court before the English seneschal of Gascony. He refused to do homage to Edward when he arrived in Gascony. Edward acted carefully, following legal forms, but eventually marched against Gaston and forced his surrender. Further legal argument followed; taking advantage of the fact that Gascony was held by the English as a fief from the French king, Gaston appealed to the *parlement* of Paris. It was not until 1278 that final agreement was reached, after which Gaston caused no further trouble. It may be that the affair gave Edward a false sense of confidence when it came to dealing with Welsh and Scottish leaders later in the reign; they were not to be brought to heel as easily as Gaston de Béarn.

Edward's first visit to Gascony as king saw a major inquiry into the feudal duties owed by the nobility to himself as duke. This was not complete by the time he left for England, but demonstrated his intention of reorganizing and reaffirming his rule. The importance he attached to the duchy was demonstrated by the fact that in 1278 he appointed two of his most important advisers, the Savoyard Otto de Grandson and the chancellor, Robert Burnell, to go there to investigate complaints against the rule of Luke de Tany, the seneschal, who was duly replaced by Jean de Grailly, a Savoyard. In the autumn of 1286 Edward himself returned to Gascony, and the energy with which the problems of the duchy were tackled testifies to the king's own vigour and determination. Feudal obligations in the Agenais were investigated. A series of charters to new towns, or *bastides*, were issued. The Jews were expelled from the duchy. Lands were purchased for the crown. Finally, in March 1289, near the end of the king's stay, a set of ordinances for the government of the duchy was drawn up at Condom. The duties of the seneschal and of the constable of Bordeaux were clearly laid out; rates of pay for officials were specified. Separate ordinances dealt with the provinces of Saintonge, Périgord, Limousin, Quercy, and the Agenais. The ordinances were specifically Gascon in character. Edward was not attempting to impose a standard administrative system on all his dominions, but there was a strong sense that he was bringing order and method to replace incoherence and individualism. What Edward could not do, however, was to alter the inconvenient situation by which he held Gascony as a fief from the French king. This was to be a major reason for the outbreak of the Anglo-French war in 1294.

The French war, 1293–1303, and marriage to Margaret of France In the first half of the reign relations with the French monarchy had been reasonably good. Edward had visited Paris in 1279, so that Queen Eleanor might do homage for the county of Ponthieu. At Amiens outstanding differences with the French, notably over the Agenais, were settled. A French request that Edward, who as duke of Aquitaine was a vassal of the French monarchy, should serve in the campaign of 1285 in Aragon created problems, but the failure of the campaign and the death of Philippe III averted crisis. In 1286 Edward did homage to the new king, Philippe IV (r. 1285–1314), at Paris, and good relations were re-established. The war with France that broke out in 1294 was, from Edward's standpoint, unexpected. He was the victim of an aggressive French monarchy, which regarded Edward, in his capacity as duke of Aquitaine, as an overmighty vassal whose subjection to French sovereignty and jurisdiction needed to be emphasized. Philippe was presented with his opportunity by a private naval war, which began in 1293 between English and Norman sailors. The involvement of some Gascons provided the French king with the opportunity to summon Edward to appear before the *parlement* of Paris. Edmund of Lancaster, Edward's brother, was sent to try to negotiate a settlement. Early in 1294 a secret agreement was reached. Edward was to marry Philippe IV's sister *Margaret (1279?–1318). Gascon hostages, fortresses, and towns were to be handed over to the French for a period, and then returned to the English. The summons to the *parlement* would be withdrawn. The English negotiators were

duped. Edward kept his part of the bargain; but the French did not withdraw the summons, and declared Gascony forfeit when Edward failed to appear.

In October 1294 the first English contingents sailed to Gascony, to achieve some success at Bayonne, though none at Bordeaux. Edward's war plans, however, extended much further than campaigning in southwestern France. On the advice of Antony (I) Bek, bishop of Durham and a long-standing supporter of the king, an elaborate series of continental alliances was planned, above all with princes in the Low Countries, Germany, and Burgundy. The main assault against Philippe IV would come from the north, not from Gascony. The English schemes prospered at first. Agreement was swiftly reached with the German king, Adolf of Nassau, while the duke of Brabant, Edward's son-in-law, readily accepted English subsidies. The counts of Gueldres and Holland joined the alliance, and the promise of the marriage of his daughter to Edward's son, together with a large subsidy, won over the count of Flanders. In 1295, however, Philippe IV succeeded in detaching the count of Flanders from the alliance, and early in the following year the count of Holland also abandoned Edward's cause. The Welsh rebellion of 1294–5, followed by the Scottish campaign in 1296, meant that the planned English campaign in concert with allies was put off until 1297. Early in that year Edward managed to win the count of Flanders over once again, and in May he added to the alliance an important group of Burgundian nobles. The alliance was at long last ready to act.

The English, meanwhile, had mixed fortunes in Gascony. A substantial expedition sailed early in 1296, led by Edmund of Lancaster, who died in June of that year. In January 1297 the earl of Lincoln suffered a significant defeat at Bellegarde, though in the following summer he was able to conduct a successful raid into French territory. The outcome of the war did not depend on these events, but on Edward's own expedition to Flanders, which eventually sailed on 22 August. By that time his allies had suffered defeat at the battle of Veurne, and the city of Lille had surrendered. The most serious fighting that Edward encountered was that between his own sailors from the Cinque Ports and those of Yarmouth, at the time of disembarkation. The small English army moved first to Bruges, and then to Ghent, but the assistance that had been hoped for from the German king never materialized, and on 9 October a truce was agreed with the French. It took time for Edward to extricate himself from the Low Countries; he faced serious riots early in February 1298 in Ghent, and there were problems in paying off his allies. He eventually returned to England in March 1298 after an ignominious campaign. It took until 1303 to agree a final peace with the French, but Edward's marriage to the French princess Margaret took place in 1299, and there was little danger of further hostilities. For both the English and the French the war had proved expensive and unrewarding. The war account for Gascony alone showed expenses approaching £360,000. The various allies were promised some

£250,000, and paid about £165,000. The Flanders campaign probably cost over £50,000.

The Great Cause and the Scottish revolt, 1286–1297 Edward's earliest experience of Scotland had probably been in the autumn of 1266, when he may have travelled to Haddington in Lothian to visit his sister *Margaret, the queen of Scots. Relations with Scotland during the first part of the reign were smooth; the thorny issue of the homage due from Alexander III to Edward was settled without much argument in 1278. Problems arose only when Edward tried to take advantage of the dynastic problems that faced Scotland on the death of Alexander in 1286. The latter's heir was his granddaughter, Margaret of Norway, and in 1290 agreement was reached for her to marry Edward's own heir, Edward of Caernarfon. Though it was agreed that Scotland should remain independent of England, Edward's actions once the treaty was agreed suggested that he intended to exercise effective lordship there. His plans were dashed by the death of Margaret in Orkney in the autumn of 1290. The right to the Scottish throne was then disputed between Robert Bruce and *John Balliol, and eventually eleven other claimants. Edward determined that the dispute should be resolved by himself, as feudal overlord of Scotland. The Scots were not prepared to accept such a claim, but in negotiations at Norham in May and June 1291 Edward obtained sufficient recognition of his rights from the competitors to the throne to be able to act. The hearings were lengthy and complex, with a long adjournment between August 1291 and June 1292. A full record was made by an English notary, John of Caen, though this was not drawn up contemporaneously. The final judgment, in November 1292, went in favour of John Balliol; his was the strongest case in law.

The resolution of the Great Cause, as the dispute to the Scottish throne became known, was followed by determined efforts by Edward to make good his claims to the superior lordship of Scotland. Appeals against judgments made in the court of the guardians of Scotland (who had ruled that kingdom between 1286 and 1292) were quickly heard. In the case of Macduff, the Scottish king himself was summoned to appear before the English parliament, which he did at Michaelmas 1293, thereby acknowledging Edward's rights of lordship. In 1294 Edward summoned King John Balliol and eighteen Scottish magnates to perform feudal service against the French, an unprecedented step. John was a weak monarch, and in 1295 effective power was taken from him by a council of twelve. The French naturally looked to Scotland as an ally against Edward in the Anglo-French war, and early in the next year a treaty was concluded. At the same time Edward was able to use the Macduff case, and King John's refusal to come to court in March 1296, as an excuse for action. At the end of March he invaded, and took Berwick.

The campaign of 1296 was a triumphant success for Edward. The Scots were defeated at Dunbar, and the expedition developed into little more than an unopposed military promenade. Scotland, it appeared, was conquered in twenty-one weeks, and its king removed ignominiously from office. The removal of the coronation stone from Scone to Westminster made it clear that this was a true conquest. The government of the country was, as far as was possible, entrusted to Englishmen. However, the victory had been too easy. In 1297 the Scots revolted. Robert Bruce (later *Robert I, king of Scots), grandson of the competitor to the throne, was one of the leaders, but the most effective resistance to the English was provided by William Wallace, a man of knightly not baronial rank, and Andrew Moray. This was a genuinely popular rebellion, and it triumphed in September when an English army under Earl Warenne was defeated at Stirling Bridge.

Victory and settlement in Scotland, 1298–1305 Edward retaliated promptly on his return from Flanders in 1298. A large army, approaching 30,000 strong, was completely victorious on 22 July over the Scottish defensive formations, or schiltroms, at Falkirk, the only major battle fought by the king himself since Evesham. Yet despite this triumph, the English were able to establish only limited control of areas around the castles they held in southern Scotland. No campaign was possible in 1299, for political reasons, and the Scots recovered Stirling Castle after a lengthy siege. In 1300, 1301, and 1303 great English armies marched north under Edward's command, but the Scots would not come to battle. Robert Bruce came over to the English side in the winter of 1301–2, but it was not until early 1304 that the majority of the Scottish leaders surrendered. The capture of Stirling Castle by Edward marked the end of this phase of the war. It appeared once more that conquest had been achieved. Edward deserves some praise for his determination, and his officials credit for the way in which a vast military enterprise had been organized. At the same time, the fact that the Scots had lost the backing of the French when the latter made peace with Edward in 1303 was an important element in the Scottish surrender. In 1305 one of the heroes of Scottish resistance, William Wallace, was finally captured, tried, and executed.

In parliament in 1305 Edward agreed a scheme for the government of Scotland. John of Brittany, the king's young nephew, was to become royal lieutenant, and English officials were given the offices of chancellor and chamberlain. Sheriffs were appointed; naturally, in the important southern part of the country they were to be Englishmen. Pairs of justices, one Englishman and one Scotsman, were nominated, and arrangements were put in hand for a review of Scottish law. The ordinance was limited in its nature, displaying no far-sighted statesmanship. No resolution was proposed to the problems of the many rival claims to land which resulted from the war, and the only indication that thought was given to the long-term future of Scotland is the fact that the country was no longer described as a kingdom, but as a land.

The revival of Scottish resistance, 1305–1307 The settlement did not last. On 10 February 1306 Robert Bruce murdered John Comyn, lord of Badenoch. Like those Welsh princes and nobles who had rebelled against Edward, Robert no doubt felt that he had been inadequately rewarded for the assistance he had given the English king, and he must have judged correctly that he had a real chance of gaining the Scottish throne for himself. Edward was astonished by what had happened, and was not in proper physical shape to respond. Forces under Aymer de Valence and Henry Percy moved into action, followed by a major army under the prince of Wales. Edward himself was ill in the summer of 1306, and moved only slowly northwards. He wintered at Lanercost Priory. The policy he adopted was ferocious. Simon Fraser, a Scot who had formerly been a knight of Edward's household, was savagely executed in London, as were other Scots. Robert I's sister Mary and the countess of Buchan, taken soon after the siege of Kildrummy Castle in September 1306, were imprisoned in cages at Roxburgh and Berwick, in full public view; a cruel and unusual punishment. Edward regarded the war as a rebellion, not as a conflict between equal and independent countries. Robert's cause was at a low ebb over the winter of 1306–7, but by May 1307 separate forces under Aymer de Valence and the earl of Gloucester were defeated in skirmishes, to Edward's fury. The king himself was in no fit state to campaign, though at Whitsun he reviewed troops at Carlisle. He finally set out for Scotland, only to die at Burgh by Sands on 7 July. He had come near to success in Scotland, or so it seemed, in 1304, but the task was beyond his capabilities in both military and political terms. He had not the flexibility of mind to develop appropriate strategies and tactics to deal with the novel style of warfare developed by Wallace and his countrymen, and, for all his experience, he had not learned how to win the support of those he aimed to dominate.

The king and the magnates: manipulating inheritances
Edward I, like all medieval kings, depended greatly on the co-operation of his magnates. He did not, however, achieve this co-operation by means of skilful patronage; rather, his policies have been described as 'masterful'. His relationship with some great men was consistently good: Henry de Lacy, earl of Lincoln, was a staunch friend and ally, and at a slightly lower level of society he could rely on such men as the Cliffords to provide consistent support in war and in council. His relationship with the earl of Gloucester, however, remained stormy from the 1260s, and the fact that no earls sailed with him for Flanders in 1297 was noted as providing an indication of the nature of the king's rule.

Edward was keen to take advantage of the accidents of family history, manipulating the rules of inheritance in his own interests when he could. He created no new earldoms, and displayed a certain reluctance to permit succession to existing ones. After the death of the countess of Aumale in 1274 the king supported a bogus claimant to the earldom, and then bought him out for a mere £100 a year, so acquiring a major inheritance for the crown. Pressure was put on the widowed countess of Devon to sell her very substantial estates to the crown, disinheriting her rightful heir, Hugh de Courtenay. Finally, in 1293, when she was on her deathbed, she was persuaded to hand over the reversions of the Isle of Wight and other estates to the king in return for £6000. When Edward married his daughter Joan of Acre to the earl of Gloucester in 1290, the earl handed his lands over to the king, receiving them back on terms that effectively disinherited his children by his first marriage, and ensuring that future earls would be members of the royal family. There were similar arrangements made in 1302 when another daughter, Elizabeth, married the young earl of Hereford. In 1306 the childless earl of Norfolk was persuaded to surrender his lands to the crown, and to receive them back on condition that they should be inherited in the strict male line of descent. This meant that their reversion to the crown on his death was virtually inevitable. Another manipulation of the rules of inheritance took place when Alice, daughter of Henry de Lacy, earl of Lincoln, married the king's nephew Thomas of Lancaster in 1294. Once the marriage had taken place, Alice's parents surrendered most of their lands to the king, to be regranted them for life. Arrangements were made to ensure that if Alice had no children, her family estates would go, not to her rightful heirs, but to the crown. The intention of these unscrupulous policies was to provide land for the royal family, not to increase the resources of the crown by building up its landed wealth.

Quo warranto and the Welsh marchers Edward's manipulation of rights of inheritance affected relatively few families. The assault between 1278 and 1290 on private rights of jurisdiction by means of writs of *quo warranto* ('by whose authority') was more extensive. The hundred rolls inquiry in 1274 showed that often there was real uncertainty over the rights by which magnates exercised rights of jurisdiction. The king first intended to challenge such rights in parliament, but by Easter 1278 it was clear that this method was not working. Other business had caused the postponement of cases. In parliament at Gloucester in 1278 a new procedure was worked out. Those claiming rights to jurisdictional franchises should set out their claims before justices on eyre, while the crown might proceed against them by means of a writ of *quo warranto*, asking them to justify their claims to exercise jurisdiction. There was much argument in the courts, particularly over claims to tenure by prescriptive right, or tenure from time out of mind. Even if a charter did exist, there might be problems over its interpretation. The campaign did make it clear that the exercise of rights of local jurisdiction was a delegation of royal authority, but there was a lack of proper clarity over what claims were acceptable. Many cases were postponed; few franchises were in practice recovered by the crown. It was perhaps only the ineffectiveness of the campaign that prevented a major confrontation between crown and magnates before 1290. In that year, soon after the king's return from Gascony, matters came to a head. Gilbert of Thornton, one of the most aggressive royal attorneys, was appointed chief justice of the king's bench, and his judgments on previously postponed cases were clear: long tenure of a franchise was not sufficient warrant in the absence of a charter. In parliament at Easter 1290 the matter was angrily discussed, and in May it was settled by the issue of the Statute of *Quo warranto*. Anyone who could show that he and his ancestors had exercised franchisal rights continuously since 1189 could have them confirmed. The issue was not finally settled, as in 1292 royal attorneys began once again challenging claims just as they had done in the past. In 1294, however, the king abandoned the inquiries, 'as a favour to his people' (Prestwich, *Edward I*, 347), and in acknowledgement of the fact that he needed their support in the French war.

Edward had not extended the *quo warranto* inquiries into the Welsh marches, no doubt partly because he needed the support of the marchers for his Welsh wars. In 1290, however, he intervened in the affairs of the march in dramatic fashion. A feud was taking place in the southern march between the earls of Gloucester and Hereford, over a castle built by the former in territory claimed by the latter. Hereford, rather than relying on the customary marcher methods of settling disputes by negotiation or by private war, appealed to the king, though when Gloucester refused to cease his raids, Hereford's men retaliated in kind. The case was heard at Abergavenny in 1291, and eventually settled at Westminster in 1292 when the two earls submitted themselves to Edward. Both men were humbled; they forfeited lands and incurred fines. The lands were soon regranted to them, and the fines were not paid, but nevertheless the incident was very significant, as it displayed the way in which Edward was prepared to cut through arguments about traditional rights and privileges. There were other cases concerning the marches. Edmund (I) de Mortimer was sentenced in 1290 to lose his liberty of Wigmore because he had tried and executed a criminal rather than handed him over to a royal official. The liberty was eventually given back to him, but the dent in his pride could not so easily be restored. For obstructing a royal sheriff Theobald de Verdon was sentenced in the same year to lose his liberty of Ewyas Lacy, though he too soon recovered his lands. Such actions directed against members of the most militarily powerful group of magnates demonstrated Edward's toughness and his determination to control the nobility.

Threats and rewards Threats might well be as effective as persuasion. When a group of magnates, headed by the earl of Arundel, refused to go to fight in Gascony in 1295, the king simply threatened that the exchequer would collect the debts that they owed to the crown, a move that had the desired effect. Yet it was noted by the chronicler Peter Langtoft that Edward did not obtain all the support that he might have had for campaigns, notably those in Wales in 1294–5 and Flanders in 1297, and this he blamed on the king's lack of generosity. Edward, however, did not wholly neglect the arts of patronage. He was generous in his grant of estates in Ireland to his friend Thomas de Clare, who received Thomond in 1276. Otto de Grandson was well rewarded for his loyal service with lands in Ireland and in the Channel Islands. The conclusion of the second Welsh war was marked by major grants to some of the leading English magnates. A substantial redistribution of estates in Scotland took place at Carlisle after the Scottish campaign of 1298, and Edward then adopted a policy of making grants of important Scottish estates before their conquest. Bothwell was promised to Aymer de Valence in 1301, a month before the castle was actually conquered. By 1302 some fifty Englishmen had been granted Scottish lands by Edward I. The king, however, was not notable for his generosity. Even so, he obtained good service from those who were devoted to him.

The crisis of 1297 The immense burden that was imposed on the realm by the wars in Wales, Scotland, and Gascony from 1294 created much resentment among Edward's subjects. Edward attempted to give his policies legitimacy by obtaining parliamentary consent. In 1294 knights of the shire were summoned with full powers (*plena potestas*) to act on behalf of their communities, and in 1295 the writs used to call knights and burgesses to what was much later termed the Model Parliament employed what became the standard formula for such summonses. In summoning the clergy in the same year the king's clerks used the phrase 'what touches all should be approved by all' ('quod omnes tangit ab omnibus approbetur'; Prestwich, *Edward I*, 451). Such devices were not enough. Opposition was first voiced at the Salisbury parliament, which met on 24 February 1297; Roger (IV) Bigod, earl of Norfolk, objected strongly to the king's plans to campaign in Flanders, while sending him and others to fight in Gascony. The issue of military service was an important theme in the growing crisis. A novel form of summons was used to request attendance at a muster in London on 7 May, extending service to all those holding at least £20 worth of land. When the muster took place, Edward asked Bigod, as marshal, and Humphrey (VI) de Bohun, earl of Hereford (d. 1298), as constable, to draw up registers of those who attended, just as if it were a normal feudal occasion. The earls refused and were dismissed. An offer of wages to all those who served with the king, made at the end of July, produced a very limited response; Edward's military plans found few supporters outside the royal household.

Added to the grievances over military services were complaints about taxation, and the prises of wool and other commodities. Prises of foodstuffs were taken by the crown in order to supply armies with victuals; Edward had greatly extended a traditional right to take goods for the use of the royal household, and there was much bitterness at the inevitable corruption that accompanied the process. In July it was even suggested in a very able statement of grievances, the *Monstraunces*, that the various royal exactions might serve as a precedent for reducing the people to a state of servitude. The complaints at this stage were essentially over the level of royal demands, rather than their unconstitutional nature. In August, however, the demands for a tax of an eighth, and for a further prise of wool, provided the opposition with fresh arguments. The clergy, led by Archbishop Winchelsey, were also bitterly opposed to Edward's actions in 1297, as a result of the way in which he had carried out his threat of outlawry if they did not pay the tax he demanded. Edward, however, achieved a reconciliation of sorts with Winchelsey on 11 July. But a demand on 20 August that the exchequer collect a new harsh levy on the church did nothing to cement this understanding.

The crisis of 1297 was characterized by attempts by both sides to explain their position publicly. On 12 August

Edward issued a long letter setting out a justification for his actions. He apologized for burdening his people so heavily, but stressed the need to bring the war to a quick conclusion. When that happened, the grievances of the people would be met. The king's case did not convince many; he sailed for Flanders with a relatively small force, largely recruited from his own household. To leave the country when civil war seemed imminent was a bold step. On the day the king was about to embark, 22 August, Bigod and Bohun appeared at the exchequer to prevent the collection of the tax of an eighth, and of the prise of wool. The news of the defeat in Scotland at Stirling Bridge in September shifted the confused political situation in favour of a settlement. The opposition's demands were almost certainly those set out in a document known as *De tallagio*, a draft of articles to be added to Magna Carta. Consent was to be obtained for taxes and for prises, the maltote was to be abolished, and those who had refused to campaign in Flanders were to be pardoned. The council, in the king's absence, agreed to grant the *Confirmatio cartarum* of 10 October. This was not added to Magna Carta, but promised that 'aids, mises and prises' would not be taken without common assent. No precedent would be made of the wartime exactions. The maltote was abolished. On 12 October promises were made that everything would be done to persuade the king to abandon the 'rancour and indignation' in which he held the earls and their associates. Edward must have been angered by the concessions, which almost certainly went further than he wished, but he had little option other than to confirm the *Confirmatio* in his own name on 5 November, and to pardon Bigod, Bohun, and their followers.

Reform and recovery, 1298–1307 Edward's reaction when he returned from Flanders in 1298 was to set up a nationwide inquiry into official corruption and malpractice. He was undoubtedly right in seeing such problems as part of the reason for the problems he had faced, but the crisis was largely the result of his determination to carry through his military plans come what may. The crisis left a lasting legacy of suspicion. In 1298 there was concern that the king would go back on his promises of the previous year. Then the question of the investigation of the boundaries of the royal forest became a test of his good faith; it was widely suspected that these had been improperly extended. The issue of the statute *De finibus levatis* in 1299 made it clear that the investigation of the boundaries would not be permitted to curtail royal rights, and when the forest charter was reissued important clauses were omitted. In 1300 Edward agreed to the issue of the *Articuli super cartas*, detailed provisions that set limits on the use of the courts of household and exchequer, and on the use of the privy seal. Sheriffs were to be elected locally, and a new procedure for the enforcement of Magna Carta, now reissued, was set out. What Edward was not prepared to do was make formal concessions on the issue of military service, as was demanded of him.

Arguments continued in parliament in 1301, when a bill highly critical of the government was submitted by a knight of the shire. Edward had to concede the demands made about the boundaries of the forests, and although no concessions were made on military service, he ceased attempting any innovations in methods of recruitment. The final years of the reign were politically relatively quiescent, even though many of the issues raised in the 1290s were still simmering. In the autumn of 1305 Edward was in a strong enough position to obtain a papal bull revoking the concessions he had made, and in the following year he reversed the disafforestations of 1301. He did not, however, go too far in trying to restore his position, and at the final parliament of the reign, summoned to Carlisle in January 1307, the main controversies were over the exactions of papal tax collectors and other papal demands. There were other problems during these years: the king became involved in a series of disputes in Durham between the bishop, his old friend Antony Bek, and the cathedral priory, which led to the seizure of the bishopric into royal hands on two occasions. Edward also had a dispute with the archbishop of York, Thomas of Corbridge, over the nomination of a royal clerk to a living. The rebuke that the archbishop received was so severe that it was said to have been the cause of his death in September 1304. Edward was a formidable man.

Physique and character In physical terms Edward was an impressive man, 6 feet 2 inches tall. His curly hair was blond in youth, dark in maturity, and white in old age. He spoke with a slight lisp, but was said to be persuasive and fluent. He possessed all the physical competence appropriate to knighthood. Edward was conventional. All the evidence indicates that he was a faithful and devoted husband to both his wives. His marriage to Eleanor of Castile, in particular, was a notably happy one; Eleanor accompanied her husband wherever possible, even on crusade, and Edward's distress at her death in 1290 was given magnificent visual expression in the famous sequence of Eleanor crosses that marked the places where her body rested on its journey from Harby in Nottinghamshire to Westminster. There were probably fourteen children of the marriage, though only one son, Edward of Caernarfon, the future *Edward II, born in 1284, survived the perils of childhood. Five daughters, Eleanor, *Joan of Acre, Margaret, *Mary of Woodstock, and Elizabeth, also survived into adulthood. With his second wife, Margaret of France, Edward had three children, *Thomas of Brotherton, *Edmund of Woodstock, and Eleanor.

Edward's religious habits were orthodox, as is demonstrated by his foundation of Vale Royal Abbey in fulfilment of a vow made when shipwreck threatened during a channel crossing in the 1260s. Accounts show that he was a regular attender at chapel services, and that he was a generous giver of alms. Little is known of his literary tastes; the only literary work from which he is known to have quoted is an obscene parody of a chivalric romance. His architectural patronage was more notable. The Eleanor crosses were very significant, as was St Stephen's Chapel, Westminster, on which work began in 1292. Edward continued his father's patronage of the painter Walter of Durham, and was probably responsible in the

1290s for extensive additions to the decoration of the Painted Chamber at Westminster.

A record of a bet Edward had with the royal laundress Matilda of Waltham suggests an amiable side to his character; other evidence, such as a payment for the repair of his daughter Elizabeth's coronet after Edward had thrown it into a fire, points to a violent temper. He was a keen huntsman, being particularly fond of falconry and hawking. He was interested in the Arthurian past, and was responsible for the translation of the bodies of Arthur and Guinevere at Glastonbury in 1278. Direct evidence for Edward's views on government is scanty. His arguments lacked sophistication; in 1297 an instruction that his people 'should do their duty toward their lord with good will, as good and loyal people ought, and are bound to do toward their liege lord in so great and high an affair' reflects his attitude well (Prestwich, *Edward I*, 564). The case he put in the same year, that 'it seems to us that we should be as free as any man to buy wool in our own country' (ibid., 563), showed a lack of understanding of the objections of those whose wool was being arbitrarily seized by royal officials. A concern that the king should not be dishonoured is a frequent theme in letters that can be closely linked to Edward. A request for the recruitment of the impossibly large number of 60,000 men in 1296 argues that he had little care for administrative detail, while correspondence with the exchequer in 1301 suggests that the king had no detailed understanding of the financial situation, though there is no doubting his overall drive and determination to push his policies through.

Reputation and achievement Edward and his reign have been subject to varied interpretations. Bishop William Stubbs saw Edward as acting on high constitutional principles; the 'English Justinian' was the nineteenth-century vision of him. Twentieth-century commentators have been less kind, with the notable exception of F. M. Powicke, whose treatment of him was very sympathetic. T. F. Tout's detailed work on royal administration brought to light the immense labour of the many clerks who worked to achieve so much under Edward; his overall view of the king was of an autocrat, who used 'the mass of the people as a check upon his hereditary foes among the greater baronage' (Tout, *Admin. hist.*, 2.190). G. O. Sayles saw Edward as arbitrary and untrustworthy both as a youth and in his later years, rather than as a man convinced that he should rule according to principles of counsel and consent. K. B. McFarlane emphasized the unreasonableness of Edward's policies towards the higher nobility. Nor, unsurprisingly, has he had a good press from Welsh and Scottish historians.

Nevertheless, Edward's achievements were most impressive. The reconstruction of royal government after the traumas of the 1260s was a major task, and the legislative changes enshrined in a series of statutes were a monumental work. The years up to 1290 were astonishingly productive. Parliament evolved rapidly, both as a mechanism through which the crown could achieve its aims, and as an occasion where petitions could be presented and wrongs corrected. In Europe the king displayed himself as a peacemaker, while his mobilization of massive military resources enabled him to destroy the independent authority of the princes of Gwynedd. Gascony was ruled far more effectively by the English than in the past, in part as a result of the king's two visits to the duchy. Edward was not, however, able to build on his achievements as he would have liked, by leading a successful crusade. Instead, in his later years he was embroiled in war. Conflict with Philippe IV of France from 1294 to 1298, which presaged the Hundred Years' War, proved expensive and frustrating; campaigns against the Scots promised success in 1296, 1298, and 1304, but Edward was never able to subject Scotland as he had done Wales. The demands of war, for manpower, supplies, and money, led to political crisis at home in 1297. The king was opposed by the leading earls, and by Archbishop Winchelsey. The crisis was not easily settled, and arguments continued in the succeeding years. There was no longer the same impetus to reform law and government. Edward's leadership in his final years was characterized by the unreliability that had dogged his reputation as a young man, and that was now combined with inflexibility. In the long term the positive achievements of the reign need to be balanced against the fact that Edward's policies had set England on a long course of war against the Scots.

Death Edward died at Burgh by Sands, having been intermittently ill for some time. At the end he was suffering from dysentery, and his determination to go north to fight the Scots was misguided; he was in no fit state to travel. His servants came to him at noon on 7 July 1307 to lift him from his bed so that he could eat; he died in their arms. The corpse was brought south, and on 27 October the funeral service took place in Westminster Abbey, conducted by his old friend, and recent adversary, Antony Bek, bishop of Durham. MICHAEL PRESTWICH

Sources *Ann. mon.* · *Bartholomaei de Cotton … Historia Anglicana*, ed. H. R. Luard, Rolls Series, 16 (1859) · E. B. Fryde, ed., *Book of prests of the king's wardrobe for 1294–5* (1962) · *Close rolls of the reign of Henry III*, 14 vols., PRO (1902–38) · *CCIR* · *CDS* · *CPR* · *Chronica Johnannis de Oxenedes*, ed. H. Ellis (1859) · W. Stubbs, ed., *Chronicles of the reigns of Edward I and Edward II*, 2 vols., Rolls Series, 76 (1882–3) · *The chronicle of Walter of Guisborough*, ed. H. Rothwell, CS, 3rd ser., 89 (1957) · F. M. Powicke and C. R. Cheney, eds., *Councils and synods with other documents relating to the English church, 1205–1313*, 2 vols. (1964) · M. Prestwich, ed., *Documents illustrating the crisis of 1297–98 in England*, CS, 4th ser., 24 (1980) · Peter of Langtoft, *Le règne d'Édouard Ier*, ed. J. C. Thiolier (Créteil, 1989) · E. L. G. Stones and G. G. Simpson, eds., *Edward I and the throne of Scotland, 1290–1296*, 2 vols. (1978) · H. R. Luard, ed., *Flores historiarum*, 3 vols., Rolls Series, 95 (1890) · Rymer, *Foedera*, new edn, vol. 1/2 · J. Topham, *Liber quotidianus contrarotulatoris garderobae: anno regni regis Edwardi primi vicesimo octavo* (1787) · Paris, *Chron.* · B. F. Byerly and C. R. Byerly, eds., *Records of the wardrobe and household, 1285–1286* (1977) · B. F. Byerly and C. R. Byerly, eds., *Records of the wardrobe and household, 1286–1289* (1986) · A. Luders and others, eds., *Statutes of the realm*, 11 vols. in 12, RC (1810–28), vol. 1 · G. W. S. Barrow, *Robert Bruce and the community of the realm of Scotland* (1965) · P. Binski, *The Painted Chamber at Westminster*, Society of Antiquaries of London Occasional Papers, new ser., 9 (1986) • R. Brown, H. M. Colvin, and A. J. Taylor, eds., *The history of the king's works*, 1 (1963) • P. Chaplais, ed., 'Some private letters of Edward I', *EngHR*, 77 (1962), 79–86 • R. R. Davies, *Conquest, coexistence, and change: Wales, 1063–1415*, History of Wales, 2 (1987) • G. L. Harriss, *King, parliament and public finance in medieval England to 1369* (1975) • S. D. Lloyd, 'The Lord Edward's crusade, 1270–2: its setting and significance', *War and government in the middle ages*, ed. J. B. Gillingham and J. C. Holt (1984) • R. S. Loomis, 'Edward I, Arthurian enthusiast', *Speculum*, 28 (1953), 114–27 • K. B. McFarlane, *The nobility of later medieval England* (1973) • J. E. Morris, *The Welsh wars of Edward I* (1901) • J. C. Parsons, *Eleanor of Castile: queen and society in thirteenth-century England* (1995) • T. F. T. Plucknett, *Legislation of Edward I* (1949) • F. M. Powicke, *King Henry III and the Lord Edward: the community of the realm in the thirteenth century*, 2 vols. (1947) • F. M. Powicke, *The thirteenth century* (1962), vol. 4 of *The Oxford history of England*, ed. G. M. Clarke, 2nd edn • M. Prestwich, *Edward I* (1988) • M. Prestwich, *War, politics, and finance under Edward I* (1972) • H. Rothwell, 'Edward I and the struggle for the charters, 1297–1305', *Studies in medieval history presented to Frederick Maurice Powicke*, ed. R. W. Hunt and others (1948), 319–32 • L. F. Salzman, *Edward I* (1968) • G. O. Sayles, *The king's parliament of England* (1975) • J. R. Studd, 'The Lord Edward and King Henry III', *BIHR*, 50 (1977), 4–19 • D. W. Sutherland, *Quo warranto proceedings in the reign of Edward I, 1278–1294* (1963) • Tout, *Admin. hist.*, vol. 2 • E. B. Fryde and others, eds., *Handbook of British chronology*, 3rd edn, Royal Historical Society Guides and Handbooks, 2 (1986)

Archives BL, Add. MSS 7965, 7966a, 8835 • PRO, accounts of the royal wardrobe and household, largely in exchequer, accounts various, E101 • PRO, Chancery miscellanea, accounts of the royal wardrobe and household, C47 • PRO, ancient correspondence, SC 1 • S. Antiquaries, Lond., wardrobe book and inventory of plate and jewels, MSS 119, 545

Likenesses corbel, 1230–70, Westminster Abbey, London • manuscript, 1297–8, PRO, memoranda roll E 368 • L. P. Boitard, line engraving, pubd 1757 (after a portrait), BM, NPG • G. Vertue, line engraving (after a portrait), NPG • manuscript illumination, BL, Cotton MS Vitellius A.xiii, fol. 6v [*see illus.*] • manuscript painting, BL, Rochester chronicle, Cotton MS Nero D.ii, fol. 191v; *see illus. in* Edward II (1284–1327) • statue, choir screen, York Minster • wax seals, BM • wax seals, King's Cam.

Edward II [of Caernarfon] (**1284–1327**), manuscript painting [kneeling before his father, Edward I]

Edward II [Edward of Caernarfon] (**1284–1327**), king of England and lord of Ireland, and duke of Aquitaine, was born at Caernarfon Castle in north Wales on 25 April 1284, the youngest child of *Edward I (1239–1307) and his first wife, *Eleanor of Castile (1241–1290).

Infancy and education At the time of Edward's birth Caernarfon Castle was still under construction. Although there is no apparent foundation for the sixteenth-century statements that the young prince was presented to the Welsh as a native-born sovereign, there is evidence that Edward I deliberately arranged for his latest child to be born at Caernarfon in order to draw, for his own political advantage, on the supposed associations of the place in Welsh legend with imperial Rome.

Edward was the youngest of at least fourteen (and possibly as many as sixteen) children of Edward I's first marriage. By the time he was born at least seven of Edward I's children were already dead, including his two elder sons, John and Henry, while a third son, Alfonso, was to die in August 1284 in his eleventh year. This left the new-born Edward of Caernarfon both as the only surviving son and as heir to the throne, and made his childhood illnesses more than usually important. In April 1290, when Edward

I was completing his plans for a new crusade, he recognized the possibility that he might not be succeeded by a male heir when he ensured the rights of succession in turn of each of his surviving daughters and any future offspring.

Despite the political importance of Edward of Caernarfon's health and welfare his childhood was to modern eyes very unsatisfactory. His mother, Eleanor, died on 28 November 1290, when her son was in his seventh year. For over three years just before this loss, between May 1286 and August 1289, both parents had been absent in Gascony. His grandmother, *Eleanor of Provence, died in June 1291; his sisters *Joan of Acre and Margaret both married in 1290, and Margaret left England to join her husband, John (II), duke of Brabant, in 1297; his eldest sister, Eleanor, married Henri, count of Bar, in 1293. The two sisters closest to him in age, Elizabeth (born in August 1282) and *Mary of Woodstock (born in March 1279), also left the family circle, one to marry the count of Holland in 1297, the other to enter the convent of Amesbury in 1285.

Little is known in any systematic way about Edward's training and education. Sir Gui de Ferre the elder, a Gascon knight who had formerly been steward to Eleanor of Provence, was '*magister* of the king's son' (his tutor in horsemanship and military exercises) from as early as 1295, or even 1293, until his death in April 1303. A toy castle was made for Edward in his early childhood, while a copy of Vegetius's *De re militari*, which was possibly made *c.*1306 for his knighting, was still in his possession in the 1320s. Although Edward seems in fact to have been strong and athletic in his youth and to have been a good horseman, he is never known to have taken part in a tournament. Lack of interest or aptitude may have been the reason, but it is just as likely that it was simply too dangerous to risk the life or health of the heir to the throne, and hence also the life and health of the kingdom itself, in such a dangerous sport. Edward's participation in and exposure to the risks of military campaigns in Scotland, both as prince and as king, were to be danger enough.

Dominican friars were members of his household from at least 1290, beginning a close spiritual and personal relationship between himself and the order that continued throughout his life. Dominican confessors were to be on intimate terms with Edward as king, while other Dominicans were closely involved in the plots to release him from captivity in 1327 and probably also in the attempts to establish for Edward a posthumous reputation for sanctity. Edward's attendance at religious ceremonies as child and man, and his regular donations of alms to religious orders were at one level no more than might be expected of a medieval king, but his relationship with the Dominicans, and Richard II's efforts to have him canonized (while certainly influenced by political considerations) suggest that Edward's piety may have been more than conventional in nature. In April 1301 he commissioned a picture of the martyrdom of Thomas Becket for the chapel of Chester Castle, and his devotion to St Thomas was to be conspicuous during his reign. In 1302 an illuminated manuscript of the life of Edward the Confessor was bought for him. Although this is consistent with the use that had been made of the cult of St Edward by both Henry III and Edward I to add prestige to the English monarchy, there is little doubt that Edward was himself greatly affected by the cult.

In 1290 the prince's mother sent her scribe Philip to join Edward at Woodstock, which may imply that Edward was better educated (or at least that a greater effort was made to educate him) than is generally thought. Edward spoke French and presumably also English (as his father had done); he was certainly capable of reading French but whether he could also write (as could his son and successor *Edward III) is unknown. It has been suggested that Edward was unable to understand Latin because he took his coronation oath in 1308 in a French form rather than the traditional Latin, and because in 1317 a papal bull thanked the archbishop of Canterbury for translating its contents into French 'so that what is the better understood may bear the richer fruit' (LPL, register of Archbishop Walter Reynolds, fol. 218). The argument is spurious, since French was more appropriate for a public gathering such as a coronation, while the convolutions of the papal chancery's Latin would probably have required explanation even to many who were well versed in the language.

The young prince Edward's earliest years were marked by the itinerant life characteristic of royal and noble families. His earliest 'public' appearances were such occasions as the entry of his six-year-old sister Mary into the convent at Amesbury in 1285, and his attendance at the marriage of his sister Margaret to the future duke of Brabant in July 1290. In late September 1290 the intended marriage alliance between Edward and Margaret (the Maid of Norway), the heir to the Scottish throne, which had been agreed in the treaty of Birgham in July, came to nothing when Margaret died. On 28 November he lost his mother, Eleanor of Castile, and gained nominal possession of the counties of Ponthieu and Montreuil in northern France, which had been her personal inheritance.

The Anglo-French war which began in 1294 led to another plan for Edward's marriage, this time with a daughter of the count of Flanders. The agreement concluded in February 1297 was to be annulled by the pope in 1298 as part of the Anglo-French peace negotiations. In 1296 Edward was in nominal command of English defences against a possible French invasion, and in the following year, at the age of thirteen, he gained his first meaningful experiences of government and of a political crisis involving the English magnates, when on 14 July 1297 the leading clergy and magnates swore fealty to Edward as his father's successor in Edward I's presence at Westminster. Edward then acted as regent of England between 22 August 1297 and 14 March 1298 while his father was absent in Flanders. On 10 October 1297 Edward made a formal offer of pardon to the opposition earls and witnessed the *Confirmatio cartarum*, aimed at defusing the crisis, on the same day. In June 1299 the treaty of Montreuil between England and France provided for the betrothal of Edward and *Isabella (1295–1358), daughter of Philippe IV of France (*r.* 1285–1314). In July 1300 Edward had his first military experience when he was present at the siege of Caerlaverock.

On 7 February 1301 Edward, now almost seventeen, was created prince of Wales and earl of Chester at the Lincoln parliament (although the title of prince was not used in official documents until May 1301). This was probably a mark of Edward I's approval of his son's achievements to date, but it was also a way of providing him with an appropriate endowment in advance of his marriage to Isabella as well as an attempt to ensure the future allegiance of the Welsh to English rule. At about the same time Edward is recorded as having acquired a copy of a book 'de gestis regum Anglie', probably Geoffrey of Monmouth's *Historia regum Britanniae*, a work which was appropriate to his new status in Wales but also a reminder of the English crown's claims to supremacy over the entire island of Britain. Edward spent most of April and May in Wales receiving the homage of his Welsh subjects. It was his only visit before he fled there in October 1326. While there is nothing to confirm the opinion of Rishanger that the Welsh of all ranks esteemed Edward as 'their rightful lord, because he derived his origin from those parts' (Rishanger, *Chronicle*, 464), the Welsh were later to show notable loyalty to Edward as king, especially during the civil war of 1321–2 and in the plots to free him after his deposition in 1327.

Relations with Edward I In the summer and autumn of 1301 Edward was in Scotland where his father hoped that he would have 'the chief honour of taming the pride of the Scots' (*CDS*, 2, no. 1949). In March 1302 he presided over a council of magnates in the absence of his father and was summoned to parliament for the first time in his own right in July and October that year. His betrothal to Isabella of France took place in May 1303. Later in 1303 he was again in Scotland and remained there until after the capture of Stirling in July 1304. On 27 September 1304 Edward was appointed to go to Amiens to do homage to Philippe IV on his father's behalf for the duchy of Aquitaine. However, this visit was cancelled when the French failed to send letters of safe conduct.

Until early 1305 Edward's career seemed to have been advancing steadily towards the inevitable succession to the throne, which could not now be long delayed. Although Edward I was never lavish with praise, he appears to have been generally satisfied with his son's progress. However on 14 June 1305, at Midhurst in Sussex, Edward quarrelled with his father's treasurer, Walter Langton. Edward I immediately came to Langton's support and banished his son from court. What was really at issue is not clear: possibly Langton's anger was roused by the extravagance of Edward's household expenses, while the prince wished to seek revenge on a powerful but unpopular royal minister. Although father and son were reconciled on 13 October 1305, significantly the feast of St Edward, full trust was never restored between them.

Piers Gaveston During the estrangement Edward was also deprived of the company of several of his close associates, one of whom was Piers *Gaveston (*d.* 1312), who had been a member of his household since 1300. Although the relationship that developed between the two young men was certainly very close (and may already have been a factor in the crisis of 1305), its exact nature is impossible to determine. An anonymous chronicler of the civil wars of Edward's reign remarked that:

> upon looking on him the son of the king immediately felt such love for him that he entered into a covenant of constancy, and bound himself with him before all other mortals with a bond of indissoluble love, firmly drawn up and fastened with a knot. (Haskins, 75)

Such comments have led to the modern assumption that their relationship was definitely sexual. The evidence for this, however, is far from clear. While some of the chroniclers' remarks about Edward II can be interpreted as implying homosexuality or bisexuality, too many of them are either much later in date or the product of hostility, or a combination of the two, and thus not acceptable at face value.

Edward II and Gaveston both married early in the reign, at a time when the closeness of their relationship was much remarked upon. While each of their marriages had a social and a political dimension, it is highly improbable that Philippe IV of France, who had an extreme aversion to homosexuality, would have allowed the marriage with Isabella, which had been under negotiation since 1298, if her future husband's sexual proclivities had been clearly proclaimed over so long a period. Nor might the young Gilbert de Clare, earl of Gloucester and Edward II's

nephew, have agreed to the marriage between his sister Margaret and Gaveston. There were children of both marriages. Gaveston's daughter Joan was born in early 1312, and Edward's son, the future Edward III, was born at Windsor on 13 November 1312, a few months after Gaveston's death, and must have been conceived while the latter was still alive. Edward II's wife, Isabella, was only twelve years old at the time of their marriage and could not have been expected to bear children much earlier than she did. Three more children were born to Edward and Isabella: *John, born at Eltham on about 15 August 1316; Eleanor, born at Woodstock on 18 June 1318; and *Joan, born in the Tower of London on 5 July 1321. There is nothing to suggest that Edward II was not the father of any of these children. Edward also had an illegitimate son Adam, who died during the Scottish campaign of 1322 and was probably born before his father's marriage in 1308 at a time when his relationship with Gaveston was already established, while Gaveston is known to have had an illegitimate daughter.

It has also been very plausibly, though not conclusively, argued by Chaplais that the two men entered into a bond of adoptive brotherhood, comparable with the relationship between David and Jonathan in the Old Testament or with the practice of brotherhood-in-arms between members of the nobility in fourteenth- and fifteenth-century Europe. But whatever the actual nature of their relationship—sexual, a formal bond, or simply a very close friendship—Gaveston was perceived as wielding a degree of influence over the king that excluded others who considered they had a right to be consulted. Both he and ultimately Edward himself were to pay the penalty for their offence.

The end of Edward I's reign Following the reconciliation with his father in October 1305 Edward was given a greater role. In April 1306 it was announced that Edward was to lead an army into Scotland to put down the revolt of Robert Bruce, recently crowned as Robert I. On 7 April Edward, who was now almost twenty-two, was granted the duchy of Aquitaine, the Isle of Oléron, and the Agenais to maintain the status of knighthood which he was to receive at Westminster on 22 May. Altogether about 300 other young men were knighted on the same occasion in a splendid ceremony, which was followed by a great feast at which Prince Edward swore that he would not sleep two nights in the same place until he had defeated Robert. In August 1306 Edward entered Scotland, but caused such devastation and showed such cruelty that he was angrily rebuked by his father.

Edward was back in England by December 1306 when he went to Dover to meet Cardinal Pedro of Spain, who was charged with completing the marriage agreement between Edward and Isabella. This was duly achieved at the Carlisle parliament in March 1307, when it was also decided that Edward should go to France in late May for his wedding. However, although Edward reached Dover he did not cross to France, but instead saw off Gaveston who in February had been ordered to leave England by a furious Edward I, after Prince Edward had apparently attempted to give him the county of Ponthieu.

King of England A new Scottish campaign had barely begun when on 7 July 1307 Edward I died near Carlisle, where Edward received the homage of the English magnates on 20 July. One of his first acts as king was to recall Gaveston, whom he created earl of Cornwall at Dumfries on 6 August. Edward then returned to England to hold a short parliament at Northampton on 13 October, for the burial of his father at Westminster Abbey on 27 October, and to make arrangements for his own marriage and coronation. He also settled old political scores by dismissing and imprisoning the treasurer, Walter Langton, who was replaced by Walter Reynolds, the keeper of Edward's household. On 1 November Gaveston married Edward's niece, Margaret de Clare, and when Edward II crossed to France, on 22 January 1308, he left Gaveston as regent of England. On 25 January Edward and Isabella were married at Boulogne in a splendid ceremony attended by Philippe IV of France and by many of the leading nobility of both kingdoms. On 31 January Edward II performed homage for the duchy of Aquitaine.

However, on the same day the bishop of Durham, the earls of Lincoln, Surrey, Pembroke, and Hereford, and others made an agreement in which they declared that since they were bound by fealty to preserve the king's honour and the rights of his crown, they wished to redress and amend anything that had been done against his honour. None of the parties to the agreement was personally hostile to the king and it is likely that they were thinking chiefly of the financial and administrative consequences of the continuing inconclusive war with Scotland, which had created serious political tensions between the king and his subjects, rather than of Edward II's own personal behaviour or even that of Gaveston. But the warning signs were there, and the benign reform programme of the Boulogne agreement was soon followed by demands for reform of a much more far-reaching and personal kind.

Edward II and Isabella returned to Dover on 7 February. On 25 February Edward was crowned at Westminster. In his oath he swore in a newly added clause to uphold 'the laws and rightful customs which the community of the realm shall have chosen' (Chrimes and Brown, 4). This was probably designed to prevent him from evading his undertakings as Edward I had done, but had obvious implications for the future. However he first of all swore to uphold the laws of St Edward (Edward the Confessor), thereby emphasizing an aspect of the royal ideology which had been growing in importance since the reign of Henry III. This clause may already have formed part of Edward I's coronation oath in 1274, but it is possible that this too was newly added in 1308. The splendour of the occasion was disturbed by the resentment of both the English and French nobles present over the prominence given by Edward to Gaveston, alike in the coronation and in the coronation festivities afterwards. This had the effect of concentrating demands for the reform of royal government around the person of Gaveston.

Demands for reform, 1308–1310 On 28 April 1308 the magnates, led by the earl of Lincoln, made a declaration that their allegiance was due to the crown rather than to the person of the king and demanded that Gaveston should be exiled and stripped of his earldom. Edward II agreed to these demands on 18 May but circumvented them in part by appointing Gaveston as his lieutenant in Ireland, and Gaveston left to take up his new post on 25 June. Edward also appealed to the pope to annul Gaveston's exile, in which he succeeded on 25 April 1309. Meanwhile in August 1308 Edward had achieved a reconciliation with the barons at Northampton. By the summer of 1309 he had persuaded a significant number of them to agree to Gaveston's return to England: he and Edward met at Chester on 27 June. In exchange for this and Gaveston's reinstatement as earl of Cornwall, Edward II was faced with further demands for reform, which were first put forward at the parliament held at Westminster in late April and accepted by him at a further parliament at Stamford in early August. Equally ominously, the absence from Stamford of *Thomas, earl of Lancaster (Edward's first cousin), was the first overt sign of Lancaster's future leadership of opposition to the king.

Edward's continuing favours to Gaveston, and his failure to observe the promised reforms, led to further demands from the magnates. The earls of Lancaster, Lincoln, Warwick, Arundel, and Oxford refused to attend a council summoned to York in October, because Gaveston would be present. The crisis came to a head in late February 1310 when the earls attended parliament at Westminster, after Edward had sent Gaveston away for safety. Finally, on 16 March, Edward was forced to bow to the magnates' threat to withdraw their allegiance from him as king and agreed to the appointment of twenty-one ordainers to draw up detailed proposals for reform by 29 September 1311 [see Lords ordainer].

While the ordainers met in London, Edward responded to a warning that the situation in Scotland was rapidly deteriorating by summoning an army to meet at Berwick on 8 September. On the pretext of their work of reform the leading earls—Lancaster, Pembroke, Hereford, and Warwick—stayed away, sending only the minimum military service required by their tenure. Edward reached Edinburgh in late October but, leaving Gaveston to campaign further north, he had returned by early November to Berwick where he remained until the end of July 1311. Meanwhile the death in February 1311 of the earl of Lincoln removed a moderating force, but brought Thomas of Lancaster to greater prominence.

The ordinances The work of the ordainers was finally distilled in a lengthy document of forty-one clauses which dealt with a wide range of grievances. In a clear reference to the Scottish campaign of 1310–11, the king was forbidden to go to war or to leave the kingdom without the consent of the baronage. The king was not to make any gifts of land or other grants without the approval of the baronage in parliament and all grants made since the appointment of the ordainers were to be revoked, until the king's debts had been paid off. Prises (the seizure of foodstuffs for royal use and taken without immediate payment), which were deeply resented, were to cease. The customs duties were to be paid directly into the exchequer and not to be collected by aliens (a reference to the Italian merchant company, the Frescobaldi of Florence); no revenues were to be collected for the direct use of the royal household, which was to be maintained by the exchequer. These provisions reflected the financial confusion into which the royal government had fallen under the pressures of the Scottish war and had their roots both in the reign of Edward I and in current practice.

However, what gave the ordinances a distinctive flavour was their insistence on 'evil and deceptive counsel' and 'evil counsellors' as causes of the troubles of the king and his kingdom: because of such influence the king's chancellor, treasurer, and all other leading officials were to be appointed with the advice and approval of the baronage in parliament, and 'all the evil counsellors' were to 'be ejected and dismissed altogether'. Gaveston was especially singled out for attention, and 'as the evident enemy of the king and of his people', he was to 'be completely exiled as well from the kingdom of England, Scotland, Ireland and Wales as from the whole lordship of our lord the king overseas as well as on this side, forever without ever returning' (*English Historical Documents*, 3.529–39).

The ordinances were sent to Edward for inspection on 3 August and formally presented in parliament at Westminster on 16 August. Edward at first refused to accept them, because they infringed his sovereignty as well as ordering Gaveston's exile. But under intense pressure he gave way, and the ordinances were published in London on 27 September. An order for the general publication of the ordinances was given on 11 October, but on 12 October Edward began diplomatic proceedings to persuade the pope to annul them. From then until 1322 a running battle over the confirmation or annulment of the ordinances was to be fought between the king and his opponents.

The death of Gaveston Although Edward was determined to recall Gaveston at the earliest opportunity, there is no evidence that the latter was with Edward at Christmas, which the king spent at Westminster. But Gaveston probably rejoined the king at Knaresborough on 13 January, and was at York on 18 January 1312 when Edward officially announced his return; he then remained with Edward until after the birth of his own daughter Margaret on 20 February. Open conflict was bound to result. Archbishop Robert Winchelsey of Canterbury summoned a council of prelates and magnates to meet at St Paul's on 13 March, when the earls of Pembroke and Surrey were appointed to pursue and arrest Gaveston. Edward was rejoined by Gaveston at York on 31 March, when Gaveston was given custody of Scarborough Castle. By mid-April they were in Newcastle, but were forced to flee from there on 4 May. Edward and Gaveston sailed to Scarborough, where Gaveston was left while Edward returned to York. Gaveston was then besieged in Scarborough, and on 19 May surrendered to the earls of Pembroke and Surrey, who gave him guarantees of his personal safety until 1 August, while further negotiations were carried out with Edward.

After a meeting with the king at York, Gaveston was placed in the personal custody of Pembroke, who took him south. But on 10 June Gaveston was seized by the earl of Warwick at Deddington in Oxfordshire, imprisoned in Warwick Castle, and on 19 June, with the approval of the earls of Lancaster, Hereford, and Arundel, was executed on Blacklow Hill near Warwick.

Crisis and recovery The death of Gaveston created an undying enmity between Edward and the earls primarily responsible, Lancaster and Warwick; Pembroke and Surrey returned permanently to the king's side; and Edward became more than ever determined to annul the ordinances. Neither side however was prepared to push the issue to open civil war. In August 1312 Edward sent envoys to the pope and to Philippe IV in the hope of enlisting their mediation, and summoned the earls to appear unarmed at Westminster to discuss the ordinances. A complex set of negotiations followed, concluded on 20 December by a treaty in which Edward agreed to pardon the opposition magnates for the death of Gaveston, in return for their submission to him, and for the restoration of royal jewels that had been captured while in Gaveston's custody. In the meantime, on 13 November, Edward and Isabella's first child, the future Edward III, was born at Windsor.

Mutual suspicion remained strong, however, causing delays in performing the terms of the treaty and contributing to the failure of the parliaments summoned for 18 March and 8 July 1313. Edward's position was strengthened by the death of Archbishop Winchelsey in May and the provision to Canterbury on 1 October of his old ally, Walter Reynolds. It was further strengthened between 23 May and 16 July when Edward and Isabella, accompanied by Pembroke and other supporters, made a state visit to Paris. On 6 June Edward and Philippe IV took the cross in Notre Dame, while on 2 July they settled many of the outstanding disputes between them over Aquitaine. Edward now had both personal and diplomatic support from his father-in-law. French and papal mediation both contributed to the political settlement between Edward and the opposition magnates who submitted to the king on 14 October and were pardoned two days later. By 28 November Edward had also obtained agreement for a campaign against his remaining opponents, the Scots, in the following June. On 12 December Edward crossed to Boulogne for a meeting at Montreuil with Philippe IV whose approval, as suzerain of Aquitaine, was required for a large papal loan to Edward secured by the revenues of the duchy. Edward returned to England on 20 December. Although the issue of the ordinances remained unresolved, Edward, by dint of persistence and the skilful use of both domestic and external political support, had achieved a great deal.

Disaster in Scotland Edward's attendance at the enthronement of Walter Reynolds at Canterbury on 17 January 1314 was another sign of his political success, but was quickly followed by news from Scotland of the fall of Roxburgh and Edinburgh castles. But the agreement by the constable of Stirling to surrender that castle if not relieved by 24 June presented Edward with a challenge which he eagerly accepted, hoping to defeat the Scots in a pitched battle. Although four earls, most notably Lancaster and Warwick, refused to join the army in person, fearing the political consequences of a royal victory, the army that advanced in Scotland in early June was a large one of about 15,000 infantry and 2000–3000 cavalry, with many experienced commanders. Properly handled, and with the necessary element of luck, the army should have been capable of defeating the much smaller Scottish army. Instead the English army, crammed into a narrow position which made cavalry deployment difficult, not quite believing that the Scots would be so bold as to attack, and plagued by rivalries and differences of opinion among its leaders, suffered a humiliating defeat at Bannockburn near Stirling on 24 June.

The English archers, who had turned a hard-fought battle into a victory at Falkirk in 1298, and were to win many future engagements, were never brought fully into action and were scattered by the small reserve force of Scottish cavalry. The English cavalry meanwhile had charged the Scottish infantry, who were armed with long pikes and drawn up in close formation (schiltroms), and were cut to pieces. Edward's nephew the earl of Gloucester, whom Edward had accused of cowardice on the previous day for wanting to delay the battle, broke ranks in his anxiety to attack, and was among those killed. The earl of Hereford, who had taken offence when Edward replaced him as constable by Gloucester on the eve of the battle, was captured, along with other leading nobles. Edward II fought bravely, and had a horse killed under him, but eventually had to be led away to safety by the earl of Pembroke, lest his capture should turn disastrous defeat into a catastrophe. Edward reached Dunbar, sailed from there to Berwick, and then moved to York, where he summoned a parliament to meet in September to discuss the Scottish threat. When parliament assembled Edward was instead forced to confirm the ordinances and change all his leading ministers.

On 2 January 1315 an elaborate funeral ceremony was staged for the body of Gaveston at the royal chapel in Kings Langley, Edward's favourite residence. When parliament met again in January and February 1315 Edward was forced to make further concessions to his opponents who demanded the strict observance of the ordinances. Then in May 1315 a Scots army, led by Edward Bruce, landed in Ireland in an attempt to seize it from English control, while in July the Scots laid siege to Carlisle. Edward held meetings with the leading magnates at Lincoln in late August, and at Doncaster in mid-December 1315, to discuss the Scottish attacks and the state of the realm in general. These prepared the way for the parliament that began at Lincoln on 27 January 1316. On 17 February Lancaster was appointed as the head of the king's council, and further measures for the enforcement of the ordinances and for administrative reform were put in train.

The conflict with Lancaster   By the end of April 1316 Lancaster had effectively given up his new role, allegedly because of Edward's refusal to accept the proposed reforms, but probably also because of his own incapacity for government. This began a new period of political instability, during which Lancaster's lack of co-operation prevented a proposed campaign against the Scots during the summer, and the king, queen, and Lancaster all supported rival candidates for the see of Durham. In November and December 1316 Edward planned to improve his position by sending to the newly elected pope, John XXII (r. 1316–34), a high-level embassy designed to win papal assistance against the Scots, to achieve financial concessions, and possibly also to obtain absolution for Edward from his oath to uphold the ordinances. On 28 March 1317 the pope lent Edward the proceeds of a clerical tenth, and on 1 May ordered a truce between England and Scotland.

On 17 March the pope had appointed two cardinals to go to England to negotiate a final peace with Scotland: in the event they were to play an even more important role in bringing about a settlement between Edward and Lancaster. Edward had been attempting to contact Lancaster since at least February 1317 but the mutual suspicions remained, and both sides gathered armed forces, on the pretext of a campaign against the Scots scheduled for September. No campaign took place, and in early October, as Edward was returning south from York, he was only narrowly dissuaded from attacking Lancaster in his castle of Pontefract.

The personal hatred between Edward and his cousin was exacerbated by the rise to prominence of a new group of royal favourites, Roger Damory, Hugh Audley, William Montagu, and Hugh *Despenser the younger (d. 1326), together with the latter's father, Hugh Despenser the elder, a long-time opponent of Lancaster. Edward had also since late 1316 entered into a series of formal contracts for service in peace and war with these and other leading magnates, including the earls of Pembroke and Hereford and Bartholomew Badlesmere. The immediate import of these was their promise to provide Edward with specified amounts of military service but they also had a clear political implication. By the autumn of 1317 Edward had therefore skilfully built up around himself a coalition composed of some individuals who were personally obnoxious to Lancaster, and of others who had no confidence in Lancaster's ability to provide political leadership, and were alarmed at the very real threat of civil war caused by the continuing enmity between Edward and his cousin. Moderate political figures such as Pembroke and Badlesmere were afraid that the behaviour of favourites such as Roger Damory, the husband of one of the heiresses to the earldom of Gloucester, would tip the balance in favour of open conflict.

It was this desire to restrain the king's current favourites, rather than an attempt to create a so-called 'middle party', that led Pembroke and Badlesmere to enter into an indenture with Damory (and possibly with others whose indentures are not extant) on 24 November 1317. The actions of Pembroke and Badlesmere had been bizarrely anticipated at Pentecost (22 May) 1317, when a woman dressed as a theatrical player had ridden into Westminster Hall, while Edward II was feasting with his magnates, and presented a letter to the king. Under questioning she revealed that she had been induced to do this by one of Edward II's own household knights who were annoyed that the king was neglecting knights who had served his father, and was promoting others 'who had not borne the heat of the day' (*Johannis de Trokelowe*, 98–9). This incident very probably arose from the marriages in late April of Roger Damory and Hugh Audley the younger to Elizabeth and Margaret de Clare, two of the three heiresses to the lands of the earldom of Gloucester, and from the partition of their inheritance which had been ordered on 17 April.

Between November 1317 and August 1318 a lengthy series of negotiations took place aimed at producing a lasting accommodation between Edward and Lancaster. Pembroke, Badlesmere, and others acted on behalf of the king, but a crucial mediating role was also played during this period by the archbishop and bishops of the province of Canterbury, the archbishop of Dublin, and the two papal envoys, cardinals Luca and Gaucelin. It was only in July, while Edward remained at Northampton, and royal envoys and ecclesiastical mediators went back and forth to Lancaster at Tutbury, that the deadlock was finally broken. It was also during this period of intense negotiations, on either 11 or about 24 June, that an impostor, John *Powderham (*d.* 1318), appeared at Oxford, claiming to be the true king, and was taken to Northampton where he was executed about 20 July. Ironically, this political embarrassment occurred as Edward was unsuccessfully attempting to persuade the pope to give approval for his reanointing with the holy oil of St Thomas of Canterbury, which had been brought to Edward's attention by an unscrupulous Dominican, Nicholas Wisbech, and which would supposedly have brought a miraculous solution to all Edward's political troubles. Edward and Lancaster finally met on 7 August to exchange the kiss of peace, and on 9 August met again at Leake, near Nottingham, where their agreement was embodied in the form of a treaty. A parliament was also summoned to York for 20 October to confirm and to amplify the terms of the treaty.

Uneasy co-existence At York the ordinances were again confirmed, the royal favourites left court at least for a time, a standing royal council was appointed, and appointments to the major offices under the crown were made or confirmed. But the political settlement was much less favourable to Lancaster than has usually been thought. Lancaster himself would not be a member of the council, while all the members of the council and the office-holders would be men sympathetic to and acceptable to Edward. However the success of this compromise would depend on how far Edward and Lancaster were truly reconciled, whether the royal favourites continued to behave more discreetly, and whether the war with Scotland could be prosecuted with greater success than in the past. Although the loss of the key border fortress of Berwick in April 1318 showed how dangerous the Scots still were, the defeat and death of Edward Bruce at Faughart

near Dundalk on 14 October removed the Scottish threat to the lordship of Ireland, and provided the first definitive military success of Edward II's reign.

Lancaster and his retainers attended the York parliament of May 1319, where it was decided to mount a campaign to recover Berwick. Although all the leading magnates, including Lancaster, answered the summons, and Edward began the siege of Berwick on 7 September 1319, the king was forced to break it off on 17 September, after a Scottish force under Sir James Douglas entered Yorkshire, and on 12 September defeated an army hastily gathered by the archbishop of York and bishop of Ely at Myton-on-Swale near York. Edward was forced to open urgent negotiations with the Scots for a truce, which was agreed for two years in late December.

Relations between Edward and Lancaster then deteriorated once more, engendered by suspicions on the king's side that Lancaster had connived in the Scots' attack and on Lancaster's side that, if Berwick had been taken, Edward would then have turned the army against him. There is also evidence that the behaviour of Hugh Despenser the younger, who had merely been one of a number of royal favourites until his appointment as chamberlain of the royal household in 1318, also contributed to the failure of the campaign of 1319. Together with his father, Hugh Despenser the elder, he was starting to achieve the control of royal favour that led to the outbreak of open civil war in 1321–2.

Lancaster failed to attend parliament at York on 20 January 1320, at which, in an unaccustomed burst of activity on the king's part, it was decided that Edward should go to France in May to perform homage for Aquitaine to Philippe V; embassies were also dispatched to Gascony and to the papal curia. It was also decided to transfer the royal administration from York, where it had been since September 1318, back to Westminster. On 19 June Edward and Isabella crossed to France where on 29 June Edward performed homage for Aquitaine and Ponthieu in the cathedral at Amiens, thereby acknowledging that he held them of the French king. A few days later, when the two kings met to renew the alliance of perpetual friendship concluded between Edward I and Philippe IV in 1303, a French councillor suggested that Edward should also swear fealty, which would have implied a more personal subordination to Philippe V. This was firmly rejected by Edward in a recorded speech which clearly represents his own views. It is an incident that suggests that, although in some situations Edward could be unduly influenced by people in whom he placed particular trust, or by his hatred of other individuals such as Lancaster, he none the less possessed greater abilities as king than are usually credited to him. Edward returned to England on 22 July and reached London on 2 August.

Edward was showing signs of an unwonted energy and initiative at this time. In a well-known letter to the pope, Bishop Thomas Cobham of Worcester remarked that the king was rising unusually early, and was contributing to the discussions of parliamentary business. The unpublished chronicle attributed to Nicholas Trivet adds that

Edward 'showed prudence in answering the petitions of the poor, and clemency as much as severity in judicial matters, to the amazement of many who were there' (BL, MS Cotton Nero D.x, fol. 110v). Despite these encouraging signs, and the further confirmation of the ordinances, there were more sinister developments. Lancaster refused to attend the parliament, and attempts to placate him during October and November were unsuccessful. One cause of Lancaster's absence was probably the growing influence of the younger Despenser. As his ambition to obtain the earldom of Gloucester in his own right became increasingly apparent, Despenser's behaviour also alienated the husbands of the other Gloucester heiresses, Roger Damory and Hugh Audley, together with other magnates with interests in the Welsh march. The turning point came on 20 October 1320 when Edward seized the lordship of Gower in south Wales and granted it to Despenser. The slide into open civil war had now begun.

The civil war On 22 February 1321 Lancaster and other unnamed magnates met at Pontefract and decided to attack the younger Despenser in Wales. Edward and Despenser left London for the danger area on 1 March, and reached Gloucester on 27 March. Edward's summons on 28 March to the earl of Hereford and his allies, who had been gathering forces on their Welsh lands, to attend a council at Gloucester on 5 April was rebuffed and on 4 May the marchers began their attacks on the lands of the two Despensers. On 24 May Lancaster and a group of northern magnates met at Pontefract and made a defensive pact. On 28 June Lancaster met Hereford and the other marcher lords at Sherburn in Elmet, where Lancaster gave his approval of the marchers' actions but apparently failed to bring about a formal alliance for future action between the marchers and the northern magnates.

On 15 May Edward had summoned a parliament to Westminster on 15 July in the hope of saving the Despensers from further attack. Although the clergy tried to mediate, when the marchers reached London on 29 July, they threatened to depose Edward unless the Despensers were expelled. Edward then agreed to exile the Despensers on 14 August, and on 20 August formally pardoned their opponents. As in the case of Gaveston, Edward's one ambition was the return of the Despensers. Taking a gamble that his enemies would not act together, Edward chose to attack Bartholomew Badlesmere, the former steward of the household, who had sided with the marchers against the Despensers earlier in 1321, but who was bitterly hated by Lancaster. Having rejoined the younger Despenser on the Isle of Thanet, Edward sent his queen to request hospitality from Badlesmere's wife at Leeds Castle in Kent. She was, as Edward hoped, refused admission on 13 October. Edward began a siege and on 31 October the castle surrendered, after the baronial army which had advanced to Kingston in Surrey had failed to intervene.

Both sides now prepared for open conflict. Lancaster summoned a meeting between himself and the marchers, which was intended to take place at Doncaster on 29 November but was probably held instead at Pontefract.

The document they drew up, generally known as the Doncaster petition, accusing Despenser of encouraging the king to attack the peers of the realm, and Edward of supporting him, was ignored by the king. Instead, on 30 November Edward gave orders for an army to join him at Cirencester on 13 December, and on 1 December a council of the province of Canterbury, attended only by the archbishop and four of the sixteen bishops, declared the Despensers' exile to be null and void. The earls of Pembroke, Richmond, and Arundel, and the king's half-brother, Edmund, earl of Kent, then concurred. Edward and his army left London on 8 December; he was in Cirencester on 25 December and reached Worcester on 31 December. Forced to make a detour because the marchers held the crossing of the Severn, Edward arrived in Shrewsbury on 14 January 1322, just as his opponents' ranks were starting to crumble. On 22 January both Roger Mortimer of Wigmore and his uncle, Roger Mortimer of Chirk, surrendered to Edward at Shrewsbury, partly because of Lancaster's failure to help his allies, but largely because a Welsh revolt led by Sir Gruffudd Llwyd had captured the Mortimers' castles on behalf of the king.

In a skilfully managed and determined campaign Edward lost no time in pursuing his remaining enemies. He left Shrewsbury on 24 January and on 6 February reached Gloucester where Maurice Berkeley and the elder Hugh Audley surrendered. As a last resort the earl of Hereford, Hugh Audley the younger, and Roger Damory fled to join Lancaster. On 11 February Edward issued safe conducts for the Despensers, and on 14 February ordered the mustering of troops at Coventry on 5 March. He also ordered Sir Andrew Harclay, the royal commander at Carlisle, to move against Lancaster and his supporters from the north. Edward left Gloucester on 18 February, captured Lancaster's castle of Kenilworth on 26 February, and arrived at Coventry on 27 February. On 3 March he was met at Lichfield by the Despensers and a large force of troops. Hearing of the king's advance, Lancaster and Hereford left Pontefract and took up defensive positions on 1 March at the river-crossing at Burton upon Trent near Lancaster's castle at Tutbury. On 10 March part of the royal army crossed the river and outflanked Lancaster and Hereford who fled to Pontefract, leaving Tutbury and the mortally wounded Roger Damory to be captured by Edward. On 11 March Edward declared Lancaster and his allies to be traitors and ordered the siege of Pontefract. Lancaster then attempted to flee to Northumberland, but only reached Boroughbridge in Yorkshire, where he was defeated by Harclay on 16 March. Hereford was killed in the battle; Lancaster was captured the next day and taken to York from where he was taken to Pontefract on 21 March, tried before the king, found guilty of treason, and beheaded outside his castle on the same day. Of the remaining contrariants, Badlesmere and twenty-six others were executed, and the Mortimers, Hugh Audley, and many more were sentenced to imprisonment, and their lands forfeited to the crown. Some former contrariants regained their lands after paying a fine, but over a hundred individuals suffered enduring losses.

The king's victory was confirmed at the parliament which began at York on 2 May 1322. The ordinances, from which Edward had been trying to escape since 1311, were formally revoked in the Statute of York, on the grounds that they improperly restrained royal power. In future any such ordinances would be null and void unless agreed in parliament, with the approval of the prelates, earls and barons, and the community of the realm. Much of the past speculation about the significance of the Statute of York is anachronistic. Edward II was seeking to restore the situation as it had been before 1310–11, rather than to introduce a new emphasis on the authority of parliament or on the role of the 'community' in its future sense of the 'commons'. No king in his hour of victory was likely to tie his hands for the future by introducing a new constitutional doctrine. However, as a way of emphasizing that the ordinances had originally been imposed upon him, and that he was not opposed to reform in principle, Edward had six clauses reissued and confirmed as 'good points'. The York parliament also confirmed the legal process against Lancaster, and formally annulled that against the two Despensers, who were rewarded with a steady stream of grants of forfeited lands; the elder Despenser also became earl of Winchester; and Harclay was given the earldom of Carlisle.

Scottish failure and domestic tyranny Edward's one remaining enemy was the king of Scots, whose forces had caused great destruction and suffering in the northern counties of England in the years since Bannockburn, as well as depriving the English government of revenue and providing a constantly renewed reminder of the humiliation of that defeat. In the summer of 1315, for example, a vast area in the north of England, equivalent to a fifth of the entire kingdom, was paying tribute to King Robert, with the tacit acceptance of Edward II, while the siege of Carlisle in July 1315 and the Scottish capture of Berwick in April 1318 threatened to deprive England of the military bases essential for its own defence and for any future counter-attack against Scotland. Lack of resources and internal political divisions had hitherto hindered any coherent and consistent English response. Now that Lancaster was dead the temptation for Edward to turn against Scotland and to avenge the long humiliation was irresistible. A Scottish campaign was therefore ordered on 25 March, barely a week after Lancaster's defeat. Edward's army finally invaded Scotland on 12 August but the Scots avoided battle by withdrawing northwards and destroying all food supplies in the path of the English army. Edward reached the vicinity of Edinburgh in late August, but was then forced to withdraw with heavy losses of men through starvation and sickness, including his own illegitimate son Adam. Edward was back at Newcastle on 10 September, having dissipated much of the military reputation he had gained through the defeat of Lancaster and his adherents.

Worse was to follow. King Robert crossed into England on 30 September with the apparent intention of capturing Edward. Although Edward knew of his approach, and tried to take precautions, the Scots surprised and routed the English forces on 'Blakehoumor' in Yorkshire on 14 October. Edward, who was nearby at Byland, was forced to flee for safety, arriving at York about 18 October, still pursued by the Scots. Meanwhile Queen Isabella, who had been left at Tynemouth Priory, now found herself cut off behind enemy lines and had to make a difficult escape by sea. The futility of Edward's policy towards Scotland was further demonstrated on 3 January 1323 when Andrew Harclay, the victor of Boroughbridge, acted on his own initiative in making a peace treaty with Robert I, recognizing Scottish independence. Although the agreement was repudiated, and Harclay was tried and executed for treason on 3 March, Edward entered into negotiations of his own. These resulted in a thirteen-year truce which was confirmed by Edward at Bishopthorpe near York on 30 May 1323. The truce had been born out of Edward's humiliation, but England was at least at peace with all her external enemies for the first time since 1294.

However, England was only superficially at peace internally. Rebels had been executed before on grounds of treason, but none of so high a rank as Thomas of Lancaster, or so closely related to the king himself: the precedent was an ominous one for the future of English political conflict. The confiscations and executions of 1322 created resentments among the surviving contrariants and the relatives of those who had perished, which were eventually bound to surface, while the loyalty of many others was to be strained to breaking point. The escape of Roger Mortimer of Wigmore from the Tower of London on 1 August 1323 was just the beginning of a process that led to Edward's downfall three years later. Although the younger Despenser was now the dominant influence on the king, who rewarded him lavishly with grants of land, there is little doubt that Edward himself was the prime mover in much of what happened. Just as his determination to defeat and destroy his enemies had inspired the Boroughbridge campaign in 1321–2, so now it dictated the ruthless zeal with which Edward and his agents exploited the confiscated lands of the contrariants for the advantage of the royal treasury.

His new revenues allowed Edward to pay off his father's debts, to fight a war with France in 1323–5 without the need for additional taxation, and to accumulate by the end of his reign a reserve of treasure of about £60,000, equivalent to a year's income. The nature of Edward's regime during his years of almost unfettered rule was aptly expressed by the author of the *Vita Edwardi secundi*:

> The harshness of the king has today increased so much that no one however great and wise dares to cross his will. Thus parliaments, colloquies, and councils decide nothing these days. For the nobles of the realm, terrified by threats and the penalties inflicted on others, let the king's will have free play. Thus today will conquers reason. For whatever pleases the king, though lacking in reason, has the force of law.
> (*Vita Edwardi secundi*, 136)

Edward, however, had a different view of his achievements in these years after 1322. In 1324 he ordered Master John St Albans to paint the walls of the Lesser Hall of Westminster Palace with scenes from the life of his father, Edward I, 'whom God assoil'. Perhaps at last Edward felt reconciled with his father, and deluded himself that in destroying his internal enemies he had somehow matched Edward I's greatness in war.

Crisis in France In October 1323 a crisis arose in Gascony when English officials destroyed the newly erected French bastide at St Sardos in the Agenais, so ending the good relations between England and France which had endured throughout the reign of Edward II and which had enabled Edward to deal more effectively with his domestic and Scottish enemies. Attempts to resolve the dispute failed and in August 1324 a French army invaded the duchy. Edward considered leading an army to Gascony in person, leaving his son Edward as regent, but instead, on 9 March 1325, Isabella was sent to Paris in order to mediate with her brother Charles IV. After further negotiations Edward finally agreed to go to France in person, to do homage to Charles IV at Beauvais on 29 August 1325. However, he then accepted Charles's offer to receive homage from Edward's eldest son, Prince Edward, provided that Edward II first transferred to him all his French lands. On 2 September Prince Edward received the counties of Ponthieu and Montreuil, and on 10 September the duchy of Aquitaine. The prince then left England on 12 September, and performed homage on 24 September at Bois-de-Vincennes near Paris, where Isabella had also been staying. Despite repeated demands from Edward, neither the prince nor his mother returned to England, and by November 1325 Isabella was openly refusing to do so until Despenser had been removed from court.

Edward and Isabella Relations between Edward and Isabella deteriorated rapidly in 1325–6. The major reason was certainly the influence that the younger Despenser exercised, both over the making of royal policy and over the king's person: whether this influence also took the form of a sexual relationship, there is no way of knowing. But there is no doubt that Despenser was driving Edward and Isabella apart. Isabella had blamed Despenser for her abandonment at Tynemouth in October 1322 and also for the seizure of her lands in September 1324, as part of the official English reaction to the French invasion of Gascony. According to the usually well-informed author of the *Vita Edwardi secundi*, Isabella declared:

> I feel that marriage is a joining together of man and woman, maintaining the undivided habit of life, and that someone has come between my husband and myself trying to break this bond; I protest that I will not return until this intruder is removed, but, discarding my marriage garment, shall assume the robes of widowhood and mourning until I am avenged of this Pharisee. (*Vita Edwardi secundi*, 143)

However, there is also a possibility that the estrangement was partly caused by Despenser's wife, Eleanor de Clare, Edward II's own niece, who was reportedly given custody of the queen and of her seal after Isabella's lands were confiscated. The Leicester chronicler, Henry Knighton, reported that while Isabella was absent in France, Eleanor was treated as if she were queen and spoke slanderously of Isabella, while a Hainault chronicler, who recorded events in England in the 1320s in great detail, even claimed that she was Edward II's mistress and that,

after her husband was executed in 1326, she was kept under surveillance in case she might be pregnant by the king.

Isabella's own sexual liaison with Roger Mortimer of Wigmore, who had fled to France after his escape in 1323, is thought to have begun in December 1325, and news of it was probably brought to England by disapproving members of her household. Edward was furious at his wife's behaviour. In a letter to Charles IV of France on 18 March he accused Isabella of keeping Mortimer's company 'in and out of house' (*CClR, 1323–1327*, 579). Chronicle reports that in 1325 Edward was petitioning the pope for a divorce are probably incorrect, but it is possible that in the summer of 1326 Edward was contemplating such a course. If reports of a sermon preached by the bishop of Hereford at Wallingford in the following December, after Isabella's landing in England, are to be believed, Edward II 'carried a knife in his hose to kill queen Isabella, and had said that if he had no other weapon he would crush her with his teeth' (Goodman, 105).

The deposition of Edward II In January and February 1326 Edward II began to take precautions against a possible invasion by France and the count of Hainault in support of Isabella and Mortimer and of the young Prince Edward, who was betrothed to the count's daughter, Philippa. Edward was greatly angered by this news and on 19 June 1326, in an echo of the scenes between himself and his own father, wrote to his son, forbidding him to marry and warning him that, unless he obeyed, 'he will ordain in such wise that Edward shall feel it all the days of his life, and that all other sons shall take example thereby of disobeying their lords and fathers' (*CClR, 1323–1327*, 577). Despite Edward II's precautions, Isabella and her supporters landed without opposition at Orwell in Suffolk on 24 September 1326. Deserted by many of his followers, on 2 October Edward fled westwards from London with the younger Despenser, probably hoping for support from Despenser's lands in south Wales, or for a Welsh revolt like the one that had defeated the Mortimers in 1322. Edward was in Gloucester on 11 October; at Chepstow on 16 October; and on 21 October he and Despenser sailed from Chepstow for the island of Lundy, possibly hoping from there to reach Ireland, but were blown into Cardiff, where they remained until 28 October. On 28 and 29 October Edward was at Despenser's great fortress of Caerphilly, but then moved farther west, to the Cistercian abbeys of Margam, where he was on 3 and 4 November, and of Neath between 5 and 10 November. On 16 November Edward and Despenser were captured at Llantrisant, between Neath and Caerphilly; Edward was taken to the earl of Leicester's castle of Monmouth, where the great seal was taken from him on 20 November, and from there to Kenilworth, where he arrived on 5 December. He remained there in Leicester's custody until after his deposition on 20 January 1327. Meanwhile on 15 October at Wallingford, Isabella and Prince Edward had proclaimed that they had come to deliver the king, the church, and the realm from the ruin caused by the tyrannies of Hugh Despenser and others; on 26 October Prince Edward was proclaimed guardian of the realm at Bristol, and retained this title until he gained control of the great seal. The elder Despenser was executed at Bristol on 27 October, the younger Despenser at Hereford on 24 November.

Although Edward II had already been threatened with deposition in 1310 and 1321, there now remained the problem of how to bring this about with some semblance of legality and consent. The parliament summoned by Prince Edward in the king's name on 28 October, met at Westminster on 7 January 1327. Edward II having refused to attend, on 13 January a set of six articles, outlining his defects as king and probably drawn up by a clerk of the bishop of Winchester, was presented to the assembly.

Edward was accused of being personally incapable of governing, of allowing himself to be led and governed by others, who advised him badly, and of refusing to remedy these defects when asked to do so by the great and wise men of the kingdom or allowing anyone else to do so; of devoting himself to unsuitable work and occupations, while neglecting the government of his kingdom; of exhibiting pride, covetousness, and cruelty; of losing, for lack of good government, the kingdom of Scotland, and other lands and lordships in Gascony and Ireland (which had been left to him in peace by his father), and of forfeiting the friendship of the king of France and of many other great men; of destroying the church and imprisoning churchmen, and of putting to death, imprisoning, exiling, and disinheriting the great men of his kingdom; of failing to observe his coronation oath through the influence of his evil counsellors; of abandoning his kingdom and doing all in his power to cause the loss both of it and of his people; and of being incorrigible and without hope of improvement. All of which was said to be so notorious that it could not be denied.

Even allowing for the vagueness of these charges, and for the simplistic nature of some of them, such as his alleged personal responsibility for the failure to hold Scotland (far from peaceful in 1307) and for the war in Ireland (in reality the scene in 1318 of one of the few definite English military successes), Edward II was clearly regarded as an incompetent ruler and as a man who could not command any respect. His government in the last resort could only be ended, not mended.

A second delegation then went to Kenilworth. On 20 January the bishop of Hereford outlined the charges against Edward and demanded that he should resign his throne in favour of his son. Under intense pressure and with great emotion, Edward finally agreed. Sir William Trussell, on behalf of parliament, formally renounced his homage to Edward, and Sir Thomas Blount, steward of the household, broke his staff of office. Prince Edward officially acceded as king on 25 January, and on 1 February 1327 was crowned at Westminster.

Imprisonment and death The former Edward II remained at Kenilworth until 2 April when he was transferred to the custody of Thomas Berkeley and John Maltravers, following a plot to free him by a Dominican, John Stoke. He was at Llanthony Abbey near Gloucester on 5 April and reached Berkeley Castle on the following day. In July a conspiracy involving another Dominican, Thomas Dunheved, and a number of other men temporarily released Edward from his dungeon in Berkeley, but it is not clear whether he was ever outside the walls of the castle. On 14 September yet another plot to release Edward, this time by a Welshman, Sir Rhys ap Gruffudd, was reported. Shortly afterwards it was announced at the Lincoln parliament that Edward had died at Berkeley on 21 September. Edward's body was removed to Gloucester for public display on 22 October, and on 20 December 1327 he was buried in St Peter's Abbey, Gloucester, in the presence of the young Edward III and Edward's widow, Isabella, to whom Edward's embalmed heart had earlier been sent. In later years Edward III erected a splendid tomb in his father's memory.

Although the official account said that Edward had died of natural causes, it was soon widely believed that he had been murdered. Murder is the most likely cause, perhaps following a conscious decision by Mortimer to rid himself of the embarrassment of a former king, or even in a moment of panic by Edward's gaolers when yet another attempt to free him was reported. However, a natural death, possibly from a pre-existing and painful condition (which might account for the lurid chronicle accounts of his death) or from ill treatment or from the mental shock of his deposition, should not be ruled out. But it was also rumoured that Edward had after all escaped from Berkeley, so much so that in March 1330 Edward's half-brother, *Edmund, earl of Kent, was executed for plotting to restore the late king. In September 1330 the pope wrote to the king and to Isabella expressing amazement that anyone could believe 'that he, for whom solemn funerals had been made, could still be alive' (*CEPR letters*, 2.499).

In September 1338 a certain William le Galeys ('the Welshman') appeared at Cologne claiming to be Edward II and was escorted to Koblenz where Edward III was then meeting the emperor, Ludwig of Bavaria. This episode may have some connection with the astonishing letter preserved in a fourteenth-century register of the French diocese of Maguelone (now Montpellier) and apparently written to Edward III between 1336 and 1338 or at the latest 1343 by Manuele Fieschi, an Italian cleric with good connections both with the English court and the papal curia who ended his career as bishop of Vercelli in Italy. According to this, Edward had wandered across Europe after his escape, visiting Ireland, England, Normandy, Avignon, Paris, Brabant, Cologne, and Milan, before ending his days as a hermit at Cecima, near Voghera in Lombardy. A tomb of earlier date which is wrongly claimed to be that of Edward II can even be seen in the nearby abbey of Sant-'Alberto di Butrio. Although there is no reason to believe that the circumstantial story told in the Fieschi letter is based on fact, the mystery remains of how and why the letter came to be written.

If some believed that Edward lived on after 1327, others wished to present him as a candidate for canonization. Such feelings were probably inspired both by a desire to counter the moves to canonize Edward's former oppon-ent, Thomas of Lancaster, and by the rumours about the hideous mode of Edward's death—his bowels burnt out with a red-hot spit or poker inserted at his anus—which were given literary expression by the unknown author of the *Brut* chronicle and by Geoffrey Baker. Some of Edward's old allies and sympathizers among the Domin-ican order may also have played a part. There is no evi-dence of any systematic attempt to have Edward canon-ized until Richard II petitioned the pope in 1385; a book of Edward II's miracles was compiled and presented to Pope Boniface IX at Florence early in 1395. The process however lapsed with Richard II's own deposition in 1399, never to be resumed.

Edward was also remembered in prayer by his old ally, Archbishop William Melton of York, by the scholars of Oriel College, his foundation in Oxford (where he is still remembered), and even by his estranged wife and queen, Isabella, who about 1336 established a chantry at Eltham for prayers for the souls of her husband and her son, John of Eltham. When she died in 1358 she was buried in the wedding mantle she had worn in 1308, and with Edward's embalmed heart over her breast.

The personality of the king With the significant exception of Geoffrey Baker, whose account of the death of Edward II seems to have been designed to give the impression that his sufferings were a sign of sanctity, contemporary and near contemporary chroniclers were universally critical of Edward, when not openly hostile to him. This in spite of the fact that he was clearly no nullity. He took his status as king very seriously, and resisted with remarkable stub-bornness any attempt to restrict the powers of the mon-archy. He was probably better educated than was once thought, and was capable of expressing himself effect-ively in public, most notably, perhaps, at Amiens in July 1320, when his refusal to perform fealty in addition to homage for Aquitaine apparently reduced Philippe V of France and his council to stunned silence. Handsome, strong, and athletic, he was an impressive figure who rode well, and appears to have acquitted himself well on the battlefield. There is certainly no reason to suppose him to have been a physical coward. He enjoyed good company, and was generous in his entertaining and in gifts to his friends. There is evidence that he had a shrewd sense of humour. At Easter 1314, when he was shown the body of St Alban which was allegedly in the possession of Ely Cath-edral, he remarked that he had seen another body of the same saint at St Albans itself only a week earlier. His reli-gious observance was regular and perhaps deeply felt, so much so that he could be taken in by a plausible story when it came from a religious source: this, perhaps com-bined with political desperation, may explain why Nich-olas Wisbech was able to persuade him between 1317 and 1318 that a reanointing with the holy oil of St Thomas of Canterbury would solve all his problems at a stroke.

However, Edward's positive qualities were more than offset by his defects. That he had no extensive experience of government before becoming king may have been as much the result of Edward I's obsession with Scotland as of any perceived lack of ability on Prince Edward's part, but it was a serious disadvantage. He engaged in activities like swimming, rowing, and digging which were con-sidered inappropriate for a king. There was a streak of cruelty and bad temper in him, which could manifest itself in fierce vindictiveness. And above all he was addicted to the company of favourites, first Gaveston and later the younger Despenser, whose behaviour created profound hostility between Edward and the English nobil-ity, and also, in the case of Despenser, between Edward and his wife. Edward probably played a larger role in the day-to-day business of government than has usually been believed, and could show great determination at moments of crisis, as in 1321–2, but the fact that his activ-ity was inclined to be sporadic and unpredictable gave ample scope for his favourites (and also for others with better intentions, like the earl of Pembroke) to exert influ-ence over him.

Reputation and significance It has long been appreciated that Edward II succeeded to a number of very serious problems bequeathed to him by his father, especially a heavy burden of debt and administrative confusion largely caused by the war with Scotland, a war which was itself already going badly but which it was politically unthinkable to abandon. And he also inherited a deep-seated distrust among his leading subjects of the monarchy's good faith in accepting and implementing demands for reform. None the less, it has been well said that 'Edward II sat down to the game of kingship with a remarkably poor hand, and he played it very badly' (*Vita Edwardi secundi*, ix). His determination to uphold royal rights and protect his favourites was taken to such an extreme that no acceptable and enduring compromise between himself and his opponents was possible. After Gaveston's execution in 1312 Edward's resolve to destroy the men responsible led ultimately to the civil war of 1321–2, and thence to his own deposition and death in 1327.

Edward's fate was vividly recalled in the reign of Rich-ard II, both by the king, who wished to canonize his great-grandfather, and by his opponents, when they threatened Richard with deposition in 1387. In later centuries an extensive literary and historiographical tradition devel-oped round Edward II. Holinshed's *Chronicles of England, Scotland and Ireland* (1578) are distinguished both by their use of unpublished source material, and by Holinshed's sympathy for Edward and his understanding of the impli-cations of Edward's overthrow for the future of the king-dom of England. But few writers had Holinshed's breadth of vision, and most concentrated on Edward and his favourites, especially Gaveston, who even played a role in French political controversy, when in 1588 Jean Boucher (drawing on the chronicles of Thomas Walsingham) dedi-cated his *Histoire tragique et memorable de Pierre de Gaverston, gentilhomme Gascon jadis le mignon d'Edouard 2 roy d'Angleterre* to another Gascon gentleman and royal intimate, the duke of Épernon, favourite, or *mignon*, of the French king Henri III (*r.* 1574–89).

Christopher Marlowe's play *Edward II*, written about 1592, is unusual in making explicit reference to a sexual relationship between king and favourite, and in the twentieth century gave rise to Derek Jarman's even more explicit 1992 film version of the play, as well as to Bertolt Brecht's adaptation of 1922–3. More frequently the nature of the relationship between the two is only hinted at, or is cited as a dreadful example of the fate that may befall kings who allow themselves to be influenced by favourites, and so become estranged from their subjects. In the seventeenth century a number of works on Edward II were produced at times of political excitement. A good example is *The History of the most Unfortunate Prince King Edward II* by Henry Cary, Viscount Falkland, which was written in 1627, at a time when Charles I was being execrated for his dependence on the duke of Buckingham, but published only in 1680, at the time of the exclusion crisis, with another edition following in 1689, immediately after the deposition of James II.

In the late nineteenth and early twentieth centuries, by contrast, serious academic study tended to ignore personalities, preferring to concentrate on the constitutional implications of Edward II's reign. Over and above the constant political crises, and the chaos and bitterness of civil war, the reign was seen by scholars such as W. Stubbs, T. F. Tout, and J. C. Davies as centring upon a struggle between king and magnates over issues of constitutional principle, with the king seeking to build up his power, and in the last resort use his household as an inner bastion of government secure from baronial control, while the magnates attempted to reform the royal administration and to manage policy in the interests of some greater ideal of responsible government. Seen in this light Edward's inadequacy as a ruler could be interpreted as a blessing—he was clearly not the man to manage an effective despotism—while the importance of parliament was regarded as having been greatly enhanced during his reign.

This 'constitutional' view of Edward's reign held sway until the 1970s, when it was challenged in detailed studies of two of the leading magnates, of Thomas of Lancaster by J. R. Maddicott (1970), and of Aymer de Valence by J. R. S. Phillips (1972). These and subsequent studies have revealed more of the complexity of the events of the reign, and have shown the importance of understanding individual behaviour and motivations. Seen in this light, many of the earlier certainties have largely dissolved. Although it is possible that the complexity of the political and administrative problems involved in governing England was becoming such as to exceed the capacity of any king, other than the most able, to control, it is arguable that the real lesson of the reign lay in the destruction of Gaveston, and in the executions, confiscations, and violent deaths that marked its closing years and continued into the new reign. The chronicler Adam Murimuth noted with bitterness that, from the execution of Lancaster in 1322 to that of Roger Mortimer in 1330, no noble condemned to death had been allowed to speak in his own

defence. The structures of English political life so far broke down in the 1320s that no magnate, and in the last resort not even the king himself, was safe. The genie of political violence, once out of the bottle, was to return to haunt the kingdom once again in the reign of Richard II, and with increasing frequency in the century that followed.

J. R. S. PHILLIPS

Sources T. F. Tout, *The place of the reign of Edward II in English history: based upon the Ford lectures delivered in the University of Oxford in 1913*, rev. H. Johnstone, 2nd edn (1936) • H. Johnstone, *Edward of Carnarvon, 1284–1307* (1946) • H. Johnstone, 'The eccentricities of Edward II', *EngHR*, 48 (1933), 264–7 • J. C. Parsons, *Eleanor of Castile: queen and society in thirteenth-century England* (1995) • M. Prestwich, *Edward I* (1988) • P. Binski, *Westminster Abbey and the Plantagenets: kingship and the representation of power, 1200–1400* (1995) • J. R. S. Phillips, *Aymer de Valence, earl of Pembroke, 1307–1324: baronial politics in the reign of Edward II* (1972) • J. R. Maddicott, *Thomas of Lancaster, 1307–1322: a study in the reign of Edward II* (1970) • J. S. Hamilton, *Piers Gaveston, earl of Cornwall, 1307–1312: politics and patronage in the reign of Edward II* (1988) • P. Chaplais, *Piers Gaveston: Edward II's adoptive brother* (1994) • M. Prestwich, 'The Ordinances of 1311 and the politics of the early fourteenth century', *Politics and crisis in fourteenth-century England*, ed. J. Taylor and W. Childs (1990), 1–18 • G. L. Harriss, *King, parliament and public finance in medieval England to 1369* (1975) • E. Lalou, 'Les négociations diplomatiques avec l'Angleterre sous le règne de Philippe le Bel', *La 'France Anglaise' au moyen âge: colloque des historiens médiévistes français et britanniques* [Poitiers 1986], 1 (1988), 325–55 [Actes du IIIe Congrès National des sociétés savantes, section d'histoire médiévale et de philologie] • E. A. R. Brown and N. F. Regalado, '*La grant feste*: Philip the Fair's celebration of the knighting of his sons in Paris at Pentecost of 1313', *City and spectacle in medieval Europe*, ed. B. A. Hanawalt and K. L. Reyerson, Medieval Studies at Minnesota, 6 (1994), 56–86 • E. A. R. Brown, 'Diplomacy, adultery, and domestic politics at the court of Philip the Fair: Queen Isabelle's mission to France in 1314', *Documenting the past: essays in medieval history presented to George Peddy Cuttino*, ed. J. S. Hamilton and P. J. Bradley (1989), 53–83 • M. Vale, *The Angevin legacy and the Hundred Years War, 1250–1340* (1990) • G. W. S. Barrow, *Robert Bruce and the community of the realm of Scotland*, 3rd edn (1988) • W. Childs, '"Welcome my brother": Edward II, John of Powderham and the chronicles, 1318', *Church and chronicle in the middle ages: essays presented to John Taylor*, ed. I. Wood and G. A. Loud (1991), 149–63 • J. R. S. Phillips, 'Edward II and the prophets', *England in the fourteenth century* [Harlaxton 1985], ed. W. M. Ormrod (1986), 189–201 • N. Fryde, *The tyranny and fall of Edward II, 1321–1326* (1979) • W. Childs, 'Finance and trade under Edward II', *Politics and crisis in fourteenth-century England*, ed. J. Taylor and W. Childs (1990), 19–37 • R. M. Haines, *The church and politics in fourteenth-century England: the career of Adam Orleton, c. 1275–1345*, Cambridge Studies in Medieval Life and Thought, 3rd ser., 10 (1978) • R. M. Haines, *Archbishop John Stratford: political revolutionary and champion of the liberties of the English church*, Pontifical Institute of Medieval Studies: Texts and Studies, 76 (1986) • M. Buck, *Politics, finance and the church in the reign of Edward II: Walter Stapeldon, treasurer of England*, Cambridge Studies in Medieval Life and Thought, 3rd ser., 19 (1983) • G. P. Cuttino and T. W. Lyman, 'Where is Edward II?', *Speculum*, 53 (1978), 522–43 • J. R. S. Phillips, 'The quest for Sir John Mandeville', *The culture of Christendom*, ed. M. A. Meyer (1993), 243–55 • J. Alexander and P. Binski, eds., *Age of chivalry: art in Plantagenet England, 1200–1400* (1987) [exhibition catalogue, RA] • L. Stone, *Sculpture in Britain: the middle ages* (1955) • C. Given-Wilson, 'Richard II, Edward II and the Lancastrian inheritance', *EngHR*, 109 (1994), 553–71 • C. Robinson, 'Was Edward the Second a degenerate?', *American Journal of Insanity*, 66 (1909–10), 445–64 • W. Stubbs, *The constitutional history of England in its origin and development*, new edn, 2 (1887) • E. Peters, *The shadow king: rex inutilis in medieval law and literature, 751–1327* (1970) • R. M.

Haines, 'Edwardus redivivus: the "afterlife" of Edward of Caernarvon', *Transactions of the Bristol and Gloucestershire Archaeological Society*, 114 (1996), 65–86 · C. Valente, 'The deposition and abdication of Edward II', *EngHR*, 113 (1998), 852–81 · Register of Archbishop Walter Reynolds, LPL · *Johannis de Trokelowe et Henrici de Blaneforde … chronica et annales*, ed. H. T. Riley, pt 3 of *Chronica monasterii S. Albani*, Rolls Series, 28 (1866) · [W. Rishanger], *The chronicle of William de Rishanger, of the barons' wars*, ed. J. O. Halliwell, CS, 15 (1840) · *Adae Murimuth continuatio chronicarum. Robertus de Avesbury de gestis mirabilibus regis Edwardi tertii*, ed. E. M. Thompson, Rolls Series, 93 (1889) · F. W. D. Brie, ed., *The Brut, or, The chronicles of England*, 2 vols., EETS, 131, 136 (1906–8) · *Chronicon Galfridi le Baker de Swynebroke*, ed. E. M. Thompson (1889) · *Chronicon Henrici Knighton, vel Cnitthon, monachi Leycestrensis*, ed. J. R. Lumby, 2 vols., Rolls Series, 92 (1889–95), vol. 1 · H. R. Luard, ed., *Flores historiarum*, 3 vols., Rolls Series, 95 (1890), vol. 3 · N. Denholm-Young, ed. and trans., *Vita Edwardi secundi* (1957) · G. L. Haskins, 'A chronicle of the civil wars of Edward II', *Speculum*, 14 (1939), 73–81 · *Willelmi capellani in Brederode postea monachi procuratoris Egmondensis chronicon*, ed. C. P. Hordijk, Werken uitgegeven door het Historisch Genootschap, 3rd ser., 20 (1904) · *Chancery records* · *CClR, 1323–7* · *CEPR letters*, vol. 2 · *CDS*, vols. 2–3 · *English historical documents*, 3, ed. H. Rothwell (1975) · S. B. Chrimes and A. L. Brown, eds., *Select documents of English constitutional history* (1964) · A. W. Goodman, ed., *Chartulary of Winchester Cathedral* (1927) · E. H. Pearce, ed., *Register of Thomas de Cobham, bishop of Worcester, 1317–1327*, Worcestershire Historical Society, 40 (1930) · J. C. Davies, *The baronial opposition to Edward II* (1918) · R. Holinshed and others, eds., *The chronicles of England, Scotland and Ireland*, 2nd edn, ed. J. Hooker, 3 vols. in 2 (1586–7) · H. Cary, *The history of the most unfortunate prince King Edward II* (1680) · J. Boucher, *Histoire tragique et memorable de Pierre de Gaverston, gentil-homme Gascon jadis le mignon d'Edouard 2. roy d'Angleterre* (1588) · E. M. Hallam, ed., *The itinerary of Edward II and his household*, List and Index Society, 211 (1984) · S. A. Moore, ed., 'Documents relating to the death and burial of King Edward II', *Archaeologia*, 50 (1887), 215–26 · PRO, accounts various, E101, E352 · BL, MS Cotton Nero D.x, fol. 110*v* [chronicle attributed to Nicholas Trivet]

Archives Archives Nationales, Paris · PRO, accounts various, E101, E352 · S. Antiquaries, Lond., wardrobe books and chamber accounts, MSS 120–122

Likenesses drawing, *c*.1327 (possibly Edward II and Isabella), Christ Church Oxf., Walter de Milemete, 'De nobilitatibus, sapientiis, et prudentiis regum', MS 92, fol. 4*v*.; repro. in E. Hallam, *The Plantagenet encyclopedia* (1996), p. 105 · wall painting, *c*.1330 (Edward II or Edward III), Longthorpe Tower, near Peterborough; repro. in E. Clive-Rous and A. Baker, 'The wall-paintings at Longthorpe Tower, near Peterborough, Northants', *Archaeologia*, 96 (1955), pl. 15, pp. 31–2, 35–8 · alabaster tomb effigy, 1330–39, Gloucester Cathedral · portrait, *c*.1330–1339 (Edward II or Edward III at his coronation), CCC Cam., MS 20, fol. 68; repro. in Alexander and Binski, eds., *Age of chivalry*, p. 201 · statue, *c*.1385 (one of thirteen royal statues from Edward the Confessor to Richard II), Westminster Hall, London · drawing, 15th cent., BL, Cotton MS, Julius E.iv, fol. 6*v*.; repro. in M. Prestwich, *Armies and warfare in the middle ages: the English experience* (1996), p. 85 · manuscript, *c*.1470–1480 (with Queen Isabella, 25 Jan 1308), BL, Jehan de Waurin, 'Chroniques d'Angleterre' (ending in 1336), Royal MS 15 E.iv, fol. 295*v* · J. Goldar, line engraving, pubd 1787 (after a tomb at Gloucester), NPG · J. Basire, line engraving (after a seal), NPG · carvings (head of Isabella), Winchelsea church; repro. in H. F. Hutchinson, *The pliant king* (1971), 134–5 · coloured illustration (kneeling before his father, Edward I), BL, Royal MS 20 A.ii, fol. 10; repro. in J. Cannon and R. A. Griffiths, *Illustrated history of the English monarchy* (1988), p. 210 · electrotype (after alabaster tomb effigy at Gloucester Cathedral), NPG · line print (after his great seal), BM; repro. in F. Sandford, *Genealogical history* (1677) · manuscript (being offered crown), BL, Royal MS 20.A.II, fol. 10 · manuscript painting (created prince of Wales by Edward I, 1301), BL, Rochester chronicle, Cotton MS Nero D.ii, fol. 191*v* [*see illus.*] · miniatures, Bibliothèque Nationale, Paris, Latin MS 8504, fols. 1*v*–2 · painted roof boss, Bristol Cathedral; repro. in E. Hallam, *The Plantagenet encyclopedia* (1996), p. 67 · silver penny, BM · stained-glass window, All Souls Oxf. · statue (on choir screen between Edward I and Edward III), York Minster; repro. in E. Hallam, *The Plantagenet encyclopedia* (1996), frontispiece · statue, choir screen, Canterbury Cathedral

Edward III

Edward III (1312–1377), king of England and lord of Ireland, and duke of Aquitaine, was the first child of *Edward II (1284–1327) and *Isabella of France (1295–1358).

Childhood Edward was born at Windsor on 12 November 1312. The queen was attended at the birth by Henri de Mondeville, surgeon to her father, Philippe IV of France (*r*. 1285–1314). Isabella herself wrote to the citizens of London to announce the birth, and the news was greeted with great celebrations. Her yeoman John Launge and his wife, Joan, the queen's lady, were later granted a joint annuity of £80 out of the fee farm of London for bringing the news to the king; the information was said to have consoled briefly Edward II for the recent loss of his friend Piers Gaveston. The prince was nursed by Margaret Chandeler and Margaret Daventry.

Edward was baptized on 16 November 1312, in St Edward's Chapel, Windsor, by the papal nuncio Arnold, cardinal-priest of Santa Prisca: his godparents included Louis, count of Évreux (the queen's brother), and John, duke of Brittany and earl of Richmond (*d*. 1334). The French contingent present at the time requested that the child be Philip after his maternal grandfather, but Edward II insisted on calling him Edward after his own father.

On 24 November 1312 the prince was granted the counties of Chester and Flint; there is no record of his formal creation as earl of Chester, but this was to be his style throughout childhood and the title under which he first received a summons to parliament in 1320. He never became prince of Wales or earl of Cornwall, though he was supported by revenues from both these lordships; he was also given control of the king's lands on the Isle of Wight. A separate household was quickly constituted for the prince, and later also provided for his younger siblings. Edward passed his first Christmas with the court at Windsor, but thereafter spent much of his time away from both his father and mother: throughout the first half of 1313, for example, he resided at Bisham.

Doubts have been expressed about the tradition reported by the late fourteenth-century Durham chronicler William Chambre that the distinguished scholar Richard Bury (*d*. 1345) acted as Edward's tutor. It is clear, however, that Bury was closely associated with the prince's administration in Chester, and was a member of his household by 1325. John Paynel, parson of Rostherne, Cheshire, is also recorded as having superintended the prince's education in letters. Edward could read and (at least to a limited extent) write Latin: he spoke French and English and, through his later experiences on the continent, was presumably able to communicate in Flemish and German. It is probable, though, that much of his youth was spent not in book learning but in perfecting the

Edward III (1312–1377), tomb effigy, late 14th cent.

knightly arts of horsemanship and skill in arms in which he was later to excel.

France, 1325–1326 Little further is known of Edward's life until the mid-1320s, when he became a pawn in the power games of his competing parents. In 1325 it was decided that Edward should be given the titles of duke of Aquitaine and count of Ponthieu in order that his father, a reigning monarch, could avoid paying homage in person to the king of France for his lands on the other side of the channel. The prince was dispatched to France and performed the required homage to Charles IV (r. 1322–8) at Vincennes on 24 September. Queen Isabella, who had already been sent to France to negotiate a settlement to the recent Anglo-French dispute in the Agenais, then took control of her son and let it be known that she had no intention of allowing him to return to England, where her enemies, the Despensers, had established such an invidious influence over her husband.

From December 1325 Edward II repeatedly demanded the return of his heir, but without success. Whereas the king had been in negotiations since 1324 for a marriage between the prince and an Aragonese or Castilian princess, the queen now proposed a match between her son and *Philippa (1310?–1369), the second daughter of William (I), count of Hainault, in return for the military assistance she needed to mount an invasion of England. Edward II was apprised of these illicit negotiations by March 1326, and sent a force to Normandy in September possibly with the intention of capturing the prince. But Isabella and her lover Roger Mortimer (d. 1330) sailed with the young Edward from Dordrecht on 23 September 1326 and landed at Orwell on the following day. Their advent signified nothing less than a direct challenge to the throne of England.

Accession, 1326–1327 Edward II, who had fled into Wales, was deemed to have abandoned his kingdom, and on 26 October 1326 the queen and her party issued a proclamation at Bristol declaring Prince Edward keeper of the realm. When the king was captured by Henry, earl of Lancaster (d. 1345), he was required to give up the great seal to Sir William Blount, who delivered it to the queen and her son at Martley near Worcester on 26 November. Thus equipped with the essential instrument of government, Isabella and Mortimer issued writs for a parliament to be held at Westminster on 14 December, later postponed to 7 January 1327. In this assembly the queen's ally, Bishop Adam Orleton (d. 1345), presented the young prince as the new king to the general approval not only of the great lords but also of the crowd of Londoners gathered outside the royal palace demanding the deposition of Edward II. Four bishops, however, refused to renounce their homage to the old king, and this resistance, coupled with obvious concern over the legality of an act of deposition, forced the queen's regime to concoct a series of articles justifying the removal of the king, and to send several deputations to Edward II, now imprisoned at Kenilworth, demanding his formal abdication.

The proclamation announcing Edward III's accession on 24 January 1327 stated that the former king had given up the throne and willed that it pass to his eldest son. Legitimacy thus established, the new reign was formally deemed to begin the next day. The king was knighted by the earl of Lancaster, and crowned by Walter Reynolds, archbishop of Canterbury, at Westminster Abbey on 1 February. Despite the speed with which the coronation was effected, it appears to have been an occasion of some ceremony: the Dunstable annals preserve what are claimed to be royal household accounts for the day recording expenditure of over £2800.

In a formal sense Edward III was deemed to have taken full control of his regime from the moment of accession. It was agreed in parliament that a council of four bishops, four earls, and six barons be appointed under the presidency of the earl of Lancaster; a quorum was to be constantly in attendance upon the new king and to give its assent to all important acts of government. Very quickly, however, Mortimer and Isabella assumed effective control of the regime and rendered this council inoperative. The king himself had virtually no opportunity for independent action.

Relations with France and Scotland, 1327–1330 The new administration inherited a very difficult military and diplomatic situation. On 31 March 1327 a humiliating treaty was sealed with France: not only was Charles IV allowed to remain in control of extensive sections of the duchy of Aquitaine occupied by his forces since 1324, but the English were also required to pay reparations of 50,000 marks for the damages inflicted in those territories during the intervening period. Then, on 31 January 1328, Charles IV of

France died without a direct male heir; when his pregnant wife gave birth to a daughter, Charles's cousin Philippe de Valois immediately had himself proclaimed king as Philippe VI. It was important that Edward III's own claim to the French throne should not be allowed to fall into abeyance, and in May the bishops of Worcester and of Coventry and Lichfield were dispatched to register the claim in Paris. Philippe, who was duly crowned at Rheims on 29 May, lost no time in demanding that Edward render homage for his lands in France, backing this up with military threats when the English prevaricated. On 26 May 1329 Edward finally set sail from Dover and on 6 June performed simple homage to Philippe for Aquitaine and Ponthieu in the choir of Amiens Cathedral, thus implicitly confirming Philippe's superior claim to the French throne.

In their relations with Scotland, Isabella and Mortimer at first maintained the stance of Edward I and Edward II, denying the kingship of Robert Bruce (Robert I) and regarding the northern kingdom as a 'land' in subjection to the English throne. The Scottish raid on Norham Castle on the very day of Edward III's coronation was little more than a warning shot to the new regime in England, and on 6 March 1327 the two sides confirmed the thirteen-year truce established in 1323. On 5 April 1327, however, a feudal summons went out for a campaign against the Scots. This offered the youthful Edward III the prospect of his first real military action. The campaign had an inauspicious start when the company of Hainaulters employed by Queen Isabella for the expedition was set upon by English archers in the streets of York and retaliated by burning sections of the city. Setting out for Durham early in July, the king and his forces spent some weeks in futile pursuit of the Scottish army that had recently entered the kingdom. On the night of 4 August Sir James Douglas launched a raid on Edward's own quarters at Stanhope Park and very nearly captured the king; the following night, when the English were properly prepared for an engagement, the Scots slipped away, causing the exasperated Edward, so it was said, to weep tears of vexation.

Thereafter the English had little choice but to open negotiations with Robert I. A formal peace was agreed at Edinburgh on 17 March 1328 and ratified on 4 May in a parliament held at Northampton. Not only did Edward III's government accept Robert's title as king of Scots; it also had to acknowledge the superiority of the existing Franco-Scottish alliance over the new Anglo-Scottish one. The Scots' promise of £20,000 in war reparations was little compensation for such humiliating terms, and the treaty of Edinburgh was to rankle with Edward III for some time: one of his earliest demonstrations of independence came in July 1328 when he refused to attend the marriage ceremony organized under the terms of the treaty between his sister Joan (d. 1362) and the infant David Bruce.

Marriage and domestic politics, 1327–1330 Meanwhile, Edward's own marriage with Philippa of Hainault, first projected in 1326, had taken place. The papal dispensation permitting the match (the couple were second cousins) was issued on 30 August 1327 and Philippa took part in a proxy marriage ceremony in November. The wedding was confirmed by William Melton, archbishop of York (d. 1340), in York Minster on 24 January 1328. The northern metropolitan cathedral was chosen only because the archbishop of Canterbury had died on 16 November 1327; it is however a touching coincidence that one of the children of this match, William of Hatfield, who died in infancy, was later buried in the north choir aisle at York.

The revolution of 1326–7 had received widespread support, but the regime of Isabella and Mortimer was highly divisive and rapidly alienated some of the most powerful men in the land. The earl of Lancaster and other magnates refused to attend the parliament held at Salisbury in October 1328, where the title of earl of March was conferred on Roger Mortimer, and rose in rebellion, though they were subsequently forced to surrender at Bedford in January 1329. In 1330 the king's uncle, Edmund, earl of Kent, who had assisted Lancaster in 1328, was arrested and executed on the grounds that he had believed his half-brother Edward II to be alive and had plotted the latter's restoration to the throne. It was against this troubled background that Edward III prepared to assume control of his own regime.

Mortimer was highly suspicious of the boy king, and, according to the charges later drawn up against him in parliament, set spies in the royal household to track his movements. The king therefore had to proceed by stealth. A letter written in late 1329 or 1330 reveals the degree of subterfuge necessary: aggrieved that he could not even secure patronage for his household servants, Edward secretly contacted Pope John XXII and indicated that the only royal correspondence sent to Avignon that reflected his personal wishes would bear the words *pater sancte* ('holy father') written in the king's own hand. Edward assured the pope that only his secretary, Richard Bury, and his close friend William Montagu (d. 1344) knew the secret password. The specimen phrase supplied on the extant letter by Edward III is the earliest existing autograph of an English king.

Edward's opportunity to seize power came late in 1330, after Mortimer had insisted on interrogating the king and his followers before a great council at Nottingham. On the night of 19 October, in the company of Montagu and a small group of personal followers, Edward entered Nottingham Castle by way of an underground passage and, after a brief struggle, arrested Mortimer and took charge of the keys of the castle. The next day the king issued a proclamation announcing that he had taken the government of the realm into his own hands; shortly before his eighteenth birthday Edward III's personal rule had begun.

Political reconciliation at home, 1330–1334 The parliament that met on 26 November 1330 witnessed not only the condemnation of Mortimer and his adherents but also the rehabilitation of the earl of Lancaster and other nobles who had fallen victim to the minority regime. The queen's offence was not addressed publicly: Isabella was simply deprived of the executive authority she had assumed as unofficial regent and granted a generous allowance. A carefully judged restraint also presumably explains the king's reluctance to punish those accused of the murder of Edward II, though it has also been suggested that he gave some credence to the rumours that his father had escaped death and fled the country.

As far as the aristocracy was concerned, political reconciliation was certainly the order of the day. The tournaments attended by the king in the spring and summer of 1330 at Dartford, Stepney, and Cheapside were important opportunities for social and political interaction between king and nobility. In the parliament of October 1331 Edward made a compact with the peers by which the latter undertook not to protect criminals from prosecution, that they would no longer disturb the law but assist the king and his agents in upholding it, and that they would not usurp the king's right of purveyance by seizing crops and foodstuffs from the peasantry.

Domestic political harmony was all the more necessary since the king was quickly faced by problems abroad. Philippe VI had begun to apply renewed pressure on Edward to perform liege homage for Aquitaine and Ponthieu. Faced with the confiscation of Saintes, Edward was forced to make a secret journey to France in April 1331, disguised as a merchant, and to acknowledge that the homage of 1329 should be considered to have been liege. Nothing was said about the restitution of the contested lands in the Agenais. In the parliament that convened at Westminster on 30 September the chancellor, John Stratford (d. 1348), asked the estates whether the matter ought to be settled by war or by negotiation. They called for diplomacy, pointing out to the king the more urgent need for military intervention in his lordship of Ireland.

War in Scotland, 1332–1336 Scotland was also demanding attention. Following the treaty of Northampton, King Robert had accepted the claims of certain English lords—notably Henry Percy, Henry Beaumont, and Thomas Wake—to lands in Scotland, but little had been done to effect restitution either under Robert or under the regime of his young son, David II, who succeeded in 1329. By 1331 the 'disinherited' were beginning to agitate for action. Beaumont in particular was responsible for bringing over from France Edward Balliol (d. 1364), who had a rival claim to the throne of Scotland, and for organizing a group of magnates who applied to Edward III for permission to invade Scotland through England. This was refused, but a degree of tacit support may have been given by the king to the subsequent seaborne expedition that sailed from Ravenser, landed at Kinghorn, and won a crushing victory over the Scots at Dupplin Moor on 11 August 1332.

The parliament that met at Westminster in September 1332 advised Edward to defer his journey to Ireland; it also suggested that Balliol, who was crowned king of Scots at Scone on 24 September, should be summoned before a parliament at York as a vassal of the English king. On 23 November Edward Balliol acknowledged that Scotland was a fief of the English crown for which he owed homage and fealty to Edward III. Both the king and the English aristocracy, however, remained ambivalent about this apparently tempting submission: lengthy discussions in the parliament that met at York in the winter of 1332–3 failed to reach a decision on the matter. In the end it was the sudden flight of Balliol into England that forced Edward III into a decision. In February 1333 writs were issued for the removal of the exchequer and the court of common pleas to York; most of the chancery staff quickly followed. The offices of state were to reside in the northern capital for five years as Edward devoted considerable time and money to the restoration of a Balliol king of Scotland.

In March 1333 Edward Balliol and his allies laid siege to Berwick; Edward III himself arrived at Tweedmouth in early May, leaving his queen at Bamburgh. The defenders of the town eventually agreed that, unless they were relieved by 20 July, they would surrender to the English army. Sir Archibald Douglas advanced on the town, but was decisively defeated at Halidon Hill on 20 July. The English took a defensive position and employed the new mixed formation of dismounted men-at-arms and archers already used at Dupplin Moor. Edward III derived considerable advantage and prestige from the victory. Berwick surrendered, a number of Scottish magnates gave homage to the English king, and Balliol was restored to the Scottish throne. In February 1334 Balliol surrendered the whole of Lothian to Edward III, and on 12 June, at Newcastle, performed liege homage to the English king for the throne of Scotland.

The formalities completed, Edward soon discovered that Scotland was by no means subdued. Balliol was quickly expelled and Edward was forced to undertake a northern campaign in the winter of 1334–5, though he spent almost the whole of this time at Roxburgh Castle. In mid-July 1335 a more ambitious campaign began, as Edward set out from Carlisle and Balliol marched from Berwick; the two armies converged near Glasgow and advanced to Perth, where a truce was eventually agreed in August. In June 1336 the king again set out from Newcastle for Perth; the campaign is chiefly notable for the heroic foray which Edward made into the highlands in July and August to raise the siege of Lochindorb and rescue Katherine, countess of Atholl, from this island castle. After returning to England to meet with a great council at Nottingham in September, Edward immediately marched north again, reaching his base at Bothwell at the end of October but retiring to Berwick in December. Edward III's interest in Scotland was already waning, and he was soon to be preoccupied with affairs in France.

The beginning of the Hundred Years' War, 1337–1340 On 24 May 1337 Philippe VI formally confiscated the duchy of Aquitaine and the county of Ponthieu on the grounds that Edward III was harbouring Philippe's cousin, brother-in-law, and mortal enemy, Robert, count of Artois. In fact, larger issues had already made war more or less inevitable: the talks over contested lands and rights in the Agenais had reached an impasse in 1334; the pope, who had been proposing a joint Anglo-French crusade, cancelled the project in March 1336, allowing Philippe VI to divert his fleet from Marseilles to the channel and menace the south coast of England; and by the spring of 1337 Edward III may already have been contemplating a revival of his own claim to the French throne. In the Westminster parliament of March 1337 the king created six new earls specifically to restock the ranks from which the crown traditionally selected its military commanders; in apparent imitation of the French monarchy he also introduced the title of duke into England by creating his eldest son, *Edward, born in 1330, duke of Cornwall. The two greatest powers in western Europe prepared themselves for war, though neither the scale nor the duration of that conflict could have been imagined on either side.

It was natural and appropriate for Edward III to use the strategy earlier adopted by Edward I during his dispute with Philippe IV in 1294–8 and look for support in the Low Countries and Germany: conventions were quickly arranged with Hainault, Gueldres, Limburg, Juliers, Brabant, the county palatine, and, in August 1337, the German emperor, Ludwig of Bavaria. Such alliances were secured only with generous offers of subsidies: the first instalments due to Edward's new allies by the end of 1337 alone totalled £124,000. Much of the king's time during 1337 and the first half of 1338 was therefore taken up in devising the means to pay for such an expensive policy: Edward borrowed heavily from Italian bankers, notably the Bardi and Peruzzi, negotiated taxes with parliament and the clergy, and manipulated the overseas trade in wool for financial gain. Such was the expenditure on the preliminaries, however, that when Edward sailed from Orwell on 16 July 1338 his government was already acutely short of money. This was to be the recurring theme of this first phase of the French war.

In August 1338 Edward set out from his base at Antwerp and travelled to Koblenz to meet Ludwig of Bavaria, who on 5 September appointed Edward vicar-general of the empire and thus, in theory, put the military resources of the entire imperial confederation at the disposal of the king of England. The relationship was, however, uneasy from the very start, and in 1341 Ludwig was to deprive Edward of the vicariate in order to enter into independent negotiations with Philippe VI. A similar ambivalence was encountered in the Low Countries: although the counts of Gueldres, Juliers, and Hainault and the duke of Brabant supported Edward's first and much delayed military expedition into the Cambrésis (which was part of the empire) in September 1339, even Guillaume d'Hainault expressed his concern about the legitimacy of crossing the border and facing Philippe de Valois within the latter's own kingdom of France.

In theory these ambiguities and problems were resolved when Edward III, who badly needed the support of the Flemish, was persuaded by Jacob van Artevelde of Ghent publicly to assume the title and arms of king of France on 26 January 1340. In practice, however, Edward's strategic position improved little. An emphatic victory over a Franco-Castilian naval force at Sluys on 24 June restored English superiority in the channel and put an end to French raids on the south coast, but Edward's first proper campaign into northern France in July 1340 failed: the siege of Tournai had to be abandoned and a nine-month truce was established at Esplechin on 25 September.

The strains of war, 1340–1341 Edward needed an explanation for his failure, and not surprisingly set upon the domestic administration. Faced with debts of some £400,000, he had already been forced to return to England in the spring of 1340 to negotiate with parliament for further supplies. The tax that resulted, a levy in kind based on the ecclesiastical tithe, was poorly administered and failed to alleviate the king's impending bankruptcy. In November, with his cousin Henry of Grosmont (d. 1361) and other English lords already in custody as hostages for the debts owed in the Low Countries, Edward departed secretly from Ghent and took ship for England. Amid scenes reminiscent of the Nottingham coup he landed unannounced at the watergate of the Tower of London early in the morning of 1 December and immediately dismissed the chancellor, Robert Stratford (d. 1362), and the treasurer, Roger Northburgh (d. 1358), and imprisoned several leading judges, chancery and exchequer clerks, and merchant financiers. Determined to demonstrate that his ministers should be answerable for their actions and not able to claim clerical immunity from the secular courts, he appointed laymen and common lawyers to the highest offices of state. Inquiries were also launched at the shire level into the maladministration of the country during the king's absence.

The real target for Edward's wrath, however, was the president of the regency council, John Stratford, archbishop of Canterbury. On 18 November, before his departure from Ghent, Edward had sent envoys to the pope claiming that Stratford had failed to supply him with funds at Tournai, intending, 'by lack of money, to see me betrayed and killed' (Déprez, 425). A war of words ensued. Edward denied Stratford admission to the parliament that assembled at Westminster on 26 April 1341, and tried to press on with a series of charges against the archbishop. But a number of the magnates insisted that Stratford be allowed to answer before his peers, and the king was sufficiently alarmed to be prepared to admit the archbishop to the council on 28 April and to full parliament on 3 May. He also agreed to issue a statute confirming the right of the great men of the realm to be tried before their peers and that the ministers of the crown should be made answerable before the Lords, to whose judgment the king would thereafter be bound.

Edward undoubtedly emerged bruised and, to some extent, chastened by this confrontation. Its political significance can, however, be exaggerated. On 1 October 1341 the king annulled the recent statute on the grounds that it infringed his prerogative and had been extracted by force. The king and the archbishop were publicly reconciled in Westminster Hall on 23 October 1341; in the parliament of 1343 Edward declared that all the charges against Stratford were annulled, and the written materials relating to the case were destroyed. He also promised to restore such sections of the statute which he had just repealed as were acceptable to him, though in the event nothing was done. The most important reason why the magnates chose not to magnify or prolong the political crisis of 1341, however, lay not in the king's personal relationship with Stratford but in the necessity for concerted action against the king's enemies in both Scotland and France.

The war resumed, 1341–1346 Edward III's neglect of affairs in the north and the resurgence of the Bruce party had meant a serious retreat for the English in Scotland. In April 1341 Edinburgh fell, and in the summer Stirling was taken. David II, who had sought refuge in France, returned to Scotland in July. This forced the king into action. He held a great council at the end of September and appointed Henry of Grosmont as lieutenant of the army of Scotland. The king himself marched north at the end of the year and spent Christmas at Melrose. But although Edward led raiding parties into the surrounding countryside, there were no significant engagements: indeed the English and Scots passed the time by holding a number of tournaments similar to those that were to be such a feature of the military experience during the ensuing war in France.

Meanwhile, the death of John (III), duke of Brittany, in April 1341, and the subsequent succession dispute, offered Edward III an important opportunity to test the value of his new title as king of France. While Philippe VI supported the claims of Charles de Blois to the duchy, Edward recognized John de Montfort; and between October 1342 and March 1343 he campaigned in Brittany on Montfort's behalf. After the latter's death in 1345, Edward III asserted his suzerainty and assumed control both of Montfort's heir, another John, and of the duchy. The Breton war of succession was one of a series of disputes within the French provinces that were to be exploited to great effect by Edward III during the middle decades of the fourteenth century.

In 1344–5 the English government prepared for a major offensive against France. The earls of Derby and Northampton were sent with expeditionary forces to Aquitaine and Brittany. Edward at first planned to revive the Flemish alliance and attack the French from the north, and he visited Flanders in July 1345 to make preparations. But the murder of Jacob van Artevelde rendered such a scheme impracticable, and Edward instead announced to his English subjects a major royal expedition to assist the royal armies in Brittany and Gascony.

Crécy and Calais, 1346–1347 Edward kept secret the exact destination of the great army gathering at Portsmouth in the spring of 1346, and it remains uncertain whether a landing in Normandy was planned in advance, or (as Sir Bartholomew Burghersh thought) decided suddenly when the fleet had already departed and was blown off its course for Gascony. The chroniclers attributed the change of policy to Sir Godfrey de Harcourt, a Norman baron who had defected to Edward's side and whose support guaranteed a safe landing at St Vaast-la-Hougue on the Cotentin peninsula on 12 July 1346. What is clear is that the ensuing campaign created considerable panic in the French camp and, no less importantly, inspired great enthusiasm among the English soldiers, who had their first real experience of the profit to be made from the indiscriminate plundering of enemy territory.

The king's army marched in three columns via Carentan and St Lô to Caen, which was taken on 27 July; because the count of Eu and the lord of Tancarville decided to defend a portion of the city, the inhabitants were slaughtered indiscriminately, and an orgy of rape and looting followed. Edward then intended to make for Rouen, but finding all the Seine bridges broken, moved southwards to Poissy, where the bridge was repaired sufficiently to secure the safe crossing of his troops on 16 August. Heading northwards, Edward crossed the Somme at the ford of Blanchetaque on 24 August, now pursued by the army of Philippe VI which had marched from Amiens to Abbeville.

The English army drew up on high ground on the right bank of the River Maie just outside the village of Crécy in the formation already used to great effect at Dupplin Moor and Halidon Hill: three divisions of dismounted men-at-arms, led by the king, the prince of Wales, and the earl of Northampton, flanked by two wings of longbowmen. The French attacked in the late afternoon of 26 August. The superior tactics of the English army and the lack of discipline among the French cavalry ensured a relatively speedy and decisive victory for Edward, and a final assault by a detachment of men-at-arms led by the duke of Lorraine on the following morning was rapidly scattered. Not least of the notable features of the battle of Crécy was the use by the English of a small number of cannon, the first recorded example in the West of the employment of such firearms in a pitched battle.

On 28 August the English forces moved off to the north and arrived before Calais on 3 September. Edward proceeded to lay siege to the town. Meanwhile, on 17 October, the Scots, who had been encouraged by Philippe VI to invade northern England, were defeated at Nevilles Cross, near Durham, and David II was taken prisoner. This, together with the improving English fortunes in Brittany and Aquitaine, provided encouraging news for the otherwise demoralized army of Calais. Dysentery and desertion both took a heavy toll on this force. But when the French abandoned hopes of raising the siege, the garrison was finally forced to submit on 3 August 1347. According to a famous story told first by Jean le Bel and repeated by Froissart, Edward had at first refused any terms to the besieged, and relented only so far as to require six of the leading townsmen to place themselves at his mercy. His stubborn resolve to put these six burghers to death was finally overborne only by the entreaties of Queen Philippa, who was pregnant. Nevertheless, most of the inhabitants of Calais were expelled, and proclamations were issued at home to encourage settlement in the town. After agreeing a truce for nine months Edward III returned to England with his army, landing at Sandwich on 12 October.

The Order of the Garter The winter and spring of 1347–8 passed in celebration. After spending Christmas at Guildford Edward hosted a series of tournaments at Westminster, Reading, Bury St Edmunds, Lichfield, Windsor, Canterbury, and Eltham. It was apparently at one of these meetings that he conceived the idea of founding a new secular order of chivalry. Earlier, in January 1344, at the conclusion of another series of tournaments, Edward had announced the establishment of a 'round table' and had begun a circular building in the upper bailey at Windsor Castle to act as its headquarters. But for some reason—possibly lack of funds—this scheme had never come to fruition. Then, in 1347–8, Edward revived the idea in modified form in an order of knighthood dedicated to the Virgin and St George. Its emblem, the garter, remains enigmatic: the later story that it represented an item of clothing dropped by the countess of Salisbury has been discredited, and it seems more likely to have been a sword belt, thus exemplifying the martial values of this new exclusive band of twenty-six knights. The college of priests and poor knights that would provide spiritual services for the order at St George's Chapel, Windsor, was formally instituted on 6 August 1348, and the Order of the Garter seems to have had its first formal meeting at Windsor on the feast of St George in 1349.

The Garter encapsulated much of the Arthurian imagery that had been such a feature of court life under both Edward I and the young Edward III. The list of founder members also makes it clear that it was intended as a permanent memorial to the victories of Crécy and Calais. But the symbolism of the order—the blue robes (rather than the traditional English royal colour of red) and the choice of the French motto *Honi soit qui mal y pense* ('Shame upon him who thinks ill of it'—a replacement for Edward III's more usual preference for English epigrams)—suggests that it was also designed to promote Edward's claim to the French throne. Certainly, in these heady times, some of Edward's English subjects thought the kingdom of France stood within his grasp and urged him not to accept a diplomatic compromise. Edward himself may have been rather more flexible, not least because the stream of complaints that confronted him in the parliaments of January and March 1348 suggested that the almost unprecedented level of military commitment experienced in 1346–7 (the army of Calais numbered as many as 32,000 men) was politically, if not economically, unsustainable.

Domestic affairs, 1348–1356 The biggest disruption to Edward's wars, however, was the demographic catastrophe suffered by England between the autumn of 1348 and the spring of 1350. The epidemic of bubonic plague known as the black death arrived in England in the summer of 1348 and reached London in October; in little over a year it killed perhaps a third of the entire population. The king, who crossed briefly to Calais on 30 November in order to complete negotiations with his new ally, Louis de Mâle, count of Flanders, understood the dangers of the plague all too well, for his daughter Joan had already succumbed to the disease at Bordeaux in August. He deliberately avoided the capital on his return to England, spending Christmas at Otford and then moving via Kings Langley (where the royal relic collection was delivered) and Windsor to Woodstock. Here he was joined by the privy seal office and some staff of the chancery. The parliament summoned for early 1349 was abandoned, and the courts

of king's bench and common pleas both adjourned for the Trinity term of 1349.

Yet government was very far from being in abeyance. On 18 June 1349 the king and council meeting at Westminster issued the ordinance of labourers, the precursor of the Statute of Labourers of 1351. The legislation aimed to respond to the acute shortage of manual labour by requiring agricultural and other workers to take up contracts in their places of residence and to accept wages pegged at pre-plague levels. Although England was not the only state to produce such measures in the aftermath of the black death, it was the only one to create a comprehensive mechanism for their enforcement: the emergence of the justices of the peace owed much to the structure developed for the implementation of the labour legislation.

Despite some small-scale military activity, the continuation of the truce with France also allowed for the resolution of some of the major political issues that had arisen from the pressures of war during the previous two decades. In 1352 the crown agreed to give up its earlier attempts to require military service on the basis of landed wealth; thereafter, in fact, most of the men-at-arms and the majority of mounted archers in English expeditionary forces were raised by voluntary contract. The Statute of Treasons of 1352 set a fairly limited definition of high treason, thus ending the arbitrary use of this charge in the royal courts. The Statute of Provisors (1351) and the Statute of *Praemunire* (1353) responded to the anti-alien sentiments of the Commons by restricting the practice of papal provision to ecclesiastical benefices in England; as a result, the crown's own patronage was significantly increased. In 1351 there was a major reform of the coinage, which for the first time successfully introduced a gold currency, in the form of the noble, into internal circulation, and created a new silver coin, the groat. In 1353 the administration effectively agreed to abandon its earlier practice of creating monopolies over wool exports by temporarily banning all English merchants from overseas trade in this commodity, encouraging foreign traders into the country, and setting up a series of domestic wool staples.

It is difficult to judge Edward's personal influence upon these and other measures for the government of England, though there is no doubt that he was active in those areas that traditionally demanded the attention of the sovereign: the audience of petitions, the dispensation of patronage, and the settlement of disputes between the great men of the realm. Perhaps Edward III's most important contribution was to select able and loyal ministers—men such as William Edington (d. 1366), John Thoresby (d. 1373), and William Shareshull (d. 1370)—who undertook much of the routine business of government through the administrative council. These ministers were also instrumental in securing from parliament an unbroken series of direct taxes from 1346 to 1355. The only serious breach that occurred between the king and his government came in 1355, when Edward brushed with his council over his decision to challenge clerical privilege and punish

Thomas Lisle, bishop of Ely (*d*. 1361), for crimes committed against the king's cousin Blanche, Lady Wake.

Wars with France and Scotland, 1349–1357 During the Christmas celebrations at Havering in December 1349 Edward received news that Calais was about to be betrayed to the French. In the company of his eldest son and a small military contingent, he left immediately for Calais, where he was able to pre-empt the treachery of the governor and defeat a French force led by Geoffroi de Charny; according to Froissart, the king fought incognito, under the banner of Sir Walter Mauny (*d*. 1372). The death of Philippe VI in August 1350 may have encouraged Edward III to plan a more ambitious invasion of France, possibly with the intention of seizing the vacant throne, but this was thwarted by a strong Castilian presence in the channel, and on 29 August the king put to sea to defeat this fleet, in the naval engagement off Winchelsea known as 'les Espagnols sur Mer'.

Although the war continued in Brittany and Aquitaine, Edward himself undertook no further campaigns in France until 1355. During the ensuing years the king was more actively occupied in diplomacy. In 1351 an alliance was effected with Charles II (Charles the Bad) of Navarre, who himself had a claim to the throne of France and was an important political figure in Normandy; in 1353 Edward also came to terms with his captive Charles de Blois and seemed about to renounce his support for the Montfort party in Brittany. Charles of Navarre subsequently defected from Edward's cause and was reconciled with Jean II. This serious setback for the English may explain why Edward III was prepared to consider Jean's proposals for a final settlement to their own dispute in the draft treaty of Guînes of 1354, by which the king of England would have obtained Aquitaine, the Loire provinces, Ponthieu, and Calais, all in full sovereignty, on condition that he renounce his claim to the French throne for ever.

In the end, however, neither side would ratify this treaty, and in 1355 Edward planned a two-pronged attack on France through Gascony and Normandy. The Gascon expedition led by the prince of Wales set sail on 14 September, but the duke of Lancaster's departure for Normandy was delayed by adverse winds and by the news that Charles of Navarre, with whom Edward had been in negotiation, had once more reached an understanding with Jean II. The army of Normandy had also to be diverted to Calais on news that the French king was threatening the town: Edward III led this expedition in person, disembarking at Calais on 2 November and marching south to within a few miles of Jean's army, though retreating without an engagement. He was then forced to leave Calais rapidly on news that Berwick had fallen to the Scots; in January 1356 Edward led his last campaign into Scotland, taking control of Berwick on 13 January and inflicting such extensive damage on Lothian that the expedition became known as 'the burnt Candlemas'.

The success of the great *chevauchée* led by Edward, the Black Prince, through southern France, which culminated in the capture of Jean II at the battle of Poitiers in September 1356, put Edward III in a very powerful negotiating position. By the end of 1356 both David II of Scotland and Jean II of France were captives of the English crown. Edward had to weigh the advantages of recognizing their titles and negotiating large ransoms for their release against claiming their thrones for himself and committing the country to further expensive wars of conquest. The settlement reached with the Scots at Berwick on 3 October 1357 was a tacit acknowledgement of the Bruce monarchy, since it fixed the terms for David II's release on the payment, by instalments, of a ransom of 100,000 marks (£66,666). Edward Balliol had surrendered his own claim to the Scottish throne to Edward III at Roxburgh on 20 January 1356, and it was now theoretically possible for the English king to demand suzerainty over a Bruce monarchy; but the treaty made no mention of English lordship over Scotland, an omission which the Scots at least regarded as a major victory.

The campaign of 1359 and the treaty of Brétigny With regard to France, Edward seems at first to have had no hesitation about ransoming—and thereby recognizing—Jean II; but he was equally determined to ensure a very substantial territorial settlement in return for his necessary renunciation of the French crown. The draft treaty of London of 1358 proposed terms not dissimilar to those eventually agreed in 1360—English sovereignty over Calais, Ponthieu, and an enlarged duchy of Aquitaine, and a ransom of 4 million gold écus (£666,666) for the release of Jean II—and it is possible that the treaty failed only because the French regency administration was unable to find the money needed for the first instalment of the ransom. By January 1359 plans were already taking shape for a new invasion of France. In the second draft treaty of London, dated 24 March 1359, the English king demanded sovereign control not only of greater Aquitaine, Ponthieu, and Calais but also of Normandy, Maine, Touraine, and Anjou and the suzerainty of Brittany, in return for his renunciation of the crown of France. This would have given Edward III control of the whole of the western seaboard of France from Calais to the Pyrenees. These terms were so outrageous that historians have normally assumed they were indeed tantamount to a declaration of war.

Edward embarked from Sandwich on 28 October and arrived at Calais on the same day. The king was accompanied by his three oldest sons and a large proportion of the English nobility and knightly class: in total the army numbered approximately 10,000 effective combatants. It advanced, in three columns, upon the city of Rheims, to which the king laid siege on 4 December. Edward III had brought a crown with him on the campaign, and evidently intended to have himself installed formally as king of France in the traditional coronation place of his Capetian ancestors. But Rheims was strongly defended. Edward made no attempt to take the city and raised the siege after only five weeks, on 11 January 1360. He then led his army on a *chevauchée* through Burgundy. This was not necessarily a deviation from the king's original plan: the duke of Burgundy was forced not only to offer a ransom of 700,000 gold écus (£116,666) for the withdrawal of the English army but also to promise, as a peer of France, that he would support Edward's coronation at some future date. Thereafter, however, the campaign lost momentum. After failing to provoke the dauphin into battle by marching on Paris, Edward led his forces off down the Loire valley. At Chartres on 13 April there was a sudden and dramatic storm in which both men and horses died; the weather throughout the winter had been exceptionally bad, and the English army was clearly weakened and demoralized. Edward had no choice but to submit to negotiations.

Talks opened at Brétigny on 1 May: the English and French kings were both represented by their eldest sons. By 8 May a draft treaty had been prepared. The ransom of Jean II was now reduced to 3 million gold écus (£500,000); Edward III was offered the territorial settlement of 1358 in return for his renunciation of the French throne. This settlement was reached, however, with no apparent reference to the kings, and its terms were provisional upon confirmation by Edward and Jean II. On 18 May Edward crossed from Honfleur, landed at Rye, and made for Westminster; the army itself returned to England via Calais. Meanwhile, the French government set about the daunting task of raising the first instalment of their king's ransom.

On 9 October Edward III landed at Calais for the ceremony of ratification. Talks were already under way, and continued for several weeks. The sticking point proved to be the renunciation clauses requiring Jean II to give up sovereignty over the ceded territories and Edward III to abjure the French crown. In the end these clauses had to be taken out of the main text of the treaty and put into a separate agreement to be effected only after the transfer of territory, which was to take place at the latest by 1 November 1361. This allowed the two sides to confirm the peace on 24 October without actually fulfilling all its terms, and for the following nine years both England and France prevaricated over carrying out their sections of the renunciations. Such delaying tactics certainly benefited the French, but it is possible that the compromise adopted at Calais was really the work of Edward III, who was dissatisfied with the terms offered at Brétigny and still clung to his more grandiose ambitions for the conquest of large parts of the kingdom of France. On the other hand, the peace was evidently popular in England, where it was ratified in parliament in January 1361 and celebrated with great ceremony by the king and royal family at Westminster Abbey.

Family settlements, 1358–1362 The resolution of conflict with Scotland and France gave Edward III the opportunity to implement the dynastic strategy towards which he had been moving for a number of years. Edward and Queen Philippa had at least twelve children between 1330 and 1355, of whom nine—five sons and four daughters—survived to maturity. By 1358, however, only one of these children, *Lionel of Antwerp, earl of Ulster (d. 1368), had been married off, and the king, who had been a father at seventeen, found himself in his late forties with a solitary granddaughter, Philippa of Ulster. In 1358–9, however, three important marriages were arranged: Princess Margaret was betrothed to John Hastings, earl of Pembroke (d.

1375); Philippa of Ulster to Edmund (III) Mortimer (d. 1381), the heir to the earldom of March; and *John of Gaunt (1340–1399) to Blanche of Lancaster, coheir of Henry of Grosmont, duke of Lancaster. These matches had important implications for Edward's lordship of the British Isles. In particular, the Ulster–March alliance was destined to create the largest landed interest in Ireland; with this in mind, Edward appointed Lionel of Antwerp lieutenant of Ireland in 1361, and in 1362 created him duke of Clarence. In the 1360s the king also revived earlier attempts to persuade the childless David II to recognize John of Gaunt, now the pre-eminent lord in the north of England, as the heir to the throne of Scotland.

Similar patterns emerged in the marriages and settlements devised for Edward's other children on the continent. John de Montfort, whom Edward was still supporting as a candidate for the duchy of Brittany, was married in 1361 to the Princess Mary; although she died shortly after the wedding, Montfort had agreed not to remarry without Edward's permission, and in 1366 took as his second wife Joan Holand, stepdaughter of Prince Edward, the Black Prince. Although Edward formally renounced the suzerainty of Brittany in 1362, the duchy could still for a few years be regarded as falling within the Plantagenet orbit. Edward also entered into negotiations for a marriage between his fourth son, *Edmund of Langley (d. 1402), and Margaret, heir to the counties of Flanders and Burgundy; these talks had reached an advanced stage by 1364. In 1362 he also pre-empted the fulfilment of the renunciation clauses of 1360 and created his eldest son prince of Aquitaine.

This series of marriages and titles negotiated or created for his children in these years suggest that Edward III was attempting to act in the same way as Henry II, employing his family to establish a confederation of Plantagenet states bound together by personal and feudal bonds. In the event, this strategy came to little: the opposition of the pro-French pope, Urban V, to the Flemish marriage was a particular setback to Edward's diplomacy, and resulted in a series of reprisals against the curia which included the reissue of the statutes of Provisors and *Praemunire* in the parliament of 1365. For some years, however, the prospect of advantageous marriages and foreign titles probably helped to satisfy the ambitions of Edward's large brood and to preserve the remarkable spirit of amity and unity that characterized the royal family in this period.

Domestic affairs, 1360–1369 In 1362 Edward III celebrated his fiftieth birthday; no doubt he had more than usual cause to celebrate this achievement, since the plague had returned to England in 1361–2 and a number of his closest companions had died. In the parliament that coincided with his birthday Edward granted a general pardon and issued an important statute defining and restricting the royal right of purveyance. These concessions were popular; they were also necessary, for the king had to ask the Commons to renew the wool subsidy, the levy charged over and above the regular customs duties, in order to pay off the considerable debts that the government claimed to have accumulated during the war years. The Commons agreed to do this, thereby drawing an important distinction between direct taxes, which could usually be levied only in wartime, and indirect taxes, which thereafter became more or less permanent. Rather less straightforward was the government's proposal, presented to parliament in 1362, for the removal of the domestic staples and the setting up of a single compulsory entrepôt for English wools in the port of Calais. The Commons could not agree on the matter, so the government proceeded unilaterally and set up the new staple of Calais in 1363. Some at least had no doubt that this was intended to benefit not the English economy but the merchant company appointed to run the staple.

Edward III's contribution to the government of the realm in the 1360s is again largely to be judged in terms of his selection and management of ministers. The commanding figure in the administration during this period was William Wykeham (d. 1404), who became keeper of the privy seal in 1363 and chancellor in 1367. However, the sureness of purpose that had characterized the government during the 1350s now seemed lacking. A notable case in point is its indecision over whether the justices of the peace should be allowed to retain the authority they had enjoyed during the 1350s to give judgments and deliver sentences: in the course of a decade these powers were successively confirmed (1362), withdrawn (1364), and finally restored (1368). There were accusations of corruption in the exchequer in 1365, and both the chief baron of the exchequer and the chief justice of king's bench were dismissed on unspecified charges. In 1368 Sir John Lee, the steward of the royal household, was imprisoned after protests over the abuse of his special judicial powers. As yet there was little sign of public disquiet over the quality of government dispensed by the crown, but such scandals at least hint at a certain loss of momentum for which the king himself may have borne some responsibility.

The war renewed, 1369–1375 The death of Jean II of France in 1364, and the succession of the dynamic and charismatic Charles V, made it increasingly less likely that the settlement of 1360 would be carried through into a lasting peace. Charles was instrumental in blocking the marriage of Edmund of Langley with the heiress of Flanders and secured Margaret's hand for his own brother, Philip the Bold, duke of Burgundy, in 1369. He also asserted his suzerainty over John, duke of Brittany, and came to terms with Charles of Navarre. The spark for the renewal of conflict, however, came from within Aquitaine. Certain of the Black Prince's new subjects defied his sovereign authority and made appeals to the *parlement* of Paris. Charles V, who had still not formally renounced the lordship of Aquitaine, summoned the prince before his court. When the latter failed to appear, he was pronounced a contumacious vassal and the duchy of Aquitaine was declared forfeit. The Brétigny settlement was thereby contravened, and the English king had no choice but to reassert his own dynastic claims in France. After consultation with parliament Edward III formally resumed the title of king of France on 11 June 1369.

English strategy in the war of 1369–75 was modelled, not surprisingly, on that of the 1340s and 1350s. But the personal and diplomatic links that had earlier allowed Edward III to intervene effectively in the northern French provinces now broke down. Furthermore English domination at sea collapsed in 1372 when the earl of Pembroke's fleet was defeated by the Castilians off La Rochelle. As a result the garrisons in Aquitaine could not be reinforced, and Charles V's forces promptly overran much of the northern part of the duchy. The English now controlled only a narrow strip of coastal territory from Bordeaux to Bayonne. The prospects of success seemed brighter in Brittany when John de Montfort renewed his alliance with the English in 1372; but in 1373 the duke himself had to take refuge in England, and the relief expedition planned under the leadership of John of Gaunt never reached Brittany, preferring instead to make a grand *chevauchée* through eastern and southern France, from Calais to Bordeaux.

Edward III was still actively engaged in military planning during this phase of the war, and despite his advanced years still seems to have aspired to leading his armies in person. In the summer of 1369 he was preparing to cross with an army to Calais, though the expedition was eventually led by John of Gaunt, the king perhaps being detained by the death of Queen Philippa on 15 August. Again, the defeat and capture of Pembroke in 1372 roused Edward—and the infirm prince of Wales—to announce a great expedition to Aquitaine, and a large army was gathered at Southampton. The king went aboard his own ship, the *Grâce de Dieu*, on 30 August 1372, having appointed his grandson, the five-year-old *Richard of Bordeaux, as nominal regent. But adverse weather conditions meant that the expedition never reached its destination, and after five weeks the king had to order the fleet to return to England. Edward was destined never to see Aquitaine; his campaigning days were now over.

In 1374–5 Pope Gregory XI offered to mediate between the kings of England and France, and a truce for one year was agreed at Bruges on 27 June 1375. Although allowing a holding operation in Aquitaine, this truce seriously compromised the English position in parts of northern France. In particular, an expeditionary force in Brittany under John de Montfort and the earl of Cambridge was obliged to break off the siege of Quimperlé and withdraw from the duchy. This tacit admission of defeat does much to explain the hostility with which the truce of Bruges was greeted by the political community in England.

Political crises, 1371–1377 The initial stages of the new war were paid for from the profits of the royal ransoms and the income from indirect taxation and clerical subsidies, and it was not until 1371 that the crown approached parliament for direct taxes. After a decade of freedom from such impositions the Commons proposed an experimental levy, designed to raise £50,000, to be collected by setting a standard charge on every parish in the land and allowing assessors to raise or lower the amount according to local circumstance. Edward had to pay a high political price for this tax, being required to dismiss the chancellor, Bishop

Wykeham, the treasurer, Thomas Brantingham, bishop of Exeter, and the keeper of the privy seal, Peter Lacy, and to replace them with laymen. Parliament—and particularly the parliamentary Commons—was thus pursuing very much the same line that the king had adopted during the earlier crisis of 1340–41; its ability to dictate the course of government is demonstrated by the fact that ecclesiastics were not appointed to the chancellorship and treasurership again until January 1377.

By 1376 the taxes authorized in the parliaments of 1371 and 1373 had all been spent and the government was desperately short of money. Despite the renewal of the truce of Bruges for a further year in 1376, the crown's finances were in so parlous a state that parliament had to be called and asked for further supplies. The Good Parliament, as contemporaries subsequently referred to it, met in April 1376. It refused to the last to authorize direct taxes, though, as in the years of peace during the 1360s, it did agree to the extension of the wool subsidy. Before it did so, however, it had carried out the most dramatic and damaging attack on royal government yet witnessed in a medieval parliament.

Edward III was too ill to attend the Good Parliament and his eldest son was to die in the course of the session, so the assembly was presided over by John of Gaunt. It may be that the king's absence made the Lords and, more specifically, the Commons less reticent about their grievances against the crown. The Commons, meeting in the chapter house of Westminster Abbey, selected Sir Peter de la Mare as their spokesman. After some delay, they secured the appointment of a new council, including the earl of March and Bishop Wykeham, both of whom had personal grievances against members of the court. Then, on 12 May, de la Mare appeared before Gaunt and, on behalf of the Commons, laid certain accusations against William Latimer, the king's chamberlain, John Neville of Raby, the steward of the household, Richard Lyons, a London merchant, and a number of other financiers. Latimer and Lyons, the principal targets of the Commons' wrath, were accused of profiting from controversial financial schemes designed to raise money for the king's coffers. Also accused was Alice *Perrers (d. 1400/01), the king's mistress, who had replaced Queen Philippa in Edward's bed and affections during the mid-1360s, and with whom the king had at least three illegitimate children. Her alleged greed, resulting from her influence at court, made her a controversial figure. The Commons' charges were heard before the Lords (thus establishing the procedure for parliamentary impeachment), and the government had no choice but to dismiss Latimer and Neville, to imprison Lyons, and to banish Alice Perrers from the king's company. By the time the session was concluded on 10 July the court was in complete disarray.

The political victory of the Good Parliament was, however, short-lived. By October 1376 the displaced courtiers had been pardoned and restored to their titles, if not to their offices. The parliament that assembled at Westminster in January 1377 proved extraordinarily amenable to Gaunt's will, accepting the reversal of the earlier impeachments and authorizing further direct taxation in the novel form of a poll tax fixed at the rate of 4d. per head on all those over the age of fourteen. As in 1341 parliament was apparently forced to accept that the crown had the right to renege on political concessions made against its will. More immediately it had to face the imminent renewal of war and the rumour of a French invasion. During this crisis it also became clear that the one element of stability in the regime—the king himself—was about to be removed.

Old age, illness, and death The first direct evidence of the king's failing health occurs in 1369, when his personal physician, John Glaston, was out of court for nine days between 13 February and 9 May 1369 'preparing medicine for the king's body' (PRO, E101/396/11). Between June 1371 and July 1372 Glaston's absences for this reason numbered sixty-seven days. Such periods of indisposition were not, however, necessarily connected with Edward's later infirmity, the precise nature of which also remains uncertain: although historians have conventionally described the aged king as senile, there is no direct evidence of dementia, and it seems most likely that his mental faculties were impaired by a series of strokes. Nor should the speed of his decline be exaggerated: at least until the mid-1370s there is evidence that he continued to take an active, if sporadic, part in the business of government.

On the other hand, Edward's commitment to this work undoubtedly waned. Already in the 1360s his movements had tended to become restricted to the south, and more particularly the south-east, of the kingdom, as he passed ever longer periods at the royal residences of Havering atte Bower, Woodstock, Sheen, Eltham, Queenborough, and particularly Windsor. Since the council increasingly tended to hold its sessions at Westminster, the centre of government consequently became somewhat dissociated from the court. Furthermore, by 1375 the convention had developed that the chamberlain of the royal household was entitled to endorse petitions received at court with notes purporting to represent the king's personal wishes. This strongly suggests that Edward had now become a mere cipher, and that both courtiers and government officials were having to maintain a fiction of active kingship.

At Whitsuntide 1376 Edward was taken from Havering to Kennington to visit the deathbed of his eldest son. About Michaelmas he himself fell seriously ill at Havering with a large abscess; in preparation for impending death he appointed trustees of his personal estates on 5 October and made his will three days later. After the abscess burst, on 3 February 1377, he rallied somewhat, and his physicians were able to find him a suitable diet of 'meat broths and … soups of best white bread done in warm goat's milk' (*Anonimalle Chronicle*, 95). On 11 February Edward was removed from Havering to Sheen; as his boat passed the palace of Westminster, where the Good Parliament was in session, all the Lords came out to cheer him. On 23 April he was also present at Windsor when a large number of young nobles and royals were knighted and two of his grandsons, Prince Richard and Henry Bolingbroke, were admitted to the Order of the Garter. But the king was taken back quickly to Sheen, and died there on 21 June 1377. Edward III's wooden funeral effigy, the earliest to survive, was probably carved from a death mask, and bears signs of the twisted face that is normally associated with a fatal stroke.

The obsequies of Edward III were performed with great solemnity. The king's body was embalmed by Roger Chandeler of London at a cost of £21 and transported from Sheen to London in a journey that took three days: no fewer than 1700 torches were used in the procession. Masses were said at St Paul's Cathedral on 28 June, in the presence of Simon Sudbury, archbishop of Canterbury, and on 4 July, when John of Gaunt and Edmund of Langley were both present. The funeral itself took place in Westminster Abbey on 5 July; the deceased king was interred on the south side of the chapel of Edward the Confessor. The tomb, which still survives, was evidently not constructed until 1386, when expenditure was recorded on the Purbeck marble used for its base; but there is no documentary evidence by which to date or to attribute the principal gilt bronze effigy, which represents Edward III in idealized form as a venerable sage, or the miniature effigies of the king's children which decorate the sides of the tomb.

Under the terms of his will Edward III left the lands he had acquired in fee or in reversions to complete the endowments established for two of his own religious foundations, the Cistercian abbey of St Mary Graces outside the Tower of London and the college of secular canons attached to St Stephen's Chapel, Westminster, and for the Dominican priory of Kings Langley, Hertfordshire, where a number of his family were buried. However, the government of Richard II attempted to use the designated estates to create a landed endowment for the new king's tutor, Sir Simon Burley (d. 1388), and it was not until 1401 that the legal wranglings were concluded and the terms of Edward's will finally fulfilled.

Image and personality Not surprisingly, Edward III was known by his contemporaries and honoured by posterity chiefly as a warrior. Although nineteenth- and early twentieth-century scholarship tended to deny him the status of a great strategist, more recent research has emphasized his abilities as a commander by stressing his active involvement in the administration of war, his ability to inspire confidence and discipline in his troops, and his extraordinary success in applying the tactics of the *chevauchée* and the mixed formation on the battlefields of France. Certainly, much of the credibility he enjoyed among the rulers and nobles of fourteenth-century Europe derived from the deference, not to say the considerable fear, shown to English armies operating on the continent.

This is not to say that Edward was interested only in feats of arms. Once regarded as somewhat boorish in his tastes, the king is now seen as a more rounded, if not necessarily more complex, individual who not only enjoyed martial sports and gambling but was also the patron of some of the finest artistic achievements of the day. In particular, his major building works provided a fit environment for courtly ritual and chivalric display and served as material statements of the grandeur of his kingship. The great rebuilding of Windsor Castle, carried out in the 1350s and 1360s, is especially important in that it shifted the royal cult of Arthur away from centres such as Glastonbury and Winchester and focused it on the king's own birthplace: thus were the contemporary allusions to Edward's role as the new Arthur given tangible and permanent expression. Other major building works were undertaken at the royal residences of Westminster, Eltham, Sheen, Leeds (in Kent), Woodstock, and Kings Langley. Queenborough, on the Isle of Sheppey, begun anew in the 1360s and intended primarily for the defence of the Thames estuary, was also lavishly equipped for royal visits. Edward may indeed have had something of a penchant for modern conveniences: it was during his reign that hot water was first piped into the king's baths at Westminster, Windsor, and Langley, and that mechanical clocks began to appear in the royal palaces.

Much of Edward III's construction of kingship, however, depended on his adherence to the rules of chivalry. The contemporary chronicler Jean le Bel of Liège paid him a very significant compliment by repeatedly prefixing his name with the epithet 'noble'; many English chroniclers followed suit, contrasting the honourable Edward with the 'tyrant' Philippe VI. In a courtly context, the chivalric code was principally maintained by lavish display and highly stylized protocol. In particular, the exalted place that Edward accorded to women was an important measure of his credibility as the model of chivalry: by rescuing the countess of Atholl, giving way to Queen Philippa's prayers at Calais, and taking on the role of champion for Lady Wake, he publicly advertised his honourable intentions towards the opposite sex. Not everyone was taken in by such posturing. The curious and convoluted story of Edward's rape of the countess of Salisbury (which was later transmuted, in suitably sanitized form, into the foundation myth of the Order of the Garter) may be dismissed as a piece of French propaganda, but it is less easy to ignore the accusations of licentiousness directed against the court by contemporary writers in England. In particular, his association with Alice Perrers did considerable harm to the king's reputation in his last years.

Posthumous reputation Nevertheless the cult of Edward III developed rapidly in the late fourteenth and early fifteenth centuries. Richard II's attempts to make peace with France and the factional domestic politics of his reign caused chroniclers and poets to hark back to the middle years of the fourteenth century as the golden age of a golden king. When Henry V reopened the war with France there was much interest in the military achievements of the king's illustrious great-grandfather, and accounts of the campaigns of Edward III and the Black Prince, such as those contained in the *Brut* chronicles, circulated in considerable numbers. Moreover, as the common root from which the Lancastrian, Yorkist, and Tudor dynasties all sprang, Edward's reputation was never jeopardized by changes in the political regime. The anonymous late sixteenth-century history play, *The Reign of King*

Edward III (which has been attributed, with some plausibility, to William Shakespeare), gave Edward's achievements in war a new relevance to contemporaries by comparing the battle of Sluys with the defeat of the Spanish Armada.

Nor did Edward's posthumous reputation depend solely on his military accomplishments. Both Henry IV and Edward IV were exhorted to behave like Edward III in their fiscal and legislative policies; and in the sixteenth and seventeenth centuries transcripts were made of the customs accounts of the 1350s to demonstrate the wealth of the monarchy and the favourable balance of trade during Edward's reign. In particular, the seventeenth century saw Edward as a constitutional king in whose reign crown and parliament had worked together for common profit: it is significant that Joshua Barnes's substantial and scholarly biography of Edward III was published in 1688, the year of the 'glorious' revolution.

In the nineteenth century attitudes changed. William Stubbs criticized Edward on three fronts: he was a voluptuary; he drained England of her wealth to subsidize irresponsible wars; and he lacked a policy, buying popularity by alienating the prerogatives of the crown and thus driving the monarchy into the constitutional paralysis that caused the Wars of the Roses. Twentieth-century scholarship, exemplified in the work of K. B. McFarlane and May McKisack, tended to be rather kinder, not least because it placed much greater emphasis on judging medieval rulers by the values of their own times. In the final assessment it remains uncertain whether Edward III can indeed be credited with an overall political strategy: he rarely indulged in grand statements of constitutional theory, and many of his acts of government were merely designed to placate a political community whose moral and material support was so vital to his military enterprises. On the other hand, with rare exceptions, he achieved enormous and remarkable success in inspiring the loyalty of his subjects: his reign marks one of the longest periods of domestic peace in the history of medieval England. Edward was one of the first of his line to make concerted and self-conscious use of a whole range of media—the proclamation, the sermon, religious ceremony, art and architecture, even his own clothing—to create an image of monarchy that advertised his purpose and commanded respect not only among the nobility but in the country at large. In particular this involved a new identity with the language of the ordinary people: it was during this reign that Middle English first began to establish itself as the spoken and written language of the élite. It is a nice irony that Edward III, who claimed the throne of France, was in certain cultural respects the first 'English' king of post-conquest England.   W. M. ORMROD

Sources M. McKisack, *The fourteenth century* (1959) · M. Prestwich, *The three Edwards* (1980) · G. L. Harriss, *King, parliament and public finance in medieval England to 1369* (1975) · W. M. Ormrod, *The reign of Edward III* (1990) · J. Le Patourel, *Feudal empires: Norman and Plantagenet* (1984) · M. Vale, *The Angevin legacy and the Hundred Years War, 1250–1340* (1990) · R. Nicholson, *Edward III and the Scots: the formative years of a military career, 1327–1335* (1965) · J. Vale, *Edward III and chivalry: chivalric society and its context, 1270–1350* (1982) · E. Déprez, *Les préliminaires de la guerre de cent ans* (1902) · J. Sumption, *The Hundred Years War*, 1 (1990) · K. Fowler, *The king's lieutenant: Henry of Grosmont, first duke of Lancaster, 1310–1361* (1969) · K. B. McFarlane, *The nobility of later medieval England* (1973) · J. Barnie, *War in medieval society: social values and the Hundred Years War* (1974) · W. A. Morris and others, eds., *The English government at work, 1327–36*, 3 vols. (1940–50) · Tout, *Admin. hist.* · N. M. Fryde, 'Edward III's removal of his ministers and judges, 1340–1', *BIHR*, 48 (1975), 149–61 · W. M. Ormrod, 'Edward III and his family', *Journal of British Studies*, 26 (1987), 398–422 · G. Holmes, *The Good Parliament* (1975) · PRO · *Œuvres de Froissart: chroniques*, ed. K. de Lettenhove, 25 vols. (Brussels, 1867–77) · V. H. Galbraith, ed., *The Anonimalle chronicle, 1333 to 1381* (1927) · *Adae Murimuth continuatio chronicarum. Robertus de Avesbury de gestis mirabilibus regis Edwardi tertii*, ed. E. M. Thompson, Rolls Series, 93 (1889) · *Chronica Johannis de Reading et anonymi Cantuariensis, 1346–1367*, ed. J. Tait (1914) · *RotP* · *Scalacronica, by Sir Thomas Gray of Heton, knight: a chronical of England and Scotland from AD MLXVI to AD MCCCLXII*, ed. J. Stevenson, Maitland Club, 40 (1836) · *Chronique de Jean le Bel*, ed. J. Viard and E. Déprez, 2 vols. (Paris, 1904–5) · J. de Trokelowe, 'Annales', in *Johannis de Trokelowe et Henrici de Blaneforde … chronica et annales*, ed. H. T. Riley, pt 3 of *Chronica monasterii S. Albani*, Rolls Series, 28 (1866), 63–127 · *Historiae Dunelmensis scriptores tres: Gaufridus de Coldingham, Robertus de Graystanes, et Willielmus de Chambre*, ed. J. Raine, SurtS, 9 (1839) · *Ann. mon.*, 3.1–420 · E. A. R. Brown, 'The prince is father of the king: the character and childhood of Philip the Fair of France', *Mediaeval Studies*, 49 (1987), 282–334 · C. G. Crump, 'The arrest of Roger Mortimer and Queen Isabel', *EngHR*, 26 (1911), 331–2 · G. P. Cuttino and T. W. Lyman, 'Where is Edward II?', *Speculum*, 53 (1978), 522–43 · R. Cazelles, *Société politique, noblesse et couronne sous Jean le Bel et Charles V* (1982) · J. Sherborne, *War, politics and culture in fourteenth-century England*, ed. A. Tuck (1994) · W. M. Ormrod, 'The personal religion of Edward III', *Speculum*, 64 (1989), 849–77 · R. Brown, H. M. Colvin, and A. J. Taylor, eds., *The history of the king's works*, 2 (1963) · C. J. Rogers, 'Edward III and the dialectics of strategy, 1327–1360', *TRHS*, 6th ser., 4 (1994), 83–102 · M. McKisack, 'Edward III and the historians', *History*, new ser., 45 (1960), 1–15 · J. Barnes, *The history … of Edward III* (1688) · W. Stubbs, *The constitutional history of England in its origin and development*, new edn, 3 vols. (1906) · D. A. L. Morgan, 'The political after-life of Edward III: the apotheosis of a warmonger', *EngHR*, 112 (1997), 856–81 · R. Proudfoot, 'The reign of King Edward the Third* (1896) and Shakespeare', *PBA*, 71 (1985), 159–85 · Rymer, *Foedera*, 2nd edn · *DNB* · E. B. Fryde and others, eds., *Handbook of British chronology*, 3rd edn, Royal Historical Society Guides and Handbooks, 2 (1986)

Archives BL, wardrobe accounts, Add. MS 46350 · PRO · S. Antiquaries, Lond., wardrobe accounts, MS 541 · University of Leicester, letters [official copies]

Likenesses manuscript illumination, 19 Sept 1343, Cambridge University muniments, charter · tomb effigy, 1360–99, Westminster Abbey, London [*see illus.*] · S. Hadley, funeral effigy, 1377, Westminster Abbey, London · oils, 17th cent., NPG · R. Smirke, engraving (after wall painting at St Stephen's Chapel, Westminster, now destroyed), repro. in J. Topham, *Some account of … St Stephen, Westminster* (1811) · choir screens, Canterbury · electrotype (after a tomb effigy), NPG · manuscript illumination, St John Cam. · manuscript illuminations, BL, Cotton MSS and Royal MSS; *see illus. in* David II (1324–1371) · statue, choir screens, York Minster · wax seal, BM

Edward IV (1442–1483), king of England and lord of Ireland, was born at Rouen, Normandy, on 28 April 1442, the second surviving child and eldest son of *Richard, third duke of York (1411–1460), and *Cecily, duchess of York (1415–1495), the daughter of Ralph *Neville, first earl of Westmorland, and Joan Beaufort.

Early life, 1442–1461 Edward probably assumed his father's title of earl of March (no patent of creation survives) late

Edward IV (1442–1483), by unknown artist

in 1445, when negotiations were under way for his marriage to a daughter of Charles VII of France. Little is known of his early childhood, but it does not seem to have been spent in the household of another lord or of the king. He and his younger brother Edmund were certainly based at their father's castle of Ludlow by spring 1454, and were probably already living there in May 1452, when one of the Kent rebels was accused of spreading the unlikely story that the earl of March (then aged ten) was coming with a great number of Welshmen. Although one chronicler claims that March was present at the first battle of St Albans, the first certain evidence of his involvement in his father's opposition to the circle around Henry VI is his flight from Ludford Bridge in October 1459. Edward accompanied his uncle the earl of Salisbury, and Salisbury's son Richard *Neville, earl of Warwick, to Calais, while York and Edmund went to Ireland. All five men were attainted in the parliament that met at Coventry the following month.

In 1460 the 'Calais earls' invaded England, landing in Kent and entering London on 2 July. On 10 July Warwick and March gained possession of Henry VI by defeating the Lancastrian army at the battle of Northampton, and returned with him to London. For the rest of the summer the earls and their allies ruled in Henry's name. The dominant figure in this arrangement was apparently Warwick, although he seems to have been careful to defer to

March, and it was March who remained in London while Warwick was in the midlands in September. Nor did Edward accompany his mother to meet York, who had landed near Chester early in September. By the time York entered London, bearing the undifferenced royal arms, it was obvious that he had resolved to claim the throne for himself. Although Edward had not been a party to the earlier meetings of York and Warwick at Waterford and Shrewsbury, he was presumably aware of his father's intentions, and it is unlikely that, as Waurin claims, he tried to persuade York to abandon them. But he may have realized that public opinion was against the duke, and he seems to have kept a low profile in the ensuing negotiations. In the end a compromise was achieved whereby York and his heirs were to succeed Henry on the king's death, and on 31 October March joined York in swearing that they would do nothing against the person or estate of the king.

It was clear, however, that this agreement, which disinherited Edward of Lancaster, the prince of Wales, would generate the immediate opposition of the queen and her circle. Edward was sent to the Welsh march to prevent the earl of Pembroke joining forces with the queen, while York and Edmund went north, where they were killed by the queen's forces at the battle of Wakefield on 30 December. Queen Margaret led her army south, defeating Warwick at the second battle of St Albans on 17 February, although she turned back without entering London. By then, March had defeated the Lancastrian forces led by Pembroke and Wiltshire at the battle of Mortimer's Cross on 2 or 3 February. He subsequently joined forces with Richard Neville in the Cotswolds, and they entered London together on 26 February. On 1 March the chancellor, Warwick's brother George Neville, declared Edward's title to the throne at a gathering at St George's Fields, reportedly to acclaim. Two days later a 'council' of Yorkist allies meeting at Baynard's Castle (the London house of the dukes of York) agreed that Edward should be king, and on the next day (4 March) Edward took his seat at Westminster and began his reign.

Securing the throne, 1461–1465 Although events in London were no doubt carefully stage-managed, Edward's accession reveals how thoroughly the situation had changed since his father had first declared his claim to the throne in the previous October. In part, this surely owed something to Edward's succession to his father. Richard of York, like Margaret of Anjou, had become too closely linked with faction for his victory to offer much hope of ending the civil war. Edward could more plausibly offer to unite the warring factions—and his readiness to welcome former Lancastrians into his service was to be a characteristic of the early months of his reign. In the short term, however, he needed to establish himself by military success. He and his allies began raising money and men immediately, and confronted the Lancastrian forces at Towton on Palm Sunday (29 March). Although the Lancastrian army was the larger, it was decisively defeated. Edward returned to London on 26 June, after a progress through the northern counties, and was crowned at Westminster two days later.

Although the thoroughness of the Yorkist victory forced the tacit acknowledgement of Edward's title by all but the most committed Lancastrians, his position was far from entirely secure. Henry VI, with his wife, had remained at York during the battle and had fled to Scotland on receiving news of the Lancastrian defeat. Edward IV, uniquely among medieval usurpers, thus began his reign with his predecessor not just alive but still at large: a situation that inevitably undermined Yorkist authority. The early years of the reign saw almost continuous military involvement in the north of England, where the Lancastrians could call on Scottish support, and in Wales. Edward himself played relatively little part in the campaigns. He did lead the great army assembled late in 1462 in response to the loss of Bamburgh, Alnwick, and Dunstanburgh, but fell ill with measles at Durham in November, and leadership passed to the earl of Warwick. In the following summer it was expected that Edward would lead a major campaign into Scotland in response to continuing Scottish support for the Lancastrians, but although practical preparations were still in train late in August, and the king moved into Yorkshire in September, no military operations followed. Edward also played no part in the campaigns of 1464, which culminated in the defeat of the Lancastrians at Hexham, followed by the surrender of the remaining Lancastrian fortresses in Northumberland, although he had, again, been making preparations to go north in person.

Military activity was only one facet of Edward's attempt to establish himself as the rightful and effective ruler of England. Another, perhaps Edward's preferred strategy, was his commitment to winning over opponents. From the outset of his reign Edward showed himself willing to take former Lancastrians into his favour, on little more than their assurances of future good behaviour. Given the narrowness of his power base in 1461, such a policy had obvious practical advantages, but it perhaps also marked a deliberate attempt by the king to restore political life to normality after the factionalism of the previous decade. The policy had some dramatic failures, most notably Sir Ralph Percy and the duke of Somerset, whom Edward took into his service in spite of their strong Lancastrian links, and who afterwards reneged. But in general men were as eager to support the *de facto* king as he was to have their backing, and it is a measure of the policy's success that in July 1465 Henry VI was finally betrayed and captured in Lancashire, the hereditary heartland of his dynasty.

Edward's marriage and its consequences, 1465–1467 Alongside Edward IV's search for domestic security went the need to secure recognition for his dynasty in Europe. In the context of the early 1460s the obvious opening for England onto the European stage was the growing tension between France, on the one side, and the dukes of Burgundy and Brittany on the other, as Louis XI attempted to exert his authority over the duchies. The value to both sides of acquiring English backing, or at least denying it to their opponents, gave Edward a European importance

that he would otherwise hardly have deserved, status that would inevitably be diminished once he had committed himself. In this respect, the fact that by the mid-1460s Edward was apparently inclining towards a Burgundian alliance, while Warwick favoured France, often taken as evidence of a growing rift between Edward and the earl, may have had its diplomatic advantages. Once it had become clear that Edward had decided for Burgundy, Charles, count of Charolais, who succeeded his father as duke in June 1467, was able to drive a hard bargain in the negotiations of 1467–8.

The Burgundian alliance was formalized in the marriage of Duke Charles (formerly Charolais) to Edward's youngest sister, Margaret: the only one of the Yorkist royal family to make a foreign marriage. Discussion of possible European brides for Edward and his brothers had been a feature of earlier diplomacy, but nothing had come of them and Edward had taken himself out of the running by his secret marriage, on 1 May 1464, to Elizabeth Grey [see Elizabeth (c.1437–1492)], the widow of John Grey who had died fighting on the Lancastrian side at the second battle of St Albans. She was the daughter of Richard Woodville, a former servant of John, duke of Bedford, who had married Bedford's widow, Jacquetta de Luxembourg, and had been made Earl Rivers in acknowledgement of his wife's standing. Socially, Edward had married beneath himself and an important diplomatic opportunity had been lost. Contemporaries evidently found the marriage surprising, and critics of the queen's family in 1470–71 put about the story that Edward had been bewitched by Jacquetta. The more usual explanation, progressively embroidered by later writers, was that Edward was sexually infatuated with Elizabeth, who made her submission conditional on marriage. Edward himself seems to have been rather embarrassed by his action. It was not until September that he broke the news of his marriage to the royal council at Reading, and on 29 September Elizabeth was formally acknowledged as queen, by being escorted into Reading Abbey by Edward's brother, *George, duke of Clarence, and Warwick.

Edward's marriage, and his delay in acknowledging it, laid him open to accusations of misjudgement and bad faith, the latter not least because his ambassadors were left negotiating a French match that had become impossible. But in discussions of the political impact of the marriage most emphasis is usually placed on the consequences of finding appropriate preferment for the new queen's family. Elizabeth brought a large, and largely unmarried, family into the royal circle: two sons from her first marriage, five brothers, and six sisters. Within two years Edward had found aristocratic husbands for five of the queen's sisters, who married the duke of Buckingham, and the heirs of the earls of Kent, Essex, and Arundel, and of Lord Herbert (later to become the earl of Pembroke). This series of marriages is unlikely to have been prompted only by the king's infatuation with his new wife. With his usual pragmatism Edward was seizing the chance to ally his dynasty more securely with the English nobility, an interpretation strengthened by the fact that he showed much less interest in finding brides for his wife's brothers, although the youngest, John, married the dowager duchess of Norfolk. The marriages consolidated links with existing allies of York, such as the Herberts and Bourchiers, and also forged new alliances with the Staffords and Fitzalans. This is not to imply that the marriages benefited only the king. By the mid-1460s Edward was sufficiently secure on the throne for marriage into the royal family to confer welcome prestige and influence, and the royal patronage that accompanied several of the marriages should probably be seen not as the king's attempt to buy the grudging acquiescence of the noble families concerned, but as the first fruits of an alliance valued by both sides.

The creation of an enlarged royal circle was, however, also to have more negative consequences. With hindsight the Woodville marriage marked a turning point in Edward's first reign, contributing to the progressive alienation of one of the king's leading allies, the earl of Warwick. This was probably not immediately apparent. Earlier in the reign Warwick had coexisted harmoniously with other close associates of the king, notably William, Lord Hastings, and Richard Fiennes, Lord Dacre, and there was no obvious reason why this state of affairs should not continue after the emergence of the Woodvilles as a new element within the royal circle. Warwick certainly made no overtly hostile response to Edward's marriage and the Crowland chronicler believed that the earl initially sought to co-operate with the queen's kindred. He escorted Elizabeth on her first formal appearance as queen and stood godfather to the first child of her marriage to Edward, born in February 1466. Even Warwick's plan to marry his daughter to Clarence, first mooted at about this time, may be evidence of the earl's wish to become part of the extended royal family, rather than a sign that he was already disaffected and was seeking allies against the Woodvilles.

The disaffection of the Nevilles, 1467–1469 Edward's response to the marriage proposal was, however, unwelcoming, and in the course of the next few years relations between the two men cooled noticeably. Warkworth, while linking that loss of affection with the king's marriage, saw June 1467, when Edward dismissed Warwick's brother George from the chancellorship, as a crucial stage in their slide into hostility, commenting 'And yett thei were acorded diverse tymes; but thei nevere loffyd togedere aftere' (Warkworth, 4). Waurin also saw 1467 as the point of no return, but for him the issue was Warwick's continuing support for an alliance with France, at a time when Edward had finally committed himself to supporting Burgundy and Brittany. But it is likely that both issues were expressions of a deeper malaise. Later events make it clear that Warwick had come to feel excluded from the circle around the king, and resented the influence it wielded.

The political tensions induced by this are reflected in the stirrings of Lancastrian activity apparent in the late 1460s. In autumn 1467 a captured Lancastrian claimed that Warwick had made contact with Margaret of Anjou,

and in the following summer another Lancastrian, Cornelius, implicated a number of prominent Londoners and Warwick's associate at Calais, John, Lord Wenlock, in his confession. None of this amounted to very much, and the persistent rumours of the involvement of Warwick and his circle were probably little more than wishful thinking on the part of Lancastrian dissidents. But that in itself is evidence of the importance attached to the earl's growing disaffection, and the government was clearly uneasy. In 1468 Edward arrested the surviving representatives of three strongly Lancastrian families: Henry Courtenay, Thomas Hungerford, and John de Vere, earl of Oxford. Courtenay and Hungerford were found guilty of plotting the king's death and executed, but Oxford, Warwick's brother-in-law, was not brought to trial—evidence, perhaps, that Edward, although aware of Warwick's manifest disillusionment with the regime, still thought him fundamentally loyal.

The Neville rebellions, 1469–1470 In 1469 Warwick finally moved into overt opposition, taking with him Edward's brother and heir, the duke of Clarence. The rebellion began obliquely. There had been unrest in the north of England from late April, and although it had been repressed for the king by Warwick's brother John, the rebels apparently regrouped in June under the leadership of 'Robin of Redesdale', who was almost certainly an associate of Warwick and probably one of the Conyers family. At this stage, however, Warwick had given no sign of support for the rebels, and Edward seems not to have regarded the rising as particularly threatening. It was only in mid-June that he decided to raise troops and go north in person, and not until July that he seems to have realized the full scale of the opposition.

On 11 July Clarence married Warwick's daughter Isabel at Calais and on the following day the two lords issued a manifesto, couched as a list of popular grievances which they had resolved to bring to the king's attention 'for the honoure and profite of oure seid sovereyn Lord, and the comune weal of alle this his realme' (Warkworth, 47). The complaints were directed at named associates of the king: Rivers and his wife, the earls of Pembroke and Devon, lords Scales and Audley, Sir John Fogge, and the queen's brothers. They were accused of forcing up taxes, to make good the financial shortfall their own rapacity had created, and of maintaining wrongdoers so that the law could not be enforced. The cure for such misgovernment, the manifesto proclaimed, was for the king to pay more attention to the counsel of the true lords of the blood, who had been estranged from the king by the circle around him.

If the 1469 rising is evaluated in terms of high politics, it is clear that Warwick and Clarence were extremely isolated, and it is difficult to see their disaffection as evidence that Edward was guilty of serious political mismanagement. In particular, although it is possible to cite examples of Woodville greed and insensitivity, hostility to the queen's family does not seem to have been a particularly effective rallying cry among the nobility and gentry at large. The extent of popular dissatisfaction with the regime is harder to assess. The rebel lords clearly expected their accusations of over-taxation and royal laxity in the area of law and order to be well received, and Warkworth confirms that criticisms of the regime were current by the late 1460s, although he stresses rather the damage Edward's policies were thought to have done to English trading interests. Warwick and Clarence apparently gained significant support as they advanced through Kent; enough, at least, to persuade London to open its gates to them and even to give them financial support. It is unlikely, however, that popular disillusionment alone would have constituted a major threat to the regime; a view which gains some support from the ease with which John Neville dispersed the early manifestations of northern unrest, before the emergence of aristocratic support for the rising.

Edward was, however, caught unprepared by the rebellion. The rebels were able to defeat the royal forces under Pembroke and Devon at the battle of Edgcote on 26 July. The king had not been present at the battle, and when news of the defeat reached him as he advanced south from Nottingham he was deserted by many of his men. He was captured by George Neville and sent as a prisoner first to Warwick Castle and later to Middleham, Yorkshire. For the next few weeks Warwick and Clarence attempted to rule England in the king's name; but the knowledge that the king was a prisoner fatally undermined their attempts, and the period was marked by a dramatic upsurge in lawlessness, including an attack by the duke of Norfolk on the Pastons' castle of Caister, and a flare-up of the dispute between the Stanleys and the Harringtons in the north-west. When there was a Lancastrian rising, led by Sir Humphrey Neville of Brancepeth, in the north, Warwick found himself unable to raise troops to deal with it, and Edward was able to reassert his freedom of action. He was at York, apparently at liberty, in the second week of September, and Humphrey Neville and his brother had been defeated and executed by the end of the month.

Edward returned to London in the middle of October. Initially he was careful not to take action against Clarence and Warwick, an approach that, as described by Polydore Vergil, has clear parallels with his policy towards the Lancastrians in the early 1460s: 'He regarded nothing more than to win again the friendship of such noble men as were now alienated from him [and] to confirm the goodwill of them that were hovering and inconstant' (Vergil, 125). The famous comment of John (II) Paston that, although Edward declared Warwick and the rest to be his best friends, 'hys howsolde men haue other langage' (Davis, 1.410) may imply hostility to Edward's approach within the royal circle rather than deception on the part of the king. But the leading rebels cannot have felt secure, particularly as the victims of the rising had included the queen's father and her brother John, and their apprehensions can only have been intensified when Edward showed himself minded to restore Henry Percy to the earldom of Northumberland, presumably as a counterweight to the Nevilles in the north. The chief beneficiaries of the Percy forfeiture had been Clarence and Warwick, and also

Warwick's younger brother John, who had remained loyal to Edward throughout his brother's move into opposition. Edward was careful to compensate John Neville with a major new holding in the south-west, where he was given the forfeited Courtenay lands previously held by another victim of the rising of 1469, Humphrey Stafford, earl of Devon. The grant was testimony to Edward's confidence that John Neville would be able to assert Yorkist authority in a notoriously disaffected region, but it represented a break with Neville's traditional interests in the north, and it was later to become apparent that Neville had resented the enforced move.

In the short term, however, John Neville remained loyal, as his brother and Clarence again moved into opposition. In the spring of 1470 the two men exploited opposition in Lincolnshire to a leading local member of Edward's household, Sir Thomas Burgh, in order to stir up a rising against the king. Contemporaries seem to have been unsure of the rebels' intentions: Warkworth implies that the aim was to restore Henry VI, while the official narrative of the rising and its suppression claims that it was Clarence who was to become king. It seems clear, at least, that Warwick and Clarence had abandoned hopes of forcing themselves on Edward, and were now contemplating removing him altogether.

Flight and recovery, 1470–1471 The rebellion was a complete failure. The Lincolnshire rebels were defeated near Empingham, and only the closest associates of Warwick and Clarence proved willing to support their lords' treason. The two noblemen and their families fled to France, where they opened negotiations with Margaret of Anjou for the restoration of Henry VI. Edward responded by sending secret messengers to Clarence, who had no reason to welcome a Lancastrian restoration. He also took steps to secure Calais and the south coast, and, with Burgundian help, blockaded the French coast. In September 1470, however, the fleet was scattered by storms, and the rebels, now reinforced by committed Lancastrians such as Jasper Tudor, and with French backing, invaded England. They were soon joined by Lord Stanley and the earl of Shrewsbury and it was a sizeable force that moved north. Edward had been in the north when the news of the invasion reached him, drawn thither by risings in the North Riding and Cumberland. He moved south only slowly, awaiting reinforcements from John Neville. What came instead was news of Neville's defection and Edward and a group of followers, including Gloucester, Hastings, and Howard, fled to the Low Countries, leaving Warwick to enter London unopposed and replace Henry VI on the throne.

Edward's arrival in Burgundian territory was a considerable embarrassment for Duke Charles. As part of the price Warwick had paid for French backing, the new regime in England was committed to support an invasion of Burgundy, and Charles's initial reaction was to keep his distance from Edward, to avoid giving the new Anglo-French alliance any excuse for taking action against him. For the early weeks of his exile Edward was dependent on the hospitality of Louis de Gruthuyse (whom he was later, after his restoration, to reward with the earldom of Winchester). It was only when Louis XI declared war on Burgundy in December 1470 that Charles abandoned his cautious neutrality and agreed to support a Yorkist invasion of England. The preparations for Edward's return were not, however, only military. In spite of the apparent thoroughness with which Edward's authority had collapsed, the restoration of Henry VI offered little to many of the political establishment left behind in England, and Edward could hope to call on their support once an invasion seemed viable. Members of the Yorkist royal family were mobilized to put pressure on Clarence to reconsider his allegiance, and messengers were sent to other possible allies, including the newly restored earl of Northumberland.

Edward returned to England in March 1471. Initial plans to land in East Anglia proved abortive, and the Yorkists finally came ashore at Ravenspur in Holderness on 14 March. The East Riding was Percy territory, and although Edward seems to have been confident of the earl's backing, the attitude of the Percy retainers was more problematic. Edward accordingly moved cautiously, initially claiming that he had come only for the duchy of York. This claim saw him safely through east Yorkshire, and as he turned south he began to be joined by allies, until by the time he had reached Nottingham his forces were large enough for a Lancastrian army under Exeter and Oxford to fall back rather than challenge him. On 3 April his forces were swelled by his conjunction with Clarence, and the Yorkist army entered London unopposed on 11 April. Edward was reunited with his queen, who during his exile had remained in Westminster sanctuary, where she had given birth to their heir, the future *Edward V, on 2 November 1470.

On Easter Sunday (14 April) Edward IV defeated Warwick's army at Barnet. On the same day Margaret of Anjou and her son Edward landed at Weymouth. She was able to rally significant support from Devon and Cornwall, and began to advance towards the Welsh march. Edward and his army aimed to intercept her before she could cross the Severn, and the two armies met at Tewkesbury on 4 May. The Yorkists were victorious and Edward of Lancaster was among those killed. This removed the argument for keeping Henry VI alive, and the Lancastrian king was killed on the night of Edward IV's victorious return to London, Yorkist claims that he died of 'pure displeasure and melencoly' (Bruce, 38) probably then, as now, commanding little credence.

The second reign: the exercise of patronage As in 1461 Edward IV's title to the throne had been confirmed by battle. But in one respect the situation in 1471 was very different. The death of Henry VI and his son meant that there was no longer an alternative king to validate opposition to the Yorkists. Contemporaries recognized as much, and Edward's restoration was followed by the reconciliation of most of the hard core of committed Lancastrians, like Sir Richard Tunstall, who had remained in opposition throughout the 1460s. The few exceptions included the Lancastrian half-blood, now represented by Jasper Tudor and his nephew Henry, and a handful of men who knew

that they had no hope of regaining their estates under York, such as John de Vere, earl of Oxford, whose lands had been used to endow the king's younger brother Richard, duke of Gloucester (afterwards *Richard III).

As a result the 'feel' of Edward's two reigns is very different. The 1470s were not without flurries of opposition, most notably in 1473, when Oxford secured French backing for an abortive invasion, but Edward looked unassailable in a way that he had not in the 1460s. The difference between the two reigns does not, however, extend to royal policy. There is no sense in which the events of 1469–71 had forced Edward to rethink his strategy, and most of the policies perceived as characteristic of the 1470s can be paralleled in the preceding decade.

Edward consistently showed himself willing to foster the power of trusted supporters, who then acted as his agents at a local level. The best-known example comes from the 1470s, with the elevation of Gloucester to be lord of the north, but Neville authority in the region had been built up in a similar way in the 1460s, and in the same decade William Herbert, later first earl of Pembroke, had become 'King Edward's master-lock' (Griffiths, 159) in south Wales. On a smaller scale, Edward adopted a similar policy towards leading members of the local gentry, many of whom had their links with the crown formalized by membership of the royal household, which was growing steadily throughout Edward's reign. Contemporaries saw the creation of this nexus of support as one of Edward's great achievements, and were particularly impressed by the fact that he knew all his servants, even those of yeoman status. Nor did the king's knowledge extend only to his own servants. It is characteristic of Edward that, in delivering a stinging rebuke to the Mowbray associate William Brandon, he was reported as saying three times in as many sentences that he understood or knew Brandon and his dealings 'well j-now' (Davis, 1.544).

Edward's reliance on his local agents was, on the whole, successful, allowing an effective mediation of royal authority, and it is striking that although his critics in 1469 attacked the power wielded by a group of Edward's allies at the centre, the role of his servants beyond the court never seems to have become a national issue. There were, inevitably, local grievances, such as the complaint that no lawyer could be found who was prepared to act against Sir Richard Croft, one of Edward's key men in Wales in the 1470s, but on the whole Edward's servants seem to have been seen as the embodiment of co-operation between king and country, rather than as an intrusive and alien force.

By contrast, many subsequent commentators have been critical of Edward's willingness to build up the power of his allies through grants of office and land, seeing it as tantamount to the creation of 'over mighty subjects'. But none of Edward's leading allies was able to turn his power fully against the crown. Warwick came nearest, but although he led his own retinue against Edward in 1469–70, most of the royal servants over whom he had been given authority by the crown refused to become involved. It is also clear that what Edward had made he could break, as is shown by the ruthless demotion of Clarence and the second earl of Pembroke. Their progressive exclusion from power points to the negative side of Edward's policy: the imperative to make things fit, even if that involved the manipulation of landed interests. The attempt to turn John Neville into a power in the south-west has already been mentioned, and Edward indulged in a whole series of reshapings of the political map in 1473–4, including the replacement of Clarence by Hastings in the north midlands and the downplaying of Gloucester's role in East Anglia in favour of the Woodville circle. Edward's decision to mediate authority in Wales, through a council associated with the prince of Wales, not only entailed the removal from the region of the second earl of Pembroke (who was instead given land in the west country), but also the exclusion of Henry Stafford, duke of Buckingham, after he came of age.

Such manipulation, which at the time went largely unchallenged, is testimony to Edward IV's authority. It is the king's destruction of his brother Clarence, however, that demonstrates this most clearly. Although Clarence had been reconciled with his brother in 1471, relations between the two men were soured by Clarence's refusal to co-operate with Edward's plans to endow Gloucester through marriage with Warwick's second daughter, Anne Neville. In the Act of Resumption of 1474 Clarence lost the duchy of Lancaster estates in the north midlands, upon which his influence in that area had rested. Whether the erosion of his power drove Clarence back into treason has been disputed; if it did, it is clear that his opposition was entirely ineffective. But in 1477 he was accused of conspiring against the crown and in the parliament of January 1478 attainted and subsequently executed. Although some later writers have tried to distinguish the hand of others behind Clarence's fall (Tudor writers favouring Gloucester; P. M. Kendall and other twentieth-century writers preferring the Woodvilles) contemporaries were in no doubt that it was Edward who destroyed his own brother. The Crowland chronicler, who found the episode deeply shocking, commented that in parliament no one spoke against the duke but the king. As the events of the previous years had shown, Clarence was an extremely isolated figure, unable to command much, if any, political support, but it is still striking that Edward was able first to dismantle the duke's power and then to remove him altogether.

Domestic policy The death of Clarence was evidence of the extent to which Edward was, by the late 1470s, master in his own kingdom, at least in the sphere of high politics. His success in the wider governmental arena has been disputed, but here too he seems to have been broadly in control in the 1470s. His most marked, and generally acknowledged, success, was financial. Throughout his reign, Edward IV explored ways of increasing his income, and although he has been criticized for allowing rigour to be tempered by favour, to level such criticism is to misinterpret his motives. Against a background of rigour, quite modest expressions of royal favour came to have a higher value than liberal gifts in a laxer regime. The most striking (and characteristic) example is Edward's use of parliamentary acts of resumption. A measure forced on Henry VI was adopted by Edward as, *inter alia*, a way of granting patronage (in the form of exemptions) at no additional cost to himself.

Edward consistently sought to maximize his income from the crown estates, and from royal rights such as wardships or ecclesiastical vacancies. To handle the revenues from these sources he developed the royal chamber (which had always had a role in storing and spending the king's own cash) as a financial agency largely independent of the exchequer, which, however, retained its traditional responsibility for other sources of royal finance, such as subsidies, customs (granted to Edward for life in 1465), and the sheriffs' farms. The chamber presumably also received the profits of Edward's trading ventures, and may also have handled the receipts from loans and 'benevolences'. No accounts survive for the Yorkist chamber, so the scale of Edward's financial achievement is unknown, but it is significant that in the 1480s he was able to meet the costs of one year of the Scottish war before resorting to parliamentary taxation. This drained his cash reserves, although it is impossible to set a value on the royal jewels and plate, and it may be that contemporaries were right in believing that Edward died a wealthy man, even though the exchequer and chamber together held only £1200 at his death.

Contemporary comment on Edward's wealth, and his means of amassing it, was ambivalent. Solvency was obviously desirable in a ruler, particularly when it allowed a king to meet his debts promptly and in cash, but there was always an underlying sense that the king's wealth was likely to be acquired at the expense of his subjects. Although Edward's efforts to increase the yield from his own estates could be seen as good housekeeping, other aspects of his financial dealings were less popular, notably his resort to benevolences (which were gifts, rather than loans, from his subjects) before the French and Scottish wars. Although the great chronicle treats the benevolences light-heartedly, with the story of a wealthy Suffolk widow who doubled her contribution in return for a royal kiss, the general perception is likely to have been closer to the view evoked by Richard III, that benevolences were 'newe and unlawfull Invencions and inordinate Covetise, ageyenst the lawe of this roialme' (Luders and others, 2.478).

Contemporaries also seem to have had reservations about the success with which Edward re-established law and order. Certainly, like any king, he took action against lawlessness that threatened political stability, and at this level seems to have been broadly successful. He imposed a settlement in the Harrington–Stanley dispute, for instance, which had threatened the good rule of the north-west. His primary weapon in such cases was his own royal authority, but he also made use of the royal council and of the constable's court, which was not only employed against traitors but against those suspected of less extreme forms of *lèse-majesté*, such as the two London goldsmiths whose dispute came to the king's attention in

1473. But contemporaries evidently felt that Edward was less active in cases that did not touch him personally, and as political unrest subsided in the 1470s, the Commons became increasingly critical of the regime's apparent failure to take action against other forms of lawlessness. They pointed the finger at 'such persones as eyther been of grete myght, or elles favoured under persones of grete power' (*RotP*, 6.8). Edward was clearly aware of the hostility to livery and maintenance, but his high-profile campaign against the system's abuses was not extended to forms of retaining that might be deemed beneficial to royal authority. Here too, rigour was moderated by the king's need to cultivate the support of those who underpinned his regime.

This sort of balancing act was inevitable in a system that ultimately rested on people rather than institutions, and Edward IV was not alone in his pragmatism. It has, however, sometimes been suggested that Edward's reliance on non-institutional structures was excessive, and that he should have done more to formalize his government, as (it is often claimed) Henry VII was to do. The extended financial role of the chamber, for instance, collapsed at Edward's death and had to be reactivated by Richard III. But it is difficult to argue that this was a weakness within Edward's own lifetime, when his active involvement in government can more plausibly be seen as a sign of royal strength.

Foreign policy Edward IV's growing security at home allowed him to contemplate military involvement abroad. He had been planning an invasion of France as early as 1468, when he obtained taxation for that purpose from parliament, but nothing had come of the proposal, and resentment at the 'wasted' tax probably fuelled the popular unrest of the following year. By 1472 the idea of war was again current. In April a body of English archers was sent to Brittany in response to an appeal from Duke François, and in September the Anglo-Breton treaty of Châteaugiron made provision for an English invasion in the following spring, although Brittany was subsequently to withdraw, and in March 1473 Edward made a truce with France. But he continued to prepare for the war, seeking money from parliament in both 1472 and 1473, and in 1474 finally securing an Anglo-Burgundian alliance against France. In July 1475 an English army crossed to France, but saw no significant military action. Charles of Burgundy proved unsupportive, and on 29 August Edward and Louis XI met on a bridge across the Somme at Picquigny and agreed terms. There was to be a truce for seven years, and the amity between the countries was to be embodied in the marriage of the dauphin Charles and Edward's eldest daughter, Elizabeth, or, if she died before reaching marriageable age, her sister Mary. In addition Louis undertook to pay Edward £15,000 immediately, and then an annual pension of £10,000.

In fact, Edward had been bought off, and there was considerable popular hostility to this latest waste of taxation. But the French pension helped Edward to do without further parliamentary taxation until 1482, when war with Scotland placed him under renewed financial pressure.

That war developed unexpectedly after a period of relatively harmonious relations between the two countries. In October 1473, as events moved towards the English invasion of France, James III and Edward had agreed a truce, which was planned to last until 1519 and which was formalized in the betrothal of the English princess, Cecily, to James's infant son and namesake, born the previous March. But in 1480 Edward complained about the increasing incidence of truces broken by the Scots and threatened war if reparation were not made. In May English military preparations were set in train, but failed to deter a large-scale raid into the east march by the earl of Angus, which prompted a counter-raid by Gloucester and Northumberland later in the year.

By this date Edward was clearly committed to war, and began to plan a major campaign for the following year, which he was to lead in person. In the event he did not go, although the planned campaign was not finally abandoned until October, and the English attack consisted of little more than a naval raid on the Firth of Forth in the spring and raids across the land border led by Gloucester later in the year. The end of 1481 brought a shift in English strategy. Edward decided to put forward James III's brother, Alexander, duke of Albany, as a rival claimant to the Scottish throne. By the treaty of Fotheringhay, agreed on 11 June 1482, England promised military backing in return for Albany's undertaking (if he won the Scottish throne) to hand over Berwick, to do homage and fealty to the king of England, and to break off relations with France.

The intention had been that Edward IV should lead the campaign of 1482 in person, but he again changed his mind and on 12 June Gloucester was put in effective control of the war. The English army, aided by the political divisions between James III and his nobility, entered Edinburgh unopposed, but then withdrew, after Gloucester had secured an agreement that gave England very little more than Berwick, which was finally surrendered to the English on 24 August. The immediate cause of Gloucester's withdrawal was Albany's decision to renounce his claim to the Scottish throne, but it is curious that the English did not take more advantage of their position of strength, particularly as his later career suggests that Gloucester, their commander, was strongly committed to the war. By the end of the year Albany had had second thoughts and was again in touch with England, but although Edward proved willing to reactivate the treaty of Fotheringhay, no military preparations had been made before Albany again made terms with his brother on 19 March, and three weeks later Edward IV was dead.

The Scottish war was pursued against the background of an increasingly complex continental situation. Charles of Burgundy had been killed at the battle of Nancy in January 1477, and his daughter and heir, Mary, had married Maximilian, the son of the emperor Friedrich III. In 1480 Edward's sister Margaret, the widow of Duke Charles, had helped to negotiate an Anglo-Burgundian alliance, a move that prompted Louis to withhold the latest instalment of Edward's pension, and probably also to encourage

Scottish infractions of the truce. Edward responded by rebuilding bridges with France, and by the summer of 1481 the relationship between the two countries was, on the face of it, much as it had been after Picquigny. For French chroniclers, Edward's motive was fear that he would lose his pension, but that is unlikely to have been the whole story. Edward was in no position to take large-scale military action against France, and he may also have hoped to return to the situation in the early 1460s, when his diplomacy had centred on the avoidance of commitment. Whatever his aims, the policy collapsed. In January 1482 Maximilian, who was unaware of the extent of the Anglo-French *rapprochement*, approached Edward for military help against France. Edward temporized, on the grounds that he was too heavily committed against Scotland to take action against France. This lack of English backing, coupled with the death of Mary of Burgundy in March 1482, drove Burgundy into the arms of France. On 23 December the two countries came to terms at the treaty of Arras, one of the conditions of which was that the dauphin should marry Maximilian's infant daughter, Margaret. Edward IV had lost his pension and his daughter Elizabeth her promised husband.

Last illness and death The apparent ineffectiveness of Edward's foreign policy in the closing years of his reign has led several commentators to suggest that the king was losing his grip on affairs. There is, however, no contemporary evidence that the king's health was failing. The apparent claim in the Canterbury records that Edward's health was giving grounds for anxiety in 1481–2 is an editorial interpolation. The king's notorious self-indulgence was indeed beginning to take a physical toll. Commines noted in 1475 that Edward (then aged thirty-three) was running to fat and looked less handsome than he had done five years previously, and the Crowland chronicler commented on his corpulence in later years. But the chronicler, significantly, coupled that comment with the assertion that there was (to the surprise of the royal circle) nothing wrong with the king's memory for detail. Certainly the king's final illness, which struck about Eastertide 1483, seems to have taken the political community by surprise.

The Crowland chronicle is noncommittal about the cause of Edward's death, which was due neither to old age nor to any identifiable disease that could not easily have been cured in a lesser man—perhaps a guarded way of saying, as French chroniclers did openly, that overindulgence in food and drink had hastened the king's demise. Mancini, by contrast, has a more circumstantial account of a chill contracted while boating on the river. The onset of illness was dramatic enough to give rise to reports that the king had died (which perhaps endorses Commines's verdict of an apoplexy), but Edward then lingered for about ten days, during which time he was able to add codicils to his will and express his wishes for the future governance of the kingdom. He died at the palace of Westminster on 9 April. After lying in state in St Stephen's Chapel, his body was taken to St George's Chapel, Windsor, where it was buried on 20 April in a chapel built for the purpose in the king's own lifetime, although his projected tomb of black marble, with a silver gilt effigy above a figure of death (presumably a cadaver), was never completed.

Family affairs Edward and Elizabeth Woodville had ten children: seven daughters and three sons. The eldest, *Elizabeth, was born in 1466 and remained Edward's heir until the birth of Edward in 1470. She was later to become the wife of Henry VII, but during her father's reign was betrothed first to George, the son of John Neville, earl of Northumberland, in 1470 as part of Edward's attempt to signal his favour for Neville, and then to the dauphin. Her sisters were Mary (1467–1482), Cecily (1469–1507), Margaret (who died shortly after her birth in 1472), Anne (1475–1510), Katherine (1479–1527), and Bridget (1480–1513). With the exception of Margaret and Bridget, all the sisters featured in Edward's diplomacy. Mary, after initially being held in reserve as a bride for the dauphin, was contracted to Frederick of Denmark in 1481. Cecily was to marry the heir of Scotland, and Anne was proposed as a bride for Philipp, the son of Margaret of Burgundy and Maximilian. None of these plans had come to anything at Edward's death, and Richard III, who undertook to find suitable husbands for his nieces, preferred to look for Englishmen of assured loyalty to himself. This was achieved only in the case of Cecily, who married Ralph Scrope, the brother of Baron Scrope of Masham. The marriage was annulled in 1486, to allow Cecily's marriage to Henry VII's half-uncle John, Viscount Welles. After his death Cecily married another Lincolnshire landowner, Thomas Kyme. But in general Henry VII seems to have been in no hurry to find husbands for his sisters-in-law, and it was not until 1495 that Anne and Katherine were married, to Thomas Howard, earl of Surrey, and William Courtenay, earl of Devon, respectively. Bridget, who never married, became a nun at Dartford.

The marriage of Edward IV's eldest son, Edward, was under discussion from 1476, and by 1481 negotiations for his marriage to Anne of Brittany were well advanced, although they had not been completed by the time of Edward IV's death. The only son of Edward IV to marry was *Richard, born in 1473, who married the Mowbray heir, Anne, in January 1478. Anne died in 1481, but Richard retained her estates: an arrangement that disinherited the two heirs general, John Howard and William Berkeley. The third son of Edward IV was George, who was born at Windsor in 1477 and died two years later.

Edward IV also had a number of extramarital relationships. According to Mancini, these were extremely numerous and short-lived, although he adds that the women were willing and Edward never resorted to force. This view of Edward as an insatiable predator may be coloured, as are some of Mancini's other claims, by a version of events deriving from Gloucester and his circle, which were set out more formally in the act of parliament of 1484 that asserted Richard's claim to the throne and presented Edward's womanizing as a political grievance. This may in turn have shaped the condemnation of Edward's behaviour that Sir Thomas More was later to put in the mouth of the duke of Buckingham. However, elsewhere in his history More offers a more detailed and less hostile account. According to this, Edward claimed three mistresses: the merriest, the wiliest, and the holiest in the realm. More only identified one, the merriest, who was Jane (actually Elizabeth) *Shore, the daughter of the London mercer John Lambert and the divorced wife of another mercer, William Shore, and he suggests that the others chose to remain nameless because of their higher social standing.

Edward is known to have had two illegitimate children. One, Arthur *Plantagenet, married Elizabeth, the daughter of John Grey, Viscount Lisle, in 1511 and was made Lord Lisle by Henry VIII in 1523. His mother is unknown, although one tradition claims her as a member of the Wayte family of Titchfield, Hampshire. Edward also had a daughter, Grace, who is mentioned as present at the deathbed of Elizabeth Woodville in 1492. Other families claimed royal bastards among their number. Isabella, the wife of John, brother of James, Lord Audley (d. 1497), was reputedly Edward's illegitimate daughter, as was Elizabeth, the wife of Sir Thomas Lumley, the son of George, Lord Lumley (d. 1507).

Reputation and significance Evaluations of Edward and his reign have fluctuated considerably over the years. Edward's contemporaries, at least among the political élite, seem to have been impressed by him, and early Tudor writers absorbed that tradition. Although no one was under any illusions about his self-indulgence (and the Crowland chronicler was evidently both relieved and surprised that he made an exemplary end), he was regarded as an able and far-sighted ruler. Much of this admiration surely derived from a perception that Edward had reasserted the authority of royal government after the disasters of the previous reign. For those who had experienced Henry VI's incompetence, and particularly the descent into civil war in the late 1450s, the sense that there was an effective king again must have been a considerable relief, and perhaps encouraged a readiness to allow that the ends justified the means. A similar view is apparent among Edward's more recent defenders, who regard his occasional ruthlessness as a necessary evil in the establishment of a 'new monarchy' (a concept first propounded by J. R. Green in 1878) which was a considerable improvement upon the old. An extension of this view sees Edward IV as a prototype Renaissance prince, whose appetites and cruelty matched those of his grandson *Henry VIII (who seems indeed to have resembled him physically).

This interpretation can shade into a much more hostile reading, derived ultimately from the French chroniclers, which sees Edward as debauched, vicious, greedy, and lazy, stirred to action only by a crisis. The difference between proponents of the two views is less the degree to which Edward's perceived vices are stressed, than an unwillingness on the part of Edward's critics to offset those vices with statesmanship. William Stubbs, who thought that Edward's regime marked a retrograde step after Lancastrian parliamentary monarchy, clearly felt that the needs of government were subordinated to,

rather than served by, Edward's cruelty and 'conspicuous talent for extortion'; a subordination made explicit in his comment that Edward enforced the law but only when that was compatible with 'the fortunes of his favourites or his own likes and dislikes' (Stubbs, 3.226). For later historians, by contrast, 'the ruthlessness of a Renaissance despot' becomes a desirable attribute when coupled with 'the strong-willed ability of a statesman' (Ross, 419).

Seeing Edward as a 'new' or proto-Renaissance monarch is, however, a false perspective. Edward's reign presents, and was no doubt intended to present, a contrast to the disastrous regime of Henry VI, but what Edward was doing was restoring the norms of medieval monarchy after their eclipse, not taking the opportunity to devise a new model of kingship. In a personal monarchy the character and aptitude of the individual king will necessarily colour his reign, but nothing in Edward's style of government constituted a break with accepted practice. Like any medieval king Edward essentially exercised his power through other people, and his readiness to enhance (or even create) and then employ the authority of trusted associates needs to be seen in that context. This meant that a good deal of government activity, for instance Edward's apparent concern to enforce his rights over such things as wardships and marriages, had to remain a matter of *ad hoc* negotiation, in which the king was inevitably involved. As a result, and in spite of his willingness to delegate local authority, Edward's own input remained essential. His achievements were thus vulnerable when he died, and would have been equally vulnerable had he simply lost his grip or his energies as he grew older.

Some writers have gone further, and argued that the Yorkist power base created by Edward was not only fragile but fundamentally flawed. According to this interpretation, developed most fully by C. D. Ross, Edward's willingness to promote his family and friends caused deep factional divisions within the Yorkist polity, particularly between the Woodvilles and others, so that the polity split along these fault lines as soon as Edward's hand was removed. It was thus Edward himself, on this reading, who was responsible for the dynastic collapse that so quickly followed his death, and his reign must be judged in the light of his failure to secure the accession of his heir.

While it is true that Edward's death did give rise to anxieties about the likely role of the Woodvilles, it is difficult to accept that hostility to the family was so profound that the deposition of Edward V was seen as preferable to allowing them influence—or even that political dislocation short of deposition was inevitable. In the immediate aftermath of Edward's death the political community seems, on the contrary, to have been anxious to preserve the *status quo*. It was the intervention of Edward's brother Gloucester that transformed the situation, and Edward IV can hardly be blamed for not foreseeing the dramatic deposition of a child king by his appointed protector. Significantly, an informed observer like the Crowland chronicler, although aware of Edward's failings (and of what was to happen after his death), was still prepared to describe the king's provisions for the future as wise.

Personality and achievement Edward IV was a successful warrior, whose victories in 1461 and 1471 were quite literally vital to his success. His repeated determination to seize the initiative, to move quickly and confront his enemies in the hope of taking them at a disadvantage, along with his readiness to take a lead on the battlefield itself, probably did as much as any tactical skills he may have possessed to enable him first to take the throne and later to recover it. Nevertheless, if Edward IV could be summed up in a single phrase, it would probably be that he was someone who liked to have all comfortable about him. His command to the sheriff of Devon in 1473 that 'ye sit still and be quiet' (Morgan, 17) could almost be the reign's leitmotif. At times this manifested itself as a preference for doing nothing. The Pastons' troubles over the Fastolf inheritance have been seen as an example of Edward's tendency to shrug his shoulders and let events take their course. His preferred mode of kingship was probably the careless affability he showed to overawed visitors to his court. But Edward's very accessibility is evidence that he knew how to say no. Although good-natured it is never suggested that he was gullible, and significantly 'counsel' is very rarely an issue in his reign. Apart from the criticism levelled by Warwick and Clarence at the circle around the king in 1469—which does not seem to have commanded general acceptance—no contemporaries made political capital out of accusations that Edward had favourites. The almost universal respect shown towards Edward's closest friend, William, Lord Hastings's, is as much a tribute to Edward's acumen as to Hastings's.

The king was his own master and did not hesitate to show it as necessary. When John (I) Paston ignored the king's commands Edward reportedly erupted: 'he made a gret a-vowe that if ye come not at the third commandement ye xulde dye therefore', although, characteristically, Edward added that he was not convinced by the accusation brought against Paston (Davis, 1.201). Such displays of temper should not be seen as empty words. Contemporaries testify to Edward's personal authority. One of his servants reportedly withdrew from court when Edward refused to recognize him in public, and retired to a nearby manor to await the king's orders. Consciousness of his power, coupled with the desire for things to be arranged for his own convenience, could make Edward overbearing and insensitive, as in his treatment of John Neville. His territorial reorderings of 1473–4 could be seen in the same light.

Comfort is not only a political concept. Edward liked luxury and was a great builder, most notably at Windsor, Greenwich, and Eltham. His projects were expensive, and contemporaries were under no illusions about Edward's desire to amass wealth (to an extent that some considered unbecoming in a king). Foreign commentators generally assumed that this meant a concomitant unwillingness to spend, and certainly Edward seems to have been eager to secure diplomatic marriages for his children at minimum cost to himself. But this should perhaps be seen, at least in part, as one facet of the marked hostility to the export of bullion which characterizes royal policy in this period. There is no suggestion that Edward was a miser in the usual sense of the word. On the contrary, he liked spending on himself and on his surroundings, and was well aware of the political significance of being seen in splendour. The absence of chamber accounts makes it difficult to reconstruct his environment in detail, but it can be glimpsed in the Crowland chronicler's description of Edward amid the splendour of his court at Christmas 1482. The latest fashions 'displayed the prince (who always stood out because of his elegant figure) like a new and incomparable spectacle set before the onlookers'. It was a royal court 'such as befitted a mighty kingdom' (Pronay and Cox, 149). ROSEMARY HORROX

Sources Chancery records · RotP, vols. 5–6 · GEC, Peerage · N. Pronay and J. Cox, eds., The Crowland chronicle continuations, 1459–1486 (1986) · The usurpation of Richard the third: Dominicus Mancinus ad Angelum Catonem de occupatione regni Anglie per Ricardum tercium libellus, ed. and trans. C. A. J. Armstrong, 2nd edn (1969) [Lat. orig., 1483, with parallel Eng. trans.] · N. Davis, ed., Paston letters and papers of the fifteenth century, 2 vols. (1971–6) · C. Ross, Edward IV (1974) · C. L. Scofield, The life and reign of Edward the Fourth, 2 vols. (1923) · R. Horrox, Richard III, a study of service, Cambridge Studies in Medieval Life and Thought, 4th ser., 11 (1989) · P. A. Johnson, Duke Richard of York, 1411–1460 (1988) · J. R. Lander, Crown and nobility, 1450–1509 (1976) · A. J. Pollard, ed., The Wars of the Roses (1995) · D. A. L. Morgan, 'The king's affinity in the polity of Yorkist England', TRHS, 5th ser., 23 (1973), 1–25 · A. Luders and others, eds., Statutes of the realm, 11 vols. in 12, RC (1810–28), vol. 2 · Memoirs of Phillipe de Commynes: the reign of Louis XI, 1461–83, trans. M. Jones, pbk edn (1972) · St Thomas More, The history of King Richard III, ed. R. S. Sylvester (1963), vol. 2 of The Yale edition of the complete works of St Thomas More · A. H. Thomas and I. D. Thornley, eds., The great chronicle of London (1938) · Recueil des croniques … par Jehan de Waurin, ed. W. Hardy and E. L. C. P. Hardy, 5 vols., Rolls Series, 39 (1864–91) · J. Warkworth, A chronicle of the first thirteen years of the reign of King Edward the Fourth, ed. J. O. Halliwell, CS, old ser., 10 (1839); repr. in Three chronicles of the reign of Edward IV (1988) · J. Bruce, ed., Historie of the arrivall of Edward IV in England, and the finall recoverye of his kingdomes from Henry VI, CS, 1 (1838); repr. in Three chronicles of the reign of Edward IV (1988) · P. Vergil, Polydore Vergil's 'English history', ed. H. Ellis, CS, 36 (1846) · W. Stubbs, The constitutional history of England in its origin and development, new edn, 3 vols. (1906) · J. R. Green, A short history of the English people (1888) · P. M. Kendall, Richard the third (1955) · R. A. Griffiths, 'Wales and the marches', Fifteenth-century England, 1399–1509, ed. S. B. Chrimes, C. D. Ross, and R. A. Griffiths (1972), 145–72

Archives PRO

Likenesses W. Neve, stained-glass window, c.1482, Canterbury Cathedral · oils, second version, 16th cent., NPG · P. Vanderbank, line engraving, pubd 1706 (after a portrait), BM, NPG · line engraving (after his great seal), BM; repr. in F. Sandford, Genealogical history of the kings of England (1677) · manuscript illumination, BL, Royal MS 19 E.v; repr. in Ross, Edward IV, pl. 2 · manuscript illumination (The dictes and sayings of the philosophers), LPL · manuscript illuminations, BL · oils, Royal Collection [see illus.]

Edward V (1470–1483), king of England and lord of Ireland, the eldest son of *Edward IV (1442–1483) and his queen, *Elizabeth (c.1437–1492), was born in Westminster sanctuary on 2 November 1470, during his father's exile and the readeption of Henry VI. He was baptized in the abbey, the abbot and prior of Westminster and Lady Scrope standing

Edward V (1470–1483), stained glass, c.1482

sponsor. After Edward IV had regained the kingdom, his son was created prince of Wales and earl of Chester on 26 June 1471, and on 3 July in the parliament chamber the lords spiritual and temporal took an oath of allegiance to him as heir to the throne. On 8 July the rule of his household and lands until he reached the age of fourteen was entrusted to a council headed by his mother, his paternal uncles the dukes of Clarence and Gloucester, and his maternal uncle Anthony Woodville, Earl Rivers. He received grants of the principality of Wales, the counties of Chester and Flint, and the duchy of Cornwall on 17 July, but enjoyed none of the revenues until November 1472, when the issues of the principality and of Chester and Flint were assigned to him. On 20 February 1473 his council was enlarged and given full powers to act in the prince's name, and on 23 September ordinances were drawn up for the good rule of the prince and his household. On 10 November John Alcock, bishop of Rochester, was given

responsibility for the prince's education and made president of his council, and Rivers was appointed his governor. The prince was named keeper of the realm on 20 June 1475, during the king's absence in France, and as a preliminary he was knighted on 18 April and made a knight of the Garter on 15 May, though a stall had been reserved for him since 1472.

From 1476 Edward's council, based at Ludlow, developed into the main agent of royal authority in Wales and the marches. At the same time the prince's territorial interests were gradually expanded to embrace the lands of the earldoms of March and Pembroke. The prince was not permanently based at Ludlow. In May 1481 he went with the king to Sandwich to review the fleet which John, Lord Howard, was leading against Scotland, and early in 1483 he was due to visit Canterbury with the queen, but an outbreak of measles in the city led to the cancellation of this visit. Various marriages were suggested for him. In 1476–7 a match with the Spanish infanta, Isabella, the daughter of Ferdinand and Isabella, was under discussion, and other suggestions included the daughter of Galeazzo Sforza, duke of Milan, and the sister of Maximilian, archduke of Austria and duke of Burgundy. In 1480 negotiations began for his marriage to Anne, the heir of Brittany, and the marriage treaty was ratified by Edward IV and François, duke of Brittany, in 1481.

Edward was at Ludlow when his father died at Windsor on 9 April 1483. Edward IV had apparently intended his son to be crowned immediately, and the coronation was fixed for 4 May. There were, however, anxieties about the degree of influence likely to be wielded by the Woodville family, who were already influential within the territories of the prince and his brother. As it made its way towards London the prince's party was intercepted at Stony Stratford by Richard, duke of Gloucester, who took possession of the prince and arrested his leading companions, including the prince's uncle Rivers and half-brother Richard Grey, claiming that the queen's family were planning to seize power by force. When news of these events reached London, the queen took sanctuary with her younger son, *Richard, duke of York, and her daughters.

Gloucester entered London with the prince on 4 May and was shortly afterwards named protector during the prince's minority—a move which seems to have met with general acceptance. For the next six weeks business continued smoothly, with preparations in train for the coronation (now postponed to 22 June) and for the meeting of parliament on 25 June. On 10 June, however, Gloucester wrote north for reinforcements, and on 13 May arrested a number of Edward IV's leading allies at a council meeting at the Tower of London, and executed one of them: the dead king's close friend William, Lord Hastings. With hindsight, this marked the beginning of Richard's moves to take the throne for himself, but at the time the possibility of such an unprecedented step seems not to have been generally believed. On 16 June Cardinal Bourchier was apparently acting in good faith when he persuaded Queen Elizabeth to surrender her second son, who joined his brother in the Tower. Later that day Gloucester sent letters postponing the coronation again to 9 November and cancelling the intended parliament. From this point government in Edward V's name began to wind down, as men awaited the beginning of a new regime. On 22 June Dr Ralph Shaw publicized Gloucester's claim to the throne in a sermon preached at Paul's Cross, and on 26 June the duke seated himself on king's bench in Westminster Hall and began his reign as *Richard III.

The speed with which Gloucester acted precluded any expression of dissent until after his coronation on 6 July, but later that month a conspiracy to rescue the princes was uncovered. The men put on trial for their part in the plot were insignificant figures, although there were undoubtedly more important figures in the background who wished to see Edward V restored. By September, however, the rebels were promoting another candidate for the throne—Henry Tudor—which strongly suggests that the princes were by this stage believed to be dead. Dominic Mancini notes that fears for their safety were being expressed even before Richard's coronation, with men bursting into tears when they spoke of the young king. He also preserves the evidence of the princes' physician, John Argentine, that Edward V anticipated his death and prepared for it with daily confession and penance. The princes' fate continues to arouse controversy. Chronicle accounts of their murder at the hands of Sir James Tyrell are inevitably speculative, and little light has been shed on their death by analysis of the bones found in the Tower in 1674 and assumed to be those of the princes. The most plausible explanation for their undoubted disappearance is that they were murdered on the orders of Richard III, late in the summer of 1483, to try to pre-empt a rising in their favour. ROSEMARY HORROX

Sources Chancery records · RotP · C. L. Scofield, The life and reign of Edward the Fourth, 2 vols. (1923) · C. Ross, Edward IV (1974) · R. Horrox, Richard III, a study of service, Cambridge Studies in Medieval Life and Thought, 4th ser., 11 (1989) · R. A. Griffiths, 'Wales and the marches', Fifteenth-century England, 1399–1509, ed. S. B. Chrimes, C. D. Ross, and R. A. Griffiths (1972), 145–72 · D. E. Lowe, 'Patronage and politics: Edward IV, the Wydevills, and the council of the prince of Wales, 1471–83', BBCS, 29 (1980–82), 545–73 · N. Orme, 'The education of Edward V', BIHR, 57 (1984), 119–30 · Canterbury city accounts · The usurpation of Richard the third: Dominicus Mancinus ad Angelum Catonem de occupatione regni Anglie per Ricardum tercium libellus, ed. and trans. C. A. J. Armstrong, 2nd edn (1969) [Lat. orig., 1483, with parallel Eng. trans.]

Archives PRO

Likenesses stained-glass window, c.1482, Canterbury Cathedral [see illus.] · stained-glass window, c.1482, St Giles Church, Little Malvern, Worcestershire · manuscript illumination (The dictes and sayings of the philosophers; with Edward IV), LPL

Edward VI (1537–1553), king of England and Ireland, was born at Hampton Court Palace on 12 October 1537, the eve of the feast of the translation of St Edward the Confessor—he was named after the royal saint—the first and only legitimate son of *Henry VIII (1491–1547). His mother, Jane Seymour [see Jane (1508/9–1537)], was Henry's third wife.

Early years, 1537–1544 Jane's rapid ascent to queenship in 1535–6, usually seen as part of the intrigues against Anne Boleyn, was assisted by her own family background and

Edward VI (1537–1553), attrib. Guillim Scrots [original, c.1550]

station at court. Her father, Sir John Seymour (1474–1536) of Wolf Hall, Savernake Forest, Wiltshire, was a knight of the body who stood high in royal favour; his connections and experience enabled him to place Jane as maid of honour to both Katherine of Aragon (from 1529) and Anne Boleyn (1532). Her mother Margery, the daughter of Sir Henry Wentworth of Nettlested, Suffolk, carried the blood royal, by virtue of her descent from Edward III's third son, Lionel, duke of Clarence. This meant that Jane Seymour and Henry VIII were related as fifth cousins, and so to enable their marriage on 19 May 1536 Archbishop Thomas Cranmer issued a dispensation 'in the third and third degrees of affinity' (Fraser, 257). Such a degree of affinity normally described not fifth but second cousins or those so related through a sexual liaison. Had one of Jane's second cousins been Henry's mistress? Henry was taking no chances. The announcement of Edward's birth reflected the same concern for legality: it was a circular letter made to look as if Jane herself had written it within hours of delivering 'a Prince conceived in moost Laufull Matrimony betwene my lord the Kinges Maiestie and us'

(Edward VI, *Remains*, 1.xxiii). After more than thirty years of what Henry had thought was mostly unlawful matrimony, the king had his heir, and he wept with joy when he first held the boy.

The prince whom the people called England's treasure was baptized by Cranmer on 15 October in Henry's newly redecorated chapel at Hampton Court. It was a ceremony accorded the utmost importance; a contemporary drawing, probably by a herald, preserves a unique visual record of the magnificence of the specially staged setting (College of Arms, London, MS M6, fol. 82, *v*). Despite plague-induced restrictions, those who made their way to the sound of trumpets in torchlit procession at midnight from the queen's bedchamber to the chapel and back probably numbered between three and four hundred—courtiers, clerics, officers of state, and foreign envoys. In train came the godfathers, Cranmer and the third duke of Norfolk; the godmother, Princess Mary [*see* Mary I (1516–1558)]; Gertrude Courtenay, marchioness of Exeter, who cradled Edward; and among others, the queen's brothers, who were to play prominent roles in the next reign: Edward *Seymour, earl of Hertford, who carried Princess Elizabeth [*see* Elizabeth I (1533–1603)] (who bore the chrism); and Hertford's brother Sir Thomas *Seymour, who held the canopy over the baby's head. At the baptism Edward was proclaimed duke of Cornwall, a dignity to which he was entitled at birth; he was never formally proclaimed prince of Wales.

On 24 October the queen died, probably not of a puerperal infection, as is commonly supposed, but of a massive 'naturall laxe', or haemorrhage, most likely caused by the retention of parts of the placenta in her womb—an oversight of the royal physicians who had banned experienced midwives from the delivery. Henry's son, however, was flourishing. The news that 'Our Prince … is in good health, and sucketh like a child of his puissance' was so important that Thomas Wriothesley, mindful of the political implications of his master's virility, conveyed it immediately to Henry's ambassadors at Paris where the king had secretly begun looking for a new consort (Edward VI, *Remains*, 1.xxv). Holbein's portrait of Edward of December 1538 or January 1539 (National Gallery of Art, Washington, DC; the preparatory drawing, Royal Collection) was intended to project a picture of the same princely vitality to a German audience at Cleves, where by that time Henry was negotiating for the hand of Anne, the duke's sister. Edward at fourteen months is shown brilliantly attired in red velvet and gold brocade holding a golden rattle, a lively, beautiful child whose 'maturity … has quite naturally been overstated' (Rowlands, 147).

The same image also bears a Latin inscription composed by Sir Richard Morrison, special envoy to Cleves: 'Little one, imitate your father and be the heir of his virtue, the world contains nothing greater … Surpass him … and none will ever surpass you' (Chapman, 44–5), words doubtless expressing, beneath the bombast, what Henry expected of Edward. Of those first charged officially with his upbringing, Edward later remembered that until he was six he 'was brought up … among the women' (Edward VI, *Chronicle*, 3). They included Margaret Bryan, Sir Francis Bryan's mother, who became 'lady mistress' of Edward's nursery in May 1538 (the post she had held in Princess Elizabeth's household); Sybil Penne, the wife of John Penne (a groom of the chamber), who became Edward's principal dry nurse in October 1538; and various 'rockers', two of whom, Jane Russell and Bridgett Forster, were receiving pensions as late as 1552. The royal nursery was peripatetic, moving to Greenwich with the court for Christmas 1537; to the king's hunting-lodge at Royston in the spring of 1538, where the townsfolk, according to an eyewitness, watched Henry 'with much mirth and joy, dallying with the Prince in his arms a long space, and so holding him in a window to the sight and comfort of all' (Chapman, 40); then on to Havering in Essex, where the air was thought healthier; thence to Waltham, Ashridge, and Enfield or Richmond in turn. Concerns in March 1539 for the security of Edward's person and the hygienic conditions of his residences prompted Henry personally to issue obsessively detailed instructions for the care of his 'moost precyous joyelle' to newly named officers of the boy's household: Sir William Sidney, chamberlain; Sir John Cornwallis, steward; a vice-chamberlain, possibly Sir Edward Baynton; and John Ryther, cofferer (Edward VI, *Remains*, 1.xxviii). Lady Bryan and Mrs Penne (whose sister was Sidney's wife) were reappointed, as were four female 'rockers'; other personnel included a physician, Dr George Owen, who also attended Edward on his deathbed in 1553, and a dean of the chapel, Dr Richard Cox, headmaster of Eton and canon of Westminster, who doubled as the prince's tutor from 1540. For the prince's amusement there was also a company of players.

Edward's first lessons with Cox were interrupted in October and November 1541 when he caught malaria at Hampton Court. According to the French ambassador, Henry hurriedly summoned 'all the doctors in the country' (Loach, 11), including his own physician, Dr William Butts, who asked the four-year-old patient if he 'felt any disposition to vomit'. Edward's answer—'Go away, fool'—signalled a youthful stubbornness that would later become ferocious (Chapman, 52). In fact, as Lady Bryan had observed, Edward was generally 'mery' and 'marvelowss plesantly desposed'. One night at Hunsdon, she said, 'The mensterels played, and hes Grace dawansed and playd so wantownly that he cowld not stend stel, and was as fol of prety toyes as ever I saw chyld in my lyf' (Edward VI, *Remains*, 1.xxxvii–xxxviii). Apart from his sisters, who generally shared his company—he is said to have favoured Mary, twenty years his senior, to Elizabeth, who was four years older—his dearest companion then was Jane Dormer, Sidney's granddaughter, 'my Jane', as Edward called her. In her adulthood Jane fondly remembered the day she spent with Edward at Ashridge in 1544, reading and dancing and playing at games; when she lost to him at cards, he consoled her with the reply: 'Now, Jane, your King is gone, I shall be good enough for you' (ibid., 1.xl). At Ashridge Edward also met Sidney's fourteen-year-old son, Henry, who later became one of his closest friends. By the early 1540s Edward's importance as royal heir found expression in the grandiose language of Tudor diplomacy: his suitability for marriage had already made him 'the greatest person in Christendom' (Fraser, 384). By the treaty of Greenwich of July 1543 he was betrothed to Mary, queen of Scots, then seven months old, but this diplomatic endeavour failed, and the consequences—war with Scotland and France—burnt themselves into his memory, as his later letters testify.

Early schooling Henry VIII's marriage to Katherine Parr in July 1543 decisively affected Edward's life, both emotionally and educationally. Queen Katherine brought Edward and his sisters into the royal household as members of an intimate family, providing Edward especially with an affection and attention that found endearing reflection in his frequent letters to her. This correspondence revealed 'a warmth and liveliness not elsewhere displayed': he addressed her familiarly as '*Mater Charissima*', 'my dearest mother', for she held 'the chief place in my heart' (Fraser, 385). Katherine's deep, supportive interest in Edward's schooling struck a grateful, responsive chord. In 1546, at the age of eight, he thanked her for directing 'unto me your loving and tender letters which do give me much comfort and encouragement to go forward in such things wherein your grace beareth me on hand that I am already entered' (James, 141).

The 'things' referred to were the formal lessons that began on the eve of Henry VIII's invasion of France. Before his departure in July 1544 Henry named Katherine regent-general of England and gave her charge of Edward's household, which he now put on a wholly new footing by disbanding the nursery and naming new officers. Sir Richard Page, a former sheriff of Surrey who had been vice-chamberlain to Henry Fitzroy and had married Hertford's mother-in-law, became Edward's chamberlain in place of Sidney. Sidney replaced Cornwallis as steward, and Sir Jasper Horsey, Anne of Cleves's former steward, became chief gentleman of Edward's newly formed privy chamber. Henry also named John Cheke, regius professor of Greek in Cambridge, to be 'a suppliment to mr. Cox' for Edward's 'bettere instruccion' (Edward VI, *Remains*, 1.xxxix). In practice Cheke became Edward's chief preceptor, Cox remaining as tutor and almoner. Joining Cheke was Roger Ascham, Princess Elizabeth's tutor, and Anthony Cooke, a learned courtier, who continued to assist Cheke upon Cox's retirement in 1550.

Cox, Cheke, Ascham, and Cooke were Cambridge-educated humanists zealously committed to evangelical reform, and under their influence Edward was brought up a protestant. Cheke, the key appointee, learned of his preferment on 10 June 1544; according to Strype, Henry entrusted to him the supervision of Edward's education and religious instruction on the recommendation of Dr William Butts, an evangelical whom Cheke likened to both a 'patron' and father. Cheke had also been the pupil and protégé of George Day, bishop of Chichester, Queen Katherine's religious mentor, friend, and almoner. Katherine showed Cheke special favour; the two are said to have been 'on particularly close terms', so much so that Ascham once confided to Cheke, 'I do not believe [the queen] will do anything without consulting you' (James, 138–9). Katherine later implied that God had made her Henry's queen in order that she might help further the evangelical cause. In the light of what was to follow, the importance of Katherine's support of Cheke's efforts as royal tutor can hardly be overstated.

Cheke's responsibilities also included 'the diligent teaching of such children as be appointed to attend' upon Edward (Edward VI, *Remains*, 1.lvi). Joining Edward in the royal classroom at various times while he was prince and king were some specially selected schoolfellows, including: his cousins Edward and Henry Seymour (Hertford's sons); Henry Sidney, whose father, William, was successively chamberlain and steward of the prince's household; John, Lord Lumley; Henry, Lord Strange, son and heir of the third earl of Derby; Henry, Lord Hastings, afterwards third earl of Huntingdon; James Butler, tenth earl of Ormond; Henry and Charles Brandon, the duke of Suffolk's sons (whose deaths in an epidemic in 1551 are said to have affected Edward greatly); and the prince's favourite, Barnaby Fitzpatrick, eldest son of the baron of Upper Ossory, with whom Edward shared an affectionate correspondence in his last years.

Between 1544 and 1547 Edward acquired under Cheke's tutelage the foundations of the sort of humanist education that Vives and Erasmus had prescribed for the ideally trained Christian prince. In December 1544 he began reading Erasmus's Latin editions of Aesop and Cato; by January 1546, according to Cox, he had memorized almost four books of Cato, Aesop's fables, 'things of the Bible', and Vives's *Satellitium*, originally written for Princess Mary. (He also owned copies of Vives's *De officio marito* and *De institutione faeminae Christianae*.) Using Erasmus's textbook, *De conscribendus epistolis*, he learned to compose formal letters in Latin by writing to Cranmer, Cox, the queen, Henry VIII, and his sisters. Copies of forty-three of these, possibly in Ascham's hand, survive from the period between 4 March 1545 and 19 September 1547 (BL, Harley MS 5087, fols. 1–18), and reveal a precocious young student's self-conscious exhibition of new learning: quotations from Vives, the classics, and scripture embellish his schoolboy salutations. He exhibited, said Cox, an extraordinary 'towardness in learning'; at Hatfield on 12 October 1546 when he began 'to learne Frenche' with Jean Belmain, a Calvinist refugee (and Cheke's nephew by marriage), it was 'with a great facilité even at hys first entre' (Edward VI, *Remains*, 1.lxxviii). He grasped 'the thinge taught hym by his schoolemasters' with 'such a spirit of capacitye', said another observer, that it was a 'wonder' to behold (ibid., 1.lxxxi).

Accession and coronation When Henry VIII died at 2 a.m. on 28 January 1547 Hertford removed Edward from Ashridge to Enfield where Princess Elizabeth was living, and there on the 29th informed him that he was king. Edward and his sister clung to each other, sobbing. His reception into London on the 31st, however, enthralled him; 'hys grace hadde great felycyte', said an eyewitness, at the roaring salute of 'a greate shotte' of guns from ships in the Thames (S. Antiquaries, Lond., MS 123, fol. 1r). Following tradition, he resided at the Tower until his coronation, which was fixed for Sunday 20 February. Meanwhile, on 31 January, Edward's councillors recognized Hertford as lord protector of the realm and governor of the king's person, 'because he was the King's uncle on his mother's side', as Edward later wrote (Edward VI, *Chronicle*, 4). On 6 February Hertford knighted Edward, and the king in turn knighted the lord mayor. On 16 February at the Tower, Edward bestowed new titles on several key councillors: Hertford became duke of Somerset, John Dudley, earl of Warwick, and Thomas Seymour, Baron Seymour of Sudeley. On the 19th, with hundreds of horsemen he rode for five hours in a grand procession to Westminster Palace, showing himself to his people, as protocol demanded, in a brilliant attire of white velvet and cloth of silver and gold, the whole thick-set with patterned knots of diamonds and pearls. A large drawing of 1785 (now at the Society of Antiquaries in London) based on a mural of 1547-8 commissioned by Edward's master of the horse, Sir Anthony Browne, provides a unique record of this procession winding its way through the streets of London; it shows the king on horseback beneath a fringed canopy, flanked by the protector and Browne. The pageants devised for the procession, described as 'perhaps the most tawdry on record' (Anglo, 294), recycled those written in 1432 by John Lydgate for another boy-king, Henry VI, with the difference that Edward's extolled Henry VIII's reform of religious 'abuses', a reformation which had freed God's 'Trewth' from heathen 'idolatrye' (Edward VI, *Remains*, 1.ccxci). Iconographically, Edward's tableaux also projected the crown's 'imperial' status, soon to be invoked by reformists; Edward himself preferred the airborne antics of a professional tumbler, laughing 'right hartely' when the acrobat 'fell uppon a fetherbed and a mattrasse' after sliding headfirst down a cable from the top of St Paul's (S. Antiquaries, Lond., MS 123, fol. 24r). At Westminster Abbey on the 20th, 'with the orgayns goinge, the quere singinge & the trumpettes' blaring in the battlements, Somerset and Cranmer together placed three crowns successively on Edward's head: St Edward's crown, the imperial crown of England, and a third made especially for him (Corpus Christi College, Cambridge, MS 105, p. 238). Walking beneath a canopy of crimson silk and cloth of gold topped by silver bells, the boy-king wore a crimson satin robe trimmed with gold silk lace costing £118 16s. 8d. and a pair of 'Sabatons' of cloth of gold. The service itself followed the Latin *ordo*, but in view of its length it was modified to accommodate Edward's age; the changes allowed Edward an occasional rest, and for his presentation to the people, he was carried about the stage in a 'litill cheyre' of crimson velvet (BL, Add. MS 9069, fol. 34v).

Of greater moment were Cranmer's and Somerset's revisions of the coronation oath, which, contrary to what has hitherto been believed, is shown by contemporary sources to have been changed in ways advertising how its amenders expected to use the crown's imperial jurisdiction over the church—the royal supremacy—to advance religious reform. The principle underlying the changes was set out in a proclamation of 31 January 1547 announcing Edward's accession, the first known proclamation in England to deal with the royal succession. As Edward had come to the throne 'fully invested … in the crown imperial of this realm', nothing was needed to confirm his authority. He was supreme head of the church by divine, not human, agency, or as Cranmer expressed it to Edward in an unprecedented coronation speech, 'Your Majesty is God's Vicegerent, and Christ's Vicar within your own Dominions' (Strype, *Cranmer*, 2.144-5). The new oath thus became a bulwark of the supremacy, not terms to which Edward VI could be held accountable. Gone were the historic promises by which kings protected the clergy and upheld law and liberty; it was for the crown to decide what in future constituted law and liberty, and for church, parliament, and people to give their consent. The oath thus gave the evangelicals the legal opening they needed to launch their reformation. Like Cranmer's speech, the coronation masques that followed were shot through with anti-papal invective: the war with Antichrist had begun.

Somerset's protectorate, 1547-1549 Full power and authority during Edward VI's minority—that is until his eighteenth birthday—supposedly fell to a council composed of the sixteen executors of his father's will, but even before Henry VIII's death, Somerset and the king's secretary, Sir William Paget, had decided to ignore the will, which Paget himself had helped Henry compose, and arrange for Somerset's preferment as protector of the realm and governor of Edward's person. The executors agreed to the move on 31 January 1547, their support secured by a shower of titles, offices, and rewards. Royal letters patent of 12 March 1547 confirmed Somerset in the offices of protector and governor, empowering him to direct the government and name a new, expanded board to accommodate those who, like his brother, had been left off the council of executors. But Sudeley envied his brother his position as Edward's governor, an office which Warwick duplicitously encouraged Sudeley to seek, saying the council would support his bid for it. Somerset rebuffed this request, angering Sudeley even more by appointing his own wife's stepbrother, Sir Michael Stanhope, to be chief gentleman, or head officer, of Edward's privy chamber (by 18 August 1548). As such, Stanhope became the king's *de facto* governor, for he controlled access to Edward's apartments and his privy purse. Assisting Stanhope in the privy chamber was Sir Richard Page, the duchess's stepfather. Sudeley, himself a gentleman of the privy chamber and lord high admiral, so resented Stanhope's and Page's authority that he refused to join Somerset's invasion of Scotland in September 1547. Somerset appeased him by appointing him one of Edward's custodians in his absence, an opportunity Sudeley used to curry favour with others close to the king, including Cheke and Sir Thomas Wroth (a gentleman usher), whom Somerset on his return temporarily suspended from office, suspecting, wrongly, that they had plotted to make Sudeley the boy's governor. Furious that Somerset had not appointed him to have 'the gou[ver]nament of the king his maiestie before so dronken a sole as Master Page' (Hatfield House,

Cecil papers, 150, fol. 104), on 24 December 1547 Sudeley forced Somerset to secure additional letters patent limiting his tenure as governor to the king's pleasure, not (as in the earlier patent) to Edward's minority. Sixty-two peers signed the new instrument.

In 1548 Sudeley sought to win Edward's affection and gain acceptance as his intimate adviser, not an implausible outcome, given the admiral's charm and bonhomie, so unlike Somerset's dour reserve. With 'a pryvye key', Sudeley gained access to the king's private apartments from the privy garden at Westminster, and with the help of John Fowler, a groom, and others whom he had bribed, he slipped into the 'ynner gallery' next to Edward's bedchamber at night and from there passed notes and pocket money to the boy. Edward denied Sudeley's claim that Somerset kept him a 'beggarly' king; 'he [Sudeley] said that I was toe bashful in my maters and that I wold not speake for my right. I said I was wel enoughe' (Bodl. Oxf., MS Ashmole 1729, fol. 9). Sudeley's nocturnal appearances backstairs—he would enter the 'privie buttrey & drynke there alone' or hang about, 'the king being at stoole', as Fowler remembered (BL, Harley MS 249, fol. 29ff.)—prompted Stanhope by August 1548 to put a special watch on all doors leading into the king's privy chamber in order to prevent Sudeley's clandestine entry. One night Sudeley found the door to Edward's bedchamber bolted; enraged, he shot dead the king's barking dog. The object of this reckless game, as Sudeley himself said, was to persuade Edward to bear 'the honor & rule of his oun doinges' (PRO, SP 10/6, fol. 33) by terminating Somerset's governorship in a writing under the king's own signature. Controlling the production of letters in Edward's hand was one of the cornerstones of Somerset's authority. Somerset discovered how close he had come to losing that control when Fowler revealed that in response to a letter he had carried from Sudeley to the king, Edward had commanded him to 'go into the litle house within where he dyned & to take the writing that lay underneth the carpet in the window there' and deliver it secretly to the admiral (BL, Harley MS 249, fol. 29ff.). Although the 'writing' was innocent enough, Somerset found such correspondence intolerable. Two of the three judges whose opinion he sought in the matter 'saied that his [Sudeley's] falte was not treason' (BL, Add. MS 48023, fol. 35); seeking to avoid a trial, Somerset none the less arranged for Sudeley's attainder in parliament and execution (20 March 1549) on fabricated charges of treason.

Somerset coldly termed his brother's beheading a matter of 'indifferent justice'; others said it foreshadowed the protector's own fall. Paget thought Somerset's decision to invade Scotland in September 1547 marked the beginning of his ruin. Though cloaked at first in the rhetoric of godly union, advancing a vision of 'thempire of greate Briteigne', Somerset's strategy sprang from proposals to garrison Scotland first advanced in 1543 and 1545; Edward's accession gave him the chance to implement his plan. But victory at Pinkie (10 September 1547) triggered war with France, and Somerset's desperate measures to pay for garrisons in both Scotland and Boulogne—debasement, sale of the chantries, and a tax on sheep—fell so far short of what was needed, that by September 1549 he had nearly bankrupted the king.

Protestant Reformation and the fall of Somerset Hailing Edward at his coronation as 'a second Josias', Cranmer had urged the king 'to see Idolatry destroyed' and 'Images removed' (Strype, *Cranmer*, 2.145). In July 1547 the council banned candles and shrines, and on 28 February 1548, images in stained-glass, wood, and stone. Within two years the rich pictorial heritage of medieval Christianity had largely disappeared, as windows were reglazed and church walls limed, and along with it such aspects of popular culture, civic and religious, as processions, mystery plays, pageants on holy days, maypoles, and church-ales. The chantries went dark, and with them the schools they had supported. Although this did not constitute the educational disaster once thought, neither was Edward VI a great patron or founder of new schools. Against a background of discontent Archbishop Cranmer produced a uniform vernacular service of worship in the first Book of Common Prayer (1549), whose enforced use sparked armed resistance in the west country in June, followed by numerous other revolts elsewhere. These uprisings signalled a breakdown of trust between Somerset and the local gentry on whom law and order depended. The protector's initial attempts to appease the commons backfired; to his colleagues, the royal pardons he issued smacked of an intolerable 'leniency'. In fact Somerset did not baulk at using force against Edward's subjects; the protestant myth of the 'good duke' was invented by William Harrison only in 1587. Somerset's problem was that the rebellions drew off soldiers he had intended for Scotland, and the cost of suppressing the revolts, when added to the charges in the north, finally outstripped his ability to pay his cash-hungry armies. When the French declared war the game was up: Somerset lacked men and money enough to foot operations on three fronts at once.

The rebellions of 1549, arguably sixteenth-century England's greatest crisis, dealt the country a staggering demographic blow, a loss of life proportionally the equivalent of about 200,000 deaths today. John Cheke's reaction to these 'tumults', his *Hurt of Sedicion* (1549), has been described as an 'odd combination of ferocity and fatherliness' (Chapman, 158); as such it stands in striking contrast to the king's own, coolly factual account of events in his 'Chronicle'. The dry, objective tone of Edward's version of the *coup d'état* of October 1549, penned in 1550, is even more remarkable, as he participated in some of the events described. Edward was in Somerset's custody at Hampton Court with Cranmer, Paget, Smith, and Cecil on 5 October when the protector heard that the:

> Council, about nineteen of them, were gathered in London, thinking to meet with [him] and to make him amend some of his disorders. He, fearing his state, … commanded the armor to be brought down out of the armory of Hampton Court, about 500 harnesses, to arm both his and my men withal, the gates of the house to be rempared, [and] people to be raised.

Although, as Edward recorded it, 'people came abundantly to the house' (Edward VI, *Chronicle*, 17), at 9 or 10 that night the protector suddenly decided to convey him to Windsor Castle, on the pretext, quite false, that the lords in London were plotting his death. One of those present later explained why Somerset's stand at Windsor collapsed so quickly: there were but 'iiij. tune of wynne and no great quantetie of Beare for suche a company' (Malkiewicz, 607), and when Edward, who had caught a cold, likened the castle to a 'prison' ('here be no galleries nor no gardens to walke in'), Paget and Cranmer persuaded the duke to negotiate a surrender (Edward VI, *Remains*, 1.cxxxi). On 11 October Somerset was arrested, and his adherents and servants removed from the king's household; two days later his offices were abolished.

Somerset's transparent use of Edward as a means of self-protection brought immediate changes in procedures for the king's 'suertie'. The first occurred officially on 15 October when Warwick 'procured by the meanes of the Archebusshoppe of Canterbury great frendes abowte the king' (BL, Add. MS 48126, fol. 15v): the marquess of Northampton, the earl of Arundel, and lords St John, Russell, and Wentworth, all councillors who with Warwick collectively replaced Somerset as governor. Additionally, four knights replaced Stanhope as 'principal' gentlemen in the privy chamber: Sir Andrew Dudley (Warwick's brother), Sir Edward Rogers, Sir Thomas Darcy, and Sir Thomas Wroth. As Edward's bodyguards, they slept armed, in rotation, on pallets outside the king's bedchamber. All had been Warwick's allies against Somerset, but in January 1550 Arundel and Rogers were dismissed for what Edward called 'crimes of suspicion': 'plucking down … bolts and locks at Westminster' and giving 'my stuff away' (Edward VI, *Chronicle*, 19). In fact Arundel had joined a plot aimed at Warwick's destruction; the conspirators included Thomas Wriothesley, the earl of Southampton, and other conservatives in religion. When Warwick heard of these intrigues he moved swiftly to augment his own and Edward's security. The result was the virtual militarization of Edward's court. Northampton was given command of sixty horse and men-of-arms, a newly created contingent of guardsmen attached to the privy chamber. Darcy became vice-chamberlain and captain of the pike-bearing yeomen of the guard whose numbers were doubled to 200. Edward, Baron Clinton, a professional soldier, was made a councillor and gentleman of the privy chamber at the head of a new force of 600 handpicked 'footmen' from the Boulogne garrison, 200 of whom were to 'attende on the Kinges person' as specially armed yeomen 'extraordinary' (Hoak, 'Privy chamber', 93). Finally, to protect Warwick and the king from a counter-coup, an élite (if short-lived) force of 850 mounted 'gendarmes' was created in February 1551, the nucleus of England's first standing army.

The education of a king King Edward's powers of observation and acuteness of mind, so evident in his account of the coup, revealed themselves most fully in his schooling as king. Building on the foundation of his earlier lessons, Cheke developed for him a curriculum in the classics based, according to Cecil, on the one Cheke had designed for St John's College, Cambridge, where Cheke had been Cecil's tutor. The core of this curriculum has been reconstructed for the period January 1548 to June 1552 from Edward's four surviving notebooks (BL, Add. MS 4724 and Arundel MS 510; Bodl. Oxf., MS Autogr. e.2 and MS Bodley 899); together they have been described as constituting 'the most complete record extant of a sixteenth-century humanist education' (Needham, 1.176). Edward began in early 1547 with Cicero's *Epistolae familiares* and Justin's Latin summary of Greek history, for which he had chorographical indices given to him at new year 1547 by Peter Olivarius, a Spanish humanist. During 1548 he copied phrases and sentences from Cicero's *Offices*, *De amicitia*, *Paradoxa Stoicorum*, and the *Tusculan Disputations*, all the while practising his italic penmanship under Ascham's instruction. For this Edward had the 1548 edition of Giovanni Battista Palatino's guide to italic, the earliest known use of such a writing book in England. In April 1548 he began composing moral essays based on aphorisms, 'one of the many preliminary exercises, or *progymnasmata*, taught in the ancient Greek schools of rhetoric' (ibid., 1.187). By 1549 Cheke had also introduced him to the dialectic, for by then Edward was turning his notes on Cicero's Catlinarian orations, for example, into his own inventive arguments in Latin. In these original disputations 'the language of the young logician is everywhere apparent': here, obviously, was a 'serious and intelligent mind at work' (ibid., 1.195–6).

Cheke had introduced Edward to Greek by mid-1549, for by then Edward possessed David Tavelegus's unique Greek grammar (1547) and Adrianus Junius's 'greke dictionarie' for which Edward paid the author £40 from his privy purse 'for dedicatinge' it to him (PRO, E 351/2932). Edward converted his newly learned Greek vocabulary into Latin, and vice versa. Recent events provided him with material for this exercise. Thus when he quoted Euripides in Greek on the evils of war, he cited examples in Latin from Henry VIII's wars in France and Scotland. At Christmas 1549 his Greek text was Aristotle's *Ethics* (the *Rhetoric* came later), and in January 1550 he was giving the Greek equivalents for words gleaned from Cicero's *De finibus*. As he followed a systematic course of reading in ever-more challenging texts—what Cheke (as quoted by Ascham) called the 'journey' through classical authors—he used his Greek–Latin word lists to compose original declamations in both languages. These declamations he delivered orally on Sundays, keeping to a rigorous, alternating schedule of 'Greek weeks' and 'Latin weeks' from January 1550 to 12 June 1552, according to which language he was using. In 1551–2 his reading in Plato's *Republic* and Cicero's *Philippics* inspired more than fifty *orationes*, or essays, in Greek alone on problems in political theory and moral philosophy. The extant texts of these and fifty-five in Latin (BL, Harley MS 5807, fols. 78–89 and Add. MS 4724) provide rare evidence of 'how a de luxe education' was then conducted (MacCulloch, *Tudor Church*, 20).

Edward read Herodotus, Thucydides, Plutarch, and

Pliny the Younger; copies of their works and Erasmus's *Colloquies* are among his school books in the British Library. For training in kingship, Cheke considered Aristotle's *Politics* to have been Edward's most important text, as it tested his ability to ground historical reasoning on moralistic precepts. Edward excelled at rhetorical argument. Since, in the humanists' ideal prescription, such reasoning best served statecraft, Cheke balanced Edward's theoretical instruction with the study of real politics. Responding to opposing classical proverbs, Edward argued, in two strikingly original essays of July 1549, both for and against the necessity of war. In one he deplored the damage wreaked by English armies overseas; in the other he glorified fighting in defence of religion, citing the evidence of what he called 'contemporary wars' (MacCulloch, *Tudor Church*, 21). Some of the later orations similarly show the topicality of Cheke's method: when Edward considered rulers whom men feared and therefore hated, he cited Henry VII and Richard III. Edward's notes of 1552 on the English occupation of France in the 1420s (BL, Cotton MS Nero C.x, fols. 94–7) may also have been a by-product of his reading in history.

Edward's laconic, self-styled 'Chronicle' of foreign and domestic events, a book of eighty-four leaves composed in English in his italic hand between March 1550 and November 1552 (BL, Cotton MS Nero C.x), was not a formal part of his schoolwork. Cheke recommended that he keep it as a practical means of acquainting himself with the affairs of the world. As such it is a unique royal document, apparently without precedent in English and European letters, and for some events, especially those at court, it is the only extant source. Although most of the information recorded—news of Kett's 'stir' in Norfolk, the landing of the Turkish navy near Naples (August 1552)—was supplied by his secretaries and clerks from the reports of others or by foreign ambassadors, the vocabulary, phrasing, and choice of subject matter is Edward's own. A few usages (for instance 'booted and spurred': Edward VI, *Chronicle*, 67) are among the first recorded in English. If the tone reveals nothing conclusive about Edward's inner life, the frequent mention of horsemen and footmen and military manoeuvres in France and the empire clearly bears witness to a Renaissance king's chief preoccupation. Substantively, his discussions of state policy are wholly derivative; the section on reform of the coinage in September 1551, for example, reflects the thinking of William Thomas, clerk of the council from April 1550, who had given him a paper on the topic at the time the council was considering the same issue. The boy's understanding of such a technical subject is nevertheless remarkable. Thomas also wrote secretly to Edward, counselling him about kingly behaviour and quoting Machiavelli to the effect that a prince must strive always to maintain a free hand. Edward's response to this advice remains unknown.

Edward's religious training was rigorous and relentless, his grasp of scripture, sure. Martin Bucer said that Edward listened with great attention while ten chapters of the Bible were read to him daily in May 1550. Edward began his own systematic, if soon abandoned, study of the Bible in 1550, blocking out twenty-seven issues for special enquiry: 'De Antichristo', 'De primatu papae', 'De idololatria', et cetera (Needham, 1.200–01). His lessons in rhetoric comprehended the same issues, as evidenced by his annotations to *De sacramento eucharistiae*, the published version of Pietro Martire Vermigli's disputation at Oxford in 1549. At twelve Edward 'was quite capable of following the theological controversies that were raging around him' (Birrell, 15–16). Reformist divines like Bucer, Thomas Becon, Hugh Latimer, and John Ponet preached weekly before him—from April 1550 they did so in the new privy garden pulpit at Westminster—expounding 'True Religion': here was the anti-papal protestant agenda, and, according to an eye-witness Edward absorbed it all, jotting down in now-lost ledgers 'every notable sentence, and specially if it touched a king' (Edward VI, *Remains*, 1.cvi). Edward's lessons with Belmain show how closely his tutorials in French served the ends of protestant pedagogy. The king's treatise in French on the papal supremacy (BL, Add. MS 5464) was inspired by John Ponet's translation of Bernardino Ochino's anti-papal *Dialogue*; Cranmer, knowing of Edward's project, may have added to the translation his own anti-papal vitriol. Composed at the age of eleven (December 1548–August 1549), Edward's treatise exhibited startling 'originality', as those around him acknowledged. His vehement denunciation of the pope ('the true son of the devil, a bad man, an Antichrist and abominable tyrant') matched the fervency of his youthful expressions of faith (MacCulloch, *Tudor Church*, 26–7). He adhered fully to the doctrine of salvation by faith, confessing elsewhere on 12 December 1548 'que chacu[n] qui croit en Iesuscrist, a mis toute sa fiancé en luy, sera sauvé: et que foy est la principale et plus notable chose qui soit en la religion chrestienne' ('that everyone who believes in Jesus Christ, and has put all his faith in him, will be saved: and that faith is the principal and most important thing there is in the Christian religion'; BL, Add. MS 9000, fols. 34v–35r). In his *orationes* of January and February 1552 Edward also defended predestination, urging that it be preached from every pulpit.

Edward's French progressed rapidly in 1550–51. His collection of French works—Louis le Roy's translations of Isocrates and Xenophon, Louis Megreit's *Grammaire française* (1550), Grafton's 1551 edition of the French–English dialogues of Pierre du Ploiche—confirm le Roy's eyewitness testimony of 1551, that he could read the language easily. Another visitor at court, François de Scèpeaux, said in 1550 that Edward could speak French well; his report that Edward also spoke Spanish and Italian cannot be confirmed. It is known only that Edward owned Pedro Mexia's *Sylva de varia lecion* (1550), 'a very popular Spanish bedside book' (Birrell, 14). His much-used copy of Robert Record's *Pathway to Knowledge*, a popular text on geometry, and an edition of Euclid (1510) clearly point towards instruction in mathematics and astronomy; one of the teachers was probably William Buckley of King's College, Cambridge, whom Cheke patronized. Edward's astronomical brass quadrant, engraved with Cheke's and Buckley's initials, was designed by Cheke and intended for use with Record's book.

It is also thought that Cheke introduced Dr John Dee to court circles, and that Dee taught Edward the mathematics of oceanic navigation. Ottuel Holinshed, a fellow of Trinity, presented Edward with a tract on the construction and use of the dial-ring, and the engraver Thomas Gemini, who made the quadrant, also made for him an astrolabe bearing the arms of Edward himself, Cheke, and the duke of Northumberland. Both the astrolabe and quadrant survive in the British Museum. Edward grew up with his father's many maps and globes. His own desks and coffers were chock-full of 'plattes' and charts, suggesting a real interest in cartography and geography. In 1549 he acquired Sebastian Cabot's new world map showing the north-west passage, and ordered that it be hung at Whitehall. Music, too, absorbed him: John Ashley taught him 'to play on the virginalles' and Philip van Wilder, the Netherlandish 'Master of His Singinge Children', the lute (Loach, 14–15). Whether Edward played the two viols that were given him is unknown.

Northumberland's regime, 1549–1553 Somerset's fall in October 1549 and the subsequent coup against the conservatives at the end of the year had left a number of offices vacant; in February 1550 Warwick secured Edward's approval for his own appointment to the offices of great master and lord president. The former gave him control of the king's household, including, crucially, the privy chamber, while the latter enabled him to supervise the council's business and membership. Though he lacked a protector's formal authority, he could now govern England as Somerset had done. Meanwhile, in November 1549, at Cranmer's bidding, Edward had approved the first of a string of new appointments to the board, all of them Warwick's men, and all of evangelical leaning. Somerset was readmitted to the council on 10 April 1550, but he resented Warwick's supremacy, and began mounting a campaign to unseat him. When Warwick (who had become duke of Northumberland on 11 October 1551) discovered the conspiracy he ruthlessly arranged for Somerset's execution, on 22 January 1552, on trumped-up charges. This and the later conspiracy to make Jane Grey queen have given Northumberland the reputation of an English 'Machiavel'. A full understanding of his aims in office, however, must also credit his considerable achievements as Edward's lord president. He abandoned Somerset's military preoccupations, ending the war in Scotland and concluding peace with France. He rescued England from financial ruin by curtailing debasement and government spending, adopting a deflationary monetary policy and liquidating the whole of Edward's overseas debt. Working hand in glove with Cecil, he rationalized the procedures of government by council, which became central to the conduct of affairs in a way that it had not been under Somerset, and in the process created the 'system' which Cecil reinstituted under Elizabeth I.

Although Cranmer remained personally cool towards Warwick, the threat posed by conservative councillors in the last months of 1549 pushed him over to the earl's side by early 1550. Cranmer's influence with Edward may help to explain Warwick's growing enthusiasm for the evangelical cause. Some radical protestants came to have doubts about the earl's religious sincerity. According to the French ambassador, who knew him well, Warwick was greedy for gain and '*avide de gloire*'—'desirous of glory' (Vertot and Villaret, 158). The French also spoke of his 'liberality', or noble courtesy, his grace and affability, his 'great presence' (Bibliothèque Nationale, Paris, MS Ancien Saint-Germain Français 15888, fols. 214–15). But whether or not such attributes could justly be squared with religious devotion, there is no doubt that Warwick, who was a fearless and accomplished soldier, radiated an unusual force of character, or charisma. He quickly won Edward VI's admiration, trust, and affection, and this helped defend him from the suspicion of others.

The secret of Warwick's power was that he took Edward seriously. He knew that he must accommodate the boy's keen intelligence and also his sovereign will, which first manifested itself in July 1550, when at the confirmation of the bishop of Gloucester (John Hooper), Edward with his own pen angrily deleted from the oath of supremacy all reference to saints. 'This was a Henry VIII in the making' (MacCulloch, *Cranmer*, 472). By October 1551 the king clearly possessed a powerful sense that he and not his council embodied royal authority: 'the number of councillors does not make our authority', he curtly reminded his lord chancellor (PRO, SP 10/13, no. 55). Various holograph 'state papers', memoranda for council business, and eyewitness accounts of the boy's speeches 'in council' seem to furnish evidence that in 1551–2 Edward stood on the threshold of power. But though the speeches were real enough, they were delivered before specially staged meetings not of the council but of a committee of councillors and others—what Edward termed his council 'for the state' (BL, Cotton MS Nero C.x, fol. 85r)—the matters propounded having already been concluded in regular meetings. The memoranda, like the speeches, were based on notes given to him by his secretaries and clerks. William Thomas confessed that he secretly passed to the king the topics in question, 'to this end, that your majesty may utter these matters as of your own study, whereby it shall have greater credit with your council' (Loades, 201). Warwick himself occasionally primed Edward for his speeches, as a French eyewitness discovered:

> he visited the King secretly at night in the King's Chamber, unseen by anyone, after all were asleep. The next day the young Prince came to his council and proposed matters as if they were his own; consequently, everyone was amazed, thinking that they proceeded from his mind and by his invention. (Bibliothèque Nationale, Paris, MS Ancien Saint-Germain Français 15888, fols. 214v–215v)

Warwick was skilfully guiding the king for his own purposes by exploiting the boy's precocious capacity for understanding the business of government. He did this with the help of his clients and confidants in the privy chamber, 'my speciall frendes', as he termed them (PRO, SP 15/4, fol. 14)—Darcy, who worked closely with Cecil as his liaison to the council; Sir John Gates, who in January

1550 took Rogers's place as one of the four 'principal' gentlemen and who succeeded Darcy as vice-chamberlain in April 1551; and the man who should perhaps be considered as in psychological terms the king's older brother, Sir Henry Sidney, one of Edward's closest boyhood friends and also Warwick's son-in-law. A gentleman of the privy chamber from April 1550, and from July 1551 one of the 'principal' gentlemen there, it was said in France that Sidney had 'acquired so great an influence near the King, that he was able to make all of his notions conform' to Warwick's. But Gates, the Frenchman averred, was the 'principal instrument which he [Warwick] used to induce the King to [do] something when he did not want it to be known that it had proceeded from himself'. Gates 'was to report back to him everything said to the King, for this Gates was continually in the [king's privy] Chamber' (Bibliothèque Nationale, Paris, MS Ancien Saint-Germain Français 15888, fols. 214v–215v).

It has been argued that Edward's signature on a series of signet warrants in 1552–3 constitutes hard evidence of the king's personal involvement in governmental affairs. In fact, the example cited, that of 14 May 1553, bears the inked impression of the wooden stamp of Edward's hand, a stamp wielded by Gates at a time when the king was dying. Such warrants form part of a 'file' of disbursements from a secret treasury that Warwick had set up in Edward's privy chamber, a cash reserve which allowed him to fund £40,000 in 'special' expenses, including pay-offs and loans to Sidney and Gates and the councillors who captained the gendarmes. Not only had Warwick restored the earlier system of rule by a privy council, he had also recognized the privy chamber as the real focus of power, even under a boy-king.

In religious affairs the king's refusal to tolerate Princess Mary's mass so enraged the emperor Charles V that it threatened to cause war with the Habsburgs; Edward's advisers urged caution. But in two remarkable confrontations in March 1551, first with Mary and then, privately, with his bishops and councillors, Edward's uncompromisingly hard line stiffened official resolve: there was to be no backing down. The episode underscored Edward's growing independence, his wilful insistence on his supremacy in the church, and, in the meeting with his clerics, his exceptional rhetorical skills. His support of Cranmer's projected *Reformatio legum ecclesiasticarum*, an abortive attempt to overhaul the canon law, supplies further evidence of this. Warwick certainly lost nothing by respecting Edward's reforming zeal; the Reformation went forward at a quickening pace. Cranmer's *Ordinal* of February 1550, which defined a protestant minister's calling, signalled a turning point in the government's relations with conservative clerics: those who refused the *Ordinal* were ousted. Within the next two years Northumberland had gutted the ranks of Catholic bishops, depriving seven who had opposed the 1549 prayer book. The forced surrenders of episcopal estates, some of which were parcelled out to the duke's cronies, eventually prompted the reformers to denounce him, some (like John Knox) in sermons at court.

In fact the crown was the main beneficiary of such spoliation. Only Edward's premature death prevented further confiscations. Doctrinally, the last year of Edward's reign marked the laying of foundations for the future: Cranmer's revised, unequivocally protestant prayer book of 1552; the forty-two articles of June 1553; and John Ponet's *A Short Catechism* (1553), which adapted the articles for use by schoolmasters.

Illness, death, and the 'Devise' for the succession (1553) The cold that Edward caught in February 1553 was said by contemporaries to have degenerated into the 'consumption', or tuberculosis, that killed him. A plausible alternative interpretation, that he died of 'a supporting pulmonary infection' which 'led to generalized septicaemia with renal failure' (Loach, 162), is challenged by a closer reading of his medical history. Edward's descent towards death arguably began on 2 April 1552, when he fell ill with what he described as measles and smallpox. Measles, it is known, suppresses immunity to tuberculosis. The surgeon who later opened the boy's chest found that 'the disease whereof his majesty died was the disease of lungs, which had in them two great ulcers, and were putrified' (Lodge, 10–11). Such cavities in the lungs 'are typical of reactivation of tuberculosis, which may be seen in adolescents'; in other words, 'Edward was obviously in close contact with at least one person who had tuberculosis, more likely before he contracted measles than after' (Holmes, Holmes, and McMurrough, 60–62). The first signs of the disease appeared at Christmas 1552; in March 1553 the Venetian envoy saw him and said that although still quite handsome, Edward was clearly dying.

It was probably about this time that Edward drafted his 'Devise' for the succession (Inner Temple, London, Petyt MS 538, vol. 47, fol. 317). Sir Edward Montague, chief justice of the common pleas, testified that 'the king by his own mouth said' that he was prepared to alter the succession because the marriage of either Princess Mary or Princess Elizabeth to a foreigner might undermine both 'the laws of this realm' and 'his proceedings in religion' (Fuller, 4.138–9). According to Montague, Edward also thought his sisters bore the 'shame' of illegitimacy. As first conceived, the 'Devise' envisioned the crown passing in succession to protestant males or, in their absence, to one of their would-be mothers who would rule not as a queen but as a 'governess' advised by an unnamed council of twenty. As governess, Edward nominated in succession Frances, duchess of Suffolk; her daughters, Jane, Katherine, and Mary Grey; and Margaret Clifford, the daughter of Frances's younger sister. As death approached, he altered this bizarre, convoluted scheme in such a way as to favour Jane exclusively: the words 'Jane's heirs masles' became 'Jane and her heirs male'. Close chronological analysis of the successive stages by which the 'Devise' was amended suggests that the original scheme was exclusively Edward's—Northumberland initially may have been unaware of its existence—but that Edward changed the words in question at the prompting of the duke or one of his men, possibly Gates. The decision to make the change was probably taken soon after the duke's son Guildford married Jane on 21 May, and certainly not later than 10 June 1553, when the doctors, following a secret consultation, gave Edward three days to live. Two unimpeachable eyewitnesses confirmed Northumberland's role, Montague and Sir John Gosnold, solicitor-general of the court of augmentations, both of whom examined the holograph 'Devise' and were personally charged by Edward on his deathbed to authenticate it under letters patent on 21 June.

Nevertheless the king's role is undeniable. When Montague on 14 June informed Edward that 'the execution of this device after the king's decease' would be treasonable, the dying king 'with sharp words and angry countenance' commanded him and all the judges to accept it. Montague complied, but only after getting the king's pardon, for he knew that as a minor, Edward could not make out a valid will and that only parliament could overturn the act of 1544 governing the succession. 'Whereunto the king said he would have this done, and after ratify it by parliament' (Fuller, 4.138–40), and on 19 June chancery began preparing writs for a new parliament to meet on 18 September. Edward regarded Jane as his spiritual sister, his only acceptable successor. Like himself, she had absorbed the 'godly learning' of the Cambridge-trained evangelical reformers, and more than his sisters in blood, she could be trusted to carry forward his Reformation. Facing what he believed would be Mary's destruction of true religion, he let death steel his conviction. Thomas Goodrich, bishop of Ely, heard his last confession. On the evening of 6 July, reportedly praying that England be defended against papistry, he died at Greenwich in the arms of Sidney and Wroth, attended by his doctors and Christopher Salmon, a groom. Nicholas Bellin of Modena made his (now-lost) funeral effigy in wax and wood in the style of Pietro Torrigiani's royal effigies. On 8 August he was buried in Westminster Abbey in a white marble vault in an unmarked grave beneath Torrigiani's altar for Henry VII's tomb. Cornelius Cure's coloured drawing of c.1573 for a tomb for Edward is evidence of Cecil's never-realized dream to build at Windsor next to Henry VIII's tomb a bronze and marble monument to England's first protestant king (Bodl. Oxf., Gough maps 45, no. 63).

The king, his court, and his reign At his accession Edward VI came into an enormous and splendid inheritance—his father's ships, tapestries, jewels, manors, and plate, as well as fifty-five palaces, more than any prince in Christendom. Arguably England's best-educated king, he held the potential of becoming in maturity the embodiment of the ideal Renaissance prince: learned, pious, chivalrous, decorous. He might have been a renowned scholar; the sweep of his intellectual interests was apparently without bounds. On a visit to court in autumn 1552 the Italian physician and philosopher Girolamo Cardano thought Edward had 'uttered his minde no lesse readely and eloquently than I could do my selfe' in a discourse in Latin on 'the uniform course and motion ... [of] starres and planets' (Edward VI, Remains, 1.ccix). It is possible that his memory was nearly photographic; it was said that he could rattle off the name of every creek, bay, and rivulet

not only in England but also in Scotland and France. Such reports had given Edward at fifteen a Europe-wide reputation for brilliance and learning. A godly saintliness was also attributed to him by his evangelical admirers at court, a reputation that transformed him even in death: rumours that he had not died circulated in Mary's reign and after. For John Foxe, Richard Grafton, and Raphael Holinshed, Edward's reputed godliness was central to their accounts of his Reformation.

Protestant hagiography was first undermined in John Hayward's The Life, and Raigne of King Edward the Sixt (1630), which presented Edward as the prisoner of duplicitous councillors, and his Reformation as born of factiousness and greed. Despite Hayward's distortions—he modelled his Life on Tacitus—later seventeenth- and eighteenth-century writers carried forward his story of factious division. Then in the late Victorian era this tradition was broken in its turn by James Anthony Froude and A. F. Pollard, who argued that even avaricious councillors might do good: Protector Somerset saved Edward's Reformation in the unlikely guise of a liberal hero. Froude and Pollard fundamentally redirected all later enquiry through their emphasis on the institutions of central government, the council and parliament; by the mid-twentieth century a personally attractive, godly king had virtually disappeared from the screen. In G. R. Elton's influential text England under the Tudors (1955) Edward was little more than an inconsequential pawn.

However, institutional histories beg the crucial question of how much and what sort of agency should be ascribed to Edward. A systematic analysis of the genesis of his 'state papers' shows him to have been at fifteen an exceptionally capable student who was following, not directing royal affairs. Had he lived, his capacity for public affairs might well have been matchless. The relative paucity of references to religion in his Chronicle enabled W. K. Jordan to ascribe to him the 'cool and secular spirit' of one primarily interested in the administrative aspects of the royal supremacy (Edward VI, Chronicle, xxii). But the supremacy for Edward was itself 'a profoundly religious concern' (MacCulloch, Tudor Church, 30). Jennifer Loach's view, that there cannot be ascribed to Edward 'any deep or informed interest in Protestant theology' (Loach, 158), largely reflects the disappearance of his notes on court sermons, and is in any case clearly contradicted by the zeal of his surviving writings on religion: in his treatise of 1549 against the papal supremacy he identified himself personally with those who had renounced idolatry, and in his proposals for remodelling the Order of the Garter of 1550–51 (BL, Harley MS 394) he rejected the mass as so much superstition, instead describing the Lord's supper as an act of remembrance.

However, it is to protestant hagiographers like John Foxe, and to Foxe's illustrator John Day, that the picture of Edward as an English Josiah, pious to the exclusion of all else, is derived: the woodcut in Foxe's Actes and Monuments (1563) of the young king listening attentively to Latimer's Lenten sermon of 1549 represents only a partial truth. The corrective is the extensive record of his participation in the lavish rituals of a very cosmopolitan court. His music-making, revels, jousts, and entertainments advertised publicly what the private, official record of his expenses confirms, that his were the interests of a prince given to magnificence and self-conscious display. The French in particular admired the elegance and taste of his courtly spectacle. He sometimes directed the masques in which he also acted a part, in costume: the Revels accounts show that at Christmas 1551 the 'plaies and pastimes' were altered 'to serve his maiesties plasure and determinacion' (Loach, 153). The extravagance of his dress and the jewels he bought for himself and others as gifts were stunning by any standard; from Flemish dealers he acquired some of the costliest gems on the European market. His patronage of art, however, was limited; he paid Bellin to work on Henry VIII's tomb then under construction at Westminster Abbey.

Edward's portraits show a grey-eyed lad of pale complexion and slight stature; he had a high shoulder blade and (according to Cardano) may have suffered weak eyesight and occasional deafness (Edward VI, Remains, 1.ccxv). What some thought a noticeably grave aspect made him seem older than he was. Myth makers like Foxe rendered him 'meek'. In his robust passion for the hunt and the martial games of the court, however, he was very much in the mould of Henry VIII. When left to himself, he matched the swordplay, jousting, and riding with long hours in self-absorbed study of fortifications and war. After critically surveying the defences at Portsmouth in person in 1552, he designed two new 'strong castellis on either side of the Haven there' (ibid., 1.81). His full-length portraits—one of c.1547 in the National Portrait Gallery by an unknown artist, and another in the Musée du Louvre attributed to Guillim Scrots, his court painter—show him striking 'unconvincing imitations' of his father's bold-legged stance. The pose was deliberate, and mirrored what Petruccio Ubaldini, an Italian humanist in Edward's employ, described as the 'contrived adulation' for the king and the rigid etiquette of his court, part of the 'theatre' of Tudor majesty (Loades, 202). All the same, his personal letters hint at a pronounced bossiness. In December 1551 he admonished his friend Barnaby Fitzpatrick to shun Catholic practices in Paris ('being brought up with me and bounden to obey my lawes'), avoid the company of women, and if he were not riding, shooting, or playing tennis (all 'honest games'), he was to give over his time to reading scripture. 'This I write', said Edward, 'to spurre yow [on]' (Edward VI, Remains, 1.69–70). Although his contemporaries attributed to him a sense of justice and mercy—court preachers cited scripture to remind him of a godly king's duty—he left no programme of socially minded reform. The story of his allegedly spontaneous gift of the royal palace of Bridewell to house the London poor was first told by Grafton in 1568 and ignored the fact that the city of London had been planning just such a scheme from about 1544.

Edward's youth and unfulfilled promise have given rise to a number of misconceptions. But in one respect, at least, image and achievement have been found to coincide, in the perception of his reign as having seen the foundations laid, with his encouragement, of one of the great transformations of English society and English-speaking culture, namely the protestant Reformation.

DALE HOAK

Sources APC, 1542–54 · S. Alford, Kingship and politics in the reign of Edward VI (2002) · T. Birrell, English monarchs and their books: from Henry VII to Charles II (1987) · M. Bush, The government policy of Protector Somerset (1975) · CSP dom., 1547–53 · H. Chapman, The last Tudor king: a study of Edward VI (1961) · The chronicle and political papers of King Edward VI, ed. W. K. Jordan (1966) · D. Hoak, The reign of Edward VI [forthcoming] · D. E. Hoak, The king's council in the reign of Edward VI (1976) · D. Hoak, 'The coronations of Edward VI, Mary I, and Elizabeth I, and the transformation of Tudor monarchy', Westminster Abbey reformed, 1540–1640, ed. C. S. Knighton and R. Mortimer (2003) · D. Hoak, 'The iconography of the crown imperial', Tudor political culture, ed. D. Hoak (1995), 54–103 · D. E. Hoak, 'Rehabilitating the duke of Northumberland: politics and political control, 1549–1553', The mid-Tudor polity, c.1540–1560, ed. J. Loach and R. Tittler (1980), 29–51 · D. Hoak, 'The king's privy chamber, 1547–1553', Tudor rule and revolution: essays for G. R. Elton from his American friends, ed. D. Guth and J. McKenna (1982), 87–108 · D. Hoak, 'The secret history of the Tudor court: the king's coffers and the king's purse, 1542–1553', Journal of British Studies, 26 (1987), 208–31 · R. Hutton, 'The local impact of the Tudor reformations', The English Reformation revised, ed. C. Haigh (1987), 114–38 · W. K. Jordan, Edward VI, 1: The young king (1968) · W. K. Jordan, Edward VI, 2: The threshold of power (1970) · Literary remains of King Edward the Sixth, ed. J. G. Nichols, 2 vols., Roxburghe Club, 75 (1857) · J. Loach, Edward VI, ed. G. Bernard and P. Williams (1999) · D. Loades, John Dudley: duke of Northumberland, 1504–1553 (1996) · D. MacCulloch, Thomas Cranmer: a life (1996) · D. MacCulloch, Tudor church militant: Edward VI and the protestant Reformation (1999) · A. J. A. Malkiewicz, 'An eye-witness's account of the coup d'état of October 1549', EngHR, 70 (1955), 600–09 · P. Needham, 'Sir John Cheke at Cambridge and court', PhD diss., Harvard U., 1971 · E. Shagan, 'Protector Somerset and the 1549 rebellions: new sources and new perspectives', EngHR, 114 (1999), 34–63 · D. MacCulloch, 'The Vita Mariae Angliae Reginae of Robert Wingfield of Brantham', Camden miscellany, XXVIII, CS, 4th ser., 29 (1984), 181–301 · A. Fraser, The wives of Henry VIII (1993) · J. Rowlands, Holbein (1985) · S. E. James, Kateryn Parr: the making of a queen (1999) · J. Strype, The life of the learned Sir John Cheke (1821) · A. Crawford, ed., Letters of the queens of England, 1100–1547 (1994) · M. Dowling, Humanism in the age of Henry VIII (1975) · S. Anglo, Spectacle, pageantry and early Tudor policy, 2nd edn (1997) · J. Strype, Memorials of the most reverend father in God Thomas Cranmer (1672) · J. Strype, Ecclesiastical memorials, 3 vols. (1822) · E. G. R. Taylor, The mathematical practitioners of Tudor and Stuart England (1954) · R. Vertot and C. Villaret, eds., Ambassades en Angleterre des messieurs de Noailles (1763) · E. Lodge, Portraits of illustrious personages of Great Britain, [new edn], 12 vols. in 6 (1835) · G. Holmes, F. Holmes, and J. McMurrough, 'The death of young King Edward VI', New England Journal of Medicine, 345 (2001), 60–62 · T. Fuller, The church history of Britain, ed. J. S. Brewer, new edn, 6 vols. (1845) · J. Foxe, Actes and monuments (1563) · P. Schramm, A history of the English coronation, trans. L. W. Legg (1937) · BL, Cotton MSS, Nero C.x; Vespasian D.xviii · BL, Harley MSS 249, 394, 5807 · BL, Add. MSS 4724, 5464, 9000, 9069, 48023, 48126, 71009 · BL, Arundel MS 510 · S. Antiquaries, Lond., MS 123 · Inner Temple Library, London, Petyt MS 538, vol. 47 · state papers domestic, Edward VI, PRO, SP 10/6, 13 · state papers domestic, addenda, Edward VI–James I, PRO, SP 15/4 · exchequer, king's remembrancer, accounts various, PRO, E 101/546/19 · lord chamberlain's department, special events, PRO, LC 2/3/2 · Cecil papers, Hatfield House, Hertfordshire, 150 · CCC Cam., MS 105 · Bodl. Oxf., MS Autogr. e.2 · Bodl. Oxf., MS Bodley 899 · Bodl. Oxf., MS Ashmole 1729 · Bodl. Oxf., Gough maps 45, no.

63 · Bibliothèque Nationale, Paris, MS Ancien Saint-Germain Français 15888 · exchequer, declared accounts, PRO, E 351/2932 · Coll. Arms, MS M6

Archives BL, school notebooks, Add. MS 4724, Arundel MS 510 · BL, letters, Harley MS 5087, fols. 1–18 [copies] · BL, 'Chronicle', Cotton MS Nero C.x · BL, Treatise against papal supremacy (1549), Add. MS 5444 · BL, proposals for remodelling the Order of the Garter, Harley MS 394 · BL, household book, Lansdowne MSS 35, 184 · BL, 'The governance of this realm …', Cotton MS, Nero C.x. fols. 113 ff. · BL, 'Reasons for establishing a mart in England', Cotton MS, Nero C.x. fols. 85 ff. · BL, 'Payments of debts beyond seas …', Lansdowne MS 1236, fol. 21 · BL, 'A summary of matters to be concluded', Lansdowne MS 1236, fols. 19–20 · BL, 'Certain articles devised and delivered …', Cotton MS Nero C.x. fols. 86–9 · BL, 'Notes on the English occupation of France …', Cotton MS Nero C.x. fols. 94–7 · Bodl. Oxf., school notebooks, MS E.2 and MS 899 · Inner Temple, London, draft of a sumptuary bill for parliament, Petyt MS 538/47, fol. 318 · Inner Temple, London, 'Devise' for the succession, Petyt MS 538/47, fol. 317 · PRO, Privy Purse expenses, Aug. 1547–Mar. 1549; Jan. 1550–Jan. 1552, E 351/2932; E 101/426/8 · PRO, memorandum for acts of parliament (23 Jan 1552), SP 10/14/no. 4

Likenesses H. Holbein, oils, 1538–9 (*Edward VI as a child*), National Gallery of Art, Washington, DC; repro. in J. Rowlands, *Holbein* (1985), pl. 32, cat. no. 70 · H. Holbein, drawing, c.1539–1540, Royal Collection · L. Horenbout, miniature, c.1541 (*Edward VI as prince of Wales*), collection of the duke of Buccleuch; repro. in *Country Life* (9 Jan 1997), 33 · H. Holbein?, drawing, c.1542, Royal Collection · oils, c.1542 (after H. Holbein), NPG · studio of G. Scrots, oils, 1543?, NPG; version V&A · oils, c.1545, Buckland Abbey, Devon · Flemish school, oils, 1546 (*Edward as prince of Wales*), Royal Collection; repro. in M. Howard, *The Tudor image* (1995), pl. 50, p. 66 · school of H. Holbein?, oils, 1546?, repro. in J. Loach, *Edward VI* (New Haven and London, 1999), dust jacket; priv. coll. · G. Scrots, oils, 1546, NPG · oils, c.1546–1547, Royal Collection; version, 1547, Petworth House, West Sussex · gold coronation medal, 1547, BM; repro. in MacCulloch, *Tudor church militant*, jacket · group portrait, oils, c.1547 (*Family of Henry VIII*), Royal Collection · oils on panel, c.1547 (*Edward VI*), NPG · school of H. Holbein, oils, 1552 (*Edward VI*), Royal Collection; repro. in Chapman, *Last Tudor king*, pl. 1 · group portrait, oils, c.1570 (*Edward VI and the Pope*), NPG · group portrait, oils, c.1570 (*Family of Henry VIII*), Sudeley Castle, Gloucestershire · group portrait, oils, 17th cent. (*Granting Bridewell Hospital charter*), King Edward's School, Whitley, Surrey · group portrait, oils, 17th cent. (*Granting Christ's Hospital charter*), Horsham, Sussex · follower of Holbein, oak panel (*Portrait of Edward, prince of Wales, aged six*), Metropolitan Museum of Art, New York; repro. in J. Rowlands, *Holbein* (1985), pl. 243, cat. no. R. 35 · attrib. G. Scrots, oils (*Edward VI*), Louvre, Paris; repro. in Loach, *Edward VI*, pl. 7 · attrib. G. Scrots, oils (after original, c.1550), Royal Collection [*see illus.*] · wax seals, BM

Edward VII (1841–1910), king of the United Kingdom of Great Britain and Ireland, and the British dominions beyond the seas, and emperor of India, was born at Buckingham Palace, London, on 9 November 1841, the first son and second child of the nine children of Queen *Victoria (1819–1901) and Prince *Albert (1819–1861). He was named Albert Edward (against the advice of the prime minister, Lord Melbourne, who preferred Edward Albert), and he was commonly known by both names, except in the family, where he was called Bertie. Insistence on the primacy of the name Albert reflected the burden of the queen's expectations which the prince was to carry until 1901, when, on ascending the throne, he declared himself Edward. He was the first heir born to a reigning sovereign since 1762, and the last to be born with privy councillors present to attest his identity (subsequently only the home

Edward VII (1841–1910), by Sir Luke Fildes, 1901–2

secretary attended). He was made prince of Wales aged one month and, against the advice of Palmerston, was also styled duke of Saxony in addition to the other usual royal titles (he habitually later travelled abroad semi-incognito as earl of Renfrew or earl of Chester, or, when king, duke of Lancaster). A strong German presence at his christening on 25 January 1842 confirmed the view of the whigs, who saw the court coming under German sway, and attested to the remarkable range of European royal relatives which was to be so important an aspect of the prince's life.

Education Albert Edward was brought up to be trilingual—in English, German, and French, with a governess for each language—but his best languages in the nursery were German and English; he found German initially the easier of the two. The Baron von Bunsen noted that the royal children 'all spoke German like their native tongue, even to one another' (Lee, 2.17). The prince's early days were supervised by Mrs Southey, his nurse, who was soon dismissed, and then by Sarah, Lady Lyttelton, who acted as governess and substitute mother (the queen being frequently pregnant and both Victoria and Albert preferring the Princess Victoria, the prince's elder sister). The prince was slow to learn, fell behind his younger siblings, and soon developed a stammer and a temper. Lady Lyttelton was a relative of William and Catherine Gladstone, whose similarly aged son, William Henry Gladstone, became the prince's playmate. The prince was taught elocution by the actor George Barley, but always had a slight German accent.

In January 1847 the prince's parents set out a detailed plan of education for their children, by which Lady Lyttelton retained a prominent role in Albert Edward's development. Victoria and Albert's intention was to ensure that the future king was as unlike his profligate Hanoverian uncles as possible, and that he was educated to the highest levels of contemporary knowledge: he was to be like Albert, able to talk to politicians and people of letters and science on their own terms. However, his educational development remained halting. On Prince Albert's instruction he was whipped (as were from time to time his sisters). When Albert Edward was six, Henry Birch, formerly a master at Eton, became his tutor and found his pupil difficult to teach. Albert arranged for an examination by George Combe, the phrenologist, who reported that the prince's cranium suggested that 'strong self-will, at times obstinacy' would be characteristic (Hibbert, 10). In 1852 Birch, whom the prince liked but who decided on a career in the church, was replaced by Frederick Waymouth Gibbs, a barrister who had been brought up with Leslie Stephen. Gibbs got no better results than Birch. It became apparent that the demanding programme of learning expected by the prince consort was counterproductive: the prince was not unintelligent, but he was not bookish or of intellectual interests. He was, in fact, quite like his mother in several respects, loth though she was to admit it. Indeed Baron Stockmar thought him 'an exaggerated copy of his mother' (ibid., 26). His fear of his overbearing father became marked. One consequence of his bad spelling and barely coherent sentence structure was that, even allowing for the destruction of papers by him and after his death, he left less by way of personal writing—letters, memoranda, diaries—than the volumes which characterized both his parents and several of his siblings. (His sketchy youthful diary was kept by parental demand, and though he maintained it until his death the entries are rarely revealing.) Within the family, the prince's position was a further source of insecurity. Victoria was undoubtedly the parents' favourite child, and, among the boys, Alfred, and later Arthur, were preferred; but when erstwhile favourites erred, Albert Edward could be brought forward. Despite Victoria's and Albert's practice of setting their children's faults and virtues off against each other (a trait which became more marked as the queen aged), Albert Edward formed close relationships with his sisters Victoria and Alice; he was profoundly saddened by the latter's early death in 1878.

Alternatives to studying In 1855 the Princess Victoria was engaged in marriage to the heir to the throne of Prussia, and in 1858 Prince Alfred was sent to sea. The prince of Wales was keen to escape from his educational routine, but his parents were unwilling to admit that their educational plan had failed. The young prince found refuge in alternatives to studying: travel, sport, and the theatre. In August 1855 he visited Paris, part of a state visit to Napoleon III, and fell under the city's spell. A continental tour in 1857 was less fun, for Albert insisted it be for 'purposes of study' (Hibbert, 23). At Köningswinter the prince kissed a pretty girl; Willy Gladstone, who was of the party, rather unfairly reported this to his father, then chancellor of the exchequer, who complained (to his wife) of 'this squalid little debauch', adding that the:

> Prince of Wales has not been educated up to his position. This sort of unworthy little indulgence is the compensation. Kept in childhood beyond his time, he is allowed to make that childhood what it should never be in a Prince, or anyone else, namely wanton. (Magnus, 21)

A further attempt by Gibbs and the Revd Charles Feral Tarver, his Latin tutor and chaplain, to encourage him in the educational routine devised by his parents took the form in 1858 of seclusion with three hand-picked companions at the White Lodge, Richmond Park. Further failure led to Gibbs's dismissal, with Robert Bruce, brother of Lord Elgin, replacing him, but as governor rather than as tutor. With the prince aged seventeen, Victoria and Albert in effect abandoned the attempt to force him into his father's cast of mind.

Oxford, Canada, Cambridge, and the army The prince was keen to join the army and was disappointed when he was gazetted a lieutenant-colonel (he had hoped to enter by passing the examination). He was created KG in November 1858, in which year he visited Berlin, staying with his sister Victoria, now married to the Crown Prince Frederick of Prussia, the noted liberal, with whom the prince formed a good relationship. The prince's education was to be completed by study at Oxford and Cambridge; attendance at these English universities was preceded by cramming at Edinburgh in August 1859 with Lyon Playfair. At Oxford he was prevented—to his irritation—by Prince Albert from living in a college, though he was entered on the books of Christ Church as a nobleman on 17 October 1859, matriculating the same day. Prince Henry (later Henry V) was the only previous prince of Wales to matriculate at Oxford (supposedly in 1398). Albert Edward lived in Frewin Court, listened to lectures, and was tutored by Herbert Fisher of Christ Church. For the first time he enjoyed his studies, doing adequately in his examinations and forming long-term friendships with the Liddell family of Christ Church and others. With Henry Chaplin (already a prominent huntsman and later a tory cabinet minister) and Frederick Johnstone (already a well-known philanderer) he began to break loose from the intellectual and moral parameters which his parents had tried to impose on him. He became a lifelong and famous smoker and developed his enthusiasm for blood sports.

The prince's assiduity at Oxford gained him some respect from his parents, though the queen at this time found her son physically repellent: 'Bertie … is not at all in good looks; his nose and mouth are too enormous and he pastes his hair down to his head, and wears his clothes frightfully—he really is anything but good looking' (Fulford, 1.245). Despite this lack of encouragement, growing confidence and maturity were seen during the prince's visit to Canada and the USA in July–November 1860, the first heir to the throne to visit either country. The idea for the visit was Prince Albert's. In Washington and New York, Albert Edward was especially successful in a context where royalty was not necessarily welcome. The tour defined the public role and character of the prince of Wales. He was genial and undidactic. He enjoyed himself and transmitted his good humour. His very absence of intellectual enquiry meant that awkward corners could be easily turned. The prince, moreover, had shown he could play a role different from that of his parents, that of the roving royal ambassador.

On his return, however, Albert Edward somewhat incongruously returned to his studies in Oxford, and then, on 19 January 1861, matriculated from Trinity College, Cambridge, where J. B. Lightfoot, the biblical scholar, was his chief tutor and he enjoyed lectures from Charles Kingsley. At his father's request—and he was the chancellor of the university—the prince lived at Madingley Hall, outside the town, though rooms in Trinity were surreptitiously put at his disposal. Where Oxford had liberated, Cambridge now rather shackled, despite fun at the amateur dramatic club and hunting. Determined to enter the army, the prince spent the summer of 1861 at army camp at the Curragh, near Dublin. Always keen on uniforms and parades, the prince found the discipline required from a participant excessive, his relative the duke of Cambridge, the commander-in-chief, reporting that he would never make a good professional soldier. At the Curragh he met Nellie Clifden, an actress, smuggled into his tent by his friends. She was indiscreet and the story was soon round London.

Marriage, Sandringham, and official exclusion The Clifden episode occurred just as the prince was being prepared for marriage to Princess *Alexandra of Schleswig-Holstein-Sonderburg-Glücksburg (1844–1925), daughter of the heir to the Danish throne; the union was largely engineered by his sister Victoria, the crown princess of Prussia, and was one about which Victoria and Albert were extremely cautious, given their pro-Prussian and consequently anti-Danish opinions about German unification. The queen was won over by the absence of suitable alternative spouses and by her view that her son must be settled as soon as possible (the prince consort's health already being in clear decline). The couple met in September 1861 at Speyer and Alexandra's beauty quickly captivated Albert Edward, who had insisted on meeting the princess before agreeing to marry her. However, an engagement had not been decided upon when, with the Clifden affair still simmering, the prince consort died on 14 December 1861, shortly after a visit to Cambridge to discuss both Nellie and Alexandra. The prince of Wales was chief mourner at his father's funeral, which, by custom, his mother did not attend. The queen blamed her son for Albert's final illness, telling her daughter: 'much as I pity I never can or shall look at him without a shudder' (letter of 27 Dec 1861; Fulford, 2.30). She wanted him out of the country, and in January 1862 sent him to Palestine and the Near East, from

which, having visited Jerusalem, Cairo, and Constantinople, he returned in June 1862. On the death of General Bruce in that month, Sir William Knollys (1797–1883) became the prince's comptroller and treasurer, a post he held until 1877. He was assisted by his son, Sir Francis Knollys (1837–1924), who in due course succeeded his father as the prince's secretary. In September 1862 the prince again met Alexandra, and their engagement was announced on 16 September. They were married in St George's Chapel, Windsor, on 10 March 1863, the scene being recorded in W. P. Frith's painting *The Marriage of the Prince of Wales, 1863* (Royal Collection). The short honeymoon was at Osborne House on the Isle of Wight.

The prince consort's death, the queen's consequent seclusion, and the prince of Wales's marriage marked an important stage in the latter's emergence as the public face of British royalty. On 5 February 1863 he took his seat in the House of Lords, where he occasionally attended and from time to time spoke. He received a civil-list annuity of £10,000, which with the revenues of the duchy of Cornwall gave him an annual income of about £100,000. He set up at Marlborough House in Pall Mall, his London home until he ascended the throne, and he bought Sandringham House in Norfolk from Charles Cowper, Palmerston's stepson. The Waleses first stayed there in March 1864. It soon became a country house as lively as the queen's residences were gloomy. An ample supply of wildfowl, especially pheasants, permitted good sporting house parties, and the prince in the 1860s established himself as a focal point of society. The queen, however, was strongly hostile to the prince's taking on public duties in Britain. She tried to maintain the code of behaviour which Albert had prescribed, which was one in which Albert was the chief male prince. The queen, as Sidney Lee put it, kept her son 'in permanent *in statu pupillari*. She claimed to regulate his actions in almost all relations of life' (*DNB*). Maintaining a sort of fiction that Albert was alive and active, she forbade the prince's presence on royal commissions and public bodies, and, despite her own almost total seclusion, he was not allowed to represent her at public occasions. The prince's Danish connections and his clear hostility to Prussia's conduct in 1864—'the conduct of the Prussians and the Austrians is really quite scandalous', he told Lord Spencer (Hibbert, 76)—placed him in political disagreement with his mother, whom he had further alarmed by travelling specially to London to meet the republican Garibaldi in April 1864. In marked contrast to the privileges accorded to Prince Leopold, who acted as his mother's confidential secretary and was given the keys to the dispatch boxes, the queen did not permit the prince of Wales to see cabinet papers or the foreign and colonial correspondence which came to the monarch and which she scrutinized with a very critical eye. He was given a précis of some of the documents. The queen told him such papers could be seen only by 'those immediately connected' with her (Magnus, 81). This exclusion was a private mark of his mother's lasting distrust of her son, one against which he unsuccessfully complained, with occasional help from politicians, particularly Gladstone, for a quarter of a century. Disraeli, especially, regarded Wales as indiscreet, a view that weighed strongly with the queen in the 1870s. Gladstone secretly sent him various documents. In 1886 the prince's friend Lord Rosebery, then foreign secretary, began sending him Foreign Office papers, and from 1892 he was allowed to see reports of cabinet meetings (but not the prime minister's letter to the queen which reported cabinet meetings).

The prince of Wales was thus given no positive royal role by his mother in the 1860s. He developed, not surprisingly, a routine which related little to her interests and was little connected to her physical movements. The queen lived at Windsor and Osborne, with a spell at Balmoral in the autumn. The prince lived in London or at Sandringham, coinciding with his mother during Cowes week in August and Deeside in October. In the spring he visited the Riviera. His routine was thus as close to the seasons of society as his mother's was distant. His absence of royal duties left him as a social icon, a role which, especially in the bohemian world of art, opera, and the theatre, he carried off with some panache, playing an important role in the planning of the Royal Albert Hall and of the Royal College of Music, and supporting the Royal Literary Fund. He moreover took on a number of public duties, including presidency of the Society of Arts (1863) and of the 1851 commissioners (1870), and chairman of the governors of Wellington College (1864).

A royal family In the course of seven years Princess Alexandra, despite bouts of rheumatic fever, bore six children. The Waleses' first child, *Albert Victor Christian Edward, duke of Clarence and Avondale (1864–1892), was born on 8 January 1864. He was followed on 3 June 1865 by George Frederick Ernest Albert (later *George V), in 1867 by *Louise Victoria Alexandra Dagmar (later princess royal and duchess of Fife), in 1868 by *Victoria Alexandra Olga Mary, who did not marry, and in 1869 by *Maud Charlotte Mary Victoria (later queen of Norway as wife of Haakon VII); the last, a boy, Alexander John, was born prematurely on 6 April 1871 and died after two days. The queen insisted on Albert Victor's being thus called, and declared that all the prince's descendants should bear the name of either Albert or Victoria. Princess Alexandra's chief delight was the rearing of her children. She was not anti-social, and always cut a splendid figure in public, but deafness and disinclination discouraged frequent attendance at public events. Alexandra enjoyed domesticity and doted on her children. The prince combined an amiable home life— despite their very different lifestyles he and Alexandra accommodated each other—with an increasingly vigorous social round. Impatient and easily bored, he moved restlessly from gambling to music-halls and elsewhere by night, from race meetings to yachting and blood sports by day. Money was soon short. Gladstone, as chancellor of the exchequer, declined to help (partly because a proposal for extra expenditure of public money would entitle the Commons to debate the prince's behaviour, partly because he thought the queen should pay the private debts of her family). The prince grew stout and was known in his circle (though not to his face) as Tum Tum.

Royal unpopularity and its resolution Concern grew among politicians at the conduct of the prince and absence of a role for him. Disraeli encouraged a successful Irish visit in 1868. When Gladstone succeeded Disraeli as prime minister in December 1868, a plan for the prince, in Ireland and elsewhere, was one of his first concerns. However, in April 1869 Gladstone learned that Sir Charles Mordaunt, bt (1836–1897), threatened to cite the prince as a co-respondent in the case for the divorce of his wife, Harriet Sarah. When the petition was filed in January 1870 Mordaunt did not cite the prince as co-respondent, but he was subpoenaed to appear as a witness, which he did on 13 February 1870. In a seven-minute hearing, he denied he had committed adultery and was not cross-examined. The hearing coincided with general criticism of the very different deportments of both the queen and the prince. The latter was several times booed in public, once on 13 June as he drove from the racecourse at the Ascot summer meeting. For the first time since the Chartists, republicanism was seriously and quite generally discussed. In December 1870 Gladstone brought forward a striking plan: the prince should become viceroy of Ireland, with a royal residence, and act almost as a constitutional monarch there in a reconstituted government structure. A long argument, over two years, ensued between prime minister and queen, with no positive result. The immediate problem of the prince's unpopularity was cured by an accident: in October 1871 he caught typhoid (the disease from which it was popularly thought his father had died) from the drains at Londesborough Lodge. A fellow guest, Lord Chesterfield, died on 1 December and the prince's condition was critical. The family assembled at Sandringham. Alfred Austin, the future poet laureate, wrote:

> Flash'd from his bed, the electric tidings came,
> He is not better; he is much the same.

The queen was informed that his death was imminent. However, the prince rallied on 11 December, and recovered. Gladstone capitalized on the situation, arranging a thanksgiving service in St Paul's Cathedral on 27 February 1872, which he persuaded the queen to attend. The royal party was cheered through the streets of London, and the bubble of republican feeling burst.

The prince's life continued in what Philip Magnus called 'its former rut' (Magnus, 125). Increasingly, however, he played the occasional role of representative of the head of state, as when he received the shah of Persia at Buckingham Palace in 1873 and accompanied him on his British tour. In 1874 he received the tsarevich at a great state banquet on 15 May in Marlborough House, the occasion being designed by Sir Frederick Leighton, with the prince dressed as Charles I, an unfortunate analogy but one which emphasized the passing of republicanism. He carried off such occasions with great aplomb, as he did the four speeches he made when visiting Birmingham on 3 November 1874. He charmed the mayor, Joseph Chamberlain, who had in 1870 moved on the fringe of the republican movement, and who from 1877 frequently visited Marlborough House. After an early catastrophe when he found it difficult to read his speech, the prince always spoke fluently from brief notes, and became known for this ability.

In India, 1875–1876 Keen to develop this quasi-regnal role, the prince in 1874 planned an Indian visit, personally co-ordinating the complex process by which royal and cabinet permission was obtained. The visit was financed by the government of India and a supplementary vote from the Commons of £112,500. The prince and his all-male party of eighteen left on 11 October 1875 (the princess of Wales disappointed at being excluded). They landed at Bombay on 8 November, the day before the prince's thirty-fourth birthday, travelled south to Goa and Ceylon, and then to Calcutta, arriving on 23 December, where a large durbar was held on 1 January 1876. They then went to Benares, Lucknow, Cawnpore, and Delhi. Over a month was spent hunting in the shadow of the Himalayas. The prince set a blistering pace and his appetite for hunting exhausted many of his party. On his first day tiger hunting he shot six tigers. The tour, reported for *The Times* by W. H. Russell, was in general very successful. The prince's easy manner with persons of all levels of society made a strong impression and went some way to assuage the racial tension prevalent in India. The prince, always hostile to any racial or religious prejudice, was strongly critical of the 'rude and rough' manner (Lee, 1.399) by which British political officers dealt with Indians. New instructions were issued by Lord Salisbury, the secretary of state, and at least one resident was recalled.

While the prince was in India, the queen persuaded Disraeli to introduce the Royal Titles Act making the British monarch emperor or empress of India. Her failure to inform her son—he read of the announcement in the newspapers—infuriated him, perhaps more than any of the many slights he felt he had endured from the queen. Also while in India news came of a further divorce case, which involved a bundle of the prince's letters and his friends lords Aylesford and Blandford. The royal party set out for Britain from Bombay on 13 March 1876. From Malta, the prince challenged Lord Randolph Churchill to a duel in France, the latter having strenuously defended his brother, Blandford, against a condemnation by the prince. Diplomacy by various members of the cabinet prevented the duel, but the quarrel with Churchill continued until 1883, when the prince formed a close friendship with Lady Randolph.

Public duties The visit to India was Albert Edward's chief political initiative until he ascended the throne. On his return he was welcomed by the award of honorary degrees and freedoms of various cities. The final year of the annual London satire *The Coming k—*, so critical in its first year (1870), ended its series with the prince ascending the throne to acclaim on his mother's abdication. Politically, the prince was of moderate Liberal inclination. Unlike his mother, he much preferred Gladstone to Disraeli, and sympathized with the former's difficulties with the queen (in 1898 he and his son, later George V, were to act as Gladstone's pallbearers in the face of strong condemnation from Queen Victoria). But the prince strongly supported Disraeli's Near Eastern policy in the late 1870s, and he urged the invasion of Egypt in 1882; he very much hoped to serve in the Egyptian expedition, but his offer was declined by the cabinet. On the other hand, in 1884 the prince had to be dissuaded from voting in the Lords in favour of the Liberal government's Representation of the People Bill (which the Lords rejected). But in 1886 he was strongly Liberal Unionist on the question of Irish home rule.

On Gladstone's invitation the prince became, in April 1881, a trustee of the British Museum; as such he supported Sunday opening and showed a special interest in the natural history collections and their move to South Kensington. In 1884 the prince was a member of Sir Charles Dilke's royal commission on the housing of working classes, the first occasion on which an heir to the throne served on a royal commission (he had already sat on two committees of the House of Lords, on the cattle plague in 1866 and on scarcity of horses in 1873). Initially he attended meetings of the commission assiduously, visiting East End slums incognito, but the death of his brother Prince Leopold and other family matters distracted him; he attended nineteen out of fifty-one meetings. He subsequently invited Henry Broadhurst, the Lib-Lab MP and a fellow commissioner, to Sandringham.

In 1891 the prince's offer to serve on the royal commission on labour relations was rejected by Lord Salisbury, but in 1892 he was appointed by Gladstone to the royal commission on the aged poor, of which Broadhurst and Joseph Arch, the trade unionist and MP, were also members. The prince attended quite regularly and asked well-informed questions of the witnesses. He was also publicly prominent as the chief active host of the guests at the 1887 jubilee of his mother's accession, as he was in 1897. His chief contribution to the jubilee of 1897 was his establishment, with the approval of the queen and the assistance of Sir Henry Charles Burdett, of the Prince of Wales's Hospital Fund for London, in which the prince took a close personal interest. With skilful fund-raising it soon became a vital fund in the prosperity of the London hospitals. In 1902 it was renamed King Edward's Hospital Fund for London (also known as the King's Fund), and in 1906 it was incorporated.

Unlike his father, the prince was an enthusiastic freemason, especially from 1870 onwards. He presided at public occasions. In 1871 he became patron of Free and Accepted Masons in Ireland during his visit there in August 1871. On 28 April 1875 he was installed as grand master of English freemasons, being elected to the office on the resignation of Lord Ripon (who had converted to Roman Catholicism). The prince quite often presided at fund-raising dinners for the masons, on one occasion raising £51,000 in an evening. On ascending the throne he retired as grand master and became protector of English freemasons, following the precedent of George IV. The prince's active sponsorship of freemasonry set a trend for the royal family of the future.

Public scandals The prince never masked his enthusiasm for beautiful women, though none outshone the beauty of his wife. He carefully confined his serious attention to married women with compliant husbands. He had no embarrassment about his liaison with Lillie *Langtry (1853–1929), whom he met in May 1877 and whose stage career he superintended. She was, in the view of one of his biographers, 'almost *maîtresse en titre*', accompanying the prince to Paris and to the Ascot races. From 1883 Frances Evelyn (Daisy) Maynard *Greville, Lady Brooke (1861–1938), a striking society beauty, was the chief focus of the prince's extra-marital attention. It became known in 1890—it was said that the news came out through the indiscretion of Daisy Brooke, the 'babbling Brooke' as she was dubbed—that the prince was present at Tranby Croft, near Doncaster, at a game of baccarat (illegal in Britain), at which Sir William Gordon-Cumming appeared to be cheating. The baccarat and the cheating outraged different sections of society. Together, they ensured a scandal. Gordon-Cumming brought an action against the five persons who claimed to have witnessed the cheating, and subpoenaed the prince as a witness. The case was heard by Lord Coleridge as lord chief justice from 1 to 9 June 1891. Sir Edward Clarke, the solicitor-general, represented Gordon-Cumming, whom he believed innocent, and was unhelpful to the prince in court. Gordon-Cumming lost the case, was dismissed from the army, and expelled from his clubs. The scandal was worse than the Mordaunt affair, for public tolerance in the 1890s was much narrower than in the 1870s, and the prince was shown up at the trial as, at the least, negligent. Furthermore, *Lady River*, a pamphlet by Mrs Gerald Paget, which was circulated privately but widely, gave details of the prince's liaison with Lady Brooke and of a quarrel with Lord and Lady Charles Beresford in which Lady Brooke and the prince were involved; it was discussed in *Truth* and other such journals. About 1894, soon after Lady Brooke became countess of Warwick and after she had begun to make her developing socialism a frequent topic of conversation with the prince, their affair cooled. In 1898 Princess Alexandra—always hitherto distant from Daisy Warwick, perhaps sensing a liaison that was more than the usual dalliance—was reconciled to her.

The prince rode out the scandals of the 1890s. The newspapers never seriously harried him, except when people of his own circle brought him to court, and the British in the 1890s had no general wish to see their future monarch fail.

Nearing the throne: the succession and international affairs
By the 1890s the prince's accession to the throne could not be far off: the jubilee of 1897 was seen as the old queen's apotheosis. The prince had not played a very prominent part in the education of his own children. In 1898 the Commons voted a capital sum of £60,000 and an increase in his annual income of £36,000 per annum to enable him to provide better for them. The eldest son, Prince Eddy, created duke of Clarence and Avondale in May 1890, was much the most problematic. He had his father's vices without his canniness. The prince sent his sons to be naval cadets on HMS *Britannia* in 1877. George blossomed in the navy; Eddy floundered. If some had from time to time questioned the appropriateness of the prince of Wales's character for that of a monarch, Eddy promised a far more daunting future. In what had become a life of considerable dissipation, Eddy suddenly, in 1890, fell in love with Princess Hélène of Orléans, a Roman Catholic and the daughter of the comte de Paris, pretender to the throne of France. The prince of Wales favoured the match; the princess was willing to join the Church of England; but Lord Salisbury, as prime minister, and the comte de Paris, for religious reasons, vetoed it. In 1891, while the prince was preoccupied with the Tranby Croft affair, Princess Alexandra brought forward Princess Mary of Teck, whose engagement to the duke of Clarence was ended by his death on 14 January 1892, his brother George thus becoming the prince of Wales's heir. The prince of Wales was more grief-stricken by this event than perhaps any other, but he must have soon been relieved at Prince George's much more obvious suitability for the throne. George was quickly engaged and married to Mary of Teck, and in June 1894 and December 1895 the succession was assured by the births of the future Edward VIII and George VI. A decade which started unhappily and uncertainly for the monarchy in fact saw its succession satisfactorily settled for the next fifty years.

In personal terms also, the decade finished well for the prince. In February 1898 he formed two liaisons which lasted the rest of his life. Sister Agnes Keyser, matron of a nursing home for army officers at 17 Grosvenor Crescent, London, was attractive and discreet. She often entertained Albert Edward, both as prince and king, to a plain dinner. Alice Frederica *Keppel (1868–1947) first entertained the prince in February 1898; she was soon his mistress, 'which was intelligible in view of the lady's good looks, vivacity and cleverness', as Lord Hardinge noted in 1910 (Magnus, 260).

As international relations deteriorated in the 1890s, the prince—one of the most cosmopolitan figures in Britain and related to most European monarchs, but now older than most of them—played an increasingly avuncular role in the European royal social scene, which remained of direct political importance, especially in Russia and Germany. The prince was on poor terms with his nephew Kaiser Wilhelm II. His stock comment on him was 'William the Great needs to learn that he is living at the end of the nineteenth century and not in the Middle Ages' (Magnus, 209). During the Kaiser's visit to Vienna in 1888 the prince of Wales believed he had been snubbed. William complained that the prince treated him as a nephew rather than as an emperor. During the Kaiser's rather successful state visit to Britain in 1889 the prince played an active and diplomatic role, despite the absence of a sufficient apology from the Kaiser for the Vienna episode, and from that point relations were superficially improved. In 1894, on the accession as tsar of Nicholas II, the prince and princess led a successful British mission to St Petersburg, being congratulated by Lord Rosebery, the prime minister, for their patriotic work. Privately the prince thought the new tsar 'weak as water' (ibid., 249).

The prince formed the view—rather earlier than many

of his compatriots—that Britain was dangerously isolated. He encouraged contacts with Portugal, and during the Venezuela incident between Britain and the USA in December 1895 sent a conciliatory telegram to America regardless of instructions from the prime minister, Lord Salisbury, to remain silent. The prince took especial care with the arrangements for the tsar's visit to Balmoral in 1896, but he was excluded from the talks held between the tsar, the queen, and the British prime minister. He also worked hard to make a success of the Kaiser's visit in November 1899, just after the start of the Second South African War. During the war the prince increased the number of his official visits. Cautious about foreign opinion, he cancelled his annual trip to the Riviera in 1900, leaving instead to stay with his wife's relatives in Denmark. On his journey thither, on 4 April 1900 in Brussels a Belgian anarchist student named Sipido fired at him through the carriage window. The stationmaster disarmed Sipido and the prince was unhurt. On the latter's return to London huge crowds greeted him, reflecting a popularity which had steadily grown during his mother's last years and was confirmed by popular reaction to the prince's remarkable racing results in 1900.

Racing and other sports From 1863, aged twenty-one, the prince attended the Derby and most of the classics. From his middle years, racing in Britain and France became his chief sporting passion. From 1880 the Jockey Club at Newmarket, to which he was elected in 1864, provided him with an apartment, and from 1885 he entertained all its members on Derby evening at Marlborough House and, after 1900, at Buckingham Palace. His colours—purple, gold braid, scarlet sleeves, black velvet cap with gold fringe—were first seen at Newmarket in 1877. His first success was Leonidas at Aldershot on 14 April 1880. He soon raced both on the flat and over fences, though always more successfully on the flat. Lord Marcus Beresford was his chief adviser. In 1883 John Porter of Kingclere became his trainer, and in 1885 the prince opened a stud at Sandringham, his mare Perdita II being an important and fecund purchase. From 1893 Richard Marsh at Egerton House, Newmarket, was the prince's and later the king's trainer. From that year the prince was successful, and sometimes very successful, and by a long way the most successful of royal owners in the nineteenth and twentieth centuries. In 1896 Persimmon won the Derby and the St Leger, and in 1897 he won the Eclipse Stakes and the Ascot Gold cup. In 1900, the prince's best year, he won the Grand National with Ambush II and, with Diamond Jubilee, the five chief races of those days (the Two Thousand Guineas, the Newmarket Stakes, the Eclipse, the Derby, and the St Leger), a remarkable achievement by any standard, making the prince the leading owner with £29,586 in winning stakes. He bred Persimmon and Diamond Jubilee at the Sandringham stud, both by St Simon out of Perdita II. Diamond Jubilee he sold to an Argentinian breeder; the skeleton of Persimmon (d. 1908 from an accident) was presented to the Natural History Museum. In an era when the Derby was the nation's chief sporting event, and easily the best attended, the prince's successes—so enthusiastically received both by himself and the huge number who backed his horses—easily outweighed the memory of the scandals in which he had been involved.

The prince was an equally enthusiastic sailor, often being on board during his yachts' races. He succeeded his father as commodore of the Royal Yacht Squadron at Cowes in 1863 and from 1874 was commodore of the Royal Thames Yacht Club. His first yacht was *Dagmar*; he subsequently raced *Hildegarde*, *Formosa*, and *Aline*. In 1892 he built a 300 ton racing cutter, *Britannia*, which won many races and served as a base when touring in the Mediterranean. The Kaiser treated the Cowes regatta in an increasingly competitive manner, almost as a test of national virility. His new yacht, *Meteor II*, outclassed *Britannia*, and the prince of Wales ceased to race in 1897.

The 'Marlborough House set' Associated with the prince's racing was the 'Marlborough House set', the circle around him who accompanied him on racing and other trips. From the 1870s the set constituted an important focus for London society. It was partly composed of raffish aristocrats, some of whom became publicly well known through the various scandals in which the prince was involved, partly of financiers and merchants, including Nathaniel Rothschild (whose peerage in 1885 was attributed to the prince of Wales), Reuben and Arthur Sassoon, Baron Maurice de Hirsch, Sir Ernest Cassel, Sir Thomas Lipton, Sir Blundell Maple, and Horace Farquhar. That some of these were Jewish attracted unfavourable comment, some of it strongly antisemitic. From an early stage, the prince 'discovered a special affinity with Jews' (Magnus, 106). Sir Anthony de Rothschild was the prince's financial adviser until his death in 1876. Other Rothschilds then advised until 1890, when Hirsch, who had met the prince in 1886, became both financial adviser and confidant until he died in 1890. His place was then filled by Cassel, Hirsch's executor, who, especially from 1897, formed a close friendship with the prince which lasted throughout the latter's reign as king. The prince enjoyed the company of rich men—some speculators like Hirsch and Cassel, others cautious financiers like the Rothschilds; some, but by no means all, of these rich men were Jews. He rather enjoyed rows with more traditional members of the British and continental nobility, who affronted the prince by cold-shouldering his friends.

Edward VII Queen Victoria died on 22 January 1901. Her son had not wished for the throne. He had expressed no frustration at his mother's long old age, only at her exclusion of him from the duties and confidences which as a prince of Wales in his fifties he thought it reasonable to expect. He at once announced that he would reign as Edward VII, explaining in an elegant impromptu speech to the privy council that the name Albert could be associated with no-one but his father. His long-serving secretary, Sir Francis Knollys, continued in post throughout his reign. The new king was almost sixty, stout and ageing, but very active. His enthusiasm for action, if not channelled, quickly became irritable boredom, and his bonhomie sometimes had a sharp edge. He was the first emperor of India. To the title king of the United Kingdom of Great Britain and Ireland, parliament added 'and of the British Dominions beyond the Seas' (1 Edw. VII c. 15). The abandoned suggestion of 'and of all the Britains [*sic*] beyond the Seas' was, however, echoed on the new sovereign's coinage, which included 'Britt : Omn : Rex'.

The prince's accession to the throne was a striking moment in the history of the British monarchy. Like Pip at the end of the film of *Great Expectations* (1946), Edward VII tore down the drapes of the Victorian court and let the light flood in. He at once reorganized the royal finances and palaces (including the removal of various busts and plaques to John Brown). His reorganization and refurbishment was aided by an act of 1901 which increased the monarch's annual income to £470,000, which, together with Sir Ernest Cassel's astute investments, made him much wealthier than his mother (taking currency fluctuations into account, Edward VII was the highest paid British monarch). Sir Francis Knollys was able to inform the commission on royal finances in 1901 that, contrary to public rumour, the new king had no debts, and was indeed, Knollys claimed, the first English monarch to ascend the throne in credit (Lee, 2.26).

The king transformed the court, which for forty years had been almost dormant as a force in metropolitan society, for unlike his mother he lived much of the year in London, and entertained or dined out almost every evening. His enthusiasm for his post was not limited to the presentation of the monarchy, skilful though he was at this aspect. Edward VII had an active sense of the royal prerogative. As we shall see, his autonomous actions in foreign policy were remarkable. In domestic politics he sought personally to supervise many aspects of royal affairs, and to this end he recovered into his own hands many offices which under his mother had been delegated, such as the supervision of the royal parks. Especially in the early years of his reign ministers, to their surprise, looked back to Queen Victoria as relatively supine in official affairs.

On 14 February 1901 Edward VII revived the practice of the monarch's personally opening the new session of parliament (a practice dormant since 1886, and performed by Victoria only six times before that). The anti-Roman Catholic declaration, required from a new sovereign on first addressing parliament, offended some contemporaries. The king's attempts to have it changed were initially unsuccessful, and his son George V was required similarly to declaim; but a new form of declaration was adopted by parliament in August 1910.

The king's coronation was arranged for 26 June 1902. Overwork, overweight, and restlessness had already lowered his reserves when in mid-June appendicitis and peritonitis were diagnosed by Sir Francis Lake; the press was informed only that the king was suffering from lumbago. He was with difficulty persuaded to disappoint the assembling crowds and dignitaries by postponing the ceremony and undergoing an operation. The operation was successfully performed on 23 June and the king was well enough to be crowned on 9 August in a shortened ceremony. To try to counter the flow of political honours and to broaden the character of national reward, the king in the spring of 1902 proposed an order of merit, with twenty-four members (and unlimited honorary foreign members), which would mark distinction in the arts, sciences, literature, and the armed forces; the order was instituted by letters patent on 23 June 1902, John Morley and G. F. Watts being among the first members. The king kept appointment to the order in his own hands and appointed some members, for example the controversial figure of Admiral Sir John Fisher, without any consultation.

Political relations, 1901–1905 Shortly after his operation the king accepted, on 11 July 1902, the resignation of Lord Salisbury as prime minister. A. J. Balfour, his successor, was not a natural companion of the king, who found Balfour's intellectual manner off-putting. They shared, however, an interest in the development of the committee of imperial defence and in motor cars (both being in the forefront of motoring), and a hostility to Irish home rule. Balfour's government was soon embroiled in a major dispute over tariff reform, in which the king took a keen interest, deploring the social injustice and danger of taxes on food and proposing on 18 August 1903 (from Marienbad) to the prime minister that the matter be referred to a royal commission. Though the delaying consequences of this would, at least in retrospect, have been welcome to Balfour, it was not, in the political circumstances, a practical suggestion. On 15 September 1903 the king learned that the prime minister's policy was to be that of retaliation, not full-scale tariff reform, but that his cabinet did not, as yet, know this. The king was at Balmoral in September 1903 when Balfour's cabinet disintegrated, and he played no direct part in the crisis. Balfour's announcement of resignations from the cabinet without prior notice to the sovereign considerably irritated the king.

Balfour's premiership was a period of continual political instability which Edward VII found wearing. He played an important part in one of the controversies: army and naval reform. The king took his role as head of the forces seriously. This was manifested in part in his obsession with uniforms and his fury when they were worn incorrectly. But the reform of the forces was a serious matter with important political implications. In 1903, prompted by Lord Esher, the king took up the cause of the introduction of an army board on the model of the Admiralty. Though he won over Lord Roberts, the commander-in-chief, and others, he found St John Brodrick, the war secretary, an opponent; when the cabinet was reshuffled in September 1903, Brodrick was unwillingly moved to the India Office. The king was annoyed when Esher declined to replace Brodrick at the War Office. The king was much impressed by the ability of John Fisher and was converted to his view of naval reform, and defence reform more generally. He supported the Fisher faction of naval reformers and strongly backed the report produced in January 1903 by Esher, Fisher, and Sir George Clarke which led to extensive reforms in the War Office and considerable extensions of the powers and role of the committee of imperial defence. In later years, the king used to monitor the dates of its meetings and complain to the Liberal cabinet when he thought them too infrequent. The king was incensed by an incident in July 1905 when H. O. Arnold-Forster, Brodrick's successor, having made an incautious remark to the Commons' public accounts committee, appeared to make a requirement rather than a request for the king speedily to sign an army order. Balfour offered to ask Arnold-Forster to resign if Esher would take over; the latter again declined.

Political relations, 1905–1908 On 4 December 1905 Arthur Balfour and his cabinet resigned. The king thought this 'unnecessary and a mistake. The formation of a new Govt. will give trouble in many ways, and I presume I shall have to send for Sir H. C.-B.' (Magnus, 346). The king sent for Campbell-Bannerman, who kissed hands on 5 December, successfully formed a cabinet (against Balfour's hopes), and won a striking victory in the general election held in January 1906. Campbell-Bannerman was in fact the first official prime minister, for by a royal warrant of 20 March 1905 the office was formally recognized when Balfour's successor was appointed, its holder taking fourth place in precedence after the royal family. Some have seen this as a diminution of royal prerogative, but recognition of the fact that the United Kingdom had a prime minister did no more than record a position which had been apparent for half a century or more.

The king worked through Knollys to ensure that the Liberal Imperialists joined the cabinet. Campbell-Bannerman, who declined the king's suggestion that he take a peerage on account of his health, was five years older than the king and in some respects almost a comrade. They both spent much time at German spas and each had a boisterous sense of humour. But the prime minister was a sturdy radical and declined to require Liberals who expressed political views disliked by the court to apologize. On the personal side, however, the king got on well with John Burns, sometimes seen as a socialist. Despite a disagreement on the number of peers to be created following the change of government, the king formed a close bond on meeting Campbell-Bannerman in August 1906 at Marienbad, to the extent of personally arranging the funeral of Lady Campbell-Bannerman when she died there during their holiday. The prime minister never recovered from his wife's death, and the absence of information from him on the cabinet's decisions became a matter of complaint on the part of the king (the prime minister was still expected to write personally to the king about cabinet and parliamentary decisions and progress). In 1906 the Education Bill foreshadowed much that was to be characteristic about the 1906 parliament: the Lords were intent on frustrating the Liberal majority in the Commons; the king made a sustained effort in November and December 1906 to play the role of mediator, but was unable to prevent the Lords' destruction of the bill. The king agreed with much of the Unionist case, but thought the Lords' action foolhardy; he resented both sides for

having, as he saw it, in their different ways brought the crown into politics. In 1907 several bills were similarly treated, including the Small Landholders (Scotland) Bill, the latter leading to a difference between the king and the cabinet as to whether the king's speech proroguing parliament should express regret that the measure had failed to pass into law; an impasse developed, solved by complete omission of the contentious paragraph.

The king was suspicious of Liberal policy towards South Africa. He complained both at the absence of consultation with him on the ending of employment of Chinese indentured labour in South Africa and at the rapidity of the decision. He felt that he received inadequate advice from the cabinet when the Cullinan diamond was offered to him by the Transvaal—a gift that caused significant dissent there. (The diamond was eventually graciously accepted: the uncut stone weighed almost 3026 carats; when cut, it substantially added to the value of the crown jewels.) Edward VII strongly supported the principle of federation in South Africa, but he disliked the appointment of Herbert Gladstone as first governor-general (he had also disliked his home secretaryship) and unsuccessfully tried to get Asquith to find an alternative.

Style and the leisure pursuits of a monarch Edward VII saw that style was critical to public perception of a modern monarchy. He followed a punctual pattern of life, partly designed to prevent his becoming bored. After spending the first part of the year in London for the opening of parliament and the season, he would visit France—usually Biarritz and its Hôtel du Palais—in March, and then cruise in the Mediterranean. During his reign he often travelled abroad as duke of Lancaster. In the summer the king spent each weekend at Sandringham, at a friend's house, or at his private apartments in the Jockey Club at Newmarket. In June he moved to Windsor Castle for the races at Ascot, then to the duke of Richmond's for Goodwood races in July. He was at Cowes for the regatta in August, and then at Hotel Weimar in Marienbad (while the queen was in Denmark with her relatives); the rest of the summer was passed in a combination of visits to friends with houses near relevant racecourses and staying in Scottish houses, but with only a shortish spell at Balmoral. Autumn saw the king much at Sandringham. He travelled chiefly by train, but increasingly also in one of his fleet of claret-coloured cars. He had a passion for the new form of transport and did much to popularize it; he took especial pride in fast driving and would instruct his chauffeur to pursue and overtake. On the Brighton road he liked to exceed 60 m.p.h. (three times the speed limit). The king remained, despite his vast size, an active sportsman: he was an occasional golfer; he kept goal in ice-hockey matches at Sandringham; and he was always an enthusiastic shot. He always attended church on Sunday morning, but for the rest of the day he relaxed the previously strict Sabbatarianism of the court, deliberately trying to introduce a continental view of Sundays. In the evening, the king enjoyed the new game of bridge (Mrs Keppel, an excellent player, being his usual partner) as well as his customary pursuits. He did not patronize the arts, except the theatre, and he liked paintings to be strictly representational. His taste in art was uncharacteristically old-fashioned. His vast appetite was legendary, and he ate a full meal at breakfast, luncheon, tea, dinner (normally twelve courses), and supper. He drank moderately, but usually smoked twelve enormous cigars and twenty cigarettes a day.

The court was thus the epitome of conspicuous consumption, and in this it set the tone of the British propertied classes in the Edwardian period, as it quickly came to be known. The apotheosis of the king's sporting life occurred on 26 May 1909 when his Minoru, ridden by Herbert Jones, won the Derby at 4–1 by half a head. He remains the only monarch to have won the race, and his victory occasioned a vast demonstration of public enthusiasm.

The king's close attention to dress and punctuality was legendary; he reprimanded incorrect dress or wrongly worn decorations without deference to rank or diplomacy, and complained bitterly and vocally when a servant, friend, politician—or the habitually unpunctual queen—was late. He was himself fairly conservative in his dress, attempting to delay the decline of the frock coat and to revive the fashion of knee breeches with evening dress. As prince of Wales he had popularized the modern dinner jacket with black tie, and as king his wearing of a tweed suit at Goodwood and a Norfolk jacket made them fashionable. From necessity he customarily wore the bottom button of his waistcoat undone and was followed in this in Britain and the empire but not on the continent or in the USA. His wearing of the Homburg felt hat on leisure occasions led to a marked change in the headgear of his male subjects, as, to a lesser degree, did his wearing of Tyrolean hats. However, his practice of creasing his trousers at the side rather than the front did not produce frequent emulation.

Scotland, Wales, and Ireland The title of Edward VII not surprisingly occasioned protest in Scotland, where he was the first Edward to hold the throne, the first three English Edwards having been excluded from Scotland by battle. His ordinal was commonly omitted in Scotland, even by the Church of Scotland in loyal addresses. Following the coronation, the king and queen made a cruise in *Victoria and Albert*, during which they visited Wales, the Isle of Man, and the west coast of Scotland; following the usual stay at Balmoral, the royal party went south via A. J. Balfour's house near Edinburgh. Even so, this was not an official tour of the non-English countries of the United Kingdom mainland and the king's attentions to Wales and Scotland were never more than routine.

The king and queen visited Ireland in July–August 1903, despite the refusal of the Dublin corporation to present the usual loyal address. He visited Maynooth College, went to Belfast, and toured parts of Ireland by motor car. In April–May 1904 he was again in Ireland, on a private visit, staying with the duke of Devonshire at Lismore and attending Punchestown and Leopardstown races. He also visited Dublin. On 10 July 1907 the king and queen opened at Dublin the International Exhibition. The king was not a home-ruler, and his reign came too late for a revival of the

various initiatives for a form of dual monarchy which he and Gladstone had unsuccessfully proposed in the 1870s.

The king and foreign policy: the tour of 1903 No British monarch of recent times came to the throne better equipped to play a constructive role in foreign affairs. The king was well travelled and well connected. He was accustomed to spend part of each year in Germany and France, and as king he continued to do so. He could speak in public in French and German. At his accession the rulers of Germany, Russia, Greece, and Portugal were his close relatives, and the circle widened when in October 1905 Prince Charles of Denmark (his son-in-law, married to his youngest daughter, Maud) was elected king of Norway as Haakon VII, and in May 1906 his niece Princess Ena married Alfonso XIII, king of Spain. The king's easy public manner made him a natural ambassador, though his ministers, accustomed perhaps to Victoria's hostility to public engagements, were slow to take advantage of this.

Edward VII's reign began just as British foreign policy began a wide-ranging and critical readjustment. Isolated during the Second South African War and nervous about strategic over-extension, Lord Lansdowne (who succeeded Lord Salisbury as foreign secretary in 1900) negotiated an agreement (normally referred to as an alliance) with Japan, signed on 30 January 1902, which markedly reduced Britain's over-extension in the Indian and Pacific oceans. This end of isolation concurred with the policy advocated by the king when prince of Wales, and he supported its negotiation, making helpful suggestions about not offending Germany at the time of the agreement's publication (Gooch and Temperley, 2.121). When the French objected to the agreement, the king minuted a dispatch: 'It shows more than ever the necessity of an agreement with Japan which naturally interferes with Russia's views and possible action' (ibid., 2.136). As the possibility of an alliance with Germany markedly diminished after the abortive negotiations in 1900, the Foreign Office turned instead to a settlement of imperial differences with France, hitherto seen by Britain as her most probable opponent, should there be a war in Europe.

In November 1902 the king was reluctantly persuaded to entertain the Kaiser at Sandringham. The visit did not go well, the king being heard to exclaim, 'Thank God, he's gone' as his nephew departed (Magnus, 307). The king then personally planned a state visit to a number of European countries, to take place in the spring of 1903, in the form of a Mediterranean cruise aboard the *Victoria and Albert*. This was to be the first state visit abroad by a British monarch since 1855. Edward VII saw it as a personal initiative and initially correspondence was carried on in complete secret, with even the queen, the king's secretary, and the cabinet kept in ignorance. Sir Edmund Monson, ambassador in Paris, told the Foreign Office that he believed the king had a direct and secret means of communication with President Loubet of France. The king refused to be accompanied on the visit by a cabinet minister or a Foreign Office adviser (the usual form, even on a non-state visit abroad), save Charles Hardinge (1858–1944), an under-secretary (Hardinge was upgraded to minister-plenipotentiary for the duration of the visit and accompanied the king on all his subsequent diplomatic forays). The visit to Portugal, Gibraltar, and Malta in April 1903 went well. The king's plan was to return via France; he had agreed to the cabinet's advice not to visit the pope in Rome. Many of the details of the tour were improvised as it proceeded; the king, to Sir Frederick Knollys's amazement, 'himself made the arrangements and supervised every detail' (ibid., 308). Despite the cabinet's strongly expressed injunction the king hoped to visit Rome, especially when he heard that British Roman Catholics would be offended if he did not. A row by telegraph between the king and the prime minister ensued, the upshot of which was that the king visited the pope informally on 29 April during his state visit to the kingdom of Italy, the first occasion on which a British or English sovereign had ever visited the pope in Rome (as prince of Wales the king had three times visited Pius IX).

The king returned via Paris—the essential purpose of his tour—where he arrived, accompanied by Sir Edmund Monson, the British ambassador, on 1 May 1903. The cabinet, already rather shaken by the row over the Vatican visit, would probably have preferred the king not to go. Although behind the scenes British and French officials were working towards what became the Anglo-French entente of 8 April 1904, relations between the officials anticipated rather than reflected cordiality between the two states. In 1889 the British government had not recognized the celebrations marking the centenary of the French Revolution. Following the Fashoda incident in 1898, the prince of Wales (as he then was) had been hissed in the streets of Paris in 1899. In 1900 he had cancelled his annual visit to the Riviera and had declined, despite the urgings of Lord Salisbury, to attend the Universal Exhibition in Paris that year. In 1903 the crowds were initially muted. The king carried off, unperturbed, several tricky moments. The audience at the Théâtre Français seemed uncertain. During the interval the king walked in the foyer; spotting Mlle Jeanne Granier, an actress whom he knew, he kissed her hand, remarking in French 'Mademoiselle, I remember applauding you in London where you represented all the grace and spirit of France.' The gesture and words went round Paris and the visit became a triumph. The king easily maintained monarchic dignity while acknowledging a republican setting. Eyre Crowe wrote in his famous Foreign Office memorandum of 1 January 1907 that the fact that the gradual evolution of good Franco-British relations, which was the best the Foreign Office could expect, 'declared itself with unexpected rapidity and unmistakable emphasis was without doubt due, in the first place, to the initiative and tactful perseverance of the King, warmly recognised and applauded on both sides of the Channel' (Gooch and Temperley, 3.398). On 6 July 1903 President Loubet and Delcassé, the French minister for foreign affairs, were, in turn, the king's guests, staying at St James's Palace. The king balanced the entente by a visit to the Kaiser at Kiel on 29 June 1904. He went on his yacht, *Victoria and Albert*, accompanied by a naval escort; the visit had been requested for Berlin, but

the Kaiser wished to show his uncle the growing German navy. The king's laughter at the Kaiser's alarm at the 'yellow peril' was not well received, and the visit confirmed a cooling in Anglo-German relations following the entente.

The visit to Paris in 1903 was the political culmination of the king's life. It was a high-risk, personal initiative. It could have done harm if it had failed; it probably did some good, though perhaps not as much as the strongly anti-German Eyre Crowe suggested. Where his mother had intervened in diplomacy forcefully against ministers but almost wholly behind the scenes, Edward VII's interventions, pushed through against unwilling ministers, were public and risky. His son, George V, was canny enough to see their dangers; his grandson, Edward VIII, was not. The king's initiatives were popularly assumed to be more influential than they were, a view given some substance by J. Holland Rose in his lectures *The Origins of the War* (1915), which A. J. Balfour privately deplored as 'a foolish piece of gossip … so far as I remember, during the year which you and I were his Ministers, he never made an important suggestion of any sort on large questions of policy' (Balfour to Lansdowne, 11 Jan 1915; Newton, 293). Balfour underestimated the king, for his 1903 visit was a policy in itself.

Russia and Germany The king followed it up by stimulating the interest of Aleksandr Izvolsky, Russian foreign minister from 1906, whom he met in Copenhagen in April 1904, in an Anglo-Russian understanding. In his prompt action—almost immediately after the signing of the French entente—the king was at least abreast, and perhaps ahead, of Foreign Office thinking, and he further encouraged the extension of the entente to Russia by strongly urging the appointment of Hardinge as Russian ambassador; Hardinge arrived in Russia in May 1904. In August 1904 (against Lansdowne's initial advice) the king sent Prince Louis of Battenberg to Russia for the christening of the Tsarevich Alexei, at which the prince had fruitful discussions with the tsar. In that year, the king's comments on the Anglo-Japanese agreement were poorly informed and required correction by the foreign secretary.

The king continued his sometimes unexpected interventions. In 1905 he made Admiral Togo, who had sunk the Russian fleet, a member of the Order of Merit, and he encouraged his son-in-law, Prince Charles of Denmark, to stand for election to the throne of Norway (though the British government was strictly neutral). An abrasive letter to the Kaiser, when the latter suggested a visit to Hamburg for a reconciliation, though hardly without provocation, gave the excuse for extensive displays of German grievance. These were to a degree palliated during the Kaiser's state visit to Britain in November 1907, which the king had helped to plan during his customary visit to Germany in August. As usual, he gave very close personal attention to the plans for the visit, which included a notable lunch at Windsor on 17 November with twenty-four royal persons present, showing the king as the central and reconciling force among European royalties, 'the Uncle of Europe'. The visit was felt by both the British and German courts to have cleared the air. Following it, the Kaiser stayed at Highcliffe Castle, where his conversation with Colonel Stuart-Wortley was noted down and published a year later in the *Daily Telegraph* (28 October 1908).

Edward VII used his relationship to the Russian court to soften its cautious attitude towards an entente with Britain. The tsar found his bonhomie hard to take, and the Kaiser with some success encouraged his cousin in the view that Edward VII was an 'arch-intriguer and arch-mischief maker'. The king declined to visit Russia in 1906, favouring the Duma which the tsar so disliked, but the Foreign Office felt that his assistance had been important in the making of the entente. Following the signing of the entente, the king planned to make a state visit in June 1908 to the tsar at Reval. News of the visit provoked British Labour and radical-Liberal hostility to what seemed like British acceptance of tsarist atrocities; a motion critical of the government was defeated by 225 votes to 59 on 4 June. Keir Hardie's comments on the king were ruled out of order by the speaker. By withdrawing invitations to Hardie, Victor Grayson, and Arthur Ponsonby to attend a royal garden party the king prolonged the affair. Ponsonby, a Liberal and the son of Victoria's secretary, made an apology, but the Labour Party, seeing the king's action as an attempt to influence the course of debates in the Commons, kept the question in the public eye, Hardie stating that he would in future attend no further royal functions. This was a rare lapse in Edward VII's handling of domestic questions and his irritability, usually kept under control with respect to public affairs, may have been increased by a bronchial condition.

The visit to Russia in June 1908 was, even so, in general regarded as a considerable success. The king, however, disconcerted his government by acting upon a memorandum from Lord Rothschild and his brothers on the persecution of Russian Jews to the extent of prodding Sir Arthur Nicolson, ambassador to Russia, to raise the question with P. A. Stolypin, the Russian chief minister. The king did not go beyond this, which upset Rothschild, but he was more forthright in response to a request for his friend Sir Ernest Cassel, who wished assistance in floating a new Russian loan: 'I rather fancy that the king did ask the Emperor to receive Cassel if he goes to Russia, and emphasised the fact of his being a Privy Counsellor', Hardinge told Knollys (13 June 1904; Magnus, 407). This initiative soon got out, giving the Kaiser the opportunity to describe his uncle as nothing but 'a jobber in stocks and shares' (ibid.). In other respects, the king's diplomacy charmed his nephew the tsar. Seizing the moment, he made Nicholas II an admiral of the (British) fleet, an unconstitutional act which disturbed the cabinet but consolidated the success of the visit. Its very success increased German fears of encirclement by the three entente powers, and in August 1908 the visit to Russia was balanced by a visit to Germany, during which a meeting at Friedrischof on 11 August 1908 pleased the Kaiser, the king shrewdly leaving to Hardinge the raising of the contentious subject of the German naval building programme. On 28 October

the *Daily Telegraph* published the Kaiser's interview, relaying his views of a year previously. His reported enthusiasm for good relations with the United Kingdom caused a storm in Germany and suspicion in Britain. The Kaiser then balanced his remarks through an interview with W. B. Hale of the *New York World*, in which he was reported as saying that Edward VII was personally corrupt and his court rotten. The Kaiser repudiated the report, but the king was thrown into a further fit of depression, telling Knollys: 'I know the E[mperor] *hates* me, and never loses an opportunity of saying so (behind my back) whilst I have always been civil and nice to him' (25 Nov 1908; ibid., 401).

The king's relations with the Kaiser were never broken off, but what had been a reasonably cordial façade became much more difficult to sustain. The episode occurred as a reciprocal state visit by the king to Berlin was being planned: 'The Foreign Office to gain their object will not care a pin what humiliation I have to put up with', the king told Knollys (ibid.). The visit, undertaken at a time when Anglo-German relations were markedly in decline, was made in February 1909. During it the king was, uniquely, accompanied by a cabinet minister, Lord Crewe, as well as by Hardinge. The visit began well, but on 10 February the king suffered a seizure during a lunch at the British embassy and the subsequent programme was curtailed. This was his last state visit.

A royal foreign policy? Edward VII was a significant but not a determining force in the making and maintenance of the ententes. All the major European powers save France had monarchs directly responsible for their countries' foreign policy. In such a context Edward VII's role as head of state and uncle of the rulers of Germany and Russia was ambivalent. He was seen in Germany as the architect of anti-German encirclement and of the policy of British entente with France and Russia. This credited Edward VII with more power than he either exercised or desired. He realized, however, much better than either the Conservative or the Liberal cabinets with which he worked, that the context of the times, and especially the character of German and Russian policy making, expected the active intervention of the British head of state and that, as long as his views accorded with those of his cabinets, he could encourage the evolution of foreign policy at both the symbolic and the familial level. Like the British governments of the time, he had no defined 'anti-German' position but, like them, he hedged his bets for as long as he could, trying to balance the entente by resuscitating when possible the former friendship with Germany. His irritation with the Kaiser made the latter task difficult and the tradition of personal diplomacy, so effective elsewhere, was, especially after 1907, a disadvantage in Anglo-German relations. It was also the case that the king energetically encouraged the promotion in the Foreign Office and in the embassies of members of the 'Hardinge gang'—the group of diplomatists associated with Charles Hardinge, including Sir Francis Bertie and Sir Arthur Nicolson, many of whom were strongly anti-German. He intervened with the Russian government on several occasions to preserve the position of Izvolsky as foreign secretary, and with the Austrian government to keep Albert Mensdorff as ambassador in London. And he was as capable as his mother of a rebuke to a cabinet minister, though he lacked that studious attention to detail which made her so hard to fob off.

Domestic affairs, 1908–1909 When Campbell-Bannerman resigned on 5 April 1908, the king incurred much adverse comment by not returning to Britain from Biarritz, thereby requiring H. H. Asquith to journey through France to kiss hands. It was a discourtesy more characteristic of Queen Victoria than Edward VII. Relations with Campbell-Bannerman had been personally good, despite the king's various complaints. Those with Asquith were much stiffer. The king thought Asquith 'deficient in manners but in nothing else' (Magnus, 421). He shared with Asquith a hostility to female suffrage—an open question in the cabinet—but he increasingly differed from him and the Liberal government on many aspects of domestic policy. However, he also thought the Unionists' ready use of their hereditary majority in the House of Lords to be a tactical error. On 12 October 1908, with Asquith's approval, he summoned Lord Lansdowne and warned him of the dangers to the Lords of excessive obstruction. The Lords threw out the Licensing Bill on 27 November, as they had already in that session mangled the third Liberal Education Bill of the parliament. The danger for the king was apparent: the Unionist peers, and indeed the Unionist Party as a whole, claimed that the non-elected elements of the constitution—the king and the House of Lords—in some way better represented the interests of the United Kingdom than its elected representatives. But in practice their view of the constitution set aside the king, even though in the hierarchy of the non-elected he was clearly first. For all the secret meetings and conferences, the Unionist leaders, when it came to the point, set the House of Lords above the king. None of his many initiatives to encourage the Unionists to caution and discretion succeeded. But this Unionist intransigence was not fully apparent in 1908. It was then clear that Unionist Lords would not heed him on a second-order bill—would they be more temperate on a really major measure? The question was quickly posed by Lloyd George's budget of 1909, and answered when the Lords rejected the consequent Finance Bill in November 1909. The king strongly disliked the government's financial proposals and wrote to Asquith to ask 'whether in framing the Budget the Cabinet took into consideration the possible (but the King hopes improbable) event of a European War'; he believed the income tax was already so high as to be potentially disastrous for landowners (Lee, 2.664). He also from the start of the Liberal government in 1905 regarded Lloyd George's comments on the behaviour of the Lords as unhelpful, and several times complained to Campbell-Bannerman about them. In 1909–10 he felt Lloyd George's speeches made it difficult for the Lords to avoid rejecting the budget, and he complained to Asquith about the chancellor's speeches at Limehouse and Newcastle.

The Lords, the Commons, and the king Even so, the king saw the rejection of the budget by the Lords as a serious mistake. Apart from its more general significance, it placed Edward VII in an extremely awkward position. Clearly ill, the king could not avoid playing an active role in the finding of a solution. It was one of those rare moments when a constitutional monarch had to do more than receive and respond to advice. The king knew of Unionist intentions from a memorandum (2 October 1909) for him written by Lord Cawdor. He discussed this with Asquith, and by agreement with the prime minister attempted to gain assent to a compromise, to which end he summoned Balfour and Lansdowne, the Unionist leaders, on 12 October 1909. He was unsuccessful in persuading them to change course, and the budget was rejected on 30 November 1909. The king agreed to Asquith's request for a dissolution, and a general election was held in the second half of January 1910. The king granted the dissolution without any request from Asquith as to his agreement to create peers should the circumstances require it. But many inferred from Asquith's speech on 10 December inaugurating the government's electoral campaign that such an agreement had been sought and granted. The Liberals had in fact raised such a question with Knollys, but the king's secretary had thought it better not to inform his master of it. Knollys believed that it would be better for the king to abdicate than create peers, a view echoed by the king, who in the winter of 1909–10 discussed the subject of abdication with close friends. The king did not threaten his cabinet with abdication but he did clarify his position by telling Asquith, through their respective secretaries, that 'the King had come to the conclusion that he would not be justified in creating new peers (say 300) until after a second general election and that he, Lord K[nollys], thought that you [Asquith] should know of this now', but that Asquith should keep it to himself (memorandum of 15 Dec 1909; Spender and Asquith, 1.261). The king followed this up on 30 January by expounding to Lord Crewe, the colonial secretary and lord privy seal, his self-devised plan to reform the Lords by restricting the voting rights of peers to 100, fifty of whom would be party nominees. After the election, which produced a stalemate between the Liberals and the Unionists but a substantial government coalition majority of about 124, the cabinet on 11 February told the king it had no immediate plans to request exercise of the royal prerogative. Asquith informed the Commons of this on 21 February, the day the king with the queen opened parliament; it was the king's last state appearance.

The king tried without success to persuade the Unionists not to vote in the Commons against the reintroduced Finance Bill. On 6 March, accompanied by Mrs Keppel, he left for Biarritz, but on 7 March he caught a cold at the theatre in Paris. On reaching Biarritz on 9 March, where he stayed at the Hôtel du Palais, with Mrs Keppel as usual in Sir Ernest Cassel's Villa Eugènie, he collapsed. The next day marked the forty-seventh wedding anniversary of the king and queen. Recovering somewhat, the king, with

Asquith's agreement, remained in Biarritz to convalesce. The Finance Bill was at last passed by the Lords, and on 14 April the Parliament Bill to modify their powers was introduced. Asquith had been strongly criticized by members of his own party and by his coalition partners for not pressing earlier for a royal guarantee to create peers; in his speech introducing the bill he stated the need to pass the bill 'in this Parliament', thereby ignoring the king's earlier demand for a second election.

It was soon clear that the Parliament Bill would be the occasion of further, and probably even more intense, constitutional conflict. A meeting at Lambeth Palace was organized by the archbishop of Canterbury, Randall Davidson, on 27 April 1910, with the king's advisers and A. J. Balfour present as leader of the Unionist Party. An agreement was reached as to Balfour's course of action should the government resign if the king rejected its advice to create peers. This was a meeting potentially perilous to the monarchy, for to plan with the opposition on the assumption that the king would reject his government's advice on a major constitutional question was to contradict the central assumption of constitutional monarchy. The decline in the king's health was not reported and he incurred considerable criticism for, as it was seen, lingering at Biarritz at such a moment of constitutional tension. Moreover, he was ill served by his advisers during his absence, the chief of whom—Knollys and Esher—risked placing the crown in a major confrontation with the House of Commons by their view that the acceptance by the king of the wishes of the majority of the Commons was a last resort to be avoided perhaps even by abdication. Asquith had protected the king by not earlier making a definite request for a guarantee to create peers; the king rather grudgingly recognized this, but his advisers did not.

Death and funeral On 27 April 1910 Edward VII returned from Biarritz to Buckingham Palace. He was still active, seeing ministers and, on 29 April, attending Wagner's *Siegfried* at Covent Garden. On 30 April he went to Sandringham, catching another cold. On 2 May he wrote the last (and unusual) entry in his long diary: 'The King dines alone.' The queen, alerted to his physical decline, returned from a visit to Corfu on 5 May. Now confined to an armchair, the king was visited by relays of friends including Mrs Keppel, whom he did not recognize and who had hysterics (the queen is said to have shaken hands with her as she arrived). The prince of Wales told his father that his horse, Witch of Air, had won the 4.15 at Kempton Park: 'Yes, I have heard of it. I am very glad' remarked the king in his last cogent utterance. Edward VII died at 11.45 p.m. on Friday 6 May 1910 at Buckingham Palace. His body lay in state in Westminster Hall from 17 to 19 May, viewed by about a quarter of a million persons. Vast crowds watched the funeral procession as a gun carriage—followed by the king's charger and Caesar, his scruffy fox terrier, and then George V, the German emperor, and eight kings—bore the coffin to Paddington Station. It was the last great roll call of monarchic Europe. The king's body was buried in the vault beneath St George's Chapel at Windsor on 20 May, by the side of his eldest son, the duke of Clarence, and not in his parents' mausoleum at Frogmore.

Edward VII in perspective Despite the brevity of his reign, Edward VII gave his name to an epoch which symbolized an escape from Victorianism. In this, the king was at one with his people and, indeed, led the emancipation with glee. Subsequently 'Edwardian' came to signify, nostalgically, the golden years of the propertied classes before the catastrophe of the First World War, but at the time it rather symbolized energy, change, and a certain brashness and vulgarity, which were on the whole welcomed rather than deplored.

Edward VII encouraged all of these. His lifestyle presupposed a strong popular acceptance of monarchy. The press, so ready to pillory Sir Charles Dilke, C. S. Parnell, and Oscar Wilde, made almost nothing of the king's mistresses. Mrs Keppel was often invited to functions at which Queen Alexandra was also present, this being the best way of ensuring his good temper; the queen bore this with outward serenity. When on his last trip to Biarritz in 1910 the king travelled openly, as usual, with Mrs Keppel, this was noted but not complained of. (When Sidney Lee in his memoir in the *Dictionary of National Biography* (1912) mildly remarked that during the constitutional crisis of 1910 the king 'was spending his annual spring holiday at Biarritz, where his time was mainly devoted to cheerful recreation', there was a flurry of protests from royal advisers (Bodl. Oxf., MS Don. c. 186).) The king's mistresses were discreet and after his death destroyed most of his letters to them; an exception was Lady Warwick, who in 1914, hard up and in debt, attempted via Frank Harris and Arthur du Cros to extract £100,000 from George V in exchange for silence; she failed, though her debts were indirectly relieved (Aronson, 265). The mistresses acted in line with the court, for lords Esher and Knollys obeyed the instruction in the king's will to destroy all his private and personal correspondences, the king having already superintended the burning of some of his correspondence as prince of Wales, in addition to parts of his mother's correspondence; moreover, all Queen Alexandra's papers were destroyed, in line with her wishes, though she died intestate (Magnus, Appendix).

Edward VII openly enjoyed being king. He appeared to act from enthusiasm rather than duty. His keenness for uniforms, decorations, and ceremonial caught one aspect of the public mood. His state portrait by Sir Luke Fildes (1901–2) with the king in his coronation robes, in a pose echoing Holbein's Henry VIII, epitomized the king's view of one aspect of himself: it presents imperial power and majesty more assertively than any royal portrait since 1830. Sir Arthur Cope's portrait (1907) of the king in his Garter robes is equally florid. This showy relish of monarchy died with Edward VII. Another, rather different, aspect of his view of royal life—his enthusiasm for the squirearchic life of Sandringham, with its tweeds and county style—was an important bequest to his son, George V, through whom it became the dominant strain of twentieth-century British royalty.

In Edward VII's hands the royal prerogative continued to be actively employed. In some respects, especially with his foreign initiatives, the king had almost as vigorous a view of the use of the prerogative as his father. He was as ready as his mother to try to affect the appointment of ministers and ambassadors, though he lacked a similar diligence in church appointments. The king stood much more in the political centre than his mother had done and he thus enabled the maintenance of monarchic popularity, though both the general elections of his reign were won by Liberal, even radical, majorities. There was no significant republican movement in the Edwardian era. The burgeoning Labour Party, though not enthusiastic, was not, as were its continental equivalents, anti-monarchic in principle, and it was only occasionally so in practice. Edward VII's influence, *The Times* noted, was 'not the same as that exercised by Queen Victoria but in some respects it was almost the stronger of the two' (7 May 1910). The king could look from his deathbed with a good deal of satisfaction at the condition in which he left the monarchy.

Even so, Edward VII was fortunate in the moment of his death. Well-meaning with respect to compromise over the constitutional conflict which characterized the final years of his reign, his inability to control the Unionists, his willingness to allow his conservatively minded advisers a rather free hand, and his caution about seeing that his elected government's will prevailed placed him in a potentially very awkward position, as George V quickly found. The conflict was not, of course, of his making, but it is hard to see that a solution of it on terms acceptable to Edward VII could have been forthcoming.

H. C. G. MATTHEW

Sources S. Lee, *King Edward VII*, 2 vols. (1925–7) · P. Magnus, *King Edward the Seventh* (1964) · C. Hibbert, *Edward VII* (1976) · A. Allfrey, *Edward VII and his Jewish court* (1991) · K. Middlemas, *The life and times of Edward VII* (1993) · T. Aronson, *The king in love: Edward VII's mistresses* (1988) · A. E. T. Watson, *King Edward VII as a sportsman…with an introduction and a chapter on 'Yachting' by Captain the Hon. Sir Seymour Fortescue…Contributions by the marquess of Ripon…Lord Walsingham, Lord Ribblesdale, and others* (1911) · E. Dicey and others, *King Edward VII: biographical and personal sketches, with anecdotes* (1910) · *Personal letters of King Edward VII*, ed. J. P. C. Sewell (1931) · *The private life of King Edward VII, prince of Wales, 1841–1901. By a member of the royal household* (1901) · W. H. Russell, *The Prince of Wales' tour: a diary in India* (1877) · G. Brook-Shepherd, *Uncle of Europe: the social and diplomatic life of Edward VII* (1975) · G. Dangerfield, *Victoria's heir: the education of a prince* (1941) · E. Legge, *King Edward in his true colours* (1912) · C. W. Stampe, *What I know* (1913) · H. Gernsheim and A. Gernsheim, *Edward VII and Queen Alexandra: a biography in word and picture* (1962) · V. Cowles, *Edward VII and his circle* (1956) · E. F. Benson, *King Edward VII* (1933) · C. W. Hill, *Edwardian Scotland* (1976) · H. Eckardstein, *Ten years at the court of St James* (1921) · *Journals and letters of Reginald, Viscount Esher*, ed. M. V. Brett and Oliver, Viscount Esher, 4 vols. (1934–8) · G. P. Gooch and H. Temperley, eds., *British documents on the origins of the war, 1898–1914*, 11 vols. in 13 (1926–38) · C. Hardinge, *Old diplomacy: the reminiscences of Lord Hardinge of Penshurst* (1947) · R. R. McLean, 'Monarchy and diplomacy in Europe, 1900–1910', DPhil, U. Sussex · H. Bernstein, *The Willy–Nicky correspondence* (1918) · P. M. Kennedy, *The rise and fall of the Anglo-German antagonism, 1860–1914* (1980) · K. Neilson, *Britain and the last tsar: British policy and Russia, 1894–1917* (1995) · S. Munz, *King Edward VII at Marienbad* (1934) · Gladstone, *Diaries* · H. C. G. Matthew, *Gladstone*, 2 vols. (1986–95); repr. in 1 vol. as *Gladstone, 1809–1898* (1997) ·

The letters of Queen Victoria, ed. A. C. Benson, Lord Esher [R. B. Brett], and G. E. Buckle, 9 vols. (1907–32) · E. Longford, *Victoria RI* (1964) · *Dearest child: letters between Queen Victoria and the princess royal, 1858–1861*, ed. R. Fulford (1964) · A. Gollin, *Balfour's burden* (1965) · R. Jenkins, *Mr Balfour's poodle* (1954) · B. K. Murray, *The people's budget, 1909/10: Lloyd George and liberal politics* (1980) · J. A. Spender and C. Asquith, *Life of Herbert Henry Asquith, Lord Oxford and Asquith*, 2 vols. [1932] · F. Ponsonby, *Recollections of three reigns* (1951) · *Fear God and dread nought: the correspondence of Admiral of the Fleet Lord Fisher of Kilverstone*, ed. A. J. Marder, 3 vols. (1952–9) · J. A. Fisher, *Memories* (1919) · B. E. C. Dugdale, *Arthur James Balfour, first earl of Balfour*, 2 vols. (1936) · J. A. Spender, *The life of the Right Hon. Sir Henry Campbell-Bannerman*, 2 vols. (1923) · J. Pope-Hennessy, *Lord Crewe, 1858–1945: the likeness of a liberal* (1955) · G. K. A. Bell, *Randall Davidson, archbishop of Canterbury*, 2 vols. (1935) · Lord Newton [T. W. Legh], *Lord Lansdowne: a biography* (1929) · F. Neilson, 'Edward VII and the entente cordiale', *American Journal of Economics and Sociology*, 16 (1956–7), 353–68; 17 (1957–8), 87–100, 179–94 · D. Souhami, *Mrs Keppel and her daughter* (1996) · F. K. Prochaska, *Philanthropy and the hospitals of London: the King's Fund, 1897–1990* (1992) · Bodl. Oxf., MS Don. c. 186

Archives PRO NIre., letters to Sir Robert Henry Meade · Royal Arch., political and private corresp. and papers; journals, engagement diaries | BL, corresp. with Arthur James Balfour, Add. MSS 49683, 49685 · BL, corresp. with Sir F. L. Bertie, Add. MSS 63011–63012 · BL, corresp. with John Burns, Add. MSS 46281 · BL, corresp. with Sir Henry Campbell-Bannerman, Add. MSS 41207–41208, 52512–52513 · BL, corresp. with Lord and Lady Carnarvon, Add. MS 60757 · BL, letters to Boyd Carpenter, Add. MSS 46721–46722 · BL, corresp. with W. E. Gladstone, loan 73 · BL, letters to Lady Holland, Add. MS 52113 · BL OIOC, letters to Lord Curzon, no. 1145 · Blair Castle, Perthshire, letters to seventh duke of Atholl · Bodl. Oxf., letters to H. W. Acland · Bodl. Oxf., corresp. with Herbert Asquith · Bodl. Oxf., letters to Benjamin Disraeli · Bodl. Oxf., corresp. with Sir C. H. Doyle and P. N. Doyle · Bodl. Oxf., corresp. with Sir William Harcourt · Bodl. Oxf., corresp. with Lord Kimberley · Bodl. Oxf., letters and telegrams to Friedrich Max Muller · Bodl. Oxf., corresp. with second earl of Selborne · CAC Cam., letters to Lord Randolph Churchill · CAC Cam., corresp. with Lord Esher · CAC Cam., letters to Lord Fisher · CAC Cam., corresp. with Reginald MacKenna · CKS, letters to Sir W. T. Knollys · CKS, letters to Edward Stanhope · College of William and Mary, Williamsburg, Virginia · CUL, corresp. with Lord Hardinge · HLRO, corresp. with fifth Earl Cadogan · Hove Central Library, Sussex, letters to Lord and Lady Wolseley · ICL, letters to Lord Playfair · LPL, corresp. with A. C. Tait · Lpool RO, corresp. with seventeenth earl of Derby · N. Yorks. CRO, letters to Lady Downe · NAM, letters to Earl Roberts · NL Aus., corresp. with Viscount Novar · NL Scot., corresp. with Lord Haldane · NL Scot., letters to Lord Minto · NL Scot., corresp., incl. with Lord Rosebery · NRA Scotland, priv. coll., letters to Lord Colville · NRA Scotland, priv. coll., letters to Lilly Langtry · priv. coll., letters to earl of Aylesford · priv. coll., letters to first duke of Westminster · PRO, corresp. with second Earl Granville, PRO 30/29 · PRO NIre., letters to James Hamilton, second duke of Abercorn · PRO NIre., letters to Lady Londonderry · Staffs. RO, letters to duchess of Sutherland · Suffolk RO, Bury St Edmunds, letters to Lady Mary Augusta · U. Birm., corresp. with Joseph Chamberlain · U. Durham, corresp. with Charles Grey · U. Southampton L., letters to Lord Palmerston · W. Sussex RO, letters to duke of Richmond · Wilts. & Swindon RO, corresp. with Sir Michael Herbert

Likenesses F. Grant, group portrait, oils, 1842, Royal Collection · E. Landseer, group portrait, oils, 1842, Royal Collection · W. C. Ross, miniature, 1846, Royal Collection · M. Thornycroft, marble bust, 1846, Royal Collection · F. X. Winterhalter, group portrait, oils, 1846, Royal Collection · F. X. Winterhalter, four oil paintings, 1846–64, Royal Collection · N. N. Burnard, marble bust, 1847, Royal Polytechnic Society, Cornwall · E. Landseer, group portrait, oils, 1847 (*The Queen sketching at Loch Laggan with the prince of Wales and the princess royal*), Royal Collection · M. Thornycroft, statuette, 1847,

Royal Collection · H. Watkins, albumen print, 1850–59, NPG · J. Barrett, oils, 1856, NPG · E. M. Ward, pencil drawing, 1857, Royal Collection · G. Richmond, pastel drawing, 1858, NPG · coloured lithograph, c.1860, NG Ire. · W. Gordon, oils, 1862, Examination Schools, Oxford · W. P. Frith, group portrait, oils, 1863 (*The marriage of the prince of Wales, 1863*), Royal Collection · H. N. O'Neil, oils, 1864, NPG · E. Detaille, group portrait, oils, 1865, Royal Collection · J. C. Horsley, group portrait, oils, 1865 (*Queen Victoria and her children*), RSA · M. Noble, marble bust, 1868, Gawsworth Hall, Cheshire · J. E. Boehm, bronze equestrian statuette, c.1872, Royal Collection · G. F. Watts, chalk drawing, c.1874, NPG · J. E. Boehm, marble bust, c.1875, Royal Collection · Count Gleichen, marble bust, 1875, Royal Collection · H. von Angeli, group portrait, oils, 1876, Royal Collection · L. Desanges, oils, 1877, United Grand Lodge of England · F. Holl, oils, 1884, Middle Temple, London · L. Tuxen, group portrait, oils, 1884, National Historical Museum, Fredericksborg, Denmark · Count Gleichen, marble bust, c.1885, Walker Art Gallery, Liverpool · F. Holl, oils, 1887, Trinity House, London · L. Tuxen, group portrait, oils, 1887 (*The royal family at the time of the jubilee*), Royal Collection · Count Gleichen, statue, 1891, Royal College of Music, London · A. Stuart-Wortley, oils, c.1893, Carlton Club, London · W. Q. Orchardson, group portrait, oils, 1897 (*The four generations*), Royal Agricultural Society, London · Chancellor of Dublin, print, 1899, NPG · M. Beerbohm, drawing, 1900, Princeton University Library · S. March, bronze bust, 1901, NPG · L. Fildes, oils, 1901–2, Royal Collection [*see illus.*] · L. Fildes, oils, second version, 1902, NPG · J. Gilbert, double portrait, oils, c.1902 (with Queen Alexandra), Royal Collection · G. W. de Saulles, bronze medal, 1902 (*Coronation 9 Aug 1902*) · J. H. F. Bacon, oils, 1903, NPG · E. A. Abbey, group portrait, oils, 1904 (*The coronation of King Edward VII, 1902*), Royal Collection · A. de Meyer, platinotype, 1904, NPG · L. Fildes, oils, 1905, RCP Lond. · H. Speed, oils, c.1905, Belfast corporation · F. Roe, pencil drawing, 1905–6, NPG · C. Forbes, oils, c.1906, Houses of Parliament, Ottawa · P. T. Cole, oils, 1907, NPG · A. S. Cope, oils, 1907, Broadlands, Hampshire · Mrs M. A. Barnett, watercolour, 1908, NPG · P. T. Cole, oils, 1908, Russell-Cotes Art Gallery and Museum, Bournemouth · attrib. W. & D. Downey, platinum print, 1908, NPG · M. Beerbohm, drawing, 1909, FM Cam. · E. J. Poynter, oils, 1909, RA · L. Tuxen, oils, 1909, National Historical Museum, Frederiksborg, Denmark · J. S. Sargent, charcoal, 1910, Royal Collection · A. Drury, marble statue, exh. RA 1912, U. Birm. · B. Mackennal, bronze statue, c.1912–1914, Waterloo Place, London · P. B. Baker, statue, c.1913, Huddersfield · H. S. Gamley, plaster bust, 1916, Scot. NPG · W. G. John, statue, 1916, Liverpool · M. Beerbohm, drawing, 1921, AM Oxf. · W. Hensel, drawing, c.1943, National Gallerie, Berlin · Ape [C. Pellegrini], caricatures, NPG · J. E. Boehm, marble statue, junction of Fleet Street and Strand, London · J. Cassidy, statue, Whitworth Park, Manchester · G. Hayter, group portrait, oils (*The christening of the prince of Wales in St George's Chapel, 1842*), Royal Collection · J. Mahoney, group portrait, watercolour, NG Ire. · J. Simpson, colour print, Scot. NPG · Spy [L. Ward], caricatures, NPG · J. Steel, plaster bust, Scot. NPG · H. Weigall, oils, Wellington College, Berkshire · photographs, NPG · photographs, U. Texas, Gernsheim collection · photographs, NPG · prints, BM, NPG, Royal Collection

Edward VIII [*later* Prince Edward, duke of Windsor] (**1894–1972**), king of Great Britain, Ireland, and the British dominions beyond the seas, and emperor of India, was born at White Lodge, Richmond Park, on 23 June 1894, the first child of the five sons and one daughter of the duke and duchess of York. His father, subsequently *George V, had become heir apparent to the throne in 1892 and became prince of Wales on the accession of Edward VII in 1901. His mother similarly became princess of Wales, and later Queen *Mary.

Youth and education The future king was given the forenames Edward Albert Christian George Andrew Patrick

David, the innovatory use of the four patron saints being intended to emphasize the representative character of the monarchy. Within the family he was always known as David. The name Albert was included at Queen Victoria's demand, but her strong request that this be his first name was not accepted (it was given as the first name to the next brother, the future *George VI). Unlike his father, who was not heir apparent from birth, David was from the start groomed by his parents to be king, though the pattern of his youth was in fact much the same as his father's.

Neither of his parents found it easy to bring up children, but the hardships of David and his brother Albert, who were educated together, are often exaggerated, at least in the context of what was common in the family life of propertied persons. Their gruff father and their remote mother provided a much more stable domestic background for the raising of their children than had Victoria and Albert and Edward and Alexandra in the two previous generations. The boys' upbringing was intentionally egalitarian, in the sense that it was as similar as circumstances allowed to that of other members of the British propertied class of the time. On the other hand, David grew up in a middle-brow context—not deliberately hostile to culture, but also not sensitive to it. He was an intelligent child, with something of his father's prodigious memory and an innate, wide-ranging curiosity which his parents failed to harness. He was bullied by his nanny and, as the eldest child, was the first target of his father's often violently expressed wrath. He himself, in his later autobiographical volumes, stated that he felt unloved, and he never seems to have wished for children of his own.

David and his siblings were initially educated at home, mostly at York Cottage, Sandringham, and Frogmore, near Windsor, and with little contact with other children. Their tutor was Henry Peter Hansell (1863–1935), chosen for his sporting abilities, who tried to compensate for the curious framework of his pupils' lives by installing a classroom at York Cottage and organizing football matches with children from the village. Hansell taught poorly: his pupils lacked basic arithmetical skills and had difficulty writing their names. Their knowledge of their own country's literature was minimal. However, from other teachers David learned French and German (and later he also became a fluent Spanish speaker).

Prince Edward (as he was officially known) was early noted for charm and good looks, attracting the attention and admiration of the epicene *éminence grise* of the court, Lord Esher, who noted in his *Journal*, 'Prince Edward as composed and clever as ever. … He has the mouth and expression of old Queen Charlotte … but the look of Weltschmerz in his eyes I cannot trace to any ancestor of the House of Hanover' (Donaldson, 20). The capacity to charm people of both sexes was to be of central importance to the prince's later life. Early photographs of the prince in his sailor suit show a slightly raffish quality, another attribute of subsequent importance (his wearing of hats was always anti-conventional).

In 1907 Prince Edward was sent to the naval college at Osborne, where he was nicknamed Sardine, and in 1909 he progressed to the Royal Naval College on HMS *Britannia* at Dartmouth, thus receiving the same education as his father, though without the presence of a chaperoning tutor, which left him and his brother Bertie open to bullying. His mother told Lord Esher that she found her son 'very sensitive, and knowing much more of his prospects and responsibilities than she thought. He is treated, however, at Osborne precisely like any other boy, both by teachers and lads' (Esher, *Journals and Letters of Reginald Viscount Esher*, 1934–8, 2.330). His education was thus that of a naval officer, useful in so far as it gave him relatively wide social experience, but intellectually limited to the concerns of a fighting service where technical competence was given a premium. As he was likely soon to be prince of Wales, it was an education of only partial relevance to his future.

As a youth the prince became a proficient player of the highland bagpipe, being taught by William Ross and Henry Forsyth. He frequently, until his later years, played a tune round the table after dinner, sometimes wearing a white kilt. His rather ponderous slow march, 'Mallorca', remains in print in the Seaforth Highlanders' standard book of music. He was later patron of the Piobaireachd Society. The prince's bagpipe playing found little favour with most of his friends, and less with his English biographers, but he was, even so, a competent exponent of the instrument, which gave him considerable pleasure.

With the death of Edward VII in May 1910 Prince Edward became heir to the throne, aged fifteen, inheriting the duchy of Cornwall and its large estates and revenues. He returned to Dartmouth, the new king hoping to defer his son's entry to public life. However, on his sixteenth birthday he was created prince of Wales (not an automatic inheritance) and was invested at Caernarfon Castle on 13 July 1911, Lloyd George as constable of the castle inventing a rather Ruritanian ceremonial which took the form of a Welsh pageant. Edward was the first prince of Wales to be invested at Caernarfon since Prince Charles in 1616 (and the evidence for that ceremony is thin). Lloyd George coached the prince to utter some sentences in Welsh.

The new prince of Wales almost immediately began his naval career, serving as midshipman in the *Hindustan*. On his return the king rather abruptly told him he had arranged for him to attend the University of Oxford. He matriculated in October 1912 and resided as an ordinary undergraduate in Magdalen College, but was chaperoned by Hansell and an equerry. Before going up to Oxford, Prince Edward made his first visit to France. At Oxford the prince was offered tutorials by Herbert Warren, president of Magdalen ('an awful old man' in the prince's view (Ziegler, 40)), and other luminaries, but Hansell had not prepared him sufficiently to be able to take advantage of a university education (however truncated) and he was chiefly affected by the social side of Magdalen life. Walter Monckton was one of the few fellow undergraduates with whom he formed a lasting friendship. During the long vacations he made two visits to Germany (staying with relatives) and one to Scandinavia. He left Oxford at the start of the war in 1914. He was right to be cautious of his tutors, for Warren astonishingly broke all confidences by publishing in *The Times* on 18 November 1914 a report giving his assessment of the prince's time in Oxford (it began: 'Bookish he will never be').

The prince in his Oxford days was still remarkably youthful-looking. His 'slight, shy, wistful figure' (Ziegler, 33) added vulnerability to his charm, and an enlisting sergeant in August 1914 might reasonably have queried his age.

The First World War Prince Edward began army life in July 1914 and found military camaraderie much more satisfying than academic life. He was commissioned in the Grenadier Guards and hoped to see action. It was, of

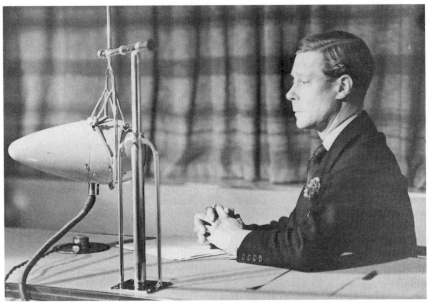

Edward VIII (1894–1972), by unknown photographer, 1936 [making the abdication broadcast on 11 December 1936]

course, out of the question that the heir to the throne could be allowed to be killed or, perhaps worse, captured, and a long process began of finding a role for the prince of Wales. A variety of activities was provided which included some real work of a non-combative sort and ambassadorial appearances among the French generals. Given the restrictions within which he was required to operate, the prince made a significant impact in two respects: he was frequently to be seen driving in a royal Daimler or, as he preferred, cycling on a green bicycle to inspect camps and encourage the troops; and by his known presence in the area of battle he associated the royal family in a direct way with the war effort, as his brother Bertie did by serving in the naval battle of Jutland. Frustrating though the prince personally found his lot in war, the state had made good use of him. He was several times in danger, and his driver was killed by shrapnel in the Daimler at Loos while the prince was visiting the front line. He toured the Middle East in 1916, meeting Australian and New Zealand troops evacuated from Gallipoli. In 1918 he was with the Canadian corps in France and after the armistice with the Australian corps in Belgium. He met many American troops. In the course of his war experience he met and dealt with (for these were not the usual royal 'visits') a far wider range of men and women than any of his recent predecessors.

Post-war years Peacetime offered a more awkward prospect for the prince of Wales. The two preceding princes of Wales had both been married early (his father while still heir apparent), and the context of royal marriages was changing. The assumption, on the part of both the future monarch and the public, that a marriage would be arranged or brokered (as had happened with the prince's father) had not wholly disappeared, but George V and Queen Mary left considerable latitude to their children in their search for spouses, and from the public's point of view there was an assumption that 'romantic love' should at least appear to play a major role. In this respect the prince was thoroughly modern. These changing assumptions set up a context of potential complexity for any heir to the throne for whom a spouse was to be both a love match and a person who fulfilled the necessary qualifications for the throne. In the army the prince developed an enthusiasm for nightlife, nightclubs, and dancing, which the style of post-war London life encouraged. He soon became a leader of fashionable London society, a more eclectic body than before the war. In this context, after several affairs, his liaison with Mrs Winifred (Freda) Dudley Ward (1894–1983) began in the spring of 1918. She was the wife, with two small daughters, of Lord Esher's grandson, William Dudley Ward (1877–1946), a Liberal MP and chamberlain of the royal household, from whom she separated; they divorced in 1931. Frances Donaldson remarks of the relationship: the prince of Wales 'was madly, passionately, *abjectly* in love with her' (Donaldson, 59). The relationship lasted until 1934, though the prince had some affairs during it. An awkward situation had swiftly been created: Mrs Dudley Ward was *maîtresse en titre*, and was treated as such, but there was no royal wife.

The quasi-egalitarian habits and manners which the prince had acquired during the war in some respects fitted popular expectations after it. They worked well in the royal tours of the empire which George V delegated to his son. He toured Newfoundland, Canada, and the United States in the summer and autumn of 1919 (and in 1922 bought Bedingfeld Ranch, near Pekisko, Alberta, Canada). His easy manner and innovative hand-shaking sessions (he was the first royal to 'press the flesh' in the modern manner) made the prince a star in the Hollywood style then just emerging. The linking of regal presence and charisma with pranks, such as turning a somersault off a diving board, exactly caught the North American spirit. In 1920 he visited Australia and New Zealand in HMS *Renown*, with similar success, and in 1921–2 India. The Congress Party boycotted the visit (made just after the Amritsar massacre and in the aftermath of the disappointment caused by the Montagu–Chelmsford reforms), but the willingness of Indian crowds to cheer him was noted by commentators. Those responsible for the prince's security (by no means as straightforward a matter in India as in Newfoundland) considerably irritated him, and there was a clear tension between what was expected of a future king–emperor and a personality that was becoming increasingly defined by a populist behaviour which deliberately cut across tradition. He was, he later concluded, 'in unconscious rebellion against my position' (Windsor, *A King's Story*, 133). A prince of Wales who was anti-establishment was likely to become a problem. Even so, the success of the tours and the popularity (at least in some quarters) of the prince's lifestyle in Britain seemed to show the extent to which traditional expectations were changing.

In Britain the prince lived an odd life of hedonism and duty. Nightclubbing and, by day, hunting, point-to-point racing (characteristically, he rode as well as watched, falling often and suffering several quite serious injuries), and frequent rounds of golf were balanced by a programme of visits. He was the first prince of Wales to find almost daily visits of a charitable sort central to his expected duties, and he did not always take well to it. Charming and successful when interested, he was prone to use his rank rather arbitrarily to disappoint, delay, or cancel when in the mood to do so. But this tendency should not be exaggerated: in general the prince was held in high regard, especially in the ex-servicemen's associations and working men's clubs, which he made his especial interest.

Like his father, the prince sympathized with the lot of working people in the 1920s, though when it came to the point he was—not surprisingly, given his upbringing—ambivalent: in 1926 he both subscribed to the miners' relief fund and lent his car to take copies of Churchill's *British Gazette* to Wales (Donaldson, 21–2). He sponsored clubs called the Feathers Clubs (with Freda Dudley Ward as chairman of the association), originally intended for the unemployed but soon more broadly based. The prince was seen as having advanced views on social questions, but these were much less well thought out than those of his brother Bertie and, by conflation with his impatient view of the establishment, tended to be exaggerated.

George V's severe illness of 1928–9 occurred while the prince was on a tour of east Africa—chiefly a visit to Happy Valley society with Lady Furness, an American, with whom he shared a fairly brief liaison. A telegram from Stanley Baldwin, the prime minister, summoned him home. Though the king recovered, it was apparent that he was entering his final years. This development seems to have encouraged the prince of Wales to intensify those aspects of his life which once king he must have known he would have had to curtail—though the precedent of Edward VII showed that the public and the political establishment could easily accommodate a *ménage à trois* consisting of a king, a queen, and a *maîtresse en titre* (Prince Edward had known Mrs Keppel well, being sixteen when Edward VII died).

Wallis Simpson The prince met Wallis Simpson [*see* Windsor, (Bessie) Wallis (1896–1986)] in the home of Lady Furness (during the latter's own affair with the prince) on 10 January 1931. She was an American citizen who in 1928 had married, as her second husband, Ernest Simpson, an American businessman then living and working in London. By 1934 the prince had cast aside both Lady Furness and Freda Dudley Ward (the latter cut off without, apparently, any personal farewell). The prince saw Mrs Simpson as his natural companion in life, both sexually and intellectually. 'To him', his closest friend during the abdication crisis observed, 'she was the perfect woman' (Birkenhead, 125). A man accustomed to get his way, when he knew what it was that he wanted, the prince of Wales seems to have thought from 1934 onwards that matters would turn out as he wished. Though he appears from an early stage to have wanted Wallis as his queen, he made no effort to test or prepare the ground, even with those whose support would be vital. Nor do those around him seem to have sounded him as to his intentions (and as his accession was clearly imminent they could not have been blamed if they had done so). Neither the prince's father nor mother seems to have raised with him either the affair or its likely result. Thus the prince of Wales's affair with Mrs Simpson, pursued with a passion evident to all who observed it, occurred in a political and constitutional limbo. Much is made of the British press's silence on the subject—but that silence provided a convenient context for discussion and resolution of which no advantage was taken by either side. Almost the only person who tried to act as a catalyst was Ernest Simpson, against whom Mrs Simpson began divorce proceedings in the summer of 1936; he pointed out to several people in London early in 1936 that he believed the new king wished to marry his wife.

Ascending the throne George V died on 20 January 1936 and the prince of Wales was proclaimed as King Edward VIII on 21 and 22 January, having flown to London from Sandringham (the first British monarch to travel by air). The new king kept guard with his brothers on the last evening of their father's lying-in-state in Westminster Hall. With George V's funeral on 28 January, which his son

did much to organize, the new reign was under way. Much was propitious: Edward VIII brought to the throne good health, modernity, and very considerable gifts of communication. He was a colourful figure in a drab era. Yet for all his modernity he had given little thought as to how he would behave as king. Though widely travelled, he had little political understanding of the complexities of the period in which he was living. George V had followed his father in letting his son see state papers, but Edward VIII once on the throne followed the precedent of Edward VII's nonchalance rather than his father's diligence with respect to papers describing policy and governmental business. Thus his ministers quickly realized that he was not seriously engaged in the processes of public business, at least in the sense that his father had always been. Partly as a consequence of this, the king had a poor perception of the relationship of his position as monarch to his ministers as his advisers. As Frances Donaldson observed, he 'had only the haziest notions of the behaviour proper to a constitutional monarch' (Donaldson, 204). This difficulty was especially evident with respect to foreign policy, where the king's sympathetic view of Nazism—a widespread interpretation of his position which he did nothing to counter—conflicted with the Baldwin government's gradual realization of the true character of Hitler's Germany. He himself remarked that the only positive pieces of advice about being king were supplied by an old courtier: 'Never miss an opportunity to relieve yourself; never miss a chance to sit down and rest your feet' (Windsor, *A King's Story*, 132).

Edward VIII inherited his father's staff and court. Godfrey Thomas, his much valued private secretary while prince of Wales, declined to become his secretary as king. This was a considerable misfortune for the new king. Instead of Thomas, after the customary six-month interim between the reigns the king appointed Sir Alexander Hardinge, previously his father's assistant secretary and with no especial association with the new king; Thomas served as assistant secretary, supported by Alan Lascelles, also from his father's secretariat (Lascelles had been on the prince's staff in the 1920s but had resigned as a result of personal differences). Lascelles was the king's speech-writer. The king's chief officials, diligent though they were in their posts, were thus, with the exception of Thomas, somewhat remote from him; they were not well placed to know his mind or give him personal advice. With respect to Hardinge, the key figure, there was 'no possibility that he [Hardinge] would achieve a working relationship with the King' (Ziegler, 258). The king's chief male cronies were G. F. Trotter (1871–1945), assistant comptroller of the household, known as G, and E. D. Metcalfe (d. 1957), known as Fruity. Metcalfe had been the prince's equerry in the early 1920s and was the king's companion during his liaison with Mrs Simpson.

Socially Edward VIII continued to behave as if he was still merely prince of Wales. He established what was in effect a second (and in his mind the chief) court at Fort Belvedere, a folly built on the border of Windsor Great Park and restored for his own use when prince of Wales. It became linked in the public mind with the abdication—just as, in the same period, Cliveden was with appeasement. Members of the royal household were excluded from Fort Belvedere, with Metcalfe acting as a go-between for all the various parties. The king's affair with Mrs Simpson was undisguised (though still almost unreported in the British press), and his informal and sometimes arbitrary behaviour was the despair of his staff. To move the monarchic establishment towards a more informal style might well have been a long-term objective, but to assume that such a change had already been made was to flout his own constituency in a dangerous way. He was pointedly warned by Cosmo Gordon Lang, archbishop of Canterbury; Lang did not explicitly mention Mrs Simpson, but the king knew the purpose of the conversation: 'That encounter was my first intimation that I might be approaching an irreconcilable conflict' (Windsor, *A King's Story*, 274). The king drew from it, however, not a political conclusion, but the hope that 'time would produce a solution' (ibid., 275).

The abdication Members of the cabinet and the archbishop of Canterbury were well aware of the foreign newspapers' coverage of the king's holiday in the Mediterranean with Mrs Simpson on the yacht *Nahlin*. Baldwin, who was never hasty and sometimes dilatory, allowed the situation to mature almost to its fullest point before he asked to see the king on 20 October 1936. Baldwin liked the king personally and had accompanied him on the tour of Canada in 1927 (which had also allowed him to see the caprice as well as the charm of the then prince of Wales). That Baldwin did not, until a late stage, perceive that the king hoped to marry Mrs Simpson was the fault of the monarch as much as of the prime minister. It is also possible that it was only on 15 October that Sir Alexander Hardinge, the king's secretary, learned of Mrs Simpson's petition for divorce, which was to be heard at Ipswich, about which he immediately told Baldwin. On 20 October Baldwin told the king of the effect press reporting would have in Britain when the self-imposed embargo was lifted, as it was bound to be, and suggested that he persuade Mrs Simpson not to pursue her divorce. He suggested she instead go abroad for six months. Though the king replied, disingenuously, that the divorce was a private matter for Mrs Simpson, Baldwin did not take the matter further and did not make an explicit warning about the king's trying to marry her. He perhaps underestimated both Edward VIII's determination and his lack of political perception. On 27 October Mrs Simpson obtained a decree nisi, and the next day Hardinge warned the duke of York (next in line to the throne) that abdication was a possibility. On 3 November—with the press still silent—the king opened parliament (the only occasion on which he did so) and made the required declaration that he was 'a faithful Protestant'. The coronation was planned for 12 May 1937, before Mrs Simpson's decree would become absolute and she would be free to marry again.

Behind the scenes various developments worsened the king's position. Two affidavits had been filed, requiring the intervention of the king's proctor, with respect to Mrs Simpson's decree nisi on grounds of collusion between the king and Mrs Simpson, a potentially very embarrassing case. On 13 November Hardinge wrote to put on record to the king the facts that the press was about to break silence and that 'the serious situation which is developing' was being discussed by Baldwin and other senior ministers. Hardinge warned of the possible resignation of the government (Donaldson, 235–6). The king was shocked by the impersonal tone of Hardinge's letter, and subsequently used Walter Monckton as his adviser. On 16 November Baldwin again requested an audience: at it, for the first time to a minister, the king stated his intention to marry Mrs Simpson. Dominion opinion—canvassed via the governors-general and directly by Baldwin and already well informed through the newspapers—was strongly hostile; Baldwin thought British opinion would also be hostile when the news finally broke. That dominion opinion was said to be so hostile was important, both because Edward VIII was the first monarch to be head of state of each dominion individually and because it was in the dominions that his modern ways had seemed so popular. In Britain he risked facing difficulties with two institutions: the Church of England, whose leaders would certainly oppose the marriage of the defender of the faith (as the king was) if his future spouse's status as a divorcee would bar him from being married in a Church of England service; and parliament, which less than a decade earlier had rejected the Church of England's modest attempt at innovation through the revised Book of Common Prayer. The king told Baldwin that if the government opposed the marriage he intended to make, he would abdicate. That night the king dined with his mother and sister, and told them of his love for Wallis Simpson and of his intention, if necessary, to abdicate—a decision repeated next day to each of his brothers.

On 18–19 November the king visited the distressed areas of south Wales, and at the Bessemer steel works at Dowlais remarked in a sentence which, in several slightly different versions, became famous: 'These works brought all these people here. Something must be done to find them work.'

The crisis having moved forward apace, there was now something of a lull. How much the king discussed these matters with Wallis Simpson is hard to know—as is the moment when he formally proposed marriage to her. A compromise was suggested by Esmond Rothermere, proprietor of the *Daily Mail*, that there be a morganatic marriage (by which Mrs Simpson would marry the king but not become queen). Ironically, though the king's marriage to someone who would be queen was not subject to the Royal Marriages Act, a morganatic marriage would require an act of parliament and would have opened the monarchy to extensive and prolonged parliamentary debate. It was very questionable whether the government could carry such a bill, and certain that it did not wish to introduce one. The king put the morganatic proposal to

Baldwin on 25 November, because of its legislative implications, and by so doing gave him title to consult the cabinet. The dominions and the opposition were formally consulted: all were agreed both that Mrs Simpson would not be suitable as queen and that a morganatic marriage was not an acceptable compromise. Of the cabinet, only Duff Cooper took a different view (suggesting all sides should defer the question until after the coronation).

Thus it was that when on 2 December the wall of press silence began to crumble (initially through reports of some remarks by A. W. F. Blunt, suffragan bishop of Bradford, to his diocesan conference) the issue had matured almost to a point of agreement between all the immediate parties: the king should abdicate. One of the few who thought he should not was Wallis Simpson, who preferred the morganatic solution and, failing that, did not find her position of *maîtresse en titre* unappealing (though she would not have countenanced a marriage of convenience by the king to another woman). On 3 December—the first day of major British press coverage—she left for Cannes. 'I am sure there is only one solution', she recorded herself as having said, 'that is for me to remove myself from the King's life. That is what I am doing now' (*The Heart has its Reasons*, 259–60). Her absence gave the king a little time and, fairly enough, emphasized how far abdication was his own choice, within the options Baldwin had described.

The king then made his only tactical intervention in the crisis: a proposal that he be allowed to go abroad as king after broadcasting to his people about his wishes, the people then, by some unstated mechanism, making their views known. Baldwin refused the broadcast as unacceptable to the cabinet: he took the view that he and the cabinet were in this instance the constitutional representatives of public opinion, though Baldwin was throughout careful not explicitly to advise the king that he should abdicate. The king, isolated with Walter Monckton at Fort Belvedere, was temporarily encouraged by an extraordinary intervention by Winston Churchill and Lord Beaverbrook, and by a phone call from Mrs Simpson, to consider fighting for his rights and to ignore his government's advice with respect to his marriage. Exhausted and by some accounts bemused, the king, through Monckton, told Baldwin on 5 December of his decision to abdicate; after several further twists and turns the instrument of abdication was signed on the morning of Thursday 10 December, witnessed by the king's three brothers, and a king's message was sent to the Commons. A plan to accompany the necessary act of parliament with a second measure making Mrs Simpson's decree immediately absolute was dropped in the light of the expected opposition.

Edward VIII's reign ceased on 11 December on his assent to the consequent statute, the same day on which James II vacated the throne in 1688. His reign had lasted 327 days, the shortest of any recognized monarch since Edward V. No longer king, he was introduced by John Reith for his broadcast that evening as his royal highness Prince Edward. Whatever the misjudgements and miscalculations he had made, his broadcast was a triumph and

remained poignant decades later. In a sentence which became immediately famous he remarked:

> you must believe me when I tell you that I have found it impossible to carry the heavy burden of responsibility and to discharge my duties as King as I would wish to do without the help and support of the woman I love.

His decision, he said, 'has been mine and mine alone' (Donaldson, 295). (The effect of his broadcast was perhaps enhanced by a censorious broadcast soon after by the archbishop of Canterbury, felt by many to have been ungenerous and ill-judged.) On the evening of his brother's broadcast George VI proposed his royal highness the duke of Windsor as his title, and so he became known from that day, the title being announced in the new king's speech to the accession council on 13 December. It was a dignified choice, though it falsely described the extent of contact which the duke was subsequently to be allowed with either the house or the castle of Windsor.

The abdication was a curious episode since the result satisfied all parties (except the Churchillites). It was of no great immediate constitutional importance for Baldwin played by the book, and the king did not challenge Baldwin's reading of it. Attempts to form a 'king's party' lacked the sustained support of the monarch. Edward VIII appears initially to have had some expectation that Mrs Simpson would become his queen. But he advanced no informed or developed case that she should do so, and he made almost no attempt thus to arrange matters with the politicians and the church. Possibly he realized from the start that that would be fruitless; certainly he lacked the political skills and acumen even to begin preparing the ground. A life founded on jumping over the official traces was not a preparation for successfully steering them.

Edward VIII was not long enough on the throne for a state portrait, though several portraits were painted of him in 1936, including one wearing his Garter robes by J. St Helier Lander (Masters Mariners' Company, London) and a portrait by W. R. Sickert for the Welsh Guards (Beaverbrook Art Gallery, Fredericton, New Brunswick), which, showing the king briskly stepping out, was a quite unusual portrait of a monarch and was painted from a photograph. Rather characteristically Edward VIII successfully insisted on his left profile being used for the new coins and postage stamps because left was his better side (the convention was that the side changed with the monarch, and George V had looked left). The stamps were issued, but he resigned the throne before any coins were issued. Though Edward VIII moved in circles in which he met some artists, and did not have his father's instinctive caution about the modern age, he was not seriously interested in the arts and made no attempt, at any stage of his life, to use his position to promote the importance of art or music.

His royal highness the duke of Windsor Though he had not discussed the possibility of abdication with his brother, or the dramatic change it would bring to him, the duke was surprised by the decisiveness with which George VI re-established royal 'normality'. An important part of this process was a pretence that the episode had never occurred. The new royal family behaved as if the Windsors did not exist, and the new king, as late as 1941, referred in his diary to the duchess as 'Mrs. S[impson]'. In fact George VI was well informed about them and kept a sharp watch, choosing, for example, the place of his exiled brother's wedding (the Château de Candé, near Tours in France). There the Windsors were married on 3 June 1937, first in the usual French civil ceremony and then according to the Church of England rite by the Revd R. A. Jardine of Darlington, who offered his services despite the Church of England's views on marriage to divorced persons. E. D. Metcalfe was best man. No member of the duke's family attended, but his mother and siblings sent telegrams, and Baldwin a kindly letter. The occasion was marred for the duke by news brought by Walter Monckton: the letters patent formally establishing the duke's title denied (with dubious legality) the duchess the prefix her royal highness—a small point *sub specie aeternitatis*, but one of great importance to all concerned on both sides. Few expected the Windsors' marriage to last, and George VI pointed out to Baldwin that HRH was a title which once given could not be removed: the fear was that the duchess would leave the duke and become a maverick HRH, conceivably even married to a fourth husband. The slight, as the duke perceived it, made him fully realize, perhaps for the first time, the extent of his exclusion.

Life after kingship The duke's financial settlement was made between him and George VI in December 1936 (as he was life tenant of Sandringham and Balmoral it was a complex matter). He received an income adequate to living fashionably in Paris with a small household, but his failure to disclose all his assets (he had in reserve a considerable fortune) left his brother and Churchill, who assisted in the negotiations, feeling duped; this episode materially contributed to the distrust with which the duke of Windsor was seen by Britain's wartime monarch and prime minister.

The Windsors had no function other than to live as a leisured, childless couple. When James II had vacated the throne great issues of principle had been the cause, a cause sustained by James's son and grandson. Comparatively Edward VIII's abdication was, as far as it could be, a private matter. Even so, there was some fear in London and Windsor that the former king would form—or have formed around him—a king's party. The duke himself seems to have expected that he would soon be given employment. It was perhaps a misjudgement that, after a short interval, he was not, for it would have brought him again within official control. The duke revived the aspect of his time which as prince of Wales he had especially enjoyed—foreign visits—and in October 1937 he and the duchess visited Germany. His stated intention was to study German solutions to unemployment, but the visit was, of course, a triumph for the Nazis who craved just this sort of recognition. The Windsors met Hitler, and the duke made 'a modified Nazi salute' and on two other occasions a full Nazi salute (Donaldson, 331–2). It used to be thought that the duke's links to Germany at this time

were merely a symptom of non-political naïvety, but recently it has been suggested that he came to see himself as a possible alternative monarch, should Britain be defeated in war, and that concern about the possibility of a king's party was no idle fear. Robert Bruce Lockhart's contemporary report catches this view: the Germans expected, Bruce Lockhart wrote, that the duke would 'come back as a social-equalising King' and inaugurate an 'English form of Fascism and alliance with Germany' (Ziegler, 392). Like his brother, the duke was a keen supporter of Neville Chamberlain; he was pessimistic about Britain's likelihood of surviving in 1940, and he favoured a negotiated peace with Hitler, a view which was not uncommon in some British circles (though not among the duke's British friends). After the war German documents were found substantiating Bruce Lockhart's view of what the Germans intended the duke's role should be. But evidence that the duke either hoped for or planned such an outcome has not been found, almost certainly because it does not exist; if it did exist, the exhaustive attention given to this episode would almost certainly have brought it to light.

In 1938 the Windsors took a long lease on the villa La Cröe at Antibes and on 24 boulevard Suchet near the Bois de Boulogne in Paris. From January 1939 the latter was intended as their usual home—the first of several addresses in that part of Paris. The duke made several other interventions in public life which confirmed his reputation as a loose cannon: he pursued a libel action arising from Geoffrey Dennis's *Coronation Commentary* (1937), though the book was largely a defence of his actions; he broadcast to America on 8 May 1939 from the battlefields of Verdun appealing for peace (just as George VI was beginning his visit to the USA); he sent a telegram to Hitler in August 1939 also appealing for peace. When war began the Windsors were at the villa La Cröe: they were brought to Britain by Lord Louis Mountbatten in HMS *Kelly*. The duke (who was still a field marshal) was offered two posts, choosing to be regional commissioner for Wales. This offer was at once dropped (perhaps his refusal had been expected), although—perhaps because—the post would have kept him in Britain. George VI 'did not like the idea' of the duke's presence in Britain: 'the sooner he went to France the better for all concerned. He is not wanted here' (George VI's diary, quoted in Rhodes James, 175). The duke thus became a member of the British military mission in France (a return to his 1914–18 work); he was a major-general for the duration of the war and was accompanied by Fruity Metcalfe.

On the fall of France in June 1940 the Windsors escaped to Madrid; they had no papers, but the duke negotiated the road blocks by calling out 'Je suis le Prince de Galles. Laissez-moi passer, s'il vous plaît' ('I am the Prince of Wales. Let me pass, please'). They subsequently moved to Lisbon at the start of July. There then occurred a plot worthy of a novel by John Buchan or a film by Alfred Hitchcock: an attempt by the Germans, organized by Ribbentrop, to kidnap the duke with a view to using him as the British Pétain, or at least to keep him in Spain with the expectation that he would support a call for peace. How justified the Germans were in believing that the Windsors would be useful to them cannot be known. Much speculation on the duke's likely actions has been based on evidence which assumes a more systematic approach to politics than was usual with him; on the other hand, the Germans evidently thought the Windsors might be a convenient way into that circle in the English establishment which thought the empire should be fighting the Russians rather than the Germans.

From his friend Winston Churchill, now prime minister, the duke requested a position in Britain and recognition for his wife by the rest of the royal family (he abstained from raising the HRH question). In Britain's 'darkest hour' Churchill had to spend much time sorting out the duke's position. The duke was offered the governorship of the Bahamas, which he accepted. Ribbentrop's attempts to persuade the Windsors not to leave neutral Portugal were counterbalanced by Monckton, and they left Lisbon for the Bahamas on 1 August 1940, reaching Nassau on 17 August. From the British point of view this was a convenient solution: the duke had a post, but was under Colonial Office control as to his statements and movements. From the Windsors' point of view the governorship seemed a chance to bid for reinstatement from an exclusion they still found hard to comprehend. Though small in population the Bahamas was not an easy posting, given all the tug and tussle of a multi-ethnic society in which the white population had the upper hand. The Windsors' time there was on balance successful, though the duke handled several incidents with lack of tact and judgement and sometimes seemed insensitive to the claims of the island's black inhabitants. On the other hand he was seen as dangerous and antagonistic by the 'Bay Street Boys' (the white traders who dominated the legislative assembly), and he tried to develop policies for agricultural improvement in the Out Islands and to diminish black unemployment. Serious riots occurred in June 1942, when the duke was in the United States. He returned promptly and reimposed order quickly by conciliating all parties and making a broadcast to the islanders which annoyed the Colonial Office by his announcement that he would seek American assistance to raise wages. The Windsors found Bahamian life tiresome, but they put on a good public show. In 1944 the duke requested a more important post, but was offered the governorship of Bermuda, which he declined. He resigned as governor of the Bahamas on 16 March 1945. Churchill had persistently but without effect tried to persuade the king to receive the duchess and to find the duke another post, such as the governorship of Madras or Ceylon. This intervention by Churchill, early in 1945, conflating the question of the duke's post with the duchess's reception, was poorly timed and counterproductive; it annoyed the king, and perhaps delayed the possibility of a degree of reconciliation. After a visit to the USA (the duke had struck up quite a regular correspondence with Roosevelt and visited the States several times during his governorship, notably in 1941 and 1942) the

Windsors returned to Paris, the duke briefly visiting Britain without the duchess. A combination of France and the USA was to be their regular routine until the duke's death. George VI made it plain that the presence of the duke and duchess in Britain would be an embarrassment, a point the duke regretfully accepted, and the duke's offer to work in 'the field of Anglo-American relations' was declined (Bloch, *Duke of Windsor's War*, 364–5). In 1952 La Cröe was sold and the Moulin de la Tuilerie, an old watermill near Paris, bought in its place. Soon after, by arrangement with the city of Paris which charged only a nominal rent, 4 rue du Champ d'Entraînement, a mansion on the Neuilly side of the Bois de Boulogne, became the Windsors' chief home (Ziegler, 534–5).

From the duke's point of view his life was lived at its fullest during his years with the duchess. The love which had drawn him into that relationship showed, on his side, no sign of diminution. Preoccupied with seeing that the duchess received adequate recognition of her status by those who met her—he insisted that guests refer to his wife as her royal highness—the duke consequently and somewhat ironically found himself the champion of status and its rights. Indeed his position depended on his status (and former status as king) being taken seriously by his coterie, and he never intended that abdication would lead to the ordinary life of a commoner. He abdicated from the throne, not from the royal family. Though he retained the charm and good looks of his youth they began to have a frozen quality, as the ageing Windsors contrasted in the photographs with Princess Elizabeth and her young family. The modish social views of the 1920s turned to reactionary convention.

As the abdication began in the late 1940s to be a distant public memory, the duke had an interest in maintaining public fascination with it. He also increasingly felt he had been unfairly treated—a charge he had not made at the time. Moreover, though the duke's income was substantial, the Windsors' lifestyle, and especially the duchess's, was expensive. Attempts to find oil on his Canadian ranch had led to significant losses and currency restrictions further complicated a life lived in several countries, and the duke sometimes pulled rank to avoid them.

A King's Story (1951) was the first book by a British monarch since 1688, apart from Queen Victoria's editions of her journals. John Gore's 'personal memoir' of George V (1941), written largely from the king's diaries at the request of George VI, was carefully discreet about 'David', but the choice of Harold Nicolson in 1948 as George V's official biographer suggested a more candid approach (in fact Nicolson's biography of 1952 was reticent with respect to David, whom Nicolson had seen from time to time since 1936). G. M. Young's biography of Baldwin was also in preparation (1952) and certain to tell the story from Baldwin's point of view. *A King's Story*, written with the help of Charles John Vincent Murphy, was thus a well-timed volume, and financially very successful. It was followed by two less substantial books, *The Crown and the People, 1902–1953* (1953), published just after the duke's niece's coronation, and *A Family Album* (1960). In 1965 a film was made of *A King's Story* by Jack Le Vien, directed by Harry Booth—a compilation of commentary by Orson Welles, interviews of the duke and duchess, and extracts from newsreels; it was nominated for best documentary in the Oscars.

In February 1952 the duke attended the funeral of George VI (they had hardly met since the latter became king). In 1953 he visited his mother before she died. He was not invited to the new queen's coronation that year. In 1966 the duke and duchess were invited by Elizabeth II to attend the unveiling of a plaque to Queen Mary, the duchess being presented to the queen. The normal informality of family life was not restored, but the taboo of non-contact was broken.

The duke aged rapidly in the late 1960s. In 1972 cancer of the throat gained ascendancy (like his brother, he had been a smoker from an early age). As he lay dying he was visited by Elizabeth II during her state visit to France. On 28 May 1972 the duke of Windsor died at his home, 4 rue du Champ d'Entraînement, Paris. His body received the panoply due to a royal prince. It lay in state, not in Westminster Hall but in St George's Chapel, Windsor, for the public to file by—which they did in unexpectedly large numbers. The funeral service was held in St George's Chapel on 5 June in the presence of the queen, the royal family, and the duchess of Windsor, and the coffin was buried in a plot beside the Royal Mausoleum at Frogmore (with provision for the duchess in due course).

Reflections on a retired monarch As long as monarchy in Britain is invested with the full fig of hereditary mystique, Edward VIII will have a bad press. In asserting private before public priorities to the extent of occasioning a constitutional crisis, he undoubtedly went far beyond what the British and imperial establishment found acceptable in a sovereign. His behaviour created a sharp royal reaction on the part of George VI and his family which prevented the evolution of the monarchy and which played a part in leading to an emphasis on family values which proved to be dangerous. But if the monarchy were to lose some of its mystique, and if the primacy of the hereditary element in monarchy weakens, then Edward VIII's priorities may come to be seen more sympathetically. Moreover it may be said of him that his values were ahead, but not very far ahead, of his time: his view of marriage to a divorcee was one increasingly favoured by his subjects and has been accommodated by most British churches in the latter part of the twentieth century—though in the 1930s it was certainly unacceptable to almost all. He himself was never party to a divorce case, and after his marriage he appears to have been strictly monogamous. As a married man the duke of Windsor was respectability personified.

It was a major difficulty for Edward VIII that, quite apart from the question of Mrs Simpson, he was not trusted by his ministers. If he had shown himself a competent monarch with respect to the handling of day-to-day business, and with a consistent and informed judgement on public affairs, his ministers might well have been willing to do much more to accommodate Mrs Simpson. But for them the Simpson affair was a symptom of a wider question mark which had arisen over his capacity to be king. In this they were surely correct: it is hard to imagine Edward VIII handling the crises such as those over the House of Lords, the First World War coalitions, and inter-war politics with any of his father's aplomb. Though it was unstated, there was therefore some elision of the question of the royal marriage with the question of the king's suitability for the throne. It is speculation to consider whether the king also took this view, and used his relationship with Mrs Simpson as a means of escape which would otherwise be denied to him; but there is little indication that he had any inclination to settle into a role of whose conventions and constrictions he was well aware. 'The fault lay not in my stars but in my genes', he later wrote of himself (Windsor, *A King's Story*, 284); however, in an interview in 1957 he remarked 'Of course I wished to be King. More, I wished to remain King' (Wheeler-Bennett, 268). The king did little to help himself tactically, but the establishment, led by Baldwin and Cosmo Gordon Lang, archbishop of Canterbury, gave the clear impression that his choice of abdication was not a choice which distressed them.

Edward VIII thus occupies an ambivalent position in the history of the British monarchy. The circumstances of his brief reign seemed to emphasize the dominance of respectability and inflexibility in inter-war British public morals, while also allowing the procedures of the constitution to demonstrate their flexibility and swift efficacy. The latter, as much as the former, caused alarm in royal circles. The fact of an abdication (as the rest of the royal family at once saw) in itself introduced in the long run alternative possible solutions to the harsh requirements imposed on those who held by the accident of birth a position whose confines they might find unacceptable. An essential point about monarchy, on the part of both sovereign and subject, was that it was not a voluntary institution: the king ruled by the accident of birth and the subject by duty obeyed the holder of the office. Abdication offered an alternative view of these relationships. If the monarch could leave the throne because he personally did not find it convenient to sit upon it, his subjects might well think that, in certain circumstances in addition to the protestant requirements already written into the constitution, they could express a view as to whether the occupant of the throne suited them. Thus the widespread and much emphasized understanding that George VI ruled unwillingly but from a sense of duty was an important counter to the possible direction that Edward VIII had set out upon.

The duke of Windsor, especially compared to the considerable number of other former monarchs of the period, behaved after 1936 with dignity and reserve in the face of what he and his wife saw as a deliberate and systematic exclusion. Few had believed the king when he said that he could not and would not live his life without Wallis Simpson, but he spoke the truth. In the long history of royal romance there are few better examples of fidelity to a person or a claim.

H. C. G. MATTHEW

Sources F. Donaldson, *Edward VIII* (1974) · P. Ziegler, *King Edward VIII: the official biography* (1990) · *DNB* · Duke of Windsor, *A king's story: the memoirs of HRH the duke of Windsor* (1951) · *Wallis and Edward: letters, 1931–1937*, ed. M. Bloch (1986) · *The heart has its reasons: the memoirs of the Duchess of Windsor* (1956) · C. Mackenzie, *The Windsor tapestry* (1938) · M. Bloch, *The duke of Windsor's war* (1982) · M. Bloch, *Operation Willi* (1984) · K. McLeod, *Battle royal: Edward VIII & George VI* (1999) · Lord Birkenhead, *Walter Monckton* (1969) · M. H. Hardinge and Lady Hardinge, *Loyal to three kings* (1967) · B. Inglis, *Abdication* (1966) · K. Rose, *King George V* (1983) · J. Pope-Hennessy, *Queen Mary* (1959) · J. H. Wheeler-Bennett, *King George VI: his life and reign* (1958) · R. Rhodes James, *A spirit undaunted: the political role of George VI* (1998) · K. Middlemas and J. Barnes, *Baldwin: a biography* (1969)
Archives Royal Arch. | BL OIOC, corresp. with Lord Curzon, 1147 · Bodl. Oxf., corresp. with Lord Monckton · CAC Cam., corresp. with Lord Esher · CUL, corresp. with Lord Hardinge · Herts. ALS, corresp. with Lady Desborough · HLRO, corresp. with Lord Beaverbrook · HLRO, corresp. with D. Lloyd George · NL Aus., corresp. with Viscount Novar · NL Scot., corresp. with Seton Gordon · Norfolk RO, letters to E. G. Buxton · PRO NIre., letters to Lady Londonderry · PRO NIre., corresp. with Lord Londonderry · Wilts. & Swindon RO, letters to earl and countess of Pembroke | FILM BFI NFTVA, 'The investiture of the prince of Wales at Caernarvon', Gaumont Graphic, 13 July 1911 · BFI NFTVA, 'Incidents during the life of the heir to the throne', 1923 · BFI NFTVA, 'King Edward abdicates', *British Paramount news*, 10 Dec 1936 · BFI NFTVA, 'Coronation crises', *March of time*, 1937 · BFI NFTVA, 'A king's story', 1965 · BFI NFTVA, 'Brothers at war: the Windsors', ITV, 1 June 1994 · BFI NFTVA, *Secret lives*, Channel 4, 16 Jan 1995 · BFI NFTVA, *Secret lives*, Channel 4, 23 Nov 1995 · BFI NFTVA, 'Edward on Edward', ITV, 23 April 1996 · BFI NFTVA, *The Windsors*, BBC2, 7 Dec 2000 · BFI NFTVA, documentary footage; news footage
Likenesses W. Q. Orchardson, pencil drawing, study, *c*.1897 (*The four generations*), Royal Collection · W. Q. Orchardson, group portrait, oils, *c*.1897–1899 (*The four generations*), Royal Agricultural Society, London · W. Q. Orchardson, study, *c*.1897–1899 (for *The four generations*), NPG · W. Strang, drawing, 1909, Royal Collection · A. S. Cope, oils, 1912, Royal Collection · F. Flameng, oils, 1912, Royal Collection · J. Lavery, group portrait, oils, 1913 (*The royal family at Buckingham Palace, 1913*), NPG; *see illus. in George V (1865–1936)* · J. Lavery, oil study, *c*.1913, NPG · J. Lavery, oils, *c*.1913, Royal Collection · H. L. Oakley, silhouette, 1919, NPG · R. G. Eves, chalk drawing, *c*.1920, NPG · R. G. Eves, miniature, *c*.1920, NPG · F. O. Salisbury, group portrait, oils, 1920 (*Burial of unknown warrior*), Palace of Westminster, London · C. Hartwell, marble bust, *c*.1920–1924, Corporation of London · F. Brooks, oils, 1921, Britannia Royal Naval College, Dartmouth · J. Collier, oils, 1921, Hall of Princes, Delhi, India · C. S. Jagger, bronze statuette, 1922, NMG Wales; version?, Graves Art Gallery, Sheffield · J. St H. Lander, oils, *c*.1922, Man. City Gall. · F. O. Salisbury, group portrait, oils, 1922 (*Marriage of Princess Mary*), Harewood House, West Yorkshire · J. St H. Lander, oils, 1925, Leeds City Art Gallery · W. Orpen, oils, 1928, Royal and Ancient Golf Club of St Andrews · W. Rothenstein, crayon drawing, 1929, Cheltenham Art Gallery and Museum · F. W. Doyle-Jones, *c*.1932, Master Mariners' Company · E. Kapp, lithograph, 1932, NPG · F. O. Salisbury, group portrait, oils, 1935 (*Jubilee service for George V*), Royal Collection · F. Kormis, bronze medal, 1936, NPG · J. St H. Lander, oils, 1936, Master Mariners' Company, London · F. O. Salisbury, oils, 1936, Belton House, Lincolnshire · W. R. Sickert, oils, 1936 (after photograph by H. J. Clemens), Beaverbrook Art Gallery, Fredericton, New Brunswick, Canada · photograph, 1936, NPG [*see illus.*] · O. H. Mavor, watercolour caricature, 1943, Dundee City Art Gallery · J. Gunn, oils, 1954, NPG · J. Gunn, oils, *c*.1954, Royal Collection · C. Beaton, photographs, NPG · Mrs Albert Broom, photographs, NPG · H. Cecil, photographs, NPG · W. & D. Downey, photograph, NPG, Royal Collection · Dunham, photographs, NPG · O. Edis, photographs · Hughes & Mullins, photographs, NPG · Nibs, Hentschel-colourtype, NPG; repro. in *VF* (21 June 1911) · J. Russell & Sons, photographs, NPG · F. O. Salisbury, group portrait, oils (*Thanksgiving service*), Guildhall, London · Vandyk, chalk drawing (after photograph?), Royal College of Music, London · Vandyk, photographs, NPG · D. Wilding, photographs, NPG

Edward Ætheling [called Edward the Exile] (*d.* **1057**), prince, was the son of *Edmund Ironside, king of England (*d.* 1016), presumably from his union in 1015 with Ealdgyth, widow of the Danelaw thegn Sigeferth. The sources on his life are thoroughly unsatisfactory. The D text of the Anglo-Saxon Chronicle says under 1057 that Cnut banished him to Hungary to betray him, that he prospered there, married Agatha, a relative of the emperor, and begot a noble family; under 1067, the same text says that Agatha was related through her mother to an Emperor Henry. Twelfth-century chroniclers are more detailed. John of Worcester says Cnut sent Edward and his brother Edmund to the Swedish king to be killed, but that he passed them to Hungary, where Edmund died and Edward married Agatha, daughter of the brother of an Emperor Henry. William of Malmesbury describes Agatha as sister of the Hungarian queen, and Ailred of Rievaulx calls her the daughter of the Hungarian king's brother, the emperor Henry, while Orderic Vitalis says Edward married the Hungarian king's daughter. The twelfth-century *Leges Edwardi Confessoris* ('Laws of Edward the Confessor'), however, has him fleeing to and marrying in Russia, which was also his destination according to Adam of Bremen, writing *c*.1070. In the 1130s the Anglo-Norman poet Gaimar was misnaming him Edgar and telling a rousing tale of his adventures, complete with dialogue.

Modern historians have had scant success with this material, which inspires little trust. Agatha was arguably the daughter of King Stephen of Hungary, or of Bruno, brother of the German Emperor Henry II, or of a half-brother of the emperor Henry III, or of none of them. Probably Edward the Exile, as he is also known, was respected in Hungary, which may say much for interest in the English monarchy; but the only certainty is his return thence to England, at his countrymen's request, in 1057, presumably because some hoped he would succeed the childless *Edward the Confessor who in 1051 or 1052 had probably promised the throne to William, duke of Normandy. Whether the Confessor really considered changing his mind in the Ætheling's favour will never be known, for the latter died on 19 April 1057, before seeing the king, and was buried at St Paul's Cathedral, leaving his wife and three children—*Edgar Ætheling, *Margaret (later queen of Scotland), and *Christina (later a nun of Romsey). M. K. LAWSON

Sources *ASC*, s.a. 1057 [text D] · *Magistri Adam Bremensis gesta Hammaburgensis ecclesiae pontificum*, ed. B. Schmeidler, 3rd edn, MGH Scriptores Rerum Germanicarum, [2] (Hanover, 1917), 114 · John of Worcester, *Chron.* · *Willelmi Malmesbiriensis monachi de gestis regum Anglorum*, ed. W. Stubbs, 2 vols., Rolls Series (1887–9) · Ordericus Vitalis, *Eccl. hist.*, 1.157; 2.180; 4.272 · F. Liebermann, ed., 'Leges Edwardi Confessoris', *Die Gesetze der Angelsachsen*, 1 (Halle, 1898), 664 · Aelredus Rievallensis [Ailred of Rievaulx], 'Genealogia regum Anglorum', *Patrologia Latina*, 195 (1855), 733–4 · R. L. Graeme Ritchie, *The Normans in Scotland* (1954) · S. D. Keynes, 'The Crowland psalter and the sons of King Edmund Ironside', *Bodleian Library*

Record, 11 (1982–5), 359–70 · *L'estoire des Engleis by Geffrei Gaimar*, ed. A. Bell, Anglo-Norman Texts, 14–16 (1960), 142–7

Edward Augustus, Prince, duke of York and Albany (1739–1767), was born on 14 March 1739 at Norfolk House, St James's Square, London, the third child and second son of *Frederick Lewis, prince of Wales (1707–1751), and his wife, *Augusta (1719–1772), daughter of Friedrich II, duke of Saxe-Gotha. He was educated with his brother the future *George III, who was only ten months older. Edward was seen by some commentators as his parents' favourite. It may be more true that in Edward's education less emphasis was placed than in George's on self-control and responsibility, and this may have shaped his later, self-centred career. In January 1757 he entered society and was frequently seen at Ranelagh and other assemblies with Frances Capel, *née* Hanbury Williams, countess of Essex (*d.* 1759). She was assumed to be his mistress and was dubbed by Horace Walpole 'Princess Edward' (Walpole, *Corr.*, 9.207). Walpole reported in May 1759 that Prince Frederick William, Edward's youngest brother, identified the courtesan Kitty Fisher as the seller of 'a sort [of oranges] that my brother Edward buys' (ibid., 237) and there were frequent rumours of Edward's involvement in sexual intrigues. Contemporaries must have seen the irony when, in January 1760, Prince Edward became patron of the Magdalen Hospital for penitent prostitutes. He later surrendered that role to Queen Charlotte, and in 1764 became president of the London Hospital.

Edward joined the navy at Portsmouth as a volunteer on 24 July 1758, encouraged by his elder brother. George seems to have believed that by associating Edward with the naval action against the French coast planned that summer the prince of Wales's court would gain credit at the expense of the ministry and of George II. The expedition, under Lieutenant-General Thomas Bligh, successfully raided Cherbourg (where Edward hosted a ball and gave 100 guineas to the poor) but an unauthorized attack on St Malo, the plan for which may have come from the prince of Wales rather than from the government, was unsuccessful, humiliating the princes. George II, who had not been informed of the attack, received the commanders frostily but commended Edward for his bravery. Edward may have sought distance from his brother after this incident. On 14 June 1759 he was appointed post captain in command of a new ship, the *Phoenix*, and served until October in the Bay of Biscay, helping to build his glamorous and valiant public image; in July his brother George wrote bitterly to John Stuart, third earl of Bute, that 'I really cannot remain immur'd at home like a girl whilst all my countrymen are preparing for the field and a brother younger than me allow'd to go in quest of the enemy' (*Correspondence of George III, Letters*, 27). In the next year Edward sought and obtained a peerage from George II without consulting the prince of Wales, to the latter's fury, becoming duke of York and Albany and earl of Ulster on 1 April 1760.

On 27 October 1760, following his brother's accession to the throne, the duke of York was sworn of the privy council and, as heir presumptive, moved into the apartments in St James's Palace previously used by his uncle the duke of Cumberland. It is unknown whether he was aware that he should have succeeded to Hanover at this point, under the terms of his father's political testament and George I's suppressed will. York was promoted to rear-admiral of the blue on 8 April 1761 but his proximity to the throne seems to have prevented him from continuing in active service. Instead he began to build a new house in Pall Mall, designed by Matthew Brettingham the elder. He spent July and August 1761 touring Yorkshire, where he received the freedoms of Scarborough and of York, proceeding to Bath and Bristol in early 1762. In May 1762, by which time it seemed certain that he would be superseded as heir to the throne by Queen Charlotte's first child, he was allowed to return to the sea. He was promoted to vice-admiral of the blue in September 1762 but resigned his command in November, at the conclusion of the war.

Unlike his uncle the duke of Cumberland, York had shown no particular interest in, or aptitude for, service life, and he spent the rest of his career in pleasure-seeking. He could have expected to be appointed bishop of Osnabrück when the nomination passed to George III as elector of Hanover in 1761 but instead the king waited until his own second son, Frederick, was born in 1763 and passed over his brother. York toured Italy between November 1763 and August 1764. His intentions seem to have been primarily social, and many of his cultivated hosts among British diplomatic representatives were unimpressed by his lack of appreciation of art. He did achieve some diplomatic success, most notably in his visit to Rome in April 1764. There he was lavishly entertained by Pope Clement XIII, courted by the Jesuits, who wanted assurances over their security in Quebec under British rule, and enjoyed playing a role in Vatican ceremonial. His stay in Rome allowed the papacy to demonstrate that it was willing to recognize the Hanoverian succession in Great Britain, which it did on the death of James Francis Edward Stuart in 1766.

York involved himself more in politics in the mid-1760s, partly through his desire to increase his income. He had been awarded £12,000 p.a. and a £16,000 grant towards a house in 1760, and £3000 from the Irish revenues in 1764, but this was not enough to maintain his establishment as he wished. It had been decided in principle that the duke of Cumberland's income could be used to benefit George III's brothers on his death, and York's burst of activity in early 1766 may well have been intended to bring in an administration that would give greater priority to his financial settlement than the beleaguered Rockingham ministry. He became a prominent member of the group of 'King's friends' led by Bute that incongruously opposed George III's ministers. On 18 February 1766 he attempted to arrange a meeting between George III and John Russell, fourth duke of Bedford, but the king refused to see Bedford. George III showed more sympathy for his brothers when York insisted that their financial settlement should be considered alongside their sister *Caroline Matilda's marriage portion in May, and a motion to that effect was carried. That year York was advanced to the rank of admiral in the navy.

York had always been fascinated by the performing arts. Some minuets in the British Library are ascribed to him. He had appreciated the company of David Garrick when their paths had crossed in Italy in 1764. He shared his enthusiasm with the circle of Sir Francis Blake Delaval, the north-east English landowner and libertine. One of the Delavals, Sarah, had married John Savile, earl of Mexborough. In February 1766, at the Mexboroughs' estate at Cannon Park in Hampshire, York infamously encouraged the actor and playwright Samuel Foote to ride his bad-tempered horse. The horse threw Foote to the ground, breaking his leg and forcing York's surgeon William Bromfield to amputate it. York's remorse secured Foote a patent to operate the Haymarket Theatre in the summer months. That autumn York commanded Garrick to play Lothario in Nicholas Rowe's *The Fair Penitent*—to Garrick's distress, as he felt he was too old for the role. York went on to play Lothario himself at a private theatre he set up at Delaval's house in James Street, Westminster. Delaval's sister Anne (1737–1812), the estranged wife of Sir William Stanhope and believed in society to be York's mistress, played Calista. Performances were given several times between December 1766 and May 1767, despite the disapproval of George III.

The king's frustration with his brother was no doubt made worse by York's maiden speech in the Lords on 22 May 1767, which was hostile to the government. York decided to spend the summer abroad and visited Brussels in July before moving on to Paris, where he was entertained by Louis XV and Queen Marie, and defied his brother's instructions by attending the French military review at Compiègne. He fell ill while travelling south at the end of August, and on 31 August arrived at Monaco, where he had been invited by Prince Honoré III. 'A malignant fever' (*London Gazette*, 29 Sept 1767) was diagnosed, his condition deteriorated, and he died at Monaco on 17 September 1767. His body was taken back to London, where he was buried on 3 November in the Henry VII chapel, Westminster Abbey.

York had no known children, although a Mr Potter wrote to him in 1766 demanding money on the grounds that Potter's wife was a discarded mistress of the duke, and her child York's. The diarist Lady Mary Coke had hoped to marry him, and after his death tried to have it believed that she had done so. Elizabeth Percy, duchess of Northumberland, wrote that York 'had great Vivacity but with a Mind so devoted to pleasure & so little regard to propriety as robb'd him of his Dignity & made him rather a trifling than an aimable Character' (*Diaries of a Duchess*, 79–80). He did, however, observe the precedents for royal conduct set by his father, Frederick, in accepting the role of patron to charitable institutions and travelling around the country when his brother considered himself tied to the seat of the executive in London. These contrasting strands of public irresponsibility and conspicuous attention to duty helped to shape the princely ethic that would be carried on by his younger brothers *William Henry and *Henry Frederick and extended by the sons of George III.

MATTHEW KILBURN

Sources Royal Arch., RA GEO 361, 362, 15823, 54251–54261, 54267, 54277, 54279–54290 · Walpole, *Corr.* · J. Brooke, *King George III* (1972) · I. Bigniamini, 'York, Edward Augustus, duke of', *A dictionary of British and Irish travellers in Italy, 1701–1800*, ed. J. Ingamells (1997) · *Report on manuscripts in various collections*, 8 vols., HMC, 55 (1901–14), vol. 2, p. 192; vol. 8, pp. 174, 177, 187–8 · P. Langford, *The first Rockingham administration, 1765–1766* (1973) · *Report on the manuscripts of Mrs Stopford-Sackville*, 1, HMC, 49 (1904), 111–12 · *The correspondence of King George the Third from 1760 to December 1783*, ed. J. Fortescue, 1 (1927), 18, 76, 273, 345–9, 472 · J. Robinson, *The Delaval papers* (c.1890), 91 · *Letters from George III to Lord Bute, 1756–1766*, ed. R. Sedgwick (1939), 15–16, 27, 41, 80–81, 239 · *The letters of David Garrick*, ed. D. M. Little and G. M. Kahrl, 3 vols. (1963), vol. 1, pp. 301–2, 393–4, 415–16, 418–19; vol. 2, pp. 421, 549–50, 559–60 · F. Askham, *The gay Delavals* (1955), 109 · W. Cooke, *Memoirs of Samuel Foote*, 3 vols. (1805), vol. 1, pp. 139–43 · *GM*, 1st ser., 9 (1739), 214 · *GM*, 1st ser., 28 (1758), 337, 449 · *GM*, 1st ser., 31 (1761), 234, 281, 331, 379–80 · *GM*, 1st ser., 32 (1762), 41, 143–4, 338 · *GM*, 1st ser., 37 (1767), 380, 427, 477, 493–4, 535 · J. Charnock, ed., *Biographia navalis*, 6 (1798), 382–5 · W. L. Clowes, *The royal navy: a history from the earliest times to the present*, 3 (1898), 193, 216, 239, 252, 563 · *The diaries of a duchess: extracts from the diaries of the first duchess of Northumberland (1716–1776)*, ed. J. Greig (1926), 79–80 · E. A. Reitan, 'The civil list, 1761–1777: problems of finance and administration', *BIHR*, 47 (1974), 186–201 · GEC, *Peerage*

Archives BL, corresp. with George Grenville, Add. MS 57822, fols. 124, 126, 129, 134 · priv. coll., corresp. with Lady Mary Coke · Royal Arch., corresp. with George III

Likenesses R. Wilson, group portrait, oils, c.1751, NPG · J. Reynolds, oils, 1758–9, Royal Collection · N. Dance, oils, 1764, Royal Collection · J. Nollekens, bust, 1766, Royal Collection · J. Reynolds, oils, 1766, Royal Collection · R. Brompton, group portrait, oils (*Edward duke of York and his friends*), Royal Collection · J. E. Liotard, drawing, Royal Collection

Edward Dafydd [Edward David] (c.1602–1678?), Welsh poet, lived in Margam in Glamorgan. Apart from his poems little is known of his life. There are a few sparse references in the records of the Margam estate and parish but even these are sometimes uncertain since at least one other person of the same name lived there during this period. One reference in Penrice and Margam MS 1282 would seem to place his date of birth c.1602. His wife was apparently named Isabell; they had at least one son. Eighteen poems are extant in contemporary manuscripts, the earliest dated 1623 and the latest 1665, and most are in his own hand. They consist chiefly of elegies and other poems in praise of his patrons among the gentry, almost all of whom lived in his own county of Glamorgan. It appears probable from estate documents in the Penrice and Margam collection that he was also a tenant farmer and that, while he would have received payment for his poems in the traditional manner, farming was his main livelihood.

Edward Dafydd's writing shows considerable mastery of the 'strict metres' and of the bardic learning in such fields as history, mythology, and genealogy. At its best it displays not only technical skill but also energy, sincerity, and facility of expression. He probably taught something of the poetic craft to a younger generation, among them his son named, in the Welsh patronymic style, Dafydd (or David) Edward. That new generation was far more limited in its metrical range and bardic skill, although one who may well have been his pupil, the Reverend David Williams (Dafydd o'r Nant), carried on some aspects of the old poetic tradition with a measure of success into the last decade of the seventeenth century. Edward Williams (Iolo Morganwg; 1747–1826), that wayward genius of a literary forger, ascribed to Edward Dafydd an exalted position in Iolo's famous invention the Gorsedd of Bards, but this belongs to the realms of fantasy. What earns Edward Dafydd his true place in the history of Welsh poetry is that he was one of the last authentic practitioners of a bardic system reaching back in an unbroken line to Taliesin and Aneirin in the sixth century.

The Margam parish register for 1678 records the burials of two persons named Edward David, one on 14 May and the other on 10 July, and it can reasonably be assumed that one of these was the poet.   JOHN RHYS

Sources J. Rhys, 'Bywyd a gwaith Edward Dafydd o Fargam a Dafydd o'r Nant, a hanes dirywiad y gyfundrefn farddol ym Morgannwg', MA diss., U. Wales, 1953 [based primarily on the MS sources 3–8 and incl. detailed references to them] · G. J. Williams, *Traddodiad llenyddol Morgannwg* (1948) · Llyfr Hir Llanharan, Cardiff Central Library, Cardiff MS, 5.44 · NL Wales, Llanover MSS B20 and B1 · NL Wales, Llanstephan MSS 148 and 164 · Cardiff Central Library, Cardiff MS, (Baglan I), 2.277 · NL Wales, Penrice and Margam MSS 1282 and 1346 · Margam parish register, Glamorgan county RO, Cardiff, 1678
Archives Cardiff Central Library, Cardiff MS, 5.44 [Llyfr Hir Llanharan] · NL Wales, Llanover MSS, B20, B1 · NL Wales, Llanstephan MSS, 148, 164

Edward of Westminster. *See* Westminster, Edward of (d. 1265); Edward, prince of Wales (1453–1471).

Edward [*née* Grant], **Catherine** (1813–1861), missionary, was born on 2 April 1813, eldest daughter of Patrick Grant (1783–1816), minister of Kirkmichael, Banffshire, and his wife, Isabella Mitchell (d. 1845). After her father's death Catherine was brought up in Edinburgh, where her mother supplemented her annuity by taking in boarders. As a young woman she was a governess in the family of Principal Nicoll of St Andrews, where she remained for eight years, and later for Lord William Douglas. She was with his family in Germany when the Disruption of 1843 took place. At the end of that year she went to live with her brother William, a Free Church of Scotland minister, in Ayr.

In 1845 Catherine and William were visited by Daniel Edward (1815–1896), a Free Church missionary who had worked among the Jews of Jassy in Moldavia since 1841. Daniel knew William Grant from their college days, renewed the acquaintance, and thus met Catherine. She shared his enthusiasm for Jewish missions and they were soon engaged. He returned to Jassy that autumn and she later went out to Germany, where they married on 25

Catherine Edward (1813–1861), by James Charles Armytage (after J. Archer)

August 1846, before going on to Moldavia. The homogeneity of the Jewish community in Jassy made the missionaries' task difficult; the few converts were generally a source of disappointment. By 1848 the mission's difficulties were compounded by the threat of war and the reality of cholera. This allowed a decent withdrawal to a new field of labour, Lemberg (Lwów) in Galicia, where the society and the surroundings were more congenial. However, it still proved impossible to establish the mission on a proper footing and in January 1852 the Austrian authorities expelled the missionaries. By this time Catherine was pregnant with the fourth of her five children and the winter journey to Breslau in Silesia proved arduous. A son was born there in March, but he did not survive and she later referred to him as her 'martyr boy'. Although the Edwards resumed their missionary work at Breslau, Catherine's part in it was reduced. On a visit to Scotland in 1852 she was described as 'so changed in appearance as … to look more like her mother than herself' (*Missionary Life*, 247); her voice had weakened and her health continued to deteriorate until her death on 21 February 1861 at Breslau (where she was also buried).

Catherine's *Memoir* contains ample evidence of the strength of her commitment to mission work but her distaste for Jews also emerges, those in Moldavia being described as 'an indolent, idle population, which is likewise detested for its cunning, fraud and filth' (*Missionary Life*, 142). The disappointments and rigours of Jassy and

Lemberg (Lwów), endured during years of child bearing, took a heavy toll on her. Her later life, despite poor health, was at least accompanied by a more tolerant attitude of mind.   LIONEL ALEXANDER RITCHIE

Sources *Missionary life among the Jews in Moldavia, Galicia and Silesia: memoir and letters of Mrs Edward* (1867) · *Fasti Scot.*, 7.715, 3.16, 6.368 · L. A. Ritchie, 'Daniel Edward (1815–1896) and the Free Church of Scotland's mission to the Jews in central Europe', *Records of the Scottish Church History Society*, 31 (2002)
Likenesses J. C. Armytage, stipple and line engraving (after J. Archer), NPG [*see illus.*] · engraving, repro. in *Missionary life*, frontispiece

Edward, Thomas (1814–1886), naturalist and shoemaker, was born on 25 December 1814 at Gosport, Hampshire, one of several children of John Edward, Fife militiaman and weaver, and Margaret Mitchell of Aberdeen. His early years were spent at Kettle, Fife, and at Aberdeen. From childhood he was passionately fond of animals, bringing home so many 'beasties' that he was frequently flogged and confined to the house. Utterly unmanageable, by the age of six he had been expelled from three schools because of his zoological pursuits and truancy. Abandoning school, he found employment at 14*d*. a week in an Aberdeen tobacco factory where his older brother worked. Two years later both boys were hired at a factory at Grandholm. Edward's walks to and from work gave further scope for natural history and this was one of the happiest times of his life. When the boy was eleven his father apprenticed him to a shoemaker in Aberdeen for six years, but Edward ran away after three because of his master's cruelty. He then worked for another cobbler but decline in trade led him to join the Aberdeenshire militia in 1831. Here he narrowly escaped punishment for leaving the ranks to chase a butterfly. Reluctant to return to shoemaking, he enlisted with the 60th rifles, but his mother's opposition led him to abandon the military. Instead, he assisted his father as beadle in North Church, King Street, Aberdeen. Edward sustained his natural history interests during this time by making a wild botanical garden, buying the *Penny Magazine*, and studying stuffed birds he saw in shop windows, and animal illustrations on bookstalls.

From 1834 Edward was employed as a shoemaker in Banff. Trade was bad and he considered emigration to America until he met and married Sophia Reid in 1837. They raised ten daughters and one son, the latter becoming a minister in the Scottish church. Although Edward earned less than 10*s*. a week, on his marriage he rented a house and for the first time had a place to keep specimens. Without friends, books, or a knowledge of scientific names, Edward developed his knowledge from direct observation, all God's creation having a 'fascinating charm' for him (Cash, 181). Edward was sober, regularly attended church, and was not a Sabbath-breaker. Night was his only free time and from 1840 to 1855 he observed nocturnal creatures, sleeping only a couple of hours outdoors at the darkest time. He thus became acquainted with the sounds and movements of wild animals and always observed before killing. His knowledge sometimes resulted from terrifying encounters, one with a polecat

Thomas Edward (1814–1886), by Sir George Reid

lasting two hours. Edward stuffed and arranged his specimens in cases he built himself, but suffered losses. Nearly a thousand labelled insects were eaten by vermin and his dried plants were spoiled by cats.

By 1845, however, Edward possessed nearly 2000 specimens and, hoping to make money, he exhibited them at the Banff fair in 1845 and 1846. His success inspired him to exhibit in Aberdeen in August 1846 in the hope that he could devote himself solely to natural history, but the exhibition failed miserably, few believing he had made the collection unaided. In debt, with a wife and five children, Edward decided to commit suicide by drowning, but an unknown bird on the beach excited his curiosity and drew his attention away from killing himself. Instead, he sold his collection, but he returned penniless to Banff, where he recommenced shoemaking.

Although Edward resolved to abandon natural history and stick to his trade, by 1847 he had resumed nocturnal collecting. He was encouraged by his wife, who was paid for cobbling work on her own account and often purchased collecting bottles for Edward. In 1850, in order to avoid being thought a poacher when collecting with a gun, he obtained a certificate signed by sixteen magistrates testifying to his interest in natural history and good character. However, disregard for his body, and a severe fall on rocks, made him unable to work for a month and forced the sale of his second collection.

By this time Edward was well known locally and had

some access to private libraries. He received encouragement from the Revd James Smith of Monquhitter, near Banff, to record his observations. Many of his natural history notes were published in the *Banffshire Journal*, and later in the *Zoologist*, *Naturalist*, and other periodicals. Smith attempted to find Edward a job preserving an ornithological collection and the Revd Alexander Boyd encouraged him to prepare lectures for a working-class audience, but both men died in 1854 and these schemes died with them. By 1858 illness had forced Edward to sell his third and best collection of birds, mosses, and marine plants. No longer capable of undergoing long expeditions or night wanderings, he devoted himself to marine zoology. His young daughters assisted him in collecting starfish and obtaining fish stomachs from fishermen. He devised home-made apparatus, although Charles Spence Bate, impressed by Edward's discoveries, sent him a simple microscope; Edward's discoveries are recorded in Bate and J. O. Westwood's *History of the British Sessile-Eyed Crustacea*, 2 vols. (1863-8), as well as in works by J. G. Jeffreys, Joshua Alder, A. M. Norman, Jonathan Couch, and others.

Edward's health was so broken by 1868 that he had to abandon collecting. He tried unsuccessfully to establish a business in photographic portraits, and continued shoemaking at home. His interests turned to the antiquities of Banff. His long-held ambition to be appointed curator of a natural history museum, despite efforts by friends such as Bate, was never fulfilled. From 1852 he did serve as curator of the Banff museum, but for only 2 guineas a year, increasing to 4 in 1864. In 1875 the museum was transferred to the Banff town council and Edward was kept on at 13 guineas. Despite quarrels in 1877, he remained in office until 1882. Edward also served as librarian of the Banff Literary Society but left the post in 1876. Although elected an associate of the Linnean Society of London in 1866, made a member of the Aberdeen Natural History Society, and awarded a diploma by the Glasgow Natural History Society, he was never invited to join the Banff Institution.

From the 1850s Edward began to attract interest as much for exemplifying the pursuit of knowledge under difficulties as for his natural history discoveries. Mentioned briefly by Samuel Smiles in *Self-Help* (1859), Edward became the subject of a full-length biography by Smiles in 1876. Although Edward had supplied an autobiographical account for James Cash's *Where there's a will there's a way!* (1873), it was Smiles's biography that brought him fame and relative fortune. The eminent naturalists J. D. Hooker, G. J. Allman, Richard Owen, and Charles Darwin backed Smiles's successful appeal to the queen for a civil-list pension of £50 a year for Edward. Little supported in Banff, in Aberdeen he was publicly presented with £333, to which he responded with an unprepared speech in broad vernacular praising his wife. This, together with Edward's later attempts to publish personal anecdotes under his own name, dismayed Smiles. In private Edward complained that he had been treated badly by great naturalists.

The Banffshire Field Club, founded in 1880, elected Edward a vice-president and he contributed several papers. In his later years he devoted himself mainly to botany. In 1885, in Dufftown with his ailing wife, despite his own weak lungs and the bad weather, he collected mosses. He died in Banff on 27 April 1886. A large number of people attended his funeral at Banff cemetery the following Friday.

ANNE SECORD

Sources S. Smiles, *Life of a Scotch naturalist: Thomas Edward* (1876); new edn (1905) • J. Cash, *Where there's a will there's a way! or, Science in the cottage* (1873), 172–214 • G. Day, *Naturalists and their investigations: Linnaeus—Edward—Cuvier—Kingsley* [1896] • 'Story of a rural naturalist', *Chambers's Journal* (31 July 1858), 79–80
Archives NL Scot., corresp. and essays | NL Scot., corresp. with David Douglas • W. Yorks. AS, Leeds, letters to Samuel Smiles
Likenesses P. Rajon, engraving, 1876 (after G. Reid), repro. in Smiles, *Life of a Scotch naturalist* (1876), frontispiece • P. Rajon, etching, 1876 (after G. Reid), BM, NPG • G. Reid, ink drawing, Scot. NPG [*see illus.*]
Wealth at death £361 13s. 10d.: confirmation, 13 Oct 1886, *CCI*

Edwardes, David (1502?–1542), physician, was probably born in Northamptonshire, and was admitted to Corpus Christi College, Oxford, on 9 August 1517. He became a probationary fellow on 1 June 1522 and was admitted BA on 16 December 1522, and MA in 1525. Made a fellow in 1524 Edwardes was lector in logic in 1521–2, and 1525–8. He was in Venice about 1525, where he, along with John Clement, William Rose, and Thomas Lupset, helped in the completion of the Aldine version of the works of Galen in Greek. It is also probable that Edwardes spent some time studying in Padua. He migrated to Cambridge in 1528; there, as a result of his Oxford MA, and his seven years' study of medicine, and on the condition of his giving a public lecture on Galen's *De differentiis febrium*, he was awarded his MD in 1529. Edwardes is credited with being responsible for the first recorded dissection of the human body in England, said to have taken place in 1531.

Edwardes published two works. *De indiciis et praecognitionibus* (1533) was dedicated to Henry, duke of Richmond, by 'medicus suus' indicating that Edwardes was his physician; in it Edwardes states that he had at one time practised in Bristol. *In anatomicen introductio luculenta et brevis* (1533) was dedicated to Henry, earl of Surrey. The preface to this work mentions that Edwardes was intending to write a complete manual of anatomy at some stage, but apparently it was never published. An English translation of *In anatomicen*, prepared by C. D. O'Malley and K. F. Russell, appeared in 1961 as *David Edwardes: Introduction to Anatomy 1532*. Edwardes died, probably in Cambridge, in 1542. It is not known if his wife, Alice, survived him.

MICHAEL BEVAN

Sources Cooper, *Ath. Cantab.*, 1.46 • Emden, *Oxf.* • A. Rook and M. Newbold, 'David Edwardes: his activities at Cambridge', *Medical History*, 19 (1975), 389–92

Edwardes [*formerly* Edwards], **George Joseph** (1855–1915), musical theatre producer, was born at Cleethorpe Road, Clee, near Great Grimsby, on 8 October 1855, the eldest son in the family of four sons and three daughters of James Edwards, comptroller of customs, and his wife, Eleanor Widdup. His parents were from Wexford in Ireland and George was brought up a Roman Catholic. After attending St James's College, Clee, without distinction, he was sent to London to cram for entry to the Royal Military Academy at Woolwich. But through his cousins the important Irish theatre managers John and Michael Gunn, he was quickly given the chance to work in the theatre world and he made his entrée into the business at the age of twenty-one with a front-of-house job at Leicester's newly constructed Royal Opera House, run by former opera tenor Eliot Galer. He soon moved to London, and through the influence of Michael Gunn, who was an important financial partner in Richard D'Oyly Carte's production house, ended up working as treasurer at the Opera Comique during the initial runs of *The Pirates of Penzance* and *Patience* (1881). When Carte shifted his operation to the Savoy Theatre in the Strand, Edwards moved with him, and he was employed as acting manager at the new theatre during the productions of *Iolanthe* (1882), *Princess Ida* (1884), and *The Mikado* (1885). On 9 July 1885 Edwardes (who had by now added an 'e' to his surname and 'Pius Nono' to his forenames) married Julia Lavinia Gwynne (1859–1934), a small-part player at the Savoy, daughter of David Putney, a publican. They had a son and three daughters.

In 1885 Edwardes left the Savoy and moved to the Gaiety Theatre. John Hollingshead, at the head of the Gaiety since its opening seventeen years earlier, and responsible for building it into one of London's most effective and popular theatres, was on the verge of retiring, and Edwardes had been chosen as his successor. The two managers worked together on the production of the Gaiety's 1885 Christmas show, *Little Jack Sheppard*, after which Hollingshead moved out and Edwardes took over the running of the theatre. In his thirty years as proprietor he was to establish the Gaiety as the single most important and popular theatre for musical productions in the world.

Hollingshead's legacy was a significant one. Not only did Edwardes inherit a theatre with a splendid reputation and an enthusiastic audience, he also inherited the beginnings of what would be a hugely popular resident company, headed by future stars Fred Leslie and Nellie Farren, and a highly profitable trend in musical plays. *Little Jack Sheppard* was the first of what became known as 'new burlesques', a full-length burlesque play (instead of one which was, as before, just one item on an evening's programme) with a score of original music rather than the second-hand songs previously used in such productions. It was also a notable hit, and Edwardes followed it up with more of the same (*Monte Cristo Jr*, *Miss Esmeralda*, *Frankenstein*, *Faust Up-To-Date*, *Ruy Blas, or The Blasé Roué*, *Carmen up-to-Data*, *Cinder-Ellen up-too-Late*) and the 'new burlesques' of the Gaiety Theatre went round the world as the young producer sent out companies through the British provinces, to America, and as far afield as Australia carrying repertoires of his shows.

Edwardes operated on numerous fronts from his headquarters at the Gaiety. While one of his companies played the Gaiety, a second toured. When the first took its latest show on the road, the other came back with a new production. Occasionally, too, he ventured with a production at another London theatre, and at other times he brought entertainments other than new burlesque into the Gaiety. On one famous occasion he mounted a pretty, second-hand comedy opera called *Dorothy* with medium success. When he went to close the show to allow his burlesquers to return, his accountant took it up, transferred it to the Prince of Wales, and turned it into the longest running London musical of the nineteenth century. Even George Edwardes didn't always get it right.

The new burlesque tradition lasted less than a decade before it transformed itself into a slightly different kind of entertainment. Fred Leslie died in 1892, Nellie Farren became disabled, and the style of show in which they had triumphed wilted. So Edwardes tried something else. He mounted a piece, at the Prince of Wales Theatre, which used all the elements of the new burlesque—the cheerful, topical comedy, the bright songs and dances, the lively display, the popular performers—but these, instead of being set in an incongruous fairytale story decked out in fantastical costumes, were used to decorate a straightforward wisp of an up-to-date, London tale. *In Town* (1892), with popular music-hall comedian Arthur Roberts and established singing star Florence St John billed large above the title, featured Roberts as a lad-about-town giving a young aristocrat a tour of the slightly naughty highlights of London high and lowish life in the style of a French revue. The tour included, of course, a visit to the theatre, and the show took in scenes on stage and backstage. *In Town* was a big success, and Edwardes moved on to produce another 'modern' piece, with a glimmer more of plot, *The Gaiety Girl*. This proved even more successful, and when Edwardes produced his first 'musical comedy' (as his 'new' genre became known) at the Gaiety, the latest trend in musical theatre became firmly established. *The Shop Girl* (1894) turned out to be even bigger than its predecessors, and the Gaiety's and Edwardes's style was fixed. It was a style which would make the Gaiety's reputation around the world.

The degree of success which he had known in his first years as a producer encouraged Edwardes to expand. While new burlesque still reigned, he went into partnership with American producer Augustin Daly to build a new theatre which they might share. Daly's Theatre opened in 1893. Daly did not share for long, and soon Edwardes was filling the new house year round. *A Gaiety Girl* ran part of its initial run at the Daly, and Edwardes subsequently mounted a twenty-year series of musical plays there. Partly by accident, the musicals which evolved at Daly's were different from those played at the Gaiety. The Daly's star team was topped by two staunchly romantic vocalists (baritone hero Hayden Coffin, soprano Marie Tempest) and the shows in which they and their successors teamed with soubrette Letty Lind, and with comic Huntley Wright (*The Geisha*, *A Greek Slave*, *San Toy*, *A Country Girl*), had a much more substantial kind of score and story than the dragonfly-weight pieces at the Gaiety. Thus, while at the turn of the century the Gaiety reigned over the 'musical comedy' theatre of its day (*My Girl*, *A Runaway Girl*, *The Circus Girl*, *The Messenger Boy*, and *The Toreador*),

Daly's Theatre was the hub of all that was best and most successful in the art of the romantic musical. It was from Daly's that came the most successful and widely played English-language musical of the century: Sidney Jones and Owen Hall's worldwide hit *The Geisha* (1896).

Edwardes's 'empire' underwent some changes in the earliest years of the twentieth century. First the old Gaiety Theatre on the Strand was condemned by the city's roadmakers, and closed on 4 July 1903. Edwardes built a new Gaiety Theatre at the Aldwych to which he transferred his operations without missing a beat. Then he expanded to take in the Adelphi Theatre as well, and there he produced a further run of musical plays, not quite like either of his other continuing sets, of which *The Quaker Girl* (1910) turned out the most memorable. He staged a variety of new pieces at the Gaiety and in other houses round the town, including some rather more book-based shows, first-rate musical comedies based on French plays (*The Spring Chicken*, *The Girl from Kay's*, *The Duchess of Dantzic*, *Kitty Grey*), and the less vertebrate, baby-blue shows of Paul Rubens (*Three Little Maids*, *Lady Madcap*). There was even an abortive attempt to bring back burlesque with *The New Aladdin*, but the main change in policy and style came as the result of a little palace revolution. Hayden Coffin and house designer Percy Anderson introduced a would-be writer friend to Edwardes, who allowed him to work on a text with his in-house team of show-makers, headed by James Tanner. The man proved a no-hoper and was eased out, but when the new Daly's show was mounted he claimed that his work had been stolen and he sued. Unwise words were said, and resentment and jealousy of Edwardes and his 'cronies', Tanner and stage director Pat Malone, and their dominant place in the musical theatre boiled over. Coffin and Anderson were dispensed with, and Edwardes soon switched to importing proven pieces from the newly resuscitated continental stage instead of having them written to order. He chose his moment well, and in the pre-1914 years he had vast successes with Messager's *Véronique* and *Les p'tites Michu*, Lehár's *Die lustige Witwe* (*The Merry Widow*) and *Der Graf von Luxemburg* (*The Count of Luxembourg*), Leo Fall's *Die Dollarprinzessin* (*The Dollar Princess*), Jean Gilbert's *Die geschiedene Frau* (*The Girl on the Train*), and Victor Jacobi's *Leányvásár* (*The Marriage Market*).

George Edwardes was still the most important figure in the British musical theatre when his final illness overtook him in 1914. He died at his home, 11 Park Square West, Regent's Park, London, on 4 October 1915 and was buried at Kensal Green on 7 October. His wife survived him. In spite of some recent reverses he was a rich man, with properties at Windsor Forest, Ogbourne in Wiltshire, and a stud farm business at Ballykisteen in co. Tipperary (he was devoted to the turf). Plans were in place for the three principal theatres under his control at the time of his death, but the structures he had set up soon collapsed without him to control them, even though his friend Bobbie Evett managed to keep Daly's afloat for some time thanks to an enormous success with *The Maid of the Mountains* (which he billed: 'George Edwardes presents …'). The musical theatre moved on to new styles of entertainment in an era which thoroughly deserved to be called post-Edwardesian, so large had he loomed over its development and international success.   KURT GÄNZL

Sources K. Gänzl, *The encyclopedia of the musical theatre*, 2 vols. (1994) • K. Gänzl, *The British musical theatre*, 2 vols. (1986) • *The Era* (1876–) • E. Reid and H. Compton, eds., *The dramatic peerage* [1891]; rev. edn [1892] • F. C. Burnand, ed., *The Catholic who's who and yearbook* (1910) • b. cert. • m. cert. • census returns, 1881
Likenesses photographs, repro. in U. Bloom, *Curtain call for the Guv'nor: a biography of George Edwardes* (1954)
Wealth at death £49,780 7s. 7d.: probate, 15 Nov 1915, CGPLA Eng. & Wales

Edwardes, Sir Herbert Benjamin (1819–1868), army and political officer in India, was born on 12 November 1819 at Frodesley, Shropshire, the second son of the Revd Benjamin Edwardes (1790/91–1823), rector of Frodesley, and his wife. On 9 July 1850 he married Emma, daughter of James Sidney of Richmond, Surrey; she survived her husband.

Early life and career in India, 1819–1845 His mother died in his infancy and Edwardes was brought up in a deeply religious household by his aunt following his father's death in 1823. From the age of ten he was educated at a private school at Richmond, Surrey, where he was undistinguished as scholar or athlete. In 1836 he started attending classes at King's College, London, studying classics and mathematics, although he was more interested in modern literature, drawing, and writing poetry, and took a prominent part in the debating society.

Edwardes obtained a direct appointment as a cadet in the Bengal infantry—after his guardians prevented him entering Oxford University to study for the bar—by personally applying to Sir Richard Jenkins, a member of the court of directors of the East India Company and a family friend. In October 1840, without having attended the East India Company's military college, Addiscombe College, Edwardes left for India and landed at Calcutta in early 1841. He served as a second lieutenant in the 1st European or Bengal fusiliers at Dinapore and then at Karnal, a frontier station, in July 1842. While at Karnal he studied hard and distinguished himself as a linguist, passing examinations in Urdu, Hindi, and Persian. In less than three years after joining his regiment he qualified for the post of interpreter, in November 1845. While his regiment was stationed at Sabathu, Edwardes wrote a series of critical essays in the *Delhi Gazette* entitled 'Brahminee Bull's letters to his cousin John Bull', discussing military, political, and social affairs in India that attracted considerable attention among the Anglo-Indian community. In particular Henry Lawrence, the resident at Nepal, was impressed by the bold political opinions and high spirit of this young subaltern. In November 1845 Sir Hugh Gough, commander-in-chief of the Indian army, selected Edwardes on the strength of these articles as a member of his personal staff. As a result Edwardes was present as aide-de-camp to Gough during the First Anglo-Sikh War at the bloody battles of Mudki on 18 December 1845, when he was wounded, and Sobraon on 10 February 1846.

The Punjab, 1845–1850 After the First Anglo-Sikh War, Edwardes obtained civil employment in 1846 when Sir

Sir Herbert Benjamin Edwardes (1819–1868), by Ross & Thomson, c.1860 [with his wife, Emma Sidney]

Henry Lawrence, who had just been appointed British Resident at Lahore to advise the durbar or council of regency, requested his services as assistant resident. Edwardes quickly established a close friendship with Lawrence and acted as his private secretary for three months at Lahore before serving in Kashmir at the court of Jammu, where he helped suppress a rebellion against the maharaja. Early in February 1847 Edwardes was detached on special duty as political agent to carry out the difficult task of collecting outstanding taxes and administering one of the outlying trans-Indus districts that had hitherto evaded paying tribute to the government at Lahore. He began work reforming the civil administration in Banu, a trans-Indus valley that bordered Afghan territory and the hills, backed by a small force of Sikh troops. He soon made a mark on the area, demolishing local fortresses, building roads, encouraging agriculture, constructing canals, settling local feuds and disagreements, and establishing considerable personal influence over the local population.

Edwardes raised, organized, and equipped a body of Pathan irregulars within a month of receiving news that the two British representatives, Patrick Alexander Vans Agnew and Lieutenant William Anderson, had been attacked at Multan in April 1848 by troops led by a rebel commander Godar Singh Mazhabi. The governor of Multan, Diwan Mulraj, was forced to lead the revolt which soon assumed serious proportions. Edwardes soon established contact with the Muslim nawab of Bahawalpur and Colonel van Cordtland, the officer commanding for the

Sikh durbar at Lahore. On 10 June Edwardes was empowered to act according to his own judgement and eight days later, with a force of irregulars and Sikh troops, routed a rebel force loyal to Mulraj at Kineyri, near Dera Ghazi Khan. After being reinforced by Lieutenant Lake, a neighbouring district officer, and troops sent by the nawab of Bahawalpur, Edwardes defeated the enemy for a second time on 3 July at Sadusam close to Multan, but during this engagement he permanently lost part of the use of his right hand when one of his pistols accidentally discharged. The diwan Mul Raj fell back upon the town and fort where he and his troops remained until General Whish and the Bombay column arrived and invested the enemy positions. Edwardes played an active role in the ensuing siege and on 22 January 1849 helped negotiate the final surrender of the rebel ruler, who was forced to surrender after the city had been captured by British troops.

Edwardes's important role in the defeat of Diwan Mulraj was quickly recognized by Sir Henry Lawrence, who declared that since the days of Clive no man had done as Edwardes. His display of initiative and military skill, without formal training, had been instrumental in defeating the rebellion. This was the zenith of Edwardes's career. From Gough and the government of India he received prompt commendation. Recommended by the Board of Control, he was promoted brevet major in September 1848 and made a CB in October 1849. The East India Company also awarded him a specially struck gold medal. In January 1850 he returned to England, where he found himself a hero and was warmly received by his native county of Shropshire. He was thanked by both houses of parliament and awarded an Oxford DCL (12 June 1850). In London and Liverpool he was entertained at civic banquets and showed his skill at public speaking. He also wrote *A Year on the Punjab Frontier* (2 vols., 1851), describing his recent actions.

Diplomacy and the Indian mutiny, 1851–1859 Edwardes soon after his appointment suggested the wisdom of negotiating a treaty with Dost Muhammad, the amir, to help improve relations with Afghanistan and ensure the security of India. Lord Dalhousie agreed to this proposal, despite opposition from Sir Henry Lawrence, then chief commissioner of the Punjab, who tried to convince Dalhousie it was futile. Dalhousie arbitrated between the two men, after backing the project, and in March 1855 a treaty of friendship was finally signed by Lawrence and Dost Muhammad; its strict non-interference clause stood the British authorities in good stead when disturbances broke out in India two years later. Despite their disagreement about the treaty, Edwardes was generally in close agreement with Sir Henry Lawrence on frontier defence. Following the conclusion of the treaty with Afghanistan, Edwardes wrote to his friend: 'After the doubts and lessons of the [past] … I have myself arrived at the conclusion that our own true military position is on our own side of the passes, just where an army must debouch upon the plain' (*DNB*). He never deviated from this view, being convinced that the best protection of British India and its interests on the frontier was 'a strong, independent, and friendly Afghanistan', and that there was a distinct feeling among the people of that country 'that the Russians are not as trustworthy as the English' (*DNB*). He also believed that the British government should seek a friendly understanding with the tsar. Following a suggestion by Edwardes the amir visited Peshawar in January 1857 and the following month signed a supplementary treaty in view of the imminent outbreak of hostilities between the Indian government and the shah of Persia. In this agreement the amir agreed he would support the British and allow a mission to reside in his country. This treaty and its predecessor proved of considerable importance when the Indian mutiny broke out, and throughout the disturbances the amir remained silent.

Shortly afterwards Edwardes's wife fell seriously ill and in March 1857 she left for England. While at Peshawar, Edwardes also took the opportunity to spread his ideas about Christianity. He was a strong supporter of evangelical work in Afghanistan and in the frontier areas, and warmly supported the founding of a mission at Peshawar in 1853, which he partly funded, run by the Church Missionary Society. Following news of the outbreak of the Indian mutiny at Meerut and Delhi on 10 and 11 May Edwardes persuaded Sir John Lawrence, brother of Henry Lawrence and the future viceroy, to sanction the raising of a levy and the formation of a mobile column in the Punjab composed of reliable troops. This force subsequently maintained order in the Punjab and ultimately powerfully aided in the overthrow of the mutineers in the south of the Sutlej. Edwardes took prompt and decisive action to maintain British authority in the area, securing points of strategic importance, disarming several disaffected native regiments, and relentlessly pursuing mutinous sepoys who had deserted. A dispute soon arose between Lawrence and Edwardes, however, after the latter in May asked to be reinforced and that part of the force destined for the siege of Delhi should be diverted for the defence of Peshawar. Lawrence refused permission, and pointed out that a possibility existed that Peshawar might have to be sacrificed in favour of holding Delhi. This statement caused considerable alarm in Peshawar, and the matter was referred to Lord Canning, the viceroy, at Calcutta who finally decreed that Peshawar should be held 'to the last'.

Last years, 1859–1868 Edwardes began to feel the strain of his long period of service in the Punjab and in September 1858 wrote that he was 'quite tired of work'. However, he was unable to leave his post for another year. In mid-1859 Edwardes finally returned to England, staying in London and Eastbourne, and the following year was urged to stand for Glasgow in the House of Commons. He declined this invitation, however, and spent two years in England. He was made a KCB on 18 May 1860, and a Cambridge LLD. While on leave Edwardes spoke regularly at religious and other meetings about spreading Christianity in India. He also undertook to write a biography of Sir Henry Lawrence at the request of his family. After his health improved Edwardes returned to the Punjab early in 1862 and was appointed commissioner of Ambala and agent for the Cis-Sutlej states. Following his return he enthusiastically urged the government of India to support publicly the propagation of Christianity in India, which arguably displayed a considerable lack of common sense and a disdain for the religious beliefs of the local population. Edwardes held this prestigious and coveted post at Ambala for three years, but his wife's and his own health deteriorated during 1864 and on 1 January 1865 he left India for the last time.

Edwardes spent most of the rest of his life in London, devoting himself to public and private charity. He was vice-president of the Church Missionary Society, supported the City Mission, and oversaw the affairs of Sir John Lawrence's family while his old chief was viceroy. He also devoted his spare time to writing a biography of the viceroy's brother, Sir Henry Lawrence, which was never completed. Edwardes was made KCSI on 24 May 1866, was promoted major-general on 22 February 1868, and was awarded a 'good conduct' pension of £100 a year.

Edwardes became deeply involved with evangelical movements, and his personal charm and skill at public speaking made him a welcome speaker of that party. He was particularly opposed to ritualism in the Anglican church. He suffered a bad attack of pleurisy in March 1868 and while recovering was offered the post of lieutenant-governor of the Punjab. However, the expected vacancy did not occur and his health relapsed. He died on 23 December 1868 in a hotel in Holles Street, Cavendish Square, London, after a severe haemorrhage. Edwardes was buried in Highgate cemetery, Middlesex. He was commemorated by a mural tablet in Westminster Abbey and a stained glass window in the chapel of King's College, London; the main town in Banu district was renamed Edwardesbad.

Edwardes was a brilliant soldier-diplomat, whose willingness to act on his own initiative at the head of an improvised force, despite his lack of formal military training, was instrumental in defeating the insurrection at Multan in 1848. Throughout his career in India he displayed considerable talent as a highly resourceful administrator, and his successful negotiation of the treaty with Afghanistan had a major impact on securing British victory during the Indian mutiny. His deeply held religious beliefs and proselytizing zeal for spreading Christianity in India, however, led him to display at times a lack of foresight and judgement.

T. R. MOREMAN

Sources E. Edwardes, *Memorials of the life and letters of Major General Sir Herbert B. Edwardes* (1886) · C. R. Low, *Soldiers of the Victorian age* (1880) · T. Holmes, *Four famous soldiers: Sir C. Napier, Hodson of Hodson's Horse, Sir W. Napier, Sir H. Edwardes* (1885) · *DNB* · H. B. Edwardes, *A year on the Punjab frontier in 1848–49*, 2 vols. (1851) · H. Morris, *Sir Herbert Edwardes: a Christian hero* (1855) · H. Edwardes, *Prospect of triumph of Christianity in India* (1866) · M. E. Yapp, *Strategies of British India: Britain, Iran and Afghanistan, 1798–1850* (1980) · J. S. Gewal, *The Sikhs of the Punjab* (1990) · C. Hibbert, *The great mutiny, India, 1857* (1978) · Boase, *Mod. Eng. biog.* · Foster, *Alum. Oxon.* · *CGPLA Eng. & Wales* (1869)

Archives BL OIOC, diary and corresp., MS Eur. E 211 · NL Wales, corresp. · Oxf. U. Mus. NH, unpublished MS relating to locusts in

India | BL OIOC, corresp. with Henry Lawrence, MS Eur. F 85 · BL OIOC, corresp. with John Lawrence, MS Eur. F 90

Likenesses S. Freeman, stipple, pubd 1850 (after Morrison), NPG · H. Moseley, oils, *c.*1850, NPG · C. Baugniet, lithograph, pubd 1858, NPG · Ross & Thomson, photograph, *c.*1860 (with his wife, Emma Sidney), NPG [*see illus.*] · Ross & Thomson, photographs, *c.*1860, NPG · W. Theed, marble monument, 1868, Westminster Abbey, London · J. H. Foley, marble bust, 1870, BL OIOC · C. Baugniet, lithograph, BM · H. Lenthall, carte-de-visite, NPG · J. Mayall, photograph, repro. in Edwardes, *Memorials of the life and letters*, frontispiece · E. Morton, lithograph (after a miniature, 1848), BL OIOC · oils, Territorial Association Centre, Shrewsbury

Wealth at death under £16,000: probate, 11 Jan 1869, *CGPLA Eng. & Wales*

Edwards, Alfred George (1848–1937), archbishop of Wales, was born on 2 November 1848 at The Bryn, a small manor house serving as the rectory of Llanymawddwy, a remote mountain parish in Merioneth. He was the youngest son of William Edwards (*d.* 1868), later vicar of Llangollen, and his wife, Sarah, daughter of Thomas Wood, of Painswick. His elder brother was Henry Thomas *Edwards.

Apart from one year (1860–61) at Llandovery College, Edwards was educated at home. In 1871 he went to Jesus College, Oxford, with an exhibition which brought up his income to £75 for his first year and £140 in his second and third. After taking his BA degree in 1874, he became second master at Llandovery, and in the following year headmaster; an appointment that he owed to his knowledge of Welsh. Edwards proved himself more than capable in his new position. After five years, the numbers had risen from 27 to 178, and a large percentage of the pupils went to the universities of Oxford and Cambridge. After eleven years of strenuous work Edwards, who had been ordained deacon in 1874 and priest in 1875, was, in 1885, appointed chaplain and secretary to Basil Jones, bishop of St David's, and became vicar of St Peter's, Carmarthen.

In 1889 Edwards was chosen bishop of St Asaph on the recommendation of Lord Salisbury. He was immediately confronted by the so-called tithe war. Nonconformist farmers were refusing to pay the tithe to the parson. Their goods were distrained and there were riots—more in the diocese of St Asaph than in any other part of the country. Edwards played an active part in the negotiations which led to the passing of the Tithe Act of 1891 by which the tithe was paid by the landlord instead of the tenant. Later he was confronted by the 'Welsh revolt' over the Education Act of 1902. The new county councils, whose members were either nonconformist or Liberal, refused to implement the act because it gave rate support to church schools. Edwards worked hard for a compromise, but he had no support from his fellow Welsh bishops and the bill he presented to the Lords in 1904 went no further than the second reading. Yet this controversy resulted in a truce between him and his old enemy, Lloyd George. Popular opinion in Wales was divided as to which of the two was the bigger liar.

Soon after, Edwards was involved in another controversy, this time over the campaign for the disestablishment and disendowment of the church in Wales, or, more

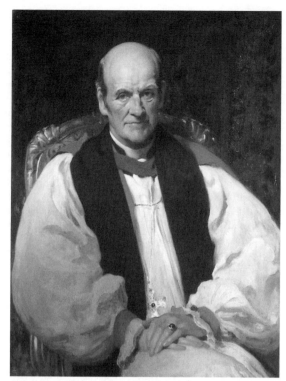

Alfred George Edwards (1848–1937), by Solomon Joseph Solomon, in or before 1924

properly, the four Welsh dioceses, then in the province of Canterbury. Well before the turn of the century, Edwards had been active in the defence of the established church in Wales.

The return of the Liberal Party to power in 1906 brought the question of the disestablishment of the Welsh church to a head, and Edwards and John Owen, bishop of St David's, found themselves leading the opposition to disestablishment. Once again the task of negotiation with political leaders was left to Edwards. Despite the outbreak of war, the bill disestablishing the church in Wales and Monmouthshire passed into law in September 1914, although in the following July disestablishment was postponed by an order in council until the end of the war. From that time onwards Edwards devoted his energies to securing better terms for the church than those which the bill had originally proposed. He was between two fires: Welsh members of parliament strongly supported the bill, while a group of Conservative Anglicans, led by Lord Robert Cecil, were demanding repeal. In the last stages Edwards maintained close contact with Lloyd George and Bonar Law, having been given complete power to act by the governing body, which had been set up for the Church in Wales in October 1917. The Welsh Church Temporalities Act, passed in August 1919, gave more generous terms. If, as it may be argued, the Church in Wales emerged from the struggle constitutionally strengthened and adequately financed, much of the credit must go to Edwards's skill as a negotiator. In 1920 Edwards received honorary degrees from the universities of Oxford, Cambridge, and Wales, and was elected an honorary fellow of his college.

On 1 June 1920 Edwards was enthroned by the archbishop of Canterbury in St Asaph Cathedral as archbishop of the new province of Wales. Prince Arthur of Connaught represented the king. Also present, a guest in the bishop's palace, was the prime minister, Lloyd George, who came to give his blessing to the church which he had helped to despoil. The new archbishop's throne was a replica of St Augustine's throne at Canterbury, an indication that Edwards could not free himself entirely from an 'establishment' frame of mind. While he owed his preferments to his knowledge of Welsh, his attitude to that language was somewhat ambivalent. It has been claimed that he relaxed the all-Welsh rule at Llandovery. He had been publicly criticized by his clergy for seeming to favour English-speaking clerics in his appointments. Yet such an attitude was not untypical of the Welsh churchmen of his day. His opposition to the appointment of E. L. Bevan as bishop of Swansea and Brecon in 1923 because he knew no Welsh may well have been on personal rather than linguistic grounds.

Edwards's remaining years were occupied with the reorganization of the church, which included the creation of two new sees, Monmouth, and Swansea and Brecon, and the consolidation of church finances. He retired in 1934.

Edwards was married three times. His first marriage, on 29 June 1875, was to Caroline Elizabeth (1851–1884), daughter of Edward Edwards, of Llangollen. They had three sons and two daughters; the second son and younger daughter died before their father. Edwards married, on 18 April 1885, secondly, Mary Laidley (1861–1912), youngest daughter of Watts John Garland, of Lisbon and Worgret, near Wareham, Dorset; they had one son, who was killed in action in 1915, and one daughter. His third wife, whom he married on 1 August 1917, was Margaret (1875–1949), daughter of John Richard Armitstead, vicar of Sandbach. Edwards died at his home, Esgopty, St Asaph, on 22 July 1937 and was buried on 27 July in St Asaph Cathedral.   A. S. DUNCAN-JONES, *rev.* O. W. JONES

Sources *The Times* (23 July 1937) · A. G. Edwards, *Memories* (1927) · G. Lerry, *Alfred George Edwards* (1940) · K. O. Morgan, *Wales in British politics, 1868–1922*, rev. edn (1970) · personal knowledge (1949, 2004) · m. certs · parish register (baptism), Llanymawddwy, Merioneth, 25 Nov 1848 · parish register (burial), St Asaph, Flintshire, 27 July 1937

Archives BL, letters to W. E. Gladstone, Add. MSS 44510–44525 · Bodl. Oxf., corresp. with Herbert Asquith · HLRO, corresp. with Andrew Bonar Law; letters to David Lloyd George · LPL, corresp. with Edward Benson · NL Wales, corresp. with Gwilym Davies · Wellcome L., letters to Sir Thomas Barlow

Likenesses W. Q. Orchardson, oils, 1897; replica, Dean Williams Library, St Asaph, Flintshire · J. St H. Lander, oils, *c.*1922, Howell's School, Denbigh, Clwyd · S. J. Solomon, oils, in or before 1924, Jesus College, Oxford [*see illus.*] · W. Stoneman, photograph, 1925, NPG · S. J. Solomon, oils, NMG Wales · photograph (*Anglican bishops*), NPG · photographs, repro. in Edwards, *Memories* · rotary photograph, postcard, NPG

Wealth at death £69,193 4*s.* 3*d.*: probate, 27 Oct 1937, *CGPLA Eng. & Wales*

Edwards, Amelia Ann Blanford (1831–1892), author and Egyptologist, was born in Colebrook Row, Islington, London, on 30 June 1831, the only child of Thomas Edwards (1786–1860), a half-pay army officer who later worked for the Provincial Bank of Ireland in London, and Alicia Walpole (*d.* 1860), eldest daughter of Robert Walpole, an Irish barrister connected with the Norfolk Walpoles. She was a lonely, quiet child who was educated at home until she was eight, by her mother and then by private tutors. She read voraciously, wrote stories, poems, and romances from an early age, and illustrated 'everything she read' (Amelia B. Edwards MS 437), becoming a skilful artist. By the age of fourteen her stories were being published in periodicals, but she had decided to devote her life to music. For seven years she worked 'with unremitting industry' (ibid.) at singing and composing vocal and instrumental scores. In 1849 she took up the guitar and the organ, and was in 1850 appointed organist at St Michael's, Wood Green, Middlesex. This was an unhappy period in her life. She was ill with typhus for many months in 1849 and then dogged by sore throats which affected her singing. In 1851 she agreed to an unsuitable engagement to a man whom she had known for several years. This alliance blighted her chances of a wished-for romance with an Irish cousin (ibid., 393). She dreaded the walk home from church with her fiancé, and resigned her appointment as organist and broke off her engagement in 1852.

Amelia Edwards taught music and worked at translating Italian poetry in the evenings. Then, in 1853, one of her short stories was published in *Eliza Cooke's Journal* and paid for. While she was in Paris with a cousin she 'resolved to be a writer' and in later life deeply regretted the years wasted on music (Amelia B. Edwards MSS). In 1854 she visited the Rhine, Paris, and Belgium, and the following year, after a time in Burgundy, returned to England to find her name 'famous' (ibid.). Her first novel, *My Brother's Wife* (1864), had been very well received and she was welcomed as a promising new author (ibid.). Between 1855 and 1880 she published nine novels, a collection of stories, *Monsieur Maurice* (1873), *A Summary of English History* (1858), a translation from the French, *A Lady's Captivity among Chinese Pirates* (1859), and *The History of France* (1858). She provided biographies for Colnaghi's *Photographic Historical Portrait Gallery* (1860) and wrote three children's books: *The Young Marquis* (1857); *Sights and Stories* (1862), about a holiday in the north of Belgium; and *The Story of Cervantes* (1863). She also prepared a volume of ballads (1865) and two anthologies of poetry (1879). Her most successful novels were *Barbara's History* (1864), which was translated into French, German, and Italian, and *Lord Brackenbury* (1880), which went through twenty editions. *Barbara's History* was likened to Charlotte Brontë's *Jane Eyre*, but without the 'coarseness': the artistically gifted heroine loves a man with a dark secret, yet learns to develop and realize her own potential.

Amelia Edwards contributed regularly to *Household Words* and *All the Year Round* (usually providing a story for Charles Dickens's Christmas numbers) and worked as

Amelia Ann Blanford Edwards (1831–1892), by Herbert Watkins, late 1850s

music, drama, and art critic and as leader writer to daily and weekly papers, including the *Morning Post*. Both her parents died in 1860, and in 1864 she moved to live with a much older widowed friend, Ellen Braysher, at Westbury-on-Trym, near Bristol (Rees, *Amelia Edwards*, 71).

Amelia Edwards was fluent in French and Italian and described herself as 'an insatiable traveller'. After bouts of work she spent sketching holidays in Europe and, in 1872, undertook the adventure, with a friend, Lucy Renshawe, through the Dolomites that she described and illustrated in *Untrodden Peaks and Unfrequented Valleys* (1873). The area was then largely unknown and inaccessible, and her enthusiasm and detailed descriptions helped open it to tourism.

In 1873 Amelia Edwards and Lucy Renshawe, dissatisfied with the weather in central France, set off for Egypt. It was a journey that changed the course of her life. She became so fascinated with Egypt that it dominated her thinking and her work for the next two decades. With other tourists whom they had met in Cairo the two women hired a *dahabiyah* and sailed to Wadi Halfa, accompanying friends met on the crossing from Italy. While at Abu Simbel the party discovered, excavated, and described in detail a previously unknown small temple with a painted chamber. Amelia Edwards and Lucy Renshawe also visited Syria, crossed the Lebanese ranges to Damascus and Baalbek, and travelled on to Constantinople (Amelia B. Edwards MS 546). On her return to England she read extensively about ancient Egypt and consulted such specialists as Dr Samuel Birch and R. S. Poole on matters of historical and archaeological detail. She was also 'led step by step to the study of hieroglyphical writing' (Edwards, *A Thousand Miles*, xiii).

With this knowledge and her own experiences she wrote her very successful *A Thousand Miles up the Nile* (1876), illustrated from her watercolours. Praised by reviewers for its 'brilliant descriptions of scenery and the exactness of its information' (*Bristol Mercury*, 16 April 1892) and as 'a delightful, gossiping book' (*The World*, 6 Feb 1877), it is still recognized as 'one of the great classics of the history of the Nile' (Crewe). She regarded it as the most important of her books and the one for which she hoped to be remembered (Amelia B. Edwards MS 477). Her studies continued and by 1878 she was contributing articles on Egyptological matters to weekly journals. In the decade before her death she contributed some hundred well-researched articles on Egypt to *The Academy* alone—for which she refused payment (R. S. Poole, *The Academy*, 28 April 1892). She corresponded regularly with various European scholars, particularly Professor Gaston Maspero, then of the École des Hautes Études in Paris.

While in Egypt, Amelia Edwards had been troubled by the neglect of the ancient monuments and the vandalism of visitors who bought up everything the local people could steal for them. At that time Mariette Pasha, the French director of excavation since 1858, was forming the national museum at Bulaq, Cairo, and clearing the great temples—some thought with more enthusiasm than care. In 1879, when Egypt came under the dual control of France and Britain, she saw an opportunity of approaching Mariette with the suggestion that a body of subscribers in Britain might be sanctioned by the new khedive to sponsor scientific excavation, preferably in the Nile delta, (James, 11). The reply gave some encouragement, for in January 1880 she wrote for support to several Egyptologists and persuaded the *Morning Post* to encourage correspondence on Egyptian topics. A number of eminent men rallied to her call, including the wealthy Sir Erasmus Wilson (whose book, *Egypt of the Past*, she updated in 1887). In June 1880 a gathering of interested parties wrote to Mariette, but he was near death and in January 1881 Maspero succeeded him. Édouard Naville, the Swiss Egyptologist, approached Maspero, who signified that he had no objection to excavations by a new English society. On 27 March 1882 the Egypt Exploration Fund (later Egypt Exploration Society) was brought into being. R. S. Poole and Amelia Edwards were elected honorary joint secretaries, and Edwards retained the post until her death in 1892. An appeal for scientific excavations produced sufficient funds to send Naville on the first excavations in January 1883. At the end of that season the khedive presented two important finds to the society which were donated to the British Museum in London. The success of this first season brought new funds and in 1884 the young archaeologist Flinders Petrie was sent to work under Maspero's direction.

Amelia Edwards worked tirelessly for the society, soliciting funds, lecturing throughout England, and writing about the progress of the fund's work. She raised sponsorship for the Egyptologist Francis Llewellyn Griffith to join Petrie. She and Poole communicated with each other constantly, but she was seldom able to attend the frequent meetings in London and felt excluded from decision making. She minded this deeply, as she had largely given up her own writing and was in some financial straits on behalf of this cause. In 1886 Poole resigned as joint secretary and Amelia Edwards took sole charge of editing and publishing the society's annual memoirs and reporting each season's finds to the press.

Amelia Edwards was a contributing member at several orientalist conferences and in 1885 read a paper in Vienna, 'The dispersion of antiquities'. She prepared articles on Egyptological topics for the new *Encyclopaedia Britannica* and its American supplement. Her translation of Maspero's *L'archéologie égyptienne* (as *Egyptian Archaeology*, 1887) had copious footnotes based on her own specialist knowledge. In the preface she stated that:

> to collect and exhibit objects of ancient art and industry is worse than idle if we do not also endeavour to disseminate some knowledge of the history of those arts and industries, and the processes employed by the artists and craftsmen of the past. (Edwards, 'Preface', vi)

She was active in other areas of both classical and biblical study, and as vice-president of the Society for the Promotion of Women's Suffrage.

The American branch of the Egypt Exploration Society soon flourished. In 1886 Smith College in Massachusetts awarded Amelia Edwards an honorary LLD, 'the first distinction of the kind ever bestowed on a woman' (*The Academy*, 24 July 1886). In 1887 Columbia College in New York also honoured her. In 1889–90 she was invited to lecture in the United States and in five months addressed some 100,000 people at about 110 meetings in 16 states, despite having broken her arm early in the tour. Her lectures were published as *Pharaohs, Fellahs and Explorers* (1892) a month before her death. She brought to her writing and lecturing on Egyptology the liveliness and vigour of the novelist, the knowledge of the scholar, and her own irrepressible sense of humour.

In October 1891, while supervising antiquities arriving from Egypt at London docks, Amelia Edwards contracted a lung infection which led to her death. She died on 15 April 1892 at 31 Royal Terrace, Weston-super-Mare, Somerset, and was buried on the 18th in the Braysher family tomb in the churchyard of St Mary, Henbury, near Bristol, her grave marked by an obelisk. Shortly before her death she was awarded a civil-list pension of £75 per year in recognition of her work. She bequeathed her Egyptological library and her own collection of antiquities (now the Edwards Library and Museum) to University College, London, where she had also founded the first ever chair devoted to Egyptology. By her choice, its first occupant was Flinders Petrie. Her other books, the original watercolours from her travels, and her personal papers she left to Somerville College, Oxford. The marble bust sculpted by Percival Ball in Rome in 1873 she bequeathed to the National Portrait Gallery, London. She was a tall, dignified woman with dark eyes and, in later years, iron-grey hair, 'with a pleasant voice and manner' (*Bradford Observer*, April 1892). Her writing makes it clear that she had a delightful sense of the ridiculous and an enjoyment of

life. Her contemporaries spoke of her charm and wit. She was naturally gifted, but worked hard at her talents, and she had the ability to make abstruse subjects come alive without losing any factual correctness.

The Egypt Exploration Society acknowledges its foundation (as the Egypt Exploration Fund) chiefly to the efforts of Amelia Edwards. It was the very first society to undertake 'the excavation of Egypt's buried places and the recovery of its records by the employment of scientific archaeological methods' (*The Work of the Egypt Exploration Fund*). In 1918 the society could pride itself that its excavations were always thoroughly investigated and recorded; the objects preserved and the site left so that subsequent explorers could resume work without difficulty; its results published fully and without delay; and its share of any finds presented to museums and institutions where its members resided. It continued to follow these standards into the late twentieth century.

Amelia Edwards is no longer remembered as a novelist and journalist, but her travel books and her contribution to Egyptology remain an enduring legacy.

DEBORAH MANLEY

Sources Somerville College, Oxford, Amelia B. Edwards MSS · obituaries of A. B. Edwards, AM Oxf., priv. coll., NRA 21/7/97 TS · T. G. H. James, ed., *Excavating in Egypt: the Egyptian Exploration Society, 1882–1982* (1982) · A. B. Edwards, *A thousand miles up the Nile* (1891); repr. (Los Angeles, 1983) · M. Bentham-Edwards, *Reminiscences* (1898) · J. Rees, *Amelia Edwards: traveller, novelist and Egyptologist* (1998) · J. Rees, *Writings on the Nile* (1995) · *The work of the Egypt Exploration Fund, 1882–1918* [n.d., *c.*1919] · A. B. Edwards, 'Preface', in G. Maspero, *Egyptian archaeology*, trans. A. B. Edwards (1887) · R. David, *The Macclesfield collection of Egyptian antiquities* (1980) · Q. Crewe, 'Introduction', in A. Edwards, *Untrodden peaks and unfrequented valleys*, new edn (1982) · R. M. Janssen, *The first hundred years: Egyptology at University College London, 1892–1992* (1992) · d. cert. · J. W. Pye, 'Painful last days of the queen of Egyptology', *KMT: a Modern Journal of Ancient Egypt*, 5/4 (1995), 77–8

Archives Egypt Exploration Society, corresp., notes, memoranda, and papers · Somerville College, Oxford, corresp. and literary papers, photographs, sketches · U. Oxf., Griffith Institute, album of Geographical material; notebook with various notes and extracts, albums containing watercolours and sketches · UCL, letters | U. Oxf., Griffith Institute, letters to Aquila Dodgson

Likenesses H. Watkins, photograph, 1856–9, NPG [*see illus.*] · oils, 1872 · P. Ball, marble bust, 1873, NPG · photograph, 1889, Saxony, New York · A. Weger, stipple (after photograph), NPG · F. R. Window, carte-de-visite, NPG · pastel drawing, Somerville College, Oxford · photographs, Somerville College, Oxford, A. M. Edwards archive

Wealth at death £8446 15s. 5d.: resworn probate, March 1893, CGPLA Eng. & Wales (1892)

Edwards, Arthur (*d.* 1743), benefactor, was elected a fellow of the Society of Antiquaries on 17 November 1725. Nothing is known of his parentage and upbringing, though his will refers to 'my brothers and sisters'. Little is known about his life, other than that he reached the rank of first major of the second troop of Horse Guards, and died in Grosvenor Street, London, on 22 June 1743.

The fire of 23 October 1731, in which the Cotton Library at Westminster was seriously damaged, prompted Edwards to bequeath £7000 to the library's trustees 'to erect and build such a house as may be most likely to preserve that library as much as can be from all accidents'.

Owing, however, to the protraction of a life interest in the legacy, the money did not become available until rebuilding work had been completed. In line with contingent instructions in the will, the bequest was appropriated to the purchase of 'such manuscripts, books of antiquities, ancient coins, medals, and other curiosities as might be worthy to increase and inlarge the said Cotton Library'. Edwards also bequeathed about 2000 printed volumes and their cases, as well as his 'pictures of King George the 1st, the Czar Peter, Oliver Cromwell, and Cosimo di Medicis the 1st, with his secretary, Bartolomeo Concini ... to be placed in the aforesaid library'.

GORDON GOODWIN, rev. DAVID BOYD HAYCOCK

Sources *GM*, 1st ser., 13 (1743), 389 · minute book, S. Antiquaries, Lond., vol. 1 · [R. Gough?], *A list of the members of the Society of Antiquaries of London, from their revival in 1717, to 19 June 1796* (1798) · E. Edwards, *Memoirs including a handbook of library economy*, 2 vols. (1859), 1.434, 460 · will, proved London, 13 July 1743, PRO, PROB 11/727, sig. 230
Archives S. Antiquaries, Lond., MS minute books
Wealth at death wealthy; bequeathed £7000 to Cotton Library; plus 2000 books and their cases: *DNB*; will, PRO, PROB 11/727, sig. 230

Edwards, Bryan (1743–1800), planter and politician, was born at Westbury, Wiltshire, on 21 May 1743, the eldest son of Bryan Edwards and his wife, Elizabeth Bayly. His father inherited a small estate of about £100 per annum which proved to be a scanty income for his large family. He undertook to augment his income by dealing in corn and malt, but with little success. He died in 1756, leaving his widow, Elizabeth, and six children in destitute circumstances. She was fortunate, however, in having two wealthy brothers in Jamaica. Zachary Bayly, the elder brother, cheerfully took the family under his wing and arranged for the education of his nephew Bryan. Before his father's death the boy was placed at the school of the Revd William Foot, a dissenting minister in Bristol. In later life Edwards recalled that, while he received no instruction in Greek and Latin, he was trained in writing, arithmetic, and English grammar. He excelled in writing essays, and the praise he received from his master gave him the first taste for correct and elegant composition.

When Edwards was put under the protection of his uncle he was removed from Foot's school and placed in a French boarding-school in Bristol, where he said he 'soon obtained the French language, and having access to a circulating library, I acquired a passion for books, which has since become the solace of my life'. In 1759 Nathaniel Bayly, Edwards's younger uncle, returned to England and took his nephew to live with him in London. They quarrelled, and after a few months Edwards was shipped off to Jamaica to his other uncle, which proved a happy and fortunate change in his life. He found Zachary Bayly the reverse of his brother, possessing an enlarged and enlightened mind and a kindly and generous disposition. Edwards soon came to regard him with more than filial affection and veneration. Bayly engaged the Revd Isaac Teale, rector of the parish of St George, to reside in his family and 'to supply by his instruction my deficiency in the learned languages' (Edwards, *History*, 1801, 1.xi–xiii).

Bryan Edwards (1743–1800), by Thomas Holloway, pubd 1800 (after Lemuel Francis Abbott)

Bayly was a man of great wealth and political and economic influence in Jamaica. He served at different times in the house of assembly for the parishes of Kingston, St George, St Mary, and St Andrew. He was a member of the island's privy council in 1762, and was custos of his home parish of St Mary in 1764. At his death in December 1769 he bequeathed to his brother Nathaniel four estates, and to his nephew three, all but one in St Mary's parish. Edwards was also bequeathed by his uncle two estates in the parish of Trelawny, and from his friend Benjamin Hume, who died in 1773, he inherited two plantations and a cattle pen in St George's parish. These were chiefly sugar and rum estates and plantations, although pimento, logwood, and fustic were produced and shipped to British markets. Conservatively estimated, these properties contained a labour force of 1500 slaves (Ingram, 2.708–15).

In 1765, at the early age of twenty-two, Edwards was elected a member of the house of assembly for the parish of St George and began his distinguished career in the political life of the colony. He also applied himself to learning the sugar plantation business, and in time was made a partner in managing his uncle's large holdings. In November 1774 he married his boyhood sweetheart, Martha, the younger daughter of Thomas Phipps, of Brook House, Westbury, Wiltshire. They had two sons, the younger of whom, Zachary Hume Edwards (b. c.1780), inherited his father's great wealth (Vendryes, 76–8).

After residing in Jamaica for more than two decades, Edwards returned to England in 1782 for a sojourn of five years. During this period he contested the parliamentary seat of Chichester in the independent interest against the duke of Richmond's nominee and was defeated at the poll by eight votes. Although he attempted to gain the seat by a petition in the Commons and by an action in the court of king's bench, he abstained from prosecuting the petition to an issue and lost his action. He returned to Jamaica in early 1787.

The last two decades of Edwards's life are significant for the role he played as a politician and historian. These years witnessed the later part of the American War of Independence and its aftermath; the French Revolution; a metis and slave revolt in French St Domingue; a maroon rebellion in Jamaica; and the campaign to abolish the Atlantic slave trade. Edwards and his fellow planters engaged in debates and enacted legislation to protest against restrictions imposed on trade and shipping between the British West Indies and the United States; they supported reform of the Atlantic slave trade, but opposed its abolition; they sought to aid French planters in St Domingue who were besieged by metis and slave insurgents; and they supported measures to suppress the maroon rebellion in Jamaica. Representing the parish of Trelawny, Edwards served on committees of the assembly to investigate and draft legislation regarding trade with the United States and Canada, to reform the Jamaican slave code, to provide aid to the planters of St Domingue, and to refute charges made by British abolitionists of widespread mistreatment of slaves in Jamaica.

In September 1791 Edwards joined a relief expedition of three or four British warships to assist the terror-stricken white inhabitants of St Domingue. His primary purpose was to collect authentic information of this once flourishing colony and write a history of the causes and consequences of the rebellion. After arriving in the harbour of Cape François the first object which arrested his attention was a dreadful scene of devastation by fire and the still smoking ruins of houses and plantations. When he approached more closely he and his companions were met by 'a crowd of spectators who, with uplifted hands and streaming eyes, gave welcome to their deliverers' (Edwards, *Historical Survey*, Preface).

On his return to Jamaica in October 1792, Edwards introduced a motion in the assembly for the granting of a large loan to the French colony. After much wrangling £10,000 was voted, but the French rejected it as altogether inadequate. Edwards was so angry at the treatment he received that he decided to leave Jamaica permanently (Vendryes, 79).

In Britain again in the autumn of 1792, Edwards settled in Southampton and became a highly successful West India merchant and the founder of a bank. In 1795 he contested the local seat for parliament and was defeated; however, at the general election in 1796 he was elected for the Cornish borough of Grampound. In parliament he was one of the 'moderate' group of West Indians who supported the slave trade with certain restrictions and the amelioration of colonial slavery, in so far as it was thought possible. Edwards was a zealous defender of the Creole planters against Wilberforce's attacks on the slave trade and slavery. He secured the repeal of that part of an act permitting slaves to be seized and sold for their masters'

debts. Such repeal enabled colonial legislatures to attach slaves to the soil as a measure of amelioration (Goveia, *Slave Society*, 34, 85).

Edwards was elected to the American Philosophical Society in 1774, and in 1797 he became a fellow of the Royal Society of Arts. He also became secretary of the Association for Promoting the Discovery of the Interior Parts of Africa, an appointment he owed to the influence of Sir Joseph Banks, the previous secretary. Banks had secured the commission for the surgeon and botanist Mungo Park to explore the Niger valley on behalf of the African Association. Edwards gave material assistance to Park in preparing the *Travels in the Interior Districts of Africa Performed … in 1795 and 1796 by Mungo Park* (1799) (Hallett, 242–5).

Edwards was a diligent and able writer of West Indian history. Of his literary works, the most important is his two-volume *History, Civil and Commercial, of the British Colonies in the West Indies*, published in London in 1793. According to Elsa Goveia, its scope is large, providing 'a complete account of the British islands—their origin and progress, their political system, their inhabitants, customs, institutions, agriculture and commerce' (Goveia, *Historiography*, 80–81). Edwards wrote that he attempted

> to describe the manners and dispositions of the present inhabitants, as influenced by climate, situation, and other local causes … an account of the African slave trade, some observations on the negro character and genius, and reflections on the system of slavery established in our colonies. (Edwards, *History*)

This classic work ran into five editions, was expanded to five volumes in the last edition, which appeared in 1819, and was translated into French, German, Dutch, Portuguese, and Italian (Ragatz, *Guide*, 164–5). In 1797 Edwards published *An Historical Survey of the French Colony in the Island of St Domingo*, recording the calamitous events that had overtaken this most valuable colony. He claimed that 300,000 inhabitants had perished and 15,000 British troops had been lost to death, desertion, and discharge. He condemned the French settlers' treatment of their slaves before the insurrection, and opposed the British campaign to conquer the colony. A French colonial official published a pamphlet in which he claimed that Edwards wrote from insufficient information. Moreover, he charged that, since Edwards was a sugar planter, he opposed British annexation of the colony because its tropical produce would compete with that of the British sugar colonies in the home market (Ragatz, *Guide*, 160–61).

In addition to these works, Edwards published a pamphlet on West Indian trade (1784), a speech on slavery made on 19 November 1789, *Poems, Written Chiefly in the West Indies* (1792), *Observations on the disposition, character, manners, and habits of life, of the maroons, and a detail of the origin, progress, and termination of the late war between these people and the white inhabitants* (1796), and *An Account of the Maroon Negroes in Jamaica and a History of the War in the West Indies*, which are included in his *An Historical Survey … of St Domingo* (Ragatz, *Guide*, 198, 282, 368, 500).

Edwards died on 16 July 1800 at his house at The Polygon, near Southampton, leaving an only son to inherit his great fortune. According to David B. Davis, he was 'the preeminent statesman-intellectual of the British West Indies'. He was a man of the enlightenment who looked to plantation slavery as the basis of his livelihood. He spoke and wrote from a colonial point of view and realized that Jamaica's survival as a sugar colony depended on the successful defence of the slave trade. Yet it must be said that he possessed great independence of mind and was not the mere mouthpiece of his interest group. He moved from the colonial assembly to a position of some power in parliament and played an important role in the slavery controversy. Beyond his own generation his reputation rests on his literary talent as a historian of the British West Indies (Davis, 185–9).   RICHARD B. SHERIDAN

Sources L. J. Ragatz, *A guide for the study of British Caribbean history, 1763–1834* (1932) • L. J. Ragatz, *The fall of the planter class in the British Caribbean, 1763–1833* (1928) • E. V. Goveia, *A study on the historiography of the British West Indies to the end of the nineteenth century* (1956) • E. V. Goveia, *Slave society in the British Leeward Islands at the end of the eighteenth century* (1965) • D. B. Davis, *The problem of slavery in the age of revolution, 1770–1823* (1975) • K. E. Ingram, *Sources of Jamaican history, 1655–1838* (1976), 2.708–16 • R. B. Sheridan, *Sugar and slavery: an economic history of the British West Indies, 1623–1775* (1974) • *GM*, 1st ser., 70 (1800) • *Lady Nugent's journal of her residence in Jamaica from 1801 to 1805*, ed. P. Wright, new edn (1966) • E. Brathwaite, *The development of Creole society in Jamaica, 1770–1820* (1971) • R. B. Sheridan, *Doctors and slaves: a medical and demographic history of slavery in the British West Indies, 1680–1834* (1985) • J. G. Wilson and J. Fiske, eds., *Appleton's cyclopaedia of American biography*, 2 (1982) • D. P. Geggus, *Slavery, war and revolution: the British occupation of Saint Domingue, 1793–1798* (1982) • H. E. Vendryes, 'Bryan Edwards, 1743–1800', *Jamaican Historical Review*, 1/1 (1945), 76–81 • R. Hallett, *The penetration of Africa: European exploration in north and west Africa to 1815* (1965), 242–5 • R. G. Thorne, 'Edwards, Bryan', HoP, *Commons* • B. Edwards, *The history, civil and commercial, of the British colonies in the West Indies*, 3rd edn, 3 vols. (1801) • B. Edwards, *An historical survey of the French colony in the island of St Domingo* (1797) • will, PRO, PROB 11/1346, sig. 593

Archives West India Reference Library, Kingston, Jamaica | RBG Kew, letters to Sir Joseph Banks

Likenesses T. Holloway, line engraving, pubd 1800 (after L. F. Abbott), BM, NPG [*see illus.*]

Edwards, (Samuel Jules) Celestine (1857?–1894),

Methodist evangelist and journal editor, was born, probably on 28 December 1857, at Burns, Dominica, in the West Indies, one of ten children. His father was a sailor, who died about 1867; little is known of his mother except that she was alive in 1894. Edwards's parents, whose first language was French, were descendants of Africans who had been sold as slaves to West Indian planters. They practised Catholicism but sent Celestine to a Wesleyan chapel school at St John, Antigua. In 1870 he stowed away aboard a French vessel bound for Guadeloupe; over the next few years he shipped before the mast and travelled the world. Eventually he settled in Britain, first in Edinburgh at the house of a Mrs McCleod, then briefly in Sunderland and Newcastle, and finally in London, where he changed address at least three times, living at Goth Street, Hackney; Palestine Place, Cambridge Road; and, in 1892, at 50 Tudor Road, South Hackney.

In Edinburgh, Edwards worked as a building labourer and joined the order of Good Templars, whereupon he discovered his talent for public speaking. He lectured initially on temperance subjects, then also 'upon my country and my people' (*Lux*, 27 Oct 1894). Concluding that men and women needed saving, not from drink only but from all their sins, he joined the Primitive Methodist church and became an evangelist. He hoped the Methodists would send him to Africa but they sent him instead to east London, which became his permanent base early in the 1880s.

In London, Edwards gained the diploma of associate from the theological school of King's College, and briefly attended the London Hospital as a medical student. He wrote at least seven religious pamphlets, attacking atheism, theosophy, and 'this worldism', and defending Christianity; he also wrote a short book on the life of Walter Hawkins, who had begun life as a slave and eventually became a bishop in Canada. He led a men's bible class every Sunday at St Andrew's Hall, Cambridge Road. He was an extraordinarily successful evangelist for the Methodists and, later, for the Christian Evidence Society (CES), speaking all over the country. A CES colleague recalled, 'I never met his equal as a lecturer … a unique personality on the platform he undoubtedly was' (*Lux*, 27 April 1895). A college friend remembered:

> There was something so unique in a black man teaching white men Christianity, and in knowing more about it than themselves, that at first one would feel inclined to be angry and resent it, but you could not. He was so happy in his method, so agreeable in his manner, so witty in his argument, so choice in his illustrations, so scathing in his remarks, that he insensibly won you to his side.   (*Lux*, 15 Dec 1894)

Although Edwards sympathized with all oppressed peoples he desired especially to help his own race. In 1892 he launched *Lux*, a Christian weekly newspaper. He aimed in part, he explained in his first issue on 6 August, to provide 'an antidote to [the] deadly poisons' spread by atheists. But *Lux* quickly became as well a megaphone for his Christian socialist, egalitarian, and—above all—anti-imperialist views, which he expressed also in his lectures for the CES. This was during the height of the socialist revival. Not surprisingly he found an audience. During a stint in Bristol he filled 'a hall with 1,000 people five nights in the week, and a much larger one three times on the Sunday' (*Lux*, 13 May 1893). As a testimony to his growing reputation, the founders of the Society for the Recognition of the Brotherhood of Man (SRBM)—Quaker activist Catherine Impey, widowed Scottish philanthropist Elizabeth Fyvie Mayo, and African-American anti-lynching crusader Ida B. Wells—asked Edwards to become general secretary of their organization and to edit its journal, *Fraternity*.

Edwards wrote most of the articles for *Fraternity* and quickly built its circulation to more than 7000. Under his stewardship the SRBM executive committee came to include Dadabhai Naoroji, leader of the south Asian community in Britain, and Alfred Webb, the Quaker Irish patriot and internationalist. Thus Edwards was not only Britain's first black editor but also one of the first in Britain to link the anti-imperialist struggles of all colonized peoples. He was also a proto-Pan-Africanist, who helped to pave the way for a slightly younger cohort of West Indian and African Britons, the men and women who organized the first Pan-African conference in London in 1900.

Edwards continued, throughout, to edit and write for *Lux*, and to support himself by lecturing for the CES. The pace was gruelling; his health collapsed. Supporters raised a fund, which enabled him to sail to the West Indies. He arrived at Bridgetown, Barbados, on 1 June 1894, and died in his brother's home on 25 July.

JONATHAN SCHNEER

Sources *Lux* (6 Aug 1892–27 April 1895) · *Fraternity* (July 1893–Sept 1894) · P. Fryer, *Staying power: the history of black people in Britain* (1989), 277–9
Likenesses photograph, repro. in *Lux* (24 July 1893)

Edwards, Charles (*b.* 1628?, *d.* in or after 1691), Welsh-language writer and preacher, was probably born in 1628 at Rhydycroesau in the parish of Llansilin, Denbighshire, one of the ten children born to Robert Edwards (*d.* 1651) and his wife, Anne, daughter of Robert Cyffin of Cynllaith. In the strange memoir that he published in 1691, *An Afflicted Man's Testimony Concerning his Troubles*, Edwards does not mention his upbringing or his early education. The book opens with him studying at Oxford. It is possible that he received his schooling at Oswestry or at Ruthin School, where David Lloyd, a former fellow of All Souls College, was warden. He could have been elected to his Bible clerkship at All Souls in 1644 through Lloyd's influence. In the summer of 1648 he was removed from the college by the puritan visitors, but by the autumn he must have satisfied them for he was given a scholarship at Jesus. In June 1649 he gained his degree, BA. Later that year, if the *Testimony* can be believed, he was 'accused as disaffected to the things then in being, and denied the Profits of the Fellowship promised [him]', a reference to the government of the day and Cromwell's ever-increasing power (Edwards, *Testimony*, 2). It is certainly not easy to judge Edwards's political or religious position at this time. According to the *Testimony* he experienced a spiritual conversion during his time at Oxford, but no date is given, and there is no way of knowing if it influenced his responses to the visitors. Nor is it known why the young man forced to leave the University of Oxford in the autumn or winter of 1649 because of his alleged disaffection with the puritan visitors was, in 1650, employed as a preacher by the approvers of the Act for the Better Propagation of the Gospel in Wales. In 1653 he was given the rich *sine cura* living of Llanrhaeadr-ym-Mochnant. Four years later he was appointed assistant to the commissioners for ejection of ministers in north Wales. But then, after the Restoration, although he swore allegiance to the king, his benefice was taken away from him in circumstances which are unclear. Whatever the truth about Llanrhaeadr, Edwards continued to live in Denbighshire until 1666 with his wife and children (it is not known how many children he had). If credence can be given to his testimony that he and his wife had lived together for sixteen years before 'she

importuned me to part with her' in 1666 'and live asunder', he married in 1650 (Edwards, *Testimony*, 9). His wife was probably the 'Mrs Abbigall Edwards, w. of Mr. Charles Edwards, Clerck' who was buried in Oswestry on 18 June 1686 (Williams, xlv). Although there is no certain proof it is more than likely that this Abigail was the daughter of Oliver Thomas (*c.*1598–1652), puritan clergyman and writer who held the living of Llanrhaeadr between 1650 and 1652.

After the separation, 'by mutual Consent', says Edwards, 'I was induced to go to *Oxford*, and afterwards to *London*' (Edwards, *Testimony*, 9). It was for the works he published in these places that he became a major figure in Welsh puritan literary history. He went to Oxford, to the university printer, to print *Ffydd ddi-ffuant* (1667), a book that he had no doubt been preparing during the previous few years. It was further changed and improved by 1671 when the second edition was published. In 1677 he returned to Oxford to print the third edition 'with Augmentation'. This was *Y ffydd ddi-ffuant, sef, Hanes y ffydd Gristianogol, a'i rhinwedd*, which became a classic of Welsh prose. To describe the slim *Ffydd ddi-ffuant* of 1667 as a part abridgement of John Foxe's magisterial *Actes and Monuments* is, perhaps, grossly insulting to the great English martyrologist but that, in essence, is what it is: a brief unbalanced 'History of the Unfeigned Faith' in the world, and in England particularly, quarried from the Bible, from Foxe, and from other sixteenth- and seventeenth-century English authors. Not only is the material of the book Foxeian, so is its mind. For the 1671 edition Edwards wrote a new section of the history of the faith among the Welsh—a section influenced by his reading of Bishop Richard Davies's epistle *ir Cembru oll* ('to all the Welsh people'), first published as the introduction to William Salesbury's translation of the New Testament, 1567, and also by his reading of Gildas's *De excidio Britanniae*, written some time before 547 and published by Polydore Vergil in 1525. From Davies and Gildas, Edwards learned to regard Wales as *Israel praesens* and to regard himself as its deuteronomic teacher–prophet cum historian. For the 1677 edition of *Y ffydd ddi-ffuant* he added another splendid section on the virtue or efficacy of the faith. Although it is a book composed in stages, the third edition of *Y ffydd ddi-ffuant* has the unity of the scripture's historical imagination. It is Edwards's definition of this as it pertains to Wales and the individual Welshman, expressed in vivid, spectacular style, that makes the book a classic.

From Oxford, after overseeing the publication of the first *Ffydd ddi-ffuant*, Edwards returned to Denbighshire, where he read Davies's epistle and was given a copy of Morris Kyffin's *Deffynniad ffydd Eglwys Loegr* (1595), the Welsh translation of Bishop Jewel's *Apologia pro ecclesia Anglicana*. In 1671, back in Oxford, he published both together as *Dad-seiniad meibion y daran* (*An Echo of the Sons of Thunder*). It was the first of many books 'of spiritual edification' (p. 5) that he prepared. In 1672 he was back again in Llansilin and district: following the declaration of indulgence of that year Edwards was licensed 'to be a gen[all] Pr: Teach[er] at Oswestree in Salop' (Williams, xxvii). By 1675 he was in London, where for the next nine years he was 'busie about the Printing of *Welch* Books' for the Welsh Trust established by Thomas Gouge and some fellow English philanthropists, with the assistance of Stephen Hughes, 'to increase the provisions of faith' among the Welsh people (Edwards, *Testimony*, 9; Williams, xxxi). These books included edited reprints of earlier excellent translations like Rowland Vaughan's translation of Lewis Bayly's *Practice of Piety*, *Yr ymarfer o dduwioldeb* (1675), and new editions of translations of contemporary English works like Richard Jones's translation of Gouge's *Christian Directions*, *Hyfforddiadau Christianogol* (1676). Edwards was also responsible for superintending the printing of the 1677–8 edition of the Welsh Bible.

During this period Edwards published a Latin pamphlet called *Hebraismorum Cambro-Britannicorum specimen* (1676), which purports to demonstrate the close connection between the Hebrew and Welsh languages, a theme first developed by Welsh authors in the sixteenth century and obviously attractive to a portrayer of Wales as *Israel praesens*. His other work of note is *Fatherly instructions: being select pieces of the writings of the primitive Christian teachers, translated into English, with an appendix, entituled Gildas Minimus* (1686). The appendix contains original sermons written by Edwards 'to disswade from Apostacy, and those other Abominations that are like to be very pernicious to these Nations, if not timely repented of' (Edwards, *Testimony*, 10).

Thereafter Edwards returned to his old neighbourhood and took a farm. In 1691 he went again to London, perhaps to publish his *Testimony*. That book ends with the date 'July 1. 1691'. That is the last mention of Charles Edwards. No one knows when he died or where he was buried.

DEREC LLWYD MORGAN

Sources D. L. Morgan, 'A critical study of the works of Charles Edwards, 1628–?1691', DPhil diss., U. Oxf., 1967 · C. Edwards, *Y ffydd ddi-ffuant*, ed. G. J. Williams (1936) · D. L. Morgan, 'Defnydd Charles Edwards o ddelweddau', *Ysgrifau Beirniadol*, 4 (1969), 47–73 · C. Edwards, *An afflicted man's testimony concerning his troubles* (1691)

Edwards, (Allen) Clement (1869–1938), trade unionist, barrister, and journalist, was born on 7 June 1869 in Knighton, Radnorshire, the third of seven children born to George Benjamin Edwards, auctioneer, master tailor, and draper, and Sarah Ellen (*née* Tudge). Both parents came from farming, nonconformist, and radical families in the border areas. Edwards, who was known as Clem, was educated at Knighton national school until the age of thirteen. Like many of his generation, he also attended evening classes (in mathematics and languages at Birkbeck Institute, London) and engaged in private study (most notably in economics and law). He was called to the bar in 1899.

Following school, Edwards worked as a clerk in a local solicitor's office. He experimented with journalism before moving to London, although he remained at heart a countryman. In London he became a Congregationalist (although a Welsh-speaking champion of nonconformist grievances, he was born into the Church of England). He studied Karl Marx and the land reformer Henry George; he

was attracted to both fiery preachers such as Charles Spurgeon and Hugh Price Hughes, and the secularist radical Charles Bradlaugh. In the late 1880s Edwards helped form a series of trade unions for unskilled workers (especially dockers). Like other radicals, he saw trade unions as a defence against cruel employers and an erratic economic system which induced personal poverty, immorality, and misery. Edwards worked both with the leading union figures Ben Tillett, J. E. Burns, and Tom Mann, and with London's religious philanthropists and Liberal campaigners. He was assistant secretary of the Dock, Wharf, and General Labourers Union, formed in 1890, and general secretary of the short-lived federation of dockland and transport unions formed in 1891.

Edwards's radical contacts enabled him to forge a career in journalism—where he exposed poverty and supported strikers' families—and to enter municipal politics, where he campaigned for better education and housing. He became labour editor of the radical London paper *The Sun* in 1893 and of *The Echo* in 1894, before moving to the *Daily News*. He stood as Progressive candidate for the London school board in 1894 (Islington) and was elected to Islington council in 1898. He stood unsuccessfully for parliament in 1895 (Tottenham) and 1900 (Denbigh Boroughs) before winning the latter seat in 1906. Defeated by just ten votes in January 1910, he was elected in December that year for the mining seat of East Glamorgan.

As a barrister, and also later in parliament, Edwards supported the legal restoration of trade union rights. As a young barrister, he quickly gained a reputation with cases involving trade unions on the south Wales circuit. He was briefed as a junior counsel by the unions when the Taff Vale and Osborne judgments threatened the trade unions' ability to engage in industrial and political action. He put the miners' case following the infamous 1913 Senghenydd pit disaster in which 439 men died. A man of strong and determined views in public and private life, he combined support for traditional Welsh radical courses with a vehement and populistic hostility to the Labour Party and to syndicalism.

During the war Edwards was a super-patriot. Like the former new union leader Ben Tillett and other Labour men from a trade union background he backed David Lloyd George, notably in efforts to prevent industrial unrest. He became a prominent figure in the National Democratic Party (NDP), a 'patriotic labour' organization. He was the party's successful parliamentary candidate for East Ham South in 1918, and the organization's chairman from 1919 to 1920. He attacked the 'unreasonable' and 'Bolshevik' actions of some unions during the post-war industrial unrest. By the end of the coalition years, this approach was losing its appeal, and although Edwards stood in 1922 for the NDP (as a supporter of the Lloyd George coalition) he was defeated.

Edwards married Fanny (*d.* 1920), daughter of Captain Emerson, the superintendent of Trinity House, Great Yarmouth, in 1890. After her death, in 1922 he married the secretary of the NDP, Alice May Parker; they had one son, John. Edwards's views and past actions did not fit easily with the now reunited Liberal Party. He remained a champion of union rights during the turmoil of the mid-1920s but drifted out of Liberal politics. He claimed to be a Liberal until 1931, when he lost faith with the party leaders and resigned his membership. He eventually retired as a barrister and died comparatively poor of cancer at Manor House Hospital, Golders Green, on 23 June 1938. He was cremated at Golders Green. Edwards's second wife worked for the London and North Eastern Railway in the 1920s and 1930s. On her husband's death the family left the ground-floor flat looking onto Hampstead Heath which had been home for some years, and lived as tenants of relations. Alice Edwards died in the 1980s. Their son, John Edwards, became a solicitor.   DUNCAN TANNER

Sources B. Nield, 'Edwards, Allen Clement', *DLB*, vol. 3 · private information (2004) · 'Election addresses' [local press] · K. O. Morgan, *Wales in British politics, 1868–1922*, 3rd edn (1980) · A. C. Edwards, *Trade unions and the law* (1904) · A. C. Edwards, 'Do trade unions limit output?', *Contemporary Review*, 81 (1902), 113–28 · K. D. Ewing, *Trade unions, the labour party and the law* (1982) · C. Tsuzuki, *Tom Mann, 1856–1941: the challenges of labour* (1991) · R. Douglas, 'The national democratic party and the British workers' league', *EngHR*, 87 (1972), 717–54 · J. Schneer, *Ben Tillett: portrait of a labour leader* (1982) · J. Shepherd, 'Labour and parliament: the lib-labs as the first working-class MPs, 1885–1906', *Currents of radicalism: popular radicalism, organised labour, and party politics in Britain, 1850–1914*, ed. E. F. Biagini and A. J. Reid (1991), 187–213 · A. J. Reid, 'Old unionism reconsidered: the radicalism of Robert Knight, 1870–1900', *Currents of radicalism: popular radicalism, organised labour, and party politics in Britain, 1850–1914*, ed. E. F. Biagini and A. Reid (1991), 214–43
Archives Mitchell L., Glas. · NRA, priv. coll., press cuttings and papers | HLRO, Lloyd George MSS
Likenesses F. Moscheles, portrait, priv. coll.

Edwards, Duncan (1936–1958). *See under* Busby Babes (*act.* 1953–1958).

Edwards, Ebenezer [Ebby] (1884–1961), trade unionist, was born on 30 July 1884 at Chevington, Northumberland, one of eleven children of William Edwards and his wife, Esther Fish. His father was president of the local miners' lodge (branch) and a freethinker. After attending elementary school, Ebby, as he was invariably known, began work in the mines in 1896, mainly at Ashington, in Northumberland. In 1908 he left the pit to take up a Northumberland miners' scholarship at Ruskin College, the college for working men at Oxford. Edwards left after ten months because of economic hardship and returned to the mines. In 1909 a student revolt at Ruskin over curriculum content led some of the students and a sacked lecturer, with the encouragement of the Miners' Federation of Great Britain (MFGB), to set up a rival institution. The Plebs League originated from this revolt and established Marxist discussion groups in many parts of the country. From this grew the National Council of Labour Colleges. Edwards sympathized with the 1909 secessionists and, influenced by Marxism, he joined the Plebs League, becoming one of the foremost advocates of radical socialism among the Northumberland miners. He was a leading advocate and practitioner of adult education in the Northumberland coalfield, helping persuade the union to send students to the Central Labour College. In 1906 he joined the Independent Labour Party but left in 1909, thereafter concentrating on union politics. In 1911 he married Alice Reed (*d.* 1961), a miner's daughter, in Gosforth.

In 1912 Edwards was elected president of the Ashington miners' lodge and identified himself with the politics of Robert Smillie, the Scottish miners' leader. An opponent of the war, Edwards was prevailed upon by the local Labour Party, in defiance of the electoral truce, to stand for Wansbeck in the by-election in May 1918. His opponent, a Coalition Liberal and non-miner, narrowly won the election; Edwards, who continued to work in the mines during the war, lost again in the general election of December 1918. Reflecting his growing reputation in the Northumberland coalfield, he was elected assistant financial secretary of the Northumberland Miners' Association in 1919, and in 1920 financial agent and secretary. In 1926 he was elected its representative on the executive of the MFGB. The events of 1926—the general strike and miners' lock-out—had a searing effect on the miners, their unions, and upon Edwards. While their defeat did not alter fundamentally his political outlook, it did lead him to adopt a more cautious political and industrial strategy. In 1928 Edwards was appointed to the committee which investigated charges made against A. J. Cook, the MFGB secretary, that he had engaged in unauthorized negotiations in 1926. Several executive members who were sympathetic to Cook refused to serve, but Edwards argued this would mean Cook would be totally exposed to his enemies.

At the May 1929 general election Edwards was elected as Labour MP for Morpeth, Robert Smillie's old seat. In parliament he concentrated on the coal industry, advocating nationalization as the cure for the industry's problems. He lost his seat in the October 1931 general election and did not stand again for parliament, concentrating on union work. Vice-president of the MFGB in 1930, he was elected president in 1931. When A. J. Cook died in November 1931 Edwards was elected his successor as MFGB secretary.

During the 1930s Edwards was, perhaps, the key figure in MFGB politics. He was a steadfast opponent of the 'non-political' unions in south Wales, Scotland, and Nottinghamshire, and worked constantly for their reintegration into the MFGB. Despite the defeat of 1926 and the economic problems of the 1930s, he believed that even in these unpropitious circumstances significant gains could be made if the objective was realistic and the correct tactics pursued. This underpinned the MFGB's strategy in the wage claim of 1935–6 which secured both a general wage increase (albeit one which varied from coalfield to coalfield) and, most importantly from Edwards's point of view, national recognition (denied since 1926) of the MFGB by the owners' association. Under the leadership of Edwards and Joseph Jones, the Yorkshire leader, the miners won over public opinion by a very effective publicity campaign, secured a huge majority for industrial action, and manoeuvred the owners into a situation where they were forced to make concessions under pressure from Baldwin's government and the big coal users, neither of which wanted a coal strike. This strategy was summed up by Edwards as 'maximum benefit for minimum sacrifice'. In 1935 he was nominated to the royal commission on safety in mines, which was appointed in response to the terrible disaster at Gresford in 1934.

Edwards was an internationalist, a committed anti-fascist, and anti-appeaser. He was treasurer and then secretary of the Miners' International Federation (a post held by his son in the 1970s), committing both that organization and MFGB to anti-fascism, both internationally and domestically. In the Second World War he strongly supported the production drive in the pits, serving on the Coal Production Council from 1940. As well as negotiating for the MFGB he was central in establishing the more unified National Union of Mineworkers (NUM), which came into being on 1 January 1945. He served as the NUM's first general secretary. In 1944 and 1945 he was chairman of the TUC, and in 1946 received the TUC's gold medal; he attended the United Mine Workers of America conference in 1944 and, in 1945, the United Nations in San Francisco. He also represented the miners and later the National Coal Board (NCB) at International Labour Office meetings.

While the NCB made no concessions to worker representation an attempt was made to show that management structures were now open to workforce influence. After a great deal of heart-searching, and a commitment from the NUM that his pension rights were secure, Edwards was appointed to the NCB in July 1946 as its labour relations member. His successor as general secretary, Arthur Horner, who frequently faced Edwards across the negotiating table (an experience Horner described as 'interesting', as Edwards knew intimately both the NUM and NCB cases), believed Edwards 'did an amazingly good job' for the miners and the industry at a very difficult time. Not only did he contribute to putting coal on a sounder footing, but miners' conditions improved. One of Edwards's first tasks was to negotiate the implementation of the miners' charter, which he had written while NUM general secretary. In common with all miners' leaders of his generation, Edwards was deeply committed to making nationalization a success. As an NUM and then NCB official, Edwards criticized indiscipline in the pits, especially unofficial strikes; he believed they undermined what the management and unions were trying to achieve. When Edwards retired from the NCB in 1953, some contemporaries felt that he had become disillusioned by his experiences.

Edwards was undoubtedly a man of the left. Not a charismatic leader in the Cook mould, he was convinced the MFGB must recreate itself so as to deal on equal terms with the employers and the state. While he was determined never to repeat the experience of 1926, he did not conclude that this entailed never striking. He also believed that while conferences laid down policy, its achievement was the responsibility of leaders, who should be permitted to modify policy according to the circumstances, subject to approval by the membership. Acutely aware of the dangers of the left–right factionalism which lurked beneath the surface of union politics,

he was well placed to bridge the gap between left and right in the union. This valuable role was acknowledged by communists and non-communists, but led to considerable ill-feeling between Edwards and Will Lawther (MFGB/NUM president) who, moving rapidly to the right in the mid-1940s, came to regard Edwards as soft on communists. Personal animosity and growing left–right factionalism may have influenced Edwards's decision to join the NCB.

Those who worked with Edwards commented on his good humour, intelligence, and calmness; and a Conservative secretary of mines contrasted favourably his tactical sense and flexibility with the coal owners' intransigence. 'Stocky, thin featured and clean-shaven, often cloth-capped, with humorous blue eyes' (DNB), he looked in many ways the archetypal miner of the period. He never forgot his origins and never accepted a knighthood, mischievously telling Arthur Horner that what put him off was seeing how Walter Citrine was always overcharged after receiving his knighthood. In retirement Edwards lived quietly with his wife; he died a month after her, at Gosforth, Newcastle upon Tyne, on 6 July 1961.

ANDREW TAYLOR

Sources *The Times* (8 July 1961) · *DLB* · R. P. Arnot, *The miners: a history of the Miners' Federation of Great Britain*, 3: … *from 1930 onwards* (1961) · R. P. Arnot, *The miners, one union, one industry: a history of the National Union of Mineworkers, 1939–46* (1979) · A. Horner, *Incorrigible rebel* (1960) · A. Moffat, *My life with the miners* (1965) · A. J. Taylor, '"Maximum benefit, minimum sacrifice": the miners' wage campaign of 1935–1936', *Historical Studies in Industrial Relations*, 2 (Sept 1996), 65–95 · Mineworkers' Federation of Great Britain, reports and proceedings · National Union of Mineworkers, reports and proceedings · *DNB*
Likenesses photograph, 1918, repro. in R. P. Arnot, *The miners: a history of the Miners' Federation* (1961), 33
Wealth at death £5603 19s. 6d.: probate, 17 Oct 1961, CGPLA Eng. & Wales

Edwards, Edward (1738–1806), painter, was born in Castle Street, Leicester Square, London, on 7 March 1738, the elder son of a chairmaker and carver from Shrewsbury and his wife, Sarah. Possibly as a result of a childhood illness, Edwards was partially crippled, and remained of small stature for the rest of his life. He was educated at a French protestant school until he was fifteen, when he began working for his father. He was subsequently employed, until the age of eighteen, by William Hallett, cabinet-maker and upholsterer, at the corner of St Martin's Lane and Long Acre, where he drew patterns for furniture. He was also enrolled at a drawing school, probably William Shipley's, situated on the Strand. In 1759 he studied at the duke of Richmond's sculpture gallery, and from 1761 at the St Martin's Lane Academy. Following his father's death in 1760 Edwards assumed responsibility for his younger sister, Sarah, and widowed mother, also Sarah. (A pencil drawing of Edwards's mother is in the British Museum, as is a self-portrait as a young man, also in pencil.) At this time Edwards took lodgings in Compton Street, Soho, where he opened an evening school for drawing. In 1763 he was employed by the print publisher John Boydell to make drawings for engravers. In 1764

Edwards was awarded a premium from the Society of Arts for the best historical picture in chiaroscuro, entitled *The Death of Tatius*, which he exhibited that year at the Free Society of Artists. He subsequently exhibited with the Incorporated Society of Artists from 1767 to 1772. On 30 January 1769 he was registered as a student at the Royal Academy Schools. He exhibited at the Royal Academy for the first time in 1771, with a portrait and a religious painting, *The Angel Appearing to Hagar and Ishmael*. In 1773 Edwards was made an associate member of the Royal Academy, and in 1788 was appointed teacher of perspective. He did not, however, become a Royal Academician. In 1774–5 Edwards made a series of grisaille wall paintings on classical themes for the North Drawing Room of the Mansion House, London, commissioned by the mayor of London, John Wilkes. For this he was paid 37 guineas.

In July 1775 Edwards, sponsored by the merchant and collector Robert Udny, travelled via France to Italy. In Florence he copied ancient sculpture and a self-portrait by Rembrandt in the Uffizi Gallery. While in Florence, Edwards also suffered an undisclosed 'misfortune' (Ingamells, 330). By the end of 1775 Edwards was in Rome. He also apparently visited a number of other unspecified Italian cities before returning to France by way of Turin and Lyons. By September 1776 he had returned to London, where he continued to exhibit large numbers of works at the Royal Academy, in a variety of genres. These included a portrait of Jonas Hanway, founder of the Marine Society (1779); *View of Brancepeth Castle near Durham* (1784); *The Angel Appearing to Gideon* (1792), *The Release of the Prisoners from Dorchester Gaol* (1796); and *Cupid and Psyche* (1800). He was also employed by the Society of Antiquaries to make a drawing from the picture in the Royal Collection, *The Interview between Henry VIII and Francis I at Calais* (artist unknown), for which he was paid 110 guineas. Edwards also worked as a mural painter. About 1781 he repaired a painted ceiling by Sir James Thornhill at Roehampton, and in 1782 he painted three decorative ceilings for the Hon Charles Hamilton at Bath. Other work included illustrations for Bell's edition of Shakespeare's plays, as well as commissions for his patron, Robert Udny. Between 1781 and 1784 he was employed by Horace Walpole to provide illustrations for his definitive edition of the *Description* of Strawberry Hill, published in 1784. A number of these drawings are now at the Lewis Walpole Library, Farmington, Connecticut.

In 1784 Walpole fell out with Edwards, who thenceforth ceased to work for him. In 1787 Edwards was in Newcastle upon Tyne, where he painted scenes for the theatre. He also made topographical drawings of Northumberland, including a view of Jesmond Dean (Eton College, Windsor). Among his most ambitious commissions at this time was *Interior view of Westminster Abbey, taken at the commemoration of Handel from the manager's box* (Yale U. CBA), which he exhibited at the Royal Academy in 1793. In 1799 Edwards was employed by Boydell to paint a single picture for the Shakspeare Gallery, a scene from *The Two Gentlemen of Verona*. A proficient etcher, in 1792 Edwards published a series of fifty-two etchings. A series of thirty-eight drawings,

Costumes of English Ladies (1781–1806) was sold at auction in 1990 (Sothebys 11 July 1990, lot 24). In 1798 Edwards was commissioned by the privy council to make a series of designs for new coinage.

Aside from his art, Edwards played the violin, composed verses, and wrote occasional works for publication. In 1781 he published a short account, based upon a paper he had presented at the Royal Society, of a hurricane that had hit Roehampton the previous year. A related drawing, showing an overturned windmill on Barnes Common, belongs to the Courtauld Institute of Art, London. In 1790 Edwards published a treatise on perspective and *A Collection of Views and Studies after Nature*. The book for which he is principally remembered, however, is *Anecdotes of Painters who have Resided or been Born in England*, intended as a supplement to Horace Walpole's *Anecdotes of Painting in England*, published in four volumes between 1762 and 1771. Edwards's book was published after his death, in 1808. An illustrated copy is in the print room of the British Museum. Edwards died on 11 December 1806 and was buried in St Pancras churchyard, London. According to a fellow academician, Edwards was 'as much a Character as any man he had ever known', whose eccentricities would 'make a History as entertaining as Don Quixotte' (Farington, *Diary*, 8.2929). Owing to Edwards's insolvency at his death, the Royal Academy awarded his surviving sister a pension. Edwards's pictures, books, and effects were sold to raise funds for her at two auctions on 30 January and 21 March 1807.

MARTIN POSTLE

Sources DNB · R. Edwards, 'Edward Edwards A.R.A. and furniture of an earlier age', *Country Life* (7 June 1930), 848–50 · S. Jeffrey, 'Paintings by Edward Edwards and William Darnell: the drawing rooms at the Mansion House', *Apollo*, 139 (1993), 303–10 · E. Edwards, *Anecdotes of painters* (1808); facs. edn (1970) · J. Ingamells, *A dictionary of British artists and travellers in Italy, 1701–1800* (1997) · Farington, *Diary* · will, GL, MS 25626/14, fols. 506v–507v
Likenesses G. Dance, pencil drawing, 1793, BM · A. Cardon, stipple (after E. Edwards), BM, NPG; repro. in Edwards, *Anecdotes of painters* · E. Edwards, self-portrait, pencil drawing, BM · D. Turner, etching (after D. Humphrey), BM, NPG
Wealth at death died in debt: Farington, *Diary*

Edwards, Edward (1803–1879), manufacturer of aquariums, was born on 23 November 1803 at Corwen, Merioneth, where he received his education. He became a draper at Bangor, Caernarvonshire, which business he carried on until 1839. In the following year he established a foundry and ironworks at Menai Bridge, which he appears to have carried on for several years with much success.

In 1864 an interest in the marine life of the Menai Strait led Edwards to study the habits and characters of fish. He attempted to create an artificial system for maintaining fish in a healthy condition, in order to study their behaviour more closely. By imitating their natural environment, Edwards succeeded in introducing improvements to the construction of aquariums that enabled the fish to thrive. His most notable improvement was his 'dark-water chamber slope-back tank', the result of a close study of the rock pools along the shores of the Menai Strait. Application of this improvement benefited the design of, and demand for, domestic aquariums, and the principle of his tank was successfully adopted by the leading museums at home and abroad. Edwards died on 13 August 1879, at the age of seventy-five, at 4 Park Hill Terrace, Upper Bangor, after an attack of hemiplegia.

ROBERT HUNT, *rev.* YOLANDA FOOTE

Sources *The Athenaeum* (6 Sept 1879), 312 · private information (1888) · *DWB* · d. cert.

Edwards, Edward (1812–1886), librarian and writer, son of Anthony Turner Edwards (1782/3–1847), builder, and Charlotte Hull (1783–1864), was born in Stepney in the East End of London on 14 December 1812. He had two sisters, Charlotte and Elizabeth, both younger. Edwards appears to have spent the first twenty years of his life entirely in the East End or City of London, certainly living at 12 Idol Lane, Great Tower Street, between 1825 and 1832. He lived subsequently at a series of central London addresses over the next two decades. Nothing is known of any formal education Edwards may have had. Some, if not the greater part, of his education was no doubt a product of his nonconformist upbringing. As a teenager, he attended the King's Weigh House chapel in Eastcheap, where, from 1829, the Revd Thomas Binney (1798–1874) had an important influence on his thinking. Edwards's education as a young man owed much to Edwin Abbott (1808–1882), headmaster of Marylebone Philological School, who taught him privately. Both Abbott and Edwards were members of a German reading circle and of the Marylebone Literary and Scientific Institution. Edwards was also a member of the Western Literary Institution in Leicester Square. In his twenties he frequently attended a small radical art and literary discussion club, the Society of Wranglers, which included the future pioneer designer of working-class housing George Godwin (1815–1888), as well as Henry Hayward, a surveyor, and his sister Margaretta Hayward (*d.* 1876), whom Edwards was to marry on 11 June 1844.

Utilitarianism and the British Museum In the 1830s Edwards became interested in three main fields: education, libraries, and industrial art. In 1836 he published, anonymously, a pamphlet entitled *Metropolitan university: remarks on the ministerial plan of a central university examining board*, in which he called for the awarding of external degrees and argued that anyone should be able to aspire to a university education. In 1838 he joined the short-lived Central Society of Education, which aimed to promote wider access to education. His beliefs in respect of education and many other social matters was thoroughly utilitarian, founded on an abhorrence of monopoly, exclusivity, and privilege, all of which he associated with the pre-modern, closed society he wished to see reformed.

Edwards's utilitarianism was similarly evident in his call for improved library provision, in terms of both increased social accessibility and greater operational efficiency. In 1836 he published *Remarks on the Minutes of Evidence Taken before the Select Committee on the British Museum*, addressed to Benjamin Hawes, a radical MP who had sat on the committee the previous year. Edwards asked why use of the museum library could not be extended to a wider class of person, suggesting longer opening hours to

help facilitate this. He also made detailed proposals, drawn from his experience as a reader in the library over the previous two years, for improvements to the book stock and to the catalogue, calling for a classed, rather than an alphabetical, arrangement. Much to the irritation of the museum's hierarchy, he repeated these proposals when asked to give evidence before the select committee when it reassembled later that year.

Edwards's radicalism was again apparent in his enthusiasm for art, and in particular its application to manufacturing. He observed the proceedings of the select committee on art and manufactures (1835–6); became honorary secretary of the Art Union of London, which he helped found (but which he left in disgrace in 1840, having squandered over £300 of the union's funds); and wrote a lengthy, authoritative book entitled *The Administrative Economy of the Fine Arts* (1840). The key objectives of his philosophy of art were, first, a desire to see greater opportunity in the production of art, requiring among other things a weakening of the monopoly position of the Royal Academy, and, second, through institutions such as libraries, museums, and schools of design, better education for the design of manufactured goods—an aspect of economic activity in which, especially in the luxury goods sector, Britain was said by many to be patently deficient.

How Edwards supported himself financially in his early adult life is largely a mystery. Having been apprenticed to his father's business at the age of fourteen, he appears to have taken no part in the building trade after the business went bankrupt in 1832. Thereafter, his only known sources of income were research and writing. Some early results of his endeavours are to be found in three publications of 1837. Edwards wrote the text to accompany the plates in *The Great Seals of England*, and spent several weeks in France researching a similar publication, *The Napoleon Medals*. While there he took the opportunity to visit a number of libraries, and to acquaint himself with French culture, society, and politics, which were to remain of lifelong interest. Edwards's talents as a researcher were also recognized by James Macarthur (1798–1867), a wealthy Australian who was in Britain to argue for political and constitutional reform for his country. To support and publicize his aims, Macarthur commissioned Edwards to research *New South Wales: its Present State and Future Prospects*, the bulk of which was eventually written by Edwards himself.

In 1838 Edwards wrote to Antonio Panizzi, the new keeper of printed books at the British Museum, repeating his earlier suggestions for improvements to the library. This initiative, together with the reputation he had gained in his appearance before the select committee on the British Museum, persuaded Panizzi to employ Edwards as an assistant cataloguer. Edwards joined the staff in 1839 and immediately became a member of a five-man committee formed to draw up a fresh set of cataloguing rules. His other main responsibility was the cataloguing of the Thomason collection of tracts and pamphlets printed during the English civil war, Commonwealth, and Restoration periods. During his employment at the museum Edwards frequently annoyed his superiors by his unpunctuality, single-mindedness, and tendency to conduct his private research in working hours.

Campaigner for public libraries In the late 1840s Edwards produced a series of papers on comparative librarianship, beginning in 1847 with 'Public libraries in London and Paris' for the *British Quarterly Review*. The following year he read a paper to the Statistical Society of London, entitled *A statistical view of the principal public libraries in Europe and the United States of North America*, which led to his election as a fellow of the society. Also in 1848, the British Museum again found itself under parliamentary scrutiny, and Edwards published an open letter to the earl of Ellesmere, chairman of the royal commission investigating the institution's affairs. This he entitled *Remarks on the paucity of libraries freely open to the public in the British Empire; together with a succinct statistical view of the existing provision of public libraries in the several states of Europe*. In each of these discourses Edwards's prime purpose was to paint a picture of retarded library provision in Britain, a state of affairs that contrasted markedly with the nation's international hegemony in the economic sphere. It was a perspective that struck a chord with radicals who pointed to the persistence of quasi-feudal social practices in cultural, political, and economic life, and who sought an on-going modernization of society, one aspect of which was increased opportunity to education through accessible libraries. One radical who shared these ideas was William Ewart MP (1798–1869), whom Edwards had first encountered when attending the select committees on the British Museum and on arts and manufactures on which Ewart had served as, respectively, member and chairman. The two had also been involved in the Art Union of London. Impressed by Edwards's criticism of the country's current state of library provision, Ewart wrote to him on 24 August 1848 suggesting the formation of a select committee to publicize the idea of establishing local public libraries sustained through a combination of local and central taxation. Edwards enthusiastically supported the idea and began to collect evidence for presentation to the inquiry.

In 1849 Edwards served as a witness at two parliamentary inquiries, giving a small amount of evidence to the royal commission on the British Museum (1848–9), commenting mainly on the progress of work for the new catalogue; but providing extensive data for the select committee on public libraries. Edwards's statistical evidence—pointing to the lamentable state of accessible library collections in Britain compared to other countries—underpinned the select committee's final report, which called for the widespread establishment of free municipal libraries. Doubts have since been cast on the integrity of Edwards's data. At the time, however, his arguments were persuasive, and did much to pave the way for Ewart's Public Libraries Act (1850), which permitted boroughs with a population of 10,000 to raise, should the ratepayers agree, a rate not exceeding ½*d.* in the pound to fund the establishment and running of a library, although not the purchase of materials.

Despite the heightened professional profile Edwards

had achieved by his contribution to the genesis of public libraries in Britain, he continued to be held in relatively low regard by British Museum superiors. His evidence to the select committee on public libraries had included a strong attack upon the museum library's standards. This, together with his long history of irresponsible behaviour in the workplace—not least his supposedly slipshod cataloguing and, in conducting his own researches, his use of museum stationery to correspond with foreign libraries—resulted in his dismissal in May 1850. Later that year, having completed some work for Salford Public Library, Edwards was appointed as librarian of the public library in Manchester, the first authority to adopt the provisions of the new Public Libraries Act. Edwards's achievements at the Manchester Free Public Library were considerable. He prepared the library for its opening in 1851 and over the next few years assembled and organized a comprehensive collection. His most strenuous efforts were directed at the building up of reference rather than lending stock, the latter containing, much to Edwards's chagrin, a large proportion of books of amusement, which proved highly popular with the library's socially diverse clientele. His professionalism was evident in the numerous detailed reports and suggestions he placed before his committee. In addition, he oversaw the establishment of two branch libraries in the city. As at the British Museum, however, Edwards often found himself in conflict with his management. Although in some respects overbearing and interfering, the corporation's library committee was none the less justified on many occasions in its criticism of Edwards: his absences were many, and his public visibility in the library was low, due to his habitual propensity for private research. Other points of friction were his inadequate salary and the reference library catalogue, for which Edwards sought standards higher than those requested by the committee. Failure to reconcile their differences resulted in the unco-operative Edwards and his committee going their separate ways: he was dismissed in 1858, and moved back to London the following year.

Literary output This second occupational failure was soon eclipsed by literary success, as Edwards entered one of the most intellectually productive stages of his life. Stripped of a secure income, he sought to earn a living through writing. The 1860s were, for Edwards, nomadic years: a time of independence and of great and varied research, but also one of uncertainty and financial anxiety. Often pursuing many projects simultaneously, he too frequently found himself juggling with deadlines and in danger of financial embarrassment; his periodic money crises were relieved by loans from friends and colleagues, selling parts of his private library, or publication of his work. Edwards's literary output exploded, beginning with the publication in 1859 of *Memoirs of Libraries*, many years in the making and probably his best-known book. Edwards wrote it essentially as a propagandist instrument: a means of fostering an awareness of libraries as a national, public resource. He did this by detailing the rich heritage of library provision since ancient times, and by providing a manual of what he called 'library economy', which included procedures for the efficient running of libraries, as well as a range of bold suggestions, the idea of a national bibliography and a proposed association of librarians among them. In the early 1860s, besides expanding previous articles on 'Police' and the 'Post Office' for the 8th edition of the *Encyclopaedia Britannica*, he also wrote several other pieces for this particular publication. These covered diverse topics, from 'Weaving' to 'Wool and the wool trade', from 'Tea and the tea trade' to 'Alexis de Tocqueville'. The latter piece included a critique of *De la démocratie en Amérique*, demonstrating Edwards's continuing interest in wider social and political issues. He went on to produce a string of major publications: *Libraries and the Founders of Libraries* (1864), which continued some of the themes covered in *Memoirs of Libraries*; *Liber monasterii de Hyda* (Rolls Series, 45, 1866); *The Life of Sir Walter Ralegh* (1868), a meticulously researched study based on primary sources, which was to win wide praise from later historians; and *Lives of the Founders of the British Museum* (1870), based on material in the Public Record Office, the Privy Council Office, and the museum's own archives. In *Free Town Libraries* (1869) Edwards returned to the subject that had dominated much of his younger life: namely, increased opportunity of access to education through the use of libraries. Unfortunately, what was intended as a cheap manual on the formation and workings of municipal public libraries became an overlong and fragmented study containing a great deal of irrelevant material on the history of libraries and on library provision in other countries. In its coverage of apparently unconnected themes, its lack of direction, and its great length, *Free Town Libraries* offers an appropriate example of Edwards's personality: an independent spirit, often reluctant to empathize with the objectives of colleagues, and frequently deficient in self-discipline, as evinced by his persistent inability to plan his personal finances.

Librarian in Oxford and later life Following this prolific period of authorship, Edwards decided, in 1869, to return to library work, having last been engaged in it in the early 1860s, when employed by the earl of Macclesfield to rearrange and catalogue his library at Shirburn Castle, Oxfordshire. Despite this long interruption Edwards's skills as a librarian were still marketable. He spent three months cataloguing the lending library of the recently inaugurated Doncaster Public Library. In 1870 he moved to Oxford to work in Queen's College preparing a new library catalogue, a task that occupied the following six years. From 1877 to 1883 he worked at the Bodleian Library calendaring the Carte papers, the results of which were so inaccurate as to prove unpublishable, highlighting therefore Edwards's limitations as a scholar. This job was supplemented by occasional employment in the library of Corpus Christi College, Oxford. His time in Oxford was one of the happiest of his life, marred only by the death of his wife in 1876. While in Oxford, Edwards radically reduced the time he devoted to research and writing, although in 1882 he was pleased to be asked to revise articles on 'Newspapers' and the 'Post Office' for the 9th edition of the *Encyclopaedia Britannica*. The energy he had also

once given to the promotion of libraries also declined, although he continued to collect material for a second edition of *Memoirs of Libraries*. He took no part in the first international conference of librarians in 1877, nor in the establishment of the Library Association of the United Kingdom that same year. He showed little interest in the association's early development. For its part, the association elected him, in 1882, an honorary member, an award usually reserved for distinguished foreign librarians. During his years in Oxford he moved further away from his radical, nonconformist origins, becoming more confirmed than ever in the righteousness of the established faith and in that brand of toryism evolving under the leadership of Disraeli, whom he much admired.

In January 1883 Edwards's tasks at the Bodleian came to an end when the library terminated his employment for reasons of economy. His work in Oxford had allowed him to live comfortably, with enough money left over to enlarge his private library and even to give to good causes such as Sunday schools, night refuges, and soup kitchens. However, at the age of seventy, and with few prospects for employment, Edwards entered retirement in a precarious financial position, with little saved, yet handicapped by an enduring profligate nature reinforced by years of good living in Oxford. Edwards left Oxford in 1883 and settled on the Isle of Wight. The remaining years of his life were marked by increasing poverty, forced as he was to live on a small civil-list pension of £80 per annum, granted to him in 1883, and money gained from the sale of the greater part of his 5000-volume private library. He took up lodgings in Niton, which he had previously visited as a tourist, but was thrown out for non-payment of rent, fortunately being taken in rent-free by a charitable Baptist clergyman and his wife. Edwards continued to work on a second edition of *Memoirs of Libraries*, going to the trouble and expense of having much of his new material set up in type. He also published, in 1885, *A Handbook to the Literature of Collective Biography*, a venture arising from his lifelong interest in biographical studies, probably his favourite reading. Towards the end of his life, however, his reading was mostly confined to devotional literature. Despite his apparently poor financial circumstances, Edwards somehow continued to mount expeditions to various parts of the island. In November 1885 he failed to return from one such excursion and was found, frost-bitten and close to death, in open country several days later. Although apparently making a good recovery, Edwards was found dead on the morning of 7 February 1886, having died in his sleep. He was buried in Niton churchyard.

Edwards's work, in particular his writings, entitle him to be regarded as a founder of modern librarianship. Notwithstanding the variety that characterized his scholarship, it is for his studies on library history and library economy, and his data on library provision at home and abroad in support of the public library movement, that he is best remembered. However, it was only in the twentieth century that his reputation as a major figure in the development of librarianship was secured; during his lifetime the contribution he made to improved library provision went largely unrecognized. It was not until 1902, when the library promoter and publisher Thomas Greenwood (1851–1908) published his biography of Edwards, that the library pioneer was rescued from oblivion. Not only did Greenwood collect as much as possible of Edwards's books, papers, manuscripts, and letters, but he also paid many of his debts, published a second edition of *Memoirs of Libraries*, and planned and financed a monument erected over Edwards's unmarked grave at Niton in 1902. These acts did much to highlight Edwards's significance in the history of librarianship, as did William Munford's 1963 biography, which improved upon Greenwood's earlier biography in terms of detail and scholarly approach. It painted a picture of an exciting, complex, and cultured, yet often stubborn and unco-operative, character, whose devotion to the cause of education through libraries was remarkable, as well as being an inspiration to later generations of professional librarians.   ALISTAIR BLACK

Sources W. A. Munford, *Edward Edwards, 1812–1886: portrait of a librarian* (1963) · T. Greenwood, *Edward Edwards* (1902) · J. L. Thornton, 'Edward Edwards, 1812–1886', in J. L. Thornton, *Selected readings in the history of librarianship* (1966), 104–14 · K. A. Manley, 'Edward Edwards: the first professional public librarian', *Library Association Record*, 88 (1986), 143–5 · H. P. McCartney, 'Edward Edwards: man of letters (first public librarian of Manchester)', *Papers of the Manchester Literary Club*, 74 (1965–8), 35–42
Archives Man. CL, Manchester Archives and Local Studies | BL, Art Union London MSS, letters to S. G. Percevall and F. J. Baigant, Add. MSS 39977, 41496 · Bodl. Oxf., Carte collection
Likenesses J. Phillip, group portrait, painting, 1848, Bury Art Gallery and Museum, Moss Street, Bury

Edwards, Edwin (1823–1879), etcher and painter, was born on 6 January 1823 in Framlingham, Suffolk, the son of Charles Edwards of Bridgham Hall, Norfolk. He was educated at Dedham, Essex, before studying law. He was admitted as a solicitor in 1845 and built up a large and successful practice as an examining proctor in the Admiralty and prerogative courts, based in Bennett's Hill and then in Knightrider Street, London. He published *Cases in the Prerogative Court with Respect to Wills* (1847), *Treatise on the Jurisdiction of the High Court of Admiralty* (1847), and *Ecclesiastical Jurisdiction* (1853).

After a trip to the Tyrol in 1859, Edwards decided to give up his legal work (which provided him with a substantial pension) to devote himself to art. For several summers, according to a French friend, he rose at 3 a.m. to catch the morning light; in the winter he worked in a specially constructed glass cabinet, dressed as a polar explorer and with his wife in attendance to clear the condensation from the windows. He worked initially in watercolours but soon turned to painting in oil and etching, the example of the French painter Alfred Legros, working on a plate at Edwards's house in Sunbury-on-Thames, inspiring him to attempt the latter medium. He became acquainted with many other French artists, including Henri Fantin-Latour (who painted a portrait of Edwards and his wife, Elizabeth Ruth, a devoted supporter of her husband's artistic career).

Edwards exhibited many works at the Royal Academy between 1861 and 1879, including sea paintings and Cornish scenes; his best-known painting was *Gainsborough's Lane* (exh. RA, 1875). He also exhibited in Paris, where his etching was much admired: his etchings, of which he made over 370 at least, included scenes of the Thames, English cathedral cities, and Cornish coast and Suffolk scenes. In 1879 he published the first part of *The Inns of Old England*, lavishly illustrated with etchings, some of which were exhibited at the Royal Academy in 1871–2; his wife edited and published the second and third parts after his death.

Edwards was a founder member of the Hogarth Club and was particularly interested in the work of the Norwich landscape painter John Crome. He died at his home, 26 Golden Square, London, on 15 September 1879; his wife survived him. An exhibition of his work was held in London at the Continental Gallery, 168 Bond Street, soon after his death.   ANNE PIMLOTT BAKER

Sources E. Duranty, 'Edwin Edwards, peintre et acquafortiste', *Gazette des Beaux-Arts*, 2nd ser., 20 (1879), 438–42 · Graves, *RA exhibitors* · *DNB* · Wood, *Vic. painters*, 3rd edn · Boase, *Mod. Eng. biog.* · *CGPLA Eng. & Wales* (1879)
Archives V&A, press cuttings collection
Likenesses H. Fantin-Latour, double portrait, oils, 1875 (with his wife), Tate collection; repro. in *Burlington Magazine*, 5 (1905) · C. S. Keene, two etchings, BM · C. S. Keene, four drawings, Tate collection
Wealth at death under £10,000: probate, 20 Oct 1879, *CGPLA Eng. & Wales*

Edwards, (Iorwerth) Eiddon Stephen (1909–1996), Egyptologist, was born on 21 July 1909 at 57 Lightfoot Road, Hornsey, London, the second of the two children of Edward Edwards (1870–1944), Persian scholar on the staff of the department of oriental manuscripts at the British Museum, and his wife, Ellen Jane, née Higgs (1870–1942), oratorio and opera singer. His parents were both Welsh, but Edwards lived for most of his life in London. He attended Merchant Taylors' School, London, where he studied classics and biblical Hebrew. He won a major open scholarship to Gonville and Caius College, Cambridge, and graduated with first-class honours in the oriental languages tripos (Hebrew and Arabic) in 1931. In 1934 he accepted an assistant keepership in the department of Egyptian and Assyrian antiquities at the British Museum. On 22 December 1938 he married (Annie) Elizabeth Lisle (b. 1912), secretary, who later performed voluntary legal work and worked for a housing trust.

Edwards's early years at the museum were spent in studying the ancient Egyptian hieroglyphic and cursive scripts and familiarizing himself with the collections, but by 1939 he had published *Hieroglyphic Texts from Egyptian Stelae*, part 8 (1939) and contributed to exhibition catalogues and learned journals. His posting in 1942 to the British embassy in Cairo enabled him to visit the major pyramid sites. After spells in Baghdad and Jerusalem, he returned to the British Museum in 1945 and completed *The Pyramids of Egypt* (1947), both a scholarly work and a bestseller, which subsequently went into several editions and was translated into many languages. In 1950 Edwards was appointed deputy keeper, and in 1955 became keeper of a new independent department of Egyptian antiquities. He spent much of the next few years modernizing the Egyptian exhibitions, promoting various museum publications, and making the department's resources accessible to outside scholars. In 1958 he was appointed as principal editor to complete the second edition of the *Cambridge Ancient History*, volumes 1 and 2 (1970–75), and performed an invaluable service to scholarship in bringing it to press. His major philological publication, *Oracular Amuletic Decrees of the Late New Kingdom* (1960), concerned some fascinating hieratic papyri designed to protect people from disease and demonic possession. By this time Edwards was a well-known and internationally respected Egyptologist; in 1962 he became a doctor of literature of Cambridge University and was elected a fellow of the British Academy, and he was created CBE for services to the British Museum in 1968.

Edwards's major claim to contemporary fame, however, was his success in persuading the Egyptian government to loan fifty of the finest treasures discovered in 1922–3 in the tomb of Tutankhamun for exhibition at the British Museum. The exhibition was opened by Elizabeth II on 29 March 1972; it attracted 1,694,000 visitors over nine months, and raised nearly £1 million for the rescue from permanent submersion of the temples on the island of Philae. No previous exhibition at the museum had been so successful with the British public, and Edwards was its main inspiration. He himself wrote the catalogue, *Treasures of Tutankhamun* (1972), later adapted for exhibitions in the United States, and in 1973 was created CMG for services to Anglo-Egyptian relations.

During his career Edwards produced over seventy learned articles, reviews, catalogues, and obituaries. He was honorary treasurer of the Egypt Exploration Society from 1949 to 1961 and vice-president from 1962 to 1988. In 1953–4 he was visiting professor at Brown University, Rhode Island, and did much service to the *Annual Egyptological Bibliography* and to the promotion of radiocarbon dating in its early years. Even after retiring from the British Museum in 1974, he continued to play an active role. From 1973 to 1980 he was a member of the joint UNESCO–Egyptian committee for the rescue of Philae, and it was he who, having noticed that the blocks of the Diocletian gate were still lying in the reservoir, arranged for a team of British and Egyptian naval divers to lift them. He also sat on international committees concerned with the future of the Egyptian Museum in Cairo and of the monuments of Giza. He was Glanville lecturer at Cambridge in 1980, and made several successful lecture tours abroad.

Of medium stature, Edwards was quick in movement, dark-haired, and clean-shaven; his eyes signalled not only the acute and critical quality of his mind, but twinkled to disclose his kindliness and sense of fun. By temperament he was a traditionalist, notable for his strong sense of loyalty and honour. Well-known as a raconteur, he enjoyed social and sporting events, especially those connected with his beloved Cambridge University. He and his wife, Elizabeth, were hospitable to colleagues and foreign scholars at their beautiful homes in Morden and later in Deddington, Oxfordshire, where he took great pleasure in his garden and in family life. Sadly, their son Philip died suddenly of leukaemia in 1968, aged twenty, in his second year at New College, Oxford, but his wife and their daughter, Lucy (*b.* 1950), a teacher, survived him. He collapsed in Marylebone Station, London, on 24 September 1996 and died the same day at St Mary's Hospital, Paddington. He was cremated at Headington, Oxford, on 11 October, and his ashes were buried in Deddington churchyard. A memorial service was held at St George's Church, Bloomsbury, London, on 1 November 1996.   H. S. SMITH

Sources T. G. H. James, 'Iorwerth Eiddon Stephen Edwards', *PBA*, 97 (1998), 273–90 · H. S. Smith, 'I. E. S. Edwards', *Journal of Egyptian Archaeology*, 84 (1998), 181–90 [incl. bibliography] · personal knowledge (2004) · private information (2004) [Elizabeth Edwards] · A. Leahy, 'Bibliography of I. E. S. Edwards (to 1986)', *Pyramid studies and other essays presented to I. E. S. Edwards*, ed. J. Baines, T. G. H. James, A. Leahy, and A. F. Shore (1988), 1–4 · *The Times* (28 Sept 1996) · *Daily Telegraph* (5 Oct 1996) · *New York Times* (7 Oct 1996) · *The Independent* (9 Oct 1996) · *The Guardian* (Oct 1996) · b. cert. · m. cert. · d. cert.
Archives SOUND BL NSA, performance recording
Likenesses photograph, repro. in *The Times* · photograph, repro. in *The Independent* · photographs, priv. coll.
Wealth at death £606,418: probate, 12 Feb 1997, *CGPLA Eng. & Wales*

Edwards, Enoch (1852–1912), trade union leader and politician, was born on 10 April 1852 in the north Staffordshire coal-mining village of Talk-o'-the-Hill, the eldest son of James Edwards, a coal-miner, and his wife, Eliza Boulton. Little is known about his private life except that he married Elizabeth Alice, daughter of Henry Rathbone, in 1875. He was educated briefly at a Primitive Methodist day school, was encouraged to read by some of the miners with whom he began to work from the age of nine, and taught at a Sunday school which had a small library attached to it.

Edwards worked at several collieries in north Staffordshire, and joined the local lodge of the North Staffordshire Miners' Association in 1870, becoming lodge treasurer within a few months, and checkweighman in 1875. Later in the same year he was made treasurer of the association, and two years later he was elected general secretary, a position that he held until his death thirty-five years later. He was the driving force behind the establishment in 1886 of the Midland Miners' Federation (which included unions in Shropshire, Staffordshire, and Warwickshire). As president of the federation from its foundation until 1912, Edwards helped to establish the Miners' Federation of Great Britain (MFGB) in 1889, and became a leading figure in the new organization. He was national treasurer from 1889 to 1904, and succeeded Ben Pickard as president from 1904 until his death in 1912. To Edwards, claimed Robert Smillie in 1912, 'more than anyone else living today, or anyone connected or who has been connected with the

Federation, is due the fact that the miners have been for some time now, absolutely solidly organised together in one body' (Arnot, 121).

Edwards was active socially and politically at local, regional, and national levels. He was a Primitive Methodist preacher, a member of the Ancient Order of Foresters, and district secretary of the Ancient Order of Shepherds. He was a member of Burslem school board (1886–95), a member, alderman, and mayor (1899–1900) of Burslem town council, a member of Staffordshire county council, a JP for Burslem (and later Stoke-on-Trent), and a member of the royal commission on mines which reported in 1909.

He was the member of parliament for Hanley from 1906 to 1912. Although he stood first for the Liberal Party and then for the Labour Party, he remained a convinced free-trade Liberal even when the MFGB affiliated to the Labour Party in 1909. He stood as a Liberal candidate, unsuccessfully in 1900 and successfully in 1906; and then stood, successfully, as a Labour candidate in the two general elections of 1910. It is significant, however, that the local press continued to describe him as a 'Lib–Lab', and that when he was adopted as Labour candidate in 1910 it was at a joint meeting of Hanley Trades Council and Hanley Liberal Association. His new Labour Party label, it has been claimed, 'made no difference at all' (Gregory, 169). Enoch Edwards died at 78 Lord Street, Southport, on 28 June 1912. JOHN BENSON

Sources R. P. Arnot, *The miners: a history of the Miners' Federation of Great Britain*, 2: … *from 1910 onwards* (1953) · H. A. Clegg, A. Fox, and A. F. Thompson, *A history of British trade unions since 1889*, 1 (1964) · *DLB* · R. Gregory, *The miners and British politics, 1906–1914* (1968) · H. Hallam, *Miners' leaders: thirty portraits and biographical sketches* (1894) · *Dod's Parliamentary Companion*
Wealth at death £3192 9s. 4d.: probate, 20 Aug 1912, CGPLA Eng. & Wales

Edwards, Sir Fleetwood Isham (1842–1910), army officer and courtier, second son of Thomas Edwards of Woodside, Harrow on the Hill, and his wife, Hester Magdalen Penelope, daughter of the Revd William Wilson, of Knowle Hall, Warwickshire, was born at Thames Ditton on 21 April 1842. Educated at Uppingham and Harrow schools, he entered the Royal Military College, Sandhurst, in 1861; on 30 June 1863 he received a commission as lieutenant in the Royal Engineers. After professional instruction at Chatham, where he was captain of the cricket eleven, Edwards was acting adjutant at Dover. From 1867 to 1869 he was private secretary and aide-de-camp to General Sir Frederick Chapman, governor of Bermuda. On 19 April 1871 he married Edith, daughter of the Revd Allan Smith-Masters of Camer, Kent and Phebe Mary Randall. She died in 1873.

After serving at Fermoy, Ireland, Edwards was appointed assistant inspector of works at the Royal Arsenal, Woolwich, in November 1870, and on 1 August 1875 became aide-de-camp to General Sir John Lintorn Simmons, inspector-general of fortifications. Promoted captain on 5 July 1877, in 1878 he accompanied his chief to the Berlin Congress, where he was noticed by Beaconsfield

and Salisbury. Appointed assistant privy purse and assistant private secretary to Queen Victoria in October 1878, he went on to become groom in waiting in 1880, an extra equerry in October 1888, and keeper of the privy purse and head of the queen's personal household in May 1895 in succession to Sir Henry Ponsonby. Promoted major on 30 June 1883, and lieutenant-colonel on 22 October 1890, he was made CB in 1882 and KCB in 1887, and a privy councillor on his retirement from the army on 12 October 1895. On 20 May 1880 he married again. His second wife was Mary, daughter of Major John Routledge Majendie and Harriet Dering. There were no children.

Edwards was one of the queen's most trusted and intimate advisers from May 1895 until her death in 1901, and was one of the executors of her will. In 1901 Edward VII made him a GCVO, a serjeant-at-arms of the House of Lords, and an extra equerry, granting him a pension. George V appointed him paymaster to the household and an extra equerry. He died at his residence, the Manor House, Lindfield, Sussex, on 14 August 1910, and was buried in Cuckfield cemetery. R. H. VETCH, *rev.* K. D. REYNOLDS

Sources W. A. Lindsay, *The royal household* (1898) · A. Ponsonby, *Henry Ponsonby, Queen Victoria's private secretary: his life from his letters* (1942) · Walford, *County families* · *WWW* · *The Times* (15 Aug 1910)
Archives BL, corresp. with R. Dalyell and Henry Campbell-Bannerman, Add. MS 41206 · Bodl. Oxf., corresp. with Lord Kimberley · W. Sussex RO, corresp. with duke of Richmond and Gordon
Likenesses portrait, Royal Collection
Wealth at death £23,674 15s. 3d.: probate, 27 Oct 1910, CGPLA Eng. & Wales

Edwards, George (1694–1773), ornithologist and artist, was born on 3 April 1694 at Stratford, West Ham, Essex, to a family of Welsh descent. He was educated at a boarding-school in Leytonstone and at Brentwood grammar school. He was then apprenticed to John Dod, a merchant of Fenchurch Street, London, whose relative Dr Nicholas had a library where Edwards read avidly. Dissatisfied with the prospect of a life in trade he returned home in 1716 to live on his patrimony and study natural history. He travelled cheaply to Norway in 1718 and to France for a long stay in 1719–20. After returning home he made coloured drawings of exotic birds, aiming at accurate portrayal. His work was admired by James Theobald FRS, who introduced him to the world of rich collectors of natural history, such as the duke of Richmond, who frequented the Royal Society.

Edwards, to his surprise, was able to find a market for his drawings: as the number of clients increased so did his prices. His chief patron was Sir Hans Sloane, president of the Royal College of Physicians. In 1733 Sloane appointed him bedell to the college, in which office he was responsible for the administration and care of the college building in Warwick Lane which held the great library of the marquess of Dorchester; Edwards styled himself keeper of the library and the job gave him a home within the college building. Encouraged by the physicians he set up his studio and used the college as a publishing house. Mark

George Edwards (1694–1773), by Johann Sebastian Müller, 1754 (after Bartholomew Dandridge)

Catesby, artist and naturalist, taught him how to etch and he prepared four volumes of his hand-coloured etchings with descriptive text under the final title of *A Natural History of Uncommon Birds*. The first volume (1743) gained him nomination for fellowship of the Royal Society, but, strangely, he withdrew his candidacy. Autobiographical details featured in the second volume (1747) and the third (1750) brought him the Copley medal of the Royal Society. In the last volume (1751) he stated that age and infirmity precluded further work.

By now Edwards had gained international fame as an ornithologist and began working with the Bartrams of Philadelphia and Linnaeus in Sweden. In 1754 he published a new edition of Catesby's book on the fauna of Carolina. He made regular presentations to the Royal Society, of which be became a fellow in 1757. The next year he published the first volume of his *Gleanings of Natural History*. The second volume appeared in 1760. In the same year he sold his entire portfolio to the marquess of Bute, resigned as bedell to the College of Physicians, and retired to a house in Plaistow. From there he still visited the college and the Royal Society and, stimulated by his drawings of South American birds captured from the French by Earl Ferrers, published a last volume of *Gleanings* in 1764. After a long decline he died in Plaistow on 23 July 1773 and was buried in West Ham churchyard. He left his property in Plaistow and West Ham to his spinster sister Ann who shared with his married sister Mary Tracy his capital of some £5000. His friend James Robson, a bookseller, disposed of his library and, in 1776, published a memorial of his life with a reprint of his contributions to the *Philosophical Transactions*. A. STUART MASON

Sources A. S. Mason, *George Edwards: the bedell and his birds* (1992) • *Some memoirs of the life and works of George Edwards* (1776) • C. E. Jackson, *Bird etchings: the illustrators and their books, 1655–1855* (1985) • *DNB*

Archives BL, natural history drawings, Add. MSS 5263–5265, 5267, 5271–5272 • RS, letter and papers • Zoological Society of London, drawings | BL, letters to Thomas Birch, Add. MSS 4305, 4443 *passim* • BL, Sloane MSS, MS 5261

Likenesses B. Dandridge, portrait, 1754 • J. S. Müller, line engraving, 1754 (after B. Dandridge), BM, NPG [*see illus.*] • Ceri, portrait, 1763 • J. S. Müller, line engraving, 1770 (after I. Gosset), BM, NPG; repro. in G. Edwards, *Essays on natural history* (1770) • I. Gosset, jasper medallion, Wedgwood Museum, Barlaston, Staffordshire • J. Miller, engraving (after Ceri, 1763) • A. Tardieu, engraving (after B. Dandridge, 1754)

Wealth at death houses in Plaistow and West Ham; £5000 in funds: will, PRO, PROB 11/990

Edwards, George (1751/2–1823), political writer, graduated with a medical degree from Edinburgh University in 1772. He lived for a while in London before settling in Barnard Castle, co. Durham about 1775, where he practised as a physician. He was an untiring propounder of political and social schemes, with a particular enthusiasm for reform of the constitution, of agricultural practice, of tax laws, and of the army. But his rhetoric tended to be more extravagant than the thoroughness or consistency of his plans would warrant. The fullest elaboration of Edwards's ideas was *The practical system of human economy … whereby we are able in one immediate simple undertaking to remove the distress, burdens, and grievances of the times, and to bring all our interests, public, private, and commercial, to their intended perfection* (1816). As suggested by this and other titles, his writings abound in the unconscious humour of the egotist deeply persuaded of his mission. Edwards regarded himself as the interpreter of God's plan for human government, explaining that 'the Almighty has destined that I should discover his true system of human economy'. He maintained that his plans for political reform would work because they were congruent with the thirteen 'laws of God and nature' he claimed to have discovered. His style was to combine such extravagant claims with ideas that whiggish reformers were championing at the time. He was much impressed by the effects of 'scientific farming' in Barnard Castle, for example; he favoured the removal of taxes on manufacturing industry (and their replacement with a general income tax) and a reduction of public expenditure. At the same time Edwards was a staunch defender of the powers of the monarchy and opposed the extension of the franchise. In his proposed 'new era', government boards were to superintend all the interests of mankind and everybody was to be actuated by truly Christian principles.

It does not appear that Edwards attracted any public attention. In later life he moved to Suffolk Street, Charing Cross, London, and died, aged seventy-one, on 17 February 1823. ADAM I. P. SMITH

Sources *GM*, 1st ser., 93/1 (1823), 569 · G. Edwards and 'Observer', *A certain way to save our country and make us a more happy and flourishing people than at any former period in our history* (1807)

Edwards, George [*alias* George Parker, G. E. Parker, Mr Wards] (**1787?–1843**), modeller and spy, was born in London, the youngest of three children of a man called Edwards and a sometime lottery keeper by the name of Gordon, whom Edwards had courted in a gin shop, according to Aylmer, one of the few biographical sources available. Details of the early life of George Edwards are sketchy, but it is said that, when his father abandoned the family, the youth helped his mother to run her lottery partnership and embarked on a career as a petty thief. By the age of eight he had been caught stealing from a grocer's shop and from a local public house. Having shown early artistic abilities he was encouraged to paint, but preferred modelling, and went on to serve a full apprenticeship with the Smithfield statuary, Chicani. In March 1808 Edwards married Eleanor Hampton, whom he physically abused and abandoned for nine months. Nothing is known of his movements from the end of his apprenticeship to his arrival in Eton some six years later, but it seems likely that his involvement in a scheme with John Castles, a government spy, to free French prisoners of war and then to betray them to the authorities for a reward belongs to this period.

About 1814 Edwards moved to Windsor and ran a modeller's shop at 50 High Street, Eton. One of his best-selling lines was a plaster likeness of Dr John Keate, the unpopular headmaster of Eton College, which was bought by the schoolboys for target practice. The writer and publisher Charles Knight, who was also a customer, remembered Edwards in his *Passages of a Working Life* as a 'diminutive animal with downcast look and stealthy face'. Another visitor was Sir Herbert Taylor, then private secretary to George III, and it was possibly through him that Edwards was invited to model busts of members of the royal family. While at Windsor, Edwards became an active member of the radical Spencean Society and managed to get his brother William, said to have been a Bow Street officer in Windsor, elected secretary. It is known that following the death in 1814 of Thomas Spence, founder of Spenceanism, the modeller was asked to supply fifteen busts to mark the occasion. Whether or not the two brothers ever shared a genuine interest in the political aims of the Spenceans remains a matter of speculation. What is beyond doubt is that by January 1818 George was willing to sell his knowledge of the society to government officials. Although Edwards and his brother were said to have incited violence among the disaffected at Spa Fields in 1817, there is no evidence that George was a government informer before 1818. After this date, however, Spenceans were closely watched.

By the time Edwards began passing information it would appear that he had left his shop in Eton, where he owed money and had lost patrons. He moved to London, establishing himself in William Hone's former premises at Fleet Street. Here, from January 1819, the radical journalist and publisher Richard Carlile was his next-door neighbour. Carlile commissioned him to make a full-length figure of Thomas Paine and also a likeness of himself, which Edwards completed while Carlile was incarcerated in the king's bench prison. Throughout this period the modeller was busily employed as a government spy, worming his way into the confidence of the Spencean Arthur Thistlewood and other malcontents, reporting his findings to Henry Hobhouse of the Home Office, and inciting violence towards government ministers. After the discovery of the Cato Street conspiracy on 23 February 1820 it was Edwards who led police to the hide-out of Thistlewood [*see* Cato Street conspirators (*act.* 1820)]. At the subsequent trial of the leading conspirators the pivotal role of Edwards as the plot's instigator and the chief supplier of weapons and ammunition was revealed. Edwards, however, was never called as a witness. He went into hiding under the name of Wards but early in May was reported to have been spotted in Cambridge. Soon afterwards Alderman Wood MP called for a Commons inquiry to investigate the government's role in the conspiracy. His motion failed, but on 23 May Edwards was indicted for high treason, and a reward of 100 guineas offered for his capture. He is described in *The Times*' notice as being 5 feet 3 inches in height, 'thin and pale-faced, with an aquiline nose, grey eyes and light brown hair'.

Meanwhile the fugitive had fled to Guernsey under the name of G. E. Parker, leaving behind his wife and four young children, who eventually joined him in July. The Home Office occasionally sent him small sums of money, but there is no record of Edwards ever having received the £1000 reward for the capture of Thistlewood. Early in August 1820 he disappeared completely from Home Office records and the evidence suggests that he emigrated with his family to Cape Colony. A George Parker, modeller, is listed as living at Green Point in 1840. A 'George Parker jun., lime-burner', also of Green Point, is listed in the same issue of the *Cape Calendar and Annual Register*. On 30 November 1843, according to a local newspaper, 'George Parker senior' died, aged fifty-six.   R. M. HEALEY

Sources E. Aylmer, *The memoirs of George Edwards* (1820) · G. T. Wilkinson, *An authentic history of the Cato Street conspiracy* (1820) · D. Johnson, *Regency revolution* (1974) · J. Stanhope, *The Cato Street conspiracy* (1962) · C. Knight, *Passages of a working life during half a century*, 3 vols. (1864–5) · G. A. Aldred, *Richard Carlile—agitator* (1941) · *The Taylor papers, being a record of certain reminiscences, letters and journals in the life of Lieut.-Gen. Sir Herbert Taylor*, ed. E. Taylor (1913) · *Dolby's debates and proceedings in parliament* (1820) · *The Times* (1820) · *South African Commercial Advertiser* (9 Dec 1843)
Archives PRO, Cato Street conspiracy MSS
Likenesses oils, 1820, GL
Wealth at death £500—property value: *South African Commercial Advertiser*, 9 Dec 1843

Edwards, Sir George (1850–1933), trade unionist and politician, was born on 5 March 1850 at Marsham in Norfolk, the son of Thomas Edwards and his wife, Mary. His father, a discharged soldier, was a bullock feeder and his mother a handloom weaver. He was the youngest of four children of his mother's second marriage. He had two older brothers and a sister, and three stepbrothers, who did not live with the family.

Sir George Edwards (1850–1933), by Claude Harris

Edwards's childhood was spent in terrible poverty, including a spell in the workhouse when his father was imprisoned for stealing turnips from a field; and the only schooling he received was at a Church of England Sunday school which he attended briefly in Marsham. At the age of six he started work scaring crows. Between 1856 and 1869 he followed a series of trades in agriculture, while working periodically as a brick maker, the trade his father followed from the mid-1840s. In 1869, in one of the most important changes in his life, he was converted to Primitive Methodism, the religious cause to which he remained attached until his death.

On 21 June 1872 Edwards married Charlotte Corke (d. 1912), who lived in Alby, Norfolk, where he had gone to work on the brick-fields. Taught to read and write by his wife, in the summer of 1873 he was taken onto the plan of Aylsham Primitive Methodist circuit as a lay preacher. He conducted his first service by learning the text (1 John: 29) and the hymns of the day by heart from his wife's dictation. Alongside his religious development he began his lifelong involvement in politics and trade unionism. In his own words, the 'terrible sufferings I had undergone in my boyhood burnt themselves into my soul like hot iron' (G. Edwards, 36), and when the first agricultural trade unions appeared in Norfolk in 1872 Edwards was an early convert. For the next fifteen years he remained a loyal and dedicated member of the rank and file, first of the local East Dereham district union and then as a member of Joseph Arch's National Agricultural Labourers' Union. He

took an active part in the election campaign of 1885, the first one at which farm labourers had the vote, and was sacked and blacklisted for his beliefs. In 1889, after a period of decline, the trade union movement revived in Norfolk and Edwards became secretary of the newly formed Norfolk Federal Union, Cromer district; and then, in 1890, full time organizer for the union. However, the continuing agricultural depression and bitter, well-organized opposition from the employers led to the total collapse of the union in 1896.

For the next ten years Edwards returned to his trade as a brick maker. In 1906, following the Liberal election victory, he was instrumental in re-forming a trade union for farmworkers. This was to become the National Union of Agricultural and Allied Workers, later the agricultural trades section of the Transport and General Workers Union. He remained secretary and organizer until 1913 when he retired, following his wife's death and his own increasing ill health, and became union president. However, his work for the union and for labourers continued. He served on the Norfolk War Agriculture Committee, and as a labourers' representative on the central wages board and the Norfolk county wages board from 1917 to 1921. In 1923 he took an active role in the bitter strike in Norfolk against wage reductions.

Alongside his union work Edwards was always active in the broader world of politics. He became in the 1870s, as he put it, 'an advanced Liberal' (G. Edwards, 43), and as such served as a parish, district, and county councillor. Unusually for her time and class, his wife, Charlotte, was also active in local politics, serving as a parish and district councillor. She made a particular mark on the Erpingham board of guardians, devoting her time and care to fighting for better conditions for women inmates, especially single mothers. In 1918 Edwards left the Liberal Party and joined the Labour Party, fighting the general election of that year as a Labour candidate for South Norfolk. He lost but was elected for the same seat at a by-election in July 1920. He made his maiden speech on 21 October 1920 on unemployment and the poor law. He lost his seat at the general election of 1922 but regained it in 1923. He was again defeated in 1924 when the 'red scare' caused nationally by the fabricated Zinoviev letter was used against him by local Conservatives to suggest that he was a long-term, if lukewarm, supporter of the Soviet Union.

Although no longer active in national politics after his defeat in 1924, Edwards, unlike Arch, remained firm in his beliefs and returned to the local sphere as a Labour alderman on Norfolk county council and as a parish councillor for Fakenham, where he had lived since 1910. In 1919 he was appointed OBE for his wartime service to agriculture, and he was given a knighthood in the 1930 birthday honours. Fittingly the citation simply said 'For services to agricultural workers'. Despite increasing ill health and constant urging from doctors and his family, Edwards continued active until the last weeks of his life. He attended the Walsingham board of guardians two weeks before his death, where he argued forcefully on a case of forcible eviction of a farmworker and his family. He died after a series of heart attacks on the evening of 6 December 1933 and was buried in Fakenham cemetery on 11 December. Although Edwards had no children, in the 1920s he adopted the son of his niece Elizabeth, Noel Kernick, who took his uncle's name.

Years of hard work and poverty left their mark on Edwards physically. Never tall, he became bent in late middle age, yet continued to cycle hundreds of miles a week on union work during the years between 1906 and 1913. In his later years he was regarded by many as a moderate within the labour movement, yet he remained absolutely unswerving in its cause and even in 1931 fought hard against what he regarded as MacDonald's 'betrayal of the whole working class movement' (N. Edwards). He also remained an active Primitive Methodist, despite the fact that his own uncompromising Christian socialism was increasingly out of place in a Church which had forgotten its radical past. He was remembered, even in the 1970s, with enormous affection and respect by the generation of Norfolk farmworkers who had grown up in the bitter years before 1930. The fact that Norfolk continued to return a Labour MP until 1970—the only rural area so to do—is perhaps some reflection of the importance of Edwards's contribution to the history of farmworkers' trade unionism and rural labour in the area.

ALUN HOWKINS

Sources G. Edwards, *From crow-scaring to Westminster* (1922) · A. Howkins, *Poor labouring men: rural radicalism in Norfolk, 1870–1923* (1985) · N. Edwards, 'Ploughboy's progress', biography, unpublished MS · P. Hollis, *Ladies elect: women in English local government, 1865–1914* (1987)
Archives Norfolk RO | U. Reading, Records of National Union of Agricultural and Allied Workers
Likenesses C. Harris, photograph, repro. in Edwards, *From crow-scaring*, frontispiece [*see illus.*]
Wealth at death £10

Edwards, George Nelson (1828–1868), physician, a son of George Edwards, surgeon, was born at Eye, Suffolk, in June 1828, and received his school education in the grammar schools of Yarmouth and Beccles. He obtained a Tancred studentship at Gonville and Caius College, Cambridge, for 1846–7, and graduated MB in 1851. After studying at St Bartholomew's Hospital, London, he obtained in 1854 the licence in medicine then given by the University of Cambridge, and in 1859 he became MD. He was elected assistant physician to St Bartholomew's Hospital in 1860, was secretary to the medical council of the hospital from 14 January 1865 to 9 February 1867, and was in 1866 elected lecturer on forensic medicine in the medical school. He also held the office of medical registrar, and he was elected physician to the hospital on 23 January 1867.

However, Edwards did not hold the post for long. One day, while doing ward rounds, he collapsed in a uraemic convulsion. He was found to have chronic Bright's disease, as a result of which he lost his sight, but so gradually that he did not know when he had totally ceased to see. He was a small man, who had been bullied at school, teased at Cambridge, and envied at St Bartholomew's for the success which was the reward of perseverance rather than of ability. He acquired a considerable practice and seemed assured of a long career when his fatal illness began. He bore it heroically, and complained just once, and then only to remark that a candidate for his post was perhaps too anxious to succeed him. He died on 6 December 1868 at his home, 20 Finsbury Square, London.

Edwards edited the first three volumes of the *St Bartholomew's Hospital Reports*, between 1865 and 1867, and published in 1862 *The Examination of the Chest in a Series of Tables*. He described two cases of poisoning by mercuric methide, the symptoms of which were then new to medicine (*St Bartholomew's Hospital Reports*, 1, 1865, 141). He also wrote the paper, 'On the value of palpation in the diagnosis of tubercular disease of the lungs' (ibid., 2, 1866, 216).

NORMAN MOORE, *rev.* MICHAEL BEVAN

Sources *St Bartholomew's Hospital Reports*, 5 (1869), 1–2 · Venn, *Alum. Cant.* · private information (1888) · *CGPLA Eng. & Wales* (1868)
Wealth at death under £2000: probate, 26 Dec 1868, *CGPLA Eng. & Wales*

Edwards, Sir (John) Goronwy (1891–1976), historian, was born on 14 May 1891 in Salford, Lancashire, the only child of John William Edwards, railway signalman, the descendant of Welsh farmers in the Vale of Clwyd, and his wife, Emma Pickering, the daughter of an English miner. The family moved back to Flintshire in 1893; the son spoke and read Welsh before he did English. He attended Halkyn national school and then Holywell county school. Edwards was a Welsh foundation scholar in modern history of Jesus College, Oxford, from 1909 and gained first class honours in history in 1913—a year late because of illness. He did research at Manchester University from 1913 to 1915, when he enlisted in the Royal Welch Fusiliers. Of his war service in France as an officer in their Pioneer battalion he did not easily speak. He was demobilized with the rank of captain, and had first shown his administrative capacity during a period as adjutant.

In 1919 Edwards was elected a fellow of Jesus College and tutor in modern history. As a tutor he was incisive, humorous, and helpful, ranging with ease from Claudius to Charles II (he had been *proxime accessit* in the Stanhope prize competition with an essay on Danby in 1913). He allowed no pretentiousness: to an undergraduate foolish enough to use the word 'transcendental' in a political thought essay he urged 'Oh no, not that. We leave that to the philosophers'. Edwards's pupils did consistently well in prize competitions and their final examination, and his help to them continued long afterwards. His university lectures, especially those on Stubbs's *Select Charters* and their unpublished sequel on fourteenth-century constitutional history, were renowned; judicious, perhaps almost too measured, but supremely clear, especially when arguing a case, they set many problems for examiners. As tutor, lecturer (officially so from 1928 to 1936 and in 1947–8), or writer, he always left a message. His three heroes were his tutor C. T. Atkinson of Exeter College, T. F. Tout, who supervised his research at Manchester, and 'the great Reginald Lane Poole', former editor of the *English Historical Review*. As joint editor of the *Review* from 1938 to 1959 Edwards more than sustained its high reputation; his

Sir (John) Goronwy Edwards (1891–1976), by Walter Stoneman, 1946

comments to would-be contributors were terse but constructive. His diligent and conscientious discharge of these and other duties undoubtedly limited his own historical work, considerable though that was.

Edwards held various offices in his college in turn; but its highest prize was denied him, as was the Oxford regius chair of modern history. In 1948 came the inevitable summons elsewhere, to the directorship of the Institute of Historical Research and a concomitant professorship of history in the University of London. The director's obligations to the institute's students (whose numbers expanded vastly) and to the learned world at large were many, but all were successfully and meticulously discharged; among them was the editorship of the institute's *Bulletin*.

Edwards's writings dominated the study of two subjects, medieval Wales and the medieval English parliament. As a Welshman who made his career in England, he saw a supreme contrast between the multiple kingship of Wales (taken over by the Normans in the *marchia Walliae*) and the strong single kingship of England; this in the thirteenth century created an omnicompetent *parliamentum* which was one root of the omnicompetence of the Commons by whom that *parliamentum* was afforced. He imparted his message mainly in numerous articles and in the introductions to his editions of texts vital for Anglo-Welsh history. His technical skill and robust common sense were equally evident in his examination of the *plena potestas* formula in the published early parliamentary

writs of summons (*Essays Presented to H. E. Salter*, 1934) and in his investigation of the record evidence for 'Edward I's castle-building in Wales' (*PBA*, 32, 1946).

Edwards was of medium height and broad in build; he had a round, cheerful face and searching eyes. His academic activities, his alertness, geniality, and sense of humour, and his exertions at golf gave little idea of the rheumatism which long troubled him. (Other interests were photography and music.) He became to many generations of Jesus men, whether historians or not, and especially perhaps to the former soldiers of two wars, increasingly the personification of the college, of which he was made an honorary fellow in 1949; his high regard for the standing of his college made English members as fervent as Welsh in their affection for its special characteristics. He served the principality, and Flintshire in particular, long and loyally, especially on the Royal Commission on the Ancient and Historical Monuments of Wales and Monmouthshire and on the Ancient Monuments Board for Wales; he was proud of being Welsh, but for Welsh nationalism he had no time. He edited leading periodicals, and presided over the Institute of Historical Research, both with distinction, at a time of special importance for historical studies. He was a shrewd, lucid, exact, and original scholar, a lively personality, and a most fair-minded man.

Edwards had been made FBA in 1943, and was given honorary doctorates by four universities and an Oxford DLitt in 1960. He was Ford's lecturer at Oxford in 1960–61, the title of his lectures being 'The second century of the English parliament' (printed in 1979). He also gave the Rhys (1944), Raleigh (1956), David Murray (1955), and Creighton (1957) lectures. He was elected FSA in 1959 and was knighted on his retirement from the Institute of Historical Research in 1960. From 1961 to 1964 he was president of the Royal Historical Society. He remained active until three months before his death.

His marriage in 1925 to Gwladys (d. 1982), daughter of the Revd William Williams (also of Halkyn), was supremely happy, and their hospitality was inexhaustible. They had no children. Edwards died in London at Queen Mary's Hospital, Roehampton, on 20 June 1976.

J. F. A. MASON, rev.

Sources *The Times* (21 June 1976) · *Archaeologia Cambrensis*, 125 (1977), 174–7 · *BIHR*, 49 (1976), 155–8 · D. Hay, 'Goronwy Edwards', *EngHR*, 91 (1976), 721–2 · J. S. Roskell, 'John Goronwy Edwards, 1891–1976', *PBA*, 64 (1978), 359–96 · *Welsh History Review / Cylchgrawn Hanes Cymru*, 8 (1976–7), 466–74 · personal knowledge (1986) · private information (1986) · *CGPLA Eng. & Wales* (1976)
Archives NL Wales, research papers | NL Wales, letters to Sir Thomas Parry-Williams
Likenesses W. Stoneman, photograph, 1946, NPG [see illus.] · B. F. Walker, pencil drawing, Jesus College, Oxford · photograph, Institute of Historical Research, London
Wealth at death £59,350: probate, 29 Oct 1976, *CGPLA Eng. & Wales*

Edwards, Henry Sutherland (1828–1906), author and journalist, was born at Hendon on 5 September 1828, the eldest in a family of three sons and three daughters of John Edwards, and his wife, Harriet Exton Teale Morris.

After an education at the Brompton grammar school and in France, where he acquired a full command of the language, Edwards began contributing to *Pasquin*, a small weekly rival of *Punch*, which lasted from August to October 1847, and to another short-lived rival of *Punch*, the *Puppet Show*, which the firm of Vizetelly started in March 1848. On the recommendation of Gilbert è Beckett he joined the staff of *Punch* in 1848, albeit briefly. Not until 1880 did he renew his association with that journal as an occasional contributor.

Edwards early collaborated with Robert Barnabas Brough in writing for the London stage an extravaganza, *Mephistopheles, or, An Ambassador from below*. He also collaborated with Augustus Septimus Mayhew in 1851, and later, in producing light dramatic pieces, including *The Goose with the Golden Eggs*, a farce (1859), and *The Four Cousins*, a comic drama (1871). Edwards meanwhile found employment in varied branches of serious journalism. He was in Paris during the *coup d'état* of 1852, and in 1856 he went to Russia as correspondent of the *Illustrated Times* to describe the coronation of Tsar Alexander II. He remained at Moscow for some time to study the language, and was soon well versed in Russian politics and literature. On 2 February 1857 he married in the English church, Moscow, Margaret, daughter of Thomas Watson, a Scottish engineer settled in Russia.

Returning to England he published *The Russians at Home* (1861), sketches of Russian life. In 1862 and 1863 he was correspondent for *The Times* in Poland and witnessed the insurrection, until his friendly relations with the insurgents led to his expulsion. His experiences were embodied in a *Private History of a Polish Insurrection* (2 vols., 1865). After revisiting Moscow and St Petersburg he produced *Polish captivity, an account of the present position of the Poles in Austria, Prussia and Russia* (2 vols., 1863). *The Times* sent him to Luxembourg in 1867, and also to accompany the German army during the Franco-Prussian War of 1870–71. His observations were collected as *The Germans in France, Notes on the Method and Conduct of the Invasion*. A close observer of Balkan affairs, he republished, in 1876, a series of papers contributed to the *Pall Mall Gazette* under the general title *The Sclavonian Provinces of Turkey*. In 1885 his *Russian Projects Against India from the Czar Peter the Great to Skobeleff* appeared. Edwards also wrote music history and criticism. A *History of Opera* (2 vols.) appeared in 1862; *The Lyrical Drama* and *Rossini and his School*, both in 1881; together with lives of Rossini (1869) and Sims Reeves (1881).

Edwards was the first editor of the *Graphic* (1869). In 1877 he launched *Portrait*, a magazine featuring photographs and biographical notices of notable figures, which ran to only fifteen numbers. He (or more probably his wife) also wrote fiction, a first novel, *The Three Louisas*, appearing in 1866. Six others followed, one drawing on Margaret Edwards's Russian childhood. The last, *The Dramatist's Dilemma* (1898), was written in collaboration with Florence Marryat. His later years were largely devoted to translations of French and Russian authors. A busy compiler to the end Edwards brought out *The Romanoffs, Tzars of Moscow*

and Emperors of Russia (1890), *Personal Recollections* (1900), and, in 1902, a life of Sir William White, English ambassador at Constantinople. He died at his house, 9 Westbourne Terrace Road, London, on 21 January 1906, and was buried at St John's cemetery, Woking. His wife survived him, and one son, Gilbert Sutherland Edwards.

[ANON.], *rev.* CHANDRIKA KAUL

Sources H. S. Edwards, *Personal recollections* (1900) • private information (1912) • H. Vizetelly, *Glances back through seventy years: autobiographical and other reminiscences*, 2 vols. (1893) • M. H. Spielmann, *The history of 'Punch'* (1895) • Grove, *Dict. mus.* • J. Sutherland, *The Longman companion to Victorian fiction* (1988)
Archives News Int. RO, papers

Edwards, Henry Thomas (1837–1884), dean of Bangor, was born on 6 September 1837 at Llanymawddwy, Merioneth, the third son of the Revd William Edwards, rector of that parish (*d.* 1868) and his wife, Sarah (*née* Wood). His youngest brother was Alfred George *Edwards (1848–1937), first archbishop of Wales. Henry was educated at home until his fifteenth year, when he entered Westminster School, where he was a Welsh 'bishop's boy' holding the Williams exhibition. He left Westminster after ten months because his father could not afford to pay the fees, and he spent two unsettled years at home. He considered an army career in India, but, changing his mind, studied under the Revd F. E. Gretton at Stamford grammar school before entering Jesus College, Oxford, in 1857. He took his BA in 1860, taught briefly at Llandovery College, and in 1861 became curate at Llangollen to his father, who being an invalid left almost sole charge of the parish to his son. He restored the church at an expense of £3000.

In 1866 Edwards was appointed vicar of the large parish of Aberdâr, where, during his residence of three years, he built a new church at Cwmaman. The bishop of Chester presented him to the important vicarage of Caernarfon in 1869, where he proved to be a great pastor in spite of indifferent health. He built St David's Church in the town. While at Caernarfon he organized a series of public meetings to protest against the exclusion of religious education from primary schools. He suffered two shattering bereavements while he was at Caernarfon. His first wife, Mary Davis, whom he had married at Aberdâr in 1867, died in August 1871, leaving one daughter, and his second wife, Anne-Dora Jones, whom he had married in 1873, died in 1875, leaving two daughters.

Edwards was appointed dean of Bangor in March 1876, when he was only thirty-eight. He amply justified his appointment: he took a foremost part, as a vigorous controversialist, in defence of the church, at a time when disestablishment was becoming a very live issue, and he especially promoted the work of the Bangor Clerical Education Society, which aimed to supply the diocese with educated clergy able to minister efficiently in the Welsh language, spoken by more than three-quarters of the population. He gained great fame as a preacher, in Welsh and English, in spite of having a harsh and unmusical voice. He was energetic in restoring Bangor Cathedral, and in a short time raised £7000, which included a substantial contribution from himself. His enthusiastic support for the University College of North Wales at Bangor is commemorated by a bust and a prize in the college.

Among Edwards's many publications, mainly sermons and disestablishment pamphlets, the most influential was a letter entitled *The Church of the Cymry*, addressed to W. E. Gladstone in January 1870, in which Edwards blamed the alienation of the great majority of the Welsh people from the established church on the appointment of English bishops in Wales. Subsequently, all bishops in Wales from then until disestablishment were Welsh-speaking. Edwards's major works were republished, with a memoir of his life, in *Wales and the Welsh Church* in 1889. He was best known to the public, however, for his onslaught on the tea-drinking habits of Victorian society, which he held to be the cause of 'the general physical deterioration of the inhabitants of these islands', although these words were apparently said in jest at a public meeting. In 1883 he suffered from sleeplessness and nervousness, and was seriously depressed; he went for a long cruise in the Mediterranean, but with little benefit to his health. He committed suicide on 24 May 1884, when he was staying with his elder brother at Ruabon vicarage, Denbighshire, and was buried at Glanadda cemetery in Bangor on 28 May. St David's Church, Bangor, was built in his memory.

G. C. BOASE, *rev.* D. T. W. PRICE

Sources H. T. Edwards, *Wales and the Welsh church* (1889) · *The Times* (26 May 1884) · *The Times* (29 May 1884) · *The Times* (11 June 1884) · R. O. Roberts, 'The life and work of Dean H. T. Thomas', MA diss., U. Wales, 1977 · R. O. Roberts, 'The life and work of Dean Henry Thomas Edwards, 1837–84', *Transactions of the Caernarvonshire Historical Society*, 40 (1979), 135–60 · J. Vyrnwy Morgan, ed., *Welsh religious leaders in the Victorian era* (1905), 58–85 · *Yr Haul* (1884), 288 · T. R. Roberts, *Eminent Welshmen: a short biographical dictionary* (1908), 73–4 · *Red Dragon*, 6 (1884), 385–404 · *ILN* (31 May 1884) · J. G. Williams, *The University College of North Wales: foundations 1884–1927* (1985), 69 · Crockford (1882) · *CGPLA Eng. & Wales* (1884)

Likenesses Annan and Swan, photograph, repro. in Edwards, *Wales and the Welsh church*, frontispiece · J. M. Griffin, bust, U. Wales, Bangor · photograph (*Mr Fradelle of Regent Street*), repro. in *ILN* · photograph, repro. in Morgan, *Welsh religious leaders*, facing p. 58

Wealth at death £4803 13s. 9d.: resworn probate, Dec 1884, *CGPLA Eng. & Wales*

Edwards, Hilton Robert Hugh (1903–1982), actor and theatre director, was born on 2 February 1903 at 1 Bathurst Mansions, 460 Holloway Road, London, the only child of Thomas George Cecil Edwards (*d.* 1910), a district magistrate in India, and his second wife, Emily Murphy (*d.* 1926), a woman of Irish descent. He lost his father at the age of seven when the unfortunate man died as a result of a pigsticking incident in India. Young Bobby Edwards, as he was then called, was educated at East Finchley grammar school, Middlesex and, briefly, at St Aloysius College, Highgate, Middlesex, a college for Roman Catholic boys.

After a brief spell in the machine-gun corps and on army reserve, Hilton Edwards began his acting career in 1921 when he was employed as assistant stage manager and walk-on actor with Charles Doran, a Shakespearian actor–manager. From this he progressed in 1922 to the Old Vic Theatre in London, where he remained for three years,

acting and singing in a number of increasingly important Shakespearian roles. The turning point in Edwards's life came in June 1927 when he was engaged by Anew MacMaster for his Intimate Theatre Company tour of Ireland. MacMaster's travelling company presented Shakespeare in the small towns of Ireland and included in the company was MacMaster's brother-in-law, Micheál *MacLiammóir (born Alfred Lee Willmore) (1899–1978).

Edwards and MacLiammóir immediately became lovers and this was the beginning of a lifelong partnership. Drawn together by a shared enthusiasm for modern theatre, they made plans during the summer of 1927 to move to Dublin and to set up a permanent company, directing and designing works of contemporary drama. The handsome and flamboyant MacLiammóir, a former child actor and self-invented Irishman, was the perfect partner and foil for the pragmatic and determined Edwards. Edwards's abilities as a director and actor were perfectly complemented by MacLiammóir's flair for acting, writing, and design. This enduring relationship as Ireland's most visible and much-loved gay couple was one of the most remarkable features of their career.

This career began on 14 October 1928 with the first Gate Theatre Studio production at the Peacock Theatre, next to W. B. Yeats's Abbey Theatre in Dublin. They presented the Irish première of Ibsen's *Peer Gynt*, with Edwards directing and also taking the title role, and with MacLiammóir as designer. They followed up the success of this first play by producing Wilde's *Salome*, another première for Irish theatre. Edwards's skill as a director was confirmed by his championship of a rejected Abbey play, Denis Johnston's *The Old Lady Says 'No'!*, which opened in June 1929. Johnston's masterpiece was the Gate Theatre Studio's greatest artistic and commercial success at this point, allowing them to find a permanent theatre in the Rotunda Assembly Rooms, an eighteenth-century hall at the north end of Dublin's O'Connell Street.

Edwards and MacLiammóir lived at 4 Harcourt Terrace in the centre of Georgian Dublin and this remained their permanent base for the rest of their lives. Over the next forty years Edwards acted and directed at the Gate Theatre. One of his most important discoveries as a director was the sixteen-year-old Orson Welles, on a visit to Dublin in 1931 as part of a European vacation and already eager to act. Edwards cast Welles in a series of plays during the Gate Theatre's winter season of 1931–2 and this began a lifelong association between Welles and the Dublin Gate Theatre. In his film version of *Othello* (1950) Welles cast Edwards as Rodrigo and MacLiammóir as Iago, the novelty of film acting for Edwards being only somewhat marred by scant payment of salary. To compensate, Welles agreed to narrate a short film, *Return to Glenascaul*, directed by Edwards and released in 1950. Edwards's other important excursion into cinema came in 1961 when he appeared in *Victim*, a ground-breaking film about homosexuality directed by Basil Dearden and starring Dirk Bogarde and Sylvia Syms. In 1958 Edwards published *The Mantle of Harlequin*, an entertaining but autobiographically uninformative account of his life and his work in the theatre.

Perhaps the greatest artistic achievement for Hilton Edwards came in 1960 with *The Importance of being Oscar*, a one-man show on the life and the writings of Oscar Wilde, devised and directed by Edwards and performed by Mac-Liammóir. This show, described by Bernard Levin as 'a beautiful flower on his [Wilde's] grave' (Fitz-Simon, 232), was a crucial text in rehabilitating Oscar Wilde for a general theatre audience. Such was its popularity that it toured in Ireland, Britain, America, South Africa, and Latin America, and was eventually televised. Edwards's talents as a director found a new medium in 1961 when he was appointed head of drama at the new Irish television station, Radio Telefís Éireann. In 1973, as a mark of affection from their adopted city, Edwards and MacLiammóir were made freemen of Dublin, and when MacLiammóir died in 1978 the president of Ireland attended the funeral and paid his respects to Edwards as acknowledged life partner and chief mourner. Edwards died of diverticulitis at the Royal City of Dublin Hospital on 18 November 1982 and was buried by MacLiammóir's side, in St Fintan's cemetery, Howth, Dublin, on 22 November. After their deaths the Gate Theatre continued to flourish as a living presence in Dublin's artistic life.　　　　EIBHEAR WALSHE

Sources C. Fitz-Simon, *The boys: a double biography* (1994) · H. Edwards, *The mantle of Harlequin* (1958) · M. O'hAodha, *The importance of being Michael* (Kerry, 1990) · M. MacLiammóir, *All for Hecuba* (1947) · H. Edwards, introduction, *The importance of being Oscar* (Dublin, 1978) · M. MacLiammóir, *Put money in thy purse* (1952)

Archives Irish Theatre Archive, Dublin · NL Ire. · Northwestern University, Chicago, Dublin Gate Theatre archive, MSS · Northwestern University, Illinois, MSS | FILM BFI NFTVA, documentary footage · BFI NFTVA, performance footage · RTE archive, television plays | SOUND BL NSA, performance recordings · Radio Telefís Éireann, Dublin, archives

Likenesses photograph, repro. in Edwards, *Mantle of Harlequin*

Wealth at death £101,192: probate, 31 March 1983, *CGPLA Éire*

Edwards, Hugh Robert Arthur (1906–1972), oarsman, was born at Westcote Barton, Oxfordshire, on 17 November 1906, the fifth of six children (and fourth son) of the Revd Robert Stephen Edwards, rector of Westcote Barton, and his wife, Annie van Mottman. He was educated at Westminster School and Christ Church, Oxford, where his studies (1925–6, 1929–31) were interrupted by a spell as a schoolmaster. Edwards married in 1934 Michele Lydia Rosemary Williams, daughter of Major John Williams of the Royal Fusiliers. They had two sons: David, who rowed for Oxford in 1958–9, and John (d. 1983), a distinguished agronomist. Edwards was commissioned in the RAF in 1931 and was promoted squadron leader in 1938. He was awarded the AFC in 1943 in recognition of his feat of airmanship in bringing home a badly damaged Hampden from one of the thousand bomber raids on Cologne, and the DFC in 1944. While commanding a squadron of Liberators on convoy escort duty he suffered the loss of three engines but successfully brought his aircraft down in the sea off the Cornish coast and escaped by sculling his rubber dinghy into the shipping lanes. His outstanding achievement, for which he was officially commended, was his command of 53 squadron, which he took over

when his brother Cecil Theodore Edwards (1905–1940) was killed. He retired from the RAF in 1956 with the rank of group captain.

Edwards was well known as a racing pilot flying his own aircraft, and was placed second in the king's cup air race in 1933. His elder brother Cecil had won the race four years earlier. It was as an oarsman, however, and later as a rowing coach, that Edwards, who was known affectionately and almost universally as Jumbo, is likely to be longest remembered. After rowing for Westminster School he gained his blue as a freshman at Oxford in 1926 (he rowed again in the losing Oxford crew of 1930), but collapsed half-way along Chiswick eyot. It was said at the time that he had outgrown his strength. In the following year, rowing for London Rowing Club, he reached the final of the Grand Challenge Cup at Henley regatta. He won the grand in 1930, and in 1931 achieved his most remarkable Henley success, never since repeated, by winning three finals in the same day.

In 1930 Edwards rowed for England and won a gold medal in the empire games in Hamilton, Canada. But the crowning achievement of his rowing career came in the Olympic games in Los Angeles in 1932. Selected to represent Great Britain in the coxless pairs, with his Christ Church partner, Lewis Clive, Edwards was called on during the Olympic regatta to take the place of a sick member of the Thames Rowing Club coxless four, and went on to win two gold medals for rowing in the same day.

Edwards coached Oxford nineteen times between 1949 and 1972, with five wins in this era when Cambridge were generally dominant. However, he undoubtedly sowed the seeds which led to Oxford's resurgence in the 1970s. He also coached Britain's Olympic eight, provided by Oxford, in 1960, and was the first national coach to the unsuccessful Nautilus scheme in 1964. As a teacher of rowing Edwards had few equals; he placed a strong emphasis on the orthodox traditions of Dr Edmond Warre. But it was as a technical innovator that he was most widely known, and aroused most controversy. Many of the technical innovations of modern rowing stemmed from Edwards, most notably perhaps the development of long oars and 'spade' blades: Edwards was among the first to appreciate that increasing boat speeds called for more severe gearing. He also pioneered 'interval training'—the practice of conditioning a crew by setting them to row a large number of repetitive short periods at full pressure, rather than longer set distances. He also introduced the use of ergometers to measure and develop physical strength, and strain gauges, accelerometers, and trace recorders to calculate work output throughout the stroke cycle. He described his methods in his autobiographical account of *The Way of a Man with a Blade* (1963).

Since Edwards was second to none in knowledge and expertise, one may wonder why his success rate was not greater. The answer perhaps lies in one flaw in his methodology. He tended to ignore one cardinal rule in experimentation—the need to hold fast to a fixed datum point. By experimenting with longer oars, wider blades, and unfamiliar training schedules, all at the same time, he vitiated logical assessment of the results. Others, following on, reaped the harvest which he had so lavishly sown.

Edwards, who included sailing among his many interests, took part in the first round Britain race in 1966. After his retirement he spent much time in teaching sailing and navigation. He collapsed on board his yacht at Hamble, and died in a Southampton hospital on 21 December 1972.   RICHARD BURNELL, rev.

Sources The Times (23 Dec 1972) · personal knowledge (1986) · private information (1986) · Old Westminsters, vol. 4 · R. Burnell, One hundred and fifty years of the Oxford and Cambridge boat race (1979) · C. Dodd, The Oxford and Cambridge boat race (1983) · CGPLA Eng. & Wales (1973)
Likenesses photograph, repro. in H. R. A. Edwards, The way of a man with a blade (1963), frontispiece
Wealth at death £54,848: probate, 21 Feb 1973, CGPLA Eng. & Wales

Edwards, Humphrey (1582–1658), politician and regicide, was a younger son of Thomas Edwards (d. 1635) of Shrewsbury and Anne, daughter of Humphrey Baskerville, alderman of London, and widow of Stephen Duckett. He was admitted to Shrewsbury School in 1615, and to Gray's Inn in 1633, although he was not called to the bar. In 1623 he married Hester (d. in or before 1658), daughter of Roger Pope of Shropshire. Appointed a gentleman pensioner on 17 February 1637, he served as a minor courtier until the outbreak of civil war, and reportedly attended Charles I during the attempted arrest of the five members in January 1642. Thereafter, he withdrew from the court, along with his close friend Sir Gregory Norton, ensuring a lasting reputation as 'a half faced cavalier' who was guilty of 'changing his party for his profit' (C. Walker). Edwards sought financial support out of the royal revenue in 1644, and was quickly named to a number of local commissions in Shropshire, Middlesex, and Westminster. As a supporter of the New Model Army he was able to secure election to parliament as a recruiter MP in 1646, as a knight of the shire for Shropshire, although his enemies later challenged the propriety of this election.

Edwards rapidly emerged as a zealous supporter of the Independents at Westminster, and became heavily involved in financial and military relations with the City of London. Such issues encouraged the presbyterian counter-revolution in 1647, during which he joined those who fled to the security of the army, and who signed the protestation against the 'forcing of the Houses'. When the Independents returned to Westminster with army support in August 1647, Edwards helped launch the investigation into the recent activity of the presbyterians, and was appointed to the reformed Westminster militia. A busy committee-man in the Commons, he played a prominent part in matters such as peace treaties with Charles I and countering royalist uprisings during the second civil war. Although absent from Westminster in early December 1648, he rapidly returned to the Commons after Pride's Purge, was added to the army committee and the committee for revenue, and played an active role in establishing

the high court of justice to try the king. He was also dispatched to examine William Prynne, in order to investigate his pamphleteering attacks upon the new regime, and reported back to the Commons on 10 January 1649. Having been named as a commissioner for the high court of justice he attended every day of the king's trial and signed the death warrant [see also Regicides].

Throughout the Rump, Edwards was among the most prominent members of the Commons, although he was never elected to the council of state. Having already displayed an interest in the sale of church lands, he was made a commissioner for the sale of bishops' lands in 1649, and for forfeited estates, and was appointed to a number of committees relating to the disposal of the king's goods and the crown lands. He was also appointed to the high court of justice to investigate insurrections in Wales in June 1651. Most controversially, he sought to secure the office of chief usher of the exchequer from Clement Walker, who had already accused Edwards of speculating in the debentures market, and who was imprisoned for his vocal opposition to the Rump. Walker described Edwards as being 'greedy of an office' after he took possession of the post in March 1650, and engaged in a bitter public dispute in which he accused Edwards not only of corruption and greed, but also of incest.

Edwards did not sit in parliament after the expulsion of the Rump, but if he opposed the protectorate he did little to alienate Cromwell or his court. He died, intestate, in 1658 and was buried on 5 August at Richmond, Surrey. His wife predeceased him, and administration of the estate, which included land bequeathed to him by his friend Sir Gregory Norton, was granted to his sister, Lucy, Lady Ottley. Such property was forfeited to the crown in 1660 for Edwards's part in the trial and execution of Charles I.

GORDON GOODWIN, rev. J. T. PEACEY

Sources C. H. Firth and R. S. Rait, eds., Acts and ordinances of the interregnum, 1642–1660, 3 vols. (1911) · JHC, 4–8 (1644–67) · CSP dom., 1649–53 · R. Tresswell and A. Vincent, The visitation of Shropshire, taken in the year 1623, ed. G. Grazebrook and J. P. Rylands, 2 vols., Harleian Society, 28–9 (1889) · E. Calvert, ed., Shrewsbury School regestum scholarium, 1562–1635: admittances and readmittances [1892] · Badminton House, Beaufort Archives, FM H2/4/1, fol. 17v · B. Worden, The Rump Parliament, 1648–1653 (1974) · D. Underdown, Pride's Purge: politics in the puritan revolution (1971) · [C. Walker], The case between Clement Walker, esq. and Humphrey Edwards, truely stated (1650) · [M. Walker], The case of Mrs M. W., the wife of Clement Walker, esq. (1650) · administration, PRO, PROB 6/34, fol. 270 · G. E. Aylmer, The state's servants: the civil service of the English republic, 1649–1660 (1973)
Wealth at death significant landowner: administration, PRO, PROB 6/34, fol. 270

Edwards, Sir Ifan ab Owen (1895–1970), educationist and founder of Urdd Gobaith Cymru, was born on 25 July 1895 at Tremaran, Llanuwchllyn, Merioneth, the second of the three children (the eldest died in infancy) of Sir Owen Morgan *Edwards (1858–1920) and his wife, Ellen Elizabeth Davies (1869–1919). His parents were both Welsh and his father was arguably the most influential Welsh cultural figure at the turn of the century. Up to 1907 he lived in turn at Tremaran and Bryn'r Aber, Llanuwchllyn, and at

3 Clarendon Villas in Oxford, where his father became fellow of Lincoln College, and tutor in history, in 1889.

Edwards was educated at the Dragon School, Oxford, and (after his father's appointment in 1907 as chief inspector of education for Wales and the family's return to live at Neuadd Wen, Llanuwchllyn) at Bala grammar school. He was a student at the University College of Wales, Aberystwyth (1912–15), and after service on the Somme (1915–18) he entered Lincoln College, Oxford, where he gained a distinction in the shortened war-service course in history in 1920. (He gained an MA degree of the University of Wales in 1925.) He taught at Dolgellau grammar school (1920), was appointed part-time tutor in the department of extra-mural studies, University College of Wales, Aberystwyth (1921), then lecturer in the college's department of education (1933) and in 1946 director of extra-mural studies. He relinquished the directorship after two years in order to devote his time to founding Urdd Gobaith Cymru, the Welsh League of Youth. On 18 July 1923 he married Eirys Mary (1897–1981), the daughter of Richard and Mary Jennetta Lloyd Phillips of Liverpool. They had two sons: Owen, controller of BBC Wales (1974–81) and director of S4C (1981–9), and Ifan Prys, chair of the Welsh Tourist Board (1984–92) and of S4C (1992–8).

'Ifan ap' or 'Syr Ifan', as he was known in Wales, was an entrepreneur and visionary of unbounded energy and determination. His inheritance from his father's estate, coupled with his wife's private means, freed him early from the constraints of employed service. But he also inherited his father's love of, and commitment to, Wales and the Welsh language. On his father's death in 1920 he took over editing *Cymru* (1920–27) and *Cymru'r Plant* (1920–50). He also edited *Cronicl yr Urdd* (1928–33), a *Cymru'r Plant* supplement, and a periodical for young people, *Y Capten* (1931–2). In the 1922 issue of *Cymru'r Plant* he announced his grand plan of founding Urdd Gobaith Cymru (Fach), a patriotic but non-political, non-partisan, and non-sectarian movement for the children and youth of Wales. The prime objective was to nurture a love of Wales, pride in the Welsh language, knowledge of the nation's culture, and a sense of Christian responsibility towards all fellow human beings. He worked indefatigably to ensure the success of the movement, enlisting faithful officers and attracting influential and generous patrons. He established an Urdd Gobaith Cymru summer camp at Llanuwchllyn (1928) and permanent camps at Llangrannog, Cardiganshire (1932), and Glan-llyn, Merioneth (1950). He inaugurated the Urdd eisteddfod in 1929, mass gymnastic displays in 1932, and cruises for adults in 1933. A camp for Welsh learners and a football league followed in 1941, an international camp in 1948, and a Celtic camp in 1949. In 1949 he also initiated the first of a series of residential courses at the Pantyfedwen centre, Borth, Cardiganshire.

Activities in all these pioneering ventures were held through the medium of Welsh. So central was Edwards's contribution, through the Urdd Gobaith Cymru movement, to the culture of Wales that according to the editor of the influential periodical *Y Ford Gron* in 1933, historians a century hence would see how crucial the Urdd's founding was to the renaissance of Wales. It was the Urdd movement that afforded Edwards an opportunity in yet another interest inherited from his father—photography and film. From 1933 onwards he filmed major Urdd events, and under the title 'The Welsh cinema' his amateur films were shown in village halls throughout Wales. In 1935 he enlisted the help of the schoolmaster dramatist J. Ellis Williams to make *Y chwarelwr*, based on the lives of the quarrymen of Blaenau Ffestiniog, Merioneth: the first film with a Welsh-language soundtrack. During winter 1935–6 the film was shown five nights a week to packed audiences throughout north Wales. There followed a series of documentary films ranging from Urdd cruises to Norway, Galicia, and Morocco to features on Welsh reels and summer camps. The film-making was part of a crusade to demonstrate that Wales and the Welsh language could meet the challenge of new modes of communication.

In 1939 a new chapter in the history of education in Wales was opened when Edwards established *Ysgol Gymraeg Aberystwyth*, the first Welsh-medium school in Wales. The school reflected his father's belief that all children should be educated through their mother tongue in an environment that drew its inspiration from a nation's culture and history. He believed that this pioneering venture in linking education to the indigenous culture and language of a country was his most important contribution to Wales. One of the great public figures of his generation, Edwards was a member of the Central Advisory Council for Education, of the court of the University of Wales and of the National Museum of Wales, and of the court and council of the University College of Wales, Aberystwyth. He was president of the Union of Teachers of Welsh Schools, vice-president of Coleg Harlech, and consecutively between 1950 and 1967 treasurer, vice-president, and president of the National Library of Wales. He served on the Council for Wales, the council of the Royal National Eisteddfod of Wales, the Pantyfedwen trust, the National Parks Commission, and the Welsh advisory committee of the National Trust. He was a director of Television Wales and the West, where he argued persuasively for the claims of the Welsh language. He served on the Llanbadarn Fawr magistrates' bench between 1941 and 1958, was short-listed as a Liberal candidate for Cardiganshire in 1945, was high sheriff for Cardiganshire in 1950, and a member of the parliament for Wales campaign in the early 1950s. Knighted in 1947, he received the medal of the Honourable Society of Cymmrodorion in 1956 and an honorary LLD degree of the University of Wales in 1959.

In 1956 the Urdd movement presented Edwards with his portrait in oils by Alfred Janes, and after his death his statue in bronze by Jonah Jones (1972) was placed alongside that of his father at Llanuwchllyn. The statue captures the tall, trim, bespectacled figure of one who made a major contribution to the revitalization of Welsh cultural awareness in the twentieth century. In addition to the periodicals already mentioned, he was co-author with

E. Tegla Davies of *Llyfr y bobl bach* (1925), editor of *A Catalogue of Star Chamber Proceedings Relating to Wales* (1929), and author of *Yr Urdd, 1922–43* (1943) and of a short autobiography, 'Clych Atgof': *Wedi Deugain Mlynedd* (1961). He contributed numerous articles to several magazines, including 'The Welsh language, its modern history and its present-day problems' in *Hesperia* (1951). Edwards died, after a long illness, on 23 January 1970 at his home, Bryneithin, Llanbadarn Road, Aberystwyth, and was buried four days later at Llanuwchllyn.   HAZEL WALFORD DAVIES

Sources R. E. Griffith, *Urdd Gobaith Cymru*, 3 vols. (1971–3) · H. W. Davies, ed., *Llythyrau Syr O. M. Edwards ac Elin Edwards, 1887–1920* (1991) · N. Isaac, *Ifan ab Owen Edwards, 1895–1970* (1972) · I. ab Owen Edwards, 'Clych atgof': *wedi deugain mlynedd* (1961) · H. Davies, ed., *Bro a bywyd: Syr O. M. Edwards, 1858–1920* (1988) · M. D. Jones, *Cymwynaswyr y Gymraeg* (1978) · G. L. Jones, *Llyfryddiaeth Ceredigion, 1600–1964: a bibliography of Cardiganshire*, 3 vols. (1967) · G. L. Jones, *Llyfryddiaeth Ceredigion: a bibliography of Cardiganshire, 1964–1968 supplement* (1970) · H. R. Davies, Introduction, *Cofio Syr Ifan* (1970) · E. D. Jones and B. F. Roberts, eds., *Y bywgraffiadur Cymreig, 1951–1970* (1997) · G. Davies, *The story of the Urdd, 1922–1972* (1973) · J. T. Jones, 'Codi Cenedl', *Y Ford Gron*, 3/5 (1932–3), 97 · *CGPLA Eng. & Wales* (1970) · b. cert. · m. cert. · d. cert. · NL Wales, Sir O. M. Edwards papers
Archives NL Wales, corresp. and papers | NL Wales, letters to Thomas Iorwerth Ellis and Annie Hughes-Griffiths · NL Wales, letters to Richard Griffith [in Welsh] · NL Wales, corresp. with W. J. Gruffydd [in Welsh] · NL Wales, corresp. with Norah Isaac · NL Wales, Urdd Gobaith Cymru collection | FILM Wales Film and Television Archive, Aberystwyth
Likenesses A. Janes, oils, 1955, priv. coll.; photograph, NL Wales · J. Jones, bronze bust, 1968, NL Wales · J. Jones, bronze statue, 1972, Llanuwchllyn, Merioneth
Wealth at death £19,117: probate, 22 June 1970, *CGPLA Eng. & Wales*

Edwards, James (1756–1816), book collector and bookseller, was born on 8 September 1756 at Halifax, Yorkshire, the second of the six sons (there were also two daughters) of William *Edwards (*bap.* 1723, *d.* 1808), bookbinder and bookseller of Halifax, and his wife, Jane Green (*d.* 1772). William Edwards's other sons were also involved in the book trade. Thomas Edwards (1762–1834) carried on the family business in Halifax after his father's death until his own retirement in 1826; and Richard Edwards (1768–1827) was a bookseller in Old Bond Street.

The firm Edwards of Halifax became known for its artistry in the execution of three bookbinding techniques: watercolour drawings, usually of landscapes, on the fore-edge of books, that become visible when the pages are fanned; Etruscan bindings in imitation of the colours and designs of Greek or Etruscan vases; and, most notably, ornamental cover designs painted on the underside of transparent vellum.

In 1784 James Edwards and his brother John(*b.* 1758), who evidently died young, were established in business by their father as Edwards & Sons, Pall Mall, London. On 28 January 1785 James Edwards was granted a patent for the under-vellum painting process. At his death, the patent was assigned or transferred to his brother Thomas.

Initially James Edwards purchased and sold at auction a number of fine private libraries of English collectors and antiquaries, but his energies were soon directed to the continent, where he made frequent trips and purchased many libraries. In 1788, with James Robson, he negotiated the purchase of the renowned Pinelli library in Venice, from which Edwards later said he 'derived ... a skill of rare and valuable books' (*Diaries of Sylvester Douglas*, 1.265). Another *coup* was the acquisition of the library called Pâris de Mayzieu, though the attribution is now known to be inaccurate. This important sale, described in *Bibliotheca elegantissima, Parisina* (Paris, 1790) and *Bibliotheca Parisiana* (London, 1791), was conducted over a period of some ninety days in 1791 at sale rooms in Conduit Street, creating great excitement among collectors.

Edwards became 'a sort of literary oracle' (Beloe, 2.279). He published both catalogues and literary works such as the sixth edition of Horace Walpole's *The Castle of Otranto* (Parma, 1791) and William Roscoe's *The Life of Lorenzo de' Medici* (1795 [1796]). Collecting for his private library, he outbid George III in 1786 at the duchess of Portland's sale for the Bedford missal (BL, Add. MS 18850), executed for John, duke of Bedford. His other prized acquisition was the 'Livy on vellum' once owned by Pope Alexander VI, the only known copy on vellum (Sweynheym and Pannartz, Rome, 1469), now in the British Library.

According to Thomas Frognall Dibdin:

> His ambition ... was truly meritorious: he travelled diligently and fearlessly abroad: he was now exploring the book-gloom of dusty monasteries, and at other times marching in the rear or the front of Bonaparte's armies in Italy: he visited almost all the principal public and private collections where he sojourned—and may be fairly said to have carried on his concerns upon a scale as original as it was bold and successful. (Dibdin, *Decameron*, 3.16–17)

At the request of his friend and client Lord Grenville, foreign secretary, Edwards, as a private citizen, journeyed to France in the summer of 1800. His letter to Grenville dated 12 August 1800 provided valuable information about the French political climate. Cordially received by the French in power, Edwards was described by a fellow Englishman as:

> both courteous and courtier-like. They who were less favourably inclined towards him, complained that his enunciation was affectedly soft, and that he had too much of the air and grimace of a Frenchman; and by the shrug of his shoulders, and his facility in speaking the language, has more than once been mistaken for a native of that country. (Beloe, 2.282)

In the autumn of 1800 Edwards made a second unofficial mission to France, this time apparently as a personal favour to the eminent collector Lord Spencer, then first lord of the Admiralty, whom Edwards had assisted in purchasing the library of Count Reviczky. Refusing monetary payment for this act of friendship, he was persuaded by Lord Spencer to accept a collection of twelve miniatures of the Stuart family.

Edwards was retired from the book trade by 1804 and resided in the neighbourhood of Old Verulam, near St Albans, Hertfordshire. He sold a portion of his private collection through Christies, between 25 and 28 April 1804, and on 10 September 1805 married Catherine Ayre Bromhead (*bap.* 1779, *d.* 1863), only daughter of the Revd Edward

Bromhead, rector of Reepham, Lincolnshire, and his wife, Catherine Ayre, with whom he had five children. About this time he acquired the rectory manor house at Harrow on the Hill, Middlesex, former home of some archbishops of Canterbury.

In declining health, Edwards permitted his library to fall under the auction hammer of his successor, Robert Harding Evans, on 5–10 April 1815. Having directed that his coffin be made of strong oak shelves from his library and expressed the wish that his youngest son might become a bookseller, Edwards died at Harrow on 2 January 1816, aged fifty-nine. His widow married the Revd Thomas Butt of Kinnersley, Shropshire, on 18 October 1820. Edwards was Dibdin's 'Rinaldo: the wealthy, the fortunate, and the heroic' (Dibdin, *Decameron*, 3.14), of whom he said 'no man ever did such wonderful things towards the acquisition of rare, beautiful, and truly classical productions in the shape of a BOKE' (ibid., 3.15).

PAGE LIFE

Sources G. E. Bentley jun., 'The bookseller as diplomat: James Edwards, Lord Grenville, and Earl Spencer in 1800', *Book Collector*, 33 (1984), 470–85 • T. W. Hanson, 'Edwards of Halifax, book-binders', *The book handbook*, 6 (1948), 329–38 • T. F. Dibdin, *The bibliographical decameron*, 3 vols. (1817) • *The diaries of Sylvester Douglas (Lord Glenbervie)*, ed. F. Bickley, 2 vols. (1928) • W. Beloe, *The sexegenarian*, 2nd edn, 2 vols. (1818) • *GM*, 1st ser., 85/1 (1815), 135, 254–5, 349 • *GM*, 1st ser., 86/1 (1816), 92, 180–81 • Nichols, *Lit. anecdotes* • Nichols, *Illustrations* • A. Rau, 'Bibliotheca parisina', *Book Collector*, 18 (1969), 307–17 • Walpole, *Corr.* • *The manuscripts of J. B. Fortescue*, 10 vols., HMC, 30 (1892–1927), 289–93 [letter from Edwards to Lord Grenville, 12 Aug 1800, quoted in Bentley, 474–81] • H. M. Nixon and M. M. Foot, *The history of decorated bookbinding in England* (1992) • B. C. Middleton, *A history of English craft bookbinding technique*, 4th rev. edn (1996) • T. F. Dibdin, *Bibliomania, or, Book-madness* (1876) • R. Edwards, 'James Edwards, Giambattista Bodoni, and the castle of Otranto: some unpublished letters', *Publishing History*, 18 (1895), 5–48
Archives Museo Bodoni, Parma, letters | BL, letters to T. Dibdin, Egerton MS 2974, fols. 31, 49 • Bodl. Oxf., SC 39196–39198; 39206; 47562–47580 • Liverpool Public Libraries, letters to William Roscoe [copies in Bodl. Oxf.]
Likenesses P. Turnerelli, sculpture, priv. coll. • F. Wilkin, miniature, priv. coll. • oils, repro. in Bentley, 'The bookseller as diplomat'; priv. coll. • photograph, priv. coll.
Wealth at death very wealthy; large personal estate: will, PRO, PROB 11/1578

Edwards, James Coster (1828–1896), terracotta manufacturer, was born at Trefnant in Denbighshire on 7 November 1828, the son of William Edwards (1797–1877) and his wife, Diana Coster (1796–1875). His father was employed as a clerk at some local coalmines, having originally moved north from Montgomeryshire to transport coal, iron, lime, and slate on the Ellesmere and Montgomeryshire canals. His mother was born at Llanymynech on the border between Shropshire and Montgomeryshire.

After an elementary education, Edwards began work as an apprentice to a draper in Wrexham, leaving to become a storekeeper at the New British Iron Company's works in Acrefair, Denbighshire. From around 1850 he was working clay deposits near Ruabon, at Cefn and Acrefair. At the age of about thirty he was involved in an unsuccessful venture in operating a smelting works. Edwards married

Elizabeth (1833–1920), daughter of Evan Edwards, a draper at Mold, on 24 May 1859. The couple had five daughters and two sons. About 1860 his father bought some coal works, and Edwards used the clay from the seams to make common bricks and earthenware, in a yard where he employed a man and two boys. He became the first to exploit fully the value of the red Ruabon marls and so helped to initiate the recovery of the local economy from the long recession caused by the decline of the iron industry. As the market for architectural and industrial ceramics developed, new works were established and, by the time of its founder's death, the firm employed nearly a thousand men in four large factories. The name of J. C. Edwards was by then widely respected among late Victorian architects and builders, and its ceramics were renowned for their durability and brilliant colours.

A works at Trefnant, located between Ruabon and Llangollen, was bought in the 1860s; it housed the production of encaustic tiles and sanitary pipes and was expanded to cover 6 acres. In 1871 or the following year Edwards took over two kilns at Penybont, to the south of Ruabon and sited by one of the richest clay reserves of the area. This claypit, so rich that it was called the 'clayworkers' Eldorado', was initially used for the manufacture of roofing tiles and facing bricks. The marls proved ideal for being pressed and fired into the bright red terracotta for which the business became famous. Terracotta, large blocks of red or buff clayware moulded with florid decoration, was used on commercial and public buildings in most industrial cities, but most widely in Birmingham, Leeds, and the towns of south Lancashire and Cheshire.

Among the most important contracts that J. C. Edwards supplied were most of the Prudential offices designed by Alfred Waterhouse and the exterior of the assize courts in Birmingham by Aston Webb and Ingress Bell, built 1887–91. For more modest buildings, a range of copings, pier caps, and other components could be ordered from catalogues. While Edwards is supposed to have designed some of the details himself, he also commissioned architects for designs. Douglas and Fordham, for example, were responsible for a range of chimney tops. The Penybont works was extended in response to growing demand, so that it incorporated forty-five kilns and provided employment for five hundred workers in 1896. In 1883 a new works was opened at Coppy, Denbigh, for the manufacture of glazed and enamelled bricks. Pottery making was introduced in the fourth of Edwards's factories, at Plas Kynaston.

After about 1890 Edwards progressively withdrew from the management of his business to pursue responsibilities as a landowner and as a figure within the county. He moved into Trevor Hall near Llangollen and purchased the adjacent West Tower estate. He held office as a justice of the peace, deputy lieutenant, and, in 1892–3, as high sheriff, in the county of Denbigh. In the spring of 1896 he went to Guernsey for a recuperative holiday, but died on 26 March at the Old Government House Hotel. He was buried at Llantysilio church, near Llangollen. His sons, James Coster Edwards (1864–1934) and E. Lloyd Edwards (1860–1956), inherited the business. Terracotta was made on a decreasing scale in the Edwardian and inter-war periods. His grandson, the son of Edward Lloyd, with the name of James Coster Lloyd Edwards (b. 1897), was groomed to take over the business but died of appendicitis in 1930. Flooring tiles and facing bricks made up the bulk of the production until the firm was sold in 1956.

MICHAEL STRATTON

Sources 'Chimney top designs: Douglas and Fordham, Architects', *British Architect*, 43 (1895), 96, 112, 148, 220 [illustrations] · 'Contemporary manufacturers and art workers: J. C. Edwards', *Building News*, 58 (1890), 533 · G. C. Lerry, 'The industries of Denbighshire … part 3: more recent developments', *Transactions of the Denbighshire Historical Society*, 8 (1959), 95–113 · 'Visits to J. C. Edwards' works', *The Builder*, 43 (16 Dec 1882) · private information (2004)
Wealth at death £56,904 1s. 5d.: probate, 11 May 1896, *CGPLA Eng. & Wales*

Edwards, James Keith O'Neill [Jimmy] (1920–1988), actor, was born on 23 March 1920 in Barnes, Surrey, the fifth of five sons and eighth of nine children of Reginald Walter Kenrick Edwards, professor of mathematics at King's College, London, and his wife, Phyllis Katherine Cowan, who was from New Zealand. He was educated at St Paul's Cathedral choir school and at King's College School, Wimbledon, where he first developed what was to become a lifelong enthusiasm for brass instruments and learned to play the trombone. In 1938 he went to St John's College, Cambridge, where he read history and developed a mock 'professor' act for the Cambridge Footlights, in which he gave a musical lecture on the trombone.

Edwards's university career was interrupted by the Second World War, and in 1939 he joined the Royal Air Force, eventually succeeding in his ambition to become a pilot. In 1944 he was flying a hazardous mission towing gliders and dropping supplies to the beleaguered troops at Arnhem when his Dakota was badly hit by a German Focke-Wulf. He made a successful landing, saving the lives of two men on board and sustaining burns to his face which he later disguised by growing the magnificent handlebar moustache that was to become his trademark. He was awarded the DFC in 1945 for his skill and bravery.

Throughout his RAF career Edwards had successfully entertained the troops with his 'professor' act, and so after demobilization in 1946 he contemplated life as an entertainer. He served his apprenticeship at London's Windmill Theatre, where he met Frank Muir, who with Denis Norden was to write his most successful comedy material. In 1948 Muir and Norden created one of Edwards's best loved characters, the bibulous belligerent Pa Glum in the BBC radio comedy programme *Take it from here*, which ran from 1948 until 1959. The programme commanded audiences of more than 20 million and made Edwards a wealthy man. He bought polo ponies, an aeroplane, and a farm in Fittleworth, Sussex, which was run by his elder brother Alan while Edwards played the local squire. Fox-hunting was one of his favourite pastimes, and he was proud to be made master of foxhounds of the Old

James Keith O'Neill [Jimmy] **Edwards** (1920–1988), by Vivienne, 1965–70

Surrey and Burstow hunt. In 1951 he was elected lord rector of Aberdeen University, an appointment he held until 1954.

From 1957 until 1977 Edwards appeared in *Does the Team Think?*, a radio panel game he had devised in which four comedians answered light-hearted questions from a studio audience. He attempted some 'straight' acting, turning in a creditable Sir Toby Belch in *Twelfth Night* and Falstaff in *The Merry Wives of Windsor* for BBC radio (both 1962). On television he found a tailor-made role in the series *Whack-o!* (1957–61 and 1971–2), in which he played the corpulent, conniving headmaster of Chiselbury School. His films included *Three Men in a Boat* (1957), *Bottoms up* (1960), *The Plank* (1979), and *It's your Move* (1982). Perhaps most surprising of all, in 1964 he stood as Conservative candidate for Paddington North, and although he did not win his seat, he polled 10,639 votes—more than his predecessor had gained.

Edwards's private life was less satisfactory. In 1958 he married Valerie, a British Overseas Airways Corporation ground steward, daughter of William Seymour, small landowner. They had no children and eventually divorced in 1969. She later told the press that on their honeymoon he had admitted that he was a homosexual 'trying to reform'. In 1976 Ramon Douglas, an Australian female impersonator, told the tabloid newspapers that for the past ten years he and Edwards had shared a 'loving relationship'. Even though he was personally devastated by the resulting publicity, Edwards found that his career did not suffer, and in 1978 he was invited to reinvent his Pa

Glum character when the Glums were revived for television. In 1984 he published his memoirs, *Six of the Best*, which followed an earlier autobiography, *Take it from me* (1953).

By the early 1980s Edwards's blustering style of comedy was going out of fashion and he concentrated on touring in plays such as *Big Bad Mouse* with his friend Eric Sykes. He spent more time in the house he had bought in Perth, Western Australia, and it was there in 1988 that he became ill with bronchial pneumonia. He returned to England and died in the Cromwell Hospital, London, on 7 July 1988. VERONICA DAVIS, rev.

Sources J. Edwards, *Take it from me* (1953) · J. Edwards, *Six of the best* (1984) · *The Times* (11 July 1988) · private information (1996) · *CGPLA Eng. & Wales* (1989)
Likenesses Vivienne, photograph, 1965–70, NPG [see illus.]
Wealth at death £241,586: probate, 10 July 1989, *CGPLA Eng. & Wales*

Edwards, John (b. 1600, d. late 1650s), university teacher and physician, was born on 27 February 1600. Educated at Merchant Taylors' School, London, he was in 1617 elected to a probationary fellowship at St John's College, Oxford, where he gained the favour of the president, William Laud.

In 1632 Laud, now bishop of London, obtained for Edwards, by 'special recommendation and request', the headmastership of Merchant Taylors' School. He resigned this post at the end of 1634, and returned to Oxford, where he served the university as proctor in the following year. In 1636 he was appointed Sedleian reader of natural philosophy, and proceeded to the degrees of BM and DM. In 1639 he defended in disputations on medicine the proposition that supper 'ought to be more copious than dinner' (*Hist. U. Oxf.*, 4: *17th-cent. Oxf.*, 527).

From the later 1630s Edwards appears to have resided in college while practising medicine in Oxford, and in 1642 was, with others, appointed by convocation to provide accommodation for soldiers sent to the city, and to obtain weapons to help defend the university. His loyalty to the king led in 1647 to his being summoned, as a delinquent, to appear before the committee of Lords and Commons for regulating the affairs of the university, and in 1648 he was placed by the university visitors for a time in custody of the provost marshal for 'manifold misdemeanours'. His fellowship was taken from him, and the office of Sedleian reader was given to Joshua Crosse of Magdalen College. He was, however, permitted to receive the payments due to the readership until Michaelmas 1649, after which he seems to have remained as a medical practitioner in Oxford until his death in the late 1650s.

C. J. ROBINSON, rev. S. E. MEALOR

Sources C. J. Robinson, ed., *A register of the scholars admitted into Merchant Taylors' School, from AD 1562 to 1874*, 2 vols. (1882–3) · M. Burrows, ed., *The register of the visitors of the University of Oxford, from AD 1647 to AD 1658*, CS, new ser., 29 (1881) · Wood, *Ath. Oxon.: Fasti* (1815), 477, 508–9 · W. H. Stevenson and H. E. Salter, *The early history of St John's College, Oxford*, OHS, new ser., 1 (1939) · *Hist. U. Oxf.* 4: *17th-cent. Oxf.*, 525, 527

Edwards, John [pseud. Siôn Treredyn] (1605/6–1656), translator, was born on the banks of the Severn at Caldicot in the Vale of Gwent 'Ile y mae Saesoniaith yn drech na'r Brittaniaith' ('a place where the English language was superior to the British'; J. Edwards, *Madruddyn y difinyddiaeth diweddaraf*, 1651, introduction). In 1624, at the age of eighteen, he matriculated from Jesus College, Oxford; he obtained his BA in 1626 and MA in 1629, in which year he was appointed to the Monmouthshire living of Llanmartin. In 1633 he was appointed to Tredunnock or Treredynog, from which he took his pseudonym of Siôn Treredyn. He held this living until he was ejected in 1649, his expulsion predating by several months the founding of the Commission for the Better Propagation of the Gospel in Wales, which subsequently installed Walter Prosser, a noted Welsh Baptist minister, at Tredunnock.

Though deprived of his living, Edwards continued to live in his former parish until his death. He completed a translation of Edward Fisher's *Marrow of Modern Divinity* into Welsh, which was published at Bristol in 1651 under the title *Madruddyn y difinyddiaeth diweddaraf*, and dedicated to a number of leading families in Gwent. The preface lamented the fact that while Welsh speakers who moved to London or Gloucester quickly picked up basic English, few academics or leading churchmen in Wales could read or write in Welsh. The purpose of the book was to remedy this defect by encouraging the production of books in the Welsh language. Unfortunately no other significant work of literature in Welsh appeared until 1701.

The book consists of a conversation between Evangelista, a minister of the gospel; Nomista, a strong supporter of the Law; Antinomista, who belittled the Law; and Neophytus, a young Christian. Later scholars have commented on the translator's problems with mutations and the gender of nouns, confirming the decline of the Welsh language in Gwent at that time.

Little is known about Edwards's personal circumstances. He died in December 1656 at Tredunnock; his will, proved at Canterbury in January 1657, mentions a wife, Elizabeth, and three daughters, Anne, Elizabeth, and Susan, who all survived him. A brother, Seth, was his executor. MARTIN E. SPEIGHT

Sources *DWB* · J. C. Morrice, *Wales in the seventeenth century* (1918), 165–6 · T. Rees, *History of protestant nonconformity in Wales* (1883), 77 · W. J. Gruffydd, *Llenyddiaeth Cymru* (1926), 128–31 · *Seren Gomer* (1901), 151 · Foster, *Alum. Oxon.* · will, PRO, PROB 11/27, sig. 42

Edwards, John (1637–1716), Church of England clergyman, was born at Hertford on 26 February 1637, the second son of Thomas *Edwards (c.1599–1648), Church of England clergyman and religious controversialist. From 1647 he attended Merchant Taylors' School under William Dugard. On 10 March 1654 he was admitted as a sizar at St John's College, Cambridge, where the president, Dr Anthony Tuckney, a presbyterian, was impressed with his conduct and abilities. After graduating BA in 1658 Edwards was admitted to a fellowship on 23 March 1659, and he proceeded MA in 1661. He was ordained as a deacon in the diocese of Lincoln on 11 September 1662 and preached the sermon at his own ordination as a priest on the 21st of that month. In 1664 he was admitted as minister of Holy Trinity, Cambridge, where his plain preaching found favour. During the plague of 1665 he is reported to have left his rooms in St John's and moved to the town in order to minister to the sick; these efforts were much praised in the parish. Soon after graduating BD in 1668 he was chosen as lecturer at Bury St Edmunds with a salary of £100 per annum, but after about a year he resigned his lectureship and returned to his college.

However, Edwards's rigid high Calvinistic views brought growing friction with Tuckney's successors at St John's, Peter Gunning, who became bishop of Chichester in 1669, and Francis Turner. He eventually resigned his fellowship and entered Trinity Hall as a fellow-commoner, performing the regular exercises in civil law. Shortly afterwards, about 1670, he became minister of St Sepulchre's, Cambridge, on the invitation of the parishioners, and married the widow of Alderman Lane, a Cambridge attorney. In 1683 he was presented by Sir Thomas Audley to the vicarage of St Peter's, Colchester, a church which the mayor and aldermen of the town were accustomed to attend. It seems that his style and views did not meet with the approval of other clergymen in the town; his wife, who was widely regarded as haughty, fell ill, and Edwards himself suffered 'an apoplectic and convulsive fit' and in 1686 returned to rural Cambridgeshire. His health did not improve, and 'bodily pains and weakness accompanying him, especially the gout, he was constrained to retire from the pulpit, and confine himself to the diffusion of his theological opinions via the press' (Kippis, 5.544). Among the vast number of his publications, the exchanges which followed Locke's issue of *The Reasonableness of Christianity* are most notable; Edwards set out his positions in *Some Thoughts Concerning the Several Causes and Occasions of Atheism* (1695), *Socinianism Unmasked* (1696), *The Socinian Creed* (1697), and *A Brief Vindication of the Fundamental Articles of the Christian Faith* (1697).

Edwards never much liked company, 'but wholly separated himself to study and contemplation'. He was 'never possessed of a library' (Kippis, 5.544) and used college libraries for rare or old books, and it seems this was the chief reason for his return to Cambridge about 1697. 'With regard to [books by] modern authors, his practice was to procure the loan of them from the booksellers' on which he made extensive notes. 'By this good husbandry, he was forced to read the works which he borrowed within the time prefixed' (Kippis, 5.545). Edwards was awarded his doctorate in 1699. His first wife died in 1701; 'after a due and decent distance of time', he married Catherine Lane (*c*.1664–1745). In 1711 the vice-chancellor of Cambridge University refused permission for a sermon delivered by Edwards at St Mary's on 5 November to be printed at the university press. This was apparently out of 'a party spirit' against the author, who was 'a zealous Whig, and who in his discourse had enlarged much on our deliverance from popery, on the blessings of the revolution and on the praises of King William' (ibid., 5.546).

Edwards died in Cambridge on 16 April 1716, leaving properties in Cambridgeshire, Hertfordshire, and Lincolnshire.   C. J. ROBINSON, *rev.* STEPHEN WRIGHT

Sources A. Kippis and others, eds., *Biographia Britannica, or, The lives of the most eminent persons who have flourished in Great Britain and Ireland*, 2nd edn, 5 vols. (1778–93), vol. 5, pp. 543–6 · H. B. Wilson, *History of Merchant Taylors' School* (1812) · Venn, *Alum. Cant.* · C. J. Robinson, ed., *A register of the scholars admitted into Merchant Taylors' School, from AD 1562 to 1874*, 2 vols. (1882–3) · will, PRO, PROB 11/558, fol. 55 · T. Baker, *History of the college of St John the Evangelist, Cambridge*, ed. J. E. B. Mayor, 2 vols. (1869)
Likenesses G. Vertue, line engraving, repro. in J. Edwards, *Theologia reformata* (1713) · R. White, line engraving, BM, NPG; repro. in J. Edwards, *Sermons on special occasions and subjects* (1698)
Wealth at death considerable property scattered across three counties: will, PRO, PROB 11/558, fol. 55

Edwards, John [*pseud.* Siôn y Potiau] (*bap.* 1699?, *d.* 1776), Welsh-language poet, may have been the son of Edward Jones who was baptized in the church of Llansanffraid Glynceiriog, Denbighshire, on 27 December 1699. Siôn reputedly abandoned his calling as a weaver, and spent seven years in London in the service of a publisher or bookseller before returning to Glynceiriog and to his family, whose lament Jonathan Hughes had expressed in his verse 'Brawd doeth fardd, bryd doi i'th fwth?' ('Wise fellow poet, when will you return to your cottage?') (Hughes). He and his wife, Elizabeth, had two sons, Abel Jones, born in 1740, and Cain Jones, probably born earlier.

The extant pieces of John Edwards, 'the Welsh Poet', are few and far between (they can be found in various manuscripts in the National Library of Wales). The few *englynion* in manuscript testify to his involvement in the informal bardic meetings or eisteddfods held in Denbighshire and the vicinity during the 1730s and 1740s. A handful of free-metre poems appeared in ballad form from the press of Richard Marsh at Wrexham. In one, composed about 1749, Siôn calls upon the Methodists to return to the state church, and urges the clergy for their part diligently and faithfully to execute their duties. He may have been an almanac writer, and he may be the Siôn o'r Glyn who was, according to Huw Jones of Llangwm, renowned for his interludes. He translated the second and third parts of John Bunyan's *Pilgrim's Progress* into Welsh—no mean feat for one who claimed not to have received a single day of schooling in his entire lifetime—and these were published in 1761 and 1768 respectively. Siôn was buried in 1776, probably on 28 August, at the church of Llansanffraid Glynceiriog.

Edwards's son, **Cain Jones** (*fl.* 1776–1795), succeeded Gwilym Howel as author of the almanac *Tymmhorol, ac wybrenol newyddion, neu, almanac newydd*, which he compiled between 1776 and 1795. In the preface to his first almanac of 1776 he promised that future issues would surpass the current number 'O herwydd ei bôd yn Fîs o Haf cyn imi gael Rhybydd i'w wneuthur' ('because summer was upon us before I was instructed to prepare it'). He kept his promise, partly (but not to the liking of all his readers) by following the example of Gwilym Howel, who considered poetry an essential ingredient in his almanacs.

Cain Jones occasionally included his own and his father's compositions (the issues of 1777, 1780, 1783), but he made the works of the Llangollen poet Jonathan Hughes a regular feature of his almanacs.   A. CYNFAEL LAKE

Sources *Y Tyst Apostolaidd* (1850), 136–8 • *Y Geninen*, 5 (1887), 75–6 • E. Rees, ed., *Libri Walliae: a catalogue of Welsh books and books printed in Wales, 1546–1820*, 2 vols. (1987) • *DWB* • C. Ashton, *Hanes llenyddiaeth Gymreig o 1651 o. C. hyd 1850* [1893] • J. H. Davies, ed., *A bibliography of Welsh ballads printed in the 18th century* (1911) [1908–11] • *Mynegai i farddoniaeth gaeth y Llawysgrifau*, University of Wales, Board of Celtic Studies, 12 vols. (1978) • J. Hughes, *Bardd a byrddau* (1778) • W. Rowlands, *Cambrian bibliography / Llyfryddiaeth y Cymry*, ed. D. S. Evans (1869) • J. Edwards, *Taith y Pererin* (1761), title-page, preface • bishop's transcripts, St Asaph, NL Wales

Edwards, John (1714–1785), Independent minister, was born in Shrewsbury of unknown parentage. He converted to Methodism under George Whitefield's preaching, and was among the first set of preachers at the Tabernacle in London in 1746. He has been identified as the author of a very rare pamphlet, *An answer to part of an anonymous pamphlet, entitled, 'Observations upon the conduct and behaviour of a certain sect, usually distinguished by the name of Methodists. By J. E.'* (1744), in reply to Edmund Gibson's unsparing denunciation of Methodism.

Edwards was a tireless itinerant evangelist who travelled throughout England, Wales, and Ireland, and a confidant of Whitefield. He wrote to Whitefield concerning a tour through the midlands:

> Oh what times and seasons we have had; souls fired with the love of God, and following the word from place to place, horse and foot, like men engaged in a war, determined to take the city by force of arms.   (Tyerman, *Life of Wesley*, 1.537)

Edwards's missionary endeavours as an itinerant evangelist in Ireland often involved violence and the threat of violence. In Dublin he was roughed up by 'the Ormond Boys', who 'recognised him as *Swaddling John*, a term of reproach applied to the Methodists in Ireland'. He was rescued as he was about to be thrown into the Liffey by their opponents, 'the Liberty Boys' (Seymour, 2.152). In 1752 Whitefield's hearers in Dublin organized a class, procured a building in Skinner Street, and received help from John Edwards, Thomas Adams, and the banker Mr Lunell, but were reprimanded by Whitefield:

> I cannot help thinking, but that you have run before the Lord, in forming yourselves into a public Society. Mr. Adams's visit was designed to be transient, and I cannot promise you any settled help from hence. I am sincere, when I profess that I do not choose to set myself at the head of any party.   (Tyerman, *Life of Whitefield*, 2.287)

How long Edwards stayed in Ireland is not known, but he may have moved to Leeds, Yorkshire, where a John Edwards was listed on the very first Wesleyan Methodist ministerial list for the Leeds circuit in 1753. However, there is no subsequent mention of Edwards as a Wesleyan minister; he may have withdrawn from Methodist societies as a result of the split in Leeds between the Calvinistic Methodists, led by John Bennet, and the Wesleyans in the early 1750s. Following the resolution at a Methodist conference held in Leeds on 22 May 1753 that 'predestinarian preachers' should be excluded from Methodist pulpits, Edwards drew off Methodists with Calvinist sympathies, taking away the greater part of the society with him, and began forming an independent congregation. They were joined by other protestant dissenters from the old Independent chapel at Call Lane, Leeds, who were dissatisfied with the 'plain, serious and practical' preaching of the Revd Thomas Whitaker (Miall, 304–5). Edwards's congregation built the White or Whitehall Chapel. George Whitefield, writing to the countess of Huntingdon on 24 September 1755 about his recent visit to Leeds, exclaimed:

> unknown to me, they had almost finished a large house, in order to form a separate congregation. If this scheme succeeds, an awful separation, I fear, will take place amongst the Societies. I have written to Mr Wesley and have done all I could to prevent it.   (Tyerman, *Life of Whitefield*, 2.352)

Edwards drew in hearers from as far as Bradford and the chapel was soon enlarged. He published *A Collection of Hymns and Spiritual Songs* (1756; rev. edn, 1769), and in 1758 edited and republished Robert Trail's 1692 book *A vindication of the protestant doctrine of justification and its preachers and professors from the unjust charge of antinomianism*, a defence of Calvinism against the charges of antinomianism and an attack on Arminianism. Perhaps his most remarkable success came with the publication of *The Christian Indeed* in 1757. Its seventh edition was published in London in 1775 under the title *The Conversion of a Mehometan to the Christian Religion*, which became a hugely successful evangelical tract in North America, reaching at least seven editions between 1791 and 1817, one of them in a German translation published in Pennsylvania.

Edwards increasingly moved in a circle of Calvinist evangelicals and former Methodists who were beginning to cohere and establish the revivified Congregationalism of the mid-eighteenth century. In July 1758 he preached at Stockport for the Revd Peter Walkden, an old protestant dissenting minister who began his ministry in 1709 and welcomed the new evangelical preaching. On this occasion he is known to have met John Bennet and Caleb Warhurst, the recently ordained minister of a new Independent church in Manchester. Whitefield was still corresponding with Edwards in late 1765, and there is surviving correspondence from 24 January 1768 between Edwards in Leeds and the itinerant evangelist Captain Jonathan Scott, who was supported by Lady Glenorchy.

Edwards's only other known publication was a fast sermon, *The Safe Retreat from Impending Judgements* (1762), preached at the outbreak of war with Spain. He died on 17 February 1785, leaving bequests to three children who are mentioned in his will of 7 February.

                                                        JONATHAN H. WESTAWAY

Sources J. G. Miall, *Congregationalism in Yorkshire* (1868), 304–5 • [A. C. H. Seymour], *The life and times of Selina, countess of Huntingdon*, 2 (1840), 149, 152–4 • L. Tyerman, *The life of the Rev. George Whitefield*, 2nd edn, 2 (1890), 111, 161, 179, 286, 287, 352, 353, 395, 396, 487, 488 • L. Tyerman, *The life and times of the Rev. John Wesley*, 4th edn, 3 vols. (1878), vol. 1, p. 537; vol. 2, p. 241 • *The works of John Wesley*, [another edn], 26, ed. F. Baker and others (1982), 507–9 • letter from

John Edwards, Leeds, to Captain Jonathan Scott, York, 24 Jan 1768, JRL, Thomas Raffles collection, MSS, MS 369–371.41 · *Wesleyan Methodism in Leeds: list of ministers stationed in the Leeds circuits from 1753 to 1882 inclusive*, [n.d.], JRL, Methodist Archives and Research Centre, MAW LH.Box 35 · J. Westaway, 'Scottish influences upon the reformed Churches in north west England, c.1689–1829: a study of the ministry within the Congregational and Presbyterian churches in Lancashire, Cumberland and Westmorland', PhD diss., University of Lancaster, 1997, 150–205 · H. D. Rack, 'Survival and revival: John Bennet, Methodism, and the Old Dissent', in K. G. Robbins, *Protestant evangelicalism: Britain, Ireland, Germany, and America, c.1750–c.1950* (1990), 1–23 · A. A. Dallimore, *George Whitefield: the life and time of the great evangelist of the eighteenth-century revival*, 2 vols. (1980), 349 · R. Tudur Jones, *Congregationalism in England, 1662–1962* (1962), 152 · A. G. Matthews, *The Congregational churches of Staffordshire* (1924?), 132 · B. Nightingale, *Lancashire nonconformity*, 6 vols. [1890–93], vol. 3, pp. 17–18 · N. Sykes, *Edmund Gibson, bishop of London, 1669–1748: a study in politics & religion in the eighteenth century* (1926), 313–17 · will, proved, 23 April 1785, Borth. Inst. · *DNB*

Archives DWL, letters to Birmingham chapel, MS 12.80, pp. 410–11 · JRL, T. Raffles collection, letter to J. Scott, English MSS 369–371.41

Likenesses J. Watson, mezzotint, pubd 1772 (after J. Russell), BM, NPG

Wealth at death £387 12s.: will, 23 April 1785, Borth. Inst.

Edwards, John [Siôn Ceiriog] (1747–1792), Welsh-language poet, was born at Crogenwladus in Glynceiriog, Denbighshire. As a young man he went to London, where he became acquainted with Owen Jones (Myfyr) and Robert Hughes (Robin Ddu o Fôn); together the three men founded Cymdeithas y Gwyneddigion, or the Venedotian Society, in 1770. Siôn Ceiriog, as he was called, wrote an *awdl* (ode) for the meeting of the society on St David's day 1778; he was its secretary in 1779–80, and its president in 1783. Apart from an elegy written on Richard Morris in 1780, for which the society awarded him an honorary medal, little of his work survives. 'He was a witty man but somewhat hot-headed and irresponsible, and his chief delight lay in "ragging" his London friends' (*DWB*).

John Edwards died suddenly, in September 1792, aged forty-five, and was buried in London. John Jones, Glan-y-gors, contributed some memorial verses to the *Geirgrawn* of June 1796, with these prefatory remarks:

> To the memory of John Edwards, Glynceiriog, in the parish of Llangollen, Denbighshire, who was generally known as Sion Ceiriog, a poet, an orator, and an astronomer, a curious historian of sea and land, a manipulator of musical instruments, a true lover of his country and of his Welsh mother tongue, who, to the great regret of his friends, died and was buried in London, September 1792.

R. M. J. JONES, *rev.* M. CLARE LOUGHLIN-CHOW

Sources *DWB* · W. D. Leathart, *The origin and progress of the Gwyneddigion Society of London* (1831), 16

Edwards, John (1750/51–1832), army officer and magistrate, was the eldest son of James Edwards, a landowner, of Old Court, near Bray, co. Wicklow, Ireland, and his wife, Anne, the second daughter of Thomas Tennison of Castle Tennison, co. Roscommon. In 1782 he married Charlotte, the fifth daughter of John Wright of Nottingham; they had five children—three boys and two girls. Edwards took a patriot line in Irish politics and became prominent in the Irish Volunteers, rising to the rank of lieutenant-colonel; he celebrated the volunteer spirit in his poem *The Patriot Soldier: a Poem* (1784). In March 1797 he raised the Bray yeoman infantry and became captain. Unlike many former volunteers who joined the Irish yeomanry, Edwards kept his independent stance, and opposed martial law in 1798. He even threatened to use his yeomen to arrest soldiers 'committing outrage under the semblance of law' (National Archives of Ireland, Rebellion MSS, 620/36/176) and considered resigning his command in protest. In late twentieth-century historiography re-interpreting the 1798 rebellion in Wicklow and Wexford, Edwards is seen as representing an enduring liberalism among the older established gentry families. His literary publications resumed in 1808 with a traditional Irish ballad and a classical tragedy, followed by two economic essays (1815, 1820). He died at Booterstown, co. Dublin, on 24 March 1832.

A. F. BLACKSTOCK

Sources J. Edwards, correspondence, NA Ire., Rebellion MSS, 620/36/176, 115, 87; 620/37/99; 620/38/63; 620/39/63, 118 · *Dublin Gazette* (28–30 March 1797) · *Dublin Gazette* (14–16 Feb 1799) · Burke, *Gen. GB* · Watt, *Bibl. Brit.* · L. Cullen, 'The United Irishmen in Wexford', *The mighty wave: the 1798 rebellion in Wexford*, ed. D. Keogh and N. Furlong (1996), 49, 51 · *GM*, 1st ser., 102/1 (1832), 478 · *DNB* · R. O'Donnell, *The rebellion in Wicklow, 1798* (1998)

Archives NA Ire., Rebellion MSS, letters to the Irish government, mostly Under-Secretary Cooke, 620 ser., vols. 36, 37, 38, 39

Edwards, John Menlove (1910–1958), rock-climber, was born on 18 June 1910 at Crossens vicarage, near Southport, the last of four children of the Revd George Zachary Edwards (1872–1934) and his wife, Helen Amelia Dawes, an art teacher.

Edwards was known as Menlove to family and friends and as J. M. Edwards to the world of rock-climbing, where, in the words of his obituary in the 1958 *Climbers' Club Journal*, he was 'a man who performed the sort of feats which become legendary'. He was born into a clerical family long concerned with social and left-wing causes. Jim Perrin's excellent biography *Menlove* deals well with this family tradition. Edwards attended Holmwood preparatory school, from where he went on scholarships to Fettes College and from there to read medicine at Liverpool University. He qualified in 1933, specializing in psychiatry, and was psychiatrist to the Liverpool Child Guidance Clinic from 1935 to 1941. He started climbing in 1930, was a founder member of the pioneering Liverpool University rock-climbing club, and within a few months was doing some of the hardest climbs in Wales and had led two new routes. By 1931 he was recognized as one of the leading climbers at work.

Edwards became famous as a discoverer of crags which had previously been unexploited or which held only a small number of routes up obvious lines of weakness. A man of great physical strength and originality of approach, he was fascinated by the exploration of rock faces which were not only steep and smooth but rotten and adorned with treacherous vegetation. He certainly put up some very hard routes on clean and sound rock but one associates him most with such crags as Clogwyn y Geifr, the Devil's Kitchen cliffs. He sought difficulty and many of his comments on climbs reflect this. Of one he wrote: 'The first part is more interesting than it looks thanks to grass and poor rock. The grey slab of the second part is disappointingly covered with large holds.' The passage of time and many subsequent climbers have of course cleaned up many of his routes, though nothing can make the Devil's Kitchen other than loose and intimidating, and the taste of climbers now is rather for aerial gymnasticism. But his best routes are still taxing and he is a legend in terms of his explorations and the boldness of his leads. He undertook, sometimes on his own and sometimes in co-operation with others, the writing of the definitive Climbers' Club guides to Cwm Idwal, Tryfan, Lliwedd, and Clogwyn d'ur Arddu. For this he had to repeat all the climbs previously done on the relevant crag and naturally he took the opportunity to put up new routes. He had a very clear idea about the way in which guidebooks should be written and was particularly successful in evoking the structure of the mountain and the relationship of the various physical features. This is also a characteristic of his other writings about mountains.

Edwards's poetry, although it has found admirers and was of great importance to him, is not of a great deal of interest, but a number of his prose works, both fictional and semi-fictional, are excellent and deserve reading both for their creation of a vivid sense of ridge and gully and space and for the analysis of the feelings of a man in thought-provoking and often perilous situations. These were published mainly in the journals of the Climbers' Club and most have been collected in *Samson*, edited by Geoffrey Sutton and Wilfrid Noyce.

It is as a climber that Edwards achieved greatness; in other matters his life was sad. He was highly thought of as a clinician but he had a frustrated ambition to produce a grand, overarching psychological system, including political and social issues and matters of belief. At the beginning of the Second World War he became a conscientious objector and felt that the world was both evil and mad. He was homosexual and his love affairs were ultimately unhappy. He became increasingly despairing and paranoid, and, after several unsuccessful attempts, took his own life at his home, The Towers, Charing, Kent, on 2 February 1958. He was cremated at Ashford crematorium and his ashes were scattered on the hillside near Hafod Owen, the cottage near Beddgelert where he lived in 1941–2.

But it is as one of the greatest climbers that Edwards will be remembered, as he was by the author of this memoir, who was a member of a rescue party in which he took part in 1941. It was necessary to bring an injured man down the Idwal Slabs, a stretch of rock about 450 feet high at an average angle of 45°. The stretcher was lowered on ropes but needed two people to hold the front end to prevent it from jamming on irregularities of the rock. The Slabs have a crack running down them from top to bottom and the man on the left handle of the stretcher descended fairly comfortably in the crack. He watched in fascination

as Edwards, wearing as was customary in those days nailed boots and, as was customary with him, boots with very few very worn and rickety nails, walked about on the smooth rock, heaving the stretcher up and down, with the ease of one crossing a drawing-room. This was probably nothing very exceptional for Edwards but for the observer it was a revelation.　　　　　DOUGLAS HEWITT

Sources J. Perrin, *Menlove: the life of John Menlove Edwards, with an appendix of his writings* (1985) · *Samson: the life and writings of Menlove Edwards*, ed. G. Sutton and W. Noyce [1960] · A. D. M. Cox, W. Noyce, and A. B. Hargreaves, *Climbers' Club Journal* (1958) · personal knowledge (2004) · private information (2004) · b. cert.
Likenesses photographs, repro. in Perrin, *Menlove* · photographs, repro. in Sutton and Noyce, *Samson*
Wealth at death £500 15s. 0d.: probate, 1 April 1958, *CGPLA Eng. & Wales*

Edwards, John Passmore (1823–1911), newspaper proprietor and philanthropist, born on 24 March 1823, at Blackwater, near Truro, Cornwall, was the second of the four sons of William Edwards and his wife, Susan Passmore. Edwards received a rudimentary education at his village school before leaving in 1835 to help his father with his various jobs as carpenter, brewer, publican, and nurseryman. He continued his studies after work, teaching himself from the cheap books he was able to buy. These endeavours were rewarded when, in 1843, he was employed as a clerk by a Truro lawyer, Henry Sewell Stokes. Edwards became interested in the Anti-Corn Law League, and in 1844 left his job to become the representative in Manchester of the *Sentinel*, a London weekly newspaper, which was part of the league's huge propaganda campaign. The experience was to confirm Edwards's adherence to Cobdenite Liberalism, but the *Sentinel* failed. To meet his debts Edwards lectured at a shilling a time for various temperance societies. Obsessively concerned with the 'drink problem', the Victorians debated the subject intensely and exhaustively. Temperance societies were among the earliest advocates of the Smilesian belief that self-help was the best means of moral regeneration, a philosophy that appealed greatly to Edwards with his nonconformist background, and his own determined and successful efforts to improve himself. With his debts discharged, in 1845 he settled in London, intending to keep himself by lecturing and journalism.

Throughout his adult life Edwards was interested in political and social reform. He was an activist and propagandist for the Early Closing Association. It became increasingly apparent that the 'moral persuasion' argument had failed so the association advocated the prohibition of alcohol. Edwards sympathized with the Chartists, but not that section that advocated the use of violence. His involvement with the peace movement lasted more than six decades. A member of the London Peace Society, he was chosen as a delegate to attend conferences at Brussels (1848), Paris (1849), and Frankfurt (1850). He was president of the Transvaal Independence Committee (1881) and of the Transvaal Committee (1901). He was a prominent member of the Political Reform Association and the Ballot

John Passmore Edwards (1823–1911), by George Frederic Watts, 1894

Society, and in 1894 was appointed president of the London Reform Association, which sought to stimulate progressive municipal legislation. He advocated the suppression of gambling and of the opium trade, the abolition of capital punishment, of flogging in the army and navy, and of the newspaper tax. In 1850 Edwards invested all his small savings in a weekly newspaper, the *Public Good*, which he wrote, printed, and published from the room where he lived in Paternoster Row. The paper sold widely but, in the end, failed, as did other journals he started— the *Biographical Magazine*, the *Peace Advocate*, the *Poetic Magazine*—which were all intended to advertise and support each other's sales. A three-year struggle ended in physical breakdown and bankruptcy. It took Edwards thirteen years to discharge his debts in full. This he largely achieved by heroic endeavours as a freelance journalist. In 1862, he purchased the *Building News*, which he turned into a success. Heartened, he acquired in 1869, again for only a nominal sum, the *Mechanics Magazine*, which proved another financial success.

In 1876, aged fifty-three, Edwards made his most ambitious newspaper purchase when he acquired *The Echo*. The first halfpenny newspaper, *The Echo* had been founded in 1868 and bought by the financier and former tory MP Baron Albert Grant in 1875. Edwards's purchase meant the return of *The Echo* to the Liberal fold, which pleased the Liberal leadership. Edwards had already stood unsuccessfully as a parliamentary candidate for Truro in 1868. He supposed he might better further those causes he espoused as a member of the Commons, and stood successfully in the Liberal interest for Salisbury in the 1880

election. Parliament proved a disappointment and he vacated his seat after two years, declaring that he had not found the Commons 'such a fruitful field of usefulness as … expected' (Koss, 1). To concentrate on his political career, Edwards, who at first had edited *The Echo* himself, had passed that task to Howard Evans, an energetic, able journalist with pronounced nonconformist sympathies. The paper continued to improve its circulation and gained commercially when it was decided to exclude horse-racing tips. In 1884 Andrew Carnegie, the Scots-American steel magnate who sought control of newspapers to disseminate his ideas on republicanism and radicalism, together with Samuel Storey, radical MP for Sunderland and proprietor of a number of local newspapers, bought a two-thirds interest in *The Echo*. The relationship was neither happy nor successful, and Edwards bought back full control in 1886, restoring Evans as editor. Edwards respected Gladstone but had never hesitated to castigate him when, as over Egypt, he supposed the Liberal leader mistaken. He now repudiated home rule. There were rumours in 1892 that Edwards was tired of *The Echo* and was seeking a purchaser. In fact, Edwards could not part with the newspaper, which had become part of his persona. 'Establishing and editing *The Echo*', he told a group of journalists in 1893, 'realised a long-cherished dream … producing a paper devoted to the public good' (*The Journalist*, 1893). Sir Robert Reid, radical MP and future lord chancellor, spoke of how he had always 'revered' *The Echo*'s 'humanitarian vision' (R. Reid to W. M. Crook, 17 Jan 1898, Bodl. Oxf., Crook papers). But new political, commercial, and journalistic pressures were fast undermining the values of an earlier generation. In 1898 Edwards sold *The Echo* to a syndicate of Liberal nonconformists. Despite their best efforts, *The Echo* finally foundered in 1905.

For many years Edwards had devoted all the profit he derived from *The Echo* to finance a programme of philanthropy. These good works were the splendid practical manifestation of his humanitarianism; his native county of Cornwall and the poorer districts of London were particular beneficiaries of his largesse. Public gifts included eight hospitals, five convalescent homes, homes for epileptics, four homes for boys, twenty-four libraries, three art galleries, a museum, and countless drinking fountains. A typical measure of his unstinting generosity was the series of financial gifts made to the Tavistock Square settlement inspired by Mrs Humphry Ward. The workers' education aspect of the settlement's work appealed particularly to Edwards as a largely self-educated man. Initially he promised Mrs Ward £4000, but eventually responded to her importuning with £14,000. As its greatest patron, the settlement appropriately bears his name. Among other public gifts, he gave to reading rooms and libraries throughout the country books and busts of literary worthies, to Oxford University an endowed scholarship, to Dundee a lifeboat, and to Woolwich a public garden. He declined offers of a knighthood from Victoria and Edward VII, but accepted honorary freedoms of five boroughs: West and East Ham, Liskeard, Falmouth, and Truro.

Edwards married Eleanor Humphreys, the daughter of an artist: his wife, son, and daughter survived him. He died at his Hampstead home, 51 Netherhall Gardens, on 22 April 1911. H. W. Massingham described Edwards as 'one of the kings of modern newspaper enterprise'. Considerable as was Edwards's contribution to Victorian journalism, he deserves to be remembered also as the archetypal Victorian self-made man and philanthropist.

A. J. A. MORRIS

Sources J. P. Edwards, *A few footprints* (1906) • S. E. Koss, *The rise and fall of the political press in Britain*, 1 (1981) • *The Times* (24 April 1911) • J. Sutherland, *Mrs Humphry Ward: eminent Victorian, pre-eminent Edwardian* (1990), 222–3 • H. W. Massingham, *The London daily press* (1892), 188–9 • P. Baynes, *John Passmore Edwards, 1823–1911: an account of his life and works* (1994)
Archives Mary Ward Centre, corresp. with Mary Augusta Ward
Likenesses G. F. Watts, oils, 1894, NPG [*see illus.*] • G. Frampton, bronze bust, *c*.1898, South London Art Gallery • Ape [C. Pellegrini], cartoon, chromolithograph, NPG; repro. in *VF* (17 Oct 1885)
Wealth at death £47,685 15*s*. 3*d*.: probate, 5 July 1911, *CGPLA Eng. & Wales*

Edwards, Jonathan (1638/9–1712), college head and religious controversialist, was born in Wrexham, Denbighshire; the identity of his parents is unknown. His entire adult life was spent at the University of Oxford. He matriculated at Christ Church in 1657, graduating BA on 28 October 1659. On 7 March 1662 he was elected fellow of Jesus College. He proceeded MA the same year and BD in 1670. Edwards seems to have been a committed and popular teacher at Jesus: in the period 1682–5, by which date he was vice-principal of the college, he taught between nine and twenty-two students each quarter, almost two-fifths of the resident student body. When John Lloyd, principal of Jesus College, was made bishop of St David's, Edwards was unanimously elected his successor on 2 November 1686; he was created DD a month later, on 1 December. He remained in office until his death over twenty-five years later. From October 1689 to October 1692 Edwards served as vice-chancellor of the university. Alongside his Oxford positions he held a number of ecclesiastical appointments over the years. He was appointed rector of Kiddington, Oxfordshire, in 1666, exchanging this for Hinton Ampner, Hampshire, in 1681. He may also have held livings in Wales: at Clynnog Fawr in Caernarvonshire and (from 1687) Llandysul in Cardiganshire. He became treasurer of Llandaff Cathedral in 1687, acting as the chapter's proctor in the convocation of 1702.

At Oxford, Edwards proved himself—as fellow, principal, and vice-chancellor—a committed tory Anglican. He preached a loyalist sermon to Charles II's parliament held in the town in 1681, and when Monmouth's rebels rose in the west country in the summer of 1685, Edwards was one of the delegates appointed by university convocation to raise a troop of scholars to defend the town. As vice-chancellor he presided over a university firm in its hostility to whiggery and any compromise with religious dissent. He was inevitably a leading figure in the phalanx of Oxford dons and graduates in the convocation of 1689 who wrecked the attempts of William III's bishops to push through their scheme for comprehending nonconformists within the Church of England. During his years as vice-chancellor he also had to negotiate whig opposition to the privileges of the university and the government's suspicions of it as a haven of Jacobites. When convocation for the province of Canterbury again sat in the spring of 1701, Edwards was a principal speaker in the Oxford- and tory-dominated lower house.

Edwards's high-church position was also expressed in his writings. In the 1690s he was a vigorous defender of traditional orthodoxy concerning the doctrine of the Trinity against attacks by Socinian sympathizers (Socinianism was a radical, anti-trinitarian theology of continental origin). For this he was hailed as 'the greatest champion against Socinianism that hath appeared of late years' (Hardy, 149). His *Preservative Against Socinianism* appeared in sections between 1693 and 1703. The intention of the first part was twofold: to sound an alarm over the fact that Socinian books had 'swarmed' in England during the latter decades of the seventeenth century, and also to attempt an analysis and critique of Socinian teaching. Edwards argued that the Socinians had dug up the old heresies of Arius, Photinus, and Pelagius, but in such a way as to form what was effectively a new religion. In the following year the second part of the *Preservative* was published. In this section Edwards dealt with Socinian opposition to traditional teaching on original sin and redemption. The third part of the *Preservative* appeared in 1697 and attempted to demonstrate that the tenets of Socinianism undermined all revealed religion. The final part of the *Preservative* was not completed until 1703. This section reflected the shifting contours of the debate, with Edwards arguing against those who took reason to be the great rule of faith and the test of revealed religion. On the completion of this final part Thomas Hearne provided *An Index to the Four Parts of Dr. Edwards' 'Preservative'* in 1703.

Edwards's other published works deal with similar issues. In 1695 he published *Remarks upon a Book Lately Published by Dr. William Sherlock*, which was a scathing attack on the controversial theologian. The book upheld Oxford University's censure of Sherlock's description of the trinitarian persons as three distinct minds and substances. It also provided a defence of the traditional scholastic language used in the explication of the doctrine. In 1702 Edwards published *The exposition given [by the bishop of Sarum] on the second article of our religion examined*, a critique of a treatise by Bishop Gilbert Burnet, which Edwards feared was Nestorian in tone (that is, holding that Christ possessed two separate persons, divine and human, rather than a single person, at once God and man). His last work, *The Doctrine of Original Sin … Asserted* was an attack on William Whitby's writings on the subject.

Edwards died in Jesus College on 20 July 1712, unmarried, aged seventy-three. In his will he left books to his college, where they form part of the Fellows' Library. He also bequeathed over £600 to the college, whose building programme he had generously supported throughout his life. His epitaph in the college chapel refers to him as one who resisted the arguments and sophistry of Socinianism.

Jonathan Edwards is sometimes confused with John *Edwards of Cambridge, his contemporary and another opponent of Socinianism. PHILIP DIXON

Sources Wood, *Ath. Oxon.*, new edn, 4.721–2 · A. Wood, *The history and antiquities of the colleges and halls in the University of Oxford*, ed. J. Gutch (1786) · J. N. L. Baker, *Jesus College, Oxford* (1971) · archives, Christ Church Oxf. · archives, Jesus College, Oxford · Foster, *Alum. Oxon.* · E. G. Hardy, *Jesus College*, College Histories series (1899) · C. E. Mallet, *A history of the University of Oxford*, 3 vols. (1924–7), vol. 2 · A. Chalmers, ed., *The general biographical dictionary*, new edn, 32 vols. (1812–17) · *Hist. U. Oxf.*, vols 4–5 · *DNB* · will, PRO, PROB 11/528, sig. 153
Wealth at death at least £640 given in bequests; also books to Jesus College, Oxford: will, 1712, PRO, PROB 11/528, sig. 153

Edwards, Jonathan (1703–1758), theologian and philosopher, was born in the east parish of Windsor, Connecticut, on 5 October 1703. He was the only son in a family of eleven children. His parents were the Revd Timothy Edwards (1669–1758) and his wife, Esther (1672–1771), daughter of the Revd Solomon Stoddard (1643–1729) of Northampton, Massachusetts.

Early life and education In his youth Edwards was nurtured and instructed in reformed theology and the practice of puritan piety. Having been fitted for college at his father's tutoring school, he was admitted in 1716 at the age of thirteen to the collegiate school (renamed Yale College in 1718). The course of study there included classical and biblical languages, logic, and natural philosophy. With the modernization of the curriculum during the years 1717–18, Edwards became familiar with the new philosophy of 'Mr. Locke and Sir Isaac Newton' (*Works*, 6.15). He became familiar with the new ideas of the scientific revolution and the early Enlightenment, which tended to diminish divine sovereignty with respect to creation, providence, and redemption and to enhance human independence, producing by degrees an estimate of humankind as more morally capable and of God as more benevolent. For the rest of his life the dialogue with these intellectual movements was an inseparable part of his philosophical and theological enterprise. Edwards received his BA degree in September 1720, and was selected to deliver the valedictory oration in that year. After graduating, Edwards continued to reside at the college for two more years, pursuing theological studies.

During the summer of 1721, when he was seventeen years old and studying toward his MA degree, Edwards underwent a religious conversion that shook his life and reshaped his whole experience and existence. As he later described it, 'the appearance of every thing was altered; there seemed to be, as it were, a calm, sweet cast, or appearance of divine glory, in almost every thing'. Many features of Edwards's thought can be traced to this signal existential moment. Among these are his *theologia gloriae*—the theology which celebrates God's majestic glory and sovereignty as evident in the coherence and beauty, order and harmony, of God's creation—and the radical notion of 'God's absolute sovereignty' (*Works*, 16.792–4). His construction of a theology of nature, or typology, interprets the physical world as a representation or a 'shadow' of the spiritual (ibid., 2.53), and his idealistic

Jonathan Edwards (1703–1758), by Thomas Trotter, pubd 1783 (after Joseph Badger, 1750)

phenomenalism, the thesis that physical objects exist only in the mind, or cannot exist unless they are perceived. After his conversion Edwards produced an impressive outpouring of writings in which he tried to convert the whole world around him and to construct it according to these newly gained religious convictions and theological persuasions. In 1722 he began his seventy resolutions, his diary, a long series of scientific and philosophical essays on natural philosophy, and his miscellanies. He started his 'Notes on the Apocalypse' in 1723 and 'Notes on scripture' in 1724.

Edwards's works on natural philosophy, among them most notably 'Of being' (1722), 'Of atoms' (1722), and 'The mind' (1724), signified the genesis of his theology of nature, or his endeavour to define anew the phenomena of nature in light of his spiritual experience to provide clear proof for his participation in the transatlantic republic of letters. Aiming to prove God's existence in his sovereign majesty and glory within the created world, Edwards attacked the dominant mechanical philosophy—the doctrine that all natural phenomena can be explained in terms of the mechanics of matter and motion alone—claiming 'there is no such thing as mechanism' if that word meant that 'bodies act each upon other, purely and properly by themselves', because 'the very being, and the manner of being, and the whole of bodies depends immediately on the divine power' (*Works*, 6.216, 235). He appropriated the atomic doctrine of the dominant mechanical philosophy of his time but Christianized it, arguing that God's infinite power is responsible for holding the 'atoms together' and that every 'atom in the universe is managed by Christ so as to be most to the advantage of the Christian' (ibid., 6.214, 13.184). Likewise he rejected the mechanistic understanding of the concept of 'natural laws', because these laws, setting up a mediating sphere between God and his creation, restricted God's infinite power and limited divine immanence within the phenomena of the world: what 'we call the laws of nature' are only 'the stated methods of God's acting with respect to bodies'. He therefore denounced mechanical philosophers who argued that God 'himself in common with his creatures' is 'subject in his acting to the same laws with inferiour being', thus dethroning God from his place as 'the head of the universe' and 'the foundation & first spring of all' (ibid., 6.216; Edwards, 'Miscellany', no. 1263).

Edwards's theology of nature signified a serious and systematic attempt to provide a plausible alternative to new European ideas that threatened traditional Christian thought and belief, and led increasingly to the disenchantment of the world. His goal was the re-enchantment of the world in the hope of demonstrating the infinite power of God's absolute sovereignty in both the 'order of nature' and the 'order of time' (Edwards, 'Miscellany', no. 704; *Works*, 1.177). Edwards's interpretation of the essential nature of reality constituted therefore a radical departure from the prevailing mechanical philosophy. Believing 'the corporeal world is to no advantage but to the spiritual', he argued that 'to find out the reasons of things in natural philosophy is only to find out the proportion of God's acting' (*Works*, 6.353–5). In this re-enchantment enterprise Edwards was not alone, as can be seen in the close affinities between his thought and that of other anti-Newtonians, such as the Irish philosopher George Berkeley (1685–1753) and, later, William Blake (1757–1827).

Early career and studies Life demanded more than intellectual activity, however, and Edwards was soon called to the ministry. In early August 1722 he accepted his first pastorate at a small English Presbyterian congregation in New York city, a position he held for eight months. There, surrounded by warm Christian fellowship but in relative intellectual and ecclesiastical isolation, he began writing his miscellanies, wide-ranging essays in which he delineated his apology for the Christian faith and articulated his response to deism, Enlightenment ideas, and contemporary scientific culture. More than any other works the miscellanies, written over a period of more than thirty years and comprising over 1400 entries, embody Edwards's spiritual and intellectual autobiography.

After his short sojourn in New York, Edwards returned to his father's house on the last day of April 1723. Except for several journeys to Boston, Norwich, and other places, he stayed at home to complete the requirements for his master's degree and to give himself vigorously to his private studies. During that time he prepared his master's thesis on the nature of justification, entitled 'A sinner is not justified in the sight of God except through the righteousness of Christ obtained by faith'. This discourse dealt with the complex of doctrines on the nature and ground of justification disputed between Calvinists and Arminians (the latter stressed confidence in human beings' ability to appeal to divine favour by human endeavour). The refutation of Arminianism occupied Edwards for the rest of his life.

Edwards delivered his thesis at the Yale commencement in September 1723 and received the MA degree. While in New York, Edwards had been invited to serve the church of the newly settled town of Bolton, Connecticut. During October 1723 he concluded the negotiations and on 11 November signed the Bolton town book, agreeing to settle as a pastor. His second pastorate lasted until May 1724. This was a highly active and creative period in Edwards's intellectual life. Apart from regularly writing entries for his collection on natural philosophy, where he continued to set forth his 'idealism', he commenced two new notebooks, one on the book of Revelation ('Notes on the Apocalypse') and the other on scripture ('Notes on scripture'), both of which he continued writing for the rest of his life.

On 21 May 1724 Edwards was elected to a tutorship at Yale College, and early the following month he took up his duties. He held this office until September 1726. Owing to the vacancy of the rectorship for the whole of this period, his position was one of special responsibilities. This appointment provided Edwards with a unique opportunity to keep abreast of the world of ideas and further develop his theological and philosophical interests. Through his renewed access to the college library he became much better acquainted with major authors in theology and philosophy, and the long list of book titles appearing in his 'Catalogue' of reading testifies to the wide range of his literary interests at this time. During this period of twenty-eight months at Yale, Edwards continued to pursue his studies and writings: he further elaborated the premises of his theology of nature by enlarging the scale of his treatise on natural philosophy and making considerable additions to the manuscript.

Edwards also began collecting materials for a work in mental philosophy, 'The mind', where he formulated his idealistic phenomenalism: 'the world, i.e. the material universe, exists nowhere but in the mind', and, given that 'all material existence is only idea', the 'world therefore is an ideal one' (*Works*, 6.350–56). His main goal in 'The mind', many of whose essays were written in response to John Locke's empiricism, was to show that the essence of reality is a matter of relationship between God and the created order. Accordingly, the principle underlying his theological teleology, or the order of being inherent in the structure of the universe, was the concept of 'Excellency'. Edwards defined this as the 'consent of being to being, or being's consent to entity', which in turn defined the relationship within the hierarchy of spirits according to their consent to the supreme being, God. 'So far as a thing consents to being in general', Edwards wrote, 'so far it consents to him', hence 'the more perfect created spirits are, the nearer do they come to their creator in this regard'.

Seeing that 'the more the consent is, and the more extensive, the greater is the excellency', therefore in 'the order of beings in the natural world, the more excellent and noble any being is, the more visible and immediate hand of God is there in bringing them into being' with 'the most noble of all' the 'soul of man' (ibid., 6.336–7; Edwards, 'Miscellany', no. 541).

Northampton pastorate In September 1726 Edwards resigned his tutorship at Yale College to become the ministerial colleague of his grandfather the Revd Solomon Stoddard. The latter, then eighty-three, was in the fifty-fifth year of his pastorate in Northampton, Massachusetts. Edwards arrived at Northampton in October, the town invited him to settle as Stoddard's colleague in November, and on 15 February 1727 he was ordained. On 28 July he was married to Sarah Pierpont (1713–1758) of New Haven, daughter of the late Revd James Pierpont (1660–1714), the first pastor in the town. They had three sons and eight daughters.

Probably in late September or early October 1728 Edwards commenced the writing of another notebook, 'Images of divine things', in which he continued to add new entries until 1756. This work contains his major statements on the exegetical discipline of typology. In contrast to traditional Christian typology—the exercise of matching biblical 'types' such as prophetic figures, events, or circumstances in the Old Testament with their 'antitypes' or fulfilment in the New—Edwards's typology comprehended not only scripture but also nature and history. For him types were found not only in the Old Testament. The phenomenal world also declared divine truths: 'the works of nature are intended and contrived of God to signify and indigitate spiritual things'. Hence the 'Book of Scripture is the interpreter of the book of nature', that is, 'declaring to us those spiritual mysteries that are indeed signified or typified in the constitution of the natural world' (*Works*, 11.66, 106).

The death of his venerable grandfather on 11 February 1729 left Edwards in charge of one of New England's most prestigious parishes. At the age of twenty-six he became the sole pastor and assumed the whole round of duties belonging to the pastorate of a large congregation in the most important town in western Massachusetts. As a consequence he gradually abandoned the treatises on natural philosophy and the mind, as his time, efforts, and interests were more fully commanded by the concerns of his ministry and as new responsibilities directed his attention more and more to the ecclesiastical affairs in his congregation. A lecture he gave in Boston in 1731, 'God glorified in the work of redemption'—a staunch defence of the Calvinist doctrine of God's absolute sovereignty as the foundation of all right doctrine—became the first of his sermons to be published, and he soon gained a reputation as a staunch defender of reformed doctrines. During this period he also became a leading member of the Hampshire Association, a local organization of clergymen, and played a significant role in 1735 in efforts to prevent the Revd Robert Breck's ordination at the church of Springfield because of his suspected Arminian sympathies.

Under Edwards's pastoral care the congregation at Northampton experienced, during the winter of 1734–5, an extraordinary manifestation of religious zeal and awakening known as the 'little revival'. Edwards's accounts of the revival, especially *A Faithful Narrative of the Surprising Work of God* (1737), circulated throughout the American colonies and in Britain, establishing him as a prominent leader in the protestant evangelical awakening. After the decline of the fervour and ferment of the revival, Edwards, struggling unremittingly to revive the halcyon days when Northampton was 'a city set on a hill' (*Works*, 4.210), preached a series of sermons in 1738, posthumously published in 1852 under the title *Charity and its Fruits, or, Christian Love as Manifested in Heart and Life*. In contrast to Francis Hutcheson and other members of the British school of moral sense philosophy, who developed the rationalist's idea of disinterested benevolence as the criterion for moral judgement, Edwards instead assessed moral matters by their 'worth in the sight of God', and claimed that without 'love to God there can be no true honor', or, conversely, that from 'love to God springs love to man' (ibid., 8.63, 137, 142). Gracious affections therefore stand above and beyond the natural affections of which all are capable, and true virtue, or divine love, stands above and beyond the disinterested benevolence that marks the ultimate achievement of natural man.

The religious revival of the 1730s left an indelible mark on Edwards. He struggled to understand the nature of divine agency in the order of time, or the essential relationship between redemptive activity and the course of history, attempting to decipher God's 'great design' in the 'affairs of redemption' and 'in the disposition of things in redemption' (Edwards, 'Miscellany', no. 547; 'God glorified', 107–8). The fruit of these efforts was a long series of thirty sermons, the 'History of the work of redemption', preached to his congregation during the spring and summer of 1739; these constituted Edwards's most systematic exposition of a philosophy of history. Against the Enlightenment refashioning of new modes of historical, secular time, which denied any theistic interpretation of the historical process, Edwards viewed history as lying exclusively in the mind of omniscient God. Taking God as the sole author of history, he argued that history has been constructed by divine providence as a special dimension of sacred, redemptive time designed solely for the accomplishment of God's work of redemption for fallen humanity. Hence it should be understood exclusively from the perspective of its maker and author. In this sacred, redemptive context, the 'pourings out of the Spirit' and its historical manifestation in the form of revival and awakening constituted the ultimate mark of divine agency in the order of time: 'from the fall of man to this day wherein we live the Work of Redemption in its effects has mainly been carried on by remarkable pourings out of the Spirit of God' at 'special seasons of mercy', or revivals (*Works*, 9.143).

The great awakening The religious situation in New England changed dramatically in 1740. In the autumn of that year George Whitefield, 'the Grand Itinerant', set all New

England aflame. Whitefield's grand tour of the British colonies (1739–41) led to an impressive pietistic revival, subsequently known as the great awakening (1740–42), that engulfed much of British America and inaugurated the revival tradition there. Edwards immediately assumed a prominent role in the extraordinary revival that shattered the harmony of the established Congregational churches in New England. Attempting to advance the cause of the revival, to save detractors from sealing their doom, and to move honest doubters to positive approval of what he regarded as the latter-day miracle, Edwards preached in July 1741 his now-famous sermon 'Sinners in the Hands of an Angry God' at Enfield, Massachusetts, where he invoked the terrifying image of the unconverted as a spider hanging by a single thread 'over the pit of hell' (Edwards, 'Sinners in the Hands of an Angry God', 97). Zealously defending the revival in his commencement address at Yale in September 1741—'The distinguishing marks of a work of the spirit of God'—Edwards defined the marks of the spirit of God's saving operations, and firmly asserted that the revival 'is undoubtedly, in the general, from the Spirit of God'. Warning those who opposed the revival as fighting against God and committing unpardonable sin against the Holy Spirit, he placed the awakening within the grand, sacred, redemptive context he had already developed in the 'History of the work of redemption', claiming that the present revival was clear evidence that 'Christ is come down from heaven into this land, in a remarkable and wonderful work of his Spirit' (*Works*, 4.260, 270).

The emotional outbursts that accompanied the great awakening became increasingly controversial, causing critics to question the legitimacy of the revivalists. By 1742 opponents of the revival, known as Old Lights to distinguish them from the pro-revival New Lights, began launching their attack. Chief among the attackers was Charles Chauncy (1705–1787) of Boston's First Church. His sermon *Enthusiasm Described and Caution'd Against* (1742) launched the first onslaught against the revival, denouncing overt enthusiasm and calling for a return to sane rational religion. In another work, *Seasonable Thoughts on the State of Religion in New England* (1743)—a compendium of horror stories about the worst emotional extravagances of the awakening—Chauncy claimed the accounts given 'about the SPIRIT's influence' are nothing but 'a *notorious* Error' (Chauncy, 319). Edwards quickly immersed himself in defending the revival as a divine work—against rationalists and conservatives alienated by its emotion and tumult, and against enthusiasts who celebrated both. Believing the revival to be a true work of the Spirit, he claimed: 'If this ben't the work of God, I have all my religion to learn over again, and know not what use to make of the Bible'. Moreover, since 'Christ gloriously triumphs at this day', New England should 'give glory to him who thus ride forth in the chariots of his salvation' (*Works*, 16.97–8).

In his answer to Chauncy's attacks, *Some Thoughts Concerning the Present Revival of Religion in New England* (1742),

Edwards's most ambitious work yet (378 pages), he asserted that the rationalistic objections to the awakening rested on false philosophy that divorced 'the affections of the soul' from the 'will'. Instead of the rationalist view of man, according to which the 'passions' are sub-rational appetites to be held in check by reason, a perspective requiring that religion seek to enlighten the mind rather than raise the affections, Edwards adopted Locke's sensationalist psychology, arguing for the direct action of God upon the heart. Edwards's *Some Thoughts* is perhaps the clearest example of his interpretation of the great awakening in terms of God's work of redemption in history. In this work his *heilsgeschichtliches* reading of human events in terms of historical progress toward a goal defined by the providence of God reached its zenith. Believing that the millennium would be inaugurated by the historical manifestation of revivals, Edwards had not only defended the awakening as the work of God's Spirit, but claimed it was 'the dawning, or forerunner of an happy state' of the 'church on earth', and hence the harbinger of the millennial age (*Works*, 4.296–7, 324).

During the awakening, and as a result of the growing controversy over 'the nature and signs of the gracious operations of God's spirit', Edwards preached (probably in 1742) a long series of sermons that became the nucleus for his fullest statement on the evangelical nature of true religion, *A Treatise Concerning Religious Affections* (1746). Like his other tracts of that period, it provides a commentary upon and defence of revivalism. Rejecting the rationalistic objections to the revival, he held that the dynamic centre of a willing acting self lies not in the intellect but in the disposition, or the 'new sense of the heart'. Striving to show how the presence of the divine Spirit shall be discerned, and to define the soul's relationship to God, Edwards was concerned in this work with the 'nature and signs' of 'gracious' affections, in contrast to things of the mind which 'are not of a saving nature'. He thus distinguished the lives of the saints beyond anything that could be achieved by natural man. The central problem addressed by this tract is what are 'the distinguishing qualifications of those that are in favour with God and entitled to his eternal reward?' He defined 'true religion' as chiefly a matter of 'holy affections' respecting divine things, and identified and provided an exhaustive account of twelve 'signs' which are 'gracious' or 'saving' (*Works*, 2.84, 89, 118–19, 272). Given that each sign served as a mark through which the presence of the divine Spirit could be known, each pointed to the activity of the Spiriting out. As a whole these signs showed the very presence of the Spirit and served as evidence of the working of divine, saving grace in the heart of the believer. God thus worked a permanent qualitative change beyond anything of which natural faculties were capable; the mind was enlightened to apprehend God and the will became disposed to love and seek God for his own sake.

In the aftermath of the awakening, Edwards sought new ways to foster religious life both in his congregation and abroad, including a plan for a worldwide 'concert of prayer'. He published his reflections on the book of Revelation in the *Humble Attempt* (1747), in which he advanced the contention, already discussed in Scotland, that a union of praying Christians would 'open the doors and windows of heaven' after the withdrawal of the Spirit. Edwards believed that the saints have good reason to unite in a 'concert' of prayer, for it seemed evident that 'the beginning of that glorious work of God's Spirit' which would culminate in 'the glory of the latter-days, is not far off' (*Works*, 5.446–7, 325, 421). In 1749, as a sequel to his earlier writings relating to the great awakening, Edwards published a life of David Brainerd (1718–1747), who had been missionary to the American Indians on the western border of Massachusetts (1743–7). In no other work did Edwards articulate the genuine necessity of spiritual life and the 'New Birth' in one man with such abundance of concrete evidence.

Closer to home, in the course of his pastoral duty at Northampton, Edwards thought it was necessary to censure publicly a large number of his parishioners for immoral practices. He consequently incurred the displeasure of some of the town's most influential families. Conflict soon developed with members of his congregation over questions of ministerial authority. Edwards provoked an open rupture with his announcement that he intended to discontinue his grandfather's practice of admitting to communion those in good standing if they could provide evidence of a work of grace in their lives. The conflict spread into town politics and into relations with neighbouring ministers, causing bitter factionalism. Edwards formally made his views on this subject known to the standing committee of the church in February 1749. Because Stoddard's system of open communion had been practised in that church for nearly half a century, it was inevitable that Edwards's attempts to revise it would give offence and that he would be removed from his duties. After several months of bitter strife, a council of ministers and laity recommended a separation between Edwards and his congregation, and Edwards's formal dismissal followed in mid-1750. A council called on 22 June 1750 voted by a bare majority to dismiss him. He preached his 'farewell sermon' nine days later.

Life and works at Stockbridge After his removal Edwards faced uncertain prospects. He supplied the vacant pulpit in Canaan, Connecticut, and was contemplating settling there. At the same time he received several offers, including one from Scotland. Then, in December 1750, he received proposals from the congregation in Stockbridge, in western Massachusetts, to become their minister; about the same time similar proposals came from the commissioners of the London Society for Propagating the Gospel in New England to become the missionary of the Housatonic Indians who resided in or near Stockbridge. During the first week of August 1751 he moved his family there. Life at Stockbridge, a mission outpost populated by a few white inhabitants and more than 250 Indian families, was very difficult, especially after the outbreak of the French and Indian War. The war came to the village in 1754 when, after a raiding party of French and Indians killed several inhabitants, the town temporarily became a garrison.

Edwards's success in Stockbridge was apparently small, but it allowed him comparative retirement for study and composition. Despite the hard circumstances on the frontier settlement, these years were perhaps Edwards's most productive. Not only did he continue his pattern of study, but he also wrote several major treatises there. Among them are his well-known works such as *Freedom of the will* (1754), which is regarded as Edwards's greatest literary achievement, *Concerning the End for which God Created the World* and *The Nature of True Virtue* (both published posthumously in 1765), and *Original Sin* (1758).

Edwards's theological standing in his own day rested significantly on his *Freedom of the will*, which was both a defence of Calvinism and an assertion of God's absolute sovereignty. He attacked the Arminians' and deists' 'grand article concerning *the freedom of the will requisite to moral agency*', or the belief that absolute self-determinacy of will was necessary to human liberty and moral virtue. If the Arminian view was correct, he believed, God's providential and redemptive economy was contingent on unpredictable actions of moral agents. Such a condition contradicts the doctrine of divine foreknowledge and the premise that God, as absolute governor of the universe, orders events according to his sovereign wisdom. Instead, Edwards argued that since 'every event' in the physical as well as the moral world 'must be ordered by God', the 'liberty of moral agents does not consist in self-determining power'. Human beings must do as they will, in accordance with their fallen nature, and they have liberty only in the sense that nothing prevents them from doing what they will in accordance with their nature. Because 'nothing in the state or acts of the will of man is contingent' but 'every event of this kind is necessary', God's foreknowledge eliminates the possibility of contingency in the world, for contingency is the antithesis of God's unlimited prescience. Given that 'the power of volition' belongs only to 'the man or the soul', there is no such thing as 'freedom of the will'. That freedom is incompatible with the individual's necessary willing of what he or she can will in accordance with a nature of self already determined (*Works*, 1.163, 431–3). In the end Edwards saw the whole spectrum of moral endeavour solely in terms of his notion of the visible saints whose character was already determined.

Edwards's *Original Sin* played its part in the larger debates between the Enlightenment belief in the innate goodness of human beings and the emphasis placed by the Reformation on human depravity. Against the revolution that took place in the Western mind during the eighteenth century regarding human beings' nature and potentialities, and the rising Enlightenment notion of human beings as fundamentally rational and benevolent, Edwards provided 'a *general defense* of that great important doctrine' of original sin. This doctrine proclaimed both the depravity of the human heart and the imputation of Adam's first sin to his posterity: all Adam's posterity is 'exposed, and justly so, to the sorrow of this life, to temporal death, and eternal ruin, unless saved by grace'. The corruption of humankind, however, cannot be accounted for by considering the sin of each individual. It is essential to the human condition based on 'the *arbitrary* constitution of the Creator' in creation (*Works*, 3.102, 395, 403).

In *The Nature of True Virtue* Edwards's goal was to define the disposition that distinguished the godly. Elaborating his definition of 'Excellency', he claimed that true 'virtue most essentially consists in benevolence to Being in general'. True virtue is a kind of beauty. In moral beings, virtuous beauty pertains to a disposition of heart and exercise of will, namely 'that consent, propensity and union of heart to Being in general', or God, 'which is immediately exercised in good will' (*Works*, 8.540). True virtue in creatures appears in the degree to which their love coincides with God's love of his creation and agrees with the end that he intended for it.

Finally, in *Concerning the End for which God Created the World*, Edwards continued to develop the notion that the whole creation is the overflowing of divine being. God's 'internal glory' consists in his knowledge, resident in his understanding, and his holiness and happiness, seated in his will; this glory is 'enlarged' by communication '*ad extra*'. The 'great and last end' of all God's works is the manifestation of 'the glory of God' as 'the effulgence' of 'light from a luminary', and in the 'creature's knowing, esteeming, loving, and rejoicing' God's glory is both 'acknowledged [and] returned' (*Works*, 8.527, 530–531).

In September 1757 Edwards received a letter from the trustees of the College of New Jersey inviting him to become the college's third president; the second incumbent, Aaron Burr, Edwards's son-in-law, had died five days previously. Edwards was a popular choice for he had been a friend of the college from its inception. His three sons had graduated from Princeton, and for several years he kept in close touch with college affairs, attending commencement regularly and usually preaching on his visits. His response of 19 October 1757 was equivocal, listing many deficiencies which might disqualify him. The trustees, brushing these objections aside, pressed him to accept without delay. Accordingly, on 8 January 1758, he preached his farewell sermon to the Housatonic Indians at Stockbridge. A few days later he departed to Princeton: he arrived on 16 February and was formally inducted into office in the same day. He preached in the college chapel and gave out questions in divinity to the senior class. These seniors spoke enthusiastically of the 'light and instruction which Mr. Edwards communicated' (Leitch, 153). One week later, on 23 February, he was inoculated for smallpox, and one month later, on 22 March, he was dead. Edwards was buried in the president's lot in Princeton cemetery beside Aaron Burr.

Reputation Jonathan Edwards was the outstanding American theologian and certainly the ablest American philosopher to write before the great period of Charles S. Peirce (1839–1914), William James (1842–1910), Josiah Royce (1855–1916), John Dewey (1859–1952), and George Santayana (1863–1952). A towering figure in the American

Calvinist tradition, Edwards sought to formulate a Calvinist moral theology and to inhibit the influence of eighteenth-century secular and benevolist moral philosophy. During his lifetime Edwards achieved prominence and reputation as a preacher, a leader of the revival, and an evangelical theologian. His thought influenced the formation of the New Divinity Men—Joseph Bellamy (1719–1790), Samuel Hopkins (1721–1803), and Jonathan Edwards (1745–1801)—who attempted to defend Calvinism from rationalist attacks and to focus upon the experience of grace as the definitive religious event. His prominence is evident in the circle of evangelists during the first half of the nineteenth century, among whom the republication of his works was influential. The second half of the century witnessed an erosion of interest in Edwards: theological and cultural liberals condemned his ideas, particularly his commitment to the notion of human depravity, and so the bicentenary of his birth produced only a small surge of interest. As a result of the cultural climate in America in the middle of the twentieth century—the depression, the rise of neo-orthodoxy, and the growing search after national origins—a renaissance of interest in Edwards's ideas occurred. Since then he has become a major figure and is recognized as one of the most original thinkers in the American experience, and his place is secure within the life of the mind in America.

Yale University Press has published a multi-volume edition of Edwards's works. His unpublished writings fill forty volumes of about 500 pages each (now mainly at the Beinecke Rare Book and Manuscript Library, Yale University). AVIHU ZAKAI

Sources *The works of Jonathan Edwards*, ed. P. Miller and others, 19 vols. (1957–2001), vols. 1–6, 8–9, 11, 13, 16 • J. Edwards, 'Miscellany', no. 541, 'Miscellany', no. 547, 'Miscellany', no. 704, 'Miscellany', no. 1263, Yale U., divinity school [typescript on disk] • J. Edwards, 'God glorified in the work of redemption', *Jonathan Edwards: basic writings*, ed. O. E. Winslow (1966), 107–8 • J. Edwards, 'Sinners in the hands of an angry God', *A Jonathan Edwards reader*, ed. J. F. Smith and others (1995), 89–105 • W. E. Anderson, introduction, *Scientific and philosophical writings*, ed. W. E. Anderson (1980), vol. 6 of *The works of Jonathan Edwards*, ed. P. Miller and others, 15 • C. Chauncy, *Seasonable thoughts on the state of religion in New England* (1743), 319 • A. Leitch, *A Princeton companion* (1919), 153
Archives Newton Center, Massachusetts, Franklin Trask Library • Yale U., Beinecke L.
Likenesses T. Trotter, engraving, pubd 1783 (after J. Badger, 1750), NPG [*see illus.*] • J. Badger, oils, Yale U. Art Gallery • J. F. Weir, portrait (after unknown artist), Yale U. Art Gallery • portrait (after J. Badger), Princeton University, New Jersey, Nassau Hall
Wealth at death estate worth approx. £1000 (apart from specie): *Works of Jonathan Edwards*, Yale U., divinity school

Edwards, Joseph (1814–1882), sculptor, was born on 5 March 1814 at Ynysgau, Merthyr Tudful, Glamorgan, the son of John Edwards, a stonecutter. Joseph assisted his father in his business, showing exceptional ability from an early age. He had a limited education at local charity schools. At seventeen Joseph sought to widen his horizons by walking through south and west Wales, spending nearly two years in Swansea where he was employed as a mason. At twenty-one, in 1835, he went to London carrying an introduction to the sculptor William Behnes who, after some hesitation, employed him. He stayed with Behnes until 1838, during which time he attended the Royal Academy Schools, winning the silver medal for best model from the antique, and exhibiting for the first time. He entered the studio of Patrick Macdowell while continuing his studies at the Royal Academy, where he won a second silver medal in 1839. By this time he was gaining commissions for portrait busts and memorials in his own right, especially from patrons connected with south Wales. He carved the monument to Henry Charles Somerset, sixth duke of Beaufort, and in 1840 he made a bust of Ivor Bertie Guest, the first of several commissions from Merthyr industrialists.

In 1843 Edwards carved *The Last Dream* (exh. RA, 1844, as 'Part of a monument at North Othrington church to the late Miss Hutton of Sowber Hill, North Allerton'; North Otterington church, Yorkshire), regarded as his early masterpiece, and John Gibson interested himself in his compatriot's work on a visit to London. Welsh intellectuals became increasingly aware of his career. Edwards was perceived to demonstrate the potential for national progress in Wales, having risen by his own efforts from humble origins to find a place in the English art world. Like Gibson, he was frequently cited in the mid-nineteenth century as an example for the young to follow. In 1855, at the Royal London Eisteddfod, he became the first Welsh artist to have a solo exhibition of his works, and in the 1860s and 1870s he moved among the London Welsh intelligentsia who exercised a strong influence on national development.

Edwards was patronized by notable establishment figures. His marble relief *Religion Consoling Justice* (1853; Dingestow, Monmouthshire) formed part of the memorial to Justice Sir John Bernard Bosanquet, and in 1854 and 1856 he was again commissioned by the Beaufort family. In 1859 he met George Virtue, whose magazine, the *Art Journal*, promoted his work, publishing engravings on several occasions. Virtue also made use of a work by Edwards for the headpiece of his *Girls Own Paper*. In 1870 the sculptor was commissioned to execute the memorial to the publisher at Walton-on-Thames cemetery.

Edwards was both a meticulous craftsman and painstaking in his artistic conceptions, which were of a mystical though fundamentally Christian nature. His *Religion*, exhibited as a plaster at the International Exhibition of 1862, became his only large-scale public sculpture in his native country, erected in marble at Cefncoedycymer cemetery ten years later (a second version is at Highgate cemetery, London). His high seriousness and dedication to art came at the expense of business considerations and he was frequently financially embarrassed. Probably for this reason, in 1846 Edwards began to work for Matthew Noble in a role which, it is clear, far exceeded that of the normal assistant. Among Edwards's papers is a list of some forty major pieces attributed to the English sculptor on which he worked at every stage from conception to completion, including the famous Wellington memorial of 1856 in Manchester. He became known in the art world as Noble's 'ghost', entering his studio at the end of the day to work

overnight, and on Sundays. On Noble's death in 1876, Edwards completed his outstanding works, for which he received minimal recompense. In 1881 Thomas Woolner, who took a dim view of Noble's practice, made application on Edwards's behalf for a Turner bequest. The Welsh sculptor was able to benefit from only one payment, since he died, unmarried, on 9 January 1882 at his home, 40 Roberts Street, Hampstead Road, London. He was buried in Highgate cemetery.   PETER LORD

Sources W. Davies, 'Joseph Edwards, sculptor', *Wales*, 2 (1895), 134–7, 193–6, 273–8, 301–3, 355–60, 403–5, 468–72, 540–43; 3 (1896), 24–9, 78–80, 138–9, 174–8, 215–18, 279–84, 374–7, 508–11 · M. H. Spielmann, 'The artist's ghost', *Magazine of Art*, 17 (1893–4), 313 · U. Wales, Bangor, Sir Isambard Owen MSS
Archives NL Wales, MSS 1639; 21272E | U. Wales, Bangor, Sir Isambard Owen MSS, c., Joseph Edwards, MSS 6095–6134
Likenesses R. T. Crawshay, photographs, 1865–75, NL Wales · W. Griffith, photograph, 1865–75, NL Wales · B. S. Marks, oils, c.1870, NMG Wales
Wealth at death £473 11s. 5d.: probate, 7 March 1882, *CGPLA Eng. & Wales*

Edwards, Joseph Robert (1908–1997), motor manufacturer and industrialist, was born on 5 July 1908 at 169 Church Road, Gorleston, Great Yarmouth, the youngest son of Walter Smith Edwards, marine engineer and later Lloyds surveyor, and his wife, Annie, *née* Wilkinson. He was educated at Great Yarmouth high school. A fascination with motor cars—this was to be lifelong—led him to break with family tradition and become the first male for four generations not to go to sea. Instead he joined the Austin Motor Company in Birmingham in 1928 as a toolmaker, and soon became a chargehand. On 13 April 1936 he married Frances Mabel Haddon Bourne (1911/12–1975), daughter of Ernest Frederick Bourne, a grocer. They had three sons and a daughter.

Edwards moved to Hercules Cycles in 1939 for promotion first to toolroom superintendent and then assistant works manager. In 1941 Leonard Lord, the Austin works director, brought him back to the key role of toolroom superintendent. Edwards then began an association with George Harriman, a Leonard Lord protégé soon to be production manager, which saw the two move up the organization in tandem. Harriman, personally charming but dominated by Lord and ultimately ineffectual, relied heavily on Edwards's directness and combativeness. A man who would happily confront a trade union dispute meeting on his own, Edwards was effective at driving through Austin's war production and its huge post-war expansion, when Britain briefly exported more cars than the United States. But as labour relations became more and more a battleground, he found himself increasingly out of step with both associations and governments. In 1956, faced with a massive downturn, Edwards, by then production director for the British Motor Corporation (formed by the merger of Austin and Morris Motors), sacked 6000 men with just a week's pay. Public outcry followed, but in spite of pressure from the Engineering Employers' Association he refused to back down and rode out a strike. Shortly afterwards Lord asked him to take over labour relations full time. But Edwards saw this as demotion. He resigned to become managing director of Pressed Steel/Fisher, which built the bodies for the British Motor Corporation.

At Pressed Steel, Edwards turned loss into profit, but started with another mass dismissal. He would claim later that his actions hastened the Redundancy Payments Act. His stay at Pressed Steel was a highlight of his career. He instituted many practices which he believed Lord had neglected at the British Motor Corporation, including properly funded research and extensive apprentice and management training. He broadened his customers to include other major car manufacturers, and even supplied Hawker Hunter jet-fighter assemblies. He also set up a successful light aircraft manufacturing company, Beagle Aircraft. In 1966 Pressed Steel was bought by British Motor Holdings, formed from the old British Motor Corporation plus Jaguar. Edwards became managing director of the new group. He was appalled by what he found. 'Nothing had happened in the twelve years I had been away. The company had unwound. There was no forward thinking' (personal knowledge). His considered view was that the company, with 115,000 employees, was beyond the management's capacity to manage. If anyone could have saved it, it was probably Edwards. With typical energy he set about change, overhauling, purchasing, and styling. But it was too late. Under pressure from the Labour government's industrial reorganization drive, which saw salvation in even larger groupings, Harriman was soon in talks with Sir Donald Stokes of Leyland. As his own and the company's health failed, the deal was done. Edwards, contemptuous of Stokes and the quality of the Leyland factories, and always uncomfortable with political involvement, declined to be involved in the ill-fated merger.

Edwards was briefly parachuted into another lame duck, the persistently lossmaking Harland and Wolff shipyard in Belfast, first as deputy chairman (1968–70), then in 1970 as chairman. He favoured a sale to the Greek shipowner Aristotle Onassis, whose tankers were built there. But after the Conservative victory in the 1970 general election yet another new initiative was devised and Edwards was replaced. Subsequently he pursued his motor interests as vice-chairman of Lucas (Industries) Ltd (1976–9), chairman of Penta Motors (1978–87), and, with particular pleasure, chairman of Canewdon Consultants (from 1986), which carried out research and development work for motor companies worldwide, with designers often drawn from teams disbanded by the new foreign owners of British companies.

Following the death of his first wife in 1975 Edwards married, on 1 May 1976, Joan Constance Mary Tattersall (*b.* 1932/3), secretary, daughter of James Henry Tattersall, an engineer. Edwards died of a heart attack in Poole, Dorset, where he had lived, on 12 June 1997. He was survived by his second wife and the children of his first marriage.

MARTIN ADENEY

Sources M. Adeney, *The motormakers* (1988) · G. Turner, *The Leyland papers* (1971) · E. Wigham, *The power to manage: a history of the Engineering Employers' Federation* (1973) · R. J. Wyatt, *The Austin* (1981) · M. Moss and J. R. Hume, *Shipbuilders to the world: 125 years of Harland and Wolff, 1861–1986* (1986) · G. T. Bloomfield, 'Harriman, Sir George William', *DBB* · *The Times* (24 June 1997) · *WWW* · b. cert. · m. certs. · d. cert. · personal knowledge (2004)
Archives SOUND BL NSA, oral history interview
Likenesses photograph, repro. in *The Times*
Wealth at death £294,029: probate, 19 Aug 1997, *CGPLA Eng. & Wales*

Edwards, Lewis (1809–1887), Calvinistic Methodist minister and college head, eldest child of a small farmer, Lewis Edward (1783–1852) and his wife, Margaret (1785–1854), was born on 27 October 1809 at Pwllcenawon, near Penllwyn in the parish of Llanbadarn Fawr, Cardiganshire. His parents were pious Methodists of conviction and the young Lewis made good use of the collection of Welsh religious and devotional classics which they possessed. His early education was at various local schools, the first kept by a superannuated old soldier, others kept by men trained at a nearby grammar school of good standing. At the school held at Penllwyn Calvinistic Methodist chapel by an uncle of his, Lewis not only began his acquaintance with Greek and Latin, but was also imbued with a deep love of learning and an appreciation of the importance of education. He extended his reading of the classics and of puritan literature at a school in Llangeitho, where he began to preach locally in 1827. His father had intended him to remain at home on the farm, but as his interest in theological questions became more apparent, a neighbour persuaded him to allow Lewis to continue his education. Following further periods at local schools, most particularly with John Evans at Aberystwyth, who gave him the use of his personal library, Edwards opened his own school in the town in 1829, and also spent some time as an assistant at Llangeitho. In 1830 he left to become a private tutor to the Lloyd family of Pendine (Pen-tywyn), near Carmarthen.

Edwards had lost none of his fervour for education. He had been accepted formally as a preacher in 1829, but the leaders of his denomination were deeply suspicious of any desire for higher education in their ministerial candidates, seeing this as a sign of pride and lack of faith in the authority of scripture. They were not to be easily persuaded to allow him to gain a college education. Permission was at last granted for him to attend University College, London, but his funds supported him only through one winter. In 1832 he took charge of the English Calvinistic Methodist church at Laugharne in Carmarthenshire, where he remained a year and a half as minister and schoolmaster, and where he was able to improve his command of English. In 1833 he enrolled at Edinburgh University, where he worked with Professor John Wilson (Christopher North), Thomas Chalmers, and James Phillans, and was enabled, through the intervention of Wilson, by whom he was highly regarded, to take his degree at the end of three, instead of four, years. He returned to Wales in 1836, the first of his denomination to have gained the degree of MA. He was ordained at Newcastle Emlyn in 1837, and shortly after, with his brother-in-law, the Revd David Charles, he opened a school at Bala to prepare students for the Welsh Calvinistic Methodist ministry. It was recognized as a denominational college in 1839, and

Lewis Edwards (1809–1887), by unknown engraver

Edwards was principal for fifty years. In January 1844 Edwards started a monthly magazine, *Yr Esboniwr*, which ran for a year.

Edwards had begun to appreciate the cultural and educational role of periodicals, when he had chanced upon a copy of *Blackwood's Edinburgh Magazine* at a printing office in Aberystwyth in 1829, which was his first introduction to English literature. At Edinburgh he had an opportunity of reading regularly the popular reviews and magazines, and of coming into contact with some of their contributors and editors. He saw the need for a similar type of publication in Welsh, which would introduce the nonconformist ministry to European and Welsh authors and to non-sectarian discussions of literary, philosophical, and theological issues. In January 1845 he founded the quarterly *Y Traethodydd* with the co-operation of Roger Edwards (no relation), and the printer Thomas Gee. The journal, which he edited for ten years, and which reflected Edwards's belief in an educated, intellectual ministry, became the vehicle for much of his work, including essays on Homer, Goethe, Kant, Coleridge, Hamilton, Mill, and Milton. It established itself as one of the best Welsh periodicals, and one that has retained its character to the present time.

Many of Edwards's essays were afterwards collected and published as *Traethodau llenyddol* (*c*.1868) and *Traethodau duwinyddol* (*c*.1872). In 1847 he set up *Y Geiniogwerth*, a monthly religious magazine which ran until 1851. His best-known work was *Athrawiaeth yr Iawn* (1860), of which an English translation appeared in 1886, and a second edition of the original, with a memoir by his son T. C.

Edwards, in 1887. *Hanes duwinyddiaeth* appeared in 1889. In 1857 he was offered the honorary degree of DD by Princeton College, USA, but he declined it. His own university offered him the same degree in 1865, and he went to Edinburgh to receive it. In 1875 his friends and admirers gave him a testimonial of £2600, which assured his future.

Edwards was an influential leader of his denomination for many years. As a consequence of his familiarity with Scottish Presbyterianism he strengthened the presbyterian pattern of his denomination, but more generally he succeeded in raising the educational standards of the nonconformist ministry and broadened the horizons of Welsh education and intellectual discussion. Likewise, his support of the Liberal candidate in the famous election of 1859 in Merioneth acted as a powerful solvent of the political quiescence hitherto so characteristic of the denomination. More contentiously, he was also responsible for a policy of establishing English-language churches within Welsh Calvinistic Methodism.

Edwards died at Bala College on 19 July 1887, and was buried on 22 July in the same grave at Llanycil, near Bala, as Thomas Charles of Bala, whose granddaughter Jane he had married on 30 December 1836. There were nine children of the marriage, one of whom, Thomas Charles Edwards, became the first principal of the University College of Wales, Aberystwyth. BRYNLEY F. ROBERTS

Sources T. Ll. Evans, *Lewis Edwards: ei fywyd a'i waith* (1967) · T. C. Edwards, *Bywyd a Llythyrau y diweddar Barch Lewis Edwards DD* (1901) · A. Llywelyn-Williams, 'Lewis Edwards ac urddas cenedl', *Ysgrifau Beirniadol*, 2 (1966), 109–22 · R. T. Jenkins, 'Dylanwad Dr. Lewis Edwards ar feddwl Cymru', *Y Traethodydd*, new ser., 19 (1931), 193–206 · J. E. C. Williams, 'Hanes cychwyn *Y Traethodydd*', *Llên Cymru*, 14 (1981–2), 111–42 · H. I. Davies, 'Y Dr. Lewis Edwards a diwinyddiaeth', *Y Traethodydd*, 3rd ser., 14 (1945), 5–14, 31–42, 120–28 · D. G. Jones, 'Y Dr. Lewis Edwards fel beirniad llenyddol a bardd', *Y Traethodydd*, 3rd ser., 14 (1945), 15–28 · *CGPLA Eng. & Wales* (1887)

Archives NL Wales, essays | NL Wales, Calvinistic Methodist MSS; corresp. and papers · NL Wales, letters to T. C. Edwards · NL Wales, corresp. with Henry Rees and Owen Thomas · NL Wales, letters to Ebenezer Thomas · NL Wales, letters to Owen Thomas

Likenesses J. Barrett, painting, 1877, United Theological College, Aberystwyth · C. A. Tomkins, engraving, 1877, NL Wales · memorial, *c*.1910, Penllwyn Chapel, Cardiganshire · engravings, NL Wales [*see illus.*] · photographs, repro. in Evans, *Lewis Edwards* · photographs, repro. in Edwards, *Bywyd a Llythyrau y diweddar Barch Lewis Edwards* · photographs, NL Wales · statue, Bala College, Bala, Merioneth

Wealth at death £3817 15*s*. 3*d*.: probate, 7 Oct 1887, *CGPLA Eng. & Wales*

Edwards, Lionel Dalhousie Robertson (1878–1966), sporting artist, was born on 9 November 1878 at Clifton, Bristol, the youngest of the eight children of Dr James Edwards (1810–1886), formerly a Chester physician, of Benarth Hall, Conwy, north Wales, and his third wife, Harriet Maine, of Kelso, Roxburghshire. He received little formal education and country pursuits engrossed him from childhood. He was initially destined for the army, a career for which he showed no aptitude, and his artistic gifts inherited from his maternal grandmother, who had been a talented pupil of George Romney, were encouraged by his mother. In his teens he received brief training, including anatomical instruction, at W. Frank Calderon's school of animal painting in Baker Street, London, and he also attended evening classes at Heatherley's Art School. While still a student he was elected a member of the London Sketch Club.

In 1898 some of Edwards's drawings of the famous wild cattle at Chillingham, Northumberland, were accepted by *Country Life*, and a further six or seven years working for periodicals in London were made endurable by frequent expeditions by bicycle, or sometimes on a borrowed horse, for a day with hounds in the home counties. In 1904, during a holiday on Exmoor, his first exhibition, held in the parish hall at Porlock, Somerset, of stag-hunting subjects was a successful sell-out.

After marriage on 20 October 1905 to Ethel Ashness-Wells (1881–1968), daughter of a brewer—a union which brought sixty years of great happiness and during which three sons and a daughter were born—Edwards and his wife first lived on the border of south Oxfordshire and then in 1909 moved to Worcestershire, where they both hunted regularly, first on borrowed mounts and then on horses of their own, a pursuit which brought him many commissions. In 1912 Edwards and his family moved to north Wales, which had been his home in his youth. During the First World War he entered the army remount service, being promoted captain in March 1915, and had, as he said, 'four years of nothing but horse'—an experience which inevitably educated his eyes for equine conformation—and on demobilization he maintained that enforced artistic abstinence had freshened his style.

By disposition Edwards was dedicated to a country way of life; hunting was his great pleasure and he saw sport with ninety-one different packs. In 1921 he moved to West Tytherley, in Hampshire, near Salisbury, and for forty-three years was a member of the Hursley hunt committee. As early as 1901 he had been made an associate of the Royal Cambrian Academy of Art, in 1926 he became a full academician, and the following year a member of the Royal Institute of Painters in Water Colours. In 1931 he exhibited at the Royal Academy *A Hunt in the Snow: the Heythrop*.

All his long life Edwards possessed immense tenacity and diligence as an artist, always carrying a sketchbook in the pocket of his riding-coat. During the 1920s he began his series of studies of different hunting countries, often in fluent watercolours, his favourite medium. Sensitive landscape backgrounds of packs as diverse in country as the Quorn (Leicestershire), the Beaufort (Gloucestershire), the Meath (Ireland), and the Devon and Somerset made these pictures memorable. He understood hunting from the inside—the implications of weather conditions, of hound work, and of horsemanship, and the esoteric niceties of costume and equipment. This knowledge, allied to his eye for a country, placed him in a unique category as a sporting artist. Whether he was depicting hunting in the shires and provinces, racing scenes at Newmarket, polo at Tidworth, or bull-fighting in Spain, he could always evoke the thrill and magic of the moment

and also capture with uncanny veracity the likeness of a horse. He painted many of the important equine heroes of his time, such as the racehorses Mahmoud, Golden Miller, Team Spirit, and Arkle.

Edwards excelled as an illustrator and much of his best work was accomplished for his own articles and books— all written in a clear, vivid style, the most important of which are *My Hunting Sketch Book* (2 vols., 1928–30), *Famous Foxhunters* (1932), *My Irish Sketch Book* (1938), *Scarlet and Corduroy* (1941), *Reminiscences of a Sporting Artist* (1947), and *Thy Servant, the Horse* (1952). His studies for the books of sporting verse by William Henry Ogilvie, published between 1922 and 1932, were outstanding.

In later years Edwards held exhibitions at the Tryon Gallery in London, the last one in 1964, and many popular prints were made from his pictures, which brought his work before a wide public. By nature courteous and modest, he was also generous to a degree to aspiring sporting painters. His perceptive insight as a dedicated countryman, combined with his graphic talent as an artist, proved a considerable influence on twentieth-century sporting art, introducing a more subtle approach with appreciation of a landscape being as vital to a composition as an eye for horse and hound. Industrious and prolific to the very end of his long life, he died on 13 April 1966 at his home, Buckholt House, in West Tytherley. He was survived by his wife.   STELLA A. WALKER, *rev.*

Sources L. Edwards, *Reminiscences of a sporting artist* (1947) · *Horse and Hound* (23 April 1966) · *The Times* (14 April 1966) · private information (1981) · *CGPLA Eng. & Wales* (1966) · J. N. P. Watson, *Lionel Edwards: master of the sporting scene* (1986) · M. Edwards, *Figures in a landscape: Lionel Edwards: a sporting artist and his family* (1986)
Likenesses photographs, repro. in Edwards, *Figures in a landscape*, 95, 188
Wealth at death £33,171: probate, 23 Aug 1966, *CGPLA Eng. & Wales*

Edwards, Mary (1705?–1743), art patron, was born in or about 1705, probably in London, the only child of Francis Edwards (*d.* 1729), of Welham Grove, Leicestershire, Ketton, Rutland, and Soho Square, London, and his wife, Anna Margaretta Vernatti (*d.* in or after 1743). Both her parents were wealthy. Francis Edwards owned property in Leicestershire, Northamptonshire, Middlesex, Essex, Hertfordshire, and Kent, and in the City of London; he also had large holdings in the New River Company, Islington, of which his nephew William Edwards was treasurer. Mary's mother was of the Dutch-born Vernatti family, which had financed and profited by the draining of fenland in Lincolnshire. When Francis Edwards died in 1729 (intestate), his widow renounced all claims to his estate in favour of Mary, who thus became his sole heir. At the age of about twenty-three, Mary Edwards was reputedly the richest woman in England, with a fortune of between £50,000 and £60,000. She proved to be a woman of spirit.

Two years later Mary Edwards fell briefly in love with Lord Anne Hamilton (*b.* 1709), an ensign in the 2nd regiment of guards and a younger son of the fourth duke of Hamilton and his second wife, Elizabeth, daughter of the fifth Baron Gerard. An announcement of the marriage of

Mary Edwards (1705?–1743), by William Hogarth, 1742

'Lord Anne Hamilton, to Miss Edwards, a very great fortune' (no precise date given) appeared in the *Gentleman's Magazine* for July 1731 (*GM*, 1, 1731, 311). The marriage itself, allegedly clandestine (and allegedly later repudiated by Mary), is often said to have taken place in the chapel of the Fleet prison; but registers of that chapel (PRO, RG 7/116) contain no record of it. Possibly a record may yet be traced elsewhere; but it seems more likely that no legal marriage ever took place. Later evidence shows that Mary Edwards never claimed to be a married woman and never styled herself Hamilton. The probability is that she defied convention in order to avoid surrendering control of her fortune to a husband. After a son was born to the couple on 4 March 1733, Mary Edwards, defying respectability, had him baptized as Gerard Anne Edwards, 'Son of Mrs Mary Edwards, Singlewom^{n}' (28 March 1733, register of baptisms, St Mary Abbots, Kensington), thus effectively declaring her child to be illegitimate. She also used her maiden name when signing a grant (dated 2 July 1733; College of Arms) extending the use of her coat and crest to Lord Anne, who briefly assumed Edwards as his middle name.

Mary Edwards lived openly with Lord Anne Hamilton for two or three years. Hogarth portrayed their infant son, Gerard, in his cradle in 1733 (Bearsted collection, Upton House, Oxfordshire), and some eighteen months later painted a *Conversation Piece* (priv. coll.) of Mary Edwards, Lord Anne, and their child on the terrace of Mary's house in Kensington, purchased in 1731 (the lease describing her as 'spinster'). Mary is depicted holding a volume of the *Spectator* open at a page of Addison's essay no. 580 on how

to rear children virtuously. This brief glimpse of domesticity was shortly followed by Mary's break with the spendthrift Lord Anne, precipitated by finding that he had appropriated £1200 of her Bank of England stock and £500 of her India stock. She acted decisively. Her lawyers drew up a deed between 'Mary Edwards, spinster, and the Hon. … Anne Hamilton, alias Anne Edwards Hamilton', signed by both parties on 22 May 1734, recounting that 'differences and disputes' had arisen between them over her bank stock, and returning it to 'Mary Edwards, of Welham, Leicester'. Lord Anne Hamilton then made his exit from her life. The fact that he married another heiress (Anna Powell, seventeen years younger than himself), legally, in October 1742, within Mary Edwards's lifetime and without charges of bigamy, contributes to the probability that no marriage between him and Mary Edwards had ever taken place.

Mary Edwards enjoyed independence for the remaining nine years of her life, mostly spent between her houses in Kensington and St James's Street. She continued her patronage to Hogarth; and here it should be noted that male short-sightedness in the past has averred that it was Mary's father rather than Mary who was Hogarth's patron. Mary Edwards bought Hogarth's painting *Southwark Fair*, of 1733, and collected his prints. She reputedly commissioned (and certainly owned) his satirical painting *Taste in High Life, or, Taste à la Mode* (priv. coll.) of *c*.1742. In that year she sat to Hogarth for the portrait (*Miss Mary Edwards*, 1742; Frick collection, New York) which has immortalized her, and which has been described by David Bindman as 'entirely the equal of *Captain Coram* [Coram Foundation, London], and … as rich in symbolism' (Bindman, 135). Hogarth portrays Mary Edwards as a woman whose stout-hearted spirit is reinforced by the presence of busts of Elizabeth I and Alfred the Great. In scarlet damask, adorned with a magnificent diamond, gold, and pearl parure with a pendant cross, one hand on a companionable spaniel, she sits beside a table which holds a globe and a scroll inscribed with a stirring challenge to defend a proud inheritance (perhaps an allusion to Elizabeth I's great Tilbury speech): 'Remember Englishmen the Laws the Rights … So dearly bought the Price of so much Contest/Transmit it careful to Posterity …'. This Mary Edwards succeeded in doing. She appears to have been devoted to her son, Gerard, and to have taken pains over his education.

Mary Edwards made her will on 13 April 1742, entailing all her property on her son and his male heirs. An 'Act for making the Exemplification of the last Will and Testament of Mary Edwards, deceased' lists all her properties (19 Geo. III c 80, House of Lords RO). She died at Kensington on 23 August 1743, aged thirty-eight. The *Gentleman's Magazine*, reporting the death of 'Miss [*sic*] Edwards, of Kensington', added that 'by her death a large Fortune comes to Gerard Anne Edwards; her son, a Minor' (*GM*, 13, 1743, 443). She had transmitted her inheritance intact. Having stipulated in her will that her funeral should be conducted privately, 'without plumes or escutcheons on my hearse', she was buried on 10 September beside her father at St Andrew's Church, Welham. Mr Cock of Covent Garden conducted sales of her personal effects: her pictures and bronzes (140 lots, including Hogarth's *Taste à la Mode* and *Southwark Fair*, a half-length portrait of Queen Elizabeth, and 'a Large Pair of Globes') on 28–29 May 1746, her plate and 'all her rich jewels' on 30 May.

JUDY EGERTON

Sources *GM*, 1st ser., 1 (1731), 311 · *GM*, 1st ser., 3 (1733), 156 · *GM*, 1st ser., 13 (1743), 443 · W. F. Noel, 'Edwards of Welham', *Rutland Magazine and County Historical Record*, 4 (1909–10), 209–12, 243–4 · E. F. Noel, *Some letters and records of the Noel family* (1910), 30–31, 44–5 · *Scots peerage*, 4.385–88 · D. Bindman, *Hogarth* (1981); repr. (1994), 134–5 · R. Paulson, *Hogarth: his life, art and times*, 2 vols. (1971), 333–7, 442–3, 446–8, 543–8 · N. Tscherny, 'An un-married woman: Mary Edwards, William Hogarth and a case of eighteenth-century British patronage', *Women and art in early modern Europe*, ed. C. Lawrence (1997), 237–54 · J. Nichols, *The history and antiquities of the county of Leicester*, 2/2 (1798), 863
Likenesses W. Hogarth, *c.*1734 (*Conversation piece*; with Lord Anne and their child), priv. coll. · W. Hogarth, portrait, 1742, Frick Collection, New York [*see illus.*]
Wealth at death reputed to have been the richest woman in England; 'by her death a large Fortune comes to [her son] Gerard Anne Edwards'

Edwards, Mary. *See* Mozeen, Mary (*b.* in or before 1724?, *d.* 1773?).

Edwards, Matilda Barbara Betham (1836–1919), writer, was born on 4 March 1836 at Westerfield, Suffolk, the fourth daughter of Edward Edwards (*c.*1808–1864), a farmer, and Barbara (1806–1848) daughter of the Revd William *Betham (1749–1839), antiquary. Her father was known as the best farmer thereabouts, and through her upbringing she coupled a deep understanding of farming with literary traditions from her mother's side, nourished from an early age by literary letters from her aunt and godmother (Mary) Matilda *Betham (1776–1852).

The young Matilda educated herself by reading in her family's library, and borrowing from the Mechanics' Institution in Ipswich, until, aged ten, she went to day school in Ipswich, where her French teacher kindled an interest in France. Her mother died when she was twelve. She spent six unhappy months as governess-pupil at a school in London, and on returning home wrote her first much acclaimed and several times republished novel, *The White House by the Sea* (1857). At least from this time onwards, she used the name Matilda Barbara Betham Edwards. She lived in south Germany and Vienna in 1862 and in Paris in 1863, improving her knowledge of German and French. *Dr Jacob*, a popular novel about an English-speaking clergyman of whom she heard while in Frankfurt, was published in 1864. On her father's death that year, she returned to Suffolk to manage the farm in partnership with her sister until her sister died in 1865.

Betham Edwards then moved to London into a circle of literary celebrities, counting among her correspondents Henry James, Frederic Harrison, Clement Shorter (who became her literary executor), and others. She earned her living writing articles for newspapers, short stories, poems, children's tales, novels, some translations, and descriptions of travel in Wales, Germany, Greece, Spain,

and Africa. She became a close friend of Barbara Leigh Smith Bodichon, journeying with her in 1867 to Algiers, and of George Eliot. Her novel *Kitty* was published in 1869. Ill health took Betham Edwards to Hastings in 1873 and after a year in Nantes in 1875 she found her distinctive voice in *A Year in Western France* (1876). From then on she travelled all over France, well prepared with introductions to farmers and agricultural experts. She became a sharply percipient writer on peasant agriculture at a time when farming in western Europe was moving from prosperity into deep depression. She wrote vividly on regional agriculture, always with the strongest sympathy for self-sufficient family farming and the pride and dignity conferred on peasants by their independence and ownership of land. Her many books on French peasant life and farming were much appreciated in France.

Betham Edwards nevertheless regarded her French books as a byway, and rested her reputation on her many novels by which her English readers also judged her. She herself regarded *Forestalled* (1880) and *Love and Marriage* (1884) as her best work, but Lord Broughton judged *Kitty* the finest novel he ever read. Frederic Harrison singled out *Kitty*, *Dr Jacob*, and *John and I* (1862) as among her best. All her fiction reflected personal experience from her childhood and family life or from her observations and historical knowledge of France and Germany. Each novel showed her gift for sharp characterization, in few words, and in many her political opinions were undisguised, particularly in *The Silvestres* (1871). First serialized in *Good Words*, its socialist views caused many readers to cancel their subscriptions to the magazine.

In 1889 Betham Edwards reissued Arthur Young's *Travels in France* (1792), silently omitting much agricultural detail, but including an attractive, well-documented biographical sketch and an arresting introduction, describing her journeys over the same ground 100 years after Young. Young's fulminations against peasant farming rang hollow when set against the obvious prosperity of a highly diversified peasant agriculture with rural industries in the 1880s and 1890s. In 1898 she published Young's *Autobiography and Correspondence*, an abbreviated version of Young's unpublished memoir and some relevant letters.

That year Betham Edwards also published her own autobiographical *Reminiscences* and another novel, *A Storm-Rent Sky*, which depicted an ordinary family's experience of revolution in France. *Lord of the Harvest* (1899), set in the Suffolk countryside before the repeal of the corn laws, was reissued in the World's Classics series in 1913. *Under the German Ban in Alsace and Lorraine* (1914) and the romantic novel *Hearts of Alsace* (1916) showed her deep interest in the personal consequences of Germany's annexation of the French-speaking territory. Her *War Poems* was published in 1918 while a second autobiographical memoir, *Mid-Victorian Memories*, appeared in 1919.

Betham Edwards was described as gentle, courteous, punctilious, and a lively conversationalist. In her youth she must have endured the discomforts of travel cheerfully, but in old age she became as exacting as royalty. She was a highly disciplined worker, extremely regular in her habits. She voiced strong prejudices against Catholicism, deep admiration for the self-sufficiency of French peasant farming, and warm sympathy for 'a loftier Socialism' than that of St Simon (M. Betham Edwards, *A Year in Western France*, 1876, 53). Her writing showed intense interest in public education, opportunities for women, cultural facilities in towns, and positivism.

No public recognition was accorded Betham Edwards in England; even her application to Gladstone for a civil-list pension was unsuccessful, but the French gave her the title *Officier de l'instruction publique de France* in 1891, making her the only English woman then so honoured. The government also awarded her a gold medal for her nine books on the country, which were exhibited at the Paris exhibition in 1908. In a career of sixty-two years, only nine passed without publication.

Still mentally alert, Matilda Betham Edwards died at 1 High Wickham, Hastings, on 4 January 1919, aged eighty-two, after suffering a stroke. Her body was cremated at Ilford crematorium five days later. She made bequests to the Ipswich and Hastings museums.   JOAN THIRSK

Sources M. Betham Edwards, *Reminiscences* (1898) · M. Betham Edwards, *Mid-Victorian memories* (1919) · *The Times* (7 Jan 1919) · will, CGPLA, ledger no. NPG 1919, DRA-ELL 63/15, p. 197 · private information (2004) [Victoria Williams, curator, Hastings Museum and Art Gallery] · BL, Add. MS 44516, fols. 101–2 [request for civil pension] · BL, Add. MS 46620, fol. 316 [publisher's agreement for novel] · J. Todd, ed., *Dictionary of British women writers* (1989) · d. cert.
Archives Hastings Library, books in her library · Hastings Museum and Art Gallery, artefacts · Ipswich Museum, artefacts · NRA, corresp. and literary papers | BLPES, letters to Frederic Harrison · U. Leeds, Brotherton L., letters to Clement Shorter · U. Reading L., letters to George Bell & Sons
Likenesses S. Grand, pastel sketch, 1911, repro. in Betham Edwards, *Mid-Victorian memories* · pastel drawing, Ipswich Borough Council Museums and Galleries · photograph, Ipswich Borough Council Museums and Galleries
Wealth at death £803 9s.: probate, 10 Feb 1919, CGPLA Eng. & Wales

Edwards [*née* Newton], **Monica Le Doux** (1912–1998), writer, was born on 8 November 1912 in Belper, Derbyshire, the second daughter and third of the four children of the Revd Harry Newton (*d.* 1939) and Beryl F. Le Doux, *née* Sargeant (*d.* 1969?). Her early education was at Beecholm College, Thornes House School, and Wakefield high school.

In 1927 Harry Newton left St Andrew's, Wakefield, for the living of Rye Harbour, Sussex. There, though her sister was sent to school and her two brothers had a tutor, Monica's education ceased. She roamed Rye Harbour, sailed with fishermen, rode shepherds' ponies, and helped at a riding school. After a year of freedom she was sent to St Brandon's School for the daughters of clergy in Bristol. Monica hated the school, but encountered a good English teacher who encouraged her to write.

In 1928 the Rye Harbour lifeboat was lost and Monica walked the shore helping to identify the bodies of the crew as they were washed up. Many of them were her friends. She wrote of this in *Storm Ahead* (1953).

One of Monica's friends was William Ferdinand (Bill) Edwards (1903–1990), a part-time fisherman, nearly ten years her senior. They worked on an acrobatic and tumbling routine which they performed between the acts at local theatres and pageants and which was pictured on postcards. Her parents felt she was too young to marry and suggested a separation until she was twenty-one. Monica obeyed, but on 10 November 1933, two days after her twenty-first birthday, she married Bill Edwards and her father officiated. They had two children, a daughter, Shelley, born in 1935, and a son, Sean, born in 1943.

By 1946 Monica, living in Send, near Woking, was hankering for country life. She bought Pitlands Farm, Thursley, Surrey, a near derelict, mainly seventeenth-century farmhouse, at an auction. They renamed it Punch Bowl Farm and Bill Edwards gave up his job as a lorry driver to make the house habitable and farm the land. Monica learned to milk and, finding herself the breadwinner, began to write the first of her thirty-five books.

In 1947 two books for children were published. *Wish for a Pony* was the first of the fifteen Rye Harbour / Romney Marsh series which drew on her girlhood experiences. Edwards always regretted that it was her most successful work and, to her indignation, labelled her as a writer of pony books. She always asserted that the ponies were only incidental in her stories of country life. *No Mistaking Corker*, the first of the eleven Punchbowl Farm series, was a disappointing second work but after it Monica seemed to find her voice: one book a year in each series followed with reliable regularity.

All her child characters were middle class and Tamzin Grey, the protagonist of the Marsh books, was, like Monica, the daughter of an absent-minded vicar. The sea and boats are central to this series covering five years in the lives of the chief characters—two boys and two girls. Their adventures include shipwreck, smuggling, and the rescue of oiled seabirds and a dolphin. Monica was delighted when she was compared with Arthur Ransome; she much admired his work and acknowledged his influence.

The Punchbowl Farm children are concerned with farming the land and the joys and tragedies of caring for their animals. Yet they also have adventures involving the supernatural (*The Spirit of Punchbowl Farm*, 1952), buried treasure (*Frenchman's Secret*, 1956), a heath fire (*Fire in the Punchbowl*, 1965), and an escaped puma (*The Wild One*, 1967).

In 1960 Monica Edwards was voted children's writer of the year, jointly with Captain W. E. Johns, the creator of Biggles. She took her writing seriously and her style improved over the years. She believed that books for children needed strong plots and careful research; she was proud of the fact that she used actual locations and real animals. She was a strong-minded person and the authorial voice is sometimes evident: the reader is told rather than left to discover and, even when death and disaster are involved, emotion is held firmly in check.

Edwards also wrote for adults. These autobiographical books convey her love of the countryside and her passion for wildlife. The first, *The Unsought Farm* (1954), described the renovation of the house and the development of her farm. It was followed by *The Cats of Punchbowl Farm* (1964) and *The Badgers of Punchbowl Farm* (1966). In 1968 Bill Edwards had a horrific tractor accident, chronicled in *The Valley and the Farm* (1971). He survived his severe head injuries but during his long spell in hospital it was decided that the farm must be sold. They were able to keep Smallbrook valley and the old orchard on which they built a bungalow, Cowdray Cross. Without the farm, Monica had more time for badger watching, reading, gardening, and travelling abroad. She was also president of the Thursley Horticultural Society. Her last book, *Badger Valley* (1976), utilized the meticulous field notes which she kept from many nights watching and photographing badgers with specially designed equipment.

Bill Edwards died in 1990. When Monica's sight began to fail and she could no longer walk in the valley, the badgers, missing her treats of raisins and peanuts, made regular visits to her at the bungalow. Monica Edwards died on 18 January 1998. Her ashes were buried with Bill's in Smallbrook valley, which she left to the Woodland Trust. There is no memorial.

The readership of Monica Edwards's children's books began to fall while she was still writing. She ascribed this to television and a changing world. Collins failed to reissue the books after the mid-1970s. Goodchild republished nine of the titles in the 1980s, but they did not appeal to the new generation of children. However, her erstwhile fans remember the books with great affection, there are many collectors, and secondhand copies are hard to find. The autobiographical books, also out of print since the late 1970s, were reissued in large print in the 1990s. Their picture of rural life in the pre-technology era is historically interesting, but the descriptions of badger watching cannot compete with the intimate photography of television's wildlife programmes.

JOSEPHINE PULLEIN-THOMPSON

Sources private information (2004) · V. K. Lindley, *Monica Le Doux Edwards*, Thursley Society (2000) · M. Edwards, *The unsought farm* (1954) · *The Times* (7 Feb 1998) · *Twentieth century children's writers* (1978) · *Contemporary authors* (1974) · Crockford (1912)
Archives FILM 'Wildlife aid'
Likenesses photographs, repro. in Edwards, *Unsought farm* · photographs, repro. in M. Edwards, *The cats of Punchbowl Farm* (1964) · photographs, repro. in M. Edwards, *The badgers of Punchbowl Farm* (1966) · photographs, repro. in M. Edwards, *The valley and the farm* (1971) · photographs, priv. coll.; repro. in M. Edwards, *Badger valley* (1976) · photographs, priv. coll.

Edwards, Sir Owen Morgan (1858–1920), literary scholar and educationist, was born on 26 December 1858 at Coed y Pry, Llanuwchllyn, Merioneth. He was the eldest of four sons of Owen Edwards, a tenant farmer, and Elizabeth (Beti), *née* Jones, a farmer's daughter. The family's material circumstances were poor but the home, chapel, and community environments were rich in their literary and spiritual impact. Edwards wrote later in lyrical terms of the beauty of the locality and his father's influence in initiating him into the lore of the countryside. He always found inspiration and consolation in nature. Welsh was the language of the home, and its religion Calvinistic Methodist,

Sir Owen Morgan Edwards (1858–1920), by Bassano, 1916

yet from about the age of nine Edwards attended the local Anglican (National Society) school, Ysgol y Llan. His experience of being forced to speak nothing but English, and consequent punishments when he lapsed, have become part of Welsh folklore. After a change of teacher he became a pupil teacher at the school. In 1874 he went to the grammar school in Bala for two terms, and thence to the theological college in Bala in 1875. Here he devoted himself to mastering a wide range of English literature in a punishing regime of work which included widespread preaching engagements. In 1880 Edwards was received into the ministry of the Calvinistic Methodist church, though with misgivings. In the same year he entered the University College at Aberystwyth. His studies included English literature, history, philosophy, and modern languages, and he became convinced of the centrality of the Welsh language in the life of the nation. The puritan ethic of extreme hard work continued to drive his subsequent studies for a London degree. He graduated with a pass degree in 1883.

In 1883 Edwards left Wales, not to return professionally for nearly a quarter of a century. He went first to Glasgow University (1883–4) where he made a reputation as a literary scholar. At the second attempt he entered Balliol College, Oxford, in the autumn of 1884, and was elected to a Brackenbury scholarship. Benjamin Jowett regarded him as the outstanding Welshman in the university. He won the Stanhope (1886), Lothian (1887), and Arnold (1888) prizes and in 1887 he graduated with first class honours in history. In 1887 and 1888 he travelled widely in Europe. In

1888 he decided not to enter the regular ministry and taught for several Oxford colleges. Having failed to win a fellowship of All Souls, he was elected to a fellowship in history at Lincoln College, Oxford, in 1889.

In 1897 Edwards applied for the post of chief inspector of schools in Wales under the Central Welsh Board, the body responsible for the new intermediate schools established under the 1889 Intermediate Education Act. The significance of his failure to be appointed, both for himself and for Welsh education, was much exaggerated subsequently. His committee work included a report to the committee of the privy council on education in 1892 which advocated the establishment of a University of Wales, and he became the first warden of the university's Guild of Graduates. In 1899, while still a fellow of Lincoln College, he succeeded Tom Ellis as Liberal MP for Merioneth but resigned the seat in 1900, having made little impact. In 1907 he returned to Wales as chief inspector of schools under the newly created Welsh department of the Board of Education. In this post he had the opportunity (within the considerable constraints imposed by the board's officials and by examining systems, as well as by the rivalry of the Central Welsh Board) to develop his philosophy of education. He had a Wordsworthian affinity with the natural environment and adapted Ruskin's belief in the moral dimension of craft labour to a Welsh context. This led him to attempt to counteract the lack of imaginative teaching and the excessive emphasis on examinations in the schools of Wales. He stressed the importance of Welsh language, history, and geography, as well as the centrality of craft subjects, to individuals and communities. He was one of the few original thinkers in the history of state education in Wales, linking a belief in child-centred education to the special circumstances of Wales.

Edwards was elected to an honorary fellowship of Lincoln College in 1908. From 1914 he strongly supported the war effort in his journals and from 1916 took an active part in recruiting soldiers from Merioneth. In the same year he was appointed to the royal commission on university education in Wales. He was knighted in 1916.

Edwards's cultural Welsh nationalism developed in the 1880s. In 1886 he and six other distinguished Welsh scholars founded the Dafydd ap Gwilym Society in Oxford to foster the language and culture of Wales. His own mission to provide reading material in limpid, accessible, elegant Welsh for the children and his idealized common folk or 'gwerin' of Wales (who, for him, were the backbone of the nation) began with books recording his continental journeys in 1887 and 1888. These constituted the early part of a phenomenal literary output, as author and editor, in which Edwards's beautifully crafted Welsh gave fresh impetus and appeal to the language which was central to his mission to counteract the Anglicization of Wales. In 1889 he became joint editor of *Cymru Fydd*, giving it a more literary emphasis in contrast to its previously political bent, but the journal ceased publication in 1890. He sought to foster the traditions, history, and literature of Wales for all classes and religious affiliations in a

monthly journal, *Cymru*, which he founded in 1891 and edited until his death. In 1892 this journal was complemented by *Cymru'r Plant*, a monthly for the children of Wales, which had similar objectives. Its fare of illustrations, stories, legends, practical information, nature study, science, and history provided a variety of secular material for children in Welsh for the first time. An English-language periodical, *Wales*, launched in 1894, lasted only three years. The following year he launched the literary quarterly *Y Llenor*, published until 1898. In 1897 he began publishing another monthly, *Heddyw*, concerned with current issues in Wales, but it survived less than a year.

In the same decade Edwards produced a prodigious output of books, including the famous *Cartrefi Cymru* (1896). This unrelenting schedule continued after 1900, starting with the *Cyfres y Fil* series which aimed to make the Welsh classics in poetry and prose accessible to the ordinary reader, and a clutch of books arising from childhood memories and his journeys around Wales. His historical approach was, similarly, to eulogize the peasantry of Wales, as in his *Wales*, published in 1901.

In 1891 Edwards married Ellen (Elin) Davies, daughter of Evan Davies, a Llanuwchllyn farmer. Her death in April 1919 provoked grief and guilt in her widower, who had always been prone to sporadic bouts of ill health. He died at Neuadd Wen, Llanuwchllyn, Merioneth, on 16 May, 1920. His first son, Owen ab Owen, born in 1892, died at the age of five. In 1895 his second son, Ifan ab Owen *Edwards (d. 1970), eventual founder of the Welsh youth movement, Urdd Gobaith Cymru, was born, and in 1898 a daughter, Hâf.

GARETH ELWYN JONES

Sources H. W. Davies, *O. M. Edwards* (1988) • H. W. Davies, ed., *Llythyrau Syr O. M. Edwards ac Elin Edwards, 1887–1920* (1991) • H. Davies, 'Divisions', *Planet*, 76 (1989), 76–81 • G. E. Jones, 'Those who can, teach', *Planet*, 76 (1989), 82–7 • W. J. Gruffydd, *Owen Morgan Edwards: Cofiant, Cyfrol I, 1858–83* (1937) • G. E. Jones, *Controls and conflicts in Welsh secondary education, 1889–1944* (1982) • J. L. Williams, *Owen Morgan Edwards, 1858–1920* (1959) • G. A. Jones, *Bywyd a gwaith Owen Morgan Edwards, 1858–1920* (1958) • R. G. Jones, *Owen M. Edwards* (1962) • E. G. Millward, 'O. M. Edwards', *Y traddodiad rhyddiaith yn yr ugeinfed ganrif*, ed. G. Bowen (1976) • W. L. Lloyd, 'Owen M. Edwards (1858–1920)', *Pioneers of Welsh education* (1964) • J. G. Williams, *The University of Wales, 1893–1939* (1997)

Archives NL Wales, literary papers and collections; papers • NL Wales, letters | NL Wales, letters to D. R. Daniels • NL Wales, letters to Davies family, Ruabon • NL Wales, letters to I. T. Davies • NL Wales, letters to T. E. Ellis • NL Wales, letters incl. to Annie Hughes-Griffiths and to Peter Hughes-Griffiths • NL Wales, corresp. with Sir John Herbert Lewis • NL Wales, letters to Owen Griffith Owen (Alafon) • NL Wales, letters to Evan Rees (Dyfed) • U. Lpool, letters to Richard Griffith

Likenesses Bassano, photograph, 1916, NPG [*see illus.*] • portrait, NL Wales

Wealth at death £17,512 0s. 8d.: administration with will, 12 Aug 1920, CGPLA Eng. & Wales

Edwards, Richard (1525–1566), poet and playwright, a native of Somerset, was born in early 1525 of unknown parents, and matriculated from Corpus Christi College, Oxford, on 11 May 1540. He graduated BA in 1544; in the same year he was elected to a probationary fellowship at Corpus and in 1546 to a full fellowship which he vacated in

1547/8. In 1548 he proceeded MA, and two years later was nominated a student of Christ Church; he vacated this studentship about 1551. In 1553 he became a gentleman of the Chapel Royal, and in 1561 was appointed master of the children of the chapel, a position he held until his death in 1566.

During the Christmas season of 1564–5 Edwards's comedy *Damon and Pithias* was performed both at court and at Lincoln's Inn, to which he had been admitted earlier in 1564. In August 1566 he composed the two-part play *Palamon and Arcite* for the entertainment of Queen Elizabeth during her visit to Oxford. It was based on Chaucer's 'The Knight's Tale' and performed on successive evenings in Christ Church hall. The young cast, drawn mainly from undergraduates in Edwards's old college, Corpus Christi, included several men who were to become notable figures, such as Toby Matthew, future archbishop of York; John Rainolds, future president of Corpus and translator of the Authorized Version of the Bible; and Miles Windsor, later Oxford antiquary, who wrote a vivid account of the queen's reactions to the play:

> The Queen laughed full heartily afterward at some of the players … and gave unto John Rainolds, a scholar of Corpus Christi College which was a player in the same play, eight old angels in reward … and when the play was ended she called for Mr. Edwards, the author, and gave him very great thanks, with promises of reward, for his pains. (Corpus Christi College, Oxford, MS 257, fols. 115–123)

Unfortunately no text of the play has survived, probably due to Edwards's sudden death two months later, on 31 October 1566, the cause of which is unknown.

Damon and Pithias, after being performed again at Merton College, Oxford, in 1568, was finally published in 1571. Edwards's only other published work, the poetic miscellany called *The Paradise of Dainty Devices*, also appeared posthumously, in 1576. This contains thirteen poems by Edwards himself, including the dirge ('When griping griefs the heart doth wound') that Shakespeare has Capulet's musicians sing in *Romeo and Juliet* (IV.v). A keyboard arrangement by Edwards for another poem in the collection, by Francis Kinwelmersh, survives, and some anonymous settings of Edwards's poems have been attributed to him. Edwards's poems and plays were highly popular during his career, and after his death he was eulogized by Barnaby Googe, George Turberville, George Puttenham, and Francis Meres. In his epitaph to Edwards published in Turberville's *Epitaphs, Songs, and Sonnets* (1567), Thomas Twyne proclaimed him to be: 'The flowre of all our realm / And *Phoenix* of our age' (fol. 78*v*).

JOHN R. ELLIOTT, JUN.

Sources Emden, *Oxf.*, vol. 4 · R. Edwards, *The paradise of dainty devices*, ed. H. E. Rollins (1927) · A. Brown, introduction, in R. Edwards, *Damon and Pythias*, ed. A. Brown and F. P. Wilson (1957) · C. E. McGee and J. Meagher, 'Preliminary checklist of Tudor and Stuart entertainments, 1558–1603', *Research Opportunities in Renaissance Drama*, 24 (1981), 51–156 · J. R. Elliott, 'Queen Elizabeth at Oxford: new light on the royal plays of 1566', *English Literary Renaissance*, 18 (1988), 218–29 · J. R. Elliott, 'Drama', *Hist. U. Oxf.* 4: 17th-cent. Oxf., 641–58 · CCC Oxf., MS 257, fols. 104–123 · *New Grove*

Edwards, Sir Robert Meredydd Wynne- (1897–1974), civil engineer, was born on 1 May 1897 at North Devon Lodge, Cheltenham, Gloucestershire, the eldest in the family of four sons and two daughters of the Revd John Rosindale Wynne-Edwards (1864–1943), schoolmaster and later headmaster of Leeds grammar school and canon of Ripon Cathedral, and his wife, Lilian Agnes Streatfield Welbank, daughter of Champion Welbank. He was educated at Giggleswick School in the West Riding of Yorkshire and at Leeds grammar school. Upon the outbreak of the First World War he joined the Royal Army Medical Corps and obtained a commission in the Royal Welch Fusiliers in October 1914. He served in France from December 1915, being mentioned in dispatches, was awarded the Military Cross and bar, appointed to the DSO in 1919, and promoted temporary major.

On demobilization in January 1919 Wynne-Edwards went to Christ Church, Oxford, where he obtained a second-class honours degree in engineering science in 1921. In July 1921 his sense of adventure took him to Canada where he accumulated much varied experience with consulting engineers and contractors in both the design and construction of harbour works, dams, bridges, deep foundations, earth moving, piling, caisson sinking, and hard- and soft-ground tunnelling. In 1924 he married Hope Elizabeth Day Fletcher, daughter of Francis Fletcher, surveyor, of Nelson, British Columbia. They had one son and three daughters.

Wynne-Edwards's period in Canada commenced with a two-year pupillage under Andrew Don Swan, consulting engineer to the Vancouver Harbour Board. In 1923 he joined a firm of contractors in Vancouver, the Sydney E. Junkins Company Ltd, which was engaged on the construction of a deep-sea reinforced concrete wharf for the Canadian Pacific Railway. Specifically he spent several years working under Austin Wilmott Earl, the terminal's director of construction. At Vancouver he often inspected work under water as a trained full-suit diver. He became a member of the American Society of Civil Engineers and studied Karl von Terzaghi's important work on the new science of soil mechanics. In 1926 he joined the Institution of Civil Engineers (ICE) as an associate member; he became a full member in 1941. In February 1928 he submitted a paper, 'Reinforced-concrete piles driven in a gravel fill at the Canadian Pacific Railway Company's new pier "B-C" at Vancouver, B.C., Canada' (*PICE*, 226, 1928), for which he was awarded a Telford premium. During his last five years in Canada he alternated between the Junkins company and the Northern Construction Company Ltd for which he acted as agent on the shield-driven sections of the Detroit (Michigan)–Windsor (Ontario) road tunnel and subsequently as subagent on the construction of a water tunnel under the First Narrows, Vancouver.

When the Canadian engineering industry collapsed in the economic slump in 1934, Wynne-Edwards returned to England. In 1935 he joined John Mowlem & Co. with the task of building an earth-bank reservoir for the Metropolitan Water Board at Chingford in Essex, using the first fleet of newly developed American earth-moving equipment to reach Britain. In 1937 a length of newly compacted bank at the reservoir collapsed. The fall was studied by young engineers of the Building Research Station who were studying soil mechanics. They proved that the slip had occurred through a bed of soft clay, for the removal of which Wynne-Edwards had pressed unsuccessfully. When elderly consultants derided this idea, he traced Terzaghi to Paris, flew over, and persuaded him to represent the firm. Terzaghi emphatically supported the Building Research Station solution and was asked to redesign the bank to suit tests on the site. He then delivered the James Forrest lecture to the ICE in May 1939: 'Soil mechanics—a new chapter in engineering science' (*Journal of the Institution of Civil Engineers*, 12, 1938–9). He was also asked to lecture at universities. These events, of which Wynne-Edwards was the catalyst, led to the rapid spread of the science of soil mechanics in Britain.

From the start of the Second World War, Wynne-Edwards's work, as deputy agent for Mowlems in building a shell-filling factory at Swynnerton in Staffordshire, so impressed the Ministry of Works that it asked his firm if he could be seconded as the ministry's director of plant for the duration of the war. His wide experience proved to be invaluable, especially when acting as the 'firm and fearless' chairman of sometimes difficult joint Anglo-American committees. He was appointed OBE for his wartime services in 1944.

In 1945, after the war, Wynne-Edwards became a director of Richard Costain Ltd, civil engineering contractors, which later joined John Brown & Co. to become Costain John Brown (CJB), of which Wynne-Edwards became managing director in 1948. It was formed essentially to break the American monopoly in the combined design and construction of oil refineries, chemical works, and other large plants both at home and abroad. Wynne-Edwards pioneered British pipe laying, especially on the Abadan–Tehran pipeline in Iran, laying up to 3 miles in a day. In 1957 the firm became wholly owned by John Brown & Co. and was renamed Constructors John Brown Ltd. In 1956 he had contributed an article, 'Contracting methods', to the centenary number of *The Engineer*. From 1960 to 1965 he also served as chairman of both the Building Research Board and the Road Research Board, for which he was appointed CBE in 1962.

Wynne-Edwards resigned as managing director of Constructors John Brown Ltd shortly before his election as the one hundredth president of the ICE for 1964–5, but he continued as a director. Always a keen supporter of the institution, he won further Telford premiums for papers in 1941–2 and 1944–5, served on a number of its committees (research, public relations, education and training, and membership), and had been elected to its council in 1950. He was also among those representing the ICE on the ICE/Association of Consulting Engineers joint committee set up to consider the revision of professional conduct rules in 1960. In his presidential address W. E., as he was known to all his colleagues, stressed the links between contracting and consulting engineers, one sign of which was his own election as president—the first serving contractor to be so honoured—and between civil engineers and the community. He also undertook concurrently to be the founder chairman of the newly formed Council of Engineering Institutions for 1964–6, and for this he was knighted in 1965. In 1966 he compiled for the Ministry of Power a report on the shortage of gas supplies in the west midlands during the winter of 1965–6.

Wynne-Edwards was an honorary member of the Institution of Structural Engineers and the American Society of Civil Engineers. He was made an honorary fellow of the University of Manchester Institute of Science and Technology in 1965, received the honorary degree of DSc at Salford University in 1966, and was president of the Manchester Technology Association in 1969. In his spare time he was a keen naturalist and read widely. After the war, though very busy professionally, he none the less found time for bee-keeping, gardening, and keeping horses for occasional hunting with the Old Surrey and Burstow hunt. He retired to Blandford Forum in Dorset but died in Promenade Hospital, Southport, Lancashire, on 22 June 1974, after an accident while visiting one of his daughters.

ROBERT SHARP

Sources personal knowledge (1986) [*DNB*] · private information (1986, 2004) · biography, Inst. CE, obituary files · *WWW* · *The Times* (26 June 1974), 20h · *The Times* (29 June 1974), 16h · presidential address, *PICE*, new ser., 30 (1964–5), 1–16 · b. cert. · d. cert. · *CGPLA Eng. & Wales* (1975)
Likenesses black and white photograph, Inst. CE
Wealth at death £11,142: probate, 17 July 1975, *CGPLA Eng. & Wales*

Edwards, Robert Walter Dudley (1909–1988), historian, was born on 4 June 1909 at 7 North Frederick Street, Dublin, the eldest of the two children of Walter Dudley Edwards (1862–1946), civil servant, and his wife, Bridget Therese McInerney (1871–1956), a nurse. His father was a Quaker, from Worcestershire, but Edwards was brought up in his mother's religion, Roman Catholicism. Apart from a brief interlude after the Easter rising of 1916, when, at her insistence, he successively attended Patrick Pearse's school, St Enda's, Rathfarnham, and its associate Scoill Bhride, at Ranalagh, he was educated at the Catholic University School. He entered University College, Dublin, in 1926, graduated in 1929, and read law for a year, again at his mother's insistence, while settling down to the study of the laws against the nonconformist churches in early modern Ireland for which he was awarded an MA in 1931.

There followed two years in London, where Edwards attended the Institute of Historical Research and, as he later delicately phrased it, learned the historian's trade after a manner that had not been possible in Dublin, where his teachers 'had had little connexion with historical research' (Edwards, 1). There he prepared the thesis on the penal laws against Catholics for which he was awarded a doctorate in 1933 by the University of London. The revised first part of this study was published in 1935 as *Church and State in Tudor Ireland*. In 1933 Edwards married Sheila O'Sullivan (formerly Julia Sullivan; 1905–1985), a teacher from Cork with interests in folklore. They had three children, Mary, Owen, and Ruth, the latter two both notable authors.

Edwards was elected to membership of the Royal Irish Academy in 1936, awarded the degree of DLitt by the National University of Ireland in 1937 for published work, and appointed to a lectureship in modern Irish history in University College, Dublin, in January 1939; he was promoted to statutory lecturer in the following year and succeeded in 1944 to the professorship, a post that he was to retain until his retirement in 1979. By that stage he had produced a significant body of both editorial and original work, notable for its wide chronological range, and become involved, in partnership with Theodore Moody, with whom he had shared lodgings in London, in a programme for the improvement of historical writing in Ireland which is commonly held to have begun the professionalization of Irish history. The two men shared not merely a concern to impose closer fidelity to the evidence and to improve scholarly practice, but also a belief in the ameliorative power of an informed understanding of the past.

The outcome was the foundation of the Ulster Society for Historical Studies. The Irish Historical Society began life separately in 1936, but the two bodies became complexly intertwined through the Irish Committee of Historical Sciences in 1937, of which Edwards was secretary, and combined to launch *Irish Historical Studies*, jointly edited by Edwards and Moody, which first appeared in March 1938. Edwards retained his joint editorship until 1957, when eye trouble forced his resignation. By then he had diverted his energy towards raising a new generation of rigorously trained historical scholars, not only by strengthening the undergraduate course and promoting research activity in University College, Dublin, but also through the foundation of the Irish Universities History Students' Association (1950) which, with its annual conference and its associated *Bulletin* (1956), performed for students the integrative function that the Ulster and Irish historical societies performed for their teachers.

A man of commanding presence and a compelling lecturer and conversationalist who revelled in paradox and allusion, taught that questions were more important than answers, and regarded shock tactics as a necessary teaching strategy, Edwards's influence owed more to personality than to example. Persistent eye trouble restricted his own research activity and for many years he eked out publications from the materials he had accumulated as a young man. Perhaps in compensation, he became increasingly concerned with the collection and preservation of the sources. In the 1970s he embarked upon a fresh constructive phase which contributed greatly to establishing the profession of archivist in Ireland. He was the main force behind the founding in 1970 of an Irish Society for Archives, which published the first issue of its *Bulletin* a year later, the initiation of a graduate diploma course in archival studies in 1972, and the creation of a department of archives in University College, Dublin, in 1970, which was designed as a research centre for the history of the modern Irish state and for which, as director until 1979, he acquired major collections of twentieth-century material.

After his retirement Edwards collaborated with Dr Mary O'Dowd in a valuable critical description of the sources of early modern Irish history, published in 1985. He had already begun to publish freely: a survey of Irish history appeared in 1972, an illustrated account of *Daniel O'Connell and his World* in 1975, and a narrative account of Tudor Ireland in 1977. These are works of indifferent quality, slackly written and unoriginal. As an obituarist noted:

> The pity is that nothing that Dudley wrote captured the flamboyance, the arrogance, the perverseness, the passion, the erudite intuition, and the theatrical instinct that made him what he was, a great performer whose exuberance irradiated 'the dismal muse of Irish history'. (Clarke, 127)

Edwards died on 5 June 1988 at his home, 21 Brendan Road, Donnybrook, Dublin, and was buried at St Fintan's cemetery, Sutton, Dublin. AIDAN CLARKE

Sources University College, Dublin, Edwards MSS · C. Cullen, 'The historical writings of Professor R. D. Edwards', *Studies in Irish history presented to R. Dudley Edwards*, ed. A. Cosgrove and D. McCartney (1979), 347–53 · R. D. Edwards, 'T. W. Moody and the origins of *Irish Historical Studies*: a biographical memoir', *Irish Historical Studies*, 26 (1988–9), 1–2 · A. Clarke, 'Robert Dudley Edwards (1909–1988)', *Irish Historical Studies*, 26 (1988–9), 121–7 · [A. C. Holland], 'Editorial: Robert Walter Dudley Edwards and a decade of archival achievements', *Irish Archives: Journal of the Irish Association for Archives*, 1 (1989), 5–9 · *The Leader* (10 Nov 1956) · personal knowledge (2004) · private information (2004)

Archives University College, Dublin, archives department, LA/22

Likenesses photographs, University College, Dublin, archives department, Edwards MSS

Edwards, Roger (1811–1886), Calvinistic Methodist minister and author, the son of Roger (1779–1831) and Elizabeth Edwards, was born at Tegid Street, Bala on 26 January 1811, the year in which the Calvinistic Methodists first assumed the power to ordain their own ministers. He grew up amid the controversy over Calvin's five great points, when figures such as Ebenezer Morris and John Elias were leading lights in the denomination. He was educated at the Revd Lewis Williams's school, Llanfachraeth, Tan-y-domen School, Bala, and the Revd Dr Stewart's school, Liverpool, before attending the Revd John Hughes's seminary at Wrexham. Between 1830 and c.1835 he held his own school at Dolgellau, and he began preaching in 1830. Following his marriage to Ellen Williams (d. 1877) on 28 September 1841, with whom he had three sons and three daughters, he was ordained in 1842 and became a minister at Mold, Flintshire.

In 1835 Edwards became editor of *Cronicl yr Oes*, probably the first Welsh-language political paper, and he continued working on it for four years, writing most of it himself. The leaders in the *Cronicl* for 1836 on the House of Lords, the ballot, and church rates were strongly radical, and they brought on Edwards the charge of socialism and sympathy with Tom Paine. From 1839 to 1874 he was secretary of the Calvinistic Methodist Association. In January 1845 the first number of the *Traethodydd* appeared, of which he was co-editor with his namesake Lewis Edwards until

1854, and after that with the Revd Owen Thomas of Liverpool until 1886. He also edited *Y Drysorfa*, a magazine founded in 1779 by Thomas Charles of Bala, from 1847 to 1886. As well as editing and translating the religious works of others, he wrote many of his own, most notably *Welsh Psalmist* (1840) and *Methodist Diary* (1843–6). He was also a poet and hymn writer, and was acclaimed as being the first to publish a serial story in Welsh in 1866. He died on 19 July 1886 at his home, Hill Grove, Mold, and was buried on 23 July in Mold public cemetery. He was survived by four of his six children, including his son, the Revd Ellis Edwards, who became headmaster of the theological college at Bala.   R. M. J. JONES, *rev.* MARI A. WILLIAMS

Sources T. M. Jones, *Cofiant y Parch. Roger Edwards* (1908) · G. T. Jones, 'Bywyd a gwaith Roger Edwards o'r Wyddgrug', MA diss., U. Wales, 1933 · W. Hobley and D. O., memoir, *Y Drysorfa*, 56 (1886), 322–5, 361–9 · *DWB*

Archives NL Wales, corresp.; notes, sermons, and papers · U. Wales, Bangor, corresp. and papers | NL Wales, Presbyterian church of Wales MSS · NL Wales, Cwrt MSS · NL Wales, letters to Lewis Edwards

Wealth at death £2867 5s. 9d.: probate, 4 Aug 1886, *CGPLA Eng. & Wales*

Edwards, Ronald Christopher [Buster] (1931–1994), robber, was born on 27 January 1931 at 41 Jeffreys Road, Lambeth, London, the son of Christopher Charles Joseph Edwards, barman, and his wife, Mary Elizabeth, *née* Gaisford. A south London boy from the Elephant and Castle, he left school at the age of fifteen to work in a local sausage factory, where he cashed in on the post-war black market by stealing meat. After a brief but felonious period serving in the RAF on national service (he served fifty-six days' detention for stealing cigarettes), he returned to his old haunts to begin his career as a professional criminal. He ran a drinking club and became an all-round thief, safecracker, and robber: a 'face' among London's thriving criminal fraternity. On 12 April 1952 he married June Rose (*b.* 1932/3), machinist, the daughter of Thomas Rothery, motor driver. They had a daughter, Nicky.

In 1962 Edwards was involved in a £62,000 robbery at the British Overseas Aircraft Corporation's headquarters, Comet House, which resulted in the capture of many of the robbery team. Edwards escaped, but in the aftermath cemented his reputation as a staunch and reliable villain by frantically seeking out defence witnesses for his colleagues. The Comet House robbers made up the core of the great train robbery 'firm', the team of professional criminals who, dressed in army uniforms, stopped the Glasgow–London mail train at Bridego Bridge, near Cheddington in rural Buckinghamshire, in the early hours of 8 August 1963, coshed the driver, Jack Mills, and stole £2,600,000. The perpetrators of the robbery escaped but left behind a wealth of forensic evidence at their base at Leatherslade Farm, and the police were soon rounding them up.

Edwards lay low, while some of his colleagues received sentences of thirty years. The Royal Mail had been violated and the majesty of both the trial and the sentences reflected this outrage. Edwards and his fellow fugitive Bruce Reynolds, realizing there would be no let-up in the

police investigation, then fled to Mexico with their families. However, the Edwards family suffered badly from homesickness and, despite the anticipated consequences, after a year on the run Edwards negotiated a deal with the police and returned to Britain. At his trial he received the 'master criminal' tag and a fifteen-year sentence, the original sentences having caused an affront among the public and sections of the press, who tended to regard the robbers as Robin Hood figures. Edwards served nine years of his sentence.

On his release Edwards ran a flower stall at Waterloo Station and appeared to have adapted to a life without crime better than many of his former colleagues, several of whom were convicted of drug-dealing, and one of whom was murdered. He skilfully pulled the wool over the eyes of the writer Piers Paul Read by exploiting the so-called military precision of the robbery, inventing the involvement of German commando leader Otto Skorzeny as the prime mover and financier. Read's *The Train Robbers* (1978) also named Edwards as the man who had coshed the train driver, but Edwards later retracted the story, explaining that he was trying to divert attention from another robber who had succeeded in escaping. Edwards's life story was made into a film, *Buster* (1988), starring Phil Collins and Julie Walters. The film led to a number of television appearances. He made just £5000 from the film itself. His £150,000 cut from the robbery was spent while a fugitive; he later reckoned to have spent half before landing in Mexico.

Towards the end of his life Edwards had money problems, and like many of his generation was apparently dissatisfied with the state of the country. On 29 November 1994 he was found hanging in his lock-up garage in Greet Street, Lambeth, London. An inquest held on 9 February 1995 returned an open verdict. He was survived by his wife and daughter.   RICHARD HOBBS

Sources P. P. Read, *The train robbers* (1978) · R. Hobbs, *Doing the business* (1988) · R. Biggs, *Odd man out* (1994) · D. Campbell, *The underworld* (1994) · *The Times* (30 Nov 1994) · *The Independent* (1 Dec 1994) · *The Guardian* (1 Dec 1994) · b. cert. · m. cert. · d. cert.

Archives FILM BFI NFTVA, documentary footage

Likenesses photograph, *c.*1981, repro. in *The Times* · photograph, 1981, repro. in *The Independent*

Edwards, Sir Ronald Stanley (1910–1976), professor of commerce and industrialist, was born on 1 May 1910 in New Southgate, London, the second of three sons (the eldest having died in childhood) of Charles Edwards, a gas fitter, and his wife, Alice Osborne. He was educated at Garfield Road primary school, Southgate, and Southgate county school, leaving after matriculation at the age of fifteen. He continued to educate himself by painstaking evening study.

Edwards's first jobs were as office boy for the Romford Gas Company and as junior clerk in a firm of accountants. Taking correspondence courses, he qualified as a certified accountant in 1930, then studied for a BCom degree by evening class and correspondence. The originality of his work led the London School of Economics (LSE) to offer him an assistant lectureship in business administration in

1935. He married Myrtle Violet, daughter of John Poplar RN, on 31 December 1936.

In the academic world Edwards found his spiritual home, publishing provocative articles, largely in the *Accountant*. In 1939, after rejection by the Royal Navy because of colour blindness, he joined the Ministry of Aircraft Production, being given plenary powers to restore production of aircraft in bombed Coventry and Birmingham. He was subsequently concerned with manpower planning, and finally with post-war industrial planning of strategic industries. All this stimulated his interest in manufacturing industry, and especially in its technology.

Edwards returned to the LSE as reader in commerce in 1946, becoming professor in 1949. Reviving a pre-war initiative, he ran postgraduate seminars in industrial administration, with short papers given by heads of large organizations; these were acclaimed as a unique meeting point between the academic and the business worlds. They continued for over twenty years, first at the LSE and then, after a break, at the London Business School. Edwards, together with H. Townshend, edited collections of these papers.

As a consequence of his wartime work in establishing a measuring and watchmaking industry, Edwards became chairman of the British Clock and Watch Manufacturers Association (1946–59), and a member of the privy council committee for scientific and industrial research (1949–54). Membership of the Clow (1948) and Herbert (1954–5) committees on electricity supply led to his becoming deputy chairman (1957–61) of the Electricity Council. However, the latter's large size and vague remit diverged from his recommendations. As his involvement with this council increased he abandoned teaching, apart from his seminars, though he was able to retain the title of professor.

Edwards's major contribution to the electricity supply industry was to apply economic analysis to its operations. He emphasized the need for a real rate of return on its huge capital outlay, for tighter financial control, for pricing related to marginal cost, and for more flexible hours combined with improved conditions for manual workers. He was the driving force behind a productivity agreement reached with the workforce, although by the time he (together with R. V. Roberts) published a book about it, much had been modified.

Edwards thought that the crucial issue was the way in which industries were run, not who owned them. He devoted nearly every lunchtime to discussing aspects of the economy with industrialists and political figures. His other activities multiplied: in addition to non-executive directorships, he was a member of the University Grants Committee (1955–64) and of the National Economic Development Council (1964–8), president of the Market Research Association (1965–9), and a governor of the London Business School, of the Administrative Staff College at Henley, and of the London School of Economics. He was appointed KBE in 1963.

Edwards's chairmanship of the committee of inquiry into the civil air transport industry (1967–9) produced a clear and readable report, readily understandable to laymen, and its major recommendations were accepted by the government. Surprisingly, perhaps, the report did not recommend immediate amalgamation of British European Airways (BEA) and the British Overseas Air Corporation (BOAC). However, Edwards became a founder member of the board of British Airways (BA), the holding company for both organizations, in 1971.

From 1968 to 1975, Edwards was chairman of the Beecham Group. He had a strong belief in the virtues of competition and enjoyed working in an increasingly international and research-based company, but he did not find quick decision-making entirely to his taste. Nevertheless, Beecham prospered under his chairmanship and championship, although government opposition prevented its proposed merger with Glaxo. Death cut short his subsequent chairmanship of British Leyland (from 1975).

Remembering his own early years, Edwards was always helpful to young people. To businessmen he seemed to have somewhat professorial mannerisms; to academics he sometimes gave the impression of being a no-nonsense, brass-tacks businessman. Yet many, from both the university world and from commerce, regarded him with affection. He was devoted to his wife and family. He loved the sea and went sailing (from Weymouth) on most of the weekends he spared from work. Music, opera, ballet, painting, and sculpture appealed to him and his wife, and they encouraged the work of younger artists. He was ambitious, yet modest, and aptly described himself as a 'builder of bridges between men's minds'.

Edwards was awarded honorary doctorates from Edinburgh (1966), Strathclyde (1973), Bath (1966), and Warwick (1973). He was also an honorary fellow of the LSE (1975). He died, unexpectedly, at the King Edward VII Hospital, Beaumont House, Beaumont Street, Marylebone, on 18 January 1976, and was survived by his wife. His ashes were scattered at sea.   MARGARET ACKRILL

Sources Edwards MSS, priv. coll. · *DNB* · L. Hannah, *Engineers, managers, and politicians: the first fifteen years of nationalised electricity supply in Britain* (1982) · *WWW* · L. Hannah, *Electricity before nationalisation: a study in the development of the electricity supply industry in Britain to 1948* (1979)
Likenesses photographs, priv. coll.
Wealth at death £208,565: probate, 3 May 1976, *CGPLA Eng. & Wales*

Edwards, Sydenham Teast (*bap.* **1768**, *d.* **1819**), botanical artist, was baptized Sydenham Edwards on 5 August 1768 at Usk, the second son in the family of seven or more children of Lloyd Pittel Edwards, schoolmaster, and his wife, Mary Reece. The physician Richard Reece (1775–1831) was his cousin. The family moved to Abergavenny about 1770 and Edwards was raised in that town. Little is known of his early life and education, although it appears that the family had strong connections with the Anglican church; his father was organist at various times in both Usk and Abergavenny, and his uncle, William Reece (*d.* 1781), was vicar of Bosbury. Edwards adopted the curious forename Teast (sometimes incorrectly spelt Teak) later in life.

Edwards obviously showed early promise as an artist. While a teenager he copied plates out of William Curtis's *Flora Londinensis* and about 1786 these were seen by a Mr Denman who was visiting Abergavenny from Hampshire; he brought them to Curtis's attention. The latter immediately sent for young Edwards to go to London to be trained and to work for him. At this time James Sowerby was the principal artist employed by Curtis in the production of his botanical publications.

After about two years' training, Edwards's work began to appear in Curtis's prestigious *Botanical Magazine*. His signature is noted first in 1788 on the drawing of a carnation. For the next twenty-seven years nearly all the plates in the journal were Edwards's work. Apparently his relationship with his employer was a good one, and the two were often to be seen out together in the country around London or on longer expeditions—the one gathering and the other sketching the specimens from life. In 1804, he was elected a fellow of the Linnean Society.

Edwards continued in the employ of the *Botanical Magazine* after William Curtis's death in 1799. He also contributed to the *Flora Londinensis* and the *New Botanic Garden* among other publications; as well as executing the drawings, he was sometimes also the engraver of the plates. His considerable output shows that he was a talented and enthusiastic artist. He obviously possessed knowledge of plant anatomy and much of his work for the *Botanical Magazine* is considered among the best scientific illustrations of the day. His relationship with the *Magazine* continued until 1815, when he started his own rival publication, the *Botanists' Register*. His talents extended beyond botany, notably as an artist of animal subjects as seen in Rees's *Cyclopaedia* and the rare part-publication *Cyanographia Britannica* (1799–1805) which contains coloured engravings of British dogs, and which he produced himself as author, artist, and publisher.

Edwards died at his home at Queen's Elms, near Brompton, on 8 February 1819, leaving a wife and daughter, and was buried in the churchyard of Chelsea Old Church where he was apparently a regular worshipper. Unfortunately his gravestone was lost in the blitz. His memorial within Chelsea Old Church reads, 'As a faithful delineator of nature, few equalled, none excelled'.

RAYMOND B. DAVIES

Sources T. H. Thomas, 'Sydenham Edwards of Usk, painter and draughtsman of natural history', *Transactions of the Cardiff Naturalists' Society*, 43 (1910), 15–19 · C. Hubbard, 'A book at random', *Kennel Gazette* (Nov 1991), 33–7 · *General indexes to the plants contained in the first fifty-three volumes … of the Botanical Magazine, to which are added a few interesting memoirs of the author, Mr W. Curtis*, ed. S. Curtis (1828) · L. T. Davies, 'Sydenham Edwards (of Usk, 1768–1819)', *Men of Monmouthshire* (1933), 83–6 · P. Joyner, *Artists in Wales, c.1740–c.1851* (1997) · R. Desmond, *A celebration of flowers: two hundred years of Curtis's Botanical Magazine* (1987) · W. Blunt and W. T. Stearn, *The art of botanical illustration* (1950) · *DWB* · *GM*, 1st ser., 89/1 (1819), 188 · Usk, bishop's transcripts, 1725–1858, NL Wales

Edwards, Thomas (*fl.* 1587–1595), poet, can probably be identified as the Thomas Edwards from Shropshire who was admitted to Lincoln's Inn from Furnivall's Inn on 16 June 1587. Further Lincoln's Inn records show Edwards sharing a chamber with John Donne's friend Christopher Brooke and, on 21 February 1589, acting as guarantor for one Edward Jones (also from Shropshire), newly admitted.

Edwards's claim to be a poet rests on two surviving copies of *Cephalus and Procris; Narcissus*, a volume registered in 1593 and published in 1595 by John Wolfe, with a dedicatory poem to Thomas Argall, who entered Lincoln's Inn in 1584–5. This is the sole evidence to link the law student with the poet. Both 'Cephalus and Procris' and 'Narcissus' are Ovidian epyllia in the tradition, for instance, of Christopher Marlowe's *Hero and Leander* and William Shakespeare's *Venus and Adonis*. 'Cephalus and Procris' is in couplets, 'Narcissus' in a seven-line stanza, and both conclude with a long envoy. The envoy to 'Narcissus' contains a string of references to other poets under aliases, including Edmund Spenser (Collyn) and Samuel Daniel (Rosamond). Among those referred to as recently dead are Thomas Watson and Marlowe (Amintas and Leander; the book was registered on 22 October 1593, only months after Marlowe's death). Other poets referred to in this section have still not been convincingly identified; it is likely that Adon is Shakespeare. Also interesting is Edwards's assertion that there is more of *The Faerie Queene* to be printed soon.

The volume did not impress contemporary critics. William Covell listed it, alongside *Zepheria*, among the 'smaller lights' of modern poetry, which would fade away when university students started fulfilling their proper poetic potential but which for the moment 'like water men pluck every passenger by the sleeve' (W. C., *Polimanteia*, [1595], sig. Q4r). The following year Thomas Nashe derided it in the context of a general assault against the poetasters associated with Gabriel Harvey and his printer, Wolfe. Nashe listed *Cephalus and Procris* with works by Barnabe Barnes and Anthony Chute, as examples of the 'Pamphlagonian' poems that Harvey had advised Wolfe to publish (*Works of Thomas Nashe*, 3.90). Nashe failed to name the author explicitly; this led earlier scholars, working before the surviving copies were rediscovered, to misattribute the authorship of the poem to Chute, the previous victim in Nashe's list.

It is tempting to identify Edwards as the Thomas Edwards who wrote Latin verse on the cities of Italy for Adrianus Romanus's 1595 *Parvum theatrum urbium* but this identification remains at the moment conjectural. Similarly, Edwards's name is too common for scholars to be sure of his career after leaving the inns of court, but some of the evidence is suggestive. A Thomas Edwards, servant to Sir John Wolley, gave bond in a legal case in March 1593 and wrote to Lady Wolley 'from the Court, March 1594'; Wolley himself had Shropshire connections. Another Thomas Edwards was involved in a lawsuit in 1599 against Donne and Brooke; Thomas Edwards the probable poet shared a chamber with Brooke, while Donne and his wife had stayed with Wolley's son Sir Francis Wolley for some years. But Edwards's later career remains at the moment obscure.

MATTHEW STEGGLE

Sources M. Eccles, *Brief lives: Tudor and Stuart authors* (1982), 46–7 · *The works of Thomas Nashe*, ed. R. B. McKerrow, 5 vols. (1904–10); repr. with corrections and notes by F. P. Wilson (1958) · C. Carmichael Stopes, 'Thomas Edwardes, author of "Cephalus and Procris" and "Narcissus"', *Modern Language Review*, 16 (1921), 209–23

Edwards, Thomas (*c*.1599–1648), Church of England clergyman and religious controversialist, was perhaps the son of Thomas Edwards (*d*. in or after 1616) of St Helen, Bishopsgate, London, and his wife, Mary (*d*. in or after 1617). He had a brother, Henry, and sisters Judith and Susanna, and Thomas and Mary Edwards had children of those names baptized in St Helen between 1607 and 1617.

Education and early clerical career In Michaelmas term 1618 Edwards, described as of London, matriculated as a pensioner from Queens' College, Cambridge. He graduated BA in 1622 (the degree was incorporated at Oxford in 1623), proceeded MA in 1625, and was ordained deacon on 18 January 1626. Queens' was then renowned for its puritan reputation, and Edwards's time in Cambridge provided the opportunity to establish spiritual ties with the godly. Among those he befriended were William Bridge and Thomas Goodwin, men from whom he turned during the debates in the 1640s over church government. Indeed Edwards's near contemporaries at Cambridge included both future allies and opponents, most notably John Goodwin, a fellow of Queens' at his arrival and one of the principal targets (and critics) of his later works. Perhaps when in 1646 Goodwin mocked Edwards's ability at grammar and translation he remembered an indifferent student from twenty years before.

Following ordination Edwards became a university preacher in Cambridge, where according to a later correspondent he was known as 'young Luther' (Edwards, *Gangraena*, 3.77). Sermon notes reveal that he delivered a conventional if awkward Calvinist doctrine on the deceptions of Satan and the fall from grace. Thomas Fuller, his contemporary at Queens', recalled that Edwards 'often was transported beyond due bounds with the *keenness* and *eagernesse* of his spirit', and this seemingly occurred during a sermon in St Andrew's Church (*The Appeal of Injured Innocence*, 1659, 3.58). In February 1628 the vice-chancellor's court heard evidence that Edwards had instructed the congregation to reject the orders of carnal humanity at moments of crisis and to follow the dictates of the conscience. Alarmed at the political implications of the doctrine, the court ordered Edwards to preach a recantation sermon and to produce a certificate confirming he had done so. The sermon was duly delivered at St Andrew's in April 1628, but soon afterwards Edwards left Cambridge, and not until May the following year was his rather qualified certificate of submission produced. Among the certificate's signatories guaranteeing his orthodoxy were, ironically, his future Independent opponents William Bridge and Thomas Goodwin. Moreover, he had clearly fallen victim to the hostile evidence and story-telling for which he and his books became notorious.

Edwards moved to London and became lecturer at St Botolph, Aldgate, where late in 1628 the parishioners celebrated his appointment with 'wine and ringers' (GL, MS 9235/2, pt 2, fol. 359*r*). Although opponents later alleged that he had been '*a great man for the Bishops and their wayes*' he vehemently and with some plausibility denied the accusation (Edwards, *Gangraena*, 1.76, first pagination). In 1629 new instructions to preachers required all lecturers to wear surplice and hood when reading the service book. Edwards was seemingly reluctant to comply, and this may have accounted for his apparent suspension by the bishop of London, William Laud. In May 1629 leading parishioners of St Botolph petitioned Laud on Edwards's behalf, stating that his preaching brought great comfort and encouraged large collections for the poor. Their efforts may have been successful, for alongside preaching at other City parishes he seemingly retained the St Botolph lectureship at least intermittently until 1636. During that year, however, he left London to become curate of All Saints', Hertford. By this time he was already married to his wife, Mary (*d*. in or after 1648): on 6 March 1637 the couple's second son, John *Edwards, was baptized at All Saints'. Opponents later claimed that Edwards lived off the wealth of his wife, but no record has been uncovered of Mary's financial standing.

Edwards returned to London in the late 1630s and possibly resided in St Helen, Bishopsgate: an Israel, son of Thomas, was baptized there in April 1642. During this period he recounted preaching '*against leaving the Church of England*' and being brought before high commission for a fast-day sermon in 1640 '*against the Bishops and their faction*' (ibid., 3, preface; 1.76, first pagination). However, no evidence has been found of his troubles with the court, a fact which highlights the modern reliance on Edwards's own words for the details of his career, particularly from the late 1630s. There is a consistent polemical thread to his life-writing characteristic of heresiographers: that of the embattled champion of the true church who has forsaken all worldly goods in a crusade against the errors of the times. Elements of this are certainly apparent in Edwards's early career, though it is open to question whether it was self-sacrifice or his intemperate character that prevented his advancement. Before 1644 he appears a peripheral figure. He failed to acquire a parochial living, and opponents later criticized his wanderings between parishes in Surrey and Essex in the mid-1640s. He was never invited to preach a parliamentary fast-day sermon or nominated to the Westminster assembly. In short, and in contrast with a number of his Cambridge contemporaries, he did not enjoy great success in his early career. Despite his self-presentation of sacrificing '*any great things for my self*', it may well be that Edwards had little choice in the matter (ibid., 3, preface).

The attack on Independency The publication in 1641 of Edwards's first work, the polemical *Reasons Against the Independent Government of Particular Congregations*, saw his emergence as an early and vociferous opponent of liberty of conscience or, as he termed it, toleration. Differences among the godly clergy on issues of church government clearly existed by this date, and Edwards was among the minority who baulked at their smoothing over. As he saw it, popery was in decline and the fruits of Reformation were now threatened by new errors in the form of Independency. Although there was no extended positive justification for presbyterian government (which was never the central theme of his writing), he contrasted the defining features of the true church, 'edification, order, peace', with the dangerous schism of Independency, which could lead only to a limitless toleration and a threat to social order (p. 12). Instead a compromise must be sought between total conformity and toleration for gathered congregations.

The *Reasons* was published before the meeting of godly clergy at the Aldermanbury home of Edmund Calamy in November 1641. There ministers agreed to a 'mutuall silence' regarding their differences over church government in the face of the common enemy of popery. Although on the fringes of the City's puritan community, Edwards attended the meeting and abided by the accord, 'though for many Reasons I desired to have been excepted' (Edwards, *Antapologia*, 241, 242). The Aldermanbury accord largely accounted for the lack of response to the *Reasons*, which prompted only a single direct reply. However, this proved an utter humiliation for Edwards, as its author was not only an uneducated separatist but a mere woman, the 'brasen-faced' Katherine Chidley (Edwards, *Gangraena*, 3.170). Asserting that the weakness of Edwards's arguments made the task of reply fitting for a woman, Chidley refuted his defence of a hierarchical church government and asserted the biblical justification for separatism before turning on the 'bloody minded man' himself (*The Justification of the Independent Churches of Christ*, 1641, 61). As one opponent remarked, surely this amounted to 'a *spetting in his face*' (Woodward, 5).

In late 1643 the publication of *An Apologeticall Narration* by the leading Independents Thomas Goodwin, Philip Nye, Sidrach Simpson, Jeremiah Burroughs, and William Bridge signified the end of the Aldermanbury accord. Their plea to parliament for acceptance of the congregational way prompted a second work from Edwards in the following July, *Antapologia, or, A Full Answer to the 'Apologeticall Narration'*. Ten times longer than the thirty-page pamphlet it refuted, *Antapologia*, in contrast with the orderly *Reasons*, was an unwieldy work that nevertheless propelled Edwards to the centre of the presbyterian campaign. He now saw an alarmingly polarized society about him, with religious, political, and military divisions between presbyterians and Independents. Moreover, the growing power of the Independents increased his anxiety about religious radicalism at a time when the issue of church government remained unsettled. There was no longer room for compromise. Edwards denied the apologists' claim to a middle way and included stories of their disruptive practices and divisions during their exile in the Netherlands. He identified Burroughs and Bridge as conformists in the 1630s, no doubt with his own sufferings in mind. The apologists, like all separatists, were nothing more than schismatics. They moved towards a separatist position before they left England and were unwilling to

take communion in a church once they had returned. Edwards also emphasized the superiority of presbyterianism, contrasting its 'beauty, order, strength' with 'the deformity, disorder, and weaknesse' of Independency (preface, sig. A1r). For it was only a presbyterian settlement that could counter 'those many errours, divisions, evils which fall out in your way' (p. 152).

Antapologia caused a great commotion, as Edwards no doubt intended. It was the longest and most controversial reply to *An Apologeticall Narration*, and one contemporary remarked that '*all the City and Parliament rings of it*' (Woodward, 2). According to Robert Baillie, the presbyterian ministers of London moved quickly to exploit this notoriety by establishing a weekly lecture for Edwards at Christ Church, Newgate. It was there that he performed his particular function in the presbyterian campaign. Never an organizational leader or a positive advocate of the specific forms of the system, he had a purely negative role, that of harrier of the sects. Christ Church, at the very heart of the City, proved the perfect platform for this task, and his tumultuous lectures to all comers became the most notorious in London. While Edwards delivered his polemics scuffles, 'insolency and disorder' would break out. He was frequently heckled and challenged to debate; on one occasion a sectary branded him a '*Rascally Rogue* [who] *deserves to be pull'd out of the Pulpit*' (Edwards, *Gangraena*, 1.107, 108). Katherine Chidley accused him of having turned the pulpit into a cockpit. All this only increased Edwards's reputation as an opponent of toleration. Moreover, as a prominent City lecturer he was at the centre of networks providing alarmist news of the sectarian threat throughout the country.

Gangraena Despite *Antapologia*'s notoriety, once again there was little direct response to Edwards, though his old foe Katherine Chidley returned to haunt him with a pamphlet. Nevertheless, as the book's author he was the natural recipient of information regarding the sects and their practices, and the stories were saved to fulfil the promise of a successive attack against Independency. By 1646 the need for such a work was all the more pressing. Despite the efforts of the orthodox, Edwards saw a land where separate congregations and heretical opinions proliferated; where Independents hampered the settlement of church government; where parliament showed little support for presbyterianism, and its victorious army was lost to the cause; and where daily printed polemics exposed divisions within the parliamentarian camp.

Edwards's response in 1646, *Gangraena*, was a composite polemic against the spread of toleration perhaps best summarized by the title-page of its third part:

> A new and higher Discovery of the Errors, Heresies, Blasphemies, and insolent Proceedings of the Sectaries of these times; with some Animadversions by way of Confutation upon many of the Errors and Heresies named. As also a particular Relation of many remarkable Stories, speciall Passages, Copies of Letters written by Sectaries … together with ten Corollaries from all forenamed Premises.

A heresiography drawing on a wide range of printed

pamphlets, oral encounters, and manuscript material, the work was equally dependent upon its host of informants. The outcome was a rambling, repetitive, disorganized text that was nevertheless a publishing sensation. Despite running to more than 800 pages, *Gangraena* was a seventeenth-century best-seller, the first part being reprinted three times in as many months. Yet its author was a poor heresiographer. Edwards's clumsy list-making and classifications give the impression of a man overwhelmed by the reality of the horrors around him, the sheer scale of his material having got out of hand. But this was not a simple catalogue of errors, and its ramshackle appearance was determined by the urgency of the context in which it was produced. *Gangraena* was part of a larger presbyterian campaign to compete with the Independents for popular support. Edwards called on the godly to organize themselves against '*Toleration* … the grand designe of the Devil', prompting them to give active support to the presbyterians (Edwards, *Gangraena*, 1.121). Although he claimed little involvement in affairs of government, all parts of the work seem timed to fit in with presbyterian agitation in the City. The first, in February, came during the presbyterians' calls on parliament for renewal of the solemn league and covenant, action against sectarianism, and effective church government; the second, in May, during the campaign for the City *remonstrance*; the third, in December, during a period of renewed hostility towards the army.

Gangraena demonstrates the existence of errors from example. In part 1 Edwards calls on his readers 'to communicate to me all the certain intelligence they have … of the Sectaries' and emphasizes his efforts to substantiate the information received (Edwards, *Gangraena*, 1.42). The work contains scandalous news of Seekers, lay preachers, atheists, dippers, Anabaptists, and Independents, though he tells surprisingly few tales of the latter, concentrating his fire on the more extremist views. Thus he describes a woman who 'denied there was any such thing as sinne, or Hell, or the Devill, or temptation, or the holy Ghost, or Scriptures' and a follower of an antinomian who declared '*That if a child of God should commit murther, he ought not to repent of it*' (ibid., 2.8, 146). The author's vociferous narrative of horror welded these descriptions together in an effort to call the innocent to action and shame and silence the guilty. Independency was the root of error and Edwards's main polemical purpose was to implicate leading Independent ministers in the spread of heresy. For toleration was protean, a slow creeping disease—a gangrene—that would corrupt the entire body if not cut off. Indeed, the attempt to categorize and contain schism with a complete list of sectarian errors only reinforced this threat; by the third part of *Gangraena*, Edwards's list had grown to almost 300 errors and was still unfinished. Similarly, part 3 contains more material than the first two parts on the New Model Army, such as a story (originating in a royalist newsbook) of soldiers urinating in a font to baptize a horse, and on political radicalism within London, reflecting growing presbyterian fears of a hostile army of Independents and their supporters within the

City. This illustrates the immediacy of Edwards's text and the way in which he shaped it to changing events.

Of course while Edwards and his supporters portrayed his book as 'a Book full of truth', his opponents branded it full of lies (Edwards, *Gangraena*, 2.44). Some twenty pamphlets directly addressed *Gangraena* soon after its publication and numerous others commented on the work and its author, quickly establishing the notoriety of the book. In part the replies fought out a battle for the truth. Edwards's allies, such as William Prynne, John Bastwick, and Robert Baillie, defended and used his book as a source for their own works, seemingly authenticating his information. For his enemies, meanwhile, his book was a litany of falsehoods, and Edwards himself the personification of an intolerant and vengeful presbyterianism. John Goodwin's initially anonymous *Cretensis, or, A Briefe Answer to an Ulcerous Treatise* (1646) was one of the earliest and most sustained attacks on part 1 of *Gangraena* and was replied to at length in part 2. This prompted Goodwin to respond with a lengthy rejoinder that also addressed *Antapologia*. The detailed attacks by Goodwin, William Walwyn, John Saltmarsh, and others prove that Edwards failed in one of his objectives, that of shattering his opponents into silence, *Gangraena* having given voice to their views just as Edwards's enemies in turn did to his.

Defeat and exile During 1647 Edwards became a symbolic figure in the struggle between the New Model Army and London presbyterianism. For many soldiers the third part of *Gangraena* was the most conspicuous component of a hostile campaign against non-presbyterians in the army and the City. Moreover, during the early months of the year this campaign had been relatively successful. The rise of the group of presbyterian MPs around Denzil Holles advocating disbandment of the New Model was an all-too obvious threat, and Edwards clearly aligned himself with the group's agenda, questioning whether it was necessary to have 'so great an Army … continued in this Kingdom' (Edwards, *Gangraena*, 3, sig. d2). In this sense *Gangraena* and its author were among the grand incendiaries in the conflict between the army and London, and it is hardly surprising to find the arguments of Edwards and his books among the regimental grievances expressed by the New Model that spring.

Unfortunately very little is known of Edwards's activities during this period. His eventual flight and the presence of leading presbyterians by his deathbed may indicate that he played a major role in the City's campaign; conversely a man of his reputation was unlikely to escape the army's wrath. His last major work, *The Casting Down of the Last and Strongest Hold of Satan*, appeared in June 1647. Although this repeated the now familiar arguments against any form of toleration, limited or unlimited, the tract's repetitiveness was offset by a more systematic approach than usual. Edwards was a frequent target in hostile pamphlets, and it may be significant that he is rarely mentioned in the presbyterians' own works. There is some evidence that he may have been ill, and opponents had of course suggested this as a likely outcome for one who spread so much poison. But ultimately whatever he did in the ill-fated attempt to raise the City against the New Model, he felt unable to remain in the country after the collapse of the presbyterians' campaign.

At some point during late summer 1647 Edwards fled to Amsterdam, where he was probably relieved to join the staunchly presbyterian English church. He kept in touch with events in London, and in November was considered for the post of pastor of his new church. However, by December he was ill and chose to record a self-vindicating and unrepentant confession of his beliefs and actions, later witnessed by his fellow presbyterian exiles William Waller and Edward Massey. He made a will on 3 February 1648 NS and died four days later at Amsterdam, where he was later buried. He was survived by his wife, who obtained probate on 25 May, and a number of his children, including the second son, John.

Reputation Edwards's funeral prompted a gathering of presbyterian exiles, who no doubt lamented the death of such a true and valiant warrior. He was committed to a reformed and comprehensive Church of England throughout his career and suffered for his beliefs at first. If his intemperate character held back his advancement during those initial years, it was the identical trait that was his making. As the presbyterians' polemist he willingly confronted the sectarian menace in the pulpit and in print. His lectures were the most talked of in London, and in *Gangraena* he produced a powerful weapon in the battle against the never ceasing threat of toleration. Of course ultimately he died disappointed but he remained, in the words of his fellow presbyterian Thomas Hall, the 'true hammer of the heretics' to the last (Birmingham Reference Library, D94/1646/I).

To his enemies Edwards and *Gangraena* were inseparable. Indeed contemporaries referred to him as Gangraena Edwards or simply as Gangraena. The personification of mid-seventeenth-century ill tolerance, he was portrayed as a rabid, lying enemy of liberty of conscience, a vindictive, evil man intent on blasting people's reputations at any cost and without justification. This image of 'shallow Edwards' was immortalized by his most famous target, John Milton, and was still prevalent among historians of civil-war radicalism during the second half of the twentieth century (*John Milton: Complete Shorter Poems*, ed. J. Cary, 1997, 295).

The question of how historians should use Edwards's catalogues remains a prevalent one. Previously his descriptions were taken at face value and used to provide vivid descriptions of the variety of radical beliefs and opinions in civil-war England. Historians gradually brought an increasing scepticism to this approach, using *Gangraena* as a source but with qualifications. This trend reached its zenith when a number of revisionist historians denounced Edwards as an unquestionably tainted source and refused to use his works as evidence. The most recent work has turned away from the problematic issue of accuracy to focus on *Gangraena* as a text, examining the manner of its construction and its place in the polemics of the mid-1640s. A central argument is that presbyterians and Independents competed for popular support in the

public arena, with Edwards a key initiator and participant in the resultant debate. This challenges the traditional image of the embattled orthodox conservative clergyman, arguing that Edwards was motivated by a positive duty to defend truth and define and refute error wherever he found it.

P. R. S. Baker

Sources A. Hughes, *Gangraena and the struggle for the English revolution* [forthcoming] · T. Edwards, *Gangraena*, 3 pts (1646); repr. (1977) [with an introduction by M. M. Goldsmith and I. Roots] · A. Hughes, '"Popular" presbyterianism in the 1640s and 1650s: the cases of Thomas Edwards and Thomas Hall', *England's long reformation, 1500–1800*, ed. N. Tyacke (1998), 235–59 · E. C. Vernon, 'The Sion College conclave and London presbyterianism during the English revolution', PhD diss., U. Cam., 1999 · T. Edwards, *Antapologia, or, A full answer to the 'Apologeticall narration'* (1644) · H. Woodward, *A short letter modestly intreating a friends judgement upon Mr Edwards his booke, he calleth an anti-apologie* (1644) · M. Tolmie, *The triumph of the saints: the separate churches of London, 1616–1649* (1977) · T. Webster, *Godly clergy in early Stuart England: the Caroline puritan movement, c.1620–1643* (1997) · V. Pearl, 'London's counter-revolution', *The interregnum: the quest for settlement, 1646–1660*, ed. G. E. Aylmer (1972); repr. (1974), 29–56 · F. J. Bremer, *Congregational communion: clerical friendship in the Anglo-American puritan community, 1610–1692* (1994) · V. Pearl, 'London puritans and Scotch Fifth Columnists: a mid-seventeenth century phenomenon', *Studies in London history presented to Philip Edmund Jones*, ed. A. E. J. Hollander and W. Kellaway (1969), 317–31 · M. Mahoney, 'Presbyterianism in the City of London, 1645–1647', *HJ*, 22 (1979), 93–114 · Tai Liu, *Puritan London: a study of religion and society in the City parishes* (1986) · P. S. Seaver, *The puritan lectureships: the politics of religious dissent, 1560–1662* (1970) · K. Lindley, *Popular politics and religion in civil war London* (1997) · I. Gentles, 'London Levellers in the English revolution: the Chidleys and their circle', *Journal of Ecclesiastical History*, 29 (1978), 281–309 · Venn, *Alum. Cant.* · *IGI* · churchwardens' accounts, St Botolph, Aldgate, London, GL, MS 9235/2, pt 2 · *DNB*

Edwards, Thomas (1651/2–1721), Church of England clergyman and orientalist, was born at Llanllechid, near Bangor in Caernarvonshire, the son of Edward Edwards. He attended school in Bangor and matriculated as a sizar at St John's College, Cambridge, on 16 March 1670 aged eighteen, graduating BA in 1674 and proceeding MA in 1677. With the support of Edmund Castell, the professor of Arabic whom he met at St John's and with whom he subsequently stayed, Edwards devoted himself to the study of oriental languages, above all Coptic. In 1685 Edwards was summoned to Oxford by John Fell to help in the publication of the Coptic New Testament on which Thomas Marshall had been working until shortly before his death in April.

Edwards was incorporated MA at Oxford on 9 July and was appointed chaplain of Christ Church. With a good reputation as a scholar he met the Arabist Edward Pococke and formed a friendship with the Huguenot refugee Pierre Allix. Fell, however, died in July 1686. Deprived of his patron Edwards made little headway with the projected publication (which was completed only in 1716 by David Wilkins). Already at Oxford, moreover, Edwards exhibited the taste for religious polemics which would inspire his later publications: on 27 November 1687, at the church of St Mary the Virgin, he preached a sermon which was found so outrageous that he had to retract it before the vice-chancellor of the university on 2 December, and Thomas Hearne recalled the incident thirty-five years later. In 1690 Edwards was appointed vicar of Badby, near Daventry, in the gift of Christ Church, and withdrew to Northamptonshire. On 29 September 1692 he married Frances Ward, a widow from Brafield, some 5 miles southeast of Northampton.

With numerous pastoral duties—he said that they would always take precedence over his scholarly activity—and with no access to Coptic manuscripts Edwards had decided to abandon his studies. But owing to Pierre Allix he received a letter in the autumn of 1695 from the French orientalist Louis Picques (like Allix a correspondent of Robert Huntington) with a list of questions about Coptic. In his reply Edwards revealed his qualities as a scholar. He also begged Picques to persuade some bishop, peer of the realm, or even the king, to obtain for him a preferment which would enable him to continue his research. Picques responded by drawing Edwards to the attention of William Lloyd, bishop of Lichfield and Coventry.

Encouraged by Lloyd, Picques, and Allix, Edwards resumed the plan he had formed with Fell of composing a Coptic dictionary. While at Oxford he had seen Marshall's copy, with his corrections, of the *Lingua Aegyptiaca restituta* published by the Jesuit Athanasius Kircher in 1643, an edition and Latin translation of a thirteenth-century Coptic–Arabic dictionary brought back from Egypt by Pietro della Valle. Although Kircher was a pioneer in the study of Coptic his knowledge of the language was imperfect. Edwards resolved to produce a better lexicon based on Kircher and the other Coptic–Arabic dictionaries at Oxford. According to Hearne, Edwards, whom he defines as 'a whimsical, crazed Man, and fickle', placed the sheets of the dictionary in alphabetical order on chairs. When a gust of wind threw them into confusion it 'put him into such a Fret that he said he would do no more, it being an ill Omen, and thereupon he threw all aside, and proceeded no farther' (*Remarks*, 7.351). Nevertheless Edwards completed his work in 1711, ending it with a brief section on Coptic grammar and an analysis of the Coptic version of the Lord's prayer. It remained in manuscript and was later acquired by the Bodleian (MS Bodl. Or. 344). Although Edwards's dictionary often improves on Kircher it can hardly be regarded as a contribution to Coptic studies. By 1711, as Edwards himself realized, the Coptic collections, notably at the Bodleian and in Paris, but also elsewhere in Europe, had expanded vastly, and it required far more than a consultation of the relatively few codices collected by Marshall to make a proper advance in the subject.

In his early years in Northamptonshire, Edwards devoted much of his time to religious polemic, producing two publications enlivened by references to *Don Quixote*. His *Discourse of praying in the spirit or against extempore prayer, with a friendly admonition to the dissenters* (1703) was written against the nonconformist argument that extempore praying had already been practised in the early church. There was, claimed Edwards, 'no such thing in the World, till Fanaticism, the Spirit of mad Error put the wild Notion into the Head, and the vile Practice into the Mouth of the English Puritans … and the Sects that have sprung from

them' (p. 15). The book extended its attack to all nonconformist practices including adult baptism. It gave great offence, drawing a sarcastic remark from Edmund Calamy in his *Defence of Moderate Non-Conformity* (1703). In 1705 Edwards published his *Diocesan Episcopacy, Proved from Holy Scripture*, which opened with a reply to Calamy. A demonstration of the antiquity of ecclesiastical hierarchy and of the apostolic succession practised by the bishops of the Church of England, it was mainly directed against *Primitive Episcopacy* (1688) by David Clarkson, a supporter of congregational (or collegial) supervision.

In 1708 Edwards was given the rectory of Aldwincle All Saints, also in Northamptonshire. He was hardly less isolated than before and in no better position to return to his studies, even if it was there that he finished his Coptic dictionary. His last work is a poem entitled *A Christmas Carol, Dedicated to the Ancient Britons that Understand English* (1715). Although it ends with a plea for a decorous celebration of Christmas, it is also intended to confute the Socinians. Edwards died at Aldwincle All Saints and was buried there on 5 September 1721. ALASTAIR HAMILTON

Sources Venn, *Alum. Cant.* · L. Picques, *Commercium literarium* (1750) · *Remarks and collections of Thomas Hearne*, ed. C. E. Doble and others, 7, OHS, 48 (1906) · *DNB* · E. Quatremère, *Recherches critiques et historiques sur la langue et la littérature de l'Égypte* (1808) · H. Carter, *A history of the Oxford University Press*, 1: *To the year 1780* (1975) · J. Bridges, *The history and antiquities of Northamptonshire*, ed. P. Whalley, 1 (1791) · *The life and times of Anthony Wood*, ed. A. Clark, 3, OHS, 26 (1894) · parish register, Badby, 29 Sept 1692, Northants. RO [marriage] · parish register, Aldwincle All Saints, 5 Sept 1721, Northants. RO [burial]
Archives Bodl. Oxf., Coptic dictionary, MS Bodl. Or. 344
Likenesses T. Murray, oils, 1712, St John Cam.

Edwards, Thomas (*d.* 1757), poet and literary editor, was descended from Welsh gentry, though the family had settled in Middlesex before his birth. Emulating his father and grandfather, both barristers, Edwards elected to study law at Lincoln's Inn, beginning in 1721, after having been tutored in the classical languages during childhood. In his *Select Collection of Poems* (1780) John Nichols declared that Edwards had been educated at Eton College and King's College, Cambridge; an anonymous letter to the *Gentleman's Magazine* in 1782, perhaps on this authority, repeated the account. There is no record, however, of Edwards's attendance at either institution. Decades later, in his *Literary Anecdotes*, Nichols reported that Edwards was only privately educated before his study of law (Nichols, *Lit. anecdotes*, 2.200). Having inherited an ample estate on his father's early death, Edwards lived mostly in retirement and, except for participating in the assizes at Buckingham until his health failed, he devoted most of his time to reading, writing poetry, and gardening. In 1740 he left his paternal estate in Pitshanger, Middlesex, and settled on a small farm at Turrick, Ellesborough, near Aylesbury, Buckinghamshire, where he stayed for the rest of his life.

By his early forties Edwards was bereft of all his siblings—four brothers and four sisters; when planning to print the sonnet addressed to his deceased family, he had originally contemplated having a portrait engraved by

Arthur Pond of himself in their company to be used as an illustration. To the end, he maintained close ties with his cousins Harvy and Lockey, and two surviving nephews and heirs—Joseph Paice and Nathaniel Mason. Apparently not a bachelor by choice, he took offence at any of the fashionable slurs on the married state and was a strong advocate of women writers. After entering Samuel Richardson's circle on the appearance of *Clarissa* in 1748, he cultivated the friendship of Hester Mulso especially and exchanged poems with her.

Edwards distinguished himself as a writer of sonnets in Miltonic form and through Daniel Wray's intercession had thirteen included in the third edition of Dodsley's *Collection of Poems* (1751). Since most of his more than fifty sonnets were circulated in manuscript among friends, public knowledge of his literary achievement was limited until the sixth edition of the *Canons* (1758) included twenty-seven sonnets not printed by Dodsley. In an era when this popular Renaissance poetic form was almost forsaken, the *Monthly Review* (1799) declared Edwards's poems 'perhaps the best modern sonnets' (p. 362). He was elected a fellow of the Society of Antiquaries on 20 October 1745.

In 1748 Edwards published *A Supplement*, a withering attack on William Warburton's edition of Shakespeare, which made him immediately a celebrity; by the time the third and expanded edition of 1750 appeared, renamed *The Canons of Criticism* (using Warburton's own phrase in the introduction to his edition), Edwards had become recognized as a champion of responsible scholarly editing of the canonical English authors. Despite Johnson's well-known defence of Warburton as a 'stately horse' being stung by a fly [Edwards] (Boswell, *Life*, 1.263), he himself deferred to Edwards's commentary as well as to Warburton's in his own edition of Shakespeare. While deriving twenty-five categories of editorial abuses, assisted by his Cambridge friend Richard Roderick, Edwards needed little more than to quote Warburton verbatim. The main target was the editor's pompous tone in exerting his authority over cruxes in Shakespeare.

Edwards made at least preliminary attempts to produce an edition of Spenser but quickly abandoned the idea after recognizing his limited resources while living in the country. A project that Richardson encouraged, a book on orthography, resulted in the playful fantasy *An Account of the Trial of the Letter Y [Upsilon], alias Y*, printed in 1753 along with the fifth edition of the *Canons* at Richardson's press. Edwards's letter-books show a considerable range of friends: Daniel Wray (who introduced him to the highly talented literati involved in the secret *Athenian Letters*, 1741, which included Philip and Charles Yorke, Thomas Birch, John Lawry, William Heberden, and Mrs Catherine Talbot, among others), Richard Owen Cambridge, Speaker Arthur Onslow and son George, Isaac Hawkins Browne, John Dyer, Lewis Crusius, John Hoadly, William Melmoth the younger, and John Wilkes.

Although he repeatedly declined the Richardsons' earnest invitations to spend his winters with them for fear of imposing an invalid on them, Edwards finally decided to accept and visit them occasionally at Parson's Green,

where after a violent attack of pleurisy he died on 3 January 1757. Edwards was buried at Ellesborough, Buckinghamshire, and his two nephews wrote an eloquent epitaph on his exemplary character.

JOHN A. DUSSINGER

Sources J. Nichols, ed., *A select collection of poems*, 6 (1780), 103–8 • Nichols, *Lit. anecdotes*, 2.200 • *GM*, 1st ser., 52 (1782), 288–9 • J. S. Watson, *The life of William Warburton, D.D.* (1863) • A. W. Evans, *Warburton and the Warburtonians: a study in some eighteenth-century controversies* (1932) • T. C. D. Eaves and B. D. Kimpel, *Samuel Richardson: a biography* (1971) • W. M. Sale, *Samuel Richardson: master printer* (1950) • Boswell, *Life*, vol. 1 • R. Dodsley, ed., *A collection of poems … by several hands*, [3rd edn], 2 (1751), 322–34 • *The letters of Samuel Johnson*, ed. B. Redford, 1 (1992) • P. Yorke and others, *Athenian letters, or, The epistolary correspondence of an agent of the king of Persia, residing at Athens during the Peloponnesian War*, ed. T. Birch, new edn, 2 vols. (1798) • *Monthly Review*, new ser., 29 (1799), 362 • *The correspondence of Samuel Richardson*, ed. A. L. Barbauld, 6 vols. (1804), vol. 3, pp. 1–139 • R. D. Havens, *The influence of Milton on English poetry* (1922) • T. Edwards, *The canons of criticism and glossary, being a supplement to Mr Warburton's edition of Shakespear to which are added the trial of the letter Y, alias Y, and sonnets*, 7th edn (1765) • *The sonnets of Thomas Edwards*, ed. D. G. Donovan (1974) • T. Edwards, *Free and candid thoughts on the doctrine of predestination* (1761) • *DNB*

Archives Bodl. Oxf., letter-book, MS 1011, MS 1012 • Bodl. Oxf., letters, MS Eng. Lett.e.92 [copies] | BL, letters to Lord Hardwicke, Add. MSS 35605–35606 • BL, letters to John Wilkes, Add. MS 30867 • V&A, Forster MSS, Richardson corresp.

Likenesses A. Pond, etching, c.1749; [lost] • A. Pond, oils, c.1749; [lost] • W. Holl, stipple, pubd 1828, BM, NPG

Wealth at death considerable; incl. four houses in Bedfordshire, Buckinghamshire, Surrey, and London; also two farms: will, PRO, PROB 11/827, fols. 83r–83v

Edwards, Thomas (1729–1785), Church of England clergyman and schoolmaster, was born at Coventry in August 1729, the son of Thomas Edwards (*b. c.*1691). Having been educated at the free grammar school in Coventry under Dr Jackson, in November 1746 he went to Cambridge, where he briefly attended St John's College. He then moved to Clare College, whence he graduated BA (1750), MA (1754), and DD (1766); he was a fellow of Clare from 1752 to 1759. He was ordained deacon in 1751 and priest in 1753 by Frederick Cornwallis, bishop of Lichfield and Coventry, to whom he dedicated his *New English Translation of the Psalms* (1755). In 1758 he was appointed master of his old school and rector of St John the Baptist, Coventry; he retained these appointments until 1779. In 1758 he was made vicar of Bablake, Coventry. On 27 November of the same year he married Ann Parrott (*d.* 1784) at St Michael's, Coventry. They had a son, Thomas *Edwards (1759?–1842), who was also a clergyman and writer on religious subjects.

In 1759 Edwards contributed *The doctrine of irresistible grace proved to have no foundation in the writings of the New Testament* to the Calvinist and Arminian debate. He disagreed with Robert Lowth over Hebrew prosody and criticized him in print in 1762. Lowth responded in *De sacra poesi Hebraeon* (1765), claiming that Edwards's treatment of syllabic weight was incompatible with metrical forms. Edwards also published various other pieces on the New Testament and some miscellaneous sermons. His principal friend was Edward Law, bishop of Carlisle.

In 1770 Edwards became vicar of Nuneaton, Warwickshire, to where he moved in 1779. A mild and benevolent man, who was fond of retirement, he died in Warwickshire in June 1785 after a long illness. He was buried at Foleshill, Warwickshire.

N. D. F. PEARCE, *rev.* EMMA MAJOR

Sources Venn, *Alum. Cant.* · ESTC · R. Lowth, *De sacra poesi Hebraeon*, trans. G. Gregory, 2 vols. (1787), 2.442–6 · will, PRO, PROB 11/1133, sig. 463 · *GM*, 1st ser., 55 (1785), 572 · Watt, *Bibl. Brit.* · Foster, *Alum. Oxon.*, *1500–1714* [Thomas Edwards, father]
Wealth at death all to son; vague references to land rents and property: will, PRO, PROB 11/1133, sig. 463

Thomas Edwards [Twm o'r Nant] (1738–1810), by unknown artist, *c.*1800–10 [detail]

Edwards, Thomas [*called* Twm o'r Nant] (1738–1810), poet, was born between 1 and 8 January 1738 in Penporchell Isaf in the parish of Llannefydd, Denbighshire, the son of Evan Edwards, a smallholder, and his wife, Mary. He became known as Twm o'r Nant on account of his parents' moving to Y Nant Isaf, near the village of Nantglyn, in the parish of Henllan, about 1741. He married Elizabeth Hughes (1738/9–1808) of Llanfair Talhaearn in 1763, and the first of the couple's three daughters was born before the end of the same year.

Twm recorded the details of his early life, and sketched his subsequent movements, in a short autobiographical tract which appeared in *Y Greal* in 1805. He mentions his meagre schooling—a few weeks at the Nantglyn Free School and a fortnight's instruction in the English tongue at Denbigh—and boasts of his exploits as a timber haulier which were unfortunately arrested when his horses fell victim to a disease and died. Further tribulations were to follow with the bankruptcy of an uncle for whom Twm had agreed to act as surety. Twm chose to outwit his debtors by leaving Denbigh, where he had settled shortly after his marriage, and fleeing first to Dolobran in Montgomeryshire and eventually to Llandeilo in Carmarthenshire where he again undertook haulage work before returning to his native county in 1786.

Twm sought to overcome his financial plight by writing interludes. His involvement with this form of popular entertainment began around 1749 when he was invited to join a local company of touring actors. By the time he was twenty Twm had written seven interludes, all of which have since disappeared. There remain in print and in manuscript seven works written between about 1766 and 1789 which the author performed throughout north Wales and which brought him, according to his own testimony, considerable pecuniary reward, enhanced by the sale of printed versions. His interludes were republished after his death—no other writer received this treatment—and six of his works appeared collectively in an Isaac Foulkes publication of 1874, *Gwaith Thomas Edwards*.

His explicit commentary on the social evils of his day helps to explain Twm's renown as an interlude writer. The unpopularity of the various taxes levied by the authorities is frequently mentioned. Landowners are castigated on account of their exorbitant rents, their greed, and their absenteeism. The representatives of the church are shown to be immoral, unconcerned with the spiritual welfare of their flocks, and unable to communicate effectively with the masses due to their lack of fluency in the Welsh language. The legal profession, central in Twm o'r Nant's personal drama of misery, is portrayed as a haven for conniving swindlers. Yet, paradoxically, Twm parades as the upholder of the social order, especially so in *Pedair colofn gwladwriaeth*, published three years prior to the French Revolution. Social tension, Twm argues, is caused not by an unjust system but rather by the inability of the individual, whatever his status, to respect his predestined place and perform his required duties.

The interludes also proclaim the author's moral and religious values. Man is shown to be at the mercy of his nature and his sins are symbolized by the two stock characters, the miser and jester, and by parallel allegorical characters. *Tri chryfion byd*, possibly Twm's last interlude, ends not with the conventional death of the former, but with his conversion. The miser's rejection of the transient serves to remind the public of a pivotal theme in the teaching of the Methodists, and also explains how Twm became *persona grata* in the eyes of the movement's leaders, who naturally despised the interlude and the lewd actions and speech of its characters. Nineteenth-century commentators were less impressed with the religious undertones in the interludes.

The most prominent interlude writers in eighteenth-century Wales were also prolific ballad writers, and Twm o'r Nant was no exception. There remain approximately 200 extant pieces in print and in manuscripts, and as many poems again in *cynghanedd*, mostly *englynion*, awaiting the services of an editor. Interestingly, scraps of poetry by two of Twm's offspring, Margaret and Lowri, survive in their father's manuscripts. The poet prepared an anthology of his works (again as part of his efforts to establish himself financially); *Gardd o gerddi* appeared in 1790, and Twm gleefully informed readers of his autobiography that he had sold 2000 copies. The strict-metre *cywyddau* in the collection bear the hallmark of hurried composition. Their style and subject matter however—his elegies and eulogies to the north Wales gentry take a prominent place—indicate that their author was well acquainted with the poetry of the *cywyddwyr* of the late middle ages. Twm himself was the proud owner of several early manuscripts which he eventually sold to the Gwyneddigion Society (the London-Welsh Society founded in 1770).

Twm o'r Nant participated in the eisteddfods held under the auspices of the same society during the latter years of the eighteenth century, but the cherished main honour eluded him, possibly as a consequence of an earlier dispute between Twm and the Gwyneddigion, which deemed the impromptu composition of its favourite, Gwallter Mechain (Walter Davies), superior to Twm's effort, in spite of the entreaties of Twm's protagonist, David Samwell, Captain James Cook's surgeon, who dubbed his hero the Cambrian Shakespeare.

Twm survived his wife by two years. He died on 1 April 1810 and was buried in the parish church of Denbigh. The Gwyneddigion funded a tablet in his memory.

A. CYNFAEL LAKE

Sources G. M. Ashton, *Hunangofiant a llythyrau Twm o'r Nant* (1964) · G. M. Ashton, 'Bywyd a gwaith Twm o'r Nant a'i le yr hanes yr anterliwt', MA diss., U. Wales, 1944 · I. Foulkes, *Gwaith Thomas Edwards (Twm o'r Nant)* (1874) · I. Foulkes, *Geirlyfr bywgraffiadol o enwogion Cymru* (1870), 274–80 · bishop's transcripts, diocese of St Asaph, parishes of Llanfair Talhaern and Denbigh
Archives NL Wales
Likenesses oils, 1800–10, NL Wales · oils, c.1800–1810, Gwynedd Archives, Caernarfon [*see illus.*] · portrait, repro. in T. R. Roberts, *Eminent Welshmen* (1908), following p. 80

Edwards, Thomas (1759?–1842), Church of England clergyman, son of Thomas *Edwards (1729–1785), and his wife, Anne Parrott, was born at Coventry, where his father was master of the free school, and rector of St John the Baptist Church. He graduated LLB from Clare College, Cambridge, in 1782. In 1787 he was a fellow of Jesus College, and took his LLD. He was ordained in 1782, and was subsequently vicar of Hinxton (1787), and Histon (1789–1808), both in Cambridgeshire, and later curate, and then rector, of Aldford, Cheshire (1788–1842), and curate of Caldecote, Hertfordshire (1812–14). His publications included *A Discourse on the Limits and Importance of Free Inquiry in Matters of Religion* (1792) and *Criticisms Relating to the Dead* (1810). N. Nisbet, rector of Tunstall, made several attacks upon Edwards's biblical criticism. Edwards died on 4 July 1842 at Aldford. [ANON.], *rev.* MARI G. ELLIS

Sources Venn, *Alum. Cant.* · C. H. Cooper, *Memorials of Cambridge* (1860) · d. cert.

Edwards, Thomas (1776/7–1845), legal writer, was the son of Thomas Edwards, master of Chelsea Academy, London. He studied at Pembroke College and then Trinity Hall, Cambridge, where he proceeded LLB in 1800 and LLD in 1805. He was also a fellow of Trinity Hall from 1805 to 1811, and was admitted advocate at Doctors' Commons in 1805. He was a reporter of Admiralty cases, and his reports were published in 1812. He was also a magistrate for the county of Surrey, and took considerable interest in social questions. He published pamphlets on the misconduct of licensing in magistrates in 1825, and on church ritual in 1835. He died at The Grove, Carshalton, on 29 October 1845. FRANCIS WATT, *rev.* JONATHAN HARRIS

Sources GM, 2nd ser., 24 (1845), 662 · Venn, *Alum. Cant.* · Watt, *Bibl. Brit.*, 1.331

Edwards, Thomas [*pseud.* Caerfallwch] (1779–1858), orthographer and lexicographer, was born at Caerfallwch, Northop, Flintshire, the son of Richard Edwards and his wife, Margaret. He was baptized at Northop on 5 March 1780. After a short period at Northop grammar school he was apprenticed, at the age of fourteen, to a saddler at Mold named Birch, in whose family he read English newspapers and books, and cultivated his taste for Welsh literature. He married Margaret Jones of Trellynian in 1800 or 1801, and with her dowry set up a saddler's shop at Northop, but it failed. After the death of his first wife, he married in 1803 a Miss Wynne of Northop, and in 1816 he married Miss Webster, also of Northop. From 1802 to 1806 he was secretary to a colliery, and was then appointed to its London office, where he became secretary to a Mr Bell, and then, in 1815, to Nathaniel M. Rothschild. He often visited Europe on business; in 1830, for example, he was sent to Germany by his firm to investigate irregularities in the princely court.

In 1838 Edwards was selected with five others, in connection with the Abergavenny eisteddfod, to improve Welsh orthography. Nothing came of this, but in 1845 Edwards published his *Analysis of Welsh Orthography*. This used William Owen Pughe's method to describe changes in sounds, and explained the meaning of prefixes and suffixes. He was for many years a member of the Cymmrodorion, and delivered many of their lectures; that on currency was afterwards published. But Edwards's most important work was his *English and Welsh Dictionary*, published in 1850, with a second edition appearing in 1864; another edition was published in the United States. His dictionary was an expansion of that by Pughe, and aimed to provide neologisms in Welsh for English industrial, economic, and scientific terms. Those generally accepted include *pwyllgor* (committee), *cyngerdd* (concert), and *nwy* (gas). Edwards's verse, including 'Adgovion', a description of his childhood, was written in the manner of Pughe; it is derivative, and is not highly regarded. His support for Catholic emancipation led to his excommunication by the Calvinistic Methodists, and he joined the Jewin Welsh Methodist Church in London. Edwards was a frequent contributor to the Welsh magazines of the day. In addition to his bardic name, Caerfallwch he used the pseudonyms T. ap Edwart ap Eurgain and Zabulonum. He died at 10 Cloudesley Square, London, on 4 July 1858, and was interred in Highgate cemetery.

R. M. J. JONES, *rev.* JOHN D. HAIGH

Sources DWB · M. Stephens, ed., *The Oxford companion to the literature of Wales* (1986) · Boase, *Mod. Eng. biog.* · E. H. Rowland, *A biographical dictionary of eminent Welshmen who flourished from 1700 to 1900* (privately printed, Wrexham, 1907) · Allibone, *Dict.*, suppl.

Edwards, Thomas Charles (1837–1900), theologian and educationist, was born at Llanycil, Bala, Merioneth, on 22 September 1837. He was the eldest son of Lewis Edwards, founder of Bala College, and through his mother he was related to Thomas Charles, organizer of the Sunday school movement in Wales. From 1852 he was educated in Bala College, graduating BA (1861) and MA (1862) from the University of London. In 1862 he matriculated at St Alban Hall, Oxford, and entered Lincoln College, Oxford, as a scholar, where he took a first class honours degree in classics in 1866, graduating MA in 1872. He was awarded a doctorate of divinity of Edinburgh University in 1887 and became the first doctor of divinity of the University of Wales in 1898.

Ordained in 1864, Edwards became one of the most powerful and scholarly of preachers in both English and Welsh. In 1866 he was inducted minister of the English Calvinistic Methodist Chapel in Liverpool and in 1867 he married Mary Roberts; they had four children. Edwards was appointed first principal of the University College of Wales in Aberystwyth in 1872. Advised by his Oxford mentors, Benjamin Jowett and Mark Pattison, he accepted the post on condition that he be allowed to continue preaching. He directed the infant college at a most difficult time, having to negotiate denominational narrowness and academic and structural problems of college government. Contemporary denominational jealousies ensured that his ordained status was often held against him and the college. His devotion to preaching has since prompted adverse judgement from the academic commentator W. J. Gruffydd but his fame as a preacher attracted students and enhanced Aberystwyth's reputation. He was the first president of the theological board of the University of Wales, and moderator of the South Wales Association in 1883 and of the general assembly in 1887.

As principal at Aberystwyth, Edwards was both teacher (for a time professor of Greek and philosophy) and administrator, and acquired a considerable reputation for his lectures. Despite his quick temper many of his students regarded him with 'unbounded admiration'. He championed academic freedom against interference by the college council and president. His was also an era of unrelenting financial pressure and he had to devote much time to cost-cutting and fund-raising. With the Aberdare report (1881) he faced the possible extinction of the college. In 1885 Edwards had to face another crisis when the college's north wing was destroyed by fire. He played a crucial role in ensuring survival by fund-raising across Wales, speaking at hundreds of meetings, and appealing to each student to remain. When, in 1889, the college received its charter it was Edwards's achievement that it was set to prosper.

In 1891 Edwards succeeded his father (who had always been the most significant influence on his son and who had died in 1887) as principal of Bala College. He did so on condition that it become a purely theological college. Furthermore, it should be open to students of other denominations, and of both sexes. The formal opening as a theological college took place in October 1891. Edwards

Thomas Charles Edwards (1837–1900), by James Russell & Sons

brought considerable prestige, with new appointments, library expansion, and more scholarships following. However, high expectations were not realized, partly because of Edwards's ill health which especially marred the years after 1897. In 1899 he resigned, but was prevailed upon to remain as principal without lecturing duties. He died at the college on 22 March 1900.

Edwards has been regarded as, potentially, one of the outstanding theological scholars of his era whose energies were usually directed elsewhere. He published notable biblical commentaries: on the first epistle to the Corinthians (1885), which earned him a European reputation, and on the epistle to the Hebrews (1888). A Welsh version of the latter appeared in 1890. *The God-Man: being the 'Davies Lecture' for 1895* was published in the same year and a Welsh version in 1897. He published his father's letters, and an account of his life, *Cofiant a llythyrau y diweddar Barch Lewis Edwards*, which appeared in 1901.

GARETH ELWYN JONES

Sources *Thomas Charles Edwards letters*, ed. T. I. Ellis, 2 vols. (1952–3) · J. E. C. Williams, 'T. C. Edwards a'i Gyfraniad i Ddiwynyddiaeth Cymru', *Diwynyddiaeth*, 25 (1974), 3–28 · D. D. Williams, *Thomas Charles Edwards* (1921) · J. P. Jones, 'Principal Thomas Charles Edwards', *Welsh religious leaders in the Victorian era*, ed. J. Vyrnwy Morgan (1905) · W. J. Gruffydd, *Owen Morgan Edwards: Cofiant* (1937) · E. L. Ellis, *The University College of Wales, Aberystwyth, 1872–1972* (1972) · R. Hughes, 'T. C. Edwards', *Yr Efrydydd* (1936–7), 27–34 · J. G. Williams, *The University of Wales foundations* (1993) · CGPLA Eng. & Wales (1900) · DNB

Archives NL Wales, corresp., notebooks, diaries, and papers; family letters, notes and papers | NL Wales, letters to D. S. Evans · NL Wales, letters to Owen Jones

Likenesses H. von Herkomer, oils, 1897, U. Wales, Aberystwyth · J. Russell & Sons, photograph, NPG [*see illus.*]

Wealth at death £9619 12s. 8d.: probate, 7 May 1900, CGPLA Eng. & Wales

Edwards, (Arthur) Trystan (1884–1973), architectural critic and town planner, was born on 10 November 1884 at The Court, Merthyr Tudful. His father, William Edwards (1850–1940), was then HM inspector of schools for the

Merthyr Tudful district and later chief inspector to the central Welsh school board; his mother was Johanna Emilie Phillipine, *née* Steinthal. Edwards was educated at Clifton College and at Hertford College, Oxford, where he took moderations in mathematics (first class, 1905) and finals in *literae humaniores* (third class, 1907).

Following pupillage with the classically minded architect Reginald Blomfield, Edwards studied civic design under S. D. Adshead at the Liverpool School of Architecture (1911–13). Here he learned ideas about town planning to which he adhered throughout his career: chiefly, an antagonism towards the rustic bias of the garden city movement and respect for the urbanity of the Georgian street. After returning to London in 1913 to work for the firm of Richardson and Gill, he soon became immersed in architectural journalism. A fine series of articles for the *Architects' and Builders' Journal* on modern classical architects was curtailed by the First World War. In 1915 Edwards volunteered as a 'hostilities only' rating in the Royal Navy, where he served for four years. He liked the service so much that he spent twelve peacetime years as a Royal Naval Volunteer Reserve rating, and considered his naval experiences one of the major cultural influences of his life. He published an autobiographical book on the subject, *Three Rows of Tape* (1929), subtitled 'a social study of the lower deck', later twice revised and republished under fresh titles.

For six years after the war Edwards worked in the housing department of the Ministry of Health. But he was increasingly taken up with aesthetics and architectural criticism. He defined his philosophy in *The Things which are Seen: a Revaluation of the Visual Arts* (1921), then worked out its implications for architecture in *Good and Bad Manners in Architecture* (1924) and *Architectural Style* (1926). These books reveal an original but conservative thinker, influenced by the aesthetic 'humanism' of the writer and architect Geoffrey Scott. Edwards's seriousness and force of argument were belied by a sprightly, journalistic style; one device he sometimes used brilliantly in articles was to make adjacent urban buildings argue with one another, so as to bring out their faults and virtues. *Good and Bad Manners in Architecture*, the best of his books, combines indignation at the destruction of the old Regent Street with a scrupulously civilized code of principles for urban design. It enjoyed some public influence. But with modernism in the wings, Edwards was writing too late to make headway with younger architects or with international opinion.

Following the slump of 1929–32 Edwards determined to propagandize for a 'national scheme of building' in the form of a plan for 100 new towns. They were to be distinguished from garden cities or 'satellite towns' by their number and ubiquity, by the substitution of 'green wedges' into city centres for the circumferential green belts hitherto advocated, and by 'a return to the continuous street convention'. The Hundred New Towns Association was founded in 1933–4 and enjoyed a modest following. Edwards and his supporters gave evidence before the Barlow, Uthwatt, and Scott inquiries which helped shape the conditions of development after the Second World War. But they had scant impact on the post-war new towns policy, because Edwards's ideas lacked any economic basis, and depended for their force on idealism plus certain propositions about the layout of housing. These propositions, set out in the pamphlet *Modern Terrace Houses* (1946), were, however, suggestive and prophetic. His urban blocks of high-density, low-rise housing following stepped sections were later to be reinvented by planners and architects ignorant of Edwards's work.

On 15 March 1947 Edwards, then sixty-two, married Margaret Meredyth Smith (1900/01–1967), daughter of Canon Frederick Charles Smith of Hailsham, Sussex. Latterly, his activity and writing were diffuse. In 1953 he published *A New Map of the World*, which contained his 'homalographic' projection, a new method for correcting the comparative areas of continents. He also proposed a scheme for the realignment of national frontiers so as to give all nations an outlet to the sea. Though he appears never to have built to his own designs, he sketched out several planning projects: a wartime scheme to create a holiday centre along a broad section of the front at Hastings; an insulated overground tunnel ('Trajan's Tunnel') to carry a relief road through Christ Church Meadow, Oxford; and a plan for extending the Palace of Westminster across Bridge Street.

Having retired to Merthyr Tudful, Edwards continued to write well into old age. He produced *Merthyr, Rhondda and 'the Valleys'* (1958), *Towards Tomorrow's Architecture* (1968), and *Second-Best Boy: the Autobiography of a Non-Speaker* (1970). The subtitle of the last book refers to Edwards's marked speech impediment. This, accompanied by a disconcerting winking of one eye, reduced the impact of his platform appearances. Nevertheless, his Celtic enthusiasm was irresistible. A little round man with a gnomish and mercurial temperament, he made up for his faltering speech by the intensity and forcefulness of his writing. He died at St Tydfil's Hospital, Merthyr Tudful, on 30 January 1973 and was cremated.

GONTRAN GOULDEN, rev. ANDREW SAINT

Sources *The Times* (31 Jan 1973) · *The Times* (3 Feb 1973) · *The Times* (14 Feb 1973) · *Building* (9 Feb 1973) · A. T. Edwards, *Second-best boy: the autobiography of a non-speaker* (1970) · personal knowledge (1986) · A. T. Edwards, *Three rows of tape* (1929) · A. T. Edwards, *Modern terrace houses* (1946) · A. T. Edwards, *A hundred new towns?* (1944) · A. T. Edwards, *Good and bad manners in architecture* (1924) · b. cert. · m. cert. · d. cert. · CGPLA Eng. & Wales (1974)

Wealth at death £5305: probate, 19 March 1974, CGPLA Eng. & Wales

Edwards, Vero Copner Wynne- (1906–1997), zoologist, was born on 4 July 1906 in Leeds, the fifth of the six children of the Revd Canon John Rosindale Wynne-Edwards, headmaster of Leeds grammar school, and his wife, Lilian Agnes, *née* Streatfeild. His love of natural history was fostered early on by his childhood at Austwick in the Yorkshire dales, during which he observed, drew, and made detailed notes on the animals and plants around him. From Leeds grammar school he went on to Rugby School,

Vero Copner Wynne-Edwards (1906–1997), by Godfrey Argent Studios, 1976

in 1919, and thence to New College, Oxford, graduating with first-class honours in zoology in 1927. There then followed a period at the Marine Biological Laboratory in Plymouth studying fish and crustacea, but also out of hours the movements of starlings to and from their roosts. His interest in population studies had taken root. On 19 December 1929 he married Jeannie Campbell Morris (b. 1904/5), a schoolteacher, and daughter of Percy Morris, architect. They had met as classmates in Oxford. There were two children of the marriage, Janet and Hugh.

After a brief period at Bristol University, Wynne-Edwards moved, in 1930, to an assistant professorship at McGill University in Montreal, Canada, making observations on seabird distribution on the voyage and on several subsequent crossings of the Atlantic. His paper on the subject earned him a Walker prize from Boston Natural History Society. He remained in Canada for fifteen years, earning a considerable reputation, and fellowship of the Royal Society of Canada, particularly for his studies of plant distribution, for which he won a second Walker prize. It is a measure of his breadth that during the war he also taught electronics to radar mechanics and assessed the fish populations of the Yukon and Mackenzie rivers for the fisheries research board of Canada. In 1946 he decided to return to the United Kingdom, where he was appointed to the regius chair of natural history at Aberdeen, remaining in that post until his retirement in 1974. Aberdeen was an ideal location for Wynne-Edwards, and

not just for his passion for skiing and hill walking, enthusiasms he maintained into his eighties. He built up a large and successful zoology department in which he fostered a variety of research projects among members of his staff, perhaps most notably that on red grouse populations in the Deeside hills. He was vice-principal of the university for two years before he retired, but his most notable administrative contribution was to the Natural Environment Research Council: he took a major role in its early years, acting as its chairman 1968–71. He was elected FRS in 1970 and appointed CBE in 1973.

Wynne, as he was universally known, was a man who attracted strong loyalties. At the time of his death he was described as an 'intellectual giant' (*Ibis*, 415) and as 'one of the 20th century's greatest scientific naturalists' (*The Independent*), even though his primary research, broad as it was, was restricted to the first two decades of his long career. It was this breadth, together with his encyclopaedic knowledge of natural history, that allowed him to develop the theory that he first set out in his book *Animal Dispersion in Relation to Social Behaviour* (1962). This book was his major academic achievement and the contribution for which he would be chiefly remembered. Prior to its publication it is probably true to say that most biologists thought rather little about the level at which natural selection acted, regarding arguments of the 'good for the species' variety as more or less interchangeable with those phrased in terms of advantage to the individual. Wynne-Edwards's book made it clear that the two were very different and would require quite distinct mechanisms to operate. What he argued was that animals behaved for the good of the species or group to which they belonged. In this way, he suggested, they avoided such undesirable consequences as exhausting their food supply. Thus individuals might, for example, forgo breeding if the size of the population was too great, and thereby ensure that it remained in balance with its food. He argued that many aspects of the behaviour of animals, from the acrobatics of flocks of starlings to the vertical migration of plankton, were what he called epideictic displays, the function of which was to assess population size so that birth-rate could be matched to death-rate. He supported this argument with a huge array of information on a wide variety of animal species, ranging from scientific studies to anecdotal observations, all of which he interpreted in its terms.

While Wynne-Edwards's thesis attracted some supporters, it was strongly criticized by others, particularly those who believed that selection acted only at the level of the individual. What would happen, they argued, if a population was above the optimal size so that individuals should not breed, and a mutant arose that did so anyway? The answer was clear. That animal's disobeying genes would spread through the population. Any influence of group selection, essential to Wynne-Edwards's ideas, would thus be overridden by selection at the level of the individual, except under a narrow and restricted range of conditions. However, this dispute was, in itself, only a transient phase: within a few years both views had been overtaken by the idea of kin selection, stressing that animals act for the good not of themselves or the group to which they belong, but of their genes.

Wynne-Edwards was a gentle and self-effacing man, not well suited to the aggressive cut and thrust of academic dispute. Yet the wiry determination that took him to the top of mountains lay firm beneath the surface. While its foundations appeared shaky to others, he was absolutely convinced of the correctness of the magnificent and self-contained edifice that he had constructed. He would quietly and patiently explain why they were wrong to any he found to differ in their opinions. He resisted the strongest of attacks. His old Oxford tutor, Charles Elton, reviewing *Animal Dispersion* for *Nature*, wrote: 'The theory is set forth with enthusiasm, often pontifically (if a bishop can wear blinkers), sometimes in a sort of Messianic exaltation which admits no other processes affecting population levels' (*Nature*, 197, 1962, 634). Some of Wynne-Edwards's writings in the 1970s betrayed the seeds of doubt, but by 1986 these had been dispelled, and he published *Evolution through Group Selection* in answer to his critics. By then all but a handful of evolution theorists had accepted the idea of kin selection, and this book received little attention.

Wynne-Edwards's persistence in advocating his theory in the face of the evidence against it was remarkable, but it should not cloud the contribution that he made. He highlighted issues that needed to be addressed, and pointed to explanations different from those considered orthodox. In so doing he presented a clear challenge to others in the field, who then went on to carry out the appropriate experiments and seek the necessary evidence. While these studies may have shown his ideas to be mistaken, the subject as a whole gained great impetus from his statement of them. He undoubtedly deserved the respect and honour in which he was widely held. He can rightly be regarded as one of the founders of the synthesis between ecology, evolution, and animal behaviour that took place in the latter half of the twentieth century.

Wynne-Edwards and his wife lived in Banchory, Aberdeenshire, in retirement. In 1996 they moved to a nursing home there, Inchmarlo House, where Wynne-Edwards died on 5 January 1997, of prostate cancer. He was cremated in Aberdeen and his ashes were scattered on Morven. He was survived by his wife, two children, seven grandchildren, and seven great-grandchildren.

P. J. B. SLATER

Sources *The Independent* (11 Jan 1997) · *Ibis*, 139 (1997), 415–18 · *Scottish Birds*, 19 (1997), 61–3 · *Yearbook of the Royal Society of Edinburgh* (1999), 183–6 · *Auk*, 116 (1999), 815–16 · *Aberdeen University Review*, 57 (1997), 149–55 · *Memoirs FRS*, 44 (1998), 471–84 · V. C. Wynne-Edwards, 'Backstage and upstage with animal dispersion', *Studying animal behavior: autobiographies of the founders*, ed. D. A. Dewsbury (1985), 486–512 · J. M. Smith, 'Vero Wynne-Edwards: an assessment of his contribution to animal behaviour', *Association for the Study of Animal Behaviour Newsletter*, 31 (1997), 12–13 · WWW · m. cert. · d. cert. · private information (2004)

Archives Queen's University, Kingston, Ontario

Likenesses Godfrey Argent Studios, photograph, 1976, RS [see illus.] · photograph, repro. in *The Independent* · photograph, repro. in *Scottish Birds* · photograph, repro. in *Aberdeen University Review* · photograph, repro. in *Memoirs FRS* · photographs, U. Aberdeen, department of zoology

Wealth at death £70,394.50: confirmation, 12 Sept 1997, CCI

Edwards, William (1719–1789), bridge-builder, youngest son of a farmer of the same name, was born in the parish of Eglwysilan, near Caerphilly, Glamorgan. The skill which he displayed in the construction of drystone walls for his father's fields early attracted notice, and at the age of twenty he was employed to build a large iron forge at Cardiff. During his stay in Cardiff, where he erected many similar buildings, he lodged with a blind baker who taught him the English language. In 1746, having in the meantime returned to Eglwysilan, he undertook to build a bridge over the River Taff. This was built on piers, but in two and a half years it was washed away by a flood which drove debris against the piers. Edwards had given sureties to a large amount that the bridge should stand for seven years, and at once set about its reconstruction. He now resolved to build a bridge of a single arch of 140 foot span. He carried out this plan; but no sooner was the arch completed than the immense pressure on the haunches of the bridge forced the keystones out of their place, compelling the demolition of the structure. In 1751 he began construction again, on a new principle of his own invention. He retained the single arch, but perforated each of the haunches with three cylindrical openings running right through, which reduced the stress on the masonry, making it perfectly secure. The bridge was finally finished in 1755, and was greatly admired. It was claimed for it that it was the longest and most beautiful bridge of a single span in the world. The success of this work procured for Edwards other contracts of the same kind, and a number of the principal bridges in south Wales were erected by him. These included three bridges over the Towy, the Usk Bridge, Betws and Llandovery bridges in Carmarthenshire, Aberafan Bridge in Glamorgan, and Glasbury Bridge, near Hay in Brecknockshire. Though none of his later efforts was more picturesque than his bridge over the Taff, they were more convenient, as the great height of the arch used in the Taff Bridge made the approaches to the summit very steep. Edwards discovered that when there was no danger of the abutments giving way it was possible to construct arches describing much smaller segments, and of far less than the customary height. His masonry was of a distinctive, archaic style, and he claimed to have been inspired by the careful study of the ruins of Caerphilly Castle, which was situated in the parish of Eglwysilan. Throughout his life he carried on the occupation of a farmer in addition to his bridge-building. He was also a nonconformist minister in his parish meeting-house, having been ordained in 1750. His sermons, which were always in the Welsh language, were considered very effective. He died at Eglwysilan in 1789, leaving six children. Three of his four sons were trained to their father's trade, and David, the second, inherited a large portion of his skill. Among the bridges built by David were that at Llandeilo over the Towy, and Newport Bridge over the Usk.

ALSAGER VIAN, *rev.* RALPH HARRINGTON

Sources R. Williams, *Enwogion Cymru: a biographical dictionary of eminent Welshmen* (1852) • B. H. Malkin, *The scenery, antiquities, and biography of South Wales* (1804) • [Clarke], *The Georgian era: memoirs of the most eminent persons*, 4 (1834)
Likenesses W. Skelton, line engraving (with a plan of Taaffe Bridge; after T. Hill), BM, NPG

Edwards, William (*bap.* 1723, *d.* 1808), bookbinder, was baptized on 6 January 1723 at St James's Church, Halifax, Yorkshire, the second of three sons of Richard Edwards, a schoolmaster.

Edwards was very successful in collecting rare books and his Halifax bookshop and bindery, facing up Old Market, which he founded about 1750, became a mecca for discerning bibliophiles. He refined the old technique of fore-edge painting by creating exquisite miniatures on the fore-edges of the pages while the books were carefully supported in a clamp, gilding them afterwards so as to conceal the painting until the pages were gently fanned. He also produced Etruscan calf bindings which usually employed a central 'tree pattern' bordered by palmettes, taken from Greek and Etruscan vases, which were lightly burned onto the leather with acid, giving a terracotta effect. He frequently completed this work with an outer border of gold tooling showing either the Greek 'key pattern' or his own distinctive marking which consisted of five short vertical bars followed by concentric circles.

Edwards married Jane Green on 4 February 1753. They raised eight children: William (1753–1786), Mary (who became Mrs Alexander), James (*b.* 1756), John (*b.* 1758), Sarah (*bap.* 1761), later Mrs Macauly, Thomas (*bap.* 1762, *d.* 1834), Joseph (*bap.* 1765, *d.* 1771), and Richard (*b.* 1768). Jane Edwards died on 24 July 1772.

His growing stock of valuable books prompted Edwards to open a large shop at 102 Pall Mall in 1784 to gain the benefit of the London market. This was run by James and John, who, with Thomas, became famous as binders and dealers in fine books. On 28 January 1785 James took out a patent for a new treatment of vellum, devised by his father, which rendered it transparent by scraping it, soaking it in a solution of pearl ash, and heavily pressing it so that a painting executed on the reverse showed through. James spent much of his time on profitable journeys in Holland and Italy buying valuable libraries, while John concentrated on Paris, where he met his death about 1791. Although there is no evidence, the supposition is that he was seen to be in possession of valuable books and guillotined as an aristocrat.

Thomas continued to work in the Halifax shop which he took over after his father, a devout member of Northgate End Chapel, died, at the shop, 2 Old Market, Halifax, on 10 January 1808, aged eighty-five. William Edwards was buried at Halifax parish church on 17 January 1808.

DEREK BRIDGE

Sources T. W. Hanson, 'Edwards of Halifax: a family of booksellers, collectors and book binders', *Transactions of the Halifax Antiquarian Society* (1912), 141–200 • C. J. Weber, *A thousand and one fore-edge paintings* (1949) • H. M. Nixon, *Five centuries of English bookbinding* (1978) • J. R. Abbey, *English bindings, 1490–1940, in the library of J. R. Abbey*, ed. G. D. Hobson (privately printed, London, 1940) • parish register (baptisms), 6 Jan 1723, St James's, Halifax, Yorkshire • parish register (burials), 17 Jan 1808, St James's, Halifax, Yorkshire • parish register (burials), 27 July 1772, St James's, Halifax, Yorkshire • *Halifax Journal* (16 Jan 1808)
Archives W. Yorks. AS, Calderdale, Calderdale District Archives, collection of bindings | W. Yorks. AS, Calderdale, Calderdale District Archives, Hanson MSS relating to the Edwards family

Edwards, William Camden (1777–1855), engraver, was born in Monmouthshire, where he probably trained to be an engraver. About 1801 he went to work for the publisher Mr Brightly of Bungay, Suffolk, for whom he engraved portraits, biblical and archaeological scenes, and illustrations for *The Pilgrim's Progress*. Following Brightly's death about 1808, Edwards went to work for Childs, another local publisher, and it was through Childs that he met Charles Fox, who later became his pupil. Edwards was very industrious, and his productions were of the most varied description; the majority of his plates were line engravings consisting mainly of portraits, this being the genre in which his reputation was established. His most popular engraved portraits were of notable figures such as Sir Joshua Reynolds, Dr Johnson, after Reynolds, Sir William Chambers, after Reynolds, Flaxman, after John Jackson, Hogarth, after himself, and Henry Fuseli, after Sir Thomas Lawrence. He also produced steel plates for the frontispiece of William Cowper's *Private Correspondence* (1824) and Matthew Henry's *Exposition of the Old and New Testament* (1844). Other noteworthy engravings by Edwards include *Milton and his Daughters*, after George Romney, and a landscape after Salvator Rosa. A complete series of his engravings and etchings was in the Dawson Turner collection (ex Puttick and Simpson, May 1859). Edwards died at Bungay on 22 August 1855, and was buried there in the cemetery of Holy Trinity Church.

L. H. CUST, rev. ASIA HAUT

Sources B. Hunnisett, *An illustrated dictionary of British steel engravers*, new edn (1989) • Redgrave, *Artists* • T. M. Rees, *Welsh painters, engravers, sculptors (1527–1911)* (1912) • *DWB* • Boase, *Mod. Eng. biog.*
Archives priv. coll.
Likenesses Mrs D. Turner, etching, 1815, priv. coll. • Mrs D. Turner and W. C. Edwarde, etching and line engraving (after J. P. Davis), BM, NPG

Edwardston, Thomas (*d.* 1396), Augustinian friar and ecclesiastic, was probably born at Edwardstone, Suffolk, in the first quarter of the fourteenth century. He entered the Augustinian order as a young man and spent much of his early career at Oxford, where he may have graduated doctor of theology. At some point, perhaps during his time at Oxford, he attracted the patronage of the court, and in 1368, as confessor to Edward III's second son, Lionel, duke of Clarence, he travelled to Italy for Clarence's marriage to Violante, daughter of Galeazzo Visconti, lord of Pavia. Clarence died on the return journey, but probably as a result of his patronage Edwardston secured further advancement, with the title of archbishop of Nazareth and suffragan duties in the diocese of Norwich. In 1374 and 1375 he also served as prior at Clare, Suffolk, the order's premier convent. He acted as suffragan for the ageing Henry Despenser, bishop of Norwich (*d.* 1406), early in 1396. None of Edwardston's theological writings survives, but Bale attributes to him a collection of sermons, determinations, and theological lectures. It was probably his reputation as a theologian and preacher that led to his pastoral appointments. He died at Clare on 20 May 1396, and was buried in the convent.   JAMES G. CLARK

Sources Emden, *Oxf.* · Bale, *Cat.*, 1.513 · Tanner, *Bibl. Brit.-Hib.*, 252 · F. M. Powicke and E. B. Fryde, eds., *Handbook of British chronology*, 2nd edn, Royal Historical Society Guides and Handbooks, 2 (1961), 267 · A. Gwynn, *The English Austin friars in the time of Wyclif* (1940)

Edwin. *See* Eadwine (*c.*586–633).

Edwin [*née* Richards], **Elizabeth Rebecca** (1771?–1854), actress, was the daughter of the actor William Talbot Richards (*d.* 1813) and his first wife, a singer and actress. Both her parents were engaged at the Crow Street Theatre, Dublin. As a child, Elizabeth Richards appeared there as Prince Arthur and other juvenile characters, including a part written especially for her by John O'Keefe in his farce *The Female Club*. She left the stage for a time to be educated, and, although there is some confusion concerning the next stage of her career, she appeared at Covent Garden on 13 November 1789, as 'Miss Richards from Margate', in Arthur Murphy's *The Citizen*. The following year she joined Tate Wilkinson's company at Hull, and played with great success in comedy. In the line of parts taken by Dorothy Jordan, Wilkinson declared her the 'very best' he had seen. 'Her face is more than pretty, it is handsome and strong featured, not unlike Bellamy's; her person is rather short, but take her altogether she is a nice little woman' (*Wandering Patentee*, 3.127).

In 1791 Elizabeth Richards married the actor John *Edwin the younger (1768–1805) and joined with her husband the mixed company of actors and amateurs assembled by the earl of Barrymore at Wargrave, Berkshire. She also appeared with her husband at the Haymarket, on 20 June 1792, when she took the part of Lucy in Henry Fielding's *The Virgin Unmasked*. She then performed in Sheffield, Edinburgh, and the private theatre in Fishamble Street, Dublin, opened by Lord Westmeath and Frederick Jones. In October 1794 she and her husband rejoined Tate Wilkinson, and appeared first in Doncaster, then in Cheltenham, and on 14 October 1797 made her début in Bath. Here, in Bristol, and in Southampton, where she became a special favourite, she took the leading characters in comedy and farce, and came under the patronage of the duchess of York.

In 1804 Frederick Jones recalled the Edwins to Dublin. Following her husband's early death in 1805, Elizabeth Edwin continued to perform in Dublin and Edinburgh. At the recommendation of Thomas Sheridan she was engaged for Drury Lane, and appeared with that company at the Lyceum on 14 October 1809, as Widow Cheerly in Andrew Cherry's *The Soldier's Daughter*. Among other comic characters, she was the original Lady Traffic in

Elizabeth Rebecca Edwin (1771?–1854), by Samuel De Wilde, 1810 [as Lady Traffic in *Riches, or, The Wife and Brother* by Sir James Bland Burges]

Riches, or, The Wife and Brother, adapted by Sir James Bland Burges. She remained at Drury Lane through 1814–15 where she was selected to recite verses in commemoration of the battle of Waterloo (3 July 1815). She then returned to Crow Street Theatre, Dublin, but records of her professional activity there are scarce. She reappeared in London in 1818 and had engagements at the Olympic, Drury Lane, the Haymarket, the Adelphi, the Surrey, and other theatres, in both London and the provinces.

At a comparatively early age Elizabeth Edwin retired from the stage with a competency. This was greatly diminished by the dishonesty of a stockbroker, who absconded to America with between £8000 and £9000, and she was forced to return again to the boards. On 13 March 1821 she played the title role in Sheridan's *The Duenna* at Drury Lane, this being announced as her first appearance in a character of that description. With rare candour she owned herself too old for her accustomed part. She performed at Drury Lane the following season, and then retired. Mrs Edwin was a pleasing comedian. Mrs C. Baron-Wilson recalled that she 'had as much talent as any woman on the stage, but she had little (if any) genius, and was a decided mannerist'. She was below average height, with a fair complexion and blue eyes. For many years she lived in obscurity. She died at her lodgings in Cadogan Street, Chelsea, on 3 August 1854.

JOSEPH KNIGHT, *rev.* K. A. CROUCH

Sources Highfill, Burnim & Langhans, *BDA* · C. B. Hogan, ed., *The London stage, 1660–1800*, pt 5: *1776–1800* (1968) · T. Wilkinson, *The wandering patentee, or, A history of the Yorkshire theatres from 1770 to the present time*, 4 vols. (1795) · Genest, *Eng. stage*, vols. 7, 9 · *Monthly Mirror* (Feb 1810) · *Monthly Mirror* (March 1810) · Mrs C. Baron-Wilson, *Our actresses*, 2 vols. (1844) · *Dramatic censor, or, critical and biographical illustration of the British stage* (1811) · A. Pasquin [J. Williams], *The life of the late earl of Barrymore, including a history of the Wargrave theatricals and original anecdotes of eminent persons*, 3rd edn (1793) · *Theatrical Inquisitor, or Literary Mirror*, 1 (1812–13) · J. W. Croker, *Histrionic epistles* (1807) · *Oxberry's Dramatic Biography*, 4/60 (1826)
Likenesses S. De Wilde, watercolour drawing, 1810, Garr. Club [*see illus.*] · Alais, engraving, *c.*1811 (as Fanny in *The clandestine marriage*) · H. R. Cook, engraving, in or before 1813 (after W. Foster) · J. Carver, engraving (as Beatrice in *Much ado about nothing*; after J. Partridge), repro. in *Theatrical Inquisitor*, 6 (1815) · S. De Wilde, oils (as Eliza in *Riches*), Garr. Club · S. De Wilde, portrait (as Albina Mandeville in *The will*), Garr. Club · S. Freeman, engraving (after De Wilde), repro. in *Monthly Mirror* (Feb 1810) · J. Rogers, engraving (as Juliana in *The honeymoon*), repro. in *Oxberry's Dramatic Biography* · engraving (as Lydia Languish in *The rivals*), repro. in *Hibernian Magazine* (1805) · prints, BM, NPG

Edwin, Sir Humphrey (1642–1707), merchant and local politician, was born at Hereford, only son (there were also two daughters) of William Edwin and his wife, Anne, of the family of Mansfield. William Edwin was a Welsh feltmaker from Llandeilo, Carmarthenshire, who moved to Hereford and became a hatter. There he prospered, becoming an alderman and (twice) mayor. The young Edwin was apprenticed to a Hereford tailor but soon went to London and established himself, probably as a wool merchant, in the parish of St Helen's, off Bishopsgate.

In or before 1670 Edwin married Elizabeth (1644/5–1714), daughter of Samuel Sambrooke, a wealthy London merchant. Their first four children, Samuel (1671–1722), Humphrey (1673–1747), Thomas (1676–1735), and Charles (1677–1756), were baptized at St Helen's Bishopsgate. There were also four daughters and a fifth son, John, possibly born when the family moved to the neighbouring parish of St Peter-le-Poer. Edwin's marriage and success in trade brought him great wealth. He owned extensive property in Westminster, and a town house at Kensington. In 1678 he was admitted a freeman of the Barber–Surgeons' Company by redemption, becoming afterwards an assistant and in 1688 master of the company; in 1694, however, he was dismissed from the office of assistant for failing to attend meetings. In 1690 he became an honorary member of the Skinners' Company, in gratitude for which he covenanted to give £10 annually to buy fuel for the residents of the Skinners' almshouses at Mile End. He served the Skinners as master in 1691.

As an avowed nonconformist Edwin came to the notice of James II, who was anxious to conciliate the dissenters in order to obtain their help in relaxing the penal laws against the Roman Catholics. Edwin also joined the Merchant Taylors' Company in anticipation of high office, and on 18 October 1687 he was sworn in as alderman of Tower ward, on the direct appointment of the king, a position he held, apart from transferring briefly to Cheap ward, until his death. On the following 18 November the king knighted him at Whitehall and a few weeks later appointed him sheriff of Glamorgan. Probably before this time he had purchased the considerable estate and house at Llanfihangel Plas in that county, to which he later added the castle and lordship of Ogmore. In 1688 Edwin was elected sheriff of London and Middlesex, and in December that year he and his co-sheriff and the aldermen attended the prince of Orange on his entry into London, and took part in the proclamation of the king and queen.

When he was elected lord mayor in 1697 Edwin was obliged to receive the sacrament in order to hold office, as prescribed by the Corporation Act; once installed, he openly proclaimed himself a dissenter by attending one of their places of worship in full civic state, preceded by the City sword and mace. It soon became common knowledge that Edwin was only one of many dissenters holding lucrative offices after submitting to this one act of conformity. But the court of aldermen, learning that he had twice attended a dissenters' meeting held in one of the lesser livery halls, attended by the City sword-bearer, passed a resolution deploring his action, and directing that the sword should not in future be carried to any such meeting.

Despite the controversies aroused by Edwin's actions he seems to have gained the approval of his fellow citizens and to have realized and fully met the difficulties of the times in which he lived. He was captain of a picked body of mounted volunteers in the City, of whom the king was colonel. He responded energetically to the order from the privy council, instructing the lord mayor and aldermen to seek out and arrest certain foreign desperadoes involved in a conspiracy to assassinate the king. In May 1698 he was unwell and, with the king's leave, retired to his house at Kensington.

Edwin died at Llanfihangel on 14 December 1707 and was buried there. His widow died in London on 22 November 1714 and on 2 December her remains were temporarily deposited at St Stephen, Coleman Street; they were later transferred to rest beside those of her husband.

ANITA MCCONNELL

Sources *DWB* · A. B. Beaven, ed., *The aldermen of the City of London, temp. Henry III–[1912]*, 2 vols. (1908–13) · J. Edwin-Cole, 'Memoir of the family of Edwin', *Herald and Genealogist*, 6 (1871), 54–62 · W. H. Cooke, ed., *Duncumb's Herefordshire* (1870) · N. Luttrell, *A brief historical relation of state affairs from September 1678 to April 1714*, 4 (1857), 386 · C. Hopper, 'The lord mayor and the dissenters', *N&Q*, 2nd ser., 4 (1857), 389 · J. F. Wadmore, *Some account of the Worshipful Company of Skinners of London* (1902)
Archives CKS

Edwin, John, the elder (1749–1790), actor and singer, was born on 10 August 1749 at Clare Market, St Clement Danes, London, the eldest of the three children of John Edwin, a watchmaker, and his wife, Hannah, the daughter of Henry Brogden, a sculptor of statues in York. His sisters were Mary and Elizabeth; the latter acted briefly and became a fortune-teller under the name Mrs Williams. His parents were well educated, and his father had a talent for

John Edwin the elder (1749–1790), by Thomas Beach, exh. RA 1790

music, which John inherited. At the age of nine he was sent to relatives near Enfield and there went to school until he was fifteen. On leaving school in 1764 he obtained a sinecure appointment, working for two hours per day, at the pensions office of the exchequer. While there he joined a 'spouting club' which met at the French Horn tavern in Wood Street, Cheapside, where he saw William Woodfall in the role of Old Mask in George Colman's *Musical Lady*. This inspired him to move into acting, and he began to practise his skills at another spouting club, The Falcon in Fetter Lane, where he became one of the managers. It was here that he met Ned Shuter, on whom he modelled his whole comic style and who ironically predicted his later success.

It was at this time that a wealthy relative, John Edwin of George Street, died leaving a sum of £50,000 to various charities. Young John may have had expectations of becoming a beneficiary of this estate, but instead he was appointed secretary to the trust and was charged with the administration of the funds. His salary was £30 per week, and he held the position for just one year. The executors gave him £500 outright, most of which he handed to his father before launching his professional career as an actor. His potential had been recognized by John Lee of Drury Lane, who engaged him at 1 guinea per week for a summer season in Manchester. Edwin made his début there (barring a possible appearance at the Haymarket as Quidnunc in a benefit performance of Arthur Murphy's *The Upholsterer*) in 1765.

Edwin's first performances in Manchester were mainly in farces, and despite his youth he played mostly old men. While there he is reputed to have had a relationship with Sophia Baddeley, whose husband, Robert, was performing in Liverpool that summer. In autumn 1765 Edwin went to Dublin, to Henry Mossop's Smock Alley Theatre, where he played Sir Philip Modelove in Susannah Centlivre's *A Bold Stroke for a Wife* and Lord Trinket in Colman's *The Jealous Wife*. His wages of 30s. per week at the theatre were so erratic that he once successfully got a friendly bailiff to arrest him in order to force Mossop to hand over £10 if he wanted that evening's performance to go ahead. The deception worked and Edwin obtained his money. He moved from Dublin to an engagement with Thomas Ryder in Waterford, and then back to England to Preston, Lancashire. By January 1767 he was apparently acting for Joseph Austin's company, playing in Bewdley, Shrewsbury, Bridgnorth, and Chester. This work must have been uninspiring, for back in London in 1768 he was on the verge of giving up acting. He was persuaded by his old friend John Lee to fill in for John Arthur, who had died during the season at Bath, and arrived at his lodgings at The Bear, Cheap Street, on 2 October 1768. On 6 October he appeared as Periwinkle in *A Bold Stroke for a Wife*, and after a while his reputation and spirit for acting began to revive.

Soon after arriving in Bath, Edwin met Mrs Sarah Walmsley, described as 'a respectable milliner of Horse Street', who took his name and became his faithful common-law wife for the next twenty years. Reports indicate that they had four children, John *Edwin the younger, Richard, David, and Sarah, but there is much discrepancy and confusion in these accounts.

Edwin spent several years building up his reputation in Bath before making his professional début in London, at the Haymarket on 19 June 1776, in an unspecified part in Samuel Foote's *The Cozeners*. He continued to perform there in a variety of roles that summer. In 1777 the Haymarket acquired a new proprietor when George Colman purchased the lease from Samuel Foote. Colman immediately cut salaries, and Edwin took issue with him, threatening not to resume his contract on account of all his travel and London living expenses. A deal was agreed which included Edwin's wife and son John, who was gaining a reputation as a singer in Bath. All three were employed at the Haymarket at 5 guineas a week, and for the next three years the Edwins spent the winter in Bath and the summer in London at the Haymarket. Among the many parts Edwin played at the Haymarket were young Gobbo in *The Merchant of Venice*, the original Wingrove in Colman's *The Suicide*, the original Carlo in Charles Dibdin's *The Gypsies*, one of the witches in *Macbeth*, the original Etiquette in M. P. Andrew's *Summer Amusement*, and the original Splash in Paul Jodrell's *A Widow and No Widow*. On 17 August 1779 for his benefit he played Scrub in George Farquhar's *The Beaux' Stratagem*, where his son John, then ten years old, spoke a monologue before the afterpiece.

During winter 1779–80 Edwin moved to Covent Garden after Harris offered him £7 per week. Touchstone in *As You Like It* (14 September 1779) was the first part he chose to play there. Other roles included Canteen in Frederick Pilon's afterpiece *The Device* and the original Silvertongue in Hannah Cowley's *The Belle's Stratagem* (22 February 1780).

As Edwin's success and popularity grew, his wages rose from £7 to £10 per week, and his benefits were unusually large. He also appeared outside London, at Dublin (1783 and 1788), Cambridge (1786), and Brighton (1789). In 1789 he created a company at Richmond, Surrey, where he played a successful season. A friendship with the playwright John O'Keeffe at this time was particularly fruitful, not only for the twenty parts written especially for him but also for the numerous lyrics O'Keeffe supplied (to music by William Shield) for the occasional songs he presented in clubs, social gatherings, and fashionable homes. The success of this collaboration prompted a popular jest at the time, which went 'when Edwin did die O'Keeffe would be damned'. Edwin became as famous for his entr'acte singing as for his acting. George Colman, one of his closest friends, referred to him as the best burletta singer that ever had been or perhaps would be: 'while he sang in a style which produced roars of laughter, there was a melody in some of the upper tones of his voice that was beautiful' (Peake, 2.10–11).

In the late 1780s Edwin had met Mary Hubbard, who became his mistress, and this led to estrangement from and acrimonious negotiations with Sarah Walmsley and their family. Edwin, in ill health through excessive drinking, his severe workload, and the stress of the separation, disowned all his family and through the press and in person tried to hinder their employment in every theatre in which he worked. Just before his death he was still having unedifying exchanges with his eldest son, John, and with Sarah over financial support for his family.

Edwin continued to perform. In 1790 he helped with the benefit of a close friend, Lee Lewes, at Rochester, after which both men went over to Paris to continue the celebration. After returning to London, on 7 April 1790 he took his last benefit at Covent Garden, playing Dromio in *The Comedy of Errors*. At the end of the mainpiece he recited his monologue *Lingo the Butler's Opinion on Men and Manners*, and also sang one of his most popular renditions, 'Four and Twenty Fiddlers All in a Row'. Two months later, on 13 June 1790, he married Mary Hubbard at St James's, Westminster.

Three weeks before his death Edwin was being strongly advised by doctors to move to Nice for health reasons. Harris, the proprietor of Covent Garden, even offered to advance money for the trip, and a vessel was chartered, but it was too late. Edwin died at his home in Bedford Street at 4.15 p.m. on 30 October 1790, at the age of forty-one, on a couch by the fire with his arm out for his wife. He was buried on the north side of St Paul's, Covent Garden, between Dr Arne and his role model Ned Shuter. He was survived by his wife, Mary, and by Sarah, who continued to act as Mrs Edwin and died on 8 June 1794, and their children.

Edwin was regarded by many contemporaries as a comic actor of genius, and later commentators have highly estimated his influence:

> To Shuter's breadth of humour Edwin added a dry, whimsical manner of taking, as it were, the audience into his confidence … he established, in the monologue, the method that was later developed by clowns such as [Joseph] Grimaldi and [Robert] Bradbury in their familiar discussions with the audience of their seeming problems and joys. (Hogan, 1.xxxvi)

TERRY ENRIGHT

Sources Genest, *Eng. stage* · R. B. Peake, *Memoirs of the Colman family*, 2 vols. (1841) · A. Pasquin [J. Williams], *The eccentricities of John Edwin, comedian: collected from his manuscripts, and enriched with several hundred original anecdotes*, 2 vols. [1791] · J. Roach, *John Edwin's jests, humours, frolics and bon mots* (1794) · J. Bernard, *Retrospections of the stage*, ed. W. B. Bernard, 2 vols. (1830) · J. Boaden, *Memoirs of Mrs Siddons*, 2 vols. (1827) · J. Boaden, *Memoirs of the life of John Philip Kemble*, 2 vols. (1825) · J. Boaden, *The life of Mrs Jordan*, 2 vols. (1831) · *Memoirs of Mrs Inchbald*, ed. J. Boaden, 2 vols. (1833) · J. Winston, ed., *A collection of memoranda, documents, play bills, newspaper cuttings, etc. relating to Drury Lane Theatre*, 23 vols. [1711–1830] · T. Gilliland, *The dramatic mirror, containing the history of the stage from the earliest period, to the present time*, 2 vols. (1808) · J. O'Keeffe, *Recollections of the life of John O'Keeffe, written by himself*, 2 vols. (1826) · *London Magazine*, 40 (June 1771) · *London Chronicle* (Sept 1779) · C. B. Hogan, ed., *The London stage, 1660–1800*, pt 5: *1776–1800* (1968) · Highfill, Burnim & Langhans, *BDA*

Archives Folger, MSS

Likenesses T. Beach, portrait, exh. RA 1790; Sothebys, 10 Nov 1993, lot 62 [*see illus.*] · engraving, *c*.1790 · T. Beach, oils (as Justice Woodcock in *Love in a village*), Garr. Club · T. Beach, oils (as Peeping Tom), Garr. Club · E. Edridge, watercolour, Garr. Club · attrib. T. Gainsborough, oils, Garr. Club · J. Roberts, two pencil drawings, Garr. Club · engraving (after *Pills to purge melancholy* by Rider) · theatrical prints, BM, NPG

Edwin, John, the younger (1768–1805), actor, was the son of the actor John *Edwin the elder (1749–1790) and his long-term partner, the Bath milliner Mrs Walmsley. Edwin junior first appeared on stage with his father at Bath in 1777. The following year he was at the Haymarket, London, as Hengist in a revival of *Bonduca* by Beaumont and Fletcher (30 July 1778). From this period, at the Haymarket or at Bath, he frequently performed with his father, his first recorded appearance in an adult role being at Covent Garden on 26 March 1788, as Dick in Murphy's *The Apprentice*, for his father's benefit. Taken up by the earl of Barrymore, who made an inseparable companion of him, Edwin directed the amateur theatricals at Wargrave, Berkshire, Barrymore's seat, for some years.

After his marriage to Elizabeth Rebecca Richards (1771?–1854) [*see* Edwin, Elizabeth Rebecca] in 1791, Edwin's career was eclipsed by that of his wife. He went with her to the Haymarket, and on 20 June 1792 appeared in *The Virgin Unmasked*, previously known as *An Old Man Taught Wisdom*, a ballad farce by Henry Fielding, in which he played Blister to the Lucy of his wife. He also accompanied her to Dublin and to Doncaster in 1794, and on most of her country tours.

Edwin was best known at Bath, where he was held in some parts equal or superior to his father. He was an excellent provincial actor, and would probably, but for his irregular life, have made a high reputation. In the roles of Lenitive in *The Prize*, Nipperkin in *The Sprigs of Laurel*, and

Mr Tag in *The Spoiled Child*, he was generally regarded as being better than any comedian who had ever played those parts. A tombstone to his memory, erected by his wife in St Werburgh's churchyard, Dublin, attributes his death to the acuteness of his sensibility: a satirical poem, *Familiar Epistles*, attributed to John Wilson Croker, had appeared in 1804, containing some stinging lines on the 'lubbard spouse' of Mrs Edwin and the degenerate son of a man 'high on the rolls of comic fame'. On reading the poem, Edwin is reported to have invited a friend to 'come and help me to destroy myself with some of the most splendid cogniac [*sic*] that I have ever exported to cheer a breaking heart'. He did not recover from the debauch thus initiated, and died in Dublin on 22 February 1805.

JOSEPH KNIGHT, *rev.* NILANJANA BANERJI

Sources P. Hartnoll, ed., *The Oxford companion to the theatre* (1951); 2nd edn (1957); 3rd edn (1967) • Adams, *Drama* • *The thespian dictionary, or, Dramatic biography of the eighteenth century* (1802) • *The thespian dictionary, or, Dramatic biography of the present age*, 2nd edn (1805) • Hall, *Dramatic ports.* • 'Memoirs of Mrs Edwin', *Monthly Mirror*, new ser., 7 (Feb 1810), 83–5 • 'Memoirs of Mrs Edwin', *Monthly Mirror*, new ser., 7 (March 1810), 188–9 • Genest, *Eng. stage* • Mrs C. Baron-Wilson, *Our actresses*, 2 vols. (1844) • T. Wilkinson, *The wandering patentee, or, A history of the Yorkshire theatres from 1770 to the present time*, 4 vols. (1795) • *DNB*

Likenesses line engraving, *c.*1780, BM; repro. in H. Fielding, *Tom Thumb* (1780) • Freeman, engraving (after a portrait by De Wilde), repro. in *Monthly Mirror* (Feb 1810), facing p. 83

Edwy. *See* Eadwig (*c.*940–959).

Edzell. For this title name *see* Lindsay, David, Lord Edzell (1551?–1610).

Eedes, John (1609–*c.*1667), Church of England clergyman, son of Nicholas Eedes, was born at Salisbury, Wiltshire. He entered Oriel College, Oxford, in 1626, when he was seventeen, and graduated BA on 3 June 1630. Having become vicar of Eastchurch on the Isle of Sheppey he was ejected from that position by the parliamentary side in the civil war and imprisoned at Ely House in London. Upon his release he was curate of Broad Chalk, Wiltshire, for about two years until, in 1652, he became vicar of Hale, Hampshire, where he continued for the rest of his life.

In 1654, identifying himself as a 'Minister of the Gospel', Eedes published *The Orthodox Doctrine Concerning Justification by Faith Asserted and Vindicated*. Attacking both William Eyre's *Vindiciae Justificationis gratuitae: Justification Without Conditions* (1654), a book endorsed by John Owen, and Richard Baxter's *Aphorisms of Justification* (1649), which Eyre had charged with Arminianism and 'popery', Eedes sought a middle ground between these authors, citing Calvin and other Reformed theologians on behalf of what he took to be the longstanding protestant view of justification. Eedes thought that Baxter erred in an Arminian and Jesuit direction, and that Eyre, a high Calvinist who taught justification from eternity, erred in an antinomian direction. For Eedes, only the elect for whom Christ died were justified, but they were not justified until they actually believed. Eedes also evinced the double covenant federal theology characteristic of mid-century Calvinists. Eedes referred to having other treatises, including a longer one

on justification, ready for the press, but they were never published. In or about 1667 Eedes was murdered by robbers in his house at Hale. He was buried in the church there.   DEWEY D. WALLACE, JUN.

Sources Wood, *Ath. Oxon.*, new edn, 3.802 • Wood, *Ath. Oxon.: Fasti* (1815), 453 • *Walker rev.* • *DNB* • J. Eedes, *The orthodox doctrine concerning justification by faith* (1654)

Eedes, Richard (*bap.* **1610**, *d.* **1686**), clergyman and ejected minister, was baptized in 1610, at an unknown date at Feckenham, Worcestershire. His father was John Eedes; his mother's name is not known.

Eedes entered Corpus Christi College, Oxford, as either a clerk or a chorister, in 1626, graduated BA in February 1629, became curate of Bishop's Cleeve, Gloucestershire, at Michaelmas 1632, and proceeded MA in 1635. He remained at Bishop's Cleeve until 1647, when he became vicar of nearby Beckford, also in Gloucestershire. He took the covenant and subscribed to the rigidly presbyterian *Gloucestershire Ministers' Testimony* of 1648. He became a member of the Worcestershire Voluntary Association of Ministers and subscribed to its agreement to pursue a course of parochial catechizing in 1656. His involvement in the association's pastoral ambitions is well caught in a letter he wrote to Richard Baxter in late 1657, much exercised with the questions of religious instruction and of who should be admitted to receive the Lord's supper (which he had suspended since he had begun a course of catechizing the ignorant) and thanking Baxter for a copy of his *Gildas Salvanus: the Reformed Pastor*. However, he explained 'I am at too great a distance to receive the Comfort, and Countenance of the Associations influence, my body beinge so weake, and my distempers so pressing, that I can not visit their neerest meeting, which is at Evesham' (Keeble and Nuttall, 1.276).

In 1656 Eedes published *Great Salvation by Jesus Christ*, a sermon on Hebrews 2: 3, following this with *Christ Exalted and Wisdom Justified*, another sermon, on 1 Peter 2: 7, in 1659. The latter contained a preface by Baxter, commending the 'excellent treasure' of Christ and wisdom to the reader. There was no obvious theological hue to Eedes's writing, but he consistently expressed the belief that any form of church government was better than none. He bitterly opposed sectarians of all kinds and defended infant baptism, the eucharist, observation of the sabbath, prayer, and the discipline imposed on the primitive church by Christ. As early as 1656 he lamented that England must mourn 'Till Cesar come who will give God his due'. Later he wrote that 'The Moses and Aron, the Magistrate and Minister, must go hand in hand if we would have the Common-wealth of Israel to prosper in the common wealth of England' (Wood, *Ath. Oxon.*, 2.79; Eedes, *Christ Exalted*, 111).

About 1658, Anthony Wood says, a parliamentarian captain who lived nearby persuaded Eedes to return to Bishop's Cleeve, where he might hope to succeed the aged Timothy Gates as rector of this rich living. There he acted unofficially as minister after—if not also before—Gates's death in 1660. On 6 June 1660 he preached a sermon on 2

Samuel 3: 36 in Gloucester at the invitation of the corporation. This was shortly afterwards published as *Great Britain's Resurrection*. It dwelled at length on the duty of all good Christians to render obedience to a king who had been restored almost miraculously to his throne by God after 'the bitter fruits of innovation and changeableness since our Land hath swarmed with Lunaticks and Phanaticks' (Eedes, *Great Britain's Resurrection*, 8). After the Act of Uniformity came into effect on 24 August 1662, 'being deceived with expectation of an idle Dispensation for his Nonconformity', Eedes 'silenced himself' (Wood, *Ath. Oxon.*, 2.792). He remained at Bishop's Cleeve, where the next known rector was admitted in November 1662, attending the services in the parish church 'as much as his age would give him leave' and apparently showing no signs of nonconformity (ibid.). At some stage he moved to Gretton in nearby Winchcombe, where he died in 1686. He was buried at Bishop's Cleeve on 6 April 1686.

ANDREW WARMINGTON

Sources Wood, *Ath. Oxon.*, 2nd edn · *Calamy rev.* · R. Eedes, *Christ exalted and wisdom justified* (1659) · R. Eedes, *Great Britain's resurrection* (1660) · C. R. Elrington, 'The survey of church livings in Gloucestershire, 1650', *Transactions of the Bristol and Gloucestershire Archaeological Society*, 83 (1964), 85–98 · *The Gloucestershire ministers testimony to the truth of Jesus Christ and to the solemn league and covenant* (1650) · R. Atkyns, *The ancient and present state of Glostershire*, 2 pts in 1 (1712) · *Calendar of the correspondence of Richard Baxter*, ed. N. H. Keeble and G. F. Nuttall, 1 (1991), 276–382 · Worcs. RO

Efa ferch Maredudd (*fl. 1300*). *See under* Gruffudd ap Rhys (*d.* 1201).

Effingham. For this title name *see* Howard, Kenneth Alexander, first earl of Effingham (1767–1845).

Egan, James (1799–1842), engraver, was born in co. Roscommon, Ireland. Of his parents, nothing is known. It seems that his success as 'undoubtedly the best artist in his particular department of the arts which Ireland has produced' (*GM*, 100) was due to his own work and abilities. In 1825 Egan was employed by S. W. Reynolds to run errands, occasionally laying mezzotint ground, after which he set himself up as a ground-layer for engravers. His plates include *Love's Reverie* (after J. R. Herbert), *Abbot Boniface* (after C. S. Newton), *The Morning after the Wreck* (after C. Bentley), *The Study* (after E. Stone), *The Mourner* (after J. M. Moore), *The Young Wife* (after S. J. Jones), *The Citation of Wycliffe* (after S. J. Jones), *The Tribunal of the Inquisition* (after S. J. Jones), *Portrait of John Lodge, Librarian at Cambridge* (after Walmisley), *Portrait of Denvil, Actor, as Manfred* (after H. Farrer), and the aquatint *Genealogical Tree of British Naval Victories* (after H. Innes). Egan's last plate was *English Hospitality in the Olden Times* (after J. G. Cattermole), considered to be 'safely classed among the most successful achievements of modern art' (ibid.). It is uncertain whether the J. Egan (*fl. c.*1841) who drew twenty-three illustrations for Mr and Mrs S. C. Hall's *Ireland: its Scenery, Character, etc.* (1841–2) is James Egan. In the eight years preceding his death Egan suffered from consumption and

related illnesses, and he died at Pentonville, London, on 2 October 1842, leaving a wife and three children, for whom a public subscription was raised at the main printsellers.

E. M. KIRWAN

Sources *GM*, 2nd ser., 19 (1843), 100 · W. G. Strickland, *A dictionary of Irish artists*, 2 vols. (1913) · Bénézit, *Dict.* · Thieme & Becker, *Allgemeines Lexikon* · Bryan, *Painters* (1903–5) · Redgrave, *Artists*
Wealth at death public subscription raised for wife and three children: *GM*

Egan, John (1754/5–1810), judge and duellist, was probably born in Charleville, co. Cork, the second son of the Revd Dr Carbery Egan (*d.* in or before 1776), professor of theology. He matriculated, as a sizar, at Trinity College, Dublin, on 23 May 1769, at the age of fourteen. He graduated BA in 1773 and LLB in 1776, and subsequently received the degree of LLD *honoris causa* in 1790. He entered the Middle Temple, London, on 8 November 1776 (prospective Irish barristers being required, at the time, to belong to an English inn of court), and was called to the Irish bar in Michaelmas term 1778.

Egan acquired a substantial legal practice, his success being at least partly attributable to his close friendship with Barry Yelverton, first Viscount Avonmore, chief baron of the Irish exchequer from 1783 to 1805. He joined Avonmore's patriot society, the Order of St Patrick, or the 'monks of the screw', whose members included Henry Flood, Henry Grattan, John Philpot Curran, and James Caulfeild, first earl of Charlemont. He was, in time, appointed king's counsel, and in 1787 he was elected a bencher of King's Inns. He apparently entertained hopes of an appointment to king's bench or the exchequer, but his only judicial appointment was to the chairmanship of Kilmainham, the title given to the judge for co. Dublin.

In addition to having an 'immense' legal practice (Barrington, *Personal Sketches*, 173), Egan was a member of the Irish House of Commons, where he sat for Ballynakill, Queen's county, from 1789 to 1790 and for Tallow, co. Waterford, from 1790 to 1800. Here he made a number of 'virulent phillipics' (*Recollections of Jonah Barrington*, 220) against the French Revolution, and numerous bold speeches against the Union with Great Britain. In February 1792 he presented a petition for Catholic relief which was rejected.

Egan was a remarkable character. Known universally as Bully Egan, he was 'an immense-sized man, as brawny, and almost as black, as a coal-porter' (Phillips, 78), and carried himself with a pronounced swagger. The younger Henry Grattan remembered him as:

a good-natured, honest, warm-hearted man,—rough in manner and grotesque in appearance; a courageous character, very hot and full of anger. His brains (so to speak) lay in his veins. He loved even the man whom he attacked; and though he said coarse things, he did not in reality mean them, or intend either injury or insult; with him abuse became a habit,—almost his dialect. (Grattan, 57–8)

Egan was party to a number of duels. During the 1783 election for co. Cork he duelled with Richard Hely-Hutchinson. He fought, among others, James Connor and his fellow barrister Roger Barrett. One opponent, Jerry

John Egan (1754/5–1810), by James Heath, pubd 1811 (after John Comerford)

(Phillips, 83), until his honour finally overbore his material need. He delivered a powerful and vitriolic condemnation of the proposed union and sat down, shouting, 'Ireland! Ireland for ever! and damn Kilmainham' (ibid.).

Egan died in 1810; according to Charles Phillips, he left nothing but the 3s. found on his mantelpiece, so hard had his political stance damaged his business. He does not seem to have married. Egan may not have attained a degree of immortality commensurate with that enjoyed by Grattan or Curran, but he was, nevertheless, a very able lawyer and politician, and one of the great characters of eighteenth-century Ireland.   NATHAN WELLS

Sources C. Phillips, *Curran and his contemporaries*, [3rd edn] (1850) • H. Grattan, *Memoirs of the life and times of the Rt Hon. Henry Grattan*, 5 vols. (1839–46), vol. 4 • Burtchaell & Sadleir, *Alum. Dubl.*, 2nd edn • *Recollections of Jonah Barrington* [1918] • J. Barrington, *Personal sketches of his own times*, 2 vols. (1827) • E. Keane, P. Beryl Phair, and T. U. Sadleir, eds., *King's Inns admission papers, 1607–1867*, IMC (1982) • H. A. C. Sturgess, ed., *Register of admissions to the Honourable Society of the Middle Temple, from the fifteenth century to the year 1944*, 1 (1949) • DNB • D. R. Plunket, *The life, letters, and speeches of Lord Plunket*, 1 (1867), vol. 1 • W. O'Regan, *Memoirs of the legal, literary and political life of … John Philpot Curran* (1817) • J. Kelly, *That damn'd thing called honour: duelling in Ireland, 1570–1860* (1995)

Likenesses J. Heath, stipple, pubd 1811 (after J. Comerford), BM, NG Ire., NPG [*see illus.*]

Wealth at death 3s.: Phillips, *Curran and his contemporaries*

Keller, was fought following a dispute at the Waterford assizes on a point of law. Just as his hot-headedness drew him into these confrontations, however, his warmheartedness ensured that they were never very serious affairs. At his duel with Curran he observed in reference to their respective sizes that 'I may as well fire at a razor's edge as at him, and he may hit me as easily as a turf-stack' (Phillips, 79), Curran suggesting that the solution might be to chalk his outline on Egan's ample frame and to dismiss any hits that were not within it. Not surprisingly, neither party was injured in the engagement, and the two remained lifelong friends.

A radical downturn in Egan's fortunes was precipitated by a brief but highly acrimonious dispute with Grattan in the Commons in 1795. Egan had criticized the administration of William Wentworth Fitzwilliam, fourth Earl Fitzwilliam, and was attacked by Grattan for inconsistency, as he had formerly supported the government. This led to a heated exchange between the two, involving considerable personal abuse. The incident was widely publicized, and such was the regard in which Grattan was held that there was an almost immediate fall in Egan's legal business. None the less, Egan was an unshakeable Irish patriot, whose courage and conviction perhaps reached their zenith at the end of his political career. At the time of the Act of Union almost the whole of Egan's income came from his chairmanship of Kilmainham, a post to which he had been appointed by the government. It was apparently made clear to him that his support for the measure would lead to considerable reward, while opposition could only redound to his detriment. Egan could be seen throughout the debates, 'writhing with some insuppressible emotion'

Egan, Pierce (1772–1849), sporting journalist and author, was probably born in London in 1772, although his death certificate gave his age in 1849 as 74. His family background is obscure, but he claimed Irish ancestry. He was based in London throughout his life but travelled widely as a sports reporter. Egan spent the early part of his working life in the printing trade and became a skilled compositor, a faculty which he exploited by liberally peppering his writings with asterisks, dashes, exclamation marks, and whatever else the font had to offer. By some accounts he married in 1812, but there is a record of someone of his name marrying, at St Marylebone, London, on 7 July 1806, Catherine Povey (a Catherine Egan was present at his death). By 1812 he was working as a compositor for George Smeeton of 139 St Martin's Lane, London, who undertook that year the serial publication of *Boxiana, or, Sketches of ancient and modern pugilism, from the days of the renowned Broughton and Slack to the heroes of the present milling era*. Although the volume was anonymously ascribed to 'one of the Fancy' it was almost certainly the work of Egan, who was already known as a racy reporter and who in time became the voice of 'the Fancy', the sporting set of fashionable society. He was soon reporting for the *Weekly Dispatch* and beginning to produce other works, such as *The Mistress of Royalty, or, The Loves of Florizel and Perdita* (1814), concerning the Prince Regent and Mary Robinson. A second volume of *Boxiana* appeared in 1818 and was openly acknowledged as Egan's work.

Egan's greatest success came in 1821, when his two characters Tom and Jerry first appeared, in *Life in London, or, The day and night scenes of Jerry Hawthorn, esq., and his elegant friend, Corinthian Tom, accompanied by Bob Logic, the Oxonian, in their rambles and sprees through the metropolis.* Its popularity was instant and unprecedented, and the demand for copies increased with every month. Its attractions lay in both content and style, for its contrasting characters and scenes, setting the misery of low life against the prodigal waste and folly of high society, were all presented with vivacious dialogue and lively description and accompanied by the excellent illustrations of the brothers George and Robert Cruikshank. Success brought imitators, pirated copies, and numerous stage versions, the most enduring of which was the one produced at the Adelphi Theatre in London in November 1821 and superintended by Robert Cruikshank. The monthly instalments of the story ended in 1822, but Egan returned to the theme in 1828, rebuking the pirates and plagiarists with his *Finish to the adventures of Tom, Jerry, and Logic, with numerous coloured illustrations by Robert Cruikshank.*

In the intervening years Egan had become deeply involved with much of contemporary sport and in particular with boxing. He not only wrote about it but sometimes also took at least a minor role in its management. He claimed a part in the arrangements for the fight in 1824 between the champion, Tom Spring, and Langan, and organized the collection from the spectators for the defeated challenger. When he left the *Weekly Dispatch* at the end of 1823 he immediately began his own sporting journal, *Pierce Egan's Life in London and Sporting Guide.* This, in turn, was shortly merged with *Bell's Life in London*, which had begun to appear in 1822; for more than fifty years the pink broadsheets of the new journal, *Bell's Life*, provided the most voluminous single record of nineteenth-century sport. A third volume of *Boxiana*, for which John Badcock was responsible, was published in 1824 and was followed by a final update in 1829. In 1832 *Pierce Egan's Book of Sports* appeared, a comprehensive if somewhat chaotic collection of material covering a wide range of contemporary sport and recreations.

By this time Egan had become disillusioned by the increasing dishonesty and double-dealing of pugilism, but he had made an invaluable contribution to its history. His descriptions of fights were full of graphic action and high drama, more bloody, it was said, than the fights themselves. He was always prepared to embellish the truth in the interests of entertainment, especially where one of the subjects was Irish and so merited particular praise. Jack Randall, for instance, was always 'the prime Irish lad', although the boxer himself never claimed to be other than a Londoner. Egan's language grew steadily more and more extravagant, larded with slang terms and exaggerations that catered for 'the Fancy' but never so specialized as to exclude others totally. Egan plunged into the language of the street and the tavern, embellishing it unashamedly and giving it an immediacy and vitality, which, however spurious, brought to his avid readers a sense of connection with life's great excitements. A simple blow to the eye that drew blood became 'the left *peeper* of Perkins napt it, and the *claret* followed' (*Pierce Egan's Book of Sports*, 1832, 25). If Wordsworth had sought to

return to the simple language of the honest countryman, Egan wanted his readers to share to the full all the sensations that city life could offer. It was both a major factor in his instant success and a reason for the fall in his popularity, once Charles Dickens had shown how it could be done with much more style and much less crudity.

Egan also wrote on other subjects. His *Account of the Trial of John Thurtell and Joseph Hunt* for the murder of William Weare in 1824 followed his daily reports of the case, and helped make it a major sensation of the day, set as it was at the sordid end of the London gaming scene. Egan's reports constituted effectively the first instance of trial by newspaper, and when the murderers were hanged at Hertford they attracted a crowd of 15,000. In addition to this and other trial reports, Egan also ventured into acknowledged fiction with *The Life of an Actor* (1824) and into verse with *The Show Folks* and *Matthew's Comic Annual* (both 1831). He also published a number of light-hearted city guide books, including *Walks through Bath* (1819) and others on Liverpool and Dublin. His most important later work was *The Pilgrims of the Thames* (1838), dedicated, by permission, to the young Queen Victoria and containing the customary lively pictures of many aspects of the city's life. However, Egan was increasingly dismissed as a mere slang writer and appears to have been somewhat less prosperous in old age. Nevertheless, his large family—the best-known of his children was the fiction writer Pierce James *Egan (1814–1880)—was said to be left comfortably placed on his death at 9 Regents Terrace, Islington, on 3 August 1849.

The claim in the *Bell's Life* obituary that Egan was 'a right-minded fellow, and was respected by all who knew him', hardly squares with the fierce jealousies which he aroused during his writing career. John Badcock, with his pretence to some learning, was vituperative in his hatred of Egan's apparently easy success, while his younger contemporary Henry Downes Miles, for all the use he was prepared to make of *Boxiana* when it suited him, was always ready with a snide remark on Egan's style and accuracy and quoted with obvious relish the Hon. Grantley Berkeley's comment on his 'low slang of Irish ruffianism' (Miles, 1.239 n.). Evaluations of Egan's work have changed with the increasing recognition in social history of the importance of sport and recreation. He is acknowledged as an invaluable source, if one to be used with caution. The obituary judgment that he was 'a historian in his way as great as Plutarch' smacks of Egan's own brand of hyperbole. What is true is that he did virtually create modern sporting journalism—with all its strengths and weaknesses.

DENNIS BRAILSFORD

Sources J. C. Reid, *Bucks and bruisers: Pierce Egan and Regency England* (1971) · J. Ford, *Prizefighting: the age of Regency boximania* (1971) · *Bell's Life in London* (12 Aug 1849) · H. D. Miles, *Pugilistica: the history of British boxing*, 3 vols. (1906) · *TLS* (17 July 1943) · d. cert. · IGI [marriage]

Archives BL, letters relating to application to the Royal Literary Fund, loan no. 96

Likenesses C. Turner, mezzotint, pubd 1823 (after G. Sharples), BM, NPG

Egan, Pierce James (1814–1880), novelist, was born in London on 19 December 1814, the son of Pierce *Egan (1772–1849), sporting journalist and author of *Life in London* (1821), and his wife, Catherine, née Povey. Egan displayed a taste for drawing at a young age, and in 1834 he was admitted to the art school of the Royal Academy. The first stage of his career was an artistic one, as he became a close frequenter of theatres, and made sketches during the performances, afterwards etching these designs, which were published as frontispieces to the plays in G. B. Davidge's Acting Drama. His most ambitious work as an artist was a series of etchings to illustrate his father's serial, *The Pilgrims of the Thames, in Search of the National* (1838), and these were so successful and promising that he might have taken a well-paid position as an illustrator, but he preferred novel writing.

Egan's novels were first issued in weekly numbers, and afterwards in volumes. Several of them contained woodcuts and etchings by the author. Historical fiction was Egan's preferred genre for his early works, particularly 'unreal and bloody stories of the Middle Ages' (Kunitz and Haycraft, 209), such as his *Wat Tyler* (1841, republished 1851), in which scenes of ghastly slaughter were interposed with romantic interludes. His *Robin Hood and Little John* (1840) was hugely popular and was reprinted many times; it started a trend that has been called 'a whole Robin Hood industry in popular fiction' (Sutherland, 209). These novels were followed by such works as *Paul Jones* (1842), a tale of a privateer, illustrated with woodcuts by Egan, and *Edward the Black Prince, or, A Tale of the Feudal Times* (c.1855). In spite of their extravagant narrations of feudal cruelty, Egan's early works were careful to avoid accusations of immorality or irreligiosity, but cannot be said to be realistic or historically accurate.

Egan contributed to the early volumes of the *Illustrated London News*, from the time of its founding in 1842, and from 7 July 1849 to the end of 1851 he edited the *Home Circle*. His stated purpose as editor of the *Home Circle* was to provide 'cheap literature' which would 'blend the moral and the instructive with the amusing' (*Home Circle*, 1, 7 July 1849, 1). He continued to write for other publications; during 1857 he became a frequent contributor to *Reynolds's Miscellany*. He then transferred himself to the *London Journal*, and made a significant contribution to its success, remaining one of its most prolific contributors until the end of his life. From 5 December 1857 to 27 November 1858, Egan contributed weekly chapters to two long-running serials: 'Flowers of the Flock' (which appeared on the *London Journal*'s front page), and 'The Snake in the Grass'. After the second serial was completed, a note from Pierce Egan to the public craved leave of absence for a brief period 'to recruit health and strength', but otherwise he was singularly unobtrusive. The subject matter of Egan's later fiction shifted from his earlier feudal extravagances to the depiction of rural scenes, characterized by sensationalism and the overt juxtaposition of contrasting ranks and classes.

In 1858 and 1859 a new proprietor of the *Journal*, in an attempt to encourage a more literary taste among the purchasers of penny miscellanies, dispensed with Egan's services and reprinted three novels by Sir Walter Scott. But the circulation of the *Journal* diminished so significantly, that Egan was again summoned to restore the popularity. This he did successfully, continuing his serial contributions until March 1880. Among his most popular works, 'The Poor Girl' was published from November 1862 to September 1863, and 'Eve, or, The Angel of Innocence', appeared in 1867. Some contemporary critics, however, felt that he veered too much towards full-blown sensationalism in works such as 'My Love Kate, or, The Dreadful Secret' (1869–70), and that his inferior 'The Poor Boy' (1870–71) was an ill-judged attempt to capitalize on his previously better-received novel of 1863.

Comparatively little is known of Egan's personal life; he was married to Charlotte Martha, née Jones, on 10 February 1844, and they had several children, including a son, yet another Pierce Egan, who was baptized on 1 December 1844 at St James's Church in London. He enjoyed a reasonable income from his work, leaving about £2000 to his executors at his death. He was a liberal in politics, and was for some time connected with the *Weekly Times*, and acted as the London correspondent for 'one of the oldest leading daily papers of the United States' (*Men of the Time*, 1875). He is deservedly accounted one of the pioneers of cheap literature. Pierce Egan died of liver disease on 6 July 1880, at Ravensbourne, Burnt Ash Hill, Lee, Kent, and was buried three days later in Highgate cemetery.

J. W. EBSWORTH, rev. MEGAN A. STEPHAN

Sources *The Athenaeum* (10 July 1880), 49–50 · S. J. Kunitz and H. Haycraft, eds., *British authors of the nineteenth century* (1936), 209 · J. Sutherland, *The Longman companion to Victorian fiction* (1988), 208–9 · *London Journal* (5 Dec 1887) · *Home Circle* (7 July 1849) · Allibone, *Dict.* · *Men of the time* (1875) · Boase, *Mod. Eng. biog.* · IGI · d. cert.
Wealth at death under £2000: probate, 9 Aug 1880, CGPLA Eng. & Wales

Egbert. See Ecgberht (639–729); Ecgberht (d. 766); Ecgberht (d. 839).

Egerton, Sir Alfred Charles Glyn (1886–1959), chemist, was born on 11 October 1886 at Glyn, Talsarnau, north Wales, the fourth son of Sir Alfred Mordaunt Egerton, comptroller to the duke of Connaught, and his wife, Mary Georgina Ormsby-Gore, elder daughter of the second Baron Harlech. His family traces its descent from Sir Thomas Egerton who was lord keeper to Elizabeth I and later lord chancellor to James I. Alfred Egerton was a direct descendant of a cadet of the family of the second earl of Bridgewater. He was educated at Eton College (1900–04) and University College, London, where he worked under Sir William Ramsay and graduated in chemistry with first-class honours in 1908. The following year he was appointed instructor at the Royal Military Academy, Woolwich.

In 1912 Egerton married Ruth Julia, daughter of Sir C. A. *Cripps, afterwards Lord Parmoor. They had no children, but adopted a nephew. The following year Egerton went to Berlin to study in Nernst's laboratory, but returned to England on the outbreak of war. He soon began work at the Ministry of Munitions, where he took part in the design

Sir Alfred Charles
Glyn Egerton
(1886–1959), by
Howard Coster,
1943

Elected FRS in 1926, he served on the council (1931–3), was physical secretary (1938–48), and received the Rumford medal (1946). He served for many years on the governing bodies of Charterhouse School and Winchester College, and was director of the Salters' Institute of Industrial Chemistry (1949–59).

Egerton was a man of wide and varied interests, a talented artist, a lover of music, a skilful and enthusiastic angler, and an experienced skier. He travelled widely and after his retirement visited many of the under-developed territories of the Commonwealth to study their problems and needs. But none of these interests diminished his love of scientific research, and he was happiest when working in his laboratory or discussing scientific matters. He received honorary degrees from the universities of Birmingham, Cairo, Nancy, and Helsinki, and fellowships of University College, London, the Imperial College of Science, and the City and Guilds College. Egerton died at Mouans-Sartoux, France, on 7 September 1959.

D. M. NEWITT, *rev.*

Sources D. M. Newitt, *Memoirs FRS*, 6 (1960), 39–64 · personal knowledge (1971) · *WW*
Archives ICL, papers · RS, corresp. and papers | CAC Cam., corresp. with A. V. Hill · Nuffield Oxf., corresp. with Lord Cherwell
Likenesses W. Stoneman, photographs, 1932–54, NPG · H. Coster, photograph, 1943, NPG [*see illus.*] · P. Annigoni, portrait, priv. coll. · H. Coster, photographs, NPG · W. Stoneman, photograph, RS
Wealth at death £69,055 6s. 3d.: probate, 19 Jan 1960, *CGPLA Eng. & Wales*

and erection of the great national explosives factories built in response to the wartime munitions crisis. After the war Egerton accepted an invitation to work in the Clarendon Laboratory at Oxford where he became a reader in thermodynamics in 1921. In 1936 he was appointed to the chair of chemical technology at the Imperial College of Science where he remained until 1952.

At Oxford Egerton carried out an extensive investigation into the vapour pressures, latent heats of vaporization, and temperature coefficients of the specific heats of a number of metals and alloys. He also began the researches into problems of combustion for which he is best known. These started with an investigation into the causes of explosive detonation, or 'knock', in the internal combustion engine. This led him by logical steps to a more general study of the mechanism of hydrocarbon oxidation, and enabled him to establish the important role played by peroxides in slow combustion. The advent of the turbo-jet engine, in which rapid and total combustion of large quantities of fuel is required, led Egerton to consider the possibility of using promoters or inhibitors to change the limits of inflammability of the fuel. He studied the propagation of flame in limit mixtures and developed a special type of burner by means of which a stationary plane flame front could be formed and its properties examined. He also carried out a detailed investigation into the oxidation of methane and was a pioneer in the use of liquid methane as a fuel in internal combustion engines.

In addition to his scientific researches and academic duties Egerton devoted much time to public service. He was a member of the advisory council of the Department of Scientific and Industrial Research, of the Fuel Research Board, and the Water Pollution Board, and chairman of the Scientific Advisory Council of the Ministry of Fuel and Power. During the Second World War he was a member of the war cabinet scientific advisory committee, and in 1942 was given the task of reorganizing the British central scientific office in Washington. He was knighted in 1943.

Egerton, Alice. *See* Spencer, Alice, countess of Derby (1559–1637).

Egerton, Charles Chandler (1798–1885), surgeon, son of Charles and Mary Egerton, was born at his father's vicarage of Thorncombe, Devon, in April 1798, and received his medical education at the then united St Thomas's and Guy's hospitals, London. In 1819 he became a member of the Royal College of Surgeons.

In June 1823 Egerton was appointed by the East India Company as assistant surgeon on the Bengal establishment to practise as an oculist, and especially to take charge of those Indo-European boys at the lower orphan school who had contracted eye disease. He dealt successfully with the epidemic there, and during his stay in India he held the first position as an oculist at the eye hospital, which was established under his own immediate care, and afterwards at the medical college hospital. In 1837 Egerton was appointed professor of surgery and clinical surgery at the Calcutta Medical College Hospital (founded 1835), and he held that position until he retired from the service in January 1847. The college, which was established mainly owing to Egerton's efforts, provided teaching of anatomy by actual dissection.

On his retirement Egerton returned to Britain and resided at Kendal Lodge, Theydon Garnon, Epping, until his death there on 4 May 1885.

JAMES DIXON, *rev.* ANITA McCONNELL

Sources E. T. Collins, *The history and traditions of the Moorfields Eye Hospital: one hundred years of ophthalmic discovery and development* (1929) · D. G. Crawford, *A history of the Indian medical service, 1600–1913*, 2 (1914), 252, 439 · D. G. Crawford, ed., *Roll of the Indian Medical Service, 1615–1930* (1930) · d. cert. · *CGPLA Eng. & Wales* (1885) · parish register (baptism), Thorncombe, Dorset, 2 May 1799
Wealth at death £29,307 12s. 8d.: probate, 11 July 1885, *CGPLA Eng. & Wales*

Egerton, Sir Charles Comyn (1848–1921), army officer, was born on 10 November 1848, the third son of Major-General Caledon Richard Egerton (1814–1874) and his wife, Margaret (*d.* 7 Sept 1900), third daughter of Alexander Cumming of the island of St Vincent. Educated at Rossall School and Sandhurst, he was commissioned ensign in the 31st foot on 8 June 1867. On 12 June 1867 he transferred to the 76th foot.

After four years in the British service Egerton decided on an Indian army career, and was accordingly posted on 30 May 1871 to the staff corps (the general list of British officers selected for the Indian army). Egerton joined the 3rd Punjab cavalry, serving first as squadron subaltern, then (from 14 July 1876) as squadron officer. On 7 August 1877 he married Anna Wellwood (*d.* 17 Dec 1890), daughter of James Lawson Hill of Edinburgh; they had three sons. On 8 June 1879 he was promoted captain, and on 15 August of that year he was appointed squadron commander.

Egerton served in the Anglo-Afghan War of 1879–80, including the march from Kabul to Kandahar, and was mentioned in dispatches. Then followed a long period of hard, incessant work in frontier operations. He was promoted major on 8 June 1887 and served as assistant adjutant-general of the Punjab frontier force during the Hazara expedition of 1888. On 30 May 1891 he was awarded the DSO. Staff duty with the Miranzai expedition followed, in which he was severely wounded; he received a brevet lieutenant-colonelcy on 1 September 1891.

On 25 November 1892 Egerton was promoted second in command of the 3rd Punjab cavalry, and on 8 June 1893 he was given the rank of full colonel. In 1894–5 he commanded the Bannu column in the Waziristan campaign, under Sir William Lockhart, receiving the CB at the end of hostilities. He was promoted colonel on 1 September 1895 and commandant of the corps of Guides on 12 October that year. In 1896 he was appointed to command the Indian contingent in the Sudan expedition under Kitchener, for his services in which he was appointed aide-de-camp to Queen Victoria on 18 November 1896.

After his return to India, Egerton was employed on the staff of the Tochi field force during the punitive expedition of 1897–8. On 1 April 1899 he was appointed commandant of the Punjab frontier force, with the rank of major-general. In 1901–2 he commanded another expedition into Waziristan. He was promoted major-general on 1 April 1902 and lieutenant-general on 28 October 1903, and was appointed KCB on 1 January 1903.

On 27 June 1903 Egerton was appointed commander of the Somaliland field force, assembled to deal with Muhammad bin Abdullah, known as the Mad Mullah. His expedition (1903–4) was successful, and he was appointed

colonel of his old regiment (now the 23rd cavalry) on 13 May 1904, and received the GCB on 24 June 1904.

On his return to India, Egerton was appointed commander of the forces in Madras, serving from 1 June 1904 to 4 February 1907. On 28 October 1906 he was promoted full general, and on 5 February 1907 he was appointed a member of the Council of India, a post which he held until his retirement on 4 February 1917. His long and varied military experience in India, especially on the frontier and in expeditions beyond its borders, gave him a position of great authority on many political and military questions. He was much interested in, and assisted much in carrying out, Kitchener's military reforms. He was made field marshal on 16 March 1917. In retirement he lived at The Staithe, Mudeford, near Christchurch, Hampshire, where he died on 20 February 1921. Like many who served on the outposts of the empire, Egerton was little known to the majority of his contemporaries in England.

F. E. WHITTON, *rev.* ALEX MAY

Sources *Army List* · *Indian Army List* · J. G. Elliott, *The frontier, 1839–1947* (1968) · *The Times* (22 Feb 1921) · A. George, *The life of Earl Kitchener* (1920) · R. Kellett, *The king's shilling: the life and times of Lord Kitchener of Khartoum* (1984) · Kelly, *Handbk* · Burke, *Peerage* · P. Magnus, *Kitchener: portrait of an imperialist* (1958) · A. Swinson, *North west frontier* (1967) · *CGPLA Eng. & Wales* (1921)
Archives NAM, MS letters, 6502–104 | NAM, letters to Earl Roberts · NAM, MS letters to Lord Roberts, 7101–23–28
Wealth at death £6686 7s. 2d.: probate, 16 April 1921, *CGPLA Eng. & Wales*

Egerton, Daniel (1772–1835), actor and theatre manager, was born in the City of London on 14 April 1772. He seems to have been trained for law, and was placed in business near Whitechapel before making his first attempt on the stage at the Royalty Theatre. It was at this point that he assumed the name Daniel Egerton. He enjoyed performing in plays of Otway and Congreve at private theatres, and played once or twice for benefits at the Haymarket. In June 1799 he made, as Captain Absolute in *The Rivals*, his first appearance at the Birmingham theatre, then under the management of the elder Macready. He remained there for two summers, playing during the winter months with Stephen Kemble in Edinburgh. On account of a sudden break between himself and the manager, Egerton opened the assembly room in Birmingham in 1800, with an entertainment of his own called *Whimsicalities*, consisting of songs, imitations, and extracts from Stevens's 'Lecture on Heads'. In November 1801, as Millamour in Arthur Murphy's *Know your Own Mind*, he made his first appearance at Newcastle, and in May 1803, as Frederick in George Colman's *The Poor Gentleman*, was first seen in Bath, where he also played Jaffier in Otway's *Venice Preserv'd* and other characters. By this period he was already married to the actress Sarah *Egerton (1782x5–1847), the daughter of Revd Peter Fisher, rector of Little Torrington, Devon, but he had quite a reputation for pursuing women nevertheless.

His first appearance in London was at Covent Garden in 1802, for the benefit of Henry Johnston, but after the departure of R. W. Elliston from Bath Egerton took over the roles there of Jaques, Lord Towneley, Mr Oakley in Colman's *The Jealous Wife*, Rolla in Sheridan's *Pizarro*, and many important parts. He left Bath in 1807, when he was engaged at the Haymarket to appear in the part of the Duke of Aranza, which was not successful. Far more felicitous was his appearance at Covent Garden in October 1809 as Lord Avondale in Thomas Morton's *The School of Reform*. In tragedy, King Henry VIII, Tullus Aufidius in *Coriolanus*, Syphax in Joseph Addison's *Cato*, and Clytus in *Alexander the Great* were regarded as his best parts. He remained a member of the Covent Garden company almost until his death, his chief occupation being the performance of secondary characters in tragedy or serious drama. While engaged at Covent Garden he assumed the management first of Sadler's Wells (1821–4) and then of the Olympic (1828). He himself acted at neither house, though his wife was a principal attraction at both. His conduct of the Olympic embroiled him for a time with the management of Covent Garden. It was, however, a failure and was soon abandoned. In July 1833, in conjunction with William Abbot, his associate at Covent Garden, he opened the Victoria Theatre, previously known as the Coburg, but in 1834 he retired from the management, ruined. He died on 22 July 1835. JOSEPH KNIGHT, *rev.* NILANJANA BANERJI

Sources 'Memoir of Mr Egerton', *Oxberry's Dramatic Biography*, 3/47 (1825) • *The Era* (15 Aug 1847) • *Era Almanack and Annual* (1872–3) • Adams, *Drama* • *The biography of the British stage, being correct narratives of the lives of all the principal actors and actresses* (1824) • *The thespian dictionary, or, Dramatic biography of the eighteenth century* (1802) • Hall, *Dramatic ports.*

Likenesses S. De Wilde, watercolour and chalk drawing, 1816, BM • portrait, repro. in Oxberry, *New English drama* (1818) • portrait, repro. in 'Memoir of Mr Egerton', *Oxberry's Dramatic Biography* • six prints, Harvard TC

Egerton [*née* Cavendish], Elizabeth, countess of Bridgewater (1626–1663), writer, second daughter of William *Cavendish, first duke of Newcastle upon Tyne (*bap.* 1593, d. 1676), and his first wife, Elizabeth Bassett (1599–1643), spent her childhood in the shelter of her father's immense wealth. From her earliest years, she was, like her siblings (and later, her prolific stepmother, Margaret *Cavendish), encouraged to write by William Cavendish, himself the author of plays, poems, advice to his pupil (the future Charles II), and manuals on horsemanship. He was also patron to such seventeenth-century writers as Ben Jonson, James Shirley, and William Davenant. The earliest of Egerton's manuscript compilations (Bodl. Oxf., MS Rawl. poet. 16; Yale University, Beinecke Library, Osborn MS b. 233), consonant with the works of the literary coterie that surrounded her cultivated father, is an anthology of poems and dramas co-authored with her sister Jane (later Lady Jane *Cheyne). The best-known section, 'The Concealed Fansyes', is a drama (present only in the Bodleian exemplar) that has, since the twentieth century, been accorded scholarly attention.

After her marriage in 1641 to John *Egerton, later second earl of Bridgewater (1623–1686), she remained, with her sisters Jane and Frances (later countess of Bolingbroke), at Welbeck, her father's Nottinghamshire seat, despite her mother's death, and even after Cavendish, an important military figure in Charles I's camp, left England for the continent with her brothers. In 1645 she and her sisters twice entertained Charles at Welbeck, where they also experienced its possession by parliamentary forces. By late 1645 she moved to Ashridge, the Egerton family seat, and was thereafter largely sheltered from the ravages of the civil war, from which the Egertons succeeded, for the most part, to distance themselves. Her very successful marriage was ended on 14 June 1663 by her sudden and dramatic death at thirty-seven while being delivered of her tenth child during a visit to her husband, who had been placed in the custody of John Ayton, gentleman usher of the black rod after being challenged to a duel by Lionel Cranfield, third earl of Middlesex. She was buried at Ashridge, Hertfordshire. Although he survived her for over twenty years, Bridgewater never remarried; ironically, his extraordinary epitaph for her (recorded most prominently by Ballard), and particularly its mention of her private writings, has brought her belated notice.

Shrouded from public view by her family during her lifetime, Egerton nevertheless claims attention today for a number of manuscripts described in family accounts though long kept in private hands. In various forms, some of these have found their way to public depositories: letters exchanged with family members (Nottingham University Library, Portland collection); the literary anthology co-written with her sister Jane in the early 1640s (Bodleian and Beinecke libraries); the deeply pious manuscripts written later in her life, her 'Loose Papers' (British and Huntington libraries); and her 'Meditations' (Hunt. L.).

Fair copies of Egerton's posthumously bound 'Loose Papers' were apparently made for each of her children. The exemplar that descended to Samuel Egerton Brydges was sold to the British Library in 1836 (Egerton MS 607). Two other fair copies remain in the possession of the family, although facsimiles of these copies are housed at the Huntington Library (EL 8376; EL 8377). The title-page of each of these three copies bears the statement in John Egerton's hand that the manuscript was 'Examined by JBridgewater', and the extent of this examination is suggested by the inclusion, in each, of four entries by him (which are attributed to him, however, in only one copy). The originally 'Loose Papers' that constitute this manuscript contain original, unobjectionable prayers and meditations, many on domestic subjects; moving meditations, or essays, composed during the illness or after the death of three of Egerton's children; and essays on marriage and widowhood that open a highly unusual window on the thinking of a seventeenth-century woman.

A partial fair copy of 'Meditations' (RB 297343), as well as a facsimile of the author's holograph of this compilation (EL 8374), is also held at the Huntington Library. Emendations, in the holograph, in John Egerton's distinctive hand, are carried over to the fair copy, providing clear evidence of his interference in his wife's work. A number of leaves in the folder containing the holograph seem to provide John Egerton's directions for copying the manuscript. That such interference was not limited to husband and wife can be shown by interpolations by the second earl in manuscripts by his oldest son, later the third earl.

BETTY S. TRAVITSKY

Sources B. S. Travitsky, *Subordination and authorship in early modern England: the case of Elizabeth Egerton and her 'loose papers'* (1999) · M. J. M. Ezell, '"To be your daughter in your pen": the social functions of literature in the writings of Lady Elizabeth Brackley and Lady Jane Cavendish', *Huntington Library Quarterly*, 51 (1988), 281–96 · N. Starr, ed., '"The concealed fansyes": a play by Lady Jane Cavendish and Lady Elizabeth Brackley', *Publications of the Modern Language Association of America*, 46 (1931), 802–38 · G. Ballard, *Memoirs of several ladies of Great Britain* (1752) · S. E. Brydges, *GM*, 1st ser., 62 (1792), 1163 [letter to Mr Urban, 21 Dec 1792] · H. Chauncy, *The historical antiquities of Hertfordshire* (1700) · R. Clutterbuck, ed., *The history and antiquities of the county of Hertford*, 3 vols. (1815–27) · H. J. Todd, *History of the college of Bonhommes, at Ashridge* (1823) · S. P. Cerasano and M. Wynne-Davies, eds., *Renaissance drama by women: texts and documents* (1996) · A. Findlay, 'Playing the "scene self" in Jane Cavendish and Elizabeth Brackley's *The concealed fancies*', *Enacting gender on the English Renaissance stage*, ed. A. Russell and V. Comensoli (1999), 154–76 · L. Hopkins, 'Judith Shakespeare's reading: teaching *The concealed fancies*', *Shakespeare Quarterly*, 47 (1996), 396–406
Archives BL, Egerton MS 607 · Bodl. Oxf., MS Rawl. poet. 16 · NRA, priv. coll., MSS | Hunt. L., Ellesmere collection · U. Nott., Portland collection · Yale U., Beinecke L., Osborn MS b. 233
Likenesses double portrait, oils (with her husband; after engraving), repro. in B. Falk, *The Bridgewater millions: a candid family history* (1942) · portraits, priv. coll.

Egerton [*née* Stanley], **Frances, countess of Bridgewater** (1583–1636), noblewoman, was born in May 1583, the second of three daughters of Ferdinando *Stanley, Lord Strange, later fifth earl of Derby (1559?–1594), and his wife, Alice *Spencer (1559–1637), daughter of Sir John Spencer of Althorp and Katherine Kytson. Her elder sister was Lady Anne Stanley (1580–1647), later successively wife of Grey *Brydges, fifth Baron Chandos, and Mervin *Touchet, second earl of Castlehaven; her younger sister was Lady Elizabeth *Stanley, later countess of Huntingdon (*bap.* 1587, *d.* 1633). Six years after the death of Lord Derby, her mother married Thomas *Egerton (1540–1617), lord keeper to Elizabeth I and lord chancellor to James I, who also created him Baron Ellesmere and Viscount Brackley. About 1601, and certainly before 24 March 1603, Lady Frances married her step-brother John *Egerton (1579–1649), the second son and heir of Thomas Egerton and his first wife, Elizabeth Ravenscroft. The young couple had fifteen children, eleven daughters and four sons, many of whom died young. Despite the lord keeper's well-known difficulty with his wife, Frances's mother, his relationship with Frances was excellent. The lengthy lawsuit waged by Ellesmere against her uncle William *Stanley, sixth earl of Derby, eventually secured for Frances a settlement of £6000 and the manors of Halse, Northamptonshire, and of Brackley, from which her father-in-law derived his second title in 1616.

Within two months of Ellesmere's death in 1617, John Egerton was created by James I first earl of Bridgewater. As countess of Bridgewater, Frances continued as a patron of the arts and an ardent book collector. A lengthy 'Catalogue of my ladies books at London, 1627, Oct. 27' (augmented in 1631 and 1632) indicates her interest in sermons (several are by John Donne, whom she knew), meditations, and theology, but also contains Aesop's fables, *Don Quixote*, and Plutarch's *Lives*, along with Sir Thomas Overbury's *Characters*, Edmund Spenser's *The Faerie Queene*, and 'Divers playes by Shakespeare' dated 1602. One of her surviving letters recounts the execution of James Franklin for complicity in the murder of Sir Thomas Overbury (Hunt., MS EL 270).

Although the countess of Bridgewater's literary connections are not as well documented as those of her sister the countess of Huntingdon, she was honoured with her mother and sisters in the verse dedication by John Davies of Hereford to *The Holy Roode*, in which he urges the four women to be constant in their religion. Thomas Newton follows his dedication of *Atropoïon delion*, a lament for the death of Elizabeth I, to the dowager countess of Derby (whom he mistakenly calls Anne) with acrostic verses to Frances and her sisters. John Attey's dedication of 1622 of *The First Booke of Ayres of Four Parts* to the earl and countess of Bridgewater indicates that he was probably music instructor to the Egerton daughters. When John Milton's *Comus* was presented in honour of Bridgewater's assumption of the lord presidency of Wales at Ludlow Castle in 1634, the countess watched her three youngest children, John, Lord Brackley [see Egerton, John, second earl of Bridgewater (1623–1686)], Thomas, and Lady Alice take the leading roles along with Henry Lawes, another music master to the family.

Through her children, the countess became connected to a wide circle of important families. Her eldest daughter became Lady Frances *Hobart (1603–1664); Lady Arabella married in 1623 Oliver *St John, fifth Baron St John of Bletso (*bap.* 1603, *d.* 1642); Lady Elizabeth married David Cecil; Lady Mary married Richard *Herbert, second Lord Herbert of Cherbury [see under Herbert, Edward]; Lady Penelope married Sir Robert Napier; Lady Katherine married the merchant and shipowner William *Courten (*d.* 1655) [see under Courten, Sir William (*c.*1568–1636)]; Lady Magdalen married Sir Gervase Cutler; and Lady Alice (*d.* 1689) married in 1652, as his third wife, Richard *Vaughan, second earl of Carbery.

Countess Frances did not live to see all her children married. She died on 11 March 1636 and was buried at the family estate at Ashridge in Little Gaddesden, Hertfordshire. On this occasion, Robert Codrington presented to her mother, the dowager countess of Derby, a lengthy funeral poem, a copy of which is in the Huntington Library (MS EL 6850; the original is still held by the family), including an elaborate acrostic for the late countess. Bridgewater outlived his wife, and died on 4 December 1649.

MARY ANN O'DONNELL

Sources Hunt. L., Ellesmere papers, Hastings papers · *CSP dom.*, 1631–3 · 'Stanley, Ferdinando', *DNB* · 'Egerton, Thomas', *DNB* · 'Egerton, John', *DNB* · GEC, *Peerage* · Burke, *Peerage* (1999) · B. Falk, *The Bridgewater millions: a candid family history* (1942) · J. Davies of Hereford, *The holy roode, or, Christ's crosse* (1609) · Milton's 'Comus',

being the Bridgewater manuscript with notes and a short family memoir, ed. A. Egerton (1910) · D. Masson, *The life of John Milton*, 7 vols. (1859–94), vol. 1, pp. 590–610 · J. Attey, *The first book of Ayres of four parts* (1622) · J. J. Bagley, *The earls of Derby 1485–1985* (1985) · B. Coward, *The Stanleys, lords Stanley and earls of Derby, 1385–1672: the origins, wealth and power of a landowning family*, Chetham Society, 3rd ser., 30 (1983) · T. Heywood, *The earls of Derby and the verse writers and poets of the 16th and 17th centuries* (1825) · R. H. Kinvig, *The Isle of Man: a social, cultural and political history* (Rutland, VT, 1975) · W. R. Parker, *Milton: a biography*, 2 vols. (1968) · *The Egerton papers*, ed. J. P. Collier (1840) · F. R. Fogle, "Such a rural queen": the countess dowager of Derby as patron', *Patronage in late Renaissance England: papers read at a Clark Library seminar, 14 May 1977*, ed. F. R. Fogle and L. A. Knafla (Los Angeles, 1983), 1–29 · F. Williams, *Index of dedications and commendatory verses in English books before 1641* (1962); Addenda, *The Library*, 30/1 (March 1975), supplement, 1–19
Archives Hunt. L., Hastings papers · Hunt. L., Ellesmere papers
Likenesses W. P. Sherlock, engraving (after unknown artist), NPG · portrait, church of St Mary, Harefield, Middlesex · portrait, repro. in Egerton, *Milton's 'Comus'*; known to be in Bridgewater House in 1910

Egerton, Lady Frances. *See* Hobart, Lady Frances (1603–1664).

Egerton, Francis, third duke of Bridgewater (1736–1803), canal promoter and colliery owner, was born on 21 May 1736 and baptized the following month at St James's, Piccadilly, London. He was the youngest of eleven children of Scroop Egerton, first duke of Bridgewater (1681–1745), eight of whom were born to his second wife, Rachel (c.1705–1777), daughter of Wriothesley Russell, second duke of Bedford, and Elizabeth, only daughter and heir of John Howland of Streatham.

Education and early life Francis was the only Egerton male child to survive until his majority, but he shared the family ailment and during his formative years was sickly and consumptive. He was educated at Dr William Pitman's boarding-school at Markyate in Hertfordshire and at Eton College. In 1745 his father died, to be succeeded by the fourth-born son, John, who died soon after; and in March 1748 Francis, aged eleven, inherited the dukedom. His guardians were his mother and a cousin, Samuel Egerton of Tatton in Cheshire.

Later in 1745 Rachel married Sir Richard Lyttelton, who was nearly half her age. Francis's childhood had been unhappy and the advent of an uncaring stepfather brought major problems. There was an attempt to stop him assuming the title on grounds of mental deficiency; fees for Eton were withheld until a chancery case was brought on his behalf; and he was so maltreated that at times he ran away or was thrown out. For a while he lived with either Samuel Egerton or the duke of Bedford, who was married to Francis's half-sister, Ann. He did eventually return home, but his continuing unhappiness brought drinking problems.

In 1753 Francis, now duke of Bridgewater, was sent on a grand tour with a tutor, Robert Wood, a renowned scholar, who later represented the Egerton family pocket borough of Brackley and became a minister of the crown. They first stayed in Paris and Lyons, but Bridgewater's drinking and escapades with a French actress brought Wood to the brink of resignation. Relations were mended and further

Francis Egerton, third duke of Bridgewater (1736–1803), by Peter Rouw, 1803

travels ensued. A visit at Bridgewater's insistence to the Languedoc Canal impressed him so much that he attended courses covering science and engineering at Lyons Academy. In 1754 they went to Italy, where Bridgewater nearly died of tuberculosis but where he also purchased works of art under Wood's guidance.

On his return to England in late 1755 Bridgewater settled down to a life of gambling and horse racing, but he must also have begun to plan his canal. In 1758 he fell in love with one of the 'beautiful Miss Gunnings', Elizabeth, the widowed duchess of Hamilton, and they became engaged, to Francis's surprise. However, Elizabeth's sister, Maria, had a scandalous public affair and the duke felt obliged to break off his engagement in November 1758 when Elizabeth refused to renounce her sister. Elizabeth soon married the future duke of Argyll; Bridgewater, hurt, soon withdrew from fashionable London society to concentrate on his estates, but not before hosting a spectacular ball in March 1759. He was never to marry.

First arterial canal Bridgewater had substantial estates in twelve counties producing an income of about £30,000 a year. The estates were run from the family home at Ashridge in Hertfordshire, but it was the improvement of the duke's property at Worsley in Lancashire that brought him fame, both for the construction of the Bridgewater Canal, the first arterial canal in England, and for the development of his collieries there. The canal brought a substantial reduction in the price of coal in Manchester and involved much spectacular engineering. This captured the public imagination, and the canal and mines became popular tourist attractions. The Bridgewater Canal inspired the English canal age, and the duke was to be called the 'father of inland navigation' (Egerton, *Transactions*, 279). He was that rare example, an aristocratic entrepreneur, commended by Arthur Young as 'one of those truly great men, who have the soul to execute what they have the genius to plan' (Young, 3.241). Bridgewater did fight his own corner, endeavouring to thwart potential competitors, but he was also motivated by a desire to improve economic conditions and by what was later termed 'utilitarian Christianity'.

The first act of parliament in March 1759 authorized a canal from inside the duke's mines at Worsley to both Salford and Hollin Ferry near Warrington. This was never built. An act in 1760 authorized a new route to Manchester, crossing the River Irwell by the Barton aqueduct, and in 1762 a branch to the Mersey at Runcorn that was later to link with the Trent and Mersey Canal was authorized in another act of parliament. The Bridgewater Canal built was that authorized in the last two acts. It was not finally completed until 1776, but the route to Manchester was open by the early 1760s, and the canal was operating commercially long before completion. There is debate over the exact roles of its makers. It was Bridgewater who provided the vision, the wealth, and the connections that saw the plans to fruition, but he had essential managerial and engineering assistance from John Gilbert, his estate steward at Worsley, and the engineer James Brindley. The Bridgewater was the only major English canal to be financed by a private individual, and its construction threatened the financial viability of the Bridgewater estates. However, by the 1780s the gamble had paid off, and returns thereafter became substantial.

The duke retained his interest in canal development. He promoted and invested in the Trent and Mersey Canal; he constructed docks for inland craft at Liverpool—the Duke's Dock—and at Runcorn; he built a branch of the Bridgewater to Leigh in the late 1790s; he negotiated with the Leeds and Liverpool Canal Company for a link; he developed passenger and goods' traffic on the Bridgewater; and he experimented with steam barges and tugs. His Hertfordshire interests led to managerial involvement in the Grand Junction Canal and to the promotion of a proposed canal to link the Lee or Stort navigations with Cambridge.

Bridgewater believed that 'A Navigation should have Coals at the Heels of it' (Egerton, *The First Part of a Letter to the Parisians*, 40), and the development of his mines at Worsley fuelled his canal construction policy which in turn allowed a massive expansion of his mining activities. His mine shafts were nearly exhausted when he began, so expansion arose from driving deeper shafts and by expanding onto adjacent estates. The Bridgewater Canal began inside the Worsley mine, to provide a water supply and to allow small boats to bring coal out of the mines for trans-shipment as containers onto canal craft, the first such underground system in Europe. Originally two navigable soughs had been driven on the same level, but once the system had proved successful another was opened on a higher level, and by 1822 another two levels had been opened below the original line, one of which had been started during the duke's lifetime. Between 1795 and 1797 Bridgewater built an inclined plane to link the two upper levels; and he was awarded a gold medal by the Society of Arts for this work and for his canal building, one of the few honours he was prepared to accept, as he scorned others.

Final years The life Bridgewater led gave rise to personal habits which shocked his aristocratic relatives, for he swore often, failed to wash regularly, and paid scant attention to the conventions of polite society. But he was well thought of by his employees, for though strict he was frequently kind, and gave better wages and conditions than most, including a properly supervised and beneficial 'truck system'. His ownership of the pocket borough of Brackley meant he could oversee canal legislation in the Commons in addition to his own attendance in the Lords, but otherwise he was not particularly active in politics. Yet he did subscribe £100,000 to the 1796 loyalty loan of William Pitt the younger.

In the last decade of his life Bridgewater began to collect paintings. He still had those bought in Italy in his youth, but he obtained many others through shrewd investment. Especially significant was his acquisition of the Orléans collection of Italian paintings first put together by Cardinal Richelieu, and he was one of the first to encourage J. W. M. Turner. The duke's will insisted that his collection remain intact, and the Bridgewater collection, added to by his heirs, was to become renowned. In this last decade he also rebuilt his London home, Cleveland House, and added to his Hertfordshire home at Ashridge, partly to house his art collection.

Survival of the Bridgewater Canal In January 1803, determined to maintain the viability of his business empire, Bridgewater made a long and complicated will setting up a trust to allow his nominee, Robert Bradshaw, to manage the canal and mines, while permitting his main heirs, George Leveson-*Gower, second marquess of Stafford and the future duke of Sutherland, and his cousin Lieutenant-General John William Egerton, to benefit greatly. His intentions were successful, for the Bridgewater Canal survived the coming of the railways, thanks to the duke's determination in setting up a proper management structure and to the efforts of those later managers, even if Bridgewater can be criticized for making insufficient provision for investment capital.

On 8 March 1803 Bridgewater died at Cleveland House, after a road accident in his coach brought on a short bout of flu; and on 16 March he was buried with his forebears at Little Gaddesden, near Ashridge, where a memorial records, 'He sent barges across fields the farmer formerly tilled'. The dukedom became extinct, but his title of earl of Bridgewater passed to his cousin John William Egerton.

K. R. FAIRCLOUGH

Sources H. Malet, *Bridgewater, the canal duke, 1736–1803* (1990) • C. T. G. Boucher, *James Brindley, engineer, 1716–1772* (1968) • V. I. Tomlinson, 'Salford activities connected with the Bridgewater Canal', *Transactions of the Lancashire and Cheshire Antiquarian Society*, 66 (1956), 51–86 • F. H. Egerton, 'Communication relative to an inclined plane', *Transactions of the (Royal) Society of Arts*, 18 (1800), 265–85 • A. Young, *A six months tour through the north of England*, 4 vols. (1770) • H. Malet, 'The duke of Bridgewater and the 18th-century energy crisis', *Journal of the Royal Society of Arts*, 123 (1974–5), 374–7 • GEC, *Peerage* • *Lord Granville Leveson Gower: private correspondence, 1781–1821*, ed. Castalia, Countess Granville [C. R. Leveson-Gower], 2nd edn, 2 vols. (1916) • F. H. Egerton, *The first part of a letter to the Parisians and the French nation …: containing a defence of the public character of his grace Francis Egerton* [1819–20] • *Catalogue of the Bridgewater collection of pictures*, 5th edn (1856) • *The parish of St James, Westminster*, 1/1, Survey of London, 29 (1960), 493–5 • B. Falk, *The Bridgewater millions: a candid family history* [1942] • C. Hadfield and G. Biddle, *The canals of north west England*, 2 vols. (1970) • C. Nickson, *History of Runcorn* (1887) • will of the duke of Bridgewater, 1836

Archives Hunt. L., corresp. and papers, some relating to canals · University of Salford, corresp. and papers | Buile Hill Mining Museum, Salford, book for Walkden Moss colliery · Herts. ALS, Ashridge House collection · Northants. RO, Bridgewater canal mine and estate papers · Salford City Archives, account book for Bridgewater Canal and other enterprises · E. Malley, 'The financial administration of the Bridgewater estate, 1780–1800', MA diss., University of Manchester, 1929 [uses manuscripts now destroyed] · Mertoun, Roxburghshire, Sutherland family estate papers

Likenesses line engravings, pubd 1766, BM, NPG · P. Rouw, wax medallion, 1803, NPG [*see illus.*] · R. Crosse, miniature (in old age), Tatton Park, Cheshire; repro. in Malet, *Bridgewater* · E. Scriven, stipple (after W. M. Craig), BM, NPG; repro. in W. Jerdan, *National portrait gallery of illustrious and eminent personages of the nineteenth century, with memoirs*, 5 vols. (1830–34) · death mask, repro. in Malet, *Bridgewater* · print, repro. in R. Whitworth, *Advantages of inland navigation* (1766)

Wealth at death approx. £600,000; plus other major bequests to Earl Gower and the Bridgewater Trust: Malet, *Bridgewater*, 166

Egerton [*formerly* Leveson-Gower], **Francis**, **first earl of Ellesmere** (1800–1857), politician and poet, was born at 21 Arlington Street, Piccadilly, London, on 1 January 1800. He was the younger son of George Granville Leveson-*Gower, second marquess of Stafford (1758–1833), politician and art patron, who was created duke of Sutherland in 1833, the year of his death, and Elizabeth, countess of Sutherland, only daughter of William Sutherland, eighteenth earl of Sutherland. Francis was at Eton College from 1811 to 1814, when he proceeded to Christ Church, Oxford. On 6 August 1819 he became a lieutenant in the Staffordshire regiment of yeomanry, and was promoted to a captaincy on 27 September in the same year. He was elected MP for Bletchingley on 19 February 1822, and commenced his public career. He also began his literary career, publishing his translations of Goethe's *Faust* and Schiller's *Song of the Bell* (1823).

Leveson-Gower married, on 18 June 1822, Harriet Catherine (1800–1866), only daughter of Charles Greville and Charlotte, eldest daughter of William, third duke of Portland. They had five sons and two daughters. His wife had literary and religious interests; she published works on the epistles and holy communion, and a *Journal of a Tour to the Holy Land* (1841), which included some of her husband's drawings.

As a liberal conservative of the Canning school, Leveson-Gower spoke eloquently on behalf of free trade well before it became a fashionable cause. He carried in the House of Commons a motion for the endowment of the Catholic clergy, and warmly supported the project of the founding of London University. On 26 June 1826 he became MP for Sutherland, was re-elected for that county in 1830, and afterwards sat for South Lancashire in the parliaments of 1835, 1837, and 1841, and until July 1846. In the meantime he held office as a lord of the Treasury (April to September 1827), under-secretary of state for the colonies (January to May 1828), chief secretary to the marquess of Anglesey, lord lieutenant of Ireland (21 June 1828 to 30 July 1830), and secretary for war (30 July to 30 November 1830). He was sworn of the privy council on 28 June 1828, and likewise for Ireland on 9 August 1828.

Francis Egerton, first earl of Ellesmere (1800–1857), by Edwin Longsden Long

On the death of his father in 1833 he assumed the surname and arms of Egerton, in place of his patronymic of Leveson-Gower. Under the will of Francis *Egerton, third duke of Bridgewater, Egerton became the owner of a property estimated at £90,000 per annum. At the commemoration at Oxford on 10 June 1834 he was created DCL, and in October 1838 he became rector of King's College, Aberdeen. He spent the winter of 1839 in the East, voyaging in his own yacht to the Mediterranean and the Holy Land. The result of his observations appeared in *Mediterranean Sketches* in 1843.

A portion of Egerton's considerable wealth was put to generous use in his support of the arts and scholarship and in building a gallery at his town residence in Cleveland Row—with easy public access—for the magnificent collection of paintings which he had inherited. On 30 June 1846 he was created Viscount Brackley and earl of Ellesmere, and on 7 February 1855 was made KG. He was first president of the Camden Society in 1838, and president of the British Association at Manchester in 1842, of the Royal Asiatic Society in 1849, and of the Royal Geographical Society, 1854–5. He was a trustee of the National Portrait Gallery and a member of the Roxburghe Club. From 1856 he was lord lieutenant of Lancashire.

Ellesmere published extensively, translating plays, histories, and romances from German and French, writing on the duke of Wellington and the Crimea, and publishing volumes of poetry, sometimes privately and sometimes quickly withdrawn. He republished selections from his journalism (eighteen articles in the *Quarterly Review*) as

Essays on History, Biography, Geography, Engineering, etc. (1858). His version of Alexandre Dumas's tragedy, *Henri III et sa cour*, entitled *Catherine of Cleves*, was performed with much success at Covent Garden, Charles Kemble and his daughter Fanny appearing in the piece.

Ellesmere died at Bridgewater House, London, on 18 February 1857, and was buried on the 26th at Worsley, near Manchester, where a monument by G. G. Scott was erected in 1860.   G. C. BOASE, *rev.* H. C. G. MATTHEW

Sources *GM*, 3rd ser., 2 (1857), 358 · *The Times* (19 Feb 1857) · *The Times* (27 Feb 1857) · J. Evans, *Lancashire authors* (1850) · *Wellesley index* · GEC, *Peerage*

Archives NA Ire., letter-books as chief secretary of Ireland · Northants. RO, corresp. · PRO NIre. · RGS, letters · Staffs. RO, bank account | BL, corresp. with Lord Aberdeen, Add. MSS 43238–43255 · BL, corresp. with W. E. Gladstone, Add. MSS 44354–44527 · BL, corresp. with Sir Robert Peel, Add. MSS 40335–40338 · Bodl. Oxf., corresp. with Sir Thomas Phillipps · Keele University Library, letters to Ralph Sneyd · Lancs. RO, corresp. with G. G. Scott · Lpool RO, letters to fourteenth earl of Derby · NA Scot., corresp. with James Lock · NL Scot., letters to duke of Sutherland · NL Scot., corresp. incl. to Lord Rutherford · NRA, priv. coll., letters to Harriet, duchess of Sutherland · PRO, corresp. with Lord John Russell, PRO30/22 · PRO NIre., corresp. with marquess of Anglesey · Staffs. RO, letters to duke of Sutherland · Trinity Cam., letters to Lord Houghton · U. Durham L., letters to Lady Grey · U. Nott. L., letters to J. E. Denison · U. Southampton L., letters to first duke of Wellington · UCL, corresp. with Sir Edwin Chadwick

Likenesses T. Phillips, group portrait, oils, 1806, Dunrobin Castle, Highland region · H. Cousins, mezzotint, pubd 1837 (after J. Bostock), BM · S. Cousins, group portrait, mezzotint, pubd 1840 (after E. Landseer; *Earl of Ellesmere and family*), BM · E. M. Ward, group portrait, oils, 1855 (*The queen investing Napoleon III with the order of the Garter*), Royal Collection · M. Noble, marble bust, 1858, NPG · M. Noble, marble effigy, 1860, St Mark's Church, Worsley, Greater Manchester · G. G. Scott, funerary monument, 1860, Worsley, Greater Manchester · F. Holl, lithograph (after G. Richmond, 1852), NPG · F. C. Lewis, stipple (after J. Slater), BM, NPG · E. L. Long, oils, NPG [*see illus.*] · D. Maclise, etching, NPG · D. Maclise, lithograph, NPG; repro. in *Fraser's Magazine* (July 1835); related drawing, V&A · J. Stephenson, line engraving (after O. de Hanara), NPG · R. Thorburn, miniature, Scot. NPG · F. W. Wilkin, lithograph, BM · portrait, repro. in *Doyle's official baronage*, 1, 679 · portrait, repro. in *ILN* (24 Jan 1846) · portrait, repro. in *Bates's Maclise portrait gallery* (1883)

Egerton, Francis Henry, eighth earl of Bridgewater (1756–1829), collector of manuscripts and patron of learning, was born on 11 November 1756, probably in London, the youngest of the three surviving children of John *Egerton (1721–1787), bishop of Durham, and his first wife, Lady Anna Sophia de Grey (*d.* 1780), daughter of Henry *Grey, duke of Kent (*bap.* 1671, *d.* 1740), lord justice, and his second wife, Sophia. He was educated at Eton College (1766–73), and at Christ Church, Oxford, where he matriculated on 27 March 1773. In 1776, having proceeded BA (23 October), Egerton was elected to a fellowship at All Souls College. He proceeded MA on 24 May 1780, and on 30 November he was appointed prebendary of Durham through his father's influence. He was obliged to resign his fellowship in 1782 on being presented to the rectory of Middle, Shropshire, by his father's cousin Francis *Egerton, third duke of Bridgewater, who in 1797 also presented him to the Shropshire rectory of Whitchurch. Far from assiduous in his parochial duties, he spent long

periods away from his parishes, both in England and abroad, pursuing a wide range of scholarly interests, and amassing a large collection of manuscripts. He was elected FRS in 1784 and FSA in 1791, but his writings on classical, historical, and technical subjects, generally published privately, exhibited steadily increasing eccentricity.

Of Egerton's classical publications, the best-received was his magnificently produced and moderately competent edition of the *Hippolytus* of Euripides, published at the Clarendon Press in 1796. He subsequently published some highly eccentric addenda and corrigenda to this edition (n.d. [1821]), including an extended footnote on natural theology which probably accounts for reports that he wrote a work on that subject. Inordinately proud of his ancestry, he published several biographical and genealogical works on the subject, the most substantial of which was a life of the distinguished Elizabethan lord chancellor, Thomas Egerton, which was described by Lord Campbell as the 'worst piece of biography' he had ever read (J. Campbell, *Lives of the Lord Chancellors*, 8 vols., 1845–69, 2.176 n.). Originally written for Andrew Kippis's edition of the *Biographia Britannica* (1778–95), the biography was issued by Egerton in numerous reprints, which contained increasing amounts of extraneous documentary material. He also published editions of several historical manuscripts, including a rather poor literal translation in French and Italian (1806) of an important early manuscript of Milton's *Comus*, which he discovered among family papers.

From about 1792 Egerton lived almost exclusively with the third duke of Bridgewater, who provided him with an apartment at Bridgewater House in Cleveland Court, London. He consequently came into contact with many of the leading politicians of the day, concerning whom he later published reminiscences in his *Family Anecdotes* (n.d. [1826?]). He also spent much time at the duke's Lancashire manor of Worsley, whence the duke was building his prototype summit-level canal to convey coal to markets in Manchester and Liverpool. His account of an inclined plane designed by the duke in the underground canals of his Lancashire mines was read in 1800 before the Society of Arts, which subsequently awarded the duke its gold medal for the invention. This important account was widely reprinted in technical journals and was published separately in French. Disappointed by the size of his inheritance on the duke's death in 1803 (£40,000), Egerton published in 1809 an announcement repudiating his previously stated intention to produce a memoir of his cousin. However, he subsequently sought to defend the duke's reputation in his chauvinistic two-part *Letter to the Parisians and the French Nation upon Inland Navigation* (n.d. [1819–20]); a proposed third part never appeared, although one of the footnotes, a disquisition on the book of Job, was published about 1823.

Having travelled to Paris in 1802 during the peace of Amiens, Egerton found himself under house arrest when hostilities were resumed, and he was not able to return to England until 1806 when Sir Joseph Banks procured his release. On 22 January 1808 he was granted the title and precedence of an earl's son, in view of his distinguished descent. Later that year he published under the title *John Bull* an anonymous millenarian pamphlet explaining what he considered to be the prophetic significance of the French revolutionary and Napoleonic wars. Shortly afterwards he obtained dispensation for absence from his clerical duties, on the grounds of ill health, and returned to Paris, where he lived for the remainder of his life. Although his health was undoubtedly poor and continued to deteriorate, he is known to have fathered five illegitimate children, at least some of whom were born while he was in Paris. Moreover, he travelled widely in pursuit of manuscripts, even during the Napoleonic wars, and was visited by and corresponded with distinguished men of learning from all over Europe. In 1814 he purchased a splendid house in the rue St Honoré, but he became embroiled in acrimonious and public exchanges over money with his brother, who had inherited a vast fortune on succeeding to the earldom of Bridgewater in 1803. Following his brother's death on 21 October 1823 Egerton succeeded as eighth earl of Bridgewater, Viscount Brackley, and Baron Ellesmere. Inheriting a life interest in his brother's estates, worth about £40,000 per annum, he lived in ever greater luxury. His odd appearance and increasingly eccentric behaviour—which reportedly included dressing his dogs to join him at dinner, and keeping game in his garden for him to shoot for 'sport'—provoked press comment in both Paris and London.

Egerton died at his residence in Paris on 11 February 1829, and his body was interred in March in the family vault at the parish church of St Peter and St Paul, Little Gaddesden, Hertfordshire. He never married, and all his titles became extinct with him. By his will, dated 25 February 1825, he disposed of a fortune of £70,000, mostly in the patronage of learning, in charitable causes, and in glorifying his family's achievements. Most famously, he bequeathed £8000 for the commissioning of a work on the 'power, wisdom, and goodness of God as manifested in the creation', the authors to be selected by the president of the Royal Society. The eight authors appointed—Thomas Chalmers, John Kidd, William Whewell, Sir Charles Bell, Peter Mark Roget, William Buckland, William Kirby, and William Prout—produced a series of eight works known as the Bridgewater Treatises (1833–6), which was extremely successful and frequently reprinted. Egerton's bequest to the British Museum of his valuable manuscripts, mainly relating to French and Italian history and literature, together with over £12,000 for their augmentation and upkeep, gave rise to the important collection that bears his name.   JONATHAN R. TOPHAM

Sources GM, 1st ser., 99/1 (1829), 558–60 · GEC, *Peerage* · B. Falk, *The Bridgewater millions: a candid family history* [1942], 185–218 · D. Coult, *A prospect of Ashridge* (1980), 170–88 · F. H. Egerton, *Catalogue of all the works of the Right Honourable Francis Henry Egerton, earl of Bridgewater* [1828] · E. Edwards, *Lives of the founders of the British Museum* (1870), 446–59 · B. Burke, *A genealogical history of the dormant, abeyant, forfeited and extinct peerages of the British empire*, new edn (1883) · Foster, *Alum. Oxon.* · *A catalogue of all graduates ... in the University of Oxford, between ... 1659 and ... 1850* (1851) · *Fasti Angl.* (Hardy), 3.312 · *LondG* (26–30 Jan 1808), 144–5 · All Souls Oxf., archives · *DNB*
Archives BL, autograph indexes to 67 vols. of Egerton MSS, Egerton MSS 3060–3085 · Herts. ALS, Ashridge II collection · Lincs. Arch., Belton House archives
Likenesses J. Heath, caricature, engraving, 1823, BM · Coupé, line engraving (after medallion by Donadio), NPG · Coupé, stipple (after F. Gérard), BM, NPG · F. P. S. Gérard, engraving, repro. in W. H. Brock, 'The selection of the authors of the Bridgewater Treatises', *Notes and Records of the Royal Society*, 21 (1966), 162–79 · oils, Durham Cathedral
Wealth at death £70,000: GM

Egerton, George. *See* Dunne, Mary Chavelita (1859–1945).

Egerton, Hugh Edward (1855–1927), historian, was born in London on 19 April 1855, the younger son of Edward Christopher Egerton (1816–1869), of Mountfield Court, Robertsbridge, Sussex, member of parliament for Macclesfield in 1852–68, and for East Cheshire in 1868–9, and under-secretary of state for foreign affairs. His mother was Lady Mary Frances (d. 1905), the elder daughter of Charles Pierrepont, the second Earl Manvers. He was descended from Thomas Egerton, Baron Ellesmere, lord chancellor, and from the first and second Earls of Bridgewater.

Egerton was educated at Rugby School and (from 1873) at Corpus Christi College, Oxford. He obtained a second class in classical moderations (1874) and a first class in *literae humaniores* (1876). He was called to the bar by the Inner Temple in 1880, and joined the North Wales and Chester circuit. On 7 July 1886 he married Margaret Alice, the daughter of Alexander Trotter, stockbroker, of Dreghorn, Midlothian; they had two sons and two daughters. His wife was a great-granddaughter of Sir Robert Strange, the engraver, and the sister of Coutts Trotter, vice-master of Trinity College, Cambridge.

In 1885 Egerton became assistant private secretary to his first cousin by marriage, Edward Stanhope, and it was his chief's promotion to be secretary of state for the colonies in 1886 which introduced Egerton to the field in which his life's work was to be done. The new imperialist mood affected Egerton, on whom the publication of J. R. Seeley's *Expansion of England* in 1883 and the imperial character of Queen Victoria's jubilee of 1887 made a strong impression. By nature a scholar rather than a politician, he soon found an appropriate vehicle for his imperialist opinions. As a member of the emigrants' information office (created in 1886 and later merged in the overseas settlement office) he helped with the preparation of an official handbook on the colonies and soon saw the need for an authoritative account of the growth of the British empire. In 1897 his *Short History of British Colonial Policy* was published. A well-researched and pioneering work, it was widely read in the dominions as well as in England, and with its publication Egerton found his métier and made his name.

A short biography of Sir Stamford Raffles (1900) and a collection of the speeches of Sir William Molesworth (1903) on colonial policy followed; and when, in 1905, a new chair of colonial history was founded at Oxford by Alfred Beit, Egerton was the obvious choice as its first occupant. He was not a popular lecturer, but his breadth of knowledge in his field, his impartial judgement, and high standards of scholarship were recognized. His useful *Federations and Unions within the British Empire* (1911) soon became a prescribed authority in the modern history syllabus at Oxford. He was at his best, however, on controversial issues, and his *Causes and Character of the American Revolution*, published in 1923, three years after his resignation of the chair, was seen as a masterpiece of clarity and learning. He also contributed to the Cambridge Modern History, and edited the *Report of the Royal Commission on the Loyalists' Claims*, and his last piece of work was an article on Joseph Chamberlain contributed to the *Dictionary of National Biography*.

Egerton was a fellow of All Souls College, Oxford, from 1906 onwards, and he held the office of sub-warden shortly before his death, which took place at 14 St Giles', Oxford, on 21 May 1927 after a long illness. His funeral was held on 24 May in the chapel of All Souls College.

R. COUPLAND, rev. NILANJANA BANERJI

Sources The Times (23 May 1927) · Foster, *Alum. Oxon.* · J. Foster, *Men-at-the-bar: a biographical hand-list of the members of the various inns of court*, 2nd edn (1885) · R. Symonds, *Oxford and empire: the last lost cause?* (1986) · Burke, *Gen. GB* · *CGPLA Eng. & Wales* (1927) · personal knowledge (1937)
Wealth at death £14,135 10s. 2d.: probate, 15 July 1927, *CGPLA Eng. & Wales*

Egerton, John, first earl of Bridgewater (1579–1649), politician and lawyer, was born on 8 June 1579, the second son of Thomas *Egerton, Baron Ellesmere and Viscount Brackley (1540–1617), and his first wife, Elizabeth (d. 1588), daughter of Thomas Ravenscroft of Bretton, Flintshire. He matriculated on 17 October 1589 from Brasenose College, Oxford, where he was a noted classical scholar and from where he graduated BA on 4 July 1594. The following year he was admitted to Lincoln's Inn, where, although he was reputedly a keen student of the law, the privileges of a son of the attorney-general (from 1596, lord keeper) seem to have excused him from formal completion of his legal training. In 1597, despite his youth, he sat as MP for Callington. Two years later, with his elder brother, Sir Thomas Egerton, he joined the earl of Essex's expedition to Ireland; he was knighted there on 8 April 1599. In August Sir Thomas was killed and about this time Sir John returned to England. On 25 September, still aged only twenty, he became in succession to his brother deputy baron of the exchequer court of the county palatine of Chester, a position he held until 21 February 1605. As MP for Shropshire in the 1601 parliament, he served on committees for business, monopolies, penal laws, and levying fines at Chester.

Probably in 1601, although possibly as early as October 1600, Egerton married Lady Frances Stanley [see Egerton, Frances (1583–1636)], second daughter of his stepmother, Alice *Spencer, dowager countess of Derby (1559–1637), and her first husband, Ferdinando *Stanley, fifth earl of Derby (1559?–1594). They established themselves at Ashridge House in Little Gaddesden, Hertfordshire, near to their parents' estate at Harefield, Middlesex, and when in

London lived in St Martin-in-the-Fields or St Giles, Cripplegate. They had four sons and seven daughters. In 1603 Egerton was apparently seriously ill: his father's letters in April refer to his 'lympinge with lame Mephiboseth' (Collier, 362, 365). However, if any permanent disability resulted, it does not seem to have hampered either his career or his leisure interests. He tilted at court and was known to his family as an 'indefatigable' bell-ringer (A. Egerton, 11). He was made a knight of the Bath on 24 July 1603, on James VI and I's arrival in England. Created MA at Oxford on 30 August 1605, he was appointed *custos rotulorum* of Shropshire the same year. In 1607 he became joint captain with his father of Lyons Castle, Denbigh.

Following his father's death on 15 March 1617, Egerton became second Viscount Brackley. In fulfilment of a promise made by James to his lord keeper and, contemporary reports had it, in response to encouragement to the king from the countess of Derby, Brackley was on 27 May raised to an earldom, that of Bridgewater. It was also said that he had to pay £20,000 to the king's favourite, George Villiers, earl of Buckingham, for the privilege. Further expense was incurred when he was sued by his sisters, Mary and Elizabeth, and their husbands, over the deposition of their late father's estates. However, his public career continued: about the same time he became a member of the council of Wales. In the 1621 parliament he was one of two peers on the standing committee for petitions, and served in that capacity through subsequent parliaments of the 1620s. He was among the legal counsel for Buckingham at his impeachment in 1624. Throughout the decade he helped to consolidate the authority of the House of Lords to try civil and criminal cases as a court of both original jurisdiction and appeal.

With the accession of Charles I, Bridgewater was initially in greater favour. He became privy councillor on 4 July 1626, and president of the council in the marches of Wales on 26 June 1631 with official residence at Ludlow Castle, Shropshire. He became lord lieutenant of Shropshire, Worcestershire, Herefordshire, Monmouthshire, and north and south Wales on 8 July 1631. A delay in taking up his seat at Ludlow was caused by the trial of the countess's brother-in-law, Mervin *Touchet, earl of Castlehaven, for incest, rape, and sodomy of his wife (the former Lady Anne Stanley) and servants in 1631; Lady Bridgewater thought that the family had been bewitched. When Bridgewater was finally installed on 12 May 1633, great festivities were held. John Milton's *Comus*, written for the occasion, was acted at Ludlow Castle on 29 September by the earl's children. They also took part in the first performance of Milton's *Arcades* at Harefield that year.

Bridgewater's legal background was quite evident with his presidency of the council in Wales. A strong advocate, he preserved its jurisdiction against neighbouring English counties and other courts. He maintained its casebooks in his own hand, presiding over an average of 1200 cases each year; most of these were civil actions, but some also involved questions of law and order. In his first prominent case, that of Marjorie Evans who appealed after a JP failed to prosecute an alleged rapist, he conducted his own investigation to find the truth, overriding the local gentry, and Evans was vindicated. He also kept personal notes of proceedings in the Star Chamber at Westminster in the 1630s. As lord lieutenant he was an efficient officer. The militia was well maintained and equipped at his own expense, and he kept detailed records of orders, collections, and disbursements.

The earl's letters reveal that by the mid-1630s he was becoming increasingly disenchanted with the royal court and its administration. When Charles I organized the rebuilding of St Paul's Cathedral in London, Bridgewater collected from 95 per cent of householders in Oswestry hundred. But when the privy council ordered the collection of ship money, he protested, resulting in few payments from the region. He also refused to censure nonconformist ministers. Asked to mobilize men for war against the Scots in July 1638, he complained that he had no useful arms or money. Asked to sell land and horses to meet his obligations, he refused.

Bridgewater joined Charles I at Newcastle in 1639, but in the next few months lived a retired life. The evidence suggests that he did not feel appreciated by Charles or the council, and disagreed with Archbishop William Laud's ecclesiastical policy. John Castle, a clerk of the privy seal, kept him apprised of court politics. Bridgewater supported Charles in the Short Parliament, defending the king in several committees, but not after the second bishops' war. Government ineptitude 'sapped his enthusiasm' for the king's cause (Hamilton, 'Earl of Bridgewater'). He seldom attended the Long Parliament. In 1641 he was impeached for removing a judge, but escaped trial with a fine. In May 1643 he was joint commissioner of array for Flintshire, Denbighshire, and Merioneth but soon afterwards he resigned his offices and withdrew to his house at Ashridge. When royalist troops under Prince Rupert occupied the area, they pillaged his house and imprisoned the servants. The Lords then granted him an order for his protection. Thereafter, there is no evidence that he assisted either side in the civil wars; his focus was on keeping his lands, family, and communities intact.

Bridgewater's income fluctuated markedly. Although he inherited an estate said to be worth £12,000, some land, such as the Ellesmere and Whitchurch estates comprising fifty-five townships and 358 tenants in northern Shropshire, was in trust for the use of his stepmother. His fortunes increased when her life interest passed with her death in 1637. For six years from 1637 he re-leased the lands, supervising the commissioners personally. Since the region had rich and fertile land, supporting mixed agriculture, he was able to increase the fines by a factor of fifteen, and more than double the rents. However, his expenses were quite high, especially those connected with his presidency of the council in Wales. He was worth about £7000 to £8000 a year by 1640 and by 1641 his income had dropped by half. Like all major landowners, he experienced difficulty collecting rents during the war, and much of his land lay in areas particularly affected. At his death, he had personal debts of £26,950, had defaulted

on several judgments against him by merchants and gentry, and had debts of £51,700 from his son-in-law William *Courten's failed merchant ventures [see under Courten, Sir William (c.1568–1636)].

The earl was generous to a fault. He contributed to Lincoln's Inn chapel, and annually to poor boxes of parishes where he owned property. In 1630, under the Book of Orders, he was one of the first poor-law commissioners to appoint overseers to levy rates for poor relief. His literary tastes encouraged him to improve the library left by his father. A prominent collector and patron of literature, numerous major works were dedicated to him and to members of his family. He also befriended and patronized the celebrated composer Henry Lawes in the 1630s and 1640s. An avid reader in his declining years, he copiously annotated the sermons and theological and political tracts that he had collected. A semi-invalid, following his wife's death on 11 March 1636 he was taken care of by his daughter Lady Alice, who never married. He died intestate on 4 December 1649, and was buried on 7 December beside his wife in Little Gaddesden church.

LOUIS A. KNAFLA

Sources B. Falk, *The Bridgewater millions, a candid family history* (1942) · GEC, *Peerage*, new edn, 2.311–12 · A. Collins, *The peerage of England*, ed. B. Longmate, 5th edn, 8 vols. (1779), vol. 2, pp. 232–5; vol. 3, pp. 193–4, 196 · J. E. Doyle, *The official baronage of England*, 1 (1886), 224–5 · *Milton's 'Comus', being the Bridgewater manuscript with notes and a short family memoir*, ed. A. Egerton (1910) · J. P. Collier, ed., *The Egerton papers*, CS, 12 (1840) · S. R. Gardiner, *History of England from the accession of James I to the outbreak of the civil war, 1603–1642*, 10 vols. (1883–4), vol. 3, p. 78; vol. 6, pp. 132, 281; vol. 7, p. 335 · J. S. Hart, *Justice upon petition: the House of Lords and the reformation of justice, 1621–1675* (1991) · R. C. Gabriel, 'Egerton, John', HoP, *Commons, 1558–1603* · *CSP dom., 1625–43* · L. Marcus, 'The milieu of Milton's *Comus*: judicial reform at Ludlow and the problem of sexual assault', *Criticism*, 25 (1983), 293–327 · E. Hopkins, 'The re-releasing of the Ellesmere estates, 1637–1642', *Agricultural History Review*, 10/1 (1962), 14–28 · E. Hopkins, 'The Bridgewater estates in north Shropshire during the civil war', *Transactions of the Shropshire Archaeological Society*, 56/3 (1961), 308–13 · C. Hamilton, 'The earl of Bridgewater and the English civil war', *History*, 75 (1990), 23–38 · C. Hamilton, 'The Bridgewater debts', *Huntington Library Quarterly*, 42/3 (1979), 217–29 · C. Russell, *Parliaments and English politics, 1621–1629* (1979) · K. Sharpe, *The personal rule of Charles I* (1992) · Rymer, *Foedera*, 2nd edn, 19.449–65 · family papers, Hunt. L., Bridgewater and Ellesmere collection · estate documents, Shrops. RRC, Bridgewater collection · Herts. ALS, Bridgewater collection · BL, Add. MS 10609 · C. G. Grayling, *The Bridgewater heritage: the story of the Bridgewater estates* (1983) · C. A. J. Skeel, *The council in the marches of Wales* (1904), 2, 129, 151, 157 · *Calendar of the manuscripts of the most hon. the marquis of Salisbury*, 24 vols., HMC, 9 (1883–1976), vols. 17, 20, 24 · *The manuscripts of Rye and Hereford corporations*, HMC, 31 (1892), 277–9 · R. E. Ruigh, *The parliament of 1624: politics and foreign policy* (1971), 187–8 · E. S. Cope and W. H. Coates, eds., *Proceedings of the Short Parliament of 1640*, CS, 4th ser., 19 (1977), 59, 76–7, 110 · BL, Sloane MS 3827 · *The letters of John Chamberlain*, ed. N. E. McClure, 2 vols. (1939), vol. 1, pp. 111, 153, 190; vol. 2, p. 65 · R. H. Clive, *Documents connected with the history of Ludlow and the lords marchers* (1841), 182–3 · G. Baker, *The history and antiquities of the county of Northampton*, 1 (1822–30), 564 · G. Ormerod, *The history of the county palatine and city of Chester*, 2nd edn, ed. T. Helsby, 1 (1882), 445 · *VCH Hertfordshire*, vol. 2 · R. Clutterbuck, ed., *The history and antiquities of the county of Hertford*, 3 vols. (1815–27)

Archives Herts. ALS, corresp. with his agent · Hunt. L., Bridgewater and Ellesmere collection · Hunt. L., corresp. and papers |

JRL, letters to Peter Legh; letter to Anne Bold • Shrops. RRC, Bridgewater collection • Shrops. RRC, corresp. and papers as president of council of the marches
Likenesses oils, Tatton Park, Cheshire • photogravure, repro. in Egerton, ed., *Milton's 'Comus'*, frontispiece • portrait, BL

Egerton, John, second earl of Bridgewater (1623–1686), politician, was born in June 1623, the third but eldest surviving son of John *Egerton, first earl of Bridgewater (1579–1649), politician, and his wife, Frances (1583–1636), second daughter and coheir of Ferdinando *Stanley, earl of Derby, and his wife, Alice *Spencer. Styled Viscount Brackley until 1649, in 1633 he entered Gray's Inn. On 18 February 1634 he and his younger brother Thomas were among the young lords and noblemen's sons who performed with the king in Carew's masque, *Coelum Britannicum*. In the same year Milton's *Arcades* was presented to his grandmother, the dowager countess of Derby, at Harefield, near Ashridge, his father's Hertfordshire country house. The masque was performed in the great hall of Ludlow Castle on Michaelmas night and John and his brother were among the noble family members who sang and spoke Milton's words to their grandmother. His sisters were pupils of Henry Lawes, who wrote music for *Arcades*. Milton's first edition of *Comus*, published in 1637 without the author's name, was dedicated by Lawes to the young Brackley. On 22 July 1641 at St James's, Clerkenwell, he married Lady Elizabeth Cavendish [see Egerton, Elizabeth (1626–1663)], second daughter of William *Cavendish, first duke of Newcastle upon Tyne, and his first wife, Elizabeth, daughter and heir of William Bassett of Blore, Staffordshire. She was devout, and a writer of poetry, songs, pastoral plays, and meditations; John seems to have been passionately attached to her.

In 1649 Brackley succeeded his father as earl of Bridgewater. Unlike his father, who had attempted to remain neutral during the civil war, the new earl was a royalist close to Archbishop Laud. Suspected of conspiring against the Commonwealth, he was arrested, imprisoned, and examined in April 1651. He was soon released on bail, giving his own bond for £10,000 and two sureties in £5000 each to appear before the privy council. In the same year Milton's *Pro populo Anglicano defensio* was published. Bridgewater possessed a copy of it, which he annotated. A strong defender of local courts, he maintained correspondence with his county JPs from the 1650s to 1685, providing information and advice as well as hearing arbitrations.

After the Restoration Bridgewater held a host of local offices including the high stewardship of Oxford University, to which he was elected on 14 May 1663, and where he was awarded the degree of MA, the high stewardship of Wycombe in 1672, and the lord lieutenancy of Buckinghamshire from 1660, Lancashire and Cheshire from 1670 to 1676, and Hertfordshire from 1681. On the national level, in 1662 he was appointed with Clarendon and the bishop of London to manage the conference between the two houses on the Act of Uniformity. Clarendon promoted him to several major offices as Bridgewater became

his protégé. In June 1663 Bridgewater accepted a challenge from the earl of Middlesex; both men were ordered into custody at black rod's house in Westminster. There Bridgewater was joined by his wife, who died in childbirth on 14 June, a loss from which, according to his epitaph, he never recovered. When David Lloyd published a sympathetic account under the title *The Countess of Bridgwater's Ghost* (1663), the earl had him imprisoned for six months. The couple had had six sons and three daughters.

Bridgewater went on to attend parliament, claiming it 'doth agree so much with my nature and disposition that I cannot find in my heart to forbear it' (Swatland, 38). On 13 February 1666 he was sworn of the privy council. Throughout the following decade he actively chaired parliamentary committees, managed joint committees, and steered religious legislation. After Clarendon's fall he alienated the courtiers and began to act with the country party. By 1675 he was part of Lord Shaftebury's 'malcontents', a strong supporter of parliamentary privileges and of the lords as a high court of judicature. In 1679 he was sworn of the new privy council, which consisted of members of both court and country parties, and which was for the exclusion of James, duke of York, in 1680. Considered an ultra Anglican, none the less he was anti-papist and sympathetic to dissenters if they would take oaths of allegiance and not engage in unlawful assemblies.

Bridgewater was plagued with financial problems throughout his life. In 1649 he had claims against him of over £200,000. In 1654 he wrote to Oliver Cromwell that he was so deep in debt that he was a prisoner in his home at Ashridge and could not appear in public. A memo of the same year reveals that he had paid off debts of £71,615 and had made marriage provisions for his sons and daughters. To do this he sold land, raised large mortgages, enclosed common fields, and borrowed heavily from relatives. All the estates settled on his son and heir John *Egerton, Viscount Brackley, at the latter's remarriage in 1673 were encumbered. Re-leasing estates in the 1650s and 1660s did not improve Bridgewater's situation because his father had already obtained high fines and low rents. The earl continued to spend lavishly on his houses and grounds and on public festivities. Correspondence with his lawyer, Sir John Halsey, reveals that he was always short of cash. Playing a careful balancing act he maintained an economic status credible for a privy councillor. He died with less land than he had inherited, but with slightly better net assets than his father had left him.

Sir Henry Chauncy, the historian of Hertfordshire, who knew him, described Bridgewater as 'adorned with a modest and grave aspect, a sweet and pleasant countenance, a comely presence'; 'a learned man' who 'delighted much in his library' (Chauncy, 2.38). The earl is said to have been a liberal patron of works of learning. Todd's *Ashridge* prints a series of instructions drawn by him for the management of his household, interesting in its detailed account and philosophy of organizing a nobleman's establishment. A sabbatarian, he exhorted his servants to be good-tempered, devout, and zealous in religious instruction. Bridgewater died at his house in the Barbican,

London, on 26 October 1686, and was buried on 4 November at Little Gaddesden, Hertfordshire. His eldest son, John, inherited the title.

FRANCIS ESPINASSE, *rev.* LOUIS A. KNAFLA

Sources B. Falk, *The Bridgewater millions: a candid family history* [1942], 61–5, 69–75 · P. Seaward, *The Cavalier Parliament and the reconstruction of the old regime, 1661–1667* (1988) · A. Swatland, *The House of Lords in the reign of Charles II* (1996) · GEC, *Peerage*, 2.311–12 · J. E. Doyle, *The official baronage of England*, 1 (1886), 225–6 · *VCH Hertfordshire*, vol. 2 · *VCH Buckinghamshire*, vol. 3 · *Milton's 'Comus', being the Bridgewater manuscript with notes and a short family memoir*, ed. A. Egerton (1910) · J. P. Collier, ed., *The Egerton papers*, CS, 12 (1840) · C. Hamilton, 'The Bridgewater debts', *Huntington Library Quarterly*, 42 (1978–9), 217–29 · C. G. Grayling, *The Bridgewater heritage: the story of the Bridgewater estates* (1983) · W. J. Hardy, ed., *Notes and extracts from the sessions rolls, 1581 to 1698* (1905) · W. Le Hardy, ed., *Calendar to the sessions books … 1619 to 1657* (1928) · W. Le Hardy, ed., *Calendar to the sessions books … 1658 to 1700* (1930) · H. Chauncy, *The historical antiquities of Hertfordshire* (1700); repr. in 2 vols., 2 (1826) · H. J. Todd, *History of the college of Bonhommes at Ashridge* (1823) · Hunt. L., Ellesmere papers · letters and papers, Herts. ALS, Bridgewater collection · corresp., lord-lieutenant of Buckinghamshire, BL, Stowe MSS 142, 324 · collected family prayers with his wife, Elizabeth's, prayers and meditations, BL, Egerton MS 607 · E. Egerton, poems and writings, Bodl. Oxf., MS Rawl. poet. 16 · D. Lloyd, *The countess of Bridgewater's ghost* (1663) · Pepys, *Diary*, vol. 8 · D. Masson, *The life of John Milton*, rev. edn, 1 (1894), 552 · J. Milton, *Arcades* (1645) · J. Milton, *Comus*, ed. H. J. Todd (1798) · *The poetical works of John Milton*, ed. H. J. Todd, 2nd edn, 1 (1809) · T. Warton, *Milton's minor poems* (1785) · W. Dugdale, *The baronage of England*, 2 vols. (1675–6), vol. 2, p. 415
Archives Hunt. L., papers | Herts. ALS, letters to John Halsey · Hunt. L., letters to Sir Richard Temple
Likenesses A. Blooteling?, mezzotint, 1680 (after W. Claret), BM · attrib. W. Claret, oils, Tatton Park, Cheshire · photogravure, repro. in Egerton, ed., *Milton's 'Comus'*, facing pp. 8, 20 · portrait, BL, Add. MS 32349, fol. 131

Egerton, John, **third earl of Bridgewater** (**1646–1701**), politician and government official, was born on 9 November 1646, the eldest surviving son of John *Egerton, second earl of Bridgewater (1623–1686), and his wife, Elizabeth *Egerton (1626–1663), second daughter of William *Cavendish, first duke of Newcastle upon Tyne, and his wife, Elizabeth.

Viscount Brackley, as Egerton was known during his father's lifetime, was made a knight of the Bath at the coronation of Charles II on 23 April 1661. He married Lady Elizabeth (1647/8–1670), daughter and heir of James Cranfield, second earl of Middlesex, and Anne, daughter and coheir of Edward Bouchier, earl of Bath, on 17 November 1664 at Bridgwater House, Barbican, in London; she died on 3 March 1670 aged twenty-two. They had one son, who died young. On 2 April 1673, at the chapel of the Charterhouse, London, he married Jane (1655–1716), eldest daughter of Charles *Paulet or Powlett, Lord St John of Basing, later first duke of Bolton, and his second wife, Mary, daughter of Emanuel *Scrope, earl of Sunderland. They had seven sons (the two eldest of whom died in a fire at Bridgwater House on 12 April 1687) and two daughters. Along with his brothers, Brackley was admitted to the Inner Temple on 20 April 1673.

Brackley held local office from 1668 as a JP and deputy lieutenant for Buckinghamshire but he resisted entering parliament, declining to be a candidate in the elections of

1679–81 and giving way to his father's commands to stand only in 1685, when he was elected for Buckinghamshire. He was an active MP, sitting on fourteen committees, and in the second session went into opposition with his father. He succeeded his father as earl of Bridgewater on 26 October 1686. He inherited the family estates, including Ashridge, near Little Gaddesden, Hertfordshire, held office as recorder of Brackley (1686–8), and succeeded his father as lord lieutenant of Buckinghamshire. In 1687, however, James II removed him from the lord lieutenancy when he opposed exempting Roman Catholics from the Test Acts and placing them in positions of authority. After the revolution of 1688 Bridgewater supported settling the crown on the prince and princess of Orange, and William III reappointed him lord lieutenant of Buckinghamshire on 4 April 1689.

Bridgewater turned his attention to national office, being sworn a member of the privy council on 7 May 1689 and appointed president of the new Board of Trade and Plantations on 17 December 1695. In March 1695 he carried one of the banners of England and France at Queen Mary's funeral. He was speaker of the House of Lords in 1697 and 1700, presiding over debates during the absence of Lord Chancellor Somers, and at the king's request prorogued parliament several times. William evidently held him in high esteem, and he appointed him first lord of the Admiralty on 22 May 1699, a position he held until his death. He also served as a lord justice during the king's absence, from June to October 1699 and June to September 1700. He was elected a governor of Charterhouse on 8 January 1700.

Bridgewater, after the fire at Bridgwater House in 1687, had moved to Red Lion Square, London, and then to St James's Square, where he died on 19 March 1701. He had a private funeral and was buried with his ancestors at Little Gaddesden on 31 March. Contemporaries remembered him as 'a just and good man, a faithful friend, and a wise counsellor' (Collins, *Peerage*, 3.194–6). He and the countess were celebrated in a novella based on their lives written in French. In an unusual trust he settled all his estates on his brothers to hold to the use of his male heirs for 1000 years, with his wife, Jane, as executor able to extend the proportion given to the use of any child at her discretion. The countess died on 23 May 1716, aged sixty, and was buried on 31 May at Little Gaddesden. Bridgewater was succeeded in the earldom by his and Jane's third but eldest surviving son, Scroop, who first thought of constructing the canals which were the foundation of the family's later great fortune and who was created duke of Bridgewater on 18 June 1720.

LOUIS A. KNAFLA

Sources B. Falk, *The Bridgewater millions: a candid family history* [1942], 75–9 · GEC, *Peerage*, new edn, 2.313 · A. Collins, *The peerage of England*, ed. B. Longmate, 5th edn, 8 vols. (1779), vol. 3, pp. 194–6 · J. E. Doyle, *The official baronage of England*, 1 (1886), 226 · J. Brydges, *The history and antiquities of Northamptonshire*, rev. edn (1812), vol. 3 · papers on trade, military, and colonies, 1690–1700, Hunt. L., Ellesmere MSS 9618–9799 · *First report*, HMC, 1/1 (1870); repr. (1874) · Inner Temple, London, MS 202, fol. 1045 · will, PRO, PROB 11/460, fol. 3 · admiralty corresp., 1693–1700, BL, Add. MSS 28878, 28886 · French novel based on Bridgewater's life, 1690s, BL, Sloane MS

1009, fols. 360–65 · M. Knights, *Politics and opinion in crisis, 1678–1681* (1994), 334 · D. H. Hosford, *Nottingham, nobles and the north: aspects of the revolution of 1688* (1976), 12, 22 · J. R. Jones, *The politics of the exclusion crisis, 1678–1683* (1961), 45–6 · J. R. Jones, *The revolution of 1688 in England* (1972), 63 · T. B. Macaulay, *The history of England from the accession of James II*, 5 vols. (1858–61), vol. 5 · W. Dugdale, *The baronage of England*, 2 vols. (1675–6), vol. 2, p. 415 · F. A. Inderwick and R. A. Roberts, eds., *A calendar of the Inner Temple records*, 3 (1901) · L. Naylor, 'Egerton, John', HoP, *Commons, 1660–90* · IGI · F. Collins, ed., *The registers and monumental inscriptions of Charterhouse chapel*, Harleian Society, Register Section, 18 (1892), 1

Archives Herts. ALS, corresp. and papers · Hunt. L., papers | Yale U., Beinecke L., letters to William Blathwayt

Likenesses J. Smith, mezzotint, 1661 (after G. Kneller), BM, NPG · oils, *c*.1675, Gov. Art Coll.; on loan to Marlborough House, London, 1979

Egerton, John (1721–1787), bishop of Durham, was born on 30 November 1721 in London, eldest son of Henry Egerton (1689/90–1746), bishop of Hereford from 1724 and sixth son to John *Egerton, third earl of Bridgewater, and his wife, Lady Elizabeth Ariana Bentinck, daughter of Hans Willem *Bentinck, first earl of Portland.

Educated at Eton College, Egerton matriculated at Oriel College, Oxford, on 20 May 1740. He took no degree before graduating BCL on 30 May 1746, but on 22 December 1745 Benjamin Hoadly ordained him priest in Grosvenor Chapel, Westminster, having deaconed him in a private ceremony the previous day. Egerton was preferred by his father to the Herefordshire rectory of Ross on 23 December that year, and on 3 January 1746 to the Hereford Cathedral prebend of Cublington. His father died that April. On 21 November 1748 Egerton married his cousin Lady Anne Sophia de Grey (*d*. 1780), daughter and coheir of Henry Grey, duke of Kent; her mother was Egerton's mother's sister. They had one daughter and three sons. The eldest son died in infancy, the other two successively became earl of Bridgewater. Their youngest son, Francis Henry *Egerton, was a renowned collector of manuscripts.

Appointed chaplain-in-ordinary to George II on 19 March 1749, Egerton became dean of Hereford on 24 July 1750. He graduated DCL by diploma on 21 May 1756. According to his son he was devoted to Ross-on-Wye, where he resided and performed the parish duties, and reluctant to become a bishop: 'he could not be prevailed upon to use any applications of his own for that purpose, and with difficulty permitted those of his friends' (Egerton, 4). He was nevertheless consecrated bishop of Bangor on 4 July 1756, retaining Ross *in commendam*. His only published works date from this period: two sermons preached before the House of Lords in 1757 and 1761, one for the Society for the Propagation of the Gospel in 1763.

Egerton is said to have declined the Irish primacy, probably in 1765. On 12 October 1768 he was translated to Lichfield and Coventry, adding a St Paul's canonry with the prebend of Wildland a few days later. When the bishop of Durham died in 1771, Egerton's poor health commended him to Lord North, who wanted the prince bishopric kept warm for his brother. Unfortunately Egerton recovered and Brownlow North had to content himself with Winchester. During his summer residences in Durham,

John Egerton (1721–1787), by unknown artist, *c*.1760

Egerton proved a hospitable and eirenic bishop. Arriving to find Durham county split by post-electoral hostilities, he succeeded in reconciling the principals and bringing them together around his table. In a deeply troubled political climate he won a reputation for strict party neutrality. The city of Durham had lost its charter in 1766 after violent political disturbances. Egerton granted a new charter on 2 October 1780, timed to avoid influencing the general election, and chose the new corporation with acclaimed even-handedness. A 1772 petition from the borough of Gateshead to begin the process of incorporation, however, he deflected.

Egerton conducted visitations in 1772, 1774, and 1778; in 1782 failing health made him delegate Northumberland to Bishop Law of Clonfert. His episcopate saw seventy-two deacons and ninety-two priests ordained, an increase on his predecessor's figures. He made generous gifts to diocesan schools and to the Newcastle Infirmary, and supported the Corporation of the Sons of the Clergy.

Egerton was a skilled negotiator: while he required enclosure arrangements to include gifts of land to the local living and secured steep increases in lease renewal fines, his fifteen years at Durham involved him in only one lawsuit, whereby he successfully denied liability for some road repair costs. He played a generous part in rebuilding the Tyne Bridge after its destruction by floods in 1771, and waived some feudal dues to facilitate a major forestry project. His diplomacy reconciled conflicting interests to secure the enclosure and drainage of 6000 acres on Walling Fen, Howdenshire, generating agricultural land, a new town, and a navigable canal.

After his wife's death in 1780, Egerton on 31 March 1782

married Mary, sister of Sir Edward Boughton, baronet. They had no children. Egerton died on 18 January 1787 at his house in Grosvenor Square, London, and was buried in St James's, Piccadilly. His second wife survived him.

E. A. VARLEY

Sources F. H. Egerton, earl of Bridgewater, 'A biographical sketch of John Egerton', in W. Hutchinson, *The history and antiquities of the county palatine of Durham*, 3 (1794), ix–xxi, iii–xiii • W. B. Maynard, 'The ecclesiastical administration of the archdeaconry of Durham, 1774–1856', PhD diss., U. Durham, 1973 • E. Hughes, *North country life in the eighteenth century*, 1 (1952) • G. Allan, *John Egerton* [undated pamphlet in Durham University Library] • *VCH Berkshire*, vol. 2 • GEC, *Peerage*, new edn • *Newcastle Courant* (27 Jan 1787) • *Newcastle Chronicle* (27 Jan 1787) • speech at Egerton's enthronement by James Douglas, subdean, and Egerton's reply [pamphlet in Durham University Library] • Foster, *Alum. Oxon.*
Archives Herts. ALS, papers, mainly charges to clergy
Likenesses oils, *c.*1760, Auckland Castle, co. Durham [*see illus.*] • F. Bartolozzi, stipple (after I. Gosset), BM, NPG • oils, Durham Cathedral • two portraits, Durham Chapter Library

Egerton [*née* Compton], **Marianne Margaret**, **Viscountess Alford** [*known as* Lady Marian Alford] (1817–1888), art patron and writer on needlework, was born on 21 June 1817 in the Casa del Pre, Naples; she lived with her parents in Rome from 1820 to 1830, mostly in the Palazzo Sciarra. She was the second child of Spencer Joshua Alwyne *Compton, second marquess of Northampton (1790–1851), eldest surviving son of Charles Compton, ninth earl and first marquess of Northampton (1760–1828), and his wife, Margaret, *née* Maclean Clephane. Her mother died in 1830 and Lady Marian returned to England with her father, who had succeeded as second marquess of Northampton in 1828. She lived chiefly at Castle Ashby, Northamptonshire. A too liberal upbringing was possibly the root of Augustus Hare's remark that 'had the real greatness and goodness that were in her been regulated and disciplined by the circumstances of her early life she would have been one of the noblest women of her century' (Hare, 6.141–2). On 10 February 1841, at St George's, Hanover Square, London, she married John Hume Cust (afterwards Egerton), Viscount Alford (1812–1851), heir to John Cust, first Earl Brownlow. Her dark hair and eyes contrasted with the white and silver of her dress trimmed with white plumage, an effect marred only by her 'rough and red complexion' (Blake, 411). To have sat for five portraits indicates a touch of vanity, for Lady Marian was 'never handsome or really good looking, her figure was imposing and carriage stately' (Paget, 1.438–9). However, she was renowned for the beauty of her feet and her well-shaped hands, plump and white, which told particularly in a large woman.

Lord Alford, who changed his surname to Egerton in 1849, died in 1851 and by 1856 his widow showed 'a little tinge of graceful melancholy, just suiting her last stage of mourning' (Mrs Hugh Wyndham, ed., *Correspondence of Sarah Spencer, Lady Lyttelton*, 1912, 416–17). Their eldest son had succeeded as second Earl Brownlow in 1853 with an income of £100,000, and Lord Clarendon had predicted accurately—if uncharitably—that Lady Marian would

Marianne Margaret Egerton, Viscountess Alford (1817–1888), by unknown artist

'make a pretty hole in the fortune' (A. L. Kennedy, ed., *My Dear Duchess*, 1956, 120). Although Brownlow, a consumptive invalid, died at Menton in 1867, his younger brother inherited the earldom and her position was assured. Lady Marian's life became that of a wealthy aristocratic widow, making the round of country visits, generous in her hospitality at palatial Gothic Ashridge Park in Hertfordshire, at Belton House in Lincolnshire, and at 11 Prince's Gate, her London house. Winters were spent partly in Rome, where she was much influenced by the calculating and masculine American sculptor Harriet Hosmer, and commissioned the *Siren* fountain and a marble bust. Her admiration for Hosmer was such that she knelt down before her, placing on her finger a heart-shaped ruby and diamond ring.

Although Lady Marian was worldly and cultivated, her extravagance was 'nicely balanced with a personal charm' (Hare, 3.368). Lacking powers of discrimination, however, she was 'easily imposed upon and was apt to find herself in embarrassing situations' (GEC, *Peerage*). Her reverence for art was sometimes excessive but winning: Elizabeth Barrett Browning thought her 'very eager about literature and art showing the least little bit of affectation and fussiness' (Surtees, 126–7). Lady Marian was a knowledgeable and generous patron, a good critic, and exhibited talent as an accomplished amateur watercolourist. Her influence in forming the Royal School of Needlework under its president, Princess Christian—with herself, a skilled embroiderer, as vice-president—was widely acknowledged. Premises were secured in London in small rooms above a Sloane Street bonnet shop. In 1873, when more space was needed, the school moved to no. 31, exchanging in 1875 for a temporary home in Exhibition Road. The same year the school embarked on an ambitious building project on the west side of the street, completed in 1903. Lady Marian's book *Needlework as Art* (1886) is still recognized as a classic in its field. By her own practical knowledge she had elevated needlework to the status of a serious art form, creating a workshop where ancient and modern stitches could be learnt, the designs of any period imitated, and the repair of old work undertaken.

In 1872 Lady Marian moved into Alford House, Prince's Gate, decorated and built by Sir Matthew Digby Wyatt from her own designs. Notable for its moulded red brick, high roof, terracotta ornaments, and conservatory built to house the *Siren* fountain bought from Hosmer's studio, its chief peculiarity lay in the placing of the kitchen on the top floor. She conducted a lively correspondence with Disraeli and Gladstone; during the Franco-Prussian War she was strongly pro Prussian. Already infirm, she died peacefully at Ashridge on 8 February 1888, following a stroke. Her son and his wife knelt beside her 'each holding a beautiful hand', and her brother, the bishop of Ely, read prayers while she whispered the responses. Though a strong advocate of cremation she was buried at Belton in a spot she had chosen. As her memorial a white Iona cross was unveiled by her son in Ashridge's village of Little Gaddesden on 21 June 1891. Beneath is a fountain and trough for horses, and on the ground below a small one for dogs.

VIRGINIA SURTEES

Sources Lincs. Arch., Cust archives, Lady Marian Alford papers · *DNB* · A. J. C. Hare, *The story of my life*, 6 vols. (1896–1900) · GEC, *Peerage* · V. Surtees, *The Ludovisi goddess: the life of Louisa, Lady Ashburton* (1984) · R. Blake, *Disraeli*, another edn (1967) · W. Paget, *Embassies of other days* (1923) · *CGPLA Eng. & Wales* (1888)
Archives Lincs. Arch., Lady Marian Alford archives | BL, letters to Gladstone · Bodl. Oxf., letters to Disraeli
Likenesses F. Grant, two oils, 1841, Belton House, Lincolnshire · E. Cali, marble bust, 1857, Belton House, Lincolnshire · G. Zobel, mezzotint, 1863 (after J. R. Swinton), BM, NPG · British school, watercolour, Belton House, Lincolnshire · oils, Belton House, Lincolnshire [*see illus.*] · photographs, NPG
Wealth at death £24,968 4*s*. 8*d*.: probate, 12 July 1888, *CGPLA Eng. & Wales*

Egerton, Sir Philip (*d*. 1698), politician, was the fifth but second surviving son of Sir Rowland Egerton, first baronet (*d*. 1646), of Oulton, Cheshire, and his wife, Bridget (*d*. 1648), daughter of Arthur *Grey, fourteenth Baron Grey of Wilton. Egerton inherited the Oulton estate on his father's death, while his elder brother, John, inherited the baronetcy and estates in Staffordshire and Northamptonshire. In 1656 he married Catherine (*d*. 1707), daughter and heir of Piers Conway of Hendre, Flintshire. They had seven children, two of whom survived to adulthood, John Egerton and Philip Egerton (*d*. 1726), rector of Astbury, Cheshire. During his career Egerton acquired more land for the estate; his business interests included (by 1685) the long-established ironworks at Tib Green, near Nantwich, Cheshire. Egerton's father had lent Charles I money at the

start of the civil war, but later co-operated with parliament, which voted him thanks for bringing news of the surrender of Pontefract in 1645.

In 1659 Egerton's career took a decisively royalist path when he raised and equipped a troop of horse in Sir George Booth's rising in favour of Charles II, for which the king rewarded him with a knighthood on 23 June 1660. That April Egerton had become a captain of the militia horse, and from 1661 was a lieutenant-colonel; he took a part in investigating and suppressing any indications of rebellion as well as enforcing the penal laws against dissenters in Cheshire. Egerton stood as a country candidate at the 1670 by-election in Cheshire against Thomas Cholmondeley of Vale Royal, the court candidate, following unsuccessful negotiations among the gentry aimed at agreeing a single candidate. Cholmondeley had also taken part in Booth's rising and had been appointed sheriff of Cheshire at the Restoration. Egerton stood down after a three-day poll, conceding the election to Cholmondeley.

In 1673 Egerton was appointed deputy lieutenant of Cheshire when his relation John Egerton, second earl of Bridgewater, was appointed lord lieutenant. Egerton continued to serve as a deputy lieutenant following the appointment of William George Richard Stanley, ninth earl of Derby, as lord lieutenant of Cheshire in 1676.

Egerton did not run in the 1678 by-election, where Henry Booth was elected without opposition. Booth, like his father, Sir George Booth, by then first Baron Delamer, had become a vocal opponent of the government. In the elections for the first Exclusion Parliament in 1679, the Cheshire gentry met and agreed that Egerton and Booth would sit without opposition. Although Shaftesbury had listed Egerton as 'Honest', Egerton voted against the Exclusion Bill and was an active member sitting on fifteen committees, including the committees on the bills for protecting the country against popery and a bill which limited the importation of Irish cattle, which was very important to Cheshire.

It is not clear whether Egerton stood for the second Exclusion Parliament, but Sir Robert Cotton, an ally of Booth and a supporter of the Exclusion Bill, was returned in his place. In the 1681 election Robert Cholmondeley, first Viscount Cholmondeley, unsuccessfully tried to organize the Cheshire gentry to support Egerton and another court candidate, Sir Robert Leycester. He ordered that his cousin Francis Cholmondeley (the brother of Thomas, whose election Egerton had contested in 1670) make sure that Cholmondeley's tenants got out to vote. Egerton was described to the king as a 'very good man' (*CSP dom.*, *1680–81*, 152). Both Egerton and Leycester were defeated. Lord Cholmondeley complained after the election that Booth and Cotton spent vast sums during the election. Booth in turn branded Egerton's supporters 'Papists', and noted with satisfaction that during the election Booth and Cotton had received respectively 1500 and 1200 votes while Leycester had about 340 and Egerton only 280 votes.

After Charles II dissolved the Oxford parliament his illegitimate son James Scott, duke of Monmouth, arranged a tour of the north-west. Egerton's rivals, such as Booth, organized demonstrations in favour of Monmouth. Egerton helped the government gather intelligence about these activities, and took part in competing 'loyal gentry meeting[s] at a hunting and other sports in the forest', with his son winning a 'tumbler' at a foot-race (*CSP dom.*, 1682, 393).

The next major local contest was the mayoral election in Chester in 1682. One of Booth's allies, Colonel Roger Whitley, lost the race, and in response the 'mobile' (*CSP dom.*, 1682, 471) rioted and broke out the windows of Egerton's new Chester house. In 1683, after the discovery of the Rye House plot, Egerton, in his role as deputy lieutenant, was active in the harassment of the local whig gentry, including searching their houses for allegedly concealed arms. Egerton also supported the replacement of the charter for the city of Chester. During the delivery of the new charter Egerton joined the mayor, Sir Thomas Grosvenor, and 'a great many other gentlemen' (Hughes, 41–2) in a great celebration. Numerous whigs, such as the former mayor Whitley, were expressly excluded from being able to hold office under the new charter.

After James II's accession Egerton was again appointed deputy lieutenant for Cheshire, and stood as a court candidate at the hotly contested 1685 election. Booth had succeeded his father as second Baron Delamer, and the whigs advanced Booth's old ally, Sir Robert Cotton, together with John Mainwaring. Egerton was paired with his rival from the 1670 election, Thomas Cholmondeley (who was already or was to be the father-in-law of Egerton's oldest surviving son, John). Mainwaring's father in his diary complained bitterly that the sheriff manipulated the election by closing the poll early. Egerton and Cholmondeley were elected with 1966 and 2099 votes, compared to Mainwaring and Cotton getting 1682 and 1552. Egerton was again an active member of the Commons, where he served on eleven committees.

Egerton retained his militia command under James II, but it is not clear whether he was removed from his post as deputy lieutenant when Derby was removed in 1687. When Derby was restored to the lord lieutenancy of Cheshire, Egerton was either confirmed or reappointed by James on 3 November 1688.

Egerton did not sit in the Convention, and instead his 1685 rivals Sir Robert Cotton and John Mainwaring represented Cheshire. He became a nonjuror and in 1690 was imprisoned in Chester Castle as a Jacobite suspect. He was implicated in the 1694 'Lancashire plot' as being prepared to rise in support of James's restoration. He was not, however, tried for treason, and died at his home at Oulton, Cheshire, on 15 August 1698. He was buried at Little Budworth, Cheshire, and was survived by his wife and two sons. At her death in 1707, his wife left money to build a school at Oulton, which she endowed with £21 per annum to support the education of eight children.

JOHN H. RAINS, III

Sources G. Ormerod, *The history of the county palatine and city of Chester*, 3 vols. (1819), vol. 2, pp. 118–20, 350–51 · G. Hampson, 'Egerton, Sir Philip', HoP, *Commons, 1660–90* · G. Hampson and B. D. Henning, 'Cheshire', HoP, *Commons, 1660–90*, 1.151–2 · J. S. Morrill, 'Parliamentary representation', *VCH Cheshire*, 2.114–27 · H. Hughes, *Cheshire and its Welsh border* (1966) · *Third report*, HMC, 2 (1872), 245 · J. P. Earwaker, 'The "progress" of the duke of Monmouth in Cheshire, in September, 1682', *Transactions of the Historic Society of Lancashire and Cheshire*, 46 (1894), 71–96 · P. de M. Grey-Egerton, 'Published letter', *Transactions of the Historic Society of Lancashire and Cheshire*, 8 (1856), 243–4 · P. de M. Grey-Egerton, 'Some remarks on the lords lieutenants of the county palatine of Chester, from the Restoration to 1690', *Proceedings and Papers of the Historic Society of Lancashire and Cheshire*, 2 (1850), 124–36 · B. G. Awty, 'Charcoal, ironmasters of Cheshire and Lancashire, 1600–1785', *Transactions of the Historic Society of Lancashire and Cheshire*, 109 (1957), 71–94 · GEC, *Baronetage*, 1.108 · *CSP dom.*, 1665–6, 8; 1670, 30; 1672–3, 598–9; 1680–81, 52, 198; 1682, 393, 471–2; 1687–9, 340 · P. de M. Grey-Egerton, 'Papers referring to elections of knights of the shire of the county palatine of Chester', *Journal of the Architectural, Archaeological, and Historical Society for the County, City, and Neighbourhood of Chester*, 1 (1857), 101–12 · Burke, *Peerage* (1999)

Archives Ches. & Chester ALSS, deeds, estate and household papers · Ches. & Chester ALSS, estate and family papers

Egerton, Sir Philip de Malpas Grey-, tenth baronet (1806–1881), palaeontologist and politician, was born on 13 November 1806, probably at his father's residence, Oulton Park, Tarporley, Cheshire. He was the eldest son of the Revd Sir Philip Grey-Egerton, ninth baronet (1767–1829), and Rebecca, daughter of Josias Du Pré of Wilton Park, Buckinghamshire. He was educated at Eton College until 1825 and then at Christ Church, Oxford, where he graduated BA in 1828. While an undergraduate Egerton (as he was known—his father assumed the name Grey-Egerton in 1825) was attracted to geology, which he studied under William Buckland and William Conybeare, and in conjunction with his college friend Viscount Cole (afterwards earl of Enniskillen) he devoted himself to the collection of fossil fish. The friends travelled together over Germany, Switzerland, and Italy in pursuit of this object, and accumulated many specimens of unique value.

In 1830 Egerton was elected member of parliament for Chester as a tory. He unsuccessfully contested the southern division of the county in 1832, but was successful in 1835. He continuously represented the division until 1868, when he was elected for West Cheshire, which he represented until his death. In 1832 he married Anna Elizabeth (d. 1882), second daughter of George J. Legh, of High Legh, Cheshire; the couple had two sons and two daughters.

While sedulously discharging his political duties, especially on committees, Egerton never ceased to add to his collection of fossil fish. Many of the fish described in the monographs of Louis Agassiz (1807–1873) and in the *Decades of the Geological Survey of Great Britain* belonged to the Egerton collection. Egerton himself contributed the descriptions in the sixth, eighth, and ninth *Decades*. He published several catalogues of his collection of fossil fish. In 1837 he produced *A systematic and stratigraphical catalogue of the fossil fish in the cabinets of Lord Cole and Sir Philip Grey Egerton*, which included references to his published figures and descriptions. He later published a greater catalogue, entitled *Alphabetical Catalogue of Type Specimens of Fossil Fishes* (1871).

From 1833 onwards Egerton contributed over eighty

memoirs or short papers, chiefly relating to fossil fish, to the Geological Society's *Transactions*, *Proceedings*, and *Journal* and to other scientific journals. He edited several memoirs published by the Camden and Chetham societies, and also issued *Papers relating to elections of knights of the shire for the county palatine of Chester, from the death of Oliver Cromwell to the accession of Queen Anne* (1852) and *A short account of the possessors of Oulton … until the accession to the baronetcy on the death of Thomas, first earl of Wilton* (1869) for private distribution.

Egerton was elected fellow of the Geological Society in 1829 and of the Royal Society in 1831, and was awarded the Wollaston medal of the Geological Society in 1873. In 1879 the Chester Society of Natural Science gave him the first Kingsley medal for his services to the society and to the literature and history of the county. He served science assiduously for many years as a member of the councils of the Royal and Geological societies, and as a trustee of the British Museum and of the Royal College of Surgeons. He was also a member of the senate of the University of London.

Egerton died at his home, 28B Albemarle Street, London, on 5 April 1881, after a very brief illness. His funeral was, by his own request, extremely simple; after expressing his wishes he concluded his instructions thus: 'I trust in God's mercy, through Jesus Christ, that the occasion may be one of rejoicing rather than of mourning'. Egerton's elder son, Philip le Belward, succeeded to the baronetcy; Lady Egerton died in 1882.

Egerton was not merely a collector but a careful scientific observer, and a good naturalist. He also had great business ability and good judgement, and was of a genial and kindly disposition, which made him very popular with political opponents. His collection of fossil fish, as well as that of Lord Enniskillen, was acquired for the British Museum (Natural History), South Kensington, London.   G. T. BETTANY, rev. YOLANDA FOOTE

Sources *Chester Chronicle* (9 April 1881) · *Nature* (21 April 1881) · R. Etheridge, *Quarterly Journal of the Geological Society*, 38 (1882), 46–8 · *PRS*, 33 (1881–2), xxii–iv · Foster, *Alum. Oxon.* · *Thom's British directory* (1873)
Archives Elgin Museum, letters to George Gordon · GS Lond., letters to Sir R. I. Murchison · NHM, letters to Albert Gunther and R. W. T. Gunther · NHM, corresp. with Richard Owen and William Clift · NLNZ, Alexander Turnbull Library, letters to Gideon Algernon Mantell
Likenesses F. C. Lewis, engraving (after G. Richmond), RS; negative, RS · F. C. Lewis, stipple (after G. Richmond), BM, NPG · Maull & Polyblank, photograph, RS · S. W. Reynolds, mezzotint (after J. Bostock), NPG
Wealth at death under £30,000: probate, 31 May 1881, CGPLA Eng. & Wales

Egerton, Sir Ralph (*b.* before **1476**, *d.* **1528**), courtier and administrator, was a younger son of Hugh Egerton of Wrinehill in Cheshire, who died in 1505, about eighty years old. His mother was possibly the Margaret Dutton whom Hugh married in 1446, but Ralph's omission from the entail of the Egerton estate suggests that he may have been the son of a second wife, also named Margaret. He was probably of age by 1496 when his father made him

independent by the gift of a wich of six leads in Nantwich, and so was born not later than 1475.

By 1501 Ralph Egerton was marshal of the hall to Prince Arthur, earl of Chester, and on the latter's death in 1502 entered the royal household as a gentleman usher in daily waiting. Earlier the same year he was at the home of his half-sister Eleanor Bassett at Blore in Staffordshire, apparently intending to be betrothed or married to her daughter Margaret (*d.* 1534), the wealthy widow of Serjeant Thomas Kebell. Margaret, however, was abducted by retainers of the Vernon family and, despite pursuit by the Bassetts and Egerton, was forcibly married to Roger, the son and heir of Sir Henry Vernon of Haddon. Margaret proved implacable and after escaping made a personal appeal to Henry VII. Eventually that and her parallel appeal to the church courts were successful and she and Ralph were dispensed to marry in 1509.

Under Henry VIII Egerton became enormously successful, benefiting particularly from grants (including the keepership of the Cheshire lordship of Ridley) lost by William Smith of the council learned, a colleague of Empson and Dudley. Egerton fought in the Greenwich barriers of June 1510 and served as standard-bearer in the 1513 invasion of France. According to the pro-Howard 'Ballate of the Battalle of Floden Feeld' (datable as 1521–44, possibly 1521–8), Egerton was in the thick of a quarrel which arose in the English camp at Tournai when the first reports of the battle received from England suggested that the Cheshire and Lancashire levies had broken and fled. When fuller reports arrived showing that this was true only on the left wing and that men from the two counties had played a vital part in the victory overall, Egerton and others from the region were rewarded. He received Ridley outright and was made standard-bearer for life; once Tournai had been captured he was knighted. He became a knight of the body and further grants followed as he continued to appear in jousts and court festivities. In all he acquired at least fifteen crown offices and three valuable leases and three annuities; when he made his will in 1520, he had more than £400 available in cash.

Egerton attended Henry at the Field of Cloth of Gold, at the meeting with Charles V at Gravelines, and during Charles's visit to England in 1522. He effectively retired as standard-bearer in 1524 and was among the king's justices sent on one of Henry VIII's periodic attempts to prop up English authority in Ireland. The mission was (somewhat optimistically) counted a success and Egerton was appointed treasurer on the council for the marches of Wales then being set up under the nominal headship of Princess Mary. Nothing is known of his activity as her treasurer, but jointly with the chamberlain of Chester he was instructed to levy the 1525 amicable grant in the county palatine. The association is piquant since a struggle was developing between Egerton and the chamberlain's son William Brereton over the succession to Sir Ralph's crown patents. The struggle was principally fought out at court but also on the ground in Cheshire with evictions enforced by violence. A particular focus of contention was the park of Shotwick-on-Dee, where Brereton attempted to impugn Egerton's title for life and eventually obtained the property after Sir Ralph's heir accepted arbitration.

Egerton's passion in his declining years was his chantry chapel at Bunbury. He had already embellished the gate-house of Ridley Hall, 'the fairest gentleman's howse of all Chestreshire' (Leland, 5.28), and the brief for the chapel is laid down in meticulous details in his will, along with its armorial plate and the description, 'The Kinges Standertberer and Thresaurer to my lady Princess' (Ives, 'Patronage', 370). He died on 9 March 1528 and was buried at Bunbury. The chapel survives (effectively stripped), as does the associated priests' house; what remains of the magnificent roof covers a nearby barn. As well as his heir, Richard, Egerton left two named bastard children and other bastard daughters whose names he could not remember. Richard's bastard son was Thomas Egerton, Lord Ellesmere.   E. W. IVES

Sources E. W. Ives, 'Patronage at the court of Henry VIII: the case of Sir Ralph Egerton of Ridley', *Bulletin of the John Rylands Library*, 52 (1970), 346–74 • G. Ormerod, *The history of the county palatine and city of Chester*, 2nd edn, ed. T. Helsby, 3 vols. (1882) • *Letters and accounts of William Brereton*, ed. E. W. Ives, Lancashire and Cheshire RS, 116 (1976) • E. W. Ives, 'Court and county palatine', *Transactions of the History Society of Lancashire and Cheshire*, 123 (1972), 1–38 • E. W. Ives, '"Against taking awaye of women": the inception and operation of the Abduction Act of 1487', *Wealth and power in Tudor England: essays presented to S. T. Bindoff*, ed. E. W. Ives, R. J. Knecht, and J. J. Scarisbrick (1978), 21–44 • F. J. Child, ed., *Popular ballads* (1889); repr. (1957), 353–62 • *The itinerary of John Leland in or about the years 1535–1543*, ed. L. Toulmin Smith, 11 pts in 5 vols. (1906–10), vol. 4, p. 3; vol. 5, p. 28 • T. Thornton, *Cheshire and the Tudor state* (2000)

Egerton [*née* Fyge; *other married name* Field], **Sarah** (1670–1723), poet, was born in London, one of the six daughters of Thomas Fyge (*d.* 1706), physician and city councilman who was descended from a landowning family of Winslow, Buckinghamshire, and his wife, Mary Beacham (*d.* 1704), of Seaton, Rutland.

Little is known of Sarah Fyge's education; however, she was certainly precocious. She claimed to have been 'scarce fourteen years' when she wrote *The Female Advocate*, her most important work, which was published in 1686. The poem, a long verse satire, was one of many responses to Robert Gould's popular verse satire, *Love Given O're* (1682). Her father objected to her poetry and sent her to live with relatives in Shenley, Buckinghamshire, about 1687. Following this banishment she was married, apparently against her will, to an attorney named Edward Field. During this marriage they lived in or near London. Edward Field was dead by the mid-1690s. In 1700 she contributed an ode on the death of John Dryden: *Luctus Britannici, or, The Tears of the British Muses*, and she also contributed to *The Nine Muses* (1700), a volume of poems by women in memory of Dryden edited by Mary Delarivier Manley, with whom she had an intense but short-lived friendship.

Some time between 1700 and 1703 Sarah married the Revd Thomas Egerton (*d.* 1720), rector of Adstock, Buckinghamshire, a second cousin about twenty years her senior, and a widower. At the time of her second marriage she was in love with Henry Pierce, an attorney's clerk and associate of her first husband. By 1703 Sarah and Thomas Egerton were embroiled in an apparently unsuccessful suit for divorce. Their marriage was notoriously unhappy. Delarivier Manley records somewhat maliciously a 'comical Combat' between the Egertons, in which Sarah throws a pie at her husband's face, and dumps butter and drink over his head while he grapples with her topknot.

In 1703 Egerton published, against her husband's wishes, *Poems on Several Occasions*. Apart from angry descriptions of the narrowness of a woman's lot, the poems also describe the poet's feelings for Pierce, whom she calls Alexis. This volume was reissued in 1706, the same year that *The Female Advocate* was reprinted bearing the date 1707. After this time information about Egerton is sparse. Her husband died in 1720, leaving her a childless widow in comfortable circumstances. She died in Winslow on 13 February 1723.   RICHARD GREENE, *rev.*

Sources [D. Manley], *Secret memoirs and manners of several persons of quality of both sexes, from the New Atalantis*, 2 vols. (1709) • M. D. Manley, *Memoirs of Europe* (1710) • J. Medoff, 'New light on Sarah Fyge (Field, Egerton)', *Tulsa Studies in Women's Literature*, 1 (1982), 155–75 • J. Todd, ed., *A dictionary of British and American women writers, 1660–1800* (1984) • R. Lonsdale, ed., *Eighteenth-century women poets: an Oxford anthology* (1989)

Egerton [*née* Fisher], **Sarah** (1782×5–1847), actress, was one of the nine children of Peter Fisher (1748/9–1803), rector of Little Torrington, Devon, and his wife, Jane (1749/50–1832). After the death of her father she took to the stage, and appeared at Bath on 3 December 1803 as Emma in John Till Allingham's *The Marriage Promise*, which performance gained her the patronage of the duchess of Devonshire and Lord Boringdon. She remained in Bath for six or seven years, playing as a rule secondary characters. Her last benefit there took place on 21 March 1809, when she played Gunilda in W. W. Dimond's *The Hero of the North* and Emmeline in John Hawkesworth's *Edgar and Emmeline*. She probably married Daniel *Egerton (1772–1835) soon afterwards. He was playing leading business in Bath, and was said to be 'in love up to his false collar'. The first recorded appearance of Mrs Egerton was at Birmingham in 1810. On 25 February 1811, as 'Mrs Egerton from Birmingham', she played Juliet at Covent Garden, but with no very conspicuous success. The roles of Marcia in *Cato*, Luciana in *The Comedy of Errors*, and Emilia in *Othello* followed during the same season, but she could not compete with the formidable opposition of Sarah Siddons and subsequently of Eliza O'Neill, and it was not until she took to melodrama that her position was assured. In October 1813 she was the original Ravina in *The Miller and his Men* by Pocock. On 8 February 1816 she took over Julia Glover's role in *Accusation*, but was reported to be equally bad in both the tragic and the comic aspects of the part.

Sarah Egerton was rescued from obscurity by a series of roles in adaptations of Scott's Waverley novels. *Guy Mannering, or, The Gipsy's Prophecy*, by Daniel Terry, was produced at Covent Garden on 12 March 1816. John Emery was originally cast for Meg Merrilies, but refused positively to take the part. Under these circumstances the management turned almost in despair to Mrs Egerton, whose success proved to be conspicuous. The role of Helen Macgregor in Pocock's *Rob Roy Macgregor, or, Auld Lang Syne* followed in 1818. Her services having been dispensed with at Covent Garden (the result of 'a pitiful economy'), she moved to the Surrey, where she played Madge Wildfire in Thomas Dibdin's *The Heart of Midlothian, or, The Lily of St Leonard's* in 1819 and then Young Norval in John Home's *Douglas*, played as a melodrama. In 1819–20 she appeared at Drury Lane, at that time under R. W. Elliston's management, as Meg Merrilies. During this and the following seasons she played a variety of roles in tragedy, melodrama, and even comedy: she was Gertrude to Kean's Hamlet, and appeared as Clementina Allspice in T. Morton's *The Way to Get Married*, and as Volumnia in *Coriolanus*, among many other characters. When, in 1821, her husband took Sadler's Wells, she appeared with conspicuous success as Joan of Arc in Edward Fitzball's drama, which was otherwise considered a miserable production. Thereafter she played in melodrama at the Olympic, also under her husband's management. Soon after Egerton's death in 1835 she retired from the stage, and accepted a pension from the Covent Garden Fund. She died at Chelsea on 3 August 1847, and was buried on 7 August in Chelsea churchyard. While she was only a third-rate actress in tragedy, she approached the first rank in melodrama.

JOSEPH KNIGHT, *rev.* J. GILLILAND

Sources Mrs C. Baron-Wilson, *Our actresses*, 2 vols. (1844) · *Theatrical Inquisitor* · 'Memoir of Mrs Egerton', *Oxberry's Dramatic Biography*, 4/62 (1826), 235–42 · Adams, *Drama* · Genest, *Eng. stage* · *The Era* (15 Aug 1847) · 'Mrs Egerton', *The biography of the British stage, being correct narratives of the lives of all the principal actors and actresses* (1824), 51–3 · W. C. Lane and N. E. Browne, eds., *A. L. A. portrait index* (1906) · Hall, *Dramatic ports.* · *Drama, or, Theatrical Pocket Magazine*, 5 (1823–4) · C. W. Boase, ed., *Registrum Collegii Exoniensis*, new edn, OHS, 27 (1894)

Likenesses S. De Wilde, watercolour and chalk drawing, 1816, BM · S. De Wilde, portrait, Garr. Club · Williams, engraving, repro. in 'Memoir of Mrs Egerton', 235 · engraving (as Meg Merrilies), repro. in *Theatrical Inquisitor*, 10 (1817) · portraits, Harvard TC · prints, BM, NPG

Egerton, Stephen (*c.*1555–1622), Church of England clergyman, was born in London, fifth son of Thomas Egerton, mercer, and his wife, Anne (*née* Langton). The chronology of his university career suggests that he was born about 1555. He graduated BA from Peterhouse, Cambridge, in 1576, proceeded MA in 1579, and secured a fellowship that year only after the intervention of Lord Burghley, and 'even against the mind of Dr Perne, then Master' (*Salisbury MSS*, 11.157). Ordained priest at Peterborough on 11 May 1581, he seems to have settled in the London liberty of St Ann Blackfriars in late 1583 or early 1584. On 4 May 1585, resigning his fellowship, he was married there to Sara (*d.* 1624), daughter of Thomas *Crooke, and by 1586 was officially described as parish lecturer.

Since the dissolution attempts by the bishops of London to exert control over the liberty had met with limited success, its ministers being appointed at the grace and favour of its lay owners, the More (or Moore) family. On 18 July 1578 John Aylmer took the draconian step of placing it under an interdict because the incumbent minister, Thomas Sperin, did not observe the Book of Common Prayer. In mid-September the interdict was relaxed when Sperin and his churchwardens agreed to do so.

It remained a partial victory. Egerton joined the nonconformist clerical conference which met secretly under the auspices of John Field, who now hoped to introduce the Book of Discipline into a programme of ecclesiastical reform, and whilst Egerton's reasons for refusing subscription to Archbishop Whitgift's articles in 1584 are preserved along with Field's, there is no evidence that he was suspended as a result. On 6 July 1588 Aylmer ordered the (unnamed) preacher, minister, and churchwardens to admit none to communion but their own parishioners, whilst at the episcopal visitation of 1589 Egerton was enjoined to administer communion himself or else assist his curate. In 1590 he was a delegate to a 'synod' at Cambridge and attended the last major London conference that same year.

Like many radical London clergy Egerton was recruited by the government to examine and refute the leaders of separatism. The conference which he and Sperin conducted in the Fleet prison with Henry Barrow and John Greenwood on 20 March 1590 survives along with the exchange of letters which followed. In 1591, pestered with unsolicited messages from Edmund Coppinger, Egerton quickly distanced himself from the former's fanatically presbyterian stratagems. This episode belies the tradition that late in 1590 he was imprisoned by Whitgift for three years. No such imprisonment is mentioned by John Strype or Benjamin Brook, whilst Egerton was listed as preacher at Blackfriars (but absent) during Aylmer's last visitation in 1592.

At about this time Egerton published a translation from the French of Matthew Virel, *A Learned and Excellent Treatise Containing All Principal Grounds of the Christian Religion*. A fourteenth edition appeared in 1635. *A Brief Method of Catechizing* (1594) achieved a forty-fourth in 1644.

In November 1596 Egerton was amongst those who successfully petitioned against the conversion of James Burbage's Blackfriars property into a playhouse. During Richard Bancroft's primary visitation in 1598 he was again ordered to observe the ceremonies. Bancroft claimed that he was the only city minister who had not 'conformed' at this time, Robert, earl of Essex, having undertaken that he should behave 'in peaceable sort' (*Salisbury MSS*, 11.154).

In the aftermath of Essex's rebellion in February 1601 Bancroft ordered the preaching of official sermons throughout the capital but, dissatisfied with Egerton's, suspended his twice-weekly lectures. When Sir Robert Cecil hinted that a satisfactory account of himself might save him from Bancroft's further attentions, Egerton penned two dignified letters, observing that he had taken the oath of supremacy five or six times and always approved the article on obedience to the civil magistrate. For his part Bancroft reminded Cecil that Egerton had been involved in 'the pretended presbyterial discipline' fifteen years before, meanly noting that he had also been 'acquainted' with Coppinger's activities, but added that if Egerton could satisfy Cecil about his 'loose dealing' he was 'after a sort for quietness, so as you undertake for him' (*Salisbury MSS*, 11.154).

Under Cecil's protection Egerton thus remained undisturbed for the rest of Bancroft's episcopate. In March 1603 he and Arthur Hildersham were amongst the chief organizers of the millenary petition to James I and, with Edward Fleetwood, prepared 'instructions' for the delegates to the Hampton Court conference. On 2 May 1604 Egerton, Fleetwood, and Anthony Wotton urged convocation to consider the revision of the prayer book.

After the promulgation of the constitutions and canons of 1604 King James insisted upon subscription to Whitgift's articles, now incorporated within them, and yet when Bancroft conducted his final visitation later that year Egerton remained undisturbed. According to Sir Thomas Posthumus Hoby, writing on 28 January 1605, Bancroft summoned the London clergy on his elevation to Canterbury in December but 'passed over' Egerton on the grounds that 'he was not to proceed against lecturers'. Yet his successor Richard Vaughan—'I fear by his grace's special directions'—now proposed to suspend him. Hoby reminded Cecil that Egerton had ministered 'twenty-two years without detection'—further evidence that he had never been imprisoned—and that since Blackfriars maintained a conforming curate he himself was not bound by law to use the prayer book (*Salisbury MSS*, 17.38).

Although there can be no doubt that Vaughan, highly sympathetic to moderate puritan aspirations, soon restored Egerton, the experience seems to have induced a mysterious, self-imposed silence on the latter for the rest of his life. Seldom mentioned in the Blackfriars records after 1604 he perhaps formally relinquished the lectureship in 1607, for Blackfriars was 'destitute of a preaching minister' in June 1608, when Hildersham recommended William Gouge (Clarke, 242).

Egerton contributed commendatory prefaces to the works of many godly writers, including Richard Rogers's *Seven Treatises* (1604). In 1615 the merchant adventurer William Jones left £1000 to be distributed to poor preachers, appointing Egerton one of three trustees. In 1620 he received a legacy from his younger sister, Anne, Lady Tyndall, whose daughter Margaret had in 1618 married John Winthrop, later governor of Massachusetts.

Egerton's original will survives, written in a steady, crabbed hand on 12 April 1622. A simple protestant preamble preceded six simple bequests: £5 each to his brother Thomas, to two female relatives, and to his servant; 40s. to the poor of Blackfriars; the residue to Sara as sole executrix. His four overseers, including William Gouge and the preacher Richard Stock, each received 20s. for a memorial ring.

Egerton died in St Ann Blackfriars and was buried there on 7 May 1622. He must have left Sara considerably better off than his will suggests for in her own, dated 19 August 1624, she left legacies totalling nearly £600, including £100 to her 'loving cousin' Margaret Winthrop. William Gouge was appointed overseer.   BRETT USHER

Sources Venn, *Alum. Cant.*, 1/2.91 · T. A. Walker, *A biographical register of Peterhouse men*, 2 (1930) · B. Burch, 'The parish of St Anne's Blackfriars, London, to 1665', *Guildhall Miscellany*, 3 (1969–71), 1–54 · R. G. Usher, ed., *The presbyterian movement in the reign of Queen Elizabeth, as illustrated by the minute book of the Dedham classis, 1582–1589*, CS, 3rd ser., 8 (1905) · *The writings of John Greenwood, 1587–1590*, ed. L. H. Carlson (1962) · *The writings of John Greenwood and Henry Barrow, 1591–1593*, ed. L. H. Carlson (1970) · *The diary of John Manningham of the Middle Temple, 1602–1603*, ed. R. P. Sorlien (Hanover, NH, 1976) · *Calendar of the manuscripts of the most hon. the marquis of Salisbury*, 11, HMC, 9 (1906) · *Calendar of the manuscripts of the most hon. the marquess of Salisbury*, 17, HMC, 9 (1938) · inhibition of Aylmer, 1588, LMA, DL/C/333, fols. 120r, 122v; DL/C/334, fol. 229r · call books of visitation, 1586–98, GL, MSS 9537/6–9 · P. S. Seaver, *The puritan lectureships: the politics of religious dissent, 1560–1662* (1970) · S. B. Babbage, *Puritanism and Richard Bancroft* (1962) · A. Walsham, '"Frantick Hacket": prophecy, sorcery, insanity, and the Elizabethan puritan movement', *HJ*, 41 (1998), 27–66 · S. Clarke, *The lives of thirty two English divines*, in *A general martyrologie*, 3rd edn (1677) · B. Brook, *The lives of the puritans*, 3 vols. (1813) · E. K. Chambers, *The Elizabethan stage*, rev. edn, 4 vols. (1951) · N. Tyacke, *The fortunes of English puritanism, 1603–1640* (1990) · original will, LMA, DL/C/419/188 · will of Sara Egerton, PRO, PROB 11/144, sig. 110, fol. 359v · A. Peel, ed., *The seconde parte of a register*, 2 vols. (1915) · P. Collinson, *The Elizabethan puritan movement* (1967) · R. Cooke, *Visitation of London, 1568*, ed. H. Stanford London and S. W. Rawlins, [new edn], 2 vols. in one, Harleian Society, 109–10 (1963) · parish register, St Ann Blackfriars, London, 7 May 1622 [burial]

Archives BL, sermon notes in Gilbert Frevile's commonplace book, Egerton MS 2877 · BL, Robert Smarte's letter-book, Sloane MS 271 · Hatfield House, Hertfordshire, Hatfield MSS, letters to Robert Cecil

Wealth at death will, LMA, DL/C/419/188 · est. £1000 in liquid capital: will, 1624, PRO, PROB 11/144, sig. 110, fol. 359v [Sara Egerton]

Egerton, Thomas, first Viscount Brackley (1540–1617),

lord chancellor, was born on 23 January 1540, the illegitimate son of Sir Richard Egerton, landowner, of Ridley, Cheshire, and a servant girl called Alice Sparke. His father's family claimed descent from Robert Fitzhugh, baron of Malpas, a contemporary of William I, and had assumed their surname from Egerton in Cheshire during the thirteenth century. One of several illegitimate siblings, Thomas Egerton was brought up in the household of Thomas Ravenscroft (d. c.1553), of Bretton, Flintshire, and his wife, Katherine.

Early career, 1556–1581 Egerton entered Brasenose College, Oxford, in 1556 and was on 31 October 1560 admitted to Lincoln's Inn, where he became caught up in a notorious Catholic circle. He escaped censure from Star Chamber in 1569, when several members of the inn were imprisoned, and produced a certificate of conformity; but his call to the bar was postponed until 1572, the same year in which Edward Coke—twelve years his junior—was called. Egerton's law books and commonplace book, which survive, bear signs of intense study in these years. Among them is a manuscript 'discourse' on statutes and their interpretation, written in the 1560s, which has been tentatively ascribed to him. By 1576 he was sufficiently established in his profession to marry his stepfather's youngest daughter, Elizabeth (d. 1588). The couple had two sons, John *Egerton, first earl of Bridgewater (1579–1649), and Sir Thomas Egerton (1574–1599). After only seven years'

Thomas Egerton, first Viscount Brackley (1540–1617), by unknown artist

call Thomas Egerton the elder became a bencher of his inn in 1579, and in 1582 he delivered the Lent reading, choosing a recent statute concerning letters patent. A good practice was established during this period, with the patronage of the Ravenscrofts and Grosvenors, kinsmen of his stepmother, William Chaderton, bishop of Chester, Henry Stanley, fourth earl of Derby, and Robert Dudley, earl of Leicester.

Solicitor-general and attorney-general, 1581–1596 Private practice continued into the 1590s, but was increasingly submerged by the duties of public office. On 26 June 1581 Egerton was appointed solicitor-general, supposedly at Elizabeth I's personal insistence. In 1582 he was elected recorder of Lichfield, Staffordshire, and in 1584 and 1586 he was returned as MP for Cheshire. He represented Reading in parliament in 1589. Since Egerton's student days the papal bull *Regnans in excelsis* of 1570 had polarized religious inclinations, and as a law officer of the crown in the 1580s he necessarily laid aside any youthful sympathies for the Catholic cause. Egerton became heavily involved in the prosecution of recusants and Jesuits, including William Vaux, third Baron Vaux, and St Edmund Campion (1581), not to mention Mary, queen of Scots (1586), Thomas Percy, sixth earl of Northumberland (1585), the Babington conspirators (1586), Philip Howard, earl of Arundel (1589), and Sir John Perrot (1592). He became in course of time a Calvinist, implacably imposed to 'the devilish doctrine of Rome' (Hunt. L., Ellesmere MS EL 459, fol. 1r). However, in 1588, and later as lord keeper of the great seal, he said that a distinction was to be made concerning recusants: 'some

are simple and led by error—those he pitied and was not forward to punish—others dangerous, wilful and seditious' (Hawarde, 164). Elizabeth Russell, dowager Baroness Russell, reported that many thought him 'an arrant hypocrite and deep dissembler' (Hunt. L., Ellesmere MS EL 46, fol. 1r). Nevertheless, his ability and judgement were widely recognized, both within the profession and at court. He became a particular friend in the 1590s of the young Robert Devereux, second earl of Essex.

Already by 1592 Egerton was spoken of as a possible lord keeper; but instead he became on 2 June 1592 attorney-general, a post he occupied for only two years. In February 1594, already the most important member of the queen's council in the marches of Wales (to which he had been appointed in 1586), he was made chamberlain of Chester and knighted. On 10 April 1594 he began his long judicial association with the court of chancery when he was appointed master of the rolls. Egerton entered into the position with characteristic zeal, and immediately set about restoring some of its prerogatives. He recovered possession of the Rolls Chapel, which had been unlawfully alienated under his predecessors, and obtained the annulment of some earlier reversionary grants of offices in his gift, though he was less successful in fighting off other interferences with his patronage and failed in his attempt to bring the public records at the Tower of London under his control. Although his efforts were largely self-interested, Egerton as head of the chancery administration was concerned at growing court interference with his department for reasons of financial gain.

Lord keeper, 1596–1617 On 6 May 1596, on the death of Sir John Puckering, Egerton was appointed to succeed him as lord keeper, being allowed to retain the mastership of the rolls until the queen should choose a successor—which she never did. Again he seems to have been Elizabeth's personal choice; and on handing over the seal on 6 May she reduced Egerton to tears with an affecting speech in which she prophesied correctly that he would be her last lord keeper. Although the appointment was not fully welcomed by the Cecils, it is said that there was no serious competitor, and the general reaction seems to have been favourable. The unprecedented conjunction of offices did little for the dispatch of business, but it put Egerton in a unique position to reform the chancery system, and he took the opportunity to improve procedure and efficiency by issuing several new practice directions and by settling an approved scale of fees. He took great pains to inform himself as to the history of chancery and Star Chamber, with a view to establishing their jurisdictions, and employed William Lambarde to collect materials from the records. It is generally supposed that Egerton's best work was achieved in the 1590s, though he was too conservative and too touchy about his own sources of income for radical reform to be contemplated.

In 1597 Egerton married as his second wife Elizabeth (*d.* 1600), daughter of Sir William More of Loseley, Surrey, and his wife, Margaret, and widow of Sir John Wolley, Latin secretary and clerk of the pipe, and of Richard Polsted. The marriage ended with Elizabeth Egerton's death only three years later in January 1600, coming close on that of Egerton's eldest son, Sir Thomas Egerton, on 23 August 1599, of wounds received while serving in Ireland with Essex. Egerton suffered the further blow of a personal betrayal by the earl, whom he had befriended in his troubles. Egerton chose as his third wife Alice *Spencer (1559–1637), literary patron, daughter of Sir John Spencer of Althorp, Northampton, and his wife, Katherine, and widow of Ferdinando Stanley, fifth earl of Derby, whom he had served as an adviser. They married in October 1600. Like his second marriage, this one produced no children. The marriage brought Egerton further wealth but untold misery. A prominent lady of the court, and a cultured patron of literature, the beautiful and wealthy dowager countess of Derby must have seemed a good match. She had been left extensive property around Brackley in Northamptonshire and in neighbouring counties, secured by chancery decree. However, she was haughty, profligate, greedy, and ill-tempered, and added greatly to her husband's burdens for the last seventeen years of his life. 'I thank God I never desired long life', wrote Egerton in 1610, 'nor ever had less cause to desire it than since this, my last marriage, for before I was never acquainted with such tempests and storms' (*CSP dom.*, *1611–18*, 527).

On the accession of James I, Egerton was reappointed lord keeper and advanced to the peerage on 21 July 1603 as Baron Ellesmere, of Ellesmere in Shropshire (where he was given a large estate), but at the king's behest relinquished the rolls in favour of the Scottish lawyer Edward Bruce. On 24 July Egerton was appointed lord chancellor, relinquishing his position as lord keeper. He presided over the chancery and Star Chamber for another fourteen years, and also conducted a number of state trials, notably those of Sir Walter Ralegh (1603), the gunpowder plotters (1605), and Robert Carr, earl of Somerset, and his wife, Frances (1616). In his judicial roles he did not always maintain a proper independence—for instance, he did not scruple to make a decree in favour of his bride-to-be in 1600, which greatly enriched himself—and in the Somerset case he was alleged by Coke to have summed up the prosecution case after the prisoner had left the bar, without referring to his defence, and adding new information which had not been given in evidence. Moreover, according to Coke, Ellesmere 'told the king that he as chancellor was keeper of the king's conscience and therefore whatsoever the king directed in any case he would decree accordingly' (CUL, MS Ii.5.21, fol. 47v). On the other hand, Ellesmere's manner of dispensing justice in ordinary cases, at any rate in his earlier years, had impressed the profession. It was during his time that the first specialist reports of chancery cases were preserved, and also the first extensive Star Chamber reports (written by John Hawarde). It may be significant that the reports end in the early years of James's reign and that few of Ellesmere's later pronouncements were preserved.

Ellesmere encouraged favourites at the bar, and was an especial patron of Sir Francis Bacon, who became the first queen's counsel-extraordinary in 1596. They worked closely together on matters of state, and Bacon—probably at his suggestion—eventually succeeded him in office. Ellesmere could be very sharp with lesser practitioners who exceeded their duty. He once promised to 'abolish and extirpate all solicitors', whom he called 'caterpillars of the common weal' (Hawarde, 45–6)—a description which he applied equally to uneducated barristers—and also proposed to reduce the number of attorneys. He was even sharper with criminal defendants, and was fond of telling them that punishments ought to be heavier than the law permitted. Slander was an especial bugbear, and in passing sentence he often remarked that in other times and places it was punished with loss of the tongue. 'Thought is free, but the tongue should be governed by knowledge' (ibid., 66).

Jurisprudence and politics Ellesmere's approach to the law was essentially conservative, and he regretted recent reforms in common-law procedure which had rendered the medieval learning as to real actions obsolete. He also attacked the king's bench latitat, which had simplified mesne process and amplified the court's business, saying that 'the original writ is the true, ancient and best course, and safest for every man to use' (Hawarde, 326). Here again, an underlying reason for his opposition was financial, in that chancery stood to lose fines on original writs. In parliament he effectively stifled a Commons proposal to abolish the incidents of tenure, which would not only have made the king financially dependent on parliament but would have struck at the roots of the feudal common law and the monarchy as Ellesmere saw it. Legislation was another matter. He said that the Statute *De donis* (1285), which made entails possible, was 'made but upon a singularity of conceit and that it had been well for the commonwealth if it had never been made' (Bryson, 306). He considered the Statute of Wills (1540), which permitted landowners to devise their lands by will, to have been 'not only the ruin of ancient families but the nurse of forgeries' (Hudson, 69). Ellesmere favoured Bacon's scheme for overhauling the statute book, removing obsolete matter and resolving ambiguities, and urged it on the parliament of 1597; but neither man was able to achieve any success with this ambition.

Even during Elizabeth's reign, Ellesmere was as much a statesman as a judge. He was a confidential adviser on domestic and foreign policy, close to the Cecils but with an independence which the queen found valuable, and was employed on diplomatic negotiations with France (1597), the states general (1598), and Denmark (1600). He was one of the few privy councillors (from 1596) who witnessed the scene in the council chamber, in July 1598, when Essex insulted the queen and she boxed his ears. Under James he became a still more valued minister and—though willing at times to question the king's decisions—increasingly aligned himself with James's absolutist conceptions of monarchy. In addressing the judges in 1604, he declared that 'the king's majesty, as it were inheritable and descended from God, hath absolute monarchical power annexed inseparably to his crown and diadem, not by common law nor statute law, but more anciently than either of them' (Hawarde, 188). His views on the constitution were expounded at length in his celebrated judgment in *Calvin's Case* (1608), which determined that persons born in Scotland after the accession of James were not aliens in England: there was one king, one allegiance. The speech took four hours to deliver and was published as a separate pamphlet in 1609. Ellesmere did not regard the king as being above the law, and he recognized the importance of a balance of power between king, lords, and commons, but his increasingly elevated position in the state placed an ever growing distance between his political thinking and that of his old profession, and he seemed unable or unwilling to understand the concerns shared by many lawyer members of parliament, and judges, at what they perceived as growing absolutism.

Ellesmere was at odds with the judiciary on a number of occasions, at least from 1604, when they opposed the king's project of a legal union between England and Scotland. He fell out with them over the use of writs of prohibition, mandamus, and certiorari, which he thought were being issued too lightly and without proper judicial supervision. Prohibitions, in particular, were depriving the ecclesiastical courts of their tithe jurisdiction, and in 1609 the judges were hauled before the privy council to explain themselves. Worst of all, king's bench was assuming a power of judicial review over governmental activities. Ellesmere was angry that Coke and his brethren had taken to reviewing the activities of municipal corporations, the provincial councils, and even the high commission, 'as if the King's Bench had a superintendency over the government itself' (Knafla, 307–8). However, the principal clash came over Ellesmere's claim as chancellor to reopen cases which had proceeded to judgment at common law. This had long been held to be illegal, since judgments were supposed to be inviolate, and in 1598 the judges in the exchequer chamber confirmed this position. Ellesmere resumed the practice of issuing decrees after judgment under the justification that his jurisdiction was concerned not with the judgment but with the conscience of the parties. In 1615 Coke released on habeas corpus a number of prisoners who had been committed by Ellesmere in cases of this kind, including Dr Barnaby Goche, master of Magdalene College, Cambridge.

One of the parties released by Coke, a rogue called Richard Glanville, embarked on the foolhardy course of trying to secure an indictment upon the Statute of *Praemunire* not only against his opponent but also against Ellesmere himself. Ellesmere made a strong complaint to James and had the matter referred to the privy council, and to the king's counsel (particularly Bacon), with a view to disgracing Coke. It was in this connection that he compiled, doubtless with Bacon's assistance, *A Breviate or Direction for the King's Learned Counsel*, a tract in defence of his disputed jurisdiction, which survives in numerous copies. In June 1616 the king, primed by Ellesmere and Bacon, sat in Star Chamber and pronounced in favour of chancery. Coke, who had become a nuisance to the government in several respects, was thrice called before the privy council, suspended from his circuits, and ordered to revise some supposed defects in his reports as set out in writing by Ellesmere. Timothy Tourneur, a young barrister, saw these proceedings as symbolic of a new form of tyranny for which Ellesmere was largely to blame:

> this is maintained by the high power of the chancellors, who persuade the king that they are solely the instruments of his prerogative, and insinuate with the king that his prerogative is transcendent to the common law; and thus in a short time they will enthral the common law (which yields all due prerogative) and by consequence the liberty of the subjects of England will be taken away, and no law practised on them but prerogative, which will be such that no one will know the extent thereof; and thus the government in a short time will lie in the hands of a small number of favourites, who will flatter the king to obtain their private ends … And if these breeding mischiefs are not redressed by parliament, the body will in a short time die in all its parts. But some say that no parliament will be held again in England—and then goodbye, ancient liberty of England. (BL, Add. MS 35957, fol. 55v, translated)

Coke perceived the threat to the rule of law even earlier. Since about 1609 he had been compiling a list of 'dangerous and absurd opinions affirmed before the king' by Ellesmere, and by 1616 the total had reached eighteen (CUL, MS Ii.5.21, fol. 47v). The first complaint was that Ellesmere had told James that he could decide cases in person without consulting the judges, a matter on which Coke had engaged in a famous altercation with the king. Others concerned questions of jurisdiction and the authority of the judges. Coke was especially exercised by the new practice—engineered by Bacon and Ellesmere—of summoning judges before the privy council to answer for their decisions, which were openly reproved by the law officers. The result drove a wedge between the king and his judges. When Ellesmere was asked to stand with the judges on these occasions, 'his continual answer was that he would not lie in the gap for any man'. These were serious accusations, but Coke was out of favour and was generally ignored by the leading jurists. In November 1616, to the horror of the profession, he was peremptorily dismissed from office. Ellesmere dragged himself from his sickbed to swear in Sir Henry Mountagu as Coke's successor, and delivered an ungracious speech warning him not to follow the example of his predecessor, whose faults he listed in detail. The Stuart form of government was set on a disastrous course.

Last years, 1610–1617 Ellesmere's last years were rendered miserable not merely by affairs of state and by his third wife but also by illness, in the form of the gout and the stone, and perhaps some form of senile dementia. He was fond of fresh air, moderate country living, and a healthy diet, and many believed that he was apt to feign illness to escape his duties, just as he claimed an aversion to the smell of molten wax to excuse himself from sealing patents to which he was opposed. He petitioned the king several times to be allowed to resign on grounds of senility, though it was widely thought in the legal profession that he clung to office through unawareness of his growing incompetence. Having begun life in circumstances then considered ignoble, he was always covetous of rewards and dignities, and finally set his heart on an earldom. On 7 November 1616, already in failing health, he was created Viscount Brackley, a title which Coke's friends deliberately mispronounced 'Break-Law'. Four months later his wish to retire was finally granted by James, supposedly on a temporary basis, with the promise of an earldom. On 3 March 1617 he surrendered the great seal to the king in person—some thought it was taken from him after he refused to affix it to a patent—and he died at York House, his London home, on 15 March. On 5 April he was buried at Dodleston, Cheshire, where he had kept his principal seat since the 1580s.

In 1610–11 Ellesmere prepared with care some 'notes and remembrances' for peace between his wife and his son, and he made his last will on 16 August 1615, 'finding no true comfort nor contentment in this miserable life, but feeling the mighty hand of God in many grievous afflictions both in body and in mind' (Hunt. L., Ellesmere MS EL 721). His 'loving wife', who was left her jointure and paraphernalia but nothing else, contested the will unsuccessfully. Most of the considerable fortune—estimated by some contemporaries at £12,000 a year—went, after provision for his daughters, to his only surviving son, Sir John Egerton, who was charged to be kind to his sister and her children, 'for I fear that after my decease they will be friendless and comfortless in this world' (ibid.). Sir John Egerton inherited the viscountcy and was soon afterwards given the earldom promised to his father. His descendant Scroop Egerton, fifth earl of Bridgewater (1681–1745), was created duke of Bridgewater in 1741.

The many panegyrics written upon Ellesmere in his lifetime, for instance by Ben Jonson, can hardly be considered objective. There was wide agreement that he was deeply learned in the law and wise in judgement, eloquent in speech, and with a pleasing voice. He liked to coin a nice phrase but did not waste words. According to his admirer William Hudson, 'the grave chancellor Ellesmere, affecting matter rather than affectation of words, tied the same to laconical brevity' (Hudson, 18). Many of Ellesmere's aphorisms have been preserved, in addition to his set speeches delivered on various occasions. On the other hand, in his later years his virtues were offset by his defects. John Chamberlain wrote, on hearing of his death, that he 'left but an indifferent name, being accounted too sour, severe, and implacable, an enemy to parliaments and the common law, only to maintain his own greatness and the exorbitant jurisdiction of his court of Chancery' (*The Letters of John Chamberlain*, ed. N. E. McClure, 2 vols., 1939, 2.65). Richard Hutton, a serjeant-at-law who became a judge in 1617, set down a similar opinion in his diary:

> he was a man of great and profound judgment, an eloquent speaker, and yet in his later times he became more choleric and opposed the jurisdiction of the common law and enlarged the jurisdiction of the Chancery, and in many things he derogated from the common law and the judges. (CUL, Add. MS 6862, fol. 126r, translated)

Tourneur, while praising his judgement and voice, said he was:

> *acerrimus propugnator* of the Chancery and Star Chamber, in a word the bane of the law; yet not for any hate he bare it, but for the love he bare to his own honour to greaten himself by the fall of others.   (BL, Add. MS 35957, fol. 81v)

Nor were Ellesmere's judicial endeavours appreciated as highly as they had been in Elizabeth's reign. A combination of overwork and decrepitude had resulted in an enormous backlog of undecided causes, which one chancery clerk in 1617 put as high as 8000. The office of lord chancellor was undoubtedly too much for one man, and the problem was not resolved until the nineteenth century; but Ellesmere had abandoned his earlier attempts to improve the chancery, and in furthering the absolutist tendencies of James for his own aggrandizement had apparently forfeited the general esteem of his profession.   J. H. BAKER

Sources L. A. Knafla, *Law and politics in Jacobean England: the tracts of Lord Chancellor Ellesmere* (1977) · HoP, *Commons, 1558–1603*, 2.79–83 · W. J. Jones, *The Elizabethan court of chancery* (1969) · J. H. Baker, *The legal profession and the common law* (1987) · F. H. Egerton, *The life and character of Thomas Egerton, Lord Ellesmere* (1806) · J. H. Baker, *Readers and readings in the inns of court and chancery*, SeldS, suppl. ser., 13 (2000) · W. H. Bryson, ed., *Cases concerning equity and the courts of equity, 1550–1660*, 2 vols., SeldS, 117–18 (2001–2), vol. 1 · *Les reportes del cases in camera stellata, 1593 to 1609, from the original ms. of John Hawarde*, ed. W. P. Baildon (privately printed, London, 1894) · W. Hudson, 'A treatise of the court of star chamber', *Collectanea juridica*, ed. F. Hargrave, 2 (1792) · GEC, *Peerage* · Foss, *Judges*, vol. 6 · J. H. Baker, *English legal manuscripts in the United States of America: a descriptive list*, 2 vols., SeldS (1985–90) · J. H. Baker, *A catalogue of English legal manuscripts in Cambridge University Library* (1996) · Hunt. L., Ellesmere MS EL 721 [copy of will]

Archives Folger, corresp. · Hatfield House, Hertfordshire, corresp. and papers · Herts. ALS, official papers and estate papers · Hunt. L., corresp. and papers, incl. papers relating to work as lord chancellor · Inner Temple, London, papers · Northants. RO, notes on royal prerogative

Likenesses oils, c.1603, NPG; at Montacute House, Somerset · oils, c.1603, Lincoln's Inn, London · oils, c.1617, Lincoln's Inn, London; version, Bodl. Oxf. · S. de Passe, engraving, 1618 · oils on panel, NPG [*see illus.*]

Egg, Augustus Leopold (1816–1863), genre and history painter, was born on 2 May 1816 at 1 Piccadilly, London, the youngest of the four children of (Jean) Joseph Egg (1775–1837), gun maker and truss maker, and his wife, Ann Stephens (c.1773–1834). Egg's father, who was born in Huningue, Alsace, and immigrated to London, was from a distinguished gun making family which included the London armourer Durs Egg (1748–1831). Egg initially attended Hall Place, Bexley, Kent (c.1828–c.1833); then, with the encouragement of the sculptor Francis Chantrey, one of his father's clients, he entered Henry Sass's academy in Bloomsbury, London, about 1834, where he learned the fundamentals of drawing. With Sass's sponsorship, Egg was formally admitted to the Royal Academy Schools in December 1836. In 1837 Egg, Richard Dadd, William Powell Frith, Henry Nelson O'Neil, and John Phillip founded the sketching club known as The Clique, a society of young artists which met weekly to draw subjects from Shakespeare and Byron and to socialize. Egg made his London début at the Society of British Artists in Suffolk Street in 1837 and at the British Institution and the RA in 1838, at the annual exhibitions in Birmingham and Liverpool in 1839, and at Manchester in 1840. His earliest works included competent but undistinguished portraits and costume pieces such as *A Spanish Girl*, which was his first work exhibited at the RA.

Beginning about 1840, after he had moved to 30 Gerrard Street, Soho, Egg began to paint literary and historical subjects. Although he was chided for a derivative style that was reminiscent of Charles Robert Leslie and other genre painters, contemporary critics also noted improved handling and strong dramatic characterization in works such as *Scene in the Boar's Head, Eastcheap* (exh. RA, 1840; exh. Sothebys, 16 July 1975) from Shakespeare's *2 Henry IV*, and *The Introduction of Sir Piercie Shafton to Halbert Glendinning* (exh. RA, 1843; Walker Art Gallery, Liverpool) from Sir Walter Scott's *The Monastery*. Several of Egg's early history paintings deal with the relationships between the sexes, such as *Cromwell Discovering his Chaplain, Jeremiah White, Making Love to his Daughter Frances* (exh. RA, 1842) and *Buckingham Rebuffed* (exh. RA, 1846; priv. coll.). Amorous dalliances and human vanity are the subjects of his costume piece *L'amante* (exh. Liverpool Academy 1840; Royal Collection) from Donizetti's opera *L'elisir d'amore*, which was purchased by Prince Albert, as well as his painting from the novel by Alain René Le Sage, *Scene from 'The Devil on Two Sticks'*, which he repeated in several versions, the most important of which (exh. RA, 1844; Tate collection) was acquired by the prominent Victorian art collector Robert Vernon. Egg submitted paintings of two different episodes from *The Taming of the Shrew* to the RA in 1847, and a third in 1860; the play was his most frequent source for the more than two dozen works which he showed at the RA during his career.

About 1847 Egg moved to Ivy Cottage, Queen's Lane, Bayswater, London, the former home of the engraver Samuel William Reynolds, and unsuccessfully stood for associateship in the RA. Goaded perhaps by this rejection, he painted a larger and graver historical composition for the RA exhibition the following year, *Queen Elizabeth Discovers she is No Longer Young* (exh. RA, 1848; priv. coll.). The work was favourably reviewed by critics for its antiquarian knowledge, dramatic invention, and execution, and he was elected an associate member of the RA in November. Egg thereafter contributed regularly to the RA annual exhibitions, alternating light-hearted subjects from literature and history with those of a more austere, sombre nature. Pictures such as *Launce's Substitute for Proteus's Dog* (exh. RA, 1849; Leicestershire Museum and Art Gallery, Leicester) from *Two Gentlemen of Verona*, a painting commissioned by Isambard Kingdom Brunel for his Shakespeare room, *Queen Henrietta Maria in Distress, Relieved by the Cardinal de Retz* (exh. RA, 1849), *Peter the Great Sees Catherine, his Future Empress, for the First Time* (exh. RA, 1850), and *Pepys's Introduction to Nell Gwynne* (exh. RA, 1851; Museum of New Mexico, Santa Fe) evince Egg's continuing preoccupation with dramatic and comic themes and the relationships between men and women.

Egg's best-known works were his moralizing paintings of the 1850s. From 1853 to 1855 he painted a diptych, *The Life and Death of Buckingham*, which won the Liverpool prize of £50 in 1855 and was originally exhibited in a single outer frame (exh. RA, 1855; Yale U. CBA). In this pair of pendant paintings, which recall William Hogarth's *Rake's Progress* series, Egg depicted the rise of George Villiers, second duke of Buckingham, and his legendary sordid demise. In another dramatic series, his famous tragic trilogy of an adulterous wife exhibited untitled at the RA in 1858 and now known as *Past and Present* (Tate collection), Egg further demonstrated his admiration for Hogarth as well as his interest in the portrayal of contemporary social issues and moral subject matter. *Past and Present* was accompanied in the RA catalogue by an imaginary diary entry which began 'August the 4th' and which served as a gloss on the events that unfolded in the visual melodrama. The three paintings in the trilogy were hung together on one line. In the central scene (*Past*) the middle-class husband has returned home from a trip and has received a letter which reveals his wife's infidelity; the wife lies prostrate on the floor, while card-castles built by their two young daughters crumble and other narrative details in the painting portend the family's impending destruction. The two wings (*Present*) take place simultaneously five years later on a moonlit night, a fortnight after the husband's death: in the second scene the two daughters—now orphans because of their father's demise and the desertion of their adulterous mother—are alone in a sparsely furnished room; in the third scene the faithless wife, with her illegitimate child wrapped in a blanket in her arms, seeks refuge under the arches of the Thames. Critics found the paintings painful and realistic, and, as the reviewer in *The Times* commented, the works were 'as tragic as any that ever held an Athenian theatre mute' ('The exhibition of the Royal Academy', 1 May 1858, 5). *Past and Present*, representative of the Victorian genre of 'problem pictures' which depicted difficult social issues, remained unsold during Egg's lifetime.

Egg continued to paint historical, literary, and modern themes in the later 1850s, including, in 1857 and 1858, two pictures from Thackeray's novel *The History of Henry Esmond* (Tate collection and Walker Art Gallery, Liverpool), and *The Night before Naseby* (exh. RA, 1858; RA) which showed Cromwell in his tent on the eve of the battle in 1645. One of Egg's most popular paintings, *The Travelling Companions* (1862, City of Birmingham Museum and Art Gallery), depicts two sisters riding in a railway carriage near Menton, on the French riviera, and suggests his evolution towards non-narrative art. He moved to The Elms, Campden Hill, Kensington, London, about 1853. On 11 April 1860 he married a solicitor's daughter, Esther Mary Browne (1823–1908), and in May of that year was elected a member of the RA.

According to many of his contemporaries, Egg was a sociable, hard-working, self-effacing, and generous man, who 'was never happy unless he was doing something for somebody' (R. Renton, *John Forster and his Friendships*, 1912, 215). His numerous literary friends included Charles Dickens and Wilkie Collins, with whom he travelled on the continent in the autumn of 1853. From 1847 to 1857 he appeared in dozens of Dickens's amateur theatricals staged throughout England and Scotland to benefit a variety of charitable causes. Egg's only painting of Dickens in character, *Charles Dickens as Sir Charles Coldstream in 'Used Up'* (Dickens House Museum, London), was based on a scene from the play by Dion Boucicault which was acted by Dickens's company between 1848 and 1852. Another painting, Egg's *Self-Portrait as a Poor Author* (1858, Trustees of the Patrick Allan Fraser of Hospitalfield Trust, Hospitalfield House, Arbroath), records Egg's role in Edward Bulwer-Lytton's comedy *Not so Bad as we Seem*, which was performed by Dickens's theatrical troupe to benefit the Guild for Literature and Art, a society founded to assist artists and writers. According to numerous sources, Egg was a creditable actor with a special sensitivity to costume and stage design. He and Dickens enjoyed a warm friendship, and Egg may have been a suitor of Dickens's sister-in-law, Georgina Hogarth. He was elected a member of the Garrick Club in 1849, where he was nominated by Charles Kean and seconded by Dickens and Thackeray. His serious interest in the theatre is evident in the subjects of many of his paintings and in the stagelike presentation of his compositions.

Egg was friendly with older artists as well as many of his own generation, and he especially extended his support to his younger colleagues. He assisted the Pre-Raphaelite painter William Holman Hunt at the beginning of his career by selling his pictures to important collectors such as John Gibbons and Thomas Fairbairn. He also personally patronized younger struggling artists, and his collection included Holman Hunt's *Claudio and Isabella* (exh. RA, 1853; Tate collection) from Shakespeare's *Measure for Measure*, and *Chatterton* (exh. RA, 1856; Tate collection), Henry Wallis's painting of the distressed poet. Because of the respect accorded him by diverse modern artists and collectors, Egg supervised the installation of modern British paintings at the Manchester Art Treasures Exhibition in 1857.

In his notes of Egg's life, Holman Hunt described Egg as a handsome man about 5 feet 7 inches tall, broad-chested and large-shouldered, with a sallow complexion, dark brown hair, brown eyes, aquiline nose, thin lips, and a large chin. He did not exhibit at the RA after 1860 due to his increasingly poor health. Throughout his mature life he sought respite from his pulmonary illnesses in the temperate climate of southern England and the Mediterranean, but he died from asthma on 26 March 1863 during a stay in Algiers. According to reports, he was buried on a hill in the new cemetery in Algiers. He was survived by his wife. His premature death was mourned by friends, including Dickens and Holman Hunt, and he was praised by writers in numerous obituaries for the inventiveness and dramatic character of his paintings and for his upright and genial personality. The contents of Egg's studio were sold at Christies on 18 and 19 May 1863.

HILARIE FABERMAN

Sources [W. H. Hunt], 'Notes of the life of Augustus L. Egg', *The Reader* (9 May 1863); (16 May 1863); (6 June 1863); (11 July 1863); (25 July 1863); (31 Oct 1863); (9 Jan 1864) · H. Faberman, 'Augustus Leopold Egg, RA (1816–1863)', PhD diss., Yale U., 1983 · *Art Journal*, 25 (1863), 87 · *The Athenaeum* (11 April 1863), 491–2 · *The Examiner* (11 April 1863), 237 · *ILN* (11 April 1863), 415 · A. Chester, 'The art of Augustus L. Egg, RA', *Windsor Magazine*, 219 (March 1913), 452–66 · 'Portraits of British artists, no. 8: Augustus Leopold Egg', *Art Union*, 9 (1847), 312 · H. Faberman, 'Augustus Leopold Egg's *Self-portrait as a poor author*', *Burlington Magazine*, 125 (1983), 224–6 · H. Faberman and P. McEvansoneya, 'Isambard Kingdom Brunel's "Shakespeare room"', *Burlington Magazine*, 137 (1995), 108–18 · H. Faberman, 'William Holman Hunt's "Notes of the life of Augustus L. Egg"', *Burlington Magazine*, 127 (1985), 86, 91 · Victoria Library, London · parish register (baptism), 1815–16, St James's, Piccadilly [VIII, 141, no. 448 [of 1816]] · parish register (marriage), 1803–9, St James's, Piccadilly [XXXVI, 111, no. 255 of 1805—Joseph Egg and Ann Stephens] · parish register (burial), 1829–37, St James's, Piccadilly [XXVII, 313, nos. 424 and 458, no. 233—Ann Stephens Egg and Joseph Egg] · b. cert. · m. cert. · parish register, St Anne's, Limehouse, London [no. 205], 11 April 1860 [marriage] · gravestone, London Road Cemetery, Brompton, London [Esther Mary Egg] · Graves, *Brit. Inst.* · Graves, *RA exhibitors* · J. Johnson, ed., *Works exhibited at the Royal Society of British Artists, 1824–1893, and the New English Art Club, 1888–1917*, 2 vols. (1975) · *CGPLA Eng. & Wales* (1863)

Archives V&A NAL, corresp. with W. T. Williams

Likenesses R. Dadd, oils, *c.*1840, Yale U. CBA · C. H. Lear, black chalk drawing, 1845, NPG · J. Smyth, line engraving, 1847 (after W. P. Frith), BM, NPG; repro. in *Art Union* (1847), facing p. 312 · W. L. Price, photograph, 1856–9, NPG · A. L. Egg, self-portrait, oils, 1858, Hospitalfield Trust, Arbroath · J. Phillip, oils, exh. RA 1859, RA · T. O. Barlow, engraving, 1865 (after J. Phillip), BM, V&A · Maull & Polyblank, photographs, 1886–9, NPG · engraving (after photograph by J. Watkins), repro. in *ILN*, 30 (2 May 1857), 417 · print, NPG

Wealth at death under £14,000: resworn probate, Jan 1864, *CGPLA Eng. & Wales* (1863)

Eginton, Francis (1736/7–1805), decorative artist, was born probably in Bilston, Staffordshire, the second son of John or William Eginton, and the grandson of Walter and Ann Eginton of Doverdale, near Droitwich, Worcestershire. He was living in Birmingham by the time of his marriage to Ann Davis (*d.* 1771) on 8 January 1759, when he was described as a chaser and engraver.

By 1764, Eginton was working for Matthew Boulton, with whom he became increasingly friendly, at the Soho Manufactory in Handsworth, near Birmingham. He was especially associated with the production of the most costly and ambitious metalwork and was variously described as an enameller, japanner, modeller, and chaser. He designed a wide range of wares in the firm's refined neo-classical style, and, in 1771, was cited as their chief designer. In 1776 he was taken into partnership with Boulton and John Fothergill for the production of silver, Sheffield plate, and ormolu, becoming the director of one of the most influential workshops in Britain.

Eginton precipitated the dissolution of the partnership in 1778, and became increasingly involved in a partnership which had been formed between his elder brother, John Eginton, Edward Jee, Boulton, and Fothergill for the production of japanned wares and mechanical paintings. The latter, apparently an invention by Francis Eginton himself, had been in production within his department for some time. The intention was to provide copies of paintings which exhibited all the qualities of an original oil painting at a fraction of the cost. These copies were either framed and sold as decorative pictures in their own right, or used as ornamental panels within interior decorative schemes on walls, ceilings, doors, or furniture. Copies were made of popular images or of decorative paintings commissioned specifically for the purpose. In spite of current research, the technique of production is still unclear. The method appears to have involved the transferring of outlines and principal colour blocks from inked-up copperplates to a prepared canvas (using inks with an additive to delay drying), which was then finished by hand in oils.

The enterprise did not bring a quick enough financial return, and from about 1780 Boulton sought to run the business down. Eginton's management was poor, and the partnership dissolved amid acrimony and losses of nearly £500. Eginton left Boulton's employment, but continued to produce mechanical paintings on his own account (using Boulton's property and equipment), later establishing a button, toy, and japanning business. From about 1781 he began experimenting with the production of painted glass, initially attempting to print enamel colours onto glass in the manner of a mechanical painting.

In 1784 Eginton moved to Prospect Hill House, Handsworth (dem. 1871), set up a range of workshops, and began developing his painted glass business in earnest. By about 1790 he was confident enough of success as a glass painter to turn the button business over to John, his son by his first marriage, who by 1800 had become sword cutler to the duke of Kent, and button maker to the dukes of Kent and Cumberland.

A modest revival of stained glass was already under way in the second half of the eighteenth century. Eginton's rapid rise to become the leading glass painter of his generation was aided both by his ready access to patronage through his experience of Boulton's ormolu and mechanical paintings business and, especially, by the influence of the architects James and Samuel Wyatt. The close involvement of the Wyatt family with Soho inevitably brought Eginton into contact with them, and this association was cemented by his marriage to Maria Wyatt (d. 1812), his second wife, who was James's cousin and Samuel's sister, on 14 October 1776.

It is probable that Eginton's first major commission, for three heraldic windows in St George's Chapel, Windsor (1786), came as a direct result of James Wyatt's patronage. Eginton subsequently supplied windows for several commissions from James and Samuel Wyatt including, among many others, Salisbury and Lichfield cathedrals (1790 and 1795); Wilton House (1805); Lord Yarborough's mausoleum at Brocklesby (1794–5); Fonthill (a massive commission placed in 1794); Canwell House, near Lichfield (1795); and St Paul's Church, Birmingham (1786–91), his finest surviving work. Other major commissions included St Asaph Cathedral (1800, partly extant, the heraldic glass in situ, some pictorial glass removed to the church of Llandegla, Denbighshire); the archiepiscopal chapel, Armagh (c.1788); the churches of Marchwiel, Denbighshire (1787), Wanstead, Essex (1790, heraldry only extant), Hatton, Warwickshire (c.1792), Sts Peter and Paul, Aston, Birmingham (1793, extant, but in imminent danger

of destruction), St Alkmund's, Shrewsbury (1795), Papplewick, Nottinghamshire (1796), and Great Barr, Staffordshire (1800). Works at major houses included Arundel Castle (c.1789–90 and 1802–6); the chapels at Wardour Castle (c.1790), Painshill, Surrey (c.1795), and Stonor Park, near Henley-on-Thames (1797–1800), the most complete surviving single commission; the library at Stourhead, Wiltshire (c.1802–5); and Stationers' Hall, London (1801). His sketches for the college chapel windows (1795–7) are in the archives of Magdalen College, Oxford.

Eginton's windows use no coloured glass, but are, in the style of the time, painted in a combination of silver stain and translucent enamels on thin, rectangular panels of clear, colourless glass. The panels are set into cast-metal frames, the manufacture of which he also supervised. He did not produce his own designs, but copied or adapted works which already existed or were specifically commissioned for the purpose. Like most late Georgian glass, Eginton's has suffered badly at the hands of more recent generations driven by a different aesthetic. Without the merit of antiquity to recommend them, many of his windows were unceremoniously destroyed during the nineteenth and twentieth centuries.

Eginton's wife, Maria, son William Raphael (1778–1834), son-in-law and long-time assistant Samuel Lowe (d. 1826), daughters Ann (who married Lowe) and Mary, were all involved in the business. During his long last illness, from c.1802, it was William Eginton and Lowe who largely completed the commissions. Eginton died at his home, Prospect Hill House, Handsworth, on 25 March 1805 and was buried in the churchyard of St Mary's, Handsworth, Staffordshire. To judge from surviving documentation, he was greatly liked and genuinely mourned: an engaging, gentle, generous, and highly skilled man, who had no head for business. Under the terms of his will, his establishment passed to his widow, Maria, but the estate was so heavily encumbered with debts (mainly to Boulton and Watt and to the Wyatt family) that any activity was severely curtailed. On the death of Ann Lowe in 1811, the business broke up, with both William Eginton and Samuel Lowe establishing successful independent careers in glass painting. Lowe bought Maria out at Prospect Hill, eventually moving to Newman Street, London, in 1818. William moved to Newhall Street in Birmingham, obtaining the warrant of glass-painter to Princess Charlotte in 1811, and remained there until his retirement in 1824.

MARTIN ELLIS

Sources W. C. Aitken, 'Francis Eginton', *Birmingham & Midland Institute, Archaeological Section, Transactions, Excursions, and Reports*, 3 (15 Feb 1872), 27–43 • [W. R. Eginton and S. Lowe], *GM*, 1st ser., 75 (1805), 387, 482–3, 606 • E. Robinson and K. R. Thompson, 'Matthew Boulton's mechanical paintings', *Burlington Magazine*, 112 (1970), 497–507 • K. Quickenden, 'Boulton and Fothergill's silversmiths', *Silver Society Journal*, 7 (1995), 342–56 • E. Benton, 'Some eminent enamellers and toy makers', *Transactions of the English Ceramic Circle*, 10 (1976–8), 118–29 • N. Goodison, *Ormolu: the work of Matthew Boulton* (1974) • Birmingham Museums and Art Gallery, Department of Art, Eginton family MSS • Birm. CL, Boulton and Watt collection • will, Lichfield Joint RO, Lichfield, B/C/11/20 Jan 1806 • 'Glass painters of Birmingham: Francis Eginton', *Journal of the British Society of Master Glass Painters*, 2/2 (Oct 1927), 63–71 •

S. Shaw, *The history and antiquities of Staffordshire*, 2 (1801) · J. M. Robinson, *The Wyatts: an architectural dynasty* (1979)
Archives Birmingham Museums and Art Gallery, corresp. and family MSS | Birm. CA, letters, etc., to Matthew Boulton
Likenesses J. Millar, oils, 1796, Birmingham Museums and Art Gallery
Wealth at death £1500; outstanding debts of more than £1700: will, B/C/11/20 Jan 1806, Lichfield Joint RO; Boulton and Watt MSS, Box 37, Bundle 10

Eginton, Francis (1775?–1823), engraver, was born in Birmingham, the son of John Eginton, an engraver, and the nephew of the glass painter Francis *Eginton. His father was one of the engravers who worked on Valentine Green's *Dusseldorf Gallery* (1793?) and, most unusually, published large sentimental stipple engravings from Birmingham in partnership with J. F. Tomkins in London. The younger Francis Eginton remained about Birmingham, working in aquatint and line, chiefly on locally published county and urban topographical and historical works of the west midlands, such as Stebbing Shaw's *The History and Antiquities of Staffordshire* (1798–1801), and straying from home only so far as to illustrate *The New Bath Guide* (1807). His contributions to James Bisset's eccentric *A poetic survey round Birmingham; with a brief description of the different curiosities and manufactories of the place, intended as a guide to strangers, accompanied by a magnificent directory* (1799) and his elegant aquatints of Matthew Boulton's *Soho* (*c.*1800) were characteristic of his pride in his place of birth, although contemporaries selected a large print of the Pont-y-Cyssyllte aqueduct as his *chef d'oeuvre*. He died on 22 October 1823 at his home, Meertown House, near Newport, Shropshire, aged forty-eight. An obituarist described him as a 'cheerful and gentlemanly companion, and much respected' (*GM*, 94). TIMOTHY CLAYTON

Sources *GM*, 1st ser., 94/1 (1824), 94

Eglesfield [Egilsfeld], **Robert** [Robert de Eglesfeld] (*c.*1295–1349), founder of Queen's College, Oxford, was the third son of John of Eglesfield and Beatrix, his wife, John having been the third son of Thomas of Eglesfield and Hawisa, his wife. John, and other members of the family, held lands in and near Eglesfield, Cumberland, the place from which they took their name, and which lay within the honour of Cockermouth. In 1316 Robert was a *valettus* in the service of Sir Anthony Lucy (*d.* 1343), lord of Cockermouth, who on 21 May in that year granted him an annuity of 20*s.* and a robe for 'services rendered and to be rendered' (Queen's College muniments, deed DY 2141). Between 1316 and 1328 Eglesfield followed a secular career, particulars of which are unknown. In this period he acquired lands of the annual value of £6 4*s.* 10½*d.* in Laleham, Littleton, and Staines, Middlesex, which in February 1328 he exchanged with Edward III for the manor of Renwick, Cumberland. He served as member for Cumberland in the parliament which met at Northampton in April 1328. At some point after this, and when he was probably already in the king's service, he decided to take orders. On 28 March 1331, the year in which he is first found referred to as a king's clerk, Edward ordered the chancellor to present him to the first void benefice in the king's gift worth over 20 marks, and

accordingly in July 1332 he was admitted to the rectory of Brough, Westmorland, said at the time of his resignation in 1344 to be worth £53 16*s.* 7*d.* p.a. Only an acolyte when admitted to Brough, Eglesfield was ordained deacon in December 1332 and priest in February 1333, in each case by the bishop of Carlisle.

Eglesfield did not reside on his cure but remained in royal service, in which he did not attain a high position but was employed occasionally on minor administrative duties, such as a visitation of the hospital of St Nicholas, Carlisle, in 1335. Still described as a king's clerk in 1342, he was by 1340 also one of Queen Philippa's chaplains. There is no evidence to support past conjecture that he took the degree of bachelor of theology at Oxford, or indeed that he studied anywhere. In November 1346 the pope, at the petition of Queen Philippa, granted him the reservation of a benefice in the gift of the bishop of Winchester, but it does not appear that he received it. In his last years he took upon himself the headship of the Oxford hall he had founded in 1341, being named as provost in deeds dated January and September 1347. He was living in the hall from March to September 1348, and is recorded as having died on 31 May 1349, the place of his death being unknown. A funeral service (*funeracio Roberti Egilsfeld*) held between October 1351 and July 1352 probably marked the reinterment of his remains in the hall's chapel, in accordance with his stated wishes.

The hall was founded, under the name of the Hall of the Queen's Scholars of Oxford, by royal licence dated 18 January 1341, but Eglesfield, in the statutes which he sealed on 10 February following, gave it the name of the Queen's Hall. During the medieval period it was referred to indifferently as Queen's Hall and as Queen's College. The founder purchased the site from his own funds, and also gave his manor of Renwick. Queen Philippa was closely associated with the foundation, and she and the king assisted in the establishment of a modest endowment of lands and appropriated churches worth at the time about £80 p.a. The queen and her successors were given the patronage of the hall, without power to appoint provosts, and without even visitatorial powers, which were given to the archbishops of York. The foundation was for three classes: fellows, chaplains, and 'poor boys', and the fellows were to be elected from MAs who were 'distinguished in moral character, poor in means, and the more suitable for the study of theology' ('Queen's College statutes', 12). A preference was to be given to men who were natives of Cumberland or Westmorland, especially those of the founder's kin. Eglesfield thought that, because of the 'devastated state, poverty and lack of letters' in those counties (ibid., 12), the occasions for exercising the preference would be rare, and the 'universality' of the university itself, which he had wished to see mirrored in his hall, not seriously impaired. Within fifty years of his death the college had turned the founder's 'preference' into a rule virtually excluding all but natives of the two named counties from the foundation. J. M. KAYE

Sources J. R. Magrath, *The Queen's College*, 2 vols. (1921) · J. R. Magrath, 'Fresh light on the family of Robert de Eglesfield, founder of the Queen's College, Oxford', *Transactions of the Cumberland and Westmorland Antiquarian and Archaeological Society*, new ser., 16 (1915–16), 239–72 · Emden, *Oxf.* · 'Queen's College statutes', *Statutes of the colleges of Oxford*, 3 vols. (1853) · *The register of John Kirkby, bishop of Carlisle, 1332–52, and the register of John Ross, bishop of Carlisle, 1325–32*, ed. R. L. Storey, 1, CYS, 79 (1993) · J. R. L. Highfield, 'The early colleges', *Hist. U. Oxf.* 1: *Early Oxf. schools*, 225–63, esp. 236–51 · J. R. Magrath, ed., *Liber obituarius aulae reginae in Oxonia*, OHS, 56 (1910) · R. H. Hodgkin, *Six centuries of an Oxford college: a history of the Queen's College, 1340–1940* (1949) · Queen's College, Oxford, muniments, long roll · Queen's College, Oxford, muniments, deed DY 2141

Archives Queen's College, Oxford, statutes, accounts, deeds
Likenesses W. Sonmans, oils, 1670, Bodl. Oxf. · oils, 1700–99, Queen's College, Oxford

Egley, William (1798–1870), miniature painter, was born at Doncaster. His father was an agent of the firm of Walkers in Eastwood, Nottinghamshire. First employed, together with his brother Thomas, as a bookkeeper by the London publisher William Darton, Egley was inspired to take up painting by visits to exhibitions in Somerset House. Entirely self-taught in his spare time, he succeeded in exhibiting portraits of Lieutenant-Colonel Sir David Ogleby and of Frederick Yates, the actor, at the Royal Academy in 1824. Having given up his other employment to concentrate on painting, and having overcome the early difficulties inherent in developing his art and network of connections, Egley became a prolific and dedicated miniaturist, exhibiting at the Royal Academy, almost every year until 1869, a total of 169 works, as well as a small number at the British Institution and at the Suffolk Street gallery of the Society of British Artists. Egley's work was distinguished by true-to-life portraiture, especially of aristocratic subjects. These included portraits of Lord Churchill (1850; among a group of five miniatures lent to the exhibition at the South Kensington Museum in 1865), and of Egley's literary friend Chevalier de Chatelain (1869). He was particularly successful in portraying children, and painted those of Don Carlos of Spain and of Prince Hohenlohe, the latter by royal commission. Egley painted miniatures in watercolour on ivory, a standard technique of the period, and he usually signed his work in full on the reverse, followed by an address and a date. Occasionally he signed in monogram on the front. An example of the latter is his portrait (1828) of Harriet, *née* Thornton, wife of John Thornton, ninth earl of Leven.

With his first wife, Sarah Maw, whom he married on 30 June 1825 at St Margaret's, King's Lynn, Norfolk, Egley had a son, William Maw Egley (*c.*1827–1916), who was also a miniaturist as well as a painter of historical works, text illustrations, and scenes from contemporary life. Among the latter, *Omnibus Life in London* (1859; Tate collection) has become particularly well known, though William Maw Egley never achieved consistent success in his own lifetime. A portrait by him of his father (British Museum) also exists. At the time of his death, on 26 February 1916, William Maw Egley was living at 32 Chiswick Lane, Chiswick, Middlesex.

A constant characteristic of William Egley's work was its fine colouring, so fine in fact that his early subjects took on a somewhat ghostly appearance as an immediate result. Egley's son, by contrast, was much criticized by contemporaries for his use of hard, almost metallic-looking, shiny colours. Both father and son apparently shared, however, a painstakingly slow approach to their work. William Egley died at his home, 8 Montagu Street, Portman Square, London, on 19 March 1870, leaving a widow, Helena Elizabeth, who was his executor. Examples of his work are in the Victoria and Albert Museum, London, and the City of Liverpool Museum.

ROBERT HARRISON, *rev.* GORDON F. MILLAR

Sources *Art Journal*, 32 (1870), 203–4 · G. Meissner, ed., *Allgemeines Künstlerlexikon: die bildenden Künstler aller Zeiten und Völker*, [new edn, 34 vols.] (Leipzig and Munich, 1983–) · Redgrave, *Artists* · D. Foskett, *A dictionary of British miniature painters*, 1 (1972), 260 · *The Times* (22 March 1870) · *The Times* (22 Feb 1916) · G. Reynolds, *Victorian painting* (1987), 96, 109 · C. Wood, *Victorian panorama* (1976), 217 · *IGI* · *DNB* · S. Redgrave, ed., *Catalogue of the special exhibition of portrait miniatures on loan* (1865) [South Kensington Museum, June 1865] · *Engraved Brit. ports.*, 1.546; 3.95 · Graves, *Brit. Inst.* · D. Foskett, *Miniatures: dictionary and guide* (1987), 417–18, 535 · Graves, *RA exhibitors*, 3 (1905), 31–5 · B. Stewart and M. Cutten, *The dictionary of portrait painters in Britain up to 1920* (1997) · CGPLA Eng. & Wales (1870) · CGPLA Eng. & Wales (1916)

Archives V&A, notebooks, account books · V&A NAL, corresp.; letters
Likenesses W. M. Egley, portrait, BM
Wealth at death under £1500: probate, 29 April 1870, *CGPLA Eng. & Wales*

Eglinton. For this title name *see* Montgomery, Hugh, first earl of Eglinton (1460?–1545); Montgomery, Hugh, third earl of Eglinton (1531?–1585); Montgomery, Alexander, sixth earl of Eglinton (1588–1661); Montgomery, Hugh, seventh earl of Eglinton (1613–1669); Montgomerie, Alexander, ninth earl of Eglinton (*c.*1660–1729); Montgomerie, Susanna, countess of Eglinton (1689/90–1780); Montgomerie, Alexander, tenth earl of Eglinton (1723–1769); Montgomerie, Archibald, eleventh earl of Eglinton (1726–1796); Montgomerie, Hugh, twelfth earl of Eglinton (1739–1819); Montgomerie, Archibald William, thirteenth earl of Eglinton and first earl of Winton (1812–1861).

Eglinton, Sir Hugh (*d.* 1376), courtier and poet, came from Ayrshire. Little is known of his early life and career, but he was probably one of five men knighted by David II in 1342, before an ill-fated raid into England, where all five were captured. He was certainly back in Scotland by 1348, when he received the relief of Meldrum, Aberdeenshire, from Robert Stewart (*d.* 1390). Despite the political rivalry which existed between King David and his heir presumptive, Eglinton appears to have prospered under both men. He was justiciar of Lothian in 1361 and six years later was named in an indenture as one of the commissioners appointed to keep order in the marches. Between 1358 and 1369 he received seven safe conducts to travel to England; he accompanied Sir Archibald Douglas (*d.* 1400) to Canterbury in 1359, presumably on a pilgrimage there. Eglinton was made bailie of Cunningham, Ayrshire, by Robert Stewart in 1367 and, following Stewart's succession as Robert II in 1371, he became a close counsellor of the king; from 1372 to 1375 he also served as an auditor of the accounts, a position which brought him into contact with John Barbour (d. 1395), author of *The Bruce*. He remained in regular receipt of fees and payments, some of them very substantial, until his death in 1376.

Eglinton was probably married twice, first to Agnes More, sister of William More of Abercorn, Linlithgowshire, and the likely mother of his daughter, Elizabeth, who married John *Montgomery of Eaglesham [*see under* Montgomery family]. His second marriage, to Egidia Stewart, half-sister of Robert II, occurred about 1365, when he was recorded as receiving one-third of his wife's annuity in respect of her former husband, James (or David) Lindsay.

Eglinton's literary reputation stems from the reference to 'The Gude Syr Hew of Eglintoun' found in William Dunbar's 'Lament for the Makaris' (1505x8). The fact that Eglinton is the first in Dunbar's basically chronological list of Scottish vernacular poets, before the unknown 'Heryot' and Andrew Wyntoun (c.1350–c.1422), lends credence to the suggestion that the two are identical. Much less convincing are the attempts to link Eglinton with the mysterious *Hucheon of the Awyle Ryale mentioned in Wyntoun's *Original Chronicle*, for the works which the chronicler attributes to Hucheon (two Arthurian gestes and a tale from the Old Testament Apocrypha) have been most plausibly identified as being of English provenance. Moreover it is unlikely that Wyntoun would have mentioned Eglinton elsewhere (as he does) without making the connection explicit. If, however, Dunbar's estimation of Eglinton's literary worth can be accepted, it offers important evidence for the cultural life of fourteenth-century Scotland. Chronicle tradition credits David II with a passion for chivalry, and it is tempting to speculate that Eglinton's compositions contributed to the chivalric ethos of his court. Whatever his subject matter, Eglinton was probably the first significant lay poet of the Scottish language.   C. EDINGTON

Sources G. Burnett and others, eds., *The exchequer rolls of Scotland*, 23 vols. (1878–1908) • *RotS* • *APS* • *CDS*, vol. 4 • *The 'Original chronicle' of Andrew of Wyntoun*, ed. F. J. Amours, 6 vols., STS, 1st ser., 50, 53–4, 56–7, 63 (1903–14) • F. J. Amours, ed., *Scottish alliterative poems in riming stanzas*, 2 vols., STS, 27 (1897); 38 (1897) • *Johannis de Fordun Scotichronicon, cum supplementis … Walteri Boweri*, ed. W. Goodall, 2 vols. (1759) • *Fifth report*, HMC, 4 (1876) • W. Fraser, *Memorials of the Montgomeries, earls of Eglinton*, 2 vols. (1859) • W. Geddie, *A bibliography of Middle Scots poets, with an introduction on the history of their reputations*, STS, 61 (1912) • *The poems of William Dunbar*, ed. J. Kinsley (1979)

Eglinton, John. *See* Magee, William Kirkpatrick (1868–1961).

Eglisham, George (*fl.* 1601–1642), physician and religious controversialist, was probably born in Scotland and was introduced at the age of three to James VI by the marquess of Hamilton (1532–1604), a friend of Eglisham's father. He was brought up with Hamilton's son, James (1589–1625), afterwards second marquess, who became his friend and patron. He was sent abroad and studied at the University of Leiden, where he probably obtained his MD degree. While there he launched an attack on the Arminian theologian Vorstius (Konrad von der Vorst; 1564–1622), whom

he accused of atheism, publishing in Delft *Hypocrisis apologetica orationis Vorstianae, cum secunda provocatione ad Conradum Vorstium missa* (1612). The preface to this work is dated from The Hague, 1 June 1612. Eglisham obtained leave from the authorities at Leiden to invite Vorstius to a public discussion, but Vorstius declined to take up the challenge.

Returning to Scotland, Eglisham was appointed one of the king's personal physicians in 1616, and continued to receive many tokens of favour from James, who, according to Eglisham, 'daily augmented them in writ, in deed; and accompanied them with gifts, patents, offices' (Eglisham). No record of these honours remains. On 13 September 1617 he married Elizabeth Downes 'in the Clink' (*CSP dom.*, 1629, 168). They had one daughter.

In 1618 Eglisham published *Duellum poeticum contendentibus G. Eglisemmio medico regio, et G. Buchanano, regio preceptore pro dignitate paraphraseos psalmi civ*. In an elaborate dedication to the king he undertook to prove that the poet and scholar George Buchanan (1506–1582) had been guilty of 'impiety towards God, perfidy to his prince, and tyranny to the muses'. Eglisham gave a pedantic verbal criticism of Buchanan's Latin version of the psalm in question, which he printed in full, with his own translation opposite. Included in the volume are a number of the author's short Latin poems and epigrams. Eglisham appealed in vain to the University of Paris to decide that Buchanan's version was inferior. He succeeded in attracting attention to himself, and drew from his colleague Arthur Johnston (1587–1641) a mock *Consilium collegii medici Parisiensis de mania G. Eglishemii* (1619), and from his friend William Barclay (1570–1630) a serious judgement on the question at issue, which he decided strongly in favour of Buchanan.

Eglisham further published in 1626 *Prodromus vindictae in ducem Buckinghamiae*, a pamphlet in which he openly accused the duke of Buckingham of having poisoned the marquess of Hamilton and the late king, and petitioned both Charles I and the parliament to have the duke put on trial. It was later translated into English as *The Forerunner of Revenge* (1642). Proceedings were instituted against Eglisham and his assistants, but he fled to Brussels. A letter of the period states that for some years he and a companion, Captain Herriot, 'coined double pistolets together, and yet both unhanged' (*CSP dom.*, 1627–8, 192). Eglisham appears to have remained in Brussels until his death.   ALSAGER VIAN, *rev.* SARAH BAKEWELL

Sources *STC, 1475–1640*, nos. 7546–8 • Wing, *STC*, E255–256CA • G. Eglisham, *Prodromus vindictae in ducem Buckinghamiae* (Frankfurt [i.e. Netherlands], 1626) • *CSP dom.*, 1627–9

Egmont. For this title name *see* Perceval, John, first earl of Egmont (1683–1748); Perceval, John, second earl of Egmont (1711–1770).

Egremont. For this title name *see* Percy, Thomas, first Baron Egremont (1422–1460); Wyndham, Charles, second earl of Egremont (1710–1763); Wyndham, George O'Brien, third earl of Egremont (1751–1837); Wyndham, John Edward

Reginald, first Baron Egremont and sixth Baron Leconfield (1920–1972).

Egremont, Sir John (*b.* 1459?, *d.* in or after **1505**), rebel, was the son of Thomas *Percy (1422–1460), the second son of Henry *Percy, second earl of Northumberland, who had been created Lord Egremont on 20 November 1449 and was killed on the Lancastrian side at the battle of Northampton on 10 July 1460. Thomas Percy is not known to have married, and although John regarded himself as his heir he never inherited the barony, which, with his use of the surname Egremont, suggests that his legitimacy was disputed. He was probably born in 1459, making him twenty-one in 1480 when he released his rights in one of his father's grants; this is the only occasion when their relationship is made explicit. By the mid-1470s, when Egremont was already a knight, he was apparently in the service of his kinsman, the earl of Northumberland, at Leconfield. In 1478 he was granted £20 by Edward IV by way of reward and in 1480 was given an annuity of £20. Richard III gave him an annuity of £40, which was the usual fee of a knight of the body, and he was described as the king's servant in March 1484 when he was granted Kempston, Bedfordshire, for his good service against the rebels in the previous year.

By May 1486 Egremont had transferred his service to Henry VII, who granted him an annuity of 40 marks from the forfeited lands of Viscount Lovell. Egremont may have hoped for his restoration to his father's barony by the new dynasty. In February 1488 he styled himself John Egremont, Lord Egremont. Restoration, however, was not forthcoming, and in 1489 Egremont rebelled. The rising, which led to the death of his cousin Henry *Percy, fourth earl of Northumberland, took place against a background of dissatisfaction with heavy royal taxation. Many writers have also seen a lingering loyalty to Richard III's memory in the unrest. Egremont, however, may have had more personal motives, if, as seems probable, Northumberland had refused him his father's land.

The unrest began at Ayton in Cleveland on 20 April 1489, under the leadership of the yeoman **Robert Chamber** (*d.* 1489), rebel, of Ayton, whom Tudor chroniclers, perhaps in confusion with a Percy servant of the same name, were later to call John à Chamber. On 28 April Chamber's men confronted and killed Northumberland at Cock Lodge in the earl's park at Topcliffe, near Thirsk. The Cleveland insurgents then joined forces with Egremont, who was at the head of rebels from the North and East Ridings, and they advanced as far south as Doncaster before falling back to York. A faction within the city opened its gates to them on 15 May. By then Henry VII was marching north, and the approach of his army's advance guard under Thomas Howard, earl of Surrey, dispersed the rebels. Egremont had already gone north to try and raise more men in Richmondshire and was able to make his escape to the court of Margaret, duchess of Burgundy, at Malines near Brussels. Chamber was among those tried by a commission of oyer and terminer which sat in York at the end of the month and was hanged.

By 1492 Egremont had made his peace with Henry VII and had returned to England. The minority of his kinsman the fifth earl of Northumberland evidently brought him greater recognition as one of the Percy family. In October 1493 he was granted the Percy manors of Isleham, Cambridgeshire, and Forston, Leicestershire, during the earl's minority and the grant, uniquely if slightly ambiguously, describes him as lord of Egremont. He was, however, never summoned to parliament, and in a list of 1492 appears among the knights rather than the barons. His uncertain status was also apparent in November 1495 when Henry VII sent him to confer with the emperor Maximilian about Perkin Warbeck. A Venetian account of the embassy refers to him as Lord Egremont, but adds that he was judged a man of not much repute because he had only ten horses with him. Egremont returned to England late the following March. His date of death is unknown, but was after 30 May 1505 when he granted his manor of Catterton, Yorkshire, to the earl of Northumberland in return for an annuity. Egremont had a sister, Mary, who married the Percy retainer John Gascoigne of Burghwallis. There is no certain evidence that Egremont himself ever married, but the Mistress Maud Egremont who was in the service of the earl of Northumberland in the early 1520s may have been his widow.   ROSEMARY HORROX

Sources Chancery records · GEC, *Peerage* · J. Gairdner, ed., *Letters and papers illustrative of the reigns of Richard III and Henry VII*, 2 vols., Rolls Series, 24 (1861–3) · M. E. James, 'The murder at Cocklodge', *The Durham University Journal*, 57 (1964–5), 80–87 · M. A. Hicks, 'The Yorkist rebellion of 1489 reconsidered', *Northern History*, 22 (1986), 39–62 · M. A. Hicks, 'Dynastic change and northern society: the career of the fourth earl of Northumberland, 1470–89', *Northern History*, 14 (1978), 78–107 · I. Arthurson, *The Perkin Warbeck conspiracy, 1491–1499* (1994) · F. Collins, ed., *Feet of fines of the Tudor period*, 1: 1486–1570, Yorkshire Archaeological and Topographical Association, 2 (1887) · J. M. W. Bean, *The estates of the Percy family, 1416–1537* (1958) · The Dodsworth transcript, W. Yorks. AS, Leeds, Yorkshire Archaeological Society, MS 282, fol. 103ᵛ · R. Grafton, *Chronicle*, 2 vols. (1809) · L. C. Attreed, ed., *The York House books, 1461–1490*, 2 vols. (1991) · L. F. Salzman, *English trade in the middle ages* (1931)

Ehret, George Dionysius (1708–1770), botanical artist, was born Georg Dionysius Ehret on 30 January 1708 at Heidelberg, Germany, the elder son of Ferdinand Christoph Ehret, gardener, and Anna Maria, both of Heidelberg. Ehret trained as a gardener, initially working on estates of German nobility, and painted flowers as a hobby, taught by his father, a good draughtsman. His first major sale of flower paintings came through Dr Christoph Joseph Trew, eminent physician and botanist of Nuremberg, who recognized his exceptional talent and became both patron and lifelong friend. Ehret sent him large batches of watercolours on the fine-quality paper Trew provided. In 1733 Trew taught Ehret the botanical importance of floral sexual organs and advised that he should show them in detail in his paintings. Many Ehret watercolours were engraved in Trew's works, such as *Hortus Nitidissimus* (1750–86) and *Plantae selectae* (1750–73), in part two of which (1751) Trew named the genus *Ehretia* after him.

During 1734 Ehret travelled in Switzerland and France, working as a gardener and selling his paintings. While at the Jardin des Plantes, Paris, he learned to use body-colour on vellum, thereafter his preferred medium. In 1735 he travelled to England with letters of introduction to patrons including Sir Hans Sloane and Philip Miller, curator of the Chelsea Physic Garden. In the spring of 1736 Ehret spent three months in the Netherlands. At the garden of rare plants of George Clifford, banker and director of the Dutch East India Company, he met the great Swedish naturalist, Carl Linnaeus, who was then formulating his new classification based on plant sexual organs. Ehret painted a *Tabella* (1736), illustrating the system, and sold engravings of it to botanists in Holland. Some of his paintings of the exotics were engraved in Linnaeus's *Hortus Cliffortianus* (1737).

Ehret returned to England to settle in Chelsea, and in 1738 married Susanna Kennet, sister of Miller's wife; two children died young, and a son, George Philip Ehret, became an apothecary at Watford, Hertfordshire. Portraits show Ehret as good-looking and fresh-complexioned, with dark hair, bushy eyebrows, cleft chin, and a wart near his mouth. Late in life he suffered eyestrain. Despite his poor English and strong German accent, he made friends easily and in society exhibited complete self-assurance.

Now firmly established as a botanical artist of distinction, Ehret spent his winters teaching ladies of the nobility and his summers painting, often travelling to record the first flowering of a new or exotic plant. He signed and dated his work, naming the subject in pre-Linnaean terms. He published a florilegium, *Plantae et papiliones rariores* (1748–62), with eighteen hand-coloured plates, drawn and engraved by himself. He fulfilled many commissions for wealthy patrons, such as 204 vellums and 4 engravings, at 1 guinea each, for Sir Richard Mead, royal physician, a task extending over four years. Taylor White, lawyer and treasurer of the Foundling Hospital, owned some 300 vellums; Ralph Willet FRS FSA, friend and executor of Ehret's will, had over 800 works. Ehret also provided plant illustrations for several travel books. His distinctive style greatly influenced his successors. His output was prodigious: more than 3000 drawings and paintings are extant in major collections.

In 1750 Ehret took the post of gardener at the Oxford Physic Garden, but resigned after a year. In 1757 he returned to London, where he lived in Park Street, Mayfair. He became a fellow of the Royal Society on 19 May 1757 and contributed notes on particular plants to *Philosophical Transactions* in 1763 and 1767. Proposed by Trew, Ehret became a member of the Leopoldina, the German Academy of Naturalists, on 10 September 1758, and he contributed to the *Nova Acta Academiae* in 1761. He died at his home in Park Street on 9 September 1770 and was buried in St Luke's churchyard, Chelsea.　　ENID SLATTER

Sources 'A memoir of Georg Dionysius Ehret … written by himself, and translated, with notes by E. S. Barton', *Proceedings of the Linnean Society of London* (1894–5), 41–58 • G. D. Ehret, autobiography with notes by C. J. Trew, NHM • G. Calmann, *Ehret, flower painter extraordinary* (1977) • R. Pulteney, *Historical and biographical sketches of the progress of botany in England*, 2 (1790), 284–93 • E. M. Slatter, *Dr Richard Mead's commission and Ehret drawings at the Wellcome Institute* (1985), 40 • C. Murdoch, *G. D. Ehret, botanical artist* (1970) • W. Blunt and W. T. Stearn, *The art of botanical illustration*, new edn (1994), 159–66 • will, PRO, PROB 11/962, sig. 429

Archives Carnegie Mellon University, Pittsburgh, Hunt Institute for Botanical Documentation • Erlangen University, Germany • FM Cam. • NHM, drawings and papers; MS autobiography • V&A | Knowsley Hall, earl of Derby's collection • Wellcome L., MS list of flowers painted for Dr R. Mead

Likenesses G. D. Ehret, self-portrait, pencil and wash, c.1740, Hamburg Kunsthalle, Germany • J. J. Haid, engraving, c.1750 (after a self-portrait by G. D. Ehret), repro. in C. J. Trew, *Plantae selectae* (1750) • G. James, oils, 1767, Linn. Soc.

Ehrlich, Georg (1897–1966), sculptor and graphic artist, was born on 22 February 1897 in Vienna, the eldest of the three children of Kurt Ehrlich of Breslau, the representative of a German coalmining company, and his wife, Rosa, who was Viennese. Kurt Ehrlich was a businessman by necessity but, like his son, a musician by inclination. Georg was allowed to leave his *Gymnasium* in Vienna at the age of fifteen and enrol in the Vienna Kunstgewerbeschule. After only three years there he was called up to the Austrian army and saw service on the Russian and Italian fronts with the rank of lieutenant until the end of the war.

During his short time at the Kunstgewerbeschule Ehrlich managed to master the techniques of etching and lithography. In 1920, in the economic misery which followed Austria's defeat, he moved to Munich and until 1925 produced many prints in those media. Despite hyperinflation they sold well to collectors and museums. The prints were shown with, and stand comparison with, the more demonstrative works of Ernst Barlach, Oskar Kokoschka, and others. They project, however, a huge sadness quite different from the bitter protest and denunciation which characterized post-war art in German-speaking countries. In Ehrlich's vision humanity is helpless. His bodies serve as frail supports for the encephalitic heads from which the soul looks out from great melancholy eyes. In real life such eyes belonged to a certain friend, the well-known actress Elizabeth Bergner, whom he first portrayed in 1921. Ehrlich included himself in some prints, satirizing his small stature and pronounced features. The writer on art Erica Tietze-Conrat, who was an intimate friend, suggested that his vision of victimized humanity was less related to post-war suffering than to his own history as the son of a frustrated and angry father.

Ehrlich returned to Vienna in 1924 and began to devote himself to sculpture. He was by no means an Orthodox Jew. Already in his graphic work he had mingled Old and New Testament and Apocryphal themes. His sculpture shows the same sense of the numinous. In it, mankind is seldom seen to be in charge of its own destiny but seems more often to be listening and waiting, sometimes despairingly. This tendency did not show itself immediately or consistently. His first prominent commission in Vienna, *Girl Carrying her Little Brother* (1933, Österreichische Galerie, Vienna), was in a Germanic tradition of realist public sculpture. In a series of heads of boys and men in the 1930s, the clean-cut features and cropped hair show a confident classicizing tendency, but in *Two Sisters* (1932, Museum der Stadt Wien) there is conventual submission and abnegation of the flesh. Ehrlich's concern for form was as great as any modernist's, as he searched for the most classical form in which to convey his subjects' interiority. Between 1928 and 1937 he exhibited in ten cities. His Viennese career was cut short by the Anschluss in March 1938, which made it dangerous for him to remain in Austria. At this time he was already in London, and his wife, Bettina Bauer (*d.* 1985), whom he had married on 27 November 1930, joined him in July of that year and brought many of his works with her.

Ehrlich made a success in London. His first exhibition in Britain was there in 1939. As early as 1944 he was commissioned by the city of Coventry to make a memorial to the victims of air raids; his figure *Pax* (1944–5) is in the city's Garden of Rest. Like other refugee artists of quality he did not fit the stereotypes of academic or modernist which competed for attention on the British post-war scene. But the distinction of his work earned him supporters in both camps, and in the world of music. He was an associate of the Royal Academy and member of the Royal Society of British Arts, and a member of the London Group, but his works were also exhibited by the Arts Council and represented in important public collections. The number of his public commissions belies the scant attention he received from critics and publicists fixated on modernism. The Ehrlichs rapidly committed themselves to Britain and Georg became a British subject in 1947. His beautiful and talented wife must have greatly helped their integration. Bettina, as she signed herself, was a painter and illustrator who also became expert in the casting and patination of her husband's bronzes.

Although his work never looked English, Ehrlich responded to the mood of post-war Britain. The contemporary angst had its reflection in his increasingly etiolated, mannerist figures, such as *Recumbent Boy* (original plaster, Museum and Art Gallery, Letchworth, Hertfordshire) which he showed at the Festival of Britain in 1951. Their melancholy grace was offset by the animal sculptures which became a feature of his London period. (Some of these are in the Tate collection.) Whether or not he intended these to appeal to British collectors, they are rooted in his childhood, when he would trudge some distance to draw the horses at a cab stand—his *Tired Horse* (1961, Bruton Gallery, Bruton, Somerset, in 1979) revives such a memory. Years later he remarked that in order to represent a horse one had for the time to *be* a horse. Indeed an element of self-portraiture runs through his whole work and becomes palpable in the last *Head of a Horse* (Scottish National Gallery of Modern Art, Edinburgh) he made in 1963–4. Other bronze portraits of mainly musical celebrities include *Benjamin Britten* (1950–52, priv. coll.).

Georg Ehrlich died on 1 July 1966 at Lucerne, Switzerland, from the heart condition which had troubled him since 1951, and he was buried in Vienna in a grave donated by the city. His widow continued to live in London and carefully to supervise the casting of his plaster and Plasticine originals until her death in 1985; there was then no one left to represent him in London, since his long-term dealers, the O'Hana Gallery, had closed. Bettina Ehrlich had therefore provided that all the originals and casts should be returned to Vienna. DOUGLAS HALL

Sources E. Tietze-Conrat, *Georg Ehrlich* (1956) · B. Ehrlich, *Georg Ehrlich* (1972) [exhibition catalogue, O'Hana Gallery, London] · private information (2004) [B. Ehrlich] · D. Hall, *Georg Ehrlich: graphic work* (1972) [exhibition catalogue, Edinburgh and Stirling universities] · F. Thorn and P. Pears, *Georg Ehrlich: Plastiken, Zeichnungen* (Munich, 1977) [exhibition catalogue, Wolfgang Ketterer, Munich] · A. Haskell and L. Goldscheider, *Georg Ehrlich* (1978–9) [exhibition catalogue, Bruton and London] · O. Kurz, *Georg Ehrlich as sculptor of animals* (1973) [exhibition catalogue, Scottish Arts Council] · *CGPLA Eng. & Wales* (1967)
Likenesses photograph, repro. in *An exhibition of sculpture by Georg Ehrlich* (1964), Arts Council, exhibition catalogue
Wealth at death £29,129: probate, 15 Feb 1967, *CGPLA Eng. & Wales*

Eichholz, Alfred (1869–1933), medical inspector of schools, was born at 196 Wilmslow Road, Fallowfield, Manchester, on 26 November 1869, the son of Adolph Eichholz, cotton merchant, formerly of Hildesheim and Hanover, and his wife, Babet Praeger of Amsterdam. He was educated at Manchester grammar school and at Emmanuel College, Cambridge, where he gained first-class honours in both parts of the natural sciences tripos (1891, 1892).

After graduating Eichholz published two papers on the palate process of the maxilla and the morphology of the limb arteries in the *Journal of Anatomy and Physiology* in 1892 and 1893 respectively. In 1893 he was elected to a fellowship at Emmanuel, becoming one of the first Jews to hold a fellowship at a Cambridge college. He married on 26 June 1895 Ruth Adler, the younger daughter of Hermann *Adler (1839–1911), the chief rabbi of the United Hebrew Congregations of the British Empire, and they were to have three sons. In 1894 the *Jewish Chronicle* commented that his engagement to the chief rabbi's daughter 'evidences anew the growing importance attached in Jewish circles in England—as it has long been abroad—to professional as distinct from commercial distinction' (*Jewish Chronicle*, 5 Oct 1894, 6). After a period as a medical student at St Bartholomew's Hospital, he graduated MB BCh at Cambridge in 1895 and was an additional demonstrator in the department of physiology at Cambridge. He declined to pursue an academic career and, gaining his Cambridge MD degree in 1898, he took up a post as one of her majesty's inspectors of schools in the same year.

Eichholz had a particular interest in the impact of economic and social conditions on the health of children, and in the effect of health on educational performance. In 1902 he compiled a brief report for the Board of Education on the education of 'feeble-minded' children in Germany ('Report of the congress on the education of feeble-minded children', *Special Reports on Educational Subjects*, vol. 9, *Parl. papers*, 1902, 27, Cd 836), and in 1903 he wrote a report on the physical condition of children attending the Johanna Street board school in Lambeth in south London ('Note on physical condition of London children in poorer districts', PRO, PC8/584). This report played a major role in the discussions which preceded the establishment of the interdepartmental committee on physical deterioration, and Eichholz's evidence to the committee exercised a decisive influence on its final recommendations. When the committee was first appointed it was widely believed that the unhealthy effects of town life were leading to a 'hereditary deterioration' in the health of the working-class population. Eichholz's evidence helped to persuade the committee that 'while there are, unfortunately, very abundant signs of physical defect traceable to neglect, poverty and ignorance', there was no evidence to show that these possessed any marked hereditary effect, and so 'there is every reason to anticipate rapid amelioration of physique so soon as improvement occurs in external conditions' ('Report of the interdepartmental committee on physical deterioration', *Parl. papers*, 1904, 32, para. 69). Among the many recommendations of the physical deterioration committee, one of the most important concerned the imposition of 'a systematised medical inspection of schoolchildren … as a public duty on every school authority' (ibid., para. 423, section 41), and in 1907 parliament passed the Education (Administrative Provisions) Act, which instructed every local education authority to make arrangements for the medical inspection of elementary schoolchildren, and gave them the power to make arrangements for medical treatment.

In view of his experience of working in schools, Eichholz might have been expected to become the board's first chief medical officer, but the government was anxious to ensure the closest possible co-ordination between the school medical service and the existing public health service, and the new post was offered to Dr George Newman, the medical officer of health for Finsbury. Eichholz was appointed with Newman, and these two, together with Dr Ralph Crowley (1869–1953) and Dr Janet Campbell (1877–1954), were largely responsible for the development of the school medical service before the First World War. During the war Eichholz also carried out a major survey of the health conditions of munitions workers, for which he was made CBE in January 1919. Later in the same year, when Newman became chief medical officer of the Ministry of Health as well as of the Board of Education, Eichholz was promoted to the post of chief medical inspector, a post which he continued to hold until his retirement in 1930.

In retirement Eichholz wrote a major report on the problems faced by deaf people in England and Wales (*A Study of the Deaf in England and Wales, 1930 to 1932*, 1933). He urged local education authorities to improve their arrangements for the early detection of hearing problems, and highlighted the importance of vocational training in giving deaf people the skills needed to maintain financial independence. He also called on the government to improve the provision of secondary education for deaf and deaf mute people, pointing out that 'there is, at present, no body of highly-educated deaf persons in the country such as would be able to voice the cause of the deaf and dumb with adequate effect from within' (p. 177). His

report was granted the unusual distinction of being published under his own name, and was cited approvingly in two Board of Education circulars (nos. 1337 and 1337a) published in the following year.

Eichholz was heavily involved in educational and philanthropic work in the Jewish community. His wife, Ruth, had been actively engaged in social work in the East End of London before their marriage, and she went on to become a prominent social worker in her own right. Eichholz himself became president of the East End Social Club for Jewish Deaf and Dumb in 1912, before becoming vice-president of the Jewish Health Organisation of Great Britain and chairman of the New West End Synagogue League of Social Service. Shortly after Eichholz's death, the chief rabbi, Dr J. H. Hertz, wrote that 'aside from his eminent educational labours in the service of the state, it is Jewish religious education that commanded his utmost devotion' (*Jewish Chronicle*, 10 Feb 1933, 12). Eichholz was chairman of the Central Committee for Jewish Education, president of the Union of Hebrew and Religion Classes, and a vice-president of the Jewish Religious Education Board. He was actively involved in local religious activities, including the Hampstead and West Ham religion classes and the West Ham Talmud Torah, and he was a past president of the Palestine Society and a member of the Maccabeans. He was also a founder member of the National Special Schools Union.

Eichholz died at his home, 26 North End House, Fitzjames Avenue, North End Road, London, on 6 February 1933, and was buried on 8 February at Willesden cemetery. He was survived by his wife. In March 1933 the national institutes of the blind and the deaf, the Scottish Association for the Deaf, and the Advisory Committee on the Welfare of the Blind launched a national appeal to raise funds in his memory. He was also commemorated by the establishment of the Alfred Eichholz Memorial Clinic and Institute of Massage and Physiotherapy in July 1934.

BERNARD HARRIS

Sources WWW · Venn, *Alum. Cant.* · *The Times* (7 Feb 1933) · *Jewish Chronicle* (10 Feb 1933) · *BMJ* (18 Feb 1933), 294–5 · *The Lancet* (18 Feb 1933) · *Jewish Chronicle* (5 Oct 1894), 6a, 7b · *Jewish Chronicle* (28 June 1895), 1a, 6b · 'Memorial to Dr Alfred Eichholz', *BMJ* (25 March 1933), 548 · 'Courage of the blind', *The Times* (7 July 1934), 9a · B. Harris, *The health of the schoolchild: a history of the school medical service in England and Wales* (1995) · A. Fitzroy, *Memoirs*, 1 [1925], 175–6 · G. Newman, *The building of a nation's health* (1939), 197–8 · *CGPLA Eng. & Wales* (1933)

Likenesses photograph, repro. in *Jewish Chronicle* (10 Feb 1933), 12 · photograph, repro. in *The Lancet*, 388

Wealth at death £1662 18s. 3d.: resworn administration, 27 March 1933, *CGPLA Eng. & Wales*

Eiffert, Philip (d. 1792), musician, joined the Royal Society of Musicians on 3 June 1750 as 'Philipp Eiffert'. His previous history is unknown. An oboist, he played regularly in London from 1765 to 1790 and occasionally in Oxford between 1754 and 1773, and has been identified with Peter Philip Eiffert, 'executor and residuary legatee of the flutist and oboist Charles Weideman, whose will was written on 24 January 1781 and proved on 5

June 1782' (Highfill, Burnim & Langhans, *BDA*). The portrait of Eiffert by Teeds names the oboist as J. Philip Eiffert; on London playbills of the 1760s his name appeared as Eisent through a printer's error. In 1779 Wilhelm Cramer, leader of the orchestra at the King's Theatre, exempted the oboist 'Einfort' (Eiffert) from his complaint that the wind players were 'insufferable' (Price, Milhous, and Hume, 185) and deserved to have their salaries reduced.

The earliest performance of Eiffert documented was in May 1758, when *Jackson's Oxford Journal* announced (13 May) that 'Mr. Eiffert, the Hautboy from London' was 'expected here on 22d' for an 'extraordinary Instrumental Concert' at the Holywell Music Room. He returned there on 4 July to perform in a 'Concert of Vocal and Instrumental Music' including 'Messrs. *Miller* and *Eiffert* from London' playing a concerto on the bassoon and oboe respectively (*Jackson's Oxford Journal*, 1 July 1758). The pair were involved in a benefit concert for Orthman, principal cellist in the Holywell band, on 21 February 1760 at the music room, when the 'Miscellaneous Concert Of Vocal and Instrumental Music' featured 'particularly, A Concerto and Solo on the Hautboy by Mr. EIFFERT, and a Concerto on the Bassoon by Mr. MILLER' (ibid., 16 Feb 1760). For the performance of Handel's *Acis and Galatea* at the Holywell Music Room on 1 July 1762 Eiffert was billed as contributing, between the acts, a 'Solo upon the Hautboy' (ibid., 26 June 1762); and, together with Miller on the bassoon, he took part in a concert of vocal and instrumental music (playing a concerto on the oboe) on 2 July at the music room.

By 1765–6 Eiffert was in the band at the King's Theatre, London. He accompanied Signora Gabrielli there in a song interpolated in act 2 of *Antigono* by Tommaso Giordani and Mattia Vento on 8 June 1776. These facts, together with Cramer's comment of 1779 and various later mentions, give the impression of a fairly continuous period of service. In 1781 the *Public Advertiser* (23 November) referred to the band at the King's Theatre, 'as usual completely magnificent … Eiffert [is] the Hautboy' (Plantinga, 38). Eiffert was still listed in the King's Theatre roster for the 1782–3 season. During 1784–90 he played in the annual Handel commemorations held at Westminster Abbey and the Pantheon. According to the records of the Royal Society of Musicians, Eiffert died in 1792. SUSAN WOLLENBERG

Sources Highfill, Burnim & Langhans, *BDA* · *Jackson's Oxford Journal* (1753–1928) · C. Price, J. Milhous, and R. D. Hume, *Italian opera in late eighteenth-century London*, 1: *The King's Theatre, Haymarket, 1778–1791* (1995) · L. Plantinga, *Clementi: his life and music* (1977), 37–8 · B. Matthews, ed., *The Royal Society of Musicians of Great Britain: list of members, 1738–1984* (1985) · Mrs R. Lane Poole, ed., *Catalogue of portraits in the possession of the university, colleges, city and county of Oxford*, 1, OHS, 57 (1912), 161 [no. 391] · *The letters of Dr Charles Burney*, ed. A. Ribeiro, 1 (1991) · C. Burney, *An account of the musical performances … in commemoration of Handel* (1785); facs. edn (Amsterdam, 1964) · J. H. Mee, *The oldest music room in Europe* (1911)
Likenesses Teeds, oils, 18th cent., U. Oxf., faculty of music; repro. in Lane Poole, *Catalogue of portraits* · C. L. Smith, group portrait, aquatint, 1782, repro. in *Letters*, ed. Ribeiro

Eilmer (*b. c.*985, *d.* after 1066), pioneer of man-powered flight, was probably born in the 980s, dying not long after 1066. He was a monk of Malmesbury and all that is known of him is told by his fellow-monk William of Malmesbury, writing *c.*1125 in his *De gestis regum Anglorum*. There is no reason to doubt the substantial accuracy of the story, probably derived directly from Eilmer, whom Malmesbury could just have known as a very old man. When Halley's comet appeared in 1066, 'portending (as they say) a change in governments', Eilmer, by then advanced in years, crouched in terror and declared 'You've come, have you? … You've come, you source of tears to many mothers. It is long since I saw you; but as I see you now you are much more terrible, for I see you brandishing the downfall of my country' (Malmesbury, chap. 225). Malmesbury tells us that in his youth Eilmer had believed the fable of Daedalus and, seeking to imitate him, fixed wings to his hands and feet. Casting off from the top of a tower, he caught a breeze and flew for 'a stade and more'. Conscious of his own temerity, and buffeted by the wind, he fell, crippling his legs and remaining thereafter an invalid. He himself attributed his fall to his forgetting to fit a tail.

Eilmer seems to have spent nearly all of his long life as a monk, and was and is distinguished only by his attempt at unpowered flight. This probably took place at some time between 1000 and 1010, assuming that he was about five years old when he saw Halley's comet for the first time in 989. Nor was it wholly unsuccessful. The distance travelled, 'a stade or more', corresponds to about 600 feet, or 200 metres, assuming that Malmesbury had in mind the Roman *stadium* of 606 feet 9 inches. It is true that the use of flexible wings requires a tail to act as a rudder, and that its absence undoubtedly contributed to Eilmer's crash landing. Curiously, a similar attempt had been made a century earlier, within western Europe but in a quite different cultural context. The fourteenth-century writer al-Makkari tells of the late ninth-century Cordovan Abu'l-Qasim Abbas ibn Firnas who tried to fly, using similar methods to Eilmer's with similar results. He hurt his back badly, for 'not knowing that birds when they alight come down upon their tails, he forgot to provide himself with one' (al-Makkari, 1.148). Perhaps Eilmer got the idea for his attempt from news of the earlier one.

This particular story of Malmesbury's had a long and independent afterlife: it was quoted by medieval chroniclers and encyclopaedists, and by early modern proponents of man-powered flight. Lynn White has noted the testimonia of Helinand of Froidmont, Alberic of Trois-Fontaines, Vincent of Beauvais, Roger Bacon, Ranulf Higden (who first misnamed the aviator 'Oliver') and the English translators of his work, Henry Knighton, John Nauclerus of Tübingen (*c.*1500), John Wilkins (1648), John Milton (1670), and John Wise (1850). Malmesbury referred to Eilmer as a good scholar for his times, which suggests that he may have been a writer, and there is a slender possibility that works ascribed to him survived until the sixteenth century. John Bale credited him with three works which are certainly of a sort that one might associate with a serious imitator of Daedalus, but are no longer known to exist. R. M. THOMSON

Sources William of Malmesbury, *Gesta regum Anglorum | The history of the English kings*, ed. and trans. R. A. B. Mynors, R. M. Thomson, and M. Winterbottom, 2 vols., OMT (1998–9) • Al-Makkari, *History of the Muhammadan dynasties in Spain*, trans. P. Gayangos, 2 vols. (1840) • J. Bale, *Illustrium Maioris Britannie scriptorum … summarium* (1548) • Bale, *Cat.* • M. Massip, 'Une victime d'aviation au onzième siècle', *Mémoires de l'Academie des Sciences, Inscriptions et belles-lettres de Toulouse*, ser. 10, 10 (1910), 199–217 • 'Eilmer of Malmesbury, an eleventh-century aviator: a case study of technological innovation, its context and tradition', L. White Jr, *Medieval religion and technology* (1978), 59–73

Einarr [Torf-Einar, Einarr Rögnvaldarson], **earl of Orkney** (*fl.* **early 890s–930s**), magnate, was the youngest son of Earl Rögnvald of Möre (*d. c.*894) and a concubine, who was said (by Rögnvald) to have been slave-born on both her father's and her mother's side. Torf-Einar was a contemporary nickname. Despite his disability of birth, Einarr was very successful in establishing the Möre dynasty's control in Orkney, and was the founder of the line of earls which continued in unbroken succession until the ending of the earldom in 1470. The story in *Orkneyinga Saga* of Earl Rögnvald's giving the earldom to his youngest son, expressing the unlikelihood that he would make much of a ruler, and saying that he was glad to get rid of him, is a variant of a common scene in Old Norse literature, the 'provocation scene'. Such a scene always foreshadows the young man in question proving himself to be the opposite of whatever has been predicted for him. Einarr promises that he will never return from the islands; he is given a fully equipped ship of twenty benches by his father, has the title of earl conferred on him by the king, and sails west for his first battle with the vikings who had been overrunning Orkney.

The circumstances by which the earldom of Orkney was established over the northern isles are not very clear, despite the clarity of the saga account. The means by which Earl Rögnvald of Möre gained control of them, and the nature of the grant he received from Harald Finehair, king of Norway, are very much in doubt, although the saga says that he was given Shetland and Orkney in compensation for the death of his son Ivar on the royal expedition to the British Isles. The *Historia Norvegiae* of *c.*1200 makes no mention of any royal grant, but records that the islands were conquered by Earl Rögnvald entirely on his own account. However, according to the saga he gave the islands to his brother, Sigurd, who was a 'forecastleman' on King Harald's ship, and Sigurd was given the title of earl by the king. These repeated pieces of information about royal grants could very easily have been added by the thirteenth-century saga writer for contemporary reasons of political correctness.

The rule in Orkney of Earl Sigurd the Mighty (*fl. c.*870–890) was remembered as the first period of conquest and expansion on the north Scottish mainland, when the earl joined forces with Thorstein the Red, son of Óláf the White and Aud the Deepminded, to overrun 'the whole of Caithness and a large part of Argyll, Moray and Ross' (*Orkneyinga Saga*, chap. 5). The story of Sigurd's death after a successful battle with the Scottish earl Mael Brigte (Melbrikta) is a famous incident in the saga. This occurred after

he was infected from a cut to his thigh caused by the projecting tooth of the dead Scot, which scratched him as the successful Norse warriors rode back home with their victims' heads strapped to their saddle bows. This incident is also interpreted as a standard literary motif, that of the 'avenging head', but this time with Celtic associations. The likelihood that Sigurd was killed on campaign is strengthened from the added detail (probably reliable) that he was buried in a mound on the banks of the River Oykel, the traditional southern boundary of Norse territory in north Scotland: perhaps indeed at Cyderhall (*Sigurðar haugr*, 'Sigurd's Mound') in Sutherland.

The period after Sigurd the Mighty's death seems to have been one of problems for the earldom: there was the rapid succession of Earl Sigurd's son Guttorm, who died after a year, and Earl Rögnvald's son Hallad (given the title of earl by King Harald), who failed to do anything about controlling the vikings who were raiding the islands and Caithness at the time. He gave up his earldom and retired back to Norway as a 'common landholder' (*hauldr*). So Einarr was faced with the task of rescuing the family's possession of the islands, and a skaldic verse records his killing two Danish vikings: 'after that he took over the island territories and became a great leader', in the words of the saga, which goes on to attempt to explain his nickname, declaring (erroneously) that he 'was the first man to dig peat for fuel' (*Orkneyinga Saga*, chap. 7). The unreliable nature of this explanation is clear when it is said that he did this at Torfnes in Scotland, which is in Easter Ross (Tarbat Ness), an area with which Einarr had no recorded connection at all. This unsatisfactory linking of nickname with placename shows clearly that by *c.*1200 it was quite unknown why the earl was called Torf-Einar.

The saga writer derived most of his information from the five skaldic verses composed by Einarr himself about his contest with Hálfdan Long-Leg, the son of Harald Finehair. Relations between the Möre family and the sons of Harald had deteriorated into a feud, which climaxed in the contest between Einarr and Hálfdan, who managed to set himself up as king in the islands for a period. Einarr's victory, and ceremonial killing of Hálfdan as an offering to Odin, is expressed in the verses as being his revenge for Hálfdan's murder of his father, Rögnvald—revenge that his brothers had failed to exact. The 'blood-eagling' of Hálfdan, described in detail by the saga writer, may derive from his misunderstanding of skaldic terminology. The verse certainly suggests that Hálfdan was buried under a stone cairn (possibly in North Ronaldsay).

Einarr's entrenched position in Orkney meant that King Harald was unable to dislodge him in a succeeding expedition to avenge Hálfdan's murder, although the king imposed a fine of 60 gold marks on the islands, which may be the only reliable fact to be gleaned from the negotiation, recorded in variant forms in different sagas. The incident was later remembered as the occasion when the Orkney farmers lost control of their family lands (their 'odal'), which they resigned to the earl, who paid the whole fine. It was also interpreted later as being the occasion when the earl lost his own right to his family 'odal' and held his earldom 'in fee' from the king. It is certainly the first of many recorded agreements between king and earl, and was looked back to later as forming a landmark in the formal association of Orkney with Norway.

It was known in the later middle ages that Einarr 'be lang tyme brukit the said Erildome, habundand in mycht and riches' ('Genealogy of the earls', 75). He seems to have been unchallenged for the remainder of his rule, and 'died in his bed' (*Orkneyinga Saga*, chap. 8), leaving three sons. His own successes in establishing his rule in the islands made him a worthy progenitor of the earldom dynasty which he firmly established, despite his slave-born mother. He is described as being tall and ugly, and was moreover one-eyed, though 'still the most keen-sighted of men' (*Orkneyinga Saga*, chap. 7): does this personal trait give a hint of Odin's mark on the one earl who has some pagan association in *Orkneyinga Saga*?

BARBARA E. CRAWFORD

Sources H. Pálsson and P. Edwards, eds. and trans., *The Orkneyinga saga: the history of the earls of Orkney* (1978) • 'Genealogy of the earls', *The Bannatyne miscellany*, ed. D. Laing, 3, Bannatyne Club, 19b (1855), 63–85 • B. E. Crawford, *Scandinavian Scotland* (1987) • E. Mundal, 'The Orkney earl and scald Torf-Einarr and his poetry', *The viking age in Caithness, Orkney and the North Atlantic*, ed. C. E. Batey, J. Jesch, and C. D. Morris (1993), 248–59 • R. Frank, 'Viking atrocity and skaldic verse, the rite of the blood-eagle', *EngHR*, 99 (1984), 332–43 • B. Almquist, 'Scandinavian and Celtic folklore contacts in the earldom of Orkney', *Saga-Book of the Viking Society*, 20 (1978–9), 80–105 • W. P. L. Thomson, *The history of Orkney* (1987)

Eineon. *See* Einion ap Gollwyn (*supp. fl.* 1093).

Einion ab Ynyr. *See* Anian (*d.* 1293).

Einion ap Gollwyn (*supp. fl.* 1093), ruler in south Wales, was the son of Gollwyn ap Gwyn, or alternatively of Cydifor ap Gollwyn (*d.* 1091), though the latter may have been his brother. According to various legends, which cannot be traced back earlier than the sixteenth century, Einion's double dealings with Rhys ab Iestyn, king of Glamorgan, against Rhys ap Tewdwr of Deheubarth played an important role in the Norman invasion of Glamorgan, reminiscent of that of Diarmait mac Murchada in the Anglo-Norman invasion of Ireland in 1169. (They are recounted in detail in the *Dictionary of National Biography*.) The earliest extant account occurs in 'The winning of the lordship of Glamorgan out of the Welshmen's hands', written by Edward Stradling (*d.* 1609) between 1561 and 1566, which survives in Cardiff, Central Library, MS 4943. David Powell (*d.* 1598) of Ruabon drew on Stradling's text but produced a variant account in his *Historie of Cambria, now called Wales*, published in 1584. Powell's version was in turn the basis of the description by Edward Williams, alias Iolo Morgannwg (*d.* 1826) in his forged chronicle now known as *Brut Aberpergwm*, published in the *Myvyrian Archaiology of Wales* (1801–7): this *Brut* was regarded as reliable by many in the nineteenth century, which explains why some scholars reproduced the account of Einion's deeds as historical fact. Einion is not mentioned in the surviving medieval chronicles, though his brother (or father) Cydifor ap Gollwyn is. Einion appears as common ancestor of various Welsh families in some late genealogies.

DAVID E. THORNTON

Sources P. C. Bartrum, ed., *Early Welsh genealogical tracts* (1966) • P. C. Bartrum, 'Pedigrees of the Welsh tribal patriarchs', *National Library of Wales Journal*, 13 (1963–4), 93–146, esp. 121 • *The historie of Cambria, now called Wales*, ed. D. Powell, trans. H. Lhoyd [H. Llwyd] (1584); repr. (1811) • O. Jones, E. Williams, and W. O. Pughe, eds., *The Myvyrian archaiology of Wales, collected out of ancient manuscripts*, new edn (1870) • L. H. Nelson, *The Normans in south Wales, 1070–1171* (1966), 101–3 • R. A. Griffiths, *Conquerors and conquered in medieval Wales* (1994), 19–29 • J. C. Davies, ed., *Episcopal acts and cognate documents relating to Welsh dioceses, 1066–1272*, 1, Historical Society of the Church in Wales, 1 (1946), 106–12 • G. Williams, ed., *Glamorgan county history*, 3: *The middle ages*, ed. T. B. Pugh (1971)

Einion Offeiriad (*d.* 1353?), grammarian, is the supposed author of the earliest extant Welsh bardic treatise ('grammar'). Neither the personal name nor the epithet (which means 'the Priest') is uncommon and not all notices of an Einion Offeiriad need refer to the same person, though the concurrence of dates and of localities, together with the literary associations revealed in them, make it inherently probable that most actually do so. Einion is the author of a eulogy, *c.*1322 or more probably *c.*1330, to Sir Rhys ap Gruffudd (*d.* 1356), one of the most powerful and wealthiest of Welsh gentry of the fourteenth century and who held extensive estates in south-west Wales. He may be the person of the same name who figures in the crown's records of Cardiganshire in the 1340s.

The earliest version of the medieval Welsh bardic grammar appears to be that found in the Red Book of Hergest (Bodl. Oxf., Jesus College MS 111, *c.*1400); a rather different version of recognizably the same treatise is found in Aberystwyth, NL Wales, Peniarth MS 20 (*c.*1330). The treatise, probably compiled in the 1330s, is anonymous but the red book version claims that three poetic metres were devised by Einion. Two of these are used in Einion's poem, the ending of which is now lost, to Sir Rhys ap Gruffudd, while the example of the third metre that appears in the treatise ends with the name Rhys ap Gruffudd and may have been taken from the conclusion of the poem. A model sentence explicating a grammatical rule in the treatise uses 'Rhys' and 'Einion' as co-ordinate subjects. All these details lend support to a seventeenth-century attribution of the treatise to Einion Offeiriad. However, the Peniarth MS 20 version attributes the three metres to Dafydd Ddu of Hiraddug and the authorship of the text is also attributed to him both in bardic tradition and in another seventeenth-century copy. His (uncertain) *floruit* is too late and he may have been responsible for a revision of the work.

The treatise contains a grammar, abridged from Donatus and Priscianus, though no direct source for the Welsh version has been discovered. Notwithstanding the importance of linguistic training in the bardic schools, its description of the alphabet, parts of speech, and syntax relates to Latin and is not relevant for Welsh, though it reflects the compiler's desire to work within the Latin grammatical tradition. In contrast, the sections on diphthongs and syllables are a highly competent and accurate analysis of aspects of Welsh phonology. These are important for Welsh prosody and the discussion probably reflects actual bardic instruction. A second section of the treatise deals with prosody—the twenty-four metres, prohibited faults (for example, in rhymes and accentuation); a third ordains how each thing which pertains to poetry is to be praised; poetic triads conclude the work. Praise had always been central to the Welsh bardic tradition and the laws had stipulated that praise of God should precede praise of kings, princes, and other patrons. The author of the treatise develops this principle in his *schema* categorizing hierarchically those, both spiritual and temporal, who are to be praised and their proper attributes. A philosophical basis both for the principle of praise and for its social function in poetry is set out. The section on the twenty-four metres was taken by successive generations of poets from the fifteenth to the nineteenth century as an authoritative statement of bardic regulations. The twenty-four metres, however, do not reflect the practice of fourteenth-century poets. The figure of twenty-four is derived from medieval number symbolism, not from bardic usage. The number is achieved by describing some metres actually being used and others adapted from them, developed from Latin prosody or newly devised; some metres in use were ignored. The metres are erroneously viewed as stanzas rather than line units combined to create a poem. The section contains genuinely archaic and established elements but in design and in comprehension of traditional prosody it is both personal and amateur. It has been described as the compilation of a clever dilettante following his own whims rather than a codification of bardic practice.

The grammar is, nevertheless, of particular significance in Welsh literary history. The traditional basis of literary patronage, and the highly formalized poetry that it nurtured, had been fatally undermined by the disappearance of princely courts following the Edwardian conquest after 1282. A number of the exemplary excerpts used in the treatise are, anomalously in view of its generally conservative clerical ambience, taken from the love and nature poems of lower orders of poets. Circulating orally, these were given enhanced status by being used to exemplify bardic practice and being written down. Combined with a new philosophical basis for poetic praise, it appears that the traditional role of poetry was being adapted in form, style, and content for a new class of patrons, the gentry, 'uchelwyr' (typified by Sir Rhys ap Gruffudd). Einion Offeiriad's treatise, by drawing on the subjects and metres of popular verse, is an element in the reorientation which led to the development of praise poetry in the *cywydd* metre *c.*1350.

The grammar was attributed by Edward Williams, 'Iolo Morganwg' (*d.* 1826), to Edern Dafod Aur, a shadowy figure whose brief classification of letters and words is found in some sixteenth-century manuscripts and who is referred to by a fifteenth-century poet.

BRYNLEY F. ROBERTS

Sources G. J. Williams and E. J. Jones, eds., *Gramadegau'r penceirddiaid* (1934) • C. W. Lewis, 'Einion Offeiriad and the bardic grammar', *A guide to Welsh literature*, ed. A. O. H. Jarman and G. R. Hughes, 2: 1282–*c.*1550 (1979), 58–87 • T. Parry, 'The Welsh metrical treatise attributed to Einion Offeiriad', *PBA*, 47 (1961), 177–95 • J. B. Smith, 'Einion Offeiriad', *BBCS*, 20 (1962–4), 339–47 • R. Bromwich, 'Gwaith Einion Offeiriad a barddoniaeth Dafydd ap Gwilym', *Ysgrifau Beirniadol*, 10 (1977), 157–80 • R. G. Gruffydd, 'Wales's second grammarian: Dafydd Ddu of Hiraddug', *PBA*, 90 (1996), 1–29 • A. T. Matonis, 'Welsh bardic grammars and the Western grammatical tradition', *Modern Philology*, 79 (1981–2), 121–45 • A. T. Matonis, 'Literary taxonomies and genre in the Welsh bardic grammars', *Zeitschrift für Celtische Philologie*, 47 (1995), 211–34 • J. Morris-Jones, 'Dosbarth Edern Dafod Aur', *Transactions of the Honourable Society of Cymmrodorion* (1923–4), 1–28 • J. Williams, ed., *Dosparth Edeyrn Davod Aur* (1856)
Archives Bodl. Oxf., Jesus College MS 111 • NL Wales, Peniarth MS 20 • U. Wales, Bangor, Bangor MS 1

Einzig, Paul (1897–1973), journalist and author, was born in Brasov, Transylvania, then a province of the Austro-Hungarian empire, on 25 August 1897, the son of Bernard Einzig, a forwarding agent, and his wife, Giselle Weisz. He was educated at the Oriental Academy of Budapest and, while still a student, turned his hand to financial journalism with some success. An 'irresistible urge to be at the centre of things', as he described it, took him to London in 1919. His specialist knowledge of Hungary's post-war communist experiment enabled him to get articles accepted by such reputed journals as *The Economist* and the *Economic Journal* almost immediately. But his initial success did not last and for a time he supplemented his earnings from journalism by working as a clerk.

Subsequently, having come to the conclusion that a degree in economics would greatly assist his progress and that it could be obtained more easily in France, Einzig moved to Paris in 1921 and two years later was granted his degree of doctor of political and economic science. Having acted as Paris correspondent for the *Financial News* of London while studying for his doctorate, he was able to persuade the paper to make him its foreign editor on his return to London in 1923.

The foundations for what was to be a highly successful writing career were thereby laid. Initially the emphasis was on journalism and more particularly financial journalism. The Lombard Street column he began to contribute to the paper in 1926 became a major feature of the financial writing scene. This was not only because of the extent and depth of its coverage; it was also because of Einzig's determination to use it for promoting what he considered good causes 'from behind the scenes'—a notable example being its role in the 1939 Czech gold scandal.

On the outbreak of the Second World War Einzig was appointed political correspondent, though he went on writing his Lombard Street column to deal with matters relating to banking and finance. When the *Financial News* was merged with the *Financial Times* in 1945 he turned down the suggestion that he should return to City affairs, it having been made clear that there would be no scope for 'campaigning' in the new setting. He stayed on as lobby correspondent until ill health forced him to accept premature retirement in 1956, his main journalistic activity thereafter being a weekly column in the *Commercial and Financial Chronicle* of New York.

The book written in 1921 as the thesis for his Paris degree apart, Einzig's first venture into authorship came in 1929 when he incorporated into a small book all available published material on gold movements—then a crucial aspect of the international financial scene—and persuaded Macmillan to publish it. Its success encouraged him to follow it up with a book on the emergent Bank for International Settlements in 1930 and a further two—*The Fight for Financial Supremacy* and *The World Economic Crisis*—in the ensuing twelve months.

Altogether Einzig wrote more than fifty books, mostly published by Macmillan though his relationship with the firm became somewhat less cordial after his book *Appeasement: before, during and after the War* (1941) caused it to be involved with him in a libel action in the early 1940s. His output, bearing in mind that it was largely concerned with matters demanding specialist knowledge, was prodigious. The books fall into two main categories—one dealing with topical issues and relying heavily on material that had already appeared in his daily articles, the other comprising works of a technical character resulting from in-depth study of their subjects. Einzig enjoyed most writing books of the first type, maintaining that his temperament was not that of a textbook writer.

The extent of Einzig's output and his tendency to exaggerate when he thought this would help to advance a cause he was prosecuting resulted in his acquiring a reputation for superficiality. He himself, never afraid to engage in self-criticism, admitted in his autobiography that some of his books had deservedly faded into oblivion. Yet it must be said that they nearly all served a useful purpose, that they were almost invariably at least moderately financially successful, and that a number of them—notably *Primitive Money* (1949) and *Dynamic Theory of Forward Exchange* (1961)—were scholarly enough to have become acknowledged works of reference.

In his autobiography, written in 1960, Einzig takes a sober view of the value of his achievements. What cannot be disputed is that he was one of the principal architects of the great advance seen in economic and financial writing since the First World War.

Naturalized in 1929, Einzig had deep affection for his adopted country and greatly admired its institutions, most of all the City. He married in 1931 Eileen Ruth, daughter of Joseph Telford Quick, stockbroker, of St Mawes, Cornwall. They had a son and a daughter. Einzig died in a London hospital on 8 May 1973.

C. GORDON TETHER, rev.

Sources P. Einzig, *In the centre of things* (1960) · *The Times* (9 May 1973) · *WWW* · personal knowledge (1986) · private information (1986) · *CGPLA Eng. & Wales* (1973) · certificate of naturalization, PRO HO 334/111, 15 Oct 1929
Archives BLPES, corresp. with editors of the *Economic Journal* · CAC Cam., corresp. and papers
Wealth at death £4330: probate, 6 July 1973, *CGPLA Eng. & Wales*

Ekarte, George Daniel [*known as* Daniels Ekarte] (1896/7–1964), minister and community worker, was born in west Africa, possibly in the Calabar region of Nigeria. His early years were spent at mission stations run by Free Church of Scotland missionaries. Impressed by what he had heard of the glories of the 'mother country', he obtained a seaman's certificate (which named him simply George Daniel) and worked his way to Britain, where he arrived probably in the early 1920s. Instead of finding glories, he found Liverpool, the city with the highest infant mortality rate in the UK, where the unemployment rate among insured workers was 28 per cent; by 1933 10 per cent of the city's population was in receipt of relief, with the poor heavily concentrated in the racially mixed Toxteth district. The census of 1911 revealed 880 residents born in India and 693 born in Africa; ethnicity was not recorded. In 1919 anti-black riots in the city resulted in the lynching of a black man for whose murder no one was arrested, though the police witnessed the incident.

Working in the local oil mills and sugar refineries, Pastor Daniels Ekarte, as he now called himself, began preaching on street corners, at a gospel hall, and at the Coloured Men's Religious Institute. He also began to visit Africans on ships and in lodging-houses and hospitals. Not satisfied with what he could accomplish this way, he approached the Church of Scotland foreign missions committee and probably also the Liverpool diocese for financial help to set up a permanent mission home. The African Churches Mission was opened in Toxteth on 7 July 1931. It became the main, if not the only, source of succour for the city's resident and itinerant black population, as well as for other local people, serving as a spartan hostel, a place of worship, and a canteen providing cheap meals and free breakfasts for the district's children. There was a scout troop and a Brownie pack, music and secondary school classes for schoolchildren, a mothers' union, and an annual children's Christmas party. The mission also served as a social services agency to which even the police referred people, especially Africans. The mission's ledger reveals the level of local poverty: money was provided for boots, winter coats, and burials, for hospital fees and for rent. During the Second World War, when Ekarte was an ARP warden, the mission also provided emergency housing. All this was accomplished with little financial support, but with help from neighbours, white and black, and donations from local shopkeepers.

During the Second World War Ekarte became involved in two controversial issues. In 1940 he actively supported a strike by African seamen, demanding higher wages and the end of the system whereby deductions were made for the shipping company's Liverpool hostel, whether the men stayed there or not. (African and other 'colonial' seamen received not only much lower wages than their European peers, but also less living space and rations on board ship.) The men's demands were ignored. The other issue was that of the 'brown babies': that is, the 650 or so children fathered by African American servicemen stationed in Britain, whose white mothers did not want to keep them.

(The American army did not permit the men to marry the mothers.) Ekarte lobbied the government for action on the children's behalf and even housed some of them at the mission. With help from the fund-raising efforts of Trinidad-born cricketer and government official Learie Constantine he tried to purchase a larger house to use as a children's home. The government did nothing; Ekarte could not raise enough funds for a home, and in a dawn raid the eight children at the mission were dragged away and dispersed around the country by Liverpool social services.

Naturally Ekarte maintained a relationship with other black organizations in the UK and, when funds permitted, he attended their meetings. The mission was visited by civil and religious African dignitaries, occasionally by MPs interested in its work, and by officials from the Colonial Office, from which it received some support. Three future African prime ministers—Hastings Banda, Jomo Kenyatta, and Kwame Nkrumah—stayed at the mission in the 1940s.

Though racial strife and discrimination in Liverpool did not decrease (there were anti-black riots in 1948), there was a huge increase in social service provisions after the war, and thus the mission lost much of its *raison d'être*. Ekarte could not raise the funds to repair the dilapidated and bomb-damaged mission buildings in Hill Street, and they were demolished by the city in 1964. Ekarte was moved to sheltered housing, at 27 Avison Tower, Princes Park, Toxteth, Liverpool, where he died of a coronary thrombosis on 12 July 1964, aged sixty-seven. He was buried on 20 July in Allerton cemetery, Liverpool. Of his wife, Lily, no details are known. MARIKA SHERWOOD

Sources M. Sherwood, *Pastor Daniels Ekarte and the African Churches Mission* (1994) · d. cert.
Archives Lpool RO, manuscripts and public relations material; papers regarding the mission
Likenesses photograph, Liverpool Life Museum · photographs, priv. colls.

Ekins, Sir Charles (1768–1855), naval officer and naval historian, son of Dr Jeffery *Ekins (1731–1791), dean of Carlisle, and his wife, Anne, daughter of Philip Baker, was born at Quainton rectory, Buckinghamshire, where his father was then rector. He entered the navy in March 1781, on the *Brunswick* (74 guns), under the Hon. Keith Stewart. In the *Brunswick* he was present in the action on the Doggerbank on 5 August 1781, and afterwards went with Captain Stewart to the *Cambridge*, which was one of the fleet under Lord Howe that relieved Gibraltar in 1782. After continuous service on the Mediterranean and home stations for the next eight years, he was promoted lieutenant on 20 October 1790. During the next five years he was mainly employed in the West Indies. Early in 1795 he came home in the *Boyne* (98 guns), bearing the flag of Sir John Jervis, and was in her when she was burnt at Spithead on 1 May. On 18 June he was promoted to the command of the sloop *Ferret* (14 guns) in the North Sea, from which he was appointed to the *Echo*, supposed to be at the Cape of Good

Hope but found, on his arrival, to have been condemned and broken up. He returned to Britain in command of one of the Dutch prizes taken in Saldanha Bay, and was advanced to post rank on 22 December 1796. In August 1797 he was appointed to the frigate *Amphitrite* (28 guns), and in her was actively employed in the West Indies until March 1801, when, after a severe attack of yellow fever, he was sent home with dispatches. He married, in 1800, a daughter of T. Parlby of Stonehall, Devon.

From 1804 to 1806 Ekins commanded the frigate *Beaulieu*, and from 1806 to 1811 the *Defence* (74 guns), in which he took part in the expedition against Copenhagen in 1807, in the operations on the coast of Portugal in 1808, and in the Baltic cruise of 1809. In September 1815 he commissioned the *Superb* (78 guns), and commanded her at the bombardment of Algiers, on 27 August 1816, when he was wounded. He afterwards, together with the other captains engaged, was nominated CB and, by the king of the Netherlands, a knight of the order of William of the Netherlands. The *Superb* was paid off in October 1818, and Ekins had no further service afloat; however, he became in course of seniority rear-admiral on 12 August 1819, vice-admiral on 22 July 1830, and admiral on 23 November 1841. He was made KCB on 8 June 1831 and GCB on 7 April 1852.

A lively controversialist, Ekins was the author of *Naval battles of Great Britain from the accession of the illustrious house of Hanover to the battle of Navarin reviewed* (1824; 2nd edn, 1828). This interesting and useful work pioneered the serious study of tactical development in English, though its value was reduced by much hearsay criticism and the lack of any reference to foreign authorities. The diagrams, too, drawn from the official dispatches, which are generally vague and frequently inaccurate, are often more remarkable for their fancy than their accuracy. Ekins wrote also a pamphlet (1824) criticizing the round stern designs of Sir Robert Seppings. He died at 69 Cadogan Place, London, on 2 July 1855. J. K. LAUGHTON, *rev.* ANDREW LAMBERT

Sources J. S. Corbett, ed., *Signals and instructions, 1776–1794*, Navy RS, 35 [1909] · J. Marshall, *Royal naval biography*, 2 (1835) · B. Tunstall, *Naval warfare in the age of sail: the evolution of fighting tactics, 1650–1815*, ed. N. Tracy (1990) · O'Byrne, *Naval biog. dict.* · Boase, *Mod. Eng. biog.* · *GM*, 2nd ser., 43 (1855)

Ekins, (Emily) Helen (1879–1964), horticulturist and educational administrator, was born on 9 November 1879 at Market Place, St Albans, the only daughter of Arthur Edward Ekins, pharmaceutical chemist, and his wife, Elizabeth Ann Childs. She matriculated from St Albans high school, where she was one of its original pupils. During the following ten years she undertook voluntary work; but in her spare time she grew plants for market, winning in the process a number of prizes at local flower shows. This experience awakened in her what was to become a lifelong interest in horticulture.

In 1909 at the age of thirty Helen Ekins became a full-time horticultural student at Studley College for Women, Warwickshire. This was the start of a lifelong association with an institution which had been established by the countess of Warwick in 1898 specifically to train women to work in horticulture. Her progress at Studley was remarkable. In the second year of her course she was elected head student and she became, in 1913, the first woman student successfully to complete the National Diploma in Horticulture preliminary examination. She was subsequently only the third woman to obtain the full diploma. Having been appointed a lecturer at Studley, Ekins then began studying on a part-time basis at Birmingham University for the newly introduced external London horticulture degree. She graduated with a BSc in 1920. At this stage she was acclaimed by the principal of Studley College, Dr Lillias Hamilton, as 'the most highly qualified man or woman in horticulture in England' (Sanecki, 18).

During the early 1920s Ekins was increasingly involved in the administrative side of the college. In 1922 she was appointed acting warden and two years later, following Dr Hamilton's premature retirement through illness, she became the principal, a position which she held until her own retirement in 1946. Under her leadership Studley College experienced a period of both modernization and expansion. New courses were introduced and examinations remodelled in line with those prevailing in other educational institutions. This was complemented by the formal adoption of a college badge which was based on the bear and ragged staff of the family crest of their patron, Lady Warwick. There was also a significant improvement in the college's financial position. In 1926, following prolonged negotiations, the Ministry of Agriculture and Fisheries formally recognized the work of the college by awarding it a grant of £1000 per annum. Ekins also made strenuous efforts to enhance the college's national reputation. This led, in 1928, to the princess royal, on behalf of Studley College, opening a prestigious exhibition at the hall of the Royal Horticultural Society in Vincent Square, London.

In early 1929, when the existing twenty-one year lease on the college estate and buildings was due to expire, a national appeal was launched to raise £20,000, in order to purchase the freehold and carry out renovations. As part of the money-raising operation the then duchess of York spent a full day at the college taking part in fundraising activities. The results of the appeal fund, run with customary efficiency and diplomacy by Helen Ekins, with the addition of a small mortgage allowed the freehold of the Studley estate to be purchased. In recognition of her pioneering role in advancing the education of women in agriculture Ekins was appointed OBE in 1934. In the later 1930s, and especially during the Second World War, the college introduced several new courses for the increasing numbers of women employed in agriculture and horticulture.

Helen Ekins, who was affectionately known as 'Ma' by her students, never married. She was of medium build, lean but not thin, with straight hair which parted to one side with a hairslide. In undertaking her role of principal in a firm but fair way, she engendered enduring respect from both staff and students. A pioneer of agricultural

and horticultural training for women, her name was synonymous with that of Studley College. Following her formal retirement in 1946 she moved to Dorset but continued to take an active interest in the welfare and development of Studley College. She was also involved in writing articles dealing with her recollections and interest in rural life.

Ekins died on 4 June 1964 at Oakfield Farm, Stevenage Road, St Ippollitts, near Hitchin, Hertfordshire, and was cremated on the 9th at Watford crematorium. She left a generous bequest, along with all her horticultural books, to her beloved Studley College. The latter unfortunately closed a mere three years after her death.

JOHN MARTIN

Sources K. Sanecki, *A short history of Studley College* (1990) · *News About the Guild* [The magazine of Studley College Guild], 66/2 (Dec 1964) · *The Times* (10 Sept 1964) · *The Times* (6 June 1964) · U. Reading, Studley College MSS · P. King, *Women rule the plot: the story of the 100 year fight to establish women's place in farm and garden* (1999) · *Studley Guild Year Book*, 11 (1993) · S. Foreman, *Loaves and fishes: an illustrated history of the ministry of agriculture, fisheries, and food, 1889–1989* (1989) · b. cert. · d. cert.
Archives U. Reading, Studley College MSS · Warks. CRO, Warwick Castle MSS
Likenesses photographs, U. Reading, Studley College MSS · photographs, repro. in Sanecki, *Short history of Studley College*
Wealth at death £9287: probate, 10 Aug 1964, *CGPLA Eng. & Wales*

Ekins, Jeffery (1731–1791), dean of Carlisle, was born on 10 June 1731 in Barton Seagrave, Northamptonshire, of which parish his father, Jeffery or Geoffrey Ekins (*bap.* 1699, *d.* 1773), was rector. He was educated at Eton College (king's scholar, 1744 election) and in 1749 was elected to King's College, Cambridge, where he matriculated in 1750 and where he was made a fellow in 1753. He graduated BA in 1755 and proceeded MA in 1758. On leaving the university he returned to Eton as an assistant master, and was tutor to Frederick Howard, fifth earl of Carlisle. He was inducted to the rectory of Quainton, Buckinghamshire, on 30 March 1761, on the presentation of his father, who had been rector there since 1732. He married in 1765 Anne, daughter of Philip Baker, of Colston, Wiltshire. She was the sister of the wife of his younger brother John Ekins (1732–1808), dean of Salisbury. Their eldest son was Admiral Sir Charles *Ekins (1768–1855); their second, Jeffery (1772–1796), was educated at Eton and King's like his father, but entered the army and died of yellow fever in the West Indies. They had two other sons and three daughters.

In 1775, after resigning Quainton, Ekins was instituted to the rich living of Morpeth, Northumberland (worth £700 a year), on the presentation of his patron the earl of Carlisle. In February 1777 he was instituted to the rectory of Sedgefield, co. Durham; in 1781 he was created DD at Cambridge. From 1780 to 1782 he was chaplain to Lord Carlisle when the latter was lord lieutenant of Ireland. In 1782 Ekins was installed as dean of Carlisle on the advancement of Dr Thomas Percy to the Irish see of Dromore.

Ekins wrote poetry throughout his life. *The loves of Medea* and Jason; a poem in three books translated from the Greek of *Apollonius Rhodius' Argonautics* was published in 1771, and a second edition appeared in 1772. A volume of poems was published in 1810. He died at Parsons Green, Middlesex, on 20 November 1791 'after a lingering illness' (*GM*, 1st ser., 61/2, 1070) and was buried at All Saints', Fulham. He was fondly remembered by a contemporary, Richard Cumberland, who wrote:

> My friend Jeffrey was, in my family, as I was in his, an intimate ever welcome; his genius was quick and brilliant, his temper sweet, and his nature mild and gentle in the extreme; I lived with him as a brother; we never had the slightest jar; nor can I recollect a moment in our lives that ever gave occasion of offence to either.   (Cumberland, 1.124)

Cumberland also expressed his admiration of Ekins's unpublished allegorical drama *Florio, or, The Pursuit of Happiness*, which does not seem to have survived.

THOMPSON COOPER, rev. ANDREW ROBINSON

Sources T. Faulkner, *An historical and topographical account of Fulham; including the hamlet of Hammersmith* (1813), 74, 75, 302 · J. Hodgson, *A history of Northumberland*, 3 pts in 7 vols. (1820–58), pt 3, vol. 2, pp. 394, 527 · *GM*, 1st ser., 61 (1791), 1070, 1239–40 · *GM*, 1st ser., 83/1 (1813), 557 · Nichols, *Illustrations*, 8.191, 267 · D. Lysons, *The environs of London*, 2nd edn, 2 vols. in 4 (1811), 2/1.369, 393 · R. Cumberland, *Memoirs of Richard Cumberland written by himself* (1806), 124 · R. A. Austen-Leigh, ed., *The Eton College register, 1753–1790* (1921) · Venn, *Alum. Cant.*

Archives Castle Howard, Yorkshire, letters to fifth earl of Carlisle, etc.

PICTURE CREDITS

Duane, Matthew (1707–1785)—
© National Portrait Gallery, London

Ducarel, Andrew Coltée (1713–1785)—
© National Portrait Gallery, London

Duckworth, Sir John Thomas, first
baronet (1748–1817)—Christie's
Images Ltd. (2004)

Du Cros, Sir Arthur Philip, first baronet
(1871–1955)—© National Portrait
Gallery, London

Ducrow, Andrew (1793–1842)—V&A
Images, The Victoria and Albert
Museum

Dudley, Ambrose, earl of Warwick
(c.1530–1590)—reproduced by
permission of the Marquess of Bath,
Longleat House, Warminster,
Wiltshire, Great Britain.
Photograph: Photographic Survey,
Courtauld Institute of Art, London

Dudley, Harold Ward (1887–1935)—
© National Portrait Gallery, London

Dudley, Sir Henry Bate, baronet (1745–
1824)—© Tate, London, 2004

Dudley, Joseph (1647–1720)—courtesy
of the Massachusetts Historical
Society

Dudley, Lettice, countess of Essex and
countess of Leicester (b. 1540,
d. 1634)—reproduced by permission
of the Marquess of Bath, Longleat
House, Warminster, Wiltshire, Great
Britain

Dudley, Robert, earl of Leicester
(1532/3–1588)—© National Portrait
Gallery, London

Dudley, Sir Robert (1574–1649)—
National Museum of Fine Arts,
Sweden

Duff, Alexander (1806–1878)—in the
collection of the Church of Scotland;
photograph courtesy the Scottish
National Portrait Gallery

Duff, Sir Mountstuart Elphinstone
Grant- (1829–1906)—© National
Portrait Gallery, London

Duff, Sir Robert William (1835–1895)—
© National Portrait Gallery, London

Duffy, Sir Charles Gavan (1816–1903)—
© National Portrait Gallery, London

Dugdale, Blanche Elizabeth Campbell
(1880–1948)—private collection /
National Portrait Gallery, London

Dugdale, Sir William (1605–1686)—
© National Portrait Gallery, London

Duigenan, Patrick (1734/5–1816)—
© National Portrait Gallery, London

Duke, Henry Edward, first Baron
Merrivale (1855–1939)—by
permission of the Masters of the
Bench of the Honourable Society of
Gray's Inn. Photograph:
Photographic Survey, Courtauld
Institute of Art, London

Dukes, Sir Paul (1889–1967)—
© reserved; collection National
Portrait Gallery, London

Dulac, Edmund (1882–1953)—
© National Portrait Gallery, London

Duleep Singh, Princess Sophia
Alexandra (1876–1948)—The
Women's Library, London
Metropolitan University

Du Maurier, Dame Daphne (1907–
1989)—© National Portrait Gallery,
London

Du Maurier, George Louis Palmella
Busson (1834–1896)—private
collection

Du Maurier, Sir Gerald Hubert Edward
Busson (1873–1934)—© National
Portrait Gallery, London

Duncan II (b. before 1072, d. 1094)—
Chapter of Durham Cathedral

Duncan, Adam, Viscount Duncan
(1731–1804)—© National Portrait
Gallery, London

Duncan, Andrew, the elder (1744–
1828)—in the collection of the
National Museums of Scotland;
photograph courtesy the Scottish
National Portrait Gallery

Duncan, Sir Andrew Rae (1884–1952)—
© National Portrait Gallery, London

Duncan, Francis (1836–1888)—
© National Portrait Gallery, London

Duncan, Henry (1774–1846)—
© National Portrait Gallery, London

Duncan, John (1794–1881)—© National
Portrait Gallery, London

Duncan, John (1805–1849)—
Ashmolean Museum, Oxford

Duncan, Sir Patrick (1870–1943)—
© National Portrait Gallery, London

Dunckley, Henry (1823–1896)—
© Manchester City Art Galleries

Duncombe, Sir Charles (bap. 1648,
d. 1711)—private collection.
Photograph: Photographic Survey,
Courtauld Institute of Art, London

Duncombe, Thomas Slingsby (1796–
1861)—© National Portrait Gallery,
London

Duncombe, William (1690–1769)—by
kind permission of the Master and
Fellows of Corpus Christi College,
Cambridge

Dundas, Henry, first Viscount Melville
(1742–1811)—private collection

Dundas, Sir James Whitley Deans
(1785–1862)—© National Portrait
Gallery, London

Dundas, Lawrence John Lumley,
second marquess of Zetland (1876–
1961)—© National Portrait Gallery,
London

Dundas, Robert, Lord Arniston
(d. 1726)—in the collection of the
Dundas-Bekker Family; photograph
courtesy the Scottish National
Portrait Gallery

Dundas, Robert Saunders, second
Viscount Melville (1771–1851)—
© National Portrait Gallery, London

Dunlop, Frances Anna (1730–1815)—
Scottish National Portrait Gallery

Dunlop, John Boyd (1840–1921)—
photograph courtesy of Dunlop
Tyres Ltd

Dunlop, Marion Wallace- (1864–1942)—
© Museum of London, neg. number
15346, ref. CL02/7448

Dunlop, William (1792–1848)—
© National Portrait Gallery, London

Dunnett, Sir (Ludovic) James (1914–
1997)—© National Portrait Gallery,
London

Dunning, John, first Baron Ashburton
(1731–1783)—Ashmolean Museum,
Oxford

Dunstan [St Dunstan] (d. 988)—© The
Bodleian Library, University of
Oxford

Dunstan, Jeffrey (1759?–1797)—
© National Portrait Gallery, London

Dunsterville, Lionel Charles (1865–
1946)—© National Portrait Gallery,
London

Dunton, (Walter) Theodore Watts-
(1832–1914)—© National Portrait
Gallery, London

Duppa, Brian (1588–1662)—Christ
Church, Oxford

Durand, Sir Henry Marion (1812–
1871)—© National Portrait Gallery,
London

Durand, Sir (Henry) Mortimer (1850–
1924)—© National Portrait Gallery,
London

D'Urban, Sir Benjamin (1777–1849)—
© National Portrait Gallery, London

Durbin, Evan Frank Mottram (1906–
1948)—© National Portrait Gallery,
London

D'Urfey, Thomas (1653?–1723)—private
collection. Photograph:
Photographic Survey, Courtauld
Institute of Art, London

Durham, Lawrence of (c.1110–1154)—
reproduced by permission of the
University of Durham

Durnford, Sir Walter (1847–1926)—by
kind permission of the Provost and
Fellows of King's College, Cambridge

Durrell, Gerald Malcolm (1925–1995)—
© Wolfgang Suschitzky / National
Portrait Gallery, London

Durrell, Lawrence George (1912–
1990)—© Mark Gerson; collection
National Portrait Gallery, London

Duse, Eleonora Giulia Amalia (1858–
1924)—Witt Library, Courtauld
Institute of Art, London

Dutt, (Rajani) Palme (1896–1974)—
© National Portrait Gallery, London

Dutt, Romesh Chunder
[Rameshchandra Datta] (1848–
1909)—© National Portrait Gallery,
London

Duveen, Joseph Joel, Baron Duveen
(1869–1939)—© National Portrait
Gallery, London

Dvořák, Antonín Leopold (1841–1904)—
Getty Images – Hulton Archive

Dwight, John (1633x6–1703)—V&A
Images, The Victoria and Albert
Museum

Dyce, William (1806–1864)—
© National Portrait Gallery, London

Dyck, Sir Anthony Van (1599–1641)—
private collection; Photograph:
Photographic Survey, Courtauld
Institute of Art, London

Dyer, George (1755–1841)—© National
Portrait Gallery, London

Dyer, Joseph Chessborough (1780–
1871)—© National Portrait Gallery,
London

Dyer, Reginald Edward Harry (1864–
1927)—© National Portrait Gallery,
London

Dyer, Sir William Turner Thiselton-
(1843–1928)—© Royal Botanic
Gardens, Kew: reproduced by kind
permission of the Director and the
Board of Trustees

Dyson, Sir Frank Watson (1868–1939)—
© National Portrait Gallery, London

Eadred (d. 955)—© Copyright The
British Museum

Eadwig Basan (fl. c.1020)—The British
Library

Eardley, Sir Culling Eardley, third
baronet (1805–1863)—Ashmolean
Museum, Oxford

Eardley, Joan Kathleen Harding (1921–
1963)—© Estate of Lady Walker

Earle, John (1598x1601–1665)—
© National Portrait Gallery, London

Earle, (Maria) Theresa (1836–1925)—
© National Portrait Gallery, London

Earwaker, John Parsons (1847–1895)—
© National Portrait Gallery, London

East, Sir Edward Hyde, first baronet
(1764–1847)—© National Portrait
Gallery, London

Eastlake, Sir Charles Lock (1793–
1865)—© Royal Academy of Arts,
London

Eaton, Daniel Isaac (bap. 1753,
d. 1814)—© National Portrait Gallery,
London

Ebsworth, Joseph Woodfall (1824–
1908)—© National Portrait Gallery,
London

Eccles, Sir John Carew (1903–1997)—by
permission of the National Library of
Australia

Ecclestone, Alan (1904–1992)—private
collection

Eddington, Sir Arthur Stanley (1882–
1944)—© National Portrait Gallery,
London

Eddington, Paul Clark (1927–1995)—
Johnny Boylan / Rex Features

Ede, James Chuter Chuter-, Baron
Chuter-Ede (1882–1965)—© National
Portrait Gallery, London

Edelman, (Israel) Maurice (1911–1975)—
© Mark Gerson; collection National
Portrait Gallery, London

Edelsten, Sir John Hereward (1891–
1966)—© National Portrait Gallery,
London

Eden, (Robert) Anthony, first earl of
Avon (1897–1977)—© Halsman Estate
/ Magnum Photos; collection
National Portrait Gallery, London

Eden, Emily (1797–1869)—© National
Portrait Gallery, London

Eden, George, earl of Auckland (1784–
1849)—© National Portrait Gallery,
London

Eden, Sir Robert, first baronet (1741–
1784)—private collection

Eden, William, first Baron Auckland
(1744–1814)—Christ Church, Oxford

Eden, Sir William, seventh baronet and
fifth baronet (1849–1915)—
© reserved; photograph National
Portrait Gallery, London

Edgar (943/4–975)—The British Library

Edge, Sir John (1841–1926)—© National Portrait Gallery, London

Edge, Selwyn Francis (1868–1940)—© National Portrait Gallery, London

Edgeworth, Francis Ysidro (1845–1926)—© National Portrait Gallery, London

Edgeworth, Henry Essex (1745–1807)—© National Portrait Gallery, London

Edgeworth, Maria (1768–1849)—© National Portrait Gallery, London

Edgeworth, Richard Lovell (1744–1817)—© National Portrait Gallery, London

Edington, William (d. 1366)—by courtesy of the Dean and Chapter of Winchester

Edis, Sir Robert William (1839–1927)—© National Portrait Gallery, London

Edmund, first earl of Lancaster and first earl of Leicester (1245–1296)—© Dean and Chapter of Westminster

Edmund, first earl of (920/21–946)—© Copyright The British Library

Edrich, William John [Bill] (1916–1986)—Getty Images – Hulton Archive

Edward [St Edward; Edward the Martyr] (c.962–978)—© Copyright The British Museum

Edward [St Edward; Edward the Confessor] (1003x5–1066)—by special permission of the City of Bayeux

Edward, prince of Wales and of Aquitaine (1330–1376)—by kind permission of the Dean and Chapter of Canterbury; photographer: Mrs Mary Tucker

Edward, Prince, duke of Kent and Strathearn (1767–1820)—© National Portrait Gallery, London

Edward I (1239–1307)—The British Library

Edward II [of Caernarfon] (1284–1327)—The British Library

Edward III (1312–1377)—© Dean and Chapter of Westminster

Edward IV (1442–1483)—The Royal Collection © 2004 HM Queen Elizabeth II

Edward V (1470–1483)—by kind permission of the Dean and Chapter of Canterbury Cathedral

Edward VI (1537–1553)—The Royal Collection © 2004 HM Queen Elizabeth II

Edward VII (1841–1910)—The Royal Collection © 2004 HM Queen Elizabeth II

Edward VIII (1894–1972)—© reserved

Edward, Catherine (1813–1861)—© National Portrait Gallery, London

Edward, Thomas (1814–1886)—Scottish National Portrait Gallery

Edwardes, Sir Herbert Benjamin (1819–1868)—© National Portrait Gallery, London

Edwards, Alfred George (1848–1937)—reproduced by kind permission of the Principal, Fellows, and Scholars of Jesus College, Oxford

Edwards, Amelia Ann Blanford (1831–1892)—© National Portrait Gallery, London

Edwards, Bryan (1743–1800)—© National Portrait Gallery, London

Edwards, George (1694–1773)—© National Portrait Gallery, London

Edwards, Sir George (1850–1933)—© National Portrait Gallery, London

Edwards, Sir (John) Goronwy (1891–1976)—© National Portrait Gallery, London

Edwards, James Keith O'Neill [Jimmy] (1920–1988)—© National Portrait Gallery, London

Edwards, John Passmore (1823–1911)—© National Portrait Gallery, London

Edwards, Jonathan (1703–1758)—© National Portrait Gallery, London

Edwards, Lewis (1809–1887)—by courtesy of the National Library of Wales

Edwards, Mary (1705?–1743)—© The Frick Collection, New York

Edwards, Sir Owen Morgan (1858–1920)—© National Portrait Gallery, London

Edwards, Thomas [Twm o'r Nant] (1738–1810)—Gwynedd Archives and Museums Service

Edwards, Thomas Charles (1837–1900)—© National Portrait Gallery, London

Edwards, Vero Copner Wynne- (1906–1997)—Godfrey Argent Studios / Royal Society

Edwin, Elizabeth Rebecca (1771?–1854)—Garrick Club / the art archive

Edwin, John, the elder (1749–1790)—photograph by courtesy Sotheby's Picture Library, London

Egan, John (1754/5–1810)—© National Portrait Gallery, London

Egerton, Sir Alfred Charles Glyn (1886–1959)—© National Portrait Gallery, London

Egerton, Francis, third duke of Bridgewater (1736–1803)—© National Portrait Gallery, London

Egerton, Francis, first earl of Ellesmere (1800–1857)—© National Portrait Gallery, London

Egerton, John (1721–1787)—by kind permission of the Lord Bishop of Durham and the Church Commissioners of England. Photograph: Photographic Survey, Courtauld Institute of Art, London

Egerton, Marianne Margaret, Viscountess Alford (1817–1888)—Belton House, The Brownlow Collection (The National Trust). Photograph: Photographic Survey, Courtauld Institute of Art, London

Egerton, Thomas, first Viscount Brackley (1540–1617)—© National Portrait Gallery, London